VideoHound's® DVD Guide (Book 1)
2000. $19.95. ISBN 1-57859-115-5

VideoHound's Golden Movie Retriever® 2002
2001. $24.95. ISBN 0-7876-5755-7

WITHDRAWN

VideoHound's®

DVD

GUIDE

BOOK 2

ISSN 1535-3478

VideoHound's® DVD GUIDE BOOK 2

Mike Mayo

GALE GROUP

THOMSON LEARNING

Detroit • New York • San Diego • San Francisco
Boston • New Haven, Conn. • Waterville, Maine
London • Munich

Copyright   © 2002 by Gale Group

Published by   Gale Group, Inc.

27500 Drake Rd.

Farmington Hills, MI 48331-3535

VideoHound and the VideoHound logo are registered trademarks of Gale Group, Inc.

Gale Group and Design is a trademark used herein under license.

Most VideoHound books are available at special quantity discounts when purchased in bulk by corporations, organizations, or groups. Customized printings, special imprints, messages, and excerpts can be produced to meet your needs. For more information, contact Special Markets Manager, Gale Group, 27500 Drake Rd., Farmington Hills, MI 48331-3535.

Art Direction   Pamela A.E. Galbreath

Library of Congress Card Number   00-043481

ISBN   0-7876-5757-3
ISSN   1535-3478

Contents

Foreword

by
Jack Hill

This is necessarily going to be a rather subjective commentary—although I'm fairly sure I can speak for many of my colleagues—from the point of view of a director who once made the kind of movies which, in their day, were expected to play one summer—or, if highly successful, might have a return engagement on the bottom half of a double bill—and then be consigned only to the memories of those who had seen them on the big screen, most likely at the local drive-in. Many of our films were knowingly too…well, let's say *intemperate* to be suitable for television release at the time. Home video was only a distant dream, and some were even skeptical that it would ever "catch on."

So it's with amazement and an admittedly shameless delight that I can now find virtually all of my films on display in DVD in video stores (including a few that I'd just as soon *not* see there), most with far better quality of picture and sound than was ever available to their original theatre audiences. And it's an even greater pleasure to know that all those little pluses and minuses that make up the digital matrix will be permanent. No more faded colors, ever again. No more bits of action or dialogue lost from careless handling of a print or deliberately excised because they offended some local censor or even a theatre owner. Now we know (well, at least we hope) that we are sharing the director's vision—for better or worse—unaltered, uncut.

Even more important may be the almost miraculous capability of digital technology to restore, or even re-create in some cases, the lost quality of a work that may only exist in a badly worn theatrical print or a 16mm reduction, with the accompanying loss of both visual and aural quality. I recently had the pleasure—courtesy of Quentin Tarantino— of supervising the restoration of my unfinished 1962 UCLA student film, *The Host,* for inclusion on the Rolling Thunder DVD release of my *Switchblade Sisters* (1975). All that existed was a much-abused 16mm. work print that even had some lines of dialogue missing from the sound track. After I (luckily) located the actress who had appeared in the film 35 years before, the technicians were even able to match the much changed timbre of her voice to that of the original recording. The missing dialogue was added, and stereo sound effects and music were layered in in a matter of days.

What a boon to cinema students it must be to be able to compare the various remakes or alternate versions of classics like *Love Affair* or *The Maltese Falcon* and see how the material was adapted to changes in social and moral values over time. (I must here point out a caveat for future writers and directors: I was recently caught out using certain identical lines of dialogue in two and even three different films—never, of course, expecting anyone to notice.)

But whether for film students or movie buffs, I think the cream of all the bells and whistles now offered on the DVD pudding is the director's commentary. Recording a commentary is nowadays standard practice almost as a part of the production schedule of a film, but what a strange sensation for those of us who are asked to comment on their work 20 or even 30 years after it was done—to watch the film once again and let the images bring back to memory the little tricks we used to get certain effects, to explain why we happened to cast a certain player, perhaps even to point out what we wish we had done differently. (Wouldn't we love to hear Mike Curtiz tell us in his tangled Hungarian accent how he dealt with Ingrid and Bogie when he was shooting *Casablanca*?)

So what does the digital future hold for home video? As of this writing, the latest sales projections estimate 27 million installed DVD players by the end of the year 2001 in the United States alone, and 52 million by the year 2005. The overseas market is already exploding as well. Many films are already being offered on DVD with dialogue tracks in multiple languages and optional subtitles. I dare say that to any filmmaker—and by that I include the players and everyone else involved in the production of a motion picture—to contemplate even a tiny fraction of such a potential audience for our work, not even considering perhaps countless generations to come, is a measure of gratification that is quite simply inexpressible. My only sadness is that some of the wonderful actors whom I once worked with—Boris Karloff, Lon Chaney Jr., Brian Donlevy, Mantan Moreland—have not remained with us long enough to share in it.

But enough of looking back. Now it's back to work on the screenplay for my next film.

—Jack Hill
June, 2001

Among Jack Hill's "intemperate" films are Pit Stop, Spider Baby, Coffy, *and* Foxy Brown. *Though his pictures have been alternately ignored and praised by critics, they have remained popular with audiences from the 1960s until today. The reason is simple: they're fast moving, funny, and entertaining.*

A number of years ago, there was a studio-connected elite circuit of homes in Hollywood, made up mostly of executives and movie stars, who maintained 35mm. projection rooms and had weekly screenings of studio prints that made the rounds. It was like a club. They'd sit around on plush sofas and sip drinks before waving to the projectionist to start the show. Access to the studio prints was the key. Not on the list? No movies. Now, after two decades of home video, DVD has given millions access to home theatres. They might not see the shows the same week they premiere, but for quality and convenience, DVD closely rivals the motion picture experience.

Everyone is familiar with the basics of DVD: it's one of the most successful new product launches, ever. For quality, it outstrips VHS and laserdiscs, and the relative low price of a DVD makes it affordable in a way laser never was; the average retail price of a laserdisc was $40, and DVDs hover between $20—$25. Early adopters bought $700 machines when there were literally only a couple of dozen titles to choose from. People now buy movies the way they might buy pocketbooks, and collectors with hundreds of DVD films on their shelves are not unusual. The ease of home video makes threading up a motion picture projector seem like far too much work; now with the ease of the tiny DVD disc, just flipping those laserdisc platters is too big an inconvenience.

Four years after its debut, DVD is finally poised to take over from VHS. The low price of the new disc has changed the marketplace; people mostly rented VHS tapes, but they purchase DVDs. Name a recent movie and chances are you can buy it on DVD. The folks who want to see last year's Eddie Murphy comedy are well-taken care of. But what's the current state of affairs for the serious collector of older movies, the people who not only want to have the films of

by

Glenn Erickson

Stanley Kubrick, but all of their favorite titles, and who also care about issues like format, extras, and image quality?

The answer is that the collector will find that many of the movies he wants are readily available, and many not. Not all movies are created equal. Trying to figure out why not a single Errol Flynn movie has become a DVD (beyond the public domain *Santa Fe Trail*), while thousands of fairly trivial made-for-video films are already out, requires a slightly deeper look at the inside of the DVD biz.

The majors each control large libraries. Columbia-TriStar, Fox, and Disney have retained their libraries fairly intact. Paramount still owns most of its films made after 1949. Universal has all of its own films, plus the early Paramounts. MGM owns most of the output of United Artists, American-International, Orion, Cannon, and Polygram, but only those MGM titles made after Ted Turner bought Metro in the mid '80s. It is Warner that currently has distribution rights to the enormous MGM library. Besides their own output, Warner also has rights to many Allied Artists films, as well as the RKO library. When you look at the small print on the label of something like *The Man Who Would Be King*, from Warner, you'll see that it's actually copyrighted by Allied Artists.

Smaller labels, such as Image Entertainment, Criterion, Anchor Bay, and Winstar, don't have large libraries and instead license titles from rights holders individually or in batches. They're also known to license titles from the majors. Criterion has long-established ties with Janus Films, a holder of many art movies. Image and Anchor Bay have both licensed product from Universal, but are very creative about finding unattached titles.

The release of a movie on DVD can be very different, depending on whether it's handled by a major or an independent. The majors, with their vast and well-oiled distribution networks, are geared to high-yield marketing. The library of a major may contain 5,000 older titles, yet only a few hundred get any kind of video release, and of those there might only be a hundred or so whose sales performance can be compared to that of a new film. The majors complain of slow sales on catalog titles, and the high cost of added-value extras; they're naturally geared toward titles for which good marketing can move millions of units. Going through the same motions to put a title in the inventory that may only sell in the low thousands, while fickle fan websites complain about tiny (to the studios, mind you) details, is not their idea of fun. That arcane title YOU LOVE might require legal research or revenue-splitting that would make it a much less attractive release than another.

What all this means is that how happy you are with a movie depends very much on who is releasing it. Some studios remaster their older films for DVD as conscientiously as they do their new product. Others organize their library into tiers, putting out movies considered of less importance with whatever video master is available. MGM is currently releasing DVDs in large numbers, but outside their "A" product, the quality of the transfer and its mastering can vary considerably. By contrast, Paramount and Columbia's output is but a trickle, but each of their titles appears to get more individual attention.

The independents often release DVDs of movies that the majors wouldn't touch, in high-quality editions. This can be frustrating, when you discover that Anchor Bay will lavish attention on every minor Hammer horror film it can acquire, whereas the major studios, who control some of the best of the Hammer films, have so far ignored them entirely for DVD. But one also has to be careful with the independents as well. They may have difficulties obtaining good materials (negatives and other printing elements) from which to make a good DVD master. Some popular public-domain films are out on two or three different labels, with quality that varies.

Anamorphic-enhanced DVDs, in the 16:9 format, take matted or letterboxed movies and squeeze them horizontally to utilize more picture area. When played back on a widescreen television they yield a startlingly superior image. At the present time this is the single most attractive DVD feature: seeing a disc in this format on a large monitor is the closest video has come to approximating a theatrical experience.

The laserdisc format championed the letterboxing of movies on video, a concept that DVD has retained. Releasing movies widescreen is still the norm, although some studios will put out "family" films only pan and scanned. With the customer base for DVDs expanding far beyond the film-collector crowd, studios are beginning to cite growing demand for full-frame product.

Widescreen is one of several features that some studios initially promised would be standard for all (applicable) titles. They started with flat and widescreen versions on each disc, along with several languages, subtitles, and closed-captioning. Economy and market concerns have altered all of this, so that determining the features of any new disc requires reading the fine print. In an attempt to standardize the programming of chapter stops, some studios have assigned a set number of chapters per disc, effectively defeating the feature as a navigation tool.

Whereas independent labels hunger for almost any movie with a known following, big studios have so far been very slow in releasing their "golden age" titles, especially those in black and white. There's very little available on stars like James Cagney, Humphrey Bogart, etc. A small company has every incentive to make an extras-loaded "special edition" of every title it releases, which leads buyers to unrealistically expect every studio release to be treated this way as well. Studios are equally proud of their product, but align their choices to performance demands, not the desires of the small fan base. Ask Turner executives about their enormous collection of RKO films, and they'll point you to cable television.

Finally, there is an elite class of blockbuster picture controlled by a small group of big-name talents whose influence exceeds the studios combined. For years now, the biggest issue on web fan sites has been the non-availability of key films by Steven Spielberg and George Lucas. Both are finally letting their big films out, but Lucas indefinitely withholding the bulk of his *Star Wars* and *Indiana Jones* franchises remains a big bone of contention. Another less stratospheric but equally controlling director is Francis Coppola, who has taken his time with the *Godfather* movies (due in October, 2001), while apparently re-inventing *Apocalypse Now* for the crowd that likes their classics better the second time around.

There is obviously a surfeit of interesting product to collect and watch while waiting for these holy-grail titles. The field of library titles that are available is heavily weighted in favor of male action movies, war movies, the Clint Eastwood pictures, etc. Perhaps because they're favored by the early-adopter, tech-oriented crowd, there are plenty of science fiction and fantasy films, and the selection of horror films in the DVD format is already far larger than what was offered on laserdisc. Older westerns are only just getting started and are rather thin. Art films are scarce but, thanks to some of the smaller houses, when you find one it is usually given a good presentation. What DVD is particularly light on are old-style studio star vehicles and Hollywood classics, as best represented by absence of *Citizen Kane,* which is rumored to be on the way.

The galling thing is that that special film YOU want is not out, when big promotions are being thrown at stuff you think is trash. Perhaps the market will drift away from the concerns of collectors. But more likely, the smaller companies will keep the studios sufficiently honest to remember the guy who wants to hear the original Australian audio track to *Mad Max,* and who won't watch a movie in a format "altered to fit his television screen." The studios have been much more generous with their cult titles on DVD than with video; just as an example, there is a possibility we'll be seeing restored versions of three of this writer's western favorites: *Man of the West, A Fistful of Dynamite,* and *Once Upon a Time in the West.*

With the price of a disc still far less than two movie tickets and parking, the DVD experience is going to remain unbeatable in the foreseeable future.

Glenn Erickson
June, 2001

Glenn Erickson is a film editor and writer with a website called DVD Savant (www.dvdtalk. com/dvdsavant/spec.html). In addition to editing DVD documentaries, he promotes film restorations and consults on film history for studios.

First question: Why isn't this book done like *VideoHound's Golden Movie Retriever* and other film guides? They incorporate new entries with the ones from previous year; you've just got one year's worth of movies on DVD here.

Answer: Size. If we had combined new entries with the old ones, this book would have been too big, too heavy, too expensive, and, if you must have it, too unattractive. We like the way it looks. We want to provide the same information about both plot and presentation quality in the same format for about the same price—corporate and individual greed being what they are. Think of this edition and the original *VideoHound's DVD Guide* as two Kevin Spaceys, not one Orson Welles. This book covers a single year's releases and contains almost as many reviews as the first edition, and that one deals with three years' material. Even now, we know we've missed some titles and we're trying to cover the omissions.

The DVD business is growing at a pace that nobody realistically anticipated, as both Jack Hill and Glenn Erickson note in their introductory comments. That growth is being expressed in two distinct areas.

First is the presentation of movies themselves. It almost goes without saying that new big-budget Hollywood studio pro-

ductions arrive on DVD looking very good. Discs are made from absolutely pristine original elements. With digital animation— *Toy Story 2,* for example—there may not even be a celluloid generation. The film goes straight from computer to disc and contains no flaws.

With older films, it's trickier, with more factors to be considered:

- Condition of the original elements. If they can be found.
- Copyright questions. Who owns the various visual and audio components?
- The amount of time, effort, and enthusiasm that people are willing to expend to bring a particular title to disc.

At one end of the spectrum, you've got *North by Northwest,* which, in essence, has been digitally "washed" from first frame to last so that the version that is on DVD now looks and sounds better (in some ways) than the prints that were distributed in 1959. At the other end are discs like *Silent Shakespeare* that bring together short films and fragments, some from the 19th century, of adaptations and scenes from the plays. The films look terrible, showing every minute of their age, with serious damage of almost every kind. Today, they have no real entertainment value and they're not particularly important in a cinematic sense, but DVD makes them available and affordable for serious students of film. In the same vein and even more ambitious is the *Treasures from the American Film Archives* four-disc collection. It brings together a disparate group of early films with accompanying text to provide historical context, providing a look at a side of the early American film that is essentially unknown outside university classrooms.

The second area in which DVD is growing is extras: the wonderful and ever-expanding variety of supplementary elements that can be packed onto a disc. The most common are:

- Screen-size options
- Languages and subtitles (often overlooked)
- Deleted and expanded scenes
- Commentary tracks

Those are the basics, at least some of which are found on most discs. We're beginning to see what might be called the "second wave" of DVD extras. New Line Films, for example, is launching its "Infinifilms" with *13 Days,* which, unfortunately, was unavailable for review. It combines a wealth of options for exploring the realities behind the fictionalized treatment of the Cuban missile crisis. NUON technology, an option on some DVD players, gives viewers similar choices on other titles.

The critical element that determines both the clarity of DVD presentation and the amount of extra features included on a disc is money. In that respect, DVD is exactly like the rest of the entertainment business. Big hits get the best treatment. A fine filmmaker like John Boorman, for example, has not had a recent blockbuster and so we see no special collections of his work. His brilliant semi-autobiographical film *Hope and Glory* arrives on DVD as a bare-bones affair from a major studio. (At the same time, his older science-fiction film *Zardoz* gets special treatment from a much smaller distributor. Read Glenn Erickson's preface for an explanation of the monetary reasons behind that difference.)

In the wider field of home entertainment, DVD is without question the superior medium for watching feature films. Within a few years, it will outstrip and replace VHS tape. Even though other technologies have been proposed for the distribution of feature films to homes, for DVD, the field ahead is clear.

High-definition broadcast television (HDTV) has been promised for years, but it remains somewhere in an ever receding future.

Video on demand (VOD), a phrase that seems to mean something different to everyone who uses it, is even farther away.

When it comes to the delivery of theatre-quality image and sound to home entertainment, DVD is the best option and the rest are not even close. (Let's not mention the deplorable and deteriorating state of theatrical presentation these days. The big chains and independents are in sad financial shape and I do not want to be accused of piling on. But the truth is that even the modest Surround system in my house delivers picture and sound that are superior to those that I often find at the local multiplex, where dinged-up prints and intermittent stereo are commonplace.)

At its best, the DVD presentation of a film can have crystalline clarity that reveals intricate detail with a new depth to the image. Sound—particularly when experienced through multi-speaker Surround speakers—can add another dimension that actually surpasses theatrical presentation. Those are the ideals, though the medium does not always live up to them. If it did, there would be no need for this book. Curiously, DVD appears to be driving the sales of high-definition 16:9 television sets. People are buying these high-end monitors ($3,000-10,000) to watch *Hannibal* and *Cast Away,* not the minimal programming, mostly sports, that the networks offer.

With the introduction of RSDL (Reverse Spiral Dual-Layer) discs that can hold twice as much information as the first DVDs that were released, and other technological developments, the quality of image and sound has risen, but many of the same problems that have always plagued the medium remain:

- Pixels or artifacts: sections of the image coalesce into visible squares.
- Flashing patterns: often found in tweed clothes or background miniblinds. When parallel lines are close together, they may flash stroboscopically or appear to pinwheel.
- Aliasing: diagonal lines break into a shallow stair-step pattern.
- Graininess and artifacts increase in large areas of solid color.
- Digital sound can pop or "clip."
- Surround sound effects, which are meant to place the viewer in the middle of the audio, may be absent or minimal in action scenes.
- As is the case with CDs, surface scratches or blemishes on a disc can cause it to hang up or malfunction in a player.

DVD has also turned home video into a collector's market, as opposed to the VHS rental market. Rental DVD remains strong, however, and it will continue to, I think, no matter how discs are priced. If you weren't willing to shell out $20 for a couple of theatre tickets to see *Mission Impossible 2,* why should you pay $20 to own it? But, when you're talking about a $3 rental, why not give it a whirl?

Something similar applies to the true "big screen" epics. Even though *Lawrence of Arabia* and *Ben Hur* have been released in impressive DVD special editions which have sold well, they still need to be seen on the largest theatre screen possible to be fully appreciated. But for many—if not most—films, DVD presents the potential for the best home viewing experience possible. And so this book attempts to help videophiles and movie fans evaluate their options.

The dozen or so reviewers who contributed are united only by their love of movies. They and I may well have questionable, dubious taste when it comes to personal preferences. We certainly bring different levels of experience and expertise to the task of commenting on movies. But no one should doubt our enthusiasm.

We expect an epiphany (or at least an epiphanette) every time we slide a disc into the player. We want to be inspired, delighted, surprised, awe-struck, horrified, thrilled, spellbound, enraptured, emboldened, appalled, transported, and transformed. Of course, we seldom achieve that state; you know that. But if you study this book, you'll learn from our mistakes and increase your chances.

—Mike Mayo
Chatham, NJ

No book like this is the product of a single individual. Without the help of many people, it would not have been possible. Perhaps the most important are the publicists who provide review copies of discs and the background press materials from which we reviewers steal so shamelessly to make ourselves sound intelligent and experienced. The following really went out of their way to make sure that we received what we needed:

Anchor Bay—Sue Procko and Maral Kaloustian

BFS Entertainment—Leigh Ross

Buena Vista Entertainment—Roger Saunden

Columbia TriStar—Jeff Kaplan

Dreamworks Home Entertainment—Cheryl Glenn

E.I. Independent—Mike Raso

Elite—Josh Davidson

HBO Home Video—Laura Freeman

Home Vision Cinema and Criterion Collection—R. O'Donnell

Image Entertainment—Marc Walkow, Garrett Lee, and Stephen Savage

Madacy—Jim Newhouse

MGM Home Entertainment—Alyssa Alison, Steve Wegner, and Julie Weitzberg

MTI—Jay Grossman and Claudia Brahms

New Concorde Home Entertainment—Tony Pines

New Line Home Entertainment—Amy Gorton

New Yorker Video—Brian Brown

Paramount—Martin Blythe and Liz Hagar

Troma—Tony Rosen and Lloyd Kaufman

Universal—Maria LaMagra and Evan Fong

USA Home Entertainment—Jeff Klein

Vanguard—Scott Thalman and Alex Xagorakis

VCI—Bea Suarez

Winstar—Kimberly Rubin, Dana Kornbluth, and Sandi Bushnell

Xenon Entertainment—Barbara Vetter

York/Maverick—Ed Baran

To all, my most sincere thanks.

VideoHound's DVD Guide would not have been possible without the following talented people:

Editor

Mike Mayo (MM), editor in chief of Video-Hound's DVD Guide, is the author of Video-Hound's War Movies, VideoHound's Horror Show, and VideoHound's Video Premieres, and is a proud contributor to VideoHound's Complete Guide to Cult Flicks and Trash Pics and Sci-Fi Experience. He has written about film and video for the Roanoke Times and the Washington Post. Mike is also the co-host on the weekly syndicated radio program "The Movie Show on Radio."

Reviewers

Carlye Archibeque (CA) rules the Independent Reviews Site (www.irs.theroadlesstraveled.org) from her castle in Los Angeles, California. Surrounded by feline subjects, she views and reviews film, and reads and writes poetry. Ms. Archibeque favors horror films and romance comedies, especially when they are combined in one film, but her only requirement for a film to be considered good is that it tell any old story in a fresh way. For a film to be considered great, "wow" must be uttered in sincerity (not disbelief) at least once during the viewing. Her film critic career began at the age of four reviewing films for family and friends. A bit of a snob, she never gave a Disney film anything more than a 2 on the Toddler scale until Tron came out. Since then she has contributed movie and music reviews to more widely known Los Angeles magazines such as No Ho Magazine, L.A. Village View, Damaged Goods, Next...Magazine, Sic Vice & Verse, and Potpourri & Roses. (She also did time writing for AOL's Big Brother 2000 web site, but doesn't like to talk about it.) She works at the Academy of Motion Picture Arts and Sciences where she learns something new about film everyday, and lives in said castle with her nerdy husband whom she captured in a cemetery on Halloween.

Mike Brantley (MB) writes about film, television, and other media for the Mobile Register newspaper on the Gulf Coast of Alabama. He and his wife Cheryl are avid collectors of cinema in every format, including DVD, laserdisc, 16mm, and even Betamax when they run across the rare garage sale find. Whenever he gets the chance, Mike rolls his own movies with a vintage Super 8 movie camera. He is webmaster of www.super8filmmaking.com, an Internet gathering place for small-gauge filmmakers.

Glenn Erickson (GE) is a film editor and writer with a website called DVD Savant (www.dvdtalk.com/dvdsavant/spec.html). In addition to editing DVD documentaries, he promotes film restorations and consults on film history for studios.

Darren Gross (DG) is a Los Angeles–based writer, film preservationist, and researcher. Born and raised in New Jersey (the tollbooth state!), he studied film production, writing, and preservation (thanks to professor William K. Everson) at New York University. He has contributed reviews and feature articles to *Video Watchdog Magazine* and *Worlds of Horror,* and is currently composing liner notes for upcoming DVD releases. Mr. Gross also contributed chapters to *The Dark Shadows Movie Book* and the *Dark Shadows Almanac Millennium Edition.* In 1999 after a two year–long, globe-spanning search, he recovered the long lost "director's cut" of *Night of Dark Shadows.* He has worked as a publicist in the Home Video arena and is currently searching for the lost footage from *House of Dark Shadows* and other films. Darren has just recently discovered some long-lost footage from another cult film, but can't reveal it yet. (What a tease!) For more information on his restoration projects, go to: www.nightofdarkshadows.com

When he is not designing and producing award-winning computer games, **Guido Henkel (GH)** spends most of his time working on www.DVDReview.com, one of the most popular DVD information websites on the Internet. He also writes for a variety of industry and consumer publications.

Donald Liebenson (DL) is a Chicago writer who writes about home entertainment for the *Chicago Tribune,* the *Los Angeles Times,* Amazon.com, and other publications.

Mike Long (ML) has a Bachelor's Degree in Film Studies from the University of North Carolina, where he began reviewing movies years ago. He also has a Master's Degree in Counseling from the University of North Carolina at Charlotte, and is a Licensed Professional Counselor. Mike has been reviewing films for DVDReview.com since March of 1999.

Jim Olenski (JO) is the owner of Thomas Video (www.thomasvideo.com) in metro Detroit, a fabulous video store that specializes in hard-to-find, cult, foreign, independent, and classic film on VHS, DVD, and laserdisc. Jim is a frequent contributor to the *VideoHound,* and his column, "Videophile," appears weekly in *Real Detroit.* Jim's pseudo-elite and sometimes abrasive critical style spawned from the same punk ethic demonstrated in his 25 years as lead guitarist for the Detroit band Cinecyde. Jim is grateful for the opportunity to write for this book, because it gave him the excuse to buy a really expensive home theatre system.

Ed Peters (EP) has a bachelor's degree in English from California State University, Northridge. His professional experience includes more than ten years in the electronic public relations industry, specializing in satellite transmission and video production. Ed was there at "the beginning," working with home video companies to promote the first "sell through" titles. The real breakthrough occurred in 1988 when he bought his first laserdisc player. (Despite upgrading several times since, his creditors still have vivid memories of the purchase.) Since March 2000, Ed has been a regular contributor to www.dvdreview.com.

Michael Pflug (MP) is a Detroit-area Internet lackey with a degree in Political Science—making him uniquely qualified to ramble on about DVDs in a concise yet indecipherable style. When not reviewing the shiny discs for DVDReview.com he can be found chasing a two-year-old, recalibrating his home theatre system for the umpteenth time, and attempting to break the land speed record in a mini-van.

Jack Sanderson (JAS) has written entertainment reviews and articles for America Online's *Entertainment Asylum,* AOL's *Kid's Asylum, Hero Magazine,* and *The Independent Review Site.* In live theatre he has made his living as an actor, and has dallied as a producer, writer, and award-winning director. Jack is currently undergoing aversion therapy for his film addiction by being force-fed bad popcorn.

Stephen Spurling (SS) lives in Chicago.

Phil Thron (PT) is a New York–based actor and filmmaker whose work is often seen in various theatre and film festivals in Manhattan. He has supplemented his raging movie addiction by various contributions to DVD Review.com, which include reviews and an extensive stint as news editor.

In the dark days before home video, **Ralph Tribbey (RJT)** brought *The Rocky Horror Picture Show* to weekly midnight screenings in a chain of small theatres that he owned and operated in Southern California. More recently, he has served in various capacities within the entertainment industry. On the publishing side of the business, he has served as managing editor for *American Video Monthly,* editor of *Video $ell Magazine,* and is currently editor and publisher of *The DVD Release Report.* On the manufacturing end of the business, he was senior vice president of marketing for West Coast Video Duplicating and is currently a consultant for Technicolor.

Michael J. Tyrkus (MJT) is an award-winning independent filmmaker, author, and editor. He has co-written and directed more than a dozen short films. As a writer and editor specializing in biographical and critical reference sources in literature and film, he has contributed to numerous references, including *The International Dictionary of Films and Filmmakers Vol 1: Films, Twentieth-Century Young Adult Writers,* and *The St. James Film Directors Encyclopedia,* edited by Andrew Sarris. He is editor of *Gay & Lesbian Biography* and co-editor of *Outstanding Lives: Profiles of Lesbians and Gay Men.* He has also served as in-house project editor for and contributor to the *The St. James Women Filmmakers Encyclopedia.* He is co-founder of Lamb-Kiss Productions and founder of CityScene Productions.

Production Editor
Carol A. Schwartz

Editor without Whom Nothing Would Be Accomplished
Chris Tomassini

The VideoHound Litter
Erin Bealmer, Christa Brelin, Joann Cerrito, Jim Craddock, Stephen Cusack, Miranda Ferrara, Kris Hart, Melissa Hill, and Margaret Mazurkiewicz

The Big Giant Hound Head
Peter Gareffa

Design Hound
Pamela A.E. Galbreath

Techno Hound
Wayne Fong

Proofreader and Former Hound
Beth Fhaner

Guy Who Spent a Lot of Time on the Phone Checking Facts
Jim Olenski

Production Hounds
Rita Wimberly, Evi Seoud, Mary Beth Trimper, and Dorothy Maki

Hype Hounds
Lauri Taylor and PJ Butland

Special Hound Markets
Inez Torbert

Typesetting
Marco Di Vita of the Graphix Group

This book attempts to review every feature-length film that was released on DVD from roughly June 2000 to June 2001. Following the criteria used for *VideoHound's Golden Movie Retriever* and the first *DVD Guide,* we don't review works that are shorter than feature length (less than one hour, for practical purposes). We don't review music discs or adult films. We have included cartoon collections and Japanese anime, along with a few worthy TV shows. The book is meant for people who like to watch movies and want to see them in the best form possible.

Each review begins with a brief plot synopsis and comment on the artistic quality of the film. Following that are remarks—some detailed, some cursory—on the technical details of image and sound. We then give each disc two ratings: one for content and one for presentation. That's something new for the VideoHound, but we—the editors, reviewers, and I—feel that the medium demands it. To explain: the content rating is based on the traditional 🦴🦴🦴🦴 to woof scale that judges the quality of the storytelling and filmmaking:

🦴🦴🦴🦴   Excellent: One of the best of its kind. You want to own this disc.

🦴🦴🦴½   Very good: Prime rental material. Perhaps worth owning.

🦴🦴🦴   Good: Well worth watching.

🦴🦴   Average: For fans of the genre or star.

🦴   Poor: Make sure the scan button is working properly.

woof   You have been warned.

The technical rating refers to the quality of image, sound, and extras:

🦴🦴🦴🦴   Excellent: Wow! The image approaches or even surpasses theatrical quality. Audio is equally spectacular. Delightful extras are imaginative and abundant.

🦴🦴🦴½   Very good: The image is noticeably sharper and brighter than videotape. The sound is crisp and clear. All the extras you could reasonably expect are present.

🦴🦴🦴   Good: Image and sound are somewhat better than tape but not really special. Extras may or may not be present.

🦴🦴   Average: Image and sound are not noticeably superior to VHS tape. Extras are minimal.

🦴   Poor: Image and sound are substandard, due either to a poor original or transfer. Extras are probably absent.

woof   What *were* they thinking?

(Other half-bone ratings indicate the individual reviewer's mixed emotions, second and third thoughts, and free-floating equivocation.)

Each review ends with a listing of the extra features, if any, included on the disc. We also comment on those extras within the review when it's appropriate.

The various sound options available on many DVDs can be confusing and intimidating to those who are not familiar with the medium. This explanation, created by Image Entertainment and included with many discs, illustrates and explains the most popular systems (used with permission):

Dolby Digital Mono

This program features a mono soundtrack encoded to an AC-3 bitstream. When played through Dolby Digital equipment, sound will be heard from the center channel speaker only.

Dolby Digital Stereo

This program features a stereo soundtrack encoded to an AC-3 bitstream. When played through Dolby Digital equipment, sound will be heard from the front left and front right speakers only.

Dolby Digital Surround

This program features a matrixed Surround soundtrack encoded to an AC-3 bitstream. When played through Dolby Digital equipment, sound will be heard from all five system speakers. The Surround information will be discrete monophonic.

Dolby Digital 4.0

This program features a discrete four-channel soundtrack encoded to an AC-3 bitstream. When played through Dolby Digital equipment, sound will be heard from all five system speakers. The Surround information will be discrete monophonic.

Dolby Digital 5.0

This program features a discrete five-channel soundtrack encoded to an AC-3 bitstream. When played through Dolby Digital

equipment, discrete sound will be heard from all five system speakers.

Dolby Digital 5.1

This program features a discrete 5.1-channel soundtrack encoded to an AC-3 bitstream. When played through Dolby Digital equipment, discrete sound will be heard from all five system speakers and a subwoofer.

PCM

This program features an uncompressed digital stereo soundtrack for improved fidelity. When played, discrete stereo sound will be heard from the front right and front left speakers.

DTS

This program features a discrete 5.1-channel soundtrack and must be played through DTS-capable equipment. When played through DTS equipment, sound will be heard from all five system speakers and a subwoofer.

The more advanced stereo Surround systems, which require extra equipment, add a dramatic dimension to newer films, but even without additional speakers and amplifiers, digital sound can be an improvement, particularly when heard through good headphones. (A headphone jack is available on many DVD players.) The soundtracks of some older films still contain static and hiss. Others have been cleaned up admirably.

Format and aspect ratios generally fall into three main categories: Full frame is the general dimensions of your TV screen (usually 1.33:1); if the original film was a different (usually wider) aspect ratio, this picture has probably been cropped or "panned and scanned." Letterboxed video offers a wide-screen presentation, with black bands across the top and bottom of the picture, to better approximate the original aspect ratio of the theatrical presentation. The anamorphic format, like letterboxing, perserves the widescreen ratio, but with higher quality. In this book, the specific aspect ratios are provided when available.

While we address the technical questions with each title, we don't obsess over them. This book is for people who like movies. Anyone who discovers the wonderful sleeper *Best Laid Plans* and criticizes the image quality is missing the point.

Like videophiles everywhere, reviewers have different tastes, different equipment, different budgets, different living arrangements. It would be wonderful if all of us—and I include readers with reviewers here—could have state-of-the-art "reference" systems like the ones used by the writers at *Widescreen Review* magazine. Those are true home theatres with high-quality widescreen monitors, powerful Surround sound systems, and, I suspect, really comfortable chairs. But that's not the case with us, and so we do not presume to make definitive judgments. Having played many of the same discs on two different DVD players through the same monitor, I know that no two systems produce precisely the same image and sound.

When you watch a disc at home, your experience may not be the same as our reviewer's. You may see more flaws or fewer. If you enjoy a movie, you're likely to be forgiving. If you don't like it, the errors are going to jump off the screen at you.

In the end, we experience films in our minds. Yes, we use our eyes and ears, but intellect and emotion are just as important.

The various reviewers are identified by their initials at the end of each review. (Please see their thumbnail biographies on page xxv.) As a group, they are superbly qualified for the job. Each of them has written about film and video for other publications, and each brings different priorities to DVD. For example, JO, who belongs to a band, pays more attention to sound than most others. DG is particularly interested in film restoration and is careful to note differences between actual running times and the times claimed by the box copy and/or other reviewers.

The one quality the reviewers share is a love of film.

Most of the entries were written from review copies of DVDs provided by the studios, but not all of them were willing to make their products available. Jim Olenski lent many discs from his store, Thomas Video, in metro Detroit (www.thomasvideo.com). Other reviewers worked from their personal libraries, and, when necessary, we rented and bought discs wherever we could find them.

Readers should pay little attention to the prices listed here. They are the retail prices suggested by the distributors. DVDs are often put on sale and, after their initial release, catalogue titles are routinely marked down.

Finally, I must admit that we weren't able to get to everything. Since the beginning of the DVD business, production and distribution have been troublesome. Even though the industry is only a few years old, it is extremely difficult to find some titles. Several discs have gone out of print after having been released in small numbers. Others have been announced but never delivered.

With each volume of the *DVD Guide,* we try to fill in the blanks and correct oversights. The book will never be perfect; we try to make it better every time out of the gate.

—MM

Alphabetization

Titles are arranged on a word-by-word basis, including articles and prepositions. Leading articles (A, An, The) are ignored in English-language titles; the equivalent foreign articles are not ignored (because so many people—not you, of course—don't recognize them as articles); thus, *The Abyss* appears in the As, but *L'Enfer* appears in the Ls. Acronyms appear alphabetically as if regular words; for example, *D.O.A.* is alphabetized as "DOA." Common abbreviations in titles file as if they were spelled out, so *Dr. Strangelove* will be alphabetized as "Doctor Strangelove" and *Mr. Nice Guy* as "Mister Nice Guy." Movie titles with numbers, such as *2001: A Space Odyssey,* are alphabetized as if the number were spelled out—so Kubrick's classic would appear in the Ts as if it were "Two Thousand and One: A Space Odyssey." Proper names in titles are alphabetized beginning with the individual's first name; for instance, *Richard Pryor: Live on the Strip* is under "R;" *Stephen King's The Tommyknockers* is under "S."

Country of Origin Codes

The country of origin codes indicate the country or countries in which a film was produced or financed. A listing of films by country may also be found in the **Category Index** under the appropriate term below.

AL	Algerian	IR	Irish
AR	Argentinian	IS	Israeli
AT	Austrian	IT	Italian
AU	Australian	JP	Japanese
BE	Belgian	KO	Korean
BR	Brazilian	LI	Lithuanian
GB	British	MA	Macedonian
CA	Canadian	MX	Mexican
CH	Chinese	NZ	New Zealand
CL	Colombian	NI	Nicaraguan
CU	Cuban	NO	Norwegian
CZ	Czech	PL	Polish
DK	Danish	PT	Portuguese
NL	Dutch	RU	Russian
PH	Filipino	SA	South African
FI	Finnish	SP	Spanish
FR	French	SW	Swedish
GE	German	SI	Swiss
GR	Greek	TU	Turkish
HK	Hong Kong	TW	Taiwanese
HU	Hungarian	VT	Vietnamese
IC	Icelandic	VZ	Venezuelan
IN	Indian	YU	Yugoslavian
IA	Iranian		

Abbreviations

No detailed technical explanations here, just a quick reference list (with a few literal definitions, for the really curious reader) for abbreviations and acronyms used in this book.

AC3	audio coding algorithm (that is, Dolby Digital)
AKA	also known as
B	black and white
B&W	black and white
C	color
CAP:	Closed captions:
Cat.	catalog (number)
CD	compact disc
CD-I	compact disc—interactive
CE	Collector's Edition
CGI	computer-generated image
CS	Collector's Series
D.P.	director of photography (cinematographer)
DC	Director's Cut
DD	Dolby Digital
DS	Dolby Surround
DTS	Digital Theater Systems (a surround audio system)
DVD	digital versatile disc
DVD-ROM	digital versatile disc—read only memory
f/x	effects
HDTV	high-definition television
LANG:	Language(s):
LD	laserdisc
min.	minute
mm.	millimeter
MPAA	Motion Picture Association of America
NOM:	Nominations:
NSL	no standard list (price)
NYR	not yet reviewed
PCM	pulse code modulation (a sound format)
RSDL	reverse spiral dual-layer
SE	Special Edition
sf	science fiction
SUB:	Subtitles:
THX	Tomlinson Holman experiment (an audio system certification)
UPC	Universal Product Code (number)
VHS	video helical scan (the predominate videotape format)

Sample Review

Each review contains up to 25 tidbits of information, as enumerated below. Please realize that we faked a bit of info in this review for demonstration purposes.

1. Title; some titles have the designation SE (Special Edition), CE (Collector's Edition), CS (Collector's Series), or DC (Director's Cut), as indicated by the distributor

2. Synopsis/review

3. Byline of reviewer; see **Contributors,** p. xxv

4. Alternative title (we faked it here)

5. Critical rating of the movie (♫ to ♫♫♫♫ or woof, ♫♫♫♫ being the ultimate praise)

6. Technical rating of DVD image, sound, and extras (using the same scale); DVDs that were not yet available for review are noted "NYR"

7. Distributor of the DVD

8. Distributor catalog number

9. Distributor UPC

10. Format and aspect ratio (more than one option may be offered)

11. Sound (again, more than one are possible)

12. Price of DVD

13. Type of DVD case

14. Language(s)

15. Subtitle(s), if any

16. Closed captions, if any

17. Special added features of the DVD

18. Other information about the DVD

19. Year movie was released

20. MPAA rating

21. Length in minutes

22. Black and white (B) or Color (C)

23. Country of origin (if other than the U.S.); see previous page for codes

24. Credits, including cast, voice cast (**V:**), director (**D:**), screenwriter (**W:**), cinematographer (**C:**), and music composer/lyricist (**M:**)

25. Awards and nominations

---

❶ Clerks

❷ Day in the life of a bored convenience store clerk (O'Halloran) and his best friend Randal, who mans the video store next door. Nothing much actually happens—other than a constant parade of crazies, a hockey game on the roof, and even a little necrophilia. Lots of scuzzy fun and non-stop offensive (and hilarious) dialogue. First-time director Smith (Silent Bob in the movie) based this low-budget ($27,575) film on his four years of tormenting customers at the convenience store where he shot on location. The big plus is that the DVD offers all the extras that first appeared on the laserdisc, including the alternate ending and deleted scenes. Unfortunately the video itself looks far worse than the VHS tape. There's so much grain that on most movies it would be unbearable; but because the film's style is so deliberately rough, that's not too aggravating. The contrast and brightness levels are good (about the same as the laserdisc), and the sound is very good, in fact almost too good when the music cuts come in. The bottom line is that, despite the picture, this DVD is worth adding to your collection even if its just for the supplemental material. ❸ —JO ❹ **AKA:** Kevin Smith's Clerks.
❺ **Movie:** ♫♫½ ❻ **DVD:** ♫♫
❼ Miramax ❽ (Cat # 17365, ❾ UPC # 717951002716). ❿ Widescreen (1.85:1) letterboxed. ⓫ Dolby Surround. ⓬ $34.98.
⓭ Keepcase. ⓮ *LANG:* English.
⓯ SUB: French, Spanish. ⓰ CAP: English.
⓱ FEATURES: 18 chapter links - Theatrical trailer - Alternate ending - Deleted scenes - Commentary: director Smith and cast members - Soul Asylum music video. ⓲ Also available as part of a "Kevin Smith" two-pack boxed set.
⓳ 1995 ⓴ (R) ㉑ 89m/ ㉒ B
㉓ US ㉔ Brian O'Halloran, Jef Anderson, Marilyn Ghiglliotti, Lisa Spoonhauer, Jason Mewes, Kevin Smith; *D:* Kevin Smith; *W:* Kevin Smith; *C:* David Klein; *A:* David Klein; *M:* Scott Angley. ㉕ Sundance Film Festival '94: Filmmakers Trophy; *NOM:* Independent Spirit Awards '95: Best First Feature, Debut Performance (Anderson), First Screenplay.

Abbott and Costello Meet Frankenstein

Bud and Lou are railroad baggage clerks in Florida where strange crates arrive for the wax museum. Dracula (Lugosi) wants to revive Frankenstein's monster (Strange) by giving him Lou's brain! Lawrence Talbot (Chaney Jr.), AKA The Wolfman, says no. It's all played for laughs, making this one of the best horror comedies, with the emphasis definitely on comedy and some cool animated effects. Universal has done its usual excellent job in bringing the title to DVD with a nice "making of" featurette about the comedians' later screen work. The image captures the fine black-and-white cinematography that the studio could create even for such modest vehicles. —MM *AKA:* Abbott and Costello Meet the Ghosts; Meet the Ghosts; The Brain of Frankenstein.
Movie: ♫♫♫ *DVD:* ♫♫♫½
Universal Studios Home Video (Cat #20572, UPC #025192057229). Full frame. Dolby Digital Mono. $26.98. Keepcase. *LANG:* English. *SUB:* French. *CAP:* English. *FEATURES:* 18 chapter links • "Abbott and Costello Meet the Monsters" featurette • Commentary: film historian Gergory W. Mank • Production photographs.
1948 83m/B Bud Abbott, Lou Costello, Lon Chaney Jr., Bela Lugosi, Glenn Strange, Lenore Aubert, Jane Randolph, Frank Ferguson, Charles Bradstreet, Howard Negley, Clarence Straight; *D:* Charles T. Barton; *W:* John Grant, Robert Lees, Frederic Rinaldo; *C:* Charles Van Enger; *M:* Frank Skinner; *V:* Vincent Price.

Abilene Town

Please see review of *Errol Flynn / Randolph Scott Double Feature.*
Movie: ♫♫♫
1946 90m/B Randolph Scott, Ann Dvorak, Edgar Buchanan, Rhonda Fleming, Lloyd Bridges; *D:* Edwin L. Marin; *W:* Harold Shumate; *C:* Archie Stout.

The Abominable Dr. Phibes

In Vincent Price's long and varied career, this may be his most enjoyable role. As a vengeful 1920s mad doctor, he's droll and virtually silent. More important to the film, he's got a fine, funny script and excellent co-stars to work with. Though Terry-Thomas, Hugh Griffith, and Joseph Cotten don't have as much to do, they contribute substantially. Add in terrific sets, costumes, jazzy music, props, and even some fair scares amid the laughs. Robert Fuest (veteran of many episodes of the original *Avengers* TV series) directs with a confident, wry tone and gives new meaning to the term "acid rain." Yes, that's Caroline Munro as the late Mrs. Phibes. Simply a delight for fans of Grand Guignol comedy. The DVD boasts a superb image. Even dim interiors reveal a fine level of detail. Mono sound is fine. It's far superior to the speaker at the drive-in where I first saw this wonder decades ago. —MM *AKA:* Dr. Phibes; The Curse of Dr. Phibes.
Movie: ♫♫♫½ *DVD:* ♫♫♫½
MGM Home Entertainment (Cat #1001540, UPC #027616858511). Widescreen (1.85:1) anamorphic. Dolby Digital Mono. $19.98. Keepcase. *LANG:* English; French; Spanish. *SUB:* French; Spanish. *CAP:* English. *FEATURES:* Trailer • 16 chapter links.
1971 (PG-13) 90m/C *GB* Vincent Price, Joseph Cotten, Hugh Griffith, Terry-Thomas, Virginia North, Susan Travers, Alex Scott, Caroline Munro, Peter Jeffrey, Peter Gilmore, Edward Burnham, Sean Bury, David Hutcheson, Maurice Kaufmann; *D:* Robert Fuest; *W:* William Goldstein, James Whiton; *C:* Norman Warwick; *M:* Basil Kirchin, Jack Nathan.

The Abominable Snowman

Underrated Hammer horror finds adventurer Tom Friend (Tucker), Dr. John Rollason (Cushing), and guide Ed Shelley (Brown) searching for the legendary Yeti. The harsh conditions cause the explorers to lose their grip and, after Shelley shoots a Yeti, Rollason suspects that the creatures can practice mind control. Anchor Bay's DVD is for most people the first opportunity to really see this movie. (The frequent AMC airings of a pan-and-scanned American print that cropped characters and scenery offscreen made the film look cramped and insubstantial.) This disc has attractive menus and the unexpected bonus of 16:9 enhancement on the Hammerscope image. It's not perfect; even with the widescreen formatting some shots look a bit soft, especially at the beginning. The less said about the feeble World of Hammer documentary the better. Redeeming the extras is an engrossing full-length commentary by director Guest and author Kneale, similar to the one on *Quatermass 2*. —MM/GE *AKA:* The Abominable Snowman of the Himalayas.
Movie: ♫♫♫ *DVD:* ♫♫♫
Anchor Bay (Cat #11076). Widescreen (2.35:1) anamorphic. $29.98. Keepcase. *LANG:* English. *FEATURES:* Commentary: Nigel Kneale, Val Guest • "World of Hammer" documentary.
1957 91m/B *GB* Peter Cushing, Forrest Tucker, Robert Brown, Richard Wattis, Maureen Connell; *D:* Val Guest; *W:* Nigel Kneale; *C:* Arthur Grant; *M:* Humphrey Searle.

The Addams Family

This one-joke movie may be short on plot, but it's filled with the graveyard humor that made Charles Addams so justly famous. The casting is truly inspired, and the relationship between Morticia (Huston) and Gomez (Julia) is so believably intense that it pulls the story over any rough spots. Ricci and Lloyd are equally excellent. The DVD presentation is powerful and stark, creating a great impression from the first seconds. With solid blacks that make the shadows of the movie more looming, and powerful highlights that never bleed. The color reproduction is faithful to the original film. The audio mix creates a wide sound field with crisp, but unexaggerated and undistorted high ends, and a good, natural-sounding frequency response. —MM/GH

Movie: 🎬🎬½ **DVD:** 🎬🎬🎬
Paramount Home Video (Cat #326897). Widescreen (1.85:1) letterboxed. Dolby Digital 5.1 Surround Stereo; Dolby Digital Stereo. $29.99. Keepcase. *LANG:* English. *FEATURES:* Theatrical trailers.
1991 (PG-13) 102m/C Anjelica Huston, Raul Julia, Christopher Lloyd, Dan Hedaya, Elizabeth Wilson, Judith Malina, Carel Struycken, Dana Ivey, Paul Benedict, Christina Ricci, Jimmy Workman, Christopher Hunt, John Franklin; *Cameos:* Marc Shaiman; *D:* Barry Sonnenfeld; *W:* Caroline Thompson, Larry Thompson; *C:* Owen Roizman; *M:* Marc Shaiman. *AWARDS:* Golden Raspberries '91: Worst Song ("Addams Groove"); *NOM:* Oscars '91: Costume Des.

The Adjuster

Videophiles tend to either love or hate Egoyan, and this early work is no exception. Insurance adjuster Noah Render's (Koteas) clients look to him for all sorts of comfort, so much so that his own identity becomes a blurred reflection of their tragedies. His wife Hera (Khanjian, Egoyan's wife) is a film censor who secretly videotapes the pornography she watches at work. Their carefully organized lives are invaded by Bubba (Chaykin) and Mimi (Rose), a wealthy couple who pass themselves off as filmmakers wanting to use the Render house as a movie set. Those familiar with *The Sweet Hereafter* and *Exotica* will not be surprised by the deliberate pace, the surreal sexiness, and the challenging approach to the material. Egoyan does not make flashy films and so the visual flaws—artifacts in panning shots across broad areas of raw earth, aliasing on bright lines—are unimportant. Surround is used effectively in the fire scenes. —MM

Movie: 🎬🎬🎬 **DVD:** 🎬🎬½
MGM Home Entertainment (Cat #1001732, UPC #027616860323). Widescreen (2.35:1) anamorphic. Dolby Digital Surround. $24.99. Keepcase. *LANG:* English. *SUB:* French; Spanish. *FEATURES:* Trailer ✦ 16 chapter links.
1991 (R) 102m/C *CA* Elias Koteas, Arsinee Khanjian, Maury Chaykin, Gabrielle Rose, David Hemblen, Jennifer Dale, Don McKellar, Raoul Trujillo; *D:* Atom Egoyan; *W:* Atom Egoyan; *C:* Paul Sarossy; *M:* Mychael Danna. *AWARDS:* Toronto-City '91: Canadian Feature Film.

The Adventures of Ichabod and Mr. Toad

Disney's wonderful animated versions of Kenneth Grahame's *The Wind in the Willows* and Washington Irving's *Legend of Sleepy Hollow* make a delightful transition

to DVD. Rathbone narrates the story of Mr. Toad, who defends himself in court after being charged with car theft. Crosby provides the voices for *Sleepy Hollow*. Only the lightest signs of wear are evident. Colors are very bright for these stories that will never lose their appeal. Add in an extra cartoon, "Lonesome Ghosts," with Mickey, Donald, and Goofy and you've got a genuine winner. —MM

Movie: 🎬🎬🎬½ **DVD:** 🎬🎬🎬½
Buena Vista Home Entertainment (Cat #19581, UPC #717951008466). Full frame. Dolby Digital Mono. $29.99. Keepcase. *LANG:* English; French; Spanish. *CAP:* English. *FEATURES:* 24 chapter links ✦ Legend of Sleepy Hollow DVD storybook ✦ Mr. Toad game ✦ Sing-along song "Lonesome Ghosts" cartoon ✦ 24 chapter links.
1949 68m/C *D:* James Nelson Algar, Clyde Geronimi; *W:* Winston Hibler, Erdman Penner, Joe Rinaldi, Ted Sears, Homer Brightman, Harry Reeves; *M:* Oliver Wallace; *V:* Eric Blore, Pat O'Malley, Jack Kinney, Bing Crosby; *Nar:* Basil Rathbone.

The Adventures of Priscilla, Queen of the Desert [MGM]

Quirky down-under musical comedy follows two drag queens (Weaving and Pearce) and a transsexual (Stamp) across the Australian Outback on their way to a gig in a small resort town. Priscilla is the name of their bus. Along the way, they encounter—and perform for—the usual assortment of colorful local characters. Strong performances, particularly by Stamp, rise above the clichés in what is basically a bitchy cross-dressing road movie that celebrates drag as art and the nonconformity of its heroes. Unfortunately, two of the film's most basic visual motifs fare very poorly on DVD. Tracking shots across the sun-baked desert are riddled with artifacts. Shots of the bright metal of the bus break up into excessive aliasing. The big flamboyant moment in Chapter 12 is virtually unwatchable. For those who love disco and Abba, the soundtrack is superb. For all others.... —MM

Movie: 🎬🎬🎬 **DVD:** 🎬🎬
MGM Home Entertainment (Cat #908409, UPC #027616840929). Widescreen letterboxed. Dolby Digital Surround Stereo. $24.99. Keepcase. *LANG:* English; French. *SUB:* French; Spanish. *CAP:* English. *FEATURES:* 32 chapter links.
1994 (R) 102m/C *AU* Terence Stamp, Hugo Weaving, Guy Pearce, Bill Hunter, Sarah Chadwick, Mark Holmes, Julia Cortez, Rebel Russell, June Marie Bennett, Alan Dargin, Al Clark, Margaret Pomeranz; *D:* Stephan Elliott; *W:* Stephan Elliott; *C:* Brian J. Breheny; *M:* Guy Gross. *AWARDS:* Oscars '94: Costume Des.; Australian Film Inst. '94: Costume Des; *NOM:* Australian Film Inst. '94: Actor (Stamp), Actor (Weaving), Cinematog., Director (Elliott), Film, Orig. Screenplay; Golden Globes '95: Actor—Mus./Comedy (Stamp), Film—

Mus./Comedy; Writers Guild '94: Orig. Screenplay.

The Adventures of Rocky & Bullwinkle

Thirty-five years after the cancellation of their TV show, Boris (Alexander), Natasha (Russo), and Fearless Leader (De Niro) are pulled out of the cartoon world by a film executive (Garofalo). As Fearless Leader plans the domination of the world by subjecting the masses to inane, zombifying TV programs, Rocky and Bullwinkle are called upon by a youthful FBI agent (Perabo) to save the world. This truly awful film features embarrassing, painful performances by all involved (De Niro has rarely been worse) and an insipid, annoying script. The opening animated sequence is passable, but the film plummets afterward and never regains anything even close to mediocrity. Several stars (Goldberg, Crystal, Goodman, Winters) appear in lame cameo roles. One wishes they hadn't. The disc is bright with strong colors and a very sharp image, but it shows slight grain throughout. The score is particularly well-recorded and the Surround track is excellent. The featurette is a fascinating artifact and well worth watching. Rarely have a cast and crew been so completely unaware of the disaster they were making. Believe it or not, the trailer actually redubs some of the lame jokes in an attempt to make the film look better. It doesn't. —DG

Movie: 🎬 **DVD:** 🎬🎬🎬
Universal Studios Home Video (Cat #20927, UPC #025192092725). Widescreen (1.85:1) anamorphic. DTS Surround 5.1; Dolby Digital 5.1. $26.98. Keepcase. *LANG:* English; French. *SUB:* English. *FEATURES:* 18 chapter links ✦ "Making of" featurette ✦ Cast and crew bios ✦ Production notes ✦ Theatrical trailers ✦ DVD-ROM: voice-activated computer software ✦ Insert card with chapter listing.
2000 (PG) 88m/C Robert De Niro, Jason Alexander, Rene Russo, Janeane Garofalo, Randy Quaid, Piper Perabo, Carl Reiner, Jonathan Winters, John Goodman, Kenan Thompson, Kel Mitchell, James Rebhorn, David Alan Grier, Norman Lloyd, Jon Polito, Whoopi Goldberg, Billy Crystal, Don Novello, Harrison Young, Dian Bachar, Paget Brewster; *D:* Des McAnuff; *W:* Kenneth Lonergan; *C:* Thomas Ackerman; *M:* Mark Mothersbaugh; *V:* June Foray, Keith Scott. *AWARDS: NOM:* Golden Raspberries '00: Worst Support. Actress (Russo).

The Adventures of Sherlock Holmes

This disc contains four episodes of the acclaimed British television series: "A Scandal in Bohemia" (with Gayle Hunnicutt as Irene Adler), "The Dancing Men," "The Naval Treaty," and "The Solitary Cyclist." The series's production values are very good, but the real appeal lies in the performances of the leads. In appearance and attitude, Jeremy Brett is second only to Basil Rathbone, and to my taste, his interpretation is often more carefully shaded. David Burke's Watson is closer to the literary original than Nigel Bruce's comic figure. Unfortunately, the image is far from perfect, most obviously in the daylight exteriors. Heavy grain and artifacts swim annoyingly in the background. Interiors and night scenes are much better. Sound is very good and the original elements have been well preserved. —MM

Movie: ♪♪½ **DVD:** ♪♪♪½
MPI Home Video (Cat #DVD7065, UPC #030306706528). Full frame. Dolby Digital Mono. $19.98. Keepcase. LANG: English. SUB: English; French; Spanish. FEATURES: 49 chapter links ☞ Series promo ☞ Photo gallery ☞ Thumbnail bios of Brett and Conan Doyle.
1985 220m/C GB Jeremy Brett, David Burke.

An Affair of Love

French love story sounds like Last Tango in Paris but really owes more to sex, lies and videotape. A nameless woman (Baye) arranges to meet a nameless man (Lopez) for afternoon sexual encounters in a hotel. Virtually all of the physical action takes place behind a closed door. The point is emotional and so, in after-the-fact monologues, she talks about what she did. Though this is not a visually demanding film, the softish image is consistently well realized. Surround effects are minimal. —MM AKA: Une Liaison Pornographique.

Movie: ♪♪½ **DVD:** ♪♪♪
New Line Home Video (Cat #N5168, UPC #794043516825). Widescreen (2.35:1) anamorphic; full frame. Dolby Digital 5.1 Surround Stereo; Dolby Digital Stereo. $24.98. Snapper. LANG: French. SUB: English. FEATURES: Talent files ☞ 12 chapter links ☞ Trailer.
2000 (R) 80m/C FR BE LU Nathalie Baye, Sergei Lopez, Paul Pavel; **D:** Frederic Fonteyne; **W:** Philippe Blasband; **C:** Virginie Saint-Martin; **M:** Andre Dziezuk, Marc Mergen, Jeannot Sanavia.

An Affair to Remember

McCarey remakes his own Love Affair, with less success. Nightclub singer Kerr and wealthy bachelor Grant discover love on an ocean liner and agree to meet six months later on top of the Empire State Building to see if their feelings are the same. Not as good as the original, but a winner of a fairy tale just the same. Notable for causing many viewers to sob uncontrollably. Affair was gathering dust on the video rental shelves until Sleepless in Seattle used it as a plot device. In 1994 real-life couple Warren Beatty and Annette Bening attempted a third Love Affair remake. For an older film, the disc is pretty sharp. The colors are another matter, ranging from weak to average, with the stronger colors bleeding a bit. The tint is never quite right with everything from fleshtones to hair colors being way off. Too bad; a romance like

this is always more enjoyable with warmer colors and the right hues. —JO

Movie: ♪♪½ **DVD:** ♪♪
20th Century Fox Home Entertainment (Cat #2000030, UPC #024543000303). Widescreen (2.35:1) letterboxed. Dolby Digital Stereo. $24.98. Keepcase. LANG: English; French. SUB: English; Spanish. CAP: English. FEATURES: 20 chapter links ☞ Theatrical trailer.
1957 115m/C Cary Grant, Deborah Kerr, Richard Denning, Cathleen Nesbitt, Neva Patterson, Robert Q. Lewis, Fortunio Bonanova, Matt Moore, Nora Marlowe, Sarah Selby; **D:** Leo McCarey; **W:** Leo McCarey, Delmer Daves, Donald Ogden Stewart; **C:** Milton Krasner; **M:** Hugo Friedhofer. AWARDS: NOM: Oscars '57: Cinematog., Costume Des., Song ("An Affair to Remember"), Score.

Affairs of Anatol

The box copy states that this silent film is adapted "from the Author of Eyes Wide Shut," and the two films tell essentially the same story of a husband who is tempted to cheat on his wife but doesn't. In this case, Anatol Spencer (Reid) casts his eye on an old flame (Hawley), a conniving country woman (Ayres), and, most memorably, Satan Synne (Daniels), whom he meets at the Devil's Cloister (sign above the door: "He Who Would Sup with the Devil Must Have a Golden Spoon."). Meanwhile, his wife Vivian (Swanson) is making plans of her own. There is a fair amount of snow on the tinted images, but overall, the film is amazingly well preserved. The new score by Brian Benison is true to the era. —MM

Movie: ♪♪♪ **DVD:** ♪♪♪
Image Entertainment (Cat #ID9225DSDVD, UPC #014381922523). Full frame. Dolby Digital Stereo. $24.99. Snapper. FEATURES: 16 chapter links.
1921 117m/B Wallace Reid, Gloria Swanson, Bebe Daniels, Wanda (Petit) Hawley, Agnes Ayres, Monte Blue, Theodore Roberts, Elliott Dexter; **D:** Cecil B. DeMille; **W:** Beulah Marie Dix; **C:** Karl Struss, Alvin Wyckoff.

AFI's 100 Years, 100 Stars

This CBS special is a pleasant little stroll down memory lane, though the title is somewhat misleading. It's really about 50 favorite older stars (25 men and 25 women) from the "classic era" (as narrator Shirley Temple Black puts it) who are ranked according to their "popularity and historical context." Ava Gardner and William Holden come in at #25; Humphrey Bogart and Katherine Hepburn share #1. Clips of the 50 "classic" stars are introduced by 50 relative whippersnappers. Neither image nor sound is extraordinary. Both are about the same as the original television broadcast. The main value of the disc is its accessibility. Each star gets a chapter. —MM

Movie: ♪♪♪ **DVD:** ♪♪½

Image Entertainment (Cat #ID9618AFDVD, UPC #014381961829). Full frame; widescreen. Dolby Digital Stereo. $24.99. Snapper. LANG: English. FEATURES: 52 links.
1999 135m/C D: Gary Smith; **W:** Richard Schickel, Marty Farrell; **Nar:** Shirley Temple.

Africa Screams / Jack and the Beanstalk

In the first feature on this double-sided disc, Abbott and Costello go on safari with a treasure map. The unheralded independent production is not bad in the stupid vein of comedy with lots of jungle slapstick and a supporting cast of familiar faces. In the second film, Lou falls asleep while babysitting and dreams he's Jack in a spoof of the famous fairy tale. Unfortunately, the disc is recommended to only the duo's most devoted fans. Both sound and image are substandard. The fuzzy black and white of Africa Screams looks like an early '50s TV broadcast. Jack was filmed in a process called "Super cine Color," emphasizing heavy reds and oranges. —MM

Movie: ♪♪ **DVD:** ♪
Madacy Entertainment (Cat #DVD9 9106, UPC #056775036492). Full frame. Dolby Digital Mono. $14.98. Keepcase. LANG: English. FEATURES: 8 chapter links each ☞ Abbott and Costello filmography and trivia.
1949 79m/B Lou Costello, Bud Abbott, Shemp Howard, Hillary Brooke, Joe Besser, Clyde Beatty, Max Baer Sr.; **D:** Charles T. Barton; **W:** Earl Baldwin; **M:** Walter Schumann.

After Life

For comparative purposes, think of a Japanese version of Wim Wenders's Wings of Desire. Kore-eda Hirokazu spins an allegorical tale of life after death. The premise: everyone gets to choose one memory from his or her life to carry into eternity. What will it be and how do you decide? The situation is handled by heavenly bureaucrats and caseworkers who gently guide the recently departed through their duties. On DVD, the image is on the darkish side, but that's entirely appropriate to the subject, and even the graininess seems to add a level of texture. Yellow subtitles are easy to read. The film may be a bit too slow and meditative for all tastes, but it will reward the patient. Don't miss the explanations in the director's profile extra. —MM AKA: Wandafuru Raifu.

Movie: ♪♪♪♪ **DVD:** ♪♪♪½
New Yorker Video (Cat #73300, UPC #717119733049). Full frame. $29.95. Keepcase. LANG: Japanese. SUB: English. FEATURES: 8 chapter links ☞ American and Japanese trailers ☞ Director bio and filmography ☞ Director's statement.
1998 118m/C JP Taketoshi Naito, Susumu Terajima, Arata, Erika Oda, Takashi Naito, Hisako Hara; **D:** Hirokazu Kore-eda; **W:** Hirokazu Kore-eda; **C:** Yutaka Yamazaki, Masayoshi Sukita; **M:** Yasuhiro Kasamatsu.

After the Storm

In the Caribbean of 1933, Arno (Bratt) finds himself working with the crooked Jean-Pierre (Assante) to dispose of a small fortune that they're not exactly supposed to possess. The plot is based on a Hemingway story but this one's a long way from the chemistry of *To Have and Have Not.* On DVD, it is an astonishingly good-looking film, particularly after one learns from the commentary track that it was shot in a mere 30 days in Belize. Image and sound are both fine; Ferland tends to take a fairly dry, technical approach with his remarks. —*MM*

Movie: 🎞️🎞️½ **DVD:** 🎞️🎞️½
Trimark Home Video (Cat #7647D, UPC #031398764724). Widescreen anamorphic. Dolby Digital 5.1 Surround. $24.99. Keepcase. *LANG:* English. *SUB:* English; French; Spanish. *FEATURES:* 30 chapter links • Commentary: Guy Ferland • Storyboards • Interviews • Trailer.
2001 (R) 103m/C Benjamin Bratt, Armand Assante, Mili Avital, Simone-Elise Girard, Stephen Lang; **D:** Guy Ferland; **W:** A.E. Hotchner; **C:** Gregory Middleton; **M:** Bill Wandel.

Aftershock

Grade Z post-apocalyptic thriller has nothing to offer. John Saxon leads the forces of repression against heroic Willy (Roberts Jr.) and space babe Sabina (Kaitan). Sound may be superior to VHS tape; image is identical. —*MM*

Movie: 🎞️½ **DVD:** 🎞️½
Image Entertainment (Cat #0VED9015 DVD, UPC #014381901528). Full frame. Dolby Digital Surround Stereo. $24.99. Snapper. *LANG:* English. *FEATURES:* 12 chapter links • Trailer.
1988 (R) 90m/C Jay Roberts Jr., Elizabeth Kaitan, Chris Mitchum, Richard Lynch, John Saxon, Russ Tamblyn, Michael Berryman, Chris De Rose, Chuck Jeffreys; **D:** Frank Harris; **W:** Michael Standing; **M:** Kevin Klinger, Bob Mamet.

Aftershock: Earthquake in New York

Typical TV disaster movie is based on a novel by Chuck Scarborough. You're introduced to a bunch of nice people (the cast is quite good); disaster strikes; death and destruction are everywhere and all that results are good deeds and rescues (rather than hysteria, looting, violence, and assorted evilness). Nifty special effects, though, and it's always fun to see a major metropolitan area trashed. Since the effects are the main element in the film worth watching, it helps that this is a good-looking disc, even though, at times, the sharpness is a hindrance since you can more easily tell something is an effect. Artifacts and grain are minimal and the colors are far better than this TV flick deserves. The Dolby Surround does a good job in conveying the necessary crunching, rumbling, and shaking to make things appear somewhat realistic. Just scan through the disc and watch the destruction. —*JO*

Movie: 🎞️🎞️½ **DVD:** 🎞️🎞️🎞️
Artisan Entertainment (Cat #10121, UPC #707729101215). Full frame. Dolby Surround. $19.98. Keepcase. *LANG:* English. *CAP:* English. *FEATURES:* 36 chapter links • Theatrical trailer • Cast and crew bios • Production notes • Earthquake preparedness information.
1999 139m/C Tom Skerritt, Sharon Lawrence, Charles S. Dutton, Lisa Nicole Carson, Cicely Tyson, Jennifer Garner, Rachel Ticotin, Frederick Weller, Erika Eleniak, Mitchell Ryan; **D:** Mikael Salomon; **W:** David Stevens, Paul Eric Meyers, Loren Boothby; **C:** Jon Joffin; **M:** Irwin Fisch.

Against All Odds

Washed-up football player Terry Brogan (Bridges) goes to Mexico to find Jessie Wyler (Ward), the wayward girlfriend of his friend Jake Wise (Woods), a professional gambler. That's the first half of a remake of 1947's *Out of the Past.* The second half suffers from odd plot lapses and it never matches the atmospheric menace of the original. The DVD image looks good enough for a film of this age, though it's far from great. The commentaries and the extras are well done but, for me, the film doesn't really deserve the attention. —*MM*

Movie: 🎞️🎞️½ **DVD:** 🎞️🎞️🎞️
Columbia Tristar Home Video (Cat #779). Widescreen (1.85:1) letterboxed. Dolby Digital Surround Stereo; Dolby Digital Stereo. $14.95. Keepcase. *LANG:* English. *SUB:* English; Spanish; Portuguese; Chinese; Korean; Thai. *FEATURES:* Commentary: director, writer • Commentary: director, cast • Music videos • 7 deleted scenes • Trailers • Talent files • 28 chapter links.
1984 (R) 122m/C Jeff Bridges, Rachel Ward, James Woods, Alex Karras, Jane Greer, Richard Widmark, Dorian Harewood, Swoosie Kurtz, Bill McKinney, Saul Rubinek; **D:** Taylor Hackford; **W:** Eric Hughes; **C:** Donald E. Thorin; **M:** Larry Carlton, Michel Colombier. *AWARDS: NOM:* Oscars '84: Song ("Against All Odds (Take a Look at Me Now)").

Agatha Christie's Poirot

This set includes two stylized films based on the writings of Agatha Christie and the adventures of her famous detective, Hercule Poirot (Suchet). In the first feature, *Lord Edgware Dies,* Poirot finds himself smitten with the actress Jane Wilkinson. When her estranged husband is murdered, Poirot must find the killer. In the second film, *The Murder of Roger Ackroyd,* Poirot again finds himself forced to solve a murder. This time out, the killing of a wealthy industrialist exposes a web of blackmail, envy, and murder. The colors are quite good on this video transfer, perfectly representing the diffused colors that are so often used on A&E programs. The audio transfer is also solid, delivering a rich, clear soundtrack with no cracks or other problems. —*MJT*

Movie: 🎞️🎞️🎞️ **DVD:** 🎞️🎞️🎞️
A & E Home Video (Cat #AAE70128, UPC #733961701289). Full frame. Dolby Digital 2.0 Stereo. $39.95. Keepcase. *LANG:* English. *FEATURES:* 22 chapter links (11 per feature).
2000 200m/C *GB*

Agnes Browne

Sentimental, old-fashioned film concerns recent widow Agnes Browne (producer/director Huston) who's trying to cope with her seven children under difficult circumstances in Dublin, 1967. She works in a market stall and has one dream—to see Tom Jones in an upcoming concert. Guess what happens. Though the image is not the sharpest you've ever seen, it's fine for the story and setting. Subtitles are a help for some of the accents. —*MM*

Movie: 🎞️🎞️½ **DVD:** 🎞️🎞️🎞️
USA Home Entertainment (Cat #963 060 103-2, UPC #696306010326). Widescreen anamorphic. Dolby Digital Surround Stereo. $24.95. Keepcase. *LANG:* English. *SUB:* French; Spanish. *CAP:* English. *FEATURES:* 17 chapter links • Talent files • Trailer.
1999 (R) 91m/C Anjelica Huston, Ray Winstone, Arno Chevrier, Marion O'Dwyer, Ciaran Owens, Tom Jones; **D:** Anjelica Huston; **W:** John Goldsmith, Brendan O'Carroll; **C:** Anthony B. Richmond; **M:** Paddy Moloney.

Aguirre, the Wrath of God

Herzog at his best, combining brilliant poetic images and an intense narrative dealing with power, irony, and death. Spanish conquistadors in 1590 search for the mythical city of gold in Peru. Instead, they descend into the hell of the jungle. Kinski is fabulous as Aguirre, succumbing to insanity while leading a continually diminishing crew in this compelling drama shot in the jungles of South America. Even with its flaws, this DVD is by far the best version released on video. There are some grain problems when jungle mists appear and some shimmering in detailed shots, but the DVD pretty much retains the original look of the film, with accurate colors and fleshtones. There's not much to the 5.1 mix but the sound is strong with particularly crisp narration. —*JO AKA:* Aguirre, der Zorn Gottes.

Movie: 🎞️🎞️🎞️🎞️ **DVD:** 🎞️🎞️🎞️
Anchor Bay (Cat #DV11099, UPC #013131109993). Full frame. Dolby Digital 5.1; Dolby Digital Mono. $29.98. Keepcase. *LANG:* English (DDmono); German (DD5.1). *SUB:* English. *FEATURES:* 25 chapter links • Theatrical trailer • Commentary: Werner Herzog • Cast and crew bios.
1972 94m/C *GE* Klaus Kinski, Ruy Guerra, Del Negro, Helena Rojo, Cecilia Rivera,

Peter Berling, Danny Ades; **D:** Werner Herzog; **W:** Werner Herzog; **C:** Thomas Mauch; **M:** Popul Vuh. *AWARDS:* Natl. Soc. Film Critics '77: Cinematog.

Air Bud [2]

Buddy is a charming, photogenic basketball-playing Golden Retriever. He escapes the clutches of an evil Party Clown (Jeter) and becomes an integral part of a young boy's family. Twelve-year-old Josh (Zegers) and his family have relocated to his mother's hometown in hopes of recovering from the death of Josh's dad in an airplane accident. Buddy is just the dog to help Josh fit in to a new town, and start to come out of his shell. Buddy becomes the team mascot and with his ability to rally the troops, he takes Josh and the Timberwolves all the way to the playoffs. Despite the great capacity for failed absurdity, *Air Bud* is a pretty good movie. The jokes are obvious and the story elements cliché, but here they work. "Ain't no rule says a dog can't play basketball." The VideoHound agrees. The bare-bones DVD exhibits the usual problems with grid patterns, clothes designs, and fast panning shots, but those aren't going to be a problem for the young fans who will love this one. On a trivial note (don't tell the kids), the dog playing Buddy postponed surgery for a week to finish filming and subsequently died of canine cancer. He was ten years old and survived by nine puppies. He was buried near his home in San Diego, and *Air Bud* was his only film appearance as Buddy. Another hound appears in the sequels. All three are available in the *Air Bud Gift Set* (cat. # 21179; $89.99). —JAS
Movie: 🐾🐾🐾 **DVD:** 🐾🐾
Buena Vista Home Entertainment (Cat #13681, UPC #717951000163). Full frame. Dolby Digital 5.1 Surround Stereo. $29.99. Keepcase. *LANG:* English. *FEATURES:* 16 chapter links • Theatrical trailer.
1997 (PG) 92m/C Kevin Zegers, Michael Jeter, Bill Cobbs, Wendy Makkena, Eric Christmas, Brendan Fletcher, Jay Brazeau, Stephen E. Miller, Nicola Cavendish; **D:** Charles Martin Smith; **W:** Paul Tamasy, Aaron Mendelsohn; **C:** Mike Southon; **M:** Brahm Wenger.

Air Bud 2: Golden Receiver

Well, *Air Bud* must have been a financial success because Disney cobbled together a sequel with the same plot but a different villain and a different sport, making this a true paint-by-numbers movie. This time, the dog plays football, and instead of a mean clown wanting Buddy for his own, an evil Russian ringmaster (Dunn) wants the sporty pooch for her circus. She's been stealing animals all over town, guaranteeing a menagerie of furry foils to close out the film's climax. Instead of a pick-up with a clown on top, the ringmaster drives an old ice cream truck. Josh's mother is dating again, and the trouble this causes him is so poorly scripted that it contains eerie

Oedipal overtones. Fortunately, Norman Bates was wrong when he said, "A boy's best friend is his mother." If you saw the first film, you know a boy's best friend is his dog. The dog playing Buddy this time out is the picture of patience; dressed for tea with Josh's little sister, or tucked into football pads and a helmet, the dog can still act. If you're looking to plop the kids in front of the TV to stay out of your hair for 90 minutes, this'll work, but there are better choices. That said, DVD looks and sounds much better than VHS tape. The film is also available in the *Air Bud Gift Set* (cat. # 21179; $89.99). —JAS
Movie: 🐾 **DVD:** 🐾🐾
Buena Vista Home Entertainment (Cat #20709, UPC #786936140019). Full frame. Dolby Digital Surround 2.0. $29.99. Keepcase. *LANG:* English; French. *CAP:* English. *FEATURES:* 17 chapter links • Production featurette.
1998 (G) 90m/C Kevin Zegers, Cynthia Stevenson, Gregory Harrison, Nora Dunn, Robert Costanzo, Tim Conway, Dick Martin, Perry Anzilotti, Suzanne Ristic, Jay Brazeau; **D:** Richard Martin; **W:** Paul Tamasy, Aaron Mendelsohn; **C:** Mike Southon; **M:** Brahm Wenger.

Air Bud 3: World Pup

Scraping the bottom of the cliché barrel for a third *Air Bud* film, this one comes out ahead of *Air Bud: Golden Receiver,* but still smells stale. In the first film, the town was less idyllic; Josh and Buddy's problems were a bit more real. Now, come the third installment, the town is perfect, Josh and Buddy are celebrities, Josh's mom gets married, and all is right in this Disney world. In an effort to freshen up the tired premise, Josh's sister Andrea has a best friend and their amateur sleuthing uncovers Buddy's love interest and their litter of pups. Josh too has a love interest, and wrestles with dating trouble and how to be cool. Puppy-nappers are after Buddy's pups; the Timberwolves are disqualified from the league; and things couldn't be worse in this perfect world of lazy contrivances. Forced into the plot, World Cup Champions Brandi Chastain, Briana Scurry, and Tisha Venturini appear inexplicably to congratulate and then recruit Buddy. What are they doing in the Midwest? Don't ask; it's a cheap movie. Despite its cheapness, it's completely innocuous to the kids to watch, and DVD is a solid step up from tape in terms of image and sound. The film is also available in the *Air Bud Gift Set* (cat. # 21179; $89.99). —JAS
Movie: 🐾 **DVD:** 🐾🐾
Buena Vista Home Entertainment (Cat #20655, UPC #786936140019). Full frame. Dolby Surround Sound. $29.99. Keepcase. *LANG:* English. *CAP:* English. *FEATURES:* 18 chapter links • Production featurette • Air Bud music video.
2000 (G) 83m/C Kevin Zegers, Dale Midkiff, Caitlin Wachs, Martin Ferrero, Duncan Regehr, Brittany Paige Bouck, Briana Scurry, Brandi Chastain, Tisha Venturini; **D:** Bill Bannerman.

Airplane!

"I can't believe you paid for this!" is the last thing heard on the commentary track. The question is, "Why not?" We've got one of the funniest movies ever made presented in its widescreen format with Surround sound. What's not to like? The picture is very crisp and clear, showing few defects on the source print. However, the image is a bit dark and displays some graininess at times. This, of course, is a direct result of the film's low-budget origins. That said, this is the best that the comic masterpiece has ever looked. The transfer shows no complications from artifacting or compression problems. The Dolby Digital 5.1 mix offers some nicely placed Surround sound effects. The razor-sharp dialogue is always clear and audible and there is no apparent hissing on the soundtrack. The only real shortcoming is the paucity of its extras. —GH/MM
Movie: 🐾🐾🐾🐾 **DVD:** 🐾🐾🐾
Paramount Home Video (Cat #01305, UPC #097360130546). Widescreen (1.85:1) anamorphic. Dolby Digital 5.1 Surround; Mono. $29.99. Keepcase. *LANG:* English; French. *SUB:* English. *FEATURES:* Commentary: writing/directing ZAZ team and producer Jon Davison • Theatrical trailer.
1980 (PG) 88m/C Jerry Zucker, Jim Abrahams, David Zucker, Robert Hays, Julie Hagerty, Lloyd Bridges, Peter Graves, Robert Stack, Kareem Abdul-Jabbar, Leslie Nielsen, Stephen Stucker, Ethel Merman, Barbara Billingsley, Lorna Patterson, Joyce Bulifant, James Hong, Maureen McGovern, Jimmie Walker; **D:** Jerry Zucker, Jim Abrahams, David Zucker; **W:** Jerry Zucker, Jim Abrahams, David Zucker; **C:** Joseph Biroc; **M:** Elmer Bernstein. *AWARDS:* Writers Guild '80: Adapt. Screenplay.

Airplane 2: The Sequel

Though some of the slapstick of the Zucker, Abrahams, and Zucker original is missing, this is an adequate effort that contains about 60% of the laughs, which is par for a sequel. The setting is the maiden voyage of the first commercial lunar shuttle with a mad bomber (Bono) aboard and other disasters involving the semi-star-studded ensemble cast. There are so many gags in the background of most scenes that the relative clarity of the DVD is a real benefit. For a film of its age, this one looks very good. Sound is O.K. —MM
Movie: 🐾🐾½ **DVD:** 🐾🐾½
Paramount Home Video (Cat #01489, UPC #097360148947). Widescreen anamorphic. Dolby Digital Mono. $29.99. Keepcase. *LANG:* English; French. *SUB:* English. *FEATURES:* 15 chapter links.
1982 (PG) 84m/C Ken Finkleman, Robert Hays, Julie Hagerty, Lloyd Bridges, Raymond Burr, Peter Graves, William Shatner, Sonny Bono, Chuck Connors, Chad Everett, Stephen Stucker, Rip Torn, Kent McCord, Sandahl Bergman, Jack Jones, John Dehner, Richard Jaeckel; **D:** Ken Fin-

kleman; **W:** Ken Finkleman; **C:** Joseph Biroc; **M:** Elmer Bernstein.

The Alamo

Old-fashioned patriotic battle epic recounts the events of the 1836 fight for independence in Texas. The usual band of diverse and contentious personalities, including Wayne as a coonskin-capped Davy Crockett, defend a small fort against a very big Mexican raiding party outside of San Antonio. Before meeting mythic death, they fight with each other, learn the meaning of life, and ultimately come to respect each other. Just to make it more entertaining, Avalon sings. Big-budget production features an impeccable musical score by Tiomkin and an impressive 7,000 extras for the Mexican army alone. Wayne reportedly received directorial assistance from John Ford, particularly during the big massacre finale. The video transfer is very good, featuring vibrant colors and crisp definition (though blacks do tend to blur in the more dimly lit scenes). The audio transfer is similarly impressive, and features clear dialogue and a lush musical score. The documentary included on the disc is a must for any Wayne fan. —*MJT*
Movie: ♪♪♪ **DVD:** ♪♪♪
MGM Home Entertainment (Cat #1001270, UPC #027616855503). Widescreen (1.85:1) letterboxed. Dolby Digital 5.1 Surround; Dolby Digital Stereo; Dolby Digital Mono. $19.98. Keepcase. *LANG:* English; French; Spanish. *SUB:* French; Spanish. *FEATURES:* 32 chapter links • "John Wayne's 'The Alamo'" documentary • Theatrical trailer.
1960 161m/C John Wayne, Richard Widmark, Laurence Harvey, Frankie Avalon, Richard Boone, Carlos Arruza, Chill Wills, Veda Ann Borg, Linda Cristal, Patrick Wayne, Joan O'Brien, Joseph Calleia, Ken Curtis, Jester Hairston, Denver Pyle, John Dierkes, Guinn "Big Boy" Williams, Olive Carey, William Henry, Hank Worden, Ruben Padilla, Jack Pennick; **D:** John Wayne; **W:** James Edward Grant; **C:** William Clothier; **M:** Dimitri Tiomkin, Paul Francis Webster; **Technical Advisor:** Jack Pennick, C. Frank Beetson Jr. *AWARDS:* Oscars '60: Sound; Golden Globes '61: Score; *NOM:* Oscars '60: Color Cinematog., Film Editing, Picture, Song ("The Green Leaves of Summer"), Support. Actor (Wills), Orig. Dramatic Score.

Alexandria Again and Forever

The third volume of director Chahine's autobiographical "Alexandria Trilogy" finds his alter ego Yehia accepting awards for his earlier work and becoming socially involved and romantically entangled. The same flaw that plagues the first two films is in evidence here—exceptionally heavy grain. It does come with the original elements, though, and it should not dissuade anyone who's interested in a serious filmmaker doing challenging work. (The other two films are *Alexandria...Why?* and *An*

Egyptian Story.) —*MM* **AKA:** Iskanderija, Kaman oue Kaman.
Movie: ♪♪♪ **DVD:** ♪♪
Winstar Home Entertainment (Cat #FLV5235, UPC #720917523521). Widescreen (1.66:1) letterboxed. $24.98. Keepcase. *LANG:* Arabic. *SUB:* English. *FEATURES:* 8 chapter links • Weblinks • DVD production credits • Filmographies and awards.
1990 105m/C EG Youssef Chahine, Zaki Abdel Wahab, Menha Batraoui, Teheya Cariocca, Amr Abdel Guelil, Yousra; **D:** Youssef Chahine; **W:** Youssef Chahine; **C:** Ingy Assolh; **M:** Mohammed Nouh.

Alexandria...Why?

Director Chahine tells a Felliniesque (in the nostalgic sense) autobiographical story of growing up in Egypt during World War II. Teenaged Yehia is heavily influenced by the American movies he sees in Alexandria, and his reality and fantasy become mixed on-screen. It's an entertaining combination but the film's heavy grain makes for a difficult image on DVD. Virtually all of the visual problems stem from the original elements. Lighting glares in several scenes and darkened theatre interiors are hard to make out. Dialogue is in both Arabic and English with subtitles at the appropriate moments. The film is the first volume of the "Alexandria Trilogy." —*MM*
Movie: ♪♪♪ **DVD:** ♪♪
Winstar Home Entertainment (Cat #FLV5233, UPC #720917523323). Widescreen (1.66:1) letterboxed. Keepcase. *LANG:* English; Arabic. *SUB:* English. *FEATURES:* 8 chapter links • Weblinks • Filmographies and awards • DVD production credits.
1978 133m/C EG Gerry Sundquist, Naglaa Fathi, Farid Shawki, Mohsen Mohiedine; **D:** Youssef Chahine; **W:** Youssef Chahine; **C:** Mohsen Nasr; **M:** Foad El Zaheri.

Alfie

In his first starring role, Caine plays a British playboy out of control in mod London. He's a despicable, unscrupulous, vile lout who uses woman after woman and then casts them aside until life catches up with him in several ways. This transfer looks about as good as any home video version could. Sound is also fine, though I prefer the original mono mix to the 5.1 Surround. It's somehow more fitting to the story and the intimate first-person narration. —*MM*
Movie: ♪♪♪½ **DVD:** ♪♪♪½
Paramount Home Video (Cat #06604, UPC #097360660449). Widescreen anamorphic. Dolby Digital 5.1 Surround Stereo; Mono. $29.99. Keepcase. *LANG:* English. *SUB:* English. *FEATURES:* 18 chapter links • Trailer.
1966 (PG) 114m/C GB Michael Caine, Shelley Winters, Millicent Martin, Vivien Merchant, Julia Foster, Jane Asher, Shirley Anne Field, Eleanor Bron, Denholm Elliott,

Alfie Bass, Graham Stark, Murray Melvin, Sydney Tafler; **D:** Lewis Gilbert; **W:** Bill Naughton; **C:** Otto Heller; **M:** Burt Bacharach, Sonny Rollins. *AWARDS:* Cannes '67: Grand Jury Prize; Golden Globes '67: Foreign Film; Natl. Bd. of Review '66: Support. Actress (Merchant); Natl. Soc. Film Critics '66: Actor (Caine); *NOM:* Oscars '66: Actor (Caine), Adapt. Screenplay, Picture, Song ("Alfie"), Support. Actress (Merchant).

Alfred Hitchcock's Bon Voyage & Aventure Malgache

Alfred Hitchcock made these two short films as propaganda pieces to aid the French cause in World War II. Sergio Leemann's detailed liner notes explain the reasons behind Hitch's efforts and the place that the films have in relation to his other work of the period. They're really recommended only to the Master's true devotees. In the first film, an RAF flier who escaped the Germans after being shot down, learns that a companion is a spy. The second involves political infighting within the resistance movement, and was too lighthearted to be of any use. Some static is audible on the soundtrack, and the image is in good shape, but is really no better than you could expect of works from the '40s. Highlighted subtitles are easy to read. —*MM*
Movie: ♪♪½ **DVD:** ♪♪½
Image Entertainment (Cat #ID4190MLSDVD, UPC #014381419023). Full frame. Dolby Digital Mono. $24.99. Snapper. *LANG:* French. *SUB:* English. *FEATURES:* 28 chapter links • Liner notes by Sergio Leemann.
1944 57m/B GB John Blythe; **D:** Alfred Hitchcock; **W:** J.O.C. Orton; **C:** Gunther Krampf.

Alice

Fascinating but disturbing interpretation of the Lewis Carroll children's classic is anything but childlike. Using stop-motion far removed from the candied visions of Harryhausen, Svankmajer places his live action *Alice* amidst slithering socks, sawdust-leaking taxidermy, and galloping fish skeletons. While the film keeps true to the book's plot, the Disney-esque elements have been taken to a surreal, illogical extreme. Fever dream does not begin to describe this gruesome journey through the looking-glass. Transfer looks sharp with stable, slightly drab colors. Exceptionally clean source elements make for a crisp image. The soundtrack is just as unnerving, with seemingly ordinary sound effects (running water, scissor snips, electrical hum) magnified to ominous proportions. Mono audio is overly bright, with intermittent hiss and occasional pops. However, given the gruesome visuals that it underscores, the "in-your-face" nature of the soundtrack seems strangely apropos. A short film, "Darkness Light Darkness," accompanies the feature. Utilizing clay animation, "DLD" re-imagines biblical creation in a small wooden room. Needless to say, Svankmajer sees the clay we come from as a sinister force all its own. Watch this DVD with the lights on. —*EP* **AKA:** Neco Z Alenky.

Movie: ♫♫½ **DVD:** ♫♫½
First Run Features (Cat #FRF909266D, UPC #720229909266). Full frame. Dolby Digital Mono. $24.99. Keepcase. *FEATURES:* 8 chapter links ▪ Special bonus short film: "Darkness Light Darkness" (7 min.).
1988 84m/C *CZ* Kristina Kohoutova; **D:** Jan Svankmajer; **W:** Jan Svankmajer; **C:** Svatopluk Maly.

Alice

Despite her outwardly perfect life—ritzy Manhattan apartment, perfect hubby (Hurt), and kids—Alice (Farrow) is troubled and prone to backaches. Those bring her to an Oriental "herbalist" whose treatments include bouts of invisibility. It's a lightweight fairy tale that Allen handles lightly until the curious conclusion. The film ends on a note that the younger, sharper, funnier filmmaker would never have considered, except in mocking tones. Perhaps his then-squeeze Farrow had clouded his mind. Softish DVD image is an accurate re-creation of the theatrical release, as I remember it. All the shades of red that Alice wears are true. At times, the score has a purposefully tinny sound. —*MM*

Movie: ♫♫½ **DVD:** ♫♫½
MGM Home Entertainment (Cat #1002024, UPC #027616862655). Widescreen anamorphic. Dolby Digital Mono. $19.98. Keepcase. *LANG:* English; French; Spanish. *SUB:* French; Spanish. *FEATURES:* 16 chapter links ▪ Trailer ▪ Booklet.
1990 (PG-13) 106m/C Mia Farrow, William Hurt, Joe Mantegna, Keye Luke, Alec Baldwin, Cybill Shepherd, Blythe Danner, Gwen Verdon, Bernadette Peters, Judy Davis, Patrick O'Neal, Julie Kavner, Caroline Aaron, Holland Taylor, Robin Bartlett, David Spielberg, Bob Balaban, Dylan O'Sullivan Farrow, Elle Macpherson; **D:** Woody Allen; **W:** Woody Allen; **C:** Carlo Di Palma. *AWARDS:* Natl. Bd. of Review '90: Actress (Farrow); *NOM:* Oscars '90: Orig. Screenplay.

Alice in Wonderland

This beautifully animated version of Carroll's tale contains some startling, frightening images, but it's served with a strange dispassion. Wynn's Mad Hatter and Holloway's Cheshire Cat may be the highlights, but the Red Queen is the stuff of childhood nightmares. The quality of the transfer is top-notch. Colors are as vibrant as the characters they illustrate, and even the rare faded shot or two can't detract from this very beautiful picture. The audio is advertised as a DD 5.0 mix, although for all intents and purposes the sound is firmly anchored to the center speaker with some ambient music and effects spreading to the sides—and even less to the rear

speakers. But the mix is nice and clean with very little hiss and is probably as good as it gets for a film this old. —*MP/MM*

Movie: ♫♫½ **DVD:** ♫♫♫
Buena Vista Home Entertainment (Cat #14372). Full frame. Dolby Digital 5.0 Surround Stereo; Dolby Digital Mono. $29.99. Keepcase. *LANG:* English; Spanish. *FEATURES:* Featurette ▪ Sing-alongs ▪ Read-along storybook ▪ Trivia game ▪ Theatrical trailer.
1951 (G) 75m/C *D:* Hamilton Luske, Wilfred Jackson, Clyde Geronimi; *V:* Kathryn Beaumont, Ed Wynn, Sterling Holloway, Jerry Colonna. *AWARDS: NOM:* Oscars '51: Scoring/Musical.

Alice's Restaurant

This version of Arlo Guthrie's autobiographical song is one of the most perceptive and honest examinations of the 1960s ever put on film. Director Penn subtly criticizes the thoughtlessness and lack of responsibility that characterized much of that era. He also tells an entertaining tale of a naive young man at a pivotal point in history. Some nicks and flecks are apparent on this print, along with some aliasing, but they're not really a problem. This has never been a highly polished production. In the same vein, to enhance the monaural sound would be wrong. The film looks and sounds the way it always has. Guthrie's commentary track is chatty and more personal than most. This is an "R"-rated version of the film, but differences between it and the theatrical "PG" are minimal. —*MM*

Movie: ♫♫♫½ **DVD:** ♫♫♫
MGM Home Entertainment (Cat #1001444, UPC #027616857644). Widescreen (1.85:1) letterboxed. Dolby Digital Mono. $19.98. Keepcase. *LANG:* English. *SUB:* French; Spanish. *CAP:* English. *FEATURES:* 16 chapter links ▪ Trailer ▪ Commentary: Arlo Guthrie.
1969 (R) 111m/C Arlo Guthrie, James Broderick, Pat Quinn, Geoff Outlaw, Pete Seeger, Lee Hays, Michael McClanathan, Tina Chen, Kathleen Dabney, William Obanhein, Graham Jarvis, M. Emmet Walsh; **D:** Arthur Penn; **W:** Arthur Penn, Venabel Herndon; **C:** Michael Nebbia; **M:** Garry Sherman, Arlo Guthrie. *AWARDS: NOM:* Oscars '69: Director (Penn).

Alien Nation

A few hundred thousand alien workers accidentally land on Earth and slowly become part of its society, although widely discriminated against. One of the "newcomers" (Patinkin) teams with a surly and bigoted human cop (Caan) to solve a racially motivated murder. An inconsistent and occasionally transparent script looks at racial conflicts and includes some humorous parallels with American society. The crisp transfer belies the film's age, and there is nary a speck of dirt, nor a noticeable amount of grain to be seen. As most of the film takes place at night, the

blacks come across as rich and true, giving the image a great sense of depth. Use of Surround is generous and the dialogue is always crisp and clear. —*MM/ML*

Movie: ♫♫½ **DVD:** ♫♫♫
20th Century Fox Home Entertainment (Cat #20011302, UPC #024543013020). Widescreen (2.35:1) anamorphic. Dolby Digital 4.0 Surround Stereo; Dolby Digital Surround; Dolby Stereo. $24.99. Keepcase. *LANG:* English; French. *SUB:* English; Spanish. *FEATURES:* Behind-the-scenes featurette ▪ Trailers and TV spots.
1988 (R) 89m/C James Caan, Mandy Patinkin, Terence Stamp, Kevyn Major Howard, Peter Jason, Jeff Kober, Leslie Bevis; **D:** Graham Baker; **W:** Rockne S. O'Bannon; **C:** Adam Greenberg; **M:** Curt Sobel.

Alien: Resurrection

After her fiery end in the last outing, Ripley (Weaver) is brought back through cloning by a team of scientists anxious to get their hands on the alien embryo that invaded her. Ripley is buffer and stranger than ever since some of her DNA gets mixed with her alien friend. Director Jeunet creates a freaky and macabre journey as the aliens get loose on the mysterious space craft Auriga, making the usual messy alien appetizers out of the new crew. Incredibly tense underwater sequence. Nobody handles atmosphere better than Jeunet. If you've seen one *Alien* DVD, you've seen them all—quality-wise that is. All four are pretty much flawless: incredible sharpness, no grain, stunning colors with no bleed, blacker-than-black blacks. It goes on, from the excellent contrast and totally consistent brightness levels to the complete lack of artifacts. The sound completes the package with clear dialogue, fine dynamics in both the music and effects, wrap-around Surround, and a house-shaking low end. Another winner. —*JO*

Movie: ♫♫♫½ **DVD:** ♫♫♫♫
20th Century Fox Home Entertainment (Cat #4110433, UPC #3 086162000768). Widescreen (2.35:1) letterboxed. Dolby Digital 5.1; Dolby Surround. $29.98. Keepcase. *LANG:* English (DD5.1; DS); French (DS). *SUB:* English; Spanish. *CAP:* English. *FEATURES:* 27 chapter links ▪ Theatrical trailer ▪ Behind-the-scenes footage ▪ "Making of" featurette ▪ Cast and crew interviews.
1997 (R) 108m/C Sigourney Weaver, Winona Ryder, Ron Perlman, Dominique Pinon, Michael Wincott, Kim Flowers, Leland Orser, Brad Dourif, Dan Hedaya, J.E. Freeman, Raymond Cruz; **D:** Jean-Pierre Jeunet; **W:** Joss Whedon; **C:** Darius Khondji; **M:** John (Gianni) Frizzell.

All About My Mother

In the mother of all chick flicks, even most of the men are women, or at least they try to be. In Madrid, Manuela (Roth) is a nurse and single mom who's devoted to her 17-year-old son Esteban (Azorin). After he's killed, she returns to her hometown of Barcelona to grieve and to take care of unfinished business involving her father (Canto), a transvestite. To find him, she goes to another transvestite friend, Agrado (San Juan). Also involved are Huma Rojo (Paredes), an emotionally troubled actress, and Sister Rosa (Cruz), a nun with problems of her own. The plotting is actually more coherent emotionally than it sounds in synopsis, but it would all fly apart if Cecilia Roth's performance weren't so strong. She doesn't hit a single false note in a demanding role, though the conclusion comes across as forced. Given the importance of her acting and the others, the lack of a dubbed version is appropriate. On the widescreen side of the disc, the subtitles are bright yellow and easy to read in the lower band of the letterbox. In general, the film looks and sounds as good as a comparable Hollywood production, though there is considerable flashing within patterns. Also, the brightest reds bleed slightly and Almodovar uses many shades of red, orange, auburn, and henna. —MM **AKA:** Todo Sobre Mi Madre.

Movie: 🎵🎵🎵 **DVD:** 🎵🎵🎵
Columbia Tristar Home Video Widescreen (1.66:1) letterboxed; full frame. Dolby Digital Surround Stereo; Dolby Digital 5.1 Surround Stereo. $24.95. Keepcase. *LANG:* Spanish. *SUB:* English; French. *FEATURES:* 28 chapter links • Isolated music score • Conversation with Almodovar • "Making of" featurette • Cast and crew thumbnail bios.
1999 (R) 102m/C *SP* Cecilia Roth, Penelope Cruz, Marisa Paredes, Eloy Azorin, Toni Canto, Antonia San Juan, Candela Pena; **D:** Pedro Almodovar; **W:** Pedro Almodovar; **C:** Alfonso Beato; **M:** Alberto Iglesias. *AWARDS:* Oscars '99: Foreign Film; British Acad. '99: Director (Almodovar), Foreign Film; Cannes '99: Director (Almodovar); Golden Globes '00: Foreign Film; L.A. Film Critics '99: Foreign Film; N.Y. Film Critics '99: Foreign Film; Broadcast Film Critics '99: Foreign Film; *NOM:* British Acad. '99: Orig. Screenplay; Ind. Spirit '00: Foreign Film.

All Creatures Great and Small

WARNING! Before watching this disc, DO NOT look at the trailer. This trailer, the only extra on the DVD, gives away most of the plot points in the movie! Based on the autobiography of James Herriot, the film is set in Yorkshire, England, 1937, where a young Herriot (Ward) has come to town to work as a veterinary assistant to Siegfried Farnon (Hopkins). Herriot soon learns that his education hasn't prepared him for the real world. Farnon is a terrible role model and the locals don't trust the newcomer. The image is very sharp, being free of grain and noise for the most part. This clear picture shows no problems with compression or artifacting. Also, there are very few obvious defects from the source print.

The Dolby Digital Stereo offers some distinction in the front channels, but the majority of dialogue, sound effects, and music are still concentrated in the center channel. —ML/MM
Movie: 🎵🎵🎵½ **DVD:** 🎵🎵🎵
Anchor Bay Full frame. Dolby Digital Stereo. $24.98. Keepcase. *LANG:* English. *FEATURES:* Trailer.
1974 92m/C *GB* Simon Ward, Anthony Hopkins, Lisa Harrow, Brian Stirner, Freddie Jones, T.P. McKenna; **D:** Claude Whatham; **W:** Hugh Whitemore; **C:** Peter Suschitzsky; **M:** Wilfred Josephs.

All Dogs Go to Heaven

In 1939 Louisiana, Charlie (Reynolds) is a gangster German Shepherd who is killed by his business partner. On the way to heaven, he discovers how to get back to Earth to seek revenge. But when he returns, he is taken in by a little girl and learns an important lesson about life. The image looks (and always has) slightly pale when compared to so much of today's overly bright animation. Grain increases in the celestial scenes. Sound is fine. This one and the sequel are fine for kids. —MM
Movie: 🎵🎵 **DVD:** 🎵🎵
MGM Home Entertainment (Cat #1001599, UPC #027616859099). Full frame. Dolby Digital Surround. $24.99. Keepcase. *LANG:* English; French. *SUB:* French; Spanish. *FEATURES:* 16 chapter links • Trailer.
1989 (G) 85m/C D: Don Bluth; **W:** Don Bluth, David N. Weiss; **M:** Ralph Burns; **V:** Burt Reynolds, Judith Barsi, Dom DeLuise, Vic Tayback, Charles Nelson Reilly, Melba Moore, Candy Devine, Loni Anderson.

All Dogs Go to Heaven 2

Sequel finds scamp Charlie (Sheen) in heaven but homesick for Earth. When bad dog Carface (Borgnine) steals Gabriel's Trumpet, Charlie is sent back to fetch it. He falls in love with sexy Irish Setter Sasha (Easton). The animation is slightly less detailed and elaborate than the original, and the pastel colors are a bit softer. Sound is better. Kids won't care either way. —MM
Movie: 🎵½ **DVD:** 🎵🎵
MGM Home Entertainment (Cat #1001600, UPC #027616859105). Full frame. Dolby Digital 5.1 Surround Stereo; Dolby Digital Surround. $24.99. Keepcase. *LANG:* English; French; Spanish. *SUB:* French; Spanish. *FEATURES:* Trailer • 16 chapter links.
1995 (G) 82m/C D: Paul Sabella, Larry Leker; **W:** Arne Olsen, Kelly Ward, Mark Young; **M:** Mark Watters, Barry Mann, Cynthia Weil; **V:** Charlie Sheen, Sheena Easton, Ernest Borgnine, Dom DeLuise, George Hearn, Bebe Neuwirth, Hamilton Camp, Wallace Shawn, Bobby DiCicco, Adam Wylie.

All I Wanna Do

The students of an exclusive and financially troubled East Coast girls' school, circa 1963, are vigorously opposed to the merger of their school with a boys' academy. So they decide to stage a protest strike. Rather typical coming-of-age tale with a notable cast of up-and-comers who briefly released in 1998 at 110 minutes under the title *Strike,* and then re-edited and released under its current title in 2000. This is one of those aggravating DVDs that pretty much forces you to watch a trailer before getting to the menu—even the scan won't work. The transfer is a rich one with deep saturated colors in the wood interiors of the school. At times a little more brightness would make viewing more comfortable There is a little artifacting when something moves quickly in the background. —JO **AKA:** The Hairy Bird; Strike!
Movie: 🎵🎵½ **DVD:** 🎵🎵🎵
Buena Vista Home Entertainment (Cat #20387, UPC #717951010001). Widescreen (1.85:1) anamorphic. Dolby Digital 5.1; Dolby Surround. $29.99. Keepcase. *LANG:* English (DS); French (DD5.1). *SUB:* Spanish. *CAP:* English. *FEATURES:* 25 chapter links.
1998 (PG-13) 94m/C Kirsten Dunst, Gaby Hoffman, Heather Matarazzo, Rachael Leigh Cook, Monica Keena, Merritt Wever, Lynn Redgrave, Vincent Kartheiser, Tom Guiry, Matthew Lawrence, Robert Bockstael; **D:** Sarah Kernochan; **W:** Sarah Kernochan; **C:** Anthony C. "Tony" Jannelli; **M:** Graeme Revell.

All the Pretty Horses

John Grady (Damon) and his friend Lacey Rawlins (Thomas) are latter-day cowboys who go to Mexico where they find work on a prosperous ranch. Grady falls for the rich man's daughter (Cruz) and their romance sets off a clash of cultures. The DVD image is essentially flawless. It's actually too crisp and sharp for the story and the setting. Director Thornton has such a good eye for spectacular landscapes that some of the exteriors will make you want to go out and buy that widescreen set. Darker interiors are properly detailed, too. The clarity of the 5.1 sound makes the attempts at dialect and accents all the more lamentable. —MM
Movie: 🎵🎵 **DVD:** 🎵🎵🎵
Columbia Tristar Home Video (Cat #04605, UPC #043396046054). Widescreen (2.35:1) anamorphic. Dolby Digital 5.1 Surround Stereo; Dolby Digital Surround. $24.99. Keepcase. *LANG:* English. *SUB:* English; French. *FEATURES:* Trailers • Filmographies • 28 chapter links.
2000 (PG-13) 117m/C Matt Damon, Penelope Cruz, Ruben Blades, Lucas Black, Henry Thomas, Robert Patrick, Julio Mechoso, Miriam Colon, Bruce Dern, Sam Shepard; **D:** Billy Bob Thornton; **W:** Ted Tally; **C:** Barry Markowitz; **M:**

Marty Stuart. *AWARDS:* Natl. Bd. of Review '00: Screenplay.

Almost Famous

Inspired by the real-life experiences of director Cameron Crowe, this drama follows 15-year-old William Miller (Fugit) as he travels with the fictional band Stillwater on their 1973 "Almost Famous Tour." Miller, assigned to write his first big article on the band for *Rolling Stone* magazine, eventually loses his virginity and some of his innocence as he becomes involved with groupie "Penny Lane" (Hudson) and lead guitarist Russell Hammond (Crudup), whose crucial interview for the magazine is inadvertently thwarted at every stop. Enjoyable but overrated film (a kind of serious *This Is Spinal Tap*) captures the period and milieu of '70s rock and roll perfectly but lacks momentum and dramatic punch. Miller, though mildly changed by his experience, frustratingly remains the same wide-eyed character at the end as he was at the beginning. The band, led by nice-guy Hammond, seems unbelievably clean, and the absence of sex and heavy drug-taking, prevalent in this era, seems curious. Hudson, though appealing, conveys none of the star power one has been led to expect. Hoffman shines in his few scenes as Miller's mentor, rock and roll critic Lester Bangs. The DVD conveys the muted tones of the film with clarity and accuracy and a slight bit of grain. The sound is crisp and involving, with the concert scenes and storm sequence given intense Surround sound effects. The extras give one a greater appreciation for the film and the inclusion of Crowe's original *Rolling Stone* articles is a brilliant and much appreciated touch. Crowe is reportedly preparing a longer cut of the film, adding several scenes to a future DVD release. —*DG*

Movie: ♫♫½ **DVD:** ♫♫♫½
DreamWorks Home Entertainment (Cat #87818, UPC #67068781823). Widescreen (1.85:1) anamorphic. DTS 5.1 Surround; Dolby Digital 5.1; Dolby Surround. $26.99. Keepcase. *LANG:* English. *SUB:* English. *FEATURES:* 24 chapter links • Theatrical trailer • "Fever Dog" music video • Cast and crew bios • Production notes • "Making of " featurette • Original *Rolling Stone* articles by Cameron Crowe • Color booklet with chapter listings and notes.
2000 (R) 202m/C Patrick Fugit, Philip Seymour Hoffman, Frances McDormand, Jason Lee, Billy Crudup, Kate Hudson, John Fedevich, Mark Kozelek, Fairuza Balk, Bijou Phillips, Anna Paquin, Noah Taylor; *D:* Cameron Crowe; *W:* Cameron Crowe; *C:* John Toll; *M:* Nancy Wilson. *AWARDS:* Oscars '00: Orig. Screenplay; Golden Globes '01: Film—Mus./Comedy, Support. Actress (Hudson); L.A. Film Critics '00: Actor (Douglas), Support. Actress (McDormand); Broadcast Film Critics '00: Adapt. Screenplay, Orig. Screenplay, Support. Actress (McDormand); *NOM:* Oscars '00: Film Editing, Support. Actress (Hudson, McDormand); Directors Guild '00: Director

(Crowe); Screen Actors Guild '00: Support. Actress (Hudson), Support. Actress (McDormand), Cast; Writers Guild '00: Orig. Screenplay.

Alvarez Kelly

Offbeat western casts Holden as the Mexican-Irish Kelly who has just sold a herd of cattle to the North during the Civil War. Union officer Steadman (O'Neal) demands that the beef be transported to Richmond. Confederate officer Widmark kidnaps Kelly in an effort to have the cattle redirected to the South. Naturally, a beautiful woman (Rule) is involved too, intensifying the fierce hatred that develops between the two. Based on a real incident, the script occasionally wanders far afield with the beef who cleverly heighten the excitement by stampeding when things get slow. Holden's sleepy performance is counterbalanced by an intense Widmark. The image ranges between very good and excellent with detail clearly visible even in black uniforms. Overall, the film has the well-tailored look of a mid-'60s big-budget studio production. —*MM*

Movie: ♫♫½ **DVD:** ♫♫½
Columbia Tristar Home Video (Cat #1199). Widescreen (2.35:1) letterboxed; full frame. Dolby Digital Mono. $24.95. Keepcase. *LANG:* English; Spanish. *SUB:* Chinese; Korean; Portuguese; Spanish; Thai. *FEATURES:* Cast and crew thumbnail bios • Trailer • 28 chapter links.
1966 109m/C William Holden, Richard Widmark, Janice Rule, Patrick O'Neal, Harry Carey Jr., Victoria Shaw, Roger C. Carmel; *D:* Edward Dmytryk; *W:* Elliott Arnold, Franklin Coen; *C:* Joe MacDonald; *M:* Johnny Green.

The Amazing Transparent Man

Please see *Indestructible Man / The Amazing Transparent Man*.
Movie: woof
1960 58m/B Douglas Kennedy, Marguerite Chapman, James Griffith, Ivan Triesault, Red Morgan, Carmel Daniel, Jonathan Ledford, Norman Smith, Patrick Cranshaw, Kevin Kelly; *D:* Edgar G. Ulmer; *W:* Dr. Jack Lewis; *C:* Meredith Nicholson; *M:* Darrell Calker.

American Beauty [SE]

Lester Burnham (Spacey) is dead. This isn't giving anything away; Lester tells you this himself in the opening narration. It's the time leading up to his death that Lester wants to remember. Lester is a middle-aged drone with a brittle, status-conscious wife, Caroline (Bening), and a sullen teenaged daughter, Jane (Birch). Lester's world is rocked when he meets Jane's Lolita-like friend, Angela (Suvari), and his fantasies find him quitting his job, pumping iron, and smoking pot with Ricky (Bentley), the voyeuristic kid next door. It's a suburban nightmare writ large with

some unexpected twists. This is a beautiful DVD to look at and listen to. The superb cinematography comes across with a great feeling of depth thanks to incredible sharpness, contrast, and brightness. Colors are strong yet refuse to bleed, even in those petal-filled sex-fantasy sequences with Suvari. Surround is used mainly for ambience but is all-enveloping, completing the near-perfect home theatre experience. —*JO*

Movie: ♫♫♫♫ **DVD:** ♫♫♫½
Universal Studios Home Video (Cat #85382, UPC #667068538229). Widescreen (2.35:1) anamorphic. Dolby Digital 5.1; Dolby Surround; DTS 5.1. $26.99. Keepcase. *LANG:* English. *SUB:* English. *CAP:* English. *FEATURES:* 28 chapter links • Behind-the-scenes documentary • Theatrical trailers • Cast and crew bios • Production notes • Commentary: Sam Mendes, Conrad L. Hall • Digital screenplay; corresponding film footage and storyboards • Storyboards • DVD-ROM features.
1999 (R) 118m/C Kevin Spacey, Annette Bening, Mena Suvari, Thora Birch, Wes Bentley, Peter Gallagher, Chris Cooper, Allison Janney, Scott Bakula, Sam Robards; *D:* Sam Mendes; *W:* Alan Ball; *C:* Conrad Hall; *M:* Thomas Newman. *AWARDS:* Oscars '99: Actor (Spacey), Cinematog., Director (Mendes), Film, Orig. Screenplay; British Acad. '99: Actor (Spacey), Actress (Bening), Cinematog., Film, Film Editing, Score; Directors Guild '99: Director (Mendes); Golden Globes '00: Director (Mendes), Film—Drama, Screenplay; L.A. Film Critics '99: Director (Mendes); Natl. Bd. of Review '99: Film; Screen Actors Guild '99: Actor (Spacey), Actress (Bening), Cast; Writers Guild '99: Orig. Screenplay; Broadcast Film Critics '99: Director (Mendes), Film, Orig. Screenplay; *NOM:* Oscars '99: Actress (Bening), Film Editing, Orig. Score; British Acad. '99: Art Dir./Set Dec., Director (Mendes), Makeup, Orig. Screenplay, Sound, Support. Actor (Bentley), Support. Actress (Birch, Suvari); Golden Globes '00: Actor—Drama (Spacey), Actress—Drama (Bening), Orig. Score; MTV Movie Awards '00: Film, Breakthrough Perf. (Bentley); Screen Actors Guild '99: Support. Actor (Cooper).

American Buffalo

Screen adaptation of Mamet's play lacks a certain spark. Junk shop owner Donny (Franz) plans to steal back a rare Buffalo-head nickel with the help of his protégé Bobby (Nelson). Teach (Hoffman), one of Donny's poker buddies and an arrogant opportunist, tries to weasel in on the plan. The action is set in director Corrente's hometown of Pawtucket and he gives the film a gritty sense of place. His sense of reverence for the material is obvious and he plays it safe. Overall, the DVD image is on the soft side, ranging between good and very good. Sound is fine, too, making the most of the abundant dialogue and fine performances. —*MM*
Movie: ♫♫½ **DVD:** ♫♫♫

MGM Home Entertainment (Cat #1001445, UPC #027616857651). Widescreen (1.85:1) anamorphic. Dolby Digital Surround Stereo. $19.98. Keepcase. *LANG:* English. *SUB:* French; Spanish. *CAP:* English. *FEATURES:* 16 chapter links ⬩ Trailer.

1995 (R) 88m/C Dustin Hoffman, Dennis Franz, Sean Nelson; *D:* Michael Corrente; *W:* David Mamet; *C:* Richard Crudo; *M:* Thomas Newman.

American Cinema: 100 Years of Filmmaking

The ten-part program is right up there with public television's best; informative, surprising and, like its subject, entertaining. Unlike most documentaries about movies, though, it goes beyond the conventional "feel-good" montage of clips from favorite films to explore how and why those clips make us feel good. The episodes are arranged thematically and chronologically, and they focus on both the business and art of the movies. The relationship between those two sides is fundamental to any understanding of American movies. Personal favorite episodes: "The Hollywood Style," "Film Noir," "The Combat Film," and "Film in the Television Age." Even though this two-disc set has a hefty price tag, it's worth it for any serious student of American film. Image quality varies with the source material, naturally, but the general level is fine. No matter, here substance is much more important than style. —*MM*

Movie: 🎵🎵🎵½ *DVD:* 🎵🎵🎵
Image Entertainment (Cat #ID9163CUDVD, UPC #014381916324). Full frame; widescreen. Dolby Digital Mono. $79.99. Keepcase. *LANG:* English. *FEATURES:* 80 chapter links.

1994 500m/C *Nar:* Robert Altman, Clint Eastwood, Harrison Ford, Spike Lee, John Lithgow, George Lucas, Sidney Lumet, Julia Roberts, Martin Scorsese, Steven Spielberg, Oliver Stone, Quentin Tarantino.

American Psycho

Streamlined version of Bret Easton Ellis's widely hated 1991 novel has Bale as '80s hotshot Wall Street exec and apparent serial killer Patrick Bateman. He epitomizes Reagan-era excess and preference for style over substance. Filmmaker Harron emphasizes the story's bleak black humor and ambiguities, though the film is certainly not going to appeal to all tastes. To my mind, it's an underrated, intelligent gem. DVD captures the sleek expensive surfaces that are the real subject and manages to avoid the flashing Venetian blinds that trouble so many discs. Sound is fine for the Bernard Herrmann-esque score and Bale's detached voice-over narration, though it's not as thunderous as some others. A commentary track might have been a real asset. The unrated version is an intriguing peek into the mind of the MPAA ratings board. The violence is essentially the same in both; one scene involving Bateman and two prostitutes is handled with a bit more discretion in the "R"-rated version. The two have the same running time. —*MM*

Movie: 🎵🎵🎵½ *DVD:* 🎵🎵🎵
Universal Studios Home Video (Cat #20722, UPC #025192072222). Widescreen (2.35:1) letterboxed. Dolby Digital 5.1 Surround Stereo. $26.98. Keepcase. *LANG:* English. *FEATURES:* 18 chapter links ⬩ Interview with Christian Bale ⬩ "Making of" featurette ⬩ Production notes ⬩ Talent files ⬩ Trailer. An unrated version is also available (cat. #20942, UPC 025192094222).

1999 (R) 103m/C Christian Bale, Willem Dafoe, Jared Leto, Reese Witherspoon, Samantha Mathis, Chloe Sevigny, Justin Theroux, Joshua Lucas, Guinevere Turner, Matt Ross, William Sage, Cara Seymour; *D:* Mary Harron; *W:* Mary Harron, Guinevere Turner; *C:* Andrzej Sekula; *M:* John Cale.

American Vampire

Post-*Buffy* video premiere is actually a nice little horror comedy. Teenager Frankie (Lussauer) has been left alone while his parents are on vacation. One night on the beach, he and his friend Bogie (Hitt) meet Moondoggie (Venokur), who promises to help them party the summer away. He soon reappears with two babes (Electra and Xavier) who appear to be undead. Frankie must turn to The Big Kahuna (West) to stop the vampires. Yes, the plot strictly follows the formula, but the effects are not bad for a low-budget production; the photography is better than it needs to be; and the humor is intentional. (The Groundlings Improv Group provides an *MST3K* style commentary track.) Image is probably a slight improvement over VHS. Sound is much better, and surf guitar legend Dick Dale makes an appearance. —*MM*

Movie: 🎵🎵½ *DVD:* 🎵🎵½
York Entertainment (Cat #YPD-1059, UPC #750723105925). Full frame. Dolby Digital 5.1 Surround Stereo; DTS Surround. $19.99. Keepcase. *LANG:* English. *SUB:* Spanish. *FEATURES:* 30 chapter links ⬩ Trailers ⬩ Talent files ⬩ CAT comic commentary track.

1997 (R) 99m/C Trevor Lissauer, Danny Hitt, Johnny Venokur, Carmen Electra, Debora Xavier, Adam West, Sydney Lassick; *D:* Luis Esteban; *W:* Rollin Jarrett; *C:* Jurgen Baum, Goran Pavicevic.

American Yakuza

Nick Davis (Mortensen) joins the American branch of the Yakuza, Japan's organized criminal underground. He rises through the ranks and is adopted into the Tendo family, though, as anyone who has seen a John Woo film knows, the situation is complicated by personal and professional loyalties. The image is only a slight improvement over tape. The same goes for sound. —*MM*

Movie: 🎵🎵½ *DVD:* 🎵🎵½
Image Entertainment (Cat #OVED9016DVD, UPC #014381901627). Full frame. Dolby Digital Surround Stereo. $24.99. Snapper. *LANG:* English. *FEATURES:* 12 chapter links ⬩ Trailer.

1994 (R) 95m/C Viggo Mortensen, Michael Nouri, Ryo Ishibashi, Franklin Ajaye; *D:* Frank Cappello; *W:* Max Strom, John Allen Nelson; *C:* Richard Clabaugh; *M:* David Williams.

The Amityville Horror

The newlywed Lutzs (Brolin and Kidder) sink everything they have into a Long Island house that turns out to be a lemon. So's the movie, but it has been incredibly popular, spawning a bevy of sequels that are even worse. The plot is standard haunted house stuff with a weak ending, and Rod Steiger munching merrily on the scenery as a priest. On the plus side, the house has a feeling of reality to it and that gritty quality is heightened by the visual quality of the DVD. It looks much better than older rental tapes. Sound is very good, too. —*MM*

Movie: 🎵½ *DVD:* 🎵🎵½
MGM Home Entertainment (Cat #1000974, UPC #027616852816). Widescreen letterboxed; full frame. Dolby Digital Mono. $24.99. Keepcase. *LANG:* English; Spanish. *SUB:* French; Spanish. *CAP:* English. *FEATURES:* Trailer ⬩ 32 chapter links.

1979 (R) 117m/C James Brolin, Margot Kidder, Rod Steiger, Don Stroud, Murray Hamilton, Helen Shaver, Amy Wright, Val Avery, Natasha Ryan, John Larch, K.C. Martel, Meeno Peluce; *D:* Stuart Rosenberg; *W:* Sandor Stern; *C:* Fred W. Koenekamp; *M:* Lalo Schifrin. *AWARDS: NOM:* Oscars '79: Orig. Score.

Amos and Andrew

Embarrassing attempt at comedy barely stops short of endorsing the racial stereotypes it tries to parody. Pulitzer Prize–winning playwright Andrew Sterling (Jackson) is mistaken for a thief when his neighbors see him for the first time in their ritzy New England resort town. The politically ambitious police chief (Coleman) compounds their mistake and then tries to bring in Amos (Cage), a jailed drifter, to cover up his mistake. The "buddy picture" conclusion is a final insult to any viewer who makes it that far, and it's doubtful that anyone watching this DVD will finish it. The full-frame image is no better than fair with heavy pixels in solid backgrounds and a dull look throughout. —*MM*

Movie: 🎵 *DVD:* 🎵½
MGM Home Entertainment (Cat #1001841, UPC #02761686115). Full frame. Dolby Digital Surround Stereo. $14.95. Keepcase. *LANG:* English; French. *SUB:* French; Spanish. *FEATURES:* 16 chapter links ⬩ Trailer.

1993 (PG-13) 96m/C Nicolas Cage, Samuel L. Jackson, Michael Lerner, Margaret Colin, Giancarlo Esposito, Dabney Coleman, Bob Balaban, Aimee Graham,

Brad Dourif, Chelcie Ross, Jodi Long; **D:** E. Max Frye; **W:** E. Max Frye; **M:** Richard Gibbs.

Amuck!

Vintage early '70s Euro-sleaze makes a belated debut on home video. Greta (Bouchet) is hired to be a secretary to world-famous author Richard Stuart (Granger). But Stuart's wife Eleanora (Neri) has designs on the young woman, and Greta has secrets of her own. The pan-and-scan image is far from perfect, with black specks and horizontal streaks. It's really no better than an import tape, but the film is such a nostalgic treat for fans of the era that it deserves at least a qualified recommendation. —*MM*
Movie: 🎵🎵🎵 **DVD:** 🎵🎵½
Luminous Film & Video (Cat #EDE 004). Full frame. $19.98. Keepcase. *LANG:* English. *FEATURES:* 8 chapter links ▪ Talent files ▪ Photo gallery ▪ Interviews with Barbara Bouchet and Rosalba Neri.
1971 98m/C *IT* Farley Granger, Barbara Bouchet, Rosalba (Sara Bay) Neri, Umberto Raho, Patrizia Viotti, Dino Mele, Petar Martinovic, Nino Segurini; **D:** Silvio Amandio; **W:** Silvio Amandio; **C:** Aldo Giordani; **M:** Teo Usuelli.

Anatomy [SE]

Medical student Paula Henning (Potente) is accepted into a prestigious Heidelberg anatomy class. She's carrying on the family tradition of her grandfather, who's dying in the hospital he built, and her father, with whom she disagrees on almost everything. But when she gets to the new university, she finds that very creepy stuff is going on. For my money, this medical horror/thriller is right up there with *Coma*. It's inventive, grotesque, and the special effects work very well. Franka Potente shows that the impression she made in *Run, Lola, Run* was no fluke. She's a terrific actress, but she sounds much better in her native German than she does in dubbed English. For non-deutschephones, unless you absolutely detest subtitles, go with the original dialogue. Both image and sound on the disc are excellent. —*MM*
AKA: Anatomie.
Movie: 🎵🎵🎵 **DVD:** 🎵🎵🎵½
Columbia Tristar Home Video (Cat #06278, UPC #043396062788). Widescreen (2.35:1) anamorphic. Dolby Digital 5.1 Surround; Dolby Digital Surround. $24.95. Keepcase. *LANG:* English; German; French. *SUB:* English; French. *FEATURES:* 28 chapter links ▪ Commentary: director (in German) ▪ 2 deleted scenes ▪ Music video.
2000 (R) 100m/C *GE* Franka Potente, Benno Furmann, Anna Loos, Holger Spechhahn, Sebastian Blomberg; **D:** Stefan Ruzowitzky; **W:** Stefan Ruzowitzky; **C:** Peter von Haller; **M:** Marius Ruhland.

Anatomy of a Murder

Considered by many to be the best courtroom drama ever made. Small-town lawyer in northern Michigan faces an explosive case as he defends an army officer who has killed a man he suspects was his philandering wife's rapist. Realistic, cynical portrayal of the court system isn't especially concerned with guilt or innocence, focusing instead on the interplay between the various courtroom characters. Classic performance by Stewart as the down-home but brilliant defense lawyer who matches wits with Scott, the sophisticated prosecutor; terse and clever direction by Preminger. This is one of those DVDs that is a must-have for any serious film collector. The black-and-white transfer is every bit up to the four-bone quality of the film itself. Only the lack of supplementals—a photo montage, set to music from the Duke Ellington score, is the only highlight—and the slightly muted sound incur the wrath of the Hound and the resulting half-bone drop in the tech rating. The picture is gorgeous with incredible contrast delivering detail rarely found in a color film. The only flaws (including the sound) on the DVD seem to be the result of the preprint material itself and are easily forgiven on this 40-year-old masterpiece. —*JO*
Movie: 🎵🎵🎵🎵 **DVD:** 🎵🎵🎵½
Columbia Tristar Home Video (Cat #07019, UPC #043396070196). Full frame. Dolby Digital Mono. $24.95. Keepcase. *LANG:* English; Spanish. *SUB:* English; Spanish; Chinese; Korean; Thai; Portuguese. *CAP:* English. *FEATURES:* 28 chapter links ▪ Theatrical trailer ▪ Talent files ▪ Production notes ▪ Photo montage: "Anatomy of a Classic" ▪ Vintage advertising.
1959 161m/B James Stewart, George C. Scott, Arthur O'Connell, Ben Gazzara, Lee Remick, Orson Bean, Eve Arden, Duke Ellington, Kathryn Grant, Murray Hamilton, Joseph Welch; **D:** Otto Preminger; **W:** Wendell Mayes; **C:** Sam Leavitt; **M:** Duke Ellington. *AWARDS:* N.Y. Film Critics '59: Actor (Stewart), Screenplay; *NOM:* Oscars '59: Actor (Stewart), Adapt. Screenplay, B&W Cinematog., Film Editing, Picture, Support. Actor (O'Connell, Scott).

Anchoress

Tale of medieval religious belief contains elements of *Return of Martin Guerre* and *Passion of Joan of Arc* with touches of Fellini and Bergman tossed in, too. Young Cristine's (Morse) faith is so strong that she follows the advice of a priest and has herself walled into a small room. The faithful then come to this "anchoress" for advice and healing. Such an odd story is just as concerned with texture and organic patterns as it is with plot. The black-and-white photography is reproduced faithfully. Details are purposefully lost in extremely dark ominous interiors. —*MM*
Movie: 🎵🎵🎵 **DVD:** 🎵🎵🎵
Vanguard International Cinema, Inc. (UPC #658769001433). Widescreen (1.66:1) letterboxed. $29.95. Keepcase. *LANG:* English. *FEATURES:* 10 chapter links.
1993 108m/B *GB BE* Natalie Morse, Christopher Eccleston, Gene Bervoets, Toyah Wilcox, Pete Postlethwaite; **D:** Chris

Newby; **W:** Judith Stanley-Smith, Christine Watkins; **C:** Michel Baudour.

And Justice for All

Dour earnestness meets surreal liberalism in Norman Jewison's 1979 indictment of the American legal system. Al Pacino, in his histrionic prime, plays Arthur Kirkland, an idealistic lawyer waging the good fight in Baltimore's criminal courts. Tapped as lead defense counsel by a respected judge (played with oily gusto by John Forsythe) accused of rape, Kirkland finds himself a pawn of unseen political forces with seemingly no possibility for either justice to prevail or his integrity to remain intact. The script by Barry Levinson (of *Diner* and *Rain Man* fame) and Valerie Curtin revels in its anti-establishment coda, embodied with characters like Judge Rayford (Jack Warden), who packs a pistol in court and eats his lunch from the outside ledge of the courthouse. The two-sided DVD offers the video in 1.85:1 anamorphic and full frame. Both transfers stem from the same exceptionally clean source. Deep, clean black levels highlight the desaturated color scheme with no film grain or blemishes detectable in each instance. Fleshtones look natural, albeit with a slightly orange tint. The letterboxed version reads compositionally better, with the characters and environment balanced within the matted frame. In full frame, the characters seem off-center and some information is lost on the sides. The monophonic sound varies widely in performance. When reproducing Dave Grusin's very '70s score, the Dolby Digital audio projects competently with occasional distortion. Dialogue is mostly clear and intelligible, but sometimes the ADR is poorly integrated. The main supplemental on the disc is a feature-length commentary by director Jewison. He tackles virtually every scene, discussing the actors' motivation or elaborating on logistical problems and offering some historical context. His comments about the scenes between Pacino and the legendary Lee Strasberg are particularly poignant. Trailers for *And Justice* and 1995's *Donnie Brasco* provide an interesting counterpoint between the younger, explosive Pacino with the more mature, but equally volatile elder Pacino. ...*And Justice for All* recalls everything dynamic about '70s cinema: provocative content, explosive acting, and its critical eye towards the American dream. With the culture suffering through numerous "trials of the century" in the last few years, *And Justice* may have been uncannily prescient. —*EP*
Movie: 🎵🎵🎵 **DVD:** 🎵🎵🎵
Columbia Tristar Home Video (Cat #05819, UPC #4339605189). Widescreen (1.85:1) anamorphic; full frame. Dolby Digital Mono. $24.95. Keepcase. *LANG:* English; French; Spanish. *SUB:* English; French; Spanish; Portuguese; Chinese; Korean; Thai. *CAP:* English. *FEATURES:* 28 chapter links ▪ Commentary: director Jewison ▪ Theatrical trailers ▪ Talent files ▪ Production notes (booklet).

1979 (R) 120m/C Al Pacino, Jack Warden, Christine Lahti, Thomas G. Waites, Craig T. Nelson, John Forsythe, Lee Strasberg, Jeffrey Tambor; **D:** Norman Jewison; **W:** Barry Levinson, Valerie Curtin; **C:** Victor Kemper; **M:** Dave Grusin. *AWARDS: NOM:* Oscars '79: Actor (Pacino), Orig. Screenplay.

And the Band Played On

Randy Shilts's monumental and controversial 1987 book on the beginnings of the AIDS epidemic is an equally controversial and earnest film. It details the intricate medical research undertaken by doctors in France and the U.S. who fought to isolate and identify the mystery virus despite government neglect, red tape, clashing egos, and lack of funding. Various aspects of gay life are shown objectively, without sensationalism. Celebrity cameos are somewhat distracting though most acquit themselves well. The script went through numerous rewrites and director Spottiswoode reportedly objected to HBO interference in the editing stage. That being the case, it's no surprise that a commentary track is lacking. In fairness, HBO seldom includes such extras, but it still might have been valuable. DVD does a fine job with the made-for-cable image. Sound is better. —*MM*
Movie: ♫♫♫ **DVD:** ♫♫½
HBO Home Video (Cat #90962, UPC #026359096228). Widescreen (1.66:1) anamorphic. Dolby Digital 5.1 Surround Stereo; Dolby Digital Surround; Mono. $19.98. Snapper. *LANG:* English; Spanish. *SUB:* English; French; Spanish. *FEATURES:* 42 chapter links.
1993 (PG-13) 140m/C Matthew Modine, Alan Alda, Ian McKellen, Lily Tomlin, Glenne Headly, Richard Masur, Saul Rubinek, Charles Martin Smith, Patrick Bauchau, Nathalie Baye, Christian Clemenson; **Cameos:** Richard Gere, David Clennon, Phil Collins, Alex Courtney, David Dukes, David Marshall Grant, Ronald Guttman, Anjelica Huston, Ken Jenkins, Richard Jenkins, Tcheky Karyo, Swoosie Kurtz, Jack Laufer, Steve Martin, Dakin Matthews, Peter McRobbie, Lawrence Monoson, B.D. Wong, Donal Logue, Jeffrey Nordling, Stephen Spinella; **D:** Roger Spottiswoode; **W:** Arnold Schulman; **C:** Paul Elliott; **M:** Carter Burwell.

Andy Warhol

This 1987 documentary chronicles the life of Andy Warhol, Pop Culture's biggest fan, from his infancy to his death. Born to a normal family life, Warhol became fascinated with Catholic saints and soon moved on to the pop icons of the '50s and '60s. He turned his fascination into a worldwide phenomenon creating mass-produced art for the masses at his workshop in New York known as the Factory. Warhol eventually realized the value of his own status as a pop icon and turned to self-portraits, filmmaking, and even music,

with his band the Velvet Underground. While Warhol's career is interesting enough to hold anyone's attention, director Kim Evans and editor Melvyn Bragg bring a style to the assembly of the clip footage and new interviews that makes the film especially pleasurable to watch. Most of the interviews and news clips are taken from old TV footage and aren't the most pristine to look at, and the sound has the familiar hiss of video in a lot of places, but overall it is well worth watching. —*CA*
Movie: ♫♫♫½ **DVD:** ♫♫
Image Entertainment (Cat #ID5807RZDVD, UPC #014381580723). Full frame. Dolby Digital Mono. $24.99. Snapper. *LANG:* English. *FEATURES:* 12 chapter links.
1988 78m/C Andy Warhol; **D:** Kim Evans.

Angel Blue

All-around nice guy Dennis (Bottoms) lives with his wife Jill (Eichhorn) and newborn child in his California hometown. He befriends newcomer Enrique (Rodriguez) and soon Enrique's daughter (Behrens) is babysitting. Dennis really should know better when his friendship with the teen turns sexual and their secret gets out. On DVD, this made-for-Lifetime channel movie is sharp and clear, showing only minor amounts of grain. There are some obvious defects from the source print, however these are minuscule. The mono soundtrack contains a slight noticeable hiss. —*ML/MM* *AKA:* My Neighbor's Daughter.
Movie: ♫♫½ **DVD:** ♫♫
Vanguard International Cinema, Inc. (Cat #50). Full frame. Dolby Digital Mono. $29.95. Keepcase. *LANG:* English.
1997 91m/C Karen Black, Sandor Tecsi, Sam Bottoms, Yeniffer Behrens, Lisa Eichhorn, Marco Rodriguez; **D:** Steven Kovacs; **W:** Steven Kovacs; **C:** Mickey Freeman; **M:** Joel Lindheimer.

Angel of the Night

This European tale of vampires and romance comes about an inch away from being really good. Rebecca inherits a villa and brings her girlfriend and her beau with her to spend the weekend. What threatens to be a typical "and then there were none" plot steps outside the box as Rebecca begins to read her family history to her friends from a dusty old book. Each story is illustrated with fun vignettes complete with cowboy vampire hunters and strip clubs that show a real sense of humor for the vampire genre. The film falls down into the pit of predictability and picks itself up several times, but the good scenes make the film worth the viewing. The cinematography and lighting are beautiful and the acting is decent though it has to work at overcoming the dubbing. The DVD looks good and the sound is good, but once again the dubbing gives it a hollow ring. —*CA* *AKA:* Nattens Engel.
Movie: ♫♫ **DVD:** ♫♫½
MTI Home Video (Cat #50034, UPC #619935403437). Widescreen. $24.98.

Keepcase. *LANG:* English dubbed. *FEATURES:* Fangoria feature • Theatrical trailer • Cast bios • Fangoria previews.
1998 (R) 98m/C **DK** Ulrich Thomsen, Maria Karlsen, Erik Holmey; **D:** Shakey Gonzaless; **W:** Shakey Gonzaless; **C:** Jacob Kusk; **M:** Soren Hyldgaard.

Angel on My Shoulder

Murdered criminal Eddie Kagle (Muni) makes a deal with the Devil (Rains) and returns to Earth for revenge as respected Judge Parker, who has been thinning Hell's waiting list and causing a labor shortage. Occupying the good judge, the crook has significant problems adjusting. It's an amusing fantasy that gives Muni one of his rare comic performances. It was co-written by Segall, who also wrote *Here Comes Mr. Jordan,* in which Rains played an angel. Overall, this is a pretty good transfer of an often harsh black-and-white original. Thin vertical scratches and other signs of wear are visible. —*MM*
Movie: ♫♫♫ **DVD:** ♫♫½
VCI Home Video (Cat #8243, UPC #089859824326). Full frame. Dolby Digital Mono. $19.99. Keepcase. *LANG:* English. *FEATURES:* "Lord Epping Returns" short film • 18 chapter links • Talent files.
1946 101m/B Paul Muni, Claude Rains, Anne Baxter, Onslow Stevens; **D:** Archie Mayo; **W:** Harry Segall; **C:** James Van Trees; **M:** Dimitri Tiomkin.

Angela's Ashes

Frank McCourt's devastating memoir covers growing up in poverty-stricken Limerick during the 1930s with an alcoholic father (Carlyle), and a mother (Watson) who's struggling to hold the family together while dealing with her own deep depression. The book had the saving graces of lyricism and wit. Unfortunately, the film misses all that and is merely bleak despite the talented cast (including the three actors who play Frank through the years). This DVD includes two commentaries that are worth a listen. McCourt's actually embellishes his story, while Parker's gets into his cinematic technique. The transfer is very accurate to the theatrical presentation. The blacks are near-perfect and, even in scenes heavy with Irish mist, the only grain around is that of the film stock. —*JO*
Movie: ♫♫½ **DVD:** ♫♫♫½
Paramount Home Video (Cat #33607, UPC #097363360742). Widescreen (1.77:1) anamorphic. Dolby Digital 5.1; Dolby Surround. $29.99. Keepcase. *LANG:* English (DD5.1); French (DS). *SUB:* English. *CAP:* English. *FEATURES:* 30 chapter links • Theatrical trailers • "Making of" featurette • Commentary: Alan Parker, Frank McCourt • Cast and crew interviews.
1999 (R) 145m/C Emily Watson, Robert Carlyle, Joe Breen, Ciaran Owens, Michael Legge, Ronnie Masterson, Pauline McLynn; **D:** Alan Parker; **W:** Robert Carlyle, Laura Jones; **C:** Michael Seresin; **M:** John Williams; **Nar:** Andrew Bennett. *AWARDS:*

NOM: Oscars '99: Orig. Score; British Acad. '99: Actress (Watson), Art Dir./Set Dec., Cinematog.; Golden Globes '00: Orig. Score.

Angels' Wild Women

The man who brought you *Dracula vs. Frankenstein* turns his attention to hippies, motorcycle babes and dudes, evil desert gurus, and mild sexual shenanigans in this drive-in classic. Producer Sherman's commentary track is a trip down memory lane. He doesn't inflate the value of these exploitation pictures but he was friends with the late director Adamson and so he treats them kindly. So will fans. This is one of the best-looking discs in the series with a superb image for a low-budget effort. —*MM*
Movie: 🎵🎵 **DVD:** 🎵🎵🎵
Troma Team Video (Cat #9025). Full frame. $19.95. Keepcase. *LANG:* English. *FEATURES:* 9 chapter links ▪ Commentary: Sam Sherman ▪ Trailers ▪ TV teaser ▪ "Producing schlock" featurette ▪ Behind-the-scenes gallery ▪ DVD credits.
1972 85m/C Kent Taylor, Regina Carrol, Ross Hagen, Maggie Bemby, Vicki Volante; **D:** Al Adamson.

Animal Factory

When first-time felon Ron Decker (Furlong) is sentenced to two years in a decaying prison, he is introduced to a world where violence is a way of life. After witnessing a riot, Ron is taken under the wing of Earl Copen (Dafoe), the main-man on the cellblock, but the younger man soon discovers that life in prison is not about rehabilitation, it's about survival. Bunker wrote the screenplay based on his novel of the same name. The video transfer reproduces colors quite well (the blues of the prison uniforms stand out in particular). Blacks too are crisp and nicely defined. The 5.1 sound mix features an excellent transfer that delivers clear dialogue, a powerful musical score, and rather intense sound effects. —*MJT*
Movie: 🎵🎵½ **DVD:** 🎵🎵🎵
Columbia Tristar Home Video (Cat #05929, UPC #043396059290). Widescreen (1.78:1) anamorphic. Dolby Digital 5.1 Surround; Dolby Digital Stereo. $29.95. Keepcase. *LANG:* English; French. *SUB:* Spanish. *FEATURES:* 28 chapter links ▪ Commentary: actor Danny Trejo, writer Edward Bunker ▪ Interviews with Buscemi, Dafoe, Furlong, Rourke ▪ Bios and filmographies ▪ Theatrical trailer.
2000 (R) 94m/C Willem Dafoe, Edward Furlong, Danny Trejo, John Heard, Mickey Rourke, Tom Arnold, Mark Boone Jr., Steve Buscemi, Seymour Cassel; **D:** Steve Buscemi; **W:** Edward Bunker, John Steppling; **C:** Phil Parmet.

Animal Instincts

Joanne (Whirry) is a bored housewife whose husband (Caulfield), a cop, discov-

ers that he gets turned on by watching her with other men. It's loosely based on the supermarket tabloid tale of the Florida call girl and her husband who kept a list of names and videotapes of her encounters with the rich and politically connected in their little town. This one's the original video premiere "erotic thriller" and it's still one of the very best because Shannon Whirry carries off her role with such intensity. Unfortunately, though, this disc is made from the "R"-rated version of the film, not the steamier unrated version. The image is essentially identical to VHS tape; sound is stronger. —*MM*
Movie: 🎵🎵 **DVD:** 🎵🎵
Studio Home Entertainment (Cat #4020). Full frame. Dolby Digital Stereo. $24.95. Keepcase. *LANG:* English. *FEATURES:* Cast and crew thumbnail bios ▪ 18 chapter links.
1992 (R) 94m/C Maxwell Caulfield, Jan-Michael Vincent, Mitch Gaylord, Shannon Whirry, Delia Sheppard, John Saxon, David Carradine; **D:** Alexander Gregory (Gregory Dark) Hippolyte; **W:** Jon Robert Samsel, Georges des Esseintes; **C:** Paul Desatoff; **M:** Joseph Smith.

Animation Greats

This collection of cartoons selected by the National Film Board of Canada runs the gamut from conventional animation, moving cut-outs, collages, and even some live action mixed with stop-motion. As a group, they're experimental in tone, but the best of the bunch (for my money), "Get a Job," could have been done by a hyper-caffeinated Tex Avery. Stereo sound is fine. There are no visual flaws worth mentioning. Contents: "The Cat Came Back," "The Big Snitt," "Special Delivery," "Getting Started," "Get a Job," "Juke Bar," "Blackfly," and "The Lump." —*MM*
Movie: 🎵🎵🎵 **DVD:** 🎵🎵🎵
Lumivision Corp. (Cat #4970). Full frame. Dolby Digital Stereo. $24.95. Keepcase. *LANG:* English. *FEATURES:* 8 chapter links.
1997 70m/C

Animation Legend: Winsor McCay

This collection of early animation is of mainly historical value. The images are heavily scratched and many of the entries are fragments of short works. But considering that the works are so old (1911–21), that they exist at all is remarkable. McCay was a genuine pioneer. Contents: Little Nemo, How a Mosquito Operates, Gertie the Dinosaur, The Sinking of the Lusitania, The Centaurs, Gertie on Tour, Flip's Circus, Big Vaudeville, The Pet, The Flying House, The Flying House (excerpt). —*MM*
Movie: 🎵🎵½ **DVD:** 🎵🎵
Lumivision Corp. (Cat #1397, UPC #724117139766). Full frame. Dolby Digital Mono. $19.99. Keepcase. *FEATURES:*

11 chapter links ▪ Liner notes by John Canemaker.
1993 100m/C

Anna and the King

In 1862, English widow and teacher Anna Leonowens (Foster) is hired by King Mongkut (Chow Yun-Fat) of Siam to introduce his 58 children to the ideas of the West. The film looks stunning and Chow is regal and charismatic despite the fact that he speaks neither Thai nor English, which he uses in the film. Foster disappoints. She's stiff, remote, and her English accent is atrocious. Also, there's nary a hint of romance. The story was previously filmed as *Anna and the King of Siam* (1946) and *The King and I* (1956). DVD makes the most of the spectacular Malaysian locations and director Tennant's commentary track is filled with details of the difficulties of the location shoot. He also has a lot to say about the use of computer-generated effects in a big-budget star vehicle. Overall, both sound and image range between very good and excellent, even in intricate silk patterns, which are often troublesome to the medium. —*MM*
Movie: 🎵🎵½ **DVD:** 🎵🎵🎵
20th Century Fox Home Entertainment (Cat #2000044, UPC #024543000440). Widescreen (2.35:1) anamorphic. Dolby Digital 5.1 Surround Stereo; Dolby Digital Surround. $29.98. Keepcase. *LANG:* English; French. *SUB:* English; Spanish. *FEATURES:* 20 chapter links ▪ 5 featurettes ▪ 6 deleted scenes ▪ Trailer ▪ Music video ▪ TV special ▪ Commentary: Andy Tennant.
1999 (PG-13) 147m/C Jodie Foster, Chow Yun-Fat, Bai Ling, Tom Felton, Syed Alwi; **D:** Andy Tennant; **W:** Steve Meerson, Peter Krikes; **C:** Caleb Deschanel; **M:** George Fenton. *AWARDS: NOM:* Oscars '99: Art Dir./Set Dec., Costume Des.; Golden Globes '00: Song ("How Can I Not Love You"), Orig. Score.

Anna Karenina

Vivien Leigh stars in a stiff version of Tolstoy's passionate story of a married woman's illicit affair with a military officer (Richardson). In spite of the exquisite costumes and the talented leads, it's still tedious. The thin sound is typical of the late 1940s, but the fluttery, wavering audio is annoying. The lack of perfect synchronization between voices and mouth movements is even more troublesome. The black-and-white image is acceptable. —*MM*
Movie: 🎵🎵½ **DVD:** 🎵½
Madacy Entertainment (Cat #99021). Full frame. Dolby Digital Mono. $9.99. Keepcase. *LANG:* English. *FEATURES:* Cast and crew thumbnail bios ▪ 9 chapter links ▪ Vivien Leigh thumbnail biography.
1948 123m/C *GB* Vivien Leigh, Ralph Richardson, Kieron Moore, Sally Ann Howes, Niall MacGinnis, Martita Hunt, Michael Gough; **D:** Julien Duvivier; **W:**

Julien Duvivier; **C:** Henri Alekan; **M:** Constant Lambert.

Annie

Stagy, big-budget adaptation of the Broadway musical, which was adapted from the comic strip, was a major financial disaster in its theatrical incarnation. Over the years, though, it has found a following on home video. Credit the fine cast and bouncy musical numbers. The DVD transfer is generally clean and stable and without obvious blemishes. Colors are faithfully reproduced, creating vibrant scenery for this entertaining musical. Blacks are solid and deep with good shadow definition. The overall level of detail of the transfer is very good. The compression is generally well done, but some pixelation is evident as are signs of edge-enhancement. Some framing problems appear in the widescreen presentation. In a few scenes the image composition cuts off people's heads at the top of the screen. In those instances, the transfer looks as if a full-frame image had been blown up and accidentally matted. The Surround track is surprisingly dynamic with very good bass reproduction, wide frequency response, and very good dynamics. —*MM/GH*
Movie: ♫♫½ **DVD:** ♫♫♫½
Columbia Tristar Home Video (Cat #05286). Widescreen (2.35:1) letterboxed; full frame. Dolby Digital Stereo. $24.99. Keepcase. *LANG:* English; French. *FEATURES:* Talent files • Trailers • Production notes • Advertising.
1982 (PG) 128m/C Aileen Quinn, Carol Burnett, Albert Finney, Bernadette Peters, Ann Reinking, Tim Curry; **D:** John Huston; **W:** Thomas Meehan; **C:** Richard Moore; **M:** Ralph Burns. *AWARDS:* Golden Raspberries '82: Worst Support. Actress (Quinn); *NOM:* Oscars '82: Art Dir./Set Dec., Orig. Song Score and/or Adapt.

Annie

Lively and amusing adaptation of the Broadway musical will make you forget that dud 1982 movie version. Scrappy urchin Annie (newcomer Morton) is incarcerated in a Depression-era orphanage run by despotic Miss Hannigan (Bates) when she's offered the chance to spend the holidays with chilly moneybags Oliver Warbucks (Garber). Naturally, Annie thaws his frosty demeanor. Able support is provided by Warbucks's faithful assistant Grace (McDonald), and Miss Hannigan's wastrel brother and his floozy Lily (Chenoweth). From the opening scene of the film, which features hundreds of snow flakes fluttering by, it's obvious that this is going to be a good-looking disc. There are a few places where pastel-colored backgrounds have a bit of grain, but overall the colors are strong and the image is sharp. The soundtrack has very little in the way of Surround effects, but the front mix is very lively (especially during songs) and features great separation. —*JO*
Movie: ♫♫♫ **DVD:** ♫♫♫½

Buena Vista Home Entertainment (Cat #19065, UPC #717951006707). Full frame. Dolby Surround. $29.99. Keepcase. *LANG:* English. *CAP:* English. *FEATURES:* 27 chapter links • Trailer.
1999 120m/C Alicia Morton, Victor Garber, Kathy Bates, Alan Cumming, Audra McDonald, Kristin Chenoweth; **Cameos:** Andrea McArdle; **D:** Rob Marshall; **W:** Irene Mecchi; **C:** Ralf Bode; **M:** Charles Strouse, Martin Charnin.

Annie Get Your Gun

Some of the lyrics may sound dated and the staging may look a bit creaky, but this is still one of the better cinematic adaptations of a Broadway musical, finally making an appearance on home video. The story revolves around the romance between Annie Oakley (Hutton) and fellow sharpshooter Frank Butler (Keel) in Buffalo Bill's Wild West Show. The big numbers—"There's No Business Like Show Business," "You Can't Get a Man with a Gun," and many others—are real showstoppers. Since the film was made before the advent of widescreen processes, it loses nothing on a conventional monitor. Beyond a few troublesome plaid and houndstooth clothing patterns, the image is excellent. The monaural sound is true to the era. Two of the outtakes are numbers by Judy Garland, who left the production for "health reasons." In short, a real winner. —*MM*
Movie: ♫♫♫ **DVD:** ♫♫♫½
Warner Home Video, Inc. (Cat #65438, UPC #012569543829). Full frame. Dolby Digital Mono. $24.98. Snapper. *LANG:* English; French. *SUB:* English; French. *FEATURES:* 36 chapter links • Susan Lucci introduction • Talent files • 4 outtakes • Notes on Broadway production • Trailer • Awards • Full-length audio version of "There's No Business Like Show Business."
1950 107m/C Betty Hutton, Howard Keel, Keenan Wynn, Louis Calhern, J. Carrol Naish, Edward Arnold, Clinton Sundberg; **D:** George Sidney; **W:** Sidney Sheldon; **C:** Charles Rosher; **M:** Irving Berlin. *AWARDS:* Oscars '50: Scoring/Musical; *NOM:* Oscars '50: Art Dir./Set Dec., Color, Color Cinematog., Film Editing.

Another Day, Another Man

Please see review of *Bad Girls Go to Hell*.
Movie: ♫♫½
1966 ?m/B Gigi Darlene, Darlene Bennett, Barbie Kemp, Mary O'Hara, Rita Bennett; **D:** Doris Wishman; **W:** Doris Wishman, Dawn Whitman; **C:** Yuri Haviv.

Another Woman

Fans of Woody Allen's serious side are the target audience here; everyone else should be wary. Marion (Rowlands) is a philosophy professor whose life begins to change when she eavesdrops on a psychiatrist. She's forced to examine her rela-

tionship with her husband (Holm) and a friend, Larry (Hackman), to whom she is attracted. Allen and director of photography Nykvist tell the story with a typically soft, autumnal focus and emphasize various shades of brown. The clean monaural soundtrack is fine for the mannered dialogue and voice-overs. —*MM*
Movie: ♫♫½ **DVD:** ♫♫
MGM Home Entertainment (Cat #1001164, UPC #027616854629). Widescreen (1.85:1) anamorphic. Dolby Digital Mono. $19.98. Keepcase. *LANG:* English; French; Spanish. *SUB:* French; Spanish. *FEATURES:* 16 chapter links • Trailer • Booklet.
1988 (PG) 81m/C Gena Rowlands, Gene Hackman, Mia Farrow, Ian Holm, Betty Buckley, Martha Plimpton, Blythe Danner, Harris Yulin, Sandy Dennis, David Ogden Stiers, John Houseman, Philip Bosco, Frances Conroy, Kenneth Welsh, Michael Kirby; **D:** Woody Allen; **W:** Woody Allen; **C:** Sven Nykvist.

Antitrust

Thriller essentially updates Grisham's *The Firm* and sets it in the world of computer geeks, with a thinly disguised Bill Gates as the villain. Young computer genius Milo Hoffman (Phillippe) is heavily recruited by the N.U.R.V. company and its boss Gary Winston (Robbins, who seems to be having a whale of a time). But to accept a job means leaving his friends. He takes the job, uncovers hints of conspiracy, and then comes to suspect everyone including girlfriend Alice (Forlani) and co-worker Lisa (Cook). The young cast handles itself well enough. On DVD, the image is everything you'd expect of a top-drawer studio-produced thriller. On his commentary track, director Howitt and editor Zach Staenberg tend toward structural remarks—how the various pieces of the film were manipulated, edited, and reworked—and the use of computer effects. —*MM*
Movie: ♫♫½ **DVD:** ♫♫♫½
MGM Home Entertainment (Cat #1001867, UPC #027616861436). Widescreen (2.35:1) anamorphic. Dolby Digital 5.1 Surround Stereo. $24.99. Keepcase. *LANG:* English; French; Spanish. *SUB:* French; Spanish. *CAP:* English. *FEATURES:* 16 chapter links • 7 deleted scenes • "Making of" featurette • Music video • Trailer • Commentary: Howitt, editor Zach Staenberg.
2000 (PG-13) 120m/C Ryan Phillippe, Tim Robbins, Rachael Leigh Cook, Claire Forlani, Douglas McFerran, Richard Roundtree, Yee Jee Tso, Tygh Runyan; **D:** Peter Howitt; **W:** Howard Franklin; **C:** John Bailey; **M:** Don Davis.

Any Given Sunday

Stone sets aside his conspiracy theories on war and politics and effectively shines an appreciative light on a different kind of battlefield to come up with his most successful and entertaining film to date. Pacino heads an all-star cast as the battered veteran coach of the Miami Sharks. He locks horns with his hot young black quarterback (Foxx) and the team's ball-busting owner (Diaz). Stone mixes an unapologetic love of the game with clear-eyed observations on commercialism, television, and the prostitution of the game by all concerned—players, staff, journalists, owners. Real pros Jim Brown and Lawrence Taylor play variations of their real selves and the supporting cast is filled with other Hall of Famers. The surprise is the way comedian Foxx holds his own with them. The game scenes are some of the most spectacular and kinetic ever put on film and Stone whips things along at such a furious pace the long film actually seems short. The DVD handles the jittery hyperactive editing well enough. In the 5.1 Surround mix, the music tracks seem to be slightly pumped up over the theatrical release. —*MM*

Movie: ♪♪♪½ **DVD:** ♪♪♪½
Warner Home Video, Inc. Widescreen letterboxed. Dolby Digital 5.1 Surround Stereo. $24.99. Snapper. *LANG:* English. *SUB:* English; French. *FEATURES:* 48 chapter links ▪ "Making of" featurette ▪ L.L. Cool J. music video ▪ Cast and crew thumbnail bios ▪ Trailer.
1999 (R) 170m/B Al Pacino, Dennis Quaid, Cameron Diaz, Jamie Foxx, Charlton Heston, James Woods, Matthew Modine, Ann-Margret, Lauren Holly, Lela Rochon, L.L. Cool J., Aaron Eckhart, Jim Brown, Bill Bellamy, Elizabeth Berkley, John C. McGinley; *D:* Oliver Stone; *W:* Oliver Stone, John Logan; *C:* Salvatore Totino; *M:* Robbie Robertson. *AWARDS: NOM:* MTV Movie Awards '00: Breakthrough Perf. (Foxx).

The Apartment

Billy Wilder tour de force with Jack Lemmon as C.C. "Bud" Baxter, a nebbish insurance clerk scaling the corporate ladder by "loaning" out his apartment to his philandering superiors. His vertical ascent through the ranks catches the watchful eye of "big boss" J.D. Sheldrake (Fred MacMurray), who seduces Baxter with even greater advancement provided he surrenders the apartment key to Sheldrake for his affairs. Turns out Sheldrake's current object of lust and Baxter's object of adoration are the same: worldly elevator operator Fran Kubelik (Shirley MacLaine, miraculously ducking under Wilder's sometimes misogynist radar). Like *City Lights* and *To Be or Not to Be* before it and *Annie Hall* after, *The Apartment* is one of those rare movie gifts: a serious comedy. Classic sight gag of Lemmon straining spaghetti with a tennis racket ironically acts as a metaphor for the screenplay's construction: for every serve of broad laughs, equal volleys of pathos hit head-on. The scene were Baxter negotiates a minefield of juggling his bosses' tryst schedule just so he can nurse his cold (Chapter 3) is priceless. The widescreen laserdisc released a few years ago exhibited aliasing in scenes with fine details (the rows of fluorescent

office lights reaching into infinity, a TV speaker grill, art frames), due to the strict adherence of the film's 2.35 aspect ratio. (This is not a criticism of letterboxing the title. Panning and scanning Wilder's Panavision images, as with the VHS version, literally destroys the narrative flow.) The DVD sports a new anamorphic transfer; however, the flickering still remains albeit to a lesser degree. The good news is the added resolution produces an extremely crisp picture, aided by deep black levels, excellent gray scale, and strong detail delineation. Mono audio is crystal-clear. Not until an hour through the film did I notice the lack of hiss on the soundtrack, making it easier to catch Wilder and I.A.L. Diamond's glorious bon mots. They don't make satires like this anymore. —*EP*

Movie: ♪♪♪½ **DVD:** ♪♪♪
MGM Home Entertainment (Cat #1002028, UPC #027616862686). Widescreen (2.35:1) anamorphic. Dolby Digital Mono. $14.95. Keepcase. *LANG:* English; French; Spanish. *SUB:* French; Spanish. *FEATURES:* 16 chapter links ▪ Theatrical trailer.
1960 125m/B Jack Lemmon, Shirley MacLaine, Fred MacMurray, Ray Walston, Jack Kruschen, Joan Shawlee, Edie Adams, Hope Holiday, David Lewis; *D:* Billy Wilder; *W:* I.A.L. Diamond, Billy Wilder; *C:* Joseph LaShelle; *M:* Adolph Deutsch. *AWARDS:* Oscars '60: Art Dir./Set Dec., B&W, Director (Wilder), Film Editing, Picture, Story & Screenplay; AFI '98: Top 100; British Acad. '60: Actor (Lemmon), Actress (MacLaine), Film; Directors Guild '60: Director (Wilder); Golden Globes '61: Actor—Mus./Comedy (Lemmon), Actress—Mus./Comedy (MacLaine), Film—Mus./Comedy, Natl. Film Reg. '94; N.Y. Film Critics '60: Director (Wilder), Film, Screenplay; *NOM:* Oscars '60: Actor (Lemmon), Actress (MacLaine), B&W Cinematog., Sound, Support. Actor (Kruschen).

The Apostate

Dennis Hopper plays yet another of those darned serial killers. This time, a young priest (Grieco) becomes involved in his murderers. The main and supporting characters are more interesting than the overly familiar story. Given the nature of the material, the dark image is unusually sharp. Various shades of black and dark gray reveal fine detail. —*MM* **AKA:** Michael Angel.
Movie: ♪♪ **DVD:** ♪♪½
HBO Home Video (Cat #91768, UPC #026359176821). Full frame. Dolby Digital Surround Stereo; Dolby Digital Stereo. $24.99. Snapper. *LANG:* English; Spanish. *SUB:* English; French; Spanish. *CAP:* English. *FEATURES:* 14 chapter links ▪ Talent files.
1998 (R) 94m/C Richard Grieco, Dennis Hopper, Kristin Minter, Frank Medrano, Michael Cole, Efrain Figueroa, Bridget Ann White; *D:* Bill Gove; *W:* Bill Gove; *C:* Reinhart Pesche; *M:* Thomas Morse.

The Arena

Ancient Romans capture beautiful barbariennes from around the world and force them to compete in gladiatorial games. Sand-and-sandals exploitation features a mostly Italian cast, including Bay who had starred in *Lady Frankenstein* the year before, but none of them can upstage the magnificent Pam Grier. On disc, sound and image are not noticeably better than they were when I first encountered this gem at the drive-in years ago. —*MM* **AKA:** Naked Warriors.
Movie: ♪♪½ **DVD:** ♪♪
New Concorde (Cat #20129). Full frame. $24.98. *LANG:* English. *FEATURES:* 24 chapter links ▪ Trailer ▪ Talent files.
1973 (R) 75m/C Margaret Markov, Pam Grier, Lucretia Love, Paul Muller, Daniel Vargas, Marie Louise, Mary Count, Rosalba (Sara Bay) Neri, Vic Karis, Sid Lawrence, Peter Cester, Anna Melita; *D:* Steve Carver; *W:* John W. Corrington, Joyce H. Corrington; *C:* Joe D'Amato; *M:* Francesco De Masi.

The Aristocats

Typically entertaining Disney animation is about the pampered pussy Duchess (Gabor) and her three kittens who are left a fortune in their mistress Madame's will. The loot goes to the butler if the cats don't survive, so he dumps them in the country, hoping they won't find their way home. The picture is very clear, and for a movie that is this old, the colors look very nice. The digital transfer does reveal some curious flaws in the source material. In some cases, you can actually see where the original drawings on the cels were either not erased or weren't covered with ink. (Pay close attention to the 'lines' in Madame's hair.) —*ML/MM*
Movie: ♪♪♪ **DVD:** ♪♪
Buena Vista Home Entertainment (Cat #19536). Full frame. Dolby Digital Stereo. $29.99. Keepcase. *LANG:* English; French; Spanish. *FEATURES:* Trailers ▪ Trivia game ▪ Read-along.
1970 78m/C *D:* Wolfgang Reitherman; *M:* George Bruns; *V:* Eva Gabor, Phil Harris, Sterling Holloway, Roddy Maude-Roxby, Bill Thompson, Hermione Baddeley, Carol Shelley, Pat Buttram, Nancy Kulp, Paul Winchell.

Around the Fire

Coming-of-age tale is set against the backdrop of Grateful Dead–style jam-band concerts. Simon (Sawa) is a poor little rich kid haunted by his mother's early death and his father's inability to emote. While away at boarding school he falls in with the neo-hippie drug culture of the Dead-heads. Soon he falls in love and turns to constant drug use. His life spirals out of control and he ends up in rehab, where he meets hard-nosed drug counselor Kate (Woodard) who's seen it all and still wants to help him. The focus shifts between Simon in rehab and the story of how he got there. Good pacing and editing keep the story rolling nicely. The script avoids the demonization of all drug culture and devotes itself to dealing with Simon's story. Sawa's acting keeps Simon from becoming a cliché. In fact, there are no slackers on the acting front, keeping this well-worn story fresh. Woodard is especially good in a role that leaves little room to breakout. There is also a fabulously funny Hunter Thompson–style scene where Simon gets to meet the LSD chemist. The color is good and the tie-dyed shirts really jump out at you. The soundtrack is fun with a lot of Bob Marley and such. —CA

Movie: 🎞🎞½ **DVD:** 🎞🎞½
A-PIX Entertainment Inc. (Cat #APX27027, UPC #783722702734). Widescreen letterboxed. Dolby 5.1 Surround. $19.98. Keepcase. *LANG:* English. *SUB:* Spanish. *FEATURES:* Interviews with director and main cast • Theatrical trailers • Weblink.
1998 (R) 107m/C Devon Sawa, Eric Mabius, Bill Smitrovich, Tara Reid, Charlaine Woodard, Michael McKeever; **D:** John Jacobsen; **W:** John Comerford, Tommy Rosen; **M:** B.C. Smith.

Around the World with Orson Welles

This disc is made up of five episodes of a '50s documentary series that Welles made for the BBC. Though far from his finest work, Welles's screen presence alone gives a lot of oomph to the rather average presentations. The shows themselves are remarkably preserved, better than a lot of movies—and this was TV! There is very little film damage and nothing in the way of jumps or jitters. The mono sound is nothing special, but is most likely an accurate representation of the original. —JO

Movie: 🎞🎞🎞 **DVD:** 🎞🎞🎞
Image Entertainment (Cat #ID5887EUDVD, UPC #014381588729). Full frame. Dolby Digital Mono. $29.99. Snapper. *LANG:* English. *FEATURES:* 26 chapter links.
1955 134m/C *GB* **D:** Orson Welles.

The Arrangement

Jake (Keskhemnu) lives in Los Angeles. Luhann (James) is in New York. They're engaged until he admits to a one-night stand and invites her to experiment herself before the wedding. When she accepts, he is not pleased. Low-budget independent production is a bit obvious and slow moving in some respects, much more sophisticated in others. The details of everyday life are well observed and ring true. Editing is zippy and the characters are treated seriously. DVD image is grainy—that comes from the original—but the score sounds distorted at times, as if it were recorded too "hot." —MM

Movie: 🎞🎞🎞 **DVD:** 🎞🎞
MTI Home Video (Cat #D7009, UPC #039414570090). Widescreen (1.66:1) letterboxed. $24.95. Keepcase. *LANG:* English. *SUB:* Spanish. *FEATURES:* 16 chapter links • 2 trailers • Talent files.

1999 (R) 90m/C Billie James, Keskhemnu; **D:** H.H. Cooper; **W:** H.H. Cooper; **C:** Douglas W. Shannon; **M:** Michael Bearden.

Arsenic and Old Lace

Set-bound but energetic adaptation of the classic Joseph Kesselring play. Easygoing drama critic Grant is caught in a sticky situation when he learns of his aunts' favorite pastime. Apparently the kind, sweet, lonely spinsters lure gentlemen to the house and serve them elderberry wine with a touch of arsenic, then bury the bodies in the cellar—a cellar which also serves as the Panama Canal for Grant's cousin (who thinks he's Theodore Roosevelt). Massey and Lorre excel in the sinister roles. The DVD for this classic doesn't just look good for a movie this age, it looks great period. The black-and-white cinematography is presented highly detailed with excellent gray-tones and tremendous depth of field. The detail remains clear even in the shadows that are so often prevalent, and the blacks are super deep without any increase in grain. The print is so free of scratches that it's hard to believe that the movie was made in the '40s. The mono sound is also very clean with no distortion or clipping, even during louder dialogue or abrupt crashing sound effects. —JO

Movie: 🎞🎞🎞🎞 **DVD:** 🎞🎞🎞½
Warner Home Video, Inc. (Cat #65025, UPC #012569502529). Full frame. Dolby Digital Mono. $19.98. Snapper. *LANG:* English. *SUB:* English; French. *CAP:* English. *FEATURES:* 37 chapter links.
1944 118m/B Cary Grant, Josephine Hull, Jean Adair, Raymond Massey, Jack Carson, Priscilla Lane, John Alexander, Edward Everett Horton, Peter Lorre, James Gleason, John Ridgely; **D:** Frank Capra; **W:** Julius J. Epstein, Philip G. Epstein; **C:** Sol Polito; **M:** Max Steiner.

Art of Fighting

Rather lame anime piece finds Ryo and Robert witnessing a mob hit, and then becoming targets themselves. When Mr. Big kidnaps Ryo's sister, their only chance to get sis back alive is to find a magic diamond and give it to Mr. Big. Plenty of action doesn't ever build up the adrenalin. The DVD is as punchless as the film itself with rather weak colors and contrast that's several notches too low. While animation usually makes for a good DVD transfer, and Central Park Media is one of the leading purveyors of the genre, it's surprising they'd even bother with this one. —JO

Movie: 🎞½ **DVD:** 🎞½
Central Park Media/U.S. Manga Corps (Cat #ID4413CTDVD, UPC #014381441321). Full frame. PCM Stereo. $24.99. Snapper. *LANG:* Japanese. *SUB:* English. *FEATURES:* 12 chapter links.
1993 46m/C *JP* **D:** Hiroshi Fukutomi; **W:** Nobuaki Kishima.

The Art of War

Disappointingly formulaic thriller has Snipes starring as top-secret U.N. operative Neil Shaw, who is framed for the assassination of a Chinese ambassador (Hong). Also involved is his boss, Eleanor Hooks (Archer), Chinese power broker David Chan (Tagawa), and interpreter Julia (Matiko), whom Shaw kidnaps to help him prove his innocence. Plot is both convoluted and obvious (you can pretty much guess what's coming) and you learn so little about the players that you won't be very interested in what happens to them. Since the plot's so messed up, the DVD does what it can to make the viewing experience more pleasurable. The entire presentation is very sharp and deeply textured with excellent blacks, contrast, and subtly detailed hues. Action sequences (the only things this film really has going for it) are accented by a superb 5.1 mix with powerful near-subsonic bass and incredible Surround tracks that totally envelope the viewer. The music is delivered with energy and great imaging, and the dialogue (which matters the least in this film) remains out front throughout. —JO

Movie: 🎞🎞 **DVD:** 🎞🎞🎞½
Warner Home Video, Inc. (Cat #18871, UPC #085391887126). Widescreen (2.35:1) anamorphic. Dolby Digital 5.1. $24.98. Snapper. *LANG:* English. *SUB:* English. *CAP:* English. *FEATURES:* 35 chapter links • Theatrical trailer.
2000 (R) 117m/C Wesley Snipes, Marie Matiko, Cary-Hiroyuki Tagawa, Anne Archer, Maury Chaykin, Michael Biehn, Donald Sutherland, Liliana Komorowska, James Hong; **D:** Christian Duguay; **W:** Wayne Beach, Simon Davis Barry; **C:** Pierre Gill; **M:** Normand Corbeil.

Ashes of Time

Mystical, brooding, and sumptuously lensed martial arts epic was filmed in mainland China, with respect paid to Sergio Leone. A swordsman, played by Tony Leung, is going blind and wants to see his wife one last time before the lights go out completely. Another, played by the other Tony Leung, possesses a magic wine that allows him to forget his haunted past. Swordsmen are hired to kill other swordsmen. The plot simmers and occasionally explodes into chaotic action peppered with sparkling geysers and such. For some reason, the picture is horribly overmatted with as much as 25% of the image missing, possibly for placement of the subtitles. In any case, a lot of shots feel very cramped. Other than that, the quality is O.K., but the feeling of the film is really lost. —JO

Movie: 🎞🎞🎞 **DVD:** 🎞½
World Video & Supply, Inc. (Cat #WVDVD1433, UPC #639518600121). Widescreen (2.2:1) letterboxed. Dolby Digital Stereo. $29.95. Keepcase. *LANG:* Chinese. *SUB:* English.
1994 95m/C *CH* Tony Leung Chiu-Wai, Tony Leung Ka-Fai; **D:** Wong Kar-Wai; **W:** Wong Kar-Wai.

The Asphyx

A 19th-century doctor (Stephens) is studying death when he discovers the Asphyx, an aura that surrounds a person just before he or she dies. He delves deeper into his research and finds the keys to immortality. However, his irresponsibility in unleashing the obscure supernatural power into the world brings a swarm of unforeseen and irreversible troubles. The extensive notes in the extras section give an overview of the problems this production ran into on its first theatrical release. The generally darkish widescreen image is good for a film of this age, with only a few dings and some aliasing along bright lines. Sound is slightly muffled and buzzy. —*MM* **AKA:** Spirit of the Dead.
Movie: 🐾🐾🐾 **DVD:** 🐾🐾½
Elite Entertainment, Inc. (Cat #97100001). Widescreen (2.35:1) letterboxed. Dolby Digital Mono. $24.99. Keepcase. *LANG:* English. *FEATURES:* 25 chapter links ▪ U.S. press art ▪ Production notes ▪ DVD credits.
1972 (PG) 98m/C *GB* Robert Stephens, Robert Powell, Jane Lapotaire, Alex Scott, Ralph Arliss, Fiona Walker, John Lawrence, Paul Bacon, Terry Scully; **D:** Peter Newbrook; **W:** Brian Comfort; **C:** Frederick A. (Freddie) Young; **M:** Bill McGuffie.

Assassin of Youth

Please see review of *Marihuana /Assassin of Youth / Reefer Madness.*
Movie: 🐾½
1935 70m/B Luana Walters, Arthur Gardner, Earl Dwire, Fern Emmett, Dorothy Short; **D:** Elmer Clifton.

Assault of the Party Nerds

Nerds throw a party to attract new pledges while the jock fraternity plots against them. Sound familiar? Made-for-video production borrows freely from *Revenge of the Nerds.* In the interviews, star Michelle Bauer remembers that the entire shoot took five days and she was six months pregnant at the time. The filmmakers' commentary track maintains the movie's cheesy tone and beer-blast sensibility. Beyond the extras, the disc is no improvement over VHS tape. What can DVD do with a poorly focused, grainy original? —*MM*
Movie: 🐾 **DVD:** 🐾½
Passport International Productions (Cat #9006, UPC #025493900620). Full frame. Dolby Digital Surround Stereo. $29.95. Keepcase. *LANG:* English. *FEATURES:* Bloopers ▪ 12 chapter links ▪ Slide show ▪ Trailer ▪ Commentary track ▪ Cast interviews ▪ Music video.
1989 (R) 82m/C Michelle (McClellan) Bauer, Linnea Quigley, Troy Donahue, Richard Gabai, C. Paul Demsey, Marc Silverberg, Robert Mann, Richard Rifkin, Deborah Roush; **D:** Richard Gabai.

Assault of the Party Nerds 2: Heavy Petting Detective

After the nerds of the first film have graduated, our hero Ritchie (director Gabai) has become a detective who's still trying to win Muffin (Bauer). On the commentary track, Gabai admits that the bedroom scene was shot at his parents' house, and that's completely appropriate for this sort of micro-budget production. Many of the extras are also included on the disc with the original. They are the only improvement over VHS tape. —*MM*
Movie: 🐾 **DVD:** 🐾½
Passport International Productions (Cat #9007, UPC #025493900729). Full frame. Dolby Digital Surround Stereo. $29.95. Keepcase. *LANG:* English. *FEATURES:* 12 chapter links ▪ Cast interviews ▪ Commentary track ▪ Behind-the-scenes featurette ▪ Tane McClure recording session ▪ Music video.
1995 87m/C Linnea Quigley, Richard Gabai, Michelle (McClellan) Bauer, Arte Johnson, Burt Ward; **D:** Richard Gabai; **W:** Richard Gabai.

Asteroid

Re-edited version of the TV miniseries emphasizes the special effects and action, which helps this routine disaster flick. Lily McKee (Sciorra) discovers that several giant asteroids are on a collision course with Kansas City. She contacts FEMA and gets hotshot director Jack Wallace (Biehn) anxious to help out (and not just with the rock problem). Of course, the citizenry freaks and one asteroid hits, but there's an even bigger one on the way. Sound is stronger than image on this disc, even in the big effects scenes. For fans of the genre only. —*MM*
Movie: 🐾🐾 **DVD:** 🐾🐾
Pioneer Entertainment (Cat #10105). Full frame. Dolby Digital Stereo. $24.98. Keepcase. *LANG:* English. *FEATURES:* 20 chapter links ▪ Asteroid factoids ▪ Slide show with audio.
1997 120m/C Michael Biehn, Annabella Sciorra, Don Franklin, Anne-Marie Johnson, Anthony Zerbe, Carlos Gomez, Jensen Daggett; **D:** Bradford May; **C:** David Hennings, Thomas Del Ruth; **M:** Shirley Walker.

The Astounding She-Monster

How could you not love this title? If only the film truly lived up to it. The box copy states that filmmaker Ashcroft received uncredited help from his "mentor" Ed Wood Jr., and that's easy to believe. All the Wood touches are here—threadbare production values, bizarre speechifying from all concerned, and an incredulous plot. The title character (Kilpatrick) is always shown with deliberately smudged focus. She's a visitor from the stars who stumbles onto the kidnapping of a socialite (Harvey) by criminals who want to "redistribute wealth." The DVD contains a very nice transfer of a very cheap movie. Even when the Astounding She-Monster isn't around, the black-and-white photography is muddy. The score is shrill and sound tends to fade in and out. All of those flaws are absolutely appropriate, even essential to any appreciation of the film. —*MM* **AKA:** Mysterious Invader.
Movie: 🐾 **DVD:** 🐾🐾
Image Entertainment (Cat #ID8698CODVD, UPC #014381869828). Full frame. Dolby Digital Mono. $24.99. Snapper. *LANG:* English. *FEATURES:* 12 chapter links ▪ Liner notes by Tom Weaver.
1958 60m/B Robert Clarke, Kenne Duncan, Marilyn Harvey, Jeanne Tatum, Shirley Kilpatrick, Ewing Miles Brown; **D:** Ronnie Ashcroft; **W:** Frank Hall; **C:** William C. Thompson; **M:** Guenther Kauer.

The Astro-Zombies

Alternative classic (co-written by Rogers from TV's *M*A*S*H*) is a legitimate contender for Worst Movie of All Time. Carradine is the scientist who's creating zombies with a taste for human flesh. Cult heroine Satana is the leader of a group of Mexican spies. The effects are delightfully silly, but be warned—the pace is slow. The DVD was made from a very good original with only minor evidence of wear. The image is bright with pale colors. Overall, the film looks much better than it ought to. —*MM* **AKA:** The Space Vampires.
Movie: 🐾 **DVD:** 🐾🐾
Image Entertainment (Cat #ID6603WEDVD, UPC #014381660326). Widescreen (1.78:1) anamorphic. Dolby Digital Mono. $24.99. Snapper. *LANG:* English. *FEATURES:* Trailer ▪ 10 chapter links.
1967 83m/C Tura Satana, Wendell Corey, John Carradine, Tom Pace, Joan Patrick, Rafael Campos, William Bagdad, Joseph Hoover, Victor Izay, Vincent Barbi, Rod Wilmoth; **D:** Ted V. Mikels; **W:** Ted V. Mikels, Wayne Rogers; **C:** Robert Maxwell; **M:** Nico Karaski.

Asylum

Four strange and chilling stories weave together in this British horror anthology film. A murderer's victim seeks retribution. A tailor seems to be collecting his bills. A man makes voodoo dolls...only to become one later on. A woman is plagued with a double. The tales are told by a doctor visiting the asylum. They're horrifying and grotesque, yet graced with far more humor than American horror films of the time. There is quite a bit of print damage on this DVD, some scratches and white flecks, and the colors are at times pretty weak. The sound doesn't fare much better, with some very noticeable distortion. It's also much thinner and more tinny than I remember from the theatre. (At times, however, that actually works to the film's advantage, enhancing the horror effect of the somewhat overused *Night on Bald Mountain* in the soundtrack.) Despite its flaws, this one's still worth adding to the collection. —*JO* **AKA:** House of Crazies.

Movie: 🦴🦴🦴 **DVD:** 🦴🦴½
Image Entertainment (Cat #ID6144TVDVD, UPC #014381614428). Full frame. Dolby Digital Mono. $24.99. Snapper. *LANG:* English. *FEATURES:* 12 chapter links.
1972 (PG) 100m/C *GB* Peter Cushing, Herbert Lom, Britt Ekland, Barbara Parkins, Patrick Magee, Barry Morse, Robert Powell, Richard Todd, Charlotte Rampling, Ann(e) Firbank, Sylvia Syms, James Villiers, Geoffrey Bayldon, Megs Jenkins; *D:* Roy Ward Baker; *W:* Robert Bloch; *C:* Denys Coop.

Asylum of Terror
Scores of unsuspecting Nashville residents visit an abandoned mental institution that has been converted into a haunted house. They soon discover that the violence and mayhem is real. This dreadful, amateurish horror flick is disjointed, poorly acted and scripted, and is mostly out-of-focus. There is no chapter menu, and the 5.1 Dolby Digital mix is wasted on some truly horrible sound recordings—think: tin can and string. The good news is that this exercise in bad moviemaking runs only one hour and 15 minutes. —*RJT*
Movie: 🦴 **DVD:** 🦴
York Entertainment (Cat #YPD-1047, UPC #730723104720). Full frame. Dolby Digital 5.1 Surround Sound. $14.98. Keepcase. *LANG:* English. *FEATURES:* 15 chapters, but no menu.
1998 75m/C Jason Petty, Kerry Wade, Melissa Young, Misty Lewis, Sixx Williams, Brandon Boyd; *D:* George Demick.

At Close Range
Based on the true story of Bruce Johnston Sr. and Jr. in Brandywine River Valley, Pennsylvania. Father (Walken) tempts his teenaged son (Penn) into pursuing criminal activities with talk of excitement and high living. Jr. soon learns that Sr. is extremely dangerous and a bit unstable, but he's still fascinated by his wealth and power. The film is sometimes overbearing and depressing, but good acting and fancy camerawork redeem it. A young cast of stars includes Masterson as the girl Penn tries to impress. Features Madonna's "Live to Tell." The video transfer tends a bit toward the muted side with poorly defined blacks, but the picture is better than VHS can provide. The audio transfer fares a bit better, although dialogue is occasionally hard to understand. —*MJT*
Movie: 🦴🦴🦴 **DVD:** 🦴🦴½
MGM Home Entertainment (Cat #1001271, UPC #027616855510). Widescreen (1.85:1) anamorphic; full frame. Dolby Digital Stereo Surround; Dolby Digital Mono. $19.98. Keepcase. *LANG:* English; French; Spanish. *SUB:* French; Spanish. *FEATURES:* 32 chapter links • Theatrical trailer.
1986 (R) 115m/C Sean Penn, Christopher Walken, Christopher Penn, Mary Stuart Masterson, Crispin Glover, Kiefer Sutherland, Candy Clark, Tracey Walter, Millie Perkins, Alan Autry, David Strathairn,

Eileen Ryan; *D:* James Foley; *W:* Nicholas Kazan; *C:* Juan Ruiz-Anchia; *M:* Patrick Leonard.

At War with the Army
Martin and Lewis's debut as a comedy team is a serviceable service comedy based on a play by James Alardice. They're recruits who become mixed up in all sorts of wild situations at their Army base. You get what you pay for with this bargain-bin disc. The thin sound distorts the score painfully during the opening credits. The black-and-white image is grainy with the expected wear and tear on the print. —*MM*
Movie: 🦴½ **DVD:** 🦴½
Digital Disc Entertainment (Cat #DDE573). Full frame. Mono. $9.99. Keepcase. *LANG:* English. *FEATURES:* 26 chapter links.
1950 93m/B Dean Martin, Jerry Lewis, Polly Bergen, Mike Kellin; *D:* Hal Walker; *W:* Fred Finklehoffe; *C:* Stuart Thompson; *M:* Jerry Livingston.

Attack of the Giant Leeches
Corman cheapie is about the titular swamp critters who suddenly decide to make human flesh their new food supply. Perturbed innkeeper plays along by forcing his wife and her lover into the murk. This sow's ear has never looked very good and DVD can't turn it into a silk purse. The image is very grainy and shows normal signs of wear for a film this old. Title is part of the *Roger Corman Retrospective, Vol. 1* triple feature. —*MM* **AKA:** The Giant Leeches; She Demons of the Swamp; Demons of the Swamp.
Movie: 🦴 **DVD:** 🦴½
SlingShot Entertainment (Cat #TDVD9114, UPC #017078911428). Full frame. Dolby Digital Mono. $19.99. Large jewelcase. *LANG:* English. *FEATURES:* 13 chapter links.
1959 62m/B Kenneth (Ken) Clark, Yvette Vickers, Gene Roth, Bruno VeSota, Michael Emmet, Tyler McVey, Jan Shepard, George Cisar, Dan White; *D:* Bernard L. Kowalski; *W:* Leo Gordon; *C:* John M. Nickolaus Jr.; *M:* Alexander Laszlo.

Attack of the Puppet People
This alternative classic from the prolific Bert I. Gordon, a rival to Ed Wood Jr. in the schlock hall of fame, will not make anyone forget *The Incredible Shrinking Man*. The insane dollmaker Dr. Franz (Hoyt) shrinks six people (including our heroes Agar and Kenny) to the size of Ken and Barbie. Can they escape the mad scientist? The dog? The rat? The effects are nostalgically charming. Light aliasing mars an otherwise pristine black-and-white print. This is a very good transfer of a very bad (but fun) movie. —*MM*
Movie: 🦴🦴 **DVD:** 🦴🦴🦴
MGM Home Entertainment (Cat #1001541, UPC #027616858528). Full frame. Dolby Digital Mono. $19.98. Keep-

case. *LANG:* English. *SUB:* French; Spanish. *CAP:* English. *FEATURES:* 16 chapter links.
1958 79m/B John Agar, John Hoyt, June Kenny; *D:* Bert I. Gordon; *W:* George Worthing Yates.

Attention Shoppers
This little film has all the ingredients to make a midnight classic, but in the end nothing mixes together quite right and the final product falls flat. Enrique Suarez (Carbonell) is an American-born Latino who plays fifth banana in a popular sitcom. His relationship with his wife is falling apart, he is about to be canned from his job, and the Latin community is not too happy with the character he portrays on TV. In what turns out to be a run of bad decisions, he goes to Texas to put in a celebrity appearance at the opening of a Big-K rather than attend his brother-in-law's wedding. One horrible, embarrassing situation after another makes Enrique realize the tenuous nature of celebrity and he goes back home with a better idea of what is valuable in life. The humor here is as dry as a Bond martini, but too often viewers find themselves feeling as uncomfortable as the lead character. There is a priceless scene with, of all people, Luke Perry, as an egomaniacal, Nietzsche-reading soap star who is opening another Big-K across town and does everything he can to undermine Enrique's self-confidence. The DVD quality is good with nice color, and the sound is acceptable for a dialogue-driven film. —*CA*
Movie: 🦴½ **DVD:** 🦴🦴½
MGM Home Entertainment (Cat #4001470, UPC #027616854797). Full frame. Dolby Digital Surround. $19.98. Keepcase. *LANG:* English; Spanish. *SUB:* French; Spanish. *CAP:* English. *FEATURES:* 28 chapter links.
1999 (R) 87m/C Nestor Carbonell, Luke Perry, Martin Mull, Kathy Najimy, Michael Lerner, Cara Buono, Lin Shaye, Casey Affleck; *D:* Philip Charles MacKenzie; *W:* Nestor Carbonell.

Attila
Made-for-TV historical adventure is a sort of lightweight *Conan*. Attilla (Butler) has long hair and a stubble. He's up against decadent Rome, represented by General Falvius Aetius (Boothe). Both production values and DVD image range between good and very good. Disc is an improvement over broadcast quality. —*MM*
Movie: 🦴🦴½ **DVD:** 🦴🦴½
USA Home Entertainment (Cat #96306 0186-2, UPC #696306018629). Widescreen (1.77:1) letterboxed. Dolby Digital 5.1 Surround Stereo; Dolby Digital Surround. $26.95. Keepcase. *LANG:* English. *FEATURES:* 25 chapter links • "Making of" featurette • Theatrical trailer • DVD-ROM photo gallery.
2001 177m/C Gerard Butler, Powers Boothe, Alice Krige, Simmone Jade MacKinnon, Tim Curry, Reg Rogers, Steven

Berkoff, Tommy Flanagan, Pauline Lynch, Liam Cunningham, Jolyon Baker, Sian Phillips, Jonathan Hyde; *D:* Dick Lowry; *W:* Robert Cochran; *C:* Steven Fierberg; *M:* Nick Glennie-Smith.

Attila 74: The Rape of Cyprus

Simply devastating. Michael Cacoyannis returned to his homeland after the 1975 Turkish invasion of Cyprus to document on film the human cost of a failed political coup and the bloody aftermath. Interviewing victims and refugees from all walks of life—mothers, fathers, children, policeman, politicians, clergy—Cacoyannis's unflinching camera lens unveils a nation drowning in tears and blood. For every scene of witnesses recounting the horrors they saw, there are equal stretches of the documentary without a single word spoken. For Cacoyannis, the silence wails as loudly as those whose lives were forever changed by the invasion. The transfer does what it can with the grainy source material shot under less than ideal circumstances. The image is as clear and sharp as the rough-looking source materials will allow. Sound is fine. An epilogue filmed by Cacoyannis 25 years later closes the documentary on a chilling, unresolved note. —*EP*

Movie: 🎜🎜🎜 *DVD:* 🎜🎜
Winstar Home Entertainment (Cat #FLV5217, UPC #720917521725). Full frame. Dolby Digital Mono. $24.99. Keepcase. *LANG:* Greek. *SUB:* English. *FEATURES:* 8 chapter links • Filmographies and awards • Production credits • Weblinks.
1975 101m/C *GR D:* Michael Cacoyannis; *C:* Sakis Maniatis; *M:* Michalis Christodoulidis; *Nar:* Michael Cacoyannis.

The Audrey Hepburn Story

When you portray a movie icon, expect the critical brickbats to fly. Sweet Hewitt does her best in the title role, but it's all surface gloss. Biopic covers 1935 to 1960 as Hepburn deals with family crises (dad's a two-timing Nazi), war years in occupied Holland, her beginnings as a dancer in England, and the first small roles. Then it's on to New York and the world of theatre and films. Along the way, there's a little romance, a marriage to Mel Ferrer (McCormack), and various re-creations of some Hepburn movie roles. The transfer is beautifully clean and without any blemishes. A tad soft at times, the image boasts powerful colors that are very faithfully reproduced, purposely adding to the romantic mystique surrounding Audrey Hepburn. The picture has very good contrast and blacks are deep and solid. The stereo soundtrack comes across nicely. —*GH/MM*

Movie: 🎜🎜 *DVD:* 🎜🎜½
Columbia Tristar Home Video (Cat #4724). Widescreen (1.78:1) anamorphic. Dolby Digital Stereo. $24.95. Keepcase. *LANG:*

English. *SUB:* English; French; Spanish. *FEATURES:* Talent file • Trailers.
2000 (PG) 133m/C Jennifer Love Hewitt, Eric McCormack, Frances Fisher, Peter Giles, Keir Dullea, Gabriel Macht, Marcel Jeannin, Swede Svensson, Michael J. Burg, Ryan Hollyman; *D:* Steve Robman; *W:* Marsha Norman; *C:* Pierre Letarte; *M:* Lawrence Shragge.

Autumn in New York

Shanghai-born actress Joan Chen, who impressed critics with her directorial debut film, *Xiu Xiu: The Sent Down Girl,* tackles her second feature, a "Hollywood Studio" production, with big-name stars. What she's come up with is a classy May/September romance between "48-year-old" restaurant owner Richard Gere and "22-year-old" Winona Ryder, the daughter of a former flame. Actually, Gere and Ryder look good together, and age doesn't really become an issue. Rather she has a bad heart, and their newfound love is doomed in the due course of time. Sad and melancholy, but beautifully rendered. Disappointing DVD presentation, with no special features, not even the film's trailer. —*RJT*

Movie: 🎜🎜½ *DVD:* 🎜🎜½
MGM Home Entertainment (Cat #1001441, UPC #027616857613). Widescreen (1.85:1) anamorphic; full frame. Dolby Digital 5.1 Surround; Dolby Digital Surround. $26.98. Keepcase. *LANG:* English; French; Spanish. *SUB:* French; Spanish. *FEATURES:* 16 chapter links.
2000 (PG-13) 104m/C Richard Gere, Winona Ryder, Anthony LaPaglia, Elaine Stritch, Vera Farmiga, Sherry Stringfield, Jill(ian) Hennessey; *D:* Joan Chen; *W:* Allison Burnett; *C:* Changwei Gu; *M:* Gabriel Yared.

Avalon

Powerful, quiet portrait of the break-up of the family unit as seen from the perspective of a Russian family settled in Baltimore at the close of World War II. Initially, the family is unified in its goals, ideologies, and social lives. Gradually, all of that disintegrates as members move to the suburbs and television replaces conversation at holiday gatherings. Levinson based the film on his own experiences and that's why the lack of any commentary track is such an obvious omission. Otherwise, both image and sound are all that you expect from a big-budget studio production. —*MM*

Movie: 🎜🎜🎜 *DVD:* 🎜🎜🎜
Columbia Tristar Home Video (Cat #05844, UPC #043396058446). Widescreen (1.85:1) anamorphic. Dolby Digital Surround Stereo. $29.95. Keepcase. *LANG:* English; French; Spanish; Portuguese. *SUB:* English; French; Spanish; Portuguese; Korean; Thai. *FEATURES:* 28 chapter links • Talent files • Trailers.
1990 (PG) 126m/C Armin Mueller-Stahl, Aidan Quinn, Elizabeth Perkins, Joan Plowright, Lou Jacobi, Leo Fuchs, Eve Gor-

don, Kevin Pollak, Israel Rubinek, Elijah Wood, Grant Gelt, Bernard Hiller; *D:* Barry Levinson; *W:* Barry Levinson; *C:* Allen Daviau; *M:* Randy Newman. *AWARDS:* Writers Guild '90: Orig. Screenplay; *NOM:* Oscars '90: Cinematog., Costume Des., Orig. Screenplay, Orig. Score.

The Avengers 1964–66

The first shows on these discs are in black and white, and they star Honor Blackman (later Pussy Galore in *Goldfinger*) as Mrs. Cathy Gale, partner to the dapper John Steed. Diana Rigg joins the series in 1965. In visual terms, the episodes look as good as anyone could expect television productions of this age to look. But, as was noted in the review in *Avengers '67* in the first edition, this series was never about dazzling images. It's about wit, style, and sex, and all three arrive intact on DVD. (Each set contains two discs; discs are also available individually.) Set 1 '64: #AAE-70070 (The White Elephant, The Little Wonders, The Wringer, Mandrake, The Secrets Broker, The Trojan Horse). Set 2 '64: #AAE-70073 (Build a Better Mousetrap, The Outside-In Man, The Charmers, Concerto, Esprit de Corps, Lobster Quadrille). Set 1 '65: #AAE-70028 (The Town of No Return, The Gravediggers, The Cybernauts, Death at Bargain Prices, Castle De'ath, The Master Minds). Set 2 '65: #AAE-70033 (The Murder Market, A Surfeit of H20, The Hour That Never Was, Dial a Deadly Number, Man-Eater of Surrey Green, Two's a Crowd, Too Many Christmas Trees). Set 1 '66: #AAE-70034 (Silent Dust, Room without a View, Small Game for Big Hunters, The Girl from Auntie, The 13th Hole, Quick-Quick-Slow Death). Set 2 '66: #AAE-70035 (The Danger Makers, A Touch of Brimstone, What the Butler Saw, The House That Jack Built, A Sense of History, How to Succeed At Murder, Honey for the Prince). —*MM*

Movie: 🎜🎜🎜🎜 *DVD:* 🎜🎜🎜
New Video Group Full frame. $44.95. Keepcase, boxed set. *LANG:* English. *FEATURES:* 7–8 chapter links per episode • Production stills galleries.
1967 m/C Patrick Macnee, Diana Rigg, Honor Blackman; *M:* Laurie Johnson.

Awakenings of the Beast

Semi-plotted horror/fantasy documents the sufferings of an LSD user who is beset with hallucinatory visions and is prone to fits of frenzied violence. Director Jose Mojica Marins (AKA Coffin Joe) steps out of his Ze do Ciaxia character in this mix of drugs and sex intercut with Mojica Marins himself on trial for his offensive movies. By the end, there is a point—that drugs aren't the cause of evil behavior—but it's a long hike. This is the kind of midnight movie that is best appreciated with a receptive crowd. It's a psychedelic interpretation of an old EC comic. In fact, a small comic book is included with the

disc. Image and thin sound are probably the best that anyone could expect of a film this old. The combination of black and white with some full color and tinted footage contains fairly few visual flaws. —*MM* *AKA:* Ritual Dos Sadicos; Ritual of the Maniacs.
Movie: ♫♫ **DVD:** ♫♫½
Fantoma Films (UPC #014381060423). Widescreen (1.66:1) letterboxed. Dolby Digital Mono. $24.99. Keepcase. *LANG:* Portuguese. *SUB:* English. *FEATURES:* 12 chapter links ● Interview with Jose Mojica Marins ● 3 trailers.
1968 93m/B *BR* Jose Mojica Marins, Sergio Hinst, Andrea Bryan, Mario Lima; **D:** Jose Mojica Marins; **W:** Jose Mojica Marins, Rubens Francisco Lucchetti; **C:** Giorgio Atilli.

Away All Boats
This is the true (well, mostly true) story of Capt. Hawks (Chandler), who leads a crew of misfits to victory about the transport USS *Belinda* during World War II in the Pacific. The battle scenes are well done but much of the day-to-day business of life on the ship is blandly realistic. Look for an early and brief appearance by Clint Eastwood. The main flaw here is the full-frame transfer. The Pacific setting loses a lot without the widescreen. Otherwise, the DVD was made from a print with only a few visible flecks and some light static on the soundtrack. —*MM*
Movie: ♫♫½ **DVD:** ♫♫
Goodtimes Entertainment (Cat #81040). Full frame. Dolby Digital Mono. $24.95. Snapper. *LANG:* English. *SUB:* French; Spanish; English. *FEATURES:* 18 chapter links.
1956 114m/B Jeff Chandler, George Nader, Richard Boone, Julie Adams, Keith Andes, Lex Barker, Clint Eastwood; **D:** Joseph Pevney; **W:** Ted Sherdeman; **C:** William H. Daniels; **M:** Frank Skinner.

The Awful Dr. Orlof
Prolific director Franco got his start with this hash of elements borrowed from Dr. Jekyll, Jack the Ripper, and Frankenstein. Trying to repair his daughter's scarred face, Dr. Orlof (Vernon) and his blind assistant Morpho (Valle) kidnap women and operate on them. The horror is uneven with some genuine creepiness and atmosphere to be found among hammy overacting, clumsy clichés, and overly talky scenes. Some brief line flashing can be traced to deliberate variations in lighting. The black-and-white photography is generally very good. This is the "full-length" version that contains a bit of nudity. —*MM* *AKA:* Gritos en la Noche; The Demon Doctor.
Movie: ♫♫½ **DVD:** ♫♫♫
Image Entertainment (Cat #ID9099BIDVD, UPC #014381909920). Widescreen (1.66:1) letterboxed. Dolby Digital Mono. $24.99. Snapper. *LANG:* English; French.

FEATURES: 12 chapter links ● Liner notes by Tim Lucas.
1962 86m/B *SP FR* Howard Vernon, Diana Lorys, Frank Wolff, Riccardo Valle, Conrado San Martin, Perla Cristal, Maria Silva, Mara Laso; **D:** Jess (Jesus) Franco; **W:** Jess (Jesus) Franco; **C:** Godofredo Pacheco; **M:** Jose Pagan, Antonio Ramirez Angel.

B. Monkey
B. (for Beatrice) (Argento) tries to leave her life of crime and drugs when she falls for Alan (Harris), a school teacher. But her ex-partners Paul (Everett) and Bruno (Rhys Meyers) want her to do one last job. Will they change her ways? Will she change Alan? This one mainly has cool Brit style and a very sexy star in place of substance. The image is fine. Glowing reds are supposed to glow. Surround is acceptable. —*MM*
Movie: ♫♫½ **DVD:** ♫♫½
Miramax Pictures Home Video (Cat #18292, UPC #717951004789). Widescreen (1.85:1) anamorphic. Dolby Digital 5.1 Surround Stereo. $24.99. Keepcase. *LANG:* English. *CAP:* English. *FEATURES:* Trailers ● 22 chapter links.
1997 (R) 91m/C *GB* Asia Argento, Jared Harris, Rupert Everett, Jonathan Rhys Meyers, Tim Woodward, Ian Hart; **D:** Michael Radford; **W:** Michael Thomas, Chloe King; **C:** Ashley Rowe; **M:** Jennie Muskett.

Babar: King of the Elephants
This is a feature-length animated film based on the popular HBO children's series. (I'm not sure if it was made before the series began.) It tells the slowly paced (much too slowly for children) story of the origin of the popular elephant. The DVD color palette is washed-out grays and tans. The unusual, catchy songs are better and the episode of the series, "An Elephant's Best Friend," is far superior—bright and fast-moving. —*ML*
Movie: ♫ **DVD:** ♫♫
HBO Home Video (Cat #91567). Full frame. Dolby Digital Stereo. $19.98. Snapper. *LANG:* English. *SUB:* English; French; Spanish. *FEATURES:* Trailer ● 1/2 hour episode "An Elephant's Best Friend."
1999 78m/C *CA FR GE* **D:** Raymond Jafelice; **W:** Raymond Jafelice, Peter Sauder.

Babette's Feast
Adaptation of an Isak Dinesen story is a simple, moving pageant-of-life fable. A group of religiously zealous villagers are taught love and forgiveness through a lavish banquet prepared by one of their housemaids, who turns out to be a world-class chef. The DVD is a virtually flawless reproduction of an often somber, softly focused image. The original Danish and French Surround soundtrack is preferable to the mono English. —*MM* *AKA:* Babettes Gaestebud.
Movie: ♫♫♫½ **DVD:** ♫♫♫

MGM Home Entertainment (Cat #1001475, UPC #027616857958). Widescreen (1.66:1) letterboxed. Dolby Digital Mono; Dolby Digital Surround Stereo. $19.98. Keepcase. *LANG:* Danish and French; English; Spanish. *SUB:* English; French; Spanish. *FEATURES:* 16 chapter links ● Trailer.
1987 102m/C *DK FR* Stephane Audran, Bibi Andersson, Bodil Kjer, Birgitte Federspiel, Jean-Philippe LaFont, Ebbe Rode, Jarl Kulle; **D:** Gabriel Axel; **W:** Gabriel Axel; **C:** Henning Kristiansen; **M:** Per Norgard; **Nar:** Ghita Norby. *AWARDS:* Oscars '87: Foreign Film; British Acad. '88: Foreign Film.

Baby Boom
Hard-charging businesswoman J.C. Wiatt (Keaton) becomes the reluctant guardian of a baby girl (an inheritance from a long-lost cousin). With great difficulty, she adjusts to life outside the New York City rat race, but a relationship with pretty-boy Sam Shepard eases the pain. The power-suited ad queen becomes a jelly-packing Vermont store owner and proud mom. The fairly harmless collection of clichés is bolstered by a good performance from the star. The disc boasts an acceptable transfer of a slightly soft-focus image. The only glaring flaw is one polka-dot tie that creates a weird stroboscopic flash whenever it moves. —*MM*
Movie: ♫♫½ **DVD:** ♫♫½
MGM Home Entertainment (Cat #1001548, UPC #027616858580). Widescreen (1.85:1) letterboxed. Dolby Digital Surround Stereo. $19.98. Keepcase. *LANG:* English; French. *SUB:* French; Spanish. *CAP:* English. *FEATURES:* 16 chapter links ● Trailer.
1987 (PG) 103m/C Diane Keaton, Sam Shepard, Harold Ramis, Sam Wanamaker, James Spader, Pat Hingle, Mary Gross, Victoria Jackson, Paxton Whitehead, Annie Golden, Dori Brenner, Robin Bartlett, Christopher Noth, Britt Leach; **D:** Charles Shyer; **W:** Charles Shyer, Nancy Meyers; **C:** William A. Fraker; **M:** Bill Conti.

Back to Back
Ex-cop Malone (Rooker) teams up with hitman Koji (Ishibashi), who's holding Malone's daughter Chelsea (Harris) hostage, to double-cross a corrupt cop and stay alive while being hunted by the Mafia. Think John Woo–light with fast-paced action. Both the full-frame image and sound are only slightly brighter than VHS tape. —*MM*
Movie: ♫♫ **DVD:** ♫♫♫
Winstar Home Entertainment (Cat #FLV5166, UPC #720917516622). Full frame. $24.98. Keepcase. *LANG:* English. *FEATURES:* 8 chapter links ● Production credits.
1996 (R) 95m/C Michael Rooker, Ryo Ishibashi, John Laughlin, Danielle Harris, Bob(cat) Goldthwait, Vincent Schiavelli; **D:** Roger Nygard; **W:** Lloyd Keith; **C:** Mark W. Gray; **M:** Walter Werzowa.

Back to God's Country / Something New

Nell Shipman is virtually unknown in America. She was a Canadian writer/producer/star of the silent era. According to the box copy, she was also a conservationist. These two films are both fast-paced romantic adventures. In *Back to God's Country,* she's a young wife who is lusted after by an evil villain. The setting is the Canadian wilderness. *Something New,* made a year later, finds her playing a writer who goes to the Mojave Desert for inspiration. She finds more romance, is kidnapped by bandits, and then is rescued by her sweetie in his Maxwell sedan. Stuntwork in both films is very good. Unfortunately, both films have suffered some serious damage in places. But what appears to be chemical burning or decomposition is mostly limited to the opening scenes. After that, it's only the expected wear that's evident. The restorers have done well with what they had to work with, re-creating the original tinting, too. —*MM*
Movie: 🎬🎬🎬 *DVD:* 🎬🎬
Image Entertainment (Cat #ID9796MLDVD, UPC #014381979626). Full frame. Dolby Digital Stereo. $24.99. Snapper. *LANG:* Silent. *SUB:* English intertitles. *FEATURES:* 18 chapter links.
1919 74m/B CA Nell Shipman, Wheeler Oakman, Wellington A. Playter, Ralph Laidlaw, Charles Arling; **D:** Nell Shipman, Ernest Shipman, David M. Hartford; **C:** Joseph Walker; **M:** Philip Carli.

Back to School

Dangerfield plays an obnoxious millionaire who enrolls in college to help his wimpy son (Gordon) achieve campus stardom. His motto seems to be "if you can't buy it, it can't be had." At first his antics embarrass his shy son, but soon everyone is clamoring to be seen with the pair and the son develops his own self-confidence. The sepia opening looks great on this DVD but the grain kicks in when color is introduced. There are black flecks intermittently throughout, indicating that the film print may be part of the problem. At times the artifacts are so bad they distort faces enough to make a character look like he jumped out of a horror film. The blacks are pretty true and this is at least a little better than the VHS version, but hardly worth the upgrade. The full-bodied sound's not bad at all, though, with tight, clean bass. —*JO*
Movie: 🎬🎬½ *DVD:* 🎬½
MGM Home Entertainment (Cat #908058, UPC #027616805829). Widescreen (1.85:1) letterboxed; full frame. Dolby Surround. $24.98. Keepcase. *LANG:* English; Spanish; French. *SUB:* Spanish; French. *CAP:* English. *FEATURES:* 32 chapter links ▪ Theatrical trailer.
1986 (PG-13) 96m/C Rodney Dangerfield, Keith Gordon, Robert Downey Jr., Sally Kellerman, Burt Young, Paxton Whitehead, Adrienne Barbeau, M. Emmet Walsh,

Severn Darden, Ned Beatty, Sam Kinison, Kurt Vonnegut Jr., Robert Picardo, Terry Farrell, Edie McClurg, Jason Hervey, William Zabka; **D:** Alan Metter; **W:** Will Aldis, Steven Kampmann, Harold Ramis, Peter Torokvei; **C:** Thomas Ackerman; **M:** Danny Elfman.

Backlash

Federal prosecutor Gina Gallagher (Needham) has gotten on the wrong side of the Colombian drug cartel. After her partner is killed, Gina works with veteran homicide detective Moe Ryan (Durning) and uncovers a government conspiracy—so maybe trusting a convict (Belushi) to protect her isn't such a bad idea. The full-frame DVD transfer is a good one, and the high contrast, combined with strong colors, keeps every scene visually energized. The biggest flaw is the odd artifact in dimmer scenes—something that shouldn't be a problem now. The soundtrack does its job as well, with an all-around lively mix containing plenty of ambience and the occasional Surround effect. —*JO* *AKA:* Justice.
Movie: 🎬🎬 *DVD:* 🎬🎬🎬
Columbia Tristar Home Video (Cat #05003, UPC #043396050037). Full frame. Dolby Digital 5.1; Dolby Surround. $24.95. Keepcase. *LANG:* English. *SUB:* English; Spanish. *CAP:* English. *FEATURES:* 28 chapter links ▪ Theatrical trailer ▪ Cast and crew bios ▪ Commentary: director Jack Ersgard, writer Patrick Ersgard.
1999 (R) 103m/C Tracey Needham, Charles Durning, James Belushi, JoBeth Williams, Patrick Ersgard, Tony Plana, Henry Silva, Warren Berlinger; **D:** Joakim (Jack) Ersgard; **W:** Patrick Ersgard.

Backstage

Absolutely nothing about this concert film will appeal to those who do not already embrace hip-hop music. It follows several rappers on a bus tour. As the title suggests, most of the action takes place away from the auditoriums—in hotels, corridors, buses, and bathrooms. The guys swear constantly, smoke a lot of dope, and brag about their various exploits. Given the raw nature of the material, it doesn't gain much beyond accessibility on DVD. —*MM*
Movie: 🎬🎬 *DVD:* 🎬🎬
Buena Vista Home Entertainment (Cat #21645, UPC #786936144673). Full frame. Dolby Digital 5.1 Surround Stereo. $29.99. Keepcase. *LANG:* English. *CAP:* English. *FEATURES:* 19 chapter links ▪ Trailer.
2000 (R) 87m/C DMX, Method Man, Jay-Z, Redman, Ja Rule, Beanie Sigel; **D:** Chris Fiore; **C:** Elena "EZ" Sorre, Mark Petersson, Lenny Santiago.

Bad Girls Go to Hell / Another Day, Another Man

This double feature tries to re-create the complete drive-in experience, right down to intermission animation ("only 3 minutes

until the 2nd feature—time to visit the concession stand!"). The two Doris Wishman films may seem tame today but they were cutting edge exploitation in the mid-'60s and their portrayal of sexual violence is still strong. In the first, a young woman (Darlene) kills a rapist and runs off to New York. The second (see separate entry for credits) concerns a woman who's forced into prostitution to pay for her husband's medical expenses. On both features, the black-and-white photography ranges between good and fair, though the films exhibit few signs of wear. Sound is acceptable. —*MM*
Movie: 🎬🎬½ *DVD:* 🎬🎬½
Image Entertainment (Cat #ID95975SW DVD, UPC #014381949727). Full frame. Dolby Digital Mono. $24.99. Snapper. *LANG:* English. *FEATURES:* 20 chapter links ▪ Theatrical trailers ▪ Gallery of exploitation ads ▪ Drive-in intermission short subjects ▪ Drive-in adult peep ad.
1965 98m/B Gigi Darlene, George La Rocque, Sam Stewart, Sandee Norman, Alan Yorke, Bernard L. Sankett, Darlene Bennett, Marlene Starr, Harold Key; **D:** Doris Wishman; **W:** Doris Wishman, Dawn Whitman; **C:** C. Davis Smith.

Bad Manners

Pompous musicologist Matt (Rubinek) returns to Boston with his razor-tongued girlfriend Kim (Feeney) to give a lecture and check in with his old girlfriend, brittle unhappy Nancy (Bedelia) and her prissy academic husband Wes (Strathairn). It's a weekend in hell for houseguests and hosts as they play not-so-adult games of truth-or-dare. The film is based on Gilman's play *Ghost in the Machine* and never really breaks free of the conventions of the stage. Actually, the commentary track with director Kaufer, Rubinek, and friends is more enjoyable than the film itself. The DVD image is good, though much of the action has an autumnal focus. —*MM*
Movie: 🎬🎬 *DVD:* 🎬🎬½
Bell Canyon Entertainment Inc. (Cat #BCE-61022, UPC #797381610224). Widescreen letterboxed. $24.98. Keepcase. *LANG:* English. *FEATURES:* Commentary track ▪ 24 chapter links ▪ Behind-the-scenes featurette ▪ Talent files.
1998 (R) 88m/C David Strathairn, Bonnie Bedelia, Saul Rubinek, Caroleen Feeney, Julie Harris; **D:** Jonathan Kaufer; **W:** David Gilman; **C:** Denis Maloney; **M:** Ira Newborn.

Bad Man's River

A Mexican revolutionary leader hires a gang of outlaws to blow up an arsenal used by the Army. That's the basis for a comic heist plot that combines elements of *Cat Ballou* with a spaghetti western. For a film this old, the image is astonishingly sharp and clear. A bit of static on the soundtrack doesn't really detract from the ludicrous dubbing, or the soundtrack, which is a marvel unto itself. According to the production notes, Walter de los Rios was famous in the '60s for his pop ditties and this score could have come straight from the Mitch Miller songbook. —MM

Movie: ♫♫ **DVD:** ♫♫♫
Parade (Cat #55286). Widescreen (2.35:1) letterboxed. Dolby Digital Mono. $17.98. Keepcase. *LANG:* English. *SUB:* Japanese. *FEATURES:* 14 chapter links • Thumbnail bios and notes.
1972 92m/C *IT SP* Lee Van Cleef, James Mason, Gina Lollobrigida; **D:** Eugenio (Gene) Martin; **W:** Philip Yordan; **C:** Alejandro Ulloa; **M:** Waldo de los Rios.

Bad Moon

Inventive werewolf tale has a good twist—one of the main characters is a German Shepherd. That's Thor (Primo), who's owned by Marjorie (Hemingway) and her young son Brett (Gamble). Marjorie invites her wayward brother Ted (Pare) to stay at her Rocky Mountain home. Out in the Orient, Ted was bitten by a wolf creature. Before long, he and Thor are forced to figure out who's top dog, as it were. Director Red sometimes shifts to a canine point of view with a slightly flattened blurred picture. The image is crisp and clear, showing practically no grain or any faults in the source print. Actually, this transfer is a nearly pristine copy of the film. The nighttime scenes show good contrast between light and dark, and never appear overlit. The soundtrack makes nice use of the Surround effects, especially during the scenes where the werewolf is stalking his prey. —MM/GH

Movie: ♫♫ **DVD:** ♫♫♫
Warner Home Video, Inc. (Cat #14910). Widescreen (2.35:1) anamorphic. Dolby Digital 5.1 Surround Stereo. $19.98. Snapper. *LANG:* English; French. *SUB:* English; French. *FEATURES:* Trailers • Talent files • Filmographies.
1996 (R) 79m/C Mariel Hemingway, Michael Pare, Mason Gamble, Ken Pogue; **D:** Eric Red; **W:** Eric Red; **C:** Jan Kiesser; **M:** Daniel Licht.

Bait

Petty thief Alvin (Foxx) winds up in the clink after a botched seafood robbery. His cellmate Jaster (Pastorelli) is the double-crossing partner of prancing archvillain Bristol (Hutchison), who has stolen $40 million in gold. Unfortunately for Alvin, Jaster winds up in the Big House in the sky before he can tell anyone where the hidden loot is stashed. Head Fed Clenteen (Morse), thinking that Alvin knows where the gold is hidden, has him unwittingly equipped with surveillance devices and springs him from the pokey. Alvin, now followed by Bristol and the feds, tries to find the stashed loot by piecing together the cryptic clues that Jaster has left him. Lots of action on a minimal (for this type of movie) budget. The audio tracks are a highlight on this DVD, especially the extremely boisterous sub-woofer track that

aggressively accents each gunshot with enough low-end resonance, resulting in a larger-than-life feel to all the action. That's not to say that the image is lacking; in fact, there is not much to complain about visually at all. When the disc is put to the test by dark nighttime scenes, it responds well with a picture that remains highly detailed, with dead-on blacks and very little grain. Foxx's commentary is worth a listen if only for the extra laughs he occasionally adds to the goings-on. —JO

Movie: ♫♫ **DVD:** ♫♫♫½
Warner Home Video, Inc. (Cat #18804, UPC #085391880424). Widescreen (2.35:1) anamorphic. Dolby Digital 5.1. $19.98. Snapper. *LANG:* English; French. *SUB:* English; French. *CAP:* English. *FEATURES:* 36 chapter links • Commentary: Jamie Foxx • Dual-layered.
2000 (R) 119m/C Jamie Foxx, Doug Hutchison, David Morse, Jamie Kennedy, Robert Pastorelli, Kimberly Elise, David Paymer, Tia Texada, Mike Epps, Nestor Serrano, Megan Dodds, Jeffrey Donovan; **D:** Antoine Fuqua; **W:** Tom Gilroy, Jeff Nathanson, Adam Scheinman, Andrew Scheinman; **C:** Tobias Schliessler; **M:** Mark Mancina.

The Balcony

French playwright Jean Genet, whose life would make for better cinema than director Joseph Strick's interpretation of his play *Le Balcon,* is strictly for the initiated and those blessed with both insight and culture. His allegorical tale of the corruption of society's elite was perhaps avant-garde filmmaking in 1963, but it is now nothing more than a star-studded curiosity, with the meaning and significance of Shelley Winters's brothel madam muted by time. The movie arrives intact, but the DVD begs for audio commentary and by the very nature of the film itself, underscores an opportunity missed. —RJT

Movie: ♫♫ **DVD:** ♫♫
Image Entertainment (Cat #ID9516RLDVD, UPC #014381951622). Full frame. Mono. $29.99. Snapper. *LANG:* English. *FEATURES:* 10 chapter links.
1963 87m/B Peter Falk, Shelley Winters, Lee Grant, Kent Smith, Peter Brocco, Ruby Dee, Jeff Corey, Leonard Nimoy, Joyce Jameson; **D:** Joseph Strick; **W:** Ben Maddow; **C:** George J. Folsey. *AWARDS: NOM:* Oscars '63: B&W Cinematog.

The Ballad of Ramblin' Jack

Seminal '60s folk singer "Ramblin' Jack" Elliott was born Elliott Adnopoz, son of a Jewish doctor in New York. But bitten by the bug of the romantic West, the young free spirit transformed himself into the spiritual heir of Woody Guthrie who, to a degree, paved the way for Bob Dylan. Along the way he had a wife and family, though he seldom saw them. His daughter Aiyana made this documentary about her father, so strict objectivity is not high on the list of the film's attributes. When

you add in a commentary track by the subject, you've got a DVD that's positively post-modern in its double-edged self-awareness. It's also entertaining, though there's not enough to recommend the film to audiences not interested in the subject or the times. DVD image is essentially equal to tape, but the extras are extensive. —MM

Movie: ♫♫♫ **DVD:** ♫♫♫
Winstar Home Entertainment (Cat #WHE3134, UPC #720917313429). Full frame. Mono. $24.98. Keepcase. *LANG:* English. *FEATURES:* 16 chapter links • DVD production credits • Trailer • Commentary: Jack Elliott • Clips from the film *Ramblin' Jack in Texas* • Discography.
2000 112m/C Jack Elliott, Arlo Guthrie, Kris Kristofferson, Pete Seeger, Odetta, Dave Van Ronk; **D:** Aiyana Elliott; **W:** Aiyana Elliott, Dick Dahl; **M:** Jack Elliott.

Bamboozled

Spike Lee's savage invective starts "in media race" with Damon Wayans as Pierre De La Croix, a TV writer who finds that institutionalized racism at the network prevents him from creating shows that document the African-American experience without resorting to stereotypes. Network boss Dunwitty (Michael Rapaport) orders the staff writers to create shows that will boost the network's ratings. Fed up, "De La" concocts a plan of conceiving the most racist, offensive show ever—*Mantan: The New Millennium Minstrel Show*—to get out of his contract. In true satirical tradition, the plan backfires and *Mantan* becomes a huge commercial and critical hit. Pierre watches in horror as his characters, "Mantan" and "Sleep 'n' Eat" become media Frankensteins, spinning his original message and ultimately the situation horribly out of control. With *Bamboozled,* writer/director Lee challenges not only the decades of racial stereotypes, but also how fame, power, and the media can seduce anyone, regardless of race, into making the wrong choices. Lee invokes the best satiric tradition when he shows an entire live studio audience in blackface and white gloves mimicking the thoroughly distasteful "catch phrases" of the show. For artistic and economic reasons, Lee shot mostly in digital video with some sequences originated on film. The 1.78:1 anamorphic transfer looks mastered from the converted film elements. There is some loss of detail and the image waivers in clarity, sometimes clear, sometimes with a soft haze. (The deleted scenes, taken directly from the source tapes, may look like video, but they are much cleaner.) The Dolby Digital 5.1 track really rocks, much more so than the matrix Surround track offered, with an aggressive sound field, directional sound effects, and effectively targeted low-frequency enhancement. The DVD boasts a full bill of fare, with director commentary, ten deleted scenes, two music videos, a theatrical trailer, and a couple of DVD-ROM features. I found the hour-long documentary informative and not at all promotional, giving historical perspective in addition to the standard behind-the-scenes glimpses. —EP

Movie: 🎞🎞🎞 **DVD:** 🎞🎞🎞
New Line Home Video (Cat #N5197, UPC #794043519727). Widescreen (1.78:1) anamorphic. Dolby Digital 5.1; Dolby Digital Surround Stereo. $24.98. Snapper. *LANG:* English. *CAP:* English. *FEATURES:* 26 chapter links • Feature-length commentary with director Spike Lee • 10 deleted scenes • "Making of" documentary • Animated art gallery • 2 music videos • Theatrical trailer • Cast and crew filmographies. DVD-ROM features: "Script to screen" film/screenplay comparison, website access.
2000 (R) 135m/C Damon Wayans, Jada Pinkett Smith, Savion Glover, Tommy Davidson, Michael Rapaport, Thomas Jefferson Byrd, Paul Mooney, Susan Batson, Mos Def, Sarah Jones, Gillian Iliana Waters; **D:** Spike Lee; **W:** Spike Lee; **C:** Ellen Kuras; **M:** Terence Blanchard.

Bananas

Intermittently hilarious (and labored) early Allen is full of the director's signature angst-ridden philosophical comedy and some inspired set pieces. Frustrated product tester Fielding Melish runs off to South America where he volunteers his support to the revolutionaries in a shaky Latin-American dictatorship and winds up a leader. On DVD—in both the full-frame and widescreen versions—the film is very grainy. It always has been. Sound is fine. —MM

Movie: 🎞🎞🎞 **DVD:** 🎞🎞½
MGM Home Entertainment (Cat #100672, UPC #027616850171). Widescreen anamorphic; full frame. Dolby Digital Mono. $24.99. Keepcase. *LANG:* English; Spanish. *SUB:* French; Spanish. *CAP:* English. *FEATURES:* 24 chapter links.
1971 (PG-13) 82m/C Woody Allen, Louise Lasser, Carlos Montalban, Howard Cosell, Charlotte Rae, Conrad Bain, Allen (Goorwitz) Garfield, Sylvester Stallone; **D:** Woody Allen; **W:** Mickey Rose, Woody Allen; **C:** Andrew M. Costikyan; **M:** Marvin Hamlisch.

Bandit Queen

Phoolan Devi (Biswas) is a female Robin Hood in modern-day India. A lower-caste woman, Devi is sold into marriage at 11, brutalized by her husband (and many others throughout the film), and eventually winds up with an equally brutal group of bandits. Only this time around, Devi takes action by aiding the group in robbing, kidnapping (and murdering) the rich and higher castes. In real life Devi surrendered to the authorities in 1983 and spent 11 years in jail. The film is based on screenwriter Sen's biography *India's Bandit Queen: The True Story of Phoolan Devi* and Devi's diaries. This film deserved a much better transfer, and looks like a DVD put out much earlier in the history of the format. The flaws are most apparent in dark scenes where the sharpness drops way

off; reds and earthtones bleed, and artifacts become noticeable. The soundtrack tries to make up for it and is near as-good-as-it-gets. The low end is rumbling but clean, and the Surround tracks are both well utilized and nicely mixed. —JO

Movie: 🎞🎞🎞 **DVD:** 🎞½
Artisan Entertainment (Cat #DVD15083, UPC #013023035195). Full frame. Dolby Digital Mono. $24.98. Keepcase. *LANG:* Hindi. *SUB:* English. *FEATURES:* 24 chapter links.
1994 119m/C GB IN Seema Biswas, Nirmal Pandey, Manoj Bajpai, Raghubir Yadav, Rajesh Vivek, Govind Namdeo; **D:** Shekhar Kapur; **W:** Mala Sen; **C:** Ashok Mehta; **M:** Nusrat Fateh Ali Khan, Roger White.

Bandits

Talk about your band on the run! Four young women form a prison rock-and-roll band called the Bandits. Their first gig on the outside is the policeman's ball, where they escape. They become folk heroes as they elude the police, and a clandestine recording they send to a music exec zooms up the charts. At first glance this DVD appears a little grainy, but it is actually the look of the film, which was grainy in the theatre. There are some very fast camera movements and music video–like cuts, as well as concert footage that goes from black-and-white to color. The transfer handles all those very well. The film uses the Surround to put you in the middle of things, rather than for effects, and does it very well. —JO

Movie: 🎞🎞🎞 **DVD:** 🎞🎞🎞
Columbia Tristar Home Video (Cat #04725, UPC #043396047259). Widescreen (1.85:1) letterboxed. Dolby Digital 5.1; Dolby Surround. $27.95. Keepcase. *LANG:* German. *SUB:* English; Spanish; French. *CAP:* German. *FEATURES:* 28 chapter links • Theatrical trailers • Commentary: director Katja von Garnier • 2 music videos.
1999 (R) 109m/C GE Katja Riemann, Jutta Hoffmann, Jasmin Tabatabai, Nicolette Krebitz, Hannes Jaenicke, Werner Schreyer; **D:** Katja von Garnier; **W:** Katja von Garnier, Uwe Wilhelm; **C:** Torsten Breuer.

The Bank Dick

Fields wrote the screenplay (using an alias) and stars in this zany comedy about a man who accidentally trips a bank robber and winds up as a guard. Fields's last major role is a classic, a worthy end to his great career. Of particular note is the frenetic cops-and-robbers chase sequence and the DVD's allowance of single frame access. As with most Criterion discs, the audio and video are as good as can be expected, considering the age of the source material. The black-and-white transfer is crisp and well defined. The soundtrack is equally impressive, with no distortion or loss of clarity. The disc is a gem in that it succeeds wildly in the greatest aspect of DVD—film preservation. —MJT **AKA:** The Bank Detective.

Movie: 🎞🎞🎞🎞 **DVD:** 🎞🎞🎞½
Criterion Collection (Cat #78, UPC #715515010627). Full frame. Dolby Digital Mono. $29.95. Keepcase. *LANG:* English. *SUB:* English. *FEATURES:* 19 chapter links.
1940 73m/B W.C. Fields, Cora Witherspoon, Una Merkel, Evelyn Del Rio, Jack Norton, Jessie Ralph, Franklin Pangborn, Shemp Howard, Grady Sutton, Russell Hicks, Richard Purcell, Reed Hadley; **D:** Edward F. (Eddie) Cline; **W:** W.C. Fields; **C:** Milton Krasner. *AWARDS:* Natl. Film Reg. '92.

Banzai Runner

California state trooper Billy Baxter (Stockwell) decides to join an exclusive desert highway road race to avenge his brother who was killed by the group. This underpowered video premiere looks and sounds no different on disc than it does on tape. —MM

Movie: 🎞 **DVD:** 🎞🎞
Image Entertainment (Cat #OVED9017DVD, UPC #014381901726). Full frame. Dolby Digital Mono. $24.99. Snapper. *LANG:* English. *FEATURES:* 12 chapter links.
1986 88m/C Dean Stockwell, John Shepherd, Charles Dierkop; **D:** John G. Thomas; **W:** Phil Harnage; **C:** Howard Wexler; **M:** Joel Goldsmith.

Bar-B-Q

A pro-ball player turned actor needs a break and heads home to have a Bar-B-Q with his girl and old homies. When word gets out the entire neighborhood shows up for the party. A lot of music and a lot of crude jokes and infantile humor make this poorly made, horribly acted film practically unwatchable. The video transfer is absolutely awful. Colors bleed everywhere and lack any definition whatsoever. The soundtrack is even worse. Although labelled as a 5.1 mix, it is little more than the same track blared through five separate speakers, which creates an annoying echo effect. Also, there is no menu control on the disc, making navigation extremely difficult. The 102-minute running time includes nearly 15 minutes of credits and what the cast and crew apparently considered humorous outtakes. —MJT

Movie: woof **DVD:** 🎞
York Entertainment (Cat #YPD-1045, UPC #750723104522). Full frame. Dolby Digital 5.1 Surround. $19.98. Keepcase. *LANG:* English. *FEATURES:* 18 chapter links.
2000 102m/C Layzie Bone, John West, Chanda Watts, Lea Griggs; **D:** Amanda Moss, John West; **W:** John West.

Barb Wire

Bizarre little hybrid is a comic book shoot-'em-up filled with pyrotechnic fight scenes, but the plot has been lifted from a more curious source: *Casablanca*. In this variation—set in Steel Harbor, the last free city in a fascist future America—Rick's Cafe is

Hammerhead, a nightclub run by the motorcycle-riding blonde bombshell Barb Wire (Anderson). The local corrupt policeman, Commander Willis (Berkeley), takes over for Claude Rains's Capt. Renault. Ilsa is now Axel (Morrison), a man from Barb's past, and Victor Laszlo is Cora D (Rowell). Instead of letters of transit, they need "retinal lenses" to evade the evil Congressionals' security scanners. And Col. Pryzer (Railsback), filling in for Maj. Strasser, will do anything to stop them, etc., etc. The DVD handles the music video–tinged visuals well enough, and the 5.1 Surround sound is more than adequate to the story. The "sexy outtakes" extra is slo-mo full-frame footage of our heroine showing off her silicone in an open bustier while some guy off camera spritzes her with water. —*MM*

Movie: ♫½ **DVD:** ♫♫½
USA Home Entertainment (Cat #639927). Widescreen (1.85:1) letterboxed. Dolby Digital 5.1 Surround Stereo; Dolby Digital Surround Stereo. $29.95. Keepcase. *LANG:* English; French. *CAP:* English. *FEATURES:* Sexy outtakes • Talent files • Trailer • Photo gallery • 16 chapter links.
1996 111m/C Pamela Anderson, Temuera Morrison, Jack Noseworthy, Victoria Rowell, Xander Berkeley, Udo Kier, Steve Railsback, Clint Howard, Tony Bill; *D:* David Hogan; *W:* Chuck Pfarrer, Ilene Chaiken; *C:* Rick Bota; *M:* Michel Colombier. *AWARDS:* Golden Raspberries '96: Worst New Star (Anderson); *NOM:* MTV Movie Awards '97: Fight (Pamela Lee/A Guy); Golden Raspberries '96: Worst Picture, Worst Screenplay, Worst Song ("Welcome to Planet Boom!").

The Barefoot Contessa

Maria Vargas's (Gardner) rise to fame in Hollywood is told in flashback by writer/director Harry Dawes (Bogart). By now, this is a fairly familiar showbiz formula, but the cast, including Edmond O'Brien who won an Oscar for his work, makes it more than worthwhile. Though the image lacks the sparkle of contemporary films, it looks very good, perhaps even excellent for a 1954 production. Surface flaws are minor and occasional. —*MM*

Movie: ♫♫♫ **DVD:** ♫♫½
MGM Home Entertainment (Cat #1002029, UPC #027616862693). Full frame. Dolby Digital Mono. $19.98. Keepcase. *LANG:* English; French. *FEATURES:* 16 chapter links • Trailer.
1954 128m/C Ava Gardner, Humphrey Bogart, Edmond O'Brien, Valentina Cortese, Rossano Brazzi; *D:* Joseph L. Mankiewicz; *W:* Joseph L. Mankiewicz; *C:* Jack Cardiff. *AWARDS:* Oscars '54: Support. Actor (O'Brien); Golden Globes '55: Support. Actor (O'Brien); *NOM:* Oscars '54: Story & Screenplay.

The Base

Army Intelligence officer Maj. John Murphy (Dacascos) is sent undercover to Fort Tillman to investigate the murder of an army operations officer. Murphy is assigned to a border patrol unit and discovers his fellow soldiers are muscling in on the Mexican/American drug trade. When he learns who's behind the operation, his cover is blown. Both image and sound are marginally better than VHS tape, but this is a generic action video premiere that gains little on DVD. —*MM*

Movie: ♫♫ **DVD:** ♫♫
Studio Home Entertainment (Cat #7245). Full frame. $24.95. Keepcase. *LANG:* English. *SUB:* Spanish. *FEATURES:* Cast and crew thumbnail bios • Commentary: Mark Lester • Trailer • 20 chapter links.
1999 (R) 101m/C Mark Dacascos, Tim Abell, Paula Trickey, Noah Blake, Frederick Coffin; *D:* Mark L. Lester; *W:* Jeff Albert, William Martell; *C:* Jacques Haitkin; *M:* Paul Zaza.

Batman Beyond: Return of the Joker

A resurrected Joker is back terrorizing Gotham and seeking revenge on an aging Bruce Wayne. But now, after the Joker brutally rips into Wayne, the new Batman Terry McGinnis is the one to take on the Clown Prince of Crime. The *Batman Beyond* series represents the finest in animated television, with excellent scripting, art, animation, and voice performances. This made-for-video feature allows for even more detail, both in story and characterization. The DVD (as well as the VHS) version features a cut version of the film, missing the rougher violence that was on the screener copies sent out before the actual release. The edits were rumored to have been in response to charges that the industry was selling violence to kids. Indeed, that original cut was pretty harsh for an animated feature, but was not out of line when compared to the Batman movies or comic books. Visually and sonically the DVD is a knockout. The colors are super vibrant with no hint of bleed, with blacks as dark and true as you can find on a DVD. The image is sharp, as well as artifact- and grain-free. Even though a direct-to-video release, there is an excellent 5.1 mix with energetic and well-used Surround tracks. A too-short (but interesting) behind-the-scenes documentary is included, but the commentary provides much more insight into the talent that went into the making of this feature. Note: Both the movie and the DVD bone rating would have been 4.0 if not for the cuts. —*JO*

Movie: ♫♫♫ **DVD:** ♫♫♫
Warner Home Video, Inc. (Cat #18173, UPC #085391817321). Full frame. Dolby Digital 5.1. $24.98. Snapper. *LANG:* English. *SUB:* English; French. *CAP:* English. *FEATURES:* 18 chapter links • Trailer • Animated character bios • Production notes • Behind-the-scenes documentary • Commentary: Curt Geda, Paul Dini, Bruce Timm, Glen Murakami • Music video Crash.
2000 70m/C *D:* Curt Geda; *V:* Will Friedle, Mark Hamill, Kevin Conroy, Melissa Joan Hart.

Batman: Mask of the Phantasm

Based on the Fox television series with the animated Batman fending off his old enemy the Joker, new enemy the Phantasm, and dreaming of his lost first love. Cartoon film noir is set in the 1940s but is filled with '90s sarcasm. Complicated storyline with a stylish dark look that may be lost on the kiddies, but adults will stay awake. If only all movies on DVD looked as good as this animated feature. This disc is stunning—extremely sharp, strong saturated colors (with no bleed), and super blacks. Flashes are near blinding and the contrast is intense throughout. If there is a weakness, it's the soundtrack, which would have benefitted from the added punch of a 5.1 mix, especially on the low end. But the Dolby Surround is no slouch and most (particularly the kiddies) probably won't notice. —*JO* **AKA:** Batman: The Animated Movie.

Movie: ♫♫♫½ **DVD:** ♫♫♫♫
Warner Home Video, Inc. (Cat #15502, UPC #085391550228). Widescreen (1.85:1) anamorphic; full frame. Dolby Surround. $19.98. Snapper. *LANG:* English; French. *SUB:* English; French. *CAP:* English. *FEATURES:* 30 chapter links • Theatrical trailer.
1993 (PG) 77m/C *D:* Eric Radomski, Bruce W. Timm; *W:* Michael Reeves, Alan Burnett, Paul Dini, Martin Pako; *M:* Shirley Walker; *V:* Kevin Conroy, Dana Delany, Mark Hamill, Stacy Keach, Hart Bochner, Abe Vigoda, Efrem Zimbalist Jr., Dick Miller.

Bats

In its theatrical release (with a "PG-13" rating) this sf/horror flick was nothing special. It arrives on home video with an "R" rating that retains more of the violence and humor, and while the 1950s formula plot doesn't break any new ground for the genre, it is funny and well constructed. Your basic mad scientist (Gunton) breeds some super-intelligent bats meant to be used as weapons by the military. They attack the residents of a remote Texas hamlet (actually Utah). It's up to the usual suspects—science babe (Meyer), sidekick (Leon), and sheriff (Phillips)—to stop them before the military types nuke the town. All of the laughs are intentional, with the possible exception of Phillips's Stetson, which threatens to fall down over his ears at any minute. As was the case with the hit *Anaconda*, the computer-generated effects are obvious, but overall these are some of the best bat monsters ever filmed. The 5.1 Surround effects are so supercharged that they are ridiculously unrealistic, but with this kind of flick, that's hardly a serious criticism. The only noticeable flaw is some flashing within the grid patterns of cyclone fencing and chicken wire. —*MM*

Movie: ♫♫♫ **DVD:** ♫♫♫
Columbia Tristar Home Video (Cat #04510, UPC #043396045101). Widescreen (2.35:1) letterboxed. Dolby Digital 5.1 Surround Stereo; Dolby Digital Surround

Stereo. $14.95. Keepcase. *LANG:* English. *SUB:* English. *FEATURES:* 28 chapter links ● Isolated music score ● Commentary: Phillips and Morneau ● "Bats Around" featurette ● Photo galleries ● Talent files ● Trailers.
1999 (R) 91m/C Lou Diamond Phillips, Dina Meyer, Bob Gunton, Leon, Carlos Jacott, Oscar Rowland, David Shawn McConnell, Marcia Dangerfield; *D:* Louis Morneau; *W:* John Logan; *C:* George Mooradian; *M:* Graeme Revell.

Battle beyond the Stars

John Sayles wrote this version of *The Magnificent Seven* set in outer space with Richard Thomas hiring warriors to defend his home planet against John Saxon. Valkyrie Sybil Danning makes the most lasting impression. Also, James Cameron worked on the special effects and James Horner supplied the score. Image transfer is on the dark side but adequate; there's a lot of dirt and negative damage, some of which appears to be built into the opticals. There are twin commentaries with writer Sayles and production manager Gale Anne Hurd. Both are fascinating. Hurd and Sayles are enthusiastic about the movie and talk openly about the business and the opportunity *Battle* represented for them. Jolly Roger Corman joins Sayles and together they visit all kinds of subjects, movies, and people related to this movie and others. —*MM/GE*
Movie: 🎵🎵½ *DVD:* 🎵🎵½
New Concorde (Cat #NH20209D, UPC #736991220997). Widescreen (1.85:1) letterboxed. Dolby Digital 5.1 Surround Stereo. $19.98. Keepcase. *LANG:* English. *FEATURES:* Commentary: Sayles, Gale Anne Hurd ● Trailer ● Production stills.
1980 (PG) 105m/C Richard Thomas, Robert Vaughn, George Peppard, Sybil Danning, Sam Jaffe, John Saxon, Darlanne Fluegel, Jeff Corey, Morgan Woodward, Marta Kristen, Ron Ross, Eric Morris; *D:* Jimmy T. Murakami; *W:* John Sayles; *C:* Daniel Lacambre; *M:* James Horner.

Battle for the Planet of the Apes

A tribe of human atomic bomb mutations are out to make life miserable for the peaceful ape tribe. The story is told primarily in flashback with the opening and closing sequences taking place in the year A.D. 2670. This is the final chapter in the five-movie simian sci-fi saga. The DVD looks pretty good, but has trouble with highly detailed shots and quick pans, where digital grain appears. Sharpness is above average and colors are strong with very little bleed—a good thing since many of the apes wear red uniforms. The backgrounds seem a little softer than in the theatre, but in this case it may help the film better hide the cheaper "non-talking" ape makeup jobs. —*JO*
Movie: 🎵🎵½ *DVD:* 🎵🎵½

20th Century Fox Home Entertainment (Cat #2000108, UPC #024543001089). Widescreen (2.35:1) letterboxed. Dolby Surround; Dolby Digital Mono. $29.95. Keepcase. *LANG:* English (DS); French (Mono). *SUB:* English; Spanish. *CAP:* English. *FEATURES:* 24 chapter links ● Theatrical trailers ● Interactive game. Also available as part of the 6-DVD "Planet of the Apes: The Evolution" box set (cat. #2000109, UPC 024543001096) for $99.95.
1973 (G) 96m/C Roddy McDowall, Lew Ayres, John Huston, Paul Williams, Claude Akins, Severn Darden, Natalie Trundy, Austin Stoker, Noah Keen, Michael Stearns, John Landis; *D:* J. Lee Thompson; *W:* John W. Corrington, Joyce H. Corrington; *C:* Richard H. Kline; *M:* Leonard Rosenman.

Battle of the Amazons

This vintage exploitation is notable for having perhaps the most inappropriate "schwing" sound effects you've ever heard. They're overemphasized in a vain attempt to compensate for the minimal props and locations. The story concerns a tribe of women who terrorize nearby villages. The high point is a brief slow-mo naked bareback ride. DVD appears to have been made from a print that was distributed by Samuel Arkoff's American International outfit. Image is very rough with green lines appearing in some scenes. It is, however, all that's called for in this case. —*MM*
Movie: 🎵🎵 *DVD:* 🎵🎵½
Luminous Film & Video Widescreen letterboxed. $19.98. Keepcase. *LANG:* English. *FEATURES:* 8 chapter links ● Talent files ● 2 trailers ● Publicity photos.
1974 (R) 92m/C *IT SP* Lucretia Love, Paolo Tedesco, Mirta Miller, Lincoln Tate, Benito Stefanelli, Genie Woods; *D:* A. Brescia; *W:* Mario Amendola, Bruno Corbucci; *C:* Fausto Rossi; *M:* Franco Micalizzi.

Battle of the Sexes

Real estate tycoon Judson (Hersholt) abandons his wife (Bennett) and home for money-hungry flapper Marie (Haver). Griffith's remake of his own 1913 film is based on the novel *The Single Standard* by Daniel Carson Goodman. As with most of Image's silent film discs, the picture quality is astounding. The black-and-white print is crisp and clear. The soundtrack is also quite well done, proving enjoyable while not overpowering. The film preservation these Image discs represent is without equal. —*MJT*
Movie: 🎵🎵 *DVD:* 🎵🎵🎵
Image Entertainment (Cat #ID9226DSDVD, UPC #014381922622). Full frame. Dolby Digital Stereo. $24.99. Snapper. *LANG:* Silent. *SUB:* English intertitles. *FEATURES:* 16 chapter links ● 32 music cues.
1928 88m/B Jean Hersholt, Phyllis Haver, Belle Bennett, Don Alvarado, William "Billy" Bakewell, Sally O'Neil; *D:* D.W. Griffith; *W:* Gerrit J. Lloyd; *C:* Billy (G.W.) Bitzer, Karl Struss.

Battle Queen 2020

In a frozen post-apocalyptic future (eternal winter after asteroid crash), Gayle (Strain) leads the downtrodden masses in a revolution against the Elites who live above ground. She's a courtesan by day, freedom fighter by night...or is it the other way around? This one is at least as good as *Battlefield Earth*. It's certainly shorter and was filmed by people who were under no illusions about what they were doing. The low-budget Canadian video-premiere was filmed on a few cramped sets and so the image gains nothing on DVD. Strain's audio commentary touted on the box copy is not on the disc. —*MM*
Movie: 🎵🎵 *DVD:* 🎵🎵
New Concorde (Cat #NH20733 D, UPC #736991473393). Full frame. Stereo. $19.98. Keepcase. *LANG:* English. *SUB:* Spanish. *FEATURES:* 24 chapter links ● Talent files ● Trailers ● Interview with Julie Strain.
1999 (R) 80m/C *CA* Julie Strain, Jeff Wincott; *D:* Daniel D'or; *W:* Michael B. Druxman, William Hulkower, William D. Bostjancic, Caron Nightengale; *C:* Billy Brao; *M:* Robert Duncan.

Battlefield Earth

Ponderous, meandering sf epic is enjoyable for all the wrong reasons. Producer Travolta is Terrell, security chief for the Psychlos, the 10-foot-tall aliens who rule the Earth in the year 3000. He plods around in massive ski boots, shoulder pads, and cat-eye contact lenses. Like everyone else on the planet, he wears ratty dreadlocks and is having a very bad hair day. Barry Pepper is the leader of the resistance forces, plucky cavemen who teach themselves how to fly jet fighters in the silly conclusion. It's difficult to say much about the image transfer. The dark inky interiors are meant to look that way. Exteriors are generally undersaturated and the matte shots are nothing special. A few of the visual effects are more effective, but the cumulative effect is one of unintentional comedy. Sound is fine; don't miss the moment near the end when Travolta hawks up an intergalactic lugie as he bellows, "Happy Hunting!" —*MM*
Movie: 🎵½ *DVD:* 🎵🎵½
Warner Home Video, Inc. (Cat #18566). Widescreen anamorphic. Dolby Digital 5.1 Surround Stereo. $19.98. Snapper. *LANG:* English; French. *SUB:* English; French. *FEATURES:* 38 chapter links ● Commentary: director Christian and production designer Tatapoulos ● Behind-the-scenes documentary ● Travolta makeup test ● Visual effects featurette ● Trailers and TV spots ● Talent files.
2000 (PG-13) 117m/C John Travolta, Barry Pepper, Forest Whitaker, Kelly Preston, Kim Coates, Richard Tyson, Sabine Karsenti; *D:* Roger Christian; *W:* J. David Shapiro, Cory Mandell; *C:* Giles Nuttgens; *M:* Elia Cmiral.

Bay of Blood

Typically confused giallo horror from the prolific Mario Bava concerns murders that take place near a bay that is scheduled to be developed. The grim image is difficult to watch. A rough original comes to disc with all of its graininess intact. Reds bleed. The darker areas of the dark scenes (and there are a lot of those) are filled with artifacts. Sound does the so-so dubbing no favors. The Image version, released under the title *Twitch of the Death Nerve*, is far superior (please see review). —*MM* **AKA:** Twitch of the Death Nerve; Last House on the Left, Part 2; Carnage.
Movie: ♪♪½ **DVD:** ♪♪½
Simitar Entertainment (Cat #7654). Widescreen (1.66:1) letterboxed. Dolby Digital 5.1 Surround Stereo. $14.98. Keepcase. *LANG:* English. *FEATURES:* 8 chapter links ▪ Production credits.
1971 (R) 87m/C *IT* Claudine Auger, Chris Avran, Isa Miranda, Laura Betti, Luigi Pistilli, Sergio Canvari, Anna M. Rosati; **D:** Mario Bava; **W:** Mario Bava, Filippo Ottoni, Joseph McLee, Gene Luotto; **C:** Mario Bava; **M:** Stelvio Cipriano.

Baywatch: Nightmare Bay / River of No Return

Two episodes of the popular syndicated television series about babes, hunks, and swimwear. The first is the pilot; the second (on the flip side) takes place partly in the California mountains. The disc may be an improvement over tape, but to someone who has never seen the show, the DVD looks just like any other made-for-TV movie. —*MM*
Movie: ♪♪½ **DVD:** ♪♪
Pioneer Entertainment (Cat #10242). Full frame. Dolby Digital Stereo. $29.98. Keepcase. *LANG:* English. *FEATURES:* 5 chapter links each.
1994 178m/C David Hasselhoff.

The Beach

Traveling in Thailand, cynical young Richard (DiCaprio) meets the manic Daffy (Carlyle), who gives him a map to a supposedly unspoiled island off the coast. It's a place with a beautiful beach and acres of marijuana. Richard then asks acquaintances Francoise (Ledoyen) and Etienne (Canet) to accompany him to the place if it exists. The story is intriguing, but in the end, the film will make many viewers uncomfortable with the way it presents thoughtless, attractive people making easy, corrupt choices. The DVD includes an alternative ending, but it's really no more satisfying than the current one. The disc does an excellent job of capturing Darius Khondji's striking cinematography, both bright ocean exteriors and firelit interiors. Sound is fine, though Carlyle's gravelly incomprehensible brogue benefits mightily from the subtitles. —*MM*
Movie: ♪♪♪ **DVD:** ♪♪♪½

20th Century Fox Home Entertainment (Cat #2000176, UPC #024543001768). Widescreen (2.35:1) letterboxed. Dolby Digital 5.1 Surround Stereo; Dolby Digital Surround Stereo. $34.98. Keepcase. *LANG:* English; French. *SUB:* English; Spanish. *FEATURES:* Commentary: Danny Boyle ▪ 9 deleted scenes ▪ Music video ▪ Storyboard gallery ▪ Theatrical trailers.
2000 (R) 120m/C Leonardo DiCaprio, Tilda Swinton, Virginie Ledoyen, Guillaume Canet, Robert Carlyle, Paterson Joseph, Peter Youngblood Hills, Jerry Swindall; **D:** Danny Boyle; **W:** John Hodge; **C:** Darius Khondji; **M:** Angelo Badalamenti.

Beach Blanket Bingo

The *ne plus ultra* of mid-'60s beach movies is sublime nostalgia for some viewers, cringe-inducing torture to others. Both Frankie and Annette are back for this fifth installment, and an incredibly young Linda Evans and Deborah Walley also make plays for our hero. Throw in a mermaid, some moon doggies, skydiving, beach parties and Buster Keaton (!) and this one moves into a class by itself. Image is soft and bright and looks better than it really needs to. DVD appears to have been made from well-maintained original elements. —*MM*
Movie: ♪♪♪ **DVD:** ♪♪½
MGM Home Entertainment (Cat #1002047, UPC #027616862846). Widescreen (2.35:1) anamorphic. Dolby Digital Mono. $14.95. Keepcase. *LANG:* English. *SUB:* French; Spanish. *FEATURES:* 16 chapter links ▪ Trailer.
1965 96m/C Frankie Avalon, Annette Funicello, Linda Evans, Don Rickles, Buster Keaton, Paul Lynde, Harvey Lembeck, Deborah Walley, John Ashley, Jody McCrea, Marta Kristen, Timothy Carey, Earl Wilson, Bobbi Shaw, Brian Wilson; **D:** William Asher; **W:** William Asher, Sher Townsend, Leo Townsend; **C:** Floyd Crosby; **M:** Les Baxter.

Beach Girls

Please see review of *The Pom Pom Girls / The Beach Girls*.
Movie: ♪
1982 (R) 91m/C Debra Blee, Val Kline, Jeana Tomasina, Adam Roarke; **D:** Patrice Townsend; **C:** Michael D. Murphy.

Beach Party

This one started the "Beach Party" series with the classic Funicello/Avalon combo. Scientist Cummings studying the mating habits of teenagers intrudes on a group of surfers, beach bums, and bikers, to his lasting regret. Typical beach party bingo, with sand, swimsuits, singing, dancing, and bare minimum in way of a plot. The video transfer features vibrant colors and blacks are crisp and solid (for the most part). There are a few signs of age, but that's forgivable. The full-frame version showcases the disc's shortcomings and, as a result, should be avoided. Also pre-

sent is a solid soundtrack, which features clear dialogue and, if you can get past the corny songs, a decent musical score. —*MJT*
Movie: ♪♪ **DVD:** ♪♪
MGM Home Entertainment (Cat #10009 75, UPC #027616852823). Full frame; widescreen (2.35:1) anamorphic. Dolby Digital Mono. $19.98. Keepcase. *LANG:* English. *SUB:* French; Spanish. *FEATURES:* 32 chapter links ▪ Theatrical trailer.
1963 101m/C Frankie Avalon, Annette Funicello, Harvey Lembeck, Robert Cummings, Dorothy Malone, Morey Amsterdam, Jody McCrea, John Ashley, Candy Johnson, Dolores Wells, Yvette Vickers, Eva Six, Brian Wilson, Vincent Price, Peter Falk, Dick Dale; **D:** William Asher; **W:** Lou Rusoff; **C:** Kay Norton; **M:** Les Baxter.

Bear in the Big Blue House: Party Time with Bear

This kid's show focuses on a group of lovable characters who live in a big, blue house. There's the show's host, Bear, a huge brown bear, who always has something nice to say. There's Tutter, the timid and anxious mouse. Pip and Pop are two purple otters who are always getting into trouble. There's a lemur named Treelo, who is very hyper and speaks with a distinct accent. A smaller female bear named Ojo also lives in the house. And finally, every episode ends with Bear conversing with Luna, the moon. (Don't ask me.) The show is aimed at young children, probably ages 3-7, and teaches lessons about sharing and socialization. The DVD contains three episodes, each dealing with a party. The image appears to have been taken directly from a video master and so it is clearer than a conventional broadcast. The vibrant colors are outstanding and make the show appealing even to the youngest children. —*ML*
Movie: ♪♪♪ **DVD:** ♪♪♪
Columbia Tristar Home Video (Cat #4726). Full frame. Dolby Digital Stereo. $24.95. Keepcase. *LANG:* English. *SUB:* English; Spanish. *FEATURES:* Interactive sing-alongs ▪ Bonus trailers.
2000 ?m/C

Bear in the Big Blue House: Shapes, Sounds & Colors

Three episodes of the Disney Channel series are aimed at the 3–7-year-old crowd. The creatures come from the Jim Henson studios and so they're cute and funny, with Tutter Mouse and Pip & Pop being the stand-outs. Although the songs are nice, none can touch the "Hey! Hey! Hey! Potty!" song from "Potty Time with Bear." The picture is incredibly crisp and clear and it's evident that the DVD was digitally transferred straight from the video master. The colors are astoundingly true, a key to holding the attention of toddlers,

and show no bleeding. The clarity of the picture adds a real depth to the image, making it almost 3-D at times. —*ML/MM*
Movie: ♪♪½ **DVD:** ♪♪♪
Columbia Tristar Home Video Full frame. $24.99. Keepcase. *LANG:* English. *SUB:* English; Spanish. *FEATURES:* Sing-alongs ☞ Bonus trailers.
2000 75m/C

The Beast

Anyone who watches many DVDs knows that large expanses of ocher dirt in bright exteriors can generate heavy pixels. That's the near-constant background for this story set during the Russian invasion of Afghanistan, but the image transfer is essentially flawless. Sound is equally good, with the Surround coming into play mostly during the shelling scenes and rumbling tank sound effects. It's also good for Mark Isham's score. The story is essentially a variation on the "lost patrol" theme with a tank in the desert (actually Israel) being hunted by guerrillas. While the plot is handled well enough, it is difficult to generate much sympathy for any of the parties involved, either the Soviets or the Afghan fundamentalists who have been in power since the end of the war. —*MM* **AKA:** The Beast of War.
Movie: ♪♪♪ **DVD:** ♪♪♪
Columbia Tristar Home Video (Cat #06200, UPC #043396062009). Widescreen (1.85:1) anamorphic; full frame. Dolby Digital Surround Stereo. $24.98. Keepcase. *LANG:* English; French; Spanish; Portuguese. *SUB:* English; French; Spanish; Portuguese; Chinese; Korean; Thai. *FEATURES:* 28 chapter links ☞ Talent files ☞ Trailers.
1988 (R) 93m/C George Dzundza, Jason Patric, Steven Bauer, Stephen Baldwin, Don Harvey, Kabir Bedi, Erik Avari, Haim Gerafi; *D:* Kevin Reynolds; *W:* William Mastrosimone; *C:* Doug Milsome; *M:* Mark Isham.

The Beast Must Die

Curious horror/action picture combines elements of *The Most Dangerous Game, Ten Little Indians,* and spy adventures with a gimmick—the "werewolf break" in Chapter 9 which gives viewers 30 seconds near the end to come up with the identity of the wolfman (or wolfwoman). Multimillionaire Tom Newcliffe (Calvin Lockhart) invites houseguests—each with a nasty secret—for a weekend at his security-enhanced country estate, and claims that one of them is a monster. The mystery side of the story demands long passages of explanatory dialogue while the action side is often reduced to pointless motion. Cushing stands out in the supporting cast. Lockhart's impressive in the lead. An archetypal '70s theme and score by Douglas Gamley is the finishing touch and it sounds terrific, even in mono. Dialogue and effects are on the thin side, though. The DVD was made from slightly worn original elements. Exteriors tend to have a soft, autumnal cast while interiors are noticeably brighter and sharper. —*MM* **AKA:** Black Werewolf.

Movie: ♪♪ **DVD:** ♪♪
Image Entertainment (Cat #ID6161TVDVD, UPC #014381616125). Widescreen (1.66:1) letterboxed. Dolby Digital Mono. $24.99. Snapper. *LANG:* English. *FEATURES:* 12 chapter links.
1975 (PG) 93m/C *GB* Peter Cushing, Calvin Lockhart, Charles Gray, Anton Diffring, Marlene Clark, Ciaran Madden, Tom Chadbon, Michael Gambon; *D:* Paul Annett; *W:* Michael Winder; *C:* Jack Hildyard; *M:* Douglas Gamley.

The Beast of Yucca Flats

Extremely cheap early nuclear protest film posits a Russian scientist (Johnson, at his imposing best) being chased by communist agents into a testing area and caught in an atomic blast. Voice-over narration is often used in place of more expensive dialogue, and though the black-and-white photography is relatively crisp, virtually the entire film seems to have been shot with day-for-night filters, giving the action a heavily shadowed look. —*MM*
Movie: ♪♪½ **DVD:** ♪♪½
Image Entertainment (Cat #ID9696CODVD, UPC #014381969627). Full frame. Dolby Digital Mono. $24.99. Snapper. *LANG:* English. *FEATURES:* 3 chapter links.
1961 53m/B Tor Johnson, Douglas Mellor, Larry Aten, Barbara Francis, Conrad Brooks, Anthony Cardoza, Bing Stafford, John Morrison; *D:* Coleman Francis; *W:* Coleman Francis; *C:* John Cagle; *M:* Irwin Nafshun, Al Remington.

The Beast That Killed Women / The Monster of Camp Sunshine

In the first half of this drive-in double feature, colonists at a Florida nudist camp are attacked by a man in a really cheap gorilla suit. Otherwise, they occupy their time with semi-naked square dancing, shuffleboard, and the always-popular volleyball. The bright colors are reproduced with no flaws beyond one striped kerchief that flashes madly. In muddy black and white, *The Monster of Camp Sunshine* looks much worse but it's a lot more fun. It must be one of the most cheaply made feature-length films ever produced. Dialogue is kept to an absolute minimum. Instead, director Ferenc Leroget uses voice-over narration and intertitle cards to tell the story of this early eco-horror-nudie-comedy. A handyman drinks contaminated water and becomes an axe-wielding maniac with a wig that would make Moe Howard weep. The big finish includes lots of stock footage of Army maneuvers along with clips from (I think) *Charge of the Light Brigade* and a Civil War movie. Must be seen to be believed. As usual, the Something Weird double feature contains oodles of extras. (To see credits for *The Monster of Camp Sunshine,* see separate entry.) —*MM*
Movie: ♪♪ **DVD:** ♪♪♪

Image Entertainment (Cat #ID0361SW DVD, UPC #014381036121). Full frame. Dolby Digital Mono. $24.99. Snapper. *LANG:* English. *FEATURES:* 22 chapter links ☞ 5 nudie shorts ☞ 3 intermission shorts ☞ "Let's Go to the Drive-In" featurette ☞ Radio spots ☞ Gallery of exploitation art.
1965 60m/C *D:* Barry Mahon; *W:* Barry Mahon; *C:* Barry Mahon.

Beat the Devil

Please see review of *Comedy Noir.*
Movie: ♪♪♪
1953 89m/C Humphrey Bogart, Gina Lollobrigida, Peter Lorre, Robert Morley, Jennifer Jones, Edward Underdown, Ivor Barnard, Bernard Lee, Marco Tulli; *D:* John Huston; *W:* John Huston, Truman Capote; *C:* Oswald Morris; *M:* Franco Mannino.

The Beatles: The Ultimate DVD Collection

This set is comprised of two features, *Help!* and *Magical Mystery Tour,* and two fine documentaries, the Maysles brothers' *The First U.S. Visit* and *You Can't Do That: The Making of "A Hard Day's Night."* The first three are reviewed in the first volume. *You Can't Do That* is their equal in every respect. It's an excellent reminiscence by most of the key participants in the creation of the Beatles' first feature. Phil Collins, who actually appeared as a teenager in the closing concert crowd, narrates, but most of the best information comes from producer Walter Sherson, writer Alun Owen, and director Richard Lester. Actor Victor Spinetti does an uncanny John Lennon imitation. For any Beatles fan, this is a wonderful addition to the library. Since so much of the material comes from the '60s, image quality varies but the majority is superb, much of it in sparkling black and white. —*MM*
Movie: ♪♪♪♪ **DVD:** ♪♪♪♪
MPI Home Video (Cat #DVD7630, UPC #030306763026). Full frame. Dolby Digital Stereo. $79.99. Boxed set. *LANG:* English; Spanish; French (on *Help!* only). *SUB:* English; Spanish; French. *FEATURES:* 15 chapter links.
2000 ?m/C

Beautiful

This is more a "movie of the week" than a feature worthy of a full-blown theatrical release, but even with this in mind, *Beautiful* somehow seems to work. Sally Field, best known for her body of acting work, makes the leap to feature film director (her other directing effort, *The Christmas Tree,* was a true TV movie). Here, Minnie Driver is a life-long beauty contest entrant, who abandons her daughter (Eisenberg) to the care of her best friend (Adams) so that she can continue to compete in the "Miss American Miss" pageant year-in and year-out. This all sounds really dark, but even when her friend is accused of murder, the film manages to plow ahead to its inevitable happy ending. DVD features a nice visual look and a quality audio presentation, but it lacks support material or audio commentary from either star (Driver) or director (Field). —RJT

Movie: 🎵🎵🎵 **DVD:** 🎵🎵½

Columbia Tristar Home Video (Cat #05609, UPC #043396056091). Widescreen (1.85:1); full frame. Dolby Digital 5.1 Surround Sound. $24.95. Keepcase. *LANG:* English. *SUB:* English; Spanish. *CAP:* English. *FEATURES:* 28 chapter links • Theatrical trailer • Bonus theatrical trailer for *28 Days* • Talent files for Sally Field, Minnie Driver, Kathleen Turner.

2000 (PG-13) 112m/C Minnie Driver, Hallie Kate Eisenberg, Joey Lauren Adams, Kathleen Turner, Leslie Stefanson, Bridgette Wilson, Kathleen Robertson, Michael McKean, Gary Collins; **D:** Sally Field; **W:** Jon Bernstein; **C:** Robert Yeoman; **M:** John (Gianni) Frizzell.

Beautiful Joe

After he catches his wife in the sack with the plumber, Joe (Connolly) decides that he's going to lead a life of adventure. First stop, Churchill Downs, where he picks a winner and catches the eye of ex-stripper Hush (Stone) who's got far too much adventure in her life. Before long, they hit the road for Vegas with gangsters on their trail. Performances are very good, and so is the evocation of the road. Plot turns are predictable. Image ranges between good and very good. One thing: wearing cat-eye sunglasses and a short reddish wig, Sharon Stone is Catherine O'Hara's twin sister. —MM

Movie: 🎵🎵½ **DVD:** 🎵🎵½

Columbia Tristar Home Video (Cat #06448, UPC #043396064485). Widescreen letterboxed. Dolby Digital 5.1 Surround Stereo; Dolby Digital Surround. $24.95. Keepcase. *LANG:* English; French. *SUB:* English; French; Spanish. *FEATURES:* 28 chapter links • Trailers • Talent files.

2000 (R) 98m/C Billy Connolly, Sharon Stone, Gil Bellows, Ian Holm, Dann Florek, Barbara Tyson; **D:** Stephen Metcalfe; **W:** Stephen Metcalfe; **C:** Thomas Ackerman.

Beautiful People

The war in Bosnia (circa 1993) comes to London when former-neighbors-turned-enemies, one a Serbian and the other a Croatian, accidentally meet on a bus and try to kill each other. This chaos leads to a variety of intersecting situations: Portia (Coleman), a doctor and daughter of a snobby Tory MP, falls for a refugee; another doctor (Farrell) counsels a pregnant refugee who wants to abort her baby, the product of rape; a druggy skinhead (Nussbaum) winds up experiencing battle firsthand. Just don't look at any of the backgrounds on the DVD and you'll do just fine. Actually they're not that bad, it's just that the foregrounds are so super sharp that things look a little weird. Dim scenes trouble the blacks and add grain. On the plus side,

there are some amazingly vibrant reds with not a hint of bleed. The DVD includes the film's trailers from Japan, Great Britain, France, the U.S., and one made for the Independent Film Channel. —JO

Movie: 🎵🎵🎵 **DVD:** 🎵🎵½

Trimark Home Video (Cat #7370D, UPC #031398737025). Widescreen (1.85:1) letterboxed. Dolby Digital 5.1. $24.99. Keepcase. *LANG:* English. *SUB:* English; Spanish; French. *FEATURES:* 24 chapter links • Theatrical trailers • IFC featurette.

1999 (R) 107m/C *GB* Charlotte Coleman, Nicholas Farrell, Danny Nussbaum, Edin Dzandzanovic, Charles Kay, Rosalind Ayres, Heather Tobias, Siobhan Redmond, Gilbert Martin, Linda Bassett, Steve Sweeney; **D:** Jasmin Dizdar; **W:** Jasmin Dizdar; **C:** Barry Ackroyd; **M:** Gary Bell.

Beauty and the Beast: The Enchanted Christmas

Compact video premiere sequel to the popular Disney animated feature is a solid cut above the norm. Actually, it's more a revision than a true sequel with a story that takes place within the action of the first film. This time the villain is Forte, a huge pipe organ (voice of Tim Curry) within the Beast's castle. All of the voice talent from the original is back with the addition of Haley Joel Osment, Paul Reubens, and Bernadette Peters. If the songs aren't as catchy as the first ones, they're very good. The same goes for the combination of traditional and computer animation. Sound is fine throughout and impressive at the big finish. —MM

Movie: 🎵🎵🎵 **DVD:** 🎵🎵🎵

Buena Vista Home Entertainment (Cat #15282). Full frame. Dolby Digital 5.1. $34.99. Keepcase. *LANG:* English; French. *SUB:* English. *FEATURES:* 17 chapter links.

1997 71m/C D: Andy Knight; **W:** Flip Kobler, Cindy Marcus, Bill Motz, Bob Roth; **M:** Rachel Portman; **V:** Robby Benson, Angela Lansbury, Tim Curry, Bernadette Peters, Paige O'Hara, Jerry Orbach, David Ogden Stiers, Paul (Pee-wee Herman) Reubens, Haley Joel Osment.

Because of You

Kyoko (Takaoka) travels from Japan to New York to find Jose (Osorio), the Cuban-American serviceman who taught the young Kyoko Latin dancing. Jose, however, has AIDS, and wishes only to be reunited with his family in Miami. Kyoko decides to drive Jose home, hoping somehow he'll come to remember their past. The foregrounds on this DVD are super sharp while the backgrounds lose a little detail, and the result is one of those discs that sometimes look more like a video game than a movie. Dim shots find both grain and a weakening of the blacks to near-gray. The colors, however, are strong and bleed very little. The stereo mix is super lively with great separation and the music sounds particularly good. Of interest are the trailers on the

disc, which include the domestic, Japanese, French, British, and the Independent Film Channel versions. —JO **AKA:** Kyoko.

Movie: 🎵🎵🎵 **DVD:** 🎵🎵½

New Concorde (Cat #NH20594 D, UPC #736991459496). Full frame. Dolby Digital Stereo. $19.98. Keepcase. *LANG:* English. *FEATURES:* 24 chapter links • Theatrical trailers • Talent files.

1995 (R) 85m/C Saki Takaoka, Carlos Osorio, Scott Whitehurst, Mauricio Bustamante, Oscar Colon, Bradford West, Angel Stephens; **D:** Ryu Murakami; **W:** Ryu Murakami; **C:** Sarah Cawley.

Bed and Board

Part four in Truffaut's Antoine series finds his young hero (Leaud) married to Christine (Jade) and tempted into an affair with Kyoko (Berghauer). Compared to other Winstar European imports, this one looks pretty good, though it was never meant to be a visual spectacle. Image is perfectly clear; colors are a bit muted. French-speakers may complain that the bright white subtitles are burned in and cannot be turned off. The letterboxing is so slight as to be almost unnoticeable. —MM **AKA:** Domicile Conjugal.

Movie: 🎵🎵 **DVD:** 🎵🎵½

Winstar Home Entertainment (Cat #5122). Widescreen (1.66:1) letterboxed. $29.98. Keepcase. *LANG:* French. *SUB:* English. *FEATURES:* Cast and crew thumbnail bios • Production notes • Trailer • Tribute to Jean-Pierre Leaud • 6 chapter links.

1970 100m/C *FR* Jean-Pierre Leaud, Claude Jade, Barbara Laage, Daniel Ceccaldi, Daniel Boulanger, Pierre Maguelon, Jacques Jouanneau, Jacques Rispal, Jacques Robiolles, Pierre Fabre, Billy Kearns, Hiroko Berghauer, Daniele Girard, Claire Duhamel, Sylvana Blasi, Claude Vega, Christian de Tiliere, Annick Asty, Marianne Piketi, Guy Pierauld, Marie Dedieu, Marie Irakane, Yvon Lec, Ernest Menzer, Christophe Vesque; **D:** Francois Truffaut; **W:** Francois Truffaut, Bernard Revon, Claude de Givray; **C:** Nestor Almendros; **M:** Antoine Duhamel.

The Bed You Sleep In

Ray (Blair) and Jean (McLaughlin) live in a small Oregon town where Ray runs a local sawmill. For the first hour of the film, we witness Ray dealing with financial hardships and indulging in his love of fly-fishing. At the one-hour mark, the plot shows up when Jean receives a letter from their daughter, accusing Ray of sexual abuse. Think a slowly paced *Twin Peaks.* Unfortunately, the image, while crisp, is also fuzzy and has a squeezed look to it. At times, the picture resembles streaming video, with a pixelated look. Also, there is some flickering during several scenes. Most of these problems occur early on in the film, and some of the later scenes are quite clear. Still, the look of the film makes one wonder if the letterbox framing is correct. The "Hi-Fi Stereo" promised on the box copy sounds more like digital mono, as most of the sound is concentrated in the center channel. There are some distinct sounds from the front channels, but not very much. There are no special features on the disc. —*GH/MM*

Movie: ♫♫½ **DVD:** ♫♫
Vanguard International Cinema, Inc. (Cat #54). Widescreen (1.85:1) letterboxed. $29.95. Keepcase. *LANG:* English.
1993 117m/C Tom Blair, Ellen McLaughlin, Kathryn Sannella; **D:** Jon Jost; **W:** Jon Jost; **C:** Jon Jost.

Bedazzled [SE]

Low-level computer geek Elliot (Fraser) needs help wooing a co-worker (O'Connor). The devil (Hurley) offers him a little help in exchange for his soul. Various scenes involve him as a pro basketball player, drug lord, and rock star, etc. The film actually has some funny moments but hunky Fraser is miscast. (Dudley Moore was much better in the original, still unavailable on disc.) La Liz is excellent. DVD is an excellent reproduction of a sparkling big-budget studio production. Hurley's red outfits glow, as they should. Sound is strong, too. —*MM*

Movie: ♫♫½ **DVD:** ♫♫♫½
20th Century Fox Home Entertainment (Cat #2000815, UPC #024543008156). Widescreen (2.35:1) anamorphic. Dolby Digital 5.1 Surround Stereo; Dolby Digital Surround Stereo. $26.98. Keepcase. *LANG:* English; French. *SUB:* English; Spanish. *FEATURES:* 2 featurettes • Extended basketball sequence • Trailer • TV spots • 2 scoring sessions • 24 chapter links • NUON features • Commentary: Harold Ramis • Commentary: Elizabeth Hurley, producer Trevor Albert.
2000 (PG-13) 105m/C Brendan Fraser, Elizabeth Hurley, Frances O'Connor, Rudolph Martin, Orlando Jones; **D:** Harold Ramis; **W:** Harold Ramis, Larry Gelbart, Peter Tolan; **C:** Bill Pope.

Bedknobs and Broomsticks

In August 1940, a novice witch (Lansbury) takes in three Cockney kids who have been sent to the English countryside during the Blitz. Along with a professor (Tomlinson), they try to find an ancient spell that will protect the country from invaders. This relatively little-known Disney combination of live action and animation is actually a sort of companion piece to *Mary Poppins*. It looks terrific for a 1971 movie with virtually no signs of wear. Image is excellent. If the 5.1 remix lacks the fullness of today's fare, it's still fine and the disc is loaded with extras. —*MM*

Movie: ♫♫♫ **DVD:** ♫♫♫½
Buena Vista Home Entertainment (Cat #19608, UPC #717951008596). Widescreen (1.66:1) anamorphic. Dolby Digital 5.1 Surround Stereo. $29.99. Keepcase. *LANG:* English. *SUB:* French. *CAP:* English. *FEATURES:* 25 chapter links • Behind-the-scenes featurette • David Tomlinson recording session • Scrapbook • Film

facts • "Step in the Right Direction" reconstruction • Trailers • "The Worm Turns" animated short • "Vanishing Prairie" animated short.
1971 (G) 117m/C Angela Lansbury, Roddy McDowall, David Tomlinson, Bruce Forsyth, Sam Jaffe; **D:** Robert Stevenson; **W:** Don DaGradi, Bill Walsh; **C:** Frank Phillips; **M:** Richard M. Sherman, Robert B. Sherman. *AWARDS:* Oscars '71: Visual FX; *NOM:* Oscars '71: Art Dir./Set Dec., Costume Des., Song ("The Age of Not Believing"), Orig. Song Score and/or Adapt.

The Bedroom Window

Architect Terry Lambert (Guttenberg) is having an affair with his boss's wife (Huppert) who witnesses an assault on another woman (McGovern) from his apartment. To keep their secret, Lambert reports the crime, but since his account is second-hand, it's flawed and he becomes a suspect. The lightweight thriller has its moments, though it's difficult to find anything that director Hanson would use years later in *L.A. Confidential*. The film comes from the time when Guttenberg seemed to star in every other movie that was released. Disc is an excellent transfer of an image that's seldom better than good. Potentially troublesome patterns are fine. —*MM*

Movie: ♫♫½ **DVD:** ♫♫♫
Anchor Bay (Cat #DV11183, UPC #013131118391). Widescreen (2.35:1) anamorphic. Dolby Digital Mono. $24.98. Keepcase. *LANG:* English. *FEATURES:* 30 chapter links • Trailer.
1987 (R) 113m/C Steve Guttenberg, Elizabeth McGovern, Isabelle Huppert, Wallace Shawn, Paul Shenar, Carl Lumbly, Frederick Coffin, Brad Greenquist; **D:** Curtis Hanson; **W:** Curtis Hanson; **C:** Gilbert Taylor; **M:** Patrick Gleeson, Michael Shrieve, Felix Mendelssohn.

Bedrooms and Hallways

Refreshing, clever social comedy is built on real characters, true wit, and great acting. Leo (McKidd) joins a men's group and stirs things up when he openly admits to being attracted to another member of the group. Leo is surprised when his interest is returned and the complications that ensue are better viewed than read here. Simon Callow plays the group's straight leader with comic undertones only the British can pull off. Tom Hollander is hilarious as Leo's best friend and lovingly flamboyant roommate. Hugo Weaving plays a real estate agent with a fetish for performing sexual acts in his client's homes. Rose Troche's interview, though interesting, is more about her film *Go Fish* and her views on cinema than anything to do with *Bedrooms and Hallways*. —*JAS*

Movie: ♫♫♫½ **DVD:** ♫♫♫
First Run Features (Cat #FRF909372D, UPC #720229909372). Full frame. $29.95. Keepcase. *LANG:* English. *FEA-*

TURES: 9 chapter links • Interview with director Rose Troche.
1998 96m/C *GB* Kevin McKidd, James Purefoy, Jennifer Ehle, Tom Hollander, Hugo Weaving, Simon Callow, Harriet Walter, Christopher Fulford, Julie Graham; **D:** Rose Troche; **W:** Robert Farrar; **C:** Ashley Rowe; **M:** Alfredo Troche.

Beethoven

Give Abel Gance credit for attempting to embrace his subject with genuine passion and unfettered romanticism. Many of the conventions of his time will strike contemporary audiences as dated—particularly the almost naive use of music—but it is unfair to dismiss the film. Beethoven is well played by Harry Bauer, who's able to make him seem like a believably real human being. The gauzy focus at the edges of the image is intentional but other flaws are not. The disc was made from an original that has been damaged with the years. Faint scratches are visible throughout, along with the occasional jump at a spliced break. Some static and crackle mar the soundtrack. The subtitles are easy-to-read bright yellow. —*MM* **AKA:** *Beethoven's Great Love; The Life and Loves of Beethoven; Un Grand Amour de Beethoven.*

Movie: ♫♫♫ **DVD:** ♫♫½
Image Entertainment (Cat #ID5742PDVD, UPC #014381574227). Full frame. Dolby Digital Mono. $24.99. Snapper. *LANG:* French. *SUB:* English. *FEATURES:* 12 chapter links.
1936 116m/B *FR* Harry Baur, Jean-Louis Barrault, Marcel Dalio; **D:** Abel Gance; **W:** Abel Gance; **C:** Marc Fossard, Robert Lefebvre.

Beethoven

Sure-fire crowd-pleaser for the small set is a virtual live-action cartoon. It opens with our hero as an indescribably cute St. Bernard puppy. After a quick series of adventures, young B. finds himself in the Newton household. Dad (Grodin) is a strict disciplinarian who isn't about to have a dog in the home. But the rest of the family falls for the pup. In the rest, the grown dog solves any problem that confronts the family, including nasty accountants and an evil vet (Jones). Some brighter reds glow but that's an inconsequential flaw to the target audience. They'll love this no-extras disc as much as the VideoHound does. —*MM*

Movie: ♫♫½ **DVD:** ♫♫
Universal Studios Home Video (Cat #20027). Full frame. $24.98. Keepcase. *LANG:* English; French; Spanish. *SUB:* Spanish; English. *FEATURES:* 16 chapter links.
1992 (PG) 89m/C Charles Grodin, Bonnie Hunt, Dean Jones, Oliver Platt, Stanley Tucci, Nicholle Tom, Christopher Castile, Sarah Rose Karr, David Duchovny, Patricia Heaton, Laurel Cronin; **D:** Brian Levant; **W:** John Hughes, Amy Holden Jones; **C:** Victor Kemper; **M:** Randy Edelman.

Beethoven's 3rd

Dad Richard Newton (Reinhold) wants to take the family on vacation and, naturally, huge St. Bernard Beethoven is coming along. Suddenly, that rented luxury RV doesn't seem very big and dad's idea of fun is lame to the kids. Of course, it's not a typical vacation anyway; seems thieves Tommy (Ciccolini) and Bill (Marsh) need to retrieve a videotape that Richard has rented. Beethoven tries to protect his family while being blamed for every little mishap. A dog's life, indeed! One time-lapse scene makes it easy to judge the DVD's image quality as the sun sets and then rises again during a long and detailed shot. The picture remains sharp and grain-free, with strong colors and contrast, and comfortable brightness throughout the entire cycle. The 5.1 track barely uses the rears and lacks some low-end oomph, but is generally pleasing to the ear. —JO
Movie: ♫♫ **DVD:** ♫♫♫½
Universal Studios Home Video (Cat #20775, UPC #025192077524). Widescreen (1.85) anamorphic. Dolby Digital 5.1; Dolby Surround. $24.98. Keepcase. *LANG:* English (DD5.1); French (DS). *CAP:* English. *FEATURES:* 18 chapter links • Theatrical trailer • Production notes • Talent files.
2000 (PG) 99m/C Judge Reinhold, Julia Sweeney, Joe Pichler, Michaela Gallo, Jamie Marsh, Michael Ciccolini, Frank Gorshin, Danielle Wiener; *D:* David Mickey Evans; *W:* Jeff Schechter; *C:* John Aronson; *M:* Philip Giffin.

Beetle Bailey / Hagar the Horrible / Betty Boop

The 12 cartoons on this collection are nothing special. Ten of them feature Beetle Bailey and the guys at Camp Swampy. They're on a par with the original *Flintstones* or any other generic Saturday morning fare. The same goes for the one Hagar installment. The updated Betty Boop is a bit more ambitious, but it's not up to the best animation. The full-frame image is no better than broadcast quality. Reds bleed throughout. The drawing is simple. —MM
Movie: ♫♫ **DVD:** ♫♫
Rhino Home Video (Cat #ID9705RHDVD, UPC #014381970524). Full frame. Dolby Digital Mono. $24.99. Snapper. *LANG:* English. *FEATURES:* 12 chapter links.
1989 103m/C

Before Night Falls

Warm, poetic biopic about the life of gay Cuban writer Reinaldo Arenas follows him from birth to death. Though Arenas is embraced as a great up-and-coming writer, as the Cuban government grows more repressive, he finds his books banned and himself jailed for a crime he didn't commit. A moving and frightening portrayal of a people trapped by a fascist government, the film is beautifully shot and realized. Bardem is excellent as Arenas, though some of his thickly accented voice-overs are a bit difficult to decipher. As the film follows a real person's life story, it seems formless and has a tendency to meander a bit. Look quick for Sean Penn as a Cuban peasant and Johnny Depp in two roles. The DVD is gorgeous, richly capturing the warm green and brownish hues of the film and the Surround sound is phenomenal, giving a believable "you are there" feeling to the film. The commentary is excellent and dissects the film in great detail. The featurettes are interesting and worthwhile; "Improper Conduct" features a real interview with Arenas, while the other two show two very different sides of director Schnabel. —DG
Movie: ♫♫♫ **DVD:** ♫♫♫♫
New Line Home Video (Cat #N5251, UPC #79404352512). Widescreen (1.85:1) anamorphic. Dolby Digital 5.1 Surround; Dolby Stereo. $24.98. Snapper. *LANG:* English; Spanish. *SUB:* English; Spanish; French. *CAP:* English. *FEATURES:* 27 chapter links • Commentary: Schnabel, Bardem, Gomez-Carriles, Burwell, Perez Grobet • Excerpt from "Improper Conduct," interview with Reinaldo Arenas • Behind-the-scenes/home movie • "Little notes on painting," artwork by Julian Schnabel • Cast and crew filmographies • Theatrical trailer.
2000 (R) 134m/C Javier Bardem, Olivier Martinez, Andrea Di Stefano, Johnny Depp, Michael Wincott, Sean Penn, Hector Babenco, Najwa Nimri; *D:* Julian Schnabel; *W:* Julian Schnabel, Lazaro Gomez Carilles, Cunningham O'Keefe; *C:* Xavier Perez Grobet, Guillermo Rosas; *M:* Carter Burwell. *AWARDS:* Ind. Spirit '01: Actor (Bardem); Natl. Bd. of Review '00: Actor (Bardem); Natl. Soc. Film Critics '00: Actor (Bardem); *NOM:* Oscars '00: Actor (Bardem); Ind. Spirit '01: Cinematog., Director (Schnabel), Film.

Behind the Planet of the Apes

If you just can't get enough of the *Planet of the Ape* series, take a look at this two-hour documentary. Host *Apes* star Roddy McDowall serves up more details on the making of the series than the average movie fan would ever want. But the *Ape* fan will appreciate all these goodies, including makeup effects, behind-the-scenes footage, and interviews with the cast and crew. In addition to the five feature films, some time is given to the TV series and more. The quality on the DVD varies tremendously due to the many different source materials. There are even some home movies thrown in. Sometimes the image is great, sometimes grainy, sometimes just plain soft. But it doesn't really matter—there's so much history here that any fan of the series will have to have this. Originally available only as part of the *Planet of the Apes: The Evolution* box set, *Behind* is now available on its own. —JO
Movie: ♫♫♫ **DVD:** ♫♫♫

20th Century Fox Home Entertainment (Cat #2000516, UPC #024543005162). Full frame. Dolby Surround. Keepcase. *LANG:* English. *SUB:* English; Spanish. *CAP:* English. *FEATURES:* 22 chapter links • Theatrical trailers • TV spot.
1998 120m/C *D:* Kevin Burns, David Comtois; *W:* Kevin Burns, David Comtois, Brian Anthony; *Nar:* Roddy McDowall.

Being There

Adaptation of Jerzy Kosinski's satiric novella about politics, the media, and our national love affair with television gave us the final great performance of comedic genius Peter Sellers. He plays Chance, an innocent middle-aged man living a sheltered life and tending garden for his benefactor. When the "old man" dies, Chance loses paradise and must fend for himself in a hostile world. An accident lands him in the care of Eve Rand (MacLaine), wife to Benjamin Rand (Douglas), terminally ill philanthropist and casual advisor to the President (Warden). Like his name, a series of happenstances quickly transforms Chance from a simple gardener to Chauncey Gardiner, sage visionary quoted by presidents and desired by the rich and powerful. Chauncey affects all in his ever-increasing orbit, completely oblivious of how he just might be the new Adam, the next step on our evolutionary ladder. Everyone is wonderful and perfectly cast; Sellers, MacLaine (at her most appealing), and Douglas (who won an Oscar for the role, winning over Robert Duvall for *Apocalypse Now*) all shine here. There is also a short but effective scene with veteran character actor Richard Basehart playing a Soviet attaché just as beguiled as his decadent Western counterparts by the nothingness of Chance. The 1.85 anamorphic transfer is better than average but not spectacular. Caleb Deschanel's cinematography is perfectly in tune with Hal Ashby's direction, understated and delicate. As such, colors are accurate and consistent without being flashy. Black levels are solid but not deep, leaving some details lost in the shadows. The image is extremely clean and free of blemishes or defects. Edge enhancement is apparent in some scenes. Fleshtones look natural and I did not detect any compression or digital artifacts during the presentation. The audio is competent enough, replicating the original mono soundtrack with adequate dynamic range and a minimum of distortion. The music, ranging from Johnny Mandel's witty piano arrangements to Brazilian artist Deodato's very '70s rendition of "Thus Spake Zarathrustra," plays well through the center channel without obscuring the dialogue or clogging the tweeter. A theatrical trailer is the disc's only extra. Presented in anamorphic widescreen, the trailer is in good physical shape and markets both the extraordinary Sellers and the film's outrageous elements. In true Jackie Chan fashion, outtakes play over the end credits. Make sure to watch them. —EP
Movie: ♫♫♫ **DVD:** ♫♫½

Warner Home Video, Inc. (Cat #938, UPC #012569093829). Widescreen (1.85:1) anamorphic. Dolby Digital Mono. $19.98. Snapper. *LANG:* English; French. *SUB:* French; Spanish; Portuguese. *CAP:* English. *FEATURES:* 36 chapter links ▪ Theatrical trailer ▪ Cast/filmmaker profiles.
1979 (PG) 130m/C Peter Sellers, Shirley MacLaine, Melvyn Douglas, Jack Warden, Richard Dysart, Richard Basehart; *D:* Hal Ashby; *W:* Jerzy Kosinski; *C:* Caleb Deschanel; *M:* Johnny Mandel. *AWARDS:* Oscars '79: Support. Actor (Douglas); Golden Globes '80: Actor—Mus./Comedy (Sellers), Support. Actor (Douglas); L.A. Film Critics '79: Support. Actor (Douglas); Natl. Bd. of Review '79: Actor (Sellers); N.Y. Film Critics '79: Support. Actor (Douglas); Natl. Soc. Film Critics '79: Cinematog.; Writers Guild '79: Adapt. Screenplay; *NOM:* Oscars '79: Actor (Sellers).

Bellyfruit

Low-budget independent production looks at the sexual initiation of three young women. Shanika is a 14-year-old foster child abandoned by her junkie mother. Aracely scandalizes her traditional Latin family when she becomes pregnant. Christina is ready to follow her mother's footsteps in a life of partying, casual sex, and drugs. Considerable voice-over is used to tell their grim stories. Generally, the image is good considering the monetary constraints the filmmakers were working under. This is not supposed to be a pretty film in any way. —MM
Movie: ♫♫½ **DVD:** ♫♫½
Vanguard International Cinema, Inc. (Cat #VF0056, UPC #658769005639). Widescreen letterboxed. $29.95. Keepcase. *LANG:* English. *FEATURES:* 12 chapter links.
1999 95m/C Kelly Vint, Tamara La Seon Bass, Tonatzin Mondragon, T.E. Russell, Michael Pena, Bonnie Dickenson, Kimberly Scott, James Dumant; *D:* Kerri Green; *W:* Kerri Green, Maria Bernhard, Suzannah Blinkoff, Janet Borrus; *C:* Peter Calvin.

Ben-Hur

The third film version of the Lee Wallace classic stars Heston in the role of Palestinian Jew Judah Ben-Hur who seeks revenge against his former friend Messala (Boyd), who had made him a galley slave. Won a record 11 Oscars, including Best Picture. The breathtaking chariot race is still unbelievably violent even in today's world of CGI effects. Superb Miklos Rozsa score. The DVD presents the film in its original 2.76:1 aspect ratio, which makes for a much smaller TV screen image (about 15% less than the more common 2.35:1 ratio) than most other films on video. It's worth it though just to see the stunning cinematic composition, which combined with the super-sharp image and highly detailed colors, delivers *Ben-Hur* to the home screen looking better than it ever has. A new 5.1 soundtrack was produced from the original elements and,

even with a few glitches due to film's age, makes the action sequences even more breathtaking, at times giving the sound as much guts as most newer films. Christopher Plummer narrates the hour-long documentary, "Ben-Hur: The Making of an Epic," which features interviews (including one with director Wyler) and some great behind-the-scenes footage. First scheduled for DVD several years ago and then cancelled (most likely due to the film's length). This Warner Home Video disc takes advantage of the DVD-18 doublesided dual-layered technology for maximum storage capacity allowing for less compression than would have been required previously. —JO
Movie: ♫♫♫½ **DVD:** ♫♫♫½
Warner Home Video, Inc. (Cat #65506, UPC #012569550629). Widescreen (2.76:1) anamorphic. Dolby Digital 5.1; Dolby Digital Stereo. $24.98. Snapper. *LANG:* English (DD5.1); French (Stereo). *SUB:* English; Spanish; French; Portuguese. *CAP:* English. *FEATURES:* 81 chapter links ▪ Theatrical trailers ▪ Talent files ▪ "Making of" documentary ▪ Photo gallery ▪ Screen tests ▪ Commentary: Charlton Heston ▪ Dual-layered.
1959 212m/C Charlton Heston, Jack Hawkins, Stephen Boyd, Haya Harareet, Hugh Griffith, Martha Scott, Sam Jaffe, Cathy O'Donnell, Finlay Currie; *D:* William Wyler; *W:* Karl Tunberg; *C:* Robert L. Surtees; *M:* Miklos Rozsa. *AWARDS:* Oscars '59: Actor (Heston), Art Dir./Set Dec., Color, Color Cinematog., Costume Des. (C), Director (Wyler), Film Editing, Picture, Sound, Support. Actor (Griffith), Orig. Dramatic Score; AFI '98: Top 100; British Acad. '59: Film; Directors Guild '59: Director (Wyler); Golden Globes '60: Director (Wyler), Film—Drama, Support. Actor (Boyd); N.Y. Film Critics '59: Film; *NOM:* Oscars '59: Adapt. Screenplay.

Beneath the Planet of the Apes

In the first sequel, another Earth astronaut passes through the same time warp and follows the same path as Taylor, through Ape City and to the ruins of the bombblasted New York subway system, where warhead-worshipping human mutants are found. For some reason, I really like the DVD's menu, where you are taken through tunnels to each feature, giving a video game–like rendering of the film. The film transfer itself looks good; a grain problem on bright mono-colored shots is the most aggravating aspect. Highly detailed shots also shimmer on occasion, but only rarely. The blacks are superb. On this one, the Dolby Surround tracks really kick out and deliver music, effects, and dialogue, with equal energy. —JO
Movie: ♫♫♫ **DVD:** ♫♫♫
20th Century Fox Home Entertainment (Cat #2000105, UPC #024543001058). Widescreen (2.35:1) letterboxed. Dolby Surround; Dolby Digital Mono. $29.95. Keepcase. *LANG:* English (DS); French (Mono). *SUB:* English; Spanish. *CAP:* Eng-

lish. *FEATURES:* 24 chapter links ▪ Theatrical trailers ▪ Photo gallery ▪ Weblink. Also available as part of the 6-DVD "Planet of the Apes: The Evolution" box set (cat. #2000109, UPC 024543001096) for $99.95.
1970 (G) 108m/C James Franciscus, Kim Hunter, Maurice Evans, Charlton Heston, James Gregory, Natalie Trundy, Jeff Corey, Linda Harrison, Victor Buono, Paul Richards, David Watson, Thomas Gomez; *D:* Ted Post; *W:* Paul Dehn; *C:* Milton Krasner; *M:* Leonard Rosenman.

Benny & Joon

A quirky, sweet story about a young girl named Joon (Masterson) who is too fantasy-driven (probably schizophrenic) to function in the real world. She lives with her bachelor brother Benny (Quinn), making grilled cheese sandwiches with an iron and decorating the house like something from *Alice in Wonderland.* She is dependent on him for her livelihood and he in turn is dependent on her to feel needed. When Joon wins an equally quirky handsome stranger (Depp) at the weekly poker game, romance ensues and a battle for control of Joon begins between Benny, who doubts his sister's ability to make informed romantic decisions, and Sam, who believes that Joon is perfect the way she is. This being a romantic comedy, the perfect solution is for the couple to find Benny a love of his own (Moore). Heels are dragged but in the end everyone is happy. The film is fun yet serious, with a good balance between showing ways that the mentally ill are different from the so-called normal people, as well as the ways that they are the same, and how, in some ways, everyone is a little crazy. Depp is adorable as Sam and does a few beautiful Chaplin/Little Tramp impersonations that are worth seeing. Masterson also does a great job of portraying a woman whose own mental instability is a mystery to her. The disc looks and sounds above average. —CA
Movie: ♫♫½ **DVD:** ♫♫½
MGM Home Entertainment (Cat #1001453, UPC #027616857736). Widescreen (1.85:1) anamorphic. Dolby Digital. $19.98. Keepcase. *LANG:* English. *SUB:* French; Spanish. *CAP:* English. *FEATURES:* 16 chapter links ▪ Commentary ▪ Deleted scenes ▪ Stunt reel ▪ Theatrical trailer ▪ Music video ▪ Costume and makeup tests.
1993 (PG) 98m/C Johnny Depp, Mary Stuart Masterson, Aidan Quinn, Julianne Moore, Oliver Platt, CCH Pounder, Dan Hedaya, Joe Grifasi, William H. Macy, Eileen Ryan; *D:* Jeremiah S. Chechik; *W:* Barry Berman; *C:* Jason Schwartzman; *M:* Rachel Portman. *AWARDS: NOM:* Golden Globes '94: Actor—Mus./Comedy (Depp); MTV Movie Awards '94: On-Screen Duo (Johnny Depp/Mary Stuart Masterson), Comedic Perf. (Depp), Song ("I'm Gonna Be 500 Miles").

Beowulf

This is a computer game/music video/ *Highlander* version of the famous poem.

It's set in a sort of medieval future. Christopher Lambert, who's getting mighty long in the tooth for this kind of thing, is the titular hero who comes to a dank castle to dispatch Grendel. The goofiest prop is a giant straight razor that looks like it might have been a sculpture by Roy Lichtenstein. The monster effects combine *Species* and *Predator*. Surround sound gives Lambert's voice an artificial rumble. DVD image looks very good, capturing a fine level of detail even in the black and dark gray interiors and the entire film is very dark. —*MM*

Movie: 🎬½ **DVD:** 🎬🎬

Buena Vista Home Entertainment (Cat #20776, UPC #717951010650). Widescreen (1.85:1) anamorphic. Dolby Digital Surround Stereo. $24.99. Keepcase. *LANG:* English. *FEATURES:* Trailer • Behind-the-scenes featurette • 22 chapter links.

1998 (R) 92m/C Christopher Lambert, Rhona Mitra, Oliver Cotton, Patricia Velasquez, Goetz Otto, Layla Roberts, Brent J. Lowe; *D:* Graham Baker; *W:* Mark Leahy, David Chappe; *C:* Christopher Faloona; *M:* Ben Watkins.

Beshkempir the Adopted Son

A slow-paced, meditative look at the life of a young boy living in a small pre-industrial town. He is forced to consider his place in the world when he learns he is adopted during a fight with a friend over a girl. While the story itself is typical fodder for the art-house crowd, it is the breathtaking cinematography that makes this film worth watching. Every shot in this film is a still life worthy of Ansel Adams. From the field of cherry trees that are shown first bare and then in full bloom to mark the season to the semi-naked rotund woman that the boys sneak a peak at, every scene inspires awe for its raw beauty. The director chose to film the present in B&W with the past exploding in brief flurries of color which, granted, seems contrived but actually brings a spark of pleasure to the viewing of the film. The transfer on the DVD is flawless and the sound is great. —*CA*

Movie: 🎬🎬 **DVD:** 🎬🎬🎬🎬

Winstar Home Entertainment (Cat #FLV5197, UPC #72091751972). Widescreen (1.85:1) letterboxed. Dolby Digital Stereo. $29.98. Keepcase. *LANG:* Kirghizstani. *SUB:* English. *FEATURES:* Theatrical trailer.

1998 81m/B *RU* Mirlan Abdykalykov; *D:* Aktan Abdykalykov; *W:* Aktan Abdykalykov, Avtandil Adikulov, Marat Sarulu; *C:* Hassan Kidirialev; *M:* Nurlan Nishanov.

Best in Show

Christopher Guest and Eugene Levy's "mockumentary" about dog shows is a gem. They exaggerate an already rarified world with very funny results. An ensemble cast takes the pooches through their paces at the Mayflower Dog Show. Fred Willard almost steals the show as the

sports announcer who doesn't quite get the point. Image and sound are all you'd expect from a major studio release. The surprise of the disc is the wealth of extras, including 17 deleted scenes with commentary. —*MM*

Movie: 🎬🎬🎬 **DVD:** 🎬🎬🎬½

Warner Home Video, Inc. (Cat #18951). Widescreen anamorphic. $24.98. Snapper. *LANG:* English; French. *SUB:* English; French. *FEATURES:* 36 chapter links • Talent files • Commentary: Christopher Guest, Eugene Levy • 17 deleted scenes • Trailer.

2000 (PG-13) 89m/C Christopher Guest, Michael McKean, Parker Posey, Eugene Levy, Catherine O'Hara, Fred Willard, Michael Hitchcock, John Michael Higgins, Jennifer Coolidge, Trevor Beckwith, Bob Balaban, Ed Begley Jr., Patrick Cranshaw, Don Lake, Larry Miller; *D:* Christopher Guest; *W:* Christopher Guest, Eugene Levy; *C:* Roberto Schaefer; *M:* C.J. Vanston. *AWARDS: NOM:* Ind. Spirit '01: Director (Guest); Writers Guild '00: Orig. Screenplay.

The Best of Boys in Love: Award Winning Gay Short Films

The sharpness of claymation makes "Achilles" the most successful transfer to DVD in this mediocre collection of gay shorts. The films in this collection fall into the usual traps of shorts: extreme situations and jokes played just for effect, and the skill level of those involved, whatever it may be, is frequently more apparent than their artistic intent. "Death in Venice, CA" is the most effective in evoking an atmosphere and tone of dangerous love, but goes awry in its tragic end. "Achilles" features incredible claymation, but skirts absurdity with its sexuality and anatomical details. "Karen Black Like Me" and "Dirty Baby Does Fire Island" are long jokes that don't sustain their laugh and the transfer to DVD reveals a grainy quality. The black-and-white "Twilight of the Gods" is well shot and occasionally touching, but occasionally contrived. Rent it, don't buy it. Some entries are widescreen; some are full frame. —*JAS*

Movie: 🎬½ **DVD:** 🎬🎬

First Run Features (Cat #FRF909389D, UPC #720229909389). Widescreen letterboxed; full frame. $29.95. Keepcase. *LANG:* English. *FEATURES:* 7 chapter links.

2000 101m/C

Best of Intimate Sessions: Vol. 2

Three episodes of the popular late-night cable series are collected on disc. Wife Lucy (Drew) spices up her marriage with voyeurism; Joy (Bodnar) discovers that she really likes younger men; and Renee (Reed) finds love in the office. Background mini-blinds flash madly. A grainy original makes for a grainy DVD. Sound is very good, though that's not really the point, is it? Volume 1, not available for review, is

also available (cat. # YPD-1009; $14.99). —*MM*

Movie: 🎬½ **DVD:** 🎬🎬

York Entertainment (Cat #YPD-1010, UPC #750723101026). Full frame. Dolby Digital 5.1 Surround Stereo. $14.99. Keepcase. *LANG:* English. *FEATURES:* 18 chapter links • Trailer.

1999 100m/C Griffin (Griffen) Drew, Jenna Bodnar, Kira Reed; *D:* Marilyn Vance; *W:* Karol Silverstein, Marcy Ronen; *C:* Kurt Albert; *M:* Herman Beeftink.

Best of the Best 3: No Turning Back / Best of the Best: Without Warning

Double feature from star/director/producer Rhee. In the first, he goes up against white racist neo-Nazis. In the second, Russian mobsters are the bad guys. Production values are acceptable, though the action scenes won't show fans anything they haven't seen before. In both, the full-frame image is maybe a hair better than VHS tape. The beefed-up Surround is relatively inoffensive. (See separate entry, *Best of the Best: Without Warning*, for credits.)—*MM*

Movie: 🎬🎬 **DVD:** 🎬🎬

Buena Vista Home Entertainment (Cat #19695, UPC #717951008718). Full frame. Dolby Digital Surround Stereo. $24.99. Keepcase. *LANG:* English. *FEATURES: No Turning Back*, 17 chapter links • *Without Warning*, 12 chapter links.

1995 (R) 102m/C Phillip Rhee, Gina Gershon, Christopher McDonald, Mark Rolston, Peter Simmons, Dee Wallace Stone; *D:* Phillip Rhee; *W:* Deborah Scott; *C:* Jerry Watson; *M:* Barry Goldberg.

Best of the Best: Especially for Kids

This string of nine films, all Academy Award winners or nominees, is presented under an "Especially for Kids!" umbrella that appears to have been chosen to assure buyers that adult material isn't going to sneak in. Not all are animated, exactly; only a few can be called traditional animation at all. None is concerned with being a "standard cartoon," and all can be called a boon to the imagination. Contents: "The Cat Came Back," "Every Child, Evolution," "Monsieur Pointu," "Christmas Cracker," "The Sand Castle," "The Tender Tale of Cinderella Penguin," "The Owl Who Married a Goose," and "Black Fly." The DVD image is clean and trim, and when you're laughing and singing along to "The Cat Came Back" (one of the greatest cartoons ever made), you aren't thinking about commentaries or context. —*GE*

Movie: 🎬🎬🎬½ **DVD:** 🎬🎬🎬½

Image Entertainment (Cat #ID0220NFDVD, UPC #014381022025). Full frame. Snapper. *LANG:* English and Inuit. *FEATURES:* 9 chapter links.

1999 82m/C

Best of the Best: Romantic Tales

All of the animated shorts in this collection are beautifully mastered, and only a couple of the very oldest show any sign of wear whatsoever. Someone should collect award-winning student films and American animated short subjects for DVD output as well...this bunch is just charming. Contents: "A Chairy Tale," "George and Rosemary," "Strings," "Bob's Birthday," "The Street," "Walking," "Pas de Deux," "The Romance of Transportation in Canada," "The Drag," "The Family that Dwelt Apart." —GE

Movie: ♫♫♫½ **DVD:** ♫♫♫½
Image Entertainment (Cat #ID0232NFDVD, UPC #01438102322). Full frame. Dolby Digital Stereo. $24.99. Snapper. *LANG:* English. *FEATURES:* 10 chapter links.
1999 97m/C

Best of the Best: Strange Tales of the Imagination

Collections of animated films from the National Film Board of Canada tend to be very good and this is one of the best. All of these were nominated for Oscars and two of them won. One of those is "Special Delivery," a blackly humorous little story from 1974 that's worth the price of the disc all by itself. Generally the image is fine, but some of these were created with fairly heavy grain. Contents: "The Big Snit," "This Is the House That Jack Built," "Special Delivery," "My Financial Career," "Neighbours," "Paradise," "Hunger," "The Bead Game," "La Salla," and "What On Earth!" —MM

Movie: ♫♫♫½ **DVD:** ♫♫½
Image Entertainment (Cat #ID0239NFDVD, UPC #014381023923). Full frame. Dolby Digital Stereo. $24.99. Snapper. *LANG:* English. *FEATURES:* 10 chapter links.
1999 90m/C

Best of the Best: Without Warning

Please see review for *Best of the Best 3*.
Movie: ♫½
1998 (R) 90m/C Phillip Rhee, Ernie Hudson, Tobin Bell, Thure Riefenstein, Chris Lemmon, Jessica Collins; *D:* Phillip Rhee; *C:* Michael D. Margulies; *M:* David Grant.

The Best of Zagreb Film: Laugh at Your Own Risk and For Children Only

Some of the cartoons in this collection are showing their age with light flecks and static in the soundtrack. Others are pristine, but criticisms about image quality are secondary to the imagination, inventiveness, and playful intelligence behind the films. The disc is divided into adult and children's halves. For my money, the two best are "Tower of Babel" and "The Devil's

Work," though there's not a loser in the bunch. Contents: The Tower of Babel, Exciting Love Story, The Devil's Work, Of Holes and Corks, Learning to Walk, Home Is the Best, Maxicat in Tennis, Maxicat in Rope, Maxicat in Door, Cow on the Moon, Strange Bird, Octave of Fear, Little and Big, Anna Goes to Buy Some Bread, Well Done Job, Krek, Maxicat in Ball of Yarn/Maxicat in Fishing. —MM

Movie: ♫♫♫ **DVD:** ♫♫½
Image Entertainment (Cat #ID9003ASDVD, UPC #014381900323). Full frame. Dolby Digital Mono. $24.99. Snapper. *FEATURES:* 16 chapter links.
19?? 109m/C YU

Betrayed

Costa-Gavras's rabid political film deals with an implausible FBI agent (Winger) infiltrating a white supremacist organization via her love affair with a handsome farmer (Berenger), who turns out to be a murderous racist. Revealing a high level of detail the non-anamorphic print creates a very pleasing image with strong and nicely delineated colors. The color balance is natural and faithfully renders fleshtones. It creates deep shadows and black while always striking a good balance with the highlights in the image. Audio is generally well produced but lacks some of the openness and dynamics of modern audio tracks. The frequency response is good. —GH/MM

Movie: ♫♫ **DVD:** ♫♫♫
MGM Home Entertainment Widescreen (1.85:1) letterboxed; full frame. Dolby Digital Stereo. $19.98. Keepcase. *LANG:* English; French; Spanish. *SUB:* French; Spanish. *FEATURES:* Trailer.
1988 (R) 112m/C Tom Berenger, Debra Winger, John Mahoney, John Heard, Albert Hall, Jeffrey DeMunn; *D:* Constantin Costa-Gavras; *W:* Joe Eszterhas; *C:* Patrick Blossier.

A Better Tomorrow, Part 1 [Anchor Bay]

Former hitmen (Lung and Yun-Fat) team up to bring down the mob boss who double-crossed them, sending one to prison and the other to the streets. Then there's the matter of the younger brother who's a cop. This is one of Woo's better Hong Kong action films, though most fans consider *The Killer* and *Hard-Boiled* (made a few years later) to be superior. DVD is an excellent reproduction of a fairly grainy image. That grain does not lead to excess artifacts or pixels. Sound curiously drops out for a few moments on the Cantonese soundtrack. Otherwise, it's fine and is more expressive than the English. —MM
AKA: Ying Huang Boon Sik; Gangland Boss.

Movie: ♫♫♫ **DVD:** ♫♫½
Anchor Bay (Cat #DV11258, UPC #013131125894). Widescreen (1.85:1) anamorphic. Dolby Digital Mono. $24.99. Keepcase. *LANG:* Cantonese; Mandarin; English. *SUB:* English. *FEATURES:* 29 chap-

ter links • Talent files • 3 versions of trailer.
1986 95m/C CH HK Chow Yun-Fat, Leslie Cheung, Ti Lung, Emily Chu, Waise Lee, John Woo; *D:* John Woo; *W:* John Woo; *C:* Wing-hang Wong; *M:* Ka-Fai Koo.

A Better Tomorrow, Part 2 [Anchor Bay]

Chow Yun-Fat's smooth-talking gangster, who was killed in Part I, returns as the dead man's unmentioned twin brother, and Woo takes his usual epic mayhem from Hong Kong to New York. Both image and sound are virtually identical to the first film, faithfully re-creating a grainy image. —MM **AKA:** Yinghung Bunsik 2.

Movie: ♫♫½ **DVD:** ♫♫½
Anchor Bay (Cat #DV11259, UPC #013131125993). Widescreen (1.85:1) anamorphic. Dolby Digital Mono. $24.99. Keepcase. *LANG:* Cantonese; English. *SUB:* English. *FEATURES:* 28 chapter links • Talent files.
1988 100m/C HK Chow Yun-Fat, Leslie Cheung; *D:* John Woo; *W:* John Woo; *M:* Joseph Koo.

A Better Way to Die

The packaging for this direct-to-DVD action/thriller promises Andre Braugher (*Duets*), Joe Pantoliano (*Risky Business*), Natasha Henstridge (*Species*), and Lou Diamond Phillips (*Courage under Fire*, *La Bamba*), but the actual star is Scott Wiper, who is also the writer and director. Make no mistake, this is an independent film, but it looks great, and surprise, surprise, it rips along and delivers the unexpected at every turn. Wiper manages to keep the "wrong man" theme on a steady course, and if given a bigger budget and a better script, we can expect to hear more from him in the future—for now, enjoy the moment, don't worry about the details of the plot, just know that Wiper is mistaken for someone else and everyone is after him. Excellent DVD presentation, which is topped off with an insightful commentary track from filmmaker Scott Wiper. —RJT
Movie: ♫♫½ **DVD:** ♫♫♫
Columbia Tristar Home Video (Cat #05980, UPC #043396059801). Widescreen (1.85:1) anamorphic. Dolby Digital 5.1 Surround; Dolby Digital Surround. $24.95. Keepcase. *LANG:* English; French; Portuguese; Spanish. *SUB:* English; French; Spanish; Portuguese; Chinese; Korean; Thai. *CAP:* English. *FEATURES:* Commentary: director Scott Wiper • 28 chapter links.
2000 (R) 101m/C Andre Braugher, Joe Pantoliano, Natasha Henstridge, Lou Diamond Phillips, Wayne Duvall, Scott Wiper; *D:* Scott Wiper; *W:* Scott Wiper.

Beware! The Blob

This sequel to the 1958 original appears to have been made for television. Actor Larry Hagman directed. He and the cast of familiar faces play the material for all of its inherent humor. The stuff, which is retrieved from the arctic by geologist Godfrey Cambridge, looks like raspberry jam and adds a reddish tint to some scenes. Overall, the image is exceptionally grainy, but all the flaws come from the inexpensively produced source material. —*MM* ***AKA:*** Son of Blob.

Movie: 🐾🐾 **DVD:** 🐾🐾

Image Entertainment (Cat #ID6609WEDVD, UPC #014381660920). Full frame. Dolby Digital Mono. $24.99. Snapper. *LANG:* English. *FEATURES:* 10 chapter links. **1972 (PG) 87m/C** Robert Walker Jr., Godfrey Cambridge, Carol Lynley, Shelley Berman, Larry Hagman, Burgess Meredith, Gerrit Graham, Dick Van Patten, Gwynne Gilford, Richard Stahl, Richard Webb, Cindy Williams; *D:* Larry Hagman; *W:* Jack Woods, Anthony Harris; *M:* Mort Garson.

The Beyond

This stylish Fulci gore classic, recently re-released to theatres by Tarantino's Rolling Thunder Pictures, is generally considered the best of Fulci's splatter flicks. It all begins in 1927 Louisiana where a warlock is brutally executed. Years later, a woman inherits a hotel, not realizing that it is built upon one of the seven doors to Hell. Filled with ultra-cool gore, puss-oozing zombies, a demon dog, and an eerie atmosphere that can't be beat. It's easy to see why this one's a cult fave. Anchor Bay has delivered another in-demand previously unavailable genre film to DVD. Somehow, they even went back to the original elements and came up with a 5.1 soundtrack for the English tracks on the disc, so that's the way to watch this one—it adds energy throughout with the climactic zombie hospital siege becoming even more intense. Visually the picture looks incredible, much sharper than expected with strong colors and deep blacks. —*JO* ***AKA:*** Seven Doors of Death.

Movie: 🐾🐾🐾½ **DVD:** 🐾🐾🐾½

Anchor Bay (Cat #DV11231, UPC #013131123197). Widescreen (2.35:1) anamorphic. Dolby Surround 5.1; Dolby Digital Mono. $29.98. Keepcase. *LANG:* English; Italian. *SUB:* English. *FEATURES:* 53 chapter links ● 3 theatrical trailers ● Commentary: David Warbeck, Catriona MacColl ● Lucio Fulci interview ● Lost pre-credit sequence ● Music video ● Stills gallery ● Liner notes by Chas Balun. **1982 (R) 88m/C** *IT* Katherine MacColl, David Warbeck, Farah Keller, Tony St. John; *D:* Lucio Fulci; *W:* Lucio Fulci, Dardano Sacchetti, Giorgio Mariuzzo; *C:* Sergio Salvati.

Beyond Atlantis

South of the Philippines, an underwater tribe is discovered. These ancient mermen kidnap landlubber women for breeding stock. The low-budget adventure actually features some nice colorful underwater photography. Although the source print itself seems to be in rather good shape and doesn't exhibit distracting defects, the picture quality of the transfer into the digital domain is rather poor. The picture seems to come from a rather low-end master source and has a washed-out look without detail. Edges and colors bleed throughout and excessive film grain adds to the rather poor look of the DVD. Every compression artifact imaginable is visible in the transfer, including pixelation, banding, dot crawl, shimmering and ringing. Tinny, thin sound is equally weak. —*GH/MM*

Movie: 🐾½ **DVD:** 🐾½

VCI Home Video (Cat #8236). Full frame. Dolby Digital Mono. $14.99. Keepcase. *LANG:* English. *FEATURES:* Thumbnail bios ● Previews.

1973 (PG) 91m/C *PH* John Ashley, Patrick Wayne, George Nader; *D:* Eddie Romero; *W:* Charles Johnson; *C:* Justo Paulino.

Beyond the Clouds

Omnibus offers four meditations on the mystery and sometimes inanity of relationships by the legendary film director Michelangelo Antonioni. The stories connect through the musings of a Director with No Name, played by John Malkovich, as he wanders Europe in search of inspiration and reflects on stories told to him. He also conjures situations from the ornate architecture and the placid countryside. Like most anthologies, some segments work, some do not. Not easy to either categorize or explain, the film takes its time in unfolding the perplexities and frustrations of what makes people come together or split apart. The first two installments suffer from languid pacing as well as a lack of focus (some might call it "realism"), but the last two more than make up for the notion that Antonioni might have lost his edge. The third story, especially, benefits from the presence of Fanny Ardant, Jean Reno, and Peter Weller. There are moments, however, when you want to just slap some of the characters out of their Euro-romantic stupor and yell, "Get over it!" The video transfer, as well as the format's increased resolution, admirably preserves the soft, pastel color scheme. The film contains a fair amount of foggy or smoky scenes, the bane of DVD authors, yet no pixelation or compression artifacts are present. Except for an odd thunderclap or ambient city noise, the Surrounds mainly contain music fill, but at least it's music from Van Morrison and U2. The English subtitles (necessary since the film is in three languages: Italian, French, and English) display within the film frame, good news for anyone with a 16 x 9 display. An hour-long documentary about the making of the film is the disc's sole supplement. Produced by Enrica Antonioni (Mrs. Michelangelo), the behind-the-scenes look sometimes gets just as arty as her hubby's features, emphasizing odd angles and jarring cuts. Yet the insights about Antonioni's working style and philosophy by Ardant, Reno, et al, rises several cuts above the advertising pabulum passed off as glimpses into the creative process. —*EP* ***AKA:*** Par-dela les Nuages.

Movie: 🐾🐾½ **DVD:** 🐾🐾🐾

Image Entertainment (Cat #ID9080SIDVD, UPC #1438190802). Widescreen (1.85:1) anamorphic. Dolby Digital Stereo Surround. $24.99. Snapper. *LANG:* English; Italian; French. *SUB:* English. *FEATURES:* 8 chapter links ● Documentary on Michelangelo Antonioni: "To Make a Film Is to Be Alive." **1995 109m/C** *IT GE FR* John Malkovich, Marcello Mastroianni, Sophie Marceau, Fanny Ardant, Vincent Perez, Jean Reno, Jeanne Moreau, Irene Jacob, Peter Weller, Chiara Caselli, Ines Sastre, Kim Rossi-Stuart; *D:* Michelangelo Antonioni, Wim Wenders; *W:* Michelangelo Antonioni, Wim Wenders, Tonino Guerra; *C:* Robby Muller, Alfio Contini; *M:* Van Morrison, Lucio Dalla, Laurent Petitgrand.

Beyond the Mat

Behind-the-scenes look at the world of professional wrestling (sports entertainment), including WWF (and its head Vince McMahon), and the riskier (and gorier) ECW. Some of the most popular stars are here—The Rock, Chyna—but the film concentrates on 30-year pro Terry Funk, legendary Mick "Mankind" Foley, and drug addict (at least at the time) Jake "The Snake" Roberts. Some unforgettable scenes include the tearful frightened looks on the faces of Mankind's kids as the Rock slams him into a bay of sound equipment. It may be an act, but the pain is brutally real. The DVD is sometimes grainy, and the sharpness varies, but no more than it did in the theatre. Footage ranges from home movies to video and the disc more than does justice to all the media. Combine the added scenes (including backstage with Mankind after a particularly bloody match) with a great commentary and you've got a DVD that shouldn't be missed, whether or not you're a fan. —*JO*

Movie: 🐾🐾🐾½ **DVD:** 🐾🐾🐾

Universal Studios Home Video (Cat #20910, UPC #025192091025). Full frame. Dolby Surround. $29.98. Keepcase. *LANG:* English. *CAP:* English. *FEATURES:* 20 chapter links ● Theatrical trailer ● Commentary: Mick Foley, Terry Funk, Barry W. Blaustein ● Production notes ● Talent files.

1999 (R) 103m/C *D:* Barry W. Blaustein; *C:* Michael Grady; *M:* Nathan Barr.

Bicentennial Man

Robin Williams is Andrew, a domestic robot of the near future. When he's purchased by the Martin family, they notice that he's different from most 'bots: he exhibits compassion and other human qualities. As time goes on, Andrew continues to develop past his programming and seeks his freedom and the pursuit of a more human form. Director Columbus opts for sentiment and empty platitudes instead of exploring the questions the film raises. Though not terrible, the DVD does nothing to make this very average movie any more entertaining. The image is generally sharp but many backgrounds are soft and the 5.1 soundtrack very seldom rises much above what a stereo mix could have accomplished. The "making of" featurette is short and not very interesting, so unless you're a gotta-have-everything Robin Williams fan, there's not really any reason to bother with this one. —JO

Movie: ♪♪½ **DVD:** ♪♪½

Buena Vista Home Entertainment (Cat #18303, UPC #717951004888). Widescreen (1.85:1) anamorphic. Dolby Digital 5.1. $32.99. Keepcase. *LANG:* English; French. *CAP:* English. *FEATURES:* 30 chapter links ● Theatrical trailer ● "Making of" featurette.

1999 (PG) 131m/C Robin Williams, Embeth Davidtz, Sam Neill, Wendy Crewson, Hallie Kate Eisenberg, Oliver Platt, Stephen Root, Lynne Thigpen, Bradley Whitford, Kiersten Warren, John Michael Higgins, George D. Wallace; **D:** Chris Columbus; **W:** Nicholas Kazan; **C:** Phil Meheux; **M:** James Horner. *AWARDS:* NOM: Oscars '99: Makeup; Golden Raspberries '99: Worst Actor (Williams).

The Big Blue [DC]

Relentlessly unrealistic tale of boyhood friends Jacques (Barr) and Enzo (Reno) who live to free dive. Enzo is the brutish, competitive type and Jacques is the shy sensitive type. When Jacques meets Johanne (Arquette), the ditzy type with a deafening biological clock, a love triangle develops among Jaques, the ocean, and the girl. In the end everyone loses except the big blue. The director's cut is longer than the original release print by 49 minutes, with the added footage raising the film's rating to an "R." Also restored is the original score by Eric Serra, which is very good. The DVD quality for this film, whose reputation thrives on the fabulous underwater photography, is disappointing. There is a distinct lack of brightness to the colors, most notably the blues. The B&W sequence at the beginning during Jaques and Enzo's childhood is far more impressive from a visual standpoint. —CA *AKA:* Le Grand Bleu.

Movie: ♪♪ **DVD:** ♪♪♪

Columbia Tristar Home Video (Cat #03927, UPC #043396039278). Widescreen (2.35:1) anamorphic. Dolby Digital 5.1; Dolby Surround. $29.95. Keepcase. *LANG:* English; French. *SUB:* English; Spanish; French. *FEATURES:* Isolated music score ● Trailers (*The Professional; The Messenger*) ● Photo gallery ● Talent files.

1988 (R) 188m/C Rosanna Arquette, Jean Reno, Jean-Marc Barr, Paul Shenar, Sergio Castellitto, Marc Duret, Griffin Dunne; **D:** Luc Besson; **W:** Luc Besson; **C:** Carlo Varini; **M:** Bill Conti. *AWARDS:* Cesar '89: Sound, Score.

Big City Blues

Reynolds and Forsythe are assassins who become involved with a hooker (Cates). Much hilarity allegedly ensues. Everyone involved has done much better work. The garish colors are about par for the video-

premiere course. Image and sound are essentially identical to VHS tape. —MM

Movie: ♪♪ **DVD:** ♪♪

Avalanche Entertainment (Cat #13996). Full frame. Dolby Digital Stereo. $24.95. Keepcase. *LANG:* English. *SUB:* Spanish. *FEATURES:* Cast and crew thumbnail bios ● Trailer ● Synopsis ● 12 chapter links ● Photo gallery ● Production notes.

1999 (R) 94m/C Burt Reynolds, William Forsythe, Georgina Cates, Giancarlo Esposito, Roger Floyd, Balthazar Getty, Arye Gross, Donovan Leitch, Roxana Zal, Amy Lyndon, Jad Mager; **D:** Clive Fleury; **W:** Clive Fleury; **C:** David Bridges; **M:** Tomas San Miguel.

The Big Country

Sea captain James McKay (Peck) heads west to marry Pat (Baker), daughter of wealthy rancher Henry Terrill (Bickford) to whom she is just a bit too attached. The Terrills and the Hannasseys, led by patriarch Rufus (Oscar-winning Ives), have a long-standing feud. McKay tries to make peace by buying another ranch, owned by school teacher Julie Maragon (Simmons). Though the genre and the epic approach are a bit dated now, the film is still hugely entertaining, though it does suffer on anything but the largest screen. The image ranges between good and very good though it is marred by some very bad aliasing, usually in the patterns of roof shingles. —MM

Movie: ♪♪♪½ **DVD:** ♪♪♪

MGM Home Entertainment (Cat #4001802, UPC #027616859013). Widescreen (2.35:1) anamorphic. Dolby Digital Mono. $19.98. Keepcase. *LANG:* English; French. *SUB:* French; Spanish. *FEATURES:* 16 chapter links ● Trailer.

1958 (R) 168m/C Gregory Peck, Charlton Heston, Burl Ives, Jean Simmons, Carroll Baker, Chuck Connors, Charles Bickford; **D:** William Wyler; **W:** Jessamyn West, Robert Wyler, James R. Webb, Sy Bartlett, Robert Wilder; **C:** Franz Planer; **M:** Jerome Moross. *AWARDS:* Oscars '58: Support. Actor (Ives); Golden Globes '59: Support. Actor (Ives); NOM: Oscars '58: Orig. Dramatic Score.

Big Deal on Madonna Street

A band of inept crooks stumble onto an elaborate jewelry store heist, but their scheming results in numerous disasters. One of the original "gang that couldn't shoot straight" comedies has never looked better on home video. This DVD has been cleaned up so that the black-and-white photography is as luminous as a contemporary rock video. Mono sound is fine, and the colloquial subtitles fit the action perfectly. A real winner, though the early '50s action looks so dated now that younger viewers may not be able to become properly involved. —MM *AKA:* The Usual Unidentified Thieves; I Soliti Ignoti; Persons Unknown.

Movie: ♪♪♪½ **DVD:** ♪♪♪♪

Criterion Collection (Cat #113, UPC #037429155424). Full frame. Dolby Digital Mono. $29.95. Keepcase. *LANG:* Italian. *SUB:* English. *FEATURES:* 25 chapter links ● Trailer ● Liner notes by Bruce Eder.

1958 90m/B IT Marcello Mastroianni, Vittorio Gassman, Claudia Cardinale, Renato Salvatori, Memmo Carotenuto, Toto, Rosanna Rory; **D:** Mario Monicelli; **W:** Mario Monicelli, Furio Scarpelli, Suso Cecchi D'Amico; **C:** Gianni Di Venanzo; **M:** Pierro Umiliani. *AWARDS:* NOM: Oscars '58: Foreign Film.

The Big Doll House

Archetypal Philippine babes-behind-bars stars Pam Grier as one of a group of tormented female inmates who decide to break out and wreak vengeance on their sadistic wardens. Considering the age and budgetary limitations under which this drive-in classic was made, the DVD looks very good. The image is clear; sound is O.K. —MM *AKA:* Women's Penitentiary 1; Women in Cages; Bamboo Dolls House.

Movie: ♪♪½ **DVD:** ♪♪½

New Concorde (Cat #20103). Full frame. $24.98. Keepcase. *LANG:* English. *FEATURES:* Roger Corman interview ● Cast and crew thumbnail bios ● Trailers.

1971 (R) 93m/C Judy Brown, Roberta Collins, Pam Grier, Brooke Mills, Pat Woodell, Sid Haig, Christianne Schmidtmer, Kathryn Loder, Jerry Frank, Charles Davis; **D:** Jack Hill; **W:** Don Spencer; **C:** Fred Conde; **M:** Les Baxter, Hall Daniels.

The Big Kahuna

The short review is Mamet in a motel as three salesmen in a Wichita hospitality suite try to finagle a huge contract for industrial lubricants from a client. The wily Larry (Spacey) has seen it all. His friend and partner Phil (DeVito) is initially willing to go along with anything he says. Young Bob (Facinelli) may be a neophyte but he's not quick to back down when his ideals are questioned. Roger Rueff's dialogue-heavy adaptation of his own play can't break free of the strict limitations of the stage, and so the movie never really moves. That said, the cast does excellent work. DVD image and sound may be a tiny improvement over VHS tape, but the bare-bones disc has no real extras. —MM

Movie: ♪♪½ **DVD:** ♪♪½

Universal Studios Home Video (Cat #20784, UPC #025192078422). Widescreen (1.85:1) anamorphic. Dolby Digital 5.1 Surround Stereo. $26.98. Keepcase. *LANG:* English. *SUB:* Spanish. *CAP:* English. *FEATURES:* 18 chapter links ● Trailer.

2000 (R) 90m/C Kevin Spacey, Danny DeVito, Peter Facinelli; **D:** John Swanbeck; **W:** Roger Rueff; **C:** Anastas Michos; **M:** Christopher Young.

Big Momma's House

Martin's attempt to beat Eddie Murphy's *Nutty Professor 2* out of the gate in the summer of 2000 became a hit. He plays an FBI agent who puts on fat makeup to fool potential witness Long into thinking that he is her long-lost grandmother. DVD re-creates the polished studio image flawlessly, of course. Sound is fine, but the most interesting feature of the disc is the commentary track by director Raja Gosnell and producer David Friendly. It's a primer on the ways that cookie-cutter movies like this are created by committees and compromise. —MM

Movie: 🎜🎜 **DVD:** 🎜🎜🎜
20th Century Fox Home Entertainment (UPC #0245543008194). Widescreen (1.85:1) anamorphic. Dolby Digital 5.1 Surround Stereo; Dolby Digital Surround. $29.98. Keepcase. *LANG:* English; French. *SUB:* English; Spanish. *FEATURES:* 20 chapter links • Deleted scenes with commentary • Outtakes and bloopers • Trailers and TV spots • 2 music videos • Commentary: director Gosnell, producer David Friendly • "Building Big Momma's House" featurette • Makeup test.
2000 (PG-13) 98m/C Martin Lawrence, Nia Long, Paul Giamatti, Terrence DaShon Howard, Anthony Anderson, Carl Wright, Ella Mitchell, Jascha Washington, Starletta DuPois, Cedric the Entertainer; **D:** Raja Gosnell; **W:** Darryl Quarles, Don Rhymer; **C:** Michael D. O'Shea; **M:** Richard Gibbs.

The Big Tease

Gay Glasgow hairdresser Crawford Mackenzie (Ferguson) thinks he's being asked to compete in the prestigious World Freestyle Hairdressing Championship being held in Los Angeles. Trailed by a documentary filmmaker, he heads to Hollywood and discovers that he's just been asked to observe. Blithely self-confident, Mackenzie decides that he will find a way to enter and to defeat the three-time champion Stig (Rasche). The good-natured campy fun goes a bit too heavy into hysterical gay stereotypes. DVD image is generally very good, particularly when you realize that the filmmakers were going for a faux documentary style. Sound is very good, too. —MM

Movie: 🎜🎜 **DVD:** 🎜🎜🎜
Warner Home Video, Inc. (Cat #17428). Widescreen; full frame. Dolby Digital 5.1 Surround Stereo. $19.98. Snapper. *LANG:* English. *SUB:* English; French. *FEATURES:* 31 chapter links • Trailer • Filmographies.
1999 (R) 86m/C *GB* Kevin Allen, Craig Ferguson, Frances Fisher, Chris Langham, Mary McCormack, Donal Logue, Larry Miller, David Rasche, Charles Napier, David Hasselhoff, Cathy Lee Crosby, Bruce Jenner, Isabella Aitken; **D:** Kevin Allen; **W:** Craig Ferguson, Sacha Gervasi; **C:** Seamus McGarvey; **M:** Mark Thomas.

Big Trouble in Little China [SE]

Russell adapts an ersatz John Wayne drawl for trucker Jack Burton in this free-falling martial arts/fantasy/action/horror comedy. It has to do with a kidnapped bride (Pai), the evil wizard/ghost David Lo Pan (Hong), gangs, monsters, gunfights, and three magical figures who wear big lampshades on their heads. It's fast action and silly dialogue spun out at a snappy Hawksian pace. This Special Edition is a big batch of goodies in a little package. A second disc has everything the *BTILC* fan wants: a pile of deleted scenes, trailers, the whole television campaign, and the original featurette. There's a pretty obnoxious music video as well. Back on disc one, the impeccably transferred feature comes with a commentary track from Carpenter and Russell, which is another one of their chummy gabfests, as much fun as the one on the old *Escape from New York* laserdisc. Carpenter has nothing to hide and Russell is charming and no-nonsense, and it's plain obvious they're having a grand time drinking beer and laughing their heads off at the fun they had 16 years ago making this thing. Carpenter offers that before Rick Richter overhauled the script, it was a western called *El Diablo*. At one point they veer so far afield that they apologize for not talking more about the movie, but we don't care, as we get to sit in the same room with them for 90 minutes. They should be proud; this is one quality movie that's a great party picture at the same time. —MM/GE

Movie: 🎜🎜🎜½ **DVD:** 🎜🎜🎜½
20th Century Fox Home Entertainment (Cat #2001438, UPC #024543014386). Widescreen (2.35:1) anamorphic. DTS Surround Stereo; Dolby Digital 5.1 Surround Stereo. $26.99. Keepcase. *LANG:* English; French. *FEATURES:* Deleted scenes • Commentary: Carpenter, Russell • Music video • Still gallery • Production notes • Magazine articles • Trailers and TV spots.
1986 (PG-13) 99m/C Kurt Russell, Suzee Pai, Dennis Dun, Kim Cattrall, James Hong, Victor Wong, Kate Burton; **D:** John Carpenter; **W:** David Weinstein, Gary Goldman, W.D. Richter; **C:** Dean Cundey; **M:** John Carpenter, Alan Howarth.

The Big Wheel

Cliché-filled story is fairly well told. An energetic Rooney is Billy Coy, who's determined to follow in his father's tracks as a race-car driver, even though old dad died in a crash. Today, the film is most enjoyable as a nostalgic look at formula filmmaking. The clarity of the disc makes the cuts between real race footage and the inserts even more obvious than they have ever been. Overall, the black-and-white photography ranges between good and very good with minor flashing in clothing patterns. There is a lot of grain in the night racing scenes. —MM

Movie: 🎜🎜½ **DVD:** 🎜🎜½
Image Entertainment (Cat #ID9651CODVD, UPC #014381965124). Full frame. Dolby Digital Mono. $24.99. Snapper. *LANG:* English. *FEATURES:* 16 chapter links.
1949 92m/B Mickey Rooney, Thomas Mitchell, Spring Byington, Mary Hatcher, Allen Jenkins, Michael O'Shea; **D:** Edward Ludwig.

Bikini Beach

Frankie (Avalon) and Dee-Dee (Funicello) are back for a third visit to the beach. This time out, they've got a British visitor, pop star Potato Bug (Avalon again in a challenging dual role), and villainous Keenan Wynn who wants to build a retirement community. When you consider how, when, and why this film was made—not to mention how little it cost—the quality of the DVD is staggering. For fans of mid '60s nostalgia. —MM

Movie: 🎜🎜½ **DVD:** 🎜🎜½
MGM Home Entertainment (Cat #1000977, UPC #027616852830). Widescreen letterboxed; full frame. Dolby Digital Mono. $14.95. Keepcase. *LANG:* English. *SUB:* French; Spanish. *FEATURES:* Trailer • 32 chapter links.
1964 100m/C Annette Funicello, Frankie Avalon, Martha Hyer, Harvey Lembeck, Don Rickles, Stevie Wonder, John Ashley, Keenan Wynn, Jody McCrea, Candy Johnson, Danielle Aubry, Meredith MacRae, Dolores Wells, Donna Loren, Timothy Carey, Boris Karloff; **D:** William Asher; **W:** William Asher, Leo Townsend, Robert Dillon; **C:** Floyd Crosby; **M:** Les Baxter.

Billy Elliot

During a long-lasting coal miner's strike in England, Billy (Bell), an 11-year-old working-class boy, finds a means of self-expression in the local ballet class. Though forbidden by his father (Lewis) from attending, his teacher (Walters) continues to tutor Billy, seeing the innate talent he possesses. A wonderfully funny and moving British drama, perfectly directed by newcomer Daldry and featuring an excellent cast and a knockout soundtrack. Walters is terrific, but the real star of this picture is 14-year-old Jamie Bell, who delivers an amazing, believable, and naturalistic performance. The dance sequences (which fuse together a mix of ballet, tap, and dramatic expression) are nothing short of brilliant. A magnificent achievement that improves with repeated viewings. The disc is bright, colorful, and sharp but there is some digital grain occasionally visible during smokier scenes and some minor print dirt in the first few minutes of the film. The Surround track is extremely satisfying and gives the riot scenes and songs some real visceral punch. The documentary is fairly slight but features some interesting behind-the-scenes footage and interviews. The DVD-ROM features are slim. —DG

AKA: Dancer.

Movie: 🎜🎜🎜½ **DVD:** 🎜🎜🎜½
Universal Studios Home Video (Cat #21134, UPC #02519211342). Wide-

screen (1.85:1) anamorphic. Dolby Digital 5.1 Surround Stereo. $24.98. Keepcase. *LANG:* English; French. *SUB:* English. *FEATURES:* 18 chapter links ▪ Insert card with chapter listing ▪ Theatrical trailer ▪ Cast and filmmaker bios ▪ Production notes ▪ "Billy Elliot: Breaking Free" featurette ▪ DVD-ROM photo gallery & info. **2000 (R) 111m/C** *GB* Jamie Bell, Julie Walters, Gary Lewis, Jamie Driven, Nicola Blackwell, Jean Heywood, Stuart Wells, Adam Cooper; *D:* Stephen Daldry; *W:* Lee Hall; *C:* Brian Tufano; *M:* Stephen Warbeck. *AWARDS:* British Acad. '00: Actor (Bell), Film, Support. Actress (Walters); *NOM:* Oscars '00: Director (Daldry), Orig. Screenplay, Support. Actress (Walters); Screen Actors Guild '00: Actor (Bell), Support. Actress (Walters), Cast; Writers Guild '00: Orig. Screenplay.

Billy's Holiday

Excessively offbeat Australian musical lacks the highly polished look of Hollywood's best, but given the setting and subject matter, it is probably not meant to have it. The subject is Billy Apples (Cullen), hangdog hardware store owner by day, hangdog jazz musician at night. His audiences regularly fall asleep, but Kate (McQuade), owner of the beauty shop down the street, still loves him. Then one night, Billy magically receives the ability to sing just like his idol, Billie Holiday. The main attractions are the likeably middle-aged stars and a soundtrack filled with big band tunes. Surround effects are fairly limited. —*MM*
Movie: ♫♫½ *DVD:* ♫♫½
Anchor Bay (Cat #DV11320, UPC #013131132090). Widescreen (1.85:1) anamorphic. Dolby Digital Surround Stereo. $29.98. Keepcase. *LANG:* English. *FEATURES:* 23 chapter links ▪ Trailer.
1995 (R) 92m/C *AU* Max Cullen, Kris McQuade, Tina Bursill, Drew Forsythe, Genevieve Lemon, Richard Roxburgh, Rachel Coopes; *D:* Richard Wherrett; *W:* Denis Whitburn; *C:* Roger Lanser.

BioHunter [SE]

The staples of Japanese animated horror—monsters bursting out of human bodies, dismemberment, and tentacles, lots of tentacles—get full play here. The story concerns a "demon virus" that turns people into ravenous beasts. Our two heroes Komada and Koshigaya are molecular biologists, one infected with the virus, who are trying to find a cure and battling grotesque monsters every step of the way. The action is graphic, but not up to the levels set by *Urotsukidoji*. The animation is slightly more detailed than most. The only minor flaw on the DVD is aliasing. Surround effects are good but not overactive. —*MM*
Movie: ♫♫½ *DVD:* ♫♫½
Urban Vision Entertainment (Cat #UV1066, UPC #638652106605). Full frame. Dolby Digital 5.1 Surround Stereo; Dolby Digital Stereo. $24.95. Keepcase. *LANG:* English; Japanese. *SUB:* English. *FEATURES:* 8

chapter links ▪ Trailers ▪ Storyboard images ▪ Website link.
1995 60m/C *JP D:* Yuzo Sato; *W:* Yoshiaki Kawajiri.

Bird

Richly textured, though sadly one-sided biography of jazz sax great Charlie Parker, from his rise to stardom to his premature death via extended heroin use. A remarkably assured, deeply imagined film from Eastwood never really shows the Bird's genius of creation. The soundtrack features Parker's own solos re-mastered from original recordings. The film's overall dark look results in a little more grain than is usually present on a Warner Home Video DVD, but at least there isn't much of an artifact problem; in fact, one has to strain to find them. Also, despite the darkness and grain, blacks are fairly true. Colors are muted but appear accurate to the theatre, with very good fleshtones. The 5.1 mix gives a fresh feel to both the Parker recordings and the incidental music by Neihaus, but due to the dramatic nature of the film, it's very rare that the rear channels come into play. When "Bird" isn't performing, the dialogue is always up front and easy to understand. The isolated music track would have been of more interest if Parker's songs were presented in their complete form, rather than exactly as in the film. —*JO*
Movie: ♫♫♫ *DVD:* ♫♫½
Warner Home Video, Inc. (Cat #11820, UPC #085391182023). Widescreen (1.85:1) anamorphic. Dolby Digital 5.1; Dolby Surround. $19.98. Snapper. *LANG:* English (DD5.1); French (DS). *SUB:* English; Spanish; French; Portuguese. *CAP:* English. *FEATURES:* 47 chapter links ▪ Theatrical trailer ▪ Talent files ▪ Isolated music track ▪ Dual-layered.
1988 (R) 160m/C Forest Whitaker, Diane Venora, Michael Zelniker, Samuel E. Wright, Keith David, Michael McGuire, James Handy, Damon Whitaker, Morgan Nagler, Peter Crook; *D:* Clint Eastwood; *W:* Joel Oliansky; *C:* Jack N. Green; *M:* Lennie Niehaus. *AWARDS:* Oscars '88: Sound; Cannes '88: Actor (Whitaker); Golden Globes '89: Director (Eastwood); N.Y. Film Critics '88: Support. Actress (Venora).

Birdman of Alcatraz

Birdman of Leavenworth is more accurate, for it was at that federal penitentiary that convicted murderer Robert Stroud, while spending decades in solitary confinement, became the world's most unlikely bird authority. Burt Lancaster is electrifying in his Oscar-nominated performance as the rock-hard Stroud, whose humanity is reawakened by his study of and care for his rapidly increasing menagerie of fine feathered friends. Also captivating in Oscar-nominated supporting roles are Telly Savalas as a fellow convict and Thelma Ritter as Stroud's indomitable mother ("I will not let them kill you," she vows). But Stroud and his birds are only part of the

story. Also compelling is Stroud's ongoing battle of wills with a crusading warden (Karl Malden) who is bent on breaking him. This classic film has been given a worthy transfer. The print is pristine and the black-and-white contrast superb (the film's cinematography was also nominated for an Oscar). —*DL*
Movie: ♫♫♫ *DVD:* ♫♫♫
MGM Home Entertainment (Cat #1001580, UPC #2761685870). Widescreen (1.66:1) letterboxed. Dolby Digital Mono. $19.98. Keepcase. *LANG:* English. *SUB:* French; Spanish. *CAP:* English. *FEATURES:* Original theatrical trailer ▪ 16 chapter links.
1962 143m/B Burt Lancaster, Karl Malden, Thelma Ritter, Betty Field, Neville Brand, Edmond O'Brien, Hugh Marlowe, Telly Savalas; *D:* John Frankenheimer; *W:* Guy Trosper; *C:* Burnett Guffey, Robert Krasker; *M:* Elmer Bernstein. *AWARDS:* British Acad. '62: Actor (Lancaster); *NOM:* Oscars '62: Actor (Lancaster), B&W Cinematog., Support. Actor (Savalas), Support. Actress (Ritter).

The Bishop's Wife [MGM]

An angel comes down to Earth at Christmas to help a young bishop, his wife, and his parishioners. Excellent performances by the cast make this an entertaining outing. The disc features a crisp, crisp transfer. However, blacks do lose definition in some scenes and some age deterioration is occasionally present (though this isn't overtly noticeable). Both the stereo and mono soundtracks reproduce dialogue, music, and sound effects quite well and exhibit no distortion. I will say that the mono track was far more impressive than the stereo one, which seemed muted and lacking in zest. —*MJT*
Movie: ♫♫♫ *DVD:* ♫♫½
MGM Home Entertainment (Cat #1001581, UPC #027616858917). Full frame. Dolby Digital Stereo; Dolby Digital Mono. $19.98. Keepcase. *LANG:* English; French; Spanish. *SUB:* French; Spanish. *FEATURES:* 16 chapter links ▪ Theatrical trailer.
1947 109m/B Cary Grant, Loretta Young, David Niven, Monty Woolley, Elsa Lanchester, James Gleason, Gladys Cooper, Regis Toomey; *D:* Henry Koster; *W:* Leonardo Bercovici, Robert Sherwood; *C:* Gregg Toland; *M:* Hugo Friedhofer. *AWARDS:* Oscars '47: Sound; *NOM:* Oscars '47: Director (Koster), Film Editing, Picture, Orig. Dramatic Score.

Black and White

Director Toback attempts to investigate white kids' fascination with black hip-hop culture by creating an intriguing combination of pseudo-documentary and urban melodrama with cameos and performances by professional celebrities alongside professional actors. In the more effective part of the film, Shields is a documentary filmmaker asking rich white kids why they're into hip-hop. This section also includes Downey as her gay husband hitting on Mike Tyson (playing himself in one of the film's strongest scenes). The part that doesn't work is the more conventional storyline involving an undercover cop (Stiller) bribing college basketball star Dean (Houston) to throw a game in an attempt to get at Dean's best friend. The sound on this hip-hop flick's DVD delivers the bass as tight and clean as anything out there. Musically, the rest of the mix is all up front too, with great dynamics and fidelity. Not much Surround, though. The visuals keep up with the sound with only a couple of problem scenes where minor artifacting occur. —JO

Movie: 🎵🎵🎵 **DVD:** 🎵🎵🎵½

Columbia Tristar Home Video (Cat #05288, UPC #043396052888). Widescreen (2.35:1) anamorphic. Dolby Digital 5.1; Dolby Surround. $28.95. Keepcase. LANG: English. SUB: English. CAP: English. FEATURES: 28 chapter links ▪ Theatrical trailers ▪ Commentary: James Toback ▪ "Making of" featurette: "James Toback's Video Diary" ▪ Deleted scenes and alternate takes ▪ Music videos.

1999 (R) 98m/C Scott Caan, Robert Downey Jr., Stacy Edwards, Gaby Hoffman, Jared Leto, Marla Maples, Joe Pantoliano, Brooke Shields, Power, Claudia Schiffer, William Lee Scott, Ben Stiller, Eddie Kaye Thomas, Elijah Wood, Mike Tyson, James Toback, Allan Houston, Kidada Jones, Bijou Phillips, Raekwon; **D:** James Toback; **W:** James Toback; **C:** David Ferrara.

Black & White

Rookie cop Chris O'Brien (Cochrane) is partnered with tough veteran female officer Nora Hugosian (Gershon), who's known for both her sexiness and her ruthless style. The two begin an affair while searching for a serial killer. And then the rookie comes across some evidence that seems to implicate his partner in the crimes. This is one of those films that was shot with a very grainy look. Unfortunately, this is one of those discs that increases the grain even further and the result is a DVD that is at times a little hard to watch. There's also a bit of bleed adding to the distortion while detracting from the otherwise accurate colors. It's still better than the VHS tape, though, and features one of the most entertaining and informative director's commentaries out there. Filmmaker wanna-bes should definitely give it a listen. Director Zeltser comes across as sincerely interested in helping those with cinematic ambitions. —JO

Movie: 🎵🎵🎵 **DVD:** 🎵🎵½

Columbia Tristar Home Video (Cat #04495, UPC #04339604495). Widescreen (1.85:1) anamorphic; full frame. Dolby Digital 5.1; Dolby Surround. $27.95. Keepcase. LANG: English (DD5.1; DS); Spanish (DS). CAP: English. FEATURES: 28 chapter links ▪ Theatrical trailer ▪ TV spot ▪ Commentary: director Yuri Zeltser ▪ Talent files.

1999 (R) 97m/C Gina Gershon, Rory Cochrane, Ron Silver, Alison Eastwood, Marshall Bell; **D:** Yuri Zeltser; **W:** Yuri Zeltser, Leon Zeltser; **C:** Phil Parmet.

Black Caesar

Tommy Gibbs (Williamson) climbs the ladder to become the head of a Harlem crime syndicate. Early "blaxploitation" picture delivers the goods with fast-paced action, cool threads, and sideburns that must be seen to be believed. The DVD image isn't as sharp as some, but it is an accurate reproduction of the original, as I remember it from the drive-in. Director Cohen's commentary is anecdotal and fascinating for fans of the genre. —MM

Movie: 🎵🎵 **DVD:** 🎵🎵½

MGM Home Entertainment (Cat #1001461, UPC #027616857811). Widescreen (1.85:1) anamorphic. Dolby Digital Mono. $14.95. Keepcase. LANG: English; Spanish. SUB: French; Spanish. FEATURES: 16 chapter links ▪ Trailer ▪ Commentary: Larry Cohen.

1973 (R) 92m/C Fred Williamson, Julius W. Harris, Val Avery, Art Lund, Gloria Hendry, James Dixon; **D:** Larry Cohen; **W:** Larry Cohen; **C:** Fenton Hamilton, James Signorelli; **M:** James Brown.

The Black Cat

Like so many Italian horrors—even those made in England—this one's a wacky, virtually plotless exercise in style over substance. The titular feline is a harmless, altogether unthreatening creature, despite the filmmakers' best attempts to persuade us otherwise. Miles (the jut-jawed and always delectably hammy Magee) is a medium who hangs out in the cemetery of an English village. Jill (Farmer) is a photographer. The aforementioned kitty is allegedly killing people. DVD represents a major step up from the older tapes that have been in circulation. The image transfer is bright and clear, doing justice to Fulci's inventive camerawork, though the cat's POV shots are still giggle-inducing. —MM AKA: Il Gatto Nero.

Movie: 🎵½ **DVD:** 🎵🎵🎵

Anchor Bay (Cat #DV11637, UPC #013131163797). Widescreen (2.35:1) anamorphic. Dolby Digital Mono. $24.99. Keepcase. LANG: English. FEATURES: 25 chapter links ▪ Fulci thumbnail bio ▪ Trailer ▪ Liner notes by Travis Crawford.

1981 92m/C IT GB Patrick Magee, Mimsy Farmer, David Warbeck, Al Cliver, Dagmar Lassander, Geoffrey Copleston, Daniela Dorio; **D:** Lucio Fulci; **W:** Lucio Fulci, Biagio Proietti; **C:** Sergio Salvati; **M:** Pino Donaggio.

Black Cat Run

Made-for-cable action flick delivers the goods. Johnny (Muldoon), a young mechanic and racer, gives chase after his girlfriend Sara Jane (Heinle) is kidnapped by vicious escaped convicts. But a deputy (Busey) thinks that Johnny is behind the

series of crimes committed by the cons. The pace is quick and the action is suitably lurid. Some aliasing is visible in the brighter exteriors. Overall, image and sound are not much better than VHS tape. —MM

Movie: 🎵🎵 **DVD:** 🎵🎵

HBO Home Video (Cat #91481). Full frame. Dolby Digital Stereo; Mono. $24.98. Snapper. LANG: English. SUB: English; Spanish; French. FEATURES: Cast and crew thumbnail bios ▪ 15 chapter links.

1998 (R) 88m/C Patrick Muldoon, Amelia Heinle, Russell Means, Kevin J. O'Connor, Peter Greene, Jake Busey; **D:** D.J. Caruso; **W:** Frank Darabont, Douglas Venturelli; **C:** Bing Sokolsky; **M:** Jeff Rona.

The Black Cauldron

In the land of Prydain, Taran, keeper of the psychic pig Hen Wen, yearns to fight in a war and do noble deeds, etc. Eventually, he must face the Horned King who wants to release an evil spirit from the titular kitchenware. Though the film doesn't have the reputation of early Disney animation or the studio's more recent work, it's not bad and compares favorably to Bakshi's Lord of the Rings. For whatever reason, the studio was not able to put a completely unmarked version on disc. The DVD displays light snow in darker scenes and some larger flaws, most noticeable in the first castle scene. 5.1 remix sounds fine. —MM

Movie: 🎵🎵🎵 **DVD:** 🎵🎵🎵

Buena Vista Home Entertainment (Cat #19607, UPC #717951008589). Widescreen (2.35:1) letterboxed. Dolby Digital 5.1 Surround Stereo; Dolby Digital Surround. $29.98. Keepcase. LANG: English; French; Spanish. CAP: English. FEATURES: 16 chapter links ▪ Quest for the Black Cauldron game ▪ Donald Duck "Trick or Treat" cartoon ▪ Still gallery ▪ Trailer.

1985 (PG) 82m/C D: Ted Berman, Richard Rich; **W:** Ted Berman, Richard Rich; **M:** Elmer Bernstein; **V:** Grant Bardsley, Susan Sheridan, John Hurt, Freddie Jones, Nigel Hawthorne, John Byner, Arthur Malet; **Nar:** John Huston.

Black Christmas

A college sorority house is besieged by an axe-murderer over the holidays. It would appear that director Clark was gearing up for Porky's as this seminal slasher flick has bits of sophomoric humor, which totally wreck the horror aspect. The image is somewhat dark in spots, but is overall pretty crisp and clear. There is some subtle grain and some noticeable defects from the source print. The digital mono audio is a disappointment, but the dialogue is clear and audible. —ML/MM AKA: Silent Night, Evil Night; Stranger in the House.

Movie: 🎵🎵 **DVD:** 🎵🎵

Critical Mass Full frame. Dolby Digital Mono. LANG: English. FEATURES: John Saxon interview ▪ Trailer ▪ Filmographies.

1975 (R) 98m/C *CA* Olivia Hussey, Keir Dullea, Margot Kidder, John Saxon; *D:* Bob (Benjamin) Clark; *W:* Roy Moore; *C:* Reginald Morris; *M:* Carl Zittrer.

Black Eagle

Pre-Glasnost anti-Soviet tale revolves around two high-kicking spies (Van Damme and Kosugi). CIA and KGB agents race to recover innovative equipment from a crashed jet fighter in the Mediterranean. The bare-bones disc is no improvement over VHS tape in either image or sound. —*MM*

Movie: ♫♫ *DVD:* ♫½
Studio Home Entertainment (Cat #4055). Full frame. Dolby Digital Mono. $24.95. Keepcase. *LANG:* English; Spanish. *FEATURES:* Cast and crew thumbnail bios ▪ Trailer ▪ 18 chapter links.
1988 (R) 93m/C Bruce Doran, Jean-Claude Van Damme, Sho Kosugi; *D:* Eric Karson; *W:* Shimon Arama; *M:* Terry Plumeri.

Black Mama, White Mama

One of the best Philippine babes-behind-bars flicks makes a belated appearance on home video on DVD. Lee (Grier), a hooker, and Karen (Markov), a revolutionary, are chained together when they escape from the prison farm where they've been incarcerated. No, it's not exactly a distaff version of *The Defiant Ones*. The film does feature one of the great shower scenes in the genre. The image is very good throughout, capturing in all its flagrant detail a wonderfully gaudy bus in Chapter 11. —*MM*

Movie: ♫♫½ *DVD:* ♫♫½
MGM Home Entertainment (Cat #1001462, UPC #027616857828). Widescreen (1.85:1) anamorphic. Dolby Digital Mono. $19.98. Keepcase. *LANG:* English; French. *SUB:* French; Spanish. *FEATURES:* 16 chapter links ▪ Trailer.
1973 (R) 87m/C Pam Grier, Margaret Markov, Sid Haig, Lynn Borden, Eddie Garcia, Vic Diaz, Zaldy Zschornack, Laurie Burton, Alona Alegre, Dindo Fernando; *D:* Eddie Romero; *W:* H.R. Christian; *C:* Justo Paulino; *M:* Harry Betts.

Black Moon Rising

Cat burglar Sam Quint (Jones) is hired by the government to steal computer evidence from a mob organization. He hides it in his experimental car, the titular Black Moon, which in turn is stolen by car thief Nina (Hamilton). The then-young cast is fine, and the script by John Carpenter rattles right along at a happy pace. DVD is a fine reproduction of a mid-budget mid-'80s action picture that contains an average amount of grain. Beefed-up 5.1 sound is not incongruous. —*MM*

Movie: ♫♫½ *DVD:* ♫♫½
Anchor Bay (Cat #DV11410, UPC #013131141092). Widescreen (1.85:1) anamorphic. Dolby Digital 5.1 Surround Stereo; Dolby Digital Surround Stereo. $24.99. Keepcase. *LANG:* English. *CAP:* English. *FEATURES:* 29 chapter links ▪ Trailers.
1986 (R) 100m/C Tommy Lee Jones, Linda Hamilton, Richard Jaeckel, Robert Vaughn; *D:* Harley Cokliss; *W:* John Carpenter; *C:* Misha (Mikhail) Suslov; *M:* Lalo Schifrin.

Black Narcissus

A group of Anglican nuns attempting to found a school and clinic in the Himalayas confront native distrust and human frailties amid spectacular scenery. At the top of their craft and the height of their creative powers, Powell and Pressburger create a sensual, disturbing, weird, magical, and magnificent movie. Its spell is not easily described. The old laserdisc of this title was a standout in the Criterion library, but the added extras on the new DVD are even better. On the commentary, Scorsese guides a frail-sounding Powell through an examination of the film. Powell is sometimes hard to understand, but what he says is as priceless. With the obvious enthusiastic input of Powell's widow and editor Thelma Schoonmaker, and Powell revivalist Martin Scorsese, Craig McCall's documentary "Painting with Light" interviews both Jack Cardiff and his Technicolor camera. —*MM/GE*

Movie: ♫♫♫♫ *DVD:* ♫♫♫♫
Criterion Collection (Cat #93, UPC #037429152126). Full frame. Dolby Digital Mono. $29.95. Keepcase. *LANG:* English. *SUB:* English. *FEATURES:* 26 chapter links ▪ Commentary: Martin Scorsese, Michael Powell ▪ "Painting with Light," documentary on the photography of Jack Cardiff ▪ Production stills ▪ Trailer.
1947 101m/C *GB* Deborah Kerr, David Farrar, Sabu, Jean Simmons, Kathleen Byron, Flora Robson, Esmond Knight, Jenny Laird, Judith Furse, May Hallitt, Nancy Roberts; *D:* Michael Powell, Emeric Pressburger; *W:* Michael Powell, Emeric Pressburger; *C:* Jack Cardiff; *M:* Brian Easdale. *AWARDS:* Oscars '47: Art Dir./Set Dec., Color, Color Cinematog.; N.Y. Film Critics '47: Actress (Kerr).

Black Robe

In 1634, a young Jesuit priest, Father Laforgue (Bluteau), journeys across the North American wilderness to bring the word of God to Canada's Huron Indians. The winter journey is brutal and perilous. He begins to question his mission after seeing the strength of the Indians' native ways. Stunning cinematography, a good script, and fine acting combine to make this one superb. Indians are portrayed in a realistic manner, but Beresford presents white culture with few redeeming qualities and blames it for the Indians' downfall. Brian Moore adapted his novel for the screen. The exteriors are filled with muted autumn and winter colors, and look fine. Darker interiors are grainy, but that's appropriate to the subject, time, and atmosphere. Sound is acceptable. —*MM*

Movie: ♫♫♫ *DVD:* ♫♫½
Trimark Home Video (Cat #6785). Widescreen (1.66:1) letterboxed; full frame. Dolby Digital Stereo. $24.99. Keepcase. *LANG:* English. *SUB:* French; Spanish. *FEATURES:* 24 chapter links ▪ Trailer ▪ Talent files.
1991 (R) 101m/C *AU CA* Lothaire Bluteau, Aden Young, Sandrine Holt, August Schellenberg, Tantoo Cardinal, Billy Two Rivers, Lawrence Bayne, Harrison Liu, Marthe Tungeon; *D:* Bruce Beresford; *W:* Brian Moore; *C:* Peter James; *M:* Georges Delerue. *AWARDS:* Australian Film Inst. '92: Cinematog.; Genie '91: Director (Beresford), Film.

Black Sabbath

The venerable Boris Karloff introduces three short films and stars as a vampire in the middle piece. The pace is slow, and each tale contains at least one solid scare. Writer/director Mario Bava's horror is based on character and situation, not graphic visual effects. This DVD contains the first "complete" version of the feature to be released on home video. As Tim Lucas recounts in his extensive liner notes, American studio officials interfered with Bava's ideas and many changes were made before the theatrical release. Those have been corrected here. The films are in a new order and the original introduction and ending are retained. The disc was created from an astonishingly clear original. The image rivals contemporary films, particularly in interiors. Exteriors are comparatively rough, but there aren't many of them. —*MM* *AKA:* I Tre Volti della Paura; Black Christmas; The Three Faces of Terror; The Three Faces of Fear; Les Trois Visages de la Peur.

Movie: ♫♫♫½ *DVD:* ♫♫♫
Image Entertainment (Cat #ID5941AODVD, UPC #014381594126). Widescreen (1.78:1) anamorphic. Dolby Digital Mono. $24.99. Snapper. *LANG:* Italian. *SUB:* English. *FEATURES:* 16 chapter links ▪ Mario Bava thumbnail bio ▪ Liner notes by Tim Lucas ▪ Photo and promotional materials gallery ▪ Karloff filmography ▪ Trailer.
1964 99m/C *IT FR* Boris Karloff, Jacqueline Pierreux, Michele Mercier, Lidia Alfonsi, Susy Andersen, Mark Damon, Rika Dialina, Glauco Onorato, Massimo Righi; *D:* Mario Bava; *W:* Mario Bava, Marcello Fondato, Alberto Bevilacqua; *C:* Ubaldo Terzano; *M:* Les Baxter.

Black Scorpion

Darcy Walker (Severance) is an ex-cop-turned-superhero who dons a scorpion mask (sort of), black vinyl bustier, fishnet hose, and superboots to fight crime and avenge her dad's death. She's got the requisite sidekick—an ex–chop shop operator (Morris)—and supervillain—the asthmatic Breathtaker (Siemaszko) who threatens to annihilate L.A. with toxic gas. It's campy, schlocky fun and that's the approach Ms.

Severance takes on her commentary track. Otherwise, disc is identical to VHS tape in image and sound. —*MM* **AKA:** Roger Corman Presents: Black Scorpion.
Movie: 🐾🐾½ **DVD:** 🐾🐾½
New Concorde (Cat #NH20510D, UPC #736991451094). Full frame. $19.98. Keepcase. *LANG:* English. *FEATURES:* 24 chapter links ▪ Joan Severance introduction ▪ Commentary: Joan Severance ▪ Thumbnail bios ▪ Trailers.
1995 (R) 92m/C Joan Severance, Garrett Morris, Casey Siemaszko, Rick Rossovich; *D:* Jonathan Winfrey; *W:* Craig J. Nevius; *C:* Geoffrey George; *M:* Kevin Kiner.

Black Scorpion 2: Ground Zero
Superhero crimefighter Darcy Walker (Severance) returns to battle the villains Prankster (Jackson) and AfterShock (Rose), who are bent on destroying the City of Angels by earthquake. Style meanders between pure comic book and standard low-budget action. Only the extras differentiate disc from tape. Image and sound are identical with exceptionally heavy grain in several scenes. —*MM* **AKA:** Black Scorpion 2: Aftershock.
Movie: 🐾🐾 **DVD:** 🐾🐾
New Concorde (Cat #NH20619D, UPC #736991461994). Full frame. $19.98. Keepcase. *LANG:* English. *FEATURES:* 24 chapter links ▪ Behind-the-scenes featurette on *Black Scorpion* TV series ▪ Thumbnail bios.
1996 (R) 85m/C Joan Severance, Whip Hubley, Stoney Jackson, Sherrie Rose, Garrett Morris; *D:* Jonathan Winfrey; *W:* Craig J. Nevius; *C:* Mark Kohl; *M:* Kevin Kiner.

Black Tight Killers
Imagine a Japanese Matt Helm movie with an Elvis impersonator in the lead. That's essentially what's going on in this gonzo adventure/comedy from the mid-'60s. Hondo (Kobayashi) is a combat photographer just back from Vietnam. He and his stewardess girlfriend (Matsubara) become involved with various gangsters in a fast-moving plot filled with such bizarre devices as Ninja chewing gum bullets. The image is nothing short of astonishing. The DVD was made from original materials that show virtually no sign of wear. The bright '60s Op art colors in costumes and set design shine forth in all their radiance. Some of the subtitles are difficult to read and they contain a few misspellings, but that's a quibble. A rare treat for fans of the era. —*MM* **AKA:** Ore Ni Sawaru to Abunaize.
Movie: 🐾🐾🐾 **DVD:** 🐾🐾🐾
Image Entertainment (Cat #ID8964VFDVD, UPC #014381896428). Widescreen (2.35:1) anamorphic. Dolby Digital Mono. $24.99. *LANG:* Japanese. *SUB:* English. *FEATURES:* 16 chapter links ▪ Liner notes by Chris D. ▪ Interview with director Yasuharu Hasebe.

1966 84m/C *JP* Akira Kobayashi, Chieko Matsubara; *D:* Yasuharu Hasebe.

Blackmale
Small-time hustlers Jimmy (Woodbine) and Luther (Pierce) bet everything on a fixed fight and lose big. Now they owe $100,000 to a loan shark. So they decide to blackmail a doctor (Rees) with an incriminating videotape and discover that their would-be mark is more dangerous than they could have imagined. With the barrage of films like this since Tarantino made his money, we should all be tired of it, but this one is sickeningly entertaining. The DVD could have used some deleted scenes or the like—with this film's attitude there must have been some goodies lying around on the cutting room floor. Picture quality is generally O.K., with a few fuzzy backgrounds causing the main complaints. The sound delivers an incredibly thumping bass, especially when one considers that there is no subwoofer out. —*JO*
Movie: 🐾🐾½ **DVD:** 🐾🐾🐾
Image Entertainment (Cat #ID9619UMDVD, UPC #014381961928). Widescreen (1.85:1) letterboxed. Dolby Surround. $24.99. Snapper. *LANG:* English. *FEATURES:* 12 chapter links.
1999 (R) 89m/C Bokeem Woodbine, Justin Pierce, Roger Rees, Sascha Knopf, Erik Todd Dellums; *D:* George Baluzy, Mike Baluzy.

Blackrock
Clichéd though dramatic saga is inspired by a true story and adapted by Enright from his play. Uncommunicative teenager Jared (Breuls) throws a bash upon the return of his best surfing bud Ricko (Lyndon). The party gets out of control and Jared witnesses a group of his mates beating and raping Tracey (Novakovitch), who's discovered dead the next morning. Her death attracts rabid media attention and divides the community while Jared is filled with guilt for doing nothing to stop the act. His conflicts increase when he realizes the extent of Ricko's involvement and he tries to decide where his loyalties lie. Definition-wise, the video transfer is very good. But the film's muted orange color scheme causes blacks to bleed somewhat. The audio is passable, though the Australian accents are a bit indecipherable from time to time. —*MJT*
Movie: 🐾🐾 **DVD:** 🐾🐾½
Vanguard International Cinema, Inc. (Cat #VF0018, UPC #658769001839). Full frame. Dolby Digital Stereo. $29.95. Keepcase. *LANG:* English. *FEATURES:* 10 chapter links.
1997 100m/C *AU* Laurence Breuls, Simon Lyndon, Linda Cropper, Rebecca Smart, David Field, Chris Haywood, Boyana Novakovitch; *D:* Steven Vidler; *W:* Nick Enright; *C:* Martin McGrath, George Greenough; *M:* Steve Kilbey. *AWARDS: NOM:* Australian Film Inst. '97: Adapt. Screen-

play, Cinematog., Film, Support. Actor (Lyndon), Support. Actress (Smart).

A Blade in the Dark
Bruno (Occhipinti) is writing the score for a horror film in a secluded villa. Why is it that all the young women who come to visit him wind up being stabbed to death? Judged as an Italian giallo horror, the film is certainly imaginative and well-made, but there's little to recommend it to those who are not already fans of the genre. As usual, Anchor Bay presents a superb image. Apparently an Italian language track was unavailable (or unusable), because this dubbed English version is far from perfect. However, its imperfections fit with the film's slightly parodic nature. —*MM* **AKA:** La Casa con la Scala Nel Buio; House of the Dark Stairway.
Movie: 🐾🐾 **DVD:** 🐾🐾½
Anchor Bay (Cat #DV11841, UPC #013131184198). Widescreen (1.85:1) anamorphic. Dolby Digital Mono. $24.99. Keepcase. *LANG:* English. *FEATURES:* Trailer ▪ Interviews with Bava and Sacchetti ▪ Talent files ▪ Liner notes by Tim Lucas.
1983 104m/C Michele (Michael) Soavi, Fabiola Toledo, Valeria Cavalli, Lara Naszinsky, Andrea Occhipinti, Anny Papa; *D:* Lamberto Bava; *W:* Dardano Sacchetti; *C:* Gianlorenzo Battaglia; *M:* Guido de Angelis, Maurizio de Angelis.

Blame It on Rio
Middle-aged Matthew (Caine) has a ridiculous fling with his best friend's (Bologna) daughter (Johnson) while on vacation with them in Rio de Janeiro. It's a remake of a French film, *One Wild Moment*, and the French tend to handle this kind of material with a finer touch than Americans. That said, all involved acquit themselves well, and Michelle Johnson is a temptation that few men could resist. DVD image is an accurate reproduction of the bright, colorful original. Much of the dialogue has a clipped, redubbed quality. —*MM*
Movie: 🐾🐾½ **DVD:** 🐾🐾½
MGM Home Entertainment (Cat #100-1844, UPC #027616861139). Widescreen (1.85:1) anamorphic. Dolby Digital Mono. $14.95. Keepcase. *LANG:* English; French; Spanish. *SUB:* French; Spanish. *CAP:* English. *FEATURES:* 16 chapter links ▪ Trailer.
1984 (R) 90m/C Michael Caine, Joseph Bologna, Demi Moore, Michelle Johnson, Valerie Harper; *D:* Stanley Donen; *W:* Charlie Peters, Larry Gelbart.

Blaze Starr Goes Nudist
The title tells what little story there is in this nudie from Doris Wishman, who rivals Ed Wood Jr. in her affinity for outré subjects and lack of filmmaking skills. Playing herself, Blaze decides to see what all this naturist stuff is about at a Florida camp. There is light static on the soundtrack and the occasional visible splice, but overall the transfer seems to be a faithful re-cre-

ation of an ultra-saturated color scheme that's heavy on reds, purples, lavenders, and oranges. —MM AKA: Blaze Starr: The Original.
Movie: ♫½ **DVD:** ♫♫
Image Entertainment (Cat #ID6008 SW DVD, UPC #014681600827). Full frame. Dolby Digital Mono. $24.99. Snapper. LANG: English. FEATURES: 12 chapter links ☛ Gallery of Doris Wishman exploitation art ☛ Trailer ☛ Vintage Blaze Starr striptease act.
1963 80m/C Blaze Starr, Russ Martine, Gene Berk; **D:** Doris Wishman.

Bless the Child
This religious thriller will probably find a more enthusiastic audience on disc than it found in theatres. Nurse Maggie O'Connor (Basinger) must raise her baby niece Cody (Coleman) after her druggie sister disappears. Years later, it appears that the girl may have special powers, and a cult leader (Sewell) is after her. Fairly familiar material is handled very nicely. The image has the glossy sheen of a big-budget Hollywood production. The same goes for the sound, though the 5.1 track sometimes makes the star's voice sound artificial and/or oddly dubbed. —MM
Movie: ♫♫♫ **DVD:** ♫♫♫
Paramount Home Video (Cat #32796, UPC #097363279648). Widescreen anamorphic. Dolby Digital 5.1 Surround Stereo; Dolby Digital Surround Stereo. $29.99. Keepcase. LANG: English; French. SUB: English. FEATURES: 10 chapter links ☛ Trailer ☛ Cast and crew interviews ☛ Commentary: director Russell and effects supervisor Hynek.
2000 (R) 110m/C Kim Basinger, Jimmy Smits, Rufus Sewell, Holliston Coleman, Christina Ricci, Michael Gaston, Lumi Cavazos, Angela Bettis, Ian Holm, Eugene Lipinski, Anne Betancourt, Dimitra Arlys; **D:** Chuck Russell; **W:** Tom Rickman, Clifford Green, Ellen Green; **C:** Peter Menzies Jr.; **M:** Christopher Young.

Blind Justice
Blinded in a Civil War battle, gunfighter Canaan (Assante) rides into a small western town where he gets into a gun battle with outlaw Alacran (Davi) and is nursed back to health by Caroline (Shue). More violence follows in an updated spaghetti western. The cast is excellent. Full-frame image ranges between good and very good. Sound is fine. A sleeper. —MM
Movie: ♫♫½ **DVD:** ♫♫½
HBO Home Video (Cat #90984, UPC #026359098420). Full frame. Dolby Digital Surround; Mono. $19.98. Snapper. LANG: English; French; Spanish. SUB: English; French; Spanish. FEATURES: 12 chapter links.
1994 (R) 85m/C Armand Assante, Elisabeth Shue, Robert Davi, Adam Baldwin; **D:** Richard Spence; **W:** Daniel Knauf; **C:** Jack Conroy; **M:** Richard Gibbs.

The Blob
The presence of Steve McQueen in his first starring role elevates this teens-vs.-menace-from-outer-space above the rest of its ilk. The humor is intentional and Burt Bacharach's bouncy theme is still infectious. By current standards, the image may appear to be lacking—it's a bit overly bright and soft—but this is as good as the film has ever looked. Or sounded. Add in two commentary tracks and the other extras, and this overachieving little cult hit deserves the careful treatment that Criterion always gives to its projects. —MM
Movie: ♫♫♫ **DVD:** ♫♫♫½
Criterion Collection (Cat #91, UPC #715515011129). Widescreen (1.66:1) anamorphic. Dolby Digital Mono. $39.95. Keepcase. LANG: English. SUB: English. FEATURES: 19 chapter links ☛ Mini-poster ☛ Commentary: producer Harris and film historian Bruce Eder ☛ Commentary: director Yeaworth Jr. and actor Fields ☛ Trailer ☛ Blob-abilia.
1958 83m/C Steve McQueen, Aneta Corsaut, Olin Howlin, Earl Rowe, Steve Chase, John Benson, Vincent Barbi; **D:** Irvin S. Yeaworth Jr.; **W:** Kate Phillips, Theodore Simonson; **C:** Thomas E. Spalding; **M:** Burt Bacharach, Hal David, Ralph Carmichael.

Blood and Black Lace
Beautiful models are being murdered and an inspector (Mitchell) is assigned to the case, but not before more gruesome killings occur. This is the Bava film that officially began the "giallo" school of horror. In his carefully prepared commentary track, critic Tim Lucas goes into the background and production of the film in the right detail. The real surprise on the disc though is the astonishingly sharp image. The film has been preserved or restored to a level of quality that's easily the equal of today's Hollywood studio releases. Colors and focus are crisp and the dual-layer disc comes with a full slate of extras. —MM AKA: Fashion House of Death; Six Women for the Murderer; Sei Donne per l'Assassino.
Movie: ♫♫♫ **DVD:** ♫♫♫½
VCI Home Video (Cat #8213, UPC #089859821325). Widescreen (1.66:1) letterboxed. Dolby Digital Mono. $29.99. Keepcase. LANG: English; French; Italian. SUB: English; Spanish. FEATURES: 15 chapter links ☛ Talent files ☛ Trailers ☛ French main titles ☛ Original American release titles ☛ Interview with Cameron Mitchell ☛ Interview with Dawne Arden ☛ Commentary: Tim Lucas ☛ Photo gallery.
1964 90m/C IT FR GE Cameron Mitchell, Eva Bartok, Mary Arden, Dante DiPaolo, Arianna Gorini, Lea Krugher, Harriet Medin, Giuliano Raffaelli, Thomas Reiner, Frank Ressel, Massimo Righi; **D:** Mario Bava; **W:** Mario Bava, Marcello Fondato, Joe Barilla; **C:** Ubaldo Terzano; **M:** Carlo Rustichelli.

Blood and Sand
Young bullfighter Juan (Rydell) is on the verge of super-stardom when he meets Dona Sol (Stone) and risks everything he has worked for. Will she destroy his one opportunity at fame? You'll be rooting for the bulls and Dona Sol all the way. The no-frills disc is identical to VHS tape in every important way. —MM
Movie: ♫♫½ **DVD:** ♫♫
Trimark Home Video (Cat #7045). Full frame. Stereo. $14.99. Keepcase. LANG: English. SUB: French; Spanish. FEATURES: Trailer ☛ 11 chapter links.
1989 (R) 96m/C Christopher Rydell, Sharon Stone, Ana Torrent, Jose-Luis De Villalonga, Simon Andrew; **D:** Javier Elorrieta; **W:** Rafael Azcona, Ricardo Franco, Thomas Fucci; **C:** Antonio Rios; **M:** Jesus Gluck.

Blood Beast Terror
An entomologist (Flemyng) transforms his daughter into a moth monster who drains her victims of blood. The local Inspector (Cushing) is hot on her trail. This kind of British silliness was handled with more clarity and sophistication by the folks at Hammer. The DVD is only an incremental improvement over tape. Both interior and exterior night scenes tend to be underlit. The graininess of the original appears to be inherent in the original, along with the faded colors. —MM AKA: The Vampire-Beast Craves Blood; Deathshead Vampire.
Movie: ♫♫ **DVD:** ♫♫
Image Entertainment (Cat #ID5888EUDVD, UPC #014381588828). Widescreen (1.66:1) letterboxed. Dolby Digital Mono. $24.99. Snapper. LANG: English. FEATURES: 12 chapter links.
1967 81m/C GB Peter Cushing, Robert Flemyng, Wanda Ventham, Vanessa Howard; **D:** Vernon Sewell; **W:** Peter Bryan; **C:** Stanley Long; **M:** Paul Ferris.

Blood Bullets Buffoons
Please see review for In the Flesh / Blood Bullets Buffoons.
1996 90m/C Amy Lynn Baxter, Zachary Winston Snygg; **D:** Zachary Winston Snygg; **W:** Zachary Winston Snygg.

Blood In . . . Blood Out: Bound by Honor
Three-hour epic about Chicano gang culture focuses on three buddies (Borrego, Bratt, and Chapa) whose lives follow different courses. Written by acclaimed poet Baca from a story by mystery master Ross Thomas, the film touches on issues of poverty, racism, drugs, and violence as they pertain to Hispanic life. The very slight letterboxing is hardly noticeable on a conventional-sized TV screen. Image ranges between very good and excellent. —MM AKA: Bound by Honor.
Movie: ♫♫♫ **DVD:** ♫♫♫
Hollywood Pictures Home Video (Cat #19694, UPC #717951008701). Widescreen (1.66:1) letterboxed. Dolby Digital Surround. $24.99. Keepcase. LANG: English. FEATURES: "Making of" featurette ☛ 32 chapter links.

1993 (R) 180m/C Damian Chapa, Jesse Borrego, Benjamin Bratt, Enrique Castillo, Victor Rivers, Delroy Lindo, Tom Towles; **D:** Taylor Hackford; **W:** Floyd Mutrux, Jimmy Santiago Baca, Jeremy Iacone; **C:** Gabriel Beristain; **M:** Bill Conti.

Blood of Ghastly Horror

A young man thinks he has a new lease on life when he is the happy recipient of a brain transplant, but his dreams are destroyed when he degenerates into a rampaging killer. On his commentary track, producer Sherman explains that the idea of the film had been floating around for years. At one time, it was to be a straight heist-thriller, but things changed, etc., explaining the numerous titles. Of the films in the Adamson-Troma series, this is one of the worst-looking. The image is exceptionally grainy. Even the sound wouldn't be out of place in a drive-in speaker. This is simply a very low-budget production. There's little DVD can do for it. —*MM* **AKA:** The Fiend with the Atomic Brain; Psycho a Go Go!; The Love Maniac; The Man with the Synthetic Brain; The Fiend with the Electronic Brain.
Movie: 🎵½ **DVD:** 🎵½
Troma Team Video (Cat #9026). Full frame. $19.95. Keepcase. *LANG:* English. *FEATURES:* 9 chapter links • Commentary: Sam Sherman • Trailers • TV teaser • "Producing schlock" featurette • Behind-the-scenes gallery • DVD credits.
1972 87m/C John Carradine, Kent Taylor, Tommy Kirk, Regina Carrol, Roy Morton, Tracey Robbins; **D:** Al Adamson; **W:** Chris Martino, Dick Poston; **C:** Vilmos Zsigmond.

Blood on the Sun

In Japan, newspaperman Nick Condon (Cagney) uncovers plans for world domination as propaganda, violence, and intrigue combine in an action adventure. The black-and-white image is fine but it lacks the sparkle of the very best studio work. Light static is audible throughout the soundtrack. —*MM*
Movie: 🎵🎵🎵 **DVD:** 🎵🎵🎵
Parade (Cat #55086). Full frame. Dolby Digital Mono. $17.98. Keepcase. *LANG:* English. *FEATURES:* 11 chapter links • Talent files and notes. Also available from Madacy (cat. #990572) for $9.99.
1945 98m/B James Cagney, Sylvia Sidney, Robert Armstrong, Wallace Ford; **D:** Frank Lloyd; **W:** Lester Cole, Nathaniel Curtis, Frank Melford; **C:** Theodor Sparkuhl; **M:** Miklos Rozsa.

Bloodfist

Jake Raye (Wilson) goes to Manila to find out who killed his brother. Typical martial arts plot is given a boost by colorful locales and good casting with Wilson and Blanks. Like most Roger Corman productions, DVD is essentially the same as VHS tape. —*MM*
Movie: 🎵🎵½ **DVD:** 🎵🎵

New Concorde (Cat #NH20338D, UPC #736991433847). Full frame. $19.98. Keepcase. *LANG:* English. *FEATURES:* 24 chapter links • Thumbnail bios • Previews.
1989 (R) 85m/C Don "The Dragon" Wilson, Rob Kaman, Billy Blanks, Kris Aguilar, Riley Bowman, Michael Shaner, Joe Mari Avellana, Marilyn Bautista; **D:** Terence H. Winkless; **W:** Robert King; **C:** Ricardo Jacques Gale; **M:** Sasha Matson.

Bloodfist 2

Jake Raye (Wilson) goes back to Manila and finds himself up against kidnapped kickboxers who are forced to fight. Image and sound are identical to VHS tape. —*MM*
Movie: 🎵🎵 **DVD:** 🎵🎵
New Concorde (Cat #NH20390D, UPC #736991439047). Full frame. $19.98. Keepcase. *LANG:* English. *FEATURES:* 24 chapter links • Previews • Thumbnail bios.
1990 (R) 85m/C Don "The Dragon" Wilson, Maurice Smith, James Warring, Timothy Baker, Richard (Rick) Hill, Rina Reyes, Kris Aguilar, Joe Mari Avellana; **D:** Andy Blumenthal; **W:** Catherine Cyran; **C:** Bruce Dorfman; **M:** Nigel Holton.

Bloodfist 3: Forced to Fight

The series jettisons the original character and setting and moves to a prison where the martial arts scenes are well-choreographed, and the cast of supporting characters, including Roundtree and Corman-regular Dean, almost steal the show. In some ways, this may be the best of the bunch. Again, image and sound are no better than tape. —*MM*
Movie: 🎵🎵🎵 **DVD:** 🎵🎵
New Concorde (Cat #NH20415D, UPC #736991441545). Full frame. $19.98. Keepcase. *LANG:* English. *FEATURES:* 24 chapter links • Previews • Thumbnail bios.
1992 (R) 90m/C Don "The Dragon" Wilson, Richard Roundtree, Laura Stockman, Richard Paul, Rick Dean, Peter "Sugarfoot" Cunningham; **D:** Oley Sassone; **W:** Allison Burnett; **C:** Rick Bota; **M:** Nigel Holton.

Bloodfist 4: Die Trying

This time out, Wilson plays a repo man who boosts the wrong car and finds the CIA, FBI, and lots of other international bad guys on his trail. Fights are handled well and the low-rent locations give the proceedings a nicely lived-in look. Like the other entries in the series, this one is identical to VHS tape. The film was remade in 2000 as *Moving Target*. (Please see review.) —*MM*
Movie: 🎵🎵½ **DVD:** 🎵🎵
New Concorde (Cat #NH20454D, UPC #736991445444). Full frame. $19.98. Keepcase. *LANG:* English. *FEATURES:* 24 chapter links • Previews • Thumbnail bios.

1992 (R) 86m/C Don "The Dragon" Wilson, Catya Sassoon, Amanda Wyss, James Tolkan, Liz Torres; **D:** Paul Ziller.

Bloodstorm: Subspecies 4

Fourth installment in the shot-on-location Transylvanian vampire series maintains the above-average production values and humor. Master vampire Radu (Hove) wants to reclaim his vast wealth and recapture fledgling vamp Michelle (Duff, who provides a commentary track in the cheeky spirit of the series). She has been taken to a creepy doctor (Dinvale) who's after the bloodstone. The DVD image is sharp, accurately reproducing director Nicolaou's strange pale color scheme. Sound, always an important element of Full Moon releases, is strong. —*MM* **AKA:** Subspecies 4; Subspecies 4: Bloodstorm—The Master's Revenge.
Movie: 🎵🎵🎵½ **DVD:** 🎵🎵🎵
Full Moon Pictures (Cat #8010). Full frame. $24.95. Jewelcase. *LANG:* English. *SUB:* English. *CAP:* English. *FEATURES:* 18 chapter links • Commentary: Nicolaou and Duff • Talent files • Videozone fan magazine • Trailers • Full Moon catalog.
1998 (R) 90m/C Anders (Tofting) Hove, Denice Duff, Jonathan Morris, Mihai Dinvale, Floriella Grappini; **D:** Ted Nicolaou; **W:** Ted Nicolaou; **C:** Adolfo Bartoli; **M:** Richard Kosinski.

Bloody Murder

Stupid-teen-campers-in-peril-from-maniac movie. This time the creepoid wears a hockey mask (sound familiar?) and has a chainsaw in place of his left arm. With such a lamo plot, even die-hard slasher fans would want better and more creative gore, but *Bloody Murder* doesn't deliver the splatter either. The quality of the DVD doesn't rise much above that of the film. When the scene dims, the blacks turn gray and the image sometimes gets so blurry that your eyes will hurt from squinting. Before viewing the movie, the "Jump to a Bloody Murder" feature sounded interesting, but once you see any frame in this film, you'll never want to see it again. —*JO*
Movie: 🎵½ **DVD:** 🎵½
Artisan Entertainment (Cat #10451, UPC #012236104513). Full frame. Dolby Digital Stereo. $29.98. Keepcase. *LANG:* English. *SUB:* Spanish. *CAP:* English. *FEATURES:* 20 chapter links • Trailer • Talent files • Commentary: director Ralph Portillo • "Jump to a Bloody Murder" feature.
1999 (R) 90m/C Michael Stone, Jessica Morris, Peter Guillemette, Patrick Cavanaugh, Christelle Ford, Tracy Pacheco, Justin Martin; **D:** Ralph Portillo; **W:** John R. Stevenson; **C:** Keith Holland; **M:** Steven Stern.

The Bloody Pit of Horror

While wife Jayne Mansfield was in Italy filming *Primitive Love*, her husband, body-

builder Hargitay, starred in this alternative epic. He plays Travis Anderson, the owner of a castle that is visited by a group of photographers and models shooting lurid paperback covers. The violent images they stage unhinge Travis and he imagines himself the reincarnation of the sadistic Crimson Executioner who's entombed in the dungeon. The film is filled with the "near nudity" so neatly spoofed in the *Austin Powers* films, but its real power is in Hargitay's wonderful and earnest performance. Not that the arrow-shooting spider isn't a kick. On DVD, the film looks much better than other more serious films of its era. The image is boldly colorful with above-average sharpness. Frank Henenlotter's informative liner notes place the film in its cinematic historical context. —*MM*
AKA: Crimson Executioner; The Red Hangman; Il Boia Scarlatto.
Movie: 🎵🎵½ **DVD:** 🎵🎵½
Image Entertainment (Cat #ID9734SW DVD, UPC #014381973426). Widescreen (1.85:1) letterboxed. Dolby Digital Mono. $24.99. Snapper. *LANG:* English. *FEATURES:* 12 chapter links • Trailer • Gallery of exploitation art • Deleted scenes • Excerpt from *Primitive Love* • Excerpt from *Cover Girl Slaughter.*
1965 87m/B *IT* Mickey Hargitay, Louise Barrett, Walter Brandi, Moa Thai, Ralph Zucker, Albert Gordon; **D:** Max (Massimo Pupillo) Hunter; **W:** Romano Migliorini, Roberto Natale; **C:** Luciano Trasatti; **M:** Gino Peguri.

Blue Ridge Fall

Parts of *A Simple Plan* are mixed with parts of *Remember the Titans* in a story of rural Southern teens who become involved in a bizarre crime. Danny Shepherd (Facinelli) is the star quarterback of the Jefferson Creek, NC, high school football team. But that doesn't stop him from being best friends with the mildly retarded Aaron (Eastman), who is bullied by his father (Arnold), a stereotypical religious maniac. Both image and sound are a step up from VHS tape, but the mid-budget production is not going to test the limits of anyone's home theatre. —*MM*
Movie: 🎵🎵½ **DVD:** 🎵🎵½
Image Entertainment (Cat #ID8801UMDVD, UPC #014381880120). Widescreen (1.85:1) letterboxed. Dolby Digital Stereo. $24.99. Snapper. *LANG:* English. *FEATURES:* 12 chapter links.
1999 (R) 99m/C Peter Facinelli, Rodney Eastman, Will Estes, Jay R. Ferguson, Tom Arnold, Amy Irving, Chris Isaak, Brent Jennings, Heather Stephens, Garvin Funches; **D:** James Rowe; **W:** James Rowe; **C:** Chris Walling; **M:** Greg Edmonson.

Blue Sky

In 1962, Carly Marshall (Lange) is an irrepressible beauty, long married to adoring but uptight military scientist Hank (Jones). Things are barely under control when they're stationed in Hawaii, but after Hank's transfer to a backwater base in Alabama, Carly's emotional mood swings go wildly out of control. Then she attracts the attention of the camp commander (Boothe). A nuclear radiation subplot proves a minor distraction. On DVD, the image ranges between good and very good, though this is not the kind of film anyone watches for visual pyrotechnics. The performances—particularly Lange's out-of-left-field Oscar-winner—are more important than polish. —*MM*
Movie: 🎵🎵🎵 **DVD:** 🎵🎵½
MGM Home Entertainment (Cat #1001535, UPC #027616858467). Widescreen (1.85:1) anamorphic. Dolby Digital Surround Stereo. $19.98. Keepcase. *LANG:* English; French; Spanish. *SUB:* French; Spanish. *CAP:* English. *FEATURES:* 16 chapter links • Trailer.
1991 (PG-13) 101m/C Jessica Lange, Tommy Lee Jones, Powers Boothe, Carrie Snodgress, Amy Locane, Chris O'Donnell, Mitchell Ryan, Dale Dye, Richard Jones; **D:** Tony Richardson; **W:** Arlene Sarner, Jerry Leichtling, Rama Laurie Stagner; **C:** Steve Yaconelli; **M:** Jack Nitzsche. *AWARDS:* Oscars '94: Actress (Lange); Golden Globes '95: Actress—Drama (Lange); L.A. Film Critics '94: Actress (Lange); *NOM:* Screen Actors Guild '94: Actress (Lange).

Blue Streak

Only hard-core Martin Lawrence fans will enjoy this formulaic buddy-cop-with-a-twist action comedy. Lawrence plays jewel thief Miles Logan, who hides a gem from his latest heist at a construction site just before he's caught. Three years later and out of jail, Logan tries to retrieve his diamond only to discover the site is now a police station. While impersonating a detective in order to sneak in and grab the stash, he accidentally catches an escaping felon and is forced to continue the charade. He's saddled with rookie partner Carlson (Wilson) and begins using his criminal knowledge to catch other crooks, including his old crony Tulley (Chappelle). Lawrence gives a good effort but all of his mugging can't save the lame material he's forced to work with. The biggest thing that hit me watching this DVD was that, even though the rear channels of the 5.1 sound were basically used for ambience and music, the mix seemed too obviously gimmicky. More like something you'd expect from a low-budget effort with 5.1 sound thrown in just for the hell of it. Other than that the DVD is what you should expect from a major studio for one of their big-budget releases. The two "making of" featurettes are pretty much overkill. —*JO*
Movie: 🎵🎵½ **DVD:** 🎵🎵🎵½
Columbia Tristar Home Video (Cat #04011, UPC #043396040113). Widescreen (1.85:1) anamorphic; full frame. Dolby Digital 5.1. $24.95. Keepcase. *LANG:* English. *SUB:* English. *CAP:* English. *FEATURES:* 28 chapter links • Theatrical trailers • 2 "making of" featurettes • Music videos • Talent files.
1999 (PG-13) 94m/C Martin Lawrence, Luke Wilson, Peter Greene, Dave Chap-
pelle, William Forsythe, Graham Beckel, Tamala Jones, Nicole Parker, Robert Miranda, Olek Krupa; **D:** Les Mayfield; **W:** Stephen Carpenter, Michael Berry, John Blumenthal; **C:** David Eggby.

Blue Tiger

Gina Hayes (Madsen) is in a drugstore with her young son when a masked gunman enters and opens fire. The boy is killed and she becomes obsessed with finding the killer. Her only clue is a blue tiger tattoo. This modestly budgeted, competent thriller gains little on DVD. The image is only a slight improvement over VHS tape. Sound is considerably better. —*MM*
Movie: 🎵🎵½ **DVD:** 🎵🎵½
Image Entertainment (Cat #0VED9018DVD, UPC #014381901825). Full frame. Dolby Digital Surround Stereo. $24.99. Snapper. *LANG:* English. *FEATURES:* 13 chapter links.
1994 (R) 88m/C Virginia Madsen, Toru Nakamura, Harry Dean Stanton, Ryo Ishibashi; **D:** Norberto Barba; **W:** Joel Soisson.

Blue Velvet

Unique, disturbing portrait exploration of the dark side of America involves innocent college student Jeffrey Beaumont (MacLachlan) who discovers a severed ear in an empty lot and is thrust into a turmoil of depravity, murder, and sexual deviance. Brutal, grotesque, and unmistakably Lynch, it is a fiercely imagined film unlike any other. Mood is enhanced by the Badalamenti soundtrack and graced by splashes of Lynchian humor. This DVD is the first really acceptable transfer of Lynch's wide, wide visuals. The telling "headlights" shots, which were cropped in half on the old Warner laserdisc, are intact here. Ditto the extremely wide composition when Jeffrey brings the stricken Dorothy into the Williams's home—the narrow sliver on the far right containing the kitchen door and Mrs. Williams is no longer cropped away. The picture is bright, the colors are pure (unlike the grainy laser), and the soundtrack rich. The review copy, however, exhibited a few odd compression artifacts. Here and there angular patterns show up briefly in solid colors, at least on the preview disc. The wide 16:9 picture has excellent clarity, but at least at one point (the very beginning of Chapter 5) a big compression error is distractingly evident. —*MM/GE*
Movie: 🎵🎵🎵½ **DVD:** 🎵🎵🎵½
MGM Home Entertainment (Cat #908059). Widescreen anamorphic. Dolby Digital Surround Stereo. $24.98. Keepcase. *LANG:* English; French. *SUB:* French; Spanish. *CAP:* English. *FEATURES:* Trailer.
1986 (R) 121m/C Kyle MacLachlan, Isabella Rossellini, Dennis Hopper, Laura Dern, Hope Lange, Jack Nance, Dean Stockwell, George Dickerson, Brad Dourif, Priscilla Pointer, Angelo Badalamenti; **D:** David Lynch; **W:** David Lynch; **C:** Frederick

Elmes; **M:** Angelo Badalamenti. *AWARDS:* Ind. Spirit '87: Actress (Rossellini); L.A. Film Critics '86: Director (Lynch), Support. Actor (Hopper); Montreal World Film Fest. '86: Support. Actor (Hopper); Natl. Soc. Film Critics '86: Cinematog., Director (Lynch), Film, Support. Actor (Hopper); *NOM:* Oscars '86: Director (Lynch).

Bluebeard

For various Oedipal reasons, Baron Kurt Von Sepper (Burton) knocks off a series of beautiful women whom he has married. Will chorine Anne (Heatherton) be the next? It's all very sexy in an early '70s sort of way. Burton, hiding behind a literal blue goatee, seems to be having fun with the silly material. The DVD image is surprisingly nice for a film of this age, particularly considering the grotesquely vibrant color scheme that emphasizes brilliant fire engine red backgrounds. —*MM*
Movie: 🎬½ **DVD:** 🎬🎬½
Anchor Bay (Cat #DV11193, UPC #013131119398). Widescreen (1.85:1) anamorphic. Dolby Digital Mono. $24.99. Keepcase. *LANG:* English. *FEATURES:* 33 chapter links ▪ Trailer ▪ Stills gallery ▪ Talent files.
1972 (R) 128m/C Richard Burton, Raquel Welch, Joey Heatherton, Nathalie Delon, Virna Lisi, Sybil Danning; **D:** Edward Dmytryk; **W:** Edward Dmytryk, Ennio de Concini, Maria Pia Fusco; **C:** Gabor Pogany; **M:** Ennio Morricone.

Blue's Big Musical Movie

Everybody wants Steve's help as Blue and her friends put together a backyard Music Show. Steve wishes he were better at finding clues and Blue's new friend Periwinkle tries to get Steve to watch her magic tricks, but there's so much to do! They have to make costumes, rehearse, build the stage, get the snacks ready, and find a singing partner for Blue. As you'll see in the behind-scenes clips, Steve acts in front of a green screen and absolutely everything he interacts with—Blue, the house, Mr. Salt, and Mrs. Pepper—is digitally inserted later. This technique works and it thrives here with the clarity the DVD provides. With gentle musical lessons, and Ray Charles voicing the character of G-Clef, this disc is sure to be a hit with the kiddies. Parents may need to be prepared for perpetual viewing. The DVD-ROM games require a DVD-compatible computer with Windows95 or higher. —*JAS* **AKA:** Blue's Clues: The Movie.
Movie: 🎬🎬🎬🎬 **DVD:** 🎬🎬🎬🎬
Paramount Home Video (Cat #83972, UPC #09736839724). Full frame. Dolby Digital Surround. $24.99. Keepcase. *LANG:* English. *SUB:* English for hearing impaired. *FEATURES:* 28 chapter links ▪ "You Can Be Anything You Want to Be" music video ▪ "There It Is" music video ▪ Backstage at Blue's Clues ▪ "Who Am I?" Guessing game ▪ 2 Blue's Clues DVD-ROM games.

2000 78m/C V: Ray Charles, Steven Burns.

Bob Dylan: Don't Look Back

This remarkable (and until now largely unseen) documentary follows Bob Dylan on a 3 1/2 week tour of England in 1965. Filmmaker D.A. Pennebaker shot more than 20 hours of 16mm. black-and-white film that were edited down to 96 minutes. It's an accurate snapshot of the times and portrait of the artist as a young man. Though much of this material has been rehashed many times since, Pennebaker was breaking new ground when he went beyond the concerts to film agents at work and the background of meeting other musicians, chatting with VIPs, dealing with semi-hysterical fans and assorted hangers-on. Though the focus is tightly on the star, whose music was new to the world then, the main supporting character is a radiant Joan Baez. The DVD also includes the famous "cue card" version of "Subterranean Homesick Blues," arguably one of the first music videos. Considering the age of the film, the image is very good. Those accustomed to wall-rattling 5.1 remixes may be disappointed with the soundtrack, but it makes every word and note completely clear. Songs: "To Ramona," "The Lonesome Death of Hattie Carroll," "It's All Over Now, Baby Blue," "Love Minus Zero/No Limit," "It Ain't Me, Babe." —*MM*
Movie: 🎬🎬🎬½ **DVD:** 🎬🎬🎬½
New Video Group (Cat #NVG-9447, UPC #767685944738). Full frame. $24.95. Keepcase. *LANG:* English. *FEATURES:* 16 chapter links ▪ Commentary: Pennebaker and tour manager Bob Neuwirth ▪ Trailer ▪ Cast and crew thumbnail bios ▪ Bob Dylan discography.
1967 95m/B Bob Dylan, Joan Baez, Donovan, Alan Price, Albert Grossman, Bob Neuwirth; **D:** D.A. Pennebaker; **C:** Howard Alk.

Bob Hope Double Feature

The two films on this disc are a solid cut above the norm for bargain basement features. Some care has been taken with the transfer. *Road to Bali* is about the same as the Brentwood release. *My Favorite Brunette* looks much better than any other version I've seen to date. It's a tough-guy parody (Alan Ladd shows up in a cameo) with Hope playing a photographer who gets tangled up with femme fatale Lamour and villainous Lorre. The black-and-white photography ranges from good to very good to excellent. The opening music has a tinny quality typical of the era but overall, the sound is acceptable. (See also individual reviews for the two movies.) —*MM*
Movie: 🎬🎬½ **DVD:** 🎬🎬🎬
Marengo Films (Cat #MRG-0016, UPC #807013001624). Full frame. $14.98. Keepcase. *LANG:* English. *FEATURES:* 6 chapter links each.
2000 ?m/C

Bob Hope: Hollywood's Brightest Star

Pay no attention to the heavy artifacts in the introduction. Those clear up in the body of the film. It's an informative, uncritical look at Bob Hope, which was produced for public television. So much of the work is made up of archival material that the image quality is widely varied throughout. Sound emphasizes the bass end of the scale, making most male voices sound like James Earl Jones. Much of the information was new to me—the first "Road" picture was meant to star George Burns and Gracie Allen—and some of the blooper moments from Hope's TV shows are really funny. Recommended for fans. —*MM*
Movie: 🎬🎬 **DVD:** 🎬🎬½
Brentwood Home Video (Cat #60995-9, UPC #090096099590). Full frame. Dolby Digital Mono. $14.98. Keepcase. *LANG:* English. *FEATURES:* 8 chapter links ▪ Bob Hope thumbnail bio and filmography.
1997 67m/C Bob Hope, Les Brown, Hy Averback, Larry Gelbart; **D:** Les Brown Jr., Tom Meshelski; **W:** Les Brown Jr.

Bob Roberts [SE]

Pseudo-documentary satire is about a 1990 Pennsylvania senatorial race between Robbins's right-wing folk singer/ entrepreneur versus Vidal's aging liberal incumbent. Roberts seems like a gee-whiz kinda guy but he'll stop at nothing to get elected and he knows a lot about political dirty tricks and, even more important, manipulating the media to get what he wants. Line to remember: "Vote first. Ask questions later." A lot of creativity went into the menus for this DVD. The film itself is labled "Documentary," the supplementals are under "Election Night" with a simulation of returns coverage, and the chapter links are the "Timeline." Pretty cool. Sure, it'd confuse my grandmother, God rest her soul, but I had fun with it. The commentaries are very entertaining, especially the contributions from Gore Vidal. And Artisan even had the decency to throw in a good transfer of the film that looks exactly like I remembered it in the theatre. —*JO*
Movie: 🎬🎬🎬½ **DVD:** 🎬🎬🎬½
Artisan Entertainment (Cat #10412, UPC #012236104124). Full frame. Dolby Surround. $24.98. Keepcase. *LANG:* English. *CAP:* English. *FEATURES:* 29 chapter links ▪ Commentary: Tim Robbins, Gore Vidal, Alex Cockburn, Jeffrey St. Clair ▪ Theatrical trailer ▪ TV spots ▪ Deleted scenes ▪ Photo gallery ▪ Talent files ▪ Dual-layered RSDL.
1992 (R) 105m/C Tim Robbins, Giancarlo Esposito, Ray Wise, Rebecca Jenkins, Harry J. Lennix, John Ottavino, Robert Stanton, Alan Rickman, Gore Vidal, Brian Doyle-Murray, Anita Gillette, David Strathairn, Susan Sarandon, James Spader, John Cusack, Fred Ward, Pamela Reed; **D:** Tim Robbins; **W:** Tim Robbins; **C:** Jean Lepine; **M:** David Robbins.

Bobby Darin: Mack Is Back!

The central part of this disc is a full-length version of a TV special that Bobby Darin taped nine months before his death in 1973. When seen with the extensive and well-chosen extras, the DVD is an introduction to the performer's career. The "Up Close and Personal" featurette is a home movie documentary of Darin's 1966 "come-back" nightclub performance. It's full-frame grainy black and white that's somehow reminiscent of *A Hard Day's Night*. Also included are three long examples of his television work (a 1961 special, appearances with Andy Williams in 1965, and with Flip Wilson in 1970), a discography and look at his movie career, including clips from the rarely seen *Pressure Point*. Even the roughest archival material looks very good. Sound is fine. —*MM*
Movie: 🐾🐾🐾 ***DVD:*** 🐾🐾🐾
Questar Video, Inc. (Cat #QD3180, UPC #033937031809). Full frame; widescreen. $24.99. Keepcase. *LANG:* English. *FEATURES:* 16 chapter links ● "Up Close and Personal" ● 3 TV appearances ● Discography ● Overview of movie career.
2000 71m/C Bobby Darin.

The Body Beneath

A vampire (Reed) in late-'60s London poses as a preacher. He has a hunchbacked servant, a wife, and three female assistants who wear gobs of blue-green makeup. The silliness is mixed with an equal amount of intentional humor. The ultra-low budget horror is harshly lit with a raw audio track. Parts of the original appear to have been chemically damaged or burned in places. —*MM* *AKA:* Vampire's Thirst.
Movie: 🐾½ ***DVD:*** 🐾½
Image Entertainment (Cat #ID9735 SW DVD, UPC #014381973525). Full frame. Dolby Digital Mono. $24.99. Snapper. *LANG:* English. *FEATURES:* 12 chapter links ● 5 trailers ● Gallery of exploitation art ● "Vapors" featurette.
1970 85m/C Gavin Reed, Jackie Skarvellis, Susan Heard, Colin Gordon; *D:* Andy Milligan.

Body Chemistry

Married sex researcher Dr. Redding (Singer) enters a passionate affair with colleague Clare Archer (Pescia). When he tries to end the relationship, she goes psycho. Sound familiar? It is, but this video premiere is also funny in all the right ways, and it works as a thriller, too. Since it was made for the small screen, grain is exceptionally heavy. Image and sound are no better than VHS tape. —*MM*
Movie: 🐾🐾🐾 ***DVD:*** 🐾🐾
New Concorde (Cat #NH20378 D, UPC #736991437890). Full frame. $9.98. Keepcase. *LANG:* English. *FEATURES:* 24 chapter links ● Talent files ● Trailers.
1990 (R) 84m/C Marc Singer, Mary Crosby, Lisa Pescia, Joseph Campanella, David

Kagen; *D:* Kristine Peterson; *W:* Jackson Barr, Thom Babbes; *C:* Phedon Papamichael; *M:* Terry Plumeri.

Body Chemistry 2: Voice of a Stranger

Dr. Clare Archer (Pescia) has taken her sex therapy to a radio show. That's how she comes to treat ex-cop Dan Pearson (Harrison). This sequel's actually not bad, mostly because it retains the original's sense of humor. On DVD, it's the best looking entry in the series, too. Image is a major improvement over the first film. You can catch Jeremy Piven and director John Landis in cameos. —*MM*
Movie: 🐾🐾½ ***DVD:*** 🐾🐾½
New Concorde (Cat #NH20378 D, UPC #736991437890). Full frame. $9.98. Keepcase. *LANG:* English. *FEATURES:* 24 chapter links ● Talent files ● Trailers.
1991 (R) 84m/C Gregory Harrison, Lisa Pescia, Morton Downey Jr., Robin Riker, Jeremy Piven, John Landis; *D:* Adam Simon; *W:* Jackson Barr, Christopher Wooden; *C:* Richard Michalak; *M:* Nigel Holton.

Body Chemistry 3: Point of Seduction

TV producer Alan Clay (producer Stevens) thinks that Clare Archer's (Shattuck) life story would make a terrific movie and his wife (Fairchild) would just love to star in it. So what if Clare is a multiple murderess? Picky, picky, picky. Image and sound quality reverts to the level of the first film. —*MM*
Movie: 🐾🐾 ***DVD:*** 🐾🐾
New Concorde (Cat #NH20483 D, UPC #736991448391). Full frame. $9.98. Keepcase. *LANG:* English. *FEATURES:* 24 chapter links ● Talent files ● Trailers.
1993 (R) 90m/C Andrew Stevens, Morgan Fairchild, Shari Shattuck; *D:* Jim Wynorski; *W:* Jackson Barr; *C:* Don E. Fauntleroy; *M:* Chuck Cirino.

Body Chemistry 4: Full Exposure

When sex therapist Clare Archer (the indefatigable Tweed picking up the torch) is accused of murder, she hires attorney Simon Mitchell (Poindexter) to represent her. Of course, she expects very personal service. The image is slightly better than *1* and *3* but not nearly as sharp as *2*. —*MM*
Movie: 🐾🐾 ***DVD:*** 🐾🐾
New Concorde (Cat #NH20532 D, UPC #736991453296). Full frame. $9.98. Keepcase. *LANG:* English. *FEATURES:* 24 chapter links ● Trailers ● Talent files.
1995 (R) 89m/C Shannon Tweed, Larry Poindexter, Andrew Stevens, Chick Vennera, Larry Manetti, Stella Stevens; *D:* Jim Wynorski; *W:* Karen Kelly; *C:* Zoran Hochstatter; *M:* Paul Di Franco.

Body Count

Professional killer Makoto (Chiba) and his partner Sybil (Nielsen) seek revenge on the New Orleans cops who set them up. Opposing them are special crime unit partners Eddie Cook (Davi) and Vinnie Rizzo (Bauer). Lots of shootouts and macho bravado. The video transfer is murky in some areas, grainy in others, and merely adequate the rest of the way. The audio is even less impressive, with muffled dialogue and sound effects. —*MJT*
Movie: 🐾½ ***DVD:*** 🐾½
Image Entertainment (Cat #ID5766UMDVD, UPC #014381576627). Full frame. Dolby 2.0 Digital Stereo. $24.99. Snapper. *LANG:* English. *FEATURES:* 10 chapter links.
1995 (R) 93m/C Sonny Chiba, Brigitte Nielsen, Robert Davi, Steven Bauer, Jan-Michael Vincent, Talun Hsu; *D:* Talun Hsu; *W:* Henry Madden; *C:* Blake T. Evans; *M:* Don Peake.

Body Shots

An ensemble of attractive twentysomethings explore sex and dating while traversing L.A. nightlife. Eight friends come to reflect on their attitudes when Sara (Reid) accuses macho football player Michael (O'Connell) of date rape. Substance doesn't measure up to style, but the filmmakers deserve credit for trying to go beyond "he said/she said" simplicities. The image is fine, but the disc's main feature is the choice it offers of full-frame and widescreen versions of "R"- and unrated versions of the film. The 5.1 mix seems to me to exaggerate the bass, as virtually all contemporary films do. Surround effects really crank up in the club scene. —*MM*
Movie: 🐾🐾½ ***DVD:*** 🐾🐾🐾½
New Line Home Video (Cat #N4982, UPC #794043498220). Widescreen (1.85:1) letterboxed; full frame. Dolby Digital 5.1 Surround Stereo; Dolby Digital Surround Stereo. $24.98. Snapper. *LANG:* English. *SUB:* English. *FEATURES:* 22 chapter links ● Talent files ● Trailer ● DVD-ROM features.
1999 (R) 102m/C Sean Patrick Flanery, Jerry O'Connell, Amanda Peet, Tara Reid, Ron Livingston, Emily Procter, Brad Rowe, Sybil Temchen; *D:* Michael Cristofer; *W:* David McKenna; *C:* Rodrigo Garcia; *M:* Mark Isham.

The Bodyguard / Dragon Princess

In the first half of this martial arts double bill, Sonny Chiba is a martial artist who's in the middle of a war between the Italian mafia and the Japanese yakuza in New York. In the second, he teaches his daughter (Shiomi) to be a great fighter. The quote from Ezekiel at the beginning of *Bodyguard* might well have been the inspiration for Samuel L. Jackson's famous speech in *Pulp Fiction*. Unfortunately, both images are poor pan and scan that look little better than a VHS dupe. (*Princess is* particularly fuzzy.) For such goofball exploitation, though, it's not a fatal flaw. —*MM*

Movie: 🎭🎭½ **DVD:** 🎭½ Diamond Entertainment Corp. (Cat #98701, UPC #011891987011). Full frame. $19.98. Keepcase. *LANG:* English. *FEATURES:* 8 chapter links • Sonny Chiba thumbnail bio • Film credits.

1976 (R) 89m/C Sonny Chiba, Aaron Banks, Bill Louie, Judy Lee; **D:** Maurice Sarli.

The Bodyguard from Beijing

This cut-rate disc is almost impossible to watch. The poor image looks like a second generation dupe. Both English and Chinese subtitles are burned in. There is no menu. Jet Li's fans should check out *The Defender* (see separate entry) instead. —*MM* **AKA:** The Defender; Zhong Nan Hai Bao Biao.

Movie: 🎭🎭 **DVD:** 🎭 Beverly Wilshire Filmworks (Cat #9705-9, UPC #026617970598). Widescreen letterboxed. Dolby Digital Mono. $9.99. Keepcase. *LANG:* Chinese. *SUB:* Chinese; English.

1994 90m/C *HK* Jet Li, Christy Chung, Kent Cheng, Ngai Sing; **D:** Corey Yuen; **W:** Gordon Chan, Kin-Chung Chan; **C:** Tom Lau.

The Bogus Witch Project

In the long and ignoble history of cheap parodies, this is surely one of the cheapest. It's a series of short films—sketches and blackouts, really—that use the premise of the original *Blair Witch* to poke fun at the movie biz. Here's the preface to one: "In August 1999, three out-of-work actors disappeared in the woods near Sherman Oaks, CA, while looking for Blair Underwood to give him a script. 24 hours later, their footage was found and turned into a vehicle for shameless self-promotion." The episode starring Pauly Shore is the weakest of the weak. The full-frame image is no better than VHS tape, and considering the deliberate roughness of the material, that's to be expected. —*MM*

Movie: 🎭 **DVD:** 🎭🎭 Trimark Home Video (Cat #VM7487D, UPC #031398748724). Full frame. $24.99. Keepcase. *LANG:* English. *SUB:* English; French; Spanish. *CAP:* English. *FEATURES:* 6 chapter links • Campfire sing-along.

2000 (R) 85m/C Pauly Shore, Michael Ian Black; **D:** Victor Kargan; **M:** Carvin Knowles.

Boiler Room

A greedy young man (Ribisi) gets in over his head when he upgrades from a suburban gambling den to a high-pressure phone sales job. He jumps at the chance to become a trainee at an up-and-coming brokerage firm filled with macho twentysomethings as ambitious as he is. When he discovers the full extent of the con that he's involved in, he has to decide whether to save himself or work with the feds. The characters and the moral choices are both exceptionally well developed. The high-powered supporting cast makes the most of some juicily profane soliloquies—most notably Affleck and Scott. Among the DVD extras is an alternate ending that's really more appropriate than the existing one. Unfortunately, the viewer cannot choose between the two. Though this kind of film doesn't gain much in visual or audio terms, DVD earns a strong recommendation over tape due to the extras. —*MM*

Movie: 🎭🎭🎭 **DVD:** 🎭🎭🎭 New Line Home Video (Cat #N5055, UPC #79404350552). Widescreen (1.85) letterboxed. Dolby Digital 5.1 Surround Stereo; Dolby Digital Surround Stereo. $24.98. Snapper. *LANG:* English. *FEATURES:* 32 chapter links • Commentary: director Younger, producer Todd, and Ribisi • Commentary: composer and isolated score • Theatrical trailer • Cast and crew filmographies • DVD-ROM features.

2000 (R) 120m/C Giovanni Ribisi, Vin Diesel, Nicky Katt, Nia Long, Scott Caan, Ron Rifkin, Jamie Kennedy, Taylor Nichols, Tom Everett Scott, Ben Affleck; **D:** Ben Younger; **W:** Ben Younger; **C:** Enrique Chediak.

Bojangles

Made-for-cable biopic of Bill "Bojangles" Robinson is strictly a by-the-numbers affair from the beginning at the funeral to the various characters who turn and address the camera to explain what they thought of the contradictory man. Gregory Hines does his usual excellent job in the lead, and the film looks very good. Production values are not lacking and the full-frame image ranges between very good and excellent. Why, then, is the disc such a bare-bones effort? No menu, no chapter links, only previews which must be scanned through before you get to the feature. Unsatisfactory. —*MM*

Movie: 🎭🎭½ **DVD:** 🎭 Showtime Networks, Inc. (UPC #73380-7213075). Full frame. Dolby Digital Stereo. $24.98. Keepcase. *LANG:* English.

2001 101m/C Gregory Hines, Peter Riegert, Kimberly Elise, Savion Glover, Maria Ricossa; **D:** Joseph Sargent; **W:** Richard Wesley, Robert P. Johnson; **C:** Donald M. Morgan; **M:** Terence Blanchard.

The Bone Yard

A weird morgue (actually a condemned hospital in Statesville, NC, according to the commentary track) is the setting for an attack by reanimated corpses. All in all, it's not a bad effort for the money. That's the approach that producer Brophy and director Cummins take on their commentary. It's recommended mostly to those who want to do the same kind of work, though if they want to top this one, they'll have to find things more frightening than Phyllis Diller and a monstrous poodle from hell. Full-frame image looks fine, but the real value of the disc is the wealth of extras. —*MM*

Movie: 🎭🎭½ **DVD:** 🎭🎭🎭 Program Power Entertainment (UPC #740178999620). Full frame. $24.99. Keepcase. *LANG:* English. *FEATURES:* 9 chapter links • Commentary: director Cummins, producer Richard F. Brophy • Interviews with Diller, Cummins, Brophy • Trailer • Creature effects gallery • Original screenplay • Publicity photo collection • Advertising materials.

1990 (R) 98m/C Ed Nelson, Deborah Rose, Norman Fell, Jim Eustermann, Denise Young, Willie Stratford Jr., Phyllis Diller; **D:** James Cummins; **W:** James Cummins; **C:** Irl Dixon; **M:** Kathleen Ann Porter, John Lee Whitener.

Book of Shadows: Blair Witch 2

Director Joe Berlinger spends most of his commentary track defending his original intentions and the director's cut of this film. That's a legitimate approach, though viewers would have been better served by having the option of actually seeing that film. As it is, this is a fair sequel to a wildly overpraised original. Five young people go out into the woods and then spend the second half of the film in a creepy loft. They are either guilty of terrible crimes or are possessed by a force of evil. DVD presents an accurate reproduction of the theatrical image and sound, but the disc really is an opportunity missed. The version of the film that Berlinger describes is much different from the one presented here. It's easy to understand how the studio and even the producers of the first film (executive producers here) would not want to further muddy the waters because more sequels and prequels are reportedly in the works. But it still would have been interesting to see what Berlinger had in mind and what he did. The two-sided disc contains the film and most extras on one side; CD of the soundtrack on the other. (The title is also available with the original *Blair Witch Project* in a three-disc boxed set, catalog #11709.) —*MM* **AKA:** Blair Witch 2.

Movie: 🎭🎭½ **DVD:** 🎭🎭🎭 Artisan Entertainment (Cat #11577, UPC #012236115779). Widescreen (1.85:1) anamorphic. Dolby Digital 5.1 Surround Stereo; Dolby Digital Surround. $24.98. Keepcase. *LANG:* English; French; Spanish. *CAP:* English. *FEATURES:* 25 chapter links • Commentary: Berlinger • Commentary: composer Carter Burwell • Production notes • Talent files • DVD-ROM features • "Secret of Esrever" features.

2000 (R) 90m/C Jeffrey Donovan, Kim Director, Tristen Skylar, Stephen Barker Turner, Erica Leerhsen; **D:** Joe Berlinger; **W:** Joe Berlinger, Dick Beebe; **C:** Nancy Schreiber; **M:** Carter Burwell. *AWARDS:* Golden Raspberries '00: Worst Remake/Sequel; *NOM:* Golden Raspberries '00: Worst Picture, Worst Screenplay.

The Book of Stars

Quiet little indie film is about coping with grief and finding the strength to go on without a happy ending. Penny (Masterson) is a disillusioned poet-turned-call-girl living in a poor inner city neighborhood with her optimistic sister Mary (Malone), who is dying of cystic fibrosis. Mary sees her sister slipping into a numb world of drugs and sex and is desperate to show her that life is worth living. Through her book of stars and good things, Mary uses art and story telling to reach Penny as well as her eclectic friendships with people like the Professor (Lindo), a prisoner pen-pal (Sweeney), and a refugee neighbor (Geary). A strong script never falls on sentimentality or information overload. Combined with some brilliant performances, especially by Malone *(Bastard Out of Carolina, Ellen Foster),* the film is a standout. The sound is good and the picture quality is above average for a work with few special effects. —*CA*
Movie: ♫♫♫ **DVD:** ♫♫½
Winstar Home Entertainment (Cat #FLV5237, UPC #720917523729). Full frame. $29.98. Keepcase. *LANG:* English. *FEATURES:* 16 chapter links ▪ Filmographies ▪ Original trailer ▪ Weblink.
1999 98m/C Mary Stuart Masterson, Jena Malone, Karl Geary, D.B. Sweeney, Delroy Lindo; *D:* Michael Miner; *W:* Tasca Shadix; *C:* James Whitaker; *M:* Richard Gibbs.

Born on the Fourth of July [2]

Riveting meditation on American life in the 1960s and the Vietnam war is based on the real experiences of Ron Kovic (Cruise), but some facts have been subtly changed and at key moments, director Stone cops out and fails to address the issues that he has raised. The film follows Kovic as he develops from naive high-school student to Marine sergeant to wheelchair-bound anti-war protestor. Unfortunately, the disc is a major disappointment. Virtually every flaw imaginable is in evidence—artifacts in bright exteriors, edge enhancement (though some of that comes from Stone's lighting choices), aliasing. Sound, on the other hand, is excellent. —*MM*
Movie: ♫♫♫ **DVD:** ♫♫
Universal Studios Home Video (Cat #20465, UPC #025192046520). Widescreen (2.35:1) letterboxed. Dolby Digital 5.1 Surround Stereo; DTS 5.1 Surround. $29.98. Keepcase. *LANG:* English. *CAP:* English. *FEATURES:* 16 chapter links.
1989 (R) 145m/C Tom Cruise, Kyra Sedgwick, Raymond J. Barry, Jerry Levine, Tom Berenger, Willem Dafoe, Frank Whaley, John Getz, Caroline Kava, Bryan Larkin, Abbie Hoffman, Stephen Baldwin, Josh Evans, Dale Dye, William Baldwin, Don "The Dragon" Wilson, Vivica A. Fox, Holly Marie Combs, Tom Sizemore, Daniel Baldwin, Ron Kovic; *Cameos:* Oliver Stone; *D:* Oliver Stone; *W:* Oliver Stone; *C:* Robert Richardson; *M:* John Williams. *AWARDS:* Oscars '89: Director (Stone), Film Editing;

Directors Guild '89: Director (Stone); Golden Globes '90: Actor—Drama (Cruise), Director (Stone), Film—Drama, Screenplay; *NOM:* Oscars '89: Actor (Cruise), Adapt. Screenplay, Cinematog., Picture, Sound, Orig. Score.

Born to Win

A New York hairdresser (Segal) with an expensive drug habit struggles through life in this uneven comedy drama. Today the film is most notable for early appearances by Hector Elizondo, Robert De Niro, and others. Unfortunately, the low-budget effort is virtually unwatchable on this barebones disc. No menu; no links. Colors are dark and faded. Grain and pixelation are heavy throughout. Sound is slightly better. —*MM* **AKA:** Addict.
Movie: ♫♫½ **DVD:** ♫½
Essex (Cat #1404). Full frame. Dolby Digital Mono. $19.95. Slipcase. *LANG:* English.
1971 (R) 90m/C George Segal, Karen Black, Paula Prentiss, Hector Elizondo, Robert De Niro, Jay Fletcher; *D:* Ivan Passer; *W:* Ivan Passer, David Scott Milton; *C:* Jack Priestley; *M:* William S. Fisher.

Bossa Nova

Three interconnected love stories are played out in Rio de Janeiro. The central one concerns Mary Ann (Irving), an American, and Pedro (Fagundes). She's a widowed teacher; he's an attorney who's separated. A very sharp DVD image does justice to well-chosen locations, top-drawer production values, and a riotous color scheme. Disc comes with all the extras including commentary track and an isolated music score. This is a very nice romance for grown ups. It deserves to find an audience on home video. —*MM*
Movie: ♫♫♫ **DVD:** ♫♫♫
Columbia Tristar Home Video (Cat #005600, UPC #043396052710). Widescreen anamorphic. Dolby Digital 5.1 Surround Stereo; Dolby Digital Surround. $29.95. Keepcase. *LANG:* English and Portuguese. *SUB:* English; Spanish; Portuguese. *FEATURES:* 28 chapter links ▪ Commentary: Bruno Barreto, Amy Irving ▪ Isolated music score ▪ Deleted scene with commentary ▪ Talent files ▪ Trailers.
1999 (R) 95m/C BR Amy Irving, Antonio Fagundes, Alexandre Borges, Debora Bloch, Pedro Cardoso, Alberto De Mendoza, Stephen Tobolowsky, Drica Moraes, Giovanna Antonelli, Rogerio Cardoso; *D:* Bruno Barreto; *W:* Alexandre Machado, Fernanda Young; *C:* Pascal Rabaud; *M:* Eumir Deodato.

Bounce

A fluffy fantasy romance about a charming but irresponsible drunkard Buddy (Affleck) who gives a responsible family man his plane ticket. This way the man can make it home in time to sell Christmas trees with his son and Buddy can stay at the airport and score with a good-looking blonde.

When the plane goes down and everyone on it dies, guilt leads Buddy to AA and the family man's wife Abbey (Paltrow). Melodrama and redemption ensue. In all fairness, Affleck and Paltrow do their mouseketeer best to sell the sincerity of the characters but the brother and sister chemistry between them makes it hard to buy. This is definitely the stuff of guilty pleasure romance viewing. The writer/director was also responsible for the screenplay for *Single White Female* and has obviously had a reverse epiphany going from cynical to saccharine over the years. One notably positive performance is Johnny Galecki, who turns in yet another second banana performance as Seth, Buddy's gay assistant, who is both witty and wise in the way of the 12 steps. The DVD looks and sounds great, though the logic of a two-disc set, gag reel aside, is questionable. Perhaps they are hoping for airport tragedy cult status? —*CA*
Movie: ♫♫ **DVD:** ♫♫♫½
Miramax Pictures Home Video (Cat #21655, UPC #786936144765). Widescreen (1.85:1) anamorphic. Dolby Digital 5.1 Surround Stereo; Dolby Digital Surround. $29.99. Keepcase. *LANG:* English; French. *SUB:* Spanish. *CAP:* English. *FEATURES:* 18 chapter links ▪ Commentary: producer, director ▪ Deleted scenes with commentary ▪ Gag reel ▪ Music video ▪ "All About Bounce" featurette.
2000 (PG-13) 105m/C Gwyneth Paltrow, Ben Affleck, Natasha Henstridge, Jennifer Grey, Tony Goldwyn, Joe Morton, David Paymer, Johnny Galecki, Alex D. Linz, Juan Garcia, Sam Robards, Julia Campbell, Michael Laskin, John Levin, David Dorfman; *D:* Don Roos; *W:* Don Roos; *C:* Robert Elswit; *M:* Mychael Danna.

The Bounty

While Mel Gibson, as mutiny leader Fletcher Christian, looks hot running around with no shirt, Anthony Hopkins, as the steel-willed Captain Bligh, is the true fire of this film. The movie covers the legendary mutiny on the HMS *Bounty.* The captain wants to stop on a lush South Sea island to pick up some exotic fruit trees and make a fortune. All goes according to plan, until the crew falls in love with the women and freedom the island provides. Bligh responds to the men's good spirits with unreasonably strong disciplinary measures resulting in the inevitable mutiny. Good script punctuated by great acting and beautiful cinematography. Missing is the harrowing journey of over 3,000 miles that Bligh sailed in a lifeboat with no navigational charts back to England. The color on the disc is very good, capturing the exotic flowers and dazzling sunsets in all of their glory, and the sound is above average. —*CA*
Movie: ♫♫♫ **DVD:** ♫♫½
MGM Home Entertainment (Cat #100-1183, UPC #027616854742). Widescreen (1.85:1) anamorphic. Dolby Digital 5.1. $19.98. Keepcase. *LANG:* English. *SUB:* Spanish; French. *CAP:* English. *FEATURES:*

32 chapter links • Original theatrical trailer.
1984 (PG) 130m/C Mel Gibson, Anthony Hopkins, Laurence Olivier, Edward Fox, Daniel Day-Lewis, Bernard Hill, Philip Davis, Liam Neeson; **D:** Roger Donaldson; **W:** Robert Bolt; **C:** Arthur Ibbetson; **M:** Vangelis.

Bounty Hunters

Rival bounty hunters and ex-lovers Jersey Bellini (Dudikoff) and B.B. Mitchell (Howard) join forces to capture bail-jumping stolen-car king Delmos (Ratner), who's also the target of mob hitmen. The gunfights and car chases are handled nicely and the whole thing is not without some humor and visual style. Widescreen image is only a slight improvement over tape, but that's due to the soft Pacific Northwest light, not the transfer. —MM
Movie: ♫♫½ **DVD:** ♫♫½
Buena Vista Home Entertainment (Cat #22831, UPC #786936156058). Widescreen (1.85:1) anamorphic. Dolby Digital Surround Stereo. $24.98. Keepcase. LANG: English. CAP: English. FEATURES: 17 chapter links • Trailers.
1996 (R) 98m/C Michael Dudikoff, Lisa Howard, Benjamin Ratner; **D:** George Erschbamer; **W:** George Erschbamer; **C:** A.J. Vesak; **M:** Norman Ornstein.

Bounty Hunters 2: Hardball

Bounty hunters Jersey Bellini (Dudikoff) and B.B. Mitchell (Howard) are back in another action flick. This time, Tony Curtis is involved, too. The plot has to do with jewel heists and revenge. Again, the image and sound are a cut above average for a video premiere, but the sense of humor is really stronger than either. —MM **AKA:** Hardball.
Movie: ♫♫½ **DVD:** ♫♫½
Buena Vista Home Entertainment (Cat #21657, UPC #786936144789). Widescreen (1.85:1) anamorphic. Dolby Digital Surround Stereo. $24.98. Keepcase. LANG: English. CAP: English. FEATURES: 20 chapter links • Trailers.
1997 (R) 97m/C Michael Dudikoff, Lisa Howard, Steve Bacic, Tony Curtis; **D:** George Erschbamer; **W:** George Erschbamer, Jeff Barmash, Michael Ellis; **C:** Brian Pearson; **M:** Leon Aronson.

Boxing Helena

At the time of its making, Jennifer Lynch's directorial debut was famous for the legal suit that was brought against Kim Basinger after she agreed to do the film and then backed out. The story is a quasi-allegorical hash of elements all revolving around Helena (Fenn), a flirtatious beauty who will have nothing to do with surgeon Nick Cavanaugh (Sands). Then an accident occurs right outside his mansion and he finds her in his control. The title then becomes literal, in a way, and that lack of subtlety turns what might have been metaphorical into an artsy skin flick. This

unrated version contains a few seconds of "male thrusting" that was too much for the MPAA ratings board. The widescreen transfer is an accurate representation of the original. Sound is acceptable. —MM
Movie: ♫♫½ **DVD:** ♫♫½
MGM Home Entertainment (Cat #1001733, UPC #027616860330). Widescreen (1.85:1) anamorphic. Dolby Digital Surround Stereo. $24.99. Keepcase. LANG: English. SUB: French; Spanish. FEATURES: 16 chapter links • Trailer.
1993 (R) 107m/C Julian Sands, Sherilyn Fenn, Bill Paxton, Kurtwood Smith, Betsy Clark, Nicolette Scorsese, Art Garfunkel, Meg Register, Bryan Smith; **D:** Jennifer Lynch; **W:** Jennifer Lynch; **C:** Bojan Bazelli; **M:** Graeme Revell. AWARDS: Golden Raspberries '93: Worst Director (Lynch).

Boy Meets Girl

A sort of French Holden Caulfield (Lavant) falls for a woman after hearing her voice and then cruises the seamier side of Paris. This is director Carax's debut. Like his more recent work, its strength is more visual than narrative. There's a bit of Lynch's Eraserhead in Carax's approach. DVD appears to be an accurate reproduction of a very good black-and-white image that's often dark and heavily shadowed. Even the clashing stripes and plaids that the characters favor make an untroubled transition. —MM
Movie: ♫♫♫ **DVD:** ♫♫♫
Winstar Home Entertainment (Cat #FLV5272, UPC #720917527222). Widescreen anamorphic. $24.99. Keepcase. LANG: French. SUB: English. FEATURES: Interview with Leos Carax • 16 chapter links • Pola X trailer • Filmographies • DVD production credits.
1984 100m/B FR Denis Lavant, Mireille Perrier, Carroll Brooks, Anna Baldaccini; **D:** Leos Carax; **W:** Leos Carax; **C:** Jean-Yves Escoffier; **M:** Jacques Pinault.

The Boys

French-Canadian comedy about ordinary guys who play amateur hockey has become a sleeper hit. "Les Boys" are sponsored by local tavern-owner Stan (Girard), who's in debt to a smalltime mobster, Meo (Lebeau). Meo strikes a deal, pitting Stan's ragtag team against his own thugs. If Stan's guys lose, Meo gets the bar. Dirty tricks abound on both sides. The formula comedy certainly plays better to audiences familiar with the game, but the male-bonding jokes are universal. To my taste, English subtitles would have been preferable to the dubbing, which sounds like it belongs in a spaghetti western. Some sound effects are punched up but the skating scenes are fairly realistic without exaggeration. The bright, softish full-frame image is generally very good. —MM **AKA:** Les Boys.
Movie: ♫♫½ **DVD:** ♫♫½
Studio Home Entertainment (Cat #7165). Full frame. Dolby Digital Stereo. $24.95. Keepcase. LANG: French; English. FEA-

TURES: 24 chapter links • Trailer • Talent files.
1997 107m/C CA Remy Girard, Marc Messier, Patrick Huard, Serge Theriault, Yvan Ponton, Dominic Philie, Patrick Labbe, Roc Lafortune, Pierre Lebeau, Paul Houde; **D:** Louis Saia; **W:** Christian Fournier; **C:** Sylvain Brault; **M:** Normand Corbeil. AWARDS: NOM: Genie '98: Actor (Girard).

Boys and Girls

Freddie Prinze Jr. is rivaling Steven Segal as the king of the three-word-title movie (She's All That, Down to You, Head over Heels). This slight romantic comedy rips off When Harry Met Sally with its story of a mismatched couple whose friendship is sorely tested after they have sex. Prinze stars as control freak Ryan. A miscast Claire Forlani is Jennifer, a free-spirit (read annoying). They run into each other over the years, quarrel, and separate ad tedium until their interminably delayed first kiss. This, as the film's tag line cautions us, "changes everything." American Pie's Jason Biggs reprises his already tiresome hapless womanizer-doofus routine. But on DVD, at least the film looks great, with a near pristine transfer and bright colors. The 5.1 Surround is also impressive. —DL
Movie: ♫♫ **DVD:** ♫♫½
Buena Vista Home Entertainment (Cat #20770, UPC #1795101059). Widescreen (1.85:1) anamorphic. Dolby Digital. $29.99. Keepcase. LANG: English; French. SUB: Spanish. CAP: English. FEATURES: 18 chapter links.
2000 (PG-13) 94m/C Freddie Prinze Jr., Claire Forlani, Jason Biggs, Heather Donahue, Alyson Hannigan, Amanda Detmer, Lisa Eichhorn; **D:** Robert Iscove; **W:** Andrew Lowery, Andrew Miller; **C:** Ralf Bode; **M:** Stewart Copeland.

The Boys Next Door

Bo (Sheen) and Roy (Caulfield) are typically alienated California high school students who go on a violent rampage out of boredom. The title sequence, focusing on other real serial killers, reinforces the film's solid basis in reality, and in the wake of more recent teen killings, it can be seen as prescient in some ways. DVD presents an excellent re-creation of a low-budget image that has never aspired to conventional Hollywood polish. It's often poorly lighted and the mono sound seems a bit hollow by today's standards. The commentary track is of the everyone-was-wise-and-wonderful variety. —MM
Movie: ♫♫♫ **DVD:** ♫♫½
Anchor Bay (Cat #DV11376, UPC #013131137699). Widescreen (1.85:1) anamorphic. Dolby Digital Mono. $24.99. Keepcase. LANG: English. CAP: English. FEATURES: Trailer • Talent files • Commentary: Penelope Spheeris • 23 chapter links.
1985 (R) 90m/C Maxwell Caulfield, Charlie Sheen, Christopher McDonald, Hank

Garrett, Patti D'Arbanville, Moon Zappa; *D:* Penelope Spheeris; *W:* Glen Morgan, James Wong; *C:* Arthur Albert; *M:* George S. Clinton.

Boyz N the Hood

Singleton's debut is an astonishing picture of four black high school students with different backgrounds, aims, and abilities trying to survive Los Angeles gangs and bigotry. Excellent acting throughout with special nods to Fishburne, Gooding Jr., and Ice Cube. It's often violent but the emotional conclusion is powerful. Both image and sound range between good and very good, accurately reflecting the theatrical release. —*MM*
Movie: ♪♪♪ *DVD:* ♪♪½
Columbia Tristar Home Video (Cat #50819). Widescreen (1.85:1) letterboxed; full frame. Dolby Digital Stereo. $29.95. Keepcase. *LANG:* English; French; Spanish. *SUB:* French; Spanish. *CAP:* English. *FEATURES:* Trailers.
1991 (R) 112m/C Laurence "Larry" Fishburne, Ice Cube, Cuba Gooding Jr., Nia Long, Morris Chestnut, Tyra Ferrell, Angela Bassett, Whitman Mayo; *D:* John Singleton; *W:* John Singleton; *C:* Charles Mills; *M:* Stanley Clarke. *AWARDS:* MTV Movie Awards '92: New Filmmaker (Singleton); *NOM:* Oscars '91: Director (Singleton), Orig. Screenplay.

Brain Dead

Low-budget but brilliantly assembled puzzle follows a brain surgeon (Pullman) who agrees to perform an experimental operation on a psychic to retrieve some corporately valuable data. That's his first mistake and it sets in motion a seemingly endless cycle of nightmares and identity alterations. It's a mind-blowing feast from original *Twilight Zone* writer Charles Beaumont. The digital transfer has rendered the picture as sharp and clear, but it has also revealed a significant amount of grain. The picture is dark at times, consistent with low-budget films of the era. The color is good, but the darkness of the picture makes the colors sometimes appear washed-out. The audio is acceptable. This transfer leaves much to be desired, but it's a definite improvement over the old VHS version and with a retail price of $14.95, it's a pretty good bargain. —*MM/ML*
Movie: ♪♪♪½ *DVD:* ♪♪½
New Concorde (Cat #20350). Full frame. Dolby Digital Mono. $14.95. Keepcase. *LANG:* English. *FEATURES:* Theatrical trailers ⬝ Thumbnail bios of Pullman, Paxton, Kennedy, Cort, Corman.
1989 (R) 85m/C Bill Pullman, Bill Paxton, Bud Cort, Patricia Charbonneau, Nicholas Pryor, George Kennedy, Brian Brophy, Lee Arenberg, Andy Wood; *D:* Adam Simon; *W:* Adam Simon, Charles Beaumont; *M:* Peter Rotter.

The Brain from Planet Arous

In one of the VideoHound's personal sf favs, an evil alien brain (that looks like a water balloon with eyes) appropriates the body of a scientist (Agar) to conquer the world, etc., etc. But his plans are thwarted by a good alien brain that likewise inhabits the body of the scientist's brave dog! A splendid time is guaranteed for all fans of '50s camp. After a few light scratches at the beginning, the rest of the film is virtually perfect. The black-and-white image looks about as good as the day it first came out of the lab. —*MM*
Movie: ♪♪♪ *DVD:* ♪♪♪
Image Entertainment (Cat #ID8694CODVD, UPC #014381869422). Full frame. Dolby Digital Mono. $24.99. Snapper. *LANG:* English. *FEATURES:* Trailer ⬝ 16 chapter links.
1957 80m/B John Agar, Joyce Meadows, Robert Fuller, Henry Travis, Bill Giorgio, Tim Graham, Thomas B(rowne). Henry, Ken Terrell; *D:* Nathan (Hertz) Juran; *W:* Ray Buffum; *C:* Jacques "Jack" Marquette; *M:* Walter Greene.

The Brain that Wouldn't Die

Though writer/director Joseph Green never reaches the heights that Ed Wood Jr. achieved, it's not for lack of trying. After a painfully slow, uneventful introduction and an off-camera car crash, a mad scientist (Herb Evers) keeps his decapitated fiancée Janey's head (Leith) alive on a tray in his lab, and then sets out to strip clubs and modeling agencies to find a suitable body for reattachment. Janey, meanwhile, has gone slightly psychotic—and who could blame her?—telepathically contacting the creature who lives in the closet. But the film really belongs to Leslie Daniels as the henchman Kurt, whose death scene is a full 2 minutes and 45 seconds of rabid, unfettered scenery chewing, which must be seen to be appreciated. Grain and blemishes appear intermittently in the black-and-white source material, but rather than detract from the presentation, they actually enhance the nostalgia effect. Black levels are solid, though there are a few instances of high-contrast levels washing out some of the details. Audio presentation performs on par with its age. —*MM/EP* *AKA:* The Head That Wouldn't Die.
Movie: ♪♪♪ *DVD:* ♪♪♪
Synapse (Cat #7). Full frame. Dolby Digital Mono. $24.98. Keepcase. *LANG:* English. *FEATURES:* Trailer ⬝ Publicity photos.
1963 92m/B Herb Evers, Virginia Leith, Adele Lamont, Leslie Daniel, Bruce Brighton, Paula Maurice; *D:* Joseph Green; *W:* Joseph Green; *C:* Stephen Hajinal; *M:* Tony Restaino.

Brainstorm

Husband-and-wife scientists (Walken and Wood) invent headphones that can record dreams, thoughts, and fantasies and allow other people to experience them by playing back the tape. Their marriage suffers when he becomes obsessed with pushing the limits of the technology. Then the government tries to exploit it. Natalie Wood died before work was completed; this is her last film. The "shared vision" scenes are presented in a 2.35:1 ratio. They were meant to be sharper than the rest of the film in its theatrical release, but have never been noticeably better. Disc is only a small improvement over VHS tape. —*MM*
Movie: ♪♪½ *DVD:* ♪♪½
Warner Home Video, Inc. (Cat #907045). Widescreen (1.85:1; 2.35:1) letterboxed. $24.98. Keepcase. *LANG:* English; French. *SUB:* French; Spanish. *CAP:* English. *FEATURES:* Trailer ⬝ 32 chapter links.
1983 (PG) 106m/C Natalie Wood, Christopher Walken, Cliff Robertson, Louise Fletcher; *D:* Douglas Trumbull; *W:* Bruce Joel Rubin; *C:* Richard Yuricich; *M:* James Horner.

Bram Stoker's Shadowbuilder

Silly horror apparently takes this title but little else from a Bram Stoker short story. Shadowbuilder (Jackson) is a demonic creature that wants to unleash hell's power upon the unsuspecting town of Grand River. But he needs 12-year-old Chris (Zegers) for your basic satanic ritual, which doesn't go over well with the local priest (Rooker) and sheriff (Thompson). The full-frame DVD image is only slightly sharper than VHS tape. Sound, however, is a solid step up. —*MM* *AKA:* Shadowbuilder.
Movie: ♪♪½ *DVD:* ♪♪½
Studio Home Entertainment (Cat #7045). Full frame. Dolby Digital Stereo. $14.95. Keepcase. *LANG:* English. *SUB:* Spanish. *FEATURES:* 18 chapter links ⬝ Commentary: director ⬝ Trailer ⬝ Talent file.
1998 (R) 101m/C Michael Rooker, Leslie Hope, Andrew Jackson, Kevin Zegers, Shawn Thompson, Tony Todd, Richard McMillan; *D:* Jamie Dixon; *W:* Michael Stokes; *C:* David Pelletier; *M:* Eckart Seeber.

The Brave One

This is a love story about a Mexican boy (Ray) and the bull that saves his life. The animal is later carted off to the bull ring by the evil padrone who claims to own him. The award-winning screenplay is credited to "Robert Rich," the then-blacklisted Dalton Trumbo. Though the bright colors are translated faithfully, the disc suffers from occasional digital jitter, and broad areas of darkness or earthtones are littered with artifacts. —*MM*
Movie: ♪♪♪ *DVD:* ♪♪
Lumivision Corp. (Cat #1697). Widescreen (2.35:1) letterboxed. Dolby Digital Stereo. $24.95. Keepcase. *LANG:* English. *CAP:* English. *FEATURES:* Trailer ⬝ Music and audio track ⬝ 18 chapter links.
1956 100m/C Michel Ray, Rodolfo Hoyos, Joi Lansing; *D:* Irving Rapper; *W:* Dalton Trumbo; *C:* Jack Cardiff; *M:* Victor Young.

Braveheart

Overachieving sword-and-kilt epic has so much celestial wattage that its many lapses and clichés are almost covered up. But despite all the awards and honors, the film is still a cold-climate gladiator flick built on a stereotyped structure and an overreliance on cinematic clichés in the clinches. That's not to say it isn't entertaining as a classy guilty pleasure. Director/producer Mel Gibson also stars as William Wallace, folk hero and savior of 14th-century Scotland, which suffers under the cruel yoke of Longshanks, King Edward I (McGoohan). On anything but the largest screen, the sprawling picture suffers. Even so, the pale gray image is first-rate—even coarsely woven materials look fine—with an excellent 5.1 mix that sounds great in the big battle scenes. A confident Gibson has relatively little to say on his commentary track. He sticks mostly to the day-to-day business of filmmaking, almost never referring to himself, and he makes a subtle variation on John Ford's advice when he says, "We adhered to history where we could but hyped it up where the legend led us." —MM

Movie: 🎬🎬🎬 **DVD:** 🎬🎬🎬
Paramount Home Video (Cat #15584, UPC #097361558448). Widescreen letterboxed. Dolby Digital 5.1 Surround Stereo; Dolby Digital Surround Stereo; Mono. $29.99. Keepcase. LANG: English; French. SUB: English. FEATURES: 22 chapter links • 2 theatrical trailers • "Making of" featurette • Commentary: director.
1995 (R) 178m/C Mel Gibson, Sophie Marceau, Patrick McGoohan, Catherine McCormack, Brendan Gleeson, James Cosmo, David O'Hara, Angus Macfadyen, Peter Hanly, Ian Bannen, Sean McGinley, Brian Cox, Stephen Billington, Barry McGovern, Alun Armstrong, Tommy Flanagan; **D:** Mel Gibson; **W:** Randall Wallace; **C:** John Toll; **M:** James Horner. AWARDS: Oscars '95: Cinematog., Director (Gibson), Makeup, Picture; British Acad. '95: Cinematog.; Golden Globes '96: Director (Gibson); MTV Movie Awards '96: Action Seq.; Writers Guild '95: Orig. Screenplay; Broadcast Film Critics '95: Director (Gibson); NOM: Oscars '95: Costume Des., Film Editing, Orig. Screenplay, Sound, Orig. Dramatic Score; British Acad. '95: Director (Gibson), Score; Directors Guild '95: Director (Gibson); Golden Globes '96: Film—Drama, Screenplay, Score; MTV Movie Awards '96: Film, Male Perf. (Gibson), Most Desirable Male (Gibson).

Breaker! Breaker!

A convoy of angry truck drivers, led by Norris, launch an assault on the corrupt and sadistic locals of a small Texas town. Goofy entry in "mad or sex-crazed trucker armed with a CB radio" genre. The video transfer is very good, or at least as good as a movie about kung-fu truck drivers

deserves to have. The colors are crisp and feature nice black definition (although some scenes show signs of deterioration). The soundtrack is decent, with the mono mix leaning towards muddied dialogue in spots. —MJT
Movie: 🎬 **DVD:** 🎬🎬½
MGM Home Entertainment (Cat #1001273, UPC #027616855534). Widescreen (1.85:1) anamorphic; full frame. Dolby Digital Mono. $19.98. Keepcase. LANG: English. SUB: French; Spanish. FEATURES: 28 chapter links.
1977 (PG) 86m/C Chuck Norris, George Murdock, Terry O'Connor, Don Gentry, Jack Nance; **D:** Don Hulette; **W:** Terry Chambers; **C:** Mario DiLeo; **M:** Don Hulette.

Breakfast of Champions

Adaptation of Kurt Vonnegut's 1973 satire on American greed and consumerism is messy and offbeat. Relentlessly upbeat salesman Dwayne Hoover (Willis) runs the most successful car dealership in middle America's Midland City. A leading citizen who stars in his own garish commercials, Dwayne has alienated his drugged-up wife (Hershey) and his aspiring lounge-singer son Bunny (Haas). Dwayne also is going nuts and his one hope lies with eccentric sf writer Kilgore Trout (Finney). And then there's his cross-dressing sales manager Harry (Nolte). This is an absolutely pristine transfer of an absolutely atrocious comedy. At least, the box claims it's a comedy. Sound is very good, too. Go figure. —MM
Movie: 🎬½ **DVD:** 🎬🎬🎬
Hollywood Pictures Home Video (Cat #20510, UPC #717951010209). Widescreen (1.85:1) letterboxed. Dolby Digital 5.1 Surround Stereo; Dolby Digital Surround Stereo. $29.99. Keepcase. LANG: English; French. FEATURES: 26 chapter links.
1998 (R) 110m/C Bruce Willis, Albert Finney, Nick Nolte, Barbara Hershey, Glenne Headly, Lukas Haas, Omar Epps, Buck Henry, Vicki Lewis, Ken Campbell, Will Patton, Chip Zien, Owen C. Wilson, Alison Eastwood, Shawnee Smith, Kurt Vonnegut Jr.; **D:** Alan Rudolph; **W:** Alan Rudolph; **C:** Elliot Davis; **M:** Mark Isham.

Breakheart Pass

Offbeat western/thriller casts Bronson as John Deakin, a mysterious stranger who may be a murderer. At least, that's what the marshal (Johnson) believes when he loads Deakin onto an army train through the Rocky Mountains. As various passengers are bumped off, the train is threatened by exterior forces. The whole thing rattles along at an engaging pace. Second unit direction was handled by legendary stuntman Yakima Canutt. The image is very good, maintaining a high level of detail in black clothes. The print exhibits only a slight amount of wear; the grain comes from the original theatrical release, if memory serves. —MM
Movie: 🎬🎬🎬 **DVD:** 🎬🎬🎬

MGM Home Entertainment (Cat #100-1274, UPC #027616855541). Widescreen anamorphic; full frame. Dolby Digital Mono. $19.98. Keepcase. LANG: English; French. SUB: French; Spanish. FEATURES: 28 chapter links • Theatrical trailer.
1976 (PG) 92m/C Charles Bronson, Ben Johnson, Richard Crenna, Jill Ireland, Charles Durning, Ed Lauter, Archie Moore, Sally Kirkland; **D:** Tom Gries; **W:** Alistair MacLean; **C:** Lucien Ballard; **M:** Jerry Goldsmith.

Breaking the Waves

Though critics have gushed over the curious tale of Bess (Watson), a religious woman from an austere northern Scotland coastal village, who marries Jan (Skarsgard), an oil rig worker, I find it a calculated, irritating work. Von Trier's nervous handheld camerawork constantly calls attention to itself. Perhaps it's his penchant for natural-looking lighting that causes the excessive grain and the artifacts that grow from it. In some scenes they are so heavy as to appear intentional. Add in a soft focus, pale watery skin tones, and heavy black clothes and you've got a disc that's unwatchable to the uninitiated. Sound is O.K. —MM
Movie: 🎬🎬½ **DVD:** 🎬🎬½
Artisan Entertainment (Cat #10048, UPC #707729100485). Widescreen (1.85:1) letterboxed. Dolby Digital Surround Stereo. $24.99. Keepcase. LANG: English. FEATURES: 40 chapter links • Production notes.
1995 (R) 152m/C DK FR Emily Watson, Stellan Skarsgard, Katrin Cartlidge, Adrian Rawlins, Jean-Marc Barr, Sandra Voe, Udo Kier, Mikkel Gaup; **D:** Lars von Trier; **W:** Lars von Trier; **C:** Robby Muller; **M:** Joachim Holbek. AWARDS: Cannes '96: Grand Jury Prize; Cesar '97: Foreign Film; N.Y. Film Critics '96: Actress (Watson), Cinematog., Director (von Trier); Natl. Soc. Film Critics '96: Actress (Watson), Cinematog., Director (von Trier), Film; NOM: Oscars '96: Actress (Watson); British Acad. '96: Actress (Watson); Golden Globes '97: Actress—Drama (Watson), Film—Drama; Ind. Spirit '97: Foreign Film.

Brian's Song

The story of the relationship between Chicago Bears star running back Gale Sayers (Williams) and teammate Brian Piccolo (Caan) is one of the great sports bio-pics, even if it was made for TV. On DVD, the image is mostly clean and clear without defects. The picture shows some grain but it's never distracting. Colors are generally vibrant and strong, although slight oversaturation is evident on occasion. Blacks are deep and solid and the shadows are nicely delineated. Mono audio sounds a bit dated with a rather narrow frequency response, giving especially the dialogue an unnatural harshness. —GH/MM
Movie: 🎬🎬🎬🎬 **DVD:** 🎬🎬🎬

Columbia Tristar Home Video (Cat #4863). Full frame. Dolby Digital Mono. $24.95. Keepcase. *LANG:* English. *SUB:* English; Spanish; Portuguese; Chinese; Korean; Thai. *FEATURES:* "Gale Sayers First and Goal" featurette • Commentary: Williams and Caan • Trailers • Talent files.

1971 (G) 74m/C James Caan, Billy Dee Williams, Jack Warden, Shelley Fabares, Judy Pace, Bernie Casey; *D:* Buzz Kulik; *W:* William Blinn; *C:* Joseph Biroc; *M:* Michel Legrand.

Bride of Re-Animator

Disappointing sequel to the cult masterpiece goes too far in all the wrong directions. Of course, the prosthetic special effects are graphic, but severed body parts have been so overused that they don't even have the power to shock anymore. The strong, flippant humor of the first film has become studied, though star Jeffrey Combs gives it his best. Worst of all, the filmmakers don't even pay attention to plot details from the original. Characters who were clearly dead and/or squashed are brought back without explanation. No, logic is not a prime consideration in cheap horror movies, but that kind of unimaginative sloppiness is an insult to fans. The two-sided disc contains the "R"-rated version of the film with commentary by the filmmakers on one side, and the unrated version on the other; both are in full-frame and widescreen. The image is rough and grainy. Only the commentary tracks make the disc superior to tape. —*MM* *AKA:* Re-Animator 2.

Movie: woof *DVD:* 🎞🎞½
Pioneer Entertainment (Cat #10317). Full frame; widescreen letterboxed. Dolby Digital Stereo. $29.98. Keepcase. *LANG:* English. *FEATURES:* Rehearsals, outtakes, deleted scenes, bloopers • Commentary: filmmakers • 20 chapter links • Featurette, "Getting Ahead in Horror."

1989 99m/C Bruce Abbott, Claude Earl Jones, Fabiana Udenio, Jeffrey Combs, Kathleen Kinmont, David Gale, Mel Stewart, Irene Forrest; *D:* Brian Yuzna; *W:* Brian Yuzna, Rick Fry, Woody Keith; *C:* Rick Fichter; *M:* Richard Band.

The Bride Wore Black

Truffaut's homage to Hitchcock comes complete with a Bernard Herrmann score. A young woman (Moreau) exacts brutal revenge on the five men who were involved in the death of her husband. The story is adapted from a Cornell Woolrich novel. The image is very good for a film of this age. Focus is a bit soft and deep blacks lack detail. Also, there is an occasional slight shift in color values within the same static shot. Sound is fine. —*MM* *AKA:* La Mariee Etait en Noir.

Movie: 🎞🎞🎞 *DVD:* 🎞🎞🎞
MGM Home Entertainment (Cat #1001476, UPC #027616857965). Widescreen (1.66:1) letterboxed. Dolby Digital Mono. $19.98. Keepcase. *LANG:* English;

French. *SUB:* English; French; Spanish. *FEATURES:* 16 chapter links • Trailer.

1968 107m/C *FR* Jeanne Moreau, Claude Rich, Jean-Claude Brialy, Michel Bouquet, Michael (Michel) Lonsdale, Charles Denner, Daniel Boulanger; *D:* Francois Truffaut; *W:* Francois Truffaut, Jean-Louis Richard; *C:* Raoul Coutard; *M:* Bernard Herrmann.

The Bridge

In 1963, Mira (Bouquet) loves to go to the movies to watch *Jules et Jim* and *West Side Story*. She has a 15-year-old son, but that doesn't stop her from entering into an affair with a visiting engineer (Berling) who's in her little town to build a bridge. Director Depardieu plays her husband, a builder who's working on the bridge. It's precisely the sort of material that the French handle so deftly and Depardieu proves that he's a competent craftsman behind the camera. DVD appears to be a completely accurate reproduction of a soft, pastel image. Sound is very good, though the story doesn't call for overpowering audio effects. The optional subtitles are easy to read. —*MM*

Movie: 🎞🎞🎞 *DVD:* 🎞🎞🎞
Winstar Home Entertainment (Cat #FLV5270, UPC #720917527024). Widescreen anamorphic. $24.98. Keepcase. *LANG:* French. *SUB:* English. *FEATURES:* 8 chapter links • Theatrical trailer • Filmographies.

2000 92m/C *FR* Carole Bouquet, Gerard Depardieu, Charles Berling; *D:* Frederic Auburtin, Gerard Depardieu; *W:* Francois Bupeyron; *C:* Pascal Ridao; *M:* Frederic Auburtin.

The Bridge at Remagen

Allies attempt to capture a vital bridge before retreating German troops destroy it. Based on real incidents and well told. The print has a few nicks here and there but on the whole is relatively clean. Colors are somewhat muted, mostly due to the drab palette used for this type of film. Brightness and contrast are good with only a few interior scenes coming across as too dark. All in all, the picture is quite good. The audio is presented in its original mono, split between the two front speakers. What's amazing about this mix is just how good the deep bass comes across. The rumble of tanks and abundant explosions all pack more punch than might be expected from a 30-year-old film. This is one of the more dynamic mono mixes I've heard. —*MP/MM*

Movie: 🎞🎞½ *DVD:* 🎞🎞½
MGM Home Entertainment Widescreen (2.35:1) letterboxed. Dolby Digital Mono. $19.98. Keepcase. *LANG:* English; French; Spanish. *SUB:* French; Spanish. *FEATURES:* Booklet • Theatrical trailer.

1969 (PG) 115m/C George Segal, Robert Vaughn, Ben Gazzara, Bradford Dillman, E.G. Marshall; *D:* John Guillermin; *W:* William Roberts; *C:* Stanley Cortez; *M:* Elmer Bernstein.

Bridge of Dragons

Dictator Tagawa, having murdered the kingdom's rightful ruler, plots to marry the country's princess (Shane) to consolidate his power. But when she escapes to join the rebel forces, human killing machine Lundgren is sent to retrieve her. Of course, he joins her side and massive explosions ensue. The DVD transfer is generally clean and without notable noise or grain. It contains a good level of detail, but some edge overenhancement is visible throughout the film, creating an image that is a little harsh looking. The frequency response and dynamics of the audio track are good. —*GH/MM*

Movie: 🎞🎞 *DVD:* 🎞🎞½
HBO Home Video (Cat #91674). Full frame. Dolby Digital Stereo. $19.98. Snapper. *LANG:* English; Spanish. *SUB:* English; French; Spanish. *FEATURES:* Talent files.

1999 (R) 91m/C Dolph Lundgren, Cary-Hiroyuki Tagawa, Gary Hudson, Scott Schwartz, Rachel Shane; *D:* Isaac Florentine; *W:* Carlton Holder; *C:* Yossi Wein; *M:* Steve Edwards.

The Bridge on the River Kwai [LE]

British POW Col. Nicholson (Guinness) and Japanese Col. Saito (Hayakawa) fight a duel of wills over the construction of a bridge in the Burmese jungle. Their conflict makes for one of the all-time great war movies. On DVD, the film finally gets the treatment it has deserved on home video. Most important is the widescreen transfer, which is able to accommodate director Lean's important two shots. But the disc handles potentially troublesome visuals—jungle scenes, water, bright sandy yards—without any serious flaws. Both the 5.1 and Surround Stereo soundtracks are a notable improvement over VHS tape. In this boxed set, the film is on one disc; the extras on a second. Of those, John Milius's appreciation is a real treat. —*MM*

Movie: 🎞🎞🎞🎞 *DVD:* 🎞🎞🎞🎞
Columbia Tristar Home Video (Cat #05747, UPC #043306057470). Widescreen (2.55:1) anamorphic. Dolby Digital 5.1 Surround Stereo; Dolby Digital Surround Stereo. $39.95. Box set. *LANG:* English; French; Portuguese; Spanish. *SUB:* English; French; Portuguese; Spanish; Chinese; Korean; Thai. *FEATURES:* 40 chapter links • Production documentary • Original featurette, "Rise and Fall of a Jungle Giant" • USC short on film appreciation introduced by William Holden • Appreciation by John Milius • Theatrical trailers • Talent files • DVD-ROM features. Also available in conventional, full-frame edition (cat. #05278; UPC 043306052789) for $24.95.

1957 161m/C *GB* William Holden, Alec Guinness, Jack Hawkins, Sessue Hayakawa, James Donald, Geoffrey Horne, Andre Morell, Ann Sears, Peter Williams, John Boxer, Percy Herbert, Harold Goodwin, Henry Okawa, Keiichiro Katsumoto, M.R.B. Chakrabandhu; *D:* David Lean; *W:* Carl Foreman, Michael Wilson; *C:* Jack

Hildyard; **M:** Malcolm Arnold; **Technical Advisor:** Maj. Gen. L.E.M. Perowne. *AWARDS:* Oscars '57: Actor (Guinness), Adapt. Screenplay, Cinematog., Director (Lean), Film Editing, Picture, Score; AFI '98: Top 100; British Acad. '57: Actor (Guinness), Film, Screenplay; Directors Guild '57: Director (Lean); Golden Globes '58: Actor—Drama (Guinness), Director (Lean), Film—Drama; Natl. Bd. of Review '57: Actor (Guinness), Director (Lean), Support. Actor (Hayakawa), Natl. Film Reg. '97; N.Y. Film Critics '57: Actor (Guinness), Director (Lean), Film; *NOM:* Oscars '57: Support. Actor (Hayakawa).

The Bridges at Toko-Ri

Though the subject is the Korean conflict, this is really a Cold War film, perhaps the archetypal Cold War film with Red-baiting politics, a strongly pro-military agenda, and an absolute blindness to the situation it addresses. If you can overlook the politics, the flying and carrier scenes are some of the very best. Both have a degree of authenticity that Hollywood seldom achieves, due in part to the full cooperation of the Navy. Comparatively few models and special effects were used. The bombing runs and the landings have a strong you-are-there quality and the filmmakers handle them with a loving attention to detail. The domestic side involving Holden and Kelly is forgettable. Grain is moderate in the seafaring scenes, and some aliasing is visible there, too. Full-frame image is not a huge improvement over a good tape. —*MM*
Movie: 🐾🐾🐾 **DVD:** 🐾🐾½
Paramount Home Video (Cat #05906, UPC #097360590647). Full frame. Dolby Digital Mono. $29.99. Keepcase. *LANG:* English; French. *FEATURES:* 16 chapter links.
1955 103m/C William Holden, Grace Kelly, Fredric March, Mickey Rooney, Robert Strauss, Earl Holliman, Keiko Awaji, Charles McGraw, Richard Shannon, Willis Bouchey; **D:** Mark Robson; **W:** Valentine Davies; **C:** Loyal Griggs; **M:** Lyn Murray. *AWARDS: NOM:* Oscars '55: Film Editing.

Brief Encounter

Based on Noel Coward's *Still Life* from *Tonight at 8:30,* two middle-aged, middle-class people meet at the railroad station and become involved in a short bittersweet romance. Set in WWII England. Intensely romantic, underscored with Rachmaninoff's Second Piano Concerto. They don't make 'em like this anymore, so Criterion has added this to their fine line of DVDs. There is some preprint damage and sight grain that can't be hidden with this sharp a transfer, but overall, *Brief Encounter* looks spectacular for its age. Excellent contrast makes for great graytones, which give superb depth to picture. The mono sound lacks low end (again due to the source material) but the dialogue is at all times clear and distinct. If you can get through the obviously (too) rehearsed commentary, there are many interesting

facts offered up on this film and others from the post-war years by film historian Bruce Eder. If this is your first Criterion DVD, be sure and watch the restoration demonstration, which shows what a difference the process makes through use of "before" and "after" clips. —*JO*
Movie: 🐾🐾🐾🐾 **DVD:** 🐾🐾🐾½
Criterion Collection (Cat #BRI140DVD, UPC #037429150726). Full frame. Dolby Digital Mono. $39.95. Keepcase. *LANG:* English. *SUB:* English. *FEATURES:* 20 chapter links • Theatrical trailer • Commentary: film historian Bruce Eder • Restoration demonstration.
1946 86m/B *GB* Celia Johnson, Trevor Howard, Stanley Holloway, Cyril Raymond, Joyce Carey, Everley Gregg, Margaret Barton, Dennis Harkin, Valentine Dyall, Marjorie Mars, Irene Handl; **D:** David Lean; **W:** Noel Coward, David Lean, Ronald Neame, Anthony Havelock-Allan; **C:** Robert Krasker. *AWARDS:* N.Y. Film Critics '46: Actress (Johnson); *NOM:* Oscars '46: Actress (Johnson), Director (Lean), Screenplay.

Bringing Out the Dead

New York City paramedic Frank Pierce (Cage), like Travis Bickle in *Taxi Driver,* is searching for redemption in a violent world. Aided by Scorsese's kinetic style, Schrader's on-tempo script, and revved up performances by Rhames and Sizemore as Pierce's partners, the movie successfully conveys the day-to-day stress of emergency units. On disc, the glare of slightly bleached colors set against the darkness of the streets makes for a beautiful but difficult color balance. The sound stage is robust and applied to perfection, immersing us in the chaotic sounds of the city and surrounding us with a great musical soundtrack. —*PT/MM*
Movie: 🐾🐾🐾½ **DVD:** 🐾🐾🐾
Paramount Home Video (Cat #335647). Widescreen (2.35:1) anamorphic. Dolby Digital 5.1 Surround Stereo; Dolby Digital Surround Stereo. $29.99. Keepcase. *LANG:* English. *FEATURES:* Theatrical trailers • Cast and crew interviews.
1999 (R) 120m/C Nicolas Cage, John Goodman, Tom Sizemore, Ving Rhames, Patricia Arquette, Marc Anthony, Mary Beth Hurt, Clifford Curtis, Nestor Serrano, Aida Turturro, Afemo Omilami, Arthur J. Nascarelli, Cynthia Roman, Cullen Oliver Johnson; **D:** Martin Scorsese; **W:** Paul Schrader; **C:** Robert Richardson; **M:** Elmer Bernstein.

The British Invasion Returns

Anyone old enough to remember the British music invasion of the mid-1960s will likely be profoundly depressed by this public television special taped at the Foxwoods Resort Casino in Connecticut. The years have taken their toll on these rock 'n' roll survivors (Gerry and the Pacemakers, Eric Burdon, Herman's Hermits, etc.) and they plow through the familiar songs

so stolidly that younger viewers will wonder how they ever became hits. At least nobody asks for a donation. —*MM*
Movie: 🐾🐾 **DVD:** 🐾🐾
Image Entertainment (Cat #ID0369CJDVD, UPC #014381036923). Full frame. Dolby Digital Stereo. $24.99. Snapper. *LANG:* English. *FEATURES:* Interviews with Peter Noone and Eric Burdon • 31 chapter links.
2000 105m/C D: Haig Papasian; **W:** Larry Rifkin.

Broken Harvest

Jimmy O'Leary remembers his youth in rural 1950s Ireland when a poor wheat harvest led to his family's financial demise and a feud between his father (Lane) and neighbor Josie McCarthy (O'Brien) threatened to destroy their lives. The men fought together for Irish independence, but the friendship dissolved when they took different sides during the ensuing civil war and then fought over Jimmy's mother Catherine (Quinn). Strong performances and the beautiful West Cork and Wicklow locations provide a nice balance against the uneven narrative, which director O'Callaghan admits on his unusually honest commentary track. He also talks about the black-and-white flashbacks which were actually shot in the 1980s for another film. The image has slightly pale exteriors and dark interiors. Those are absolutely appropriate for the story and setting, but they lack Hollywood polish. —*MM*
Movie: 🐾🐾🐾 **DVD:** 🐾🐾🐾
VCI Home Video (Cat #8239, UPC #089859823923). Widescreen letterboxed. Stereo. $24.98. Keepcase. *LANG:* English. *FEATURES:* Trailer • Talent files • Intro, closing remarks, commentary: Maurice O'Callaghan • 18 chapter links.
1994 101m/C *IR* Colin Lane, Niall O'Brien, Marian Quinn, Darren McHugh, Joy Florish, Joe Jeffers, Pete O'Reilly, Michael Crowley; **D:** Maurice O'Callaghan; **W:** Maurice O'Callaghan; **C:** Jack Conroy; **M:** Patrick Cassidy.

The Broken Hearts Club

Aspiring photographer Dennis (Olyphant) and his group of friends all work at a restaurant called "Jack of Broken Hearts" run by warm, fatherly Jack (Mahoney) who treats the group more like a family. As newly "out" gay boy, Kevin (Keegan) joins their midst. The guys find themselves struggling with their hopes, dreams, and relationship woes while trying to show Kevin what it means to be gay. A warm, funny, and immensely likable gay comedy with wonderful (and believable) performances and a well-written script. Director Berlanti's debut film shows promise as he deftly blends comedy and tragedy with moving results. The disc features a gorgeous, colorful transfer of the Super35 original except for some minor instances of ghosting during some of the red darkroom sequences. (Because the film was shot Super35, the full-frame version shows more picture information than the widescreen version.) The sound is crisp with the music track given the most substantial Surround effects. The commentary track is affectionate and entertaining, and the deleted scenes are essential viewing. Though the theatrical trailer (which was awful) is promised on the packaging, it is actually a home-video commercial. The disc loses a notch for grainy, artifact-filled menu screens. —*DG*

Movie: ♪♪♪½ **DVD:** ♪♪♪½
Columbia Tristar Home Video (Cat #05611, UPC #043396056114). Widescreen (2.35:1) anamorphic; full frame. Dolby Digital 5.1; Dolby Surround. $29.95. Keepcase. *LANG:* English; French. *SUB:* English; French. *CAP:* English. *FEATURES:* Commentary: Greg Berlanti, co-producer Mickey Liddell • Deleted scenes with optional commentary • 28 chapter links • Color insert with chapter listings.
2000 (R) 94m/C Dean Cain, John Mahoney, Timothy Olyphant, Andrew Keegan, Nia Long, Zach Braff, Matt McGrath, Billy Porter, Justin Theroux, Mary McCormack; **D:** Greg Berlanti; **W:** Greg Berlanti; **C:** Paul Elliott; **M:** Christophe Beck.

Broken Vessels

Watch this disc with *Bringing Out the Dead* and you'll take 911 off the speed dial. Scorsese's take on paramedics depicts one who cares too much. The California emergency medical technicians here become unhinged by a cold drug-induced indifference. Tom (London) is pulled into a downward spiral by his crazed partner Jimmy (Field), who smokes heroin and feels up unconscious girls while on break from saving lives. Excellent debut from producer/director Ziehl. Sound is fine, though unspectacular. The clear image ranges between good and very good, though some scenes are purposefully distorted. The film was a hit on the festival circuit and will do well on DVD. Only quibble: no commentary track. —*MM*

Movie: ♪♪♪ **DVD:** ♪♪♪
A-PIX Entertainment Inc. (Cat #APX27011, UPC #783722701133). Widescreen letterboxed. Stereo. $19.98. Keepcase. *LANG:* English. *FEATURES:* 12 chapter links • Trailers • Filmographies.
1998 (R) 90m/C Todd Field, Jason London, Roxana Zal, Susan Traylor, James Hong, Patrick Cranshaw, William Smith, Dave Baer; **D:** Scott Ziehl; **W:** Scott Ziehl, Dave Baer, John McMahon; **C:** Antonio Calvache.

Bronco Billy

Eastwood stars as a New Jersey shoe clerk who has decided to fulfill his dreams of the heroic west by founding a rag-tag Wild West show. Locke's one-note performance as the spoiled wealthy heiress who joins up is a problem. The film's charm is as ragged as the acts, but its heart is definitely in the right place and it comes across as a labor of love. The general aura of autumnal nostalgia has never made for a sharp image, so the widescreen option

is the main advantage of disc over tape. —*MM*

Movie: ♪♪½ **DVD:** ♪♪½
Warner Home Video, Inc. (Cat #18588). Widescreen; full frame. Dolby Digital Surround. $19.98. Snapper. *LANG:* English. *SUB:* English; French. *FEATURES:* 32 chapter links • Talent files.
1980 (PG) 117m/C Clint Eastwood, Sondra Locke, Bill McKinney, Scatman Crothers, Sam Bottoms, Geoffrey Lewis, Dan Vadis, Sierra Pecheur; **D:** Clint Eastwood; **W:** Dennis Hackin; **C:** David Worth; **M:** Steve Dorff.

Brother Cadfael: The Devil's Novice

Brother Cadfael (Jacobi) is a 12th-century monk and former Crusader who seems always to find himself in the midst of a mystery in Shrewsbury Abbey. Here he comes to the defense of the order's newest novice who has confessed to murdering his visiting kinsman, the king's own chaplain, in a fit of madness. While the story may seem to be a straightforward whodunit, the era in which it takes place is used for more than mere window dressing as the ensuing investigation delves into the corruption of the clergy and the role of superstition in everyday life. The period details are quite accurate and firmly anchor the production in 12th-century Britain. While the made-for-TV image is fairly good, the deficiency of the source materials is apparent in the soft nature of the picture and lack of shadow details. Colors are a bit on the drab side as well but that's surely a result of the 12th-century color palette consisting almost exclusively of dark browns and grays. The video quality is never a distraction but it isn't leaps and bounds better than what the over-the-air TV broadcasts look like. The stereo sound is clear but lacks dynamic range. —*MP/MM*

Movie: ♪♪♪ **DVD:** ♪♪½
Acorn Media Publishing (Cat #AMP-4053, UPC #05496140539). Full frame. Dolby Digital Stereo. $19.95. Keepcase. *LANG:* English. *CAP:* English. *FEATURES:* Audio interview with Jacobi • Ellis Peters bio • Production photos • Cadfael episode index • Derek Jacobi thumbnail bio.
1994 75m/C *GB* Derek Jacobi; **D:** Herbert Wise; **W:** Christopher Russell.

The Brothers McMullen

Festival hit finds three Irish-American brothers suddenly living under the same Long Island roof for the first time since childhood. Eldest Jack (Mulcahy) is a stolid high school basketball coach married to teacher Molly (Britton) who's ready to have children. Cynical middle brother Barry (Burns), a writer, has just broken up with free-spirited Ann (McKay), and earnest young Patrick (McGlone) is engaged to Jewish girlfriend Susan (Albert). All three find their romantic relationships and their belief in each other tested. Performances

are fine and much of the film was made in the house where Burns grew up. On his commentary track, he talks about the problems that an essentially no-budget ($25,000) independent production faced, and the visual shortcomings are apparent on the disc. The image ranges between fair and good and there's little that DVD can or should do to improve it. Sound is fine. The title is also available as part of the "Stories from Long Island" boxed set. —*MM*

Movie: ♪♪♪ **DVD:** ♪♪½
20th Century Fox Home Entertainment (Cat #2000568, UPC #024543005681). Widescreen (1.85:1) anamorphic; full frame. Dolby Digital Stereo; Mono. $29.98. Keepcase. *LANG:* English; French. *SUB:* English; Spanish. *FEATURES:* 20 chapter links • Commentary: director • Ed Burns weblink • Trailer.
1994 (R) 98m/C Edward Burns, Jack Mulcahy, Mike McGlone, Connie Britton, Shari Albert, Elizabeth P. McKay, Maxine Bahns, Jennifer Jostyn, Catharine Bolt, Peter Johansen; **D:** Edward Burns; **W:** Edward Burns; **C:** Dick Fisher; **M:** Seamus Egan. *AWARDS:* Ind. Spirit '96: First Feature; Sundance '95: Grand Jury Prize.

The Brutal Truth

Group of high school friends get together for a 10-year reunion at a secluded mountain cabin for a weekend of fun, but then learn that one of the gang, Emily (Applegate), has committed suicide. This leads to the inevitable arguments, self-examination, and revealed secrets; a *Big Chill* for the angst-ridden grunge generation. The video transfer is adequate, with crisp colors and fairly well-defined blacks. A few scenes, however, suffer from bleeding (especially during the sepia-tinted flashbacks). The soundtrack is decent, although the lack of a Surround sound remix is a disappointment. —*MJT*

Movie: ♪♪ **DVD:** ♪♪½
Image Entertainment (Cat #ID9359UM-DVD, UPC #014381935929). Full frame. Dolby Digital Stereo. $24.99. Snapper. *LANG:* English. *FEATURES:* 10 chapter links.
1999 (R) 89m/C Christina Applegate, Justin Lazard, Johnathon Schaech, Moon Zappa, Paul Gleason, Molly Ringwald, Leslie Horan; **D:** Cameron Thor.

The Brylcreem Boys

In September 1941, Canadian pilot Miles Keogh (Campbell) and his crew are forced to bail out of their plane. They land in neutral southern Ireland, where they're interned in the local POW camp run by Sean O'Brien (Byrne). The camp holds both Allies and Germans—separated by only a thin wire fence. Keogh figures it's his patriotic duty to try to escape as does German officer Rudolph von Stegenbeck (Macfadyen), and problems compound when both soldiers are let out on day-release passes and, naturally, fall for the same lovely local colleen, Mattie (Butler). It's pleasant but unmemorable.

The video transfer is quite good. The muted colors of the POW camp lose no definition or crispness. Other colors prove bright and vibrant as well. The soundtrack, however, is often quiet and hard to discern, which makes dialogue especially hard to understand. —*MJT*

Movie: 🎬🎬 **DVD:** 🎬🎬½
Winstar Home Entertainment (Cat #FLV5156, UPC #720917515625). Full frame. Dolby Digital Stereo. $24.98. Keepcase. *LANG:* English. *FEATURES:* 8 chapter links • Theatrical trailer • Filmographies and awards • Production credits • Weblinks.
1996 (PG-13) 105m/C *GB* Bill Campbell, Angus Macfadyen, William McNamara, Gabriel Byrne, Jean Butler, Joe McGann, Oliver Tobias, Gordon John Sinclair; *D:* Terence Ryan; *W:* Terence Ryan, Jamie Brown; *C:* Gerry Lively; *M:* Richard Hartley.

Bubblegum Crisis Tokyo 2040

Standard anime feature comes from a TV series about four young women in a future Tokyo who don mechanical armor and become the Knight Sabers. As such, they fight against evil robots, capitalists, etc. Image has the brightness typical of the genre. It moves well and the sound is very good. —*MM*

Movie: 🎬🎬 **DVD:** 🎬🎬
A.D.V. Films (Cat #DV/DBG/001, UPC #702727001826). Full frame. Dolby Digital Surround Stereo; Dolby Digital Stereo. $24.98. Keepcase. *LANG:* English; Spanish; Japanese. *SUB:* English. *FEATURES:* 16 chapter links.
2000 120m/C *JP* **D:** Hiroki Hayashi; *M:* Kouichi Korenaga.

A Bucket of Blood

Cult favorite Dick Miller stars as a sculptor with a peculiar talent for lifelike artwork. Corman fans will see thematic similarities to *Little Shop of Horrors*. The horror spoof does create goofy beatnik atmosphere. The image suffers brief intermittent registration problems and considerable grain throughout. (What do you expect from a movie made in five days?) Light static abounds. Title is part of the *Roger Corman Retrospective, Vol. 1* triple feature. —*MM*

Movie: 🎬🎬🎬 **DVD:** 🎬🎬
SlingShot Entertainment (Cat #TDVD9114, UPC #017078911428). Full frame. Dolby Digital Mono. $19.99. Large jewelcase. *LANG:* English. *FEATURES:* 12 chapter links.
1959 66m/B Dick Miller, Barboura Morris, Antony Carbone, Julian Burton, Ed Nelson, Bert Convy, Judy Bamber, John Brinkley, Myrtle Domerel, John Herman Shaner, Bruno VeSota; *D:* Roger Corman; *W:* Charles B. Griffith; *C:* John Marquette; *M:* Fred Katz.

Buddy

Tedious, saccharine kid's movie does little more than demonstrate the self-evident fact that gorillas make poor house pets. The addition of four obnoxious chimpanzees for comic relief is no help at all. Rene Russo plays an eccentric 1920s New York socialite who tries to raise a gorilla in her home. The animal is played by a team of actors in ape suits and puppeteers manipulating facial expressions. The clarity of DVD makes their efforts all the more obvious to any adults who make it that far. Surround is restrained. —*MM*

Movie: 🎬½ **DVD:** 🎬🎬🎬
Columbia Tristar Home Video (Cat #05617, UPC #043396056176). Widescreen (2.35:1) anamorphic; full frame. Dolby Digital 5.0 Surround Stereo; Dolby Digital Surround. $24.95. Keepcase. *LANG:* English; French; Spanish; Portuguese. *SUB:* English; French; Spanish; Portuguese; Chinese; Korean; Thai. *FEATURES:* 18 chapter links • "Making of" featurette • Trailers • Talent files.
1997 (PG) 84m/C Rene Russo, Robbie Coltrane, Irma P. Hall, Alan Cumming, Paul (Pee-wee Herman) Reubens; *D:* Caroline Thompson; *W:* Caroline Thompson; *C:* Steve Mason; *M:* Elmer Bernstein.

Buffalo Bill & the Indians

Robert Altman's perennially underrated historical pastiche belongs on the shelf beside *McCabe & Mrs. Miller* and *Little Big Man* (or it will whenever those two are released on DVD). Paul Newman is excellent playing the famous Wild West character as a charlatan and shameless exemplar of encroaching imperialism. He's surrounded by a first-rate supporting cast. The rough DVD image appears to be an accurate re-creation of the theatrical release, as I remember it. Sound is acceptable, but what could a 5.1 remix have done for Altman's wonderful overlapping dialogue? And in a perfect world where DVDs were granted commentary tracks on the basis of merit, not profit, the director and star would be on hand to reminisce. So if this disc represents something of an opportunity missed, it is good to see the film get another chance. —*MM* *AKA:* Sitting Bull's History Lesson.

Movie: 🎬🎬🎬½ **DVD:** 🎬🎬🎬
MGM Home Entertainment (Cat #1001834, UPC #027616861047). Widescreen (2.35:1) letterboxed. Dolby Digital Mono. $19.98. Keepcase. *LANG:* English. *SUB:* French; Spanish. *FEATURES:* 16 chapter links • Trailers • "From the Prairie to the Palace" original featurette.
1976 (PG) 135m/C Paul Newman, Geraldine Chaplin, Joel Grey, Will Sampson, Harvey Keitel, Burt Lancaster, Kevin McCarthy; *D:* Robert Altman; *W:* Robert Altman, Alan Rudolph; *M:* Richard Baskin.

Bulldog Drummond Escapes

World War I vet turned hero-for-hire Drummond (an incredibly young Milland) aided by his pal Algy (Denny), rescues beautiful heiress Phyllis Clavering (Angel) from spies then falls in love with her. Considerable wear is evident in the first reels but that clears up. Grain shows up in the foggy scenes. Those flaws come from the original, not the transfer. The title is available as part of *Bulldog Drummond Double Feature*. —*MM*

Movie: 🎬🎬 **DVD:** 🎬🎬½
Image Entertainment (Cat #ID4555JFDVD, UPC #014381455526). Full frame. Dolby Digital Mono. $24.99. Snapper. *LANG:* English. *FEATURES:* 8 chapter links.
1937 67m/B Ray Milland, Heather Angel, Reginald Denny, Guy Standing, Porter Hall, E.E. Clive; *D:* James Hogan; *W:* Edward T. Lowe; *C:* Victor Milner.

Bulldog Drummond's Secret Police

On the eve of his marriage, Bulldog Drummond (Howard) is called upon to track down a mad scientist in a moldy old castle. This is the shortest (54 minutes) and most swiftly paced film in the series. It's also much sharper black and white than the first film on this double bill. Leo G. Carroll plays three villains. —*MM*

Movie: 🎬🎬🎬 **DVD:** 🎬🎬🎬
Image Entertainment (Cat #ID4555JFDVD, UPC #014381455526). Full frame. Dolby Digital Mono. $24.99. Snapper. *LANG:* English. *FEATURES:* 8 chapter links.
1939 54m/B John Howard, Heather Angel, H.B. Warner, Reginald Denny, E.E. Clive, Leo G. Carroll; *D:* James Hogan; *W:* Garnett Weston; *C:* Merritt B. Gerstad.

Bulletproof

Nary an ounce of originality is to be found anywhere here. From the clichéd premise to the rigidly stereotyped characters to the no-surprises plot, it's a generic cop-buddy picture. But the stars work well together, generating a few real laughs, and cinematographer-turned-director Ernest Dickerson gives the action a funky off-center look. Keats (Wayans) is an L.A. undercover cop who's spent a year knocking around with Moses (Sandler), a flunky for Colton (Caan), a drug kingpin and used car magnate. When the big drug bust goes bad, Moses is enraged to learn that Keats has set him up. The chase is on. Dickerson's careful photography makes for an astonishingly sharp image. The disc really sparkles. It looks clearer than the theatrical release. Surround Stereo is excellent, too. —*MM*

Movie: 🎬🎬½ **DVD:** 🎬🎬🎬
Universal Studios Home Video (Cat #20276). Widescreen (2.35:1) letterboxed. $24.98. Keepcase. *LANG:* English; French. *SUB:* Spanish. *FEATURES:* Cast and crew thumbnail bios • Production notes • Trailer • 16 chapter links.
1996 (R) 85m/C Damon Wayans, Adam Sandler, James Caan, Kristen Wilson, James Farentino, Bill Nunn, Mark Roberts, Xander Berkeley, Allen Covert, Jeep Swenson, Larry McCoy; *D:* Ernest R. Dickerson; *W:* Joe Gayton, Lewis Colick; *C:* Steven Bernstein; *M:* Elmer Bernstein. *AWARDS:*

NOM: Golden Raspberries '96: Worst Actor (Sandler).

Burlesque on Carmen

Please see review for *Carmen / The Cheat*.
Movie: 🎵🎵
1916 30m/B Charlie Chaplin, Ben Turpin, Edna Purviance; *D:* Charlie Chaplin; *W:* Charlie Chaplin.

Bus Stop

In one of her first bids to be taken seriously as an actress, Marilyn Monroe succeeds, by and large, in adding a human dimension to the character of the dim-witted but adorable dance hall girl, Cherie. Murray, in his screen debut, has to deal with a more broadly written and less-likeable character. Previous video and broadcast versions of this one have been notable for depressingly faded color. DVD looks fine, and with the proper letterboxing, the showcase scene of Marilyn trying to sing in the honky-tonk bar, awkwardly kicking switches to change her mood lighting, works much better. *—MM/GE* **AKA:** The Wrong Kind of Girl.
Movie: 🎵🎵🎵 *DVD:* 🎵🎵🎵½
20th Century Fox Home Entertainment (Cat #2001448, UPC #024543014485). Widescreen (1.85:1) anamorphic. Dolby Digital 4.0 Surround; Mono. $24.98. Keepcase. *LANG:* English; French. *FEATURES:* Gallery of lobby cards.
1956 96m/C Marilyn Monroe, Arthur O'Connell, Hope Lange, Don Murray, Betty Field, Max (Casey Adams) Showalter, Hans Conried, Eileen Heckart; *D:* Joshua Logan; *W:* George Axelrod; *C:* Milton Krasner; *M:* Cyril Mockridge, Alfred Newman. *AWARDS: NOM:* Oscars '56: Support. Actor (Murray).

Buster Keaton Rides Again / The Railrodder

What a wonderful double feature! *The Railrodder* is a short film from 1965 starring Buster Keaton. In his familiar hat, he takes a trip across Canada on a small self-propelled railroad car. It's another silent role firmly in the tradition of his great early work. While that film was being shot, a longer "making of" black-and-white featurette was made. Together, they are a terrific portrait of the comedian near the end of his career. I'm sure there are flaws on the disc, but I didn't notice and I don't care to know about them. This DVD belongs in any fan's collection. *—MM*
Movie: 🎵🎵🎵🎵 *DVD:* 🎵🎵🎵🎵
Image Entertainment (Cat #ID0240NFDVD, UPC #014381024029). Full frame. Dolby Digital Mono. $24.99. Snapper. *LANG:* Silent. *FEATURES:* 18 chapter links.
1965 81m/C Buster Keaton, Gerald Potterton; *D:* John Spotton; *W:* Donald Brittain; *C:* John Spotton.

Bustin' Loose

A teacher (Tyson) persuades a reluctant ex-con (Pryor) to drive a bus load of misplaced kids across the country to their school. The stars are fine but the disc is substandard. It was made from an original with some dings, but the amount of artifacts in areas of bright sky or other solid colors is unacceptable. *—MM*
Movie: 🎵🎵🎵 *DVD:* 🎵
Goodtimes Entertainment (Cat #81047). Full frame. $14.99. Snapper. *LANG:* English. *SUB:* English; French; Spanish. *FEATURES:* 18 chapter links.
1981 (R) 94m/C Richard Pryor, Cicely Tyson, Robert Christian, George Coe, Bill Quinn; *D:* Oz Scott; *W:* Lonnie Elder III, Richard Pryor; *C:* Dennis Dalzell; *M:* Roberta Flack, Mark Davis.

But I'm a Cheerleader

The funny premise isn't quite enough for a full-length comedy. Megan (Lyonne) is a popular cheerleader, with a boyfriend. But her family and friends are convinced that she's really a lesbian, so she is sent to a deprogramming center run by Mary (Moriarty) and Mike (Rupaul Charles, here appearing as a man). Once at the center, Megan realizes that she is a lesbian and begins to fall for Graham (Duvall). After the main joke of the deprogramming center has been established, the film runs out of gas. The picture is crisp and clear, with only a fine amount of grain. The film is filled with bright pastel colors, mostly pinks and blues, and these come across beautifully on the DVD transfer. The dialogue is clear and audible in the 2-channel mix, and there is no obvious hiss. However, the only real Surround sound usage comes during the many musical cues. *—ML/MM*
Movie: 🎵🎵 *DVD:* 🎵🎵½
Universal Studios Home Video (Cat #20987). Widescreen (1.85:1) anamorphic. Dolby Digital Surround Stereo. $24.98. Keepcase. *LANG:* English. *FEATURES:* Theatrical trailer.
1999 (R) 81m/C Natasha Lyonne, Clea DuVall, Cathy Moriarty, RuPaul, Bud Cort, Mink Stole, Julie Delpy, Eddie Cibrian; *D:* Jamie Babbit; *W:* Jamie Babbit, Brian Wayne Peterson; *C:* Jules Labarthe; *M:* Pat Irwin.

Butterfield 8

A seedy film of the John O'Hara novel about a prostitute who wants to go straight and settle down. Taylor won an Oscar, perhaps because she was ill and had lost in the two previous years in more deserving roles. Not a great DVD, but certainly not a bad one. The fleshtones often seem a little warm, but other than that, the colors are mostly true, and even the intense reds in the opening credits don't bleed much. Although the sound seems a little crisp (almost tinny), there's none of the distortion or clipping that often shows up during loud dialogue or noises. *—JO*
Movie: 🎵🎵½ *DVD:* 🎵🎵🎵

Warner Home Video, Inc. (Cat #65244, UPC #012569524422). Widescreen (2.35:1) anamorphic; full frame. Dolby Digital Mono. $19.98. Snapper. *LANG:* English; French. *SUB:* English; French. *CAP:* English. *FEATURES:* 32 chapter links ● Theatrical trailer.
1960 108m/C Elizabeth Taylor, Laurence Harvey, Eddie Fisher, Dina Merrill, Mildred Dunnock, Betty Field, Susan Oliver, Kay Medford; *D:* Daniel Mann; *W:* John Michael Hayes, Charles Schnee; *C:* Joseph Ruttenberg. *AWARDS:* Oscars '60: Actress (Taylor); *NOM:* Oscars '60: Color Cinematog.

Butterfly

Young Moncho (Lozano) grows up in 1930s Spain and is guided by teacher Don Gregorio (Gomez). This kind of languidly paced coming-of-age story is almost never found in American theatrical releases these days. Europeans tend to treat the material with more seriousness. Director Jose Cuerda's work is solidly in the tradition of Fellini and Truffaut. The DVD image is very good overall, with only a little meaningless aliasing. Sound is fine. *—MM*
AKA: La Lengua de las Mariposas.
Movie: 🎵🎵🎵 *DVD:* 🎵🎵🎵
Miramax Pictures Home Video (Cat #21644, UPC #786936144666). Widescreen (2.35:1) anamorphic. Dolby Digital Surround. $32.99. Keepcase. *LANG:* French; Spanish. *SUB:* English. *FEATURES:* 21 chapter links.
2000 (R) 94m/C SP Fernando Gomez, Manuel Lozano, Uxia Blanco; *D:* Jose Luis Cuerda; *W:* Rafael Azcona; *C:* Javier Salmones; *M:* Alejandro Amenabar.

Buzz Lightyear of Star Command: The Adventure Begins

Young fans may be surprised to see that in his first solo outing, the hero of *Toy Story* is conventionally drawn by hand, not computer-generated. The image is still fine and, more importantly, the rapid-fire pace and humor are both intact. The story's standard space-opera fare (Buzz vs. Emperor Zurg) with nice Surround effects to heighten the action scenes. Sound is very good. The comparative lack of extras indicates that this is not one of the studio's most ambitious video-premiere sequels. *—MM*
Movie: 🎵🎵🎵 *DVD:* 🎵🎵🎵
Buena Vista Home Entertainment (Cat #19574, UPC #717951008404). Widescreen (1.78:1) letterboxed. Dolby Digital 5.1 Surround Stereo. $29.99. Keepcase. *LANG:* English. *CAP:* English. *FEATURES:* 20 chapter links ● Rogue's Gallery game ● Star Command trivia game ● Digital comic book.
2000 (G) 70m/C *D:* Ted Stones; *W:* Mark McCorkle, Robert Schooley, Bill Motz, Bob Roth; *M:* Adam Berry; *V:* Tim Allen, Wayne Knight, Larry Miller, Nicole Sullivan, Stephen Furst, Diedrich Bader, Patrick Warburton.

Call of the Wild

Charlton Heston stars in this adaptation of Jack London's famous novel of survival—by both men and dogs—in the Alaskan wilderness. It was filmed in Finland but a DVD viewer would be hard pressed to recognize the landscape or anything else in this substandard presentation. The ghostly image looks like a copy of a second-generation EP VHS dupe. Sound quality is equally lacking. There's not even a menu. —*MM*

Movie: ♫♫ **DVD:** woof
Essex (Cat #1005). Full frame. Mono. $10.97. Slipcase. *LANG:* English.
1972 (PG) 105m/C Charlton Heston, Michele Mercier, George Eastman; **D:** Ken Annakin; **W:** Harry Alan Towers, Hubert Frank; **C:** John Cabrera; **M:** Carlo Rustichelli.

Camille Claudel

Lushly romantic film explores the French art world at the turn of the century when it was exploding with new forms, and independence for women was unheard of. Sculptor Claudel's (Adjani at her loveliest) tragic love for art, Auguste Rodin (Depardieu), and independence clash. The film is overlong in the telling, and, unfortunately, far from perfect on disc. The image is riddled with problems—heavy aliasing in night scenes and artifacts in bright daylight exteriors, particularly noticeable in fast pans. Black clothes lack definition. —*MM*

Movie: ♫♫♫ **DVD:** ♫♫
MGM Home Entertainment (Cat #10011477, UPC #027616857972). Widescreen (2.35:1) letterboxed. Dolby Digital Surround Stereo. $19.98. Keepcase. *LANG:* French. *SUB:* English; French; Spanish. *FEATURES:* 16 chapter links.
1989 (R) 149m/C FR Isabelle Adjani, Gerard Depardieu, Laurent Grevill, Alain Cuny, Madeleine Robinson, Katrine Boorman, Daniele Lebrun; **D:** Bruno Nuytten; **W:** Bruno Nuytten, Marilyn Goldin; **C:** Pierre Lhomme; **M:** Gabriel Yared. *AWARDS:* Cesar '89: Actress (Adjani), Art Dir./Set Dec., Cinematog., Costume Des., Film; *NOM:* Oscars '89: Actress (Adjani), Foreign Film.

Canadian Bacon

Regrettably amateurish satire (with some sharp observations and heartfelt nastiness) serves as the feature film debut for Moore, who irritated many with *Roger and Me*. Title refers to the military code name for a campaign to whip up anti-Canadian hysteria and justify a U.S. invasion of its neighbor to the north. Evil political advisor Pollack convinces well-meaning but inept President Alda that it's just the thing to get the poll numbers up and to reinvigorate defense industries. Ugly Americans abound, at the expense of polite Canadians, eh? Overall, the image is fine; there aren't even any artifacts to be found in the mist around Niagara Falls. Surround is serviceable. —*MM*

Movie: ♫♫ **DVD:** ♫♫½

MGM Home Entertainment (Cat #1001847, UPC #027616861153). Widescreen (1.85:1) anamorphic. Dolby Digital Surround. $14.95. Keepcase. *LANG:* English; Spanish. *SUB:* French; Spanish. *FEATURES:* 16 chapter links • Trailer.
1994 (PG) 110m/C Alan Alda, Kevin Pollak, John Candy, Rhea Perlman, Rip Torn, Bill Nunn, Kevin J. O'Connor, Steven Wright, G.D. Spradlin, James Belushi, Wallace Shawn, Dan Aykroyd; **Cameos:** Michael Moore; **D:** Michael Moore; **W:** Michael Moore; **C:** Haskell Wexler; **M:** Elmer Bernstein, Peter Bernstein.

Candy

Relic from the most excessive days of the '60s makes a belated debut on home video. The hysterical adaptation of Terry Southern's novel was pilloried during its theatrical run and time has proved the critics right. The movie is simply a mess, though it is certainly an enjoyable mess, at least at times. Candy (Aulin) is a doe-eyed blonde who's lusted after by all she meets, including but not limited to a drunken poet (Burton, who is the spitting image of Bill Murray), a horny Mexican gardener (Starr), a monomaniacal surgeon (Coburn), and a bogus mystic (Brando, who seems to understand the humor better than most). DVD image is close to perfect, but the filmmakers' trippy approach to their work doesn't really require perfection in any sense. Mono sound is appropriately dated. —*MM*

Movie: ♫♫ **DVD:** ♫♫½
Anchor Bay (Cat #DV11070, UPC #013131107098). Widescreen (1.85:1) anamorphic. Dolby Digital Mono. $24.99. Keepcase. *LANG:* English. *FEATURES:* Trailer • Radio spots • Still gallery • 25 chapter links.
1968 (R) 124m/C FR IT Ewa Aulin, Marlon Brando, Charles Aznavour, Richard Burton, Ringo Starr, James Coburn, Walter Matthau, John Huston, John Astin, Elsa Martinelli, Anita Pallenberg, "Sugar Ray" Robinson; **D:** Christian Marquand; **W:** Buck Henry; **C:** Giuseppe Rotunno.

Cannibal Ferox

Cannibal movies are an acquired taste, as it were, and among aficionados, this one is considered to be the best. It's about several North Americans (druggies and students) who go into the South American jungle where they encounter various primitive people and assorted unspeakable acts are perpetrated. At one key point on the commentary track, star John Morghen admits that he's ashamed of the film. It's the same sort of stuff that Hershell Gordon Lewis did, but with slightly better effects. On disc, the film looks better than anyone should expect. A lot of care and work went into the transfer. Still, it's strictly drive-in fare. —*MM* *AKA:* Make Them Die Slowly.

Movie: ♫½ **DVD:** ♫♫½

Image Entertainment (Cat #9656, UPC #014381965629). Widescreen (1.85:1) letterboxed. Dolby Digital Stereo. $24.99. Keepcase. *LANG:* English. *FEATURES:* 50 chapter links • Commentary: Umberto Lenzi, John Morghen • 3 trailers • DVD credits • Stills gallery • Liner notes by Bill Landis • Interview with Lenzi • Lenzi filmography.
1984 93m/C IT John Morghen, Venantino Venantini, Brian Redford, Zora Kerova; **D:** Umberto Lenzi; **W:** Umberto Lenzi.

Cannonball Run

Lots of stars, lots of great cars, no more plot than absolutely necessary to keep them running from one side of the country to the other. Reynolds and DeLuise disguise themselves as paramedics to win an illegal street race. Softish image is an accurate reflection of the original. Exteriors are a bit grainy, as they have always been. The best part of the disc is the commentary by director Needham and producer Albert Ruddy. It's old home week for them, and they sound genuinely affectionate toward this lightweight period piece. —*MM*

Movie: ♫♫ **DVD:** ♫♫½
HBO Home Video (Cat #90609). Widescreen. Dolby Digital 5.1 Surround Stereo; Dolby Digital Surround. $14.98. Snapper. *LANG:* English. *SUB:* English; French; Spanish. *FEATURES:* 20 chapter links • Talent files • Commentary: Needham, Albert Ruddy.
1981 (PG) 95m/C Burt Reynolds, Farrah Fawcett, Roger Moore, Dom DeLuise, Dean Martin, Sammy Davis Jr., Jack Elam, Adrienne Barbeau, Peter Fonda, Molly Picon, Bert Convy, Jamie Farr; **D:** Hal Needham; **W:** Brock Yates; **C:** Michael C. Butler; **M:** Al Capps.

The Canterville Ghost

British TV adaptation of Oscar Wilde's oft-filmed story casts Ian Richardson as the ghost whose ancestral home is bought by an American millionaire (Saxon) whose family refuses to be frightened by the apparition. The soft, grainy image is typical of British productions. So are the excellent writing and acting, though English interpretations of American accents still sound a bit strange. No matter, the story is a proven favorite (at least for me) and the stereo is put to good use in the dark-and-stormy-night scenes. —*MM*

Movie: ♫♫♫ **DVD:** ♫♫½
BFS Video (Cat #98671-D, UPC #066805916717). Full frame. Dolby Digital Stereo. $29.98. Keepcase. *LANG:* English. *FEATURES:* 12 chapter links.
1998 90m/C GB Ian Richardson, Celia Imrie, Pauline Quirke, Rik Mayall, Ian McNeice, Donald Sinden, Edna Dore, Sara-Jane Potts, James D'Arcy, Rolf Saxon; **D:** Crispin Reece; **W:** Olivia Hetreed; **C:** David Higgs; **M:** Tony Flynn.

Captain Kidd

This isn't the place to look if you want an historically accurate look at the life of Captain Kidd. But fans of the swashbuckling genre should get what they're after as Laughton goes for the gusto and has an obviously good time to boot. Kidd masquerades as a shipbuilder to escort a treasure-filled boat into dangerous waters where the fun begins. Most likely the preprint material is responsible for the flaws with this DVD. While the black-and-white image is usually pretty sharp and there is little grain, there are lines and flecks throughout most of the film. The sound is often slightly muffled, but that may be a result of noise reduction. Overall, a very enjoyable disc. —*JO*
Movie: *♪♪♪* **DVD:** *♪♪♪*
Troma Team Video (Cat #ROAN AED-2045, UPC #785604204527). Full frame. Dolby Digital Mono. $19.95. Keepcase. *LANG:* English. *FEATURES:* 14 chapter links.
1945 83m/B Charles Laughton, John Carradine, Randolph Scott, Reginald Owen, Gilbert Roland, Barbara Britton, John Qualen, Sheldon Leonard; *D:* Rowland V. Lee; *W:* Norman Reilly Raine; *C:* Archie Stout. *AWARDS: NOM: Oscars '45:* Orig. Dramatic Score.

Captive

Strapped for cash, adman Joe Goodis (Grieco) elects to go along with co-worker Juliette Lorraine's (Croze) nutty scheme to kidnap their boss's (Greene) bratty son. It's difficult to work up much involvement in such a story. Basically, it's an average Canadian video premiere. DVD image is not superior to VHS tape. Surround sound is well utilized, mostly for ambient effects. —*MM*
Movie: *♪♪* **DVD:** *♪♪*
York Entertainment (Cat #YPD-1062, UPC #750723106229). Full frame. DTS Surround Stereo; Dolby Digital 5.1 Surround Stereo. $14.99. Keepcase. *LANG:* English. *SUB:* Spanish. *FEATURES:* 30 chapter links ☞ Trailers.
2000 90m/C *CA* Richard Grieco, Michele Greene, Marie Josee Croze; *D:* Matt Dorff; *W:* Mark David Perry; *C:* Georges Archambault; *M:* Marty Simon.

Car Wash

An L.A. car wash gives new meaning to the term soap-opera when it becomes the setting for a series of vaguely interrelated comic bits about the owners of dirty cars and those who hose them down. Think *Grand Hotel* with disco and hot wax. The budget is small but the comic talent is huge, with Ajaye turning in particularly fine work. His entrance beneath the mushroom cloud of a huge Afro is a defining moment of '70s cinema. Since this is a low-budget comedy, it has always been on the rough side and DVD can't help much. The image is grainy and the screen pattern in the background of the locker room is particularly troublesome. Lots of aliasing in the brightwork of the cars. Even with

mono, however, the soundtrack is great. —*MM*
Movie: *♪♪♪* **DVD:** *♪♪*
Goodtimes Entertainment (Cat #81008). Full frame. Dolby Digital Mono. $19.98. Keepcase. *LANG:* English. *FEATURES:* 18 chapter links.
1976 (PG) 97m/C Franklin Ajaye, Sully Boyer, Richard Brestoff, George Carlin, Richard Pryor, Melanie Mayron, Ivan Dixon, Antonio Fargas; *D:* Michael A. Schultz; *W:* Joel Schumacher; *C:* Frank Stanley; *M:* Norman Whitfield.

Caracara

Ridiculous flick stars Henstridge as ornithologist Rachel Sutherland, who agrees to allow the FBI to use her apartment for a stakeout and falls for agent David MacMillan (Schaech). Then she learns she's been duped—her "guests" are actually assassins planning to kill Nelson Mandela. Boring would-be spy movie never takes off despite all Henstridge's feathered friends. Another DVD that looks terrific, with excellent sharpness, vibrant colors, true blacks—the works. And the Dolby Surround is not bad with decent bass, fidelity, and even a little work for the Surround track. The problem is...who cares. This is the sort of movie that you only watch if you've got a job to do. —*JO*
Movie: *♪½* **DVD:** *♪♪♪*
HBO Home Video (Cat #91706, UPC #026351706217). Full frame. Dolby Surround; Dolby Digital Mono. $14.98. Snapper. *LANG:* English; Spanish. *SUB:* English; Spanish; French. *CAP:* English. *FEATURES:* 13 chapter links ☞ Talent files.
2000 (R) 93m/C Natasha Henstridge, Johnathon Schaech, David McIlwraith, Lauren Hutton; *D:* Graeme Clifford; *W:* Craig Smith; *C:* Bill Wong.

Carmen / The Cheat

This Cecil B. DeMille double feature will show contemporary viewers why the man who made *The Ten Commandments* had such a reputation. The first film tells the familiar story of lust and betrayal with opera star Geraldine Farrar in the lead. The second is darker. It's about Edith Hardy (Ward), a beautiful social climber who becomes involved financially with Arakau (Hayakawa), a sinister Asian. The story is pretty lurid and ends with an incredible scene. Finally, the disc also contains Charlie Chaplin's *Burlesque on Carmen*, a sharp parody that he made a month after DeMille's film. It's the roughest of the three. The two features show hardly any signs of wear and have the original tinting. —*MM*
Movie: *♪♪♪* **DVD:** *♪♪♪*
Image Entertainment (Cat #ID9227DS DVD, UPC #014381922721). Full frame. Dolby Digital Stereo. $24.99. Snapper. *LANG:* Silent. *SUB:* English intertitles. *FEATURES:* 23 chapter links.
1915 57m/B Geraldine Farrar, Wallace Reid, Pedro de Cordoba; *D:* Cecil B.

DeMille; *W:* William C. deMille; *C:* Alvin Wyckoff; *M:* Hugo Riesenfeld.

Carmen Miranda: Bananas Is My Business

Fellow Brazilian Solberg's documentary about the legendary Miranda features rare film clips, newsreel footage, interviews with friends and family, and even home movies. It also throws in lots of politics along the way with regard to Miranda's relation to her native country. This DVD has one of the slowest-moving and clunkiest menus ever. As with most documentaries, there is such a large variety of source material that it's hard to pinpoint just how good the DVD transfer is. It does seem that at all points the image is never quite sharp enough and there is usually a bit of grain, although not as much as we've come to expect from a lot of Winstar DVDs. —*JO*
Movie: *♪♪½* **DVD:** *♪½*
Winstar Home Entertainment (Cat #FLV5025, UPC #720917502526). Full frame. Dolby Digital Stereo. $19.98. Keepcase. *LANG:* English. *SUB:* English; Portuguese. *FEATURES:* 12 chapter links ☞ Production notes ☞ Trailer ☞ Filmographies.
1995 92m/C Alice Faye, Rita Moreno, Cesar Romero; *D:* Helena Solberg; *W:* Helena Solberg; *C:* Tomasz Magierski; *Nar:* Helena Solberg.

Carnosaur

This is one of the more ambitious, successful, and better-looking films from the Corman assembly line. Nobody will mistake these dinosaurs for the creatures from *Jurassic Park*, but they're not bad and the film has a wicked sense of humor. Genetic scientist Dr. Jane Tiptree (Ladd) is hatching diabolic experiments with chickens when things go slightly awry at the lab. Disc is only a slight improvement over tape. Sound is better, but this is an enjoyable horror movie on any medium, and I like the in-your-face menu. —*MM*
Movie: *♪♪♪* **DVD:** *♪♪½*
New Concorde (Cat #NH20444D, UPC #736991444447). Full frame. Stereo. $19.98. Keepcase. *LANG:* English. *FEATURES:* Trailers ☞ Thumbnail bios ☞ 24 chapter links.
1993 (R) 82m/C Diane Ladd, Raphael Sbarge, Jennifer Runyon, Harrison Page, Clint Howard, Ned Bellamy; *D:* Adam Simon; *W:* Adam Simon; *C:* Keith Holland; *M:* Nigel Holton.

Carnosaur 2

Technicians investigating a super-secret military installation that's about to blow up discover that dinosaurs are loose inside. The real inspiration for this sequel is James Cameron's *Aliens*. Image may be a slight improvement on VHS tape, but no more. —*MM*
Movie: *♪♪* **DVD:** *♪♪*

New Concorde (Cat #20496). Full frame. $19.98. Keepcase. *LANG:* English. *FEATURES:* 24 chapter links ● Trailers ● Talent files.
1994 (R) 90m/C John Savage, Cliff DeYoung, Arabella Holzbog, Ryan Thomas Johnson; *D:* Louis Morneau.

Carnosaur 3: Primal Species

Terrorists get a big surprise when the cargo of the truck they hijack turns out to be three hungry dinosaurs who make snacks out of them and the Special Forces troops who are after the bad guys. The film actually looks pretty good for a 3. Disc is essentially identical to tape; sound is a bit better. —*MM*
Movie: 🐾🐾 *DVD:* 🐾🐾
New Concorde (Cat #NH20586D, UPC #736991458642). Full frame. Stereo. $19.98. Keepcase. *LANG:* English. *FEATURES:* 24 chapter links ● Thumbnail bios ● Trailers.
1996 82m/C Scott Valentine, Janet Gunn, Rick Dean, Rodger Halstead, Tony Peck; *D:* Jonathan Winfrey; *C:* Andrea V. Rossotto; *M:* Kevin Kiner.

Cartoon Crazys: Banned & Censored

The main value in this collection lies in its brief history of the Hays Office and motion picture censorship, and in its revelation of the racism that was so widespread in America and in the movie business. Beyond the casual slurs aimed at black characters, the sexual innuendo is mild by contemporary standards. The 13 cartoons are in desperate need of restoration, though it's difficult to see why anyone would bother. The official objection to one Betty Boop cartoon is "making it appropriate and portraying positive the drugging of the entire city of New York without their knowledge or approval." Contents: "Be Human," "Booby Traps," "Ha Ha Ha!," "Cupid Gets His Man," "Opening Night," "Scrub Me Momma with a Boogie Beat," "Spies," "Fresh Vegetable Mystery," "Making Stars," "Christmas Night," "In a Cartoon Studio," "Easy Does It." —*MM*
Movie: 🐾🐾 *DVD:* 🐾🐾
Winstar Home Entertainment (Cat #WHE73118, UPC #720917311821). Full frame. Dolby Digital Surround Stereo; Dolby Digital Stereo. $24.98. Keepcase. *LANG:* English. *FEATURES:* 13 chapter links ● DVD production credits.
2000 110m/C

Cartoon Crazys Comic Book Heroes

The popular anthology series continues with more of the familiar Superman and Popeye entries along with some curiosities, like Dodo, the Kid from Outer Space, and Tobor the 8th Man. Given the nature of this material from decades past (mostly '40s and '50s), these cartoons are likely

to be of most interest to nostalgic adults. Kids weaned on computer-generated animation will be a hard sell. Contents: "Underground World," "Electronic Earthquake" (Superman); "I Don't Scare," "Out to Punch" (Popeye); "The Kid from Outer Space" (Dodo); "Toonervukke Trolley"; "Seapreme Court" (Little Audrey); "Suddenly It's Spring" (Raggedy Ann); "The Funniest Living American" (Betty Boop and Henry); "The Case of the Numbers Gang" (Tobor the 8th Man); "Little Nemo." —*MM*
Movie: 🐾🐾½ *DVD:* 🐾🐾½
Winstar Home Entertainment (Cat #WHE73078, UPC #720917307824). Full frame. Dolby Digital Stereo. $19.98. Keepcase. *LANG:* English. *FEATURES:* 16 chapter links.
2000 100m/C

Cartoon Crazys Spooky Toons

The age is showing on several of these cartoons and that's not surprising considering their age. Image and sound quality is on a par with the other discs in the series. Contents: "There's Good Boos Tonight," "Fright to the Finish," "Jasper in a Jam," "The Lunar Luger," "Balloon Land," "Spooking About Africa," "The Scared Crows," "The Huffless Puffless Dragon," "Is My Palm Read," "Wot a Night," "Ouija Board." —*MM*
Movie: 🐾🐾½ *DVD:* 🐾🐾½
Winstar Home Entertainment (Cat #WHE73111, UPC #720917311128). Full frame. Dolby Digital Stereo. $19.98. Keepcase. *LANG:* English.
2000 90m/C

Cartoon Crazys: The Great Animation Studios: Famous Studios

Famous Studios was Paramount's answer to Warner Bros. cartoons and Disney animation. It was never really in the same league, as these cartoons demonstrate. The main characters are Little Lulu, Casper the Friendly Ghost, and Baby Huey. They're not nearly as detailed as other Winstar collections with poor focus, heavy grain, and smeary colors. Contents: "Bargain Counter Attack," "Quack A Doodle Doo," "Self-Made Mongrel," "Base Brawl," "Out to Punch," "Seapreme Court," "Golden State," "A-Haunting We Will Go," "Suddenly It's Spring," "Scout with the Gout," "The Mild West," "Scrappily Married." —*MM*
Movie: 🐾🐾 *DVD:* 🐾🐾
Winstar Home Entertainment (Cat #WHE73119, UPC #72091731192). Full frame. Dolby Digital Surround Stereo; Dolby Digital Stereo. $24.98. Keepcase. *LANG:* English. *FEATURES:* 12 chapter links ● Studio history (text).
2000 ?m/C

Cartoon Noir

The title might make one expect the animations to be about detectives or crime, but they're not. In this case the noir refers to an attitude and a mood. There's nary a joke to be had in any of these six works. They aren't about standard entertainment values. Avid animation fans might find a treasure here, whereas those looking for pretty pictures or cuteness on any level will be left out in the noir, so to speak. The plots range from depictions of alien abductions to necrophilic bestiality, to alienation and angst. Overall image and sound quality is good. Contents: "Abductees," "Ape," "Club of the Discarded," "Gentle Spirit," "Joy Street," "The Story of the Cat and the Moon." —*GE/MM*
Movie: 🐾🐾½ *DVD:* 🐾🐾½
First Run Features (Cat #FRF909488D, UPC #720229909488). Full frame. $29.95. Snapper.
2000 ?m/C

Casper's Haunted Christmas

Direct-to-video sequel doesn't attempt the mix of live-action and cartoons that was used in the 1995 film. Instead, like *Toy Story,* it is done completely with computer animation. The result is sterile with a hard plastic quality that sparkles on DVD. Sound is equally bright and polished, too, and much of the humor is on target. The story has to do with the Friendly Ghost being ordered to scare at least one person before Christmas Day. —*MM*
Movie: 🐾🐾 *DVD:* 🐾🐾🐾
Universal Studios Home Video (Cat #20921, UPC #025192092121). Widescreen (1.78:1) anamorphic; full frame. Dolby Digital 5.1 Surround Stereo. $24.98. Keepcase. *LANG:* English. *SUB:* French. *CAP:* English. *FEATURES:* 18 chapter links ● "Making of" featurette ● Talent files ● DVD-ROM features.
2000 (G) 80m/C D: Owen Hurley; *W:* Ian Boothby, Roger Fredericks; *M:* Randy Travis, Robert Buckley; *V:* Brendon Ryan Barrett, Scott McNeil.

The Cassandra Crossing

European terrorists try to infest a luxury train with the plague. The proverbial all-star cast hangs in the balance. On disc, the mid-'70s clothes and baroque hairdos shine forth in all their embarrassing brightness. Martin Sheen suffers particular humiliation in that regard. Overall, the image ranges between good and very good, particularly for a film of this age. —*MM*
Movie: 🐾½ *DVD:* 🐾🐾½
Pioneer Entertainment (Cat #10305). Widescreen (1.85:1) letterboxed. Dolby Digital Stereo. $24.98. Keepcase. *LANG:* English. *FEATURES:* 24 chapter links.
1976 (R) 129m/C *GB* Sophia Loren, Richard Harris, Ava Gardner, Burt Lancaster, Martin Sheen, Ingrid Thulin, Lee Stras-

berg, John Phillip Law, Lionel Stander, O.J. Simpson, Ann Turkel, Alida Valli; **D:** George P. Cosmatos; **W:** George P. Cosmatos, Tom Mankiewicz; **C:** Ennio Guarnieri; **M:** Jerry Goldsmith.

Castaway

Chuck Noland (Hanks) is a Fed Ex guy who's stranded on a desert island for several years after a plane crash. From that slender premise, Robert Zemeckis and Tom Hanks weave an elaborate (but simple) story about loneliness. For much of the film, the only human character is Hanks. But as the voluminous extras (most included on the second of this two-disc set) show, that isolation was largely a creation of the computer. The film is actually more enjoyable if you don't know the details of the special effects and so I advise that you leave them to a second viewing. It could almost go without saying that the DVD image is flawless, and the DTS sound is much more effective than the theatrical aural presentation. The big scenes—the crash, leaving the island—are considerably more powerful with the enhanced sound effects. Much is made of that part of the film on the commentary track by sound designer Randy Thom. He, director Zemeckis, and visual effects supervisors Ken Ralston and Carrey Villegas tend to talk about the more technical aspects of the production. That's also the approach of the "Special Effects vignettes" in the second disc. Again, though, watch the film before dipping into those. —*MM*
Movie: 🎬🎬🎬½ **DVD:** 🎬🎬🎬🎬
20th Century Fox Home Entertainment (Cat #2001790, UPC #024543017905). Widescreen anamorphic. DTS ES, Dolby Digital EX, Dolby Digital Surround. $29.98. Keepcase. *LANG:* English; French. *SUB:* Spanish. *CAP:* English. *FEATURES:* 32 chapter links ▪ Commentary: filmmakers ▪ 4 "making of" featurettes ▪ 6 special effects vignettes ▪ Video and stills galleries ▪ Charlie Rose interview with Tom Hanks ▪ Trailers and TV spots.
2000 (PG-13) 143m/C Tom Hanks, Helen Hunt, Nick Searcy, Michael Forest, Viveka Davis, Christopher Noth, Geoffrey Blake, Jenifer Lewis, David Allan Brooks, Nan Martin; **D:** Robert Zemeckis; **W:** William Broyles Jr.; **C:** Don Burgess; **M:** Alan Silvestri.

Cat Ballou [SE]

In 1894, schoolmarm Catherine Ballou (Fonda) turns outlaw with the help of the drunken gunfighter Kid Shelleen (Marvin, who also plays the silver-nosed evil-twin Tim Strawn). The cheery spoof of westerns also features Cole and Kaye as a one-of-a-kind Greek chorus. The Motion Picture Academy seldom gives Oscars for comic roles, and so Marvin's Best Actor is all the more well-deserved. On disc, the image is every bit as sharp as it was in the initial theatrical release. The curious sound mix makes some of the voice dubbing seem

artificial, but, if memory serves, that too goes back to the original. —*MM*
Movie: 🎬🎬🎬½ **DVD:** 🎬🎬🎬
Columbia Tristar Home Video (Cat #04864). Widescreen letterboxed; full frame. Dolby Digital Mono. $24.95. Keepcase. *LANG:* English. *SUB:* English; Spanish; Portuguese; Chinese; Korean; Thai. *FEATURES:* 28 chapter links ▪ Commentary: Callan and Hickman ▪ "Making of" featurette ▪ Cast and crew thumbnail bios ▪ Original trailers and ads.
1965 96m/C Jane Fonda, Lee Marvin, Michael Callan, Dwayne Hickman, Reginald Denny, Nat King Cole, Stubby Kaye; **D:** Elliot Silverstein; **W:** Frank Pierson; **C:** Jack Marta; **M:** Frank DeVol. *AWARDS:* Oscars '65: Actor (Marvin); Berlin Intl. Film Fest. '65: Actor (Marvin); British Acad. '65: Actor (Marvin); Golden Globes '66: Actor—Mus./Comedy (Marvin); Natl. Bd. of Review '65: Actor (Marvin); *NOM:* Oscars '65: Adapt. Score, Adapt. Screenplay, Film Editing, Song ("The Ballad of Cat Ballou").

Cat Women of the Moon

Scientists—including noir icon Marie Windsor—take a tiny plastic spaceship to the Moon where they discover a big spider puppet and a race of women in leotards. DVD makes the black-and-white image so sharp that the strings holding the spider up are clearly visible and that only enhances the charms of this alternative classic. The film was made in 3-D but it's presented here in a conventional image and without the excessive grain that often accompanies the shift to 2-D. —*MM* **AKA:** Rocket to the Moon.
Movie: 🎬🎬½ **DVD:** 🎬🎬½
Image Entertainment (Cat #ID8603CO-DVD, UPC #014381860320). Full frame. Dolby Digital Mono. $24.99. Snapper. *LANG:* English. *FEATURES:* 17 chapter links ▪ Trailer.
1953 65m/B Sonny Tufts, Victor Jory, Marie Windsor, Bill Phipps, Douglas Fowley, Carol Brewster, Suzanne Alexander, Susan Morrow, Ellye Marshall, Bette Arlen, Judy W, Roxann Delman; **D:** Arthur Hilton; **W:** Roy Hamilton; **C:** William F. Whitley; **M:** Elmer Bernstein.

Catch-22

At one point in their back-slapping commentary track, director Mike Nichols admits to Steven Soderbergh that this is really not his kind of movie. He's right. The essence of Joseph Heller's brilliant satire finally evades the filmmakers, though Buck Henry is as faithful to the original as any screenwriter could be. Yossarian (Arkin) is a bombardier stationed on a Mediterranean island during World War II. He's sure that everyone's out to kill him, and he wants to go home. But the surrounding all-star cast won't let him. This DVD is perhaps the best the film has ever looked and sounded. The addition of the 5.1 Surround track works wonders during

the shots of the bombers lining up and taking off. During those scenes, when they turn to technical matters, Nichols and Soderbergh are at their best. (Don't miss their revelation of how the plane crash in Chapter 12 was accomplished.) —*MM*
Movie: 🎬🎬½ **DVD:** 🎬🎬🎬½
Paramount Home Video (Cat #06924, UPC #097360692440). Widescreen anamorphic. Dolby Digital 5.1 Surround Stereo; Mono. $29.99. Keepcase. *LANG:* English; French. *SUB:* English. *FEATURES:* 22 chapter links ▪ Trailer ▪ Photo gallery ▪ Commentary: Nichols, Steven Soderbergh.
1970 (R) 121m/C Alan Arkin, Martin Balsam, Art Garfunkel, Jon Voight, Richard Benjamin, Buck Henry, Bob Newhart, Paula Prentiss, Martin Sheen, Charles Grodin, Anthony Perkins, Orson Welles, Jack Gilford, Bob Balaban, Susanne Benton, Norman Fell, Austin Pendleton, Peter Bonerz, Jon Korkes, Collin Wilcox-Paxton, John Brent; **D:** Mike Nichols; **W:** Buck Henry; **C:** David Watkin.

Catherine Cookson's The Cinder Path

In Northumberland, England, 1913, Charlie MacFell (Owen) has been tyrannized by his father for years. A series of events leads him into a bad marriage (to Catherine Zeta-Jones) and then to the trenches of World War I. Like so many British television productions, solid character-based storytelling is more important than flashy visuals or action. The image is dark and grainy, again familiar to fans of *Masterpiece Theatre*, who are the target audience for this one, too. It's essentially identical to tape. —*MM* **AKA:** The Cinder Path.
Movie: 🎬🎬🎬 **DVD:** 🎬🎬½
BFS Video (Cat #30003-D, UPC #066805300035). Full frame. Dolby Digital Mono. $29.98. Keepcase. *LANG:* English. *FEATURES:* 12 chapter links.
1994 145m/C *GB* Lloyd Owen, Catherine Zeta-Jones, Maria Miles, Antony Byrne, Tom Bell; **D:** Simon Langton; **W:** Alan Seymour; **M:** Barrington Pheloung.

Catherine Cookson's The Secret

Complex historical thriller is based on Catherine Cookson's *The Harrogate Secret*. In 19th-century England, Freddie Musgrave (Buchanan) has to work through secrets hidden in his own past as a runner and messenger for criminals. Anonymous letters, diamonds, and the like are involved in the British made-for-TV film. Image quality varies from shot to shot. Overall, it's as grainy as most English imports. Sound is fine. —*MM* **AKA:** The Secret.
Movie: 🎬🎬🎬 **DVD:** 🎬🎬
BFS Video (Cat #30048-D, UPC #066805300486). Full frame. Dolby Digital Mono. $29.98. Keepcase. *LANG:* English. *FEATURES:* 12 chapter links.
2000 156m/C *GB* Colin Buchanan, June Whitfield, Stephen Moyer, Hannah Yelland, Clare Higgins; **D:** Alan Grint; **W:** T.R. Bowen; **C:** Allan Pyrah; **M:** Colin Towns.

Cave of the Living Dead

Dashing Interpol Inspector Doren (Adrian Hoven) is called in to investigate the murders of several young women in an isolated village. He finds a mysterious professor, his beautiful assistant, an old crone with all the answers, and many an irate villager. Oh yeah, and all those undead people living under the castle. There is a fun '60s hip quality to this film, and a few gem scenes, but overall the story is typical vampire fare and not worth viewing unless you're a fan of the genre. The transfer looks like it came from a print, not a negative, and while the sound is a little less than average, the dubbing is fairly inoffensive. Shot in sepia tone. —CA **AKA:** Der Fluch Der Gruenen Augen; Night of the Vampire; The Curse of Green Eyes.
Movie: 🎗️½ **DVD:** 🎗️½
Image Entertainment (Cat #ID8190GDVD, UPC #014381819020). Widescreen letterboxed. Dolby Mono. $24.99. Snapper. *LANG:* German; English. *FEATURES:* 10 chapter links.
1965 87m/B *GE YU* Adrian Hoven, Erika Remberg, Carl Mohner, Wolfgang Preiss, Karin (Karen) Field, John Kitzmiller, Akos Von Rathony; **D:** Akos Von Rathony; **W:** C.V. Rock; **C:** Hrvoje Saric.

Cecil B. Demented

Waters returns to a more hard-edged satire with this indictment against the studio system. Dorff is Cecil B. Demented, indie auteur who, along with his band of cinema terrorists, wreaks havoc on Hollywood. They kidnap A-list actress Honey Whitlock (Griffith) and force her to appear in their film—in doing so, making her the poster child for their cause. Punish bad film! No English-language remakes of foreign film! Death to those who are cinematically incorrect! Will appeal more to fans of Waters's very early work than to those who enjoyed *Serial Mom* or *Hairspray*. For the DVD, the film is given a 5.1 soundtrack, but hardly any use is made of the rear Surround tracks. The dialogue that comes from the center speaker is generally very crisp, with some instances of harshness which borders on distortion, while the right and left speakers emit the score. A full-blown 5.1 mix would have detracted from the character and message of the film, so the sound should not really be considered flawed. The picture is very sharp and detailed with problems only showing up in the darkest of scenes, where some detail is lost and the usually defined colors show a little bleed. The highlight of the disc is Waters's commentary, which is full of mostly entertaining jokes and on-the-set anecdotes, as well as his insights on how hard it is to get his kind of movie made. Also included is the HBO "making of" documentary "Canned Ham: Cecil B. Demented," featuring interviews with Waters and crew. —JO
Movie: 🎗️🎗️🎗️ **DVD:** 🎗️🎗️🎗️

Artisan Entertainment (Cat #11358, UPC #012236113584). Widescreen (1.77:1) anamorphic. Dolby Digital 5.1. $24.98. Keepcase. *LANG:* English. *CAP:* English. *FEATURES:* 24 chapter links ▪ Theatrical trailer ▪ Talent files ▪ Production notes ▪ Commentary: director John Waters ▪ "Making of" featurette: "Canned Ham."
2000 (R) 88m/C Stephen Dorff, Melanie Griffith, Jack Noseworthy, Alicia Witt, Larry Gilliard Jr., Adrian Grenier, Patty (Patricia Campbell) Hearst, Ricki Lake, Mink Stole, Robert Stevens, Basil Poledouris, Maggie Gyllenhaal, Eric M. Barry, Zenzele Uzoma, Erika Lynn Rupli, Kevin Nealon, Eric Roberts; **D:** John Waters; **W:** John Waters; **M:** Zoe Poledouris. *AWARDS: NOM:* Golden Raspberries '00: Worst Actress (Griffith).

The Cell

It's difficult to understand why this slight, trite thriller caused such controversy during its theatrical release. Yes, the film contains violent images, but it is so clichéd that they lack any real power. Add in Jennifer Lopez as the obligatory science-babe and Vincent D'Onofrio as yet another serial killer and you've got a piece of bloody fluff from the studio that brought you the *Nightmare on Elm Street* movies. The title of the accompanying documentary, "Style As Substance," is the tip-off to director Tarsan Singh's approach and his semicoherent commentary erases all doubts that he should be taken seriously. That said, the DVD looks and sounds very good. So what? —MM
Movie: 🎗️🎗️ **DVD:** 🎗️🎗️🎗️
New Line Home Video (Cat #N5150, UPC #79404351502). Widescreen (2.4:1) anamorphic. Dolby Digital 5.1 Surround Stereo; Dolby Digital Surround Stereo. $24.99. Snapper. *LANG:* English. *SUB:* English. *CAP:* English. *FEATURES:* Commentary: director Singh ▪ 8 deleted scenes ▪ 22 chapter links ▪ Isolated score ▪ Behind-the-scenes featurette ▪ Theatrical trailers ▪ Filmographies ▪ DVD-ROM game and other features.
2000 (R) 110m/C Jennifer Lopez, Vince Vaughn, Vincent D'Onofrio, Marianne Jean-Baptiste, Dylan Baker, Jake Weber, Patrick Bauchau, James Gammon, Tara Subkoff, Gareth Williams, Colton James; **D:** Tarsem; **W:** Mark Protosevich; **C:** Paul Laufer; **M:** Howard Shore.

The Cement Garden

Fatherless 15-year-old Jack (Robertson) and 16-year-old sister Julie (Gainsbourg) are afraid that they and their two younger siblings Sue (Coulthard) and Tom (Birkin) will be taken into foster care after their mother dies at home. So they bury her in the basement and try to assume normal family life. Not that this works for long—Jack and Julie give into an incestuous fascination and the household (and the film) slowly sinks into chaotic squalor. Yellowish light gives the entire production a dirty, gritty, grim quality that is difficult to appre-

ciate. DVD appears to reproduce the original image with regrettable accuracy. —MM
Movie: 🎗️🎗️ **DVD:** 🎗️🎗️½
New Yorker Video (Cat #62000, UPC #717119620042). Full frame. $29.99. Keepcase. *LANG:* English. *FEATURES:* 13 chapter links ▪ Talent files ▪ Production notes ▪ Weblinks ▪ Trailer.
1993 105m/C *FR GE GB* Charlotte Gainsbourg, Andrew Robertson, Alice Coulthard, Ned Birkin, Sinead Cusack, Hanns Zischler, Jochen Horst; **D:** Andrew Birkin; **W:** Andrew Birkin; **C:** Stephen Blackman; **M:** Ed Shearmur.

Center Stage

Realistic tale of the demanding world of a group of ballet students who have achieved their dream of entry in to the ABT academy and now strive to be accepted into the company. Along the way to this new goal, they confront affairs, bulimia, tears, triumph, and some really good dance sequences. Directed by Nicholas Hynter (*The Madness of King George, The Crucible*) and written by Carol Heikkinen, who also wrote the quirky *Empire Records,* this film could be trite for anyone who lived through the *Fame* years, but will be loved by anyone who lives to dance. Really sharp, saturated colors add nicely to the costume sequences with the reds and blacks holding their own against the creamy skin of the ballerinas. —CA
Movie: 🎗️½ **DVD:** 🎗️🎗️🎗️
Columbia Tristar Home Video (Cat #05425, UPC #043396054257). Widescreen (2.35:1) letterboxed. Dolby Digital Surround. $24.95. Keepcase. *LANG:* English; French. *SUB:* English; French. *FEATURES:* 28 chapter links ▪ Director's commentary ▪ Mandy Moore music video "I Wanna Be with You" ▪ Extended dance sequences ▪ Deleted scenes ▪ "Making of" featurette ▪ Isolated music score ▪ Theatrical trailers ▪ Talent files.
2000 (PG-13) 116m/C Peter Gallagher, Ethan Stiefel, Amanda Schull, Sascha Radetsky, Susan May Pratt, Ilia Kulik, Donna Murphy, Zoe Saldana, Debra Monk, Julie Kent, Eion Bailey, Shakiem Evans, Victor Anthony, Elizabeth Hubbard, Priscilla Lopez; **D:** Nicholas Hytner; **W:** Carol Heikkinen; **C:** Geoffrey Simpson; **M:** George Fenton.

Chained Heat 3: Hell Mountain

The *Chained Heat* in the title refers to a two-picture series of babes-behind-bars exploitation flicks. This one is set in a post-apocalyptic future where said babes are kidnapped and forced to work in mines—and to change clothes as often as possible. Both the outdoor action sequences and the soft-core scenes are standard-issue stuff for the genre. The grainy image is no improvement over VHS tape. —MM
Movie: 🎗️🎗️ **DVD:** 🎗️🎗️
MTI Home Video (Cat #1064, UPC #039414510645). Full frame. $24.95.

Keepcase. *LANG:* English. *SUB:* Spanish. *FEATURES:* 20 chapter links ▪ Trailers.
1998 (R) 97m/C Bentley Mitchum, Kate Rodger, Christopher Clarke, Karel Augusta, Noelle Balfour, Jack Scalia, Sarah Douglas; *D:* Mike Rohl; *W:* Chris Hyde; *C:* David Frazee; *M:* Peter Allen.

Chang: A Drama of the Wilderness

A farmer and his family have settled a small patch of ground on the edge of the jungle and struggle for survival against numerous wild animals. The climactic elephant stampede is still thrilling. Shot on location in Siam. Picture quality suffers a bit with this transfer; most noticeable are the lighter colors, which tend to bleed and flare quite a bit, but this is probably a result of the age and state of the film. The musical soundtrack appropriately sets the mood. However, the real gem of the disc is the informative and entertaining commentary by Rudy Behlmer. —*MJT*
Movie: ♫♫♫½ *DVD:* ♫♫♫
Image Entertainment (Cat #ID5922MLSDVD, UPC #014381592221). Full frame. Dolby Digital Stereo. $29.99. Snapper. *LANG:* Silent. *FEATURES:* 14 chapter links ▪ Commentary: film historian Rudy Behlmer ▪ Color test ▪ Production essay ▪ Original press kit.
1927 67m/B D: Merian C. Cooper, Ernest B. Schoedsack; *W:* Merian C. Cooper, Ernest B. Schoedsack; *C:* Ernest B. Schoedsack.

The Changeling

Composer John Russell (Scott) moves into an old house and discovers that he shares the place with a ghost. Scares are less important than atmosphere and characters. The source print is remarkably free from any defects or blemishes for a work of this age. The picture is very crisp and clear, although this does reveal some grain during the snowbound opening. Overall, this is a very nice video transfer, but the uneven audio leaves more to be desired. Keep the volume control handy at all times. —*ML/MM*
Movie: ♫♫½ *DVD:* ♫♫½
HBO Home Video (Cat #90630). Widescreen (1.85:1) anamorphic. Dolby Digital Surround Stereo. $19.98. Snapper. *LANG:* English. *SUB:* English; French; Spanish. *FEATURES:* Talent files.
1980 (R) 114m/C *CA* George C. Scott, Trish Van Devere, John Russell, Melvyn Douglas, Jean Marsh, John Colicos, Barry Morse, Roberta Maxwell, James B. Douglas; *D:* Peter Medak; *W:* William Gray, Diana Maddox; *C:* John Coquillon. *AWARDS:* Genie '80: Film.

Charlie's Angels

The '70s series is translated to the big screen with tongue-in-cheek humor, cheesy effects, and wire-work fight scenes. Natalie (Diaz), Alex (Liu), and Dylan (producer Barrymore) are the updat-

ed heroines; Bosley (Murray) is their loyal assistant. The action zips along at a frantic pace and contains dozens of hip self-referential jokes. The sense of self-congratulation continues into the extras where the featurette on director McG is a shameless ego massage. DVD appears to be an absolutely accurate reproduction of a riotous *Austin Powers* color scheme. The screen often looks like an explosion in a paint factory. It's well matched by a hyperactive 5.1 Surround track. —*MM*
Movie: ♫♫ *DVD:* ♫♫♫
Columbia Tristar Home Video (Cat #06017, UPC #043396060173). Widescreen (2.35:1) anamorphic. Dolby Digital 5.1 Surround Stereo; Dolby Digital Surround. $27.95. Keepcase. *LANG:* English; French. *SUB:* English; French. *FEATURES:* 3 "making of" featurettes ▪ Outtakes and bloopers ▪ 2 music videos ▪ 28 chapter links ▪ Trailers ▪ Talent files ▪ Production notes ▪ Weblink ▪ Deleted and extended scenes ▪ Commentary: director McG, cinematographer Russell Carpenter.
2000 (PG-13) 99m/C Drew Barrymore, Cameron Diaz, Lucy Alexis Liu, Bill Murray, Tim Curry, Sam Rockwell, Kelly Lynch, Crispin Glover, Matt LeBlanc, L.L. Cool J., Tom Green, Luke Wilson, Sean Whalen, Alex Trebek; *D:* McG; *W:* John August, Ryan Rowe, Ed Soloman; *C:* Russell Carpenter; *M:* Ed Shearmur; *V:* John Forsythe.

Charlie's Angels: Angels Undercover

The DVD contains two episodes from the original TV series, "To Kill an Angel" and "Night of the Strangler," featuring the original cast. Given the age of the material it is hardly surprising to see that the films are actually very grainy—something nobody would have noticed during the 1976 broadcast. The print also contains a few occasional speckles, but these never become overly noticeable. The color reproduction is faithful, nicely restoring the slightly subdued '70s look of the production. Skin tones are always presented nicely and faithful, creating an overall natural-looking quality. Blacks are deep and solid and never lose their definition. The result is an image that looks slightly dated, but is otherwise in good condition. The compression is flawless without any hints of artifacts. —*GH/MM*
Movie: ♫½ *DVD:* ♫♫
Columbia Tristar Home Video Full frame. Mono. $24.95. Keepcase. *LANG:* English; Spanish. *FEATURES:* Featurette ▪ Trailer for 2000 theatrical film.
1976 100m/C Kate Jackson, Farrah Fawcett, Jaclyn Smith, David Doyle.

Charlotte's Web

E.B. White's wonderful story about the friendship between a spider (voice of Reynolds) and a pig (Gibson) is given barely adequate treatment by the Hanna-Barbera studios. The characters lack the detail and depth that today's audiences expect of animation. DVD exhibits very

slight signs of wear in faint speckles. Otherwise, it's fine, but this is no *Babe*. —*MM*
Movie: ♫♫½ *DVD:* ♫♫
Paramount Home Video (Cat #15645, UPC #097361564548). Widescreen anamorphic. Dolby Digital Mono. $24.99. Keepcase. *LANG:* English; French. *SUB:* English. *FEATURES:* 15 chapter links ▪ Trailer ▪ "Meet the Animals" game.
1973 (G) 94m/C D: Charles A. Nichols, Iwao Takamoto; *W:* Earl Hamner; *M:* Irwin Kostal; *V:* Pamelyn Ferdin, Danny Bonaduce, Agnes Moorehead, Debbie Reynolds, Agnes Moorehead, Paul Lynde, Henry Gibson; *Nar:* Rex Allan.

Charming Billy

Why does Billy Starkman (Hayden) pick up a hunting rifle, climb to the top of a water tower, and begin shooting? That's the question the film tries to answer and it does a very good job. If it isn't as ambitious as Bogdanovich's *Targets*, it comes closer to the despair that drives such acts. The commentary track by director Pace, Hayden, and the producers is the main attraction. They approach the task with enthusiasm and talk at length about the problems of independent filmmaking. DVD image is riddled with heavy grain throughout and rough dark colors that seem to come from the original. —*MM*
Movie: ♫♫♫ *DVD:* ♫♫♫
Winstar Home Entertainment (Cat #FLV5263, UPC #720917526324). Widescreen letterboxed. $24.98. Keepcase. *LANG:* English. *FEATURES:* 16 chapter links ▪ Production credits ▪ Commentary: Pace, Hayden, producers Tom Rondinella, Joseph Infantolino.
1999 80m/C Michael Hayden, Sally Murphy, Tony Mockus Sr., Chelcie Ross; *D:* William R. Pace; *W:* William R. Pace; *C:* William Newell; *M:* David Barkley.

Chasers

Gruff Navy petty officer Rock Reilly (Berenger) and his conniving partner Eddie Devane (McNamara) are stuck escorting maximum security prisoner Toni Johnson (Eleniak) to a Charleston naval base. She turns out to be a knockout blonde whose sole purpose is to escape. Director Hopper does his usual journeyman work. His evocation of that wonderfully tacky South Carolina beach milieu is first-rate. The image is generally good and without noticeable flaws. There are a few specks in the print and some grain is evident, but overall, the transfer features good level of detail and natural looking colors. Audio is well integrated and makes good use of the Surround channels. —*GH/MM*
Movie: ♫♫ *DVD:* ♫♫½
Warner Home Video, Inc. (Cat #13363). Widescreen (1.85:1) anamorphic. Dolby Digital 5.1 Surround Stereo. $19.98. Snapper. *LANG:* English; French. *SUB:* English; French; Spanish; Portuguese. *FEATURES:* Behind-the-scenes featurette ▪ Talent files ▪ Trailers.

1994 (R) 100m/C Tom Berenger, William McNamara, Erika Eleniak, Gary Busey, Crispin Glover, Dean Stockwell, Seymour Cassel, Frederic Forrest, Marilu Henner, Dennis Hopper; **D:** Dennis Hopper; **W:** Joe Batteer, John Rice, Dan Gilroy; **C:** Ueli Steiger; **M:** Dwight Yoakam, Pete Anderson.

Chasing Amy

Holden (Affleck) and best friend Banky (Lee), New Jersey comic book artists, attend a convention where Holden is immediately attracted to fellow artist Alyssa (Adams). His ego is quickly deflated when Alyssa lets him know she's a lesbian. They try for friendship, head into a rocky romance, and then Holden discovers Alyssa has had a wild heterosexual past, which pushes all the right (or wrong) emotional buttons. Writer/director Smith supplies his trademark sharp dialogue, and the leads contribute fine performances. In an introduction, Smith admits that the DVD is a copy of the Criterion laser edition. The two even share a commentary track which, rather embarrassingly, begins with Smith vehemently cursing the then-emerging medium of DVD. It could go without saying that Criterion has done its usual splendid job with a flawless image and a full slate of well-chosen extras. —MM
Movie: 🦴🦴🦴 **DVD:** 🦴🦴🦴🦴
Criterion Collection (Cat #75, UPC #71795-1002372). Widescreen (1.85:1) anamorphic. Dolby Digital 5.1 Surround Stereo. $39.95. Keepcase. *LANG:* English. *SUB:* English. *FEATURES:* 25 chapter links • 10 deleted scenes • Trailer • Introduction by Kevin Smith • Commentary: Smith, Affleck, Mewes, producers Mosier & Hawk, et al.
1997 (R) 113m/C Ben Affleck, Joey Lauren Adams, Jason Lee, Dwight Ewell, Jason Mewes, Kevin Smith, Matt Damon; **D:** Kevin Smith; **W:** Kevin Smith; **C:** David Klein; **M:** David Pirner. *AWARDS:* Ind. Spirit '97: Screenplay, Support. Actor (Lee); *NOM:* Golden Globes '98: Actress—Mus./Comedy (Adams); Ind. Spirit '98: Film; MTV Movie Awards '98: Breakthrough Perf. (Adams), Kiss (Joey Lauren Adams/Carmen Llywellyn).

The Cheat

Please see review for *Carmen / The Cheat.*
Movie: 🦴🦴🦴
1915 55m/B Jack Dean, James Neill, Dana Ong, Hazel Childers, Fannie Ward, Sessue Hayakawa; **D:** Cecil B. DeMille; **W:** Alvin Wyckoff, Hector Turnbull. *AWARDS:* Natl. Film Reg. '93.

Cheaters

Think of this as the flip side of all the inspirational teacher flicks you've seen. In this fact-based made-for-cable story, Mr. Plecki (Daniels) has a tough time recruiting members for an academic decathlon team at his Chicago inner-city high school. He gets help from an unlikely source,

bright student Jolie Fitch (Malone, who's astonishingly good). When they gain access to a sheet of answers, what do they do? Writer/director Stockwell is at his best exploring the complexities of that question—the balance between expediency and ethics—and in the process he makes a film that's much more intelligent and funny than comparable big-screen efforts. The disc is virtually flawless with a properly detailed full-frame image. Trust me, this is one of the best sleepers around. —MM
Movie: 🦴🦴🦴½ **DVD:** 🦴🦴🦴½
HBO Home Video (Cat #91709, UPC #026359170928). Full frame. Dolby Digital Surround Stereo; Mono. $19.98. Snapper. *LANG:* English; Spanish. *SUB:* English; Spanish; French. *FEATURES:* 16 chapter links • Talent files.
2000 (R) 106m/C Jeff Daniels, Jena Malone, Paul Sorvino, Luke Edwards, Blake Heron; **D:** John Stockwell; **W:** John Stockwell; **C:** David Hennings; **M:** Paul Haslinger.

Cheech and Chong: Still Smokin'

Still smokin'? Well, not really. More like still trying to make a buck. Veteran marijuana-dazed comedy duo travel to Amsterdam to raise funds for a bankrupt film festival group by hosting a dope-a-thon. Lots of concert footage is used in an attempt to hold the slim plot together. Only for serious fans of the dopin' duo. The video transfer is adequate at best. Colors are distinct, though blacks tend to bleed and lose definition. The soundtrack fares a bit better with the reproduction of nice, crisp dialogue and a not-too-muddied musical score. —MJT **AKA:** Still Smokin'.
Movie: 🦴½ **DVD:** 🦴🦴
Paramount Home Video (Cat #02315, UPC #097360231526). Widescreen (1.66:1) anamorphic. Dolby Digital Mono. $29.99. Keepcase. *LANG:* English. *SUB:* English. *FEATURES:* 12 chapter links • Theatrical trailer.
1983 (R) 91m/C Richard "Cheech" Marin, Thomas Chong; **D:** Thomas Chong; **W:** Richard "Cheech" Marin, Thomas Chong; **C:** Harvey Harrison; **M:** George S. Clinton.

Cheech and Chong's Up in Smoke

A pair of free-spirited burn-outs team up for a tongue-in-cheek spoof of sex, drugs, and rock and roll. First and probably the best of the dopey duo's cinematic adventures was a boxoffice bonanza when released and remains a cult favorite. The video transfer is sufficient, with nice color definition (although blacks do appear muddied at times). The 5.1 soundtrack is similarly acceptable. The extras on the disc are informative and make it a better-than-average collection, although they are probably only of interest to a Cheech and Chong devotee. —MJT **AKA:** Up in Smoke.
Movie: 🦴🦴½ **DVD:** 🦴🦴🦴

Paramount Home Video (Cat #08966, UPC #097360896626). Widescreen (1.85:1) anamorphic. Dolby Digital 5.1 Surround; restored Dolby Digital Mono. $29.99. Keepcase. *LANG:* English. *SUB:* English. *FEATURES:* 11 chapter links • Commentary: Cheech Marin, director Lou Adler • Deleted scenes with commentary • Theatrical trailer.
1979 (R) 87m/C Richard "Cheech" Marin, Thomas Chong, Stacy Keach, Tom Skerritt, Edie Adams, Strother Martin, Cheryl "Rainbeaux" Smith; **D:** Lou Adler; **W:** Richard "Cheech" Marin, Thomas Chong; **C:** Gene Polito.

Cherry Falls / Terror Tract

This double feature is a treat for horror fans. In the first, a serial killer stalks the little Virginia town of Cherry Falls. All the victims are virgins. Hmmm? What are the high school students to do? More specifically, what will Sheriff Marken's (Biehn) daughter Jody (Murphy) and her persistent boyfriend do? The final result reflects both *Heathers* and *Scream*. In the second film, real estate agent Bob Carter (Ritter) shows a young couple three houses. Each comes with a nasty story about the previous owners. The humor here is a nasty mix of Tim Burton and David Lynch. Production values on both films are very good for video premieres. On DVD, then, image is more than adequate but not great. Sound is fine in the second film; subtitles would be very helpful for the whispered conversations in the first. Though the double bill makes for an economical package, the films deserve better. —MM
Movie: 🦴🦴½ **DVD:** 🦴🦴🦴
USA Home Entertainment (Cat #96306-0185-2). Widescreen. Stereo. $19.95. Keepcase. *LANG:* English. *FEATURES:* 12 chapter links each.
2000 (R) 100m/C Jay Mohr, Michael Biehn, Brittany Murphy, Candy Clark, Gabriel Mann, Keram Malicki-Sanchez, Jesse Bradford; **D:** Geoffrey Wright; **W:** Ken Selden; **C:** Anthony B. Richmond; **M:** Walter Werzowa.

Cherry 2000

Uneven futuristic adventure begins when Sam Treadwell (Andrews) short-circuits his robot girlfriend (Gidley). A replacement body for that model can be found only in the wilderness of the Zone, so he hires tracker E. Johnson (Griffith) to take him there. The disc captures the film's off-putting color scheme with unfortunate accuracy, including our heroine's virulent red hair. —MM
Movie: 🦴🦴 **DVD:** 🦴🦴½
MGM Home Entertainment (Cat #1001549, UPC #027616858597). Widescreen (1.85:1) anamorphic. Dolby Digital Surround Stereo; Mono. $19.98. Keepcase. *LANG:* English; French. *SUB:* French; Spanish. *CAP:* English. *FEATURES:* 16 chapter links • "Making of" documentary • Trailer.

1988 (PG-13) 94m/C Melanie Griffith, David Andrews, Ben Johnson, Tim Thomerson, Michael C. Gwynne, Pamela Gidley; **D:** Steve DeJarnatt; **W:** Michael Almereyda; **C:** Jacques Haitkin; **M:** Basil Poledouris.

Chicken Run

Peter Lord and Nick Park retell *The Great Escape* on Mrs. Tweedy's chicken farm. That's where the plucky Ginger (Sawalha) leads her fellow fowl in a series of escape attempts. All are futile until the rooster Rocky (Gibson) sails in from the other side of the fence. He claims that he can fly and that he can teach the others. The stop-motion animation is altogether wonderful, and it makes the transfer to DVD with absolute clarity. The film looks sharper and sounds better on DVD than it does in most theatres. Add in a veritable flock of extras and you've got a disc that kids will watch over and over. Adults may not love it as often, but they will enjoy. —*MM*
Movie: ♫♫♫♫ **DVD:** ♫♫♫♫
DreamWorks Home Entertainment (Cat #86453, UPC #667068645323). Widescreen (1.85:1) letterboxed. Dolby Digital 5.1 Surround Stereo; DTS 5.1. $26.99. Keepcase. *LANG:* English. *SUB:* English. *FEATURES:* 24 chapter links • Commentary: Lord and Park • 2 "making of" featurettes • Readalong story • DVD-ROM features • Production notes • Talent file.
2000 (G) 86m/C *GB* **D:** Nick Park, Peter Lord; **W:** Karey Kirkpatrick; **M:** John Powell, Harry Gregson-Williams; **V:** Mel Gibson, Julia Sawalha, Miranda Richardson, Jane Horrocks, Tony Haygarth, Timothy Spall, Imelda Staunton, Phil Daniels, Benjamin Whitrow, Lynn Ferguson.

Children of a Lesser God

Based on the play by Mark Medoff, this sensitive film deals with John Leeds (Hurt), an unorthodox speech teacher at a school for the deaf who falls in love with Sarah (Matlin), a beautiful and rebellious ex-student. The image has always been romantically soft, enhancing the appeal of the attractive leads and the Washington state setting. DVD does nothing to sharpen it. To have done anything to the monaural sound would have subverted Medoff's points. —*MM*
Movie: ♫♫♫ **DVD:** ♫♫½
Paramount Home Video (Cat #01839, UPC #097650183948). Widescreen anamorphic. Dolby Digital Mono. $29.99. Keepcase. *LANG:* English; French. *SUB:* English. *FEATURES:* 17 chapter links.
1986 (R) 119m/C William Hurt, Marlee Matlin, Piper Laurie, Philip Bosco, E. Katherine Kerr; **D:** Randa Haines; **W:** Hesper Anderson, Mark Medoff; **C:** John Seale; **M:** Michael Convertino. *AWARDS:* Oscars '86: Actress (Matlin); Golden Globes '87: Actress—Drama (Matlin); *NOM:* Oscars '86: Actor (Hurt), Adapt. Screenplay, Picture, Support. Actress (Laurie).

Children of the Corn

So-so adaptation of a fair Stephen King story has been the basis for three sequels to date. Go figure. The film begins with a familiar premise—city couple (Horton and Hamilton) stop in remote rural town and find it deserted. What happened to the inhabitants? Director Fritz Kiersch does a fair job of establishing his eerie atmosphere. He doesn't fare as well with a cast of child actors who are either shrill, exaggerated monsters or overly cute moppets. They can't handle writer George Goldsmith's stilted biblical language and they shouldn't have been expected to. When the big critter finally shows up—a scene which King describes in two sentences—he doesn't work too well, either. The image is very clear and sharp, showing only some slight grain and very little noise. The picture is bright and the colors are very rich and true. The 5.1 sound mix is impressive, offering a very nice Surround sound field and deep bass, which brings the explosions to life. —*MM/ML*
Movie: ♫♫ **DVD:** ♫♫♫
Anchor Bay (UPC #013131125795). Widescreen (1.85:1) anamorphic. Dolby Digital 5.1 Surround Stereo. $24.98. Keepcase. *LANG:* English. *FEATURES:* Trailer.
1984 (R) 93m/C Peter Horton, Linda Hamilton, R.G. Armstrong, John Franklin, Courtney Gains, Robbie Kiger; **D:** Fritz Kiersch; **W:** George Goldsmith; **C:** Raoul Lomas; **M:** Jonathan Elias.

China O'Brien

Gorgeous police officer China (Rothrock) returns home for a little R&R and finds that she has to kick some major butt, instead. Typical martial arts action is handled with little style. Both the fight choreography and the acting are amateurish. The slight amount of clarity that's added on DVD does the film no favors. —*MM*
Movie: ♫♫ **DVD:** ♫♫
Studio Home Entertainment (Cat #4010). Full frame. $24.95. Keepcase. *LANG:* English; Spanish. *CAP:* English. *FEATURES:* Trailer • 18 chapter links • Talent files.
1988 (R) 90m/C Cynthia Rothrock, Richard Norton, Patrick Adamson, David Blackwell, Steven Kerby, Robert Tiller, Lainie Watts, Keith Cooke; **D:** Robert Clouse; **W:** Robert Clouse; **C:** Kent Wakeford; **M:** Paul Antonelli.

Chinese Ghost Story II

Chinese horror-romance continues with Ning Tsai-shen (Leslie Cheung) and Nieh Hsiao-tsing (Joey Wong) battling more inventive special effects. Early scenes have the slightly faded, transparent look of so many Hong Kong imports. Later the image improves considerably, though some aliasing appears along bright lines and hex errors in the subtitles add unintended humor. —*MM*

Movie: ♫♫½ **DVD:** ♫♫½
Tai Seng Video Marketing (Cat #MS/DVD/101/98). Widescreen letterboxed. Dolby Digital 5.1 Surround Stereo. $49.95. Keepcase. *LANG:* Cantonese; Mandarin. *SUB:* Bahasa Malaysian & Indonesian; Chinese Simplified & Traditional; English; Japanese; Korean; Thai. *FEATURES:* Cast and crew thumbnail bios • Production notes • Trailer • 9 chapter links • Synopsis.
1990 103m/C *HK* Leslie Cheung, Joey Wong, Wu Ma, Jacky Cheung, Michelle Reis, Waise Lee; **D:** Ching Siu Tung.

Chinese Ghost Story III

A hundred years after the end of *Part II*, a monk (Leung) and a ghost (Wong) fight supernatural forces. All of the flaws found in *II* are here. They're not at all serious to fans of Hong Kong horror/comedy. —*MM*
Movie: ♫♫ **DVD:** ♫♫
Tai Seng Video Marketing (Cat #MS/DVD013/98). Widescreen letterboxed. Dolby Digital 5.1 Surround Stereo. $49.95. Keepcase. *LANG:* Cantonese; Mandarin. *SUB:* English; Simplified & Traditional Chinese; Korean; Thai; Bahasa Indonesia & Malaysia. *FEATURES:* Cast and crew thumbnail bios • Production notes • Trailer • 9 chapter links.
1991 106m/C *HK* Joey Wong, Tony Leung Chiu-Wai, Jacky Cheung; **D:** Ching Siu Tung; **W:** Roy Szeto, Tsui Hark; **C:** Moon-Tong Lau.

A Chinese Ghost Story: The Tsui Hark Animation

A mix of conventional animation and computer graphics is used in this colorful and energetic adaptation of the '80s Hong Kong Action series. Ning is unable to forget the girl of his dreams (whom he has only seen once) as he wanders from town to town collecting gold for his masters. He meets and falls in love with Shine, a ghost, who is being hunted by several odd "ghostbusters," intent on sending Shine back to where she came from. Labeled a Tsui Hark animation, the film is as entertaining as any of Hark's live-action productions and, unlike many anime, has nothing too offensive for the kiddies. The DVD is near perfect and the only thing that comes close to being a problem is a slight grain that invades some of the incredibly detailed backgrounds. The colors are stunning, the blacks are bold and true, and the soundtrack, though only stereo, is full bodied with great separation and imaging. The packaging says that the film is presented full frame but it's actually letterboxed to 1.77:1. —*JO*
Movie: ♫♫♫½ **DVD:** ♫♫♫½
Pioneer Entertainment (Cat #PEAD-010, UPC #013023033498). Widescreen (1.77:1) letterboxed. Dolby Digital Stereo. $29.98. Keepcase. *LANG:* Cantonese. *SUB:* English. *FEATURES:* 9 chapter links

• Theatrical trailer • Interview with director Tsui Hark.
1997 84m/C *HK* **W:** Tsui Hark; **M:** Ricky Ho.

Choices

A deaf athlete (Carafotes) is alienated after being banned from the football team. The film is noteworthy as the screen debut of Demi Moore in a supporting role. The DVD also has the dubious distinction of being one of the worst ever made. No menu. The image is filled with heavy artifacts. It's a poor reproduction of a deeply flawed and inexpensive original. Impossible to watch. —*MM*
Movie: ♪½ **DVD:** woof
Essex (Cat #1002). Full frame. $10.97. Keepcase. *LANG:* English.
1981 90m/C Paul Carafotes, Victor French, Lelia Goldoni, Val Avery, Dennis Patrick, Demi Moore; **D:** Rami Alon; **W:** Rami Alon; **C:** Hanania Baer; **M:** Christopher Stone.

A Christmas Carol

The Alastair Sim version of the Dickens classic is considered the best by some. Personally, I prefer the 1984 George C. Scott, but this is certainly a faithful adaptation of the story. Some wear is evident from the original print, but overall the DVD looks good. It's as grainy and thin-sounding as most non-Hollywood features of its era. None-too-faint static is audible on the soundtrack, too. The two-sided disc contains the original black-and-white film, along with a colorized version which has the bilious look that afflicts all victims of that particular form of cinematic bastardization. —*MM* *AKA:* Scrooge.
Movie: ♪♪♪½ **DVD:** ♪♪½
VCI Home Video (Cat #8215). Full frame. Dolby Digital Mono. $19.99. Keepcase. *LANG:* English. *FEATURES:* Max Fleischer cartoon "Rudolph the Red-Nosed Reindeer" • Introduction and afterword by Patrick McNee • Cast and crew thumbnail bios • Production notes • 20 chapter links. Title is also available in a colorized version (cat. # 8201) for $29.99.
1951 86m/B *GB* Alastair Sim, Kathleen Harrison, Jack Warner, Michael Hordern, Patrick Macnee, Mervyn Johns, Hermione Baddeley, Clifford Mollison, George Cole, Carol Marsh, Miles Malleson, Ernest Thesiger, Hattie Jacques, Peter Bull, Hugh Dempster; **D:** Brian Desmond Hurst; **W:** Noel Langley; **C:** C.M. Pennington-Richards; **M:** Richard Addinsell.

A Christmas Carol

Oft-told tale does have the advantage of Stewart (who has performed a one-man stage production of the Dickens saga as well as recording an audiobook) as the miserly Scrooge, who has a change of heart when visited by the ghosts of Christmas past, present, and future. It also has a strong supporting cast and special effects that enhance but don't overwhelm.

Overall the DVD is pretty strong visually, although the brightness of the outdoor scenes tends to be a little harsh and a slight bit of grain is introduced. A similar aggravation is that during the numerous CGI sequences, the picture softens and doesn't quite match the non-CGI scenes, a flaw that is a result of the original production and not the DVD itself. Most of the time, the image is quite sharp with good color and excellent blacks. The Dolby Surround track for the most part sounds like a stereo mix with only occasional use of the rear Surround, and that's mostly for musical ambience. —*JO*
Movie: ♪♪½ **DVD:** ♪♪½
Warner Home Video, Inc. (Cat #T8161, UPC #053939815129). Full frame. Dolby Surround. $19.98. Snapper. *LANG:* English. *SUB:* English; French. *CAP:* English. *FEATURES:* 25 chapter links • Behind-the-scenes documentary.
1999 120m/C Patrick Stewart, Richard E. Grant, Joel Grey, Saskia Reeves, Desmond Barrit, Bernard Lloyd, Tim Potter, Ben Tibber, Dominic West, Trevor Peacock, Liz Smith, Elizabeth Spriggs, Laura Fraser, Celia Imrie; **D:** David Hugh Jones; **W:** Peter Barnes; **C:** Ian Wilson; **M:** Stephen Warbeck.

Chuck & Buck

Sweet-natured festival hit revolves around the relationship between Chuck (Weitz) and Buck (writer White), childhood friends who have grown in opposite directions. Buck has a curious obsession with Chuck's life that is not completely appropriate. This is such a low-budget independent production that the image is absolutely nothing special. The disc's best features are the extras, and perhaps the most interesting of those is a second commentary track by director's assistant Ruben Fleischer and key grip Doug Kieffer. They really do provide an "insider's view" of the day-to-day business of the unglamourous grunt work side of the business. —*MM*
Movie: ♪♪♪ **DVD:** ♪♪½
Artisan Entertainment (Cat #11356, UPC #012236113560). Widescreen anamorphic. Dolby Digital Surround Stereo. $24.98. Keepcase. *LANG:* English. *CAP:* English. *FEATURES:* 32 chapter links • Commentary: director Miguel Arteta and Mike White • Commentary: director's assistant Ruben Fleischer, key grip Doug Kieffer • Trailer • Deleted scenes • Production notes • "The Games We Used to Play" • Talent files.
2000 (R) 99m/C Mike White, Chris Weitz, Paul Weitz, Lupe Ontiveros, Paul Sand, Beth Colt, Maya Rudolph, Mary Wigmore, Gino Buccola; **D:** Miguel Arteta; **W:** Mike White; **C:** Chuy Chavez; **M:** Joey Waronker. *AWARDS:* Natl. Bd. of Review '00: Support. Actress (Ontiveros); *NOM:* Ind. Spirit '01: Director (Arteta), Screenplay, Support. Actress (Ontiveros), Debut Perf. (White).

C.H.U.D.

Two of Hollywood's favorite political causes—homelessness and toxic waste—com-

bine to create a so-so variation on a standard monster story. A photographer (Heard) and an activist (Stern) try to convince corrupt officials to tell the truth about a series of disappearances. The makeup effects are good and director Douglas Cheek wisely keeps his monsters out of full sight most of the time. Watch for John Goodman and Jay Thomas briefly at the end. The image is clear and sharp, showing little grain or noise. There are some minor defects from the source print, but these are of little consequence. The colors are quite nicely presented, as fleshtones look natural and the glowing green ooze for the monsters looks very good. The audio on this DVD is a Dolby Digital Mono track; while this renders clear and audible dialogue, it takes some of the punch out of the musical stings and the explosions. —*MM/ML*
Movie: ♪♪½ **DVD:** ♪♪½
Anchor Bay (UPC #013131132397). Widescreen (1.77:1) anamorphic. Dolby Digital Mono. $24.98. Keepcase. *LANG:* English. *FEATURES:* Commentary: Cheek, Abbot, Stern, Heard, and Curry • Trailer • Stills gallery.
1984 (R) 90m/C John Heard, Daniel Stern, Christopher Curry, Kim Greist, John Goodman, Jay Thomas, Eddie Jones, Sam McMurray, Justin Hall, Cordis Heard, Michael O'Hare, Vic Polizos; **D:** Douglas Cheek; **W:** Parnell Hall; **C:** Peter Stein; **M:** David A. Hughes.

The Cider House Rules

Homer Wells (Maguire) grows up in the St. Clouds, Maine, orphanage, with his mentor, Dr. Larch (Caine) teaching Homer everything about caring for the children, delivering babies, and performing (illegal) abortions (which Homer refuses to do). But in 1943, when flyboy Wally (Rudd) shows up with girlfriend Candy (Theron), Homer gets his chance to see something of the world. He winds up an apple picker and, when Wally returns to the war, Candy's new beau. But Homer has a lot to learn about making—and living by—your own rules. Irving wrote his first screenplay from his novel. Most striking in the DVD transfer of the film are the colors, which are highly detailed and accurate—the scenes in the orchard are gorgeous. The other elements of the image are equally impressive: sharp image; super-true blacks; vivid contrast and comfortable brightness; and not a hint of digital grain or artifacts. There isn't much in the way of Surround effects, but it really doesn't have a negative effect on this film. The commentary is excellent, with author Irving's insights on the film, and his feelings on Hallstrom's input, being the most interesting. Unfortunately, the "making of" featurette is a little lame, coming across as more of a film highlight reel. —*JO*
Movie: ♪♪♪½ **DVD:** ♪♪♪½
Buena Vista Home Entertainment (Cat #18306, UPC #717952004918). Widescreen (2.35:1) anamorphic. Dolby Digital

5.0 Surround. $32.99. Keepcase. *LANG:* English; French. *SUB:* Spanish. *CAP:* English. *FEATURES:* 37 chapter links • Theatrical trailer • TV spots • Talent files • Commentary: Hallstrom, Irving, producer Richard N. Gladstein • "Making of" featurette.

1999 (PG-13) 125m/C Tobey Maguire, Charlize Theron, Michael Caine, Delroy Lindo, Paul Rudd, Erykah Badu, Kathy Baker, Jane Alexander, Kieran Culkin, Kate Nelligan, K. Todd Freeman, Heavy D, J.K. Simmons, John Irving; **D:** Lasse Hallstrom; **W:** John Irving; **C:** Oliver Stapleton; **M:** Rachel Portman. *AWARDS:* Oscars '99: Adapt. Screenplay, Support. Actor (Caine); Screen Actors Guild '99: Support. Actor (Caine); *NOM:* Oscars '99: Art Dir./Set Dec., Director (Hallstrom), Film, Film Editing, Orig. Score; British Acad. '99: Support. Actor (Caine); Golden Globes '00: Screenplay, Support. Actor (Caine); Screen Actors Guild '99: Cast; Writers Guild '99: Adapt. Screenplay.

CinderElmo

The Cinderella story is retold with Elmo and all of your favorite Sesame Street characters. Guest appearances are provided by French Stewart and Keri Russell, Oliver Platt and Kathy Najimy. Clear and with strong colors, the image on this DVD is sure to please young and old alike. The black level is very good and highlights are always warm and well-balanced. Audio is well produced and always understandable, with a rather good frequency response. It is lacking a bit in the lower ends however. —*GH*

Movie: ♫♫♫ **DVD:** ♫♫♫
Sony Wonder Full frame. Dolby Digital Stereo. $19.99. Keepcase. *LANG:* English. *SUB:* English; Spanish. *FEATURES:* Behind-the-scenes footage • Trivia game • Highlights.

2000 65m/C French Stewart, Keri Russell, Oliver Platt, Kathy Najimy; **V:** Frank Oz.

Cinema Combat: Hollywood Goes to War

Documentary produced by Fox Television and American Movie Classics is a superb introduction to the various ways that the movies have used war. The producers combine newsreel and other actual film with Hollywood studio interpretations of the same and similar events. Their purpose is to show how the two have influenced each other, with an emphasis on propaganda. Clips come from *Wings, Triumph of the Will, Guadalcanal Diary, Apocalypse Now,* and several others. I recommend it without question to anyone who's interested in war films. Naturally, image quality varies with the source material but this is generally excellent. The oldest footage (the 1898 sinking of the *Maine* in Havana harbor) looks rough as does much of the material from World War I, but don't let that dissuade you. —*MM*

Movie: ♫♫♫½ **DVD:** ♫♫♫
Image Entertainment (Cat #ID8764FSDVD, UPC #014381876420). Full frame. Dolby Digital Stereo. $24.99. Snapper. *LANG:* English. *FEATURES:* 16 chapter links.

1998 101m/C D: Edith Becker; **W:** Dorothy Rompalske; **Nar:** Martin Sheen.

Cinema's Dark Side Collection

This collection of three lesser-known films noir (well, semi-noir) is fascinating for fans. The version of *Impact* is essentially the same as the Image disc. (Please see review.) *The Second Woman* is *Rebecca*-redux from the opening voice-over narration. Robert Young is an architect who may do terrible things during bouts of depression that lead to black-outs. In *They Made Me a Criminal,* John Garfield is a boxer who's led to believe that he killed a man while he was drunk. Director Busby Berkeley was more famous for his opulent musicals. Defects are relatively minor in all three—faint vertical scratches, hiss on the soundtrack of *Criminal.* As a group, they look and sound remarkably good for films of their age. —*MM*

Movie: ♫♫♫ **DVD:** ♫♫♫
SlingShot Entertainment (Cat #TDVD9852, UPC #017078985221). Full frame. Dolby Digital Mono. $24.99. Large jewelcase. *LANG:* English. *FEATURES:* 43 chapter links.

2000 ?m/C

Circus

Leo (Hannah) and Lily (Janssen) are your average British criminals looking for one last score so they can retire and drink margaritas. They are easily drawn into an intricate mobster scam that, naturally, involves lots of guns, violence, and betrayals. Comparisons to *Lock, Stock and 2 Smoking Barrels* are not out of place. On DVD, the British production looks and sounds superb. The image is exceptionally well detailed. Sound is fine. —*MM*

Movie: ♫♫♫ **DVD:** ♫♫♫½
Columbia Tristar Home Video (Cat #05076, UPC #043396050761). Widescreen (1.85:1) anamorphic. Dolby Digital 5.1 Surround Stereo; Dolby Surround Stereo. $24.95. Keepcase. *LANG:* English; French. *SUB:* English; French; Spanish; Portuguese; Chinese; Korean; Thai. *FEATURES:* 28 chapter links • Commentary: producer, writer • "Making of" featurette • Deleted scenes • Talent files • Theatrical trailers.

2000 (R) 95m/C *GB* John Hannah, Famke Janssen, Peter Stormare, Brian Conley, Eddie Izzard, Fred Ward, Amanda Donohoe, Ian Burfield, Tommy (Tiny) Lister, Neil Stuke; **D:** Rob Walker; **W:** David Logan; **C:** Ben Seresin; **M:** Simon Boswell.

Citizen X

Viktor Burakov (Rea) is a beleaguered forensics expert in rural Russia who realizes that a serial killer is responsible for the mutilated bodies of children he is examining. But party officials refuse to admit that such creatures can exist in the Soviet Union. (The story is based on events that took place in the 1980s.) Burakov's only ally is Col. Fetisov (Sutherland), who's adept at political maneuvering, but it takes them eight frustrating years to bring the grisly killer to justice. The film was made for cable in Budapest, Hungary, and so the full-frame image gains little on DVD, beyond the sound and subtitle options. —*MM*

Movie: ♫♫♫ **DVD:** ♫♫½
HBO Home Video (Cat #91185). Full frame. Dolby Digital Surround Stereo; Mono. $19.98. Snapper. *LANG:* English. *SUB:* English; French; Spanish. *FEATURES:* 16 chapter links • Talent files.

1995 (R) 100m/C Stephen Rea, Donald Sutherland, Jeffrey DeMunn, John Wood, Joss Ackland, Max von Sydow, Ralph Nossek, Imelda Staunton, Radu Amzulrescu, Czeskaw Grocholski, Ion Caramitru, Andras Balint, Tusse Silberg; **D:** Chris Gerolmo; **W:** Chris Gerolmo; **C:** Robert Fraisse; **M:** Randy Edelman.

City of Industry

Small-timers Lee Egan (Hutton) and Jorge Montana (Dominguez) have planned a Palm Springs jewel store robbery. Skip Kovich (Dorff) is brought in to drive. Lee's brother Roy (Keitel) arrives by bus to fill out the gang, and that's all that anyone should know about what's going to happen. Writer Ken Solarz and director John Irvin provide one surprising jolt early on, and to reveal it would spoil the rest. The image ranges between very good and excellent; Surround is used sparingly but effectively. In short, this is an unassuming noir sleeper that's much more enjoyable than many more heavily hyped star vehicles. Seek it out. —*MM*

Movie: ♫♫♫ **DVD:** ♫♫♫
MGM Home Entertainment (Cat #1001550, UPC #027616858603). Widescreen (1.85:1) anamorphic. Dolby Digital Surround Stereo. $19.98. Keepcase. *LANG:* English; French. *SUB:* French; Spanish. *CAP:* English. *FEATURES:* 16 chapter links • Trailer.

1996 (R) 97m/C Harvey Keitel, Stephen Dorff, Famke Janssen, Timothy Hutton, Michael Jai White, Wade Dominguez, Reno Wilson; **D:** John Irvin; **W:** Ken Solarz; **C:** Thomas Burstyn; **M:** Stephen Endelman.

City of Women

Those who are not in tune with the Maestro's sexual preoccupations may not be amused by this curious little fantasy that can almost be seen as a continuation of *8 1/2.* It begins with Snaporaz (Mastroianni) drowsing on a train. He may have an erotic encounter with a mysterious woman and then he impulsively follows her into the woods where he finds himself in a feminist theme park replete with roller rink and screening room. It's a delightfully bawdy if lesser work in the Fellini canon. DVD

image ranges between very good and excellent though it has always been on the soft side. Sound is fine; the optional subtitles are easy to read. —*MM* **AKA:** La Citte delle Donne.
Movie: ♫♫♫½ **DVD:** ♫♫♫
New Yorker Video (Cat #DVD 32000, UPC #717119320041). Widescreen letterboxed. $29.95. Keepcase. *LANG:* Italian. *SUB:* English. *FEATURES:* 20 chapter links • Talent files • Promotional short • "Making of" featurette • Photo gallery.
1981 (R) 140m/C *IT* Marcello Mastroianni, Ettore Manni, Anna Prucnall, Bernice Stegers; **D:** Federico Fellini; **W:** Federico Fellini; **C:** Giuseppe Rotunno; **M:** Luis Bacalov.

City Slickers

Three middle-aged New Yorkers go to a cattle ranch for a vacation that turns into an arduous character-building ordeal. Crystal, Stern, and Kirby are fine in the leads, but Jack Palance won a Best Supporting Actor Oscar for his performance as Curly, the wise, salty old cowpoke. Slater is fetching as the lone female vacationer on the cattle drive. Boxoffice hit makes a respectable if unspectacular transition to DVD with an image that captures the wide western landscapes without any noticeable flaws. Sound is fine, but again, nothing memorable. —*MM*
Movie: ♫♫♫ **DVD:** ♫♫½
MGM Home Entertainment (Cat #100 1825, UPC #027616860958). Widescreen (1.85:1) anamorphic. Dolby Digital Surround. Mono. $19.98. Keepcase. *LANG:* English; French. *SUB:* French; Spanish. *FEATURES:* 16 chapter links • Trailer.
1991 (PG-13) 114m/C Billy Crystal, Daniel Stern, Bruno Kirby, Patricia Wettig, Helen Slater, Jack Palance, Noble Willingham, Tracey Walter, Josh Mostel, David Paymer, Bill Henderson, Jeffrey Tambor, Phill Lewis, Kyle Secor, Yeardley Smith, Jayne Meadows; **D:** Ron Underwood; **W:** Lowell Ganz, Babaloo Mandel; **C:** Dean Semler; **M:** Marc Shaiman. *AWARDS:* Oscars '91: Support. Actor (Palance); Golden Globes '92: Support. Actor (Palance); MTV Movie Awards '92: Comedic Perf. (Crystal).

The Claim

Visually stunning but meandering western is an adaptation of Thomas Hardy's *The Mayor of Casterbridge*. In the spectacular Sierra Nevada mountains, a railroad representative (Bentley) has to decide where the line will build a station. At the same time, the town's mayor (Mullan) is shocked by the arrival of two women (Kinski and Polley). The evocation of a wintry frontier town is as strong as Robert Altman's in *McCabe & Mrs. Miller*. Moody exteriors look fine and so do the carefully illuminated interiors. Sound is fine, too. Somehow, this one missed a theatrical audience. It ought to do well on home video. Recommended. —*MM*

Movie: ♫♫♫ **DVD:** ♫♫♫
MGM Home Entertainment (Cat #10 01840, UPC #027616861108). Widescreen (2.35:1) anamorphic. Dolby Digital 5.1 Surround Stereo. $26.98. Keepcase. *LANG:* English; Spanish. *SUB:* French; Spanish. *FEATURES:* 16 chapter links • Trailer.
2000 (R) 120m/C Peter Mullan, Nastassia Kinski, Sarah Polley, Wes Bentley, Milla Jovovich, Sean McGinley, Julian Richings; **D:** Michael Winterbottom; **W:** Frank Cottrell-Boyce; **C:** Alwin Kuchler; **M:** Michael Nyman.

The Clan of the Cave Bear

A scrawny cavegirl (Hannah) is taken by Neanderthals after her mom is swallowed up by an earthquake. (Really!) Hannah is lifeless as the primitive gamine, and the film is similarly DOA. Despite a script by John Sayles, from Jean Auel's popular novel, it's ponderous and only unintentionally funny. Some artifacts appear in bright water and snowfields. They are a welcome distraction from the ludicrous Neanderthal makeup. —*MM*
Movie: ♫½ **DVD:** ♫♫½
Warner Home Video, Inc. (Cat #13753). Widescreen (2.35:1) letterboxed; full frame. Dolby Digital Stereo. $19.98. Snapper. *LANG:* English. *SUB:* French. *CAP:* English. *FEATURES:* 31 chapter links.
1986 (R) 100m/C Daryl Hannah, James Remar, Pamela Reed, John Doolittle, Thomas G. Waites; **D:** Michael Chapman; **W:** John Sayles; **C:** Jan De Bont; **M:** Alan Silvestri. *AWARDS: NOM:* Oscars '86: Makeup.

Class

Prep-school student Skip (Lowe) discovers that his mother (Bissett) is the lover whom his shy roommate (McCarthy) has bragged about. Everyone in the cast was slumming in this crude teen sex comedy. The clarity of the Dolby mono somehow makes voices sound poorly dubbed. Overall, the image is thin with blacks that lack definition. It's a so-so transfer of a so-so movie. —*MM*
Movie: ♫♫ **DVD:** ♫♫
MGM Home Entertainment (Cat #100 1184, UPC #027616854759). Widescreen anamorphic; full frame. Dolby Digital Mono. $19.98. Keepcase. *LANG:* English; Spanish. *SUB:* French; Spanish. *FEATURES:* 9 chapter links.
1983 (R) 98m/C Jacqueline Bisset, Rob Lowe, Andrew McCarthy, Cliff Robertson, John Cusack, Stuart Margolin, Casey Siemaszko; **D:** Lewis John Carlino; **W:** Jim Kouf, David Greenwalt; **C:** Ric Waite; **M:** Elmer Bernstein.

Cleopatra

Victorious Julius Caesar (Harrison) pursues the defeated Pompey to Alexandria, where civil war is threatened between Cleopatra (Taylor) and her brother, who are

supposed to be harmonious joint rulers. Seduced by Cleopatra's allure, Caesar takes her for his lover and chooses her side of the matter. All would be settled, if it were not for the entrance of Marc Antony (Burton) into the picture. Hours follow of engrossing court intrigue, romantic double-crosses, barge seductions, and wars waged to appease the pride of spurned romance, all with the enigmatic Cleopatra at the center. Visual interest and depth effects seem to be handled more by color than by lighting itself; Egypt and Rome look to have been bathed in ever-present kleig lights. It's hard to find a shadow in the interiors—where's all that light coming from? On DVD, this sumptuous look is almost an asset—the picture practically pops off the screen, and with the extra detail of 16:9 enhancement, you can find yourself studying the tones of Taylor's skin or the perfect complexion of her face. The show looks that good. Fox has wisely put this four-hour, eight-minute monster on two discs, and it pays off with a good fat bit rate to keep the image from deteriorating. The third disc is chock-full of goodies for special edition fans: the new documentary; a featurette from the time of the film's release; premiere footage; commentaries by two of Mankeiwicz's sons, Martin Landau, and Jack Brodsky; and galleries of stills, design, and costume concept art. —*GE*
Movie: ♫♫♫ **DVD:** ♫♫♫½
20th Century Fox Home Entertainment (Cat #20011483, UPC #024543014836). Widescreen (2.35:1) anamorphic. Dolby Digital 5.1 Surround Stereo; Dolby Digital Surround. $26.98. Keepcase. *LANG:* English; French. *CAP:* English. *FEATURES:* 52 chapter links • Commentary: Chris and Tom Mankeiwicz, Martin Landau, Jack Brodsky • Stills gallery • 2 documentaries • Archival footage.
1963 248m/C Elizabeth Taylor, Richard Burton, Rex Harrison, Roddy McDowall, Martin Landau, Pamela Brown, Michael Hordern, Kenneth Haigh, Andrew Keir, Hume Cronyn, Carroll O'Connor; **D:** Joseph L. Mankeiwicz; **W:** Joseph L. Mankeiwicz; **C:** Leon Shamroy; **M:** Alex North. *AWARDS:* Oscars '63: Art Dir./Set Dec., Color, Color Cinematog., Costume Des. (C), Visual FX; Natl. Bd. of Review '63: Actor (Harrison); *NOM:* Oscars '63: Actor (Harrison), Film Editing, Picture, Sound, Orig. Score.

Clerks Uncensored

Underrated and underappreciated animated version of Smith's *Clerks*. While the two episodes that actually found their way onto network television made the show look like little more than an ego project, the additional four episodes collected on these discs prove that the show is a vital addition to the Kevin Smith canon. The video transfer is excellent and features crisp colors and extremely well-defined blacks. The soundtrack reproduces the original broadcast quality quite admirably. As with most Kevin Smith discs, the extras are astounding in both amount and quali-

ty. Of particular note are the "animatics" that follow the creative process of each episode through early drawings and animations. Although the commentary track and the introductions to each episode provided by Jay and Silent Bob are thoroughly enjoyable, you should be aware that the raunchy content therein is responsible for the disc's rating. —*MJT* **AKA:** Clerks: The Animated Series.
Movie: ♫♫♫ **DVD:** ♫♫♫½
Miramax Pictures Home Video (Cat #21707, UPC #786936145335). Full frame. Dolby Digital Surround. $29.99. Keepcase. *LANG:* English. *FEATURES:* 25 chapter links ▪ Intros to each episode by Jay and Silent Bob ▪ Animatics ▪ Commentary: Kevin Smith, Scott Mosier, Dave Mandel ▪ Commentary: Chris Bailey, Brian O'Halloran, Jeff Anderson, Jason Mewes ▪ Character development featurette ▪ "The Clerks Style" featurette ▪ "Super Bowl" TV spot ▪ Film festival trailer ▪ DVD-ROM: script/storyboard synch. viewer, character profiles, weblink.
2000 (R) 130m/C V: Jeff Anderson, Brian O'Halloran, Jason Mewes, Kevin Smith, Alec Baldwin.

Cliffhanger [2 CS]

Expert mountain climber Gabe Walker (Stallone) is pressed into service when criminal mastermind Eric Qualen (Lithgow) steals a load of cash from the Denver Mint and then loses it. The mountain settings are vertiginously well realized, and much of the stuntwork is exceptional. The plot, however, is poor. Every high-altitude movie cliché you've ever seen is dusted off and recycled: the avalanche, the landslide, the cave filled with bats, the loose suspension bridge, the fraying rope. On their commentary track, Stallone and Harlin try to treat this piffle seriously. The DVD image is very good. Aliasing in bright exteriors is often a problem for the medium but it's not here. Sound is first-rate, too, and the extras are well chosen. —*MM*
Movie: ♫♫♫ **DVD:** ♫♫♫
Columbia Tristar Home Video (Cat #52232, UPC #043396522329). Widescreen (2.35:1) anamorphic. Dolby Digital 5.1 Surround Stereo; Dolby Digital Surround Stereo. $29.95. Keepcase. *LANG:* English; Spanish; Portuguese. *SUB:* English; Spanish; Portuguese; Cantonese. *FEATURES:* 28 chapter links ▪ Commentary: Harlin and Stallone ▪ Technical commentary track ▪ "Making of" featurette ▪ Special effects: how it was done ▪ Two deleted scenes ▪ Storyboard comparisons ▪ Photo galleries ▪ Trailers ▪ Talent files.
1993 (R) 113m/C Sylvester Stallone, John Lithgow, Michael Rooker, Janine Turner, Rex Linn, Caroline Goodall, Leon, Paul Winfield, Ralph Waite, Craig Fairbrass, Michelle Joyner, Max Perlich; **D:** Renny Harlin; **W:** Sylvester Stallone, Michael France; **C:** Alex Thomson; **M:** Trevor Jones. *AWARDS:* NOM: Oscars '93: Sound, Sound FX Editing, Visual FX; MTV Movie Awards '94: Action Seq.

Clockin' Green

Ultra-low-budget action picture doesn't measure up to even the lowest standards. The story of two black women (Sylvester and Joyce) who rob banks features semi-professional acting and pitiful production values. The weapons sound like toy cap pistols. Colors shift within the same shot. Heavy grain and pixelation is visible throughout the no-frills (not even a menu) disc. —*MM*
Movie: ♫ **DVD:** woof
York Entertainment (Cat #YPD-1035, UPC #750723103525). Full frame. $19.98. Keepcase. *LANG:* English.
2000 ?m/C Ella Joyce, Joyce Sylvester, Charles Weldon; **D:** Juney Smith.

Close Encounters of the Third Kind [CE]

This Collector's Edition of Steven Spielberg's first-contact epic comes in an impressive, strangely constructed package made mostly of card stock that doesn't look too durable. Disc one is the movie, which is very handsomely presented with excellent sound and image. Disc two has the extras, several trailers, a worn-looking original featurette, and a 1997 documentary done for the laserdisc of the 2nd Special Edition, which received a very limited release. (Owners of the old Criterion boxset laserdisc are advised to hang on to it, for this DVD has none of its still galleries or effects interviews.) The best extras on the DVD are the deleted scenes. Almost all would have helped the movie. The Nearys' visit to a neighborhood picnic looks a little forced and too critical of the suburbanites, but Roy Neary's (Dreyfuss) adventures on the night of the blackouts are great. The documentary also has some deleted scene bits that are rarely seen—all of them very interesting, especially all of the failed attempts at filming aliens, and Neary entering the Mothership floating on wires. To be honest, even when I watch this "final" version I'm confused by what's there and what's not, and what version it was in. Spielberg very clearly says (in 1997) that showing the inside of the Mothership was a mistake. In 1980 he behaved as if it were the greatest idea ever. There's something to be said for the old "one movie, one negative" rule. —*GE*
Movie: ♫♫♫½ **DVD:** ♫♫♫½
Columbia Tristar Home Video (Cat #12649, UPC #043396126497). Widescreen (2.35:1) anamorphic. Dolby Digital 5.1 Surround Stereo; DTS Surround Stereo. $27.98. Special packaging. *LANG:* English; French; Spanish; Portuguese. *SUB:* English; French; Spanish; Portuguese; Chinese; Korean; Thai. *FEATURES:* "Making of" documentary ▪ Original featurette ▪ 11 deleted scenes (some workprint) ▪ Trailers ▪ Filmographies.
1977 (PG) 152m/C Richard Dreyfuss, Teri Garr, Melinda Dillon, Francois Truffaut, Bob Balaban, Cary Guffey, J. Patrick McNamara; **D:** Steven Spielberg; **W:** Steven Spiel-

berg; **C:** Vilmos Zsigmond; **M:** John Williams. *AWARDS:* Oscars '77: Cinematog., Sound FX Editing; AFI '98: Top 100; NOM: Oscars '77: Art Dir./Set Dec., Director (Spielberg), Film Editing, Sound, Support. Actress (Dillon), Orig. Score.

Clue

The popular board game's characters must unravel a night of murder at a spooky Victorian mansion. The entire cast seems to be subsisting on sugar, with wild eyes and frantic movements the order of the day. Butler Curry best survives the uneven script and direction. Warren is appealing too. The theatrical version played with three alternative endings; video versions contain all three. Some grain is visible on occasion during the presentation but apart from that, the print is in perfect condition and the transfer features a very high level of detail even in the many dark scenes. It is great to see that the transfer has strong blacks with good definition throughout. Never do you lose details in the shadows and with the good highlights, the transfer always looks pleasing and balanced. Colors nicely reproduce the quirky and warm atmosphere of the film that is highly reminiscent of classic detective stories, and fleshtones are always natural. Both mono language tracks are equally well produced and, despite their lack of spatial integration, sound rather natural. —*GH/MM*
Movie: ♫♫½ **DVD:** ♫♫½
Paramount Home Video (Cat #18407). Widescreen (1.85:1) anamorphic. Dolby Digital Mono. $29.99. Keepcase. *LANG:* English; French. *FEATURES:* Trailer.
1985 (PG) 96m/C Lesley Ann Warren, Tim Curry, Martin Mull, Madeline Kahn, Michael McKean, Christopher Lloyd, Eileen Brennan, Howard Hesseman, Lee Ving, Jane Wiedlin, Colleen Camp, Bill Henderson; **D:** Jonathan Lynn; **W:** John Landis, Jonathan Lynn; **C:** Victor Kemper; **M:** John Morris.

Cockfighter

Frank Mansfield (Oates) has taken a vow of silence until one of his birds wins the "championship" of cockfighting. He does provide voice-over narration to this rarely seen curiosity. But if you listen to that, you'll miss an excellent commentary track from director Hellman, production assistant Steven Gaydos, and Dennis Bartok. They spend much of their time talking about the film's curious background and history, and the documentary nature of the production. It's certainly one of Warren Oates's best roles and they give him the full credit he deserves. The DVD image is remarkably good for a Roger Corman–produced film that's more than a quarter century old. —*MM* **AKA:** Gamblin' Man; Born to Kill; Wild Drifters.
Movie: ♫♫♫ **DVD:** ♫♫♫
Anchor Bay (Cat #DV11318, UPC #013131131895). Widescreen (1.77:1) anamorphic. Dolby Digital Mono. $24.99.

Keepcase. *LANG:* English. *FEATURES:* Commentary: Hellman, Gaydos, Bartok • Liner notes by Steven Davies • Trailer • TV spot • 54-minute Warren Oates featurette • Talent files.
1974 (R) 84m/C Warren Oates, Harry Dean Stanton, Richard B. Shull, Troy Donahue, Millie Perkins, Robert Earl Jones, Warren Finnerty, Ed Begley Jr., Charles Willeford; *D:* Monte Hellman; *W:* Charles Willeford; *C:* Nestor Almendros; *M:* Michael Franks.

Coffy

In the role that made her a star, Pam Grier plays Coffy, a nurse who takes revenge on the drug pushers who hooked her little sister. On his commentary track, Jack Hill talks about the many contributions that she made to the script and her overall importance to the collaborative effort. All of the grain in the image comes from the original. Mono sound is weak. —*MM*
Movie: ♫♫♫ *DVD:* ♫♫½
MGM Home Entertainment (Cat #1001463, UPC #027616857835). Widescreen (1.85:1) letterboxed. Dolby Digital Mono. $19.98. Keepcase. *LANG:* English; French; Spanish. *SUB:* French; Spanish. *FEATURES:* 16 chapter links • Trailer • Commentary: Jack Hill.
1973 (R) 91m/C Pam Grier, Booker Bradshaw, Robert DoQui, Allan Arbus; *D:* Jack Hill; *W:* Jack Hill; *C:* Paul Lohmann; *M:* Roy Ayers.

Cold Blooded

A serial killer is at work in an unnamed city (Calgary) in the middle of a bitter winter. A reporter gets a tip that says the police themselves may be involved. Grain is heavy but acceptable in this video premiere. Script avoids the most egregious clichés of the genre, and it's generally well acted. Most importantly, the cold sense of place is very strong. DVD image and sound are equal to tape. —*MM*
Movie: ♫♫½ *DVD:* ♫♫
MTI Home Video (Cat #BE50038, UPC #619935403833). Full frame. $24.95. Keepcase. *LANG:* English. *SUB:* Spanish. *FEATURES:* 20 chapter links • Trailers • Talent files.
2000 (R) 94m/C Michael Moriarty, Patti LuPone, John Kapelos, Gloria Reuben; *D:* Randy Bradshaw; *W:* Ian Adams; *C:* Dean Bennett; *M:* Tim McCauley.

Cold Sweat

A brutal drug trader (Bronson) takes violent revenge after his wife (Ullman) is captured by a drug boss's moronic henchmen. Typical Bronson flick boasts superior supporting cast with Ullman and Mason, but mediocre writing and direction. This slapdash bargain-bin disc is atrocious at any price. No menu. The dim dark image is much worse than a substandard VHS tape. —*MM AKA:* L'Uomo Dalle Due Ombre; De la Part des Copains.
Movie: ♫♫ *DVD:* woof

Essex (Cat #1006). Full frame. Dolby Digital Mono. $10.97. Slipcase. *LANG:* English.
1971 (PG) 94m/C *IT FR* Charles Bronson, Jill Ireland, Liv Ullmann, James Mason; *D:* Terence Young; *W:* Albert Simonin, Shimon Wincelberg; *C:* Jean Rabier; *M:* Michel Magne.

The Colony

Aliens planning an Earth invasion decide to test humankind by abducting four people and observing their survival skills. The formulaic plot is leavened by some humor, but not enough. The film was made for the Sci-Fi Channel and so its unsurprising production values gain nothing from an adequate digital transfer. Neither image nor sound is appreciably superior to broadcast TV. —*MM*
Movie: ♫½ *DVD:* ♫½
Trimark Home Video (Cat #6892). Full frame. Dolby Digital Stereo. $24.99. Keepcase. *LANG:* English. *SUB:* French; Spanish. *FEATURES:* Trailer.
1998 (R) 94m/C Isabella Hofmann, Michael Weatherly, Cristi Conaway, Eric Allen Kramer, Jeff Kober, James Avery, Clare Salstrom; *D:* Peter Geiger; *W:* Peter Geiger, Richard Kletter; *C:* Zoltan David; *M:* Paul Rabjohns.

Colorz of Rage

Give writer/producer/director/star Resteghini credit for good intentions and an ability to create good characters. His story of an interracial relationship between Tony (Resteghini) and Debbie (Richards) covers familiar ground, but the New York locations have a gritty feel that's accentuated by the rough production values. The film is such a low-budget affair that it really gains little on DVD. A commentary track would have been a welcome addition. —*MM*
Movie: ♫♫½ *DVD:* ♫♫
A-PIX Entertainment Inc. (Cat #APX27035, UPC #783722703533). Full frame. Dolby Digital Stereo. $19.98. Keepcase. *LANG:* English. *SUB:* Spanish. *FEATURES:* 12 chapter links • Trailers.
1997 91m/C Dale Resteghini, Nicki Richards, Cheryl "Pepsii" Riley, Don Wallace; *D:* Dale Resteghini; *W:* Dale Resteghini; *C:* Martin Ahlgren; *M:* Tony Prendatt.

Come and Get It

Howard Hawks and William Wyler directed this adaptation of the Edna Ferber novel about lumber king Barney Glasgow (Arnold) battling his son (McCrea) for the love of Lotta Morgan (Farmer, in her most important role). Though some artifacts are visible in high-contrast snow scenes and one plaid top flashes, this is a first-rate disc with excellent black-and-white photography. Some of the explosions and logging scenes have a sense of reality that today's computer-enhanced wonders cannot approach. Sound is fine. —*MM AKA:* Roaring Timber.

Movie: ♫♫♫½ *DVD:* ♫♫♫
HBO Home Video (Cat #90660). Full frame. Mono; Stereo. $24.98. Snapper. *LANG:* English; German; Italian. *SUB:* French; Spanish. *FEATURES:* Cast and crew thumbnail bios • Trailer • 22 chapter links.
1936 99m/B Frances Farmer, Edward Arnold, Joel McCrea, Walter Brennan, Andrea Leeds, Charles Halton; *D:* William Wyler, Howard Hawks; *W:* Jules Furthman, Jane Murfin; *C:* Rudolph Mate, Gregg Toland; *M:* Alfred Newman. *AWARDS:* Oscars '36: Support. Actor (Brennan); *NOM:* Oscars '36: Film Editing.

Comedy Noir

In the first half of this double bill, John Huston's *Beat the Devil*, each person on a slow boat to Africa has a scheme to beat the other passengers to the uranium-rich land which they all hope to claim. This unusual black comedy did not fare well when released theatrically but over the years, it has become the epitome of spy spoofs. It is by far the better-looking of these two. The low-contrast black-and-white photography is generally good. A light hiss is audible throughout and sound tends to be thin. Performances are terrific. Lubitsch's *That Uncertain Feeling* is all but unwatchable. From minor registration problems in the opening credits, things get worse with a very muddy image riddled with heavy artifacts. (See separate entries for credits.) Both titles are available from other distributors. —*MM*
Movie: ♫♫½ *DVD:* ♫♫
SlingShot Entertainment (Cat #DVD9115, UPC #017078911527). Full frame. Dolby Digital Mono. $19.99. Large jewelcase. *LANG:* English. *FEATURES:* 35 chapter links.
2000 ?m/C

Comic Act

The world of London stand-up comedy is the setting for a surprisingly sexy look at life beyond the microphone. Gus (Schneider) and Jay (Mullarkey) are struggling until Alex (Webster) joins their act. Her combination of intelligence and unembarrassed sexuality makes them a hit with audiences, and with that come all the temptations (and all the clichés) of show business. Yes, the same story has been told countless times, but this version is fresh and energetic. Most of the time, the DVD image is excellent. Well-lighted interiors are exceptionally sharp. One T-shirt gets a bit psychedelic, but that's a minor flaw in a serious sleeper. —*MM*
Movie: ♫♫♫ *DVD:* ♫♫♫
Image Entertainment (Cat #ID8758SIDVD, UPC #014381875829). Widescreen (1.85:1) letterboxed. Dolby Digital Surround Stereo. $24.99. Snapper. *LANG:* English. *FEATURES:* 12 chapter links.
2000 107m/C Stephen Moyer, Neil Mullarkey, David Schneider, Suki Webster, Magnus Hastings; *D:* Jack Hazan; *W:* Jack

Hazan, David Mingay; *C:* Richard Branczik; *M:* Patrick Gowers.

Coming Soon

Perhaps the chickest chick-flick ever made is about one young woman's search for her first orgasm. Teen Stream Hodsell (Root) goes to a fancy Manhattan prep school but her life is far from perfect. There's the sex thing and then there's her hippie mom (Farrow), school, etc. Actually, as director Burson says on the commentary track, the film's checkered history is easily as interesting as the story. She sounds a bit naive when she talks about the problems she had cutting the film down for an "R" rating. It's no secret that the ratings board is much more conservative with sexual material than it is with violence, and her protestations are hard to take at face value. Otherwise, she and Root are chatty, giggly, and tend toward the "everyone-was-wonderful" approach. The disc itself has no trouble handling the film's bright, clashing color scheme. Sound is very good. —*MM*
Movie: 🎵🎵½ *DVD:* 🎵🎵🎵
Image Entertainment (Cat #ID9496UMUM DVD, UPC #014381949629). Widescreen (1.85:1) letterboxed. Dolby Digital Surround Stereo. $24.99. Snapper. *LANG:* English. *FEATURES:* 24 chapter links ▪ Commentary: Colette Burson and Bonnie Root ▪ Theatrical trailer ▪ Cast interviews ▪ Lyrics to "Love a Woman."
1999 96m/C Gaby Hoffman, Tricia Vessey, Ryan Reynolds, Bonnie Root, James Roday, Spalding Gray, Mia Farrow, Ryan O'Neal, Peter Bogdanovich, Leslie Lyles, Yasmine Bleeth; *D:* Colette Burson; *W:* Colette Burson, Kate Robin; *C:* Joaquin Baca-Asay.

Communion [CE]

After a bunch of those all-too-familiar UFO-style lights surround the cottage that Streiber and his family are vacationing in, Streiber becomes convinced that they have been abducted by aliens. When his behavior becomes more and more manic and excessive, he visits a shrink where his repressed memories are brought to the surface and visualized on the screen, delivering at least a few good thrills. A serious adaptation of the purportedly non-fictional best-seller by Streiber about his family's traumatic experiences. This is one of Elite's best-looking DVDs, and includes a great supplementary section; the super commentary track with director Mora and William J. Birnes of *UFO Magazine* delves into the reality of UFOs and abduction. The image is sharp and colors are bold and saturated without ever a hint of bleed. Fleshtones are dead-on. The 5.1 mix is excellent, with not that much in the way of bombastic Surround effects, but almost constant use of the rears for natural (and unnatural) ambience. Clapton's surprisingly dark score is reproduced with fine dynamics and excellent fidelity. In the sup-

plementals, the "actual" footage of a surgical removal of an alien implant adds to the overall atmosphere of the disc and most of the outtakes are extended versions of scenes used in the film. A great package from Elite. —*JO*
Movie: 🎵🎵½ *DVD:* 🎵🎵🎵½
Elite Entertainment, Inc. (Cat #EE2666, UPC #790594266622). Widescreen (2.35:1) anamorphic. Dolby Digital 5.1. $29.95. Keepcase. *LANG:* English. *FEATURES:* 14 chapter links ▪ Theatrical trailer ▪ Commentary: Philippe Mora ▪ Commentary: William J. Birnes, publisher of *UFO Magazine* ▪ Outtakes ▪ Behind-the-scenes footage ▪ Footage of an alien implant removal.
1989 (R) 103m/C Christopher Walken, Lindsay Crouse, Frances Sternhagen, Joel Carlson, Andreas Katsulas, Basil Hoffman; *D:* Philippe Mora; *M:* Eric Clapton.

The Complete Superman Collection

Most if not all of these cartoons have appeared on other discs, but this appears to be the best version—in image if not sound, which tends to become muddled in parts of the score. But the picture is so clear that even kids might enjoy them. Nostalgic adults will certainly get a kick. Side-by-side comparison to some of the Winstar versions gives this one a slight edge. They're arranged in order of theatrical release. Contents: "Superman" (pilot film), "The Mechanical Monsters," "Billion Dollar Limited," "The Arctic Giant," "The Bulleteers," "The Magnetic Telescope," "Electric Earthquake," "Volcano," "Terror on the Midway," "Japoteurs," "Showdown," "Eleventh Hour," "Destruction Inc.," "The Mummy Strikes," "Jungle Drums," "The Underground World," and "Secret Agent." —*MM*
Movie: 🎵🎵½ *DVD:* 🎵🎵🎵
Image Entertainment (Cat #ID9574BK DVD, UPC #014381957426). Full frame. Dolby Digital Mono. $24.99. Snapper. *LANG:* English.
1943 ?m/C

Conan the Barbarian [2 CE]

Milius injects his own warrior spirit in to this fine sword and sorcery tale featuring graphic brutality, believably choreographed swordplay, and excellent production values. Conan's (Schwarzenegger) parents are killed and he's enslaved. But hardship doesn't kill him (it just makes him stronger), so when he is set free he can seek revenge and retrieve the sword bequeathed to him by his father. Bergman is great as the Queen of Thieves, and Arnold more than holds his muscular own, while injecting his sense of humor throughout. Jones is dandy as usual. This DVD is such an improvement over the first edition that it could easily have been a 4-bone wonder (the image quality is excellent) if they had come up with some sort of Surround mix. Of course, nobody would

have seriously griped about it until being jaded by the work Anchor Bay has done on those '70s Italian genre flicks. As it is, the sound is still an improvement over that of the earlier disc and all the slicing and dicing is delivered with more than enough fidelity. The commentary won't win any awards, but Arnold is entertaining while Milius makes it clear where his heart is. —*JO*
Movie: 🎵🎵🎵½ *DVD:* 🎵🎵🎵½
Universal Studios Home Video (Cat #20564, UPC #025192056420). Widescreen (2.35:1) anamorphic. Stereo. $29.95. Keepcase. *LANG:* English. *SUB:* French. *CAP:* English. *FEATURES:* 16 chapter links ▪ Theatrical trailers ▪ Deleted scenes ▪ "Making of" featurette ▪ Commentary: director John Milius, Arnold Schwarzenegger ▪ Special effects ▪ The Conan Archives ▪ Dual-layered RSDL. Extended 129-minute version.
1982 (R) 115m/C Arnold Schwarzenegger, James Earl Jones, Max von Sydow, Sandahl Bergman, Mako, Ben Davidson, Valerie Quennessen, Cassandra Gaviola, William Smith; *D:* John Milius; *W:* John Milius, Oliver Stone; *C:* Duke Callaghan, John Cabrera; *M:* Basil Poledouris.

Coneheads

Of all the features that have come from *SNL* skits, this may be the least appreciated and it's certainly one of the most enjoyable. Aykroyd and Curtin reprise their roles as Beldar and Prymaat, the couple from the planet Remulak who are just trying to fit in on Earth. Newman, who created the role of teenaged daughter Connie, appears as Beldar's sister, while Burke takes over as Connie. Look for lots of familiar faces in cameos. On disc, the film is as rough-looking as it always has been. No serious flaws appear in the image transfer. —*MM*
Movie: 🎵🎵 *DVD:* 🎵🎵🎵
Paramount Home Video (Cat #32874, UPC #097363287445). Widescreen anamorphic. Dolby Digital 5.1 Surround Stereo; Dolby Digital Surround. $24.99. Keepcase. *LANG:* English; French. *SUB:* English. *FEATURES:* 13 chapter links ▪ Trailer.
1993 (PG) 86m/C Dan Aykroyd, Jane Curtin, Laraine Newman, Jason Alexander, Michelle Burke, Chris Farley, Michael Richards, Lisa Jane Persky, Sinbad, Shishir Kurup, Michael McKean, Phil Hartman, David Spade, Dave Thomas, Jan Hooks, Chris Rock, Adam Sandler, Julia Sweeney, Danielle Aykroyd; *D:* Steven Barron; *W:* Tom Davis, Bonnie Turner, Terry Turner, Dan Aykroyd; *C:* Francis Kenny; *M:* David Newman.

The Confession

Slick lawyer Roy Bleakie (Baldwin) suffers a crisis of conscience with the case of Harry Fertig (Kingsley), who has killed the three people he regards as responsible for the death of his young son. Harry wants to plead guilty and accept responsibility. Roy has been promised a job as D.A. if he can get Harry to plead temporary insanity. But there's still more to the case. Fine performances from a first-rate cast raise this one above the usual level of courtroom drama. The disc, however, is not a significant improvement over VHS tape. The image is acceptable but lacks the finest level of detail. —MM

Movie: 🎬🎬 **DVD:** 🎬🎬½
Studio Home Entertainment (Cat #7255). Full frame. Dolby Digital Surround Stereo. $28.97. Keepcase. *LANG:* English. *SUB:* Spanish. *FEATURES:* Baldwin and Kingsley thumbnail bios • 9 chapter links • Trailer.
1998 (R) 114m/C Alec Baldwin, Ben Kingsley, Amy Irving, Jay O. Sanders, Kevin Conway, Anne Twomey, Christopher Lawford, Boyd Gaines, Christopher Noth; *D:* David Hugh Jones; *W:* David Black; *C:* Mike Fash; *M:* Mychael Danna.

Confessions of Sorority Girls

Sometime in the early '60s, wicked Sabrina (Luner) shows up at college and takes it by storm. Will she steal Rita's (Milano) beau? That's the least of her schemes. The villainy is played strictly for campy laughs and the film is never as trashy as its title suggests. It's obvious that the low-budget production was made quickly. DVD does no favors to the garish Tiki Bar color scheme. Heavy pixels show up in the darker scenes, but so what? —MM

Movie: 🎬🎬½ **DVD:** 🎬🎬½
Buena Vista Home Entertainment (Cat #21629, UPC #786936144529). Full frame. Dolby Digital Stereo. $32.99. Keepcase. *LANG:* English. *SUB:* English. *FEATURES:* 20 chapter links • Dimension previews.
2000 (PG-13) 83m/C Jamie Luner, Alyssa Milano, Bette Rae; *D:* Uli Edel.

Conquest of the Planet of the Apes

The apes turn the tables on the human Earth population when they lead a revolt against their cruel masters in the distant year of 1990. Sure, there are plenty of clichés—but the story drags you along. The fourth film in the series, this is the weakest of the five discs. Along with the shimmer in the detailed longshots that appears on three of the other DVDs in the series, there is also some bleed in the reds through most of the film. The sound is also a little tinny at times with slight high-end distortion. Still, also like the other DVD presentations, this one still looks better than the Fox VHS edition and even their corresponding letterboxed laserdisc release. —JO

Movie: 🎬🎬½ **DVD:** 🎬🎬🎬
20th Century Fox Home Entertainment (Cat #2000107, UPC #024543001072). Widescreen (2.35:1) letterboxed. Dolby Surround. $29.95. Keepcase. *LANG:* English; French. *SUB:* English; Spanish. *CAP:* English. *FEATURES:* 21 chapter links • Theatrical trailers • Weblink. Also avail-

able as part of the 6-DVD "Planet of the Apes: The Evolution" box set (cat. #2000109, UPC 024543001096) for $99.95.
1972 (PG) 87m/C Roddy McDowall, Don Murray, Ricardo Montalban, Natalie Trundy, Severn Darden, Hari Rhodes, Asa Maynor, Gordon Jump, John Randolph, H.M. Wynant, Lou Wagner; *D:* J. Lee Thompson; *W:* Paul Dehn; *C:* Bruce Surtees; *M:* Tom Scott.

The Contender

Liberal senator Laine Hanson (Allen) is poised to be appointed the first woman vice president, but evil conservative congressman Shelly Runyon (Oldman) will do anything to derail her nomination, even if it means smearing her with allegations of pre-marital sexual escapades. Parts of the film work extremely well, particularly the political maneuvering, but the viewer has to take the story with huge grains of salt. Could a woman or a man reach the Senate after having run for various public offices without the accusations having been made public before? Also, one key plot element is much too obvious, and throughout, the filmmakers' liberal political bias is so blatant that even viewers of similar sentiments will wish it had been handled more deftly. That said, the DVD image is every bit as sharp as the theatrical release and the various Surround tracks are much stronger. —MM

Movie: 🎬🎬🎬 **DVD:** 🎬🎬🎬
DreamWorks Home Entertainment (Cat #87809, UPC #667068780925). Widescreen (1.85:1) anamorphic. DTS 5.1 Surround Stereo; Dolby Digital 5.1 Surround Stereo; DD Surround. $26.99. Keepcase. *LANG:* English. *SUB:* English. *CAP:* English. *FEATURES:* 20 chapter links • 10 deleted scenes with commentary • Commentary: director Rod Lurie, Joan Allen • Behind-the-scenes featurette • Trailer • Production notes • Talent files.
2000 (R) 127m/C Joan Allen, Gary Oldman, Jeff Bridges, Sam Elliott, Christian Slater, William L. Petersen, Philip Baker Hall, Saul Rubinek; *D:* Rod Lurie; *W:* Rod Lurie; *C:* Denis Maloney; *M:* Lawrence Nash Groupe. *AWARDS: NOM:* Oscars '00: Actress (Allen), Support. Actor (Bridges); Ind. Spirit '01: Actress (Allen), Support. Actor (Oldman); Screen Actors Guild '00: Actress (Allen), Support. Actor (Bridges, Oldman).

The Contract

Former black ops specialist Luc (Imbault) is making a living as a private sector assassin and is teaching the trade to his daughter Hannah (Black). When dad is killed in a set-up, she wants revenge against the man behind the deed—Presidential candidate J. Hamon (Williams), who wants his own questionable past to stay hidden. Low-budget image is so grainy that the night scenes are riddled with artifacts. Overall, DVD is no better than tape. —MM

Movie: 🎬🎬½ **DVD:** 🎬🎬
MTI Home Video (Cat #1061, UPC #039414510614). Full frame. $24.95. Keepcase. *LANG:* English. *SUB:* Spanish. *FEATURES:* 20 chapter links • Trailers • Talent files.
1998 (R) 90m/C Billy Dee Williams, Johanna Black, Laurent Imbault; *D:* K.C. Bascombe.

The Conversation

Francis Ford Coppola's other early masterpiece has been largely overlooked by audiences, probably because it was made between the two *Godfather* films. It's a tightly made, complex story of Harry (Hackman), a surveillance expert who becomes increasingly uneasy about his current job. Before it's over, the film becomes a meditation on privacy, responsibility, and guilt. A scene-by-scene comparison of the DVD with the full-frame laserdisc reveals just how far the technology has advanced. The difference between the two is almost immeasurable. Though this is not a particularly demanding film in visual terms, the DVD image has depths of texture and detail that are only hinted at on laser. The 5.1 remix is far superior to the original and, in this case, completely justified by the story. On his commentary track, Coppola is quick to admit the influence of *Blow Up*. For his part, editor Walter Murch isn't as loquacious, but both filmmakers are low-keyed and perceptive. The disc belongs in the library of any collector. —MM

Movie: 🎬🎬🎬🎬 **DVD:** 🎬🎬🎬🎬
Paramount Home Video (Cat #02307, UPC #097360230741). Widescreen anamorphic. Dolby Digital 5.1 Surround Stereo; Dolby Digital Mono. $29.99. Keepcase. *LANG:* English; French. *SUB:* English. *FEATURES:* 12 chapter links • Commentary: Francis Ford Coppola and Walter Murch • "Close-Up on 'The Conversation'" featurette • Trailer.
1974 (PG) 113m/C Gene Hackman, John Cazale, Frederic Forrest, Allen (Goorwitz) Garfield, Cindy Williams, Robert Duvall, Teri Garr, Michael Higgins, Elizabeth McRae, Harrison Ford; *D:* Francis Ford Coppola; *W:* Francis Ford Coppola; *C:* Bill Butler; *M:* David Shire. *AWARDS:* Cannes '74: Film; Natl. Bd. of Review '74: Actor (Hackman), Director (Coppola), Natl. Film Reg. '95; Natl. Soc. Film Critics '74: Director (Coppola); *NOM:* Oscars '74: Orig. Screenplay, Picture, Sound.

The Cook, the Thief, His Wife & Her Lover

Peter Greenaway's brilliant and challenging (it caused the creation of the "NC-17" rating) tale of love, lust, gluttony, and hate has never looked or sounded so good on home video. It's a sensual feast of bizarre characters in exotic costumes with big splashes of primary colors. The action takes place on vast expressionistic sets and it's played out over a lovely haunting score by Michael Nyman. It's an unsettling

combination of the beautiful and the repugnant. There may be some flaws on the DVD, but I missed them because Greenaway's magic works so well on me. The disc would have earned a four-bone technical rating if the director could have been persuaded to provide a commentary track, and if a separate music-only track had been available. Those are quibbles, though. The film is a masterpiece. —*MM*
Movie: 🦴🦴🦴🦴 **DVD:** 🦴🦴🦴½
Anchor Bay (Cat #DV11391, UPC #013131139198). Widescreen (2.35:1) anamorphic. Dolby Digital Surround Stereo. $29.95. Keepcase. *LANG:* English. *FEATURES:* 30 chapter links ☞ Trailers.
1990 (R) 123m/C *GB* Richard Bohringer, Michael Gambon, Helen Mirren, Alan Howard, Tim Roth; **D:** Peter Greenaway; **W:** Peter Greenaway; **C:** Sacha Vierny; **M:** Michael Nyman.

Cooley High
Black Chicago high school students go through the rites of passage in their senior year of 1964. The film is smart, funny, and well made. The grain in the image comes from the original elements and does not result in excessive artifacts. The great Motown soundtrack deserves a stereo remix. Overall, disc is identical to tape. —*MM*
Movie: 🦴🦴🦴 **DVD:** 🦴🦴
MGM Home Entertainment (Cat #907989, UPC #027616798923). Full frame. Dolby Digital Mono. $24.99. Keepcase. *LANG:* English; French. *SUB:* English; French. *FEATURES:* 32 chapter links.
1975 (PG) 107m/C Glynn Turman, Lawrence-Hilton Jacobs, Garrett Morris, Cynthia Davis; **D:** Michael A. Schultz; **W:** Eric Monte.

The Coroner
Dr. Leon Urasky (St. Louis) is both a coroner and a serial killer. He chooses lawyer Emma Santiago (Longenecker) as a victim, but she is no pushover. The horror/thriller has some humor, a few nice moments, and it's generally well acted. Unfortunately, the DVD is filled with heavy artifacts in bright exteriors and night scenes. —*MM*
Movie: 🦴🦴½ **DVD:** 🦴🦴
New Concorde (Cat #NH20629D, UPC #736991462946). Full frame. Stereo. $19.98. Keepcase. *LANG:* English. *SUB:* Spanish. *FEATURES:* 24 chapter links ☞ Talent files ☞ Trailers ☞ Booklet on Roger Corman.
1998 (R) 75m/C Jane Longenecker, Dean St. Louis; **D:** Juan A. Mas; **W:** Geralyn Ruane; **C:** Charles "Chip" Schneer.

The Cosmic Man
An alien "cosmonaut" (Carradine) arrives on Earth in a giant beachball with a message of peace and understanding. It's essentially *Day the Earth Stood Still* without the budget, but interesting nonetheless. On DVD, the black-and-white photography remains crisp with good levels of

detail. The monaural soundtrack sounds better when Carradine orates in that big rolling voice. Don't miss the trailer. It's not really faithful to the spirit of the film, but it's certainly fun on its own. —*MM*
Movie: 🦴🦴🦴 **DVD:** 🦴🦴🦴
Image Entertainment (Cat #ID8702CO DVD, UPC #014381870220). Full frame. Dolby Digital Mono. $24.99. Snapper. *LANG:* English. *FEATURES:* 12 chapter links ☞ Theatrical trailer.
1959 72m/B Bruce (Herman Brix) Bennett, John Carradine, Angela Greene, Paul Langton, Scotty Morrow; **D:** Herbert Greene; **W:** Arthur C. Pierce; **C:** John F. Warren; **M:** Paul Sawtell, Bert Shefter.

Cotton Comes to Harlem
In his directorial debut, Ossie Davis adapts Chester Himes's novel. Cambridge and St. Jacques star as Harlem plainclothes detectives "Gravedigger" Jones and "Coffin Ed" Johnson, who suspect that a preacher's (Lockhart) back-to-Africa scheme is a scam. The action is brightened by a rude, raucous sense of humor. The Harlem locations have a real sense of authenticity on this disc, which also captures the aggressive color scheme. Some aliasing is bothersome along chrome trim lines and the sound is unimpressive. —*MM*
Movie: 🦴🦴🦴 **DVD:** 🦴🦴½
MGM Home Entertainment (Cat #100-1464, UPC #027616857842). Full frame. Dolby Digital Mono. $19.98. Keepcase. *LANG:* English. *SUB:* French; Spanish. *FEATURES:* 16 chapter links ☞ Trailer.
1970 (R) 97m/C Godfrey Cambridge, Raymond St. Jacques, Calvin Lockhart, Judy Pace, Redd Foxx, John Anderson, Emily Yancy, J.D. Cannon, Teddy Wilson, Eugene Roche, Cleavon Little, Lou Jacobi; **D:** Ossie Davis; **W:** Ossie Davis; **C:** Gerald Hirschfeld; **M:** Galt MacDermot.

Cotton Mary
Tedious, dreary, and frustrating are only a sampling of the words that can be tagged to producer/director Ismail Merchant's effort. Since he is an Indian-born filmmaker, one would expect a more insightful look at the difficulties of life in the early 1950s for Anglo-Indians living in the newly created India. Sadly, that's not what's been delivered here; instead it's a minor story about an insane Anglo-Indian nurse and her corruption of a British household, whose matriarch (Scacchi) seems oblivious to everything around her. Serviceable DVD presentation lacks extras, but then the film doesn't deserve more. —*RJT*
Movie: 🦴½ **DVD:** 🦴🦴½
Universal Studios Home Video (Cat #20979, UPC #025192097928). Widescreen (1.85:1). Dolby Digital Surround. $24.98. Keepcase. *LANG:* English. *SUB:* English; French. *CAP:* English; French. *FEATURES:* 18 chapter links ☞ Theatrical trailer.
1999 (R) 124m/C *GB* Madhur Jaffrey, Greta Scacchi, James Wilby, Neena Gupta,

Sakina Jaffrey, Gemma Jones, Sarah Badel, Joanna David, Riyu Bajaj, Prayag Raj; **D:** Ismail Merchant; **W:** Alexandra Viets; **C:** Pierre Lhomme; **M:** Richard Robbins.

A Couch in New York
This romantic comedy was directed and written by the French and is proof that some French ideas just don't translate into English. Beatrice (Binoche), a dancer who lives in Paris, is tired of the pursuit of countless suitors and answers an ad to switch apartments with Henry (Hurt). He's a famous psychoanalyst who lives in New York and is being driven crazy by his elite clientele. Hijinks ensue as Henry's clients mistake Beatrice for his substitute shrink and Beatrice's boyfriends mistake him for a threat. Henry comes home early and learns that she is impersonating an analyst, but is so enchanted with her that he becomes a client. Binoche is charming and does her best to appear smitten with Hurt, but in the end she has a better chance of achieving chemistry with Henry's golden retriever. The main problem with the film, aside from the overused plot device, is that absolutely no sparks fly between Binoche and Hurt. Even the most contrived of romantic comedies can survive if the leads are a little spicy with each other. The soundtrack is lovely, but the picture looks as if the original film were overlit and the transfer looks washed-out. —*CA* **AKA:** Un Divan a New York.
Movie: 🦴½ **DVD:** 🦴½
Winstar Home Entertainment (Cat #05290, UPC #043396052901). Widescreen letterboxed. $24.98. Keepcase. *LANG:* English; French. *SUB:* English; French. *FEATURES:* 8 chapter links ☞ Bonus trailers *(Stuart Little; Baby Geniuses)* ☞ Star and director bios ☞ Photo gallery.
1995 (R) 104m/C *FR BE GE* William Hurt, Juliette Binoche, Paul Guilfoyle, Stephanie Buttle, Richard Jenkins, Kent Broadhurst, Henry Bean, Barbara Garrick; **D:** Chantal Akerman; **W:** Chantal Akerman, Jean-Louis Benoit; **C:** Dietrich Lohmann; **M:** Paolo Conte, Sonia Atherton.

Coup de Torchon
In 1938 French West Africa, police chief Lucien Cordier (Noiret) is consistently harassed by his community, particularly by the town pimp. But then Lucien discovers just how much power he really has and the lamb becomes a murderous wolf. The film is based on Jim Thompson's novel *Pop. 1280* and is required viewing for all noir fans. The anamorphic-enhanced image is accurate in its subdued color, and the sound, especially the infrequent but effective Phillipe Sarde music, is well-rendered. Extras include a trailer and some interviews with director Tavernier. He's a published authority on film history as well as an accomplished director but you have to concentrate to understand him through his accent. English subtitles are not burned in. —*MM/GE* **AKA:** Clean Slate.
Movie: 🦴🦴🦴½ **DVD:** 🦴🦴🦴½

Criterion Collection (Cat #106, UPC #037429149829). Widescreen (1.78:1) anamorphic. Dolby Digital Mono. $29.95. Keepcase. *LANG:* French. *SUB:* English. *FEATURES:* Trailer ● Director interview ● Clips from alternate ending.
1981 128m/C *FR* Philippe Noiret, Isabelle Huppert, Guy Marchand, Stephane Audran, Eddy Mitchell, Jean-Pierre Marielle, Irene Skobline; *D:* Bertrand Tavernier; *W:* Bertrand Tavernier; *C:* Pierre William Glenn; *M:* Philippe Sarde. *AWARDS: NOM:* Oscars '82: Foreign Film.

Coyote Ugly

Empty-headed but somewhat enjoyable cheap-thrills film is about a young girl named Violet (Piper Perabo) who leaves her hometown and goes to the Big Apple to pursue her dream of becoming a songwriter. Along the way she gets a job at Coyote Ugly, a bar owned by a gorgeous blonde and serviced by equally attractive blondes and brunettes who insult the customers, throw ice on troublemakers, and dance on the bar, occasionally setting it on fire. Violet doesn't want to work there because she is so nice and the bar is so rowdy, but she has to pay the bills (sniff). To make a long story short, she ends up with everything she ever wanted. In all fairness Perabo makes the most of her clichéd role as the small town girl. Her ability to look truly taken aback by the goings-on at the bar mark her as a great actress, and she has a fine sense of comedic timing. All the dance sequences are amazing and fun, but still don't fill in for a good story. The disc looks and sounds great. —CA
Movie: 🎶🎶 **DVD:** 🎶🎶🎶
Buena Vista Home Entertainment (Cat #21627, UPC #786936144505). Widescreen (2.35:1) anamorphic. Dolby Digital 5.1 Surround; DTS 5.1. $29.99. Keepcase. *LANG:* English; French. *SUB:* Spanish. *CAP:* English. *FEATURES:* 28 chapter links ● Theatrical trailer ● Lee Ann Rimes music video ● Behind-the-scenes featurette ● Hottest Moments Reel ● Commentary: producer, director, and Coyotes.
2000 (PG-13) 94m/C Piper Perabo, Maria Bello, Tyra Banks, John Goodman, Melanie Lynskey, Ellen Cleghorne, Bud Cort, Izabella Miko, Bridget Moynahan, Adam Garcia, Del Pentacost, Michael Weston; *D:* David McNally; *W:* Todd Graff, Kevin Smith, Gina Wendkos; *C:* Amir M. Mokri; *M:* Trevor Horn.

The Cradle Will Rock

Robbins's attempt to capture the artistic/political fervor of New York in the mid-'30s is exuberant to a fault. He admits up front that it is "a (mostly) true story." Theatrical collaborators Orson Welles (a flamboyant Macfadyen) and John Houseman (Elwes) agree to produce Marc Blitzstein's (Azaria) new political musical *Cradle Will Rock* for their Federal Theatre Company. Right-wing political interference closes the theatre on opening night but Welles leads his company to another venue in Manhattan. The dramatic circumstances create a

unique success in the history of American theatre. The film is a lavish production that looks terrific on disc. Focus is sharp enough (but not too sharp); colors have a muted richness suitable for period nostalgia. The film is quirky enough that it failed to find a receptive audience in theatrical release. It will become a favorite on home video. —MM
Movie: 🎶🎶🎶½ **DVD:** 🎶🎶🎶½
Buena Vista Home Entertainment (Cat #18288, UPC #717951004765). Widescreen (2.35:1) anamorphic. Dolby Digital 5.0 Surround Stereo. $32.99. Keepcase. *LANG:* English. *FEATURES:* 28 chapter links ● "Making of" featurette ● Trailers.
1999 (R) 133m/C Angus Macfadyen, Cary Elwes, Hank Azaria, Cherry Jones, Ruben Blades, Joan Cusack, John Cusack, Philip Baker Hall, Bill Murray, Vanessa Redgrave, Susan Sarandon, Jamey Sheridan, John Turturro, Emily Watson, Bob Balaban, Paul Giamatti, Barnard Hughes, Barbara Sukowa, John Carpenter, Gretchen Mol, Harris Yulin; *D:* Tim Robbins; *W:* Tim Robbins; *C:* Jean-Yves Escoffier; *M:* David Robbins.

Crazy in Alabama

If they greenlighted this southern-fried mess, then they're crazy in Hollywood too. Lucille (Griffith) is an unbalanced aging southern belle who decapitates her husband and heads off to fulfill her dream of becoming a Hollywood star. She also takes his severed noggin with her, although it is a little talkative. Woven through this bizarre storyline is another that focuses on Lucille's nephew Peejoe back home in Alabama as he stands up to a bigoted sheriff, helps protest for civil rights, and meets Martin Luther King. Banderas's directorial debut is fine technically, but veers wildly all over the road as far as content goes. With the sharpness and vibrant colors (the Las Vegas neons are stunning) displayed on this DVD, it was surprising that so many of the blacks pale out to gray in dimmer scenes. And there are enough of those dimmer scenes to knock the rating down a notch. No complaints about the sound, though; good Surround is used with the energetic mix that really comes to life on the assorted songs—the theme from the TV show *Bewitched* is a killer. —JO
Movie: 🎶🎶½ **DVD:** 🎶🎶½
Columbia Tristar Home Video (Cat #02977, UPC #043396029774). Widescreen (2.35:1) anamorphic. Dolby Digital 5.1; Dolby Surround. $24.95. Keepcase. *LANG:* English. *CAP:* English. *FEATURES:* 28 chapter links ● Theatrical trailers ● Talent files ● Commentary: director Antonio Banderas, Melanie Griffith ● Deleted scenes with narration ● Blooper reel ● Photo montage ● "Making of" featurette.
1999 (PG-13) 111m/C Melanie Griffith, David Morse, Lucas Black, Cathy Moriarty, Meat Loaf Aday, Rod Steiger, Richard Schiff, John Beasley, Robert Wagner, Noah Emmerich, Sandra Seacat, Paul Ben-Victor, Brad Beyer, Fannie Flagg, Elizabeth Perkins, Linda Hart, Paul Mazursky, William

Converse-Roberts, Holmes Osborne, David Speck; *D:* Antonio Banderas; *W:* Mark Childress; *C:* Julio Macat; *M:* Mark Snow. *AWARDS: NOM:* Golden Raspberries '99: Worst Actress (Griffith).

The Crazysitter

Edie (D'Angelo), a petty thief recently released from jail, is hired by the clueless Paul (Begley) and Treva (Kane) Van Ardsdale to look after their nasty twin children Jason (Bluhm) and Bea (Duncan) while the parents are on vacation. When the kids act up, she decides to sell them. The overstated comedy actually manages to make *Home Alone* look subtle. Well, sort of subtle. Image actually looks pretty sharp for a Corman production. DVD is still only a marginal improvement over tape. —MM
Movie: 🎶🎶½ **DVD:** 🎶🎶
New Concorde (Cat #NH20497D, UPC #736991349797). Full frame. Stereo. $19.98. Keepcase. *LANG:* English. *FEATURES:* 24 chapter links ● Thumbnail bios ● Trailers.
1994 (PG-13) 92m/C Beverly D'Angelo, Ed Begley Jr., Carol Kane, Phil Hartman, Brady Bluhm, Rachel Duncan, Nell Carter, Steve Landesburg; *D:* Michael James McDonald; *W:* Michael James McDonald; *C:* Christopher Baffa; *M:* David Wurst, Eric Wurst.

The Creeps

Librarian Anna (Griffin) hires a detective (Lauer) to get back the original manuscript of Mary Shelley's *Frankenstein*, which has been stolen by a mildly mad scientist, Berber (Moynihan). He's using manuscripts and a crackpot lab to bring fictional monsters back to life. His experiment goes awry and the results are midget versions of Dracula (Fondacaro), Frankenstein's Monster (Wellington), the Werewolf (Simanton), and the Mummy (Smith). It's a typical Full Moon production—low-budget, O.K. makeup, good effects, juvenile humor. The image is slightly sharper than VHS, but this is such a dark production that any difference is minimal. The double-sided disc contains voluminous extras (mostly trailers for other Full Moon releases) on the flip side. —MM
Movie: 🎶🎶 **DVD:** 🎶🎶½
Full Moon Pictures (Cat #8026). Full frame. Dolby Digital Stereo. $24.98. Keepcase. *LANG:* English. *FEATURES:* Cast and crew thumbnail bios ● Blooper reel ● Trailers ● Videozone magazine "making of" featurette.
1997 (PG-13) 80m/C Phil Fondacaro, Rhonda Griffin, Justin Lauer, Bill Moynihan, Kristin Norton, Jon Simanton, Joe Smith, Thomas Wellington; *D:* Charles Band; *W:* Benjamin Carr; *C:* Adolfo Bartoli; *M:* Carl Dante.

Creepshow 2

Sequel anthology is second-tier material from Stephen King and screenwriter George Romero. All three stories lack interesting twists, depending instead on good production values and middling effects. George Kennedy and Dorothy Lamour deal with a vengeful wooden Indian in one. In the second, four teenagers are trapped by a lake-dwelling blob. In the third, a socialite (Lois Chiles) is involved in a hit-and-run accident. Actually, the menus that re-create the animated connecting material are the most interesting part of the disc. Image and sound are better than tape, but only moderately. —*MM*

Movie: 🎬 **DVD:** 🎬🎬
Anchor Bay (Cat #DV11419, UPC #013131141993). Widescreen (1.85:1) anamorphic. Dolby Digital Mono. $24.99. Keepcase. *LANG:* English. *CAP:* English. *FEATURES:* Trailer • Stills gallery • 23 chapter links.
1987 (R) 92m/C Lois Chiles, George Kennedy, Dorothy Lamour, Tom Savini, Domenick John, Frank S. Salsedo, Holt McCallany, David Holbrook, Page Hannah, Daniel Beer, Stephen King, Paul Satterfield, Jeremy Green, Tom Wright; *D:* Michael Gornick; *W:* George A. Romero; *C:* Richard Hart, Tom Hurwitz; *M:* Les Reed, Rick Wakeman.

The Crew

Bobby (Dreyfuss), "Bats," (Reynolds), "The Brick" (Hedaya), and "Mouth" (Cassel) are grumpy old goodfellas—gangsters living in retirement at a South Beach hotel in Miami. But when they face eviction because the place has become so popular, they decide to stage a murder in the lobby to decrease its desirability. That leads to a string of comic crimes involving kidnapping. Carrie Moss shines in a small role as Bobby's long-lost daughter who's a cop. The film looks fine on DVD. Soft tropical pastels are no problem and even the aliasing in bright sunlit scenes is kept to a minimum. Don't miss the parody of the famous nightclub entrance from *Goodfellas* in chapter five. This is a better comedy than its lackluster theatrical reception might lead you to believe. The "action overload" feature is a montage of the film's action scenes. —*MM*

Movie: 🎬🎬🎬 **DVD:** 🎬🎬🎬
Buena Vista Home Entertainment (Cat #21652, UPC #786936144734). Widescreen (1.85:1) anamorphic. Dolby Digital 5.1 Surround Stereo. $32.99. Keepcase. *LANG:* English. *CAP:* English. *FEATURES:* "Making of" featurette • "Action overload" • Trailers • Talent files • 32 chapter links.
2000 (PG-13) 88m/C Richard Dreyfuss, Burt Reynolds, Dan Hedaya, Seymour Cassel, Carrie-Anne Moss, Jennifer Tilly, Lainie Kazan, Miguel Sandoval, Jeremy Piven, Casey Siemaszko, Matt Borlenghi, Jeremy Ratchford, Mike Moroff, Billy Jayne Young, Jose Zuniga; *D:* Michael Dinner; *W:* Barry Fanaro; *C:* Juan Ruiz-Anchia; *M:* Steve Bartek.

Crime and Punishment in Suburbia

Despite the title, this curious little thriller actually owes as much to *Heathers* as it does to Dostoyevsky. The central character is abused manipulative cheerleader Rosanne Skolnik (Keena) whose parents (Ironside and Barkin) are one of the screen's most unhappy couples. Throw in a jock boyfriend (DeBello) and an obsessive young photographer (Kartheiser) and the ingredients are in place. Yes, it's a bit derivative of all the other dark-side-of-suburbia tales, but director Schmidt makes a credible debut. The only serious visual flaw is aliasing along the lines of shingles on a roof. Otherwise, DVD handles the generally dark image quite well. Sound is O.K. —*MM*

Movie: 🎬🎬🎬 **DVD:** 🎬🎬🎬½
MGM Home Entertainment (Cat #100-1442, UPC #027616857620). Widescreen (1.85:1) anamorphic; full frame. Dolby Digital 5.1 Surround Stereo; Dolby Digital Surround. $24.98. Keepcase. *LANG:* English; French; Spanish. *SUB:* French; Spanish. *FEATURES:* 16 chapter links • Commentary: Rob Schmidt, Michael Ironside.
2000 (R) 98m/C Monica Keena, Vincent Kartheiser, Ellen Barkin, Michael Ironside, Jeffrey Wright, Larry Gross, James DeBello; *D:* Michael Brook, Rob Schmidt; *W:* Bobby Bukowski.

Crime Story

Police Inspector Jackie Chan tries to crack a kidnapping case that involves his faithless partner (Cheng). As usual, the stunts and action sequences are the real point, but this is one of the most polished of Chan's Asian films. The unusually well-photographed image is very good, actually excellent for a Hong Kong import. Even the dubbing is a cut above the norm. Only flaw worth noting is what appear to be streaks made by a marker pen across a few frames. A must for fans. —*MM* **AKA:** Hard to Die.

Movie: 🎬🎬🎬 **DVD:** 🎬🎬🎬
Buena Vista Home Entertainment (Cat #20309, UPC #717951009890). Widescreen (1.85:1) letterboxed. Dolby Digital Mono. $29.99. Keepcase. *LANG:* English. *SUB:* English. *FEATURES:* 22 chapter links.
1993 (R) 104m/C Jackie Chan, Kent Cheng, Law Hang Kang, Christine Ng; *D:* Kirk Wong; *C:* Arthur Wong, Ardy Lam.

Crime Story: The Complete Saga

Nostalgically kitschy television film is set in Chicago, circa 1963. Lt. Mike Torrello (Farina) wages war with gangster Ray Luca (Denison) on the city streets in a stylized battlefield of justice, revenge, and murder. This pilot feature launched the cult classic television series. Although the video transfer features some stunning clarity with brighter colors (especially in daylight scenes), darker scenes are poorly defined and some are just plain awful. Blacks have little if any definition and the overall look tends toward the grainy side. The soundtrack fares a bit better and is high-lighted by clear, discernible music and dialogue. —*MJT*

Movie: 🎬🎬🎬 **DVD:** 🎬🎬
Anchor Bay (Cat #DV11245, UPC #013131124590). Full frame. Dolby Digital Mono. $24.98. Keepcase. *LANG:* English. *FEATURES:* 23 chapter links.
1986 96m/C Dennis Farina, Anthony John (Tony) Denison, Bill Smitrovich, Steve Ryan, Bill Campbell, Paul Butler, Stephen Lang, Darlanne Fluegel; *D:* Abel Ferrara; *W:* David Burke; *C:* James A. Contner.

Crimes & Misdemeanors [MGM]

One of Allen's most mature films explores a range of moral ambiguities through the parallel and interlocking stories of a nebbish filmmaker—who agrees to make a profile of a smug Hollywood television comic and then sabotages it—and an esteemed ophthalmologist who is threatened with exposure by his neurotic mistress. If there's any real difference between this MGM edition and the Image edition (reviewed in the first place), I couldn't see it. This is an anamorphic transfer, though, so it's certainly preferable for those with widescreen monitors. —*MM*

Movie: 🎬🎬🎬 **DVD:** 🎬🎬🎬
MGM Home Entertainment (Cat #1002025, UPC #027616862662). Widescreen (1.85:1) anamorphic. Dolby Digital Mono. $19.98. Keepcase. *LANG:* English; French; Spanish. *SUB:* French; Spanish. *FEATURES:* 16 chapter links • Trailer • Booklet.
1989 (PG-13) 104m/C Martin Landau, Woody Allen, Alan Alda, Mia Farrow, Joanna Gleason, Anjelica Huston, Jerry Orbach, Sam Waterston, Claire Bloom, Jenny Nichols, Caroline Aaron, Daryl Hannah, Nora Ephron, Jerry Zaks; *D:* Woody Allen; *W:* Woody Allen; *C:* Sven Nykvist. *AWARDS:* Natl. Bd. of Review '89: Support. Actor (Alda); N.Y. Film Critics '89: Support. Actor (Alda); Writers Guild '89: Orig. Screenplay; *NOM:* Oscars '89: Director (Allen), Orig. Screenplay, Support. Actor (Landau).

Criminals

Often disturbing view of crime that catches lawbreakers in the act ranges from a church elder with his hand in the till to a blood-chilling gang beating. Also includes real-life interrogations, confessions, and interviews with rapists, prostitutes, murderers, armed robbers, and drug dealers. Director Strick spent six months filming with police in New York, California, and Minnesota to get the footage for this film. Both video and audio are limited by their respective source materials since the film is culled together from a variety of sources. In essence, they are as good as they can be; think *Cops* without the budget. —*MJT*

Movie: 🎬🎬🎬 **DVD:** 🎬🎬½
Image Entertainment (Cat #ID9517RLDVD, UPC #014381951721). Full frame. Dolby

Digital Mono. $24.99. Snapper. *LANG:* English. *FEATURES:* 11 chapter links.
1997 74m/C D: Joseph Strick; **W:** C. K. Williams.

The Crimson Code

Serial killer stories are a dime a dozen and this one adds little to the overworked genre beyond a good cast. This time out, the murderers are being murdered and FBI agent Chandler (Muldoon) is on the case. On his commentary track, director Jeremy Haft takes a fairly technical approach, focusing on the problems of location shooting in a cold climate. (Winnipeg, Canada, stands in for Minnesota.) The full-frame image with a frozen bluish cast is a slight improvement over tape. —*MM*
Movie: 🎵🎵 *DVD:* 🎵🎵½
Artisan Entertainment (Cat #11357, UPC #012236113577). Full frame. Dolby Digital 5.1 Surround Stereo; Dolby Digital Surround Stereo. $24.99. Keepcase. *LANG:* English. *CAP:* English. *FEATURES:* 20 chapter links • Commentary: Jeremy Haft • Trailer • Talent files.
2000 (R) 90m/C Patrick Muldoon, Cathy Moriarty, C. Thomas Howell, Fred Ward, Tim Thomerson; **D:** Jeremy Haft; **W:** Alex Metcalf; **C:** Ian Elkin; **M:** Ken Williams.

Critical Care

Spader is a doctor in a high-tech intensive care unit. He must deal with such ethical questions as euthanasia, insurance scams, and a drunken administrator (Brooks) whose only concern is hospital profits. Two sisters (Sedgwick and Martindale) fight over the fate of their terminally ill, near-vegetable father. Spader finds his career on the line after sleeping with Sedgwick and backing her attempts to pull the plug. Given the meatiness of the subject, Lumet could have made a much more scathing satire. Schwartz's script is lame even for a first-time effort. Image and sound are good, but the film has never been extra sharp in either department. —*MM*
Movie: 🎵½ *DVD:* 🎵🎵½
Artisan Entertainment (Cat #60464). Widescreen (1.85:1) letterboxed; full frame. Dolby Digital 5.1 Surround Stereo. $29.98. Snapper. *LANG:* English. *SUB:* Spanish. *FEATURES:* Production notes • Trailer • Talent files • Featurette • 36 chapter links.
1997 (R) 105m/C James Spader, Albert Brooks, Kyra Sedgwick, Helen Mirren, Margo Martindale, Jeffrey Wright, Wallace Shawn, Anne Bancroft, Philip Bosco, Edward Herrmann, Colm Feore, James Lally, Al Waxman, Harvey Atkin; **D:** Sidney Lumet; **W:** Steven S. Schwartz; **C:** David Watkin; **M:** Michael Convertino. *AWARDS:* NOM: Ind. Spirit '98: First Screenplay.

Crocodile

An awful *Jaws* clone about a killer crocodile that stalks a group of sex-crazed teenagers on vacation (there's even a sheriff that no one will listen to, a seasoned crocodile hunter with a score to settle, etc.). It's sad to see a director like Hooper trying to regain form with schlock like this. The disc's video transfer is decent and features bright colors and crisp blacks. The sound transfer is acceptable and packs a few scary moments, but it is often muddied and the musical score is unnecessarily amplified throughout. The "making of" featurette amounts to little more than a glorified backslapping for the filmmakers, the highlight of which is Hooper's recounting of his glory days directing *The Texas Chainsaw Massacre*. —*MJT*
Movie: 🎵½ *DVD:* 🎵🎵½
Trimark Home Video (Cat #VM-7517D, UPC #031398751724). Widescreen (1.78:1) letterboxed. Dolby Digital 5.1 Surround Sound. $24.99. Keepcase. *LANG:* English. *SUB:* English; Spanish; French. *FEATURES:* 24 chapter links • "The Making of Crocodile" featurette • Theatrical trailer.
2000 (R) 94m/C Chris Solari, Mark McLaughlin, Caitlin Martin, Julie Mintz, Sommer Knight; **D:** Tobe Hooper; **W:** Michael D. Weiss, Adam Gierasch, Jace Anderson; **C:** Eliot Rockett.

Cross My Heart and Hope to Die

Young Otto (Garfalk) is an average misfit kid until he comes to the attention of the mischief-making Frank (Kornstad), who is the catalyst for Otto to get into various kinds of trouble and to be initiated into the complexities of sex. Burned in subtitles are clear and easy to read on a halftone background. The image is unusually pale, or is that just all of those blue-white skin tones? Blacks and browns tend to be unforgivingly harsh. —*MM* **AKA:** Ti Kniver I Hjertet.
Movie: 🎵🎵 *DVD:* 🎵🎵½
Vanguard International Cinema, Inc. (Cat #VF0012, UPC #658769001235). Widescreen (1.66:1) letterboxed. $29.95. Keepcase. *LANG:* Norwegian. *SUB:* English. *FEATURES:* 10 chapter links.
1994 96m/C *NO* Martin Dahl Garfalk, Jan Devo Kornstad; **D:** Marius Holst; **W:** Marius Holst; **C:** Philip Ogaard; **M:** Kjetil Bjerkestrand, Magne Furuholmen.

Crouching Tiger, Hidden Dragon

In 19th-century China a warrior priest (Chow Yun-Fat), a woman warrior he loves (Michelle Yeoh), and a princess (Zhang Ziyi) are brought together by a fabulous sword, the Green Destiny. That simple synopsis could be applied to any number of martial arts movies, but few of them are made with such care and money. That said, it should be noted that director Ang Lee is not alone in his ambitions. Fans of Hong Kong imports know that *The Bride with White Hair* (reviewed in first edition) treats similar ideas with much more energy, imagination, speed, and spirit. On a second viewing, the acting from the leads gains even more depth, particularly Yun-Fat and Yeoh. Though their English dubbing is above average, subtitles and original language track and subtitles are still recommended. DVD image is, if anything, a bit sharper than theatrical release (though I base that on a less-than-perfect experience at a neighborhood quadriplex); sound is a solid step up. Both the dusty wilderness scenes and the impressive bamboo wire work in Chapter 25 look fine. On their commentary track Ang Lee and producer/writer James Schamus take a lighter tone than the film itself, and they often wander off track. The overly busy menu is cool. —*MM*
Movie: 🎵🎵🎵 *DVD:* 🎵🎵🎵½
Columbia Tristar Home Video (Cat #05990, UPC #043396059900). Widescreen anamorphic. Dolby Digital 5.1 Surround Stereo; Dolby Digital Surround. $27.96. Keepcase. *LANG:* English; Mandarin; French. *SUB:* English; French. *FEATURES:* 28 chapter links • Trailers • Conversation with Michelle Yeoh • "Making of" featurette • Commentary: Ang Lee, James Schamus • Photo montage • Filmographies.
2000 120m/C Chow Yun-Fat, Michelle Yeoh, Zhang Ziyi, Chang Chen, Cheng Pei-Pei, Lung Sihung; **D:** Ang Lee; **W:** James Schamus, Wang Hui Ling, Tsai Kuo Jung; **C:** Peter Pau; **M:** Tan Dun. *AWARDS:* Oscars '00: Art Dir./Set Dec., Cinematog., Foreign Film, Orig. Score; British Acad. '00: Director (Lee), Foreign Film, Score; Directors Guild '00: Director (Lee); Golden Globes '01: Director (Lee), Foreign Film; Ind. Spirit '01: Director (Lee), Film, Support. Actress (Ziyi); L.A. Film Critics '00: Cinematog., Film, Score; Natl. Bd. of Review '00: Foreign Film; N.Y. Film Critics '00: Cinematog.; Broadcast Film Critics '00: Foreign Film; *NOM:* Oscars '00: Adapt. Screenplay, Costume Des., Director (Lee), Film, Film Editing, Song ("A Love Before Time"); Writers Guild '00: Adapt. Screenplay.

Croupier

Jack Manfred (Owen) is a would-be novelist who falls back on his professional skills as a roulette croupier and blackjack dealer when he can't arrange a book deal. He takes a job at a London casino that leads to a very tricky plot which is virtually impossible to decipher completely on only one viewing. That's just one of the film's many pleasures. The characters are very strong (to be expected, since writer Mayersburg is also responsible for *The Man Who Fell to Earth* and *Merry Christmas, Mr. Lawrence*), and the story has a lived-in sense of realism that few films realize. (Director Hodges made the original and similar *Get Carter*.) DVD is something of a surprise because both image and sound are far superior to the theatrical release. The only thing lacking here is a commentary track, but that could be cured with a Special Edition. This one certainly deserves it. —*MM*
Movie: 🎵🎵🎵½ *DVD:* 🎵🎵🎵
Image Entertainment (Cat #ID0596SL DVD). Widescreen. Dolby Digital Stereo.

$24.99. Snapper. *LANG:* English. *FEA-TURES:* 12 chapter links.
1997 91m/C *GB* Clive Owen, Alex Kingston, Kate Hardie, Gina McKee, Nicholas Ball, Nick Reding; *D:* Mike Hodges; *W:* Paul Mayersberg; *C:* Mike Garfath; *M:* Simon Fisher Turner.

The Crow: Salvation

This surprisingly good sequel premiered on home video instead of in theatres but don't let that scare you away. The stylish and somber film tells the tale of Alex Corvis (Mabius) who is wrongly executed for the murder of his girlfriend (O'Keefe) and returns from the dead (with the help of an otherworldly crow) to seek vengeance against the dirty cops responsible. Nalluri directs the grisly proceedings with much visual panache and is ably abetted by a capable lead cast who brings this tragic, poetic, and exciting tale to life. Unfortunately the villains are so repellent and sleazy that they are almost cartoonish, which is at odds with the tone of the film. The DVD is an absolute knockout; the picture is razor sharp and clear despite the dark and smoky look of the film. The Surround sound is exemplary, giving the loud songs their desired punch and Beltrami's driving, moving score the foreground presence it deserves. The featurettes are brief but excellent and include behind-the-scenes clips. The audio commentary is informative and interesting, ping-ponging back and forth between the various production members who discuss the origin of the production, onset changes, design ideas, and character motivation. —*DG*
Movie: 🎬🎬 *DVD:* 🎬🎬🎬🎬
Buena Vista Home Entertainment (Cat #21463, UPC #78693614274). Widescreen (1.85:1) anamorphic. DTS Dolby Digital Surround 5.1; Dolby Digital Surround. $29.99. Keepcase. *LANG:* English. *SUB:* English. *CAP:* English. *FEATURES:* 18 chapter links ⚫ Insert card/chapter listing ⚫ Behind-the-scenes featurette ⚫ Behind-the-makeup featurette ⚫ Production design image gallery ⚫ "Who's That Bird?" featurette ⚫ Commentary: Nalluri, Mabius, Jeff Most, Beltrami, Maia Javan ⚫ DVD-ROM screenplay/ film viewer ⚫ Weblinks.
2000 (R) 102m/C Eric Mabius, Kirsten Dunst, Fred Ward, Jodi Lyn O'Keefe, William Atherton, Dale Midkiff, Grant Shaud; *D:* Bharat Nalluri; *W:* Chip Johannessen; *C:* Carolyn Chen; *M:* Marco Beltrami.

Crucible of Terror

Mad sculptor (Raven) covers beautiful models with hot wax then encases them in plaster and bronze. It's every bit as trite and poorly done as it sounds. Curiously, though, the DVD provides an excellent image with no signs of wear worth noting. —*MM*
Movie: 🐶 *DVD:* 🎬🎬½
Image Entertainment (Cat #ID6147TVDVD, UPC #014381614725). Full frame. Dolby Digital Mono. $24.99. Snapper. *LANG:*

English; Spanish. *FEATURES:* 16 chapter links ⚫ Music and sound effects track.
1972 95m/C *GB* Mike Raven, Mary Maude, James Bolam, John Arnatt, Ronald Lacey, Judy Matheson, Me Me Lay, Melissa Stribling, Beth Morris; *D:* Ted Hooker; *W:* Ted Hooker, Tom Parkinson; *C:* Peter Newbrook.

The Crush

Fourteen-year-old temptress Silverstone (in her debut) develops an obsessive crush on handsome 28-year-old Elwes, who rents her family's guest house. It's a pubescent variation on the standard "killer blonde" formula originated in *Fatal Attraction, Basic Instinct,* and all the rest, without enough style or inventiveness to separate it from the pack. The cast is attractive; the production values a thin cut above the norm; exploitative elements are kept to a minimum. The widescreen DVD image is only a slight improvement over tape. —*MM*
Movie: 🎬½ *DVD:* 🎬🎬½
Warner Home Video, Inc. Widescreen letterboxed. $24.95. Snapper. *LANG:* English. *SUB:* English; French; Spanish. *FEATURES:* 25 chapter links ⚫ Cast thumbnail bios.
1993 (R) 89m/C Cary Elwes, Alicia Silverstone, Jennifer Rubin, Kurtwood Smith, Gwynyth Walsh, Amber Benson; *D:* Alan Shapiro; *W:* Alan Shapiro; *C:* Bruce Surtees; *M:* Graeme Revell. *AWARDS:* MTV Movie Awards '94: Breakthrough Perf. (Silverstone), Villain (Silverstone).

A Cry in the Wild

Fourteen-year-old Brian Robeson (Rushton) must find his way back to civilization after he's the lone survivor of a small plane crash in the Canadian woods. Think a combination of *Never Cry Wolf* and *Castaway* but without the fancy special effects. Nature photography is good and the image is generally fine for a Corman production. The full-frame DVD image is still only a slight improvement over tape. —*MM*
Movie: 🎬🎬½ *DVD:* 🎬🎬½
New Concorde (Cat #NH20365 D, UPC #736991236592). Full frame. Stereo. $14.98. Keepcase. *LANG:* English. *FEATURES:* 24 chapter links ⚫ Talent files ⚫ Trailers.
1990 (PG) 93m/C Jared Rushton, Ned Beatty, Pamela Sue Martin, Stephen Meadows; *D:* Mark Griffiths; *W:* Catherine Cyran.

Cry Uncle

Comic mystery follows a plump private eye (Garfield) who investigates a blackmailing case involving a film of orgies in which he participated. Even for Troma, this one's pretty strange. The remastered film looks about as sharp as could be expected for low-budget early '70s exploitation. It's rough, pale, and hollow-sounding. —*MM*
Movie: 🎬½ *DVD:* 🎬🎬
Troma Team Video (Cat #9950). Widescreen (1.66:1) letterboxed. $24.95.

Keepcase. *LANG:* English. *FEATURES:* Intro by Troma president Lloyd Kaufman ⚫ Commentary: Avildsen, Odell, Garfield, Kaufman ⚫ The usual "Tromatic" extras ⚫ Crew interviews ⚫ Trailers.
1971 (R) 85m/C Allen (Goorwitz) Garfield, Paul Sorvino, Devin Goldenberg, Madeleine Le Roux; *D:* John G. Avildsen; *W:* David Odell; *C:* John G. Avildsen; *M:* Harper Mckay.

Cujo

Cujo, a rabid St. Bernard, traps a mother and her son (Dee Wallace Stone and Danny Pintauro) in the family Pinto, which has just died at a remote farmhouse. The characters are colorful and though the film is a bit too long, the dog attacks are harrowing. Cujo is easily as frightening as any of author Stephen King's supernatural monsters. With artifacts and pixels littering any large bright area of solid color and a soft grainy image, the barebones DVD is no improvement over VHS tape. —*MM*
Movie: 🎬🎬🎬½ *DVD:* 🎬🎬½
Artisan Entertainment (Cat #10022, UPC #017153100228). Full frame. $24.99. Keepcase. *LANG:* English. *FEATURES:* 27 chapter links.
1983 (R) 94m/C Dee Wallace Stone, Daniel Hugh-Kelly, Danny Pintauro, Ed Lauter, Christopher Stone, Kaiulani Lee, Mills Watson, Jerry Hardin, Billy Jacoby, Sandy Ward; *D:* Lewis Teague; *W:* Lauren Currier, Don Carlos Dunaway; *C:* Jan De Bont; *M:* Charles Bernstein.

The Curious Dr. Humpp

A short review can barely describe this legendary '60s Argentinian exploitation. A mad scientist (Barbero) has his monster (with a light in his forehead) kidnap people engaged in sex. Dr. H extracts their libidos to preserve his youth. According to Frank Henenlotter's liner notes, the sexual content was enhanced with inserts of American actors, but those are neatly integrated with the other footage and fit perfectly into the loosey-goosey plot. Remarkably, the black-and-white photography looks good, and the disc appears to have been made from a pristine original. (That is the only sense in which the word "pristine" could be used here.) Sound is all that the funky score needs. Of the extras, the three short films are most bizarre. —*MM*
Movie: 🎬🎬🎬 *DVD:* 🎬🎬🎬
Image Entertainment (Cat #ID9736SW DVD, UPC #014381973624). Full frame. Dolby Digital Mono. $24.99. Snapper. *LANG:* English. *FEATURES:* 12 chapter links ⚫ 3 exploitation shorts ⚫ Alternate title sequence ⚫ Trailers, TV, and radio spots ⚫ Gallery of exploitation art.
1970 87m/B *AR* Ricardo Bauleo, Aldo Barbero; *D:* Emilio Vieyra; *W:* Emilio Vieyra, Raul Zorrilla; *C:* Anibal Gonzalez Paz; *M:* Victor Buchino.

Curse of the Puppet Master: The Human Experiment

The little guys are back after a four-year break. This time, they're trying to prevent their new master, the evil Dr. Magrew, from transforming more victims into living dolls. The director "Victoria Sloan" is really Dave DeCoteau. DVD boasts a slightly better image than the earlier installments. Disc is also available as part of the *Puppet Master Collection* boxed set. —*MM*
Movie: 🎞🎞 **DVD:** 🎞🎞
Full Moon Pictures (Cat #FUM-DV 8061, UPC #763843806160). Full frame. $16.99. Keepcase. *LANG:* English. *FEATURES:* 24 chapter links • Behind-the-scenes Videozone magazine • Trailers.
1998 (R) 90m/C George Peck, Emily Harrison, Michael Guerin, Robert Donovan; *D:* David DeCoteau; *W:* Benjamin Carr; *C:* Howard Wexler; *M:* Richard Band.

The Curve

Think *Dead Man on Campus* since you've got basically the same premise. College roommates Tim (Lillard), Rand (Batinkoff), and Chris (Vartan) learn that the student myth is true at their small university. Should a roomie commit suicide, the survivors receive an automatic 4.0 for the semester. So Tim offs Rand and has Chris help him cover things up. Naturally nothing works out as expected, and it's not nearly as clever as it's trying to be, though some of the humor is sharp. The image is generally good. It's not a major step up from VHS tape, but it's all that the production demands. —*MM* **AKA:** Dead Man's Curve.
Movie: 🎞🎞 **DVD:** 🎞🎞½
Trimark Home Video (Cat #7092). Widescreen letterboxed. Dolby Digital Stereo. $24.99. Keepcase. *LANG:* English. *FEATURES:* Trailers • 30 chapter links.
1997 (R) 90m/C Matthew Lillard, Michael Vartan, Randall Batinkoff, Keri Russell, Dana Delany, Tamara Craig Thomas, Anthony Griffin, Bo Dietle, Kevin Huff, Henry Stozier; *D:* Dan Rosen; *W:* Dan Rosen; *C:* Joey Forsyte.

Cut

With her acting career on the skids, Vanessa (Ringwald) decides to accept the invitation from a group of young filmmakers to complete the horror film *Hot Blooded,* which she began 12 years before. (Production was halted when the leading man killed the director.) Since then, anyone who has attempted to finish the film has met a gruesome end. For my money, this one's got a meaner and more realistic streak than the similar *Scream* entries, though perhaps the presence of Molly Ringwald in such a curious role colors my opinion. The image of this Australian production is nothing special, but the English subtitles are a help with some of those growly accents. To access the previews, click on the Trimark logo on the main menu. —*MM*

Movie: 🎞🎞½ **DVD:** 🎞🎞
Trimark Home Video (Cat #7549D, UPC #031398754923). Widescreen letterboxed. Dolby Digital Stereo. $24.99. Keepcase. *LANG:* English. *SUB:* English; French; Spanish. *FEATURES:* 24 chapter links • Previews.
2000 (R) 82m/C Molly Ringwald, Jessica Napier, Simon Bossell, Kylie Minogue; *D:* Kimble Rendall; *W:* Dave Warner; *C:* David Foreman; *M:* Guy Gross.

Cut Throats Nine

Violent, bizarre spaghetti western owes something to *Treasure of the Sierra Madre.* Elaborate circumstances force a soldier to chain himself and his beautiful daughter to the prisoners he has been escorting to the stockade. The setting is snow-covered mountains. The struggle for survival changes when they realize that the chains are made of gold. Though the harsh image cannot be compared to contemporary studio releases, the DVD looks pretty good for an import of this age. Sound is acceptable. —*MM*
Movie: 🎞🎞½ **DVD:** 🎞🎞
Luminous Film & Video (Cat #EDE-03). Widescreen letterboxed. $19.98. Keepcase. *LANG:* English. *FEATURES:* Talent files • 8 chapter links • Trailers • Publicity stills.
1972 90m/C *SP* Emma Cohen, Robert Hundar, Alberto Dalbes, Manuel Tejada, Antonio Iranzo; *D:* Joaquin Luis Romero Marchent; *W:* Santiago Moncada, Jaoquin Romero Hernandez, Joaquin Luis Romero Marchent; *C:* Luis Cuadrado; *M:* Carmelo A. Bernaola.

Cutaway

Undercover cop Vic Cooper (Baldwin) infiltrates a professional sky-diving team that may be involved with drug smuggling in Florida. The leader, Redline (Berenger), is a charismatic fellow and Turbo (Rodman) might also be in on the scheme. Actually, the plot is no more important than some fairly spectacular aerial footage. DVD does a good job with the normally sharp image. Colors in the bright jump suits remain true. Sound is very good. —*MM*
Movie: 🎞🎞½ **DVD:** 🎞🎞🎞
Artisan Entertainment (Cat #11495, UPC #012236114956). Widescreen anamorphic. Dolby Digital Surround Stereo. $24.98. Snapper. *LANG:* English. *CAP:* English. *FEATURES:* 15 chapter links • Commentary: Baldwin, Bahns • Commentary: Guy Manos • Trailer • Talent files • Production notes.
2000 (R) 104m/C Tom Berenger, Stephen Baldwin, Dennis Rodman, Maxine Bahns, Casper Van Dien, Ron Silver; *D:* Guy Manos; *W:* Guy Manos, Greg Manos; *C:* Gerry Lively.

The Cutting Edge

Spoiled figure skater Kate's (Kelly) quest for Olympic gold is seriously hampered by her inability to be civil with any of her part-

ners. In a final effort to snag a medal, she teams up with injured hockey player Doug (Sweeney). This crowd-pleaser is saddled with a formulaic plot, but it succeeds because the two leads strike such sparks. The image is sharp but hazy at times, and scratches and white-spots are evident from the source print. The colors come across well, as the fleshtones look natural and the costumes stand out against the ice. For the most part the audio stays in the center and front channels, with the Surround sound speakers being used primarily for musical cues and audience noise. The dialogue is clear and audible, and there is no hiss on the soundtrack. —*MM/ML*
Movie: 🎞🎞🎞 **DVD:** 🎞🎞🎞
MGM Home Entertainment (UPC #027616857743). Widescreen (1.85:1) anamorphic. Dolby Digital Surround. $19.98. Keepcase. *LANG:* English; French. *SUB:* French; Spanish. *FEATURES:* Trailer.
1992 (PG) 101m/C D.B. Sweeney, Moira Kelly, Roy Dotrice, Terry O'Quinn, Dwier Brown, Rachelle Ottley, Jo Jo Starbuck; *D:* Paul Michael Glaser; *W:* Tony Gilroy; *C:* Elliot Davis; *M:* Patrick Williams.

Cyberotica

The Computer Escapes company sells virtual reality vacations to several attractive young women who have sexual fantasies. This is amateur shot-on-video soft-core, little better than home movies. Image quality is equal to *America's Funniest Home Videos,* but you gotta love the scene where the tiger tattoo on one girl's butt complements her partner's leopard skin briefs. Now, that's attention to detail. —*MM*
Movie: 🎞 **DVD:** 🎞
El Independent Cinema (Cat #sc-1005-dvd, UPC #612385100598). Full frame. $19.98. Keepcase. *LANG:* English. *FEATURES:* 9 chapter links • Trailers • Extra scenes.
2000 110m/C Kim Evans, Marie Hopkins, Jill Mandell, Ross Stewart, Patty Wilson, Bill Beyn, Mary Vautin; *D:* John Kain; *W:* Ann Taylor; *C:* John March; *M:* Kenton Lee.

Cyborg

When a really bad movie plumbs the depths of its own badness and comes up smiling, it's called an alternative classic. This is just such a film. It is the *Mommie Dearest* of post-apocalyptic thrillers. From its redundant beginning to characters named for guitars to the clichéd conclusion, it is filled with one glorious goof after another. Van Damme does his splits, etc. Grain increases noticeably in the special effects scenes, and several clothing patterns flash horribly. The flaws come from the original but they're still bothersome. —*MM*
Movie: 🎞🎞 **DVD:** 🎞
MGM Home Entertainment (Cat #906-561). Widescreen (1.85:1) letterboxed; full frame. Dolby Digital Stereo. $24.98. Slipcase. *LANG:* English; French. *SUB:* French; Spanish. *CAP:* English. *FEATURES:* Trailer • 21 chapter links.

1989 (R) 85m/C Jean-Claude Van Damme, Deborah Richter, Vincent Klyn, Dayle Haddon, Alex Daniels, Terrie Batson, Janice Graser, Jackson "Rock" Pinckney; **D:** Albert Pyun; **W:** Kitty Chalmers; **C:** Philip Alan Waters; **M:** Kevin Bassinson.

Cyrano de Bergerac

This silent version of Edmond Rostand's novel (and the play) is one of the most remarkable works of its era. Much of it is so dated that it's recommended more to serious students of film than to fans. But anyone will be astonished at the early Pathé Stencil Color process. As the liner notes explain, it was essentially a frame-by-frame hand-tinting similar to silk screen. The result is much more delicate than Technicolor or any of today's processes. Though the original contains some scratches and stains, this DVD looks very good. Credit goes to film historian David Shepard. —*MM*
Movie: 🐾🐾🐾½ **DVD:** 🐾🐾🐾½
Image Entertainment (Cat #ID9410SDVD, UPC #014381941029). Full frame. Dolby Digital Stereo. $24.99. Snapper. *LANG:* Silent. *SUB:* English intertitles. *FEATURES:* 16 chapter links.
1925 114m/C *IT FR* Pierre Magnier, Linda Moglia, Angelo Ferrari; **D:** Augusto Genina; **M:** Carlo Moser.

Da Hip Hop Witch

This disc is not so much a parody of *Blair Witch Project* as a collection of rap artists' unscripted monologues about a woman who is doing terrible things to them. It also marks the return to the screen of Vanilla Ice, last seen in the abominable *Cool As Ice*. The shot-on-video footage is deliberately unpolished and poorly focused. Fans of the music are the target audience. It is inconceivable that anyone else would make it through more than five minutes of this vanity project. Image and sound are identical to VHS tape. —*MM*
Movie: 🐾 **DVD:** 🐾
A-PIX Entertainment Inc. (Cat #APX27031, UPC #783722703137). Full frame. Dolby Digital 5.1 Surround Stereo. $19.98. Keepcase. *LANG:* English. *SUB:* Spanish. *FEATURES:* 15 chapter links ▪ Commentary: Resteghini ▪ Behind-the-scenes footage.
2000 (R) 93m/C Stacii Jae Johnson, Dale Resteghini, Pras, Killah Priest, Spliff Star, Mobb Deep, (Marshall Mathers) Eminem, Rock, Colleen (Ann) (Vitamin C) Fitzpatrick; **D:** Dale Resteghini; **W:** Dale Resteghini.

Dakota

Troubled half-breed teen (Phillips) works for a rancher (Cummins), romances his daughter (Norton), and befriends his crippled 12-year-old son (Burton) in a well-meaning and predictable drama. The DVD image is very sharp and clear, showing only a slight amount of grain at times. The mono mix yields clear and audible dialogue without any hiss or background noise. —*MM/ML*

Movie: 🐾🐾 **DVD:** 🐾🐾½
Anchor Bay (Cat #11379). Widescreen (1.85:1) anamorphic. Dolby Digital Mono. $29.98. Keepcase. *LANG:* English. *FEATURES:* Trailer.
1988 (PG) 96m/C Lou Diamond Phillips, Dee Dee Norton, Eli Cummins, Herta Ware, Jordan Burton; **D:** Fred Holmes; **C:** James W. Wrenn.

Dame Edna's Neighbourhood Watch 2

Australian-born Barry Humphries has struck a cultural gold mine in England with his *Dame Edna's Neighbourhood Watch*. It's a simple television show in which "he" (dressed in outrageous drag outfits) selects three members of the studio audience (with his "Purple Possum Picker"—a strand of gladiolas) to participate in a quiz where the contestants can win "fabulous" prizes. The catch is, one of the "random" picks has had her house ransacked by Dame Edna's minions and is in for 20 minutes of public embarrassment and verbal jibs at the hands of the devilish witty cross-dressing queen. This DVD presents six show episodes which are best watched and enjoyed one at a time over a period of several viewings. They tend to be somewhat repetitious if viewed all at once—after all, Dame Edna is a persona that should be savored in small doses, not devoured in one sitting. Image and sound are acceptable. —*RJT*
Movie: 🐾🐾 **DVD:** 🐾🐾½
Image Entertainment (Cat #ID9596AGDVD, UPC #014381959628). Full frame. Dolby Digital Surround Stereo. $24.99. Snapper. *LANG:* English. *FEATURES:* 6 show episodes with 7 chapter markers each.
1992 ?m/C *GB* Barry Humphries.

Damien: Omen 2

Teenaged son of Satan (Jonathan Scott-Taylor) goes off to military school where Lance Henriksen is the Staff Sergeant of Satan. The relative subtlety of the first film is nowhere to be found. In its place is clichéd Hollywood nonsense involving a crow that apparently scares people to death. The best supernatural stories of this school use the religious element much more sparingly. The basic problem here is poor writing—in both plot and character development—so the presence of star William Holden is mostly wasted. An overreliance on Jerry Goldsmith's hyperventilating music doesn't help either. DVD presents a very good widescreen image. The studio has taken some care with it, providing more extras than the film really deserves. The film is also available as part of *The Omen Collection* boxed set. —*MM*
Movie: 🐾 **DVD:** 🐾🐾½
20th Century Fox Home Entertainment (Cat #2000449, UPC #024543004493). Widescreen (2.35:1) anamorphic. Dolby Digital Surround; Mono. $29.98. Keepcase. *LANG:* English; French. *SUB:* English; Spanish. *FEATURES:* 20 chapter links ▪

Commentary: producer Harvey Bernhard, DVD producer J.M. Kenney ▪ Trailer.
1978 (R) 110m/C William Holden, Lee Grant, Lew Ayres, Robert Foxworth, Sylvia Sidney, Lance Henriksen, Jonathan Scott-Taylor, Nicholas Pryor, Allan Arbus, Meshach Taylor; **D:** Don Taylor; **W:** Mike Hodges; **C:** Bill Butler; **M:** Jerry Goldsmith.

Damn the Defiant

Adventure abounds as Captain Crawford (Guinness) of the HMS *Defiant* finds himself up against the French (in the Napoleonic wars), his vicious second-in-command Scott-Padget (Bogarde), and a mutinous crew. It's grand stuff with a rare degree of attention paid to historical detail. The same care appears to have gone into the DVD transfer. The image is sharp and bright, coming from either a carefully preserved or well-restored original. The choice of image sizes is another plus. —*MM* **AKA:** HMS Defiant.
Movie: 🐾🐾🐾½ **DVD:** 🐾🐾🐾½
Columbia Tristar Home Video (Cat #08259, UPC #043396082595). Widescreen (2.35:1) anamorphic; full frame. Dolby Digital Mono. $24.95. Keepcase. *LANG:* English. *SUB:* English; French; Spanish; Portuguese, Chinese, Korean, Thai. *FEATURES:* 28 chapter links ▪ Vintage advertising ▪ Talent files ▪ Trailers ▪ Production notes.
1962 101m/C *GB* Alec Guinness, Dirk Bogarde, Maurice Denham, Anthony Quayle; **D:** Lewis Gilbert; **W:** Nigel Kneale, Edmund H. North; **C:** Christopher Challis; **M:** Clifton Parker.

Dance with a Stranger

Marilyn Monroe lookalike Ruth Ellis (Richardson) gained notoriety as the last woman to be executed in Great Britain. This emotional and sometimes violent film mirrors the sensationalism produced in the 1950s. It follows Ruth's pre-trial life and her perpetual struggle to maintain her independence. The period setting is evoked with muted, slightly smoky colors in the interiors, and a pale look to many exteriors. According to the box copy, lenses from the 1950s were used to heighten that feeling of authenticity. Perhaps that accounts for the soft quality of the image. Mono sound is fine. —*MM*
Movie: 🐾🐾🐾½ **DVD:** 🐾🐾½
MGM Home Entertainment (Cat #1001 447, UPC #027616857675). Widescreen (1.66:1) letterboxed. Dolby Digital Mono. $19.98. Keepcase. *LANG:* English. *SUB:* French; Spanish. *CAP:* English. *FEATURES:* 16 chapter links ▪ Alternate ending ▪ Trailer.
1985 (R) 101m/C *GB* Miranda Richardson, Rupert Everett, Ian Holm, Joanne Whalley, Matthew Carroll, Tom Chadbon, Jane Bertish, David Troughton, Paul Mooney, Stratford Johns, Susan Kyd, Leslie Manville, Sallie-Anne Field, Martin Murphy, Michael Jenn, Daniel Massey; **D:** Mike Newell; **W:** Shelagh Delaney; **C:** Peter Hannan; **M:** Richard Hartley. *AWARDS:* Cannes '85: Film.

Dance with the Devil

Perdita Durango (Perez) is ready to kill someone—anyone—when she meets Romeo Doloroso (Bardem) at a border crossing. She's got her reasons and Romeo, a bank robber/smuggler/sorcerer, is just the guy to help her realize her ambitions. But he has already betrayed one partner (Segura) and he's got to deliver a truckload of human fetuses to a gangster in Las Vegas. (It has something to do with cosmetics research.) He and Perdita still find time to kidnap a couple of wide-eyed caricatured American teenagers, Duane (Cross) and Estelle (Graham). At her leisure, Perdita can decide which one she wants to murder. Meanwhile, DEA agent Woody Dumas (Gandolfini) is on their trail, and an assassin is after him. Fans will spot elements of *The Getaway; Faster, Pussycat! Kill! Kill!; El Mariachi;* and *From Dusk Till Dawn.* The combination of violence, humor, and sex in this Spanish-Mexican-American production goes well beyond conventional limits. DVD looks fine but the widescreen image is the only visual improvement over tape. This is such crazy material that a commentary track is definitely called for. But that's not likely to happen unless director de la Iglesia has a commercial hit in America. —*MM* **AKA:** Perdita Durango.
Movie: 🎬🎬🎬 **DVD:** 🎬🎬½
A-PIX Entertainment Inc. (Cat #27015). Widescreen letterboxed. Dolby Digital 5.1 Surround Stereo. $19.98. Keepcase. *LANG:* English. *SUB:* Spanish. *FEATURES:* Trailers • Filmographies • 20 chapter links.
1997 (R) 126m/C *MX SP* Rosie Perez, Javier Bardem, Harley Cross, Aimee Graham, Don Stroud, James Gandolfini, Santiago Segura, Screamin' Jay Hawkins, Alex Cox, Carlos Bardem; **D:** Alex de la Iglesia; **W:** Alex de la Iglesia, Barry Gifford, Jorge Guerricaechevarria, David Trueba; **C:** Flavio Martinez Labiano; **M:** Simon Boswell.

Dancer in the Dark

Utterly devastating story of Selma, a young factory worker who is going blind due to a genetic disease. To save her son from the same affliction, she makes an incredible sacrifice that ultimately brings her to tragedy. Deneuve is wonderful and Morse's performance (and character) will haunt you. Bjork is fine as Selma, but her greatest contribution to the film is her song writing. Director Von Trier gives the film an intentionally grainy look with oversaturated, bleeding colors for the fantasy dream sequences. Powerful but perhaps too reminiscent of Von Trier's *Breaking the Waves* and a bit hard to take at times. Incredibly depressing and not for all audiences, but lovers of art films will definitely find much to appreciate here. The disc is perfect, handling the variant looks of the film with sharpness and clarity. The extras are exhaustive and exhausting; the audio commentaries are rich and interesting, answering every question one could have about the film. The featurettes offer interesting interviews, behind-the-scenes footage, and alternate cuts of some of the musical numbers are included. Unfortunately the longer version of the "107 Steps" (which was shown when the film premiered at Cannes) is not included here. The song-only access to the film is an appreciated extra. —*DG*
Movie: 🎬🎬🎬½ **DVD:** 🎬🎬🎬½
New Line Home Video (Cat #N5199, UPC #79404351992). Widescreen (2.35:1) anamorphic. DTS Surround Sound; Dolby Digital 5.1. $24.98. Snapper. *LANG:* English. *SUB:* English. *CAP:* English. *FEATURES:* 30 chapter links • Commentary: Von Trier, Vibeke Windelov, Peter Hjorth, Per Kirkeby • Commentary: Vincent Paterson • "100 Cameras: Capturing Lars Von Trier's Vision" documentary • "Choreography: Creating Vincent Paterson's Dance Sequences" documentary • Selma's Music: song access to the film • Alternate scenes • Cast and crew filmographies • Original theatrical trailer • DVD-ROM link to website.
1999 (R) 141m/C *DK SW FR* Bjork, Catherine Deneuve, David Morse, Peter Stormare, Cara Seymour, Joel Grey, Vincent Paterson, Vladica Kostic, Jean-Marc Barr, Udo Kier, Zeljko Ivanek; **D:** Lars von Trier; **W:** Lars von Trier; **C:** Robby Muller; **M:** Bjork. *AWARDS:* Cannes '00: Actress, Film; Ind. Spirit '01: Foreign Film; *NOM:* Oscars '00: Song ("I've Seen It All").

Dangerous Curves

Lawyer John Burnsides (Carradine) sets off to find Stella Crosby (Bahns), a woman from his past. It turns out that she's involved with various thugs and a missing $4 million. The comic thriller has some nice moments. Image is no better than tape, in part because the gray Irish light tends to soften shapes. —*MM*
Movie: 🎬🎬½ **DVD:** 🎬🎬
New Concorde (Cat #NH20752D, UPC #736991475243). Full frame. $19.99. Keepcase. *LANG:* English. *FEATURES:* 24 chapter links • Trailers • Talent files.
1999 (R) 85m/C Robert Carradine, David Carradine, Maxine Bahns, Marina Carradine; **D:** Jeremiah Cullinane; **W:** Christopher Wood; **C:** Laurence Manly; **M:** Siobhan Cleary.

Darkdrive

On the commentary track, director Roth describes this sci-fi actioner as a digital remake of *Jacob's Ladder* inspired by "An Occurrence at Owl Creek Bridge." It's also a low-budget film that gains little visually on DVD, and the filmmakers make no attempt to hide its deficiencies. In fact, their testy "MST3K" approach to the picture is a refreshing counterpoint to the orgy of self-congratulation that normally accompanies such enterprises. —*MM*
Movie: 🎬🎬 **DVD:** 🎬🎬½
MTI Home Video (Cat #7003). Full frame. Dolby Digital Stereo. $24.95. Keepcase. *LANG:* English. *FEATURES:* 9 chapter links • Commentary • Talent files • Production slides • DVD credits.
1998 (R) 100m/C Ken Olandt, Julie Benz, Claire Stansfield, Carlo Scandiuzzi; **D:** Phillip J. Roth; **W:** Alec Carlin; **C:** Andres Garreton; **M:** Jim Goodwin.

Darkroom

Economically made psycho killer thriller is a fair little video premiere. The crazy-guy-with-camera bit has been used countless times and not much new is done with it here. The flowing '80s hairdos are more memorable. The full-frame disc is not appreciably superior to VHS tape. —*MM*
Movie: 🎬½ **DVD:** 🎬½
Simitar Entertainment (Cat #7607). Full frame. Dolby Digital Stereo. $14.98. Keepcase. *LANG:* English. *FEATURES:* 8 chapter links • Producer filmography • 2 Simitar trailers.
1990 90m/C Jill Pierce, Jeffrey Allen Arbaugh, Sara Lee Wade, Aaron Teich; **D:** Terrence O'Hara.

Darkside Blues

Japanese animation presents yet another bleak vision of the near future. The title character, Darkside, is a mopey Byronic figure. The imaginative plot contains some fairly sadistic violence, though it is not excessive compared to other works in the genre. Sound is fine. The image has a pale, overly bright look that causes large areas of white to glow. It is intentional. —*MM*
Movie: 🎬🎬 **DVD:** 🎬🎬½
Central Park Media/U.S. Manga Corps (Cat #1827). Full frame. Dolby Digital Surround Stereo; Dolby Digital Stereo. $26.97. Keepcase. *LANG:* Japanese; English. *SUB:* English. *CAP:* English. *FEATURES:* 10 chapter links • Weblink • Voice cast listing.
1999 83m/C *JP* **D:** Yoshimichi Furukawa; **V:** Akira Natsuki, Hideyuki Hori.

Daughter of Horror / Dementia

A young woman finds herself involved with a porcine mobster who resembles her abusive father. Trouble is, dad's dead and daughter dearest abetted his departure. Obscure venture into expressionism was banned ten times by the New York State Board of Censors. The *Dementia* title was re-edited to *Daughter of Horror* and narration by Ed McMahon was added. This smart DVD contains both versions. *Dementia* is said to be taken from the original negative, and *Daughter* from a print. Both look exceptionally good, with the original having the edge on quality, although it's not completely free of speckles either. —*MM/GE* **AKA:** Dementia.
Movie: 🎬🎬🎬½ **DVD:** 🎬🎬🎬
Kino on Video (UPC #738329018528). Full frame. $29.95. Keepcase. *LANG:* English. *FEATURES:* "Dementia: A Case Study," illustrated essay on the making of the film • Trailer • Press book • Stills gallery.

1955 60m/B Adrienne Barrett, Ben Roseman, Richard Barron, Ed Hinkle, Lucille Howland, Angelo Rossitto, Bruno VeSota; **D:** John Parker; **W:** John Parker; **C:** William C. Thompson; **M:** George Antheil; **V:** Marni Nixon; **Nar:** Ed McMahon.

DaVinci's War

Frank DaVinci's (Travolta) sister is murdered and he wants revenge. So he hooks up with a professional killer (Nouri) and a group of homeless Vietnam vets and gets the firepower he needs to blow away the bad guys. Actually, the standard-issue plot is enlivened by some fairly interesting characters. DVD might be a hair more detailed than VHS tape, but only that. —*MM*
Movie: ♫♫½ **DVD:** ♫♫
Image Entertainment (Cat #OVE9020DVD, UPC #014381902020). Full frame. Dolby Digital Stereo. $24.99. Snapper. *LANG:* English. *FEATURES:* 12 chapter links • Trailers.
1992 (R) 94m/C Joey Travolta, Michael Nouri, Vanity, Richard Foronjy, Branscombe Richmond, Sam Jones, Jack Bannon, Brian Robbins, James Russo; **D:** Raymond Martino; **W:** Raymond Martino; **M:** Jeff Lass.

Dawn Rider / Trail Beyond

In the first feature, Wayne is a cowboy out for revenge on the gang that murdered his dad. In the second, the Duke and sidekick (Beery Jr.) head for Canada to find a girl and a goldmine. The first film is simply unwatchable—muddy, filled with static and artifacts. The second is better but the opening credits jitter in the frame. For the most devoted fans only, and not a bargain even at the price. —*MM*
Movie: ♫♫ **DVD:** ♫
Madacy Entertainment (Cat #DVD-9-9003-3, UPC #056775002299). Full frame. Dolby Digital Mono. $9.99. Keepcase. *LANG:* English. *FEATURES:* 8 chapter links • John Wayne filmography 1945–56 • Trivia quiz. Disc is also available in "The John Wayne Collection" (cat. #DVD-9-9003; UPC 056775001995).
1935 60m/B John Wayne, Marion Burns, Yakima Canutt; **D:** Robert North Bradbury.

A Day in Black and White

This film is a series of discussions about race and other matters. Very little happens beyond people talking to, at, and around each other. At the center is a conversation between Mike (Perrineau) and his friend Richard (DeSando) about a speech that Mike is supposed to write for his girlfriend Nicole (Swift), a teacher. Mike is black; Richard and Nicole are white. Director Hall is more interested in the areas of accommodation and understanding than in confrontation, and throughout he displays a strong sense of humor. Given the static nature of the material, it gains little on DVD beyond the commentary track by director Hall, director of photography Konczals, and editor Laskas. —*MM*
Movie: ♫♫½ **DVD:** ♫♫
Xenon Entertainment (Cat #4091DVD, UPC #000799409121). Full frame. $19.98. Keepcase. *LANG:* English. *FEATURES:* 12 chapter links • Trailers • Commentary.
2001 85m/C Harold Perrineau Jr., Anthony De Sando, Francie Swift; **D:** Desmond Hall; **W:** Desmond Hall; **C:** Peter Konczal; **M:** Loris Holland.

Day of the Animals

Nature goes wild when a depleted ozone layer has exposed them to radiation, turning Bambi and Bugs into ravaging beasts. Unaware of the transformation, a group of backpackers—many familiar faces from television—trek into Sierras and are set upon by critters in completely unpersuasive attack scenes. It's all much too silly to be remotely frightening. The disc is a slapdash full-frame transfer of a low-budget widescreen '70s drive-in horror. Without a menu, the disc is no different from VHS tape. —*MM* **AKA:** Something Is Out There.
Movie: ♫ **DVD:** ♫
Digital Versatile Disc Ltd. (Cat #144). Full frame. $19.95. *LANG:* English.
1977 (PG) 95m/C Christopher George, Leslie Nielsen, Lynda Day George, Richard Jaeckel, Michael Ansara, Ruth Roman, Jon Cedar, Susan Backlinie, Andrew Stevens, Gil Lamb; **D:** William Girdler; **W:** William W. Norton Sr.; **C:** Robert Sorrentino; **M:** Lalo Schifrin.

The Day the Earth Caught Fire

The Earth is knocked out of its orbit and sent hurtling toward the sun when nuclear testing is done simultaneously at the North and South Poles. This British sleeper is one of the best examples of intelligent '60s SF. DVD is virtually pristine. Even the bookend tinted scenes look fine. Image and sound are excellent, but the best part of the disc is the commentary by director Guest and journalist Ted Newsom, who guides the talk in the right directions. —*MM*
Movie: ♫♫♫½ **DVD:** ♫♫♫½
Anchor Bay (Cat #DV11429, UPC #013131142990). Widescreen (2.35:1) anamorphic. Dolby Digital Mono. $24.98. Keepcase. *LANG:* English. *FEATURES:* 22 chapter links • Trailer • Radio and TV spots • Commentary: Val Guest, Ted Newsom • Still gallery • Val Guest thumbnail bio.
1961 95m/B Janet Munro, Edward Judd, Leo McKern; **D:** Val Guest; **W:** Wolf Mankowitz, Val Guest; **C:** Harry Waxman; **M:** Stanley Black. *AWARDS:* British Acad. '61: Screenplay.

The Daytrippers

Happily married Eliza (Davis) lives on Long Island while husband Louis (Tucci) goes to work in Manhattan. Then she finds what might be a love letter addressed to him. Her "helpful" mom Rita (Meara) suggests they seek out Louis to find the truth. Dad (McNamara) packs them up in the family station wagon along with sister Jo (Posey) and Jo's beau Carl (Schreiber) and off they all head to the city where a day and night of adventures await. The transfer faithfully captures the undersaturated colors and minimal lighting usually associated with low-budget filmmaking. Black levels provide adequate shadow definition, but details lack depth and some scenes look soft. Fleshtones are natural during the daytime scenes, only to take on a pasty quality during nighttime scenes. The source is blemish-free, exhibiting a few instances where the image gets very grainy. (With faces constantly spilling over the edge of the frame, releasing the film as a full-frame DVD seems a bit short-sighted, though.) The dialogue-driven soundtrack, presented in Dolby Digital 2.0, does a satisfactory job of imaging an active sound field. —*EP/MM*
Movie: ♫♫♫ **DVD:** ♫♫½
Columbia Tristar Home Video (Cat #4744). Full frame. Dolby Digital Stereo. $24.99. Keepcase. *LANG:* English. *SUB:* English; French; Spanish. *FEATURES:* Trailer • Talent files.
1996 88m/C Hope Davis, Anne Meara, Parker Posey, Liev Schreiber, Pat McNamara, Stanley Tucci, Campbell Scott, Marcia Gay Harden, Andy Brown; **D:** Greg Mottola; **W:** Greg Mottola; **C:** John Inwood.

Deacon Brodie

British made-for-TV movie about the character who was the basis for Dr. Jekyll and Mr. Hyde is similar to *Tom Jones* in its setting and bawdy humor. In 1788 Edinburgh, Brodie (Connolly) is a larger-than-life character who consorts with hookers (McCormack) and enjoys other pleasures of life until he's framed for a crime and sentenced to be hanged on the very gallows that he designed. Veteran director Saville keeps things moving nicely and he got a fine lusty performance from his star. The full-frame image is no real improvement over tape. Sound is very good. —*MM*
Movie: ♫♫♫ **DVD:** ♫♫½
BFS Video (Cat #99958-D, UPC #0668 05919589). Full frame. Dolby Digital Mono. $29.98. Keepcase. *LANG:* English. *FEATURES:* 12 chapter links.
1998 90m/C *GB* Billy Connolly, Patrick Malahide, Catherine McCormack, Lorcan Cranitch; **D:** Philip Saville; **W:** Simon Donald; **C:** Ivan Strasburg; **M:** Simon Boswell.

Dead and Buried

Anyone unfamiliar with this rarely seen shocker is in for a real treat. It's one of the best sleepers around, filled with jolts and surprises. James Farentino is the sheriff of Potters Bluff, a New England seaside town where bizarre events are taking place, and seem somehow to involve his sweet wife (Anderson) and the garrulous undertaker/coroner (Albertson).

The film combines a series of genuinely horrifying images with macabre humor and a cold, fog-shrouded atmosphere. Lots of familiar faces in the supporting cast. On this import disc, the film is presented in a non-anamorphic widescreen and is letterboxed at 1.66:1. The framing appears to be fairly accurate, although there is some warping at the edge of the screen at times. The DVD image is so grainy that the grain seems to move and have a life of its own. Picture quality is inconsistent, and some of the scenes are very dark, while others are very bright, bordering on white-hot at times and others are fine. Dialogue is clear and audible, although volume noticeably dips at times, and there are audible pops from the soundtrack during the last third of the film. —MM/GH

Movie: 🐶🐶🐶🐶 **DVD:** 🐶🐶
Dragon Video Widescreen (1.66:1) letterboxed. Dolby Digital Mono. LANG: English; German. SUB: German; Dutch. FEATURES: Theatrical trailer ▪ Filmographies.
1981 (R) 95m/C James Farentino, Jack Albertson, Melody Anderson, Lisa Blount, Bill Quinn, Michael Pataki, Robert Englund, Barry Corbin, Lisa Marie; **D:** Gary Sherman; **W:** Dan O'Bannon, Ronald Shusett; **C:** Steven Poster; **M:** Joe Renzetti.

Dead Are Alive

Alcoholic archaeologist Jason (Cord) has come to Italy to search for Etruscan ruins near the home of orchestral conductor Nicos (John Marley) and his wife Myra (Samantha Eggar), Jason's ex-lover. Soon after he opens an Etruscan tomb, a series of violent murders begin. The above-average giallo shocker is much better than director Crispino's more popular Autopsy. DVD image quality is a mix of good and bad. The source print from which the digital transfer was made was in very bad shape. There is a green scratch running down the center of the frame for the majority of the film and a green hair in the lower left-hand corner. Throughout the film, scratches and blemishes abound. Also, many obvious edits and jumps suggest missing footage. Yet, the image shows very little grain, and the colors are only slightly washed-out. Mono sound gives clear and audible dialogue. However, the soundtrack was recorded a bit loud, so there is some distortion, accompanied by pops and hissing throughout the film. —ML

Movie: 🐶🐶½ **DVD:** 🐶🐶½
Luminous Film & Video Widescreen (2.35:1) letterboxed. Dolby Digital Mono. $19.98. Keepcase. LANG: English. FEATURES: Talent files ▪ Photo gallery ▪ Press book reproduction.
1972 103m/C IT Alex Cord, Samantha Eggar, John Marley, Nadja Tiller, Horst Frank, Enzo Tarascio; **D:** Armando Crispino; **W:** Armando Crispino, Lucio Battistrada; **C:** Erico Menczer; **M:** Riz Ortolani.

Dead Man

Depp wanders through the 19th-century west as William Blake, an Ohio accountant who runs afoul of the law. He is saved by an American Indian named Nobody (Farmer), who envisions him as the famous English poet. The two try to stay one step ahead of the hired guns and lawmen out to get them. The action is sporadic as Jarmusch is equally interested in polished visuals that that transferred beautifully to DVD. The black-and-white photography is evocative and richly textured. Sound is very good for Young's equally strong score. Jarmusch is something of an acquired taste but this is as good a place as any for the uninitiated to give him a try. —MM

Movie: 🐶🐶🐶 **DVD:** 🐶🐶🐶½
Miramax Pictures Home Video (Cat #21364, UPC #786936141788). Widescreen (1.78:1) anamorphic. Dolby Digital Surround Stereo. $32.99. Keepcase. LANG: English. SUB: French. FEATURES: 19 chapter links ▪ Deleted scenes and outtakes ▪ Trailer ▪ Music video ▪ Previews.
1995 (R) 121m/B Johnny Depp, Gary Farmer, Lance Henriksen, Michael Wincott, Mili Avital, Crispin Glover, Gabriel Byrne, Iggy Pop, Billy Bob Thornton, Jared Harris, Jimmie Ray Weeks, Mark Bringleson, John Hurt, Alfred Molina, Robert Mitchum; **D:** Jim Jarmusch; **W:** Jim Jarmusch; **C:** Robby Muller; **M:** Neil Young. AWARDS: N.Y. Film Critics '96: Cinematog.; Natl. Soc. Film Critics '96: Cinematog; NOM: Ind. Spirit '97: Cinematog., Film, Screenplay, Support. Actor (Farmer).

Dead Man Walking

The story of a nun whose anti-death penalty beliefs put her in moral crisis is based on a truth. Sarandon stars as Sister Helen Prejean, a nun who develops a relationship with death-row murderer Poncelet (Penn). She's unwavering in her Christian beliefs even though he shows no remorse for the two young lovers he murdered. Penn's performance is one of his best while writer/director Robbins presents both sides of the issue. The DVD transfer is clean and does not exhibit any notable signs of film defects or digital artifacting. Only the slightest hint of edge-enhancement is evident to give the image a sharper look. Color delineation is flawless without noise or bleeding, nicely reproducing the somber, yet sometimes stark and carefully crafted, color scheme of the movie. Both language tracks are well produced with good spatial integration and without noise. The Surround field is used sparingly. —GH/MM

Movie: 🐶🐶🐶½ **DVD:** 🐶🐶🐶
MGM Home Entertainment (Cat #9078 49). Widescreen (1.85:1) letterboxed; full frame. Dolby Digital Surround Stereo. $24.98. Keepcase. LANG: English; French. SUB: English; Spanish. FEATURES: Commentary: Robbins ▪ Theatrical trailer.
1995 (R) 122m/C Susan Sarandon, Sean Penn, Robert Prosky, Raymond J. Barry, R. Lee Ermey, Celia Weston, Lois Smith, Scott Wilson, Roberta Maxwell, Margo Martindale, Barton Heyman, Larry Pine; **D:** Tim Robbins; **W:** Tim Robbins; **C:** Roger Deakins; **M:** David Robbins. AWARDS: Oscars '95: Actress (Sarandon); Ind. Spirit '96: Actor (Penn); Screen Actors Guild '95: Actress (Sarandon); NOM: Oscars '95: Actor (Penn), Director (Robbins), Song ("Dead Man Walking"); Australian Film Inst. '96: Foreign Film; Golden Globes '96: Actor—Drama (Penn), Actress—Drama (Sarandon), Screenplay; Ind. Spirit '96: Support. Actress (Weston); MTV Movie Awards '96: Female Perf. (Sarandon); Screen Actors Guild '95: Actor (Penn).

Dead Men Don't Wear Plaid

Martin is hilarious as a private detective who encounters a bizarre assortment of suspects while trying to find the truth about a scientist's death. He is ingeniously interspliced with clips from old Warner Bros. films allowing him to share the screen with Bogie, Bette Davis, Alan Ladd, Burt Lancaster, Ava Gardner, and others. There are no compression artifacts visible anywhere in the film and shadow details are usually very good. It is surprising how well most of the older footage holds up against the newly shot scenes. Unfortunately, in some of the older footage, a distinct hiss is audible. —MM

Movie: 🐶🐶🐶 **DVD:** 🐶🐶½
Universal Studios Home Video (Cat #20523). Widescreen (1.85:1) letterboxed. Dolby Digital Mono. $24.98. Keepcase. LANG: English. SUB: English; French; Spanish. FEATURES: Trailer ▪ Film highlights ▪ Talent files ▪ Production notes ▪ Weblinks.
1982 (PG) 89m/B Steve Martin, Rachel Ward, Reni Santoni, George Gaynes, Frank McCarthy, Carl Reiner; **D:** Carl Reiner; **W:** Steve Martin, Carl Reiner; **C:** Michael Chapman; **M:** Miklos Rozsa.

The Dead Next Door

Homage/continuation of Romero's zombie films takes place in a world where zombies have run rampant and are very common. (They were the result of an experiment, which got out of control.) To deal with this problem with the undead, the government has created "The Zombie Squad": specially trained soldiers who try to eradicate the zombie hordes. Writer/director/producer J.R. Bookwalter has crafted a very complex film, with several subplots, and doesn't let his limited budget stop him from telling his story. The digital transfer is both a blessing and a curse. The movie was shot on Super 8mm (yes, you read that right), thus the image from the DVD is full-frame. The picture is clear and sharp, offering nice colors and remaining stable throughout the film. The dark scenes never get overly dark, and the action is always visible. Unfortunately, the transfer has also revealed a noticeable amount of grain and many defects from the source print. Also, it is now evident when a shot is slightly out of focus. Those of you who have become accustomed to the pristine, reference-quality releases from the major studios may find this transfer to be sorely lacking in quality, but those of us who have seen the old VHS transfer of *The Dead Next Door* know just how good this version is. The sound is mainly limited to the front and center channels, although there are occasional sound effects and musical cues from the rear speakers. —ML

Movie: ♫♫½ **DVD:** ♫♫½
Tempe Entertainment (Cat #SR1001). Full frame. Dolby Digital Surround. $19.99. Keepcase. *LANG:* English. *FEATURES:* Trailer. **1989 84m/C** Scott Spiegel, Peter Terry, Michael Grossi, Len Kowalewich, J.R. Bookwalter; *D:* J.R. Bookwalter; *W:* J.R. Bookwalter.

Dead of Night

Leo Rook (Adamson) is a psycho who collects the severed heads of his victims as trophies. He's aboard the prison ship Hyperion, which is transporting criminals to a remote island off the English coast. He escapes and soon is terrorizing the inhabitants of a lighthouse on the desolate Gehenna Rocks. It's crude and gory and it's all been done before. The picture is crisp and clear for the most part. As all of the action takes place at night, in the dark, the DVD does a fine job of reproducing the blacks, making the lit areas stand out very well. The audio is another story entirely. Music and sound effects are mixed very loudly, while the dialogue is barely audible. Keep the volume control handy. Add in the thick British accents of some of the actors, and you've got dialogue that is practically undecipherable. —ML/MM **AKA:** *Lighthouse.*

Movie: ♫ **DVD:** ♫♫
Image Entertainment (Cat #ID9358UM DVD, UPC #014381935820). Full frame. Dolby Digital Stereo. $24.99. Snapper. *LANG:* English. *FEATURES:* Trailer • 12 chapter links.
1999 (R) 95m/C *GB* Chris(topher) Adamson, James Purefoy, Rachel Shelley, Paul Brooke, Don Warrington, Chris Dunne, Bob Goody, Pat Kelman; *D:* Simon Hunter; *W:* Simon Hunter; *C:* Tony Imi; *M:* Debbie Wiseman.

Dead Waters

This Euro-horror is essentially a homage to Dario Argento. The screen is filled with dripping water; the camera prowls relentlessly; the plot makes little sense. Instead, this slow story of a young English woman's (Salter) journey to a Crimean nunnery is filled with grotesque images and faces. Atmosphere is more important than graphic gore, which is kept to a minimum. This barebones (no menu) disc offers slight, if any, improvement over VHS tape. —MM **AKA:** *Dark Waters.*

Movie: ♫♫½ **DVD:** ♫♫
York Entertainment (Cat #YPD-1048, UPC #750723104829). Full frame. $14.99. Keepcase. *LANG:* English. *FEATURES:* 16 chapter links.

1994 94m/C *IT RU GB* Louise Salter, Venera Simmons, Maria Kapnist, Anna Rose Phipps; *D:* Mariano Baino; *W:* Mariano Baino, Andrew Bark; *C:* Alex Howe; *M:* Igor Clark.

Dead Zone

John Smith (Walken) comes out of a five-year coma to find that he has unwanted psychic powers. Though Walken has gone on to create characters of much more flamboyant weirdness, this is one of his early defining roles, and he receives excellent support from Lom as a sympathetic doctor and Sheen as a chest-thumping maniacal villain. Such key details as a murderer's bedroom that reflects his madness are carefully chosen, and a suicide is about as frightening as any put on film. The Surround effects are particularly effective in snow scenes. The image is very sharp. Some detail is lost in the darkest scenes, but that has always been the case. A commentary track by Cronenberg and King could have been illuminating. —MM

Movie: ♫♫♫½ **DVD:** ♫♫♫
Paramount Home Video (Cat #01646, UPC #097360164640). Widescreen anamorphic. Dolby Digital 5.1 Surround Stereo; Dolby Digital Surround Stereo. $29.99. Keepcase. *LANG:* English; French. *SUB:* English. *FEATURES:* 16 chapter links • Trailer.
1983 (R) 104m/C Christopher Walken, Brooke Adams, Tom Skerritt, Martin Sheen, Herbert Lom, Anthony Zerbe, Colleen Dewhurst; *D:* David Cronenberg; *W:* Jeffrey Boam; *C:* Mark Irwin; *M:* Michael Kamen.

Deadbeat at Dawn

Goose (writer/director Van Bebber) is just your average gang-leader who enjoys selling drugs and having knife-fights with rival gangs in the local cemetery. But when his girlfriend Christy (Megan Murphy) threatens to leave him, Goose decides to quit the gang and lead a more normal life. But first he must do one more drug deal. Van Bebber definitely shows a flair for action filmmaking. Stuntwork is fine and he gives the film a kinetic energy that is only occasionally undone by sloppy editing. However, the story and tone of the film leave much to be desired. The whole gang/revenge plot is far from original and the unappealing characters do despicable things. The digital transfer reveals some flaws in the source print, but no major ones. The color balancing appears to be accurate and image is never dark. The audio mix offers clear sound, but with little depth or range. —ML

Movie: ♫♫ **DVD:** ♫♫½
Synapse (Cat #SYNA4). Full frame. Dolby Digital Mono. $29.95. Keepcase. *LANG:* English. *FEATURES:* Commentary: Van Bebber • "Chunkblower" promotional trailer • "My Sweet Satan" short film • Skinny Puppy music video.

1988 80m/C Jim Van Bebber, Megan Murphy, Paul Harper, Ric Walker; *D:* Jim Van Bebber; *W:* Jim Van Bebber.

Deadly Beauty: Snow's Secret Life

Well-shot and educational documentary about snow, the animals that adapt to it, and the reason for and damage caused by avalanches. Filled with many interesting tidbits, and visually exciting recordings of staged avalanches, it is well-produced, but some of the interviewees' near-fetishistic obsession with snow produces strange moments. In addition, the narration tends to oversell the material, as if desperately trying to convince us of the importance of the subject matter. While it certainly is interesting, some of the re-creations of snow-disasters and one man's account of a tragedy seem designed to underline the importance of the film. (There may be a whole substructure of life adapted to snow environments, but as the narrator ponders about "snow's long-term plan for mankind," you wonder if you're listening to the prologue of a science-fiction film.) The DVD is bright and clear with some minor digital artifacts visible during footage that has been manually slowed down. The sound is acceptable but undistinguished for a 5.1 track. The "additional avalanche footage and interviews" supposedly included on the disc, fails to materialize, and the running time is only 52 minutes (62, if you include a montage section of winter animal footage), not 90 as stated. —DG

Movie: ♫♫½ **DVD:** ♫♫♫
Image Entertainment (Cat #TE0566DVD, UPC #01438105662). Full frame. Dolby Digital 5.1. $24.98. Keepcase. *LANG:* English. *FEATURES:* 21 chapter links • Still gallery • Montage of additional snow footage.
2001 52m/C *W:* Doug Hajicek; *C:* Steve Kroschel, Doug Hajicek, Scott Olson, Dan Nyberg, Lynn Rogers, Mark Peterson, Dean Hansen.

Deadly Weapons

Chesty Morgan (billed here as "Zsa Zsa"), she of the 73-inch bust, takes on gangsters with only her two God-given talents. (Hint: think smothering.) Director Doris Wishman is the female answer to Ed Wood Jr. and this is some of her strangest work. Her camera is often inexplicably attracted to ashtrays. It's difficult to say much about the image quality since so many of the interiors are so poorly lit and the exteriors are so boring. Sound is equally rudimentary. Porn star Harry Reems appears briefly. —MM

Movie: ♫ **DVD:** ♫♫
Image Entertainment (Cat #ID6034SW DVD, UPC #014381603422). Full frame. Dolby Digital Mono. $24.99. Snapper. *LANG:* English. *FEATURES:* 12 chapter links • "Breast development" featurette • Trailers • Gallery of exploitation art.

1970 (R) 90m/C Chesty Morgan, Harry (Herbert Streicher) Reems, Greg Reynolds, Saul Meth, Phillip Stahl, Mitchell Fredericks, Denise Purcell, John McMohon; **D:** Doris Wishman; **W:** J.J. Kendall; **C:** Juan Fernandez.

Deal of a Lifetime

This direct-to-video teen comedy is sheer hell to sit through. Michael Goorjian stars as hapless high schooler Henry Spooner, who (yawn) yearns for popular cheerleader Laurie Petler (Shiri Appleby). Enter the Devil's henchman (the usually resourceful Kevin Pollak, who does all he can to give this feeble film some life), making the standard wishes-for-soul offer. The sound is adequate, but picture quality only fair. Darker scenes are particularly grainy. With no extras, this DVD is anything but a good "Deal." —DL

Movie: 🐾 **DVD:** 🐾
MGM Home Entertainment (Cat #1001089, UPC #2761685389). Full frame. Dolby Digital. $19.98. Keepcase. *LANG:* English. *SUB:* French; Spanish. *FEATURES:* 32 chapter links.
1999 (PG) 95m/C Kevin Pollak, Michael Goorjian, Shiri Appleby, Jennifer Rubin; **D:** Paul Levine; **W:** Katharine R. Sloan; **C:** Denise Brassard; **M:** Amotz Plessner.

Dear Santa

Unspeakably sappy seasonal supernatural comedy is a low-budget version of *The Santa Claus.* Used-car salesman Gordon (Green) is transformed into the red-suited "jolly old elf" and then must fulfill his duties. The production values are strictly straight-to-video, and the clarity of sound does no favors to the treacly score. You have been warned. —MM

Movie: 🐾 **DVD:** 🐾½
Image Entertainment (Cat #8789). Full frame. Dolby Digital Stereo. $24.99. Snapper. *LANG:* English. *FEATURES:* Trailer ▪ 12 chapter links.
1998 (G) 87m/C D.L. Green, Debra Rich, Harrison Myers, Richard Gabai; **D:** Peter Stewart; **W:** Hamilton Underwood; **C:** Theo Angell.

Death and the Compass

Those who are familiar with the Borges story upon which this film is loosely based are the very ones who will not appreciate it. Director Alex Cox has imposed an MTV sensibility—jittery editing, intrusive handheld camerawork, distorted sound, acidic-looking color mixed with black and white, extreme violence treated as comedy—upon a literary detective tale. In his liner notes, Cox explains the project's tangled roots and release schedule. (It was made as a 50-minute film for the BBC with extra footage filmed later to flesh it out to feature length.) Cast is exemplary, but the final result is a disappointment. DVD appears to be an accurate reproduction of Cox's original intentions. Sound is fine. —MM

Movie: 🐾½ **DVD:** 🐾🐾½
Anchor Bay (Cat #DV11394, UPC #0131 31139495). Widescreen (1.78:1) anamorphic. Dolby Digital Surround. $24.98. Keepcase. *LANG:* English. *FEATURES:* Commentary: Alex Cox, composer Dan Wool ▪ Short film, "Spiderwebs" ▪ 19 chapter links ▪ Liner notes by Cox.
1996 86m/C *MX* Peter Boyle, Christopher Eccleston, Miguel Sandoval, Pedro Armendariz Jr.; **D:** Alex Cox; **W:** Alex Cox; **C:** Miguel Garzon; **M:** Pray for Rain.

Death Mask

Screenwriter, executive producer, and star James Best plays Wilbur Johnson, a vengeful carnival worker who was abused and disfigured as a child. He becomes friends with Angel (Linnea Quigley), a sideshow dancer. After hearing Wilbur's story, she takes him to the swamp, where he meets a witch (Brigitte Hill) who gives him the titular "Death Mask." It causes violent and painful death to Wilbur's enemies when he dons the mask, so Wilbur goes on a killing spree. Then it's up to Angel to convince her to stop. Best hams it up in every scene and Quigley proves that she's still willing to take her clothes off whenever necessary. The film doesn't aim to be anything more than campy fun, and on that point, it delivers. The image is clear, but somewhat grainy and a little blurry at times. The garish hues of the carnival come across as very rich and true. There is some noticeable hissing on the soundtrack at times, but otherwise the dialogue is clear and audible. —ML

Movie: 🐾🐾½ **DVD:** 🐾🐾
MTI Home Video (Cat #1047, UPC #039 414510348). Full frame. Dolby Digital Mono. $19.95. Keepcase. *LANG:* English. *FEATURES:* "Making of" featurette ▪ Trailer ▪ Deleted scene and outtakes ▪ Previews ▪ Trivia game.
1998 97m/C James Best, Linnea Quigley, Brigitte Hill; **D:** Steve Latshaw; **W:** James Best.

Death on the Nile

Agatha Christie's Hercule Poirot (Ustinov) is called upon to interrupt his vacation to uncover the murderer of an heiress aboard a steamer cruising down the Nile. The ensemble cast does fine work, as does composer Nino Rota. Both image and sound are equal to the bright elegance of this little bauble. —MM

Movie: 🐾🐾½ **DVD:** 🐾🐾½
Anchor Bay (Cat #DV11428, UPC #01313 1142891). Widescreen (1.85:1) anamorphic. Dolby Digital Mono. $24.98. Keepcase. *LANG:* English. *FEATURES:* "Making of" featurette ▪ Talent files ▪ 28 chapter links ▪ Interview with Peter Ustinov ▪ Interview with Jane Birkin ▪ Trailer.
1978 (PG) 135m/C *GB* Peter Ustinov, Jane Birkin, Lois Chiles, Bette Davis, Mia Farrow, David Niven, Olivia Hussey, Angela Lansbury, Jack Warden, Maggie Smith, George Kennedy, Simon MacCorkindale, Harry Andrews, Jon Finch; **D:** John Guiller-min; **W:** Anthony Shaffer; **C:** Jack Cardiff; **M:** Nino Rota. *AWARDS:* Oscars '78: Costume Des.; Natl. Bd. of Review '78: Support. Actress (Lansbury).

Death Sentence

When a woman juror (Leachman) on a murder case finds out that the wrong man is on trial, she is stalked by the real killer in this made-for-TV movie. It's difficult to tell where the heavy grain ends and the artifacts begin in the dark scenes. Conventional interiors fare little better. The disc appears to have been made from a banged-up original. Sound is exceptionally scratchy and poor. No menu or chapter links. Notable only for a good cast, including an early role for Nolte. —MM *AKA:* Murder One.

Movie: 🐾½ **DVD:** 🐾
Essex (Cat #1401). Full frame. Dolby Digital Mono. $10.97. Keepcase. *LANG:* English.
1974 74m/C Cloris Leachman, Laurence Luckinbill, Nick Nolte, William Schallert; **D:** E.W. Swackhamer; **M:** Laurence Rosenthal.

Death Warrant

Van Damme whams and bams a little less than usual in this cop-behind-bars testosterone fest. As Canadian Mountie Burke undercover in a prison where inmates are perishing under mysterious circumstances, the pectorally perfect star is on the brink of figuring out the scheme when an inmate transferee threatens his cover. The violence is appropriately gratuitous, though director Sarafian handles it with some flashy visuals. The prison interiors are re-created well enough. Surround effects are pumped up for the fight scenes. —MM

Movie: 🐾🐾 **DVD:** 🐾🐾½
MGM Home Entertainment (Cat #1001551, UPC #027616858610). Widescreen (1.85:1) anamorphic. Dolby Digital Surround Stereo. $19.98. Keepcase. *LANG:* English; French. *SUB:* French; Spanish. *CAP:* English. *FEATURES:* 16 chapter links.
1990 (R) 111m/C Jean-Claude Van Damme, Robert Guillaume, Cynthia Gibb, George Dickerson, Patrick Kilpatrick; **D:** Deran Sarafian; **W:** David S. Goyer; **C:** Russell Carpenter; **M:** Gary Chang.

Death Wish

The film that launched a fistful of lesser (much lesser) sequels and thousands of imitators is really more nuanced than its reputation. Middle-aged New York liberal Paul Kersey (Bronson) becomes a vigilante avenger after his wife and daughter are brutally attacked. (One of the attackers is Jeff Goldblum and what was meant to be horrifying in the mid '70s comes across as comically overblown.) The night scenes on city streets are as harsh-looking on disc as they have ever been. Throughout the film, the autumnal auburns and blacks are as grim as the story. The DVD is an accurate re-creation of the original. —MM

Movie: ♪♪½ **DVD:** ♪♪½
Paramount Home Video (Cat #08774, UPC #097360877441). Widescreen anamorphic. Dolby Digital Mono. $29.99. Keepcase. *LANG:* English; French. *SUB:* English. *FEATURES:* 14 chapter links.
1974 (R) 93m/C Charles Bronson, Vincent Gardenia, William Redfield, Hope Lange, Jeff Goldblum, Stuart Margolin, Olympia Dukakis; *D:* Michael Winner; *W:* Wendell Mayes; *C:* Arthur Ornitz; *M:* Herbie Hancock.

Death Wish 5: The Face of Death

Paul Kersey (Bronson) returns to vigilantism when his clothing manufacturer fiancée Olivia (Down) has her business threatened by mobsters, one of whom turns out to be her sadistic ex (Parks). Bronson looks understandably bored with the rehashed material and grisly violence. Beyond the beefed-up sound, the disc is no different from VHS tape. —*MM*
Movie: ♪ **DVD:** ♪♪
Trimark Home Video (Cat #6919). Full frame. $14.99. Keepcase. *LANG:* English. *SUB:* French; Spanish. *CAP:* English. *FEATURES:* Trailer ● 30 chapter links.
1994 (R) 95m/C Charles Bronson, Lesley-Anne Down, Michael Parks, Kenneth Welsh; *D:* Allan Goldstein; *W:* Allan Goldstein; *C:* Curtis Petersen; *M:* Terry Plumeri.

December 7th: The Pearl Harbor Story

The famous "lost" feature about the bombing of Pearl Harbor made by John Ford and cinematographer Gregg Toland is only the beginning of this ambitious disc. It contains both versions of *Dec. 7th*—the radically shortened version that won a best short film Oscar in 1943 and the feature-length cut that appeared on home video in 1991. The longer edition is a curious piece of fantasy propaganda. DVD also contains Frank Capra's *Know Your Enemy: Japan*, a wild, virulent, hour-long bit of propaganda made for the War Department. It's a companion piece to his *Why We Fight* series and it ought to serve as a real eye-opener to contemporary audiences about racial attitudes of the 1940s. Image quality for those and the other extras is no better than the source material with lots of scratches and occasional registration problems. New bright yellow titles and credits have been added to fill in gaps. For war movie fans, this one's a real treasure chest. —*MM*
Movie: ♪♪♪ **DVD:** ♪♪½
VCI Home Video (Cat #507, UPC #089859 050725). Full frame. Dolby Digital Mono. $19.99. Keepcase. *LANG:* English. *FEATURES:* 23 chapter links ● Commentary: 4 Pearl Harbor veterans ● 2 Pearl Harbor newsreels ● Japanese TV newsstory on 1995 theatrical screening of *Dec. 7th.*
1943 206m/B Walter Huston, Harry Davenport; *D:* John Ford; *C:* Gregg Toland; *M:* Alfred Newman.

Deep in the Heart (of Texas)

Two British documentary filmmakers, Robert (Cranham) and his wife Kate (Root), take an assignment for British television to interview Texans. They choose the capital of Austin and the eccentric locals provide the requisite color, but the couple are undergoing their own personal crisis which keeps interfering with their work. DVD image is very sharp and clear, showing practically no grain, nor any defects from the source print. The colors are reproduced quite nicely, and the flesh-tones all appear very natural. The framing seems accurate and there are no artifacting problems. The 2-channel Surround soundtrack offers clear and audible dialogue, along with a solid bass response. The rear speakers offer some sound effects and some nicely done musical cues. Box copy promises "Behind the scenes look director's commentary!" There is no audio commentary track on the DVD that I could find, so I can only imagine that this is referring to the "Making of" segment, as it does include behind-the-scenes footage and comments from the director. —*MM/ML*
Movie: ♪♪ **DVD:** ♪♪½
Vanguard International Cinema, Inc. (UPC #658769011838). Widescreen (1.66:1) letterboxed. Dolby Digital Surround Stereo. $29.99. Keepcase. *LANG:* English. *FEATURES:* "Making of" featurette ● 2 deleted scenes ● Trailer.
1998 90m/C Kenneth Cranham, Amanda Root; *D:* Stephen Purvis; *W:* Tom Huckabee, Stephen Purvis, Jesse Sublett; *C:* Thomas Flores Alcala; *M:* Joe Ellen Doering, George Doering.

Deepstar Six

This one appeared during the 15-minutes of popularity for low-budget underwater horrors inspired by *The Abyss*. Same plot: scientists at the seafloor upset a prehistoric creature. The only distinction here is that this critter may be the least frightening construction of latex and foam rubber ever to be placed in front of a camera. Full-frame image is indistinguishable from VHS tape. —*MM*
Movie: ♪ **DVD:** ♪♪
Artisan Entertainment (Cat #11516, UPC #012236115168). Full frame. Dolby Digital Surround Stereo. $24.99. Keepcase. *LANG:* English. *CAP:* English. *FEATURES:* 24 chapter links.
1989 (R) 97m/C Taurean Blacque, Nancy Everhard, Greg Evigan, Miguel Ferrer, Matt McCoy, Nia Peeples, Cindy Pickett, Marius Weyers, Thom Bray, Elya Baskin; *D:* Sean S. Cunningham; *W:* Lewis Abernathy, Geof Miller; *C:* Mac Ahlberg; *M:* Harry Manfredini.

The Defender

Beijing bodyguard John Chang (Li) is hired to protect pampered rich girl Michelle (Chung), who's the witness to a murder. John also has to deal with the revenge

plans of an ex-soldier whose brother John has killed. Below par for Li on every level, including the script and the action, which is lame and far too infrequent. With all the far superior Jet Li titles out there, this is at best good for one viewing. The DVD quality matches up pretty well with the film itself. Not too bad, but nothing special (no supplementals either). Detail and sharpness are good but on many occasions grain comes in and takes the image down a notch. At several points minor artifacting joins in. Even in the whup-ass scenes the Surround tracks get very little use. There is plenty of bass and dynamics to the 5.1 track but it pretty much stays all up front. —*JO* **AKA:** The Bodyguard from Beijing; Zhong Nan Hai Bao Biao.
Movie: ♪♪♪ **DVD:** ♪♪♪
Buena Vista Home Entertainment (Cat #20708, UPC #717951010490). Widescreen (1.85:1) letterboxed. Dolby Digital 5.1 Surround Stereo. $29.99. Keepcase. *LANG:* English. *CAP:* English. *FEATURES:* 19 chapter links.
1994 (R) 93m/C *HK* Jet Li, Christy Chung, Kent Cheng, Ngai Sing; *D:* Corey Yuen; *W:* Gordon Chan, Kin-Chung Chan; *C:* Tom Lau.

Defending Your Life

Albert Brooks writes, directs, and stars in this slyly optimistic 1991 comedy, billed as "the first real story of what happens after you die." Brooks plays Daniel Miller, a thirtyish advertising executive living a lonely existence in Los Angeles. Crashing his new BMW into a bus, Miller arrives in Judgment City, where the food is the best you've ever had and you can eat as much as you want without any side effects. The only hitches are your stay lasts five days and you must defend your life. Daniel has to prove he has overcome his fears enough to progress to the next level of existence. If he can't, it's back to Earth for another go around. There's a defender (Rip Torn, pitch perfect here), a prosecutor (Lee Grant) and a judge (in this case, two). The evidence is presented as "clips" from his life, with both sides arguing how Daniel acted bravely or cowardly. Brooks's neurotic shtick works best in measured doses. As with his characters in *Modern Romance* or *Lost in America*, Brooks's Daniel still has that know-it-all vibe. However, when faced with the moments when he should have said "no" instead of "yes," there is an instant sympathetic connection to those moments in our lives that we took the paths of least resistance. The 1.85 anamorphic transfer far surpasses the laserdisc in clarity and resolution. Colors are a bit muted, but solidly rendered. Deep blacks contribute to excellent detail delineation, down to counting the peas and carrots on Daniel's plate. Fleshtones are natural looking, even in the few night scenes. The Dolby Digital Surround soundtrack exhibits good dynamic range and even a little LFE kick in some of the musical passages. Surround activity is occasional but pleasing. The only supplemental materials consist of a theatrical trailer and some cast notes. A commentary track by Brooks would have made the disc priceless. —*EP*

Movie: 🎬🎬🎬 **DVD:** 🎬🎬🎬
Warner Home Video, Inc. (Cat #12049, UPC #085391204923). Widescreen (1.85:1) anamorphic. Dolby Digital Surround Stereo. $19.98. Snapper. *LANG:* English; French. *SUB:* French; Spanish; Portuguese. *CAP:* English. *FEATURES:* 32 chapter links • Theatrical trailer • Cast/filmmaker profiles.
1991 (PG) 112m/C Albert Brooks, Meryl Streep, Rip Torn, Lee Grant, Buck Henry, George D. Wallace, Lillian Lehman, Peter Schuck, Susan Walters; *D:* Albert Brooks; *W:* Albert Brooks; *C:* Allen Daviau; *M:* Michael Gore.

The Defilers

The original "roughie" is about two '60s dudes (Mabe and Eden) who kidnap and imprison a young woman (Jannson) in their basement for sex. It's repulsive stuff, but as producer Friedman says on the commentary track, the allure is the "forbiddenness" of the subject matter. DVD exhibits some flashing in shingle patterns, but the general level of the image is remarkable for a low-budget independent production of this age. The black-and-white photography is surprisingly well preserved. Title is available with *Scum of the Earth* on a drive-in double feature. —*MM*

Movie: 🎬🎬 **DVD:** 🎬🎬½
Image Entertainment (Cat #ID9749SW DVD, UPC #014381974928). Full frame. Dolby Digital Mono. $24.99. Snapper. *LANG:* English. *FEATURES:* 12 chapter links • "Let's Go to the Drive-in" short with Julie Andrews • Commentary: Dave Friedman, Mike Vraney • 2 nudie shorts • 3 intermission reels • Gallery of exploitation art • Trailers.
1965 (R) 69m/B Byron Mabe, Jerome (Jerry Stallion) Eden, Mae Johnson; *D:* David Friedman.

Delivered

Comic book artist Will Sherman (Strickland) is having to deliver pizzas to keep body and soul together; his girlfriend Clair (Stefanson) has left him; and an insane killer (Eldard) thinks that the ideas Will records on a microcassette recorder have real merit. Several of the elements in this black little comedy are too familiar, but the film is made with imagination and real wit. DVD presents a very good image for a low-to mid-budget production. Sound is acceptable. —*MM* *AKA:* Death by Pizza.

Movie: 🎬🎬🎬 **DVD:** 🎬🎬🎬
Winstar Home Entertainment (Cat #FLV 5159, UPC #720917515922). Widescreen anamorphic. $24.98. Keepcase. *LANG:* English. *FEATURES:* 6 chapter links • DVD production credits • Talent files • Trailer.
1998 (R) 90m/C David Strickland, Ron Eldard, Leslie Stefanson, Scott Bairstow, Nicky Katt, Jillian Armenante, Bob Morrisey, Mark Berry; *D:* Guy Ferland; *W:* Andrew Liotta, Lawrence Trilling; *C:* Shane Kelly; *M:* Nicholas Pike.

The Delivery

Euro crime/road flick combines a little Tarantino with a little John Woo and tosses in a dash of *Run, Lola, Run*. The result is derivative but entertaining enough for a target audience that never mistakes it for anything serious. Down and out in Amsterdam, Anna (Bretoniere), Alfred (Van Huet), and Guy (Douglas) agree to drive a multi-million dollar load of Ecstasy pills to Barcelona in a Volvo station wagon. They must follow an absurdly complex route, which is needed to provide the skeleton of a plot that eventually involves terrorism, revenge, and kidnapping. On disc, the production has a dark look that doubtlessly comes from the original. It's meant to have that grim, dirt-streaked feeling. Dolby stereo is fine for the techno-pop score. —*MM*

Movie: 🎬🎬½ **DVD:** 🎬🎬🎬
Trimark Home Video (Cat #VM7432D, UPC #031398743224). Widescreen letterboxed. Dolby Digital Stereo. $24.99. Keepcase. *LANG:* English. *SUB:* English; French; Spanish. *FEATURES:* 24 chapter links • "Making of" featurette • Deleted scenes • Commentary: director.
1999 (R) 100m/C *NL BE* Fredja Van Huet, Freddy Douglas, Auriele Meriel, Rik Launspach, Esmee De La Bretoniere, Jonathan Harvey, Hidde Maas, Christopher Simon; *D:* Roel Reine; *W:* David Hilton; *C:* Jan van den Nieuwenhuyzen.

Delta Force

Fact-based (very loosely) story has the anti-terrorist Delta Force led by Norris and Marvin saving the day when an American airliner is hijacked in Athens. It's a standard jingoistic revenge fantasy. Disc is identical to tape. —*MM*

Movie: 🎬🎬 **DVD:** 🎬🎬
MGM Home Entertainment (Cat #4001163, UPC #027616852892). Full frame. Dolby Digital Surround. $24.99. Keepcase. *LANG:* English. *SUB:* French; Spanish. *CAP:* English. *FEATURES:* 24 chapter links • Trailer.
1986 (R) 125m/C Lee Marvin, Chuck Norris, Shelley Winters, Martin Balsam, George Kennedy, Hanna Schygulla, Susan Strasberg, Bo Svenson, Joey Bishop, Lainie Kazan, Robert Forster, Robert Vaughn, Kim Delaney; *D:* Menahem Golan; *W:* James Bruner; *C:* David Gurfinkel; *M:* Alan Silvestri.

Delta Force 2: Operation Stranglehold

Col. Scott McCoy (Norris) leads the Delta Force against drug dealers led by Ramon Cota (Drago). The same story has been told with just as much energy and imagination in hundreds of video premieres. The cartoonish violence gains nothing on this full-frame DVD. It's identical to tape in every way. —*MM*

Movie: 🎬½ **DVD:** 🎬🎬
MGM Home Entertainment (Cat #4001165, UPC #027616852908). Full frame. Dolby Digital Surround Stereo. $24.99. Keepcase. *LANG:* English. *SUB:* French; Spanish. *CAP:* English. *FEATURES:* 16 chapter links • Trailer.
1990 (R) 110m/C John P. Ryan, Chuck Norris, Billy Drago, Richard Jaeckel, Paul Perri; *D:* Aaron Norris; *W:* Lee Reynolds; *C:* Joao Fernandes; *M:* Frederic Talgorn.

Dementia

Please see *Daughter of Horror / Dementia*.
1955/C

Dementia

Wild-eyed sexual thriller owes a bit to *Diabolique*. Recovering from a breakdown, wealthy Kathrine (Bursiel) becomes friendly with her outpatient nurse Luisa (Sanchez). Then Luisa's smarmy ex-husband Sonny (Schulze) shows up and things get twisty. Production values are not top drawer and the cast is not well known, but director Keith keeps things moving nicely. The DVD image ranges from fair to very good depending on the lighting. Sound is good. —*MM*

Movie: 🎬½ **DVD:** 🎬
Image Entertainment (Cat #ID8907YODVD, UPC #014381890723). Widescreen (1.85:1) letterboxed. Dolby Digital Surround Stereo. $24.99. Snapper. *LANG:* English. *FEATURES:* 12 chapter links.
1998 85m/C Marisol Padilla Sanchez, Patricia Bursiel, Matt Schulze, Azura Skye, Matthew Sullivan, Jesus Nebot, Susan Davis; *D:* Woody Keith; *W:* Woody Keith, R.G. Fry; *C:* David Trulli; *M:* Karl Preusser.

Dementia 13

Comparing Francis Ford Coppola's Gothic debut to the other low-budget Corman productions of the early 1960s, it's easy to see hints of the genius that would follow. Coppola tells a fairly simple story of ghosts and greed with pretty blonde Louise (Anders) trying to pry loose some of the Haloran family fortune from the possibly demented matriarch (Dunn). At least, that's the way things begin. It's obvious that Coppola is using Hitchcock's *Psycho* as his model. A key watery moment may be the first homage to the shower scene. More significantly, though, he shows a solid understanding of his medium—how to combine character, dialogue, sound, and image to tell a good story. And to scare an audience. Even if he'd never made another film, this one would have a following today. This disc was made from a scratchy print. A constant hiss is audible; the murky black-and-white image is about the same as VHS tape, though the film has never been particularly crisp. —*MM* *AKA:* The Haunted and the Hunted.

Movie: 🎬🎬🎬 **DVD:** 🎬🎬
Madacy Entertainment (Cat #990602, UPC #05677502049). Full frame. Dolby Digital Mono. $9.99. Keepcase. *LANG:* English.

FEATURES: Thumbnail bio of Francis Ford Coppola • Trivia • 8 chapter links. **1963 75m/B** William Campbell, Luana Anders, Bart Patton, Patrick Magee, Barbara Dowling, Ethne Dunn, Mary Mitchell, Karl Schanzer; **D:** Francis Ford Coppola; **W:** Francis Ford Coppola; **C:** Charles Hannawalt; **M:** Ronald Stein.

Demetrius and the Gladiators

Early Cinemascope sequel to *The Robe* follows Demetrius (droopy faced Victor Mature) as he is thrown into the gladiatorial arena for refusing to reveal the whereabouts of Jesus's robe. Messalina (Hayward), intrigued by him, sets about a series of obstacles to test his Christian faith. Enjoyable, fast-paced sequel is more camp than pious, though it's refreshing to see Demetrius lose his faith and confront his beliefs. Jay Robinson as Caligula overacts shamelessly, devouring even more scenery than he did in *The Robe*. Look closer for a barely glimpsed Woody Strode, who can be seen during the gladiator school sequence (which strongly prefigures similar scenes in *Spartacus*). The disc is very widely framed but still trims a sliver off of the sides. The image is sharp but pale and exceedingly grainy with occasional aliasing and visible print dirt. The multi-channel sound is acceptable for an older track, but the volume levels vary as the film progresses. The packaging and typeface seem to be designed to fool the consumer that this is *Gladiator*. It isn't. —DG
Movie: 🎜🎜½ **DVD:** 🎜🎜
20th Century Fox Home Entertainment (Cat #2001177, UPC #02454301177). Widescreen (2.55:1) anamorphic. Dolby Digital 4.0 Surround; Dolby Stereo. $24.98. Keepcase. *LANG:* English; French. *SUB:* English; Spanish. *CAP:* English. *FEATURES:* Theatrical trailer in English, German, French, Spanish • Trailers from other Fox releases.
1954 101m/C Victor Mature, Susan Hayward, Michael Rennie, Debra Paget, Anne Bancroft, Jay Robinson, Barry Jones, Richard Egan, William Marshall, Ernest Borgnine; **D:** Delmer Daves; **W:** Philip Dunne; **C:** Milton Krasner.

Demon City Shinjuku

Japanese anime begins with two men battling against dark forces. One is killed, allowing his rival to turn Shinjuku into a city of monsters inhabited only by those lawless enough to live among the remains of the dead, plus the occasional demon. When an official is kidnapped, his daughter Sayaka and martial arts student Kyoya go into the dark part of the city to save him and the world, as is so often the case in these movies. The so-so animation is not particularly detailed or energetic. Sound is superior to tape, and the choice of languages is a significant improvement, but the image is about the same. —MM
Movie: 🎜🎜 **DVD:** 🎜🎜

Central Park Media/U.S. Manga Corps (Cat #1732). Full frame. Dolby Digital 5.1 Surround Stereo. $29.95. Keepcase. *LANG:* Japanese; English. *SUB:* English. *FEATURES:* Character notes • Trailer • 24 chapter links.
1993 82m/C *JP* **D:** Yoshiaki Kawajiri; **W:** Kaori Okamura.

Dersu Uzala

A Russian captain (Solomin) in Siberia befriends Derzu (Munzuk), a crusty resourceful Mongolian hunter. Kurosawa made the acclaimed film in Russia at the invitation of the Soviet government. Unfortunately, his majestic photography of a vanishing wilderness is undercut by an imperfect transfer to disc. Heavy artifacts are visible in large areas of dirt or brown leaves. Scratches are abundant as is aliasing along bright lines. The film deserves better. —MM
Movie: 🎜🎜🎜½ **DVD:** 🎜🎜
Kino on Video (Cat #K172DVD, UPC #738 329017224). Widescreen (2.35:1) letterboxed. Dolby Digital Mono. $39.99. Snapper. *LANG:* Russian. *SUB:* English. *FEATURES:* 27 chapter links • U.S. trailer.
1975 140m/C *JP RU* Yuri Solomin, Maxim Munzuk; **D:** Akira Kurosawa; **W:** Akira Kurosawa, Yuri Nagibin; **C:** Asakazu Nakai, Yuri Gantman, Fyodor Dobronravov; **M:** Isaak Shvartz. *AWARDS:* Oscars '75: Foreign Film.

Desert Hearts

Professor Vivian Bell (Shaver) goes to Reno, Nevada, in 1959 for a quick divorce. She slowly becomes involved in a lesbian relationship with free-spirited casino waitress Cay Rivvers (Charbonneau). In her commentary track, director Donna Deitch is quick to note her affinity for the similarly themed *The Misfits*, and to say that she was attempting to tell a different version of the story. She takes obvious pride in the work that she put into this independent production. On DVD, the film looks remarkably sharp for a relatively low-budget work. Sound is thoroughly adequate for a period piece. —MM
Movie: 🎜🎜🎜 **DVD:** 🎜🎜🎜
MGM Home Entertainment (Cat #1001 448, UPC #027616857682). Widescreen (1.85:1) letterboxed. Dolby Digital Mono. $19.98. Keepcase. *LANG:* English. *SUB:* French; Spanish. *CAP:* English. *FEATURES:* 16 chapter links • Commentary: Donna Deitch • Trailer.
1986 (R) 93m/C Helen Shaver, Audra Lindley, Patricia Charbonneau, Andra Akers, Dean Butler, Jeffrey Tambor, Denise Crosby, Gwen Welles; **D:** Donna Deitch; **W:** Natalie Cooper; **C:** Robert Elswit.

Desert Thunder

Retired Air Force pilot Lee Miller (Baldwin) rejoins the action when he's called in to lead a commando mission against an Iraqi terrorist. Considering the meager budget, director Wynorski gets some decent explo-

sions and aerial sequences, many probably borrowed from other Corman productions. Image and sound are identical to tape. —MM
Movie: 🎜🎜 **DVD:** 🎜🎜
New Concorde (Cat #NH20757 D, UPC #736991475748). Full frame. $19.95. Keepcase. *LANG:* English. *SUB:* Spanish. *FEATURES:* 24 chapter links • Talent files • Trailers.
1999 (R) 88m/C Daniel Baldwin, Richard Tyson, Richard Portnow, Stacy Haiduk; **D:** Jim Wynorski; **W:** Lenny Juliano.

Desert Winds

Weird little fantastical romance finds Jackie (Graham), who lives in the New Mexican desert, regularly communicating with nature on the rocky plateau. She once heard the voice of Eugene (Nickles), who lives 500 miles away in Arizona, thanks to a rare phenomenon known as a wind tunnel. Seven years later, he returns. The picture is very crisp and relatively free of grain, with the exception of some shots, which appear to be stock footage. The desert locations display very muted colors, but the night scenes show a very true black which exhibits no saturation or pixelation. The disc shows no signs of compression problems or artifacting. The Surround mix is used wisely throughout. In the desert conversation scenes, the voice of the person who isn't on-screen comes from the front and rear speakers, to subtly simulate an echo effect. —GH/MM
Movie: 🎜🎜 **DVD:** 🎜🎜
Vanguard International Cinema, Inc. (Cat #VF0036, UPC #65876003635). Full frame. Dolby Digital Stereo. $29.95. Keepcase. *LANG:* English.
1995 97m/C Heather Graham, Michael A. Nickles, Grace Zabriskie, Jack Kehler, Adam Ant; **D:** Michael A. Nickles; **W:** Michael A. Nickles; **C:** Denis Maloney; **M:** James McVay.

Desperately Seeking Susan

Bored New Jersey housewife Roberta (Arquette) reads the personals and becomes obsessed with the relationship between two lovers who arrange their trysts through the columns. She decides to attend a meeting, but suffers accident-induced amnesia and thinks that she is Susan, the free-spirited woman of the ads. Meanwhile, the real Susan (Madonna) is being hunted by an assassin (Patton). From that point, the screwball comedy spins in all sorts of interesting directions. The performances are excellent, but for the movie's most devoted female fans, the main attraction of the disc is the commentary track with director Seidelman, studio executive Barbara Boyle, and producers Midge Sanford and Sarah Pillsbury. They take the entire concept of "chick flick" to a new, rarified level. The alternative ending is a few more minutes of footage that originally followed the current conclusion. It was properly jettisoned but makes a nice

extra. The image is actually very nice, a bit better than I remember the theatrical release and fine for a work of this age. Even the mono sound is good. This one's a personal favorite and I'm glad to see that it's being treated properly. —*MM*
Movie: 🎬🎬🎬½ **DVD:** 🎬🎬
MGM Home Entertainment (Cat #1000757, UPC #027616850799). Widescreen anamorphic; full frame. Dolby Digital Mono. $24.99. Keepcase. *LANG:* English. *SUB:* French; Spanish. *CAP:* English. *FEATURES:* Alternate ending • Director/producer commentary track • 24 chapter links • Trailer.
1985 (PG-13) 104m/C Rosanna Arquette, Madonna, Aidan Quinn, Mark Blum, Robert Joy, Laurie Metcalf, Steven Wright, John Turturro, Will Patton, Richard Hell, Annie Golden, Ann Magnuson, Richard Edson; *D:* Susan Seidelman; *W:* Leora Barish; *C:* Edward Lachman; *M:* Thomas Newman. *AWARDS:* British Acad. '85: Support. Actress (Arquette); Natl. Bd. of Review '85: Support. Actress (Arquette).

Destination Vegas
Smart, funny road thriller belies its modest budget. Young attorney Missy (Sommerfield) is too idealistic for her own good. The partners in her law firm decide to get rid of her when she becomes inconvenient and she finds herself on the run across the desert with only the rough-edged Texas (Duhamel) on her side, and two hitmen on their trail. The image is remarkably sharp for a Corman production. Sound is fine, too. This one's a real sleeper. —*MM*
Movie: 🎬🎬🎬 **DVD:** 🎬🎬½
New Concorde (Cat #NH20771 D, UPC #736991477193). Full frame. Stereo. $19.95. Keepcase. *LANG:* English. *SUB:* Spanish. *FEATURES:* 24 chapter links • Trailers • Talent files.
1995 (R) 78m/C Jennifer Sommerfield, Claude Duhamel, Stephen Polk, Richard Lynch; *D:* Paul Wynne; *W:* Paul Wynne; *C:* William H. Molina; *M:* Peter Tomashek.

Destiny
Fritz Lang's silent fantasy is a version of the myth of Orpheus. Death takes a young man on the eve of his wedding, but agrees to return him if his fiancée can save three lives. In terms of style, it's really closer to Dreyer's *Vampyr* than to Lang's own *M*. Some damage has been done to the print but this version is eminently watchable. Some credit goes to film historian David Shepard. —*MM* **AKA:** *Der Mude Tod.*
Movie: 🎬🎬🎬 **DVD:** 🎬🎬🎬
Image Entertainment (Cat #ID9411DS DVD, UPC #014381941128). Full frame. Dolby Digital Stereo. $24.99. Snapper. *LANG:* Silent. *SUB:* English intertitles. *FEATURES:* 12 chapter links.
1921 99m/B *GE* Lil Dagover, Rudolf Klein-Rogge, Bernhard Goetzke, Walther Janssen, Eduard von Winterstein, Paul Biensfieldt; *D:* Fritz Lang; *W:* Thea von Harbou; *C:* Fritz Arno Wagner, Erich Nitzschmann, Hermann Saalfrank.

Detention
Urban drama about black Baltimore teens and their teacher earns more credit for intention than for execution. Both the writing and acting are earnest, right-minded, and inspirational, but the conflicts are blatant, the characters are broadly written, and the acting by an attractive young cast is often less than persuasive. —*MM*
Movie: 🎬🎬½ **DVD:** 🎬🎬
MTI Home Video (Cat #5033, UPC #6199 35403338). Full frame. $24.95. Keepcase. *LANG:* English. *FEATURES:* 20 chapter links • Previews • Talent files.
1998 83m/C Justin Black, Charisse Brown, Reginald Davis, John Hall, Keisha Harvin, Kiatenai, Darryl Wharton; *D:* Darryl Wharton; *W:* Darryl Wharton; *C:* Boots Shelton; *M:* Camara Kambon.

Deterrence
Engrossing one-room thriller is set during the presidential campaign of 2008. Unelected VP Walter Emerson (Pollak) became prez when the incumbent died. Campaigning in the Colorado primary, he and his staff (and a TV crew) are stranded in a mountain diner. Watching CNN, they learn that the Iraqis have invaded Kuwait. When Emerson threatens to nuke Baghdad, the situation quickly escalates. Writer/director Lurie combines the best elements of *Fail Safe* and Orson Welles's radio version of *War of the Worlds*. Yes, the situation is artificial, but it's so neatly constructed that it works beautifully on DVD. Neither image nor sound are particularly challenging for the medium. The main improvement over tape is Lurie's commentary track. —*MM*
Movie: 🎬🎬🎬 **DVD:** 🎬🎬🎬
Paramount Home Video (Cat #33818, UPC #097363381846). Widescreen letterboxed. Dolby Digital Surround Stereo. $29.99. Keepcase. *LANG:* English. *CAP:* English. *FEATURES:* 14 chapter links • Trailer • Commentary: Rob Lurie.
2000 (R) 101m/C Kevin Pollak, Timothy Hutton, Sheryl Lee Ralph, Sean Astin, Clotilde Courau, Badja (Medu) Djola, Mark Thompson; *D:* Rod Lurie; *W:* Rod Lurie; *C:* Frank Perl; *M:* Lawrence Nash Groupe.

Detour
One of the all-time great B-noirs makes an appropriately flawed debut on DVD. Mopey pianist Al (Neal) hitches across country to rejoin his fiancée and he runs across Vera (Savage), a woman with a massive chip on her shoulder. Things go seriously wrong. Yes, it's contrived, but so what? That last twist is a real jolt. According to the box copy, the disc has been made from original nitrate masters. It's still filled with scratches (heavy at times), mangled sprocket holes that cause the image to waver and jump in the frame, and a near-constant bothersome hiss. At the same time, deep blacks are detailed and so are foggy grays. The transfer is also sharp enough to make it obvious that Neal's hands never touch a keyboard. —*MM*

Movie: 🎬🎬🎬½ **DVD:** 🎬🎬
Image Entertainment (Cat #ID8708CODVD, UPC #014381870824). Full frame. Dolby Digital Mono. $24.99. Snapper. *LANG:* English. *FEATURES:* 12 chapter links.
1946 67m/B Tom Neal, Ann Savage, Claudia Drake, Edmund MacDonald, Tim Ryan, Esther Howard, Don Brodie, Pat Gleason; *D:* Edgar G. Ulmer; *W:* Martin Goldsmith; *C:* Benjamin (Ben H.) Kline; *M:* Leo Erddoy. *AWARDS:* Natl. Film Reg. '92.

Detroit 9000
Two Detroit cops, one white (Rocco) and one black (Rhodes), investigate a robbery that takes place at a black politician's classy fund-raiser. The thieves are so heavily covered by coveralls, gloves, and masks that nobody can tell what race they are. The result is a classic of blaxploitation. The action is fast, unpredictable, and sexy. On DVD, this low-budget exercise looks no better than it ever has, not that that's a problem. The often harshly lit image is grainy but no extra artifacts are added, even in the many night exteriors. —*MM* **AKA:** Detroit Heat.
Movie: 🎬🎬🎬 **DVD:** 🎬🎬
Miramax Pictures Home Video (Cat #21362, UPC #786936141764). Widescreen (1.85:1) anamorphic. Dolby Digital Mono. $24.99. Keepcase. *LANG:* English. *FEATURES:* 24 chapter links.
1973 (R) 106m/C Alex Rocco, Scatman Crothers, Hari Rhodes, Lonette McKee, Herbert Jefferson Jr.; *D:* Arthur Marks; *W:* Orville H. Hampton; *C:* Harry J. May; *M:* Luchi De Jesus.

Deuce Bigalow: Male Gigolo
Schneider tries to enter the low-brow leading man territory now occupied by Adam Sandler (who exec produced) as Deuce Bigalow, a hapless tropical fish caretaker turned hapless gigolo. When Deuce is asked to nurse a stereotypically ethnic gigolo's fish to health, he proceeds to practically destroy his house and subsequently take over his "business" to pay for the repairs. With the help of pimp T.J. (Griffin), Deuce finds a clientele and the secret that the women want compassion, not sex. The gags (mostly of the tasteless, toilet humor variety) are very hit and miss, but they should play well to the intended audience of adolescent boys. This is a near-perfect DVD transfer with super-vivid colors, flawlessly true blacks, and an incredibly sharp picture. It is also one of those annoying Buena Vista DVDs that tries to force you to watch trailers from other BV titles, by having them start as soon as the DVD is loaded and disabling the scan button. The soundtrack is an uninventive mix, but every bit of dialogue is distinct, the music is full, and there are some nicely placed Surround effects (the fish tank destruction is pretty splashy). —*JO*
Movie: 🎬🎬½ **DVD:** 🎬🎬🎬½
Buena Vista Home Entertainment (Cat #20054, UPC #717951009289). Wide-

screen (1.85:1) anamorphic. Dolby Digital 5.1. $32.99. Keepcase. *LANG:* English. *CAP:* English. *FEATURES:* 28 chapter links ▪ Theatrical trailer ▪ Behind-the-scenes featurette ▪ Storyboard-to-scene comparisons.

1999 (R) 86m/C Rob Schneider, William Forsythe, Eddie Griffin, Oded Fehr, Gail O'Grady, Richard Riehle, Jacqueline Obradors; *D:* Mike Mitchell; *W:* Rob Schneider, Harris Goldberg; *C:* Peter Collister; *M:* Teddy Castellucci.

The Devil & Max Devlin

A good cast wanders aimlessly in this lesser family fantasy from Disney. After he's run over by a bus full of Hare Krishnas, nasty Max Devlin (Gould) strikes a bargain with Barney Satin (Cosby), a midlevel manager in hell, and gets a second chance. He must persuade three innocents to sell their souls. The image quality varies with the original. Some scenes are soft and misty while others are much brighter and sharper. The only real improvement over VHS tape is the choice of image size. —*MM*

Movie: 🐾½ **DVD:** 🐾🐾
Anchor Bay (Cat #DV11181, UPC #01313 1118193). Widescreen (1.85:1) anamorphic; full frame. Dolby Digital Mono. $24.98. Keepcase. *LANG:* English. *FEATURES:* 19 chapter links.

1981 (PG) 95m/C Elliott Gould, Bill Cosby, Susan Anspach, Adam Rich, Julie Budd; *D:* Steven Hilliard Stern; *W:* Jimmy Sangster; *C:* Howard Schwartz; *M:* Marvin Hamlisch, Buddy (Norman Dale) Baker.

The Devil Rides Out

Many consider this to be Hammer's finest achievement and I agree, though several other of the studio's films rate serious consideration. This one's a solid witchcraft tale written by Richard Matheson. In 1925, the Duc de Richleau (Lee), a "good" warlock, and the evil Mocata (Gray) battle each other over de Richleau's friend Simon (Mower). Some of the effects are a little dated now, but director Terence Fisher builds suspense through a stately pace. Production values are highlighted by the usual excellent sets and a fleet of vintage cars. Lee's performance is one of his strongest in a conventionally heroic role. He takes center stage on the commentary track with co-star Sarah Lawson and critic Marcus Stern in assistance. Lee sounds authoritative and even takes some credit for the film's being produced. (He was familiar with Dennis Wheatley's novel.) My only criticism is that the commentary audio has a boomy, hollow quality, as if it had been recorded in a large room. —*MM*
AKA: The Devil's Bride.

Movie: 🐾🐾🐾½ **DVD:** 🐾🐾🐾½
Anchor Bay (Cat #013131066692, UPC #DV10666). Widescreen (1.66:1) anamorphic. Dolby Digital 5.1 Surround Stereo; Dolby Digital Surround; Mono. $24.98. Keepcase. *LANG:* English; French. FEA-

TURES: Commentary: Christopher Lee, Sarah Lawson, Marcus Stern ▪ Trailers ▪ 22 chapter links ▪ World of Hammer episode.

1968 95m/C *GB* Christopher Lee, Charles Gray, Nike Arrighi, Leon Greene, Patrick Mower, Gwen Ffrangcon Davies, Sarah Lawson, Paul Eddington; *D:* Terence Fisher; *W:* Richard Matheson; *C:* Arthur Grant; *M:* James Bernard.

Devil's Island

Touted as a brutal black comedy, this film is almost painful in the abuse of its characters. The story centers on a family in 1950s Iceland who are so poor that they live in a makeshift squatters' village with other poor families in the timber huts left behind on a deserted American military base. The story opens with one of the brood, a young blonde, marrying an American serviceman and leaving for America. She leaves behind two sons, a daughter, and her parents. She sends for her favored son (the aptly named Baddi), a brash ego-driven hunk of a man-child, to visit her in the States, leaving her good son, Danni, behind. Baddi returns from his trip full of himself sporting a leather jacket, ducktail, and incredibly clichéd American mannerisms. He immediately begins to raise hell in his small community, abusing his siblings and his grandfather, who supports the family, by drinking and acting like a spoiled brat. There is a small undercurrent theme about the modernization that is taking place in Iceland, but not enough to make the film worthy as a social statement. The picture and sound are about average, but the acting and cinematography are first-rate. —*CA* *AKA:* Djoflaeyjan.

Movie: 🐾🐾 **DVD:** 🐾🐾½
Winstar Home Entertainment (Cat #FLV 5211, UPC #720917521121). Full frame. Dolby Digital Stereo. $29.98. Keepcase. *LANG:* Icelandic. *SUB:* English. *FEATURES:* Filmographies ▪ Web access.

1996 103m/C *IC* Gisli Halldorsson, Baltasar Kormakur, Sveinn Geirsson, Sigurveig Jonsdottir; *D:* Fridrik Thor Fridriksson; *W:* Einar Karason; *C:* Ari Kristinsson; *M:* Hilmar Orn Jilmarsson.

Diabolique

Remake of the 1955 French noir classic, updated for '90s sensibilities, finds timid teacher Mia (Adjani) married to overbearing school head Guy (Palminteri), who's having an affair with fellow teacher Nicole (Stone). The two women, who loathe Guy equally, plot to kill him. But when a P.I. (Bates) investigates, it seems possible that Guy isn't dead after all. If you're having trouble accessorizing with leopard skin, watch Stone. Otherwise, watch the superior original. The usually publicity-hungry Stone refused to have anything to do with this picture after its release due to a spat with director Chechik. If you didn't see *Diabolique* at the theatre, you might think that the DVD looks a little soft. Truth

is, it looks pretty much like the big-screen version, which played around with a lot of filters and muted colors to convey a stylized noir look. When the colors do punch through, they are saturated and highly detailed. The 5.1 sound is more than respectable but hardly a showpiece. The occasional effect is nicely mixed to the split Surround channels and the subwoofer's presence is felt when needed but never obtrusive. —*JO*

Movie: 🐾🐾 **DVD:** 🐾🐾🐾½
Warner Home Video, Inc. (Cat #14204, UPC #085391420422). Widescreen (1.85:1) anamorphic. Dolby Digital 5.1. $19.98. Snapper. *LANG:* English; French. *SUB:* English; Spanish; French. *CAP:* English. *FEATURES:* 30 chapter links ▪ Theatrical trailer ▪ Talent files ▪ Behind-the-scenes featurette.

1996 (R) 105m/C Sharon Stone, Isabelle Adjani, Chazz Palminteri, Kathy Bates, Spalding Gray, Shirley Knight, Adam Hann-Byrd, Allen (Goorwitz) Garfield; *D:* Jeremiah S. Chechik; *W:* Don Roos; *C:* Peter James; *M:* Randy Edelman.

Diamond Run

Heist thriller produced mostly in Vermont is a satisfactory video premiere. Megan Marlow (Ljoka) manages to steal a load of diamonds from the original thieves and then finds herself on the run from an explosives expert (Gleek) who's very good at blowing things up. And that's what the film does best, too. The explosions are first-rate. Acting and plot don't fare as well. DVD image is the equal of tape in every respect. —*MM*

Movie: 🐾🐾 **DVD:** 🐾🐾
MTI Home Video (Cat #1044, UPC #03941 4510447). Full frame. $24.95. Keepcase. *LANG:* English. *SUB:* Spanish. *FEATURES:* 20 chapter links ▪ Trailers ▪ Talent files.

2000 (R) 98m/C Richard Lynch, Linda Ljoka, Michael J. Valentine, Fred Gleek, Peter Harrington; *D:* David Giancola; *W:* Marty Poole, Derrick J. Costa; *C:* John McAleer.

Diamondbacks

The Diamondbacks of the title are a militia group (led by O'Keeffe) that manages to take control of a space shuttle from the ground. A NASA engineer (Lottimer) must stop them. This is an acceptable low-budget video-premiere thriller with a deliberate pace and staging, but some O.K. effects. The image might be a hair brighter than VHS tape, but the difference is meaningless. —*MM*

Movie: 🐾🐾 **DVD:** 🐾🐾
York Entertainment (Cat #1008). Full frame. Dolby Digital 5.1 Surround Stereo. $24.98. Keepcase. *LANG:* English. *SUB:* Spanish. *FEATURES:* Cast and crew thumbnail bios ▪ Trailer ▪ Behind-the-scenes featurette ▪ 25 chapter links.

1999 90m/C Miles O'Keeffe, Chris Mitchum, Timothy Bottoms, Eb Lottimer; *D:* Bernard Salzman.

Diamonds

Douglas lends both dignity and humor to his first screen role since recovering from a stroke. He is Harry Agrensky, a one-time boxing champ (recovering from a stroke) who wants to live as independently as possible. He claims to have a fortune in diamonds, given to him by a mobster, hidden away in Reno and bullies his estranged son Lance (Aykroyd) and his grandson Michael (Allred) to go on a road trip and retrieve them. There are various adventures and bonding moments along the way and Douglas is reunited with Bacall (as a Nevada madam), with whom he worked in 1950's *Young Man with a Horn*. The video transfer features nice, crisp colors and impressive definition. Some clarity is lost, however, on darker scenes but thankfully that doesn't prove too distracting. The soundtrack is crisp and dialogue is solid. The featurette on Douglas is, on the surface, informative and entertaining. But it quickly becomes little more than a glorified trailer for the main feature. Surely, there are people better suited to discuss Douglas's life and career than the cast and crew of *Diamonds*. —*MJT*
Movie: 🎵🎵½ **DVD:** 🎵🎵🎵
Miramax Pictures Home Video (Cat #18318, UPC #717951005045). Widescreen (1.85:1) anamorphic. Dolby Digital 5.1 Surround; Dolby Digital 2.0. $29.99. Keepcase. *LANG:* English; French. *SUB:* English. *FEATURES:* 29 chapter links ● Cast and crew bios ● "The Life and Times of Kirk Douglas" featurette.
1999 (PG-13) 90m/C Kirk Douglas, Dan Aykroyd, Corbin Allred, Lauren Bacall, Kurt Fuller, Jenny McCarthy, John Landis, Mariah O'Brien; **D:** John Mallory Asher; **W:** Allan Aaron Katz; **C:** Paul Elliott; **M:** Joel Goldsmith.

Diamonds Are Forever [SE]

007 once again battles Blofeld, this time in Las Vegas where Bond must foil a plot to destroy Washington with a space-based laser. (Was this a prototype for the Strategic Defense Initiative?) Fabulous stunts include Bond's wild drive through the streets of Vegas in a Mustang Mach 1. The commentary track explains the famous continuity error in the chase, and a deleted scene shows the stunt as it was originally meant to be seen. Connery returned to play Bond in this one after being offered the then record-setting salary of $1 million. MGM has done its usual bang-up job with the special edition. Image and mono sound are tip-top. The disc is filled with the extras collectors expect. —*MM*
Movie: 🎵🎵🎵½ **DVD:** 🎵🎵🎵½
MGM Home Entertainment (Cat #4001181, UPC #027616853929). Widescreen (2.35:1) anamorphic. Dolby Digital Mono. $26.98. Keepcase. *LANG:* English. *SUB:* French; Spanish. *CAP:* English. *FEATURES:* 32 chapter links ● 5 TV spots ● 4 deleted scenes ● 3 radio spots ● 2 trailers

● "Inside *Diamonds Are Forever*" featurette ● Cubby Broccoli featurette ● Commentary: director Hamilton and cast members ● "Making of" booklet.
1971 (PG) 120m/C *GB* Sean Connery, Jill St. John, Charles Gray, Bruce Cabot, Jimmy Dean, Lana Wood, Bruce Glover, Putter Smith, Norman Burton, Joseph Furst, Bernard Lee, Desmond Llewelyn, Laurence Naismith, Leonard Barr, Lois Maxwell, Margaret Lacey, Joe Robinson, Donna Garrat, Trina Parks; **D:** Guy Hamilton; **W:** Tom Mankiewicz; **C:** Ted Moore; **M:** John Barry. *AWARDS: NOM:* Oscars '71: Sound.

Diary of a Chambermaid

Celestine (Moreau), a sexy young Parisienne, takes a job at a provincial estate and finds herself drawn into the owners' world of decadence and hypocrisy. It's vintage Buñuelian social satire that encompasses both personal and political themes. Criterion has done yet another superb job on the film. It arrives on DVD with a near flawless black-and-white image that renders fine detail much more sharply than color can. Optional subtitles are easy to read, and, in an area that's often overlooked, the menu is clear and intuitive. The main extra is a long interview with Buñuel's collaborator Jean-Claude Carriere recorded in 2000. —*MM* **AKA:** *Le Journal d'une Femme de Chambre; Il Diario di una Cameriera.*
Movie: 🎵🎵🎵½ **DVD:** 🎵🎵🎵🎵
Criterion Collection (Cat #117, UPC #0374 29158118). Widescreen (2.35:1) anamorphic. Dolby Digital Mono. $30.00. Keepcase. *LANG:* French. *SUB:* English. *FEATURES:* 32 chapter links ● Trailer ● Interview with Jean-Claude Carriere (8 links) ● Carriere bio ● Liner notes by Michael Anderson.
1964 97m/C *FR* Jeanne Moreau, Michel Piccoli, Georges Geret, Francoise Lugagne, Daniel Ivernel; **D:** Luis Bunuel; **W:** Luis Bunuel, Jean-Claude Carriere; **C:** Roger Fellous.

Diary of a Serial Killer

Down-on-his-luck journalist Nelson Keece (Busey) witnesses a murder and then is invited by the killer, Stefan (Vosloo), to conduct an exclusive interview. Stefan keeps killing and Nelson keeps writing, but the cops (including Madsen) come to think that Nelson is the killer. Then Stefan targets Nelson's girlfriend Juliette (Campbell). Perhaps the most disturbing image in this video premiere is Busey in drag smoking a cigar—not a pretty sight in any medium. Overall, image is not substantially better than VHS. —*MM*
Movie: 🎵🎵 **DVD:** 🎵🎵
Simitar Entertainment (Cat #7424). Full frame. Dolby Digital 5.1 Surround Stereo. $14.98. Keepcase. *LANG:* English. *FEATURES:* Cast and crew thumbnail bios ● 8 chapter links.
1997 (R) 92m/C Gary Busey, Arnold Vosloo, Michael Madsen, Julia Campbell;

D: Alan Jacobs; **W:** Jennifer Badham-Stewart; **C:** Keith L. Smith; **M:** Steve Edwards.

Dick

Deft, imaginative satire puts forth the theory that two dizzy teenaged girls (Dunst and Williams) caused the downfall of Richard Nixon (Hedaya). They bump into all of the major Watergate players including Liddy (Shearer), Haldeman (Foley), Dean (Breuer), Woodward (Ferrell), and Bernstein (McCulloch), for whom they become the famous "Deep Throat." The writing is sharp and the period details all ring true. The picture is very clear and the source print is free from any obvious defects. The film is filled with the many garish colors of the '70s and the color balancing is excellent on the DVD. The audio mix is a bit flat at times, but otherwise, sounds very good. —*ML/MM*
Movie: 🎵🎵🎵 **DVD:** 🎵🎵🎵
Columbia Tristar Home Video (Cat #4001). Widescreen (1.85:1) anamorphic; full frame. Dolby Digital 5.1 Surround Stereo. $24.95. Keepcase. *LANG:* English. *SUB:* English. *FEATURES:* Commentary: director Fleming and writer Longin ● Bloopers ● Deleted scene ● Isolated score.
1999 (PG-13) 95m/C Kirsten Dunst, Michelle Williams, Dan Hedaya, Will Ferrell, Dave Foley, Harry Shearer, Jim Breuer, Bruce McCulloch, Devon Gummersall, Ted McGinley, Ryan Reynolds, Saul Rubinek, Teri Garr, G.D. Spradlin, Ana Gasteyer; **D:** Andrew Fleming; **W:** Andrew Fleming, Sheryl Longin; **C:** Alexander Grusynski; **M:** John Debney.

Die! Die! Die!

Fellow crooks and lovers Macy (Bako) and Frank (Grieco) doublecross each other in a low-budget thriller. Image and sound, however, are a cut above the norm for this sort of thing. —*MM*
Movie: 🎵🎵½ **DVD:** 🎵🎵½
New Concorde (Cat #NH20774 D, UPC #736991377493). Full frame. Stereo. $19.98. Keepcase. *LANG:* English. *SUB:* Spanish. *FEATURES:* 24 chapter links ● Talent files ● Trailers.
2000 (PG-13) 82m/C Brigitte Bako, Richard Grieco, Greg Evigan; **D:** Gordon McLennan; **W:** Vincent Monton; **C:** Mark Dobrescu; **M:** Ross Nykiforuk.

Die, Monster, Die!

Typical American-International Gothic is a bit underpowered and lacking in real scares compared to A-I's best. Steve Reinhart (Adams) goes to rural England to visit his sweetie Susan (Farmer). The suspicious villagers won't tell him the way to her father's (Karloff) estate. He finds it to be a blighted wasteland. The pace plods and Karloff has a relatively ineffectual role. The plot is based on H.P. Lovecraft's "The Color Out of Space." Overall, the DVD image is very good. So is the mono sound but the pace is still stodgy. —*MM* **AKA:** *Monster of Terror.*

Movie: 🎵🎵 **DVD:** 🎵🎵½
MGM Home Entertainment (Cat #1001542, UPC #027616858535). Widescreen (2.35:1) anamorphic. Dolby Digital Mono. $19.98. Keepcase. *LANG:* English; French. *SUB:* French; Spanish. *CAP:* English. *FEATURES:* 16 chapter links • Trailer.
1965 80m/C *GB* Boris Karloff, Nick Adams, Suzan Farmer, Patrick Magee, Freda Jackson, Terence de Marney, Leslie Dwyer, Paul Farrell; *D:* Daniel Haller; *W:* Jerry Sohl; *C:* Paul Beeson; *M:* Don Banks.

Die Screaming, Marianne

About to turn 21, Marianne (George) is on the run from assassins hired by her father (Genn), a corrupt judge. Why? Because she will inherit a fat Swiss bank account. The crisp image does justice to the very bright colors of those early '70s clothes and presents the regrettable haircuts in all their shame. —*MM* **AKA:** Die, Beautiful Marianne.
Movie: 🎵🎵 **DVD:** 🎵🎵🎵
Image Entertainment (Cat #ID9348EUDVD, UPC #014381934823). Full frame. Dolby Digital Mono. $24.99. Snapper. *LANG:* English. *FEATURES:* 12 chapter links.
1973 81m/C *GB* Michael Rennie, Susan George, Karin Dor, Leo Genn; *D:* Pete Walker; *W:* Murray Smith; *C:* Norman G. Langley; *M:* Cyril Ornadel.

Digging to China

Hutton's directorial debut is a sentimental '60s story of a sweet friendship between misfits—precocious 10-year-old Harriet (Wood) and mentally handicapped 30-year-old Ricky (Bacon). Harriet's alcoholic mom (Moriarty) runs a motel in rural New Hampshire with Harriet's slutty older sister Gwen (Masterson). Ricky winds up at the motel with his dying mother Leah (Seldes), who is taking him to an institution when her car breaks down. Bacon's performance may be accurate, but it's still uncomfortable. (He makes Dustin Hoffman's work in *Rain Man* seem understated.) That said, the film's emotions are honest. On DVD, the pale color scheme seems to be accurate. Sound is fine for a period piece. —*MM*
Movie: 🎵🎵½ **DVD:** 🎵🎵½
Winstar Home Entertainment (Cat #5140). Widescreen letterboxed. Dolby Digital Surround Stereo. $24.98. Keepcase. *LANG:* English. *FEATURES:* 8 chapter links • Talent files • Trailer • Awards and credits.
1998 (PG) 98m/C Evan Rachel Wood, Kevin Bacon, Mary Stuart Masterson, Cathy Moriarty, Marian Seldes; *D:* Timothy Hutton; *W:* Karen Janszen; *C:* Jorgen Persson; *M:* Cynthia Miller.

Digimon: The Movie

The title refers to "digital monster" the way "Pokemon" refers to "pocket monster" and these cute critters obviously came from the same source. So did the cute kids who must protect the digital

world, etc., etc. It's standard anime fare, presented here with a very clear image and bright colors. —*MM*
Movie: 🎵🎵 **DVD:** 🎵🎵½
20th Century Fox Home Entertainment (Cat #2001134, UPC #024520011347). Full frame. Dolby Digital 5.1 Surround Stereo; Dolby Digital Surround. $24.98. Keepcase. *LANG:* English. *SUB:* English; Spanish. *FEATURES:* 20 chapter links • Trailer • Music video.
2000 (PG) 83m/C *D:* Takaaki Yamashita, Hisashi Nakayama, Masahiro Aizawa, Jeff Nimoy, Bob Buchholz; *W:* Jeff Nimoy, Bob Buchholz; *M:* Udi Harpaz, Amotz Plessner.

Dilemma

On Death Row, Rudy Salazar (Trejo) volunteers to be a bone-marrow donor to a sick child. LAPD detective Quin (Howell) realizes that it's a set-up for an escape and he's right. Then the cops have to catch Salazar again, but they can't kill him without sacrificing the kid. Similar material was handled much more effectively in the underrated *Desperate Measures*. The image here is well-above average for a modestly budgeted thriller. Sound is exaggerated. —*MM*
Movie: 🎵🎵½ **DVD:** 🎵🎵½
Image Entertainment (Cat #ID8908YODVD, UPC #014381890822). Full frame. Dolby Digital Stereo. $24.99. Snapper. *LANG:* English. *FEATURES:* 10 chapter links.
1997 87m/C C. Thomas Howell, Danny Trejo, Sofia Shinas; *D:* Erik Larsen; *W:* Ira Israel, Chuck Conaway; *C:* Mark Melville; *M:* Albritton McClain.

Dillinger

Warren Oates has one of his best starring roles as America's most famous gangster, and he's backed up by a superb supporting cast that includes Geoffrey Lewis, Harry Dean Stanton, Richard Dreyfuss, and Ben Johnson as G-Man Melvin Purvis. Cloris Leachman is fine as "the Lady in Red." Both the softness of the image and the heavy grain come from the original. There's some slight surface damage, too. —*MM*
Movie: 🎵🎵🎵 **DVD:** 🎵🎵½
MGM Home Entertainment (Cat #1000 985). Widescreen. $19.98. Keepcase. *LANG:* English. *CAP:* English. *FEATURES:* 32 chapter links.
1973 (R) 106m/C Warren Oates, Michelle Phillips, Richard Dreyfuss, Cloris Leachman, Ben Johnson, Harry Dean Stanton; *D:* John Milius; *W:* John Milius; *C:* Jules Brenner; *M:* Barry DeVorzon.

The Dinner Game

Smug publisher Pierre (Lhermitte) dines weekly with equally smug friends, their entertainment being to see who can bring the biggest fool as a dinner guest. This nasty joke gets the turnabout it deserves when Pierre intends to bring bumbling Francois (Villeret) to the party, only to have the man proceed to wreck Pierre's life

before they even get there—all while Francois maintains his own sweet dignity. Not as memorable as writer/director Veber's *La Cage aux Folles* but almost as funny. Lhermitte is superb as the yuppie sleazebag Pierre. This DVD, though it doesn't offer any extras other than the trailer, looks great. The colors are strong and the image is sharp. What's really unique about this low-exposure film is that preprint itself is far cleaner than those used for many other titles in the foreign film genre. Not much happens on the soundtrack, but both the French and English (dubbed) dialogue is very crisp and clean. The subtitles are easy to read as well. —*JO* **AKA:** Le Diner de Cons.
Movie: 🎵🎵🎵 **DVD:** 🎵🎵🎵
Universal Studios Home Video (Cat #20706, UPC #025192070624). Widescreen (2.35:1) anamorphic. Dolby Surround. $24.98. Keepcase. *LANG:* French. *SUB:* English. *FEATURES:* 20 chapter links • Theatrical trailer.
1998 (PG-13) 82m/C *FR* Thierry Lhermitte, Jacques Villeret, Alexandra Vandernoot, Catherine Frot, Francis Huster, Daniel Prevost; *D:* Francis Veber; *W:* Francis Veber; *C:* Luciano Tovoli; *M:* Vladimir Cosma. *AWARDS:* Cesar '99: Actor (Villeret), Support. Actor (Prevost), Writing.

Dinosaur [CE]

Young iguanodon Aladar is separated from his parents (when he's still in the shell). He's raised by lemurs on an isolated island and must discover his heritage as a meteor crash threatens to destroy his world. The ambitious animation attempts to combine computer-generated characters with conventionally photographed real natural settings. On this two-disc set, the fusion of the two approaches is seamless. Both image and sound are astonishingly bright and clear. But that very clarity highlights the spotless, antiseptic quality of computer animation. The TheatreVision voice-over narration describes the action for the visually impaired. For animation fans, though, the highlight of this set is the second disc, which is packed with almost three hours of background material that covers virtually every part of the filmmaking process. Disney is known for delivering the goods with their big releases. This is one of the studio's best to date. —*MM*
Movie: 🎵🎵🎵 **DVD:** 🎵🎵🎵🎵
Buena Vista Home Entertainment (Cat #21924, UPC #786936147728). Widescreen (1.85:1) anamorphic. Dolby Digital 5.1 Surround Stereo; DTS Surround. $39.99. Keepcase. *LANG:* English; French. *CAP:* English. *FEATURES:* 27 chapter links • 2 commentary tracks; isolated sound effects track • DVD-ROM features • Film fact fossil dig; dinosaur facts • "Aladar's Adventure" • Dino Search game • Development of *Dinosaur* • Dinosaur design featurette • Concept art; character design; computer animation tests • Creating a prehistoric world • Special effects featurette; music and sound

design featurette • Story reel; progression reels • 3-D workbook • Publicity material • Audio mix demonstration • Abandoned sequences • "Easter eggs."
2000 (PG) 82m/C D: Ralph Zondag, Eric Leighton; **W:** John Harrison, Robert Nelson Jacobs; **M:** James Newton Howard; **V:** Julianna Margulies, Alfre Woodard, D.B. Sweeney, Ossie Davis, Della Reese, Max Casella, Samuel E. Wright, Joan Plowright, Hayden Panettiere, Peter Siragusa.

Dinosaur Valley Girls

Hollywood action hero Tony Markham finds a magic stone that hurls him back in time to a prehistoric world populated by model dinosaurs and babes in animal print bikinis. Yes, silicone meets saurian! It's all every bit as frivolous as it sounds. Beyond the extensive extras, included on the flip side of the disc, image and sound are essentially identical to VHS tape. —*MM*
Movie: 🎵½ **DVD:** 🎵
El Independent Cinema (Cat #sc-1009-dvd, UPC #612385100994). Full frame. $19.98. Keepcase. *LANG:* English. *FEATURES:* "Making of" featurette • Screen tests • Deleted scenes • Commentary: director • Trailers.
1996 94m/C Karen Black, William D. Russell, Ron Jeffries, Jeff Rector, Griffin (Griffen) Drew, Ed Fury; **D:** Don Glut; **W:** Don Glut.

Dinosaurus!

American engineers set off underwater blasts that release two dinosaurs and a Neanderthal man from the ocean floor. Electrical storm, lightning strikes—you know the drill. The loopy period piece benefits from intentional humor and stop-motion critters that are slightly more realistic and frightening than Barney. In fact, the resurrected T-Rex is almost the same color. Coincidence? The DVD is exceptionally sharp for a film of this age. The negative was well preserved and carefully transferred to disc. First-rate drive-in fare for all ages. —*MM*
Movie: 🎵½ **DVD:** 🎵🎵🎵
Image Entertainment (Cat #ID6605WEDVD, UPC #014381660524). Widescreen (2.35:1) anamorphic. Dolby Digital Mono. $24.99. Snapper. *LANG:* English. *FEATURES:* 16 chapter links • Liner notes by Tom Weaver • Trailer • Poster gallery.
1960 85m/C Ward Ramsey, Kristina Hanson, Paul Lukather, Fred Engelberg; **D:** Irvin S. Yeaworth Jr.; **W:** Dan E. Weisburd, Jean Yeaworth; **C:** Stanley Cortez; **M:** Ronald Stein.

Diplomatic Siege

The U.S. Embassy is taken over by Serbian terrorists who demand that foreign forces clear out of Bosnia or they'll kill their hostages. But General Buck Swain (Berenger) decides to get rid of the Serbs instead. And just to keep things interesting, CIA ops Steve Parker (Weller) and Erica Long (Hannah) are in the embassy

basement trying to defuse a bomb. The DVD does nothing to add to the presentation of this so-so thriller. Color accuracy seems to come and go and the dimmer scenes lose a lot of detail. More contrast and better lighting, please. On a DVD, the one thing that you can usually count on (even in a low-budget shoot 'em up) is a beefed-up 5.1 soundtrack to accent even the mildest of action. In fact, sometimes it's way overdone. But not so here. Actually, there ought to be a law about an action film being released with such lamo gunshots. Not that every movie can sound like *Dirty Harry*, but every time someone pulls the trigger, it's a flashback to a childhood cap gun. —*JO* *AKA:* Enemy of My Enemy.
Movie: 🎵🎵 **DVD:** 🎵½
Trimark Home Video (Cat #VM7323D, UPC #031398732327). Widescreen (1.85:1) anamorphic. Dolby Digital 5.1. $24.99. Keepcase. *LANG:* English. *SUB:* English; Spanish; French. *CAP:* English. *FEATURES:* 24 chapter links • Trailer.
1999 (R) 94m/C Tom Berenger, Daryl Hannah, Peter Weller; **D:** Gustavo Graef-Marino; **W:** Robert Boris, Kevin Bernhardt, Sam Bernard, Mark Amin; **C:** Steven Wacks; **M:** Terry Plumeri.

Dirty Duck

Grubby-looking adult cartoon is rude and crude, but also fairly pointless. Willard, a lonely insurance adjuster, meets Dirty Duck who promises to make him a success with women. Creator Charles Swenson went on to make *Rugrats*, and, difficult as it may be to believe, the grotesque style of that popular children's series is a huge step up from this work. It's minimalist animation that really is hard to take in a feature-length work. DVD accentuates the existing grain to present a rough image. —*MM*
Movie: 🎵 **DVD:** 🎵🎵
New Concorde (Cat #NH2143UD, UPC #736991614390). Full frame. $19.98. Keepcase. *LANG:* English. *FEATURES:* 20 chapter links • Thumbnail bios • Trailers.
1975 (X) 70m/C D: Charles Swenson; **W:** Charles Swenson; **M:** Howard Kaylan, Mark Volman.

Dirty Pictures

This version of the controversy surrounding an exhibit of photographs by Robert Mapplethorpe in Cincinnati in 1990 is intelligent, imaginative entertainment. The filmmakers blend real footage of President George Bush, Senator Jesse Helms, and others with a re-creation of the trial. James Woods is the museum director who sponsors the show; Craig T. Nelson is the sheriff who shuts it down. The film's ideological point of view is completely clear, but it is more nuanced and complex than many theatrical releases. Since the production was made for cable, the image loses nothing on DVD. Image is excellent. Extras are lacking, though. A gallery of

Mapplethorpe's work would have been instructive. (They are on-screen during the opening credits.) —*MM*
Movie: 🎵🎵🎵½ **DVD:** 🎵🎵🎵
MGM Home Entertainment (Cat #1000 792, UPC #027616851130). Full frame. Dolby Digital Surround Stereo. $19.98. Keepcase. *LANG:* English. *SUB:* French; Spanish. *FEATURES:* 32 chapter links.
2000 (R) 104m/C James Woods, Diana Scarwid, Craig T. Nelson, Leon Pownall, David Huband, Judah Katz, R.D. Reid, Matt North; **D:** Frank Pierson; **W:** Ilene Chaiken; **C:** Hiro Narita; **M:** Mark Snow.

Dirty Work

You'll notice that star and ex-SNL newsguy MacDonald isn't even trying to act here; he's just doing his not-very-funny deadpan routine with a different name. Mitch (MacDonald) and Sam (Lange) are two losers who can't keep a job but have a talent for petty revenge. When Sam's father (Warden) has a heart attack, the boys decide to open a business specializing in dirty deeds done dirt cheap to pay for a transplant. Although the premise is good, the tricks are mostly of the junior high variety and don't seem quite dirty enough. Look for several unbilled cameos including Adam Sandler, John Goodman, and the late Chris Farley. Production values are typical of a feature made for a TV comedian, so the film gains little on DVD. It's really no different from a widescreen tape. —*MM*
Movie: 🎵½ **DVD:** 🎵🎵
MGM Home Entertainment (Cat #907 248). Widescreen (1.85:1) anamorphic. Dolby Digital 5.1 Surround Stereo. $24.98. Keepcase. *LANG:* English; French. *SUB:* French. *CAP:* English. *FEATURES:* Trailer • 44 chapter links.
1997 (PG-13) 81m/C Norm MacDonald, Artie Lange, Chevy Chase, Don Rickles, Jack Warden, Traylor Howard, Christopher McDonald, Chris Farley, Gary Coleman, Ken Norton, John Goodman, Adam Sandler; **D:** Bob Saget; **W:** Fred Wolf; **C:** Arthur Albert; **M:** Richard Gibbs.

The Discreet Charm of the Bourgeoisie

Frequently uproarious comedy by the master of the surreal, Luis Buñuel. Constructed around three middle-class couples' constantly frustrated attempts to have dinner, the film takes place over several days and features several outlandish (and two bone-chilling and creepy) fantasy sequences. A completely successful art film that gets funnier on repeated viewings. A highlight: the local priest who also works as a union-waged gardener. Gorgeous, colorful disc occasionally features some source-print dirt and clumsy grammar in the subtitle translation. The sound is crisp and excellent. The disc features two documentaries of variable quality: *Speaking of Buñuel* is feature length, thorough, and beautifully photographed, but dull and seemingly endless. "The Castaway on the Street of Providence," a short collection of footage shot of Buñuel and his friends over the years, is more successful but not as pristine. An absolute must. —DG **AKA:** Le Charme Discret de la Bourgeoisie.

Movie: 🐶🐶🐶½ **DVD:** 🐶🐶🐶½

Criterion Collection (Cat #102, UPC #037 42915462). Widescreen (1.85:1) anamorphic. Dolby Digital Mono. $39.95. Keepcase (2-disc). *LANG:* French; Spanish. *SUB:* English. *FEATURES:* "The Castaway on the Street of Providence," 24-minute documentary ▪ Theatrical trailer ▪ Buñuel filmography ▪ *Speaking of Buñuel,* a new 98-minute documentary ▪ Insert booklet with notes ▪ 21 chapter links (feature), 36 chapter links (documentary).

1972 (R) 100m/C *FR* Milena Vukotic, Fernando Rey, Delphine Seyrig, Jean-Pierre Cassel, Bulle Ogier, Michel Piccoli, Stephane Audran, Luis Bunuel; *D:* Luis Bunuel; *W:* Luis Bunuel, Jean-Claude Carriere; *C:* Edmond Richard. *AWARDS:* Oscars '72: Foreign Film; British Acad. '73: Actress (Seyrig), Screenplay; Natl. Soc. Film Critics '72: Director (Bunuel), Film; *NOM:* Oscars '72: Story & Screenplay.

Dish Dogs

Morgan (Astin) and Jason (Lillard) are philosopher-surfers who wash dishes for a living and have vowed to remain single. Then they go to a strip joint where they meet Shannon Elizabeth. Much of the action is too talky, but this junior grade *Good Will Hunting* certainly has its moments. Image is as good as you'll see on such a modestly budgeted picture. Same for sound. —MM

Movie: 🐶🐶½ **DVD:** 🐶🐶🐶½

Trimark Home Video (Cat #7410D, UPC #031398741022). Widescreen letterboxed. Dolby Digital Stereo. $24.99. Keepcase. *LANG:* English. *SUB:* English; French; Spanish. *CAP:* English. *FEATURES:* 24 chapter links ▪ Music video ▪ Trailer ▪ Blooper/outtakes reel ▪ Photo gallery with commentary by director Kubilos.

1998 (R) 96m/C Matthew Lillard, Sean Astin, Shannon Elizabeth, Maitland Ward, Brian Dennehy, Richard Moll; *D:* Bob (Robert) Kubilos; *W:* Ashley Scott Meyers, Nathan Ives; *C:* Mark Vicente; *M:* Herman Beeftink.

Disney's The Kid

Cynical image consultant Russ Duritz (Willis) comes face to face with his eight-year-old self (Breslin), who is upset to learn that he is going to grow up to have such an empty life. It's typical Disney fantasy stuff that's handled deftly by a very talented cast, with Lily Tomlin turning in strong support. The studio does its usual fine job, delivering a disc that has no visual flaws worth noting, and a well-chosen roster of extras. The 5.1 sound is fine if unspectacular. —MM

Movie: 🐶🐶🐶 **DVD:** 🐶🐶🐶

Buena Vista Home Entertainment (Cat #19690, UPC #717951008664). Widescreen (1.85:1) anamorphic. Dolby Digital 5.1 Surround Stereo. $29.99. Keepcase. *LANG:* English; French; Spanish. *SUB:* Spanish. *CAP:* English. *FEATURES:* 24 chapter links ▪ Conversation with Jon Turteltaub ▪ Turteltaub bio ▪ Commentary: Turteltaub, Spencer Breslin ▪ Trailers ▪ "Making of" featurette from Breslin's point of view.

2000 (PG) 104m/C Bruce Willis, Emily Mortimer, Jean Smart, Spencer Breslin, Chi McBride, Lily Tomlin, Dana Ivey, Daniel von Bargen; *D:* Jon Turteltaub; *W:* Audrey Wells; *C:* Peter Menzies Jr.; *M:* Jerry Goldsmith.

Divided We Stand

Naïve college student Jennice (Lisa) joins the Black Student Coalition and soon accuses one of the leaders (Robey) of rape. Another student, Troy (Jarrod), knows the truth and is pressured to remain silent. Heavy grain generates heavy digital artifacts even in conventional interiors, but flashy visuals are not the point of this independent production. It looks at tensions within the black community that are seldom addressed on film. If director Jarrod is a bit too earnest, he is trying to tell a good story. His film earns a qualified recommendation. —MM

Movie: 🐶🐶½ **DVD:** 🐶🐶

MTI Home Video (Cat #7006, UPC #039-414570069). Widescreen (1.66:1) letterboxed. $24.95. Keepcase. *LANG:* English. *FEATURES:* 20 chapter links ▪ Talent files ▪ Trailers.

2000 (R) 81m/C Andrea Lisa, Crayton Robey, J.R. Jarrod; *D:* J.R. Jarrod; *W:* J.R. Jarrod; *C:* Joan Crawford; *M:* Charles D. Jackson, Sherwood Seward, Derek Seward.

Divine Trash

This documentary takes a roughly chronological look at the first years of director John Waters's career. The structure is standard: home movies, interviews with parents and friends, clips from the filmmaker at work. Those who are familiar only with the films—*Pink Flamingos, Female Trouble,* etc.—will probably be surprised at what a nice, normal person Waters really is, though admittedly, he has his preoccupations and he chooses to deal with them in unusual ways. On DVD, much of the image is purposefully rough, reflecting the subject material, but some heavy pixelation is visible in conventional interiors. Sound is fine. —MM

Movie: 🐶🐶🐶 **DVD:** 🐶🐶½

Winstar Home Entertainment (Cat #FLV 5226, UPC #720917052267). Widescreen letterboxed. $24.98. Snapper. *LANG:* English. *FEATURES:* 8 chapter links ▪ Weblink ▪ Filmographies ▪ Production credits.

1998 96m/C *D:* Steve Yeager; *W:* Steve Yeager, Kevin Heffernan; *M:* Don Barto.

Do the Right Thing [2]

An uncompromising, brutal comedy about the racial tensions surrounding a white-owned pizzeria in the Bed-Stuy section of Brooklyn on the hottest day of the summer, and the violence that eventually erupts. Lee's coming-of-age film is ambivalent and, for the most part, hilarious. Thought-provoking film provoked intense discussion at the time of its release and retains all of its power more than a decade later. *Do the Right Thing* truly deserves a full-blown special edition treatment, and Criterion has given it the works. The anamorphic transfer is miles above even the finest laserdisc ever produced; it is incredibly sharp with colors that precisely replicate the original theatrical presentation. Besides the Dolby Surround, there is also an uncompressed PCM stereo track which, when played through high-end equipment, offers stunning dynamics and truly distortion-free fidelity. Disc one in the set contains the film and the engrossing commentary in which the participants discuss not only the film, but the state of society itself. It's one of the most powerful commentaries ever recorded, and deserves repeated listening. The second disc contains "The Making of *Do the Right Thing,*" a superb hour-long documentary by filmmaker Claire Bourne, a good deal of behind-the-scenes footage shot by Lee himself, and many more very worthwhile extras. —JO

Movie: 🐶🐶🐶🐶 **DVD:** 🐶🐶🐶🐶

Criterion Collection (Cat #CC1561DVD, UPC #715515011228). Widescreen (1.85) anamorphic. Dolby Surround; PCM Stereo. $29.95. Keepcase. *LANG:* English. *SUB:* English. *FEATURES:* 32 chapter links ▪ Theatrical trailer ▪ TV spots ▪ "Making of" documentary ▪ Commentary: Spike Lee, Ernest Dickerson, Wynn Thomas, Joie Lee ▪ Public Enemy music video "Fight the Power" ▪ Behind-the-scenes footage ▪ Intro by Spike Lee ▪ Storyboards for the riot sequence ▪ Interview with editor Barry Brown ▪ 1989 Cannes press conference with Spike Lee and cast.

1989 (R) 120m/C Spike Lee, Danny Aiello, Richard Edson, Ruby Dee, Ossie Davis, Giancarlo Esposito, Bill Nunn, John Turturro, John Savage, Rosie Perez, Frankie Faison; *D:* Spike Lee; *W:* Spike Lee; *C:* Ernest R. Dickerson; *M:* Bill Lee. *AWARDS:* L.A. Film Critics '89: Director (Lee), Film, Support. Actor (Aiello), Natl. Film Reg. '99; N.Y. Film Critics '89: Cinematog; *NOM:* Oscars '89: Orig. Screenplay, Support. Actor (Aiello).

D.O.A. [Roan]

A man is given a lethal, slow-acting poison. As his time runs out, he obsessively attempts to find his murderer and to learn why someone would want to kill him. O'Brien's performance is at times manic and at others frantic, but always dead-on, and there are plenty of twists and turns to keep you guessing. The film has been remade several times, but the claustrophobic tension generated by director Mate's ultra-realism has never been matched by its successors. This Roan

DVD is certainly a vast improvement over the many earlier home video releases of the title. There is still some ghosting on the high-contrast lines and the picture softens here and there (mainly near the end of the film). The sound is harsh and occasionally scratchy. Intermittent film scratches do appear (not unexpected in a 50-year-old movie), but for the most part the black-and-white image is more than satisfactory. —JO

Movie: 🎵🎵🎵½ **DVD:** 🎵🎵½
Roan Group (Cat #AED-2032, UPC #78560 4203223). Full frame. Dolby Digital Mono. $19.99. Keepcase. *LANG:* English. *FEATURES:* 18 chapter links.
1949 83m/B Edmond O'Brien, Pamela Britton, Luther Adler, Neville Brand, Beverly Garland, Lynne Baggett, William Ching, Henry Hart, Laurette Luez, Virginia Lee, Jess Kirkpatrick, Cay Forrester, Michael Ross; *D:* Rudolph Mate; *W:* Russell Rouse, Clarence Green; *C:* Ernest Laszlo; *M:* Dimitri Tiomkin.

Doctor Dolittle

Eighteenth-century veterinarian Dr. Dolittle (Harrison) dreams of teaching animals to speak. Somehow, the real spirit of Hugh Lofting's stories doesn't make it to the screen, though this opulent, almost three-hour production certainly doesn't stint on anything. The film marks the end of the big-budget musical. This DVD re-creates the theatrical experience down to the overture and the exit music. The image captures the bright, vivid colors, and even the remixed sound doesn't seem out of place. —MM

Movie: 🎵🎵 **DVD:** 🎵🎵½
Universal Studios Home Video (Cat #2000 494, UPC #024543004943). Widescreen (1.85:1) anamorphic. Dolby Digital 4.0 Surround; Dolby Digital Stereo. Mono. $29.98. Keepcase. *LANG:* English; French. *SUB:* English; Spanish. *FEATURES:* Trailer • 36 chapter links.
1967 151m/C Rex Harrison, Samantha Eggar, Anthony Newley, Richard Attenborough, Geoffrey Holder, Peter Bull; *D:* Richard Fleischer; *W:* Leslie Bricusse; *C:* Robert L. Surtees; *M:* Leslie Bricusse. *AWARDS:* Oscars '67: Song ("Talk to the Animals"), Visual FX; Golden Globes '68: Support. Actor (Attenborough); *NOM:* Oscars '67: Art Dir./Set Dec., Cinematog., Film Editing, Picture, Sound, Orig. Score.

Dr. Frankenstein's Castle of Freaks

Forgettable (though not forgivable) horror film about the crackpot Count Frankenstein (Brazzi), whose latest creature is a goofy, dome-headed Neanderthal man cleverly named Goliath. Typical of monsters, Goliath also has the hots for Frankenstein's new squeeze, Krista (Royce), who likes to bathe in milk. Things turn ugly, however, when Genz, a horny necrophilic dwarf, is expelled from the castle and promptly makes friends with Ook, another Neanderthal man who just hap-

pens to be passing through town. Out for revenge, Genz lets Goliath loose to go head to pointy-head with Ook in a good old-fashioned monster rumble. Most colors on this transfer lack definition. In fact, the whole film has the muted look of appearing colorized. Blacks also lack any definition and tend to bleed quite a bit. The sound is discernible but is ultimately unimpressive. An odd assortment of pseudo-erotic horror vignettes make for an interesting lesson in history and save this disc from the junk pile. —MJT

Movie: 🎵½ **DVD:** 🎵🎵
Image Entertainment (Cat #ID9737SW DVD, UPC #014381973723). Full frame. Dolby Digital Mono. $24.99. Snapper. *LANG:* English. *FEATURES:* 16 chapter links • Theatrical trailer • Short subject "The Monster and the Maiden" • Short subject "Frankenstein and the Naughty Nurse" • Gallery of exploitation art • Horrorama radio-spot rarities.
1974 (PG) 90m/C *IT* Rossano Brazzi, Michael Dunn, Edmund Purdom, Christiane Royce, Simone Blondell; *D:* Robert (Dick Randall) Oliver; *W:* William Rose, Mark Smith, Robert Spano; *C:* Mario Mancini.

Dr. Giggles

A cast of allegedly young characters lifted from a dead-teenager slasher flick is transplanted to an escaped-lunatic plot. Dr. Rendell (Drake) is said wacko who goes back to his hometown after the breakout to reopen his practice, killing the locals with medical devices, including a giant Band Aid. The jokes are grisly and grim. Even though this one debuted on video, it's solidly in the Universal tradition of slickly made, energetic horror. Director Coto makes a limited budget look extravagant and the film makes a fine transition to DVD with a very good image. A commentary track would not have been out of place. —MM

Movie: 🎵🎵🎵 **DVD:** 🎵🎵½
Goodtimes Entertainment (Cat #81024). Full frame. Dolby Digital Surround Stereo. $19.98. Snapper. *LANG:* English. *SUB:* French; Spanish. *CAP:* English. *FEATURES:* Production notes • 18 chapter links.
1992 (R) 96m/C Larry Drake, Holly Marie Combs, Glenn Quinn, Keith Diamond, Cliff DeYoung; *D:* Manny Coto; *W:* Manny Coto, Graeme Whifler; *C:* Rob Draper; *M:* Brian May.

Dr. Goldfoot and the Bikini Machine

A mad scientist (Price at his hammy best) employs gorgeous female robots to seduce the wealthy and powerful, thereby allowing him to take over the world. The long-forgotten title song is sung by The Supremes. There's some terribly bad aliasing in the opening pan across the Golden Gate Bridge, along with madly flashing '60s plaids throughout, but otherwise the image is fine. The numerous gold lamé bikinis are reproduced flawlessly. —MM

Movie: 🎵🎵½ **DVD:** 🎵🎵½
MGM Home Entertainment (Cat #1002 049, UPC #027616862860). Widescreen (2.35:1) letterboxed. Dolby Digital Mono. $14.95. Keepcase. *LANG:* English; Spanish. *SUB:* French; Spanish. *FEATURES:* 16 chapter links • Trailer.
1966 90m/C Vincent Price, Frankie Avalon, Dwayne Hickman, Annette Funicello, Susan Hart, Kay Elkhardt, Fred Clark, Deanna Lund, Deborah Walley; *D:* Norman Taurog; *M:* Les Baxter.

Doctor Phibes Rises Again

Ostensible sequel is really a baroque re-creation of the original with humor that's even more tongue-in-cheek. (Sample dialogue: "I don't know about his body, but we should give his head a decent burial.") An introduction goes back over the key points of the first film wherein Dr. Phibes (Price) eludes capture by draining his blood and replacing it with embalming fluid. To rise again, he simply reverses the process. The new plot finds Phibes and Darius Biederbeck (Quarry) heading to Egypt to discover the secret of eternal life at the Temple of Ibiskis, etc., etc. Amazingly, Quarry's flamboyance matches Price's. The presence of Hugh Griffith, Terry Thomas, and all too briefly, Beryl Reid, helps too. Fiona Lewis, Valli Kemp, and Caroline Munro provide delightful window dressing. The DVD image is a small step down from the first film. It lacks some sharpness and detail, but appears to be an accurate re-creation of the original. —MM

Movie: 🎵🎵🎵½ **DVD:** 🎵🎵½
MGM Home Entertainment (Cat #1001 543, UPC #027616858542). Widescreen (1.85:1) anamorphic. Dolby Digital Mono. $19.98. Keepcase. *LANG:* English; French; Spanish. *SUB:* French; Spanish. *CAP:* English. *FEATURES:* 16 chapter links • Trailer.
1972 (PG) 89m/C *GB* Vincent Price, Robert Quarry, Peter Cushing, Beryl Reid, Hugh Griffith, Terry-Thomas, Valli Kemp, Peter Jeffrey, Fiona Lewis, Caroline Munro; *D:* Robert Fuest; *W:* Robert Fuest, Robert Blees; *C:* Alex Thomson; *M:* John Gale.

Dr. Strangelove, or: How I Learned to Stop Worrying and Love the Bomb [2 SE]

The minor technical problems noted in the review of the first DVD edition of this masterpiece have been cleared up, though in truth, the film has always been grainy and minor evidence of wear is evident. In many scenes—the interiors of the B-52, the attack on the air base—image quality is supposed to be less than stellar. And it's beside the point to be overly critical of that side of the film. The performances, the biting wit, and even the suspense are undiminished. Perhaps the most valuable extra on the disc is the "making of" featurette, which clears up (or attempts to) many of the stories and rumors that surround the film. Yes, Peter Sellers was to play four parts, but an accident forced him out of the role that Slim Pickens took over. The pie-fight finale was not seriously considered. It had been deleted before the assassination of President Kennedy. The rest of the details from one-time producer James Harris, production designer Ken Adams, and art director Peter Murton are fascinating. It's highly recommended to all of Kubrick's fans. Also, click down the menu to highlight the top of the globe to find an "Easter egg." —*MM*

Movie: 𝄞𝄞𝄞𝄞 **DVD:** 𝄞𝄞𝄞𝄞
Columbia Tristar Home Video (Cat #06187, UPC #043396061873). Full frame. Dolby Digital Mono. $29.95. Keepcase. *LANG:* English; French; Spanish. *SUB:* English; French; Spanish; Portuguese; Chinese; Korean; Thai. *FEATURES:* 28 chapter links ▪ "Making of" featurette ▪ "Art of Stanley Kubrick from Short Films to *Dr. Strangelove*" ▪ Publicity interviews with Sellers and Scott ▪ Original advertising material ▪ Talent files ▪ Production notes.
1964 93m/B *GB* Peter Sellers, George C. Scott, Sterling Hayden, Keenan Wynn, Slim Pickens, James Earl Jones, Peter Bull, Tracy Reed, Shane Rimmer, Glenn Beck, Gordon Tanner, Frank Berry, Jack Creley; **D:** Stanley Kubrick; **W:** Stanley Kubrick, Terry Southern, Peter George; **C:** Gilbert Taylor; **M:** Laurie Johnson. *AWARDS:* AFI '98: Top 100; British Acad. '64: Film, Natl. Film Reg. '89; N.Y. Film Critics '64: Director (Kubrick); *NOM:* Oscars '64: Actor (Sellers), Adapt. Screenplay, Director (Kubrick), Picture.

Dr. T & the Women

Though this comedy was poorly received in theatrical release, the director's fans may be more generous to the home video version. After all, even at less than his best, Altman is better than most. Richard Gere plays the title character, a Houston gynecologist popular with high society matrons. His "women" include a troubled wife (Fawcett) and a golf pro (Hunt). For an Altman film, this one boasts a very flashy image, appropriate for a wealthy Texas milieu, that's re-created flawlessly on disc. Sound is fine. —*MM*

Movie: 𝄞𝄞𝄞 **DVD:** 𝄞𝄞𝄞
Artisan Entertainment (Cat #11548, UPC #012236115489). Widescreen (2.35:1) letterboxed. Dolby Digital 5.1 Surround Stereo. $24.99. Keepcase. *LANG:* English. *CAP:* English. *FEATURES:* 34 chapter links ▪ Altman interview ▪ "Making of" featurette ▪ Trailer and TV spots ▪ Talent files ▪ Production notes.
2000 (R) 122m/C Richard Gere, Farrah Fawcett, Kate Hudson, Helen Hunt, Lee Grant, Liv Tyler, Shelley Long, Laura Dern, Tara Reid; **D:** Robert Altman; **W:** Anne Rapp; **C:** Jan Kiesser; **M:** Lyle Lovett.

Dogma

Smith packs a lot into his brave, controversial comedy on Catholicism and, as a

Catholic himself, illustrates that he has some issues about his religion. He vents with a film that's both devilishly funny and agonizingly boring. A great cast does his dirty work, including Affleck and Damon as two cast-out angels with a plan to re-enter heaven. Rock plays an angry apostle, Hayek is a muse turned stripper, and Rickman is the voice of God informing an abortion worker (Fiorentino) that she's to stop the angel. The first half is loaded with on-target jokes, but laughs are hard to find in the second hour, which falls victim to excessive religious yakety-schmakety. Smith's a talented screenwriter; unfortunately, this time out, it's his directing that's really a sin. *Dogma* may actually look better on this DVD than it did in the theatre. The blacks are as deep and dark as any, yet even in dark scenes, the image remains detailed. Color shadings seem even more subtly defined than on the big screen, and when combined with the excellent sharpness, the result is very pleasing to the eye. The super-clean bass adds good bottom to the music, and the rest of the 5.1 mix is also dead-on, with the Surround tracks used sparingly but effectively. *Dogma* is still not a great movie, but it's a great DVD. —*JO*

Movie: 𝄞𝄞½ **DVD:** 𝄞𝄞𝄞𝄞
Columbia Tristar Home Video (Cat #04891, UPC #043396048911). Widescreen (2.35:1) anamorphic. Dolby Digital 5.1; Stereo. $24.95. Keepcase. *LANG:* English (DD5.1); French (Stereo). *SUB:* English; Spanish; French. *CAP:* English. *FEATURES:* 28 chapter links ▪ Theatrical trailers ▪ Talent files.
1999 (R) 125m/C Ben Affleck, Matt Damon, Linda Fiorentino, Chris Rock, Salma Hayek, Jason Lee, George Carlin, Alan Rickman, Jason Mewes, Janeane Garofalo, Kevin Smith, Alanis Morissette, Bud Cort, Jeff Anderson, Guinevere Turner; **D:** Kevin Smith; **W:** Kevin Smith; **C:** Robert Yeoman; **M:** Howard Shore. *AWARDS:* *NOM:* Ind. Spirit '00: Screenplay; Golden Raspberries '99: Worst Support. Actress (Hayek).

Dolphins

Any IMAX production loses a lot on anything smaller than those gigantic screens, but this touchy-feely documentary is dazzlingly sharp on a conventional TV. The underwater footage has that smooth blue tranquility while all of the ocean-going and dry-land scenes sparkle. Sound is fine, too. This one will really impress your friends with the brightness of the picture. The image is so impressive that the disc was nominated for several video awards in 2000. —*MM*

Movie: 𝄞𝄞½ **DVD:** 𝄞𝄞𝄞½
Image Entertainment (Cat #ID9889MVDVD, UPC #014381988925). Full frame. Dolby Digital 5.1 Surround Stereo; DTS Surround. $24.99. Snapper. *LANG:* English; French; Spanish. *SUB:* French; Spanish. *CAP:* English. *FEATURES:* 24 chapter links ▪ "Making of" feature ▪ Trailers ▪ DVD-ROM features ▪ Talent files.

2000 89m/C **D:** Greg Macgillivray; **W:** Tim Cahill, Steve Judson; **M:** Sting, Steve Wood; **Nar:** Pierce Brosnan.

Donnie Brasco [2]

Al Pacino is terrific as the aging mid-level Brooklyn Mafioso, Lefty Ruffiero, who befriends young Donnie Brasco (Depp), an undercover FBI agent infiltrating the mob. The doomed friendship between the two men is the filmmakers' real subject. The stars share the screen comfortably and do some of their best work. For Pacino, it's a restrained performance, largely lacking glamour and thunder. The DVD transfer accurately reflects the film's gritty look and feeling. Lefty's ugly winter coat presents the occasional problem, but that's a minor flaw. Newell's soft-spoken commentary track is keyed to story and characters. His comments on the deleted scenes are worth listening to. —*MM*

Movie: 𝄞𝄞𝄞½ **DVD:** 𝄞𝄞𝄞½
Columbia Tristar Home Video (Cat #05272, UPC #043396052727). Widescreen (2.35:1) anamorphic. Dolby Digital 5.0 Surround Stereo; Dolby Digital Surround Stereo. $24.95. Keepcase. *LANG:* English; French; Spanish. *SUB:* English; French; Spanish. *FEATURES:* 28 chapter links ▪ 2 featurettes ▪ 5 deleted scenes ▪ Isolated score ▪ Talent files ▪ Trailer ▪ DVD-ROM features ▪ Commentary: director.
1996 (R) 126m/C Johnny Depp, Al Pacino, Anne Heche, Michael Madsen, Bruno Kirby, James Russo, Zeljko Ivanek, Gerry Becker, Zach Grenier, Robert Miano; **D:** Mike Newell; **W:** Paul Attanasio; **C:** Peter Sova; **M:** Patrick Doyle. *AWARDS:* Natl. Bd. of Review '97: Support. Actress (Heche); *NOM:* Oscars '97: Adapt. Screenplay; Writers Guild '97: Adapt. Screenplay.

Donovan's Brain

Dr. Patrick Cory (Ayres) maintains the still-living brain of an otherwise deceased millionaire. But the brain has a mind of its own and begins to control the doctor psychically! Adaptation of Curt Siodmak's novel works much more effectively than it sounds. DVD presents a terrific black-and-white image. I noted no flaws worth mentioning. —*MM*

Movie: 𝄞𝄞 **DVD:** 𝄞𝄞½
MGM Home Entertainment (Cat #100 2048, UPC #027616862853). Full frame. Dolby Digital Mono. $14.95. Keepcase. *LANG:* English; Spanish. *SUB:* French; Spanish. *FEATURES:* 16 chapter links ▪ Trailer.
1953 85m/B Lew Ayres, Gene Evans, Nancy Davis, Steve Brodie; **D:** Felix Feist; **C:** Joseph Biroc.

Donovan's Reef

Two World War II buddies, Guns (Wayne) and Boats (Marvin), meet every year on a Pacific island to engage in a bar-brawl. Then a proper Bostonian (Allen) arrives to find her dad (Romero), who has fathered a brood of lovable half-castes. Ford is at his most lighthearted here. DVD is made from an exceptionally well-preserved original. There may be a few artifacts in the long shots of ocean and surf, but they're inconsequential. —*MM*

Movie: 𝄢𝄢𝄢 **DVD:** 𝄢𝄢𝄢
Paramount Home Video (Cat #06220, UPC #09360622041). Widescreen anamorphic. Dolby Digital Mono. $29.95. Keepcase. *LANG:* English; French. *SUB:* English. *FEATURES:* Trailer ☞ 17 chapter links.
1963 109m/C John Wayne, Lee Marvin, Jack Warden, Elizabeth Allen, Dorothy Lamour, Mike Mazurki, Cesar Romero; *D:* John Ford; *W:* James Edward Grant, Frank Nugent; *C:* William Clothier; *M:* Cyril Mockridge.

Don't Answer the Phone

Deeply troubled photographer stalks and attacks the patients of a beautiful radio talk-show host. The dim image is no better than fair, though that's really about all that could be expected of an aged low-budget horror. —*MM* *AKA:* The Hollywood Strangler.

Movie: 𝄢 **DVD:** 𝄢½
Rhino Home Video (Cat #5740). Full frame. $14.95. Snapper. *LANG:* English. *FEATURES:* Cast and crew thumbnail bios ☞ 6 chapter links ☞ Stills.
1980 (R) 94m/C James Westmoreland, Flo Gerrish, Ben Frank; *D:* Robert Hammer; *W:* Robert Hammer, Michael Castle; *C:* James L. Carter; *M:* Byron Allred.

Don't Go in the House

Long-dormant psychosis is brought to life by the death of a young man's mother. Of all of the *Don't* horrors, this is arguably the worst. It's certainly one of the most cheaply made and that shows. The disc doesn't even contain a menu. Image is underlit and dim throughout. No better than tape. —*MM*

Movie: 𝄢 **DVD:** 𝄢
Digital Versatile Disc Ltd. (Cat #147). Full frame. Dolby Digital Surround Stereo. $19.95. Keepcase. *LANG:* English.
1980 (R) 90m/C Dan Grimaldi, Robert Osth, Ruth Dardick; *D:* Joseph Ellison; *W:* Joseph Ellison, Ellen Hammill; *C:* Oliver Wood; *M:* Richard Einhorn.

Don't Let Me Die on a Sunday

Bizarre, disturbing wallow in Parisian depravity begins in a morgue. That's where attendant Ben (Barr) meets Teresa (Bouchez). The details of that encounter will not be recounted, but the two begin a downward spiral into joyless sex, angst, alienation, and despair. Not surprisingly, the image is a little harsh at times, but that is the point. Otherwise, the DVD image is excellent. Not for the fainthearted. —*MM*

Movie: 𝄢𝄢½ **DVD:** 𝄢𝄢𝄢½
First Run Features (Cat #FRF90956, UPC #720229909563). Widescreen letter-

boxed. $29.95. Keepcase. *LANG:* French. *SUB:* English. *FEATURES:* 8 chapter links ☞ First Run Features previews ☞ Photo gallery.
1999 86m/C *FR* Elodie Bouchez, Jean-Marc Barr, Martin Petitguyot, Patrick Catalifo, Gerard Loussine, Jeanne Casilas, Florence Darel; *D:* Didier Le Pecheur; *W:* Didier Le Pecheur; *C:* Denis Rouden; *M:* Philippe Cohen-Solal.

Don't Mess with My Sister!

A married New York junkyard worker falls in love with a belly dancer he meets at a party. The affair leads to murder and subsequently, revenge. An interesting, offbeat film from the director of *I Spit on Your Grave.* Fans may be disappointed at the low level of gore and nudity, but at least another rapist (in this case, would-be) bites the dust in the spirit of *Spit.* This Elite presentation not only makes *Don't Mess with My Sister* look better than it ever has, it makes it look like it had a much bigger budget. The colors seem a little enhanced (for the better) and the film has an overall richer look. Sharpness is good and there is no evidence of digital grain—only the grain from the film itself. Elite has also ensured that the sound is clean and undistorted even if not spectacular. It's also listed as stereo on the package but sounds completely mono. The extra footage is mainly just gab, but does explain a few things about a couple of the characters. —*JO*

Movie: 𝄢𝄢½ **DVD:** 𝄢𝄢𝄢
Elite Entertainment, Inc. (Cat #EE7478, UPC #790594747824). Widescreen (1.85:1) anamorphic. Stereo. $24.95. Keepcase. *LANG:* English. *FEATURES:* 12 chapter links ☞ Theatrical trailer ☞ Never-before-seen footage.
1985 90m/C Joe Perce, Jeannine Lemay, Jack Gurci, Peter Sapienza, Laura Lanfranchi; *D:* Mier Zarchi.

Don't Tell Mom the Babysitter's Dead

With Mother traveling to Australia, the titular situation leaves a houseful of teenagers and pre-teens with the whole summer to themselves. To earn enough money to keep them afloat, eldest Sue Ellen (Applegate) cons her way into a white-collar business job. Her metalhead brother parties hearty. Do you think they learn some valuable lessons about personal responsibility? The DVD presents an adequate transfer of a softish image filled with bright reds and hot pinks. Dolby Surround adds a deep rumble to the energetic score. —*MM*

Movie: 𝄢𝄢 **DVD:** 𝄢𝄢𝄢
HBO Home Video (Cat #90637, UPC #026359003725). Widescreen anamorphic. Dolby Digital Surround Stereo; Dolby Digital Stereo. $24.98. Snapper. *LANG:* English. *SUB:* English; French; Spanish. *FEATURES:* 20 chapter links ☞ Trailer ☞ TV spots.

1991 (PG-13) 105m/C Christina Applegate, Keith Coogan, Joanna Cassidy, John Getz, Josh Charles, Concetta Tomei, Eda Reiss Merin; *D:* Stephen Herek; *W:* Neil Landau, Tara Ison; *C:* Tim Suhrstedt; *M:* David Newman.

Don't Torture a Duckling

Though the title sounds like a comedy, this is a horror film about the murders of young boys in a Sicilian village. Newspaperman Andrea Martelli (Milian) investigates the crimes as the suspicious locals take revenge on a couple of outcasts. He has the help of the sexy Patrizia (Bouchet). The material is actually handled with restraint, considering the extremes to which Fulci would go. What's most remarkable, though, is the condition of the image. This one looks and sounds exceptional for a work of its age. Considering the spotty release it has enjoyed over the years, it's good to see the film finally getting the treatment it deserves. —*MM* *AKA:* Non Si Sevizia un Paperino.

Movie: 𝄢𝄢½ **DVD:** 𝄢𝄢𝄢
Anchor Bay (Cat #DV11103, UPC #01313 1110395). Widescreen (2.35:1) anamorphic. Dolby Digital Mono. $24.98. Keepcase. *LANG:* English. *FEATURES:* 27 chapter links ☞ Fulci thumbnail bio.
1972 102m/C *IT* Tomas Milian, Barbara Bouchet, Irene Papas, Florinda Bolkan, Marc Porel; *D:* Lucio Fulci; *W:* Lucio Fulci, Robert Gianviti; *C:* Sergio d'Offizi; *M:* Riz Ortolani.

The Doors [2 SE]

Image and sound on this special edition appear to be the same as the earlier Artisan release (cat. #60451) reviewed in the first edition. Of the plateful of new extras, the most interesting are Stone's commentary track and 14 deleted scenes. The "cinematographic moments" feature is essentially notes on cinematography. Most of the extras are on a second disc. —*MM*

Movie: 𝄢𝄢½ **DVD:** 𝄢𝄢𝄢½
Artisan Entertainment (Cat #10810, UPC #012236108108). Widescreen (2.35:1) letterboxed. Dolby Digital 5.1 Surround Stereo. $34.98. Keepcase. *LANG:* English. *CAP:* English. *FEATURES:* 36 chapter links ☞ Commentary: Stone ☞ Jump to song feature ☞ Talent files ☞ Trailer and teaser ☞ Production notes ☞ "Road to Excess" featurette ☞ 14 deleted scenes with introduction ☞ "Cinematographic moments."
1991 (R) 138m/C Val Kilmer, Meg Ryan, Kevin Dillon, Kyle MacLachlan, Frank Whaley, Michael Madsen, Kathleen Quinlan, Crispin Glover, Josh Evans, John Densmore, William Jordan, Mimi Rogers, Paul Williams, Bill Graham, Billy Vera, William Kunstler, Wes Studi, Costas Mandylor, Billy Idol, Michael Wincott, Dennis Burkley; *D:* Oliver Stone; *W:* Oliver Stone, Ralph Thomas, Randy Johnson, J. Randall Johnson; *C:* Robert Richardson.

Dope Case Pending

Extremely low-budget urban action picture revolves around Devon King (Prime Time), who's got a bright future in athletics ahead of him until the cops are called to a party at his house and he's arrested for drug possession. It's a downward spiral from there on. Everything about the film is substandard. Semi-professional writing, acting, and directing. Both focus and sound are iffy from scene to scene. Aliasing along bright lines is about as excessive as I've ever seen. —MM

Movie: 🎬 **DVD:** 🎬

York Entertainment (Cat #YPD-1056, UPC #750723105628). Full frame. Dolby Digital 5.1 Surround Stereo. $14.99. *LANG:* English. *FEATURES:* 15 chapter links.

2000 91m/C Prime Time, Thinline, Kid Frost, Coolio, Sean Levert, Tony Dorian; **D:** Patrick McKnight, Jeff Williams; **W:** Patrick McKnight; **C:** Steve Van Dyne; **M:** Prime Time.

Double Agent 73

The title refers to star Chesty Morgan's amazing bust size. Here, she's a secret agent who has a camera/bomb implanted in her...oh, never mind. The result is more curiosity than exploitation. Director Doris Wishman doesn't care about the plot and neither should you. Like *Deadly Weapons,* the DVD was made from an accurate reproduction of an appallingly inept original. Lighting is atrocious; so is the focus. Ditto sound. —MM

Movie: 🎬 **DVD:** 🎬🎬

Image Entertainment (Cat #ID6035SW DVD, UPC #014381603521). Full frame. Dolby Digital Mono. $24.99. Snapper. *LANG:* English. *FEATURES:* "Big Big Bust" featurette • 12 chapter links • Trailers • Gallery of exploitation art.

1980 (R) 73m/C Chesty Morgan, Frank Silvano, Saul Meth, Jill Harris, Louis Burdi, Peter Petrillo, Cooper Kent; **D:** Doris Wishman; **W:** Doris Wishman, Judy J. Kushner; **C:** Yuri Haviv.

Double Dragon

Generally harmless brain candy based on the video game finds orphaned brothers Jimmy (Dacascos) and Billy (Wolf) living in the rubble of post-earthquake L.A., circa 2007. They have half of a mystical dragon amulet. Obsessed mogul Koga Shuko (Patrick), who has the other half, is after them. Seems he needs the whole thing to control its vast power. Non-stop action will keep the kiddies amused. The image is bright and clean. Sound is fine. —MM

Movie: 🎬🎬½ **DVD:** 🎬🎬½

Goodtimes Entertainment (Cat #81032). Widescreen (1.66:1) letterboxed. Dolby Digital 5.1 Surround Stereo. $19.98. Snapper. *LANG:* English. *SUB:* French; Spanish. *CAP:* English. *FEATURES:* 18 chapter links.

1994 (PG-13) 96m/C Scott Wolf, Mark Dacascos, Robert Patrick, Alyssa Milano, Kristina Malandro Wagner, Julia Nickson-Soul; **D:** Jim Yukich; **W:** Michael Paul

Davis, Peter Gould; **C:** Gary B. Kibbe; **M:** Jay Ferguson.

Double Impact

Van Damme does the twins-separated-as-kids thing. Beverly Hills fitness instructor Chad and cigar-chomping smuggler Alex are reunited in Hong Kong to fight gangsters, avenge their parents' murders, etc. You know the drill. Image and sound are slightly superior to VHS tape, and given the quality of the material, that's all that's called for. —MM

Movie: 🎬🎬 **DVD:** 🎬🎬

MGM Home Entertainment (Cat #10015 52, UPC #027616858627). Widescreen (1.85:1) anamorphic. Dolby Digital Surround Stereo. $19.98. Keepcase. *LANG:* English. *SUB:* French; Spanish. *CAP:* English. *FEATURES:* 16 chapter links • Trailer.

1991 (R) 107m/C Jean-Claude Van Damme, Cory Everson, Geoffrey Lewis; **D:** Sheldon Lettich; **W:** Jean-Claude Van Damme, Sheldon Lettich; **C:** Richard H. Kline; **M:** Arthur Kempel.

Double Parked

Lovely Rita, meter maid and single mom, tries to protect her son from assorted temptations including delinquent classmates and sex. Callie Thorne is very good in the lead. The rest of this festival hit isn't as strong. DVD is an accurate reproduction of an O.K. low- to mid-budget independent production with pale colors and harsh lighting. Carefully polished images are not the point. Characters are. —MM

Movie: 🎬🎬½ **DVD:** 🎬🎬½

Winstar Home Entertainment (Cat #FLV52 75, UPC #720917527529). Widescreen letterboxed. $24.99. Keepcase. *LANG:* English. *FEATURES:* 16 chapter links • Production credits • Trailer • Filmographies.

2000 98m/C Callie (Calliope) Thorne, Rufus Read, Noah Fleiss, William Sage, Anthony De Sando, Eileen Galindro, Michelle Hurd, P.J. Brown; **D:** Stephen Kinsella; **W:** Stephen Kinsella, Paul Solberg; **C:** Jim Denault; **M:** Craig Hazen, David Wolfert.

Double Suicide

Married paper merchant Jihei (Kichiemon Nakamura) falls helplessly in love with prostitute Koharu (Shima Iwashita). This adaptation of a famous puppet play by Monzarmon Chikamatsu works on several levels of "reality." It's too stylized for all viewers but those who appreciate Japanese films should give it a try. DVD presents a minutely detailed black-and-white image that appears to capture every shade of gray accurately. There is some shimmering within tight horizontal lines in one shot, but almost all of the intricate kimono patterns are fine. Monaural sound does justice to the strong spare score. —MM *AKA:* Shinju Ten No Amijima.

Movie: 🎬🎬🎬 **DVD:** 🎬🎬🎬

Criterion Collection (Cat #104, UPC #0374 29149621). Full frame. Dolby Digital

Mono. $29.95. Keepcase. *LANG:* Japanese. *SUB:* English. *FEATURES:* 18 chapter links • Liner notes by Claire Johnston.

1969 105m/B JP Kichiemon Nakamura, Shima Iwashita, Yusuke Takita, Hosei Komatsu; **D:** Masahiro Shinoda; **W:** Masahiro Shinoda, Toru Takemitsu, Taeko Tomioka; **C:** Toichiro Narushima; **M:** Toru Takemitsu.

Down to You

Light romantic comedy has appealing leads and a predictable plot (and references to about a gazillion similar movies). Aspiring chef Al (Prinze Jr.) and artist Imogen (Stiles) are immediately smitten when they meet at the campus dive. The relationship develops at headlong speed but then they both realize neither of them is ready for a lifelong commitment. So, do they just split or try being friends or slow things down or what? All right, so nobody's interested in a "making of" for the film much less the music video. At least the transfer is a good one, and if you want to suffer (O.K., that's an exaggeration) through this fluff, you'll be treated to an extremely sharp image with strong saturated colors that remain natural, vibrant, and bleed-free. Blacks are true and inky and strong contrast keeps the details vivid. The sound is fairly unspectacular but does the job by delivering the dialogue clearly and out front, and really kicking in for some of the music. —JO

Movie: 🎬🎬½ **DVD:** 🎬🎬🎬½

Miramax Pictures Home Video (Cat #19301, UPC #717951007421). Widescreen (1.85:1) anamorphic. Dolby Digital 5.1; Dolby Surround. $29.99. Keepcase. *LANG:* English (DD5.1); French (DS). *SUB:* Spanish. *CAP:* English. *FEATURES:* 26 chapter links • "Making of" featurette • Music video "It All Comes Down to You" • Behind-the-scenes of the music video.

2000 (PG-13) 92m/C Freddie Prinze Jr., Julia Stiles, Selma Blair, Shawn Hatosy, Zak Orth, Rosario Dawson, Henry Winkler, Ashton Kutcher, Lucie Arnaz; **D:** Kris Isacsson; **W:** Kris Isacsson; **C:** Robert Yeoman; **M:** Edmund Choi.

Downhill Willie

Goodhearted doofus Willie Jones (Coogan) enters an international extreme ski competition, hoping to win the $500,000 purse and save the airplane repair shop where he apprentices. If you enjoy scatological slapstick and misogyny, you will not be disappointed. Some of the actors' accents are so bad the only way you can tell their nationality is from the background music. Even the stolen jokes fall flat: one sight gag blatantly apes *Dumb and Dumber* and the spa scene is a disastrously unfunny "homage" to a certain noisy scene from *Blazing Saddles.* To its credit, the well-filmed skiing scenes spark some energy. All the pity, since the filmmakers thought it prudent to graft a lame teenage wet dream scenario onto genuinely exciting ski footage. The full-frame transfer looks decent, with clear, sharp images and good detail depth. Mono soundtrack plays well enough. For anyone interested, a trailer, biographies of the cast, and weblinks are included. Be warned: this isn't a movie; it's a tax shelter. —*EP*

Movie: 🐾½ **DVD:** 🐾🐾🐾
Fox/Lorber Home Video (Cat #FLV5169, UPC #2091751692). Full frame. Dolby Digital Mono. $24.98. Snapper. *LANG:* English. *FEATURES:* 8 chapter links ✏ Trailer ✏ Filmographies ✏ Weblinks.
1996 (PG) 90m/C Keith Coogan, Staci Keanan, Lochlan Monroe, Estelle Harris, Fred Stoller, Lee Reherman; *D:* David Mitchell; *W:* Stephanie Cedar; *C:* David Pelletier; *M:* Norman Orenstein.

Dracula / Strange Case of Dr. Jekyll & Mr. Hyde

Palance shines as the squinty-eyed Count, and the noble Dr. Jekyll and the evil Hyde in this two-sided double feature. Both made-for-TV features come from producer Dan Curtis, creator of the *Dark Shadows* series. Unfortunately, the films are virtually unwatchable on disc. Overly dark, the transfer of a less-than-perfect master never gives you the chance to really see anything in an image riddled with compression artifacts that range from banding to out-of-control pixelation. —*GH/MM* **AKA:** Bram Stoker's Dracula.

Movie: 🐾🐾½ **DVD:** 🐾
MPI Home Video (Cat #DVD6353, UPC #030306635323). Full frame. $24.98. Keepcase. *LANG:* English; Spanish (Dracula). *SUB:* English; French (both); Spanish (Dracula). *FEATURES:* Interviews with Palance and Curtis ✏ *Dracula* European theatrical trailer ✏ 52 chapter links.
1973 105m/C Jack Palance, Simon Ward, Fiona Lewis, Nigel Davenport, Pamela Brown, Penelope Horner, Murray Brown, Virginia Wetherell, Sarah Douglas, Barbara Lindley; *D:* Dan Curtis; *W:* Richard Matheson; *C:* Oswald Morris; *M:* Wojciech Kilar.

Dracula vs. Frankenstein

Typically impoverished Adamson drive-in fare is notable for trippy period clothes, the final appearances of Lon Chaney Jr. and J. Carrol Naishe, and one scene of Regina Carrol's Las Vegas lounge act. The title creatures themselves have seldom looked more laughable. TV veteran Jim Davis shows up briefly as a dime-store Dirty Harry. Despite the early "GP" (now a "PG") rating and lack of sexual activity, the film has the mindset and atmosphere of a late '60s skin flick. That's what it looks like on DVD, too, though in truth, the disc is a bit easier to watch than older tapes that are virtually opaque. —*MM* **AKA:** Blood of Frankenstein; They're Coming to Get You; Dracula Contra Frankenstein; The Revenge of Dracula; Satan's Bloody Freaks.

Movie: woof **DVD:** 🐾🐾
Troma Team Video (Cat #9027, UPC #790 357902736). Full frame. $19.98. Keep-

case. *LANG:* English. *FEATURES:* 9 chapter links ✏ Sam Sherman intro ✏ Commentary: Sam Sherman ✏ 4 deleted scenes ✏ Trailer ✏ TV teaser ✏ Credits.
1971 (PG) 90m/C *SP* J. Carrol Naish, Lon Chaney Jr., Regina Carrol, Russ Tamblyn, Jim Davis, Anthony Eisley, Zandor Vorkov, John Bloom, Angelo Rossitto, Forrest J Ackerman; *D:* Al Adamson; *W:* William Pugsley, Sam M. Sherman; *C:* Paul Glickman, Gary Graver; *M:* William Lava.

The Dragon Chronicles

Epic fantasy action takes you into the spiritual world of kung fu, where three sisters fight for ultimate power and domination. There appear to be some registration problems with the source print, as the image jitters slightly on the outside in some scenes. Audio tracks are rather well produced with some good Surround effects and unobtrusive ambient Surround information throughout. Subtitles have been burned into the film and are not optional. Since Chinese and English subtitles have to share screen space, the letters are very small and they appear and disappear very rapidly. —*GH*

Movie: 🐾🐾½ **DVD:** 🐾
Tai Seng Video Marketing (Cat #35454). Widescreen (2.35:1) letterboxed. Dolby Digital 5.1 Surround Stereo. $29.95. Keepcase. *LANG:* Cantonese; Mandarin. *SUB:* Chinese; English. *FEATURES:* Trailers.
1994 96m/C *HK* Brigitte (Lin Chinag-hsia) Lin, Ching Has, Cheung Man, Gong Li; *D:* Andy (Wing Keung Chien) Chin.

Dragon Princess

Please see review of *The Bodyguard / Dragon Princess.*
Movie: 🐾
1981 (R) 90m/C *JP* Sonny Chiba, Sue Shiomi; *D:* Hiro Matsuda, Yutaki Kodair; *M:* Shinsuke Kikuchi.

Dragonheart: A New Beginning

A young stable boy (Masterson) discovers Drake (voice by Benson), a baby dragon and the last of its kind. Surprisingly, the quality of this video premiere varies quite a bit. While some shots show significant signs of film grain, others are absolutely stable and beautifully clean. The color reproduction of the film is good. Blacks are deep and solid, giving the image good visual depth. Highlights appear slightly underexposed, creating a somewhat dull-looking image that lacks solid white. Fleshtones show some signs of red overemphasis, but it is never distracting from the actual presentation. Audio is clean and free of any distortion. Surround usage is good and rather active, giving the movie a good, lively feel. —*GH/MM*

Movie: 🐾🐾 **DVD:** 🐾🐾½
Universal Studios Home Video (Cat #206 79). Full frame. Dolby Digital 5.1 Surround Stereo; Dolby Digital Stereo. $24.98.

Keepcase. *LANG:* English; French. *FEATURES:* "Making of" documentary ✏ Featurettes ✏ Trailer ✏ Production notes.
2000 (PG) 85m/C Christopher K. Masterson, Henry O, Harry Van Gorkum, John Woodnutt, Rona Figueroa, Ken Shorter; *D:* Doug Lefler; *W:* Shari Goodhartz; *C:* Buzz Feitshans IV; *V:* Robby Benson.

Dralion

Cirque Du Soleil's production toured the world to constantly sold-out houses. And once again they have managed to up the ante with a production that is as entertaining as it is hypnotic. Filled with beautiful costumes, fantastic music, mesmerizing characters, and spectacular acts, *Dralion* has an Asian theme and it freely mixes Chinese and Japanese influences. The image is stellar in its quality with beautiful sharpness and magnificent colors that bring the entire beauty of the production to life. The blacks are deep and at no point is there any distracting unbalance in the picture. Violaine Corradi's beautiful score—once again blending Chinese and Japanese themes—is very rhythmic with a varying degree of textures, enchantingly performed and sung. It adds immensely to the overall flair of the circus act and the 5.1 Dolby Digital mix is wide with very good dynamics. —*GH*

Movie: 🐾🐾🐾½ **DVD:** 🐾🐾🐾🐾
Columbia Tristar Home Video (Cat #06105, UPC #043396061057). Widescreen (1.78:1) anamorphic. Dolby Digital 5.1 Surround Stereo. $24.95. Keepcase. *LANG:* English; French. *FEATURES:* "Making of" featurette ✏ Multi-angle performances ✏ Trailers ✏ 16 chapter links.
2000 89m/C *D:* David Mallet; *M:* Violaine Corradi.

Dressed to Kill

Holmes and Watson (Rathbone and Bruce) find that a series of music boxes holds the key to plates stolen from the Bank of England. The plot's a bit thin but even in their final appearances in the roles, the stars are a delight. The image is at best fair; same for sound. The disc is part of the *Evening with Sherlock Holmes* boxed set. (See also review for *Woman in Green / Dressed to Kill.*) —*MM*

Movie: 🐾🐾½ **DVD:** 🐾🐾
FOCUSfilm (Cat #FF7385, UPC #6830707 38525). Full frame.$69.99. Keepcase. *LANG:* English. *FEATURES:* 12 chapter links ✏ Episodes 9-15 of "New Adventures of Sherlock Holmes" radio show ✏ Photo gallery.
1946 72m/B Basil Rathbone, Nigel Bruce, Patricia Morison, Edmund Breon, Tom Dillon; *D:* Roy William Neill; *W:* Frank Gruber, Leonard Lee; *C:* Maury Gertsman; *M:* Hans J. Salter.

The Drifter

Julia (Delaney) impulsively picks up a hunky hitchhiker (O'Keeffe) and enjoys a one-night stand in a motel. But the guy turns out to be, perhaps, a bit unhinged.

The same material has been used in countless "erotic thrillers," but this one handles it fairly well. The graininess of the image suits the material, but it does not make for a particularly crisp DVD. Image and sound are no better than tape. —*MM*
Movie: 🐶🐶½ **DVD:** 🐶🐶
New Concorde (Cat #NH20304D, UPC #736991430495). Full frame. $19.98. Keepcase. *LANG:* English. *FEATURES:* Thumbnail bios ● 24 chapter links ● Trailers.
1988 (R) 90m/C Kim Delaney, Timothy Bottoms, Miles O'Keeffe, Al Shannon, Thomas Wagner, Larry Brand; **D:** Larry Brand; **W:** Larry Brand; **C:** David Sperling; **M:** Rick Conrad.

Drive-in Discs, Vol. 1

This disc re-creates the full drive-in experience. It uses the 5.1 to create "Distorto Sound," which reduces dialogue and music to the static-filled whispers that came from the speaker you hung from the car window. Now they come from the front left speaker. Intermittent sound effects of footsteps crunching across gravel and car engines are added in all the Surround speakers. If you choose to play the DVD straight through, it begins with the national anthem, then goes through cartoons, ads for the snack bar, dancing hotdogs, PSAs, etc. The films—*Screaming Skull* and *Giant Leeches* (please see individual reviews)—look very rough; they always have and always will. —*MM*
Movie: 🐶🐶 **DVD:** 🐶🐶🐶½
Elite Entertainment, Inc. (Cat #EE3748, UPC #790594374822). Widescreen (1.85:1) anamorphic; full frame. Dolby Digital 5.1 Surround Stereo. $29.98. Keepcase. *LANG:* English. *FEATURES:* 16 chapter links ● DVD credits ● 2 cartoons ● Vintage drive-in materials.
2000 ?m/C

Drive Me Crazy

Nicole (Hart) and Chase (Grenier) have grown up next door to each other and attend the same high school, but that's all they think they have in common. Pep-rallying Nicole yearns to date BMOC Brad (Carpenter), but he's only interested in a rival cheerleader. Slacker-type Chase just wants to hang out at the coffeehouse with his animal activist girlfriend Dulcie (Larter), but he gets dumped hard. They conspire to win their dream dates to the prom by pretending to be a couple and provoke jealousy. As the two grow closer, they inevitably fall in love. Unfortunately, they don't do it in a very entertaining or amusing manner. Slow-paced, unfunny, and trite is no way to go through life, son. For a Fox DVD this one's sub-par. Image quality ranges from sharp to soft, dark scenes introduce grain, and even the colors are inconsistent. Those dark scenes also suffer from occasional minor artifacting. The sound is good enough and when the rock songs come on there is plenty of guts to them. Unfortunately, it doesn't really matter that much. —*JO*

Movie: 🐶🐶 **DVD:** 🐶½
20th Century Fox Home Entertainment (Cat #2000033, UPC #024543000334). Widescreen (1.85:1) anamorphic. Dolby Digital 5.1; Dolby Surround. $34.98. Keepcase. *LANG:* English (DD5.1; DS); French (DS). *SUB:* English; Spanish. *FEATURES:* 16 chapter links ● Theatrical trailer ● TV spots ● Music videos.
1999 (PG-13) 91m/C Melissa Joan Hart, Adrian Grenier, Stephen Collins, Faye Grant, Susan May Pratt, Kris Park, Mark Webber, Ali Larter, Mark Metcalf, William Converse-Roberts; **D:** John Schultz; **W:** Rob Thomas; **C:** Kees Van Oostrum; **M:** Greg Kendall.

Drop Dead Rock

Hindenburg, an atrocious young rock band, decides to abduct its idol Spazz-O, but his manager (Adam Ant) doesn't want to pay the ransom; he's ready to hire a hitman to get rid of his obnoxious client. It's every bit as unfunny on the screen as it sounds in synopsis. DVD provides a near-perfect reproduction of a loud, painful color scheme. —*MM*
Movie: 🐶🐶 **DVD:** 🐶🐶
Pioneer Entertainment (Cat #10293). Full frame. Dolby Digital Surround Stereo. $24.98. Keepcase. *LANG:* English. *FEATURES:* 19 chapter links.
1995 93m/C Adam Ant, Deborah Harry, Soshana Ami, Eddie Brill, Ian Maynard; **D:** Adam Dubin; **W:** Adam Dubin, Ric Menello; **C:** David Hausen; **M:** John Hill.

Drop Zone

Routine action-thriller finds U.S. Marshal Pete Nessip (Snipes) and his brother Terry (Warner) assigned to protect drug cartel snitch Earl Leedy (Jeter). Their plane is hijacked by Moncrief (Busey), who parachutes off with Leedy. Nessip must go undercover in the world of sky-diving with the aid of ex-con cutie Jessie (Butler). The plot holes would accommodate a 747 but the stunts are good and Snipes is never less than professional. Image is seldom better than good; sound is only fair. —*MM*
Movie: 🐶🐶½ **DVD:** 🐶🐶
Paramount Home Video (Cat #327347). Widescreen (2.35:1) letterboxed. Dolby Digital 5.1 Surround Stereo; Dolby Digital Surround Stereo. $29.99. Keepcase. *LANG:* English; French. *FEATURES:* Trailer ● 19 chapter links.
1994 (R) 101m/C Wesley Snipes, Gary Busey, Yancy Butler, Michael Jeter, Corin "Corky" Nemec, Kyle Secor, Luca Bercovici, Malcolm Jamal Warner, Rex Linn, Grace Zabriskie, Sam Hennings, Claire Stansfield, Mickey Jones, Andy Romano; **D:** John Badham; **W:** John Bishop, Peter Barsocchini; **C:** Roy Wagner; **M:** Hans Zimmer.

Drowning Mona

Strident comedy focuses on the low-IQ denizens of small town Verplanck, New York, where everybody still drives a Yugo (the town was a test market). Nasty Mona

Dearly (Midler) drives her car into the Hudson River and drowns. It's murder and Chief Wyatt Rash (DeVito) must investigate. He's not lacking in suspects since Mona was the most hated woman in the community. Everyone in the cast looks like they're enjoying themselves, and though this is not the laugh riot you'd expect from this crew, you should enjoy yourself too. The image on this DVD is just what it should be on a new film. Fleshtones, and the rest of the color spectrum, are perfect. Blacks are deep and true but never hide the details. And the pic is grain-free and sharp. The soundtrack features plenty of deep clean bass, and the Surround provides ambience throughout and kicks in strongly when called upon. The commentary by director Gomez is one not to be missed, as some of his stories are as funny as the film itself. —*JO*
Movie: 🐶🐶½ **DVD:** 🐶🐶🐶🐶
Columbia Tristar Home Video (Cat #05056, UPC #043396050563). Widescreen (1.85:1) anamorphic; full frame. Dolby Digital 5.1; Dolby Surround. $24.95. Keepcase. *LANG:* English; French. *SUB:* English; Spanish; French. *CAP:* English. *FEATURES:* 28 chapter links ● Theatrical trailers ● Commentary: Nick Gomez ● Talent files ● Deleted scenes with director's commentary.
2000 (PG-13) 95m/C Danny DeVito, Bette Midler, Jamie Lee Curtis, Casey Affleck, Neve Campbell, William Fichtner, Peter Dobson, Marcus Thomas, Kathleen Wilhoite, Tracey Walter, Paul Ben-Victor, Paul Schulze, Mark Pellegrino; **D:** Nick Gomez; **W:** Peter Steinfeld; **C:** Bruce Douglas Johnson; **M:** Michael Tavera.

Drugstore Cowboy

Gus Van Sant takes a grim, uncompromising look at a pack of early-'70s drugstore-robbing junkies as they look to score. Brushes with the law and tragedy encourage them to change their ways but the trap seems impossible to leave. The well-crafted work reflects the "me generation" era, though some will see it as a glamorization of drug use. Van Sant and star Dillon try to correct that on their commentary track, recorded ten years after they made the film. It's the most valuable extra on the disc. Image and sound are fine, particularly considering the budget. —*MM*
Movie: 🐶🐶🐶½ **DVD:** 🐶🐶🐶½
Artisan Entertainment (Cat #60497). Widescreen (1.85:1) letterboxed. Dolby Digital Stereo. $29.98. Keepcase. *LANG:* English. *FEATURES:* Commentary: Van Sant and Dillon ● Theatrical trailers ● Production notes ● Talent files ● 35 chapter links ● Documentary ● TV spot.
1989 (R) 100m/C Matt Dillon, Kelly Lynch, James Remar, James LeGros, Heather Graham, William S. Burroughs, Beah Richards, Grace Zabriskie, Max Perlich; **D:** Gus Van Sant; **W:** Gus Van Sant, Daniel Yost; **C:** Robert Yeoman; **M:** Elliot Goldenthal. *AWARDS:* Ind. Spirit '90: Actor (Dillon), Cinematog., Screenplay, Support. Actor (Perlich); L.A. Film Critics '89:

Duets

Karaoke is the unlikely subject of this road comedy, which was filmed almost entirely in Vancouver. That's one of the things that director Bruce Paltrow and producer Kevin Jones say on their unusually forthright and personal commentary track. (Perhaps that's why Buena Vista saw fit to run a disclaimer before it stating that the men are not speaking for the studio.) The story concerns a group of characters, played by an accomplished ensemble cast, who are trying to win a $5,000 singing prize. Image is fine, though nothing special. Sound is more than many of the songs require. Still, this is an amiable little movie with an impressive number of extras on the disc. —MM
Movie: 🎵🎵½ **DVD:** 🎵🎵🎵½
Hollywood Pictures Home Video (Cat #21650, UPC #786936144710). Widescreen (1.85:1) anamorphic. Dolby Digital 5.1 Surround Stereo. $32.99. Keepcase. LANG: English. SUB: English. FEATURES: 3 deleted scenes • Previews • Multiple-angle music video • Commentary: Bruce Paltrow, Kevin Jones.
2000 (R) 112m/C Gwyneth Paltrow, Maria Bello, Scott Speedman, Andre Braugher, Paul Giamatti, Huey Lewis, Marian Seldes, Kiersten Warren, Angie Phillips, Angie Dickinson; **D:** Bruce Paltrow; **W:** John Byrum; **C:** Paul Sarossy; **M:** David Newman.

Dune

Cable's Sci-Fi Channel's international production of Frank Herbert's novel is a fairly satisfying attempt with some very prominent strengths and a few weaknesses. The consensus from literary Dune fans is mixed but basically positive. If nothing else, the 265-minute running time allows for a fuller reading of the text. Young Paul Atreides (Newman) relocates with his family to Arrakis, only to find his destiny lies with an indigenous, blue-eyed race of desert dwellers called the Fremen. They live in a symbiotic relationship with a species of colossal worms that "swim" through the sands like segmented ocean liners. The main asset here is the unifying vision of cameraman Vittorio Storaro. Don't let his indigestible essay (an extra on the disc) on the cinematic theory behind his artistic decisions fool you; Dune is very nicely photographed, and a number of scenes (the climactic confrontation in the throne room) rival anything Storaro has photographed for clarity of image. There's an aspect ratio on the packaging that's somewhat misleading. The diagram makes it look as if there are two formats of the film on the discs, and that one of them is 16:9 enhanced, but all there is is a letterboxed 4:3. —GE **AKA:** Frank Herbert's Dune.
Movie: 🎵🎵🎵 **DVD:** 🎵🎵🎵½

Artisan Entertainment (Cat #11517, UPC #012236115175). Widescreen (1.78:1) letterboxed. $24.98. Snapper. LANG: English. FEATURES: "Making of" documentary.
2000 270m/C Alec Newman, William Hurt, Saskia Reeves, Ian McNeice, P. H. Moriarty, Julie Cox, Matt Keeslar, Giancarlo Giannini, Barbara Kodetova, Robert Russell, Miljen Kreka Kljakovic; **D:** John Harrison; **W:** John Harrison; **C:** Vittorio Storaro, Harry B. Miller III; **M:** Graeme Revell.

Dungeons and Dragons

Risible adventure film (produced about 15 years too late) is based on the ground-breaking role-playing fantasy game. Evil sorcerer Profion (Jeremy Irons) schemes to acquire a powerful scepter that can control red dragons. At the same time, a group of misfit adventurers set out to find the object and give it to young Empress Savina (Thora Birch), who wants to erase class distinctions in her kingdom. It's filled with action and colorful characters, but the story is weak (and unfortunately reminiscent of Star Wars: Episode 1—The Phantom Menace) and the acting is atrocious. Jeremy Irons delivers what must be the worst performance of his career, with a constant display of shouting, eye rolling, and scenery chewing that makes his character more laughable than menacing. His blue lipstick–wearing assistant is even more ridiculous. Birch is miserably miscast and conveys none of the grandeur and power her character is supposed to have. Wayans and Arenberg are O.K. but the less said about the rest of the main cast, the better. A plot twist intended to give the film a serious edge fails miserably and the ending is a confusing muddle. The CGI effects are colorful, but completely unbelievable and jar with the location scenery. Look quick for Tom Baker (Doctor Who) as an elf. The disc is a nice package and features a sharp and colorful transfer of the film, only marred by some moderate grain. The Surround track is sweeping, exciting, and crisp. The documentaries are thorough and interesting, giving a nice look at the special effects and a brief history of role-playing games. Also included are many deleted scenes (including an outtake of Irons looking less than thrilled) and an alternate ending, which are interesting and worth viewing. The two audio commentaries are playful, amusing, and filled with behind-the-scenes info and anecdotes. The Baldur's Gate II demo included on the DVD-ROM is appreciated but incredibly difficult to play. Overall, it's worth a look, just for the supplements and commentary alone. —DG
Movie: 🎵½ **DVD:** 🎵🎵🎵½
New Line Home Video (Cat #N5245, UPC #79404352452). Widescreen (1.85:1) anamorphic. Dolby Digital 5.1 Surround; Dolby Stereo. $24.98. Snapper. LANG: English. SUB: English. CAP: English. FEATURES: 2 commentaries: Solomon, Milsome, Whalin, Dave Arneson • "Let the Games Begin" documentary • Behind-

the-scenes featurette • Deleted scenes with optional commentary • Special effects deconstruction • DVD-ROM demo of Baldur's Gate II • DVD-ROM printable role-playing game • 20 chapter links.
2000 (PG-13) 107m/C Justin Whalin, Marlon Wayans, Jeremy Irons, Thora Birch, Zoe McLellan, Kristen Wilson, Lee Arenberg, Bruce Payne, Richard O'Brien, Tom Baker, Robert Miano; **D:** Courtney Solomon; **W:** Topper Lilien, Carroll Cartwright; **C:** Doug Milsome; **M:** Justin Caine Burnett.

The Eagle Has Landed

Nazi colonels Radl (Duvall) and Steiner (Caine) commission IRA agent Devlin (Sutherland) to kill Prime Minister Winston Churchill. Director Sturges focuses more on character than action. The film is presented in a non-anamorphic letterboxed format framed at roughly 2.35:1. I say roughly because the image actually seems to have been stretched a bit resulting in an aspect ratio closer to 2.00:1. The image is generally good with nice colors and sharpness but there are many blemishes and imperfections on the source materials and blacks tend to come across more as shades of gray. Audio is a fairly subdued DD 2.0 mix. The package indicates that this is a Surround mix but my receiver didn't recognize it as such and I heard no activity from the rear speakers. —MP/MM
Movie: 🎵🎵🎵 **DVD:** 🎵🎵½
Artisan Entertainment (Cat #10419). Widescreen letterboxed. Dolby Digital Surround Stereo. $14.98. Keepcase. LANG: English. FEATURES: Talent files • Winston Churchill thumbnail bio.
1977 (PG) 123m/C Michael Caine, Donald Sutherland, Robert Duvall, Larry Hagman, Jenny Agutter, Donald Pleasence, Treat Williams, Anthony Quayle; **D:** John Sturges; **W:** Tom Mankiewicz; **C:** Anthony B. Richmond; **M:** Lalo Schifrin.

Earthly Possessions

Sarandon can't really pass for a drab housewife but she does her best in this made-for-cable adaptation of Anne Tyler's novel. She's Charlotte Emory, the very sheltered wife of a small-town minister (Sanders), who longs for a break from her tedious routine. She gets her chance when she's taken hostage by would-be bank robber Jake Simms Jr. (Dorff), who suffers from impulse control problems and continual bad luck. Their fortunes change when he forces her to go on the road with him (he wants to see his pregnant girlfriend) and they form an increasingly close bond. The image is very good, probably better than the original broadcast. Sound is much better. —MM
Movie: 🎵🎵½ **DVD:** 🎵🎵½
HBO Home Video (Cat #91475). Full frame. Dolby Digital Stereo. $24.98. Snapper. LANG: English; French. SUB: French; Spanish. CAP: English. FEATURES: Cast and crew thumbnail bios • 17 chapter links.

1999 (R) 120m/C Susan Sarandon, Stephen Dorff, Jay O. Sanders, Elissabeth Moss, Margo Martindale; **D:** James Lapine; **W:** Steven Rogers; **C:** David Franco; **M:** Stephen Endelman.

East Is East

Culture clash comedy is set in 1971 in the northern working-class community of Salford, England. Pakistani immigrant George Khan (Puri) is the would-be stern patriarch to a brood of six sons and one daughter. While he wants to raise his kids traditionally, they're rebelling. Especially in the marriage department: despite his own long marriage to the English Ella (Bassett), George tries to arrange marriages to fellow Pakistanis for his two eldest sons, with disastrous results. Story is swift-paced, definitely not politically correct, and is told in amusingly broad strokes. Based on Khan-Din's play. An exceptional video transfer is highlighted by particularly vibrant colors and crisp, well-defined blacks. A similarly impressive soundtrack features clear, understandable dialogue (the dialects are the viewer's only stumbling block) and a lush musical score. —*MJT*
Movie: ♪♪♪ **DVD:** ♪♪♪½
Miramax Pictures Home Video (Cat #20768, UPC #717951010575). Widescreen (1.85:1) anamorphic. Dolby Digital 5.1 Surround Stereo. $29.99. Keepcase. *LANG:* English. *SUB:* English. *FEATURES:* 19 chapter links • Theatrical trailer.
1999 (R) 96m/C *GB* Om Puri, Linda Bassett, Archie Panjabi, Chris Bisson, Jimi Mistry, Ian Aspinall, Jordan Routledge, Raji James; **D:** Damien O'Donnell; **W:** Ayub Khan-Din; **C:** Brian Tufano; **M:** Deborah Mollison. *AWARDS:* British Acad. '99: Film; *NOM:* British Acad. '99: Actor (Puri), Actress (Bassett), Adapt. Screenplay.

East–West

An intense semi-epic story of a man who repatriates to Russia from France after Stalin's invitation to all Russian citizens to return to the mother country in 1946. He brings his French wife Marie and their young son with him to what he believes will be a good life in his homeland. From the moment they step off the boat, it is clear that the expatriates have been lured to Russia to be killed or locked up for being spies and traitors. However, Alexei (Menshikov) is a respected doctor and negotiates for the lives of his son and wife by promising his loyalty to the Party. He is also a proud man, and never lets his wife know about his Faustian bargain. Even after she repeatedly tries to find ways to escape (that endanger her life and his standing), he keeps his intentions and feelings secret. The film manages to capture the paranoia inherent in living in a society where you can't trust your neighbor, or possibly even your husband or wife. In an interesting twist, while Alexei seems to be the weak link in the relationship most of the time, in the end he proves to be far more trustworthy and loyal than his

wife, and sacrifices himself to save both her and his son. This is a truly good film, worth watching for the historical background as well as for the well fleshed-out characters. The DVD transfer is beautiful and shows off the rich textures and colors of the sets and costumes and the sound is also very good. —*CA* **AKA:** Est-Ouest.
Movie: ♪♪♪½ **DVD:** ♪♪♪½
Columbia Tristar Home Video (Cat #05077, UPC #043396050778). Widescreen (1.85:1) anamorphic. Dolby Digital Surround; Dolby Digital 5.1 Surround. $29.95. Keepcase. *LANG:* French; Russian. *SUB:* English; French. *CAP:* English. *FEATURES:* 28 chapter links • Commentary: director, writer • Theatrical trailer • Separate score audio track • Cast and crew bios.
1999 (PG-13) 125m/C *FR* Sandrine Bonnaire, Oleg Menshikov, Sergei Bodrov Jr., Catherine Deneuve, Tatiana Dogileva; **D:** Regis Wargnier; **W:** Regis Wargnier, Sergei Bodrov, Rustam Ibragimbekov, Louis Gardel; **C:** Laurent Dailland; **M:** Patrick Doyle. *AWARDS: NOM:* Oscars '99: Foreign Film.

Eastern Condors

At the end of the Vietnam war, a band of Chinese convicts are recruited by the U.S. Army (and promised their freedom) if they can destroy an ammunition dump before the North Vietnamese can make use of it. This Hong Kong remake of *The Dirty Dozen* (with nods to *Deer Hunter* and *Mission: Impossible*) has the requisite levels of high energy and violence and some super action scenes. The image displays some evidence of wear with heavy artifacts in bright exteriors. Other scenes have the shimmering quality typical of Hong Kong imports. Surround is nothing special. —*MM*
Movie: ♪♪½ **DVD:** ♪♪
Tai Seng Video Marketing (Cat #2104). Widescreen letterboxed. Dolby Digital 5.1 Surround Stereo. $49.95. Keepcase. *LANG:* Cantonese; Mandarin. *SUB:* Bahasia Mal. & Ind.; Simp. & Trad. Chinese; English; Japanese; Korean; Vietnamese; Thai. *FEATURES:* Cast and crew thumbnail bios • Trailer • 8 chapter links.
1987 94m/C *HK* Sammo Hung, Joyce Godenzi, Yuen Biao, Haing S. Ngor; **D:** Sammo Hung.

Tha Eastsidaz

Drug dealer Killa Pop (Snoop Dog) is framed by his lieutenant Crackle (Tray Deee) and sent to the slammer where he plots escape and revenge. It's violent wish fulfillment for would-be gangstas and rapper wanna-bes. Acting and writing are amateurish. Film appears to have been shot on video. Image displays all the flaws of the medium: heavy artifacts and aliasing. Sound is unexceptional throughout but drops down a notch to poor in the action scenes. —*MM*
Movie: ♪ **DVD:** ♪
Xenon Entertainment (Cat #XEXX 4084 DVD, UPC #000799408421). Full frame.

$19.98. Keepcase. *LANG:* English. *SUB:* Spanish. *FEATURES:* 17 chapter links • Trailers • Bloopers.
2000 (R) 90m/C Snoop Dogg, Tray Deee, Goldie Loc, Darryl Brunson; **D:** Michael Martin; **C:** Michael Martin, Matt Faw; **M:** Tommy Coster.

Eat Your Heart Out

Young chef Daniel (Oliver) is an overnight success with a cooking show. In short order, he acquires a new agent (San Giacomo) and forgets his roommate Sam (Segall). The cast is attractive; the romantic entanglements are predictable. The full-frame image and stereo sound aren't really superior to VHS tape. —*MM*
Movie: ♪♪ **DVD:** ♪♪
Pioneer Entertainment (Cat #10234). Full frame. Stereo. $19.98. Keepcase. *LANG:* English. *FEATURES:* Trailer • 25 chapter links.
1996 (R) 96m/C Christian Oliver, Laura San Giacomo, Pamela Segall, Linda Hunt; **D:** Felix Adlon; **W:** Felix Adlon; **C:** Judy Irola; **M:** Alex Wurman.

Ecstasy of the Angels

Interesting, though somewhat confusing erotic tale of a group of militant extremists who realize that they've been betrayed by their own organization when a nocturnal weapons raid on a U.S. Army base goes awry. Their delicate internal balance of trust and friendship splinters apart and their already fragile, idealistic young psyches quickly disintegrate into a morass of sexual paranoia, violent recrimination, and sadistic torture that completely destroys their ability to function as an organization. Though the video transfer faithfully reproduces most light colors, many are washed-out and hard on the eyes. Similarly, blacks and other darker colors have almost no solid definition. All this makes for a mostly unimpressive transfer. The sound transfer delivers as clear a track as a mono mix can. The interview with Wakamatsu included on the disc is interesting enough, though I would have preferred a subtitle translation as opposed to the dubbed English version provided (the singular setting becomes a bit tiresome after 30 minutes as well). One interesting note, this interview is also included on the *Go, Go Second Time Virgin* disc. —*MJT*
Movie: ♪♪½ **DVD:** ♪♪½
Image Entertainment (Cat #ID8965VFDVD, UPC #014381896527). Widescreen (1.66:1) anamorphic. Dolby Digital Mono. $24.99. Snapper. *LANG:* Japanese. *SUB:* English. *FEATURES:* 12 chapter links • Interview with director Koji Wakamatsu.
1972 88m/C *JP* Ken Yoshizawa, Rie Yokoyama, Yuki Arasa, Masao Adachi; **D:** Koji Wakamatsu; **W:** Izuru Deguchi.

Eden

Frustrated, Multiple Sclerosis–afflicted housewife Helen (Going) deals with the physical and emotional limitations of her life with dreams of astral projection. Husband Bill (Walsh) is a prep school teacher who doesn't want her to work even though she reaches one of his problem students (Flanery) more effectively than he does. First-time director Goldberg won a Sundance competition for his screenplay, but can't quite deliver on its promise. A tight budget and too many unanswered questions keep this one on the intriguing but ultimately disappointing level. The barebones DVD does a more than adequate job with the soft-focus period ('60s) setting. Sound is acceptable. —MM

Movie: 🎬🎬 **DVD:** 🎬🎬½
Winstar Home Entertainment (Cat #5135). Full frame. Dolby Digital Stereo. $29.98. Keepcase. *LANG:* English. *FEATURES:* 8 chapter links.
1998 (R) 106m/C Joanna Going, Dylan Walsh, Sean Patrick Flanery; **D:** Howard Goldberg; **W:** Howard Goldberg; **C:** Hubert Taczanowski; **M:** Brad Fiedel.

Edgar Ulmer Collection, Vol. 1

Impressive double-feature disc features *The Strange Woman* and *Moon over Harlem*. Both films have been digitally restored and especially in the case of *The Strange Woman*, the result is simply stunning. For a low-budget movie from 1946, this film looks breathtakingly sharp and well defined. Although some defects in the film print are visible, for the most part the presentation is a great experience. The film itself is a gripping story about a Scarlett O'Hara–like woman who is very determined to make a better life at any cost; a better life for herself, and more importantly, for other people. *Moon over Harlem* is an ethnic picture from 1939 that stars jazz legend Sidney Bechet. Although the film is in decidedly worse shape than *The Strange Woman*, the quality is still much better than you would expect from such an old movie that was shot for only $8,000. —GH

Movie: 🎬🎬🎬 **DVD:** 🎬🎬🎬½
All Day Entertainment (Cat #69891). Full frame. Dolby Digital Mono. $29.99. Keepcase. *LANG:* English. *FEATURES:* Photo gallery • Interview.
2000 170m/C

Edvard Grieg: What Price Immortality?

Curious biopic examines the life of composer Edvard Grieg (Scheia and Brammer at different times) through his music and the voice-over narration of Derek Jacobi. There is no dialogue. As the scenes are acted out, Grieg's compositions are played and our narrator fills in the details. The DVD image looks fine, and the music is terrific. (Crank up the 5.1 and you can really irritate your heavy-metal neighbors.) It's a curiously detached way to approach the subject. Those who are already familiar with the man will appreciate the film more than most others. —MM

Movie: 🎬🎬½ **DVD:** 🎬🎬🎬

Image Entertainment (Cat #ID9256RADVD, UPC #014381925623). Widescreen (1.78:1) anamorphic. Dolby Digital 5.1 Surround Stereo; Dolby Digital Surround Stereo. $24.99. Snapper. *LANG:* English. *FEATURES:* 10 chapter links.
2000 70m/C Staffan Scheia, Philip Brammer, Claudia Zohner, Sabine Oberhorner; **D:** Thomas Olofsson; **W:** Thomas Olofsson, Ture Rangstrom, Johanna Olofsson; **Nar:** Derek Jacobi.

Edward Scissorhands [SE]

From the opening credits, it's clear that this story takes place within a cinematic snowglobe. Tim Burton's take on *Pinocchio* is a combination of fantasy, myth, fairy tale, and horror that ought not to work at all, but does, splendidly. Vincent Price is the Inventor who creates Edward (Depp) but dies before he can give the boy human hands, leaving him with blades for fingers. (Stan Winston created those effects.) The Avon lady (Wiest) brings Edward down from his black hilltop castle to the pastel 'burbs below where he falls in love with her daughter Kim (Ryder). Price's brief role, virtually a cameo, is a fitting coda to his career in the field, and on his low-keyed commentary track, Burton highlights the actor's importance to his budding career. Danny Elfman's score is one of his best and he has a commentary track of his own. I could find no visual or aural flaws on the disc. It is particularly recommended to younger viewers who have possibly seen the film only on pan-and-scan VHS tape. This is one of Burton's best. —MM

Movie: 🎬🎬🎬½ **DVD:** 🎬🎬🎬½
20th Century Fox Home Entertainment (Cat #2000537, UPC #024543005377). Widescreen (1.85:1) letterboxed. Dolby Digital 4.0 Surround Stereo; Dolby Digital Surround Stereo. $29.98. Keepcase. *LANG:* English; French. *SUB:* Spanish. *CAP:* English. *FEATURES:* 24 chapter links • Commentary: Burton and Elfman • Theatrical trailer and TV spots • Concept art • "Making of" featurette. This is the "10th Anniversary Edition."
1990 (PG-13) 100m/C Johnny Depp, Winona Ryder, Dianne Wiest, Vincent Price, Anthony Michael Hall, Alan Arkin, Kathy Baker, Conchata Ferrell, Caroline Aaron, Dick Anthony Williams, Robert Oliveri, John Davidson; **D:** Tim Burton; **W:** Tim Burton, Caroline Thompson; **C:** Stefan Czapsky; **M:** Danny Elfman. *AWARDS:* NOM: Oscars '90: Makeup.

An Egyptian Story

The second volume of Chahine's "Alexandria Trilogy" finds director Yehia grown and suffering heart problems. That leads a fantasy confrontation with his ideals (à la *All That Jazz*). Again, Chahine's combination of fantasy and reality is masterful. If only the disc matched his work. The image is dark and filled with artifacts that seem to come from the existing grain of the

image. Subtitles are provided for the Arabic sections of dialogue. (The other two films are *Alexandria Why?* and *Alexandria Again and Forever*.) —MM **AKA:** Hadduta Misriya.

Movie: 🎬🎬🎬 **DVD:** 🎬🎬
Winstar Home Entertainment (Cat #FLV5234, UPC #720917523422). Widescreen (1.66:1) letterboxed. $24.98. Keepcase. *LANG:* English; Arabic. *SUB:* English. *FEATURES:* 8 chapter links • Weblinks • DVD production credits • Filmographies and awards.
1982 127m/C EG Mohiel Dine, Nour El Chef, Oussama Nadir, Magda El Khatib; **D:** Youssef Chahine; **W:** Youssef Chahine; **C:** Mohsen Nasr; **M:** Gamal Salama.

8 1/2 Women

Peter Greenaway's films (*The Cook, the Thief, His Wife and Her Lover*, *The Draughtsman's Contract*) are definitely an acquired taste, and this is probably not the place for the uninitiated to pick it up. As the title suggests, it is in part an homage to Fellini's *8 1/2* about a businessman (Standing) who embarks on a series of sexual adventures after the death of his wife. His son (Delamere) joins him. Greenaway splashes garish, challenging, often harsh colors across the screen. If those weren't enough, he fills the frame with clashing patterns and extremes of bright and dim lighting. The image, then, is often far from perfect, as it is supposed to be. —MM

Movie: 🎬🎬🎬 **DVD:** 🎬🎬🎬
Universal Studios Home Video (Cat #20712, UPC #025192071225). Widescreen (1.66:1) anamorphic. Dolby Digital Surround Stereo. $24.95. Keepcase. *LANG:* English. *CAP:* English. *FEATURES:* 18 chapter links • Trailer.
1999 (R) 122m/C GB John Standing, Vivian Wu, Annie Shizuka Inoh, Matthew Delamere, Toni Collette, Amanda Plummer, Manna Fujiwara, Barbara Sarafian, Polly Walker, Karina Mano, Natacha Amal; **D:** Peter Greenaway; **W:** Peter Greenaway; **C:** Sacha Vierny.

Eight Men Out

Adaptation of Eliot Asinof's book is a moving, full-bodied account of the infamous 1919 "Black Sox" scandal in which members of the Chicago White Sox teamed to throw the World Series for $80,000. A dirge of lost innocence, this is among Sayles's best films, making the lack of a commentary track all the more glaring. The actual baseball scenes are first-rate, and an ensemble cast (most of whom were on the cusp of fame when the film was made) is superb. That's Sayles as Ring Lardner. The soft focus and pastel color scheme of a period piece are reproduced without flaw on DVD. Mono sound is fine for the story, but again, why isn't there a commentary track? Maybe someday. —MM

Movie: 🎬🎬🎬½ **DVD:** 🎬🎬🎬
MGM Home Entertainment (Cat #100187, UPC #027616860972). Widescreen

(1.85:1) anamorphic. Dolby Digital Mono. $19.98. Keepcase. *LANG:* English; French; Spanish. *SUB:* French; Spanish. *FEATURES:* 16 chapter links ● Trailer.
1988 (PG) 121m/C John Cusack, D.B. Sweeney, Perry Lang, Jace Alexander, Bill Irwin, Clifton James, Michael Rooker, Michael Lerner, Christopher Lloyd, Studs Terkel, David Strathairn, Charlie Sheen, Kevin Tighe, John Mahoney, John Sayles, Gordon Clapp, Richard Edson, James Read, Don Harvey, John Anderson, Maggie Renzi, Michael Mantell, Nancy Travis, Michael Laskin; *D:* John Sayles; *W:* John Sayles; *C:* Robert Richardson; *M:* Mason Daring.

El Diablo

Young teacher Billy Ray Smith (Edwards) finds that the west is wilder than he expected when one of his students is kidnapped by an outlaw. With the help of Thomas Van Lee (Gossett Jr.), he sets off in pursuit. Comic western may not equal *Cat Ballou*, but it's a game attempt with some nice funny moments. The made-for-cable production looks very good on DVD. Even some complicated interiors are re-created flawlessly. Ditto the often-troublesome dusty exteriors. —*MM*
Movie: ♪♪½ *DVD:* ♪♪½
HBO Home Video (Cat #90435, UPC #026 359043529). Widescreen anamorphic. Dolby Digital Surround; Mono. $19.98. Keepcase. *LANG:* English; Spanish. *SUB:* English; French; Spanish. *FEATURES:* 14 chapter links.
1990 (PG-13) 107m/C Louis Gossett Jr., Anthony Edwards, John Glover, Robert Beltran, M.C. Gainey, Miguel Sandoval, Sarah Trigger, Joe Pantoliano; *D:* Peter Markle; *W:* John Carpenter, Bill Phillips; *C:* Ron Garcia; *M:* William Olvis.

The Element of Crime

In a monochromatic, post-holocaust future, a detective tracks down a serial killer of young girls. Made in Denmark, this minor festival favorite features an impressive directorial debut and awaits cult status. The video transfer of the sepia-toned original is sharp and clear and very impressive. The yellow/orange color scheme of the film is reproduced admirably (although this palette does occasionally lead to a slight loss of definition with some blacks and other dark colors—but this is easily overlooked). The mono track, while not outstanding, is passable and features dialogue and music which are devoid of distortion. The excellent documentary on director von Trier raises the value of the supplements above the average mark. —*MJT* **AKA:** Forbrydelsens Element.
Movie: ♪♪½ *DVD:* ♪♪♪
Criterion Collection (Cat #80, UPC #03742 9149423). Widescreen (1.85:1) anamorphic. Dolby Digital Mono. $39.95. Keepcase. *LANG:* English. *SUB:* English. *FEATURES:* 18 chapter links ● "Tranceformer: A Portrait of Lars von Trier" documentary feature ● Theatrical trailer.
1984 104m/C *DK* Michael Elphick, Esmond Knight, Jerold Wells, Meme Lei,

Astrid Henning-Jensen, Preben Leerdorff-Rye, Gotha Andersen; *D:* Lars von Trier; *W:* Lars von Trier, Niels Vorsel; *C:* Tom Elling; *M:* Bo Holten.

Element of Doubt

Beth Murray (McKee) introduces herself by sitting down in front of a video camera and telling us that she is going to describe how her life turned into a nightmare. It all has to do with her ambitious husband Richard (Havers), whose actions have become increasingly strange. This British TV production shares some visual and thematic elements with the American hit *What Lies Beneath* and delivers solid suspense with very good work from a talented cast. The image is unusually clear and sharp. Sound is fine. —*MM*
Movie: ♪♪♪ *DVD:* ♪♪♪
BFS Video (Cat #98676-D, UPC #066805 916762). Full frame. Dolby Digital Mono. $29.98. Keepcase. *LANG:* English. *FEATURES:* 12 chapter links.
1996 90m/C *GB* Nigel Havers, Gina McKee, Polly Adams, Judy Parfitt, Sarah Berger, Michael Jayston, Dennis Lill, Robert Reynolds; *D:* Christopher Morahan; *C:* Brian Tufano; *M:* Stephen Warbeck.

An Elephant Called Slowly

In a sequel of sorts to the 1966 hit *Born Free*, Virginia McKenna and Bill Travers star as an English couple who trek to Africa to meet game warden George Adamson (here playing himself). Once in Africa, they are introduced to a menagerie of animals, such as lions and hippos. Along the way, the meet Pole Pole (Swahili for "Slowly"), a baby elephant who adopts McKenna and Travers and attempts to travel with them. The first 20 minutes are rather slow, but the last 70 are very watchable with gorgeous cinematography and astounding nature shots. The image is crystal clear and razor sharp, with hardly a speck of grain visible; quite a feat, considering that the bulk of the film takes place outside in the bright African sun. There are no obvious artifacting or compression problems, and only a couple of scenes look a bit washed-out. The mono soundtrack is serviceable. —*ML*
Movie: ♪♪½ *DVD:* ♪♪♪
Anchor Bay (Cat #DV11371, UPC #01313 1137194). Full frame. Dolby Digital Mono. $24.98. Keepcase. *LANG:* English. *FEATURES:* Trailer.
1969 (G) 91m/C *GB* Virginia McKenna, Bill Travers, George Adamson, Joab Collins, Vinay Inambar, Ali Twaha; *D:* James Hill; *W:* Bill Travers, James Hill; *C:* Simon Trevor; *M:* Howard Blake, Bert Kaempfert.

Elephant Parts

This video album by ex-Monkee Michael Nesmith was the first of its kind when released in 1981. Nesmith blends musical numbers with a load of still-funny com-

edy skits. The DVD release has added footage that was not in the original video release, although it may be hard for some to pick out. Compared to most DVDs, the image is kind of soft, but when compared to the older VHS tape the image is actually improved, with colors being at times circus-like bright. (The softness of the disc will be evident if you access the press clippings in the supplemental section and try to read them.) The stereo sound is also conveyed with much more crispness and imaging than before. The big challenge on the disc is to attempt to listen to Nesmith's rambling stream-of-consciousness commentary which, although intermittently funny, might be better appreciated as an entity of its own, without the distraction of the unrelated visuals. —*JO*
Movie: ♪♪♪ *DVD:* ♪♪
DVD International (Cat #DVD107114, UPC #647715071422). Full frame. Stereo. $24.95. Keepcase. *LANG:* English. *FEATURES:* 41 chapter links ● Talent files ● Photo gallery ● Press clippings ● Commentary ● Discography.
1981 60m/C Michael Nesmith, Bill Martin; *D:* William Dear; *W:* William Dear, Michael Nesmith, Bill Martin.

Embryo

Average sci-fi drama about a scientist (Hudson) who uses raw genetic material to produce a beautiful woman (Carrera) with ghastly results. This is one of the worst-looking DVDs released to date. The image is dim and fuzzy. Night scenes are particularly bad, and even ordinary interiors are substandard. —*MM* **AKA:** Created to Kill.
Movie: ♪♪ *DVD:* woof
Passport International Productions (Cat #710). Full frame. $14.99. Keepcase. *LANG:* English. *FEATURES:* Trailers ● 12 chapter links.
1976 (PG) 108m/C Rock Hudson, Barbara Carrera, Diane Ladd, Roddy McDowall, Ann Schedeen, John Elerick, Dr. Joyce Brothers; *D:* Ralph Nelson; *W:* Anita Doohan, Jack W. Thomas; *C:* Fred W. Koenekamp; *M:* Gil Melle.

The Emerald Forest

A young boy (Charley Boorman, son of the director) is kidnapped by a primitive Amazon tribe while his family is traveling in the Brazilian jungle. Ten years later, his father (Booth) learns that the boy might still be alive and goes in search of him. To some viewers, the idealized views of tribal societies and environmentalism will be off-putting but the film succeeds as a first-rate adventure, and the disc does justice to Boorman's lush visual sense. On DVD, jungle backgrounds can dissolve into featureless green abstraction but they remain well detailed here. Surround sound could have been emphasized more but that's a personal quibble. Recommended. —*MM*
Movie: ♪♪♪ *DVD:* ♪♪♪
MGM Home Entertainment (Cat #1001 536, UPC #027616858474). Widescreen

(2.35:1) anamorphic. Dolby Digital Surround Stereo. $19.98. Keepcase. *LANG:* English. *SUB:* French; Spanish. *CAP:* English. *FEATURES:* 16 chapter links • Trailer.
1985 (R) 113m/C Powers Boothe, Meg Foster, Charley Boorman, Dira Pass, Rui Polonah; *D:* John Boorman; *W:* Rospo Pallenberg; *C:* Philippe Rousselot.

Emmanuelle: First Contact

This appears to be another compilation of half-hour episodes of the late-night cable series. New Orleans, the Nile, and Paris (or establishing shots thereof) are the settings for soft-core sex scenes. There's also a spaceship that looks like it belongs on *MST3K*'s Satellite of Love. Image is about equal to tape, though this is one of the grainiest DVDs you'll ever see. —*MM*
Movie: 🐾🐾 **DVD:** 🐾🐾
New Concorde (Cat #NH20568 D, UPC #736991656840). Full frame. Stereo. $14.99. Keepcase. *LANG:* English. *FEATURES:* 24 chapter links • Talent files • Trailers • "Emmanuelle story" (text).
1999 (R) 93m/C Krista Allen.

Emmanuelle in Space: A World of Desire

Feature is a combination of episodes from the long-lived late-night cable series. Emmanuelle (Allen) orbits the Earth in an alien spaceship. She pops back to the surface of the planet for soft-core romps while her fellow travelers share the experiences through little headset gizmos. Production values range between cheap and very good. Many of the conventionally filmed scenes are exceptionally grainy, but that grain disappears in shot-on-video sequences. Overall, though, DVD image is identical to tape. —*MM*
Movie: 🐾🐾 **DVD:** 🐾🐾
New Concorde (Cat #NH2596U D, UPC #736991656994). Full frame. Stereo. $19.99. Keepcase. *LANG:* English. *FEATURES:* 24 chapter links • Talent files • Trailers.
1999 92m/C Krista Allen, Paul Michael Robinson, Debra Beatty, PS. Sono; *D:* L.L. Shapira; *W:* Noel Harrison; *C:* Andrea Rosotto; *M:* Tim Wynn.

The Emperor and the Assassin

Sumptuous historical drama (and a complicated storyline) concerns a united China's first emperor. In 320 B.C., China is a collection of seven rival kingdoms with Ying Zheng, the King of Qin (Xuejian) obsessed with uniting the country and then dividing it into provinces for proper ruling (with himself as supreme head). Naturally, this means war. Also involved is his lover, Lady Zhao (Li), who plans a fake assassination attempt to aid Zheng. But the assassin she chooses, Jing Ke (Fengyi), is trying to reform and things

don't go exactly according to plan. Remember—power corrupts. With such a large number of Hong Kong films being transferred to DVD from inferior source material, it's great to see this one get the proper treatment. Starting with what looks like a pristine print, Columbia Tristar has delivered a near-perfect transfer with far richer colors and sharper image than just about all of the Tai Seng DVDs, which comprise a very large portion of that genre's releases. This is a beautiful film to look at and the DVD presents it with excellent detail and an incredible feeling of depth. The Dolby Surround is amazing, with as much low end as most 5.1 mixes. At times, the interaction between the front and Surround channels was so intense that it made me replay scenes to see if there were somehow separate right and left rear channels (which there aren't in Dolby Surround). The commentary track by director Kaige provides character, plot, and filmmaking insight delivered by a man who is truly excited about his craft. —*JO*
Movie: 🐾🐾🐾 **DVD:** 🐾🐾🐾½
Columbia Tristar Home Video (Cat #05045, UPC #043396050457). Widescreen (1.85:1) anamorphic. Dolby Surround. $29.95. Keepcase. *LANG:* Mandarin; Spanish. *SUB:* English; Spanish; French. *FEATURES:* 28 chapter links • Theatrical trailers • Talent files • Production notes • Commentary: Chen Kaige.
1999 (R) 161m/C CH Li Xuejian, Gong Li, Zhang Fengyi, Wang Zhiwen, Sun Zhou, Chen Kaige; *D:* Chen Kaige; *W:* Chen Kaige, Wang Peigong; *C:* Zhao Fei; *M:* Zhao Jiping.

The Emperor's New Groove [SE]

Delightful Disney animation actually owes more to Warner Bros. Looney Tunes than to the studio's other animated features. (Think *Duck Dodgers in the 24 1/2th Century!*) This is a fast-paced, wickedly funny story set in a vaguely South American mythic past. Spoiled rotten emperor Kusko (voice of Spade) is transformed into a llama by the witch Yzma (Kitt). The four-legged ruler must turn to peasant Pacha (Goodman) for help. The two-disc set contains every imaginable extra. They're actually longer than the film itself! Also included is a third disc with a CD-ROM promotional game for the feature *Atlantis*. It could go without saying that both image and sound are flawless; the creative use of the 5.1 tracks is particularly good. —*MM*
Movie: 🐾🐾🐾½ **DVD:** 🐾🐾🐾½
Buena Vista Home Entertainment (Cat #22311, UPC #786936150926). Widescreen (1.66:1) anamorphic. Dolby Digital 5.1 Surround Stereo; DTS 5.1 Surround. $29.99. Keepcase. *LANG:* English; French. *CAP:* English. *FEATURES:* 28 chapter links • Commentary: filmmakers • Music video • Video game • DVD-ROM features • Behind-the-scenes studio tour (85 min.) • "Making of" featurette on music video.

2000 (G) 79m/C *D:* Mark Dindal; *W:* Dave Reynolds; *M:* John Debney; *V:* David Spade, John Goodman, Eartha Kitt, Patrick Warburton, Wendie Malick, Patti Deutsch, John Fiedler, Kellyann Kelso, Eli Russell Linnetz. *AWARDS:* Broadcast Film Critics '00: Song ("My Funny Friend and Me"); *NOM:* Oscars '00: Song ("My Funny Friend and Me").

Empire Records

A then-unknown ensemble cast a few years from stardom is the main attraction in this frantic film that's about half as funny and hip as it's trying to be. Joe (LaPaglia) is the manager of an independent record store that will be bought by a faceless conglomerate unless he and his young-and-crisis-prone staff can come up with the cash within 24 hours. Disc gets the nod over tape for the widescreen image and 5.1 Surround track. —*MM*
Movie: 🐾🐾½ **DVD:** 🐾🐾½
Warner Home Video, Inc. (Cat #14169, UPC #085391416920). Widescreen anamorphic. Dolby Digital 5.1 Surround Stereo. $19.98. Snapper. *LANG:* English; French. *SUB:* English; French; Portuguese; Spanish. *FEATURES:* 28 chapter links • Talent files • Trailer.
1995 (PG-13) 91m/C Anthony LaPaglia, Rory Cochrane, Liv Tyler, Renee Zellweger, Johnny Whitworth, Robin Tunney, Ethan (Randall) Embry, Maxwell Caulfield, Debi Mazar; *D:* Allan Moyle; *W:* Carol Heikkinen; *C:* Walt Lloyd; *M:* Mitchell Leib.

The End

Sonny (Reynolds) discovers that he has a terminal illness. He elects not to prolong his suffering and attempts various tried-and-true methods for shuffling off this mortal coil. Schizophrenic Marlon (DeLuise) is all too ready to help him. Directing himself, Reynolds smirks a bit too much, but the comedy has its moments. On this no-frills DVD, it looks pretty good for a film of its age. Sound is no different from VHS tape. —*MM*
Movie: 🐾🐾½ **DVD:** 🐾🐾½
MGM Home Entertainment (Cat #100153, UPC #027616858634). Widescreen (1.85:1) letterboxed. Dolby Digital Mono. $19.98. Keepcase. *LANG:* English; French; Spanish. *SUB:* French; Spanish. *CAP:* English. *FEATURES:* 16 chapter links • Trailer.
1978 (R) 100m/C Burt Reynolds, Sally Field, Dom DeLuise, Carl Reiner, Joanne Woodward, Robby Benson, Kristy McNichol, Norman Fell, Pat O'Brien, Myrna Loy, David Steinberg; *D:* Burt Reynolds; *W:* Jerry Belson; *C:* Bobby Byrne; *M:* Paul Williams.

End of the Affair

In World War II London, Sarah (Kerr), the wife of a British civil servant (Cushing), falls in love with her neighbor Maurice (Johnson). The two make plans for their future together, but suddenly and mysteriously, Sarah brings the affair to an end. Broken splices and grain are evident throughout the film. Certain scenes also exhibit quite a bit of dust and scratch marks, giving away the movie's age. For some reason, the anamorphic widescreen presentation also exhibits discoloration problems that are not evident in the full-frame transfer of the movie. Some shots have a greenish tint. Given the film's age it is hardly surprising that the soundtrack has a very harsh and thin quality that also exhibits quite a bit of sibilance. The music score comes across as distorted in many instances, as do certain lines of dialogue. —GH/MM

Movie: 🎬🎬 **DVD:** 🎬🎬

Columbia Tristar Home Video (Cat #04950). Widescreen (1.85:1) anamorphic; full frame. Dolby Digital Mono. $24.95. Keepcase. *LANG:* English. *SUB:* English; Spanish; Portuguese; Chinese; Korean; Thai. *FEATURES:* Featurette ▪ Talent files ▪ Trailers ▪ Production notes.

1955 105m/B *GB* Deborah Kerr, Van Johnson, John Mills, Peter Cushing; *D:* Edward Dmytryk; *W:* Lenore Coffee; *C:* Wilkie Cooper; *M:* Benjamin Frankel.

The End of the Affair

During the blitz of WWII, married Londoner Sarah Miles (Moore) suddenly breaks off her affair with writer Maurice Bendrix (Fiennes). An unexpected meeting with her husband, Henry (Rea), leads Bendrix to believe Sarah is having a new affair and he hires a detective (Hart) to follow her. Instead, Bendrix discovers her reasons for breaking off with him and her spiritual reawakening. Compellingly adult drama about love, faith, and moral dilemmas is based on the 1955 novel by Graham Greene. This is a beautiful transfer of a beautifully lensed film. Subtle differences in color shadings are accurate, and though the picture may at times seem soft, it is also a true representation of the theatrical release and the film's use of softness for effect. The 5.1 sound is always full and the exploding bombs are frighteningly realistic. The "making of" featurette is ridiculously short (seven minutes) and yet still manages to bore. Director Jordan's interesting commentary compares the film to the original novel—insightful as to why some changes must often be made when going from print to celluloid and offers much about the technical aspects of filmmaking. On the other side, Moore's banal commentary does little more than praise the work of her cinematic teammates. —JO

Movie: 🎬🎬🎬 **DVD:** 🎬🎬🎬½

Columbia Tristar Home Video (Cat #04745, UPC #043396047457). Widescreen (1.85:1) anamorphic; full frame. Dolby Digital 5.1. $27.95. Keepcase. *LANG:* English. *SUB:* English. *CAP:* English. *FEATURES:* 28 chapter links ▪ Theatrical trailers ▪ Talent files ▪ Production notes ▪ "Making of" featurette ▪ Commentaries: Neil Jordan, Julian Moore ▪ Isolated music score.

1999 (R) 101m/C *GB* Ralph Fiennes, Julianne Moore, Stephen Rea, Ian Hart, Sam Bould, Jason Isaacs; *D:* Neil Jordan; *W:* Neil Jordan; *C:* Roger Pratt; *M:* Michael Nyman. *AWARDS:* British Acad. '99: Adapt. Screenplay; *NOM:* Oscars '99: Actress (Moore), Cinematog.; British Acad. '99: Actor (Fiennes), Actress (Moore), Art Dir./Set Dec., Cinematog., Costume Des., Director (Jordan), Film, Makeup, Orig. Score; Golden Globes '00: Actress—Drama (Moore), Director (Jordan), Film—Drama, Orig. Score; Screen Actors Guild '99: Actress (Moore).

Endless Night

An ambitious young chauffeur (Oscarsson) dreams of building a dream house after he romances an American heiress (Mills). How ambitious is he? Given the often bloodless nature of Agatha Christie's work, this adaptation is a little spicy and experimental. The *Vertigo*-like score by Bernard Herrmann is a tip-off. Anchor Bay has done its usual excellent work, delivering a nearly perfect image that belies the film's age. —MM *AKA:* Agatha Christie's Endless Night.

Movie: 🎬🎬½ **DVD:** 🎬🎬🎬

Anchor Bay (Cat #DV11627, UPC #01313 1162790). Widescreen (1.77:1) anamorphic. Dolby Digital Mono. $24.98. Keepcase. *LANG:* English. *FEATURES:* Trailer ▪ 30 chapter links.

1971 95m/C *GB* Hayley Mills, Hywel Bennett, Britt Ekland, George Sanders, Per Oscarsson, Peter Bowles; *D:* Sidney Gilliat; *W:* Sidney Gilliat; *C:* Harry Waxman; *M:* Bernard Herrmann.

The Entertainer

An empire lay in ruins; an emperor surveys a domain that exists only in his mind. "The Entertainer" is playwright John Osborne's poison-pen eulogy of the British Empire filtered through the destructive pipe dreams of music hall hack Archie Rice in late 1950s England. Vainly trying to gain the fame his ailing father once possessed, he mortgages his family's happiness and potentially his freedom (Archie always remarks being one step ahead of the "tax man") in raising money for a "comeback" show that will never happen. Laurence Olivier does not play Archie; he IS Archie in every delusional gesture, every flat joke. Check out Chapter 15: with a simple wave of his hand, Olivier epitomizes Archie's loathing—for his audience and himself. The 1.66 widescreen transfer may not boast anamorphic enhancement, but with images this crisp and sharp, any objections should be silenced quickly. The source print is jaw-droppingly immaculate. Deep black levels and superb detail delineation make for an all-out stunning picture. The mono soundtrack understandably exhibits some hiss but the lack of crackles or pops means the audio is as perfect as the video. Looks like the price for a pristine presentation is no goodies: the disc is completely free of extras; the omission cost it half a bone in the Hound's technical rating. Despite the caveat, the title is a must for anyone who appreciates good storytelling or great acting. —EP

Movie: 🎬🎬🎬½ **DVD:** 🎬🎬½

MGM Home Entertainment (Cat #1002 060, UPC #027616862709). Widescreen (1.66:1) letterboxed. Dolby Digital Mono. $14.95. Keepcase. *LANG:* English. *SUB:* French; Spanish. *FEATURES:* 16 chapter links.

1960 104m/B *GB* Laurence Olivier, Brenda de Banzie, Roger Livesey, Joan Plowright, Daniel Massey, Alan Bates, Shirley Anne Field, Albert Finney, Thora Hird; *D:* Tony Richardson; *W:* Nigel Kneale, John Osborne; *C:* Oswald Morris; *M:* John Addison. *AWARDS: NOM:* Oscars '60: Actor (Olivier).

Erin Brockovich

Desperate for a job, single mom Erin Brockovich (Roberts) bullies her way into a file clerk position at the small law office of Ed Masry (Finney), where her salty language, take-no-prisoners attitude, and scanty outfits unnerve her co-workers. Everyone comes around when she investigates shady corporate dealings leading to a multi-million dollar settlement against a public utility over contaminated water. Fans of director Soderbergh's *Out of Sight* and *The Limey* may have been disappointed in this more conventional film, but it is a genuine crowd-pleaser. DVD doesn't do much to improve the film's dusty ochre color scheme, but the image is an accurate re-creation of the theatrical release. The disc's main assets are the deleted scenes, 30 minutes of them, with Soderbergh's comments. He provides a fine explanation of the editing process that provides a balance of pace, character development, and action. But why no commentary track on the film itself? That might have explained how the car accident in chapter two was accomplished. —MM

Movie: 🎬🎬🎬 **DVD:** 🎬🎬🎬

Universal Studios Home Video (Cat #20783, UPC #025192078323). Widescreen (1.85:1) anamorphic. Dolby Digital 5.1 Surround Stereo; Dolby Digital Surround Stereo. $26.98. Keepcase. *LANG:* English; French. *SUB:* English. *FEATURES:* 44 chapter links ▪ "Making of" featurette ▪ Theatrical trailer ▪ Production notes ▪ Talent files ▪ Deleted scenes ▪ DVD-ROM features.

2000 (R) 131m/C Julia Roberts, Albert Finney, Aaron Eckhart, Marg Helgenberger, Cherry Jones, Veanne Cox, Conchata Ferrell, Tracey Walter, Peter Coyote; *D:* Steven Soderbergh; *W:* Susannah Grant; *C:* Edward Lachman; *M:* Thomas Newman.

The Erotic Adventures of Zorro

Semi-legendary soft-core (verging on hard in one scene) comedy is a genuine treat for fans of early '70s drive-in fare. It retells the familiar story of the foppish Don Diego (Frey), who is transformed by the dashing swordsman at night. The DVD image is bright, garish, and slightly on the

soft side. Given the film's budget and age, it looks remarkably good. Friedman's commentary track is, as usual, good-humored and comfortable. —*MM*
Movie: 🦴🦴 **DVD:** 🦴🦴½
Image Entertainment (Cat #ID6036SW DVD, UPC #014381603620). Full frame. Dolby Digital Mono. $24.99. Snapper. *LANG:* English. *FEATURES:* 16 chapter links ● Commentary: producer Dave Friedman ● Trailers ● 1930s short film, "Scarred Face" ● Gallery of exploitation art.
1972 102m/C Douglas Frey, Robyn Whitting, Penny Boran, John Alderman, Robert W. Cresse; *D:* Robert Freeman; *W:* David Friedman.

The Erotic Ghost

Doris (Caine) is a bored housewife who is seduced by a ghost (Parks) and a couple of female demons who have little horns glued to their foreheads. This is another ultra–low budget soft-core exploitation from a studio that specializes in the field. The difference here is slightly higher production values in the love scenes, and one long scene that verges on hard-core. Only the extras differentiate DVD from VHS. —*MM*
Movie: 🦴🦴 **DVD:** 🦴🦴
El Independent Cinema (Cat #sc-1016dvd, UPC #612385101694). Full frame. $19.98. Keepcase. *LANG:* English. *FEATURES:* Cast interviews ● Behind-the-scenes featurette ● Trailers ● Weblinks.
2000 90m/C Tammy Parks, Darian Caine, Victoria Vega, Debbie Rochon; *D:* John Bacchus; *W:* John Bacchus; *C:* Giorgyorgy Benaskovich.

Erotic Survivor

As long as cheap-looking originals like *Blair Witch Project* and the TV show *Survivor* are hits, the guys at E.I. Independent will have no trouble making cheap-looking soft-core (verging on hard) knockoffs. They took some video cameras into the woods and rounded up their usual starlets for al fresco mud wrestling, etc. Extras are all that separates the DVD from tape. —*MM*
Movie: 🦴 **DVD:** 🦴
El Independent Cinema (Cat #sc-1014-dvd, UPC #612385101496). Full frame. $19.98. Keepcase. *LANG:* English. *FEATURES:* 23 chapter links ● Interview with Darian Caine ● Trailers ● Behind-the-scenes featurette.
2000 90m/C Darian Caine, Jade DuBoir, Misty Mundae, Esmerelda Della Rocco, Debbie Rochon; *D:* John Bacchus; *W:* John Bacchus.

The Erotic Witch Project [CE]

Inevitable low-budget parody has three tattooed "college girls" going out into the New Jersey woods to learn the truth about the "erotic witch." The results are soft-core lesbian sex scenes shot on video in a tent, with the brief appearance of a guy in a gorilla suit. Neither image nor sound is appreciably superior to VHS tape; they're not really supposed to be. This is a

double-sided disc with the feature on one side, extras on the other. —*MM*
Movie: 🦴 **DVD:** 🦴🦴
El Independent Cinema (Cat #sc-1003-dvd, UPC #612385100390). Full frame. Dolby Digital Stereo. $19.95. Keepcase. *LANG:* English. *FEATURES:* 22 chapter links ● Behind-the-scenes featurette ● Stills gallery ● Trailers.
1999 90m/C Katie Keane, Darian Caine, Victoria Vega; *D:* John Bacchus; *W:* John Bacchus, Michael Beckerman, Joe Ned, Clancy Fitzsimmons; *C:* Giorgyorgy Benaskovich.

Erotic Witch Project 2: Book of Seduction

The producers of the first film spoof the sequel using the same props (including the gorilla suit) and attitude. Results are the same, too. Image quality is equal to tape. Disc boasts more extras. —*MM*
Movie: 🦴½ **DVD:** 🦴½
El Independent Cinema (Cat #sc-1017-dvd, UPC #612385101793). Full frame. $19.98. Keepcase. *LANG:* English. *FEATURES:* 18 chapter links ● Behind-the-scenes featurette ● Trailers.
2000 110m/C Darian Caine, Katie Jordan, A.J. Kahn, Allanah Rhodes; *D:* John Bacchus; *W:* Michael Beckerman, Joe Ned, Clancy Fitzsimmons, John Bacchus; *C:* Giorgyorgy Benaskovich.

Errol Flynn / Randolph Scott Double Feature

The two features on this disc vary widely. In *Abilene Town*, Scott is the fair-minded sheriff who's trying to keep the peace between the churchgoing settlers and the wild cattlemen. He also finds time to participate in a romantic triangle with dance hall chanteuse Dvorak and devout heart-of-gold Fleming. Overall, the image ranges between fair and good with some scratches and snow, and adequate mono sound. *Santa Fe Trail* looks much better with sharp black-and-white photography that's virtually blemish-free. In it, future Civil War figures J.E.B. Stuart (Flynn), Custer (Reagan) and others begin their military careers in the fight for "bloody Kansas." Historically inaccurate but loads of fun. —*MM*
Movie: 🦴🦴½ **DVD:** 🦴🦴½
Marengo Films (Cat #MRG-0005, UPC #80 7013000528). Full frame. $14.98. Keepcase. *LANG:* English. *FEATURES:* 6 chapter links each.
2000 200m/C

Escape from Hell

Scantily clad women fight, shower, and try to escape from a jungle prison. It's prototypical "babes behind bars," with a rough grainy image that gains little on DVD. Interiors are adequately detailed and sweaty, but the dubbing sounds like it was done on another planet. —*MM* **AKA:** Hellfire on Ice, Part 2: Escape from Hell; Femmine Infernali.

Movie: 🦴 **DVD:** 🦴½
Troma Team Video (Cat #9992, UPC #790 357999231). Full frame. $24.95. Keepcase. *LANG:* English. *FEATURES:* 8 chapter links ● Lloyd Kaufman thumbnail bio ● Trailers ● Other "Tromatic" extras.
1989 ?m/C IT SP Anthony Steffen, Ajita Wilson; *D:* Edward (Edoardo Mulargia) Muller.

Escape from New York

In a ruined future (well, 1997), a walled-off Manhattan is a huge maximum security prison. When terrorists crash Air Force One there, the President (Pleasence) is taken hostage. Bank robber Snake Plissken (Russell) is sent in to rescue him. In many ways, this perennial audience favorite established the ground rules for the sf action blockbusters (*Terminator, Total Recall,* etc.) that have followed. The DVD lacks a sharp focus, but this is a dark film. It looks about as good as it could. The Surround remix sounds fine without calling too much attention to itself. A commentary track by Carpenter and Russell could have been a nice extra. —*MM*
Movie: 🦴🦴🦴½ **DVD:** 🦴🦴🦴
MGM Home Entertainment (Cat #1001 186, UPC #027616854773). Widescreen anamorphic; full frame. Dolby Digital Surround Stereo. $19.98. Keepcase. *LANG:* English. *SUB:* French; Spanish. *FEATURES:* 32 chapter links.
1981 (R) 99m/C Kurt Russell, Lee Van Cleef, Ernest Borgnine, Donald Pleasence, Isaac Hayes, Adrienne Barbeau, Harry Dean Stanton, Season Hubley, Tom Atkins, Charles Cyphers, George "Buck" Flower; *D:* John Carpenter; *W:* John Carpenter, Nick Castle; *C:* Dean Cundey; *M:* John Carpenter; *V:* Jamie Lee Curtis.

Escape from the Planet of the Apes

Reprising their roles as intelligent, English-speaking apes, McDowall and Hunter flee their world before it's destroyed, and travel back in time to present-day America. In L.A. they become the subjects of a relentless search by the fearful population, much like humans Charlton Heston and James Franciscus were targeted for experimentation and destruction in simian society in the earlier entries. A grim and dark entry in the series that nonetheless manages to retain some humor. Like the other *Ape* films, *Escape* has been given a super transfer and the image beats the Fox letterboxed laserdisc in every department. Most noticeable is the improvement in the color, which is much more saturated and totally free of bleed. The disc is also very sharp and both contrast and brightness levels are vastly improved. The 5.1 mix is new to the film and offers up crisp distinct dialogue and good low end, although very little in the way of Surround effects. —*JO*
Movie: 🦴🦴🦴 **DVD:** 🦴🦴🦴½

20th Century Fox Home Entertainment (Cat #2000791, UPC #024543001065). Widescreen (2.35:1) letterboxed. Dolby Digital 5.1; Dolby Surround. $29.98. Keepcase. *LANG:* English; French. *SUB:* English; Spanish. *CAP:* English. *FEATURES:* 24 chapter links • Theatrical trailers • Photo gallery.
1971 (G) 98m/C Roddy McDowall, Kim Hunter, Sal Mineo, Ricardo Montalban, William Windom, Bradford Dillman, Natalie Trundy, Eric (Hans Gudegast) Braeden, Jason Evers, Harry Lauter, John Randolph, M. Emmet Walsh; *D:* Don Taylor; *W:* Paul Dehn; *C:* Joseph Biroc; *M:* Jerry Goldsmith.

Escape under Pressure

The generic title turns out to have a literal element in this made-for-cable *Die Hard*-on-a-Greek-ferry. It all has to do with a valuable statue that Chloe (Miller) is interested in. She and husband John (Lowe) are having marital difficulties. Bad guys take over ferry—you know the drill. Beyond the usual aliasing problems, the disc has an uncommonly sharp image. That makes it all the more obvious when the computer-generated effects kick in. —*MM*
Movie: 🎵🎵 **DVD:** 🎵🎵½
HBO Home Video (Cat #91713, UPC #026 35917321). Full frame. Dolby Digital Surround Stereo; Dolby Digital Mono. $19.98. Snapper. *LANG:* English; Spanish. *SUB:* English; French; Spanish. *FEATURES:* 14 chapter links • Talent files.
2000 (R) 90m/C Rob Lowe, Larisa Miller, Craig Wasson, Harry Van Gorkum, Stanley Kamel; *D:* Jean Pellerin; *W:* James Christopher; *C:* Richard Clabaugh.

Essex Boys

Though the box copy compares this crime drama to *Reservoir Dogs*, it's really closer to another terrific English film, *The Long Good Friday,* in its pace and intensity. Fans will also see hints of *The Sopranos* and *Croupier* too. Jason Locke (Bean) hasn't been out of the slammer for half a day before he has begun to exact brutal revenge on the friends he holds responsible for his being locked up. His ambitious wife Lisa (Kingston) is waiting for him and he has hired young Billy (Creed-Mills), our narrator, to drive for him. Jason has more scores to settle, both professional and personal, and deals to do. Thankfully, the film lacks the stylistic excesses so popular with young directors. Instead, Terry Winsor tells this loosely based-on-truth story (but it's sometimes hard to follow) with a steady hand and fully realized, flawed characters. Bare-bones DVD delivers a superb image, even with the soft gray British light. Subtitles would help the thick muttered accents. Make an effort to find this one; it's a lot of fun. —*MM*
Movie: 🎵🎵🎵½ **DVD:** 🎵🎵🎵
Miramax Pictures Home Video (Cat #228 97, UPC #786936156676). Widescreen (1.85:1) anamorphic. Dolby Digital 5.1 Surround. $32.99. Keepcase. *LANG:* English. *SUB:* English. *FEATURES:* 17 chapter links.

1999 (R) 102m/C *GB* Charlie Creed-Miles, Sean Bean, Tom Wilkinson, Alex Kingston, Larry Lamb, Terence Rigby, Billy Murray, Amelia Lowdell; *D:* Terry Winsor; *W:* Terry Winsor, Jeff Pope; *C:* John Daly; *M:* Colin Towns.

Eternal Love

Marcus (Barrymore), a hunter in the Swiss Alps (actually the Canadian Rockies), refuses to give up his rifle during the war of 1806 when French soldiers take over his village. He's also deeply in love with Ciglia (Horn), but he's such a hunk that the temptress Pia sets her sights on him. This version of the film, preserved by the UCLA Film and Television Archive and the Mary Pickford Foundation, adds some sound effects. The image ranges between very good and excellent, particularly considering the age of the work. Even in full-frame black and white, some of the mountain scenery is incredible. —*MM*
Movie: 🎵🎵🎵 **DVD:** 🎵🎵½
Image Entertainment (Cat #ID9198MLSD-VD, UPC #014381919820). Full frame. Dolby Digital Mono. $24.99. Snapper. *LANG:* Silent. *SUB:* English intertitles. *FEATURES:* 12 chapter links.
1929 71m/B John Barrymore, Camilla Horn, Hobart Bosworth; *D:* Ernst Lubitsch; *W:* Hans Kraly; *C:* Oliver Marsh.

Evangeline

This adaptation of the famous Henry Wadsworth Longfellow poem is about as dated as its source material. The acting is florid; the storytelling conventions seem funny. But Dolores Del Rio is still lovely. The disc was made from a well-restored image. There is a slight hiss on the soundtrack. —*MM*
Movie: 🎵🎵½ **DVD:** 🎵🎵½
Image Entertainment (Cat #ID9527MLSD-VD, UPC #014381952728). Full frame. Dolby Digital Mono. $24.99. Snapper. *LANG:* Silent. *SUB:* English intertitles. *FEATURES:* 11 chapter links.
1929 90m/B Dolores Del Rio, Roland (Walter Goss) Drew, Alec B. Francis, George F. Marion Sr., Donald Reed; *D:* Edwin Carewe; *W:* Finis Fox; *C:* Robert B. Kurrle; *M:* Hugo Riesenfeld, Philip Carli.

The Evening Star

Wretched sequel to *Terms of Endearment* exaggerates everything that was honest and funny about the original and turns it into a bizarre parody. The central problem is obvious from the beginning: the main character in the first film, Debra Winger's Emma, is dead. What was a well-balanced ensemble piece is now focused on one character, megalomaniacal Houston grand dame Aurora Greenway, furiously overplayed by Shirley MacLaine. The DVD retains the original softish image that is a perfect match for the treacly score. —*MM*
Movie: woof **DVD:** 🎵🎵½
Paramount Home Video (Cat #32902, UPC #097363290247). Widescreen anamorphic. Dolby Digital 5.1 Surround Stereo;

Dolby Digital Surround Stereo. $24.99. Keepcase. *LANG:* English. *SUB:* English. *FEATURES:* 34 chapter links • Trailer • Commentary: director Robert Harling.
1996 (PG-13) 128m/C Shirley MacLaine, Juliette Lewis, George Newbern, MacKenzie Astin, Bill Paxton, Miranda Richardson, Marion Ross, Ben Johnson, Donald Moffat, Scott Wolf, China Kantner, Jack Nicholson; *D:* Robert Harling; *W:* Robert Harling; *C:* Don Burgess; *M:* William Ross. *AWARDS:* NOM: Golden Globes '97: Support. Actress (Ross).

An Evening with Sherlock Holmes

Four public domain titles (*Dressed to Kill, Sherlock Holmes and the Secret Weapon, Terror by Night, The Woman in Green*) make up this boxed set. (Please see individual reviews.) Image and sound are no better than you'd expect for works of such age and (even for their time) modest budgets. Fine print on the box admits as much but still, some care has gone into the collection. The liner notes contain nice bits of Sherlockian trivia. One disc, *Terror by Night,* also has a filmed interview with Sir Arthur Conan Doyle, and each has several episodes of the "New Adventures of Sherlock Holmes" radio show. —*MM*
Movie: 🎵🎵 **DVD:** 🎵🎵½
FOCUSfilm (Cat #FF7437, UPC #6830707 43727). Full frame. $69.99. Keepcase boxed set. *LANG:* English.
2000 ?m/C

Everything You Always Wanted to Know about Sex (But Were Afraid to Ask)

Allen's most laugh-out-loud funny comedy remains a bawdy incorrect gem. (It's impossible to imagine anyone today having the courage to make fun of bestiality the way Allen and Wilder do in one segment.) The final bit is genuinely inspired. The image is as rough and grainy as it has always been, and it's hard to believe that a commentary track could have added anything, though I am curious as to what Allen might have to say now. Sound is fine. —*MM*
Movie: 🎵🎵🎵½ **DVD:** 🎵🎵½
MGM Home Entertainment (Cat #100006 73, UPC #027616850188). Widescreen anamorphic; full frame. Dolby Digital Mono. $24.99. Keepcase. *LANG:* English; Spanish. *SUB:* French; Spanish. *CAP:* English. *FEATURES:* 32 chapter links • Liner notes.
1972 (R) 88m/C Woody Allen, John Carradine, Lou Jacobi, Louise Lasser, Anthony Quayle, Geoffrey Holder, Lynn Redgrave, Tony Randall, Burt Reynolds, Gene Wilder, Robert Walden, Jay Robinson; *D:* Woody Allen; *W:* Woody Allen; *C:* David M. Walsh; *M:* Mundell Lowe.

Evil Dead 2: Dead by Dawn [2 THX]

This second DVD edition corrects the only flaw in the first—the addition of a com-

mentary track by writer/director Sam Raimi, writer Scott Spiegel, star Bruce Campbell, and makeup effects artist Greg Nicotero. Image is equal to the first disc (reviewed in the first edition of this book). Sound is superior, as are the extras. —*MM*
Movie: 🎬🎬🎬 **DVD:** 🎬🎬🎬½
Anchor Bay (Cat #DV11188, UPC #01313 1118896). Widescreen (1.85:1) anamorphic; full frame. Dolby Digital 5.1 Surround Stereo; Dolby Digital Surround. $24.98. Keepcase. *LANG:* English. *FEATURES:* Commentary ▪ 24 chapter links ▪ "The Gore the Merrier" featurette ▪ Video game preview ▪ Stills gallery ▪ Talent files.
1987 (R) 84m/C Bruce Campbell, Sarah Berry, Dan Hicks, Kassie Wesley, Theodore (Ted) Raimi, Denise Bixler, Richard Domeier, Scott Spiegel, Josh Becker, Lou Hancock; *Cameos:* Sam Raimi; *D:* Sam Raimi; *W:* Sam Raimi, Scott Spiegel; *C:* Peter Deming; *M:* Joseph LoDuca.

Evil Dead Trap
Nami (Miyuki Ono), a Japanese late-night TV show host, is sent a tape that appears to show a brutal murder. Her cheap boss refuses to do anything, but she and her female crew decide to follow up on the tape and find the location where it was made. What follows in an abandoned factory owes much to Argento with even more visceral sex and violence. Director Ikeda's camera is almost never still. The script combines supernatural elements with a realistic setting and believable characters. The image is generally good and the print is mostly free of scratches or other blemishes though soft and washed-out at times. Some registration problems are evident, causing the image to jitter visibly on occasion. The transfer shows good and solid blacks, although shadow definition is somewhat lost. The film has been compressed quite well, although the innate film grain introduces occasional pixelation artifacts. Mono sound is clean and clear without notable defects. —*MM/GH*
Movie: 🎬🎬🎬½ **DVD:** 🎬🎬🎬
Synapse (Cat #9). Widescreen (1.85:1) letterboxed. Dolby Digital Mono. $29.98. Snapper. *LANG:* Japanese. *SUB:* English. *FEATURES:* Commentary: director ▪ Theatrical trailer.
1988 90m/C *JP* Miyuki Ono, Fumi Katsuragi, Hitomi Kobayashi, Eriko Nakagawa; *D:* Toshiharu Ikeda; *W:* Takashi Ishii.

Evil under the Sun
An opulent beach resort on Majorca is the setting for a murder that Hercule Poirot (Ustinov) must solve. Writing, acting, and production values are on a par with the other Christie adaptations of the '70s and '80s, and those are all very high. The DVD image ranges between very good and excellent; sound is average or a bit better. —*MM*
Movie: 🎬🎬 **DVD:** 🎬🎬🎬
Anchor Bay (Cat #DV11624, UPC #01313 1162493). Widescreen (1.77:1) anamorphic. Dolby Digital Mono. $24.98. Keep-

case. *LANG:* English. *FEATURES:* "Making of" featurette ▪ Trailer ▪ Talent files ▪ 25 chapter links.
1982 (PG) 112m/C *GB* Peter Ustinov, Jane Birkin, Maggie Smith, Colin Blakely, Roddy McDowall, Diana Rigg, Sylvia Miles, James Mason, Nicholas Clay; *D:* Guy Hamilton; *W:* Anthony Shaffer; *C:* Christopher Challis; *M:* Cole Porter.

Excellent Cadavers
Giovanni Falcone (Palminteri) was an incorruptible Italian prosecutor who took on the Mafia in Sicily in the 1980s. By the end of the decade, and with the help of informer Tommaso Buscetta (Abraham), Falcone had 300 convictions and sealed his own grim fate. Title refers to the corpses of public officials who challenged the mobsters. This is a very hard DVD to watch, with artifacts appearing almost constantly. Because of that, it's hard to say how sharp the image is. The Dolby Surround is the only worthwhile feature of the disc. The dialogue is always crystal clear and when action and gunplay occur, there is substantial low end and better Surround than expected from a TV movie. Still, the sound can't make up for the poor quality DVD. Watch the VHS version. —*JO*
Movie: 🎬🎬½ **DVD:** 🎬
HBO Home Video (Cat #91473, UPC #026 359147326). Full frame. Dolby Surround; Mono. $14.98. Snapper. *LANG:* English; Spanish. *SUB:* English; Spanish; French. *CAP:* English. *FEATURES:* 14 chapter links ▪ Talent files.
1999 (R) 86m/C Chazz Palminteri, F. Murray Abraham, Anna Galiena; *D:* Ricardo Tognazzi; *W:* Peter Pruce; *M:* Joseph Vitarelli.

Extramarital
A magazine editor (Fahey) assigns reporter Elizabeth Barton (Lords) to investigate a woman whose affair with a mystery man turns deadly. It's a fairly standard video-premiere erotic thriller that certainly doesn't test the limits of the genre. A competent cast handles the familiar material with ease. The bare-bones (no menu) disc is identical to VHS tape in every respect. —*MM*
Movie: 🎬🎬 **DVD:** 🎬🎬
Sunland Studios (Cat #281). Full frame. $24.99. Keepcase. *LANG:* English.
1998 (R) 90m/C Jeff Fahey, Traci Lords, Brian Bloom, Maria Diaz; *D:* Yael Russcol.

Eye of the Beholder
Disengaged surveillance expert known only as "The Eye" (McGregor) works for British intelligence out of their embassy in Washington. His latest assignment is to keep track of blackmailing Joanna (Judd), who turns out to be a psychotic serial killer of many identities. This must provide some strange turn-on, since instead of calling the cops, he proceeds to track her cross-country, protecting her from capture. Judd's an attractive femme fatale but the picture makes little sense and soon falls

into the jaw-dropping, I-don't-believe-what-I'm-seeing category. Some of this film's excellent sound editing could have been enhanced by better use of the DVD's 5.1 tracks. Unfortunately, that didn't happen and the mix seems limited to the front channels. The image transfer is very clean and sharp with little grain and no artifacts. Director Elliott's fine use of color, although not as flamboyant as in his *Priscilla, Queen of the Desert,* is accurately presented with subtle and detailed hues. —*JO*
Movie: 🎬 **DVD:** 🎬🎬½
Columbia Tristar Home Video (Cat #05052, UPC #043396050525). Widescreen (2.35:1) anamorphic; full frame. Dolby Digital 5.1; Dolby Surround. $24.95. Keepcase. *LANG:* English. *SUB:* English; Spanish; French. *CAP:* English. *FEATURES:* 28 chapter links ▪ Theatrical trailers ▪ Talent files ▪ Production notes ▪ Commentary: Stephan Elliott.
1999 (R) 101m/C Ewan McGregor, Ashley Judd, Patrick Bergin, k.d. lang, Jason Priestley, Genevieve Bujold; *D:* Stephan Elliott; *W:* Stephan Elliott; *C:* Guy Dufaux; *M:* Marius De Vries.

Eye of the Killer
Unimaginative formulaic thriller has psychic cop (Sutherland) on the trail of a serial killer. DVD has no trouble with a fairly simple image and a subdued color scheme of mostly grays and blues. Sound is O.K. —*MM*
Movie: 🎬🎬 **DVD:** 🎬🎬½
Trimark Home Video (Cat #7470D, UPC #031398747024). Widescreen letterboxed. Dolby Digital Stereo. $24.99. Keepcase. *LANG:* English. *SUB:* English; French; Spanish. *FEATURES:* 24 chapter links ▪ Trailer.
1999 (R) 100m/C Kiefer Sutherland, Henry Czerny, Polly Walker, Gary Hudson; *D:* Paul Marcus; *W:* Jeff Miller; *C:* Brian Pearson; *M:* Michael Hoenig.

Eyes of Laura Mars
This '70s thriller was one of the first to combine the psychic heroine (Dunaway) with the serial killer. It also boasts a very nice cast and a title song by Barbra Streisand. Though the image is unexceptional, it looks fine for a film of its age. Fans of the cast with conventional-sized monitors are advised to go with the full-frame version. Director Kershner's commentary track is geared toward story and storytelling techniques. —*MM*
Movie: 🎬🎬½ **DVD:** 🎬🎬½
Columbia Tristar Home Video (Cat #2847). Widescreen (1.85:1) anamorphic; full frame. Dolby Digital Mono. $14.95. Keepcase. *LANG:* English. *SUB:* English; Spanish; Portuguese; Chinese; Korean; Thai. *FEATURES:* 28 chapter links ▪ Commentary: Irvin Kershner ▪ "Making of" featurette ▪ Photo gallery ▪ Talent files ▪ Trailers.
1978 (R) 104m/C Faye Dunaway, Tommy Lee Jones, Brad Dourif, Rene Auberjonois, Raul Julia, Darlanne Fluegel, Michael Tuck-

er; **D:** Irvin Kershner; **W:** John Carpenter, David Zelag Goodman; **C:** Victor Kemper.

The Eyes of Tammy Faye

Documentary examines the eventful life of a not-particularly interesting woman, Tammy Faye Bakker Messner. She was most famous for being married to televangelist Jim Bakker when their PTL ministry went belly up. Since much of the story is told through static interviews and television news footage, the image is nothing special. Neither is the sound, though the choice of RuPaul Charles as narrator is inspired. The film was a hit on the festival circuit, and is recommended to that audience. —MM

Movie: 🐾🐾½ **DVD:** 🐾🐾
Universal Studios Home Video (Cat #211 31, UPC #025192113123). Full frame. Dolby Digital Surround Stereo. $24.98. Keepcase. *LANG:* English. *SUB:* English. *FEATURES:* 18 chapter links ▪ Trailer.
2000 (PG-13) 79m/C Tammy Faye Bakker, Jim Bakker; **D:** Fenton Bailey, Randy Barbato; **Nar:** RuPaul.

F/X

Hollywood special effects expert Rollie Tyler (Brown) is contracted by the government to fake an assassination to protect a mob enforcer. After completing the assignment, he finds that he took part in a real crime and that the shady feds are out to kill him. The plot may not survive a strict logic test, but the ride is certainly a lot of fun. Even though the disc lacks many extras, it looks very sharp—somehow better than I remember the theatrical release. Sound is fine. —MM

Movie: 🐾🐾🐾 **DVD:** 🐾🐾🐾
MGM Home Entertainment (Cat #1000 756). Widescreen letterboxed; full frame. Dolby Digital Surround Stereo; Mono. $19.98. Keepcase. *LANG:* English; Spanish. *SUB:* French; Spanish. *FEATURES:* Trailer ▪ 28 chapter links.
1986 (R) 109m/C Bryan Brown, Cliff DeYoung, Diane Venora, Brian Dennehy, Jerry Orbach, Mason Adams, Joe Grifasi, Martha Gehman, Angela Bassett; **D:** Robert Mandel; **W:** Robert T. Megginson, Gregory Fleeman; **C:** Miroslav Ondricek; **M:** Bill Conti.

F/X 2: The Deadly Art of Illusion

Weak follow-up finds special effects specialist Rollie Tyler (Brown) set to pull off just one more illusion for the cops. His girlfriend's (Ticotin) ex is a policeman who wants help in trapping a serial killer. Detective McCarthy (Dennehy) is involved, too. DVD image is very sharp for a film of this age and virtually without signs of wear. Sound is very good, too. —MM

Movie: 🐾🐾 **DVD:** 🐾🐾🐾
MGM Home Entertainment (Cat #908169, UPC #027616816924). Widescreen letterboxed; full frame. Dolby Digital Surround

Stereo. $24.99. Keepcase. *LANG:* English. *SUB:* French; Spanish. *CAP:* English. *FEATURES:* Trailer ▪ 24 chapter links ▪ Liner notes.
1991 (PG-13) 107m/C Bryan Brown, Brian Dennehy, Rachel Ticotin, Philip Bosco, Joanna Gleason; **D:** Richard Franklin; **W:** Bill Condon; **C:** Victor Kemper; **M:** Michael Boddicker, Lalo Schifrin.

Fail-Safe

Grim, clinical unfolding of a nuclear nightmare. When a computer malfunction mistakenly transmits the "go code" for American planes to bomb Moscow, both American and Russian military commands fight the clock and ingrained prejudices in frantic effort to recall planes and prevent Armageddon. Lean direction by Sidney Lumet and Walter Bernstein's keen script (adapted from a novel by Eugene Burdick and Harvey Wheeler) weave an authentic atmosphere of how world leaders might face the unthinkable. Sterling, all-star cast lends weight and substance to the dire proceedings, particularly Walter Matthau as a blindly hawkish political scientist and Henry Fonda as the President, slowly running out of options. Glibly referred to as the "serious *Dr. Strangelove*," *Fail-Safe* wears its political and humanitarian intentions squarely on its sleeve. It retains its power to captivate precisely because of those qualities. The DVD offers a crisp transfer, the black-and-white images exhibiting good gray scale. Deep blacks and careful mastering yield excellent shadow and detail delineation, with no discernible digital or compression artifacts. Mono soundtrack is fine for its age, despite a few peaks. Numerous supplements make this disc a virtual document of the film: an illuminating Sidney Lumet running commentary, a behind-the-scenes feature boasting new video interviews with Lumet, screenwriter Bernstein, and Dan O'Herlihy, and theatrical trailers for *Fail-Safe* (looking just as good as the feature), and other Columbia Tristar war-theme titles including *Das Boot* and *Guns of Navarone*. A must have for any DVD library. —EP

Movie: 🐾🐾🐾½ **DVD:** 🐾🐾🐾🐾½
Columbia Tristar Home Video (Cat #05424, UPC #4339605424). Widescreen (1.85:1) anamorphic. Dolby Digital Mono. $24.95. Keepcase. *LANG:* English; French; Spanish. *SUB:* English; French; Spanish; Portuguese; Chinese; Korean; Thai. *CAP:* English. *FEATURES:* 28 chapter links ▪ Featurette: *Fail-Safe* Revisited ▪ Commentary: director Lumet ▪ Theatrical trailers ▪ Talent files ▪ Production notes (booklet).
1964 111m/B Henry Fonda, Dan O'Herlihy, Walter Matthau, Larry Hagman, Fritz Weaver, Dom DeLuise; **D:** Sidney Lumet; **W:** Walter Bernstein; **C:** Gerald Hirschfeld.

Fair Game

Deliverance meets *Mad Max* in the Australian outback as three loathsome poach-

ers attack Jessica (Delaney), who's living alone on a farm. The film delivers the cheap thrills of good, fast-paced exploitation. It's such a rough dusty image that any difference between disc and tape is minimal. —MM

Movie: 🐾🐾 **DVD:** 🐾🐾
Vanguard International Cinema, Inc. (Cat #VF0072, UPC #658769007237). Full frame. $29.95. Keepcase. *LANG:* English. *FEATURES:* 12 chapter links.
1985 83m/C *AU* Cassandra Delaney, Peter Ford, David Sandford, Gary Who; **D:** Mario Andreacchio; **W:** Rob George; **C:** Andrew Lesnie; **M:** Ashley Irwin.

Fair Game

What is insanely jealous businessman (Henry) to do when his girlfriend (Styler) jilts him? He does what any of us would do—he locks her in her spacious apartment with an irate mamba, of course. The action is so well photographed and staged that you can suspend your disbelief until the end, when it does go too far. A welcome streak of unexpected humor runs throughout, but Moroder's here-comes-the-snake music is more irritating than frightening. Henry's unhinged villain is a scene-stealing delight. The often grainy image is indistinguishable from VHS tape. —MM

AKA: Mamba Snakes.
Movie: 🐾🐾½ **DVD:** 🐾🐾
Image Entertainment (Cat #OVED9021 DVD, UPC #014381022129). Full frame. Dolby Digital Stereo. $24.99. Snapper. *LANG:* English. *FEATURES:* 12 chapter links.
1989 (R) 81m/C *IT* Gregg Henry, Trudie Styler, Bill Moseley; **D:** Mario Orfini; **W:** Mario Orfini, Linda Ravera; **C:** Dante Spinotti; **M:** Giorgio Moroder.

Fall of the House of Usher

This Expressionist avant-garde feature is one of the few that gained enough attention to be released in the United States. A young Luis Buñuel was director Jean Epstein's assistant on the movie, but upstarts Buñuel and Salvador Dali probably looked on Epstein's fussy pictorial literalism with disdain, taking notes for their own provocative *An Andalusian Dog*. In a wind-blown castle on a haunted moor, Roderick Usher (Debucourt) paints portraits of his wife Madelaine (Gance), claiming that she is more alive in his art than in real life. Middle-aged visitor Allan (Charles Lamy) sees her wandering the halls, sickly and forlorn, and it is true that as Roderick's portraits become more vivid, she seems to wane in vitality. As a horror film, this one doesn't come near Murnau's *Nosferatu* or Dreyer's *Vampyr*, both of which integrate their fantastic effects into great horror themes. But it is an impressive experimental film in the cinema-study sense. The DVD is sourced from a preserved 35mm master print. The transfer is fine for a film of this vintage, except for patches of white specks that look like some kind of authoring flaw, as they crop

up in a few scenes with lower than normal contrast. The intertitles are in the original French, a nice touch, so Jean Pierre Aumont translates them in English...but with an accent so thick one must concentrate to follow them. —*GE* **AKA:** La Chute de la Maison Usher.
Movie: 🐾🐾½ **DVD:** 🐾🐾
All Day Entertainment (Cat #ADED0618 DVD, UPC #014381061826). Full frame. $24.98. Snapper. *LANG:* Silent. *SUB:* French intertitles.
1928 48m/B *FR* Marguerite Gance, Jean Debucourt, Charles Lamy; **D:** Jean Epstein; **W:** Jean Epstein; **C:** Georges Lucas, Jean Lucas. *AWARDS:* Natl. Film Reg. '00.

The Fall of the House of Usher
The first Roger Corman/Vincent Price Poe adaptation depicts the collapse of the famous estate due to madness and revenge. Terrific sets, solid direction, and one of Price's most restrained performances. This DVD is worlds away from the seriously flawed full-frame tapes that have been in distribution. Image is very good. Mono sound is fine, and Corman's commentary is to the point. —*MM* **AKA:** House of Usher.
Movie: 🐾🐾🐾 **DVD:** 🐾🐾🐾
MGM Home Entertainment (Cat #1002 050, UPC #027616862877). Widescreen (2.35:1) anamorphic. Dolby Digital Mono. $24.95. Keepcase. *LANG:* English; French. *SUB:* French; Spanish. *CAP:* English. *FEATURES:* 16 chapter links • Trailer • Commentary: Roger Corman.
1960 85m/C Vincent Price, Myrna Fahey, Mark Damon, Harry Ellerbe, Bill Borzage, Nadajan; **D:** Roger Corman; **W:** Richard Matheson; **C:** Floyd Crosby; **M:** Les Baxter.

Fall Time
Offbeat crime drama is set in small-town Minnesota, circa 1957. Three high schoolers set in motion a prank that turns bad when they pull up in front of the local bank. David (Arquette), Joe (Blechman), and Tim (London) intend to stage a mock robbery—but a real robbery is in progress and the teens wind up hostages of creepy criminals Florence (Rourke) and Leon (Baldwin). Though aliasing is extreme along bright lines of chrome trim, the overall image is good. Sound is very good. —*MM* **AKA:** Falltime.
Movie: 🐾🐾½ **DVD:** 🐾🐾½
Pioneer Entertainment (Cat #10267). Full frame. Dolby Digital Stereo. $24.98. Keepcase. *LANG:* English. *FEATURES:* Trailer • 17 chapter links.
1994 (R) 88m/C Mickey Rourke, Stephen Baldwin, Jason London, David Arquette, Jonah Blechman, Sheryl Lee; **D:** Paul Warner; **W:** Steve Alden, Paul Skemp; **C:** Mark J. Gordon; **M:** Hummie Mann.

Fallen Angel
Soft-core Playboy production is a faux noir story of a private eye (Keefe), who

becomes involved with the wife (Philips) of a mobster. Many cigarettes are smoked while light cuts through Venetian blinds. Though the setting is allegedly the 1940s, period details are sketchy or non-existent. With soft focus and colors and thin sound, the DVD is not a significant improvement over VHS tape. Genre stalwart Buck Flower appears as a bartender. —*MM*
Movie: 🐾 **DVD:** 🐾🐾
Image Entertainment (Cat #ID8909YODVD, UPC #014381890921). Full frame. Dolby Digital Stereo. $19.99. Snapper. *LANG:* English. *FEATURES:* 12 chapter links.
1999 100m/C James Patrick Keefe, Samantha Phillips, I (Ai) Wan, Thomas Adams, Kevin Wickham, George "Buck" Flower; **D:** John Quinn; **W:** John Quinn; **C:** Andrea V. Rossotto; **M:** John Boegehold.

Falling for a Dancer
When young Elizabeth Sullivan (Dermot-Walsh) gets pregnant after a brief affair with an actor, there's not much she can do. In the Ireland of 1937, she is forced by her family into a marriage with a drunken widower and resigns herself until she finds love again. The soft focus and pale colors of British television productions are fine for such a romantic story. Sound is acceptable. —*MM*
Movie: 🐾🐾🐾 **DVD:** 🐾🐾½
BFS Video (Cat #96100-D, UPC #0668059 11002). Full frame. Dolby Digital Mono. $39.98. Keepcase boxed set. *LANG:* English. *FEATURES:* 24 chapter links.
1998 200m/C *GB* Elisabeth Dermot-Walsh, Dermot Crowley, Liam Cunningham, Rory Murray, Brian McGrath, Maureen O'Brien, Colin Farrell; **D:** Richard Standeven; **W:** Deirdre Purcell; **C:** Kevin Rowley; **M:** Stephen McKeon.

Family Enforcer
Please see review of *Great Mafia Movies*.
AKA: Death Collector.
Movie: 🐾
1976 (R) 82m/C Joe Cortese, Lou Criscuola, Joe Pesci, Anne Johns, Keith Davis; **D:** Ralph De Vito; **W:** Ralph De Vito; **C:** Bob Bailin.

Family of Cops 2: Breach of Faith
Sequel to 1995 made-for-TV movie shows it's tough to be a Jewish cop in Milwaukee with four grown children involved with or aspiring to be in law enforcement. This chapter finds police inspector Paul Fein (Charles Bronson) and his family battling Russian mobsters while investigating the murder of a priest. FC2 offers an uneven but occasionally interesting cops-and-robbers plot while further exploring the hook begun in the first installment of patriarch Fein juggling familial, professional, and religious responsibilities. Bronson is the only reason to watch this disc; he's the glue that keeps the proceedings from melting into a puddle of "A Quinn Martin Production" clichés. Given its small-

screen origins, the full-frame video transfer is pleasing enough with clean color rendition and accurate fleshtones. Mono sound is fine. —*EP* **AKA:** Breach of Faith: A Family of Cops 2.
Movie: 🐾🐾½ **DVD:** 🐾🐾½
Trimark Home Video (Cat #VM7534D, UPC #3139875342). Full frame. Dolby Digital Mono. $19.99. Keepcase. *LANG:* English. *SUB:* English; Spanish. *FEATURES:* 24 chapter links • Trailers.
1997 (PG-13) 90m/C Charles Bronson, Joe Penny, Diane Ladd, Sebastian Spence, Angela Featherstone, Barbara Williams, Andrew Jackson, Matt Birman, Kim Weeks, David Hemblen, Mimi Kuzyk, Real Andrews; **D:** David Greene; **W:** Joel Basberg; **C:** Ronald Orieux; **M:** Peter Manning Robinson.

Family of Cops 3
Third and, so far, final chapter in the law-keeping Fein family saga. While it may not have the same closure as Luke unmasking Vader or Indiana Jones riding off into the sunset with his dad, *FC3* does seem to resolve a few of the lingering plot threads from the second chapter. This go-around, Milwaukee once more seethes as the deaths of a socialite couple triggers a chain of events, uncovering drug money laundering and a hotbed of political corruption. By now, the formula is set: cross cut family issues with a gunfight every half-hour and have at least one scene in a strip club. Just like the first two, Bronson's thoroughly pro delivery saves the made-for-TV movie from its own TV-ness and by the end credits, I actually looked forward to episode four. The transfer exhibits the same color fidelity as the previous disc, yet intermittently suffers pixelation artifacts. The mono soundtrack adequately projects. —*EP*
Movie: 🐾🐾½ **DVD:** 🐾🐾½
Trimark Home Video (Cat #VM7533D, UPC #3139875332). Full frame. Dolby Digital Mono. $19.99. Keepcase. *LANG:* English. *SUB:* English; Spanish. *FEATURES:* 24 chapter links • Trailers.
1998 (PG-13) 90m/C Charles Bronson, Joe Penny, Kim Weeks, Sebastian Spence, Barbara Williams, Torri Higginson, Nikki DeBoer; **D:** Sheldon Larry; **W:** Noah Jubelirer; **C:** Bert Dunk.

Family Plot
A phony psychic and her cab-driving boyfriend try to find the lost illegitimate heir to the "Rainbird" fortune. At the same time the man they seek (Devane, who is unaware of his family ties) and his girlfriend (Black) are kidnapping esteemed locals to acquire priceless jewels. Hitchcock's last film is a slight but funny affair with charismatic leads and excellent turns by Devane and Black. Hitchcock's use of rear-projection is quite dated (as it was even at the time of release) but the out-of-control car sequence is still thrilling and hilarious. The disc is colorful and sharp but very grainy, soft, and appears to be

made from an older transfer. The sound is clear and the music has lots of presence, but it's a fairly undistinguished mono track. Like the other titles in the series, this one features an excellent documentary with fascinating interviews and rare behind-the-scenes footage. The other tidbits included make it a very satisfying package. —DG

Movie: ♫♫½ **DVD:** ♫♫½
Universal Studios Home Video (Cat #20659, UPC #025192065927). Widescreen (1.85:1) anamorphic. Dolby Digital Mono. $29.98. Keepcase. *LANG:* English; French. *SUB:* English; Spanish. *FEATURES:* 18 chapter links • Insert card with chapter listing • Cast and filmmaker bios • Production notes • Theatrical trailer • "Plotting Family Plot," a making-of documentary • Photo and poster gallery • Storyboards for the chase scene.
1976 (PG) 120m/C Karen Black, Bruce Dern, Barbara Harris, William Devane, Ed Lauter, Katherine Helmond, Cathleen Nesbitt, Warren Kemmerling, Edith Atwater, William Prince, Nicholas Colasanto, Alfred Hitchcock; **D:** Alfred Hitchcock; **W:** Ernest Lehman; **C:** Leonard J. South; **M:** John Williams.

A Family Thing

Give Robert Duvall and James Earl Jones a good script with decent characters to play, and the rest of any film is almost an afterthought. That's the case here, but for all the "chemistry" between the two stars, there's little dramatic tension or conflict in their story once the premise has been established. Duvall is a Southerner who, on the death of the woman he believed to be his mother, learns that his real mother was black; and that Jones, a Chicago cop, is his half-brother. As their Aunt T, Irma P. Hall almost steals the film. Beyond some aliasing in pan shots, image is fine. Surround effects are used subtly, but then, nothing about the movie is flashy. A commentary by writers Thornton and Epperson might have been enlightening. —MM

Movie: ♫♫♫ **DVD:** ♫♫½
MGM Home Entertainment (Cat #10018 28, UPC #027616860989). Widescreen (2.35:1) anamorphic. Dolby Digital 5.1 Surround Stereo; Dolby Digital Surround. $14.95. Keepcase. *LANG:* English; French. *SUB:* French; Spanish. *FEATURES:* 16 chapter links • Trailer.
1996 (PG-13) 109m/C Robert Duvall, James Earl Jones, Irma P. Hall, Michael Beach, Grace Zabriskie, Regina Taylor, Mary Jackson, Paula Marshall, Jim Harrell; **D:** Richard Pearce; **W:** Billy Bob Thornton, Tom Epperson; **C:** Fred Murphy.

Fanatic

Location filming at the Cannes festival and a gossipy peek at the business side of the industry are the main attractions here. Cabbie Vinny Durand (Spinell) is a semi-crazed fan of Jana Bates (Munro) and a would-be filmmaker. Does he go to France to stalk the star or to make a movie deal? Whichever, someone is slicing and dicing Jana's associates. Spinell's sweaty, voyeuristic obsession seems quite real and sick, but the ideas and the writing are better than the overall execution. The film never really rises above the level of the genre and the DVD image is not a significant improvement over VHS tape. —MM **AKA:** The Last Horror Film.

Movie: ♫♫ **DVD:** ♫♫
Troma Team Video (Cat #9991, UPC #790 357999132). Full frame. $24.95. Keepcase. *LANG:* English. *FEATURES:* 8 chapter links • Trailers • Other Tromatic extras.
1982 (R) 87m/C Caroline Munro, Joe Spinell, Judd Hamilton, Devin Goldenberg, David Winters; **D:** David Winters; **W:** Tom Klassen, Judd Hamilton, David Winters; **C:** Thomas Denove; **M:** Jesse Frederick.

The Fantasia Anthology

Deluxe set includes *Fantasia* (1940) and *Fantasia/2000* (2000) as well as a third disc of additional features. Included in this exhaustive look at the 60-year history of both films are detailed storyboards, concept art, character designs, special effects, etc. This disc (like the others in the set) features an amazing picture that reproduces the myriad colors used to create these films fantastically. The sound remastering on the set is also darn close to perfect. Definitely a must-have set for any DVD collection. Includes an indispensable map to all DVD features. —MJT

Movie: ♫♫♫♫ **DVD:** ♫♫♫♫
Buena Vista Home Entertainment (Cat #21269, UPC #786936141030). Widescreen (1.85:1) anamorphic; full frame. Dolby Digital 5.1 Surround; DD 5.0 Surround; DTS 5.1; DTS Surround. $69.99. Box set. *LANG:* English; French. *FEATURES:* **Fantasia:** In-depth exploration of segments • Special effects • Still frame galleries: "The Art of *Fantasia*" • Publicity material (trailers/posters) • Pencil tests of unused animation • Exclusive Disney segments • Bios of the filmmakers • Historical context of each musical piece • "The *Fantasia* That Never Was" • Still frame art: "Flight of the Bumble Bee," "Mosquito," "Baby Ballet" • Original theatrical trailer • **Fantasia 2000:** Behind-the-scenes featurette • Interviews with the filmmakers • Production progression demonstrations • Deleted animation; alternate versions; abandoned concepts • Publicity material (trailers/posters), original trailer • Historical context of each musical piece.
2000 356m/C

Fantasia/2000

Lightweight continuation of Disney's 1940 film hangs on to Mickey Mouse's popular "The Sorcerer's Apprentice" and adds seven new animated sequences of varying charm with celebrity introductions. Probably the most fun sequence is Saint-Saens "Carnival of the Animals" with a yo-yoing flamingo. The DVD image is pristine, showing no grain, noise, or artifacting. Colors simply leap off of the screen—reds and frosty blues, which never bleed together or look saturated. The various animation styles present several different color palettes, and they're all equally beautiful. Both the Dolby 5.1 and DTS tracks sound equally grand, offering a wide dynamic range which allows the music to fill the speakers and envelope the viewer. For a good example of the dynamic Surround sound on the title, check out the beginning of Chapter 13 as the sound of Mickey Mouse searching for Donald moves about the room. The title is also available on the 3-disc "Fantasia Anthology." —MM/ML

Movie: ♫♫♫ **DVD:** ♫♫♫½
Buena Vista Home Entertainment (Cat #19571, UPC #717951008374). Widescreen (1.85:1) anamorphic. Dolby Digital 5.1 Surround Stereo; DTS. $29.99. Keepcase. *LANG:* English; French. *FEATURES:* Audio commentaries • Animated shorts "Melody," "Toot, Whistle, Plunk, and Boom" • "Making of" featurette.
2000 (G) 75m/C D: Hendel Butoy, Eric Goldberg, James Nelson Algar, Gaetan Brizzi, Paul Brizzi, Pixote Hunt, Francis Glebas.

Fantastic Voyage

Please see review of *Voyage to the Bottom of the Sea / Fantastic Voyage.* **AKA:** Microscopia; Strange Journey.

Movie: ♫♫♫
1966 100m/C Stephen Boyd, Edmond O'Brien, Raquel Welch, Arthur Kennedy, Donald Pleasence, Arthur O'Connell, William Redfield, James Brolin, Barry Coe, Brendan Fitzgerald, Shelby Grant, Ken Scott; **D:** Richard Fleischer; **W:** Harry Kleiner; **C:** Ernest Laszlo; **M:** Leonard Rosenman. *AWARDS:* Oscars '66: Art Dir./Set Dec., Color, Visual FX; *NOM:* Oscars '66: Color Cinematog., Film Editing.

The Fantasy Film Worlds of George Pal

Pure pleasure for fantasy film and sci-fi buffs, this tribute to visionary George Pal boasts a treasure trove of classic film clips (*7 Faces of Dr. Lao, The Time Machine* and *War of the Worlds*) and illuminating interviews with Pal and those who worked with and were inspired by him. With "a twinkle in his eye and a twinkle in his brain," Pal pioneered stop-motion animation and was the founding father of the modern science fiction and fantasy film genres. The source materials are of varying quality, but Pal's state-of-the-art magic has not lost its sense of awe-inspiring wonder. In the fairly extensive extras, animator Wah Chang demonstrates a hand puppet used in *The Seven Faces of Dr. Lao* —DL

Movie: ♫♫♫½ **DVD:** ♫♫♫
Image Entertainment (Cat #ID5866ALDVD, UPC #014381586626). Full frame. Dolby Digital Mono. $24.99. Snapper. *LANG:* English. *FEATURES:* Theatrical trailers • Interviews: Pal and animators Ward Kimball, Phil Kellison, Bob Baker • Kinescopes •

Home movies • Production photo and art gallery • *Doc Savage: Man of Bronze* promotional excerpts • Puppet demonstration • 22 chapter links.
1986 93m/C Robert Bloch, Chesley Bonestell, Ray Bradbury, Wah Chang, Tony Curtis, Jim Danforth, Joe Dante, Roy Edward Disney, Barbara Eden, Duke Goldstone, Ray Harryhausen, Charlton Heston, Walter Lantz, Janet Leigh, Tony Randall, Ann Robinson, Gene Roddenberry, Russ Tamblyn, Rod Taylor, Gene Warren, Robert Wise, Alan Young; *D:* Arnold Leibovit; *W:* Arnold Leibovit; *Nar:* Paul Frees.

Fantasy Mission Force
Apparently, the title is meant to be taken literally. In this indescribably silly action comedy, Japanese troops capture an international group of generals (some in Civil War—era uniforms). An invasion of Canada is underway. Jackie is, I think, part of a group trying to rescue them. UN troops wear kilts; others wear armor. Like so many bargain-bin discs, this one exhibits every flaw imaginable. It is much worse than most bad VHS tapes. —*MM*
Movie: 🎵🎵 *DVD:* woof
Madacy Entertainment (Cat #DVD9-9207-1). Full frame. $9.98. Keepcase. *LANG:* English. *FEATURES:* 9 chapter links.
1984 90m/C *HK* Jackie Chan, Brigitte (Lin Chinag-hsia) Lin, Adam Cheng, Jimmy Wang Yu; *D:* Yen Ping Chu.

The Fantasy Worlds of Irwin Allen
Originally broadcast on the Sci-Fi Channel, the homage documents the man responsible for such '60s sci-fi TV fare as *Lost in Space, Time Tunnel, Land of the Giants,* and such disaster films as *The Poseidon Adventure* and *The Towering Inferno.* Space alumni June Lockhart and Bill Mumy guide us through generous servings of clips, behind-the-scenes footage, and reminiscences. Image quality is good for the shot-on-video interviews and wrap-arounds by Mumy and Lockhart. The archival sources look clean with surprisingly strong color fidelity and detail. As many of his theatrical ventures were widescreen, the clips and trailers in the documentary are similarly letterboxed. Audio provides ample levels for clean playback. —*EP/MM*
Movie: 🎵🎵🎵 *DVD:* 🎵🎵½
Image Entertainment (Cat #8765). Full frame. Dolby Digital Mono. $29.99. Snapper. *LANG:* English. *FEATURES:* Featurettes.
1995 95m/C June Lockhart, Billy Mumy, Barbara Eden, David Hedison, Lee Meriwether, Roddy McDowall, James Darren, Robert Wagner.

The Far Pavilions
This 1984 miniseries is based on M.M. Kaye's popular book of forbidden love in colonial India between junior British officer Ash (Cross) and Indian princess Anjuli (Amy Irving, in the most grievous case of ethnic miscasting since John Wayne por-

trayed Genghis Khan). The two-disc period epic is rich with enough incident to keep romance fans intrigued, and boasts a distinguished supporting cast, including Omar Sharif, Sir John Gielgud, Christopher Lee, and a young Rupert Everett. Picture quality is scratchy and dull. —*DL* *AKA:* Blade of Steel.
Movie: 🎵🎵½ *DVD:* 🎵🎵
Acorn Media Publishing (Cat #AMP-4274, UPC #054961427499). Full frame. Dolby Digital. $39.95. Keepcase. *LANG:* English. *FEATURES:* M.M. Kaye bio • Books by M.M. Kaye • Production notes • 45 chapter links.
1984 108m/C *GB* Ben Cross, Amy Irving, Omar Sharif, Benedict Taylor, Rossano Brazzi, Christopher Lee, John Gielgud, Rupert Everett; *D:* Peter Duffell; *C:* Jack Cardiff; *M:* Carl Davis.

A Farewell to Arms
Please see review of *Gary Cooper Double Feature.* —*MM*
Movie: 🎵🎵🎵
1932 85m/B Helen Hayes, Gary Cooper, Adolphe Menjou, Mary Philips, Jack LaRue, Blanche Frederici; *D:* Frank Borzage; *W:* Oliver H.P Garrett, Benjamin Glazer; *C:* Charles B(ryant) Lang Jr. *AWARDS:* Oscars '33: Cinematog., Sound; *NOM:* Oscars '33: Picture.

Farinelli
A movie to make men cringe floridly depicts the complex professional and personal ties of 18th-century opera composer Riccardo Broschi (Lo Verso) and his younger brother Carlo (Dionisi), a celebrated castrato singer under the stage name "Farinelli." (In part, because of an early church prohibition against women singing in public, boys were castrated before puberty to preserve their pure soprano voices while vocal power and agility grew.) Castrati were the glam rock stars of their day and that's how their world is presented here. Perhaps we should be thankful that a 5.1 remix wasn't done on the castrato voice heard here. It's an electronic mixture of counter-tenor Derek Lee Ragin and soprano Ewa Mallas Godlewska. The image is excellent, preserving the slightly muted color scheme of the ornate sets and costumes—particularly the many shades of red—from overpowering everything else. Details are easy to make out in heavy black clothes. —*MM* *AKA:* Farinelli the Castrato; Farinelli Il Castrato.
Movie: 🎵🎵 *DVD:* 🎵🎵🎵
Columbia Tristar Home Video (Cat #10629, UPC #043396106291). Widescreen (1.85:1) anamorphic. Dolby Digital Surround Stereo. $24.95. Keepcase. *LANG:* Italian; French. *SUB:* English; Spanish; French. *FEATURES:* 28 chapter links • Trailers • Talent files • Production notes.
1994 (R) 110m/C *FR IT BE* Stefano Dionisi, Enrico Lo Verso, Jeroen Krabbe, Elsa Zylberstein, Caroline Cellier, Omero Antonutti, Jacques Boudet; *D:* Gerard Corbiau; *W:* Gerard Corbiau, Andree Corbiau,

Marcel Beaulieu; *C:* Walther Vanden Ende; *M:* Christopher Rousset. *AWARDS:* Cesar '95: Art Dir./Set Dec., Sound; Golden Globes '95: Foreign Film; *NOM:* Oscars '94: Foreign Film.

Farscape, Vol. 2
"Exodus from Genesis" and "Throne for a Loss," two episodes of the colorful Sci-Fi Channel space opera, are presented on a dual-layer DVD. The image quality is superb. The full-frame transfer is absolutely clean and without any speckles or blemishes. Colors are saturated, creating the right atmosphere. Blacks are very deep, giving the image visual depth. The compression of the material is meticulous and entirely without flaws. There is not a hint of compression artifacting, not a sign of edge-enhancement, and no other digital artifact. The disc is a prime example of how great contemporary television productions can look on DVD, and it creates an image that is significantly more detailed than any of the garble coming down your cable or DSS channels. A full-blown 5.1 audio track makes very aggressive use of the Surround channels. The brightest sounds and the lowest basses are all nicely reproduced, creating a powerful voluminous mix that matches the film. —*GH*
Movie: 🎵🎵🎵 *DVD:* 🎵🎵🎵½
A.D.V. Films (UPC #702727009723). Full frame. Dolby Digital 5.1 Surround Stereo; Dolby Digital Surround. $24.98. Keepcase. *LANG:* English. *FEATURES:* Commentary: Brian Henson, Virginia Hey • Commentary: Ben Browder, Claudia Black • Video profile • Image gallery.
2000 ?m/C

Farscape, Vol. 3
If mutant Muppets took over the starship *Enterprise,* the result might be *Farscape,* exceptionally well-produced science-fiction aimed squarely at fans. The creators wisely limit their scope and don't try to do too much with too little. In some episodes, such as "Back and Back and Back to the Future," that can lead to a slight sense of claustrophobia with a few characters who do not leave a few sets. But in "Thank God It's Friday...Again" things open up to include a city and surrounding countryside. In both, the writing is sharp, intelligent, and funny. DVD image is flawless, looking much better than most broadcasts. The 5.1 Surround is exceptionally active. My one criticism: Why do so many of the alien characters have funny noses? *Farscape, Vol. 1* (cat. #DFS/001; $24.98) is also available, but has not yet been reviewed. I'd be surprised if it differed from the other two discs in image or sound. —*MM*
Movie: 🎵🎵🎵 *DVD:* 🎵🎵🎵½
A.D.V. Films (Cat #DFS/003, UPC #70272 7009822). Full frame. Dolby Digital 5.1 Surround Stereo; Dolby Digital Surround. $24.98. Keepcase. *LANG:* English. *FEATURES:* 8 chapter links • Commentary • Video profile of Zhaan, Delvian priestess

- Image gallery • Conceptual drawings
- Weblinks.

2001 100m/C Ben Browder, Claudia Black, Virginia Hey, Anthony Simcoe; **D:** Rowan Woods; **W:** Babs Greyhosky, David Wilks; **C:** Craig Barden; **V:** Jonathan Hardy, Lani Tupu.

Fast Times at Ridgemont High

Teens at a Southern California high school revel in sex, drugs, and rock 'n' roll. A full complement of student types meet at the Mall—that great suburban microcosm percolating with angst-ridden teen trials—to contemplate losing their virginity, plot skipping homeroom, and move inexorably closer to the end of adolescence. The talented young cast became household names: Sean Penn is most excellent as Spicolli, the surfer dude who antagonizes teacher Walston. This widescreen transfer perfectly restores the movie's original color schemes. Those subtle qualities got lost in previous video incarnations. The monaural sound quality is good, although the frequency response is somewhat limited with no notable bass extension. —*GH/MM*
Movie: 🎵🎵🎵 **DVD:** 🎵🎵½
Universal Studios Home Video (Cat #20530). Widescreen (1.85:1) anamorphic. Dolby Digital Mono. $29.98. Keepcase. *LANG:* English. *SUB:* English; French. *FEATURES:* Commentary • Documentary • Video map • Musical highlights • Theatrical trailer.
1982 (R) 91m/C Sean Penn, Jennifer Jason Leigh, Judge Reinhold, Robert Romanus, Brian Backer, Phoebe Cates, Ray Walston, Scott Thomson, Vincent Schiavelli, Amanda Wyss, Forest Whitaker, Kelli Maroney, Eric Stoltz, Pamela Springsteen, James Russo, Martin Brest, Anthony Edwards, Nicolas Cage; **D:** Amy Heckerling; **W:** Cameron Crowe; **C:** Matthew F. Leonetti.

Fatal Beauty

Undercover LAPD cop Rita Rizzoli (Goldberg) tracks down a drug dealer selling cocaine (from which the title is taken). Mike Marshak (Elliott), the bad guy's bodyguard, tries to help. The film tiptoes around the interracial romance between the two that is suggested. For a mid-level studio production that was only moderately popular at the boxoffice, the DVD looks very good. Sound is adequate. —*MM*
Movie: 🎵🎵 **DVD:** 🎵🎵½
MGM Home Entertainment (Cat #1001 554, UPC #027616858641). Widescreen (1.85:1) letterboxed. Dolby Digital Surround Stereo. $19.98. Keepcase. *LANG:* English; French; Spanish. *SUB:* French; Spanish. *CAP:* English. *FEATURES:* 16 chapter links • Theatrical trailer.
1987 (R) 104m/C Whoopi Goldberg, Sam Elliott, Ruben Blades, Harris Yulin, Richard "Cheech" Marin, Brad Dourif; **D:** Tom Holland; **W:** Hilary Henkin, Dean Riesner; **C:** David M. Walsh; **M:** Harold Faltermeyer.

Father of the Bride Part II

Is it a sequel to a remake or a remake of a sequel? Sweetly sentimental update of the 1951 film *Father's Little Dividend* finds George Banks (Martin) once again thrown for a loop—first by his beloved daughter Annie's (Williams) pregnancy and then by wife Nina's (Keaton) announcement that they are about to become parents again themselves. Short adds to the comedic mayhem as the party planner. The image is generally good looking, with a reasonably sharp picture with good color saturation, although the lack of anamorphic enhancement will be problematic for some. However, occasional pixelation and infrequent damage (nicks and scratches) to the original film element mar the presentation slightly. Dialogue is clear and distinct, which is about all you can ask of most comedy soundtracks. The trailer and two featurettes are fun, but the back of the case implies a bonus feature that is not present: the packaging promises an audio commentary track with Martin and Short, but that extra doesn't seem to exist on the disc. —*MB*
Movie: 🎵🎵½ **DVD:** 🎵🎵🎵
Buena Vista Home Entertainment (Cat #18336, UPC #717951005175). Widescreen (1.85:1) letterboxed. Dolby Digital 5.0. $32.99. Keepcase. *LANG:* English; French. *SUB:* Spanish. *CAP:* English. *FEATURES:* 20 chapter links • Theatrical trailer • Production featurettes.
1995 (PG) 106m/C Steve Martin, Diane Keaton, Kimberly Williams, Martin Short, George Newbern, Kieran Culkin, Peter Michael Goetz, Kate McGregor Stewart, Eugene Levy, B.D. Wong, Jane Adams; **D:** Charles Shyer; **W:** Nancy Meyers, Charles Shyer; **C:** William A. Fraker; **M:** Alan Silvestri. *AWARDS:* NOM: Golden Globes '96: Actor—Mus./Comedy (Martin).

Father's Little Dividend

Tracy expects a little peace and quiet now that he has successfully married off daughter Taylor in this charming sequel to *Father of the Bride*. However, he's quickly disillusioned by the news that he'll soon be a grandfather—a prospect that causes nothing but dismay. The DVD image is very good, though the print exhibits a few nicks. Sound is thin and wavery but Tracy's voice-over narration comes through nice and strong. —*MM*
Movie: 🎵🎵🎵 **DVD:** 🎵🎵
Madacy Entertainment (Cat #99014, UPC #056775005092). Full frame. Dolby Digital Mono. $9.99. Keepcase. *LANG:* English. *FEATURES:* Spencer Tracy thumbnail bio • Production credits • 9 chapter links.
1951 82m/B Spencer Tracy, Joan Bennett, Elizabeth Taylor, Don Taylor, Billie Burke, Russ Tamblyn, Moroni Olsen; **D:** Vincente Minnelli; **W:** Frances Goodrich, Albert Hackett; **C:** John Alton; **M:** Albert Sendry.

Fay Wray Collection

The first feature on the disc, *The Most Dangerous Game* isn't as sharp as the Criterion Collection edition and the audio is marred by a constant background hiss. The second, *Vampire Bat*, looks better but is still flawed with vertical lines and flecks. The cast is the main reason to see this otherwise stodgy tale of bats infesting a small town, and the series of murders that ensue. Melvyn Douglas is at his suave best as the skeptical hero. Lionel Atwill is fine as the villainous mad scientist. Dwight Frye's character is a caricature of Renfield. Fay Wray isn't given nearly enough to do. Too much comic chit-chat doesn't help the short film, though it does have a few eerie moments. —*MM*
Movie: 🎵🎵🎵 **DVD:** 🎵🎵½
SlingShot Entertainment (Cat #TDVD9125, UPC #017078912524). Full frame. Dolby Digital Mono. $19.99. Large jewelbox. *LANG:* English. *FEATURES:* 17 chapter links (Game) • 14 chapter links (Bat).
2000 ?m/C

Fear City

A psycho is stalking New York strippers and it's up to booking agent Matt Rossi (Berenger) to stop him before he goes after Rossi's ex-girlfriend Loretta (Griffith). It's another wallow in the seething underbelly of the Big Apple for director Ferrara, who has plumbed the depths before. The image is very good despite (or because of) the grain, which is a part of the visual fabric of the story. It's not excessive in the night scenes until the big violent finish, when it appears to be intentional. For more on the film's history on home video, check out the liner notes by VideoHound contributor Jim Olenski on the reverse side of the sleeve. —*MM*
Movie: 🎵🎵 **DVD:** 🎵🎵
Anchor Bay (Cat #DV11450, UPC #01313 145090). Widescreen (1.85:1) anamorphic. Dolby Digital Mono. $24.99. Keepcase. *LANG:* English. *FEATURES:* 28 chapter links • Trailer • Liner notes by Jim Olenski.
1985 (R) 93m/C Billy Dee Williams, Tom Berenger, Jack Scalia, Melanie Griffith, Rae Dawn Chong, Joe Santos, Maria Conchita Alonso, Rossano Brazzi; **D:** Abel Ferrara; **W:** Nicholas St. John; **C:** James (Momel) Lemmo; **M:** Dick Halligan.

Fear Runs Silent

This is a strange movie that doesn't know if it is a "horrible beast in the forest eating teenagers" film, or a psychological thriller about the internal mental struggle of a sexually abused girl who is fighting the monsters that haunt her inner child. If they had stuck with the later plotline this could have been a really interesting, inventive film. However, in the end the filmmakers chose to fall on the soft cushy pillow of those who have come before them and we are left with a hodge-podge of a film that makes no sense from either viewpoint. The disc looks and sounds good but not great. —*CA*

Movie: 🎬 **DVD:** 🎬½

Artist View Entertainment (Cat #8107, UPC #039414581072). Full frame. $24.95. Keepcase. *LANG:* English (with reservations). *SUB:* Spanish. *FEATURES:* Cast Bios • Trailers.

1999 (R) 90m/C Stacy Keach, Billy Dee Williams, Dan Lauria, Bobby Jacoby, Suzanne Davis, Ethan Erickson, Elizabeth Low; *D:* Serge Rodnunsky; *W:* Serge Rodnunsky; *C:* Pierre Chemaly.

Fellini Satyricon

Fellini's episodic journey through pre-Christian pagan decadence is a surreal hell that's fetid, swollen, and about to burst. "What caused the decadence?" the film's Felliniesque poet asks. "Lust of money," he answers. Plot, however, is much less important than the images, and these are some of the strongest in a body of work that's filled with indelible images. The underground human hive destroyed by an earthquake, a huge seafaring barge in the snow, the temple of the hermaphrodite, the minotaur's city. On one level, it's a progression from darkness to light in a world filled with grotesques, suicide, dismemberment, impotence, and fart jokes. MGM has already distributed an excellent widescreen tape so this bare-bones DVD is not a huge improvement. A bit of very light snow crops up intermittently. There are no artifacts in the smoke that's used in almost every scene, but I'm such a fan of the film that I could have missed them. Though the English dubbed version is better than most and is recommended to those who really detest subtitles, the original Italian still sounds better. —*MM* **AKA:** Satyricon.

Movie: 🎬🎬🎬🎬 **DVD:** 🎬🎬🎬

MGM Home Entertainment (Cat #1001 740, UPC #027616860408). Widescreen (2.35:1) anamorphic. Dolby Digital Mono. $24.99. Keepcase. *LANG:* English; Italian. *SUB:* English; French; Spanish. *FEATURES:* 16 chapter links • Trailer.

1969 (R) 129m/C IT FR Martin Potter, Capucine, Hiram Keller, Salvo Randone, Max Born, Alain Cuny; *D:* Federico Fellini; *W:* Federico Fellini, Barnardino Zapponi; *C:* Giuseppe Rotunno; *M:* Nino Rota. *AWARDS:* NOM: Oscars '70: Director (Fellini).

Female Convict Scorpion— Jailhouse 41

According to Chris D.'s liner notes, this is the second in a series of Japanese exploitation films based on comic books. It's a tough-minded, extremely violent feminist prison melodrama. Forget the Philippine babes-behind-bars template. Our heroine Matsu (Meiko Kaji) takes on Terminator-like implacability as she refuses to knuckle under to inmates, warden, or guards. (The reasons behind her incarceration in a prison camp come from the first film.) Though the pace is slow, the static images of retribution are still shocking. The garish DVD image is better than

should be expected for a film of this age, budget, and intent. The mono sound has been heightened so that the gritty sound of a footstep on a stone floor takes on harsh intensity. —*MM* **AKA:** Joshuu Sasori—Dai 41 Sakkyobo.

Movie: 🎬🎬½ **DVD:** 🎬🎬½

Image Entertainment (Cat #ID8966VFDVD, UPC #014381896626). Widescreen (2:35:1) anamorphic. Dolby Digital Mono. $24.99. Snapper. *LANG:* Japanese. *SUB:* English. *FEATURES:* 12 chapter links • Liner notes by Chris D. • Theatrical trailer.

1972 89m/C JP Meiko Kaji, Kayoko Shiraishi, Fumio Watanabe, Hiroko Isayama; *D:* Shunya Ito; *W:* Shunya Ito, Hiro Matsuda, Norio Konami; *M:* Shinsuke Kikuchi.

Female Vampire

According to Tim Lucas's extensive liner notes, this DVD is the first time that Jess Franco's erotic horror film has been available in its intended form on home video. (Other versions with varying amounts of violence and sexual explicitness are available as *The Bare Breasted Contessa* and *Erotikill*.) It's a contemporary story with the Contessa Irina (Romay) living in a hotel and feeding on those who pass through. Though the film broke new ground in the amount of flesh exposed, it's tame and slow by more recent standards. The DVD was made from original elements that have been dinged up a bit. Compared to other Franco releases in this series, the image is about average; not as crisp as the best, but watchable. The material is recommended only to horror fans with an interest in the history of the genre. —*MM* **AKA:** Erotikill; The Loves of Irina; Les Avaleuses; The Bare Breasted Contessa.

Movie: 🎬🎬 **DVD:** 🎬🎬

Image Entertainment (Cat #ID9105BIDVD, UPC #014381910520). Widescreen (2.35:1) letterboxed. Mono. $24.99. Snapper. *LANG:* English; French. *FEATURES:* 12 chapter links • Alternate scenes from the *Erotikill* edition • Theatrical trailer.

1973 95m/C FR SP GE Lina Romay, Monica Swin, Jack Taylor, Alice Arno; *D:* Jess (Jesus) Franco; *C:* Jess (Jesus) Franco; *M:* Daniel White.

Femalien

A strange alien being, composed of pure light energy, travels to Earth and assumes corporal form (Taylor) so she can once again experience sexual pleasure. She sure does, in some enthusiastic soft-core scenes. Given the production values of this video premiere, the only advantage of disc over tape lies in accessibility and the extras, which are mostly advertisements for other Surrender Cinema products. —*MM*

Movie: 🎬🎬 **DVD:** 🎬🎬

Full Moon Pictures (Cat #8007, UPC #763 843800762). Full frame. $24.98. Keepcase. *LANG:* English. *FEATURES:* 18 chapter links • Surrender Cinema promotional materials.

1996 (R) 90m/C Vanessa Taylor, Jacqueline Lovell, Matt Schue; *D:* Cybil Richards,

David DeCoteau; *W:* Cybil Richards, David DeCoteau.

Femalien 2

Two aliens follow Kara (Taylor) to Earth to learn what she knows of humans' physical pleasure. The soft-core action isn't nearly as fresh or energetic as it was in the first film. The grainy DVD image is no different from tape and that's none too good. Pedestrian. —*MM*

Movie: 🎬½ **DVD:** 🎬½

Full Moon Pictures (Cat #8052). Full frame. $24.98. *LANG:* English. *FEATURES:* 18 chapter links • Trailers and promos.

1998 93m/C Vanessa Taylor, Debra Summers, Bethany Lorraine, Josh Edwards, Summer Leeds, Damian Wells; *D:* Cybil Richards, David DeCoteau; *W:* Cybil Richards, David DeCoteau; *C:* Gary Graver; *M:* Wayne Scott Joness.

Ferngully 2: The Magical Rescue

Evil Poachers (are there any good ones?) steal the baby animals from the enchanted rainforest, Ferngully. Fairy guy Pips and his pals, the Beetle Boys, head out to the human world to save their friends. Crysta and the other magical creatures stay behind to restore their forest after a devastating fire. Magic saves the day. Surprised? The head poacher is a poor rip-off of the McLeach character from the superior Disney flick *Rescuers Down Under.* The comedic bat, Batty Koda, voiced by Robin Williams in the first *Ferngully,* is voiced by a lackluster facsimile in this sequel. The clarity of the DVD reveals the flatness of the cheap animation. No-brainer dialogue, simple ideas, and tolerable music make this disc O.K. for very young viewers. Those over the age of 10 are not likely to be entertained for long. —*JAS*

Movie: 🎬 **DVD:** 🎬🎬🎬

CBS/Fox Video (Cat #ID9167CUDVD, UPC #014381916720). Full frame. $24.99. Snapper. *LANG:* English. *FEATURES:* 16 chapter links.

1997 (G) ?m/C

Fever Pitch

Paul (Firth) is a veteran English teacher at the British equivalent of an American high school. Sarah (Gemmell) is brand new. They take an immediate dislike to each other, but her friend predicts, "I've seen this movie. You're going to wind up shagging on the carpet." The problem is Paul's addiction to football (British soccer). The film flashes back and forth in time to explain his attraction to the game. The film was made for British television and so glossy production values are less important than character development. Reds tend to be fuzzy and night scenes lack fine detail. Image and sound are only a small step above VHS tape. —*MM*

Movie: 🎬🎬½ **DVD:** 🎬🎬

Trimark Home Video (Cat #7496D). Widescreen. Dolby Digital Stereo. $24.99.

Keepcase. *LANG:* English. *SUB:* English; French; Spanish. *FEATURES:* 24 chapter links.
1996 (R) 103m/C *GB* Colin Firth, Ruth Gemmell, Neil Pearson, Mark Strong, Holly Aird, Ken Stott, Stephen Rea, Lorraine Ashbourne; *D:* David Evans; *W:* Nick Hornby; *C:* Chris Seager; *M:* Neil MacColl, Boo Hewerdine.

The Field

After an absence from the big screen, intense and nearly over-the-top Harris won acclaim as an iron-willed peasant fighting to retain a patch of Irish land he has tended all his life, now offered for sale to a wealthy American. His uncompromising stand divides his community in this glowing adaptation of John B. Keane's play, an allegory of Ireland's internal problems. Unfortunately, it is difficult to appreciate some of his performance because the muttered dialogue and thick accents are often incomprehensible. (This is a film that was meant for subtitles.) Image is only fair, with dark interiors that lack detail. Both flaws come from the original, not the transfer. —*MM*
Movie: 🎬🎬🎬½ *DVD:* 🎬½
Pioneer Entertainment (Cat #10113). Full frame. $24.98. Keepcase. *LANG:* English. *FEATURES:* 18 chapter links.
1990 (PG-13) 113m/C *GB* Richard Harris, Tom Berenger, John Hurt, Sean Bean, Brenda Fricker, Frances Tomelty, John Cowley, Sean McGinley, Jenny Conroy; *D:* Jim Sheridan; *W:* Jim Sheridan; *C:* Jack Conroy; *M:* Elmer Bernstein. *AWARDS: NOM:* Oscars '90: Actor (Harris).

Fiend without a Face

At an American military base deep in the Canadian wilderness, a series of horrific deaths stun the nearby village and rally the local townspeople against the installation, forcing the Army to investigate the fatalities and find an answer that will exonerate the base's atomic experiments conducted there. Eventually, the sinister truth emerges: a local scientist has been siphoning power off the reactor, creating an army of invisible thought-eating creatures or "mental vampires." A sudden burst of power gives them the visual form of motile brains complete with spinal stems and spindly antennae. The inevitable showdown between humanity and science run amok at a lone country house is a bounty of jolting stop-motion images and revolting sound effects. The script does a better-than-average job of sucking the viewer in, following events coolly and logically with minimal interjections about meddling with the unknown. Thompson, Parker, and Reeves give believability to their roles precisely because the whole affair, except for the gory finale, underplays in direction, script, and action. When the creatures appear, there is nothing subtle about them: they move with disquieting patience, strike indiscriminately, and when they take a bullet, the blood oozes and gurgles freely. While the source shows some blemishes, the transfer displays exceptional detail delineation and depth, down to the lobes (yuck!) on the creatures. Black levels are deep and solid, with occasional high contrast. The matting looks somewhere between a 1.66 and a 1.78 aspect ratio, with a complete lack of digital or compression artifacts. The Dolby Digital mono soundtrack plays back sharp and distortion-free, replicating every slurp and every crunch with unsettling accuracy. Extras are plentiful on the disc, analyzing the cultural, social, and historical factors that spawned the film. Weaver's Q&A commentary with Gordon draws out interesting ruminations including how the film became part of a Parliamentary discussion about the failure of censorship in England! Fun animated menus trumpet the different sections including "Exploitation!" for the publicity materials and "It Came From" for the illustrated essay examining *Fiend's* place within the science-fiction/horror genre. Vintage newspaper advertisements and eight lobby cards are highlighted in their own individual still-frame galleries. *Fiend* and four other horror/science-fiction movies from producer Gordon comprise the "Trailers" section, varying in visual quality from strikingly clean to low contrast to just plain beat-up. The curators at Criterion have done *Fiend* proud with this very respectful DVD, adding the title to a collection that houses *Amarcord, Brazil, Kwaidan,* and *The Third Man.* Go figure. —*EP*
Movie: 🎬🎬🎬 *DVD:* 🎬🎬🎬
Criterion Collection (Cat #92, UPC #1551501132). Widescreen (1.66) anamorphic. Dolby Digital Mono. $39.95. Keepcase. *LANG:* English. *CAP:* English. *FEATURES:* 15 chapter links • Commentary: executive producer Richard Gordon, genre writer Tom Weaver • Illustrated essay on British sci-fi/horror films • Theatrical trailers from Gordon films • Rare photographs and ephemera with commentary • Vintage advertisements and lobby cards.
1958 77m/B Marshall Thompson, Kim Parker, Terence (Terry) Kilburn, Michael Balfour, Gil Winfield, Shane Cordell, Kynaston Reeves; *D:* Arthur Crabtree; *W:* Herbert J. Leder; *C:* Lionel Banes; *M:* Buxton Orr.

Fight for the Title

Please see review of *Great Boxing Movies.*
Movie: 🎬🎬
1957 30m/C Michael Landon, George Brenlin; *D:* Eric Kenton.

The Fighter

Please see review of *Great Boxing Movies.*
AKA: The First Time.
Movie: 🎬🎬🎬
1952 78m/B Richard Conte, Vanessa Brown, Lee J. Cobb, Frank Silvera, Roberta Haynes, Hugh Sanders, Claire Carleton, Martin Garralaga; *D:* Herbert Kline; *W:* Herbert Kline, Aben Kandel; *C:* Floyd Crosby, James Wong Howe; *M:* Vicente Gomez.

The Filth and the Fury

British punk anarchists The Sex Pistols get their documentary due. Combines new and old footage and interviews of the (surviving) band members. Even though John "Johnny Rotten" Lydon's face is always in the shadows, you can hear the tears as he emotionally talks about ex–band mate Sid Vicious, who died from a heroin overdose. Director Temple previously covered the group in 1980's *The Great Rock 'n' Roll Swindle,* which was told from the viewpoint of their former manager, Malcolm McLaren. Hey, this is punk rock; even if the image quality on the disc totally sucked (which it doesn't), it would still be worth adding to the collection. As it is, it appears that the various source materials are presented accurately with just about all the elements being, at the very least, watchable. The sound is adequate if not spectacular. As interesting as *The Filth and the Fury* itself is the documentary "Un-defining Punk" (which is also included on the disc) in which several now middle-aged New York Punkers provide real insight into what was really going on in the late '70s punk rock scene. —*JO*
Movie: 🎬🎬🎬 *DVD:* 🎬🎬🎬
New Line Home Video (Cat #N5086, UPC #79404350862). Widescreen (1.85:1) anamorphic. Stereo. $24.98. Snapper. *LANG:* English. *SUB:* English. *CAP:* English. *FEATURES:* 20 chapter links • Theatrical trailer • Documentary: "Un-defining Punk" • Commentary: Julien Temple.
1999 (R) 105m/C *GB D:* Julien Temple.

Final Destination

Teenager Alex (Sawa) predicts that a plane filled with classmates will explode. It does but he and some others manage to make it off the plane beforehand. Things get interesting (and a little philosophical) when the survivors start dying. Seems Death feels cheated and is getting even. Typical body count slasher genre gets a twist from the machinations of fate. A film full of dark scenes, oodles of vividly red blood, and that big plane explosion, all presented without flaw. No grain, no bleed (except the intentional gory stuff), and no artifacts. The sound is all it should be and every crash and explosion can be felt throughout the house. There are two main commentary tracks with the first by director Wong, his co-writers, and his editor supplying tons of technical info, and the second featuring several of the actors having a good time as they anecdotally talk about their experience. Walker's ominous score is provided on an isolated track where she also supplies a third commentary (this one's about the music) during lulls in the music. The short documentary "A Look at Test Screenings" is as interesting as the film itself to those interested in the industry. It details the significant changes that the story went through, including a new $2 million ending, after the first audiences saw the film. Based on interviews with New Line studio executives, it's a telling look at the relationship between art and commerce in the movie business. —JO/MM

Movie: 🎵🎵🎵 **DVD:** 🎵🎵🎵🎵

New Line Home Video (Cat #N5061, UPC #794043506123). Widescreen (1.85:1) anamorphic. Dolby Digital 5.1; Dolby Surround. $24.98. Snapper. *LANG:* English. *SUB:* English. *CAP:* English. *FEATURES:* 19 chapter links ✷ Theatrical trailer ✷ Deleted scenes and alternate ending ✷ Commentary: James Wong, Glen Morgan, James Coblentz, Jeffrey Reddick ✷ Commentary: Devon Sawa, Kerr Smith, Kristin Cloke, Chad E. Donella ✷ Documentaries: *Test screenings; Premonitions* ✷ Isolated music score with commentary by composer Shirley Walker ✷ Dual-layered RSDL.

2000 (R) 97m/C Devon Sawa, Ali Larter, Kristen (Kristin) Cloke, Daniel Roebuck, Roger Guenveur Smith, Chad E. Donella, Seann William Scott, Tony Todd, Kerr Smith, Amanda Detmer; *D:* James Wong; *W:* Glen Morgan, James Wong, Jeffrey Reddick; *C:* Robert McLachlan; *M:* Shirley Walker.

Final Payback

A cast of faded TV stars long since past their prime time (Richard Grieco of *21 Jump Street,* Corbin Bernsen of *L.A. Law,* Martin Kove of *Cagney and Lacey,* Priscilla Barnes of *Three's Company*) collect their paychecks for this ineptly directed thriller that leaves no direct-to-video cliché unturned. Grieco stars as an ex-cop who finds himself "pushed over the fence" after he is framed for the murder of the police chief's wife. Gee, you think the police chief himself (B-movie vet John Saxon) may be involved in the conspiracy? No nudity and only one car explosion. Why bother? Considering the production values, the DVD transfer is adequate. —DL

Movie: woof **DVD:** woof

York Entertainment (Cat #929, UPC #5072 309293). Full frame. DTS Digital Surround; 5.1 Surround. $14.98. Keepcase. *LANG:* English. *SUB:* Spanish. *FEATURES:* Filmographies ✷ Trailers ✷ 25 chapter links.

1999 102m/C Richard Grieco, Corbin Bernsen, Martin Kove, Priscilla Barnes, John Saxon; *D:* Art Camacho.

Final Voyage

Die Hard on an ocean liner with a few computer effects attempting to re-create *Titanic.* Ignore the plot—terrorists led by Ice-T taking over the USS *Britannica*—and listen to the cheeky commentary track by director Jim Wynorski and star Claudia Christian. It's way more fun than the movie itself. As she says, this one's about "action and mammary glands." When our commentators are not wandering far afield, as they often do when the pace lags, as it often does, they point out continuity errors and sound like they're having a grand time. Otherwise, image is equal to tape. —MM

Movie: 🎵🎵 **DVD:** 🎵🎵½

Artisan Entertainment (Cat #10588, UPC #012236105985). Full frame. Dolby Digital 5.1 Surround Stereo; Dolby Digital Stereo. $9.99. Keepcase. *LANG:* English. *CAP:* English. *FEATURES:* 20 chapter links ✷ Trailers ✷ Talent files ✷ Commentary: Jay Andrews and Claudia Christian.

1999 (R) 95m/C Ice-T, Dylan Walsh, Erika Eleniak, Claudia Christian, Ric(k) Ducommun; *D:* Jim Wynorski; *W:* Jim Wynorski, J. Everitt Morley; *C:* Ken Blakey; *M:* David Wurst, Eric Wurst.

Finding Forrester

Co-producer Sean Connery stars as a Salinger-esque writer who has retired to his Brooklyn apartment after early success. After some curious plot contortions, he becomes a mentor to young Jamal Wallace (Brown), who wants to write but is tempted by basketball and other more worldly ambitions. All of the expected heartstrings are tugged, though the two stars—particularly Brown in a terrific debut—handle their earnest roles extremely well. Disc is a faithful re-creation of Van Sant's muted color scheme and focus. Both are matched by a nicely understated score. —MM

Movie: 🎵🎵🎵 **DVD:** 🎵🎵🎵

Columbia Tristar Home Video (Cat #05989, UPC #043396059894). Widescreen anamorphic. Dolby Digital Surround Stereo; Dolby Digital Stereo. $24.95. Keepcase. *LANG:* English; French. *SUB:* English; French. *FEATURES:* 28 chapter links ✷ "Making of" featurette ✷ "Found: Rob Brown" featurette ✷ Deleted choir scenes ✷ Filmographies ✷ Trailers.

2000 (PG-13) 133m/C Anna Paquin, Sean Connery, Robert Brown, F. Murray Abraham, Busta Rhymes, April Grace, Michael Nouri; *D:* Gus Van Sant; *W:* Mike Rich; *C:* Harris Savides; *M:* Hal Willner.

Fire

Two sisters-in-law in New Delhi form a relationship of increasing intimacy, which eventually comes into conflict with strict Hindu culture. Radha (Azmi) is married to Ashok (Kharbanda), a video store clerk who has taken a vow of celibacy under the teachings of a scruffy swami. Sita (Das) is married to Ashok's brother Jatin (Jaaferi), who is openly having an affair with a Chinese-Canadian woman. As her frustration grows, the younger Sita acts on her attraction to Radha. A short film included on the disc examines the outrage and protest that Deepa Mehta's film sparked, and her reaction to it. Though much of the dialogue is in "Hinglish," English with occasional Hindi phrases, the film's emotions are completely understandable. On disc, the film lacks the polish and careful lighting of a Hollywood production, but the image appears to have been reproduced accurately. —MM

Movie: 🎵🎵🎵 **DVD:** 🎵🎵½

New Yorker Video (Cat #65300, UPC #717119653040). Widescreen (1.85:1) letterboxed. $29.95. Snapper. *LANG:* English.

1996 104m/C *CA* Shabana Azmi, Nandita Das, Kulbashan Kharbanda, Jaaved Jaaferi, Ranjit (Chaudry) Chowdhry, Kushal Rekhi; *D:* Deepa Mehta; *W:* Deepa Mehta; *C:* Giles Nuttgens; *M:* A.R. Rahman.

Fire over England

Young naval officer (Olivier) volunteers to spy at the Spanish court to learn the plans for the invasion of his native England and to identify the traitors among the English nobility. He arouses the romantic interest of his queen, Elizabeth I, one of her ladies, and a Spanish noblewoman who helps with his mission. Later he leads the fleet to victory over the huge Spanish armada. The first on-screen pairing of Olivier and Leigh is just one of the many virtues of this entertaining swashbuckler. The black-and-white photography is very good. Evidence of wear ranges between faint and heavy. Snow and breaks are apparent. Some static and wavering plagues the soundtrack. But don't let those dissuade you; this one's a winner. —MM

Movie: 🎵🎵🎵½ **DVD:** 🎵🎵½

Lumivision Corp. (Cat #298). Full frame. Mono. $19.95. Keepcase. *LANG:* English. *FEATURES:* 30 chapter links.

1937 81m/B *GB* Flora Robson, Raymond Massey, Laurence Olivier, Vivien Leigh, Leslie Banks, James Mason; *D:* William K. Howard; *W:* Clemence Dane, Sergei Nolbandov; *C:* James Wong Howe; *M:* Richard Addinsell.

Fireworks

Writer/director/star Kitano's work is an idiosyncratic mixture of drama, comedy, violence, and sentiment. Nishi (Kitano) is a tough police detective whose wife Miyuki (Kishimoto) is dying from leukemia. He's visiting her in the hospital when his partner Horibe (Osugi) is gunned down. Deciding to get justice on his own terms, Nishi quits the force and robs a bank. Kitano is an unusually visual director—those are his paintings in the film and art gallery extra—and DVD reproduces his striking approach with no significant flaws. The easy-to-read subtitles also translate signs, graffiti, and other important visual information. John Woo fans who haven't discovered this guy are the target audience. —MM **AKA:** Hana-Bi.

Movie: 🎵🎵🎵 **DVD:** 🎵🎵🎵

New Yorker Video (Cat #66600, UPC #717 119666040). Widescreen letterboxed. $29.95. Keepcase. *LANG:* Japanese. *SUB:* English. *FEATURES:* 5 chapter links ✷ 2 trailers ✷ Gallery ✷ Talent files ✷ Behind-the-scenes featurette.

1997 103m/C *JP* Takeshi "Beat" Kitano, Kayoko Kishimoto, Ren Osugi, Susumu Terajima, Tetsu Watanabe; *D:* Takeshi "Beat" Kitano; *W:* Takeshi "Beat" Kitano; *C:* Hideo Yamamoto; *M:* Joe Hisaishi. *AWARDS: NOM:* Ind. Spirit '99: Foreign Film.

The Firing Line

A Central American government hires a mercenary rebel-buster (Brown) to squash

insurgents. Everything's great until he agrees with the rebels' cause and trains them to fight. The indefatigable Shannon Tweed is along for window dressing. Video premiere lives up to its generic title. Bare-bones DVD is no improvement whatsoever over VHS tape. —*MM*
Movie: ♫½ **DVD:** ♫♫
Tapeworm Video Distributors (Cat #313). Full frame. $19.95. Keepcase. *LANG:* English. *FEATURES:* 15 chapter links.
1991 93m/C Reb Brown, Shannon Tweed, Michael Monty, Kathlena Marie, Melvin Davidson, Carl Terry, Andy Jacobson; **D:** John Gale; **W:** John Gale, Sonny Sanders; **C:** Carl Sommers; **M:** Martia Manuel.

The First 9 1/2 Weeks
Prequel to *9 1/2 Weeks* finds investor Matt Wade (Mercurio) trying to close the biggest deal of his career with eccentric New Orleans businessman Francois Dubois (McDowell) while engaging in some kinky tricks with the man's wife (Bellar). It's familiar erotic thriller material that might look a degree better on disc than on VHS tape, but only that. —*MM*
Movie: ♫½ **DVD:** ♫♫
Studio Home Entertainment (Cat #7085). Full frame. Dolby Digital Stereo. $24.95. Keepcase. *LANG:* English. *SUB:* Spanish. *FEATURES:* 18 chapter links • Talent files • Trailer.
1998 (R) 99m/C Paul Mercurio, Clara Bellar, Malcolm McDowell, Frederic Forrest, Dennis Burkley, James Black, Anna Jacyszyn, William Keane, Richard Durden; **D:** Alexander Wright; **W:** Alexander Wright; **C:** John Tarver; **M:** Norman Orenstein.

First Spaceship on Venus
In 1985 (as imagined in 1960) eight scientists from various countries set out for Venus and find the remains of an advanced civilization that perished because of nuclear weapons. Curious film combines elements of a conventional space opera with serious anti-nuclear ideas. On DVD, image and sound are both very good for a genre piece of this age. A few minor nicks are visible within the supersaturated Technicolor image, and the clear sound makes the bad dubbing even more enjoyable. —*MM* **AKA:** Der Schweigende Stern; Milczaca Gwiazda.
Movie: ♫♫½ **DVD:** ♫♫½
Image Entertainment (Cat #ID8709CO DVD, UPC #014381870923). Widescreen (2.35:1) letterboxed. Dolby Digital Mono. $24.99. Snapper. *LANG:* English. *FEATURES:* 17 chapter links • Trailer.
1960 78m/C GE PL Yoko Tani, Oldrich Lukes, Ignacy Machowski, Julius Ongewe, Michal Postnikow, Kurt Rackelmann, Gunther Simon, Tang-Hua-Ta, Lucyna Winnicka; **D:** Kurt Maetzig; **C:** Joachim Hasler.

The First to Go
Impulsive Adam (Galligan) is the first of his crowd to get engaged. His four best

friends don't approve and decide to change his mind during their annual Catalina vacation. But his new fiancée Carrie (Holloman) decides to come along, too. Very similar material has been the basis for several recent comedies and this is about par for the course. DVD image is identical to tape; sound is worse. An intrusively loud but otherwise mediocre rock soundtrack necessitates near constant volume adjustment to understand the dialogue and keep the score from cracking the plaster. —*MM*
Movie: ♫♫ **DVD:** ♫♫
MTI Home Video (Cat #1057DVD, UPC #039414510577). Full frame. $24.95. Keepcase. *LANG:* English. *SUB:* Spanish. *FEATURES:* 20 chapter links • Talent files • Previews.
1997 (PG-13) 91m/C Zach Galligan, Laurel Holloman, Mark Harmon, Corin "Corky" Nemec, Steve Parlavecchio, Jennifer Jostyn, Lisanne Falk; **D:** John Jacobs.

The Fisher King
In derelict-infested Manhattan, Jack (Bridges), a down-and-out radio talk show host, meets Parry (Williams), a crazed vagabond who's obsessed with medieval history and the search for the holy grail. The two share an event in their past that might hold the key to their mutual redemption. It's a curious tale, alternately fascinating and infuriating, and that makes the lack of a director's commentary track a glaring omission. The often busy and difficult image is handled without any serious problems. Likewise, the sound is accurate but unimpressive. —*MM*
Movie: ♫♫♫ **DVD:** ♫♫½
Columbia Tristar Home Video (Cat #70619). Widescreen (1.85:1) anamorphic. Dolby Digital Surround Stereo. $14.95. Keepcase. *LANG:* English. *SUB:* English. *FEATURES:* 28 chapter links.
1991 (R) 138m/C Robin Williams, Jeff Bridges, Amanda Plummer, Mercedes Ruehl, Michael Jeter, Harry Shearer, John de Lancie, Kathy Najimy, David Hyde Pierce; **D:** Terry Gilliam; **W:** Richard LaGravenese; **C:** Roger Pratt; **M:** George Fenton. *AWARDS:* Oscars '91: Support. Actress (Ruehl); Golden Globes '92: Actor—Mus./Comedy (Williams), Support. Actress (Ruehl); L.A. Film Critics '91: Actress (Ruehl); *NOM:* Oscars '91: Actor (Williams), Art Dir./Set Dec., Orig. Screenplay, Orig. Score.

Fist of the North Star
Legendary warrior Kenshiro (Daniels) returns from the grave to avenge the death of his father (McDowell) and restore his North Star clan. He must battle the evil Lord Shin (Mandylor) and his henchmen in a post-apocalyptic future. This is the live action version of an animated feature, both based on the comic book. With intermittent white flecks, the full-frame image is seldom much better than good. It's only a modest improvement over VHS tape. —*MM*

Movie: ♫♫½ **DVD:** ♫♫½
Winstar Home Entertainment (Cat #5139). Full frame. Dolby Digital Surround Stereo. $24.98. Keepcase. *LANG:* English. *FEATURES:* 8 chapter links • Production credits • Filmographies and awards.
1995 (R) 90m/C Gary Daniels, Costas Mandylor, Christopher Penn, Julie Brown, Malcolm McDowell, Melvin Van Peebles, Isako Washio; **D:** Tony Randel; **W:** Tony Randel; **C:** Jacques Haitkin; **M:** Christopher Stone.

Five Dolls for an August Moon
A group of investment speculators try to talk scientist Gerry Farrell (Berger) into selling them the rights to a new formula, while at a wild weekend retreat on an isolated island. As the competitors try to cheat one another with secret bids, Farrell seems disinterested, and tempers rise with the stakes. The wives and girlfriends along for the fun and games feel the tension as their men stray, or try to get them to use sex to close a deal. But once the murders begin, the possibility of anyone trusting anyone is left far behind. Allegedly a professional assignment given Bava with just two days' notice, the film is a fair murder mystery in which even this director's visual tricks can't sustain interest. The cast of connivers is interchangeable and hard to keep straight, and in some cases more easily identifiable by their now-hideous 1970 fashions than their faces. This is one of the better-looking discs in Image Entertainment's Mario Bava Collection. The widescreen (but not enhanced) image is brightly colored and free of most wear, and the only real dirt on view would seem to be built-into the optical titles. Having an Italian language track with removable English titles, and an English dub track to choose from, covers all preferences. —*GE*
Movie: ♫♫ **DVD:** ♫♫♫
Image Entertainment (Cat #ID0736IXDVD, UPC #014381073621). Widescreen (1.85:1) letterboxed. Dolby Digital Mono. $24.98. Snapper. *LANG:* Italian; English. *SUB:* English. *FEATURES:* Liner notes by Tim Lucas • Isolated music and effects track • Trailers.
1970 78m/C IT William Berger, Ira von Furstenberg, Edwige Fenech, Howard (Renato Rossini) Ross, Helena Ronee, Teodoro Corra, Ely Galleani, Edith Meloni, Mauro Bosco, Maurice Poli; **D:** Mario Bava; **W:** Mario di Nardo; **C:** Antonio Rinaldi; **M:** Pierro Umiliani.

Five Easy Pieces
Nicholson's superb acting brings to life this character study of a talented musician who has given up a promising career and now works on the oil rigs. After 20 years, he returns home to attempt one last communication with his dying father and perhaps, reconcile himself to his fear of failure and desire for greatness. Black, Anspach, and Bush create especial-

ly memorable characters. Visually, this is a great DVD transfer. With the exception of a couple of jittery scenes (which are in the film itself) where there are slight artifacts, the image is sharp and near perfect. Just one look at Struthers's exuberant sex scene shows how accurate the fleshtones are. The sound is a bit disappointing, not because it's mono, but because there is some slight wow and flutter to it. It would also have been nice to have had some supplemental features to go along with this contemporary American classic. Still, a must-have for the collection. —JO

Movie: 🎬🎬🎬🎬 **DVD:** 🎬🎬🎬
Columbia Tristar Home Video (Cat #09659, UPC #043396096592). Widescreen (1.85:1) anamorphic; full frame. Mono. $14.95. Keepcase. *LANG:* English. *SUB:* English; Spanish; Portuguese; Chinese; Korean; Thai. *CAP:* English. *FEATURES:* 28 chapter links • Theatrical trailer • Talent files • Production notes.
1970 (R) 98m/C Jack Nicholson, Karen Black, Susan Anspach, Lois Smith, Billy Green Bush, Fannie Flagg, Ralph Waite, Sally Struthers, Helena Kallianiotes, Richard Stahl, Lorna Thayer; **D:** Bob Rafelson; **W:** Adrien (Carole Eastman) Joyce, Bob Rafelson; **C:** Laszlo Kovacs. *AWARDS:* Golden Globes '71: Support. Actress (Black), Natl. Bd. of Review '70: Support. Actress (Black); N.Y. Film Critics '70: Director (Rafelson), Film, Support. Actress (Black); Natl. Soc. Film Critics '70: Support. Actress (Smith); *NOM:* Oscars '70: Actor (Nicholson), Picture, Story & Screenplay, Support. Actress (Black).

The Five Senses

Five urbanites are linked by a missing child and their physical senses. Massage therapist Ruth (Rose) is losing her sense of touch; cake baker Rona (Parker) has an impaired sense of taste; house-cleaner Robert (MacIvor) believes that his acute sense of smell will lead to love; ophthalmologist Richard (Volter) is losing his hearing; and teenager Rachel (Litz) is drawn into spying games (sight) via a voyeur. It's surprisingly accessible given the complex construct. Each story is warm, witty, and well-acted. Recommended to fans of *The Red Violin* and *Exotica*. On disc, the image is so sharp that fine textures are clearly visible. The sound isn't overpowering but it has similar depth and complexity. Highly recommended. —MM
Movie: 🎬🎬🎬½ **DVD:** 🎬🎬🎬½
New Line Home Video (Cat #N5157, UPC #794043515729). Widescreen (1.85:1) anamorphic; full frame. Dolby Digital Surround Stereo. $24.98. Snapper. *LANG:* English; French. *SUB:* English. *FEATURES:* 20 chapter links • Talent files • Trailer • DVD-ROM features.
1999 105m/C CA Mary-Louise Parker, Phillipe Volter, Gabrielle Rose, Daniel MacIvor, Molly Parker, Pascale Bussieres, Marco Leonardi, Brendan Fletcher, Nadia Litz; **D:** Jeremy Podeswa; **W:** Jeremy Podeswa; **C:** Gregory Middleton; **M:** Alex Pauk, Alexina Louie. *AWARDS:* Genie '99:

Director (Podeswa); Toronto-City '99: Canadian Feature Film; *NOM:* Genie '99: Actor (MacIvor), Actress (Parker), Cinematog., Film, Screenplay.

The 5000 Fingers of Dr. T

In Dr. Seuss's first live-action movie, young Bart (Rettig) dreams of a fantastic world where the evil Dr. Terwilliger (Conried) holds hundreds of boys captive in his castle and forces them to take piano lessons. Worse yet, he's got Bart's mom (Healy) and wants her to marry him! The rollerskating twins connected at the beard are a visual highlight. The film has always been dim and grainy and the DVD is no exception. Only the extras—including a cartoon that's a bit of an "Easter egg" (click on the icon of Gerald McBoing-Boing)—differentiate disc from tape. —MM
Movie: 🎬🎬🎬 **DVD:** 🎬🎬
Columbia Tristar Home Video (Cat #058 36, UPC #043396058361). Full frame. Dolby Digital Mono. $24.99. Keepcase. *LANG:* English; French; Spanish. *SUB:* English; French; Spanish. *FEATURES:* Trailers • 26 chapter links • Cartoon "Gerald McBoing-Boing's Symphony."
1953 (G) 88m/C Peter Lind Hayes, Mary Healy, Tommy Rettig, Hans Conried, Noel Cravat; **D:** Roy Rowland; **W:** Theodore "Dr. Seuss" Geisel, Allan Scott; **C:** Franz Planer; **M:** Frederick "Friedrich" Hollander, Hans J. Salter. *AWARDS: NOM:* Oscars '53: Scoring/Musical.

Flash Gordon: Space Soldiers

This dual-layer disc contains all 13 episodes of the Buster Crabbe/Charles Middleton *Flash Gordon* serial from Chapter 1, "The Planet of Peril" to 13, "Rocketing to Earth." Although some defects are visible in the film print, the transfer is generally clean. Occasional registration problems cause the image to jitter slightly, but considering the film's age, the quality of the material on this DVD is quite amazing. Audio sounds fine, given the technical limitations and aging of these episodes. Some distortion is evident but the noise floor is surprisingly low, bringing the oftentimes frantically entertaining episodes back to full life. —GH
Movie: 🎬🎬🎬 **DVD:** 🎬🎬🎬
Image Entertainment (Cat #8961). Full frame. Dolby Digital Mono. $29.99. Snapper. *LANG:* English.
1936 245m/B Buster Crabbe, Jean Rogers, Frank Shannon, Charles Middleton, Priscilla Lawson, Jack Lipson, Basil Dickey, Ella O'Neill, George Plympton; **D:** Frederick Stephani; **W:** Frederick Stephani; **C:** Jerome Ash, Richard Fryer.

Flashfire

The torching of an apartment building and the murder of a cop seem unrelated until troubled detective Jack Flinder (Zane) becomes involved. Soon, he and murder

witness Lisa (Minter) are on the run from the arsonists and crooked police. The bare-bones disc is essentially identical to VHS tape. —MM
Movie: 🎬🎬½ **DVD:** 🎬🎬
Trimark Home Video (Cat #7047). Full frame. Stereo. $14.99. Keepcase. *LANG:* English. *FEATURES:* Trailer • 11 chapter links.
1994 (R) 88m/C Billy Zane, Kristin Minter, Louis Gossett Jr.; **D:** Elliot Silverstein; **W:** John Warren, Dan York; **C:** Albert J. Dunk; **M:** Sylvester Levay.

Flawless

Former New York cop Walt Koontz (De Niro) lives across the hall from nosily outrageous drag queen Rusty (Hoffman). The odd couple have a mutual animosity that's put to the test when Walt suffers a stroke and his doctor recommends that he take singing lessons to help him recover the ability to speak. He makes an offer to Rusty who needs the cash and before long they're bonding. Virtually free of defects, the DVD transfer is clean and mostly without grain, and nicely restores the atmospheric camerawork and lighting of the movie. Colors are strong and finely delineated without oversaturation or bleeding. The audio is well integrated and dialogue is always understandable. —GH/MM
Movie: 🎬🎬½ **DVD:** 🎬🎬½
MGM Home Entertainment (Cat #9084 02). Widescreen (1.85:1) anamorphic. Dolby Digital 5.1 Surround Stereo; Dolby Digital Surround Stereo. $24.98. Keepcase. *LANG:* English; Spanish. *SUB:* French; Spanish. *FEATURES:* Theatrical trailer.
1999 (R) 111m/C Robert De Niro, Philip Seymour Hoffman, Barry Miller, Chris Bauer, Skipp Sudduth, Wanda De Jesus, Daphne Rubin-Vega, Rory Cochrane; **D:** Joel Schumacher; **W:** Joel Schumacher; **C:** Declan Quinn; **M:** Bruce Roberts. *AWARDS: NOM:* Screen Actors Guild '99: Actor (Hoffman).

Fled

Charles Piper (Fishburne) and Luke Dodge (Baldwin) are combative prison escapees who need to find a stash of cash in Atlanta and a computer disk that could save them from both the Cuban mob and the cops. Bombshell Cora (Hayek) decides to help the duo and tries to get steamy with Piper. Lots of chases and shooting; not much sense. The climactic battle takes place in a sightseeing gondola at Georgia's Stone Mountain. The image is very good; Surround sound ranges between good and very good. —MM
Movie: 🎬🎬 **DVD:** 🎬🎬½
MGM Home Entertainment (Cat #906 278). Widescreen anamorphic. Dolby Digital 5.1 Surround Stereo. Keepcase. *LANG:* English; French. *SUB:* French. *FEATURES:* Trailer • 44 chapter links.
1996 (R) 98m/C Laurence "Larry" Fishburne, Stephen Baldwin, Salma Hayek, Will Patton, Robert John Burke; **D:** Kevin Hooks; **W:** Preston A. Whitmore II; **C:** Matthew F. Leonetti; **M:** Graeme Revell.

Flesh Gordon 2: Flesh Gordon Meets the Cosmic Cheerleaders

Emperor Wang (Hunt) threatens the universe with his powerful Impotence Ray. Flesh (Murdocco), Dale (Kelly), and Dr. Flexi Jerkoff (Travis) do battle with a belt of farting asteroids and other weirdos. Director Ziehm delivers this one on a frayed shoestring of less than $1 million, but manages to improve on the visual quality of the original. The scatological humor is the basis for this "unrated" version. Is it the added clarity of DVD that makes the costumes and sets look so much sillier, or has that always been true? Whatever the case, image appears a bit sharper than tape. —MM
Movie: ♪♪½ **DVD:** ♪♪½
New Concorde (Cat #NH2488UD, UPC #736991648890). Full frame. Stereo. $19.98. Keepcase. *LANG:* English. *FEATURES:* 24 chapter links • Trailers • Thumbnail bios.
1990 98m/C *CA* Vince Murdocco, Tony Travis, William Dennis Hunt, Robyn Kelly, Morgan Fox, Melissa Mounds; **D:** Howard Ziehm; **W:** Howard Ziehm; **C:** Danny Nowak.

The Flintstones in Viva Rock Vegas

In a prequel to the 1994 film, a young Fred (Addy) and his best pal Barney (Baldwin) take their girlfriends Wilma (Johnson) and Betty (Krakowski) on a would-be romantic weekend to Rock Vegas. There's a whole lot going on, as runaway society girl Wilma is being wooed by playboy Chip Rockefeller (Gibson), Chip's trying to bankrupt and frame Fred, and the Great Gazoo (Cumming) is on hand to observe earthly mating habits. Everything is appropriately cartoonish, including the story and the acting. Unfortunately, the only ones who'll be entertained are the ones who are too young to remember the original series. The best thing about the film is the way it looks and the DVD delivers it fully intact to the home screen. Colors are exceptionally rich and vivid, and combined with the high (but not harsh) contrast, totally conveys the required live-action cartoon feel. The blacks are incredibly deep but that high contrast and very consistent brightness ensures that details are never lost in the shadows. The soundtracks are mixed nicely with the DTS sound being a bit cleaner on the low end. Both the DTS and the DD5.1 feature strong dynamics, full fidelity, and superb separation that comes into play both on the music mix and the surprisingly energetic Surround mix. —JO
Movie: ♪♪ **DVD:** ♪♪♪½
Universal Studios Home Video (Cat #20919, UPC #025192091926). Widescreen (1.85:1) anamorphic. Dolby Digital 5.1; DTS 5.1; Dolby Surround. $24.98. Keepcase. *LANG:* English; French. *CAP:* English. *FEATURES:* 18 chapter links • Theatrical trailer • Talent files • Production notes • "Making of" featurette.

2000 (PG) 90m/C Mark Addy, Kristen Johnston, Stephen Baldwin, Jane Krakowski, Thomas Gibson, Joan Collins, Alan Cumming, Harvey Korman, Alex Meneses; **D:** Brian Levant; **W:** Harry Elfont, Deborah Kaplan, Jim Cash, Jack Epps Jr.; **C:** Jamie Anderson; **M:** David Newman.

Floating

Teen Van's (Reedus) life is in shambles: father's disabled; mom's gone. He hangs with slackers and gets into trouble until he meets Doug (Lowe), who seems to have everything that Van lacks—athleticism, loving family, money. But there's a secret that turns out to be not so surprising. Neither is the conclusion. The full-frame image looks good, with only minor aliasing, but it's a slight improvement over tape. —MM
Movie: ♪♪ **DVD:** ♪♪♪½
Winstar Home Entertainment (Cat #FLV5260, UPC #720917526027). Full frame. $24.98. Keepcase. *LANG:* English. *FEATURES:* 16 chapter links • Filmographies • Production credits.
1997 91m/C Norman Reedus, Chad Lowe, Will Lyman, Jonathan Quint, Josh Marchette, Sybil Temchen; **D:** William Roth; **W:** William Roth; **C:** Wolfgang Held; **M:** David Mansfield.

The Florentine

A decaying steel town is home to a bar called The Florentine, its owner Whitey (Madsen), and the usual drinking denizens. But with profits sinking, Whitey may lose his livelihood. And then there's his sister Molly's (Madsen) problems. Her wedding to Frankie (Perry) is in jeopardy because of a con man (Belushi) and her ex-fiancé, Teddy (Sizemore), who's back in town. Despite having almost too many plot elements to keep track of, *The Florentine* remains a solid drama. The DVD manages to look only a slight bit better than its VHS counterpart. The image is a little sharper but there is a small amount of grain present throughout the disc. Colors are drab, most likely just a representation of the film itself since the fleshtones do appear fairly natural. The soundtrack delivers the dialogue well, but not much is demonstrated by the stereo mix. —JO
Movie: ♪♪♪ **DVD:** ♪♪
Monarch Home Video (Cat #7555, UPC #729352075550). Full frame. Stereo. $19.98. Keepcase. *LANG:* English. *FEATURES:* 24 chapter links.
1998 (R) 104m/C Michael Madsen, Virginia Madsen, Luke Perry, Tom Sizemore, James Belushi, Mary Stuart Masterson, Christopher Penn; **D:** Nick Stagliano.

Flowers in the Attic

Would-be horror/thriller is based on V.C. Andrews best-seller about four young siblings locked up in their family's old mansion by their grandmother (Fletcher) with their mother's (Tennant) selfish acquiescence. Chickenhearted, clumsy adaptation

skimps on the novel's trashier elements. The image is exceptionally grainy, but the transfer appears not to add any additional artifacts. Most viewers would be hard pressed to see or hear any difference from a widescreen tape. —MM
Movie: ♪½ **DVD:** ♪½
Anchor Bay (Cat #DV11325, UPC #01313 1132595). Widescreen (1.85:1) anamorphic. Dolby Digital Mono. $24.98. Keepcase. *LANG:* English. *CAP:* English. *FEATURES:* Trailer • 27 chapter links.
1987 (PG-13) 93m/C Victoria Tennant, Kristy Swanson, Louise Fletcher, Jeb Stuart Adams; **D:** Jeffrey Bloom; **W:** Jeffrey Bloom; **C:** Gil Hubbs; **M:** Christopher Young.

Fluke

Ghost meets *Beethoven* as Tom (Modine) is murdered in an arranged auto accident and is reincarnated as a newborn puppy. (No, the VideoHound is not making this up.) He returns to his wife and son (Travis and Pomeranc) to protect them from his evil former partner (Stoltz) and battles such puppy perils as cosmetic testing labs and dog catchers along the way. The same kids who are moved by the squishy sentimentality may find the scenes involving animal abuse troubling. Full-frame image and sound are a notch or two above videotape. —MM
Movie: ♪♪ **DVD:** ♪♪½
MGM Home Entertainment (Cat #1001601, UPC #027616859112). Full frame. Dolby Digital Surround; Mono. $24.99. Keepcase. *LANG:* English; French; Spanish. *SUB:* French; Spanish. *CAP:* English. *FEATURES:* Trailer • 16 chapter links.
1995 (PG) 96m/C Matthew Modine, Nancy Travis, Eric Stoltz, Max Pomeranc, Ron Perlman, Jon Polito, Bill Cobbs, Frederico Pacifici, Collin Wilcox-Paxton; **D:** Carlo Carlei; **W:** James Carrington, Carlo Carlei; **C:** Raffaele Mertes; **M:** Carlo Siliotto; **V:** Samuel L. Jackson.

The Fly / Return of the Fly

The historic, chillingly original '50s sci-fi tale about a hapless scientist experimenting with teleportation who accidentally gets anatomically confused with a housefly. Clavell's excellent script tells the tale in flashback, building the tension until the horror is revealed and wrapping things up with one of the most memorable endings in genre history. A true classic with much higher production values than most horror films of the era, and this 2.35:1 anamorphic transfer conveys the richness as no other home video transfer ever has (even Fox's own letterboxed laserdisc). Given the age of the film, the DVD rendering of *The Fly* is superb with excellent sharpness and colors that, though most likely faded since the original theatrical release, are fairly strong and enjoyable to look at. Source material damage is minimal and the only grain visible on the disc is from the original film stock. The transfer of the black-

and-white *Return of the Fly* is equally well done with excellent sharpness, deep blacks, and nicely graduated graytones. Some minor ghosting occasionally occurs around bright whites, but the film remains enjoyable to watch. Both films have been given the Surround treatment, which works much better with the original film than its sequel, for which the included mono track is preferable. —*JO*
Movie: 🦴🦴🦴 **DVD:** 🦴🦴🦴
20th Century Fox Home Entertainment (Cat #2000454, UPC #024543004547). Widescreen (2.35:1) anamorphic. Dolby Digital 4.0; Dolby Surround; Mono. $24.98. Keepcase. *LANG:* English; French. *SUB:* English; Spanish. *CAP:* English. *FEATURES:* 25 chapter links ▪ Theatrical trailer.
1958 94m/C David Hedison, Patricia Owens, Vincent Price, Herbert Marshall, Kathleen Freeman, Betty Lou Gerson, Charles Herbert; *D:* Kurt Neumann; *W:* James Clavell; *C:* Karl Struss; *M:* Paul Sawtell.

The Fly / The Fly 2

David Cronenberg's sensitive humanistic remake of the 1958 original is in some ways superior. Seth Brundle (Goldblum) experiments with teleportation and has his genetic code combined with a house-fly. The result is equally shocking and thought-provoking. The sequel is, expectedly, about half as good. On DVD, it's easy to see the difference in the amount of care and money that went into the two films. Where the first has a well-detailed image, even in the many dark scenes with their gray-brown color scheme, the second is not nearly as sharp. There is a slight increase in grain with some of the special effects shots, but that can be traced to the original elements. Limited Surround effects are used well. —*MM*
Movie: 🦴🦴½ **DVD:** 🦴🦴🦴½
20th Century Fox Home Entertainment (Cat #2000457, UPC #024543004578). Widescreen (1.85:1) anamorphic. Dolby Digital 5.1 Surround Stereo; Dolby Digital Surround. $24.98. Keepcase. *LANG:* English; French. *SUB:* English; Spanish. *FEATURES:* 24 chapter links ▪ Trailers.
1986 (R) 96m/C Jeff Goldblum, Geena Davis, John Getz, Joy Boushel, Les Carlson; *D:* David Cronenberg; *W:* David Cronenberg, Charles Edward Pogue; *C:* Mark Irwin; *M:* Howard Shore. *AWARDS:* Oscars '86: Makeup.

The Fly 2

Please see review for *The Fly / The Fly 2.*
Movie: 🦴½
1989 (R) 105m/C Eric Stoltz, Daphne Zuniga, Lee Richardson, John Getz, Harley Cross; *D:* Chris Walas; *W:* Ken Wheat, Frank Darabont, Mick Garris, Jim Wheat; *C:* Robin Vidgeon; *M:* Christopher Young.

The Flying Deuces / Utopia

Ollie's broken heart lands Laurel and Hardy in the Foreign Legion. The comic pair escape a firing squad only to suffer a plane crash that results in Hardy's reincarnation as a horse. The musical interlude with a Laurel soft shoe while Hardy sings "Shine On, Harvest Moon" is one of the film's highlights. A few light scratches mar a print that wasn't very crisp to begin with. Sound is about what you'd expect from a film this old. Title is available on a double feature with *Utopia.* —*MM* **AKA:** Flying Aces.
Movie: 🦴🦴🦴 **DVD:** 🦴½
Madacy Entertainment (Cat #99113, UPC #056775037192). Full frame. Dolby Digital Mono. $12.98. Keepcase. *LANG:* English. *FEATURES:* Stan Laurel thumbnail bio ▪ 8 chapter links ▪ Trivia ▪ Laurel and Hardy filmography.
1939 65m/B Stan Laurel, Oliver Hardy, Jean Parker, Reginald Gardiner, James Finlayson; *D:* Edward Sutherland; *W:* Ralph Spence, Charles R. Rogers, Harry Langdon, Alfred Schiller; *C:* Elmer Dyer, Art Lloyd; *M:* Leo Shuken, John Leopold.

The Flying Saucer

Russian and U.S. agents clash while searching for a flying saucer in Alaska. Mike (producer/director/co-writer/star Conrad) leads the good guys. Box copy claims that this is the first "flying saucer" movie, and one could argue that this is a prototype for *The X-Files.* The main flaw—a horribly discordant score—probably comes from the original. Minor registration problems and light dust and snow are evident, too. Overall, though, the film has been nicely preserved and could not be expected to look any better on disc. —*MM*
Movie: 🦴🦴½ **DVD:** 🦴🦴½
Image Entertainment (Cat #ID8711CODVD, UPC #014381871128). Full frame. Dolby Digital Mono. $24.99. Snapper. *LANG:* English. *FEATURES:* Trailer ▪ 12 chapter links.
1950 71m/B Mikel Conrad, Pat Garrison, Hanz von Teuffen; *D:* Mikel Conrad; *W:* Howard Irving Young, Mikel Conrad; *C:* Philip Tannura; *M:* Darrell Calker.

Flynn

Australian production details the eventful early years of the Tazmanian-born Errol Flynn (Pearce) before he becomes the swashbuckling hero of Hollywood. His sexual exploits get him kicked out of school and he makes his way as bum, gigolo, thief, and gold hunter. The full-frame image is no real improvement over VHS tape. Sound is distinctly better. —*MM* **AKA:** My Forgotten Man.
Movie: 🦴🦴 **DVD:** 🦴🦴
Vanguard International Cinema, Inc. (Cat #VF0008, UPC #658769000832). Full frame. $29.95. Keepcase. *LANG:* English. *FEATURES:* 10 chapter links.
1996 96m/C *AU* Guy Pearce, Claudia Karvan, Steven Berkoff; *D:* Frank Howson; *W:* Frank Howson; *C:* John Wheeler; *M:* Anthony Marinelli.

Flypaper

Parking-lot bigshot Marvin (Loggia) and his younger associate Jack (Brolly) help out junkie Natalie (Frost), who's being pressured by thuggish Bobby Ray (Sheffer), who has also kidnapped Dot (Liu). At the same time, a vengeful woman (Douglas) is getting the goods on her two-timing fiancé (McGinley). He and several other characters suffer horrible physical pain in this unstable comedy-drama. Writer/director Hoch mixes equal amounts of *Reservoir Dogs* and *Magnolia.* Results are definitely mixed. The too-talky film earns high marks for unpredictability, low marks for broad overacting. The full-frame DVD image is not much better than VHS tape with heavy aliasing evident in almost all bright daylight scenes. Stereo sound is acceptable. —*MM*
Movie: 🦴🦴½ **DVD:** 🦴🦴
Trimark Home Video (Cat #7365D, UPC #031398736523). Full frame. Dolby Digital Stereo. $24.99. Keepcase. *LANG:* English. *SUB:* English; French; Spanish. *FEATURES:* 30 chapter links.
1997 (R) 111m/C Robert Loggia, Sadie Frost, Craig Sheffer, Shane Brolly, Lucy Alexis Liu, James Wilder, Illeana Douglas, Talisa Soto, John C. McGinley; *D:* Klaus Hoch; *W:* Klaus Hoch; *C:* Jurgen Baum; *M:* Peter Manning Robinson.

Foolish Wives

Reconstruction of Erich Von Stroheim's lavish 1922 film concerns the corrupt practices of a counterfeit count (Stroheim) and his two mistresses, living a decadent existence on a villa near Monte Carlo. Posing as deposed Russian expatriates, they fund their parasitic existence by feeding off the wealthy but dazed throngs streaming into the gambling mecca. Per the legendary perfectionism of Stroheim, the film teems with details that reveal the moral ennui of a society confused and stunned by the devastation of the Great War. Stroheim's Count Karamzin is thoroughly despicable, whether using a hand mirror to spy on a woman undressing or comically rubbing on a hunchback's hump for good luck at the roulette wheel. Yet it was another Stroheim performance of depravity and sophistication that rightfully earned him the billing "The Man You Love to Hate!" because audiences could safely identify with his loathsome but imperious characters. Between painting the plot on so epic a canvas and watching Stroheim strut his oily stuff with such gleeful mastery, it's understandable that the first cut of the film ran over eight hours! The DVD contains the general release version that runs a little over two hours (a rendering that Stroheim complained was nothing but "bones."). Whenever watching silent movies, one must separate judging the transfer from its source. The disc does an excellent job in bringing an 80-year-old negative to the digital realm, but the master is plagued with blemishes, splices, breaks, and repaired negative shrinkage. The liner notes, incorporating both historical and technical facts, explain how some of the various processes employed to restore the original length affected image quality, like slowing down the projection speed by a third to extend scenes initially edited down to a few frames. Contrast varies widely, sometimes yielding moments of sharpness with quite a bit of detail, then sinking into an inky, muddy black-and-white image. The tinting in certain scenes (i.e. a golden hue to signify daytime, a bluish cast for night, etc.) sometimes washes out detail delineation. The Dolby Digital audio, consisting of a newly recorded piano accompaniment score by Philip Carli, is fine. —EP

Movie: ♫♫♫½ **DVD:** ♫♫♫
Image Entertainment (Cat #ID9414DS DVD, UPC #1438194142). Full frame. Dolby Digital Stereo. $24.99. Snapper. *LANG:* Silent. *FEATURES:* 12 chapter links.
1922 141m/B Erich von Stroheim, Mae Busch, Maud(e) (Ford) George, Cesare Gravina, Harrison Ford; *D:* Erich von Stroheim; *W:* Erich von Stroheim; *C:* William H. Daniels; *M:* Sigmund Romberg.

Footsteps

Reporter Jason Drake (Chapa) witnesses a murder and is romanced by the sultry photographer Amber (Lombard). Standard video thriller does have a serious angle concerning child abuse, but DVD presentation is undone by a grossly substandard image. Soft, grainy picture looks much worse than most cheaply produced videotapes. —MM **AKA:** Expose.
Movie: ♫♫ **DVD:** ♫
MTI Home Video (Cat #1072, UPC #03941 4510720). Full frame. $19.98. Keepcase. *LANG:* English. *SUB:* Spanish. *FEATURES:* 20 chapter links • Thumbnail bios • Previews.
1998 (R) 93m/C Damian Chapa, Karina Lombard, Tom Schanley, Maria Conchita Alonso, Steven Schub, Sandra Bernhard, Tippi Hedren; *D:* Daphna Edwards; *W:* Daphna Edwards; *C:* David J. Miller; *M:* Alex Wurman.

For Hire

Suffering with cancer and with a pregnant wife, Chicago cabbie Mitch Lawrence (Lowe) is desperate for money. He agrees to kill an associate of famous writer Lou Webber (Mantegna) for $50,000. From that premise, the thriller takes some inventive twists. Cast, script, and image are above average. Though the full-frame image is only a slight improvement over VHS tape, the disc is worth watching. —MM
Movie: ♫♫½ **DVD:** ♫♫½
Pioneer Entertainment (Cat #10249). Full frame. Dolby Digital Surround Stereo. $19.98. Keepcase. *LANG:* English. *FEATURES:* 19 chapter links • Trailer.
1998 96m/C Rob Lowe, Joe Mantegna, Dominic Philie, Bronwen Black; *D:* Jean Pellerin; *M:* Alan Reeves.

For Love of the Game

The baseball glove has long been a velvet one for Costner. In his third baseball outing, he moderately scores as veteran Detroit Tigers pitcher Billy Chapel, facing a crossroad in his professional and personal life. In 1-2-3 manner, he learns that the team he's played on for 20 years has been sold, the new owners want to trade him, and his longtime girlfriend, Jane (Preston), is dumping him prior to an important game with the Yankees. Magically, he's this close to pitching a perfect game, as the last five years of his life flash before him. Sudsy, predictable romance overshadows the game action, but harder-edged Raimi, with his own love for the game, injects some striking visual flair. Costner pitched a fit against the studio for editing out his infamous penis shot to insure a kid-friendly rating. The best supplemental Universal could have included on this DVD would have been a mini-movie of just the visually energetic baseball scenes with all the other B.S. cut out. The deleted scenes are fine, but offer nothing more than we've come to expect on a DVD release. The transfer is pretty sharp and colors are vibrant and accurate. During a few of the game sequences, the subwoofer and Surround tracks really kick in, making the viewer actually feel the frenzied stadium atmosphere. Most of the time there's mainly ambience for the Poledouris score and not much else. —JO
Movie: ♫♫½ **DVD:** ♫♫♫
Universal Studios Home Video (Cat #20684, UPC #025192068423). Widescreen (2.35:1) anamorphic. Dolby Digital 5.1; Dolby Surround. $26.98. Keepcase. *LANG:* English; French. *CAP:* English. *FEATURES:* 18 chapter links • Theatrical trailer • Deleted scenes • "Spotlight on Location" featurette • "The History of the Perfect Game" featurette • "On the Mound" trivia game.
1999 (PG-13) 137m/C Kevin Costner, Kelly Preston, John C. Reilly, Jena Malone, Brian Cox, J.K. Simmons, Bill Rogers, Vin Scully, Carmine D. Giovinazzo, Hugh Ross, Steve Lyons; *D:* Sam Raimi; *W:* Dana Stevens; *C:* John Bailey; *M:* Basil Poledouris. *AWARDS: NOM:* Golden Raspberries '99: Worst Actor (Costner).

For Love or Country: The Arturo Sandoval Story

After meeting one of his idols, American Dizzy Gillespie (Dutton), trumpeter Arturo Sandoval (co-producer Garcia) decides to leave Cuba, where the government tries to control his music. But defection is not easy. Though the fact-based film lacks intense narrative drive and suspense, it looks very good and the soundtrack is terrific. Production values are exceptional for a made-for-cable feature and DVD presents an image that ranges between very good and excellent. Surround sound is superb. —MM
Movie: ♫♫½ **DVD:** ♫♫♫
HBO Home Video (Cat #91769, UPC #026 359176920). Widescreen letterboxed. Dolby Digital 5.1 Surround Stereo; Dolby Digital Surround; Mono. $24.99. Snapper. *LANG:* English; Spanish. *SUB:* English; French; Spanish. *CAP:* English. *FEATURES:* 15 chapter links • Talent files • Behind-the-scenes featurette.
2000 (PG-13) 120m/C Andy Garcia, Mia Maestro, Charles S. Dutton, David Paymer, Gloria Estefan, Tomas Milian, Freddy Rodriguez, Jose Zuniga, Steven Bauer, Fionnula Flanagan, Michael O'Hagan; *D:* Joseph Sargent; *W:* Timothy J. Sexton; *C:* Donald M. Morgan; *M:* Arturo Sandoval.

For Pete's Sake

Early on in his commentary, director Peter Yates admits that this little comedy was conceived as a vehicle for a young Barbara Streisand to show that she could make a movie without singing. Then she did the theme song. It's a frivolous comedy about Henrietta's (Babs) efforts to raise enough money to put her husband (Sarrazin) through school. Those involve loan sharks, a madame, and cattle rustling in New York City. The well-preserved image looks fine for a film of this age. —MM **AKA:** July Pork Bellies.
Movie: ♫♫½ **DVD:** ♫♫♫
Columbia Tristar Home Video (Cat #05814, UPC #043396058149). Widescreen (1.85:1) anamorphic; full frame. Dolby Digital Mono. $19.95. Keepcase. *LANG:* English; French. *SUB:* English; French; Spanish; Portuguese; Chinese; Korean; Thai. *FEATURES:* 28 chapter links • Commentary: Peter Yates • Talent files • Trailers.
1974 (PG) 90m/C Barbra Streisand, Michael Sarrazin, Estelle Parsons, William Redfield, Molly Picon; *D:* Peter Yates; *W:* Stanley Shapiro, Maurice Richlin; *C:* Laszlo Kovacs; *M:* Artie Butler.

For the Boys

Midler stars as Dixie Leonard, a gutsy singer-comedienne who hooks up with Eddie Sparks (Caan) to become one of America's favorite USO singing, dancing, and comedy teams. The movie spans 50 years and three wars and raises such issues as the blacklist and the role of politics in show business. Midler's performance is by far the strongest aspect of the film. Like the theatrical release, the DVD presents an image that is carefully calculated to a specific degree of softness. In the "present day" scenes, the lack of sharp focus camouflages the stars' "old" makeup. In the flashbacks, it makes for a mistily nostalgic past. Sound is better, emphasizing the musical numbers and the fine Dave Grusin score. —MM
Movie: ♫♫ **DVD:** ♫♫½
20th Century Fox Home Entertainment (Cat #2001377, UPC #024543013778). Widescreen (1.85:1) letterboxed. Dolby Digital 4.1 Surround Stereo; Dolby Digital Surround; Mono. $24.99. Keepcase. *LANG:* English; French. *SUB:* English; French. *FEATURES:* Trailers and TV spots • 18 chapter links.
1991 (R) 120m/C Bette Midler, James Caan, George Segal, Patrick O'Neal, Christopher Rydell, Arye Gross, Norman Fell, Rosemary Murphy, Dori Brenner, Bud

Yorkin, Jack Sheldon, Melissa Manchester, Brandon Call, Arliss Howard; **D:** Mark Rydell; **W:** Marshall Brickman, Neal Jimenez, Lindy Laub; **C:** Stephen Goldblatt; **M:** Dave Grusin. *AWARDS:* Golden Globes '92: Actress—Mus./Comedy (Midler); *NOM:* Oscars '91: Actress (Midler).

Forever Mine

Paul Schrader's curious erotic thriller is a riff on themes found in *Body Heat* and *Out of the Past*. In the 1970s, Alan (Fiennes) and Ella (Mol) had a white-hot affair that was broken up by her husband Mark (Liotta) in a particularly brutal way. Flash forward 14 years when Alan returns. If the plot doesn't completely hold together, Schrader tells the story beautifully. On his commentary track, he sticks mostly to technical matters—the use of colored gels, camera placement, and working with actors. DVD appears to be an accurate re-creation of an image that ranges between pastel softness, hard focus, and carefully diffused light. —MM
Movie: 🎬🎬🎬 **DVD:** 🎬🎬🎬
MGM Home Entertainment (Cat #100-1816, UPC #027616860866). Widescreen (2.35:1) anamorphic. Dolby Digital Surround Stereo. $24.99. Keepcase. *LANG:* English. *SUB:* English; French; Spanish. *FEATURES:* 24 chapter links ▪ Commentary: Paul Schrader.
1999 (R) 117m/C Joseph Fiennes, Ray Liotta, Gretchen Mol, Vincent Laresca; **D:** Paul Schrader; **W:** Paul Schrader; **C:** John Bailey; **M:** Angelo Badalamenti.

Forever Together

Thirteen-year-old Danny (Bryan Burke, *True Friends*), discovers that he is falling in love with his childhood friend, Julia (Michelle Trachtenberg, *Harriet the Spy*), and seeks the advice of a sax-playing cemetery apparition (Ralph Macchio). Diane Ladd does an odd turn as Burke's old-country/Italian grandmother, whose relationship with visions from the past neatly fall into place by film's end. Slight, feel-good family-targeted effort is populated by talented actors given little to do. Neither image nor sound is different from VHS tape. —RJT **AKA:** Can't Be Heaven.
Movie: 🎬🎬 **DVD:** 🎬🎬
A-PIX Entertainment Inc. (Cat #APX27832, UPC #783722703236). Full frame. Dolby Digital Stereo. $19.98. Keepcase. *LANG:* English. *SUB:* Spanish. *FEATURES:* 14 chapter markers ▪ Video trailer.
2000 (PG) 88m/C Michelle Trachtenberg, Rachel Ticotin, Ralph Macchio, Bryan Burke, Matt McCoy, Diane Ladd, Garry Marshall; **D:** Richard S. Friedman.

Forgotten Silver

Jackson's mockumentary finds the director and co-director Botes "discovering" the lost films of Colin McKenzie, a pioneering New Zealand filmmaker of the early 1900s. These include his epic *Salome*. The entire escapade is fiction, but

Leonard Maltin, Sam Neill, and Miramax honcho Harvey Weinstein are completely believable playing themselves. The humor is so good-natured that any criticism is pointless. And it's also pointless to criticize the quality of the DVD image since so much of the film is made of deliberately "distressed" footage, which is all the more enjoyable for its authentic quality. That said, to anyone not interested in the early days of movie making, the whole enterprise is pointless. —MM
Movie: 🎬🎬🎬 **DVD:** 🎬🎬½
First Run Features (Cat #FRF909549D, UPC #720229909549). Widescreen (1.66:1) letterboxed. $29.95. Keepcase. *LANG:* English. *FEATURES:* Deleted scenes ▪ Interviews with Jackson, Botes, cast, and crew ▪ Special effects test shots ▪ Commentary: director ▪ 9 chapter links.
1996 70m/C *NZ* Costa Botes, Sam Neill, Leonard Maltin, Harvey Weinstein, John O'Shea, Hannah McKenzie, Lindsay Shelton, Johnny Morris, Marguerite Hurst; **D:** Peter Jackson, Costa Botes; **W:** Peter Jackson, Costa Botes, Robert Sarkies; **C:** Alun Bollinger; **Nar:** Jeffrey Thomas.

Fort Apache, the Bronx

When this film was released, nobody realized how influential it would be, but virtually every TV cop show since—from *Hill St. Blues* to *NYPD Blue*—borrows liberally. Newman is at his understated best as Murphy, a plainclothes officer who goes up against every kind of criminal and crazy and, of course, his superiors in an attempt to maintain what order he can in a rough community. Artifacts are rife in panning shots of brickwork and rubble, but that's hardly a flaw given the bleak tone of the film. Sound is fine. —MM
Movie: 🎬🎬🎬 **DVD:** 🎬🎬½
HBO Home Video (Cat #90610, UPC #026 359061028). Widescreen letterboxed. $19.98. Snapper. *LANG:* English. *FEATURES:* 28 chapter links ▪ Talent files.
1981 (R) 123m/C Paul Newman, Ed Asner, Ken Wahl, Danny Aiello, Rachel Ticotin, Pam Grier, Kathleen Beller; **D:** Daniel Petrie; **W:** Heywood Gould; **C:** John Alcott; **M:** Jonathan Tunick.

42nd Street

During the depression, a Broadway musical producer (Baxter) faces numerous problems in his efforts to reach a successful opening night. Made in pre-code Hollywood, *42nd Street* is loaded with innuendo and is much grittier than later musicals choreographed by Berkeley would be, and as a result, seems far less dated while still retaining a campy charm. This Warner DVD is pretty amazing, especially when compared to the earlier home video versions of the film. Plenty of sharpness and detail, excellent contrast and brightness, and deep blacks with bright whites. The depth of field is excellent, making the elaborately staged numbers that much more impressive. The sound

has been cleaned up quite a bit; the high end is very clear and there is far more low end than expected in a film of this age. Rounding out the disc are three short documentaries contemporary to the era, the last of which takes us on a tour of a studio, showing the at-the-time state-of-the-art audio recording equipment. —JO
Movie: 🎬🎬🎬 **DVD:** 🎬🎬🎬
Warner Home Video, Inc. (Cat #65001, UPC #012569500129). Full frame. Dolby Digital Mono. $19.98. Snapper. *LANG:* English. *SUB:* English; French. *CAP:* English. *FEATURES:* 28 chapter links ▪ Theatrical trailer ▪ 3 Vintage documentary shorts ▪ Notes on Busby Berkeley.
1933 89m/B Warner Baxter, Ruby Keeler, Bebe Daniels, George Brent, Dick Powell, Guy Kibbee, Ginger Rogers, Una Merkel, Busby Berkeley, Ned Sparks, George E. Stone; **D:** Lloyd Bacon; **W:** Rian James, James Seymour; **M:** Harry Warren, Al Dubin. *AWARDS:* Natl. Film Reg. '98; *NOM:* Oscars '33: Picture, Sound.

Four Little Girls

On September 15, 1963, Birmingham, Alabama, the so-called "Magic City," was shaken when the 16th St. Baptist Church was bombed. This horrific act claimed the lives of four young choir members, one age 11, the others 14. In this Academy Award–nominated documentary, Spike Lee brings all his artistry and rage to bear on telling this story that was both tragedy and a turning point. The "perverted and terrible crime," notes Walter Cronkite, awakened the nation to "the real nature" of racial hatred, and galvanized the burgeoning Civil Rights movement. In a masterful use of archival footage, Lee puts the bombing in historical context, and in heartbreaking interviews with family members and friends, puts a human face on the victims of this appalling crime. This DVD presentation has no chapter links. The film is best appreciated uninterrupted. Considering the vintage materials, the transfer is impeccable. The soundtrack, too, does justice to this wrenching film that ranks among Lee's very best and most vital films. —DL
Movie: 🎬🎬🎬½ **DVD:** 🎬🎬🎬½
HBO Home Video (Cat #91478, UPC #263 5914782). Widescreen (2.35:1) anamorphic. Dolby Digital Stereo. $19.98. Snapper. *LANG:* English. *CAP:* English. *FEATURES:* "The Making of *4 Little Girls*" ▪ Spike Lee bio ▪ Epilogue ▪ Weblinks.
1997 102m/C D: Spike Lee; **C:** Ellen Kuras; **M:** Terence Blanchard. *AWARDS:* Broadcast Film Critics '97: Feature Doc; *NOM:* Oscars '96: Feature Doc.

The Four Musketeers

Continuation of *The Three Musketeers*, filmed at the same time, is a lavish swashbuckler that jaunts from France to England to Italy, following the adventures of D'Artagnan (York) and cohorts (Reed, Finlay, Chamberlain). Both pictures give an amusing depiction of 17th-century Europe as envisioned by director Lester and writer/historian Fraser. Curiously, the credits on this DVD are in French, and, like the first film, the image seems to have been slightly cropped on the sides in the transfer to disc. It also has a faded, flat look that reveals its age. Both *Musketeer* films are prime candidates for restoration. —*MM* **AKA:** The Revenge of Milady.

Movie: 🎜🎜🎜 ***DVD:*** 🎜🎜½

Winstar Home Entertainment (Cat #5030). Widescreen (1.66:1) letterboxed. Dolby Digital Mono. $29.98. Keepcase. *LANG:* English. *FEATURES:* Cast and crew thumbnail bios ▪ Production notes ▪ 12 chapter links.

1975 (PG) 108m/C Michael York, Oliver Reed, Richard Chamberlain, Frank Finlay, Raquel Welch, Christopher Lee, Faye Dunaway, Jean-Pierre Cassel, Geraldine Chaplin, Simon Ward, Charlton Heston, Roy Kinnear, Nicole Calfan; ***D:*** Richard Lester; ***W:*** George MacDonald Fraser; ***C:*** David Watkin; ***M:*** Lalo Schifrin. *AWARDS: NOM:* Oscars '75: Costume Des.

Four Sided Triangle

Two mad scientists find their friendship threatened when they discover that they are both in love with the same woman. So they do what anyone would do in this situation—they invent a machine and duplicate her. A pristine video transfer enhances this otherwise forgettable film. The blacks are crisp and well-defined. The soundtrack is adequate while occasionally producing some rather tinny sounding dialogue. —*MJT*

Movie: 🎜 ***DVD:*** 🎜🎜🎜

Anchor Bay (Cat #DV11075, UPC #01313 1107593). Full frame. Dolby Digital Mono. $29.98. Keepcase. *LANG:* English. *FEATURES:* 15 chapter links ▪ *World of Hammer* episode "The Curse of Frankenstein."

1953 81m/B *GB* James Hayter, Barbara Payton, Stephen Murray, John Van Eyssen, Percy Marmont; ***D:*** Terence Fisher; ***W:*** Terence Fisher, Paul Tabori; ***C:*** Reg Wyer; ***M:*** Malcolm Arnold.

Four Times That Night

Though he's known for his work in horror, Mario Bava also made one sex comedy and it's not a bad little movie, though its appeal is mostly nostalgia. Technically, it's a *Rashomon* story with the events of one night told from different points of view. What happens when Gianni (Halsey) takes the lovely Tina (Girodano) to his bachelor pad? Is it date rape or does she seduce him? The DVD was made from a lightly scratched print and some static is audible on the soundtrack. Those detract some from the wild colors and the groovy soundtrack, but the film is still grand stuff for '60s fans. The shagadelic apartment must be seen to be believed. Don't pass up Tim Lucas's informative liner notes. —*MM* **AKA:** Quante Volte...Quella Notte.

Movie: 🎜🎜 ***DVD:*** 🎜🎜½

Image Entertainment (Cat #ALF9856DVD, UPC #014381985627). Widescreen (1.85:1)

anamorphic. Dolby Digital Mono. $24.99. Snapper. *LANG:* Italian. *SUB:* English. *FEATURES:* 10 chapter links ▪ Bava thumbnail bio and filmography ▪ Photo and stills gallery ▪ Liner notes by Tim Lucas.

1969 (R) 83m/C *IT* Brett Halsey, Daniela Giordano, Pascale Petit, Brigitte Skay; ***D:*** Mario Bava; ***M:*** Lallo Gori.

The 4th Floor

A well-produced thriller (which is becoming a pay cable perennial) featuring a good cast and excellent photography. After her aunt dies, Jane (Lewis) moves into her apartment to have some space from her boyfriend (Hurt). After receiving a series of increasingly hostile and demanding notes from her unseen downstairs neighbor, Jane becomes paranoid about her fellow tenants and begins to fear for her life. Suspenseful and involving with some nice Hitchcockian twists, but it's marred by an unfortunately cryptic ending. The disc is absolutely gorgeous, perfectly conveying the gold and brownish tones of the film with rich, detailed blacks and excellent flesh tones. The Surround sound is highly satisfying, crisp, and involving, and the commentary is good, though one wishes a member of the cast had been included. —*DG*

Movie: 🎜🎜 ***DVD:*** 🎜🎜🎜½

A-PIX Entertainment Inc. (Cat #APX27025, UPC #783722702536). Widescreen (1.85:1) letterbox; full frame. Dolby Digital 5.0; Dolby Digital Stereo. $24.98. Keepcase. *LANG:* English. *SUB:* Spanish. *FEATURES:* 16 chapter links ▪ Insert card with chapter listing ▪ Alternate ending ▪ Commentary: Josh Klausner, Tricia Cooke, Timothy Galvin.

1999 (R) 90m/C Juliette Lewis, William Hurt, Austin Pendleton, Shelley Duvall, Artie Lange, Tobin Bell; ***D:*** Josh Klausner; ***W:*** Josh Klausner; ***C:*** Michael Slovis; ***M:*** Brian Tyler.

The 4th Man

Steeped in saturated colors and jet black comedy, Verhoeven's nouveau noir mystery enjoyed considerable art house success and was his entrée to Hollywood, but it was not released theatrically until 1984. From the exceptionally creepy beginning of a black widow spider in close-up, the story is stylishly lit and strange. Reve (Krabbe) is an alcoholic bisexual Catholic writer who becomes the hypotenuse of a love triangle involving Herman, a young man he encounters at a railway station, and his lover Christine (Soutendijk), who owns the Sphinx beauty salon and whose last three husbands died mysteriously. DVD does the ambitious film justice. Verhoeven's commentary is relaxed and informative. The original elements have been well preserved (or restored) and I could see no problems with the transfer to disc. This one will remind people that there's more to the director than *Showgirls*. —*MM* **AKA:** Die Vierde Man.

Movie: 🎜🎜🎜½ ***DVD:*** 🎜🎜🎜½

Anchor Bay (Cat #DV11251, UPC #0131 31125191). Widescreen (1.66:1) anamorphic. Dolby Digital Mono. $24.98. Keepcase. *LANG:* Dutch. *SUB:* English. *FEATURES:* Trailer ▪ Commentary: Paul Verhoeven ▪ Storyboard art ▪ 25 chapter links ▪ Liner notes by Mark Wickum.

1979 102m/C *NL* Jeroen Krabbe, Renee Soutendijk, Thom Hoffman, Jon (John) DeVries, Geert De Jong; ***D:*** Paul Verhoeven; ***W:*** Gerard Soeteman; ***C:*** Jan De Bont; ***M:*** Loek Dikker. *AWARDS:* L.A. Film Critics '84: Foreign Film.

The Fox and the Hound

Disney animators spin a sweet story of the friendship between a fox and a hound who meet as young pups and swear allegiance to one another. But they are separated and meet again as grown-ups who see each other as natural enemies. Unfortunately, the film fares poorly on DVD. The picture is very grainy throughout the majority of the film and the colors are washed-out. Whenever there is a close-up of a character, the picture suddenly gets muddy, fuzzy, and grainy simultaneously, as if the picture were being squeezed. Also, the digital transfer reveals a great many flaws in the source print. Notice the strange blueish/purple line that is always around Widow Tweed. In contrast, the Dolby Surround Sound is satisfactory, offering some nice rear channel sound during the chase scenes. —*ML/MM*

Movie: 🎜🎜🎜 ***DVD:*** 🎜½

Buena Vista Home Entertainment (Cat #18453). Full frame. Dolby Surround. $29.99. Keepcase. *LANG:* English; French; Spanish. *SUB:* English. *FEATURES:* Read-along ▪ Trivia game ▪ Theatrical trailer.

1981 (G) 83m/C *D:* Art Stevens, Ted Berman, Richard Rich; ***W:*** Art Stevens, Peter Young, Steve Hulett, Earl Kress, Vance Gerry, Laury Clemmons, Dave Michener, Burny Mattinson; ***M:*** Buddy (Norman Dale) Baker; ***V:*** Mickey Rooney, Kurt Russell, Pearl Bailey, Jack Albertson, Sandy Duncan, Jeanette Nolan, Pat Buttram, John Fiedler, John McIntire, Richard Bakalyan, Paul Winchell, Keith Mitchell, Corey Feldman.

Foxfire

Think *The Craft* without the hocus pocus. Lusty Legs Sadovsky (Jolie) is the liberated drifter who empowers a quartet of abused teens to take action against their molester, who's also their biology teacher. This adaptation of a Joyce Carol Oates's novel written in the 1950s suffers from time warp, most notably when the girls expose their teacher's behavior to the principal and he promptly suspends them. After some bonding and tattooing in an abandoned house, the story descends into the more masculine and mundane territory of car chases, kidnapping, and gunplay. The filmmakers rather timidly back away from the leather-clad Legs's obvious lesbianism and her relationship with the

adoring Maddy (Burress). The young cast's inexperience doesn't help matters. DVD delivers a very good image and sound, even in some shadowy interiors. —*MM*
Movie: 🎬🎬 **DVD:** 🎬🎬½
Columbia Tristar Home Video (Cat #80992, UPC #043396809925). Widescreen (2.35:1) anamorphic. Dolby Digital Surround Stereo. $24.99. Keepcase. *LANG:* English. *SUB:* English; Spanish. *FEATURES:* 28 chapter links • Trailers • Angelina Jolie talent file.
1996 (R) 102m/C Angelina Jolie, John Diehl, Jenny Lewis, Cathy Moriarty, Richard Beymer, Hedy Burress, Jenny Shimizu, Sarah Rosenberg, Peter Facinelli; *D:* Annette Haywood-Carter; *W:* Elizabeth White; *C:* Newton Thomas (Tom) Sigel; *M:* Michel Colombier.

Foxy Brown

In this sequel to *Coffy* Pam Grier plays essentially the same character with a different name. This time out, she's looking for vengeance on the criminals who killed her beau. As Hill says in his commentary track, this time they decided to go completely over the top with plot and action and they certainly succeeded. On DVD the image is one of the sharpest of the early '70s exploitation pictures. Monaural sound is weak. —*MM*
Movie: 🎬🎬🎬 **DVD:** 🎬🎬🎬
MGM Home Entertainment (Cat #1001 465, UPC #027616857859). Widescreen (1.85:1) anamorphic. Dolby Digital Mono. $14.95. Keepcase. *LANG:* English. *SUB:* French; Spanish. *FEATURES:* 16 chapter links • Commentary: Jack Hill • Trailer.
1974 (R) 92m/C Pam Grier, Terry Carter, Antonio Fargas, Kathryn Loder; *D:* Jack Hill; *W:* Jack Hill; *C:* Brick Marquard; *M:* Willie Hutch.

Frances

Frances Farmer (Lange) is the beautiful and talented screen actress of the 1930s and '40s who was driven to a mental breakdown by bad luck, drug and alcohol abuse, a neurotic domineering mother, despicable mental health care, and her own stubbornness. The film isn't nearly as bleak as it sounds in synopsis because Lange understands the character from the inside out and never allows her to become melodramatic or weak. Disc provides an acceptable widescreen transfer that's not really much better than tape. Heavy artifacts fill any scene with a bright sky. Some voice dubbing—even Lange's in certain scenes—sounds detached and doesn't quite synch up with mouth movements. If memory serves, that comes from the original material. —*MM*
Movie: 🎬🎬🎬 **DVD:** 🎬🎬
Republic Pictures Home Video (Cat #11189). Widescreen letterboxed. $24.98. Keepcase. *LANG:* English. *FEATURES:* 40 chapter links.
1982 134m/C Jessica Lange, Kim Stanley, Sam Shepard, Jeffrey DeMunn, Gerald S. O'Loughlin, Chris Pennock, John Randolph, Lane Smith; *D:* Graeme Clifford; *W:*

Christopher DeVore, Nicholas Kazan, Eric Bergren; *C:* Laszlo Kovacs; *M:* John Barry. *AWARDS: NOM:* Oscars '82: Actress (Lange), Support. Actress (Stanley).

Frank and Jesse

Another revisionist western finds outlaw Jesse James (Lowe) brooding about his violent existence while brother Frank (Paxton) keeps the gang together and they all try to avoid capture by the vengeful Alan Pinkerton (Atherton) and his detective agency. If the occasionally anachronistic dialogue isn't enough to put you off, Lowe's bad Southern accent will finish the job. Overall, the stereo sound is superior to the image, which is marred by heavy artifacts in both dark interiors and bright sunlit exteriors. —*MM*
Movie: 🎬🎬 **DVD:** 🎬🎬
Trimark Home Video (Cat #7395). Widescreen anamorphic. Dolby Digital Stereo. $14.98. Keepcase. *LANG:* English. *SUB:* French; Spanish. *CAP:* English. *FEATURES:* Cast and crew thumbnail bios • Trailer • 30 chapter links.
1994 (R) 106m/C Rob Lowe, Bill Paxton, Randy Travis, William Atherton, Alexis Arquette; *D:* Robert Boris; *W:* Robert Boris; *C:* Walt Lloyd; *M:* Mark McKenzie.

Frankenstein Created Woman

In Hammer's fourth take on the Frankenstein story, traditional lab scenes are replaced with less expensive "soul" translocations, though the filmmakers retain an ongoing fascination with decapitations. Oddly, the story has a warmth that's often lacking in the genre, and it's aimed at a younger audience, reflecting the changes that were going on when it was made. The image transfer is very clean, with strong colors and good contrast. Blacks are deep and solid, giving the image plenty of visual depth. The compression is flawless without any compression artifacts, leaving the highly detailed image fully intact. Despite its technical limitations, the mono audio comes across as very lively. The dynamic range is surprisingly good, creating an experience that is pleasing and never overly harsh. —*MM/GH* *AKA:* Frankenstein Made Woman.
Movie: 🎬🎬🎬 **DVD:** 🎬🎬🎬
Anchor Bay (Cat #11190). Widescreen (1.66:1) anamorphic. Dolby Digital Mono. $29.98. Keepcase. *LANG:* English. *FEATURES:* "World of Hammer" episode • Trailers and TV spots.
1966 86m/C Peter Cushing, Susan Denberg, Thorley Walters, Robert Morris, Duncan Lamont, Peter Blythe, Alan McNaughton, Peter Madden, Barry Warren, Derek Fowlds; *D:* Terence Fisher; *W:* John (Anthony Hinds) Elder; *C:* Arthur Grant.

Frankenstein's Daughter

Scientist Carter Morton (Felix Locher) should have done a better background check on his assistant Oliver Frank. He's

really a Frankenstein, and he's subverting Morton's experiments to rid the world of disease by injecting a serum into Morton's unsuspecting niece, who is transformed into a hideous, bushy-eyebrowed monster. Hardly the "macabre nightmare to a teenage world of rock and roll emotion," as the accompanying trailer promises. Unlike *I Was a Teenage Werewolf* with Michael Landon, this grade-Z teensploitation film doesn't even offer any "before they were stars" kicks, although as the affectionate liner notes point out, leading lady Sandra Knight was married to Jack Nicholson in the 1960s. More care may have been lavished on this pristine transfer than in the making of this made-for-$60,000 quickie. —*DL* *AKA:* She Monster of the Night.
Movie: 🎬🎬 **DVD:** 🎬🎬
Image Entertainment (Cat #ID8627CO DVD, UPC #014381862720). Full frame. Dolby Digital Mono. $24.99. Snapper. *LANG:* English. *FEATURES:* Still gallery • Liner notes by Tom Weaver • Theatrical trailer • 10 chapter links.
1958 85m/B John Ashley, Sandra Knight, Donald Murphy, Felix Locher, Sally Todd, Harry Wilson; *D:* Richard Cunha; *C:* Meredith Nicholson; *M:* Nicholas Carras.

Frankie and Johnny

Formula Elvis musical from the summer of 1966; served up strictly for Presley fans. Elvis (Johnny) is teamed with *Beverly Hillbillies* television star Donna Douglas (Frankie) as performers on a Mississippi River showboat. While they profess their love for each other, Frankie vows that she will never fully commit to Johnny until he gives up his gambling ways. Thirteen musical numbers, including the title song, move the "conflict" between the lovers along to a requisite happy ending. DVD presentation fails to focus on its core audience, namely Elvis fans. It lacks not only support materials (stills, behind-the-scenes, bios, etc.), but English titles for the song lyrics. This seems strange for a musical, especially so when the choice was made to provide the viewer with French and Spanish titles. —*RJT*
Movie: 🎬🎬 **DVD:** 🎬🎬
MGM Home Entertainment (Cat #1001 845, UPC #027616861146). Widescreen (1.66:1) letterboxed. Dolby Digital Stereo. $14.95. Keepcase. *LANG:* English; French. *SUB:* French; Spanish. *CAP:* French; Spanish. *FEATURES:* 16 chapter markers • Theatrical trailer.
1965 88m/C Elvis Presley, Donna Douglas, Harry (Henry) Morgan, Audrey Christie, Anthony Eisley, Sue Ane Langdon, Robert Strauss, Nancy Kovack; *D:* Fred de Cordova.

Freejack

Futuristic thriller is set in 2009 when pollution, a hole in the ozone layer, and the financial gap between social classes have grown to such horrific proportions that the rich pillage the past to find bodies to replace their own. Estevez is a young race-

car driver whose sudden death makes him an ideal candidate for this bizarre brand of surgery. Once transported to the future, he becomes a "Freejack" on the run for his life. A good cast including Jagger, Hopkins, and Russo edges this one up a notch. On disc, sound is a more significant improvement over image. —MM
Movie: ♪♪½ **DVD:** ♪♪½
Warner Home Video, Inc. (Cat #16373). Widescreen (2.35:1) letterboxed. Dolby Digital 5.1 Surround Stereo. $19.98. Snapper. *LANG:* English; French. *SUB:* English; French; Spanish. *FEATURES:* 6 chapter links ▪ Trailer.
1992 (R) 110m/C Emilio Estevez, Mick Jagger, Rene Russo, Anthony Hopkins, Jonathan Banks, David Johansen, Amanda Plummer, Grand Bush, Frankie Faison, Esai Morales, John Shea; *D:* Geoff Murphy; *W:* Dan Gilroy, Ronald Shusett, Steven Pressfield; *C:* Amir M. Mokri; *M:* Michael Boddicker, Trevor Jones.

Frenzy

After being fired from his job, the temperamental Blaney finds himself hunted by the police for a recent series of rape and strangulation murders. Good, but not great, late-period Hitchcock is filled with brilliant camerawork and sequences, but an awkward story structure. Though filled with very black humor (and some very disgusting food!), this is probably the most gruesome and morbid of the director's films. The murders are still chilling and the acting is top-notch. Finch successfully carries off a very difficult role. The disc is absolutely stunning: fleshtones are perfect; the color is bright and vivid; and the picture is so clear, it nearly seems 3-D at times. The sound is clear with the music given the most presence. The extras are extremely satisfying and the documentary is perfect. It offers a rare chance to see Hitchcock actually directing and features excellent interviews with the cast and crew. An absolute must for Hitchcock fans and scholars. —DG
Movie: ♪♪♪ **DVD:** ♪♪♪♪
Universal Studios Home Video (Cat #20661, UPC #025192066122). Widescreen (1.85:1) anamorphic. Dolby Digital Mono. $29.98. Keepcase. *LANG:* English; French. *SUB:* English; Spanish. *FEATURES:* 18 chapter links ▪ Insert card with chapter listing ▪ Cast and filmmaker bios ▪ Production notes ▪ Theatrical trailer ▪ "Making of" documentary, "The Story of *Frenzy*" ▪ Photo and poster gallery.
1972 (R) 116m/C GB Jon Finch, Barry Foster, Barbara Leigh-Hunt, Anna Massey, Alec McCowen, Vivien Merchant, Billie Whitelaw, Jean Marsh, Bernard Cribbins, Michael Bates, Rita Webb, Jimmy Gardner, Clive Swift, Madge Ryan, George Tovey, Noel Johnson; *D:* Alfred Hitchcock; *W:* Anthony Shaffer; *C:* Gilbert Taylor; *M:* Ronald Goodwin.

Frequency

In 1999, New York cop John Sullivan (Caviezel) finds that he can communicate with his dead father Frank (Quaid) in 1969 through dad's old ham radio. Since Frank was a fireman who was killed in a warehouse fire almost exactly 30 years earlier, John is able to give him advice that saves his life. In the process, though, they alter something else and now a serial killer is back at work. Yes, that synopsis sounds far too screwy to be entertaining, but the story works beautifully—as long as you don't ask too many questions, particularly in the last reel. The film looks and sounds very good on DVD, particularly the evocative domestic interiors. The commentary tracks are excellent, too. —MM
Movie: ♪♪♪ **DVD:** ♪♪♪♪½
New Line Home Video (Cat #N5058, UPC #794043505829). Widescreen (2.35:1) anamorphic. Dolby Digital 5.1 Surround Stereo; Dolby Digital Surround. $24.98. Snapper. *LANG:* English. *SUB:* English. *CAP:* English. *FEATURES:* 21 chapter links ▪ Deleted scenes ▪ Commentary ▪ Commentary: Hoblit ▪ Commentary: actor Noah Emmerich and writer/producer Toby Emmerich ▪ Isolated score ▪ Trailer ▪ DVD-ROM features.
2000 (PG-13) 117m/C Dennis Quaid, James Caviezel, Elizabeth Mitchell, Andre Braugher, Shawn Doyle, Noah Emmerich, Jordan Bridges, Melissa Errico, Daniel Henson; *W:* Toby Emmerich; *C:* Alan Kivilo; *M:* Michael Kamen.

Friday Foster

Pam Grier plays another variation on the strong, willful heroine that made her a star of "blaxploitation" cinema but the action is relatively tame. This time out, she's a photographer who investigates an assassination attempt and uncovers a conspiracy against black politicians. The DVD looks fine. Potentially troublesome striped patterns are fine and only minor signs of wear are visible. —MM
Movie: ♪♪ **DVD:** ♪♪½
MGM Home Entertainment (Cat #1001466, UPC #027616857866). Widescreen (1.85:1) letterboxed. Dolby Digital Mono. $19.98. Keepcase. *LANG:* English; French; Spanish. *SUB:* French; Spanish. *FEATURES:* 16 chapter links ▪ Trailer.
1975 (R) 90m/C Pam Grier, Yaphet Kotto, Thalmus Rasulala, Carl Weathers, Godfrey Cambridge; *D:* Arthur Marks; *W:* Orville H. Hampton; *C:* Harry J. May; *M:* Luchi De Jesus.

Friday the 13th, Part 3

Originally filmed in 3-D, this entry in the series has always looked bad on home video. DVD manages to correct the extra graininess, but is that really an improvement? The film is really notable only for Jason's acquisition of his trademark hockey mask. Though some claim this is the worst of the films, I think that honor goes to *Part 8*. —MM
Movie: woof **DVD:** ♪♪
Paramount Home Video (Cat #01539, UPC #097360153941). Widescreen letterboxed. Dolby Digital Mono. $29.99. Keepcase. *LANG:* English; French. *SUB:* English. *FEATURES:* 14 chapter links ▪ Trailer.

1982 (R) 96m/C Dana Kimmell, Paul Kratka, Richard Brooker, Catherine Parks, Jeffrey Rogers, Tracie Savage, Larry Zerner; *D:* Steve Miner; *W:* Martin Kitrosser, Carol Watson; *C:* Gerald Feil.

Friday the 13th, Part 4: The Final Chapter

All this dissembling title has to offer is the sight of a pubescent Corey Feldman, and strengthened intentionally comic elements. Beyond those dubious virtues, it's more of the same old slice-and-dice. The mediocre production values are reflected in a disc that's only a slight improvement over VHS tape. —MM
Movie: woof **DVD:** ♪♪
Paramount Home Video (Cat #01765, UPC #097360176544). Widescreen letterboxed. Dolby Digital Mono. $29.99. Keepcase. *LANG:* English; French. *SUB:* English. *FEATURES:* 14 chapter links ▪ Theatrical trailer.
1984 (R) 90m/C Erich Anderson, Judie Aronson, Kimberly Beck, Peter Barton, Tom Everett, Corey Feldman, Crispin Glover, Richard Brooker; *D:* Joseph Zito; *W:* Barney Cohen; *C:* Joao Fernandes.

Friendly Persuasion

Earnest, solidly acted tale about a peaceful Quaker family struggling to remain true to its ideals in spite of the Civil War which touches their farm life in southern Indiana. Cooper and McGuire are excellent as the parents with Perkins fine as the son who's worried that he's using his religion to hide his cowardice. DVD image is very nice for a film of this age. It's a bit soft but colors are true with no real signs of wear. The "Wide Wide World" extra is a visit to the set during production. —MM **AKA:** Except for Me and Thee.
Movie: ♪♪♪ **DVD:** ♪♪½
Warner Home Video, Inc. (Cat #16693). Widescreen (1.66:1) letterboxed. Dolby Digital Mono. $19.98. Snapper. *LANG:* English; French. *SUB:* English; French. *FEATURES:* Talent files ▪ 1957 *Wide Wide World* TV show with Dave Garroway ▪ Production notes ▪ Awards ▪ 37 chapter links ▪ Trailer.
1956 140m/C Gary Cooper, Dorothy McGuire, Anthony Perkins, Marjorie Main, Charles Halton; *D:* William Wyler; *W:* Michael Wilson; *C:* Ellsworth Fredericks; *M:* Dimitri Tiomkin. *AWARDS:* Cannes '57: Film; *NOM:* Oscars '56: Adapt. Screenplay, Director (Wyler), Picture, Song ("Friendly Persuasion (Thee I Love)"), Sound, Support. Actor (Perkins).

Fright Night

Perhaps the best of the vampires-in-the-'burbs flicks makes fine use of all the conventions of the sub-genre and combines them with first-rate effects. Teenaged Charlie (Ragsdale) can't persuade anyone that his new neighbor Jerry Dandridge (Sarandon) is undead. His girlfriend Amy (Bearse) thinks Charlie's being a jerk. Making his debut, director Holland treats his young characters more honestly than many "serious" filmmakers. The nightclub scene is a brilliant set piece, but note the neat smaller touches. Dandridge makes his entrance drinking a Bloody Mary. Before an attack he whistles an offhand bar of "Strangers In the Night." Stephen Geoffreys's Beavis & Butthead–inspired Evil Ed is terrific. So is Roddy McDowall as the hambone horror host, but the film belongs to Sarandon. DVD presents a very nice image, even in the dark scenes and there are a lot of those. Sound is fine if not overpowering. —MM

Movie: ♫♫♫½ *DVD:* ♫♫♫
Columbia Tristar Home Video (Cat #5629). Widescreen (2.35:1) letterboxed; full frame. Dolby Digital Stereo. $14.95. Keepcase. *LANG:* English; French; Portuguese. *SUB:* English; French; Portuguese; Spanish; Chinese; Korean; Thai. *FEATURES:* Trailers • 28 chapter links.
1985 (R) 106m/C William Ragsdale, Chris Sarandon, Amanda Bearse, Roddy McDowall, Stephen Geoffreys, Jonathan Stark, Dorothy Fielding, Art Evans; *D:* Tom Holland; *W:* Tom Holland; *C:* Jan Kiesser; *M:* Brad Fiedel.

The Frightened Woman

Wealthy Sayer (LeRoy) gets his sexual kicks by playing master and slave in his villa outside Rome. When his regular call girl isn't available, he lures a young journalist (Lassander) into his kinky games. Though the film is less explicit than the similarly themed *9 1/2 Weeks*, its weirdness feels more authentic. Part of that certainly is due to the damaged quality of the original. The soundtrack is filled with static. The image has a dingy yellow tinge that seems to come from age, though other scenes are tinted pink. —MM

Movie: ♫♫ *DVD:* ♫♫
First Run Features (Cat #FRF909358D, UPC #720229909358). Widescreen letterboxed. $29.95. Keepcase. *LANG:* English. *FEATURES:* 8 chapter links • Trailer.
1971 90m/C *IT* Phillippe LeRoy, Dagmar Lassander; *D:* Piero Schivazappa; *W:* Piero Schivazappa; *M:* Stelvio Cipriano.

Frightmare

Edmund and Dorothy, a seemingly quiet British couple, indulge in one unsettling habit—they're cannibals. But, after years of therapy in an institution, they're pronounced sane by a judge, and move to a secluded farmhouse. Overall, the DVD image ranges from excellent to good, though later reels exhibit flecks and other signs of wear. (This is not the 1981 *Frightmare* starring Ferdy Mayne.) —MM *AKA:* Frightmare 2.

Movie: ♫♫½ *DVD:* ♫♫♫
Image Entertainment (Cat #ID9346EUDVD, UPC #014381934625). Full frame. Dolby Digital Mono. $24.99. Snapper. *LANG:* English. *FEATURES:* 12 chapter links.
1974 (R) 86m/C *GB* Deborah Fairfax, Kim Butcher, Rupert Davies, Sheila Keith; *D:*

Pete Walker; *W:* David McGillivray; *C:* Peter Jessop; *M:* Stanley Myers.

From a Whisper to a Scream

This three-part made-for-television documentary traces the history of Irish popular music from 1950 and the "showbands" who were essentially the only form of entertainment in a country that lacked most electronic media. It then follows the rise of the likes of Van Morrison, Bob Geldof, U2, and the rest. Archival footage has a delicately (and apparently purposefully) distressed look. The contemporary stuff is very good. Sound is all that it needs to be. Very good for fans and for those who are only casually interested. —MM

Movie: ♫♫♫ *DVD:* ♫♫♫
Winstar Home Entertainment (Cat #73125, UPC #720917312521). Widescreen anamorphic. Stereo. $29.98. Keepcase. *LANG:* English. *FEATURES:* 24 chapter links • Extra interview footage • Discographies • Production credits.
2000 155m/C *D:* David Heffernan.

From Dusk Till Dawn [2 CS]

Escaped cons Seth and Richie Gecko (Clooney and Tarantino) pick up an ex-preacher (Keitel) and his two kids (Lewis and Liu) as hostages en route to their Mexican rendezvous spot, a raunchy biker joint run (unbenownst to them) by vampires. Feels like two movies in one, as Rodriguez's and Tarantino's styles don't necessarily mesh as much as they coexist. The first half features Tarantino's gift for snappy dialogue and somewhat sympathetic scumbags while the gory barroom finale shows off Rodriguez's testosterone-driven mastery of go-for-broke action and juicy violence. For a letterboxed transfer, this disc looks great. The image is super-sharp and colors are saturated to the point just this side of where they would bleed. During the climactic extended showdown there is some artifacting, although minor. The 5.1 mix really shows off Rodriguez's use of exaggerated sound effects and the house will be a-shakin' with the ultra-realistic gunfire. The two-disc set is loaded with supplementals including *Full Tilt Boogie*, a feature-length documentary on the making of *From Dusk Till Dawn*. When director Sarah Kelly isn't leering with her camera at that Clooney guy, the film is pretty interesting, even though it concentrates more on personalities than the technical aspects of making *Dusk*. Some of the deleted material is pretty flipped out and shouldn't be missed. As expected, the commentary is nearly all Tarantino, with mild-mannered Rodriguez managing to interject here and there. It's the same commentary that was used on the Collector's Edition laserdisc and worth a listen. —JO

Movie: ♫♫♫ *DVD:* ♫♫♫
Buena Vista Home Entertainment (Cat #18631, UPC #717951005786). Wide-

screen (1.85:1) letterboxed. Dolby Digital 5.1; Dolby Surround. $32.99. Keepcase. *LANG:* English; French. *SUB:* Spanish. *CAP:* English. *FEATURES:* 26 chapter links • Theatrical trailer • TV spots • Talent files • Deleted scenes and alternate takes • 2 "making of" featurettes • Commentary: Robert Rodriguez, Quentin Tarantino • Outtakes • Photo gallery • *Full Tilt Boogie*, feature–length documentary • Music videos.
1995 (R) 108m/C George Clooney, Quentin Tarantino, Harvey Keitel, Juliette Lewis, Ernest Liu, Fred Williamson, Richard "Cheech" Marin, Salma Hayek, Michael Parks, Tom Savini, Kelly Preston, John Saxon, Danny Trejo; *D:* Robert Rodriguez; *W:* Quentin Tarantino; *C:* Guillermo Navarro; *M:* Graeme Revell. *AWARDS:* MTV Movie Awards '96: Breakthrough Perf. (Clooney); *NOM:* Golden Raspberries '96: Worst Support. Actor (Tarantino).

From Mao to Mozart: Isaac Stern in China

American movies are full of phony stories about "inspirational" music teachers—the magic of this film is that you see the real thing happening before your very eyes. The Academy Award–winning documentary is nothing less than superlative. In 1979, violinist Isaac Stern was invited to China on a cultural visit, a month-long trip to Beijing and Shanghai. The soul and center of the film is the time spent watching Stern coach and inspire the Chinese students, some of whom seem little older than tots, yet play with intense professionalism. A consummate teacher, he seems to inspire them to stop being simply technical masters and to put their heart and emotion into their playing. The DVD is a quality product. The (16mm?) image is always bright and clear, making one wonder how they captured all those intimate musical moments without intruding on the drama. —GE/MM

Movie: ♫♫♫½ *DVD:* ♫♫♫½
New Video Group (Cat #NVG-9473, UPC #767685947333). Full frame. $24.95. Keepcase. *LANG:* English. *FEATURES:* "Musical Encounters" documentary • "The Gentleman from Shanghai" documentary.
1980 84m/C Isaac Stern, David Golub; *D:* Murray Lerner; *Nar:* Tan Shuzhen. *AWARDS:* Oscars '80: Feature Doc.

From Russia with Love [2 SE]

The main extra on this "special edition" is a knowledgeable, dry, well-rehearsed commentary track featuring director Terence Young. The other fillips are nice window dressing for my own favorite in the series. Image and sound are identical to the standard edition. —MM

Movie: ♫♫♫♫ *DVD:* ♫♫♫♫
MGM Home Entertainment (Cat #100103, UPC #027616853936). Widescreen anamorphic. Dolby Digital Mono. $26.98.

Keepcase. *LANG:* English; Spanish. *SUB:* French; Spanish. *CAP:* English. *FEATURES:* Commentary • "Inside *From Russia with Love*" documentary • Harry Saltzman documentary • Animated boat chase storyboard sequence • Trailers, TV, and radio spots • "Making of" booklet.
1963 (PG) 125m/C *GB* Sean Connery, Daniela Bianchi, Pedro Armendariz Sr., Lotte Lenya, Robert Shaw, Eunice Gayson, Walter Gotell, Lois Maxwell, Bernard Lee, Desmond Llewelyn, Nadja Regin, Alizia Gur, Martine Beswick, Leila; *D:* Terence Young; *W:* Johanna Harwood, Richard Maibaum; *C:* Ted Moore; *M:* John Barry.

Frostbiter: Wrath of the Wendigo

What's worse than a Troma movie? A Troma movie with pretensions. This one's based on an underground comic book. The plot involves some liquor guzzlin', rifle totin' hunters desecratin' the resting place of the Wendigo, a blood-thirsty snow spirit. Writer/director Chaney salutes *Evil Dead II* with our heroes battling demons in an isolated cabin buried deep in the frozen Michigan woods. Stop-motion effects and old hag prosthetics attempt, albeit vainly, to elevate Troma's standard zero production values to "one." Comes up short, although the chili monster (no joke) almost makes up for the low-budget shenanigans. Even the patented Troma gratuitous nudity gets short shrift here. (The cover touts the DVD as "The Director's Cut." What, did Lloyd Kaufman butcher it for its theatrical run?) The transfer solidly renders the myriad lighting effects, whether the bluish pall during the Wendigo attack scenes or the ever-present gushes of red during the more sanguinary moments. The daytime winter shots look remarkably crisp and clear, almost convincing us we're watching an actual movie. Surround sound is adequate, serving up a quirky soundtrack with songs by Ron Asheton (star of the film and former lead guitarist for Iggy Pop), Elvis Hitler, and the "chili monster" theme by Randall & Allan Lynch. —*EP*
Movie: 🦴 *DVD:* 🦴🦴
Troma Team Video (Cat #9017, UPC #9035790173). Full frame. Dolby Digital Stereo Surround. $24.99. Keepcase. *LANG:* English. *FEATURES:* 10 chapter links • Theatrical trailer • "Frostbiter" Sales Promo • Intro by Lloyd Kaufman • 3 "Coming Distractions" Trailers • *Frostbiter* comic book excerpts • 2 music videos • "True Legend of the Wendigo."
1994 (R) 90m/C Ron Asheton, Lori Baker, Patrick Butler, Devlin Burton; *D:* Tom Chaney; *W:* Tom Chaney; *C:* Tom Chaney.

Fruits of Passion: The Story of "O" Continued

O (Illiers) goes to China and becomes a slave at a brothel because she and Sir Stephen (Kinski) feel that if she can pleasure many men, then she will love him

even more. (What?!) In the meantime, he is seeing another woman (Dombasle). O is subjected to many cruelties, but comes to befriend some of the other employees. Illiers is very good and of course, Kinski is scary as hell. (Do we really need to see him naked?) This one's a perfect appetizer for those who are looking for a soft-core film that offers something a little different. The picture is very crisp and clear, showing only minimal defects in the source print. The colors are somewhat muted and some scenes appear dark, but this is typical of a foreign film from the eighties and most likely has nothing to do with a flaw in the transfer. —*ML/MM* *AKA:* Les Fruits de la Passion; The Story of "O" Continued; Shina Ningyo.
Movie: 🦴🦴 *DVD:* 🦴🦴½
Anchor Bay (Cat #11080). Widescreen (1.66:1) anamorphic. Dolby Digital Mono. $29.98. Keepcase. *LANG:* English; French. *SUB:* English. *FEATURES:* Klaus Kinski bio.
1982 82m/C *FR JP* Klaus Kinski, Arielle Dombasle, Isabelle Illiers; *D:* Shuji Terayama.

Fugitive Champion

Gangsters bust motor-cross champion Jake McKnight (Mayer) out of a chain-gang so that he can search for his kidnapped daughter, a participant in an Internet sex site. The silly plot is a framework upon which to hang some inventive lively chase scenes. Standard action for a video premiere with a generic title. The DVD is essentially identical to VHS tape in image and sound. —*MM*
Movie: 🦴🦴 *DVD:* 🦴🦴
Image Entertainment (Cat #ID8910YODVD, UPC #014381891027). Full frame. Dolby Digital Stereo. $24.99. Snapper. *LANG:* English. *FEATURES:* 12 chapter links.
1999 94m/C Chip Mayer, Charlene Blaine, Thomas Burr, Carlos Cervantes; *D:* Max Kleven; *W:* Steven Baio, Jack Burkhead Jr.; *C:* Jason C. Poteet; *M:* Ennio di Berardo.

Full Disclosure

Thriller works with some interesting political ideas and clichéd characters. Hard-bitten-newspaperman-with-a-drinking-problem John McWhirter (Ward) digs up a tip on the murder of a prominent pro-Israeli activist. Before long, he finds that he has been targeted by a hitwoman (Miller), the CIA, the FBI, and probably the PTA. Then there's the involvement of a Palestinian posing as a Peruvian (Ticotin). Like the overachieving cast, both the full-frame image and Surround sound are well above average for a video premiere. —*MM*
Movie: 🦴🦴½ *DVD:* 🦴🦴½
Image Entertainment (Cat #OVED0555 DVD, UPC #014381055528). Full frame. Dolby Digital 5.1 Surround Stereo; Dolby Digital Surround. $24.98. Keepcase. *LANG:* English. *FEATURES:* 12 chapter links • Isolated music and effects track.
2000 (R) 137m/C Fred Ward, Christopher Plummer, Penelope Ann Miller, Rachel Ticotin, Virginia Madsen, Kim Coates,

Nicholas Campbell, Dan Lauria, Roberta Maxwell; *D:* John Bradshaw; *W:* Tony Johnston; *C:* Barry Stone; *M:* Claude Desjardins, Eric N. Robertson.

Fun & Fancy Free

Combined live-action and animation feature is made of two segments: "Bongo," with Dinah Shore narrating the story of a circus bear who escapes into the woods, and "Mickey and Beanstalk," where the famous rodent is joined by Goofy and Donald in search of a singing harp in the Giant's castle. The film marks Disney's last performance as the voice of Mickey. The studio has done its usual splendid job of preservation and/or restoration. The selection of extras is very good. Though the colors are not as bright as contemporary animation, the film looks fine...no, it looks great for 1947. —*MM*
Movie: 🦴🦴🦴 *DVD:* 🦴🦴🦴
Buena Vista Home Entertainment (Cat #19693, UPC #717951008695). Full frame. Dolby Digital Mono. $29.99. Keepcase. *LANG:* English; French; Spanish. *SUB:* English. *FEATURES:* DVD storybook • Trivia game • Disney's Mambo #5 by Lou Bega • Behind-the-scenes featurette • 24 chapter links.
1947 (G) 73m/C *D:* Jack Kinney, Hamilton Luske, William M. Morgan; *C:* Charles P. Boyle; *M:* Paul J. Smith, Oliver Wallace, Eliot Daniel; *V:* Walt Disney, Cliff Edwards, Billy Gilbert, Clarence Nash, Anita Gordon; *Nar:* Edgar Bergen, Dinah Shore.

Fusion One

DVD is a fine medium for this collection of short films. They're easily accessible from the menu and each is introduced by a brief written description of the contents. As a group, these are low-budget independent productions that depend more on intelligence and innovation than on sterling production values. Though some, such as "Every Night and Twice on Sunday" and "Flying with the Angels," are stylistically sophisticated, they are also rough. Short works are something of an acquired taste and so these won't appeal to all videophiles, but I recommend to anyone with a sense of adventure. Contents: "Animated Corpse," "Dinner," "Every Night and Twice on Sunday," "Flying with the Angels," "Iceman," "Hidden Child," "The Passage," "Today's Life," "Zitlover." —*MM*
Movie: 🦴🦴🦴 *DVD:* 🦴🦴🦴
Indie DVD (Cat #00019, UPC #80269500 0194). Full frame; widescreen (1.85:1) letterboxed. Dolby Digital 5.1 Surround Stereo. $24.95. Keepcase. *LANG:* English. *FEATURES:* 10 chapter links • Commentary.
2000 ?m/C

Galaxy Quest

Affectionate spoof of TV sci-fi treats fans' obsessions and love seriously. The obvious inspiration is *Star Trek*. At a convention, the actors from the campy '70s space series *Galaxy Quest* are taken for real space-traveling heroes by naive aliens who take the episodes as "historical documents" and need them to aid in an intergalactic war. They whisk the troupe off to a galaxy far, far away. Naturally, the incredulous "crew" is ill-prepared for their mission. Playful acting includes Allen's vain leader Nesmith, blonde bosomy babe DeMarco (Weaver), and cynical Brit Dane (Rickman). The DVD contains all the extras anyone could want, save a director's commentary. Both image and sound are exemplary, but only the most obsessed fan could watch the entire film with the "Thermian" soundtrack. The "Omega 13" special feature can be accessed only after one has watched the film. The menu is particularly cool. —*MM*

Movie: 🐾🐾🐾 **DVD:** 🐾🐾🐾½
DreamWorks Home Entertainment (Cat #86017, UPC #667068601725). Widescreen (2.35:1) letterboxed. Dolby Digital 5.1 Surround Stereo; Dolby Digital 2.0 Surround Stereo. $26.98. Keepcase. *LANG:* English; Thermian. *CAP:* English. *FEATURES:* 20 chapter links • "Making of" featurette • 7 outtakes • Cast and crew thumbnail bios • Production notes.
1999 (PG) 104m/C Tim Allen, Sigourney Weaver, Alan Rickman, Tony Shalhoub, Sam Rockwell, Darryl (Chill) Mitchell, Robin Sachs, Enrico Colantoni; **D:** Dean Parisot; **W:** David Howard, Robert Gordon; **C:** Jerzy Zielinski; **M:** David Newman.

The Garden of Allah

Arriving by train in a colorful, harmless North Africa full of Arabian horses, impeccably attired Arabs and exotic night spots, virginal Domini Enfilden (Marlene Dietrich, in something like 40 costume changes) falls for the sullen, neurotic Boris Androvsky (Charles Boyer, looking and behaving amazingly like Johnny Depp). He's a Trappist monk of the sworn-to-silence and penury type, escaped from a local monastery on a desperate quest to find passion in his life. They are soon married and on an illogical honeymoon in the desert wastes, all courtesy of suave Arab(?) potentate Count Anteoni (Basil Rathbone, just looking lost). All is smoldering romance (in tents, not intense) until a French legionnaire (Alan Marshal) spills the beans about Boris's broken vows. Not only has Boris double-crossed God, but the Monastery is failing because in his absence they cannot brew their famous liqueur, of which only Boris knows the recipe. How will Domini and Boris resolve this impasse of faith and love? Anchor Bay's DVD is an amazingly beautiful presentation. The film was made as a very early 3-strip Technicolor feature and it appears to be in perfect shape. The colors leap off the screen; the art directors were apparently advised to chuck realism out the nearest minaret and make this Arab fantasyland the most colorful place on Earth. —*GE*

Movie: 🐾🐾🐾 **DVD:** 🐾🐾🐾½
Anchor Bay (Cat #DV11329, UPC #01313 1132991). Full frame. Dolby Digital Mono.

$29.98. Keepcase. *LANG:* English. *FEATURES:* 20 chapter links.
1936 85m/C Alan Marshal, Marlene Dietrich, Charles Boyer, Basil Rathbone, Sir C. Aubrey Smith, Tilly Losch, Joseph Schildkraut, Henry (Kleinbach) Brandon, John Carradine; **D:** Richard Boleslawski; **W:** W.P. Lipscomb, Lynn Riggs; **C:** William Howard Greene; **M:** Max Steiner. *AWARDS: NOM:* Oscars '36: Score.

Gary Cooper Double Feature

These two public domain features are in better shape than most budget discs. *Meet John Doe* boasts a fair to good image, comparable to the Image Entertainment edition. (Please see review.) *A Farewell to Arms,* almost a decade older, is rougher and darker. On both, sound is acceptable. —*MM*

Movie: 🐾🐾½ **DVD:** 🐾🐾½
Marengo Films (Cat #MRG-0007, UPC #807013000726). Full frame. $14.98. Keepcase. *LANG:* English. *FEATURES:* 6 chapter links each.
2000 m/C

Gasaraki 1: The Summoning

Yet another Japanese animated TV series makes a debut on DVD. This one features huge robots, explosions, war, and a familial structure that's so complex it takes a flow chart in the liner notes to keep the characters straight. This appears to be a very good reproduction of a fairly ambitious work. The drawing is well detailed and the image is visually flawless. The same care was taken with the English voice track, which sounds as emotional as the Japanese. —*MM*

Movie: 🐾🐾½ **DVD:** 🐾🐾🐾
A.D.V. Films (Cat #DVDGK/001, UPC #702 727005220). Full frame. Dolby Digital Stereo. $24.99. Keepcase. *LANG:* Japanese; English. *SUB:* English. *FEATURES:* 16 chapter links • Interview with Ryosuke Takahashi • Episode production sheets • Glossary of terms • Gasaraki memos • Liner flow chart • DVD credits.
2000 100m/C *JP* **D:** Ryosuke Takahashi.

The Gay Deceivers

Unmistakably grounded in the '60s, the performances of this comedy are still fresh, but the script is a little stale. Danny (Coughlin) and Elliot (Casey) are two straight guys who avoid the draft by posing as a loving couple. When an army Colonel appears to be investigating the duo, they move into a gay apartment complex to carry on their scam. Naturally, hilarity ensues. The jokes are stereotype-based and show no true skill from the writer or director. Unfortunately, the film is credited with ruining the careers of its leads. Students of gay cinema or those with a sense of nostalgia for more "closeted times" may find it of interest. In terms of image quality, the disc is about equal to VHS

tape, though the film has never been available on home video. —*JAS*

Movie: 🐾🐾 **DVD:** 🐾🐾
Image Entertainment (Cat #ID6748CQ DVD, UPC #014381674828). Full frame. $24.99. Snapper. *LANG:* English. *FEATURES:* 12 chapters.
1969 (R) 97m/C Kevin Coughlin, Lawrence Casey, Brooke Bundy; **D:** Bruce Kessler; **W:** Gil Lasky, Jerome Wish; **C:** Richard C. Glouner; **M:** Stu Phillips.

The Gay Desperado

Movie-loving Mexican bandits kidnap opera singer Chivo (Martini) and an American and his fiancée (Lupino). Various romantic entanglements are the result. The film is a very light comedy. Today's audiences may be surprised at how visually sophisticated it is. The filmmakers' attitudes toward their own medium are positively postmodern. The full-frame image is very good—for a 1936 release, it's incredible. Sound is fine. —*MM*

Movie: 🐾🐾🐾 **DVD:** 🐾🐾½
Image Entertainment (Cat #ID9199MLSD-VD, UPC #014381919929). Full frame. Dolby Digital Mono. $24.99. Snapper. *LANG:* English. *FEATURES:* 14 chapter links.
1936 85m/B Leo Carrillo, Ida Lupino, Harold Huber, Nino Martini, Stanley Fields, Mischa Auer; **D:** Rouben Mamoulian; **W:** Wallace Smith; **C:** Lucien N. Andriot; **M:** Alfred Newman.

Gen-X Cops

Hong Kong police break a ring of smugglers who are selling a massive shipment of explosives. But the cops then lose the goods to major criminal, Akatura (Nakamura). So a rebellious trio of young cops go undercover and discover the bad guy has very sinister plans. What the film lacks in plot is more than made up for by the high-energy action sequences and generally good performances from an unfamiliar cast. The DVD further enhances the positives by delivering a near-perfect visual presentation of the film. The image is very sharp and the colors remain strong but never oversaturated. Deep blacks are complemented by excellent contrast, giving the film a bold but true feel. The soundtrack itself is pretty engaging, with occasional Surround effects, but lacks the gutsy overblown gunshots that come with bigger-budget Hollywood-produced action films. The DVD excels with its supplementals, including nearly an hour's worth of deleted scenes and an above-average and often exciting "making of" featurette offering numerous interviews and an in-your-face look at how some of the stunts were done. —*JO AKA:* Tejing Xinrenlei.

Movie: 🐾🐾 **DVD:** 🐾🐾🐾
Columbia Tristar Home Video (Cat #05026, UPC #043396050266). Widescreen (1.85:1) anamorphic. Dolby Digital 5.1; Stereo. $24.95. Keepcase. *LANG:* English; Cantonese. *SUB:* English; French. *CAP:* English. *FEATURES:* 28 chapter links • Theatrical trailer • Deleted scenes • "Making of" featurette.

1999 (R) 113m/C HK Nicholas Tse, Stephen Fung, Sam Lee, Grace Kip, Toru Nakamura, Jackie Chan; **D:** Benny Chan; **W:** Benny Chan; **C:** Arthur Wong.

Generator 1: Gawl

In 2007, Japanese teens must deal with all of the expected problems of adolescence while saving the world from the forces of evil, giant tentacled monsters, etc. Like all ADV animated films, this one is very bright and sharp. Sound is good, too, even the English dialogue track. The disc contains three episodes of the TV series. —MM

Movie: 🎵🎵½ **DVD:** 🎵🎵½
A.D.V. Films (Cat #DVD66/001, UPC #702 727013928). Full frame. $24.99. Keepcase. LANG: English; Japanese. SUB: English. FEATURES: 15 chapter links ☞ Trailer ☞ Character and creature sketches ☞ DVD credits.
2000 90m/C JP **D:** Seiji Mizushima; **C:** Kohtaro Yokoyama; **M:** Norimasa Yamanaka.

Gentlemen Prefer Blondes

Amusing satire involves two show-business girls (Russell and Monroe) from Little Rock trying to make it big in Paris. Seeking rich husbands or diamonds, their capers land them in police court. The film's plot is basically a re-tread of any of umpteen musical comedies about gold-digging girls on a madcap romantic cruise, but with Charles Lederer's racy script there are surprises to be had if one pays attention. The DVD transfer does a good job of approximating the gaudy candy colors and saturated flesh tones of the original prints. The red lipstick and sequined, crimson gowns are so vibrant, you may want to subdue the color. The legendary "Diamonds Are a Girl's Best Friend" number has never looked better. —MM/GE

Movie: 🎵🎵🎵 **DVD:** 🎵🎵🎵½
20th Century Fox Home Entertainment (Cat #2001424, UPC #024543014249). Full frame. Stereo; Mono. $24.98. Keepcase. LANG: English; French. FEATURES: MovieTone News short ☞ Trailers.
1953 91m/C Marilyn Monroe, Jane Russell, Charles Coburn, Elliott Reid, Tommy Noonan, George Winslow; **D:** Howard Hawks; **W:** Charles Lederer; **C:** Harry Wild; **M:** Leo Robin, Jule Styne, Lionel Newman.

Get Carter

Tough and stylish crime drama that has gained in stature since its release. Small-timer London hood Jack Carter (Caine) arrives in Newcastle determined to find out who killed his brother. After meeting local crime boss Cyril Kinnear (Osborne), Carter is told to go back home and leave things alone. But he doesn't and things (and the film) don't turn out exactly as expected. Caine shows just how ruthless he can make a character. Hey, this DVD could look like total crap and the film would still be more enjoyable to watch than the Stallone remake—but don't

worry, it doesn't. The transfer is very good and the only flaws are the result of the preprint material. The colors are slightly faded, but that actually works well for the noirish look of the film, and since they're not pushed, bleed is never a problem. Overall, the image is very sharp with good blacks and only a hint of grain. The mono sound delivers the goods clearly and is only a little thinner than you'd like. The commentary is as interesting as you'd expect from veteran filmmakers reflecting on the earlier stages of their careers. —JO

Movie: 🎵🎵🎵½ **DVD:** 🎵🎵🎵½
Warner Home Video, Inc. (Cat #65400, UPC #012569540026). Widescreen (1.85:1) anamorphic. Mono. $24.98. Snapper. LANG: English. SUB: English; French. CAP: English. FEATURES: 32 chapter links ☞ 2 theatrical trailers ☞ Commentary: Michael Caine, Mike Hodges, Wolfgang Suschitzky ☞ Isolated music score ☞ Michael Caine bio.
1971 (R) 112m/C GB Michael Caine, Ian Hendry, John Osborne, Geraldine Moffatt, Glynn Edwards, Dorothy White, Petra Markham, Bryan Mosley, Britt Ekland, Tony Beckley, George Sewell, Alun Armstrong, Bernard Hepton, Terence Rigby; **D:** Mike Hodges; **W:** Mike Hodges; **C:** Wolfgang Suschitzky; **M:** Roy Budd.

Get Carter

You don't have to read too deeply between the lines of director Stephen Kay's commentary track to find the source of this remake's many problems. He was brought in fairly late in the process, after several producers had been muddying the waters. (Nine people have some kind of production credit, along with three organizations.) The confusing story concerns Jack Carter (Stallone), Las Vegas muscle, who goes to Seattle to find out how his brother died. DVD re-creates the impenetrable black-green color scheme, the funky look, and hyperactive editing with appalling accuracy. Find the 1971 original. Surround sound does nice things with the interesting score. —MM

Movie: 🎵🎵 **DVD:** 🎵🎵
Warner Home Video, Inc. (Cat #18583, UPC #085391858324). Widescreen letterboxed. Dolby Digital 5.1 Surround Stereo. $24.98. Snapper. LANG: English; French; Spanish. SUB: English; French; Spanish. FEATURES: 29 chapter links ☞ 2 trailers ☞ Talent files ☞ Commentary: director Stephen Kay ☞ Deleted scenes.
2000 (R) 104m/C Sylvester Stallone, Michael Caine, Rachael Leigh Cook, Alan Cumming, Miranda Richardson, Mickey Rourke, John C. McGinley, Rhona Mitra, John Strong, John Cassini, Garwin Sanford, Gretchen Mol; **D:** Stephen Kay; **W:** David McKenna; **C:** Mauro Fiore; **M:** Tyler Bates. AWARDS: NOM: Golden Raspberries '00: Worst Remake/Sequel, Worst Actor (Stallone).

Get On the Bus

Lee looks at the personal side of the Million Man March through a fictional group of men

who board a bus in south central Los Angeles and head for Washington, D.C. Lee and writer Bythewood ignore the event itself and focus on the men—their reasons for participating and their interaction. Standouts in the ensemble include Dutton as the attentive bus driver, a brash young actor (Braugher), a likeable old man (Davis, who should have been nominated for an Oscar), an absentee father (Byrd) and his potentially delinquent son (Bonds), and a cop (Smith). On the commentary track, Lee is his usual opinionated, confrontational self. The film was shot in Super 16mm, not the conventional 35mm, and perhaps because of it, some grain is visible. For this kind of story, it is not a problem. Also, since so much of the film takes place on the bus and is told through close-ups, the full-frame version is recommended over the widescreen for those with conventional-sized monitors. —MM

Movie: 🎵🎵🎵 **DVD:** 🎵🎵🎵
Columbia Tristar Home Video (Cat #05833, UPC #043396058330). Widescreen (1.85:1) anamorphic; full frame. Dolby Digital 5.0 Surround Stereo; Dolby Digital Surround. $24.95. Keepcase. LANG: English; French. SUB: English; French; Spanish. FEATURES: 28 chapter links ☞ Talent files ☞ Commentary: Lee.
1996 (R) 122m/C Andre Braugher, Ossie Davis, Charles S. Dutton, De'Aundre Bonds, Gabriel Casseus, Albert Hall, Hill Harper, Harry J. Lennix, Bernie Mac, Wendell Pierce, Roger Guenveur Smith, Isaiah Washington, Steve White, Thomas Jefferson Byrd, Richard Belzer, Randy Quaid; **D:** Spike Lee; **W:** Reggie Rock Bythewood; **C:** Elliot Davis; **M:** Terence Blanchard.

Getting Even with Dad

The combination of a pubescent Macaulay Culkin and Ted Danson wearing a ponytail is enough to send any intelligent moviegoer screaming in terror from the theatre or video store. But that's exactly what this dubious comedy has to offer. Danson is a bumbling crook who is redeemed by the son from whom he has been separated for years. Surround sound is superior to tape; image is not. —MM

Movie: 🎵 **DVD:** 🎵🎵
MGM Home Entertainment (Cat #10016 02, UPC #027616859129). Full frame. Dolby Digital Surround Stereo. $24.99. Keepcase. LANG: English; French; Spanish. SUB: French; Spanish. CAP: English. FEATURES: Trailer ☞ 16 chapter links.
1994 (PG) 108m/C Macaulay Culkin, Ted Danson, Glenne Headly, Hector Elizondo, Saul Rubinek, Gailard Sartain, Kathleen Wilhoite, Sam McMurray; **D:** Howard Deutch; **W:** Tom S. Parker, Jim Jennewein; **C:** Tim Suhrstedt; **M:** Miles Goodman. AWARDS: NOM: Golden Raspberries '94: Worst Actor (Culkin).

Getting Gertie's Garter

This silly little number passed for a sex farce in the mid-'40s. Scientist Ken

(O'Keefe) is chagrined when he's called upon to testify in court about a jeweled garter that he gave to his former girlfriend Gertie (the gorgeous McDonald). What will his wife (Ryan) and the prestigious Society of Scientific Research think? DVD presents an accurate rendering of a fairly good black-and-white original. Sound is unexceptional. —MM

Movie: 🎵🎵🎵 **DVD:** 🎵🎵

VCI Home Video (Cat #8259, UPC #0898 59825927). Full frame. Dolby Digital Mono. $19.99. Keepcase. LANG: English. FEATURES: 18 chapter links • Talent files • "Pretty Dolly" short comedy (1942).

1945 74m/B Dennis O'Keefe, Marie McDonald, Barry Sullivan, Binnie Barnes, Sheila Ryan, J. Carrol Naish, Jerome Cowan; **D:** Allan Dwan; **C:** Charles Lawton Jr.

Gettysburg

Civil War buff Ted Turner originally intended Shaara's Pulitzer Prize-winning novel *The Killer Angels* to be adapted as a miniseries for his TNT network, but opted for a big-screen release instead. The film marks the first time a film crew has been allowed to film battle scenes on the Gettysburg National Military Park battlefield. The greatest battle of the war and the bloodiest in U.S. history is realistically staged by more than 5,000 Civil War re-enactors. The cast concentrates on the human cost of the war, with Daniels particularly noteworthy as the scholarly Colonel Chamberlain, determined to hold Little Round Top for the Union. Last film role for Jordan, to whom the movie is codedicated. The full-scale re-creation of Pickett's Charge is believed to be the largest period scale motion-picture sequence filmed in North America since D.W. Griffith's *Birth of a Nation*. The DVD is only slightly above average with a picture that is far too often a little soft and has even more problems during darker scenes, where detail is lost and grain added. The audio almost makes up for it with thundering renditions of cannon and rifle fire, good (but not excessive) use of Surround for ambience and selected effects, and a superb mix of the fine score by Edelman. The disc really excels in the supplemental department with the documentary, "The Battle of Gettysburg," narrated by Leslie Neilsen, making for a good orientation before viewing the actual film. The "making of" documentary gives additional historical info and when combined with the battlefield maps, the entire scope of the event comes into perspective. —JO

Movie: 🎵🎵🎵½ **DVD:** 🎵🎵🎵

Warner Home Video, Inc. (Cat #05393961 4926, UPC #053939613926). Widescreen (1.77:1) anamorphic. Dolby Digital 5.0. $24.98. Snapper. LANG: English (DD5.0); French (Stereo). SUB: English (DD5.0); French (Stereo). CAP: English. FEATURES: 81 chapter links • Theatrical trailer • Talent files • "Making of" documentary • Vintage documentary: "The Battle of Gettysburg" • Commentary: R. F. Maxwell, K. Van Ostrum, J. M. Mcpherson, C. Syn-

monds • TV spots • Battlefield maps • Dual-layered.

1993 (PG) 254m/C Jeff Daniels, Martin Sheen, Tom Berenger, Sam Elliott, Richard Jordan, Stephen Lang, Kevin Conway, C. Thomas Howell, Maxwell Caulfield, Andrew Prine, James Lancaster, Royce D. Applegate, Brian Mallon, Cooper Huckabee, Bo Brinkman, Kieran Mulroney, Patrick Gorman, William Morgan Sheppard, James Patrick Stuart, Tim Ruddy, Joseph Fuqua, Ivan Kane, Warren Burton, MacIntyre Dixon, George Lazenby, Alex Harvey, John Diehl, John Rothman, Richard Anderson, Bill Campbell, David Carpenter, Donal Logue, Dwier Brown, Mark Moses, Ken Burns, Ted Turner; **D:** Ronald F. Maxwell; **W:** Ronald F. Maxwell; **C:** Kees Van Oostrum; **M:** Randy Edelman.

Ghost

The top grosser of 1990 makes a properly impressive debut on disc. Swayze is an investment banker who's murdered but whose spirit remains on earth to protect his sweetie Moore from the unscrupulous (and lecherous) Goldwyn. Whoopi Goldberg's Oscar-winning comic psychic provides the energy that keeps the whole thing from collapsing into its own romanticism. It is an engaging piece of escapism that looks fine on DVD. The glossy image is all that a big-budget Hollywood movie ought to be. Sound is better than theatrical. —MM

Movie: 🎵🎵🎵 **DVD:** 🎵🎵🎵½

Paramount Home Video (Cat #32004, UPC #097363200444). Widescreen anamorphic. Dolby Digital 5.1 Surround Stereo; Dolby Digital Surround. $24.99. Keepcase. LANG: English; French. SUB: English. FEATURES: 16 chapter links • Retrospective featurette • Commentary: Zucker, Rubin • Trailer.

1990 (PG-13) 127m/C Patrick Swayze, Demi Moore, Whoopi Goldberg, Tony Goldwyn, Rick Aviles, Vincent Schiavelli, Gail Boggs, Armelia McQueen, Phil Leeds; **D:** Jerry Zucker; **W:** Bruce Joel Rubin; **C:** Adam Greenberg; **M:** Maurice Jarre. AWARDS: Oscars '90: Orig. Screenplay, Support. Actress (Goldberg); British Acad. '90: Support. Actress (Goldberg); Golden Globes '91: Support. Actress (Goldberg); NOM: Oscars '90: Film Editing, Picture, Orig. Score.

Ghost Chase

A young filmmaker desperate for funds inherits his dead grandfather's clock, from which issues the ghost of the deceased's butler. The spectral retainer aids in a search for the departed's secret fortune. It's neither scary nor funny but it did launch the career of the director of *Independence Day* and *Stargate*. The film was made on a minuscule budget and that shows, with an image that's grainy and heavy on the artifacts. No better than tape. —MM

Movie: 🎵½ **DVD:** 🎵🎵

Image Entertainment (Cat #OVE9022DVD, UPC #014381902228). Full frame. Dolby Digital Mono. $24.99. Snapper. LANG: English. FEATURES: 12 chapter links.

1988 (PG-13) 89m/C Jason Lively, Jill Whitlow, Tim McDaniel, Paul Gleason, Chuck "Porky" Mitchell; **D:** Roland Emmerich; **W:** Roland Emmerich, Oliver Eberle; **C:** Karl Walter Lindenlaub.

Ghost Dog: The Way of the Samurai

Jarmusch takes a Far Eastern approach to the Mob-hit man genre with *Dog*, whose title character, a contract killer played excellently by Whitaker, pledges himself to small-time hood Louie in the tradition of the Samurai after Louie saves his life. When one of his hits goes wrong, Ghost Dog is targeted for elimination, which leads to many dead bodies. Like most Jarmusch offerings, this one's quirky, disjointed, and not for everyone, but Whitaker's performance and the offbeat humor make up for a lot. The DVD release is pretty good, with a sharp image and good fleshtones. The color and overall feel could have been improved with just a touch more contrast. At times the Surround really kicks in and the sound is very good throughout with excellent imaging. The highlights of the supplementals are the deleted scenes, some of which are out-and-out hilarious, which is not to say the documentary featurette won't hold your interest—it will. —JO

Movie: 🎵🎵🎵 **DVD:** 🎵🎵🎵

Artisan Entertainment (Cat #10352, UPC #012236103523). Widescreen (1.85:1) anamorphic. Dolby Digital 5.1. $24.98. Keepcase. LANG: English. CAP: English. FEATURES: 27 chapter links • Trailers and TV spots • Deleted scenes • Documentary: "The Odyssey: The Journey into the Life of a Samurai" • Deleted scenes • Talent files • Isolated music score • Music video.

1999 (R) 116m/C Forest Whitaker, Cliff Gorman, Henry Silva, John Tormey, Isaach de Bankole, Tricia Vessey, Victor Argo, Gene Ruffini, Richard Portnow, Camille Winbush; **D:** Jim Jarmusch; **W:** Jim Jarmusch; **C:** Robby Muller.

Ghosts on the Loose

Lugosi made nine films for Monograph Pictures from 1941 to 1944, according to the on-screen liner notes—which are better-written than the film itself. "It'd be easy to find better movies, but almost impossible to find pictures more beloved by film buffs." The notes may overstate it a bit, but the slapstick antics and silly frights presented here will be of interest to fans of Lugosi and The East Side Kids, AKA the Bowery Boys. Lugosi worked with The East Side Kids previously in 1941's *Spooks Run Wild*. That one made money, so future pairings were assured. This one involves some silliness with Nazi spies. The image and sound are in rough shape, as should be expected of a title of this vintage,

which no doubt suffered decades of neglect. Extras are minimal, but the on-screen essay is informative. —MB **AKA:** The East Side Kids Meet Bela Lugosi; Ghosts in the Night.
Movie: 🎵½ **DVD:** 🎵🎵
Troma Team Video (Cat #AED2041, UPC #785604204121). Full frame. Dolby Digital Mono. $19.95. Keepcase. *LANG:* English. *FEATURES:* 9 chapter links ▪ Film notes.
1943 67m/B Bela Lugosi, Leo Gorcey, Huntz Hall, Bobby Jordan, Ava Gardner, Rick Vallin, Billy (William) Benedict, Stanley Clements, Bobby Stone, Bill Bates; **D:** William Beaudine; **W:** Kenneth Higgins; **C:** Mack Stengler.

Gia

Made-for-cable biopic begins with the corpse of Gia Carangi (Jolie) being made up. What follows is a swiftly paced look at the live-fast-die-young-of-AIDS-leave-a-pretty-corpse existence of a self-destructive supermodel who's essentially not very interesting but who checked out at an opportune time. It is undeniably sexy, and Jolie delivers a strong, confident performance. DVD provides a slight improvement visually, but the addition of Surround is actually a detriment. It punches up the bass in the score so much that it's intrusive to the downbeat story. The French stereo soundtrack is more in tune with the rest of the film. —MM
Movie: 🎵🎵½ **DVD:** 🎵🎵🎵
HBO Home Video (Cat #91390). Full frame. Dolby Digital Surround Stereo; Stereo; Mono. $19.98. Snapper. *LANG:* English; French; Spanish. *SUB:* English; French; Spanish. *FEATURES:* 15 chapter links ▪ Talent files ▪ Photo gallery.
1998 (R) 120m/C Angelina Jolie, Mercedes Ruehl, Kylie Travis, Faye Dunaway, Elizabeth Mitchell, Louis Giambalvo, John Considine, Scott Cohen; **D:** Michael Cristofer; **W:** Michael Cristofer, Jay McInerney; **C:** Rodrigo Garcia; **M:** Terence Blanchard.

Giant from the Unknown

A classic 1950s low-budget monster fest. Within the first two minutes of this film, the phrases "Something strange is goin' on around here," "It ain't natural," and "Did you see what happened to Kukla's chicken coop?" are uttered with intense sincerity, and the fabulous absurdity only continues to grow. A small town is experiencing a string of horrible murders and the handsome, young rock collector visiting from out of town is suspected. Then a professor and his buxom blonde daughter show up. Together with the rock collector they go to Devils Craig to look for the bones of a giant Spanish Conquistador, who they find is actually very fleshy having been in suspended animation for 500 years because he was buried in a special type of rock well, you get the idea. Horror on a low budget

ensues and the rock collector and the blonde live happily ever after. The unintentionally funny dialogue and awkward acting make it a must-see for die-hard late-night horror fans. The transfer looks really good with only minimal artifacts; the trailer, however is as bad as old film gets, but still fun to watch. The mono sound is a little hollow but not bad enough to distract anyone who puts the disc in the machine in the first place. —CA
Movie: 🎵🎵 **DVD:** 🎵🎵½
Image Entertainment (Cat #ID8710C0DVD, UPC #01438187102). Full frame. Dolby Digital Mono. $24.99. Snapper. *LANG:* English. *FEATURES:* 12 chapter links ▪ Theatrical trailer.
1958 80m/B Edward Kemmer, Buddy Baer, Bob Steele, Sally Fraser, Morris Ankrum; **D:** Richard Cunha; **W:** Ralph Brooke, Frank Hart Taussig; **C:** Richard Cunha; **M:** Albert Glasser.

Gilda

In the middle of an overripe disaster of a plot, Rita Hayworth creates a searing icon of cinematic sexuality. Her attempted striptease in the dark silk evening dress to "Put the Blame on Mame" is one of those moments that nobody forgets. If only the rest of the film were its equal. Down and out in Buenos Aires, Johnny Farrell (Ford) goes to work for casino owner Ballin Mundson (Macready). But Johnny has a past with the boss's new wife Gilda (Hayworth). The love triangle is too silly to be described, as is Mundson's plan to rule the world by cornering the tungsten market. The bizarre dialogue highlights the story's inherent frailty. No matter, Hayworth's performance is the centerpiece and it shines forth brilliantly on DVD. Minor flecks are visible but they do nothing to detract from the richly detailed black-and-white photography. The image transfer does justice to the work of director of photography Rudolph Maté and art directors Stephen Goosson and Van Nest Polglase. And, of course, the immortal Rita. The sound is fine, but the movie is really more enjoyable with the volume turned all the way down. —MM
Movie: 🎵🎵🎵½ **DVD:** 🎵🎵🎵½
Columbia Tristar Home Video (Cat #28999, UPC #043396028999944). Full frame. Dolby Digital Mono. $29.95. Keepcase. *LANG:* English; French; Portuguese; Spanish. *SUB:* English; French; Portuguese; Spanish; Chinese; Korean; Thai. *FEATURES:* 28 chapter links ▪ Rita Hayworth featurette ▪ Talent files ▪ Trailer ▪ Original advertising.
1946 110m/B Rita Hayworth, Glenn Ford, George Macready, Joseph Calleia, Steven Geray; **D:** Charles Vidor; **W:** Jo Eisinger, Marion Parsonnet; **C:** Rudolph Mate.

Gimme Shelter

In 1969, the Rolling Stones were touring America and the last ten days of this tour—which included a show at Madison Square Garden and a free show at Altamont Speedway in San Francisco—were

captured by a film crew. However, what started out to be a simple documentary about a rock 'n' roll band turned into one of the most disturbing and fascinating chronicles of desire and disaster in rock 'n' roll history. At the Altamont free concert, the group would use members of the Hell's Angels as bouncers around the stage. Six songs into their set, a man in the crowd pulled a gun and fired at the stage. He was quickly disarmed and then stabbed to death by one of the Angels. The film begins at the Madison Square Garden show and cuts between the band playing and the members of the band in the cutting room putting together the very documentary you're watching. From the beginning you are told what happened at Altamont and it is fascinating to watch Mick Jagger and Charlie Watts decompress as they watch the footage. The documentary takes its time in showing you how the events came to pass (including footage of attorney Melvin Belli negotiating the deal for the speedway) that brought everyone to the pinnacle event. The mark of a good documentary is to show events in as non-partisan a way as possible, and this is a great documentary. Intertwined with the tension of the Altamont situation are several full live performances of some of the Stones' most famous songs, including "Jumpin' Jack Flash" and "Sympathy for the Devil." Watching the live footage, it's easy to understand the worship the band has inspired within its fan base when you see the young Mick Jagger of 1969 strutting his stuff. There is also one song each from Ike and Tina Turner (from Madison Square Garden), The Jefferson Airplane, and The Flying Burrito Brothers (both from Altamont). The direction and cinematography are fabulous, unabashedly capturing the crowd at both shows in all their drugged-out star-struck glory, and the band members in their alternately egotistical and befuddled states over their fame, their art, and what it all leads to. Overall, this is both a fabulous concert film and a thought-provoking documentary. The DVD has been re-mastered from the camera original and looks great (one of the extras is about the restoration process), however, the additional footage looks like it's taken from clips that have been stored in someone's garage. The sound has also been re-mastered and is incredibly good. —CA
Movie: 🎵🎵🎵🎵 **DVD:** 🎵🎵🎵½
Criterion Collection (Cat #99, UPC #03742 9154526). Full frame. Dolby Digital 5.1 Surround; Dolby Digital Stereo. $39.95. Keepcase. *LANG:* English. *CAP:* English. *FEATURES:* 27 chapter links ▪ Theatrical trailer ▪ Still photo gallery ▪ Commentary: directors ▪ Additional footage ▪ Production notes ▪ 44-page booklet.
1970 91m/C Mick Jagger, Keith Richards, Charlie Watts, Bill Wyman, Mick Taylor, Marty Balin, Grace Slick, Paul Kantner, Jerry Garcia, David Crosby, Stephen Stills, Graham Nash, Tina Turner, Ike Turner, Melvin Belli, Bill Graham; **D:** David Maysles, Albert Maysles, Charlotte Zwerlin; **C:** Haskell Wexler; **M:** Rolling Stones.

Girl

Give the filmmakers credit for avoiding the exploitative elements of this story of Andrea's (Swain) coming-of-age. As a graduating senior, she has to make choices between going to a good college or becoming a groupie to rocker Todd (Flanery). The world that she and her friends inhabit is strictly the Hollywood version of teen rebelliousness and music. Similarly, the cast is really too attractive to be believable, though younger audiences may be more forgiving of that side. The DVD looks and sounds fine for a production that's only a step or so above made-for-cable quality, particularly in the scenes with the band. —*MM*

Movie: ♪♪ **DVD:** ♪♪½
Columbia Tristar Home Video Widescreen letterboxed; full frame. Dolby Digital 5.1 Surround Stereo. $24.95. Keepcase. *LANG:* English. *SUB:* English; French; Spanish. *FEATURES:* 28 chapter links ☞ "Making of" featurette ☞ Cast and crew thumbnail bios ☞ Commentary: director and cast.
1998 (R) 99m/C Dominique Swain, Sean Patrick Flanery, Tara Reid, Summer Phoenix, Selma Blair, Channon Roe, Portia de Rossi, Christopher K. Masterson, Rosemary Forsyth, James Karen; ***D:*** Jonathan Kahn; ***W:*** David E. Tolchinsky; ***C:*** Tami Reiker; ***M:*** Michael Tavera.

Girl Explores Girl: The Alien Encounter [CE]

Low-budget sf erotica is standard stuff about aliens who arrive on Earth to observe mating habits, etc., etc. The love scenes are about as graphic as they can be this side of hard-core. Production values lead a lot to be desired and the extras are all that separate the disc from VHS tape. —*MM*

Movie: ♪ **DVD:** ♪♪
El Independent Cinema (Cat #1004, UPC #612385100499). Full frame. $19.98. Keepcase. *LANG:* English. *FEATURES:* 16 chapter links ☞ Photo gallery ☞ Cast interviews ☞ "Making of" documentary.
2000 90m/C Katie Keane, Darian Caine, Victoria Vega, Natalia Ashe; ***D:*** John Bacchus; ***W:*** John Bacchus, Michael Beckerman, Joe Ned; ***C:*** Clancy Fitzsimmons, Jay Kestrel.

Girl Gang

Please see review of *Violent Years*.
1954 60m/B Joanne Arnold, Timothy Farrell, Harry Keatan, Lou Monson, Mary Lou O'Connor; ***D:*** Robert Derteno.

Girl in Black

Pavlo (Horne), a young writer vacationing on the island of Hydra, falls in love with the sad-eyed Marina (Lambetti). As their love blossoms, Marina and Pavlo battle local hostility towards the family, once prominent in the community but now disgraced, as well as bitter jealousies from Marina's jilted lover Christos (Foundas). Writer/director Cacoyannis offers another passionate slice of (1950s) contemporary Greek life, this time merging Sophoclean tragedy with Shakespearean structure. He knows how to make the terrain magnify his weighty explorations of forbidden love and fatal resentments; a star-crossed love drenched in Hellenic sunlight. Transfer offers a crisp image with the occasional surface blemish. Some of the nighttime scenes lose detail, but the daytime moments look exceedingly clear and sharp. Mono sound is decent, with few instances of brightness and distortion. On the whole, a step above VHS but nothing to write to Athens about. —*EP* ***AKA:*** To Koritsi Me Ta Mavra.

Movie: ♪♪½ **DVD:** ♪♪
Winstar Home Entertainment (Cat #FLV5 216, UPC #720917521626). Full frame. Dolby Digital Mono. $24.98. Keepcase. *LANG:* Greek. *SUB:* English. *FEATURES:* 8 chapter links ☞ Filmographies and awards ☞ Production credits ☞ Weblinks.
1956 100m/B *GR* Ellie Lambetti, Eleni Zafirou, Georges Foundas, Dimitri Horne, Stefanos Stratigos; ***D:*** Michael Cacoyannis; ***W:*** Michael Cacoyannis; ***C:*** Walter Lassally; ***M:*** Manos Hadjidakis.

Girl, Interrupted

Ryder stars as neurotic 18-year-old Susanna who, after making a halfhearted suicide attempt, is diagnosed with borderline personality disorder. So, in 1967, she's sent to Claymoore, a psychiatric hospital outside Boston, where she'll spend the next two years. There, Susanna meets some young women who are truly disturbed, including compelling sociopath Lisa (Jolie). Yes, the story's predictable but it's also touching—just don't expect the fireworks of *One Flew over a Cuckoo's Nest. Girl Interrupted* is given a nice rendering by Columbia TriStar on this DVD. The transfer is top-notch with excellent sharpness, solid blacks, and strong, vibrant colors that make the institution look like a much nicer place than it must have been. The included deleted scenes are, for the most part, deservedly left out of the film with the exception being an extended version of the cab ride to the asylum where Ryder surrealistically sees herself. Director Mangold provides an excellent commentary, giving details on shot setups and conceptual problem solving, not to mention philosophizing about mental health. Unfortunately, the short "making of" documentary comes off more promotional than sincere and its interview with author Kaysen feels way too abbreviated. —*JO*

Movie: ♪♪♪ **DVD:** ♪♪♪
Columbia Tristar Home Video (Cat #04746, UPC #043396047464). Widescreen (1.85:1) anamorphic. Dolby Digital 5.1; Dolby Surround. $24.95. Keepcase. *LANG:* English. *SUB:* English. *CAP:* English. *FEATURES:* 28 chapter links ☞ Theatrical trailers ☞ Talent files ☞ Production notes ☞ Commentary: director James Mangold ☞ "Making of" featurette ☞ Isolated music score.
1999 (R) 127m/C Winona Ryder, Angelina Jolie, Vanessa Redgrave, Whoopi Goldberg, Clea DuVall, Brittany Murphy, Elissabeth Moss, Jared Leto, Jeffrey Tambor, Mary Kay Place; ***D:*** James Mangold; ***W:*** James Mangold, Anna Hamilton Phelan, Lisa Loomer; ***C:*** Jack N. Green; ***M:*** Mychael Danna. *AWARDS:* Oscars '99: Support. Actress (Jolie); Golden Globes '00: Support. Actress (Jolie); Screen Actors Guild '99: Support. Actress (Jolie); Broadcast Film Critics '99: Support. Actress (Jolie); *NOM:* Screen Actors Guild '99: Support. Actress (Jolie).

The Girl Who Knew Too Much

Ten years ago in Italy a string of "alphabet murders" began on "A" and ended on "C." Now a pretty young American named Nora Davis (Roman) is visiting a family friend in Italy. When the friend dies and Nora goes for help—in the middle of the night, in the rain, wearing only a raincoat, alone, through an empty plaza—she witnesses a murder that happened ten years ago or does she? She shouldn't worry, though, because handsome young Dr. Marcello Bassi (Saxon, speaking fluent Italian) wants to help her. Typically fun and frightening Bava fare with the script, cinematography, and direction working much more smoothly than usual. The DVD looks like it was mastered from a used print and suffers for it. There are scratches and dust particles on some of the frames, and the sound is muddy at times. Overall, it is still a very watchable print and a worthwhile film for old-time horror and suspense fans. —*CA* ***AKA:*** La Ragazza Che Sapeva Troppo; The Evil Eye.

Movie: ♪♪½ **DVD:** ♪½
Image Entertainment (Cat #ID5943AODVD, UPC #014381594324). Widescreen (1.66:1) letterboxed. Dolby Digital Mono. $24.99. Snapper. *LANG:* Italian. *SUB:* English. *FEATURES:* 10 chapter links ☞ Theatrical trailer ☞ Cast and crew bios and filmographies ☞ Production notes ☞ Photo gallery of posters and lobby cards.
1963 86m/B *IT* Leticia Roman, John Saxon, Valentina Cortese, Robert Buchanan; ***D:*** Mario Bava; ***W:*** Mario Bava, Ennio de Concini, Mino Guerrini; ***C:*** Mario Bava.

Girlfight

Diana (Rodriguez) is a high school senior with a bad temper and a penchant for trouble. Her single dad encourages her brother to work out with a boxing trainer but refuses to allow his daughter to participate. She decides to train anyway. On the way to a championship, she falls in love with another amateur and has to decide where her priorities are. On her anecdotal commentary track, director Kusama spends much of her time talking about the limits of a $1 million budget (provided by John Sayles and the Independent Film

Channel). DVD image is fine; actually, it's excellent for a picture made under these conditions. —*MM*

Movie: 🎵🎵½ **DVD:** 🎵🎵🎵½

Columbia Tristar Home Video (Cat #05668, UPC #043396056688). Widescreen letterboxed; full frame. Dolby Digital 5.1 Surround Stereo; Dolby Digital Surround. $24.95. Keepcase. *LANG:* English; French. *SUB:* English; French; Spanish. *FEATURES:* 28 chapter links ● "Making of" featurette ● Commentary: Karyn Kusama ● Talent files ● Trailers.

1999 (R) 90m/C Jamie Tirelli, Michelle Rodriguez, Santiago Douglas, Ray Santiago, Elisa Bacanegra, Paul Calderon, John Sayles; **D:** Karyn Kusama; **W:** Karyn Kusama; **C:** Patrick Cady; **M:** Theodore Shapiro. *AWARDS:* Ind. Spirit '01: Debut Perf. (Rodriguez); Sundance '00: Director (Kusama), Grand Jury Prize; *NOM:* Ind. Spirit '01: First Feature.

Girls Just Want to Have Fun

Army brat Janey (Parker) moves to Chicago where she becomes pals with the free-spirited Lynne (Hunt), who persuades her to audition for a TV dance show. The hokey and predictable musical is most notable for the early efforts of the two stars. The DVD image is very crisp and clear, showing no defects from the source print or overt noise. There is some sight grain on the image and some scenes are slightly darker than others, but the colors (yes, those '80s neon colors) look very good. The dialogue is audible and clear, with no hissing on the track. The Surround creates a nice sound field, but some of the songs (and there is a lot of music in this dance movie) sound a bit tinny and lack the needed amount of bass. Of course, this may have more to do with the way this wimpy '80s music was recorded than the transfer itself. —*ML/MM*

Movie: 🎵🎵½ **DVD:** 🎵🎵½

Anchor Bay (UPC #01313131125795). Widescreen (1.85:1) letterboxed; full frame. Dolby Digital 5.1 Surround Stereo. $24.98. Keepcase. *LANG:* English. *FEATURES:* Trailer.

1985 (PG) 90m/C Sarah Jessica Parker, Helen Hunt, Ed Lauter, Holly Gagnier, Morgan Woodward, Lee Montgomery, Shannen Doherty, Biff Yeager; **D:** Alan Metter; **W:** Janice Hirsch, Amy Spies; **C:** Thomas Ackerman; **M:** Thomas Newman.

Gladiator

Teen fantasy of boxing follows Tommy Riley (Marshall), a suburbanite transplanted to the inner city. To help pay off his father's gambling debts, he becomes involved with shady boxing promoters (Loggia and Dennehy), who thrive on pitting different races against each other in illegal boxing matches. Eventually, Riley must get into the ring with his friend Lincoln (Gooding). Before it's over, all of your favorite clichés have been trotted out. The DVD does a good job with potentially diffi-

cult material. Much of the action is set in dark, dingy interiors where the level of detail is very good. The pale colors are true to the original. Sound ranges between good and very good. —*MM*

Movie: 🎵½ **DVD:** 🎵🎵½

Columbia Tristar Home Video (Cat #94569, UPC #043396945692). Full frame; widescreen (1.85:1) letterboxed. Dolby Digital Surround Stereo; Mono. $24.95. Keepcase. *LANG:* English; Spanish. *SUB:* English; French; Spanish; Portuguese; Chinese; Korean; Thai. *FEATURES:* 28 chapter links ● Talent files ● Trailers.

1992 (R) 98m/C Cuba Gooding Jr., James Marshall, Robert Loggia, Ossie Davis, Brian Dennehy, Cara Buono, John Heard, Jon Seda, Lance Slaughter; **D:** Rowdy Herrington; **W:** Lyle Kessler, Robert Mark Kamen; **C:** Tak Fujimoto; **M:** Brad Fiedel.

Gladiator

Though any synopsis makes this epic sound like conventional sword-and-sandals stuff, it's really a fine, subtle, moving updating of *Spartacus* and *Ben-Hur*. Maximus (Crowe) is a Roman general who runs afoul of the mad Commodus (Phoenix), and eventually becomes a fighter in the Roman Coliseum. Beneath the spectacle, the acting is first-rate. The clarity of DVD makes the use of computer-generated effects all the more obvious in some scenes, and aliasing is a little bothersome, too. Those are quibbles. The disc looks fine, from the cool opening blues in the German forest to the dust-brown middle section and finally dry reds. The Surround mix is one of the best sound fields created to date. The commentary track is a careful balance between technical questions and matters of character. The rest of the extensive extras are on a second RSDL disc. (Director Scott's best line, on a deleted scene, "Our Christians in the Colosseum—well, I cut this out because I don't think the lion ate the child very well.") *AWARDS:* VSDA DVD Festival 2000: Best Video Transfer, Best Audio Presentation, Best of Show—Theatrical. —*MM*

Movie: 🎵🎵🎵½ **DVD:** 🎵🎵🎵½

DreamWorks Home Entertainment (Cat #86386, UPC #667068720426). Widescreen (2.35:1) anamorphic. Dolby Digital Surround DD 5.1 Surround Stereo; DTS 6.1 Surround. $29.99. Keepcase. *LANG:* English. *SUB:* English. *CAP:* English. *FEATURES:* 28 chapter links ● Commentary: Scott, Mathieson, Scalia ● "Making of" featurettes ● Deleted scenes ● Interview with composer Hans Zimmer ● Production diary by Spencer Treat Clark ● Trailers and TV spots ● Production notes and filmographies ● Stills gallery.

2000 (R) 154m/C Russell Crowe, Joaquin Rafael (Leaf) Phoenix, Connie Nielsen, Djimon Hounsou, Ralph Moeller, Derek Jacobi, Oliver Reed, Richard Harris, David Schofield, John Shrapnel, Tomas Arana, Spencer (Treat) Clark, Tommy Flanagan, David Hemmings, Sven-Ole Thorsen;

D: Ridley Scott; **W:** David Franzoni, John Logan, William Nicholson; **C:** John Mathieson; **M:** Hans Zimmer.

Gladiator Eroticus

The guys at E.I. Independent specialize in spoofing mainstream hits with their ultra-low budget soft-core filmed in New Jersey. That approach works fine for things like *Survivor* and *Blair Witch Project*. It's more difficult to make fun of the multimillion-dollar special effects of *Gladiator*, but they do pretty well with some of the cheesiest CGI effects you'll ever see. As for the movie itself: a bunch of young folks in and out of togas romp around in a grassy field. On her commentary track, one of the stars mentions the large number of bugs that were involved. The shot-on-video production gains nothing but the extras on DVD. —*MM*

Movie: 🎵🎵 **DVD:** 🎵½

EI Independent Cinema (Cat #sc-1015-dvd, UPC #612385101595). Full frame. $19.98. Keepcase. *LANG:* English. *FEATURES:* Trailers ● Behind-the-scenes featurette ● Debbie Rochon interview ● Misty Mundae interview ● Weblinks.

2000 110m/C Darian Caine, Misty Mundae, Jade DuBoir, Victoria Vega, Heidi Christine, Debbie Rochon, Katie Jordan, A.J. Kahn; **D:** John Bacchus; **W:** John Bacchus.

Gladiators: Bloodsport of the Colosseum

Historically accurate and interesting (more so if you are obsessed with Russell Crowe in *Gladiator*) portrait of gladiators and their way of life. Narration is provided by noted actor David Hemmings. I don't think I've ever run across a more yellow picture than the one on this disc. The mix of distorted film and video makes for a poor-man's cable historical documentary. Certainly the awful state of some of the archival footage used in the film does nothing to alleviate any of the disc's problems. The soundtrack fares a bit better than the picture and features clear and discernible dialogue. The additional featurettes included on the disc are actually a bit more engaging and enjoyable than the actual program. They range from a look at the Colosseum to a treatise on the portrayal of gladiators in Hollywood. —*MJT*

Movie: 🎵🎵½ **DVD:** 🎵🎵½

Questar Video, Inc. (Cat #QD3216, UPC #033937032165). Full frame. Dolby Digital Mono. $24.95. Keepcase. *LANG:* English. *FEATURES:* 12 chapter links ● "Colosseum, House of Terror" featurette ● "Flamma, Gladiator Superstar" featurette ● "Gladiators of Hollywood" featurette ● "Training Killers" featurette ● "Fighting Men of the Arena" featurette ● "Fearful Facts" featurette.

2000 58m/C D: Rolf Forsberg, Marco De Stefanis; **W:** Rolf Forsberg; **C:** Aldo Zappala, Gianenrico Bianchi; **Nar:** David Hemmings.

Glastonbury: The Movie

Began in 1970 as an English version of "Woodstock," the three-day Glastonbury festival (1995 version presented here) has evolved into a well-organized, laid-back excuse to bask in the sun and be mellow while counter-culture and alternative bands bang away. This documentary is a meandering, unscripted look at three days in the English countryside with alternative rock bands. Presentation is strictly for the initiated. —RJT

Movie: ♫♫ **DVD:** ♫♫

Image Entertainment (Cat #ID8717NB DVD, UPC #014381871722). Widescreen. Dolby Digital 5.1 Surround Stereo; Dolby Digital Stereo. $24.99. Snapper. *LANG:* English. *FEATURES:* 28 chapter markers.

1995 101m/C D: William Beaton, Lisa Lake, Robin Mahoney, Matthew Salkeld, Michael Sarne.

Glory [2 SE]

Edward Zwick's masterful Civil War film receives the treatment that due with this superb special edition. The first of the two-disc set contains the widescreen version of the film with video commentary from the director and stars Broderick and Freeman. The second disc has the full-frame version with the traditional commentary track, along with the other extras. It should go without saying that image and sound on both are first-rate, and anyone who has not seen the film should certainly experience it first with the version that best suits the individual video system. The impressive battle scenes—some of the most realistic ever filmed—will lose a lot on a small monitor and so the full-frame option may be preferable. On a later viewing, listen to the intelligent commentary. The two deleted scenes are particularly instructive. This special edition belongs in every video library. —MM

Movie: ♫♫♫♫ **DVD:** ♫♫♫♫

Columbia Tristar Home Video (Cat #04183, UPC #043396041837). Widescreen (1.85:1) anamorphic; full frame. Dolby Digital 5.1 Surround Stereo; Dolby Digital Surround Stereo. $29.95. Keepcase. *LANG:* English; French; Spanish; Portuguese. *SUB:* English; French; Spanish; Portuguese; Chinese; Korean; Thai. *FEATURES:* 28 chapter links ● Video commentary by Zwick, Broderick, Freeman ● "Voices of Glory" featurette ● "Making of" featurette ● Documentary "The True Story of Glory Continues" ● Talent files ● Trailers ● Two deleted scenes.

1989 (R) 122m/C Matthew Broderick, Morgan Freeman, Denzel Washington, Cary Elwes, Jihmi Kennedy, Andre Braugher, John Finn, Donovan Leitch, John David (J.D.) Cullum, Bob Gunton, Jane Alexander, Raymond St. Jacques, Cliff DeYoung, Alan North, Jay O. Sanders, Richard Riehle, Ethan Phillips, RonReaco Lee, Peter Michael Goetz; **D:** Edward Zwick; **W:** Kevin Jarre, Marshall Herskovitz; **C:** Freddie Francis; **M:** James Horner. *AWARDS:* Oscars

'89: Cinematog., Sound, Support. Actor (Washington); Golden Globes '90: Support. Actor (Washington); *NOM:* Oscars '89: Art Dir./Set Dec., Film Editing.

Go for Broke!

Please see review of *Legendary WWII Movies*.

Movie: ♫♫½

1951 92m/B Van Johnson, Gianna Maria Canale, Warner Anderson, Lane Nakano, George Miki; **D:** Robert Pirosh; **C:** Paul Vogel. *AWARDS: NOM:* Oscars '51: Story & Screenplay.

Go, Go Second Time Virgin

More soft-core porn from Japan's infamous director recounts the story of two damned and abused teenagers who meet and fall in love after a rape on a Tokyo rooftop. The video transfer features nice definition in the more colorful scenes. But in the black-and-white scenes (which unfortunately make up most of the film), blacks are poorly defined and detract from the picture's otherwise sharp quality. Clear dialogue and crisp ambient sounds and music are delivered by a decent sound transfer. The interview with Wakamatsu included on the disc is interesting enough, though I would have preferred a subtitled translation as opposed to the dubbed English version provided. This interview is also included on the *Ecstasy of the Angels* disc. —MJT

Image Entertainment (Cat #ID8967VFDVD, UPC #014381896725). Widescreen (2.35:1) anamorphic. Dolby Digital Mono. $24.99. Snapper. *LANG:* Japanese. *SUB:* English. *FEATURES:* 11 chapter links ● Interview with director Koji Wakamatsu.

Movie: ♫♫½ **DVD:** ♫♫½

1969 65m/C *JP* Mimi Kozakura, Michio Akiyama; **D:** Koji Wakamatsu; **W:** Izuru Deguchi; **C:** Hideo Ito.

The Godfather DVD Collection

Perhaps the most eagerly anticipated of all American films (well, two of them, anyway) arrive on DVD on October 9, 2001. Francis Ford Coppola's three *Godfather* films are being packaged as a unit, not separately. The first and third films are each on a single disc; *Godfather 2* is on two discs. Extras (over three hours) are on a fifth. Even though the collection was not available for review as this book went to press, I'm comfortable giving it a four-bone technical rating. —MM

Movie: ♫♫♫♫ **DVD:** ♫♫♫♫

Paramount Home Video (Cat #15647). Widescreen anamorphic. Dolby Digital 5.1 Surround Stereo; Mono. $74.95. Keepcase boxed set. *LANG:* English; French. *SUB:* English. *FEATURES:* Commentary: Francis Ford Coppola ● "Francis Coppola's Notebook" featurette ● "On Location" featurette with production designer Dean Tavoularis ● "The Godfather Family:

A Look Inside" featurette ● 1971 behind-the-scenes featurette ● 2 "Music of the Godfather" featurettes on Carmine Coppola and Nino Rota ● "Cinematography of the Godfather" featurette with Gordon Willis ● Storyboards from *2* and *3* ● "Corleone Family Tree" character and cast bios ● Trailers ● Talent files ● Photo galleries ● Academy Award acceptance speeches.

1972 (R) 175m/C Marlon Brando, Al Pacino, Robert Duvall, James Caan, Diane Keaton, John Cazale, Talia Shire, Richard Conte, Richard S. Castellano, Abe Vigoda, Alex Rocco, Sterling Hayden, John Marley, Al Lettieri, Sofia Coppola, Al Martino, Morgana King; **D:** Francis Ford Coppola; **W:** Mario Puzo, Francis Ford Coppola; **C:** Gordon Willis; **M:** Nino Rota. *AWARDS:* Oscars '72: Actor (Brando), Adapt. Screenplay, Picture; AFI '98: Top 100; Directors Guild '72: Director (Coppola); Golden Globes '73: Actor—Drama (Brando), Director (Coppola), Film—Drama, Screenplay, Score; Natl. Bd. of Review '72: Support. Actor (Pacino), Natl. Film Reg. '90; N.Y. Film Critics '72: Support. Actor (Duvall); Natl. Soc. Film Critics '72: Actor (Pacino); Writers Guild '72: Adapt. Screenplay; *NOM:* Oscars '72: Costume Des., Director (Coppola), Film Editing, Sound, Support. Actor (Caan, Duvall, Pacino).

The Godfather, Part 2

Please see review for *The Godfather DVD Collection*.

Movie: ♫♫♫♫

1974 (R) 200m/C Dominic Chianese, Frank Sivero, Gianni Russo, Peter Donat, Al Pacino, Robert De Niro, Diane Keaton, Robert Duvall, James Caan, Danny Aiello, John Cazale, Lee Strasberg, Talia Shire, Michael V. Gazzo, Troy Donahue, Joe Spinell, Abe Vigoda, Marianna Hill, Fay Spain, G.D. Spradlin, Bruno Kirby, Harry Dean Stanton, Roger Corman, Kathleen Beller, John Aprea, Morgana King; **D:** Francis Ford Coppola; **W:** Mario Puzo, Francis Ford Coppola; **C:** Gordon Willis; **M:** Nino Rota, Carmine Coppola. *AWARDS:* Oscars '74: Adapt. Screenplay, Art Dir./Set Dec., Director (Coppola), Picture, Support. Actor (De Niro), Orig. Dramatic Score; AFI '98: Top 100; Directors Guild '74: Director (Coppola), Natl. Film Reg. '93; Natl. Soc. Film Critics '74: Director (Coppola); Writers Guild '74: Adapt. Screenplay; *NOM:* Oscars '74: Actor (Pacino), Costume Des., Support. Actor (Gazzo, Strasberg), Support. Actress (Shire); Natl. Soc. Film Critics '74: Cinematog.

The Godfather, Part 3

Please see review for *The Godfather DVD Collection*.

Movie: ♫♫♫

1990 (R) 170m/C Al Pacino, Diane Keaton, Andy Garcia, Joe Mantegna, George Hamilton, Talia Shire, Sofia Coppola, Eli Wallach, Don Novello, Bridget Fonda, John Savage, Al Martino, Raf Vallone, Franc D'Ambrosio, Donal Donnelly, Richard

Bright, Helmut Berger; **D:** Francis Ford Coppola; **W:** Mario Puzo, Francis Ford Coppola; **C:** Gordon Willis; **M:** Nino Rota, Carmine Coppola. *AWARDS:* Golden Raspberries '90: Worst Support. Actress (Coppola), Worst New Star (Coppola); *NOM:* Oscars '90: Art Dir./Set Dec., Cinematog., Director (Coppola), Film Editing, Picture, Song ("Promise Me You'll Remember"), Support. Actor (Garcia).

God's Comedy

Joao (writer/director Monteiro), the dour aging manager of the Paradise ice-cream store, fantasizes about the young women who work for him as he experiments with new flavors. With the arrival of Joaninha (Teixeira), he is able to combine the two in a way that's reminiscent of Almodovar and Fellini. At almost three hours, though, this curious sex comedy is not for everyone. DVD image is excellent, capturing lighting that's much more subtle than American audiences are accustomed to. Burned in subtitles are large and easy to read. —*MM* **AKA:** A Comedia de Deus.
Movie: 🎵🎵🎵 *DVD:* 🎵🎵🎵
Image Entertainment (Cat #ID0278SIDVD, UPC #014381027822). Widescreen (1.66:1) letterboxed. Dolby Digital Mono. $24.99. Snapper. *LANG:* Portuguese. *SUB:* English. *FEATURES:* 20 chapter links.
1995 163m/C *PT* Joao Cesar Monteiro, Claudia Teixeira, Manuela de Freitas, Raquel Ascensao, Saraiva Serrano; **D:** Joao Cesar Monteiro; **W:** Joao Cesar Monteiro; **C:** Mario Barroso.

Godzilla 2000

After his big-budget American incarnation, the original Japanese Godzilla returns to his roots, snapping power lines, dancing the Funky Chicken on buildings, and, more importantly, saving the Earth from alien invaders who are hiding in a big rock. For sheer juvenile enjoyment, this is one of the best in the series. The violence is kept to a level that's acceptable for most kids, and as the filmmakers explain on their fascinating commentary track, the story has been streamlined and exposition has been added to make the plot understandable for young American audiences. Actually, the commentary is one of the best in recent years. DVD director Mike Schlesinger, editor Mike Mahoney, and sound editor Darren Paskal stay on the subject as they detail the changes they wrought in the original, and explain what they were trying to accomplish with their work. Highly recommended to fans of the character and the genre. —*MM*
Movie: 🎵🎵🎵 *DVD:* 🎵🎵🎵½
Columbia Tristar Home Video (Cat #05667). Widescreen. Dolby Digital. $24.99. Keepcase. *LANG:* English. *SUB:* English; French. *FEATURES:* 28 chapter links • Behind-the-scenes featurette • Trailers • Talent files • Commentary: Mike Schlesinger, Mike Mahoney, Darren Paskal.
1999 (PG) 97m/C *JP* Takehiro Murata, Shiro Sano, Hiroshi Abe, Naomi Nishida,

Mayu Suzuki; **D:** Takao Okawara; **W:** Hiroshi Kashiwabara, Waturu Mimura; **C:** Katsuhiro Kato; **M:** Takayuki Hattori.

Gold of the Amazon Women

Ludicrous jungle adventure isn't nearly ludicrous enough. After being attacked in New York by female archers in leather bikinis, an adventurer (Svenson) is given a map and heads for darkest Africa where he finds the titular babes. The action is strictly on the made-for-TV level. In the lead, Svenson is very blonde, and as the Queen of the Amazons, Anita Ekberg is just a tad pudgy. The disc was made from a damaged print, but that's the least of its problems. —*MM* **AKA:** Amazon Women.
Movie: 🎵½ *DVD:* 🎵½
Image Entertainment (Cat #ALF9855DVD, UPC #014381985528). Full frame. Dolby Digital Mono. $24.95. Snapper. *LANG:* English. *FEATURES:* 12 chapter links.
1979 94m/C Bo Svenson, Anita Ekberg, Bond Gideon, Donald Pleasence; **D:** Mark L. Lester; **W:** Stanley Ralph Ross; **C:** David Quaid; **M:** Gil Melle.

Golden Voyage of Sinbad

In the mysterious ancient land of Lemuria, Sinbad (Law) and his crew encounter magical and mystical creatures. A six-armed statue and a ship's figurehead come to life. The fight between a griffin and a cyclops/centaur is perhaps the finest moment. Harryhausen's effects aren't quite as superb as they are in *Jason and the Argonauts* but they're fine, and Caroline Munro is delightful eye candy. Increased grain is apparent in the stop-motion animation scenes, but that has always been the case. Best feature of the disc is the choice of screen sizes. —*MM*
Movie: 🎵🎵🎵 *DVD:* 🎵🎵½
Columbia Tristar Home Video (Cat #04747, UPC #043396047471). Widescreen (1.85:1) anamorphic; full frame. Dolby Digital Mono. $24.95. Keepcase. *LANG:* English; Portuguese. *SUB:* English; Spanish; Portuguese; Chinese; Korean; Thai. *FEATURES:* 28 chapter links • 3 featurettes • Vintage advertising • Trailer • Talent files.
1973 (G) 105m/C John Phillip Law, Caroline Munro, Tom Baker, Douglas Wilmer, Martin Shaw, John David Garfield, Gregoire Aslan; **D:** Gordon Hessler; **W:** Brian Clemens; **C:** Ted Moore; **M:** Miklos Rozsa.

Gone in 60 Seconds

While running his own auto salvage business in southern California, H.B. "Toby" Halicki decided to make a movie about car thieves. Being the do-it-yourselfer that he was, he wrote, produced, directed, starred in, and stunt drove for the over-the-top automotive love-fest that became a smash drive-in hit in 1974. (Pay no attention to the Nic Cage remake.) Over the course of the movie, 93 different cars are

destroyed. The DVD's quality is nothing short of amazing given the film's age. Sharpness is rock-solid with even the finest details coming through clearly on screen. Heck, even the garish patterns on everyone's vintage clothing come through crystal clear with no artifacting or shimmering evident on those extra-wide lapels. Colors, while very stable as well, do display that unique '70s feel that is evident in many movies from that time period. There is also a fair amount of grain evident and nighttime scenes suffer from the lack of decent black levels. The 2.0 Dolby mix has clear dialogue and sound but very little range. The 5.1 track adds nice directionality and provides the soundtrack with a much fuller lower end, and the DTS track offers even greater range and better directionality. It also enhances even the subtlest of sound effects. In one scene a hammer is dropped on the chop-shop floor; in the Dolby Digital mix it hits with a thud while in the DTS mix the sharp ringing of metal on concrete reverberates across the front soundstage and fades slowly into the background. —*MP*
Movie: 🎵🎵🎵 *DVD:* 🎵🎵🎵½
Navarre Corp. Widescreen (1.85:1) letterboxed. Dolby Digital 5.1 Surround Stereo; DTS; Dolby Digital Surround Stereo. $19.98. *LANG:* English. *FEATURES:* Commentary • Deleted scenes • Interviews • Photo gallery • Trailers.
1974 105m/C H.B. Halicki, Marion Busia, George Cole, James McIntyre, Jerry Daugirda; **D:** H.B. Halicki; **W:** H.B. Halicki; **C:** Jack Vacek; **M:** Philip Kachaturian.

Gone in 60 Seconds

Fun but frivolous descent in Bruckheimer madness comes complete with bad dialogue, pointless storylines, and some really cool, loud, death-defying, digitally enhanced car chases. "Memphis" Raines (Cage) left a life as the Jedi Master of car thieves in Los Angeles, and now must return to save his kid brother (Ribisi). Raines and his newly assembled team of old-time crack car thieves, including an ex-girlfriend (Jolie) and youngster hood friends of Ribisi, must steal 50 exotic cars in 24 hours. After this clumsily constructed storyline is put in place, the fun begins with exotic cars caressed lovingly by the camera and by the actors, and high-speed car chases set in impossible locations. One of the best extras is the ability to watch only the car chases narrated by the mechanical effects guys, and this way you only have to watch the whole story once. A beautiful disc with fabulous color (you can see that the cinematographer longed for sepia tone shots), and the sound is so good it seems like Surround on regular TVs. —*CA*
Movie: 🎵🎵 *DVD:* 🎵🎵🎵½
Buena Vista Home Entertainment (Cat #19606, UPC #717951008572). Widescreen (2.35:1) anamorphic. Dolby Digital 5.1 Surround. $29.99. Keepcase. *LANG:* English; French; Spanish. *SUB:* Spanish. *CAP:* English. *FEATURES:* 32 chapter links

• Theatrical trailer • Jerry Bruckheimer interview • Music video • Chase scenes with commentary • Behind-the-scenes featurette exclusive to the DVD. **2000 (PG-13) 117m/C** Nicolas Cage, Angelina Jolie, Giovanni Ribisi, Robert Duvall, Scott Caan, Vinnie Jones, Will Patton, Delroy Lindo, Chi McBride, Christopher Eccleston, Timothy Olyphant, William Lee Scott, Frances Fisher, Grace Zabriskie, James Duval, TJ Cross, Arye Gross, Bodhi (Pine) Elfman, Percy (Master P) Miller; **D:** Dominic Sena; **W:** Scott Rosenberg; **C:** Paul Cameron; **M:** Trevor Rabin.

A Good Baby

A surprisingly well made, intelligently scripted, and professionally acted story of big dreams and small towns. David Strathairn is Truman Lester, a sleazy traveling salesman with a warped sense of religion who works the small towns of the South. He is surprised to learn that the girl he's been seeing in one of his towns is pregnant when she comes to meet him in a secluded backwoods area. As they argue she goes into labor. Sometime later, the town loner Raymond Toker (Thomas) finds an abandoned baby girl in the woods. As he wanders around town looking for the parents of the baby, everyone slowly becomes multi-dimensional. We learn everyone's dirty secrets but realize that the minor wrongs committed by the people in the town are nothing compared to the true evil that stalks the orphaned child. In the end, those whose lives have been touched by the child confront the evil and win with a stroke of backwoods justice. This is by no means a great film but it is certainly worthy of viewing. The color on the disc is great with lots of lush backwoods greens and browns courtesy of Denault, who also shot *Boys Don't Cry* and the pixelated *Nadja*. The sound is average. —CA
Movie: 𝄞𝄞½ **DVD:** 𝄞𝄞𝄞
Winstar Home Entertainment (Cat #FLV5 256, UPC #7 20917 52562 4). Full frame. Dolby Digital 5.1 Surround. $24.99. Keepcase. *LANG:* English. *FEATURES:* 16 chapter links • Filmographies • Weblink.
1999 98m/C Henry Thomas, David Strathairn, Cara Seymour, Danny Nelson; **D:** Katherine Dieckmann; **W:** Katherine Dieckmann, Leon Rooke; **C:** Jim Denault; **M:** David Mansfield.

Good Morning

One of Ozu's first color efforts, *Good Morning* is a light social comedy revolving around two young Japanese boys who try to talk their parents into buying them one of those new-fangled television sets. Dad feels that the boob tube will dull the senses of the Japanese youth (imagine that!); the kids feel that there's too much small talk going on. Ozu keeps the camera at kids' eye-level, emphasizing the sympathetic perspective of the children and giving a unique look to the film. Bold colors populate the screen and Ozu keeps the story whimsical while commenting on Japanese society (very much like Juzo Itami would years later). The characters are well-fleshed out and likable. Criterion's DVD is another excellent transfer of an important film. The colors appear as rich as they probably were upon the film's initial release four decades ago. Blacks and contrasts are good, making for excellent detail in all lighting conditions. No artifacts or noticeable grain. The mono sound is a little tinny and there are some preprint related glitches, but all in all another very fine Criterion edition. No supplementals. —JO **AKA:** Ohayo.
Movie: 𝄞𝄞𝄞 **DVD:** 𝄞𝄞𝄞
Criterion Collection (Cat #60, UPC #03742 9149720). Full frame. Dolby Digital Mono. $29.95. Keepcase. *LANG:* Japanese. *SUB:* English. *FEATURES:* 24 chapter links.
1959 94m/C JP Masahiko Shimazu, Koji Shigaragi, Chishu Ryu, Kuniko Miyake; **D:** Yasujiro Ozu; **W:** Yasujiro Ozu, Kogo Noda; **C:** Yushun Atsuta; **M:** Toshiro Mayuzumi.

Good News

A vintage Comden-Green musical about the love problems of a college football star, who will flunk out if he doesn't pass French exams. Allyson plays the female Poindexter who must help the lame-brain jock make the grade. Second feature from director Walters who went on such classic musicals as *Easter Parade* and *The Unsinkable Molly Brown*. Revamping of the 1937 Broadway smash features the unlikely sight of Lawford in a song-and-dance role. "Pass that Peace Pipe" garnered a nomination for Best Song. The DVD is not as sharp as one would like, but does feature bright, vibrant color and fairly true blacks. There is grain present throughout that seems to be more of a digital addition than a representation of older film stock. The mono sound is free of distortion and more full-bodied than some found on the discs of other films from this era. One only wishes that the musical number "An Easier Way," with its energetic performance by Allyson, could have been re-incorporated into the film. At least the deleted song is included in the supplementals. —JO
Movie: 𝄞𝄞𝄞 **DVD:** 𝄞𝄞½
Warner Home Video, Inc. (Cat #65193, UPC #012569519329). Full frame. Dolby Digital Mono. $19.98. Snapper. *LANG:* English. *SUB:* English; French. *CAP:* English. *FEATURES:* 32 chapter links • Theatrical trailer • Production notes • Excerpts from *Good News* (1930) • Deleted musical number "An Easier Way."
1947 92m/C June Allyson, Peter Lawford, Joan McCracken, Mel Torme; **D:** Charles Walters; **W:** Betty Comden; **C:** Charles E. Schoenbaum; **M:** Hugh Martin, Ralph Blane, Roger Edens. *AWARDS:* NOM: Oscars '47: Song ("Pass That Peace Pipe").

Goodbye America

Though the box art leads you to believe that this is a military action flick, it's really a bit more serious minded. It concerns relations between service personnel and locals as the Navy is closing its last base in the Philippines. The ensemble cast is working with some of the same themes that made *An Officer and a Gentleman* such a hit. This one's not nearly as successful but it has its moments. Full-frame DVD image is a slight improvement over VHS tape; sound is not. —MM
Movie: 𝄞𝄞½ **DVD:** 𝄞𝄞½
MTI Home Video (Cat #BE50020DVD, UPC #619935402034). Full frame. $24.95. Keepcase. *LANG:* English. *SUB:* Spanish. *FEATURES:* 20 chapter links • Talent files • Previews.
1997 (R) 115m/C Michael York, Corin "Corky" Nemec, Rae Dawn Chong, Alexis Arquette, James Brolin, Wolfgang Bodison, John Haymes Newton, Maureen Flannigan; **D:** Thierry Notz; **W:** Ricardo Lee, Frederick Bailey; **C:** Sharon Meir.

The Gore-Gore Girls

Splatter horror director Lewis's final film follows a detective's search for a madman who is mutilating and murdering young go-go dancers. The methods employed are inventive, disgusting and, of course, bloody. On his commentary track, Lewis sounds less happy with this one than with many of his others. DVD image is acceptable, though the original has always been harsh and darkly lit in some scenes, overly bright in others. —MM **AKA:** Blood Orgy.
Movie: 𝄞 **DVD:** 𝄞𝄞
Image Entertainment (Cat #ID6041SW DVD, UPC #014381604122). Full frame. Dolby Digital Mono. $24.99. Snapper. *LANG:* English. *FEATURES:* 12 chapter links • Commentary: Mike Vraney, Herschell Gordon Lewis, Jimmy Maslin • Short gore film, "Love Goddess of Blood Island" • Herschell Gordon Lewis gallery of exploitation art.
1972 84m/C Frank Kress, Amy Farrel, Hedda Lubin, Henny Youngman, Russ Badger, Nora Alexis, Phil Laurensen, Frank Rice, Jackie Kroeger, Corlee Bew, Emily Mason, Lena Bousman, Ray Sager; **D:** Herschell Gordon Lewis; **W:** Alan J. Dachman; **C:** Alex Ameri.

Gorgeous

This Jackie Chan effort is more romantic comedy than the furious action comedy the star has become so famous for. Nonetheless, it wouldn't really be a Jackie Chan movie without any fights, right? Get ready for some very cool—albeit very different—fighting sequences. Most of it is body work without overly flashy action stunts. Breathtakingly executed, these showcases of martial arts are nothing short of mesmerizing once again, with a good portion of humor. One caveat: the film has actually been cut by 22 minutes compared to its original Chinese counterpart, making it less desirable than the original version released in Hong Kong. Colors are strong and absolutely natural, also rendering skin tones very faithfully.

Audio quality is good. The disc defaults to the Cantonese language track with English subtitles. —GH/MM **AKA:** Glass Bottle; Bor Lei Jun.

Movie: 🎬🎬🎬 **DVD:** 🎬🎬🎬
Columbia Tristar Home Video (Cat #5054). Widescreen (2.35:1) letterboxed. Dolby Digital 5.1 Surround Stereo. $24.95. Keepcase. *LANG:* Cantonese; English. *SUB:* English. *FEATURES:* Commentary • Jackie Chan • Featurette • Music video • Talent files.
1999 (PG-13) 99m/C *HK* Jackie Chan, Tony Leung Chiu-Wai, Qi Shu, Hsein-Chi Jen; **D:** Vincent Kok; **W:** Vincent Kok; **C:** Man Po Cheung; **M:** Dang-Yi Wong.

Gorgo

An undersea explosion off the coast of Ireland brings to the surface a prehistoric monster (played both by a guy in a goofy suit and a full-sized statue). It's captured and taken to a London circus until its irate mom appears. The Brit version of *Godzilla* may lack a certain cheesiness, but it's certainly fun for fans of the genre. DVD image is often harsh and dark, but that's the way it's always looked, as I remember from theatrical screenings. —MM

Movie: 🎬🎬½ **DVD:** 🎬🎬
VCI Home Video (Cat #8203, UPC #08985 9829328). Widescreen (1.66:1) letterboxed. Dolby Digital Mono. $19.99. Keepcase. *LANG:* English. *FEATURES:* Behind-the-scenes featurette • Photo gallery • Talent files • Trailers • 18 chapter links.
1961 76m/C *GB* Bill Travers, William Sylvester, Vincent Winter, Bruce Seton, Christopher Rhodes; **D:** Eugene Lourie; **W:** Robert L. Richards, Daniel James; **C:** Frederick A. (Freddie) Young; **M:** Angelo Francesco Lavagnino.

Gorky Park

When three faceless corpses are found in Moscow's Gorky Park, militia Inspector Arkady Renko (Hurt) has few clues. But why is the KGB so interested? It's a fine police procedural that's well-acted by an excellent cast. The widescreen transfer is really all that the disc has to offer. Beyond that, sound and image are only a slight improvement over VHS tape. —MM

Movie: 🎬🎬🎬 **DVD:** 🎬🎬½
MGM Home Entertainment (Cat #1001276, UPC #027616855565). Widescreen anamorphic. Dolby Digital Mono. $19.98. Keepcase. *LANG:* English; French; Spanish. *SUB:* English; French; Spanish. *FEATURES:* 36 chapter links • Theatrical trailer.
1983 (R) 127m/C William Hurt, Lee Marvin, Brian Dennehy, Joanna Pacula; **D:** Michael Apted; **W:** Dennis Potter; **C:** Ralf Bode; **M:** James Horner.

The Gospel According to Philip K. Dick

Philip K. Dick is a personal guru to hundreds of thousands of ardent fans. His sf writings range from clever short stories in the '50s, to visionary novels in the '60s

and '70s that are still unsurpassed in intelligence, insight, and just plain genius. This DVD turns out to be not a full-out documentary, but a well-intentioned 95-minute collection of talking-head testimony, aimed at people who already know something about the author. The interviewees include a couple of well-known writers and speculative magazine editors, as well as personal friends and associates of Dick. The information they have is mostly personal opinion of things already on the record about the controversial aspects of Dick's life—his paranoia, the break-in to his house, his avowed spiritual visions. Dick wrote about these visions endlessly towards the end of his life. Unfortunately, the interviewees have nothing to offer about these matters except unfocused opinions. The final negatives are the technical inconsistencies. The interviews were shot on digital video, and look O.K., but the audio is all over the place. Several speakers border on inaudible. There are no subs or closed captioning to help out with this, so concentration is needed to understand all of what's being heard. The editing looks rushed, as does the music. There is a droning techno track under most of the show, interrupted by emotional piano music to accompany accounts of the author's death. The amateurishness would be forgiven in a minute if the film had some real academic content or insight to its subject. —GE

Movie: 🎬½ **DVD:** 🎬½
First Run Features (Cat #FRF909655D, UPC #720229909655). Full frame. $29.95. Snapper. *LANG:* English. *FEATURES:* "Dicktionary" of terms • Interviews with filmmaker • Photo gallery • "Bonus footage" (just another animated segment of Dick talking).
2000 95m/C D: Andy Massagli, Mark Steensland; **C:** Andy Massagli, Mark Steensland.

Gossip

College roommates Derrick (Marsden), Jones (Headey), and Travis (Reedus) decide to do their communications class thesis on gossip, and start a false rumor about a couple, Naomi and Beau (Hudson and Jackson) having sex. Despite its somewhat hackneyed premise, the film is well-written and falls apart only during its far-fetched finale. The picture is extremely sharp and clear, showing no noise or grain. This nearly perfect image offers a wide array of colors, which are all presented very naturally and realistically. The movie features many "rave-like" party scenes that are awash in various hues and these come across very well. The 5.1 sound is equally impressive during these scenes, as the bass-heavy music sounds very good. The audio mix has a wide dynamic range and sound field. Dialogue is clear and audible and the volume is consistently well-balanced. On the commentary track Guggenheim and Marsden do a fine job of delivering anecdotes, behind-the-scenes

tidbits, and, of course, gossip about the production of the film. —ML/MM

Movie: 🎬🎬🎬 **DVD:** 🎬🎬🎬½
Warner Home Video, Inc. (Cat #18324). Widescreen (2.35:1) letterboxed. Dolby Digital 5.1 Surround Stereo. $19.98. Snapper. *LANG:* English; French. *SUB:* English; French. *FEATURES:* Commentary • Deleted scenes • Music videos • Alternate footage and ending • Trailer • Talent files.
1999 (R) 91m/C James Marsden, Lena Headey, Norman Reedus, Kate Hudson, Joshua Jackson, Marisa Coughlan, Edward James Olmos, Sharon Lawrence, Eric Bogosian; **D:** Davis Guggenheim; **W:** Gregory Poirier, Theresa Rebeck; **C:** Andrzej Bartkowiak; **M:** Graeme Revell.

Gothic

Mary Shelley (Richardson), her stepsister Clair (Cyr), Lord Byron (Byrne), and Percy Shelley (Sands) spend the night in a Swiss villa telling each other ghost stories, gulping laudanum, and fooling around. Their dreams and realizations of the night will color the rest of their lives, and lead to the novel *Frankenstein*. Director Russell gives his wildest excesses full rein. The video transfer displays numerous problems. For starters, the full-frame image looks as if it was mastered from a much worn print. Speckles appear throughout, starting at the credits. The garish colors of the film, for the most part, are well represented, but the transfer lacks sharpness and detail. Compression artifacts are present, as is quite a bit of film grain. The audio serves Thomas Dolby's bombastic music score well enough, but dialogue at times seems overly produced and not at all naturally integrated within the environment. —EP/MM

Movie: 🎬🎬🎬 **DVD:** 🎬½
Pioneer Entertainment (Cat #10361). Full frame. Dolby Digital Stereo. $24.98. Keepcase. *LANG:* English. *FEATURES:* Trailers.
1987 (R) 87m/C Julian Sands, Gabriel Byrne, Timothy Spall, Natasha Richardson, Myriam Cyr; **D:** Ken Russell; **W:** Stephen Volk; **C:** Mike Southon; **M:** Thomas Dolby.

Gotti

Made-for-cable biopic follows the career of the New York mobster know as the "Teflon Don." Gotti's (Assante) mentor is Neil Dellacroce (Quinn), underboss to the aging head of the Gambino crime family. When Gambino (Lawrence) dies, Gotti is incensed that Paul Castellano (Sarafian) is named as family successor and eventually has him killed. He then grabs power (and lots of tabloid headlines), manages to beat his first federal racketeering rap, but is brought down with the aid of his own underboss, Sammy the Bull (Forsythe), whom the feds get into court. The DVD shows off a lot of detail in the brighter scenes but becomes grainier in the darker sequences where there is also a tendency for reds bleed. The tint leans too much to the red as well, and fleshtones are slightly

off. Some artifacting occurs in longer detailed shots. Well-lit interior shots are sharper and do convey a lot of depth, so it's hard to nail down the real culprit (DVD authoring or preprint) for the flaws in the image. Like many visually so-so DVDs, the soundtrack nearly comes to the rescue. In this case, the Dolby Surround is surprisingly full and lively, with the rear track contributing frequently and the overall mix satisfying for both music and dialogue. —JO
Movie: 🎵🎵½ **DVD:** 🎵🎵½
HBO Home Video (Cat #91286, UPC #026 359128662). Full frame. Dolby Surround; Dolby Digital Mono; Dolby Digital Stereo. $19.98. Snapper. *LANG:* English; Spanish; French. *SUB:* English; Spanish; French. *CAP:* English. *FEATURES:* 15 chapter links ▪ Talent files.
1996 (R) 118m/C Armand Assante, William Forsythe, Anthony Quinn, Richard Sarafian, Vincent Pastore, Robert Miranda, Frank Vincent, Marc Lawrence, Al Waxman, Alberta Watson, Silvio Oliviero, Nigel Bennett; **D:** Robert Harmon; **W:** Steve Shagan; **C:** Alan Kivilo; **M:** Mark Isham.

Goya in Bordeaux

As an old, sick man Goya (Rabal) remembers the wild creative days of his youth, particularly his passionate affair with the Duchess of Alba (Verdu). This is a lavish production, filled with sumptuous sets and costumes. It's also a fairly standard biopic that settles back on clichés in the second half. The image is on the soft side, but that's as it should be. The bright yellow subtitles are fitted into the lower letterbox. Sound is excellent. —MM
Movie: 🎵🎵 **DVD:** 🎵🎵½
Columbia Tristar Home Video (Cat #05745, UPC #043396057456). Widescreen (2:1) anamorphic. Dolby Digital 5.1 Surround Stereo; Dolby Digital Surround. $29.95. Keepcase. *LANG:* Spanish. *SUB:* English; Spanish. *FEATURES:* 28 chapter links ▪ Trailers ▪ Talent files.
2000 (R) 105m/C *SP IT* Francesco Rabal, Jose Coronado, Maribel Verdu, Daphne Fernandez; **D:** Carlos Saura; **W:** Carlos Saura; **C:** Vittorio Storaro; **M:** Roque Banos.

Grand Canyon

Diverse group of Los Angelenos are thrown together through chance encounters while coping with urban chaos and familial pressures. The main focus is the growing friendship between an immigration lawyer (Kline) and a tow-truck driver (Glover) who meet when Kline's car breaks down in a bad neighborhood. First-rate performances by the cast make up for the numerous moral messages that often lack subtlety. DVD image looks much as I remember the theatrical release. Sound is very good, too, but considering the amount of talent that was at hand on both sides of the camera, a commentary track could have been a valuable extra. —MM
Movie: 🎵🎵🎵 **DVD:** 🎵🎵🎵

20th Century Fox Home Entertainment (Cat #2001248, UPC #024543012481). Widescreen (2.35:1) anamorphic. Dolby Digital 4.0 Surround; Dolby Digital Surround. $24.99. Keepcase. *LANG:* English; French. *SUB:* English; Spanish. *FEATURES:* "Making of" featurette ▪ 32 chapter links ▪ Trailers.
1991 (R) 134m/C Danny Glover, Kevin Kline, Steve Martin, Mary McDonnell, Mary-Louise Parker, Alfre Woodard, Jeremy Sisto, Tina Lifford, Patrick Malone, Mary Ellen Trainor; **D:** Lawrence Kasdan; **W:** Lawrence Kasdan, Meg Kasdan; **C:** Owen Roizman; **M:** James Newton Howard. *AWARDS: NOM:* Oscars '91: Orig. Screenplay.

The Grandfather

Charming, yet oddly emotional film weaves familial relationships and deceit around the story of old Count Albrit, who returns home to Spain after many years abroad. Upon meeting his two charming young granddaughters, he discovers that one of the girls is not his true heir. The video transfer shows some grain and tends to lose clarity on some darker scenes. On the whole, however, the picture is suitably reproduced. An above average soundtrack features skillfully reproduces music and dialogue. —MJT **AKA:** El Abuelo.
Movie: 🎵🎵🎵 **DVD:** 🎵🎵
Miramax Pictures Home Video (Cat #18308, UPC #717951004932). Widescreen (1.85:1) anamorphic. Dolby Digital Surround. $29.99. Keepcase. *LANG:* Spanish. *SUB:* English. *CAP:* English. *FEATURES:* 29 chapter links ▪ Theatrical trailer ▪ Additional Miramax trailers.
1998 (PG) 145m/C *SP* Fernando Fernan-Gomez, Cayetana Guillen Cuervo, Rafael Alonso, Augustin Gonzalez; **D:** Jose Luis Garci; **W:** Jose Luis Garci, Horacio Valcarcel; **C:** R(aul) P. Cubero; **M:** Manuel Balboa. *AWARDS: NOM:* Oscars '98: Foreign Film.

Grave of the Fireflies

This film is a perfect example of the Japanese ability to use animation to make serious films rather than just animated stories. The story is set in the countryside outside of Tokyo, just after the Japanese surrender of World War II. It follows the surprisingly dark tale of two orphans, an older brother, Seita, and his younger sister, Setsuko, who are left to starve by the adults around them while their society collapses in upon itself. A brutally frank telling of the flip side of human nature that can rear its head during tragedy. Don't put this on expecting the usual anime fare of scantily clad women and big explosions, and keep plenty of tissue on hand. The color and clarity of the animation are clean and clear and the sound is crisp. —CA **AKA:** Hotaru no Haka.
Movie: 🎵🎵🎵 **DVD:** 🎵🎵½
Central Park Media/U.S. Manga Corps (Cat #CPMD1729, UPC #719987172920). Widescreen. Dolby Digital Stereo. $29.95. Keepcase. *LANG:* English; Japanese. *SUB:* English. *FEATURES:* 24 chapter links ▪

Historical background ▪ Additional anime trailers.
1988 88m/C *JP* **D:** Isao Takahata; **W:** Isao Takahata.

Greaser's Palace

Beguiling satire filters *The Greatest Story Ever Told* through a Sergio Leone–like western landscape. Allan Arbus stars as the zoot-suited Jessy who runs afoul of town boss Seaweedhead Greaser while on a journey to Jerusalem "where the agent Morris awaits." Chutzpah meets '70s counter-culture as writer/director Robert Downey Sr. slaughters one sacred cow after another, from the Stigmata as a show-stopper to the Holy Ghost depicted as a guy wearing a bed sheet with holes cut out for eyes. Aside from a few speckles and blemishes, source material is remarkably clean. The video transfer exhibits good color detail, yet some scenes suffer from high contrast washout. Edge enhancement is apparent, but the clean, sharper-than-sharp images serve only to highlight the desolation of the terrain and the town's bizarre inhabitants, including a pre–*Fantasy Island* Herve Villechaize! Mono soundtrack is fine. Go with the crazy flow and find yourself both mystified and exhilarated. *Greaser's Palace* is a time capsule well worth visiting. —EP
AKA: Zoot Suit Jesus.
Movie: 🎵🎵🎵 **DVD:** 🎵🎵🎵½
Image Entertainment (Cat #ID6783CQ DVD, UPC #1438167832). Widescreen (1.85:1) letterboxed. Dolby Digital Mono. $24.99. Snapper. *LANG:* English. *FEATURES:* 12 chapter links.
1972 91m/C Albert Henderson, Allan Arbus, Michael Sullivan, Luana Anders, James Antonio, Ronald Nealy, Larry Moyer, John Paul Hudson, Herve Villechaize; **D:** Robert Downey; **W:** Robert Downey; **C:** Peter Powell; **M:** Jack Nitzsche.

The Great Alaska Train Adventure

Train and travel buffs will want to get on board for this single-disc collection of two episodes from the PBS series *America's Scenic Railway Journeys*. From "Anchorage to Seward" and "Anchorage to Fairbanks," experience America's "last frontier" from the privileged vantage point of the Alaska Railway. Along these scenic routes strewn with Alaskan history, you'll experience parts of the state that can only be seen via train. The crystal clear images of snowy peaks, pristine waters, and frolicking killer whales and sea lions are breathtaking. James Coburn narrates. —DL
Movie: 🎵🎵🎵 **DVD:** 🎵🎵🎵
Acorn Media Publishing (Cat #37319, UPC #054961373192). Full frame. Dolby Digital. $29.95. Keepcase. *LANG:* English. *FEATURES:* Historical photos ▪ Alaska Railroad trip information and weblink ▪ 12 chapter links.
19?? 108m/C *Nar:* James Coburn.

Great Animation Studios: Fleischer Studios

The Fleischer Studios were always considered something less than Disney or Warner Bros. Though their work is comparable and was probably as popular and innovative in its day, the cartoons don't have the same emotional connection. These works are representative. The most familiar characters are Betty Boop and Popeye. The black-and-white films tend to have held up to the aging process better than the supersaturated colors. That may be a personal prejudice; I am a fan of good black-and-white photography. In the same vein, I find the beefed-up Dolby stereo a bit of overkill. Contents: "Tantalizing Fly," "Bubbles," "Betty Boop's Ker-Choo," "More Pep," "Song of the Birds," "Little Swee' Pea," "Grampy's Indoor Outing," "Small Fry," and "Aladdin's Wonderful Lamp." —*MM*
Movie: 🎞🎞½ *DVD:* 🎞🎞½
Winstar Home Entertainment (Cat #WHE7 3104, UPC #720917310428). Full frame. Dolby Digital Stereo. $24.99. Keepcase. *LANG:* English. *FEATURES:* 12 chapter links ➤ History of studio (text) ➤ DVD credits.
2000 90m/C

Great Baseball Movies

This version of *The Jackie Robinson Story* isn't nearly as sharp as the MGM release. (Please see review.) *It's Good to Be Alive* is a made-for-TV bio-pic about Roy Campanella, the catcher who was left a quadriplegic after a car accident. In the third film, *Headin' Home,* Babe Ruth plays an idealized version of himself. It's silent with an orchestral accompaniment and is the oldest and worst-looking of the trio. As a group, they're not really superior to tape in either image or sound. Note: The chapter links do not take you to the beginning of the second and third features. —*MM*
Movie: 🎞🎞 *DVD:* 🎞🎞
BFS Video (Cat #30091-D, UPC #0668053 00912). Full frame. Dolby Digital Mono. $9.98. Keepcase. *LANG:* English. *SUB:* English intertitles in *Headin' Home.* *FEATURES:* 12 chapter links.
2000 ?m/C

Great Boxing Movies

Coley Wallace looks amazingly like the real "Brown Bomber" in *The Joe Louis Story.* Unfortunately, this disc was made from a damaged print that's missing bits of footage and is filled with spots, snow, and vertical streaks. In *The Fighter,* a Mexican patriot (Conte) comes to America and falls for a co-revolutionary. Flashbacks show the destruction of his family and village, and his pugilistic experience. (It's adapted from Jack London's story "The Mexican.") The disc ends with a short (27-minute) television film, *Fight for the Title,* starring a young Michael Landon. Overall, the image ranges between poor and fair. Sound is about the same. Most problems come from damaged originals, not the transfer. Disc is a bare-bones affair without chapter links. —*MM*
Movie: 🎞🎞 *DVD:* 🎞½
BFS Video (Cat #30092-D, UPC #0668053 00929). Full frame. Dolby Digital Mono. $9.98. Keepcase. *LANG:* English.
2000 ?m/C

The Great Lover

Hotshot reporter Freddie Hunter (Hope) has chaperoned a troop of young scouts on a trip to France. Returning on a luxury ocean liner, he runs into a murderous gambler (Young), a lovely duchess (Fleming), and murder. Vintage comic vehicle is terrific for the star's fans who will appreciate the cameo by Jack Benny. The dark and slightly muddy black-and-white image is acceptable for a film of its age. The soundtrack contains faint static throughout. —*MM*
Movie: 🎞🎞🎞 *DVD:* 🎞🎞
Brentwood Home Video (Cat #60981-9, UPC #090096098197). Full frame. Dolby Digital Mono. $14.98. Keepcase. *LANG:* English. *FEATURES:* 8 chapter links ➤ Bob Hope thumbnail bio and filmography.
1949 80m/B Bob Hope, Rhonda Fleming, Roland Young, Roland Culver, George Reeves, Jim Backus, Jack Benny; **D:** Alexander Hall; **W:** Edmund Beloin, Melville Shavelson, Jack Rose; **C:** Charles B(ryant) Lang Jr.

Great Mafia Movies

In *Honor Thy Father,* a made-for-TV adaptation of Gay Talese's book, the everyday life of a real-life Mafia family is seen through the eyes of Bill Bonanno (Bologna), son of mob chieftain Joe Bonanno. *Family Enforcer* is about a small-time hood (Pesci) bent on becoming the best in his business. In *Mob War,* boxer Jake La Motta, the subject of *Raging Bull,* appears as godfather Don Ricci. All three features are very dark and grainy—indistinguishable from VHS tape. Same goes for sound. —*MM*
Movie: 🎞🎞 *DVD:* 🎞🎞
BFS Video (Cat #30094-D, UPC #0668053 00943). Full frame. Dolby Digital Mono. $9.95. Keepcase. *LANG:* English. *FEATURES:* 12 chapter links.
2000 ?m/C

The Greatest Story Ever Told [SE]

Max von Sydow takes a nicely restrained approach to the role of Jesus Christ in this international all-star epic. On the other hand, Charlton Heston's bombastic John the Baptist is an unrepentant scenery-devouring machine. And then there are Shelley Winters, Pat Boone, John Wayne, and many many more. Director Stevens tells the story through some nicely composed visuals that make a solid transition to DVD. The restoration has removed virtually all signs of wear. Special effects, matte shots, locations, and sets are first-rate. But on anything but the largest home monitor, the opening crawl credits are impossible to read. Alfred Newman's score drenches the entire production in cloying sanctity. The extras are on a second disc. —*MM*
Movie: 🎞🎞 *DVD:* 🎞🎞🎞½
MGM Home Entertainment (Cat #10015 84, UPC #027616858948). Widescreen (2.35:1) anamorphic. Dolby Digital 5.1 Surround Stereo; Dolby Digital Surround. $26.98. Keepcase. *LANG:* English; French. *SUB:* French; Spanish. *CAP:* English. *FEATURES:* 32 chapter links ➤ 2 "making of" documentaries ➤ Deleted scenes and music ➤ Photo gallery ➤ Trailer.
1965 196m/C Max von Sydow, Charlton Heston, Sidney Poitier, Claude Rains, Jose Ferrer, Telly Savalas, Angela Lansbury, Dorothy McGuire, John Wayne, Donald Pleasence, Carroll Baker, Van Heflin, Robert Loggia, Shelley Winters, Ed Wynn, Roddy McDowall, Pat Boone; **D:** George Stevens; **W:** George Stevens, James Lee Barrett; **C:** William Mellor, Loyal Griggs; **M:** Alfred Newman. *AWARDS: NOM:* Oscars '65: Art Dir./Set Dec., Color, Color Cinematog., Costume Des. (C), Orig. Score.

Grey Owl

Interesting old-fashioned bio-pic is based on the story of Archie Grey Owl (Brosnan), an Ojibway trapper in 1930s Canada who changes his occupation and becomes an early environmentalist and celebrity lecturer and writer. Only after his death does the truth come out. The transfer features lush and strong colors, nicely reproducing the hues and shades of the outdoors in which the movie is mostly set. Blacks are deep and solid and highlights are well balanced to create a good-looking picture. The 5.1 mixes are very well integrated, producing a wide sound field with good spatial effects. —*GH/MM*
Movie: 🎞🎞½ *DVD:* 🎞🎞🎞
Columbia Tristar Home Video (Cat #4722). Widescreen (2.35:1) anamorphic. Dolby Digital 5.1 Surround Stereo. $14.95. Keepcase. *LANG:* English; French. *SUB:* English; Spanish. *FEATURES:* 2 commentary tracks ➤ 2 featurettes ➤ Shorts ➤ Interviews ➤ Trailers ➤ Screenplay.
1999 (PG-13) 117m/C *GB CA* Pierce Brosnan, Annie Galipeau, Vlasta Vrana, Nathaniel Arcand, David Fox, Charles Powell, Renee Asherson, Stephenie Cole, Graham Greene; **D:** Richard Attenborough; **W:** William Nicholson; **C:** Roger Pratt; **M:** George Fenton. *AWARDS:* Genie '99: Costume Des.

Grind

Just out of the joint, Eddie Dolan (Crudup) moves in with brother Terry (Schulze) and sister-in-law Janey (Shelly) in New Jersey. He gets a dull factory job and fixes up old cars to go drag racing on weekends—as well as helping out Terry, who has a sideline working for a car theft ring. Since gorgeous Eddie works nights, he and sulky stay-at-home-with-the-baby Janey get to be real close daytime buddies. The paint-by-numbers Garden State plot is brightened by some decent acting. No-frills full-frame disc, however, offers no improvement over tape. —*MM*

Movie: 🎬🎬 **DVD:** 🎬🎬

Winstar Home Entertainment (Cat #FLV5 264, UPC #720917526423). Full frame. $24.98. Keepcase. *LANG:* English. *FEATURES:* 12 chapter links • Filmographies • Trailer.

1996 96m/C Billy Crudup, Adrienne Shelly, Paul Schulze, Frank Vincent, Saul Stein, Amanda Peet, Steven Beach, Tim Devlin; **D:** Chris Kentis; **W:** Chris Kentis, Laura Lau; **C:** Stephen Kazmierski; **M:** Brian Kelly.

The Grissom Gang

Remake of the 1948 British film *No Orchids for Miss Blandish* has a young Midwestern heiress (Darby) kidnapped by a family of grotesques, led by a sadistic mother. The ransom gets lost in a series of bizarre events and the young lady appears to be falling for the moronic Slim (Wilson). Director Aldrich blends extreme violence with dark humor and a nasty appreciation of these characters. Every face that's shown in close-up is sweaty—really sweaty and pale. Some artifacts show up in bright areas of sky and in the darker night scenes. Minor surface wear is not really a problem. For fans of *Hush, Hush, Sweet Charlotte.* —*MM*

Movie: 🎬🎬🎬 **DVD:** 🎬🎬🎬

Anchor Bay (Cat #DV11206, UPC #01313 1120691). Widescreen (1.85:1) letterboxed; full frame. Dolby Digital Mono. $24.99. Keepcase. *LANG:* English. *FEATURES:* 24 chapter links.

1971 (R) 127m/C Kim Darby, Scott Wilson, Tony Musante, Ralph Waite, Connie Stevens, Robert Lansing, Wesley Addy; **D:** Robert Aldrich; **W:** Leon Griffiths; **C:** Joseph Biroc; **M:** Gerald Fried.

Groove

Editor Greg Harrison's directorial debut is an economically paced examination of the "rave" scene. It features a terrific ensemble cast, but at heart, the film is an old-fashioned boy-meets-girl romance. The setting is an abandoned building on a San Francisco pier. That's where the squarish David (Linklater) is attending his first rave. Leyla (Glaudini) has perhaps been to too many. Over the course of the night they and the other rave kids go through a series of changes fueled by drugs, emotion, and sexual indecision. In another time, the same story with more limited sexual roles and consciousness-altering substances could have been told about a homecoming dance or spring break. The changes and discoveries the characters make have not changed. Even though the film was made on a restricted budget—actually shot in Super 16mm.—it looks very good on DVD. Though the bulk of the action takes place under extreme conditions of lasers, strobes, and other colored lights, the image is consistently clear and well-

detailed. The near-constant music (also available on an isolated track) makes full use of the 5.1 Surround field. The dialogue is sometimes difficult to understand (intentionally, I suspect). Subtitles are helpful. Add in a full plate of extras and the disc is one of the best. —*MM*

Movie: 🎬🎬🎬½ **DVD:** 🎬🎬🎬🎬

Columbia Tristar Home Video (Cat #05612, UPC #043396056121). Widescreen (1.85:1) anamorphic; full frame. Dolby Digital 5.1 Surround Stereo; Dolby Digital Surround Stereo. $24.95. Keepcase. *LANG:* English; French. *SUB:* English; French. *FEATURES:* Commentary: Harrrison, producer, and cinematographer • Deleted and extended scenes with commentary • Music video • Link to website • Cast auditions • Talent files • Trailers • Photo gallery • Behind-the-scenes featurette • Camera tests.

2000 (R) 86m/C Steve Van Wormer, Lola Glaudini, Hamish Linklater, Denny Kirkwood, Rachel True, MacKenzie Firgens, Nick Offerman, Ari Gold; **D:** Greg Harrison; **W:** Greg Harrison; **C:** Matthew Irving.

The Groundstar Conspiracy

Predating *The X-Files* by decades, this thriller begins with an explosion at a government installation. Only John Wells (Sarrazin) escapes alive and he can't remember what happened. Investigator Tuxan (Peppard) has reasons to be suspicious about him. Things move nicely enough. The plot's familiarity comes from the many imitators that have followed. DVD was made from a very well-preserved original. It looks exceptionally good for an early '70s production. —*MM*

Movie: 🎬🎬🎬 **DVD:** 🎬🎬½

Anchor Bay (Cat #DV11247, UPC #01313 1124798). Widescreen (2.35:1) anamorphic; full frame. Dolby Digital Mono. $24.99. Keepcase. *LANG:* English. *FEATURES:* 26 chapter links.

1972 (PG) 96m/C CA George Peppard, Michael Sarrazin, Christine Belford, Cliff Potts, James Olson, Tim O'Connor, James McEachin, Alan Oppenheimer; **D:** Lamont Johnson; **W:** Matthew Howard; **C:** Michael Reed; **M:** Paul Hoffert.

Gruesome Twosome

Another guts/cannibalism/mutilation funfest by Lewis, about someone who's marketing the hair of some very recently (and suspiciously) deceased college coeds. The video transfer is adequate, though it retains the look of a 1960s-era film suffering from the ravages of time. All that can be said of the audio is that it is clear and discernable. Probably the most enjoyable aspect of this otherwise forgettable disc is the commentary track. Director Lewis provides a candid, bare-bones look at shock-cinema filmmaking at its, er, finest. —*MJT*

Movie: 🎬 **DVD:** 🎬🎬

Image Entertainment (Cat #ID6061SW DVD, UPC #014381606126). Full frame. Dolby Digital Mono. $24.99. Snapper.

LANG: English. *FEATURES:* 12 chapter links • Commentary: director Herschell Gordon Lewis • Theatrical trailer • Archival short subject: "Wigs-O-Rama" • Herschell Gordon Lewis Gallery of Exploitation Art.

1967 75m/C Elizabeth Davis, Gretchen Wells, Chris Martell, Rodney Bedell, Ronnie Cass, Karl Stoeber, Dianne Wilhite, Andrea Barr, Dianne Raymond, Sherry Robinson, Barrie Walton, Michael Lewis, Ray Sager; **D:** Herschell Gordon Lewis; **W:** Allison Louise Downe; **C:** Roy Collodi; **M:** Larry Wellington.

Guantanamera

Famous singer Yoyita returns to her hometown of Guantanamo for the first time in 50 years, is reunited with her first sweetheart, and promptly dies. Her niece Georgina (Ibarra) comes to take her remains back to Havana. Her husband Adolfo (Cruz), an oafish Communist Party worker, has devised a bizarre relay system to save gasoline while transporting corpses. Also in the caravan is Mariano (Perugorria), a former student of Georgina who has a crush on her. Directors Alea and Tabio celebrate the lives of everyday Cubans and skewer bumbling government bureaucrats. The DVD image is soft, but clear enough for this tropical tale that depends more on mood and character than brilliant visuals. Sound, like the picture, is about the same as tape. —*MM*

Movie: 🎬🎬🎬 **DVD:** 🎬🎬

New Yorker Video (Cat #68600, UPC #717 119686048). Full frame. $29.95. Keepcase. *LANG:* Spanish. *SUB:* English. *FEATURES:* 10 chapter links • Talent files • Trailer.

1995 104m/C CU Carlos Cruz, Mirta Ibarra, Jorge Perugorria, Raul Eguren, Pedro Fernandez; **D:** Tomas Gutierrez Alea, Juan Carlos Tabio; **W:** Tomas Gutierrez Alea, Juan Carlos Tabio, Eliseo Alberto Diego; **C:** Hans Burman; **M:** Jose Nieto.

Gulliver's Travels [Image]

This version of Max Fleischer's feature-length cartoon looks about the same as the Winstar edition, reviewed in the first volume of this book. It's bright, but not sharp enough to hold the interest of most kids who expect animation to be fast-moving and brilliant. Some static is audible on the soundtrack and the music is a bit reedy. —*MM*

Movie: 🎬🎬½ **DVD:** 🎬🎬🎬

Image Entertainment (Cat #HRS9447, UPC #014381944723). Full frame. Mono. $24.99. Snapper. *LANG:* English. *FEATURES:* 9 chapter links • "It's a Hap-Hap-Happy Day" short cartoon.

1939 74m/C D: Dave Fleischer; **W:** Dan Gordon, Tedd Pierce, Edmond Seward, Izzy Sparber; **C:** Charles Schettler; **V:** Lanny Ross, Jessica Dragonette. *AWARDS:* NOM: Oscars '39: Song ("Faithful Forever"), Orig. Score.

Gumboots

In the tradition of *Riverdance* and *Stomp,* this stage show turns a particular kind of dance into popular entertainment. In this case, it is the rhythmic stomping and singing of South African mine laborers. The disc is a recording of a stage performance at the Playhouse Theatre, London, so it gains little in terms of image. Sound is another story. Surround puts you in the middle of the performers, which is sometimes disconcerting. At one loud moment, the combination of whistles and DTS was enough to scare the cat. —*MM*
Movie: 🎬🎬½ **DVD:** 🎬🎬🎬
Image Entertainment (Cat #ID0314WZDVD, UPC #014381031423). Full frame. DTS Surround Stereo; Dolby Digital 5.1 Surround Stereo; DD Stereo. $24.99. Keepcase. *LANG:* English. *FEATURES:* 21 chapter links, feature ● 9 chapter links, documentary ● "The Gumboots Story" documentary.
2000 53m/C *GB*

Gummo

The off-putting image on the box art is an all-too accurate preview of the contents. Novice director Korine (writer of *Kids*) would have us believe that this is a portrait of the seething underbelly of small-town heartland America. It's really more a series of grisly images than a cohesive narrative set in Xenia, Ohio. Characters are thin and scabrous; humor is absent. Surround sound makes the moist voice-over narration even harder to take. —*MM*
Movie: woof **DVD:** 🎬🎬
New Line Home Video (Cat #N5236, UPC #794043523625). Widescreen (1.85:1) anamorphic. Dolby Digital Surround. $24.99. Snapper. *LANG:* English. *FEATURES:* Talent files ● Photo gallery ● 27 chapter links.
1997 (R) 88m/C Chloe Sevigny, Jacob Reynolds, Jacob Sewell, Nick Sutton, Carisa Bara, Darby Dougherty, Max Perlich, Linda Manz; *D:* Harmony Korine; *W:* Harmony Korine; *C:* Jean-Yves Escoffier.

Gun Shy

Liam Neeson is a D.E.A. agent, already suffering from job stress, who finds himself embroiled in an undercover sting operation involving the mob (represented by Oliver Platt) and a Colombian drug cartel. He's in therapy and has gastrointestinal problems to boot, so his life is pretty much in the "shitter," so to speak. But things take a turn for the better when nurse Judy (Sandra Bullock) brings hope and a "ray of sunshine" into his life—now all he has to do is survive all the double-crossing partners to the deal and find true happiness. First-time director Eric Blakeney will perhaps learn from this experience. Throwing in everything, including the kitchen sink, doesn't always make for a better film experience. The film swings from comedy to horrific violence, and in the process fails to establish an acceptable tone. Even the arrival of Bullock, well

into the story, seems like another last-minute decision to spice things up. Image and sound are fine though neither is noteworthy. —*RJT*
Movie: 🎬🎬½ **DVD:** 🎬🎬½
Hollywood Pictures Home Video (Cat #20269, UPC #717951009814). Widescreen (1.85:1) anamorphic. Dolby Digital 5.1 Surround. $29.99. Keepcase. *LANG:* English. *SUB:* English. *CAP:* English. *FEATURES:* 24 chapter links ● Theatrical trailer ● Four cross-promotional trailers.
2000 (R) 102m/C Liam Neeson, Oliver Platt, Sandra Bullock, Jose Zuniga, Richard Schiff, Andrew Lauer, Mitch Pileggi, Paul Ben-Victor, Mary McCormack, Frank Vincent, Michael Mantell, Louis Giambalvo, Gregg Daniel, Michael Delorenzo; *D:* Eric Blakeney; *W:* Eric Blakeney; *C:* Tom Richmond; *M:* Rolfe Kent.

Gun Smith Cats: Bulletproof

Bizarre Japanese anime combines the familiar big-eyed girls with a Chicago setting and a fetishistic attitude toward firearms. Rally and Minnie May are the titular gunsmiths who drive a vintage Shelby GT-500 and are dragooned by the AFT into helping capture bad guys. Lots of stuff blows up and many many bullets are fired. If these episodes of a TV series don't exactly test the limits of animation, they do go in an odd direction. Drawing is very nice. The image is up to ADV's high standards. It's essentially flawless. The violence might not recommend this one to younger viewers, but it's certainly not adult material. Contents: "Neutral Zone," "Swing High," "High Speed Edge." —*MM*
Movie: 🎬🎬½ **DVD:** 🎬🎬🎬
A.D.V. Films (Cat #DGS/001, UPC #70272 7006722). Full frame. Dolby Digital Stereo. $24.99. Keepcase. *LANG:* English; Japanese. *SUB:* English. *FEATURES:* 18 chapter links ● "Making of" featurette ● Trailers ● Credit-less opening sequence.
1995 90m/C *JP D:* Takeshi Mori; *W:* Atsuji Kaneko; *M:* Peter Erskine.

Gung Ho!

Please see review of *Legendary WWII Movies.*
Movie: 🎬🎬
1943 88m/B Robert Mitchum, Randolph Scott, Noah Beery Jr., Alan Curtis, Grace McDonald; *D:* Ray Enright; *C:* Milton Krasner.

Guys and Dolls

New York gambler Sky Masterson takes a bet that he can romance a Salvation Army lady. Based on the stories of Damon Runyon with Blaine, Kaye, Pully, and Silver re-creating their roles from the Broadway hit. Sinatra plays Nathan Detroit, who runs a floating crap game even as his fiancée demands that he get out of the business. Features several outstanding songs. Brando's not-always-convincing musical debut. MGM has released a non-anamorphic DVD

transfer of the film, and even so it proves to be very sharp with vibrant colors that even at their boldest do not bleed. Contrast and brightness levels are very comfortable and blacks are near perfect, although it seems like some detail is lost in darker sequences. The film has been given the 5.1 treatment and, though the Surround effects are pretty much nonexistent, the musical numbers sound great and the dialogue is clear and up front. —*JO*
Movie: 🎬🎬🎬 **DVD:** 🎬🎬🎬
MGM Home Entertainment (Cat #908093, UPC #027616809322). Widescreen (1.85:1) letterboxed. Dolby Digital 5.1; Dolby Surround. $24.98. Keepcase. *LANG:* English; Spanish; French. *SUB:* Spanish; French. *CAP:* English. *FEATURES:* 32 chapter links ● Theatrical trailer ● Booklet.
1955 150m/C Marlon Brando, Jean Simmons, Frank Sinatra, Vivian Blaine, Stubby Kaye, Sheldon Leonard, Veda Ann Borg, Regis Toomey; *D:* Joseph L. Mankiewicz; *W:* Joseph L. Mankiewicz; *C:* Harry Stradling Sr.; *M:* Frank Loesser. *AWARDS:* Golden Globes '56: Actress—Mus./Comedy (Simmons), Film—Mus./Comedy; *NOM:* Oscars '55: Art Dir./Set Dec., Color, Color Cinematog., Costume Des. (C), Scoring/Musical.

Half Japanese: The Band Who Would Be King

It's hard to believe that this is a documentary, not a mockumentary. The film follows the alternative-rock band Half Japanese through an 18-year period as they work their way into obscurity. (Don't worry if you haven't heard of them. I doubt that many people have.) The film focuses on Jad and David Fair, the brothers who started the group in Ann Arbor, Michigan, in 1975, and features interviews with the various members of the band (the lineup has changed over the years) and some archival footage. There are also interviews with record executives and corporate insiders, who give their perspectives. The film is made up of many video sources, but most (except for the home movies) appear clear with some slight graininess at times. The audio offers every shrill note with digital clarity. —*ML/MM*
Movie: 🎬🎬 **DVD:** 🎬🎬½
Vanguard International Cinema, Inc. (Cat #VF0002, UPC #658769000238). Full frame. Dolby Digital Stereo. $24.95. Keepcase. *LANG:* English. *FEATURES:* Commentary ● "Live in Hell" video ● TV shot excerpt.
1992 89m/C Jad Fair, David Fair, Penn Jillette, Moe (Maureen) Tucker, Gerard Cosloy.

The Hallelujah Trail

A major hangfire, this John Sturges super-western takes the simple comedy idea of Alexander MacKendrick's *Tight Little Island* and stretches it into an overlong, repetitive farce. A dozen fine players fight honorably against a weak script in which the deadpan narrator gets the most laughs. A whiskey shortage in Denver has thirsty miners praying for the safe arrival of a wagon train full of booze. Calvary officer Lancaster is caught between the locals, equally thirsty Indians, and the temperance agitator (Lee Remick) who demands the shipment be seized and destroyed. A director with an enviable string of westerns to his credit, Sturges demonstrates a knack for slapstick, and Lancaster, Remick, and Hutton are excellent, yet the obviousness of the jokes and the slow pacing of too many subplots bog them all down, and the fun wears out long before the finish. One can't help but think that the temperance march/massacre at the beginning of *The Wild Bunch* was Sam Peckinpah's answer to this "cute" vision of the West. Listed at a roadshow length of 165 minutes, the DVD appears to be the shorter general release version, its Ultra Panavision dimensions cropped down to 2.35:1. It would also seem to be the same transfer used on the laserdisc from the early '90s, and the lack of anamorphic enhancement doesn't help. Also, 16 chapter stops are insufficient for such a long title. The stereo audio mix is clear but unremarkable. —*GE*

Movie: 𝄞𝄞𝄞 **DVD:** 𝄞𝄞𝄞
MGM Home Entertainment (Cat #1001 592, UPC #027616859020). Widescreen (2.35:1) letterboxed. Dolby Digital 5.1. $19.98. Keepcase. *LANG:* English; French. *SUB:* French; Spanish. *CAP:* English. *FEATURES:* 16 chapter links ● Theatrical trailer.
1965 166m/C Burt Lancaster, Lee Remick, Jim Hutton, Pamela Tiffin, Donald Pleasence, Brian Keith, Martin Landau; *D:* John Sturges; *W:* John Gay; *C:* Robert L. Surtees; *M:* Elmer Bernstein; *Nar:* John Dehner.

Halloween 5: The Revenge of Michael Myers

Eclipsed only by 6 as the worst of the bunch, this entry was bad enough to put the series on hiatus for six years. But for overall lack of originality and contempt for its audience, this one remains noteworthy. It contains a few attempts at intentional comedy and it inexcusably involves a psychic child in the proceedings. On disc, image is acceptable and the 5.1 sound is much better, but it does nothing to improve the film itself. —*MM*

Movie: woof **DVD:** 𝄞𝄞½
Anchor Bay (Cat #DV11218, UPC #01313 1121896). Widescreen (1.85:1) anamorphic; full frame. Dolby Digital 5.1 Surround Stereo; Dolby Digital Surround Stereo. $24.99. Keepcase. *LANG:* English. *CAP:* English. *FEATURES:* Liner notes by Michael Felsher ● 26 chapter links ● "Inside Halloween 5" featurette ● Trailer.
1989 (R) 96m/C Donald Pleasence, Ellie Cornell, Danielle Harris, Don Shanks, Betty Carvalho, Beau Starr, Wendy Kaplan, Jeffrey Landman; *D:* Dominique Othenin-Girard; *W:* Dominique Othenin-Girard, Shem Bitterman, Michael Jacobs; *C:* Rob Draper; *M:* John Carpenter, Alan Howarth.

Hamlet

Classic, cinematic adaptation of Shakespeare's play about a Danish prince who avenges the murder of his father at great cost to himself and those around him. Richly evocative and extremely atmospheric (with exquisite black-and-white photography) and featuring a near-perfect cast. Olivier is mostly exquisite, but has a tendency to chew the scenery. Peter Cushing is wonderful as Osric and Felix Aylmer is a perfect Polonius. Though several famous speeches and subplots were not utilized in this film version (in place of Rosencrantz and Guildenstern, we get a pirate battle!), it is an admirably tight and beautifully realized rendering of the story. It also features the creepiest ghost of any adaptation, bar none. The disc is beautiful, sharp, and clear with rich contrasts and clean mono sound. Unfortunately, while most dirt and print damage has been digitally cleaned up, there are still quite a few tiny spots and scratches. (Warning: the disc this reviewer screened had an audio glitch; it defaulted to a non-existent channel and had to be manually switched on the remote control in order to hear the film!) The essay is excellent. —*DG*

Movie: 𝄞𝄞𝄞½ **DVD:** 𝄞𝄞𝄞
Criterion Collection (Cat #HAM020, UPC #03742912842). Full frame. Dolby Digital Mono. $29.95. Keepcase. *LANG:* English. *SUB:* English. *CAP:* English. *FEATURES:* Insert booklet with notes ● 27 chapter links.
1948 153m/B *GB* Laurence Olivier, Basil Sydney, Felix Aylmer, Jean Simmons, Stanley Holloway, Peter Cushing, Christopher Lee, Eileen Herlie, John Laurie, Esmond Knight, Anthony Quayle; *D:* Laurence Olivier; *W:* Alan Dent; *C:* Desmond Dickinson; *M:* William Walton; *V:* John Gielgud. *AWARDS:* Oscars '48: Actor (Olivier), Art Dir./Set Dec., B&W, Costume Des. (B&W), Picture; British Acad. '48: Film; Golden Globes '49: Actor—Drama (Olivier); N.Y. Film Critics '48: Actor (Olivier); *NOM:* Oscars '48: Director (Olivier), Support. Actress (Simmons), Orig. Dramatic Score.

Hamlet

The attempt to modernize this Shakespeare tale suffers from a truncated script, bad acting, and hyperactive direction. Its promising conceit of setting the story in the world of corporate America is smothered by the decision of writer/director Almereyda to shorten the play. With no time for personalities to develop, we are left with caricatures instead of characters, and Shakespeare's triumph is reduced to glittery family melodrama. Ethan Hawke pouts his way through the role of the world's most famous mama's boy. Where Hamlet should be a roller coaster of emotion, his performance is strictly one note, and while brooding may get lots of chicks, it doesn't sell Shakespeare. He comes across as a moody, spoiled brat rather than a son devastated by the loss of his father. Styles's Ophelia has lost most of her dialogue, but if her few utterances of

Elizabethan English are any example, in this case we should be grateful. The bright spots in the film are the calculated art direction by Jeanne Develle, who did the cold sets for *American Psycho*, and the performances by Sam Shepard as Hamlet's father and Liev Schreiber as Laertes. Shepard manages to rise above the loss of dialogue and bring a sense of dignity and spectral creepiness to the dead king. Schreiber seems to be in a different film altogether, giving a true performance of Shakespeare, rather than running through it like his hair was on fire as Bill Murray does in his turn as Polonius. For some reason, Almereyda also chooses to speed through the final fight sequence and add some modern hardware, but it doesn't work. Let's just say that bungee cords and Shakespeare don't mix. For modernized Shakespeare, stick with DiCaprio's *Romeo + Juliet* or McKellan's *Richard III*. For good renderings of *Hamlet* on film, the crown prince is still Olivier followed closely by Branaugh with Gibson pulling up the rear. As, it seems, with all truly horrible big budget flops, the DVD has excellent color and sound. —*CA*

Movie: 𝄞½ **DVD:** 𝄞𝄞𝄞½
Miramax Pictures Home Video (Cat #18314, UPC #717951004994). Widescreen (1.85:1) anamorphic. Dolby Digital 5.1 Surround. $32.99. Keepcase. *LANG:* English. *CAP:* English. *FEATURES:* 22 chapter links ● Theatrical trailers.
2000 (R) 111m/C Ethan Hawke, Kyle MacLachlan, Sam Shepard, Diane Venora, Bill Murray, Julia Stiles, Liev Schreiber, Karl Geary, Paula Malcomson, Steve Zahn, Dechen Thurman, Jeffrey Wright, Paul Bartel, Rome Neal, Casey Affleck; *D:* Michael Almereyda; *W:* Michael Almereyda; *C:* John de Borman; *M:* Carter Burwell. *AWARDS: NOM:* Ind. Spirit '01: Cinematog.

Hanging Up

Strident, schmaltzy comedy revolves around cantankerous dying Lou (Matthau), father of Eve (Ryan), Georgia (Keaton), and Maddy (Kudrow). They check in by phone but duck out on responsibilities as sibling rivalry rears its head. The combination of comedy and darker undertones is brought to life by a very good cast. The source print from which the transfer has been struck is very clean and without defects or blemishes. The image is highly detailed and brings out the best of the photography, which utilizes soft filters to create faded backgrounds that give the movie a very soft and warm look. Both the 5.1 and Surround tracks are well produced. The discrete 5.1 mix seems somewhat more expansive and with its dedicated bass extension has a little more weight. —*GH/MM*

Movie: 𝄞½ **DVD:** 𝄞𝄞𝄞
Columbia Tristar Home Video (Cat #4748). Full frame; widescreen (1.85:1) anamorphic. Dolby Digital 5.1 Surround Stereo; Dolby Digital Surround Stereo. $24.95. Keepcase. *LANG:* English. *FEATURES:* Documentary ● Isolated score ● Deleted scenes ● Gag reel ● Trailer.

1999 (PG-13) 93m/C Meg Ryan, Diane Keaton, Lisa Kudrow, Walter Matthau, Adam Arkin, Cloris Leachman, Jesse James, Duke Moosekian, Ann Bortolotti; **D:** Diane Keaton; **W:** Delia Ephron, Nora Ephron; **C:** Howard Atherton; **M:** David Hirschfelder.

Hangman

Another of those mischievous serial killers is at work and detective Nick Roos (Phillips) thinks that it's a copycat of one who committed suicide years before. Unstable psychiatrist Grace Mitchell (Amick) is a witness and possibly a suspect. Give the filmmakers credit for treating the familiar material with some ingenuity and coming up with an interesting twist. DVD makes very good use of the Surround tracks. Image is equally sharp. Something of a sleeper. —*MM*
Movie: 🎵🎵½ **DVD:** 🎵🎵🎵
Columbia Tristar Home Video (Cat #064 49, UPC #043396064492). Full frame; widescreen (1.85:1) letterboxed. Dolby Digital 5.1 Surround Stereo; Dolby Digital Surround Stereo. $24.98. Keepcase. *LANG:* English; French; Spanish; Portuguese. *SUB:* English; French; Spanish; Portuguese; Chinese; Korean; Thai. *FEATURES:* 28 chapter links ▪ Talent files ▪ Trailers.
2000 (R) 96m/C Lou Diamond Phillips, Madchen Amick, Dan Lauria, Mark Wilson, Vincent Coraza; **D:** Ken Girotti; **W:** Vladimir Nemirovsky; **C:** Gerald Packer; **M:** Steven Stern.

Hangmen Also Die

Lang's anti-Nazi propaganda was inspired by (and rushed into production to capitalize on) the actual May 1942 assassination of Reinhard Heydrich. Franz Svoboda is the member of the Czech resistance who shoots the "Hangman." The Nazis seek revenge and set about executing citizens, aided by the traitorous Emil (Lockhart). DVD is a very good presentation of a film whose original elements are probably long gone. The majority of it is clear and sharp, with some minimal damage here and there. It plays better than many an older title in the catalogs of the big studios. Mono sound is good but a little low. —*GE/MM*
Movie: 🎵🎵½ **DVD:** 🎵🎵½
Kino on Video (UPC #738329014322). Full frame. Mono. $29.95. Keepcase. *LANG:* English.
1942 134m/B Brian Donlevy, Gene Lockhart, Walter Brennan, Anna Lee, Dennis O'Keefe, Alexander Granach, Jonathan Hale, Margaret Wycherly, Hans von Twardowski; **D:** Fritz Lang; **W:** John Wexley; **C:** James Wong Howe; **M:** Hanns Eisler. *AWARDS: NOM:* Oscars '43: Orig. Dramatic Score.

Hannibal

If Ridley Scott's adaptation of Thomas Harris's novel isn't as deeply subversive as the fiction, it probably goes as far as it could within the restrictions of the American movie industry. It certainly pushes the limits of an "R"-rating, and it does so with style, nerve, and humor. A second viewing reveals just how restrained the on-screen violence is. The film begins with FBI agent Clarice Starling (Moore, in a fine steely performance) being relegated to obscurity or worse by her corrupt superior Krendler (Liotta). Dr. Lechter (Hopkins) is living happily in Florence, Italy, until another corruptible cop, Pazzi (Giannini) suspects his identity and tries to sell the information to Mason Verger (Oldman), one of the doctor's victims who survived. Verger is a disfigured monster who has plotted a revenge so sadistic that he makes Lechter look good. The deleted and alternate scenes don't really change the film; not even the two other endings—one shown, one described, neither close to Harris's. On his commentary track, Scott is typically dry and to the point. He stresses character and storytelling over cast and anecdote. For those, go to the second disc, which contains most of the extras. Scott is more interested in the basics of cinematic narrative; how and when to deliver information that keeps the viewer engaged. DVD image and sound are the best that a major studio can deliver for a major release. The only flaw is the inescapable pause at the layer shift between chapters 16 and 17. —*MM*
Movie: 🎵🎵🎵½ **DVD:** 🎵🎵🎵🎵
MGM Home Entertainment (Cat #1002 321, UPC #027616865403). Widescreen (1.85:1) anamorphic. DTS Surround; Dolby Digital 5.1 Surround. $29.98. Keepcase. *LANG:* English; French; Spanish. *SUB:* English; French; Spanish. *FEATURES:* "Breaking the Silence," 5 "making of" featurettes ▪ "Anatomy of a Shoot-Out," multi-angle breakdown of fish market scene ▪ "Ridleygrams" storyboarding featurette ▪ Title design ▪ 14 deleted and alternate scenes with optional commentary ▪ Marketing gallery ▪ Talent files ▪ Production notes ▪ DVD credits ▪ Commentary: director ▪ 32 chapter links ▪ Trailers.
2001 (R) 131m/C Anthony Hopkins, Julianne Moore, Gary Oldman, Ray Liotta, Frankie Faison, Giancarlo Giannini, Francesca Neri, Zeljko Ivanek, Hazelle Goodman, David Andrews, Francis Guinan, Enrico Lo Verso; **D:** Ridley Scott; **W:** David Mamet, Steven Zaillian; **C:** John Mathieson; **M:** Hans Zimmer.

Hans Christian Andersen [20th Century Fox]

Danny Kaye stars in a sentimental tale about the famous storyteller. This edition is essentially identical to the disc previously released by HBO. Colors are deeply saturated but the image is only a slight improvement over VHS tape. —*MM*
Movie: 🎵🎵 **DVD:** 🎵🎵½
20th Century Fox Home Entertainment (Cat #1001603, UPC #027616859136). Full frame. Dolby Digital Mono. $24.99. Keepcase. *LANG:* English; French; Span-

ish. *SUB:* French; Spanish. *CAP:* English. *FEATURES:* 16 chapter links ▪ Trailer.
1952 112m/C Danny Kaye, Farley Granger, Zizi Jeanmarie, Joey Walsh; **D:** Charles Vidor; **W:** Moss Hart; **C:** Harry Stradling Sr.; **M:** Frank Loesser. *AWARDS: NOM:* Oscars '52: Art Dir./Set Dec., Color, Color Cinematog., Costume Des. (C), Song ("Thumbelina"), Sound, Scoring/Musical.

Hard-Boiled [Winstar]

The Winstar edition of John Woo's other action masterpiece is a slight but definite improvement over the Criterion laserdisc. It features new larger yellow subtitles and a new commentary track by Woo and producer Terrence Chang. Though I have not seen the Criterion DVD (reviewed in first edition), this version is excellent. —*MM*
AKA: Lashou Shentan.
Movie: 🎵🎵🎵½ **DVD:** 🎵🎵🎵½
Winstar Home Entertainment (Cat #FLV5 224, UPC #720917522425). Widescreen (1.85:1) letterboxed. Mono. $29.98. Keepcase. *LANG:* Cantonese; English. *SUB:* English. *FEATURES:* 30 chapter links ▪ Notes by David Chute ▪ Talent files ▪ Production credits ▪ Commentary: Woo and Terrence Chang. Also available as half of a boxed set (cat. # FLV5243) with *The Killer*.
1992 126m/C *HK* Chow Yun-Fat, Tony Leung Chiu-Wai, Philip Chan, Anthony Wong, Teresa Mo, Bowie Lam, Hoi-Shan Kwan, Philip Kwok, John Woo; **D:** John Woo; **W:** Barry Wong, John Woo; **C:** Wing-Heng Wang; **M:** Michael Gibbs.

Hard Core Logo

Mockumentary focuses on a group of Canadian veteran punk rockers who, at thirtysomething, have reunited for one last concert, to benefit Bucky Haight. He's their pal who has just had both legs amputated; or was it only one leg? Whatever, the not-quite-legendary Vancouver band is so pleased by the gig that the guys decide to head back on the road for one last shot at the brass ring, trailed by director McDonald's film crew. Inserts reveal the ego trips that drove them apart before. DVD really gives the film too good a look. Image is nice and crisp; 5.1 Surround is so strong it will drive non-punk fans nuts. —*MM*
Movie: 🎵🎵½ **DVD:** 🎵🎵🎵
Miramax Pictures Home Video (Cat #18535, UPC #717951005526). Widescreen (1.85:1) anamorphic. Dolby Digital 5.1 Surround Stereo. $32.99. Keepcase. *LANG:* English. *SUB:* English. *FEATURES:* 23 chapter links ▪ Trailers.
1996 (R) 96m/C *CA* Hugh Dillon, Callum Keith Rennie, John Pyper-Ferguson, Bernie Coulson; **D:** Bruce McDonald; **W:** Noel S. Baker; **C:** Danny Nowak; **M:** Shaun Tozer. *AWARDS:* Genie '96: Song ("Swamp Baby, Who the Hell Do You Think You Are?"); *NOM:* Genie '96: Adapt. Screenplay, Director (McDonald), Film, Film Editing, Sound.

Hard Eight

Performances are the highlight of this low-key story set in Reno, Nevada. Sydney (Hall) is a professional gambler who decides to take under his wing the destitute John (Reilly) and teach him the trade. John falls for waitress/hooker Clementine (Paltrow), but there has to be a snake in this gambler's paradise and it shows up in the form of the scary Jimmy (Jackson). The dim John befriends him despite Sydney's warnings. Film looks fine on DVD, and director Anderson gets a double commentary track for his debut. Those who have listened to him talk about *Magnolia* and *Boogie Nights* won't be surprised or shocked by his repeated reliance on the "f-word." Apparently he learned it from his dad. Image and sound are fine. —MM **AKA:** Sydney.
Movie: 🎵🎵🎵 **DVD:** 🎵🎵🎵
Columbia Tristar Home Video (Cat #81039). Widescreen (2.35:1) anamorphic; full frame. Dolby Digital Stereo. $27.95. Keepcase. *LANG:* English. *FEATURES:* Deleted scene ▪ Three Sundance Institute lab scenes ▪ Cast and crew thumbnail bios ▪ Commentary: Anderson, cast ▪ Commentary: Anderson, cast, crew ▪ Talent files ▪ 27 chapter links.
1996 (R) 101m/C Philip Baker Hall, John C. Reilly, Gwyneth Paltrow, Samuel L. Jackson, F. William Parker, Philip Seymour Hoffman, Nathanael Cooper, Wynn White, Robert Ridgely, Michael J. Rowe, Kathleen Campbell, Melora Walters; **D:** Paul Thomas Anderson; **W:** Paul Thomas Anderson; **C:** Robert Elswit; **M:** Michael Penn, Jon Brion. *AWARDS: NOM:* Ind. Spirit '98: Actor (Hall), Cinematog., First Feature, Support. Actor (Jackson), First Screenplay.

Hardcase and Fist

By-the-numbers video premiere has cop Bud McCall (Prior) framed and sent to prison where he's a marked man. The plot rattles along from fistfight to shoot-out to explosion. This is such a low-budget exercise that it gains little on DVD. The image is just as harsh as it has always been. —MM
Movie: 🎵½ **DVD:** 🎵½
Image Entertainment (Cat #OVE9023DVD, UPC #014381902327). Widescreen (1.85:1) letterboxed. Dolby Digital Mono. $24.99. Keepcase. *LANG:* English. *FEATURES:* 12 chapter links ▪ Trailer.
1989 (R) 92m/C Maureen Lavette, Ted Prior, Tony Zarindast, Christine Lunde, Carter Wong; **D:** Tony Zarindast; **W:** Tony Zarindast, Bud Fleischer; **C:** Robert Hayes; **M:** Matthew Tucciarone, Tom Tucciarone.

The Harder They Come

A poor Jamaican youth becomes a success with a hit reggae record after he has turned to a life of crime. Songs, which are blended nicely into the framework of the film, include "You Can Get It If You Really Want It" and "Sitting in Limbo." The video transfer is adequate, although darker colors have virtually no definition. This, however, could be the fault of the original negative. The sound transfer is quite impressive (it is, by far, one of the better mono tracks that I have heard). The disc's extras provide a wealth of information on the film and its subject matter. —MJT
Movie: 🎵🎵½ **DVD:** 🎵🎵🎵
Criterion Collection (Cat #83, UPC #71551 5010825). Widescreen (1.66:1) letterboxed. Dolby Digital Mono. $39.95. Keepcase. *LANG:* English. *SUB:* English. *FEATURES:* 26 chapter links ▪ Commentary: director Perry Henzell, star Jimmy Cliff ▪ Video interview with Island Records founder Chris Blackwell ▪ Illustrated biodiscographies on the film's contributing musicians.
1972 (R) 93m/C *JM* Jimmy Cliff, Janet Barkley, Carl Bradshaw, Bobby Charlton, Ras Daniel Hartman, Basil Keane, Winston Stona; **D:** Perry Henzell; **W:** Perry Henzell, Trevor D. Rhone; **C:** Peter Jessop, David McDonald; **M:** Desmond Dekker, Jimmy Cliff.

Harley Davidson and the Marlboro Man

Complete misfire is a sort of rehash of *Butch Cassidy and the Sundance Kid* with Harley (Rourke) and Marl (Johnson) transformed from pop culture corporate icons to near-future outlaws. Out of the most noble intentions, they rob a bank and find that it's a front for drug money. The stars mumble, posture, and mope. The DVD is a faithful re-creation of the theatrical image, but that should not be taken as a recommendation. —MM
Movie: 🎵 **DVD:** 🎵🎵
MGM Home Entertainment (Cat #1001 556, UPC #027616858665). Widescreen (1.85:1) anamorphic. Dolby Digital Surround Stereo; Mono. $19.98. Keepcase. *LANG:* English; French; Spanish. *SUB:* French; Spanish. *CAP:* English. *FEATURES:* 16 chapter links ▪ Trailer.
1991 (R) 98m/C Mickey Rourke, Don Johnson, Chelsea Field, Tom Sizemore, Vanessa Williams, Robert Ginty, Daniel Baldwin; **D:** Simon Wincer; **W:** Don Michael Paul; **C:** David Eggby; **M:** Basil Poledouris.

Harold and Maude

Cult classic pairs Cort as a deadpan disillusioned 20-year-old obsessed with suicide (his staged attempts are a highlight) and a loveable Gordon as a fun-loving 80-year-old eccentric. They meet at a funeral (a mutual hobby), and develop a taboo romantic relationship, in which they explore the tired theme of the meaning of life with a fresh perspective. The script was originally the 20-minute long graduate thesis of UCLA student Higgins, who showed it to his landlady, wife of film producer Lewis. The biggest improvement Paramount has made to this classic cult fave is to give it a 5.1 soundtrack on their DVD release (they have also been kind enough to include the original mono if you're so inclined). The new sound gives a lot more power to the Cat Stevens songs, as well as opening up the entire film with a new dimensionality without sounding gimmicky. As for the image, it is slightly sharper than the Paramount letterboxed laserdisc, but is still a little pale as on the laser. Blacks are true and shadow detail is good with no increase in grain in darker sequences. —JO
Movie: 🎵🎵🎵🎵 **DVD:** 🎵🎵🎵
Paramount Home Video (Cat #080427, UPC #097360804270). Widescreen (1.85:1) anamorphic. Dolby Digital 5.1; Dolby Digital Mono. $29.99. Keepcase. *LANG:* English; French. *SUB:* English. *CAP:* English. *FEATURES:* 26 chapter links ▪ 2 theatrical trailers.
1971 (PG) 92m/C Ruth Gordon, Bud Cort, Cyril Cusack, Vivian Pickles, Charles Tyner, Ellen Geer, Eric Christmas, G(eorge) Wood, Gordon Devol; **D:** Hal Ashby; **W:** Colin Higgins; **C:** John A. Alonzo; **M:** Cat Stevens. *AWARDS:* Natl. Film Reg. '97.

Harvey

Everybody's favorite rabbit movie makes a splendid debut on DVD. Stewart plays Elwood P. Dowd, a gentle soul who takes an occasional drink and is happy to call Harvey his friend. Harvey is a six-foot tall white rabbit who's invisible to some, much to the dismay of Elwood's sister Veta Louise (Oscar-winning Hull). The disc includes the introduction that Stewart recorded for the 1990 videotape release. Happily, many of the visuals that tend to give digital discs problems are well handled here. The most obvious is the tweed suit that Elwood wears. Only the slightest flash is visible within the pattern and you've got to look hard to spot it. The black-and-white photography is some of the best that Hollywood ever created. It's absolutely perfect for the whimsical atmosphere the film creates. So is the monaural sound. This one belongs in the collection of every Stewart fan. —MM
Movie: 🎵🎵🎵½ **DVD:** 🎵🎵🎵½
Universal Studios Home Video (Cat #20336, UPC #025192033636). Full frame. Dolby Digital Mono. $29.98. Keepcase. *LANG:* English; Spanish. *SUB:* French. *CAP:* English. *FEATURES:* 18 chapter links ▪ Production notes ▪ Jimmy Stewart intro ▪ Trailer ▪ Talent files.
1950 104m/B James Stewart, Josephine Hull, Victoria Horne, Peggy Dow, Cecil Kellaway, Charles Drake, Jesse White, Wallace Ford, Nana Bryant; **D:** Henry Koster; **W:** Oscar Brodney; **C:** William H. Daniels; **M:** Frank Skinner. *AWARDS:* Oscars '50: Support. Actress (Hull); Golden Globes '51: Support. Actress (Hull); *NOM:* Oscars '50: Actor (Stewart).

Hatchet for the Honeymoon

This Bava slasher has some moments of sheer genius, including the film's opening on a train as the killer takes the life of a bride getting ready for her first night of wedded bliss. (Shades of this opening can be seen almost ten years later in George Romero's *Martin*.) From the beginning, we know who the killer is, mostly because he tells us everything he knows about himself in voice-over. John (Forsyth) realizes he's being bad when he chops up newlywed women and buries them in the green house, but he can't stop himself because with every swing of the hatchet, more details of his mother's murder are revealed. The poor guy is finally forced to kill his wife in what is undoubtedly one of the most utterly bizarre and clever cleaver scenes in Italian horror cinema. The dubbed dialogue makes the sound a bit muddy and the transfer is less than perfect, but given the age and the origin of the film, it is forgivable. —*CA* **AKA:** Blood Brides; Una Hacha para la Luna de Miel; Il Rosso Segmo della Follia; An Axe for the Honeymoon; The Red Sign of Madness. **Movie:** 🎬🎬 **DVD:** 🎬½

Image Entertainment (Cat #1D7307EU DVD, UPC #014381730320). Widescreen (1.66:1) letterboxed. Dolby Digital Mono. $24.99. Snapper. *LANG:* English. *FEATURES:* 10 chapter links • Cast and crew bios • Filmographies • Extensive liner notes.

1970 90m/C *SP IT* Stephen Forsyth, Dagmar Lassander, Laura Betti, Gerard Tichy, Femi Benussi, Luciano Pigozzi, Jesus Puente; **D:** Mario Bava; **W:** Mario Bava, Santiago Moncada, Mario Musy; **C:** Mario Bava; **M:** Santa Maria Romitelli.

The Head Mistress
Please see review of *The Notorious Daughter of Fanny Hill*.
Movie: 🎬🎬
1968 70m/C Marsha Jordan, Victor Brant, Julia Blackburn; **D:** Byron Mabe; **W:** David Friedman.

Headin' Home
Please see review of *Great Baseball Movies*.
Movie: 🎬🎬½
1924 56m/B Babe Ruth.

Heart of Light
Strangely captivating film revolves around the conflict between cultural traditions and modernization in Dutch-conquered Greenland. The indigenous population faced with little more than liquor and rock music to replace centuries of tribal customs is slowly imploding. Rasmus, a Greenland native, faces intense disgrace beyond his role as the town drunk when his youngest son goes on a suicidal killing rampage in his small town. The ostracism resulting from the killings, along with his difficult relationship with his older son and his own fear about his place in the modern world, drive Rasmus to go on a pilgrimage to the icy inland on a broken-down dogsled. Along the way he meets a mystical hermit who leads him on a path toward reconciliation with his living family as well

as his dead ancestors. While the story is simple, it is also engrossing. Powerful in message as well as medium, it is a good film for anyone willing to relax and let the story unfold. Shot on location in temperatures well below freezing, the vast icescapes make for a breathtaking story backdrop. The disc is slightly above average in color and clarity and the sound is good. —*CA* **AKA:** Lysets Hjerte.
Movie: 🎬🎬🎬 **DVD:** 🎬🎬½

Vanguard International Cinema, Inc. (UPC #658769004236). Full frame. $29.95. Keepcase. *LANG:* Dutch; Inuit. *SUB:* English. *FEATURES:* 12 chapter links • Documentaries • Trailer • Photo gallery.

1997 92m/C *DK* Rasmus Lyberth, Anda Kristensen, Vivi Nielsen, Niels Platow; **D:** Jacob Gronlykke; **W:** Jacob Gronlykke; **C:** Dan Laustsen; **M:** Joachim Holbek.

Heaven and Earth
Like most Oliver Stone films, this one is long, ambitious, engrossing, political, and flawed. The third volume of his Vietnam trilogy is based on the life of Le Ly Hayslip, a Vietnamese woman who saw the war and its aftermath from several sides, and wrote two books about her experiences. She's a strong character and her portrayal on-screen by newcomer Hiep Thi Le is remarkably effective. The conclusion is long and talky. Throughout, Stone makes his points, then feels it necessary to underline, explain, and embroider. The deleted scenes indicate that he wanted a version that was longer still, and Stone admits as much on his passionate, informative commentary track. Image is strong, particularly in the idealized bucolic scenes. —*MM*
Movie: 🎬🎬🎬 **DVD:** 🎬🎬🎬

Warner Home Video, Inc. (Cat #18533, UPC #085391853329). Widescreen anamorphic. Dolby Digital 5.1 Surround Stereo; Dolby Digital Surround. $24.98. Snapper. *LANG:* English; French. *SUB:* Portuguese; Spanish; French; English. *FEATURES:* 47 chapter links • Commentary: Stone • Talent files • Deleted scenes • Trailer.

1993 (R) 142m/C Hiep Thi Le, Tommy Lee Jones, Joan Chen, Haing S. Ngor, Debbie Reynolds, Conchata Ferrell, Dustin Nguyen, Liem Whatley, Dale Dye; **D:** Oliver Stone; **W:** Oliver Stone; **C:** Robert Richardson; **M:** Kitaro. *AWARDS:* Golden Globes '94: Score.

Heaven's Burning
Fast-paced road movie contains some unexpected twists. Midori (Kudoh) is a young Japanese woman honeymooning in Sydney with new hubby Yukio (Isomura). She fakes her own kidnapping to take off with her lover (who doesn't show). Then she gets caught in the middle of a bank robbery gone bad and becomes the sort-of hostage of Colin (Crowe), who takes off across Australia pursued by cops, angry ex-partners, and a husband looking for revenge. Overall, both image and sound

are on a par with Hollywood productions. A little aliasing in bright sunlit exteriors is not a serious problem. DVD can do little with Crowe's unfortunate Elvisian sideburns. For a relatively unknown title, the disc contains voluminous extras. —*MM*
Movie: 🎬🎬🎬 **DVD:** 🎬🎬🎬

Trimark Home Video (Cat #7519D, UPC #031398751922). Widescreen letterboxed. Dolby Digital Stereo. $24.99. Keepcase. *LANG:* English. *SUB:* English; French; Spanish. *CAP:* English. *FEATURES:* Talent files • 24 chapter links • Director's short films • Script to screen comparisons • Deleted scenes • Cast and crew interviews • Trailer • Production commentary.

1997 (R) 96m/C *AU* Youki Kudoh, Russell Crowe, Kenji Isomura, Ray Barrett, Robert Mammone, Petru Gheorghiu, Matthew Dyktynski, Anthony Phelan, Colin Hay, Susan Prior, Norman Kaye; **D:** Craig Lahiff; **W:** Louis Nowra; **C:** Brian J. Breheny; **M:** Michael Atkinson.

Heaven's Fire
Criminal mastermind Quentin (Prochnow) tries to steal currency engraving plates from a treasury building in Seattle (actually British Columbia), but a heroic security guard, Dean (Roberts), and his family stand in the way. Some fairly well-handled pyrotechnics recall *Die Hard*, but the formulaic plot of this made-for-TV thriller does not. Generally, the image is a notch above broadcast quality. Sound is several notches better. Some pixels creep in during cloudy, rainy exteriors. If nothing else, the disc proves that independent labels can produce discs that look and sound as good as the major studios. —*MM*
Movie: 🎬🎬 **DVD:** 🎬🎬🎬

York Entertainment (Cat #YPD-1070, UPC #750723107028). Full frame. DTS 5.1 Surround; Dolby Digital 5.1 Surround Stereo. $19.99. Keepcase. *LANG:* English. *SUB:* Spanish. *FEATURES:* 30 chapter links • Trailers • Filmographies.

2000 91m/C Eric Roberts, Juergen Prochnow, Cali Timmins; **D:** David Warry-Smith; **W:** Rob Kerchner, Charles Philip Moore; **C:** Gordon Verheul; **M:** Deddy Tzur.

Heavy Metal 2000 [SE]
The sequel to the 1981 animated film is a moderate step down. The animation is sharp enough, but the story lacks imagination and it's fairly tame. (The best Japanese anime is much more outrageous.) The plot concerns a vengeful female warrior (voice of Strain) who's trying to rescue her sister from a madman (Ironside) who's out to find the secret of eternal life, etc. Where the original broke boundaries for the levels of sex and violence in cartoon form, this one barely earns its "R" rating. The animation is a combination of computer-generated and hand-drawn sequences, both handled with ease on DVD, but neither is particularly outstanding. The

rumbly 5.1 Surround effects are impressive. —*MM*
Movie: 🎬🎬 **DVD:** 🎬🎬½
Columbia Tristar Home Video (Cat #05267, UPC #043396052673). Widescreen (1.85:1) letterboxed. Dolby Digital 5.1 Surround Stereo; Dolby Digital Surround Stereo. $24.95. Keepcase. *LANG:* English. *SUB:* English; French; Spanish; Portuguese. *FEATURES:* 28 chapter links ▪ Julie Strain featurette ▪ Voice talent featurette ▪ Isolated music score.
2000 (R) 88m/C **D:** Michael Coldewey, Michel Lemire; **W:** Robert Payne Cabeen; **C:** Bruno Philip; **M:** Frederic Talgorn; **V:** Julie Strain, Michael Ironside, Billy Idol, Sonja Ball.

Heavy Traffic

Bawdy, crude, and frequently hilarious portrait of various down-and-out characters eking out a living in New York's mean streets. Bakshi's animated tale is filled to the brim with over-the-top violence, sex, and gruesome characters and is certainly not for the politically correct. Though its style and dialogue are (naturally) dated, its innovative use of live-action backgrounds and wrap-around scenes makes it an interesting curiosity. Enjoyable and amusing to those with a taste for adult animation and definitely not for children. Though sources denote both "X"- and "R"-rated versions of this film, it was most likely changed after an appeal, as this print doesn't seem cut and matches the running time noted in most references. The disc is sharp and colorful and the full-frame transfer rarely seems cropped. The sound is acceptable, but flat and muddy, making some lines of dialogue difficult to discern. This is most likely due to the gritty, low-budget nature of the production and the original dialogue recording. —*DG*
Movie: 🎬🎬½ **DVD:** 🎬🎬🎬
MGM Home Entertainment (Cat #1000-979, UPC #02761685285). Full frame. Dolby Digital Mono. $19.98. Keepcase. *LANG:* English. *SUB:* French; Spanish. *CAP:* English. *FEATURES:* Theatrical trailer ▪ 16 chapter links ▪ Insert card with chapter listing.
1973 77m/C Joseph Kaufmann, Beverly Hope Atkinson, Michael Brandon, Frank DeKova, Terri Haven, Mary Dean Lauria, Lillian Adams, Jamie Farr, Robert Easton; **D:** Ralph Bakshi; **W:** Ralph Bakshi; **C:** Ted C. Bemiller, Gregg Heschong; **M:** Ed Bogas.

Height of the Sky

In rural Arkansas, 1935, the poor Jones family farms a small plot of land, which they rent from the rich Caldwells. When Gabriel Jones (Moninger) succumbs to tuberculosis, family patriarch Wendel Jones (Stewart) decides to hide Gabriel in an old cabin thereby leaving the strong-willed Leora (Weedon) in charge of the family. Jennifer must convince Mr. Caldwell (Palazzo) that all is well on their farm while she covers for her father's absence. How much truth is there to the story co-written,

produced, and directed by Lyn Clinton, cousin of President Bill Clinton? The picture is crisp and relatively free from grain or film defects. The sunsplashed daytime shots are clear, giving us a great feeling for the dry and dusty conditions on the farm. Dialogue is always audible and well balanced but there is little action from the Surround speakers. There are no extras on the DVD, which is disappointing. This DVD could have benefited from an audio commentary or a documentary to shed some light on any factual basis to the story. —*EP*
Movie: 🎬🎬½ **DVD:** 🎬🎬½
Vanguard International Cinema, Inc. (Cat #VF0045, UPC #658769004434). Widescreen (1.85:1) letterboxed. Dolby Digital Surround Stereo. $29.95. Keepcase. *LANG:* English.
1999 116m/C Grant Moninger, Evan Palazzo, Jackie Stewart, Jennifer Weedon; **D:** Lyn Clinton; **W:** Lyn Clinton; **C:** John R. Zilles; **M:** Boris Zelkin.

Held Up

Engaged couple Foxx and Long are having a hard time staying together after they have a fight when Foxx becomes a hostage during a botched convenience store robbery in a sleepy southwestern town. Broad comedy works in all the black-guy-meets-white-yokels gags, but they've all been done better by funnier writers. Foxx has some appeal, but not enough to overcome this mess. It could've been worse: Rob Schneider bailed after four days of filming. The DVD transfer is as inconsistent as the film. Sharpness comes and goes and there is even some source material damage like that usually associated with older movies. Some pixelation occurs during some of the detailed and scenic outdoor shots. At least the color remains consistently strong and fairly accurate. The disc also features one of those seemingly just-for-the-hell-of-it 5.1 mixes where the Surround channels only come alive every now and then during the music. —*JO* **AKA:** Inconvenienced.
Movie: 🎬½ **DVD:** 🎬🎬
Trimark Home Video (Cat #VM7419D, UPC #031398741923). Widescreen (1.85:1) letterboxed. Dolby Digital 5.1. $24.99. Keepcase. *LANG:* English. *SUB:* English; Spanish; French. *CAP:* English. *FEATURES:* 24 chapter links ▪ Theatrical trailer ▪ Interview with Jamie Foxx.
2000 (PG-13) 88m/C Jamie Foxx, Nia Long, Jake Busey, John Cullum, Barry Corbin, Eduardo Yanez, Mike Wiles, Sarah Paulson, Julie Hagerty; **D:** Steve Rash; **W:** Jeff Eastin; **C:** David Makin; **M:** Robert Folk.

Hell Is for Heroes

Steve McQueen leads a young ensemble cast in a taut war drama about a squad of Americans on the Siegfried Line near the end of World War II. They're outmanned by the Germans facing them, but the Nazis might not know that. Writer Robert Pirosh is better known for the much more famous

(and bigger budgeted) *Battleground*. Director Siegel makes this one tough, brutal, and short. He also got some of the sharpest black-and-white cinematography you'll ever see. Even the mono sound is crisp. This is one of the great "lost" war films. A superb discovery for any fan who's missed it. —*MM*
Movie: 🎬🎬🎬½ **DVD:** 🎬🎬🎬½
Paramount Home Video (Cat #06116, UPC #097360611649). Widescreen anamorphic. Dolby Digital Mono. $24.98. Keepcase. *LANG:* English or French. *SUB:* English. *FEATURES:* 15 chapter links.
1962 90m/B Steve McQueen, Bobby Darin, Fess Parker, Harry Guardino, James Coburn, Mike Kellin, Nick Adams, Bob Newhart, L.Q. (Justus E. McQueen) Jones, Don Haggerty, Joseph Hoover, Michele Montau, Bill Mullikin; **D:** Donald Siegel; **W:** Robert Pirosh, Richard Carr; **C:** Harold Lipstein; **M:** Leonard Rosenman.

Hellblock 13

Anthology of three low-budget short horror tales is told with grainy, raw-edged energy and a distinct regional flavor. Tara (Debbie Rochon) writes stories while she's on Death Row and shows them to her stolid guard (Gunnar Hansen, Leatherface from *Texas Chainsaw Massacre*). Rochon brings a welcome note of humor to what might have been your basic madwoman stereotype. The individual films get better and funnier as they go along. The full-frame DVD image is not a marked improvement over VHS tape. Neither is the sound. —*MM*
Movie: 🎬🎬½ **DVD:** 🎬🎬
Troma Team Video (Cat #9983, UPC #790 357998333). Full frame. $24.99. Keepcase. *LANG:* English. *FEATURES:* 9 chapter links ▪ DVD credits ▪ Radiation March.
1997 91m/C Debbie Rochon, Gunnar Hansen, J.J. North, Jennifer Peluso, David G. Holland; **D:** Paul Talbot; **W:** Paul Talbot, Jeff Miller, Michael R. Smith.

Hellraiser [2]

Author Clive Barker makes a credible directorial debut in this tale of ultimate pleasure and pain. Those come from the Cenobites, five creatures who are conjured up by an intricate puzzle box, and who descend upon a damaged family (Robinson, Higgins, Laurence). Though the tricky story is bloody, it doesn't wallow in gore after the graphic introduction. On their commentary track, Barker, Laurence, and moderator Pete Atkins talk about the structure of horror. Their approach, 15 years after they made the film, is nostalgic and professional. It could go without saying that the quality of the image is excellent. The 5.1 sound is an improvement over the theatrical release. —*MM*
Movie: 🎬🎬🎬 **DVD:** 🎬🎬🎬🎬
Anchor Bay (Cat #DV11232, UPC #01313 1123296). Widescreen (1.85:1) anamorphic. Dolby Digital 5.1 Surround Stereo. $24.99. Keepcase. *LANG:* English. *CAP:* English. *FEATURES:* 28 chapter links ▪ "Resurrection" featurette ▪ Trailer ▪

Stills gallery • Commentary: Barker, Laurence, and Atkins.
1987 (R) 94m/C *GB* Andrew (Andy) Robinson, Clare Higgins, Ashley Laurence, Sean Chapman, Oliver Smith, Robert Hines, Doug Bradley, Nicholas Vince, Dave Atkins; *D:* Clive Barker; *W:* Clive Barker; *C:* Robin Vidgeon; *M:* Christopher Young.

Hell's Kitchen NYC

Ex-con Johnny Miles (Phifer) returns home to New York's notorious Hell's Kitchen after serving five years for a crime he did not commit, only to face grudges, guns, and the ramifications of his violent past. More or less a redemption drama, the film benefits from a good cast, especially Jolie as a revenge-driven street urchin and Arquette as her drugged-out mom. Despite the trappings of his "convict-into-street angel" role, Phifer exudes a quiet strength that never seems out of place, even when the action gets hysterical. Director Cinciripini scores points in creating scenes of drug addiction that invoke a kind of horrific absurdity, guiding seemingly over-the-top moments with a sure hand and a rock-solid purpose. It's in the more preachy aspects of his script where he loses control, the rising saccharine quotient potentially diluting the potency of his worthwhile message. The full-frame transfer is clean enough with stable colors, but offers no discernible benefit from watching it on videotape. The Surround soundtrack is surprisingly active, teeming with the blare of sirens, gunshots, and ever-present traffic noise, mixing in a judicious amount of bass when appropriate. —*EP*
Movie: ♫♫½ **DVD:** ♫♫½
Image Entertainment (Cat #ID8808UM DVD, UPC #1438188082). Full frame. Dolby Digital Stereo Surround. $24.99. Snapper. *LANG:* English. *FEATURES:* 12 chapter links.
1997 (R) 101m/C Rosanna Arquette, William Forsythe, Michael Spiller, Angelina Jolie, Mekhi Phifer; *D:* Tony Cinciripini; *W:* Tony Cinciripini; *C:* Derek Wiesehahn; *M:* Tony Cinciripini, Nat Robinson.

Hendrix

Standard made-for-TV biopic begins with an interview that Jimi Hendrix (Harris) gave late in his life and immediately flashes back to his father (Harewood) giving him his first guitar. The body of the film irritatingly mixes black-and-white and color footage, videotape and film. The sound does no justice to the music and the film itself never captures the tumultuous times. Full-frame image is little better than tape. —*MM*
Movie: ♫♫ **DVD:** ♫♫
MGM Home Entertainment (Cat #100015 34, UPC #027616858450). Full frame. Dolby Digital Surround Stereo. $24.99. Keepcase. *LANG:* English. *SUB:* French; Spanish. *CAP:* English. *FEATURES:* 16 chapter links.
2000 (R) 103m/C Wood Harris, Vivica A. Fox, Billy Zane, Christian Potenza, Dorian

Harewood, Kris Holdenried, Christopher Ralph, Michie Mee; *D:* Leon Ichaso; *W:* Art Washington, Hal Roberts, Butch Stein; *C:* Claudio Chea; *M:* Daniel Licht.

Henry V

Kenneth Branagh's interpretation of Shakespeare's history of the warrior-king is stirring stuff. It's only on a second or third viewing that you realize how economically he was working. He could afford neither masses of extras nor the physical space to film the sweeping battle scenes that Laurence Olivier staged in another time. Instead, Branagh takes Kurasawa's *Seven Samurai* for his model. The battle of Agincourt is staged in mud and rain where the focus is on individual fights and graphic sound effects. It's in those scenes that the Surround effects really kick in, and so does Patrick Doyle's stirring score. (By the way, that's him singing right after the battle.) The only visual flaw worth noting is a tendency toward artifacts in areas of bright mist. Some might criticize the disc for the lack of a commentary track, but who could talk over the Bard? This is an excellent version of a terrific film. —*MM*
Movie: ♫♫♫♫ **DVD:** ♫♫♫
20th Century Fox Home Entertainment (Cat #1000681, UPC #027616850126). Widescreen anamorphic. Dolby Digital Surround Stereo. $24.99. Keepcase. *LANG:* English. *SUB:* French; Spanish. *CAP:* English. *FEATURES:* 36 chapter links • Trailer • Liner notes.
1989 138m/C *GB* Kenneth Branagh, Derek Jacobi, Brian Blessed, Alec McCowen, Ian Holm, Richard Briers, Robert Stephens, Robbie Coltrane, Christian Bale, Judi Dench, Paul Scofield, Michael Maloney, Emma Thompson, Patrick Doyle, Richard Clifford, Richard Easton, Paul Gregory, Harold Innocent, Charles Kay, Geraldine McEwan, Christopher Ravenscroft, John Sessions, Simon Shepherd, Jay Villiers, Danny Webb; *D:* Kenneth Branagh; *W:* Kenneth Branagh; *C:* Kenneth Macmillan; *M:* Patrick Doyle. *AWARDS:* Oscars '89: Costume Des.; British Acad. '89: Director (Branagh); Natl. Bd. of Review '89: Director (Branagh); *NOM:* Oscars '89: Actor (Branagh), Director (Branagh).

Her Name Is Cat

Yet another Hong Kong hitwoman (Almen Wong) agrees to yet another "last job" before retiring...fans know the drill. Explosions and slo-mo shoot outs are plentiful, though the fight choreography isn't going to make anyone forget John Woo or Ringo Lam. DVD image has the blue, overly bright, thin quality found in so many Hong Kong imports. Dubbing is a cut above a spaghetti western, but only a very small cut. —*MM*
Movie: ♫♫½ **DVD:** ♫♫
MTI Home Video (Cat #1056, UPC #03941 4510560). Widescreen letterboxed. $24.95. Keepcase. *LANG:* English. *SUB:*

Spanish. *FEATURES:* 20 chapter links • Trailer • Talent files.
1999 (R) 94m/C *HK* Michael Wong, Almen Wong, Kent Masters King; *D:* Clarence (Fok) Ford; *W:* Wong Jing.

Hercules in New York

In the motion picture debut of Schwarzenegger, his voice is dubbed, and he's billed in the opening titles as Arnold Strong "Mr. Universe." It's not only his first movie, but it's his worst. Still, the whole affair can also be described as 250 pounds of stupid, lighthearted fun. Schwarzenegger, AKA Strong, is a Herculean mass of muscles sent by dad Zeus to Manhattan, where he ends up a professional wrestling superstar. There are scratches here and there, there is grain everywhere, and the theatrical widescreen compositions have not been preserved. But, truthfully, the image is significantly better here than any other time this "Herc" misadventure has shown up on TV or video monitors. Besides, the film's looks are not its biggest problems. The main reason to seek out this DVD (we're talking only to Schwarzenegger fans here) is that the disc provides an optional soundtrack that features the Schwarzenegger's own voice, before dubbing obliterated his heavy Austrian accent. The non-dubbed version is from the international release, and it is otherwise unavailable on American video releases or on American TV. The Dolby Digital 2.0 mono soundtrack is not bad, with no easily detectable hiss nor distortion and perfectly clear dialogue. The menus look good, but the included trailers are heavily damaged. —*MB* **AKA:** Hercules: The Movie; Hercules Goes Bananas.
Movie: ♫½ **DVD:** ♫♫
Trimark Home Video (Cat #VM7483D, UPC #031398748328). Full frame. Dolby Digital 2.0 Mono. $19.99. Keepcase. *LANG:* English; Spanish; French; German. *SUB:* English; Spanish; French. *CAP:* English. *FEATURES:* 24 chapter links • Theatrical trailers • Optional audio from international release.
1970 (G) 93m/C Arnold Schwarzenegger, Arnold Stang, Deborah Loomis, James Karen, Ernest Graves, Taina Elg; *D:* Arthur Seidelman; *W:* Aubrey Wisberg; *C:* Leo Lebowitz; *M:* John Balamos.

Here on Earth

What begins as a cliché about a teenage love triangle evolves into a tale of selfless love and dying young. Spoiled, yet misunderstood rich kid Kelley (Klein) is sentenced to spend the summer rebuilding a restaurant he helped burn down after a drag race with local boy Jasper (Hartnett). The triangle soon ensues with Kelley, Jasper, and Samantha (Sobieski). Good performances by the principles and the adult supporting cast (Rooker, Greenwood) give the plain script some flavor. Director Piznarski's past credits include episodes of *My So-Called Life,* which no doubt gave him a leg up on working with a young cast.

A good movie for adolescents who haven't seen the dying heroine plot device before. The color is fabulous on the DVD with great saturation and transitions from brights to darks. —CA

Movie: ♫♫ **DVD:** ♫♫½
20th Century Fox Home Entertainment (Cat #2000622, UPC #024543006220). Widescreen (1.85:1) anamorphic. Dolby Digital 5.1; Dolby Surround. $29.98. Keepcase. *LANG:* English. *SUB:* English; Spanish; French. *CAP:* English. *FEATURES:* 20 chapter links • Jessica Simpson music video "Where You Are" • Original theatrical trailer.
2000 (PG-13) 96m/C Chris Klein, Leelee Sobieski, Josh Hartnett, Michael Rooker, Annie Corley, Bruce Greenwood, Annette O'Toole, Stuart Wilson; *D:* Mark Piznarski; *W:* Michael Seitzman; *C:* Michael D. O'Shea; *M:* Andrea Morricone.

Hideaway

Following what would otherwise be a fatal car crash, Hatch Harrison (Goldblum) is brought back from the other side. The side effect for Harrison—other than the ability to keep breathing—is the ability to psychically connect with Vassago (Sisto), a sadistic serial killer of young girls. Vassago eyes Harrison's teenage daughter, Regina (Silverstone), as his next victim. Film is a weak adaptation of a Dean R. Koontz novel bogged down by a hodge-podge of a script. On the plus side are the special effects, particularly shots of spirits floating down a cosmic vortex. Though generally sharp, the video is annoyingly soft on occasion. Sound is just fine, with ample opportunity for Surround speakers to do their thing. Some might find director Leonard's commentary track more interesting than his movie. —MB

Movie: ♫½ **DVD:** ♫♫♫
Columbia Tristar Home Video (Cat #05273, UPC #043396052734). Widescreen (2.35:1) anamorphic; full frame. Dolby Digital 5.1. $24.95. Keepcase. *LANG:* English; Spanish; French; Portuguese. *SUB:* English; Spanish; French; Portuguese; Chinese; Korean; Thai. *CAP:* English. *FEATURES:* 28 chapter links • Commentary: director • Alternate ending • "Making of" featurette • Talent files.
1994 (R) 103m/C Jeff Goldblum, Christine Lahti, Alicia Silverstone, Jeremy Sisto, Rae Dawn Chong; *D:* Brett Leonard; *W:* Andrew Kevin Walker, Neal Jimenez; *C:* Gale Tattersall; *M:* Trevor Jones.

High Fidelity

Frears, Cusack, and the writing team from *Grosse Pointe Blank* successfully bring Nick Hornby's 1995 novel to the screen, transplanting it to Chicago from London in the process. Cusack is Rob, a stuck-in-adolescence record store owner who just broke up with Laura (Hjejle), his long-time live-in love. This gets him to thinking about his Top Five All-Time Breakups. Cue flashbacks. Cusack does his usual fine job, but co-stars Black and Louiso take over when-

ever they're on-screen. The image is very crisp and clear, displaying no noise or grain. Frears shot the film using a realistic color palette, so the picture gives us very natural skintones and nighttime scenes, with no bleeding of the colors. While the 5.1 mix doesn't offer a very wide sound field, the dialogue is always clear and audible and the ever-present music in the film comes across as crystal clear. —ML/MM

Movie: ♫♫♫½ **DVD:** ♫♫♫½
Buena Vista Home Entertainment (Cat #20349). Widescreen (1.85:1) anamorphic. Dolby Digital 5.1 Surround Stereo. $32.99. Keepcase. *LANG:* English. *SUB:* English; Spanish. *FEATURES:* 9 deleted scenes • Interviews with Cusack and Frears • Theatrical trailer.
2000 (R) 113m/C John Cusack, Todd Louiso, Jack Black, Iben Hjejle, Tim Robbins, Joan Cusack, Lisa Bonet, Catherine Zeta-Jones, Lili Taylor, Natasha Gregson Wagner, Sara Gilbert, Chris Rehmann, Ben Carr, Joelle Carter, Bruce Springsteen; *D:* Stephen Frears; *W:* John Cusack, D.V. DeVincentis, Steve Pink, Scott Rosenberg; *C:* Seamus McGarvey; *M:* Howard Shore.

High School High

Hard-to-get-through comedy features idealistic teacher Richard Clark (Lovitz) leaving the private school world for notorious inner-city Marion Barry High. This school is so bad it has its own cemetery (it's a parody, folks), but Clark is determined to get through to the kids. *Clockers* star Phifer shows up as a helpful student. Penned by David Zucker of *Airplane!* fame, so don't expect a *Mr. Holland's Opus*. If you just have to have this turkey, the DVD won't disappoint with its excellent sharpness and highly detailed, accurate colors. True blacks and punchy contrast give the film more guts than its script. Even the 5.1 sound is a winner with good low end, excellent fidelity, and surprisingly active Surround tracks. It doesn't make the flick any funnier, but at least makes it worth turning on your AV receiver. Thankfully, there are no supplementals. —JO

Movie: ♫♫ **DVD:** ♫♫♫
Columbia Tristar Home Video (Cat #824 89, UPC #043396724898). Widescreen (1.85:1) anamorphic. Dolby Digital 5.1; Dolby Surround. $27.95. Keepcase. *LANG:* English; Spanish; French. *SUB:* English; Spanish; French. *CAP:* English. *FEATURES:* 28 chapter links • Theatrical trailer.
1996 (PG-13) 86m/C Jon Lovitz, Tia Carrere, Mekhi Phifer, Louise Fletcher, Malinda Williams; *D:* Hart Bochner; *W:* Pat Proft, David Zucker, Robert Locash; *C:* Vernon Layton; *M:* Ira Newborn.

Highlander: Endgame

Some might reasonably have expected that the title *Highlander: The Final Dimension* carries the implied guarantee that it is the last of the popular series. Not a chance. The immortals are back in the

most polished and visually sophisticated of the films. The time-traveling plot is familiar stuff. Connor (Lambert) and Duncan (Paul, from the TV series) battle the forces of evil led by Kell (Payne), etc., etc. The premise is so loose and loopy that the producers can do whatever they want with it, and they do keep things imaginative and romantic in a bodice-ripper vein. The action scenes are jazzed with some very nice effects, and the beefy Surround mix really adds a lot. For fans who just can't get enough, the two-disc set also contains an early rough version of the film. —MM

Movie: ♫♫½ **DVD:** ♫♫♫
Buena Vista Home Entertainment (Cat #21 661, UPC #786936144833). Widescreen (1.85:1) anamorphic. Dolby Digital 5.1 Surround. $29.99. Keepcase. *LANG:* English. *SUB:* English. *FEATURES:* 13 chapter links (feature) • 12 chapter links (rough version) • 3 deleted scenes • Commentary: producers Davis, Panzer, and Gross; editor Ferretti • Behind-the-scenes featurette • Visual effects: a historical progression • DVD-ROM features. Title is also available with Spanish subtitles.
2000 (R) 101m/C Christopher Lambert, Adrian Paul, Bruce Payne, Lisa Barbuscia, Peter Wingfield, Jim Byrnes, Donnie Yen, Beatie Edney, Sheila Gish; *D:* Douglas Aarniokoski; *W:* Joel Soisson; *C:* Doug Milsome; *M:* Stephen Graziano.

Highlander: The Final Dimension

This is a fitting third chapter in the goofball sword-and-sorcery series. Like the first two, it's built around excellent but uninspired special effects, bad acting, and a story that doesn't even attempt to make sense. Immortal warrior Conner MacLeod (Lambert) battles master illusionist Kane (Van Peebles), who seeks to rule the world. Aiding MacLeod in more ways than one is science-babe Alex Smith (Unger), who discovers that Kane was once buried beneath a mystical mountain with three other immortal warriors (they're everywhere!) some 300 years before. The "exclusive director's cut!" video contains some sexual material left out of the theatrical release. Aliasing and artifacts are visible during the brightest snow and desert scenes. The 5.1 kicks in for the big effects numbers. —MM *AKA:* Highlander 3: The Magician; Highlander 3: The Sorcerer.

Movie: ♫♫ **DVD:** ♫♫½
Buena Vista Home Entertainment (Cat #14374). Widescreen (2.35:1) letterboxed. Dolby Digital Stereo. $29.99. Keepcase. *LANG:* English. *CAP:* English. *FEATURES:* 19 chapter links.
1994 (R) 99m/C Christopher Lambert, Mario Van Peebles, Deborah Kara Unger, Mako; *D:* Andrew Morahan; *W:* Paul Ohl; *C:* Steven Chivers; *M:* J. Peter Robinson.

The Highway Man

Middle-aged Frank Drake (McHattie) is running telephone scams and winds up being framed by his nasty boss (Gossett) for fraud and is then accused of murder. Into this mess strolls Ziggy (Harris), who thinks Frank is her daddy, along with her boyfriend/thief Breakfast (Priestley), who's just made a big score. It plays like two separate stories that never quite come together. Without speckles, grain, or blemishes, the transfer comes from a clean source. Colors in the transfers are strong and nicely rendered, while blacks are deep and solid. The film has an intentionally cold look with lots of steel-blue hues. Audio has been well produced and sounds very natural. —MM

Movie: 🐾🐾 **DVD:** 🐾🐾½
Studio Home Entertainment (Cat #7355). Widescreen (1.85:1) letterboxed. Dolby Digital 5.1 Surround Stereo; Dolby Digital Stereo. $24.95. Keepcase. *LANG:* English. *SUB:* Spanish. *FEATURES:* Commentary • Featurette • Trailer • Talent files.
1999 (R) 97m/C Jason Priestley, Louis Gossett Jr., Stephen McHattie, Laura Harris, Callum Keith Rennie, Gordon Michael Woolvett, Bernie Coulson; *D:* Keoni Waxman; *W:* Richard Beattie.

Hillbillys in a Haunted House

If reels of the TV show *Hee Haw* were mixed in with *Frankenstein Meets the Wolf Man* or any of the lesser Universal horror movies, the result would look a lot like this. Two country singers and their manager (an incredibly cantilevered Joi Lansing) en route to Nashville run into a group of "foreign spies" (including Rathbone, Carradine, and Chaney Jr.) and a guy in a gorilla suit at a fake haunted house. Entertainment value is completely camp. The film is surprisingly clear and sharp on DVD. It looks very good for a work of this age. —MM *AKA:* Hillbillies in a Haunted House.

Movie: 🐾🐾½ **DVD:** 🐾🐾
VCI Home Video (Cat #8234, UPC #0898 59823428). Full frame. $24.99. Keepcase. *LANG:* English. *FEATURES:* 18 chapter links • Previews.
1967 88m/C Ferlin Husky, Joi Lansing, Don Bowman, John Carradine, Lon Chaney Jr., Basil Rathbone, Merle Haggard, Sonny James, Linda Ho, Molly Bee, George Barrows; *D:* Jean Yarbrough; *W:* Duke Yelton; *C:* Vaughn Wilkins; *M:* Hal Borne.

Hip Hop 2000

Movies about hip hop tend to be rough looking, but this one is so amateurish that it's barely watchable. It combines interviews with such music stars as Ice-T with a fictional story involving the theft of songs and narration by Rudy Ray Moore. Image is fuzzily focused and grainy. Some scenes are widescreen; others are full frame. A rental disc froze in chapter seven. Sometimes you get lucky. —MM

Movie: woof **DVD:** 🐾
Delta/Laserlight (Cat #7011, UPC #0394 14570113). Widescreen; full frame. $24.98. Keepcase. *LANG:* English. *FEATURES:* 20 chapter links • Trailers •

Separate interviews with Ice-T, Too $hort, and Dolomite • Talent files.
2000 (R) 104m/C Desi Arnez Hines II, Temple Poteat, Marvin Jordan, Marvin Jordan; *D:* Will Anderson; *W:* Will Anderson, Jumad Pinkney; *C:* Edgar Arellano; *Nar:* Rudy Ray Moore.

Holiday Heart

Warmhearted, politically correct tale is done in by its good intentions and a predictable plot. Holiday Heart (Rhames) is the most popular singer at a female impersonators bar. (The sight of him lip-synching "Baby Love" in full Diana Ross drag regalia is not soon forgot.) By day, he is a choirmaster at a black evangelical church. He is still mourning the death of his companion, a policeman. Then he meets Niki (Reynolds), lovely little daughter of a drug-addicted mom (Woodard), and invites them to move into his half-empty house. Performances are fine, particularly by Rhames. Full-frame image is little better than tape and the Surround is given only a limited workout. The language and subtitle options are the only improvements. —MM

Movie: 🐾🐾 **DVD:** 🐾🐾
MGM Home Entertainment (Cat #10018 17, UPC #027616860873). Full frame. Dolby Digital Surround Stereo. $24.99. Keepcase. *LANG:* English; French; Spanish. *SUB:* French; Spanish. *FEATURES:* 16 chapter links.
2000 (R) 97m/C Ving Rhames, Alfre Woodard, Mykelti Williamson, Jesika Reynolds; *D:* Robert Thompson; *W:* Cheryl L. West; *C:* Jan Kiesser; *M:* Stephen James Taylor.

The Hollow Man [SE]

The main flaw in this rehash of *The Invisible Man* is that the title character, Dr. Sebastian Caine (Bacon), is too crazy too soon. Director Verhoeven tacitly admits as much in his commentary on the deleted rape scene, which made little sense in the theatrical release. As a collection of inventive special effects, the film is still enjoyable enough, though much more could have been done with the first-rate cast and premise. Of the numerous extras, perhaps the most interesting are the "picture within picture" scenes, which show how body suits were used to create various effects in different scenes. Within the film, quite a bit of grain is evident, giving the image a fairly soft look. Color reproduction is good and faithful with deep solid blacks. The transfer shows some signs of edge-enhancement, but it never gets to the point of being distracting. No notable compression artifacts are evident in the presentation. Like most modern multi-channel mixes, the 5.1 Surround track can be used to show off the format's capabilities. —MM/GH

Movie: 🐾🐾½ **DVD:** 🐾🐾🐾½
Columbia Tristar Home Video (Cat #050 72, UPC #043396050723). Widescreen (1.85:1) anamorphic. Dolby Digital 5.1 Surround Stereo; Dolby Digital Surround

Stereo. $24.95. Keepcase. *LANG:* English; French. *SUB:* English; French. *FEATURES:* 28 chapter links • Commentary: Verhoeven, Bacon, and Marlowe • 15 behind-the-scenes featurettes • 3 deleted scenes • 3 "picture within picture" comparisons • DVD-ROM weblinks • Talent files • Production notes • Isolated score with Jerry Goldsmith commentary • "Making of" featurette.
2000 (R) 114m/C Kevin Bacon, Elisabeth Shue, Josh Brolin, William Devane, Kim Dickens, Greg Grunberg, Mary Jo Randle, Joey Slotnick; *D:* Paul Verhoeven; *W:* Andrew Marlowe; *C:* Jost Vacano; *M:* Jerry Goldsmith.

Hollywood Boulevard

One of Roger Corman's best and funniest gets the treatment it deserves on DVD. On their commentary track, the filmmakers admit that it's essentially a "home movie" mostly cobbled together from pieces of other films. That said, it's also an affectionately autobiographical film about a young woman (Rialson) who arrives in Hollywood on a bus and quickly finds work in the low-budget exploitation business. That's the premise and, later on, there's even a plot (sort of), but it never gets in the way. Directors Dante and Arkush and producer Davison made a movie about making movies for Roger Corman. The "cutting room floor" extra is simply more previews. The widescreen image is as rough as it has ever been, but at least it's widescreen. —MM

Movie: 🐾🐾🐾 **DVD:** 🐾🐾🐾
New Concorde (Cat #NH20154D, UPC #73 6991415492). Widescreen letterboxed. Surround. $19.98. Keepcase. *LANG:* English. *FEATURES:* 24 chapter links • Commentary: Joe Dante, Allan Arkush, Jon Davison • Trailers • Thumbnail bios.
1976 (R) 93m/C Candice Rialson, Mary Woronov, Rita George, Jonathan Kaplan, Jeffrey Kramer, Dick Miller, Paul Bartel, Charles B. Griffith, Richard Doran; *D:* Joe Dante, Allan Arkush; *W:* Patrick Hobby; *C:* Jamie Anderson; *M:* Andrew Stein.

The Hollywood Knights

Cheap imitation of *American Graffiti* is not without its funny moments. Beverly Hills teens, lead by Newbomb Turk (Wuhl), are displeased that their hangout—Tubby's Drive-in—is being shut down by those no-fun adults. So they decide to retaliate. Set on Halloween Night, 1965. Good fun if at times a bit confusing. Columbia has done an excellent job with their DVD transfer of *The Hollywood Knights,* which made its first legitimate appearance on home video with this disc and the concurrent Columbia VHS release. Most notable is the color, which is very saturated and natural with almost no bleed. There is some occasional grain, but it is so rare that you have to look for it, and the image is extremely sharp—as sharp as most good transfers of more recent films. Columbia has included three audio tracks: the original mono; Dolby Surround; and the expected Dolby Digital 5.1. The mono seems to work best with the film since the 5.1 sounds totally synthetic and maybe a little distorted, and the Dolby Surround is only a little better. The 5.1 mix might just be a marketing ploy since there are some consumers who refuse to buy a DVD that does not have one. —JO

Movie: 🎵🎵 **DVD:** 🎵🎵🎵
Columbia Tristar Home Video (Cat #218 94, UPC #043396218949). Widescreen (1.85:1) letterboxed. Dolby Digital 5.1; Dolby Surround; Mono. $24.95. Keepcase. *LANG:* English; Spanish. *SUB:* English; Spanish; French. *CAP:* English. *FEATURES:* 28 chapter links ● Trailers ● Talent files ● Production notes ● Commentary: Director Floyd Mutrux.
1980 (R) 91m/C Robert Wuhl, Michelle Pfeiffer, Tony Danza, Fran Drescher, Leigh French, Gary (Rand) Graham, James Jeter, Stuart Pankin, Gailard Sartain, Mike Binder, T.K. Carter, Moosie Drier, Debra Feuer, Garry Goodrow, Joyce Hyser, Roberta Wallach, Doris Hargrave, Walter Janovitz, Art LaFleur, Glenn Withrow, Sandy Helberg; **D:** Floyd Mutrux; **W:** Floyd Mutrux; **C:** William A. Fraker.

Hollywood Vice Sqaud

Years before reality TV, the script bug bit the real-life chief of the Hollywood Vice Squad and he tried to turn real events into a comedy/drama/exploitation picture. Not surprisingly, the finished film doesn't succeed as any of them. The storylines involve child pornography, prostitution, and gambling. DVD image is strictly low-budget and grainy, exactly like VHS tape and the theatrical release. —MM

Movie: 🎵🎵 **DVD:** 🎵🎵
Image Entertainment (Cat #OVE9025DVD, UPC #014381902525). Full frame. Dolby Digital Mono. $24.99. Snapper. *LANG:* English. *FEATURES:* 13 chapter links ● Trailer.
1986 (R) 90m/C Trish Van Devere, Ronny Cox, Frank Gorshin, Leon Isaac Kennedy, Carrie Fisher, Ben Frank, Robin Wright Penn; **D:** Penelope Spheeris; **W:** James J. Docherty; **M:** Michael Convertino.

Holy Smoke

Free-spirited Ruth (Winslet) finds spiritual enlightenment in India, terrifying her parents. They lure her back to Australia where they have hired PJ Walters (Keitel) to deprogram her. Let the psycho-sexual games begin. Complex characters are undermined by Campion's typically strident style. Extremely dark interiors don't have much detail or definition and they probably never did. Many exteriors mirror the characters' troubled emotional states and so they're tinted with brownish hues. Sound is very good. —MM

Movie: 🎵🎵 **DVD:** 🎵🎵

Miramax Pictures Home Video (Cat #182 93, UPC #717951004796). Widescreen (1.85:1) anamorphic. Dolby Digital 5.1 Surround Stereo; Dolby Digital Surround. $29.99. Keepcase. *LANG:* English; French. *SUB:* Spanish. *CAP:* English. *FEATURES:* 29 chapter links.
1999 (R) 114m/C *AU* Harvey Keitel, Kate Winslet, Julie Hamilton, Tim Robertson, Sophie Lee, Pam Grier, Paul Goddard, Daniel Wyllie; **D:** Jane Campion; **W:** Jane Campion, Anna Campion; **C:** Dion Beebe; **M:** Angelo Badalamenti.

Home for Christmas

Twelve-year-old Susan Ferris (Love Hewitt) has run away from her wicked stepmom (Morris) who hires a bounty hunter (Hesseman) to bring her back—for a half a million bucks. When he does, she refuses to pay and accuses him of kidnapping. The film looks very good for a Corman production, as director Wynorski notes in his commentary track. The presence of the young star earns the disc its special treatment, but it's still an entertaining kid's adventure. Image and sound are about the same as tape; the extras make a difference. —MM *AKA:* Little Miss Millions.

Movie: 🎵🎵½ **DVD:** 🎵🎵🎵
New Concorde (Cat #NH20765, UPC #736 991276543). Full frame. Stereo. $19.98. Keepcase. *LANG:* English. *FEATURES:* 24 chapter links ● Booklet ● Trailers ● Thumbnail bios ● Commentary: Jim Wynorski.
1993 (PG) 90m/C Howard Hesseman, Anita Morris, Jennifer Love Hewitt; **D:** Jim Wynorski; **W:** Jim Wynorski, R.J. Robertson; **C:** Zoran Hochstatter; **M:** Joel Goldsmith.

A Home of Our Own

In 1962, Frances Lacey (Bates), widowed mother of six, decides to move her brood from Los Angeles to someplace—anyplace—better and heads off, "sorta north and sorta east." They wind up in Idaho in an unfinished house that's little more than a semi-walled foundation. It's owned by the lonely Mr. Moon (Oh), and what follows is a very tough winter. Bates, as usual, is nothing short of superb. Furlong delivers narration as the eldest son. DVD provides an excellent reproduction of the theatrical image. It's properly detailed with a very strong sense of place. The score benefits from the Surround effects. But this semi-autobiographical story cries out for a commentary track, ideally by writer Duncan and director Bill. —MM

Movie: 🎵🎵🎵½ **DVD:** 🎵🎵🎵
MGM Home Entertainment (Cat #10018 48, UPC #027616861160). Widescreen (1.85:1) letterboxed. Dolby Digital Surround. $14.95. Keepcase. *LANG:* English. *SUB:* French; Spanish. *FEATURES:* 16 chapter links ● Trailer.
1993 (PG-13) 104m/C Kathy Bates, Edward Furlong, Soon-Teck Oh, Amy Sakasitz, Tony Campisi; **D:** Tony Bill; **W:** Patrick Duncan.

Homegrown

Engaging comedy-noir has three dense Northern California pot growers (Thornton, Azaria, Phillippe) witness their boss's (Lithgow) murder. Seeing this as a bad omen, they take off with the crop to the operation's packaging department and decide to carry on as if the boss is still alive. Amid many cameos (Danson, Curtis) they set up a big deal with a seemingly laid-back wholesaler (Bon Jovi). Performances are surprisingly good all around and most of the pot-head comedy works. The DVD is rather average and not quite up to the quality of the film. Sharpness is good but drops off during highly detailed shots. Same for the color, which is pretty good except in darker scenes where some bleed occurs and the blacks become slightly grainy. Very little use is made of the 5.1 mix, which at its best adds ambience, mainly to the music. —JO

Movie: 🎵🎵🎵 **DVD:** 🎵🎵½
Columbia Tristar Home Video (Cat #25329, UPC #043396253292). Widescreen (1.85:1) anamorphic. Dolby Digital 5.1; Dolby Surround. $27.95. Keepcase. *LANG:* English; Spanish; French. *SUB:* English; Spanish; French. *CAP:* English. *FEATURES:* 28 chapter links ● Theatrical trailer.
1997 (R) 101m/C Billy Bob Thornton, Hank Azaria, Ryan Phillippe, Kelly Lynch, Jon Bon Jovi, John Lithgow, Jon Tenney, Matt Clark; **Cameos:** Ted Danson, Jamie Lee Curtis, Judge Reinhold; **D:** Stephen Gyllenhaal; **W:** Stephen Gyllenhaal, Nicholas Kazan; **C:** Greg Gardiner; **M:** Trevor Rabin.

Homicide: The Movie

Former Homicide Shift Commander Al Biardello (Kotto) is running for mayor of Baltimore on a platform of drug-legalization. At an Inner Harbor photo-op, he is shot. His former and fellow cops work to catch the shooter as he is treated at the hospital. This made-for-TV movie, like the series, uses a combination of film and video, and DVD is an accurate reproduction of an often offputting image. The series is one of the most intense ever broadcast and the film captures it at its best. Particularly recommended to knowledgeable fans. —MM

Movie: 🎵🎵🎵 **DVD:** 🎵🎵🎵
Trimark Home Video (Cat #VM7649D, UPC #031398764922). Full frame. Stereo. $24.99. Keepcase. *LANG:* English. *SUB:* English; Spanish. *FEATURES:* 30 chapter links.
2000 (PG-13) 89m/C Yaphet Kotto, Andre Braugher, Kyle Secor, Richard Belzer, Giancarlo Esposito, Peter Gerety, Clark Johnson, Zeljko Ivanek, Michael Michele, Reed Edward Diamond, Michelle Forbes, Isabella Hofmann, Melissa Leo, Callie (Calliope) Thorne, Jon Seda, Max Perlich, Jason Priestley, Daniel Baldwin, Ned Beatty, Jon Polito, Toni Lewis; **D:** Jean De Segonzac; **W:** Eric Overmyer, Tom Fontana, James Yoshimura; **C:** Jean De Segonzac; **M:** Douglas J. Cuomo.

Honey & Ashes

This story of women attempting to break free in a patriarchal society is frustrating. Opening French voice-over is not translated and when the Arabic dialogue is subtitled, the words are small and difficult. In a North African Islamic country, young Leila is punished by her strict father for seeing a boyfriend. Naima has studied medicine but is expected to enter an arranged marriage. A third woman, Amina, is beaten by her husband. The full-frame image is rough with harsh colors. The no-frills disc is not a real improvement over tape, but still should find an audience. —*MM* **AKA:** Miel et Cendres.

Movie: 🎬🎬½ *DVD:* 🎬🎬
Vanguard International Cinema, Inc. (Cat #1-892649-88-8, UPC #658769010633). Full frame. $29.95. Keepcase. *LANG:* French and Arabic. *SUB:* English. *FEATURES:* 12 chapter links.
1996 80m/C *SI* Nozha Khouadra, Amel Hedhili, Samia Mzali, Lara Chaouachi, Naji Najeh, Slim Larnaout, Jamel Sassi; *D:* Nadia Fares; *W:* Nadia Fares, Yves Kropf; *C:* Ismael Ramirez; *M:* Slim Larnaout, Jean-Francois Bovard, Mami Azairez.

Honor Among Thieves

Two former mercenaries (Bronson and Delon) reteam for a robbery that doesn't come off as planned. It's not as swiftly paced as others in the Bronson canon, though that's the least of the disc's problems. It is one of the worst DVDs ever made. Judging by the look of it, this one could have been copied from a third generation VHS dupe. No menu; positively unwatchable. —*MM* **AKA:** Farewell, Friend.
Movie: 🎬½ *DVD:* woof
Essex (Cat #1403). Full frame. Dolby Digital Stereo. $10.97. Slipcase. *LANG:* English.
1968 (R) 115m/C *FR IT* Charles Bronson, Alain Delon, Brigitte Fossey, Olga Georges-Picot, Bernard Fresson; *D:* Jean Herman; *W:* Sebastien Japrisot; *C:* Jean-Jacques Tarbes; *M:* Francois de Roubaix.

Honor Thy Father

Please see review of *Great Mafia Movies.*
Movie: 🎬🎬
1973 97m/C Raf Vallone, Richard S. Castellano, Brenda Vaccaro, Joseph Bologna; *D:* Paul Wendkos; *M:* George Duning.

Hoodlum

Highly fictionalized tale of '30s gangster "Bumpy" Johnson (Fishburne) who refuses to allow Dutch Schultz (Roth) and Lucky Luciano (Garcia) to muscle into the Harlem numbers racket. Director Duke makes the proceedings nice to look at, and DVD is an accurate re-creation of the theatrical image. This being a period piece, image tends toward soft, nostalgic focus and pastel colors. Sound is very nice, too, but the cast is the point here.

Roth is ruthless and Garcia is smooth, but the show belongs to Fishburne. —*MM*
AKA: Gangster; Hoods.
Movie: 🎬🎬🎬 *DVD:* 🎬🎬🎬
MGM Home Entertainment (Cat #9069 95). Widescreen letterboxed; full frame. $14.95. Keepcase. *LANG:* English; French. *SUB:* English; French; Spanish. *FEATURES:* 32 chapter links • Trailer.
1996 (R) 130m/C Laurence "Larry" Fishburne, Tim Roth, Andy Garcia, Vanessa Williams, Cicely Tyson, Clarence Williams III, William Atherton, Chi McBride, Richard Bradford, Loretta Devine, Queen Latifah, Paul Benjamin, Mike Starr, Beau Starr, Joe Guzaldo, Ed O'Ross; *D:* Bill Duke; *W:* Chris Brancato; *C:* Frank Tidy; *M:* Elmer Bernstein.

Hope and Glory

John Boorman turns his memories of WWII London into a complex, sensitive, and rigorously unsentimental film. Seven-year-old Bill's (Rice-Edwards) life is turned upside down by the announcement of war on September 3, 1939. Father (Hayman) volunteers; mother (Miles) must deal with the awakening sexuality of her daughter (Davis), balance the ration books, and make it to the bomb shelter in the middle of the night. Seen through the boy's eyes, war creates a playground of collectible shrapnel and wild imaginings. Mono sound is fine for the film, though the option of Surround might have been nice. Image is excellent. But if ever a film cried out for a commentary track, this is it. Boorman is one of the most intelligent filmmakers in the business and this is a particularly personal work. For now though, we can continue to hope that studio executives will come to their senses and give this film the treatment it deserves. —*MM*
Movie: 🎬🎬🎬🎬 *DVD:* 🎬🎬🎬
MGM Home Entertainment (Cat #10020 42, UPC #027616862792). Widescreen (1.78:1) letterboxed. Dolby Digital Mono. $19.98. Keepcase. *LANG:* English; French. *SUB:* French; Spanish. *FEATURES:* 16 chapter links.
1987 (PG-13) 97m/C *GB* Sebastian Rice-Edwards, Geraldine Muir, Sarah Miles, Sammi Davis, David Hayman, Derrick O'Connor, Susan Wooldridge, Jean-Marc Barr, Ian Bannen, Jill Baker, Charley Boorman, Annie Leon, Katrine Boorman, Gerald James, Amelda Brown, Colin Higgins; *D:* John Boorman; *W:* John Boorman; *C:* Philippe Rousselot; *M:* Peter Martin. *AWARDS:* British Acad. '87: Film, Support. Actress (Wooldridge); Golden Globes '88: Film—Mus./Comedy; L.A. Film Critics '87: Director (Boorman), Film, Screenplay; Natl. Soc. Film Critics '87: Cinematog., Director (Boorman), Film, Screenplay; *NOM:* Oscars '87: Art Dir./Set Dec., Cinematog., Director (Boorman), Orig. Screenplay, Picture.

The Horrible Dr. Bones

Dr. Bones (Igus) is a record producer who gives the young Urban Protectors band

their big break, but it turns out that he's exploiting them in a supernatural scheme involving human sacrifice and zombies. The plotting is amateurish. Some of the effects have shock value. The low-budget horror doesn't rise much above the studio's bare-bones production, but the image is clear and the sound is strong. The voluminous extras on the B-side of the disc are previews for other Full Moon productions and ads for their merchandise. —*MM*
Movie: 🎬🎬 *DVD:* 🎬🎬½
Full Moon Pictures (Cat #FUM-DV8055, UPC #763843805569). Widescreen letterboxed. $19.98. Keepcase. *LANG:* English. *FEATURES:* 16 chapter links • "Making of" featurette • 44 trailers • Igus thumbnail bio.
2000 (R) 72m/C Darrow Igus, Larry Bates, Sarah Scott, Rhonda Claebaut, Nathaniel Lamar; *D:* Art Carnage; *W:* Raymond Forchon; *C:* Adolfo Bartoli.

Horror Hotel

In an early role, Christopher Lee is Prof. Driscoll who sends young Nan Barlow (Stevenson) off for some primary research in Whitewood, Mass., where a witch was burned centuries before. With its lovely black-and-white photography and fog-shrouded atmosphere, the film really is a "lost" milestone of the 1960s that was influential on many of the Gothic horrors of later decades. This is a very dark film, but blacks are generally true. The few flecks and scratches are to be expected on a film of this age. —*MM* **AKA:** The City of the Dead.
Movie: 🎬🎬½ *DVD:* 🎬🎬🎬
Troma Team Video (Cat #AED-2047, UPC #785604204725). Widescreen (1.66:1). Dolby Digital Mono. $19.95. Keepcase. *LANG:* English. *FEATURES:* 11 chapter links • Christopher Lee interview • Background information.
1960 76m/B *GB* Christopher Lee, Patricia Jessel, Betta St. John, Dennis Lotis, Venetia Stevenson, Valentine Dyall; *D:* John Llewellyn Moxey; *W:* George L. Baxt; *C:* Desmond Dickinson.

Horrors of Spider Island

Gary (D'Arcy, who claims to have co-directed) is a Hollywood talent scout who accompanies a troupe of showgirls to Singapore. Their plane crashes (offscreen) in the Pacific and they find themselves stranded on an island with crab-sized spider puppets. After he's bitten, Gary becomes a monster. The effects are about as persuasive as the cast's acting abilities. The result is a skinless skinflick that was actually a German production. Frank Henenlotter details the film's curious history in fine liner notes. Some light static is audible but the black-and-white image ranges between good and very good. —*MM* **AKA:** It's Hot in Paradise; Ein Toter Hing im Netz; A Corpse Hangs in the Web.
Movie: 🎬🎬½ *DVD:* 🎬🎬🎬

Image Entertainment (Cat #ID9739SW DVD, UPC #014381973921). Full frame. Dolby Digital Mono. $24.99. Snapper. *LANG:* English. *FEATURES:* 12 chapter links • 3 short tame stripper films • Gallery of exploitation art.

1959 77m/C *GE* Alexander D'Arcy, Ursula Lederstger, Barbara Valentin, Harold Maresch, Helga Franck; *D:* Fritz Bottger; *W:* Fritz Bottger.

The Horse Soldiers

The only feature-length film John Ford made about the Civil War is far from his best work. Even so, it has some worthwhile moments and is loosely based on two historical incidents, Grierson's Raid and the Battle of New Market. Union Col. Marlowe (Wayne) leads a raid 300 miles behind Confederate lines to destroy a railway junction. He has an unpersuasive conflict with the unit's doctor (Holden) and an equally unpersuasive romance with a Southern Scarlett-wanna-be (Towers). The battle scenes are by far the best parts. Given the film's age, the flat look of the color is not surprising. DVD is still an improvement over VHS tape. —*MM*

Movie: 🐾🐾½ *DVD:* 🐾🐾½
MGM Home Entertainment (Cat #100185, UPC #027616861054). Widescreen (1.66:1) letterboxed. Dolby Digital Mono. $14.95. Keepcase. *LANG:* English; Spanish. *SUB:* French; Spanish. *FEATURES:* 16 chapter links • Trailer.

1959 114m/C John Wayne, William Holden, Hoot Gibson, Constance Towers, Russell Simpson, Strother Martin, Anna Lee, Judson Pratt, Denver Pyle, Jack Pennick, Althea Gibson, William Forrest, Willis Bouchey, Bing Russell, Ken Curtis, O.Z. Whitehead, Walter Reed, Hank Worden, Carleton Young, Cliff Lyons; *D:* John Ford; *W:* John Lee Mahin, Martin Rackin; *C:* William Clothier; *M:* David Buttolph.

Hot Boyz

A Master P Film—shouldn't that say it all. Plenty of bad acting (mostly by rappers) accompanies Master P's bad directing, making this an experience to avoid. Nice kid Kool (Sikk the Shocker) vows revenge on the dirty cop who pummeled his girlfriend to death, and turns gangsta, forming the Hot Boyz gang. Lots of shooting and smacking around ensues. The Artisan DVD is on a par with the film itself. The image is as soft as the plot is lame and the Surround in the Dolby Surround only comes into play a couple of times through the entire film. What's more, even the front stereo mix of the action and non-stop rap songs fails to offer much in the way of left/right separation effects. There is enough bass, however, and both the songs and the gunfire shake things up at least a little. Artisan gave this waste of time a $29.98 list price and didn't include one music video (or any supplementals) on the disc, even though rap label No Limit seems to be behind things. —*JO*

Movie: 🐾 *DVD:* 🐾½

Artisan Entertainment (Cat #10947, UPC #012236109471). Full frame. Dolby Surround. $29.98. Keepcase. *LANG:* English. *CAP:* English. *FEATURES:* 31 chapter links • Theatrical trailer • Talent files.

1999 (R) m/C

Hot Vampire Nights

Miami vampire Mina (Jones) calls a late night talk show and attempts to seduce the female host. This horror might be fairly erotic but the image is so poor with excessive grain in the blue night scenes that it's pretty much impossible to tell. Substandard. —*MM*

Movie: 🐾 *DVD:* 🐾
El Independent Cinema (Cat #1006, UPC #612385100697). Full frame. $19.98. Keepcase. *LANG:* English. *FEATURES:* 12 chapter links • Interview with Shelly Jones • Photo gallery • Trailers.

2000 90m/C Shelly Jones, Katelyn Gold, Dominique, Beth Linhart, Allegra, Anita Hayes; *D:* Will Danahur; *W:* Charlton Byrnes.

H.O.T.S.

Several ex-Playboy Playmates star in this teen-sex comedy that predates *Porky's* by several years. It's very frivolous and, compared to contemporary approaches to similar material, fairly tame and sweet-natured. Writer Caffaro was famous for her series of *Ginger* exploitation films. The DVD image is an accurate re-creation of a fuzzily focused original. But why no director's commentary? —*MM* *AKA:* T & A Academy.

Movie: 🐾🐾½ *DVD:* 🐾🐾🐾
Anchor Bay (Cat #DV11186, UPC #013131118698). Widescreen (1.85:1) anamorphic. Dolby Digital Mono. $24.99. Keepcase. *LANG:* English. *CAP:* English. *FEATURES:* 28 chapter links • Trailer.

1979 (R) 95m/C Susan Kiger, Lisa London, Kimberly Cameron, Danny Bonaduce, Steve Bond; *D:* Gerald Seth Sindell; *W:* Cheri Caffaro, Joan Buchanan; *C:* Harvey Genkins; *M:* David Davis.

The House by the Cemetery [Diamond]

Forget the videotape that was released in the U.S. under the same title. This is the uncut version of Lucio Fulci's 1981 film. Dr. Boyle (Malco), his wife Lucy (Fulci regular MacColl), and their son Bob (Frezza, who sounds as if his voice was dubbed by a 34-year old woman) move to the Freudstein Mansion where the doc will continue research begun by a deceased colleague. Basement doors lock themselves, bats attack, murders occur, and there's a tombstone in the middle of the living room. As with most of Fulci's work, this one sounds better on paper than it really is. The picture is clear and very sharp, showing a very fine amount of grain. There are some obvious defects from the source print, such as dirt on the film and noticeable

splices. The bottom line is that for a second-generation copy of a low-budget Italian film, the image looks pretty good. Dialogue is clear and audible, with a slightly noticeable hiss on the soundtrack. The incredibly annoying music also comes across quite well. —*ML* *AKA:* Quella Villa Accanto Al Cimitero.

Movie: 🐾🐾½ *DVD:* 🐾🐾½
Diamond Entertainment Corp. Widescreen (2.35:1) letterboxed. Dolby Digital Stereo. $7.99. *LANG:* English. *FEATURES:* Fulci bio.

1983 (R) 84m/C *IT* Katherine MacColl, Paolo Malco, Giovanni Frezza; *D:* Lucio Fulci; *W:* Lucio Fulci, Dardano Sacchetti; *C:* Sergio Salvati; *M:* Walter Rizzati.

The House by the Cemetery [Anchor Bay]

A family moves to the titular house and finds that the owner is buried inside, though he may not be officially dead. The violence may not be as extensive as it is in other Fulci films, but this is certainly some of his most intense work, beginning with a knife through a head and getting worse. Since some of the action involves children, it's pretty hard to take. But the plotting is so far removed from reality that it's difficult to treat any of this work seriously. (Admittedly, graphic Italian horror has never been my cup of gore.) As usual, Anchor Bay's DVD image is crystalline. The excellent sound makes the English dubbing more obvious than it has been on tape, but that doesn't really get in the way of Fulci's true intentions. The disc also comes with a cool, zippy menu. —*MM* *AKA:* Quella Villa Accanto Al Cimitero.

Movie: 🐾🐾 *DVD:* 🐾🐾🐾
Anchor Bay (Cat #DV11530, UPC #013131153095). Widescreen (2.35:1) anamorphic. Dolby Digital Surround. $24.99. Keepcase. *LANG:* English. *FEATURES:* 25 chapter links • Liner notes by Michael Felsher • Trailers • TV spot • Stills gallery • Talent files.

1983 (R) 84m/C *IT* Katherine MacColl, Paolo Malco, Giovanni Frezza; *D:* Lucio Fulci; *W:* Lucio Fulci, Dardano Sacchetti; *C:* Sergio Salvati; *M:* Walter Rizzati.

House of Games

An engrossing tale of tightly strung psychiatrist Margaret Ford (Crouse) who is taken on the ride of her life by a group of con men led by Mike (Mantegna). In the end we realize it has actually been a voyage of self-discovery toward coming to terms with her own manipulative personality. Mantegna is fabulous as the smoldering grifter who woos Margaret into doing anything he wants her to because, in the end, she wants to. Whether he has made her want to, or she has made him make her want to, is but one of the many questions raised by the story. Crouse (Mamet's wife at the time) is ice cold in her role, perfectly coifed with a mind that seems as organized as her office. Multi-layered as a good soufflé, the story has something for

everyone. Written by David Mamet *(The Spanish Prisoner, State and Main)* who is a playwright by trade, this was his directorial debut. His skill with the details of the theatre translate beautifully to film with every word of dialogue and every movement of the players carefully crafted. This may be the one flaw in the film, that it is too studied and precise. The disc looks and sounds better than the average VHS. —CA
Movie: ♪♪♪½ **DVD:** ♪♪½
MGM Home Entertainment (Cat #10012 77, UPC #027616855572). Full frame; widescreen anamorphic. Dolby Digital Mono. $19.98. Keepcase. *LANG:* English; French; Spanish. *SUB:* Spanish; French. *FEATURES:* 24 chapter links ☛ Theatrical trailer.
1987 (R) 102m/C Joe Mantegna, Lindsay Crouse, Lilia Skala, J.T. Walsh, Meshach Taylor, Ricky Jay, Mike Nussbaum, Willo Hausman; **D:** David Mamet; **W:** David Mamet; **C:** Juan Ruiz-Anchia; **M:** Alaric Jans.

House of Mirth

Lily Bart (Anderson), a ravishing young woman in New York at the turn of the century, is on the search for a wealthy husband, but she falls in love with Lawrence Selden (Stoltz), who doesn't live up to certain social expectations. It's an adaptation of Edith Wharton's novel. The transfer is very clean and without the slightest blemish. Colors are vibrant and lively, nicely recreating the film's ambitious and lush settings. A number of scenes feature a pastel palette with many gray tones, but this is an intentional, stylistic device employed by the director. Blacks are very deep and never break up, giving the image immaculate shadow detail. The level of detail is extremely high, creating a flawless presentation of the film. The compression is also without flaws, and no hints of artifacting are evident anywhere on the disc. Audio presentation is very good and well rounded, with a natural-sounding frequency response that contains solid deep bass and very clear high ends free of distortion. —GH
Movie: ♪♪♪ **DVD:** ♪♪♪♪½
Columbia Tristar Home Video (Cat #064 55, UPC #043396064553). Widescreen (2.35:1) anamorphic. Dolby Digital 5.1 Surround Stereo; Dolby Digital Surround. $29.95. Keepcase. *LANG:* English. *FEATURES:* Commentary: Terence Davies ☛ Deleted scenes with optional commentary ☛ Trailers ☛ Filmographies.
2000 (PG-13) 140m/C *GB* Gillian Anderson, Eric Stoltz, Dan Aykroyd, Eleanor Bron, Terry Kinney, Anthony LaPaglia, Laura Linney, Jodhi May, Elizabeth McGovern; **D:** Terence Davies; **W:** Terence Davies; **C:** Remi Adefarasin.

The House of Seven Corpses

This trite horror movie within a horror movie might be good at 3 a.m. when you're having trouble sleeping, but in the harsh light of day it is little more than a cut-and-paste of clichéd scenes from ten other clichéd films. A film crew goes to shoot a script about a family that was massacred in the house where the murders took place and, to everyone's great shock, people start dying. The transfer is washed-out and fuzzy and the sound is average. —CA
Movie: ♪ **DVD:** ♪♪
Image Entertainment (Cat #1D6159TV DVD, UPC #014381615920). Widescreen letterboxed. Dolby Mono. $24.99. Snapper. *LANG:* English; Spanish. *FEATURES:* 12 chapter links ☛ Theatrical trailer.
1973 (PG) 90m/C John Ireland, Faith Domergue, John Carradine, Carole Wells; **D:** Paul Harrison; **W:** Paul Harrison, Thomas J. Kelly.

The House on Sorority Row

Hey kiddies, school's out and seven sorority sisters plan to throw one last party, knowing full well that their housemother frowns upon such things. When their fun is ruined, the girls decide to scare the housemom with a gun mostly filled with blanks. Soon she's dead and the girls are being stalked, hacked, sliced, skewered, and otherwise made uncomfortable. Less than harrowing but loads-o-fun when you're in the mood for a good old-fashioned slasher. It looks like Elite showed more respect to the movie than the keepers of the film themselves. There doesn't seem to be any transfer-related problems and the only distractions are some film scratches and flicks. Colors are somewhat blah but appear accurate to the theatre, and the overall transfer is very sharp and detailed. There is an occasional warble on the soundtrack but most of that comes after the film is over. The only supplemental you'll get is a trailer. —JO **AKA:** House of Evil; Seven Sisters.
Movie: ♪♪½ **DVD:** ♪♪½
Elite Entertainment, Inc. (Cat #EE4678, UPC #790594467821). Widescreen (1.85:1) anamorphic. Stereo. $24.95. Keepcase. *LANG:* English. *FEATURES:* 15 chapter links ☛ Theatrical trailer.
1983 90m/C Eileen Davidson, Kate McNeil, Robin Meloy, Lois Kelso Hunt, Christopher Lawrence, Janis Zido; **D:** Mark Rosman; **W:** Mark Rosman; **C:** Tim Suhrstedt; **M:** Richard Band.

House Party

Lighthearted hip-hop comedy is a throwback to the teen flicks of the '50s. After his father (Harris) grounds him, Kid (Reid) resorts to all sorts of schemes to get to his friend Play's (Martin) party. The DVD image is very good, but the disc's strongest suit is the sound, which does justice to some energetic dance numbers. —MM
Movie: ♪♪♪ **DVD:** ♪♪♪
New Line Home Video (Cat #N4854, UPC #794043485428). Widescreen (1.85:1) anamorphic; full frame. Dolby Digital 5.1 Surround Stereo; Dolby Digital Surround Stereo. $24.98. Snapper. *LANG:* English. *SUB:* English. *FEATURES:* 27 chapter links ☛ Trailer ☛ Talent files.
1990 (R) 100m/C Christopher Reid, Christopher Martin, Martin Lawrence, Tisha Campbell, Paul Anthony, A.J. (Anthony) Johnson, Robin Harris; **D:** Reginald (Reggie) Hudlin; **W:** Reginald (Reggie) Hudlin; **C:** Peter Deming; **M:** Marcus Miller. *AWARDS:* Sundance '90: Cinematog.

House Party 2: The Pajama Jam

At Harris University, Kid 'N' Play try to come up with Kid's overdue tuition by holding a campus "jammie jam." For a sequel, it's not bad. Technical quality of the disc is virtually identical to the first. —MM
Movie: ♪♪½ **DVD:** ♪♪♪
New Line Home Video (Cat #N4855, UPC #794043485527). Widescreen (1.85:1) anamorphic; full frame. Dolby Digital 5.1 Surround Stereo; Dolby Digital Surround Stereo. $24.99. Snapper. *LANG:* English. *SUB:* English. *FEATURES:* 26 chapter links ☛ Trailer ☛ Talent files.
1991 (R) 94m/C Christopher Reid, Christopher Martin, Tisha Campbell, Iman, Queen Latifah, Georg Stanford Brown, Martin Lawrence, Eugene Allen, George Anthony Bell, Kamron, Tony Burton, Helen Martin, William Schallert; **D:** Doug McHenry, George Jackson; **W:** Rusty Cundieff, Daryl G. Nickens; **M:** Vassal Benford.

House Party 3

This time out, the excuse for a rap party is Kid's (Reid) impending marriage. The results are about what you'd expect from any movie with a "3" at the end of the title. The disc looks and sounds as good as the first two, however. —MM
Movie: ♪ **DVD:** ♪♪♪
New Line Home Video (Cat #N4856, UPC #794043485626). Widescreen (1.85:1) anamorphic; full frame. Dolby Digital 5.1 Surround Stereo; Dolby Digital Surround. $24.99. Snapper. *LANG:* English. *SUB:* English. *FEATURES:* 19 chapter links ☛ Trailer ☛ Talent files.
1994 (R) 93m/C Christopher Reid, Christopher Martin, Angela Means, Tisha Campbell, Bernie Mac, Barbara (Lee) Edwards, Michael Colyar, David Edwards, Betty Lester, Chris Tucker; **D:** Eric Meza; **W:** Takashi Bufford; **M:** David Allen Jones.

How Green Was My Valley

Compelling story of the trials and tribulations of a Welsh mining family, from the youthful perspective of the youngest child (played by a 13-year-old McDowall). Spans 50 years, from the turn of the century, when coal mining was a difficult but fairpaying way of life, and ends, after unionization, strikes, deaths, and child abuse, with the demise of a town and its culture. Considered by many to be director Ford's finest work. When WWII prevented shooting on location, producer Zanuck built a facsimile Welsh valley in California (although Ford, born Sean Aloysius O'Fearna, was said to have been thinking of his story as taking place in Ireland rather than Wales). The DVD transfer of this black-and-white classic is near perfect. It's a good thing, since the film won an Academy Award for Best Cinematography, and anything less would be an insult. The image is very sharp, graytones are subtly varied, and the great contrast level makes for an incredibly vivid picture with astounding depth and detail. To complete the viewing enjoyment is a crisp soundtrack ensuring that every piece of dialogue will be heard. Even with the lack of supplementals (the "photo gallery" amounts to less than one roll of film), this is a worthwhile investment. —JO

Movie: ♪♪♪½ **DVD:** ♪♪♪½
Fox/Lorber Home Video (Cat #2000031, UPC #024543000310). Full frame. Mono. $24.98. Keepcase. *LANG:* English; French. *SUB:* English; Spanish. *CAP:* English. *FEATURES:* 10 chapter links • Theatrical trailer • Photo gallery.
1941 118m/C Walter Pidgeon, Maureen O'Hara, Donald Crisp, Anna Lee, Roddy McDowall, John Loder, Sara Allgood, Barry Fitzgerald, Patric Knowles, Rhys Williams, Arthur Shields, Ann E. Todd, Mae Marsh; **D:** John Ford; **W:** Philip Dunne; **C:** Arthur C. Miller; **M:** Alfred Newman; **Nar:** Irving Pichel. *AWARDS:* Oscars '41: B&W Cinematog., Director (Ford), Picture, Support. Actor (Crisp), Natl. Film Reg. '90; N.Y. Film Critics '41: Director (Ford); *NOM:* Oscars '41: Film Editing, Screenplay, Sound, Support. Actress (Allgood), Orig. Dramatic Score.

How to Commit Marriage

Hope and Wyman have been married for 20 years when they decide to divorce—just when their daughter (Cameron) decides to marry her boyfriend (Matheson, playing an early version of Otter in *Animal House*). His father (Gleason) tries to stop the marriage, fails, but sticks around to cause trouble. Subplots abound, many revolving around the generational conflicts of the 1960s. Though this is not the best work for any of the older stars, it's still fine for their fans. The DVD was created from a near flawless original. The image is excellent, though darks are slightly oversaturated and fleshtones are pale. Sound is acceptable. —MM
Movie: ♪♪½ **DVD:** ♪♪½
Brentwood Home Video (Cat #60987-9, UPC #090096098791). Full frame. Dolby Digital Mono. $14.98. Keepcase. *LANG:* English. *FEATURES:* 8 chapter links • Bob Hope thumbnail bio and filmography.
1969 (PG) 96m/C Bob Hope, Jane Wyman, Jackie Gleason, Joanna Cameron, Tim Matheson, Beatrice Arthur, Leslie Nielsen, Tina Louise, Paul Stewart, Prof. Irwin Corey; **D:** Norman Panama; **W:** Ben Starr, Michael Kanin; **C:** Charles B(ryant) Lang Jr.; **M:** Joseph J. Lilley.

How to Marry a Millionaire

Three models (Bacall, Grable, Monroe) pool their money and rent a lavish apartment in a campaign to trap millionaire husbands. Clever performances by the three salvage a vehicle intended primarily to bolster Monroe's career. It was also the first movie to be filmed in CinemaScope and boy, is this wide. In its first year or so, the 'Scope process was 2:55 to one, and this disc retains much of that width, so a big screen is almost mandatory to appreciate this one. At about 31 minutes in, in Chapter 8, Marilyn walks to a mirror and hovers there for a few seconds, watching six clones of herself spread across the CinemaScope acreage. This image most likely got applause all on its own. —MM/GE
Movie: ♪♪♪ **DVD:** ♪♪♪½
20th Century Fox Home Entertainment (Cat #2001427, UPC #024543014270). Widescreen (2.55:1) anamorphic. Dolby Digital 4.0 Surround Stereo; Stereo; Mono. $24.98. Keepcase. *LANG:* English; French. *FEATURES:* MovieTone News "Premiere with the Stars" short • Trailers.
1953 96m/C Lauren Bacall, Marilyn Monroe, Betty Grable, William Powell, David Wayne, Cameron Mitchell; **D:** Jean Negulesco; **W:** Nunnally Johnson; **C:** Joe MacDonald; **M:** Alfred Newman. *AWARDS: NOM:* Oscars '53: Costume Des. (C).

Human Traffic

Surreal inner dialogue and what-if fantasy sequences highlighted by fabulous music and fashion are the backdrop for a story about nothing more than a weekend in the life of five friends who trudge through their work weeks in order to get to the weekends. When the weekend comes they hang out, take drugs, dance, and search for meaning in their lives, and in the case of two of the friends, find love. The thing that keeps this movie from being like every film about youth looking for meaning in the world is that these characters seem fine with the fact that they may never find it. Another thing that separates this story from the typical fare is that there is no real trauma associated with the wild weekend antics. A couple falls in love, another bickers, no one dies. These are characters who seem comfortable with real life, and it is a pleasant surprise to see a film that shows real life to be interesting. This is a visually colorful film and the DVD quality is up to the task. The sound is also great. —CA
Movie: ♪♪♪½ **DVD:** ♪♪♪
Miramax Pictures Home Video (Cat #212 77, UPC #786936141115). Widescreen (1.85:1) anamorphic. Dolby Digital 5.1 Surround. $32.99. Keepcase. *LANG:* English. *FEATURES:* 23 chapter links • Theatrical trailer.
1999 (R) 84m/C GB John Simm, Lorraine Pilkington, Shaun Parkes, Nicola Reynolds, Danny Dyer, Dean Davies; **D:** Justin Kerrigan; **W:** Justin Kerrigan; **C:** David Bennett; **M:** Matthew Herbert, Rob Mellow.

Humanity

Director Bruno Dumont's controversial, indulgent French drama plays like two and a half hours of art-film hell. Detective Pharaon De Winter (Schotte, strongly resembling the comic strip character "Ziggy"), upset over the rape and murder of an 11-year-old girl, somberly views the world around him. That's all there is in this dull, torturous drama. The identity of the murderer is pretty obvious, and most viewers will figure it out in the first half-hour, especially since there's barely any detective work on display. It's hard to believe that the not-too-bright, overly sensitive Pharaon is a police detective and his constant moping and never-ending "introspective" stares will make you want to strangle him. Pointless, pretentious, glacially slow and with a few graphic sex scenes and extremely vulgar "gynecological" shots. A film more interesting to read about than to actually watch. Perhaps it would have worked if cut down to a 15-minute short film.... The packaging lists several rave reviews from critics whose opinions will now be regarded as dubious. The disc is sharp and captures the muted hues, but the wider shots are subject to digital artifacting and there's severe color shifting whenever faces move across the screen. The soundtrack is clear and pleasing. Also included is a ridiculous trailer that tries to sell it as a thriller. Anyone who sees it based on that trailer probably won't make it through the first hour. The interview with Dumont is more focused on his general views of cinema and how he works than on the specifics on this film. Few will care enough after seeing this film to watch it anyway. —DG
AKA: L'Humanite.
Movie: woof **DVD:** ♪♪
Fox/Lorber Home Video (Cat #FLV5262, UPC #72091752622). Widescreen (2.35:1) anamorphic. Dolby Stereo Surround. $24.98. Keepcase. *LANG:* French. *SUB:* English. *FEATURES:* Trailer • 16 chapter links • Interview with Dumont • Weblink.
1999 142m/C FR Emmanuel Schotte, Severine Caneele, Philippe Tullier, Ghislain Ghesquiere, Ginette Allegre; **D:** Bruno Dumont; **W:** Bruno Dumont; **C:** Yves Cape; **M:** Richard Cuvillier. *AWARDS:* Cannes '99: Actor (Schotte), Actress (Caneele), Grand Jury Prize.

The Hurricane

Moving, albeit truncated account of the true story of middleweight boxing champ Rubin "Hurricane" Carter (Washington—in peak professional and physical form), who was falsely accused and convicted of murder and who spent 20 years in prison. Anchored by an transcendent performance by Washington, pic came under fire for its liberal rearrangement of the facts behind the case (something addressed by Jewison's DVD commentary). Carter was immortalized in Bob Dylan's 1976 protest song, "Hurricane." This is a good-looking DVD that pretty much delivers the film exactly as it looked and sounded on the

big screen. The picture looks great throughout and, though there is nothing spectacular to the sound mix (like a lot of dramatic films), it's full bodied and dynamic, with the dialogue always out front and intelligible. The included featurette is made up of interviews with the real-life counterparts (including Carter) of the film's characters adding extra believability to the portrayals. Jewison's commentary reflects his years of experience in getting what he wants from his actors. —JO *AKA:* Lazarus and the Hurricane.
Movie: ♪♪♪½ **DVD:** ♪♪♪
Universal Studios Home Video (Cat #207 19, UPC #025192071928). Widescreen (1.85:1) anamorphic. Dolby Digital 5.1; Dolby Surround. $29.98. Keepcase. *LANG:* English (DD5.1); French (DS). *CAP:* English. *FEATURES:* 20 chapter links • Theatrical trailer • Talent files • Production notes • "Making of" featurette • Deleted scenes • Commentary: Norman Jewison • Dual-layered • DVD-ROM features.
1999 (R) 125m/B Denzel Washington, Vicellous Reon Shannon, Deborah Kara Unger, Liev Schreiber, John Hannah, David Paymer, Dan Hedaya, Debbi Morgan, Clancy Brown, Harris Yulin, Vincent Pastore, Rod Steiger; *D:* Norman Jewison; *W:* Armyan Bernstein, Dan Gordon; *C:* Roger Deakins; *M:* Christopher Young. *AWARDS:* Golden Globes '00: Actor—Drama (Washington); *NOM:* Oscars '99: Actor (Washington); Golden Globes '00: Director (Jewison), Film—Drama; Screen Actors Guild '99: Actor (Washington).

Hysterical

Odd attempt at horror parody features the Hudson Brothers and involves a haunted lighthouse occupied by the vengeful spirit of a wronged woman (Newmar). Image and sound are weaker than most VHS tapes, but given the semi-professional nature of the production, that's no surprise. —MM
Movie: ♪ **DVD:** woof
Image Entertainment (Cat #0VED9026 DVD, UPC #014381902624). Full frame. Dolby Digital Mono. $24.99. Snapper. *LANG:* English. *FEATURES:* 13 chapter links • Trailer.
1983 (PG) 86m/C Brett Hudson, William (Bill) Hudson, Mark Hudson, Cindy Pickett, Richard Kiel, Julie Newmar, Bud Cort; *D:* Chris Bearde; *W:* Trace Johnston, Brett Hudson, William (Bill) Hudson, Mark Hudson; *C:* Thomas Del Ruth; *M:* Robert Alcivar.

I, Claudius

DVD can do little to improve the image of this excellent BBC miniseries, but it does present an opportunity to revisit some splendid acting in a very classy soap opera. The boxed set also includes a documentary of the uncompleted 1937 film version of Robert Graves's novel. The pale colors and dim lighting come from the original, not the transfer. The image ranges between fair and good. The monaural soundtrack is fine for Derek Jacobi's confessional voice-over narration. —MM
Movie: ♪♪♪♪ **DVD:** ♪♪½
Image Entertainment (Cat #ID9187CU DVD, UPC #014381918724). Full frame. Dolby Digital Mono. $89.99. Boxed set keepcase. *LANG:* English. *FEATURES:* 116 chapter links • "The Epic That Never Was" documentary (71 min.).
1991 669m/C *GB* Sian Phillips, Brian Blessed, Derek Jacobi, Margaret Tyzack, John Hurt, George Baker, Patrick Stewart, Sheila White; *D:* Herbert Wise; *W:* Jack Pulman.

I Dreamed of Africa

Adaptation of the autobiography of Kuki Gallman (Basinger) tells the story of her move to Kenya with her new husband. Once settled in, she sees how cruel poachers destroy the country's wildlife and drain the valuable animal resources. She becomes an animal rights activist, and, like many others before her, faces the harshness of life and politics as her opposition attempts to break her. The widescreen presentation is generally good looking, but the transfer appears surprisingly soft and lacking detail in many instances. Edge-enhancement has been applied to the transfer, creating visible ringing artifacts in many shots, and many of the nighttime shots appear washed-out. The heavily cropped pan-and-scan version diminishes much of the film's articulate photography. The compression has been done carefully and the transfer is free of pixelation or other compression artifacts for the most part. Surround usage is very active and discrete sound effects can be found almost throughout the film, creating a bustling and lively ambience. —GH/MM
Movie: ♪♪½ **DVD:** ♪♪♪
Columbia Tristar Home Video (Cat #4606). Full frame; widescreen (2.35:1) anamorphic. Dolby Digital 5.1 Surround Stereo; Dolby Digital Stereo. $29.95. Keepcase. *LANG:* English. *FEATURES:* "Making of" documentary • Isolated score • Trailer • Talent files • Production notes.
2000 (PG-13) 114m/C Kim Basinger, Vincent Perez, Eva Marie Saint, Daniel Craig, Lance Reddick, Liam Aiken, Garrett Strommen; *D:* Hugh Hudson; *W:* Paula Milne, Susan Shilliday; *C:* Bernard Lutic; *M:* Maurice Jarre.

I Know Where I'm Going

Young Joan (Hiller) believes that money can buy happiness and is on the verge of marrying a rich old man until she meets a handsome naval officer (Livesey) out on the Hebrides (Livesey) out on the Hebrides. Criterion does its usual top-notch job on the disc. The black-and-white photography is extra-sharp in conventional interiors. Some unavoidable grain appears in the many foggy scenes. Extras are well chosen. —MM
Movie: ♪♪♪ **DVD:** ♪♪♪½
Criterion Collection (Cat #94, UPC #03742 9154427). Full frame. Dolby Digital Mono.

$39.95. Keepcase. *LANG:* English. *SUB:* English. *FEATURES:* 23 chapter links • Commentary: film historian Ian Christie • Behind-the-scenes stills • Home movies • Clips from *The Edge of the World* • "Making of" documentary • Photo essay.
1945 91m/B *GB* Roger Livesey, Wendy Hiller, Finlay Currie, Pamela Brown, George Carney, Walter Hudd; *D:* Michael Powell, Emeric Pressburger; *W:* Michael Powell, Emeric Pressburger; *C:* Erwin Hillier; *M:* Allan Gray.

I Like the Girls Who Do

The New Jersey exploitation video label is importing soft-core European flicks from the early 1970s and repackaging them for a new audience. This German effort about a young man's efforts to seduce seven women to win his inheritance is on a par with such contemporary American productions as *Boob Tube* and *If You Don't Stop It You'll Go Blind*. It's pointless to criticize image and sound. They've never been exemplary; the disc appears to be a faithful re-creation of the original. The accompanying short feature, "Peeping in a Girl's Dormitory," looks like it was videotaped in someone's suburban basement by a libidinous teenager. —MM *AKA:* Liebesjagd durch 7 Betten.
Movie: ♪♪ **DVD:** ♪♪
EI Independent Cinema (Cat #sc-2202-dvd, UPC #612385220296). Full frame. $19.98. Snapper. *FEATURES:* 24 chapter links • Trailers • "Peeping in a Girl's Dormitory" short feature.
1973 80m/C *GE* Alexander Allerson, Bea Baldur, Birgit Bergen, Helga Konig; *D:* Hans Billian; *W:* Hans Billian, Werner Hauff; *C:* Heinz Holscher; *M:* Karl Bette.

I Married a Strange Person

Newlywed Keri is getting the "worse" of the "for-better-or-worse" part of the marital vows when hubby Grant suddenly develops the ability to will his fantasies to life thanks to an odd growth on his neck, including some bizarre sexual adventures. Plympton's animated tale is imaginative and, with considerable offensive (but fun) images, certainly for adults only. There's not much to say about this DVD. The picture is acceptable but not exceptional. Most other animated features have a sharper picture and more vibrant colors but, even with not having seen the film in the theatre, I have to assume that the DVD presentation matches the big screen. The sound is only mono. With all the action that takes place in fantasyland, and all the re-mixed and synthesized 5.1 tracks out there, at least stereo could have been simulated. A Plympton commentary would have been nice as well (or at least an interview), just to hear where the hell he gets these bizarre ideas. Even without the add-ons, however, it's Bill Plympton on DVD and still worth owning. —JO

Movie: ♫♫♫ **DVD:** ♫♫½
Universal Studios Home Video (Cat #207
68, UPC #025192076824). Widescreen.
Dolby Digital Mono. $24.98. Keepcase.
LANG: English. *CAP:* English. *FEATURES:* 16
chapter links ☞ Theatrical trailer.
1997 (R) 73m/C D: Bill Plympton; **W:** Bill
Plympton, P.C. Vey; **M:** Maureen McEl-
heron; **V:** Christopher Cooke, Charis
Michelsen, Tom Larson, Richard Spore.

I Shot Andy Warhol

Based on a true story, this black comedy
focuses on the 15 minutes of fame
achieved by Valerie Solanas (Taylor), the
woman who shot pop artist Andy Warhol
(Harris) in 1968. Taylor makes Solanas a
compelling, if unattractive figure. In her
feature debut, Harron does a wonderful
job of re-creating the drugged-out world
Warhol and his cohorts inhabit. (She takes
a similar approach in the underrated *American Psycho*.) The film will not wow viewers
with striking visuals, but the disc appears
to be an accurate re-creation of a serious
independent production. Highly recommended. —*MM*
Movie: ♫♫♫ **DVD:** ♫♫½
MGM Home Entertainment (Cat #10014
49, UPC #027616857699). Widescreen
(1.85:1) anamorphic. Dolby Digital Sur-
round Stereo. $19.98. Keepcase. *LANG:*
English; Spanish. *SUB:* French; Spanish.
CAP: English. *FEATURES:* 16 chapter links
☞ Trailer.
1996 (R) 100m/C Lili Taylor, Jared Harris,
Stephen Dorff, Martha Plimpton, Donovan
Leitch, Tahnee Welch, Michael Imperioli,
Lothaire Bluteau, Anna Thompson, Peter
Friedman, Jill(ian) Hennessey, Craig
Chester, James Lyons, Reginald Rodgers,
Jamie Harrold, Edoardo Ballerini, Lynn
Cohen, Myriam Cyr, Isabel Gillies, Eric
Mabius; **D:** Mary Harron; **W:** Mary Harron,
Daniel Minahan; **C:** Ellen Kuras; **M:** John
Cale. *AWARDS: NOM:* Ind. Spirit '97: First
Feature.

I Spit on Your Corpse

This inspired exploitation title is actually a
variation on *Faster, Pussycat! Kill! Kill!* Two
mob hit women (including Spelvin in a non-
porn role) run amok in the desert terrorizing any man who crosses them. As producer Sherman says on the commentary
track, this is a road movie that was
designed specifically for the drive-in. It has
been preserved or restored to near-mint
condition. Sound is nothing special but
the image is very good. —*MM* **AKA:** Girls
for Rent.
Movie: ♫♫♫ **DVD:** ♫♫½
Troma Team Video (Cat #9028, UPC #790
357902835). Full frame. $24.99. Keep-
case. *LANG:* English. *FEATURES:* 9 chapter
links ☞ Intro and commentary: producer
Samuel Sherman ☞ "Producing schlock"
featurette ☞ Trailers ☞ Stills gallery.
1974 (R) 90m/C Georgina Spelvin, Susan
McIver, Kent Taylor, Rosalind Miles, Pres-

ton Pierce, Robert "Bob" Livingston; **D:** Al
Adamson.

I Spy

Two episodes of the famous '60s series
are on this disc, "A Few Miles West of
Nowhere" and "The Trouble with Temple."
Incredibly young Bill Cosby and Robert
Culp play globe-trotting spies who pose as
a trainer and tennis pro. Production values
are strictly broadcast TV quality so the
disc gains nothing visually. One striped T-
shirt flashes crazily in medium shots. The
films are an interesting historical snapshot, though. To date, 12 more discs have
been released in combinations of two and
four episodes. —*MM*
Movie: ♫♫ **DVD:** ♫♫
Image Entertainment (Cat #ID5021BR
DVD, UPC #014381502121). Full frame.
Dolby Digital Mono. $14.98. Snapper.
LANG: English. *FEATURES:* 20 chapter
links.
1965 101m/C Bill Cosby, Robert Culp,
Andrew Duggan, Carol Wayne, Jack Cassidy.

I, Zombie

A young British writer (Aspen) is bitten by
a seriously wounded woman and acquires
a taste for human flesh. Actually, as the
filmmakers state in their forthright commentary, the human flesh is bits of dough-
nut. For comparative purposes, think of
Romero's *Martin*. There's nothing that DVD
can do to improve this low-budget image.
The film's heavy grain leads to severe pixels, artifacts, and still images that swim.
The best thing about the disc is the commentary track, which outlines the hazards
and difficulties that young filmmakers
face. It took more than four years to make
this less-than-epic labor of love. —*MM*
Movie: ♫♫½ **DVD:** ♫♫½
MTI Home Video (Cat #BP50022DVD, UPC
#619935002234). Full frame. $24.98.
Keepcase. *LANG:* English. *FEATURES:* 10
chapter links ☞ Behind-the-scenes fea-
turette ☞ Preview of *Lady of the Lake* ☞
Commentary: Andrew Parkinson, Gile
Aspen, Tudor Davies.
1999 85m/C Gile Aspen, Ellen Softley,
Dean Sipling; **D:** Andrew Parkinson; **W:**
Andrew Parkinson.

Ice Castles

Lexie Winston's (Johnson) dreams of an
Olympic figure-skating medal are dashed
when she is blinded in a freak accident
(which is really funny to those who are not
into the spirit of this dim-witted heart-
warmer), but her old sweetie Nick Peterson (Benson) provides the strength, love,
and encouragement to help her overcome,
etc., etc. It's all far too sappy, but on disc
it looks as good as anyone could reasonably expect for a film of this age. —*MM*
Movie: ♫♫ **DVD:** ♫♫½
Columbia Tristar Home Video (Cat #062
02, UPC #043396062023). Widescreen
(1.85:1) anamorphic. Dolby Digital Mono.

$24.98. Keepcase. *LANG:* English; French;
Spanish; Portuguese. *SUB:* English;
French; Spanish; Portuguese; Chinese;
Korean; Thai. *FEATURES:* Talent files ☞
Trailers ☞ 28 chapter links.
1979 (PG) 110m/C Robby Benson, Lynn-
Holly Johnson, Tom Skerritt, Colleen
Dewhurst, Jennifer Warren, David Huff-
man; **D:** Donald Wrye; **W:** Donald Wrye,
Gary L. Bain; **C:** Bill Butler; **M:** Marvin
Hamlisch. *AWARDS: NOM:* Oscars '79:
Song ("Theme from Ice Castles-Through
the Eyes of Love").

Ice from the Sun

Filmmaker Eric Stanze says, with appropriately mixed emotions, that this is the low-
est-budgeted film to be released on DVD
to date. He's probably right, but in the
wake of *Blair Witch*, horror fans seem to
be willing to take chances, and this one
ought to find an audience. Shot on Super
8mm, it is a loose, semi-linear narrative
about Alison (Midgett), a troubled young
woman, and the Presence (Vivona), a
supernatural being of some ill-defined
sort. On their commentary track, Stanze
and sound designer Matt Meyer talk about
the strict limitations they were working
under and the many compromises they
had to make. On the cast track, the actors
focus more on the mundane details of the
shoot. Both tracks reveal young people
who were learning on the job. It's impossible to judge the DVD by conventional standards. The image is rough and grainy and
often intentionally off-putting. Same goes
for the disorienting sound field dominated
by a loud punk rock score. Certainly not to
all tastes, but I recommend it to horror
fans who are looking for something different and challenging. —*MM*
Movie: ♫♫½ **DVD:** ♫♫½
Salt City Video Productions (Cat #CEDVD5
504). Full frame. Stereo. $24.95. Keep-
case. *LANG:* English. *FEATURES:* 6 chapter
links ☞ Trailers ☞ Stills gallery ☞ Commentary: Stanze and Meyer ☞ Cast commentary track.
2000 116m/C Ramona Midgett, Angela
Zimmerly, Todd Tevlin, Jason Christ, Tommy
Biondo, Jo Palermo, D.J. Vivona; **D:** Eric
Stanze; **W:** Eric Stanze; **C:** David Berliner;
M: Matt Meyer, Brian McClelland.

Idle Hands

Pothead slacker Anton (Sawa) finds that
his very idle hand is possessed by a
demon, making him do things he doesn't
want to, like killing his friends Mick
(Green) and Pnub (Henson). When Anton
removes the offending appendage, it sets
out to terrorize his girlfriend Molly (Alba).
With the help of a Druid priestess (Fox)
and his now undead friends, Anton must
stop the hand from taking Molly's soul to
hell. Laughs are just as important as
scares. DVD captures the off-putting color
scheme (borrowed from Argento's
Suspiria) all too well. On his commentary
track, director Flender sounds surprised
that he's been allowed to play with the

grown-ups. He and his cast members don't take their job too seriously. —*MM*
Movie: 🎵🎵 **DVD:** 🎵🎵🎵
Columbia Tristar Home Video (Cat #3931). Widescreen (1.85:1) anamorphic; full frame. Dolby Digital 5.1 Surround Stereo; Dolby Digital Surround. $14.95. Keepcase. *LANG:* English. *SUB:* English. *FEATURES:* 28 chapter links ⚬ Storyboard comparisons ⚬ Deleted scene ⚬ "Making of" featurette ⚬ Trailers ⚬ Talent files.
1999 (R) 90m/C Devon Sawa, Seth Green, Elden (Ratliff) Henson, Jessica Alba, Christopher Hunt, Vivica A. Fox, Jack Noseworthy, Sean Whalen, Nicholas Sadler, Fred Willard, Katie Wright, Connie Ray; *D:* Rodman Flender; *W:* Terri Hughes, Ron Milbauer; *C:* Christopher Baffa; *M:* Graeme Revell.

If Lucy Fell

Ludicrous premise has psychotherapist Lucy (Parker) bent on realizing a 10-year-old pact with longtime friend Joe (writer/director Shaeffer) that stipulates they both jump off the Brooklyn Bridge if neither one has found true love by age 30. With the big day approaching, Lucy takes a desperate shot with eccentric performance artist Bwick (Stiller) while Joe finally asks the object of his desire, stunning neighbor Jane (stunning Macpherson) to a show of his paintings. Casting is solid and the film can be seen as a warm-up for *Sex and the City,* though it's something of a comedown from Shaeffer's debut, *My Life's in Turn-around.* Overall, the image is good but not great, but that's less important than the sparkling dialogue. In this case, fans of the cast should consider going with the full-frame version. —*MM*
Movie: 🎵🎵½ **DVD:** 🎵🎵🎵
Columbia Tristar Home Video (Cat #058 35, UPC #043396058354). Widescreen (1.85:1) anamorphic; full frame. Dolby Digital Surround Stereo. $29.95. Keepcase. *LANG:* English; French; Spanish; Portuguese. *SUB:* English; French; Spanish; Portuguese; Korean; Thai. *FEATURES:* 28 chapter links ⚬ Talent files ⚬ Trailers.
1995 (R) 92m/C Sarah Jessica Parker, Eric Schaeffer, Ben Stiller, Elle Macpherson, James Rebhorn, Dominic Luchese; *D:* Eric Schaeffer; *W:* Eric Schaeffer, Tony Spiridakis; *C:* Ron Fortunato; *M:* Amanda Kravat, Charles Pettis.

If These Walls Could Talk 2

Sequel to the popular made-for-cable movie continues to examine the lives of women. Here the focus is on lesbianism as experienced in one house over the course of three decades. In "1961," Vanessa Redgrave must deal with the emotional and legal repercussions of the death of her companion Marian Seldes. "1972" finds free-spirited hippie Michele Williams forcing her own kind of non-conformity onto Chloe Sevigny. By "2000" Ellen DeGeneres and Sharon Stone decide to have a baby. Overall, image and sound

quality are a slight improvement over cablecast. —*MM*
Movie: 🎵🎵🎵 **DVD:** 🎵🎵🎵
HBO Home Video (Cat #91707). Full frame. Dolby Surround Stereo. $19.98. Snapper. *LANG:* English; Spanish. *SUB:* English; French; Spanish. *FEATURES:* 15 chapter links.
2000 (R) 96m/C Vanessa Redgrave, Marian Seldes, Paul Giamatti, Elizabeth Perkins, Michelle Williams, Chloe Sevigny, Nia Long, Natasha Lyonne, Heather McComb, Sharon Stone, Ellen DeGeneres, Regina King, Kathy Najimy, Mitchell Anderson, George Newbern, Amy Carlson; *D:* Jane Anderson, Martha Coolidge, Anne Heche, Alex Sichel; *W:* Jane Anderson, Sylvia Sichel, Anne Heche; *C:* Paul Elliott, Robbie Greenberg, Peter Deming; *M:* Basil Poledouris.

Iguana

Oberlus (McGill), a deformed sailor with lizardlike features, creates his own slave civilization on a remote island. The period piece is slow, thoughtful, and serious. The DVD image is very clear and sharp, showing no overt grain or noise interference. Audio offers clear and articulate dialogue from the center and front speakers, with nice ambient sound effects and subtle musical cues from the rear speakers. The real bonus feature is an audio commentary featuring director Monte Hellman, writer Steven Gaydos, and star Everett McGill, moderated by Dennis Bartok of the American Cinematheque. While this is at once loose and fun-spirited, it is also very serious, matching the tone of the film. —*MM/ML*
Movie: 🎵🎵🎵 **DVD:** 🎵🎵🎵
Anchor Bay (UPC #013131131796). Widescreen (1.77:1) anamorphic. Dolby Digital Stereo. $24.98. Keepcase. *LANG:* English. *FEATURES:* Commentary ⚬ Director bio.
1989 88m/C *SI IT* Everett McGill, Michael Madsen, Joseph Culp, Fabio Teste; *D:* Monte Hellman; *W:* Monte Hellman, Jaime Comas Gil, Steven Gaydos; *C:* Josep Civit.

Il Bidone

Three Italian conmen led by Crawford pull off capers in Rome. Dark overtones permeate one of Fellini's early efforts. Greed, isolation, and family are the themes the maestro examines in a funny, tragic story of redemption. The presentation is inconsistent, both in the source print and the transfer. The first reel, for instance, is rife with problems; a great deal of scratching and grain are visible in some reels while others are very clean. If this is due to the print, then some restoration work was sorely needed. Still, this is the best presentation yet available on home video. The mono sound is about as good as we're going to get from an old Italian film. The only soundtrack is the original Italian with English subtitles, so anyone looking for a dubbed version (shame on you!) is out of luck. The yellow subtitles are very easy to

read and I wish more companies would use them. —*PT/MM* **AKA:** The Swindle.
Movie: 🎵🎵🎵 **DVD:** 🎵🎵
Image Entertainment (Cat #8446, UPC #014381844627). Full frame. Dolby Digital Mono. $24.99. Snapper. *LANG:* Italian. *SUB:* English. *FEATURES:* 12 chapter links.
1955 92m/C *IT* Broderick Crawford, Giulietta Masina, Richard Basehart, Franco Fabrizi; *D:* Federico Fellini; *W:* Federico Fellini, Tullio Pinelli, Ennio Flaiano; *C:* Otello Martelli; *M:* Nino Rota.

I'll Be Home for Christmas

Snotty college kid Jake (Thomas) wants to teach his dad a lesson by boycotting Christmas and stealing away to Mexico with his girlfriend (Biel). Why? Jake thinks dad remarried too soon after the death of his mother. But Jake is bribed home with pop's prized Porsche (now there's a lesson for the kiddies) if he can arrive for Christmas Eve dinner. A series of absurd mishaps ensue (almost all of which occur because Jake is a lying, cheating jerk) and he makes his way cross-country glued inside a Santa suit. The characters are superficial and annoying in this run-of-the-mill holiday stinker. Even so, it looks terrific on disc with an excellent, well-detailed image. Sound is equally fine. —*MM*
Movie: 🎵½ **DVD:** 🎵🎵½
Buena Vista Home Entertainment (Cat #17596). Widescreen (1.85:1) letterboxed. Dolby Digital 5.1 Surround Stereo. $29.99. Keepcase. *LANG:* English; French. *SUB:* English. *FEATURES:* 17 chapter links ⚬ Trailer.
1998 (PG) 86m/C Jonathan Taylor Thomas, Jessica Biel, Adam LaVorgna, Gary Cole, Eve Gordon, Sean O'Bryan, Andrew Lauer; *D:* Arlene Sanford; *W:* Harris Goldberg, Tom Nursall; *C:* Hiro Narita; *M:* John Debney.

Ill-Gotten Gains

In 1896, slaves being held in the hold of a ship off the coast of Africa revolt. The black-and-white film mixes a realistic look at the particulars of the trade in human beings with a magical element (Eartha Kitt gives voice to an animated spirit) and depictions of violence and depravity that verge on exploitation. The black-and-white photography makes an impressive transition to DVD, as does a full-bodied sound field. Some faint artifacts are visible in the large areas of heavy shadow, and there are many of those. —*MM*
Movie: 🎵🎵½ **DVD:** 🎵🎵🎵
Xenon Entertainment (Cat #4071, UPC #000799417133). Full frame. Dolby Digital Mono. $14.95. Keepcase. *LANG:* English. *FEATURES:* Elvis Mitchell radio interview with director Joel Ben Marsden ⚬ Separate soundtrack ⚬ Theatrical trailer ⚬ 16 chapter links.
1997 (R) 106m/B Djimon Hounsou, Akosua Busia, De'Aundre Bonds, Reg E. Cathey; *D:* Joel B. Marsden; *W:* Joel B. Marsden; *C:* Ben Kufrin; *M:* Keith Bilder-

beck, Mike Baum, Tina Meeks; **V:** Eartha Kitt.

I'll Never Forget What's 'Isname

To some tastes, this overwrought and long-unseen comedy from the swinging '60s will be completely dated with characters whose mindsets are totally alien. Protagonist Andrew Quint (Reed) is a piggish young ad executive who tries to leave his even more piggish boss (Welles), and his two mistresses, though he's not sure he wants to divorce his wife. Why? He wants to go back to do something meaningful with his life, something like working for a literary magazine. It's actually a long midlife crisis (though the phrase did not exist when the film was made) that set standards for frankness in its sexual material. The DVD image is very good, and the mono sound is fine, too. The best feature of the disc is director Winner's anecdotal commentary track, which is a long reminiscence of those singular days. As one character in the film says, "Everything's so extraordinarily available." —*MM*
Movie: 🎵🎵🎵 **DVD:** 🎵🎵🎵
Anchor Bay (Cat #DV10988, UPC #01313 1098891). Widescreen (1.85:1) anamorphic. Mono. $29.98. Keepcase. *LANG:* English. *FEATURES:* 27 chapter links • Commentary: Michael Winner • Talent files • Stills gallery.
1967 99m/C Oliver Reed, Orson Welles, Carol White, Marianne Faithfull, Michael Hordern, Frank Finlay; **D:** Michael Winner; **W:** Peter Draper; **C:** Otto Heller; **M:** Francis Lai.

I'll Remember April

Loosely based on actual reports of Japanese submarines patrolling the Pacific during WWII, this coming-of-age morality tale about following your heart details the adventures of four ten-year-old California boys who find a Japanese sailor washed up on the beach. When the sailor rescues one of the boys from drowning, their actions become more emotional than patriotic. The video transfer is actually quite good and features crisp colors and solid blacks (the lack of a superb digital transfer does lead to some bleeding, but it is negligible). Crisp and understandable dialogue highlights a solid, though not spectacular, sound transfer. The disc also includes a passable commentary track, but director Clark does leave long pauses throughout as he apparently stops to enjoy his own film. —*MJT*
Movie: 🎵🎵½ **DVD:** 🎵🎵🎵
Pioneer Entertainment (Cat #PEAD-11508, UPC #013023150898). Full frame. Dolby Surround Sound. $24.98. Keepcase. *LANG:* English. *FEATURES:* 17 chapter links • Commentary: director Bob Clark • Theatrical trailer.
1999 90m/C Haley Joel Osment, Trevor Morgan, Richard Taylor Olson, Yuki Tokuhiro, Mark Harmon, Pam Dawber, Noriyuki "Pat" Morita, Yuji Okumoto, Troy Evans,

Paul Dooley; **D:** Bob (Benjamin) Clark; **W:** Mark Sanderson; **C:** Stephen Katz; **M:** Paul Zaza.

Illuminata

Comedy-drama about a struggling theatre troupe in turn-of-the-(19th) century New York is a Turturro family affair. Tuccio (director John) is the company's playwright—in love with manager/leading lady Rachel (John's wife Borowitz) and worried about the reception of his new work. Also involved are self-centered diva Celimene (Sarandon), foppish critic Bevalaqua (Walken), and the unlikely object of his affections, clown Marco (Irwin). Turturro is accompanied on his commentary track by his son Amadeo and they're quick to point out the family babysitter's cameo. The young boy's participation may be good for familial relations but it's irritating. DVD image is very good. It handles the darkened theatre interiors and bright shiny fabrics without problem. Sound doesn't exactly give the Surround a workout but it's fine for the material. —*MM*
Movie: 🎵🎵½ **DVD:** 🎵🎵🎵
Artisan Entertainment (Cat #10031, UPC #012236100317). Widescreen (1.85:1) letterboxed. Dolby Digital Surround. $29.99. Keepcase. *LANG:* English. *CAP:* English. *FEATURES:* 28 chapter links • Commentary: John and Amadeo Turturro • Talent files • Trailer • Three deleted scenes and one extended scene • Production notes.
1998 (R) 111m/C John Turturro, Katherine Borowitz, Christopher Walken, Susan Sarandon, Beverly D'Angelo, Bill Irwin, Rufus Sewell, Georgina Cates, Ben Gazzara, Donal McCann, Aida Turturro, Matthew Sussman, Leo Bassi; **D:** John Turturro; **W:** John Turturro, Brandon Cole; **C:** Harris Savides; **M:** William Bolcom, Arnold Black.

Ilsa, Harem Keeper of the Oil Sheiks

The second entry in the "Ilsa" series is set in "never-never time," according to the commentators, and it was filmed in Glendale. Ignore the fact that everybody's favorite villainess (Thorne) was killed off at the end of the first film. She's up to a new set of sadistic games and this time Arabs have replaced Nazis as the bad guys. (Remember that it was made during an oil crisis.) The filmmakers also tell us that for this sequel they had a ten-day shooting schedule (as opposed to nine for *She Wolf*). Image quality is about the same. The best thing about the disc is the commentary track. —*MM*
Movie: 🎵🎵 **DVD:** 🎵🎵🎵½
Anchor Bay (Cat #DV11106, UPC #01313 1110692). Widescreen (1.66:1) letterboxed. Dolby Digital Mono. $24.99. Keepcase. *LANG:* English; French. *FEATURES:* 32 chapter links • Trailer • Talent files • Commentary: Thorne, Howard Maurer, Edmonds, Martin Lewis.

1976 (R) 90m/C Dyanne Thorne, Michael Thayer, Victor Alexander, Elke Von, Sharon Kelly, Haji, Tanya Boyd, Marilyn Joy, Bobby Woods; **D:** Don Edmonds; **W:** Langton Stafford; **C:** Dean Cundey, Glenn Roland.

Ilsa, She-Wolf of the SS

The inclusion of a commentary track moderated by British humorist Martin Lewis is an inspired addition to this infamous (and perennially popular) piece of exploitation. Talking with director, producer Dave Friedman, and star Dyanne Thorne, he sets just the right tone and the four of them are a font of wonderful trivia. For example, the film was made on sets left over from TV's *Hogan's Heroes* on a lot where *The Little Rascals* and parts of *Gone with the Wind* were shot. With their commentary, the whole thing has a certain "Springtime for Hitler" attitude. The story concerns obscene medical experiments and other acts of torture in a prison camp. The disc was made from well-preserved original elements. For low-budget early '70s fare, the image is excellent. It certainly looks better than it did when I last saw it at a drive-in. —*MM*
Movie: 🎵🎵 **DVD:** 🎵🎵🎵
Anchor Bay (Cat #DV11105, UPC #01313 1110593). Widescreen (1.66:1) anamorphic. Dolby Digital Mono. $24.99. Keepcase. *LANG:* English. *FEATURES:* 27 chapter links • Commentary: Thorne, Edmonds, producer David F. Friedman, Martin Lewis • Talent files • Trailer.
1974 (R) 45m/C Dyanne Thorne, Greg Knoph, Sharon Kelly, Uschi Digart, Sandy Richman; **D:** Don Edmonds; **W:** Jonah Royston.

Ilsa, the Wicked Warden

The commentators explain that this film was never meant to be an "Ilsa" picture. According to the star and director they were tricked by the producers into thinking that they were making a story that had to do with Bruce Li in the Bermuda Triangle. Star Dyanne Thorne's character was to be called Wanda or Greta, and she was under different titles, but it hardly mattered since so many people in the cast spoke different languages. In any case, prolific horror director Jess Franco took the helm and the result was about snuff films made at a women's prison in South America. Visually, the disc isn't quite as sharp as the first two. It is, however, just as energetic, sexy, and sleazy. —*MM* *AKA:* Ilsa, the Absolute Power; Greta the Mad Butcher.
Movie: 🎵🎵 **DVD:** 🎵🎵🎵
Anchor Bay (Cat #DV11107, UPC #0131 31110791). Widescreen (1.66:1) anamorphic. Dolby Digital Mono. $24.99. Keepcase. *LANG:* English. *FEATURES:* 28 chapter links • Trailer • Talent files • Commentary: Thorne, Howard Maurer, Martin Lewis.
1978 (R) 90m/C Dyanne Thorne, Lina Romay, Tania Busselier, Howard Maurer,

Jess (Jesus) Franco; **D:** Jess (Jesus) Franco; **W:** Erwin C. Dietrich, Jess (Jesus) Franco; **C:** Ruedi Kuttel; **M:** Walter Baumgartner.

I'm Gonna Git You Sucka

Parody of '70s "blaxploitation" films is laced with outright belly laughs. Jack Spade (director Keenen Wayans) is the decorated returning veteran who must avenge the death of his brother Junebug who was crushed by his gold jewelry. DVD image is very good and so is the sound for a modestly budgeted spoof. —MM
Movie: 🐶🐶🐶 **DVD:** 🐶🐶½
MGM Home Entertainment (Cat #10014 67, UPC #027616857873). Widescreen (1.85:1) letterboxed. Dolby Digital Surround Stereo. $14.95. Keepcase. LANG: English. SUB: French; Spanish. FEATURES: 16 chapter links • Trailer.
1988 (R) 89m/C Keenen Ivory Wayans, Bernie Casey, Steve James, Isaac Hayes, Jim Brown, Ja'net DuBois, Dawnn Lewis, Anne-Marie Johnson, John Vernon, Antonio Fargas, Eve Plumb, Clu Gulager, Kadeem Hardison, Damon Wayans, Gary Owens, Clarence Williams III, David Alan Grier, Kim Wayans, Robin Harris, Chris Rock, Jester Hairston, Eugene Glazer, Peggy Lipton, Robert Townsend; **D:** Keenen Ivory Wayans; **W:** Keenen Ivory Wayans; **C:** Tom Richmond; **M:** David Michael Frank.

I'm Losing You

Confusing story has too many shocks and no point of view, stranding a good ensemble cast. TV producer Perry Krohn (Langella) learns that he is dying of cancer. His wife Diantha (Jens) takes the news badly as do his wayward children Bertie (McCarthy) and Rachel (Arquette). But it seems everyone has a doom-laden revelation to deal with. Image ranges between very good and excellent with only minor aliasing. Sound is good to very good. —MM
Movie: 🐶🐶 **DVD:** 🐶🐶🐶
Studio Home Entertainment (Cat #7325). Widescreen (1.85:1) letterboxed. Dolby Digital Surround Stereo. $24.95. Keepcase. LANG: English. SUB: Spanish. FEATURES: Cast and crew thumbnail bios • Commentary: Wagner, Arquette • 20 chapter links.
1998 (R) 102m/C Frank Langella, Salome Jens, Rosanna Arquette, Andrew McCarthy, Amanda Donohoe, Elizabeth Perkins, Gina Gershon, Buck Henry, Ed Begley Jr.; **D:** Bruce Wagner; **W:** Bruce Wagner; **C:** Rob Sweeney; **M:** Daniel Catan.

Imaginary Crimes

Ray Weiler (Keitel) is a well-meaning salesman with dreams beyond his reach. After the death of his wife (Lynch), he must raise his two daughters. But gifted teen Sonya (Balk) resents being her younger sister Greta's (Moss) maternal anchor and she's not crazy about her father's fruitless schemes. The performances by Keitel and Balk are extraordinary. DVD image is about what you'd expect for a period ('60s) piece. Sound is fine. —MM
Movie: 🐶🐶🐶 **DVD:** 🐶🐶
Warner Home Video, Inc. (Cat #13739, UPC #085391373926). Widescreen letterboxed. Dolby Digital 5.1 Surround Stereo. $19.98. Snapper. LANG: English. FEATURES: Trailers • Talent files • 34 chapter links.
1994 (PG) 106m/C Harvey Keitel, Fairuza Balk, Kelly Lynch, Vincent D'Onofrio, Elissabeth Moss, Diane Baker, Christopher Penn, Seymour Cassel, Annette O'Toole; **D:** Tony Drazan; **W:** Kristine Johnson, Davia Nelson; **C:** John Campbell; **M:** Stephen Endelman.

Immoral Tales

Director Walerian Borowczyk is best known for his notorious sexual fantasy, The Beast. This collection of four short films follows the same themes. It describes sexual desire in different settings and times. Two cousins become lovers on a trip to a really cold and nasty-looking beach; a Renaissance girl masturbates to a religious text; Countess Elizabeth Bathory bathes in the blood of virgins; and the Borgias do their thing. The on-screen sexual goings-on are not particularly shocking by today's standards (they're no more explicit than late-night cable) but the addition of the religious element is more controversial. DVD appears to be an accurate reproduction of a less-than-stellar original. The soft image is not very artfully lit and the action has a static quality. Subtitles are burned in and easy to read. —MM
AKA: Contes Immoraux.
Movie: 🐶🐶 **DVD:** 🐶
Anchor Bay (Cat #DV11079, UPC #01313 1107999). Widescreen (1.66:1) anamorphic. Dolby Digital Mono. $24.99. Keepcase. LANG: English; French. SUB: English. FEATURES: 21 chapter links • Trailer • Walerian Borowczyk thumbnail bio.
1974 103m/C FR Paloma Picasso, Lise Danvers, Fabrice Luchini, Charlotta Alexandra, Pascale Christophe, Florence Bellamy, Jacopo Berinzini, Lorenzo Berinzini; **D:** Walerian Borowczyk; **W:** Andre Pieyre de Mandiargues; **C:** Bernard Daillencourt, Guy Durban, Noel Very.

Immortal Battalion

Please see review of Legendary WWII Movies. **AKA:** The Way Ahead.
Movie: 🐶🐶🐶
1944 89m/B GB David Niven, Stanley Holloway, Reginald Tate, Raymond Huntley, William Hartnell, James Donald, Peter Ustinov, John Laurie, Leslie Dwyer, Hugh Burden, Jimmy Hanley, Leo Genn, Renee Asherson, Mary Jerrold, Tessie O'Shea, Raymond Lovell, A.E. Matthews, Jack Watling; **D:** Carol Reed; **W:** Eric Ambler, Peter Ustinov; **C:** Guy Green; **M:** William Alwyn.

Immortality

The vampire undergoes yet another postmodern twist. Steven Griscz (Law looking unusually unkempt) is a medical researcher in London who stops Maria (Fox) from committing suicide and then sets out to seduce her. When he's convinced she's in love with him, he kills her and takes her blood. His next conquest and would-be victim is Anne (Lowensohn), but she's reluctant to commit. The material never quite comes together either as horror or as a psychological thriller. The DVD looks and sounds very good though the darkish image is not particularly demanding. —MM **AKA:** The Wisdom of Crocodiles.
Movie: 🐶🐶½ **DVD:** 🐶🐶🐶
Miramax Pictures Home Video (Cat #183 11, UPC #717951004963). Widescreen (1.85:1) anamorphic. Dolby Digital 5.1 Surround Stereo; Dolby Digital Surround Stereo. $32.99. Keepcase. LANG: English; French. CAP: English. FEATURES: 16 chapter links • Trailer • Behind-the-scenes featurette.
1998 (R) 98m/C GB Jude Law, Elina Lowensohn, Timothy Spall, Kerry Fox, Jack Davenport, Colin Salmon; **D:** Po Chich Leong; **W:** Paul Hoffman; **C:** Oliver Curtis; **M:** John Lunn, Orlando Gough.

The Impossible Spy

This made-for-cable spy thriller tells the remarkable true story of Egyptian-born Israeli Elie Cohen (John Shea), a self-described "ordinary man" with an ordinary job who is reluctantly recruited by the Mossad, Israel's elite secret service organization, to spy on Syria. He leads an increasingly dangerous double life as a husband and father in Israel and a rising star businessman in Syria, where he gains access to the top echelons of government. Eli Wallach co-stars as Cohen's supervisor. A gripping film is ill-served by this DVD, which offers no extras. Image quality is mediocre. —DL
Movie: 🐶🐶🐶 **DVD:** 🐶
SlingShot Entertainment (Cat #9856, UPC #1707898562). Full frame. Dolby Digital. $19.99. Keepcase. LANG: English. FEATURES: Weblink • 14 chapter links.
1987 96m/C GB John Shea, Eli Wallach, Michal Bat-Adam, Rami Danon, Sasson Gabray, Chaim Girafi; **D:** Jim Goddard; **M:** Richard Hartley.

In Country

A Kentucky high school student (Lloyd) searches for her father, killed in Vietnam. Willis plays her uncle, a veteran still struggling to accept his own survival and crippled with memories. Disc exhibits the main problem that plagued the medium in its infancy—heavy artifacts in bright scenes. Otherwise, the full-frame image is not a significant improvement over VHS. —MM
Movie: 🐶🐶½ **DVD:** 🐶🐶

Warner Home Video, Inc. (Cat #11888). Full frame. $19.98. Snapper. *LANG:* English. *CAP:* English. *FEATURES:* 29 chapters. **1989 (R) 116m/C** Bruce Willis, Emily Lloyd, Joan Allen, Kevin Anderson, Richard Hamilton, Judith Ivey, Peggy Rea, John Terry, Patricia Richardson, Jim Beaver; *D:* Norman Jewison; *W:* Frank Pierson, Cynthia Cidre; *C:* Russell Boyd; *M:* James Horner.

The In Crowd

Combination of *Beverly Hills, 90210* and *Wild Things* revolves around the spoiled rich kids who spend the summer at the Cliffmont Country Club. They're led by the beautiful but cold Brittany Foster (Ward). Fresh-faced newcomer Adrien Williams (Heuring) has just been released from a mental hospital, and her job at the club will be her first step at rejoining society. Why is Brittany so drawn to Adrien and what plans does she have? Unfortunately, the characters are interchangeable, uninteresting cardboard cutouts, so it's hard to muster up much interest. On disc, the disappointing film is dressed up in a nice package. The picture is very nice with a clear, very sharp image free of any noise or distortion. Actually, the digital transfer works against the film in Chapter 10, when a "day-for-night" shot becomes headache inducing. Surround sound is average. The stars' chatty commentary track is actually more enjoyable than the film. *—ML*
Movie: 🎵½ *DVD:* 🎵🎵🎵
Warner Home Video, Inc. Widescreen (1.85:1) anamorphic. Dolby Digital 5.1 Surround Stereo. $24.95. Snapper. *LANG:* English. *SUB:* English; French. *FEATURES:* Commentary • Deleted scenes • Isolated score • Trailers • Photo gallery • Talent files.
2000 (PG-13) 98m/C Susan Ward, Lori Heuring, Matthew Settle, Nathan Bexton, Tess Harper, Laurie Fortier, Kim Murphy; *D:* Mary Lambert; *W:* Mark Gibson, Philip Halprin; *C:* Tom Priestley; *M:* Jeff Rona.

In God's Hands

Three surfers (Dorian, George, and Liu) travel the world in search of the perfect wave. Disjointed, plot-deprived but beautifully shot flick has the trio busting out of prison (why they're there to begin with is never explained) to begin their quest from Madagascar to Bali to Hawaii. One finds love with a girl from Ipanema; another contracts malaria; the third succumbs to the surf. What happens to whom doesn't much matter because as actors, these guys are great surfers. Besides, the story is just connective tissue for the surfing scenes. Gnarly. A few artifacts are visible in the brightest white foam of the waves, but that's picky. This is some of the most spectacular wave footage ever captured on film. Surround sound is terrific in those scenes too. In short, director Zalman King does for surfing what he does for sex in his *Red Shoes Diaries* series and other video erotica. *—MM*
Movie: 🎵🎵 *DVD:* 🎵🎵🎵½
Columbia Tristar Home Video (Cat #217 49, UPC #043396217492). Full frame; widescreen (2.35:1) anamorphic. Dolby Digital Surround Stereo. $29.95. Keepcase. *LANG:* English; French. *SUB:* French. *FEATURES:* Trailer • 28 chapter links.
1998 (PG-13) 98m/C Patrick Shane Dorian, Matt George, Matty Liu, Brion James, Shaun Thompson, Maylin Pultar, Bret Michaels, Brian L. Keaulana, Darrick Doerner; *D:* Zalman King; *W:* Zalman King, Matt George; *C:* John Aronson.

In Harm's Way

Overdone story revolves around two naval officers (Wayne and Douglas) and their response to the Japanese attack on Pearl Harbor. Even the superb cast members (and there are plenty of them) can't overcome the interminable length and overly intricate plot. DVD enables us who missed the show in the theatres to finally see it in its widescreen glory. It's been mostly pan and scanned on TV and home video. Image and sound are excellent. The extras are great. The featurette has a bunch of interesting outtakes and behind-the-scenes material. It's supposed to be immature to laugh at a natural accent, but Otto Preminger's is a hoot, narrating and appearing on-screen in the trailers. His readings of the hyped ad copy are fall-down funny. He wasn't exaggerating his voice when he played Mr. Freeze on television's *Batman*. *—MM/GE*
Movie: 🎵🎵 *DVD:* 🎵🎵🎵
Paramount Home Video (Cat #06418, UPC #097360641844). Widescreen (2.35:1) anamorphic. Dolby Digital 5.1 Surround Stereo; Dolby Digital Surround. $29.99. Keepcase. *LANG:* English. *SUB:* English. *FEATURES:* 24 chapter links • 3 trailers • "Making of" featurette.
1965 165m/B John Wayne, Kirk Douglas, Tom Tryon, Patricia Neal, Paula Prentiss, Brandon de Wilde, Burgess Meredith, Stanley Holloway, Henry Fonda, Dana Andrews, Franchot Tone, Jill Haworth, George Kennedy, Carroll O'Connor, Patrick O'Neal, Slim Pickens, Bruce Cabot, Larry Hagman, Hugh O'Brian, Jim Mitchum, Barbara Bouchet, Stewart Moss, Tod Andrews; *D:* Otto Preminger; *W:* Wendell Mayes; *C:* Loyal Griggs; *M:* Jerry Goldsmith. *AWARDS:* British Acad. '65: Actress (Neal); *NOM:* Oscars '65: B&W Cinematog.

In Pursuit

Lawyer Rick Alvarez (Baldwin) is falsely accuse of murder and has to break out of prison to clear himself. He's helped by his lawyer (Lassez) and a sympathetic guard (Coolio). On the other side is a treacherous detective (Schiffer). The plot is wildly imaginative, but this one may go down in cinematic history for containing perhaps the worst sex scene ever put on film. It involves Baldwin, uber-babe Schiffer, and a folding aluminum ladder. The image is marred by the usual aliasing in certain stripes, but overall it can be rated between good and very good. Sound is fine. *—MM*
Movie: 🎵🎵½ *DVD:* 🎵🎵
Paramount Home Video (Cat #86029, UPC #097368602946). Widescreen letterboxed. Dolby Digital 5.1 Surround Stereo; Dolby Digital Surround. $29.99. Keepcase. *LANG:* English. *FEATURES:* 16 chapter links • Commentary: Peter Pistor, John Penney • Trailer • Stills gallery • Talent files.
2000 (R) 91m/C Daniel Baldwin, Claudia Schiffer, Coolio, Sarah Lassez, Dean Stockwell; *D:* Peter Pistor; *W:* Peter Pistor, John Penney; *C:* Richard Crudo.

In Pursuit of Honor

The story of five American cavalry soldiers who find themselves and their horses being phased out of the Army in 1935 is based on truth. Ordered by Gen. Douglas MacArthur to destroy 500 horses, Sgt. Libby (Johnson) and Lt. Buxton (Sheffer) instead try to outrun a tank division and get the horses to safety in Canada. Film is told in muted colors that are accurately reproduced. Pixelation is notable for its absence in the many dusty scenes. A solid sleeper. *—MM*
Movie: 🎵🎵🎵 *DVD:* 🎵🎵🎵
HBO Home Video (Cat #91229, UPC #026 35912927). Widescreen letterboxed. Dolby Digital Surround; Stereo; Mono. $19.98. Snapper. *LANG:* English; French; Spanish. *SUB:* English; French; Spanish. *FEATURES:* 13 chapter links • Talent files.
1995 (PG-13) 110m/C Don Johnson, Craig Sheffer, Gabrielle Anwar, Bob Gunton, Rod Steiger, James B. Sikking, John Dennis Johnston, Robert Coleby; *D:* Ken Olin; *W:* Dennis Lynton Clark; *C:* Stephen Windon; *M:* John Debney.

In the Beginning...

Made-for-TV production retells the first books of the Bible from the Garden of Eden to the return of the Israelites with Moses. Production values are well above average and so the image looks very good. Sound is a real improvement where Surround effects give the voice of God an appropriately threatening rumble. *—MM*
Movie: 🎵🎵 *DVD:* 🎵🎵
Artisan Entertainment (Cat #11359, UPC #70772911359). Full frame. Dolby Digital Surround Stereo. $24.98. Keepcase. *LANG:* English. *CAP:* English. *FEATURES:* 37 chapter links • "Making of" featurette.
2000 168m/C Martin Landau, Jacqueline Bisset, Bill Campbell, Eddie Cibrian, Frederick Weller, Alan Bates, Steven Berkoff, Geraldine Chaplin, Amanda Donohoe, Christopher Lee, Art Malik, Rachael Stirling, Diana Rigg; *D:* Kevin Connor; *W:* John Goldsmith; *C:* Elemer Ragalyi; *M:* Ken Thorne.

In the Flesh / Blood Bullets Buffoons

Despite the box art, title, and the studio's reputation for soft-core exploitation, this documentary is mainly interviews with women who perform in strip clubs (and one who does hard-core work). They talk about what they do and why (money). Amy Lynn seems pretty ordinary; Ashlyn Gere is more defensive. Since the interviews and stage acts were shot on video, the image is so rough as to be barely watchable. Much more interesting really is the disc's second feature, *Blood Bullets Buffoons*. In it, sex-obsessed Jack Winston (producer/writer/director Zachary Snygg) is arrested in a drug bust. Later, he breaks out of jail to get even with the people who let him take the rap. Within that loose narrative structure, Snygg flashes back to black-and-white scenes involving Jack and his girlfriend Natasha (Lynn again). Cutting against the exploitation grain, she's a relatively "realistic" character who keeps her clothes on while strippers bump and grind in other scenes. She's also a surprisingly effective actress who makes the most out of a good role. The rest is a combination of slapstick and offbeat verbal humor. Though the DVD image isn't that much better than tape, the film earns a VideoHound rating of three bones. —*MM*
Movie: 🦴🦴🦴 **DVD:** 🦴🦴
El Independent Cinema (Cat #1012-dvd, UPC #612385101298). Full frame. $19.95. Keepcase. *LANG:* English. *FEATURES:* 11 chapter links • 6 strip acts • Interviews.
2000 ?m/C D: Michael G. Leonard, Sean K. Donnellan; **W:** Michael G. Leonard, Sean K. Donnellan.

In the Heat of the Night

A wealthy industrialist is murdered in the small Mississippi town of Sparta. Initially, Philadelphia police detective Virgil Tibbs (Poitier) is a suspect, but it soon becomes clear to the sheriff (Steiger, who won an Oscar for his role) that the black man is better equipped to solve the crime than he and his own undereducated, underpaid force are. Powerful script manages to handle the mystery elements while working with the larger themes of racism and social justice. On their commentary track, director Jewison and director of photography Wexler talk about those issues and the practical matters of making a challenging film on a modest budget. They give a lot of credit to editor Hal Ashby and they fill their talk with the right details. (The film was made in Sparta, Illinois, because it looked right and they could shoot the water tower.) Image quality is absolutely first-rate. The disc looks better than the print I saw at a film festival a few years ago. Mono sound is acceptable. —*MM*
Movie: 🦴🦴🦴½ **DVD:** 🦴🦴🦴½
MGM Home Entertainment (Cat #10014 72, UPC #027616857927). Widescreen (1.85:1) anamorphic. Dolby Digital Mono. $19.98. Keepcase. *LANG:* English; French; Spanish. *SUB:* French; Spanish. *CAP:* Eng-lish. *FEATURES:* 16 chapter links • Commentary: Jewison, Wexler, Grant, Steiger • Trailer.
1967 109m/C Sidney Poitier, Rod Steiger, Warren Oates, Lee Grant; **D:** Norman Jewison; **W:** Stirling Silliphant; **C:** Haskell Wexler; **M:** Quincy Jones. *AWARDS:* Oscars '67: Actor (Steiger), Adapt. Screenplay, Film Editing, Picture, Sound; British Acad. '67: Actor (Steiger); Golden Globes '68: Actor—Drama (Steiger), Film—Drama, Screenplay; N.Y. Film Critics '67: Actor (Steiger), Director (Nichols), Film; Natl. Soc. Film Critics '67: Actor (Steiger), Cinematog; *NOM:* Oscars '67: Director (Jewison).

In the Line of Fire [2 SE]

Eastwood is the Secret Service agent who goes up against would-be presidential assassin Malkovich. The image and sound of this "special edition" may be slightly improved over the earlier release (cat. #52315, reviewed in first edition). The real difference here is a full plate of extras beginning with a cool new menu, a commentary track by director Petersen and DVD producer J.M. Kinney, and four featurettes. It's easy to see why the deleted scenes were deleted. —*MM*
Movie: 🦴🦴🦴½ **DVD:** 🦴🦴🦴½
Columbia Tristar Home Video (Cat #523 17, UPC #043396523173). Widescreen (2.35:1) anamorphic. Dolby Digital 5.1 Surround Stereo; Dolby Digital Surround Stereo. $29.95. Keepcase. *LANG:* English; French; Spanish; Portuguese. *SUB:* English; French; Spanish; Portuguese; Chinese; Korean; Thai. *FEATURES:* 28 chapter links • "Ultimate Sacrifice" featurette • "Catching the Counterfeiters" featurette • "How'd They Do That?" featurette • "Behind the Scenes with the Secret Service" featurette • 5 deleted scenes • Talent files • Commentary: director • Trailers.
1993 (R) 128m/C Clint Eastwood, John Malkovich, Rene Russo, Dylan McDermott, Gary Cole, Fred Dalton Thompson, John Mahoney, Gregory Alan Williams; **D:** Wolfgang Petersen; **W:** Jeff Maguire; **C:** John Bailey; **M:** Ennio Morricone. *AWARDS: NOM:* Oscars '93: Film Editing, Orig. Screenplay, Support. Actor (Malkovich); British Acad. '93: Orig. Screenplay, Support. Actor (Malkovich); Golden Globes '94: Support. Actor (Malkovich); MTV Movie Awards '94: Villain (Malkovich); Writers Guild '93: Orig. Screenplay.

In This House of Brede

Sophisticated London widow Phillipa Talbot (Rigg) turns her back on her worldly life to become a cloistered Benedictine nun. Diana Rigg is, as always, outstanding as a woman struggling to deal with the discipline of faith. This adaptation of the Rumer Godden novel was made for television. The full-frame image is slightly better than broadcast quality, but only just. The nuns' habits are an undetailed area of black in most lighting conditions. —*MM*
Movie: 🦴🦴🦴 **DVD:** 🦴🦴
VCI Home Video (Cat #8235, UPC #08985 9823527). Full frame. Dolby Digital Mono. $19.99. Keepcase. *LANG:* English. *FEATURES:* 18 chapter links • Talent files • Previews.
1975 105m/C Diana Rigg, Pamela Brown, Gwen Watford, Denis Quilley, Judi Bowker; **D:** George Schaefer; **M:** Peter Matz.

Incubus

Leslie Stevens, the oddball writer/producer who created the television series *The Outer Limits,* also made this "lost Esperanto masterpiece." In the land of Nomen Tuum, Marc (Shatner) lives a happy existence with his sister Arndis (Atman), trying to forget his war experiences. But evil forces are afoot in the form of a pair of succubi, whose Earthly mission is simply to harvest corrupt men. Ambitious phantom Kia (Ames) makes the mistake of seducing a Good man, Marc, and falling in love with him. In retribution, her superior Amael (Hardt) dispatches an Incubus (Milos Milos, AKA Milosevicz) to attack the innocent Arndis. Why would anyone want to shoot a movie in Esperanto, that living-dead generic romance-based language promoted by the United Nations as a possible One-World universal tongue? Answer: to aestheticize and abstract the "text" of the movie. Ever notice how foreign films are slightly distanced by the language barrier? We have to read the movie, an active role, instead of just passively watching it, and reading words actually makes us more susceptible to ideas than watching literal actors saying literal lines. The film plays at a perceptual remove, where even a silly story seems more serious. The DVD is made from the same good master used for the VHS tape. Conrad Hall's very interesting photography looks simply terrific, making us want to see those great old *Outer Limits* episodes again. The extras on the DVD will make VHS purchasers want to revisit the title. A video interview is provided with producer Taylor and cameramen Conrad Hall and Bill Fraker; it's terribly edited but interesting anyway. The best extra is an entire second copy of the film, the French-subtitled version, which, if you read French, has the advantage of not having the obscuring black boxes that sometimes hide actors' mouths. —*GE*
Movie: 🦴🦴🦴½ **DVD:** 🦴🦴🦴½
Winstar Home Entertainment (Cat #FLV5 274, UPC #720917527420). Full frame. $24.98. Keepcase. *LANG:* Esperanto. *SUB:* English; French. *FEATURES:* Commentary: William Shatner • Commentary: Anthony Taylor, Conrad L. Hall, William Fraker • Interview with Taylor, Hall, Fraker • Weblinks.
1965 76m/B William Shatner, Allyson Ames, Eloise Hardt, Ann Atmar, Robert Fortier, Milos Milos; **D:** Leslie Stevens; **W:**

Leslie Stevens; **C:** Conrad Hall; **M:** Dominic Frontiere.

The Indestructible Man / The Amazing Transparent Man

Near the end of his career, an alcoholic Chaney gamely made his way through this low-budget horror as a gangster who is electrocuted and brought back to life. The second feature is a lesser work from cult-fav director Edward James Ulmer, made at the Texas State Fair. It's presented in widescreen and looks much better than *Indestructible,* which is as muddy as a bad tape. —*MM*

Movie: 🐾½ **DVD:** 🐾🐾½
Roan Group (Cat #2007). Full frame; widescreen letterboxed. $29.95. Keepcase. *LANG:* English. *FEATURES:* 14 chapter links each.

1956 70m/B Ross Elliott, Ken Terrell, Robert Shayne, Lon Chaney Jr., Marian Carr, Max (Casey Adams) Showalter; **D:** Jack Pollexfen; **W:** Sue Bradford, Vy Russell; **C:** John L. "Jack" Russell; **M:** Albert Glasser.

The Indian Tomb

Considered by some critics to be one of the greatest film epics ever made, *The Indian Tomb* tells the story of Ayan (Veidt), the Maharajah of Eschnapur who has lost his wife, Princess Savitri, to the handsome British officer MacAllan. When Ayan plans his revenge, the yogi Ramigani prophesies the Maharajah's downfall and all hell breaks loose. Definitely one of the forefathers of *Raiders of the Lost Ark.* The video transfer is adequate given the age of the film. However, scratches and skips are prevalent throughout the disc, though the color tinting does help to draw attention away from this (as it does the occasionally murky blacks). The new musical score is quite good and sets an appropriate mood and tone throughout. —*MJT* **AKA:** The Mission of the Yogi; The Tiger of Eschanapur.

Movie: 🐾🐾🐾 **DVD:** 🐾🐾🐾½
Image Entertainment (Cat #ID9363MQ DVD, UPC #014381936322). Full frame. Dolby Digital Stereo. $29.99. Snapper. *LANG:* Silent. *SUB:* English intertitles. *FEATURES:* 20 chapter links.

1921 212m/B *GE* Conrad Veidt, Paul Richter, Olaf Fönss, Mia May, Bernhard Goetzke, Lya de Putti, Erna Morena; **D:** Joe May; **W:** Fritz Lang; **C:** Werner Brandes.

Inferno

Jack Conley awakens in the middle of the desert with no idea who he is or what's happened to him. Taken in by a reclusive artist, Jack suffers violent flashbacks as he tries to piece together his identity, only remembering that he had a lot of money in his possession and it's gone. Things take a turn for the worse when two of Jack's former associates track him down and he learns the dangerous truth about himself. The image on the DVD ranges from very good to below average; although for the most part it stays fairly sharp, the colors seem to change at random, with flesh-tones occasionally turning out-and-out pink. There's also a lot of grain and even the preprint has a lot of imperfections, something that is acceptable only in a much older film. The sound doesn't get much better, but is at least consistent, with crisp out-front dialogue but very little low end during effects (gunshots and such), resulting in a overall cheap feel to the film. —*JO*

Movie: 🐾🐾½ **DVD:** 🐾🐾½
Trimark Home Video (Cat #7361D, UPC #031398736127). Widescreen (1.85:1) letterboxed. Dolby Surround. $24.99. Keepcase. *LANG:* English; Spanish. *SUB:* English; Spanish. *CAP:* English. *FEATURES:* 24 chapter links • Trailer.

1999 (R) 94m/C Ray Liotta, Gloria Reuben, Armin Mueller-Stahl; **D:** Harley Cokliss; **C:** Stephen McNutt; **M:** Fred Mollin.

Inhumanity

Serial killer thriller is indescribably inept. Though the lead performances are mostly all right, supporting work is amateur. The film is padded with shots of traffic and buildings in Dallas. Lighting, writing, and directing are substandard. From chapter to chapter, the image changes from full frame to widescreen. Scratches and other signs of wear are evident throughout. —*MM*

Movie: 🐾 **DVD:** 🐾
York Entertainment (Cat #YPD-1061, UPC #750723106120). Widescreen; full frame. Dolby Digital 5.1 Surround Stereo. $14.99. Keepcase. *LANG:* English. *FEATURES:* 30 chapter links • Talent files • Trailers.

2000 90m/C Todd Bridges, Faizon Love, Carl Jackson, Georgia Foy, Billy Davis; **D:** Carl Jackson; **W:** Carl Jackson; **C:** Kurt Ugland; **M:** Damon Criswell.

The Inland Sea

Donald Ritchie, an American living in Japan, narrates a meditative documentary about travel and the nature of the expatriate. The documentary re-creates a journey he took 30 years before. His observations on Japanese culture past and present are mixed with gloomy predictions for the future and his ideas on sex and religion. Throughout, the humor is dry. This DVD is even sharper than the laserdisc edition. Recommended. —*MM*

Movie: 🐾🐾🐾½ **DVD:** 🐾🐾🐾
Image Entertainment (Cat #ID4540JFDVD, UPC #014381454024). Full frame. Dolby Digital Stereo. $24.99. Snapper. *LANG:* English.

1993 56m/C D: Lucille Carra; **C:** Hiro Narita; **M:** Toru Takemitsu; **Nar:** Donald Ritchie.

Inn of 1000 Sins

Silly sex comedy is about Albert (Hamm) who works at a hotel and makes sure that the female guests get everything that they want. The full-frame image is as soft and grainy as you'd expect from a mid-'70s import. The extra short film looks much much worse. —*MM* **AKA:** Ein Echter Hausfrauenfreund; Room Service; Happy Gigolo.

Movie: 🐾 **DVD:** 🐾🐾
El Independent Cinema (Cat #sc-2201-dvd, UPC #612385220197). Full frame. $19.98. Snapper. *LANG:* English. *FEATURES:* 16 chapter links • "The Vibrating Maid" short film • Trailers.

1975 73m/C Peter Hamm, Margaret Rose Keil, Eva Gross, Rose Gardner, Al Price, Elfriede Gerstl, Gisela Kraus, Michaela Roos; **D:** Ilja Nutrof; **W:** Nanni DeLollis; **C:** Gery Werner.

Inseminoid

Vile, repulsive, dim-witted imitation of *Alien* manages to disgust and bore in almost equal measures. On an archeological expedition to a distant planet, archeo-astronaut Judy Geeson is impregnated by a creature with glowing green liquid. As her stomach swells, she bumps off her dim-witted companions. In any given situation, if there's something stupid that these one-dimensional characters can do, they will do it. The special effects aren't special, and the general level of sets and props is marked by the motorcycle helmets meant to pass for space helmets. The image tends to range between good and very good, but with all the tinting, smoke, and deliberately dark interiors, this is such a funny-looking film that it gains little beyond the widescreen transfer. —*MM* **AKA:** Horror Planet.

Movie: woof **DVD:** 🐾🐾
Elite Entertainment, Inc. (Cat #4674). Widescreen (2.35:1) letterboxed. Dolby Digital Stereo. $24.95. Keepcase. *LANG:* English. *FEATURES:* 20 chapter links • Trailer.

1980 (R) 93m/C *GB* Robin Clarke, Jennifer Ashley, Stephanie Beacham, Judy Geeson, Stephen Grives, Victoria Tennant; **D:** Norman J. Warren; **W:** Gloria Maley, Nick Maley; **C:** John Metcalfe; **M:** John Scott.

The Inside Man

Double agents struggle to find a submarine-detecting laser device. The Swedish film is based on true incidents in which a Soviet sub ran aground in Sweden. The disc looks much worse than a bad tape. It's a bare-bones affair with no menu. —*MM*

Movie: 🐾🐾½ **DVD:** woof
Essex (Cat #1010). Full frame. $10.97. Slipcase. *LANG:* English.

1984 90m/C *SW* Dennis Hopper, Hardy Kruger, Gosta Ekman Jr., David Wilson; **D:** Tom Clegg; **W:** Alan Plater; **C:** Jorgen Persson; **M:** Stefan Nilsson.

The Inspector General

Danny Kaye provides the comedy and musical ditties in this over-the-top screen adaptation of Nikolai Gogol's play, *The Government Inspector*. Kaye stars as Georgi, a good-natured but buffoonish Russian peasant who is mistaken for the Inspector General—an all powerful, but unknown individual who is feared by all. Traveling sideshow entrepreneur Yakov (Walter Slezak) is quick to take advantage of the village's mistake, while Leza (Barbara Bates) falls for Georgi regardless of his status in life. Songs, dance, and a happy ending—who could ask for more? DVD presentation comes as something of a surprise. The picture quality, all things considered, is fresh, if somewhat on the light pastel side throughout. The sound is good. Only drawbacks are the lack of a chapter menu and subtitles. —*RJT* **AKA:** Happy Times.

Movie: ♫♫½ **DVD:** ♫♫½
Roan Group (Cat #AED-2049, UPC #78560 4204923). Full frame. Dolby Surround Stereo. $19.98. Keepcase. *LANG:* English. *FEATURES:* 11 chapter markers, but no menu access ☛ Film bios (Danny Kaye, Walter Slezak, Barbara Bates) ☛ Film background (notes about the film's production) ☛ Trailers: *White Zombie, Rage at Dawn, The Outlaw*.
1949 103m/C Danny Kaye, Walter Slezak, Barbara Bates, Elsa Lanchester, Gene Lockhart, Walter Catlett, Alan Hale; **D:** Henry Koster; **W:** Harry Kurnitz, Philip Rapp; **C:** Elwood "Woody" Bredell; **M:** Johnny Green. *AWARDS:* Golden Globes '50: Score.

Interceptor Force

Straightforward tale of a close-knit commando force saddled with two computer nerds who go in search of a hostile alien that has landed in a small town in Mexico run by a hard-drinking drug lord. Lots of gunfire and kung fu ensues. The acting, production quality, and story are all competent, and the opening title sequence is fun. Brad Dourif, who is credited second in the film titles but is absent from the DVD box credit, sleepwalks through a small role he probably took to pay off his car. Some decent TV-quality alien effects break up the gunfire. The transfer is amazingly clear and crisp and the sound is good. All this adds up to a fun Friday night rental. —*CA*

Movie: ♫♫ **DVD:** ♫♫♫½
York Entertainment (Cat #YPD1028, UPC #750723102825). Widescreen (1.85:1) letterboxed; full frame. Dolby 5.1 Surround. $24.98. Keepcase. *LANG:* English. *SUB:* Spanish. *CAP:* English. *FEATURES:* 28 chapter links ☛ Theatrical trailer ☛ Cast bios.
1999 (R) 91m/C Olivier Gruner, Brad Dourif, Glenn Plummer, Ernie Hudson, Ken Olandt, Angel Boris, Holly Fields; **D:** Phillip J. Roth; **W:** Phillip J. Roth, Martin Lazarus.

Interiors

Woody Allen tries his hand at Ingmar Bergman with a drama about three neurotic sisters coping with the dissolution of their family. When Father (Marshall)

decides to leave mentally unbalanced Mother (Page) for a divorcee, the daughters (Keaton, Griffith, and Hurt) are shocked and bewildered. It's every bit as depressing and humorless as it sounds, but performances are fine all around. Gordon Willis's elegant, static camerawork doesn't test the limits of DVD image quality. Same for sound. Those with conventional-sized televisions will probably choose the full-frame version. —*MM*

Movie: ♫♫♫ **DVD:** ♫♫½
20th Century Fox Home Entertainment (Cat #1000793, UPC #027616851147). Widescreen anamorphic; full frame. Dolby Digital Mono. $24.99. Keepcase. *LANG:* English; Spanish. *SUB:* French; Spanish. *CAP:* English. *FEATURES:* 28 chapter links ☛ Trailer ☛ Liner notes.
1978 (R) 95m/C Diane Keaton, Mary Beth Hurt, E.G. Marshall, Geraldine Page, Richard Jordan, Sam Waterston, Kristin Griffith, Maureen Stapleton; **D:** Woody Allen; **W:** Woody Allen; **C:** Gordon Willis. *AWARDS:* British Acad. '78: Support. Actress (Page); L.A. Film Critics '78: Support. Actress (Stapleton); *NOM:* Oscars '78: Actress (Page), Art Dir./Set Dec., Director (Allen), Orig. Screenplay, Support. Actress (Stapleton).

Intern

Ignore the box art. This story of Jocelyn Bennett (Swain), an intern at a fashion magazine, is not erotic. It's a sharp satire of the industry, along the lines of *How to Succeed in Business without Really Trying*, where characters are likely to burst into song. Unfortunately, the film was made with tons of intelligence, ambition, and talent, but not much money. It has a made-on-the-fly look with pale colors that are no better than VHS tape. —*MM*

Movie: ♫♫♫½ **DVD:** ♫♫
York Entertainment (Cat #YPD-1046, UPC #750723104621). Full frame. Dolby Digital 5.1 Surround Stereo. $14.99. Keepcase. *LANG:* English. *SUB:* English. *FEATURES:* 30 chapter links ☛ Filmographies ☛ 3 trailers.
2000 93m/C Dominique Swain, Benjamin Pullen, Peggy Lipton, Joan Rivers, David Deblinger, Dwight Ewell, Billy Porter, Anna Thompson, Paulina Porizkova, Kathy Griffin; **D:** Michael Lange; **W:** Caroline Doyle, Jill Kopelman; **C:** Rodney Charters; **M:** Jimmy Harry.

Internal Affairs

Wild, sexually charged action piece follows an LAPD Internal Affairs officer (Garcia) who becomes obsessed with uncovering a sleazy, corrupt street cop (Gere). It all becomes pretty illogical before it's over, but the performances and bizarre humor are terrific. Gere's creepy degenerate is one of his best and strangest roles. Image ranges between good and very good. Sound is not exceptional but both are appropriate to this tricky, noirish tale. —*MM*

Movie: ♫♫½ **DVD:** ♫♫♫

Paramount Home Video (Cat #322457). Widescreen (1.85:1) letterboxed. Dolby Digital 5.1 Surround Stereo; Dolby Digital Surround Stereo. $29.99. Keepcase. *LANG:* English; French. *CAP:* English. *FEATURES:* 13 chapter links.
1990 (R) 114m/C Richard Gere, Andy Garcia, Laurie Metcalf, Ron Vawter, Marco Rodriguez, Nancy Travis, William Baldwin, Richard Bradford, Annabella Sciorra, Michael Beach; **D:** Mike Figgis; **W:** Henry Bean; **C:** John A. Alonzo; **M:** Brian Banks, Mike Figgis.

The Interview

Eddie Fleming (Weaving) is a seemingly ordinary man who's awakened when armed police burst into his apartment and haul him to headquarters for questioning. His interrogators are the tenacious Det. Steele (Martin) and his thuggish younger partner Prior (Jeffery). At first, the subject seems to be a stolen car but something more serious is going on, and even the cops themselves are not above suspicion. Comparisons to *The Usual Suspects* are hard to ignore, but this is a genuine Aussie original. Given the nature of the material, it gains little in visual terms on DVD. The real attraction comes in the extensive extras. Don't listen to Monahan's commentary until you've watched the film straight through. —*MM*

Movie: ♫♫♫½ **DVD:** ♫♫♫½
New Yorker Video (Cat #80801, UPC #717 119808143). Widescreen letterboxed. $24.98. Keepcase. *LANG:* English. *FEATURES:* 22 chapter links ☛ Trailer ☛ Press kit ☛ Deleted scenes ☛ Alternate ending ☛ Commentary: Craig Monahan.
1998 101m/C *AU* Hugo Weaving, Tony Martin, Aaron Jeffery, Paul Sonkkila, Michael Caton, Peter McCauley; **D:** Craig Monahan; **W:** Craig Monahan, Gordon Davie; **C:** Simon Duggan; **M:** David Hirschfelder. *AWARDS:* Australian Film Inst. '98: Actor (Weaving), Film, Orig. Screenplay; *NOM:* Australian Film Inst. '98: Cinematog., Director (Monahan), Orig. Score.

The Intruder

In the segregated South, opportunist-provocateur Adam Cramer (Shatner) slips into the small Southern town of Caxton just before the start of the school year and goes to work stirring up hatred and bigotry among the white locals. The new integration laws decree that blacks may attend the same schools as whites, which the population, taking the law-abiding lead of newspaperman Tom McDaniel (Maxwell), had more or less accepted. Cramer enlists the support of local bigshot bigot Verne Shipman (Emhardt), while inflaming the hostility already present in the local layabouts. He also finds time to court a married woman in his rooming house (Cooper) while her salesman husband (Gordon) is away, and also put the moves on McDaniel's teenaged daughter Ella (Lunsford). With speeches that incite near-riots, Cramer's intimidation tactics quickly

incite a flurry of Klan activity, because even the most casually "nice" white citizen on the street is resolutely against integration. The only law is a do-nothing sheriff who is practically part of the mob himself. Before the issue is resolved, Caxton will be thrown into a racial firestorm of fear, hatred, and vicious violence. The black-and-white image appears to come from a print that has seen some wear, but it is intact and plays well. One brief shot has been replaced with a bad-looking dupe, and that's it. The fluid camerawork in the real streets and rural shanty towns is well served on the DVD, and the audio is clear, especially for location sound on a low-budget film. (I'm assuming all those local accents are genuine.) —GE **AKA:** Shame; I Hate Your Guts; The Stranger.
Movie: 🎞🎞½ ***DVD:*** 🎞🎞🎞
New Concorde (Cat #NH20051 D, UPC #736991305199). Full frame. $14.98. Keepcase. *LANG:* English. *FEATURES:* Trailer ▪ Shatner-Corman interview.
1961 84m/B William Shatner, Frank Maxwell, Jeanne Cooper, Robert Emhardt, Leo Gordon, Charles Beaumont, Beverly Lunsford, William F. Nolan, George Clayton Johnson; ***D:*** Roger Corman; ***W:*** Charles Beaumont; ***C:*** Taylor Byars; ***M:*** Herman Stein.

Inventing the Abbotts

An appealing cast populates this sleepy, bittersweet coming-of-age story set in 1957 small-town Illinois. Alice (Going), Eleanor (Connelly), and Pamela (Tyler) are the lovely daughters of wealthy Lloyd Abbott (Patton) who's determined that they'll marry well despite the temptations offered by the two working-class Holt boys. Surly stud Jacey (Crudup) holds a grudge against Lloyd for possibly cheating his deceased father in a business deal and causing whispers about his schoolteacher mother Helen (Baker), while sweet-natured younger brother Doug (Phoenix) has his romantic ideas fixed on Pamela who loves him in return. DVD does all it can with the hazy, good-old-days image. Sound is fine. —MM
Movie: 🎞🎞🎞 ***DVD:*** 🎞🎞🎞
20th Century Fox Home Entertainment (Cat #2001215, UPC #024543012153). Widescreen (2.35:1) anamorphic. Dolby Digital 5.1 Surround Stereo; Dolby Digital Surround. $24.99. Keepcase. *LANG:* English; French. *SUB:* English; Spanish. *FEATURES:* Trailers ▪ "Making of" featurette ▪ 28 chapter links.
1997 (R) 110m/C Billy Crudup, Joaquin Rafael (Leaf) Phoenix, Liv Tyler, Will Patton, Kathy Baker, Jennifer Connelly, Joanna Going, Barbara Williams; ***D:*** Pat O'Connor; ***W:*** Ken Hixon; ***C:*** Kenneth Macmillan; ***M:*** Michael Kamen.

The Invisible Man

The vintage horror-fest based on H.G. Wells's novella about a scientist whose formula for invisibility slowly drives him insane. His mind definitely wandering, he

plans to use his recipe to rule the world. Rains's first role; though his body doesn't appear until the final scene, his voice characterization is magnificent. The visual detail is excellent, setting standards that are imitated because they are difficult to surpass. It appears that Universal could not come up with as good a source material for this presentation as it had for some of their other monster classics. As a result, the DVD is limited by film scratches and other defects, and the image is also softer than one would like. Still, the disc does its best, delivering good gray tones, brightness, and contrast, combined with very good mono sound. The documentary doesn't give enough information about filming *The Invisible Man* and its exceptional effects, and instead seems more concerned with promoting other Universal titles. Behlmer's commentary is more interesting on the technical end, but it would have been nice to see the two (visuals and audio) combined. —JO
Movie: 🎞🎞🎞½ ***DVD:*** 🎞🎞🎞½
Universal Studios Home Video (Cat #20766, UPC #025192076626). Full frame. Dolby Digital Mono. $29.98. Keepcase. *LANG:* English. *SUB:* Spanish; French. *CAP:* English. *FEATURES:* 18 chapter links ▪ Talent files ▪ Production notes ▪ Photo gallery ▪ Documentary featurette ▪ Commentary: film historian Rudy Behlmer ▪ Dual-layered.
1933 71m/B Claude Rains, Gloria Stuart, Dudley Digges, William Harrigan, Una O'Connor, E.E. Clive, Dwight Frye, Henry Travers, Holmes Herbert, John Carradine, Walter Brennan; ***D:*** James Whale; ***W:*** R.C. Sherriff; ***C:*** Arthur Edeson.

Invisible Mom

Dad (Livingston) invents an invisibility potion that his 10-year-old son thinks will make him popular at school. But his protective Mom (Wallace Stone) swallows the concoction instead. The special effects break no new ground but this is pleasant family fare. Disc is interchangeable with VHS tape. —MM
Movie: 🎞🎞½ ***DVD:*** 🎞🎞½
New Concorde (Cat #NH20597D, UPC #736991259799). Full frame. Stereo. $19.98. Keepcase. *LANG:* English. *FEATURES:* 24 chapter links ▪ Thumbnail bios ▪ Trailers.
1996 (PG) 82m/C Dee Wallace Stone, Barry Livingston, Trenton Knight, Russ Tamblyn, Stella Stevens; ***D:*** Fred Olen Ray; ***W:*** William Martell; ***C:*** Gary Graver; ***M:*** Jeff Walton.

Irene Dunne Romance Classics

Love Affair and *Penny Serenade* are the two public domain features on this disc. They're fine films (please see individual reviews), but there's nothing special about the transfer. —MM
Movie: 🎞🎞🎞 ***DVD:*** 🎞🎞
SlingShot Entertainment (Cat #TDVD9118, UPC #017078911824). Full frame. Dolby

Digital Mono. $19.99. Large jewelcase. *LANG:* English. *FEATURES:* 38 chapter links ▪ Weblinks.
2000 ?m/C

Isaac Asimov's Nightfall

With its six suns, the planet Aeon has no night. But when astronomical predictions call for the first darkness, the inhabitants react in different ways. This version of the famous science-fiction story is certainly more successful than the abysmal 1988 adaptation. Image and sound range between good and very good. Cast is good, too. —MM **AKA:** Nightfall.
Movie: 🎞🎞½ ***DVD:*** 🎞🎞½
New Concorde (Cat #NH20755 D, UPC #736991475595). Full frame. Stereo. $19.99. Keepcase. *LANG:* English. *FEATURES:* 24 chapter links ▪ Talent files ▪ Trailers.
2000 (R) 85m/C David Carradine, Jennifer Burns, Joseph Hodge; ***D:*** Gwyneth Gibby; ***W:*** Gwyneth Gibby, John W. Corrington, Michael B. Druxman; ***C:*** Abhik Mukhopadhyay; ***M:*** Nicolas Tenbroek, Brad Segal.

Isn't She Great

Kitsch biopic about trash novelist queen Jacqueline Susann (Midler) and her quest for fame starts out as biographical gloss, but the narrative shifts into mid gear when she starts down her literary path...specifically, the talk gets dirty. Midler appropriately chews the sets and Lane, as manager/husband/eternal cheerleader Irving Mansfield, doles out the saccharine moments. Paul Rudnick's script, based on a magazine article, should have been far more vinegary given the subject. The supporting cast fares better, with David Hyde Pierce as Susann's exasperated editor and Stockard Channing stealing the movie as Florence, Jackie's boozy floozy pal. The DVD offers anamorphic widescreen and full-frame viewing options. Both transfers display immaculate, pristine images. Even when the production design populates the frame with pink typewriters or orange Day-Glo office chairs, colors are natural looking and accurate, never oversaturated. Details come across sharp and clear, with only a minimum of grain present during the soft-focus (i.e. warm and fuzzy) moments. Direct comparison between both formats yields no vast differences in screen information. The widescreen version exhibits more room on the sides, but other than sneaking in more mutton-chop sideburns and feather boas, the framing is practically identical. The Dolby Digital 5.1 soundtrack punches up Burt Bacharach's retro music score and houses approximately a few discrete Surround effects. Otherwise, audio is strictly dialogue-driven. Less schmaltz and more sharp-tongued barbs (a la *All About Eve*) might have provided some needed juice. In all, the film is even more shallow than a Susann novel and not nearly as fun. —EP
Movie: 🎞🎞 ***DVD:*** 🎞🎞🎞

Universal Studios Home Video (Cat #207 08, UPC #2519207082). Widescreen (1.85:1) anamorphic; full frame. Dolby Digital 5.1. $26.98. Keepcase. *LANG:* English. *SUB:* French. *CAP:* English. *FEATURES:* 18 chapter links • Theatrical trailer • Filmographies • Production notes • Universal weblink.

2000 (R) 96m/C Bette Midler, Nathan Lane, Stockard Channing, David Hyde Pierce, John Cleese, John Larroquette, Amanda Peet; *D:* Andrew Bergman; *W:* Paul Rudnick; *C:* Karl Walter Lindenlaub; *M:* Burt Bacharach.

It Could Happen to You

NYC cop Charlie Lang (Cage) doesn't have any change to leave coffee shop waitress Yvonne (Fonda) a tip, so he promises to split his lottery ticket with her. When he nets $4 million, he makes good on the promise, much to the chagrin of his upwardly mobile wife (Perez). Capra-corn for the X-crowd is pleasant dinnertime diversion as Cage and Perez shine as henpecked nice guy and the wife committed to making him miserable. Don't look for the diner on your next trip to NYC; it was specially built in TriBeCa and dismantled after the shoot. The warm colors of this romantic comedy are presented very nicely on the DVD. Many sequences in the film have a dreamy soft-focus look to them, and though sometimes that kind of hazy look can wreak havoc during DVD authoring, it's never a problem on this disc. Though used only for ambience, the Surround tracks add nice dimension to the score, which is already enhanced by the excellent separation of the front tracks. Overall, a good no-frills DVD. —*JO* *AKA:* Cop Tips Waitress $2 Million.

Movie: ♪♪½ *DVD:* ♪♪♪
Columbia Tristar Home Video (Cat #728 19, UPC #043396728196). Widescreen (1.85:1) anamorphic. Dolby Digital 5.1; Dolby Surround. $27.95. Keepcase. *LANG:* English; Spanish; French. *SUB:* English; Spanish; French. *CAP:* English. *FEATURES:* 28 chapter links • Theatrical trailer.

1994 (PG) 101m/C Bridget Fonda, Nicolas Cage, Rosie Perez, Red Buttons, Isaac Hayes, Seymour Cassel, Stanley Tucci, J.E. Freeman, Richard Jenkins, Ann Dowd, Wendell Pierce, Angela Pietropinto; *D:* Andrew Bergman; *W:* Andrew Bergman, Jane Anderson; *C:* Caleb Deschanel; *M:* Carter Burwell.

Italian Movie

Pizza joint owner Leonardo (DellaFemina) decides to become a male escort to pay off his gambling debts to Angelo (Gandolfini) and to support his large family. Things get complicated, but never as funny as they're supposed to be. As his wife, model Benedetti is incongruously gorgeous. Gandolfini's performance is a prototype for Tony Soprano. The rough-looking low-budget production is not a real improvement over VHS tape. —*MM*

Movie: ♪♪ *DVD:* ♪♪
Vanguard International Cinema, Inc. (UPC #658769006032). Full frame. $29.95. Keepcase. *LANG:* English. *FEATURES:* 12 chapter links.

1993 95m/C Michael DellaFemina, Rita Moreno, James Gandolfini, Caprice Benedetti; *D:* Roberto Monticello.

The Italians

This Discovery Channel documentary is essentially a promotional travelogue. It's a combination of artfully staged "real" footage and re-creations, all extremely complimentary and designed to persuade the viewer to visit Italy. Chapter titles tell the story: "Ferrari," "Favignana: Island of Life and Death," "Venice," "Italian Alps," "Pantelleria: Island of the Wind." Both photography and sound are superb. Beyond some aliasing in the grillwork of a vintage sports car and in fast pans, the image is strikingly clear, bright, and sharp. Surround sound is equally imaginative with thumping music and effects. —*MM*

Movie: ♪♪ *DVD:* ♪♪♪
A-PIX Entertainment Inc. (Cat #UPX72030, UPC #71102720302). Widescreen. Dolby Digital 5.1 Surround Stereo; DTS Surround; DD Surround Stereo. $19.98. Keepcase. *LANG:* English. *FEATURES:* 9 chapter links.

2000 104m/C *D:* William Livingston; *W:* Jeanne Rawlings Livingston; *C:* William Livingston; *M:* Frank Ferrucci; *Nar:* Linda Hunt.

It's Good to Be Alive

Please see review of *Great Baseball Movies.*

Movie: ♪♪½
1974 100m/C Ramon Bieri, Joe De Santis, Paul Winfield, Ruby Dee, Louis Gossett Jr.; *D:* Michael Landon; *M:* Michel Legrand.

It's Raining on Santiago

Helvio Soto's version of the coup that overthrew Chile's President Salvador Allende unapologetically takes the side of the socialists. Despite the box copy's claim that the film contains a "shocking revelation" of U.S. involvement, the participation of Henry Kissinger, the CIA, and the Nixon administration has been public knowledge for many years. That makes it no less shameful. The most useful comparison is to Costa-Gavras's *Z.* Soto employs a deliberately documentary approach that results in excessive grain and artifacts in exteriors. Interiors fare somewhat better, but polish is not what the filmmakers were aiming for. Burned in subtitles are easy to read. —*MM* *AKA:* Il Pleut sur Santiago.

Movie: ♪♪♪ *DVD:* ♪♪½
Image Entertainment (Cat #ID9081SIDVD, UPC #014381908121). Widescreen (1.66:1) letterboxed. Dolby Digital Mono. $24.99. Snapper. *LANG:* Spanish. *SUB:* English. *FEATURES:* 16 chapter links.

1974 113m/C *FR* Jean-Louis Trintignant, Bernard Fresson, Andre Dussollier, Bibi Andersson, Annie Giradot; *D:* Helvio Soto; *W:* Helvio Soto; *C:* Georges Barsky.

It's the Rage

Ensemble drama wears its anti-gun politics on its sleeve. In the opening scene, boorish Warren (Daniels) shoots a man in his living room. His wife (Allen) leaves him and goes to work for a reclusive billionaire (Sinise). Warren's lawyer (Braugher) is having problems with his gay lover (Schwimmer) because he's also attracted to a kleptomaniacal hooker (Paquin), who has a murderous brother (Ribisi). About-to-retire cop (Forster) watches them with bemused detachment. Some of the humorous moments meant to be light come across as silly; others are surreal. The DVD looks very good, but the 5.1 Surround enhancement makes everyone sound like James Earl Jones. Cheryl Wheeler's closing theme, "If It Were Up to Me," actually has more to say about gun violence than the film does. —*MM* *AKA:* All the Rage.

Movie: ♪♪♪ *DVD:* ♪♪½
Columbia Tristar Home Video (Cat #052 65, UPC #043396052659). Widescreen (1.85:1) letterboxed. Dolby Digital 5.1 Surround Stereo. $24.95. Keepcase. *LANG:* English. *SUB:* Spanish. *CAP:* English. *FEATURES:* 28 chapter links • Commentary: director James D. Stern • Cast and crew thumbnail bios • "Making of" featurette • Trailer.

1999 (R) 97m/C Jeff Daniels, Joan Allen, Andre Braugher, David Schwimmer, Anna Paquin, Giovanni Ribisi, Gary Sinise, Josh Brolin, Robert Forster, Bokeem Woodbine; *D:* James D. Stern; *W:* Keith Reddin; *C:* Alex Nepomniaschy; *M:* Mark Mothersbaugh.

Ivory Tower

Anthony Daytona (Van Horn) is a hotshot marketing exec in charge of launching a new computer product. But this new boss (Ironside) arrives and immediately Anthony's career, the project, and the company itself are in jeopardy. The image is sharp at times, a bit blurry and soft at others. The colors appear true for the most part, although there are some scenes which have a slightly washed-out look to them. The film's original aspect ratio is unknown, but some scenes do appear to be somewhat "squeezed." Surround mix offers clear and audible dialogue, along with some musical cues and ambient sound from the rear speakers. —*MM/ML*

Movie: ♪♪ *DVD:* ♪♪
Vanguard International Cinema, Inc. (Cat #VF0112, UPC #658769011234). Full frame. Dolby Digital Surround. $29.95. Keepcase. *LANG:* English.

1997 107m/C Patrick Van Horn, James Wilder, Kari Wuhrer, Michael Ironside, Donna Pescow, Keith Coogan, Ian Buchanan; *D:* Darin Ferriola; *W:* Darin Ferriola; *C:* Maida Sussman.

Jack & the Beanstalk

See review for *Africa Screams / Jack and the Beanstalk*.
Movie: 🐾🐾
1952 78m/C Bud Abbott, Lou Costello, Buddy Baer, Dorothy Ford, Barbara Brown, William Farnum; *D:* Jean Yarbrough; *W:* Nathaniel Curtis; *C:* George Robinson; *M:* Heinz Roemheld.

The Jack Bull

Cusack's father adapted a 19th-century German novel, *Michael Kohlhaas*, by Heinrich Von Kleist, into an American western set in Wyoming. Myrl Redding (Cusack) is a peaceful horse trader who demands justice when Ballard (Jones), a wealthy landowner, beats two of Redding's horses and his Indian caretaker. Since Ballard has the local law in his pocket, Redding gets no satisfaction and turns to vigilante tactics. The Surround mix unnaturally overemphasizes commonplace sounds so that a boot dropping on a wooden floor sounds like the prelude to an earthquake. With a muted color scheme, disc is only a scant improvement over tape. —*MM*
Movie: 🐾🐾½ *DVD:* 🐾🐾½
HBO Home Video (Cat #91574). Full frame. Dolby Digital Surround Stereo; Mono. $24.98. Snapper. *LANG:* English; Spanish. *SUB:* French; Spanish. *CAP:* English. *FEATURES:* Cast and crew thumbnail bios ▪ "Making of" featurette ▪ 19 chapter links ▪ Trailer.
1999 (R) 120m/C John Cusack, L.Q. (Justus E. McQueen) Jones, John Goodman, Rodney A. Grant, Miranda Otto, John C. McGinley, John Savage, Jay O. Sanders, Scott Wilson, Drake Bell, Glenn Morshower, Ken Pogue; *D:* John Badham; *W:* Dick Cusack; *C:* Gale Tattersall; *M:* Lennie Niehaus.

Jack Frost 2: Revenge of the Mutant Killer Snowman

If you thought the killer snowman possessed by the spirit of a serial killer had perished in the first film, then you don't know Jack about the direct-to-video business. Where there's a will, there's a franchise. This crudely—albeit resourcefully—made sequel resurrects the screen's most improbable boogie man, who heads for a tropical resort (not the most ideal haunting grounds for a snowman) to settle the score with Sheriff Sam who is on his second honeymoon. Along the way, Jack Frost dispenses with hapless castaways and the usual assortment of bikini-clad bimbos, all expendable. With the introduction of Jack's progeny, the horror literally snowballs. An uneven blend of clumsily staged slasher and amateurishly acted slapstick sequences. Writer/director Michael Cooney supplies a breezy and entertaining commentary in which he assures us, "It's all right to laugh at the movie." I think he meant "with" the movie. The film was shot on high-definition video. The transfer is

clean, but the image is soft. The sound is adequate. —*DL*
Movie: 🐾🐾 *DVD:* 🐾🐾½
A-PIX Entertainment Inc. (Cat #APX27037, UPC #8372270373). Widescreen anamorphic. Dolby 5.1 Surround Sound. $19.98. Keepcase. *LANG:* English. *SUB:* Spanish. *FEATURES:* Behind-the-scenes ▪ Director's interview ▪ Commentary: director ▪ Music video spoof ▪ Trailers ▪ 14 chapter links.
2000 (R) 91m/C Christopher Allport, David Allan Brooks, Chip Heller, Eileen Seeley, Adrienne Barbeau; *D:* Michael Cooney; *W:* Michael Cooney.

The Jackie Robinson Story

The famous baseball player plays himself in telling the story of his rise through UCLA athletics to become the first black player in the major league. Though the script seems naïve at key moments, it is a product of its time and attempts to deal honestly with racism. This disc looks much better than any of the public domain versions that are distributed by the bargain labels. A few faint signs of wear are visible in a crisp black-and-white image. —*MM*
Movie: 🐾🐾½ *DVD:* 🐾🐾½
MGM Home Entertainment (Cat #100185, UPC #027616858955). Full frame. Dolby Digital Mono. $24.99. Keepcase. *LANG:* English. *SUB:* French; Spanish. *CAP:* English. *FEATURES:* 16 chapter links.
1950 76m/B Jackie Robinson, Ruby Dee, Minor Watson, Louise Beavers, Richard Lane, Harry Shannon, Joel Fluellen, Ben Lessy; *D:* Alfred E. Green; *W:* Arthur Mann, Lawrence Taylor; *C:* Ernest Laszlo; *M:* David Chudnow.

Jackson County Jail

While driving across country, ad woman Dinah (Mimieux) is robbed, imprisoned, and raped by a deputy. She kills him and flees with another prisoner (Jones) in one of the all-time great drive-in adventures. Curiously, the audio on the disc sounds like it might have come straight from one of those speakers you hang on the window. It's hissy and hard to understand, and so it complements the grainy image. Both come from the original elements and are appropriate. —*MM*
Movie: 🐾🐾🐾 *DVD:* 🐾🐾½
New Concorde (Cat #NH20156D, UPC #736991415690). Full frame. Stereo. $19.98. Keepcase. *LANG:* English. *FEATURES:* 24 chapter links ▪ Leonard Maltin—Roger Corman interview ▪ Thumbnail bios ▪ Trailers.
1976 (R) 84m/C Yvette Mimieux, Tommy Lee Jones, Robert Carradine, Severn Darden, Howard Hesseman, Mary Woronov, Ed Marshall, Cliff Emmich, Betty Thomas; *D:* Michael Miller; *W:* Donald Stewart; *C:* Bruce Logan; *M:* Loren Newkirk.

The Jagged Edge

The beautiful wife of newspaper editor Jack Forester (Bridges) is killed. The police

finger Jack for the murder. Attorney Teddy Barnes (Close) is brought in to defend him and falls in love. Taut thriller will keep you guessing. The difference in image quality between the full-frame and widescreen transfers on this double-sided disc is quite striking, most likely because the full-frame presentation stems from an older source, while the anamorphic widescreen presentation comes from a new high-resolution transfer. The full-frame version exhibits visible signs of noise and grain; colors are muted, if not pale; and the level of detail in the image is average at best. However, the widescreen is a highly detailed transfer that is free of grain and shows rather good color reproduction and well-defined edges. Fleshtones are natural and although some slight signs of edge-enhancement are evident, the transfer has a beautifully natural look. —*GH/MM*
Movie: 🐾🐾½ *DVD:* 🐾🐾½
Columbia Tristar Home Video (Cat #5919). Widescreen (1.85:1) anamorphic; full frame. Dolby Digital Stereo. $24.95. Keepcase. *LANG:* English. *SUB:* Spanish; Portuguese; Chinese; Korean; Thai. *FEATURES:* Trailers ▪ Talent files ▪ Production notes.
1985 (R) 108m/C Jeff Bridges, Glenn Close, Robert Loggia, Peter Coyote, John Dehner, Leigh Taylor-Young, Lance Henriksen, James Karen, Karen Austin, Michael Dorn, Guy Boyd, Marshall Colt, Louis Giambalvo; *D:* Richard Marquand; *W:* Joe Eszterhas; *C:* Matthew F. Leonetti; *M:* John Barry. *AWARDS:* NOM: Oscars '85: Support. Actor (Loggia).

Jake Speed

Alleged parody of action films is pretty tame stuff. Paperback hero Jake Speed (producer Crawford) is hired by an American family to find the teenaged daughter who has been kidnapped by white slavers. With his sidekick Remo (Christopher) kicking him in the side, Jake is off to the rescue. There's not much to say about a so-so image that has never looked very good on theatre screens or on tape. Sound is fine. —*MM*
Movie: 🐾½ *DVD:* 🐾½
Anchor Bay (Cat #DV11374, UPC #013131137491). Widescreen (1.85:1) anamorphic. Dolby Digital Stereo. $24.99. Keepcase. *LANG:* English. *FEATURES:* 30 chapter links ▪ Trailers.
1986 (PG) 93m/C Wayne Crawford, John Hurt, Karen Kopins, Dennis Christopher; *D:* Andrew Lane; *W:* Wayne Crawford; *C:* Bryan Loftus; *M:* Mark Snow.

James and the Giant Peach

This feature is one of the great overlooked kid's films of all time. An all-star cast and a brilliant adaptation of Roald Dahl's book of the same name make this a must-own for any children's collection. Fans of the book may bristle at the differences between the film and the novel, but each stands on its own. Young James (voice of

Terry) escapes the clutches of his evil guardians, Aunt Spike (Lumley) and Aunt Sponge (Margolyes) when an Old Man (Postlethwaite) gives him a bag of magic crocodile tongues. James spills the bag and the magic tongues cause a peach to grow to enormous proportions. Inside the peach reside giant insects; the Grasshopper (Callow), the Spider (Sarandon), the Centipede (Dreyfuss), the Glowworm (Margolyes, again), and the Earthworm (Thewlis) are all happy to meet James. James and his insect pals travel across the Atlantic, having many adventures and learning many lessons along the way (lessons that are generally rarely contained within children's films). The crispness of the DVD image coupled with stop animation is amazing. Check out the slow-motion feature on your player with this movie. You'll see the staggering smoothness of the motion. Putting that together with camera movement requires a meticulous director. Henry Selick, the expert director of *The Nightmare before Christmas,* uses that same animation technique for the journey part of the film. Randy Newman's songs and music are superb. Karey Kirkpatrick, Jonathan Roberts, and Steven Bloom wrote the screenplay, providing tension, wit, and characters with depth. Adults will enjoy it as much as kids will. Is there a downside? Well, it may be a bit scary for the young ones, but everyone lives and only the Aunts come out the worse for wear. But they deserve it! —*JAS*
Movie: 🐾🐾🐾🐾 **DVD:** 🐾🐾🐾🐾
Buena Vista Home Entertainment (Cat #20 100, UPC #717951009388). Widescreen (1.66:1) anamorphic. Dolby Digital 5.1 Surround Sound. $29.99. Keepcase. *LANG:* Spanish; French; English. *SUB:* Spanish. *CAP:* English. *FEATURES:* 20 chapter links ➠ Still frame gallery of concept art and puppet designs ➠ "Good News" music video performed by Randy Newman ➠ Theatrical trailer.
1996 (PG) 80m/C D: Henry Selick; **C:** Pete Kozachik, Hiro Narita; **M:** Randy Newman; **V:** Paul Terry, Pete Postlethwaite, Joanna Lumley, Miriam Margolyes, Richard Dreyfuss, Susan Sarandon, David Thewlis, Simon Callow, Jane Leeves. *AWARDS: NOM:* Oscars '96: Orig. Score.

James Dean: Live Fast, Die Young

Unnecessary made-for-TV biopic casts jut-jawed Casper Van Dien as the famous '50s star whose brief career, flamboyant life, and death on the brink of superstardom made him an instant and enduring legend. In his final screen role, Robert Mitchum plays George Stevens, director of *Giant.* This version contains a few moments of nudity that are too racy for broadcast television, but the slender production values remain unchanged. DVD image and sound are little better than VHS tape. —*MM AKA:* James Dean: Race with Destiny.
Movie: 🐾🐾 **DVD:** 🐾🐾

York Entertainment (Cat #YPD-1003, UPC #750723100326). Full frame. Dolby Digital 5.1 Surround Stereo. $24.99. Keepcase. *LANG:* English. *SUB:* Spanish. *FEATURES:* 25 chapter links ➠ Cast filmographies ➠ Trailer.
1997 105m/C Casper Van Dien, Robert Mitchum, Mike Connors, Carrie Mitchum, Diane Ladd, Connie Stevens, Monique Parent, Casey Kasem, Joseph Campanella; **D:** Marti Rustam; **W:** Dan Sefton; **C:** Gary Graver, Irv Goodnoff.

Jane & the Lost City

Silly British farce is based on a comic strip character who made her debut in the 1930s and is famous for not keeping her clothes on. (In this "PG"-rated incarnation, she's not exactly naughty.) During World War II, Jane (Hughes) stumbles across ancient cities, diamonds, treasures, Nazis, and a stalwart hero (Jones). The low-budget campiness has such a deliberately soft focus that it looks as if much of the film was shot through gauze. Very light signs of wear are evident. —*MM*
Movie: 🐾🐾 **DVD:** 🐾🐾½
Anchor Bay (Cat #DV11375, UPC #013131 137590). Widescreen (1.66:1) anamorphic. Dolby Digital Surround Stereo. $24.99. Keepcase. *LANG:* English. *FEATURES:* 30 chapter links ➠ Trailer.
1987 (PG) 94m/C *GB* Kristen Hughes, Maud Adams, Sam Jones; **D:** Terry Marcel; **W:** Mervyn Haisman; **C:** Paul Beeson; **M:** Harry Robertson.

Jason and the Argonauts

Elaborate retelling of the Greek myth of Jason and his quest for the golden fleece. Young Prince Jason (London) has had his heritage usurped by his evil Uncle Pelias (Hopper in braids), who has killed Jason's father and taken his throne. To reclaim it, Jason must retrieve the magical golden fleece from distant Colchis and bring it to Pelias. So Jason assembles the usual motley crew of would-be heroes and sets sail on the Argos for uncharted waters and numerous adventures. The overall look of the DVD is very good, although there are many scenes where the image is a bit soft, mostly during the effects sequences. Colors are somewhat paler than other fantasy flicks, but the original showing on TV had the same look. There is never a hint of artifacts, even during the action scenes featuring fast, non-stop movement. This lively fantasy adventure could have been much enhanced by a more elaborate sound mix. As it is, the Dolby Surround hardly ever makes use of the rear track and not even the front speakers demonstrate much in the way of separation effects. Included on the disc is a short "making of" featurette that seems obviously made to promote rather inform. —*JO*
Movie: 🐾🐾🐾 **DVD:** 🐾🐾½
Artisan Entertainment (Cat #10638, UPC #707729106388). Full frame. Dolby Surround. $19.98. Keepcase. *LANG:* English.

CAP: English. *FEATURES:* 35 chapter links ➠ Talent files ➠ "Making of" featurette.
2000 179m/C Jason London, Dennis Hopper, Angus Macfadyen, Olivia Williams, Brian Thompson, Adrian Lester, Derek Jacobi, Jolene Blalock, Frank Langella, Natasha Henstridge, Ciaran Hinds, Kieran O'Brien, Charles Cartmell; **D:** Nick Willing; **W:** Matthew Faulk, Mark Skeet; **C:** Sergei Kozlov; **M:** Simon Boswell.

Jaws [CE]

Technical problems turned what might have been nothing more than another monster movie into one of the best. The tales about the difficulties with "Bruce," the mechanical shark, are the stuff of Hollywood legend. When Bruce didn't work, young director Spielberg was forced to shoot around it and to suggest what he couldn't show. In the process, every scene set on or near the ocean became doubly suspenseful. Even in bright daylight, the surface of the water is hiding a creature that comes straight from our collective nightmares. The two main settings—the island village of Amity and the fishing boat—are well realized. The script wisely jettisons the needless subplots from Peter Benchley's novel and focuses on the three protagonists—the sheriff (Scheider), the scientist (Dreyfuss), and the salt (Shaw)—as they hunt for the shark. If the telling of the story is a bit stilted and formal, it was good enough to keep thousands of people out of the ocean during the summer of '75. John Williams's ominous here-comes-the-shark theme and soaring score add immeasurably. The DVD image is about as sharp as anyone could expect of a mid-'70s movie. It's still grainy in some exteriors and the mechanical shark is even more blatantly obvious than it's been before. The 5.1 Surround mix is an improvement over the original. —*MM*
Movie: 🐾🐾🐾🐾 **DVD:** 🐾🐾🐾
Universal Studios Home Video (Cat #20912, UPC #025192091223). Widescreen (2.35:1) letterboxed. Dolby Digital 5.1 Surround Stereo. $26.99. Keepcase. *LANG:* English. *SUB:* French. *CAP:* English. *FEATURES:* 20 chapter links ➠ "Making of" featurette ➠ Deleted scenes and outtakes ➠ Shark information ➠ Production photos ➠ Trivia game.
1975 (PG) 124m/C Roy Scheider, Robert Shaw, Richard Dreyfuss, Lorraine Gary, Murray Hamilton, Carl Gottlieb, Peter Benchley; **D:** Steven Spielberg; **W:** Carl Gottlieb, Peter Benchley; **C:** Bill Butler; **M:** John Williams. *AWARDS:* Oscars '75: Film Editing, Sound, Orig. Score; AFI '98: Top 100; Golden Globes '76: Score; *NOM:* Oscars '75: Picture.

Jaws: The Revenge

Third sequel finds Mrs. Brody (Gary) pursued the world over by a seemingly personally motivated Great White. The home video version includes footage not seen in the theatrical release. Another altogether inferior entry in the downwardly spiraling

series. Stereo soundtrack does nice things with all the watery effects, but image suffers from artifacts on the wide stretches of ocean. —*MM*
Movie: 🎵 **DVD:** 🎵🎵
Goodtimes Entertainment (Cat #81030). Widescreen (1.85:1) letterboxed. Dolby Digital Stereo. $19.98. Snapper. *LANG:* English. *SUB:* French; Spanish. *CAP:* English. *FEATURES:* 18 chapter links.
1987 (PG-13) 87m/C Lorraine Gary, Lance Guest, Karen Young, Mario Van Peebles, Michael Caine, Judith Barsi, Lynn Whitfield; *D:* Joseph Sargent; *W:* Michael deGuzman; *C:* John McPherson; *M:* Michael Small.

Jazz on a Summer's Day
In 1958, still photographer Bert Stern turned to motion pictures with this documentary of the Newport, Rhode Island, Jazz Festival. It's a terrific work that was an obvious influence on the rock films of the following decade, *Monterey Pop* and *Woodstock*. Stern combines footage of the crowd and town—mostly shot with telephoto lenses—with the performers. The 5.1 Surround mix is not too active and it should not be. The music from Louis Armstrong, Monk, Chuck Berry, Mahalia Jackson, and others sounds just fine. (I should admit that I'm a fan of '50s and '60s jazz. Those who do not appreciate it won't be as taken with the film.) The image is almost unbelievably clear and blemish-free for a film this old. Chapter breaks and menus are not broken down in traditional numerical order, but by individual musicians and "reflections." The film is valuable if it's seen simply as a snapshot of wealthy mid-century America at play. Add in the terrific music and it's one of the very best. Highest recommendation. —*MM*
Movie: 🎵🎵🎵🎵 **DVD:** 🎵🎵🎵🎵
New Yorker Video (Cat #16500, UPC #717 119165048). Full frame. $29.95. Keepcase. *LANG:* English. *FEATURES:* Production notes • Liner interview with Stern and Ronald Ramsland • 30-minute short film, "A Summer's Day with Bert Stern."
1959 85m/C *D:* Bert Stern; *C:* Bert Stern, Courtney Hafela, Ray Phealan. *AWARDS:* Natl. Film Reg. '99.

Jean de Florette
A single spring in drought-ridden Provence, France, is blocked by two scheming countrymen (Montand and Auteuil). They await the imminent failure of the farm nearby, inherited by a city-born hunchback (Depardieu), whose chances for survival fade without water for his crops. The devastating story is undermined, to a degree, by a less-than-perfect DVD. The film shares the same problems that plague its sequel, *Manon of the Spring*. Artifacts are heavy in virtually all brightly lit exteriors. The problem is most apparent in shots of dirt fields, roofs, any large solid-colored field. Sound is fine. —*MM*
Movie: 🎵🎵🎵½ **DVD:** 🎵½

MGM Home Entertainment (Cat #10014 78, UPC #027616857989). Widescreen (2.35:1) letterboxed. Dolby Digital Surround Stereo. $19.95. Keepcase. *LANG:* French. *SUB:* English; French; Spanish. *FEATURES:* 16 chapter links • Trailer.
1987 (PG) 122m/C *FR* Gerard Depardieu, Yves Montand, Daniel Auteuil, Elisabeth Depardieu, Ernestine Mazurowna, Margarita Lozano, Armand Meffre; *D:* Claude Berri; *W:* Claude Berri, Gerard Brach; *C:* Bruno Nuytten; *M:* Jean-Claude Petit. *AWARDS:* British Acad. '87: Adapt. Screenplay, Film, Support. Actor (Auteuil); Cesar '87: Actor (Auteuil), Support. Actress (Beart).

Jerome
Wade Hampton (Pillsbury) works in a machine shop and dreams of visiting artsy little Jerome, Arizona. One day, he punches out his time card before lunch and leaves. On the road he meets Jane (Malick), who seems to have the freedom he is seeking. This is a slowly paced road movie. It works through quirky characters, not bold action, and so it is not to all tastes. DVD image is acceptable; the grain appears to come from the original. Stereo sound is employed nicely. —*MM*
Movie: 🎵🎵🎵 **DVD:** 🎵🎵½
Vanguard International Cinema, Inc. (UPC #658769012231). Widescreen (1.66:1) letterboxed. Stereo. $29.95. Keepcase. *LANG:* English. *FEATURES:* 12 chapter links • Trailer.
1998 91m/C Wendie Malick, Drew Pillsbury, Scott McKenna, Beth Kennedy, James Keeley; *D:* Thomas Johnston, David Elton, Eric Tignini; *W:* Thomas Johnston, David Elton, Eric Tignini; *C:* Gina DeGirolamo.

Jerry and Tom
Offbeat tale of wise, fatherly Tom (Mantegna) who trains his dopey young partner, Jerry (Rockwell) in the ways of mob assassinations. Spanning 10 years, the film is essentially a series of long vignettes which focus on the two performing hits or cleaning up after them. Fine acting by all involved with extra marks given to Durning and Danson who bring their small roles to memorable life. Likable, if somewhat static (at times it almost seems like a filmed play) black comedy improves with repeated viewings. Worth a look, especially to admirers of Mamet or Tarantino, or those who admire dialogue over action. Look quick for director/character actor Rubinek in a small role late in the film. The DVD (lamely marketed as a *Sopranos* rip-off, but actually pre-dating it) is a near-flawless, handsome transfer of the film with well-utilized, involving Surround effects. Recommended. —*DG*
Movie: 🎵🎵🎵 **DVD:** 🎵🎵🎵🎵
Miramax Pictures Home Video (Cat #185 40, UPC #717954100554). Widescreen (1.85:1) anamorphic. Dolby Surround 5.1; Dolby Surround 2.0. $29.99. Keepcase. *LANG:* English; Spanish. *CAP:* English. *FEATURES:* 15 chapter links • Insert card with chapter listing.

1998 (R) 97m/C Joe Mantegna, Sam Rockwell, Maury Chaykin, Charles Durning, Peter Riegert, William H. Macy, Ted Danson; *D:* Saul Rubinek; *W:* Rick Cleveland; *C:* Paul Sarossy; *M:* David Buchbinder.

Jesus
TV miniseries makes an admirable transition to disc. This version of the biblical stories is something of a throwback to the epics of the '50s and '60s. Jeremy Sisto makes a valiant attempt to turn the title role into a believably real human character, but the attempt comes with a whiff of sanctity that is difficult for skeptics to swallow. The DVD image is exceptionally strong, though in the later chapters, artifacts show up in bright exteriors. Sound is not quite as impressive as the picture. Perhaps the most curious extra is a letter from the Pope. How many discs can boast that? —*MM*
Movie: 🎵🎵½ **DVD:** 🎵🎵🎵
Trimark Home Video (Cat #7386D, UPC #031398738626). Full frame. Dolby Digital Stereo. $29.99. Keepcase. *LANG:* English. *SUB:* English; French; Spanish. *FEATURES:* 36 chapter links • Soundtrack interviews • Letter from the Pope • Music video.
2000 174m/C Jeremy Sisto, Jacqueline Bisset, Armin Mueller-Stahl, Debra Messing, Gary Oldman, Jeroen Krabbe, David O'Hara, G.W. Bailey, Thomas Lockyer, Luca Zingaretti, Stefania Rocca, Claudio Amendola; *D:* Roger Young; *W:* Suzette Couture; *C:* Raffaele Mertes; *M:* Patrick Williams.

Jesus Christ Superstar
This new version updates the Tim Rice–Andrew Lloyd Webber rock opera for the MTV generation. The musical numbers have a rock video look and feel. The production is based on a stage version and so it doesn't feel or look like a real film. (Comparisons to the similar *Joseph and the Technicolor Dreamcoat* DVD are not out of place, though this one is more ambitious.) The carefully crafted image looks very good. I could see no glaring problems with the transfer. The 5.1 mix does wonders for the familiar music. —*MM*
Movie: 🎵🎵½ **DVD:** 🎵🎵½
Universal Studios Home Video (Cat #211 56, UPC #025192115622). Widescreen (1.78:1) anamorphic. Dolby Digital 5.1 Surround Stereo. $29.98. Keepcase. *LANG:* English. *SUB:* French. *CAP:* English. *FEATURES:* "Making of" featurette • Trailer • Production notes • Talent files • 23 chapter links.
2000 112m/C Glenn Carter, Jerome Pradon, Renee Castle, Rik Mayall; *D:* Nick Morris, Gale Edwards; *W:* Tim Rice, Andrew Lloyd Webber; *C:* Nicholas D. Knowland, Andrew Van Laast; *M:* Simon Lee, Tim Rice, Andrew Lloyd Webber.

Jesus' Son
A marvelously told tale revolves around a young man in the '70s. Full of magical real-

ism and drugs, he journeys toward a better understanding of himself and the world around him with all the grace of a wounded gazelle. Narrated by the lead character named FH (Crudup), which are the initials of an unmentionable nickname given him by an angry boyfriend who finds him necking with his girlfriend (Morton), the story meanders purposely towards its goal much as FH meanders towards his own salvation. The title begs the question of FH's place in the world as a son of Christ, but also hints at how lost a true son of such a successful father might be. Crudup and Morton are heartbreaking as a couple who love each other more than life, but also love drugs more than each other. As FH, Crudup is a haze of befuddlement and longing as he goes from one misadventure to another in search of the intangible notion of happiness. The amazing acting and script keep the film from being another drug-addict-from-the-gutter-to-grace story. There are fine drop-in performances by the likes of Holly Hunter, Jack Black, and Denis Leary, but they never distract from the overall power of the film to stand on its own. The cinematography is beautiful and the wide landscapes are captured well on the DVD. Sound quality is also good. —CA
Movie: 🐾🐾🐾½ *DVD:* 🐾🐾🐾
Universal Studios Home Video (Cat #21103, UPC #025192110320). Widescreen (2.35:1) anamorphic. Dolby Digital Surround. $24.98. Keepcase. *LANG:* English. *CAP:* English. *FEATURES:* 18 chapter links ☛ Theatrical trailer.
1999 (R) 109m/C Billy Crudup, Samantha Morton, Denis Leary, Holly Hunter, Dennis Hopper, Jack Black, Will Patton, Greg Germann; *D:* Alison Maclean; *W:* Elizabeth Cuthrell, David Urrutia, Oren Moverman; *C:* Adam Kimmel; *M:* Joe Henry. *AWARDS: NOM:* Ind. Spirit '01: Actor (Crudup).

Jet Li's The Enforcer [Buena Vista]

Kung Wei (Jet Li) is an undercover cop who'd rather spend time with his young son, a budding martial artist. Also involved are his ailing wife and a sympathetic fellow officer (Anita Mui). Action scenes are mixed with more serious moments. This dubbed version of the film improves considerably over the previously released Tai Seng disc. Image and sound range between good and very good. —MM *AKA:* The Enforcer; My Father Is a Hero; Letter to Daddy; Gei Ba Ba de Xin.
Movie: 🐾🐾½ *DVD:* 🐾🐾🐾
Buena Vista Home Entertainment (Cat #18534, UPC #717951005519). Widescreen (1.85:1) anamorphic. Dolby Digital 5.1 Surround Stereo. $24.99. Keepcase. *LANG:* English. *CAP:* English. *FEATURES:* 22 chapter links ☛ Trailers.
1995 100m/C *HK* Jet Li, Anita Mui, Damian Lau, Tse Miu, Rongguang Yu, Ngai Sing; *D:* Corey Yuen.

Jew-boy Levi

When Levi, the Jewish cattle dealer, makes his annual trip to a remote farming village hoping to conduct his business and win the hand of farmer Horger's lovely daughter, Lisbeth, he finds that Nazism has polluted the town. Based on the stage play by Thomas Strittmatter. The disc features an above-average video transfer that boasts bright, vibrant colors, particularly in the numerous scenes set amidst nature. Unfortunately, blacks and darker colors do lose definition and are quite bland in the interiors. The audio transfer features crisp, easy-to-understand dialogue (which can sometimes be forgotten with discs of foreign film). —MJT *AKA:* Viehjud Levi.
Movie: 🐾🐾🐾 *DVD:* 🐾🐾🐾
Image Entertainment (Cat #ID9603SIDVD, UPC #014381960327). Widescreen (1.85:1) letterboxed. Dolby Digital Surround. $24.99. Snapper. *LANG:* German. *SUB:* English. *FEATURES:* 16 chapter links.
1998 90m/C *GE SI AT* Bruno Cathomas, Caroline Eber, Ulrich Noethen, Martina Gedeck, Bernd Michael Lade, Georg Olschewski, Eva Mattes; *D:* Didi Danquart; *W:* Didi Danquart, Martina Docker; *C:* Johann Feindt.

Joan the Woman

Cecil B. DeMille's epic has been largely forgotten. As Robert S. Birchard explains in his liner notes, the film was not a commercial success in its theatrical release, but it is not without superior moments. In telling the story of Joan of Arc (Farrar), DeMille and his assistants staged some spectacular battle scenes that are comparable to Griffith's work in *Birth of a Nation*. Today, the film's value is almost entirely historical, and educational for students of the silent era. It's long with many dated conventions, and it is difficult to listen to the ponderous organ score for more than two hours. DVD does an excellent job of re-creating the black-and-white and tinted images—particularly the "Handschiegl" color process used in the final flames. The expected registration and wear problems are evident, but for practical purposes, the whole film is in very good shape. —MM
Movie: 🐾🐾🐾 *DVD:* 🐾🐾½
Image Entertainment (Cat #ID0509DSDVD, UPC #014381050929). Full frame. Dolby Digital Stereo. $24.99. Snapper. *LANG:* Silent. *SUB:* English intertitles. *FEATURES:* 16 chapter links ☛ Liner notes by Robert S. Birchard.
1916 137m/B Geraldine Farrar, Wallace Reid, Raymond Hatton, Hobart Bosworth; *D:* Cecil B. DeMille; *W:* Jeanie Macpherson; *C:* Alvin Wyckoff; *M:* William Furst.

Joe Gould's Secret

New Yorker magazine writer Joe Mitchell's (Tucci) articles are about the interesting people he meets throughout the city. Mitchell becomes aware of an eccentric, Harvard-educated homeless vagabond named Joe Gould (Holm), who has been writing a book for the last several years called the *Oral History of Our Time*. The legendary book is supposedly three times longer than the Bible and is essentially a catalogue of dialogue exchanges heard throughout everyday life, which Gould has written down. Fascinated by the tale, Mitchell tracks Gould down and quickly becomes his friend and biographer, composing feature articles about him while trying to get the *Oral History* reclaimed from its secret location and published. Based on a true story, this fairly somber film captures the feeling of 1940s bohemian New York vividly and believably. The strong cast brings the story to life, but the film (like Joe Gould) loses momentum in the second half and seldom penetrates below the surface of the two lead characters. The sumptuous disc conveys the warm, gray tones of the period with sharpness and clarity. There is some occasional grain in some of the darker scenes, but it's probably an aspect of the low-light photography. The sound is clean but average. —DG
Movie: 🐾🐾🐾 *DVD:* 🐾🐾🐾½
USA Home Entertainment (Cat #96306013 22, UPC #696306013228). Widescreen (1.85:1) anamorphic. Dolby 5.1 Surround Stereo; Dolby Surround. $24.95. Keepcase. *LANG:* English. *SUB:* English. *CAP:* English. *FEATURES:* Featurette ☛ Theatrical trailer ☛ Cast and director bios ☛ 21 chapter links ☛ Color booklet with notes.
2000 (R) 108m/C Stanley Tucci, Ian Holm, Hope Davis, Patricia Clarkson, Steve Martin, Susan Sarandon, Celia Weston, Allan Corduner, Alice Drummond, Julie Halston, Hallee Hirsh, Ben Jones, John Tormey, David Wohl, Patrick Tovatt, Sarah Hyland; *D:* Stanley Tucci; *W:* Howard A. Rodman, Stanley Tucci; *C:* Maryse Alberti; *M:* Evan Lurie.

The Joe Louis Story

Please see review of *Great Boxing Movies*.
Movie: 🐾🐾
1953 88m/B Coley Wallace, Paul Stewart, Hilda Simms, Albert "Poppy" Popwell; *D:* Robert Gordon; *W:* Robert Sylvester; *C:* Joseph Brun; *M:* George Bassman.

Johnny B.

Johnny B (editor/producer/director Brooks) is a self-centered loser on the streets of Chicago (which, with the occasional palm tree, looks suspiciously like the streets of L.A.). A combination of family pressures and his discovery of corruption in local government turns him around. Unfortunately, the exceptionally low budget undercuts many of Brooks's angry efforts. On DVD, the film is so grainy and riddled with artifacts that it's difficult to appreciate. Sound is on a par with VHS tape. —MM
Movie: 🐾🐾½ *DVD:* 🐾½
MTI Home Video (Cat #BE50037DVD, UPC #619935403734). Full frame. $24.95. Keepcase. *LANG:* English. *FEATURES:* 20 chapter links ☛ Trailers ☛ Talent files.
2000 (R) 98m/C Richard Brooks, Vonetta McGee, Richard Gant, Kent Masters King; *D:* Richard Brooks; *W:* Gwendolyn J. Lester; *C:* Pancho Gonzales.

Johnny 100 Pesos

Seventeen-year-old Johnny Garcia (Araiza) walks into a video store that's a front for an illegal currency exchange operation. He's the advance man for a group of crooks. But before they can rob the place, the cops show up and a hostage situation ensues. Then the TV cameras appear and the whole thing turns into a mediastorm while the Chilean authorities try to take control. Director Graef-Marino makes some very good political points and he tells the fact-based story with dry humor. The full-frame DVD image is only a slight improvement (if any) over VHS tape. —MM **Movie:** 🎵🎵🎵½ **DVD:** 🎵🎵½
Winstar Home Entertainment (Cat #LFV5231, UPC #720917523125). Full frame. $24.98. Keepcase. *LANG:* Spanish. *SUB:* English. *FEATURES:* 8 chapter links • Production credits • Talent files • Weblinks. **1993 90m/C** Armando Araiza, Patricia Rivera, Willy Semler, Sergio Hernandez; *D:* Gustavo Graef-Marino; *W:* Gustavo Graef-Marino, Gerardo Caceres; *C:* Jose Luis Arredondo; *M:* Andres Pollak.

The Joint Is Jumpin'

Once-over-lightly documentary is aimed at young fans who have just discovered the joys of swing music and swing dancing. It's a production of the Canadian government and the Bravo cable channel so it sticks close to the mainstream, and is focused more on current practitioners— Big Bad Voodoo Daddy, Brian Setzer Orchestra—than the original creators— Duke, Count, Benny, and so many more. Sound is more important than image here and this one makes the most of some very good music, new and old. —MM **Movie:** 🎵🎵½ **DVD:** 🎵🎵½
Image Entertainment (Cat #ID9694CDDVD, UPC #014381969429). Full frame. Dolby Digital 5.1 Surround Stereo; Dolby Digital Stereo. $24.99. Snapper. *LANG:* English. *FEATURES:* 22 chapter links. **2000 94m/C** *D:* Mark Hall; *W:* Tanja Crouch; *C:* Jack Lawrence; *Nar:* Ian MacLean.

Joseph and the Amazing Technicolor Dreamcoat

This video premiere is something more than a filmed stage presentation of the Webber-Rice musical, but something less than a real movie. It begins with a school assembly hall where the narrator (Friedman) bursts into song and tells the biblical story of Joseph (Osmond). Then the scene shifts to soundstages. The catchy songs often seem to be on the verge of morphing into *Cats* or *Phantom of the Opera*. Overall, the production values are good and the DVD transfer is excellent. Though the box copy proclaims the transfer to be "widescreen," the 1.55:1 letterboxing is barely noticeable. Sound is excellent. —MM **Movie:** 🎵🎵½ **DVD:** 🎵🎵🎵
Universal Studios Home Video (Cat #207 14, UPC #025192071423). Widescreen (1.55:1) letterboxed. Dolby Digital 5.1 Surround Stereo; DTS Surround Stereo. $29.98. Keepcase. *LANG:* English. *SUB:* French. *CAP:* English. *FEATURES:* 23 chapter links • "Making of" featurette • Production notes and history • Talent files. **2000 78m/C** Donny Osmond, Richard Attenborough, Joan Collins, Maria Friedman; *D:* David Mallet, Steven Pimlott; *C:* Nicholas D. Knowland; *M:* Andrew Lloyd Webber, Tim Rice.

Joseph: King of Dreams

The creators of *Prince of Egypt* have made an incredibly ambitious and polished video premiere. The story of Joseph (voice of Affleck) takes liberties with the version in Genesis, but is faithful to the spirit of the story and would be seen as sacrilegious by only the most literal-minded. It's bright, colorful, and imaginative in all the right ways. The detail and craftsmanship of the animation are on a par with Disney's best theatrical work. True, the songs lack a certain catchiness, but that's a comparatively small flaw. Of course, image and sound are flawless. —MM **Movie:** 🎵🎵🎵 **DVD:** 🎵🎵🎵½
DreamWorks Home Entertainment (Cat #86452, UPC #667068645224). Widescreen (1.85:1) anamorphic. Dolby Digital 5.1 Surround Stereo. $26.99. Keepcase. *LANG:* English. *FEATURES:* 18 chapter links • Read-along version of story • 3 sing-along songs • Trivia game • Storyboard sequence with directors' commentary • Production notes • DVD-ROM features • Talent files • Trailer. **2000 75m/C** *D:* Rob LaDuca, Robert Ramirez; *W:* Eugenia Bostwick-Singer, Raymond Singer, Joe Stillman, Marshall Goldberg; *V:* Ben Affleck, Mark Hamill, Steven Weber, Judith Light, Jodi Benson, James Eckhouse, Maureen McGovern, Dan Castellaneta.

The Josephine Baker Story

Made-for-cable biopic tells the story of exotic entertainer/activist Josephine Baker (Whitfield), a black woman from St. Louis who found superstardom in pre-WWII Europe, but repeated racism and rejection in her home country. At times the treatment is clichéd and turns her eventful life into a standard rise-and-fall showbiz tale, but a great cast and lavish scope pull it through. Whitfield re-creates Baker's scandalous (and topless) routines, including the famous "banana dance." Carol Dennis dubs her singing. Image is a slight improvement over cablecast or tape. Sound is much better, particularly in the jazzy musical numbers. —MM **Movie:** 🎵🎵🎵½ **DVD:** 🎵🎵½
HBO Home Video (Cat #90571, UPC #026 359057120). Widescreen (1.66:1) letterboxed. Dolby Digital 5.1 Surround Stereo; Dolby Digital Surround; Mono. $14.98.
Snapper. *LANG:* English; French; Spanish. *CAP:* English. *FEATURES:* 16 chapter links. **1990 (R) 129m/C** Lynn Whitfield, Ruben Blades, David Dukes, Craig T. Nelson, Louis Gossett Jr., Kene Holliday, Vivian Bonnell; *D:* Brian Gibson; *M:* Ralph Burns.

Joy House

French director Rene Clement, perhaps best known for his early *Forbidden Games* and *Purple Noon*, or the big budget *Is Paris Burning?*, serves up a delicious game of cat (figuratively, if not literally) and mouse in this 1964 sleight of hand. Alain Delon, under a death sentence and on the run for seducing a gangster's moll, takes refuge in a church in the south of France. He is hired by the church's rich benefactor, Lola Albright and her young cousin, Jane Fonda, to be their live-in chauffeur. Little does he know, but his perfect hideout is more akin to a cage, where the "felines" toy with him before revealing their real motives for hiring him. Clever little film with nice acting turns and featuring Fonda as a seductress is often more style than substance. DVD arrives with both French and English language options, but no subtitles. Desired features, such as a commentary track or production bios, are nonexistent, but the black-and-white film transfer is from source material in reasonably good shape. —RJT **AKA:** The Love Cage; Les Felins. **Movie:** 🎵🎵½ **DVD:** 🎵🎵½
Image Entertainment (Cat #ID9230SIDVD, UPC #014381923025). Widescreen (2.35:1) anamorphic. Mono. $24.99. Snapper. *LANG:* French; English. *FEATURES:* 12 chapter links. **1964 98m/B** Jane Fonda, Alain Delon, Lola Albright; *D:* Rene Clement; *W:* Rene Clement; *C:* Henri Decae; *M:* Lalo Schifrin.

Juice

Four Harlem teens try to earn respect ("juice") in their neighborhood. Q (Epps), an aspiring DJ, is talked into a robbery by his friends, but everything takes a turn for the worse when one of them, Bishop (Shakur), gets a pistol. The gritty look and feel of the film comes naturally to cinematographer Dickerson in his directorial debut. DVD accurately re-creates the theatrical image as I remember it. Sound is much stronger. A director's commentary track might have been illuminating. —MM **Movie:** 🎵🎵🎵 **DVD:** 🎵🎵🎵
Paramount Home Video (Cat #32758, UPC #097363275848). Widescreen anamorphic. Dolby Digital 5.1 Surround Stereo; Dolby Digital Surround Stereo. $29.99. Keepcase. *LANG:* English. *SUB:* English. *FEATURES:* 11 chapter links. **1992 (R) 95m/C** Omar Epps, Jermaine "Huggy" Hopkins, Tupac Shakur, Khalil Kain, Cindy Herron, Vincent Laresca, Samuel L. Jackson; *D:* Ernest R. Dickerson; *W:* Gerard Brown, Ernest R. Dickerson; *C:* Larry Banks.

Julien Donkey-boy

Excruciatingly awful, repellent documentary-styled geek show follows a family of dysfunctional caricatures over several days. Julien, a mentally ill and highly annoying young man, mumbles and shouts incoherent nonsense as the film crawls from pointless scene to pointless scene. Extremely tedious with intentionally grainy, blurry headache-inducing images, it's one of the "Dogma 95" films, and should, I hope, ring the death-knell for that pretentious movement. Renowned director (and eccentric raconteur) Herzog's presence in the film is appreciated, but whoever convinced him to appear in this mess should be strung up. It's doubtful that many audience members would make it to the end of the film and frankly, most would probably prefer to scrub a bus station toilet than sit through this again. As for the disc, there's not much DVD can do for such a thoroughly miserable-looking video-originated film; if anything it only serves to heighten the film's silver dollar–sized grain and smeary inconsistent colors. Sound is also poor, but again due to the original production material. —DG
Movie: woof **DVD:** ♪½
New Line Home Video (Cat #N4988, UPC #79404349882). Widescreen (1.85:1) anamorphic. Dolby Digital 2.0. $24.98. Snapper. *LANG:* English. *SUB:* English. *CAP:* English. *FEATURES:* "The Confession of Julien Donkey-Boy" featurette ▪ 2 deleted Scenes ▪ 20 chapter links ▪ Theatrical trailer ▪ Cast and crew filmographies.
1999 (R) 101m/C Ewen Bremner, Chloe Sevigny, Werner Herzog, Evan Neumann, Joyce Korine, Chrissy Kobylak, Alvin Law; *D:* Harmony Korine; *W:* Harmony Korine; *C:* Anthony Dod Mantle. *AWARDS: NOM:* Ind. Spirit '00: Cinematog., Director (Korine).

Jurassic Park [CE]

In making an absolutely spectacular dinosaur film, that elusive Hollywood "chemistry" works to perfection... and, near perfection. First, the monsters created by Dennis Muren, Stan Winston, and Michael Lantieri with live-action, stop-motion animation and computer-generated digital images are magnificent. Second, the script puts a cast of interesting stock figures through a series of adrenaline-pumping adventures. Finally, director Spielberg mixes image and sound deftly, and keeps the whole thing zipping right along at a potboiler pace, though his tendency toward oversweetness bubbles close to the surface a time or two. Even so, for some younger horror fans, this movie will generate nightmares that might last for years. The DVD comes in two editions, DTS and Dolby. The DTS features superior sound and fewer extras. Along with the features listed below, the Dolby version contains rough footage of pre-production meetings, location scouting, a Foley sound effects demonstration, production art archives, storyboards (including the original ending), and an early version of the kitchen scene. Combined,

those approximate a commentary track. On both versions, image and sound are excellent, though some critics have claimed that they can detect some visual flaws in the DTS. I could not spot any significant difference. However, collectors should be careful to choose the proper version. Even though the DTS also contains a Dolby 5.1 soundtrack, the extras on the Dolby edition make it the preferred choice for anyone without DTS or for those who find scant difference between DTS and Dolby 5.1. —MM
Movie: ♪♪♪½ **DVD:** ♪♪♪½
Universal Studios Home Video (Cat #200 32, UPC #025192003226). Widescreen (1.85:1) letterboxed. Dolby Digital 5.1 Surround Stereo; DD Surround Stereo; DTS 5.1 Surround. $26.98. Keepcase. *LANG:* English; French. *SUB:* Spanish; French. *CAP:* English. *FEATURES:* 20 chapter links ▪ "Making of" featurette ▪ Trailers for three *Jurassic Park* films ▪ Dinosaur encyclopedia ▪ Production notes ▪ Talent files ▪ DVD-ROM features. DTS 5.1 (cat. #20787, UPC 025192078729). Also available with *The Lost World*, cat. #20789 ($53.98) and #20983 ($119.98).
1993 (PG-13) 127m/C Sam Neill, Laura Dern, Jeff Goldblum, Richard Attenborough, Bob Peck, Martin Ferrero, B.D. Wong, Joseph Mazzello, Ariana Richards, Samuel L. Jackson, Wayne Knight; *D:* Steven Spielberg; *W:* David Koepp, Michael Crichton; *C:* Dean Cundey; *M:* John Williams; *V:* Richard Kiley. *AWARDS:* Oscars '93: Sound, Sound FX Editing, Visual FX; *NOM:* MTV Movie Awards '94: Film, Villain (T-Rex), Action Seq.

Just Looking

During the summer of 1955, libidinous teenager Lenny (Merriman) pledges to observe two adults having sex. Forced to stay with his aunt and uncle in Queens, Lenny finds that he's very close to achieving his goal. Well-performed coming-of-age story (which isn't exactly fresh) is warmly and affectionately told. There are a few clunky bits and the act of watching 14-year-olds slobbering about sex is a bit unsettling. The disc is sharp, but overly grainy and a bit pale. (In the commentary track, Alexander mentions a blanket that's supposed to be pink, but it only appears off-white here.) The sound is crisp and pleasing. The commentary is led by the producer and editor, and focuses primarily on the technical behind-the-scenes aspects of production, but it does offer a satisfying look at the effort that went into the film. Director Alexander ends the commentary on a very amusing note. —DG
AKA: Cherry Pink.
Movie: ♪♪½ **DVD:** ♪♪♪
Columbia Tristar Home Video (Cat #05982, UPC #04339605982). Widescreen (1.85:1) anamorphic; full frame. Dolby Surround Stereo. $29.95. Keepcase. *LANG:* English. *SUB:* English. *CAP:* English. *FEATURES:* Commentary: Alexander, producer Jean Doumanian, editor Norman Hollyn ▪ Deleted scenes with commentary ▪ Theatrical trail-

ers ▪ 28 chapter links ▪ Insert card with chapter listing. The disc only lists the widescreen version, but full frame is also included.
1999 (R) 97m/C Ryan Merriman, Gretchen Mol, Patti LuPone, Peter Onorati, Ilana Levine, Richard V. Licata, John Bolger; *D:* Jason Alexander; *W:* Marshall Karp; *C:* Fred Schuler.

K-911

Ten years after the original film, Belushi returns to his role of LAPD detective Dooley, along with his German shepherd partner Jerry Lee. The aging duo are now reluctantly partnered with a younger K-9 unit—no-nonsense detective Welles (Tucci) and her partner, a Doberman named Zeus. DVD presentation is clean and razor sharp, without any defects. The color reproduction on this disc is flawless, nicely rendering the many outdoor settings as well as interiors, also faithfully reproducing fleshtones. —GH/MM
Movie: ♪♪½ **DVD:** ♪♪½
Universal Studios Home Video (Cat #205 71). Widescreen (1.78:1) anamorphic. Dolby Digital 5.0 Surround Stereo; Dolby Digital Surround Stereo. $24.98. Keepcase. *LANG:* English; French. *SUB:* English. *FEATURES:* Production notes.
1999 (PG-13) 91m/C James Belushi, James Handy, Christine Tucci, Wade Andrew Williams, J.J. Johnston, Vincent Castellanos; *D:* Charles Kanganis; *W:* Gary Scott Thompson; *C:* George Mooradian; *M:* Steve Edwards.

The Karate Kid

Teenaged Daniel (Macchio) learns that martial arts mean more than using his fists when Mr. Miyagi (Morita), a handyman, agrees to teach him to fight. Their friendship is more important to the film than the action scenes. It's similar to the successful formula that director Avildsen worked with in *Rocky,* and it's effective. The various language options are all that differentiate disc from VHS tape. Image is about the same. —MM
Movie: ♪♪♪ **DVD:** ♪♪
Columbia Tristar Home Video (Cat #04069, UPC #043396040694). Full frame. Dolby Digital Surround Stereo. $24.99. Keepcase. *LANG:* English; French; Spanish. *CAP:* English. *FEATURES:* Trailers ▪ 28 chapter links.
1984 (PG) 126m/C Ralph Macchio, Noriyuki "Pat" Morita, Elisabeth Shue, Randee Heller, Martin Kove, Chad McQueen, William Zabka; *D:* John G. Avildsen; *W:* Robert Mark Kamen; *M:* Bill Conti. *AWARDS: NOM:* Oscars '84: Support. Actor (Morita).

Kayla: A Cry in the Wilderness

Synopsis sounds like a standard boy-and-his-dog story. Young Sam (Fennell) hasn't come to terms with his mother's (Booth) remarriage years after the disappearance of his explorer father. With the help of a wild dog, Kayla, and a girl, Jaynie (Henderson), he grows up. It's much better than that with a well-realized sense of place (Quebec) and solid production values. DVD delivers an excellent image, in both muffled interiors and bright, snowy exteriors. This is an excellent film for kids and their families. —MM

Movie: 🎵🎵🎵 **DVD:** 🎵🎵🎵
Questar Video, Inc. (Cat #QD3174). Full frame. $24.95. Keepcase. *LANG:* English. *FEATURES:* 18 chapter links • Family discussion topics • Quebec featurette • About Elizabeth Van Steenwyk (audio).
2000 96m/C Tod Fennell, Meredith Henderson, Bronwyn Booth, Henry Czerny; *D:* Nicholas (Nick) Kendall; *W:* Peter Behrens; *C:* John Berrie; *M:* Milan Kymlicka.

Keeping the Faith
Childhood friends Jake (Stiller), a rabbi, and Brian (Norton), a priest, are assigned to posts in their New York neighborhood. All is well, until third childhood friend Anna (Elfman) comes to town. The tomboy has blossomed and both Jake and Brian are instantly attracted to her. Unfortunately, the film tries to do too much and, with a running time of more than two hours, it's too long. The image is very sharp and clear, showing no defects on the source print or grain. The colors are very well balanced, and given the natural, shooting style of the film, the tones all appear very realistic. The 5.1 soundtrack presents clean and clear dialogue and gives a nice presentation to Bernstein's score. There isn't a great deal of Surround action. —ML/MM

Movie: 🎵🎵½ **DVD:** 🎵🎵🎵
Buena Vista Home Entertainment (Cat #20769). Widescreen (1.85:1) anamorphic. Dolby Digital 5.1 Surround Stereo. $29.99. Keepcase. *LANG:* English. *SUB:* English. *FEATURES:* Commentary: Edward Norton and writer/producer Stuart Blumberg • 10 deleted scenes • Gag reel • Theatrical trailer • Talent files.
2000 (PG-13) 127m/C Edward Norton, Ben Stiller, Jenna Elfman, Anne Bancroft, Eli Wallach, Milos Forman, Ron Rifkin, Holland Taylor, Rena Sofer, Lisa Edelstein, Bodhi (Pine) Elfman; *D:* Edward Norton; *W:* Stuart Blumberg; *C:* Anastas Michos; *M:* Elmer Bernstein.

Kelly's Heroes
A misfit band of soldier/crooks are led by Eastwood to steal a fortune in gold from behind German lines toward the end of World War II. Fine work from the supporting cast, particularly Sutherland and MacLeod. The image is very sharp with deep, accurate colors. Brightness and contrast are both solid, providing fine detail in even the darkest of scenes. Some slight wear and tear of the film elements is present, along with a bit of grain in a few scenes, but on the whole this is a great transfer and the movie has never looked this good on home video. The

soundtrack is a brand-new 5.1 remastering of the original mono mix which, unfortunately for the sake of audio purists, is not available on the DVD. The musical score has clearly benefited the most from this new mix. Dialogue and sound effects are very firmly anchored to the center channel, with only an occasional burst of sound spreading across the full set of speakers. —MP/MM

Movie: 🎵🎵🎵 **DVD:** 🎵🎵🎵
Warner Home Video, Inc. (Cat #65156). Widescreen (2.35:1) anamorphic. Dolby Digital 5.1 Surround Stereo. $24.98. Snapper. *LANG:* English; French. *SUB:* English; French. *FEATURES:* Trailer.
1970 (PG) 145m/C Clint Eastwood, Donald Sutherland, Telly Savalas, Gavin MacLeod, Don Rickles, Carroll O'Connor, Stuart Margolin, Harry Dean Stanton, Jeff Morris, Richard (Dick) Davalos, Perry Lopez, Tom Troupe, Len Lesser, David Hurst, George Savalas, Tom Signorelli; *D:* Brian G. Hutton; *W:* Troy Kennedy Martin; *C:* Gabriel Figueroa; *M:* Lalo Schifrin.

The Kentuckian
Frontiersman Big Eli (Lancaster) and his young son Little Eli (MacDonald) make their way from Kentucky to Texas. On their journey they encounter fighting mountaineers and other adventures. It's the kind of larger-than-life role that Lancaster built his early career on. There's no serious wear, so the film looks as good as could be expected of a mid-'50s work. Sound, however, has a curious muffled quality. The film is Lancaster's directorial debut and the first big-screen work for Matthau. —MM

Movie: 🎵🎵½ **DVD:** 🎵🎵½
MGM Home Entertainment (Cat #10018 36, UPC #027616861061). Widescreen (2.35:1) anamorphic. Dolby Digital Mono. $14.95. Keepcase. *LANG:* English; French; Spanish. *SUB:* French; Spanish. *FEATURES:* 16 chapter links • Trailer (full frame).
1955 104m/C Burt Lancaster, Walter Matthau, Diana Lynn, John McIntire, Dianne Foster, Una Merkel, John Carradine; *D:* Burt Lancaster; *C:* Ernest Laszlo.

Kept
Architecture student Kyle Griffin (Oliver) enters into an ill-advised affair with his boss's wife Barbara Weldon (Von Flotow). When detective Jack Moisier (Ice-T) suspects that she's involved with a murder, Kyle is a suspect, too. If plot and execution owe a slight debt to *Basic Instinct*, the director handles the material with some style. And he wrapped it in a slick package that arrives on DVD with no serious flaws and an unusually large number of extras for a video premiere. Fans of the genre should take a look. —MM

Movie: 🎵🎵🎵 **DVD:** 🎵🎵🎵
Columbia Tristar Home Video (Cat #06607, UPC #043396066076). Widescreen (1.85:1) letterboxed. Dolby Digital 5.1 Surround Stereo; Dolby Digital Surround. $24.95. Keepcase. *LANG:* English; French.

SUB: English; Spanish. *FEATURES:* 28 chapter links • Deleted scenes • Trailer • Commentary: director, cast • Talent files • Photo gallery.
2001 (R) 98m/C Ice-T, Yvette Nipar, Christian Oliver, Paul Michael Robinson, Michelle Von Flotow, Laura Rose, Art Hingle; *D:* Fred Olen Ray; *W:* Richard Uhug, Kimberly A. Ray; *C:* Theo Angell; *M:* Herman Jackson, Michael van Blum, Barry Taylor.

Kicked in the Head
This is the story of Redmond (Corrigan) and his search for the meaning of life. Yawn. Along the way he interacts with his loser uncle (Woods), the neighborhood girl who carries a torch for him (Taylor), and a sultry stewardess (Fiorentino) who gives women a bad name. Some scenes are fun and/or funny, but nothing links them together in a way to make you care whether Redmond finds the meaning of life or his next meal. The image and sound quality are slightly above VHS standards. —CA

Movie: 🎵½ **DVD:** 🎵🎵🎵
Image Entertainment (Cat #ID9169 CU DVD, UPC #014381916928). Full frame. Dolby Digital Stereo. $24.99. Snapper. *LANG:* English. *CAP:* English. *FEATURES:* 12 chapter links.
1997 (R) 97m/C Kevin Corrigan, Linda Fiorentino, James Woods, Lili Taylor, Michael Rapaport, Burt Young, Olek Krupa; *D:* Matthew Harrison; *W:* Matthew Harrison, Kevin Corrigan; *C:* John Thomas, Howard Krupa; *M:* Stephen Endelman.

The Kid with the X-Ray Eyes
Yes, it's a kid's version of *The Immoral Mr. Teas*, Russ Meyer's early nudie flick. This version has none of that naughtiness. Instead, it recycles action footage from old Roger Corman movies. The story has to do with imaginative 12-year-old Bobby (Berfield), who discovers a pair of goggles that allow him to see through clothes and skin—all the way down to the skeleton if he adjusts them right. His uncle Chuck (Carradine) thinks they should use them to find stuff buried in the sand on the beach. Crooks and spies are involved too. It's good-natured fun for the short set. Image and sound are only a slight improvement over VHS tape. —MM

Movie: 🎵🎵½ **DVD:** 🎵🎵½
New Concorde (Cat #NH20746 D, UPC #736991274693). Full frame. Stereo. $14.98. Keepcase. *LANG:* English. *FEATURES:* 24 chapter links • Trailers • Talent files.
1999 (PG) 84m/C Justin Berfield, Robert Carradine, Mark Collie, Diane Salinger, Griffin (Griffen) Drew, Brinke Stevens; *D:* Sherman Scott; *W:* Sean O'Bannon; *C:* Theo Angell; *M:* Jay Bolton.

The Kidnapping of the President
The U.S. President (Holbrook) is taken hostage by a South American terrorist

(Fernandes). Jerry O'Connor (Shatner) of the Secret Service is on the ball trying to recover the big guy. A well-integrated subplot has the VP (Johnson) involved in a scandal. The thriller looks very dated now, but it still plays well. Full-frame image is no better than tape. —MM

Movie: 🎵🎵½ **DVD:** 🎵🎵
Rhino Home Video (Cat #R2 976646, UPC #603497664627). Full frame. $9.99. Snapper. *LANG:* English. *FEATURES:* 12 chapter links.
1980 (R) 113m/C *CA* William Shatner, Hal Holbrook, Van Johnson, Ava Gardner, Miguel Fernandes; **D:** George Mendeluk.

Kids Return

Director Takeshi Kitano tells his stories methodically. In this movie, two juvenile delinquents travel through their youth in skewed adult lives, skewed for Japanese culture anyway. The pair skip class, extort money from classmates, and make fun of others, all in service to bolstering their egos. Down this path lie the melancholy musings of a director/writer who questions what defense there is against a society that judges the value of each person on his or her position in the world. Masaru and Shinji understand early on that they are not destined for the respect and honor garnered by the best of Japanese society. It's hard to have great honor in a society without also manufacturing examples of dishonorable lives. Shinji becomes a boxer and learns how to advance himself by getting away with cheating. Masaru joins a local yakuza gang. His advancement is harder. Toward the end, the two friends join forces again to become a stand-up comedy team and again, are failures. But maybe they are happy doing what they want. Takeshi Kitano's film is ultimately an art-house flick that puts a social thesis before entertainment. If you're looking to be entertained, move along. The quality of the transfer from film to DVD has a bit to be desired. The digital format reveals the occasional coarseness of the film. If you want to feel like you've done a little sociological lab work on Japanese society, pop it in the player. —JAS

Movie: 🎵🎵 **DVD:** 🎵🎵🎵
Image Entertainment (Cat #ID9528KDVD, UPC #014381952827). Widescreen (1.85:1) letterboxed. Dolby Digital Stereo. $29.99. Snapper. *LANG:* Japanese. *SUB:* English. *FEATURES:* 16 chapter links.
1996 107m/C *JP* Mansanobu Ando, Ken Kaneko; **D:** Takeshi "Beat" Kitano; **W:** Takeshi "Beat" Kitano; **C:** Katsumi Yanagishima; **M:** Joe Hisaishi.

Kill Me Again

Director Dahl whips up a neat contemporary noir in the James M. Cain school. Femme fatale Fay (Whalley) asks Reno detective Jack (Kilmer, then her real husband) to fake her death. That sets them against her psycho-thug boyfriend (Madsen) and the cops. It's great stuff for fans, but given the spectacular mountain set-

ting, why is the DVD full frame? Image looks fine with some excellent night scenes in Reno; sound is better, but the film is good enough to rate a widescreen option. —MM

Movie: 🎵🎵🎵 **DVD:** 🎵🎵½
MGM Home Entertainment (Cat #1001278, UPC #027616855589). Full frame. Dolby Digital Surround Stereo; Mono. $19.98. Keepcase. *LANG:* English; French. *SUB:* French; Spanish. *FEATURES:* Trailer ▪ 24 chapter links.
1989 (R) 93m/C Val Kilmer, Joanne Whalley, Michael Madsen, Jonathan (Jon Francis) Gries, Bibi Besch; **D:** John Dahl; **W:** John Dahl, David Warfield; **C:** Jacques Steyn.

Kill Shot

If two trucks loaded with episodes of *Beverly Hills 90210* and *Baywatch* smashed together in a head-on collision, a can of film containing this little trifle might roll out. It's all about attractive young things who go to college and live in a glitzy Malibu beach high-rise where they play volleyball and dodge assassins (Scalia). Despite the box art, Denise Richards has a virtual cameo. Full-frame image is equal to VHS tape; production values are strictly TV with the addition of a little skin. —MM

Movie: 🎵 **DVD:** 🎵🎵
Paramount Home Video (Cat #87475, UPC #097368747548). Full frame. Dolby Digital 5.1 Surround Stereo; Dolby Digital Surround. $29.99. Keepcase. *LANG:* English. *SUB:* English; Spanish. *FEATURES:* Talent files ▪ Trailer ▪ Behind-the-scenes featurette ▪ 20 chapter links.
2001 (R) 92m/C Casper Van Dien, Jack Scalia, Sally Kellerman, Elliott Gould, Denise Richards, Jacqueline Collen, Catherine Lazo; **D:** Nelson McCormick; **W:** Gianni Russo; **C:** Larry Blanford; **M:** Timothy S. Jones.

The Killer [Winstar]

The Winstar edition of John Woo's action masterpiece is slightly sharper than the Criterion laserdisc. It also features new larger yellow subtitles and a new commentary track by the director. The disc is also available as half of a boxed set (cat. #FLV5243) with *Hard Boiled*. —MM **AKA:** Die Xue Shuang Xiong.

Movie: 🎵🎵🎵½ **DVD:** 🎵🎵🎵½
Winstar Home Entertainment (Cat #FLV5223, UPC #720917522326). Widescreen (1.85:1) letterboxed. Mono. $29.98. Keepcase. *LANG:* Cantonese; English. *SUB:* English. *FEATURES:* 30 chapter links ▪ Notes by David Chute ▪ Talent files ▪ Production credits ▪ Commentary: Woo.
1990 110m/C *HK* Chow Yun-Fat, Sally Yeh, Danny Lee, Kenneth Tsang, Chu Kong, Fui-On Shing; **D:** John Woo; **W:** John Woo; **C:** Wing-hang Wong, Peter Pau; **M:** Lowell Lo.

Killers

Four young people try to skim the cream off a drug deal in an abandoned ware-

house. They're trapped when gangsters with pony tails, guns, and bad attitudes show up. Actually, this video premiere makes a lot out of its modest budget. Acting is acceptable and director Latt uses colored lights effectively to make his single set look interesting. It's such a dark film (literally and figuratively) that grain and artifacts are heavy throughout. Sound is very good. —MM

Movie: 🎵🎵🎵 **DVD:** 🎵🎵🎵
MTI Home Video (Cat #229). Full frame. Dolby Digital 5.1 Surround Stereo. $29.99. Keepcase. *LANG:* English. *FEATURES:* Commentary: director David Michael Latt ▪ Cast and crew thumbnail bios ▪ Trailers ▪ 2 deleted scenes ▪ 2 alternate endings ▪ DVD production credits ▪ Production stills ▪ 9 chapter links.
1997 (R) 86m/C Kim Little, Scott Carson, Anastasia Martino, Paul Logan; **D:** David Michael Latt, David Michael Latt.

Killer's Kiss

A boxer and a dancer set out to start a new life together after he saves her from an attempted rape. Gritty second feature from Kubrick was financed by family and friends and shows signs of his budding talent. This short (67-minute) feature exhibits only a few signs of wear. For the most part, its grainy black-and-white photography arrives on disc looking very good. The mono sound is fine for a film of this age. Required viewing for Kubrick fans. —MM

Movie: 🎵🎵½ **DVD:** 🎵🎵🎵
MGM Home Entertainment (Cat #907707, UPC #027616779721). Full frame. Dolby Digital Mono. $24.98. Keepcase. *LANG:* English. *SUB:* English; French. *FEATURES:* Theatrical trailer ▪ 20 chapter links.
1955 67m/C Frank Silvera, Jamie Smith, Irene Kane, Jerry Jarret; **D:** Stanley Kubrick; **W:** Stanley Kubrick; **C:** Stanley Kubrick; **M:** Gerald Fried.

The Killing of a Chinese Bookie

Gazzara runs a Sunset Strip nightclub and is in hock to loan sharks. When he can't come up with the cash, he's offered a deal—get rid of a troublesome Chinese bookie and all debts will be forgiven. But it turns out the bookie is highly connected in the Asian mob and nothing goes as planned. Cassavetes's improv technique makes for a self-indulgent and endless film. The picture transfer is decent, but darker-lit scenes are grainy and lack definition to the point of being distracting. Other than that, the disc looks fine. The soundtrack is crisp, providing clear and understandable dialogue, though it lacks a lush depth. —MJT

Movie: 🎵🎵 **DVD:** 🎵½
Pioneer Entertainment (Cat #PSE-99-102, UPC #013023017993). Full frame. Dolby Digital Stereo. $24.98. Keepcase. *LANG:* English. *FEATURES:* 16 chapter links.
1976 (R) 109m/C Ben Gazzara, Jean-Pierre Cassel, Zizi Johari, Soto Joe Hugh, Robert Phillips, Timothy Carey, Morgan

Woodward; **D:** John Cassavetes; **W:** John Cassavetes; **C:** Frederick Elmes.

Killing Zoe

American safecracker Zed (Stoltz) travels to Paris for a little rest, relaxation, and robbery. At the request of childhood friend Eric (Anglade), he involves himself in an ill-conceived daylight bank heist but not before enjoying a night with a local call girl (Delpy) and some heroin-induced debauchery with the other members of the gang. The next day, things go wrong. The widescreen image is no better than good, but it seems to be an accurate reproduction of the original. —*MM*
Movie: 🎬🎬½ **DVD:** 🎬🎬½
Artisan Entertainment (Cat #60499, UPC #012236604990). Widescreen (1.85:1) anamorphic. Dolby Digital Surround Stereo. $24.98. Keepcase. *LANG:* English. *CAP:* English. *FEATURES:* 28 chapter links • Trailer • Production notes.
1994 (R) 97m/C Eric Stoltz, Julie Delpy, Jean-Hugues Anglade, Gary Kemp, Bruce Ramsay, Kario Salem, Carlo Scandiuzzi; **D:** Roger Roberts Avary; **W:** Roger Roberts Avary; **C:** Tom Richmond.

King and Country

Aristocratic army officer Capt. Hargreaves (Bogarde) serves as the defense lawyer for troubled Private Arthur Hamp (Courtenay), whose wartime experiences have caused him to desert. At first, Hargreaves ignores the uneducated Hamp's obvious shell-shock, but soon begins to feel sympathy for his confused client. Director Losey shows the effects of war, rather than the experience of combat, and provides a sincere and bitter condemnation of military mentality. The full-frame image is fine, but sound is lacking. The harmonica score is often distorted and off-key. Some dialogue and voice-overs are difficult to understand and there are no captions or subtitles. —*MM*
Movie: 🎬🎬🎬 **DVD:** 🎬🎬
VCI Home Video (Cat #8249, UPC #08985 9824920). Full frame. Dolby Digital Mono. $19.99. Keepcase. *LANG:* English. *FEATURES:* 12 chapter links • Trailers • Talent files.
1964 86m/B *GB* Dirk Bogarde, Tom Courtenay, Leo McKern, Barry Foster, James Villiers, Peter Copley; **D:** Joseph Losey; **W:** Evan Jones; **C:** Denys Coop; **M:** Larry Adler. *AWARDS:* British Acad. '64: Film.

King of New York

Drug czar Frank White (Walken), recently returned from a prison sabbatical, regains control of his New York drug empire with the aid of a loyal network of black dealers. How? Call it dangerous charisma, an inexplicable sympatico. Headquartered in Manhattan's chic Plaza hotel, he ruthlessly orchestrates the drug machine, while funneling the profits into a Bronx hospital for the poor. As inscrutable as White him-

self, Walken makes the drug czar's power tangible, believable, yet never fathomable. Directed with no-punches-pulled grit and style by Ferrara. *King of New York* is one of my favorite cinematic indulgences and I immediately sold my laserdisc when the DVD announced. Big mistake. The image is overall soft and whenever the scene is dark (and that's quite often), there are more artifacts than I've seen on an Artisan DVD release. The colors are somewhat improved over the LD, but nothing can make up for Ferrara's slick look being ruined by the lack of sharpness. Oh well, with the lack of extras on the DVD, and the propensity for special-edition re-dos, Artisan will most likely kick out another version shortly, and maybe this time they'll get it right. —*JO*
Movie: 🎬🎬🎬 **DVD:** 🎬
Artisan Entertainment (Cat #60477, UPC #012236604778). Widescreen (1.85:1) letterboxed. Dolby Surround. $24.98. Keepcase. *LANG:* English. *CAP:* English. *FEATURES:* 27 chapter links • Theatrical trailer • TV spots • Schooly D music video.
1990 (R) 106m/C Christopher Walken, Laurence "Larry" Fishburne, David Caruso, Victor Argo, Wesley Snipes, Janet (Johnson) Julian, Joey Chin, Giancarlo Esposito, Steve Buscemi; **D:** Abel Ferrara; **W:** Nicholas St. John; **C:** Bojan Bazelli; **M:** Joe Delia.

Kiss Me Deadly

Aldrich's loose adaptation of Mickey Spillane's novel has been overpraised by many. It's a loopy work powered by Ralph Meeker's interpretation of Mike Hammer as a brutish thug. One night he picks up a hitchhiker (Leachman). She's murdered and he sets out to solve a Byzantine plot that arrives at a famously bizarre conclusion. During the many years that the film was unavailable, it became the subject of some controversy due to changes in that ending. DVD presents both versions. Overall, the image is very good with true inky blacks in the numerous night scenes. —*MM*
Movie: 🎬🎬½ **DVD:** 🎬🎬🎬
MGM Home Entertainment (Cat #10020 61, UPC #027616862914). Widescreen (1.66:1) letterboxed. Dolby Digital Mono. $19.98. Keepcase. *LANG:* English. *SUB:* French; Spanish. *CAP:* English. *FEATURES:* Alternate ending • 16 chapter links • Trailer.
1955 105m/B Ralph Meeker, Albert Dekker, Paul Stewart, Wesley Addy, Cloris Leachman, Strother Martin, Marjorie Bennett, Jack Elam, Maxine Cooper, Gaby Rodgers, Nick Dennis, Jack Lambert, Percy Helton; **D:** Robert Aldrich; **W:** A.I. Bezzerides; **C:** Ernest Laszlo; **M:** Frank DeVol. *AWARDS:* Natl. Film Reg. '99.

Kiss Me, Guido

Heterosexual and handsome Frankie (Scotti) is a Bronx-born-and-raised pizza maker and De Niro wanna-be who's not too bright. Apartment hunting in Manhat-

tan, he thinks an ad listing "GWM" stands for "guy with money" and mistakenly moves in with gay actor Warren (Barrile). Pokes fun at both Italian-American and gay stereotypes without offending or canonizing either group. Director Vitale and an excellent if largely unknown cast inject enough energy and humor to rise above the often predictable story. Low-budget independent sex farce offers a promising start for first-time filmmaker Vitale. The video transfer is solid, although browns and blacks do lose definition in a few scattered scenes. Similarly, the soundtrack is generally decent, though the 5.1 mix occasionally amounts to little more than a louder version of the original Surround Sound mix. At the start of the disc's commentary track, director Vitale seems ill-at-ease and does little more than describe the film while watching it. But, he does get into a groove and manages to provide some behind-the-scenes info and other amusing anecdotes as the film continues. —*MJT*
Movie: 🎬🎬½ **DVD:** 🎬🎬🎬
Paramount Home Video (Cat #33572, UPC #097363357247). Widescreen (1.85:1) anamorphic. Dolby Digital 5.1 Surround Sound; Dolby Digital Surround Sound. $29.99. Keepcase. *LANG:* English. *SUB:* English. *FEATURES:* 12 chapter links • Commentary: director Tony Vitale.
1997 (R) 90m/C Nick Scotti, Anthony Barrile, Craig Chester, Anthony De Sando, Christopher Lawford, Molly Price; **D:** Tony Vitale; **W:** Tony Vitale; **C:** Claudia Raschke; **M:** Randall Poster.

Kiss of Fire

What sounds like a dozen other erotic video premieres is actually a well-acted character study. Claudine (Applegate) is a lap dancer who tries to leave that life when she falls for a guy (Dionisi). The image is generally good to very good but director Tibaldi indulges in too much music video flashiness. Sound is very good. —*MM* **AKA:** *Claudine's Return.*
Movie: 🎬🎬½ **DVD:** 🎬🎬½
Miramax Pictures Home Video (Cat #185 46, UPC #717951005601). Widescreen (2.35:1) anamorphic. Dolby Digital Surround Stereo. $29.99. Keepcase. *LANG:* English. *FEATURES:* 29 chapter links.
1998 (R) 92m/C Stefano Dionisi, Christina Applegate, Matt Clark, Gabriel Mann, Perry Anzilotti, Tom Nowicki; **D:** Antonio Tibaldi; **W:** Antonio Tibaldi, Heidi A. Hall; **C:** Luca Bigazzi; **M:** Michel Colombier.

Kiss Shot

Goldberg is a struggling single mom who loses her job but still must make the mortgage payments. She becomes a waitress but realizes it isn't going to pay enough so she tries her hand as a pool hustler. Franz is the promoter who finances her; Harewood is the pool-shooting playboy whose romantic advances are destroying her concentration. DVD image and sound are identical to tape. —*MM*

Movie: 🎵🎵 *DVD:* 🎵🎵
Studio Home Entertainment (Cat #4065). Full frame. $24.95. Keepcase. *LANG:* English. *FEATURES:* Trailer • Production notes • 18 chapter links.
1989 88m/C Whoopi Goldberg, Dennis Franz, Dorian Harewood, David Marciano, Teddy Wilson; *D:* Jerry London; *C:* Chuy Elizondo; *M:* Steve Dorff.

Kiss the Sky

Though the synopsis makes this sound like an erotic thriller, it's a well-made drama based on character. Suffering from simultaneous mid-life crises, Jeff (Petersen) and Marty (Cole) head off on a business trip to the Philippines. Attempting to recapture their lost youth, both of them fall for Andy (Lee), a high-spirited Oxford grad. DVD image is fine but doesn't really improve much on VHS tape. The 5.1 sound does a lot more for the Leonard Cohen songs in the score. —*MM*
Movie: 🎵🎵½ *DVD:* 🎵🎵½
20th Century Fox Home Entertainment (Cat #908499, UPC #027616849922). Full frame. Dolby Digital 5.1 Surround Stereo. $24.99. Keepcase. *LANG:* English. *SUB:* French; Spanish. *CAP:* English. *FEATURES:* 28 chapter links.
1998 (R) 105m/C William L. Petersen, Gary Cole, Sheryl Lee, Terence Stamp, Patricia Charbonneau, Season Hubley; *D:* Roger Young; *W:* Eric Lerner; *C:* Donald M. Morgan; *M:* Patrick Williams.

Kiss Toledo Goodbye

Amusing, well-acted story about a small town boy named Kevin (Rapaport) who suddenly finds out that his real father, Sal (Forrester), is a mob boss. The scene where Kevin confronts his mother, a ditzy Nancy Allen, and she tells him about his conception is rewardingly humorous. When his newfound dad is blown up with a car bomb, Kevin must step in to help find out who put the hit out on poppa. Flanked by a detail of bodyguards headed by Christopher Walken, Kevin juggles his work responsibilities and his girlfriend (Taylor), all while being shot at by a wide assortment of assassins. This is not a great film by any standards, but would be an enjoyable way to pass an evening. The sound and picture quality are better than average. —*CA*
Movie: 🎵🎵½ *DVD:* 🎵🎵½
A-PIX Entertainment Inc. (Cat #APX27029, UPC #783722702932). Full frame. Dolby Digital 5.1 Surround. $19.98. Keepcase. *LANG:* English. *SUB:* Spanish. *FEATURES:* Chapter links • Theatrical trailer • Filmographies.
2000 (R) 96m/C Michael Rapaport, Christine Taylor, Christopher Walken, Robert Forster, Nancy Allen, Paul Ben-Victor, Bill Smitrovich; *D:* Lyndon Chubbuck; *W:* Robert Easter; *C:* Frank Byers; *M:* Phil Marshall.

Kisses in the Dark

Four award-winning short films are collected here. "Coriolis Effect" finds two dare-devil tornado-chasers falling in love. "Solly's Diner" has a vagrant becoming a hero during a hold-up. In "Looping," an egotistic Italian director decides in the middle of shooting his big-budget Mafia musical that the material isn't worthy of him. "Joe" finds his solace in his daily routine in a psych ward until an interloper disturbs his refuge. Given the different budgets that the filmmakers had to work with and their intentions, the image quality in the quartet ranges from poor to very good. Sound is fine throughout. Recommended for something different. —*MM*
Movie: 🎵🎵🎵½ *DVD:* 🎵🎵🎵
Vanguard International Cinema, Inc. (UPC #658769009033). Widescreen letterboxed; full frame. $29.98. Keepcase. *LANG:* English. *FEATURES:* 14 chapter links.
1997 75m/C Jennifer Rubin, James Wilder, Dana Ashbrook, Corinne Bohrer, Katherine Wallach, Ronald Guttman, Quentin Tarantino; *D:* Larry Hankin, Louis Venosta, Roger Paradiso, Sasha Wolf; *W:* Louis Venosta, Roger Paradiso, Sasha Wolf.

Klash

Photographer Stoney (Esposito) is sent to Kingston, Jamaica, to shoot pictures of a reggae concert. He meets up with old flame Blossom (Guy) and becomes involved in her scheme to steal the ticket money. Director Parker makes the most of the atmosphere of tropical miasma and so the image is deliberately softened and the many night scenes are kept dark. The full-frame image is no better than VHS tape. The music sounds very nice and there is a lot of it. —*MM*
Movie: 🎵🎵½ *DVD:* 🎵🎵
Xenon Entertainment (Cat #4073). Full frame. $19.95. Keepcase. *LANG:* English. *FEATURES:* 12 chapter links • Behind-the-scenes featurette • Trailer.
1995 (R) 90m/C Carl Bradshaw, Paul Campbell, Giancarlo Esposito, Jasmine Guy, Stafford Ashani, Lucien Chen, Cedella Marley; *D:* Bill Parker; *W:* Bill Parker, Peter Allen; *C:* Bill Parker; *M:* Olivia "Babsy" Grange.

Knight Moves

Another of those pesky serial killers is at work, this time at a chess tournament. Could master Sanderson (Lambert) have anything to do with the killings? Will he fall for beautiful police psychologist Kathy Sheppard (Lane)? The image is washed-out and shadowy, about what you'd expect for such derivative material. It's not much of a step up from a widescreen tape. —*MM*
Movie: 🎵🎵 *DVD:* 🎵🎵
Artisan Entertainment (Cat #11514, UPC #017153115147). Widescreen letterboxed. Dolby Digital Surround. $24.98. Keepcase. *LANG:* English. *CAP:* English. *FEATURES:* 25 chapter links.
1993 (R) 105m/C Christopher Lambert, Diane Lane, Tom Skerritt, Daniel Baldwin; *D:* Carl Schenkel; *W:* Brad Mirman; *C:* Dietrich Lohmann; *M:* Anne Dudley.

Knightriders

Billy (a commanding Harris in his first starring role) leads a group of motorcyclists who compete in jousting tournaments at a traveling Renaissance Faire. George Romero's curious study of the conflicts between art and commerce has become an enduring audience favorite. On the commentary track, he admits that the film is also a personal favorite (along with *Martin*). The image does not gain much on disc. This has always been a rough-looking grainy work; it should be. Since Romero is joined by his wife Christine, actors John Amplas and Tom Savini (also special effects), and film historian Chris Stavrakis, their conversation tends to be an old-home-week affair, as they point out friends and family and reminisce about the production. —*MM*
Movie: 🎵🎵🎵 *DVD:* 🎵🎵🎵
Anchor Bay (Cat #DV10966, UPC #013131 099690). Widescreen (1.85:1) anamorphic. Dolby Digital Mono. $24.99. Keepcase. *LANG:* English. *FEATURES:* 30 chapter links • Liner notes by Michael Felsher • Commentary: Romero, cast and crew • Behind-the-scenes home movies • Trailer • TV spots.
1981 (R) 145m/C Ed Harris, Gary Lahti, Tom Savini, Amy Ingersoll; *D:* George A. Romero; *W:* George A. Romero; *C:* Michael Gornick; *M:* Donald Rubinstein.

Know Your Enemy: Japan

Please see review for *Dec. 7th: The Pearl Harbor Story*.
1945 63m/B *D:* Frank Capra; *Nar:* John Huston, Dana Andrews.

Komodo

Komodo dragons are pretty impressive in the wild. On DVD, they're not as frightening as the velociraptors in *Jurassic Park*, but they're much more believable than the nutty effects in *Anaconda*, and the entire film is an acceptable little horror. Most of the budget was spent on animatronic/computer-generated effects. An extremely small cast goes through the motions to keep the standard-issue plot moving along in the first half. The second half is much livelier. The setting is an island off North Carolina (actually Australia) where the evil oil company is trying to hide the existence of the titular critters who slobber poisonous drool. Said critters are trying to kill and eat six people stranded there. The image is sharp and reveals proper details in the many night scenes. Surround effects are nice, if limited. —*MM*
Movie: 🎵🎵½ *DVD:* 🎵🎵🎵
Studio Home Entertainment (Cat #7465). Widescreen (1.78:1) letterboxed. Dolby Digital 5.1 Surround Stereo; Dolby Digital Surround Stereo. $28.52. Keepcase. *LANG:* English; French. *SUB:* Spanish. *FEATURES:* Talent files • Commentary: director Lantieri • Trivia game • Notes.
1999 (PG-13) 85m/C *AU* Kevin Zegers, Nina Landis, Jill(ian) Hennessey, Paul

Gleeson, Billy Burke; **D:** Michael Lantieri; **W:** Hans Bauer, Craig Mitchell; **C:** David Burr; **M:** John Debney.

Kronos

A giant robot from space drains the Earth of all its energy resources. Nothing can stop the machine, not even the H-bomb, and mankind's fate seems to be sealed! The DVD itself is not 16x9 enhanced but manages to nonetheless render a very detailed image. The source print is mostly clear and only occasional dust marks are visible. The image is stable with only the slightest registration problems. The black-and-white transfer offers solid, deep blacks and good highlights. The film has very good contrast, never overexposing the whites, but instead creating a very nice fall-off, running the entire gamut of gray shades. Compression has been done very well without notable compression artifacts. Without sibilance or distortion, the monaural sound has much more natural frequency response than you'd expect. This can be attributed to the rather high bit-rate applied for the audio presentation, which manages perfectly to reproduce the film's original sonic presentation. —*GH/MM*
Movie: 🎵🎵½ **DVD:** 🎵🎵½
Image Entertainment (Cat #8602, UPC #014381860221). Widescreen (2.35:1) letterboxed. Dolby Digital Mono. $24.99. Snapper. *LANG:* English. *FEATURES:* Trailer • 16 chapter links.
1957 78m/B Jeff Morrow, Barbara Lawrence, John Emery; **D:** Kurt Neumann; **W:** Lawrence Louis Goldman; **C:** Karl Struss; **M:** Paul Sawtell, Bert Shefter.

Krull [SE]

Likeable fantasy adventure is set in a world inhabited by creatures of myth and magic. A prince (Marshall) embarks on a quest to find a weapon called the Glaive and then to rescue his young bride (Anthony). The dopey dialogue could be a textbook for the worst clichés of the genre. That said, the image is very good and the special effects look almost as good as the computer-generated wonders that are commonplace today. Sound is fine. The behind-the-scenes commentary is taken from a *Cinefantastique* magazine article. —*MM*
Movie: 🎵🎵 **DVD:** 🎵🎵🎵½
Columbia Tristar Home Video (Cat #05890, UPC #043396058903). Widescreen (2.35:1) anamorphic. Dolby Digital 5.1 Surround Stereo; Dolby Digital Surround. $24.95. Keepcase. *LANG:* English; French; Spanish; Portuguese. *SUB:* English; French; Spanish; Portuguese; Chinese; Korean; Thai. *FEATURES:* 28 chapter links • Commentary: Yates, Marshall, Anthony, editor Ray Lovejoy • "Making of" featurette • Photo galleries • Talent files • Production notes.
1983 (PG) 121m/C *GB* Ken Marshall, Lysette Anthony, Freddie Jones, Francesca Annis, Liam Neeson; **D:** Peter Yates; **W:**

Stafford Sherman; **C:** Peter Suschitzsky; **M:** James Horner.

Kwaidan

A haunting, stylized quartet of supernatural stories, each with a surprise ending is adapted from the work of Lafcadio Hearn, an American author who lived in Japan just before the turn of the century. The visual effects are splendid. Another fine disc from Criterion (big surprise). Both audio and video tracks are extremely well transferred. The only complaint I have is the occasional loss of definition with some of the darker colors throughout the film. Other than that, the video is wonderful, featuring vibrant colors that really stand out and add to the beautiful photography. —*MJT*
Movie: 🎵🎵🎵🎵 **DVD:** 🎵🎵🎵
Criterion Collection (Cat #90, UPC #03742 9152027). Widescreen (2.35:1) anamorphic. Dolby Digital Mono. $29.95. Keepcase. *LANG:* Japanese. *SUB:* English. *FEATURES:* 28 chapter links • Theatrical trailer.
1964 164m/C *JP* Michiyo Aratama, Rentaro Mikuni, Katsuo Nakamura, Keiko Kishi, Tatsuya Nakadai, Takashi Shimura; **D:** Masaki Kobayashi; **W:** Yoko Mizuki; **C:** Yoshio Miyajima; **M:** Toru Takemitsu. *AWARDS:* Cannes '65: Grand Jury Prize; *NOM:* Oscars '65: Foreign Film.

La Cucaracha

Ex–office worker Walter Pool (Roberts) has gone to Mexico to become a novelist. Instead, he's a drunk who's practically immobilized by night terrors. Then the local big-shot (de Almeida) suddenly offers Walter a wad of money to kill somebody. Naturally, things go wrong, as they always do in these south-of-the-border noirs. That's how director Perez describes the story in his informative, enjoyable commentary track. The filmmakers couldn't afford to go to Mexico so the film was made in L.A., over the course of 18 cold days in December. The full-frame image is often dark and seldom improves on tape, so the extras are the key here. —*MM*
Movie: 🎵🎵🎵 **DVD:** 🎵🎵🎵
Paramount Home Video (Cat #839757, UPC #097368397576). Full frame. Dolby Digital 5.1 Surround Stereo; Dolby Digital Surround. $29.99. Keepcase. *LANG:* English. *SUB:* English; Spanish. *FEATURES:* 20 chapter links • Commentary: Jack Perez, Eric Roberts • Trailer • Talent files.
1999 (R) 95m/C Eric Roberts, Joaquin de Almeida, Tara Crespo, James McManus; **D:** Jack Perez; **W:** James McManus; **C:** Shawn Maurer; **M:** Martin Davich.

La Femme Nikita [MGM]

Stylish French noir version of Pygmalion. Having killed a cop during a drugstore theft gone awry, young French sociopath Nikita (Parillaud) is reprieved from a death sentence in order to enroll in a government fin-

ishing school, of sorts. Trained in etiquette and assassination, she's released after three years, and starts a new life with a new beau, all the while carrying out agency-mandated assassinations. Parillaud is excellent as the once-amoral street urchin transformed into a woman of depth and sensitivity—a bitterly ironic moral evolution for a contract killer. Remade as the pointless *Point of No Return* and followed by a cable TV series. An above-average video transfer does justice to the rich palette of colors used to create the film's unbelievable look. (It is easy to forgive the few darkly lit scenes where blacks lose a bit of definition.) The 5.1 English sound mix, however, is a major disappointment, with an awful dub that is merely amplified over the original soundtrack. The French track is much better and should be the listener's choice. A word to the wise: the so-called "collectible booklet" is actually a one-page pamphlet. —*MJT*
Movie: 🎵🎵🎵 **DVD:** 🎵🎵
MGM Home Entertainment (Cat #10010 88, UPC #027616853882). Widescreen (2.35:1) anamorphic. Dolby Digital 5.1 Surround Sound; Dolby Digital Stereo Surround. $19.98. Keepcase. *LANG:* English; French. *SUB:* English; French; Spanish. *FEATURES:* 32 chapter links • Theatrical trailer • Collectible booklet.
1991 (R) 117m/C *FR* Anne Parillaud, Jean-Hugues Anglade, Tcheky Karyo, Jeanne Moreau, Jean Reno, Jean Bouise; **D:** Luc Besson; **W:** Luc Besson; **C:** Thierry Arbogast; **M:** Eric Serra. *AWARDS:* Cesar '91: Actress (Parillaud).

La Grande Bouffe

In an ode to excess in all its forms, four middle-aged men (Mastroianni, Tognazzi, Piccoli, Noiret) meet at a secluded mansion for one last weekend to feast on gourmet food, prostitutes, and a full-figured fun-loving school teacher. No, the film is not to all tastes—it is rated "NC-17"—but it takes such joy in vulgarity that it's hard not to enjoy the ride, at least for a while. Virtually all of the action takes place in dim rooms or autumnal exteriors so the DVD image is not particularly special in visual terms. It's an excellent transfer of a dark original. —*MM* **AKA:** The Blow-Out.
Movie: 🎵🎵🎵 **DVD:** 🎵🎵½
Image Entertainment (Cat #ID4779SIDVD, UPC #014381477924). Full frame. Dolby Digital Mono. $24.99. Snapper. *LANG:* French. *SUB:* English. *FEATURES:* 14 chapter links.
1973 (NC-17) 125m/C *FR* Marcello Mastroianni, Philippe Noiret, Michel Piccoli, Ugo Tognazzi, Andrea Ferreol; **D:** Marco Ferreri; **W:** Marco Ferreri, Rafael Azcona; **C:** Mario Vulpiani; **M:** Philippe Sarde.

La Guerre Est Finie

Alain Resnais's understated suspense film makes a belated debut on home video. It's the story of Diego (Montand), a revolutionary who comes to wonder if he can still fight the good fight against the

fascists who control Spain. Montand, one of the most deceptively effortless actors ever to appear on-screen, is a commanding presence in this low-keyed exercise. On DVD, this is not the most sharply detailed black-and-white photography you'll ever see, but the film has been exceptionally well preserved. Some minor registration problems are negligible. The bright yellow subtitles are easy to read, and dubbed English is also available. —*MM*
AKA: The War Is Over; Kriget ar Slut.
Movie: 🎬🎬🎬½ *DVD:* 🎬🎬🎬
Image Entertainment (Cat #ID0246OFDVD, UPC #014381024623). Widescreen (1.66:1) anamorphic. Dolby Digital Mono. $24.99. Snapper. *LANG:* English; French. *SUB:* English. *FEATURES:* 16 chapter links.
1966 121m/C *FR SW* Yves Montand, Michel Piccoli, Ingrid Thulin, Genevieve Bujold, Jean Daste, Dominique Rozan, Jean-Francois Remi; *D:* Alain Resnais; *W:* Jorge Semprun; *C:* Sacha Vierny; *M:* Giovanni Fusco; *Nar:* Jorge Semprun.

La Separation

Pierre (Auteuil) and Anne (Huppert) share a long-term relationship and a young son. What they no longer seem to have is any passion for each other as they go through their daily routines. Anne decides to have an affair but doesn't see why it should break up the household. Pierre thinks otherwise. The film is focused on everyday lives of middle-class people in an understated way that the French seem to handle so well. Burned-in subtitles are very easy to read. Otherwise, the image is not markedly superior to tape. —*MM*
Movie: 🎬🎬🎬 *DVD:* 🎬🎬½
Winstar Home Entertainment (Cat #5123). Widescreen (1.85:1) letterboxed. $29.98. Keepcase. *LANG:* French. *SUB:* English. *FEATURES:* Cast and crew thumbnail bios • Production notes • Trailer • 6 chapter links.
1998 85m/C *FR* Daniel Auteuil, Isabelle Huppert, Karin Viard, Jerome Deschamps; *D:* Christian Vincent; *W:* Christian Vincent, Dan Franck; *C:* Denis Lenoir.

The Ladies Man

Yet another *Saturday Night Live* skit is expanded to feature length with less-than-perfect results. Leon Phelps (Meadows) is a self-appointed expert on sex who dispenses advice on his late-night Chicago radio show. He doesn't know the difference between chlamydia and clam chowder and so he is regularly fired. Then he gets a letter from an old love asking him to come back. Meadows is completely comfortable as Leon and the movie does have some very funny moments. On DVD, the film looks as good as you'd expect a polished studio production to look. If only the story were as consistent as the image. —*MM*
Movie: 🎬🎬 *DVD:* 🎬🎬½
Paramount Home Video (Cat #33764, UPC #0973633766446). Widescreen anamorphic. Dolby Digital 5.1 Surround Stereo;

Dolby Digital Surround. $29.99. Keepcase. *LANG:* English; French. *SUB:* English. *FEATURES:* 18 chapter links • Interviews • Trailer.
2000 (R) 84m/C Tim Meadows, Will Ferrell, Tiffani-Amber Thiessen, Billy Dee Williams, Karyn Parsons, Lee Evans, John Witherspoon, Eugene Levy, Tamala Jones, Julianne Moore, Sean Thibodeau; *D:* Reginald (Reggie) Hudlin; *W:* Tim Meadows, Dennis McNicholas, Andrew Steele; *C:* Johnny E. Jensen; *M:* Marcus Miller.

Lady and the Tramp 2: Scamp's Adventure

The Disney organization knows how to make direct-to-video sequels to its theatrical animation. Even the most devoted fan of the original is likely to be pleased with one, and kids who have just discovered *Lady and the Tramp* will love it. The animation re-creates the idealized turn-of-the-century small-town American setting, and the characters are a natural extension of the first film. As generations of comic-page readers already know, Scamp (voice of Wolf) is the "son" of Tramp (Bennett) and Lady (Benson). Like his father, he wants to be a free-wheeling dog-about-town. But he has a loving family, and he has to live by the rules of the house. So Scamp rebels and takes up with a pack of junkyard dogs led by Buster (Palminteri). He's ready to run wild until he is smitten by the cute Angel (Milano). All of the voices are handled very well and the film avoids the excessive cuteness that can make this kind of animated feature insufferable for adults. If there are any flaws in the DVD image, I could not spot them. The drawing is bright and sharp without the hardness that comes from computer animation. Surround effects are neatly integrated into the music and story, too. Add in a full slate of extras—including three Pluto cartoons from the 1940s—and you've got a superb, overachieving disc. —*MM*
Movie: 🎬🎬🎬½ *DVD:* 🎬🎬🎬🎬
Buena Vista Home Entertainment (Cat #21 228, UPC #786936140491). Widescreen (1.66:1) anamorphic. DTS 5.1 Surround; Dolby Digital 5.1 Surround Stereo. $29.99. Keepcase. *LANG:* English; French; Spanish. *CAP:* English. *FEATURES:* 24 chapter links • 3 Disney cartoons • "Making of" featurette • Commentary: Rooney, Roussel, Trenbirth • Hide and seek game.
2001 (G) 70m/C *D:* Darrell Rooney, Jeannine Roussel; *W:* Bill Motz, Bob Roth; *M:* Danny Troob, Melissa Manchester, Norman Gimbel; *V:* Scott Wolf, Alyssa Milano, Jodi Benson, Bill Fagerbakke, Don Knotts, Cathy Moriarty, Chazz Palminteri, Bronson Pinchot, Mickey Rooney, Kath Soucie, Jeff Bennett.

Lady Dragon

A woman (Rothrock) and her husband are viciously attacked and only she survives. Found by an old man, she learns a number of martial arts tricks and sets out for revenge. Standard-issue martial arts plot

gains nothing on DVD. Image is identical to tape. Sound may be a slight improvement. —*MM*
Movie: 🎬🎬 *DVD:* 🎬🎬
Studio Home Entertainment (Cat #4070). Full frame. $24.95. Keepcase. *LANG:* English. *FEATURES:* Cast and crew thumbnail bios • Trailer • 18 chapter links.
1992 (R) 89m/C Cynthia Rothrock, Richard Norton, Robert Ginty, Bella Esperance, Hengko Tornando; *D:* David Worth; *W:* David Worth; *C:* David Worth; *M:* Jim West.

The Lady from Shanghai

Welles's first true film noir is a glorious mess. He plays Mike O'Hara, an innocent who's lured into a tangle of deception involving Elsa Bannister (Hayworth, once Mrs. Welles) and her crippled husband Arthur (Sloane). O'Hara's hired to work on their yacht. The scene moves from New York to Mexico to San Francisco, ending in the famous hall-of-mirrors confrontation. The bizarre plot is preposterous from beginning to end, so viewers unfamiliar with Welles are advised to ignore it as much as possible. Focus instead on Hayworth's shimmering blonde glamour and the supporting cast of grotesques. The DVD image contains a few intermittent flecks. The digital sound is clear but falsely full in some scenes. Accents, including Welles's own faux brogue, are exaggerated and that exaggeration is heightened by the distortion. If this one doesn't equal *Touch of Evil*, it belongs in the library of every Welles fan. —*MM*
Movie: 🎬🎬🎬 *DVD:* 🎬🎬🎬
Columbia Tristar Home Video (Cat #04859, UPC #043396048591). Full frame. Dolby Digital Mono. $24.95. Keepcase. *LANG:* English; French; Spanish; Portuguese. *SUB:* English; Spanish; French; Portuguese; Chinese; Korean; Thai. *CAP:* English. *FEATURES:* Featurette by Peter Bogdanovich • Commentary: Peter Bogdanovich • 28 chapter links • Advertising material and trailer • Production notes • Cast and crew thumbnail bios.
1948 87m/B Orson Welles, Rita Hayworth, Everett Sloane, Glenn Anders, Ted de Corsia, Erskine Sanford, Gus Schilling; *D:* Orson Welles; *W:* Orson Welles; *C:* Charles Lawton Jr.; *M:* Heinz Roemheld.

The Lady in White

Small-town ghost story begins when young Haas is locked in school one night and is visited by the ghost of a little girl who wants his help in solving her murder. Well-developed characters, interesting style, and a suspenseful plot make for a sometimes slow but well-done horror film. On his commentary track, auteur Laloggia talks at length about the autobiographical nature of the project. DVD appears to be a faithful re-creation of a soft-focus nostalgic original. The amount of extras indicate the care that was taken with the transfer to disc. —*MM*

Movie: ♪♪♪ **DVD:** ♪♪½

Elite Entertainment, Inc. (Cat #5240). Widescreen (1.85:1) letterboxed. Dolby Digital 5.1 Surround Stereo. $29.95. Keepcase. *LANG:* English. *FEATURES:* Deleted scenes • Commentary: director/writer Frank Laloggia • 3 soundtrack suites with notes • "Making of" featurette • Trailer and promotional material • 29 chapter links • Stills gallery.
1988 (PG-13) 92m/C Lukas Haas, Len Cariou, Alex Rocco, Katherine Helmond, Jason Presson, Renata Vanni, Angelo Bertolini, Jared Rushton, Joelle Jacob; **D:** Frank Laloggia; **W:** Frank Laloggia; **C:** Russell Carpenter; **M:** Frank Laloggia.

The Land Before Time

Lushly animated children's film follows five orphaned baby dinosaurs who band together to find the Great Valley, a paradise where they might live safely. It works with the same parental separation theme as Bluth's *American Tail*. Followed by a series of video premiere sequels. The heavy grain in this early disc seems to come from the original material. It's not a huge improvement over tape but that won't matter to the target audience. —*MM*
Movie: ♪♪♪ **DVD:** ♪♪½
Universal Studios Home Video (Cat #20278). Full frame. $24.98. Keepcase. *LANG:* English; French; Spanish. *FEATURES:* 16 chapter links.
1988 (G) 67m/C D: Don Bluth; **W:** Stu Krieger; **M:** James Horner; **V:** Pat Hingle, Helen Shaver, Gabriel Damon, Candice Houston, Burke Barnes, Judith Barsi, Will Ryan.

Land Before Time 7: The Stone of Cold Fire

In the seventh installment of the popular kid's series, the young dinosaurs Littlefoot, Cera, Spike, Ducky, and Petrie go off in search of a meteor that only Littlefoot saw. Petrie's disreputable uncle Pterano eggs them on. The moral lessons are simple; the animation is bright; the story moves quickly. In short, the movie delivers exactly what its young fans want to see. The pidgin English dialogue will be hard for adults to take. The image is very good, though the detail of the art is not equal to the best in the field. 5.1 delivers impressively rumbling effects. —*MM*
Movie: ♪♪ **DVD:** ♪♪½
Universal Studios Home Video (Cat #20920, UPC #025192092022). Full frame. Dolby Digital 5.1 Surround Stereo. $24.98. Keepcase. *LANG:* English; French. *SUB:* English. *FEATURES:* 18 chapter links • DVD-ROM features.
2000 (G) 75m/C D: Charles Grosvenor; **W:** Len Uhley; **V:** Jeff Bennett, Anndi McAfee, Rob Paulsen, Thomas Dekker, Aria Noelle Curzon.

Laser Mission

When it is discovered that the Soviets have laser weapon capabilities, an agent (Lee) is given the task of destroying the thingy but he is kidnapped by the scientist (Borgnine) who developed it. This may be an adequate presentation of an exceptionally poor original. It's grainy and poorly lit. The rental disc I watched kept freezing and skipping. —*MM*
Movie: ♪♪½ **DVD:** ♪
Diamond Entertainment Corp. (Cat #98002). Full frame. Dolby Digital Stereo. $6.99. Keepcase. *LANG:* English. *FEATURES:* 4 chapter links • Talent files.
1990 83m/C Brandon Lee, Debi Monahan, Ernest Borgnine, Werner Pochat, Graham Clarke, Maureen Lahoud, Pierre Knoessen; **D:** Beau Davis; **M:** David Knopfler.

The Last Best Sunday

Joseph (Spain), a Mexican-American teenager, snaps after he's beaten up by two racist thugs in the little farm town of Pickley, California. He steals a shotgun and kills the pair, then hides out in a home that he thinks is abandoned. But Lolly (Bettis) is staying there alone while her parents are away for the weekend. At first, she is his hostage but that changes quickly. Writer Karen Kelly and director Don Most create their characters and conflicts with broad brushstrokes, but they avoid exploitation. DVD presents a generally well-photographed image with a rough, unsophisticated independent feeling. —*MM*
Movie: ♪♪½ **DVD:** ♪♪
Vanguard International Cinema, Inc. (Cat #1-892649-86-1, UPC #658769010237). Widescreen (1.66:1) letterboxed. $29.95. Keepcase. *LANG:* English. *FEATURES:* 12 chapter links.
1998 101m/C Douglas Spain, Angela Bettis, Kim Darby, William Lucking, Marion Ross, Craig Wasson, Daniel Beer; **D:** Donny Most; **W:** Karen Kelly; **C:** Zoran Hochstatter; **M:** Tim Westergren.

The Last Great Adventure

DVD contains a three-part documentary about the race to be the first person to circumnavigate the Earth in a hot-air balloon. The main players are billionaire Richard Branson, Swiss psychiatrist Bertrand Piccard, and American businessman Steve Fossett. Naturally, the image quality varies with the source material and most of it is no better than broadcast quality. Same for sound. —*MM*
Movie: ♪♪½ **DVD:** ♪♪
BFS Video (Cat #30049-D, UPC #066805300493). Full frame. Dolby Digital Mono. $29.98. Keepcase. *LANG:* English. *FEATURES:* 18 chapter links.
1999 160m/C D: Garfield Kennedy; **W:** Garfield Kennedy; **Nar:** Sean Barrett.

The Last Lieutenant

Aging Thor Espedal (Skjonberg) has just retired from the Merchant Marines and returned home to his beloved wife Anna (Tellefsen). But the year is 1940 and the Germans are invading the country. So the ex-cavalry lieutenant gets his old uniform out of mothballs and enlists. He finds the army in complete disarray but is able to cobble together a group of volunteers to hold a key mountain pass. On DVD, interiors are carefully lit and almost flawless. Problems appear in exteriors where bad artifacts and aliasing are evident. Sound is good. Subtitles have been placed with some care. Based on a true story. —*MM* *AKA:* The Second Lieutenant; Secondloitnanten.
Movie: ♪♪♪½ **DVD:** ♪♪
Vanguard International Cinema, Inc. (UPC #658769006438). Widescreen letterboxed. $29.95. Keepcase. *LANG:* Norwegian. *SUB:* English. *FEATURES:* 12 chapter links.
1994 102m/C *NO* Espen Skjonberg, Bjorn Sundquist, Rut Tellefsen, Gard B. Eidsvold, Lars Andreas Larssen; **D:** Hans Petter Moland; **W:** Hans Petter Moland, Axel Hellstenius; **C:** Harald Gunnar Paalgard; **M:** Randall Meyers.

The Last Marshal

Cole McCleary (Glenn) is a hard-bitten Texas Marshal who hates every racial, ethnic, and sexual group imaginable. After a botched hostage-rescue, he becomes the target of a Miami drug dealer (Forsythe). The villains and the action are both hamfistedly overstated, but the cast does more than capable work. Image is about equal to VHS tape, save very bad pixelation in some exteriors. Sound mix sometimes overpowers voices with music. —*MM*
Movie: ♪♪ **DVD:** ♪♪
York Entertainment (Cat #YPD-1038, UPC #750723103822). Full frame. $14.99. Keepcase. *LANG:* English. *SUB:* Spanish. *FEATURES:* 28 chapter links • Trailers • Behind-the-scenes featurette.
1999 (R) 102m/C Scott Glenn, Constance Marie, Randall Batinkoff, Vincent Castellanos, John Ortiz, Raymond Cruz, William Forsythe, Lisa Boyle; **D:** Mike Kirton.

The Last of the Blonde Bombshells

In England during World War II, the Blonde Bombshells was a hot all-girl dance band. Decades later, after the death of her husband, sax player Elizabeth (Dench) tries to arrange a reunion. With a superb cast, this made-for-cable production is a solid sleeper. It looks and sounds every bit as good as contemporary theatrical releases. The script is much smarter and funnier. Recommended. —*MM*
Movie: ♪♪♪½ **DVD:** ♪♪♪
HBO Home Video (Cat #91711, UPC #026359171123). Widescreen anamorphic. Dolby Digital Surround Stereo; Dolby Digital Stereo. $19.98. Snapper. *LANG:* English; Spanish. *SUB:* English; French; Spanish. *FEATURES:* 13 chapter links.
2000 (PG-13) 80m/C Judi Dench, Ian Holm, Olympia Dukakis, Leslie Caron, Cleo Laine, Joan Sims, Billie Whitelaw, June Whitfield, Felicity Dean, Valentine Pelka, Millie Findlay; **D:** Gilles Mackinnon; **W:** Alan Plater; **C:** Richard Greatrex; **M:** John Keane.

The Last of the Mohicans

Color tints enhance this silent version of the James Fenimore Cooper rouser. Beery is the villainous Magua, with Bedford memorable as the lovely Cora and Roscoe as the brave Uncas. Fine action sequences, including the Huron massacre at Fort Henry. Director credit was shared when Tourneur suffered an on-set injury and was off for three months. Like all silent films transferred to DVD, this disc benefits a great deal. The picture is crisp and clear. The added color tinting is not a distraction and does, in fact, seem to cover up a few minor flaws. There is a registration problem with some excessive "bouncing" in the picture, and the matted black border on the right side of my screen occasionally features a digital blue hue. The soundtrack proves nice and clear. —MJT

Movie: 🎵🎵🎵 **DVD:** 🎵🎵½
SlingShot Entertainment (Cat #DVD9851, UPC #017078985122). Full frame. Dolby Digital Stereo. $19.99. Super jewelbox. *LANG:* Silent. *SUB:* English intertitles. *FEATURES:* 15 chapter links • Weblinks.
1920 75m/B Wallace Beery, Barbara Bedford, Albert Roscoe, Lillian Hall-Davis, Henry Woodward, James Gordon, George Hackathorne, Harry Lorraine, Nelson McDowell, Theodore Lorch, Boris Karloff; **D:** Maurice Tourneur, Clarence Brown; **W:** Robert Dillon; **C:** Charles Van Enger. *AWARDS:* Natl. Film Reg. '95.

The Last of the Mohicans

Like *Casablanca,* this streamlined adaptation of the famous novel is really more a love story than a war story. Mostly, it's a vehicle for two sleek stars. Hawkeye (Day-Lewis) is a Samurai in buckskins; Cora (Stowe) is the English aristocrat's daughter who comes into her own during the French and Indian War. The action is swiftly paced and Wes Studi is a memorable villain. This "director's expanded edition" is three minutes longer than the theatrical release. The additions are not structurally significant. The DVD image faithfully recreates the soft mossy greens and blues of the North Carolina mountain settings. The shadows are the same deliberately murky black pools that they have always been. Some non-English dialogue is subtitled in the lower bar of the letterbox. Though the 5.1 mix is not overly active, it's fine for this Oscar-winning sound. Too bad Michael Mann couldn't be persuaded to do a commentary track. —MM

Movie: 🎵🎵🎵 **DVD:** 🎵🎵🎵½
20th Century Fox Home Entertainment (Cat #4112891, UPC #086162128912). Widescreen (2.35:1) letterboxed. Dolby Digital 5.1 Surround Stereo; Dolby Digital Surround Stereo. $34.98. Keepcase. *LANG:* English; French. *SUB:* English; Spanish. *FEATURES:* 32 chapter links.
1992 (R) 114m/C Daniel Day-Lewis, Madeleine Stowe, Wes Studi, Russell

Means, Eric Schweig, Jodhi May, Steven Waddington, Maurice Roeves, Colm Meaney, Patrice Chereau, Pete Postlethwaite, Terry Kinney, Tracey Ellis, Dennis Banks, Dylan Baker; **D:** Michael Mann; **W:** Christopher Crowe, Michael Mann; **C:** Dante Spinotti; **M:** Trevor Jones, Randy Edelman. *AWARDS:* Oscars '92: Sound.

The Last Picture Show [DC]

Slice of life/nostalgic farewell to an innocent age is based on Larry McMurtry's novel. Set in Archer City, a backwater Texas town, most of the story plays out at the local hangout run by ex-cowboy Sam the Lion (Johnson). Bridges is hooked up with spoiled local belle Shepherd, while Bottoms, the sensitive guy, is having an affair with the coach's neglected wife (Leachman). Disillusionment, confusion, and the only movie theatre in town is about to close its doors for good. The transfer exhibits some noise and some slight speckles, but is otherwise free of defects. The DVD image is generally very good, striking the right visual balance that ranges from deep blacks to well-defined highlights. The mono soundtrack that has been well transferred without noise or notable distortion. It is natural sound and understandable. This is the 126-minute director's cut of the film. —GH/MM

Movie: 🎵🎵🎵🎵 **DVD:** 🎵🎵🎵½
Columbia Tristar Home Video (Cat #50429, UPC #043396504295). Widescreen (1.85:1) anamorphic. Dolby Digital Mono. $27.95. Keepcase. *LANG:* English. *SUB:* English; Spanish; Portuguese; Korean; Mandarin; Thai. *FEATURES:* Documentary • Talent files • Featurette • Theatrical trailers.
1971 (R) 126m/B Jeff Bridges, Timothy Bottoms, Ben Johnson, Cloris Leachman, Cybill Shepherd, Ellen Burstyn, Eileen Brennan, Clu Gulager, Sharon Taggart, Randy Quaid, Sam Bottoms, John Hillerman; **D:** Peter Bogdanovich; **W:** Larry McMurtry, Peter Bogdanovich; **C:** Robert L. Surtees. *AWARDS:* Oscars '71: Support. Actor (Johnson), Support. Actress (Leachman); British Acad. '72: Screenplay, Support. Actor (Johnson), Support. Actress (Leachman); Golden Globes '72: Support. Actor (Johnson); Natl. Bd. of Review '71: Support. Actor (Johnson), Support. Actress (Leachman), Natl. Film Reg. '98; N.Y. Film Critics '71: Screenplay, Support. Actor (Johnson), Support. Actress (Burstyn); Natl. Soc. Film Critics '71: Support. Actress (Burstyn); *NOM:* Oscars '71: Adapt. Screenplay, Cinematog., Director (Bogdanovich), Picture, Support. Actor (Bridges), Support. Actress (Burstyn).

Last Resort

A married furniture executive (Grodin) unknowingly takes his family on a vacation to a sex-saturated Club Med–type holiday spot. Not much hilarity ensues. The crazy clashing clothing patterns and red-orange-green color scheme are much too clear on

DVD, though the image is essentially the same as VHS tape. —MM *AKA:* She Knew No Other Way.

Movie: 🎵🎵 **DVD:** 🎵🎵
New Concorde (Cat #NH20276D, UPC #736991427693). Full frame. $19.98. Keepcase. *LANG:* English. *FEATURES:* 20 chapter links • Talent files • Previews.
1986 (R) 80m/C Charles Grodin, Robin Pearson Rose, John Aston, Ellen Blake, Megan Mullally, Christopher Ames, Jon Lovitz, Scott Nemes, Gerrit Graham, Mario Van Peebles, Phil Hartman, Mimi Lieber, Steve Levitt; **D:** Zane Buzby; **W:** Jeff Buhai; **C:** Stephen M. Katz, Alex Nepomniaschy; **M:** Steven Nelson, Thom Sharp.

The Last September

The setting is a ritzy estate in County Cork, Ireland, circa 1920, and the players form a capable cast that includes Oscar-winner Smith. Hawes plays 19-year-old Lois, who is struggling with her yearnings for love and freedom amid the demise of the Anglo-Irish aristocracy in Ireland. She is being courted by a British Army captain. But when she discovers a childhood friend who has become a Irish freedom fighter hiding out on the estate, she becomes intrigued by him. Though some will find the drama based upon Elizabeth Bowen's novel absorbing, others will not abide the deliberate, almost plodding pace. Non-anamorphic transfer steals from the technical rating. Still, the picture when displayed on non-widescreen monitors is beautiful, showing off the gorgeous Irish countryside and nice cinematography. Sound is fine, but this is not a disc to challenge your subwoofer. —MB

Movie: 🎵🎵½ **DVD:** 🎵🎵🎵
Trimark Home Video (Cat #VM7440D, UPC #031398744023). Widescreen (1.85:1) letterboxed. Dolby Digital 5.1. $24.99. Keepcase. *LANG:* English. *SUB:* English; Spanish; French. *CAP:* English. *FEATURES:* 24 chapter links • Trailer • Director and actor interviews • Dramatic reading.
1999 (R) 103m/C *IR GB FR* Maggie Smith, Michael Gambon, Keeley Hawes, David Tennant, Gary Lydon, Fiona Shaw, Lambert Wilson, Jane Birkin, Jonathan Slinger, Richard Roxburgh; **D:** Deborah Warner; **W:** John Banville; **C:** Slawomir Idziak; **M:** Zbigniew Preisner.

The Last Stop

Colorado state trooper Jake (Beach) is stranded by a blizzard at the Last Stop Motel and Diner. Also trapped are his old flame Nancy (McGowan), a black trucker, a couple of drunken rednecks, and a slime-ball and his much younger girlfriend. Then Fritz (Prochnow), the owner of the place, finds a body and a bag of cash. This a competent little mystery that looks fine on DVD, but the best part of the disc is director Malone's commentary. He focuses on the tricks of lower-budget film work—how to use colors and smoky light to make a small room look larger; how to turn two motel room sets into four. Anyone who's

trying to work in that side of the business ought to listen and take notes. —*MM*
Movie: 🎬🎬🎬 ***DVD:*** 🎬🎬🎬½ Studio Home Entertainment (Cat #7525). Widescreen letterboxed. Dolby Digital 5.1 Surround; Dolby Digital Surround. $19.98. Keepcase. *LANG:* English. *SUB:* Spanish. *FEATURES:* 20 chapter links ▪ Trailer ▪ Interviews ▪ Talent files ▪ Commentary: Mark Malone.
1999 (R) 94m/C *CA* Adam Beach, Juergen Prochnow, Rose McGowan, Callum Keith Rennie, Winston Rekert; *D:* Mark Malone; *W:* Bart Sumner; *C:* Tony Westman; *M:* Terry Frewer.

The Last Temptation of Christ

Scorsese's controversial adaptation of the Nikos Kazantzakis novel portrays Christ in his last year as an ordinary Israelite. He's tormented by divine doubt, the voice of God, and is given the ultimate temptation by Satan—come down from the cross and truly live life as a man. The controversy engulfing the film, as it was heavily protested and widely banned, tended to divert attention from what is an exceptional statement of religious and artistic vision, and ultimately a profoundly reverent reflection of faith. Excellent score by Peter Gabriel. This Criterion DVD looks better than their own widescreen laserdisc edition. In fact, the colors are markedly improved, with even more detailed and varied hues reflecting the beautifully realistic cinematography. With this release you really can almost taste the dust of the desert. The DVD is also sharper than the LD, which was a very good-looking laserdisc. The 5.1 sound's main improvement is the subwoofer track, which gives more energy to Gabriel's score, serving to propel the film along during what some might call the slower set-up scenes. Like most Criterion Collection issues, this is a must-have for the library. —*JO*
Movie: 🎬🎬🎬🎬 ***DVD:*** 🎬🎬🎬½ Criterion Collection (Cat #70, UPC #71551 5010528). Widescreen (1.85:1) anamorphic. Dolby Digital 5.1. $39.95. Keepcase. *LANG:* English. *SUB:* English. *FEATURES:* 30 chapter links ▪ Commentary: Martin Scorsese, Willem Dafoe, Paul Schrader, Jay Cocks ▪ Production stills ▪ Costume designs ▪ Location production footage ▪ Interview with composer Peter Gabriel.
1988 (R) 164m/C *CA* Willem Dafoe, Harvey Keitel, Barbara Hershey, Harry Dean Stanton, Andre Gregory, David Bowie, Verna Bloom, Juliette Caton, John Lurie, Roberts Blossom, Irvin Kershner, Barry Miller, Tomas Arana, Nehemiah Persoff, Paul Herman, Illeana Douglas; *D:* Martin Scorsese; *W:* Paul Schrader; *C:* Michael Ballhaus; *M:* Peter Gabriel. *AWARDS:* NOM: Oscars '88: Director (Scorsese).

The Last Time I Saw Paris

A successful writer (Johnson) reminisces about his love affair with a wealthy American girl (Taylor) in post–World War II Paris. Considering the level of talent on both sides of the camera—director Richard Brooks working with a script based on a Fitzgerald story by the Epstein brothers (*Casablanca*)—the result is a bit disappointing. The disc comes from a substandard original. The Technicolor blacks and reds are too heavy; lighter greens and blues are faded. Color values shift within the same shot. The image ranges between poor and fair. Sound is nothing special. —*MM*
Movie: 🎬🎬½ ***DVD:*** 🎬🎬 Madacy Entertainment (Cat #99028, UPC #056775006495). Full frame. Dolby Digital Mono. $9.99. Keepcase. *LANG:* English. *FEATURES:* Elizabeth Taylor thumbnail bio ▪ Trivia ▪ Production credits ▪ 9 chapter links.
1954 116m/C Elizabeth Taylor, Van Johnson, Walter Pidgeon, Roger Moore, Donna Reed, Eva Gabor; *D:* Richard Brooks; *W:* Richard Brooks, Julius J. Epstein, Philip G. Epstein; *C:* Joseph Ruttenberg; *M:* Conrad Salinger.

The Last Valley

A scholar (Sharif) tries to protect a pristine 17th-century Swiss valley, untouched by the Thirty Years War, from marauding mercenaries led by Caine. Period action with an intellectual twist has been praised by many historians as an unusually accurate portrayal of a confusing and often overlooked war. Unfortunately, the disc is riddled with problems. Pixels, artifacts, and almost every other visual flaw crop up in bright exteriors. They may come from heavy grain in the original, but this is still an unusually poor image for an Anchor Bay release. —*MM*
Movie: 🎬🎬 ***DVD:*** 🎬🎬 Anchor Bay (Cat #10984). Widescreen (2.21:1) letterboxed. Dolby Digital Stereo. $24.98. Keepcase. *LANG:* English. *FEATURES:* 18 chapter links.
1971 (PG) 128m/C Michael Caine, Omar Sharif, Florinda Bolkan, Nigel Davenport, Per Oscarsson, Arthur O'Connell; *D:* James Clavell; *W:* James Clavell; *C:* John Wilcox; *M:* John Barry.

The Lathe of Heaven

In a late 20th-century future suffocating from pollution, George Orr (Davison) visits a dream specialist. He then dreams of a world free from war, pestilence, and overpopulation. At times, the dreams come true but they have disastrous side effects. The technical bone rating here is based on the restorative work that went into this long-unavailable title, which was made for public television. An on-screen prologue admits that the original master has been lost and the disc was made from imperfect 2" videotape. The image and sound are no better than a worn VHS tape. —*MM*
Movie: 🎬🎬🎬 ***DVD:*** 🎬🎬 New Video Group (Cat #NVG-9467, UPC #767685946732). Full frame. Dolby Digital Stereo. $24.98. Keepcase. *LANG:* English. *FEATURES:* 12 chapter links ▪ 1999 interview by Bill Moyers with Ursula K. LeGuin ▪ LeGuin thumbnail bio.
1980 100m/C Bruce Davison, Kevin Conway, Margaret Avery, Peyton E. Park; *D:* David Loxton, Fred Barzyk; *W:* Roger E. Swaybill, Diane English; *C:* Robbie Greenberg; *M:* Michael Small.

L'Avventura

On his commentary track, historian Gene Youngblood mounts a relentless defense of this film as one of the genuine masterpieces of world cinema. Those not already on board may think that he protests too much, but, in this instance, that's his job. Antonioni's influential story of alienation and angst has been imitated often in the years since. It remains an effective minimalist exercise in narrative. The story concerns the disappearance of a wealthy young woman and the affair between her lover and best friend. Criterion's restoration of the black-and-white image results in a visually flawless DVD. English translation of the optional subtitles is a solid step up from most. The film is on one disc; most of the extras are on the other, and they are extensive. —*MM* *AKA:* The Adventure.
Movie: 🎬🎬🎬½ ***DVD:*** 🎬🎬🎬🎬 Criterion Collection (Cat #98, UPC #03742 9156025). Widescreen (1.77:1) anamorphic. Dolby Digital Mono. $39.95. Keepcase. *LANG:* Italian. *SUB:* English. *FEATURES:* 35 chapter links ▪ 1989 commentary track by film historian Gene Youngblood ▪ "Antonioni: Documents and Testimonials" documentary (16 chapter links) ▪ Antonioni essays read by Jack Nicholson (3 links) ▪ Trailer ▪ Restoration demonstration.
1960 145m/C *IT* Monica Vitti, Gabriele Ferzetti, Lea Massari, Dominique Blanchar, James Addams; *D:* Michelangelo Antonioni; *W:* Tonino Guerra, Michelangelo Antonioni; *C:* Aldo Scavarda; *M:* Giovanni Fusco. *AWARDS:* Cannes '60: Special Jury Prize.

Law and Disorder

Willie (O'Connor) and Sy (Borgnine), two average New Yorkers, become fed up with the rising crime rate in their neighborhood and form an auxiliary police force. It's a semi-comic take on the same emotions and social conditions that inspired the original *Death Wish,* and as such, it's an accurate depiction of the city in the early '70s. It's also a fine vehicle for the two stars. The disc was made from very good original elements, but it has the rough quality of so many made-on-location '70s movies. And then there are the clothes. Don't look too closely at Borgnine's clashing polyester patterns and colors. Almost all of his combinations are truly hideous. —*MM*
Movie: 🎬🎬🎬 ***DVD:*** 🎬🎬 Anchor Bay (Cat #DV11244, UPC #013131 124491). Widescreen (1.85:1) anamorphic. Dolby Digital Mono. $24.99. Keepcase. *LANG:* English; French. *FEATURES:* 25

chapter links ▪ Trailer ▪ TV spots ▪ Talent files.
1974 (R) 103m/C Carroll O'Connor, Ernest Borgnine, Ann Wedgeworth, Anita Dangler, Leslie Ackerman, Karen Black, Jack Kehoe; **D:** Ivan Passer; **W:** Ivan Passer, William Richert, Kenneth Harris Fishman; **C:** Arthur Ornitz; **M:** Angelo Badalamenti.

Lawless Frontier / Randy Rides Alone

The first feature on this disc looks like it was copied from a bad tape. Zip through it to the second, which looks much better but is still only a fair version of one of Wayne's early B-movies. Sound is poor. Both titles are in public domain. —*MM*
Movie: ♪ **DVD:** ♪
Madacy Entertainment (Cat #DVD-9003-4, UPC #056775002398). Full frame. Dolby Digital Mono. $9.99. Keepcase. *LANG:* English. *FEATURES:* 8 chapter links ▪ John Wayne filmography 1956–65 ▪ Trivia quiz. Also available in *The John Wayne Collection* (cat. # DVD-9-9003; UPC 056775001995).
1935 53m/B John Wayne, George "Gabby" Hayes, Sheila Terry, Earl Dwire; **D:** Robert North Bradbury.

Lawrence of Arabia

One of the greatest, if not *the* greatest film ever made. Rich, powerful, and exquisitely cinematic, *Lawrence* remains a pinnacle in the art of visual storytelling. O'Toole brings the legendary, contradictory T. E. Lawrence to vivid life in the role that (deservedly) made his career. Bolt's script manages to be literate, funny, and faithful as it conveys the real-life adventures of the famous low-ranking British military man who became a unifying figure (and near-messiah) to the scattered and feuding Bedouin tribes. Lean's mastery of the art form (while always stunning) has never been better than it is here. It's one classic scene after another in this visually stunning, beautifully scored tapestry of a film. Lean and editor Anne Coates edit the film to perfection, delicately balancing perfectly timed long-takes and rapidly cut battle scenes into a masterpiece of pacing. Without hyperbole, this film really needs to be experienced in 70mm on a huge screen to give justice to Freddie Young's poetic, beautifully composed photography. Though trimmed several times over the years, it was restored in 1989 by Robert Harris and Jim Painten to a close approximation of its original length. An additional 2 1/2–minute scene that needed to be restored (the first part of the scene where Allenby convinces Lawrence to return to Arabia) could not be finished at that time and unfortunately is still not included on this DVD edition. Curiously enough, Harris and Painten are snubbed throughout the supplements for this two-disc set as well as in Laurent Bouzereau's "making of" documentary, which is fascinating, informative, and otherwise exemplary. The beautifully packaged set includes a well-written booklet with background on T.E. Lawrence and the film, along with several well-worn though interesting original 1962 featurettes. The film has been treated to a new transfer that is sharp and vivid overall. There are a few instances of shimmering and some slight chemical stains are occasionally visible in the transfer print, but the image itself is mostly stunning. The disc's 5.1 Surround track is the preferred option, though one must choose it before viewing as it is not the default setting. This vivid, involving track helps bring the video experience that much closer to the theatrical one. A gem. —*DG*
Movie: ♪♪♪♪ **DVD:** ♪♪♪½
Columbia Tristar Home Video (Cat #05832, UPC #04339605832). Widescreen (2.20:1) anamorphic. Dolby Digital 5.1, Dolby Stereo Surround. $39.95. Library-bound 2-disc keepcase. *LANG:* English; French; Spanish; Portuguese. *SUB:* English; French; Spanish; Portuguese; Chinese; Korean; Thai. *CAP:* English. *FEATURES:* 56 chapter links ▪ Conversation with Steven Spielberg ▪ "Maan, Jordan: The Camels Are Cast" featurette ▪ "In Search of Lawrence" featurette ▪ "Romance of Arabia" featurette ▪ "Wind, Sand and Star: The Making of a Classic" featurette ▪ "The Making of *Lawrence of Arabia*" documentary ▪ Original newsreel footage of the New York premiere ▪ Theatrical trailer and other trailers ▪ Cast and crew bios ▪ Color insert booklet replica of original 1962 souvenir booklet ▪ Advertising campaign gallery ▪ DVD-ROM: interactive map of the Middle East, historic photographs.
1962 (PG) 221m/C *GB* Peter O'Toole, Omar Sharif, Anthony Quinn, Alec Guinness, Jack Hawkins, Claude Rains, Anthony Quayle, Arthur Kennedy, Jose Ferrer, Michel Ray, Norman Rossington, John Ruddock, Donald Wolfit; **D:** David Lean; **W:** Robert Bolt, Michael Wilson; **C:** Frederick A. (Freddie) Young; **M:** Maurice Jarre. *AWARDS:* Oscars '62: Art Dir./Set Dec., Color, Color Cinematog.; Director (Lean), Film Editing, Picture, Sound, Orig. Score; AFI '98: Top 100; British Acad. '62: Actor (O'Toole), Film, Screenplay; Directors Guild '62: Director (Lean); Golden Globes '63: Director (Lean), Film—Drama, Support. Actor (Sharif); Natl. Bd. of Review '62: Director (Lean), Natl. Film Reg. '91; *NOM:* Oscars '62: Actor (O'Toole), Adapt. Screenplay, Support. Actor (Sharif).

Left Behind: The Movie

Ace TV newsman Buck Williams (Cameron) is on hand for a sneak attack on Israel. Right after it, devout Christians and innocent children mysteriously vanish. The film is a dramatization of the novels based on a conservative Christian interpretation of the Book of Revelation. As entertainment, it's heavy handed at every level—plotting, acting, writing, directing. The CGI special effects are obvious. The DVD displays artifacts, aliasing, and edge enhancement, making the disc only a notch or two superior to a good VHS tape. —*MM*
Movie: ♪ **DVD:** ♪♪
Cloud Ten Pictures (UPC #7456380019 36). Full frame. $29.99. Keepcase. *LANG:* English. *FEATURES:* 14 chapter links ▪ "Making of" documentary ▪ Music list ▪ Videos ▪ Weblinks ▪ Proselytizing promotional spot.
2000 95m/C Kirk Cameron, Brad Johnson, Chelsea Noble; **D:** Vic Savin; **W:** Alan B. McElroy, Clarence Gilyard Jr., Joe Goodman; **C:** George Tirl.

The Legend

This film has been available under the title *Fong Sai Yuk* on a substandard disc. This version corrects all of the flaws—well, most of them—and allows western audiences to experience Jet Li's masterpiece as it should be. Fong Sai Yuk is a Chinese folk hero and Li plays him with a rare combination of humor, physical grace, and athleticism. Purists might decry the lack of original Chinese dialogue, but the dubbing is very good. Image quality is superb; the 5.1 Surround only slightly less so. Grand stuff for action fans. —*MM* **AKA:** Fong Sai Yuk; The Legend of Fong Sai-Yuk; Fong Shi Yu.
Movie: ♪♪♪½ **DVD:** ♪♪♪½
Buena Vista Home Entertainment (Cat #21595, UPC #786936144116). Widescreen (1.85:1) letterboxed. Dolby Digital 5.1 Surround Stereo. $32.99. Keepcase. *LANG:* English. *CAP:* English. *FEATURES:* 21 chapter links.
1993 (R) 95m/C *HK* Jet Li, Michelle Reis, Adam Cheng, Chu Kong, Josephine Siao; **D:** Corey Yuen; **W:** Kung-Yung Chai, Jiang-Chung Change; **C:** Jingle Ma; **M:** Romeo Diaz, James Wong.

The Legend of Bagger Vance

Damon plays a once-promising white southern boy with a talent for golf and for wooing Charlize Theron. World War II and the Germans change all that, and he returns to his hometown a broken man who turns his back on his privileged life and on Charlize. Like any good southern belle, she takes it in stride. And when her daddy, the owner of the state's largest golf course, dies and leaves her in debt, she puts on her most fluctuating southern accent and sets out to get the two biggest golf names of the time to play a tournament at the failing course. This all leads to Damon's inevitable entry into the game, the appearance of mystical caddy Bagger Vance, and the big showdown on the grassy knoll. Will Smith is captivating, as usual, as Vance, but the rest of the cast and the script are strictly cookie cutter fare. The lush southern scenery looks great on the disc and the colors are fairly sharp. The sound is above average. —*CA*
Movie: ♪♪ **DVD:** ♪♪♪½
DreamWorks Home Entertainment (Cat #86398, UPC #667068639827). Widescreen (1.85:1) anamorphic. Dolby Digital 5.1; Dolby Digital Surround 2.0. $26.99. Keepcase. *LANG:* English. *SUB:* English.

CAP: English. FEATURES: 20 chapter links • Commentary: director • Production featurette • Theatrical teaser and trailer • Production notes • Cast and filmmaker bios.
2000 (PG-13) 127m/C Matt Damon, Will Smith, Charlize Theron, Jack Lemmon, Bruce McGill, Lane Smith, Harve Presnell, Peter Gerety, Michael O'Neill, Thomas Jay Ryan, Joel Gretsch, J. Michael Moncrief; **D:** Robert Redford; **W:** Jeremy Leven; **C:** Michael Ballhaus; **M:** Rachel Portman.

The Legend of Drunken Master

Folk hero Wong Fei-hong (Chan) saves priceless antiquities from being smuggled out of pre–World War I China. The catch: he can fight only when he's loaded. The film contains some of the most incredible fight sequences of the star's long career. The routines are meticulously timed and dazzlingly imaginative, particularly in the last reels. Of course, the outtakes are the highlight. Those who have seen only the import discs and tapes will be happily surprised at the quality of the image. The DVD looks terrific. Purists may decry the lack of Chinese sound tracks, but the dubbing is very good. Personally, I think it's not a flaw in an action movie. The 5.1 Surround works well with the fight choreography. —MM AKA: Drunken Master 2; Tsuui Kun 2.
Movie: ♪♪♪½ **DVD:** ♪♪♪½
Buena Vista Home Entertainment (Cat #22366, UPC #786936151268). Widescreen (2.35:1) anamorphic. Dolby Digital 5.1 Surround Stereo. $32.99. Keepcase. LANG: English; French. CAP: English. FEATURES: 16 chapter links • Jackie Chan interview.
1994 (R) 102m/C Jackie Chan, Lau Kar Leung, Anita Mui, Ti Lung, Andy Lau; **D:** Lau Kar Leung; **W:** Edward Tang; **C:** Yiutsou Cheung, Tong-Leung Cheung, Jingle Ma, Man-Wan Wong; **M:** Michael Wandmacher.

Legendary WWII Movies

In the first feature, Gung Ho, Carlson's Raiders are a specially trained unit of Marine jungle fighters determined to retake the Pacific island of Makin. It's an early role for Robert Mitchum. Inexperienced lieutenant Van Johnson heads up a special attack force made up of Japanese Americans in Go for Broke! The film follows the unit from training in Mississippi to fighting in the European theatre. David Niven does the same for a disparate group of Brits in The Immortal Battalion, one of the finest "unit pictures" to come out of the war. Neither image nor sound is much to write home about with any of these, but they are three excellent films, and at this price, the disc is a real bargain. —MM
Movie: ♪♪♪ **DVD:** ♪♪
BFS Video (Cat #83953-D, UPC #0668058 19537). Full frame. Dolby Digital Mono.

$9.95. Keepcase. LANG: English. FEATURES: 12 chapter links.
2000 ?m/C

Legends of the Fall [2 SE]

This "special edition" builds upon the film's first release on DVD (reviewed in the first edition). New language and subtitle tracks have been added; the widescreen transfer is anamorphic and two commentary tracks—one with Zwick and Pitt, a second with cinematographer John Toll and production designer Lully Kilvert—are included, along with an isolated track for James Horner's woozy score and three deleted scenes with commentary. —MM
Movie: ♪♪ **DVD:** ♪♪♪½
Columbia Tristar Home Video (Cat #78727, UPC #043396787278). Widescreen (1.85) anamorphic. Dolby Digital 5.1 Surround Stereo; Dolby Digital Stereo. $24.98. Keepcase. LANG: English; French; Spanish; Portuguese. SUB: English; French; Spanish; Portuguese; Chinese; Korean; Thai. FEATURES: 28 chapter links • 3 deleted scenes • Production design featurette • Original featurette • 2 commentary tracks • Talent files • Trailers • Isolated score.
1994 (R) 134m/C Brad Pitt, Aidan Quinn, Julia Ormond, Anthony Hopkins, Henry Thomas, Gordon Tootoosis, Tantoo Cardinal, Karina Lombard, Paul Desmond, Kenneth Welsh; **D:** Edward Zwick; **W:** Susan Shilliday, William D. Wittliff; **C:** John Toll; **M:** James Horner. AWARDS: Oscars '94: Cinematog; NOM: Oscars '94: Art Dir./Set Dec., Sound; Golden Globes '95: Actor—Drama (Pitt), Director (Zwick), Film—Drama, Score.

The Lemon Drop Kid

This is the second version of the Damon Runyon chestnut about Sidney Melbourne (Hope), a racetrack bookie who must recover the gangster's money that he lost on a bet. It's also one of Hope's best comedies and this DVD was made from an excellent original. The black-and-white image is very good. The songs sound fine, even in mono. —MM
Movie: ♪♪♪ **DVD:** ♪♪♪
Brentwood Home Video (Cat #60979-9, UPC #090096097992). Full frame. Dolby Digital Mono. $14.98. Keepcase. LANG: English. FEATURES: 8 chapter links • Bob Hope thumbnail bio and filmography.
1951 91m/B Bob Hope, Lloyd Nolan, Fred Clark, Marilyn Maxwell, Jane Darwell, Andrea King, William Frawley, Jay C. Flippen, Harry Bellaver; **D:** Sidney Lanfield; **W:** Frank Tashlin, Edmund Hartmann, Robert O'Brien; **C:** Daniel F. Fapp; **M:** Ray Evans, Jay Livingston, Victor Young.

The Lemon Sisters

Three women (Keaton, Kane, and Grody), friends since childhood, struggle to buy their own club. They juggle the men in their lives with less success. Such

actresses as these should have been given more to work with in this prototypical chick-flick. The DVD image ranges between good and very good with an intentionally soft focus. The limited vocal talents of the leads are all too apparent, but again, that's intentional. —MM
Movie: ♪♪ **DVD:** ♪♪½
Anchor Bay (Cat #DV11538, UPC #013131 153897). Widescreen (1.85:1) anamorphic. Dolby Digital Surround Stereo. $24.98. Keepcase. LANG: English. FEATURES: 25 chapter links • Trailer.
1990 (PG-13) 93m/C Diane Keaton, Carol Kane, Kathryn Grody, Elliott Gould, Ruben Blades, Aidan Quinn; **D:** Joyce Chopra; **W:** Jeremy Pikser; **C:** Bobby Byrne; **M:** Dick Hyman.

L'Ennui

Martin (Berling), a fortysomething writer, embarks upon an affair with plump 17-year-old Cecilia (Guillemin). With its theme and French setting, the film is easily comparable to Last Tango in Paris. For my money, it's much better in its examination of obsession and physical desire, and it's not nearly as self-indulgent. The two leads, particularly Guillemin, are excellent and the depiction of physical acts is forthright and honest. Since the film is exploring dark ideas, there is little that DVD can do with the harsh images. Almost all of the action is underlit, by American standards, but the disc appears to be an accurate re-creation of the original. English subtitles are easy to read and burned in. —MM
Movie: ♪♪♪ **DVD:** ♪♪♪½
Winstar Home Entertainment (Cat #FLV 5259, UPC #720917525921). Widescreen letterboxed. $24.99. Keepcase. LANG: French. SUB: English. FEATURES: 16 chapter links • 2 trailers • Filmographies • Production credits.
1998 120m/C FR Charles Berling, Sophie Guillemin, Arielle Dombasle, Robert Kramer, Tom Ouedraoge; **D:** Cedric Kahn; **W:** Cedric Kahn, Laurence Ferreira Barbosa; **C:** Pascal Marti.

Leon, the Professional

This DVD is the longer "international" version of Leon, which was released theatrically in America in 1994 (as The Professional) and has been available only on laserdisc. With an extra 24 minutes, it really is a different film. Though the level of violence is intensified, the main difference is in the complex relationship between Leon (Reno), a professional hitman or "cleaner," and 12-year-old Mathilda (Portman). She comes to him for help after her family (including her baby brother) is killed by corrupt DEA agent Stansfield (Oldman) and his men. The result is a superb action film with real heart. Leon is cut from the same cloth as Chow Yun-Fat's Killer. If Portman's willful, manipulative, mercurial preteen temptress makes viewers uncomfortable, she is an honest compelling character. The 5.1 Surround effects really kick in during the big gun battles. Visually, the disc is fine, except for one very irritating flash in a striped blouse. —*MM* **AKA:** The Professional.

Movie: 🎵🎵🎵½ **DVD:** 🎵🎵🎵½
Columbia Tristar Home Video (Cat #04730, UPC #043396047303). Widescreen (2.35:1) letterboxed. Dolby Digital 5.1 Surround Stereo; Dolby Surround Stereo. $24.95. Keepcase. *LANG:* English. *SUB:* English; Spanish; French; Portuguese. *FEATURES:* 28 chapter links ▪ Isolated music score ▪ Cast and crew thumbnail bios ▪ Trailers.
1994 133m/C *FR* Jean Reno, Natalie Portman, Gary Oldman, Danny Aiello, Michael Badalucco, Ellen Greene; **D:** Luc Besson; **W:** Luc Besson; **C:** Thierry Arbogast; **M:** Eric Serra. *AWARDS: NOM:* Cesar '94: Actor (Reno), Director (Besson), Film.

Leprechaun 2

Low-budget sequel is a definite step down from this none-too-wonderful original. On his 2,000th birthday, the grody little critter (Davis) gets "to claim his bride" if she sneezes three times. L.A. babe Bridget (Durkin) is the lucky gal. The nasty make-up and the ridiculous fake Irish legends are the same; the sadistic sexual angle is new and unneeded. One scene directly quotes Tod Browning's *Freaks*. Widescreen image is an improvement over VHS tape. So is the stereo sound. —*MM*

Movie: 🎵 **DVD:** 🎵🎵½
Trimark Home Video (Cat #6918). Widescreen anamorphic. Dolby Digital Stereo. $14.99. Keepcase. *LANG:* English. *SUB:* French; Spanish. *FEATURES:* 24 chapter links.
1994 (R) 85m/C Warwick Davis, Sandy Baron, Adam Biesk, James Lancaster, Clint Howard, Kimmy Robertson, Charlie Heath, Shevonne Durkin; **D:** Rodman Flender; **W:** Turi Meyer, Al Septien; **C:** Jane Castle; **M:** Jonathan Elias.

Leprechaun 3

Third entry pays virtually no attention to the predecessors and moves the setting to Las Vegas where innocent student Scott (Gatins) and magician Tammy (Armstrong) come up against the short green guy (Davis). While director Brian Trenchard-Smith does a fine job with the characters and the Vegas exteriors, his budget is too meager to re-create the frenzied, full-frontal electronic assault of a casino floor. Veteran Michael Callan almost steals the show as the casino owner. Full-frame image is no better than tape. —*MM*

Movie: 🎵🎵½ **DVD:** 🎵🎵
Trimark Home Video (Cat #VM7560D, UPC #031398756026). Full frame. Stereo. $24.99. Keepcase. *LANG:* English; Spanish. *SUB:* English; French; Spanish. *FEATURES:* 24 chapter links ▪ Trailer.
1995 (R) 93m/C Warwick Davis, John Gatins, Michael Callan, Caroline Williams, Lee Armstrong; **D:** Brian Trenchard-Smith; **W:** Brian Dubos; **C:** David Lewis; **M:** Dennis Michael Tenney.

Leprechaun 4: In Space

Slapdash entry has virtually nothing to do with the others in the equally slapdash series. Sometime in an unspecified future, on the planet Ithacon, our short ugly villain (Davis) persuades a buxom blonde princess (Carlton) to marry him by promising to make her wealthy. (Hey, he's not the first.) Actually, the whole concept is an excuse for humor, intentional but not very funny, and O.K. effects, some involving penises and big bugs. Image and sound are identical to VHS. —*MM*

Movie: 🎵 **DVD:** 🎵🎵
Trimark Home Video (Cat #VM7561D, UPC #031398756125). Full frame. Stereo. $24.95. Keepcase. *LANG:* English; Spanish. *SUB:* English; French; Spanish. *FEATURES:* 24 chapter links ▪ Trailer.
1996 (R) 98m/C Warwick Davis, Rebekah Carlton, Brent Jasmer, Debbe Dunning, Rebecca Cross, Tim Colceri; **D:** Brian Trenchard-Smith; **W:** Dennis Pratt; **C:** David Lewis; **M:** Dennis Michael Tenney.

Leprechaun 5: In the Hood

Rivaling *Witchcraft* as the worst direct-to-video franchise, the *Leprechaun* series hits a new low. Warwick Davis (a long, long way from *Willow*) returns as the rhyming homicidal Leprechaun, who runs amuck in Compton, California, after he is reawakened by three unwitting aspiring rappers ripping off a ruthless record producer (Ice-T). The title is about as clever as this rather tame urban horrorshow gets, although props are due for whoever came up with the Zombie Fly Girls ("Lep in the Hood!" they moan. "Gonna do no good."). The DVD is cursed by the film's poor production values, and the image is hazy. Consider yourselves warned. —*DL*

Movie: 🎵 **DVD:** 🎵🎵
Trimark Home Video (Cat #VM7285D, UPC #031398728528). Full frame. Dolby Stereo. $24.99. Keepcase. *LANG:* English. *SUB:* English; French; Spanish. *FEATURES:* Trailer ▪ Trimark trailers ▪ 24 chapter links.
1999 (R) 91m/C Warwick Davis, Ice-T; **D:** Robert Spera.

Les Miserables

Yet another adaptation of the Victor Hugo novel. Paroled convict Jean Valjean (Neeson) is chased by police inspector Javert (Rush) while factory worker Fantine (Thurman) turns to prostitution to survive. Director August chooses to begin this tale after Valjean's trial and imprisonment for petty theft and until the final third of the film, he doesn't really deal with the political upheaval of the time. It's not as sweeping or grand as other versions, but what this one lacks in scope, it makes up for with top-notch performances (especially by Neeson and Rush) and more careful study of the characters themselves. The film looks good on disc, though the image

is not ultra-sharp. Dark gray and black clothes display a very good level of detail. The 5.1 is used nicely in crowd scenes and more subtly to provide slight echoing effects in others. —*MM*

Movie: 🎵🎵🎵 **DVD:** 🎵🎵🎵
Columbia Tristar Home Video (Cat #23999, UPC #043396239999). Widescreen (2.35:1) letterboxed. Dolby Digital 5.1 Surround Stereo. $29.95. Keepcase. *LANG:* English; French. *SUB:* French. *CAP:* English. *FEATURES:* Trailer ▪ 28 chapter links.
1997 (PG-13) 134m/C Liam Neeson, Geoffrey Rush, Uma Thurman, Claire Danes, Paris Vaughan, Reine Brynolfsson, Hans Matheson, Mimi Newman; **D:** Bille August; **W:** Rafael Yglesias; **C:** Jorgen Persson; **M:** Basil Poledouris.

A Lesson before Dying

Cheadle is impressive as idealistic teacher Grant Wiggins, who has a one-room school for black children in 1948 Louisiana. He's reluctantly pressed into service by his formidable Aunt Lou (Tyson) and her friend Miss Emma (Hall), who want him to bring some dignity to the life of Jefferson (Phifer), who is awaiting execution for a crime he didn't commit. Without any compression artifacts, the movie literally blossoms on DVD. Neither the nighttime scenes nor the dimly lit interior shots cause any compression artifacts and always maintain a very high level of detail. Taken from a clean print without notable speckles or dust, the image looks absolutely gorgeous. Powerful colors, deep, solid shadows, and balanced highlights make it a great experience. Audio is equally strong, with dialogue that is well integrated and never drowned out by the music or the sound effects. The frequency response is wide with a good and neutral sounding low end, as well as brilliant high ends. —*GH/MM*

Movie: 🎵🎵🎵 **DVD:** 🎵🎵🎵
HBO Home Video (Cat #91570). Full frame. Dolby Digital Stereo. $19.98. Snapper. *LANG:* English; Spanish. *SUB:* English; French; Spanish. *FEATURES:* Talent files.
1999 (PG-13) 100m/C Don Cheadle, Cicely Tyson, Mekhi Phifer, Irma P. Hall, Brent Jennings, Lisa Arrindell Anderson, Frank Hoyt Taylor; **D:** Joseph Sargent; **W:** Ann Peacock; **C:** Donald M. Morgan; **M:** Ernest Troost.

Let Sleeping Corpses Lie

England's answer to *Night of the Living Dead* is more polished and has a more pronounced environmental edge. George (Lovelock) and Edna (Galbo) are the heroes who must confront the cannibalistic animated corpses. If the film lacks the single-mindedness and originality of Romero's work, it's an accurate snapshot of the early 1970s with appropriately gruesome special effects. The widescreen image is very good, apparently transferred from virtually pristine original elements.

Surround sound is equally vivid. The title has had a well-deserved cult reputation in this country for decades. —MM *AKA:* The Living Dead at Manchester Morgue.
Movie: 🎬🎬½ *DVD:* 🎬🎬½
Anchor Bay (Cat #DV11154, UPC #013131115499). Widescreen (1.85:1) anamorphic. Dolby Digital 5.1 Surround Stereo. $29.98. Keepcase. *LANG:* English. *FEATURES:* 26 chapter links ● Interview with Grau ● TV and radio spots ● Stills gallery ● Liner notes by N.J. Burrell. Also available in limited edition with 24-page booklet and toe tag for $39.98 (Cat #DV11311, UPC #013131131199).
1974 93m/C *GB* Ray Lovelock, Christine Galbo, Arthur Kennedy; *D:* Jorge Grau; *W:* Alessandro Continenza, Marcello Coscia; *M:* Giuliano Sorgini.

Let the Devil Wear Black

Loose retelling of *Hamlet* is set in a contemporary L.A. of Armani and BMWs. It turns out to be an oddly engaging experiment. After the death of his dad (Sarandon), Jack (co-producer/writer Penner) learns that his uncle Carl (Sheridan) is planning to marry his mother (Bisset). What will this mean to the family business of bars and strip joints? His possibly pregnant girlfriend Julia (Parker) is too spacey to be of much help, and Jack is suspicious of her dad (Hall). Director Title lets the pace meander a bit. It's slow, disjointed, and very dark visually. Because the production design is heavy with blacks and deep reds, the DVD image is only a fractional improvement over tape. Sound is not much improved either. Even so, the film deserves at least a look from fans of avant-garde Shakespeare. —MM
Movie: 🎬🎬🎬 *DVD:* 🎬🎬
A-PIX Entertainment Inc. (Cat #APX27023, UPC #783722702338). Full frame. Dolby Digital 5.1 Surround Stereo. $24.98. Keepcase. *LANG:* English. *SUB:* Spanish. *FEATURES:* 14 chapter links ● Behind-the-scenes footage ● Trailers.
1999 (R) 89m/C Jonathan Penner, Jacqueline Bisset, Jamey Sheridan, Mary-Louise Parker, Philip Baker Hall, Jonathan Banks, Maury Chaykin, Chris Sarandon, Joanna Gleason; *D:* Stacy Title; *W:* Jonathan Penner, Stacy Title; *C:* James Whitaker; *M:* Barklie K. Griggs; *E:* Luis Colina; *A:* Catherine Tarver.

Lethal Seduction

Local crime boss Gus Gruman (Estevez) is rapidly losing friends and associates to a sexually oriented serial killer. And there's obsessed cop Trent Jacobson (Mitchum) who's determined to solve the crimes. The one clue is a mystery brunette seen leaving a crime scene. Julie Strain plays a hitwoman in this shot-on-video production. It is quite possibly the cheapest-looking work reviewed in this book. It's so poorly lit, acted, and edited that any comments

on the technical merits of the DVD are pointless. —MM *AKA:* Lethal Betrayal.
Movie: woof *DVD:* woof
El Independent Cinema (Cat #so-5237-dvd, UPC #612385523793). Full frame. $19.98. Keepcase. *LANG:* English. *FEATURES:* 26 chapter links ● "Hangin' with Julie" featurette ● "Making of" documentary.
1997 110m/C Julie Strain, Chris Mitchum, Joe Estevez, Joette Rhodes, David Michie, Susan Alexander, Patrick De Fazio, James Dupee, Allen Arkus, Chuck Gale, Tyler Mason, Jim O'Brien, Frederick P. Watkins; *D:* Frederick P. Watkins; *W:* Scott (S.M. Magruder) Murphy, Frederick P. Watkins; *C:* Robert Dracup; *M:* Kristopher Carter; *E:* Scott (S.M. Magruder) Murphy, Frederick P. Watkins; *A:* Richard O. Burst Jr.

Lewis and Clark and George

Lewis (Xuereb) is an illiterate psycho killer; Clark (Gunther) is a white-collar criminal. They escape from prison and set out to find a gold mine in the desert. George (McGowan) is a mute snake thief—that is, she's a mute who steals a snake, not a woman who steals silent serpents—who tries to cut herself into the action. It's too-familiar stuff for fans of road movies with big '60s cars, lots of guns, and a strained sense of humor. Director McCall confuses the smoking of cigarettes for emotion and the snap of a Zippo lighter with real drama. The DVD exhibits heavy aliasing in bright chrome. Sound is adequate. —MM
Movie: 🎬🎬 *DVD:* 🎬🎬½
Winstar Home Entertainment (Cat #FLV5163, UPC #720917516325). Widescreen (1.85:1) letterboxed. Dolby Digital Surround Stereo. $24.98. Keepcase. *LANG:* English. *FEATURES:* 12 chapter links ● Talent files ● Trailer ● Production credits.
1997 (R) 84m/C Salvator Xuereb, Dan Gunther, Rose McGowan, Art LaFleur, Aki Aleong, James Brolin, Paul Bartel; *D:* Rod McCall; *W:* Rod McCall; *C:* Mike Mayers; *M:* Ben Vaughn.

Liberty Heights

Levinson returns to Baltimore (for the fourth time) for his 1954 coming-of-age/family drama with a focus on the city's Jewish community and the Kurtzman family in particular. Nate (Mantegna) has a two-bit numbers racket and a failing burlesque house; college son Van (Brody) falls for a shiksa (Murphy) while high schooler Ben (Foster) is captivated by Sylvia (Johnson), the first black student in his class. It may be too early for Bob Dylan, but the times were a-changin' indeed and Levinson takes an unsentimental if heartfelt look at his past. The source print is virtually free of defects and blemishes and with a very high level of detail, the image quality of the transfer is very good. Colors are generally well rendered with powerful hues and good saturation, although the contrast of the presentation seems a little low at times,

resulting in a very dark image. Especially during night scenes the transfer seems a tad too dark with shadows losing definition, shrouding the entire image in blackness. Surround usage is limited to a number of scenes where the ambience is given a nice spatial integration, but for the most part, the movie's audio is firmly located in the center channel. Dialogue is well integrated and placed in the mix without distortion or sibilance, always held at an understandable level. The movie's '50s music is also presented in an isolated audio track that is presented in a 5.1 mix. However, since these are original mono numbers, the spatial possibilities are mostly used to beef up the overall quality of the songs rather than create new multichannel mixes of the songs. —GH/MM
Movie: 🎬🎬½ *DVD:* 🎬🎬½
Warner Home Video, Inc. (Cat #18019). Widescreen (1.85:1) anamorphic. Dolby Digital 5.1 Surround Stereo. $24.98. Snapper. *LANG:* English. *SUB:* English; French. *FEATURES:* Interviews ● Deleted scenes ● Isolated score ● Production notes.
1999 (R) 127m/C Adrien Brody, Joe Mantegna, Ben Foster, Bebe Neuwirth, Rebekah Johnson, Orlando Jones, Frania Rubinek, David Krumholtz, Richard Kline, Vincent Guastaferro, Carolyn Murphy, Justin Chambers, James Pickens Jr., Anthony Anderson, Kiersten Warren; *D:* Barry Levinson; *W:* Barry Levinson; *C:* Christopher Doyle; *M:* Andrea Morricone.

Life According to Muriel

After her husband leaves the family, Laura (Villami) takes her young daughter Muriel (Camiletti), our narrator, to the country. They're taken in by hotel owner Mirta (Estevez). Bonding ensues. The DVD image is so rough that it's no improvement over VHS tape. Sound is marginally better. Though the menu is so simple it might be called rudimentary, it is virtually impossible to navigate. —MM *AKA:* La Vida Segun Muriel.
Movie: 🎬🎬 *DVD:* 🎬🎬
Vanguard International Cinema, Inc. (UPC #658769004830). Full frame. $29.98. Keepcase. *LANG:* Spanish. *SUB:* English. *FEATURES:* 12 chapter links.
1997 97m/C *AR* Ines Estevez, Jorge Perugorria, Florencia Camiletti, Federico Olivera, Soledad Villamil; *D:* Eduardo Milewicz; *W:* Eduardo Milewicz, Susana Silvestre; *C:* Esteban Sapir; *M:* Bob Telson.

The Life Before This

On one level, this is a sort of Canadian *Pulp Fiction* that begins and ends with a coffee shop shoot-out. Between those two bookends, the plot flashes back to six overlapping stories that follow 44 characters and what happened to them during the 12 hours before. It's very loosely based on a true incident. The film was made with the participation of Canadian television, so the full-frame ratio is correct. Director Ciccoritti uses some interesting visual effects for transitions, but overall the image is probably not a large step up from tape. Accessibility is a greater asset. A commentary track might have been interesting. Curiously, the film is very similar in plot and construction to *October 22* copyrighted a year earlier. —*MM*

Movie: 🎬🎬🎬 **DVD:** 🎬🎬½

Image Entertainment (Cat #OVED0322 DVD, UPC #014381032222). Full frame. Dolby Digital Surround Stereo. $24.99. Snapper. *LANG:* English. *FEATURES:* 12 chapter links.

1999 92m/C *CA* Leslie Hope, David Hewlett, Joel S. Keller, Jacob Tierney, Alberta Watson, Jennifer Dale, Dan Lett, Catherine O'Hara, Martha Burns, Joe Pantoliano, Sarah Polley, Stephen Rea, Callum Keith Rennie; *D:* Gerard Ciccoritti; *W:* Semi Chellas; *C:* Norayr Kasper; *M:* Ron Sures. *AWARDS:* Genie '99: Support. Actress (O'Hara).

The Life of Jesus

Small-town ennui, teenage angst, and racism...avec pommes frites. Twenty-year-old Freddy is an unemployed epileptic who constantly hangs out with his equally jobless friends, joyriding through the tiny streets and across the sparse French countryside. Without even a conversation between them, they spend their days just withering away. When an Arab family moves into the neighborhood and the eldest son, Kadder, starts courting Marie, Freddy's girlfriend, resentment and anger boil over for a fateful confrontation. The trouble with dramatizing tedium is that eventually the viewer gets just as bored as the characters. Even for 96 minutes, the film seems padded with incessant shots of scooters shuffling down the rue, parents who say even less than their kids, and the gang just sitting around, waiting for the next fade out. I suppose the title refers to suffering, that Freddy endures emotional as well as physical pain. With characters so vacuous it's difficult to muster any sympathy for their situation. The transfer also suffers; high contrast levels sometimes wash out the few colors used. The image is sharp enough, but aliasing pops up in long shots with fine detail (brick walls, gates), which anamorphic enhancement would have helped alleviate. Mono sound occasionally peaks, but otherwise is fine. —*EP* *AKA:* La Vie de Jesus.

Movie: 🎬🎬 **DVD:** 🎬🎬

Fox/Lorber Home Video (Cat #FLV5071, UPC #720971507125). Widescreen (2.35: 1) letterboxed. Dolby Digital Mono. $29.98. Keepcase. *LANG:* French. *SUB:* English. *FEATURES:* 8 chapter links • Trailer • Production credits • Theatrical trailer.

1996 96m/C *FR* David Douche, Marjorie Cottreel, Kader Chaatouf, Samuel Boidin, Genevieve Cottreel; *D:* Bruno Dumont; *W:* Bruno Dumont; *C:* Philippe Van Leeuw; *M:* Richard Cuvillier.

Life with Father

Based on the writings of Clarence Day Jr., this is the story of his childhood in 1880s New York City. It's a delightful (but dated)

saga of a stern, loving father (Powell) and his relationship with his knowing wife (Dunne) and four sons. The disc was made from poor original elements. The color is pale. The wavering sound tends to screech in the higher ranges. —*MM*

Movie: 🎬🎬🎬½ **DVD:** 🎬

Madacy Entertainment (Cat #99013, UPC #056775004996). Full frame. Dolby Digital Mono. $9.99. Keepcase. *LANG:* English. *FEATURES:* Production notes • Trivia • William Powell thumbnail bio • 9 chapter links.

1947 118m/C William Powell, Irene Dunne, Elizabeth Taylor, Edmund Gwenn, ZaSu Pitts, Jimmy Lydon, Martin Milner; *D:* Michael Curtiz; *W:* Donald Ogden Stewart; *C:* William V. Skall, J. Peverell Marley; *M:* Max Steiner. *AWARDS:* Golden Globes '48: Score; N.Y. Film Critics '47: Actor (Powell); *NOM:* Oscars '47: Actor (Powell), Art Dir./Set Dec., Color, Color Cinematog., Orig. Dramatic Score.

The Lifestyle

This astonishing documentary gives swingers—adults who engage in group sex and various other acts with their spouses—a chance to talk about what they do without judgment. Some of the acts are shown, but most of the running time is simply people talking about what they do and why. What makes the film so unusual is that these folks are so profoundly ordinary. They're mostly from the suburbs. (Some of their parties also include karaoke singing and potluck dinners.) The film is also really funny in the most unexpected places and ways. DVD presents a very sharp image that's probably only marginally superior to VHS tape, but the disc also includes more than 45 minutes of extra footage. Of the extras, be sure to read the production notes. They are illuminating. —*MM*

Movie: 🎬🎬🎬 **DVD:** 🎬🎬🎬

Winstar Home Entertainment (Cat #FLV5261, UPC #720971526133). Widescreen letterboxed. $24.98. Keepcase. *LANG:* English. *FEATURES:* 16 chapter links • Thumbnail bios • Production notes • Outtakes.

1999 121m/C *D:* David Schisgall; *C:* Peter Hawkins; *M:* Byron Estep, Eddie Sperry.

Light It Up

When their favorite high school teacher (Nelson) is unfairly suspended, a group of fed-up students led by jock Lester (Raymond) stage a sit-in. After a confrontational security guard (Whitaker) is shot, the students take him and the crumbling school building hostage. Despite the implausibility of the plot, it works. The DVD transfer is absolutely clean and without a hint of noise or grain. Highly detailed, the image holds up to even the most scrutinizing examination. With its wide frequency response, the 5.1 sound is dynamic and natural throughout. A good bass extension gives the track power while the high end is clear and never

appears overemphasized. Dialogue is always understandable and clear, however, some signs of distortion were evident, most likely a result of the original voice recording. —*GH/MM*

Movie: 🎬🎬🎬 **DVD:** 🎬🎬🎬½

20th Century Fox Home Entertainment (Cat #2000041). Widescreen (1.85:1) anamorphic. Dolby Digital 5.1 Surround Stereo; Dolby Digital Stereo. $29.98. Keepcase. *LANG:* English. *SUB:* English; Spanish. *FEATURES:* Music videos • "Making of" featurette • Theatrical trailer.

1999 (R) 99m/C Forest Whitaker, Judd Nelson, Sara Gilbert, Rosario Dawson, Usher Raymond, Robert Ri'chard, Fredro Starr, Glynn Turman, Clifton (Gonzalez) Collins Jr., Vic Polizos, Vanessa L(ynne) Williams; *D:* Craig Bolotin; *W:* Craig Bolotin; *C:* Elliot Davis; *M:* Harry Gregson-Williams.

Lightning Jack

It's a western comedy, but they left out the laughs. Lightning Jack Kane (Hogan) is a publicity-seeking gunslinger who loses his entire gang when a bank robbery goes bad. When he takes a hostage (Gooding) on his next (solo) robbery attempt, he winds up with a mute partner instead. Clichés run rampant, and the running gags (including aging Kane's surreptitious use of eyeglasses so he can see his shooting targets) fall flat. Bland and boring all around, this flick tries—and fails—to draw from the same well as Hogan's *Crocodile Dundee*. The DVD picture suffers from too-frequent shimmering whenever the background imagery is busy, and dark scenes are flat and muddy. The 2.0 Surround soundtrack is nothing to brag about, either. The extras are more than sufficiently generous for this title. —*MB*

Movie: 🎬½ **DVD:** 🎬½

HBO Home Video (Cat #91143, UPC #026359114328). Widescreen (1.85:1) letterboxed. Dolby Surround 2.0. $19.98. Snapper. *LANG:* English; Spanish. *SUB:* English; French; Spanish. *CAP:* English. *FEATURES:* 16 chapter links • Cast and crew bios and filmographies • Theatrical trailer • TV spots • Featurette.

1994 (PG-13) 93m/C Paul Hogan, Cuba Gooding Jr., Beverly D'Angelo, Kamala Dawson, Pat Hingle, Richard Riehle, Frank McRae, Roger Daltrey, L.Q. (Justus E. McQueen) Jones, Max Cullen; *D:* Simon Wincer; *W:* Paul Hogan; *C:* David Eggby; *M:* Bruce Rowland.

Lilian's Story

Aging Lilian (Cracknell) has just been released after spending 40 years in a mental institution. She was placed there as an adolescent by her controlling, possessive father. The haunted Lilian is given a room at a residential hotel in Sydney's red-light district where the local prostitutes look out for her and she spends her days wandering the streets. Flashbacks reveal what led the high-strung young Lilian (Collette) to her incarceration. Colors are so harsh on this DVD that the film is downright difficult to watch. A heavily shadowed exterior, for example, is almost impossible to make out. The flaws appear to come from the original. —*MM*

Movie: 🎬🎬½ **DVD:** 🎬🎬
Vanguard International Cinema, Inc. (Cat #1-89264904602, UPC #658769002836). Widescreen (1.66:1) letterboxed. $29.95. Keepcase. *LANG:* English. *FEATURES:* 12 chapter links.
1995 94m/C *AU* Ruth Cracknell, Barry Otto, Toni Collette, John Flaus, Essie Davis, Susie Lindemann, Anne Louise Lambert, Iris Shand; *D:* Jerzy Domaradzki; *W:* Steve Wright; *C:* Slawomir Idziak; *M:* Cezary Skubiszewski. *AWARDS:* Australian Film Inst. '95: Support. Actress (Collette).

Lilies of the Field

Amen! Sidney Poitier became the first African American to win an Academy Award for Best Actor for his spirit-lifting performance as Homer Smith, an itinerant handyman who is reluctantly recruited by a stern Mother Superior to build a "shapel" on an impoverished desert convent. This is a lovely little film; a simple story, simply told with little sentimental flourish. Lilia Skala is wonderful as the iron-willed Mother. The battle of the Bibles and Homer's English lessons to the German-speaking nuns are classic scenes. *Lilies* really blossoms on DVD with a near–picture perfect transfer. It would have been illuminating to hear Poitier's reflections on his groundbreaking role, so the absence of a commentary or interview, or even footage of his historic Oscar acceptance speech, is a disappointment. —*DL*

Movie: 🎬🎬🎬 **DVD:** 🎬🎬🎬½
MGM Home Entertainment (Cat #10015 86, UPC #2761685896). Widescreen letterboxed. Dolby Digital Mono. $19.95. Keepcase. *LANG:* English. *SUB:* French; Spanish. *CAP:* English. *FEATURES:* Original theatrical trailer ● 16 chapter links.
1963 94m/B Sidney Poitier, Lilia Skala, Lisa Mann, Isa Crino, Stanley Adams; *D:* Ralph Nelson; *W:* James Poe; *C:* Ernest Haller; *M:* Jerry Goldsmith. *AWARDS:* Oscars '63: Actor (Poitier); Berlin Intl. Film Fest. '63: Actor (Poitier); Golden Globes '64: Actor—Drama (Poitier); *NOM:* Oscars '63: Adapt. Screenplay, B&W Cinematog., Picture, Support. Actress (Skala).

Lingerie

This two-part British TV series takes a revealing, uplifting look at women's underwear. All right, there is a little bit about men's underwear, but that's what the scanforward button is for. The producers take an appropriately lighthearted approach. Cleavage, they tell us, "is the hot topic of the season," and they ask the question: "Where's the 'ooh' factor when it comes to knickers?" For Americans, the programs are also a vocabulary lesson on English slang for unmentionables. Both image and sound are a step up from broadcast quality. —*MM*

Movie: 🎬🎬🎬 **DVD:** 🎬🎬½

Image Entertainment (Cat #ID0546ITDVD, UPC #014381054620). Full frame. Dolby Digital Stereo. $24.99. Snapper. *LANG:* English. *FEATURES:* 16 chapter links.
2001 96m/C *D:* Sophie Paul; *M:* David McEwan; *Nar:* Janet Ellis.

The Lion in Winter

Medieval monarch Henry II (O'Toole) and his wife Eleanor of Aquitaine (Hepburn) match wits over the succession of the English throne and much else in this fast-paced adaptation of James Goldman's play. The family, including grown sons and visiting royalty, are united for the Christmas holidays fraught with tension, rapidly shifting allegiances, and layers of psychological manipulation. Superb dialogue and perfectly realized characterizations. Screen debut for both Hopkins and Dalton. DVD boasts an excellent image for a film of this age, but the real surprise here is director Anthony Harvey's commentary track. Recorded 35 years after the fact, it's one of the most fascinating you'll hear. He's confident, and he chooses to recount the right details. —*MM*

Movie: 🎬🎬🎬🎬 **DVD:** 🎬🎬🎬½
MGM Home Entertainment (Cat #10015 87, UPC #027616858979). Widescreen (2.35:1) anamorphic. Dolby Digital Mono. $19.98. Keepcase. *LANG:* English. *SUB:* French; Spanish. *FEATURES:* 16 chapter links ● Commentary: Anthony Harvey ● Trailer.
1968 (PG) 134m/C Peter O'Toole, Katharine Hepburn, Jane Merrow, Nigel Terry, Timothy Dalton, Anthony Hopkins, John Castle, Nigel Stock; *D:* Anthony Harvey; *W:* James Goldman; *M:* John Barry. *AWARDS:* Oscars '68: Actress (Hepburn), Adapt. Screenplay, Orig. Score; Directors Guild '68: Director (Harvey); Golden Globes '69: Actor—Drama (O'Toole); Film—Drama; N.Y. Film Critics '68: Film; *NOM:* Oscars '68: Actor (O'Toole), Costume Des., Director (Harvey), Picture.

The List

The legal community is thrown into panic when call girl Gabrielle Michelle (Amick) is arrested and threatens to make public her list of clients. Judge Richard Miller (O'Neal) doesn't know how much to reveal and how much to conceal. It's a fairly standard video thriller that gains nothing on DVD. Image is identical to VHS tape. —*MM*

Movie: 🎬🎬 **DVD:** 🎬🎬
York Entertainment (Cat #YPD-1044, UPC #750723104423). Full frame. Dolby Digital 5.1 Surround Stereo. $14.99. Keepcase. *LANG:* English. *SUB:* Spanish. *FEATURES:* 30 chapter links ● Trailers ● Filmographies.
1999 (R) 93m/C Madchen Amick, Ryan O'Neal, Roc Lafortune, Ben Gazzara; *D:* Sylvain Guy; *W:* Sylvain Guy; *C:* Yves Belanger; *M:* Louis Babin.

A Little Bit of Soul

Godfrey Usher (Rush) is an ambitious politician whose present position is that of

federal treasurer, a job he has no clue about. He's married to Grace Michael (Mitchell), the head of a philanthropic foundation. Scientist Richard Shorkinghorm (Wenham) and his rival, ex-lover Kate Haslett (O'Connor), have both applied for funding from the foundation and are invited to the Usher/Michael home for a weekend. Offbeat comedy falters, but it is not the fault of the performers. The picture is very clear, with some slight grain at times. The digital transfer does reveal some slight flaws in the source material, but these are minor. Audio offers a well-balanced soundtrack with occasional action from the rear speakers. —*ML/MM*

Movie: 🎬🎬½ **DVD:** 🎬🎬½
Vanguard International Cinema, Inc. (Cat #VANF4). Widescreen (1.85:1) letterboxed. Dolby Digital Stereo. $29.95. Keepcase. *LANG:* English.
1997 (R) 83m/C *AU* Geoffrey Rush, David Wenham, Frances O'Connor, Heather Mitchell, John Gaden, Kerry Walker; *D:* Peter Duncan; *W:* Peter Duncan; *C:* Martin McGrath; *M:* Nigel Westlake. *AWARDS:* *NOM:* Australian Film Inst. '98: Support. Actor (Rush).

Little Fugitive

Lennie (Brewster) has just turned 12 years old and is looking forward to spending a day enjoying the Coney Island amusements with his Brooklyn pals. But his plans are dashed when his single mom must leave home on an emergency errand, leaving Lennie in charge of his 7-year-old brother, Joey (Andrusco). A prank goes awry when Joey becomes convinced he has murdered his brother. So the tyke takes off and winds up wandering lost around Coney Island, leaving his brother to spend the weekend in worry. Regarded as one of the more influential independent American movies of the early 1950s, *Little Fugitive* actually benefits from a handheld camera and non-pro performers. On the commentary track, one of the directors explains how the movie was actually shot as a silent film, with all the dialogue and other sounds added later. The clarity of the DVD image makes the loosely synched lips apparent, but they don't detract from the enjoyment of the story. The mono soundtrack is quite serviceable. —*MB*

Movie: 🎬🎬🎬 **DVD:** 🎬🎬🎬
Image Entertainment (Cat #K121DVD, UPC #7-38329-01212-0). Full frame. Dolby Digital 2.0. $29.99. Snapper. *LANG:* English. *FEATURES:* 12 chapter links ● Commentary: director Engel ● Original theatrical trailer.
1953 80m/C Richie Andrusco, Ricky Brewster, Winnifred Cushing, Jay Williams; *D:* Morris Engel, Ruth Orkin, Ray Ashley; *W:* Ray Ashley; *C:* Morris Engel; *M:* Eddy Manson. *AWARDS:* Natl. Film Reg. '97.

Little Lord Fauntleroy

Beloved Hollywood favorite tells Frances Hodgson Burnett's story of a fatherless American boy (Bartholomew) who discovers he's the heir to a British dukedom. In many ways, this one is so dated that it's difficult to enjoy today. (The idea of a boy calling his mother "dearest" is more than a little odd.) The excellent black-and-white image is a bit on the dark side, and so some grain creeps in, but that comes from the original elements, not the transfer. *—MM*

Movie: 🎬🎬🎬½ **DVD:** 📀📀½
Anchor Bay (Cat #DV11330, UPC #013131 133097). Full frame. Dolby Digital Mono. $24.99. Keepcase. *LANG:* English. *FEATURES:* 24 chapter links • Trailer • TV spot.
1936 102m/B Freddie Bartholomew, Sir C. Aubrey Smith, Mickey Rooney, Dolores Costello, Jessie Ralph, Guy Kibbee; *D:* John Cromwell; *W:* Hugh Walpole; *C:* Charles Rosher; *M:* Max Steiner.

The Little Mermaid 2: Return to the Sea

Ariel and Prince Eric are married and have a daughter, Melody. However, they have kept her mermaid heritage a secret, which is revealed when it's discovered that the evil sea-witch Morgana wants to use Melody to take control of the ocean from King Triton. It's gotta be hard to screw up the transfer of an animated feature to DVD. This disc is no exception. The colors are so vibrant and the image so sharp that there are times the image looks 3-D (it's not). There's absolutely no bleed, grain, or artifacts. The sound is full and there is almost constant use of the Surround tracks, although the mix at times feels contrived, but the kids won't know the difference. They'll also be entertained by the two games on the disc. Adults will find the classic Disney cartoon "Merbabies" much more entertaining than *LMII* even if the colors are a little pale and the overall image quality is several notches down from the main feature. *—JO*

Movie: 🎬🎬 **DVD:** 📀📀📀½
Buena Vista Home Entertainment (Cat #19 303, UPC #7179510077445). Widescreen (1.66:1) letterboxed. Dolby Digital 5.1. $29.99. Keepcase. *LANG:* English; Spanish; French. *CAP:* English. *FEATURES:* 19 chapter links • "Merbabies" (Disney classic cartoon) • Trivia game • "What Am I" game • *The Little Mermaid II* DVD storybook.
2000 (G) 75m/C *D:* Jim Kammerud; *W:* Elizabeth Anderson, Temple Matthews; *M:* Michael Silversher, Patty Silversher; *V:* Jodi Benson, Pat Carroll, Buddy Hackett, Samuel E. Wright, Christopher Daniel Barnes.

Little Nicky

Every 10,000 years Satan's (Harvey Keitel) reign in hell is up for renewal and it's that time again. However, two of his sons (Rhys Ifans and Tom "Tiny" Lister Jr.) have other plans, and it falls to his third son, Nicky (Sandler), a complete idiot, to restore the balance between good and evil, and his father to his throne. Crude, unbelievably bad comedy (even by Adam Sandler's standards) is now rumored to be used to torture film critics in hell. Terrible

film effort is given the royal treatment on DVD, including bonus menu features that are unlocked by highlighting the "halo" above Adam Sandler's head, which is located in the Special Features sub-menu. Click left, down, and then right on your DVD remote to turn the halo gold, then click the halo and a series of "pop-up" menus will become available during the movie. Before going through this process, if you click on the halo, a special sneak preview of *Lord of the Rings* will play. *—RJT*

Movie: 🎬½ **DVD:** 📀📀📀
New Line Home Video (Cat #5160, UPC #794043516023). Widescreen (1.85:1) anamorphic. Dolby Digital 5.1 Surround Stereo; Dolby Digital Surround. $24.98. Keepcase. *LANG:* English. *FEATURES:* 18 chapter markers • Commentary: Sandler, director Steven Brill, co-writer Tim Herlihy • Commentary: Michael McKean, Jon Lovitz, Kevin Nealon, Henry Winkler • 21 deleted scenes • Theatrical trailer • Behind-the-scenes documentary "Adam Sandler Goes to Hell" • Heavy Metal documentary "Satan's Top 40" • "School of Hard Knocks" music video by P.O.D.
2000 (PG-13) 93m/C Adam Sandler, Rhys Ifans, Tommy (Tiny) Lister, Harvey Keitel, Patricia Arquette, Allen Covert, Blake Clark, Rodney Dangerfield, Kevin Nealon, Reese Witherspoon, Lewis Arquette, Dana Carvey, Jon Lovitz, Michael McKean, Quentin Tarantino, Carl Weathers, Rob Schneider, Clint Howard, Ellen Cleghorne, Fred Wolf; *Cameos:* Dan Marino, Henry Winkler, Regis Philbin, Ozzy Osbourne, Bill Walton; *D:* Steven Brill; *W:* Adam Sandler, Steven Brill, Tim Herlihy; *C:* Theo van de Sande; *M:* Teddy Castellucci; *V:* Robert Smigel. *AWARDS: NOM:* Golden Raspberries '00: Worst Picture, Worst Actor (Sandler), Worst Support. Actress (Arquette), Worst Screenplay.

The Little Princess

Ten-year-old Shirley Temple, in her first Technicolor film, wrings every tear out of this Victorian melodrama about a pampered but plucky young girl who goes from little princess to penniless, put-upon servant at a harsh all-girls school when her officer father disappears during the Boer Wars. This tailor-made vehicle was supposed to be for Temple what *The Wizard of Oz* was for Judy Garland. The source material shows minor damage, but nothing to detract from this lavishly mounted production based on Frances Hodgson Burnett's classic book. *—DL*

Movie: 🎬🎬🎬 **DVD:** 📀📀📀
SlingShot Entertainment (Cat #9821, UPC #017078982121). Full frame. Dolby Digital. $19.99. Keepcase. *LANG:* English. *FEATURES:* Theatrical trailer • Public service ad for the American Red Cross • 20 chapter links.
1939 (G) 91m/B Shirley Temple, Richard Greene, Anita Louise, Ian Hunter, Cesar Romero, Arthur Treacher, Sybil Jason, Miles Mander, Marcia Mae Jones, E.E. Clive; *D:* Walter Lang; *W:* Ethel Hill, Walter Ferris; *C:* Arthur C. Miller; *M:* Walter Bullock.

The Little Vampire

Young Tony Thompson (Lipnicki) and his family have relocated from California to Scotland. One day he sees a vampire. Of course, no one believes the outsider. But then he manages to save the vampire boy's life, and they become friends. He dives into a world of myths and lore and sets out to help the vampires to find their eternal peace. Significant grain and mosquitoing are evident in a number of shots. Still the image is stable and absolutely clean and without any blemishes. The 5.1 track is big and dynamic, featuring a wide sound field with a very wide frequency response. *—GH*

Movie: 🎬🎬½ **DVD:** 📀📀½
New Line Home Video (UPC #794043516 320). Widescreen (1.85:1) anamorphic; full frame. Dolby Digital 5.1 Surround Stereo; Dolby Digital Surround. $24.98. Snapper. *LANG:* English. *FEATURES:* 3 animated games • Jokes and recipes • Trailer • Talent files.
2000 (PG) 91m/C Jonathan Lipnicki, Richard E. Grant, Alice Krige, Jim Carter; *D:* Uli Edel; *W:* Karey Kirkpatrick, Larry Wilson; *C:* Bernd Heinl; *M:* Nigel Clarke, Michael Csanyi-Wills.

Little Women [2 SE]

Beloved story of the March women is beautifully portrayed in a solid production that blends a seamless screenplay with an excellent cast, authentic period costumes, and lovely cinematography and music. Ryder, perfectly cast as the unconventional Jo, is also the strongest of the sisters: domestically inclined Meg (Alvarado), the fragile Beth (Danes), and the youngest, mischievous Amy (the delightful Dunst) who grows up into a sedate young lady (Mathis). Charming adaptation remains faithful to the spirit of the Alcott classic while adding contemporary touches. Fittingly brought to the big screen by producer Denise Di Novi, writer/co-producer Swicord, and director Armstrong. This is an impressively lit and photographed film that features a rich soft-focus look. The DVD accurately delivers all the subtle hues of the color cinematography and, despite that soft look, is amazingly sharp, without a trace of digital grain or pixelation. Being dialogue driven, there's not much as far as Surround effects, but the 5.1 soundtrack adds superb dimension to the excellent score (also featured on an isolated track), while making sure that every word is distinctly heard. There are plenty of supplementals on the disc (including a rather lame short "making of" featurette) but most worthwhile is the commentary by director Armstrong, which contains plenty of info on the details that give the film such a warm feel, including set construction and use of color. *—JO*

Movie: 🎬🎬🎬🎬 **DVD:** 📀📀📀📀
Columbia Tristar Home Video (Cat #05044, UPC #043396050440). Widescreen (1.85:1) anamorphic. Dolby Digital 5.1; Dolby Surround; Stereo. $27.95. Keepcase. *LANG:* English; Spanish; French. *SUB:* Eng-

lish; Spanish; Korean; Thai; Portuguese. *CAP:* English. *FEATURES:* 28 chapter links ▪ Theatrical trailer ▪ Talent files ▪ Production notes ▪ "Making of" featurette ▪ Commentary: director Gillian Armstrong ▪ Deleted scenes with commentary ▪ Two trivia games ▪ Isolated music score ▪ Costume gallery with commentary.
1994 (PG) 118m/C Winona Ryder, Gabriel Byrne, Trini Alvarado, Samantha Mathis, Kirsten Dunst, Claire Danes, Christian Bale, Eric Stoltz, John Neville, Mary Wickes, Susan Sarandon; *D:* Gillian Armstrong; *W:* Robin Swicord; *C:* Geoffrey Simpson; *M:* Thomas Newman. *AWARDS: NOM:* Oscars '94: Actress (Ryder), Costume Des., Orig. Score; Writers Guild '94: Adapt. Screenplay.

Live Flesh

This entry from quirky Castillian Almodovar spans a generation to tell a sobering but erotic tale of love and vengeance. Young Victor (Rabal) meets Elena (Neri) not knowing she's a junkie, and a few hours later mistakenly shoots David (Javier Bardem), the cop who's come to arrest her. After six years in prison, Victor returns to restart the romance and even the score, only to find that the wheelchair-bound David is now Elena's husband.... Another of Almodovar's essays in obsessive love, this smoldering thriller has fewer of his trademark mannerisms but captivates with its tight story and genuinely sexy setpieces. His extravagant visual excess is reserved for the allegorical beginning and end, which use a pair of emergency births in the street 20 years apart, to link the cyclical inevitability of passion's mark on us all. To the film's credit, people coming to it for the "hot" sex will be seduced by its intense drama. Stargazers will note the presence of heartthrob Cruz and Brando-ish Bardem before they made it big. The image is rich and sensual, and the 2.35:1 compositions are far superior to the previous VHS release. The soundtrack of flamenco vocals and other Latin music is a concert in itself. *—GE* *AKA:* Carne Tremula.
Movie: 🎵🎵🎵½ *DVD:* 🎵🎵🎵
MGM Home Entertainment (Cat #10017 42, UPC #027616860422). Widescreen (2.35:1) anamorphic. Dolby Digital 5.1. $19.98. Keepcase. *LANG:* Castillian Spanish. *SUB:* English; French; Spanish. *CAP:* English. *FEATURES:* 16 chapter links ▪ Trailer.
1997 (R) 100m/C FR SP Javier Bardem, Francesca Neri, Angela Molina, Liberto Rabal, Jose Sancho, Penelope Cruz, Pilar Bardem, Alex Angulo; *D:* Pedro Almodovar; *W:* Pedro Almodovar, Ray Loriga, Jorge Guerricaechevarria; *C:* Alfonso Beato; *M:* Alberto Iglesias. *AWARDS: NOM:* British Acad. '98: Foreign Film.

The Living Daylights

After being used as a pawn in a fake Russian defector plot, our man Bond (Dalton) tracks down an international arms and opium smuggling ring. Dalton is excellent

in his debut, a rousing, refreshing cosmopolitan shoot-'em-up. This is actually one of the best entries in the series and on DVD, it looks as sharp as you'd expect. The disc contains all the usual Bondian extras, including a carefully edited commentary track. The deleted "magic carpet" scene is slow and rough. Had it been in the finished film, a lot of work would have been done. Image and sound are, of course, first-rate. The DVD is also available as part of the *James Bond Collection, Vol. 3* (UPC 027616853912). *—MM*
Movie: 🎵🎵🎵 *DVD:* 🎵🎵🎵
MGM Home Entertainment (Cat #10010 94, UPC #027616853943). Widescreen anamorphic. Dolby Digital 5.1 Surround Stereo; Dolby Digital Surround. $26.98. Keepcase. *LANG:* English; Spanish. *SUB:* French; Spanish. *FEATURES:* 36 chapter links ▪ Booklet ▪ Deleted scene ▪ Music video ▪ "Making of" music video featurette ▪ 3 trailers ▪ 2 documentary featurettes ▪ Commentary: director, cast.
1987 (PG) 130m/C Timothy Dalton, Maryam D'Abo, Jeroen Krabbe, John Rhys-Davies, Robert Brown, Joe Don Baker, Desmond Llewelyn, Art Malik, Geoffrey Keen, Walter Gotell, Andreas Wisniewski; *D:* John Glen; *W:* Richard Maibaum, Michael G. Wilson; *C:* Alec Mills; *M:* John Barry.

Local Hero

Riegert is a representative of a huge oil company who endeavors to buy a sleepy Scottish fishing village for excavation, and finds himself hypnotized by the place and its crusty denizens. When troubled Texas tycoon Lancaster sees the place, he is similarly entranced. Low-key, charmingly offbeat comedy set the standard for all of the imports that have followed it across the Atlantic and stress quirky characters, poetic landscapes, and locale. The soft-focus image—perfect for the story—doesn't really gain much on DVD. It's fairly grainy. Sound is good. *—MM*
Movie: 🎵🎵🎵🎵 *DVD:* 🎵🎵½
Warner Home Video, Inc. (Cat #11307). Widescreen anamorphic; full frame. Dolby Digital Mono. $14.98. Snapper. *LANG:* English. *SUB:* English; French. *FEATURES:* 35 chapter links ▪ Trailer.
1983 (PG) 112m/C GB Peter Riegert, Denis Lawson, Burt Lancaster, Fulton Mackay, Jenny Seagrove, Peter Capaldi, Norman Chancer; *D:* Bill Forsyth; *W:* Bill Forsyth; *C:* Chris Menges; *M:* Mark Knopfler. *AWARDS:* British Acad. '83: Director (Forsyth); N.Y. Film Critics '83: Screenplay; Natl. Soc. Film Critics '83: Screenplay.

Lock, Stock and 2 Smoking Barrels

Plot twist–laden British caper comedy plays like Tarantino and crumpets. Four dim hoods—Bacon (Statham), Soap (Fletcher), Eddy (Moran), and Tom (Flemyng)—pool their ill-gotten gains so that Eddy can play in a high-stakes card game. They don't know that the game is fixed

and they wind up owing gambler Hatchet Harry (Moriarty) 500,000 pounds. They then plan to rob a drug-dealing neighbor who's also planning a robbery of his own. Throw in a wandering pair of antique shotguns and you have the recipe for a cap-poppin' good time. Rock star Sting appears as the pub-owning father of one of the lads. It's impossible to judge the image by the usual standards because director Ritchie chooses to give the film a yellowish cast with harsh, acid-dark shadows. This appears to be an accurate transfer. Subtitles are welcome and so is the cockney rhyming slang glossary. *—MM*
Movie: 🎵🎵🎵 *DVD:* 🎵🎵🎵
USA Home Entertainment (Cat #59391, UPC #044005939125). Full frame; widescreen (1.85:1) letterboxed. Dolby Digital 5.1 Surround Stereo. $24.95. Keepcase. *LANG:* English. *SUB:* French; Spanish. *FEATURES:* Cast and crew thumbnail bios ▪ Trailers ▪ "Making of" featurette ▪ 17 chapter links ▪ Cockney rhyming slang glossary.
1998 (R) 105m/C GB Jason Flemyng, Dexter Fletcher, Nick Moran, Jason Statham, Steven Mackintosh, Vinnie Jones, Sting, Lenny McLean, P. H. Moriarty, Steve Sweeney, Frank Harper, Stephen Marcus; *D:* Guy Ritchie; *W:* Guy Ritchie; *C:* Tim Maurice-Jones; *M:* David A. Hughes, John Murphy. *AWARDS:* MTV Movie Awards '99: New Filmmaker (Ritchie); *NOM:* British Acad. '98: Film, Film Editing.

Lockdown

Charged with his partner's murder, a San Jose detective is sent to the big house. This cut-rate video premiere is no better than its generic title. Aliasing is heavy. *—MM*
Movie: 🎵 *DVD:* 🎵
Image Entertainment (Cat #0VED9027 DVD, UPC #014381902723). Full frame. Dolby Digital Stereo. $24.99. Snapper. *LANG:* English. *FEATURES:* 12 chapter links.
1990 90m/C Joe Estevez, Mike Farrell, Richard Lynch; *D:* Frank Harris.

Lolida 2000

In the future, all sexual activity is prohibited (bummer). Lolida (Lovell) works for an organization that destroys sexual material, but three particular stories get her all hot and bothered. The title was changed from *Lolita 2000,* as if anyone would find a meaningful connection to Vladimir Nabokov. Beyond the extras, which are mostly promotional material for other Surrender Cinema releases, the disc is identical to VHS tape—soft-focused image, bright edge enhancement. *—MM* *AKA:* Lolita 2000.
Movie: 🎵 *DVD:* 🎵🎵
Full Moon Pictures (Cat #8011, UPC #763 843801165). Full frame. $24.95. *LANG:* English. *FEATURES:* 29 chapter links ▪ Trailers ▪ Surrender Cinema promotions ▪ Weblink.
1997 90m/C Jacqueline Lovell, Gabriella Hall, Eric Acsell; *D:* Sybil Richards.

Lolita

Middle-aged college professor Humbert Humbert (Irons) becomes obsessed with nymphet Lolita (Swain), even to the point of marrying her mother Charlotte (Griffith). Later, the older man and the teenaged girl set off on a road trip that leads them to another older man, Quilty (Langella). Director Lyne is no stranger to controversy, but charges of kiddie porn are misplaced. (Why did Trimark feel it necessary to put a disclaimer before his commentary track?) This is an exceptionally well-made film about passion and obsession. DVD is a fine reproduction of a soft pastel image meant to evoke the past. The 5.1 sound field doesn't detract from Irons's voice-over. —MM
Movie: 🎵🎵🎵 **DVD:** 🎵🎵🎵½
Trimark Home Video (Cat #7193, UPC #03 1398719335). Widescreen letterboxed. Dolby Digital 5.1 Surround Stereo. $24.99. Keepcase. *LANG:* English. *FEATURES:* 30 chapter links • 8 deleted scenes • Screen tests • Script-to-scene • Featurette • Trailer.
1997 (R) 137m/C Jeremy Irons, Melanie Griffith, Frank Langella, Dominique Swain, Suzanne Shepherd, Keith Reddin, Erin J. Dean, Ben Silverstone; *D:* Adrian Lyne; *W:* Stephen Schiff; *C:* Howard Atherton; *M:* Ennio Morricone. *AWARDS: NOM:* MTV Movie Awards '99: Kiss (Jeremy Irons/Dominique Swain).

Lone Justice 2

Ned Blessing (Johnson) and his friend Crecencia (Avalos) return home to find that the nasty Borgers are terrorizing the town. Straight away, they set about righting wrongs, defending the defenseless, etc., etc. Wes Studi appears all too briefly in a supporting role. Slight aliasing and edge enhancement are visible but overall, image and sound are identical to VHS tape. Made-for-TV production gains little on this no-frills DVD. —MM **AKA:** Ned Blessing: The Story of My Life and Times.
Movie: 🎵🎵 **DVD:** 🎵🎵
Image Entertainment (Cat #ID5605FMDVD, UPC #014381560527). Full frame. Dolby Digital Stereo. $24.99. Snapper. *LANG:* English. *FEATURES:* 12 chapter links.
1993 (PG-13) 93m/C Brad Johnson, Luis Avalos, Wes Studi, Bill McKinney, Brenda Bakke, Julius Tennon, Richard Riehle, Gregory Scott Cummins, Rob Campbell, Rusty Schwimmer; *D:* Jack Bender; *W:* William D. Wittliff; *C:* Neil Roach; *M:* David Bell.

Lone Justice 3: Showdown at Plum Creek

Ex-outlaw-turned-sheriff Ned Blessing (Johnson) discovers the body of the previous sheriff has disappeared from its grave; Big Emma has taken over the saloon and wants Blessing out of town; and Oscar Wilde is coming for a visit. The three re-edited stories are taken from a miniseries. Production values really don't rise

above the made-for-TV level and the DVD image is not much better than VHS tape. —MM
Movie: 🎵🎵½ **DVD:** 🎵🎵
Image Entertainment (Cat #ID5606FMDVD, UPC #014381560626). Full frame. Dolby Digital Mono. $24.99. Snapper. *LANG:* English. *FEATURES:* 12 chapter links.
1996 (PG) 94m/C Brad Johnson, Wes Studi, Brenda Bakke, William Sanderson, Luis Avalos, Rusty Schwimmer, Stephen Fry; *D:* Jack Bender, Dan Lerner, David Hemmings; *W:* Stephen Harrigan; *C:* Neil Roach.

The Long Riders

The Jesse James outlaw legend gets a critical rework from master action storyteller Walter Hill *(Warriors, 48 HRS)* who uses real-life brothers Carradine, Keach, Quaid, and Guest to portray members of the James–Younger bank-robbing band. Hill makes some interesting choices in presenting a by-the-numbers retelling of the gang's exploits—Jesse (played by James Keach) is often indecisive, portrayed as cold and not particularly bright; his brother Frank (Stacy Keach) is warmer; and their cohort Cole Younger (David Carradine) comes off as the real brains of the outfit. Highlights include Cole's side trip to Texas; the disastrous North Field, Minnesota, foray; and the not-unexpected assassination of Jesse by brothers Charlie and Bob Ford (Christopher and Nicholas Guest). Although the DVD arrives with a nice widescreen transfer, the overall presentation must be viewed as an opportunity missed. The unique casting of brothers in legendary roles has been ignored as indicated by the lack of commentary support. "Special Features" have been limited to the film's original theatrical trailer. —RJT
Movie: 🎵🎵🎵 **DVD:** 🎵🎵½
MGM Home Entertainment (Cat #10015 93, UPC #027616859037). Widescreen (1.85:1) anamorphic. Dolby Digital Stereo. $19.98. Keepcase. *LANG:* English; French. *SUB:* French; Spanish. *FEATURES:* 16 chapter links • Theatrical trailer.
1980 (R) 100m/C Stacy Keach, James Keach, Randy Quaid, Dennis Quaid, David Carradine, Keith Carradine, Robert Carradine, Christopher Guest, Nicholas Guest, Pamela Reed, Savannah Smith, James Whitmore Jr., Harry Carey Jr.; *D:* Walter Hill; *W:* Stacy Keach, James Keach, Bill Bryden; *C:* Ric Waite; *M:* Ry Cooder.

The Long Way Home

This documentary examines the migration of European Jews to Palestine in the years following World War II. The archival footage of the liberation of the concentration camp at Dachau, though not the most graphic that was filmed, is still horrifying. Overall, the quality of the older film is very good. The music, however, is overwrought at key moments. The images and strong narration by Morgan Freeman need no embellishment. —MM
Movie: 🎵🎵🎵 **DVD:** 🎵🎵½

Vanguard International Cinema, Inc. (Cat #1-892649-53-5, UPC #658769003833). Full frame. $29.95. Keepcase. *LANG:* English. *FEATURES:* 12 chapter links.
1997 120m/C D: Mark Jonathan Harris; **W:** Mark Jonathan Harris; **C:** Don Lenzer; **M:** Lee Holdridge; **Nar:** Morgan Freeman, Ed Asner, Martin Landau, Michael York, Miriam Margolyes, David Paymer, Nina Siemaszko, Helen Slater. *AWARDS:* Oscars '97: Feature Doc.

The Longest Yard

Burt Reynolds was at the top of his game when he starred in Robert Aldrich's way-brutal "guy movie" classic about a disgraced pro football quarterback who is arrested after manhandling his girlfriend and taking her car for a joy ride. He gets a chance at redemption when he leads a misfit team of convicts against the guards. But he finds himself at the mercy of corrupt warden Eddie Albert. Print quality is good, save for minor speckling. The colors are mostly rich. The widescreen presentation preserves the film's theatrical aspect ratio and does full justice to the editing, which was nominated for an Oscar. This DVD is penalized for not providing any extras, but the film itself—one of Burt's very best—more than carries the ball. —DL
Movie: 🎵🎵🎵½ **DVD:** 🎵🎵
Paramount Home Video (Cat #08708, UPC #9736087084). Widescreen anamorphic. Dolby Digital Mono. $24.99. Keepcase. *LANG:* English; French. *SUB:* English. *CAP:* English. *FEATURES:* 16 chapter links.
1974 (R) 121m/C Burt Reynolds, Eddie Albert, Bernadette Peters, Ed Lauter, Richard Kiel; *D:* Robert Aldrich; *W:* Tracy Keenan Wynn; *C:* Joseph Biroc; *M:* Frank DeVol. *AWARDS:* Golden Globes '75: Film—Mus./Comedy; *NOM:* Oscars '74: Film Editing.

Longtime Companion

Though not the first, but probably the best, *Longtime Companion* can certainly be credited with inspiring the genre of AIDS films that peppered the '90s. In Craig Lucas's script, several different couples struggle with an unknown disease and strive to maintain their lives in the face of fear, loathing, and the willful ignorance inspired by prejudice that the society around them adopts. The story captures the drama of everyday life as magnified by illness. The characters—unlike most gay films—are defined by their feelings, their jobs, their moral fiber, and personal struggles and not just the fact that they're gay. In the early '80s, the *New York Times* refused to acknowledge gay relationships in its obituaries column, and thus coined the phrase "longtime companion." The plot follows the characters through the evolution, growth, and tribulations of their relationships, peppered with human foibles, and the evolving of the AIDS crisis. If you're looking for an educational drama about people with AIDS, skip Hollywood's glassy-eyed *Philadelphia*, and opt for this independent. The DVD is no frills with mediocre sound and no extras beyond the trailer. —*JAS*

Movie: 🐾🐾🐾🐾 **DVD:** 🐾🐾½
MGM Home Entertainment (Cat #4001608, UPC #027616857705). Widescreen (1.85:1) letterboxed. Dolby Digital. $19.99. Keepcase. *LANG:* English. *SUB:* French; Spanish. *FEATURES:* Original theatrical trailer.
1990 (R) 100m/C Stephen Caffrey, Patrick Cassidy, Brian Cousins, Bruce Davison, John Dossett, Mark Lamos, Dermot Mulroney, Mary-Louise Parker, Michael Schoeffling, Campbell Scott, Robert Joy, Brad O'Hara; *D:* Norman Rene; *W:* Craig Lucas; *C:* Tony Jennelli. *AWARDS:* Golden Globes '91: Support. Actor (Davison); Ind. Spirit '91: Support. Actor (Davison); N.Y. Film Critics '90: Support. Actor (Davison); Natl. Soc. Film Critics '90: Support. Actor (Davison); Sundance '90: Aud. Award; *NOM:* Oscars '90: Support. Actor (Davison).

Look Who's Talking, Too

Fluffy sequel uses the initially clever but unbelievable conceit that Amy Heckerling knows what babies are saying. Mikey's parents (Alley and Travolta) are having marital troubles and are forced to sing songs about toilet training. The only one who seems to get the irony is Rosanne, whose voice betrays a kind of "I can't believe this is happening" tone most of the time. It's hard to accept, when watching this mindless parade of toilet jokes, that Heckerling brought us *Fast Times at Ridgemont High*. The sad thing is that this is an amazing transfer with color that would hold up under a microscope and sound that calls to you from the kitchen. —*CA*

Movie: 🐾½ **DVD:** 🐾🐾🐾½
Columbia Tristar Home Video (Cat #05425, UPC #043396054257). Widescreen (1.85:1) letterboxed; full frame. Dolby Digital Surround. $24.95. Keepcase. *LANG:* English; French; Spanish; Portuguese. *SUB:* English; French; Spanish; Portuguese; Chinese; Korean; Thai. *FEATURES:* 28 chapter links • Bonus trailers *(Stuart Little; Baby Geniuses)* • Star and director bios • Photo gallery.
1990 (PG-13) 81m/C Kirstie Alley, John Travolta, Olympia Dukakis, Elias Koteas; *D:* Amy Heckerling; *W:* Amy Heckerling, Neal Israel; *C:* Thomas Del Ruth; *M:* David Kitay; *V:* Bruce Willis, Mel Brooks, Damon Wayans, Roseanne.

Lord Edgeware Dies

Please see review of *Agatha Christie's Poirot.* —*MJT*
(Cat #AAE70129, UPC #733961701296).
1999 100m/C *GB* David Suchet, Philip Jackson, Hugh Fraser, Pauline Moran, Dominic Guard, Christopher Guard, Helen Grace, Fiona Allen, John Castle, Lesley Nightingale, Hannah Yelland, Tim Steed; *D:* Brian Farnham; *W:* Anthony Horowitz; *C:* Chris O'Dell; *M:* Christopher Gunning.

The Lords of Flatbush

Four street toughs battle against their own maturation and responsibilities in 1950s Brooklyn. Winkler introduces the leather-clad hood he's made a career of and Stallone introduces a character not unlike Rocky. Interesting slice of life. The image on this DVD is very sub-standard for a Columbia Tristar release, but based on the previous VHS and laserdisc releases, the original source material must be the real problem. The color is very weak, with the actors all looking so pale that you'd swear they were vampires. Grain is present all the way through, but again it looks film-related and not of the digital variety. The mono sound is somewhat harsh so you might not want to really crank this one up. When the preprint is the problem, it's hard to rate the DVD on its own merits; but even with all the flaws, if you want to own the film, buy it on DVD. —*JO*

Movie: 🐾🐾½ **DVD:** 🐾🐾½
Columbia Tristar Home Video (Cat #04540, UPC #043396045408). Widescreen (1.85:1) anamorphic; full frame. Dolby Digital Mono. $27.95. Keepcase. *LANG:* English. *SUB:* English; Spanish; Portuguese; Chinese; Korean; Thai. *CAP:* English. *FEATURES:* 28 chapter links • Theatrical trailer • Talent files • Production notes.
1974 (PG) 88m/C Sylvester Stallone, Perry King, Henry Winkler, Susan Blakely, Armand Assante, Paul Mace; *D:* Stephen Verona, Martin Davidson; *M:* Joseph Brooks.

Loser

College comedy finds nerdy Midwesterner Biggs branded a loser by his dorm mates at New York University. He's also pining over beauty Suvari, who's having an affair with heartless prof Kinnear. Writer/director Heckerling's trademark sympathy for the adolescent outcast is intact, but this outing is missing the insight, subtlety, and (most importantly) the fun of her earlier efforts. Biggs and Suvari give passable performances, but Kinnear is the bright spot. For such a recent film, the preprint used for the DVD is a little disappointing. However, the digital transfer is a good one that remains well defined even when a scene is dimly lit. Colors are very vibrant and the outdoor shots of New York are at times very exhilarating. The Surround tracks very rarely join in and most music and dialogue is front speaker only. The rock soundtrack comes through thumpingly loud and clear, and the Surround really kicks in for a concert in the middle of the film. Be sure and watch the Wheatus music video "Teenage Dirtbag," which naturally incorporates clips from the film but is much better done than most. —*JO*

Movie: 🐾🐾 **DVD:** 🐾🐾🐾
Columbia Tristar Home Video (Cat #05068, UPC #043396050686). Widescreen (1.85:1) anamorphic; full frame. Dolby Digital 5.1; Dolby Surround; Stereo. $24.95. Keepcase. *LANG:* English; Spanish; French; Portuguese. *SUB:* English; Spanish; French; Chinese; Korean; Thai; Portuguese. *CAP:*

English. *FEATURES:* 28 chapter links • Theatrical trailer • Talent files • Production notes • Wheatus music video "Teenage Dirtbag."
2000 (PG-13) 95m/C Jason Biggs, Mena Suvari, Greg Kinnear, Zak Orth, Dan Aykroyd, Tom Sadoski, Jimmi Simpson, Colleen Camp, Robert Miano, Andy Dick, David Spade, Steven Wright, Taylor Negron, Andrea Martin, Scott Thompson; *D:* Amy Heckerling; *W:* Amy Heckerling; *C:* Rob Hahn; *M:* David Kitay.

Losin' It

Four teens (including a young Cruise) travel across the Mexican border to Tijuana on a journey to lose their virginity. On the way, they pick up a married woman (Long) who's in desperate need of a divorce. It's almost impossible to believe that the cast survived this lame comedy and that the director went on to make *L.A. Confidential*. Disc is really no better than tape with a full-frame image and uninspired sound. —*MM*

Movie: 🐾🐾 **DVD:** 🐾🐾
MGM Home Entertainment (Cat #1001557, UPC #027616858672). Full frame. Dolby Digital Mono. $14.98. Keepcase. *LANG:* English; Spanish. *SUB:* French; Spanish. *CAP:* English. *FEATURES:* 16 chapter links • Trailer.
1982 (R) 104m/C Tom Cruise, John Stockwell, Shelley Long, Jackie Earle Haley, John P. Navin Jr.; *D:* Curtis Hanson; *W:* Bill W.L. Norton; *C:* Gilbert Taylor; *M:* Kenneth Wannberg.

The Loss of Sexual Innocence

Figgis's ambitious film follows the fall from grace (literally of Adam and Eve), and the nature of sex, love, jealousy, and violence. Unfortunately, this turns out to be less-than-scintillating material. Interspersed with scenes from the Garden of Eden story is that of dissatisfied filmmaker Nic (Sands), as he relives his past and ponders his unhappy present. This art-house film is gorgeous on DVD. The image is crystal clear and even with Figgis's occasionally unusual lighting, the DVD remains grain and artifact free. The DVD is also able to convey all the subtleties of the color composition of the film. For a Dolby Surround mix, there is an amazing amount of ambience from the rear and lively separation effects up front to help immerse the viewer in the film. If you're a film student (and even if you're not), be sure and give the film a second look, this time with the commentary on, as Figgis gives plenty of details about both his ideas and the technical aspects of the film. —*JO*

Movie: 🐾🐾🐾 **DVD:** 🐾🐾🐾
Columbia Tristar Home Video (Cat #04013, UPC #043396040137). Widescreen (1.78:1) letterboxed. Dolby Surround; Stereo. $27.95. Keepcase. *LANG:* English (DS); Spanish (Stereo). *SUB:* English; French. *CAP:* English. *FEATURES:* 28 chapter links • Commentary: director Mike Figgis.

1998 (R) 101m/C Julian Sands, Saffron Burrows, Stefano Dionisi, Jonathan Rhys Meyers, Kelly Macdonald, Femi Ogumbanjo, Hanne Klintoe, Johanna Torrel, George Moktar, John Cowey; *D:* Mike Figgis; *W:* Mike Figgis; *C:* Benoit Delhomme; *M:* Mike Figgis.

Lost in America

Neurotic advertising man David Howard (Brooks) has sold his house in anticipation of a big career move at his Los Angeles agency. He's also driving his wife Linda (Hagerty) half-nuts with his incessant second-guessing and insecure obsessions. When the promotion meeting turns out to be a sideways shift to the New York office, David flips out, insults his boss, and gets himself escorted from the building by security. Making a rash decision to "drop out" like the fantasy in the movie *Easy Rider,* David gets Linda to quit her job too. They head for Las Vegas in a large motorhome, to renew their marriage vows and sleep under the stars. But a nice hotel sounds like a better plan for the exhausted couple, so they stay the night in a casino-hotel.... DVD image is clean and handsome, beautifully transferred in bright 16:9. The audio track is simply dialogue about 90% of the time, but is also free of flaws. *—GE*
Movie: 🐾🐾🐾½ *DVD:* 🐾🐾🐾½
Warner Home Video, Inc. (Cat #11460, UPC #085391146025). Widescreen (1.78:1) anamorphic. $19.98. Snapper. *LANG:* English. *FEATURES:* Trailer.
1985 (R) 91m/C Albert Brooks, Julie Hagerty, Michael Greene, Tom Tarpey, Garry Marshall, Art Frankel; *D:* Albert Brooks; *W:* Albert Brooks, Monica Johnson; *M:* Arthur B. Rubinstein. *AWARDS:* Natl. Soc. Film Critics '85: Screenplay.

Lost Souls

Dull, portentous horror film features Ryder as a once-possessed young woman who informs a young author (Chaplin) that he is about to become the antichrist. As his relationship with her grows stronger, he discovers a large conspiracy orchestrated by his loved ones to bring about the apocalypse. Derivate and ugly, this directorial debut by Kaminski (a brilliant cinematographer) is unnecessarily stylized, convoluted, and predictable. The whole film is shot in an intentionally grainy, color-muted style that is both tedious and unflattering to the actors. A big buildup to nothing, the ending is a real letdown. The commentary features the usual production anecdotes, but Kaminski frequently rambles and admits he bears no true passion for the genre. The disc accurately conveys the grain and lack of color of the photography, and the Surround sound has lots of presence. *—DG*
Movie: 🐾 *DVD:* 🐾🐾🐾
New Line Home Video (Cat #N5207, UPC #79404352072). Widescreen (2.35:1) anamorphic. DTS Dolby Surround 5.1; Dolby Stereo Surround. $24.98. Snapper. *LANG:* English. *SUB:* English. *CAP:* English. *FEATURES:* 20 chapter links ☛ Commentary:

Kaminski, Fiore ☛ Deleted scenes with optional commentary ☛ Cast and crew filmographies ☛ Theatrical trailer. DVD-ROM features: screenplay/film viewer, weblinks.
2000 (R) 98m/C Winona Ryder, Ben Chaplin, John Hurt, Elias Koteas, John Diehl, W. Earl Brown, Sarah Wynter, Philip Baker Hall, Brian Reddy, John Beasley, Victor Slezak, Brad Greenquist; *D:* Janusz Kaminski; *W:* Pierce Gardner, Betsy Stahl; *C:* Mauro Fiore; *M:* Jan A.P. Kaczmarek.

The Lost Weekend

Heartrending Hollywood masterpiece depicts a single weekend in the life of a writer (Milland) who cannot believe he's an alcoholic. Except for a pat ending, it's an uncompromising, startlingly harsh treatment with Milland giving one of the industry's bravest lead performances ever. It's still a remarkable piece of work from all concerned. The disc's only flaw comes from the source material. The photography lacks the razor-sharpness that the best black and white could achieve only a few years later. It is, however, the best that could be done about the writing and acting are the point, anyway. *—MM*
Movie: 🐾🐾🐾🐾 *DVD:* 🐾🐾🐾½
Universal Studios Home Video (Cat #211 53, UPC #025192115325). Full frame. Dolby Digital Mono. $29.99. Keepcase. *LANG:* English. *SUB:* French; Spanish. *CAP:* English. *FEATURES:* 18 chapter links ☛ Trailer ☛ Production notes ☛ Talent files.
1945 100m/B Ray Milland, Jane Wyman, Phillip Terry, Howard da Silva, Doris Dowling, Frank Faylen, Mary Young; *D:* Billy Wilder; *W:* Charles Brackett, Billy Wilder; *C:* John Seitz; *M:* Miklos Rozsa. *AWARDS:* Oscars '45: Actor (Milland), Director (Wilder), Picture, Screenplay; Cannes '46: Actor (Milland), Film; Golden Globes '46: Actor—Drama (Milland), Director (Wilder), Film—Drama; Natl. Bd. of Review '45: Actor (Milland); N.Y. Film Critics '45: Actor (Milland), Director (Wilder), Film; *NOM:* Oscars '45: B&W Cinematog., Film Editing, Orig. Dramatic Score.

The Lost World [Image]

Forget the public domain copies of this silent masterpiece. This restored version eliminates them from any serious consideration. First, the film has been returned to something like its original running length of 93 minutes. (Most other discs and tapes are about an hour long.) Though the image is far from perfect with obvious signs of wear, it is much better than existing versions and restores the original tinting. Of the various sound options available, the newly recorded 5.1 score by the Alloy Orchestra is my choice. The DVD also comes with a booklet that's a re-creation of an original souvenir program. This one belongs in the library of any serious science-fiction and stop-motion animation fan. *—MM*
Movie: 🐾🐾🐾½ *DVD:* 🐾🐾🐾½
Image Entertainment (Cat #ID0319DSDVD, UPC #014381031928). Full frame. Dolby

Digital 5.1 Surround Stereo; Dolby Digital Surround. $24.99. Keepcase. *LANG:* Silent. *SUB:* English intertitles. *FEATURES:* 18 chapter links ☛ Promotional booklet ☛ Commentary: Roy Pilot, author of *The Annotated Lost World* ☛ New score by the Alloy Orchestra ☛ Traditional score by Robert Israel ☛ Production stills and art gallery ☛ Images from *The Annotated Lost World.*
1925 93m/B Wallace Beery, Lewis Stone, Bessie Love, Lloyd Hughes; *D:* Harry Hoyt; *W:* Marion Fairfax; *C:* Arthur Edeson. *AWARDS:* Natl. Film Reg. '98.

The Lost World: Jurassic Park 2 [CE]

Clumsily plotted sequel has more dinosaurs, tinier dinosaurs, faster dinosaurs, cuter dinosaurs, and hungrier dinosaurs than the first film. It also has some spectacular action sequences (Chapter 14 is a brilliant set piece) and a ridiculous ending that falls apart completely. Two competing groups—noble scientists and nasty hunters—go to another island where dinosaurs flourish. Before it's over, a T-Rex is running amok on the mainland. Naturally, the DVD image and sound range between very good and excellent, though much of the action is deliberately dark. The extras are extensive, but be warned that the disc comes in two different editions. The DTS version (cat. # 20788) does not contain the deleted scenes and several other extras that are found on the Dolby 5.1 version. *—MM AKA:* Jurassic Park 2.
Movie: 🐾🐾½ *DVD:* 🐾🐾🐾½
Universal Studios Home Video (Cat #200 52, UPC #025192005220). Widescreen (1.85:1) anamorphic. Dolby Digital 5.1 Surround Stereo; Dolby Digital Surround Stereo. $26.98. Keepcase. *LANG:* English; French. *SUB:* Spanish. *CAP:* English. *FEATURES:* "Making of" featurette ☛ Two deleted scenes ☛ Illustrations and conceptual drawings ☛ Storyboards ☛ Models ☛ World of Jurassic Park ☛ Magic of ILM ☛ Trailers for 3 *Jurassic Park* films ☛ Dinosaur encyclopedia ☛ Talent files ☛ Posters and toys ☛ DVD-ROM features ☛ DVD newsletter.
1997 (PG-13) 129m/C Jeff Goldblum, Julianne Moore, Vince Vaughn, Richard Attenborough, Arliss Howard, Pete Postlethwaite, Peter Stormare, Vanessa Lee Chester, Richard Schiff, Harvey Jason, Thomas F. Duffy, Ariana Richards, Joseph Mazzello; *D:* Steven Spielberg; *W:* David Koepp; *C:* Janusz Kaminski; *M:* John Williams. *AWARDS: NOM:* Oscars '97: Visual FX; MTV Movie Awards '98: Action Seq.; Golden Raspberries '97: Worst Remake/Sequel, Worst Screenplay.

Louis Prima: The Wildest!

This biography and appreciation of Louis Prima focuses on his music and undeniable showmanship. Prima's career roughly follows the rise and fall of big-band jazz.

He wrote the standard "Sing, Sing, Sing" and late in his life he gave voice to "King Louie," the orangutan in Disney's *The Jungle Book.* In between, he wrote many hits and performed with groups of varying size and talent. Today, he may be remembered best for his work with his wife, singer Keely Smith. DVD image is very good for a documentary. There is some visible damage to the original elements but overall, it looks fine. Mono sound is crisp and appropriate to the times. —*MM*

Movie: 🎬🎬🎬 **DVD:** 🎬🎬🎬

Image Entertainment (Cat #ID0535BUDVD, UPC #014381053524). Full frame. Dolby Digital Mono. $24.99. Keepcase. *LANG:* English. *FEATURES:* 5 extra interviews ▪ Songs: "Sing, Sing, Sing," "Robin Hood," "Please No Squeeza Da Banana" ▪ Videos: "Basin Street Blues," "Oh, Babe," "Waitin on the Robert E Lee" ▪ 16 chapter links.

1999 80m/C Louis Prima, Keely Smith; *D:* Don McGlynn; *C:* Steven Wacks, Randy Drummond, Alex Vlacos.

Loulou

Nelly (Huppert) leaves her middle-class husband when she meets Loulou (Depardieu), a charming stud in a leather jacket. The resulting erotic attraction is played out in bawdy detail. DVD appears to be an accurate reproduction of the original. Underlit scenes—mostly night exteriors—tend to be very grainy and hard to see. Interiors are stronger though they usually lack the flattering light of Hollywood productions. Optional subtitles are easy to read. —*MM*

Movie: 🎬🎬🎬½ **DVD:** 🎬🎬

New Yorker Video (Cat #30701, UPC #717119307042). Widescreen letterboxed. $29.95. Keepcase. *LANG:* French. *SUB:* English. *FEATURES:* 15 chapter links ▪ Liner notes by Maurice Pialat ▪ Trailer ▪ Pialat filmography.

1980 (R) 110m/C *FR* Isabelle Huppert, Gerard Depardieu, Guy Marchand; *D:* Maurice Pialat; *W:* Maurice Pialat, Arlette Langmann; *C:* Pierre William Glenn; *M:* Philippe Sarde.

Love Affair

Multi-Kleenex weepie has inspired countless romantic dreams of true love atop the Empire State Building. Dunn and Boyer fall in love aboard a ship bound for New York, but they're both involved. They agree to meet later to see if their feelings hold true but tragedy intervenes. Excellent comedy/drama is witty at first, more subdued later with plenty of romance and melodrama and an attractive cast. Reportedly, this public domain version lacks the original score. It's a typically rough image that's really no better than VHS tape. The title is also available on the "Irene Dunne Romance Classics" double feature. —*MM*

Movie: 🎬🎬🎬½ **DVD:** 🎬🎬

Madacy Entertainment (Cat #9-9017, UPC #056775005399). Full frame. Dolby Digital Mono. $9.99. Keepcase. *LANG:* English.

FEATURES: 9 chapter links ▪ Irene Dunne thumbnail bio ▪ Lobby card.

1939 87m/B Irene Dunne, Charles Boyer, Maria Ouspenskaya, Lee Bowman, Astrid Allwyn, Maurice Moscovich, Scotty Beckett, Joan Leslie, Gerald Mohr, Dell Henderson, Carol Hughes; *D:* Leo McCarey; *W:* Leo McCarey, Delmer Daves, Donald Ogden Stewart; *C:* Rudolph Mate; *M:* Roy Webb. *AWARDS:* NOM: Oscars '39: Actress (Dunne), Picture, Song ("Wishing"), Story, Support. Actress (Ouspenskaya).

Love After Love

Curious film looks at sex and relationships among thirtysomething professionals in Paris. Lola (Huppert), a successful romance novelist, is suffering a crisis in both her career and love life. She's involved with two men who, in turn, are involved with different women who happen to have borne them children. The movie starts off with so much mate switching and secret sexual rendezvous that by the second half you don't really care who Lola winds up with. The filmmakers use a pale black and white to show Lola's imagined scenes. It's a nice match for the muted color scheme of the rest of the film. Overall, the image is fine, if unspectacular. Yellow subtitles are burned in. —*MM* **AKA:** Apres l'Amour.

Movie: 🎬🎬 **DVD:** 🎬🎬½

Winstar Home Entertainment (Cat #5114). Full frame. $29.98. Keepcase. *LANG:* French. *SUB:* English. *FEATURES:* Cast and crew thumbnail bios ▪ Production notes ▪ 6 chapter links ▪ Trailer.

1994 104m/C *FR* Isabelle Huppert, Hippolyte Girardot, Lio; *D:* Diane Kurys; *W:* Diane Kurys, Antoine Lacomblez; *C:* Fabio Conversi; *M:* Yves Simon, Serge Perathone, Jannick Top.

Love and Death

Boris Grushenko (Allen) has been condemned to death and remembers his life in 19th-century Russia. Along the way, he has conversations with Death and falls in love with his beautiful cousin Sonja (Keaton). Though relatively little known (compared to his other work), Allen's parody of Russian novels is really funny. It's also one of the better looking of his early films on disc. The bucolic exteriors are fine and some of the interiors are properly opulent. Mono sound is acceptable. —*MM*

Movie: 🎬🎬🎬½ **DVD:** 🎬🎬🎬

MGM Home Entertainment (Cat #100006 83, UPC #027616850140). Widescreen anamorphic; full frame. Dolby Digital Mono. $24.99. Keepcase. *LANG:* English; Spanish. *SUB:* French; Spanish. *CAP:* English. *FEATURES:* 24 chapter links ▪ Liner notes.

1975 (PG) 89m/C Woody Allen, Diane Keaton, Georges Adel, Despo Diamantidou, Frank Adu, Harold Gould; *D:* Woody Allen; *W:* Woody Allen; *C:* Ghislan Cloquet.

Love by Appointment

Though the box copy claims that this is a "sexy overseas romp," it's really an

ensemble piece about a classy Italian bordello, focusing both on the staff and the customers. Some of the characters are interesting, but the film has an unfocused quality. Many fine scratches are visible but overall, the sharpness of the image and lighting are very good for a film of this age. —*MM*

Movie: 🎬🎬½ **DVD:** 🎬🎬½

Image Entertainment (Cat #ALF9857DVD, UPC #013481985726). Widescreen (1.85:1) letterboxed. Dolby Digital Mono. $24.99. Snapper. *LANG:* English. *FEATURES:* 12 chapter links.

1976 96m/C *IT* Ernest Borgnine, Robert Alda, Francoise Fabian, Corinne Clery; *D:* Armando Nannuzzi; *M:* Riz Ortolani.

Love Field

Pfeiffer is a Jackie Kennedy–obsessed hairdresser who decides to travel by bus to Washington, D.C., when she learns of President Kennedy's assassination. Along the way, she becomes involved in an interracial friendship with the secretive Haysbert (a woefully underused character actor) who's traveling with his young daughter. Basically, the DVD does a standard job with a mistily focused pastel image that's meant to make us nostalgic for the early '60s. It's only a slight improvement over VHS tape. —*MM*

Movie: 🎬🎬½ **DVD:** 🎬🎬½

MGM Home Entertainment (Cat #10014 55, UPC #027616857750). Widescreen (1.85:1) letterboxed. Dolby Digital Surround Stereo. $19.98. Keepcase. *LANG:* English; French. *SUB:* French; Spanish. *CAP:* English. *FEATURES:* 16 chapter links ▪ Trailer.

1991 (PG-13) 104m/C Michelle Pfeiffer, Dennis Haysbert, Stephanie McFadden, Brian Kerwin, Louise Latham, Peggy Rea, Beth Grant, Cooper Huckabee, Mark Miller, Johnny Rae McGhee; *D:* Jonathan Kaplan; *W:* Don Roos; *C:* Ralf Bode; *M:* Jerry Goldsmith. *AWARDS:* NOM: Oscars '92: Actress (Pfeiffer).

Love, Honour & Obey

The writing, directing, and acting team of Dominic Anciano and Ray Burdis are back for their second feature film (*Final Cut* being their first), and it's a winner. Jude Law brings childhood friend Johnny Lee Miller ("Crash Override" of *Hackers* fame) into the family business—the mob! Miller, a seemingly meek mailman, moves quickly from mail theft to murder and sets in motion a war between rival gangs in the process. One is immediately reminded of director Guy Ritchie's *Lock, Stock and 2 Smoking Barrels,* as this film covers similar ground and is played in much the same tone, with rapid shifts between comedy and bloody mayhem. Image and sound are acceptable but this DVD begs for an audio commentary from the directing duo. Also note, as a hint of the way in which the quirky team works, all the characters share the same first name as the actors who play them. —*RJT*

Movie: ♪♪♪ **DVD:** ♪♪½
Trimark Home Video (Cat #VM 7628D, UPC #031398762829). Widescreen (1.85:1) letterboxed. Dolby Digital Surround. $24.99. Keepcase. *LANG:* English. *SUB:* English; French; Spanish. *CAP:* English. *FEATURES:* 24 chapter links ● Theatrical trailer ● Bonus trailers for *Xchange* and *Once in the Life.*
2000 95m/C *GB* Jonny Lee Miller, Jude Law, Ray Winstone, Sadie Frost, Sean Pertwee, Kathy Burke, Rhys Ifans, Laila Morse, Dominic Anciano, Ray Burdis; **D:** Dominic Anciano, Ray Burdis; **W:** Dominic Anciano, Ray Burdis; **C:** John Ward.

Love Kills

A con man (Van Peebles) pretends to be masseuse to con sexy widowed trophy wife (Warren) out of millions on the orders of his psychotic girlfriend (Devine). The only things that stand in his way are the slimy stepson (Leitch), his gang of drugged out slackers, and the Third Reich's answer to grandmothers (Fletcher). Loretta Devine is fun as the electric saw-wielding nurse/girlfriend and Daniel Baldwin is amusing as a Columbo-style police detective. Written and directed by Van Peebles, who cut his teeth directing episodes of *21 Jump Street,* this film doesn't have anywhere near the social conscience of *Panther* or *New Jack City,* but the script and acting are decent. The picture is better in quality than most videos and the sound is good. —*CA*
Movie: ♪♪½ **DVD:** ♪♪½
Image Entertainment (Cat #ID9360UMD-VD, UPC #014381936020). Widescreen (2.35:1) letterboxed. Dolby Digital Surround. $24.99. Snapper. *LANG:* English. *FEATURES:* 12 chapter links.
1998 (R) 97m/C Mario Van Peebles, Lesley Ann Warren, Daniel Baldwin, Donovan Leitch, Louise Fletcher, Loretta Devine, Melvin Van Peebles, Susan Ruttan, Alexis Arquette; **D:** Mario Van Peebles; **W:** Mario Van Peebles; **C:** George Mooradian.

Love Letters

A young public radio disc jockey (Curtis) falls under the spell of a box of love letters written to her mother. Reading them, she learns that her mother led a double life with a lover, and she finds herself retracing those steps with a married man (Keach). Similar material has been the basis for countless "erotic thrillers," but it's treated seriously here. Disc is an accurate reproduction of an appallingly dark, harsh original. Added to that, the soundtrack contains an irritating intermittent hiss. No better than tape. —*MM* **AKA:** Passion Play; My Love Letters.
Movie: ♪♪ **DVD:** ♪♪
New Concorde (Cat #NH20249D, UPC #736991424999). Full frame. Stereo. $19.98. Keepcase. *LANG:* English. *FEATURES:* 24 chapter links ● Thumbnail bios ● Trailers.
1983 (R) 102m/C Jamie Lee Curtis, Amy Madigan, Bud Cort, Matt Clark, Bonnie Bartlett, Sally Kirkland, James Keach; **D:** Amy Holden Jones; **W:** Amy Holden Jones; **C:** Alec Hirschfeld; **M:** Ralph Jones.

The Love Master

Comedian Craig Shoemaker stars as himself in this unconventional comedy mostly cut together from an Arizona stand-up performance. Offscreen and flashback vignettes flesh things out a bit, but it's the stand-up material that is the meat of the movie. When it gets going, it has quite a bit of funny stuff, as Shoemaker slips into various characters, including an all-too-realistic Barney Fife, Vagina Man, and the title character. Wendt plays Shoemaker's therapist, and Fawcett is his dream date. Don't expect high production values, but you will laugh. The 1.33:1 framing of the DVD is uncomfortably tight, with close-ups particularly claustrophobic. Fleshtones seem off quite a bit as well, with a tendency toward red on a properly calibrated display. The image overall is disappointingly soft. The Dolby Digital Mono track no doubt is true to the source material, and hearing every word of the dialogue is never a problem. There aren't any extras. —*MB*
Movie: ♪♪½ **DVD:** ♪½
Image Entertainment (Cat #ID0247LMDVD, UPC #014381024722). Full frame. Dolby Digital Mono. $24.99. Snapper. *LANG:* English. *FEATURES:* 12 chapter links.
1997 ?m/C Craig Shoemaker, George Wendt, Farrah Fawcett; **D:** Marius Balchunas.

Love Stinks

Apparently designed as an antidote to the date movie, this joyless "unromantic" comedy gives off a few rank fumes of its own. Writer Seth Winnick (Stewart) meets Chelsea (Wilson) at the wedding of his pals Larry (Bellamy) and Holly (Banks). After he's lured into Chelsea's clutches, she begins to take over his life while dropping hints that he should pop the big question. Eventually, she sues for palimony. Stewart attempts to rise above the material with his excellent comic timing. The transfer appears to be a little soft at times, but is great looking nonetheless, with good color delineation and a solid black level that gives the picture a great sense of depth. —*GH/MM*
Movie: ♪½ **DVD:** ♪♪♪
Columbia Tristar Home Video (Cat #4554). Widescreen (1.85:1) anamorphic. Dolby Digital Surround Stereo. $24.95. Keepcase. *LANG:* English. *FEATURES:* Commentary ● Production notes ● Trailers.
1999 (R) 94m/C French Stewart, Bridgette Wilson, Tyra Banks, Bill Bellamy, Steve Hytner, Jason Bateman, Tiffani-Amber Thiessen; **D:** Jeff Franklin; **W:** Jeff Franklin; **C:** Uta Briesewitz; **M:** Bennett Salvay.

Love Story

O'Neal's the son of Boston's upper crust at Harvard; McGraw's the daughter of a poor Italian on scholarship at Radcliffe. They meet; they fall in love but only briefly. Time has rendered the arch performances and the infamous tagline "Love means never having to say you're sorry" comical, though I must admit that I have never bought into this mushball. That said, the DVD image looks very good for a film of this age. It displays no real signs of wear, and Arthur Hiller provides a fine commentary track. —*MM*
Movie: ♪♪½ **DVD:** ♪♪♪
Paramount Home Video (Cat #08006, UPC #097360800647). Widescreen anamorphic. Dolby Digital Mono. $24.99. Keepcase. *LANG:* English; French. *SUB:* English. *FEATURES:* 18 chapter links ● Trailer ● Retrospective featurette ● Commentary: Arthur Hiller.
1970 (PG) 100m/C Ryan O'Neal, Ali MacGraw, Ray Milland, John Marley, Tommy Lee Jones; **D:** Arthur Hiller; **W:** Erich Segal; **C:** Richard Kratina; **M:** Francis Lai. *AWARDS:* Oscars '70: Orig. Score; Golden Globes '71: Actress—Drama (MacGraw), Director (Hiller), Film—Drama, Screenplay, Score; *NOM:* Oscars '70: Actor (O'Neal), Actress (MacGraw), Director (Hiller), Picture, Story & Screenplay, Support. Actor (Marley).

Lovers and Liars

A romantic adventure in Rome turns into a symphony of mishaps when the man (Giannini) forgets to tell the woman (Hawn) that he is married. This substandard disc appears to have been made from a well-worn tape. Image is dark and unfocused; sound is scratchy. —*MM* **AKA:** Travels with Anita; A Trip with Anita.
Movie: ♪♪ **DVD:** woof
Tapeworm Video Distributors (Cat #1735). Full frame. $19.95. Keepcase. *LANG:* English. *FEATURES:* 8 chapter links.
1981 (R) 93m/C *IT* Goldie Hawn, Giancarlo Giannini, Laura Betti; **D:** Mario Monicelli; **W:** Mario Monicelli, Paul Zimmerman; **C:** Tonino Delli Colli; **M:** Ennio Morricone.

Love's Labour's Lost

The King of Navarre (Alessandro Nivola) and three pals (Kenneth Branagh, Matthew Lillard, Adrian Lester) swear off women while pursuing their studies. Enter a French princess (Alicia Silverstone) and her ladies-in-waiting (Natascha McElhone, Carmen Ejogo, and Emily Mortimer). The stage is set for...a 1930s musical? Kenneth Branagh audaciously sets William Shakespeare's romantic comedy (heavily abridged) to the songs of, among others, George Gershwin and Cole Porter. At what point did this seem like a good idea? Not since *At Long Last Love* or *Cop Rock* has there been a more misguided attempt to revive the Hollywood musical (a *Dirty Dancing* rendition of "Let's Face the Music and Dance" is a cheeky low point). The cast exhibits high spirits, but the strain shows in the song and dance numbers. Scene-stealer Nathan Lane shows how it's done with his rendition of "There's No Business Like

Show Business." Not much labor seems to have gone into this DVD. The widescreen presentation is welcome (nothing spoils the rhythm of a musical number like pan and scan). Sound and picture are adequate. The image is soft at times, but overall, the colors are vibrant. —DL
Movie: 🎞🎞 **DVD:** 🎞🎞½
Miramax Pictures Home Video (Cat #18317, UPC #1795100502). Widescreen (2.35:1) anamorphic. Dolby Digital; 5.1 Surround. $32.99. Keepcase. *LANG:* English. *SUB:* English. *FEATURES:* Behind-the-scenes featurette ▪ Deleted scenes ▪ Outtakes ▪ 20 chapter links.
2000 (PG) 93m/C *GB* Kenneth Branagh, Alicia Silverstone, Natascha McElhone, Alessandro Nivola, Matthew Lillard, Nathan Lane, Timothy Spall, Geraldine McEwan, Carmen Ejogo, Adrian Lester, Emily Mortimer, Richard Briers, Stefania Rocca, Jimmy Yuill; *D:* Kenneth Branagh; *W:* Kenneth Branagh; *C:* Alex Thomson; *M:* Patrick Doyle.

The Loves of Carmen
Adaptation of the Prosper Merrimee novel about a tempestuous Spanish gypsy (Hayworth) and the soldier (Ford) who loves her. Hayworth is great to look at. On DVD, the Technicolor is rich and vivid, bringing back memories of these glory cinema days with its lush production designs. The disc's black level is solid with deep shadows and balanced highlights. The monaural audio track is surprisingly clear. The frequency response is good without overemphasis on the high end, and a rather good bass extension. —GH/MM
Movie: 🎞🎞½ **DVD:** 🎞🎞🎞
Columbia Tristar Home Video (Cat #8649). Full frame. Dolby Digital Mono. $27.95. Keepcase. *LANG:* English; Spanish; Portuguese. *SUB:* English; Spanish; Portuguese; Chinese; Thai. *FEATURES:* Rita Hayworth featurette ▪ Vintage advertising ▪ Trailers.
1948 98m/C Rita Hayworth, Glenn Ford, Ron Randell, Victor Jory, Arnold Moss, Luther Adler, Joseph Buloff; *D:* Charles Vidor; *W:* Helen Deutsch; *C:* William E. Snyder; *M:* Mario Castelnuovo-Tedesco. *AWARDS: NOM:* Oscars '48: Color Cinematog.

Loving Jezebel
If anything, writer/director Kwyn Bader's *Loving Jezebel* proves that Hill Harper (*The Skulls, In Too Deep,* etc.) is a terrific talent. The problem is, even at a mere 88 minutes, Bader's film seems long and even Harper can't act his way out of a weak and contrived script. The gist of the story is that he, Hill Harper, has a track record for falling in love with his friends' and other men's girlfriends—the theme of many a sit-com—with consistently bad results. Of course you have to give Harper credit for one thing—he has excellent taste in women, as all of his "girlfriends" are eye-candy super models. DVD is a bare-bones effort, but nevertheless nicely delivered. —RJT

Movie: 🎞🎞 **DVD:** 🎞🎞½
Universal Studios Home Video (Cat #212 56, UPC #025192125621). Widescreen (1.85:1) letterboxed. Dolby Digital Surround Stereo. $24.99. Keepcase. *LANG:* English. *SUB:* English; French. *CAP:* English; French. *FEATURES:* 18 chapter markers ▪ Trailer.
1999 (R) 88m/C Hill Harper, Laurel Holloman, Nicole Ari Parker, Sandrine Holt, David Moscow, Elisa Donovan, Phylicia Rashad; *D:* Kwyn Bader; *W:* Kwyn Bader; *C:* Horacio Marquinez; *M:* Tony Prendatt.

Lower Level
While working late, an attractive business woman (Gracen) becomes trapped in an office building by her psychotic secret admirer. The video transfer is quite good, featuring crisp colors and nicely defined blacks. The soundtrack is also well done. It's just a shame that such a nice effort is wasted on a none-too-great movie. —MJT
Movie: 🎞 **DVD:** 🎞🎞
Image Entertainment (Cat #OVED9028DVD, UPC #014381902822). Full frame. Dolby Digital Surround. $24.99. Snapper. *LANG:* English. *FEATURES:* 12 chapter links ▪ Theatrical trailer.
1991 (R) 88m/C David Bradley, Elizabeth (Ward) Gracen, Jeff Yagher; *D:* Kristine Peterson; *W:* Joel Soisson; *C:* Wally Pfister; *M:* Terry Plumeri.

Lucinda's Spell
If Anne Rice and Mel Brooks teamed up to make a sexy horror movie, they might come up with something like this wild romp. It's an energetic B-movie with a '60s drive-in feel and an uncertain tone that veers from comic to serious to bawdy. Jason (writer/director Jacob) is a direct descendent of Merlin who is scheduled to conceive a magical offspring on the Eve of Beltane. All the witches in New Orleans want to be the lucky girl. Lucinda (Fulton) is a hooker with a heart of gold and a history with Jason. It's difficult to judge the DVD from the promotional copy. It suffers from extreme aliasing and artifacts. The graininess in the night scenes is heavy. The bass is boosted so high in the score that some voices and accents are impossible to understand. Remember, though, that this is a movie made with more imagination and enthusiasm than money and polish. It's not supposed to be slick. —MM
Movie: 🎞🎞½ **DVD:** 🎞🎞
A.D.V. Films (Cat #ADVI701382). Widescreen letterboxed. Dolby Digital Stereo. $29.98. Keepcase. *LANG:* English. *FEATURES:* 20 chapter links ▪ "Making of" featurette ▪ Promotional TV spots ▪ Trailer.
2000 (R) 105m/C Jon Jacobs, Christina (Kristina) Fulton, Shanna Betz, Leon Herbert, Angie Green, Alix Koromzay, J.C. Brandy, John El, Fatt Natt; *D:* Jon Jacobs; *W:* Jon Jacobs; *C:* Jaime Reynoso; *M:* Niki Jack.

Lucky Numbers
In Harrisburg, Pennsylvania, 1988, TV weatherman Russ Richards (Travolta) and TV lotto-ball babe Crystal LaTroy (Kudrow) cook up a scheme to rig the state lottery. The comedy certainly has its moments, but it's hard to overcome the feeling of superiority that the filmmakers have toward the characters and their world. The DVD certainly captures the second-rate quality that the film is trying to achieve. Image is a faithful re-creation of the theatrical release. Director Ephron's commentary is careful and on the sparse side. —MM
Movie: 🎞🎞½ **DVD:** 🎞🎞🎞
Paramount Home Video (Cat #33695, UPC #097363369547). Widescreen anamorphic. Dolby Digital 5.1 Surround Stereo; Dolby Surround Stereo. $29.99. Keepcase. *LANG:* English; French. *SUB:* English. *FEATURES:* 16 chapter links ▪ Trailer ▪ Cast and crew interviews ▪ Commentary: Nora Ephron.
2000 (R) 105m/C John Travolta, Lisa Kudrow, Tim Roth, Ed O'Neill, Michael Rapaport, Darryl (Chill) Mitchell, Bill Pullman, Richard Schiff, Michael Moore, Michael Weston, Sam McMurray; *D:* Nora Ephron; *W:* Adam Resnick; *C:* John Lindley; *M:* George Fenton.

Lucky Texan
Please see review for *Winds of the Wasteland / The Lucky Texan.*
Movie: 🎞½
1934 61m/B John Wayne, George "Gabby" Hayes, Yakima Canutt; *D:* Robert North Bradbury; *W:* Robert North Bradbury; *C:* Archie Stout.

Lust for Frankenstein
Franco regular Lina Romay stars as Moira Frankenstein, daughter of Dr. Frankenstein. She has visions of her dead father (who looks like he should be in a grunge band), and he urges her to play his heavy metal records. After listening, she leaves her apartment and goes to a villa where she finds her father's last creation, a creature called Goddess (Bauer), who's a lot like the "Bride of Frankenstein" except that she's naked and needs fresh blood to survive. This is quite convenient, as Goddess murders anyone to whom Moira is sexually attracted. Most of the movie was shot on film, but at times, it changes to video. Here, Franco adds weird photographic effects, which make it resemble an '80s music video. The DVD contains two versions of the film, the American cut and the European version, which runs eight minutes longer. Those eight minutes mainly consist of sex scenes, which push the boundaries of what most would consider soft-core. The image is clear and the colors are good, but there is a fine sheen of grain visible throughout the feature. During the shot-on-video scenes, the grain is a bit diminished, and the colors improve somewhat. Mono audio offers dialogue that is audible for the most part. However, some of the sound effects and music are

a bit distorted. Also, there is a hiss on the track. —ML

Movie: 🐾🐾 **DVD:** 🐾🐾
El Independent Cinema (Cat #5236). Widescreen (1.5:1) letterboxed. Dolby Digital Mono. $19.95. LANG: English. FEATURES: Behind-the-scenes featurette • Interview with Michelle Bauer • Trailers.
1988 82m/C Lina Romay, Michelle (McClellan) Bauer; **D:** Jess (Jesus) Franco.

Lust in the Dust

When part of a treasure map is found on the derriere of Rosie Velez (Divine), the hunt is on for the other half. The comedy western travels to the sleepy village of Chile Verde and the ridiculous turns comically corrupt. Divine and co-star Kazan swap dirty double-entendres while Tab Hunter and Henry Silva hunt for the gold. The transfer is sharp and clear. Colors just burst, from blue skies to white rolling clouds to the ultra-crimson main title credits. Blacks are solid, but contrast is sometimes too high, losing details in the shadows. Film grain pops up, mainly during night scenes. Fleshtones are a little sun-baked (expected) but natural, the source elements look pristine (the only inconsistencies appear in few mismatched stock shots), and, while edge enhancement is evident, no digital or compression artifacts mar the image. Sound is less impressive. The two-channel Dolby Digital mono audio suffers from low dynamic range and overmodulation. —MM/EP

Movie: 🐾🐾½ **DVD:** 🐾🐾🐾
Anchor Bay (Cat #DV11316, UPC #013131 13169). Widescreen (2.35:1) anamorphic. Dolby Digital Mono. $24.99. Keepcase. LANG: English. FEATURES: Trailer • "Making of" featurette • Talent files.
1985 (R) 85m/C Tab Hunter, Divine, Lainie Kazan, Geoffrey Lewis, Henry Silva, Cesar Romero, Lainie Gallego, Courtney Gains, Woody Strode, Pedro Gonzalez-Gonzalez; **D:** Paul Bartel; **W:** Philip John Taylor; **C:** Paul Lohmann; **M:** Peter Matz.

Ma Vie en Rose

Talk about gender identification issues! Berliner's debut portrays seven-year-old misfit Ludovic (DuFresne) who is convinced that he's really a girl and likes to dress in girl's clothes and to play with dolls. His close-knit family tries to believe that it's a childhood eccentricity that Ludovic will grow out of. But when the child decides he's going to marry Jerome (Riviere), the boy next door, and stages a mock wedding ceremony, things get a bit dicey. Jerome's father is the straitlaced Albert (Hanssens) who happens to be Ludovic's dad's (Ecoffey) boss, and he's not nearly so understanding. Neither are the other neighbors in the conservative Parisian suburb. DuFresne is excellent in the lead. DVD handles the candy-bright color scheme very well, particularly in the fantasy sequences. Overall, the film is as sharp as a comparable Hollywood comedy/drama. —MM **AKA:** My Life in Pink.

Movie: 🐾🐾🐾 **DVD:** 🐾🐾½
Columbia Tristar Home Video (Cat #03951, UPC #043396039513). Widescreen (1.85:1) letterboxed. Dolby Digital Surround Stereo. $24.95. Keepcase. LANG: French. SUB: English; French; Spanish. FEATURES: 28 chapter links • Production notes.
1997 (R) 90m/C BE FR GB Georges DuFresne, Jean-Philippe Ecoffey, Michele Laroque, Daniel Hanssens, Julien Riviere, Helene Vincent, Laurence Bibot, Jean-Francois Galotte, Caroline Baehr, Marie Bunuel; **D:** Alain Berliner; **W:** Alain Berliner, Chris Vander Stappen; **C:** Yves Cape; **M:** Dominique Dalcan. AWARDS: Golden Globes '98: Foreign Film; NOM: British Acad. '97: Foreign Film.

Maborosi

Yumiko (Esumi) has a contented life in Osaka with her husband Ikuo (Asano) and their newborn son. Yet, inexplicably, her husband commits suicide one night. Later, a neighbor helps her with an arranged marriage to prosperous widower Tamio (Naitoh) who lives in a remote fishing village, but Ikuo's death still haunts her. Director Kore-eda Hirokazu is more a painter than a strong narrative storyteller. He lingers on still scenes of exquisite composition—two small figures on a shadowed bridge, rain on a car window, the sound of the wipers, faint light on a flight of stairs, a procession of figures across a field. The image is heavily shadowed and dark compared to Hollywood features. The harsh lighting sometimes distorts shapes instead of revealing them, but those are not flaws. The clear white subtitles are presented within the image, not in the narrow lower letterbox. —MM **AKA:** Mirage; Maboroshi no Hikari.

Movie: 🐾🐾🐾½ **DVD:** 🐾🐾🐾
New Yorker Video (Cat #66500, UPC #717 119065043). Widescreen letterboxed. $29.95. Keepcase. LANG: Japanese. SUB: English. FEATURES: Trailers • 11 chapter links • Kore-eda Hirokazu profile, filmography, and comments (text).
1995 110m/C JP Makiko Esumi, Takashi Naito, Tadanobu Asano, Gohki Kashiyama; **D:** Hirokazu Kore-eda; **W:** Yoshihisa Ogita; **C:** Masao Nakabori; **M:** Chen Ming-Chang.

Macabre

This little-known Italian horror is a genuine sleeper for fans. Lamberto Bava, son of Mario Bava, makes an impressive debut with a relatively controlled story and some inventively gruesome shocks. It begins with Jane (Stegers) leaving her young children alone when she goes off for some afternoon delight with her lover. A double catastrophe follows and things get much worse later. The rough image is all anyone could reasonably expect of a mid-budget import more than 20 years old. Signs of wear are negligible. This one has been well preserved and restored. —MM **AKA:** Frozen Terror.

Movie: 🐾🐾🐾 **DVD:** 🐾🐾½
Anchor Bay (Cat #DV11528, UPC #013131 152890). Widescreen (1.85:1) anamorphic. Dolby Digital Mono. $24.99. Keepcase. LANG: English. FEATURES: 28 chapter links • Trailer • Lamberto Bava thumbnail bio • "A Head for Horror" short film.
1980 90m/C Bernice Stegers, Stanko Molnar, Veronica Zinny, Roberto Posse; **D:** Lamberto Bava; **W:** Lamberto Bava, Antonio Avati; **C:** Franco Delli Colli.

Mach 2

Standard-issue video premiere thriller casts ex–football player Bosworth as Air Force Captain Jack Tyree who is the only one who can save a hijacked Concorde airliner. The film would hardly rate a recommendation if it weren't for one inspired extra—the commentary track by director Raymond and co-star Shannon Whirry. They have a wonderful, irreverent time with the material, and provide some genuine insights into the nuts and bolts of low-budget action filmmaking. Image and sound are a definite cut above VHS. —MM

Movie: 🐾🐾½ **DVD:** 🐾🐾🐾
Paramount Home Video (Cat #86030, UPC #097368603042). Widescreen anamorphic. Dolby Digital 5.1 Surround Stereo; Dolby Digital Surround. $29.99. Keepcase. LANG: English. SUB: Spanish; English. FEATURES: 20 chapter links • Commentary: Edward Raymond, Shannon Whirry.
2000 (R) 94m/C Brian Bosworth, Michael Dorn, Shannon Whirry, Cliff Robertson, Lance Guest, Bruce Weitz; **D:** Ed Raymond; **W:** Steve Latshaw; **C:** Thomas Callaway; **M:** Eric Wurst, David Wurst.

The Mad Butcher

Viennese butcher Otto Lehman (Buono) is placed in an asylum for three years after bludgeoning a customer unconscious with two pounds of meat. Released into the care of his perpetually nagging wife, he returns to his shop and moves into the small room above it. When his wife threatens to send him back to the asylum, Lehman strangles her in a frenzy and grinds her up into sausages. As circumstances (and the popularity of the sausages) place more victims in the butcher's path, a nosy American reporter and a bored police chief try to uncover Lehman's secret. Amusing, though limp and cheap black comedy serves up liberal amounts of nudity and very little gore. The gruesome scenario is successfully communicated entirely by suggestion and implication and Buono enjoyably plays Lehman with the same heavy-lidded, hoity, expansive charm he perfected as "King Tut" in the '60s *Batman* TV show. Though Buono provides his own voice, this European co-production is sprinkled with some very awkward post-synched dialogue and except for a few hastily grabbed exteriors, is mostly restricted to a few small sets. The film has probably never looked better than it does on this razor sharp, extremely colorful transfer. Despite a few brief moments of color instability (due to aging in the original source material) this is a highly satisfying transfer, adding much more visual polish to this micro-budgeted quickie. Rounding off the disc is a satisfying smorgasbord of extras and rare cannibalism-themed shorts. The actual on-screen title is *Meat Is Meat*, an alternate title. —*DG* **AKA:** The Mad Butcher of Vienna; The Strangler of Vienna; The Vienna Strangler; Der Wurger kommt auf leisen Socken; Lo Strangolatore di Vienna; Meat Is Meat.

Movie: ♫♫ **DVD:** ♫♫♫
Image Entertainment (Cat #ID97425SW DVD, UPC #01438197422). Widescreen (1.85:1). Dolby Digital Mono. $24.99. Snapper. *LANG:* English. *FEATURES:* Theatrical trailer ▪ Additional trailers ▪ "Cannibal Island" short subject ▪ "Cannibal Massage" short subject ▪ Gallery of promotional art ▪ Radio spots ▪ 12 chapter links.
1972 (R) 82m/C *IT* Victor Buono, Karin (Karen) Field, Brad Harris; ***D:*** Guido Zurli.

Madadayo

Kurosawa's last film spans several years and tells the warm relationship between a well-loved professor and the group of students that have become his friends. A nice companion piece to *Ikiru*, this episodic Japanese film is funny, heartbreaking, and touching. A sequence featuring a lost cat is simply devastating. A perfect choice for Kurosawa's final work, this film at times seems as a near biographical summation of the man. One must applaud any artistic work that conveys such a feeling of warmth and hope for humanity. The charming and beautiful movie, unreleased in the U.S. for almost ten years, features a recognizable cast of recent Kurosawa regulars. The disc is colorful and sharp, though some scenes are a tad soft and display digital grain. The lack of 16x9 enhancement on such a colorful film is a disappointment. The sound is extremely well recorded and involving, though a couple of loud passages of dialogue tended to distort. There are only a few storyboard illustrations but they are beautiful. —*DG*
Movie: ♫♫♫ **DVD:** ♫♫♫
Fox/Lorber Home Video (Cat #FLV5265, UPC #72091752652). Widescreen (1.85:1) letterboxed. Dolby Surround. $24.98. Keepcase. *LANG:* Japanese. *SUB:* English. *FEATURES:* Filmographies ▪ Trailer ▪ Storyboards ▪ 16 chapter links.
1992 134m/C *JP* Tatsuya Matsumura; ***D:*** Akira Kurosawa; ***W:*** Akira Kurosawa; ***C:*** Takao Saito, Masaharu Ueda; ***M:*** Shinichiro Ikebe.

Madeline

Adaptation of Ludwig Bemelmans's 1939 children's book opens with the animation of the familiar illustrations. Madeline (Jones) and her 11 classmates are under the care of Miss Clavel (McDormand) in a delightfully stylized Paris. Some fans of the book have criticized the film for not living up to expectations. Those who approach the film without preconceptions will be entertained. At least I was, though, admittedly the presence of Frances McDormand (who can do no wrong) is a major plus. DVD image is as neat and nicely scrubbed as you'd expect for a studio-produced children's story. —*MM*
Movie: ♫♫♫ **DVD:** ♫♫♫
Columbia Tristar Home Video (Cat #02718, UPC #043396027183). Widescreen (1.85:1) anamorphic; full frame. Dolby Digital 5.1 Surround; Dolby Digital Surround. $24.98. Keepcase. *LANG:* English. *SUB:* English. *FEATURES:* 28 chapter links ▪ Photo gallery ▪ Trailer ▪ 1952 "Madeline" cartoon.
1998 (PG) 90m/C Hatty Jones, Frances McDormand, Nigel Hawthorne, Ben Daniels, Arturo Venegas, Stephane Audran, Katia Caballero; ***D:*** Daisy von Scherler Mayer; ***W:*** Marc Levin, Jennifer Flacket, Chris Weitz, Paul Weitz; ***C:*** Pierre Aim; ***M:*** Michel Legrand.

Madman

Camp leader (Fredericks) prompts terror when he revives the legend of axe murderer Madman Marz, who will reappear if anyone calls his name. You can take it from there. The only real surprise is a four-minute hot-tub scene in which the young lovers go round and round as if trapped in a whirlpool! Bizarre! The DVD image is clear and sharp, showing only a subtle amount of grain at times. Unfortunately, the digital clarity of this transfer does uncover some flaws in the source print. Several shots have vertical scratches running through them. It gives the viewer the feeling of being in a movie theatre where someone has cut the screen open. There are also some noticeable white spots and scratches. Still, these are minor complaints, given the age and relative obscurity of the film. Mono sound lacks the ambient quality of a Surround sound mix. However, this may be a good thing, considering how annoying the "electronic score" is. —*MM/ML*
Movie: ♫ **DVD:** ♫
Anchor Bay (Cat #DV11613, UPC #013131 161397). Widescreen (1.77:1) anamorphic. Dolby Digital Mono. $24.98. Keepcase. *LANG:* English. *FEATURES:* Commentary: Giannone, Sales, Fish, Ehlers ▪ Trailers ▪ TV spots.
1982 (R) 89m/C Carl Fredericks, Alexis Dubin, Tony Fish, Paul Ehlers; ***D:*** Joe Giannone; ***W:*** Joe Giannone, Gary Sales; ***C:*** James (Momel) Lemmo; ***M:*** Gary Sales, Stephen Horelick.

The Madness of King George

The Madness of King George ponders the question: what happens to the body politic when it gets sick? King George III may still rule England in 1788, but with the loss of the American colonies, Parliament slowly draining away his royal governing powers, and court intrigue everywhere...well, at least he's still got his health, right? Actually he may be losing his mind, spouting obscenities and running down the palace halls half naked. The royal physicians are stumped and the conniving Prince of Wales (Everett) wants dad declared incompetent so he can rule. An outside chance by Dr. Willis (Holm) offers hope for a cure, employing very radical (i.e. sadistic) treatments. Adapting the 1991 stage play *The Madness of George III*, playwright/screenwriter Alan Bennett and stage-turned-screen director Nicholas Hytner never let the action stray too far from Hawthorne's luminous performance as the increasingly mad monarch. Hawthorne reprises the role he originated on stage, shape-shifting from devoted husband to babbling paranoiac to frightened child, sometimes within the same scene. The anamorphic transfer far exceeds the widescreen laserdisc release in image depth and clarity. Scenes shot with smoke diffusion or low lighting read much clearer on the DVD. Colors are stable and accurate. The bright reds on the royals' and military costumes remain rock solid on the DVD, where there is occasional chroma noise on the laserdisc. The laserdisc does contain a discrete Dolby Digital track whereas the DVD sports a Dolby Surround matrix soundtrack. Aurally, there is little difference between the two formats since the sound mix does not showcase discrete sound effect pans or low-frequency enhancement. Both offer ample audio levels and clear, intelligible dialogue (necessary for a stage-driven screenplay). The DVD ups the ante by including the theatrical trailer. —*EP*
Movie: ♫♫♫½ **DVD:** ♫♫½
MGM Home Entertainment (Cat #10020 43, UPC #0-27616-86280-8). Widescreen (1.85:1) anamorphic. Dolby Digital Surround Stereo. $14.95. Keepcase. *LANG:* English. *SUB:* French; Spanish. *FEATURES:* 16 chapter links ▪ Theatrical trailer.
1994 (R) 110m/C *GB* Nigel Hawthorne, Helen Mirren, Ian Holm, Rupert Everett, Amanda Donohoe, Rupert Graves, Julian Wadham, John Wood, Julian Rhind-Tutt, Jim Carter; ***D:*** Nicholas Hytner; ***W:*** Alan Bennett; ***C:*** Andrew Dunn; ***M:*** George Fenton. *AWARDS:* Oscars '94: Art Dir./Set Dec.; British Acad. '95: Actor (Hawthorne); Cannes '95: Actress (Mirren); *NOM:* Oscars '94: Actor (Hawthorne), Adapt. Screenplay, Support. Actress (Mirren); British Acad. '95: Actress (Mirren), Adapt. Screenplay, Cinematog., Director (Hytner), Film, Support. Actor (Holm), Score; Writers Guild '94: Adapt. Screenplay.

Madron

If you make a spaghetti western in Israel, is it a matzo western? If so, that's what this one is. The generic plot involves Sister Mary (Caron), a nun who's stranded in the desert after her minimalist three-wagon train is attacked by Apaches wearing some of the worst wigs you've ever seen. Madron (Boone) is the gunslinger who helps her. There are lots of artifacts in the bright exteriors. Voices often sound muffled. Overall, disc is equal to tape. —*MM*
Movie: ♫♫ **DVD:** ♫♫

VCI Home Video (Cat #8206, UPC #08985 9820625). Full frame. Dolby Digital Mono. $19.99. Snapper. *LANG:* English. *FEATURES:* 12 chapter links • Talent files.
1970 (PG) 93m/C Richard Boone, Leslie Caron, Paul Smith; *D:* Jerry Hopper; *W:* Edward Chappell, Lee McMahon; *C:* Marcel Grignon, Adam Greenberg; *M:* Riz Ortolani. *AWARDS: NOM:* Oscars '70: Song ("Till Love Touches Your Life").

Mafia!

Director Abrahams returns to the *Airplane* well once again as he takes aim at the crime movies of Coppola and Scorsese. As usual, the results are hit and miss, with the joke machine gun set on full auto. Plot follows the *Godfather* trilogy most closely with Bridges (in his last film) as klutzy and flatulent patriarch Vincenzo Cortino. His sons, sensitive war hero Anthony (Mohr) and hot-tempered Joey (Burke) wrestle for control of the keystone kriminal empire after pop checks out. Basically, the actors' jobs are to remain deadpan in the midst of shenanigans and far too many fart jokes. The disc is not a significant improvement over tape, but it is actually a little funnier to watch with the English captions explaining the jokes. By the way, the on-screen title retains the original *Jane Austen's Mafia!* —MM **AKA:** Jane Austen's Mafia!.
Movie: 🎜🎜 *DVD:* 🎜🎜
Buena Vista Home Entertainment (Cat #16320). Widescreen. Dolby Digital Surround Stereo. $29.99. Keepcase. *LANG:* English. *CAP:* English. *FEATURES:* 14 chapter links • "Making of" featurette.
1998 (PG-13) 87m/C Lloyd Bridges, Jay Mohr, Billy Burke, Olympia Dukakis, Christina Applegate, Pamela Gidley, Tony LoBianco, Joe Viterelli, Vincent Pastore, Jason Fuchs; *D:* Jim Abrahams; *W:* Jim Abrahams, Michael McManus, Greg Norberg; *C:* Pierre Letarte; *M:* John (Gianni) Frizzell.

The Magical Legend of the Leprechauns

Good fantasy finds American business-man Jack Woods (Quaid) sent to a remote part of Ireland where he happens to save the life of leprechaun, Seamus Muldoon (Meaney), which puts the "little person" in his debt. While Jack tries to romance neighbor Kathleen (Brady), the leprechauns are getting into a fracas with their enemies, the Trooping Fairies, leading to a battle and Jack's involvement. Unlike some of the recent fantasy films made for TV that feature excessive CGI effects, *Leprechauns*'s image is pretty sharp and stays that way even during those effects sequences. The colors are at times near-spectacular and almost always vibrant with no noticeable bleed. The Dolby Surround is also much better than some of the other TV films in this genre—good separation and imaging up front and substantial use of the rear Surround track. For extras, there are some filmed interviews with the cast and a very

short "making of" featurette that doesn't delve enough into the special effects as most would like. —JO
Movie: 🎜🎜½ *DVD:* 🎜🎜
Artisan Entertainment (Cat #10129, UPC #707729101291). Full frame. Dolby Surround. $19.98. Keepcase. *LANG:* English. *CAP:* English. *FEATURES:* 42 chapter links • Trailer • Talent files • Production notes • "Making of" featurette • Actors interviews.
1999 139m/C Randy Quaid, Colm Meaney, Orla Brady, Whoopi Goldberg, Roger Daltrey, Daniel Betts, Zoe Wanamaker, Caroline Carver, Kieran Culkin, Frank Finlay, Phyllida Law; *D:* John Henderson; *W:* Peter Barnes; *C:* Clive Tickner; *M:* Richard Harvey.

The Magnificent Seven

A peasant village in Northern Mexico decides to hire Americans to ward off the depredations of bandit chieftain Calvera (Wallach). Unemployed Gunslinger Chris (Brynner), just in from Dodge City, recruits six more out-of work gun hands. For $20 and room and board, they mosey on South of the Rio Grande, just seven to defend against Calvera's 40 thieves. Everyone compares this film with its model, *Seven Samurai*, when there isn't really any comparison between the two. The Kurosawa fantasy was considered too American, with its anachronistic "dialogue" between the farmer and samurai classes. The John Sturges remake is the perfect John Kennedy fantasy: a world where American know-how and firepower reaches out to other nations with a good example and lots of guns, rids them of their oppressors, and earns their eternal respect. MGM's DVD is a good show. The image is a huge improvement over the 1993 laserdisc in clarity and color, though grain is visible in some shots. The commentary track is by producer Walter Mirisch (who is proud as pumpkins over this goldmine of a movie), a jovial James Coburn, the youthful-sounding Eli Wallach, and assistant director (and later Steve McQueen producing partner) Robert Relyea. The track is an easy listen, doesn't bog down in details, yet offers a constantly changing set of viewpoints and anecdotes on the making of the film. Also, after watching the "Guns for Hire" documentary, in which Horst Bucholz admits to shooting himself in the leg with a blank, take a close look at the lightning-fast draw that Steve McQueen performs in the first faceoff with Calvera. Steve's first shot clearly goes off a split-frame after clearing the holster—straight into the ground! —GE
Movie: 🎜🎜🎜🎜 *DVD:* 🎜🎜🎜
MGM Home Entertainment (Cat #10018 37). Widescreen (2.35:1) anamorphic. $24.98. Snapper. *LANG:* English. *FEATURES:* 16 chapter links • Documentary, "Guns for Hire" • 2 trailers • Commentary: producer Walter Mirisch.
1960 126m/C Yul Brynner, Steve McQueen, Robert Vaughn, James Coburn,

Charles Bronson, Horst Buchholz, Eli Wallach, Brad Dexter; *D:* John Sturges; *W:* William Roberts; *C:* Charles B(ryant) Lang Jr.; *M:* Elmer Bernstein. *AWARDS: NOM:* Oscars '60: Orig. Dramatic Score.

Magnolia

Bad dads are the subject of this long, surreal, frantic, indulgent look into a 24-hour series of interlocking stories with an excellent ensemble cast. "These strange things happen all the time" our narrator explains and writer/director Anderson spends the next three hours trying to prove it. Jimmy Gator (Hall) and Earl Partridge (Robards) are both dying and estranged from their children—Jimmy's coke-addicted daughter (Walters) and Earl's flashy motivational speaker son Frank (Cruise, who is frighteningly good). Earl's trophy wife Linda (Moore) is having a slow-motion breakdown but he's being cared for by kind-hearted nurse Phil (Hoffman). And then there's a long-running game show and its past and present whiz kids (including Macy), and a cop (Reilly) who falls for Jimmy's daughter, and a rain of frogs, and everybody bursting into song. The film's main and near-constant flaw is the repetitious use of profanity. It becomes understandable when you watch the "making of" documentary and learn that Anderson is thoughtlessly, casually foul-mouthed. The clarity of DVD sound heightens the film's other flaw. Anderson often steps on action and characters with intrusive music. The image on the dual-layered disc is flawless. With some judicious trimming, this one could have been a masterpiece. (The film is on one disc; all the extras are on a second.) —MM
Movie: 🎜🎜🎜 *DVD:* 🎜🎜🎜
New Line Home Video (Cat #N5029, UPC #794043502927). Widescreen (2.4:1) letterboxed. Dolby Digital 5.1 Surround Stereo; Dolby Digital Surround Stereo. $30.98. Boxed slipcase. *LANG:* English. *SUB:* English. *FEATURES:* 12 chapter links • Frank Mackey seminar and infomercial • Trailer, TV spots, and teaser • "Save Me" music video • "Making of" documentary.
1999 (R) 188m/C Jason Robards Jr., Julianne Moore, Tom Cruise, Philip Seymour Hoffman, Philip Baker Hall, Melora Walters, John C. Reilly, Melinda Dillon, William H. Macy, Michael Bowen, Jeremy Blackman, Emmanuel Johnson; *D:* Paul Thomas Anderson; *W:* Paul Thomas Anderson; *C:* Robert Elswit; *M:* Jon Brion, Aimee Mann. *AWARDS:* Golden Globes '00: Support. Actor (Cruise); Natl. Bd. of Review '99: Support. Actor (Hoffman), Support. Actress (Moore); *NOM:* Oscars '99: Orig. Screenplay, Song ("Save Me"), Support. Actor (Cruise); Golden Globes '00: Song ("Save Me"); Screen Actors Guild '99: Support. Actor (Cruise), Support. Actress (Moore), Cast; Writers Guild '99: Orig. Screenplay.

Mailer on Mailer

Intelligent, well-made PBS documentary affords Mailer the opportunity to spew his opinion on the past 60 years of politics, race, and popular culture. Compiled from over 20 hours of interviews with Mailer, the film also includes rare archival footage as well as never-before-seen photographs and original manuscripts from the author's archives. The video transfer is decent and features both solid colors and well-defined blacks. Some archival footage, however, shows signs of age (but that goes with the territory). The soundtrack is clear and easy to understand but is nothing spectacular. —*MJT*

Movie: 🎵🎵½ **DVD:** 🎵🎵
Winstar Home Entertainment (Cat #WHE73 115, UPC #720917311524). Widescreen (1.78:1) letterboxed. Dolby Digital Stereo. $24.98. Keepcase. *LANG:* English. *FEATURES:* 10 chapter links • Bibliography • Filmography • Weblinks.
2000 90m/C Norman Mailer; **D:** Richard Copans, Stan Neumann; **C:** Richard Copans, Stan Neumann.

Make Mine Music

Originally released in 1946 as a feature-length follow-up to the pre-war and more elaborate *Fantasia,* this animated film from Walt Disney features the collaborative work of five directors (including Hamilton Luske, who worked on *Fantasia*) operating under the production supervision of Joe Grant (also a writer on *Fantasia*). What survives for this DVD presentation are nine of the ten animated shorts which comprised the original feature (the opening seven-minute sequence titled "The Martins and the Coys" has been excised for some odd reason). As a bonus, three classic Disney cartoons, "The Band Concert" (1935), "Music Land" (1935), and "Farmyard Symphony" (1938) have been added to this DVD release. Despite the missing sequence, the nine remaining samples of Disney animation are to be treasured. Their collective style, timing, satirical jabs, and music are every bit the equal to the best work produced by the studio today. Included are: "Blue Bayou," "All the Cats Join In," "Without You," "Casey at the Bat," "Two Silhouettes," "Peter and the Wolf," "After You've Gone," "Johnny Fedora and Alice Bluebonnet," and "The Whale Who Wanted to Sing at the Met." An otherwise magnificent DVD production is marred by an infuriating menu interface, which includes commercials for other Disney product (hint: just keep hitting the "skip" button to get to the main program menu). —*RJT*

Movie: 🎵🎵🎵 **DVD:** 🎵🎵🎵
Buena Vista Home Entertainment (Cat #19604, UPC #717951008558). Full frame. Dolby Digital Stereo. $29.99. Keepcase. *LANG:* English; Spanish. *SUB:* English. *CAP:* English. *FEATURES:* 10 chapter links.
1946 67m/C D: Clyde Geronimi, Jack Kinney, Hamilton Luske, Joshua Meador, Robert Cormack.

Malice [MGM]

If it weren't bad enough that a series of murders has occurred on the campus of his little college, Dean Safian (Pullman) also has to put up with problems restoring his Victorian house, an ailing wife (Kidman), and an overbearing surgeon (Baldwin). Actually, these are the prime elements in an inventive little thriller that stretches credulity but is still entertaining. (Look for a young Gwyneth Paltrow in a small role.) Much of the action takes place in dark interiors that lack detail, but the image has always looked that way. Sound is acceptable. —*MM*

Movie: 🎵🎵🎵 **DVD:** 🎵🎵🎵
MGM Home Entertainment (Cat #10011 87, UPC #027616854780). Widescreen anamorphic; full frame. Dolby Digital Surround Stereo. $19.98. Keepcase. *LANG:* English; French; Spanish. *CAP:* English. *FEATURES:* 28 chapter links • Trailer.
1993 (R) 107m/C Alec Baldwin, Nicole Kidman, Bill Pullman, Bebe Neuwirth, Anne Bancroft, George C. Scott, Peter Gallagher, Josef Sommer, Gwyneth Paltrow; **D:** Harold Becker; **W:** Aaron Sorkin, Scott Frank; **C:** Gordon Willis; **M:** Jerry Goldsmith.

The Maltese Falcon

After his partner is murdered, San Francisco detective Sam Spade (Bogart, in a career-defining role) sets out to find the killer and the famous "dingus," a fabulous jewel-encrusted statue. Also in the hunt are Gutman (Greenstreet), his gunsel (Cook Jr.), Joel Cairo (Lorre), and Brigid O'Shaunessey (Astor)—perhaps the greatest rogues' gallery in all of crime film or fiction. Despite some light signs of wear, DVD is a superb presentation. The many shades of black are as nicely detailed as I've ever seen them and I've watched this film on just about every medium, from late-show broadcasts to film festival screenings. The "casebook" extra is a look at Bogart's career through trailers. Mono sound is fine. —*MM*

Movie: 🎵🎵🎵🎵 **DVD:** 🎵🎵🎵
Warner Home Video, Inc. (Cat #65012, UPC #012569501225). Full frame. Dolby Digital Mono. $19.98. Snapper. *LANG:* English. *SUB:* English; French. *FEATURES:* 28 chapter links • A history of mystery (text) • Casebook.
1941 101m/B Humphrey Bogart, Mary Astor, Peter Lorre, Sydney Greenstreet, Ward Bond, Barton MacLane, Gladys George, Lee Patrick, Elisha Cook Jr., Jerome Cowan, Walter Huston; **D:** John Huston; **W:** John Huston; **C:** Arthur Edeson; **M:** Adolph Deutsch. *AWARDS:* AFI '98: Top 100, Natl. Film Reg. '89; *NOM:* Oscars '41: Picture, Screenplay, Support. Actor (Greenstreet).

Man Called Hero

After the success of *The Storm Riders,* fans of Hong Kong cinema had been eagerly awaiting movies that would be somewhat in the same vein, and the answer came in the form of *A Man Called Hero.* This slowly paced action film based on a long running comic boasts a great cast, fine martial arts, and stunning visu-als. However, without proper knowledge of the comic, the story is disjointed. The computer-generated effects are of varying quality, some spectacular, most not. The climactic fight on top of the Statue of Liberty appears more like a scene from a computer game than an actual movie sequence. The print is clean and without blemishes or speckles and has a good level of detail. Colors are very naturally reproduced, capturing the beautiful photography of America's '30s. Compression left some noticeable artifacts that are most evident in banding effects. Surround effects are used aggressively and the entire track has a natural-sounding quality with good bass extension. —*GH/MM*

Movie: 🎵🎵½ **DVD:** 🎵🎵½
Tai Seng Video Marketing (Cat #75984). Widescreen (2.35:1) letterboxed. Dolby Digital 5.1 Surround Stereo. $54.95. Keepcase. *LANG:* Cantonese; Mandarin. *SUB:* English; Chinese. *FEATURES:* "Making of" featurette • Trailers • Talent files.
1999 108m/C *HK* Ekin Cheng, Qi Shu, Nicholas Tse, Kristy Yang; **D:** Andrew Lau; **W:** Manfred Wong; **C:** Andrew Lau.

A Man for All Seasons

Sterling, heavily Oscar-honored biographical drama concerns the life and martyrdom of 16th-century Chancellor of England, Sir Thomas More (Scofield). The story revolves around his personal conflict when King Henry VIII (Shaw) seeks a divorce so he can wed his mistress—events that ultimately lead the monarch to bolt from the Pope and declare himself head of the Church of England. Few-frills disc presents an image that is very good for a film of this age. —*MM*

Movie: 🎵🎵🎵½ **DVD:** 🎵🎵½
Columbia Tristar Home Video (Cat #03256, UPC #043396032569). Widescreen (1.85:1) letterboxed; full frame. $24.98. Keepcase. *LANG:* English. *FEATURES:* 28 chapter links • Trailer.
1966 (G) 120m/C *GB* Paul Scofield, Robert Shaw, Orson Welles, Wendy Hiller, Susannah York, John Hurt, Nigel Davenport, Vanessa Redgrave; **D:** Fred Zinnemann; **W:** Constance Willis, Robert Bolt; **C:** Ted Moore; **M:** Georges Delerue. *AWARDS:* Oscars '66: Actor (Scofield), Adapt. Screenplay, Color Cinematog., Costume Des. (C), Director (Zinnemann), Picture; British Acad. '67: Actor (Scofield), Film, Screenplay; Directors Guild '66: Director (Zinnemann); Golden Globes '67: Actor—Drama (Scofield), Director (Zinnemann), Film—Drama, Screenplay; Natl. Bd. of Review '66: Actor (Scofield), Director (Zinnemann), Support. Actor (Shaw); N.Y. Film Critics '66: Actor (Scofield), Director (Zinnemann), Film, Screenplay; *NOM:* Oscars '66: Support. Actor (Shaw), Support. Actress (Hiller).

The Man from Laramie

Aging cattle baron Alec Waggoman (Crisp) who is going blind, worries about which of

his two sons should inherit his giant ranch. Into this tension-filled familial atmosphere rides Lockhart (Stewart), a cow-herder obsessed with hunting down the men who sold guns to the Indians who killed his brother. Tough, brutal western is the best of the Stewart-Mann collaborations. Few video transfers vintage 1955 look this good, given the fading of filmstocks that usually takes place. Only an occasional scratch and a reddish cast to a few scenes show any sign of aging. The prime visual joy of '50s westerns were their broad panoramic vistas, so beautifully filmed at dawn and dusk, a pleasure that can't be understood watching these films in crummy 16mm on flat TV screens. The DVD is 16:9 enhanced, lending enhanced clarity to both azure skies and Stewart's giant, nervous blue eyes. With its simple but rich stereophonic track, this disc turns a widescreen video monitor into an old-fashioned Technicolor Saturday matinee. —*MM/GE*
Movie: ♪♪♪½ **DVD:** ♪♪♪½
Columbia Tristar Home Video (Cat #4170). Widescreen (2.35:1) anamorphic; full frame. Dolby Digital Surround Stereo. $24.95. Keepcase. *LANG:* English; Spanish. *SUB:* French; Portuguese; Spanish; Chinese; Korean; Thai. *FEATURES:* Poster graphic ▪ Trailer.
1955 104m/B James Stewart, Arthur Kennedy, Donald Crisp, Alex Nicol, Cathy O'Donnell, Aline MacMahon, Wallace Ford, Jack Elam; *D:* Anthony Mann; *W:* Philip Yordan; *C:* Charles B(ryant) Lang Jr.; *M:* George Duning.

The Man from Planet X

Making a belated arrival on home video is this prototypical low-budget first-contact tale. All the elements are there—reporter, aging scientist, his nubile daughter, crafty associate—but the setting is Scotland. Not that it matters, because virtually all of the action takes place on sets. (The box copy says that they were left over from the Ingrid Bergman *Joan of Arc*.) Models are used for establishing landscape shots. The black-and-white image is dark throughout with considerable grain that probably comes from the original. —*MM*
Movie: ♪♪ **DVD:** ♪♪
MGM Home Entertainment (Cat #10015 46, UPC #027616858566). Full frame. Dolby Digital Mono. $19.98. Keepcase. *LANG:* English. *SUB:* French; Spanish. *FEATURES:* 16 chapter links ▪ Trailer.
1951 71m/B Robert Clarke, Margaret Field, William Schallert; *D:* Edgar G. Ulmer; *W:* Aubrey Wisberg, Jack Pollexfen; *C:* John L. "Jack" Russell; *M:* Charles Koff.

Man from Utah / Sagebrush Trail

In the first film on this double-bill, the Duke makes an entrance as a singing cowboy (with an atrociously dubbed voice by someone else) and then tangles with the crooked sponsor of some rodeo

events. On the second feature—his second western—he's wrongly accused of killing a man and has to bust out of the hoosegow to clear his name. Stuntwork by the great Yakima Canutt. Image quality on the first film is rough, but acceptable for a low-budget B-movie. The second feature looks like it was dubbed from a third-generation VHS tape at slow speed and is completely unwatchable. —*MM*
Movie: ♪♪ **DVD:** ♪
Madacy Entertainment (Cat #990031, UPC #056775002091). Full frame. Dolby Digital Mono. $9.99. Keepcase. *LANG:* English. *FEATURES:* 8 chapter links ▪ Thumbnail bios of John Wayne, Gabby Hayes, John Ford ▪ John Wayne filmography 1926–35.
1934 55m/B John Wayne, George "Gabby" Hayes, Polly Ann Young, Yakima Canutt, Lafe (Lafayette) McKee; *D:* Robert North Bradbury; *W:* Lindsley Parsons; *C:* Archie Stout.

The Man Who Knew Too Much

Hitchcock's remake of his 1934 film is not considered one of his best. An American couple Ben and Jo McKenna (Stewart and Day) vacationing in North Africa with their young son become entangled in international espionage, abduction, and assassination. DVD represents a vast improvement over the earlier full-frame Universal laserdisc. Colors are much truer and sharper. Even the mono sound is much better. Though there may have been some temptation for a Surround remix of Bernard Herrmann's grand score, that would have been wrong. The studio has done its usual fine work with the packaging of extras, including a long "making of" featurette. —*MM*
Movie: ♪♪♪ **DVD:** ♪♪♪
Universal Studios Home Video (Cat #204 19, UPC #025192041921). Widescreen (1.85:1) anamorphic. Dolby Digital Mono. $29.98. Keepcase. *LANG:* English. *SUB:* Spanish. *CAP:* English. *FEATURES:* 18 chapter links ▪ "Making of" featurette ▪ Production photos and notes ▪ Trailers ▪ Talent bios.
1956 (PG) 120m/C James Stewart, Doris Day, Brenda de Banzie, Bernard Miles, Ralph Truman, Daniel Gelin, Alan Mowbray, Carolyn Jones, Hillary Brooke; *D:* Alfred Hitchcock; *W:* John Michael Hayes; *C:* Robert Burks; *M:* Bernard Herrmann. *AWARDS:* Oscars '56: Song ("Que Sera, Sera").

The Man Who Loved Women

Intelligent, sensitive bachelor Bertrand Morane (Denner) writes his memoirs and recalls the many, many, many women he has loved. Truffaut couples sophistication and lightheartedness, the thrill of the chase and, when it leads to an accidental death, the wondering what's-it-all-about-Bertrand in the mourning after. The image is very good compared to other '70s imports, though it lacks the sparkle of similar Hollywood studio productions.

Mono sound is more than adequate. —*MM* *AKA:* L'Homme Qui Aimait les Femmes.
Movie: ♪♪♪½ **DVD:** ♪♪♪
MGM Home Entertainment (Cat #10014 79, UPC #027616857996). Widescreen (1.66) letterboxed. Dolby Digital Mono. $19.98. Keepcase. *LANG:* French; Spanish. *SUB:* English; French; Spanish. *FEATURES:* 16 chapter links.
1977 119m/C *FR* Charles Denner, Brigitte Fossey, Leslie Caron, Nelly Borgeaud, Genevieve Fontanel, Nathalie Baye, Sabine Glaser; *D:* Francois Truffaut; *W:* Francois Truffaut, Suzanne Schiffman, Michel Fermaud; *C:* Nestor Almendros; *M:* Maurice Jaubert.

The Man Who Shot Liberty Valance

Ford's last great western has aged beautifully. The cast is perfect and the story is strong. Rance Stoddard (Stewart) is an idealistic young lawyer who wants to rid the wild town of Shinbone of its wildest citizen, Liberty Valance (Marvin). Tom Donofan (Wayne) is the old-style cowboy who stands between the two. The superb black-and-white image is re-created flawlessly on DVD. I could tell little difference between the 5.1 Surround track and the mono, but I didn't give the new sound much of a chance. This is a no-frills disc that belongs in every library. —*MM*
Movie: ♪♪♪½ **DVD:** ♪♪♪
Paramount Home Video (Cat #06114, UPC #097360611441). Widescreen anamorphic. Dolby Digital 5.1 Surround Stereo; Dolby Digital Mono. $29.99. Keepcase. *LANG:* English. *SUB:* English. *FEATURES:* 15 chapter links ▪ Trailer.
1962 123m/B James Stewart, John Wayne, Vera Miles, Lee Marvin, Edmond O'Brien, Andy Devine, Woody Strode, Ken Murray, Jeanette Nolan, John Qualen, Strother Martin, Lee Van Cleef, John Carradine, Carleton Young, Willis Bouchey, Denver Pyle, Robert F. Simon, O.Z. Whitehead, Paul Birch, Joseph Hoover, Earle Hodgins, Jack Pennick; *D:* John Ford; *W:* James Warner Bellah, Willis Goldbeck; *C:* William Clothier; *M:* Cyril Mockridge, Alfred Newman. *AWARDS:* NOM: Oscars '62: Costume Des. (B&W).

Manhattan

Isaac Davis (Allen) is a successful TV writer who wants to be taken as a serious writer. He struggles through a series of relationships, including one with high school senior Tracy (Hemingway) and another with Mary (Keaton), who's also involved with his best friend Yale (Murphy). It's a scathingly serious and comic view of relationships in urban America and intellectual neuroses. It's also a striking valentine to New York. Gordon Willis's beautiful photography has never looked better on home video. This is some of the best black and white you'll ever see. Mono sound is acceptable, but why not at least a stereo remix for the Gershwin score? —*MM*

Movie: ✂✂✂✂ **DVD:** ✂✂✂½
MGM Home Entertainment (Cat #10007 95, UPC #027616851154). Widescreen anamorphic. Dolby Digital Mono. $24.99. Keepcase. *LANG:* English; Spanish. *SUB:* French; Spanish. *CAP:* English. *FEATURES:* 24 chapter links ▪ Liner notes ▪ Trailer.
1979 (R) 96m/B Woody Allen, Diane Keaton, Meryl Streep, Mariel Hemingway, Michael Murphy, Wallace Shawn, Anne Byrne, Tisa Farrow, Mark Linn-Baker, David Rasche, Karen Allen; *D:* Woody Allen; *W:* Woody Allen, Marshall Brickman; *C:* Gordon Willis; *M:* George Gershwin. *AWARDS:* British Acad. '79: Film, Screenplay; Cesar '80: Foreign Film; L.A. Film Critics '79: Support. Actress (Streep); N.Y. Film Critics '79: Director (Allen), Support. Actress (Streep); Natl. Soc. Film Critics '79: Director (Allen), Support. Actress (Streep); *NOM:* Oscars '79: Orig. Screenplay, Support. Actress (Hemingway).

Manhattan Baby
An archeologist and his family uncover all sorts of weird stuff in an Egyptian tomb. When they return to New York, his little girl appears to be possessed, or something to that effect. Though the film contains considerably less gore than one usually finds in a Fulci horror, this is perhaps his loopiest plot. Image, however, is excellent. Even the desert daylight exteriors, which can give even the best discs problems with artifacts, are flawless. —*MM*
Movie: ✂✂ **DVD:** ✂✂✂
Anchor Bay (Cat #DV11842, UPC #013131 184297). Widescreen (2.35:1) anamorphic. Dolby Digital Mono. $24.99. Keepcase. *LANG:* English. *FEATURES:* 24 chapter links ▪ Trailer ▪ Interview with writer Dardano Sacchetti ▪ Talent files ▪ Liner notes by Michael Felsher.
1982 90m/C *IT* Christopher Connelly, Martha Taylor, Brigitta Boccoli, Giovanni Frezza, Lucio Fulci; *D:* Lucio Fulci; *W:* Elisa Briganti, Dardano Sacchetti; *C:* Guglielmo Mancori; *M:* Fabio Frizzi.

Maniac Nurses Find Ecstasy
Even by Troma standards, this one's scraping the bottom of the barrel. The nearly non-existent plot is an excuse to present several young women dressed in nurse uniforms and underwear while holding various weapons. The sense of energy that's needed for good exploitation is lacking. Neither image or sound is an improvement over VHS tape, and both are poor. Even the Tromatic extras are on the skimpy side. —*MM*
Movie: ✂ **DVD:** ✂½
Troma Team Video (Cat #9994, UPC #7903 57999439). Full frame. $24.95. Keepcase. *LANG:* English. *FEATURES:* 9 chapter links ▪ Troma trailer reel ▪ Credits.
1994 80m/C Susanna Makay, Hajni Brown, Nicole A. Gyony, Csilia Farago; *D:* Harry M. (Leon P. Howard) Love; *W:* Harry M. (Leon P. Howard) Love.

Manon of the Spring
In this excellent sequel to *Jean de Florette,* the adult daughter (Beart) of the dead hunchback discovers who blocked up the spring on her father's land. She plots her revenge, which proves greater than she could ever imagine. Montand is astonishing and Beart's beauty is breathtaking. Bright sunlit exteriors are a real problem for this DVD. Those scenes are filled with swimming artifacts. Otherwise, the image is very good with a fine level of detail. Surround effects are minimal. —*MM AKA:* Manon des Sources; Jean de Florette 2.
Movie: ✂✂✂ **DVD:** ✂✂✂½
MGM Home Entertainment (Cat #10014 80, UPC #027616858009). Widescreen (2.35:1) letterboxed. Dolby Digital Surround Stereo. $19.98. Keepcase. *LANG:* French. *SUB:* English; French; Spanish. *FEATURES:* 16 chapter links ▪ Trailer.
1987 (PG) 113m/C *FR* Yves Montand, Daniel Auteuil, Emmanuelle Beart, Hippolyte Girardot, Margarita Lozano, Elisabeth Depardieu, Yvonne Gamy, Armand Meffre, Gabriel Bacquier; *D:* Claude Berri; *W:* Claude Berri, Gerard Brach; *C:* Bruno Nuytten; *M:* Jean-Claude Petit, Roger Legrand.

Manoushe, The Story of a Gypsy Love
Curious fantasy is almost impossible to describe. It begins with the funeral of what appears to be a gypsy leader, then flashes back to his youth and marriage. It's a surreal *Alice in Wonderland* sort of tale with supernatural spirits and the like. Though the box copy claims English dialogue, I could not decipher the language. No subtitles are available. The story appears to be told through image, dance, music and gesture. Colors are extremely harsh throughout. DVD appears to be an accurate reproduction of the gaudy image. Stereo sound is fine. —*MM*
Movie: ✂✂ **DVD:** ✂✂
Vanguard International Cinema, Inc. (Cat #1-892649-97-7, UPC #658769011036). Full frame. $29.95. Keepcase. *FEATURES:* 12 chapter links.
1998 73m/C Drica Moraes, Lelia Abramo, Candido Pires, Breno Moroni; *D:* Luiz Begazo; *W:* Luiz Begazo; *C:* Helio Silva; *M:* Paco de Lucia.

Mansfield Park
Jane Austen's novel gets a revisionist updating from filmmaker Patricia Rozema. It's not so much that Rozema has reworked the life and times of Fanny Price (played here by Frances O'Connor) at her relative's country estate in England in the early 1800s, but that she's borrowed heavily from Austen's own journals and essays to "overlay" a greater confidence onto the character. The results are mixed. If you fancy the pastoral pacing of *Sense and Sensibility* and *Emma,* then *Mansfield Park,* and Fanny Price's film-long decision between Edmund Bertram (Jonny Lee Miller) and Henry Crawford (Alessandro

Nivola) will be your cup o' tea. Image and sound are fine. Irritating and unfriendly viewer interface for this DVD presentation is more than offset by an informative audio commentary from director Patricia Rozema. —*RJT*
Movie: ✂✂½ **DVD:** ✂✂½
Buena Vista Home Entertainment (Cat #18305, UPC #717951004901). Widescreen (1.85:1) anamorphic. Dolby Digital 5.0 Surround. $29.99. Keepcase. *LANG:* English; French. *SUB:* English. *CAP:* English. *FEATURES:* Commentary: director Rozema ▪ 30 chapter links.
1999 (PG-13) 110m/C Frances O'Connor, Jonny Lee Miller, Alessandro Nivola, Embeth Davidtz, Harold Pinter, Lindsay Duncan, Sheila Gish, Justine Waddell, Victoria Hamilton, James Purefoy, Hugh Bonneville; *D:* Patricia Rozema; *W:* Patricia Rozema; *C:* Michael Coulter; *M:* Lesley Barber.

Mantis in Lace
In 1968 this was one hot little number on the exploitation circuit. Today, the groovy dialogue is the main attraction. Lila (Stewart) is a topless dancer who takes men back to her warehouse lair, drops acid, freaks out, and kills them during sex. For a film this cheaply made and this old, the disc is in remarkable shape. Colors are vivid, particularly in the nutty trip sequences. Blacks in the often-dark interiors aren't muddy. Mono sound is fine. The producers have thoughtfully included more minutes of outtakes than the original running time. Be warned: the bizarre theme song may induce flashbacks. —*MM AKA:* Lila.
Movie: ✂✂✂ **DVD:** ✂✂✂
Image Entertainment (Cat #ID9743SW DVD, UPC #014381974324). Full frame. Dolby Digital Mono. $24.95. Snapper. *LANG:* English. *FEATURES:* 16 chapter links ▪ Outtakes ▪ Alternate psychedelic murder sequence ▪ Trailers ▪ Short film, "LSD: Trip or Trap!" ▪ Short film, "Alice Goes to Acidland" ▪ Short film, "Girl in a Cage" ▪ Gallery of exploitation art ▪ Harry Novak radio spots.
1968 (R) 68m/C Susan Stewart, Steve Vincent, M.K. Evans, Vic Lance, Pat (Barringer) Barrington, Janu Wine, Stuart Lancaster, John Carrol, Judith Crane, Cheryl Trepton; *D:* William Rotsler; *W:* Sanford White; *C:* Laszlo Kovacs; *M:* Frank A. Coe.

A Map of the World
An excellent cast works with a tough story based on the novel by Jane Hamilton. Flinty would-be farm wife/mom Alice Goodwin (Weaver) hasn't endeared herself to her Wisconsin community. But she's a good deal more vulnerable than anyone suspects as her life begins to fall apart. First, there's an accident involving her neighbor Theresa's (Moore) daughter. Then a shocking charge of sexual abuse in her role as a school nurse lands her in jail. Uneven script is part family drama, part prison drama, part courtroom drama, part melodrama, and all those dramas

don't make for a completely coherent whole. At first, the image is on the soft side—the kind of look that Hollywood usually chooses to depict rural life. Later, it becomes somewhat sharper. Sound is very good, highlighting Pat Metheny's fine score. —MM

Movie: 🎬🎬½ **DVD:** 🎬🎬½
USA Home Entertainment (Cat #963 060 092 2, UPC #696306000921). Widescreen anamorphic. Dolby Digital Surround Stereo. $24.98. Keepcase. *LANG:* English. *SUB:* English. *FEATURES:* Trailer • Featurette • Talent files • 28 chapter links.
1999 (R) 125m/C Sigourney Weaver, David Strathairn, Julianne Moore, Ron Lea, Arliss Howard, Chloe Sevigny, Louise Fletcher; *D:* Scott Elliott; *W:* Peter Hedges, Polly Platt; *C:* Seamus McGarvey; *M:* Pat Metheny. *AWARDS:* Natl. Bd. of Review '99: Support. Actress (Moore); *NOM:* Golden Globes '00: Actress—Drama (Weaver).

March of the Wooden Soldiers

The Mother Goose tale about the secret life of Christmas toys stars Laurel and Hardy as Santa's helpers who must save Toyland from the wicked Barnaby. The clarity of DVD only heightens the abomination that is "colorization." (The film was made in black and white and this image simply looks wrong.) Sound is fine; its thin quality is a product of the times. —MM *AKA:* Babes in Toyland.
Movie: 🎬🎬🎬 **DVD:** 🎬🎬
Goodtimes Entertainment (Cat #81056). Full frame. $14.99. Snapper. *LANG:* English. *SUB:* English; Spanish. *FEATURES:* Stan Laurel home movie • Oliver Hardy interview • 18 chapter links • Production notes • Trailer.
1934 73m/B Stan Laurel, Oliver Hardy, Charlotte Henry, Henry (Kleinbach) Brandon, Felix Knight, Jean Darling, Johnny Downs, Marie Wilson; *D:* Charles R. Rogers, Gus Meins; *W:* Frank Butler, Nick Grinde; *C:* Art Lloyd, Francis Corby.

Marihuana / Assassin of Youth / Reefer Madness

Three marijuana-scare flicks from the 1930s sustain this pot-filled package, which also includes a moronic exposé of the Egyptian drug trade, excerpts from a silent western and many other goodies. *Marihuana* is the one to show your friends: incompetently made, addle-brained about its subject, and with an unbelievable amount of nudity for its time, it can't fail to shock. *Assassin of Youth* is the least campy, with comparatively high production values and even jokes that work. Love that motor scooter-riding harridan! The infamous *Reefer Madness* seems dull after *Marihuana,* but the best-known scenes are priceless. The prints are all badly damaged if perfectly watchable, more so than you might reasonably expect from these ancient roadshow oddi-

ties; *Reefer* is scratchy and blotchy, but still looks sharper than any other available version. The sound was badly recorded in the first place, so expect nothing better than the originals. The menus are lovingly crafted, with gorgeous animated effects. Beware the "commentary" for *Marihuana,* which is really an extemporaneous interview with Friedman that barely touches on the film. —SS *AKA:* Marijuana: The Devil's Weed; Marijuana, Weed with Roots in Hell.
Movie: 🎬🎬🎬 **DVD:** 🎬🎬🎬
Image Entertainment (Cat #ID9744SWDVD, UPC #014381974423). Full frame. Dolby Digital Mono. $29.99. Snapper. *LANG:* English. *FEATURES:* 36 chapter links • Theatrical trailers • Commentary: exploitation producer David F. Friedman • Dwain Esper's short documentary, "Sinister Menace" (1930) • Clip from *High on the Range* (1924) • Clip from *Wages of Sin* (1938) • Gallery of drug-scare exploitation art • Drug-scare radio spots. The print used for *Reefer Madness* is entitled *Doped Youth.*
1936 57m/B Harley Wood, Hugh McArthur, Pat Carlyle, Dorothy Dehn, Paul Ellis, Richard Erskine; *D:* Dwain Esper; *W:* Rex Elgin, Hildegarde Stadie; *C:* Roland Price.

Marilyn Monroe: The Diamond Collection

This boxed set contains the features *Bus Stop, Gentlemen Prefer Blondes, How to Marry a Millionaire, Seven Year Itch, There's No Business Like Show Business,* and the AMC documentary *Marilyn Monroe: The Final Days* (please see individual reviews). The restoration demonstrations on each disc deserve a close look. Obviously proud of their fine work on this set, Fox here has the maturity to do real comparisons with previous video masters. Even more dramatically shown is the role played by digital video cleanup, when a second comparison is made between the restored film element, and the final video. All manner of scratches, splotches, printing irregularities, digs, and other blemishes have been eliminated. Yes, the film has to some extent been "repainted," but it just plain looks great. —GE
Movie: 🎬🎬🎬½ **DVD:** 🎬🎬🎬½
20th Century Fox Home Entertainment (Cat #2001402, UPC #024543014027). Widescreen; full frame. $99.98. Boxed set, keepcase. *LANG:* English.
2000 ?m/C

Marilyn Monroe: The Final Days

This is one of the best documentaries that the AMC channel has produced. The unedited footage from the aborted *Something's Gotta Give* has been shown in ghoulish glimpses and bits for 40 years, but here we get an honest and thorough look at the entire set of raw dailies. In almost every take, Marilyn comes off as disoriented and strained, incapable of good work, for whatever reason. It's a good documentary, with frank discussions of the kind of sticky production intrigues

that studios usually avoid in favor of publicity pap. The movie was intended as a remake of *My Favorite Wife,* and eventually done as *Move Over, Darling,* with Doris Day. Playing a woman with children for the first time might have begun a great central section for Monroe's career, but as the dailies make very clear, her performance is forced and distracted, not quite as pathetic as Judy Garland's for *Annie Get Your Gun,* but just as useless. —GE
Movie: 🎬🎬🎬½ **DVD:** 🎬🎬🎬½
20th Century Fox Home Entertainment (Cat #2001410). Full frame. Stereo. $24.98. Keepcase. *LANG:* English.
2000 120m/C Cyd Charisse, Walter Bernstein, Henry Weinstein; *D:* Patty Ivins; *Nar:* James Coburn.

The Marquise of O

Poetic, ponderous adaptation of a Heinrich von Kleist novella about faith and redemption during the Franco-Prussian war. During an attack on their home, the widowed Marquise of O (Edith Clever) is saved from an attempted rape by "the Count," a Russian officer (Bruno Ganz). Several months later, she finds herself mysteriously pregnant. Unable to recall the circumstances and with mounting pressure from her family to name the father, the Marquise faces the hypocrisy of her family's religious beliefs as well as the Count's suspicious insistence on marrying her immediately. It's a *Masterpiece Theatre*–style adaptation, complete with elevated language and everyone walking slowly in elaborate costumes. The premise is intriguing, if ultimately baffling in its resolution. The transfer ranks slightly above videotape, primarily due to DVD's increased resolution. The source is clean enough with colors fighting through a semi-sepia haze enveloping the entire film. Mono sound is O.K. —EP *AKA:* Die Marquise Von O.
Movie: 🎬🎬½ **DVD:** 🎬🎬½
Winstar Home Entertainment (Cat #FLV52 38, UPC #720917523828). Full frame. Dolby Digital Mono. $24.99. Keepcase. *LANG:* German. *SUB:* English. *FEATURES:* 8 chapter links • Filmographies and awards • Production credits • Weblinks.
1976 (PG) 102m/C *FR GE* Edith Clever, Bruno Ganz, Peter Luhr, Edda Seipel, Otto Sander, Ruth Drexel; *D:* Eric Rohmer; *W:* Eric Rohmer; *C:* Nestor Almendros.

The Marriage Circle

This classic silent film always gets high praise among critics for its portrayal of two marriages teetering on the brink of collapse and running headlong into each other. Professor Stock (beautifully played by Aldophe Menjou) and Mizzi are trapped in a loveless marriage. She is young and hard to please, and he is a gentleman of the highest order longing for peace and quiet. When Mizzi meets Dr. Braun, her best friend's husband, she decides to get even with her own husband, and a comedy of errors begins. Well-constructed scenes coupled with seasoned silent film stars

make the film entertaining. The disc is struck from masters and looks decent but not perfect. (A run through a digital restoration would do it a world of good.) The sound is very good, as all that was needed was a music score, which has been mastered into stereo. —CA
Movie: 🎬🎬½ **DVD:** 🎬½
Image Entertainment (Cat #ID9415DSDVD, UPC #01438194152). Full frame. Dolby Digital Stereo. $24.99. Snapper. *LANG:* Silent. *SUB:* English intertitles. *FEATURES:* 12 chapter links.
1924 90m/B Florence Vidor, Monte Blue, Marie Prevost, Creighton Hale, Adolphe Menjou, Harry Myers, Dale Fuller; **D:** Ernst Lubitsch; **W:** Paul Bern; **C:** Charles Van Enger.

Married to the Mob
After the murder of her husband (Baldwin), Mafia widow Angela (Pfeiffer) tries to escape mob life, but ends up fighting off the amorous advances of the current boss (Stockwell), while being wooed by an undercover cop (Modine). A snappy script and a spry performance by a striking Pfeiffer make this one very easy to enjoy. DVD image is essentially flawless. The slightly muted color scheme looks exactly as I remember it from the theatrical release. Use of 5.1 is limited but inventive. —MM
Movie: 🎬🎬🎬½ **DVD:** 🎬🎬🎬
MGM Home Entertainment (Cat #10006 85, UPC #027616850164). Widescreen anamorphic; full frame. Dolby Digital Surround Stereo; Mono. $24.99. Keepcase. *LANG:* English; Spanish. *SUB:* French; Spanish. *CAP:* English. *FEATURES:* 32 chapter links • Liner notes • Trailer.
1988 (R) 102m/C Michelle Pfeiffer, Dean Stockwell, Alec Baldwin, Matthew Modine, Mercedes Ruehl, Anthony J. Nici, Joan Cusack, Ellen Foley, Chris Isaak, Trey Wilson, Charles Napier, Tracey Walter, Al Lewis, Nancy Travis, David Johansen, Jonathan Demme; **D:** Jonathan Demme; **W:** Mark Burns, Barry Strugatz; **C:** Tak Fujimoto; **M:** David Byrne. *AWARDS:* N.Y. Film Critics '88: Support. Actor (Stockwell); Natl. Soc. Film Critics '88: Support. Actor (Stockwell), Support. Actress (Ruehl); *NOM:* Oscars '88: Support. Actor (Stockwell).

The Married Virgin
One of the earliest films in which Valentino appeared in a featured role prior to *The Four Horsemen of the Apocalypse* and *The Sheik*. Count Roberto di Fraccini (Valentino) is a fortune hunter having an affair with Ethel Spencer McMillan (Kirkham), wife of wealthy older businessman Fiske McMillan (Jobson). After the couple unsuccessfully plot to blackmail McMillan, the Count tells his lover's daughter, Mary (Sisson), that in return for her hand in marriage (and her dowry), he will save her father from a life in prison. The print of this film is in a pretty bad state, but the disc does an admirable job of preserving what's left. The color tinting is essentially a toning up of the original black-and-white

negative. The soundtrack is well-done though it tends to be a bit loud during some scenes. —MJT
Movie: 🎬🎬 **DVD:** 🎬🎬½
Image Entertainment (Cat #ID9704DSDVD, UPC #014381970425). Full frame. Dolby Digital Stereo. $24.99. Snapper. *LANG:* Silent. *FEATURES:* 10 chapter links • 10-minute extract of 1919 film *Eyes of Youth* • Pathe Newsreel: "Valentino Dead." 1926.
1918 71m/B Rudolph Valentino, Kathleen Kirkham, Edward Jobson, Vera Sisson, Frank Newburg; **D:** Joe Maxwell; **W:** Hayden Talbott.

Martin
Martin (Amplas) is a very disturbed young man who believes that is he an 84-year-old vampire. His uncle Cuda (Maazel) from the old country believes him and wants to save Martin's soul and then to destroy him. Whatever the truth, Martin is killing people. If he uses drugs and razorblades instead of hypnotic gazes and fangs, the results are the same. In the end, Romero's story is about being human. With its grainy color, closely observed Braddock (Pennsylvania) locations, and characters thoroughly stripped of conventional movie glamour, the film certainly doesn't pick up any polish on DVD. It does have a commentary track. Personally, I would have preferred a solo Romero talking about the character and his relation to conventional horror. Instead, he has the star and makeup effects man Tom Savini along for help and their approach is much more conversational. Perhaps the most interesting point they bring up is a three-hour 16mm. version of the film that is missing and presumed stolen. They're willing to pay for its return. —MM
Movie: 🎬🎬🎬🎬 **DVD:** 🎬🎬🎬½
Anchor Bay (Cat #DV10997, UPC #013131 099799). Full frame. Dolby Digital Mono. $24.99. Keepcase. *LANG:* English. *FEATURES:* 22 chapter links • Trailer • Commentary: Romero, Amplas, Tom Savini • Liner notes by Michael Felsher.
1977 (R) 96m/C John Amplas, Lincoln Maazel, Christine Forrest, Elayne Nadeau, Tom Savini, Sarah Venable, George A. Romero, Fran Middleton; **D:** George A. Romero; **W:** George A. Romero; **C:** Michael Gornick; **M:** Donald Rubinstein.

Marty
Marty (Borgnine) is a painfully shy bachelor who feels trapped in a pointless life of family squabbles. When he falls in love with Clara (Blair), a teacher, he also finds the strength to break out of what he sees as a pointless existence. Borgnine won an Oscar for what is certainly his best work. DVD captures the tremendous shot-on-location feel of the film. The occasional fleck flits across the screen, but the overall image is excellent. Mono sound is fine for the dialogue-driven story. —MM
Movie: 🎬🎬🎬½ **DVD:** 🎬🎬🎬
MGM Home Entertainment (Cat #10020 62, UPC #027616862921). Full frame. Dolby Digital Mono. $19.98. Keepcase.

LANG: English; French; Spanish. *SUB:* French; Spanish. *FEATURES:* 16 chapter links • Trailer.
1955 91m/B Ernest Borgnine, Betsy Blair, Joe Mantell, Esther Minciotti, Jerry Paris, Karen Steele, Augusta Ciolli, Frank Sutton, Walter Kelley, Robin Morse; **D:** Delbert Mann; **W:** Paddy Chayefsky; **C:** Joseph LaShelle; **M:** Roy Webb, Harry Warren. *AWARDS:* Oscars '55: Actor (Borgnine), Director (Mann), Picture, Screenplay; British Acad. '55: Actor (Borgnine), Actress (Blair); Directors Guild '55: Director (Mann); Golden Globes '56: Actor—Drama (Borgnine); Natl. Bd. of Review '55: Actor (Borgnine), Natl. Film Reg. '94; N.Y. Film Critics '55: Actor (Borgnine), Film; *NOM:* Oscars '55: Art Dir./Set Dec., B&W, B&W Cinematog., Support. Actor (Mantell), Support. Actress (Blair).

Mary Poppins [2 SE]
Only a few extras differentiate this "Gold Edition" from the previously released disc, reviewed in the first edition. The French and Spanish language tracks are new, along with a couple of featurettes and a trivia game. Julie Andrews's performance is still one of her very best and the film remains a favorite. —MM
Movie: 🎬🎬🎬½ **DVD:** 🎬🎬🎬🎬
Buena Vista Home Entertainment (Cat #20 221, UPC #717951009753). Widescreen (1.85:1) letterboxed. Dolby Digital 5.1 Surround Stereo; Dolby Digital Mono. $29.99. Keepcase. *LANG:* English; French; Spanish. *CAP:* English. *FEATURES:* 24 chapter links • Trailers • "Making of" featurette • "World premiere" featurette • Trivia game.
1964 139m/C Julie Andrews, Dick Van Dyke, Ed Wynn, Hermione Baddeley, David Tomlinson, Glynis Johns, Karen Dotrice, Matthew Garber; **D:** Robert Stevenson; **W:** Bill Walsh, Whip Wilson; **C:** Edward Colman; **M:** Richard M. Sherman, Robert B. Sherman. *AWARDS:* Oscars '64: Actress (Andrews), Film Editing, Song ("Chim Chim Cher-ee"), Visual FX, Orig. Score; Golden Globes '65: Actress—Mus./Comedy (Andrews); *NOM:* Oscars '64: Adapt. Screenplay, Art Dir./Set Dec., Color, Color Cinematog., Costume Des. (C), Director (Stevenson), Picture, Sound, Orig. Score.

Mary Reilly
Mary (Roberts) is an innocent maid whose employer happens to be the infamous Dr. Jekyll (Malkovich). They both seem to be employed by Dr. Freud in this dank, dreary psychosexual thriller. Mary is torn between the repressed affection of the doctor and the oily sexuality of his alter ego, who conjures up images of her abusive father. Reuniting the crew and some of the cast of *Dangerous Liaisons* (Glenn Close also appears as a bawdy brothel owner), they fail to reach their previous heights. Most of the gloomy sets will make you wish you were wearing galoshes. Columbia TriStar has done an incredible job in transferring this extremely dark film to DVD. The scene is almost always composed of either a

foggy exterior haze or a dimly lit interior. Very rarely does the DVD falter and, for the most part, the image remains as sharp as in the theatre; there are a couple instances of minor artifacts but nothing you can't live with. Colors are also accurate to the theatrical presentation and are very subdued, consisting mostly of deep reds and browns, but no bleed. The 5.0 sound is very impressive and the Surround tracks add some fairly creepy ambience to the proceedings. —*JO*

Movie: ♫♫ **DVD:** ♫♫♫
Columbia Tristar Home Video (Cat #11052, UPC #043396110526). Widescreen (1.85:1) anamorphic. Dolby Digital 5.0; Dolby Surround; Stereo. $14.95. Keepcase. *LANG:* English; Spanish; French; Portuguese. *SUB:* English; Spanish; French; Chinese; Korean; Thai; Portuguese. *CAP:* English. *FEATURES:* 28 chapter links • Theatrical trailer • Talent files • Production notes • "Making of" featurette.
1995 (R) 108m/C Julia Roberts, John Malkovich, George Cole, Michael Gambon, Kathy Staff, Glenn Close, Michael Sheen, Bronagh Gallagher, Linda Bassett, Henry Goodman, Ciaran Hinds, Sasha Hanav; **D:** Stephen Frears; **W:** Christopher Hampton; **C:** Philippe Rousselot; **M:** George Fenton. *AWARDS: NOM:* Golden Raspberries '96: Worst Actress (Roberts), Worst Director (Frears).

Master with Cracked Fingers

Jackie Chan's first feature is an abominable low-budget martial arts flick which, reportedly, sat on a shelf until he became a star. Then it was re-edited and footage of a double was inserted. Whatever the truth, this disc contains virtually every flaw that can be found in the medium. First it was made from a seriously damaged original, full of grain and scratches. The musical score is so distorted it will drive you screaming from the television and is probably painful to dogs. This is the worst DVD I have attempted to watch. —*MM* **AKA:** Snake Fist Fighter.

Movie: ♫♫ **DVD:** woof
Madacy Entertainment Widescreen (1.66:1) letterboxed. Keepcase. *LANG:* English. *FEATURES:* 10 chapter links • Listing of Jackie Chan's injuries • Listing of Jackie Chan's songs • Explanation of martial arts styles.
1971 (R) 83m/C *HK* Jackie Chan; **D:** Chin Hsin.

Masters of Russian Animation, Vol. 2

These short films (ranging in length from 5 to 17 minutes) were made between 1969 and '78. There's no unifying theme or style. They're mostly experimental, though they do tell strong stories. "The Firing Range" is a relatively realistic, intelligent sf that might have been an influence on more recent Japanese anime. "Contact" could have been a lost chapter of the Beatles *Yellow Submarine,* with Nino Rota's

music from *The Godfather.* The films have been well preserved or restored. Image quality is very good in most, excellent in a few. Contents: "Seasons" (1969), "Ballerina on the Boat" (1969), "Armoire" (1970), "Battle at Kerzhenets" (1971), "Butterfly" (1972), "Island" (1973), "Fox and Rabbit" (1973), "Heron and Crane" (1974), "Hedgehog in the Fog" (1974), "Crane Feathers" (1977), "Firing Range" (1977), and "Contact" (1978). —*MM*
Movie: ♫♫♫ **DVD:** ♫♫♫
Image Entertainment (Cat #ID5526FJDVD, UPC #014381552621). Full frame. Dolby Digital Mono. $24.99. Snapper. *LANG:* Russian. *SUB:* English. *FEATURES:* 12 chapter links • Liner notes by Oleg Vidov and Joan Borsten.
1997 ?m/C *RU*

Masters of Russian Animation, Vol. 3

Echoes of the work of Maurice Sendak, Monty Python, and even *Heavy Metal* magazine (not the naughty parts) can be seen in these short films. Most are conventional animation but some are stop-motion. My only quibble: some of the subtitles are too small and too close to the bottom of the screen. Contents: "Tale of Tales" (1979), "Hunt" (1979), "Last Hunt" (1982), "There Once Was a Dog" (1982), "Travels of an Ant" (1983), "Lion and Ox" (1983), "Wolf and Calf" (1984), "Cabaret" (1984), "Old Stair" (1985), "King's Sandwich" (1985), and "About Sidorov" (1985). —*MM*
Movie: ♫♫♫ **DVD:** ♫♫♫
Image Entertainment (Cat #ID5527FJDVD, UPC #014381552720). Full frame. Dolby Digital Mono. $24.00. Snapper. *LANG:* Russian. *SUB:* English. *FEATURES:* 12 chapter links • Liner notes by Oleg Vidov and Joan Borsten.
1997 ?m/C *RU*

Masters of Russian Animation, Vol. 4

The images are a bit sharper here than in previous volumes, doubtless because these are newer films. They tend not to be as bright as their American counterparts, though the DVD appears to be a faithful re-creation of sometimes eccentric lighting. Both "Big Underground Ball" and "Alter Ego" are very dark. Some live action is mixed in with the conventional and stop-motion animation. Contents: "Door" (1986), "Boy Is a Boy" (1986), "Liberated Don Quixote" (1987), "Martinko" (1987), "Big Underground Ball" (1987), "Cat and Clown" (1988), "Dream" (1988), "Kele" (1988), "Alter Ego" (1989), "Girlfriend" (1989), "Croak x Croak" (1990), and "Cat and Company" (1990). —*MM*
Movie: ♫♫♫ **DVD:** ♫♫♫
Image Entertainment (Cat #ID5528FJDVD, UPC #014381552829). Full frame. Dolby Digital Mono. $24.99. Snapper. *LANG:* Russian. *SUB:* English. *FEATURES:* 12 chapter links • Liner notes by Oleg Vidov and Joan Borsten.
1997 ?m/C *RU*

A Matter of Dignity

With her once-rich family at the brink of bankruptcy, Chloe (Lambetti) agrees to marry a Greek-American millionaire as an act of self-sacrifice. When she truly falls in love with another man, she embarks on a painful journey of self-discovery, questioning the shallowness of her upbringing and confronting her ultimate destiny. The film's anchor is Lambetti's chameleon performance; one moment playing the blasé, unattainable socialite and the next those amazingly doleful eyes transmitting the pain of a daughter torn between duty and dignity. As with most Cacoyannis films, passions are always at fever pitch. This time out, though, he found the perfect embodiment of Greece's past and (then) present in both Chloe and Lambetti. Transfer suffers from a few blemishes and speckles, otherwise the full-frame presentation affords sharp, clear images. Shadow delineation is wanting, with details all but lost in low-light scenes. Mono sound exhibits adequate dynamic range but glitches, hiss, and occasional peaks interfere. —*EP* **AKA:** To Telefteo Psemma.
Movie: ♫♫½ **DVD:** ♫♫
Winstar Home Entertainment (Cat #FLV5215, UPC #720917521527). Full frame. Dolby Digital Mono. $24.99. Keepcase. *LANG:* Greek. *SUB:* English. *FEATURES:* 8 chapter links • Filmographies and awards • Production credits • Weblinks.
1957 104m/B *GR* Georges Pappas, Ellie Lambetti, Athena Michaelidou, Eleni Zafirou; **D:** Michael Cacoyannis; **W:** Michael Cacoyannis; **C:** Walter Lassally; **M:** Manos Hadjidakis.

Mauvais Sang

Film falls squarely into the category of "never really sure where it's going or where it's been." It tells the story of Alex (Lavant), the teenage son of a murdered criminal who is enlisted by two former associates of his father to steal a valuable serum for an AIDS-like disease. Alex's life becomes complicated when he falls in love with one of the associates' young mistress (Binoche). The video transfer proves merely adequate; bright colors are reproduced faithfully while others tend to be murky. Consequently, the overall effect of the disc is bland and rather subdued. The soundtrack is reasonably understandable, but a good deal of it is muffled and that tends to be distracting. The short interview with director Carax is intriguing and enjoyable, if a bit on the eclectic side. —*MJT* **AKA:** Bad Blood.
Movie: ♫♫½ **DVD:** ♫♫
Winstar Home Entertainment (Cat #FLV5271, UPC #720917527123). Widescreen (1.66:1) anamorphic. Dolby Digital Stereo. $24.98. Keepcase. *LANG:* French. *SUB:* English. *FEATURES:* 16 chapter links • Production credits and filmographies • Interview with director Leos Carax • Outtakes • *Pola X* theatrical trailer • Weblinks.
1986 125m/C *FR* Michel Piccoli, Denis Lavant, Juliette Binoche, Hans Meyer, Julie Delpy, Carroll Brooks, Serge Reggiani,

Hugo Pratt, Mireille Perrier; **D:** Leos Carax; **W:** Leos Carax; **C:** Jean-Yves Escoffier; **M:** Serge Reggiani, Charles Aznavour.

Maximum Overdrive

Writer Stephen King's directorial debut is a self-described "moron movie" but that doesn't mean that it's not fun in a garish, grease-stained, destructive way. After the Earth passes through the tail of a comet, machines take on lives of their own and turn on people. A group led by Emilio Estevez is trapped by trucks at the Dixie Boy Diner. The DVD image is good, but not much better than a widescreen tape. Surround sound is much better for fans of diesel exhaust and the AC-DC soundtrack. *—MM*

Movie: ♫♫ **DVD:** ♫♫
Anchor Bay (Cat #DV11384, UPC #013131 138498). Widescreen (2.35:1) anamorphic. Dolby Digital 5.1 Surround Stereo. $24.99. Keepcase. LANG: English. CAP: English. FEATURES: 30 chapter links ▪ Stephen King thumbnail bio ▪ Trailer.
1986 (R) 97m/C Emilio Estevez, Pat Hingle, Laura Harrington, Christopher Murney, Yeardley Smith, Stephen King; **D:** Stephen King; **W:** Stephen King; **C:** Armando Nannuzzi; **M:** AC-DC.

Maximum Risk

Once again (after *Double Impact*) Van Damme in a déjà vu storyline plays identical twins—a good French guy and a bad Russian guy—and when the Russkie is killed, his bro takes over his life to find out whodunit. Since sexy Henstridge is the late sib's squeeze, it could be worse. Hong Kong director Lam brings along all of his trademark fast-paced chases, explosions, and fights, so the film is energetic to a fault. DVD captures the frantic action with an image that ranges from good to very good. Same for sound. *—MM*

Movie: ♫♫½ **DVD:** ♫♫½
Columbia Tristar Home Video (Cat #27419, UPC #043396274198). Widescreen (2.35:1) letterboxed; full frame. Dolby Digital 5.1 Surround Stereo; Dolby Digital Surround. $24.98. Keepcase. LANG: English; French; Spanish. SUB: English; French; Spanish. FEATURES: Trailer ▪ 28 chapter links.
1996 (R) 100m/C Jean-Claude Van Damme, Natasha Henstridge, Jean-Hugues Anglade, Stephane Audran, Paul Ben-Victor, Zach Grenier, Frank Senger; **D:** Ringo Lam; **W:** Larry Ferguson; **C:** Alexander Grusynski; **M:** Robert Folk.

Maze

Even when judged by the loosey-goosey standards of anime, this one's pretty nutty. Even though this collection of three episodes of a series begins at the beginning, it seems to be in medias res, with a band of heroes who regularly switch identities squared off against vaguely religious bad guys and assorted monsters. The animation is a bit more stylized than most, and of about average clarity. Violence is

very bloody, and the film contains some nudity and snickering sexual material. To my taste, it's too silly for adults and too graphic for kids. Full-frame image might be a slight improvement over tape, but not by much. *—MM*

Movie: ♫♫ **DVD:** ♫♫½
Central Park Media/U.S. Manga Corps (Cat #6080, UPC #795243608020). Full frame. Dolby Digital Stereo. $24.99. Keepcase. LANG: English; Japanese. SUB: English; Japanese. FEATURES: 9 chapter links ▪ DVD-ROM features ▪ Trailer.
1996 85m/C JP **W:** Katsumi Hasegawa.

The McCullochs

Texas millionaire J. J. McCulloch (Tucker) is the kind of domineering patriarch whose kids wind up hating him and destroying their own lives. Stereotypical family saga set in 1949 is directed by Max Baer of *The Beverly Hillbillies* fame. The video looks good and features nice color definition (though some darker colors are muted). The soundtrack is adequate as well, though there is the occasional muffled line. *—MJT* **AKA:** The Wild McCullochs.

Movie: ♫½ **DVD:** ♫♫½
Anchor Bay (Cat #DV10994, UPC #013131 099492). Widescreen (1.85:1) anamorphic. Dolby Digital Mono. $24.98. Keepcase. LANG: English. FEATURES: 18 chapter links ▪ Theatrical trailer ▪ Talent bios.
1975 (PG) 93m/C Forrest Tucker, Julie Adams, Janice Heiden, Max Baer Jr., Don Grady, Chip Hand, Dennis Redfield, William Demarest, Harold J. Stone, Vito Scotti, James Gammon, Mike Mazurki; **D:** Max Baer Jr.; **W:** Max Baer Jr.; **C:** Fred W. Koenekamp; **M:** Ernest Gold.

Me Myself I

Pamela Drury (Griffiths) is a successful Sydney journalist who's also single, in her late 30s, and depressed by both situations. She moans about not marrying her long-ago beau Robert Dickson (Roberts) and, lo and behold, Pam's whisked into the life she could have had—marriage and mother of three in the suburbs. Of course, this Pam doesn't have a clue as to how her new life runs, which makes for some comic mileage. But it's the appealing Griffiths who holds all the unlikely yet clichéd situations together. The picture transfer is fantastic; colors are crisp and there is no bleeding or loss in clarity of darker colors whatsoever. Similarly, the 5.1 soundtrack is also quite good. Dialogue is crisp and additional soundtrack material is also impressive (other sound mixes on the disc lack the depth of this one). The audio commentary by director Karmel is both entertaining and insightful. *—MJT*

Movie: ♫♫ **DVD:** ♫♫♫
Columbia Tristar Home Video (Cat #05274, UPC #043396052741). Widescreen (1.85:1) anamorphic. Dolby Digital 5.1 Surround Sound; Dolby Surround Sound. $29.95. Keepcase. LANG: English; French. SUB: English; French. FEATURES: 28 chapter links ▪ Commentary: director Pip

Karmel ▪ Cast and crew bios ▪ Theatrical trailer.
1999 (R) 104m/C *AU* Rachel Griffiths, David Roberts, Sandy Winton; **D:** Pip Karmel; **W:** Pip Karmel; **C:** Graeme Lind; **M:** Charlie Chan.

Mean Guns

Lots of mayhem will redeem this silly plot for the action fan. Moon (Ice-T) lures 100 assassins to a new unopened prison with the promise of $10 million for the last three men standing. Lou (Lambert) and Marcus (Halsey) are his rivals. The extreme care taken with this video premiere is evidenced by the typographical error in the introductory newspaper story, "A new prinson opens tomorrow." Fleck and grain make the unsaturated image identical to tape. Colors are bleached almost to black and white. *—MM*

Movie: ♫♫ **DVD:** ♫♫
Trimark Home Video (Cat #6839). Full frame. Dolby Digital Surround Stereo. $24.99. Keepcase. LANG: English. SUB: French; Spanish. CAP: English. FEATURES: Trailers ▪ Talent files ▪ 8 chapter links.
1997 (R) 90m/C Ice-T, Christopher Lambert, Michael Halsey, Deborah Van Valkenburgh, Tina Cote, Yuji Okumoto; **D:** Albert Pyun; **W:** Andrew Witham, Nat Whitcomb; **C:** George Mooradian; **M:** Tony Riparetti.

Mean Season

A vicious mass murderer makes Miami crime reporter Mal Anderson (Russell) his confidante during a series of killings. In time, his intentions become clear as the tensions and headlines grow with each gruesome slaying. Varying degrees of responsibility are part of the story and that helps to raise the film above the norm for the overworked serial-killer subgenre. Russell turns in another fine understated performance. DVD image ranges between very good and excellent. Mono sound is fine for the story. *—MM*

Movie: ♫♫♫ **DVD:** ♫♫♫
MGM Home Entertainment (Cat #10018 49, UPC #027616861177). Widescreen (1.85:1) letterboxed. Dolby Digital Mono. $14.95. Keepcase. LANG: English; French; Spanish. SUB: French; Spanish. FEATURES: 16 chapter links ▪ Trailer.
1985 (R) 106m/C Kurt Russell, Mariel Hemingway, Richard Jordan, Richard Masur, Andy Garcia, Joe Pantoliano, Richard Bradford, William Smith; **D:** Phillip Borsos; **W:** Christopher Crowe; **M:** Lalo Schifrin.

The Meanest Men in the West

Two criminal half-brothers (Bronson and Marvin) battle frontier law and each other in a made-for-TV production that combines two episodes of the *Virginian* series. Given the modest production values and evident wear, it's no surprise that neither image nor sound improves on VHS tape. The film

is the television debut of director Samuel Fuller. —*MM*
Movie: ♫ **DVD:** ♫½
Goodtimes Entertainment (Cat #81017). Full frame. $19.98. Snapper. *LANG:* English. *SUB:* French; Spanish. *CAP:* English. *FEATURES:* 18 chapter links.
1976 (PG) 92m/C Charles Bronson, Lee Marvin, Lee J. Cobb, James Drury, Albert Salmi, Charles Grodin; *D:* Samuel Fuller; *W:* Charles S. Dubin; *C:* Lionel Lindon, Alric Edens; *M:* Hal Mooney.

Meet John Doe [Image]

This is the cleanest version of Capra's film available on disc to date. The image is still fuzzy by contemporary standards, but compared to other works of its era, it looks and sounds very good. Several other editions of the public domain title are also available. —*MM*
Movie: ♫♫♫ **DVD:** ♫♫½
Image Entertainment (Cat #HRS9449, UPC #014381944921). Full frame. $24.99. Snapper. *LANG:* English. *FEATURES:* 7 chapter links.
1941 123m/B Gary Cooper, Barbara Stanwyck, Edward Arnold, James Gleason, Walter Brennan, Spring Byington, Gene Lockhart, Regis Toomey, Ann Doran, Rod La Rocque; *D:* Frank Capra; *W:* Robert Riskin; *C:* George Barnes; *M:* Dimitri Tiomkin. *AWARDS: NOM:* Oscars '41: Story.

Meet the Parents

There's a mean streak in this sleeper hit comedy. Greg Focker (Stiller) must gain the approval of Jack Byrnes (De Niro) before he can propose to daughter Pam (Polo). During a weekend visit with the family, everything goes wrong—from white lies to electrocution. The curious chemistry between Stiller and De Niro accounts for much of the film's popularity. Comments about image and sound quality are unnecessary. This one looks as good as a big-budget release can look, and the disc comes with a full raft of extras. The commentary track by director Roach and editor Poll is more technically oriented than the cast track. —*MM*
Movie: ♫♫♫ **DVD:** ♫♫♫½
Universal Studios Home Video (Cat #211 33). Widescreen (1.85:1) anamorphic. DTS 5.1 Surround; Dolby Digital 5.1 Surround. $29.98. Keepcase. *LANG:* English; French. *SUB:* English. *FEATURES:* 20 chapter links ● Deleted scenes and outtakes ● Commentary: Roach, Poll ● Commentary: Stiller, De Niro, Roach, producer Rosenthal ● Lie detector test ● Forecaster game ● Production notes ● Talent files ● Trailer ● DVD-ROM features.
2000 (PG-13) 108m/C Ben Stiller, Robert De Niro, Teri Polo, Blythe Danner, James Rebhorn, Jon Abrahams, Owen C. Wilson, Phyllis George, Kali Rocha, Tom McCarthy, Nicole DeHuff; *D:* Jay Roach; *W:* Jim Herzfeld, John Hamburg; *C:* Peter James; *M:* Randy Newman. *AWARDS: NOM:* Oscars '00: Song ("A Fool in Love").

Mein Kampf: Hitler's Rise and Fall

Much of this documentary is made of footage filmed by German SS troops. Taking the title of Hitler's autobiography, it begins with a thumbnail history of the origins of Nazism and then goes on to show the horrors of the war in Europe. Visually, the black-and-white footage is not much better than tape, with the expected wear visible throughout. It's much better than the second feature on the disc, "Adolf Hitler," which is so fuzzy and filled with registration difficulties that it's barely watchable. —*MM*
Movie: ♫♫♫ **DVD:** ♫♫½
VCI Home Video (Cat #8253, UPC #08985 9825323). Full frame. Dolby Digital Mono. $19.99. Keepcase. *LANG:* English. *FEATURES:* 18 chapter links ● Trailers ● Photo gallery ● Historical notes.
1960 117m/B *D:* Erwin Leiser; *W:* Erwin Leiser.

Melody Time

Walt Disney's post-war (released in 1948), feature-length animated anthology would not have been created in today's politically correct creative climate. Fortunately, the DVD presentation arrives almost intact (the "Peco Bill" sequence got "tweaked" a bit), but references to God, the power of prayer, and the Bible managed to avoid the PC scissors. Classic segments include: "The Legend of Johnny Appleseed," "Little Toot," and "Pecos Bill," along with such wonders as the tender "Once Upon a Wintertime," the upbeat "Bumble Boogie," and back-to-back animation gems, "Trees" and "Blame It on the Samba." Three classic cartoons from the Walt Disney library have been added as bonus features to round out the presentation: "Casey Bats Again" (1954), "Donald Applecore" (1952), and "Lambert the Sheepish Lion" (1952). A magnificent animation treasure is marred by an irritating and poorly designed menu interface. This can be overcome by pressing the "skip" button several times once the disc loads to finally get to the main menu. —*RJT*
Movie: ♫♫♫ **DVD:** ♫♫♫
Buena Vista Home Entertainment (Cat #19603, UPC #717951008541). Full frame. Dolby Digital Surround Stereo. $29.99. Keepcase. *LANG:* English; Spanish; French. *SUB:* English; Spanish for "Trees" segment only. *CAP:* English. *FEATURES:* 9 chapter markers ● 3 bonus cartoons.
1948 75m/C *D:* Clyde Geronimi; *V:* Dennis Day, Ethel Smith, Buddy Clark, Bob Nolan, The Andrews Sisters, Frances Langford.

Men in Black [CS]

Charm, wit, and some outrageous insect-based aliens make a winning, if somewhat dry cosmic combination. Agents Kay (Jones) and Jay (Smith) are top-secret government operatives assigned to investigate alien visitations on Earth. They must stop terrorist extraterrestrial D'Onofrio from instigating an intergalactic disaster.

This first-rate DVD makes the most of the film's special effects and even the lower-priced "Collector's Series" contains oodles of extras. (The more expensive, double-disc "limited edition" cat. 05291 has even more.) If anything, both image and 5.1 sound are superior to the theatrical experience. I could find no flaws, even in the many dark scenes. The commentary track by Jones and Sonnenfeld is done *MST3K*-style with front-row silhouettes. A separate DTS stereo Collector's Series is also available. —*MM* **AKA:** MIB.
Movie: ♫♫♫ **DVD:** ♫♫♫½
Columbia Tristar Home Video (Cat #82659, UPC #043396826595). Widescreen (1.85:1) letterboxed. Dolby Digital 5.1 Surround Stereo; Dolby Digital Surround Stereo. $29.99. Keepcase. *LANG:* English; French. *SUB:* English; French; Spanish. *FEATURES:* 27 chapter links ● Visual commentary: Jones and Sonnenfeld ● Booklet ● Deconstruction of tunnel scene ● Extended and alternate scenes ● "Making of" documentary ● Music video ● Production notes, storyboards, and trailers.
1997 (PG-13) 98m/C Tommy Lee Jones, Will Smith, Linda Fiorentino, Rip Torn, Vincent D'Onofrio, Tony Shalhoub, Carel Struycken, Sergio Calderon, Siobhan Fallon; *D:* Barry Sonnenfeld; *W:* Edward Solomon; *C:* Don Peterman; *M:* Danny Elfman. *AWARDS:* Oscars '97: Makeup; MTV Movie Awards '98: Song ("Men in Black"), Fight (Will Smith/alien); *NOM:* Oscars '97: Art Dir./Set Dec., Orig. Mus./Comedy Score; Golden Globes '98: Film—Mus./Comedy; MTV Movie Awards '98: Film, On-Screen Duo (Tommy Lee Jones/Will Smith), Comedic Perf. (Smith).

Men of Honor

Inspired by his poor-farmer father, Carl Brashear (Gooding) determines to make something of his life. The film (based on a true story) follows his struggle as he fights racism to become a Navy diver. Brashear's instructor, Sunday (De Niro), initially fights against him, but eventually becomes his ally. After Brashear undergoes a crippling accident, Sunday helps him recuperate to prove that he can still continue his career as a diver. This epic drama tells a thrilling, moving story in the grand Hollywood tradition. Sunday's transition seems a bit abrupt, and the occasional cliché jars, but Gooding Jr. and the rest of the cast are excellent. De Niro's performance is fairly strong, but his hammy racist Southern cracker shtick (which he's been doing ad nauseam since *Cape Fear*) is becoming a bit tired. The disc does justice to the beautiful photography with a splendid, stunning transfer. The Surround sound is rich, well recorded, and exciting. The deleted scenes are interesting and the alternate ending (which is really an epilogue) is fascinating, but was wisely discarded. Fans of the film will enjoy the treasure trove of extras provided on the disc. The audio commentary is excellent and filled with fascinating details and historical information. —*DG* **AKA:** Navy Diver.

Movie: ♪♪♪ *DVD:* ♪♪♪♪
CBS/Fox Video (Cat #2001665, UPC #024 54301665). Widescreen (2.35:1) anamorphic. Dolby Digital 5.1; Dolby Surround. $29.98. Keepcase. *LANG:* English; French. *SUB:* English; Spanish. *CAP:* English. *FEATURES:* 18 chapter links • Insert card with chapter listings • Alternate ending • Deleted scenes • Animated storyboard • Commentary: Tillman Jr., Gooding, producer Robert Teitel • "Making of" featurette • "Master Chief: A Tribute to Carl Brashear" documentary • "Win" Music Video • Theatrical trailer and TV spots. **2000 (R) 129m/C** Cuba Gooding Jr., Robert De Niro, Charlize Theron, David Keith, Michael Rapaport, Hal Holbrook, Powers Boothe, Aunjanue Ellis, Joshua Leonard, David Conrad, Glynn Turman, Holt McCallany, Lonette McKee, Carl Lumbly; *D:* George Tillman Jr.; *W:* Scott Marshall Smith; *C:* Anthony B. Richmond; *M:* Mark Isham.

Men of War
Judging by the box art, this appears to be just another formula shoot-'em-up, but John Sayles has written a typically humanistic yet fast-moving script. Ex–Special Forces mercenary Nick Gunner (Lundgren) is recruited off a snowy Chicago street to put together a small team to destabilize the government of a small island somewhere in the China Sea, though his slick corporate employers are coy about their reasons. In a sequence pulled straight from *The Seven Samurai*, he puts together the usual motley crew of colorfully offbeat characters. Before they reach the island, they run afoul of Gunner's old enemy Keefer (Goddard), a scenery-chomping, bare-chested villain who really cuts loose and steals the film. The result is a genuine sleeper. The widescreen DVD image and Surround sound are both far superior to VHS tape. —*MM*
Movie: ♪♪♪½ *DVD:* ♪♪♪½
Buena Vista Home Entertainment (Cat #21 355, UPC #786936141757). Widescreen (2.35:1) anamorphic. Dolby Digital Surround. $29.99. Keepcase. *LANG:* English. *CAP:* English. *FEATURES:* 19 chapter links. **1994 (R) 102m/C** Dolph Lundgren, Charlotte Lewis, B.D. Wong, Anthony John (Tony) Denison, Tim Guinee, Don Harvey, Tommy (Tiny) Lister, Trevor Goddard, Kevin Tighe; *D:* Perry Lang; *W:* John Sayles, Ethan Reiff, Cyrus Voris; *C:* Ronn Schmidt; *M:* Gerald Gouriet.

Mercy
Catherine Baker (Barkin) is a hard-drinking homicide detective investigating a serial killer with sexual kinks. Bombshell Vickie Kittrie (Wilson) reveals that each female victim belonged to an exclusive club that likes to experiment with the wilder side of life. And all the victims were patients of psychotherapist Dominick Broussard (Sands). Image quality of the widescreen presentation is of the highest quality; the full-frame version is also very good.

Although the film exhibits a bit of grain in select scenes, the DVD creates a very pleasant and stable image that is highly detailed. Colors are strong and nicely delineated with natural fleshtones. The blacks are deep and solid without breaking up, giving the image a good visual depth. Highlights are balanced and never overexposed, adding to the natural look. Audio is well produced and makes good use of the Surround capabilities both in action scenes and more quiet moments. —*GH/MM*
Movie: ♪♪ *DVD:* ♪♪♪
Columbia Tristar Home Video (Cat #5080). Widescreen (2.35:1) anamorphic; full frame. Dolby Digital Stereo. $24.95. Keepcase. *LANG:* English. *SUB:* English; Spanish; Chinese; Thai. *FEATURES:* Theatrical trailer • Talent files. **2000 (R) 94m/C** Ellen Barkin, Peta Wilson, Julian Sands, Wendy Crewson, Karen Young, Marshall Bell, Stephen Baldwin, Beau Starr, Bill MacDonald, Stewart Bick; *D:* Damian Harris; *W:* Damian Harris; *C:* Manuel Teran; *M:* B.C. Smith.

Mermaids
Mrs. Flax (Cher) is the flamboyant mother of two who hightails out of town whenever a relationship threatens to turn serious. Having moved some 18 times, her daughters Charlotte (Ryder), 15, and Kate (Ricci), 8, are a little the worse for the psychological wear. Charlotte aspires to be a nun, though she's Jewish; Kate holds her breath under water. Then Mrs. Flax meets Mr. Landsky (Hoskins). With the notable exception of Cher's blowsy approach, the acting in this multi-generational coming-of-age story is fine. On DVD, the softish image is never as bright as it could be, but that's not completely inappropriate for a '60s period piece. Sound is fine. —*MM*
Movie: ♪♪½ *DVD:* ♪♪
MGM Home Entertainment (Cat #10015 37, UPC #027616858481). Widescreen (1.85:1) anamorphic. Dolby Digital Surround Stereo; Mono. $19.98. Keepcase. *LANG:* English; French; Spanish. *SUB:* French; Spanish. *CAP:* English. *FEATURES:* 16 chapter links • Trailer. **1990 (PG-13) 110m/C** Cher, Winona Ryder, Bob Hoskins, Christina Ricci, Michael Schoeffling, Caroline McWilliams, Jan Miner; *D:* Richard Benjamin; *W:* June Roberts; *C:* Howard Atherton; *M:* Jack Nitzsche. *AWARDS:* Natl. Bd. of Review '90: Support. Actress (Ryder).

A Merry War
Insipid tale of self centered Englishman Comstock (Grant), who decides he wants to leave his regular job behind and become a poet. Rosemary (Bonham Carter) is his long-suffering girlfriend who, along with his sister, holds a job and tries to keep Comstock from sinking too low. He, however embraces lowness and finally decides to come back to the middle class only when Rosemary gets pregnant. Based on a story by George Orwell, the tale manages to make both the pursuit of

art and the better life seem ridiculous. Grant is always a pleasure to watch and makes the movie bearable. The transfer on this disc is amazingly crisp, clear, and sharp. If only the story were as well. —*CA*
AKA: Keep the Aspidistra Flying.
Movie: ♪♪½ *DVD:* ♪♪♪½
DVD International (Cat #DVDI0720, UPC #647715072023). Widescreen (1.85:1) letterboxed. $29.98. Keepcase. *LANG:* English. *FEATURES:* 20 chapter links • Commentary with producer and screenwriter • Cast and crew bios • Audio interview with composer • Isolated soundtrack • George Orwell background • Original U.S. and U.K. trailers. **1997 101m/C** Richard E. Grant, Helena Bonham Carter, Julian Wadham, Jim Carter, Harriet Walter, Liz Smith, Barbara Leigh-Hunt; *D:* Robert Bierman; *W:* Alan Plater; *C:* Giles Nuttgens; *M:* Mike Batt.

Mesa of Lost Women
A horrible little tale about Dr. Arana (Coogan) who creates a species of buxom tarantula women to well, we're not really not sure what the master plan is, but the giant spider puppet that attacks the doomed passengers of a plane crash is a not-to-be-missed look at special effects before computers. Also keep an eye out for camera shadows and stock footage. The transfer elements look like they were hidden under the giant spider puppet and the sound is fuzzy. Rental fare for hard-core lovers of drive-in classics. —*CA AKA:* Lost Women; Lost Women of Zarpa.
Movie: ♪ *DVD:* ♪½
Image Entertainment (Cat #ID8695C0DVD, UPC #014381869521). Full frame. Dolby Digital Mono. $24.99. Snapper. *LANG:* English. *FEATURES:* 12 chapter links • Theatrical trailer. **1952 70m/B** Jackie Coogan, Richard Travis, Allan Nixon, Mary Hill, Robert Knapp, Tandra Quinn, Lyle Talbot, Katherine Victor, Angelo Rossitto, Dolores Fuller; *D:* Ron Ormond, Herbert Tevos; *W:* Herbert Tevos; *C:* Gilbert Warrenton, Karl Struss; *M:* Hoyt Curtin.

Mesmerized
Based on the work by Jerzy Skolimowski, the film dramatizes the Victoria Thompson murder case in 1880s New Zealand. A teenaged orphan girl (Foster) marries an older man (Lithgow) and decides after years of abuse to kill him through hypnosis. The story is unengaging, though the lovely New Zealand landscape serves as a fitting contrast to the ominous tone. The so-so image of the no-frills disc is identical to VHS tape. —*MM AKA:* Shocked.
Movie: ♪♪ *DVD:* ♪
Tapeworm Video Distributors (Cat #2732). Full frame. $19.95. Keepcase. *LANG:* English. *FEATURES:* 10 chapter links. **1984 90m/C** *GB NZ AU* John Lithgow, Jodie Foster, Michael Murphy, Dan Shor, Harry Andrews; *D:* Michael Laughlin; *W:* Michael Laughlin; *C:* Louis Horvath; *M:* Georges Delerue.

The Messenger: The Story of Joan of Arc

Besson's take on the legendary 15th-century French teen martyr Joan of Arc (Jovovich) leans heavily on gory battle scenes, stylish cinematography, and spectacle to tell her story. After seeing her sister murdered and raped (actually in that order) by English soldiers, Joan begins to hear heavenly voices that tell her that she must free her country and king from the invaders. After a visit with the Dauphin, several bloody battles ensue. Joan is eventually captured, and put on trial for sorcery and heresy. Awaiting her fate, she has conversations with a character that is actually billed as her Conscience (Hoffman), which brings up questions in her mind whether she was really divinely inspired or merely a cake du fruit. This is a gorgeous DVD to view. The colors are saturated but completely natural. The detail and depth of field is stunning, particularly in the battle scenes. Blacks are so dark they meld to the black borders. The 5.1 sound completes the experience, at times opening the massive battlefields by putting the viewer in the midst of the clanging steel and death cries of the warriors; and at others amplifying the ambience inside a fortress's stone walls. The score is also delivered with energy or subtlety, depending on what the moment requires. Watch the included documentary to get a better perspective on the brutal times portrayed in the film. —JO

Movie: 🎬🎬🎬 **DVD:** 🎬🎬🎬🎬
Columbia Tristar Home Video (Cat #04607, UPC #043396046078). Widescreen (2.35:1) anamorphic. Dolby Digital 5.1; Dolby Surround. $27.95. Keepcase. *LANG:* English. *SUB:* English. *CAP:* English. *FEATURES:* 28 chapter links • Theatrical trailers • Talent files • Isolated music score • Documentary, "The Messenger: The Search for the Real Joan of Arc."
1999 (R) 148m/C Milla Jovovich, John Malkovich, Faye Dunaway, Dustin Hoffman, Pascal Greggory, Vincent Cassel, Tcheky Karyo, Richard Ridings, Desmond Harrington; **D:** Luc Besson; **W:** Luc Besson, Andrew Birkin; **C:** Thierry Arbogast; **M:** Eric Serra. *AWARDS: NOM:* Golden Raspberries '99: Worst Actress (Jovovich).

Meteor

American and Soviet scientists attempt to save the Earth from a fast-approaching meteor in this disaster dud. Destruction ravages parts of Hong Kong and the Big Apple. The transfer exhibits quite a bit of grain and occasional blemishes, and it is obvious from the presentation that the film could have used a restorative clean-up. Colors are well defined with deep blacks and good highlights, but the disc constantly exhibits a slight overemphasis of red tones. Signs of edge-enhancement are evident in select scenes. Mono audio sounds thin and breathless. —GH/MM

Movie: woof **DVD:** 🎬🎬
MGM Home Entertainment (UPC #027616 837424). Widescreen (2.35:1) letterboxed.

Dolby Digital Mono. $19.98. Keepcase. *LANG:* English. *SUB:* English; French; Spanish. *FEATURES:* Theatrical trailer.
1979 (PG) 107m/C Sean Connery, Natalie Wood, Karl Malden, Brian Keith, Martin Landau, Trevor Howard, Henry Fonda, Joseph Campanella, Richard Dysart; **D:** Ronald Neame; **W:** Stanley Mann; **C:** Paul Lohmann; **M:** Laurence Rosenthal. *AWARDS: NOM:* Oscars '79: Sound.

Midaq Alley

The title street is the focal point for a series of interrelated stories set in Mexico City. A father worries about his son's homosexuality; a young woman (Hayek) about to be married is tempted into prostitution; another lonely woman is attracted to a younger man. Both image and sound are excellent, easily the equal of similarly serious Hollywood dramas. Yellow English subtitles are burned in. —MM **AKA:** The Alley of Miracles; El Callejon de los Milagros.
Movie: 🎬🎬🎬 **DVD:** 🎬🎬🎬
Winstar Home Entertainment (Cat #5142). Full frame. $19.98. Keepcase. *LANG:* Spanish. *SUB:* English. *FEATURES:* 12 chapter links • Production credits • Awards • Filmographies.
1995 140m/C MX Ernesto Cruz, Maria Rojo, Salma Hayek, Bruno Bichir, Claudio Obregon, Delia Casanova, Margarita Sanz, Juan Manuel Bernal, Luis Felipe Tovar, Daniel Gimenez Cacho; **D:** Jorge Fons; **W:** Vicente Lenero; **C:** Carlos Marcovich; **M:** Lucia Alvarez.

Midnight

Jury foreman Edward Weldon's (Heggie) daughter Stella (Fox) is romantically involved with gangster Garboni (Bogart), who's interested in a particular case involving a woman who shot her lover. Though the story never really breaks free of its roots on the stage, it remains a timely meditation on the differences between a strict interpretation of the law and real justice. Though the film has been distributed under the title *Call It Murder* (in a bootleg edition, according to the box copy), this edition was made from an original master and it is in remarkable shape for a film so old. A few white specks are visible, and the sound has the thin quality of the era but the disc still earns a rating of good to very good. —MM **AKA:** Call It Murder.
Movie: 🎬🎬½ **DVD:** 🎬🎬½
Image Entertainment (Cat #ID5833DSDVD, UPC #014381583328). Full frame. Dolby Digital Stereo. $24.99. Snapper. *LANG:* English. *FEATURES:* 12 chapter links.
1934 74m/B Humphrey Bogart, Sidney (Sydney) Fox, O.P. Heggie, Henry Hull, Richard Whorf, Margaret Wycherly, Lynne Overman; **D:** Chester Erskine; **W:** Chester Erskine.

Midnight Confessions

Provocative nighttime DJ Vannesse (Hoyt) lures her listeners into revealing their sex-

ual fantasies. But when an obsessed fan begins killing women, her involvement is questioned by a police detective (Lynch). Full-frame image is a step down from tape. Large inexplicable areas of artifacts pop up from time to time. —MM
Movie: 🎬 **DVD:** 🎬
Digital Versatile Disc Ltd. (Cat #705). Full frame. $24.95. Keepcase. *LANG:* English.
1995 (R) 98m/C Carol Hoyt, Julie Strain, Monique Parent, Richard Lynch; **D:** Allan Shustak; **W:** Jake Jacobs, Allan Shustak, Marc Cushman, Timothy O'Rawe; **C:** Tom Frazier; **M:** Scott Singer.

Midnight Dancers

Three brothers are trapped in a world of exotic dancing and prostitution in Manila. While slightly exotic, it is more schlock than shock as far as gay films go. Banned in the Philippines, it's laughable in the realm of American film and falls just short of good soft porn, if there is such a thing. Basically, scenes of gyrating young Filipino men in briefs are interspersed with flaccid attempts at drama. The bad acting and pathetic dance numbers may send you running to *Showgirls* for refuge. Neither image nor sound is noticeably superior to VHS tape. —JAS
Movie: 🎬 **DVD:** 🎬🎬
First Run Features (Cat #NL, UPC #720229 909280). Full frame. $29.95. Keepcase. *LANG:* Filipino. *SUB:* English. *FEATURES:* 9 chapter links.
1994 115m/C PH Alex Del Rosario, Gandong Cervantes, Laurence David, Perla Bautista, Soxy Topacio; **D:** Mel Chionglo; **W:** Ricardo Lee; **C:** George Tutanes; **M:** Nonong Buenoamino.

The Midnight Hour

Made-for-TV horror comedy features a veritable who's who of Hollywood has-beens, but is not without its charms. Teenagers in Pitchford, Massachusetts, unknowingly release the vampire-witch Lucinda, who rises from the grave and summons her undead minions. Before long, the entire town has been werewolf/vampire/zombiefied and it's up to young Phil, and his new undead girlfriend, Sandy, to set things right. Surprisingly, the picture quality is quite good. The image is sharp, colors are solid, and only a few blemishes pop up here and there. The audio is a fairly subdued 2.0 Surround mix that is free from distortion but certainly won't tax your system by any means. Again, though, it's more than adequate considering the source materials. —MP/MM
Movie: 🎬 **DVD:** 🎬🎬½
Anchor Bay (Cat #11533). Full frame. Dolby Digital Stereo. $24.98. Keepcase. *LANG:* English.
1986 97m/C Shari Belafonte, LeVar Burton, Lee Montgomery, Dick Van Patten, Kevin McCarthy, Jonelle Allen, Peter DeLuise, Dedee Pfeiffer, Mark Blankfield; **D:** Jack Bender; **C:** Rexford Metz; **M:** Brad Fiedel.

Midnight Tease / Midnight Tease 2

Dancers are being murdered at the Club Fugazi, and stripper Samantha (Leigh) is having bad dreams. Is she the killer or the next victim? In the sequel, Jan Brennan (Kelley) goes undercover—as it were—at a strip club, to find out who killed her sister. The first film is actually an above-average video premiere, but the limitations of the budget give it an extremely grainy look that generates excessive artifacts in several scenes. The sequel isn't nearly as good a film but it looks better. Go figure. —MM
Movie: 🎬🎬½ **DVD:** 🎬½
New Concorde (Cat #NH5007D, UPC #736 991650077). Full frame. $19.98. Keepcase. *LANG:* English. *FEATURES:* 24 chapter links each • Trailers • Thumbnail bios.
1994 87m/C Cassandra Leigh, Rachel Reed, Edmund Halley, Ashlie Rhey, Todd Joseph; *D:* Scott Levy; *W:* Daniella Purcell; *C:* Dan E. Toback; *M:* Christopher Lennertz.

Midnight Tease 2

Please see review above.
Movie: 🎬
1995 (R) 93m/C Kimberly Kelley, Tane McClure, Ross Hagen; *D:* Richard Styles; *W:* Richard Styles; *C:* Gary Graver.

Mifune

Kresten (Berthelsen) has successfully hidden his roots from his new bride and his business associates, but when his father dies he must return to his ramshackle farm in the woods and care for his developmentally retarded brother. Across town, Liva (Hjejle), a feisty hooker, has run afoul of her pimp for peeing on the carpet of her latest john, the man who kicked her younger brother out of school. When Kresten finds himself overwhelmed at the farm, and Liva looks to get out of town quick, he hires her to be the new housekeeper and well-tensioned romance ensues. As typical as the story sounds, the writer never allows the characters to get comfortable enough in their roles to fall into clichés. The actors all bring a charm and empathy to their characters that make the viewer part of this strange little family. Though the end of the tale is inevitable, we find a certain satisfaction in the final redemption. It is worth noting that this is one in a series of films made by Dogma 95, a group of filmmakers who have vowed to use natural lights, sets, props, and clothing for their films. The farmhouse in which the film is shot was "as is" and all the actors did their own clothing and makeup. The director's commentary on the disc goes into this in more detail and is very interesting. Natural lighting must be great in Holland because the cinematography is beautiful. The color and clarity on the disc is well above average and the sound is good. —CA *AKA:* Mifunes Sidste Sang; Mifune's Last Song.
Movie: 🎬🎬½ **DVD:** 🎬🎬🎬

Columbia Tristar Home Video (Cat #05390, UPC #043396053908). Full frame. Dolby Digital Mono. $29.95. Keepcase. *LANG:* Danish. *SUB:* French; English; Spanish. *FEATURES:* 28 chapter links • Theatrical trailer • Commentary: director (in English).
1999 (R) 102m/C *DK* Iben Hjejle, Anders W. Berthelsen, Jesper Asholt, Emil Tarding, Anders (Tofting) Hove, Sofie Graboel, Paprika Steen, Mette Bratlann; *D:* Soeren Kragh-Jacobsen; *W:* Soeren Kragh-Jacobsen, Anders Thomas Jensen; *C:* Anthony Dod Mantle; *M:* Karl Bille, Christian Sievert.

The Mighty Peking Man

Quentin Tarantino's Rolling Thunder organization brings us this epically bizarre rip-off of *King Kong*. The title character is a guy in a moth-eaten gorilla suit who destroys sets of miniature villages and cities. It all has to do with the love of his life, a fetching blonde (Kraft) who runs around in a skimpy leather bikini. According to other sources (*Asian Cult Cinema* by Thomas Weisser), this disc is made from the European version of the film which contains fleeting nudity and a different ending. The frantic energy, delirious pace, and high-camp humor are the main attractions, though. The film is never boring and the humor is played for all it's worth. Minor surface wear is evident but the low-budget image has never been any great shakes. Besides, the many flaws are part of the fun. —MM *AKA:* Goliathon.
Movie: 🎬🎬🎬½ **DVD:** 🎬🎬🎬
Miramax Pictures Home Video (Cat #182 85, UPC #717951004758). Widescreen (2.35:1) anamorphic. Dolby Digital Mono. $29.99. Keepcase. *LANG:* English. *CAP:* English. *FEATURES:* 15 chapter links • Trailer.
1977 (PG-13) 91m/C *HK* Evelyn Kraft, Danny Lee, Chen Cheng-Fen; *D:* Ho Meng-Hua; *W:* Yi Kuang; *C:* Tsao Hui-Chi, Wu Cho-Hua; *M:* De Wolfe, Chuen Yung-Yu.

The Mighty Quinn

While investigating the murder of a rich white guy, Jamaican Police Chief Xavier Quinn (Washington) becomes convinced that the prime suspect, his childhood friend Maubee (Townsend), is innocent. The star is fine but the use of a double to make up for his lack of martial arts skills is appallingly apparent. The DVD image ranges between fair and very good. Some of the brighter reds and hot pinks bleed. Sound is fine. —MM
Movie: 🎬🎬½ **DVD:** 🎬🎬½
MGM Home Entertainment (Cat #10015 58, UPC #027616858689). Widescreen (1.85:1) letterboxed. Dolby Digital Surround Stereo; Mono. $19.98. Keepcase. *LANG:* English; French. *SUB:* French; Spanish. *FEATURES:* 16 chapter links • Trailer.
1989 (R) 98m/C Denzel Washington, Robert Townsend, James Fox, Mimi Rogers, M. Emmet Walsh, Sheryl Lee Ralph, Esther Rolle, Art Evans, Norman Beaton, Keye Luke; *D:* Carl Schenkel; *W:*

Hampton Fancher; *C:* Jacques Steyn; *M:* Anne Dudley.

Mikey

In the evil-child sub-genre, this is a relatively weak but expensively staged entry. It lacks the emotional power of *The Other* and the strong performance of Patty McCormack in *The Bad Seed*. Even though he's offed his entire family before the first ten minutes, Mikey (Bonsall) isn't believably threatening. He's a troubled, manipulative psychoboy who's a young version of *The Stepfather*. The adult character actors do well with the unsurprising script. The extras are all that differentiate the DVD from tape. —MM
Movie: 🎬 **DVD:** 🎬🎬
Studio Home Entertainment (Cat #4045). Full frame. $24.95. *LANG:* English. *FEATURES:* 18 chapter links • Filmographies • Trailer.
1992 (R) 92m/C Brian Bonsall, John Diehl, Lyman Ward, Josie Bissett, Ashley Laurence, Mimi (Meyer) Craven, Whitby Hertford; *D:* Dennis Dimster; *W:* Jonathan Glassner; *C:* Thomas Jewett; *M:* Tim Truman.

The Million Dollar Hotel

Wem Wenders and an ensemble cast attempt to work some of the same material handled so well in *American Beauty* and *Magnolia*. Story revolves around the suicide (by jumping from the roof) of Tom Tom (Davies). Mel Gibson plays Skinner, a literally stiff-necked FBI agent; he wears a heavy metal brace. On DVD, the film generally looks terrific, with a sharp, dark-toned image that's marred only by some artifacts in tight intricate patterns of tile and the like. Sound is good, too. On their soft-spoken commentary track, director Wenders and rocker Bono stress the positive, not the many controversies that surrounded the theatrical release, where Gibson was less than completely complimentary about the project to the press. —MM
Movie: 🎬🎬🎬 **DVD:** 🎬🎬🎬
Studio Home Entertainment (Cat #7705). Widescreen anamorphic. Dolby Digital 5.1 Surround Stereo. $24.99. Keepcase. *LANG:* English. *SUB:* English; French; Spanish. *FEATURES:* 30 chapter links • Interviews • Trailer • Commentary: Wenders and Bono • Behind-the-scenes footage.
1999 (R) 122m/C Conrad Roberts, Mel Gibson, Jeremy Davies, Milla Jovovich, Jimmy Smits, Peter Stormare, Amanda Plummer, Gloria Stuart, Tom Bower, Donal Logue, Bud Cort, Julian Sands, Tim Roth, Richard Edson, Harris Yulin, Charlaine Woodard; *D:* Wim Wenders; *W:* Nicholas Klein; *C:* Phedon Papamichael; *M:* Brian Eno, Bono, Daniel Lanois, John Hassell.

The Millionaire's Express

Chin Fong-Tin (director Hung) returns to his village and hopes to save it with a plan

to derail the local train, which carries a large number of wealthy passengers. This crazed martial arts comedy has the sensibility of a spaghetti western and a zippy pace. Sammo Hung is a gifted comedian and he does some very good work here. This is one of the better-looking Hong Kong imports. The 5.1 Surround is nicely employed, too. —*MM* *AKA:* Shanghai Express; Fu Gui Lie Che.
Movie: ♪♪½ *DVD:* ♪♪½
Tai Seng Video Marketing (Cat #5374). Widescreen letterboxed. Dolby Digital 5.1 Surround Stereo. $49.95. Keepcase. *LANG:* Cantonese; Mandarin. *SUB:* Bahasa Ind. & Mal.; Chinese Simp. & Trad.; English; Japanese; Korean; Thai; Vietnamese. *FEATURES:* 8 chapter links ▪ Talent files ▪ Trailers.
1986 107m/C *HK* Sammo Hung, Yuen Biao, Cynthia Rothrock, Richard Norton, Yukari Oshima; *D:* Sammo Hung; *W:* Sammo Hung.

Milo

Four young girls are lured to the home of creepy kid Milo (Metchik) where one of them is murdered. Sixteen years later, the girls are reunited, and it appears that the psycho-kid is still around. The filmmakers attempt to do some interesting things with the standard slasher/stalker formula, and the actors, particularly Jostyn and Schiavelli, are fine, but there's really not enough that's original to recommend the film beyond horror circles. On disc, sound enjoys more of an improvement than image, which is only slightly better than tape. —*MM*
Movie: ♪♪½ *DVD:* ♪♪½
Studio Home Entertainment (Cat #7075). Full frame. Dolby Digital Stereo. $24.95. Keepcase. *LANG:* English. *SUB:* Spanish. *FEATURES:* Cast and crew thumbnail bios ▪ Trailer ▪ 12 chapter links.
1998 (R) 94m/C Jennifer Jostyn, Maya McLaughlin, Asher Metchik, Paula Cale, Vincent Schiavelli, Antonio Fargas, Rae'ven (Alyia Larrymore) Kelly, Walter Olkewicz; *D:* Pascal Franchot; *W:* Craig Mitchell; *C:* Yuri Neyman; *M:* Kevin Manthei.

The Minus Man

Van Seigert (Wilson) is the blandest, nicest serial killer you're ever likely to meet. A drifter, he has settled in a small California town where he boards with a troubled married couple, Doug (Cox) and Jane (Ruehl), who come to think of the ever-smiling Van as a surrogate son. Van befriends lonely Ferrin (Garofalo) and calmly proceeds to off the locals. Eerie thriller offers no explanations for Van's behavior, which makes it all the creepier. On DVD, the picture is quite clear, showing only some minor defects in the source material. The framing is accurate and the colors on the disc are very nice. Audio is adequate throughout, but really excels during a hallucination sequence at the one hour and two minute mark, where strange sounds fill the rear speakers. Also, don't

miss the theatrical trailer on the DVD. It's a must-see. —*ML/MM*
Movie: ♪♪ *DVD:* ♪♪♪
Artisan Entertainment (Cat #10165). Widescreen (1.85:1) anamorphic. Dolby Digital 5.1 Surround Stereo. $19.98. Keepcase. *LANG:* English. *FEATURES:* Theatrical trailer ▪ Video trailer ▪ Talent files ▪ Production notes ▪ Serial killer information.
1999 (R) 112m/C Owen C. Wilson, Brian Cox, Mercedes Ruehl, Janeane Garofalo, Dwight Yoakam, Dennis Haysbert, Eric Mabius, Sheryl Crow, Larry Miller; *D:* Hampton Fancher; *W:* Hampton Fancher; *C:* Bobby Bukowski; *M:* Marco Beltrami.

Mio in the Land of Faraway

Living with his tyrannical grandmother, young Bosse (Pickard) finds himself transported to a magic land where he is known as Mio and finds his father (Bottoms). Compared to similar big-budget Hollywood children's fantasies, this Norwegian/Swedish production features so-so special effects and acting. A very young Christian Bale steals the show as the best friend. Image is acceptable; sound is a bit better. —*MM* *AKA:* The Land of Faraway; Mio min Mio.
Movie: ♪♪ *DVD:* ♪♪
Anchor Bay (Cat #DV11321, UPC #013131 132199). Widescreen (1.85:1) anamorphic. Dolby Digital Surround Stereo. $24.98. Keepcase. *LANG:* English. *FEATURES:* 25 chapter links ▪ Trailer.
1987 (PG) 99m/C *SW NO* Timothy Bottoms, Susannah York, Christopher Lee, Nicholas Pickard, Christian Bale; *D:* Vladimir Grammatikov; *W:* William Aldridge; *M:* Benny Andersson, Bjorn Ulvaes.

The Miracle Worker

Film depicts the unconventional methods that teacher Anne Sullivan (Bancroft) used to help the deaf and blind Helen Keller (Duke) adjust to the world around her and shows the relationship that built between the two courageous women. An intense, moving experience. William Gibson adapted his own play for the screen. The excellent video transfer showcases nice, crisp definition. This is, quite simply, the best this film has ever looked for home viewing. Some scenes are a bit grayer than they should be, but these instances are negligible. The soundtrack features clear and understandable dialogue as well as a decent musical score. The only flaw with the disc, apart from the lack of substantial extras, is the quality of the theatrical trailer provided. The state of the trailer is so atrocious it seems to have been pulled from the dumpster of a film archive somewhere. —*MJT*
Movie: ♪♪♪½ *DVD:* ♪♪½
MGM Home Entertainment (Cat #10015 88, UPC #027616858986). Widescreen (1.66:1) letterboxed. Dolby Digital Mono. $19.98. Keepcase. *LANG:* English; French;

Spanish. *SUB:* French; Spanish. *FEATURES:* 16 chapter links ▪ Theatrical trailer.
1962 107m/B Anne Bancroft, Patty Duke, Victor Jory, Inga Swenson, Andrew Prine, Beah Richards; *D:* Arthur Penn; *W:* William Gibson; *C:* Ernesto Caparros; *M:* Laurence Rosenthal. *AWARDS:* Oscars '62: Actress (Bancroft), Support. Actress (Duke); British Acad. '62: Actress (Bancroft); Natl. Bd. of Review '62: Actress (Bancroft); *NOM:* Oscars '62: Adapt. Screenplay, Costume Des. (B&W), Director (Penn).

The Miracle Worker

Hallie Kate Eisenberg and Alison Elliott aren't going to make anyone forget Patty Duke and Anne Bancroft, but they do acceptable work in this made-for-TV adaptation of the famous story. Softish image is only a slight improvement over VHS tape and broadcast. —*MM*
Movie: ♪♪½ *DVD:* ♪♪½
Buena Vista Home Entertainment (Cat #22 730, UPC #786936154924). Full frame. Dolby Digital Surround Stereo. $29.99. Keepcase. *LANG:* English. *CAP:* English. *FEATURES:* 26 chapter links.
2000 90m/C Hallie Kate Eisenberg, Alison Elliott, David Strathairn, Lucas Black, Kate Greenhouse; *D:* Nadia Tass; *W:* Monte Merrick; *C:* David Parker; *M:* William Goldstein.

The Mirror Crack'd

In one of the best screen adaptations of Agatha Christie, Miss Marple (Lansbury) must deduce the identity of a killer while a troupe of American movie stars are shooting a film in her quaint little village. A veteran cast is in fine form with formulaic but thoroughly enjoyable material. The image is excellent, showing virtually no wear for a film this old. Mono sound is acceptable and that's all that's needed. —*MM*
Movie: ♪♪♪ *DVD:* ♪♪♪
Anchor Bay (Cat #DV11432, UPC #013131 143294). Widescreen (1.85:1) anamorphic. Dolby Digital Mono. $24.98. Keepcase. *LANG:* English. *FEATURES:* 27 chapter links ▪ Trailer ▪ TV spots ▪ Talent files.
1980 (PG) 105m/C *GB* Angela Lansbury, Wendy Morgan, Margaret Courtenay, Charles Gray, Maureen Bennett, Carolyn Pickles, Elizabeth Taylor, Rock Hudson, Kim Novak, Tony Curtis, Edward Fox, Geraldine Chaplin, Pierce Brosnan; *D:* Guy Hamilton; *W:* Barry Sandler; *C:* Christopher Challis; *M:* John Cameron.

Mirror, Mirror

Curious feminist horror borrows liberally from *Beetlejuice, The Amityville Horror, Carrie,* and several other Stephen King works. Oddball newcomer Megan (Rainbow Harvest) has a hard time adjusting to high school in a small town. An antique mirror gives her supernatural powers that she uses to entice cute boys and to exact revenge upon the more popular girls. The pale, heavily grained image is essentially

identical to VHS tape. Stereo sound is superior. —*MM*
Movie: ♫♫½ **DVD:** ♫♫
Anchor Bay (Cat #DV11248, UPC #013131 124897). Full frame. Dolby Digital Stereo. $24.99. Keepcase. *LANG:* English. *FEATURES:* 24 chapter links.
1990 (R) 105m/C Karen Black, Rainbow Harvest, Kristin Dattilo-Hayward, Ricky Paull Goldin, Yvonne De Carlo, William Sanderson, Charlie Spradling, Ann Hearn, Stephen Tobolowsky; *D:* Marina Sargenti; *W:* Marina Sargenti; *C:* Robert Brinkmann; *M:* Jimmy Lifton.

Mirror, Mirror 2: Raven Dance

Silly sequel has yet another teenaged girl (Wells) falling under the thrall of a magic mirror. The effects range from a guy in a silly rubber suit to some really good, inventive work done with lights and computers. The violence is too outlandish to be offensive. A cast of horror vets including Roddy McDowall, Sally Kellerman, William Sanderson, Veronica Cartwright, and several continuity errors are part of the fun, too. Full-frame image is no improvement over VHS. —*MM*
Movie: ♫½ **DVD:** ♫♫
Anchor Bay (Cat #DV11249, UPC #013131 124996). Full frame. Dolby Digital Stereo. $24.99. Keepcase. *LANG:* English. *FEATURES:* 24 chapter links.
1994 (R) 91m/C Tracy Wells, Roddy McDowall, Sally Kellerman, Veronica Cartwright, William Sanderson, Lois Nettleton; *D:* Jimmy Lifton; *W:* Jimmy Lifton, Virginia Perfili; *C:* Troy Cook; *M:* Jimmy Lifton.

Mirror, Mirror 3: The Voyeur

This alternative wonder begins with a ritual suicide (sort of) by Cassandra (Parent) because she can't be with her lover Anthony (co-producer Drago) while her drug-dealing husband has stashed a briefcase full of cash in the living room of the empty mansion where they live. The recurring image of two raw rotisserie chickens—apparently meant to represent the lovers—is an appropriately daft touch. The two directors might have been making different movies that were inexplicably intermixed. Sound and image are identical to VHS tape. —*MM*
Movie: ♫½ **DVD:** ♫♫
Anchor Bay (Cat #DV11250, UPC #013131 125092). Full frame. Dolby Digital Stereo. $24.99. Keepcase. *LANG:* English. *FEATURES:* 18 chapter links.
1996 91m/C Billy Drago, Monique Parent, David Naughton, Mark Ruffalo, Elizabeth Baldwin, Richard Cansino; *D:* Rachel Gordon, Virginia Perfili; *W:* Steve Tymon; *C:* Nils Erickson.

Misery

Author Paul Sheldon (Caan) decides to quit writing a popular series of novels and kills off his character Misery Chastain. A freak automobile accident in a Colorado blizzard leaves him helpless and in the care of Annie Wilkes (Bates), who claims to be his "number one fan." She's also a psychotic killer and Kathy Bates won an Oscar for her carefully modulated performance. Caan is almost as good in a much less flashy part. The whole film is one of the better adaptations of Stephen King. Chapter 21 contains one of the most frightening moments you'll ever see. Generally, the DVD image is fine. Some problems crop with a flashing plaid jacket, and some mild artifacts intrude in the brightest snow scenes. This is such a superb horror film that commentary tracks are definitely called for. —*MM*
Movie: ♫♫♫½ **DVD:** ♫♫½
MGM Home Entertainment (Cat #1000833). Widescreen letterboxed; full frame. Dolby Digital Surround. $19.98. Keepcase. *LANG:* English. *FEATURES:* 25 chapter links • Trailer • Teaser.
1990 (R) 107m/C James Caan, Kathy Bates, Lauren Bacall, Richard Farnsworth, Frances Sternhagen, Graham Jarvis; *D:* Rob Reiner; *W:* William Goldman; *C:* Barry Sonnenfeld; *M:* Marc Shaiman. *AWARDS:* Oscars '90: Actress (Bates); Golden Globes '91: Actress—Drama (Bates).

The Misfits

A burnt-out divorcee (Monroe) befriends an aging cowboy (Gable), a mechanic (Wallach), and a rodeo rider (Clift), and finds herself on a mustang roundup with them. Black-and-white image is excellent throughout. Younger viewers might expect more punch from the soundtrack in the final scenes, but it's an accurate re-creation of the original. What's really missing here is a commentary track by a film historian who could have provided some background about the importance of the film in the careers of all concerned, particularly Gable and Monroe, who were making their final screen appearances. The stories surrounding the making of the picture are the stuff of legend and some of them are even true. —*MM*
Movie: ♫♫♫ **DVD:** ♫♫♫
MGM Home Entertainment (Cat #100020 63, UPC #027616862938). Widescreen (1.85:1) letterboxed. Dolby Digital Mono. $19.98. Keepcase. *LANG:* English; French; Spanish. *SUB:* French; Spanish. *FEATURES:* 16 chapter links • Trailer.
1961 124m/B Clark Gable, Marilyn Monroe, Montgomery Clift, Thelma Ritter, Eli Wallach, James Barton, Estelle Winwood; *D:* John Huston; *W:* Arthur Miller; *C:* Russell Metty; *M:* Alex North.

Miss Congeniality

The sleeper mega-hit makes a suitably splashy appearance on DVD with all the extras. FBI agent Gracie Hart (producer Bullock) impersonates a contestant at the Miss United States pageant to catch a mad bomber. It's an action-comedy with the emphasis on comedy, where the star reveals an unexpected talent for slapstick timing. Add in a smart script with some very nice moments for the likes of Michael Caine, William Shatner, and Candice Bergen. Image and sound, of course, are excellent. On their commentary track, Sandra Bullock and writer/co-producer Marc Lawrence take a very lighthearted approach. Director Petrie is more technically oriented on his. Mainstream Hollywood movies are seldom this much fun. —*MM*
Movie: ♫♫♫ **DVD:** ♫♫♫½
Warner Home Video, Inc. (Cat #18976). Widescreen anamorphic. $26.98. Snapper. *LANG:* English; French. *SUB:* English; French. *FEATURES:* 34 chapter links • Commentary: Sandra Bullock, Marc Lawrence • Commentary: Donald Petrie • 2 documentaries • Talent files • Trailer.
2000 (PG-13) 111m/C Sandra Bullock, Benjamin Bratt, Michael Caine, William Shatner, Ernie Hudson, Candice Bergen, Heather Burns, Melissa De Sousa, Steve Monroe, John DiResta, Jennifer Gareis, Wendy Raquel Robinson; *D:* Donald Petrie; *W:* Donald Petrie, Marc Lawrence; *C:* Laszlo Kovacs; *M:* Ed Shearmur.

Missile to the Moon

Remake of *Cat Women of the Moon* is archetypal '50s sci-fi. A semi-mad scientist has a moon rocket in the backyard. Just as he's ready to test it, a couple of escaped convicts show up. Off they go to the moon where they find rock monsters (Chapter 7) and space babes (Chapter 8), played by a bevy of "international beauty contest winners." Overall, the black-and-white image is very sharp and crisp, but one hounds-tooth jacket strobes madly whenever it moves in medium or long shots. Sound is fine. —*MM*
Movie: ♫♫½ **DVD:** ♫♫½
Image Entertainment (Cat #ID8687CODVD, UPC #014381868722). Full frame. Dolby Digital Mono. $24.99. Snapper. *LANG:* English. *FEATURES:* 16 chapter links • Photo gallery.
1959 78m/B Gary Clarke, Cathy Downs, K.T. Stevens, Laurie Mitchell, Michael Whalen, Nina Bara, Richard Travis, Tommy Cook, Marjorie Hellen; *D:* Richard Cunha; *W:* Vincent Fotre, H.E. Barrie; *C:* Meredith Nicholson; *M:* Nicholas Carras.

Missing in Action

Perhaps the most egregious and jingoistic of the Vietnamese-are-still-holding-Americans action flicks that appeared in the '80s makes a shaky transition to DVD. The image is so grainy that even simple background wallpaper is littered with artifacts in some scenes. Well below average in all respects. —*MM*
Movie: ♫ **DVD:** ♫
20th Century Fox Home Entertainment (Cat #1000759, UPC #027616850805). Widescreen letterboxed; full frame. Dolby Digital Mono. $24.99. Keepcase. *LANG:* English. *SUB:* French; Spanish. *CAP:* English. *FEATURES:* Trailer • 28 chapter links.
1984 (R) 101m/C Chuck Norris, M. Emmet Walsh; *D:* Joseph Zito; *W:* James Bruner; *C:* Joao Fernandes; *M:* Jay Chattaway.

The Mission

A Hong Kong mobster hires five gunmen to be his bodyguards. Everything's cool until one of them has an affair with the boss's wife. Director To revisits Tarantino-Woo territory. Most of the guys have bad haircuts and all of them have big pistols. Image is on the muted side compared to most Hong Kong imports with heavy aliasing and thin sound that's pumped up in the shootouts. Subtitles are located in the lower letterbox. —*MM* **AKA:** Cheung Fo.
Movie: ♫♫½ **DVD:** ♫♫
Tai Seng Video Marketing (Cat #252, UPC #4890391102522). Widescreen letterboxed. Dolby Digital 5.1 Surround Stereo; Dolby Digital Surround. $29.95. Keepcase. *LANG:* Cantonese; Mandarin. *SUB:* Traditional Chinese; Simplified Chinese; English. *FEATURES:* 9 chapter links • Trailer.
1999 84m/C *HK* Anthony Wong, Frances Ng, Roy Cheung, Simon Yam, Jackie Lui, Lam Suet; **D:** Johnny To; **W:** Nai-Hoi Yau.

Mission: Impossible 2

Screenwriter Robert Towne has admitted that his job was to figure out a plot upon which to hang several existing action sequences. He probably did as good a job as anyone could have, but the result is still a ridiculous concoction (even when compared to the ridiculous first film) about a lethal virus and its cure. Ethan Hunt (Cruise) handles most of the derring-do solo, making the film more akin to James Bond than the TV series. As thief and love-interest Nyah Hall, Thandie Newton looks fetching in tight T-shirts. Some excellent landscapes—Australia, Monument Valley—are really more important. On DVD, the action sequences benefit hugely from the 5.1 Surround mix that kicks in hard during the chase sequences. Watching the rest of the film at a normal volume level, the screaming motorcycles and other vehicles will push you back in your seat as they slam across the screen. The only technical flaw is a slightly clunky menu. Image, of course, is fine and the extras are suitably voluminous, but in the end this disc is all flash and no substance. It's particularly disappointing to fans of director Woo's fine early work. —*MM*
Movie: ♫ **DVD:** ♫♫♫
Paramount Home Video (Cat #33487, UPC #09736334874). Widescreen anamorphic. Dolby Digital 5.1 Surround Stereo; Dolby Digital Surround Stereo. $29.99. Keepcase. *LANG:* English; French. *SUB:* English. *FEATURES:* 17 chapter links • Commentary: John Woo • Stunts featurette • Action sequences featurette • "Making of" featurette • Alternative title sequence • Metallica music video • MTV stunt double parody • DVD-ROM features.
2000 (PG-13) 125m/C Tom Cruise, Anthony Hopkins, Dougray Scott, Thandie Newton, Ving Rhames, Brendan Gleeson, John Polson, Richard Roxburgh, Rade Serbedzija; **D:** John Woo; **W:** Robert Towne; **C:** Jeffrey L. Kimball; **M:** Hans Zimmer.

Mission to Mars

When the first manned flight to Mars ends in disaster, leaving Commander Luke Graham (Cheadle) the only survivor, NASA sends a rescue mission with his best friend Jim (Sinise), married astronauts Woody (Robbins) and Terri (Nielsen), and generic tech guy Phil (O'Connell). On the way, they encounter problems you've seen in dozens of better sf flicks. On the planet, they fine the New Age-y touchy-feely secrets of creation. The digital transfer has rendered the image crisp and clear, showing no defects in the source print. Also, the image shows no noise, artifacting, or grain. The 5.1 EX mix is simply delightful with a rich sound field and good dynamic range. —*ML/MM*
Movie: ♫ **DVD:** ♫♫♫
Buena Vista Home Entertainment (Cat #19573). Widescreen (2.35:1). Dolby Digital 5.1 Surround Stereo; Dolby Digital Surround Stereo. $29.99. Keepcase. *LANG:* English; French; Spanish. *FEATURES:* Tech. commentary: D.P., visual effects supervisors, production designer • Special effects documentary • Art gallery • Theatrical trailer.
2000 (PG) 112m/C Tim Robbins, Gary Sinise, Don Cheadle, Connie Nielsen, Jerry O'Connell, Kim Delaney, Elise Neal, Peter Outerbridge, Jill Teed, Kavan Smith; **D:** Brian DePalma; **W:** Jim Thomas, John Thomas, Graham Yost; **C:** Stephen Burum; **M:** Ennio Morricone.

Mississippi Burning [MGM]

When three civil rights activists go missing in Mississippi, 1964, FBI agents Anderson (Hackman) and Ward (Dafoe) head up the investigation. In yet another Hollywood attempt to depict racial conflict, white characters save the day while black characters provide background. Image transfer is generally clean and without blemishes, such as scratches or mars. The result is a bold and solid picture with very deep blacks and solid shadows. Colors are slightly muted, as Parker had designed the film, and contrast is generally very good. However, some edge-enhancement is evident in the transfer, introducing a look that features unnaturally harsh edges. Sadly, the transfer also has some issues with the color space as a result of the compression of the material and many of the subtle nuances in the transfer are lost to compression artifacts. Color banding and pixelation are clearly showing in many shots, making this release truly a mixed bag. —*MM/GH*
Movie: ♫♫♫ **DVD:** ♫♫½
MGM Home Entertainment (Cat #100180 29, UPC #027616860996). Widescreen (1.85:1) anamorphic. Dolby Digital Surround; Mono. $19.98. Keepcase. *LANG:* English; French; Spanish. *SUB:* French; Spanish. *FEATURES:* 16 chapter links • Commentary: Alan Parker • Trailer.
1988 (R) 127m/C Gene Hackman, Willem Dafoe, Frances McDormand, Brad Dourif, R. Lee Ermey, Gailard Sartain, Stephen Tobolowsky, Michael Rooker, Pruitt Taylor Vince, Badja (Medu) Djola, Kevin Dunn, Frankie Faison, Tom Mason, Park Overall; **D:** Alan Parker; **W:** Chris Gerolmo; **C:** Peter Biziou; **M:** Trevor Jones. *AWARDS:* Oscars '88: Cinematog.; Berlin Intl. Film Fest. '88: Actor (Hackman); Natl. Bd. of Review '88: Actor (Hackman), Director (Parker), Support. Actress (McDormand); *NOM:* Oscars '88: Actor (Hackman), Director (Parker), Film Editing, Picture, Sound, Support. Actress (McDormand).

Mississippi Mermaid

Truffaut generally succeeds in merging his own directorial style with Hitchcockian suspense, but this is not one of his best. Millionaire tobacco planter Louis Mahé (Belmondo) looks for a bride in the personals and finds Julie Rouselle (Deneuve), but what is the secret that she brings with her? Like *The Bride Wore Black,* the story is based on a Cornell Woolrich novel. The DVD looks about as good as most 1969 films, though exteriors are marred by some aliasing and artifacts. —*MM* **AKA:** Le Sirene du Mississippi.
Movie: ♫♫♫ **DVD:** ♫♫
MGM Home Entertainment (Cat #100148 1, UPC #027616858016). Widescreen (2.35:1) letterboxed. Dolby Digital Mono. $19.98. Keepcase. *LANG:* French. *SUB:* English; French; Spanish. *FEATURES:* 16 chapter links • Trailer.
1969 (PG) 110m/C *FR IT* Jean-Paul Belmondo, Catherine Deneuve, Michel Bouquet, Nelly Borgeaud, Marcel Berbert, Martine Ferriere; **D:** Francois Truffaut; **W:** Francois Truffaut; **C:** Denys Clerval; **M:** Antoine Duhamel.

Mr. Accident

Star Serious is Roger Crumpkin, accident-prone maintenance man at a massive egg processing plant. He falls in love with the boss's girlfriend Sunday Valentine (Dallimore) and discovers a dastardly plan. I find Serious's goodhearted slapstick hugely funny—much more than the bathroom antics that are so popular in American films now. Given the chaotic bilious color scheme that Serious employs, it's difficult to comment on the image. (I don't even want to think about it.) Sound is very good. —*MM*
Movie: ♫♫♫ **DVD:** ♫♫½
MGM Home Entertainment (Cat #100144 43, UPC #027616857637). Widescreen (1.85:1) anamorphic; full frame. Dolby Digital 5.1 Surround Stereo; Dolby Surround Stereo. $19.98. Keepcase. *LANG:* English; French; Spanish. *SUB:* French; Spanish. *FEATURES:* 16 chapter links • Trailer.
1999 (PG-13) 89m/C *AU* Yahoo Serious, David Field, Helen Dallimore, Grant Piro, Jeanette Cronin; **D:** Yahoo Serious; **W:** Yahoo Serious; **C:** Steve Arnold; **M:** Nerida Tyson-Chew.

Mr. & Mrs. Bridge

Ivory's adaptation of Evan S. Connell's novel painstakingly portrays an upper mid-

dle-class family struggling to survive within an emotional vacuum in '30s and '40s Kansas City. Newman and Woodward, as Walter and Ivory Bridge, bring a wealth of experience and insight to their characters. This is one of Newman's most subtle and nuanced performances, worthy of comparison to *The Verdict*. DVD delivers an excellent image that's much sharper than most period pieces. Sound is acceptable. —*MM*
Movie: 🎵🎵🎵🎵 **DVD:** 🎵🎵🎵
HBO Home Video (Cat #90533, UPC #026 359053320). Widescreen (4:3) letterboxed. Dolby Digital Surround Stereo. $24.98. Snapper. *LANG:* English. *SUB:* English; French; Spanish. *FEATURES:* Talent files • 19 chapter links.
1990 (PG-13) 127m/C Joanne Woodward, Paul Newman, Kyra Sedgwick, Blythe Danner, Simon Callow, Diane Kagan, Robert Sean Leonard, Saundra McClain, Margaret Welsh, Austin Pendleton, Gale Garnett, Remak Ramsay; *D:* James Ivory; *W:* Ruth Prawer Jhabvala; *C:* Tony Pierce-Roberts; *M:* Richard Robbins. *AWARDS:* N.Y. Film Critics '90: Actress (Woodward), Screenplay; *NOM:* Oscars '90: Actress (Woodward).

Mr. Death: The Rise and Fall of Fred A. Leuchter, Jr.

The DVD incarnation of Errol Morris's excellent film is an opportunity missed. On disc he (or the studio) might have used a commentary track to answer some of the criticisms that have been leveled at the documentary. It tells the story of Fred Leuchter, an unassuming little man who is brought down by an inflated sense of his expertise. As a self-taught expert in the mechanics of state-conducted executions, he is enlisted by Holocaust deniers to bolster their ridiculous theories. The sight of him pounding away with hammer and chisel at the walls and floors of German gas chambers is stomach-turning. Morris has been chastised for not coming down more heavily against his subject. Instead, he effectively lets Leuchter hang himself (as it were), but that reticence is still unsatisfying to the viewer. His own comments or footage of follow-up material might have added much. The visual quality of the image varies considerably. Since much of the source material is essentially handheld home videos, the film has a curious *Blair Witch* quality. —*MM*
Movie: 🎵🎵🎵 **DVD:** 🎵🎵🎵
Universal Studios Home Video (Cat #207 17, UPC #025192071720). Widescreen (1.85:1) letterboxed. Dolby Digital Surround Stereo. $24.99. Keepcase. *LANG:* English. *FEATURES:* 20 chapter links • Theatrical trailer.
1999 (PG-13) 92m/C *D:* Errol Morris; *C:* Peter Donahue; *M:* Caleb Sampson.

Mr. Hulot's Holiday

Tati's pipe-smoking, bumbling, and absolutely endearing comedic character makes his debut in this 1953 French com-edy. Tati directs himself starring as Monsieur Hulot, who takes a holiday at a seaside resort where his presence provokes an endless series of minor catastrophes. The slapstick is exactingly choreographed, and a good bit of the humor is quite subtle. This is gentle slapstick for sophisticated audiences. The black-and-white image, presented in its original 1.33:1 framing, is relatively free of blemishes. Both the French and English soundtracks are mono and are clear and distinct with little discernible noise. There is very little dialogue (none in the first 11 minutes, in fact), so it matters little which soundtrack you choose. In either case, the frequent use of relaxed jazz music that was contemporary to 1953 adds charm and class. The English track was actually created by Tati. The Criterion packaging boasts a new and improved English subtitle translation. Extras include an early short film starring Tati. A video introduction by Terry Jones of Monty Python fame helps put modern audiences in the right frame of mind to admire Tati's antics. Followed by *Mon Oncle* (1958), *Playtime* (1967), and *Trafic* (1971). —*MB* *AKA:* Les Vacances de Monsieur Hulot; Monsieur Hulot's Holiday.
Movie: 🎵🎵🎵½ **DVD:** 🎵🎵🎵½
Criterion Collection (Cat #HUL040, UPC #037429155721). Full frame. Dolby Digital Mono. $29.95. Keepcase. *LANG:* English; French. *SUB:* English. *FEATURES:* 21 chapter links • Intro by Terry Jones • Rene Clement's 1936 short film "Soigne ton gauche," starring Tati.
1953 86m/B FR Jacques Tati, Natalie Pascaud, Michelle Rolia; *D:* Jacques Tati; *W:* Jacques Tati, Henri Marquet, Jacques Lagrange, Pierre Aubert. *AWARDS: NOM:* Oscars '55: Story & Screenplay.

Mister Johnson

In 1923 Africa, an educated black man working for the British magistrate constantly finds himself in trouble, thanks to backfiring schemes. The highly enjoyable film from the director of *Driving Miss Daisy* suffers only from the underdevelopment of the intriguing lead character. Some surface wear is visible throughout and the image is never better than VHS tape. Sound may be a touch superior, but only that. —*MM*
Movie: 🎵🎵🎵 **DVD:** 🎵🎵
UAV Entertainment (Cat #40099). Full frame. Dolby Digital Stereo. $19.99. Snapper. *LANG:* English. *FEATURES:* Trailers • 9 chapter links.
1991 (PG-13) 105m/C Pierce Brosnan, Edward Woodward, Maynard Eziashi, Beatie Edney, Denis Quilley, Nick Reding; *D:* Bruce Beresford; *W:* Bruce Beresford, William Boyd; *C:* Peter James; *M:* Georges Delerue.

Mr. Jones

Head case Jones (Gere) is a charmer who gets a rush from walking on a high beam at a construction site, yet is prone to bad moods when he fails to remember his own name. Once again, the psychiatrist (Olin) falls in love with her patient. The DVD image is highly detailed and devoid of any compression artifacts. All in all, this is a great-looking and stable transfer. Colors are natural and powerful with faithfully rendered fleshtones and deep shadows that always maintain every bit of detail. The soundtrack is well integrated and natural, creating a restrained Surround field. —*GH/MM*
Movie: 🎵½ **DVD:** 🎵🎵½
Columbia Tristar Home Video (Cat #4525). Widescreen (1.85:1) anamorphic; full frame. Dolby Digital Surround Stereo; Dolby Digital Mono. $27.95. Keepcase. *LANG:* English; Spanish; Portuguese. *SUB:* English; Spanish; Portuguese; Mandarin; Thai; Korean. *FEATURES:* Talent files.
1993 (R) 110m/C Richard Gere, Lena Olin, Anne Bancroft, Tom Irwin, Delroy Lindo, Bruce Altman, Lauren Tom; *D:* Mike Figgis; *W:* Michael Cristofer, Eric Roth; *C:* Juan Ruiz-Anchia; *M:* Maurice Jarre.

Mr. Wonderful

Bittersweet look at love and romance begins with divorced Con Edison worker Gus (Dillon) hard up for cash and trying to marry off his ex-wife Lee (Sciorra). He wants to use the alimony money he's been paying her to invest in a bowling alley with his buddies. But as soon as it looks like he is succeeding, he falls in love with her again. Director Minghella made this sophomore effort between his cult hit debut, *Truly, Madly, Deeply*, and *The English Patient*. It's well worth a look. Image and sound are all you'd expect from a mid-level studio effort. Given the nature of the material, the full-frame version of the image is fine for most conventional TV screens. —*MM*
Movie: 🎵🎵🎵 **DVD:** 🎵🎵🎵
Warner Home Video, Inc. (Cat #12988). Widescreen (1.85:1) letterboxed; full frame. Dolby Digital Stereo. $19.98. Snapper. *LANG:* English. *SUB:* French. *CAP:* English. *FEATURES:* 31 chapter links.
1993 (PG-13) 99m/C Matt Dillon, Annabella Sciorra, William Hurt, Mary-Louise Parker, Luis Guzman, Dan Hedaya, Vincent D'Onofrio; *D:* Anthony Minghella; *W:* Amy Schor, Vicki Polon; *C:* Geoffrey Simpson; *M:* Michael Gore.

Mistress

A weak script undoes a formidable cast in a behind-the-scenes look at movie making. Wuhl plays Marvin Landisman, a failed writer/director who's approached by has-been producer Jack Roth (Landau), who says he's found a backer to finance a movie from one of Marvin's old scripts. It turns out that Roth has three men (De Niro, Aiello, and Wallach) ready to finance the project as long as each of their mistresses, who all have acting ambitions, gets the starring role. Double-dealing at a bargain-basement level sets up the rest of this listless comedy. You'd be hard pressed to find any real difference between this full-frame image and VHS tape. —*MM*

Movie: 🦴🦴 **DVD:** 🦴🦴
Pioneer Entertainment (Cat #DVD9864). Full frame. Dolby Digital Stereo. $24.98. Keepcase. *LANG:* English. *CAP:* English. *FEATURES:* 18 chapter links.
1991 (R) 100m/C Robert Wuhl, Martin Landau, Robert De Niro, Eli Wallach, Danny Aiello, Sheryl Lee Ralph, Jean Smart, Tuesday Weld, Jace Alexander, Laurie Metcalf, Christopher Walken, Ernest Borgnine; *D:* Barry Primus; *W:* J.F. Lawton, Barry Primus; *C:* Sven Kirsten; *M:* Galt MacDermot.

Mistress Frankenstein [CE]

Micro-budget horror parody is a short step above hard-core in production values, intention, and execution. In the spirit of burlesque, dopey comic scenes are interspersed with lesbian love scenes. Tattoos, piercings, and recent surgical scars are much in evidence. Aliasing is also a problem. —*MM*

Movie: 🦴 **DVD:** 🦴
El Independent Cinema (Cat #1011, UPC #612385101199). Full frame. $19.98. Keepcase. *LANG:* English. *FEATURES:* 15 chapter links • Behind-the-scenes featurette • Producer's home video reel • Weblinks.
2000 90m/C Victoria Vega, Darian Caine, Heidi Christine; *D:* John Bacchus; *W:* John Bacchus, Michael Beckerman, Clancy Fitzsimmons, Joe Ned.

Mistress of Seduction

Dracula's daughter Vamparina is a lesbian vampire in this erotic horror that scrapes the bottom of the barrel with exceptionally poor production values. On disc, skin tones have a particularly unattractive pallor. —*MM*

Movie: 🦴 **DVD:** 🦴
El Independent Cinema (Cat #1007, UPC #612385100796). Full frame. $19.98. Keepcase. *LANG:* English. *FEATURES:* 18 chapter links • Outtakes • Audition footage • Insert card • Photo gallery • Trailers.
2000 90m/C Alysabeth Clements, Gentle Fritz, Michele Tebow; *D:* Michele Pacitto; *W:* Michele Pacitto.

Mo' Better Blues

One of Lee's more conventional outings contains few of the flourishes and innovations that have made his features so remarkable, and concentrates instead on a solid storyline. Bleek Gilliam (Washington) is a jazz trumpeter whose life is so devoted to his music that everyone around him suffers for it. (The plot is loosely based on Lee's father Bill, who worked on the score with Branford Marsalis.) The ending is unconventional and unsatisfying, but Lee's stories have often been stronger in the telling than in the resolution. DVD cannot boast the sharpest image you'll ever see.

The club scenes, in particular, have a softness about them. They're still cool, though, and the cast is superb. Sound is very good. —*MM*

Movie: 🦴🦴🦴 **DVD:** 🦴🦴🦴
Universal Studios Home Video (Cat #205 36, UPC #025192053627). Widescreen (1.78:1) anamorphic. Dolby Digital Surround Stereo. $29.99. Keepcase. *LANG:* English; French; Spanish. *CAP:* English. *FEATURES:* Trailer • 18 chapter links • Production notes • Talent files.
1990 (R) 129m/C Denzel Washington, Spike Lee, Joie Lee, Wesley Snipes, Cynda Williams, Giancarlo Esposito, Robin Harris, Bill Nunn, John Turturro, Dick Anthony Williams, Ruben Blades, Nicholas Turturro, Samuel L. Jackson, Abbey Lincoln, Tracy C. Johns, Joe Seneca; *D:* Spike Lee; *W:* Spike Lee; *C:* Ernest R. Dickerson; *M:* Bill Lee, Branford Marsalis.

Mob War [BFS]

Please see review of *Great Mafia Movies*. Also available from Simitar (cat.#7392); reviewed in volume 1.
Movie: 🦴½
1988 (R) 96m/C John Christian, David Henry Keller, Jake La Motta, Johnny Stumper; *D:* J. Christian Ingvordsen; *W:* J. Christian Ingvordsen, John Weiner; *C:* Steven Kaman.

Moby Dick

This adaptation of Melville's masterpiece features a commanding Gregory Peck as Captain Ahab. His obsession with the great white whale may be a bit overstated, but that's the nature of obsession and Peck makes it work. Full-frame DVD image is not a huge improvement over VHS tape. The muddy nature of the colors comes from the original and it fits the story's somber, stormy mood. There's a marked increase in grain during the action and special effects scenes. Sound is on the thin side. —*MM*

Movie: 🦴🦴🦴 **DVD:** 🦴🦴
MGM Home Entertainment (Cat #10020 64, UPC #027616862945). Full frame. Dolby Digital Mono. $19.98. Keepcase. *LANG:* English; French; Spanish. *SUB:* French; Spanish. *FEATURES:* 16 chapter links • Trailer.
1956 116m/C Gregory Peck, Richard Basehart, Orson Welles, Leo Genn, Harry Andrews, Friedrich Ledebur; *D:* John Huston; *W:* Ray Bradbury, John Huston; *C:* Oswald Morris. *AWARDS:* Natl. Bd. of Review '56: Director (Huston); N.Y. Film Critics '56: Director (Huston).

Mohawk

A cowboy and an Indian woman try to stop a war between Indian tribes and fanatical landowners. Perhaps the most interesting feature of the disc is the "Critical Comments" feature which quotes the *VideoHound Golden Movie Retriever*, among other sources, all of which are completely unfavorable. Light snow is intermittent

throughout. Colors are nice and bright, making the disc a bit better than a good tape. —*MM*

Movie: 🦴½ **DVD:** 🦴🦴
Parade (Cat #55156). Full frame. Dolby Digital Mono. $17.98. Keepcase. *LANG:* English. *SUB:* Japanese. *FEATURES:* 12 chapter links • Talent files • Critical comments.
1956 80m/C Rita Gam, Neville Brand, Scott Brady, Lori Nelson; *D:* Kurt Neumann; *W:* Maurice Geraghty, Milton Krims; *C:* Karl Struss; *M:* Edward L. Alperson Jr.

Moll Flanders [MGM]

Writer/director Densham takes only the title character and the 18th-century London setting from Daniel Defoe's 1922 novel in his telling of spirited heroine Moll Flanders's (Wright) life. Orphaned Moll eventually finds herself working at the brothel of the greedy, scheming Mrs. Allworthy (Channing). Her life as a prostitute leads her to drink and near suicide—despite the unwavering friendship of Hibble (Freeman), Allworthy's dignified servant—until she falls for an impoverished artist (Lynch) and briefly finds happiness. Wright and Freeman's strong performances hold everything together, but it does get dreary. DVD delivers a nice image, emphasizing browns and grays. Focus is properly soft for a costume drama. Sound is good. —*MM*

Movie: 🦴🦴½ **DVD:** 🦴🦴🦴
MGM Home Entertainment (Cat #10014 57, UPC #027616857774). Widescreen (2.35:1) anamorphic. Dolby Digital 5.1 Surround Stereo. $19.98. Keepcase. *LANG:* English. *SUB:* French; Spanish. *FEATURES:* 16 chapter links • Trailer.
1996 (PG-13) 120m/C Robin Wright Penn, Morgan Freeman, Stockard Channing, John Lynch, Brenda Fricker, Aisling Corcoran, Geraldine James, Jim Sheridan, Jeremy Brett, Britta Smith, Ger Ryan; *D:* Pen Densham; *W:* Pen Densham; *C:* David Tattersall; *M:* Mark Mancina.

Mommy [SE]

Murderous mom (McCormack) will do anything for her daughter (Lemieux). McCormack is best known for her starring role in *The Bad Seed* and the film is a sort of sequel that was made in Muscatine, Iowa. DVD presents an image that's no different from VHS tape, save the commentary track, and that reflects the homespun nature of the production. Chapters are not accessible through the menu. —*MM*

Movie: 🦴🦴 **DVD:** 🦴🦴
Roan Group (Cat #2013). Full frame. Dolby Digital Stereo. $19.95. Keepcase. *LANG:* English. *FEATURES:* Commentary: Collins, editor Phil Dingdelein, McCormack, Lemieux • Trailer • Interview with Patty McCormack.
1995 89m/C Patty McCormack, Majel Barrett, Jason Miller, Brinke Stevens, Rachel Lemieux, Mickey Spillane, Michael Cornelison, Sarah Jane Miller; *D:* Max Allan Collins; *W:* Max Allan Collins; *C:* Phillip W. Dingdelein; *M:* Richard Lowry.

Mon Oncle

When Tati reprises his role as Monsieur Hulot, who made his first appearance in *Mr. Hulot's Holiday*, he does so to provide a contrast to the mechanized modern world. The comedic action is split between Hulot's down-to-earth, old-world neighborhood and the sterile, futuristic existence of his sister's family, the Arpels. They live in a clean, orderly, and antiseptic household with all the latest conveniences—not the least alarming of which is a gaudy fountain meant to impress visitors. The Jetsons would be right at home in the place. Hulot, meanwhile, lives in an old part of town, where horse-drawn carriages share the street with a street sweeper who never manages to sweep any streets. The funniest scenes occur as Hulot attempts to fit into the modern world, either at the Arpel home or at Arpel's plastic hose factory. The film is a delightfully sophisticated satire of modern life that still has much to say to audiences living in the 21st century. The mono soundtrack is quite good, with no hiss, and is serviceable both for the French dialogue and for the music. The 1.33:1 image is marred by very few blemishes, and the colors look as vivid as if the film was exposed yesterday. There is quite a contrast between the two palettes — the rich earth tones used in Hulot's neighborhood, and the sterile pastels and blues of the modern side of town. —*MB* AKA: My Uncle; My Uncle, Mr. Hulot.
Movie: ♪♪♪♪ **DVD:** ♪♪♪½
Criterion Collection (Cat #0NC030, UPC #037429155929). Full frame. Dolby Digital Mono. $29.95. Keepcase. *LANG:* French. *SUB:* English. *FEATURES:* 26 chapter links • Video intro by Terry Hones • "L'Ecole des Facteurs," 1947 short film directed by and starring Tati • New and improved English subtitle translation.
1958 110m/C *FR* Jacques Tati, Jean-Pierre Zola, Adrienne Serrantie, Alain Bacourt; *D:* Jacques Tati; *C:* Jean (Yves, Georges) Bourgoin. *AWARDS:* Oscars '58: Foreign Film; Cannes '58: Grand Jury Prize; N.Y. Film Critics '58: Foreign Film.

Mon Oncle d'Amerique

Three characters try to find success of varying kinds in Paris, interspersed with ironic lectures by Prof. Henri Labroit about the biology that impels human behavior. Their disappointments lead them to dream of a legendary American uncle who could make their desires come true. Viewers expecting the level of brightness and detail found in Hollywood comedies will be disappointed, but the DVD image is comparable to other European imports of the same vintage. The yellow subtitles are clear throughout. —*MM* AKA: Les Somnambules.
Movie: ♪♪♪½ **DVD:** ♪♪½
New Yorker Video (Cat #17000, UPC #717119170042). Full frame. $29.95. Keepcase. *LANG:* French. *SUB:* English. *FEATURES:* 14 chapter links • Resnais and Gruault filmographies.

1980 (PG) 123m/C *FR* Gerard Depardieu, Nicole Garcia, Roger-Pierre, Marie DuBois; *D:* Alain Resnais; *W:* Jean Gruault; *C:* Sacha Vierny; *M:* Arie Dzierlatka. *AWARDS:* Cannes '80: Grand Jury Prize; N.Y. Film Critics '80: Foreign Film; *NOM:* Oscars '80: Orig. Screenplay.

Mona Lisa

Jordan tells a wonderful, sad, sensitive story of a romantic, small-time hood who gets personally involved with the welfare and bad company of the high-priced whore he's been hired to chauffeur about from job to job. Hoskins is especially touching and Caine is chilling as a suave gangster. Fine film debut for Tyson. Gritty and realistic, beautifully filmed, with deep characters backed by the excellent performances. Though this letterboxed transfer is far from the sharpest that Criterion has to offer, it still looks very good. The film's noirish look is partially the result of the faded look of the colors, and the disc duplicates the theatrical look with excellent contrast and super blacks. There are a few instances of very minor artifacting, but nothing that detracts from the enjoyment of the film. The extremely crisp mono soundtrack makes understanding the heavy Cockney accents far less work than it could be. Criterion discs feature some of the finest of commentaries and this is no exception, with Hoskins and Jordan discussing the film with both intelligence and emotion. —*JO*
Movie: ♪♪♪½ **DVD:** ♪♪♪
Criterion Collection (Cat #107, UPC #715515012027). Widescreen (1.77:1) letterboxed. Dolby Digital Mono. $39.95. Keepcase. *LANG:* English. *SUB:* English. *FEATURES:* 25 chapter links • Theatrical trailer • Commentary: director Neil Jordan, actor Bob Hoskins.
1986 (R) 104m/C *GB* Bob Hoskins, Cathy Tyson, Michael Caine, Clarke Peters, Kate Hardie, Robbie Coltrane, Zoe Nathenson, Sammi Davis, Rod Bedall, Joe Brown, Pauline Melville; *D:* Neil Jordan; *W:* David Leland, Neil Jordan; *C:* Roger Pratt; *M:* Michael Kamen. *AWARDS:* British Acad. '86: Actor (Hoskins); Cannes '86: Actor (Hoskins); Golden Globes '87: Actor—Drama (Hoskins); L.A. Film Critics '86: Actor (Hoskins), Support. Actress (Tyson); N.Y. Film Critics '86: Actor (Hoskins); Natl. Soc. Film Critics '86: Actor (Hoskins); *NOM:* Oscars '86: Actor (Hoskins).

Monkey Shines

Romero's horror is firmly based in reality. When an accident leaves law student Allan Mann (Beghe) a quadriplegic, his friend Geoffrey (Pankow) arranges for a special monkey, Ella (Boo), to be trained to help him with the tasks most people take for granted. Also on hand when Allan and Boo become psychically linked are an overprotective mother (Van Patten) and an ill-tempered nurse (Forrest). At its best, the film makes everyday horror, claustrophobia, and helpless anger seem real. An enraged

supermonkey is much less frightening than well-intentioned, manipulative friends and relatives. The image is very good; equal, as I remember it, to the theatrical release. Same for sound. —*MM* AKA: Monkey Shines: An Experiment in Fear; Ella.
Movie: ♪♪♪ **DVD:** ♪♪♪
20th Century Fox Home Entertainment (Cat #907865, UPC #027616786524). Widescreen anamorphic; full frame. Dolby Digital Surround Stereo. $24.99. Keepcase. *LANG:* English; French. *SUB:* English; French. *FEATURES:* 36 chapter links • Liner notes.
1988 (R) 108m/C Jason Beghe, John Pankow, Kate McNeil, Christine Forrest, Stephen Root, Joyce Van Patten, Stanley Tucci, Janine Turner; *D:* George A. Romero; *W:* George A. Romero; *C:* James A. Contner; *M:* David Shire.

Monsoon

Ambitious project from director Mundhra (known best for his erotic thrillers) is set in Goa, India. That's where Kenneth Blake (Tyson) and his fiancée Sally Stephens (McCoy) go to visit his friend (McShane). But in a previous incarnation Kenneth was a lover of Leela (Brodie), who's now married to the local drug lord Miranda (Grover). Their centuries-spanning affair causes the usual complications. Local color is actually much more interesting and the film looks very sharp. The full-frame image is only slightly better than VHS tape, but sound is much improved. —*MM*
Movie: ♪♪ **DVD:** ♪♪½
Tapeworm Video Distributors (Cat #1232). Full frame. Dolby Digital 5.1 Surround Stereo. $24.95. Keepcase. *LANG:* English; Hindi. *SUB:* English; Spanish. *FEATURES:* Trailer • 24 chapter links • Music video • 24 chapter links.
1997 96m/C Richard Tyson, Matt McCoy, Gulsham Grover, Jenny McShane, Doug Jeffery, Helen Brodie; *D:* Jag Mundhra; *C:* Blain Brown; *M:* Alan Dermot Derosian.

Monster from Green Hell

Dr. Brady (Davis) sends up an experimental rocket containing various animals to see how they react to radiation. The craft crashes in the African jungle and big bug critters are the result. The film utilizes lots of stock footage and the model monster (which looks a little like a giant katydid) is about the least frightening ever put on film. Some light scratches are visible but generally the image is very good for a black-and-white film of this vintage. —*MM*
Movie: ♪♪½ **DVD:** ♪♪½
Image Entertainment (Cat #ID8689CODVD, UPC #014381868920). Full frame. Dolby Digital Mono. $24.99. Keepcase. *LANG:* English. *FEATURES:* 12 chapter links.
1958 71m/B Jim Davis, Robert E. (Bob) Griffin, Barbara Turner, Eduardo Ciannelli; *D:* Kenneth Crane; *W:* Endre Bohem, Louis Vittes; *C:* Ray Flin; *M:* Albert Glasser.

The Monster of Camp Sunshine

Please see *The Beast That Killed Women / The Monster of Camp Sunshine.*

1964 74m/B Harrison Peebles, Deborah Spray, Sally Parfait, James Gatsby, Ron Cheney Jr.; **D:** Ferenc Leroget; **W:** Ferenc Leroget.

Monty Python and the Holy Grail

For many fans (including me), this is the best long-form work that the Pythons ever did. The jokes start in the credits and seldom slow down. The assault on Arthurian legends contains the famous Trojan Rabbit, shrubbery, moose, and more. The disc is an accurate reproduction of an unexceptional original image. Any more visual polish would be unnecessary to the troupe's inspired, intelligent humor. Would a commentary track have been a valuable addition? I doubt it. Mono sound is acceptable. —*MM*

Movie: 🎬🎬🎬½ **DVD:** 🎬🎬🎬
Columbia Tristar Home Video (Cat #3065). Widescreen (1.85:1) letterboxed. Dolby Digital Mono. $24.95. Keepcase. *LANG:* English. *SUB:* English; French; Spanish. *FEATURES:* 28 chapter links ☛ Trailers.
1975 (PG) 90m/C *GB* Graham Chapman, John Cleese, Terry Gilliam, Eric Idle, Terry Jones, Michael Palin, Carol Cleveland, Connie Booth, Neil Innes, Patsy Kensit; **D:** Terry Gilliam, Terry Jones; **W:** Graham Chapman, John Cleese, Terry Gilliam, Eric Idle, Terry Jones, Michael Palin; **C:** Terry Bedford; **M:** De Wolfe, Neil Innes.

Moon over Harlem

Please see review for *Edgar Ulmer Collection, Vol. 1.*
Movie: 🎬½
1939 67m/B Bud Harris, Cora Green, Alec Lovejoy, Sidney Bechet; **D:** Edgar G. Ulmer.

Moonlight and Valentino

To help her recover from the death of her husband, Rebecca (Perkins) turns to the comfort of flaky neighbor Sylvie (Goldberg), self-destructive sis Lucy (Paltrow), and overbearing ex-stepmother Alberta (Turner). Together, they sit around and spout some of the most contrived and clichéd "woman talk" ("Chicken soup is the most womanly thing on the face of the planet") in recent film history. The finale, a hokey ritual in a cemetery, will have you pulling out hair, not hankies. Rock star Bon Jovi makes his screen debut as the beefcake (discussion of his butt takes up about two-thirds of the dialogue) who puts the fire back into Rebecca's life. Not for the estrogen impaired. Overall, the pastel color scheme makes a smooth transition to DVD. The soft-focus image is very good. So is the sound. —*MM*
Movie: 🎬🎬 **DVD:** 🎬🎬½

MGM Home Entertainment (Cat #1001538, UPC #027616858498). Widescreen (2.35:1) letterboxed. Dolby Digital Surround Stereo. $19.98. Keepcase. *LANG:* English; French. *SUB:* French; Spanish. *CAP:* English. *FEATURES:* 16 chapter links ☛ Trailer.
1995 (R) 104m/C Elizabeth Perkins, Whoopi Goldberg, Gwyneth Paltrow, Kathleen Turner, Jon Bon Jovi, Jeremy Sisto, Josef Sommer, Peter Coyote; **D:** David Anspaugh; **W:** Ellen Simon; **C:** Julio Macat; **M:** Howard Shore.

The Most Dangerous Game [Madacy]

Please see review for *Fay Wray Collection.*
AKA: The Hounds of Zaroff.
Movie: 🎬🎬🎬
1932 78m/B Joel McCrea, Fay Wray, Leslie Banks, Robert Armstrong, Noble Johnson; **D:** Ernest B. Schoedsack, Irving Pichel; **W:** James A. Creelman; **C:** Henry W. Gerrard; **M:** Max Steiner.

Mother

Yes, you will shake your head in recognition of that parent-child bond. Twice-divorced writer John Henderson (Brooks) decides it's all Mom's fault he has problems with women, so he decides to move back home and figure out what went wrong. Mom Beatrice (Reynolds) is exasperated and married younger brother Jeff (Morrow) winds up jealous of mom's attentions to his sibling. Reynolds's first feature film in 25 years. The video provides a very dark, disappointing transfer. Not only do darker colors lack definition, but most of the film suffers from the subdued transfer and seems rather muted. Fortunately, the 5.1 mix redeems the disc to a certain extent, with crisp dialogue and wonderfully reproduced ambient sounds and music. The lack of any additional features beyond the obligatory trailer are also a major disappointment. —*MJT*
Movie: 🎬🎬🎬 **DVD:** 🎬🎬
Paramount Home Video (Cat #33247, UPC #097363324744). Widescreen (1.85:1) anamorphic. Dolby Digital 5.1 Surround Sound; Dolby Surround Sound. $29.99. Keepcase. *LANG:* English; French. *SUB:* English. *FEATURES:* 24 chapter links ☛ Theatrical trailer.
1996 (PG-13) 104m/C Albert Brooks, Debbie Reynolds, Rob Morrow, Lisa Kudrow, John C. McGinley, Isabel Glasser, Peter White; **D:** Albert Brooks; **W:** Albert Brooks, Monica Johnson; **C:** Lajos Koltai; **M:** Marc Shaiman. *AWARDS:* N.Y. Film Critics '96: Screenplay; Natl. Soc. Film Critics '96: Screenplay; *NOM:* Golden Globes '97: Actress—Mus./Comedy (Reynolds).

Mother and Son

Slow-paced, dreamlike story about a dedicated son's (Ananishnov) caring for his dying mother (Geyer) in their old house in the country. She wishes to go outside—he carries her along a path in the woods and they recall their childhood. She eventually

goes back to her bed where they discuss death and she falls asleep, never to waken. The video transfer is acceptable, though colors seem muted throughout (this may have more to do with the cinematography than the disc) and blacks tend to lose definition in darker scenes. The soundtrack is really quite good, with nicely reproduced natural sound and an otherworldly representation of dialogue that is perfectly in tune with the surreal style of the film. —*MJT* **AKA:** Mat i Syn; Mutter und Sohn.
Movie: 🎬🎬 **DVD:** 🎬🎬
Fox/Lorber Home Video (Cat #FLV5242, UPC #720917524221). Full frame. Dolby Digital Stereo. $29.98. Keepcase. *LANG:* Russian. *SUB:* English. *FEATURES:* Filmographies ☛ Production credits ☛ Weblinks.
1997 73m/C *RU GE* Gudrun Geyer, Alexi Ananishnov; **D:** Alexander Sokurov; **W:** Yuri Arabov; **C:** Aleksei Federov; **M:** Otmar Nussio.

Mother Night

Keith Gordon's overlooked masterpiece finally gets some of the recognition it deserves on DVD. The film is based on Kurt Vonnegut Jr.'s novel about an American playwright, Howard W. Campbell Jr. (Nolte), who becomes a Nazi propagandist and (perhaps) an American spy. He tells the tale from memory as he awaits trial in an Israeli prison. On his intelligent commentary track, Gordon takes a mostly technical approach, recounting details of the filming (all done in Montreal). Sound and image are both first-rate, though admittedly this one is a personal favorite and I'm apt to overlook any flaws. —*MM*
Movie: 🎬🎬🎬🎬 **DVD:** 🎬🎬🎬🎬
New Line Home Video (Cat #N5023, UPC #794043502323). Widescreen (1.85:1) anamorphic. Dolby Digital 5.1 Surround Stereo; Dolby Digital Surround Stereo. $24.98. Snapper. *LANG:* English; French. *SUB:* English; French. *FEATURES:* 21 chapter links ☛ Commentary: Keith Gordon, writer Robert Weide ☛ Commentary: Nick Nolte ☛ Interview with Kurt Vonnegut Jr. and Nick Nolte ☛ 8 deleted scenes ☛ Eichman trial featurette ☛ Trailer ☛ Talent files.
1996 (R) 113m/C Nick Nolte, Sheryl Lee, Alan Arkin, John Goodman, Kirsten Dunst, David Strathairn, Arye Gross, Frankie Faison, Bernard Behrens; **D:** Keith Gordon; **W:** Robert B. Weide; **C:** Tom Richmond; **M:** Michael Convertino; **V:** Henry Gibson.

Mother's Boys

Estranged mother Curtis attempts to reunite with the family she abandoned only to be snubbed, inspiring in her a ruthless effort to win back the children and to oust father Gallagher's new live-in girlfriend Whalley-Kilmer. With an almost psychotic devotion, she terrorizes everyone in the family. The overly familiar material is extremely well photographed, so the DVD looks terrific. Sound is a notch lower. —*MM*
Movie: 🎬🎬 **DVD:** 🎬🎬½
Miramax Pictures Home Video (Cat #164 50). Widescreen. Dolby Digital Surround

Stereo. $29.99. Keepcase. *LANG:* English. *CAP:* English. *FEATURES:* 19 chapter links. **1994 (R) 96m/C** Jamie Lee Curtis, Peter Gallagher, Joanne Whalley, Luke Edwards, Vanessa Redgrave, Colin Ward, Joss Ackland, Paul Guilfoyle, John C. McGinley, J.E. Freeman, Ken Lerner, Lorraine Toussaint, Joey Zimmerman, Jill Freedman; *D:* Yves Simoneau; *W:* Richard Hawley, Barry Schneider; *C:* Elliot Davis; *M:* George S. Clinton.

Mother's Day [DC]

How does one adequately review a Troma movie? It's like critiquing a fast-food restaurant or a microwaveable meal as real food. Suffice to say that this one is everything one expects from Troma. It is rude, crude, and delights in stereotypes and women's breasts. The plot is simple: a backwoods mother is training her two dumb virile sons to be the best murders and rapists they can be. Enter three middle-aged women on their annual reunion vacation in the woods, and you have a recipe for minced meat. The men abuse the women to the cheers and direction of Mother, and then the women turn the tables on the backwoods trio towards the end of the film. While the revenge sequences don't quite meet *I Spit on Your Grave* standards, the revenge is sweet and there is a truly bizarre suffocation scene at the end. The picture and sound are both worthy of late-night TV. —*CA*
Movie: 🎵 *DVD:* 🎵🎵
Troma Team Video (Cat #9016, UPC #790357901630). Full frame. $24.99. Keepcase. *LANG:* English. *FEATURES:* 10 chapter links • Commentary: director Charles Kaufman • Interview with filmmakers • Troma's Guide to Mother's Day Shopping • Theatrical trailer and additional trailers.
1980 98m/C Tiana Pierce, Nancy Hendrickson, Deborah Luce, Holden McGuire, Billy Ray McQuade, Rose Ross; *D:* Charles Kaufman; *W:* Charles Kaufman, Warren Leight; *C:* Joseph Mangine; *M:* Phil Gallo, Clem Vicari Jr.

Mountains of the Moon

Sprawling adventure details the obsessive search for the source of the Nile conducted by famed Victorian rogue/explorer Sir Richard Burton (Bergin) and cohort John Hanning Speke (Glen) in the late 1800s. Director Rafelson, better known for more personal films such as *Five Easy Pieces* and *The King of Marvin Gardens*, shows considerable skill with the spectacular scenery, epic images, and some realistically shocking violence. DVD appears to handle the extremes of light and darkness as well as the original. Artifacts appear in the expected places (large, bright areas of dirt, for example) and some bits of fluff are occasionally caught in the frame. A Surround remix of the sound to heighten the action scenes would be a good idea, too. Those minor flaws notwithstanding, this is a terrific sleeper. —*MM*

Movie: 🎵🎵🎵½ *DVD:* 🎵🎵🎵
Pioneer Entertainment (Cat #DVD68915 WS). Widescreen letterboxed. Stereo. $24.98. Keepcase. *LANG:* English. *FEATURES:* 29 chapter links • Featurette.
1990 (R) 140m/C Patrick Bergin, Iain Glen, Fiona Shaw, Richard E. Grant, Peter Vaughan, Roger Rees, Bernard Hill, Anna Massey, Leslie Phillips, John Savident, James Villiers, Delroy Lindo, Roshan Seth; *D:* Bob Rafelson; *W:* Bob Rafelson; *C:* Roger Deakins; *M:* Michael Small.

Mountaintop Motel Massacre

A resort motel's lunatic hostess Evelyn (Chappell) routinely slaughters guests. Sub-par horror features atrocious acting and sets that appear to be collapsing around the cast. The image is sharp and clear, far superior to older tapes, showing only a fine sheen of grain. The colors are fine, although they are slightly washed-out in some scenes. Mono soundtrack provides adequate reproduction of the dialogue and sound effects. —*MM/ML*
Movie: 🎵 *DVD:* 🎵🎵½
Anchor Bay (Cat #DV11403). Widescreen (1.66:1) anamorphic. Dolby Digital Mono. $24.98. Keepcase. *LANG:* English. *FEATURES:* Trailer.
1986 (R) 95m/C Bill Thurman, Anna Chappell, Will Mitchell; *D:* Jim McCullough; *W:* Jim McCullough Jr.; *C:* Joseph M. Wilcots; *M:* Ron Di Lulio.

The Mouse on the Moon

Sort-of sequel to *The Mouse That Roared* lacks the presence of Peter Sellers but maintains the whimsical tone of the original. The prime minister (Moody) of the Duchy of Grand Fenwick asks for American aid in setting up a space program. (Actually, he wants the money for indoor plumbing.) When it turns out that the local wine is actually rocket fuel, his amiable goof of a son (Cribbins) fulfills his lifelong dream of becoming an astronaut. The mild spoof of cold war politics lacks the anarchic spirit that director Lester has brought to *Help!* and his *Musketeer* films. The main flaw on the disc is an imperfect framing of the widescreen version, which crops both sides of the image. Both picture and sound are a bit dim at the beginning, though they brighten later. —*MM*
Movie: 🎵🎵🎵 *DVD:* 🎵🎵½
MGM Home Entertainment (Cat #1001280, UPC #027616855596). Widescreen (1.66:1) letterboxed; full frame. Dolby Digital Mono. $19.98. Keepcase. *LANG:* English; French; Spanish. *SUB:* English; French; Spanish. *FEATURES:* Trailer • 24 chapter links.
1962 85m/C *GB* Margaret Rutherford, Ron Moody, Bernard Cribbins, Terry-Thomas, June Ritchie, David Kosoff; *D:* Richard Lester; *W:* Michael Pertwee; *C:* Wilkie Cooper; *M:* Ron Grainer.

Moving Target

Ray (Wilson) is framed for a murder and must battle both terrorists and Irish cops to clear his name. If the story sounds familiar, it's because the film is a remake of Don "The Dragon" Wilson's *Blood Fist 4*. This time, though, the production values are higher and the whole film looks much better. Disc delivers a very nice image. Wilson's commentary track is required listening for his fans. —*MM*
Movie: 🎵🎵🎵 *DVD:* 🎵🎵🎵
New Concorde (Cat #NH20762 D, UPC #736991476295). Full frame. Stereo. $19.99. Keepcase. *LANG:* English. *FEATURES:* 24 chapter links • Trailers • Talent files.
2000 (R) 86m/C Don "The Dragon" Wilson, Bill Murphy, Hilary Kavanagh, Terry McMahon, Eileen McCloskey, Lisa Duane; *D:* Paul Ziller; *W:* Paul Ziller; *C:* Yoram Astrakhan; *M:* Derek Gleeson.

The Mummy

Universal has done its usual excellent job with the third of its original horror hits. If the film itself doesn't have the scares of *Dracula* or *Frankenstein*, it features one of Karloff's best performances, a sleek art-deco look, and some memorable sets, which would be reused often in the following years. Both image and sound are first-rate, with less wear than you'd expect to see in a film of this age. The extras are comparable to the others in the "Classic Monster Collection." —*MM*
Movie: 🎵🎵🎵½ *DVD:* 🎵🎵🎵🎵
Universal Studios Home Video (Cat #20327, UPC #025192032721). Full frame. Dolby Digital 2.0. $29.98. Snapper. *LANG:* English. *SUB:* French. *FEATURES:* Production notes • Cast and crew thumbnail bios • Weblinks • "Mummy Dearest" documentary by David Skal • Commentary: film historian Paul M. Jensen • Original theatrical trailer • The Mummy Archives.
1932 72m/B Boris Karloff, Zita Johann, David Manners, Edward Van Sloan, Arthur Byron, Bramwell Fletcher, Noble Johnson, Leonard Mudie, Henry Victor; *D:* Karl Freund; *W:* John Lloyd Balderston; *C:* Charles Stumar.

The Mummy [2 SE]

The studio has created this "ultimate" edition in an unalloyed bid to cash in on the theatrical release of the sequel. It corrects the shortcomings of the first DVD (reviewed in the first edition of this book) by including both widescreen and full-frame versions on two discs. It eliminates some extras and adds others, such as two new commentary tracks. According to other sources, the material concerning *The Mummy Returns* gives away important plot points. —*MM*
Movie: 🎵🎵🎵 *DVD:* 🎵🎵🎵½
Universal Studios Home Video (Cat #21258, UPC #025192125829). Widescreen (2.35:1) anamorphic; full frame. Dolby 5.1 Surround (English); Dolby Surround (French). $29.98. Keepcase. *LANG:* Eng-

lish. *SUB:* English; French; Spanish. *FEA-TURES:* 18 chapter links, feature ● Commentary: director Stephen, editor Bob Ducsay ● Commentary: Brendan Fraser ● Commentary: Oded Fehr, Kevin J. O'Connor, Arnold Vosloo ● "Building a Better Mummy," 40-min. documentary ● Egyptology 101 (factoids) ● Talent files ● Production notes (press kit) ● Three deleted scenes ● Storyboard comparison ● Photo montage ● Pharaoh lineage ● *The Mummy Returns* trailer and highlights. DVD-ROM drive features include "The Mummy Game," screensavers, Universal weblinks. **1999 (PG-13) 124m/C** Brendan Fraser, Rachel Weisz, Arnold Vosloo, John Hannah, Kevin J. O'Connor, Jonathan Hyde, Oded Fehr, Erik Avari, Tuc Watkins, Stephen Dunham, Corey Johnson, Bernard Fox, Aharon Ipale, Omid Djalili, Patricia Velasquez; *D:* Stephen Sommers; *W:* Stephen Sommers; *C:* Adrian Biddle; *M:* Jerry Goldsmith. *AWARDS: NOM:* Oscars '99: Sound; MTV Movie Awards '00: Action Seq.

The Mummy's Shroud

Hammer's next-to-last Mummy horror is a handsomely produced but tepid affair. The plot trots out the familiar elements—British archeological dig led by Sr. Basil Walden (Morell) discovers the remains of Pharaoh Kah-to-Bey; hieroglyphics from the shroud are read aloud...you know the drill. Lots of talk, comparatively little action. DVD presents an excellent production of a well-photographed original. Mono sound is O.K. —*MM*
Movie: ♪♪ *DVD:* ♪♪½
Anchor Bay (Cat #DV10676, UPC #01313 1067699). Widescreen (1.66:1) anamorphic. Dolby Digital Mono. $24.99. Keepcase. *LANG:* English. *FEATURES:* 25 chapter links.
1967 90m/C *GB* Andre Morrell, John Phillips, David Buck, Elizabeth Sellars; *D:* John Gilling; *W:* John Gilling; *C:* Arthur Grant; *M:* Don Banks.

Munster, Go Home!

The familiar characters from the 1960s TV series inherit an English estate. The film is nothing but an extended version of a below-average sitcom with the expected poor production values. Beyond the subtitles, disc is identical to tape. —*MM*
Movie: ♪ *DVD:* ♪♪
Goodtimes Entertainment (Cat #81041). Full frame. $14.99. Snapper. *LANG:* English. *SUB:* English; French; Spanish. *FEATURES:* 18 chapter links.
1966 96m/C Fred Gwynne, Yvonne De Carlo, Al Lewis, Butch Patrick, Debbie Watson, Terry-Thomas, Hermione Gingold, Robert Pine, John Carradine, Bernard Fox, Richard Dawson, Arthur Malet; *D:* Earl Bellamy; *W:* Joe Connelly, Bob Mosher, George Tibbles; *C:* Benjamin (Ben H.) Kline; *M:* Jack Marshall.

The Munsters' Revenge

TV movie is based on the continuing adventures of the '60s comedy series characters. Herman, Lily, and Grandpa have to contend with robot replicas of themselves which were created by a flaky scientist. Like the first film, this one is no real improvement over VHS tape. —*MM*
Movie: ♪ *DVD:* ♪♪
Goodtimes Entertainment (Cat #81041). Full frame. Dolby Digital Mono. $19.98. Snapper. *LANG:* English; French; Spanish. *SUB:* French; Spanish. *CAP:* English. *FEATURES:* 18 chapter links.
1981 96m/C Fred Gwynne, Yvonne De Carlo, Al Lewis, Jo McDonnel, Sid Caesar, Ezra Stone, Howard Morris, Bob Hastings, K.C. Martel; *D:* Don Weis; *M:* Vic Mizzy.

Murder in the First

Hours after leaving a three-year stint of medieval solitary confinement at Alcatraz, petty thief Henri Young (Bacon) kills the inmate who ratted him out. Rookie lawyer James Stamphill (Slater) defends Young by putting the institution and the warden (Oldman) on trial. Performances are uniformly excellent but they're undermined by Rocco's irritating show-off direction and a script that relies on some weak clichés. That said, the image is very good and the Surround sound makes for a more effective viewing experience than the theatrical release. —*MM*
Movie: ♪♪½ *DVD:* ♪♪♪
Warner Home Video, Inc. (Cat #13895). Widescreen anamorphic; full frame. Dolby Digital Surround Stereo. $14.98. Snapper. *LANG:* English; French. *SUB:* English; French. *FEATURES:* 38 chapter links.
1995 (R) 123m/C Christian Slater, Kevin Bacon, Gary Oldman, Embeth Davidtz, William H. Macy, Stephen Tobolowsky, Brad Dourif, R. Lee Ermey, Mia Kirshner, Stefan Gierasch, Kyra Sedgwick; *D:* Marc Rocco; *W:* Dan Gordon; *C:* Fred Murphy; *M:* Christopher Young. *AWARDS:* Broadcast Film Critics '95: Actor (Bacon); *NOM:* Screen Actors Guild '95: Support. Actor (Bacon).

The Murder of Roger Ackroyd

Please see review of *Agatha Christie's Poirot.* —*MJT*
(Cat #AAE70130, UPC #733961701302).
1999 100m/C *GB* David Suchet, Philip Jackson, Vivien Heilbron, Malcolm Terris, Oliver Ford Davies, Roger Frost, Jamie Bamber, Selina Cadell; *D:* Andrew Grieve; *W:* Clive Exton; *C:* Chris O'Dell; *M:* Christopher Gunning.

Music of the Heart [CS]

Divorced Roberta Guaspari (Streep) leaves suburbia with her two young sons to teach music in a Harlem public school with 50 violins that she purchased herself. Eventually her work becomes the landmark East Harlem Violin Program. Despite numerous obstacles, the students make it to Carnegie Hall. Streep gives another fine performance in a very familiar story. All the stops have been pulled out for this two-disc Collector's Series edition. The numerous extras include the documentary, "Small Worlds," upon which the fictionalized feature was based. Overall, the image is very good—befitting a big budget studio release—and sound is better. —*MM* *AKA:* 50 Violins.
Movie: ♪♪½ *DVD:* ♪♪♪
Miramax Pictures Home Video (Cat #183 10, UPC #717951004956). Widescreen (1.85:1) anamorphic. Dolby Digital 5.1 Surround Stereo. $39.99. Keepcase. *LANG:* English; French. *CAP:* English. *FEATURES:* 41 chapter links ● Deleted scenes ● 4 featurettes ● Music video ● Trailer ● Talent files ● Sound bites ● Commentary: director Craven, producer Marianne Maddalena ● "Small Worlds" documentary.
1999 (PG) 124m/C Meryl Streep, Angela Bassett, Aidan Quinn, Gloria Estefan, Cloris Leachman, Kieran Culkin, Charlie Hofheimer, Jay O. Sanders, Josh Pais; *D:* Wes Craven; *W:* Pamela Gray; *C:* Peter Deming; *M:* Mason Daring. *AWARDS: NOM:* Oscars '99: Actress (Streep), Song ("Music of My Heart"); Golden Globes '00: Actress—Drama (Streep); Screen Actors Guild '99: Actress (Streep).

Mutant

Nifty little zombie (sort of) flick featuring car designer Hauser and his brother being run off the road in Hicksville, USA, where Hopkins is the local sheriff. Luckily for us fans of the living-dead genre, there's a nasty little toxic waste dump nearby, and corpses are being reanimated and going after the living. Unfortunately for us fans of the living-dead genre, these dead guys have no desire to eat human flesh and instead kill their victims by sucking on their hands, a method which provides markedly less gore. The cool thing is that the zombies are not the usual slow-moving dopes, but instead seem chock-full of energy. Another argument for the proper disposal of hazardous waste. The image is slightly soft most of the time, colors are weak, and there is a definite grain all the way through. There's also occasional pixelation during some of the numerous hazy scenes. The sound is clear enough, but despite being a stereo mix, is very one dimensional. Given the low budget of the film (and Elite's reputation for doing the best they can), the flaws are most likely the result of the original preprint material, and the DVD is an incredible improvement over the previous VHS release. —*JO AKA:* Night Shadows.
Movie: ♪♪½ *DVD:* ♪♪½
Elite Entertainment, Inc. (Cat #EE6882, UPC #790594688226). Widescreen (1.85:1) anamorphic. Stereo. $24.95. Keepcase. *LANG:* English. *FEATURES:* 14 chapter links ● Theatrical trailer.
1983 (R) 100m/C Wings Hauser, Bo Hopkins, Jennifer Warren, Lee Montgomery; *D:*

John Cardos; **W:** Michael Jones; **C:** Alfred Taylor; **M:** Richard Band.

MVP: Most Valuable Primate

Jack is a young chimpanzee who has been taught sign language and is capable of many things that would typically be considered "human." When his mentor dies, Jack is sold to a laboratory but he ends up in the snowy regions of Canada where he befriends two young children—outsiders like himself. The image is clear, although in a number of scenes excessive grain is visible that results in a loss of detail. There is also a notable overenhancement of red evident in many parts of the film, creating a look that feels unnatural at times. The lack of scratches or other blemishes in the transfer still creates a good-looking presentation. The 5.1 track is surprisingly active and balanced, and makes very good use of the Surround channels. —GH

Movie: 🎬🎬 **DVD:** 🎬🎬
Warner Home Video, Inc. (UPC #08539373 0826). Full frame. Dolby Digital 5.1 Surround Stereo; Dolby Digital Surround. $24.98. Snapper. LANG: English; French. FEATURES: Commentary • Documentary • Theatrical trailer.
2000 (PG) 91m/C Kevin Zegers, Ric(k) Ducommun, Oliver Muirhead, Jamie Renee Smith; **D:** Robert Vince; **W:** Robert Vince, Anne Vince; **C:** Glen Winter; **M:** Brahm Wenger.

My Best Fiend

The relationship between filmmaker Werner Herzog and Klaus Kinski is the subject of this documentary. During Herzog's childhood, the extroverted eccentric actor lived in the same house in Munich, leaving remarkable memories in the young man's mind. The film follows them from adolescence to their collaborations in *Nosferatu*, *Aguirre*, *Fitzcarraldo*, and others. Unflinching, raw, and uncensored, the film shows the many sides of Kinski, from the philosophical to the vulgar, and at the same time describes the rather unique working relationship that grew between the two men. The material used comes from a variety of sources, including '70s television footage, and is varied in image quality. The entire presentation is absolutely clean, however, without flaws or blemishes. Although some of the raw behind-the-scenes material contains distortion—Kinski loved to yell, curse, and scream in fury—the audio is well integrated and absolutely sufficient for the subject matter, helping to paint an untamed image of the actor. —GH/MM **AKA:** Mein Liebster Fiend.

Movie: 🎬🎬🎬 **DVD:** 🎬🎬🎬
Anchor Bay (Cat #DV11236, UPC #013131 123692). Widescreen (1.77:1) anamorphic. Dolby Digital Surround Stereo. $29.98. Keepcase. LANG: German; English. SUB: English. FEATURES: Theatrical trailer.

1999 95m/C *GE GB* Werner Herzog, Klaus Kinski; **D:** Werner Herzog; **C:** Peter Zeitlinger; **Nar:** Werner Herzog.

My Cousin Vinny

Vinny Gambini (Pesci), a lawyer who took the bar exam six times before he passed, goes to Wahzoo City, Alabama (actually Georgia), to defend his cousin and a friend when they're accused of killing a convenience store clerk. Gold chains, Brooklyn accents, and his fiancée's (Tomei) tight leather outfits don't go over well with a conservative judge (Gwynn). The movie turned out to be a surprise commercial hit and won a deserved Oscar for Marisa Tomei. On his commentary track, director Lynn is fairly restrained. He's more interested in the filmmaking process than in gossip and he admits his own culture shock at coming from England to shoot in the South. The widescreen image ranges between very good and excellent and Lynn does use the entire screen. Pan-and-scan tapes lose a lot. —MM

Movie: 🎬🎬🎬 **DVD:** 🎬🎬🎬
20th Century Fox Home Entertainment (Cat #2000531, UPC #024543005315). Widescreen (1.85:1) anamorphic. Dolby Digital Surround Stereo. $24.98. Keepcase. LANG: English; French. SUB: English; Spanish. FEATURES: 24 chapter links • TV spots • Trailers • Commentary: director.
1992 (R) 120m/C Joe Pesci, Ralph Macchio, Marisa Tomei, Mitchell Whitfield, Fred Gwynne, Lane Smith, Austin Pendleton, Bruce McGill; **D:** Jonathan Lynn; **W:** Dale Launer; **C:** Peter Deming; **M:** Randy Edelman. AWARDS: Oscars '92: Support. Actress (Tomei); MTV Movie Awards '93: Breakthrough Perf. (Tomei).

My Dog Skip

This is just the kind of movie people are talking about when they complain that there's no family friendly movies being made anymore. In 1940s Mississippi, awkward only child Willie (Muniz) sees his life change when, over the protests of his overprotective father (Bacon), he gets a puppy, Skip, for his ninth birthday. Amid much nostalgia and sentiment, Willie learns to be more outgoing and has many coming-of-age moments. Even if some of the plot elements are weak, the look and feel of the period is captured well, and Muniz does a fine job, although no human is likely to compete with the pooch, anyway. Kids will love the antics of Skip, and adults will enjoy having their hearts and memories tugged. Based on the book by Willie Morris. All in all, another good-looking transfer from Warner. The image is crystal clear except in some of the bright outdoor scenes, where minimal digital grain is introduced. Colors are bold, saturated, and accurate, appearing natural at all times. The 5.1 mix isn't really needed (the Surround tracks are heard only in a couple of scenes) but it's nice having the added dimensionality and solid low end for the score. Both commentaries on the

disc are worthwhile: Russell's reveals quite a bit about his enthusiasm and the making of the film and Muniz's is amusing and short, not running the length of the film. —JO

Movie: 🎬🎬🎬½ **DVD:** 🎬🎬🎬½
Warner Home Video, Inc. (Cat #18286, UPC #08539182862). Widescreen anamorphic. Dolby Digital 5.1. $19.98. Snapper. LANG: English; French. SUB: English; French. CAP: English.
1999 (PG) 95m/C Frankie Muniz, Diane Lane, Kevin Bacon, Luke Wilson, Caitlin Wachs, Bradley Coryell, Daylan Honeycutt, Cody Linley; **D:** Jay Russell; **W:** Gail Gilchriest; **C:** James L. Carter; **M:** William Ross; **Nar:** Harry Connick Jr.

My Favorite Brunette

This disc fares poorly when compared to the Marengo edition of the film on the *Bob Hope Double Feature*. (Please see review.) Muddy transfer. So-so sound. —MM

Movie: 🎬🎬½ **DVD:** 🎬
Madacy Entertainment (Cat #DVD-9-9024, UPC #056775006099). Full frame. Dolby Digital Mono. $9.98. Snapper. LANG: English. FEATURES: 9 chapter links • Trivia • Bob Hope thumbnail bio.
1947 85m/B Bob Hope, Dorothy Lamour, Peter Lorre, Lon Chaney Jr., Alan Ladd, Reginald Denny, Bing Crosby; **D:** Elliott Nugent; **W:** Edmund Beloin, Jack Rose; **C:** Lionel Lindon; **M:** Robert Emmett Dolan.

My 5 Wives

Rodney Dangerfield fans are the target audience for this rough-hewn comedy that the star co-wrote. He plays L.A. real estate tycoon Monty Peterson, who has just finished his third divorce when a land deal in Utah leads to his marriage to three nubile Mormon cutie-pies. Two more sign on as a gangster (Stiller) tries to steal the place. Curiously, the sexual jokes are relatively tame compared to the excesses of so many teen comedies. This is a low-budget production and DVD can do little to polish the image. Sound is fine for Dangerfield's delivery. —MM

Movie: 🎬🎬 **DVD:** 🎬🎬
Artisan Entertainment (Cat #10806, UPC #012236108061). Widescreen (1.77:1) anamorphic. Dolby Digital Surround Stereo. $24.98. Keepcase. LANG: English. CAP: English. FEATURES: 30 chapter links • Trailer • Interview • Talent files • Production notes.
2000 (R) 100m/C Rodney Dangerfield, Andrew Dice Clay, John Byner, Molly Shannon, Jerry Stiller, John Pinette, Emmanuelle Vaugier, Fred Keating, Kate Luyben, Judy Tylor, Angelika Baran, Anita Brown; **D:** Sidney J. Furie; **W:** Rodney Dangerfield, Harry Basil; **C:** Curtis Petersen; **M:** Robert Carli.

My Life

Maudlin, sometimes depressing production preaches the power of a well-examined life. From the beginning we know that

PR guy Bob Jones (Keaton) has been diagnosed with cancer and will probably die before the birth of his first child. He makes a series of videotapes of himself so that his son will know who he was. Kidman has relatively little to do as his wife. This kind of glossy, undemanding material really gains little on DVD. Surround sound does nice things with John Barry's score. Image is about the same as tape. —*MM*
Movie: 🎵🎵½ **DVD:** 🎵🎵
Columbia Tristar Home Video (Cat #05853, UPC #043396058538). Widescreen letterboxed; full frame. Dolby Digital Surround; Mono. $24.99. Keepcase. *LANG:* English; French; Spanish. *SUB:* English; French; Spanish. *FEATURES:* Talent files • Trailer • 28 chapter links.
1993 (PG-13) 114m/C Michael Keaton, Nicole Kidman, Haing S. Ngor, Bradley Whitford, Queen Latifah, Michael Constantine, Toni Sawyer, Rebecca Schull, Lee Garlington; *D:* Bruce Joel Rubin; *W:* Bruce Joel Rubin; *C:* Peter James; *M:* John Barry.

My Mom's a Werewolf

An average suburban mother (Blakely) gets involved with a dashing stranger and soon, to her terror, begins to turn into a werewolf. Her daughter is sooooo embarrassed. Both sound and the full-frame image are identical to VHS tape. —*MM*
Movie: 🎵½ **DVD:** 🎵½
Rhino Home Video (Cat #5741). Full frame. Snapper. $14.95. *LANG:* English; Spanish. *FEATURES:* 6 chapter links • Stills • Cast bios.
1989 (PG) 90m/C Susan Blakely, John Saxon, John Schuck, Katrina Caspary, Ruth Buzzi, Marilyn McCoo, Marcia Wallace, Diana Barrows; *D:* Michael Fischa; *W:* Mark Pirro; *C:* Bryan England; *M:* Dana Walden, Barry Fasman.

My Sex Life... Or How I Got into an Argument

French writer and director Arnaud Desplechin proves that whining is not strictly an American trait. His lead Gen-X character Paul (Amalric) manages to sustain the whine through three separate relationships and three hours of screen time. He's a professional student, who after ten years of living with an unmotivated girlfriend Esther (Devos), decides that he's not happy and not making much progress. Three hours later he still is unhappy, now alone, and has made little progress in defining his life—oh well. A frustrating film as Desplechin lacks the discipline to cut his vision to a manageable length. A meandering script, with too many superfluous characters, takes this simple story to marathon lengths. A featureless DVD presentation with "burned-in" English subtitles and no optional features, coupled with only eight chapter stops for a three hour movie, only adds to the viewing frustration created by director Desplechin and

his unruly script. —*RJT* *AKA:* Ma Vie Sexuelle...Comment Je Me Suis Dispute.
Movie: 🎵🎵 **DVD:** 🎵🎵
Winstar Home Entertainment (Cat #FLV5229, UPC #720917522920). Widescreen. Dolby Digital Stereo. $24.98. Keepcase. *LANG:* French. *SUB:* English. *CAP:* English. *FEATURES:* 8 chapter links • Filmographies and cast list.
1996 178m/C *FR* Mathieu Amalric, Marianne (Cuau) Denicourt, Emmanuelle Devos, Emmanuel Salinger, Jeanne Balibar, Michel Vuillermoz; *D:* Arnaud Desplechin; *W:* Arnaud Desplechin, Emmanuel Bourdieu; *C:* Eric Gautier; *M:* Krishna Levy.

My Son, the Vampire

Irish scullery maid Mother Riley runs afoul of the malevolent Professor Van Hussen (Lugosi), who fancies himself a vampire and desires world domination. When a mix-up lands the irrepressible housekeeper in the clutches of Van Hussen and his creepy gang, "the Vampire" gets more than he bargained for. Mother Riley stumbles upon his nefarious plans and tries to stop him. Slap-"shtick" reigns supreme here, whether it's Mother Riley landing legs up in a barrel of flour or the requisite sped-up car chase. With her bulbous face and constant barrage of spoonerisms, Riley's simple physical being supposedly constitutes the entire joke behind the character and her antics, especially when interacting with authority, no doubt connoted the skewering of the upper classes in English music-hall revues. The sharp-looking transfer sports deep blacks and a higher-than-expected degree of detail delineation. With a few instances of speckling and occasional incongruous splices, the source for the most part is in surprisingly good condition. Mono sound is adequate, the infrequent hiss and pop not too distracting. Only extra is a theatrical trailer, devoid of any clips and instead selling Allan Sherman (he composed and performed the film's title song, for me the only bright spot in the movie) to potential audiences. If you are a fan of the series, the DVD should vindicate your devotion. For the rest of us, it's a feeble relic. —*EP* *AKA:* Old Mother Riley Meets the Vampire; The Vampire and the Robot; Vampire over London; Mother Riley Meets the Vampire.
Movie: 🎵 **DVD:** 🎵🎵🎵½
Image Entertainment (Cat #ID06608WE DVD, UPC #14381660892). Full frame. Dolby Digital Mono. $24.99. Snapper. *LANG:* English. *FEATURES:* 16 chapter links • Theatrical trailer.
1952 72m/B *GB* Bela Lugosi, Arthur Lucan, Dora Bryan, Richard Wattis; *D:* John Gilling; *W:* Val Valentine; *C:* Stanley Pavey.

My Teacher's Wife

Updated version of *My Tutor* throws a few complications into the younger boy/older woman romance. Todd Boomer (London) needs help to pass calculus to get into college. His tutor Vicki Mueller (Carrere)

turns out to be a babe and the wife of his evil math teacher (McDonald). The full-frame DVD image is good to very good but not really much better than tape. The animated interludes are drawn by Bill Plympton. —*MM*
Movie: 🎵🎵 **DVD:** 🎵🎵
Trimark Home Video (Cat #6911). Full frame. Stereo. $24.99. Snapper. *LANG:* English. *SUB:* English; French; Spanish. *CAP:* English. *FEATURES:* 30 chapter links • Trailer.
1995 (R) 90m/C Tia Carrere, Jason London, Christopher McDonald, Leslie Lyles, Zak Orth, Jeffrey Tambor, Randy Pearlstein; *D:* Bruce Leddy; *W:* Bruce Leddy, Seth Greenland; *C:* Zoltan David; *M:* Kevin Gilbert.

Mystery, Alaska

Sports Illustrated writer (and ex-local) Charles Danner (Azaria) does a feature on his hometown's weekly cutthroat hockey game. The piece draws interest and as a publicity stunt, the New York Rangers fly into remote Mystery, Alaska, for an exhibition game. Then the aging team captain and sheriff John Biebe (Crowe) is asked to step aside for young phenom Stevie Weeks (Northcott). Yes, it's pretty predictable but that's not a fatal flaw in sports comedies. Potentially troublesome snowy exteriors don't display enough artifacts to be annoying. Sound is very good, too. A solid sleeper. —*MM*
Movie: 🎵🎵🎵 **DVD:** 🎵🎵🎵
Hollywood Pictures Home Video (Cat #18291, UPC #717951004772). Widescreen (2.35:1) anamorphic. Dolby Digital 5.1 Surround Stereo. $32.99. Keepcase. *LANG:* English; French. *CAP:* English. *FEATURES:* 30 chapter links • "Making of" featurette • Trailer.
1999 (R) 118m/C Russell Crowe, Hank Azaria, Mary McCormack, Burt Reynolds, Ron Eldard, Lolita (David) Davidovich, Colm Meaney, Maury Chaykin, Ryan Northcott, Scott Grimes, Judith Ivey, Rachel Wilson, Mike Myers; *Cameos:* Little Richard; *D:* Jay Roach; *W:* David E. Kelley, Sean O'Byrne; *C:* Peter Deming; *M:* Carter Burwell.

Mystery of the Necronomicon

This anime owes much more to *Urotsukodoji* than to H.P. Lovecraft, though it appropriates the horror master's famous book of evil. The plot is a Grand Guignol mixture of violence and sex set at a snowbound mountain ski resort where a group of characters, including our hero detective Suzusaki (voices of Nakamura and Wilson in Japanese and English), are trapped with a mad murderer. This is not the brightest or the sharpest animation you'll ever see. It's not a significant improvement over tape. Sound is better, particularly the option of Japanese or English dialogue. The two are equally expressive. —*MM*
Movie: 🎵🎵½ **DVD:** 🎵🎵½
Central Park Media/U.S. Manga Corps (Cat #A18D-2043, UPC #719987204324). Full

frame. Dolby Digital Stereo. $29.95. Keep-case. *LANG:* Japanese; English. *SUB:* English. *FEATURES:* 8 chapter links • Character sketches • Storyboards • Anime art form featurette • Previews • DVD-ROM features.
2000 (NC-17) 120m/C *JP* **D:** Hideki Takayama; **W:** Ryo Saga; **M:** Kazuhiko Izu, Hiroaki Sano; **V:** Hidetoshi Nakamura, Tom Wilson, Yoko Asada, Tara Jane.

Mystic Pizza

Intelligent coming-of-age drama centers on two sisters, Daisy (Roberts) and Kat (Gish), and their best friend Jojo (Taylor) as they struggle with their hopes, loves, and family rivalries in the small town of Mystic, Connecticut. At times, it's predictable, but there are enough unexpected moments to keep interest high. During the theatrical release, newcomer Roberts got most of the attention, but her co-stars are just as winning. DVD has a very good image. Some of the night scenes appear overly dark, but, as I remember them, they've always looked that way. Sound is fine. —*MM*
Movie: ♫♫♫½ **DVD:** ♫♫♫
MGM Home Entertainment (Cat #100145 8, UPC #027616857781). Widescreen (1.85:1) anamorphic. Dolby Digital Surround Stereo; Mono. $19.98. Keepcase. *LANG:* English; French; Spanish. *SUB:* French; Spanish. *FEATURES:* Trailer • 16 chapter links.
1988 (R) 101m/C Annabeth Gish, Julia Roberts, Lili Taylor, Vincent D'Onofrio, William R. Moses, Adam Storke, Conchata Ferrell, Joanna Merlin, Matt Damon; **D:** Donald Petrie; **W:** Amy Holden Jones, Perry Howze, Alfred Uhry; **C:** Tim Suhrstedt; **M:** David McHugh. *AWARDS:* Ind. Spirit '89: First Feature.

The Myth of Fingerprints

Four adult siblings and their various partners return to their New England home to spend Thanksgiving with their parents. As with most movie families of upper–middle class status, old resentments and issues abound. Freundlich's debut doesn't go for a grand conclusion or startling revelation. Depending on your taste for pat endings and easy answers, that could be the film's greatest asset or a reason not to bother. Excellent performances by a great cast should have a bearing on your decision. The DVD image is clean throughout with grain visible in only a handful of scenes. Although the color balance appears quite natural, there is a slight oversaturation in the red tones, which may have been done purposely to create a warmer-looking image, especially in the cozy indoor environments. The Surround mix is clean and free of noise. The frequency response is very natural, creating an ambience that is always appropriate and warm. —*GH/MM*
Movie: ♫♫½ **DVD:** ♫♫♫
Columbia Tristar Home Video (Cat #4750). Widescreen (1.85:1) anamorphic. Dolby

Digital Surround Stereo. $27.95. Keepcase. *LANG:* English. *SUB:* English; Spanish; Portuguese; Chinese; Korean; Thai. *FEATURES:* Commentary: Freundlich and cinematographer Stephen Kazmierski • Trailers • Talent files.
1997 (R) 91m/C Blythe Danner, Roy Scheider, Julianne Moore, Noah Wyle, Michael Vartan, Laurel Holloman, Hope Davis, Brian Kerwin, James LeGros; **D:** Bart Freundlich; **W:** Bart Freundlich; **C:** Stephen Kazmierski; **M:** David Bridie, John Phillips. *AWARDS: NOM:* Ind. Spirit '98: Support. Actor (Scheider).

The Naked Gun: From the Files of Police Squad

More hysterical satire from the creators of *Airplane.* The short-lived television cop spoof *Police Squad* moves to the big screen and has Lt. Drebin uncover a plot to assassinate Queen Elizabeth while she is visiting Los Angeles. Nearly nonstop gags and pratfalls provide lots of laughs. Nielsen is perfect as Drebin and the supporting cast is strong; cameos abound. As you'd expect, this DVD blows away all earlier home video versions. The transfer is so clear that many more print flaws show up than did on the previous editions. Colors and contrast are very good. Only occasional Surround effects are used, but the 5.1 mix sounds great and the all-important dialogue is better heard than ever. One big highlight on the disc is the commentary, which is outright hilarious on its own, often at the expense of O.J. One only wishes that some of the outtakes talked about were included on the disc, but the commentary more than makes up for it. —*JO*
Movie: ♫♫♫ **DVD:** ♫♫♫
Paramount Home Video (Cat #321007, UPC #097363210078). Widescreen (1.85:1) anamorphic. Dolby Digital 5.1; Dolby Digital Mono. $24.99. Keepcase. *LANG:* English; French. *SUB:* English. *CAP:* English. *FEATURES:* 27 chapter links • Theatrical trailer • Commentary: David Zucker, Robert Weiss, Peter Tilden.
1988 (PG-13) 85m/C Leslie Nielsen, Ricardo Montalban, Priscilla Presley, George Kennedy, O.J. Simpson, Nancy Marchand, John Houseman; **Cameos:** Weird Al Yankovic, Reggie Jackson, Dr. Joyce Brothers; **D:** David Zucker; **W:** Jerry Zucker, Jim Abrahams, Pat Proft, David Zucker; **M:** Ira Newborn.

Naked Gun 2 1/2: The Smell of Fear

Lt. Drebin returns to rescue the world from a faulty energy policy devised by the White House and oil-lords. A notch down from the original entry, but still a hilarious cop parody. Nielsen has his character down to a tee, and there's a laugh every minute. The second in the series gets another fine transfer to DVD and this time preprint damage is pretty much nonexistent. The picture seems to be a little softer, but

there is slightly more color and a touch more contrast, giving a fresher look to the film. As with the first, there is a new 5.1 mix for the DVD and in this case, a lot more use is made of the Surround channels, though nothing as aggressive as one would find on the typical Schwarzenegger flick. Also, like the first, the commentary is nearly as funny as the film itself and, unlike most of these tracks, worth more than one listen. —*JO*
Movie: ♫♫½ **DVD:** ♫♫♫
Paramount Home Video (Cat #323657, UPC #097363236573). Widescreen (1.85:1) anamorphic. Dolby Digital 5.1. $24.99. Keepcase. *LANG:* English. *SUB:* English. *FEATURES:* 15 chapter links • Theatrical trailers • Commentary: David Zucker, Robert Weiss, Peter Tilden.
1991 (PG-13) 85m/C Leslie Nielsen, Priscilla Presley, George Kennedy, O.J. Simpson, Robert Goulet, Richard Griffiths, Jacqueline Brookes, Lloyd Bochner, Tim O'Connor, Peter Mark Richman; **Cameos:** Mel Torme, Eva Gabor, Weird Al Yankovic; **D:** David Zucker; **W:** David Zucker, Pat Proft; **M:** Ira Newborn.

Naked Gun 33 1/3: The Final Insult

Ever dumb, crass, and crude, Lt. Drebin returns to the force from retirement to lead an investigation into terrorist activities in Hollywood. Lots of current events jokes—dated as soon as they hit the screen. This one returns the series to the level of the original and is sure to satisfy fans with a taste for bad puns. Watch for cameos, especially at the "Oscars." The picture quality on this DVD jumps up a notch from the first two in the series, even though there is an occasional artifact. This time around the preprint is perfect, and the image is solidly sharp throughout. Colors are also a touch more vibrant and there is never a hint of bleed. Again, not much use is made of the Surrounds, but the 5.1 audio is substantially improved over both laser and VHS versions of the film. With this concluding entry to the *Naked Gun* trilogy comes another absolutely hilarious commentary track which, as did the others, offers far more in the way of chuckles and personality than in technical talk. All three DVDs are worth adding to the collection, even if only for the three commentaries...and the movies aren't bad either. —*JO*
Movie: ♫♫♫ **DVD:** ♫♫♫½
Paramount Home Video (Cat #327857, UPC #097363278542). Widescreen (1.85:1) anamorphic. Dolby Digital 5.1; Dolby Surround. $24.99. Keepcase. *LANG:* English; French. *SUB:* English. *CAP:* English. *FEATURES:* 17 chapter links • Theatrical trailer • Commentary: David Zucker, Robert Weiss, Peter Segal, Michael Ewing.
1994 (PG-13) 90m/C Leslie Nielsen, Priscilla Presley, O.J. Simpson, Fred Ward, George Kennedy, Gary Cooper, Kathleen Freeman, Raquel Welch; **Cameos:** Pia Zadora, James Earl Jones, Weird Al Yankovic, Ann B. Davis; **D:** Peter Segal; **W:**

Robert Locash, David Zucker, Pat Proft; **M:** Ira Newborn. *AWARDS:* Golden Raspberries '94: Worst Support. Actor (Simpson), Worst New Star (Smith).

Naked Killer

Kitty (Yau) is trying to avenge her father's murderer when she is befriended by Cindy (Madoka), a professional hitwoman who teaches her the tricks of the trade. Things become more complicated when policeman Tinam (Yam) falls for Kitty. The violence in this archetypal bizarro Hong Kong action flick is straight out of a comic book. Think John Woo with PMS and on acid. The DVD image is on a par with most HK imports. It's on the harsh side with softish reds. The goofy dubbing is part of the fun for those on the right wavelength. —*MM*
AKA: Chiklo Gouyeung.
Movie: ♫♫ **DVD:** ♫♫½
Tai Seng Video Marketing (Cat #57974). Widescreen letterboxed. Dolby Digital 5.1 Surround Stereo. $49.95. Keepcase. *LANG:* English. *SUB:* English. *FEATURES:* Trailer ● 9 chapter links.
1992 86m/C *HK* Chingmy Yau, Simon Yam, Carrie Ng, Kelly Yao, Svenvara Madoka; **D:** Clarence Fok Yiu Leung; **W:** Jing Wong; **C:** Peter Pau, William Yim; **M:** Lowell Lo.

Napoleon

Cute kiddie-pic is aimed at lovers of small furry animals. Golden retriever pup Muffin thinks of himself as Napoleon because he is so brave and adventurous. If only his mom would let him be free. He gets his chance when he's accidentally lifted aloft in a balloon and lands in Sydney, Australia. From there, it's off to the outback to find his wild relatives, the dingoes. The complexity and wit of *Babe* is completely absent. Disc may be a step down from VHS tape because artifacts are so heavy in exterior panning shots. —*MM*
Movie: ♫♫ **DVD:** ♫♫
MGM Home Entertainment (Cat #10016 04, UPC #027616859143). Full frame. Dolby Digital Surround Stereo. $24.99. Keepcase. *LANG:* English; Spanish. *SUB:* French; Spanish. *CAP:* English. *FEATURES:* 16 chapter links ● Trailer.
1996 (G) 81m/C *AU JP* **D:** Mario Andreacchio; **W:** Mario Andreacchio, Mark Saltzman; **C:** Roger Dowling; **M:** Bill Conti; **V:** Jamie Croft, Philip Quast, Carole Skinner, Anne Louise Lambert, David Argue, Joan Rivers, Steven Vidler, Susan Lyons.

Nashville

Altman and Tewkesbury's brilliant tapestry follows the lives of 24 people during a political campaign/music festival in Nashville. From the opening credits, the film repeatedly blurs reality and fiction with seemingly extraneous vignettes and actors playing themselves (Elliott Gould and Julie Christie). In turns, it's funny, touching, and poignant—always fascinating. On DVD, the film looks better than it did when I last saw it on the big screen at a festival some

years ago. Altman's commentary is one of his best and that's about as good as they come. If the enhanced soundtrack heightens the mediocrity of some of the songs, well, that's always been true. One of the greats. —*MM*
Movie: ♫♫♫♫ **DVD:** ♫♫♫♫
Paramount Home Video (Cat #08821, UPC #097360882179). Widescreen anamorphic. Dolby Digital 5.1 Surround Stereo. $29.99. Keepcase. *LANG:* English. *SUB:* English. *FEATURES:* 17 chapter links ● Trailer ● Commentary: Robert Altman ● Interview with Altman.
1975 (R) 159m/C Keith Carradine, Lily Tomlin, Henry Gibson, Ronee Blakley, Keenan Wynn, David Arkin, Geraldine Chaplin, Lauren Hutton, Shelley Duvall, Barbara Harris, Allen (Goorwitz) Garfield, Karen Black, Christina Raines, Michael Murphy, Ned Beatty, Barbara Baxley, Scott Glenn, Jeff Goldblum, Gwen Welles, Bert Remsen, Robert DoQui, Elliott Gould, Julie Christie; **D:** Robert Altman; **W:** Joan Tewkesbury; **C:** Paul Lohmann; **M:** Richard Baskin. *AWARDS:* Oscars '75: Song ("I'm Easy"); Golden Globes '76: Song ("I'm Easy"); Natl. Bd. of Review '75: Director (Altman), Support. Actress (Blakley), Natl. Film Reg. '92; N.Y. Film Critics '75: Director (Altman), Film, Support. Actress (Tomlin); Natl. Soc. Film Critics '75: Director (Altman), Film, Support. Actor (Gibson), Support. Actress (Tomlin); *NOM:* Oscars '75: Director (Altman), Picture, Support. Actress (Blakley, Tomlin).

National Lampoon's Golf Punks

In debt to gamblers, Al Oliver (Arnold) hires on as a golf instructor to a group of misfit, geeky kids. By the end, they enter a prestigious tournament. This may not be the worst movie ever to be associated with the "National Lampoon" label, but it's certainly one of the cheapest looking. The soft fuzzy image is much worse than most tapes, though that may come from the low-budget original. Substandard in every way. —*MM*
Movie: ♫ **DVD:** ♫
Avalanche Entertainment (Cat #13978). Full frame. Dolby Digital Stereo. $24.95. Keepcase. *LANG:* English. *SUB:* Spanish. *FEATURES:* 12 chapter links ● Photo gallery ● Tom Arnold thumbnail bio ● Synopsis.
1999 (PG-13) 95m/C *CA* Tom Arnold, James Kirk, Rene Tardif; **D:** Harvey Frost; **W:** Jill Mazursky; **C:** Patrick Williams; **M:** Richard Bronskill.

The Natural

The years have been kind to Barry Levinson's adaptation of Bernard Malamud's novel of baseball and myth. Roy Hobbs's (Redford) gift for baseball sets him apart and attracts women who prove to be the undoing of his youthful career. But he gets a second chance as an overaged rookie. For my money, this is the perfect Hollywood sports movie (though the city of Buf-

falo, N.Y., deserves a lot of credit, too). It's beautifully cast and acted. Director and star understand the material on an elemental level. The soft nostalgic look of the film translates well to disc. My only criticisms are two omissions: 1) a commentary track by Levinson and 2) a separate audio track for Randy Newman's score, another personal favorite. —*MM*
Movie: ♫♫♫♫ **DVD:** ♫♫♫½
Columbia Tristar Home Video (Cat #04609, UPC #043396046092). Widescreen (1.85:1) anamorphic. Dolby Digital 4.0 Surround; Dolby Digital Surround. $24.95. Keepcase. *LANG:* English; French; Spanish; Portuguese. *SUB:* English; French; Spanish; Portuguese; Chinese; Korean; Thai. *FEATURES:* 28 chapter links ● Documentary with Cal Ripkin Jr. ● Trailers ● Talent files ● Production notes.
1984 (PG) 134m/C Robert Redford, Glenn Close, Robert Duvall, Kim Basinger, Wilford Brimley, Barbara Hershey, Richard Farnsworth, Robert Prosky, Darren McGavin, Joe Don Baker, Michael Madsen; **D:** Barry Levinson; **W:** Roger Towne, Phil Dusenberry; **C:** Caleb Deschanel; **M:** Randy Newman. *AWARDS:* NOM: Oscars '84: Art Dir./Set Dec., Cinematog., Support. Actress (Close), Orig. Score.

Natural Born Killers [DC]

Like almost all of Stone's films, this one is compelling, stylistically rich, and seriously flawed. Told with the pace and look of a rock video, it's a two-hour hallucination of violence—*A Clockwork Orange* taken to the nth degree. The director means it to be a parody of contemporary attitudes toward celebrity criminals (Harrelson and Lewis). But the film falls victim to its own excesses and has nothing new to say about the subject. In the end, Stone exploits the very exploitation he claims to deplore. Not surprisingly, his commentary track is defensive in tone. In an opening disclaimer, Trimark even dissociates itself from those opinions. Image and sound are both faithful re-creations of the theatrical release. On anything but the largest home theatre screen, however, the film loses much of its aggressive power. —*MM*
Movie: ♫♫ **DVD:** ♫♫♫½
Trimark Home Video (Cat #VM7292D, UPC #031398729228). Widescreen (1.85:1) letterboxed. $24.99. Keepcase. *SUB:* English; French; Spanish. *FEATURES:* Deleted scenes ● Commentary: director ● Alternative ending ● "Making of" featurette ● Trailer.
1994 (R) 121m/C Woody Harrelson, Robert Downey Jr., Juliette Lewis, Tommy Lee Jones, Ashley Judd, Tom Sizemore, Rodney Dangerfield, Rachel Ticotin, Arliss Howard, Russell Means, Denis Leary, Steven Wright, Pruitt Taylor Vince, Dale Dye; **D:** Oliver Stone; **W:** Oliver Stone; **C:** Robert Richardson; **M:** Trent Reznor. *AWARDS:* NOM: Golden Globes '95: Director (Stone); MTV Movie Awards '95: On-Screen Duo (Woody Harrelson/Juliette Lewis), Kiss (Woody Harrelson/Juliette Lewis).

Nautilus

In the year 2099, the Earth is an ecological ruin. But the captain (Norton) of an experimental submarine believes that he can take the craft back in time a full century and correct a key mistake that ruined his present. His daughter (Jaenicke), a commando, is on hand to help. The computer effects are O.K. for low-budget science fiction; the tacky submarine sets are not. Overall, DVD image is no improvement over tape. Menu is kind of nice. —MM
Movie: ♫♫½ **DVD:** ♫♫
MTI Home Video (Cat #BE50028DVDS, UPC #619935402836). Full frame. $24.95. Keepcase. *LANG:* English. *SUB:* Spanish. *FEATURES:* 20 chapter links • Trailers • Talent files.
1999 (R) 90m/C Richard Norton, Hannes Jaenicke, Miranda Wolfe.

The Navigator

Creative time travel story revolves around a 14th-century boy with visionary powers who leads a group of men from his village away from the plague by tunneling through the Earth and into late 20th-century New Zealand. It plays better than it reads with some intriguing visual effects. The dark image—black and white, color, and tinted—is on the soft side, with heavy grain in some night scenes. It's really not much better than tape, but strong visuals are not the point. Same for sound. —MM
Movie: ♫♫♫ **DVD:** ♫♫
Hen's Tooth Video (Cat #4045, UPC #7597 31404525). Full frame. $24.95. Keepcase. *LANG:* English. *FEATURES:* 12 chapter links.
1988 (PG) 92m/C *NZ* Hamish McFarlane, Bruce Lyons, Chris Haywood, Marshall Napier, Noel Appleby, Paul Livingston, Sarah Pierse; **D:** Vincent Ward; **W:** Vincent Ward. *AWARDS:* Australian Film Inst. '88: Cinematog., Director (Ward), Film.

Navy SEALS [MGM]

Macho Navy commandos, whose regular work is rescuing hostages from Middle Eastern underground organizations, find a stash of deadly weapons. They spend the balance of the movie attempting to destroy the arsenal. Sheen chews the scenery as the crazy member of the team. The image is good enough for such a mindless exercise in explosives, but the sound is comparatively weak. —MM
Movie: ♫½ **DVD:** ♫♫
MGM Home Entertainment (Cat #10015 59, UPC #027616858696). Widescreen (1.85:1) anamorphic. Dolby Digital Surround Stereo. $19.98. Keepcase. *LANG:* English; French. *SUB:* French; Spanish. *CAP:* English. *FEATURES:* 16 chapter links • Trailer.
1990 (R) 113m/C Charlie Sheen, Michael Biehn, Joanne Whalley, Rick Rossovich, Cyril O'Reilly, Bill Paxton, Dennis Haysbert, Paul Sanchez, Ron Joseph, Nicholas Kadi; **D:** Lewis Teague; **W:** Gary Goldman; **C:** John A. Alonzo; **M:** Sylvester Levay.

Necessary Roughness

Coach Ed Gennero (Elizondo) takes over the Texas State Fighting Armadillos after the school is put on NCAA probation. His quarterback (Bakula) is a 34-year-old who never got to play at the college level. The rest of the team is the usual collection of misfits (including comedian Sinbad and swimsuit babe Ireland). Is there any chance that they will be able to beat their hated rivals in the final game? The film follows the sports formula down to the last jot and tittle, but it's a comfortable formula. DVD really doesn't bring much to this amiable shaggy dog. On disc, it looks about the same as it did in the theatre. —MM
Movie: ♫♫½ **DVD:** ♫♫½
Paramount Home Video (Cat #32597, UPC #097363259749). Widescreen anamorphic. Dolby Digital 5.1 Surround Stereo; Dolby Digital Surround Stereo. $24.99. Keepcase. *LANG:* English; French. *SUB:* English. *FEATURES:* 15 chapter links.
1991 (PG-13) 108m/C Scott Bakula, Robert Loggia, Harley Jane Kozak, Sinbad, Hector Elizondo, Kathy Ireland, Jason Bateman; **D:** Stan Dragoti; **W:** Rick Natkin, David Fuller; **C:** Peter Stein; **M:** Bill Conti.

Necromancer: Satan's Servant

After Julie (Cayton) is raped by two students, she contacts a sorceress and takes supernatural revenge with the aid of a demon. DVD offers no real improvement over VHS tape. —MM
Movie: ♫♫ **DVD:** ♫♫
Image Entertainment (Cat #OVED6833DVD, UPC #014381683325). Full frame. Dolby Digital Stereo. $24.99. Snapper. *LANG:* English. *FEATURES:* 12 chapter links.
1988 (R) 90m/C Elizabeth (Kaitan) Cayton, Russ Tamblyn, Rhonda Dorton; **D:** Dusty Nelson; **W:** William T. Naud; **C:** Eric Cayla, Richard Clabaugh; **M:** Kevin Klinger, Bob Mamet, Gary Stockdale.

Neon Genesis Evangelion Collection

In yet another post-apocalyptic animated future, mankind fights against giant mechanical beings, mass destruction, monsters, robots, and lots of explosions. It's up to teens to save the world, all with a disco soundtrack. The full-frame image is very clear and bright. The English dialogue track is more emotional and detailed than most. Disc contains four episodes of the TV series. —MM **AKA:** Shin Seiki Evangelion.
Movie: ♫♫ **DVD:** ♫♫½
A.D.V. Films (Cat #DVDEV/001, UPC #702 727001123). Full frame. Dolby Digital Stereo. $29.98. Keepcase. *LANG:* English; French; Spanish; Japanese. *SUB:* English. *FEATURES:* 16 chapter links • Character bios • DVD credits.
1999 120m/C *JP* **D:** Hideaki Anno; **W:** Hideaki Anno; **C:** Yoichi Kuroda; **M:** Shiroh Sagisu.

Neurotica: Middle–Age Spread and Other Life Crises

Here's another winner from the National Film Board of Canada. Some of these short animated films have been collected in other of their *Best of the Best...* discs. (Please see individual reviews.) These cartoons are aimed at adults. Two of them— "Bob's Birthday" and "Special Delivery"— are Oscar winners and three others are nominees. Full-frame image and sound are excellent. Contents: "Bob's Birthday," "No Problem," "George and Rosemary," "Strings," "The Big Snit," "Shyness," "Getting Started," "Special Delivery," "Get a Job," "Why Me?" and "Scant Sanity." —MM
Movie: ♫♫♫½ **DVD:** ♫♫♫
Image Entertainment (Cat #ID0242NFDVD, UPC #014381024227). Full frame. Dolby Digital Surround Stereo. $24.99. Snapper. *LANG:* English. *FEATURES:* 11 chapter links.
1997 113m/C *CA*

Never Cry Wolf

A young biologist (Smith) is sent to the Arctic to study the behavior and habitation of wolves, and then becomes deeply involved with their lives. The image is, on the whole, very good, though it does tend to go a bit soft in places. The transfer is fairly clean with only the occasional nick or blemish. Surprisingly, the video handles the vast expanse of whiteness that comes from filming in a snowbound setting very well and black levels are also accurate. While never reaching very high, or dipping very low, the audio is well balanced. —MP/MM
Movie: ♫♫♫½ **DVD:** ♫♫♫
Anchor Bay (Cat #10990). Widescreen (1.85:1) letterboxed. Dolby Digital Stereo. $24.98. Keepcase. *LANG:* English.
1983 (PG) 105m/C Charles Martin Smith, Brian Dennehy, Samson Jorah; **D:** Carroll Ballard; **W:** Curtis Hanson, Sam Hamm; **C:** Hiro Narita; **M:** Mark Isham. *AWARDS:* Natl. Soc. Film Critics '83: Cinematog; *NOM:* Oscars '83: Sound.

Never Too Late

Olive (Leachman), Rose (Dukakis), Joseph (Rubes), and Woody (Lapointe) meet at the funeral of a mutual friend. They come to realize that he was bilked out of his life savings by the manager (Craven) of his retirement home. Despite their advanced years, they decide to seek their own financial justice. Low-budget Canadian production gains nothing on DVD. Image and sound are identical to tape. —MM
Movie: ♫♫ **DVD:** ♫♫
MTI Home Video (Cat #BE50021, UPC #619935202139). Full frame. $24.95. Keepcase. *LANG:* English. *FEATURES:* 20 chapter links • Trailers • Talent files.
1998 (PG) 90m/C *CA* Cloris Leachman, Olympia Dukakis, Jan Rubes, Jean Lapointe; **D:** Giles Walker; **C:** Savas Kalogeras.

The New Adventures of Pippi Longstocking

After she is separated from her father, spunky, impulsive Pippi moves into a small town, causing "charming," free-spirited havoc wherever she goes. Irritating children's film with poor, arbitrary musical numbers. A supporting cast of recognizable character actors is thoroughly wasted. Oddly enough, Pippi's endless tapestry of lies and fantasy reminded this reviewer of Warren Oates's character from *Two Lane Blacktop*. Hmmm? Pippi's annoying behavior will probably influence misbehavior in young kids and you'll never get the stupid theme song out of your head. It's about as much fun as babysitting the neighbor's brats. The DVD is colorful but grainy with a clear though undistinguished stereo soundtrack and awfully grainy menus. You've been warned. —DG
Movie: ♫½ **DVD:** ♫♫♫
Columbia Tristar Home Video (Cat #05986, UPC #04339605986). Full frame. Dolby Surround. $19.95. Keepcase. *LANG:* English; Spanish. *SUB:* English; Spanish; French. *CAP:* English. *FEATURES:* Talent bios • Trailers • 28 chapter links • Insert card with chapter listing.
1988 (G) 101m/C Tami Erin, Eileen Brennan, Dennis Dugan, Dianne Hull, George DiCenzo, John Schuck, Dick Van Patten; **D:** Ken Annakin; **W:** Ken Annakin; **C:** Roland Smith; **M:** Misha Segal.

The New Eve

Camille (Viard in an astonishing performance) is a hard-partying Parisienne whose hedonistic life is changed when she meets Alexis (Rajot). He's a political activist, married with a couple of kids—not at all the sort of drugged-up playboy she is used to. Their rocky relationship is both sexual and emotional. This French import looks astonishingly good. The image with its bright challenging color scheme is every bit as sharp as a Hollywood studio production. Sound is fine, too. —MM **AKA:** La Nouvelle Eve.
Movie: ♫♫♫ **DVD:** ♫♫♫
Image Entertainment (Cat #ID8761SIDVD, UPC #014381876123). Widescreen (1.78:1) anamorphic. Dolby Digital Surround Stereo. $24.99. Snapper. *LANG:* French. *SUB:* English. *FEATURES:* 12 chapter links.
1998 (R) 90m/C *FR* Karin Viard, Pierre-Loup Rajot, Catherine Frot, Sergei Lopez, Mireille Roussel, Nozha Khouadra; **D:** Catherine Corsini; **W:** Catherine Corsini, Marc Syrigas; **C:** Agnes Godard.

New Legend of Shaolin

Historical martial arts stars Jet Li as Hung Shi Kwan who with his prepubescent son (Xie Miao) is involved in a series of adventures. Li commands the screen, as he almost always does, but he has poor material to work with. There's little to rec-ommend the film, beyond his fight scenes. DVD image is riddled with speckles and show. Small subtitles are burned in and filled with hex errors. —MM
Movie: ♫♫ **DVD:** ♫½
Tai Seng Video Marketing (Cat #35744, UPC #601643357447). Widescreen letterboxed. $19.99. Keepcase. *LANG:* Cantonese; Mandarin. *SUB:* English. *FEATURES:* 9 chapter links • 4 trailers.
1996 97m/C *HK* Jet Li, Chingmy Yau, Deannie Yip; **D:** Wong Jing; **W:** Wong Jing.

News from the West

Thirteen short films are essentially performance art pieces. As a group, they are non-sequential combinations of word and image, heavily influenced by "slam" poetry. In his introduction, writer/director Dwight Marcus says "what Los Angeles is about is an energy that we feel that has to do with rupture and disjuncture." I have no idea what that means, but the filmmaker certainly is passionate about it. Comment on image quality is pointless since so many of the short films (some only a few seconds long) have an intentionally distressed look. The Surround elements are used mostly for shock and surprise. —MM
Movie: ♫♫♫ **DVD:** ♫♫♫
SlingShot Entertainment (Cat #9841, UPC #017078984125). Full frame. Dolby Digital 5.1 Surround Stereo; Dolby Digital Stereo. Large jewelcase. *LANG:* English. *FEATURES:* 13 chapter links.
19?? 45m/C D: Dwight Marcus; **W:** Dwight Marcus.

Newsbreak

An overqualified cast is trapped in an underpowered thriller. Reporter John McNamara (Rooker) looks into a story involving civic corruption and people start dying. This ultra-low-budget production appears to have been shot partly on video. Image quality varies from shot to shot, seldom rising above fair. Sound is so poorly recorded that some conversations are impossible to make out. —MM
Movie: ♫ **DVD:** ♫½
MTI Home Video (Cat #8103, UPC #03941 4581034). Full frame. $24.95. Keepcase. *LANG:* English. *FEATURES:* 20 chapter links • Talent files • Trailers.
2000 (R) 95m/C Michael Rooker, Judge Reinhold, Robert Culp, Kelly Miller, Kim Darby, Noelle Parker; **D:** Serge Rodnunsky; **W:** Serge Rodnunsky, Paul Tarantino; **C:** Howard Wexler; **M:** Evan Evans.

The Next Best Thing

Heterosexual Abby (Madonna) and homosexual Robert (Everett), who are best friends, have a drunken tryst that results in a strapping baby boy. Thus begins the poster family for alternative lifestyles. But what starts out as a happy comedy turns amazingly dark and mean spirited when Abby finds true love with an investment banker from New York (Bratt) and sues for sole custody of the love child. Overall, the script is uneven and is saved only by Schlesinger's direction and Everett's ability to deftly travel between comedy and drama. Madonna's self-conscious acting style makes Abby a cardboard cut out of a biological clock with really good hair. The sound quality is better than average but the picture quality is not as good as it could be. —CA
Movie: ♫½ **DVD:** ♫♫
Paramount Home Video (Cat #33422, UPC #09736334224). Widescreen letterboxed. Dolby Surround. $29.99. Keepcase. *LANG:* English; French. *SUB:* English. *FEATURES:* 22 chapter links • Madonna *American Pie* video • Theatrical trailer • Exclusive interviews with stars and producer.
2000 (PG-13) 108m/C Madonna, Rupert Everett, Benjamin Bratt, Michael Vartan, Josef Sommer, Lynn Redgrave, Malcolm Stumpf, Neil Patrick Harris, Illeana Douglas, Mark Valley, Stacy Edwards; **D:** John Schlesinger; **W:** Tom Ropelewski; **C:** Elliot Davis; **M:** Gabriel Yared.

Next Friday [Platinum Series]

Amiable, meandering sequel to 1995's surprise hit *Friday* finds Craig (producer/writer Ice Cube) fleeing to the suburbs to escape Debo (Lister), who's broken out of prison (by tying sheets together) and is looking for payback. The level and tone of humor are set by jokes involving marijuana and dog poop. Not for all tastes, but Ice Cube is a genuine movie star and makes the most of the material. With its bright color scheme, the film looks and sounds fine, but, for once, the menu is almost as much fun as the work it introduces. It's complex, inventive, a little difficult to figure out but still enjoyable. The extras are equally imaginative, including an option to watch storyboard drawings in a corner of the screen. —MM
Movie: ♫♫♫ **DVD:** ♫♫♫
New Line Home Video (Cat #N5036, UPC #794043503627). Widescreen (1.85:1) anamorphic. Dolby Digital 5.1 Surround Stereo. $24.98. Snapper. *LANG:* English. *SUB:* English; Spanish. *FEATURES:* 20 chapter links • Commentary: Ice Cube and Steve Carr • Trailers • Music videos • Alternate ending • Blooper reel • Storyboard drawings • Blooper reel • Audition tape • Behind-the-scenes featurette • DVD-ROM features.
2000 (R) 93m/C Ice Cube, Tommy (Tiny) Lister, John Witherspoon, Justin Pierce, Jacob Vargas, Lobo Sebastian, R. Molina, Tamala Jones, Mike Epps, Don "DC" Curry, Lisa Rodriguez, Kym E. Whitley, Amy Hill, Robin Allen; **D:** Steve Carr; **W:** Ice Cube; **C:** Christopher Baffa; **M:** Terence Blanchard. *AWARDS: NOM:* MTV Movie Awards '00: Comedic Perf. (Ice Cube).

The Next Step

A Chorus Line meets *Red Shoe Diaries*. Nick Mendez (Negron) is a 35-year-old Broadway dancer who's feeling the wear-and-tear of his profession. A practiced seducer, he does have a devoted girlfriend in ex-dancer turned physical therapist Amy (Moreu), but he's also intimate with fellow dancer Heidi (Faye). Amy's impending move for a new job and his own diminishing prospects force Nick to examine his life. Negron is a former Broadway dancer and offers a compelling performance in a story that is ripe with showbiz clichés. The image is clear and sharp, but it is noticeably dark at times. This transfer does reveal some minor defects from the source print, but it is free of noise or any artifacting problems. The audio is a complete nightmare, however. The mono soundtrack is woefully unbalanced, with the dialogue being very soft and the music being very loud. So, whenever a dance number begins, you'll find yourself reaching for the remote control, lest the cat get scared and flee from the room. —ML/MM

Movie: 🎬🎬½ **DVD:** 🎬🎬½
Vanguard International Cinema, Inc. (UPC #658769007039). Widescreen (1.85:1) letterboxed. Dolby Digital Mono. $29.95. Keepcase. *LANG:* English. *FEATURES:* 12 chapter links.
1995 97m/C Rick Negron, Kristin Moreu, Denise Faye, Taylor Nichols; **D:** Christian Faber; **W:** Aaron Reed; **C:** Zack Winestine; **M:** Mio Morales, Brian Otto, Roni Skies.

Next Stop, Wonderland

Brad Anderson is the writer, director, and film editor here, a combination that pretty much defines independent filmmaking. A nice cast, coupled with an interesting concept, ultimately gets bogged down in rush hour traffic. Hope Davis and Alan Gelfant live, work, and dream about better things in Boston; she's a nurse who has dropped out of medical school, and he's the son of a plumber, who aspires to be a marine biologist. They seem perfect for each other, and Anderson is constantly nudging us in that direction, but they spend virtually the entire film crossing paths before riding the Boston subway to the "end of the line," Wonderland. It would have been nice to hear a commentary track from the multi-tasked filmmaker. Anderson's insights into the choices he's made may have proved to be interesting, especially from the point of view of a true independent filmmaker. But sadly, this DVD arrives featureless. Otherwise, image and sound are fine. —RJT

Movie: 🎬🎬½ **DVD:** 🎬🎬½
Buena Vista Home Entertainment (Cat #18 530, UPC #717951005472). Widescreen (1.85:1) anamorphic. AC3 - 5.1 Dolby Digital Surround Sound. $29.99. Keepcase. *LANG:* English. *SUB:* English; Spanish. *CAP:* English. *FEATURES:* 23 chapter links • Cross-promotional trailer for *Guinevere.*
1998 (R) 96m/C Hope Davis, Alan Gelfant, Holland Taylor, Robert Klein, Cara Buono, Jose Zuniga, Phil Hoffman, Lyn Vaus, Larry Gilliard Jr., Victor Argo, Roger Rees, Robert Stanton; **D:** Brad Anderson; **W:** Brad Anderson, Lyn Vaus; **C:** Uta Briesewitz; **M:** Claudio Ragazzi.

Nice Guys Sleep Alone

Overachieving independent romantic comedy finds nice guy Carter (O'Bryan) hearing those three dreaded words "let's be friends" at the end of each date. He has resolved to take a new approach when he meets Maggie (Temchen), a vet recently arrived in Louisville from New York. The complications that keep the plot moving are familiar, and Carter's rival Robert (Murray) is such a swine that it's impossible any intelligent woman would pay attention to him, no matter how rich he is. But the characters are engaging, especially Carter's stepsister Erin (Marcil), and the film has its heart in the right place. For a low-budget production, this one looks very good on disc. Neither image nor sound is extraordinary, but the extras are well-chosen. Hollywood studios typically spend much more money on this sort of entertainment and deliver much less. —MM

Movie: 🎬🎬🎬 **DVD:** 🎬🎬🎬
Lunacy Productions (UPC #07335481645 4). Widescreen letterboxed. $19.95. Keepcase. *LANG:* English. *FEATURES:* 16 chapter links • Director's intro • Commentary • Behind-the-scenes featurette • Deleted scenes and outtakes • Photo gallery • Trailers • Cast interviews.
1999 (R) 92m/C Sean O'Bryan, Sybil Temchen, Vanessa Marcil, Blake Steury, Christopher Murray, Morgan Fairchild, William Sanderson; **D:** Stu Pollard; **W:** Stu Pollard; **C:** Nathan Hope.

Nick of Time

Real-time thriller begins at noon in Los Angeles' Union Station where two threatening figures, Mr. Smith (Walker) and Ms. Jones (Maffia), are looking for a victim. When they spot accountant Gene Watson (Depp) and his young daughter Lynn (Chase), they know they've found their mark. They take the little girl and force Gene into a choice. They give him a revolver and a photograph of a woman (Mason) who will be coming to a nearby hotel. If he doesn't shoot her by 1:30, they'll kill his little girl. The clock is ticking and they're watching. Image ranges from very good to excellent, capturing the film's distinctive visuals. Sound is fine but the lack of a director's commentary track is an opportunity missed. The production was innovative enough to deserve some special attention despite its lack of theatrical popularity. —MM

Movie: 🎬🎬🎬 **DVD:** 🎬🎬🎬
Paramount Home Video (Cat #330417, UPC #097363304173). Widescreen anamorphic. Dolby Digital 5.1 Surround Stereo; Dolby Digital Surround Stereo. $29.99. Keepcase. *LANG:* English; French. *FEATURES:* 17 chapter links • Trailer.
1995 (R) 98m/C Johnny Depp, Christopher Walken, Charles S. Dutton, Peter Strauss, Roma Maffia, Gloria Reuben, Marsha Mason, Courtney Chase, Bill Smitrovich, G.D. Spradlin; **D:** John Badham; **W:** Patrick Duncan; **C:** Roy Wagner; **M:** Arthur B. Rubinstein.

A Night in the Life of Jimmy Reardon

A high school Casanova watches his friends leave for expensive schools while he contemplates a trip to Hawaii with his rich girlfriend, a ruse to avoid the dull business school his father has picked out. Well photographed, but acting leaves something to be desired. Based on director Richert's novel *Aren't You Even Going to Kiss Me Good-bye?* The video is solid, delivering crisp colors and well-defined blacks. The 5.1 mix is impressive, while the 2.0 mix tends to be muddied at times. —MJT

Movie: 🎬½ **DVD:** 🎬🎬🎬
Image Entertainment (Cat #ID9171CUDVD, UPC #014381917123). Widescreen (1.85:1) anamorphic. Dolby Digital 5.1 Surround; Dolby Digital Stereo. $24.99. Snapper. *LANG:* English. *FEATURES:* 14 chapter links.
1988 (R) 95m/C River Phoenix, Meredith Salenger, Matthew Perry, Louanne, Ione Skye, Ann Magnuson, Paul Koslo, Jane Hallaren, Jason Court; **D:** William Richert; **W:** William Richert; **C:** John J. Connor; **M:** Elmer Bernstein, Bill Conti.

Night of the Living Dead [Madacy]

The public domain cult fav horror gains little or nothing on this bargain-basement disc. The story of the recently deceased who rise from the grave to attack and eat the living in the Pennsylvania countryside has never been any great shakes in visual terms. Here, the black and white is pale, grainy, and washed-out. Sound is wavery. —MM **AKA:** Night of the Flesh Eaters; Night of the Anubis.

Movie: 🎬🎬🎬½ **DVD:** 🎬½
Madacy Entertainment (Cat #DVD-9-9019, UPC #056775004699). Full frame. $9.99. Keepcase. *LANG:* English. *FEATURES:* 9 chapter links • Duane Jones thumbnail bio.
1968 90m/B Judith O'Dea, Duane Jones, Karl Hardman, Marilyn Eastman, Keith Wayne, Judith Ridley, Russell Streiner, Bill "Chilly Billy" Cardille, John A. Russo, Kyra Schon, Bill (William Heinzman) Hinzman, John Simpson, Vincent Survinski, George A. Romero; **D:** George A. Romero; **W:** John A. Russo, George A. Romero; **C:** George A. Romero. *AWARDS:* Natl. Film Reg. '99.

Night of the Living Dead [Elite]

Seven people desperate to stay alive barricade themselves inside a remote farmhouse on the night when dead bodies return to life with a huge appetite for human flesh. More than three decades after *NOTLD* was made on a shoestring budget in Pittsburgh, the black-and-white tale of impossible terror remains one of the scariest, most gruesome films ever made. Its virtues are that it's claustrophobic, terrifying, gruesome, extreme, and, yes, quite humorous. The virtues of the DVD from Elite are its nearly pristine transfer from the original B&W 16mm film negative, which benefits the DVD with fine

grain, deep blacks, and moody contrast. Very occasionally a frame will appear to freeze on the screen for a brief moment, but this is because frames in the original film were irreparably damaged and had to be replaced to keep the soundtrack in synch. It's only mildly distracting and does not seriously hinder the enjoyment of the otherwise superb image. The mono soundtrack can be harsh, but its cheapness adds to the movie more so than the new soundtrack created later and thankfully not included on this disc. NOTLD has never looked this good at home, and numerous low-cost editions on DVD and VHS should be avoided even if they're free. If you only own one DVD of NOTLD, this is the one to have—although completists may also consider collecting the Anchor Bay 30th anniversary DVD. But the definitive Elite DVD is the only place to find a good-looking original cut of the movie that has the original soundtrack intact. There are two very superior audio commentary tracks included on the Elite disc. The first is more technically oriented, with director Romero, co-screenwriter John Russo, and cast members Karl Hardman and Marilyn Eastman. The other, more playful track features cast members Hinzman, O'Dea, Wayne, Schon, Streiner, and Survinski. The parody short film "Night of the Living Bread" is amusing, but probably doesn't warrant repeat viewing. Same with the vintage TV commercials. NOTLD, which was remade in 1990, was followed by sequels Dawn of the Dead (1979) and Day of the Dead (1985). —MB **AKA:** Night of the Flesh Eaters; Night of the Anubis.
Movie: 🦴🦴🦴½ **DVD:** 🦴🦴🦴½
Elite Entertainment, Inc. (Cat #EE1116, UPC #790594111625). Full frame. Dolby Digital Mono. $29.95. Keepcase. LANG: English. FEATURES: 31 chapter links ▪ THX-approved transfer ▪ 2 commentary tracks ▪ Theatrical trailer ▪ "Night of the Living Bread" short film parody ▪ Television commercials.
1968 90m/B Judith O'Dea, Duane Jones, Karl Hardman, Marilyn Eastman, Keith Wayne, Judith Ridley, Russell Streiner, Bill "Chilly Billy" Cardille, John A. Russo, Kyra Schon, Bill (William Heinzman) Hinzman, John Simpson, Vincent Survinski, George A. Romero; **D:** George A. Romero; **W:** John A. Russo, George A. Romero; **C:** George A. Romero. AWARDS: Natl. Film Reg. '99.

Night of the Living Dead [LE Anchor Bay]

To celebrate the 30th anniversary of this seminal horror film, several of the original filmmakers (sans George Romero) decided to film more than 15 minutes of new scenes and to redo all of the music cues in the original to generally screw the whole thing up. This whole disc is just such a complete mess from beginning to end that it hardly seems worthwhile to explain it in detail. Suffice it to say that whomever came up with the idea of a special edition of this film should have his or her idea-

making privileges revoked. First, the added scenes are amateur horror-show fare at best, with 1990s actors thrust into an obviously 1960s film. They seem to have been added solely for the gross-out factor. Then, the soundtrack truly pulls the disc to the bottom. Not only have they redone the entire musical score with an annoying blend of synthesizers and digitized sounds, but the filmmakers have tried to redo all of the film's ADR work just so they could put Dolby Digital 5.1 on the box (the poor quality of which is evidenced in badly missed sounds cues and a score that sounds as if it were added from somebody's home CD player, with the pause button pressed repeatedly). Also included on the disc is the original 90-minute cut of the film, to which the aforementioned abomination of a soundtrack has been added, making the disc an even greater disappointment. (Couldn't they have just cleaned up the old mono soundtrack? That would have made this disc something truly worthwhile instead of a complete waste of money.) The real tragedy here is that the video transfer is superb. This is the best this film has ever looked but, sadly, the other tinkering done to it negates any good that may have come from its remastering. The result is a thoroughly un-enjoyable bastardization of a true American classic. The Elite DVD has a different set of extras and the original cut of the movie. Other, low-priced and low-quality editions of NOTLD on DVD and VHS should be avoided. —MJT/MB **AKA:** Night of the Flesh Eaters; Night of the Anubis.
Movie: 🦴 **DVD:** 🦴🦴½
Anchor Bay (Cat #DV10951, UPC #013131 095197). Full frame. Dolby Digital 5.1 Surround Sound. $34.98. Keepcase. LANG: English. FEATURES: 30th Anniversary Edition with more than 15 minutes of new scenes ▪ 1998 Edition of original film with new musical score ▪ 30th Anniversary Edition, 30 chapter links ▪ 1998 Edition, 24 chapter links ▪ 30th Anniversary behind-the-scenes featurette ▪ 30th Anniversary theatrical trailer ▪ 30th Anniversary still gallery ▪ Commentary: Russo, Hinzman, Streiner, Michelucci ▪ Scene from the Bill Hinzman feature Flesh Eater ▪ "Dance of the Dead" music video ▪ 32-page, 4-color collector's booklet ▪ Original motion picture soundtrack CD.
1968 90m/B Judith O'Dea, Duane Jones, Karl Hardman, Marilyn Eastman, Keith Wayne, Judith Ridley, Russell Streiner, Bill "Chilly Billy" Cardille, John A. Russo, Kyra Schon, Bill (William Heinzman) Hinzman, John Simpson, Vincent Survinski, George A. Romero; **D:** George A. Romero; **W:** John A. Russo, George A. Romero; **C:** George A. Romero. AWARDS: Natl. Film Reg. '99.

Night of the Living Dead

Director Savini dares to remake George Romero's zombie classic and actually makes it work. Sure, it's not as scary as the original, but nonetheless provides a few jumps, plenty of gore (this time in

color), and a slightly different ending that works as well. Same basic plot though: A bunch of people are trapped in a farmhouse and attacked by ghouls with eating disorders. As in Romero's, the tension is multiplied by personality conflicts and, yeah, they still gotta shoot those dead suckers in the head. On DVD the film looks better than both the previous VHS and laserdisc releases, but still manages to retain the intentional low-budget look. The lack of a 5.1 mix is hardly noticeable as the Dolby Surround maintains energetic ambience accented by strong and dynamic separation effects. The included featurette, "The Dead Walk," and Savini's commentary provide much insight into the makeup, the gore, and even the politics behind the remake. —JO
Movie: 🦴🦴½ **DVD:** 🦴🦴🦴
Columbia Tristar Home Video (Cat #77179, UPC #043396771796). Widescreen (1.85:1) anamorphic; full frame. Dolby Surround; Mono. $19.95. Keepcase. LANG: English (DS); Portuguese (Mono). SUB: English; Spanish; Chinese; Korean; Thai; Portuguese. CAP: English. FEATURES: 28 chapter links ▪ Theatrical trailer ▪ Talent files ▪ Production notes ▪ "Making of" featurette, "The Dead Walk" ▪ Commentary: director Tom Savini.
1990 (R) 92m/C Tony Todd, Patricia Tallman, Tom Towles, William Butler, Bill Moseley, McKee Anderson, Kate Finneran, Bill "Chilly Billy" Cardille; **D:** Tom Savini; **W:** George A. Romero, John A. Russo; **C:** Frank Prinzi; **M:** Paul McCollough.

The Nightmare before Christmas [2 SE]

Is this a Halloween classic, a new Christmas annual, or a demented musical? No matter, this stop-motion treat about Jack Skellington, the Pumpkin King, and his "tinkering" with Christmas (with good intentions of course) is a wonder to behold from the creative mind of Tim Burton. This nightmare can be viewed over and over again, with some new nugget mined each time—move over Grinch, you've got company. Near-perfect DVD special edition, with audio commentary from director Henry Selick (Monkeybone), loads of bonus features, and two delightfully wicked shorts from Tim Burton. "Vincent" is a stop-motion short narrated by Vincent Price (six minutes in length featuring a kid who resembles Burton himself), and "Frankenweenie" is a separate mini black-and-white feature (29 minutes) starring Shelly Duvall, Daniel Stern, and Barret Oliver (Cocoon) as the latest incarnation of Victor Frankenstein. **AKA:** Tim Burton's The Nightmare before Christmas.
Movie: 🦴🦴🦴½ **DVD:** 🦴🦴🦴½
Buena Vista Home Entertainment (Cat #20 102, UPC #717951009395). Widescreen (1.66:1) letterboxed. Dolby Digital 5.1 Surround; DTS 5.1 Surround. $29.99. Keepcase. LANG: English; French. SUB: English. CAP: English. FEATURES: Commentary: director Henry Selick ▪ Short: "Vincent"

(narrated by Vincent Price) • Short: "Frankenweenie" • 20 chapter markers • 4 deleted scenes • "Making of" featurette • Still frame gallery.
1993 (PG) 75m/C D: Henry Selick; **W:** Caroline Thompson, Tim Burton, Michael McDowell; **C:** Pete Kozachik; **M:** Danny Elfman; **V:** Danny Elfman, Chris Sarandon, Catherine O'Hara, William Hickey, Ken Page, Ed Ivory, Paul (Pee-wee Herman) Reubens, Glenn Shadix. *AWARDS: NOM:* Oscars '93: Visual FX; Golden Globes '94: Score.

Nightwatch

Director Ole Bornedal got it right the first time with this fine creepy thriller. Martin (Waldau) is a student who takes a job as a night watchman at a hospital and morgue while someone is killing prostitutes. Is everyone around him really that strange and threatening, or has the job changed him? This version is infinitely superior to Bornedal's 1998 American remake. Image and sound are excellent but the best part of the disc is the director's soft-spoken (almost whispered) commentary track. He sticks mostly to matters of character, style, and actors. A true sleeper. —*MM*
Movie: 🎝🎝🎝½ **DVD:** 🎝🎝🎝½
Anchor Bay (Cat #DV11313, UPC #013131 131390). Widescreen (1.85:1) anamorphic. Dolby Digital 5.1 Surround Stereo. $24.98. Keepcase. *LANG:* Danish. *SUB:* English. *FEATURES:* Commentary: Ole Bornedal • Trailer • 26 chapter links.
1994 107m/C Nikolaj Waldau, Sofie Graaboel, Kim Bodnia, Lotte Andersen, Ulf Pilgaard, Stig Hoffmeyer; **D:** Ole Bornedal; **W:** Ole Bornedal; **C:** Dan Laustsen; **M:** Joachim Holbek.

Nightwatch

Law student Martin (McGregor) takes a job as a night watchman in a morgue at the same time that a serial killer is murdering prostitutes. As if that weren't enough, he has to deal with a creepy cop (Nolte) who suspects him, a sadistic friend (Brolin) who likes to scare him on the job, and a boss (Dourif) who doesn't like him. Adapted by director Bornedal from his Dutch film *Nattevagten*, this one has some creepy moments but the whole thing is disjointed, and the characters relatively unsympathetic. Fans of *Seven* are the target audience. DVD is an excellent re-creation of the original. It's much more watchable than the full-frame tape. —*MM*
Movie: 🎝🎝 **DVD:** 🎝🎝
Buena Vista Home Entertainment (Cat #15 280, UPC #717951000743). Widescreen (2.35:1) anamorphic. Dolby Digital 5.1 Surround Stereo. $29.99. Keepcase. *LANG:* English; French. *FEATURES:* 16 chapter links • Trailers.
1996 (R) 101m/C Ewan McGregor, Nick Nolte, Patricia Arquette, Josh Brolin, John C. Reilly, Brad Dourif, Lonny (Loni) Chapman, Alix Koromzay, Lauren Graham; **D:** Ole Bornedal; **W:** Ole Bornedal, Steven Soderbergh; **C:** Dan Laustsen; **M:** Joachim Holbek.

Nine Months

Flagrant overacting, contrived emotions, heavy-handed direction, and sticky sentimentality pretty much doom this family comedy. Happily single Sam (Grant) has a successful child psychology practice, a beautiful girlfriend (Moore) and a Porsche. Then she becomes pregnant and when he sees how the couple (Arnold and Cusack) with children from hell are living, he has doubts. The image is every bit as good as it needs to be for this kind of predictable warm and fuzzy material. —*MM*
Movie: 🎝🎝 **DVD:** 🎝🎝
20th Century Fox Home Entertainment (Cat #2001368, UPC #024543013686). Widescreen (2.35:1) anamorphic. Dolby Digital 5.1 Surround Stereo; Dolby Digital Surround. $24.98. Keepcase. *LANG:* English; French. *SUB:* English; Spanish. *FEATURES:* Trailers and TV spots • 28 chapter links.
1995 (PG-13) 103m/C Hugh Grant, Julianne Moore, Tom Arnold, Joan Cusack, Jeff Goldblum, Robin Williams; **D:** Chris Columbus; **W:** Chris Columbus; **C:** Donald McAlpine; **M:** Hans Zimmer.

9 to 5

Caricature of large corporations and women in the workplace may have lost some of its topicality, but it remains a very funny movie. Coleman is terrific as the overbearing male chauvinist boss who keeps his female employees under his thumb. Then an office manager (Tomlin), a secretary (Parton), and a newly hired employee (Fonda) conspire to kidnap the guy and run the company without him. Image looks fine for a film this old. For my money, the original mono soundtrack is more suited to the action than the Surround remix. I suppose a commentary track from the three stars would have been too much to ask for. —*MM*
Movie: 🎝🎝🎝 **DVD:** 🎝🎝½
20th Century Fox Home Entertainment (Cat #2001371, UPC #024543013716). Widescreen (1.85:1) anamorphic. Dolby Digital Surround Stereo; Dolby Digital Mono. $24.98. Keepcase. *LANG:* English; French. *SUB:* English; Spanish. *FEATURES:* Trailers • Still gallery • 18 chapter links.
1980 (PG) 111m/C Jane Fonda, Lily Tomlin, Dolly Parton, Dabney Coleman, Sterling Hayden, Norma Donaldson; **D:** Colin Higgins; **W:** Patricia Resnick; **C:** Reynaldo Villalobos; **M:** Charles Fox. *AWARDS: NOM:* Oscars '80: Song ("Nine to Five").

The Ninth Gate

Less-than-scrupulous rare-book dealer Dean Corso (Depp) is hired by wealthy publishing mogul Balkan (Langella) to find and authenticate three copies of a 17th-century book that supposedly holds the secrets to conjuring up the devil. Naturally, he encounters many spooky and deadly people along the way. Depp is perfectly cast as the sleazy bookworm, but the glacial pace and lack of dramatic tension are troublesome. On his commentary track, Polanski doesn't sound too excited about it, either. That said, the softish image is re-created very nicely. Sound is equally good. —*MM*
Movie: 🎝🎝 **DVD:** 🎝🎝🎝
Artisan Entertainment (Cat #60747). Widescreen (2.35:1) anamorphic. Dolby Digital 5.1 Surround Stereo. $24.98. Keepcase. *LANG:* English. *FEATURES:* 30 chapter links • Isolated music score • Commentary: Polanski • Talent files • Production notes • Storyboard sequences • Satanic drawings.
1999 (R) 127m/C *FR SP* Johnny Depp, Frank Langella, Lena Olin, Emmanuelle Seigner, Barbara Jefford, Jack Taylor, James Russo, Jose Lopez Rodero; **D:** Roman Polanski; **W:** Roman Polanski, John Brownjohn, Enrique Urbizu; **C:** Darius Khondji; **M:** Wojciech Kilar.

Ninth Street

Filmmaker Kevin Willmott takes his inspiration from Spike Lee's *Do the Right Thing*. The story concerns a black neighborhood in mid-1970s Junction City, Kansas. It's a rough street of gin joints, gambling dens, and hookers catering to the nearby Army base, Ft. Riley. Our narrator Bebo (Washington) is a wino who spends most of his time sitting on a nasty-looking sofa on the sidewalk with his friend Huddie (Willmott), a fellow street-corner philosopher. Story is less important than an ensemble cast, including Sheen as a priest, and an evocation of the times. Soft black-and-white image is so grainy that pixelation is extreme in some scenes. Sound is fine; the jazz-blues score is better. —*MM*
Movie: 🎝🎝½ **DVD:** 🎝🎝
Ideal Enterprises/Video (Cat #80522). Full frame. $14.98. Slipcase. *LANG:* English. *FEATURES:* 8 chapter links.
1998 (R) 98m/B Kevin Willmott, Don Washington, Nadine Griffith, Byron Myrick, Isaac Hayes, Kaycee Moore, Martin Sheen, Queen Bey; **D:** Kevin Willmott, Tim Rebman; **W:** Kevin Willmott; **C:** Troy Paddock; **M:** Wayne Hawkins.

No Code of Conduct

Predictable, violent, vice-squad vs. drug czar fare directed by ex-Poison frontman Michaels. Only Martin Sheen saves the film and its excessive violence and stupidity from oblivion (though not by much). The disc features a very poor-qality picture. Most colors have little definition and blacks are blurry to the point of making images unidentifiable. The sound mix is adequate, but music and sound effects fare much better than dialogue, which is often tinny and somewhat muffled. —*MJT*
Movie: 🎝½ **DVD:** 🎝½
Buena Vista Home Entertainment (Cat #20 649, UPC #717951010452). Widescreen (1.85:1) anamorphic. Dolby Digital 5.1 Surround. $32.99. Keepcase. *LANG:* English. *CAP:* English. *FEATURES:* 24 chapter links.
1998 (R) 90m/C Mark Dacascos, Joe Estevez, Charlie Sheen, Martin Sheen, Courtney Gains, Paul Gleason, Joe Lando, Meredith Salenger, Bret Michaels; **D:** Bret

Michaels; **W:** Charlie Sheen, Bret Michaels, Bill Gucwa, Ed Masterson; **C:** Adam Kane; **M:** Bret Michaels.

No Dessert Dad, 'Til You Mow the Lawn

Suburban parents Ken and Carol Cochran (Hays and Kerns) are harassed at home by their annoying offspring Justin, Monica, and Tyler. When the folks try hypnosis tapes to quit smoking, the kids discover that by doctoring the tapes, they can plant suggestions that lead to parental perks. It's every bit as slight and silly as it sounds. DVD delivers an image that's only a mild improvement over VHS. —*MM*
Movie: 🎬🎬 **DVD:** 🎬🎬½
New Concorde (Cat #NH20476 D, UPC #73 6991247697). Full frame. Stereo. $14.98. Keepcase. *LANG:* English. *FEATURES:* 24 chapter links ▪ Talent files ▪ Trailers.
1994 (PG) 80m/C Robert Hays, Joanna (Joanna DeVarona) Kerns, Joshua Schaefer, Allison Meek, Jimmy Marsden, Richard Moll, Larry Linville; **D:** Howard McCain.

No Looking Back

Small-town 30ish waitress Claudia (Holly) is about to settle for a boring life with her decent-but-dull boyfriend Michael (Bon Jovi) when her ne'er-do-well former beau Charlie (Burns) comes home looking to relive the glory days. Burns stays with the working-class, northeastern setting but goes for drama this time. With themes of economic hopelessness and a yearning to escape, Burns is aiming at a cinematic distillation of Bruce Springsteen's music. He admits as much in his commentary track, which like his others, focuses on the nuts and bolts side of filmmaking. Overall, the image here looks very good, easily equaling *She's the One*. Sound is very good too. The title is also available as part of the "Stories from Long Island" boxed set. —*MM* **AKA:** *Long Time, Nothing New.*
Movie: 🎬🎬½ **DVD:** 🎬🎬🎬
USA Home Entertainment (Cat #963 060 129-2, UPC #696306012924). Widescreen anamorphic. Dolby Digital 5.1 Surround Stereo; Dolby Digital Surround. $24.95. Keepcase. *LANG:* English. *CAP:* English. *FEATURES:* 24 chapter links ▪ Director's commentary ▪ Talent files ▪ Trailer.
1998 (R) 96m/C Lauren Holly, Edward Burns, Jon Bon Jovi, Blythe Danner, Connie Britton; **D:** Edward Burns; **W:** Edward Burns; **C:** Frank Prinzi; **M:** Joe Delia.

No Safe Haven

CIA agent Clete Harris (Hauser) seeks revenge against the gangsters who killed his family in this by-the-numbers video premiere. The normally reliable Hauser, who co-wrote the script, can do little to elevate the pedestrian material. DVD is absolutely no improvement over VHS tape in any respect. —*MM*
Movie: 🎬½ **DVD:** 🎬½
Image Entertainment (Cat #OVED9031DVD, UPC #014381903126). Full frame. Dolby

Digital Stereo. $24.99. Snapper. *LANG:* English. *FEATURES:* 12 chapter links.
1987 (R) 92m/C Wings Hauser, Marina Rice, Robert Tessier; **D:** Ronnie Rondell; **W:** Nancy Locke, Wings Hauser; **C:** Steve McWilliams; **M:** Joel Goldsmith.

No Way Out

Career Navy Lt. Tom Farrell (Costner) is involved with a beautiful sexy woman (Young) who is murdered. Turns out she was also the mistress of the Secretary of Defense (Hackman), Farrell's boss. Assigned to investigate the murder, he finds himself to be the chief suspect. The tight thriller is based on 1948's *The Big Clock* with a surprise ending. The quality of the video transfer is average at best. Without clean-up, the transfer contains signs of wear and tear, as well as a number of grainy scenes. Slight pixelation is evident almost throughout, and the application of edge-enhancement leaves visible ringing artifacts in the image. Color reproduction is generally good without oversaturation or noticeable bleeding. Skin tones are naturally rendered, while blacks are restored faithfully without losing detail in the shadows. The audio is clean and without major background noise, but the dialogue sounds overly compressed and thin. —*GH/MM*
Movie: 🎬🎬🎬 **DVD:** 🎬🎬
MGM Home Entertainment (Cat #98436). Widescreen (1.85:1) letterboxed; full frame. Dolby Digital Surround Stereo; Dolby Digital Mono. $24.98. Keepcase. *LANG:* English; Spanish. *SUB:* French; Spanish. *FEATURES:* Theatrical trailer.
1987 (R) 114m/C Kevin Costner, Sean Young, Gene Hackman, Will Patton, Howard Duff, George Dzundza, Iman, Chris D, Marshall Bell, Jason Bernard, Fred Dalton Thompson, David Paymer, Eugene Glazer; **D:** Roger Donaldson; **W:** Robert Garland; **C:** John Alcott; **M:** Maurice Jarre.

Noah's Ark

Made-for-TV epic of the Old Testament story doesn't exactly stay close to its biblical roots. It's eccentric, special effects–laden, and bordering on the irreverent. Noah (Voight) builds his ark, gathers the animals (and his family), watches as the world is destroyed, and survives the 40 days and nights of flooding. In conventional scenes, image ranges between very good and excellent, but that clarity of the medium highlights the shortcomings of the CGI effects. —*MM*
Movie: 🎬🎬 **DVD:** 🎬🎬
Hallmark Home Entertainment (Cat #700 73). Full frame. Dolby Digital Surround Stereo. $19.98. Keepcase. *LANG:* English. *FEATURES:* Production notes ▪ Trailer ▪ Cast and crew thumbnail bios ▪ Game ▪ 48 chapter links.
1999 178m/C Jon Voight, Mary Steenburgen, F. Murray Abraham, Carol Kane, James Coburn, Jonathan Cake, Alexis Denisof, Emily Mortimer, Sydney Poitier, Sonya Walger; **D:** John Irvin; **W:** Peter

Barnes; **C:** Mike Molloy; **M:** Paul Grabowsky.

Norma Rae

Poor, uneducated textile worker Norma Rae (Field) joins forces with a New York labor organizer (Liebman) to unionize the reluctant workers at a Southern mill. At the film's release, Field was a surprise with her fully developed character's strength, humor, and beauty. Her Oscar was well deserved. This has never been (nor should it be) a polished film, but this widescreen transfer does highlight the excellent work that director Ritt and director of photography John Alonzo did with their handheld camerawork. Somehow, even in the deafening mill scenes, the mono sound seems better to me than the Surround remix. Those who are not already familiar with the film may well disagree. —*MM*
Movie: 🎬🎬🎬 **DVD:** 🎬🎬½
20th Century Fox Home Entertainment (Cat #2001374, UPC #024543013747). Widescreen (2.35:1) anamorphic. Dolby Digital Surround Stereo; Dolby Digital Mono. $24.98. Keepcase. *LANG:* English; French; Spanish. *SUB:* English; Spanish. *FEATURES:* Trailers ▪ "Backstory: Norma Rae" featurette ▪ 32 chapter links.
1979 (PG) 114m/C Sally Field, Ron Leibman, Beau Bridges, Pat Hingle; **D:** Martin Ritt; **W:** Harriet Frank Jr., Irving Ravetch; **C:** John A. Alonzo; **M:** David Shire. *AWARDS:* Oscars '79: Actress (Field), Song ("It Goes Like It Goes"); Cannes '79: Actress (Field); Golden Globes '80: Actress—Drama (Field); L.A. Film Critics '79: Actress (Field); Natl. Bd. of Review '79: Actress (Field); N.Y. Film Critics '79: Actress (Field); Natl. Soc. Film Critics '79: Actress (Field); *NOM:* Oscars '79: Adapt. Screenplay, Picture.

North by Northwest

Hitchcock's most ambitious and enjoyable romantic thriller finally gets the treatment it deserves on home video. Cary Grant is the slick New York ad man who's kidnapped by spies (Mason and Landau), falls for a femme fatale (Saint), is attacked by a biplane, and finally makes a memorable escape across Mt. Rushmore. The DVD extras are well chosen but the real highlight here is the image. Those accustomed to the hard-edged clarity of computer-enhanced effects may think that the DVD is soft, but the film looks better than it has in years. Theatrical prints available before the 1998 restoration had faded horribly. A shot-by-shot comparison to the MGM laserdisc (but not the Criterion Collection) reveals just how poorly served the film has been by earlier editions. Perhaps the most striking differences are visible in the crop duster scene where Grant's skin turned blue before and the big finish, which was too murky to reveal any detail. The 5.1 Surround remix sounds fine, and given the liveliness of the action and Bernard Herrmann's score (available on a separate track), it doesn't seem forced or anachronistic. A personal favorite and a disc that belongs in every collection. —MM

Movie: 🐾🐾🐾🐾 **DVD:** 🐾🐾🐾🐾
Warner Home Video, Inc. (Cat #65016, UPC #012569501621). Widescreen anamorphic. Dolby Digital 5.1 Surround Stereo; Dolby Digital Mono. $24.98. Snapper. *LANG:* English; French. *SUB:* English; French. *FEATURES:* 46 chapter links • Trailers and TV spots • Commentary: Ernest Lehman • "Making of" featurette • Stills gallery • Isolated score.
1959 136m/C Cary Grant, Eva Marie Saint, James Mason, Leo G. Carroll, Martin Landau, Jessie Royce Landis, Philip Ober, Adam Williams, Josephine Hutchinson, Edward Platt; **D:** Alfred Hitchcock; **W:** Ernest Lehman; **C:** Robert Burks; **M:** Bernard Herrmann. *AWARDS:* AFI '98: Top 100, Natl. Film Reg. '95; *NOM:* Oscars '59: Art Dir./Set Dec., Color, Film Editing, Story & Screenplay.

North Dallas Forty
The film that *On Any Sunday* wanted to be, this rowdy and still hard-hitting adaptation of Peter Gent's novel is in a league of its own. Nick Nolte stars as Phil Elliott, a former star wide receiver now relegated to the bench by his Bible-quoting coach (the great G.D. Spradlin, the fallen senator in *The Godfather Part II*), who resents Elliott's "lack of seriousness." He becomes increasingly disenchanted with boardroom politics, player abuse, and other hypocrisies. Mac Davis, never better, is quarterback Seth Maxwell, a party-on good ol' boy who knows how the game is played on and off the field. Print quality is clean, but image quality varies. Skin tones in particular are on the orange side. The restored mono soundtrack is preferable to the 5.1 presentation. But Paramount really dropped the ball by not providing extras that would enhance appreciation and enjoyment of one of the best sports movies ever made. —DL

Movie: 🐾🐾🐾 **DVD:** 🐾🐾
Paramount Home Video (Cat #08773, UPC #9736087734). Widescreen anamorphic. Dolby Digital Mono; Dolby Digital 5.1 Surround. $24.99. Keepcase. *LANG:* English. *SUB:* English. *FEATURES:* 20 chapter links.
1979 (R) 119m/C Nick Nolte, Mac Davis, Charles Durning, Bo Svenson, Brian Dennehy, John Matuszak, Dayle Haddon, Steve Forrest, Dabney Coleman, G.D. Spradlin; **D:** Ted Kotcheff; **W:** Ted Kotcheff, Frank Yablans; **C:** Paul Lohmann; **M:** John Scott.

Northanger Abbey
Catherine (Schlesinger) is a young woman addicted to romance novels of dark secrets, sinister castles, dashing heroes, and helpless women. When the handsome Henry Tilney (Firth) invites her to his ancestral home, it seems all of her fantasies have come to life. BBC adaptation of Jane Austen's parody of the popular Gothic romances of her day is a bit on the

tepid side. The misty, grainy DVD image is no better than broadcast quality. —MM

Movie: 🐾🐾½ **DVD:** 🐾🐾½
BFS Video (Cat #99909-D, UPC #0668059 19091). Full frame. Dolby Digital Mono. $29.98. Keepcase. *LANG:* English. *FEATURES:* 12 chapter links.
1987 90m/C *GB* Peter Firth, Katherine Schlesinger, Googie Withers, Robert Hardy; **D:** Giles Foster; **W:** Maggie Wadey; **C:** Nat Crosby; **M:** Ilona Sekacz.

Nosferatu [2]
The main differences between this edition and the earlier Image release (cat. # ID4 098DSDVD) are the addition of a new orchestral score in 5.0 Surround composed and performed by the Silent Orchestra, and supplemental material augmenting Lokke Heiss's commentary. There's also a nicely creepy menu. Picture is excellent for a film of this age. The new score sounds grand, and though Timothy Howard's organ score may be more authentic, I prefer the new music. The "Nosferatu Tour" extra compares the locations used in the film to their current appearance. —MM *AKA:* Nosferatu, Eine Symphonie des Grauens; Nosferatu, A Symphony of Terror; Nosferatu, A Symphony of Horror; Nosferatu, the Vampire; Terror of Dracula; Die Zwolfte Stunde.

Movie: 🐾🐾🐾🐾 **DVD:** 🐾🐾🐾½
Image Entertainment (Cat #ID0277DSDVD, UPC #014381027723). Full frame. Dolby Digital 5.0 Surround Stereo; Dolby Digital Stereo. $24.99. Snapper. *LANG:* Silent. *SUB:* English intertitles. *FEATURES:* 12 chapter links • Audio essay by Lokke Heiss • "Nosferatu Tour" • Phantom carriage ride • Art and stills gallery.
1922 63m/B *GE* Max Schreck, Alexander Granach, Gustav von Wagenheim, Greta Schroder, John Gottowt, Ruth Landshoff, G.H. Schnell; **D:** F.W. Murnau; **W:** Henrik Galeen; **C:** Fritz Arno Wagner, Gunther Krampf.

Not of This Earth
Remake is true to the 1957 original in intention and execution. Traci Lords is the nurse who unwittingly assists an intergalactic vampire who's collecting blood donations for his home planet. On the commentary track, director Wynorski and star Lenny Juliano take a lighthearted approach, happily pointing out such mistakes as the crew's reflection in a car door. The combination of the clarity of the image and their talk somehow magnifies the wonderful cheesiness of the whole thing. —MM

Movie: 🐾🐾🐾 **DVD:** 🐾🐾½
New Concorde (Cat #NH20313D, UPC #73 6991431393). Full frame. Dolby Stereo. $19.98. Keepcase. *LANG:* English. *FEATURES:* 24 chapter links • Thumbnail bios • Trailers • Commentary: Jim Wynorski, Lenny Juliano.
1988 (R) 92m/C Traci Lords, Arthur Roberts, Lenny Juliano, Rebecca Perle, Ace Mask, Roger Lodge, Michael Delano,

Monique Gabrielle, Becky Le Beau; **D:** Jim Wynorski; **W:** Jim Wynorski, R.J. Robertson, Charles B. Griffith, Mark Hanna; **C:** Zoran Hochstatter; **M:** Chuck Cirino.

Nothin' 2 Lose
Kwame (Brian Hooks, *3 Strikes*) can't bring himself to commit to marriage with his girlfriend, Yasmine (Shani Bayete). He prefers to spend his time hanging with his friends, gambling on playground basketball games, and chattering illiterate gibberish about all things inane. Racist language serves for humor, women serve as objects, and the "men" lack only a banjo and tambourine to be minstrel show fools in what proves to be a sad excuse for an urban comedy. All involved sooner or later become pathetic caricatures of real human beings. DVD presentation lacks the basics, like a menu. Although marked with 17 chapters, there is no reference for their selection other than the "skip" button on the remote. Picture quality is acceptable, with soundtrack uneven throughout. —RJT

Movie: 🐾½ **DVD:** 🐾🐾
York Entertainment (Cat #YPD-1033, UPC #750723103327). Full frame. AC3 - 5.1 Dolby Digital Surround Sound. $14.99. Keepcase. *LANG:* English. *FEATURES:* 17 chapters, but no menu to access chapters.
2000 ?m/C Brian Hooks, Shani Bayete, Cedric Pendleton, Crystal Sessoms, Michael A. LeMelle, Martin C. Jones, Rodney J. Hobbs, Sekenia Williams, Malik Jones; **D:** Barry Bowles; **W:** Barry Bowles.

The Notorious Daughter of Fanny Hill / Head Mistress
Kissey Hill (Walker) is the titular daughter who hosts assorted gentlemen in her establishment, which is apparently made up of two rooms. Producer Friedman is known for keeping costs down and he demonstrates it here. The second feature, *Head Mistress,* is allegedly based on two stories from Boccaccio's *Decameron.* Whatever; it's an excuse for legendary Marsha Jordan to strut her stuff as the head of a medieval girl's school, which miraculously has modern tile fixtures. On the commentary track, Friedman brags about the old house he found to use as the sole location. On DVD, both films look good, but *Notorious* is exceptional with very bright colors and accurate skin tones (which, after all, are really most important). It has been beautifully preserved and remastered. There are much more expensive studio releases from 1966 that don't look half as good. *Head Mistress* isn't as sharply focused or as bright. Both films feature numerous naked backs. —MM

Movie: 🐾🐾 **DVD:** 🐾🐾🐾
Image Entertainment (Cat #ID9745SWDVD, UPC #014381974522). Full frame. Dolby Digital Mono. $24.99. Snapper. *LANG:* English. *FEATURES:* 20 chapter links • "Naughty Bits" short films and previews •

Gallery of exploitation art • Commentary: Friedman, Mike Vraney • Radio spots.
1966 72m/C Stacy Walker, Leigh Cochran, Ginger Hale, Orlando Fenwick; *D:* Peter Perry; *W:* David Friedman; *C:* Art Radford; *M:* Chet Moore.

Nude on the Moon

Two-man lunar expedition discovers that the moon is inhabited by topless babes (and a few guys), who wear deely-bopper antennae instead of tops. Groovy theme song, "I'm Mooning Over You, My Little Moon Doll." The early nudie was made by Doris Wishman. The DVD image may be a little sharper and brighter than the VHS tape, but not much. —*MM*
Movie: 🎵½ *DVD:* 🎵🎵
Image Entertainment (Cat #ID6065SWDVD, UPC #014381606522). Full frame. Dolby Digital Mono. $24.99. Snapper. *LANG:* English. *FEATURES:* 12 chapter links • Gallery of exploitation art • Trailer • Short film "Cosmic Striptease."
1961 83m/C Shelby Livingston, Pat Reilly; *D:* Doris Wishman; *W:* Doris Wishman; *C:* Raymond Phelan; *M:* Daniel Hart.

Nunsense 2: The Sequel

This is a filmed stage performance that was made for the A&E network. It's more of the same jokes and routines from the Little Sisters of Hoboken led by their Mother Superior (McClanahan). Those who have not had the benefit of a Catholic upbringing will not appreciate most of the humor. Image and sound are what you'd expect from the source material. They're the equal of a clear cable broadcast. —*MM*
Movie: 🎵🎵 *DVD:* 🎵🎵
Image Entertainment (Cat #ID9494DLDVD, UPC #014381949421). Full frame. Dolby Digital Stereo. $24.99. Snapper. *LANG:* English. *FEATURES:* 24 chapter links.
1994 109m/C Rue McClanahan, Christian Anderson, Semina De Laurentis, Christine Toy, Terri White; *D:* Dan Goggin, David Stern; *W:* Dan Goggin; *M:* Michael Rice.

Nuremberg

TV miniseries lacks the nuanced complexity of the Stanley Kramer–Abby Mann *Judgment at Nuremberg*. This one takes as its subject the more important Nazi figures, notably Herman Goering (well played by Cox). Alec Baldwin is the American lawyer sent to prosecute him. Overall, the film has solid production values and the DVD re-creates the image without problems. Sound is less successful. Too often, Baldwin's growly bass voice is muddied. —*MM*
Movie: 🎵🎵½ *DVD:* 🎵🎵
Warner Home Video, Inc. (Cat #T8345, UPC #053939834529). Widescreen anamorphic. Dolby Digital Surround Stereo. $24.98. Snapper. *LANG:* English. *SUB:* English; French. *FEATURES:* Talent files • 54 chapter links • 2 behind-the-scenes featurettes • Trailer.

2000 200m/C Alec Baldwin, Jill(ian) Hennessey, Brian Cox, Michael Ironside, Christopher Plummer, Matt Craven, Max von Sydow, Len Cariou, Len Doncheff, Herbert Knaup; *D:* Yves Simoneau; *W:* David W. Rintels; *C:* Alan Dostie; *M:* Richard Gregoire.

Nurse Betty

Waitress Betty (Zellweger) never, ever misses an episode of her favorite soap opera—even when her car-salesman husband is being scalped and murdered by a couple of thugs in the living room. That gruesome crime, which comes to pass when the not-too-bright hubby attempts to sell stolen drugs back to the outfit they were stolen from, sends Betty into fantasy land—and on a cross-continental trip to Hollywood to find the true love of her life, Dr. David Ravell (Kinnear). Unfortunately, he doesn't exist outside the soap-opera world she watches on television. She is quite impressionable, however. The movie makes a generally good impression with only a few rough spots here and there to spoil the fun. Dark and violent subject matter is offset by Zellweger's light-natured, Doris Day–style performance. Witty, cutting dialogue helps, too. Freeman and Rock are effective as the hitman duo following Betty's trail. The disc looks and sounds great, although there is no anamorphic enhancement. There is an abundance of extras to keep the DVD in your player an extra evening or two. Then you can pop it into your PC to view the shooting script. —*MB*
Movie: 🎵🎵🎵 *DVD:* 🎵🎵🎵½
USA Home Entertainment (Cat #96306018 02, UPC #696306018025). Widescreen (1.85:1) letterboxed. Dolby Digital 5.1 Surround Stereo. $26.98. Keepcase. *LANG:* English. *CAP:* English. *FEATURES:* 36 chapter links • 2 commentary tracks with director, cast, crew • Theatrical trailer • 6 promotional spots • "A Reason to Love" original soap opera episodes • Deleted scenes • Hidden bonus features. DVD-ROM features: theatrical teaser, website, final shooting script.
2000 (R) 110m/C Renee Zellweger, Morgan Freeman, Chris Rock, Greg Kinnear, Aaron Eckhart, Crispin Glover, Allison Janney, Pruitt Taylor Vince, Kathleen Wilhoite, Harriet Harris, Susan Barnes, Sheila Kelley, Steven Culp; *D:* Neil LaBute; *W:* John C. Richards; *C:* Jean-Yves Escoffier; *M:* Rolfe Kent. *AWARDS:* Golden Globes '01: Actress—Mus./Comedy (Zellweger).

The Nutty Professor

Long before Eddie Murphy made these same Jekyll-and-Hyde comedic roles his own in the 1996 remake, Lewis was the original nutty professor of the screen. Easily Lewis's best film (so you know it's especially admired in France!), this farce is about a nerdy, snaggletoothed college professor who through a scientific misadventure creates a potion that transforms himself into the swaggering, playboy singer Buddy Love. The mild-mannered chemistry professor's alter-ego has an irresistible attraction to women,

which gets him into trouble. Lewis has repeatedly denied the slick character is a Dean Martin parody, but you can judge that for yourself. Lewis fans rejoice, because the film has never looked or sounded better on home video. The new transfer, enhanced for 16:9 TV sets, looks great on any screen, large or small. The brightly hued concoctions bubbling over in the professor's laboratory pop right out of the picture. The remixed audio tracks, though perhaps not true to the original release prints, especially benefit the fun score. Don't expect much in the way of Surround sound, however. The included featurette is a minimal, but welcome extra. —*MB*
Movie: 🎵🎵🎵 *DVD:* 🎵🎵🎵
Paramount Home Video (Cat #06712, UPC #097360671247). Widescreen (1.85:1) anamorphic. Dolby Digital 5.1. $29.98. Keepcase. *LANG:* English; French. *SUB:* English. *FEATURES:* 15 chapter links • "Paramount in the '50s" retrospective featurette.
1963 107m/C Jerry Lewis, Stella Stevens, Del Moore, Kathleen Freeman, Howard Morris, Les Brown, Med Flory, Norman Alden, Milton Frome, Buddy Lester, Henry Gibson; *D:* Jerry Lewis; *W:* Bill Richmond, Jerry Lewis; *C:* Wallace Kelley; *M:* Walter Scharf.

Nutty Professor 2: The Klumps [1 CE]

Stunning achievement in mediocre lowbrow humor. Sherman Klump discovers that his alter ego, Buddy Love, is living in the form of renegade DNA in his body and decides to isolate and remove the undesirable material before Love can ruin his budding relationship with a fellow DNA specialist (Jackson). When Buddy Love's DNA escapes and crosses with that of a Beagle dog, fart jokes, impotence jokes, and sex with hamster jokes abound. Murphy again plays Sherman Klump and Buddy Love as well as the whole flatulent Klump clan to hyperactive perfection. The DVD has beautiful color and is crystal clear, and the sound is also great. —*CA*
Movie: woof *DVD:* 🎵🎵🎵½
Universal Studios Home Video (Cat #209 22, UPC #025192092220). Widescreen (1.85:1) anamorphic. Dolby Digital 5.1 Surround. $26.98. Keepcase. *LANG:* English; French. *CAP:* English. *FEATURES:* 20 chapter links • Deleted scenes • Commentary • Cast and crew bios • Music videos • Trailer.
2000 (PG-13) 105m/C Eddie Murphy, Janet Jackson, Anna Maria Horsford, Melinda McGraw, Richard Gant, John Ales, Larry Miller, Chris Elliott, Earl Boen, Kathleen Freeman, Charles Napier, Jamal Mixon, Nikki Cox; *D:* Peter Segal; *W:* Barry W. Blaustein, David Sheffield, Chris Weitz, Paul Weitz, Steve Oedekerk; *C:* Dean Semler; *M:* David Newman.

Nutty Professor 2: The Klumps [2 Uncensored]

The only major difference is that this new "Director's Cut" includes two-minutes

worth of footage that was deemed too risqué and actually earned the film an "R" rating. The transfer looks basically the same as the first DVD release. The same can be said of the Dolby Digital 5.1 tracks, which mirrors the quality of the soundtrack found on the prior disc. A new addition here is the DTS 5.1 soundtrack. This track adds a slightly better sound field and some improved bass response when compared to the Dolby track, but there really isn't that great a difference. Also three new music videos from Sisqo, Musiq, and Jay-Z, have been added. There is a brief "Janet Jackson Wardrobe Test" in which we see Janet wearing Mama Klump's wedding dress. The last new extra feature is an Eddie Murphy makeup test from the original 1996 *Nutty Professor* film, which is absolutely hilarious. —*ML*
Movie: ♫ **DVD:** ♫♫♫
Universal Studios Home Video (Cat #212 67). Widescreen (1.85:1) anamorphic. Dolby Digital 5.1 Surround Stereo; DTS Surround. $26.98. Keepcase. *LANG:* English. *SUB:* English; French. *FEATURES:* Music videos ▪ Janet Jackson wardrobe test ▪ Eddie Murphy makeup test.
2000 (R) 105m/C Eddie Murphy, Janet Jackson, Anna Maria Horsford, Melinda McGraw, Richard Gant, John Ales, Larry Miller, Chris Elliott, Earl Boen, Kathleen Freeman, Charles Napier, Jamal Mixon, Nikki Cox; **D:** Peter Segal; **W:** Barry W. Blaustein, David Sheffield, Chris Weitz, Paul Weitz, Steve Oedekerk; **C:** Dean Semler; **M:** David Newman.

A Nymphoid Barbarian in Dinosaur Hell [SE]

Typically low-budget, unembarrassed schlock from Troma revolves around a post-apocalyptic babe in a leather bikini. The highlight of this disc is director Brett Piper's commentary track. He's much more honest and a lot funnier than 99% of the Hollywood guys who approach the same task as if it were a sacrament. Otherwise, image and sound are equal to tape. —*MM*
Movie: ♫ **DVD:** ♫♫♫
Troma Team Video (Cat #10268). Full frame. Dolby Digital Stereo. $24.95. Keepcase. *LANG:* English. *FEATURES:* Commentary: director Brett Piper ▪ Many Tromatic extras ▪ Photos ▪ Trailer ▪ DVD credits ▪ Interviews ▪ 9 chapter links.
1994 90m/C Linda Corwin, Paul Guzzi; **D:** Bret Piper; **W:** Bret Piper.

O Brother Where Art Thou?

Joel and Ethan Coen retell Homer's *Odyssey* in the South of the 1930s. That's where Everett (Clooney), Pete (Turturro), and Delmar (Nelson) escape from a chain gang and embark on a search for treasure and Everett's wife (Hunter). It is a wonderfully picaresque adventure with striking visual touches. Some critics think that the

Coens overplay their hand when they try to make the Klan figures of fun. To me, it fits the brothers' offbeat mythic humor. DVD recreates the theatrical image—color with a sepia tone—beautifully. DTS Surround is very strong. (The first gunshot will really surprise you, particularly if you're near the left rear speaker.) The only thing that's missing here is a commentary track. —*MM*
Movie: ♫♫♫ **DVD:** ♫♫♫½
Buena Vista Home Entertainment (Cat #21 654, UPC #786936144758). Widescreen anamorphic. DTS Surround; Dolby Digital 5.1; Dolby Digital Surround. $29.99. Keepcase. *LANG:* English. *SUB:* English; Spanish. *FEATURES:* 24 chapter links ▪ Trailer ▪ Music video ▪ Storyboard comparison.
2000 (PG-13) 103m/C George Clooney, Tim Blake Nelson, John Turturro, Holly Hunter; **D:** Joel Coen; **W:** Ethan Coen, Joel Coen; **C:** Roger Deakins; **M:** T Bone Burnett. *AWARDS:* Golden Globes '01: Actor—Mus./Comedy (Clooney); *NOM:* Oscars '00: Adapt. Screenplay, Cinematog.

Oasis of the Zombies

The story has to do with a World War II treasure hidden at an oasis where the titular characters are still hanging around. The zombie makeup is so lame that it makes the slow travelogue scenes look good. The obvious inspirations are Romero's *Living Dead* movies and deOssorio's *Blind Dead*, but this doesn't measure up. DVD is a solid step up from the various tapes that have been in distribution for years, under the inspired title *Bloodsucking Nazi Zombies*, but the added clarity only makes the atrocious zombie effects even sillier. Light signs of wear are not a problem. —*MM*
AKA: Bloodsucking Nazi Zombies; Treasure of the Living Dead.
Movie: woof **DVD:** ♫♫
Image Entertainment (Cat #ID9107BIDVD, UPC #014381910728). Widescreen (1.66:1) anamorphic. Dolby Digital Mono. $24.99. Snapper. *LANG:* English; French. *FEATURES:* 12 chapter links.
1982 75m/C *SP FR* Manuel Gelin, France Jordan, Jeff Montgomery, Miriam Landson, Eric Saint-Just, Caroline Audret, Henry Lambert; **D:** Jess (Jesus) Franco; **W:** A. L. Mariaux.

The Object of Beauty

Two Americans (Malkovich and MacDowell) trapped in Europe by their love of pleasure and their lack of money, bicker over whether to sell their one object of value—a tiny Henry Moore sculpture. When it disappears, their relationship is challenged. Excellent acting and telling direction force an examination of one's own values. The full-frame image on this no-frills disc is identical to VHS tape. —*MM*
Movie: ♫♫♫ **DVD:** ♫♫
Pioneer Entertainment (Cat #DVD68948). Full frame. Dolby Digital Surround Stereo. $24.98. Keepcase. *LANG:* English. *FEATURES:* 20 chapter links.

1991 (R) 105m/C Andie MacDowell, John Malkovich, Joss Ackland, Lolita (David) Davidovich, Peter Riegert, Bill Paterson, Rudi Davies, Ricci Harnett; **D:** Michael Lindsay-Hogg; **W:** Michael Lindsay-Hogg; **C:** David Watkin; **M:** Tom Bahler.

October 22

Fred Golan and Richard Schenkman's film begins and ends with a shootout, just like *The Life Before This*, a Canadian film. With their circular structures and ensemble casts, the two are remarkably similar, though this one has the earlier copyright. Similarities to *Pulp Fiction* and *Magnolia* are also easy to see. This is a much more modest production that follows eight Los Angelenos during the course of the day leading up to the dramatic conclusion. In this case, the full-frame image and stereo sound offer only a scant improvement over VHS tape. —*MM*
Movie: ♫♫½ **DVD:** ♫♫
Image Entertainment (Cat #ID6274NGDVD, UPC #014381627428). Full frame. Dolby Digital Stereo. $24.99. Snapper. *LANG:* English. *FEATURES:* 12 chapter links ▪ Trailer.
1998 (R) ?m/C Tate Donovan, Ernie Hudson, Colm Meaney, Michael Pare, Amanda Plummer, Donna Murphy, Richard Schenkman; **D:** Richard Schenkman.

Octopus

Overachieving little video premiere contains enough elements for two regular movies. First we've got our CIA agent (Harrington) who must shepherd a terrorist (Isyanov) back to America for justice. Then there's the captain (Beecroft) of the submarine they use to transport the villain. And there's the science-babe (Lowery) who explains that they're traveling through the "Devil's Eye," which would explain the titular giant octopus, and before it's all over, we've also got the cruise liner and the time bomb. On DVD, the computer generated effects are no more (or less) laughable than they were in *Anaconda*. Sound is acceptable, too, but the best things about the movie are its energy and intentional humor. —*MM*
Movie: ♫♫½ **DVD:** ♫♫½
Trimark Home Video (Cat #7501D, UPC #031398750123). Widescreen (1.66:1) letterboxed. Dolby Digital 5.1 Surround Stereo. $24.99. Keepcase. *LANG:* English. *SUB:* English; French; Spanish. *FEATURES:* "Making of" featurette ▪ Trailers.
2000 (PG-13) 99m/C Carolyn Lowery, David Beecroft, Jay Harrington, Ravil Isyanov; **D:** John Eyres; **W:** Michael D. Weiss; **C:** Adolfo Bartoli; **M:** Marco Marinangelo.

Octopussy

When a crazed Russian general (Berkoff) engineers a plan to launch a nuclear attack against NATO forces in Europe, Bond (Moore) enlists the help of mercenary Octopussy (Adams) and her scantily

clad female army to prevent the Cold Threat, as well as defeat the megalomaniac Kamal (Jourdan), to make the world safe once again for...sex. The weak plot is aided by a couple of ducky set pieces, including the pre-credit teaser involving a lethal mini-jet, Bond as the quarry in a jungle manhunt ("Most Dangerous Bond?"), and hand-to-hand combat on the outside of an airplane. Transfer reads sharp and clear, with smooth colors and superb detail definition. The Dolby Digital Surround audio possesses excellent dynamic range with very active rear channels. In keeping with the other Bond DVDs, *Octopussy* is no slouch on supplements. Two entertaining documentaries, a commentary track with director John Glen, trailers, and animated storyboards for two scenes (mixing sketches and film clips) covers every conceivable filmmaking aspect. There's a real kick in hearing everyone talk about the controversy over the title or just reminiscing with a bemused twinkle in their eye. Check out Chapter 33; it contains one of the greatest lines in any Bond movie (hint: it's just one word, but the way Kamal utters it is priceless). The film is also available as part of *The James Bond Collection, Vol. 3* (cat. # 1001091). —*EP*
Movie: 🎬🎬½ **DVD:** 🎬🎬🎬
MGM Home Entertainment (Cat #100110 95, UPC #027616853950). Widescreen (2.35) anamorphic. Dolby Digital Stereo Surround. $26.98. Keepcase. *LANG:* French. *SUB:* French; Spanish. *FEATURES:* 36 chapter links ▪ Commentary ▪ "Inside *Octopussy*" documentary ▪ "Designing Bond—Peter Lamont" documentary ▪ Animated storyboard sequences ▪ Music video ▪ Theatrical trailers ▪ Collectible booklet.
1983 (PG) 140m/C *GB* Roger Moore, Maud Adams, Louis Jourdan, Kristina Wayborn, Kabir Bedi, Steven Berkoff; **D:** John Glen; **W:** Michael G. Wilson; **C:** Alan Hume; **M:** John Barry.

The Odd Couple
Two divorced men with completely opposite personalities move in together. Lemmon's obsession with neatness drives slob Matthau up the wall, and their inability to see eye-to-eye results in many hysterical escapades. A Hollywood rarity, the film is actually better in some ways than Neil Simon's original Broadway version. This disc is adequate. That's it, just adequate. The video delivers a better-than-VHS picture, but blacks are poorly defined and are lost in dimly lit scenes. The audio transfer is a bit more impressive, though it sounds as though it wasn't really re-mixed but merely made louder. Quite a disappointing treatment for such a great film. —*MJT*
Movie: 🎬🎬🎬½ **DVD:** 🎬🎬½
Paramount Home Video (Cat #08026, UPC #097360802641). Widescreen (2.35:1) anamorphic. Dolby Digital 5.1 Surround; Dolby Digital Mono. $29.99. Keepcase. *LANG:* English; French. *SUB:* English. *FEATURES:* 16 chapter links ▪ Theatrical trailer.
1968 (G) 106m/C Jack Lemmon, Walter Matthau, Herb Edelman, John Fiedler,

Monica Evans, Carol Shelley; **D:** Gene Saks; **W:** Neil Simon; **C:** Robert B. Hauser. *AWARDS: NOM:* Oscars '68: Adapt. Screenplay, Film Editing.

Of Human Bondage
Please see review of *Pre-Code Hollywood: Vol.1.*
Movie: 🎬🎬🎬
1934 84m/B Bette Davis, Leslie Howard, Frances Dee, Reginald Owen, Reginald Denny, Alan Hale; **D:** John Cromwell; **W:** Lester Cohen; **C:** Henry W. Gerrard; **M:** Max Steiner.

An Officer and a Gentleman
Zack Mayo (Gere) enters Officer Candidate School because he doesn't know what else to do with his life. Exposed to the harsh discipline of Sgt. Foley (Gossett) and the love of a local girl (Winger), he is transformed. Such a collection of clichés ought not to work at all, but the film has become a perennial audience favorite because the performances, writing, and direction are so sharp. Director Hackford's commentary track (recorded 19 years after he made the film) is both gossipy (in a nice nostalgic way) and technical. The DVD image is certainly not the sharpest you'll ever see, but it is an accurate reproduction of the original with no significant flaws. Worth owning. —*MM*
Movie: 🎬🎬🎬½ **DVD:** 🎬🎬½
Paramount Home Video (Cat #01467, UPC #097360146721). Widescreen anamorphic. Dolby Digital Mono. $24.99. Keepcase. *LANG:* English. *SUB:* English. *CAP:* English. *FEATURES:* 15 chapter links ▪ Commentary: Taylor Hackford ▪ Trailer.
1982 (R) 126m/C Richard Gere, Louis Gossett Jr., David Keith, Lisa Eilbacher, Debra Winger, David Caruso, Robert Loggia, Lisa Blount; **D:** Taylor Hackford; **W:** Douglas Day Stewart; **C:** Donald E. Thorin; **M:** Jack Nitzsche. *AWARDS:* Oscars '82: Song ("Up Where We Belong"), Support. Actor (Gossett); Golden Globes '83: Song ("Up Where We Belong"), Support. Actor (Gossett); *NOM:* Oscars '82: Actress (Winger), Film Editing, Orig. Screenplay, Orig. Score.

The Old Man and the Sea
Cuban fisherman Santiago hooks a giant marlin and battles sharks and the sea to bring his trophy home. Tracy's performance as the tough, aging fisherman garnered him his sixth Academy Award nomination and Tiomkin's beautiful score was an Oscar winner. The Warner DVD is not bad at all for a film of this vintage. The image is fairly sharp; often the matted-in backgrounds are softer than the balance of the image, but that, and what grain there is, appears to be from the original film itself and not an addition of the technology. Fleshtones are accurate and overall the color is vibrant and detailed. There

is a small amount of distortion on the high end and louder portions of the soundtrack, but never enough to be a problem. The included documentary deals with the author himself with footage filmed during the actual production. —*JO*
Movie: 🎬🎬🎬½ **DVD:** 🎬🎬🎬
Warner Home Video, Inc. (Cat #14158, UPC #085391415824). Widescreen (1.85:1) anamorphic. Dolby Digital Mono. $19.98. Snapper. *LANG:* English; French. *SUB:* English; French. *FEATURES:* 26 chapter links ▪ Theatrical trailer ▪ Behind-the-scenes documentary "The Legend and the Sea."
1958 86m/C Spencer Tracy, Felipe Pazos, Harry Bellaver, Don Diamond, Don Blackman, Joey Ray; **D:** John Sturges; **W:** Peter Viertel; **C:** James Wong Howe, Floyd Crosby; **M:** Dimitri Tiomkin. *AWARDS:* Oscars '59: Orig. Score (Tiomkin); *NOM:* Oscars '59: Actor (Tracy), Cinematog. (Howe).

The Omega Code
This entry in the God-vs.-Devil steel cage apocalypse smackdown genre was financed by the Christian cable network, TBN. In one corner, representing the Good, is motivational speaker Gillen Lane (Van Dien), who believes that hidden truths may be discovered by applying mathematical equations to sections of the Bible. In the other corner, representing Evil, is Stone Alexander (York), AKA the Antichrist, who uses the hidden codes to take over a one-world government. DVD image quality is sufficient to reveal the deficiencies of the CGI effects and the overacting by all concerned. There's really little about the film to recommend it beyond the audience of conservative Christians for whom it is intended. —*MM*
Movie: 🎬½ **DVD:** 🎬🎬
Goodtimes Entertainment (Cat #05-810 62). Widescreen letterboxed. Dolby Digital 5.1 Surround Stereo; Dolby Digital Surround. $24.99. Keepcase. *LANG:* English. *SUB:* English. *FEATURES:* "What is the Omega Code?" text explanation ▪ "Making of" featurette ▪ Talent files ▪ Production notes ▪ Trailers ▪ 24 chapter links.
1999 (PG-13) 99m/C Casper Van Dien, Michael York, Catherine Oxenberg, Michael Ironside, Jan Triska, William Hootkins, Robert Ito, Janet Carroll, Gregory Wagrowski, Devon Odessa, George Coe, Robert F. Lyons; **D:** Robert Marcarelli; **W:** Stephan Bliss, Hollis Barton; **C:** Carlos Gonzalez; **M:** Harry Manfredini.

The Omen [SE]
Hollywood's most successful supernatural series combines biblical horror with a political element. (Remember that the first film was made right after Watergate.) It's a first-rate potboiler in which Evil is incarnated in a rosy-cheeked little cherub. His spooky nanny—effectively underplayed by Billie Whitelaw—is a lethal Mary Poppins who's given in to the dark side of the force. The plot is filled with inventive twists and shocks and a welcome restraint in the effects department. Even without the extras, this

DVD is a huge improvement over the poor pan-and-scan tape that has been in distribution for years. This image appears to have been perfectly preserved or restored. It's old home week on the commentary track where director Donner and editor Baird remember their work fondly. A treat for fans, the film is also available in *The Omen Collection* boxed set. —*MM* **AKA:** *Birthmark.*
Movie: ♫♫♫ **DVD:** ♫♫♫½
20th Century Fox Home Entertainment (Cat #200448, UPC #024543004486). Widescreen (2.35:1) anamorphic. Stereo; Mono. $29.98. Keepcase. *LANG:* English; French. *SUB:* English; Spanish. *FEATURES:* 20 chapter links • Composer Jerry Goldsmith on four favorite themes • "Curse or Coincidence" featurette • "Making of" featurette • Commentary: Donner, Stuart Baird • Trailer.
1976 (R) 111m/C Gregory Peck, Lee Remick, Harvey Stephens, Billie Whitelaw, David Warner, Holly Palance, Robert Rietty, Patrick Troughton, Martin Benson, Leo McKern, Richard Donner; *D:* Richard Donner; *W:* David Seltzer; *C:* Gilbert Taylor; *M:* Jerry Goldsmith. *AWARDS:* Oscars '76: Orig. Score; *NOM:* Oscars '76: Song ("Ave Satani").

Omen 3: The Final Conflict

The series returns to an approximation of its former level of quality for the third entry. Sam Neill makes the most of a well-written role. He carries off potentially hilarious dialogue with absolute conviction and believability, giving the adult Damien a strong streak of Nixonian bravado. The gruesome effects and stunts are better, too, particularly a long fox hunt scene. The plot is strong and the film ends on a note of religio-cinematic excess worthy of Cecil B. DeMille. Graham Baker's commentary is more restrained than the others. Image and sound quality are excellent. The title is also available as part of *The Omen Collection* boxed set. —*MM* **AKA:** *The Final Conflict.*
Movie: ♫♫♫ **DVD:** ♫♫½
20th Century Fox Home Entertainment (Cat #2000450, UPC #024543004509). Widescreen (2.35:1) anamorphic. Dolby Digital Surround Stereo; Mono. $29.98. Keepcase. *LANG:* English; French. *SUB:* English; Spanish. *FEATURES:* 20 chapter links • Commentary: Graham Baker • Trailers.
1981 (R) 108m/C Sam Neill, Lisa Harrow, Barnaby Holm, Rossano Brazzi, Don Gordon, Mason Adams, Robert Arden, Marc Boyle, Tommy Duggan, Richard Oldfield, Arwen Holm; *D:* Graham Baker; *W:* Andrew Birkin; *C:* Phil Meheux, Robert Paynter; *M:* Jerry Goldsmith.

Omen 4: The Awakening

Please see review for *The Omen Collection.*
Movie: ♫♫
1991 97m/C Faye Grant, Michael Woods, Michael Lerner, Asia Vieira; *D:* Jorge Montesi, Dominique Othenin-Girard.

The Omen Collection

This four-disc boxed set contains the first three theatrical films—*The Omen, Damien: The Omen II, The Omen 3: The Final Conflict*—and the made-for-TV *Omen 4: The Awakening*. In it, we learn that Damien had a daughter, Delia. (That would make her the granddaughter of Satan, right?) She's taken in by a clueless couple and plans to move her adoptive dad, a Senator, into the White House. Fans of the earlier films are under no obligation to see it. —*MM*
Movie: ♫♫♫ **DVD:** ♫♫♫
20th Century Fox Home Entertainment (Cat #2000451, UPC #024543004516). Widescreen anamorphic. Dolby Digital 4.0 Surround; Dolby Digital Surround; Dolby Digital Stereo. $99.98. Keepcase boxed set. *LANG:* English; French. *SUB:* English; Spanish. *FEATURES:* 28 chapter links (for *IV*) • Trailers.
2000 ?m/C

On the Border

Familiar neo-noir revolves around a bank heist. Ex-bank robber Jake (Van Dien) is now a security guard. Kristin (Roos) entices him into a plot involving Brown, Baldwin, and Mitchum. The humor is intentional, and the Texas locations are well utilized. More importantly, particularly on disc, director Misiorowski and director of photography Sher take some care and deliver a really crisp, sharp image. They use extreme close-ups to good effect in the love scenes. Overall, this is an overachieving video premiere. —*MM*
Movie: ♫♫½ **DVD:** ♫♫½
Image Entertainment (Cat #ID6275NGDVD, UPC #014381627527). Full frame. Dolby Digital Stereo. $24.99. Snapper. *LANG:* English. *FEATURES:* 16 chapter links • Trailer.
1998 (R) 103m/C Casper Van Dien, Bryan Brown, Bentley Mitchum, Camilla Overbye Roos, Rochelle Swanson, Daniel Baldwin; *D:* Bob Misiorowski; *W:* Josh Olson; *C:* Lawrence Sher; *M:* Serge Colbert.

Once Upon a Time in China

Jet Li stars as legendary Chinese hero Wong Fei-hung who defends his country against the Western foreigners who are trying to exploit it. This is one of the seminal Hong Kong historical action films, and this edition is an excellent place for fans of *Crouching Tiger Hidden Dragon* to learn about its roots. The reason is an excellent commentary track by critic and martial artist Ric Meyers, who explains the conventions of Chinese films to the uninitiated. The DVD was made from the Media Asia original that is also distributed by Tai Seng. Some aliasing is visible but that's not a significant problem. Recommended. —*MM* **AKA:** *Wong Fei-hung.*
Movie: ♫♫♫½ **DVD:** ♫♫♫½
Columbia Tristar Home Video (Cat #05672, UPC #043396056725). Widescreen (2.35:1) letterboxed. Dolby Digital Stereo. $24.95. Keepcase. *LANG:* Cantonese; Mandarin;

English. *SUB:* English; French; Spanish. *FEATURES:* 28 chapter links • Commentary: Ric Meyers • Trailers • Talent files.
1991 128m/C *HK* Jet Li, Yuen Biao, Jacky Cheung, Rosamund Kwan, Kent Cheng; *D:* Tsui Hark; *W:* Tsui Hark; *C:* Arthur Wong, David Chung; *M:* James Wong.

Once Upon a Time...When We Were Colored

Actor Reid makes a fine directorial debut with the story of a black youngster growing up parentless in '50s Mississippi. His family faces the usual troubles of the time including poor wages and white bigotry, but manages to provide a positive and loving home life for him. The adaptation of Clifton Taulbert's autobiographical book is nostalgic, sensitive, and heartwarming. DVD heightens the dusty, auburn-tinted color scheme that Reid uses to burnish his nostalgia. A good commentary track could have been a valuable addition. —*MM*
Movie: ♫♫♫ **DVD:** ♫♫♫
Republic Pictures Home Video (Cat #39506). Widescreen (1.85:1) letterboxed. Dolby Digital Stereo. $24.98. Keepcase. *LANG:* English. *FEATURES:* Trailer • 36 chapter links.
1995 (PG) 112m/C Al Freeman Jr., Paula Kelly, Phylicia Rashad, Polly Bergen, Richard Roundtree, Charles Taylor, Willie Norwood Jr., Damon Hines, Leon; *D:* Tim Reid; *W:* Paul Cooper; *C:* Johnny Simmons; *M:* Steve Tyrell; *Nar:* Phill Lewis.

One Day in September

Kevin MacDonald does not go for subtlety in this look back at the Palestinian attack on Israeli athletes at the 1972 Munich Olympics. In the opening scenes, he shows us film shot at the wedding of an Israeli fencer and clips from a promotional travelogue for the city of Munich. He also interviews the only surviving terrorist and gets his side of the events. The director's unashamed biases aside, the film is a remarkable piece of work. It also looks very good on DVD. As expected, the new footage is fine, but much of the archival material appears to have been well preserved or restored. Highly recommended. —*MM*
Movie: ♫♫♫ **DVD:** ♫♫♫
Columbia Tristar Home Video (Cat #06358, UPC #043396063587). Widescreen (1.78:1) letterboxed. Dolby Digital Surround. $24.99. Keepcase. *LANG:* English; German. *SUB:* English. *FEATURES:* 28 chapter links • Talent files • Trailers.
1999 (R) 91m/C *D:* Kevin MacDonald; *C:* Alwin Kuchler, Neve Cunningham; *Nar:* Michael Douglas.

187

Jackson plays a Brooklyn high school teacher who is brutally attacked by one of his students. His physical scars are healed, but his emotional state is marred

as he takes some pretty unorthodox teaching methods to a troubled L.A. school. The dark psychological drama is driven by a powerful performance from the star. The DVD transfer is generally clean and without defects, but quite a bit of edge-enhancement is visible, giving the entire movie an artificially sharpened look, which also results in ringing artifacts. The color balance is natural and warm with deep blacks and good highlights. The audio is well produced and makes aggressive use of the Surrounds. The bass extension on the disc is noticeably exaggerated, giving many of the scenes an unnaturally "fat" tone, sometimes completely overpowering other ambient sound effects. —GH/MM
Movie: 🐾🐾½ **DVD:** 🐾🐾🐾
Warner Home Video, Inc. (Cat #15432). Widescreen (1.85:1) anamorphic; full frame. Dolby Digital 5.1 Surround Stereo; Dolby Digital Surround Stereo. $19.98. Snapper. *LANG:* English; French. *FEATURES:* Commentary • Trailer.
1997 (R) 119m/C Samuel L. Jackson, John Heard, Kelly Rowan, Clifton (Gonzalez) Collins Jr., Tony Plana, Lobo Sebastian, Jack Kehler, Demetrius Navarro, Karina Arroyave; *D:* Kevin Reynolds; *W:* Scott Yagemann; *C:* Ericson Core.

One-Eyed Jacks

Often engaging but lengthy psychological western focuses on an outlaw (Brando) who seeks to settle the score with a former partner (Malden) who has become a lawman. Great acting by all, particularly Brando, who took over from original director Stanley Kubrick midway through the filming. The photography is wonderful, but you can't really tell it from this bargain basement DVD. The color is faded; the widescreen image is cropped; the score fades in and out; and the image is marred by the occasional large artifact. —MM
Movie: 🐾🐾🐾½ **DVD:** 🐾½
Madacy Entertainment (Cat #DVD-9-9018, UPC #056775005498). Full frame. $9.98. Keepcase. *LANG:* English. *FEATURES:* 9 chapter links • Marlon Brando thumbnail bio • Production credits.
1961 141m/C Marlon Brando, Karl Malden, Katy Jurado, Elisha Cook Jr., Slim Pickens, Ben Johnson, Pina Pellicer, Timothy Carey; *D:* Marlon Brando; *W:* Calder Willingham; *C:* Charles B(ryant) Lang Jr. *AWARDS:* NOM: Oscars '61: Color Cinematog.

One False Move

Black psycho Pluto (Beach), his white-trash partner Ray (Thornton, who also wrote), and Ray's biracial lover Fantasia (Williams) pull off a horrifying murder-burglary and head from L.A. to Arkansas. Two L.A. cops and the local sheriff (Paxton) are waiting for them. The film follows those two converging plotlines to a fine Hitchcockian conclusion. This thriller is one of the best sleepers around. DVD wisely provides both widescreen and full-frame versions, but the main attraction is director Franklin's excellent, no-nonsense com-

mentary track. It's worth a second viewing just to listen to his explanation of the film's genesis and his work with the cast. Both image and sound are excellent re-creations of the original theatrical release. —MM
Movie: 🐾🐾🐾½ **DVD:** 🐾🐾🐾½
Columbia Tristar Home Video (Cat #911 79). Widescreen anamorphic; full frame. Dolby Digital Surround. $29.95. Keepcase. *LANG:* English; Spanish. *SUB:* English; Spanish. *FEATURES:* Trailers • 28 chapter links • Commentary: Carl Franklin.
1991 (R) 105m/C Bill Paxton, Cynda Williams, Michael Beach, Jim Metzler, Earl Billings, Billy Bob Thornton, Natalie Canerday, Robert Ginnaven, Robert Anthony Bell, Kevin Hunter; *D:* Carl Franklin; *W:* Billy Bob Thornton, Tom Epperson; *C:* James L. Carter; *M:* Peter Haycock, Derek Holt. *AWARDS:* Ind. Spirit '93: Director (Franklin); MTV Movie Awards '93: New Filmmaker (Franklin).

One Good Turn

Solid little thriller from video veteran Tony Randel delivers the goods. Matt (Von Dohlen) and his wife Laura (Amis) have things going their way until Matt runs into Simon (Remar), a man who saved his life 12 years before but has since fallen on hard times. The rest of the action comes from well-realized characters. The full-frame image is only a scant improvement over VHS tape, but the unpredictable film is recommended to fans on any medium. —MM
Movie: 🐾🐾🐾 **DVD:** 🐾🐾
Winstar Home Entertainment (Cat #24.98, UPC #720917517322). Full frame. Dolby Digital Stereo. $24.99. Keepcase. *LANG:* English. *FEATURES:* 8 chapter links • Trailer • Filmographies • DVD credits • DVD-ROM weblink.
1995 (R) 90m/C Lenny Von Dohlen, James Remar, Suzy Amis, John Savage; *D:* Tony Randel; *W:* Jim Piddock; *C:* Jacques Haitkin; *M:* Joel Goldsmith.

102 Dalmatians

Cruella De Vil (Close) has been cured of her obsession with fur and puppies, but once she is released from the looney-bin, she's back up to her old tricks. This is less a sequel than a recapitulation of the original. Like the first film, it's visually sharp and DVD captures that eye-popping quality. Sound is equally impressive. The commentary track by director Lima and several animal trainers tends toward the details of critter control and filmmaking tricks. —MM
Movie: 🐾🐾½ **DVD:** 🐾🐾🐾½
Buena Vista Home Entertainment (Cat #22755, UPC #786936155099). Widescreen (1.85:1) anamorphic. Dolby Digital 5.1 Surround Stereo; DTS 5.1 Surround Stereo. $29.98. Keepcase. *LANG:* English; French; Spanish. *SUB:* Spanish. *FEATURES:* 42 chapter links • Deleted scene • Commentary • Deleted scene and outtakes • 3 behind-the-scenes featurettes • "Dalmatians 101" featurette.

2000 (G) 100m/C Glenn Close, Gerard Depardieu, Ioan Gruffudd, Tim McInnery, Ian Richardson, Ben Crompton, Jim Carter, Ron Cook, David Horovitch, Timothy West, Alice Evans, Carol MacReady; *D:* Kevin Lima; *W:* Bob Tzudiker, Noni White, Kristen Buckley, Brian Regan; *C:* Adrian Biddle; *M:* David Newman; *V:* Eric Idle. *AWARDS:* NOM: Oscars '00: Costume Des.

One Man's Justice

Army drill sergeant John North (Bosworth) heads for the streets of Venice, California, to get the drug-dealing gun-running scum who killed his wife and daughter. Throw in a streetwise 10-year-old and all the usual suspects are in place. Lots of bullets and explosions. Image ranges between good and very good, which makes the Boz's thespianic shortcomings all the more glaring. —MM
Movie: 🐾🐾½ **DVD:** 🐾🐾
Artisan Entertainment (Cat #10515). Widescreen (1.85:1) letterboxed. Dolby Digital Surround Stereo. $24.98. Keepcase. *LANG:* English. *FEATURES:* 30 chapter links • Trailer.
1995 (R) 100m/C Brian Bosworth, Bruce Payne, Jeff Kober, DeJuan Guy, Hammer; *D:* Kurt Wimmer; *W:* Steven Selling; *C:* Jurgen Baum, John Huneck; *M:* Anthony Marinelli.

Onegin

It's a Fiennes family affair with Martha assuming directorial duties, brother Magnus providing the score, and Ralph starring as the titular 18th-century Russian aristocrat. The cynical sophisticate inherits a vast country estate where he befriends his young neighbor Lensky (Stephens) and his feather-brained fiancée, Olga (Headey). But Onegin is intrigued by Olga's older sister, lovely innocent Tatyana (Tyler), though he rejects her impulsive romantic gestures. This isn't the only mistake he makes and all of them cost him dearly. The St. Petersburg locations give the film a strong sense of place, but the lugubrious pace is a near-fatal flaw. Image is seldom better than good with heavy black clothes rendered virtually featureless. Surround is limited. —MM
Movie: 🐾🐾 **DVD:** 🐾🐾½
Studio Home Entertainment (Cat #7515). Widescreen (1.85:1) anamorphic. Dolby Digital Stereo. $28.52. Keepcase. *LANG:* English; French; Spanish. *SUB:* Spanish. *FEATURES:* 24 chapter links • Commentary: director • Trivia game • Talent files • Trailers.
1999 106m/C GB Ralph Fiennes, Liv Tyler, Toby Stephens, Lena Headey, Martin Donovan, Alun Armstrong, Harriet Walter, Irene Worth, Francesca Annis; *D:* Martha Fiennes; *W:* Peter Ettedgui, Michael Ignatieff; *C:* Remi Adefarasin; *M:* Magnus Fiennes. *AWARDS:* NOM: British Acad. '99: Film.

Only Angels Have Wings

Melodramatic adventure about a broken-down Peruvian airmail service whose pilots

must fly over a terrifying (and very high) mountain to deliver the goods. Spectacular flying sequences—look mom, no computer here. Large cast adds to the love tension between Grant, a pilot, Arthur, a showgirl at the saloon, and Hayworth, Grant's former lover. Mitchell adds to the comradery factor as Grant's buddy. Nominated for special effects, a category recognized by the Academy that year for the first time. Some film damage does little to spoil the effect of seeing this fine film's equally fine transfer to DVD. The black-and-white cinematography is highly detailed; the depth of field is often stunning; and the image always extremely sharp, even when the occasional preprint flaw does pop up. The mono soundtrack has some of the expected vintage harshness, but is overall very crisp, making the dialogue easy to understand. The supplemental section is limited but the "vintage advertising" section includes many beautiful and original lobby cards and posters. —JO
Movie: ♫♫♫♫ **DVD:** ♫♫♫½
Columbia Tristar Home Video (Cat #09469, UPC #043396094697). Full frame. Dolby Digital Mono. $27.95. Keepcase. *LANG:* English; Spanish; Chinese; Korean; Thai; Portuguese. *FEATURES:* 28 chapter links ▪ Theatrical trailer ▪ Talent files ▪ Vintage advertising.
1939 121m/B Cary Grant, Thomas Mitchell, Richard Barthelmess, Jean Arthur, Noah Beery Jr., Rita Hayworth, Sig Rumann, John Carroll, Allyn Joslyn; **D:** Howard Hawks; **W:** Jules Furthman; **C:** Joseph Walker; **M:** Dimitri Tiomkin. *AWARDS: NOM:* Oscars '39: B&W Cinematog.

Opening Night
Very long study of an actress (Rowlands) and the play she's about to open on Broadway. Backstage turmoil increases her own insecurities and the bad luck persists when an adoring fan dies in an accident on opening night. Performances carry this neurotic epic along, including director Cassavetes as Rowland's co-star and Blondell as the playwright. Unfortunately, the producers elected to spread the running time over two sides, so the disc must be flipped over before the end. The O.K. image gains little over VHS tape because Cassavettes was trying to achieve a minimalist realistic look with deliberately unflattering light. —MM
Movie: ♫♫½ **DVD:** ♫♫
Pioneer Entertainment (Cat #PSE-98-160). Full frame. Mono. $24.98. Keepcase. *LANG:* English. *FEATURES:* 11 chapter links.
1977 (PG-13) 144m/C Gena Rowlands, John Cassavetes, Joan Blondell, Ben Gazzara, Paul Stewart, Zohra Lampert, Laura Johnson; **D:** John Cassavetes; **W:** John Cassavetes; **C:** Frederick Elmes; **M:** Bo Harwood.

The Organization
This marks Sidney Poitier's third (and, to date, final) portrayal of detective Virgil Tibbs, first seen in *In the Heat of the Night*. By now, the detective is married (to

McNair) and has a family. The mystery revolves around a drug-smuggling ring with a vigilante group. The most glaring problem with the image is one plaid jacket that flashes like mad in medium shots. Beyond that, the image is good but not hugely superior to VHS tape. —MM
Movie: ♫♫♫ **DVD:** ♫♫½
MGM Home Entertainment (Cat #1001473, UPC #027616857934). Widescreen (1.85:1) letterboxed. Dolby Digital Mono. $19.98. Keepcase. *LANG:* English. *SUB:* French; Spanish. *CAP:* English. *FEATURES:* 16 chapter links ▪ Trailer.
1971 (PG) 108m/C Sidney Poitier, Barbara McNair, Sheree North, Raul Julia; **D:** Don Medford; **W:** James R. Webb; **C:** Joseph Biroc; **M:** Gil Melle.

Original Kings of Comedy
Spike Lee produced and directed this concert film of four black stand-up comedians—Steve Harvey, D.L. Hughley, Cedric the Entertainer, and Bernie Mac—performing at the Charlotte, North Carolina, Coliseum. Their act is loud, raunchy, profane, racist, and funny. DVD does a particularly good job of re-creating the feeling of a large auditorium. Lee uses the Surround mix to add in what sound like natural echoes. The disc is not supposed to be visually polished. Stage lighting is bright and harsh, but this is an accurate re-creation of the theatrical image. —MM
Movie: ♫♫♫ **DVD:** ♫♫♫
Paramount Home Video (Cat #33924, UPC #097363392446). Widescreen anamorphic. Dolby Digital 5.1 Surround Stereo; Dolby Digital Surround Stereo. $29.99. Keepcase. *LANG:* English. *SUB:* English. *FEATURES:* 13 chapter links ▪ 7 bonus scenes ▪ Music video ▪ Trailer.
2000 (R) 115m/C D.L. Hughley, Cedric the Entertainer, Bernie Mac, Steve Harvey; **D:** Spike Lee; **C:** Malik Hassan Sayeed.

Origins of Film
This three-disc boxed set earns its fourbone rating for historical importance, not entertainment value, though contemporary viewers may be surprised at the sophistication of early filmmakers. (Maurice Tourneur's *Alias Jimmy Valentine* employs an elaborate maze-like set.) The purpose of this collection is to make available works that many viewers may never have heard of. Two parts of the collection—African American Cinema and First Women Filmmakers—have never been seen widely. Some of the films have been thought lost for years. As a group, the level of quality is very good. Wavering distortion and signs of wear are apparent throughout, but great care has been taken to be sure that the films were transferred to disc at the proper projection speed. The originals come from the Library of Congress. Contents: The African American Cinema: "Within Our Gates" (1919), "The Scar of Shame" (1926), "Noble Sissle and Eubie Blake" (1923). Origins of American

Animation (21 animated short films, 1900–1921). Origins of the Fantasy Feature: "The Patchwork Girl of Oz" (1914), "A Florida Enchantment" (1914). America's First Women Filmmakers: "How Men Propose" (1913), "Matrimony's Speed Limit" (1913), "A House Divided" (1913), "Too Wise Wives" (1921). Origins of the Gangster Film: "The Narrow Road" (1912), "Alias Jimmy Valentine" (1915). —MM
Movie: ♫♫♫♫ **DVD:** ♫♫♫½
Image Entertainment (Cat #ID9807UMDVD, UPC #014381980721). Full frame. Dolby Digital Stereo. $79.99. Keepcase boxed set. *LANG:* Silent. *SUB:* English intertitles. *FEATURES:* 82 chapter links ▪ Piano score by Philip Carli ▪ Liner notes by Scott Simmon.
2000 564m/C

The Other Side of Sunday
A small town in 1959 Norway is the setting for a quirky coming-of-age comedy. Maria (Theisen) is the eldest daughter of conservative priest Johannes (Sundquist). Fun isn't part of his religion but puberty is hitting Maria hard and she longs to join in with the livelier crowd of her school friend Brigit (Salvesen) who listens to rock 'n' roll, wears makeup, and makes out with boys. Maria finds a compassionate listener in Mrs. Tunheim (Riise), who urges the girl to think for herself. The image is on the softish side of this import, and darker scenes tend toward graininess, but both image and sound are appropriate to the story and nostalgic mood. —MM **AKA:** Sondagsengler.
Movie: ♫♫½ **DVD:** ♫♫½
Winstar Home Entertainment (Cat #FLV5213, UPC #720917521329). Full frame. Dolby Digital Stereo. $24.98. Keepcase. *LANG:* Norwegian. *SUB:* English. *FEATURES:* 12 chapter links ▪ Production credits ▪ Filmographies and awards.
1996 103m/C NO Marie Theisen, Bjorn Sundquist, Hildegunn Riise, Sylvia Salvesen; **D:** Berit Nesheim; **W:** Berit Nesheim, Lasse Glomm; **C:** Arne Borsheim; **M:** Geir Bohren, Bent Aserud. *AWARDS: NOM:* Oscars '96: Foreign Film.

Our Lips Are Sealed
Mary-Kate and Ashley Olsen join the Witness Protection Program and are sent to Australia where the allegedly adorable duo finds adventures, etc. Image is no better than tape, but the disc is filled with extras, all that any fan could ask for, including a commentary track laboriously read by the twins. —MM
Movie: ♫
Warner Home Video, Inc. (Cat #37236, UPC #085393723620). Full frame. Dolby Digital 5.1 Surround Stereo; Dolby Digital Surround. $24.99. Snapper. *LANG:* English; Spanish. *SUB:* English; French; Spanish. *FEATURES:* 25 chapter links ▪ Intro by Mary-Kate and Ashley ▪ Commentary: Mary-Kate and Ashley ▪ Behind-the-scenes featurette ▪ "Bridgewalk" featurette ▪ "Film Fashion" featurette.

2000 (G) 90m/C Mary-Kate Olsen, Ashley Olsen; **D:** Craig Shapiro; **W:** Craig Shapiro, Elizabeth Kruger; **C:** David Lewis; **M:** Christopher Brady.

Our Town

Based on the Thornton Wilder play, the film tells the story of several generations of residents of Grover's Corner, which is kind of a Lake Wobegone of the 1930s. The daily lives and habits of the people are told to the viewer by the narrator who finally centers the story on the romance of Emily (Scott) and George (Holden). After they marry, Emily becomes ill during childbirth, causing her spirit to visit the cemetery where she talks to all the other residents of Grover's Corner who came before her. Life, death, mortality, and materialism are all dealt with. The movie is not faithful to the play's ending, leaving the moral of Wilder's original intention sitting outside the stage door. The picture is not very good and the sound is a scratchy mono. The extras are very cool, especially "The Wizard's Apprentice," which could also stand some real digital remastering of both picture and sound. —CA
Movie: ♫♫½ **DVD:** ♫
FOCUSfilm (Cat #FF8696, UPC #6830708 69625). Full frame. Mono. $24.95. Keepcase. *LANG:* English. *FEATURES:* 13 chapter links ⬤ Audio of Lux radio version of the story ⬤ Short "The Wizard's Apprentice" (1930) ⬤ Propaganda film "The Town."
1940 90m/B Martha Scott, William Holden, Thomas Mitchell, Fay Bainter, Guy Kibbee, Beulah Bondi, Frank Craven; **D:** Sam Wood; **W:** Harry Chandlee, Frank Craven; **C:** Bert Glennon; **M:** Aaron Copland. *AWARDS: NOM:* Oscars '40: Actress (Scott), Picture, Sound, Score.

Out Kold

Boxer Slim (Stubblefield) goes to work as muscle for pimp Goldie (Ice-T) and promptly falls in love with Goldie's favorite 'ho. Not a good move. This is an extremely low-budget action flick with slow, studied action scenes and minimal special effects. The pale image is exceptionally grainy. Sound may be an improvement over tape. —MM
Movie: ♫♫ **DVD:** ♫♫
York Entertainment (Cat #YPD-1083, UPC #750723108322). Full frame. Dolby Digital 5.1 Surround. $19.99. Keepcase. *LANG:* English. *SUB:* English; Spanish. *FEATURES:* 19 chapter links ⬤ Trailers ⬤ Filmographies ⬤ Behind-the-scenes featurette.
2000 85m/C Clifford Stubblefield, Ice-T, Kool Moe Dee, Tommy (Tiny) Lister; **D:** Detrich McClure; **W:** Detrich McClure; **C:** Lynda Cohen.

Outlaw Justice

Aging gunslingers Nelson and Kristofferson meet up with their buddy Tritt to avenge the death of their old partner Jennings. Nothing new storywise but the cast

is certainly comfortable with the material. The image on this no frills disc (not even a menu) is a very slight improvement over tape. —MM
Movie: ♫♫½ **DVD:** ♫♫
Sunland Studios (Cat #360). Full frame. $24.99. Keepcase. *LANG:* English. *FEATURES:* Trailers.
1998 (R) 94m/C Kris Kristofferson, Willie Nelson, Sancho Garcia, Travis Tritt, Chad Willet, Waylon Jennings; **D:** Bill Corcoran; **W:** Gene Quintano; **C:** Federico Ribes; **M:** Jay Gruska.

Outside the Law / Shadows

In the first half of this double feature, Lon Chaney plays the dual roles of villainous Black Mike Sylva and the kindly Ah Wing in San Francisco. The film is an early collaboration with director Tod Browning. He's Chinese again in *Shadows*, where he's washed ashore in the small town of Urkey after a storm at sea. In both, his ability to work with makeup and to use body language to express emotion are extraordinary. Both films have been damaged. Beyond the expected wear and registration problems, chemical damage is visible down the left side of parts of *Outside*. Some static is audible along with the added sound effects and orchestral score. *Shadows* has never been as sharp, and the organ music is not as pleasing, either. —MM
Movie: ♫♫½ **DVD:** ♫♫
Image Entertainment (Cat #ID5838DSDVD, UPC #014381583823). Full frame. Dolby Digital Mono. $24.99. Snapper. *LANG:* Silent. *SUB:* English intertitles. *FEATURES:* 14 chapter links *Outside the Law* ⬤ 12 chapter links *Shadows*.
1921 77m/B Lon Chaney Sr., Priscilla Dean, Ralph Lewis, Wheeler Oakman; **D:** Tod Browning; **W:** Lucien Hubbard; **C:** William Fildew.

Painted Skin

Historical supernatural tale concerns a ghost (Joey Wang) who's trapped on Earth and must paint her skin to pass among humans. The evil Demon King is responsible. Sammo Hung co-stars as a monk. Colors are pale and some faint scratches are visible throughout. DVD is not a major improvement over VHS tape. Subs are small and burned in. —MM **AKA:** Hua Pi Zhi Yinyang Fawang.
Movie: ♫♫ **DVD:** ♫♫
Tai Seng Video Marketing (Cat #89454, UPC #601643894546). Widescreen letterboxed. Stereo. $24.95. Keepcase. *LANG:* Cantonese; Mandarin. *SUB:* English; Chinese. *FEATURES:* 9 chapter links ⬤ Trailers.
1993 93m/C *HK* Adam Cheng, Joey Wang, Sammo Hung; **D:** King Hu; **W:** King Hu, Chang A. Cheng; **C:** Stephen Yip; **M:** Ng Tai Kong.

Pal Joey

Musical comedy about an opportunistic singer who courts a wealthy socialite in

hopes that she will finance his nightclub. His play results in comedic complications. Stellar choreography, fine direction, and beautiful costumes complement performances headed by Hayworth and Sinatra. Oscar overlooked his pal Joey when awards were handed out. Songs include some of Rodgers and Hart's best; based on John O'Hara's book and play. With most DVDs, the serious viewer will opt for the widescreen presentation but since *Pal Joey* was filmed with a 1.33:1 aspect ratio, the full-frame version is the more accurate. However, the widescreen does feel more theatrical, even if there is some information lost on the top and bottom. On both, the picture is fairly sharp in bright scenes but when the lights go down the grain level comes up a little and the blacks tend to fade to gray. Colors are somewhat dull and the whole image could use a shot of contrast. Like some other Columbia TriStar classic releases, the supplementals consist of the theatrical trailer (in this case a cool one), some cast and director notes, and some photos and posters in the "vintage advertising" section. —JO
Movie: ♫♫♫ **DVD:** ♫♫½
Columbia Tristar Home Video (Cat #07989, UPC #043396079892). Widescreen (1.85:1) anamorphic; full frame. Mono. $27.95. Keepcase. *LANG:* English; Portuguese. *SUB:* English; Spanish; Chinese; Korean; Thai; Portuguese. *CAP:* English. *FEATURES:* 28 chapter links ⬤ Theatrical trailer ⬤ Talent files ⬤ Vintage advertising.
1957 109m/C Frank Sinatra, Rita Hayworth, Kim Novak, Barbara Nichols, Hank Henry, Elizabeth Patterson; **D:** George Sidney; **W:** Dorothy Kingsley; **C:** Harold Lipstein; **M:** Richard Rodgers, Lorenz Hart. *AWARDS:* Golden Globes '58: Actor—Mus./Comedy (Sinatra); *NOM:* Oscars '57: Art Dir./Set Dec., Costume Des., Film Editing, Sound.

The Pallbearer

You probably liked this one better when it was called *The Graduate*. The Schwimmer vehicle shares some key plot points but lacks any cultural significance. He plays Tom, a whiny guy who's asked to be a pallbearer for an old high school classmate he can't quite remember. He's then seduced by Tom's mom (Hershey), while trying to rekindle a romance with the wan Julie DeMarco (Paltrow), an old classmate who can't quite remember him. The spurned older woman then exacts her revenge. Good performances make it watchable but only for fans of the cast. The no-frills disc is essentially identical to tape with adequate image and sound. —MM
Movie: ♫♫ **DVD:** ♫♫
Miramax Pictures Home Video (Cat #1750 3). Widescreen (1.85:1) letterboxed. Dolby Digital Stereo. $29.99. Keepcase. *LANG:* English. *FEATURES:* 16 chapter links.
1995 (PG-13) 98m/C David Schwimmer, Gwyneth Paltrow, Barbara Hershey, Michael Rapaport, Carol Kane, Toni Collette, Michael Vartan; **D:** Matt Reeves; **W:** Matt Reeves, Jason Katims; **C:** Robert Elswit; **M:** Stewart Copeland.

The Pallisers

This 4-DVD box set features the first 8 episodes of the 26-episode BBC miniseries. Based on the six "political" novels of the great Victorian author, Anthony Trollope, the full series explores the rise of the Palliser dynasty and contains enough political intrigue, romance, scandal, and drama to give any present-day soap opera a run for its money. The main characters are Plantagenet Palliser (Latham) and Lady Glencora (Hampshire), whose politically expedient marriage lays the groundwork for three generations of Palliser power. The series benefits greatly from the better-than-average acting and immaculate costumes and sets that fully transport the viewer to the drawing rooms and sculptured gardens of Victorian England. Sadly, the years have not been kind to the work. Shot on both film and video, the quality of the picture fluctuates greatly. Some scenes are very vibrant and full of color while others are muted and scarred by video noise and other imperfections inherent in the poor source materials. It is not unwatchable by any means and is about on par with an average VHS tape in terms of overall quality. The audio is better. It presents the dialogue in a clear and hiss-free manner—most important for such a prose-laden presentation. *—MP/MM*

Movie: 🎬🎬🎬 **DVD:** 🎬🎬½

Acorn Media Publishing (Cat #AMP-4088, UPC #054961408894). Full frame. Dolby Digital Stereo. $79.95. Keepcase. *LANG:* English. *FEATURES:* 36-page viewer's guide • Susan Hampshire interview • Thumbnail bio of Anthony Trollope.

1974 400m/C *GB* Susan Hampshire, Philip Latham, Anthony Andrews, Roland Culver, Donal McCann, John Hallam, Derek Jacobi, Roger Livesey, Mel Martin, Anna Massey, Barbara Murray, Stuart Wilson.

Pancho Villa

Savalas has the lead in this fictional account of the famous Mexican revolutionary. He leads his men in a raid on an American fort after being hoodwinked in an arms deal. Connors tries to hold the fort against him. The finale, in which two trains crash head-on, is the most exciting event in the film. Image displays some flecks and snow, and the score sounds awful in the credits. The softish image appears to be an accurate transfer of the original. *—MM*

Movie: 🎬½ **DVD:** 🎬🎬

Parade (Cat #55306). Widescreen letterboxed. $17.98. Keepcase. *LANG:* English. *SUB:* Japanese. *FEATURES:* Cast and crew thumbnail bios • 13 chapter links • Critical comments.

1972 (PG) 92m/C *SP* Telly Savalas, Clint Walker, Anne Francis, Chuck Connors, Angel Del Pozo, Luis Davila; **D:** Eugenio (Gene) Martin; **W:** Julian Zimet; **C:** Alejandro Ulloa; **M:** Anton Abril.

The Pandora Project

Intelligence agent Bill Stenwick (Tyson) goes bad and steals a super secret weapon that kills people but leaves objects intact. John Lacy (Baldwin) has to find it before his impending marriage to anchorbabe Wendy Lane (Eleniak). This standard-issue video premiere gains little on disc. The only improvement over VHS tape is the dubious inclusion of wisely deleted scenes. *—MM*

Movie: 🎬½ **DVD:** 🎬🎬

Pioneer Entertainment (Cat #10127, UPC #013023012790). Full frame. Stereo. $19.98. Keepcase. *LANG:* English. *FEATURES:* 17 chapter links • 6 deleted scenes.

1998 (R) 89m/C Daniel Baldwin, Erika Eleniak, Richard Tyson, Tony Todd, Jeff Yagher, Bo Jackson, Robert Hegyes; **D:** John Terlesky, Jim Wynorski; **W:** John Terlesky; **C:** Andrea V. Rossotto; **M:** Deddy Tzur.

Panther

Father and son Van Peebles's collaboration is an Oliver Stone fictionalization of history. They portray the founders of the Black Panther party as idealistic and blameless Marxist revolutionaries. Bobby Seale (Vance) and Huey Newton (Chong) simply exercise their constitutional right to bear arms against the Oakland, California, police department, which they see as an occupying army. In 1967, one of their first recruits is Judge (Hardison), a Vietnam vet. He's also signed up by police detective Brimmer (Baker) as an informer, and by Huey as a double agent against the cops. At the same time, FBI director J. Edgar Hoover (Dysart) declares the Panthers a threat to national security and launches the COINTELPRO operation against them. Brief passages from actual COINTELPRO documents are used to punctuate the film. Neither the real nor the imagined figures emerge as believable characters. The film never gets beneath the loud sloganeering rhetoric of the times to reveal genuine characters. DVD presents a good to very good image that's an accurate transfer of a mid-budget production. *—MM*

Movie: 🎬🎬 **DVD:** 🎬🎬½

USA Home Entertainment (Cat #636309, UPC #780063630924). Widescreen (1.85:1) letterboxed; full frame. Dolby Digital Surround Stereo. $29.95. Keepcase. *LANG:* English. *SUB:* French. *FEATURES:* Cast and crew thumbnail bios • Trailer • 24 chapter links.

1995 (R) 124m/C Kadeem Hardison, Marcus Chong, Courtney B. Vance, Bokeem Woodbine, Joe Don Baker, Anthony Griffith, Nefertiti, James Russo, Richard Dysart, M. Emmet Walsh, Mario Van Peebles; **D:** Mario Van Peebles; **W:** Melvin Van Peebles; **C:** Edward Pei; **M:** Stanley Clarke.

Paper Bullets

Generic action flick pits cynical veteran cop John Rourke (Russo) against Chinese gangsters who kill his friends, kidnap his son, etc. Russo has perfected a grizzled look. He and an overqualified supporting cast are the main attractions here. Fights and chases are mediocre and one character's pidgin English is borderline offensive. DVD image is no improvement over tape; sound is exceptionally poor. *—MM*

Movie: 🎬½ **DVD:** 🎬½

MTI Home Video (Cat #8106, UPC #03941 4581065). Full frame. $24.95. Keepcase. *LANG:* English. *SUB:* Spanish. *FEATURES:* 20 chapter links • Talent files.

1999 (R) 95m/C James Russo, William McNamara, Ernie Hudson, Nicole Bilderback, Jeff Wincott, Francois Chan; **D:** Serge Rodnunsky; **W:** Serge Rodnunsky; **C:** Greg Patterson; **M:** Jeff Walton.

A Paper Wedding

A middle-aged literature professor with a dead-end career and equally dead-end romance with a married man is persuaded by her lawyer sister to marry a Chilean political refugee to avoid his deportation. Of course, they must fool an immigration official and their "fake" marriage does turn into a romance, but this is no lighthearted *Green Card.* Bujold shines. The video transfer is extremely washed-out, with very little in the way of vibrant colors or definition making the film appear much older than it is. The soundtrack it also nothing spectacular, though is does feature understandable dialogue. *—MJT* **AKA:** *Les Noces de Papier.*

Movie: 🎬🎬🎬 **DVD:** 🎬🎬

Triton Multimedia (Cat #TDVD9130, UPC #017078913026). Full frame. Dolby Digital. $19.99. Super jewelbox. *LANG:* French; Spanish. *SUB:* English. *FEATURES:* 16 chapter links • PC-friendly Internet technology.

1989 90m/C *CA* Genevieve Bujold, Manuel Aranguiz, Dorothee Berryman; **D:** Michel Brault; **C:** Sylvain Brault.

Paradise Road

Fleeing the invasion of Singapore at the beginning of World War II, a group of British, American, and Australian women straggle to the shore of Sumatra after their ship is bombed. They're taken prisoner by the Japanese and herded into a jungle camp. Mrs. Pargiter (Close) becomes their unofficial leader, and eventually helps to form a singing group that keeps their spirits up. The film is based on real incidents—some handled with more detail in the excellent *Three Came Home* (not yet available on disc). The ensemble cast is excellent and the women allow themselves to be photographed in some realistically unflattering conditions. (This is probably the least glamorous work many of them will ever do.) The widescreen transfer captures that aspect much better than previous tapes, and the 5.1 Surround is well utilized in the important singing sequences. One quibble: a commentary track or an extra explaining the differences between the film and the real events is called for. *—MM*

Movie: 🎬🎬🎬 **DVD:** 🎬🎬🎬

20th Century Fox Home Entertainment (Cat #2001218, UPC #024543012184). Widescreen (2.35:1) anamorphic. Dolby Digital

5.1 Surround Stereo; Dolby Digital Surround. $24.99. Keepcase. *LANG:* English; French. *SUB:* English; Spanish. *FEATURES:* Trailers ☞ 20 chapter links.
1997 (R) 115m/C Glenn Close, Frances McDormand, Julianna Margulies, Pauline Collins, Jennifer Ehle, Elizabeth Spriggs, Tessa Humphries, Sab Shimono, Cate Blanchett, Wendy Hughes, Johanna Ter Steege, Pamela Rabe, Clyde Kusatsu, Stan(ford) Egi, Susie Porter, Lisa Hensley, Penne Hackforth-Jones, Pauline Chan; *D:* Bruce Beresford; *W:* Bruce Beresford, David Giles, Martin Meader; *C:* Peter James; *M:* Margareth Dryburgh, Ross Edwards.

The Parallax View
A reporter (Beatty) tries to disprove a report that states that a presidential candidate's assassination was not a conspiracy. As he digs deeper and deeper, he uncovers more than he bargained for and becomes a pawn in the conspirators' further plans. Beatty is excellent and the conspiracy is never less than believable. Lesser-known political thriller deserves to be more widely seen. Image is generally good with only the occasional problem (flashing patterns in a Panama hat, etc.). Same for sound. —*MM*
Movie: 🎬🎬🎬½ *DVD:* 🎬🎬½
Paramount Home Video (Cat #86707, UPC #097360867077). Widescreen (2.35:1) letterboxed. Dolby Digital Mono. $29.99. Keepcase. *LANG:* English; French. *FEATURES:* Trailer ☞ 15 chapter links.
1974 (R) 102m/C Warren Beatty, Hume Cronyn, William Daniels, Paula Prentiss, Kenneth Mars, Bill McKinney, Anthony Zerbe, Walter McGinn; *D:* Alan J. Pakula; *W:* David Giler, Lorenzo Semple Jr.; *C:* Gordon Willis; *M:* Michael Small. *AWARDS:* Natl. Soc. Film Critics '74: Cinematog.

Parasite
An early appearance by an incredibly young Demi Moore and a blatant rip-off of the famous "chest-buster" moment from *Alien* are about all this slow-moving B-movie has to offer. Paul Dean (Robert Glaudini) is the post-apocalyptic scientist who has developed a species of parasitic critter and tries to destroy his work, but not before one of them gets inside him. Off he goes to a desert town to figure out how to kill it before it kills him. That's a fair premise but director Charles Band lets the action wander down some uninteresting sidetracks, and it's pretty slow throughout. Originally filmed in 3-D, the image is absolutely no improvement over VHS tape. —*MM*
Movie: 🎬🎬 *DVD:* 🎬🎬
Full Moon Pictures (Cat #8008). Full frame. $24.98. Jewelcase. *LANG:* English. *FEATURES:* Trailers ☞ Talent files ☞ 22 chapter links.
1982 (R) 90m/C Bob Glaudini, Demi Moore, Luca Bercovici, Cherie Currie, Gale Robbins, James Davidson, Al Fann, Cheryl "Rainbeaux" Smith, Vivian Blaine; *D:*

Charles Band; *W:* Alan J. Adler, Frank Levering, Michael Shoob; *C:* Mac Ahlberg; *M:* Richard Band.

Parasite
A college professor (Gaffney) becomes involved with a psychic while he's trying to line up a large grant. This ultra–low budget video premiere gains nothing on DVD. The echoing sound, poor acting, and excessively grainy image are no better than tape. This title is not to be confused with the 1982 *Parasite* starring Demi Moore. —*MM*
Movie: 🎬½ *DVD:* 🎬½
Digital Media Ltd. (DML) (Cat #004113, UPC #619543004132). Full frame. Keepcase. *LANG:* English. *FEATURES:* 6 chapter links.
1995 90m/C David Gaffney, Julia Matias, Robert Gerard, David Akin, Marissa Hall; *D:* Andy Froemke; *W:* Patrick Roddy; *C:* David Wing; *M:* Kristopher Carter.

Paris Holiday
Actor Robert Hunter (Hope, who also wrote the story) heads for Paris to buy a novel by a noted author. He becomes involved with alluring diplomat Ann McCall (Hyer) and sexy spy Zara (Ekberg). Hope is a bit restrained, compared to some of his other comic work. Though the disc was made from excellent original elements, the image is dark, particularly in some of the night scenes and interiors. Black clothes become solid shapes without detail. Sound is very good. —*MM*
Movie: 🎬🎬½ *DVD:* 🎬🎬
Brentwood Home Video (Cat #60985-9, UPC #090096098593). Full frame. Dolby Digital Mono. $14.98. Keepcase. *LANG:* English. *FEATURES:* 8 chapter links ☞ Bob Hope thumbnail bio and filmography.
1957 100m/C Bob Hope, Fernandel, Anita Ekberg, Martha Hyer, Preston Sturges; *D:* Gerd Oswald; *W:* Edmund Beloin, Dean Reisner; *C:* Roger Hubert.

Park City: The Sundance Collection
This DVD is a collection of five short films. Though they range widely in subject matter and tone, they share a low-budget independent production look. Image quality ranges between poor and good; same for sound. The real value of the disc lies in availability—since these works are so rarely screened—and accessibility of individual films. Contents: "Hollywood (& Vine)," "Jimmy Walks Away," "Among Others," "Love Bites," and "Man About Town." (The last two are favorites.) —*MM*
Movie: 🎬🎬🎬½ *DVD:* 🎬🎬½
Vanguard International Cinema, Inc. (UPC #658769012033). Widescreen; full frame. $29.95. Keepcase. *LANG:* English. *FEATURES:* 16 chapter links.
2001 77m/C *D:* Kris Isacsson, Gregory Russin, Eric Weinrib, Trac Vu, Michael Horowitz, Colburn Tseng.

Parting Glances
Filmmaker Bill Sherwood's *Parting Glances* is standing the test of time. The story follows Michael (Ganoung) for one day as he copes with his lover being transferred to Africa, the going-away party thrown by their friend Joan (Kinney), and making meals for his ex-lover Nick (Buscemi), who is living with AIDS. It's a pity Sherwood died in 1990, because his script and direction succeed in being touching and honest without manipulating the audience or relying on star turns, perhaps the first gay heart-warmer. The DVD quality has retained the warmth of film, but without any of the videotape's flaws. —*JAS*
Movie: 🎬🎬🎬 *DVD:* 🎬🎬
First Run Features (Cat #FRF909204D, UPC #720229909294). Full frame. $29.95. Keepcase. *LANG:* English. *FEATURES:* 9 chapter Listings ☞ Production notes and cast photos.
1986 (R) 90m/C John Bolger, Richard Ganoung, Steve Buscemi, Adam Nathan, Patrick Tull, Kathy Kinney; *D:* Bill Sherwood; *W:* Bill Sherwood; *C:* Jacek Laskus.

Party
Leonor (Silveira) and her husband Rogerio (Samora) throw a garden party at their posh villa. An older couple, Michel (Piccoli) and Irene (Papas) engage them in long conversations about a variety of subjects. After a windstorm drives everyone indoors, they talk some more. Almost all of the second half is illuminated by a fireplace. Even the daylight exteriors lack sparkle so DVD gains nothing over tape. Burned in subtitles are easy to read. —*MM*
Movie: 🎬🎬½ *DVD:* 🎬🎬
Image Entertainment (Cat #ID0312SIDVD, UPC #014381031225). Full frame. Dolby Digital Mono. $24.99. Snapper. *LANG:* Portuguese. *SUB:* English. *FEATURES:* 10 chapter links.
1996 91m/C *FR PT* Leonor Silveira, Michel Piccoli, Rogerio Samora, Irene Papas; *D:* Manoel de Oliveira; *W:* Manoel de Oliveira, Augustina Bessa-Luis; *C:* Renato Berta.

A Passage to India
Ambitious adaptation of E.M. Forster's complex novel about relations between Brits and Indians in the 1920s centers on a young British woman's (Davis) accusations that an Indian doctor (Bannerjee) raped her while serving as a guide in some rather ominous caves. The story isn't nearly as compelling as director Lean's best work (*Lawrence of Arabia*, *Bridge on the River Kwai*). It's still a sumptuous production that makes a successful transition to disc. The image is excellent with carefully lit night scenes showing a rare degree of detail. If the Surround sound isn't as spectacular as more recent epics, it is accurate to my memory. The "Reflections of David Lean" extra is excerpts from a television interview. —*MM*
Movie: 🎬🎬🎬 *DVD:* 🎬🎬🎬

Columbia Tristar Home Video (Cat #05852, UPC #043396058521). Widescreen (1.85:1) anamorphic. Dolby Digital Surround Stereo. $29.95. Keepcase. *LANG:* English; French; Spanish. *SUB:* English; French; Spanish. *FEATURES:* 28 chapter links • Trailers • Reflections of David Lean • Talent files.
1984 (PG) 163m/C *GB* Peggy Ashcroft, Alec Guinness, James Fox, Judy Davis, Victor Banerjee, Nigel Havers; *D:* David Lean; *W:* David Lean; *C:* Ernest Day; *M:* Maurice Jarre. *AWARDS:* Oscars '84: Support. Actress (Ashcroft), Orig. Score; British Acad. '85: Actress (Ashcroft); Golden Globes '85: Foreign Film, Support. Actress (Ashcroft), Score; L.A. Film Critics '84: Support. Actress (Ashcroft); Natl. Bd. of Review '84: Actor (Banerjee), Actress (Ashcroft), Director (Lean); N.Y. Film Critics '84: Actress (Ashcroft), Director (Lean), Film; *NOM:* Oscars '84: Actress (Davis), Adapt. Screenplay, Art Dir./Set Dec., Cinematog., Costume Des., Director (Lean), Film Editing, Picture, Sound.

Passenger 57

No-frills direction and energetic performances from the leads elevate this standard action picture. Anti-terrorist specialist John Cutter (Snipes) has left the business following his wife's murder, but just happens to be aboard the airplane that's transporting evil terrorist Charles Rane (Payne) to Los Angeles for trial. Fans need to know nothing more to complete the plot. The stunts and fights are farfetched and athletic. The 5.1 pumps up the score and sound effects in those scenes, too. Even though the image is slightly pale and soft, the film looks as good as it needs to look. All of the extras but the trailer are text. —*MM*
Movie: ♪♪♪ **DVD:** ♪♪♪
Warner Home Video, Inc. (Cat #12569). Widescreen (2.35:1) anamorphic; full frame. Dolby Digital 5.1 Surround Stereo. $19.98. Snapper. *LANG:* English; French. *SUB:* English; French. *FEATURES:* 29 chapter links • Behind-the-scenes featurette • Airplane and hijacking films • Talent files.
1992 (R) 84m/C Wesley Snipes, Bruce Payne, Tom Sizemore, Alex Datcher, Bruce Greenwood, Robert Hooks, Elizabeth Hurley, Michael Horse; *D:* Kevin Hooks; *W:* Dan Gordon, David Loughery; *C:* Mark Irwin; *M:* Stanley Clarke.

Passion & Romance: Double or Nothing

Late-night cable eroticism gains nothing on DVD. Romance novelist Kathleen Connelly (May) dreams up encounters involving a bookstore, a blackjack dealer, a hypnotist, and actors. The color scheme emphasizes soft glowing reds and pale milky skin tones. The full-frame image is not really different from tape or broadcast. —*MM*
Movie: ♪♪½ **DVD:** ♪♪½
Image Entertainment (Cat #ALAD9896DVD, UPC #014381989625). Full frame. Dolby

Digital Stereo. $24.99. Snapper. *LANG:* English. *FEATURES:* 10 chapter links.
2000 86m/C Traci May, Gabriella Hall, Robert Donovan, Chris St. James, Glen Hill, Howard Lockie; *D:* Antonia Keeler; *W:* Glenda Rafelli; *C:* Todd Baron; *M:* Ace Edwards.

Passion & Romance: Scandal

A Georgia gubernatorial election is the flimsy excuse for a series of soft-core sexual encounters which all take place in one motel, thereby eliminating costly sets and lighting. This is strictly late-night cable fare that looks no better than broadcast or tape. —*MM*
Movie: ♪ **DVD:** ♪♪
Image Entertainment (Cat #ALAD9899DVD, UPC #014381989922). Full frame. Dolby Digital Stereo. $24.99. Snapper. *LANG:* English. *FEATURES:* 10 chapter links.
1997 85m/C Traci May, Robert Donovan, Gabriella Hall, Kira Lee, Wesley O'Brian, Thad Geer; *D:* Jill Hayworth; *W:* Harriette Lewiston; *C:* Wolfgang Bolle; *M:* Ace Edwards.

The Passion of Ayn Rand

Made-for-cable biopic opens in the standard fashion at the funeral of Ayn Rand (Mirren) and then examines her life through the prism of her relationship with a younger couple (Delpy and Stoltz) and her husband (Fonda). The star's performance is the key here. The image is not much better than broadcast or tape quality. The extra feature labeled "philosophy" is described on the box copy as "Fascinating philosophy or definition on objectivism." —*MM*
Movie: ♪♪½ **DVD:** ♪♪½
Showtime Networks, Inc. (Cat #SHO1035, UPC #758445103526). Full frame. Stereo. $24.98. Keepcase. *LANG:* English. *CAP:* English. *FEATURES:* 12 chapter links • Talent files • Photo gallery • Ayn Rand weblinks • Rand quote.
1999 104m/C Helen Mirren, Eric Stoltz, Julie Delpy, Peter Fonda, Tom McCamus, Sybil Temchen, Don McKellar, David Ferry; *D:* Christopher Menaul; *W:* Howard Korder, Mary Gallagher; *C:* Ronald Orieux; *M:* Jeff Beal.

Pat and Mike

War of the sexes rages in this comedy about leathery sports promoter Mike Conovan who futilely attempts to train a woman for athletic competition. Tracy and Hepburn have fine chemistry, but supporting players contribute as well, as does the Academy Award—nominated script by Gordon and Kanin. Watch for Ray as a dumb lug and the first on-screen appearance of Bronson (then Charles Buchinski) as a crook. The print shows a little wear but nothing to ruin the aforementioned chemistry or overall enjoyment of this riotous classic. Despite a little film grain, image is

generally very sharp and detailed. Blacks are dead-on and the varied graytones, combined with excellent contrast, give a rich look to the screwball proceedings. The aged mono soundtrack is a little tinny but is free of distortion, allowing for a crisp delivery of the dialogue and Raksin's score. —*JO*
Movie: ♪♪♪½ **DVD:** ♪♪♪
Warner Home Video, Inc. (Cat #65164, UPC #012569516427). Full frame. Dolby Digital Mono. $19.98. Snapper. *LANG:* English. *SUB:* English; French. *CAP:* English. *FEATURES:* 33 chapter links • 2 theatrical trailers • Production notes.
1952 95m/B Spencer Tracy, Katharine Hepburn, Aldo Ray, Jim Backus, William Ching, Sammy White, Phyllis Povah, Charles Bronson, Chuck Connors, Mae Clarke, Carl "Alfalfa" Switzer; *D:* George Cukor; *W:* Garson Kanin, Ruth Gordon; *C:* William H. Daniels; *M:* David Raksin. *AWARDS: NOM:* Oscars '52: Story & Screenplay.

The Patriot

Benjamin Martin (Gibson), veteran of the French and Indian War, wants to raise his family in peace on his South Carolina plantation during the Revolution. But his son (Ledger) is hot to join the fight and Martin is forced to choose sides. Seen simply as a star vehicle, the film is acceptable entertainment. It has virtually nothing to say about the Revolutionary War. The evil Brit villain (Isaacs) is a caricature and the film's view of 18th-century American racial relations is pure Hollywood nonsense. The softish image, often further blurred by smoky light, gains little on DVD. The Surround effects call attention to themselves in the big battle scenes. To reach the deleted scenes, look for a nearly invisible arrow near the top of the "special features" menu. It takes you to the second page. —*MM*
Movie: ♪♪♪ **DVD:** ♪♪♪
Columbia Tristar Home Video (Cat #05731, UPC #043396057319). Widescreen (2.35:1) anamorphic. Dolby Digital 5.1 Surround Stereo; Dolby Digital Surround Stereo. $19.95. Keepcase. *LANG:* English; French. *SUB:* English; French. *FEATURES:* 28 chapter links • Commentary; Emmerich and Devlin • Visual effects featurette • Deleted scenes • Photo galleries • Production notes • Trailers • Talent files • DVD-ROM weblink.
2000 (R) 164m/C Mel Gibson, Heath Ledger, Jason Isaacs, Chris Cooper, Tcheky Karyo, Joely Richardson, Tom Wilkinson, Donal Logue, Rene Auberjonois, Adam Baldwin, Leon Rippy; *D:* Roland Emmerich; *W:* Robert Rodat; *C:* Caleb Deschanel; *M:* John Williams.

Peace Hotel

After an opening scene of a gangland massacre, Chow Yun-Fat founds a sanctuary for those fleeing various enemies. The violence is extreme and borrows much from the Italian westerns of Sergio Leone and Sergio Corbucci. Unfortunately, the subtitles are so goofy that they're unintentionally humorous. DVD image has a dusty brown cast in many scenes. It looks pretty good for an import, but you've seen better. —MM

Movie: 🎵🎵½ **DVD:** 🎵🎵
Tai Seng Video Marketing (Cat #41454). Widescreen (1.66:1) letterboxed. $49.95. Keepcase. *LANG:* Cantonese; Mandarin. *SUB:* English; Korean; Malaysian; Japanese; Vietnamese; Indonesian; Thai. *FEATURES:* 9 chapter links • Talent files • Trailers.
1995 89m/C *HK* Chow Yun-Fat, Cecilia Yip, Lawrence Ng, Chin Ho; *D:* Kai-Fai Wai; *W:* Kai-Fai Wai; *C:* Wing-hang Wong; *M:* Cacine Wong, Healthy Poon.

Peach / A Bitter Song
Two short films star Lucy Lawless, from TV's *Xena*. In the first, she plays a sexy lesbian tow-truck driver. In "A Bitter Song," she's a nurse who helps a young girl in a hospital. The DVD also includes "Lavender Limelight," a documentary about lesbian filmmakers. The final feature is the sharpest looking of the three; at least, the original elements are. Many of the clips have that grainy, on-the-fly indie-prod look, and there's nothing DVD can (or should) do about it. —MM
Movie: 🎵🎵 **DVD:** 🎵🎵
First Run Features (Cat #FRF909099D, UPC #720229909099). Full frame. $29.95. Keepcase. *LANG:* English. *FEATURES:* 9 chapter links.
1995 95m/C Lucy Lawless, Tania Simon; *D:* Christine Parker; *W:* Christine Parker; *C:* Stuart Dryburgh.

Pearl Harbor
Two-disc set offers up three original documentaries focusing on Pearl Harbor and other aspects of the American involvement in WWII. The first feature is "Tora, Tora, Tora: The True Story of Pearl Harbor." Similar to its namesake feature film, "Tora" examines the events surrounding the Pearl Harbor attack in chronological order. The program opens with a brief overview of the political, economic, and military realities of the region in 1941 and ends with some rumination over the lessons learned from this attack and a very brief summary of the rest of the war. But the bulk of the feature deals with the events that occurred on the morning of December 7, 1941. Using archival footage, present-day views of the Pearl Harbor area, computer animation, and countless first-person accounts and interviews, the film presents a very engaging and even-handed account of the attack. Those who fought in WWII are becoming fewer and fewer so the interviews with American and Japanese veterans are particularly valuable. The second disc contains two programs: "Admiral Chester Nimitz: Thunder of the Pacific" and "America's Five-Star Heroes." The Admiral Nimitz documentary offers a very balanced account of the life

of the low-key naval commander who helped to engineer the defeat of the Japanese Empire. The second offers a somewhat less in-depth look at other key American military commanders in WWII. The newly shot video is uniformly excellent with a nice, sharp picture and well-balanced colors. Obviously the stock footage exhibits a wide range in terms of quality but this is to be expected. The picture is nothing fancy but it's more than adequate for this type of program. Same goes for sound. Press releases and even the History Channel website claim that the program "Military Blunders: Pearl Harbor," as well as an in-depth technical manual containing schematics of the aircraft and naval ships involved in the battle, are included in the DVD set. Alas, these promising-sounding extras are nowhere to be found. —MM/MP
Movie: 🎵🎵½ **DVD:** 🎵🎵
A & E Home Video (Cat #AAE-70215). Full frame. Dolby Digital Stereo. $29.95. Keepcase. *LANG:* English. *FEATURES:* "Pearl Harbor Facts" (text).
2000 150m/C

Pearl Harbor: December 7, 1941
This two-disc set contains the short version of *December 7*, the Oscar-winning documentary made by John Ford and Greg Toland; *Know Your Enemy*, a propaganda film made by Frank Capra; and *Kamikaze*, a 1951 documentary. Image and sound on all three are extremely poor, with all of the flaws coming from the original elements, which were not that good to begin with and have seen considerable wear. Image is harsh, high-contrast, low-detail black and white. Considerable static is audible throughout. Extras are minimal, including the "Exherpts" from the Honolulu Star. —MM
Movie: 🎵🎵 **DVD:** 🎵½
Madacy Entertainment (Cat #DVD9 9238-1, -2, UPC #056775068096). Full frame. $19.98. Keepcase. *LANG:* English. *FEATURES:* 16 chapter links • Trivia game • Historical thumbnails • Photo gallery.
2000 220m/C

The Pebble and the Penguin
Animated musical follows Hubie (Short), a shy romantic penguin who must present his lady love Marina (Golden) with a beautiful pebble to win her hand (or should that be wing?) before the villainous Drake (Curry) can claim her. Hubie is helped by a cantankerous new friend (Belushi) he meets when stranded on a boat to Tahiti. Together the two race back to Antarctica fighting enemies and the elements along the way. The film is based on a true mating custom of the Adeli penguins, and the story is satisfying for younger viewers but without the animation magic necessary for adult audiences. Beware of the sugary Manilow tunes. Image is soft—softer than I remember it from the theatrical release—about the same as tape. —MM

Movie: 🎵🎵½ **DVD:** 🎵🎵
MGM Home Entertainment (Cat #905403). Full frame. Dolby Digital 5.1 Surround Stereo. $24.98. Keepcase. *LANG:* English. *SUB:* English; French; Spanish. *FEATURES:* Trailer • 24 chapter links.
1994 (G) 74m/C *D:* Don Bluth; *W:* Rachel Koretsky, Steve Whitestone; *M:* Barry Manilow, Bruce Sussman, Mark Watters; *V:* Martin Short, Annie Golden, Tim Curry, James Belushi; *Nar:* Shani Wallis.

Penitentiary
Realistic story follows a black fighter (Kennedy) who survives his incarceration by winning bouts against other prisoners. It's an unusually well-made work for a low-budget effort. Exceptionally heavy grain crops up in many exteriors. Not surprisingly, the prison interiors are dark and rough. Overall, the image is dull. Fanaka's commentary track is not one of the most illuminating. —MM
Movie: 🎵🎵½ **DVD:** 🎵🎵½
Xenon Entertainment (Cat #1035). Widescreen letterboxed. $19.95. Keepcase. *LANG:* English. *FEATURES:* Trailers • Commentary: director Jamaa Fanaka • 12 chapter links.
1979 (R) 99m/C Leon Isaac Kennedy, Jamaa Fanaka, Badja (Medu) Djola, Chuck "Porky" Mitchell; *D:* Jamaa Fanaka; *W:* Jamaa Fanaka; *C:* Marty Ollstein.

Penitentiary 2
Disappointing sequel finds welterweight fighter "Too Sweet" (Kennedy) going after his arch-enemy "Half Dead" (Hudson), who murdered his girlfriend. On his lethargic commentary track, director Fanaka says that the film was largely financed by his family. The budget was small, and so the rough DVD image is no more than a modest improvement over tape. —MM
Movie: 🎵 **DVD:** 🎵🎵½
Xenon Entertainment (Cat #1036). Widescreen letterboxed. $19.95. Keepcase. *LANG:* English. *FEATURES:* 12 chapter links • Commentary: Jamaa Fanaka • Trailers.
1982 (R) 108m/C Leon Isaac Kennedy, Mr. T, Leif Erickson, Ernie Hudson, Glynn Turman; *D:* Jamaa Fanaka; *W:* Jamaa Fanaka; *C:* Stephen Posey; *M:* Jack Wheaton.

Penny Serenade
Newlyweds (Grant and Dunne) adopt a child but tragedy awaits. The stars and typically professional direction make the familiar material moving if a bit long in the telling. Minor registration problems and light static on the soundtrack are typical of films from the '40s. Overall, the image is no better than fair. The title is also available as part of the "Irene Dunne Romance Classics" double feature. —MM
Movie: 🎵🎵🎵 **DVD:** 🎵🎵
Madacy Entertainment (Cat #9-9015, UPC #056775005191). Full frame. Dolby Digital Mono. $9.99. Keepcase. *LANG:* English.

FEATURES: 9 chapter links ☞ Poster ☞ Cary Grant thumbnail bio.
1941 120m/B Cary Grant, Irene Dunne, Beulah Bondi, Edgar Buchanan, Ann Doran, Wallis (Clarke) Clark; **D:** George Stevens; **W:** Morrie Ryskind; **C:** Joseph Walker; **M:** W. Franke Harling. *AWARDS: NOM:* Oscars '41: Actor (Grant).

People of the Wind

Poignant, yet pointless examination of the annual trek of the Bakhtiari nomads from their winter pastures in southwestern Iran through the Zardeh Kuh mountain range to their summer pastures. Nominated for an Oscar for Best Documentary in 1976 (losing to *Harlan County U.S.A.*), the film depicts the timeless struggle for survival of Bakhtiari people. It takes on deeper meaning when one realizes that their land was the focal point of the devastating war in the 1980s between Iran and neighboring Iraq. Considering the difficulties of filming in such a remote area, the film to DVD presentation holds up reasonably well. Viewing options are limited, with no subtitle options or supporting menu features. —*RJT*
Movie: 🎵🎵½ *DVD:* 🎵🎵
Image Entertainment (Cat #ID9223MLSD-VD, UPC #014381922325). Widescreen (1.85:1) letterboxed. Dolby Digital Stereo. $29.99. Snapper. *LANG:* English narration. *SUB:* Some English. *FEATURES:* 16 chapter links.
1976 110m/C D: Anthony Howarth; **Nar:** James Mason.

Perceval

It's difficult to describe Rohmer's extremely stylized interpretation of Chretien de Troyes's unfinished 12th-century poem. Imagine the local community theatre version of *Camelot* complete with cardboard sets and wooden acting. Now imagine it in French. Young Welsh knight Perceval (Luchini) comes to a mysterious castle where he sees a vision of the Holy Grail, although he doesn't recognize it. DVD appears to be an accurate re-creation of what is essentially a staged play. Any further comment on the clarity of the visuals is unnecessary. —*MM*
AKA: Perceval Le Gallois.
Movie: 🎵🎵 *DVD:* 🎵🎵
Winstar Home Entertainment (Cat #FLV52 39, UPC #720917523927). Full frame. $24.98. Keepcase. *LANG:* French. *SUB:* English. *FEATURES:* 8 chapter links ☞ Production credits ☞ Filmographies and awards.
1978 140m/C FR Fabrice Luchini, Andre Dussollier, Arielle Dombasle, Marie-Christine Barrault; **D:** Eric Rohmer; **W:** Eric Rohmer; **C:** Nestor Almendros.

The Perfect Husband

Wealthy womanizer Milan (Roth) is shocked when his old friend Franz (Firth) shows up on his doorstep. (Milan has just participated in a duel, you see.) It's Prague, 1900, and Milan is haunted by memories of an affair he had with Franz's wife years before.

It is unclear what Franz knows about it. Performances are the key here, and the action is unusually sexy for a period piece. The film is an international production made for British television. Image is identical to tape. Some interiors are so dark that they simply swallow up characters in black or brown clothes. Sound is fine. —*MM* **AKA:** El Marido Perfecto.
Movie: 🎵🎵🎵 *DVD:* 🎵🎵
BFS Video (Cat #30002-D, UPC #0668053 00028). Full frame. Dolby Digital Mono. $29.98. Keepcase. *LANG:* English. *FEATURES:* 12 chapter links.
1992 90m/C SP GB Tim Roth, Peter Firth, Aitana Sanchez-Gijon, Ana Belen; **D:** Beda Docampo Feijoo; **W:** Beda Docampo Feijoo, Juan Bautista Stagnaro; **C:** Frantisek Uldrich; **M:** Jose Nieto.

The Perfect Nanny

Formula thriller combines elements of *Nurse Betty* with *Hand That Rocks the Cradle*. Andrea McBride (Nelson) is a disturbed, suicidal young woman who decides that Dr. James Lewis (Boxleitner) is perfect for her. He's a wealthy widower with a young daughter (Barron) and a great house. She assumes a false identity to worm her way into the family and then sets about getting rid of anyone who gets in her way. DVD provides such a sharply detailed image that it's easy to spot the retractable tip in one of the carving knives that Andrea uses. Sound is fine. —*MM*
Movie: 🎵🎵 *DVD:* 🎵🎵🎵
York Entertainment (Cat #YPD-1098, UPC #750723109824). Full frame. Stereo. $14.99. Keepcase. *LANG:* English. *SUB:* Spanish. *FEATURES:* 30 chapter links ☞ Behind-the-scenes featurette ☞ Trailers.
2000 90m/C Tracy Nelson, Bruce Boxleitner, Dana Barron, Susan Blakely, Katherine Helmond; **D:** Rob Malenfant; **W:** Victor Schiller, Christine Conradt, Richard Gilbert Hill; **C:** Don E. Fauntleroy; **M:** Richard Bowers.

Perfect Profile

This independently produced Texas basketball drama stars pro player Nancy Lieberman as a woman who joins a men's team. It's really too amateurish to need any critical comment. The bare-bones (no menu) DVD appears to have been made from very poor original elements. The image is scratchy and poorly focused. —*MM*
Movie: 🎵 *DVD:* 🎵
Digital Versatile Disc Ltd. (Cat #114). Full frame. $19.95. Keepcase. *LANG:* English.
1990 87m/C Nancy Lieberman, Tom Campitelli, Bruce Anderson, Nancy Buechler, Rocky Patterson, Rob Slyker; **D:** Jim Harris; **C:** Brian Hooper; **M:** Greg Krochta.

The Perfect Storm

Fishermen go up against special effects and the effects win in a fact-based adventure that pushes all of the right buttons. Clooney and Wahlberg are very good as the captain and mate of the fishing boat

Andrea Gail that sailed into the teeth of one of the most powerful storms ever to hit the Atlantic. If anything, the effects look even sharper on DVD than they do in theatre, though, of course, the big wave featured in the advertising art loses considerable power on any home theatre. Sound is just as good. —*MM*
Movie: 🎵🎵🎵 *DVD:* 🎵🎵🎵
Warner Home Video, Inc. (Cat #18584, UPC #085391858423). Widescreen anamorphic. Dolby Digital 5.1 Surround Stereo. $24.98. Snapper. *LANG:* English; French. *SUB:* English; French. *FEATURES:* 39 chapter links ☞ 3 commentary tracks ☞ 3 "making of" documentaries ☞ Photo montage ☞ Art gallery ☞ Talent files ☞ Trailer ☞ Storyboard gallery ☞ DVD-ROM features.
2000 (PG-13) 129m/C George Clooney, Mark Wahlberg, Mary Elizabeth Mastrantonio, John C. Reilly, Diane Lane, William Fichtner, Allen Payne, John Hawkes, Karen Allen, Bob Gunton, Cherry Jones, Christopher McDonald, Dash Mihok, Josh Hopkins, Michael Ironside, Janet Wright, Rusty Schwimmer; **D:** Wolfgang Petersen; **W:** William D. Wittliff; **C:** John Seale; **M:** James Horner.

Perfect Tenant

A surprisingly good way to pass a mindless afternoon. Jessica (Purl) is haunted by the memory of a childhood molestation. The teacher who molested her committed suicide on Christmas Eve after being found out, and was discovered hanging from the rafter by his son, Daniel (Caulfield). Daniel believes that Jessica lied and is responsible for his father's death. So, after his release from an asylum, he tracks Jessica down, kills her current renter so he can live in the apartment behind her house, and begins a cat and mouse game worth $250,000. The flashback scenes are amazingly effective in capturing the trauma of molestation without being exploitative. Caulfield and Purl completely sell their characters, and Tracy Nelson has a marvelous little part as Caulfield's girlfriend from the asylum. On the downside, Earl Holliman is a complete waste as Jessica's father. The picture quality is good and clean and the sound is also good. —*CA*
Movie: 🎵🎵½ *DVD:* 🎵🎵
Trimark Home Video (Cat #7404D, UPC #031398740421). Widescreen. Dolby Digital Stereo. $24.99. Keepcase. *LANG:* English. *SUB:* English; Spanish. *FEATURES:* 24 chapter links ☞ Trailer.
1999 (R) 93m/C Linda Purl, Maxwell Caulfield, Tracy Nelson, Earl Holliman, Melissa Behr, Stacy Hogue; **D:** Doug Campbell; **W:** Jim Vines, M. Todd Bonin; **C:** M. David Mullen.

Pet Sematary

Lewis and Rachel Creed (Midkiff and Crosby) and their two kids move into a Maine country house on a busy road. Jud (Gwynne) warns them that it won't be safe for the family cat. The road has claimed

so many animals that there's a *Pet Sematary* in the forest. Deeper in the forest, there's another cemetery with a darker purpose. Stephen King's version of "The Monkey's Paw" is one of his most frightening novels, and Mary Lambert's film, made from his script, is one of the best adaptations of his work. It's a shame they were not persuaded to record a commentary track for this DVD. Otherwise, image and sound are first-rate, but an opportunity has been missed. —*MM*
Movie: ♫♫♫½ **DVD:** ♫♫♫
Paramount Home Video (Cat #01949, UPC #097360194944). Widescreen anamorphic. Dolby Digital 5.1 Surround Stereo; Dolby Digital Surround. $24.99. Keepcase. *LANG:* English; French. *SUB:* English. *FEATURES:* 19 chapter links.
1989 (R) 103m/C Dale Midkiff, Fred Gwynne, Denise Crosby, Blaze Berdahl, Brad Greenquist, Miko Hughes, Stephen King; **D:** Mary Lambert; **W:** Stephen King; **C:** Peter Stein; **M:** Elliot Goldenthal.

Pete's Dragon
Elliott, an enormous bumbling occasionally invisible animated dragon, becomes friends with poor orphan Pete in a Maine seaside village. The pioneering combination of live-action and animation looks pretty primitive in the wake of *Roger Rabbit* and so many other films. All shots containing animation are heavily grained and matte lines are easy to see. Both of those come from the original, not the transfer to disc. In the conventional shots, some of the supersaturated colors (mostly the reds) are oddly bright. Personally, I think the Donald Duck cartoon (included as an extra) is much better. —*MM*
Movie: ♫♫½ **DVD:** ♫♫½
Buena Vista Home Entertainment (Cat #19576, UPC #717951008428). Widescreen (1.66:1) anamorphic. Dolby Digital 5.1 Surround Stereo. $29.99. Keepcase. *LANG:* English. *SUB:* French. *CAP:* English. *FEATURES:* 24 chapter links ● "Where's Elliott" game ● Stills gallery ● Trailers ● Film facts ● "Men, Monsters and Mysteries," short cartoon ● "Lighthouse Keeping," Donald Duck cartoon ● "Disney Family Album" excerpt ● "Plausible Impossibility" animation excerpt.
1977 (G) 128m/C Helen Reddy, Shelley Winters, Mickey Rooney, Jim Dale, Red Buttons, Sean Marshall, Jim Backus, Jeff Conaway; **D:** Don Chaffey; **W:** Malcolm Marmorstein; **C:** Frank Phillips; **M:** Irwin Kostal; **V:** Charlie Callas. *AWARDS: NOM:* Oscars '77: Song ("Candle on the Water"), Orig. Song Score and/or Adapt.

Phantasm 4: Oblivion
At least this sequel can boast the original's lead actors, which allows for footage from the first movie to be used in telling a typically (for this series) unhinged story. The Tall Man (Scrimm) is still transporting corpses and Mike (Baldwin) is becoming one of the evil guy's minions, but time travel takes him back to the Tall Man's origins

and he tries to take care of the problem at the source. Curiously, advances in special effects hurt the film. On DVD, dozens of CGI flying chrome balls—clear as they may be—aren't nearly as impressive as the older ones that were created through conventional effects. Other than that, the image is fine. —*MM*
Movie: ♫♫½ **DVD:** ♫♫½
MGM Home Entertainment (Cat #100083 4, UPC #027616851406). Full frame; widescreen anamorphic. Dolby Digital 5.1 Surround Stereo. $19.98. Keepcase. *LANG:* English. *SUB:* French; Spanish. *FEATURES:* Trailer ● 20 chapter links.
1998 (R) 90m/C Angus Scrimm, A. Michael Baldwin, Reggie Bannister, Bill Thornbury, Bob Ivy; **D:** Don A. Coscarelli; **W:** Don A. Coscarelli; **C:** Chris Chomyn; **M:** Christopher Stone.

The Phantom of the Opera
Claude Rains, one of the most versatile and effortless actors ever to grace the screen, is a thoroughly sympathetic Phantom, but this expensive production is a failure as a horror film. Far too much time is spent on the trivial romantic triangle and light opera performances. Tellingly, in the credits, Rains gets third billing after Nelson Eddy and Susanna Foster. The allegedly frightening elements are largely reduced to silliness involving a cape and a broad-brimmed hat. Even the chandelier, unmasking, and sewer scenes are disappointing. In visual terms, the DVD is an accurate, softish re-creation of the early 3-strip Technicolor print, but the real value lies in the extras. The "Opera Ghost" featurette is really a short history of the several cinematic versions of Gaston Leroux's famous story. It also includes comments by Rains's daughter Jessica. —*MM*
Movie: ♫♫ **DVD:** ♫♫♫
Universal Studios Home Video (Cat #207 67, UPC #025192076725). Full frame. Dolby Digital Mono. $26.98. Keepcase. *LANG:* English. *SUB:* French. *CAP:* English. *FEATURES:* "The Opera Ghost" featurette ● 18 chapter links ● Commentary: film historian Scott McQueen ● Production photographs.
1943 92m/C Nelson Eddy, Susanna Foster, Claude Rains, Edgar Barrier, Leo Carrillo, Hume Cronyn, J. Edward Bromberg; **D:** Arthur Lubin; **W:** Samuel Hoffenstein, Eric Taylor; **C:** Hal Mohr, William Howard Greene; **M:** Edward Ward. *AWARDS:* Oscars '43: Color Cinematog; *NOM:* Oscars '43: Sound, Scoring/Musical.

The Phantom Planet
An astronaut crashlands on an asteroid and discovers a race of tiny people living there. Having breathed the atmosphere, he shrinks to their diminutive size and aids them in their war against brutal invaders. Infamously peculiar. The disc's video transfer is merely adequate. It shows its age rather blatantly with wear and tear and often muddied blacks (a cardinal sin for a

black-and-white film). As far as mono tracks go, this one is acceptable (or, at least the dialogue is understandable). —*MJT*
Movie: ♫½ **DVD:** ♫
Image Entertainment (Cat #ID8699CODVD, UPC #014381869927). Full frame. Dolby Digital Mono. $24.99. Snapper. *LANG:* English. *FEATURES:* 16 chapter links ● Additional trailers for other Image Entertainment titles.
1961 82m/B Dean Fredericks, Coleen Gray, Tony Dexter, Dolores Faith, Francis X. Bushman, Richard Kiel; **D:** William Marshall; **W:** Fred De Gorter, Fred Gebhardt, William Telaak; **C:** Elwood J. Nicholson; **M:** Hayes Pagel.

Phenomenon— The Lost Archives: Noah's Ark Found?/Tunguska/ Stolen Glory
These three TV documentaries borrow heavily from *The X-Files* in choice of subjects, point of view, visual motifs, and almost total lack of hard evidence for their wild and wooly theories. Computer-generated illustrations of theories suffice in many cases. The episodes "investigate" the discovery of Noah's Ark, the explosion in Tunguska, and a Russian cosmonaut. The overall quality of the image is no better than broadcast, particularly in the archival footage. Some of the original studio footage is exceptionally crisp. —*MM*
Movie: ♫♫ **DVD:** ♫♫
Image Entertainment (Cat #ID7150LBDVD, UPC #014381715026). Full frame. Dolby Digital Stereo. $24.99. Keepcase. *LANG:* English. *FEATURES:* 18 chapter links.
1999 137m/C W: Harvey C. Kirk, Scott Stillman; **C:** Barbu Marion; **M:** Joey D. Vieira, David Siebels; **Nar:** Bill Rogers.

Phenomenon— The Lost Archives: Up for Sale/ Heavy Watergate
The second volume of episodes from a syndicated TV series quotes no less an authority than Jules Verne to buttress its claims that "cold fusion" is a virtually limitless source of cheap energy that's being kept from us by greedy bureaucrats and other evil-doers. Image and sound quality are the same as the first disc. —*MM*
Movie: ♫♫ **DVD:** ♫♫
Image Entertainment (Cat #ID0569LBDVD, UPC #014381056921). Full frame. Dolby Digital Stereo. $24.99. Snapper. *LANG:* English. *FEATURES:* 12 chapter links.
1999 92m/C W: Harvey C. Kirk, Scott Stillman; **C:** Barbu Marion; **M:** Joey D. Vieira, David Siebels; **Nar:** Bill Rogers.

The Philadelphia Experiment
In 1943 the Navy conducts an experiment to make a battleship invisible. But something goes wrong and two sailors, David

(Pare) and Jimmy (DiCicco) are sent forward in time to the year 1984. They're trapped in a future they don't understand. After a misunderstanding/kidnapping, they enlist the help of Allison (Allen). The digital transfer offers an image that is very crisp and clear, but does show a slight bit of noise and some minor defects from the source print. There is a subtle level of grain visible throughout the film, which worsens during certain scenes. Audio is very good but unspectacular. —*ML/MM*

Movie: 🐾🐾½ *DVD:* 🐾🐾½

Anchor Bay (Cat #11234). Widescreen (1.85:1) letterboxed. Dolby Digital 5.1 Surround Stereo; Dolby Digital Stereo. $24.98. Keepcase. *LANG:* English. *FEATURES:* Theatrical trailer.

1984 (PG) 101m/C Michael Pare, Nancy Allen, Eric Christmas, Bobby DiCicco; *D:* Stewart Raffill; *W:* Don Jakoby; *C:* Dick Bush; *M:* Kenneth Wannberg.

Picasso

This documentary uses several of Picasso's paintings along with footage of places where he lived and worked to provide an introduction to the artist. It is a very good place for the novice to start. Baussy-Oulianoff has not made a film for art professionals or the sophisticated museum goer. It's meant for a large popular audience and he keeps the material interesting. Even though the image is exceptionally clear, it will make you want to see the original pictures, not videos of them. —*MM*

Movie: 🐾🐾½ *DVD:* 🐾🐾½

Image Entertainment (Cat #ID9295RADVD, UPC #014381929522). Full frame. Dolby Digital Stereo. $24.99. Snapper. *LANG:* English. *FEATURES:* 10 chapter links.

1985 81m/C *W:* Jean Michel Michelena; *Nar:* Feodor Atkine, Nelly Borgeaud.

Pick a Card

David and Batia, two overweight lovers, leave their small hometown of Afula and try to make it in the big city of Tel Aviv. This is an offbeat (very offbeat) romantic comedy that's a bit difficult for the uninitiated. Both sound and image have the harsh, rough-edged quality that you expect with independently produced imports. Burned-in white subtitles are moderately easy to read. —*MM* *AKA:* Afula Express.

Movie: 🐾🐾🐾 *DVD:* 🐾🐾

Vanguard International Cinema, Inc. (Cat #1-892649-89-6, UPC #658769010435). Widescreen (1.66:1) letterboxed. $29.95. Keepcase. *LANG:* Hebrew. *SUB:* English. *FEATURES:* 12 chapter links.

1997 (PG-13) 94m/C *IS* Zvika Hadar, Esti Zakheim, Aryeh Moskona, Orli Perl; *D:* Julie Shles; *W:* Amit Leor; *C:* Itzik Portal; *M:* Yuval Shafrir.

Picking Up the Pieces

The title of this curious comedy is all too literal. It begins with a butcher (Allen) in El Nino, New Mexico, picking up the pieces of his wife's body after they bounce out of the bed of his pick-up truck. (He's just killed

her and hacked her up, you see.) He misses one hand though, and the next day, a blind woman trips over it. She miraculously regains her sight and decides that it must be the hand of the virgin. (Are you laughing yet?) Unfortunately, director Arau is closer to his disastrous *Walk in the Clouds* than the inspired *Like Water for Chocolate*. A talented cast has little to do. Even so, the DVD image is first-rate. Even difficult night shots are carefully lit. Use of Surround is limited but effective. —*MM*

Movie: 🐾🐾 *DVD:* 🐾🐾🐾

Artisan Entertainment (Cat #10802, UPC #012236108023). Widescreen (2:1) anamorphic. Dolby Digital 5.1 Surround; Dolby Digital Surround. $24.98. Keepcase. *LANG:* English; Spanish. *SUB:* English. *FEATURES:* Commentary: Alfonso Arau • "Making of" featurette • Cast interviews • Thumbnail bios and filmographies • Photo gallery • Trivia game.

1999 (R) 95m/C Woody Allen, David Schwimmer, Maria Grazia Cucinotta, Kiefer Sutherland, Sharon Stone, Alfonso Arau, Richard "Cheech" Marin, Lou Diamond Phillips, Danny De La Paz, Andy Dick, Fran Drescher, Joseph Gordon-Levitt, Elliott Gould, Eddie Griffin, Lupe Ontiveros; *D:* Alfonso Arau; *W:* Bill Wilson; *C:* Vittorio Storaro; *M:* Ruy Folguera.

Picnic

A down-on-his-luck drifter (Holden) wanders into a Midwestern farm town in time for the Labor Day picnic, where he puts some moves on his best friend's (Robertson) fiancée (Novak). On disc, the big-budget mid-'50s production probably looks about as good as it could. Minor artifacts are visible in a few of the busiest brightest exteriors, and tight patterns flash at the wrong angles. Overall, the softish, grainy image is typical of films of that era. Sound is fine for the famous theme song. The leads, at their most attractive, are the point. —*MM*

Movie: 🐾🐾🐾½ *DVD:* 🐾🐾½

Columbia Tristar Home Video (Cat #828 79). Widescreen (2.35:1) anamorphic; full frame. Dolby Digital Surround Stereo. $24.95. Keepcase. *LANG:* English; Spanish; Portuguese. *SUB:* English; Spanish; Portuguese; Chinese; Korean; Thai. *FEATURES:* 28 chapter links • Photo montage • Vintage advertising • Talent files • Trailers.

1955 113m/C William Holden, Kim Novak, Rosalind Russell, Susan Strasberg, Arthur O'Connell, Cliff Robertson, Betty Field, Verna Felton, Reta Shaw, Nick Adams, Phyllis Newman, Raymond Bailey; *D:* Joshua Logan; *W:* Daniel Taradash; *C:* James Wong Howe; *M:* George Duning. *AWARDS:* Oscars '55: Art Dir./Set Dec., Color, Film Editing; Golden Globes '56: Director (Logan); *NOM:* Oscars '55: Director (Logan), Picture, Support. Actor (O'Connell), Orig. Dramatic Score.

Picture Windows

Three short cable movies are inspired by works of art. "Soir Bleu" is about an affair at the circus. "Song of Songs" is about infi-

delity and "Language of the Heart" finds a young ballerina involved with a street musician and an older man. Accessibility to the individual films is the only improvement over tape. Same for sound. —*MM*

Movie: 🐾🐾 *DVD:* 🐾🐾

Pioneer Entertainment (Cat #DVD75163). Full frame. Dolby Digital Stereo. $24.98. Keepcase. *LANG:* English. *FEATURES:* 18 chapter links.

1995 95m/C Alan Arkin, George Segal, Brooke Adams, Sally Kirkland; *D:* Norman Jewison, Peter Bogdanovich, Jonathan Kaplan.

Pinocchio

This version of the story is presented as a play within a play. Danny Kaye is both Collodi, the actor, and Gepetto, the woodcarver. Sandy Duncan is the former's daughter and the latter's creation. The made-for-TV production appears to have been videotaped with a reddish color scheme. Image is strictly broadcast quality. For fans of the cast only. —*MM*

Movie: 🐾🐾½ *DVD:* 🐾🐾

VCI Home Video (Cat #8251, UPC #08985 9825125). Full frame. Dolby Digital Mono. $19.99. Keepcase. *LANG:* English. *FEATURES:* 21 chapter links • Talent files.

1976 76m/C Danny Kaye, Sandy Duncan, Flip Wilson, Liz Torres, Clive Revill; *D:* Ron Field, Sid Smith; *M:* Billy Barnes.

The Pit and the Pendulum

Corman, Price, and Matheson's second foray into Poe country (after *Fall of the House of Usher*) lacks the restraint of that film. The first half is fairly talky and stilted, but they really cut loose in the second half with an extended torture sequence that is some of the finest work Corman has ever done. Both image and mono sound are very good. So is Corman's commentary track. I admire the seriousness with which he treats the picture. —*MM*

Movie: 🐾🐾🐾 *DVD:* 🐾🐾🐾½

MGM Home Entertainment (Cat #10020 51, UPC #027616862884). Widescreen (2.35:1) letterboxed. Dolby Digital Mono. $19.95. Keepcase. *LANG:* English; French. *SUB:* French; Spanish. *CAP:* English. *FEATURES:* 16 chapter links • Commentary: Roger Corman • Trailer • Prologue.

1961 80m/C Vincent Price, John Kerr, Barbara Steele, Luana Anders, Antony Carbone, Charles Victor, Lynn Bernay, Patrick Westwood; *D:* Roger Corman; *W:* Richard Matheson; *C:* Floyd Crosby; *M:* Les Baxter.

Pit Stop

On his commentary track, director Jack Hill admits that he made this movie quickly to capitalize on the short-lived phenomenon of figure-8 racing, where the shape of the track guarantees many crashes. Brian Donlevy is the promoter who involves young racers Sid Haig and Dick Davalos in his plans. The black-and-white photography is astonishingly sharp and detailed for a low-budget film. (That black and white kept the film from wide distribution in the 1960s.) Sound is fine. It's time this long-delayed sleeper finds an audience on home video. —MM

Movie: 🎬🎬🎬 **DVD:** 🎬🎬🎬
Anchor Bay (Cat #DV11185, UPC #013131 118599). Widescreen (1.66:1) anamorphic. Dolby Digital Mono. $24.99. Keepcase. *LANG:* English. *FEATURES:* 28 chapter links ∙ Trailers ∙ "Making of" documentary ∙ Jack Hill thumbnail bio ∙ Commentary: Jack Hill, Johnny Legend.
1967 91m/B Brian Donlevy, Richard (Dick) Davalos, Ellen Burstyn, Sid Haig, Beverly Washburn; *D:* Jack Hill; *W:* Jack Hill; *C:* Austin McKinney.

Pitch Black

David Twohy's superb sf horror spins familiar elements into gold. After a spaceship crashlands on a desert planet (Queensland, Australia), the survivors find that the other inhabitants are cave-dwelling velociraptor-like monsters. When the triple suns go into eclipse, the humans become prey. The characters are well-developed and flawed, with star Vin Diesel's Riddick worthy of a place alongside the original Terminator. The critters, created by production designer Patrick Tatopoulos, are believably scary. Twohy overexposes his daylight exteriors to give the first half of the film a deliberately harsh look. DVD handles both extremes of light and darkness with no important flaws. The 5.1 sound is only so-so, but that restraint suits Twohy's purposes. This is an economical film without an ounce of fat, both in its "R"- and unrated versions. (The latter contains a bit more violence.) A sequel is in the works. —MM

Movie: 🎬🎬🎬½ **DVD:** 🎬🎬🎬½
Universal Studios Home Video (Cat #211 10, UPC #025192110627). Widescreen (2.35:1) letterboxed. Dolby Digital 5.1 Surround Stereo; DTS Stereo. $26.98. Keepcase. *LANG:* English; French. *SUB:* English; French. *FEATURES:* 18 chapter links ∙ Commentary: David Twohy, Vin Diesel, Cole Hauser ∙ Commentary: Twohy, producer Engelman, Peter Chiang ∙ Raveworld "Pitch Black" event ∙ Theatrical trailers. Also available in an unrated version at 112 minutes (cat. #21106, UPC 025192111020).
2000 (R) 108m/C Vin Diesel, Radha Mitchell, Cole Hauser, Keith David, Lewis Fitz-Gerald, John Moore, Simon Burke, Claudia Black, Rhiana Griffith; *D:* David N. Twohy, Jim Wheat, Ken Wheat; *W:* David N. Twohy; *C:* David Eggby; *M:* Graeme Revell.

Pixote

Director Hector Babenco prefaces this film with a personal introduction highlighting the reality behind his grim story of the life of street children in Sao Paolo, Brazil. "Pixote" (slang for "Peewee") (Fernando Ramos Da Silva) is a ten-year-old orphan who escapes from the authorities and makes an early start as a criminal. It's graphic, depressing, and all too accurate. Judged by standards of American enter-

tainment, the image is no better than poor, but it's completely right for the story. Heavy grain generates artifacts in many scenes. Burned-in subtitles are easy to read. —MM **AKA:** Pixote: A Lei do Mais Fraco.

Movie: 🎬🎬🎬🎬 **DVD:** 🎬🎬½
New Yorker Video (Cat #40400, UPC #717 119404048). Full frame. $29.95. Keepcase. *LANG:* Portuguese. *SUB:* English. *FEATURES:* 12 chapter links ∙ Babenco talent file.
1981 127m/C *BR* Fernando Ramos Da Silva, Marilia Pera, Jorge Juliao, Gilberto Moura, Jose Nilson dos Santos, Edilson Lino; *D:* Hector Babenco; *W:* Hector Babenco; *C:* Rodolfo Sanchez; *M:* John Neschling. *AWARDS:* L.A. Film Critics '81: Foreign Film; N.Y. Film Critics '81: Foreign Film; Natl. Soc. Film Critics '81: Actress (Pera).

Plain Jane

David Bruce (Whately) is promoted by the gas company to a managerial position in London, 1911. With the newfound prosperity, he and his wife are able to hire a live-in maid, Jane (Cunniffe). Both he and his son from a previous marriage fall for her. The film was made for British television so the material is handled tastefully. DVD image is of broadcast quality, but it has no problems with brickwork patterns that can be difficult for the medium. —MM

Movie: 🎬🎬🎬 **DVD:** 🎬🎬
BFS Video (Cat #30098-D, UPC #0668053 00981). Full frame. Dolby Digital Mono. $29.98. Keepcase. *LANG:* English. *FEATURES:* Production photos ∙ 12 chapter links.
2000 155m/C *GB* Kevin Whately, Leslie Manville, Emma Cunniffe, Keith Barron, Celia Imrie, Corin Redgrave, Jason Hughes; *D:* John Woods; *W:* Lucy Gannon; *C:* John McGlashan; *M:* Ray Russell.

Plan 9 from Outer Space [Passport Video]

Widely "lauded" as the worst movie ever, Wood's anti-masterpiece is well chronicled with numerous documentaries, websites, and even college classes. That such an astonishingly inept movie is so widely loved rather than loathed is a phenomenon in itself. It should be no surprise, then, that there is more than one DVD release. This is not the one to get, if for no other reason than Passport Video superimposed a "PIP" logo in the bottom right corner of the screen throughout the feature and bonus materials. Otherwise, the picture quality is good enough and the mono sound is just what you would expect from a bottom-budget flick from 1956. The other Region 1 *Plan 9* DVD—the one from Image Entertainment—has better box art and a better documentary, called *Flying Saucers over Hollywood: The Plan 9 Companion*. Given that both discs are priced the same and the Passport edition is marred by the "PIP" logo, the Image disc would seem to be a no-brainer as the one

to purchase. Still, collectors may want to consider the "The Ed Wood Story" on the disc from Passport Video. It consists of half a dozen interviews with people who knew or worked with Wood or starred in Tim Burton's 1994 biopic *Ed Wood*. There are new or vintage interviews with Johnny Depp and Martin Landau, who both starred in Burton's *Ed Wood*, as well as Wood's wife and actress Dolores Fuller, Vampira, Lugosi and his son, and friend Johnny Legend recalling Johnson. Trailers of several Wood films also are included, whereas they are not present on the otherwise superior Image disc. —MB **AKA:** Grave Robbers from Outer Space.

Movie: 🎬🎬🎬 **DVD:** 🎬½
Passport International Productions (Cat #DVD 700, UPC #025493070026). Full frame. Dolby Digital Mono. $24.99. Keepcase. *LANG:* English. *FEATURES:* 12 chapter links ∙ "The Ed Wood Story" ∙ Trailers for other Ed Wood films.
1956 78m/B Bela Lugosi, Tor Johnson, Lyle Talbot, Vampira, Gregory Walcott, Tom (George Duryea) Keene, Dudley Manlove, Mona McKinnon, Duke Moore, Joanna Lee, Bunny Breckinridge, Criswell, Carl Anthony, Paul Marco, Norma McCarty, David DeMering, Bill Ash, Conrad Brooks, Tom Mason, Edward D. Wood Jr.; *D:* Edward D. Wood Jr.; *W:* Edward D. Wood Jr.; *C:* William C. Thompson; *M:* Trevor Duncan, Van Phillips, James Stevens, Bruce Campbell.

Planes, Trains & Automobiles

One-joke Hughes comedy is redeemed by inspired casting of Martin and Candy in two of their best roles. On his way home to Chicago for Thanksgiving, straitlaced Neal Page (Martin) crosses paths with boorish salesman Del Griffith (Candy). The latterday Odd Couple runs into every obstacle imaginable on an extended road trip. Hughes manages to balance comedy (much of it coarse) and genuine emotion. Over the years, this has become a real favorite. Though DVD cannot do much for the so-so image, it's all the film needs. 5.1 is restrained. —MM

Movie: 🎬🎬🎬½ **DVD:** 🎬🎬🎬
Paramount Home Video (Cat #32036, UPC #097363203629). Widescreen anamorphic. Dolby Digital 5.1 Surround Stereo. $29.99. Keepcase. *LANG:* English. *SUB:* English. *FEATURES:* 27 chapter links.
1987 (R) 93m/C Steve Martin, John Candy, Edie McClurg, Kevin Bacon, Michael McKean, William Windom, Laila Robins, Martin Ferrero, Charles Tyner, Dylan Baker, Ben Stein, Lyman Ward; *D:* John Hughes; *W:* John Hughes; *C:* Don Peterman; *M:* Ira Newborn.

Planet of the Apes

Astronauts crashland on a planet where apes are masters and humans are merely brute animals. Superior science fiction with sociological implications is marred only by unnecessary humor. Chuck delivers one of his more plausible performances. Superb ape makeup creates realistic pseudo-simians of McDowall, Hunter, Evans, Whitmore, and Daly. Adapted from Pierre Boulle's novel *Monkey Planet*. From the color extravaganza as our hero's spaceship travels through the portal in time, it's obvious that there will be no problems with colors on this DVD; they're boldly saturated without a hint of bleed, and from the fleshtones it's clear that they're also very natural. The sharpness of the disc is also very good, and this is not even an anamorphic transfer! If you look real hard there are a few very minor artifacts that won't be noticed if you blink at the right time. The new 5.1 mix is a vast improvement over what was released on either the VHS hi-fi or letterboxed laserdisc versions, even if it could have used an occasional boost to the low end. When buying the *Planet of the Apes: The Evolution* box set, you get the free documentary *Behind the Planet of the Apes,* with plenty of extra information, but it would have been nice to have included a few more extras on this, the first and best of the *Ape* series. Still, definitely worth the bucks. —*JO*

Movie: ♪♪♪½ **DVD:** ♪♪♪
20th Century Fox Home Entertainment (Cat #2000791, UPC #024543007913). Widescreen (2.35:1) letterboxed. Dolby Digital 5.1; Dolby Surround. $29.98. Keepcase. *LANG:* English. *SUB:* English; Spanish. *CAP:* English. *FEATURES:* 24 chapter links • Theatrical trailers • Photo gallery.
1968 (G) 112m/C Charlton Heston, Roddy McDowall, Kim Hunter, Maurice Evans, Linda Harrison, James Whitmore, James Daly; *D:* Franklin J. Schaffner; *W:* Rod Serling, Michael Wilson; *C:* Leon Shamroy; *M:* Jerry Goldsmith. *AWARDS: NOM:* Oscars '68: Costume Des., Orig. Score.

Platoon [2 SE]

MGM improves only slightly upon the earlier Artisan DVD release of Oliver Stone's semi-autobiographical Vietnam film. The three main extras—commentaries by Stone and advisor Captain Dale Dye and the "Tour of the Inferno" documentary—are also on the Artisan DVD release. Image may be a hair better. —*MM*

Movie: ♪♪♪ **DVD:** ♪♪♪½
MGM Home Entertainment (Cat #1002044, UPC #027616862815). Widescreen (1.85:1) anamorphic. Dolby Digital 5.1 Surround Stereo. $24.98. Keepcase. *LANG:* English; French; Spanish. *SUB:* French; Spanish. *CAP:* English. *FEATURES:* 32 chapter links • "Tour of the Inferno" documentary • Commentary: Oliver Stone • Commentary: Capt. Dale Dye • TV spots • Poster art • Trailer.
1986 (R) 113m/C Charlie Sheen, Willem Dafoe, Tom Berenger, Francesco Quinn, Forest Whitaker, John C. McGinley, Kevin Dillon, Richard Edson, Reggie Johnson, Keith David, Johnny Depp, Dale Dye, Mark Moses, Chris Pederson, David Neidorf,

Tony Todd, Ivan Kane, Paul Sanchez, Corey Glover, Oliver Stone; *D:* Oliver Stone; *W:* Oliver Stone; *C:* Robert Richardson; *M:* Georges Delerue. *AWARDS:* Oscars '86: Director (Stone), Film Editing, Picture, Sound; AFI '98: Top 100; British Acad. '87: Director (Stone); Directors Guild '86: Director (Stone); Golden Globes '87: Director (Stone), Film—Drama, Support. Actor (Berenger); Ind. Spirit '87: Cinematog., Director (Stone), Film, Screenplay; *NOM:* Oscars '86: Cinematog., Orig. Screenplay, Support. Actor (Berenger, Dafoe).

Play It to the Bone

Harrelson and Banderas are fading boxers and best friends Vince and Cesar, who unexpectedly wind up against each other. Since they need to get to Vegas, Cesar's girlfriend (and Vince's ex) Grace (Davidovich) agrees to drive them. Along the way, she uses her wiles to whip up the competitive juices. It works, as the brutal fight sequence shows. The transfer could not look better. Deep, solid blacks capture details like the fairy-tale neon of the Vegas skyline and the grandeur of the Mojave Desert. Color fidelity is dead-on, whether highlighting the boxers' shiny red gloves, or contrasting a lime-green GTO racing along the desert landscape. Other than a few instances of edge enhancement, the transfer is about as picture-perfect as the format can achieve. The Dolby Digital audio may not give home theatre systems a vigorous workout, but makes effective use of the discrete audio palette. —*EP/MM*

Movie: ♪♪ **DVD:** ♪♪♪
Buena Vista Home Entertainment (Cat #20152). Widescreen (2.35:1) anamorphic. Dolby Digital 5.1 Surround Stereo. $32.99. Keepcase. *LANG:* English; French. *FEATURES:* Trailers • Production featurette.
1999 (R) 124m/C Woody Harrelson, Antonio Banderas, Lolita (David) Davidovich, Lucy Alexis Liu, Tom Sizemore, Robert Wagner, Richard Masur, Willie Garson, Cylk Cozart, Jack Carter; *D:* Ron Shelton; *W:* Ron Shelton; *C:* Mark Vargo; *M:* Alex Wurman.

Playing Mona Lisa

An uneven but pleasantly amusing story of a girl (Witt) who is at a crossroads in her life. Her chosen career as a classical pianist seems to be slipping out of her hands when her boyfriend proposes to her while drunk, forgets the next morning, and then breaks up with her. An earthquake damages her beautiful San Francisco apartment forcing her to move back in with her parents, where she firmly launches into a flurry of food binging and recreational drugs. The people closest to her, a quirky friend (Langton) who throws wild theme parties, her wacky mid-life crisis–impaired parents (Gould and Thomas), and her gay piano teacher (Fierstein) all try to help her as much as they can, considering their own messy lives. In a refreshing move, she comes out of her funk all by herself and takes charge of her

life. Stilted as it all sounds, the film carries off the wackiness of the story and its characters smoothly and enjoyably. There are also some classic scenes; one where her parents unwittingly drop acid and are enraptured by everything from the lace tablecloth to the textured carpet is priceless. The disc looks and sounds great with the wild color scheme of twentysomething fashion leaping off the screen and sticking its tongue out at you. —*CA*

Movie: ♪♪ **DVD:** ♪♪♪½
Buena Vista Home Entertainment (Cat #22598, UPC #786936153699). Widescreen (1.85:1) anamorphic. Dolby Digital Surround. $32.99. Keepcase. *LANG:* English. *CAP:* English.
2000 (R) 97m/C Alicia Witt, Ivan Sergei, Brooke Langton, Johnny Galecki, Elliott Gould, Marlo Thomas, Harvey Fierstein, Molly Hagan, Estelle Harris, Sandra Bernhard, Shannon Finn; *D:* Matthew Huffman; *W:* Marni Freedman, Carlos De Los Rios; *C:* James Glennon.

Plenty

Difficult but worthwhile film finds Streep in top form as a former member of the French Resistance. Upon returning to England, she finds life at home increasingly tedious and banal, and begins to fear that her finest hours may be behind her. Gielgud is flawless as the aging career diplomat. Adapting the play to the screen, David Hare presents an allegory of British decline. Image is good verging on very good, accurately reflecting the original. Sound is good but not exceptional. —*MM*

Movie: ♪♪½ **DVD:** ♪♪½
Republic Pictures Home Video (Cat #11190, UPC #017153111903). Widescreen (1.85:1) anamorphic. Dolby Digital Surround Stereo. $24.98. Keepcase. *LANG:* English. *CAP:* English. *FEATURES:* 32 chapter links.
1985 (R) 119m/C Meryl Streep, Tracey Ullman, Sting, John Gielgud, Charles Dance, Ian McKellen, Sam Neill, Burt Kwouk; *D:* Fred Schepisi; *W:* David Hare; *C:* Ian Baker; *M:* Bruce Smeaton. *AWARDS:* L.A. Film Critics '85: Support. Actor (Gielgud); Natl. Soc. Film Critics '85: Support. Actor (Gielgud).

Plump Fiction

This movie proves that when you want to make fun of Quentin Tarantino, you should stick to his truly horrible acting. Instead, this spoof attacks his already over-the-top characters from *Pulp Fiction, Reservoir Dogs,* and *Natural Born Killers.* Julius (Davenport) and Jimmy (Dinello) are the loser hit men. Mimi (Brown) is the gangster's wife who has a substance abuse problem, but it's not cocaine—it's food! She's fat, get it? Intersecting storylines feature Nicky (Glave) and Vallory (Segall, doing a dead-on Juliette Lewis) as "Natural Blonde Killers." The only redeeming scene is that of Kane Picoy as "Christopher Walken character" doing an uncanny impersonation of the king of psychos. The commentary track by director Koherr and producers Clifton and Roberts is almost as much fun as the movie itself. Early on, they agree that they owe actress Sandra Bernhard a "gret of datitude" for her participation. —*MM*

Movie: 🎬🎬½ **DVD:** 🎬🎬½

Rhino Home Video (Cat #4467). Full frame. $24.95. Snapper. *LANG:* English. *FEATURES:* Commentary: Mark Roberts, Bob Koherr, Patrick Clifton ▪ Interviews with Julie Brown, Mark Roberts ▪ Trailer ▪ 21 chapter links.

1997 (R) 82m/C Tommy Davidson, Julie Brown, Sandra Bernhard, Paul Dinello, Dan Castellaneta, Colleen Camp, Pamela Segall, Kevin Meaney, Matthew Glave, Jennifer Rubin, Robert Costanzo, Phillipe Bergerone; *D:* Bob Koherr; *W:* Bob Koherr; *C:* Rex Nicholson; *M:* Michael Muhlfriedel.

Pocahontas

It's 1607 and spirited Powhatan maiden Pocahontas (voice of Bedard) and settler Captain John Smith (Gibson) strike an unlikely but doomed romance. Lovely Poca, a virtual post-adolescent Native American superbabe, introduces the roguish captain to the wonders of unspoiled nature and serves as peacemaker in the clash of European and Native American cultures. Right. The picture is very crisp and the colors look very good. Unfortunately, the digital transfer has revealed some significant grain in some of the source elements. Whenever a character's face is shown, a great deal of graininess is evident in their facial features. Otherwise, any shot that doesn't contain a close-up displays only limited grain. The audio mix is bold and satisfying, with songs that sound very good. The dialogue and sound effects have been mixed together very nicely. The DVD also contains "Theatre Vision" for the visually impaired. This option adds a female voice to the soundtrack which describes the on-screen action. —*ML/MM*

Movie: 🎬🎬½ **DVD:** 🎬🎬🎬

Buena Vista Home Entertainment (Cat #19598). Widescreen (1.66:1) letterboxed. Dolby Digital 5.1 Surround Stereo. $29.99. Keepcase. *LANG:* English; French; Spanish. *SUB:* English. *FEATURES:* Theatrical trailer ▪ Read-along ▪ Trivia game ▪ Music videos ▪ Educational handbook.

1995 (G) 90m/C *D:* Mike Gabriel, Eric Goldberg; *W:* Carl Binder, Susannah Grant, Philip LaZebnik; *M:* Alan Menken, Stephen Schwartz; *V:* Irene Bedard, Judy Kuhn, Mel Gibson, Joe Baker, Christian Bale, Billy Connolly, James Apaumut Fall, Linda Hunt, John Kassir, Danny Mann, Bill Cobbs, David Ogden Stiers, Michelle St. John, Gordon Tootoosis, Frank Welker. *AWARDS:* Oscars '95: Song ("Colors of the Wind"), Orig. Score; Golden Globes '96: Song ("Colors of the Wind"); *NOM:* Golden Globes '96: Score.

Pocahontas 2: Journey to a New World

Video premiere sequel boasts very good, clear animation, though style and story are much simpler than the studio's theatrical fare. The nasty Ratcliffe is still up to no good and persuades the King to send an armada against American Indians. Pocahontas (voice of Kuhn) becomes a diplomat who goes to England to stop it. The 5.1 Surround is particularly well integrated, using the score to heighten the more kinetic musical numbers. —*MM*

Movie: 🎬🎬½ **DVD:** 🎬🎬🎬½

Buena Vista Home Entertainment (Cat #19 598, UPC #71951008497). Widescreen (1.66:1) anamorphic. Dolby Digital 5.1 Surround Stereo; Dolby Digital Surround. $24.99. Keepcase. *LANG:* English; French. *SUB:* Spanish. *CAP:* English. *FEATURES:* 23 chapter links ▪ Trivia game ▪ DVD storybook ▪ "Little Hiawatha" cartoon.

1998 72m/C *D:* Bradley Raymond, Tom Ellery; *W:* Cindy Marcus, Allen Estrin, Flip Kobler; *M:* Lennie Niehaus, Marty Panzer, Larry Grossman; *V:* Irene Bedard, David Ogden Stiers, Donal Gibson, Billy Zane, Jean Stapleton, Finola Hughes, Judy Kuhn, Jim (Jonah) Cummings, Linda Hunt.

Poetic Justice

The literal nature of the title is emblematic of director Singleton's heavy hand. Justice (Jackson, in her movie debut, for better or worse) gives up college plans to follow a career in cosmetology after her boyfriend's murder. She copes with her loss by writing poetry (provided by Maya Angelou) and meets postal worker Lucky (Shakur) and goes on a road trip with their unpleasant friends. The director's commentary track, done from memory, is not particularly illuminating. Image and sound are slightly above average, but neither is really worth a strong recommendation. —*MM*

Movie: 🎬🎬 **DVD:** 🎬🎬½

Columbia Tristar Home Video (Cat #52399, UPC #043396523999). Widescreen (1.85:1) anamorphic; full frame. Dolby Digital Stereo. $24.95. Keepcase. *LANG:* English; French; Spanish. *SUB:* Spanish. *FEATURES:* 28 chapter links ▪ Talent files ▪ Commentary: Singleton ▪ Trailers.

1993 (R) 109m/C Janet Jackson, Tupac Shakur, Tyra Ferrell, Regina King, Joe Torry, Norma Donaldson; *D:* John Singleton; *W:* John Singleton; *C:* Peter Collister; *M:* Stanley Clarke. *AWARDS:* MTV Movie Awards '94: Female Perf. (Jackson), Most Desirable Female (Jackson); Golden Raspberries '93: Worst New Star (Jackson); *NOM:* Oscars '93: Song ("Again"); Golden Globes '94: Song ("Again").

Pokemon the Movie 2000: The Power of One

A group of strange round little creatures who coo some kind of baby talk fall down a hole in the Earth and enter a place where there are more sort of like them. The colors are bright; the sound is loud and I could detect no serious flaws. But I defy any adult to voluntarily watch this puddle of animated mush from beginning to end without hitting the scan forward button on the remote. The bold colors will give you a headache if the obnoxious infantile squealings haven't already driven you totally berserk and you take a sledgehammer to the DVD player and...calm down, Mayo. It's only a movie, it's only a movie.... —*MM* *AKA:* Poketto Monsutaa: Maboroshi No Pokemon X: Lugia Bakudan.

Movie: 🎬 **DVD:** 🎬🎬½

Warner Home Video, Inc. (Cat #18620, UPC #085391862024). Full frame. Dolby Digital 5.1 Surround Stereo. $19.98. Snapper. *LANG:* English; French. *SUB:* English; French; Spanish. *FEATURES:* 2 trailers ▪ 2 chapter links ▪ Music videos ▪ "Making of" soundtrack.

2000 (G) 103m/C JP *D:* Kunihiko Yuyama, Michael Haigney; *W:* Michael Haigney, Takeshi Shudo; *M:* Ralph Schuckett, John Loeffler.

Pola X

Pierre (Depardieu) lives in a glorious chateau with his mother Marie (Catherine Deneuve), with whom he has an undefined but curiously incestuous relationship. He commutes daily to another glorious chateau to make love to his delicate, sweet fiancée Lucie (Chuillot). Together they share an undefined but curiously ambisexual relationship with his moody cousin Thibault (Lucas). Enter Isabelle (Golubyova), a mysterious woman Pierre has dreamed about and who claims to be his sister. The trendiest, and most limiting aspect of the film is the sex. There's always time for some moody nudity by all the actresses involved, and the "hot" sex 'twixt Depardieu and Golubyova is an "X"-rated hard-core encounter that overpowers most of the scenes around it, making the drama seem even less real. DVD sounds terrific, but has some drawbacks in the image department. It looks as if an insufficient bit rate has made the frequent dark and purposely defocused shots grainy and full of mottled smearing. Even some of the exteriors shot in the beautiful French countryside seem to fluctuate in brightness and sharpness. —*GE/MM*

Movie: 🎬🎬½ **DVD:** 🎬🎬½

Winstar Home Entertainment (Cat #FLV52 69, UPC #720917526928). Widescreen. Dolby Digital 5.1 Surround Stereo. $24.98. Keepcase. *LANG:* French. *SUB:* English. *FEATURES:* Commentary: Depardieu ▪ 2 behind-the-scenes featurettes ▪ Deleted scenes.

1999 134m/C FR Guillaume Depardieu, Katerina Golubeva, Catherine Deneuve, Delphine Chuillot, Laurent Lucas; *D:* Leos Carax; *W:* Leos Carax, Jean-Pol Fargeau, Lauren Sedofsky; *C:* Eric Gautier; *M:* Scott Walker.

Poldark

Made-for-TV production picks up the story of Ross and Demelza Poldark and their family from where the 1970s' BBC series ended. It's 1810 and Ross spends most of his time in London as a Member of Parliament while at the Cornwall home,

Demelza deals with the continuing Warleggan feud. Son Jeremy struggles to keep the mine going and daughter Clowance is in the throes of her first romance. DVD image is no better than broadcast or videotape. —MM

Movie: 🎵🎵🎵 **DVD:** 🎵🎵
BFS Video (Cat #94311-D, UPC #0668059 13112). Full frame. Dolby Digital Mono. $29.98. Keepcase. *LANG:* English. *FEATURES:* 12 chapter links.
1996 105m/C GB John Bowe, Mel Martin, Ioan Gruffudd, Mike Attwell, Kelly Reilly, Hans Matheson, Amanda Ryan, Nicholas Gleaves, Gabrielle Lloyd, Sarah Carpenter; **D:** Richard Laxton; **W:** Robin Mukbarjee; **C:** Rex Maidment; **M:** Ian Hughes.

The Pom Pom Girls / The Beach Girls

In *Pom Pom,* high school seniors, intent on having one last fling before graduation, get involved in crazy antics, clumsy romances, and football rivalries. The cast is a veritable "who's who" of mid-'70s drive-in faves. In *Beach,* serious Sarah lets her two rowdy buds invite about 50 of their closest friends for an impromptu party at her uncle Carl's beach house. Every ten minutes or so, a top comes off. Both films look identical to VHS tape, and both were made from prints that had seen some wear. —MM

Movie: 🎵🎵½ **DVD:** 🎵🎵
Rhino Home Video (Cat #2053). Full frame. $19.95. Keepcase. *LANG:* English; Spanish (*Pom Pom* only). *FEATURES:* 6 chapter links each • Talent files • Stills.
1976 90m/C Robert Carradine, Jennifer Ashley, Michael Mullins, Cheryl "Rainbeaux" Smith, Dianne Lee Hart, Lisa Reeves, Bill Adler; **D:** Joseph Ruben; **W:** Joseph Ruben; **C:** Stephen M. Katz; **M:** Michael Lloyd.

The Pompatus of Love

Remember the Steve Miller song, "The Joker"?—the one with the line about the "pompatus of love"—well, that's where the title comes from. The four protagonists (Cryer, Guinee, Pasdar, and Oliensis) of this ensemble drama don't understand it and the line comes to represent the mystery of women. They're bright and literate and they don't have a clue about love or how to grow up. Naturally, the women they know— or meet—are too smart for them. The extras are pretty much tacked on to this disc. The deleted scenes look very rough and the filmmakers' ideas and memories are not incorporated into a conventional commentary track. Image and sound are not notably superior to tape. —MM

Movie: 🎵🎵🎵 **DVD:** 🎵🎵½
Winstar Home Entertainment (Cat #5138, UPC #720917513829). Full frame. $24.98. Keepcase. *LANG:* English. *FEATURES:* 8 chapter links • Talent files • Awards • Production credits • Deleted scenes.
1995 (R) 99m/C Jon Cryer, Tim Guinee, Adrian Pasdar, Adam Oliensis, Kristen Wilson, Dana Wheeler-Nicholson, Paige Turco, Mia Sara, Kristin Scott Thomas, Arabella Field, Jennifer Tilly, Roscoe Lee Browne; **D:** Richard Schenkman; **W:** Jon Cryer, Adam Oliensis, Richard Schenkman; **C:** Russell Fine; **M:** John Hill.

Pop & Me

Recently divorced and realizing that he is in the last third of his life, Richard Roe decides to take a trip around the world. His son, filmmaker Chris Roe, sees the trip as a chance to have an all-expense-paid documentary shoot. Richard agrees to take his son along and they decide the subject of the documentary will be interviews with fathers and sons all over the world about their relationships with each other. The result is a remarkable journey into the meaning of love and devotion. Along the way, Chris and Richard define and refine their relationship, breaking apart and coming back together stronger than ever. A fantastic documentary for fathers and sons, and the women who have to put up with them. There is also a sad, revealing interview with Julian Lennon about his relationship with his father (an extended version is in the extras) as well as many other surprisingly poignant and emotional tales from countless men around the world that show the trials and tribulations of parenthood to be universal. The footage is shaky at times due to the mostly hand-held cameras and the sound and picture quality reflect the usual limitations of documentaries shot on the road. —CA

Movie: 🎵🎵🎵½ **DVD:** 🎵🎵
MGM Home Entertainment (Cat #40015 07, UPC #027616855633). Full frame. Dolby Digital Stereo Surround. $19.98. Keepcase. *LANG:* English. *SUB:* Spanish; French. *FEATURES:* 28 chapter links • Commentary: filmmakers • Extended interview with Julian Lennon • Deleted scenes.
1999 (PG-13) 92m/C D: Chris Roe; **W:** Chris Roe, Erik Arnesen, Juliann Jannus, Mark Kornweibel, Jesse Negron, Richard Roe; **C:** Chris Roe, Erik Arnesen; **M:** Stephen Edwards, Mazatl Galindo.

The Pope of Greenwich Village

Two low-level New York criminals (Rourke and Roberts) team up with an aging safecracker (McMillan) to pull off a big job. They don't know that they're ripping off a genuine wiseguy (Young). All of the cast members, plus Geraldine Page, are excellent in a story that's more character study than caper flick. The odd nicks and specks are visible and the expected aliasing pops up on auto trimwork, but for the most part, the DVD image is very good. Mono sound is fine for the modest story. —MM

Movie: 🎵🎵🎵 **DVD:** 🎵🎵½
MGM Home Entertainment (Cat #10018 30, UPC #027616861009). Widescreen (1.85:1) letterboxed. Dolby Digital Mono. $19.98. Keepcase. *LANG:* English; French; Spanish. *SUB:* French; Spanish. *FEATURES:* 16 chapter links • Trailer.

1984 (R) 122m/C Eric Roberts, Mickey Rourke, Daryl Hannah, Geraldine Page, Tony Musante, M. Emmet Walsh, Kenneth McMillan, Burt Young, Jack Kehoe, Philip Bosco, Val Avery, Joe Grifasi, Tony DiBenedetto; **D:** Stuart Rosenberg; **W:** Vincent Patrick; **C:** John Bailey; **M:** Dave Grusin. *AWARDS: NOM:* Oscars '84: Support. Actress (Page).

Porky's / Porky's 2: The Next Day

From these modest (though commercially successful) roots came more recent teen comedies focused on sex. These two, set in 1950s Florida, are about the boys (though none of the actors who play them look to be a day less than 30) of Angel Beach High School and their lackluster love lives. Though both films have been critically pilloried, any fair-minded reviewer will have to admit that the scene in the original, where gym teacher Nancy Parsons tries to identify the "tallywhacker" she caught spying in the girl's shower room (chapters 18 and 19), is inspired comedy. The sequel is a sequel. The double-sided disc contains absolutely faithful re-creations of low-budget originals. —MM

Movie: 🎵🎵½ **DVD:** 🎵🎵🎵½
20th Century Fox Home Entertainment (Cat #2001174, UPC #024543011743). Widescreen (1.85:1) anamorphic. Dolby Digital Surround; Mono. $24.99. Keepcase. *LANG:* English; French. *SUB:* English. *FEATURES:* 20 chapter links, (*Porky's*) • 24 chapter links, (*Porky's II*) • Trailers.
1982 (R) 94m/C CA Dan Monahan, Wyatt Knight, Scott Colomby, Tony Ganios, Mark Herrier, Cyril O'Reilly, Roger Wilson, Alex Karras, Kim Cattrall, Kaki Hunter, Nancy Parsons, Boyd Gaines, Douglas McGrath, Susan Clark, Art Hindle, Wayne Maunder, Chuck "Porky" Mitchell, Eric Christmas, Bob (Benjamin) Clark; **D:** Bob (Benjamin) Clark; **W:** Bob (Benjamin) Clark; **C:** Reginald Morris; **M:** Paul Zaza, Carl Zittrer.

Porky's 2: The Next Day

Please see review for *Porky's / Porky's 2: The Next Day.*
Movie: 🎵🎵
1983 (R) 100m/C CA Bill Wiley, Dan Monahan, Wyatt Knight, Cyril O'Reilly, Roger Wilson, Tony Ganios, Mark Herrier, Scott Colomby, Kaki Hunter, Nancy Parsons, Eric Christmas, Art Hindle; **D:** Bob (Benjamin) Clark; **W:** Alan Ormsby, Bob (Benjamin) Clark, Roger E. Swaybill; **C:** Reginald Morris; **M:** Carl Zittrer.

The Portrait

O.K. erotic horror video premiere begins when wallflower Crystal (Bodner) meets a Byronic photographer (Williams). He takes naughty pictures, which put her in touch with her inner slut and release all sorts of tendencies. It's fairly standard heavy-breathing stuff. The low-budget image is exceptionally grainy with heavy artifacts

even in conventional interiors. DVD is no improvement over tape. The supporting cast is filled with familiar faces and bodies who are dolled up in some of the silliest costumes you'll ever see. —*MM*
Movie: 🐾½ *DVD:* 🐾½
MTI Home Video (Cat #1062, UPC #03941 4510621). Full frame. $24.95. Keepcase. *LANG:* English. *FEATURES:* 20 chapter links ▪ Talent files ▪ Trailers.
1999 (R) 85m/C Gabriella Hall, Jenna Bodnar, Avalon Anders, Christopher Johnston; *D:* David Goldner; *W:* David Goldner; *C:* Rocky Dijon.

Portrait of Jennie
Struggling artist Eben Adams (Cotten) is inspired by and smitten with a strange and beautiful young girl (Jones) who may be the spirit of a dead woman. A fine cast works wonders with what could have been a forgettable story. DVD presentation is terrific. In the 1980s, a laserdisc was announced and abruptly cancelled, for a lack of decent source materials. The picture here really pops. In the spirit of its original presentation, Anchor Bay has retained the tinting of the final reel, which plays in a ghostly green, and a breathtaking ending color view of the eponymous portrait in a museum being admired by a pre-teen Anne Francis (now there's a bit of romance out-of-time to ponder). —*MM/GE*
AKA: Jennie; Tidal Wave.
Movie: 🐾🐾🐾½ *DVD:* 🐾🐾🐾½
Anchor Bay (Cat #11268, UPC #01313112 6891). Full frame. Dolby Digital Mono. $14.98. Keepcase. *LANG:* English. *FEATURES:* Theatrical trailer.
1948 86m/B Joseph Cotten, Jennifer Jones, Cecil Kellaway, Ethel Barrymore, David Wayne, Lillian Gish, Henry Hull, Florence Bates, Felix Bressart, Anne Francis; *D:* William Dieterle; *W:* Leonardo Bercovici, Peter Berneis, Paul Osborn; *C:* Joseph August; *M:* Dimitri Tiomkin. *AWARDS:* Venice Film Fest. '49: Actor (Cotten); *NOM:* Oscars '48: B&W Cinematog.

A Portrait of the Artist As a Young Man
An excellent cast highlights this moving, lyrical adaptation of the author's autobiography, told through the character of Stephen Dedalus. Joyce's characterizations, words, and scenes are beautifully translated to the medium of film. The video transfer displays some decent color definition, but it cannot overcome the state of the source material, which shows many cracks and flaws throughout. This would be forgivable if not for the badly distorted soundtrack, which proves a real chore to understand. —*MJT*
Movie: 🐾🐾🐾 *DVD:* 🐾🐾½
Image Entertainment (Cat #ID9519RLDVD, UPC #014381951929). Full frame. Dolby Digital Mono. $29.99. Snapper. *LANG:* English. *FEATURES:* 10 chapter links.
1977 92m/C John Gielgud, T.P. McKenna, Bosco Hogan; *D:* Joseph Strick; *W:* Judith Rascoe; *C:* Stuart Hetherington.

Portraits Chinois
Ada (Bonham Carter) and Paul are trendy young things who have just moved into a swanky Paris apartment. They and their equally young and trendy pals reveal their relationship issues in an ensemble piece that's difficult to become involved with. The main reason is an image that is unpleasantly grim and harsh. Very dark colors lack all detail. Skin tones are pallid. All of the image flaws come from the original, not the transfer. —*MM* *AKA:* Shadow Play.
Movie: 🐾🐾 *DVD:* 🐾🐾
Vanguard International Cinema, Inc. (Cat #1-892649-63-2, UPC #658769005837). Widescreen letterboxed. $29.95. Keepcase. *LANG:* French. *SUB:* English. *FEATURES:* 12 chapter links.
1996 105m/C *FR* Helena Bonham Carter, Jean-Philippe Ecoffey, Romane Bohringer, Sergio Castellitto, Marie Trintignant, Elsa Zylberstein, Yvan Attal, Miki Manojlovic, Jean-Claude Brialy; *D:* Martine Dugowson; *W:* Martine Dugowson, Peter Chase; *C:* Vincenzo Marano; *M:* Peter Chase.

Positive I.D.
First, do not read the box copy of this fiercely original thriller. The less you know about the plot, the more you'll enjoy it. On the surface, Julie Kenner (Rascoe, in a fearless performance) has an ordinary suburban life: split-level, Volvo, hubby, two blonde daughters. But there's a frightening trauma in her past and it is revealed only by degrees. By the end, this is a compelling, involving feminist noir. It's one of the best sleepers around, and this DVD presents it very nicely. The image looks good for a 1980s independent production. Mono sound has been punched up, too, but the real strengths are the story and terrific work by the star. —*MM*
Movie: 🐾🐾🐾½ *DVD:* 🐾🐾🐾
Anchor Bay (Cat #DV11246, UPC #013131 124699). Widescreen (1.66:1) anamorphic. Dolby Digital Mono. $24.99. Keepcase. *LANG:* English. *FEATURES:* 28 chapter links ▪ Trailer.
1987 (R) 96m/C Stephanie Rascoe, John Davies, Steve Fromholz; *D:* Andy Anderson; *W:* Andy Anderson; *C:* Paul Barton.

Posse
Though it's carrying some racial and political baggage, Van Peebles's "black" western is a rip-roaring shoot-'em-up. It has no more to do with the historical "truth" of the Old West than Sergio Leone's operatic concoctions do. In fact, the film borrows heavily from Leone's work; a clip from *Once Upon a Time in the West* shows up in the closing credits. The story also lifts elements from *The Wild Bunch* and *The Magnificent Seven,* but the real inspiration is *Raiders of the Lost Ark* with the exaggerated looks and pace of a music video, and appropriately shallow characters. Jessie Lee (Van Peebles) leads a group of Spanish American war veterans to Freemanville, a troubled community founded by former slaves. Both wide and full images

re-create Van Peebles's color palette, which tends toward orange and amber tints. Sound is fine. A commentary track would have been welcome. —*MM*
Movie: 🐾🐾½ *DVD:* 🐾🐾½
USA Home Entertainment (Cat #88115, UPC #044008811527). Widescreen (2.35:1) letterboxed; full frame. Dolby Digital Stereo. $29.95. Keepcase. *LANG:* English; French. *CAP:* English. *FEATURES:* Cast and crew thumbnail bios ▪ Trailer ▪ 16 chapter links.
1993 (R) 113m/C Mario Van Peebles, Stephen Baldwin, Charles Lane, Tommy (Tiny) Lister, Big Daddy Kane, Billy Zane, Blair Underwood, Tone Loc, Salli Richardson, Reginald (Reggie) Hudlin, Richard Edson, Reginald Vel Johnson, Warrington Hudlin; *Cameos:* Melvin Van Peebles, Pam Grier, Isaac Hayes, Robert Hooks, Richard Jordan, Paul Bartel, Nipsey Russell, Woody Strode, Aaron Neville, Stephen J. Cannell; *D:* Mario Van Peebles; *W:* Sy Richardson, Dario Scardapane; *C:* Peter Menzies Jr.; *M:* Michel Colombier.

Possession
Returned from a long mission, a secret agent (Neill) notices that his wife (Adjani) is acting strange. And why not? She's about to give birth to a manifestation of evil that is within her. This Euro-horror is gory, hysterical, intellectual, and bizarre. The picture is very crisp and clear, with only some mild defects in the source print (mainly scratches) noticeable. The bottom line is that this doesn't look like a European horror film from 1981. The dialogue and sound effects are well mixed, but it's still almost impossible to understand a word that Isabelle Adjani says. —*ML/MM*
Movie: 🐾🐾🐾 *DVD:* 🐾🐾🐾
Anchor Bay (Cat #11116). Widescreen (1.66:1) anamorphic. Dolby Digital Mono. $29.98. Keepcase. *LANG:* English. *FEATURES:* Theatrical trailer ▪ Talent files ▪ Commentary: director Andrzej Zulawski and biographer Dan Bird.
1981 (R) 123m/C *FR GE* Isabelle Adjani, Sam Neill, Heinz Bennent, Margit Carstensen, Shaun Lawtor; *D:* Andrzej Zulawski; *W:* Andrzej Zulawski, Frederic Tuten; *C:* Bruno Nuytten; *M:* Andrezej Korzynski. *AWARDS:* Cesar '82: Actress (Adjani).

Postcards from the Edge
Fisher adapts her best-selling novel, tamed and tempered, for the big screen with a hugely talented cast. Streep is very fine as a delightfully harried actress struggling with her career, her drug problem, and her competitive, overwhelming show-biz mother (MacLaine). DVD image looks pristine, and the delicate sound work is intact. Enjoying this one is not a problem. On the commentary track, Carrie Fisher conversationally cops to all kinds of naughty behavior. Originally, Debbie Reynolds was going to play "herself." There were also cut scenes with Jerry Orbach as the Father, and John Cusack as a friend from rehab.

Fisher is fun to listen to, and very open about her past drug habits. (After listening to her, you want to know what a conversation between her and Brenda Vaccaro would sound like.) Although Carrie's jokey-bitterness comes through, she's quick to say that the mother character was exaggerated for the purposes of drama; Debbie Reynolds never poured vodka into her breakfast. —*MM/GE*

Movie: 🎵🎵🎵 **DVD:** 🎵🎵🎵½
Columbia Tristar Home Video (Cat #05848, UPC #043396058484). Widescreen (1.78:1) anamorphic. $24.98. Keepcase. *LANG:* English. *FEATURES:* Commentary • Production notes • Trailers.
1990 (R) 101m/C Meryl Streep, Shirley MacLaine, Dennis Quaid, Gene Hackman, Richard Dreyfuss, Rob Reiner, Mary Wickes, Conrad Bain, Annette Bening, Michael Ontkean, Dana Ivey, Robin Bartlett, Anthony Heald, Oliver Platt, CCH Pounder; **D:** Mike Nichols; **W:** Carrie Fisher; **C:** Michael Ballhaus; **M:** Shel Silverstein, Carly Simon, Stephen Sondheim, Howard Shore, Paul Shaffer, Gilda Radner. *AWARDS: NOM:* Oscars '90: Actress (Streep), Song ("I'm Checkin' Out").

Postmortem

In Scotland, cop-turned-writer James McGregor (Sheen, here billed as "Charles") runs across another of those serial killers. Seems like you can't slap a disc into a DVD player these days without running into one of those guys. At first, he's a suspect but then he helps the local cops, etc., etc. The material is all too familiar. The *Seven* clone has a dark, carefully grubby look with a softish image that's a scant improvement over tape. —*MM*

Movie: 🎵🎵 **DVD:** 🎵🎵
Studio Home Entertainment (Cat #7005). Full frame. Dolby Digital Stereo. $24.95. Keepcase. *LANG:* English. *SUB:* Spanish. *FEATURES:* Cast and crew thumbnail bios • 18 chapter links • Trailer.
1998 (R) 105m/C Charlie Sheen, Michael Halsey, Stephen McCole, Gary Lewis, Hazel Ann Crawford; **D:** Albert Pyun; **W:** John Lamb; **C:** George Mooradian; **M:** Tony Riparetti.

Pot o' Gold

Stewart plays Jimmy Haksell, a young man who signs on with a struggling band and falls for the singer, Molly (Goddard at her loveliest). He convinces his music-hating uncle, who has a radio program, to let the band perform during a giveaway show he has concocted. This is a trifle, the stars notwithstanding. The title is in public domain, so many inferior DVDs are in distribution. The Image edition is by far the best. The disc was made from excellent original materials. The black-and-white image ranges between good and very good. The mono sound is less successful, but it's fine for a film of this vintage. —*MM AKA:* The Golden Hour.
Movie: 🎵🎵 **DVD:** 🎵🎵½

Image Entertainment (Cat #ID5837DS DVD, UPC #014381583724). Full frame. Dolby Digital Mono. $19.95. Snapper. *LANG:* English. *FEATURES:* 12 chapter links. Also available from Madacy (cat. #DVD-9-9030) for $9.95.
1941 87m/B Paulette Goddard, James Stewart, Charles Winninger, Horace Heidt, Art Carney; **D:** George Marshall; **W:** Walter DeLeon; **C:** Hal Mohr.

Power

In a study of corporate/political manipulation, Gere plays an amoral media consultant who works with various candidates and finally discovers his conscience. A fine cast can't find the energy to make this one great, though it was ahead of its time in dealing with intriguing ideas. Lumet fared much better with similar material in *Network*. The softish DVD image flatters an attractive cast, but the disc is not significantly superior to tape. —*MM*

Movie: 🎵🎵½ **DVD:** 🎵🎵½
Warner Home Video, Inc. (Cat #401). Full frame. Dolby Digital Mono. $14.98. Snapper. *LANG:* English; French. *CAP:* English. *FEATURES:* 30 chapter links.
1986 (R) 111m/C Richard Gere, Julie Christie, E.G. Marshall, Gene Hackman, Beatrice Straight, Kate Capshaw, Denzel Washington, Fritz Weaver, Michael Learned, E. Katherine Kerr, Polly Rowles, Matt Salinger, J.T. Walsh; **D:** Sidney Lumet; **W:** David Himmelstein; **C:** Andrzej Bartkowiak; **M:** Cy Coleman.

Pre-Code Hollywood: Vol. 1, "Of Human Bondage"

The first film version of Somerset Maugham's great novel finds a young, handicapped medical student (Howard) falling in love with a crude cockney waitress (Davis) in a mutually destructive affair. It established Davis's persona as a tough, domineering woman. No-frills (not even a menu) disc cannot really improve much on tape, though both image and sound are good for a work of this age. (See separate entry for credits.) —*MM*

Movie: 🎵🎵🎵 **DVD:** 🎵🎵
Roan Group (Cat #2004). Full frame. $39.95. Keepcase. *LANG:* English. *FEATURES:* 19 chapter links.
1934 m/C

Predator [20th Century Fox]

This is the best home video version of one of the most accomplished modern sf adventure films, arguably the best from Schwarzenegger. The flaws of the earlier letterboxed DVD (cat. #4109068, reviewed in first edition) have been eliminated. In visual terms, this one is as crisply detailed as the theatrical release, even in the busy jungle scenes. Surround sound is far superior on even a modest home theatre system. All that's missing is a director's com-

mentary track explaining how some of those neat effects were accomplished. —*MM*

Movie: 🎵🎵🎵½ **DVD:** 🎵🎵🎵½
20th Century Fox Home Entertainment (Cat #2001085, UPC #024543010852). Widescreen (1.85:1) anamorphic. DTS Surround Stereo; Dolby 5.1 Surround Stereo; Dolby Surround Stereo. $29.98. Keepcase. *LANG:* English; French. *SUB:* English; Spanish. *FEATURES:* 25 chapter links • Trailer.
1987 (R) 107m/C Arnold Schwarzenegger, Jesse Ventura, Sonny Landham, Bill Duke, Elpidia Carrillo, Carl Weathers, R.G. Armstrong, Richard Chaves, Shane Black, Kevin Peter Hall; **D:** John McTiernan; **W:** Jim Thomas, John Thomas; **C:** Donald McAlpine; **M:** Alan Silvestri.

Prelude to a Kiss

To appreciate this curious romantic fantasy, you have to forgive a lot in the first 15–20 minutes. That prolonged introduction comes across as cute, perky, and far, far too talky, but it sets up some serious themes. Free-spirited bartender Rita (Ryan) and straitlaced Peter (Baldwin) marry after a whirlwind courtship. At the wedding reception, Rita kisses an old man (Walker) and something very unusual happens. All three stars do fine work in its resolution. Though this does not feel like a filmed play, it's not a particularly striking work in visual terms and so it doesn't gain much on DVD. Image is good if unexceptional. Same for sound. —*MM*

Movie: 🎵🎵🎵 **DVD:** 🎵🎵
20th Century Fox Home Entertainment (Cat #2000885, UPC #024543008859). Widescreen (1.85:1) anamorphic. Dolby Digital 4.0 Surround; Dolby Digital Surround. $24.99. Keepcase. *LANG:* English; French. *SUB:* English; Spanish. *FEATURES:* Trailers • 20 chapter links.
1992 (PG-13) 106m/C Alec Baldwin, Meg Ryan, Sydney Walker, Ned Beatty, Patty Duke, Kathy Bates, Stanley Tucci; **D:** Norman Rene; **W:** Craig Lucas; **C:** Stefan Czapsky; **M:** Howard Shore.

Premonition

Tabloid reporters Morley Allen (Lloyd) and Ali Caine (Preston) discover that strange forces are behind a series of unexplained murders. Yes, it's another trip to *X-Files* land. The supernatural thriller also shows the influence of *Seven* in its broody, interesting visuals. The polished image belies what must have been a fairly modest budget. Director Wilding, a veteran of several video premieres, knows what he's doing and explains it well in a technically oriented commentary track. Something of a sleeper. —*MM*

Movie: 🎵🎵½ **DVD:** 🎵🎵½
Artisan Entertainment (Cat #10637, UPC #012236106371). Full frame. Dolby Digital 5.1 Surround Stereo; Dolby Digital Surround. $24.99. Keepcase. *LANG:* English. *CAP:* English. *FEATURES:* 20 chapter links • Trailer • Talent files • Commentary: Gavin Wilding.

1999 (R) 93m/C Christopher Lloyd, Adrian Paul, Cynthia Preston, Blu Mankuma; **D:** Gavin Wilding; **W:** Gavin Wilding, Raul Inglis, John Fairley; **C:** Glen Winter.

Pretty Village, Pretty Flame

Powerful story of the Bosnian conflict is based on a true incident. The story flashes from the days of Yugoslavian unity under Marshal Tito to 1992 when members of a Serbian patrol are trapped (along with an American journalist) by Muslim militiamen in a tunnel connecting Zagreb and Belgrade with no hope for escape. Compared to American productions, this image looks very rough with harsh colors. It appears to be an accurate reproduction of the original and this is not a story that intends to be attractive in any way. —MM **AKA:** Lepa Sela, Lepo Gore.
Movie: ♫♫♫ **DVD:** ♫♫
Winstar Home Entertainment (Cat #5027, UPC #720917502724). Widescreen (1.78: 1) letterboxed. Dolby Digital Stereo. $29.98. Keepcase. *LANG:* Serbo-Croatian. *SUB:* English. *FEATURES:* Production notes • Trailer • Awards • 12 chapter links.
1996 125m/C Dragan Bjelogric, Nikola Kojo, Bata Zivojinovic, Dragan Maksimovic, Zoran Cvijanovic, Nikola Pejakovic, Lisa Moncure; **D:** Srdjan Dragojevic; **W:** Srdjan Dragojevic, Vanja Bulic, Nikola Pejakovic; **C:** Dusan Joksimovic; **M:** Lazar Ristovski.

Price of Glory

Good solid writing and acting make this story of a father's attempt to correct the mistakes of his childhood by controlling the lives of his sons above average. Arturo (Smits) was cheated out of a boxing title as a young man and is determined to make all three of his sons champion boxers to redeem his honor. He controls his sons with the whip of family loyalty and each son reacts to Arturo's control in his own unique way: one turns to drugs, another to his girlfriend, and the youngest becomes the boxer that his father wants him to be to the exclusion of any life of his own. The talented Smits frees Arturo's character out of the stereotypical Latino father box and releases the soul of a man so haunted by the ghosts of the past that he can't see the vulnerability of his own children. The picture and sound are above video quality, but not extraordinary. —CA
Movie: ♫♫♫ **DVD:** ♫♫♫½
New Line Home Video (Cat #N5083, UPC #794043508325). Widescreen; full frame. Dolby Digital 5.1 Surround. $24.98. Snapper. *LANG:* English. *FEATURES:* 31 chapter links • Commentary: director • Deleted scenes with commentary • Theatrical trailer.
2000 (PG-13) 118m/C Jimmy Smits, Jon Seda, Clifton (Gonzalez) Collins Jr., Maria Del Mar, Sal Lopez, Louis Mandylor, Paul Rodriguez, Ron Perlman, Danielle Camastra, Ernesto Hernandez; **D:** Carlos Avila; **W:** Phil Berger; **C:** Alfonso Beato; **M:** Joseph Julian Gonzalez.

The Prince and the Pauper

Many of the cast and crew of *The Three Musketeers* turn in equally spirited work in this adaptation of Mark Twain's novel with rowdy tongue-in-cheek humor, sharp satire, and knockabout action scenes. When an English prince and a street urchin (Lester twice) discover that they're virtual twins, they trade places and have to find their way back to their proper roles. The cast is very good, particularly veterans Heston, Harrison, and Reed. Image is generally flawless, though the disc I watched had an inexplicable freeze in chapter two. Sound is less than stellar. —MM **AKA:** Crossed Swords.
Movie: ♫♫♫ **DVD:** ♫♫½
Anchor Bay (Cat #DV11110, UPC #013131111095). Widescreen (2.35:1) anamorphic; full frame. Dolby Digital Mono. $24.99. Keepcase. *LANG:* English. *FEATURES:* 24 chapter links.
1978 (PG) 113m/C *GB* Oliver Reed, Raquel Welch, Mark Lester, Ernest Borgnine, George C. Scott, Rex Harrison, Charlton Heston, Sybil Danning; **D:** Richard Fleischer; **W:** Berta Dominguez, George MacDonald Fraser, Pierre Spengler; **C:** Jack Cardiff; **M:** Maurice Jarre.

Prince of Central Park

When JJ (Nasso) chooses the streets of New York over his foster mother (Moriarty), he learns to live by a new set of rules. While seeking shelter in Central Park, he discovers a world ruled by a frightening eccentric (Keitel). One couple (Turner and Aiello) has a chance to save the child, but their past may prevent them. The video transfer is nicely done; colors are well-defined and blacks are sharp. The audio is also decent with virtually no lost dialogue to speak of. —MJT
Movie: ♫♫½ **DVD:** ♫♫♫
Trimark Home Video (Cat #VM 7537D, UPC #031398753728). Widescreen (1.85:1) letterboxed. Dolby Surround. $24.99. Keepcase. *LANG:* English. *SUB:* English; Spanish; French. *FEATURES:* 18 chapter links • Theatrical trailer gallery • Synopsis • Cast and crew bios • Production notes.
2000 (PG-13) 105m/C Frank Nasso, Kathleen Turner, Danny Aiello, Harvey Keitel, Cathy Moriarty, Lauren Velez, Jerry Orbach, Tina Holmes; **D:** John Leekley; **W:** John Leekley; **C:** Jonathan Herron; **M:** Theodore Shapiro.

The Princess Bride

Goldman's update of an archetypal fairy tale (as told by Peter Falk) is crammed with all the elements. The adventurously irreverent love story revolves around a beautiful maiden (Penn) and her young swain (Elwes) as they battle the evils of the mythical kingdom of Florin to be reunited with one another. Great dueling scenes and offbeat satire make this fun for adults as well as children. The softish image is appropriate for the material, and it's certainly acceptable for a no-frills disc. A more elaborate edition is reportedly in the works. —MM
Movie: ♫♫♫½ **DVD:** ♫♫½
MGM Home Entertainment (Cat #636861). Widescreen letterboxed; full frame. $29.95. Keepcase. *LANG:* English; Spanish. *SUB:* French; Spanish. *FEATURES:* 28 chapter links • Theatrical trailer.
1987 (PG) 98m/C Cary Elwes, Mandy Patinkin, Robin Wright Penn, Wallace Shawn, Peter Falk, Andre the Giant, Chris Sarandon, Christopher Guest, Billy Crystal, Carol Kane, Fred Savage, Peter Cook, Mel Smith; **D:** Rob Reiner; **W:** William Goldman; **C:** Adrian Biddle; **M:** Mark Knopfler. *AWARDS: NOM:* Oscars '87: Song ("Storybook Love").

Princess Caraboo

This unusual, true story of a mysterious oriental "Princess" who is adopted and exploited by a well-to-do English family in the 1800s is engaging and thoughtful, but falls just short of the enchantment for which it strives. This is not for lack of talent, as literally every role is filled by a top-notch English actor, with winsome American Phoebe Cates as the gibberish-speaking, tattooed "heathen," joined by John Lithgow's stuffy academic, and an unusually subdued Kevin Kline as a Greek butler. Except for pompous banker Jim Broadbent, who concentrates on money-making schemes, most every male in the cast becomes enamored of Caraboo, with young publisher Stephen Rea the one most deeply smitten. Wendy Hughes carries the heart of the show as the woman who goes out of her way to be kind to this very unusual, cigar-smoking young lady whom nobody can understand. If anything, the film is too subdued for its own good. Although the mystery carries great interest, and a possible death sentence for Caraboo if she proves to be a charlatan, the film shrinks from needed dramatic confrontations and seems content to settle for mild social comment. Only teenaged girls are likely to get worked up over her predicament. The word "anamorphic" is prominent on the packaging, but Columbia Tristar's DVD is a disappointing cropped full-frame presentation. It's also not quite up to their usual high standards picture-wise, with the blacks looking a bit muddy. The trailer mostly proves that this was a difficult film to market without spoiling its fragile premise. —GE
Movie: ♫♫♫½ **DVD:** ♫♫½
Columbia Tristar Home Video (Cat #06293, UPC #043396062931). Full frame. Dolby Digital. $19.95. Keepcase. *LANG:* English; French; Spanish. *SUB:* English; French; Spanish; Chinese; Korean; Thai. *CAP:* English. *FEATURES:* Theatrical trailer • Talent files.
1994 (PG) 97m/C Phoebe Cates, Stephen Rea, John Lithgow, Kevin Kline, Jim Broadbent, Wendy Hughes, Peter Eyre, Jacqueline Pearce, John Lynch, John Sessions, Arkie Whiteley, John Wells; **D:** Michael Austin; **W:** Michael Austin, John Wells; **C:** Freddie Francis; **M:** Richard Hartley.

Princess Mononoke

Stunning animated feature by Japanese master Hayao Miyazaki is a bit too long and much too graphic for small children, but it's a must-see for everyone else, particularly fans of Kurasawa's interpretations of Shakespeare. Prince Ashitaka (Crudup) must find a way to lift a curse placed upon him after he kills a rampaging forest god. Part of the secret lies in Iron Town, led by the avaricious Lady Eboshi (Driver). Her opposite number is Princess Mononoke (Danes), who was raised by wolves. Also on hand are a politically savvy monk voiced by Thornton (who observes "When you're going to kill a god, let someone else do the dirty work") and Gillian Anderson as a wolf god. On DVD, the careful voice dubbing makes the English version just as expressive as the Japanese. The captions are quick and colloquial while the subtitles are a literal translation of the original dialogue. The image is excellent and if the 5.1 mix isn't as active as some, it does the job. In limited theatrical release, the film failed to find much of an audience. It should be much more popular on disc. —MM
Movie: 🎬🎬🎬½ **DVD:** 🎬🎬🎬½
Miramax Pictures Home Video (Cat #193 00, UPC #717951007414). Widescreen (1.85:1) anamorphic. Dolby Digital 5.1 Surround Stereo. $32.99. Keepcase. *LANG:* English; French; Japanese. *SUB:* English. *CAP:* English. *FEATURES:* 25 chapter links ● "Making of" featurette ● Trailer.
1998 (PG-13) 133m/C D: Hayao Miyazaki; **W:** Neil Gaiman; **M:** Joe Hisaishi; **V:** Claire Danes, Billy Crudup, Minnie Driver, Gillian Anderson, Jada Pinkett Smith, Billy Bob Thornton.

The Prisoner

Even though the cover of this bizarre import says *Jackie Chan Is The Prisoner,* he doesn't even show up for the first 20 minutes or so. Actually, the film is something of an ensemble piece that cheerfully borrows from American prison movies (most blatantly *Cool Hand Luke*) between action scenes. The freewheeling plot has Jackie, Sammo Hung, and Tony Leung battling fellow prisoners and corrupt officials. The monochromatic gray of most of the settings makes for an acceptably detailed but dull image. Surround effects pick up in the action scenes. —MM **AKA:** Jackie Chan Is the Prisoner; Huo Shao Dao.
Movie: 🎬🎬 **DVD:** 🎬🎬½
Columbia Tristar Home Video (Cat #06083, UPC #043396060838). Widescreen (1.85:1) letterboxed. Dolby Digital 5.1 Surround Stereo; Dolby Digital Surround. $24.95. Keepcase. *LANG:* English; French. *SUB:* English; Spanish. *FEATURES:* 28 chapter links ● Commentary: martial arts expert Phillip Rhee ● Trailer ● Talent files.
1990 (R) 94m/C *HK* Jackie Chan, Sammo Hung, Tony Leung Ka-Fai; **D:** Yen Ping Chu; **W:** Fu Lai, Yeh Yuen Chiao; **C:** Chan Wing Su; **M:** Eckart Seeber.

Prisoner Maria: The Movie

Japanese variation on *La Femme Nikita,* finds Maria (Aota) in the slammer for offing the drug-dealer who killed her husband. She's recruited by a secret government agency into a work-release program as an assassin. The combination of sex and violence, including fairly graphic rape, is much stronger than you find in similar American productions. The dark image is seldom better than fair, but DVD appears to be an accurate re-creation of the original. Optional subtitles are bright and easy to read. —MM
Movie: 🎬½ **DVD:** 🎬½
Media Blasters (Cat #TSDVD-0181, UPC #631595018127). Widescreen letterboxed. Dolby Digital Stereo. $24.95. Keepcase. *LANG:* English; Japanese. *SUB:* English. *FEATURES:* 8 chapter links ● 4 previews.
1995 90m/C *JP* Noriko Aota; **D:** Shuji Kataoka; **W:** Keiju Nagasawa; **M:** Takashi Nakagawa.

The Private Eyes [SE]

Light and uneven comedic romp follows the bungling Conway and Knotts as they investigate a pair of murders committed at Morley Manor (actually, the Biltmore estate in North Carolina). They're led on a merry chase through secret passageways to a meeting with a ghostly adversary. Though the movie is light on plot and most of the dialogue feels improvised—Conway admits that the film was written in two days!—seeing the stars in action together is worth the price of admission alone. The image is clear and sharp, and shows only a slight amount of grain. There is some fuzziness around the edges of the frame, but this is minimal. The picture is somewhat dark at certain spots in the film, but this doesn't affect the color scheme, which comes across very well. The audio mix offers clear and audible dialogue, which is important, as both Conway and Knotts have a tendency to mumble. —ML/MM
Movie: 🎬🎬🎬 **DVD:** 🎬🎬½
Hen's Tooth Video Full frame. Dolby Digital Stereo. $29.98. Keepcase. *LANG:* English. *FEATURES:* Commentary: Conway and Elliott ● Theatrical trailer ● Production photos.
1980 (PG) 91m/C Don Knotts, Tim Conway, Trisha Noble, Bernard Fox; **D:** Lang Elliott; **W:** John Myhers, Tim Conway; **C:** Jacques Haitkin; **M:** Peter Matz.

Private Navy of Sgt. O'Farrell

Serviceable World War II service comedy casts Hope as the titular NCO who must salvage a cargo ship full of beer that was sunk by the Japanese. He also tries to get some nurses assigned to the remote Pacific island where he's stationed. But Phyllis Diller proves to be a poor morale booster. The film doesn't come close to the "Road" comedies, but it's still worth a mild recommendation to the star's fans. The DVD captures the riotous '60s color scheme with appalling accuracy. Gina Lollobrigida's introduction on a psychedelic beach blanket is a moment worthy of *Austin Powers.* Unfortunately, some distracting artifacts appear on her chest during the bikini scene. —MM
Movie: 🎬🎬 **DVD:** 🎬🎬½
Brentwood Home Video (Cat #60986-9, UPC #090096098692). Full frame. Dolby Digital Mono. $14.98. Keepcase. *LANG:* English. *FEATURES:* 8 chapter links ● Bob Hope thumbnail bio.
1968 92m/C Bob Hope, Phyllis Diller, Jeffrey Hunter, Dick Sargent, Mako, Gina Lollobrigida; **D:** Frank Tashlin; **W:** Frank Tashlin; **C:** Alan Stenvold.

The Prodigy

Well-intentioned but farfetched drama posits that Nathan Jones (Earl), an illiterate 12-year-old black boy, is "adopted" by a fraternity and enrolled as a student as a child prodigy. Sounds like an after-school special gone tragically awry. Heavy aliasing in the exteriors makes the image no better than VHS tape. Sound is slightly better. —MM
Movie: 🎬🎬 **DVD:** 🎬🎬
Vanguard International Cinema, Inc. (UPC #658769003437). Full frame. Stereo. $29.98. Keepcase. *LANG:* English. *FEATURES:* 12 chapter links.
1998 104m/C Robert Foreman, Jeremy Isiah Earl, Jennifer Rochester; **D:** Edward T. McDougal; **W:** Edward T. McDougal, Dale Chapman, Christopher Panneck; **C:** Ben Kufrin.

Project A

This period piece has several excellent physical routines. As Dragon Ma, a coast guard officer in 19th-century Hong Kong, Jackie Chan (who also directed) performs some of his most ingenious stunts, and pays overt homage to one of his greatest influences, Harold Lloyd. Unfortunately, those very action scenes are more heavily grained than other sequences. Sound is acceptable on this bare-bones disc. —MM **AKA:** Jackie Chan's Project A; A Gai Waak.
Movie: 🎬🎬½ **DVD:** 🎬🎬
Buena Vista Home Entertainment (Cat #18 319, UPC #717951005069). Widescreen (2.35:1) letterboxed. Dolby Digital 5.1 Surround Stereo. $29.99. Keepcase. *LANG:* English. *CAP:* English. *FEATURES:* 18 chapter links.
1983 (PG-13) 105m/C *HK* Jackie Chan, Sammo Hung, Yuen Biao; **D:** Jackie Chan; **W:** Edward Tang, Jackie Chan; **M:** Nicholas Rivera.

Project A-ko

Set in the near future, this Japanese animated feature concerns teenagers with strange powers, an alien spaceship, and lots of action. Seventeen-year-old A-ko possesses superhuman strength and a ditzy sidekick, C-ko. B-ko, the spoiled daughter of a rich business tycoon, decides to fight A-ko for C-ko's companionship. Meanwhile, the alien ship approacheth. So-so big-eyed girl animation contains excessive aliasing and is not much better than VHS tape. —*MM*

Movie: 🦴🦴 **DVD:** 🦴🦴
Image Entertainment (Cat #4640, UPC #014381464023). Widescreen (1.85:1) letterboxed. Dolby Digital Stereo. $24.99. Snapper. *LANG:* Japanese; English. *SUB:* English. *FEATURES:* 16 chapter links.
1986 86m/C *JP D:* Katsuhiko Nishijima; **W:** Tomoko Kawasaki.

The Prophet's Game

Vaguely interesting serial killer drama with Dennis Hopper as Seattle homicide detective Vincent Swan. Swan's retirement hits a bump when he is faced with the possibility that he killed the wrong man years before when the "prophet's game" killings begin again in Los Angeles. Manipulated to the city of angels by the possible copy cat's correspondence, Swan is teamed with a token female detective (Zimbalist) and harassed by the chief of detectives (Penny). Told to keep out of the way of the real police, they, of course, investigate on their own. Sondra Locke has an especially disturbing role as one of the killers. The color quality of the disc is good though the blacks aren't as clear as they could be. —*CA*

Movie: 🦴½ **DVD:** 🦴🦴½
York Entertainment (Cat #YPD1057, UPC #5072310572). Full frame. Dolby Digital 5.1 Surround. $14.99. Keepcase. *LANG:* English. *SUB:* Spanish. *FEATURES:* 12 chapter links ▪ Cast and crew bios and filmographies ▪ Theatrical trailer.
1999 (R) 107m/C Dennis Hopper, Geoffrey Lewis, Stephanie Zimbalist, Joe Penny, Greg Lauren, Shannon Whirry, Michael Dorn, Don Swayze, Robert Ginty, Sondra Locke; **D:** David Worth; **W:** Carol Chrest; **C:** David Worth.

The Proposal

Terry Martin (Nick Moran of *Lock, Stock and 2 Smoking Barrels* fame, whose British accent is remarkably changed into that of a gravel-voiced American for this role) is an undercover cop hot on the trail of mob boss Simon Bacig (played by Stephen Lang). When he needs a wife for a social occasion hosted by his target, he is forced to recruit a policewoman for the deception (Esposito) and then finds his cover ultimately blown when his new "wife" reveals an agenda of her own. Independent director Richard Gale provides a marvelous audio commentary, which reveals the tricks of low-budget filmmaking, and aids in resolving the screenplay shortcomings. An irritating menu interface marks this DVD release, which is the only real technical negative. —*RJT*

Movie: 🦴🦴½ **DVD:** 🦴🦴🦴
Buena Vista Home Entertainment (Cat #21 680, UPC #786936145052). Widescreen (1.85) anamorphic. Dolby Digital Surround Stereo. $32.99. Keepcase. *LANG:* English. *SUB:* English. *CAP:* English. *FEATURES:* 19 chapter markers ▪ Commentary: director Richard Gale ▪ "Making of *The Proposal*" ▪ Trailer ▪ 7 cross-promotional trailers.
2000 (R) 90m/C Nick Moran, Jennifer Esposito, Stephen Lang, William B. Davis; **D:** Richard Gale; **W:** Maurice Hurley; **C:** Curtis Petersen; **M:** Joseph Conlan.

Psycho Sisters

As children, Jackie (North) and Jane (Lynn) witness shocking events that traumatize them into the titular killers. Actually, after seeing so many young women pursued by homicidal maniacs, it's nice that a couple of them get to turn the tables. This low-budget horror has developed a strong cult following. The enclosed booklet explains its curious history. This is actually the second version. On disc, image and sound are both much better than most of E.I.'s releases. Recommended to fans of the genre. —*MM*

Movie: 🦴🦴½ **DVD:** 🦴🦴½
EI Independent Cinema (Cat #so-5029-dvd, UPC #612385502996). Full frame. $19.98. Keepcase. *LANG:* English. *FEATURES:* 33 chapter links ▪ Deleted scenes ▪ 2 featurettes ▪ Short film, "H.P. Lovecraft's The Lost Child" ▪ Profile of director Pete Jacelone ▪ Trailers ▪ Booklet.
1998 90m/C J.J. North, Theresa Lynn; **D:** Pete Jacelone; **W:** Pete Jacelone, James L. Edwards; **C:** Timothy Healy.

Psychomania

The venerable George Sanders's final film is a nutty horror/comedy about a British motorcycle gang, *The Living Dead,* that learns how to return from the grave. Their leader persuades them to commit suicide and then to terrorize the countryside. Our first problem here is the costuming. Having the gang name printed in hot pink on their black leather jackets somehow sends the wrong message. And then the skull graphics they wear on their helmets make them look like cartoon dragonflies. Is that a fashion statement an undead outlaw biker gang really wants to make? The whole thing simply cries out for *MST3K* treatment. The DVD sound and image are about average for a low-budget flick of this age. —*MM* **AKA:** The Death Wheelers.

Movie: 🦴🦴 **DVD:** 🦴🦴
Image Entertainment (Cat #ID6173TVDVD, UPC #014381617320). Widescreen (1.66:1) letterboxed. Dolby Digital Mono. $24.99. Snapper. *LANG:* English; Spanish. *FEATURES:* 12 chapter links.
1973 (R) 89m/C *GB* George Sanders, Beryl Reid, Nicky Henson, Mary Laroche, Patrick Holt; **D:** Don Sharp; **W:** Arnaud d'Usseau; **C:** Ted Moore.

Pumpkinhead

When his young son is accidentally killed by thoughtless dirtbikers, Ed Harley (Henriksen) calls up a grotesque monster (Tom Woodruff Jr. in terrific makeup) for vengeance. But as soon as the conflicts are being engaged, first-time director Winston gives the story a serious twist, refusing to take the easy, expected path. In Henriksen's long career, this is one of his most complex roles and the whole film is one of the unrecognized greats. Unfortunately, you'll be hard-pressed to recognize that in this DVD, which is no better than VHS tape. Sound may be an improvement, but a widescreen version is called for. —*MM* **AKA:** Vengeance: The Demon.

Movie: 🦴🦴🦴 **DVD:** 🦴🦴
MGM Home Entertainment (Cat #10008 35, UPC #027616851512). Full frame. Dolby Digital Surround Stereo. $24.99. Keepcase. *LANG:* English. *SUB:* French; Spanish. *CAP:* English. *FEATURES:* 20 chapter links ▪ Trailer.
1988 (R) 89m/C Lance Henriksen, John DiAquino, Kerry Remsen, Matthew Hurley, Jeff East, Kimberly Ross, Cynthia Bain, Joel Hoffman, Florence Schauffler, George "Buck" Flower, Tom Woodruff Jr.; **D:** Stan Winston; **W:** Mark Patrick Carducci, Gary Gerani; **C:** Bojan Bazelli; **M:** Richard Stone.

Puppet Master

The first installment of Full Moon's most popular series is a slickly made, Stephen King–sort of story about a haunted hotel filled with psychics and murderous marionettes. The action begins well with a suspenseful opening sequence but fades steadily after that. The special effects are acceptable and the production values are high throughout, but the image is very grainy, plot is uninvolving, and the characters are flat. Even so, six more features have been produced over the years. Curiously, when this series began in the late '80s, producer Charles Band anticipated many of the extras that are now commonplace on DVDs and so disc does not offer that much more than the tapes. Neither image nor sound is much better, either. The menu is kind of cool, though. All of the films are available in a boxed *Puppet Master Collection.* —*MM*

Movie: 🦴🦴½ **DVD:** 🦴🦴
Full Moon Pictures (Cat #FUM-DV 8056, UPC #763843805668). Full frame. $16.99. Keepcase. *LANG:* English. *FEATURES:* 17 chapter links ▪ Filmographies ▪ Behind-the-scenes Videozone magazine ▪ Trailer.
1989 (R) 90m/C Paul LeMat, Jimmie F. Skaggs, Irene Miracle, Robyn Frates, Barbara Crampton, William Hickey, Matt Roe, Kathryn O'Reilly; **D:** David Schmoeller; **W:** Joseph G. Collodi; **C:** Sergio Salvati; **M:** Richard Band.

Puppet Master 2

The murderous puppets are back, this time in a hotel, where they're trying to resurrect their late creator. The relative clarity of DVD somehow intensifies the rough quality of the photography. Like the other entries, disc is not a great improvement over tape. —*MM*

Movie: 🦴🦴 **DVD:** 🦴🦴

Full Moon Pictures (Cat #FUM-DV 8057, UPC #763843805767). Full frame. $16.99. Keepcase. *LANG:* English. *FEATURES:* 21 chapter links • Behind-the-scenes Videozone magazine • Talent files • Trailers.
1990 (R) 90m/C Elizabeth MacLellan, Collin Bernsen, Greg Webb, Charlie Spradling, Nita Talbot, Steve Welles, Jeff Weston; *D:* David Allen; *W:* David Pabian; *C:* Thomas Denove; *M:* Richard Band.

Puppet Master 3: Toulon's Revenge

Prequel sets the puppets against the Nazis in pre-war Germany. The weapon-hungry Third Reich tries to wrest the secrets of artificial life from sorcerer Andre Toulon, who sics his creations on them. Toulon's the good guy here, one of the many contradictions in the series. Again, DVD equals but does not really surpass tape. —*MM*
Movie: 𝄞𝄞 *DVD:* 𝄞𝄞
Full Moon Pictures (Cat #FUM-DV 8058, UPC #763843805866). Full frame. $16.99. Keepcase. *LANG:* English. *FEATURES:* 18 chapter links • Behind-the-scenes Videozone magazine • Trailer • Talent files.
1990 (R) 86m/C Guy Rolfe, Ian Abercrombie, Sarah Douglas, Richard Lynch, Walter Gotell; *D:* David DeCoteau; *W:* C. Courtney Joyner; *C:* Adolfo Bartoli; *M:* Richard Band.

Puppet Master 4

Decapitron is added to the evil puppets line-up while they engage some other pint-sized creatures (these mostly created by some nice enough stop-motion effects) that derive their power from the same eternal force as the originals. Both image and sound are a slight improvement over the previous installments, though neither is that much better than VHS. —*MM*
Movie: 𝄞𝄞 *DVD:* 𝄞𝄞
Full Moon Pictures (Cat #FUM-DV 8059, UPC #763843805965). Full frame. $16.99. Keepcase. *LANG:* English. *FEATURES:* 18 chapter links • Behind-the-scenes Videozone magazine • Trailers • Talent files.
1993 (R) 80m/C Gordon Currie, Chandra West, Jason Adams, Teresa Hill, Guy Rolfe; *D:* Jeff Burr; *W:* Todd Henschell, Steven E. Carr, Jo Duffy, Douglas Aarniokoski, Keith Payson; *M:* Richard Band.

Puppet Master 5: The Latest Chapter

Originally, this one was subtitled "The Final Chapter," but since the puppet-based horrors continued to be profitable, "Final" became "Latest." The story has to do with other bad guys who mean to do harm to the nasty little puppets. The differences are superficial. It's more of the same on DVD or tape. —*MM*
Movie: 𝄞𝄞 *DVD:* 𝄞𝄞
Full Moon Pictures (Cat #FUM-DV 8060, UPC #763843806061). Full frame.

$16.99. Keepcase. *LANG:* English. *FEATURES:* 18 chapter links • Behind-the-scenes Videozone magazine • Trailers.
1994 81m/C Gordon Currie, Chandra West, Ian Ogilvy, Teresa Hill, Nicholas Guest, Willard Pugh, Diane McBain, Kaz Garas, Guy Rolfe; *D:* Jeff Burr; *W:* Douglas Aarniokoski, Jo Duffy, Todd Henschell, Keith Payson, Steven E. Karr; *C:* Adolfo Bartoli; *M:* Richard Band.

Puppet Master Collection

This boxed set brings together all seven of the *Puppet Master* films along with a disc of (count 'em!) 45 trailers for Full Moon releases. Contain your excitement. —*MM*
Movie: 𝄞𝄞 *DVD:* 𝄞𝄞
Full Moon Pictures (Cat #FUM-DV 8054, UPC #763843805460). Full frame. $99.98. Keepcase boxed set. *LANG:* English.
2000 m/C

The Puppetoon Movie

Compilation of George Pal's famous Puppetoon cartoons from the 1940s marks his stature as an animation pioneer and innovator. Hosted by Gumby, Pokey, Speedy Alka Seltzer, and Arnie the Dinosaur in newly directed scenes, the disc includes 12 shorts not available on previous versions of the film. The DVD delivers a decent video transfer though some of the shorts are in a worse state than others. On the whole, the picture features nice, vibrant colors and well-defined blacks. The audio is similar to the video transfer in that age is the one factor that hinders its performance. —*MJT*
Movie: 𝄞𝄞½ *DVD:* 𝄞𝄞𝄞
Image Entertainment (Cat #ID5865ALDVD, UPC #014381586527). Full frame. Dolby Digital Stereo. $29.99. Snapper. *LANG:* English. *FEATURES:* 24 chapter links • Interview with Puppetoon animator Bob Baker • Production photo gallery • Theatrical trailer • Archival video footage of George Pal • *The Fantasy Film Worlds of George Pal* trailer/photo gallery.
1987 (G) 80m/C *D:* Arnold Leibovit; *M:* Buddy (Norman Dale) Baker.

Pusher

Violent thriller was the debut of 24-year-old Refn. Frank (Bodnia) and his buddy Tonny (Mikkelsen) sell heroin in Copenhagen. Their supplier is Milo (Buric), a Serbian gangster to whom Frank owes money. Things get worse when Frank dumps his latest supply before being arrested. If he doesn't pay Milo, he's a dead man. Filmed entirely using handheld cameras, natural lighting, and real locations, the video is understandably not of the highest quality—accurately conveying a pseudo-documentary feel. The image is very grainy but color, sharpness, and black level are surprisingly good. The transfer itself is free from nicks, scratches, or other blemishes. The 5.1 mix is enveloping, but a bit harsh,

with dynamic effects and a pulsing soundtrack that spreads across all of the speakers. There isn't much in the way of deep bass but on the whole the sound mix is in keeping with the film's realistic intent and is quite good. —*MP/MM*
Movie: 𝄞𝄞 *DVD:* 𝄞𝄞
Anchor Bay (Cat #11315). Widescreen (1.66:1) anamorphic. Dolby Digital 5.1 Surround Stereo; Dolby Digital Surround Stereo. $29.98. Keepcase. *LANG:* Danish. *SUB:* English. *FEATURES:* Commentary • Featurette and TV spot • Trailer • Talent files.
1996 105m/C *DK* Kim Bodnia, Zlatko Buric, Mads Mikkelsen, Laura Drasbaek, Slavko Labovic, Lisbeth Rasmussen; *D:* Nicolas Winding Refn; *W:* Nicolas Winding Refn, Jens Dahl; *C:* Morten Soborg; *M:* Povl Kristian Mortensen.

Pygmalion

Oscar-winning film adaptation of Shaw's play about a cockney flower-girl who is transformed into a "lady" under the guidance of a stuffy phonetics professor. Shaw himself aided in writing the script in this superbly acted comedy that would be adapted into the musical *My Fair Lady*, first on Broadway in 1956 and for the screen in 1964. Though there are not any extras at all on this DVD, Criterion has done another masterful job of restoring and transferring this classic film. *Pygmalion* looks far better than it ever did on the earlier Embassy Home Video VHS or laserdisc editions, despite the fact that the DVD's sharper image contributes to making the celluloid flaws more visible. There is plenty of detail, deep rich blacks, bright whites, and very good contrast. As expected the sound is nothing spectacular but very crisp and fairly clean. —*JO*
Movie: 𝄞𝄞𝄞½ *DVD:* 𝄞𝄞𝄞
Criterion Collection (Cat #85, UPC #03742 9141822). Full frame. Dolby Digital Mono. $29.95. Keepcase. *LANG:* English. *SUB:* English. *FEATURES:* 16 chapter links.
1938 96m/B *GB* Leslie Howard, Wendy Hiller, Wilfred Lawson, Marie Lohr, Scott Sunderland, David Tree, Everley Gregg, Leueen McGrath, Jean Cadell, Eileen Beldon, Frank Atkinson, O.B. Clarence, Esme Percy, Violet Vanbrugh, Iris Hoey, Viola Tree, Irene Browne, Kate Cutler, Cathleen Nesbitt, Cecil Trouncer, Stephen Murray, Wally Patch, H.F. Maltby; *D:* Anthony Asquith, Leslie Howard; *W:* W.P. Lipscomb, Anatole de Grunwald, Cecil Lewis, Ian Dalrymple, George Bernard Shaw; *C:* Harry Stradling Sr. *AWARDS:* Oscars '38: Screenplay; Venice Film Fest. '38: Actor (Howard); *NOM:* Oscars '38: Actor (Howard), Actress (Hiller), Picture.

Python

Surprisingly, it took Hollywood four full years to re-hash the surprise hit, *Anaconda*. This time, though, the setting is suburbia, not the Amazon jungle. That's where a huge computer-generated snake is running amok. Robert Englund is the mad scientist who created it; Casper Van Dien is the special agent who must catch it. It's light material meant to be taken lightly. It's almost pointless to criticize the clarity of the DVD image because the effects—like those in *Anaconda*—are so obvious that they're not really meant to be "realistic" in any conventional sense. Sound is fine, too. —*MM*

Movie: 🎞🎞½ **DVD:** 🎞🎞🎞
20th Century Fox Home Entertainment (Cat #2001141, UPC #024543011415). Widescreen (1.85:1) anamorphic. Dolby Digital 5.1 Surround Stereo; Dolby Digital Surround. $29.98. Keepcase. *LANG:* English. *SUB:* English; Spanish. *FEATURES:* 20 chapter links • Outtakes • Trailers • Talent files • Commentary: Richard Clabaugh, Andrew Hoffman, Kevin Little.
2000 (R) 90m/C Robert Englund, Casper Van Dien, Jenny McCarthy, Wil Wheaton, Frayne Rosenoff; *D:* Richard Clabaugh; *W:* Chris Neal, Gary Hershberger, Paul J.M. Bogh; *C:* Patrick Rousseau; *M:* David J. Nelsen.

Q: The Movie

Low-budget teen comedy follows that favorite formula: the parents leave teenaged Cedric (Hooks) home alone. He decides to throw a barbecue to raise money. Throwaway little movie gains little in terms of image or sound on DVD. All the expected flaws make an appearance—washed-out color, heavy grain that leads to even heavier artifacts, extreme aliasing. But what do you expect from a film that was made for $13,000 in eight days? That's what director Bowles says on the commentary track, which is instructive for young filmmakers interested in the low/no-budget side of the business. —*MM*
Movie: 🎞🎞 **DVD:** 🎞🎞
Xenon Entertainment (Cat #XE XX-407 2DVD). Full frame. $14.95. Keepcase. *LANG:* English. *FEATURES:* 21 chapter links • Commentary: Barry Bowles and Brian Hooks.
1999 (R) 85m/C Brian Hooks, N.D. Brown; *D:* Barry Bowles; *W:* Barry Bowles; *C:* Marc Lyons; *M:* Horace Washington.

Quackser Fortune Has a Cousin in the Bronx

When horse-drawn carts are replaced by delivery trucks, an Irish fertilizer salesman (Wilder) realizes that his livelihood is disappearing. At the same time, though, he meets an exchange student (Kidder) from the U.S. who finds herself attracted to this unlearned but not unknowing man. It's an original, offbeat love story that's nicely cast. The pale image is on a par with others of its time. DVD was made from an original with light surface damage and a faint hiss on the soundtrack. —*MM* *AKA:* Fun Loving.
Movie: 🎞🎞🎞 **DVD:** 🎞🎞
VCI Home Video (Cat #8216). Widescreen (1.66:1) letterboxed. Dolby Digital Mono. $24.99. Keepcase. *LANG:* English. *FEATURES:* Cast and crew thumbnail bios • Trailer • 23 chapter links.

1970 (R) 88m/C *IR* Gene Wilder, Margot Kidder, Eileen Colgan, May Ollis, Seamus Ford, Danny Cummins, Liz Davis; *D:* Waris Hussein; *W:* Gabriel Walsh; *C:* Gilbert Taylor; *M:* Michael Dress.

The Quarry

John Lynch plays "The Man" in this slow-paced character study of small-town life in South Africa, and the cost of redemption. A fugitive, "The Man," kills a gay Baptist pastor and assumes his position as the new pastor in a small town. When he arrives at the new church, "The Man" is well received by the townsfolk and surprises himself with how well he performs his duties. Local law enforcement arrests two thieves for the murder he committed. "The Man" then struggles with his guilt and the comfort of his new ill-gotten position. This is one of First Run Features' better transfers to DVD from film. The only programming flaw: this movie is long enough that it should have more than nine chapter selections in the menu. English subtitles appear when characters speak another language. —*JAS*
Movie: 🎞🎞🎞 **DVD:** 🎞🎞🎞
First Run Features (Cat #FRF 909440D, UPC #720229909440). Widescreen letterboxed. Dolby. $29.95. Keepcase. *LANG:* English. *CAP:* English. *FEATURES:* 9 chapter links.
1998 112m/C *SA* John Lynch, Serge-Henri Valcke, Jonny Phillips, Oscar Petersen, Jody Abrahams, Sylvia Esau; *D:* Marion Hansel; *W:* Marion Hansel; *C:* Bernard Lutic; *M:* Takashi Kako.

Quatermass 2

Professor Quatermass is once again faced with an alien threat in this, the second of the series of films inspired by the British radio series and produced by Hammer Studios. In the follow up to *The Quatermass Experiment,* the professor discovers a mysterious facility that has a more than coincidental likeness to his moon base design. Upon further investigation, things get strange and it soon seems that all of England and possibly the world is threatened by alien mind control and environmental disaster as the unknown enemy makes the Earth fit for invasion. Highlights include a satirical turn on the villagers storming the castle and a giant slimy, spinach-like creature to boo at towards the end. This is another fantastic transfer in Anchor Bay's Hammer Collection series. The 1957 black-and-white film is a little washed-out, but there are no dust speckles or scratches and the mono sound has been remastered for the better. —*CA* *AKA:* Enemy from Space.
Movie: 🎞🎞½ **DVD:** 🎞🎞🎞
Anchor Bay (Cat #DV110077, UPC #013131 1107791). Widescreen (1.37:1) letterboxed. Mono. $29.98. Keepcase. *LANG:* English. *FEATURES:* Commentary: director Val Guest, writer Nigel Kneale • Photo gallery • Exclusive *World of Hammer* episode.
1957 84m/B *GB* Brian Donlevy, John Longden, Sidney James, Bryan Forbes,

William Franklyn, Vera Day, John Van Eyssen, Michael Ripper, Michael Balfour; *D:* Val Guest; *W:* Val Guest, Nigel Kneale; *C:* Gerald Gibbs; *M:* James Bernard.

Queens of Comedy

This "sort of" companion piece to Spike Lee's *Original Kings of Comedy* is a concert recorded at the Orpheum Theatre in Memphis starring four black stand-up comediennes—Miss Laura Hayes, Adel Givens, Sommore, and Mo'Nique. Like their male counterparts, they're rude, sexy, raunchy, racist, and funny. The film isn't as elaborate as Lee's. Both image and sound are very good, accurate re-creations of a brightly lit stage show. —*MM*
Movie: 🎞🎞½ **DVD:** 🎞🎞½
Pioneer Entertainment (Cat #86048, UPC #097368604841). Full frame. Dolby Digital 5.1 Surround Stereo; Dolby Digital Surround Stereo. $29.99. Keepcase. *LANG:* English. *SUB:* English. *FEATURES:* 11 links • Bonus scenes • Soundtrack spot.
2001 (R) 79m/C Adele Givens, Mo'Nique, Miss Laura Hayes, Sommore; *D:* Steve Purcell.

Quicksand

Mechanic Dan Brady (Rooney) takes $20 from his boss's cash register, intending to return it. But he meets the right bad girl (Cagney), and all the wrong things happen. The result is a compact, effective little noir that looks great. The image is nearly perfect but why was the sound recorded so softly? You've got to crank up the volume to understand the dialogue. Don't miss the dishy background information. —*MM*
Movie: 🎞🎞🎞 **DVD:** 🎞🎞🎞
Troma Team Video (Cat #AED-2046, UPC #785604204626). Full frame. Dolby Digital Mono. $24.99. Keepcase. *LANG:* English. *FEATURES:* 12 chapter links • Background information • Credits.
1950 79m/B Mickey Rooney, Peter Lorre, Jeanne Cagney; *D:* Irving Pichel; *W:* Robert Smith; *C:* Lionel Linden; *M:* Louis Gruenberg.

Quidam

Cirque du Soleil's patented combination of theatre, circus, and performance art comes up with another winner. This one, recorded in Amsterdam, takes part of its inspiration from the paintings of Rene Magritte. The acts are spectacular. DVD image ranges between very good and excellent, despite the fact that this is a filmed performance with an audience. Music is very strong, too. —*MM*
Movie: 🎞🎞🎞½ **DVD:** 🎞🎞🎞½
Columbia Tristar Home Video (Cat #04225, UPC #043396042254). Widescreen (1.77:1) letterboxed. Dolby Digital 5.1 Surround Stereo; Dolby Digital Surround. $27.95. Keepcase. *LANG:* French. *SUB:* English; French; Spanish; Portuguese; Chinese; Korean; Thai. *FEATURES:* 12 chapter links.
1999 90m/C *D:* Franco Dragone; *M:* Benoit Jutras.

Quiet Days in Hollywood

Written and directed by European Josef Rusnak (*The Thirteenth Floor*), this film is all sex and no passion. A series of vignettes starts with 17-year-old hooker Lolita (Swank) and links one story to another until we end up back with her on Hollywood Boulevard. While the Lolita sections could have been made into a passable *Pretty Woman* rip-off, the addition of stories to make the links run smoothly leads to a coldly calculated storyline that leaves little care for the characters. The film is populated mostly with what seems to be acting school minions. Hillary Swank and Chad Lowe are the only bright spots. Good sound and average picture. —*CA*
AKA: The Way We Are.
Movie: 🎬½ *DVD:* 🎬🎬
Image Entertainment (Cat #OVED9677 DVD, UPC #014381967722). Full frame. Dolby Digital 5.1 Surround. $24.99. Snapper. *LANG:* English. *FEATURES:* 8 chapter links.
1997 (R) 95m/C Peter Dobson, Chad Lowe, Steven Mailer, Darryl (Chill) Mitchell, Bill Cusack, Meta Golding, Hillary Swank, Natasha Gregson Wagner; **D:** Josef Rusnak; **W:** Josef Rusnak; **C:** Dietrich Lohmann; **M:** Harold Kloser.

Quills

A fabulously told morality tale about the double-edged blade of free speech. Rush plays de Sade as pervert with an almost childish belief that the truth will set you free coupled with a devilish ability to force people to look deeply into themselves. Winslet is Madeleine, the maid at Charenton, where the Marquis is being kept. She smuggles out his manuscripts because she believes that the immorality he sets to paper can keep people from acting out. This film came out the same year as the bloated *Gladiator* and it is his role as the asylum's resident priest, Abbe Coulmier, which should have garnered Joaquin Phoenix his Oscar nomination. As the Abbe, Phoenix is a tightly wrapped ball of conflict. He truly likes the Marquis and is frustrated that he can't make him understand the need to behave, and he truly loves Madeleine but is bound by his vows to God. The Abbe's life is further complicated when the King sends Dr. Royer-Collard (Caine) to Charenton after another of the Marquis's manuscripts gets out of the asylum. Royer-Collard is a hypocrite and a sadist of the most above-board variety and a dangerous man to have in charge. The beliefs of the characters barrel along at top speed toward each other and eventually the toll must be paid. De Sade of all people is the one who learns the hardest lesson about the power of words and the responsibility of the truth. Excellently acted, beautifully scripted and luscious to look at, *Quills* is a near-perfect film. The extras on the disc are all good, most notably the screenwriter commentary with Wright, who also wrote the stage play. His

discussion of how he changed the script for film is interesting. The color on the disc is fabulous, and all the blacks take on the feel of velvet. The sound is also very good. —*CA*
Movie: 🎬🎬🎬½ *DVD:* 🎬🎬🎬½
20th Century Fox Home Entertainment (Cat #2001662, UPC #024543016625). Widescreen (1.85:1) anamorphic. Dolby Digital Surround; Dolby Digital 5.1 Surround. $29.98. Keepcase. *LANG:* English; French. *SUB:* English; Spanish. *CAP:* English. *FEATURES:* "Marquis on the Marquee" featurette • "Creating Charenton" featurette • "Dressing the Part" featurette • Theatrical and TV trailers • Commentary: screenwriter.
2000 (R) 123m/C Geoffrey Rush, Kate Winslet, Joaquin Rafael (Leaf) Phoenix, Michael Caine; **D:** Philip Kaufman; **W:** Doug Wright; **C:** Rogier Stoffers; **M:** Stephen Warbeck. *AWARDS:* Natl. Bd. of Review '00: Film, Support. Actor (Phoenix); *NOM:* Oscars '00: Actor (Rush), Art Dir./Set Dec., Costume Des.; Screen Actors Guild '00: Actor (Rush), Support. Actress (Winslet).

Rabid

This combination of medical, sexual, and mechanical horrors provides an early look at some of the themes director David Cronenberg would explore more fully in other films. In a triumph of casting, adult star Marilyn Chambers is Rose, a motorcycle accident victim whose skin grafts mutate, turning her into a vampiric carrier of a new strain of rabies. Image appears to be an accurate reproduction of the original, which contains visible specks of dust on a lens or filter in some exteriors. Interiors are much clearer. A commentary track by the director is called for. —*MM* **AKA:** Rage.
Movie: 🎬🎬🎬 *DVD:* 🎬🎬
New Concorde (Cat #NH20173D, UPC #736991417397). Full frame. $19.98. Keepcase. *LANG:* English. *FEATURES:* 24 chapter links • Thumbnail bios • Trailers.
1977 (R) 90m/C *CA* Marilyn Chambers, Frank Moore, Joe Silver, Howard Ryshpan, Patricia Gage, Susan Roman, Roger Periard, Victor Desy; **D:** David Cronenberg; **W:** David Cronenberg; **C:** Rene Verzier.

Race Against Time

Made-for-TV sf posits a near future (2018) where body parts may be sold for extra cash. James Gabriel (Roberts) signs on to pay for his son's desperately needed operation. But the evil corporation behind the scheme is up to even more nefarious schemes. For those who can forget a Monty Python skit based on the same premise, it's pretty standard stuff and video veteran Roberts is better than the material demands. The clarity of DVD makes the shortcomings of the visual effects more pronounced. Otherwise, image is good to very good; Surround sound is very good. —*MM*
Movie: 🎬🎬 *DVD:* 🎬🎬½

Warner Home Video, Inc. (Cat #T8347, UPC #053939834727). Widescreen anamorphic. Dolby Digital Surround Stereo. $19.98. Snapper. *LANG:* English. *SUB:* English; French. *FEATURES:* 26 chapter links • Talent files • 2 behind-the-scenes featurettes • Trailer.
2000 90m/C Eric Roberts, Cary Elwes, Sarah Wynter, Chris Sarandon; **D:** Geoff Murphy.

Race to Freedom: The Story of the Underground Railroad

In 1850, four fugitive slaves struggle to get from North Carolina to the safety of Canada through a network of safe-houses and people willing to risk smuggling them to asylum. The made-for-cable production is identical to VHS tape in every important way. —*MM*
Movie: 🎬🎬½ *DVD:* 🎬🎬
Xenon Entertainment (Cat #XE XX-1522 DVD, UPC #000799152225). Full frame. $19.98. Keepcase. *LANG:* English. *FEATURES:* Trailers • 18 chapter links.
1994 90m/C *CA* Courtney B. Vance, Janet Bailey, Glynn Turman, Tim Reid, Michael Riley, Dawnn Lewis, Ron White, Alfre Woodard; **D:** Don McBrearty; **W:** Nancy Trite Botkin, Diana Braithwaite; **M:** Christopher Dedrick.

Railrodder

Please see review for *Buster Keaton Rides Again / The Railrodder*.
Movie: 🎬🎬🎬
1965 25m/C Buster Keaton; **D:** Gerald Potterton.

Rain

Milestone does a fine job adapting Somerset Maugham's tale of a puritanical minister's attempt to reclaim a "fallen woman" (Crawford) on the Pacific island of Pago Pago. The stars are excellent and, for the most part, the DVD is too. It exhibits a few speckles and registration problems up front, but conventional interiors are crisp and properly detailed. —*MM*
Movie: 🎬🎬🎬 *DVD:* 🎬🎬🎬
Image Entertainment (Cat #ID9683PQDVD, UPC #014381968323). Full frame. Dolby Digital Mono. $24.99. Snapper. *LANG:* English. *FEATURES:* 12 chapter links.
1932 92m/B Joan Crawford, Walter Huston, William Gargan, Guy Kibbee, Beulah Bondi, Walter Catlett; **D:** Lewis Milestone; **W:** Maxwell Anderson; **C:** Oliver Marsh; **M:** Alfred Newman.

A Raisin in the Sun

A black family tries to make a better life for themselves in an all-white Chicago neighborhood. The characters are played realistically and make for a moving story. Each person struggles with doing what he or she must while maintaining dignity and sense of self. The DVD transfer is one of the best made to date of a black-and-white feature—clear and clean, almost entirely without speckles or scratches. Audio frequency response is noticeably limited, though, especially in the lower ends, giving the entire track a rather harsh-sounding quality. —GH/MM

Movie: ♫♫♫♫ **DVD:** ♫♫♫½
Columbia Tristar Home Video (Cat #919). Widescreen (1.85:1) anamorphic; full frame. Dolby Digital Mono. $24.95. Keepcase. *LANG:* English. *SUB:* English; Spanish; Portuguese; Chinese; Korean; Thai. *FEATURES:* Production notes ⮚ Trailer.
1961 128m/B Diana Sands, John Fiedler, Ivan Dixon, Louis Gossett Jr., Sidney Poitier, Claudia McNeil, Ruby Dee; **D:** Daniel Petrie; **W:** Lorraine Hansberry; **C:** Charles Lawton Jr.; **M:** Laurence Rosenthal. *AWARDS:* Natl. Bd. of Review '61: Support. Actress (Dee).

Raising the Mammoth

Breathtaking Discovery Channel documentary follows a French expedition discovering and excavating the remains of a mammoth from the icy grip of the Arctic Circle. Shot on video, the production has a surprisingly natural look and is mostly free of video artifacts. No noise distracts from the experience and the colors in the film are well balanced and always very well saturated. Blacks are good and solid and highlights never bleed. Color delineation is perfect and since the presentation is free of any compression artifacts, the film looks noticeably better on this DVD than it did during its TV broadcast. —GH/MM

Movie: ♫♫♫ **DVD:** ♫♫♫
Artisan Entertainment (Cat #10599). Full frame. Dolby Digital Stereo. $19.98. Keepcase. *LANG:* English. *FEATURES:* Fact file ⮚ Scientist bios ⮚ Text interview with the French Explorer Bernard Buigues ⮚ Timeline.
2000 120m/C *Nar:* Jeff Bridges.

Rambling Rose [2 SE]

Rose (Dern) is a beautiful, sexually active girl with a hard past and a soft heart, all traits that would be O.K. in modern times but that were less than desirable in a young woman in the 1930s. She comes to care for the children of "Mother" (Ladd) and "Daddy" (Duvall). Daddy has issues with Rose's sexuality, which borders on nymphomania, but Mother senses the good in Rose while still seeing the bad. She loves and nurtures her despite Rose's constant breaking of the house rules and even though she has a crush on Daddy. However, it is Buddy (Haas), the adolescent son of the family, who is most touched by the girl. This is partially due to Buddy's raging hormones but there is also an affinity between Buddy, who is smarter than his peers, and Rose, who is also separated from her peers by difference. Bittersweet to the end, none of the characters manage to understand each other com-

pletely, and decide to make do with finding the love and compassion necessary to accept one another. Directed by Martha Coolidge *(Valley Girl, Real Genius),* the script is amazing, deftly handling issues about the differences in acceptability of male and female sexuality without being overbearing. Both Dern and Ladd earned well-deserved Oscar nominations for their roles in the film. The color on the disc is good but the clarity is average (a little fuzzy around the images) and the sound is good. —CA

Movie: ♫♫ **DVD:** ♫♫½
Pioneer Entertainment (Cat #DVD6900WS, UPC #013023014398). Widescreen (1.85:1) letterbox. Dolby Digital Stereo. $29.98. Keepcase. *LANG:* English. *FEATURES:* 32 chapter links ⮚ Commentary: director ⮚ Alternate ending ⮚ Cast and crew bios ⮚ Production notes.
1991 (R) 115m/C Laura Dern, Diane Ladd, Robert Duvall, Lukas Haas, John Heard, Kevin Conway, Robert John Burke, Lisa Jakub, Evan Lockwood; **D:** Martha Coolidge; **W:** Calder Willingham; **C:** Johnny E. Jensen; **M:** Elmer Bernstein. *AWARDS:* Ind. Spirit '92: Director (Coolidge), Film, Support. Actress (Ladd); *NOM:* Oscars '91: Actress (Dern), Support. Actress (Ladd).

Rancho Deluxe

Offbeat western spoof stars Bridges and Waterston as two carefree cowpokes and features music by Buffet, who also appears. While the mono track reproduces dialogue and sound effects quite well, the video transfer falls a bit short. The picture is quite grainy throughout and blacks tend to bleed. In fact, some darker-lit scenes are overrun by shadows. Overall, however, far worse discs have been made for far better movies. —MJT

Movie: ♫♫♫ **DVD:** ♫♫½
MGM Home Entertainment (Cat #100127 5, UPC #027616855558). Widescreen (1.85:1) anamorphic; full frame. Dolby Digital Mono. $19.98. Keepcase. *LANG:* English; French. *SUB:* French; Spanish. *FEATURES:* 28 chapter links ⮚ Theatrical trailer.
1975 93m/C Jeff Bridges, Sam Waterston, Elizabeth Ashley, Charlene Dallas, Clifton James, Slim Pickens, Harry Dean Stanton, Richard Bright, Jimmy Buffett; **D:** Frank Perry; **W:** Thomas McGuane; **C:** William A. Fraker; **M:** Jimmy Buffett.

Randy Rides Alone

Please see review for *Lawless Frontier / Randy Rides Alone.*
Movie: ♫♫
1934 53m/B John Wayne, Alberta Vaughn, George "Gabby" Hayes; **D:** Harry Fraser; **W:** Lindsley Parsons.

Rangers

This low-budget video premiere is pretty much the standard bang-bang boom-boom American commandos vs. Arab terrorists, but the commentary track by director Jim

Wynorski (working under the name Jay Andrews) and Matt McCoy is a lot of fun. They talk about how Wynorksi liberally borrowed footage from his other films to economize and how Corbin Bernsen, who gets star billing, made such a brief appearance at the filming that he told the valet not to turn off his car. Beyond that, image and sound are only a scant improvement over tape. —MM

Movie: ♫♫ **DVD:** ♫♫½
20th Century Fox Home Entertainment (Cat #2001740, UPC #024543017400). Widescreen anamorphic. Dolby Digital 5.1 Surround Stereo. $24.99. Keepcase. *LANG:* English. *SUB:* English; Spanish. *FEATURES:* Commentary: Wynorski, McCoy ⮚ Talent files ⮚ Trailer ⮚ 20 chapter links.
2000 (R) 100m/C Matt McCoy, Glenn Plummer, Corbin Bernsen, Dartanyan Edmonds, Rene Rivera, **D:** Jim Wynorski; **W:** Steve Latshaw; **C:** Ken Blakey; **M:** David Wurst, Eric Wurst.

Ratas, Ratones, Rateros

Quentin Tarantino and all the other American directors who try to tell stories of petty criminals and their world would kill to achieve the authenticity that director Sebastian Cordero delivers in almost every frame of this quickly paced realistic thriller. Angel (Valencia) and Salvador (Bustos) involve themselves in various sordid activities to get out of their lives of crushing poverty in Ecuador. The film is exceptionally well made. Overall, the image quality is good, but to be any more polished would have defeated the film's gritty purpose. Comparisons to the original *El Mariachi* are not out of order. The title translates "rodents." —MM *AKA:* Rodents.

Movie: ♫♫♫ **DVD:** ♫♫½
Vanguard International Cinema, Inc. (UPC #658769011630). Widescreen (1.66:1) letterboxed. $29.95. Keepcase. *LANG:* Spanish. *SUB:* English. *FEATURES:* Trailer ⮚ 12 chapter links.
1999 107m/C Marco Bustos, Carlos Valencia, Simon Brauer, Cristina Davila; **D:** Sebastian Cordero; **W:** Sebastian Cordero; **C:** Matthew Jensen; **M:** Sergio Sacoto-Arias.

Rated X

Brothers Emilio Estevez (who also directed) and Charlie Sheen play Jim and Artie Mitchell, the original San Francisco porntrepreneurs who made millions from *Behind the Green Door* and other adult films. This is hardly the *Boogie Nights* version of the business. It's more forthright and violent. As you might expect, the brothers joke a lot on their commentary track, but, personally, I doubt Estevez's protestations that he was surprised that the MPAA refused to give his cut of the film an "R" rating. Much of the reason is in chapter three. It's exactly the sort of sexual scene that the ratings board always objects to, and everyone in the business knows it. Much of the commentary is devoted to the corners that have to be cut to work within a tight budget. (The film is also available in an "R"-rated version.) —MM

Movie: 🎵🎵½ **DVD:** 🎵🎵🎵
Showtime Networks, Inc. (Cat #SHO1031, UPC #758445103210). Full frame. Dolby Digital Surround Stereo. $24.98. Keepcase. *LANG:* English. *FEATURES:* Interviews ☞ Commentary: Estevez, Sheen ☞ Still gallery ☞ Filmographies ☞ 24 chapter links.
2000 (R) 114m/C Emilio Estevez, Charlie Sheen, Megan Ward, Danielle Brett, Rafer Weigel, Terry O'Quinn, Nikki DeBoer, Peter Bogdanovich, Tracy Hutson; **D:** Emilio Estevez; **W:** Norman Snider, Anne Meredith, David Hollander; **C:** Paul Sarossy; **M:** Tyler Bates.

Ready to Rumble
Sanitation workers and best buds Gordie (Arquette) and Sean (Caan) decide to mastermind the comeback of their favorite wrestler, Jimmy "the King" King (Platt). The reason he needs a comeback is that promoter Titus Sinclair (Pantoliano) has decided that he's outlasted his usefulness. Arquette and wrestling are annoying enough individually, but put 'em together and it's almost too painful to watch. The two buddies make Bill and Ted look like Rhodes scholars, and it's not like there's any point to further parodying the "sport" of wrestling. The DVD's vivid colors enhance the comic-book feel of the film and the power-packed soundtrack delivers the assorted punches, crunches, and body slams with so much in-your-face energy that it almost overcomes the film's weaknesses—almost. The commentary to a movie like this should have been naturally over-the-top, but even when it approaches that level, the delivery seems a bit strained. —JO

Movie: 🎵🎵 **DVD:** 🎵🎵🎵½
Warner Home Video, Inc. (Cat #18621, UPC #085391862123). Widescreen letterboxed. Dolby Digital 5.1. $19.98. Snapper. *LANG:* English; French. *SUB:* English; French. *CAP:* English. *FEATURES:* 35 chapter links ☞ Theatrical trailer ☞ Talent files ☞ Commentary: David Arquette, Scott Caan, Ahmet Zappa ☞ Behind-the-scenes footage ☞ Interview gallery ☞ Dual-layered RSDL.
2000 (PG-13) 100m/C David Arquette, Scott Caan, Oliver Platt, Rose McGowan, Joe Pantoliano, Martin Landau, Richard Lineback, Chris Owen, Kathleen Freeman, Lewis Arquette, Diamond Dallas Page; **D:** Brian Robbins; **W:** Steven Brill; **C:** Clark Mathis; **M:** George S. Clinton.

The Real Blonde
Entertaining ensemble piece daringly exposes the business side of show business through a disillusioned actor, his beleaguered girlfriend, and Bob (Caulfield), a successful soap star searching for a peroxide-free blonde in New York. The main focus is on feuding couple Joe and Mary (Modine and Keener), but that angle

is undercut by the industry mania that surrounds them. Intelligent writing and caustic wit provide a few memorable scenes, such as the "Il Piano" debate in a crowded restaurant over a thinly veiled "acclaimed independent film" and Bob's resolution to his blonde quest. Modine also revs things up in an emotional improv. Thomas stands out from the crowd as a pretentious fashion photographer. Befitting the glitzy show-biz/ad-biz world, the image is exceptionally sharp. Sound is good, not great. —MM

Movie: 🎵🎵½ **DVD:** 🎵🎵🎵
Paramount Home Video (Cat #334947, UPC #097363349471). Widescreen letterboxed. Dolby Digital 5.1 Surround Stereo. $29.99. Keepcase. *LANG:* English; French. *CAP:* English. *FEATURES:* Trailer ☞ 29 chapter links.
1997 (R) 105m/C Matthew Modine, Catherine Keener, Daryl Hannah, Maxwell Caulfield, Elizabeth Berkley, Marlo Thomas, Buck Henry, Bridgette Wilson, Christopher Lloyd, Kathleen Turner, Denis Leary, Steve Buscemi; **D:** Tom DiCillo; **W:** Tom DiCillo; **C:** Frank Prinzi; **M:** Jim Farmer.

Real Life
This is Albert Brooks's directorial debut and was produced by punk director Penelope Spheeris (*Wayne's World*). Inspired by the documentary on the Loud family, Brooks presents a story about a filmmaker intent on making a film about "real life." In a montage worthy of Woody Allen, Brooks uses the most modern-day psychobabble tests (for 1978) to choose the perfect family. When push comes to shove and two families vie for the coveted slot, he picks the one that lives in the warmer climate. From the beginning, everything the crew does influences the family. While Mrs. Yeager (McCain) is perfectly willing to talk about her cramps at the dinner table for the film crew, Mr. Yeager (Grodin) is intent on presenting his family as perfect. The documentary begins to go downhill when Mrs. Yeager gets a crush on Brooks. The project hits full downward spiral when the black psychiatrist with whom Brooks has been arguing abandons ship and begins a series of tabloid articles accusing mind control. The ending goes a little over the top, as do most Brooks films, only because the storyline is so bizarre that there is little else he can do but go wild. The sound is mono and the picture is average, but this is a script-driven film and the average sound and picture don't really do any harm. —CA

Movie: 🎵🎵½ **DVD:** 🎵🎵
Paramount Home Video (Cat #01287, UPC #097360128741). Widescreen anamorphic. Dolby Digital Mono. $29.99. Keepcase. *LANG:* English. *CAP:* English. *FEATURES:* 15 chapter links.
1979 (R) 99m/C Charles Grodin, Frances Lee McCain, Albert Brooks; **D:** Albert Brooks; **W:** Monica Johnson, Harry Shearer, Albert Brooks; **C:** Eric Saarinen; **M:** Mort Lindsey.

Rear Window
Hitchcock's masterpiece of voyeurism has never been his most polished in visual terms. Given the technological limitations of the time, it may have been the best possible, but it still has a grainy quality that cannot be erased by the pioneering restoration work by Robert A. Harris and James Katz. The story concerns a newspaper photographer (Stewart) with a broken leg whose world is confined to the courtyard he can see from his apartment window, and the limited views he has of the other apartments that face onto it. He becomes convinced that one neighbor (Burr) has killed his wife. He persuades his socialite girlfriend (Kelly) and lippy nurse (Ritter) to help him prove it. DVD is an accurate re-creation of the restored version that played in theatres in the 1980s. Actually it looks a little sharper to me. Sound is certainly stronger. —MM

Movie: 🎵🎵🎵🎵 **DVD:** 🎵🎵🎵🎵½
Universal Studios Home Video (Cat #203 95, UPC #025192039522). Widescreen (1.66:1) anamorphic. Dolby Digital Mono. $29.99. Keepcase. *LANG:* English; French. *SUB:* Spanish. *CAP:* English. *FEATURES:* "Making of and restoration of" featurette ☞ Conversation with screenwriter John Michael Hayes ☞ 2 trailers ☞ Production notes ☞ Talent files ☞ DVD-ROM features.
1954 112m/C James Stewart, Grace Kelly, Thelma Ritter, Wendell Corey, Raymond Burr, Judith Evelyn; **D:** Alfred Hitchcock; **W:** John Michael Hayes; **C:** Robert Burks; **M:** Franz Waxman. *AWARDS:* AFI '98: Top 100, Natl. Film Reg. '97; *NOM:* Oscars '54: Color Cinematog., Director (Hitchcock), Screenplay, Sound.

Reboot: Season III
Computer-generated animated series is set inside a computer game and so it looks like a computer game. For what it is, the image is exceptionally bright and free of digital errors. I am not a fan of this kind of animation, but I must admit that this comes close to the level of clarity found in *Toy Story 2*. Of course, this one contains all of the explosions and ray guns that the audience expects. Contents: "To Mend and Defend," "Between a Raccoon and a Hard Place," "Firewall," "Game Over." —MM

Movie: 🎵🎵🎵 **DVD:** 🎵🎵🎵
A.D.V. Films (Cat #DVDRB/001, UPC #702727013324). Full frame. Dolby Digital Stereo. $24.99. Keepcase. *LANG:* English. *FEATURES:* Season I and II overview ☞ Character and animation background ☞ Trailers ☞ 20 chapter links.
1997 90m/C W: Marv Wolfman.

The Red Dwarf
Melodramatic fantasy about love-starved dwarf Lucien Lhotte (Thual) is Felliniesque in its sentimentality, cast, setting, and affinity for the grotesque. He's a law clerk who is summoned by aging opera singer Countess Paola Bendoni (Ekberg) to help with her divorce and then becomes her improbable lover. He is also innocently

loved by Isis (Gauzy), a circus acrobat. The black-and-white image picks up some artifacts and distortion in quick pans during the darkest moments. Aliasing can appear then, too. Subtitles are burned in. —*MM*

Movie: 🎦🎦 **DVD:** 🎦🎦½
Columbia Tristar Home Video (Cat #4731). Widescreen (1.77:1) letterboxed. Dolby Digital Surround. $27.95. Keepcase. *LANG:* French. *SUB:* English. *FEATURES:* Trailers ➥ 28 chapter links.
1999 (R) 101m/B *FR* Anita Ekberg, Jean-Yves Thual, Dyna Gauzy, Arno Chevrier; *D:* Yvan Le Moine; *W:* Yvan Le Moine; *C:* Danny Elsen; *M:* Alexei Shelegin, Daniel Brandt.

Red Letters

Professor Peter Burke's (Coyote) penchant for dalliance with his students has already gotten him fired from one job. In a new town with a fresh start, he stumbles across erotic letters from Lydia (Kinski), who's been convicted of murder. Much of the plot is predictable in this thriller, but, as the cast suggests, it's a solid cut above average. Acting is very good and director Battersby gives the soft blue-gray image a luxurious look, heightening its symbolic use of red. Sound is fine, too. —*MM*

Movie: 🎦🎦½ **DVD:** 🎦🎦½
Pioneer Entertainment (Cat #86031, UPC #097368603141). Widescreen anamorphic. Dolby Digital 5.1 Surround Stereo; Dolby Digital Surround Stereo. $29.99. Keepcase. *LANG:* English. *SUB:* Spanish. *CAP:* English. *FEATURES:* 16 chapter links ➥ Trailer ➥ Talent files ➥ Stills gallery ➥ Commentary: Battersby, Hughes, Fierberg.
2000 (R) 102m/C Peter Coyote, Nastassia Kinski, Fairuza Balk, Jeremy Piven, Ernie Hudson, Udo Kier; *D:* Bradley Battersby; *W:* Bradley Battersby, Tom Hughes; *C:* Steven Fierberg.

Red Planet

Twenty first–century Earth is dying. Starved of food and water, mankind has to look in space for new supply sources and a trip to Mars is initiated. The mission goes awry when the ship's robot malfunctions and attacks the crew. Then the survivors find that the red planet is not uninhabited. The print is without any flaws or blemishes, creating a perfectly stable and clean presentation. The image reveals an incredible amount of detail, which brings out the best of the movie's production design and its cinematography. Colors are incredibly rich, yet never oversaturated, and with its deep blacks, the transfer renders an image that is very dimensional with plenty of visual depth. No compression artifacts are evident anywhere in the transfer. 5.1 Surround is equally impressive. —*GH*

Movie: 🎦🎦 **DVD:** 🎦🎦🎦
Warner Home Video, Inc. (Cat #18954, UPC #085391895428). Widescreen (2.35:1) anamorphic. Dolby Digital 5.1 Surround Stereo. $19.99. Snapper. *LANG:* English; French. *SUB:* English; French. *FEATURES:* 8 deleted scenes ➥ Talent files.

2000 (PG-13) 110m/C Val Kilmer, Tom Sizemore, Carrie-Anne Moss, Benjamin Bratt, Simon Baker, Terence Stamp; *D:* Antony Hoffman; *W:* Jonathan Lemkin, Chuck Pfarrer.

Red Scorpion

Soviet Lt. Nikolai (Lundgren) travels to Africa where he is to assassinate the leader of a rebel group. Will he succeed or will he switch sides? Poor acting and directing all around make this a strictly run-of-the-mill video premiere action flick. Disc is no improvement in either image or sound. Extras are minimal. —*MM*

Movie: 🎦 **DVD:** 🎦🎦
Simitar Entertainment (Cat #7388). Full frame. Dolby Digital 5.1 Surround Stereo. $19.98. Keepcase. *LANG:* English. *FEATURES:* Dolph Lundgren filmography ➥ Production facts ➥ 8 chapter links.
1989 (R) 102m/C Dolph Lundgren, M. Emmet Walsh, Al White, T.P. McKenna, Carmen Argenziano, Brion James, Regopstann; *D:* Joseph Zito; *W:* Arne Olsen, Jack Abramoff, Robert Abramoff; *C:* Joao Fernandes; *M:* Jay Chattaway.

Red Shoe Diaries: Four on the Floor

The late-night cable series continues on DVD with three more stories concerning a psychiatrist and her patient, two couples stranded on a rainy night, and the meeting of a rap star and a dancer. The soft-focus eroticism gains little on disc beyond the extras. Contents: "The Psychiatrist," "Four on the Floor," "Emily's Dance." —*MM*

Movie: 🎦🎦 **DVD:** 🎦🎦½
Showtime Networks, Inc. (Cat #SHO5007, UPC #758445500721). Full frame. Stereo. $24.98. Keepcase. *LANG:* English; Spanish. *FEATURES:* Photo gallery ➥ Featurette ➥ Diary entries ➥ Filmographies ➥ Credits ➥ Weblinks.
1996 85m/C Denise Crosby, Georges Corraface, Christopher Atkins, Nick Corri, David Duchovny, Demetra Hampton, Rachel Palieri, Freedom Williams, Marry Morrow, Kent Masters-King; *D:* Rafael Eisenman, Zalman King, David Womark; *W:* Richard Baskin, Nellie Allard, Joelle Bentolila; *C:* Etienne Fauduet, Manuel Teran, Marco Mazzei; *M:* George S. Clinton.

Red Shoe Diaries: Luscious Lola

Perhaps because these entries in the late-night series are newer, the quality of the image is noticeably sharper than it has been on other DVDs. In these three stories, shy Mimi (Phillips) fantasizes about winning her dream guy; a sailor on shore leave winds up with more women than he can handle; and a young woman toys with men. Focus tends toward the soft side with warm reds and browns predominate in the color schemes. Sound is fine. —*MM*

Movie: 🎦🎦½ **DVD:** 🎦🎦½
Showtime Networks, Inc. (Cat #SHO5008, UPC #758445500820). Full frame. Stereo.

$17.99. Keepcase. *LANG:* English. *FEATURES:* Trivia game ➥ Photo gallery ➥ 2 deleted scenes and an interview with Zalman King ➥ Diary (text) ➥ Filmographies ➥ Credits ➥ Weblinks ➥ 27 chapter links.
2000 87m/C Bobbie Phillips, Michael C. Bendetti, Christina (Kristina) Fulton, Perrey Reeves, Ernie Banks, John Enos, Joseph Whipp, David Duchovny, Andrew Bilgore, Heidi Mark, Michael Reilly Burke; *D:* Zalman King, Stephen Halbert; *W:* John Enos, Chloe King, Pascal Franchot, Elize D'Haene; *C:* Eagle Egilsson, David Stockton; *M:* George S. Clinton.

Red Shoe Diaries: Strip Poker

In terms of image and sound, this collection of the cable series is equal to the others. Improvements over broadcast and tape are mostly in the extras. Contents: "Strip Poker," "Slow Train," "Hard Labor." —*MM*

Movie: 🎦🎦 **DVD:** 🎦🎦½
Showtime Networks, Inc. (Cat #SHO5018, UPC #758445501827). Full frame. Stereo. $24.98. Keepcase. *LANG:* English. *FEATURES:* Trivia game ➥ Hotel du Voyeur photo gallery ➥ Red Shoe character profiles ➥ Filmographies ➥ Credits ➥ 27 chapter links.
1996 87m/C Athena Massey, Jennifer Ciesar, Carolyn Seymour, David Duchovny, Anfisa Nezinskaya, Larisa Tipikina, Andrew Calder, Mark Suelke, Maximo Morrone; *D:* Zalman King, Rafael Eisenman; *W:* Zalman King, Patricia Louisianna Knop, Julie Marie Myatt, Elize D'Haene; *C:* Eagle Egilsson, Alexei Rodionov; *M:* George S. Clinton.

Red Shoe Diaries: Swimming Naked

The mother of all late-night cable series is still the artsiest. As such, these stories about a lifeguard, a skydiver, and a dancer are told with lots of smoke and gauzy focus. Neither seems to cause any excess artifacts or pixels. Image may be slightly better than cable or VHS tape. Sound is very good, emphasizing the confessional nature of the voice-over narration. The "Madame Red Shoe Speaks" extra is a sort of "MST3K" silhouette who comments on parts of the action. Contents: "Swimming Naked," "Jump," "Tears." —*MM*

Movie: 🎦🎦½ **DVD:** 🎦🎦½
Showtime Networks, Inc. (Cat #SHO5017, UPC #758445501728). Full frame. Stereo. $24.98. Keepcase. *LANG:* English. *FEATURES:* 27 chapter links ➥ Trivia game ➥ Photo gallery ➥ "Madame Red Shoe Speaks" ➥ Swimmer's poem ➥ Previews ➥ Filmographies.
2000 83m/C Michael Woods, Cyia Batten, Carolyn Seymour, Arabella Holzbog, David Duchovny, Kristi Frank, Omry Reznik, Sonya Ryzy-Ryski, Todd Gordon, Daniel Ezralow; *D:* Zalman King, Rafael Eisenman; *W:* Zalman King, Melanie Finn, Chloe King, Katarina Wittich, Kathryn MacQuarrie; *C:* Eagle Egilsson, David Knaus; *M:* George S. Clinton.

Reefer Madness

Considered serious at the time of its release, this low-budget depiction of the horrors of marijuana has become an underground comedy favorite. Overwrought acting and an equally lurid script contribute to the fun. On DVD, both black-and-white image and sound are fuzzy. Also available on *Marihuana / Assassin of Youth / Reefer Madness* (see separate review). —*MM*
AKA: Tell Your Children; Dope Addict; Doped Youth; Love Madness; The Burning Question.
Movie: 🐾🐾½ **DVD:** 🐾
Madacy Entertainment (Cat #99026, UPC #056775006297). Full frame. Dolby Digital Mono. $9.99. Keepcase. *LANG:* English. *FEATURES:* Dave O'Brien thumbnail bio • 9 chapter links • Production credits.
1938 (PG) 67m/B Dave O'Brien, Dorothy Short, Warren McCollum, Lillian Miles, Thelma White, Carleton Young, Josef Forte, Harry Harvey Jr., Pat Royale; **D:** Louis Gasnier; **W:** Paul Franklin, Arthur Hoerl; **C:** Jack Greenhalgh; **M:** Abe Meyer.

Reform School Girls

Satiric raucous send-up of the women-behind-bars film, complete with tough lesbian wardens, brutal lesbian guards, sadistic lesbian inmates, and a single, newly convicted heterosexual heroine. Plasmatic Wendy O. Williams is the toughest kid on the block and throws her all into her energetic if amateurish performance. Overdone, over-campy, and exploitative (just what you want in a B-movie of this sort) with plenty of catfights, though some may be disappointed in the lack of nudity in the second half of the film. Anchor Bay does it again with a splendid DVD transfer of one of our favorite obscure films. The colors are bright and suffer very little bleed, even though most of the film takes place in the dark of the prison. The mono sound isn't one to rumble the house, but delivers crisp dialogue and as much fidelity as can usually be found on such a low-budget gem. Director De Simone's commentary (accompanied by Lewis, who is credited as being a humorist) is anecdotal and amazingly funny, yet still manages to convey many informative tidbits about the making of the film. —*JO*
Movie: 🐾🐾🐾 **DVD:** 🐾🐾🐾
Anchor Bay (Cat #DV11326, UPC #013131 132694). Widescreen (1.85:1) anamorphic. Dolby Digital Mono. $24.98. Keepcase. *LANG:* English. *CAP:* English. *FEATURES:* 28 chapter links • Theatrical trailer • Stills gallery • Talent files • Commentary: director Tom De Simone, Martin Lewis.
1986 (R) 94m/C Linda Carol, Wendy O. Williams, Pat Ast, Sybil Danning, Charlotte McGinnis, Sherri Stoner; **D:** Tom De Simone; **W:** Tom De Simone; **C:** Howard Wexler.

Reindeer Games

The prospect of a roll in the hay with Ashley (Theron) is more than just-released jail-bird Rudy (Affleck) can resist. She thinks he is her incarcerated pen pal (Frain), who was Rudy's cellmate. So does her murderous brother (Sinise) and he wants Rudy to mastermind the knockover of an Indian-run casino in Michigan's Upper Peninsula on Christmas Eve. Confused yet? It gets much more complicated before it's over. As of this writing, only the theatrical version is available on DVD. (The VHS "director's cut," 20 minutes longer, is actually much better and much funnier and is scheduled to be released on DVD.) On disc, the cold interiors and hard-bitten characters look very good. When the image gets grainy, it is supposed to. Surround effects kick in nicely during the big finish. Director Frankenheimer, as usual, provides intelligent commentary. —*MM*
Movie: 🐾🐾½ **DVD:** 🐾🐾🐾
Buena Vista Home Entertainment (Cat #18 321, UPC #717951004970). Widescreen (2.35:1) anamorphic; full frame. Dolby Digital 5.1 Surround Stereo. $29.99. Keepcase. *LANG:* English; French. *SUB:* English; Spanish. *FEATURES:* 20 chapter links • Commentary: Frankenheimer • Behind-the-scenes featurette • Trailer.
2000 (R) 98m/C Ben Affleck, Charlize Theron, Gary Sinise, Clarence Williams III, Dennis Farina, Donal Logue, James Frain, Isaac Hayes, Danny Trejo; **D:** John Frankenheimer; **W:** Ehren Kruger; **C:** Alan Caso; **M:** Alan Silvestri.

Relative Values

Adaptation of a Noel Coward play is as flat as day-old champagne. In 1953, the Earl of Marshwood (Atterton) scandalizes British society when he announces that he's going to marry American movie star Miranda Frayle (Tripplehorn). His mother (Andrews) and her ex- (Baldwin) try to disrupt their plans. Though Julie Andrews floats through the proceedings like an angel, nobody's going to forget *The Philadelphia Story*. The film translates poorly to DVD, but all of its flaws seem to come from the original. Fairly harsh saturated colors lack detail. Sound is better, though the use of Surround elements is limited. —*MM*
Movie: 🐾🐾 **DVD:** 🐾🐾
Image Entertainment (Cat #OVED0325DVD, UPC #014381032529). Widescreen (1.85:1) anamorphic. Dolby Digital 5.1 Surround Stereo; Dolby Digital Surround Stereo. $24.99. Snapper. *LANG:* English. *FEATURES:* 16 chapter links • Trailer.
1999 (PG-13) 92m/C *GB* Julie Andrews, Edward Atterton, Jeanne Tripplehorn, William Baldwin, Sophie Thompson, Colin Firth, Stephen Fry; **D:** Eric Styles; **W:** Paul Rattigan, Michael Walker; **C:** Jimmy Dibling; **M:** John Debney.

Rembrandt

Laughton is at his most enjoyably theatrical with this portrayal of the great painter. Elsa Lanchester is the servant girl he turns to after the death of his wife. Intermittent specks and snow are visible throughout the film, and light static is often audible, but the DVD still looks very good for 1936. —*MM*
Movie: 🐾🐾🐾 **DVD:** 🐾🐾½
MGM Home Entertainment (Cat #10020 65, UPC #027616862952). Full frame. Dolby Digital Mono. $19.98. Keepcase. *LANG:* English. *SUB:* French; Spanish. *FEATURES:* 16 chapter links • Trailer.
1936 86m/B *GB* Charles Laughton, Elsa Lanchester, Gertrude Lawrence, Walter Hudd; **D:** Alexander Korda; **C:** Georges Perinal.

Rembrandt Films' Greatest Hits

If the Prague-based cartoon studio Rembrandt Films is remembered for anything these days, it's for the repellant "Tom and Jerry" shorts it produced for MGM/UA in the 1960s. Forgotten is the impressive if melancholy work included in this collection, most of it directed by Gene Deitch. "Munro," a sharp, hilarious military satire based on a Jules Feiffer story, is easily the highlight of the disc. But this DVD will win the company no new fans. The prints vary in quality: the Nudnik shorts are the sharpest-looking, while other films are faded and dirty with smeary-looking colors. The transfer from video masters is awful, with rolling bars particularly visible when the screen goes black between films. Sound quality is generally crisp, though the audio level is much too low. There are no extras, and the running time is a miserly 59 minutes. The packaging provides skimpy information: Deitch is mentioned only on a sticker affixed to the shrink wrap. Contents: "Munro," "The Frozen Logger," four "Self-Help" shorts, "Anatole," "Terr'ble Tessie" (series pilot), "Big Sam & Punky" (series pilot), and three "Nudnik" shorts. —*SS*
Movie: 🐾🐾½ **DVD:** 🐾
Image Entertainment (Cat #ID9000ASDVD, UPC #014381900022). Full frame. Dolby Digital Mono. $24.99. Snapper. *LANG:* English. *FEATURES:* 12 chapter links.
2000 59m/C D: Gene Deitch.

Remember the Titans

Unrelentingly uplifting, based-on-a-true-story sports movie hammers all the right emotional buttons. In 1971, Virginia schools are desegregated and black coach Herman Boone (Washington) is sent to Alexandria's T.C. Williams high school and promoted over the popular white coach Bill Yoast (Patton). Will he be able to calm the strife and lead his multi-racial team to the state championship? You do not need three guesses. DVD re-creates the inspirational image flawlessly and this big-budget studio production looks terrific. The DTS soundtrack is far superior to the theatre where I saw the film. Perhaps the most interesting extra is a commentary track by the real Boone and Yoast. A full-frame version of the film is also available. —*MM*
Movie: 🐾🐾🐾 **DVD:** 🐾🐾🐾½
Buena Vista Home Entertainment (Cat #21 651, UPC #786936144727). Widescreen

(2.35:1) anamorphic. DTS Surround; Dolby Digital 5.1 Surround Stereo. $29.99. Keepcase. *LANG:* English; French. *CAP:* English. *FEATURES:* 32 chapter links • 3 "making of" featurettes • 6 deleted scenes • Commentary: Herman Boone, Bill Yoast • Commentary: Yakin, producer Jerry Bruckheimer, Howard.
2000 (PG) 114m/C Denzel Washington, Will Patton, Donald Adeosun Faison, Wood Harris, Ethan Suplee, Nicole Parker, Hayden Panettiere, Catherine Bosworth, Ryan Hurst, Kip Pardue, Craig Kirkwood, Burgess Jenkins, Earl C. Poitier, Ryan Gosling; *D:* Boaz Yakin; *W:* Gregory Allen Howard; *C:* Philippe Rousselot; *M:* Trevor Rabin.

Remembering the Cosmos Flower

The reaction of a small Japanese town to a young girl with AIDS is the subject of this well-meaning and sometimes preachy film. Akiko has been in South America for seven years. When she returns with her mother to Japan, only her friend Natsumi will offer any support. DVD image appears to be an accurate reproduction of a slightly soft-focused original. Both production values and theme are roughly equivalent to a good American made-for-TV movie. —*MM*
Movie: 🎬🎬½ *DVD:* 🎬🎬½
Vanguard International Cinema, Inc. (Cat #VF0024, UPC #658796002430). Widescreen letterboxed. $29.95. Keepcase. *LANG:* Japanese. *SUB:* English. *FEATURES:* 10 chapter links.
1999 103m/C *JP* Mari Natsuki, Megumi Matsushita, Akane Oda, Kai Shishido; *D:* Junichi Suzuki; *W:* Junichi Suzuki, Tetsutomo Kosugi; *C:* Kaz Tanaka; *M:* Mamoru Samurakouchi.

The Replacements

An NFL players' strike finds coach Hackman stuck with a bunch of scab players, including washed-up quarterback Shane Falco (Reeves) and never-was receiver Clifford Franklin (Jones). If you can get past the fact that the heroes are scabs, this silly cliché-fest still isn't very good. It's better than it oughta be, but only because of Hackman's presence and Jones's comic talents. The odd assortment of misfits and goofballs is occasionally amusing, but nothing you haven't seen in all the other "rag-tag-team-fights-the-odds" sports comedies. Based on the 1987 strike when players filling in for the Washington Redskins won three straight games. Well, there's really no reason to put out a bad DVD so here's another so-so film that gets the showpiece treatment with a flawless transfer to the digital format. The image is so sharp you could cut yourself and the colors incredibly vibrant with not a hint of bleed. The 5.1 mix is energetic and the Surround really kicks in during gameplay and crowd scenes. When a player gets hit, the bass track makes sure the viewer actually feels it. One of the documentaries on the disc is from the HBO First Look series while the other, "Making the Plays: An Actor's Guide to Football," shows how the performers had to prepare for their pummeling by real-life footballers. —*JO*
Movie: 🎬🎬½ *DVD:* 🎬🎬🎬🎬
Warner Home Video, Inc. (Cat #18585, UPC #085391858522). Widescreen (1.85:1) anamorphic. Dolby Digital 5.1. $24.98. Snapper. *LANG:* English; French. *SUB:* English; French. *CAP:* English. *FEATURES:* 40 chapter links • Theatrical trailer • Talent files • 2 behind-the-scenes documentaries • Commentary: director Howard Deutch • Dual-layered.
2000 (PG-13) 105m/C Keanu Reeves, Gene Hackman, Jon Favreau, Orlando Jones, Jack Warden, Brooke Langton, Rhys Ifans, Brett Cullen, Gailard Sartain, Art LaFleur, Faizon Love, Michael "Bear" Taliferro, Troy Winbush, Michael Jace, Ace Yonamine, David Denman, Keith David, Michael Jace; *Cameos:* Pat Summerall, John Madden; *D:* Howard Deutch; *W:* Vince McKewin; *C:* Tak Fujimoto; *M:* Alan Silvestri.

Repo Man

The brilliant cult hit makes a brilliant transition to disc with a full load of extras and an image transfer that puts previous tapes to shame. Emilio Estevez is Otto, a disenchanted punk rocker who becomes a car repossession agent under the none-too-tender tutelage of Bud (Stanton). The other main plot ingredient is a '64 Chevy Malibu that's come to a sun-blasted L.A. straight from Roswell, New Mexico, with something bizarre in the trunk. Several government agents, who prefigure *The X-Files* by a couple of decades, are also involved. Alex Cox's film has never been visually sophisticated—it was made on an obviously limited budget—and so the sharp image and remixed stereo sound are a treat. Anchor Bay, famous for giving the best genre titles serious treatment on disc, has outdone itself with this DVD. From the cool metal box to the separate soundtrack CD, they've loaded the package with extras. —*MM*
Movie: 🎬🎬🎬½ *DVD:* 🎬🎬🎬½
Anchor Bay (Cat #11158, UPC #013131122992). Widescreen (1.85:1) letterboxed. Dolby Digital 5.1 Surround Stereo. $29.98. Metal box. *LANG:* English. *FEATURES:* 20 chapter links • Commentary: Cox, executive producer Michael Nesmith, and others • Theatrical and video trailers • Cast and crew thumbnail bios • Soundtrack CD • Production notes booklet.
1983 (R) 93m/C Emilio Estevez, Harry Dean Stanton, Sy Richardson, Tracey Walter, Olivia Barash, Fox Harris, Jennifer Balgobin, Vonetta McGee, Angelique Pettyjohn, Biff Yeager; *D:* Alex Cox; *W:* Alex Cox; *C:* Robby Muller; *M:* Tito Larriva, Iggy Pop.

Requiem for a Dream

Darren Aronofsky's adaptation of Hubert Selby's novel is essentially a horror film about addiction. It follows a year in the life of four people: Sara (Burstyn), her son Harry (Leto), his girlfriend Marion (Connelly), and his friend Tyrone (Wayans). Each of them has an obsession and their inability to deal with it leads to depravity and ruin. It's not a pretty story, in any way, but Aronofsky tells it beautifully. He is a gifted filmmaker and he uses the medium of DVD to make the disc superior to the theatrical experience. First and most important is his commentary track, where he explains what he's doing and why. It's one of the most informative and carefully done you'll ever listen to. The extra sharp clarity of the image does justice to the innovative techniques he employs. Unlike so many younger filmmakers, he is not showing off. He's trying to tell a difficult, serious story as best he can, and he succeeds. To skip the motivational intro, just hit the menu button. Also, be warned that many Blockbuster stores carry only an inferior "R"-rated version of the film. —*MM*
Movie: 🎬🎬🎬🎬 *DVD:* 🎬🎬🎬🎬
Artisan Entertainment (Cat #11567). Widescreen anamorphic. Dolby Digital 5.1 Surround Stereo. $24.98. Keepcase. *LANG:* English. *FEATURES:* 33 chapter links • Commentary: Darren Aronofsky • Commentary: director of photography Matthew Libatique • "Making of" featurette • Anatomy of a scene featurette • "Memories, Dreams and Addictions" featurette • Trailers • Talent files • Production notes • 9 deleted scenes with commentary.
2000 102m/C Jared Leto, Ellen Burstyn, Jennifer Connelly, Marlon Wayans, Christopher McDonald, Louise Lasser, Keith David, Sean Gullette; *D:* Darren Aronofsky; *W:* Darren Aronofsky, Hubert Selby Jr.; *C:* Matthew Libatique; *M:* Clint Mansell. *AWARDS:* Ind. Spirit '01: Actress (Burstyn), Cinematog; *NOM:* Oscars '00: Actress (Burstyn); Ind. Spirit '01: Director (Aronofsky), Film, Support. Actress (Connelly); Screen Actors Guild '00: Actress (Burstyn).

The Rescuers Down Under

Heroic mice Bernard and Bianca protect a young boy and a rare golden eagle from a poacher. The great bird closely resembles the logo of Republic Pictures. A few artifacts are noticeable in bright clouds, but that is hardly enough to bother the target audience with this one. Sound is very good, too. —*MM*
Movie: 🎬🎬🎬 *DVD:* 🎬🎬🎬
Buena Vista Home Entertainment (Cat #18667, UPC #717951005809). Widescreen (1.66:1) anamorphic. Dolby Digital 4.0 Surround Stereo; Dolby Digital Surround. $24.99. Keepcase. *LANG:* English; French; Spanish. *CAP:* English. *FEATURES:* 16 chapter links • Trailers • Trivia game • DVD storybook.
1990 (G) 77m/C *D:* Hendel Butoy, Mike Gabriel; *W:* Jim Cox, Karey Kirkpatrick, Joe Ranft, Byron Simpson; *M:* Bruce Broughton; *V:* Bob Newhart, Eva Gabor, John Candy, Tristan Rogers, George C. Scott, Frank Welker, Adam Ryen.

Restaurant

What starts out as a self-obsessed story about a group of wanna-be theatre actors working in an upscale bar and restaurant in New York soon turns into a self-possessed story about overcoming your past even when the future is unclear. Chris Calloway (Brody) is an up-and-coming playwright whose current play is based on the break-up of his last relationship. While trying to write an ending to the story that makes sense, he meets a new girl, leaves his job, and loses his best friend. This is a slow burn that catches your interest and reels you in. Only after it's over do you realize how well the story was constructed. The same writing/directing team was responsible for the underwatched *Ten Benny*, which also starred Brody. The disc looks good and the sound is above average, which makes all those Karaoke scenes much more enjoyable. —CA

Movie: 🎬🎬½ **DVD:** 🎬🎬
York Entertainment (Cat #YPD 1037, UPC #750723103723). Widescreen. Dolby Digital 5.1 Surround. $14.98. Keepcase. *LANG:* English. *FEATURES:* 30 chapter links • Commentary: director • Theatrical trailer • Deleted scenes • Filmographies • Behind-the-scenes featurette.
1998 (R) 107m/C Adrien Brody, Elise Neal, David Moscow, Simon Baker, Catherine Kellner, Malcolm Jamal Warner, Lauryn Hill, John Carroll Lynch, Sybil Temchen, Vonte Sweet, Michael Stoyanov; **D:** Eric Bross; **W:** Tom Cudworth; **C:** Horacio Marquinez; **M:** Theodore Shapiro.

Restraining Order
Lawyer Robert Woodfield (Roberts) witnesses his client committing a murder. As a result of the attorney/client privileges he decides to construct an airtight case with his opposition in court to convict the killer. But before long, his friend is killed and his wife seems to be the next target. The image shows occasional blemishes and dirt but is generally clean. Although the opening shot is a bit grainy, the majority of the film is without noise or grain. Audio is generally clean. —GH/MM
Movie: 🎬🎬½ **DVD:** 🎬🎬½
Artisan Entertainment (UPC #012236106340). Full frame. Dolby Digital 5.1 Surround Stereo; Dolby Digital Surround Stereo. $24.98. Keepcase. *LANG:* English. *FEATURES:* Commentary • Talent files.
1999 (R) 95m/C Eric Roberts, Hannes Jaenicke, Tatjana Patitz, Dean Stockwell; **D:** Lee H. Katzin; **W:** John Jarrell; **M:** David Wurst, Eric Wurst.

Retro Puppet Master
Most recent entry in the "Puppet Master" series is officially the first, finding a young Toulon in pre-WWI Paris, where he falls in love with the daughter of the Swiss ambassador. Of course, the puppets and other mini-critters are involved too. Overall, image is the clearest of the series with some very nice special effects. DVD is a slight improvement over tape. Maybe. Disc is also available as part of the *Puppet Master Collection* boxed set. —MM
Movie: 🎬🎬 **DVD:** 🎬🎬

Full Moon Pictures (Cat #FUM-DV, UPC #76 3843806269). Full frame. $16.99. Keepcase. *LANG:* English. *FEATURES:* 18 chapter links • Behind-the-scenes Videozone magazine • Trailers.
1999 (PG-13) 90m/C Guy Rolfe, Greg Sestero, Brigitta Dau, Jack Donner, Stephen Blackehart; **D:** Joseph Tennent; **W:** Benjamin Carr; **C:** Viorel Sergovici Jr.; **M:** John Massari.

Return of the Fly
The son of the scientist who discovered how to move matter through space (with horrific results) decides to continue his father's work, but does so against his uncle's wishes. He soon duplicates his dad's experiments with similar results. More graphic but with a much weaker script, this B-movie sequel to *The Fly* doesn't buzz like the original. Available on DVD with *The Fly* (1958); please see that review for DVD details. —JO
Movie: 🎬🎬½
1959 80m/B Vincent Price, Brett Halsey, John Sutton, Dan Seymour, David Frankham, Danielle De Metz, Ed Wolff; **D:** Edward L. Bernds; **W:** Edward L. Bernds, Brydon Baker.

Return of the Magnificent Seven
By-the-numbers sequel finds Chris (Brynner) gathering more gunfighters to defend a village against the outlaw Lorca (Fernandez). The ensemble star power of the first film is notably absent. What's left is a standard western action picture. On DVD image is fine, but the soundtrack is abysmal. Static is near constant and is very heavy in the quiet moments. —MM
AKA: Return of the Seven.
Movie: 🎬🎬 **DVD:** 🎬🎬
MGM Home Entertainment (Cat #1001838, UPC #027616861085). Widescreen (2.35:1) anamorphic. Dolby Digital Mono. $19.98. Keepcase. *LANG:* English; French; Spanish. *SUB:* French; Spanish. *CAP:* English. *FEATURES:* 16 chapter links • Trailer.
1966 97m/C Yul Brynner, Warren Oates, Robert Fuller, Claude Akins, Julian Mateos, Elisa Montes, Emilio Fernandez; **D:** Burt Kennedy; **W:** Larry Cohen; **C:** Paul Vogel; **M:** Elmer Bernstein. *AWARDS: NOM:* Oscars '66: Adapt. Score.

Return to Me
A light, fluffy romantic comedy about a widower, Bob (Duchovny) who falls in love with the recipient of his dead wife's heart, Grace (Driver). While this seems strange story material for a romantic comedy, the issue of donor transplants is handled beautifully. The script by Bonnie Hunt (who also directed) and Don Lake avoids cliché hospital dialogue and allows montage to tell the tale of one life being traded for another. The best thing in the entire film is the relationship between the two old guys (O'Connor and Loggia) who run the Italian-Irish restaurant and bar where Grace

works for her grandfather (O'Connor). One of the more enjoyable deleted scenes included on any disc lately has the older members of the cast singing "Danny Boy." The disc looks and sounds better than average. —CA
Movie: 🎬🎬½ **DVD:** 🎬🎬🎬
MGM Home Entertainment (Cat #4001174, UPC #027616853417). Widescreen anamorphic. Dolby Digital 5.1 Surround. $26.98. Keepcase. *LANG:* English; Spanish. *SUB:* Spanish; French. *CAP:* English. *FEATURES:* 32 chapter links • Commentary: writers Lake and Hunt • Deleted scenes • Music videos.
2000 (PG) 113m/C David Duchovny, Minnie Driver, James Belushi, Bonnie Hunt, Carroll O'Connor, Robert Loggia, David Alan Grier, Joely Richardson, Eddie Jones, Marianne Muellerleile, William Bronder; **D:** Bonnie Hunt; **W:** Bonnie Hunt, Don Lake; **C:** Laszlo Kovacs; **M:** Nicholas Pike.

Revelation
In the continuing adventures based on the *Left Behind* novels (a conservative Christian interpretation of the Book of Revelation), a counter-terrorism expert (Fahey) goes up against a Messiah (Mancuso) out to rule the world, etc., etc. Like the other films in the series, the DVD exhibits a good image though the entire production lacks the professionalism of the best Hollywood escapism. —MM
Movie: 🎬 **DVD:** 🎬🎬
Cloud Ten Pictures (UPC #74563800130). Full frame. $29.99. Keepcase. *LANG:* English. *FEATURES:* 8 chapter links • Talent files • Trailers • Theme song • 700 Club interview • Weblinks.
2000 97m/C Jeff Fahey, Nick Mancuso, Carol Alt, Leigh Lewis; **D:** Andre Van Heerden; **W:** Peter LaLonde, Paul LaLonde; **C:** George Tirl.

The Rich Man's Wife
Modern noir strands unhappy wife Josie (Berry) on Martha's Vineyard without her loathsome spouse (McDonald), where she makes the mistake of confiding her marital woes to sympathetic, yet obviously deranged stranger Cole (Greene). She tells Cole sometimes she wishes her husband were dead. Poof! Before you can say "foreshadowing," hubby's murdered and she's the prime suspect. Increasingly nutso Cole stalks our heroine, seemingly innocent, but possibly not as blameless as she appears. Failed mystery/thriller delivers little of either and the attempt at a *Strangers on a Train* premise and a *Usual Suspects*-type ending fail miserably. The video transfer is quite good, yet not quite spectacular (highlighted by well-defined colors and blacks). The soundtrack is also impressive (particularly the musical score), although some quieter dialogue tends to be a bit muffled. —MJT
Movie: 🎬½ **DVD:** 🎬🎬
Hollywood Pictures Home Video (Cat #185 33, UPC #717951005502). Widescreen (1.85:1) letterboxed. Dolby Digital 2.0 Sur-

round. $29.99. Keepcase. *LANG:* English. *SUB:* Spanish. *CAP:* English. *FEATURES:* 19 chapter links ◦ Theatrical trailer ◦ Additional Hollywood Pictures trailers.
1996 (R) 95m/C Halle Berry, Christopher McDonald, Clive Owen, Peter Greene, Charles Hallahan, Frankie Faison, Clea Lewis; *D:* Amy Holden Jones; *W:* Amy Holden Jones; *C:* Haskell Wexler; *M:* John Frizzell.

Ride in the Whirlwind

Jack Nicholson co-produced and wrote the screenplay for this decidedly offbeat realistic western. He plays one of three cowboys who are taken for outlaws and hunted by a vigilante group. The film has been carefully restored to virtually pristine condition. The sharp image captures director Hellman's evocation of Utah landscapes and the equally strong characters. (Harry Dean Stanton and Rupert Crosse stand out in a small ensemble.) Sound is very good, though it is mostly limited to enhanced natural sounds of wind and water. On the commentary track, Hellman takes justifiable pride in his work. The same creative team also made *The Shooting.* —MM
Movie: 🎬🎬🎬 *DVD:* 🎬🎬🎬½
VCI Home Video (Cat #8230, UPC #08985 9823022). Widescreen anamorphic. Dolby Digital Mono. $29.99. Keepcase. *LANG:* English. *FEATURES:* 12 chapter links ◦ Commentary: Hellman, Perkins, Dennis Bartok ◦ Photo gallery ◦ Review by Quentin Tarantino ◦ Trailers ◦ Talent files.
1966 83m/C Jack Nicholson, Cameron Mitchell, Millie Perkins, Katherine Squire, Harry Dean Stanton, Rupert Crosse; *D:* Monte Hellman; *W:* Jack Nicholson; *M:* Robert Jackson Drasnin.

Ride with the Devil

Ang Lee attempts to combine the adventurousness of *The Outlaw Josey Wales* with the seriousness of *Glory* in this story of the Civil War as it was fought on the Missouri-Kansas border. It was a guerrilla conflict without clear divisions. Some scenes do generate excitement, but overall, the casting of pretty young things Ulrich, Maquire, and pop star Jewel in the leads is unfortunate. That said, the disc looks very good, handling some potentially difficult exteriors without flaws. 5.1 Surround is used effectively in the action and battle scenes. —MM
Movie: 🎬🎬 *DVD:* 🎬🎬🎬
Universal Studios Home Video (Cat #207 74, UPC #025192077425). Widescreen (2.35:1) anamorphic. Dolby Digital 5.1 Surround Stereo. $24.98. Keepcase. *LANG:* English. *SUB:* French. *CAP:* English. *FEATURES:* 18 chapter links ◦ Jewel music video ◦ Trailer ◦ Production notes ◦ Talent files ◦ Weblink.
1999 (R) 139m/C Tobey Maguire, Skeet Ulrich, Jeffrey Wright, Jewel, Simon Baker, Jonathan Rhys Meyers, James Caviezel, Tom Guiry, Tom Wilkinson, Jonathan Bran-

dis, John Ales, Matthew Faber, Steven Mailer, Zach Grenier, Margo Martindale, Mark Ruffalo, Celia Weston; *D:* Ang Lee; *W:* James Schamus; *C:* Frederick Elmes; *M:* Mychael Danna.

Riders of Destiny / Star Packer

The first feature on the disc is far too grubby and poorly focused to endure. Skip through it to the second, which looks better but is still flawed. Wayne is a marshal in that one. Both early films are short B-movies. Even considering the modicum of extras, the DVD is only slightly superior to tape. —MM
Movie: 🎬 *DVD:* 🎬
Madacy Entertainment (Cat #DVD-9-9003-2, UPC #056775002190). Full frame. Dolby Digital Mono. $9.99. Keepcase. *LANG:* English. *FEATURES:* 8 chapter links ◦ John Wayne filmography 1936–45 ◦ Trivia quiz. Also available in "The John Wayne Collection" (cat. #DVD-9-9003; UPC 056775001995).
1933 59m/B John Wayne, George "Gabby" Hayes, Cecilia Parker, Forrest Taylor, Al "Fuzzy" St. John; *D:* Robert North Bradbury; *W:* Robert North Bradbury; *C:* Archie Stout.

Rififi

This legendary French crime masterpiece was the first film in several years from blacklisted U.S. director Dassin and was a well-deserved success. Imitated endlessly in the years since, this film tells the simple, but brilliantly told tale of Tony (Jean Servais), who was recently released from jail, and his associates, who design and orchestrate the elaborate robbery of a jewelry store. To reveal more would be unthinkable. Though lauded for its nerve-wracking, classic, near silent break-in scene, the film is much more than an exercise in style and cinematic technique. All the characters and their respective wives and girlfriends are delineated with crystal clarity, and the story is never short of gripping. Rarely have gangsters been portrayed with such humanity. In this one, you truly root for the "bad guys." An absolute must. Dassin can be seen in the film as the quaint Italian safecracker. The disc is excellent, with a sharp and clear picture, never seeming contrasty or over-bright. The sound is clear, but thin and flat, typical of a foreign film from this era. The dubbing does a fairly good job of conveying the dialogue, but the original French dialogue is the way to go with this one. The interview is interesting and informative and the design drawings are beautiful. —DG *AKA:* Du Rififi Chez les Hommes.
Movie: 🎬🎬🎬½ *DVD:* 🎬🎬🎬
Criterion Collection (Cat #115, UPC #0374 2915562). Full frame. Dolby Digital Mono. $29.95. Keepcase. *LANG:* French; English. *SUB:* English. *FEATURES:* Interview with director Jules Dassin ◦ Still and set design gallery ◦ U.S. theatrical trailer ◦

Production notes ◦ Booklet with essay ◦ 24 chapter links.
1954 115m/B *FR* Jean Servais, Carl Mohner, Robert Manuel, Jules Dassin; *D:* Jules Dassin; *W:* Jules Dassin; *C:* Philippe Agostini; *M:* Georges Auric. *AWARDS:* Cannes '55: Director (Dassin).

The Right Temptation

When one is drawn to a film because of, say, the star (in this case, dreamy wide-eyed Rebecca DeMornay), there comes a point during the presentation when the question "why?" must be confronted. Exactly "why" are we watching this, and "why" for crying-out-loud has DeMornay been reduced to appearing in such drivel? As for a plot, she's a former cop turned private detective, who has been hired by Dana Delany to follow her husband, Keifer Sutherland, to see if he's having an affair. Bad writing, bad acting, and strictly by-the-numbers direction from TV director Lyndon Chubbuck follow. Hint: Sutherland will have an affair. Can you hazard a guess with whom? The DVD presentation is far better than the content it delivers—the viewer has the option of watching a truly dreadful movie either widescreen or full frame, and with a choice of subtitles. —RJT
Movie: 🎬🎬 *DVD:* 🎬🎬🎬½
Columbia Tristar Home Video (Cat #05981, UPC #043396059818). Widescreen (1.85:1); full frame. 5.1 Dolby Digital Surround Sound; Dolby Digital Surround. $24.95. Keepcase. *LANG:* English. *SUB:* English; Spanish; Chinese. *CAP:* English; Spanish; Chinese. *FEATURES:* Talent files ◦ Trailer ◦ 28 chapter links.
2000 (R) 93m/C Kiefer Sutherland, Rebecca DeMornay, Dana Delany, Adam Baldwin; *D:* Lyndon Chubbuck.

Rikyu

In 16th-century Japan, Rikyu is a Buddhist priest who elevates the tea ceremony to an art form. To him it is a spiritual experience, to his master, Lord Hideyoshi Toilyotomi, the ruler of Japan, mastery of the ceremony is a matter of prestige. Conflict arises between Rikyu's ideal of profound simplicity, symbolized by the ceremony, and Toilyotomi's planned conquest of China, which Rikyu opposes. The video transfer on this disc is horrid. With bleeding, washed-out colors, this ten-year-old film looks as though it was mastered from a decaying 30-year-old print. The soundtrack fares better and features clear, understandable dialogue. —MJT
Movie: 🎬🎬🎬 *DVD:* 🎬🎬
SlingShot Entertainment (Cat #SDVD9129, UPC #017078912920). Full frame. Dolby Digital. $19.99. Super jewelbox. *LANG:* Japanese. *SUB:* English. *FEATURES:* 16 chapter links ◦ Theatrical trailers for *Chasing Rain, Dreams of Flight* ◦ Weblinks.
1990 116m/C *JP* Rentaro Mikuni, Tsutomu Yamazaki; *D:* Hiroshi Teshigahara; *W:* Hiroshi Teshigahara, Genpei Akasegawa; *C:* Fujio Morita; *M:* Toru Takemitsu.

Ring of Bright Water

Adaptation of Gavin Maxwell's autobiography is actually a very well-done children's film about an otter. The film's stars also made *Born Free*. Acting is fine but the real stars are the superb nature photography and a well-realized Scottish setting. Anchor Bay's DVD has the kind of quality we're coming to expect from that label. The sound is clear, and widescreen-enhancement presents the scenery and wildlife with a bright and vivid picture. If only the major studios would give their libraries the kind of attention afforded these "unaffiliated" movies! —MM/GE

Movie: 🎵🎵🎵 **DVD:** 🎵🎵🎵½
Anchor Bay (Cat #11182). Widescreen (1.78:1) anamorphic. Dolby Digital Mono. $24.98. Keepcase. *LANG:* English. *FEATURES:* Trailer.
1969 (G) 107m/C *GB* Bill Travers, Virginia McKenna, Peter Jeffrey, Archie Duncan; **D:** Jack Couffer; **W:** Jack Couffer, Bill Travers; **C:** Wolfgang Suschitzky; **M:** Frank Cordell.

The Ring Virus

This horror tale began as a series of novels, and was then transformed into a TV movie. After that, a feature film was made in 1998, which solidified *The Ring* as Japan's horror champ. Since that time, there have been several sequels, a TV miniseries, a video game, and a series of knock-offs. This Korean film is an almost exact duplicate of the Japanese film *The Ring*, but with some slight changes here and there. The basic story remains intact. The film opens with the mysterious death of a young girl. The victim's aunt, Sun-joo (Shin Eun-Kyoung), investigates the death and discovers that her niece wasn't the only victim. She finds that the teens had viewed a strange videotape, which bears a warning that anyone who views the tape will die in one week. Sun-joo then enlists an eccentric physician Dr. Choi (Jeong Jin-Young) to aid her in her investigation. Soon, they find themselves involved in a mystery, which will lead them across the country in search of a mysterious woman with long black hair. The picture is very sharp and clear, showing only a small amount of grain. However, there are noticeable defects from the source print, with scratches and white dots being evident throughout. The color reproduction is quite good, with the blues and greens adding a great amount of depth. The 5.1 soundtrack works quite well. The film is often quiet, only to have a musical sting or strange sound effect rip through the Surround sound speakers. The dialogue is clear, although it gets a bit quiet at times. The subtitles are white and very easy to read, but it seems that towards the end, all of the helping verbs went on strike, so things get a bit jumbled. Overall though, this is a competently done DVD. —ML

Movie: 🎵🎵½ **DVD:** 🎵🎵½
Bitwin Co. Ltd. Widescreen (1.85:1) anamorphic. Dolby Digital 5.1 Surround Stereo; Dolby Digital Surround. $21.95. Keepcase. *LANG:* Korean. *SUB:* English; Japanese.

1999 110m/C Shin Eun-Kyoung, Jeong Jin-Young, Bae Doo-Na, Kim Chang-Wan; **D:** Kim Dong-Bin.

The River

Farmers battle a river whose flood threatens their land. Spacek, as always, is strong and believable as the wife and mother, but Gibson falters. Beautiful photography is not enough to save the third in an onslaught of early '80s films dramatizing the plight of the small farmer. Both *Country* and *Places in the Heart* managed to convey important messages less cloyingly. The clarity of DVD makes it abundantly clear that much of the film was made on soundstages. It lacks the necessary grit in the big scenes. Sound is fine. —MM

Movie: 🎵🎵 **DVD:** 🎵🎵½
Universal Studios Home Video (Cat #204 27, UPC #025192042720). Widescreen (1.85:1) anamorphic. Dolby Digital 5.1 Surround Stereo; Dolby Digital Surround. $26.98. Keepcase. *LANG:* English; French. *SUB:* Spanish. *CAP:* English. *FEATURES:* Cast and crew thumbnail bios • Trailer • Production notes • 18 chapter links • Weblinks.
1984 (PG) 124m/C Mel Gibson, Sissy Spacek, Scott Glenn, Billy Green Bush; **D:** Mark Rydell; **W:** Julian Barry, Robert Dillon; **C:** Vilmos Zsigmond; **M:** John Williams. *AWARDS: NOM:* Oscars '84: Actress (Spacek), Cinematog., Sound, Orig. Score.

River's Edge

Drug-addled high school student strangles his girlfriend and casually displays the corpse to his apathetic group of friends, who leave the murder unreported for days. Harrowing and gripping; based on a true story. Aging biker Hopper is splendid. The disc features a well-done yet flawed video transfer. It includes crisp colors and nicely defined blacks, but some colors come across as merely bland and severely muted. The decent mono soundtrack features crisp, clear dialogue and sound effects. —MJT

Movie: 🎵🎵🎵 **DVD:** 🎵🎵½
MGM Home Entertainment (Cat #10014 51, UPC #027616857712). Widescreen (1.85:1) anamorphic. Dolby Digital Mono. $19.95. Keepcase. *LANG:* English. *SUB:* French; Spanish. *FEATURES:* 16 chapter links • Theatrical trailer.
1987 (R) 99m/C Keanu Reeves, Crispin Glover, Daniel Roebuck, Joshua John Miller, Dennis Hopper, Ione Skye, Roxana Zal, Tom Bower, Constance Forslund, Leo Rossi, Jim Metzler; **D:** Tim Hunter; **W:** Neal Jimenez; **C:** Frederick Elmes; **M:** Jurgen Knieper. *AWARDS:* Ind. Spirit '88: Film, Screenplay; Sundance '87: Special Jury Prize.

Road Movie

Cult favorite about a pair of brutish truck drivers (Bostwick and Drivas) who pick up a prostitute (Baff) on a trip across America. Baff delivers an emotional performance as the beaten and furious hooker who, after being abused and rejected, seeks her revenge. The video transfer shows pronounced signs of age deterioration. Colors lack distinction, darker ones tend to bleed, and cracks and burns are noticeable throughout the film. Similarly, the soundtrack is often muffled and hard to understand. —MJT

Movie: 🎵🎵½ **DVD:** 🎵🎵
Image Entertainment (Cat #ID9520RLDVD, UPC #014381952025). Widescreen (1.85:1) anamorphic. Dolby Digital Mono. $29.99. Snapper. *LANG:* English. *FEATURES:* 12 chapter links.
1972 82m/C Barry Bostwick, Robert Drivas, Regina Baff; **D:** Joseph Strick; **W:** Judith Rascoe; **C:** Don Lenzer.

The Road to Bali

Sixth in the Hope & Crosby series, the only color entry, is a keeper. The guys are competing for the love of Princess Lala (Lamour) on a trek from Australia to Bali where they meet cannibals and other perils, including Humphrey Bogart. The image ranges between good and very good with only minor aliasing and a slightly soft color image. Mono sound is fine. (See also *Bob Hope Double Feature*.) —MM

Movie: 🎵🎵🎵 **DVD:** 🎵🎵🎵
Brentwood Home Video (Cat #60983-9, UPC #090096098395). Full frame. Dolby Digital Mono. $14.98. Keepcase. *LANG:* English. *FEATURES:* 8 chapter links • Bob Hope filmography and thumbnail bio.
1953 90m/C Bob Hope, Bing Crosby, Dorothy Lamour, Murvyn Vye, Ralph Moody, Jane Russell, Jerry Lewis, Dean Martin, Carolyn Jones; **D:** Hal Walker; **W:** Frank Butler, Hal Kanter, William Morrow; **C:** George Barnes.

The Road to El Dorado

Funny, satisfying animated adventure in the Disney style. Roguish con artists Miguel (Branagh) and Tulio (Kline) escape from Spanish conqueror Cortez's ship with his trusty war-horse Altivo and a map to the legendary city of El Dorado (literally the "Golden One"). Arriving on the shores before Cortez, the two quickly find the opulent city and are mistaken for gods. Caught between the bloodthirsty Tzekel-Kan (Assante) and the fatherly Chief (Olmos), they befriend young pickpocket Chel (Perez) and must decide whether to rob the city and run or stay in paradise. Meanwhile, Cortez's army is on the march. Visually opulent, colorful, and delightful, this is a film that holds up admirably to repeated viewings. It's fast-paced and filled with enough well-timed gags to please adults as well as children. Elton John's songs are a mixed bag though, from the excellent to the average. The DVD is a jam-packed set featuring an excellent transfer with eye-popping colors (the opening sequence is inspired and stunning). There is an instance or two of blue haloing around figures during fast-paced action, but it rarely distracts. The DVD-ROM features are fun and well designed, but the real highlight is the audio commentary. Directors Bergeron and Paul provide a fascinating and fast-paced account of the making of a modern animated film, discussing the recording sessions, alternate endings, and character designs. The commentary alone makes it a must-have for animation students. —*DG*

Movie: 🎵🎵🎵 **DVD:** 🎵🎵🎵½
DreamWorks Home Entertainment (Cat #86545, UPC #667068654523). Widescreen (1.85:1) anamorphic. DTS Surround 5.1; Dolby Digital 5.1; Dolby Surround. $26.99. Keepcase. *LANG:* English. *SUB:* English. *CAP:* English. *FEATURES:* 28 chapter links • Color booklet • Commentary: directors Eric "Bibo" Bergeron and Don Paul • Elton John music video • Theatrical trailer • Cast and crew bios • Production notes • Read-a-long picture story featurette • DVD-ROM: PC Game demo, brain teasers, games, coloring pages.
2000 (PG) 90m/C D: Eric Bergeron, Don Paul; **W:** Ted Elliott, Terry Rossio; **M:** Elton John, Hans Zimmer, John Powell, Tim Rice; **V:** Kevin Kline, Kenneth Branagh, Rosie Perez, Armand Assante, Edward James Olmos; **Nar:** Elton John.

The Road to Rio

The wisecracking duo of Hope and Crosby travel to Rio De Janeiro to prevent Maria de Andrade (Lamour) from going through a marriage arranged by her evil aunt (Sondergaard). The DVD appears to have been made from a pristine original. The black-and-white photography ranges from very good to excellent with only minor aliasing and flashing in Bing's polka dot bowtie. Sound is good for a film of this age. Belongs in every fan's video library. —*MM*

Movie: 🎵🎵🎵½ **DVD:** 🎵🎵🎵
Brentwood Home Video (Cat #60980-9, UPC #090096098098). Full frame. Dolby Digital Mono. $14.98. Keepcase. *LANG:* English. *FEATURES:* 8 chapter links.
1947 100m/B Bing Crosby, Bob Hope, Dorothy Lamour, Gale Sondergaard, Frank Faylen, The Andrews Sisters; **D:** Norman Z. McLeod; **W:** Jack Rose; **C:** Ernest Laszlo. *AWARDS: NOM:* Oscars '47: Orig. Dramatic Score.

Road Trip

Four college buddies set off on an 1,800-mile drive from Ithaca, New York, to Austin, Texas, to retrieve an incriminating pornographic videotape that Josh (Meyer) has mistakenly mailed to his girlfriend. The comedy is lightweight, surprisingly fun, and not nearly as crude or cruel as it could have been. Documentary filmmaker Todd Phillips gives the film a great look and a nice pace. The transfer here is very well done; the image displays no distortion or signs of artifacting. There are no signs of damage to the source print and the overall image comes across as very clear. DTS and 5.1 are equally strong, as the wide dynamic range makes good use of Surround sound and the constant

music on the track is nicely modulated, giving a hefty amount of work to the subwoofer. The dialogue is clear and audible. —*ML/MM*

Movie: 🎵🎵½ **DVD:** 🎵🎵🎵
DreamWorks Home Entertainment (Cat #86395, UPC #667068639520). Widescreen (1.85:1) anamorphic. Dolby Digital 5.1 Surround Stereo; DTS 5.1; Dolby Digital Surround Stereo. $26.99. Keepcase. *LANG:* English. *SUB:* English. *FEATURES:* Deleted scenes • Music video • Talent files • Production notes • Behind-the-scenes featurette • 24 chapter links. Film is also available in an unrated version.
2000 (R) 91m/C Breckin Meyer, Seann William Scott, Rachel Blanchard, DJ Qualls, Fred Ward, Andy Dick, Paulo Costanzo, Tom Green, Amy Smart, Anthony Rapp, Ethan Suplee; **D:** Todd Phillips; **W:** Todd Phillips, Scot Armstrong; **C:** Mark Irwin; **M:** Mike Simpson.

Robert Louis Stevenson's The Game of Death

In 1899 England, emotionally troubled Capt. Henry Joyce (Morrissey) considers killing himself. He and his friend Capt. May (Shuke) meet the equally suicidal Shaw (Bettany), who takes them to a secret club run by the mysterious Bourne (Pryce). Its members want to die and both victim and murderer are selected by drawing cards. DVD image is far superior to the run-of-the-mill Corman production. Same for sound. Director Samuels's commentary track is a bit star-struck, but it's also a revealing glimpse at the movie business as seen by a talented young woman who ought to have very good things in store for her. —*MM* **AKA:** The Suicide Club; The Game of Death; Robert Louis Stevenson's The Suicide Club.

Movie: 🎵🎵🎵 **DVD:** 🎵🎵🎵
New Concorde (Cat #NH20756 D, UPC #73 6991475694). Widescreen letterboxed. Stereo. $19.99. Keepcase. *LANG:* English. *SUB:* Spanish. *FEATURES:* 24 chapter links • Talent files • Commentary: director • Trailers.
1999 (R) 89m/C David Morrissey, Jonathan Pryce, Paul Bettany, Neil Stuke, Catherine Siggins; **D:** Rachel Samuels; **W:** Lev L. Spiro; **C:** Chris Manley; **M:** Adrian Johnston.

Robin Hood

This time, the Sherwood Forest crowd is portrayed by appropriate cartoon animals. Hence, Robin is a fox; Little John a bear; etc. Good family fare but not as memorable as other Disney features. The picture is very crisp and only shows minor grain. The best thing about this release are the colors. They literally leap off of the screen. Every character wears a different color costume, and these never bleed together, but remain vibrant. While some minor defects in the animation are made evident by the digital transfer, the overall

effect is very impressive. Compared to the lovely visual presentation, the mono audio tracks are anti-climactic and leave much to be desired. —*ML/MM*

Movie: 🎵🎵🎵 **DVD:** 🎵🎵🎵
Buena Vista Home Entertainment (Cat #19692). Full frame. Dolby Digital Mono. $29.99. Keepcase. *LANG:* English; French; Spanish. *FEATURES:* Storybook • Trivia game • Sing-along • Mickey Mouse short.
1973 83m/C D: Wolfgang Reitherman; **M:** George Bruns; **V:** Roger Miller, Brian Bedford, Monica Evans, Phil Harris, Andy Devine, Carol Shelley, Peter Ustinov, Terry-Thomas, Pat Buttram, George Lindsey, Ken Curtis. *AWARDS: NOM:* Oscars '73: Song ("Love").

Robot Monster

Whacked out cheapie ranks alongside *Plan 9 from Outer Space* as one of the worst films in creation. Standard low-budget invasion/annihilation plot is dubiously enriched with a Lawrence Welk–style automatic soap bubble machine and an ersatz E.T. patched together from a cheesy gorilla suit and diving helmet with glued-on TV rabbit ears. The long shots of "Ro-Man" sauntering through rocky terrain or the ludicrous "pantomime" love scene between the romantic interests defy serious description or narrative credibility. Biggest kick is the early music score by a pre–*Ten Commandments* Elmer Bernstein. The transfer is a knockout, as far as low-budget gimmick movies go (the film was released in 3-D, as well as "flat"). Deep black levels and consistent gray scale make for a highly detailed, crisp picture. Except for light speckling, the source materials are surprisingly clean. Mono sound here is less successful, with constant hiss and inept ADR. Look for the silhouette of an arm holding up a jet model at 24:26. Far out, man. —*EP* **AKA:** Monster from Mars; Monsters from the Moon.

Movie: 🎵🎵 **DVD:** 🎵🎵🎵½
Image Entertainment (Cat #ID8703CODVD, UPC #014381870329). Full frame. $24.99. Snapper. *LANG:* English. *FEATURES:* 12 chapter links • Theatrical trailer.
1953 84m/B George Nader, Claudia Barrett, Gregory Moffett, Selena Royle, John Mylong, George Barrows; **D:** Phil Tucker; **W:** Wyott Ordung; **C:** Jack Greenhalgh; **M:** Elmer Bernstein; **V:** John Brown.

Robotech: First Contact

Hailed by many as the single best anime space opera series, *Robotech* is finally available on DVD. It contains a number of science-fiction elements, ranging from *Battletech* to *Star Wars*—including the title theme—and combines them to a gripping series of furious adventures in a futuristic world where robots are powerful foes, and aliens as real as the air that we breathe. In chronological order these first six episodes mark the beginning of the series and set up the premise as events unfold after the crash of a space battleship onto Macross Island. Occasional registration problems cause the image to waver noticeably and occasional speckles and scratches mar the print. Grain is noticeable throughout, giving the image a bit of a rough look with fairly soft edges, that differs from the extremely sharp and slick look of some other recent anime releases. Audio is clean and without hiss or noise, but has a noticeably limited frequency response with underemphasized low ends. —GH

Movie: ♪♪½ **DVD:** ♪♪½
A.D.V. Films (Cat #DVDRT/001). Full frame. Dolby Digital Surround. $24.99. Keepcase. *LANG:* English. *FEATURES:* Previews.
2000 150m/C *JP*

The Rock [Criterion]

A chemical weapons expert (Cage) teams up with an incarcerated British officer (Connery) to infiltrate Alcatraz and stop a disgruntled Marine General (Harris) who has chemical weapons aimed at San Francisco. Riveting, exciting big-budget Hollywood action yarn with chase sequences and explosions to spare nicely balanced with a three-dimensional villain and some thought-provoking ideas. Connery is at his wry-humored best, and Harris is excellent as the well-intentioned bad guy. Forget all other editions of the film; Criterion's is an absolute knockout across the board. Featuring one of the clearest, eye-popping picture transfers and a speaker-blasting Surround track, this transfer is one of the finest ever presented on DVD. The interview with producer Bruckheimer is a bit dull, but the rest of the featurettes are interesting and worthwhile. The commentary (which was assembled for the laserdisc) seems to have been edited from several solo recording sessions, but is funny, interesting, and filled with fascinating behind-the-scenes stories. Highly recommended. —DG

Movie: ♪♪♪ **DVD:** ♪♪♪♪
Criterion Collection (Cat #108, UPC #7869 3615042). Widescreen (2.35:1) anamorphic. DTS; Dolby Digital 5.1. $39.99. Keepcase (2-disc). *LANG:* English. *SUB:* English. *FEATURES:* 32 chapter links • Insert booklet with notes • Outtakes • Commentary: Bay, Cage, Harris, Bruckheimer, technical advisor • Interview with Jerry Bruckheimer • Analysis of dive sequence special effects • "Movie Magic" episode on the special effects • Theatrical trailer and TV spots • Storyboards, production designs, stills • Premiere at Alcatraz • Excerpts from "Secrets of Alcatraz" • Do's and don'ts of Hollywood gunplay.
1996 (R) 136m/C Nicolas Cage, Sean Connery, Ed Harris, Michael Biehn, William Forsythe, David Morse, John Spencer, John C. McGinley, Tony Todd, Bokeem Woodbine, Danny Nucci, Vanessa Marcil, Claire Forlani, Gregory Sporleder; **D:** Michael Bay; **W:** Jonathan Hensleigh; **C:** John Schwartzman; **M:** Nick Glennie-Smith.

AWARDS: MTV Movie Awards '97: On-Screen Duo (Sean Connery/Nicolas Cage); *NOM:* Oscars '96: Sound; MTV Movie Awards '97: Film, Action Seq.

Rock-a-Doodle

Little Edmond is knocked out during a storm and has an Elvis-influenced vision. He sees Chanticleer, the sun-raising rooster, tricked into neglecting his duties by an evil barnyard owl. Humiliated and scorned, the earnest young bird leaves the farm and winds up in a Las Vegas–like city as an Elvis-impersonating singer (complete with pompadour), where he meets with success and all its trappings. It's all mildly amusing but bland by today's standards of animation, with music that is certainly nothing to crow about. The mixture of animation and live-action has a fairly soft focus and the animated scenes are on the dim side. As a result, the film gains little on DVD. —MM

Movie: ♪♪½ **DVD:** ♪♪
HBO Home Video (Cat #90701). Full frame. Dolby Digital 5.1 Surround Stereo; Dolby Digital Surround; Stereo. $24.98. Keepcase. *LANG:* English; French; Spanish. *FEATURES:* Trailer • 14 chapter links.
1992 (G) 77m/C D: Don Bluth; **W:** David N. Weiss; **M:** Robert Folk; **V:** Glen Campbell, Christopher Plummer, Phil Harris, Sandy Duncan, Ellen Greene, Charles Nelson Reilly, Eddie Deezen, Toby Scott Granger, Sorrell Booke.

Rocketship X-M

A lunar mission goes awry and the crew lands on Mars, where they discover ancient ruins and warnings of nuclear catastrophe. It's well acted, nicely photographed, and the script came from an uncredited Dalton Trumbo. DVD is made from great elements. The audio is almost perfect, with some intermittent light distortion. The picture has a scratch here and there but otherwise looks mint. The sepia-toned Mars sequence looks more orange than sepia brown, as if timed to match video copies of *The Angry Red Planet.* It still looks fine; the matte painting sequence with the domed ruins in the background looks particularly good. Collectors are going to want this one. —MM/GE *AKA:* Expedition Moon.
Movie: ♪♪½ **DVD:** ♪♪♪½
Image Entertainment (Cat #8693). Full frame. Dolby Digital Mono. $24.99. Snapper. *LANG:* English. *FEATURES:* Trailer.
1950 77m/B Lloyd Bridges, Osa Massen, John Emery, Hugh O'Brian, Noah Beery Jr.; **D:** Kurt Neumann; **W:** Kurt Neumann, Dalton Trumbo; **C:** Karl Struss; **M:** Ferde Grofe Jr.

Rocky [2 SE]

This "special edition" corrects the flaws in the first DVD release (enumerated by Mike Brantley in the first edition of this book). The widescreen transfer cannot add any polish to the rough-edged original image.

The disc is an accurate re-creation of the original. Though younger audiences may prefer the Surround remix, the mono still sounds better to me, and it seems more appropriate to the story. The commentary tracks are revealing; Stallone has his own separate piece. On the group conversation accompanying the film, someone (I wasn't sure which voice it was) notes how easy the young Stallone was to work with on the film, and then adds that it was not the case on *Rocky 5.* The film is also available as part of the *Rocky* boxed set (UPC #027616860378; $89.98). —MM
Movie: ♪♪♪½ **DVD:** ♪♪♪
MGM Home Entertainment (Cat #1001736, UPC #027616860361). Widescreen (1.85: 1) anamorphic. Dolby Digital 5.1 Surround; Mono. $24.98. Keepcase. *LANG:* English; French; Spanish. *SUB:* French; Spanish. *FEATURES:* 25 chapter links • Commentary: Avildsen, Winkler, Chartoff, Shire, Young • Video commentary by Stallone • 3 featurettes • Original trailers • Original advertising materials.
1976 (PG) 125m/C Sylvester Stallone, Talia Shire, Burgess Meredith, Burt Young, Carl Weathers; **D:** John G. Avildsen; **W:** Sylvester Stallone; **C:** James A. Crabe; **M:** Bill Conti. *AWARDS:* Oscars '76: Director (Avildsen), Film Editing, Picture; AFI '98: Top 100; Directors Guild '76: Director (Avildsen); Golden Globes '77: Film—Drama; L.A. Film Critics '76: Film; Natl. Bd. of Review '76: Support. Actress (Shire); N.Y. Film Critics '76: Support. Actress (Shire); *NOM:* Oscars '76: Actor (Stallone), Actress (Shire), Orig. Screenplay, Song ("Gonna Fly Now"), Sound, Support. Actor (Meredith, Young).

The Rocky Horror Picture Show

They really emptied the attic of *Rocky Horror* material for this ambitious two-disc set. It contains three versions of the film, the U.S. and U.K. releases, plus creator Richard O'Brien's original conception with the "black-and-white" introduction. (It's available as an "Easter egg": from the Main Menu, highlight "scene selection" then hit the left arrow on the remote, highlighting a pair of lips in the lower left corner, then hit "Enter.") Also available are two versions of the midnight theatrical experience; one with a separate audio track that makes good use of the Surround channels; the other with a prompt that cuts to film of an experienced audience at key moments. Those are on the first disc. The second contains more than a dozen deleted scenes, alternate takes and musical numbers, specials, trailers, etc. Naturally, image and sound are first-rate, and the captions allow you finally to figure out those lyrics that everyone else seems to understand. —MM
Movie: ♪♪♪♪ **DVD:** ♪♪♪♪
20th Century Fox Home Entertainment (Cat #20000574, UPC #024543005742). Widescreen (1.66:1) anamorphic. Dolby Digital 5.1 Surround Stereo; Dolby Mono. $29.98. Boxed slipcase. *LANG:* English.

SUB: English; Spanish. *FEATURES:* 35 chapter links (U.S. version); 36 links (U.K.) ➠ Multiview theatre experience ➠ Deleted scenes ➠ 30-minute documentary ➠ VH-1 "Behind the Music" special ➠ Talent files ➠ DVD-ROM features ➠ Commentary: Richard O'Brien, Patricia Quinn. **1975 (R) 105m/C** *GB* Tim Curry, Susan Sarandon, Barry Bostwick, Little Nell, Richard O'Brien, Patricia Quinn, Jonathan Adams, Peter Hinwood, Meat Loaf Aday, Charles Gray, Koo Stark; *D:* Jim Sharman; *W:* Jim Sharman, Richard O'Brien; *C:* Peter Suschitzsky; *M:* Richard Hartley, Richard O'Brien.

Roger Corman Retrospective, Vol. 1

Three of Roger Corman's better early efforts are collected. Please see individual reviews of *Attack of the Giant Leeches, The Wasp Woman,* and *A Bucket of Blood.* —MM
Movie: 🎬🎬 *DVD:* 🎬🎬
SlingShot Entertainment (Cat #TDVD9114, UPC #017078911428). Full frame. $19.99. Large jewelcase. *LANG:* English.
2000 ?m/C

Rome: Power & Glory

At the 3rd Divi Awards for DVDs, this fine set won the Best Educational/Documentary competition over entries that are much more well-known. The reason is that these two discs are a superb presentation of the series that first aired on The Learning Channel. Beyond the excellent visual and audio presentation, DVD offers easy accessibility to various points in the programs. Of the extras, the timeline may be the most useful for those who have trouble keeping names and dates straight. The computer-generated reconstructions of famous structures as they were in their heyday compared to their current condition are also illuminating. This is history for people who think they don't like history. —MM
Movie: 🎬🎬🎬½ *DVD:* 🎬🎬🎬🎬
Questar Video, Inc. (Cat #QD3082-DVD, UPC #033937030826). Widescreen (1.66:1) letterboxed. Stereo. $44.95. Keepcase. *LANG:* English. *FEATURES:* 36 chapter links ➠ 6 virtual reconstructions ➠ Timeline ➠ Thumbnail bios of the 12 Caesars.
1999 312m/C *D:* Graham Townsley, Lynn Dougherty, Neil Barrett; *W:* Graham Townsley, Lynn Dougherty, Neil Barrett; *Nar:* Peter Coyote.

Romeo Must Die

Romance is decidedly secondary to action in this kung fu/hip-hop hybrid. After an overextended (but flashy) credits sequence, the story kicks in. Black crime lord Isaak O'Day (a magnetic Lindo) and Asian crime boss Ch'u Sing (O) are maintaining an uneasy truce in order to do a mega-business deal. Then Sing's useless younger son is killed and soon O'Day's son bites the dust as well. Into the mix springs good guy/ex-cop Han Sing (Li), who's out to avenge his brother's death,

and lovely Trish O'Day (Aaliyah), who wants the same for her brother. The action sequences are frequent and frequently amazing and Li has minimal English dialogue to worry about. There's also humor, including Li's introduction to touch football. The most distinguishing element of this DVD is the incredibly loud and noisy 5.1 track, which places too much emphasis on the effects tracks, at times so much that some dialogue is covered up. Cranking the center speaker a little makes things better; nonetheless, it's kind of aggravating. On the plus side, the subwoofer track is plenty powerful and helps to propel action nicely along, especially when combined with the Surround tracks, which get plenty of use in the mix. The picture is very sharp with plenty of detail and the blacks are dark and true. A unique feature is the use of numerous short featurettes, each one concentrating on a different element in the film and filled with behind-the-scenes footage. —JO
Movie: 🎬🎬½ *DVD:* 🎬🎬🎬½
Warner Home Video, Inc. (Cat #18128, UPC #085391812821). Widescreen (2.35:1) anamorphic. Dolby Digital 5.1. $24.98. Snapper. *LANG:* English; French. *CAP:* English. *FEATURES:* 39 chapter links ➠ 2 theatrical trailers ➠ 13 behind-the-scenes documentaries ➠ 3 music videos ➠ Talent files.
2000 (R) 115m/C Jet Li, Aaliyah, Delroy Lindo, Henry O, Isaiah Washington, Russell Wong, DMX, DB Woodside, Edoardo Ballerini, Anthony Anderson, Jon Kit Lee, Francoise Yip; *D:* Andrzej Bartkowiak; *W:* Eric Bernt, John Jarrell; *C:* Glen MacPherson; *M:* Stanley Clarke, Timbaland.

Romero

Julia is riveting as the Salvadoran archbishop who championed his destitute congregation despite considerable political opposition. If the film's leftist politics are a bit blatant, they are also carefully and intelligently presented. Beyond the dual-language option, the film gains little on DVD. The full-frame image is essentially identical to VHS tape. —MM
Movie: 🎬🎬½ *DVD:* 🎬🎬½
Trimark Home Video (Cat #7462D, UPC #031398746225). Full frame. Dolby Digital Stereo. $24.95. Keepcase. *LANG:* English; Spanish. *SUB:* English; French; Spanish. *FEATURES:* Behind-the-scenes featurette ➠ Trailer.
1989 102m/C Raul Julia, Richard Jordan, Ana Alicia, Eddie Velez, Alejandro Bracho, Tony Plana, Lucy Reina, Harold Gould, Al Ruscio, Robert Viharo; *D:* John Duigan; *W:* John Sacret Young; *C:* Geoff Burton; *M:* Gabriel Yared.

Romper Stomper [SE]

Violent confrontations between Australian skinheads and the Vietnamese immigrant community are mixed with a disturbed love story. Suburban rich girl Gabe (McKenzie) is drawn to the charismatic leader Hando

(Crowe) and his friend Davey (Pollock). The first half is by far the stronger. The second is more conventional and less satisfying. On his commentary track and in interviews included as extras, director Wright addresses the controversy the film sparked, and he's not nearly as defensive as you might expect. The restored widescreen image is a massive improvement over previously available full-frame tapes, though it retains the cold blue tint that Wright chooses to use. Sound makes an equally impressive leap forward. That said, the violence is comparable to *Clockwork Orange* and the film is not recommended to all viewers. Most of the extras are located on a second disc. —MM
Movie: 🎬🎬🎬½ *DVD:* 🎬🎬🎬½
20th Century Fox Home Entertainment (Cat #2001102, UPC #024543011026). Widescreen (1.85:1) anamorphic. DTS; Dolby Digital 5.1 Surround Stereo; Dolby Digital Stereo. $26.98. Keepcase. *LANG:* English. *CAP:* English. *FEATURES:* 24 chapter links ➠ Commentary: Geoffrey Wright ➠ Interviews with Wright ➠ Film restoration demonstration ➠ Talent files ➠ Separate music track ➠ Press clippings (text).
1992 (R) 85m/C *AU* Russell Crowe, Jacqueline McKenzie, Daniel Pollock; *D:* Geoffrey Wright; *W:* Geoffrey Wright; *C:* Ron Hagen; *M:* John Clifford White. *AWARDS:* Australian Film Inst. '92: Actor (Crowe), Sound, Score.

A Room with a View

In this Merchant/Ivory comedy of manners, Bonham Carter's Lucy Honeychurch is a proper, yet idealistic young Edwardian woman who is visiting scenic Florence with her chaperone Aunt Charlotte (Smith). An engaging adaptation of E.M. Forster's novel of wit and romance, the story puts Charlotte on high alert when Lucy is kissed by an improper suitor. She removes her niece from Florence, returning Lucy to London where she is to marry a gentleman of society. But Feisty Lucy rejects dashing George Emerson (Sands) for supercilious Cecil Vyse (Day Lewis), then repents and finds (presumably) eternal passion. The scenery is superb, and so is the supporting cast. Truly romantic, and there's much humor too. The music of Puccini is appropriately lush in the remixed Dolby Digital tracks, but this isn't the disc to show off your subwoofer. Visually, perfectionists will be disappointed that an old video master was used in lieu of commissioning a pristine new transfer for the digital age. Detail suffers significantly on large screens. Another bummer: no extras to speak of. —MB
Movie: 🎬🎬🎬🎬 *DVD:* 🎬🎬
Image Entertainment (Cat #ID9172CUDVD, UPC #014381917222). Widescreen (1.85:1) letterboxed. Dolby Digital 5.1. $24.98. Snapper. *LANG:* English. *FEATURES:* 15 chapter links.
1986 117m/C *GB* Helena Bonham Carter, Julian Sands, Denholm Elliott, Maggie Smith, Judi Dench, Simon Callow, Daniel Day-Lewis, Rupert Graves, Rosemary

Leach; **D:** James Ivory; **W:** Ruth Prawer Jhabvala; **C:** Tony Pierce-Roberts; **M:** Richard Robbins. *AWARDS:* Oscars '86: Adapt. Screenplay, Art Dir./Set Dec., Costume Des.; British Acad. '86: Actress (Smith), Film, Support. Actress (Dench); Golden Globes '87: Support. Actress (Smith); Ind. Spirit '87: Foreign Film; Natl. Bd. of Review '86: Support. Actor (Day-Lewis); N.Y. Film Critics '86: Cinematog., Support. Actor (Day-Lewis); Writers Guild '86: Adapt. Screenplay; *NOM:* Oscars '86: Cinematog., Director (Ivory), Picture, Support. Actor (Elliott), Support. Actress (Smith).

Roots of Rhythm

This two and a half-hour PBS documentary provides what even many devotees of Latin American music don't have—a good overview of where it came from. Harry Belafonte hosts and narrates a dizzying three-part analysis of cultural and musical sources for modern Latin rock, offering short history lessons and visiting still-vibrant Cuban neighborhoods, where traditional roots still flourish. Old 78rpm records are heard for some near-lost recordings, while important trends, from the '20s decade-long prohibition party in Havana, to the rise of Cuban-American music in the '80s, are fully covered. Belafonte, a man who must share Dick Clark's secret of eternal good looks, is obviously excited about the topic and his enthusiasm is infectious. When he is shown visiting Cuba and watching street performers, it's true interest in his face, and not just a photo op. Color and especially sound are very good; just be prepared for the usual range of quality in the aged film clips and older video sources. —*GE*
Movie: ♫♫♫½ **DVD:** ♫♫♫
New Video Group (Cat #NVG 9476, UPC #767685947630). Full frame. Dolby Digital Surround. $24.95. Keepcase. *LANG:* English. *FEATURES:* 18 chapter links • Credits.
1999 ?m/C D: Howard P. Dratch, Eugene Rosow; **W:** Howard P. Dratch, Eugene Rosow, Linda Post; **C:** Les Blank; **M:** Gloria Estefan, Tito Puente, Dizzy Gillespie, Desi Arnaz Sr., Celia Cruz, Ruben Blades, Xavier Cugat, Carmen Miranda.

Rope

Hitchcock's first color feature probably looks as good as it possibly could on this disc. A few faded spots appear early on and overall, the image has a curious tinted quality. There's also faint noise on the soundtrack audible during more quiet moments. Now forget those criticisms and appreciate the master's great "gimmick" film. The story of a "perfect murder" committed by Granger and Dall (loosely based on Loeb and Leopold) is presented as one long "take." Hitchcock used pans through black to disguise the 10-minute limitation imposed by the amount of film the camera would hold. The entire film takes place inside an apartment set. —*MM*

Movie: ♫♫♫½ **DVD:** ♫♫♫½
Universal Studios Home Video (Cat #20671, UPC #025192067129). Full frame. Dolby Digital Mono. $29.99. Keepcase. *LANG:* English; French; Spanish. *CAP:* English. *FEATURES:* "Making of" featurette • Production photos and notes • Trailers • DVD-ROM features • 18 chapter links.
1948 (PG) 81m/C James Stewart, John Dall, Farley Granger, Cedric Hardwicke, Constance Collier; **D:** Alfred Hitchcock; **W:** Arthur Laurents; **C:** William V. Skall, Joseph Valentine; **M:** David Buttolph.

Rosemary's Baby

Rosemary (Farrow) and her ambitious actor husband (Cassavettes) move into a spooky New York apartment building and the weirdness progresses steadily. This brilliant combination of soap-opera and horror is a real crowd-pleaser. On DVD, the film doesn't have the sparkle of more recent big-budget studio productions, but it looks fine for its age. The clarity of the audio makes the flattish dubbing even more obvious than it has been before. On their retrospective interviews, producer Robert Evans and Polanski mostly round up the usual suspects. Since so much of the film comes directly from Ira Levin's novel, it's a shame that he was not included in the talk. —*MM*
Movie: ♫♫♫♫ **DVD:** ♫♫♫
Paramount Home Video (Cat #06831, UPC #097360683172). Widescreen anamorphic. Dolby Digital Mono. $29.99. Keepcase. *LANG:* English; French. *SUB:* English. *FEATURES:* 32 chapter links • "Making of" featurette • Retrospective interviews with Robert Evans and Roman Polanski.
1968 (R) 134m/C Mia Farrow, John Cassavetes, Ruth Gordon, Sidney Blackmer, Maurice Evans, Patsy Kelly, Elisha Cook Jr., Ralph Bellamy, Charles Grodin, Hanna Landy, Emmaline Henry, William Castle; **D:** Roman Polanski; **W:** Roman Polanski; **C:** William A. Fraker; **M:** Krzysztof Komeda; **V:** Tony Curtis. *AWARDS:* Oscars '68: Support. Actress (Gordon); Golden Globes '69: Support. Actress (Gordon); *NOM:* Oscars '68: Adapt. Screenplay.

Rouge

Supernatural love story follows a spectral woman (Mui) who is finally reunited with the man of her dreams (Cheung). The DVD image is about average for a Hong Kong import. Conventional day exteriors and interiors are O.K., but night exteriors are filled with artifacts and heavy grain. Sound is fine. —*MM* *AKA:* Yanzhi Kou.
Movie: ♫♫½ **DVD:** ♫♫
Tai Seng Video Marketing Widescreen letterboxed. Dolby Digital 5.1 Surround Stereo. $49.95. Keepcase. *LANG:* Cantonese; Mandarin. *SUB:* Trad. & Simpl. Chinese; English; Japanese; Korean; Bahasa Mal. & Ind.; Thai; Spanish. *FEATURES:* 9 chapter links • Talent files • Synopsis • Awards.
1987 99m/C *HK* Anita Mui, Leslie Cheung, Alex Man, Emily Chu; **D:** Stanley

Kwan; **W:** Lei Bik Wah, Chiu Tai An-Ping; **C:** Bill Wong; **M:** Michael Lai.

Roughnecks Starship Troopers Chronicles the Pluto Campaign

Animated feature is a collection of episodes of the TV series. Curiously, this version of future war is closer in spirit and character to Robert Heinlein's fiction than the live-action feature by Paul Verhoeven, who produces. The computer-created animation is more detailed than comparable Japanese anime, but it's not up to the level of detail set by *Toy Story 2*. Darker scenes are littered with heavy artifacts. 5.1 mix gives the action an overemphatic fullness. —*MM*
Movie: ♫♫½ **DVD:** ♫♫½
Columbia Tristar Home Video (Cat #06174, UPC #043396061743). Full frame. Dolby Digital 5.1 Surround Stereo; Dolby Digital Surround. $24.95. Keepcase. *LANG:* English; French; Spanish; Portuguese. *SUB:* English; French; Spanish; Portuguese; Chinese; Korean; Thai. *FEATURES:* 28 chapter links • Photo gallery • Trailers.
1999 (PG) 96m/C D: Audu Paden, Christopher Berkeley, David Hartman, Jay Oliva, Sam Liu.

Row Your Boat

Ex-con Jamey Meadows (Bon Jovi) took the fall for his crooked brother (Forsythe). He tries to go straight, working as a census counter where he meets the lovely Chun Hua (Bai Ling) who has even more problems than he does. The pace drags a bit, but the cast is certainly attractive and their performances are strong. The film looks good, too. The bright image might gain a bit of sharpness over VHS tape. Sound is much better. —*MM*
Movie: ♫♫ **DVD:** ♫♫
York Entertainment (Cat #YPD-1065, UPC #750723106526). Full frame. Dolby Digital 5.1 Surround Stereo. $19.95. Keepcase. *LANG:* English; Chinese. *SUB:* English; Spanish. *FEATURES:* 30 chapter links • Trailers • Filmographies.
1998 106m/C Jon Bon Jovi, William Forsythe, Bai Ling, Jill(ian) Hennessey, John Ventimiglia; **D:** Sollace Mitchell; **W:** Sollace Mitchell; **C:** Michael Barrow, Zoltan David; **M:** Phil Ramone.

The Rowdy Girls

Sharp-shooting Velvet (the indefatigable Tweed) disguises herself as a nun and meets up with bullwhip-wielding wild woman Mick (Strain) and runaway bride Sara (Brooks) on a trip across the Western plains. It's vintage Troma, though the image, particularly the interiors, look unusually well detailed. The treat of the disc is the commentary track with Strain and writer/producer India Allen. It's really funny and irreverent. —*MM*
Movie: ♫♫ **DVD:** ♫♫♫
Troma Team Video (Cat #9001, UPC #7903 57900138). Full frame. $24.99. Keep-

case. *LANG:* English. *FEATURES:* 12 chapter links ▪ Commentary: Julie Strain, India Allen, Mark Adams ▪ Production stills ▪ Troma studio tour ▪ Trailers. Title is also available in "R"-rated version (cat. #9002, UPC 790357900237).
2000 88m/C Shannon Tweed, Julie Strain, Deanna Brooks, Laszlo Vargo; *D:* Steve Nevius; *W:* India Allen.

Roxanne

Martin's reinterpretation of *Cyrano de Bergerac* is one of his finest screen appearances. The romantic triangle consists of a small-town firechief (Martin) who has a huge nose, a shy fireman (Rossovich), and the astronomer (Hannah) they both love. Don't miss Chapter 12, where Martin creates wonderful nose jokes. The whole film works beautifully, though it doesn't really gain much on DVD. This has never been a particularly strong movie in visual terms. The choice of full-frame or widescreen versions is probably the most important advantage of disc over tape. A commentary track by Martin might have been very good. —*MM*
Movie: 🎜🎜🎜 *DVD:* 🎜🎜🎜
Columbia Tristar Home Video (Cat #8539). Widescreen (2.35:1) anamorphic; full frame. Dolby Digital Surround. $24.95. Keepcase. *LANG:* English; French. *SUB:* English; French. *FEATURES:* 28 chapter links.
1987 (PG) 107m/C Steve Martin, Daryl Hannah, Rick Rossovich, Shelley Duvall, Michael J. Pollard, Fred Willard, John Kapelos, Max Alexander, Damon Wayans, Matt Lattanzi, Kevin Nealon; *D:* Fred Schepisi; *W:* Steve Martin; *C:* Ian Baker; *M:* Bruce Smeaton. *AWARDS:* L.A. Film Critics '87: Actor (Martin); Natl. Soc. Film Critics '87: Actor (Martin); Writers Guild '87: Adapt. Screenplay.

R.P.M.

Luke (Arquette) and Claudia (Janssen) are rival car thieves who are going after the same vintage machines in Europe. The scenery, the cars, and the women are easy on the eyes, and Arquette is not quite as irritating as he can be. Overall, image and sound range between fair and good. —*MM*
Movie: 🎜🎜 *DVD:* 🎜🎜½
Pioneer Entertainment (Cat #83978, UPC #097368397842). Full frame. Dolby Digital Stereo. $24.99. Keepcase. *LANG:* English. *SUB:* Spanish. *FEATURES:* 16 chapter links ▪ Talent files ▪ Trivia game ▪ Trailer.
1997 (R) 91m/C David Arquette, Famke Janssen, Emmanuelle Seigner, Jerry Hall; *D:* Ian Sharp; *C:* Harvey Harrison; *M:* Alan Lisk.

Ruckus

Traumatized Vietnam vet Kyle Hanson (Benedict) uses his Ranger training to defend himself when he's attacked by rednecks in a small Alabama town. The overwrought performances and lurid presentation make *First Blood* (which was released later, though David Morrell's novel had been around for some time) look positively

elegant. Veterans Farnsworth and Johnson are a bit out of place. On DVD, this drive-in material is still exceptionally grainy, as it should be. —*MM* *AKA:* The Loner.
Movie: 🎜🎜 *DVD:* 🎜🎜
Anchor Bay (Cat #DV11187, UPC #013131 118797). Widescreen (2.35:1) anamorphic. Dolby Digital Mono. $24.99. Keepcase. *LANG:* English. *FEATURES:* 22 chapter links ▪ Commentary: Max Kleven, Dirk Benedict, Linda Blair.
1981 (PG) 91m/C Dirk Benedict, Linda Blair, Ben Johnson, Richard Farnsworth, Matt Clark; *D:* Max Kleven; *W:* Max Kleven; *C:* Don Burgess; *M:* Willie Nelson.

Rudy [SE]

Likeable, true story about a little guy who triumphs over big odds. Daniel "Rudy" Ruettiger (Astin) dreams of playing football for Notre Dame, no matter how farfetched the dream. He's a mediocre student, physically unsuitable for big-time college ball, but sheer determination helps him attain his dream. Astin delivers an engaging performance and is backed up by a good supporting cast. Sentimental story stretches the truth with typical shameless Hollywood manipulation, but is still entertaining. From the director and writer of another David-beats-Goliath sports film, *Hoosiers*. The video transfer is quite impressive, with well-defined colors and crisp blacks. The new 5.1 soundtrack is equally well done, particularly during the football sequences. Of the extras, probably the most interesting is the featurette on the "real" Rudy (though it amounts to little more than Rudy narrating his life as we watch clips from the film). —*MJT*
Movie: 🎜🎜½ *DVD:* 🎜🎜🎜
Columbia Tristar Home Video (Cat #53727, UPC #043396537279). Widescreen (1.66:1) letterboxed. Dolby Digital 5.1; Dolby Digital 2.0 Surround. $24.95. Keepcase. *LANG:* English; Spanish. *SUB:* English; French; Spanish; Chinese; Korean; Thai. *FEATURES:* 28 chapter links ▪ "Rudy: The Real Story" featurette ▪ Original featurette ▪ "First Down with Sean Astin" featurette ▪ Isolated music score ▪ Bonus trailers ▪ Talent files.
1993 (PG) 112m/C Sean Astin, Ned Beatty, Charles S. Dutton, Lili Taylor, Robert Prosky, Jason Miller, Ron Dean, Chelcie Ross, Jon Favreau, Greta Lind, Scott Benjaminson, Christopher Reed; *D:* David Anspaugh; *W:* Angelo Pizzo; *C:* Oliver Wood; *M:* Jerry Goldsmith.

Rudyard Kipling's the Second Jungle Book: Mowgli and Baloo

Kid's adventure is lively enough to entertain the short set, who aren't likely to be overly critical of the so-so image. Jamie Williams is our young hero who must battle the villain Roddy McDowall. Considerable grain and excess artifacts are rampant in bright scenes; color values change noticeably in cuts from exteriors to sets to special effects shots. Sound is acceptable.

—*MM* *AKA:* Jungle Book 2; Mowgli and Baloo: Jungle Book 2; The Second Jungle Book: Mowgli and Baloo.
Movie: 🎜🎜 *DVD:* 🎜🎜½
Columbia Tristar Home Video (Cat #05988, UPC #043396059887). Full frame; widescreen (2.35:1) letterboxed. Dolby Digital Surround Stereo; Mono. $24.95. Keepcase. *LANG:* English; Spanish; Portuguese. *SUB:* English; Spanish; Portuguese. *FEATURES:* Trailers ▪ Talent files ▪ 28 chapter links.
1997 (PG) 88m/C Jamie Williams, Bill Campbell, Roddy McDowall, Cornelia Hayes O'Herlihy, David Paul Francis, Gulsham Grover, Dyrk Ashton, B.J. Hogg, Amy Robbins, Hal Fowler; *D:* Duncan McLachlan; *W:* Bayard Johnson, Matthew Horton; *C:* Adolfo Bartoli; *M:* John Scott.

Rugrats in Paris: The Movie

The series' sense of humor kicks in with the opening menu where Angelica tells you to hurry up and make a choice, already. Then the film itself begins with a quick funny parody of the opening of *The Godfather*. After that, the Pickle family is off to France where they find more jokes about peeing, barfing, etc. Adults in tune with the series' sensibility will be well entertained. Of course, so will the kids. Image appears to be a flawless re-creation of the theatrical release, which is not as bright and flashy as much contemporary animation. The disc contains enough extras to satisfy the target audience. —*MM*
Movie: 🎜🎜🎜 *DVD:* 🎜🎜🎜
Paramount Home Video (Cat #33672, UPC #097363367246). Widescreen anamorphic. Dolby Digital 5.1 Surround Stereo; Dolby Digital Surround. $29.99. Keepcase. *LANG:* English; French. *SUB:* English. *FEATURES:* 10 chapter links ▪ 2 alternate endings ▪ Sound effects showcase ▪ "Who Let the Dogs Out?" music video ▪ Trailers and promos ▪ DVD-ROM links.
2000 (G) 80m/C *D:* Stig Bergqvist, Paul Demeyer; *W:* David N. Weiss, Jill Gorey, Barbara Herndon, Kate Boutilier; *M:* Mark Mothersbaugh; *V:* Elizabeth (E.G. Dailey) Daily, Christine Cavanaugh, Susan Sarandon, Jack Riley, Michael Bell, Melanie Chartoff, Tara Charendoff, Kath Soucie, John Lithgow, Debbie Reynolds, Mako, James D. Stern, Cheryl Chase, Julia Kato, Lisa McClowry.

Rules of Engagement

Court-martial drama is single-mindedly pro-military. (Why not? It was written by ex-Secretary of the Navy James Webb.) Marine Colonel Terry Childers (Jackson) is accused of illegally giving orders that result in the deaths of women and children during the rescue of American diplomats from Yemen. He asks his old friend Colonel Hays Hodges (Jones) to defend him. DVD doesn't add much to the courtroom scenes, but in the Vietnam introduction and the other battle scenes, the 5.1 mix is put to effective use. Director Friedkin copies some of the devices first seen in *Saving Private Ryan* in the combat sequences. They're bloody, horrifying, and graphic. —MM

Movie: 🎬🎬½ **DVD:** 🎬🎬🎬

Paramount Home Video (Cat #33217, UPC #09363321743). Widescreen anamorphic. Dolby Digital 5.1 Surround Stereo; Dolby Digital Surround Stereo. $29.99. Keepcase. *LANG:* English; French. *CAP:* English. *FEATURES:* 15 chapter links • Cast and crew interviews • Friedkin commentary track • Behind-the-scenes featurette.

2000 (R) 128m/C Samuel L. Jackson, Tommy Lee Jones, Guy Pearce, Bruce Greenwood, Blair Underwood, Philip Baker Hall, Anne Archer, Ben Kingsley, Mark Feuerstein, Dale Dye; *D:* William Friedkin; *W:* Stephen Gaghan; *C:* Nicola Pecorini, William A. Fraker; *M:* Mark Isham.

Runaway

Sci-fi silliness freely mixes *The French Connection, Blade Runner,* and *Vertigo* with flavorless results. Tom Selleck stars as Jack Ramsay, sergeant in an elite police unit that chases down "runaway" robots in an undetermined future (which managed to keep the very '80s teased manes). Super-arch-criminal scientist Charles Luther (Gene Simmons, sans KISS make-up) masterminds a wave of terrorism by turning domesticated machines into assassins and dispatching electronic cockroaches that spit acid and explode. Of course, it's up to Jack's savvy with dis-arming homicidal toasters to save the day. Writer/director Crichton's good-as-gold touch with mixing science and melodrama seems to have eluded him here. Unlike *Jurassic Park* or even *Westworld,* the tech-nology just isn't that special and the cop clichés (Ramsay constantly chewed out by his perpetually irked chief, or Ramsay as the lonely single parent who finally finds love) drown any possibility of accepting this mechanical piffle on purely dramatic terms. For example, Jack has a problem with heights. Guess where the final show-down takes place? (I won't spoil the sur-prise.) The 2.35 anamorphic transfer exhibits a clean, solid image. Contrast is a little high, though, sometimes washing out the already de-saturated hues. Unless let-terboxing is the absolute bane of your video watching existence, avoid the pan-and-scan version also available on the two-sided disc. Audio imaging is virtually the same on both the four-channel dis-crete and two-channel matrix Surround soundtracks. Other than completing a Tom Selleck or Michael Crichton DVD library, reasons to pick up this disc are few. —EP

Movie: 🎬🎬 **DVD:** 🎬🎬🎬

Columbia Tristar Home Video (Cat #04699, UPC #4339604699). Widescreen (2.35:1) anamorphic; full frame. Dolby Digital 4.0 Stereo; Dolby Digital Surround Stereo. $24.95. Keepcase. *LANG:* Spanish; Por-tuguese (mono). *SUB:* Spanish; Por-tuguese; Chinese; Korean; Thai. *CAP:* Eng-lish. *FEATURES:* 28 chapter links • Theatrical trailers • Talent files.

1984 (PG-13) 100m/C Tom Selleck, Cyn-thia Rhodes, Gene Simmons, Stan Shaw, Kirstie Alley; *D:* Michael Crichton; *W:* Michael Crichton; *C:* John A. Alonzo; *M:* Jerry Goldsmith.

Running Free

Inspiring story of the friendship between an orphaned servant boy and an aban-doned colt named Lucky who is destined for a life of hard labor. Their quest for freedom from their proscribed lives cre-ates a visually stunning tale about the tri-umph of the human spirit. The video transfer is fantastic with bright, vibrant colors and crisply defined blacks and shadows. The audio transfer is equally impressive and features nice clear dia-logue and a lush musical score. The lack of substantial extras is the only thing that detracts from this disc. —MJT

Movie: 🎬🎬🎬 **DVD:** 🎬🎬🎬

Columbia Tristar Home Video (Cat #04169, UPC #043396041691). Widescreen (2.35: 1) letterboxed; full frame. Dolby Digital 5.1 Surround; Dolby Digital 2.0 Surround. $24.95. Keepcase. *LANG:* English; Span-ish; Portuguese. *SUB:* English; French; Spanish; Portuguese; Chinese; Korean; Thai. *FEATURES:* 28 chapter links • The-atrical trailers • Isolated music score • Talent files.

2000 (G) 85m/C Chase Moore, Jan Decleir, Arie Verveen, Maria Geelbooi, Lukas Haas; *D:* Sergei Bodrov; *W:* Jeanne Rosen-berg; *C:* Dan Laustsen; *M:* Nicola Piovani.

Running out of Time

Antonio (Gomez) is a Basque terrorist who's been assigned to set a bomb in a city. Upon moving there, he finds himself living next to Charo (Gabriel), a junkie hooker. Much to the distress of his com-rades, the two fall in love. Director Uribe manages to balance complex politics with suspense and a frank sexuality in a man-ner that's never seen in American movies. Though the image is pale and lacking the brightness of Hollywood productions, the DVD seems to be an accurate reproduc-tion of the original, and the film's look complements the story and tone. Purists may fault the burned-in subtitles. I do not. This one's a genuine sleeper that's worth seeking out. —MM *AKA:* Dias Contados; Numbered Days.

Movie: 🎬🎬🎬 **DVD:** 🎬🎬🎬

New Yorker Video (Cat #80400, UPC #717 119804046). Widescreen. $29.99. Keep-case. *LANG:* Spanish. *SUB:* English. *FEA-TURES:* Trailer • "Making of" featurette • Interview with Ruth Gabriel • 6 chap-ter links.

1994 93m/C *SP* Carmelo Gomez, Ruth Gabriel, Javier Bardem, Karra Elejalde, Candela Pena; *D:* Imanol Uribe; *W:* Imanol Uribe; *C:* Javier Aguirresarobe; *M:* Jose Nieto.

Running out of Time

Jewel thief Andy (Lau) knows that he has only two weeks to live. He goes ahead and

pulls a job that sets him against Sean (Wan), a canny police negotiator. Director Johnny To employs some flashy visuals in this overachieving crime movie and he got first-rate performances from his leads, particularly Lau Ching Wan, a tremendous character actor. The DVD suffers from a bit of aliasing and that bleached-out look that's typical of so many Hong Kong imports. Sound is fine. The menu has a tendency to freeze. —MM

Movie: 🎬🎬🎬 **DVD:** 🎬🎬½

Tai Seng Video Marketing (Cat #245, UPC #4890391102454). Widescreen letter-boxed. Dolby Digital 5.1 Surround Stereo. $29.95. Keepcase. *LANG:* Cantonese; Mandarin. *SUB:* Traditional & Simplified Chi-nese; English; Thai. *FEATURES:* 9 chapter links • Previews.

1999 89m/C *HK* Andy Lau, Lau Ching Wan, Waise Lee, Hui Siu Hung, Yoyo Mung; *D:* Johnny To; *W:* Yau Nai Hoi; *C:* Cheng Siu Keung; *M:* Wong Ying Wah.

Saboteur

Along with *The 39 Steps,* this film estab-lished the ground rules for the modern thriller. Barry Kane (Cummings) is wrongly accused of sabotaging the Los Angeles airplane factory where he works. With the police on his trail, he sets off on a cross-country chase to find the real spies and clear his name. It ends with the famous sequence on the Statue of Liberty. If the black-and-white photography isn't as sharp as some, it's fine for this story, which maintains its entertainment value. I've seen the film theatrically and on tape and this is as good as the image has ever looked. Universal has done its usual superb job with the extras. The disc belongs in every Hitchcock fan's collec-tion. —MM

Movie: 🎬🎬🎬½ **DVD:** 🎬🎬🎬½

Universal Studios Home Video (Cat #20673, UPC #025192067327). Full frame. Dolby Digital Mono. $29.99. Keep-case. *LANG:* English. *SUB:* French; Spanish. *CAP:* English. *FEATURES:* 18 chapter links • "Making of" documentary • Story-boards • Hitchcock sketches • Produc-tion photographs and notes • Talent files.

1942 108m/B Priscilla Lane, Robert Cummings, Otto Kruger, Alan Baxter, Nor-man Lloyd, Charles Halton; *D:* Alfred Hitch-cock; *W:* Alfred Hitchcock, Peter Viertel; *C:* Joseph Valentine; *M:* Frank Skinner.

Sagebrush Trail

Please see review for *Man from Utah / Sagebush Trail.*

Movie: 🎬🎬🎬

1933 53m/B John Wayne, Yakima Canutt, Wally Wales; *D:* Armand Schaefer; *W:* Lind-sley Parsons; *C:* Archie Stout.

The St. Francisville Experiment

Blair Witch rip-off that takes about 30 min-utes to get going but eventually delivers a few genuine scares. The digital video used to create the faux-documentary look of the film is its biggest hindrance. Several images throughout appear horribly pixelated. For the most part, however, colors are reproduced adequately. The video motif of this pseudo-documentary consequently affects the sound quality in a rather negative way, especially in action scenes where it becomes little more than white noise. Sadly, the supplements are a feeble attempt to maintain the illusion that the film is nonfiction and ultimately add nothing to the disc's value. —*MJT*

Movie: ♫♫½ **DVD:** ♫♫
Trimark Home Video (Cat #VM#7507D, UPC #031398750757). Full frame. Dolby Digital Stereo. $24.99. Keepcase. *LANG:* English. *SUB:* English; Spanish; French. *FEATURES:* 24 chapter links • Interviews with cast (in character) • Theatrical trailer • "How to Conduct Your Own Experiment" section.
2000 (PG-13) 79m/C Tim Baldini, Madison Charap, Ryan Larson, Paul Palmer, Paul James, Paul Salamoff, Troy Taylor; **D:** Tim Thompson.

Saint Jack
Jack Flowers (Gazzarra) is a small-time American expatriate pimp in Singapore. He has a dream of opening the best whorehouse in town. His plans lead him in several strange directions and bring him into contact with a colorful cast of characters. On his commentary track, Bogdanovich indulges in his customary name-dropping. The image is unusually clear for a Corman production, making the disc a solid step up from tape. —*MM*

Movie: ♫♫♫ **DVD:** ♫♫½
New Concorde (Cat #NH20197D, UPC #73 6991419797). Widescreen letterboxed. $19.98. Keepcase. *LANG:* English. *FEATURES:* 24 chapter links • Commentary: Peter Bogdanovich • Trailers • Thumbnail bios.
1979 (R) 112m/C Ben Gazzara, Denholm Elliott, Joss Ackland, George Lazenby, Peter Bogdanovich; **D:** Peter Bogdanovich; **W:** Peter Bogdanovich; **C:** Robby Muller.

Salome's Last Dance
Surreal, theatrical adaptation of the Wilde play is typically flamboyant Russell. The play was never produced in Wilde's lifetime and so Russell imagines a private performance for the poet, where all excesses are realized. It's typically fevered stuff. DVD image is not a significant improvement over VHS tape. The key is the director's commentary, which is worth the price of the disc, alone. In talking about a proposed production that Wilde wanted to do with Sarah Bernhardt, he says, "the mind boggles as to how she would have danced the Dance of the Seven Veils with her wooden leg; also, I think, she was 63 at the time." —*MM*

Movie: ♫♫♫ **DVD:** ♫♫½
Pioneer Entertainment (Cat #DVD6029). Full frame. $29.98. Keepcase. *LANG:* English. *FEATURES:* Commentary: Ken Russell • Trailers • 12 chapter links.

1988 (R) 113m/C Glenda Jackson, Stratford Johns, Nickolas Grace, Douglas Hodge, Imogen Millais Scott; **D:** Ken Russell; **W:** Ken Russell; **C:** Harvey Harrison.

Salt of the Earth
Finally available in America after being suppressed for years, this controversial film was made by a group of blacklisted filmmakers during the McCarthy era when it was deemed anti-American communist propaganda. The story deals with the anti-Hispanic racial strife that occurs in a New Mexico zinc mine where union workers organize a strike. The unabashedly pro-labor tale looks very good on DVD. Beyond a few registration problems and some static on the soundtrack, the black-and-white photography shines. —*MM*

Movie: ♫♫♫½ **DVD:** ♫♫♫
Pioneer Entertainment (Cat #DVD1005, UPC #013023002593). Full frame. Dolby Digital Mono. $24.98. Keepcase. *LANG:* English. *FEATURES:* Cast and crew thumbnail bios • Production timeline • Trailer • 29 chapter links • Photo gallery • DVD credits • Editing notes • Shooting schedule • Hollywood Ten featurette.
1954 94m/B Rosaura Revueltas, Will Geer, David Wolfe; **D:** Herbert Biberman; **W:** Michael Wilson; **C:** Stanley Meredith, Leonard Stark; **M:** Sol Kaplan. *AWARDS:* Natl. Film Reg. '92.

Saludos Amigos
Two years before releasing *The Three Caballeros,* Disney released a collection of work done as research in South America. *Saludos Amigos* is a collection of four cartoons intermingled with live-action footage from the Disney expedition. First Donald Duck visits Lake Titicaca and makes a splash as a typical American tourist. After that comes the story of the young airplane, Pedro. Pedro must fly the mail over the mountains by himself because his father is too sick to fly. Back on the ground, Goofy gets gussied-up as a Gaucho for some horse-driven antics. For the finale Donald meets Jose Carioca, another sample of Disney's gentrification of a great character from someone else's rich culture. Jose Carioca introduces Donald to the Latin beat, and their fast friendship clearly lead to the deal that co-stars these birds in *Three Caballeros.* The color quality on the DVD is terrific and kids will love the classic animation sequences, which far outweigh the live-action fillers. With its light exploration of the people and geography of South America, *Saludos Amigos* could even pass as educational. Adult fans of animation will enjoy the live-action presentations of the animator's inspirations. —*JAS*

Movie: ♫♫♫ **DVD:** ♫♫♫
Buena Vista Home Entertainment (Cat #19602, UPC #717951008534). Full frame. Dolby Mono. $29.99. Keepcase. *LANG:* English; Spanish. *CAP:* English. *FEATURES:* 9 chapter links • Theatrical trailer • Mini feature, "South of the Border with Disney."

1943 42m/C D: Norman Ferguson, Wilfred Jackson, Jack Kinney, Hamilton Luske, Bill Roberts.

Salvador [SE]
Oliver Stone's unflinching document about photojournalist Richard Boyle's tribulations in civil war-torn El Salvador still devastates 16 years after its release. Woods plays the sleazy, opportunistic Boyle with a minimum of sympathy but manages to wring out compassion for the character by the finish. Boyle seizes an opportunity to cover the civil war in El Salvador purely as a means to make some quick cash and perhaps get that one shot that turns you into a hot commodity. Through his lens, Boyle witnesses the germinating seeds of another Vietnam, down to the civilian casualties and the unstoppable influx of American "trainers." Some of Stone's trademark narrative flaws creep into the film (i.e. women as virginal or vaginal, characters spouting political or philosophical tracts instead of dialogue), but I would go so far to say this was the last time Stone's passion for a subject held par with his storytelling style. The 1.85:1 anamorphic transfer is, in a word, awesome. Colors are accurate, constant, and vibrant, depending on the specific needs of Robert Richardson's complex cinematography. Deep blacks, flawless source elements, and superb detail delineation make for an exceptional clear image, reading like a 35mm print fresh from the lab. I imagine this is how the film looked in the theatre: smooth, solid, and clean. The remixed 5.1 track at first plays mostly like standard Surround, with a narrow front sound stage and little to no rear channel action. Then, about halfway through, the sound field breaks wide open with directional sound effects, aggressive LFE enhancement, and an enveloping aural presence. The special edition features include commentary by director Stone, a retrospective documentary, more than 25 minutes of deleted scenes (of work-print quality), a still gallery, and the original theatrical trailer. Compelling and honest to the point of language, "Into the Valley of Death" is an hour-long hindsight examination of the making of the film. Including interviews with the real Richard Boyle, Oliver Stone, James Woods, James Belushi, and even the former U.S. Ambassador to El Salvador (his character figures prominently in the story). Produced by Charles Kiselyak (migrating from the special edition laserdiscs he produced for *Platoon, The Doors,* and *Amadeus*), the documentary offers surprisingly candid reminiscences about the difficulties on the set, filmmaking chutzpah (Stone tried to convince the Salvadoran government to let him shoot there by sending a doctored script), and especially Ambassador Robert White's chilling recollections of real events. Funny, profane, and engrossing, *Valley of Death* in some ways tops the movie. In tone, temperament, and execution, the DVD is as close to perfection as the format can achieve. —*EP*

Movie: 🎬🎬🎬½ **DVD:** 🎬🎬🎬🎬
MGM Home Entertainment (Cat #10020 45, UPC #027616862822). Widescreen (1.85:1) anamorphic. Dolby Digital 5.1. $24.98. Keepcase. *LANG:* English. *SUB:* French; Spanish. *CAP:* English. *FEATURES:* 24 chapter links • "Into the Valley of Death" documentary • Commentary: director Oliver Stone • Deleted scenes • Photo gallery • Original theatrical trailer.
1986 (R) 123m/C James Woods, James Belushi, John Savage, Michael Murphy, Elpidia Carrillo, Cynthia Gibb, Tony Plana, Colby Chester, Will MacMillan, Jose Carlos Ruiz, Jorge Luke, Juan Fernandez, Valerie Wildman; **D:** Oliver Stone; **W:** Oliver Stone, Richard Boyle; **C:** Robert Richardson; **M:** Georges Delerue. *AWARDS:* Ind. Spirit '87: Actor (Woods); *NOM:* Oscars '86: Actor (Woods), Orig. Screenplay.

Samurai X: The Movie

This animated film deals with some of the same characters as *Samurai X Trust*. It's set in 1879 when a corrupt government is trying to deal with the arrival of arrogant Westerners and the technological changes that they bring with them. It's a subject that's central to many Asian films, both live action and anime. The main characters here are two warriors, Kenshin Himura and Takimi Shigure, and most of the violence is highly stylized. The image is extremely bright. Night scenes are carefully detailed in many shades of gray. English soundtrack isn't bad but is not as expressive as the Japanese. —*MM*
Movie: 🎬🎬½ **DVD:** 🎬🎬🎬
A.D.V. Films (Cat #DVDSX/003, UPC #702 727004421). Widescreen (1.66:1) letterboxed. Dolby Digital Stereo. $24.99. Keepcase. *LANG:* English; Japanese. *SUB:* English. *FEATURES:* 6 chapter links • Trailers.
1995 90m/C *JP* **D:** Hatuki Tsuji; **W:** Yukiyoshi Ohashi; **M:** Taro Iwashiro.

Samurai X Trust

Animated martial arts film is cut from the same cloth as Kurosawa's samurai films. There is some historical basis for the 19th-century story of Shinta, who is renamed Kenshin and becomes an assassin under the tutelage of swordsman Hiko. The image has the bright, translucent quality seen in so much of the better anime. Attention to historical detail is mixed with fairly graphic violence. English soundtrack makes more use of the subwoofer than the Japanese and sounds more exaggerated. —*MM*
Movie: 🎬🎬🎬 **DVD:** 🎬🎬🎬
A.D.V. Films (Cat #DVDSX/001, UPC #702 727004322). Full frame. Dolby Digital Stereo. $29.98. Keepcase. *LANG:* English; Japanese. *SUB:* English; Japanese. *FEATURES:* 8 chapter links • Trailers • Character introductions • Historical background notes.
1999 60m/C *JP* **D:** Kazuhiro Furuhashi; **W:** Masashi Furuhashi; **M:** Taku Iwasaki.

The Sand Pebbles

Navy machinist Jake Holcomb (McQueen) is transferred to the gunboat *San Pablo* on the Yangtze River in 1926. He falls in love with missionary Shirley Eckert (Bergen), and as he becomes aware of the political climate of American imperialism, he finds himself at odds with his command structure. The film can easily be seen as an early criticism of American policy in Vietnam. His performance won McQueen an Oscar nomination. The glowing DVD image transfer brings out the beauty of Joe McDonald's photography and retains the shadow-on-shadow feel of the many night scenes. This is not the original roadshow print, which ran a full reel longer than what we saw in the neighborhood theatres, but it includes Jerry Goldsmith's opening, closing, and brief intermission music. There's also a full-length commentary track with Robert Wise, Candice Bergen, Mako, and an uncredited Richard Crenna. It's scene-specific and well cut. Wise and Crenna talk about the production in Taiwan and building the boat (overlapping a bit here and there), and Mako has funny things to say about most of the cast. They all remember Steve McQueen with praise and cautious remarks about his loner personality. Bergen is on the track the least, but is quite open about her youth and the fact that it was only her second picture. Wise appears to become a bit confused at least once, when he talks about submitting the script on the same day as hearing that Bobby Kennedy had been shot, which happened two years after the film was released. —*MM/GE*
Movie: 🎬🎬🎬½ **DVD:** 🎬🎬🎬½
20th Century Fox Home Entertainment (Cat #2001308, UPC #024543013082). Widescreen (2.35:1) anamorphic. $24.98. Keepcase. *LANG:* English. *FEATURES:* Commentary • Trailer • Radio spots • Audio featurettes.
1966 193m/C Steve McQueen, Richard Crenna, Richard Attenborough, Candice Bergen, Marayat Andriane, Mako, Larry Gates, Gavin MacLeod, Simon Oakland, James Hong, Richard Loo, Barney Phillips, Tommy Lee, Ford Rainey, Walter Reed, Gus Trikonis, Joe Turkel, Glenn Wilder; **D:** Robert Wise; **W:** Robert Anderson; **C:** Joe MacDonald; **M:** Jerry Goldsmith; *Technical Advisor:* Harley Misiner. *AWARDS:* Golden Globes '67: Support. Actor (Attenborough); *NOM:* Oscars '66: Actor (McQueen), Art Dir./Set Dec., Color, Color Cinematog., Film Editing, Picture, Sound, Support. Actor (Mako), Orig. Score.

Santa Claus: The Movie

From the producers of *Superman* comes this bloated special effects extravaganza (best appreciated in widescreen) starring David Huddleston as a goodhearted, toy-giving man who is anointed the "chosen one" by elves and sets up shop at the North Pole. Dudley Moore brings all his elfin charm to the role of Patch, a well-intentioned, forward-thinking elf whose ideas about speeding up production lead to disaster. John Lithgow hams it up as BZ, an evil, cigar-chomping toymaker who uses the disgraced Patch to improve his image. This falls short of family classic status, but kids will love Santa's workshop, the elves, and the scenes of Santa's flying sleigh. The video transfer is impeccable; the image merry and bright. Click on the reindeer on the main menu screen for a hidden "Easter egg." —*DL*
Movie: 🎬🎬½ **DVD:** 🎬🎬🎬
Anchor Bay (Cat #DV11239, UPC #01313 1123999). Widescreen (2.35:1) letterboxed. Dolby Digital Stereo. $24.98. Keepcase. *LANG:* English. *CAP:* English. *FEATURES:* Commentary: director Jeannot Szwarc • "Making of" featurette • U.S. and foreign theatrical trailers • Talent bios • 24 chapter links.
1985 (PG) 112m/C Dudley Moore, John Lithgow, David Huddleston, Judy Cornwell, Burgess Meredith; **D:** Jeannot Szwarc; **W:** David Newman; **C:** Arthur Ibbetson; **M:** Henry Mancini.

Santa Claws

B-movie queen Raven Quinn (Rochon) has become the object of murderer Wayne's (Kramer) obsession. He dresses up as the jolly fat man and dispatches anyone who stands between them. The leads do good work with material that attempts to deal with relatively realistic characters in a genre piece. There is not much that DVD can do with the low-budget image, however. The film is very grainy and all of the reds glow brightly. The extras (on the flip side) are all that differentiate the disc from VHS tape. —*MM*
Movie: 🎬🎬 **DVD:** 🎬🎬
El Independent Cinema (Cat #so-5031-dvd, UPC #612385503191). Full frame. $19.98. Keepcase. *LANG:* English. *FEATURES:* 30 chapter links • Outtakes • Promos • Trailers • "Scream Queens Naked Christmas" featurette.
1996 85m/C Debbie Rochon, Grant Kramer, John Mowod, Marilyn Eastman, Julie Wallace; **D:** John A. Russo; **W:** John A. Russo; **C:** Bill (William Heinzman) Hinzman; **M:** Paul McCollough.

Santa Fe Trail

Please see review for *Errol Flynn / Randolph Scott Double Feature*.
1979 17m/C

Satan's Sadists

Tamblyn and his biker gang terrorize folks in the Southern California desert, including a retired cop, a Vietnam vet, and a trio of vacationing coeds. Even compared to Adamson's other work, this one is very violent. On his commentary track, producer Sherman admits as much. On DVD, the image is neither as good as the best of the Adamson films, nor as bad-looking as the worst. Sound is acceptable. —*MM*
Movie: 🎬🎬 **DVD:** 🎬🎬

Troma Team Video (Cat #9024). Full frame. $19.95. Keepcase. *LANG:* English. *FEATURES:* 9 chapter links ▪ Commentary: Sam Sherman ▪ Trailers ▪ TV teaser ▪ "Producing schlock" featurette ▪ Behind-the-scenes gallery ▪ DVD credits ▪ Regina Carroll radio interview.
1969 (R) 88m/C Russ Tamblyn, Regina Carrol, Gary Kent, Jackie Taylor, John Cardos, Kent Taylor, Robert Dix, Scott Brady, Evelyn Frank, Greydon Clark, Bill Bonner, Bobby Clark, Yvonne Stewart, Cheryl Anne, Randee Lynn, Bambi Allen, Breck Warwick; *D:* Al Adamson; *W:* Dennis Wayne; *C:* Gary Graver; *M:* Harley Hatcher.

Saturday the 14th

Purported parody of various horror genres involves a mansion that John (Benjamin) and Mary (Prentiss) inherit. The film is so poorly made that it's neither funny nor scary. Some flecks and snow are visible, but they're not a problem considering that this is such a rough low-budget image. —*MM*
Movie: 🎵½ **DVD:** 🎵½
New Concorde (Cat #NH20225D, UPC #73 6991222595). Full frame. $19.98. Keepcase. *LANG:* English. *FEATURES:* Trailers ▪ Thumbnail bios ▪ 24 chapter links.
1981 (PG) 91m/C Richard Benjamin, Paula Prentiss, Severn Darden, Jeffrey Tambor, Kari Michaelsen, Kevin Brando, Rosemary DeCamp, Stacy Keach; *D:* Howard R. Cohen; *W:* Howard R. Cohen, Jeff Begun; *C:* Daniel Lacambre; *M:* Parmer Fuller.

Saturday the 14th Strikes Back

Lame sequel keeps the name but loses the storyline and characters from the equally lame original. It concerns a vampire (Stonebrook) who wants to make young Eddie (Presson) the leader of the undead. The image is a solid step up from the first film, making this one about equal to tape. Actually, the box illustration by Gahan Wilson is the best thing about the disc. —*MM*
Movie: 🎵½ **DVD:** 🎵🎵
New Concorde (Cat #NH20305D, UPC #73 6991230590). Full frame. $19.98. Keepcase. *LANG:* English. *FEATURES:* 24 chapter links ▪ Trailers ▪ Thumbnail bios.
1988 91m/C Ray Walston, Avery Schreiber, Patty McCormack, Julianne McNamara, Rhonda Aldrich, Daniel Will-Harris, Joseph Ruskin, Pamela Stonebrook, Phil Leeds, Jason Presson, Michael Berryman, Victoria Morsell; *D:* Howard R. Cohen; *W:* Howard R. Cohen; *C:* Levie Isaacks; *M:* Parmer Fuller.

Save the Last Dance

White middle-class Sara (Stiles) suddenly finds herself attending an inner-city Chicago high school after her mother dies. There's she's befriended by Chenille (Washington), and falls for Chenille's hottie brother Derek (Thomas). They share an interest in dance and each other. A triumph of casting that caught two attractive stars on the rise turned this one into a solid sleeper hit in its theatrical release, and it will doubtless be just as popular on DVD. Image and sound are all you'd expect of a big-budget, highly profitable new studio release. The extras amount to a full roundup of the usual suspects. —*MM*
Movie: 🎵🎵½ **DVD:** 🎵🎵🎵½
Paramount Home Video (Cat #33455, UPC #097363345541). Widescreen anamorphic. Dolby Digital 5.1 Surround; Dolby Digital Surround. $29.99. Keepcase. *LANG:* English; French. *SUB:* English. *FEATURES:* 18 chapter links ▪ Commentary: director Thomas Carter ▪ 4 deleted scenes ▪ "Making of" featurette ▪ Interviews ▪ Music video ▪ Trailer.
2001 (PG-13) 112m/C Julia Stiles, Sean Patrick Thomas, Fredro Starr, Kerry Washington, Terry Kinney, Bianca Lawson, Garland Whitt; *D:* Thomas Carter; *W:* Duane Adler, Cheryl Edwards; *C:* Robbie Greenberg; *M:* Mark Isham.

Saving Grace

Light British comedy falls firmly into that subgenre of towns-full-of-quirky-characters, with a strong dash of doper humor. When recently widowed Grace (Blethyn) realizes how impoverished she is, her handyman Matthew (writer Ferguson) persuades her to turn the greenhouse into a pot factory. The DVD image is crystal clear and very sharp, showing no noise or artifacting problems. Nor is there any overt grain or defects from the source print, creating a beautiful presentation. The 5.1 mix offers clear dialogue and does a wonderful job of presenting the lovely score by Mark Russell. The two commentaries have some funny moments, but they come across as very dry and lack spontaneity. —*ML/MM*
Movie: 🎵🎵🎵 **DVD:** 🎵🎵🎵
New Line Home Video (UPC #7940435142 27). Widescreen (2.35:1) anamorphic; full frame. Dolby Digital 5.1 Surround Stereo. $24.98. Snapper. *LANG:* English. *SUB:* English. *FEATURES:* Commentary: Blethyn, Ferguson, Cole ▪ Commentary: Cole, Ferguson, Crowdy ▪ Trailer ▪ Filmographies.
2000 (R) 93m/C *GB* Brenda Blethyn, Craig Ferguson, Martin Clunes, Tcheky Karyo, Jamie Foreman, Valerie Edmond, Tristan Sturrock; *D:* Nigel Cole; *W:* Craig Ferguson, Mark Crowdy; *C:* John de Borman.

Saviour of the Soul 2

Sequel to the 1992 film is a fantasy romantic comedy with an emphasis on silliness. Andy Lau and Rosamund Kwan play lovers who are kept apart by supernatural forces. It involves lots of wirework and ridiculous action scenes. Focus is generally soft and dreamy. The pale image is only a small improvement over tape and will be familiar to anyone who has watched many Hong Kong imports. —*MM*
Movie: 🎵🎵 **DVD:** 🎵🎵
Tai Seng Video Marketing (Cat #5275, UPC #4895024904221). Widescreen letterboxed. Dolby Digital Mono. $24.95. Keepcase. *LANG:* Cantonese; Mandarin. *SUB:* Trad. & Simpl. Chinese; English. *FEATURES:* 8 chapter links ▪ Trailers ▪ Andy Lau thumbnail bio.
1992 90m/C *CH* Andy Lau, Rosamund Kwan, Corey Yuen, Shirley Kwan; *D:* Corey Yuen, David (Dai Wei) Lai; *W:* Yip Kwong Kim, Chan Kin Chung; *C:* Lee Tak Wai, Lau Mun Tong, Leung Chi Ming; *M:* To Chi Chee.

Say Amen, Somebody

Celebration of gospel music does not try to glamorize its subject or make the music something it is not. Much of the film was shot in churches without the exotic lighting and editing techniques that many have come to expect of music documentaries. This one is about the music and the people who sing it. Neither image nor sound are much of an improvement over VHS tape, but the film is a valuable look, well worth watching on any medium. A Surround remix would have been completely inappropriate. —*MM*
Movie: 🎵🎵🎵½ **DVD:** 🎵🎵½
Xenon Entertainment (Cat #XE XP 3032 DVD, UPC #000799303221). Full frame. $19.98. Keepcase. *LANG:* English. *FEATURES:* 15 chapter links ▪ Trailers.
1980 (G) 100m/C Willie May Ford Smith, Thomas A. Dorsey, Sallie Martin, Delois Barrett Cambell; *D:* George T. Nierenberg; *C:* Edward Lachman, Don Lenzer.

Scandal: The Big Turn On

Private eye (Coleman) is hired for a divorce case which is nothing but a flimsy frame upon which to hang several mediocre soft-core sex scenes. The producer is also responsible for the *Emmanuelle* TV series. This effort has the grainy production values of late-night cable fare and the mindset to match. —*MM*
Movie: 🎵 **DVD:** 🎵🎵
Image Entertainment (Cat #ALA9901DVD, UPC #014381990126). Full frame. Dolby Digital Stereo. $24.99. Snapper. *LANG:* English. *FEATURES:* 12 chapter links.
1999 80m/C Jesse Coleman, Robert Donovan, Shauna O'Brien, Kim (Kimberly Dawn) Dawson; *D:* Howie Hoax; *W:* Sierra King; *C:* Howard Wexler.

Scarlet Empress

One of von Sternberg's greatest films tells the story of Catherine the Great and her rise to power. Dietrich stars as the beautiful royal wife who outwits her foolish husband Peter (Jaffe) to become empress of Russia. Incredibly rich decor is a visual feast for the eye, as perfectionist von Sternberg fussed over every detail. Dietrich is excellent as Catherine, and von Sternberg's mastery of lighting and camerawork makes for a highly extravagant film. Criterion often tackles some pretty rough projects, and taking on the restoration and digital transfer of this 1934 film was definitely no piece of cake. Their DVD is pretty amazing to look at, despite the fact that the image is far grainier than generally expected for the format. Sharpness is generally good and contrast is mostly fairly strong, although the film lacks the punchy detail found in many older black-and-white films. Most likely this is the best that anyone could have done with whatever film elements Criterion had to work with. The supplemental section includes a very good British documentary in which Von Sternberg explains lighting techniques to film students. —JO

Movie: 🎵🎵🎵½ **DVD:** 🎵🎵🎵
Criterion Collection (Cat #CC1569D, UPC #715515011822). Full frame. Dolby Digital Mono. $29.95. Keepcase. *LANG:* English. *SUB:* English. *FEATURES:* 19 chapter links • BBC documentary "The World of Josef von Sternberg" • Production stills • Lobby cards • Von Sternberg tribute.
1934 110m/B Marlene Dietrich, John Lodge, Sam Jaffe, Louise Dresser, Maria Sieber, Sir C. Aubrey Smith, Ruthelma Stevens, Olive Tell; *D:* Josef von Sternberg; *W:* Manuel Komroff; *C:* Bert Glennon.

The Scarlet Pimpernel

The title character (Howard), supposedly a dandy of the English court, assumes a dual identity to outwit the French Republicans and aid innocent aristocrats during the French Revolution. Fine adaptation of Baroness Orczy's novel is full of daring exploits, period costumes, intrigue, etc. The DVD image is acceptable, considering the age of the original, but a near-constant background hiss makes the film hard to listen to. —MM

Movie: 🎵🎵🎵½ **DVD:** 🎵🎵
Madacy Entertainment (Cat #99023). Full frame. Dolby Digital Mono. $9.99. Keepcase. *LANG:* English. *FEATURES:* Production credits • Leslie Howard thumbnail bio.
1934 95m/B *GB* Leslie Howard, Joan Gardner, Merle Oberon, Raymond Massey, Anthony Bushell, Nigel Bruce, Bramwell Fletcher, Walter Rilla, O.B. Clarence, Ernest Milton, Edmund Breon, Melville Cooper, Gibb McLaughlin, Morland Graham, Allan Jeayes; *D:* Harold Young; *W:* Robert Sherwood, Arthur Wimperis, Lajos Biro; *C:* Harold Rosson; *M:* Arthur Benjamin.

Scary Movie

The Wayans brothers do to horror films what ZAZ did *Airport* movies. They parody every element imaginable and throw a wide net to cover other genres as well. Their humor is so tasteless and raunchy that the film became a surprise summer blockbuster. Image transfer is good, albeit unspectacular. It's clear, showing no flaws from the source print or overt noise, but it is also a bit dark in places. The opening scene, in particular, looked rather grainy and hazy, but these defects don't continue throughout the film. Audio shows a nice dynamic range, but doesn't come close to other recent Disney offerings. —MM/ML

Movie: 🎵🎵🎵 **DVD:** 🎵🎵🎵
Miramax Pictures Home Video (Cat #18300, UPC #717951004857). Widescreen (2.35:1) anamorphic. Dolby Digital 5.1 Surround Stereo. $32.99. Keepcase. *LANG:* English; French. *SUB:* English; Spanish. *FEATURES:* Trailer • "Making of" featurette • 6 deleted scenes • DVD-ROM materials.
2000 (R) 85m/C Keenen Ivory Wayans, Marlon Wayans, Shawn Wayans, Carmen Electra, Jon Abrahams, Shannon Elizabeth, Lochlyn Munro, Cheri Oteri, Anna Faris, Regina Hall, Kurt Fuller, David Lander, Dave Sheridan, Dan Joffre; *D:* Keenen Ivory Wayans; *W:* Marlon Wayans, Shawn Wayans; *C:* Francis Kenny; *M:* David Kitay.

Scene at the Sea

Scene at the Sea is just that, a very long meditation on the ocean and silence. One day while doing his route as a garbage collector, deaf mute Shigeru finds a broken surfboard, and thus is born the seed in his mind that he could surf. He fixes the board and hits the waves. While at the beach he meets a deaf mute girl and love is in the air. Their relationship develops and evolves through the time they spend together in silence. Shigeru turns out to be a natural on the surfboard, and various characters lend their support to his efforts, while others ignore him to the point of not tapping him on the shoulder when judges call his name to hit the surf in a competition. All this surfing detracts from his work, and soon he may be out of job. Another girl takes interest in him, threatening his relationship with the deaf mute girl. The phases of the moon seem faster than the pace of this film. If you're looking for a way to acclimate yourself to subtitles, this may be a great starter film, because dialogue occurs once every five to ten minutes. The digital transfer shows the expanse and composition of each shot, making for great visual storytelling, even if the telling is methodical. Director Takeshi Kitano has a fan-base in Japan, but his films seem to be too pensive for the standard American film appetite. —JAS *AKA:* Ano Natsu, Ichigan Shizukana Umi.

Movie: 🎵🎵 **DVD:** 🎵🎵
Image Entertainment (Cat #ID9529KIDVD, UPC #014381952926). Widescreen (1.78:1) letterboxed. Dolby Digital Stereo. $29.99. Snapper. *LANG:* Japanese. *SUB:* English. *FEATURES:* 15 chapter links.
1991 101m/C *JP* Kuroudo Maki, Hiroko Oshima, Sabu Kawahara; *D:* Takeshi "Beat" Kitano; *W:* Takeshi "Beat" Kitano.

School Daze

Lee's second outing is a rambunctious comedy (with a message, of course) set during homecoming weekend at Mission College. He sketches in a series of conflicts between lighter-skinned "wannabees" and darker, self-proclaimed "jigaboos" who are proud of their African heritage; between politically active students and apathetic fraternity brothers; between students and townspeople; between manipulators and the manipulated. Lee doesn't have as much to say on this commentary track as he does on others. Image and sound are very good on both versions of the film. Visual flaws are negligible. —MM

Movie: 🎵🎵🎵 **DVD:** 🎵🎵🎵
Columbia Tristar Home Video (Cat #05834, UPC #043396058347). Widescreen anamorphic; full frame. Dolby Digital Surround Stereo. $24.95. Keepcase. *LANG:* English; French. *SUB:* English; French; Spanish. *FEATURES:* 28 chapter links • Talent files • Trailers.
1988 (R) 114m/C Spike Lee, Laurence "Larry" Fishburne, Giancarlo Esposito, Tisha Campbell, Ossie Davis, Joe Seneca, Art Evans, Ellen Holly, Branford Marsalis, Bill Nunn, Kadeem Hardison, Darryl M. Bell, Joie Lee, Tyra Ferrell, Jasmine Guy, Gregg Burge, Kasi Lemmons, Samuel L. Jackson, Phyllis Hyman, James Bond III; *D:* Spike Lee; *W:* Spike Lee; *C:* Ernest R. Dickerson; *M:* Bill Lee.

School's Out

The last sentence describing this film on the back of the DVD box says, "Their fight for survival is the ultimate final exam." Multiply the cheese factor on that by ten, mix in equal parts *Scream* and *Urban Legend,* season with some horrible dubbing and you have *School's Out.* Nuff said. Basically, there's a college graduation party. Some of the students wander off to pull a graduation prank in the deserted school on the same night that a homicidal maniac who killed his last victim in the school escapes from an asylum. Say it again, "escapes from an asylum." The picture quality is very good and the cinematography and lighting are to die for. The sound is average. —CA

Movie: woof **DVD:** 🎵🎵½
MTI Home Video (Cat #1071, UPC #039414510713). Full frame. Dolby Digital Stereo. $24.95. Keepcase. *LANG:* English dubbed. *SUB:* Spanish. *FEATURES:* Fangoria section • Trailers.
1999 90m/C *GE* Katharina Wackernagel, Marlene Meyer-Dunker, Nils Nellessen, Niels Bruno Schmidt; *D:* Robert Sigl; *W:* Kai Meyer; *C:* Sven Kirsten.

Scooby-Doo and the Alien Invaders

Scooby-Doo, Shaggy, and the Mystery, Inc. crew take on UFOs, a possible government cover-up, and a couple of good-looking babes in this recent addition to the "Scooby-Doo" adventure series. The gang gets stranded in an out-of-the-way town that houses a secret government research station. When one of the locals claims to have been abducted by aliens, the gang starts an investigation, are soon chased by some nasty aliens themselves, and eventually land aboard a UFO. Plenty of fun for Scooby-Doo fans. The animation on this direct-to-video feature is improved from the original series and its transfer to DVD is colorful and crisp. The Dolby Surround stays active all the way through with pretty good low end and quite a bit coming from the rear mono Surround track. One of the "making of" featurettes goes behind-the-scenes to interview the animators and voice talent while the other one gets into the making of a Scooby-Doo video game. Both should hold the interest of adults who may not be into the cartoon itself. —JO

Movie: ♫♫½ **DVD:** ♫♫♫
Warner Home Video, Inc. (Cat #H1533, UPC #014764153322). Full frame. Dolby Surround. $24.98. Snapper. *LANG:* English. *CAP:* English. *FEATURES:* 24 chapter links • 10 trailers • 2 "making of" featurettes • Scooby's Steps to Solving a Mystery • "Talent" files.

2000 74m/C V: Mark Hamill, Kevin M. Richardson, B.J. Ward, Frank Welker, Jennifer Hale, Scott Innes.

The Scorpio Factor

Murder and mayhem follow a microchip heist. Shady Nora Foxx (Wilson) is in the middle of an overly elaborate plot that's set in Central America and Europe. Image is exceptionally grainy—it comes from the original and leads to mild artifacts. Barebones disc lacks a menu or chapter links. —MM

Movie: ♫♫ **DVD:** ♫♫
Digital Versatile Disc Ltd. (Cat #116). Full frame. $19.95. Keepcase. *LANG:* English.

1990 87m/C Attila Bertalan, David Nerman, Wendy Dawn Wilson; **D:** Michel Waehniuc; **W:** Carole Sauve, June Pinheiro; **C:** Bruno Philip; **M:** Richard Gresko.

Scream 3 [CS]

The filmmakers swear that this series is indeed only a trilogy. Good thing because, while entertaining enough, this third film is showing wear. Sidney is working as a crisis counselor and living in blessed anonymity in northern California. However, the actors involved in *Stab 3* are being offed and it ties in to her mother's mysterious past, so Sid is forced to resurface. Ambitious Gale (Cox Arquette) returns as does dopey Dewey (Arquette) and newcomer LAPD detective Kincaid (Dempsey) tries to figure out if there are any film rules that will help him catch a killer. This disc delivers superior picture quality. Although some darker scenes tend to lose definition in their blacks and other colors (a detriment to a horror film set primarily amidst shadows), it hardly seems any worse than when it played in theatres. The soundtrack is similarly impressive and delivers crisp dialogue, powerful music, and superb sound effects. Although the extras on the disc are bountiful, sometimes less is more. For example, deleted scenes are occasionally no more than digitized footage with quality which is no better than tape. But the amount of material and the splendid commentary track more than make up for any shortcomings. —MJT

Movie: ♫♫½ **DVD:** ♫♫♫
Buena Vista Home Entertainment (Cat #18 304, UPC #717951004895). Widescreen (2.35:1) anamorphic. Dolby Digital 5.1 Surround Sound. $29.99. Keepcase. *LANG:* English; French. *SUB:* Spanish. *FEATURES:* 29 chapter links • Outtakes • Behind-the-scenes from all three *Scream* films • Commentary: director Wes Craven and crew • Deleted scenes with commentary by Craven and crew • Alternate ending with commentary by Craven and crew • TV spots and theatrical trailer • International trailer • Creed music video • Cast and crew bios.

2000 (R) 116m/C Neve Campbell, David Arquette, Courteney Cox Arquette, Patrick Dempsey, Scott Foley, Lance Henriksen, Matt Keeslar, Jenny McCarthy, Emily Mortimer, Parker Posey, Deon Richmond, Patrick Warburton, Liev Schreiber, Heather Matarazzo, Jamie Kennedy, Carrie Fisher, Kevin Smith, Jason Mewes, Roger Corman; **D:** Wes Craven; **W:** Ehren Kruger; **C:** Peter Deming; **M:** Marco Beltrami. *AWARDS:* NOM: MTV Movie Awards '00: Female Perf. (Campbell), Comedic Perf. (Posey).

The Screaming Skull

Please see review of *Drive-In Discs, Vol. One.* —MM

Movie: ♫½
1958 68m/B William (Bill) Hudson, Peggy Webber, Toni Johnson, Russ Conway, Alex Nicol; **D:** Alex Nicol; **M:** Ernest Gold.

Screw Loose

Comedy features a nice storyline but the banal humor, crude direction, and poor acting sadly turn it into an uninspired event. Mel Brooks plays Jake, a mental patient who is kidnapped by the son (Greggio) of an old war buddy and taken to Italy where the slapstick becomes predictable. The image is generally clean although some serious speckles are visible during the opening credits. Faithful color reproduction has a natural look throughout. The 5.1 mix makes good use of the Surround channels, particularly for music. —GH/MM
AKA: Svitati.

Movie: ♫½ **DVD:** ♫♫½
Columbia Tristar Home Video (Cat #05284, UPC #043396052840). Widescreen (1.85:1) anamorphic. Dolby Digital 5.1 Surround Stereo; Dolby Digital Surround. $24.95. Keepcase. *LANG:* English. *CAP:* English. *FEATURES:* Talent files • Trailers • 28 chapter links.

1999 (R) 85m/C *IT* Mel Brooks, Ezio Greggio, Gianfranco Barra, Julie Condra, Randi Ingerman; **D:** Ezio Greggio; **W:** Rudy DeLuca, Steve Haberman; **C:** Luca Robecchi.

Screwed

Chauffeur Willard Fillmore (MacDonald) kidnaps his bitchy boss's (Stritch) evil little dog, but things get so screwed up, she thinks that Fillmore has been snatched. Is it just that MacDonald is so unfunny or is it the fact that there have been so many mean-spirited comedies that use canines as the butt of their jokes? Whatever the case, the VideoHound is not amused. Even so, the widescreen image and sound are everything you could ask of a studio comedy. —MM

Movie: ♫ **DVD:** ♫♫½
Universal Studios Home Video (Cat #209 30, UPC #025192093029). Widescreen (1.85:1) anamorphic. Dolby Digital 5.1 Surround Stereo. $24.99. Keepcase. *LANG:* English. *SUB:* English; French. *FEATURES:* 18 chapter links • Production notes • Talent files • Trailer.

2000 (PG-13) 82m/C Norm MacDonald, Elaine Stritch, Danny DeVito, Dave Chappelle, Daniel Benzali, Sherman Hemsley, Malcolm Stewart; **D:** Scott Alexander, Larry Karaszewski; **W:** Scott Alexander, Larry Karaszewski; **C:** Robert Brinkmann; **M:** Michel Colombier.

Scrooged

Somewhat disjointed version of the Dickens's classic revolves around a callous TV executive (Murray) staging *A Christmas Carol*, who is visited by the three ghosts (among them a terrific Kane) and sees the light. It is a bit heavy-handed but funny, particularly for Murray's fans. The widescreen image looks very nice. All that's missing here is a commentary track, but since this one has never really found an audience, that's asking a lot. —MM

Movie: ♫♫♫ **DVD:** ♫♫½
Paramount Home Video (Cat #320547). Widescreen (1.85:1) anamorphic. Dolby Digital 5.1 Surround Stereo; Dolby Digital Surround Stereo. $29.99. Keepcase. *LANG:* English; French. *SUB:* English. *CAP:* English. *FEATURES:* 12 chapter links.

1988 (PG-13) 101m/C Bill Murray, Carol Kane, John Forsythe, David Johansen, Bob(cat) Goldthwait, Karen Allen, Michael J. Pollard, Brian Doyle-Murray, Alfre Woodard, John Glover, Robert Mitchum, Buddy Hackett, Robert Goulet, Jamie Farr, Mary Lou Retton, Lee Majors; **D:** Richard Donner; **W:** Mitch Glazer, Michael O'Donoghue; **C:** Michael Chapman; **M:** Danny Elfman.

Scum of the Earth

The second title on this "drive-in double feature" is an early '60s skin flick about innocent young Kim (Miles), who is cruelly tricked into posing topless for a photographer and is then blackmailed into a downward spiral of sleaze that ends in murder and suicide. The film features much of the cast and crew of director Lewis's *Blood Feast*. The black-and-white image is fairly soft and grainy, not nearly as sharp as the first feature, *The Defilers*. —MM

Movie: ♫½ **DVD:** ♫♫
Image Entertainment (Cat #ID9749SW DVD, UPC #014381974928). Full frame. Dolby Digital Mono. $24.99. Snapper. *LANG:* English. *FEATURES:* 8 chapter links • "Let's Go to the Drive-in" short with Julie Andrews • Commentary: Dave Friedman, Mike Vraney • 2 nudie shorts • 3

intermission reels • Gallery of exploitation art • Trailers.
1963 73m/B Vicki (Allison Louise Downe) Miles, Lawrence Wood, Mal Arnold, Thomas Sweetwood, Sandy Sinclair; **D:** Herschell Gordon Lewis; **W:** Herschell Gordon Lewis.

Seamless

The rave scene has been the subject of several recent films, but this one doesn't measure up to *Go*, *Groove*, or *The Delivery*. As director Debrah Lemattre and cinematographer Denise Brassard admit on their unusually candid commentary track, they and their Japanese backers were really more interested in the business of vintage clothes. They shaped the look of the film with images from fashion magazines, and that explains the lack of conventional narrative drive. And, as they also explain, extra footage was filmed after they had left the project and so the end result has some interesting moments, but nothing more. Conventional interiors are acceptable visually. The usual heavy grain and artifacts appear in location night scenes. DVD is an accurate reproduction of a deliberately unpolished original. Sound is acceptable. —*MM*
Movie: 🎵🎵 **DVD:** 🎵🎵½
Artisan Entertainment (Cat #11561, UPC #012236115618). Full frame. Dolby Digital 5.1 Surround Stereo; Dolby Digital Surround. $24.98. Snapper. *LANG:* English. *FEATURES:* 20 chapter links • Trailer • Talent files • Commentary: director Debrah Lemattre, cinematographer Denise Brassard.
2000 (R) 91m/C Shannon Elizabeth, Peter Alexander, Melinda Scherwinski, Broc Benedict; **D:** Debra Lemattre; **C:** Denise Brassard; **M:** Mamoru Mochizuki.

Search and Destroy

Complex, semi-experimental story finds bankrupt businessman Martin Mirkheim (Dunne) trying to overcome his financial woes by making a film based on a book by self-help guru Dr. Luther Waxling (Hopper). Of course, since Martin's broke, he first has to find someone willing to invest in his venture. A shady duo (Walken and Turturro) does just that and leaves him with more problems. This tediously stagy adaptation of Howard Korders's play is the directorial debut for artist Salle. About the best that can be said of the DVD image is that it's interesting. We were spared a commentary track. —*MM*
Movie: 🎵🎵 **DVD:** 🎵🎵
Pioneer Entertainment (Cat #10498). Full frame. Dolby Digital Surround. $24.95. Keepcase. *LANG:* English. *FEATURES:* 20 chapter links.
1994 (R) 91m/C Griffin Dunne, Dennis Hopper, Rosanna Arquette, Christopher Walken, John Turturro, Illeana Douglas, Ethan Hawke; **Cameos:** Martin Scorsese; **D:** David Salle; **W:** Michael Almereyda; **C:** Michael Spiller, Bobby Bukowski; **M:** Elmer Bernstein.

The Second Woman

Please see review of *Cinema's Dark Side Collection*. **AKA:** *Here Lies Love*; *Twelve Miles Out*.
Movie: 🎵🎵½
1951 91m/B Robert Young, Betsy Drake, John Sutton; **D:** James V. Kern; **W:** Mort Briskin, Robert Smith; **C:** Hal Mohr.

Secret Games

An unhappily married woman (Brin) searches for relief from her restrictive but wealthy marriage. She becomes a member of the "Afternoon Demitasse," an exclusive brothel where society dames tart themselves up and fulfill their fantasies. Then one of her customers (Hewitt) turns out to be a psycho. Don't you just hate when that happens? Director Hippolyte understands this kind of classy soft-core stuff perfectly and handles it well. DVD image may be a slight improvement over tape, but with the gauzy romantic focus, it's hard to say. —*MM*
Movie: 🎵🎵½ **DVD:** 🎵🎵
Studio Home Entertainment (Cat #4040). Full frame. Stereo. $24.95. Keepcase. *LANG:* English. *FEATURES:* Cast and crew thumbnail bios • Trailer • 18 chapter links.
1992 (R) 90m/C Martin Hewitt, Michele Brin, Delia Sheppard, Billy Drago; **D:** Alexander Gregory (Gregory Dark) Hippolyte; **W:** Georges des Esseintes; **C:** Wally Pfister, Thomas Denove; **M:** Joseph Smith.

The Secret KGB UFO Files

Documentary tracks alien encounter and abduction accounts from Russia. Most of the material presented stems from low-resolution and low-quality source material, so don't expect anything fancy. The image is washed-out, often fuzzy, and riddled with compression artifacts. The overall quality is no better than that of an average VHS tape. Audio, surprisingly, is well done. —*GH*
Movie: 🎵½ **DVD:** 🎵½
Madacy Entertainment (Cat #99120). Full frame. Dolby Digital Stereo. $14.98. Keepcase. *LANG:* English. *FEATURES:* Trivia • Bios.
1999 100m/C

The Secret of Anastasia

Animated version of the oft-filmed story of the lost Russian princess is strictly second-rate stuff. The animation looks like bad Hanna-Barbera with extremely simple characters and bad writing. DVD is no better than VHS tape. The shorter second feature, "Snow White and the Magic Mirror," is the same. —*MM*
Movie: 🎵 **DVD:** 🎵
UAV Entertainment (Cat #40089). Full frame. $24.98. Snapper. *LANG:* English. *CAP:* English. *FEATURES:* 9 chapter links • Trailer. The title is also available from United American Video (cat. #40089) for $9.99.
1997 ?m/C

The Secret of NIMH 2

By-the-numbers animated sequel concerns the further adventures of the Brisby family of mice whose intelligence was enhanced at the National Institute of Mental Health. The characters are handled well enough, and the image is certainly clear and sharp but the drawing lacks intricacy. It's essentially the same as tape. —*MM*
Movie: 🎵🎵 **DVD:** 🎵🎵
MGM Home Entertainment (Cat #1001608, UPC #027616859181). Full frame. Dolby Digital 5.1 Surround Stereo; Dolby Digital Surround. $24.99. Keepcase. *LANG:* English; French; Spanish. *SUB:* French; Spanish. *CAP:* English. *FEATURES:* 16 chapter links.
1998 (G) 68m/C D: Dick Sebast; **W:** Sam Graham, Chris Hubbell; **M:** Lee Holdridge; **V:** Ralph Macchio, Eric Idle, Dom DeLuise, Harvey Korman, Peter MacNicol, William H. Macy, Andrea Martin, Meshach Taylor.

Secrets of the Heart

Javi (Erburu) grows up in a provincial town in Spain in the 1960s. Director Armendariz isn't as flamboyd as Fellini in *Amarcord* but his intentions are similar. The DVD image, which appears to be an accurate reproduction of the original, is generally soft with somewhat underlit interiors. The bold white subtitles are easy to read. —*MM* **AKA:** *Secretos del Corazon*.
Movie: 🎵🎵🎵 **DVD:** 🎵🎵½
New Yorker Video (UPC #717119789046). Widescreen (1.66:1) letterboxed. $29.95. Keepcase. *LANG:* Spanish. *SUB:* English. *FEATURES:* 18 chapter links.
1997 108m/C *SP* Carmelo Gomez, Charo Lopez, Andoni Erburu, Silvia Munt, Alvaro Nagore; **D:** Montxo Armendariz; **W:** Montxo Armendariz; **C:** Javier Aguirresarobe. *AWARDS:* NOM: Oscars '97: Foreign Film.

Semi-Tough

Likeable social satire is very loosely based on Dan Jenkins's best-seller about two pro football buddies (Reynolds and Kristofferson) who are both in love with their team owner's (Preston) daughter (Clayburgh). Romantic comedy, parodic self-help programs, sports jokes, zany hijinks—they're all there, but not enough of any. DVD image is seldom better than good; sound is thin but appropriate for the film's era. —*MM*
Movie: 🎵🎵½ **DVD:** 🎵🎵
MGM Home Entertainment (Cat #1001831, UPC #027616861016). Widescreen (1.85:1) letterboxed. Dolby Digital Mono. $14.98. Keepcase. *LANG:* English; Spanish. *SUB:* French; Spanish. *FEATURES:* 16 chapter links • Trailer.
1977 (R) 107m/C Burt Reynolds, Kris Kristofferson, Jill Clayburgh, Lotte Lenya, Robert Preston, Bert Convy, Richard Masur, Carl Weathers, Brian Dennehy, John Matuszak, Ron Silver; **D:** Michael Ritchie; **W:** Walter Bernstein.

The Sentinel

Big-budget horror borrows freely from *Rosemary's Baby* and *The Exorcist*—too freely, really—but it's still entertaining in a mainstream vein with a few solid scares. Supermodel Alison Parker (Raines) is going through serious personal problems which are revealed in hamfisted flashback when she moves into a new Brooklyn brownstone and meets her "very strange" neighbors. For openers, they may be ghosts, but cops Eli Wallach and Christopher Walken suspect that all may not be kosher with Alison and her fiancé Michael (Sarandon). The apartment building's sense of reality helps considerably. The big spooky finish directly quotes Tod Browning's *Freaks*. The pale image is an accurate reflection of the original, but the full-frame image is not a significant improvement over tape. —*MM*

Movie: 🎞🎞🎞 **DVD:** 🎞🎞

Goodtimes Entertainment (Cat #81044). Full frame. $14.99. Snapper. *LANG:* English. *SUB:* English; French; Spanish. *FEATURES:* 18 chapter links ▪ Production notes.

1976 (R) 92m/C Chris Sarandon, Christina Raines, Ava Gardner, Jose Ferrer, Sylvia Miles, John Carradine, Burgess Meredith, Tom Berenger, Beverly D'Angelo, Jeff Goldblum, Arthur Kennedy, Deborah Raffin, Eli Wallach, Christopher Walken; *D:* Michael Winner; *W:* Michael Winner, Jeffrey Konvitz; *C:* Richard Kratina; *M:* Gil Melle.

September

Woody does (groan) Bergman again with a shuttered claustrophobic drama about six unhappy people trying to verbalize their feelings in a dark summer house in Vermont. Well acted and interesting at first, but the whining and angst attacks eventually give way to boredom. DVD image and sound are only a slight improvement over VHS tape. —*MM*

Movie: 🎞🎞 **DVD:** 🎞🎞

MGM Home Entertainment (Cat #1001180, UPC #027616854711). Widescreen (1.85:1) anamorphic. Dolby Digital Mono. $19.98. Keepcase. *LANG:* English; French; Spanish. *SUB:* French; Spanish. *CAP:* English. *FEATURES:* 16 chapter links ▪ Trailer ▪ Booklet.

1988 (PG-13) 82m/C Mia Farrow, Dianne Wiest, Denholm Elliott, Sam Waterston, Elaine Stritch, Jack Warden; *D:* Woody Allen; *W:* Woody Allen; *C:* Carlo Di Palma; *M:* Art Tatum.

Sergei Eisenstein: Autobiography

Documentary examines life and career of the most famous of Russian film directors. As big a name as any in the silent era, with the possible exception of D.W. Griffith himself, Eisenstein left a screen legacy that includes *Strike* (1924), *Battleship Potemkin* (1925), and *October* (1928). *Potemkin* is the most famous of his cinematic creations. Based upon Eisenstein's memoirs, the documentary boasts clips from his films as well as those of his key contemporaries. That's because *Autobiography* marks not only the anniversary of Eisenstein's birth, but also

the 100th year of cinema. The audio and video are about what you would expect, with vintage clips looking plenty vintage. Disappointing is the complete omission of extra features. This is a bare-bones DVD, but film history buffs and scholars will appreciate the content. —*MB*

Movie: 🎞🎞🎞 **DVD:** 🎞🎞

Image Entertainment (Cat #ID5381IADVD, UPC #014381538120). Full frame (1.33:1). Dolby Digital Mono. $24.99. Snapper. *LANG:* Russian. *SUB:* English. *FEATURES:* 15 chapter links.

1996 90m/C RU Sergei Eisenstein; *D:* Oleg Kovalov; *Nar:* Aleksei German.

Sergei Eisenstein: Mexican Fantasy

During the 1930s, Soviet director Eisenstein started work on what would become known as his lost masterpiece, which was to be about Mexico—a cinematic study of the nation and its people. But, due to circumstances beyond his control, the hours and hours of footage he shot for the film were taken away from him. He died in 1948, never able to revisit his footage or the project. It was a half-century after his death when film restorers rescued Eisenstein's material and assembled it into the film now available on DVD. What exists now is interesting, although surely it does not represent the film Eisenstein would have exactly made, given there was no script or input from the deceased filmmaker. A master of the editing process, Eisenstein wasn't around to edit his footage, or to make notes on what others have done with it. So, what was released to theatres in 1998 and on DVD in 2001 is something else entirely—a compilation of footage, basically. Part documentary with no aim, part story with no narrative, the result is rather a mess. What is redeeming about the project is that it allows anyone to see Eisenstein's beautiful images on-screen. It creates wonder about what sort of film he would have made of them. The black-and-white cinematography looks great, with not too many examples of wear considering the age and heritage of the elements. The soundtrack is rather amateurish, but that is the fault of the restorers and assemblers, not the DVD maker. This title screams out for either a making-of documentary, an Eisenstein biography, or at least an on-screen essay to explain what it's all about and how it came to be. Unfortunately, there are no extras to be had. —*MB*

Movie: 🎞🎞½ **DVD:** 🎞🎞½

Image Entertainment (Cat #ID9848IADVD, UPC #014381984828). Full frame. Dolby Digital Stereo. $24.99. Snapper. *LANG:* Russian. *SUB:* English. *FEATURES:* 15 chapter links.

1998 100m/C *D:* Oleg Kovalov; *W:* Oleg Kovalov, Sergei Eisenstein.

Sergio Lapel's Drawing Blood

Artist/vampire Diana (Spinella) fulfills her artistic visions with blood instead of oils

or watercolors. Her human slave Edmond (Wilson) supplies a constant flow of "models" until he meets homeless prostitute Dee (Smith) and decides to take control of his life. Edmond also has his hands full keeping his ever-horny dad (Palatta) out of trouble. The Troma label says it all: non-existent production values, mediocre acting, plenty of flowing red stuff, and ample female exposure (although this time there's a genuine narrative logic to all the nudity). The video transfer does what it can with the grainy photography and overly diffused lighting, the image most of the time looking like they forgot to polish the lens. The mono soundtrack projects each neck crack or open vein spurt at strong levels. Where Troma puts the majors to shame is that they know how to stuff a DVD properly. Deleted scenes, bloopers, trailers, two audio commentary tracks, still and storyboard galleries, and interactive games all reside within the dual-layer disc. The cast commentary sounds like a frat party while the filmmakers on a separate track attempt some justification for their actions. I think the marketing guys cooked up the tag line "Blood is thicker than water-color!" and some yutz got stuck with having to build a movie around it. *South Park* fans take note: one of the trailers is for Trey Parker and Matt Stone's lyric ode to frontier anthropophagi, *Cannibal: The Musical.* —*EP* **AKA:** *Drawing Blood.*

Movie: 🎞 **DVD:** 🎞🎞

Troma Team Video (Cat #ID8808UMDVD, UPC #9035799873). Full frame. Dolby Digital Mono. $24.95. Keepcase. *LANG:* English. *FEATURES:* 11 chapter links ▪ 2 commentary tracks by cast and crew ▪ 7 deleted scenes ▪ Blooper reel ▪ 5 "Coming Distractions" trailers ▪ Interactive games: "Dismember Lloyd" and "Where in the World Is Toxie?" ▪ Storyboard gallery ▪ Production stills gallery ▪ Music video "Troma Rap" by Julie Strain.

1999 90m/C Kirk Wilson, Larry Palatta, Dawn Spinella, Leo Otero, Erin Smith; *D:* Sergio Lapel; *W:* Noel Anderson; *C:* Shawn Lewallen.

The Serpent's Kiss

Dutch garden designer Chrome (McGregor) comes to Thomas Smithers's (Postlethwaite) country estate to create a masterpiece. But he is really working for Fitzmaurice (Grant), who lusts after Mrs. Smithers (Scacchi). It's slightly reminiscent of *Dangerous Liasons,* with similarly arch characters and conflicts. DVD image is everything that's needed for a period piece. English subs are helpful in deciphering some of the accents. —*MM*

Movie: 🎞🎞½ **DVD:** 🎞🎞½

MGM Home Entertainment (Cat #1001811, UPC #027616860828). Widescreen (1.85:1) letterboxed. Dolby Digital Surround Stereo. $24.98. Keepcase. *LANG:* English. *SUB:* English; French; Spanish. *FEATURES:* 30 chapter links.

1997 (R) 110m/C GB FR Ewan McGregor, Greta Scacchi, Pete Postlethwaite, Richard E. Grant, Carmen Chaplin, Donal McCann,

Charley Boorman; **D:** Philippe Rousselot; **W:** Tim Rose Price; **C:** Jean-Francois Robin; **M:** Goran Bregovic.

The Settlement

Con men Jerry (Fichtner) and Pat (O'Reilly) have made a bundle buying life insurance policies from the terminally ill. But business has hit a slump when they meet Barbara (McGillis) who claims to have a $2 million policy and only weeks to live. The film soon becomes a question of who's scamming who. Image and sound are nothing special on this disc, but the cast certainly is. These are three of the best character actors in the business and they have a grand time with some very funny lines. Recommended. *—MM*
Movie: 🎬🎬🎬 **DVD:** 🎬🎬
MTI Home Video (Cat #BE50036DVD, UPC #619935403635). Full frame. $24.95. Keepcase. *LANG:* English. *SUB:* Spanish. *FEATURES:* 20 chapter links ● Trailers ● Talent files.
1999 92m/C Kelly McGillis, John C. Reilly, William Fichtner, Dan Castellaneta, David Rasche; **D:** Mark Steilen; **C:** Judy Irola; **M:** Brian Tyler.

Seven [2 SE]

If this grim thriller can't make you jump, you're dead, and you won't be the only one. Arrogant, ignorant detective David Mills (Pitt) is newly partnered with erudite old-timer William Somerset (Freeman) and they're stuck with the bizarre case of a morbidly obese man who was forced to eat himself to death. The weary Somerset is certain it's just the beginning and he's right—the non-buddy duo are on the trail of a serial killer who uses the seven deadly sins (gluttony, greed, sloth, pride, lust, envy, and wrath) as his modus operandi. Since most of the film is shot in dark, grimy, and unrelenting rainy circumstances, much of the grotesqueness of the murders is left to the viewer's imagination—which will be in overdrive. This is, without a doubt, one of the best DVD sets available (easily a standard in any collection). The remastered picture delivers such sharp blacks that the details within shadows are clearly visible (You can even see individual droplets of the film's ever-present rain). The soundtrack is equally amazing, featuring stunning music cues and crisp dialogue and sound effects. As for the extras, they are nothing short of awesome. *—MJT* **AKA:** Se7en.
Movie: 🎬🎬🎬 **DVD:** 🎬🎬🎬
New Line Home Video (Cat #N4997, UPC #794043499722). Widescreen (2.40:1) anamorphic. Dolby Digital 5.1 Surround; DDS Surround; Dolby EX 5.1; DTS ES 6.1. $29.95. Slipcase. *LANG:* English. *SUB:* English; French. *FEATURES:* 37 chapter links ● Commentary: David Fincher, Brad Pitt, Morgan Freeman ● Dyer, Fincher, Walker, Francis-Bruce, studio exec De Luca ● Dyer, Fincher, Francis-Bruce, Darius Khondji, Arthur Max ● Dyer, Fincher, Howard Shore, Ren Klyce; also 5.1 music and effects cues

● Deleted scenes and extended takes ● Alternate endings with animated storyboards and commentary: Fincher ● Opening title sequence exploration ● Multiple animated galleries ● Original theatrical trailer and electronic press kit ● Filmographies ● "Mastering for the Home Theater" featurette. "John Doe" website with links to his photo gallery, several "fan sites," reading list, exploration of the deadly sins; printable script.
1995 (R) 127m/C Brad Pitt, Morgan Freeman, Gwyneth Paltrow, Kevin Spacey, R. Lee Ermey, Richard Roundtree, John C. McGinley, Julie Araskog, Reg E. Cathey, Peter Crombie; **D:** David Fincher; **W:** Andrew Kevin Walker; **C:** Darius Khondji; **M:** Howard Shore. *AWARDS:* MTV Movie Awards '96: Film, Most Desirable Male (Pitt), Villain (Spacey); Natl. Bd. of Review '95: Support. Actor (Spacey); N.Y. Film Critics '95: Support. Actor (Spacey); Broadcast Film Critics '95: Support. Actor (Spacey); *NOM:* Oscars '95: Film Editing; British Acad. '95: Orig. Screenplay; MTV Movie Awards '96: On-Screen Duo (Brad Pitt/Morgan Freeman).

Seven Days in May

Topical '60s Cold War thriller is the best of its breed and still gripping. An American general (Lancaster) plans a military takeover because he considers the President's (March) pacifism traitorous. Douglas is the colonel who stumbles onto the plot. The black-and-white transfer is marvelous. The video image displays solid black levels with a minimum of grain. Detail and shadow delineation are sharp and clear. With the exception of a stirring Jerry Goldsmith score, the mono soundtrack is mainly dialogue-driven. The Dolby Digital audio shows remarkable fidelity, revealing nary a crackle or a pop. Frankenheimer's commentary is engaging and informative, as his always are. *—EP/MM*
Movie: 🎬🎬🎬½ **DVD:** 🎬🎬🎬½
Warner Home Video, Inc. (Cat #15243). Widescreen (1.85:1) anamorphic. Dolby Digital Mono. $24.98. Snapper. *LANG:* English. *SUB:* English; French. *FEATURES:* Commentary: director ● Theatrical trailer ● Production notes.
1964 117m/B Burt Lancaster, Kirk Douglas, Edmond O'Brien, Fredric March, Ava Gardner, John Houseman; **D:** John Frankenheimer; **W:** Rod Serling; **C:** Ellsworth Fredericks; **M:** Jerry Goldsmith. *AWARDS:* Golden Globes '65: Support. Actor (O'Brien); *NOM:* Oscars '64: Art Dir./Set Dec., B&W, Support. Actor (O'Brien).

7 Faces of Dr. Lao

Dr. Lao (Randall) is the proprietor of a magical circus that changes the lives of the residents of a small western town. Marvelous special effects and makeup (by William Tuttle, who created the many characters Randall plays). *Twilight Zone* veteran writer Charles Beaumont adapted Charles Finney's excellent novel. The image has been nicely preserved. The softness and grain come from the original. *—MM*

Movie: 🎬🎬🎬 **DVD:** 🎬🎬½
Warner Home Video, Inc. (Cat #65172, UPC #012569517226). Widescreen anamorphic; full frame. Dolby Digital Mono. $19.98. Snapper. *LANG:* English. *SUB:* English; French. *FEATURES:* 24 chapter links ● Talent files ● "William Tuttle, Makeup Artist" featurette ● Awards ● Trailer.
1963 101m/C Tony Randall, Barbara Eden, Arthur O'Connell, Lee Patrick, Noah Beery Jr., John Qualen, John Ericson, Royal Dano; **D:** George Pal; **W:** Charles Beaumont; **C:** Robert J. Bronner; **M:** Leigh Harline.

Seven Girlfriends

After a freak accident involving an old flame (Leighton), Jesse (Daly) is forced to reexamine his various relationships with women and sets out to visit all of his ex-girlfriends. He and they find him wanting. It's a well-written, clever, and (by today's theatrical standards) tasteful and sophisticated comedy with an attractive cast. A nice evening's rental, if you're in the mood. Image and spectacular Surround effects are relatively unimportant in this kind of film, so it gains little on disc beyond two commentary tracks and the other extras. *—MM*
Movie: 🎬🎬½ **DVD:** 🎬🎬🎬
Trimark Home Video (Cat #7573D, UPC #03139875732). Widescreen letterboxed. Dolby Digital 5.1 Surround Stereo. $24.99. Keepcase. *LANG:* English. *SUB:* English; French; Spanish. *FEATURES:* 24 chapter links ● Gag reel ● Storyboards ● Photo gallery ● Commentary: director Lazarus ● Commentary: director Lazarus, Tim Daly, and producer Bruce Opper.
2000 (R) 100m/C Timothy Daly, Laura Leighton, Mimi Rogers, Olivia D'Abo, Jami Gertz, Elizabeth Pena, Melora Hardin, Arye Gross, Katy Selverstone; **D:** Paul Lazarus; **W:** Paul Lazarus, Stephen Gregg; **C:** Don E. Fauntleroy; **M:** Christopher Tyng.

The Seven Little Foys

Bob Hope is at his best as Eddie Foy, head of the famed vaudevillian troupe. The highlight of the disc is chapter five, where Foy shares the stage with George M. Cohan (Cagney). Actually, they share a table for a spirited dance routine. The color image has been well preserved and so the DVD contains no significant flaws. Sound is fine, too. *—MM*
Movie: 🎬🎬🎬 **DVD:** 🎬🎬🎬
Brentwood Home Video (Cat #60984-9, UPC #090096098494). Full frame. Dolby Digital Mono. $14.98. Keepcase. *LANG:* English. *FEATURES:* 8 chapter links ● Bob Hope thumbnail bio and filmography.
1955 95m/C Bob Hope, Milly Vitale, George Tobias, Angela Clark, James Cagney; **D:** Melville Shavelson; **W:** Jack Rose, Melville Shavelson. *AWARDS: NOM:* Oscars '55: Story & Screenplay.

The Seven Year Itch

Stunning blonde model (Monroe) moves upstairs just as happily married guy Ewell's

wife leaves for a long vacation. He gets itchy. This DVD corrects a major flaw in all previous video editions. Every time one of Tom Ewell's fantasies began or ended in older copies, a jolting color and grain shift would occur across a splice. You can still see them here, but just barely. —*GE*
Movie: 🎬🎬🎬 **DVD:** 🎬🎬🎬½
20th Century Fox Home Entertainment (Cat #2001421, UPC #024543014218). Widescreen (2.55:1) anamorphic. Dolby Digital 3.0; Stereo; Mono. $24.98. Keepcase. *LANG:* English; French. *FEATURES:* MovieTone News short • Behind-the-scenes featurette • 2 deleted scenes • Extension of the famous subway grate scene • Trailers.
1955 105m/C Marilyn Monroe, Tom Ewell, Evelyn Keyes, Sonny Tufts, Victor Moore, Doro Merande, Robert Strauss, Oscar Homolka, Carolyn Jones; **D:** Billy Wilder; **W:** Billy Wilder, George Axelrod; **C:** Milton Krasner; **M:** Alfred Newman. *AWARDS:* Golden Globes '56: Actor—Mus./Comedy (Ewell).

The '70s

What can you say about a decade that started with the Kent State shootings and ended with the election of Ronald Regan? Apparently 170 minutes' worth would be the answer. This ambitious mini series struggles as it tries to fit a history lesson into an entertaining block of film. Certain lessons have to be taught: feminism, the Nixon era, black rights, and as a result the characters have to follow the storyline rather than vice versa. Couple that with a male lead (Rowe) who is as exciting as damp white bread and the result is a film that falls short of its goal. However, *The '70s* is still worth watching from a historical perspective, and anyone who grew up in the decade when "Disco was King" will be surprised at all the historical events they lived through. The story follows four college friends as they maneuver through the history lesson. Good use of music and smooth integration of film clips keep the plot moving along. Color and clarity on the DVD are better than average, which manages to make all those '70s clothes even more frightening than usual. —*CA*
Movie: 🎬🎬 **DVD:** 🎬🎬
Trimark Home Video (Cat #VM7383D, UPC #03398738329). Full frame. Stereo. $24.99. Keepcase. *LANG:* English. *SUB:* English; Spanish. *CAP:* English. *FEATURES:* 36 chapter links • Cast and celebrity interviews.
2000 170m/C Brad Rowe, Guy Torry, Vinessa Shaw, Amy Smart, Kathryn Harrold, Graham Beckel, Tina Lifford, Chandra West, Robert Joy, Jeanetta Arnette, Michael Easton, Peggy Lipton; **D:** Peter Werner; **W:** Mitch Brian, Kevin Willmott; **C:** Neil Roach; **M:** Peter Manning Robinson.

Sex and the City: The Complete Second Season

All 18 episodes constituting the entire second season of the popular Home Box Office series *Sex and the City* are on this three small platter set. Sarah Jessica Parker stars as Carrie Bradshaw, sex columnist and single Manhattanite ever on the prowl for Mr. Right. The show chronicles her emotional and physical travails in the Big Apple as well as the sexual adventures of her ever-present friends: wide-eyed innocent Charlotte (Kristen Davis), cynical Miranda (Cynthia Nixon), and very sexually liberated Samantha (Kim Cattrall). The set is divided between three DVDs, each containing six episodes. The teleplays run approximately 28 minutes and cover such rocky romantic terrain as Viagra, tantric sex workshops, infidelity, and cemetery dates, with humor and compassion. Favorite episodes include: "Was It Good for You?" (#17, disc three) where the four take a class on how to make better love, "Four Women and a Funeral" (#5, disc one) about funeral "etiquette," and "The Awful Truth" (#2, disc one) which answers once and for all if honesty is the best policy when dating. With so many choices, a poorly designed DVD would have been hell to navigate. Not so here. A preview option is available (mostly on-air promos) with direct access to the episode should one choose to watch. In the "Special Features" section of each disc, the entire 18-episode line-up is offered, with preview option and instant access (if it is not on the disc being played, the text instructs which disc contains the desired episode). The DVD image is crisp and clear. Ditto with the stereo audio. —*EP*
Movie: 🎬🎬½ **DVD:** 🎬🎬½
HBO Home Video (Cat #99248, UPC #026359924828). Full frame. Dolby Digital Surround Stereo; Dolby Digital Mono. $49.98. Clear plastic foldout keepcase (3 discs). *LANG:* English; Spanish (DD Mono). *SUB:* English; French. *FEATURES:* 18 chapter links (6 per disc) • Season index (each disc) • Cast and filmmaker profiles (disc one) • Awards profiles (disc two) • Featurette (disc three) • TV Promo spots (disc three) • DVD-ROM features: website access.
2000 540m/C Sarah Jessica Parker, Kim Cattrall, Kristen Davis, Cynthia Nixon, Christopher Noth; **W:** Darren Star; **C:** Stuart Dryburgh; **M:** Douglas J. Cuomo.

Sex Files: Ancient Desires

The image may be slightly superior to *Digital Desires* but the intention and the budget are precisely the same. This time, the gimmick linking the soft-core scenes is a mummy queen. Nothing new. —*MM*
Movie: 🎬½ **DVD:** 🎬½
Image Entertainment (Cat #ALAD9900DVD, UPC #014381990027). Full frame. Dolby Digital Stereo. $24.95. Snapper. *LANG:* English. *FEATURES:* 12 chapter links.
1999 87m/C Daniel Anderson, Jenna Bodnar, Stephen Curtis, Regina Russell; **D:** Clinton J. Williams; **W:** Jay Woelfel; **C:** Howard Wexler.

Sex Files: Digital Sex

Inevitable low-budget parody has a pair of agents on the trail of the spies who stole a gizmo that allows one person to record and play back physical sensations. A series of poorly lit soft-core sex scenes follows. The producers are known for their late-night cable fare and that's exactly what this is. The exceptionally grainy image is identical to tape. —*MM*
Movie: 🎬 **DVD:** 🎬🎬
Image Entertainment (Cat #ALAD9897DVD, UPC #014381989724). Full frame. Dolby Digital Mono. $24.99. Snapper. *LANG:* English. *FEATURES:* 12 chapter links.
1998 79m/C Lauren Hays, Alicia Anne, Thad Geer, C. Johnston, James Edwards, Jeff Davis, Todd Eckert; **D:** Ellen Evans; **W:** Debra Black; **C:** Rocky Dijon; **M:** Ace Edwards.

Sextette

Lavish film revolves around an aging star who is constantly interrupted by former spouses and well-wishers while on a honeymoon with her sixth husband. West unwisely came out of retirement for this last film, based on her own novel. It's exquisitely embarrassing to watch, though it gains nothing on DVD. Both sound and image are very poor; substandard compared to VHS. —*MM*
Movie: woof **DVD:** 🎬
Rhino Home Video (Cat #R2 976612, UPC #603497661220). Full frame. $9.99. Snapper. *LANG:* English. *FEATURES:* 13 chapter links.
1978 (PG) 91m/C Mae West, Timothy Dalton, Ringo Starr, George Hamilton, Dom DeLuise, Tony Curtis, Alice Cooper, Keith Moon, George Raft, Rona Barrett, Walter Pidgeon, Regis Philbin; **D:** Ken Hughes; **W:** Herbert Baker; **C:** James A. Crabe; **M:** Artie Butler.

Shadow of a Doubt

Hitchcock always claimed that this film was his personal favorite and many fans of his early work agree. Uncle Charlie (Cotten) goes to visit family in the little town of Santa Rosa. His niece (Wright), named Charlie after him, slowly comes to suspect that he's a wanted murderer—and he's aware of her suspicions. The story is so beautifully acted and tightly constructed that it's more enjoyable on the second or third viewing. Some minor wear is apparent at first, along with a little noise on the soundtrack but both clear up quickly. The digital transfer has been done so carefully that tight patterns of light and shadow over clothing textures are not a problem, save mild flashing in one window-pane jacket. Black-and-white photography is very good. —*MM*
Movie: 🎬🎬🎬½ **DVD:** 🎬🎬🎬½
Universal Studios Home Video (Cat #20672, UPC #025192067228). Full frame. Dolby Digital Mono. $29.99. Keepcase. *LANG:* English; Spanish. *SUB:* French. *CAP:* English. *FEATURES:* 18 chapter links • "Making of" documentary • Trailer • Pro-

duction drawings and photographs • Talent files • Trailer.

1943 108m/B Teresa Wright, Joseph Cotten, Hume Cronyn, MacDonald Carey, Henry Travers, Wallace Ford; **D:** Alfred Hitchcock; **W:** Thornton Wilder, Sally Benson, Alma Reville; **C:** Joseph Valentine; **M:** Dimitri Tiomkin. *AWARDS:* Natl. Film Reg. '91; *NOM:* Oscars '43: Story.

Shadow of Chinatown

A mad scientist creates a wave of murder and terror in Chinatown in this 15-part serial. Given the age of the film, defects in the print are inevitable, as are other blemishes that come with the aging process. Whirlwind tried to salvage these problems by applying a good dose of digital noise reduction to the film—a good dose too much for my taste, because not much of the original image is left. The picture is extremely soft as a result of the digital process, and no details are distinguishable. The noise reduction creates ghosting artifacts, which further blur all movement in the images. At the same time, the film shows serious registration problems, resulting in an unstable and constantly wavering presentation. The contrast in this black-and-white presentation is a tad too harsh, creating impenetrable shadows and glaring highlights that often appear overexposed, although much of that may be a result of the age of the film and the film stock it was shot on. The image also appears to be incorrectly framed, as the opening and closing credits are visibly shifted to the left. The audio sounds muddy and through the audio noise reduction process, all high ends have been removed with it, making much of the dialogue indistinguishable. When every "s" sound is turned into a distorted "f," it simply becomes hard to follow the presentation. —*GH*

Movie: ♪♪½ **DVD:** ♪½
Whirlwind Media (Cat #2022). Full frame. Dolby Digital Mono. $24.95. Keepcase. *LANG:* English. *FEATURES:* 2-disc set.

1936 70m/B Bela Lugosi, Bruce (Herman Brix) Bennett, Joan Barclay, Luana Walters, Maurice Liu, William Buchanan; **D:** Robert F. "Bob" Hill.

Shadow of the Eagle

Former flying ace Craig McCoy (Wayne) is accused of being a master criminal known as "The Eagle." He's using his flying skills (which include skywriting that borders on calligraphy) to threaten a corrupt corporation. Can Wayne really be our villain? This hokey 12-part serial has the thin, tinny sound typical of the early 1930s. The black-and-white photography ranges between poor and fair. Flaws come from the original elements. —*MM*

Movie: ♪½ **DVD:** ♪
Marengo Films (Cat #MRG-0015, UPC #80 7013001525). Full frame. $14.98. Snapper. *LANG:* English. *FEATURES:* 6 chapter links.

1932 226m/B John Wayne, Dorothy Gulliver, Walter Miller; **D:** Ford Beebe.

Shadow of the Vampire

E. Elias Merhige imagines that when the great director F.W. Murnau (Malkovich) was trying to make the silent masterpiece *Nosferatu*, his leading man, Max Schreck (Dafoe) really was a vampire. From that premise, he spins out a terrific movie about movies. He largely takes that tack on his commentary track, too. He sounds like he's equal parts filmmaker and film fan. The often-dark image is excellent and the disc is packed with extras. Horror fans who thought this one was too "mainstream" in its theatrical release will be happily surprised. —*MM*

Movie: ♪♪♪ **DVD:** ♪♪♪½
Universal Studios Home Video Widescreen (2.35:1) anamorphic. Dolby Digital Surround; DTS Surround. $26.98. Keepcase. *LANG:* English; French. *CAP:* English. *FEATURES:* 18 chapter links • Commentary: E. Elias Merhige • "Making of" featurette • Interviews with Dafoe, Merhige, producer Nicolas Cage • Makeup application montage • Production photos • Trailers • Production notes • Talent files.

2000 93m/C *GB* John Malkovich, Willem Dafoe, Catherine McCormack, Cary Elwes, Eddie Izzard, Udo Kier, Ronan Vibert, Aden (John) Gillett; **D:** Edmund Elias Merhige; **W:** Steven Katz; **C:** Lou Bogue; **M:** Dan Jones. *AWARDS:* L.A. Film Critics '00: Support. Actor (Dafoe); *NOM:* Oscars '00: Makeup, Support. Actor (Dafoe); Ind. Spirit '01: Cinematog.; Screen Actors Guild '00: Support. Actor (Dafoe).

Shadow Raiders, Vol. 1: Uncommon Hero

Tekla, the metallic princess, is the sole survivor of an attack on her planet, Tek. She is aided by a stone miner, Graveheart, who's looking for ice. (That's right. He is a miner who is made out of stone.) Computer-generated characters are fine for this kind of animation. They and their environment are bright and hard-edged. The explosive action is familiar stuff. DVD image is flawless. Contents: "Behold the Beast," "On the Rocks," "Born in Fire," "Bad to the Bone." —*MM*

Movie: ♪♪ **DVD:** ♪♪♪
A.D.V. Films (Cat #DSR/001, UPC #70272 7010729). Full frame. Dolby Digital Stereo. $24.99. Keepcase. *LANG:* English. *FEATURES:* 16 chapter links • Character thumbnail bios • Animation models • Trailers.

1998 90m/C *CA* **D:** Colin Davies, Phil Mitchell; **W:** Len Wein.

The Shadow Riders

Two brothers, Mac (Selleck) and Del (Elliot), who fought on opposite sides of the Civil War return home to find their sister and Del's fiancée (Ross) kidnapped by a renegade Confederate officer who plans to use

them as ransom in a prisoner exchange. The brothers break their uncle (Johnson) out of jail and set out to rescue her. Some minor print damage is evident, but that's not really serious considering the made-for-television production values. —*MM* **AKA:** Louis L'Amour's "The Shadow Riders."

Movie: ♪♪ **DVD:** ♪♪
Trimark Home Video (Cat #6906). Full frame. Stereo. $24.99. Keepcase. *LANG:* English. *SUB:* French; Spanish. *CAP:* English. *FEATURES:* Cast and crew thumbnail bios • Trailer • 24 chapter links.

1982 (PG) 96m/C Tom Selleck, Sam Elliott, Ben Johnson, Katharine Ross, Jeffery Osterhage, Gene Evans, R.G. Armstrong, Marshall Teague, Dominique Dunne, Jeanetta Arnette; **D:** Andrew V. McLaglen; **W:** Jim Byrnes; **C:** Jack Whitman; **M:** Jerrold Immel.

Shadows

Please see review for *Outside the Law / Shadows.*

Movie: ♪♪
1922 70m/B Lon Chaney Sr., Harrison Ford; **D:** Tom Forman; **W:** Eve Unsell, Hope Loring; **C:** Harry Perry; **M:** Gaylord Carter.

Shadows and Fog

Offbeat, unpredictable Allen film is little more than an exercise in expressionistic visual stylings. The action revolves around a clerk (Allen) who is awakened in the middle of the night to join a vigilante group hunting for a killer. Carlo DiPalma's black-and-white cinematography is stunning, but this is no *Third Man*. DVD manages to handle all that fog and all those shadows without many serious flaws. —*MM*

Movie: ♪♪ **DVD:** ♪♪½
MGM Home Entertainment (Cat #100118 1, UPC #027616854728). Widescreen (1.85:1) anamorphic. Dolby Digital Mono. $14.98. Keepcase. *LANG:* English; French; Spanish. *SUB:* French; Spanish. *CAP:* English. *FEATURES:* 16 chapter links • Trailer • Booklet.

1992 (PG-13) 85m/B Woody Allen, Kathy Bates, John Cusack, Mia Farrow, Jodie Foster, Fred Gwynne, Julie Kavner, Madonna, John Malkovich, Kenneth Mars, Kate Nelligan, Donald Pleasence, Lily Tomlin, Philip Bosco, Robert Joy, Wallace Shawn, Kurtwood Smith, Josef Sommer, David Ogden Stiers, Michael Kirby, Anne Lange; **D:** Woody Allen; **W:** Woody Allen; **C:** Carlo Di Palma.

Shaft

He's a complicated man and no one understands him but Armani. That seems to be the style-over-substance approach that John Singleton takes to this sequel-update of the 1971 original. This John Shaft (Jackson) is the nephew of the first (Roundtree, who appears in a cameo). He's also a police detective who tries to find a missing witness (Colette), who can finger a wealthy racist murderer (Bale, doing a riff on the role he played in *Ameri-*

can Psycho). He and Jeffrey Wright as an Hispanic hoodlum almost steal the spotlight from Jackson, who exudes just the right amount of cool. DVD handles the many potentially difficult night exteriors on city streets with no problems. Sound is fine. —MM **AKA:** Shaft Returns.
Movie: 🎬🎬 **DVD:** 🎬🎬🎬
Paramount (Cat #33619, UPC #09736336 1947). Widescreen anamorphic. Dolby Digital 5.1 Surround Stereo; Dolby Digital Surround. $29.99. Snapper. *LANG:* English; French. *SUB:* English. *FEATURES:* 12 chapter links ● 2 music videos ● Cast and crew interviews ● "Making of" featurette ● Trailer.
2000 (R) 98m/C Samuel L. Jackson, Christian Bale, Vanessa L(ynne) Williams, Jeffrey Wright, Philip Bosco, Toni Collette, Angela Pietropinto, Dan Hedaya, Josef Sommer, Richard Roundtree, Ruben Santiago-Hudson, Lynne Thigpen, Pat Hingle, Busta Rhymes, Mekhi Phifer, Zach Grenier, Catherine Kellner, Isaac Hayes, Lee Tergesen; **D:** John Singleton; **W:** Richard Price; **C:** Stuart Dryburgh; **M:** Isaac Hayes, David Arnold.

Shaft in Africa

The third film in the original series is actually the sharpest looking on DVD. Image is particularly bright and crisp for an early '70s production; mono sound is only O.K. The film itself is a surprising winner. New York detective John Shaft (Roundtree) is kidnapped and eventually hired to shut down a virtual slave ring that smuggles workers from Africa to Europe. The action has a certain James Bond flavor. It moves quickly but maintains a strong sense of place. This late arrival on home video is a genuine sleeper. —MM
Movie: 🎬🎬🎬 **DVD:** 🎬🎬🎬
Warner Home Video, Inc. (Cat #65302). Widescreen letterboxed; full frame. Dolby Digital Mono. $14.95. Snapper. *LANG:* English; French. *SUB:* English; French. *FEATURES:* 30 chapter links ● Trailers ● Talent files.
1973 (R) 112m/C Richard Roundtree, Frank Finlay, Vonetta McGee, Neda Arneric, Jacques Marin; **D:** John Guillermin; **W:** Stirling Silliphant.

Shaft's Big Score

First sequel finds New York detective John Shaft (Roundtree) mediating among several mobsters while investigating a friend's murder. Lots of action and an exciting Brooklyn chase scene involving, cars, helicopters, and boats, but none of it really measures up to the original, or to the third, *Shaft in Africa*. This DVD image isn't nearly as sharp as *Africa* either. It's a nicely plotted mystery, but nothing more. —MM
Movie: 🎬🎬½ **DVD:** 🎬🎬½
Warner Home Video, Inc. (Cat #65198). Widescreen letterboxed; full frame. Dolby Digital Mono. $14.98. Snapper. *LANG:* English; French. *SUB:* English; French. *FEATURES:* 30 chapter links ● Talent files ● Trailers.
1972 (R) 105m/C Richard Roundtree, Moses Gunn, Joseph Macolo, Drew Bundi Brown, Wally Taylor, Kathy Imrie, Julius W. Harris, Rosalind Miles, Joe Santos; **D:** Gordon Parks; **W:** Ernest Tidyman; **M:** Gordon Parks.

Shag: The Movie

In 1963 our four heroines have just graduated from Spartansburg (SC) High. Luanne (Hannah) has told her mother that she wants to take an "educational" trip to study historic Ft. Sumter. Mom hands over the keys to a red Cadillac convertible. Her friends Pudge (Gish) and Melaina (Fonda) know that they're really headed to Myrtle Beach. But that's a surprise for Carson (Cates). Many adventures (too many, really) involving boys, beer, and dancing follow. The film avoids exploitation elements, but it never really captures the feeling of Myrtle Beach in the mid-'60s. The Madras shorts and the bouffant hairdos look right, but there was more to it than that, a sense of freedom and rebellion that's only hinted at here. The great Myrtle Beach movie has yet to be made, but this one's a fair shot. Image is every bit as good as the theatrical release, as I remember it; sound is superior. By the way, the title refers to a dance; it has nothing to do with *Austin Powers*. —MM
Movie: 🎬🎬🎬 **DVD:** 🎬🎬½
MGM Home Entertainment (Cat #10018 51, UPC #027616861191). Widescreen (1.85:1) letterboxed. Dolby Digital Surround Stereo. $19.98. Keepcase. *LANG:* English. *SUB:* French; Spanish. *CAP:* English. *FEATURES:* 16 chapter links ● Trailer.
1989 (PG) 96m/C Phoebe Cates, Annabeth Gish, Bridget Fonda, Page Hannah, Scott Coffey, Robert Rusler, Tyrone Power Jr., Jeff Yagher, Carrie Hamilton, Shirley Anne Field, Leilani Sarelle Ferrer; **D:** Zelda Barron; **W:** Robin Swicord, Lanier Laney, Terry Sweeney; **C:** Peter Macdonald.

Shakes the Clown

Offbeat comedy chronicles the rise and fall of Shakes (Goldthwait), an alcoholic clown wandering the streets of the all-clown town of Palookaville. Framed for the murder of his boss by his archrival Binky, Shakes takes it on the lam. The transfer is highly detailed for the most part and maintains every bit of information from the very clean source print. Without defects or blemishes, the image has very good black level, while highlights are always well-balanced. Color delineation is very good, rendering hues and shades strongly but without oversaturation. Surround effects are restrained. —GH/MM
Movie: 🎬🎬½ **DVD:** 🎬🎬½
Columbia Tristar Home Video (Cat #4062). Widescreen (1.85:1) anamorphic. Dolby Digital Surround Stereo; Dolby Digital Stereo. $24.95. Keepcase. *LANG:* English; Spanish. *SUB:* English; Spanish. *FEATURES:* Theatrical trailers ● Talent files ● Production notes.
1992 (R) 83m/C Bob(cat) Goldthwait, Julie Brown, Blake Clark, Adam Sandler, Tom Kenny, Sydney Lassick, Paul Dooley, Tim Kazurinsky, Florence Henderson, LaWanda Page; **Cameos:** Robin Williams; **D:** Bob(cat) Goldthwait; **W:** Bob(cat) Goldthwait; **C:** Bobby Bukowski, Elliot Davis.

Shane

Shane (Ladd), a retired gunfighter, comes to the aid of a homestead family (Heflin, Arthur, and de Wilde). The romantic figure becomes the young boy's idol, but the film is more interested in the human side of heroes. Despite changes in conventions and style, it remains one of the most watchable of the early '50s westerns. The cast is excellent. If the commentary track is a bit too enthusiastic, that's to be expected from George Stevens Jr., son of the producer/director, and associate producer Moffat. The bright image transfer to disc is near perfect. The conclusion is dark, as it is meant to be. —MM
Movie: 🎬🎬🎬½ **DVD:** 🎬🎬🎬½
Pioneer Entertainment (Cat #06522, UPC #097360652277). Full frame. Dolby Digital Stereo; Mono. $29.99. Keepcase. *LANG:* English; French. *SUB:* English. *FEATURES:* 16 chapter links ● Trailer ● Commentary: George Stevens Jr., Ivan Moffat.
1953 117m/C Alan Ladd, Jean Arthur, Van Heflin, Brandon de Wilde, Jack Palance, Ben Johnson, Elisha Cook Jr., Edgar Buchanan, Emile Meyer; **D:** George Stevens; **W:** Jack Sher; **C:** Loyal Griggs; **M:** Victor Young. *AWARDS:* Oscars '53: Color Cinematog.; AFI '98: Top 100; Natl. Bd. of Review '53: Director (Stevens), Natl. Film Reg. '93; *NOM:* Oscars '53: Director (Stevens), Picture, Screenplay, Support. Actor (de Wilde, Palance).

Shanghai Noon

Jackie plays a Chinese Imperial Guard who is sent to the Wild American West to rescue captive Princess Pei Pei (Liu). Unfamiliar with the language, the customs, and the country, he soon teams up with Roy O'Bannon (Wilson), a local desperado. Before he knows it, Chan becomes known as the Shanghai Kid, and with a $1000 reward on his head, is on the run from the law. The image is clear and entirely free of blemishes or scratches. Colors are beautifully vibrant, creating a bold and colorful presentation. Blacks are deep and solid without ever losing detail, not even in the most dimly lit interior shots. Skin tones are rendered naturally. Compression is flawless without a hint of compression artifacting. The 5.1 mix is dynamic and aggressive. —GH/MM
Movie: 🎬🎬🎬 **DVD:** 🎬🎬🎬½
Artisan Entertainment (Cat #20771). Widescreen (2.35:1) anamorphic. Dolby Digital 5.1 Surround Stereo; Dolby Digital Surround Stereo. $29.99. Keepcase. *LANG:* English. *FEATURES:* Featurettes ● 7 deleted scenes ● Trivia game ● Photo gallery ● Commentary: Chan, Wilson, Deyl.
2000 (PG-13) 110m/C Jackie Chan, Lucy Alexis Liu, Owen C. Wilson, Roger Yuan, Xander Berkeley, Jason Connery, Henry O, Walton Goggins, Russ Badger, Rafael

Baez, Brandon Merrill; **D:** Tom Dey; **W:** Alfred Gough, Miles Millar; **C:** Dan Mindel; **M:** Randy Edelman.

Shark Attack 2

Formulaic sequel lacks the sparkling clarity that made the original video premiere such a surprise on disc. This one's more of the same old same old with genetically enhanced mutant Great White Sharks chomping down on anyone who gets in the ocean. The 5.1 Surround is actually more impressive than the visuals but all of the crunchy, toothy sound effects don't make the models and computer effects any more persuasive. —MM
Movie: 🎵🎵 **DVD:** 🎵🎵
Trimark Home Video (Cat #7566D, UPC #031398756620). Widescreen letterboxed. Dolby Digital 5.1 Surround Stereo. $24.99. Keepcase. *LANG:* English. *SUB:* English; Spanish; French. *FEATURES:* 24 chapter links • Trailers.
2000 (R) 93m/C Nikita Ager, Daniel Alexander, Thorsten Kaye, Danny Kei; **D:** David Worth, Yossi Wein; **W:** William Hooke, Scott Devine; **M:** Mark Morgan.

Sharpe's Battle

Sharpe (Bean) must prepare the Royal Irish company, led by Lord Kiely (Durr) and accustomed only to ceremonial duties, for their first battle. Meanwhile, Kiely's wife (Byrne) goes to Sharpe for help with a personal matter, and then there's more trouble with the French. For image and sound comments, please see review of *Sharpe's Rifles.* —MM
Movie: 🎵🎵½ **DVD:** 🎵🎵½
BFS Video (Cat #98606-D, UPC #0668059 16069). Full frame. Dolby Digital Mono. $19.98. Keepcase. *LANG:* English. *FEATURES:* 12 chapter links.
1994 100m/C *GB* Sean Bean, Daragh O'Malley, Hugh Fraser, Jason Durr, Allie Byrne; **D:** Tom Clegg; **W:** Russell Lewis.

Sharpe's Company

Sharpe (Bean) sets out to rescue his Spanish lover Teresa (Serna) and their infant daughter, trapped in the French-held city of Badajoz, which is about to be stormed by the Brits. To make matters worse, Sharpe must also deal with the machinations of underhanded madman Sgt. Obadiah Hakeswill (Postlethwaite), an old enemy with a grudge. For image and sound comments, please see review of *Sharpe's Rifles.* —MM
Movie: 🎵🎵½ **DVD:** 🎵🎵½
BFS Video (Cat #98598-D, UPC #0668059 15987). Full frame. Dolby Digital Mono. $19.98. Keepcase. *LANG:* English. *FEATURES:* 12 chapter links.
1994 100m/C *GB* Sean Bean, Assumpta Serna, Daragh O'Malley, Pete Postlethwaite, Hugh Fraser, Clive Francis, Louise Germaine; **D:** Tom Clegg; **W:** Charles Wood.

Sharpe's Eagle

Sharpe (Bean) and his band of sharpshooters are once again in the thick of the battle against Napoleon's troops, but this time they have the misfortune to be led by the imbecilic Sir Henry Simmerson (Cochrane). Thanks to his incompetence and cowardice, the regimental colors are captured, and an officer Sharpe admires is killed. Setting out for revenge, Sharpe is determined to capture the French mascot, a carved golden eagle, and to settle some personal scores. For image and sound comments, please see review of *Sharpe's Rifles.* —MM
Movie: 🎵🎵½ **DVD:** 🎵🎵½
BFS Video (Cat #98580-D, UPC #0668059 15802). Full frame. Dolby Digital Mono. $19.98. Keepcase. *LANG:* English. *FEATURES:* 12 chapter links.
1993 100m/C *GB* Sean Bean, Assumpta Serna, Brian Cox, David Troughton, Daragh O'Malley, Michael Cochrane, Katia Caballero; **D:** Tom Clegg; **W:** Eoghan Harris; **C:** Ivan Strasburg; **M:** Dominic Muldowney.

Sharpe's Enemy

Sharpe (Bean) is sent to a mountain stronghold, held by a band of deserters, to ransom Isabella (Hurley), the bride of an English colonel, Sir Augustus Farthindale (Child). But the evil Hakeswill (Postlethwaite) is leading the criminals and refuses to make things easy for our hero—nor will the French troops leave the English soldiers in peace. For image and sound comments, please see review of *Sharpe's Rifles.* —MM
Movie: 🎵🎵½ **DVD:** 🎵🎵½
BFS Video (Cat #98599-D, UPC #0668059 15994). Full frame. Dolby Digital Mono. $19.98. Keepcase. *LANG:* English. *FEATURES:* 12 chapter links.
1994 100m/C *GB* Sean Bean, Assumpta Serna, Pete Postlethwaite, Daragh O'Malley, Hugh Fraser, Elizabeth Hurley, Michael Byrne, Jeremy Child, Nicholas Rowe; **D:** Tom Clegg; **W:** Eoghan Harris.

Sharpe's Gold

Circa 1813, Richard Sharpe (Bean) has been promoted to Major—still leading his band of renegade sharpshooters. This time, they're assigned to trade rifles for deserters held by the partisans, and to search for Aztec gold as Wellington (Fraser) prepares to push into France. Sharpe must also protect Wellington's cousin Bess (Linehan) and her daughter Ellie (Ashbourne) as they search for Bess's missing husband. For image and sound comments, please see review of *Sharpe's Rifles.* —MM
Movie: 🎵🎵½ **DVD:** 🎵🎵½
BFS Video (Cat #98605-D, UPC #0668059 16052). Full frame. Dolby Digital Mono. $19.98. Keepcase. *LANG:* English. *FEATURES:* 12 chapter links.
1994 100m/C *GB* Sean Bean, Daragh O'Malley, Hugh Fraser, Rosaleen Linehan,

Jayne Ashbourne, Abel Folk, Peter Eyre; **D:** Tom Clegg; **W:** Nigel Kneale.

Sharpe's Honour

Sharpe (Bean) becomes a pawn of French spy Pierre Ducos when he's forced to cross enemy lines disguised as a Spanish rebel, and to defend himself against allegations of dishonor. As usual, our man is unable to resist the attractions of the Marquesa Dorada (Krige), who's also part of the Frenchman's nefarious plan. For image and sound comments, please see review of *Sharpe's Rifles.* —MM
Movie: 🎵🎵½ **DVD:** 🎵🎵½
BFS Video (Cat #98604-D, UPC #0668059 16045). Full frame. Dolby Digital Mono. $19.98. Keepcase. *LANG:* English. *FEATURES:* 12 chapter links.
1994 100m/C *GB* Sean Bean, Daragh O'Malley, Alice Krige, Hugh Fraser, Michael Byrne, Ron Cook; **D:** Tom Clegg; **W:** Colin MacDonald.

Sharpe's Justice

Having cleared his name, Richard Sharpe (Bean) returns to England and is ordered north where he's to command the local militia. But Sharpe soon has to decide whether to support the local gentry or the working class in a time of unrest. For image and sound comments, please see review of *Sharpe's Rifles.* —MM
Movie: 🎵🎵½ **DVD:** 🎵🎵½
BFS Video (Cat #98645-D, UPC #0668059 16458). Full frame. Dolby Digital Mono. $19.98. Keepcase. *LANG:* English. *FEATURES:* 12 chapter links.
1997 100m/C *GB* Sean Bean, Daragh O'Malley, Abigail Cruttenden, Alexis Denisof, Douglas Henshall, Caroline Langrishe, Philip Glenister; **D:** Tom Clegg.

Sharpe's Mission

Sharpe (Bean) joins with Col. Brand (Strong) and his men to blow up an ammunition depot as Wellington continues his invasion of France. But Brand arouses Sharpe's suspicions that the supposedly heroic British officer is actually a French spy. For image and sound comments, please see review of *Sharpe's Rifles.* —MM
Movie: 🎵🎵½ **DVD:** 🎵🎵½
BFS Video (Cat #98631-D, UPC #0668059 16311). Full frame. Dolby Digital Mono. $19.98. Keepcase. *LANG:* English. *FEATURES:* 12 chapter links.
1996 100m/C *GB* Sean Bean, Daragh O'Malley, Hugh Fraser, James Laurenson, Mark Strong, Abigail Cruttenden; **D:** Tom Clegg; **W:** Eoghan Harris.

Sharpe's Regiment

Wellington prepares for the invasion of France in June 1813, but the South Essex battalion needs more men. So Sharpe (Bean) and Harper (O'Malley) are sent back to London for recruits and to uncover corruption in high places. For image and

sound comments, please see review of *Sharpe's Rifles.* —*MM*
Movie: 🎶🎶½ **DVD:** 🎶🎶½
BFS Video (Cat #98629-D, UPC #0668059 16298). Full frame. Dolby Digital Mono. $19.98. Keepcase. *LANG:* English. *FEATURES:* 12 chapter links.
1996 100m/C *GB* Sean Bean, Daragh O'Malley, Nicholas Farrell, Michael Cochrane, Abigail Cruttenden, Caroline Langrishe, James Laurenson; *D:* Tom Clegg; *W:* Eoghan Harris.

Sharpe's Revenge

The Peninsular War is over but Sharpe (Bean) is accused of stealing Napoleon's treasures by his old enemy, the spy Ducos. Abandoned by his wife when he's convicted of the crime, Sharpe escapes from prison and crosses post-war France in search of the truth. For image and sound comments, please see review of *Sharpe's Rifles.* —*MM*
Movie: 🎶🎶½ **DVD:** 🎶🎶½
BFS Video (Cat #98644-D, UPC #0668059 16441). Full frame. Dolby Digital Mono. $19.98. Keepcase. *LANG:* English. *FEATURES:* 12 chapter links.
1997 100m/C *GB* Sean Bean, Daragh O'Malley, Abigail Cruttenden, Feodor Atkine, Alexis Denisof, Cecile Paoli, Philip Whitchurch; *D:* Tom Clegg; *W:* Eoghan Harris.

Sharpe's Rifles

Swashbuckling heroics dominate as the Duke of Wellington's British soldiers battle Napoleon's French forces in the 1809 Peninsula War (fought in Spain and Portugal). Common soldier Richard Sharpe (Bean) receives a field commission and is given the unenviable task of leading a group of malcontent sharpshooters on a secret mission to aid Spanish allies. But the guerilla leader is the lovely Teresa (Serna). The producers aim at a relatively high degree of accuracy in historical detail, and Bean is a stouthearted hero. Production values are very good for a TV production. DVD image is on the soft side but that comes from the original. The transfer to disc seems to have created no new problems. Smoke, which is nearly constant in the battle scenes, does not create excessive artifacts. Blacks, particularly in clothing, tend to lose detail in dim interiors. Sound is a notch better, making the use of electric guitars (which strike me as anachronistic) in the score all the more glaring. —*MM*
Movie: 🎶🎶🎶 **DVD:** 🎶🎶
BFS Video (Cat #98579-D, UPC #0668059 15796). Full frame. Dolby Digital Mono. $29.98. Keepcase. *LANG:* English. *FEATURES:* 12 chapter links.
1993 100m/C *GB* Sean Bean, Assumpta Serna, Brian Cox, David Troughton, Daragh O'Malley, Julian Fellowes, Timothy Bentinck, Simon Andreu, Michael Mears, John Tams, Jason Salkey, Paul Trussell; *D:* Tom Clegg; *W:* Eoghan Harris; *C:* Ivan Strasburg; *M:* Dominic Muldowney.

Sharpe's Siege

In the winter of 1813, Napoleon Bonaparte sends his best spy, Maj. Ducos (Atkine), to find out where Wellington plans to invade France. The newly married Sharpe (Bean) must leave his ailing wife Jane (Cruttenden) and capture a French fort while preventing Ducos's treachery. For image and sound comments, please see review of *Sharpe's Rifles.* —*MM*
Movie: 🎶🎶½ **DVD:** 🎶🎶½
BFS Video (Cat #98630-D, UPC #0668059 16304). Full frame. Dolby Digital Mono. $19.98. Keepcase. *LANG:* English. *FEATURES:* 12 chapter links.
1996 100m/C *GB* Sean Bean, Daragh O'Malley, Hugh Fraser, Abigail Cruttenden, James Laurenson, Feodor Atkine; *D:* Tom Clegg; *W:* Eoghan Harris.

Sharpe's Sword

Sharpe (Bean) is sent to protect Wellington's top spy El Mirador, and finds himself up against Napoleon's top swordsman, Col. Leroux (Fierry). When Sharpe's wounded, it's up to Lass (Mortimer), a young mute convent girl, to save our hero. For image and sound comments, please see review of *Sharpe's Rifles.* —*MM*
Movie: 🎶🎶½ **DVD:** 🎶🎶½
BFS Video (Cat #98607-D, UPC #0668059 16076). Full frame. Dolby Digital Mono. $19.98. Keepcase. *LANG:* English. *FEATURES:* 12 chapter links.
1994 100m/C *GB* Sean Bean, Daragh O'Malley, Patrick Fierry, Emily Mortimer, John Kavanagh; *D:* Tom Clegg; *W:* Eoghan Harris.

Sharpe's Waterloo

Sharpe's (Bean) making a new life with new love Lucille (Paoli) at their French chateau. But when Napoleon returns from exile, Sharpe returns to the army and the Chosen Men to organize a defense before the battle of Waterloo. For image and sound comments, please see review of *Sharpe's Rifles.* —*MM*
Movie: 🎶🎶½ **DVD:** 🎶🎶½
BFS Video (Cat #98646-D, UPC #0668059 16465). Full frame. Dolby Digital Mono. $19.98. Keepcase. *LANG:* English. *FEATURES:* 12 chapter links.
1997 100m/C *GB* Sean Bean, Daragh O'Malley, Hugh Fraser, Cecile Paoli, Alexis Denisof, Paul Bettany; *D:* Tom Clegg.

She Demons

Gilligan's Island meets *I was a '50s Mutant Teenage Something.* When stormy weather shipwrecks a group of treasure hunters on an uncharted island, the lack of amenities is the least of their worries. They also happen upon the secret laboratory of a sadistic ex-Nazi scientist conducting experiments on the locals (who happen to be a tribe of gorgeous women), turning them into snaggle-toothed, feral "she-demons." Irish McCalla (best known as TV's original *Sheena, Queen of the Jungle*) plays a spoiled heiress who finds the inner

reserve to not only resist the slimy advances of lecherous SS officers but learns there are more important things than daddy's money. An inconceivable slumgullion stew mixing forgotten Nazis, island babes with Frankenstein faces, an Asian character telling Chinese jokes and, of course, blossoming love. The full-frame image is crisp enough, but the print used for the transfer must have been dragged across the floor every day for the last 43 years. Splices, speckling, even projectionist marks find their way into the presentation. Audio sounds tinny and crackly, in the best drive-in squawk-box tradition. As always, the unbridled chutzpah of the theatrical trailer makes the movie seem like a bolt from the heavens. How can anyone resist a film where "three strangers stumble upon a green hell?" —*EP*
Movie: 🐶🐶🐶🐶 **DVD:** 🎶½
Image Entertainment (Cat #ID9810CODVD, UPC #01438198105). Full frame. Dolby Digital Mono. $24.99. Snapper. *LANG:* English. *FEATURES:* 12 chapter links ⬥ Theatrical trailer.
1958 68m/B Irish McCalla, Tod Griffin, Victor Sen Yung, Rudolph Anders, Tod Andrews, Gene Roth, Bill Coontz, Billy Dix; *D:* Richard Cunha; *W:* Richard Cunha, H.E. Barrie; *C:* Meredith Nicholson; *M:* Nicholas Carras.

She–Freak

In the opening moments of his commentary, writer/producer Dave Friedman admits that he saw Tod Browning's *Freaks* when he was nine years old (from the projection booth!) and it made a profound impression on him. This loose remake doesn't have the power of the original but it is an accurate look behind the scenes of a traveling carnival. Jade (Brennen) is the cynical femme fatale who tries to take over the show. The image is astonishingly good. DVD was made from original elements that show virtually no signs of wear. Colors are appropriately bright and vivid. Sound is fine. —*MM* *AKA:* Alley of Nightmares.
Movie: 🎶🎶 **DVD:** 🎶🎶🎶
Image Entertainment (Cat #ID6062SW DVD, UPC #014381606225). Full frame. Dolby Digital Mono. $24.95. Snapper. *LANG:* English. *FEATURES:* 17 chapter links ⬥ Trailer ⬥ Commentary: Dave Friedman, Mike Vraney ⬥ Side show short film ⬥ Gallery of exploitation art.
1967 87m/C Claire Brennan, Lynn Courtney, Bill McKinney, Lee Raymond, Madame Lee, Claude Smith, Ben Moore; *D:* Byron Mabe; *W:* David Friedman; *C:* William G. Troiano; *M:* Billy Allen.

She Killed in Ecstasy

Jess Franco's version of *The Bride Wore Black* is much more explicit sexually, but it's comparatively restrained for him. Soledad Miranda plays a young woman who vows revenge on the four people who drove her lover to suicide. There is a fair amount of light surface damage on the print and some intermittent static on the soundtrack, but on DVD, the film looks remarkably good for a 1970 work and the period soundtrack is terrific. Recommended to the director's fans. —*MM*

Movie: 🎬🎬½ **DVD:** 🎬🎬
Synapse (Cat #SFD0010, UPC #65493030 1098). Widescreen (1.66:1) letterboxed. Dolby Digital Mono. $29.98. Keepcase. *LANG:* German. *SUB:* English. *FEATURES:* 17 chapter links.
1970 80m/C SP Soledad Miranda, Paul Muller, Howard Vernon; **D:** Jess (Jesus) Franco; **W:** Jess (Jesus) Franco; **M:** Mannfred Hubler, Siegfried Schwab.

Sheba, Baby

Private detective Sheba Shayne (Grier) heads to Louisville where someone is threatening her father and his loan company. This one's not nearly as much fun as the similar work that the star did with director Jack Hill. On disc, the image is not as clear as those films, either, and the mono sound could use beefing up. —*MM*

Movie: 🎬🎬 **DVD:** 🎬🎬
MGM Home Entertainment (Cat #10014 68, UPC #027616857880). Widescreen (1.85:1) anamorphic. Dolby Digital Mono. $14.95. Keepcase. *LANG:* English. *SUB:* French; Spanish. *FEATURES:* 16 chapter links • Trailer.
1975 (PG) 90m/C Pam Grier, Rudy Challenger, Austin Stoker, D'Urville Martin, Charles Kissinger; **D:** William Girdler; **W:** William Girdler; **C:** William Asman; **M:** Alex Brown, Alex Brown.

Sherlock Holmes and the Secret Weapon

In an adaptation of *The Dancing Men*, Holmes and Watson (Rathbone and Bruce) battle the evil Moriarity (Atwill) to save the British war effort. This is a good (but not great) entry in the series, with a gripping wartime setting. Hoey is fun as the bumbling Inspector Lestrade. As is the case with the other entries in this series, the DVD image ranges from fair to good with light static audible on the soundtrack. The disc is part of the "Evening with Sherlock Holmes" boxed set. —*MM* **AKA:** Secret Weapon.

Movie: 🎬🎬🎬 **DVD:** 🎬🎬
FOCUSfilm (Cat #FF7479, UPC #6830707 47923). Full frame. $69.99. Keepcase. *LANG:* English. *FEATURES:* 12 chapter links • Episodes 16-23 of *New Adventures of Sherlock Holmes* radio show • Photo gallery.
1942 68m/B Basil Rathbone, Nigel Bruce, Karen Verne, William Post Jr., Dennis Hoey, Holmes Herbert, Mary Gordon, Henry Victor, Philip Van Zandt, George Eldredge, Leslie Denison, James Craven, Paul Fix, Hugh Herbert, Lionel Atwill; **D:** Roy William Neill; **W:** W. Scott Darling; **C:** Lester White; **M:** Frank Skinner.

She's Having a Baby

Quirky tale of soul mates Jake and Kristy (Bacon and McGovern) who marry young and are forced to face the relationship negotiation process with little more than their good intentions. Jake is not sure the whole marriage thing is for him, but Kristy is sure she wants to have a baby. Jake is tempted by a fantasy girl (Lorca), and Kristy starts dropping her birth control pills down the sink. Funnier than it sounds. Alec Baldwin is also great as Jake's sleazy friend who simultaneously tempts Jake with the wild life and tries to seduce Kristy. Will true love prevail? Well, this is a John Hughes film. Less than average picture quality for a DVD, but decent sound quality. —*CA*

Movie: 🎬🎬🎬 **DVD:** 🎬🎬
Paramount Home Video (Cat #32027, UPC #09736320274). Widescreen anamorphic. Dolby Digital 5.1 Surround. $29.99. Keepcase. *LANG:* English; French. *SUB:* English. *FEATURES:* 16 chapter links • Theatrical trailer.
1988 (PG-13) 106m/C Kevin Bacon, Elizabeth McGovern, William Windom, Paul Gleason, Alec Baldwin, Cathryn Damon, Holland Taylor, James Ray, Isabel Lorca, Dennis Dugan, Edie McClurg, John Ashton; **D:** John Hughes; **W:** John Hughes; **C:** Don Peterman; **M:** Stewart Copeland.

She's So Lovely

Bizarre, oddly dramatic comedy in the John Cassavetes style (based on an unproduced script directed by his son) features tremendous, improvisational performances by all involved. It's told in two parts. The first section tells of the love between down-and-out losers Eddie (Penn) and Maureen (Wright Penn—virtually unrecognizable in this role), which ends when Penn runs amok and is committed to a mental institution. Ten years later, Maureen is happily married to Joey (Travolta) when Eddie is released. As Eddie returns to reclaim his wife, Joey starts to feel his hold slip over his family and must do whatever it takes to keep his life together. Though occasionally unfocused and awkwardly stylized, this thoroughly unpredictable movie delivers some wonderfully genuine moments of unexpected comedy and pathos. The disc is razor sharp and visually perfect, capturing the intentionally different lighting styles of the film with smooth clarity. As it's predominantly a dialogue picture, the Surround track is limited to the brief explosions of violence and music but is satisfying. The extras are appreciated, but one wishes that some information about the genesis of the picture had been included. The theatrical trailer (which showed how completely stymied Miramax was about how to sell this film) is not included. —*DG* **AKA:** She's De Lovely; Call It Love.

Movie: 🎬🎬🎬 **DVD:** 🎬🎬🎬½
Miramax Pictures Home Video (Cat #213 48, UPC #78693614168). Widescreen (2.35:1) anamorphic. Dolby Digital 5.1. $29.99. Keepcase. *LANG:* English; French. *SUB:* English. *CAP:* English. *FEATURES:* "John Cassavetes: A Discussion" • "An Actor's Look at Cassavetes" • 16 chapter links • Insert card with chapter listing • Video trailers for other releases.
1997 (R) 97m/C Sean Penn, Robin Wright Penn, John Travolta, Harry Dean Stanton, Debi Mazar, James Gandolfini, Gena Rowlands, Kelsey Mulrooney, David Thornton, Susan Traylor, Chloe Webb, Burt Young; **D:** Nick Cassavetes; **W:** John Cassavetes; **C:** Thierry Arbogast; **M:** Joseph Vitarelli. *AWARDS:* Cannes '97: Actor (Penn); *NOM:* Screen Actors Guild '97: Actress (Wright Penn).

She's the One

If Burns's debut, *The Brothers McMullen*, has a flaw, it's an overly sweet sentimentality. He corrects that with a brilliant sophomore effort that's sharp and smart. The subject is the Fitzpatrick men and their inability to deal with women. Taxi driver Mickey (Burns) is attracted to a passenger (Bahns). His younger brother Francis's (McGlone) marriage to Rene (Aniston) is cracking apart because he's having an affair with Heather (Diaz), Mickey's former flame. Their father (Mahoney) is the worst of the bunch. DVD shows how much difference a few million dollars can make. On his commentary track, Burns tells us that *Brothers* was made for $25,000. This one cost $3 million, still a comparatively modest sum, but the film looks worlds better. Any visual flaws are insignificant compared to the character-driven material. Surround is fine for Tom Petty's superb score. The film is also available as part of the "Stories from Long Island" boxed set. —*MM*

Movie: 🎬🎬🎬½ **DVD:** 🎬🎬🎬
20th Century Fox Home Entertainment (Cat #2000571, UPC #024543005711). Widescreen (1.85:1) anamorphic; full frame. Dolby Digital 4.0 Surround Stereo; Dolby Digital Surround Stereo. $29.99. Keepcase. *LANG:* English; French. *SUB:* English; Spanish. *FEATURES:* 24 chapter links • Commentary: director • Music video • Trailers • Ed Burns weblink.
1996 (R) 95m/C Edward Burns, Mike McGlone, Jennifer Aniston, Cameron Diaz, Maxine Bahns, John Mahoney, Leslie Mann, George McCowan, Amanda Peet, Anita Gillette, Frank Vincent; **D:** Edward Burns; **W:** Edward Burns; **C:** Frank Prinzi; **M:** Tom Petty.

The Shooting

Bent on revenge, a mysterious woman (Perkins) persuades a former bounty hunter (Oates) to escort her across the desert. This offbeat small film is filled with strong performances from the leads and co-producer Nicholson. It was made concurrently with *Ride in the Whirlwind* with the same crew and overlapping casts. On DVD, the two films share the same strengths—superb image transfer, fine sound, knowledgeable nostalgic commentary. Not to mention the bang-up surprise ending. —*MM*

Movie: 🎬🎬🎬½ **DVD:** 🎬🎬🎬
VCI Home Video (Cat #8229, UPC #08985 9822926). Widescreen anamorphic. Dolby

Digital Mono. $29.95. Keepcase. *LANG:* English. *FEATURES:* 12 talent links ▪ Talent files ▪ Commentary: Hellman, Perkins, Dennis Bartok ▪ Trailers.
1966 82m/C Warren Oates, Millie Perkins, Jack Nicholson, Will Hutchins; *D:* Monte Hellman; *W:* Adrien (Carole Eastman) Joyce; *C:* Gregory Sandor; *M:* Richard Markowitz.

Shriek If You Know What I Did Last Friday the 13th

Dumb, harmless assembly of exceedingly lame groaners and sight gags is designed to spoof *Scream*-type horror films. Cross plays "Dawson Deery," a new student at Bulimia High School, which is being plagued by a masked, robed serial killer offing members of the student body. In typical fashion, Arnold plays the mall security guard trying to find the killer, Thiessen plays the nosy reporter, Strong is the terminal virgin, and Rex the brain-dead muscle head. The gags are unending (spoofing everything from *Christine* to *Grease*) and there's an amusing moment or two, but this is strictly for the desperate. If you must, rent *Scary Movie* instead. Look for Simon Rex singing "Greased Frightenin'" for a true comedic low point. Many screen and TV personalities of yore appear in embarrassing cameos. The disc is sharp, colorful, and a notch above the tape but displays some minor digital grain. The sound is fine, but undemanding. —*DG*
Movie: 🎵 **DVD:** 🎵🎵🎵
Trimark Home Video (Cat #7878D, UPC #03139875782). Widescreen (1.85:1) anamorphic. Dolby Surround. $24.99. Keepcase. *LANG:* English. *SUB:* English; French; Spanish. *CAP:* English. *FEATURES:* 24 chapter links ▪ Theatrical trailer.
2000 (R) 86m/C Harley Cross, Tiffani-Amber Thiessen, Coolio, Tom Arnold, Julie Benz, Aimee Graham, Majandra Delfino, Shirley Jones, Rose Marie, Mink Stole, Simon Rex, Danny Strong; *D:* John Blanchard; *W:* Sue Bailey, Joe Nelms; *C:* David J. Miller; *M:* Tyler Bates.

Sid & Nancy [MGM]

The tragic, brutal, true love story of The Sex Pistols' Sid Vicious (Oldman) and American groupie Nancy Spungen (Webb) comes from the director of *Repo Man*. Remarkable lead performances power a very dark story that manages to be funny at times. The film is depressing but engrossing with no appreciation of punk music or sympathy for the self-destructive way of life required. Oldman and Webb are superb. This is a bare-bones edition (the Criterion edition is better supplement-wise), but a decent disc nonetheless. The video transfer is well done, with bright vibrant colors and only a slight loss of definition with some blacks. The audio delivers clear, crisp dialogue and a powerful musical score. —*MJT* **AKA:** Sid & Nancy: Love Kills.
Movie: 🎵🎵🎵½ **DVD:** 🎵🎵🎵

MGM Home Entertainment (Cat #10012 81, UPC #027616855602). Widescreen (1.66:1) letterboxed. Dolby Digital Surround. $19.98. Keepcase. *LANG:* English. *SUB:* French; Spanish. *FEATURES:* 32 chapter links ▪ Theatrical trailer.
1986 (R) 111m/C *GB* Gary Oldman, Chloe Webb, Debbie Bishop, David Hayman, Andrew Schofield, Tony London, Xander Berkeley, Biff Yeager, Courtney Love, Iggy Pop; *D:* Alex Cox; *W:* Alex Cox, Abbe Wool; *C:* Roger Deakins; *M:* The Pogues, Pray for Rain, Joe Strummer. *AWARDS:* Natl. Soc. Film Critics '86: Actress (Webb).

Sideshow

The Full Moon take on *Something Wicked This Way Comes* is an exercise in makeup effects (created by Gabe Bartalos). Five teens go to a sideshow and find more than they expected. The film was made very cheaply on a few dark sets and so the image gains nothing over tape on DVD. Still, this one looks pretty good compared to the studio's older releases. —*MM*
Movie: 🎵🎵 **DVD:** 🎵🎵
Full Moon Pictures (Cat #FUM-DV 8065, UPC #763843806566). Full frame. $16.99. Keepcase. *LANG:* English. *FEATURES:* 17 chapter links ▪ Trailer ▪ Weblink ▪ Talent files.
2000 (R) 90m/C Michael Amos, Jamie Martz, Scott Clark, Jessica Keenan, Phil Fondacaro, Jeana Blackman, G. Gordon Baer, Brinke Stevens; *D:* Fred Olen Ray; *W:* Benjamin Carr; *C:* Mac Ahlberg.

The Sign of Four

Sherlock Holmes (Richardson) takes on a strange case when a young woman (Lunghi) receives a mysterious jewel in the mail. Though the filmmakers take considerable liberties with Conan Doyle's story, they're true to the spirit of Holmes. Richardson is excellent in the lead and David Healy's Watson is one of the best, much closer to the original fictional character than the often-buffoonish clown who has so often appeared on-screen. There's not really much DVD can do to improve the soft quality of the made-for-TV image. It ranges between good and very good and is a bit better than tape. —*MM*
Movie: 🎵🎵🎵 **DVD:** 🎵🎵½
Image Entertainment (Cat #ID6628ZFDVD, UPC #014381662825). Full frame. Dolby Digital Mono. $24.99. Snapper. *LANG:* English. *FEATURES:* 18 chapter links ▪ Liner notes by Richard Valley.
1983 97m/C *GB* Ian Richardson, David Healy, Thorley Walters, Cherie Lunghi; *D:* Desmond Davis; *W:* Charles Edward Pogue; *C:* Denis Lewiston; *M:* Harry Rabinowitz.

Silent Shakespeare

These very early films are of historical value. A prologue admits that the disc was created from damaged original elements. In fact, some of them are little more than individual scenes or snippets only a few

minutes long. But every generation has its interpretations of the Bard, and these are lively, if nothing else. Damage and wear are extensive in some; very light in others. Contents: "King John" (1899), "The Tempest" (1908), "A Midsummer Night's Dream" (1909), "Twelfth Night" (1910), "The Merchant of Venice" (1910), and "Richard III" (1911). —*MM*
Movie: 🎵🎵½ **DVD:** 🎵🎵
Image Entertainment (Cat #ID9224MLSD-VD, UPC #014381922424). Full frame. Dolby Digital Stereo. $24.99. Snapper. *LANG:* Silent. *SUB:* English intertitles. *FEATURES:* 8 chapter links.
2000 89m/B

Silverado [SE]

Affectionate pastiche of western clichés has everything a viewer could ask for—except Indians. Straightforward plot has four virtuous cowboys (Kline, Glenn, Glover, Costner) rise up against a crooked lawman (Dennehy) in a blaze of six guns. Curiously, this "collector's edition" lacks many of the features that have been available on laser. But the usual suspects have been rounded up—except a director's commentary—and overall image and sound are fine. —*MM*
Movie: 🎵🎵🎵 **DVD:** 🎵🎵🎵
Columbia Tristar Home Video (Cat #04281, UPC #043396042810). Widescreen. Dolby Digital 5.1 Surround Stereo; Dolby Digital Surround. $24.99. Keepcase. *LANG:* English; Spanish; Portuguese. *SUB:* English; Spanish; Portuguese; Chinese; Korean; Thai. *FEATURES:* "Making of" featurette ▪ Talent files ▪ Trailer ▪ 28 chapter links.
1985 (PG-13) 132m/C Kevin Kline, Scott Glenn, Kevin Costner, Danny Glover, Brian Dennehy, Linda Hunt, John Cleese, Jeff Goldblum, Rosanna Arquette, Jeff Fahey; *D:* Lawrence Kasdan; *W:* Lawrence Kasdan; *C:* John Bailey; *M:* Bruce Broughton. *AWARDS:* NOM: Oscars '85: Sound, Orig. Score.

Simpatico

An excellent cast wades through a muddled script. Adapted from the Sam Shepard play, *Simpatico* defies pithy summary, but here goes: Nolte plays Vinnie, who has been blackmailing affluent horse breeder Carter (Bridges) regarding their involvement in a race fixing and extortion scam from two decades earlier. Vinnie threatens to fess up, which brings Carter out to California to confront him. Vinnie then swipes Carter's rental car, takes his plane ticket, and flies back to Kentucky to confront their first victim (Finney) as well as look up Carter's wife Rosie (Stone), who was in on the initial con. Confused yet? Guilt and geldings might make for good Sturm und Drang on the stage, but adapters Matthew Warchus (who also directs) and David Nicholls struggle in making the transition to celluloid credibility. Incessant flashbacks (to the point of nausea) and some implausible plot mechanics (Vinnie may have Carter's plane ticket, but don't they check IDs at the airport?) undermine the compelling performances of the film's acting quintet (add Catherine Keener as Nolte's girlfriend, unwittingly dragged into the jumble). The anamorphic transfer could not look better: deep blacks, solid colors, excellent detail delineation, all mastered from a flawless source. A full-frame version is available, which isn't cropped too heavy and works on its own merits. The 5.1 sound is very good, even if it doesn't take complete advantage of the discrete audio palette. A stereo Surround track juices up the rear speakers a notch, especially when filled with Stewart Copeland's evocative score. —*EP*

Movie: ♫♫½ **DVD:** ♫♫♫½
New Line Home Video (Cat #N5043, UPC #9404550432). Widescreen (1.85:1) anamorphic; full frame. Dolby Digital 5.1; Dolby Digital Surround Stereo. $24.98. Snapper. *LANG:* English. *FEATURES:* 28 chapter links • Original theatrical trailer • Cast and crew filmographies.
1999 (R) 106m/C Nick Nolte, Sharon Stone, Jeff Bridges, Catherine Keener, Albert Finney, Shawn Hatosy, Kimberly Williams, Liam Waite; *D:* Matthew Warchus; *W:* Matthew Warchus, David Nicholls; *C:* John Toll; *M:* Stewart Copeland.

Sin: The Movie

In the 21st century, the city of Freeport teeters on the verge of collapse. The Hardcorps, led by Colonel John Blade, are the only force fighting for justice. A series of unexplained kidnappings reveals an elaborate puzzle involving the villain Elexis Sinclaire. As with most animation titles (yes, I'm aware that there are exceptions), the DVD format really showcases the art form. Colors are vibrant and blacks are crisp and extremely well defined. The two sound transfers are also equally well done, delivering decent sound effects and clear, understandable dialogue. —*MJT*

Movie: ♫♫½ **DVD:** ♫♫♫
A.D.V. Films (Cat #DVDSN/001, UPC #702 727013720). Full frame. Dolby Digital Stereo. $29.98. Keepcase. *LANG:* English; Japanese. *SUB:* English. *FEATURES:* 8 chapter links • Behind-the-scenes interviews • Production portfolio • Character bios • Theatrical trailer • Additional ADV trailers.
1998 60m/C *JP D:* Yasunori Urata; *W:* Ryoma Kaneko, Kensei Date.

Sinbad and the Eye of the Tiger

This time around, Wayne is Sinbad the Sailor on a quest to find sorcerer Melanthius, who can reverse the spell that has turned his friend Prince Kassim into a stop-motion animated baboon. Sinbad must face the usual quota of Harryhausen's wondrous creatures including a troglodyte, a giant walrus, the Minotaur, and a saber-tooth tiger, not to mention a horde of insect-like demons. Don't bother to think about the plot (or the wooden acting), just sit back and enjoy the still-entertaining special effects and the fleshy performance by Seymour decked out in

belly-dancing attire. Taryn Power shows off a bit as well. One problem with doing such a good job transferring a Harryhausen film to DVD is that everything is so sharp and defined. It's not like we don't know how the stop-motion is done, but with such a sharp transfer, some of the magic is lost when the composite elements are so obvious. Even the colors, which are overall very good, lessen in intensity in many of the shots. But still, this is a great disc and the film has never looked better. The blacks are incredibly deep and subtle shading in the colors are very well defined. Fleshtones are very natural. The sound is only mono but the music is delivered with good fidelity while allowing the dialogue to remain crisp, and both lack any discernable distortion. The "Ray Harryhausen Chronicles" is a very enjoyable 60-minute retrospective on his career. —*JO*

Movie: ♫♫ **DVD:** ♫♫♫
Columbia Tristar Home Video (Cat #04469, UPC #043396044692). Widescreen (1.85:1) anamorphic. Dolby Digital Mono. $29.95. Keepcase. *LANG:* English. *SUB:* English; Spanish; Chinese; Korean; Thai; Portuguese. *CAP:* English. *FEATURES:* 28 chapter links • Theatrical trailer • Talent files • Production notes • "Ray Harryhausen Chronicles" • Featurette: "This Is Dynamation."
1977 (G) 113m/C *GB* Patrick Wayne, Jane Seymour, Taryn Power, Margaret Whiting; *D:* Sam Wanamaker; *W:* Beverley Cross; *C:* Ted Moore; *M:* Roy Budd.

Sinbad: Beyond the Veil of Mists

Kids who are accustomed to computer-generated animation on television and video games may be more tolerant of this animated feature. To my taste, the flat voices match uninspired, unemotional characters. The story has to do with Princess Serena's attempts to save her father from an evil wizard. Computer art is bright and false-looking. The 3-D that the box copy promises is not evident to me. —*MM*

Movie: ♫½ **DVD:** ♫½
Trimark Home Video (Cat #7480D, UPC #031398748021). Widescreen letterboxed. Stereo. $24.99. Keepcase. *LANG:* English. *SUB:* English; French; Spanish. *FEATURES:* 24 chapter links.
2000 (G) 85m/C *D:* Alan Jacobs, Evan C. Ricks; *W:* Jeff Wolverton; *M:* Andy Hill; *V:* Brendan Fraser, Jennifer Hale, Leonard Nimoy, John Rhys-Davies, Mark Hamill.

A Single Girl

This sufficiently engaging, somewhat experimental film chronicles a brief period in the life of Valerie, a young Parisian woman played by Ledoyen. As the story unfolds in real time, Valerie learns she is pregnant and must tell her boyfriend. Also, she starts a room service job at a four-star hotel. What *A Single Girl* is really about are the choices Valerie must make at this crossroads in her life. This film would not have worked with a lead player not as capable as Ledoyen, who

through an emotional rollercoaster ride manages to keep the movie on its feet and our eyes on the screen. The letterboxed image really is 1.85:1, despite the false labeling on the packaging that claims 1.66:1. The non-anamorphic video transfer is acceptable, though overall it is soft and is occasionally marred by dirty and damaged film elements. Again, the package labeling appears wrong when it claims a stereo soundtrack, but the film's mono track presented as Dolby Digital 2.0 sounds just fine. Subtitles are not optional but instead are permanently burned into the image—a clear indication this transfer was not made especially for DVD. The so-called extras are nothing to brag about. —*MB* *AKA:* La Fille Seule.

Movie: ♫♫½ **DVD:** ♫♫
Winstar Home Entertainment (Cat #FLV52 30, UPC #720917523026). Widescreen (1.85:1) letterboxed. Dolby Digital Stereo. $24.98. Keepcase. *LANG:* French. *SUB:* English. *FEATURES:* 8 chapter links • Filmographies and awards • Weblink.
1996 90m/C *FR* Virginie Ledoyen, Benoit Magimel, Vera Briole, Dominique Valadie; *D:* Benoit Jacquot; *W:* Benoit Jacquot, Jerome Beaujour; *C:* Caroline Champetier; *M:* Kvarteto Mesta Prahi.

Sister, Sister

A Congressional aide (Stoltz) on vacation in Louisiana takes a room in an old mansion. He gradually discovers the secret of the house and its resident sisters (Ivey and Leigh). Dark Southern Gothic ultimately collapses under its stereotypical story. The image is a bit soft, and does show some fine grain. There are also minor defects—lines and spots—visible on the source print. Still, given the low-budget roots of this film, the image is clear and you won't find a better presentation of this film. The 5.1 soundtrack improves on the image. Director Condon reveals at the beginning of his talk that he has no intention of doing a scene-specific commentary. Instead, he tells the backstory of how the film was made and then critiques the film and describes why it doesn't work! —*MM/ML*

Movie: ♫♫ **DVD:** ♫♫½
Anchor Bay (UPC #013131132397). Widescreen (2.35:1) anamorphic. Dolby Digital 5.1 Surround Stereo. $24.98. Keepcase. *LANG:* English. *FEATURES:* Commentary • Deleted scenes • Director bio.
1987 (R) 91m/C Eric Stoltz, Judith Ivey, Jennifer Jason Leigh, Dennis Lipscomb, Anne Pitoniak, Natalija Nogulich; *D:* Bill Condon; *W:* Ginny Cerrella, Bill Condon, Joel Cohen; *M:* Richard Einhorn.

Sisters

In De Palma's first ode to Hitchcock, Margot Kidder plays Siamese twins, Dominique and Danielle, who have been surgically separated late in life. Dominique, the evil twin, died as a result of the surgery, but lives on in the mind of Danielle, the kinder gentler psychotic of the two.

Danielle commits a murder, which is witnessed by an investigative reporter (Salt) from her window across the street. De Palma's use of split screen creates some amazing real-time suspense scenes. Simultaneous scenes—the police approaching Danielle's apartment and the murder scene being cleaned up—truly create an "edge of your seat" feeling. With parts of *Rear Window* and *Frenzy* present, the film is ultimately successful more because of its obvious homage elements rather than its own skill, but keep in mind that it was a freshman attempt by De Palma. The color on the disc is good overall, but the transfer is a little cloudy and speckled. The mono sound is not as good as it could be and it gives the film a hollow sounding quality. —*CA*
Movie: ♫♫ **DVD:** ♫½
Criterion Collection (Cat #89, UPC #715515 011020). Widescreen anamorphic. Dolby Digital Mono. $29.95. Keepcase. *LANG:* English. *SUB:* English. *FEATURES:* De Palma's *Village Voice* essay on composer Herrmann ➤ De Palma's 1973 print interview on the making of the film ➤ "Rare Study of Siamese Twins in the Soviet" article ➤ Press book excerpts ➤ Production stills ➤ Extensive liner note booklet.
1973 (R) 93m/C Margot Kidder, Charles Durning, Barnard Hughes, Jennifer Salt, William Finley, Lisle Wilson, Mary Davenport, Dolph Sweet; *D:* Brian DePalma; *W:* Brian DePalma, Louisa Rose; *C:* Gregory Sandor; *M:* Bernard Herrmann.

Six Degrees of Separation

Based on a true story and the play by John Guare, the film tells the tale of several upper-class New York city couples who are duped by a young street hustler (Smith), who pretends to be the son of Sidney Poitier. Sutherland and Channing become fascinated as they try to find out the identity and motive of the hustler. A frequently hilarious comedy with a strong dramatic core. Though it occasionally shows its stage origins, it still delivers an interesting and moving dissection of upper-class values. The acting is mostly excellent, though Smith's long-winded speech would only have fooled the extremely naïve. The disc looks sharp but is subject to digital grain and noise in wider shots and occasional bits of print dirt. The sound is superb with a richly recorded dialogue and music track. The widescreen framing (shot Super35) reveals more on the periphery but less on the bottom than the full-frame version. —*DG*
Movie: ♫♫♫½ **DVD:** ♫♫♫
MGM Home Entertainment (Cat #10008 41, UPC #02761685157). Widescreen (2.35:1) anamorphic; full frame. Dolby Digital 5.1. $19.98. Keepcase. *LANG:* English; Spanish. *SUB:* French; Spanish. *CAP:* English. *FEATURES:* Color booklet with notes ➤ Theatrical trailer ➤ 28 chapter links. Double-sided disc has widescreen and standard versions on either side but is inappropriately labeled as to which side is which.

1993 (R) 112m/C Stockard Channing, Will Smith, Donald Sutherland, Mary Beth Hurt, Bruce Davison, Ian McKellen, Richard Masur, Anthony Michael Hall, Heather Graham, Eric Thal, Anthony Rapp, Osgood Perkins II, Kitty Carlisle Hart, Catherine Kellner; *D:* Fred Schepisi; *W:* John Guare; *C:* Ian Baker; *M:* Jerry Goldsmith. *AWARDS: NOM:* Oscars '93: Actress (Channing); Golden Globes '94: Actress—Mus./Comedy (Channing).

The 6th Day

In the near future, Adam (Schwarzenegger) learns that he has been cloned and the evil corporation (is there ever any other kind of corporation in sf?) that did it is out to kill him. Actually, the film is better than its less-than-stellar theatrical record indicates. Performances and effects are fine. The DVD presents excellent image and sound, faithfully re-creating a polished big-budget studio production. A commentary track from Spottiswoode and Schwarzenegger might have been enlightening. —*MM*
Movie: ♫♫♫½ **DVD:** ♫♫♫½
Columbia Tristar Home Video (Cat #05074, UPC #043396050747). Widescreen (2.35:1) anamorphic. Dolby Digital 5.1 Surround Stereo; Dolby Digital Surround. $27.96. Keepcase. *LANG:* English; French. *SUB:* English; French. *FEATURES:* 28 chapter links ➤ 2 "making-of" featurettes ➤ Isolated music score with commentary by composer Trevor Rabin ➤ Three storyboard comparisons ➤ Theatrical trailers ➤ Digitally mastered audio and anamorphic video ➤ RePet infomercial and TV spot ➤ Production notes ➤ Talent files.
2000 (PG-13) 124m/C Arnold Schwarzenegger, Tony Goldwyn, Sarah Wynter, Michael Rooker, Robert Duvall, Michael Rapaport, Wendy Crewson, Rodney Rowland, Ken Pogue, Wanda Cannon, Christopher Lawford, Terry Crews, Colin Cunningham, Taylor Anne Reid, Jennifer Gareis, Don McManus, Steve Bacic; *D:* Roger Spottiswoode; *W:* Cormac Wibberly, Marianne S. Wibberly; *C:* Pierre Mignot; *M:* Trevor Rabin. *AWARDS: NOM:* Golden Raspberries '00: Worst Actor (Schwarzenegger).

The Skulls

Slick entry in the teen-paranoia-adults-are-bad subgenre is underwritten and overdirected. Luke (Jackson) is an ambitious poor kid who wants to get into the Skulls secret society to pay his way through law school so that he can become a public defender and represent the poor and downtrodden. His ideals are tested when his best friend Will (Harper) is found dead after snooping into Skull business. The plot quickly degenerates into a series of twists, each more improbable than the one before. The filmmakers' desire for a "PG-13" rating kept them from turning the material into a guilty pleasure. Both image and sound on the dual-layered disc are fine but unexceptional. —*MM*
Movie: ♫♫ **DVD:** ♫♫♫

Universal Studios Home Video (Cat #207 82, UPC #025192078224). Widescreen (1.85:1) anamorphic. Dolby Digital 5.1 Surround Stereo; Dolby Digital Surround Stereo. $26.98. Keepcase. *LANG:* English; French. *CAP:* English. *FEATURES:* 18 chapter links ➤ Commentary: director Rob Cohen ➤ Deleted scenes with commentary ➤ "Making of" featurette ➤ Theatrical trailer ➤ Talent files.
2000 (PG-13) 106m/C Joshua Jackson, Paul Walker, Hill Harper, Leslie Bibb, Christopher McDonald, Steve Harris, William L. Petersen, Craig T. Nelson; *D:* Rob Cohen; *W:* John Pogue; *C:* Shane Hurlbut; *M:* Randy Edelman.

Slaughterhouse

Buddy (Barton), a rotund, pig-loving redneck, maims, kills, and eats several victims. This is latter-day drive-in material that gains little on DVD. Image and sound are meant to be rough; they're fine for an independently produced splatter flick. And the disc is as stuffed with extras as a sausage. It contains virtually everything you can imagine connected with the film. The commentary track is good, and so is the featurette devoted to the financing and distribution of low-budget movies. —*MM*
Movie: ♫♫ **DVD:** ♫♫♫
Program Power Entertainment (UPC #7401 78999224). Full frame. Stereo. $19.98. Keepcase. *LANG:* English. *FEATURES:* 9 chapter links ➤ Deleted scenes ➤ Trailers and TV spots ➤ "Making of" featurette ➤ "Financing and Distribution" featurette ➤ Publicity materials ➤ DVD-ROM features ➤ Commentary: writer/director, producer, production designer ➤ Newspaper clippings.
1987 (R) 87m/C Joe Barton, Sherry Bendorf, Don Barrett, Bill Brinsfield; *D:* Rick Roessler; *W:* Rick Roessler; *C:* Richard Benda.

Slaughter's Big Ripoff

Sequel to *Slaughter* finds the title character (Brown) once again battling the mob, only this time the bad guys are led by ex–*Tonight Show* sidekick McMahon! The heavy grain in night scenes seems to come from the original, but the whole enterprise lacks the energy of the best '70s exploitation flicks. —*MM*
Movie: ♫½ **DVD:** ♫½
MGM Home Entertainment (Cat #10014 70, UPC #027616857903). Widescreen (2.35:1) anamorphic. Dolby Digital Mono. $19.98. Keepcase. *LANG:* English; French. *SUB:* French; Spanish. *FEATURES:* 16 chapter links ➤ Trailer.
1973 (R) 92m/C Jim Brown, Brock Peters, Don Stroud, Ed McMahon, Art Metrano, Gloria Hendry; *D:* Gordon Douglas; *W:* Charles Johnson; *C:* Charles F. Wheeler; *M:* James Brown, Fred Wesley.

Sleepaway Camp

Crazed killer hacks away at the inhabitants of a peaceful summer camp in a run-

of-the-mill slasher notable only for the absence of nudity and gore, and a twist ending. Think of a cross between *Friday the 13th* and the Bill Murray comedy *Meatballs*. The digital transfer is very crisp and clear and surprisingly, shows no flaws in the source print, except for some lines on the film in Chapter 19. Also, there is little grain in the print, save for one night scene near the end. The colors are true, but a bit washed-out at times. The commentary is by writer/director Robert Hiltzik, star Felissa Rose, and Sleepawaycampmovies.com webmaster Jeff Hayes. —ML/MM
Movie: ♫ **DVD:** ♫♫½
Anchor Bay (Cat #11194). Widescreen (1.85:1) anamorphic. $24.98. Keepcase. *LANG:* English. *FEATURES:* Commentary • Trailer.
1983 (R) 88m/C Mike Kellin, Jonathan Tiersten, Felissa Rose, Christopher Collet; **D:** Robert Hiltzik; **W:** Robert Hiltzik; **C:** Benjamin Davis; **M:** Edward Bilous.

Sleeper

Hapless nerd Miles Monroe (Allen) is revived in 2173, 200 years after he was cryogenically frozen. Poet Luna (Keaton) is part of a team of rebellious scientists who are working against a dictator. This is one of the best of Allen's early works. Don't miss the famous "orgasmatron" scene. Image ranges from fair to good—about what you'd expect from a work of this age and budget. The main benefit of disc over tape is the screen ratio option. —MM
Movie: ♫♫♫½ **DVD:** ♫♫½
MGM Home Entertainment (Cat #10006 84, UPC #027616850157). Widescreen anamorphic; full frame. Dolby Digital Mono. $24.99. Keepcase. *LANG:* English; Spanish. *SUB:* French; Spanish. *CAP:* English. *FEATURES:* 24 chapter links • Liner notes • Trailer.
1973 (PG) 88m/C Woody Allen, Diane Keaton, John Beck, Howard Cosell; **D:** Woody Allen; **W:** Marshall Brickman, Woody Allen; **C:** David M. Walsh; **M:** Woody Allen.

Sleepwalkers

Arguably King's worst film work is about shape-shifting monsters who feed on the life force of virgins and are vulnerable only to cat scratches. The incestuous mother Mary (Krige) and son Charles (Krause) set their sights on young Tanya (Amick). King's script meanders through pointless chitchat scenes. Unless something is blowing up or bleeding right in front of director Mick Garris's camera, he doesn't know how to photograph it. At one point, he tosses in close-ups of knees. The only cast member who doesn't shame him- or herself is Sparks, who plays Clovis, the brave cat. The DVD image is slightly better than VHS tape, making the silly special effects that much sillier. —MM **AKA:** Stephen King's Sleepwalkers.
Movie: woof **DVD:** ♫♫½
Columbia Tristar Home Video (Cat #05815, UPC #043396058156). Widescreen anamorphic; full frame. Dolby Digital Surround

Stereo; Mono. $24.95. Keepcase. *LANG:* English; French; Spanish. *SUB:* English; French; Spanish; Portuguese; Chinese; Korean; Thai. *FEATURES:* 28 chapter links • Talent files • Production notes.
1992 (R) 91m/C Brian Krause, Madchen Amick, Alice Krige, Jim Haynie, Cindy Pickett, Lyman Ward, Ron Perlman, Stephen King, Tobe Hooper, Mark Hamill, Glenn Shadix, Joe Dante, Clive Barker, John Landis, Dan Martin; **D:** Mick Garris; **W:** Stephen King; **C:** Rodney Charters; **M:** Nicholas Pike.

Slippery When Wet

Bruce Brown's *(The Endless Summer)* first film was made in 1958 for $5,000. It's a simple documentary that follows five young guys on a surfing trip to Hawaii. The grain in the image is inherent. The jokes are hokey; the surf photography has certainly been surpassed by the sophisticated technology that's employed today, but as a snapshot of the innocent nascent surf culture, it is still valuable. —MM
Movie: ♫♫½ **DVD:** ♫♫
Image Entertainment (Cat #ID8791OTDVD, UPC #014381879124). Full frame. Dolby Digital Mono. $24.99. Snapper. *LANG:* English. *FEATURES:* 15 chapter links.
1958 73m/C D: Bruce Brown; **W:** Bruce Brown; **C:** Bruce Brown; **M:** Bud Shank.

Slugs

A small-town health inspector discovers that spilled toxic waste is being consumed by the local slug population, and it's turning them into huge (by slug standards) toothy monsters that can invade any building through the water system. The DVD image is on the darkish side and no better than average, but this one does everything that you want a cheap eco-horror movie to do. Sound is O.K. —MM
Movie: ♫♫½ **DVD:** ♫♫½
Anchor Bay (Cat #DV11159, UPC #013131 115994). Widescreen (1.85:1) anamorphic. Dolby Digital Mono. $24.99. Keepcase. *LANG:* English. *FEATURES:* 25 chapter links • Trailer.
1987 (R) 90m/C Michael Garfield, Kim Terry, Philip Machale, Alicia Moro, Santiago Alvarez, Emilio Linder, Concha Cuetos; **D:** J(uan) Piquer Simon; **W:** J(uan) Piquer Simon; **C:** Julio Bragado; **M:** Tim Souster.

Slumber Party Massacre

A psychotic killer (Villela) with a power drill terrorizes a slumber party for high school girls. The made-by-women (director Amy Jones and writer Rita Mae Brown) slasher flick is contrived and forced but not always unfunny. The image is clear, but the digital transfer reveals many defects in the source material. The opening daylight scenes appear very grainy, but this grain is less noticeable during the nighttime shots, which constitute the bulk of the film. Once those shots begin, the picture improves,

giving us an image that is miles ahead of older tapes. Audio is adequate. —ML/MM
Movie: ♫ **DVD:** ♫♫½
New Concorde (Cat #20208). Widescreen (1.85:1) letterboxed. Dolby Digital Mono. $14.98. Keepcase. *LANG:* English. *FEATURES:* Talent files • Trailers.
1982 (R) 84m/C Michele Michaels, Robin Stille, Andre Honore, Michael Villela, Debra Deliso, Gina Mari, Brinke Stevens, Jean Vargas, Ryan Kennedy; **D:** Amy Holden Jones; **W:** Rita Mae Brown; **C:** Stephen Posey; **M:** Ralph Jones.

Slumber Party Massacre 2

Babes in lingerie face yet another madman with access to power tools. About the best that can be said is that the sequel is faithful to the spirit and sleaziness of the original. Beyond the minimal extras, DVD is no different from tape. —MM
Movie: woof **DVD:** ♫♫
New Concorde (Cat #NH20413 D, UPC #736991441392). Full frame. $14.98. Keepcase. *LANG:* English. *FEATURES:* 24 chapter links • Trailers • Talent files.
1987 75m/C Crystal Bernard, Kimberly McArthur, Juliette Cummins, Patrick Lowe; **D:** Deborah Brock; **W:** Deborah Brock; **C:** Thomas Callaway; **M:** Richard Ian Cox.

Slumber Party Massacre 3

The blood's a little bloodier; the babes are a little bustier. Otherwise, it's more of the same old same old. DVD is identical to tape. —MM
Movie: woof **DVD:** ♫♫
New Concorde (Cat #NH20392 D, UPC #73 6991439290). Full frame. $14.98. Keepcase. *LANG:* English. *FEATURES:* 24 chapter links • Talent files • Trailers.
1990 (R) 76m/C Keely Christian, Brittain Frye, Michael (M.K.) Harris, David Greenle, Hope Marie Carlton, Maria Ford; **D:** Sally Mattison; **W:** Catherine Cyran; **C:** Jurgen Baum; **M:** Jaime Sheriff.

Small Change

Pudgy, timid Desmouceaux and scruffy, neglected Goldman lead a whole pack of heart-warming tykes. It's a realistically and tenderly portrayed testament to the great director's belief in childhood as a "state of grace." Criticized for sentimentality, *Small Change* followed Truffaut's gloomy *The Story of Adele H.* Steven Spielberg suggested the English translation of *L'Argent de Poche.* Bright and vibrant colors are occasionally present on the video transfer, but a lack of definition of blacks tends to lead to an overall bland look. The merely adequate soundtrack features understandable (though occasionally muffled) dialogue. —MJT **AKA:** L'Argent de Poche.
Movie: ♫♫♫♫ **DVD:** ♫♫
MGM Home Entertainment (Cat #10014 83, UPC #027616858023). Widescreen (1.66:1) letterboxed. Dolby Digital Mono. $19.98. Keepcase. *LANG:* French; Span-

ish. *SUB:* English; French; Spanish. *FEA-TURES:* 16 chapter links.
1976 (PG) 104m/C *FR* Geory Desmouceaux, Philippe Goldman, Jean-Francois Stevenin, Chantal Mercier, Claudio Deluca, Frank Deluca, Richard Golfier, Laurent Devlaeminck, Francis Devlaeminck, Sylvie Grezel, Pascale Bruchon, Nicole Felix, Francois Truffaut; *D:* Francois Truffaut; *W:* Suzanne Schiffman, Francois Truffaut; *C:* Pierre William Glenn; *M:* Maurice Jaubert.

Small Time Crooks

Ex-con Ray (Allen), his wife Frenchy (Ullman), and three hapless pals (Lovitz, Rapaport, Darrow) plan an elaborate bank heist that goes completely wrong, but they wind up as millionaires anyway. Hugh Grant is an art dealer who tries to take advantage of their quest for respectability. Too many of the marital squabbles sound like leftovers from a *Honeymooners* script, and the other laughs are spotty. DVD looks fine, but striking visuals have never been Allen's forte. Mono sound is fine for the dialogue and jazz score. —*MM*
Movie: ♫♫ *DVD:* ♫♫½
DreamWorks Home Entertainment (Cat #86402, UPC #667068640229). Widescreen (1.85:1) anamorphic. Dolby Digital Mono. $26.99. Keepcase. *LANG:* English. *SUB:* English. *FEATURES:* 24 chapter links ▪ Production notes ▪ Talent files ▪ Trailer.
2000 (PG) 94m/C Woody Allen, Tracey Ullman, Hugh Grant, Jon Lovitz, Michael Rapaport, Elaine May, Tony Darrow, Elaine Stritch, George Grizzard; *D:* Woody Allen; *W:* Woody Allen; *C:* Fei Zhao.

Smilla's Sense of Snow

Offbeat thriller starts off well but fails to sustain the suspense of the novel upon which it is based. Solitary scientist Smilla Jasperson (Ormond) is an expert on snow and ice. When the body of a six-year-old, whom she has begrudgingly befriended, is discovered at their apartment building, she believes the boy was murdered. She begins an investigation that leads to a mining company and its suspicious boss Tork (Harris). Location cinematography in Greenland and Denmark is particularly impressive on disc. The image is of above-average sharpness and the many shades of blue become absolutely frigid before it's over. The 5.1 mix is active both in the big effects scenes and more conventional action. —*MM*
Movie: ♫♫ *DVD:* ♫♫♫
20th Century Fox Home Entertainment (Cat #2001221, UPC #024543012214). Widescreen (2.35:1) anamorphic. Dolby Digital 5.1 Surround Stereo; Dolby Digital Surround. $24.98. Keepcase. *LANG:* English; French. *SUB:* English; Spanish. *FEATURES:* 32 chapter links ▪ Trailers ▪ Featurette.
1996 (R) 121m/C *GE DK SW* Julia Ormond, Gabriel Byrne, Richard Harris, Vanessa Redgrave, Robert Loggia, Jim Broadbent, Mario Adorf, Bob Peck, Tom Wilkinson, Peter Capaldi, Emma Croft, Clip-

per Miano; *D:* Bille August; *W:* Ann Biderman; *C:* Jorgen Persson; *M:* Hans Zimmer, Harry Gregson-Williams.

Sniper

Sgt. Beckett (Berenger) is a sniper who has been sent to Panama (actually Australia) to assassinate a politician. Also assigned to the mission is Miller (Zane), a newcomer who knows his rifles but not his jungles. The buddy/action formula works well enough. DVD delivers a very sharp image that's equal to the theatrical release as I remember it. Sound is fine. —*MM*
Movie: ♫♫½ *DVD:* ♫♫½
Columbia Tristar Home Video (Cat #70759, UPC #043396707597). Full frame; widescreen (1.85:1) letterboxed. Dolby Digital Surround Stereo. $14.99. Keepcase. *LANG:* English; French. *SUB:* English; French. *FEATURES:* 28 chapter links ▪ Trailer.
1992 (R) 99m/C Tom Berenger, Billy Zane, J.T. Walsh, Aden Young, Ken Radley, Reinaldo Arenas, Carlos Alvarez, Roy Edmonds, Dale Dye; *D:* Luis Llosa; *W:* Michael Frost Beckner, Crash Leyland; *C:* Bill Butler; *M:* Gary Chang.

Snow Day

In the Nickelodeon-produced feature, kids rule and grown-ups are fools. On that rare day when roads are blocked by snow and school is out, Hal (Webber) goes after the girl of his dreams. His little sister Natalie (Chriqui) goes up against the evil Snowplowman (Elliott) to try to create a second Snow Day, the goal being to have two in a row. Their father (Chase) is the local weatherman and is having trouble of his own, while their mom (Smart) tries to work from home. Chevy Chase reaffirms his position on the Hollywood "B-List" of actors and Jean Smart sparkles again, but in vain. Overall, innocuous fodder for kids. The dual storylines represent an effort to entertain a wide age of kids, with pratfalls as the frosting. The running commentary from the director and screenwriters is pointless, unscripted, and rarely funny, despite their attempts at witty banter. They keep a running tally, and just so you don't have to check it out, we'll tell you: The final tally was three kisses and six fart jokes. We lost count of tiny skips on the DVD. For smooth viewing, check out the videotape. —*JAS*
Movie: ♫♫½ *DVD:* ♫♫
Paramount Home Video (Cat #33664, UPC #09736336644). Widescreen anamorphic. Dolby Digital. $29.99. Keepcase. *LANG:* English; French. *SUB:* English. *FEATURES:* 16 chapter links ▪ Cast and Crew interviews ▪ Featurette: Snow Day Scoop ▪ Commentary: director Koch, writers McCrobb and Viscardi.
2000 (PG) 89m/C Chevy Chase, Chris Elliott, Mark Webber, Jean Smart, Schuyler Fisk, Iggy Pop, Pam Grier, John Schneider, Emmanuelle Chriqui; *D:* Chris Koch; *W:* Will McRobb, Chris Viscardi; *C:* Robbie Greenberg; *M:* Steve Bartek.

Snow Falling on Cedars

Visually beautiful adaptation of David Guterson's novel is still dull. In 1954, journalist and vet Ishmael Chambers (Hawke) confronts his past when he's assigned to report on the trial of Japanese-American Kazuo Miyamoto (Yune), who's accused of murdering a fellow fisherman (Thal) in a small community north of Puget Sound. Kazuo just happens to be married to Ishmael's former flame, Hatsue (Kudoh). Lots of impressionistic flashbacks complicate matters while the story meanders along. On disc, the deep dark colors are handled well, with the shadows contrasting nicely with the snow. The picture is clear, showing little signs of grain or defects in the source material. The 5.1 audio mix is particularly well used. Early on, we are introduced to the groaning noise of a boat at sea. Later, during the courtroom scenes, this noise is replayed (presumably, it's the snow settling on the roof of the courthouse. The discreet (and discrete) Dolby mix makes this added audio bonus noticeable, but not overwhelming. —*ML/MM*
Movie: ♫♫ *DVD:* ♫♫♫½
Universal Studios Home Video (Cat #20558, UPC #025192055829). Widescreen (2.35:1) anamorphic. Dolby Digital 5.1 Surround Stereo. $24.98. Keepcase. *LANG:* English; French. *SUB:* English. *FEATURES:* Commentary: Scott Hicks ▪ Documentary ▪ Deleted scenes ▪ Theatrical trailer ▪ Production notes ▪ Talent files.
1999 (PG-13) 128m/C Ethan Hawke, Youki Kudoh, Rick Yune, Sam Shepard, Max von Sydow, James Cromwell, James Rebhorn, Richard Jenkins, Eric Thal, Celia Weston, Max Wright; *D:* Scott Hicks; *W:* Scott Hicks, Ronald Bass; *C:* Robert Richardson; *M:* James Newton Howard. *AWARDS: NOM:* Oscars '99: Cinematog.

The Snows of Kilimanjaro

Called by Hemingway "The Snows of Zanuck," referring to the great producer, this film is actually an artful pastiche of several Hemingway short stories and novels. The title story acts as a framing device, in which the life of a successful writer (Peck) is seen through his fevered flashbacks as he and his rich wife (Hayward), while on safari, await a doctor to save his gangrenous leg. The Technicolor image is grainy with a reddish tinge, but it's acceptable for a film of this age. So is the sound. —*MM*
Movie: ♫♫♫ *DVD:* ♫♫
Madacy Entertainment (Cat #99027, UPC #056775006396). Full frame. $9.99. Keepcase. *LANG:* English. *FEATURES:* Gregory Peck thumbnail bio ▪ 9 chapter links ▪ Production credits ▪ Trivia. Also available from United American Video (cat. #40105) for $9.99.
1952 117m/C Gregory Peck, Susan Hayward, Ava Gardner, Hildegarde Neff, Leo G. Carroll, Torin Thatcher, Ava Norring, Helene Stanley, Marcel Dalio, Vincente Gomez,

Richard Allen, Leonard Carey; **D:** Henry King; **W:** Casey Robinson; **C:** Leon Shamroy; **M:** Bernard Herrmann. *AWARDS: NOM:* Oscars '52: Art Dir./Set Dec., Color, Color Cinematog.

Social Misfits

Twelve troubled teenagers, including our narrator Skylar (co-writer Tann), are sent to Camp Resurrection outside Fresno for a weekend of "re-education." The film claims to be based on events that took place on March 14, 1997, but this alternative boot-camp seems to consist mostly of unsupervised psycho-drama as each of the kids tells his or her story. The whole thing is produced with more enthusiasm than experience or talent. (Note the visible camera shadows.) Production values are minimal but adequate to the subject matter. Harsh colors and some physical damage to the original elements make the image about the same as VHS tape. —*MM*
Movie: ♫♫ **DVD:** ♫♫
York Entertainment (Cat #YPD-1104, UPC #750723110424). Full frame. Dolby Digital 5.1 Surround Stereo. $19.99. Keepcase. *LANG:* English. *SUB:* Spanish. *FEATURES:* Trailers • 30 chapter links.
2000 91m/C Boris Cabrera, Le'Mark Cruise, Gabriel Damon, Isait de la Fuente, Ryan Francis, Bev Land, Eric Gray, Paul Gleason, Tyronne Tann; **D:** Rene Villar-Rios; **W:** Le'Mark Cruise, Tyronne Tann; **C:** Eric Leach; **M:** William Richter.

Sol Bianca: The Legacy

Wild and wooly computer-generated animation borrows from a number of sources—most obviously the first *Heavy Metal* film—but it is an original. The story has to do with spacefarers and a young orphaned stowaway. The plot is a wildly imaginative mix of science-fiction, "realistic" and metaphysical elements. Even by manga standards, it's way out there. The image is excellent, and lacks the hardness that so much of the brighter computer art has. Heavy pixels in the scenes of memory are intentional. Sound is very good and so is the English language track. Two episodes: "The Emblem" and "Memories." —*MM*
Movie: ♫♫♫ **DVD:** ♫♫♫
Pioneer Entertainment (Cat #PIDA-238TV, UPC #013023033894). Full frame. Dolby Digital 5.1 Surround Stereo; Dolby Digital Surround. $24.98. Keepcase. *LANG:* English; Japanese. *SUB:* English. *FEATURES:* 12 chapter links • Music video • Ship animation tests • Character designs • Trailer • DVD credits.
1990 60m/C *JP* **D:** Hiroyuki Ochi; **W:** Hideki Mitsui; **M:** Seikou Nagaoka.

Soldier of Orange

Three friends—Erik (Hauer), Alex (de Lint), and Guus (Krabbe)—take different paths when the Germans invade their native Holland during World War II. That's the basis for an ambitious epic (nearly 3 hours) examination of moral complexities in wartime. This is the film that made international careers for its stars and director Verhoeven. He provides an excellent commentary track, too, looking back at the film with fondness. DVD image is virtually pristine. There is a slight harshness to some colors, but the picture looks very good for a European import from the late 1970s. Actually, it looks much better than many Hollywood releases of the time. Sound is fine. This one is strongly recommended to war movie fans who might have missed it. —*MM* *AKA:* Soldaat van Oranje.
Movie: ♫♫♫½ **DVD:** ♫♫♫½
Anchor Bay (Cat #DV11253, UPC #013131125399). Widescreen (1.66:1) anamorphic. Dolby Digital Mono. $24.99. Keepcase. *LANG:* Dutch. *SUB:* English. *FEATURES:* 32 chapter links • Trailer • Commentary: Verhoeven • Still gallery • Talent files.
1978 144m/C *NL* Derek De Lint, Rutger Hauer, Jeroen Krabbe, Edward Fox, Susan Penhaligon; **D:** Paul Verhoeven; **W:** Paul Verhoeven, Gerard Soeteman, Kees Holierhoek; **C:** Jan De Bont; **M:** Roger van Otterloo. *AWARDS:* L.A. Film Critics '79: Foreign Film.

A Soldier's Story

During World War II, Capt. Davenport (Rollins Jr.), a black Army attorney, is sent to Ft. Neal, Louisiana, to investigate the murder of Sgt. Waters (Caesar), who was roundly hated by almost everyone. Charles Fuller's adaptation of his Pulitzer prize–winning play examines racism within and outside of the service. The sense of place is so strong, along with the well-constructed murder mystery, that the film never feels like it's restricted by the limits of the stage. Both image and sound are very good, but the real star of the disc is director Jewison's assured commentary track. If it's not as expansive as his discussions of *In the Heat of the Night*, it's still worth listening to. —*MM*
Movie: ♫♫♫ **DVD:** ♫♫♫½
Columbia Tristar Home Video (Cat #4089). Widescreen (1.85:1) anamorphic; full frame. Dolby Digital Surround Stereo. $14.95. Keepcase. *LANG:* English; Spanish. *SUB:* English; Spanish; Portuguese; Chinese; Korean; Thai. *FEATURES:* "Making of" documentary • Trailers • Commentary: Norman Jewison • 28 chapter links.
1984 (PG) 101m/C Howard E. Rollins Jr., Adolph Caesar, Denzel Washington, Patti LaBelle, Robert Townsend, Scott Paulin, Wings Hauser, Art Evans, Larry Riley, David Alan Grier; **D:** Norman Jewison; **W:** Charles Fuller; **C:** Russell Boyd; **M:** Herbie Hancock. *AWARDS:* L.A. Film Critics '84: Support. Actor (Caesar); *NOM:* Oscars '84: Adapt. Screenplay, Picture, Support. Actor (Caesar).

Solomon and Gaenor

A touching, but predictable, story of two lovers from different cultures in 1911 Wales. Gaenor (Roberts) is Welsh and Christian, Solomon (Gruffudd) is the seriously Jewish son of a Russian Jew who fled the pogroms in Europe. The film's predictability is overcome by the heartfelt performances and the incredible landscapes where the story takes place. Lovers of romance novels and Shakespeare plays will enjoy this film. The disc sounds good and the visuals are beautiful with crisp greens, reds, and blacks abounding. —*CA*
Movie: ♫♫½ **DVD:** ♫♫♫½
Columbia Tristar Home Video (Cat #05665, UPC #043396056657). Widescreen (1.66:1) letterboxed. Dolby Digital Surround. $29.95. Keepcase. *LANG:* English; Welsh; Yiddish. *SUB:* English. *FEATURES:* 28 chapter links • Commentary: director • Theatrical trailer • Cast and crew bios.
1998 (R) 103m/C *GB* Ioan Gruffudd, Nia Roberts, Mark Lewis Jones, William Thomas, Maureen Lipman, David Horovitch; **D:** Paul Morrison; **W:** Paul Morrison; **C:** Nina Kellgren; **M:** Ilona Sekacz. *AWARDS: NOM:* Oscars '99: Foreign Film.

Some Like It Hot [SE]

In prohibition-era Chicago, jazz musicians Joe (Curtis) and Jerry (Lemmon) have to hotfoot it out of town after they witness a St. Valentine's Day–style gang massacre. They disguise themselves as women and join Sweet Sue and Her Society Syncopators all-girl band heading to Miami by train. From that basis, one of Hollywood's greatest comedies springs forth. This has always been a very nice-looking black-and-white film. If there were any serious flaws on the disc I didn't notice them, but this one still makes me laugh a lot, and so I might have missed them. Marilyn still is at her absolute sexiest in those sequined dresses; her various problems are all too evident in other scenes. The extra features are not as extensive as those found on some special editions, but in this case, they're gilding on a near-perfect lily anyway. The "Virtual Hall of Memories" is a collection of clips taken from the film itself and behind-the-scenes photographs, some in color. This DVD belongs in every collection. —*MM*
Movie: ♫♫♫♫ **DVD:** ♫♫♫♫
MGM Home Entertainment (Cat #1001589, UPC #027616858993). Widescreen (1.66:1) letterboxed. Dolby Digital 5.1 Surround Stereo; Mono. $24.98. Keepcase. *LANG:* English; French; Spanish. *SUB:* French; Spanish. *FEATURES:* 16 chapter links • "Look Back" with Tony Curtis and Leonard Maltin • All-girl band featurette • "Virtual Hall of Memories" vignettes • Original pressbook photos • Trailers.
1959 120m/B Marilyn Monroe, Tony Curtis, Jack Lemmon, George Raft, Pat O'Brien, Nehemiah Persoff, Joe E. Brown, Joan Shawlee, Mike Mazurki; **D:** Billy Wilder; **W:** Billy Wilder, I.A.L. Diamond; **C:** Charles B(ryant) Lang Jr.; **M:** Adolph Deutsch. *AWARDS:* Oscars '59: Costume Des. (B&W); AFI '98: Top 100; British Acad. '59: Actor (Lemmon); Golden Globes '60: Actor—Mus./Comedy (Lem-

mon), Actress—Mus./Comedy (Monroe), Film—Mus./Comedy, Natl. Film Reg. '89; *NOM:* Oscars '59: Actor (Lemmon), Adapt. Screenplay, Art Dir./Set Dec., B&W, B&W Cinematog., Director (Wilder).

Somebody Has to Shoot the Picture

Photographer Paul Marish (Scheider) is hired by convicted cop killer Ray Eames (Howard) to take a picture of his execution. Hours before the event, Marish uncovers evidence that leads him to believe Eames is innocent. He then embarks on a race against time. Adapted for cable by Doug Magee from his book *Slow Coming Dark.* The full-frame image is no better than tape, but this is a solid sleeper on any medium. —*MM*
Movie: 🎵🎵🎵 *DVD:* 🎵🎵
Goodtimes Entertainment (Cat #81038, UPC #018713810380). Full frame. Dolby Digital Stereo. $19.98. Snapper. *LANG:* English. *SUB:* French; Spanish. *CAP:* English. *FEATURES:* 18 chapter links.
1990 (R) 104m/C Roy Scheider, Bonnie Bedelia, Robert Carradine, Andre Braugher, Arliss Howard; *D:* Frank Pierson; *W:* Doug Magee; *C:* Bojan Bazelli; *M:* James Newton Howard.

Something More

In the late 1990s, several romantic comedies followed the formula established by *Swingers:* A young guy hangs out with his pals while trying to find a woman to love. His friends are sort of jerky and provide no help; women treat him poorly. In this Canadian entry, the guy is played by Michael Goorjian and the girl is Chandra West. They're pleasant enough but the surrounding material is thin. Full-frame image is little different from VHS tape. Sound is only a slight improvement. —*MM*
Movie: 🎵🎵 *DVD:* 🎵🎵
Image Entertainment (Cat #OVED0324DVD, UPC #014381032420). Full frame. Dolby Digital 5.1 Surround Stereo; Dolby Digital Stereo. $24.95. Keepcase. *LANG:* English. *FEATURES:* Trailer.
1999 (R) 97m/C Michael Goorjian, Chandra West, David Lovgren, Jennifer Beals, Tom Cavanagh; *D:* Rob King; *W:* Peter Bryant; *C:* Jon Kranhouse; *M:* Rob Bryanton.

Something New

Please see review for *Back to God's Country / Something New.*
1920 57m/B Nell Shipman, Bert Van Tuyle, L.M. Wells; *D:* Nell Shipman, Bert Van Tuyle; *W:* Nell Shipman, Bert Van Tuyle; *C:* Joseph Walker; *M:* Philip Carli.

Something Weird

An electrical accident scars Cronin Mitchell's (McCabe) face and gives him psychic powers. A witch (Lee) casts a spell that makes everyone see him as normal but he must become her lover. She can do the same spell-thingy for herself, appearing as a beautiful blonde when she's really a hag with groddy blue skin and snaggle teeth. If all that sounds nutty, wait until the moment in Chapter 8 when a man is attacked by his bedsheets. It's a moment reminiscent of Bela Lugosi fighting the rubber octopus in Ed Wood's *Bride of the Monster.* The film, from which the distributor took its name, is not in perfect shape. The color is rough and some breaks are visible. The score is such a nutty collection of noises that any comment on sound is superfluous. —*MM*
Movie: 🎵🎵½ *DVD:* 🎵🎵½
Image Entertainment (Cat #ID6091SW DVD, UPC #014381609127). Widescreen letterboxed. Dolby Digital Mono. $24.99. Snapper. *LANG:* English. *FEATURES:* 12 chapter links ● 2 LSD shorts ● Singalong ● Commentary: H.G. Lewis, Mike Vraney ● Gallery of exploitation art.
1968 80m/C Tony McCabe, Elizabeth Lee, William Brooker, Mudite Arums, Taed Heil, Lawrence Wood, Larry Wellington, Roy Colodi, Jeffrey Allen, Stan Dale, Richard Nilsson, Carolyn Smith, Norm Lenet, Louis Newman, Dick Gaffield, Janet Charlton, Lee Ahsmann, Roger Papsch, Daniel Carrington; *D:* Herschell Gordon Lewis; *W:* James F. Hurley; *C:* Herschell Gordon Lewis, Andy Romanoff.

Something Wild

Imagine a Crosby/Hope road movie where Dorothy Lamour brings the handcuffs and *Something Wild* comes into focus. Milquetoast business executive Charlie Driggs (Daniels) fancies himself a rebel by not paying coffee shop checks and stealing candy bars. When real recklessness enters his life in the form of sexy Lulu (Griffith), Charlie embarks on a rowdy, possibly life-altering journey. *Something Wild* finds director Demme in a playful mood, filling Charlie's voyage of discovery with (then) alternative music references and glimpses of a Reagan-era society that Charlie's blind belief in the American way helped create. Griffith vamps it to the hilt, clad in a Louise Brooks haircut—and nothing else. The movie also put Ray Liotta on the map, as Lulu's maniac ex-con husband. He did such a good job with the role, he's been playing it ever since. Look for cameos from filmmakers John Sayles and John Waters. (Waters's bit is a hoot.) The transfer looks quite good. The image is clean as the proverbial whistle and colors are solid, if a bit drab (probably due more to how it was shot than how it was mastered). The stereo Surround is full-bodied and energetic, frequently engaging the rear channels for music fill and ambience. Crank up the volume during "Wild Thing." —*EP*
Movie: 🎵🎵½ *DVD:* 🎵🎵½
MGM Home Entertainment (Cat #1002046, UPC #027616862839). Widescreen (1.85:1) anamorphic. Dolby Digital Surround Stereo; Dolby Digital Mono. $19.98. Keepcase. *LANG:* English; Spanish (DDM). *SUB:* French; Spanish. *FEATURES:* 16 chapter links ● Theatrical Trailer.

1986 (R) 113m/C Jeff Daniels, Melanie Griffith, Ray Liotta, Margaret Colin, Tracey Walter, Dana Peru, Jack Gilpin, Su Tissue, Kenneth Utt, Sister Carol East, John Sayles, John Waters, Charles Napier; *D:* Jonathan Demme; *W:* E. Max Frye; *C:* Tak Fujimoto; *M:* Rosemary Paul, John Cale, Laurie Anderson, David Byrne.

Son of Gascogne

This exceptionally French comedy revolves around a young man (Colin) who is taken for the son of famous New Wave director Gascogne. Assorted Gallic film folk (Laszlo Szabo, Marie-France Pisier, Stephane Audran) appear as themselves. It's a sweet-natured, charming film, but the grainy image is no better than an old tape. Fault the original, not the transfer to disc. —*MM* *AKA:* *Les Fils de Gascogne.*
Movie: 🎵🎵½ *DVD:* 🎵🎵
Vanguard International Cinema, Inc. (Cat #1-892649-65-9, UPC #658769006230). Widescreen (1.66:1) letterboxed. $29.95. Keepcase. *LANG:* French. *SUB:* English. *FEATURES:* 12 chapter links.
1995 106m/C *FR* Gregoire Colin, Jean Claude Dreyfus, Dinara Droukarova, Bernadette LaFont, Alexandra Stewart, Stephane Audran, Jean-Claude Brialy, Bulle Ogier, Marie-France Pisier, Anemone, Patrice Leconte, Marina Vlady; *D:* Pascal Aubier; *W:* Pascal Aubier, Patrick Modiano; *C:* Jean-Jacques Flori; *M:* Angelo Zurzulo.

Son of Paleface

Hilarious sequel finds Harvard-educated Junior Potter (Hope again) heading west to claim his inheritance while special agent Roy Rogers (playing himself) and Trigger hunt for the outlaw Mike (Russell). It's all wonderfully silly, though the film does contain virtually every stereotype and insult that Hollywood has visited upon American Indians. DVD reproduces the Technicolor image with remarkable fidelity. The film looks very good. Sound is good, too. Recommended. —*MM*
Movie: 🎵🎵🎵½ *DVD:* 🎵🎵🎵
Brentwood Home Video (Cat #60982-9, UPC #090096098296). Full frame. Dolby Digital Mono. $14.98. Keepcase. *LANG:* English. *FEATURES:* 8 chapter links ● Bob Hope filmography and thumbnail bio.
1952 95m/C Bob Hope, Jane Russell, Roy Rogers, Douglass Dumbrille, Iron Eyes Cody, Bill Williams, Harry von Zell; *D:* Frank Tashlin; *W:* Frank Tashlin, Joseph Quillan, Robert L. Welch; *C:* Harry Wild. *AWARDS: NOM:* Oscars '52: Song ("Am I in Love").

Sons of Katie Elder

Mid-1960s transition western, terribly miscast, but amiable and enjoyable for fans of the genre. John Wayne, a legendary gunfighter, is the eldest son of the recently deceased Katie Elder. Returning to his Texas homestead for the funeral, he soon discovers that his mother died in poverty and that his father's cattle ranch is now owned by the shifty James Gregory (*The*

Manchurian Candidate) and his sniveling son Dennis Hopper. He teams with his estranged brothers, Dean Martin, Earl Holliman, and Michael Anderson Jr. to bring the land-grabbers to justice. Nice DVD presentation, enhanced for 16x9, but the disc lacks extras. —*RJT*

Movie: 🎬🎬½ **DVD:** 🎬🎬½
Paramount Home Video (Cat #06729, UPC #097360672947). Widescreen (2.35:1) anamorphic. Dolby Digital Stereo. $29.99. Keepcase. *LANG:* English; French. *SUB:* English. *CAP:* English. *FEATURES:* 16 chapter markers ▪ Theatrical trailer.
1965 122m/C John Wayne, Dean Martin, Earl Holliman, Michael Anderson Jr., Martha Hyer, George Kennedy, Dennis Hopper, Paul Fix, James Gregory; *D:* Henry Hathaway; *W:* Harry Essex, Allan Weiss, William Wright; *C:* Lucien Ballard; *M:* Elmer Bernstein.

The Sopranos: The Complete First Season

The real subject of HBO's hit series is New Jersey mob boss Tony Soprano (Gandolfini) and the women in his life: wife Carmela (Falco), shrink Dr. Melfi (Bracco), teenage daughter Meadow (Sisler) and, most of all, mother Livia (Marchand), an aging half-mad matriarch whose sole purpose in life is to bring trouble to those around her. Not that Tony needs more trouble. The show has been roundly condemned for its graphic violence and refusal to apply conventional morality to these characters. Meanwhile, audiences love it, and more will discover it on home video. This 4-disc set is a distinct improvement over the broadcast version. First, Surround sound is used for good effect in more dramatic moments. Second, the widescreen version simply looks better. If some scenes seem overly dark, that's the way they've always looked. Most importantly, the DVDs afford dedicated viewers the chance to go back and experience the show in big two-, three-, and four-hour gulps if they choose. That holds particularly true for the final three episodes that build to several strong climaxes. Highly recommended. —*MM*

Movie: 🎬🎬🎬🎬 **DVD:** 🎬🎬🎬🎬
HBO Home Video (Cat #99273, UPC #026 359927324). Widescreen anamorphic. Dolby Digital 5.1 Surround Stereo; Dolby Digital Surround Stereo; Mono. $99.98. Boxed set. *LANG:* English; Spanish. *CAP:* English. *FEATURES:* 78 chapter links ▪ 2 "making of" featurettes ▪ Interview with series creator David Chase by Peter Bogdanovich ▪ Weblinks ▪ Awards ▪ Talent files.
2000 680m/C James Gandolfini, Lorraine Bracco, Edie Falco, Michael Imperioli, Dominic Chianese, Vincent Pastore, Nancy Marchand, Stevie Van Zandt, Robert Iler, Jamie-Lynn Sisler.

Sorcerer Hunters: Magical Encounters

This first release, in what is going to be a series of discs, contains seven episodes

from Satoru Akahori's acclaimed animated fantasy series. The furious stories, solid characters, and villains, combined with the fast-paced effects animation make for great entertainment. The prints that were used for the transfer are clean and without notable defects or blemishes, and the images are rich-looking and powerful. The color reproduction is immaculate, nicely delineating the stark colors without any bleeding. Edges are incredibly sharp throughout, creating an image that is always sharp and perfectly brings the fine lines of the animation to the screen. Blacks are absolutely solid and without any noise, making this a beautiful presentation to watch. The original Japanese language track is preferable to the stiff, emotionless English. Both tracks have a good frequency response and a natural reproduction of the voices. The easy-listening music that accompanies the films is also well produced, although a tad too loud at times, compared to the dialogue. —*GH*

Movie: 🎬🎬🎬 **DVD:** 🎬🎬🎬
A.D.V. Films (Cat #DSH001, UPC #702727 008528). Full frame. Dolby Digital Surround Stereo. $24.99. Keepcase. *LANG:* English; Japanese. *SUB:* English. *FEATURES:* Character bios ▪ Trailer.
2000 165m/C *JP* *W:* Satoru Akahori.

Sorority House Massacre

Beth (O'Neill) visits her sorority pals but is troubled by premonitions of violence. Could a knife-wielding psycho have escaped from a nearby asylum? Substandard slasher stuff. The barebones disc is no improvement over tape in either image or sound. —*MM*

Movie: woof **DVD:** 🎬🎬
New Concorde (Cat #NH20272 D, UPC #73 6991427297). Full frame. $14.98. Keepcase. *LANG:* English. *FEATURES:* 24 chapter links ▪ Talent files ▪ Trailers.
1986 (R) 74m/C Angela O'Neill, Wendy Martel, Pamela Ross, Nicole Rio; *D:* Carol Frank; *W:* Carol Frank; *C:* Marc Reshovsky; *M:* Michael Wetherwax.

Sorority House Massacre 2: Nighty Nightmare

The only difference between the sequel and the original is a notable decrease in the quality of the image. It's even grainier than the first. Director Wynorksi is known for making movies cheap and quick, and this is one of his cheapest. DVD is no improvement over tape. —*MM*

Movie: woof **DVD:** 🎬
New Concorde (Cat #NH20310 D, UPC #73 6991431096). Full frame. $14.98. Keepcase. *LANG:* English. *FEATURES:* 24 chapter links ▪ Talent files ▪ Trailers.
1992 80m/C Melissa Moore, Robin Harris, Stacia Zhivago, Dana Bentley; *D:* Jim Wynorski; *W:* James B. Rogers, Bob Sheridan; *M:* Chuck Cirino.

The Sorrow and the Pity

Max Ophuls's massive documentary is one of the most important works of world film. He combines interviews with archival footage—much of it German propaganda newsreels—to create a "Chronicle of a French city under the Occupation," as the subtitle puts it. His point throughout is what has been called "the banality of evil," how everyday people, to varying degrees, aligned themselves with Nazism or acquiesced to the horrors of the Third Reich. Since the film has been out of print on home video for years and difficult to find, the primary benefit of this DVD is simple availability. Any visual flaws are irrelevant and always have been. This is simply a staggering work, not "easy" to watch in any sense of the word, but as memories fade, even more important than it has ever been. —*MM*

Movie: 🎬🎬🎬🎬 **DVD:** 🎬🎬🎬🎬
Image Entertainment (Cat #ID9526MLSD-VD, UPC #014381952629). Widescreen letterboxed. Dolby Digital Mono. $49.99. Two-disc keepcase. *LANG:* French; German. *SUB:* English. *FEATURES:* 30 chapter links ▪ Trailer.
1971 265m/B *FR* Pierre Mendes-France, Sir Anthony Eden, Dr. Claude Levy, Denis Rake, Louis Grave, Maurice Chevalier; *D:* Marcel Ophuls; *C:* Mandre Gazut, Jurgen Thieme.

Soul of the Game

Television movie follows the lives of three talented players in the Negro League during the 1945 season as they await the potential integration of baseball. Brooklyn Dodgers general manager Branch Rickey (Herrmann) has his scouts focusing on three men in particular: flashy, aging pitcher Satchel Paige (Lindo), mentally unstable catcher Josh Gibson (Williamson), and the young, college-educated Jackie Robinson (Underwood). Manages to resist melodrama through terrific performances. The excellent video transfer showcases bright, crisp colors and extremely sharp blacks (although some very dark-lit scenes show a loss of definition). A similarly decent sound transfer delivers crisp and clear dialogue in addition to a well-done soundtrack. —*MJT*

Movie: 🎬🎬🎬 **DVD:** 🎬🎬½
HBO Home Video (Cat #91309, UPC #026359130922). Widescreen (1.85:1) anamorphic. Dolby Surround Sound; Dolby Mono. $19.98. Snapper. *LANG:* English; French; Spanish. *SUB:* English; French; Spanish. *FEATURES:* 16 chapter links ▪ Cast and crew bios.
1996 (PG-13) 105m/C Delroy Lindo, Mykelti Williamson, Blair Underwood, Edward Herrmann, R. Lee Ermey, Gina Ravera, Salli Richardson, Obba Babatunde, Brent Jennings; *D:* Kevin Rodney Sullivan; *W:* David Himmelstein; *C:* Sandi Sissel; *M:* Lee Holdridge.

The Souler Opposite

Barry Singer (Meloni) is an L.A. stand-up comic who has had troubles with women

since he was an adolescent. (Who hasn't?) He thinks that things might be changing when he meets waitress Thea (Maloney). On his commentary track, writer/director Kalmenson admits that the story is largely autobiographical. Only the happy parts are fictional, he claims. Overall, this is a nice romantic comedy with its heart (and its head) in the right place. For a low-budget film, it's competently made. Disc image is not a huge improvement over tape. Unfortunately, the commentary track sounds slightly distorted, as if Kalmenson were working too close to the mike or was recorded too loud. —MM
Movie: 🎦🎦🎦 **DVD:** 🎦🎦½
MTI Home Video (Cat #1063, UPC #03941 4510638). Widescreen letterboxed. $24.95. Keepcase. *LANG:* English. *SUB:* Spanish. *FEATURES:* 20 chapter links ● Talent files ● Trailers ● Commentary: Bill Kalmenson.
1997 (R) 104m/C Christopher Meloni, Timothy Busfield, Janel Moloney, Allison Mackie, John Putch, Rutanya Alda, Steve Landesburg; **D:** Bill Kalmenson; **W:** Bill Kalmenson; **C:** Amit Bhattacharya; **M:** Peter Himmelman.

The Sound of Music [Five Star Collection]

Critic Judith Crist may have been too harsh when she dismissed this film as "the sound of marshmallows," but it's still far too saccharine for some tastes. That said, the spectacular location footage and Julie Andrews at her most winning and effervescent certainly cannot be dismissed. The musical tells the story of the Von Trapp family and their escape from the Nazis just before World War II. The studio pulled out all the stops for this edition. The only significant visual flaw is some curious "swelling" of the image during the credits. Sound is very good and the decision to include an isolated score, minus the singing voices, with director Wise's commentary track will appeal to fans of Rodgers and Hammerstein. Though Wise is a bit stiff at first, he warms to the task and sounds knowledgeable and comfortable throughout. Most of the extras are on a second RSDL disc. —MM
Movie: 🎦🎦½ **DVD:** 🎦🎦🎦½
20th Century Fox Home Entertainment (Cat #2000037, UPC #024543000372). Widescreen (2.20:1) anamorphic. Dolby Digital 4.1 Surround Stereo; Dolby Digital Surround. $29.99. Keepcase. *LANG:* English; French. *SUB:* English; Spanish. *FEATURES:* 61 chapter links (feature) ● 30 chapter links (extras) ● Booklet ● Location interviews ● Audio featurettes on Daniel Truhitte and Ernest Lehman ● Previews, radio and TV spots ● "Making of" featurette ● Feature-length documentary ● Isolated score and director's commentary ● Extensive background material.
1965 174m/C Julie Andrews, Christopher Plummer, Eleanor Parker, Peggy Wood, Charmian Carr, Heather Menzies, Marni Nixon, Richard Haydn, Anna Lee, Norma Varden, Nicholas Hammond, Angela

Cartwright, Portia Nelson, Duane Chase, Debbie Turner, Kym Karath; **D:** Robert Wise; **W:** Ernest Lehman; **C:** Ted D. McCord; **M:** Richard Rodgers, Oscar Hammerstein. *AWARDS:* Oscars '65: Adapt. Score, Director (Wise); Film Editing, Picture, Sound; AFI '98: Top 100; Directors Guild '65: Director (Wise); Golden Globes '66: Actress—Mus./Comedy (Andrews); Film—Mus./Comedy; *NOM:* Oscars '65: Actress (Andrews), Art Dir./Set Dec., Color, Color Cinematog., Costume Des. (C), Support. Actress (Wood).

Sour Grapes

Seinfeld co-creator David's feature directorial debut has cousins Evan (Weber) and Richie (Bierko) feuding over an Atlantic City slot machine jackpot. Evan, a successful surgeon, lends Richie, an extroverted loser, two quarters for one last pull on the slots. Of course, Richie wins $436,000. Escalating revenge schemes, petty greed, and quirky small talk scream sitcom episode. So do the production values, lighting, and staging. There's not really enough here to justify 90 minutes of screen time. The no-frills, full-frame DVD image is no better than tape. —MM
Movie: 🎦🎦 **DVD:** 🎦🎦
Warner Home Video, Inc. (Cat #2532). Full frame. Dolby Surround Stereo. $14.98. Snapper. *LANG:* English. *FEATURES:* 28 chapter links.
1998 (R) 91m/C Steven Weber, Craig Bierko, Karen Sillas, Matt Keeslar, Robyn Peterman, Jennifer Leigh Warren, Richard Gant, James MacDonald, Philip Baker Hall, Ann Guilbert; **D:** Larry David; **W:** Larry David; **C:** Victor Hammer.

The Source

This documentary essentially does for the Beats what *32 Short Films about Glenn Gould* does for the pianist. But Chuck Workman commingles live readings and interviews with staged performances. To anyone who's not interested in the literary scene of the 1940s and '50s, it will probably be of little entertainment value, but for those who appreciate Kerouac, Ginzberg, Burroughs, and the rest, it's a treat. Much of the footage is taken from television and other sources so the film is no great shakes in visual terms. DVD does seem to re-create the image faithfully, and the 1.66:1 letterbox is virtually invisible. Sound is fine for the subject matter. —MM
Movie: 🎦🎦🎦 **DVD:** 🎦🎦🎦
Winstar Home Entertainment (Cat #FLV52 25, UPC #720917522524). Widescreen (1.66:1) letterboxed. $24.98. Keepcase. *LANG:* English. *FEATURES:* 8 chapter links ● Filmographies and awards ● Weblink ● Trailer.
1996 89m/C Johnny Depp, Dennis Hopper, John Turturro; **D:** Chuck Workman; **W:** Chuck Workman; **C:** Tom Hurwitz, Don Lenzer; **M:** David Amram, Philip Glass.

South Central

Give writer/director Anderson credit for trying to inject notes of reality into an otherwise stereotypical life-'n-the-hood story. Bobby, a young black gang leader, spends years in prison then tries to find a way out for his young son and drug-addicted wife. The Surround mix lacks real punch and the bronze-tinted full-frame image appears to be an accurate re-creation of a modestly budgeted theatrical release. —MM
Movie: 🎦🎦 **DVD:** 🎦🎦
Warner Home Video, Inc. (Cat #12594). Full frame. Dolby Digital Surround Stereo. $14.98. Snapper. *LANG:* English. *FEATURES:* 31 chapter links.
1992 (R) 99m/C Glenn Plummer, Carl Lumbly, Christian Coleman, LaRita Shelby, Byron Keith Minns; **D:** Steve (Stephen M.) Anderson; **W:** Steve (Stephen M.) Anderson; **C:** Charlie Lieberman; **M:** Tim Truman.

Southern Comfort

Director Walter Hill delivers the goods in this offbeat survival saga about a Louisiana National Guard infantry squad lost in the swamps and stalked by Cajun locals. Keith Carradine, Powers Boothe, Peter Coyote, and Fred Ward are outgunned, lost, and ill-prepared for a battle to the death with some backwoods boys—chilling, effective, and one of Hill's most underrated efforts. DVD arrives sans features, but is attractively priced and the presentation looks sharp. —RJT
Movie: 🎦🎦🎦 **DVD:** 🎦🎦½
MGM Home Entertainment (Cat #10018 52, UPC #027616861297). Widescreen (1.85:1) anamorphic. Dolby Digital Surround Stereo. $14.95. Keepcase. *LANG:* English; French. *SUB:* French; Spanish. *CAP:* French; Spanish. *FEATURES:* 16 chapter markers ● Theatrical trailer.
1981 (R) 106m/C Ned Dowd, Powers Boothe, Keith Carradine, Fred Ward, Franklyn Seales, Brion James, T.K. Carter, Peter Coyote; **D:** Walter Hill; **W:** David Giler, Michael Kane, Walter Hill; **M:** Ry Cooder.

Space Cowboys

Director Eastwood plays a retired Air Force officer who was passed over for the astronaut training program. But now NASA needs his expertise when an ailing '60s satellite that he designed poses a threat if it crashes into Earth. He agrees to go up to fix it if he can bring along three equally codgerly buddies (Jones, Garner, Sutherland). The four of them give every appearance of having a wonderful time making this outlandish adventure, and so it becomes something more than movie star vs. computer effects. Of course, DVD handles all of the special effects without problem and, again, Surround sound is superior to theatrical presentation. —MM
Movie: 🎦🎦🎦½ **DVD:** 🎦🎦🎦
Warner Home Video, Inc. (Cat #18722, UPC #085391872221). Widescreen anamorphic. Dolby Digital 5.1 Surround; Dolby Digital Surround. $24.98. Snapper. *LANG:* English; French. *SUB:* English; French. *FEA-

TURES: 36 chapter links • Talent files • Jay Leno interview and routine • Editing featurette.
2000 (PG-13) 123m/C Clint Eastwood, Tommy Lee Jones, James Garner, James Cromwell, Donald Sutherland, Marcia Gay Harden, Loren Dean, William Devane, Rade Serbedzija, Courtney B. Vance, Barbara Babcock, Blair Brown; *D:* Clint Eastwood; *W:* Ken Kaufman, Howard Klausner; *C:* Jack N. Green; *M:* Lennie Niehaus. *AWARDS: NOM:* Oscars '00: Sound FX Editing.

Space-Thing

On his commentary track, producer David Friedman proudly boasts that this sf exploitation is so bad that "it makes *Plan 9* look like *Citizen Kane*," and he's not exaggerating. If this weren't a nudie flick, it would be much more widely known and appreciated (if that's the right word). As it is, the film has been remarkably popular. It's essentially a couple of barebones sets meant to suggest the inside of a space-craft where the guys and gals seldom miss a chance to disrobe and indulge in mid-'60s naughtiness. The DVD image is astonishingly sharp with bright colors. It appears to have been made from a carefully preserved (or restored) original. Mono sound is O.K. —*MM*
Movie: ♫ **DVD:** ♫♫♫
Image Entertainment (Cat #ID6067SW DVD, UPC #014381606720). Full frame. Dolby Digital Mono. $24.99. Snapper. *LANG:* English. *FEATURES:* 12 chapter links • Trailer • 2 archival shorts • Gallery of exploitation art • Commentary: producer Friedman, Mike Vraney.
1967 69m/C D: Byron Mabe.

Spaceways

Britain: We have a problem! Howard Duff stars as Dr. Stephen Mitchell, an American scientist at work at a cloistered, top-secret base in England. He is accused of murdering his unfaithful wife and her lover, and disposing of their bodies by launching them into space aboard a satellite. The only way to prove his innocence is to board the next rocket and retrieve the satellite. Like our hero, this modest thriller—part murder-mystery and part sci-fi thriller—doesn't really blast off until about an hour in. But genre fans will note that this is the first science-fiction film produced by England's Hammer Studios, and that the director is Terence Fisher, who went on to direct some of the studio's signature films *(Dracula, Revenge of Frankenstein)*. Not the sort of film to be a top priority for film preservation, *Spaceways* has been given a decent DVD transfer. The source material exhibits speckles, but the black-and-white contrast is good. The sound, too, is adequate, with minimal hiss and distortion. —*DL*
Movie: ♫♫½ **DVD:** ♫♫½
Image Entertainment (Cat #ID9216CODVD, UPC #1438192162). Full frame. Dolby Digital Mono. $24.99. Snapper. *LANG:* Eng-

lish. *FEATURES:* Theatrical trailer • 15 chapter links.
1953 76m/B Howard Duff, Eva Bartok, Ceclie Cheyreau, Andrew Osborn; *D:* Terence Fisher; *W:* Richard H. Landau, Paul Tabori; *C:* Reg Wyer; *M:* Ivor Stanley.

Spartacus [Criterion]

The true story of a gladiator who leads other slaves in a rebellion against the power of Rome in 73 B.C. The rebellion is put down and the rebels are crucified. Douglas, whose political leanings are amply on display herein, also served as executive producer, surrounding himself with the best talent available. Magnificent climactic battle scene features 8,000 real live Spanish soldiers to stunning effect. A boxoffice triumph that gave Kubrick much-desired financial independence. Though the Universal DVD of *Spartacus* is no slouch, this fine release by Criterion slightly improves on the sharpness and delivers colors a bit more vibrant than its predecessor. While the image quality itself may not warrant trashing (or at least trading in) your Universal copy, the loaded supplemental section may make up your mind. The main commentary track features stars Douglas and Ustinov, and a few others relating making of stories (some scene specific), while the second expresses screenwriter Trumbo's dissatisfaction with the finished project through his notes. When combined with the blacklist documentary, "The Hollywood Ten," (included on the second disc of the set), Trumbo's original ideological metaphor is easier to understand. There's plenty more to look at, including deleted scenes and some great behind-the-scenes footage, and most of it shouldn't be missed. —*JO*
Movie: ♫♫♫♫ **DVD:** ♫♫♫♫
Criterion Collection (Cat #CC1568DV, UPC #715515011723). Widescreen (2.2:1) anamorphic. Dolby Digital 5.1; Dolby Surround; Stereo; Dolby Digital Mono. $49.95. Keepcase. *LANG:* English. *SUB:* English. *FEATURES:* 46 chapter links • Theatrical trailer • Commentary: Kirk Douglas, Peter Ustinov, others • Scene-by-scene analysis by screenwriter Dalton Trumbo • Additional Alex North score compositions • 2 interviews with Peter Ustinov • Jean Simmons interview • Deleted scenes • Documentary: "The Hollywood Ten" • Blacklist documents • Sketches by director Kubrick • Production stills; lobby cards; posters; print ads; comic book • Original storyboards.
1960 (PG-13) 196m/C Kirk Douglas, Laurence Olivier, Jean Simmons, Tony Curtis, Charles Laughton, Herbert Lom, Nina Foch, Woody Strode, Peter Ustinov, John Gavin, John Ireland, Charles McGraw, Joanna Barnes; *D:* Stanley Kubrick; *W:* Dalton Trumbo; *C:* Russell Metty; *M:* Alex North. *AWARDS:* Oscars '60: Art Dir./Set Dec., Color, Color Cinematog., Costume Des. (C), Support. Actor (Ustinov); Golden Globes '61: Film—Drama; *NOM:* Oscars '60: Film Editing, Orig. Dramatic Score.

The Specials

This is the movie that *Mystery Men* wanted to be. It's a smart comic book spoof that depends on good acting and well-written characters. The Specials are the sixth or seventh greatest team of superheroes in the business. Headquarters is a suburban house in Silver Lake. Their immediate goal—if they can quit bickering among themselves—is to get a line of action figures on the market. There is nothing special about the DVD image, and there should not be; that's part of the joke. The main attraction on the disc is the commentary track with director Mazin, writer/star Gunn, producer Mark Altman, and visual effects supervisor Mojo. —*MM*
Movie: ♫♫♫ **DVD:** ♫♫½
Pioneer Entertainment (Cat #PEAD11518, UPC #013023151895). Widescreen anamorphic. Dolby Digital Surround Stereo. $24.98. Keepcase. *LANG:* English. *FEATURES:* 15 chapter links • Commentary: Mazin, Gunn, Altman, Mojo • Deleted scenes • Toy commercial • Wedding video • Trailer • Photo gallery.
2000 89m/C Rob Lowe, Jamie Kennedy, Thomas Haden Church, Paget Brewster, Judy Greer, James Gunn, Sean Gunn, Jordan Ladd, Kelly Coffield; *D:* Craig Mazin; *W:* James Gunn; *C:* Eliot Rockett; *M:* Brian Langsbard, Spring Aspers.

Speed Racer: The Movie

No, it's not the live-action version you've been dreaming of...it's two classic *Speed Racer* episodes put together and passed off as a movie. It was released in theatres as a late-night feature with "Colonel Bleep." The "Colonel Bleep" episode is hidden. If you want to watch it, you'll have to answer all the trivia questions first. The first episode is "The Car Hater." Mr. Trotter hates cars because his son was killed in one, and he does his best to make others feel that automobiles are weapons. When his daughter befriends Speed and Trixie, it becomes too much for him and he hires men to sabotage Pop Racer's factory. The second episode is "The Race Against the Mammoth Car." Inspector Detector is looking for a large quantity of stolen gold. What vehicle in the race could be big enough to hide such a large quantity of gold? Hmm? This episode also features the appearance of Speed's long-lost brother, Racer X. The color reproduction on this DVD is sharp; it couldn't be better. Missing from the disc is an uncut version of the show's title sequence. The audio commentary by voice-over actors Peter Fernandez and Corinne Orr is amusing for a while, but Orr's sickly sweetness sours it and even Fernandez shows signs of being annoyed with her. It's worth listening to for trivia sake, and the actors' unbounded deluded egos are a rare oddity. —*JAS*
Movie: ♫♫♫ **DVD:** ♫♫♫♫
Artisan Entertainment (Cat #DVD11521). Full frame. Dolby Digital. $19.98. Keepcase. *LANG:* English with Japanese mouthing. *FEA-*

TURES: 3 chapter links • Mach 5 demo • Commentary: Peter Fernandez, Corinne Orr • Speed Racer music video.
19?? 80m/C V: Peter Fernandez, Corinne Orr.

Spiders

Throwback to the "big bug" sci-fi horrors of the 1950s also borrows heavily from *The X-Files.* College reporter Marci (Parrilla) and a couple of her pals sneak into a desert military base in time to witness the secret landing of a space shuttle. On board is a spider that has been injected with alien DNA and is doing absolutely disgusting things. It all ends with an arachnid attack on Phoenix! Can the city be saved? Overall, the effects at the beginning are much more effective than the ones at the end, but the film has enough humor to overcome that flaw. Image ranges between excellent and very good. Ditto sound. *—MM*
Movie: 🐾🐾½ **DVD:** 🐾🐾🐾
Trimark Home Video (Cat #7577D, UPC #031398757726). Widescreen letterboxed. Dolby Digital 5.1 Surround Stereo. $24.99. Keepcase. *LANG:* English. *SUB:* English; French; Spanish. *FEATURES:* 24 chapter links • "Making of" featurette.
2000 (R) 93m/C David Carpenter, Lana Parrilla; *D:* Gary Jones.

The Spiral Staircase

Helen Capel (McGuire), mute since a childhood trauma, works in a creepy Gothic mansion for Mrs. Warren (Barrymore) and may be the next victim of a murderer who preys on women with disabilities. Excellent performances all around and a plot with elements that remain popular today make this one a fine suspense/horror/thriller. (Take your pick.) Anchor Bay has done its usual excellent job presenting a virtually flawless black-and-white image. Mono sound is fine. *—MM*
Movie: 🐾🐾🐾½ **DVD:** 🐾🐾🐾
Anchor Bay (Cat #DV11192, UPC #013131 119299). Full frame. Dolby Digital Mono. $24.99. Keepcase. *LANG:* English. *FEATURES:* 20 chapter links • Trailer.
1946 83m/B Dorothy McGuire, George Brent, Ethel Barrymore, Kent Smith, Rhonda Fleming, Gordon Oliver, Elsa Lanchester, Sara Allgood; *D:* Robert Siodmak; *W:* Mel Dinelli; *C:* Nicholas Musuraca; *M:* Roy Webb. *AWARDS: NOM:* Oscars '46: Support. Actress (Barrymore).

Splash

A beautiful mermaid (Hannah) ventures into New York City in search of a man (Hanks) she's rescued twice when he's fallen overboard. Charming performances by the then-young leads with scene-stealing support from Candy as the ne'er-do-well big brother and sure direction by Howard give this love story just enough slapstick. Don't miss the lobster scene. The DVD image is no great shakes. All the usual suspects show up—flashing Venet-

ian blinds, artifacts in bright beach and ocean scenes—and sound is O.K. Such an important comedy deserves better treatment. A restored special edition with commentary is in order. *—MM*
Movie: 🐾🐾🐾 **DVD:** 🐾🐾
Buena Vista Home Entertainment (Cat #16535). Widescreen letterboxed. Dolby Digital Surround Stereo. $29.99. Keepcase. *LANG:* English; French. *CAP:* English. *FEATURES:* 20 chapter links.
1984 (PG) 109m/C Tom Hanks, Daryl Hannah, Eugene Levy, John Candy, Dody Goodman, Shecky Greene, Richard B. Shull, Bobby DiCicco, Howard Morris; *D:* Ron Howard; *W:* Babaloo Mandel, Lowell Ganz; *C:* Don Peterman; *M:* Lee Holdridge. *AWARDS:* Natl. Soc. Film Critics '84: Screenplay; *NOM:* Oscars '84: Orig. Screenplay.

Splendor

Nineties screwball comedy revolves around an unconventional sexual arrangement. Veronica (Robertson) is an aspiring L.A. actress who falls for two men on opposite ends of the sexual spectrum. Abel (Schaech) is a freelance music critic who's intelligent and handsome, while punk rock drummer Zed (Kesslar) is dumb but really sexy. Eventually both move in with her and prove to be more immature than the lady herself. Enter wealthy TV director Ernest (Mabius). It's surprisingly sweet for director Araki. DVD handles his challengingly bright and energetic color scheme without any serious flaws. The Surround is properly thumpy in the right moments. *—MM*
Movie: 🐾🐾½ **DVD:** 🐾🐾🐾
Columbia Tristar Home Video (Cat #4384, UPC #043396043848). Widescreen (1.85:1) letterboxed. Dolby Digital 5.1 Surround Stereo. $27.95. Keepcase. *LANG:* English; Portuguese; Spanish. *SUB:* French; Portuguese; Spanish. *CAP:* English. *FEATURES:* Cast and crew thumbnail bios • Trailer • 28 chapter links.
1999 (R) 93m/C Kathleen Robertson, Johnathon Schaech, Matt Keeslar, Eric Mabius, Kelly Macdonald; *D:* Gregg Araki; *W:* Gregg Araki; *C:* Jim Fealy; *M:* Daniel Licht.

Spooky Encounters

Writer/director/star Samo Hung is Cheung, a simple-minded braggart who takes a bet to spend one night in a haunted temple. But it's a set-up. His unfaithful wife's lover hires an evil sorcerer to raise the dead. The film covers practically the entire palette of Chinese horror, including hopping vampires and flesh-eating zombies, along with flying undead and plenty of black magic. Samo pulls the film off easily, using his trademark humor to soften the horrific edge. The transfer is generally good, although a number of speckles and scratches are evident in the print used. The film also shows quite a bit of grain, but neither is overly distracting. Once the film gets in to the realm of the "ghostly" supernatural, colors are bold and well sat-

urated. The translation is good and mostly without notable errors. *—GH* **AKA:** Encounters of the Spooky Kind.
Movie: 🐾🐾½ **DVD:** 🐾🐾½
Tai Seng Video Marketing (UPC #6016430 21744). Widescreen (2.35:1) letterboxed. Dolby Digital 5.1 Surround Stereo. $29.95. Keepcase. *LANG:* Mandarin; Cantonese. *SUB:* English. *FEATURES:* Trailers • Production notes.
1980 94m/C HK Sammo Hung, Chung Fat; *D:* Sammo Hung; *W:* Sammo Hung.

Stalked

Macedonian transplant Aleksandr (Ognenovski) wakes up to an American nightmare, finding himself the target of a small town's wrath when framed for murder. Mayhem ensues, but not without those forced moments of pathos, romance, and testosterone-infused male bonding. Writer/director/star Ognenovski retreads the formula from early Stallone, Schwarzenegger, and Van Damme films: an outsider trapped in a hostile environment with only his wits and a few hundred rounds to protect him. Here, the clichés pile up faster than the body count. Add abysmal dialogue, casting misfires (like the actor with a thick Russian accent playing the mayor of a small American town), and fight scenes rife with punches that don't connect, and we are in the presence of a potential Ed Wood for the action crowd. Colors on the full-frame DVD look blanched. Pixelation artifacts occasionally appear, exacerbated by the soft focus photography. Surround sound is adequate with sporadic rear channel activity. Sublime schlock, any way you slice it. *—EP*
Movie: woof **DVD:** 🐾🐾
Image Entertainment (Cat #ID8911YODVD, UPC #1438189112). Full frame. Dolby Digital Surround. $24.99. Snapper. *LANG:* English. *FEATURES:* 12 chapter links.
1999 93m/C Jorgo Ognenovski, Meto Jovanovski, Lisa Marie Wilson; *D:* Jorgo Ognenovski; *W:* Jorgo Ognenovski, Mary Quijano; *C:* Ricardo Jacques Gale.

Stand by Me [2 SE]

A sentimental, observant adaptation of the Stephen King novella *The Body.* Four 12-year-olds trek into the Oregon wilderness to find the body of a missing boy and to learn about death and personal courage. Told as a reminiscence by narrator "author" Dreyfuss with solid performances from all four child actors. Too much gratuitous obscenity, but a very good, gratifying film from can't-miss director Reiner. This is the second time that Columbia TriStar has released *Stand by Me* on DVD. This edition is a huge improvement thanks to a new anamorphic transfer. The image is much sharper, although some of the brighter outdoor scenes have noticeable if slight grain. When it comes to color, there is no comparison, and scenic shots are vibrant and often stunning. Darker scenes remain very detailed with excellent blacks and contrast throughout. The mono sound is never

distorted, but is nonetheless a little disappointing since at the very least a stereo mix would have been cool with all the golden oldies used in the soundtrack. The "making of" featurette, *Walking the Tracks: The Summer of Stand by Me,* is an amazing documentary that covers more than just the production of the film. Highlights include most of the cast sharing thoughts about their late co-star River Phoenix, and Stephen King himself giving his opinion of the film. As you would expect, Reiner's commentary is nearly as entertaining as the movie. —*JO*
Movie: 🎬🎬🎬½ **DVD:** 🎬🎬🎬
Columbia Tristar Home Video (Cat #05517, UPC #043396055179). Widescreen (1.85: 1) anamorphic. Mono. $29.95. Keepcase. *LANG:* English; Spanish; French; Portuguese. *SUB:* English; Spanish; French; Chinese; Korean; Thai; Portuguese. *CAP:* English. *FEATURES:* 28 chapter links • Theatrical trailer • Talent files • Production notes • Commentary: director Rob Reiner • "Making of" featurette • Isolated music score • Music video "Stand by Me."
1986 (R) 87m/C River Phoenix, Wil Wheaton, Jerry O'Connell, Corey Feldman, Kiefer Sutherland, Richard Dreyfuss, Casey Siemaszko, John Cusack; *D:* Rob Reiner; *W:* Raynold Gideon; *C:* Thomas Del Ruth; *M:* Jack Nitzsche. *AWARDS: NOM:* Oscars '86: Adapt. Screenplay.

A Star Is Born

Aging actor helps a young actress to fame. She becomes his wife, but alcoholism and failure are too much for him. She honors his memory. Remake of the 1937 classic was Garland's triumph, a superb and varied performance. Newly restored version reinstates over 20 minutes of long-missing footage, including three Garland musical numbers. This is the way to see this classic. The image is not flawless (due to the age of the film) but the colors are improved from the Warner laserdisc and the picture is much sharper than ever before. The odd dark scene has some shimmering and grain, but not such that it ruins the enjoyment of the film. The 5.1 sound is amazing. Again, the age of the film prevents it from being perfect, but the fidelity is stunningly improved. Side one presents the feature and side two is chock-full of supplementals, including a black-and-white presentation of the film's original premiere. The alternate versions of "The Man That Got Away" are interesting to watch (but not as good as the version used in the film) and the deleted song, "When My Sugar Walks down the Street," is only a portion of the song. —*JO*
Movie: 🎬🎬🎬½ **DVD:** 🎬🎬🎬½
Warner Home Video, Inc. (Cat #17588, UPC #085391758822). Widescreen (2.35: 1) anamorphic. Dolby Digital 5.1. $24.98. Snapper. *LANG:* English. *SUB:* English; French. *CAP:* English. *FEATURES:* 54 chapter links • Theatrical trailers for the 1937, 1954, and 1976 films • 3 alternate versions of "The Man That Got Away" • Deleted scenes—audio only • Deleted song, "When My Sugar Walks down the Street" • Production notes • Documentary with newsreel footage • Dual-layered.
1954 (PG) 175m/C Judy Garland, James Mason, Jack Carson, Tommy Noonan, Charles Bickford, Emerson Treacy, Charles Halton; *D:* George Cukor; *W:* Moss Hart; *C:* Sam Leavitt; *M:* Harold Arlen, Ira Gershwin. *AWARDS:* Golden Globes '55: Actor—Mus./Comedy (Mason), Actress—Mus./Comedy (Garland); *NOM:* Oscars '54: Actor (Mason), Actress (Garland), Art Dir./Set Dec., Color, Costume Des. (C), Song ("The Man That Got Away"), Scoring/Musical.

The Star Packer

Please see review of *Riders of Destiny / Star Packer.*
Movie: 🎬🎬
1934 53m/B John Wayne, George "Gabby" Hayes, Earl Dwire, Yakima Canutt; *D:* Robert North Bradbury; *W:* Robert North Bradbury; *C:* Archie Stout.

Star Trek 2: The Wrath of Khan

Picking up from the 1967 Star Trek episode "Space Seed," Admiral James T. Kirk and the crew of the *Enterprise* must battle Khan, an old foe out for revenge. Warm and comradely in the nostalgic mode of its successors. Introduced Kirk's former lover and unknown son to the series plot, as well as Mr. Spock's "death," which led to the next sequel (1984's *The Search for Spock*). The Paramount DVD offers some of the truest and darkest blacks of any DVD. During some of the space scenes it is impossible to see where the anamorphic picture ends and the black screen begins. Colors are also accurate and remain vibrant throughout, enhanced by excellent contrast that keeps shadow details high. The main flaws are occasional softness and some scratches and flecks from the source material. The 5.1 mix could have used a bit more low end during some of the effects sequences and the Surround channels are rarely used. Also, Horner's score seems to lack some energy. On the plus side, the dialogue is usually crystal clear and mostly up front. —*JO*
Movie: 🎬🎬🎬 **DVD:** 🎬🎬🎬
Paramount Home Video (Cat #011807, UPC #097360118070). Widescreen (2.35: 1) anamorphic. Dolby Digital 5.1; Dolby Surround. $29.99. Keepcase. *LANG:* English; French. *SUB:* English. *CAP:* English. *FEATURES:* 17 chapter links • Theatrical trailer.
1982 (PG) 113m/C William Shatner, Leonard Nimoy, Ricardo Montalban, DeForest Kelley, Nichelle Nichols, James Doohan, George Takei, Walter Koenig, Kirstie Alley, Merritt Butrick, Paul Winfield, Bibi Besch; *D:* Nicholas Meyer; *W:* Jack Sowards; *C:* Gayne Rescher; *M:* James Horner.

Stargate SG-1: Season 1

This five-disc boxed set contains the first season of the TV series based on the 1994 theatrical release. The story involves extraterrestrials who favor an ancient Egyptian look, soldiers, and a big wheel that serves as the frame for neat-o CGI effects. Richard Dean Anderson takes over the Kurt Russell role. Production values are very good for television, and an above-average image does them justice. Sound is very good, too. The set consists of 21 episodes including the pilot, which is rated "R" for a bit of nudity. —*MM*
Movie: 🎬🎬½ **DVD:** 🎬🎬½
MGM Home Entertainment (Cat #10016 07, UPC #027616859174). Widescreen (1.78:1) anamorphic. Dolby Digital Surround Stereo. $89.95. Boxed set. *LANG:* English; French; Spanish. *SUB:* French; Spanish. *FEATURES:* Costume design featurette • Trailers • Cast and crew featurette • "Gen. Hammond" featurette • Behind-the-scenes featurette • "Capt. Carter" featurette.
1997 981m/C Richard Dean Anderson, Michael Shanks, Amanda Tapping, Christopher Judge.

Starry Night

The inspiration for this curious fantasy seems to come as much from Don McLean's song "Vincent" as it does from the real work of Vincent Van Gogh. A magic potion brings him to contemporary America for a brief time to see how the paintings, which were neglected in his lifetime, have become universally respected. Unfortunately, the DVD image is flat and soft, and the voices sound like they are poorly dubbed. And the very idea of the passionate Van Gogh at the Rose Bowl Parade is simply too abhorrent to contemplate. —*MM*
Movie: 🎬🎬 **DVD:** 🎬🎬
Universal Studios Home Video (Cat #211 18, UPC #025192111822). Full frame. Dolby Digital Surround Stereo. $24.98. Keepcase. *LANG:* English. *SUB:* French. *CAP:* English. *FEATURES:* 18 chapter links • "Making of" featurette • Production notes • Historical overview of Van Gogh • Commentary: Paul Davids, David W. Smith.
1999 (PG-13) 98m/C Abbott Alexander, Lisa Waltz, Sally Kirkland, Lou Wagner; *D:* Paul Davids; *W:* Paul Davids; *C:* David W. Smith; *M:* Brad Warnaar.

Steal This Movie!

This is a fabulous film based on the life of Abbie Hoffman that fell prey to poor marketing and distribution and never got the theatrical attention it deserved. The writing, directing, and editing work together with wit and humor to tell the story of a man who was an intellectual, a manic depressive, a womanizer, and a revolutionary. Hoffman was famous in his time

for creating a series of publicity stunts and practical jokes that kept several government agencies on their toes. The most famous was his gathering of over 20,000 activists to circle the Pentagon, with claims that they would levitate it and then perform an exorcism on the building to cast out the evil within. He was also one of the first '60s radicals to start drawing attention to the Counter Intelligence Program the government put together to keep tabs on and discredit political activists. The story begins in the early '60s, with Hoffman running the "Free Store" and being hounded by the FBI. It goes through his trial as one of the Chicago 7, and ends with his surrender after going underground for years after the trial to avoid prison time. The story never loses its ability to maintain viewer interest in the political activities of the times and an incredible performance by Vincent D'Onofrio in the lead role brings a humanity to Hoffman that could be lost in the hands of a lesser actor. D'Onofrio's delivery of Hoffman's eloquent, intelligent pleas during the Chicago 7 and subsequent trials on the vibrant nature of the American Constitution are awe-inspiring. The extras on the disc include an interview with other Chicago 7 defendants Tom Hayden (yes, that guy who was married to Jane Fonda) and Bobby Seale, a black activist who was chained and gagged during the trial after demanding the right to cross-examine his accusers. The color and sound are above average and the soundtrack is fabulous. —*CA*
AKA: *Abbie.*
Movie: 🎵🎵🎵🎵 **DVD:** 🎵🎵🎵
Trimark Home Video (Cat #VM#7567D, UPC #031398756729). Widescreen. Dolby Digital 5.1 Surround. $24.99. Keepcase. *LANG:* English. *SUB:* French; English; Spanish. *FEATURES:* 30 chapter links ▪ Interviews with actors, subjects, crew ▪ Deleted scenes ▪ Pig for President spots.
2000 (R) 111m/C Vincent D'Onofrio, Janeane Garofalo, Jeanne Tripplehorn, Donal Logue, Kevin Pollak, Kevin Corrigan, Troy Garity, Alan Van Sprang; **D:** Robert Greenwald; **W:** Bruce Graham; **C:** Denis Lenoir; **M:** Mader.

Steel Dawn

Another *Mad Max* clone finds a leather-clad warrior wielding his sword over lots of presumably post-apocalyptic desert terrain. Swayze made this unfortunate choice right after the release of *Dirty Dancing.* The grainy image is absolutely no improvement over tape, and there's no need for it to be. —*MM*
Movie: 🎵🎵½ **DVD:** 🎵🎵½
Artisan Entertainment (Cat #10399, UPC #012236103998). Full frame. Dolby Digital Surround Stereo. $12.99. Keepcase. *LANG:* English. *FEATURES:* 30 chapter links.
1987 (R) 90m/C Patrick Swayze, Lisa Niemi, Christopher Neame, Brett Hool, Brion James, Anthony Zerbe; **D:** Lance Hool; **W:** Doug Lefler; **C:** George Tirl; **M:** Brian May.

Steel Magnolias

Julia Roberts plays a young woman stricken with severe diabetes who chooses to live her life to the fullest despite her bad health. Much of the action revolves around a Louisiana beauty shop where the women get together to discuss the goings-on of their lives. Sweet, poignant, often hilarious, and sometimes overwrought story is based by R. Harling on his partially autobiographical play. MacLaine is funny as a bitter divorcee; Parton is sexy and fun as the hairdresser. But Field and Roberts go over the deep end and make it a weepy chick flick. The DVD image is O.K. and nobody should complain that the sound has not been redone for 5.1 Surround. It would only make those bad Southern accents sound worse. —*MM*
Movie: 🎵🎵🎵 **DVD:** 🎵🎵½
Columbia Tristar Home Video (Cat #702 47). Widescreen letterboxed. Dolby Digital Stereo. $24.95. Keepcase. *LANG:* English; Spanish; Portuguese. *SUB:* English; Spanish; Portuguese; Chinese; Korean; Thai. *FEATURES:* 28 chapter links ▪ Isolated music score ▪ Commentary: director ▪ Trailers ▪ Cast and crew thumbnail bios ▪ 5 deleted scenes ▪ "In Full Bloom" featurette.
1989 (PG) 118m/C Sally Field, Dolly Parton, Shirley MacLaine, Daryl Hannah, Olympia Dukakis, Julia Roberts, Tom Skerritt, Sam Shepard, Dylan McDermott, Kevin J. O'Connor, Bill McCutcheon, Ann Wedgeworth, Janine Turner; **D:** Herbert Ross; **W:** Robert Harling; **C:** John A. Alonzo; **M:** Georges Delerue. *AWARDS:* Golden Globes '90: Support. Actress (Roberts); *NOM:* Oscars '89: Support. Actress (Roberts).

Steele's Law

Loner cop John Steele (Williamson) is forced to take the law into his own hands to track down an insane international assassin from Chicago to Dallas. This exceptionally low-budget video premiere gains nothing on DVD. It's identical to tape with a trailer at the beginning that you must fast forward through. It cannot be skipped. No menu. —*MM*
Movie: 🎵🎵 **DVD:** 🎵
Digital Versatile Disc Ltd. (Cat #115, UPC #066479101150). Full frame. Mono. $19.95. Keepcase. *LANG:* English. *FEATURES:* Trailers.
1991 (R) 90m/C Fred Williamson, Bo Svenson, Doran Inghram, Phyllis Cicero; **D:** Fred Williamson; **W:** Charles Eric Johnson; **C:** David Blood; **M:** Mike Logan.

Stella

Melina Mercouri plays Stella, a mercurial spirit in 1950s Athens who defies conventional morality and lives life on her own terms. Bouncing from timid lover Aleko (Alexandrikis) to hot-blooded soccer player Milto (Fountas), Stella's passion for independence faces its greatest threat when Milto forces a marriage proposal on her. Writer/director Cacoyannis goes for a realism similar to the British "kitchen sink" dramas, tackling social mores and sexual politics of the era. We also get an early glimpse of Mercouri's unique sultry earthiness, with her gloriously throaty voice, typified in films like *Never on Sunday* and *Topkapi.* I would have been more involved in the drama had it not been for the shoddy technical performance of the disc. Practically every manner of film deficiency plagues the transfer: registration problems, defects on the source print, and inconsistent contrast levels never let up for the entire full-frame presentation. The audio is just as rough, with glitches, pops, and hiss strewn throughout. Ample levels make for clear dialogue, but distortion increased in direct proportion to the volume of the bouzouki music. Plenty of other DVDs in the marketplace offer crisp monochromatic video and clean soundtracks, making this entry's deficiencies all the more perplexing. Was anyone around when they authored this DVD, or did they just set the machine on autopilot and go out for a burger? —*EP*
Movie: 🎵🎵½ **DVD:** 🎵
Winstar Home Entertainment (Cat #FLV52 14, UPC #720917521428). Full frame. Dolby Digital Mono. Keepcase. *LANG:* Greek. *SUB:* English. *FEATURES:* 8 chapter links ▪ Filmographies and awards ▪ Production credits ▪ Weblinks.
1955 94m/B *GR* Melina Mercouri, Yiorgo Fountas, Aiekos Alexandrikis, Sophia Vembo; **D:** Michael Cacoyannis; **W:** Michael Cacoyannis; **C:** Costa Theodorides; **M:** Manos Hadjidakis.

The Stendahl Syndrome

Rome police detective Anna Manni (Asia Argento, daughter of the director) has an extreme hallucinatory reaction to artwork. While visiting a gallery she collapses and is assisted by Alfredo (Kretschmann), who turns out to be the very serial rapist-killer she has been searching for. After that, the action gets pretty bizarre, even for Argento. This is one of his more successful works, but the full-frame image is not really much sharper than the VHS tape. The extensive extras are the real difference. —*MM* **AKA:** *La Sindrome di Stendhal.*
Movie: 🎵🎵🎵 **DVD:** 🎵🎵½
Troma Team Video (Cat #9982, UPC #7903 57998234). Full frame. $24.99. Keepcase. *LANG:* English. *FEATURES:* 11 chapter links ▪ Talent files ▪ 4 interviews ▪ Stills ▪ Trailers.
1995 118m/C *IT* Asia Argento, Thomas Kretschmann, Marco Leonardi, Luigi Diberti, Paolo Bonacelli, John Quentin; **D:** Dario Argento; **W:** Dario Argento; **C:** Giuseppe Rotunno; **M:** Ennio Morricone.

The Stepdaughter

This is a good-looking, well-acted film that has absolutely no reason to exist. Karen (Roth) is the vindictive daughter given up at birth by Maggie Conner (Pickett). Using the name Susan so she won't be recognized, she has tracked down her birth mother with the intention of killing her and marrying her husband (Gerard). The film is not bloody or quirky enough to merit late-night screenings, and the script and story are not good enough to make it a real film. The disc, however, looks great with good color and nice sound. —*CA*

Movie: ♪ **DVD:** ♪♪
Trimark Home Video (Cat #VM7572D, UPC #031398757221). Widescreen. Dolby Digital Stereo. $24.99. Keepcase. *LANG:* English. *SUB:* French; Spanish; English. *FEATURES:* Theatrical trailer.
2000 (R) 92m/C Andrea Roth, Lisa Dean Ryan, Jaimz Woolvett, Cindy Pickett, Gary Hudson, Gil Gerard, Matt Farnsworth, Lee Dawson; *D:* Peter Paul Liapis; *W:* Richard Dana; *C:* Maximo Munzi.

Stomp Out Loud

The producers of the popular stage show move some of the action to the streets and rooftops of New York. Those are combined with numbers inside the theatre where the performers create rhythmic "music" with found objects. Generally the image is excellent, though in the first scene, aliasing is horrendous. Sound is just as important and it is very good. —*MM*

Movie: ♪♪½ **DVD:** ♪♪½
HBO Home Video (Cat #91484, UPC #026359148422). Full frame. Dolby Digital 5.1 Surround Stereo. $14.98. Snapper. *LANG:* English. *FEATURES:* 14 chapter links • "Making of" featurette • History of the production • Photo gallery • Awards.
1998 55m/C Luke Cresswell, Fraser Morrison, Nick Dwyer, Carl Smith, David Olrod, Sarah Jane Eddy, Thesus Gerard, Fiona Wilkes; *D:* Steve McNicholas, Luke Cresswell; *C:* Christopher Lanzenberg.

Stonebrook

A poor college student (Rowe) runs con-jobs to pay for tuition with the help of his nerdy but clever roommate (Green). As the two get involved in a crime syndicate run by the oily Alexander Tali (Kamel), they end up over-their-heads and tangled in a web of murder, deceit, and treachery. A predictable thriller that is strictly by-the-numbers and marred by too many contrivances and muddled twists. The cast delivers fine performances, but Green is completely unconvincing as the manipulative nerd. The final twist is laughable and ridiculous, and will most likely have audiences throwing popcorn back at the TV screen. Overall, it's a fairly harmless, but undistinguished time-waster. The no-frills DVD, though not 16x9, is a gorgeous transfer of the film, visually clear and free of artifacts. The sound is crisp and impressive. —*DG*

Movie: ♪♪ **DVD:** ♪♪♪♪
MGM Home Entertainment (Cat #10008 31, UPC #02761685137). Widescreen (1.85:1) letterboxed. Dolby Digital Surround. $19.98. Keepcase. *LANG:* English. *SUB:* French; Spanish. *CAP:* English. *FEATURES:* 32 chapter links • Insert card with chapter listing.

1998 (PG-13) 90m/C Seth Green, Brad Rowe, Zoe McLellan, William Mesnik, Stanley Kamel; *D:* Byron W. Thompson; *W:* Steven Robert Morris; *C:* John Tarver; *M:* Dean Grinsfelder.

Stories from Long Island

Please see reviews of *The Brothers McMullen*, *She's the One*, and *No Looking Back*. —*MM*

Movie: ♪♪♪½ **DVD:** ♪♪♪
20th Century Fox Home Entertainment (Cat #2000986, UPC #024543009863). Widescreen anamorphic; full frame. $69.98. Boxed set. *LANG:* English.
2000 ?m/C

Stories from My Childhood

There is a world of enchanting animation outside the Disney domain, but it is rare that American audiences get to see it. This collection offers a look at the exquisite and wondrous work created by the artists of Soyuzmultfilm, said to be Russia's premier animation studio. "The Snow Queen" features the voice of Kathleen Turner as the lonely and reclusive Snow Queen, who, "hurt by a burning love, became cold as ice." "The Wild Swans" is another Hans Christian Andersen fairy tale. "Alice and the Mystery of the Third Planet" recalls the psychedelia of "Yellow Submarine." The colors are vivid, but the source material exhibits surface scratches and fleeting discolorations. —*DL* **AKA:** Mikhail Baryshnikov's Stories from My Childhood.

Movie: ♪♪♪ **DVD:** ♪♪½
Image Entertainment (Cat #1D5521FJDVD, UPC #014381552126). Full frame. Dolby Digital. $24.99. Snapper. *LANG:* English; French; Spanish. *FEATURES:* 28 chapter links.
1998 ?m/C V: Kathleen Turner, Laura San Giacomo, Kirsten Dunst, Cathy Moriarty, JoBeth Williams, James Coburn, James Belushi, Harvey Fierstein.

Stories from My Childhood, Vol. 3

Third volume of short animated works from the Russian studio Soyuzmultfilm is imaginative and more stylized than similar American fare. It also contains less movement and is more reliant on voice-over narration (provided here by the likes of Sarah Jessica Parker, Martin Sheen, Bobcat Goldthwait, and Kathleen Turner). Image quality varies between good and very good, with heavily saturated colors. Contents: "Cinderella," "House on Chicken Legs," "Wishes Come True," and "The Last Petal." —*MM* **AKA:** Mikhail Baryshnikov's Stories from My Childhood, Vol. 3.

Movie: ♪♪♪ **DVD:** ♪♪½
Image Entertainment (Cat #1D523FJDVD, UPC #014381552124). Full frame. Dolby Digital Stereo. $24.99. Snapper. *LANG:*

English; French; Spanish. *FEATURES:* 28 chapter links.
1999 120m/C V: Sarah Jessica Parker, Martin Sheen, Bob(cat) Goldthwait, Kathleen Turner.

Stormswept

On a dark and stormy night in Louisiana, a group of young people making a film are trapped in a haunted mansion. An evil, sexy spirit lives in the place and a mysterious blonde (Kinmont) is camped out in the basement. It's acceptable soft-core fluff. This independently produced video premiere has always had a grainy look and so it gains nothing on DVD. —*MM*

Movie: ♪♪ **DVD:** ♪♪
MTI Home Video (Cat #1034, UPC #03941 4510348). Full frame. $24.95. Keepcase. *LANG:* English. *FEATURES:* 20 chapter links • Trailers • Talent files.
1995 94m/C Julie Hughes, Melissa Moore, Kathleen Kinmont, Justin Carroll, Lorissa McComas, Ed Wasser, Kim Kopf, Hunt Scarritt; *D:* David Marsh; *W:* David Marsh.

The Story of Adele H.

Adele Hugo (Adjani), daughter of novelist Victor, falls in love with an English soldier (Robinson). Her love leads to obsession and, when he refuses her, madness. Nestor Almendros's careful photography has suffered somewhat over the years. Grain and artifacts are visible in the very dark night scenes; light flecks and snow in lighter interiors. Colors are pale, reflecting the period mood. —*MM* **AKA:** L'Histoire d'Adele H.

Movie: ♪♪♪ **DVD:** ♪♪
MGM Home Entertainment (Cat #10014 84, UPC #027616858030). Widescreen (1.66:1) letterboxed. Dolby Digital Mono. $19.98. Keepcase. *LANG:* French. *SUB:* English; French; Spanish. *FEATURES:* 16 chapter links.
1975 (PG) 97m/C FR Isabelle Adjani, Bruce Robinson, Sylvia Marriott; *D:* Francois Truffaut; *W:* Suzanne Schiffman, Jean Gruault; *C:* Nestor Almendros; *M:* Maurice Jaubert. *AWARDS:* Natl. Bd. of Review '75: Actress (Adjani); N.Y. Film Critics '75: Actress (Adjani), Screenplay; Natl. Soc. Film Critics '75: Actress (Adjani); *NOM:* Oscars '75: Actress (Adjani).

The Story of Jacob & Joseph

Fine biblical drama finds brothers Jacob and Esau fighting over their birthright, tearing apart their family for 20 years. When the brothers reconcile, it's only to cast an envious eye on youngest brother Joseph whom they sell into slavery. Acting, direction, and script are well above average for a made-for-TV production. The full-frame image and mono sound are also completely clear. —*MM*

Movie: ♪♪♪ **DVD:** ♪♪½
Columbia Tristar Home Video (Cat #05846, UPC #043396058460). Full frame. Dolby

Digital Mono. $24.99. Keepcase. *LANG:* English; French. *SUB:* English; French; Spanish; Portuguese; Chinese; Korean; Thai. *FEATURES:* 28 chapter links • Talent files • Trailers.
1974 (R) 96m/C Keith Michell, Tony LoBianco, Julian Glover, Colleen Dewhurst, Herschel Bernardi, Harry Andrews; *D:* Michael Cacoyannis; *W:* Ernest Kinoy; *M:* Mikis Theodorakis; *Nar:* Alan Bates.

The Story of O: The Series

The long-form adaptation of Pauline Reage's famous S&M fantasy novel has been a perennial hit on late-night cable TV. It's fairly faithful to the source material and relatively explicit but well within soft-core boundaries. The breathless voice-over narration is really much hotter. Overall, the production values are less-than-stellar and so the dim, grainy DVD image is no better than the source material. The extras, language choices, and director's commentary are all that separates the disc from VHS tape. Each disc contains two hour-long episodes. There are five discs in the series. —MM
Movie: 🎵🎵 **DVD:** 🎵
BRI Video (Cat #BRIDVD113, UPC #79406 1011319). Full frame. $29.98. Keepcase. *LANG:* English; German. *FEATURES:* 4 chapter links • Commentary: director • Booklet • Production notes • Photo gallery • Trailer.
1992 60m/C Claudia Crepeda, Paulo Reis, Nelson Freitas, Gabriela Alves; *D:* Ron Williams; *W:* Eric Rochat.

Straight out of Compton

Stereotype-riddled saga of a tough Compton local, Henry "Hen" Alabaster, and his plan to score some big-time cash and start his own record company. He targets a racist politician named Drake Norelli who's made a fortune laundering mob money. The whole thing seems to want to deliver the meaningful message that "you can't escape your past," but it's lost amidst a mess of clichés and offensive stereotypes. The video transfer is awful; colors are nondescript and blacks are poorly defined (which is probably the result of the graininess of the original negative). The sound is equally horrid, with muffled dialogue and distorted sound effects (which is probably not helped by the atrocious original sound recording—complete with howling winds and other noticeable flaws). —MJT
Movie: 🎵🎵½ **DVD:** 🎵
York Entertainment (Cat #YPD-1059, UPC #750723105925). Full frame. Dolby Digital 5.1 Surround Sound. $14.99. Keepcase. *LANG:* English. *SUB:* Spanish. *FEATURES:* 30 chapter links • Theatrical trailer • Additional York Entertainment trailers.
2000 ?m/C Ryan Combs, Johnny DeaRenzo, Jules Dupree, Sean Epps; *D:* Ryan Combs; *W:* Ryan Combs; *C:* Eric Green.

The Straight Story

This beautiful, heartfelt, and tender film tells the real-life story of 73-year-old Alvin Straight (Farnsworth) who travels from Iowa to Wisconsin on a riding lawnmower to visit his sick brother. Farnsworth's performance is simply stunning; rich, affectionate, and moving. Lynch directs with tremendous sensitivity, creating a film closer in feeling to his *The Elephant Man* than his darker, more challenging works. The disc features a satisfying transfer with stunning colors, but there are a few specs of dirt visible from the transfer print. The Surround sound is fantastic and perfectly conveys Lynch's rich, involving soundscape, as well as Badalamenti's sweeping, haunting music. Still, given the breathtaking use of widescreen, this is a film best appreciated on the big screen. At Lynch's insistence, there are no chapter stops on the disc. —DG
Movie: 🎵🎵🎵🎵 **DVD:** 🎵🎵🎵½
Buena Vista Home Entertainment (Cat #20452, UPC #717951010117). Widescreen (2.35:1) anamorphic. Dolby Digital 5.1. $32.99. Keepcase. *LANG:* English. *SUB:* English. *CAP:* English. *FEATURES:* Theatrical trailer • Insert card.
1999 (G) 111m/C Richard Farnsworth, Harry Dean Stanton, Sissy Spacek; *D:* David Lynch; *W:* John Roach; *C:* Freddie Francis; *M:* Angelo Badalamenti. *AWARDS:* Ind. Spirit '00: Actor (Farnsworth); N.Y. Film Critics '99: Actor (Farnsworth), Cinematog; *NOM:* Oscars '99: Actor (Farnsworth); Golden Globes '00: Actor—Drama (Farnsworth), Orig. Score; Ind. Spirit '00: Director (Lynch), Film, First Screenplay.

Straight to Hell

Imagine the Three Stooges starring in *Reservoir Dogs* set in a Sergio Leone desert town and you've got a good handle on Alex Cox's intentions here. The comedy is extremely broad in this post-modern punk spaghetti gangster oat-opera. Overall, the DVD image is good but not great. The lack of depth and detail come from the original, not the transfer. —MM
Movie: 🎵½ **DVD:** 🎵🎵
Anchor Bay (Cat #DV11314, UPC #013131 131499). Widescreen (1.85:1) anamorphic. Dolby Digital Mono. $24.99. Keepcase. *LANG:* English. *FEATURES:* 27 chapter links • Commentary: Alex Cox, Dick Rude • "Back to Hell" documentary • Video promo, "The Good, the Bad and the Ugly" by the Pogues.
1987 (R) 86m/C Dennis Hopper, Joe Strummer, Elvis Costello, Grace Jones, Jim Jarmusch, Dick Rude, Courtney Love, Sy Richardson, Biff Yeager, Xander Berkeley, Shane McGowan; *D:* Alex Cox; *W:* Alex Cox, Dick Rude; *C:* Tom Richmond; *M:* The Pogues, Pray for Rain.

Strange Case of Dr. Jekyll & Mr. Hyde

Please see review of *Dracula / The Strange Case of Dr. Jekyll & Mr. Hyde.*
Movie: 🎵🎵

1968 128m/C Jack Palance, Leo Genn, Oscar Homolka, Billie Whitelaw, Denholm Elliott; *D:* Charles Jarrott; *M:* Robert Cobert.

The Strange Love of Martha Ivers

Douglas is good in his screen debut as the wimpy spouse of unscrupulous Martha (Stanwyck). She shines as a woman who must stay with him because of a crime she committed long ago. This film noir has been restored to a remarkable degree. The black-and-white image shows some light fading in a few spots, but for the most part it looks very good. Sound is fine. —MM
Movie: 🎵🎵🎵 **DVD:** 🎵🎵🎵
Image Entertainment (Cat #HRS9459, UPC #014381949528). Full frame. Dolby Digital Mono. $24.99. Snapper. *LANG:* English. *FEATURES:* 9 chapter links.
1946 117m/B Barbara Stanwyck, Van Heflin, Kirk Douglas, Lizabeth Scott, Judith Anderson; *D:* Lewis Milestone; *W:* Robert Rossen; *C:* Victor Milner; *M:* Miklos Rozsa. *AWARDS: NOM:* Oscars '46: Story.

The Strange Woman

Please see review for *Edgar Ulmer Collection, Vol. 1.*
Movie: 🎵🎵
1946 100m/B Hedy Lamarr, George Sanders, Louis Hayward, Gene Lockhart, Hillary Brooke, June Storey; *D:* Edgar G. Ulmer; *W:* Herb Meadow; *C:* Lucien N. Andriot; *M:* Carmen Dragon.

The Stranger from Venus

Reworking of ideas from *Day the Earth Stood Still* is a bit slow in the telling, but well acted by a mostly British cast. A nameless Venusian (Dantine) arrives and heals Susan North (Neal) of injuries suffered in a car crash. He then worries about the fate of the planet. Special effects won't knock anybody's socks off now. A few vertical scratches and intermittent static are the only problems with this very good black-and-white image. —MM
AKA: Immediate Disaster; The Venusian.
Movie: 🎵🎵½ **DVD:** 🎵🎵½
Image Entertainment (Cat #ID9600CODVD, UPC #014381960020). Full frame. Dolby Digital Mono. $24.99. Snapper. *LANG:* English. *FEATURES:* 14 chapter links.
1954 78m/B Patricia Neal, Helmut Dantine, Derek Bond; *D:* Bob Balaban; *W:* Hans Jacoby; *C:* Ken Talbot; *M:* Eric Spear.

Strawberry Fields

Unsettled 16-year-old Irene (Nakamura) sees visions of the ghost of her dead sister, and those lead her back to her parents' incarceration in an internment camp for Japanese Americans during World War II. This is a curious road movie. It was made on a low budget but looks very good. Some minor aliasing is the only visual problem. Otherwise, image is fine and so is the sound, particularly for the clear voice-over narration. —*MM*

Movie: 🐾🐾🐾 **DVD:** 🐾🐾🐾
Vanguard International Cinema, Inc. (Cat #1-892649-74-8, UPC #658769006636). Widescreen (1.66:1) letterboxed. $29.95. Keepcase. *LANG:* English. *FEATURES:* 10 chapter links.
1997 86m/C Suzy Nakamura, James Sie, Chris Tashima, Marilyn Tokuda, Reiko Mathieu, Peter Yoshida, Heather Yoshimura, Takayo Fischer; *D:* Rea Tajiri; *W:* Rea Tajiri, Kerri Sakamoto; *C:* Zack Winestine; *M:* Bundy Brown.

Street Gun

Small-time hood Joe Webster (Pagel) pines for some sense of accomplishment in his life. A tip from his hustler-friend lands Joe in the good graces of the local crime boss. As he ingratiates himself into his new malevolent world, the shadows yield betrayal, murder, and no place to hide. Potentially interesting premise is botched, with co-writer/director Milloy aping John Woo gun pyrotechnics and *Reservoir Dogs* attitude (a Woo rip-off once removed). There is also the thorny dilemma of rooting for a hero who aspires to be an exceptional thug. Transfer is clean and detailed, exhibiting strong colors. Edge enhancement apparent in some places. The audio is a little shrill with many instances of spitty dialogue. For those with enough stamina to make it to the end, there's a trailer for your troubles. —*EP*

Movie: 🐾 **DVD:** 🐾🐾🐾
Image Entertainment (Cat #ID6399NGDVD, UPC #1438163392). Full frame. Dolby Digital Stereo. $24.99. Snapper. *LANG:* English. *FEATURES:* 16 chapter links ☛ Trailer.
1996 92m/C Justin Pagel, Scott Cooke, Michael Egan; *D:* Travis Milloy; *W:* Travis Milloy, Timothy Lee; *C:* Joel King.

Street Scene

Based on a Pulitzer Prize–winning play, the film charts the ebbs and flows of life in a 1930s New York tenement during a hot summer day. Both temperatures and eyebrows rise when the residents chat openly about the latest scandals in their community, particularly the tribulations of the Maurrant family. Director Vidor, in collusion with cinematographer George Barnes, creates an energetic atmosphere while honoring the confined stage. Rice's dialogue must have shocked both stage and movie audiences in its day (he adapted the screenplay for the Samuel Goldwyn production), with middle-class characters passing the day by passing judgment on anyone within their cross hairs, rumors whispered by a bored, sweltering Greek chorus. Numerous speckles and scratches plague the source elements. The DVD does what it can under the circumstances. Contrast levels vary, one moment exhibiting a pristine image with sharp detail delineation, only to have the next scene blur amid murky blacks and visible film grain. The mono soundtrack is fine, with

the occasional distortions to remind the viewer of its age. Perhaps not ground-breaking enough for modern audiences, this title should find interest among Vidor and Goldwyn aficionados. —*EP*

Movie: 🐾🐾🐾 **DVD:** 🐾🐾½
Image Entertainment (Cat #ID9059VMDVD, UPC #1438190592). Full frame. Dolby Digital Mono. $24.99. Snapper. *LANG:* English. *FEATURES:* 11 chapter links.
1931 80m/B Sylvia Sidney, William "Buster" Collier Jr., Estelle Taylor, Beulah Bondi, David Landau; *D:* King Vidor; *W:* Elmer Rice; *C:* George Barnes; *M:* Alfred Newman.

Striptease

Carl Hiaasen's political/crime comedy novel is transformed into an inept star vehicle for Demi Moore, and her limitations have seldom been more apparent. She plays Erin Grant, a plucky mom whose no-good rotten ex- (Patrick) has won custody of their little daughter. To earn enough to pay her lawyer's fees, she is cruelly forced to be a dancer at the Eager Beaver strip joint. That's where Congressman Dilbeck (Reynolds) first sees her and falls in love. At the same time, he brains another patron with a champagne bottle and sets in motion a plot that attempts to combine pathos with slapstick, suspense, and stripping. The inclusion of extra footage of the star dancing topless is not nearly enough to earn a recommendation. Even though it looks and sounds fine on DVD, this is an atrocious film on any medium at any length. —*MM*

Movie: woof **DVD:** 🐾🐾
Warner Home Video, Inc. (Cat #2569). Widescreen letterboxed; full frame. Dolby Digital Surround Stereo. $19.98. Snapper. *LANG:* English; French. *SUB:* French. *CAP:* English. *FEATURES:* 25 chapter links.
1996 (R) 115m/C Demi Moore, Burt Reynolds, Ving Rhames, Armand Assante, Robert Patrick, Rumer Willis; *D:* Andrew Bergman; *W:* Andrew Bergman; *C:* Stephen Goldblatt; *M:* Howard Shore. *AWARDS:* Golden Raspberries '96: Worst Picture, Worst Actress (Moore), Worst Director (Bergman), Worst Screenplay, Worst Song ("Pussy, Pussy, Pussy (Whose Kitty Cat Are You?)"); *NOM:* Golden Raspberries '96: Worst Support. Actor (Reynolds).

Stuart Saves His Family

It's difficult to make a movie about irritating characters without making an irritating movie, and that's exactly what this expanded *SNL* skit is. Irritating. Fired from his self-help show, new-age self-help guru Stuart Smalley (Franken) returns home to help his messed-up family sort out their problems and an inheritance. The nonplot gives Stuart a chance to do his 12-step shtick. The DVD image is fine for a mainstream Hollywood production. Personally, I find it impossible to believe that anyone could voluntarily watch the whole thing without hitting the scan-forward button. —*MM*

Movie: 🐾 **DVD:** 🐾🐾
Paramount Home Video (Cat #33065, UPC #097363306542). Widescreen anamorphic. Dolby Digital 5.1 Surround Stereo; Dolby Digital Surround. $29.99. Keepcase. *LANG:* English; French. *FEATURES:* Trailer ☛ 24 chapter links.
1994 (PG-13) 97m/C Al Franken, Laura San Giacomo, Vincent D'Onofrio, Shirley Knight, Harris Yulin, Julia Sweeney, Aaron Lustig, Darrell Larson, Camille Saviola, Gerrit Graham, Theodore (Ted) Raimi, Joe Flaherty; *D:* Harold Ramis; *W:* Al Franken; *C:* Lauro Escorel; *M:* Marc Shaiman.

The Stuff

The titular "Stuff" is a dessert treat that is quickly becoming the most popular confection in the country. It's low in calories and tastes great, but nobody knows just what it is. It also has a life of its own. Director Cohen uses it as a platform to satirize the fads that sweep America. His commentary track is very entertaining. Given the age and low budget of the film, the picture is surprisingly crisp and clear. There are some infrequent defects from the source print visible and a slight amount of grain. Mono sound is adequate with no hiss. —*ML/MM*

Movie: 🐾🐾 **DVD:** 🐾🐾½
Anchor Bay (Cat #11263). Widescreen (1.85:1) anamorphic. Dolby Digital Mono. $24.98. Keepcase. *LANG:* English. *FEATURES:* Commentary: Larry Cohen ☛ Theatrical trailer.
1985 (R) 93m/C Michael Moriarty, Andrea Marcovicci, Garrett Morris, Paul Sorvino, Danny Aiello, Brooke Adams, Patrick O'Neal, Alexander Scourby, Scott Bloom, James Dixon, Tammy Grimes, Clara Peller, Abe Vigoda; *D:* Larry Cohen; *W:* Larry Cohen; *C:* Paul Glickman; *M:* Anthony Guefen.

Submerged

The audio commentary by director Ed Raymond is much more entertaining than the actual film, a direct-to-video actioner designed to stoke the DVD product pipeline. Terrorists hijack and intentionally sink an airplane containing a computer board that controls a satellite capable of launching a nuclear holocaust. Of interest only for those wondering what Dennis Weaver is up to these days. Raymond is a pseudonym for resourceful poverty-row director Fred Olen Ray, who to his credit, has stocked the cast with great character actors, including Tim Thomerson and Fred Williamson (top-billed Coolio gets maybe five minutes of screen time as a most unreliable security guard). The film's imperfections are only heightened on DVD. Some dark, interior scenes are grainy. Special effects sequences look even cheesier than they do on video. —*DL*

Movie: 🐾 **DVD:** 🐾🐾🐾
Paramount Home Video (Cat #82050, UPC #097368205048). Widescreen. Dolby Digital; 5.1 Surround; Dolby Surround. $29.99. Keepcase. *LANG:* English. *SUB:* English; Spanish. *FEATURES:* Commentary: Ed Ray-

mond ● Bios and filmographies of cast and filmmakers ● Theatrical trailer ● 20 chapter links.
2000 (R) 95m/C Coolio, Nicole Eggert, Fred Williamson, Dennis Weaver, Maxwell Caulfield, Brent Huff, Tim Thomerson, Fred Williamson; **D:** Ed Raymond; **W:** Steve Latshaw; **C:** Thomas Callaway.

The Substitute 4: Failure Is Not an Option

Inexplicably, this series has lasted for four installments. Here, cop Karl Thomasson (Williams) poses as a teacher at a military academy where young neo-Nazis are taking over. Image is no better than it has to be for a low- to mid-budget video premiere. The most interesting part of the disc is director Robert Radler's to-the-point commentary track. He doesn't make the film out to be anything more than it is, and he has some interesting things to say about the business where cable broadcast and home video are important considerations. Image is good, with heavy grain appearing in low-light interiors. —*MM*
Movie: 🎞️🎞️ *DVD:* 🎞️🎞️½
Artisan Entertainment (Cat #11735, UPC #012236117353). Widescreen (1.77:1) anamorphic. Dolby Digital 5.1 Surround Stereo; Dolby Digital Surround. $24.98. Keepcase. *LANG:* English. *FEATURES:* 24 chapter links ● 2 deleted scenes ● Photo gallery ● Talent files ● Production notes.
2000 (R) 91m/C Treat Williams, Angie Everhart, Bill Nunn, Tim Abell, Simon Rhee, Patrick Kilpatrick, Michael Weatherly, Grayson Fricke; **D:** Robert Radler; **W:** Dan Gurskis; **C:** Richard Rawlings; **M:** Steve Edwards.

Suburbia

When a group of punk rockers move into a condemned suburban development, they become the targets of a vigilante group. On her commentary track, director Spheeris talks about the autobiographical elements and factual details that underpin her work. That does not make the film any more successful as drama. It's a low-budget, needlessly violent exercise in nihilism. On DVD it looks bad; it's supposed to look bad—looking bad is the point. —*MM* *AKA:* The Wild Side.
Movie: 🎞️ *DVD:* 🎞️🎞️½
New Concorde (Cat #NH20248D, UPC #736991424890). Full frame. $19.98. Keepcase. *LANG:* English. *FEATURES:* 24 chapter links ● Trailers ● Commentary: Penelope Spheeris ● Thumbnail bios.
1983 (R) 99m/C Chris Pederson, Bill Coyne, Jennifer Clay, Timothy Eric O'Brien, Andrew Pece, Don Allen; **D:** Penelope Spheeris; **W:** Penelope Spheeris; **C:** Tim Suhrstedt; **M:** Alex Gibson.

Suddenly, Last Summer

The years have transformed this overripe melon of a melodrama into an alternative classic. The hyperventilating dialogue (perpetrated by Tennessee Williams and abetted by Gore Vidal) is matched by flamboyant overacting. Both begin on a high, hysterical note and intensify straight through to the famously bizarre conclusion. In 1937 New Orleans, a handsome young brain surgeon (Clift) is summoned by the wealthy widow Mrs. Venable (Hepburn) to perform a lobotomy on her niece Cathy (Taylor at her most voluptuous). Why? Because Cathy was involved with Mrs. V's son Sebastian's mysterious and unsavory death on a Mediterranean island. Hepburn, who appears to be playing a caricature of her older self, received an inexplicable Oscar nomination for her work. Clift never completely recovered from the auto accident he'd suffered two years before and is a bit too diffident and twitchy. Still, the ensemble scenery chewing is a wonder to behold. The DVD image does justice to cinematographer Jack Hildyard's carefully detailed black-and-white work—both the jungle-like garden interiors and the sun-blasted finale. —*MM*
Movie: 🎞️🎞️🎞️ *DVD:* 🎞️🎞️🎞️
Columbia Tristar Home Video (Cat #4752). Widescreen; full frame. Dolby Digital Mono. $24.95. Keepcase. *LANG:* English. *SUB:* English; Spanish; Portuguese; Korean; Thai; Chinese. *FEATURES:* 28 chapter links ● Photo montage ● Ads ● Trailer ● Cast and crew thumbnail bios.
1959 114m/B Elizabeth Taylor, Katharine Hepburn, Montgomery Clift, Mercedes McCambridge, Albert Dekker; **D:** Joseph L. Mankiewicz; **W:** Gore Vidal; **C:** Jack Hildyard; **M:** Malcolm Arnold. *AWARDS:* Golden Globes '60: Actress—Drama (Taylor); *NOM:* Oscars '59: Actress (Hepburn), Actress (Taylor), Art Dir./Set Dec., B&W.

Sudie & Simpson

Heart-tugging story is set in 1940s Georgia. Twelve-year-old white Sudie's (Gilbert) forbidden friendship with Simpson (Gossett Jr.), an adult black man, provides fodder for a lot of talk in their small town. Racial barriers finally cause Simpson to be accused of child molestation. The story is based on Sara Flanigan Carter's autobiographical novel. The made-for-cable production gains little on DVD. Image and sound are essentially identical to VHS. —*MM*
Movie: 🎞️🎞️🎞️ *DVD:* 🎞️🎞️
Xenon Entertainment (Cat #XE XX 4089 DVD, UPC #000799408926). Full frame. $19.98. Keepcase. *LANG:* English. *FEATURES:* 18 chapter links ● Trailers.
1990 95m/C Sara Gilbert, Louis Gossett Jr., Frances Fisher, John M. Jackson, Paige Danahy, Ken Strong; **D:** Joan Tewkesbury; **W:** Sara Flanigan Carter, Ken Koser; **C:** Mario DiLeo; **M:** Michel Colombier.

Summer Rental

Candy plays a stressed-out air-traffic controller who takes the wife and kids for a month on the beach in Florida. Of course, everything possible goes wrong. The star could bring something to the weakest of plots and this one needs all the help it can get. The first half struggles and the second is weaker. The image is no improvement over a widescreen tape. Ditto sound. —*MM*
Movie: 🎞️🎞️ *DVD:* 🎞️🎞️
Paramount Home Video (Cat #01785, UPC #097360178548). Widescreen anamorphic. Dolby Digital Mono. $24.99. Keepcase. *LANG:* English; French. *SUB:* English. *FEATURES:* 12 chapter links ● Trailer.
1985 (PG) 87m/C John Candy, Rip Torn, Richard Crenna, Karen Austin, Kerri Green, John Larroquette, Pierrino Mascarino; **D:** Carl Reiner; **W:** Mark Reisman, Jeremy Stevens; **C:** Ric Waite; **M:** Alan Silvestri.

A Summer's Tale

The third of the "Four Seasons" series is typical Rohmer—talky, understated, sexy, unhurried. Over the course of a summer, grad student Gaspard (Poupaud) must choose among three delightful young women who are attracted to him: Margot (Langlet), Solene (Simon), and Lena (Nolin). All of us should be faced with such problems. The film looks much better and sharper than Rohmer's older work available on disc. Some artifacts are visible in bright exterior tracking shots and even more in some night scenes, but those are relatively meaningless to this kind of languid character study. The yellow subtitles are easy to read and are not burned in. —*MM* *AKA:* Conte d'Ete.
Movie: 🎞️🎞️🎞️ *DVD:* 🎞️🎞️🎞️
Winstar Home Entertainment (Cat #FLV5240, UPC #720917524023). Full frame. $24.98. Keepcase. *LANG:* French. *SUB:* English. *FEATURES:* 16 chapter links ● Filmographies and awards ● Production credits.
1996 133m/C *FR* Melvil Poupaud, Amanda Langlet, Aurelia Nolin, Gwenaelle Simon; **D:** Eric Rohmer; **W:** Eric Rohmer; **C:** Diane Baratier; **M:** Sebastien Erms, Philippe Eidel.

Sunshine

Sprawling look at four generations of an assimilated Hungarian-Jewish family covers a lot of time at the expense of cohesiveness and character. The title refers to the health tonic that makes the family fortune and is a pun on the family's original name, Sonnenschein. Fiennes turns up in three roles as the family prospers in Budapest by changing their name to avoid the anti-Semetic society—eventually converting to Catholicism. It does not protect them, however, from the Nazi holocaust and the turbulent post-war period leading to the Hungarian revolution. On DVD there is a very slight loss of detail in heavy black clothes, but that's inevitable. Reds are crisp throughout, particularly toward the end when the color is more important. This is a sumptuous, ambitious production that really needs to be seen on the largest screen possible. —*MM*
Movie: 🎞️🎞️🎞️ *DVD:* 🎞️🎞️🎞️
Paramount Home Video (Cat #33880, UPC #097363388043). Widescreen anamor-

phic. Dolby Digital 5.1 Surround Stereo; Dolby Digital Surround. $29.99. Keepcase. *LANG:* English. *SUB:* English. *FEATURES:* 29 chapter links.

1999 (R) 180m/C *CA HU* Ralph Fiennes, Rosemary Harris, Rachel Weisz, Jennifer Ehle, Molly Parker, Deborah Kara Unger, James Frain, William Hurt, John Neville, Miriam Margolyes, Mark Strong; *D:* Istvan Szabo; *W:* Istvan Szabo, Israel Horovitz; *C:* Lajos Koltai; *M:* Maurice Jarre. *AWARDS:* Genie '99: Film; *NOM:* Genie '99: Actor (Fiennes), Actress (Harris, Ehle), Director (Szabo), Support. Actor (Frain, Hurt), Support. Actress (Weisz, Unger), Orig. Score.

Supergirl

Anchor Bay has built its reputation on restoring lesser-known titles to their best possible shape, even when the individual films might seem, at first blush, not to deserve such treatment. That's what many said about this "limited edition" of a spin-off sequel that has never been particularly popular with general audiences, comic book fans, or critics. And even though it is far from perfect and very much a product of its time, the film is an enjoyable comedy. Helen Slater, an excellent actress who's never quite found the right role, is the title character, Superman's niece. Faye Dunaway camps it up to a fare-thee-well as the evil Selena who has possession of a magical paperweight upon which the very fate of the world depends. The DVD contains both the 124-minute "international" version of the film and the 138-minute "director's cut." Both are so sharp on DVD that the wires are visible in some of the flying scenes. Sound is fine, even the mono on the longer version. Recommended mostly to fans of the cast and those curious big-budget sf epics of the early '80s. —*MM*

Movie: 🎵🎵½ **DVD:** 🎵🎵🎵½
Anchor Bay (Cat #DV11109, UPC #013131 110999). Widescreen (2.35:1) letterboxed. Dolby Digital 5.1 Surround Stereo; Dolby Digital Mono. $24.99. Keepcase. *LANG:* English. *FEATURES:* 24 chapter links ● Booklet ● "Making of" featurette ● Storyboards ● Stills gallery ● Cast and crew thumbnail bios ● Commentary: director Szwarc and consultant Scott Michael Bosco ● Trailers and TV spots.

1984 (PG) 114m/C *GB* Faye Dunaway, Helen Slater, Peter O'Toole, Mia Farrow, Brenda Vaccaro, Marc McClure, Simon Ward, Hart Bochner, Maureen Teefy, David Healy, Matt Frewer; *D:* Jeannot Szwarc; *W:* David Odell; *C:* Alan Hume; *M:* Jerry Goldsmith.

Superman: The Movie

Possibly the greatest comic book-to-film adaptation ever made, this ambitious, exhilarating thrill-ride treats the story of the "man of steel" as classic Americana. The movie, told in three different tones and styles (the cold formal world of Krypton, the warm farmland community of Smallville, and the crime-ridden world of Metrop-

olis) establishes his origin of Superman and launches him into his first major confrontation with evil genius Lex Luthor. The casting is pitch-perfect, with Hackman, Beatty, and Perrine effective (albeit hilarious) foils to the straight and narrow Superman. Brando manages to be both otherworldly and affectionate: his farewell speech to Jor-El beautifully performed. The real star of this film (obviously) is Christopher Reeve—simply the greatest Superman the screen has ever seen. The chemistry between Reeve and the charming Kidder (who fought mildly during production) is stunning and completely convincing. Watch for uncredited cameos by Kirk Alyn, who first played Superman on the big screen, and Noel Neill, who played Lois Lane on the 1950s TV series. Williams's sweeping and pulse-pounding score (whose main theme sounds curiously like the old Universal logo music) cannot be underrated. While the flying sequences are still exhilarating, some of the model effects near the end are pretty dated. The disc is absolutely gorgeous: sharp, clear, and colorful—a major improvement over the dark, ugly laserdisc. Many effects shots have been digitally cleaned up and some optical work has been restored to its intended brilliance. There are some minor instances of digital grain, but this is most likely due to the intentionally soft smoky look featured in the photography. The 5.1 Surround remix is a knockout, giving the film (especially the legendary opening titles) incredible sweep and presence. Originally released at 143 minutes, this version restores 9 minutes of crucial scenes to the film. A version was released to ABC-TV as a two-part event several years back which had a running time of around 166 minutes (discounting recap, duplicate opening, and end title sequences). While there has been some griping that this disc does not include those extra 12 minutes, this cut (which eliminates some of the padding in the TV version) plays the best out of all three. One wishes those bits had been included as a supplement, though. The documentaries are fascinating, informative, and feature new interviews, some vintage behind-the-scenes footage, and hilarious effects tests (who ever thought we'd ever get a chance to see those?). The music outtakes are interesting and one of them features a brief snippet of Williams cuing the orchestra before the main theme starts. The two deleted scenes (though rightfully removed) are hilarious and in excellent condition. The commentary track by Donner and friend Tom Mankiewicz, who didn't get proper credit for scripting the movie, is a gas—although it assumes familiarity on the part of the viewer of some of the behind-the-scenes turmoil that troubled this production. The screen tests are a hoot. Only complaint? The snapper packaging seems cheap next to what is used for other special-edition discs of this caliber. Followed by three sequels, all of which are available on DVD separately or in a boxed set with the first film. —*DG/MB*

Movie: 🎵🎵🎵½ **DVD:** 🎵🎵🎵½

Warner Home Video, Inc. (Cat #1013, UPC #012569101326). Widescreen (2.35:1) anamorphic. Dolby Digital 5.1. $24.99. Snapper. *LANG:* English. *SUB:* English; French; Spanish; Portuguese. *CAP:* English. *FEATURES:* 44 chapter links ● 2 deleted scenes ● Commentary: Donner, writer Tom Mankiewicz ● 3 new behind-the-scenes documentaries ● Theatrical trailers and TV spot ● Music-only audio track ● Screen tests ● DVD-ROM storyboard/scene comparisons.

1978 (PG) 152m/C Christopher Reeve, Margot Kidder, Marlon Brando, Gene Hackman, Glenn Ford, Susannah York, Ned Beatty, Valerie Perrine, Jackie Cooper, Marc McClure, Trevor Howard, Sarah Douglas, Terence Stamp, Jack O'Halloran, Phyllis Thaxter; *D:* Richard Donner; *W:* Mario Puzo, Robert Benton, David Newman; *C:* Geoffrey Unsworth; *M:* John Williams. *AWARDS:* Oscars '78: Visual FX; *NOM:* Oscars '78: Film Editing, Sound, Orig. Score.

Superman 2

The three Kryptonian villains (as seen in the first film) are accidentally released from their imprisonment in the Phantom Zone by an atomic shockwave. Arriving on Earth, they discover they all have superpowers equal to those of Superman and quickly bring the world to its knees. Thrilling sequel provides wall-to-wall excitement, but misses some of the awe and epic wonder of the first film. The strong dramatic conflict (Superman giving up his powers to be able to consummate his relationship with Lois Lane) at its center makes some of the dark development of the story even more gripping. The troubled production occasionally shows some of its rough edges: Hackman's obvious body double, the disappearance of a few characters, and dialogue relooped by a Hackman impersonator. Richard Donner actually directed much of the sequel's footage while making *Superman: The Movie.* At the time, both films were to be completed simultaneously, but producers abandoned those plans when money got tight. Later, they fired Donner from *Superman 2,* and the film was completed by Richard Lester, who had the script revised and re-shot some of Donner's scenes and discarded many others. Donner is uncredited. Overall, it's a satisfying affair miles ahead of the two inferior sequels to follow, and Reeve is excellent. The DVD is quite a disappointment after the superlative treatment lavished upon the first film. The film has not been restored at all, and it shows. Fortunately, a new anamorphic video transfer was done, but the picture shows wear and tear in the source elements, and the 2.0 soundtrack with lackluster frequency response is nothing to boast about. Most disappointing is the lack of extras as compared to what's on the first movie's DVD. Fortunately, this is reflected in a lower price. Warner missed an opportunity to tell the tumultuous behind-the-scenes story of this sequel by not commissioning a documentary. —*MB/DG*

Movie: ♪♪♪ **DVD:** ♪♪♪
Warner Home Video, Inc. (Cat #11120, UPC #08539111202). Widescreen (2.35:1) anamorphic. Dolby Surround Stereo. $19.98. Snapper. *LANG:* English; French. *SUB:* English; French; Spanish; Portugese. *CAP:* English. *FEATURES:* 37 chapter links • Theatrical trailer • Talent bios.
1980 (PG) 128m/C Christopher Reeve, Margot Kidder, Gene Hackman, Ned Beatty, Jackie Cooper, Sarah Douglas, Jack O'Halloran, Susannah York, Marc McClure, Terence Stamp, Valerie Perrine, E.G. Marshall; *D:* Richard Lester; *W:* Mario Puzo, David Newman; *C:* Geoffrey Unsworth, Robert Paynter; *M:* John Williams.

Superman 3

Computer whiz Gus Gorman (Pryor) teams with an evil businessman (Robert Vaughn, at his slimy best) to take over the world. After an attempt to kill Superman with artificial Kryptonite fails, the evildoers build a gigantic supercomputer with the intention of killing the "Last Son of Krypton" for good. Uneven, to say the least, with some hit-and-miss special effects work. Though amusing, Pryor's presence here betrays a complete lack of confidence from the producers and the de-emphasis on Superman's role in the story leaves this one lacking. Margot Kidder (looking even more charming than in *2*) only appears briefly, and is sorely missed. O'Toole returns as Lana Lang (as in *1*) but the character and her story are weak. An opening homage to silent gag slapstick is fairly funny but awkward and out of place. The "evil Superman" scenes and the battle with his alter ego Clark Kent are high points and make this passable viewing. The disc is sharp, clean, and colorful, and the widescreen framing is a tremendous improvement over the unwatchable pan and scan version. It could be just a tad wider, though, as evidenced in two very widely framed scenes that just barely capture the characters on the outer edge. The sound is fine but lacking in strong channel separation for a Surround track. Like the *Superman 2* disc, this one, unfortunately, does not include any of the scenes shot for TV (19 minutes, including a title sequence not played over the opening scenes) either in the film or as an extra. The trailer is interesting and includes a few unfinished effects shots. The filmographies are less than adequate, and feature only Reeve, Pryor, and Lester. —*DG*
Movie: ♪♪ **DVD:** ♪♪♪½
Warner Home Video, Inc. (Cat #11320, UPC #08539113202). Widescreen (2.35:1) anamorphic. Dolby Surround Stereo. $19.98. Snapper. *LANG:* English; French. *SUB:* English; French; Spanish; Portugese. *CAP:* English. *FEATURES:* 39 chapter links • Theatrical trailer • Cast and crew filmographies.
1983 (PG) 123m/C Christopher Reeve, Richard Pryor, Annette O'Toole, Jackie Cooper, Margot Kidder, Marc McClure, Annie Ross, Robert Vaughn; *D:* Richard Lester; *W:* David Newman; *M:* John Williams.

Superman 4: The Quest for Peace

After a young child writes to him, Superman vows to rid the world of nuclear weapons, and save the Earth from its own destruction. At the same time, Lex Luthor (Hackman) escapes from a chain gang with the help of his "Valley" accented nephew (Cryer) and creates a "Nuclear Man" (Mark Pillow, in yellow, honeycomb-patterned tights, '80s soap opera hair, Luthor's voice, and long gold fingernails) to ruin Superman's plan. Awful, embarrassing sequel has its heart in the right place but is totally undone by shoddy effects work, a truly lame villain, a lack of momentum, and some miserable comedy. Ned Beatty's Otis is sorely missed. The producers successfully destroyed the franchise with this one. (Fourteen years without a Superman film? Someone's asleep at the wheel.) The disc is colorful and clear but very grainy and the soundtrack has no Surround presence at all. Like the other releases of the Superman sequels, this one doesn't include any of the footage inserted into TV broadcasts (about two minutes) nor any of the footage from the longer unreleased 134-minute version. Those extra perks might have made this worth having as a curio, but without them it's just a waste. —*DG*
Movie: ♪½ **DVD:** ♪♪♪
Warner Home Video, Inc. (Cat #11757, UPC #085391175728). Widescreen (2.35:1) anamorphic. Dolby Stereo Surround. $19.98. Snapper. *LANG:* English; French. *SUB:* English; Spanish; French; Portugese. *FEATURES:* Theatrical trailer • 29 chapter links.
1987 (PG) 90m/C Christopher Reeve, Gene Hackman, Jon Cryer, Marc McClure, Margot Kidder, Mariel Hemingway, Sam Wanamaker; *D:* Sidney J. Furie; *W:* Mark Rosenthal; *M:* John Williams; *V:* Susannah York.

Supernova

Troubled sf action/effects flick spent a year sitting on the shelf, and was reportedly re-edited by Francis Ford Coppola to a "PG-13" rating. Director Walter Hill removed his name from the film, which has been re-reedited to an "R" rating for home video. It's still a relatively attractive mess. Nick Vanzant (Spader) is stuck piloting a 22nd-century medical rescue spacecraft after the original captain (Forster) is killed. The craft receives a distress call and makes the mistake of rescuing Karl (Facinelli), who has a device that looks like a crystal bowling pin and might bring about the destruction of the universe. Bummer. It's hard to take any of the action seriously when the characters wear what appear to be down-filled spacesuits that make them look like Michelin tire people. On DVD, the sophisticated visuals are more interesting than cool, and they display excessive aliasing. The beefed-up Surround mix is intrusive. —*MM*
Movie: ♪♪ **DVD:** ♪♪½
MGM Home Entertainment (Cat #100083 32). Widescreen letterboxed. Dolby Digital

5.1 Surround Stereo. $26.99. Snapper. *LANG:* English; Spanish. *SUB:* English; Spanish. *FEATURES:* 24 chapter links • Trailer • Deleted scenes.
1999 (PG-13) 91m/C James Spader, Angela Bassett, Robin Tunney, Peter Facinelli, Lou Diamond Phillips, Wilson Cruz, Robert Forster; *D:* Walter Hill; *W:* David Campbell Wilson; *C:* Lloyd Ahern II; *M:* David Williams.

Superstar: The Life and Times of Andy Warhol

Early on in his commentary track, Chuck Workman states that he's interested in images—physical images created by artists and illusory images that are taken for substance. Both are completely appropriate to this ironic, kinetic documentary. It's a rollicking look at the wild era Warhol inspired and exploited. Interviewees range from Warhol cohorts like Dennis Hopper to proud executives at the Campbell Soup plant. One highlight: a Warhol guest shot on *The Love Boat*. On DVD, the original material looks fine. The clips from TV broadcasts are intentionally weak. —*MM*
Movie: ♪♪♪½ **DVD:** ♪♪♪½
Winstar Home Entertainment (Cat #WHE73 116, UPC #720917311623). Full frame. $24.98. Keepcase. *LANG:* English. *FEATURES:* 16 chapter links • Commentary: Chuck Workman • Production credits • Music credits • Filmographies.
1990 87m/C Tom Wolfe, Sylvia Miles, David Hockney, Taylor Mead, Dennis Hopper; *D:* Chuck Workman; *W:* Chuck Workman; *C:* Burleigh Wartes.

Support Your Local Gunfighter

Garner plays western conman Latigo Smith as a variation on Brett Maverick. He comes to the small town of Purgatory and is taken for a notorious gunfighter. Elam is the bumbling sidekick and Pleshette is the heavily armed love interest. The cliché-filled western is a lot of fun with plenty of familiar faces in the cast. DVD appears to be an accurate reproduction of an exceptionally grainy original, particularly in the night scenes. Sound is fine. —*MM*
Movie: ♪♪♪ **DVD:** ♪♪½
MGM Home Entertainment (Cat #100015 95, UPC #027616859051). Widescreen (1.85:1) letterboxed. Dolby Digital Mono. $19.98. Keepcase. *LANG:* English; Spanish. *SUB:* French; Spanish. *CAP:* English. *FEATURES:* 16 chapter links • Trailer.
1971 (G) 92m/C James Garner, Jack Elam, Suzanne Pleshette, Harry (Henry) Morgan, Dub Taylor, John Dehner, Joan Blondell, Ellen Corby, Henry Jones; *D:* Burt Kennedy; *W:* James Edward Grant; *C:* Harry Stradling Jr.; *M:* Jack Elliott, Allyn Ferguson.

Surfing Hollow Days

Bruce Brown's (*The Endless Summer*) film is a free-form documentary that follows

several surfers to beaches in Hawaii, Australia, New Zealand, Texas, Mexico, and Florida. The images are unpolished; the enthusiasm of all concerned is unfeigned. At the time the film was made, 1961, surfing was just being embraced by the larger popular culture and so the film has a certain "end of an innocent era" feeling. It's also a valuable historical piece. —*MM*
Movie: 🎵🎵½ **DVD:** 🎵🎵
Image Entertainment (Cat #ID8794OTDVD, UPC #014381879421). Full frame. Dolby Digital Mono. $24.99. Snapper. *LANG:* English. *FEATURES:* 18 chapter links.
1961 84m/C D: Bruce Brown; **W:** Bruce Brown; **C:** Bruce Brown.

Suture

Clay Arlington (Haysbert) arrives in Phoenix, Arizona, on a bus. Vincent Towers (Harris) meets him. Clay's a construction worker; Vincent drives a Bentley. They met only recently at their father's funeral and both comment on their resemblance. The thing is...Clay's black; Vincent's white. The police suspect that Vincent may have had something to do with his wealthy father's death, and that's the beginning of a carefully paced Hitchcockian suspense tale. The only thing missing on this striking disc is a commentary track, which would have been more useful and informative than most. As it is, Greg Gardiner's striking black-and-white photography is re-created flawlessly. Recommended for adventurous videophiles. —*MM*
Movie: 🎵🎵🎵½ **DVD:** 🎵🎵🎵½
MGM Home Entertainment (Cat #1001452, UPC #027616857729). Widescreen (2.35:1) letterboxed. Dolby Digital Mono. $19.98. Keepcase. *LANG:* English. *SUB:* French; Spanish. *FEATURES:* 16 chapter links • Trailer.
1993 96m/B Dennis Haysbert, Sab Shimono, Mel Harris, Michael (M.K.) Harris, Dina Merrill, David Graf, Fran Ryan; **D:** Scott McGehee, David Siegel; **W:** Scott McGehee, David Siegel; **C:** Greg Gardiner; **M:** Cary Berger. *AWARDS:* Sundance '94: Cinematog; *NOM:* Ind. Spirit '95: Cinematog., First Feature.

Swamp Thing

Dr. Alec Holland (Wise) is turned into a half-vegetable monster with remarkable regenerative powers when the evil Arcane (Jourdan, having a whale of a time) tries to steal his research. Government agent Cable (Barbeau) is caught between the two. Director Craven, better known for his work in horror, shows a fine touch for camp humor. Grain leads to artifacts in some scenes, but overall, this one looks all right for a low-budget monster movie based on a DC comic book. Some sources report that this DVD was made from a European version of the film which contains a few seconds of extra nudity. Further viewings and research are certainly warranted. —*MM*
Movie: 🎵🎵🎵 **DVD:** 🎵🎵½

MGM Home Entertainment (Cat #100083 6, UPC #027616851529). Widescreen letterboxed; full frame. Dolby Digital Mono. $24.99. Keepcase. *LANG:* English; Spanish. *SUB:* French; Spanish. *CAP:* English. *FEATURES:* 28 chapter links • Liner notes • Trailer.
1982 (PG) 91m/C Adrienne Barbeau, Louis Jourdan, Ray Wise, Dick Durock; **D:** Wes Craven; **W:** Wes Craven; **C:** Robbie Greenberg; **M:** Harry Manfredini.

Sweet and Lowdown

Slight jazzy comedy set in the '30s traces the up-and-down career of fictional musician Emmet Ray (Penn), who's haunted by the fact that he's the second-best jazz guitarist in the world (after Django Reinhardt). Except for his talent, Emmet is a rat who abandons the mute Hattie (Morton) for wealthy writer Blanche (Thurman). The overall look of the DVD is of a piece with director Allen's other period work. He uses a faux documentary style, exaggerating a sepia/orange tint and giving the image a purposefully soft feel. Though it probably would have been wrong to overinflate the soundtrack, the mono soundtrack is too restrained. —*MM*
Movie: 🎵🎵½ **DVD:** 🎵🎵½
Columbia Tristar Home Video (Cat #4757). Widescreen (1.85:1) letterboxed; full frame. Dolby Digital Mono. $29.95. Keepcase. *LANG:* English; French. *SUB:* English; French; Spanish. *FEATURES:* 28 chapter links • Cast and crew thumbnail bios • Trailers.
1999 (PG-13) 95m/C Sean Penn, Samantha Morton, Uma Thurman, Brian Markinson, Anthony LaPaglia, Gretchen Mol, Vincent Guastaferro, John Waters, James Urbaniak, Constance Schulman, Kellie Overbey, Michael Sprague, Woody Allen; **D:** Woody Allen; **W:** Woody Allen; **C:** Zhao Fei; **M:** Dick Hyman. *AWARDS: NOM:* Oscars '99: Actor (Penn), Support. Actress (Morton); Golden Globes '00: Actor—Mus./Comedy (Penn), Support. Actress (Morton).

Sweet Revenge

It promises much, delivers on occasion, but for the most part this cable-television adaptation of playwright Alan Ayckbourn's *The Revengers' Comedies* is too smug, too slight, and too British for its own good. In a different take on Hitchcock's classic *Strangers on a Train*, dueling suicides Sam Neill and Helena Bonham Carter intrude upon each other's late-night attempt on London's Tower Bridge, and before Neill realizes it, he's agreed to a goofball revenge pact with Bonham Carter. She eagerly sets out to rid Neill of his tormentor (Steve Coogan), while Neill blissfully settles in to the lifestyle of the idle rich, from which Carter springs. It quickly becomes apparent that Neill has no intention of carrying out his end of the "bargain," if he ever understood that such a bargain actually existed in the first place, as he becomes enamored with Carter's would-be nemesis

Kristin Scott Thomas. Black humor, murder most foul, and bad manners (read: "bad form") follow. Serviceable DVD presentation, with optional English subtitles, but not much more—the six cross-promotional trailers seem out of place somehow. —*RT*
AKA: The Revengers' Comedies.
Movie: 🎵🎵 **DVD:** 🎵🎵½
Buena Vista Home Entertainment (Cat #18549, UPC #717951005625). Widescreen (1.85:1) anamorphic. Dolby Digital. $32.99. Keepcase. *LANG:* English. *SUB:* English. *CAP:* English. *FEATURES:* 25 chapter links • 6 cross-promotional trailers.
1998 82m/C *GB FR* Sam Neill, Helena Bonham Carter, Kristin Scott Thomas, Martin Clunes, Rupert Graves, Steve Coogan, John Wood, Liz Smith, Charlotte Coleman; **D:** Malcolm Mowbray; **W:** Malcolm Mowbray; **C:** Romain Winding; **M:** Alexandre Desplat.

Sweet Smell of Success

Ruthless New York gossip columnist J.J. Hunsecker (Lancaster, in perhaps the most chilling role of his career) and scheming press agent Sidney Falco (Curtis) cook up a plot to frame and ruin a jazz musician (Milner) who's in love with J.J.'s sister (Harrison). That's the core of this brilliant noir, but it will always be remembered for the sizzling staccato dialogue from Ernest Lehman. Any Surround enhancement would have detracted from it. Mono sound is fine. Light signs of wear are visible but it's unimportant. James Wong Howe's inky black-and-white photography looks terrific. Despite the lack of extras, buy this one. —*MM*
Movie: 🎵🎵🎵🎵 **DVD:** 🎵🎵🎵
MGM Home Entertainment (Cat #1002066, UPC #027616862969). Widescreen (1.66:1) letterboxed. Dolby Digital Mono. $19.98. Keepcase. *LANG:* English; French. *SUB:* French; Spanish. *FEATURES:* 16 chapter links • Trailer.
1957 96m/C Burt Lancaster, Tony Curtis, Martin Milner, Barbara Nichols, Sam Levene, Susan Harrison; **D:** Alexander MacKendrick; **W:** Ernest Lehman, Clifford Odets; **C:** James Wong Howe; **M:** Elmer Bernstein. *AWARDS:* Natl. Film Reg. '93.

Switch

When Steve Brooks (King) is murdered by not one, but three of the women he's two-timed and dumped at a hot tub "party," his soul goes to purgatory and confronts God. Not sure he is fit for heaven, but not wanting to damn him to hell, God decides that Steve should be sent back to Earth and if he can find one woman who truly loves him for who he is, then he can get into heaven. He agrees but on his way back to Earth, the devil adds one clause, that he must come back as a woman. Steve comes back not only as a woman, but a gorgeous leggy blonde woman (Barkin). Suddenly s/he's being hit on by every man s/he meets, including his best friend (Smits). This is one of Blake

Edwards's better films. It's not as outrageously funny as the "Pink Panther" films, but it has its moments and in typical Edwards fashion manages to slip in some social commentary along with the laughs. When a fur coat-clad JoBeth Williams saunters toward her limo, she is accosted by a woman who asks her sincerely, "Do you know how many animals had to die to make that coat?" She replies with equal sincerity, "Do you know how many rich animals I had to sleep with to get it?" This is a film about duality and understanding that there are two sides to every story. The disc itself is a little above average in both picture and sound quality. —CA

Movie: 🎬🎬🎬 **DVD:** 🎬🎬🎬
HBO Home Video (Cat #90550, UPC #026 359055027). Widescreen (2.35:1) letterboxed. Dolby Surround. $24.98. Snapper. *LANG:* English; French; Spanish. *SUB:* English; French; Spanish. *FEATURES:* 20 chapter links • Theatrical trailer • Filmographies • Cast and crew bios.
1991 (R) 104m/C Ellen Barkin, Jimmy Smits, JoBeth Williams, Lorraine Bracco, Perry King, Bruce Payne, Tony Roberts; *D:* Blake Edwards; *W:* Blake Edwards; *C:* Dick Bush; *M:* Henry Mancini.

Switchblade Sisters

Fast-paced, campy thrills about a rough-and-tumble girl gang that is torn about by perceived betrayals during their conflict with another gang. A drive-in classic all the way, kicked up a few extra notches thanks to its colorful, polished cinematography, unforgettable characters (check out Monica Gayle's butterfly embroidered eye-patch!), strange situations, and bizarre, hilarious dialogue. Partly inspired by *Othello!* The disc is gorgeous, giving the film a gloss it most assuredly did not have on ill-lit drive-in theatre screens. One only wishes it had been 16x9 enhanced. The sound is vivid and clean, but fairly undistinguished. The extra trailers and shorts only add to the enjoyment, but Tarantino steals the commentary from director Hill, interrupts him constantly, and ends up coming off like an impatient, impetuous geek. One of Tarantino's "Rolling Thunder" cult releases. —DG
AKA: The Jezebels; Playgirl Gang.
Movie: 🎬🎬🎬 **DVD:** 🎬🎬🎬½
Miramax Pictures Home Video (Cat #164 55, UPC #71795100159). Widescreen (1.85:1) letterboxed. Dolby Digital Mono. $29.99. Keepcase. *LANG:* English. *SUB:* English. *CAP:* English. *FEATURES:* Commentary: Jack Hill, Quentin Tarantino • Intro/outro with Quentin Tarantino • 8 other Jack Hill trailers • "The Host," student film by Jack Hill • Clips and reviews from *Spider Baby* • Clips from *Pit Stop* • 18 chapter links • Insert card with chapter listing.
1975 91m/C Robbie Lee, Joanne Nail, Monica Gayle, Kitty Bruce, Asher Brauner, Chase Newhart, Marlene Clark, Janice Karman, Don Stark, Kate Murtagh, Bill Adler; *D:* Jack Hill; *W:* F.X. Maier; *C:* Stephen M. Katz; *M:* Les Baxter, Medusa, Chuck Day, Richard Person.

The Sword in the Stone

The Disney version of the first volume of T.H. White's *The Once and Future King* wherein King Arthur, as a boy, is instructed in the ways of the world by Merlin and Archimedes the owl. Although not in the Disney masterpiece fold, the film boasts the usual superior animation and a gripping mythological tale. What's up with the "full frame" release? Don't worry; you're not missing any picture. Although the film originally was exhibited in a widescreen theatrical format, the animation was composed and photographed at a 1.33:1 aspect ratio and then matted for theatres. The transfer is stunning, with brilliantly saturated colors and deep blacks. It's an old movie, but the transfer seems free of nicks and scratches usually associated with vintage titles. The soundtrack is basically stereo, although a few notes from the musical score are thrown to the Surround channels. You'll hear some hiss and the occasional dropout, so understand this is a nearly 40-year-old soundtrack—not a state-of-the-art 5.1 master as the packaging may suggest. The extras are quite generous and will bring many hours of enjoyment for young and old viewers alike. —MB
Movie: 🎬🎬🎬 **DVD:** 🎬🎬🎬
Buena Vista Home Entertainment (Cat #19691, UPC #717951008671). Full frame. Dolby Digital 5.1. $29.99. Keepcase. *LANG:* English; Spanish; French. *CAP:* English. *FEATURES:* 17 chapter links • "Knight for a Day" animated short starring Goofy • "Brave Little Tailor" animated short starring Mickey Mouse • "Music Magic: The Sherman Brothers" including the song "The Magic Key" • "All About Magic," 1957 TV show hosted by Walt Disney • Scrapbook still galleries • Film facts • Sing-along: "Higitus Figitus," "That's What Makes the World Go Round."
1963 (G) 79m/C *D:* Wolfgang Reitherman; *W:* Bill Peet; *M:* George Bruns; *V:* Ricky Sorenson, Sebastian Cabot, Karl Swenson, Junius Matthews, Alan Napier, Norman Alden, Martha Wentworth, Barbara Jo Allen. *AWARDS: NOM:* Oscars '63: Adapt. Score.

Take Me Out to the Ball Game

Williams manages a baseball team, locks horns with second baseman Denis Ryan (Sinatra) and short stop Eddie O'Brien (Kelly), and wins them over with song. Naturally, there's a water ballet scene. It's a little contrived and forced but enjoyable thanks to Berkeley's often exciting direction of the musical numbers. Romance and song a-plenty. This Warner DVD looks pretty amazing, especially when you consider the age of the film. In fact, it's hard to believe that the film would have looked much better when the original Technicolor prints were first projected on the big screen—O.K., there are a few minor scratches and flecks here and there, but the DVD transfer is very sharp with colors

that appear accurate to Technicolor films of the era. Blacks stay true all the way through and the contrast gives the color more punch than expected. The mono sound is pretty clean, and though there isn't much on the low end, music and dialogue both sound great. Be sure and watch the two deleted songs, "Baby Doll" and "Boys and Girls Like You and Me." —JO **AKA:** Everybody's Cheering.
Movie: 🎬🎬½ **DVD:** 🎬🎬½
Warner Home Video, Inc. (Cat #65119, UPC #012569511927). Full frame. Dolby Digital Mono. $24.98. Snapper. *LANG:* English. *SUB:* English; French. *CAP:* English. *FEATURES:* 30 chapter links • 3 theatrical trailers • Talent files • 2 deleted musical numbers.
1949 93m/C Frank Sinatra, Gene Kelly, Esther Williams, Jules Munshin, Betty Garrett, Edward Arnold, Tom Dugan, Richard Lane; *D:* Busby Berkeley; *W:* Harry Tugend, George Wells; *C:* George J. Folsey; *M:* Roger Edens.

The Taking of Pelham One Two Three

A hijack team led by the ruthless Shaw seizes a New York City subway car and holds 17 passengers for one million dollars ransom. Fine cast and pacing keep things on the edge. For the most part, the video image displays good color fidelity, as befitting the less saturated color processes embraced by filmmakers in the 1970s. However, the transfer suffers from edge enhancements, varying degrees of contrast (noticeable in some of the dark tunnel scenes), and excessive grain, all of which occur only intermittently during the presentation. The mono soundtrack also shows its age. —EP/MM
Movie: 🎬🎬🎬 **DVD:** 🎬🎬½
MGM Home Entertainment (UPC #027616 837523). Widescreen (2.35:1) letterboxed. Dolby Digital Mono. $19.98. Keepcase. *LANG:* English; French; Spanish. *SUB:* English; French; Spanish. *FEATURES:* Theatrical trailer • Booklet.
1974 (R) 105m/C Robert Shaw, Walter Matthau, Martin Balsam, Hector Elizondo, James Broderick, Earl Hindman, Dick O'Neill, Jerry Stiller, Tony Roberts, Doris Roberts, Kenneth McMillan, Julius W. Harris, Sal Viscuso; *D:* Joseph Sargent; *W:* Peter Stone; *C:* Owen Roizman; *M:* David Shire.

The Talented Mr. Ripley

Anthony Minghella's adaptation of Patricia Highsmith's novel (previously filmed as *Purple Noon* in 1960) is beautiful but overlong. This time around, Damon takes over the role of Ripley, a poor nobody who is mistakenly sent to Italy in 1958 to persuade rich playboy Dickie Greenleaf (Law) to return to the bosom of his family in New York. Only the more the emotionally needy Ripley sees of Dickie's sybaritic lifestyle, the more he wants it for himself. The opulent locations and period sets are shown off in all their sumptuousness in this DVD, which makes the most of the top-drawer production values. Sound is equally excellent, though this is not the kind of picture that pushes the limits of 5.1 Surround. If only the filmmakers had managed to trim it to less than 2 hours. —MM

Movie: ♫♫♫ **DVD:** ♫♫♫½
Paramount Home Video (Cat #33142, UPC #097363314271). Widescreen anamorphic. Dolby Digital 5.1 Surround Stereo; Dolby Digital Surround. $29.99. Keepcase. *LANG:* English; French. *CAP:* English. *FEATURES:* 25 chapter links • Cast and crew interviews • Commentary: Minghella • Trailers • "Making of" featurette • Music videos • "Making of" soundtrack featurette.
1999 (R) 139m/C Matt Damon, Jude Law, Gwyneth Paltrow, Cate Blanchett, Philip Seymour Hoffman, Jack Davenport, James Rebhorn, Sergio Rubini, Philip Baker Hall, Lisa Eichhorn, Stefania Rocca; **D:** Anthony Minghella; **W:** Anthony Minghella; **C:** John Seale; **M:** Gabriel Yared. *AWARDS:* Natl. Bd. of Review '99: Best Director (Minghella), Support. Actor (Hoffman); British Acad. '99: Support. Actor (Law); *NOM:* Golden Globes '00: Film—Drama, Actor—Drama (Damon), Support. Actor (Law), Orig. Score, Director (Minghella); Writers Guild '99: Adapt. Screenplay; Oscars '99: Support. Actor (Law), Adapt. Screenplay, Art Dir./Set Dec., Orig. Score, Costume Des; British Acad. '99: Film, Adapt. Screenplay, Director (Minghella), Support. Actress (Blanchett), Cinematog., Orig. Score; MTV Movie Awards '00: Best Villain (Damon).

Tales of Terror

Three tales of terror based on stories by Edgar Allan Poe from the noted series of Corman/Price collaborations: "Morella," "The Black Cat," and the "The Case of M. Valdemar." Price stars in all three segments and is excellent as the bitter resentful alcoholic husband in "Morella," "Cat" delivers some excellent dark humor, and "Valdemar" has a genuinely creepy ending. Screenplay by Matheson takes more than a few artistic liberties, but still retains the Gothic spirit of their source. Beautiful-looking film despite the budget limitations. MGM's DVD delivers a sharp and detailed image with strong colors that remain accurate most of the time (indicating a film problem rather than a video problem). The fleshtones occasionally edge toward pink but are most often very natural. If you're inclined to watch the full-frame side of the disc, you'll get a much softer image with very noticeable grain in many scenes. The mono soundtrack has no problem delivering crisp distinct dialogue but is overall very listless, possibly detracting from the Les Baxter score. —JO
AKA: Poe's Tales of Terror.
Movie: ♫♫½ **DVD:** ♫♫♫½
MGM Home Entertainment (Cat #1000987, UPC #027616852939). Widescreen (2.35:1) anamorphic; full frame. Dolby Digital Mono. $19.98. Keepcase. *LANG:* English.

SUB: Spanish; French. *CAP:* English. *FEATURES:* 20 chapter links • Theatrical trailer.
1962 90m/C Vincent Price, Peter Lorre, Basil Rathbone, Debra Paget, Joyce Jameson, Maggie Pierce, Leona Gage, Edmund Cobb; **D:** Roger Corman; **W:** Richard Matheson; **C:** Floyd Crosby; **M:** Les Baxter.

Talk Radio

Spend two nights with Barry Champlain's (Bogosian) live call-in radio show, "Night Talk." He often insults his callers, and almost always feels superior to them. His special joy is baiting the boneheaded neo-Nazis who phone in to argue, but his anger is scattershot, and it can turn into self-loathing and doubt. Much of the action takes place in the studio—a strange world of dim light and disembodied voices near the top of a high-rise office building. The setting is not particularly challenging visually and so the DVD is not significantly superior to VHS tape. Unfortunately, Stone madly overdirects the material. Half of his boogie-woogie camerawork would have been more than enough. Sound is not very good either; Bogosian's voice has a curiously artificial quality which I do not remember from the theatrical release. —MM
Movie: ♫♫♫ **DVD:** ♫♫½
Universal Studios Home Video (Cat #20908, UPC #025192090820). Widescreen (1.85:1) anamorphic. Dolby Digital Surround Stereo. $24.98. Keepcase. *LANG:* English. *SUB:* French; Spanish. *CAP:* English. *FEATURES:* 18 chapter links • Talent files • Production notes.
1988 (R) 110m/C Eric Bogosian, Alec Baldwin, Ellen Greene, John Pankow, John C. McGinley, Michael Wincott, Leslie Hope; **D:** Oliver Stone; **W:** Eric Bogosian, Oliver Stone; **C:** Robert Richardson; **M:** Stewart Copeland.

The Taming of the Shrew

Zeffirelli's lavish production of Shakespeare's trenchant comedy shrewdly casts Burton and Taylor as the battling Petruchio and Katherine. At the time the film was made, the superstar duo were having their own marital problems, giving all of the sparring—both verbal and physical—a double layer of meaning. The colors seem a bit faded on this DVD, or were they always that muted? A Surround remix might brighten the big crowd and party scenes, and Nino Rota's score certainly deserves it. —MM
Movie: ♫♫♫½ **DVD:** ♫♫♫
Columbia Tristar Home Video (Cat #1109). Widescreen (2.35:1) letterboxed. Dolby Digital Mono. $27.95. Keepcase. *LANG:* English; Portuguese; Spanish. *SUB:* Chinese; Korean; Portuguese; Spanish; Thai. *CAP:* English. *FEATURES:* Cast and crew thumbnail bios • Production notes • Trailers • 28 chapter links.
1967 122m/C IT Elizabeth Taylor, Richard Burton, Michael York, Michael Hordern, Cyril Cusack; **D:** Franco Zeffirelli; **W:** Franco Zeffirelli; **C:** Oswald Morris; **M:** Nino

Rota. *AWARDS: NOM:* Oscars '67: Art Dir./Set Dec., Costume Des.

Tank Girl

In the year 2033, a comet's impact has turned Earth into a desert. All water resources are controlled by the fascist-like Department of Water and Power, headed by evil baddie Kesslee (McDowell). After a punk rogue's (Petty) friends are wiped out by a DWP attack, she is captured and enslaved. Enlisting the help of a mechanic (Watts), a small army of genetic human-kangaroo crossbreeds, and armed to the teeth, the ragtag group attacks the DWP in an effort to overthrow their rule. Based on the British comic strip, this colorful and energetic adaptation (featuring brief animated segments and a musical number!) is entertaining, but strictly hit and miss. Petty is perfect as the quirky, amusing, empowered, and downright strange "Tank Girl," but the middle sags and the ending is confusing and abrupt. The disc is sharp and colorful, and the soundtrack has lots of Surround punch. Unfortunately, though the film had several scenes removed before final cut, none of them are included on this DVD. —DG
Movie: ♫♫ **DVD:** ♫♫♫
MGM Home Entertainment (Cat #1001735, UPC #02761686035). Widescreen (2.35:1) anamorphic. Dolby Digital 5.1. $19.98. Keepcase. *LANG:* English; French; Spanish. *SUB:* French; Spanish. *CAP:* English. *FEATURES:* Theatrical trailer • 16 chapter links • Insert card with chapter listing.
1994 (R) 104m/C Lori Petty, Malcolm McDowell, Ice-T, Naomi Watts, Jeff Kober, Reg E. Cathey, Scott Coffey, Ann Cusack, Don Harvey, Brian Wimmer, Stacey Linn Ramsower, Iggy Pop, Ann Magnuson; **D:** Rachel Talalay; **W:** Tedi Sarafian; **C:** Gale Tattersall; **M:** Graeme Revell.

The Tao of Steve

The Sundance hit plays beautifully on DVD. It's a romantic comedy based on quirky characters. Dex (Logue) is an overweight, somewhat overbearing guy who is somehow attractive to women. His secret is living by the "rules of Steve," as in Steve McQueen. The explanation of those rules is a large part of the picture's charm. Just as important is Syd (Greer Goodman, sister of director Jenniphr), a woman from his past who seems immune to his gift. Their hesitant relationship is played out on New Mexico locations that have a soft-focused, orange-gold cast. The image of the modestly budgeted production is fine if unspectacular. The film works through the chemistry of the cast. On the commentary track, both Goodmans, Logue, and co-writer North come across as likeable pals who are remembering a very pleasant experience that involved many friends and family members. North, by the way, appears on-screen to Logue's right in the poker scene, and all

agree that the story is very autobiographical. Highly recommended. —*MM*
Movie: 🎬🎬🎬½ **DVD:** 🎬🎬🎬½
Columbia Tristar Home Video (Cat #05664, UPC #043396056640). Widescreen (1.85:1) anamorphic. Dolby Digital Surround. $24.95. Keepcase. *LANG:* English. *SUB:* English; French; Spanish. *FEATURES:* 28 chapter links ● Commentary: cast and crew ● Trailers ● Talent files ● Weblink to "The Steve Test."
2000 (R) 87m/C Donal Logue, Greer Goodman, Kimo Wills, Ayelet Kaznelson, David Aaron Baker, Nina Jaroslaw; *D:* Jenniphr Goodman; *W:* Greer Goodman, Jenniphr Goodman, Duncan North; *C:* Teodoro Maniaci; *M:* Joe Delia.

Tap Dogs

Performance of Dein Perry's high-energy *Tap Dogs* show was recorded live at the Lyric Theatre, London. Solid video transfer boasts nice color definition (though some darker colors lack crispness in some scenes). The audio transfer is also well done, reproducing the sounds of the performance in such a way as to not become annoying. —*MJT*
Movie: 🎬🎬½ **DVD:** 🎬🎬🎬
Image Entertainment (Cat #ID9188CUDVD, UPC #014381918823). Widescreen (1.78:1) letterboxed. Dolby Digital Stereo. $24.99. Snapper. *LANG:* English. *FEATURES:* 16 chapter links.
1998 75m/C Dein Perry, Darren Disney, Drew Kaluski; *D:* Aubrey Powell.

Tapeheads

Silly, sophomoric sexy comedy stars Cusack and Robbins as Ivan and Josh, two wanna-be rock-video producers who strike it big and then find more problems. The film contains cameos by many musical stars, including Ted Nugent, "Weird Al" Yankovic, and Monkee Michael Nesmith (who was also executive producer, and provides a commentary track with production designer Catherine Hardwicke and director/co-writer Bill Fishman). The image is very clear, showing only a slight bit of grain, and very little noise. The color scheme on the image is very impressive, as the film features a wide spectrum of vivid colors in the costuming. We get natural-looking fleshtones and realistic reds and greens. The 5.1 mix offers a nice sound field, with liberal use of Surround for music cues and sound effects. The nearly constant music in the film sounds good, but doesn't offer a great deal of bass response. —*MM/ML*
Movie: 🎬🎬½ **DVD:** 🎬🎬🎬
Anchor Bay (Cat #DV11238, UPC #013131123890). Widescreen (1.85:1) anamorphic. Dolby Digital 5.1 Surround Stereo. $24.99. Keepcase. *LANG:* English. *FEATURES:* Commentary: Michael Nesmith, Catherine Hardwicke, Bill Fishman.
1989 (R) 93m/C John Cusack, Tim Robbins, Mary Crosby, Connie Stevens, Susan Tyrrell, Lyle Alzado, Don Cornelius, Katy Boyer, Doug McClure, Clu Gulager, Jessica Walter, Stiv Bators, Sam Moore, Junior Walker, Martha Quinn, Ted Nugent, Weird Al Yankovic, Bob(cat) Goldthwait, Michael Nesmith, Xander Berkeley, Bojan Bazelli; *D:* Bill Fishman; *W:* Bill Fishman, Peter McCarthy; *C:* Bojan Bazelli.

Tarzan and the Lost City

Gorgeous South African locations are a decided plus in this routine hero/adventure story. Lord Greystoke, AKA Tarzan (Van Dien) returns to Africa from England to save his home from mercenaries hunting the Lost City of Opar. Spunky fiancée Jane (March) heads to the jungle after her Ape Man and gets into (and out of) trouble with bad guy Nigel Ravens (Waddington). The effects aren't much but Van Dien looks good in a loincloth and the action moves swiftly. DVD image ranges between good and very good. Even with the enhancement of Surround stereo, the yell doesn't resonate like the original. —*MM*
AKA: Tarzan and Jane; Greystoke 2: Tarzan and Jane.
Movie: 🎬🎬½ **DVD:** 🎬🎬½
Warner Home Video, Inc. (Cat #16647). Widescreen letterboxed. Dolby Digital Surround Stereo. $14.98. Snapper. *LANG:* English; French. *CAP:* English. *FEATURES:* 29 chapter links.
1998 (PG) 84m/C Casper Van Dien, Jane March, Steven Waddington, Winston Ntshona, Rapulana Seiphemo, Ian Roberts; *D:* Carl Schenkel; *W:* Bayard Johnson, J. Anderson Black; *C:* Paul Gilpin; *M:* Christopher Franke.

A Taste of Blood

Gore-meister Lewis's vampire film is actually fairly restrained when compared to *2000 Maniacs* and *Blood Feast*. When John Stone (Rogers) drinks brandy containing the blood of Count Dracula, he turns into a green-faced killer bent on revenge against the ancestors of…oh, never mind. The astonishing thing here is the pristine quality of the disc. It looks like it came out of the lab yesterday. Reds and oranges are bright and true. Lewis and Mike Vraney spin out another engaging commentary track. —*MM*
Movie: 🎬½ **DVD:** 🎬🎬🎬
Image Entertainment (Cat #ID6096SWDVD, UPC #014381609622). Full frame. Dolby Digital Mono. $24.99. Snapper. *LANG:* English. *FEATURES:* 16 chapter links ● Exploitation art gallery ● Silent nudie short, "Nightmare at Elm Manor" ● Commentary: H.G. Lewis, Mike Vraney.
1967 118m/C Bill Rogers, Elizabeth Wilkinson, Thomas Wood, Lawrence Tobin; *D:* Herschell Gordon Lewis; *W:* Donald Stanford; *C:* Andy Romanoff.

Teaserama

The value of this collection of burlesque numbers is historic. The box copy admits as much with "Warning: This Program Contains Mild Nudity." Technically, it contains no nudity. You can see more skin exposed on a public beach and catch more sexy moves on the sidelines of an NFL game than you'll find here. As producer Dave Friedman explains in his commentary track, this is a faithful re-creation of an early '50s burlesque show with comedians and Spanish dancers interspersed among the ecdysiasts. The reddish image displays lots of scratches at the beginning but that clears up quickly. One criticism: someone keeps hitting the microphone during the commentary. —*MM*
Movie: 🎬🎬 **DVD:** 🎬🎬½
Image Entertainment (Cat #ID6098SWDVD, UPC #014381609820). Full frame. Dolby Digital Mono. $24.98. Snapper. *LANG:* English. *FEATURES:* 16 chapter links ● Commentary: Dave Friedman, Mike Vraney.
1955 67m/C Bettie (Betty) Page, Tempest Storm, Joe E. Ross, Trudy Wayne, Vickie Lynn, Dave Starr; *D:* Irving Klaw; *C:* Michael Slifka.

Teenage Catgirls in Heat

On their lighthearted commentary track, the filmmakers admit that they had originally titled this Texas-produced horror simply *Catgirls*. It was the good folks at Troma who came up with the modifiers that turns it into an inspired piece of exploitation. If the film doesn't quite live up (or down) to it, that's not too surprising. It is a nice, silly little horror and nobody involved takes it very seriously. Bright scenes are littered with heavy artifacts, but that's not a problem with such low-budget material. —*MM*
Movie: 🎬🎬 **DVD:** 🎬🎬
Troma Team Video (Cat #9988, UPC #790357998838). Full frame. $24.99. Keepcase. *LANG:* English. *FEATURES:* 10 chapter links ● Commentary: director, producer ● Stills ● Trailers ● DVD credits.
2000 90m/C Gary Graves, Carrie Vanston, Dave Cox; *D:* Scott Perry; *W:* Scott Perry, Grace Smith; *C:* Thad Halci; *M:* Randy Buck, Nenad Vugrinec.

Teenage Doll

Vintage Corman exploitation features good girl Barbara (Kennedy), who's tired of being good and gets mixed up with gangs—the Black Widows and the Vandals. She even manages to set off a war by accidentally killing a "hot gang chick." The DVD image is dark because so much of the action takes place at night but it looks just fine. In fact, it's probably better than it was when the first audiences saw it at the drive-in. Blacks are nice and crisp. Walter Green's jazzy score is completely cool. Even the menu is neat. —*MM*
Movie: 🎬🎬🎬 **DVD:** 🎬🎬🎬
Image Entertainment (Cat #ID9809CODVD, UPC #014381980929). Full frame. Dolby Digital Mono. $24.99. Snapper. *LANG:* English. *FEATURES:* Trailer ● 12 chapter links.
1957 71m/B Fay Spain, John Brinkley, June Kenney, Collette Jackson, Barbara Wilson, Ed Nelson, Richard Devon, Ziva Rodann, Barboura Morris, Bruno VeSota;

D: Roger Corman; **W:** Charles B. Griffith; **C:** Floyd Crosby; **M:** Walter Greene.

Teenage Gang Debs / Teenage Strangler

Several DVD labels have produced "drive-in double feature" discs. This may be the best of the breed, because the films actually live up to their lurid titles. In the first, Terry Fiori (Conti) works her way to the top of "The Rebels" gang. The fevered plot involves guy-fights, girl-fights, bongos, motorcycles, and vandalism. The hipster dialogue is a wonder all on its own. The second is almost certainly the most famous teen horror-musical ever made in Huntington, West Virginia. Who's attacking young women and strangling them with their stockings? Could it be the creepy janitor? *Gang Debs* is photographed in fairly muddy black and white. *Strangler* is in color, though the color values shift abruptly a couple of times in chapters 4 and 5. Both images are seldom better than fair. Sound is O.K. in the first, not so good in the second. The "Let's Go to the Drive-In" option allows the viewer the full ozoner experience of four hours of entertainment beginning with the "5 minutes till showtime" countdown. —*MM*
Movie: 🐹🐹🐹 **DVD:** 🐹🐹
Image Entertainment (Cat #ID9752SWDVD, UPC #014381975222). Full frame. Dolby Digital Mono. $24.99. Snapper. *LANG:* English. *FEATURES:* 24 chapter links ▪ Trailers ▪ Archival shorts ▪ Gallery of drive-in exploitation art.
1966 77m/B Diana Conti, Linda Gale, Eileen Scott, Sandra Kane, Robin Nolan, Linda Cambi, Sue McManus, Geri Tyler, Joey Naudic, John Batis, Tom Yourk, Thomas Andrisano, George Winship, Doug Mitchell, Tom Eldred, Frank Spinella, Alec Primrose, Gene Marrin, Lyn Kennedy, Janet Banzet; **D:** Sande N. Johnsen; **W:** Hy Cahl; **C:** Harry Petricek; **M:** Steve Karmen.

Teenage Monster

Typical 1950s exploitation monster film about a simple boy turned into a wolf-like monster by a meteor, complete with bad acting, shoddy production values, and...oh well, you get the idea. An adequate video transfer is not aided by the blemishes and flaws apparent in the film's original negative. Blacks tend to lose sharpness in some scenes but, overall, it could be worse. The mono soundtrack transfer is as good as an awful sci-fi film from 1957 deserves to be. —*MJT* **AKA:** Meteor Monster.
Movie: 🐹 **DVD:** 🐹½
Image Entertainment (Cat #ID9775CODVD, UPC #014381977523). Full frame. Dolby Digital Mono. $24.99. Snapper. *LANG:* English. *FEATURES:* 12 chapter links ▪ Theatrical trailer.
1957 65m/B Gilbert Perkins, Stephen Parker, Anne Gwynne, Stuart Wade, Gloria Castillo, Chuck Courtney; **D:** Jacques "Jack" Marquette; **W:** Ray Buffum; **C:** Taylor Byars.

Teenage Strangler

Please see review of *Teenage Gang Debs / Teenage Strangler.*
Movie: 🐺🐺🐺
1964 61m/C Bill A. Bloom, Jo Canterbury, John Ensign, Jim Asp, Johnny Haymer, Bill Mills, Ron Ormond; **D:** Bill Posner; **W:** Clark Davis; **C:** Fred Singer; **M:** Danny Dean.

Teenagers from Outer Space

Derek (Love, a dead ringer for Harry Connick Jr.) is the young alien who rebels against his unfeeling elders who want to use Earth as a breeding ground for their food source, giant lobsters. Derek rents a room from Betty's (Anderson) kindly grandpa and saves the planet. He also discovers really cool cars, sharp clothes, and sex...well, as much sex as you could discover in a 1959 movie. This near-perfect example of its kind looks very sharp on DVD with an almost flawless reproduction of some very good black-and-white photography. That clarity makes the goofy effects even more wonderful. —*MM* **AKA:** The Gargon Terror.
Movie: 🐹🐹🐹½ **DVD:** 🐹🐹🐹
Image Entertainment (Cat #ID8691CODVD, UPC #014381869125). Full frame. Dolby Digital Mono. $24.99. Snapper. *LANG:* English. *FEATURES:* 16 chapter links ▪ Liner notes by Richard Valley ▪ Trailer.
1959 86m/B Tom Graeff, Dawn Anderson, Harvey B. Dunn, Bryant Grant, Thomas Lockyer, King Moody, Bob Williams; **D:** Tom Graeff; **W:** Tom Graeff; **C:** Tom Graeff; **M:** Tom Graeff.

Telling You

A tedious cliché-ridden tale of two high school buddies, Phil and Howard (Facineili and Lillard), who have now graduated from college and are working at the local pizzeria. They spend a great deal of time ducking behind the counter to avoid girls they knew in college and high school so the girls won't know that they are pizza boys. There is a running commentary from the characters on destiny and the one that got away, but nothing ever takes off. Small strings of the story would have made an interesting movie, but it seems like the writer never made a real decision about what the point of the film was or who the lead was until the last 15 minutes of the film. The acting is decent and it's well shot. The disc has some red color problems, most noticeably Jennie Garth's glowing red lipstick in the bar scene, but it looks decent overall, and the sound is average. —*CA*
Movie: 🐹 **DVD:** 🐹🐹
Buena Vista Home Entertainment (Cat #20238, UPC #717951009760). Widescreen (1.85:1) anamorphic. Stereo. $29.99. Keepcase. *LANG:* English. *FEATURES:* 26 chapter links.
1998 (R) 94m/C Peter Facinelli, Dash Mihok, Matthew Lillard, Jennifer Love

Hewitt, Richard Libertini, Robert DeFranco, Frank Medrano, Jennifer Jostyn, Rick Rossovich, Jennie Garth; **D:** Robert DeFranco; **W:** Robert DeFranco, Marc Palmieri; **C:** Mark Doering-Powell; **M:** Russ Landau.

Tender Flesh

Unashamed exercise in sleaze from the prolific Jess Franco is worth noting for only one scene wherein a woman urinates on camera. Beyond that dubious distinction, it's yet another unfocused variation on *The Most Dangerous Game.* Image and sound are indistinguishable from VHS tape. —*MM*
Movie: 🐺🐺🐺 **DVD:** 🐹🐹
El Independent Cinema (Cat #sc-1008-dvd, UPC #612385100895). Full frame. $19.98. Keepcase. *LANG:* English. *FEATURES:* 18 chapter links ▪ "Making of" featurette ▪ Amber Smith video shoot ▪ Trailers ▪ Stills gallery.
2000 90m/C *SP* Lina Romay, Amber Smith, Monique Parent; **D:** Jess (Jesus) Franco; **W:** Jess (Jesus) Franco.

Tender Mercies

A down-and-out country singer (Duvall) finds his life redeemed by the love of a good woman (Harper). Aided by Horton Foote's script, Duvall, Harper, and Barkin keep this material from being simplistic and sentimental. Duvall wrote and performed the songs in his Oscar-winning performance. There's little DVD can do to sharpen the soft-focused, pastoral images, nor should it. Sound is fine for the simple material. —*MM*
Movie: 🐹🐹🐹 **DVD:** 🐹🐹½
Republic Pictures Home Video (Cat #39003, UPC #017153111910). Widescreen (1.85:1) anamorphic. Dolby Digital Surround Stereo. $24.98. Keepcase. *LANG:* English. *FEATURES:* 29 chapter links.
1983 (PG) 88m/C Robert Duvall, Tess Harper, Betty Buckley, Ellen Barkin, Wilford Brimley; **D:** Bruce Beresford; **W:** Horton Foote; **C:** Russell Boyd; **M:** George Dreyfus. *AWARDS:* Oscars '83: Actor (Duvall), Orig. Screenplay; Golden Globes '83: Actor—Drama (Duvall); L.A. Film Critics '83: Actor (Duvall); N.Y. Film Critics '83: Actor (Duvall); Writers Guild '83: Orig. Screenplay; *NOM:* Oscars '83: Director (Beresford), Picture, Song ("Over You").

Tenebre

In Rome, American horror novelist Peter Neal (Anthony Franciosa) finds that someone is copying passages from his book *Tenebre* in real razor murders. The rest of the plot is complicated and pretty much dispensable. It serves merely as a clunky, coincidence-driven device to string together a series of sexual and violent images that often involve beautiful women in some stage of undress. The silliness of that side of the film is balanced against Argento's inventive camerawork, which alternates between careful attention to extreme close-up detail and long, complex

tracking and crane shots. Don't miss the famous apartment building shot in Chapter 7. On the commentary track, Argento says that it took three days to prepare and shoot. The image is superb; the 5.1 remix is used very effectively in the big scenes. I'm not Argento's biggest fan but this is a very nice disc. —*MM* **AKA:** Unsane.
Movie: 🎬🎬½ **DVD:** 🎬🎬🎬½
Anchor Bay (Cat #DV10727, UPC #013131 072792). Widescreen (1.85:1) letterboxed. Dolby Digital 5.1 Surround Stereo; Mono. $24.98. Keepcase. *LANG:* English; Italian. *FEATURES:* 20 chapter links • Commentary: Argento, composer Simonetti, journalist Loris Curci • 2 behind-the-scenes segments • Alternate end credits music • Trailer. This film has also been released in America, in a shorter version, as *Unsane*.
1982 101m/C *IT* Anthony (Tony) Franciosa, John Saxon, Daria Nicolodi, Giuliano Gemma, Christian Borromeo, Mirella D'Angelo, Veronica Lario, Ania Pieroni, Carola Stagnaro, John Steiner, Lara Wendell; **D:** Dario Argento; **W:** Dario Argento; **C:** Luciano Tovoli; **M:** The Goblins, Claudio Simonetti.

10th Victim

In a 21st-century society where legalized murder is used as a form of aggression management, Marcello (Mastroianni) and Caroline (Andress) play The Big Game. They're both ace hunters (her most famous kill is accomplished with a double-barreled bra) and now they are trying to kill each other. This DVD may be the first time the film has been shown in its original Italian language, a factor that elevates its clever script a few notches in the science-fiction genre of satirical, dysfunctional futures. The 16:9 image looks good, if not great, but it's due more to the lackadaisical original photography than any transfer flaw (lots of ugly shots in direct sunlight, with dark faces). The film comes with both Italian and English tracks, and English subtitles. Andress doesn't appear to do her voice in either version, so the Italian is preferable. It makes the film come off as a classier show when Mastroianni doesn't speak with a voice from a Saturday morning cartoon. —*GE/MM* **AKA:** La Decima Vittima; La Dixieme Victime.
Movie: 🎬🎬🎬 **DVD:** 🎬🎬🎬
Anchor Bay (Cat #DV11112, UPC #013132 222293). Widescreen anamorphic. $29.98. Keepcase. *LANG:* Italian; English. *SUB:* English.
1965 92m/C *IT* Ursula Andress, Marcello Mastroianni, Elsa Martinelli, Salvo Randone, Massimo Serato; **D:** Elio Petri; **W:** Elio Petri, Tonino Guerra, Ennio Flaiano, Giorgio Salvioni; **C:** Gianni Di Venanzo; **M:** Piero Piccioni.

Termination Man

Lackluster video premiere lives up (or down) to its generic title. When Serbian terrorists threaten with nerve gas, it's up to secret agents Pope (Railsback) and Delilah (Massey) to stop them. The Euro-pean production gains nothing on disc. Image and sound are equal to tape. —*MM*
Movie: 🎬½ **DVD:** 🎬½
New Concorde (Cat #NH20677D, UPC #73 6991467798). Full frame. $19.98. Keepcase. *LANG:* English. *FEATURES:* Trailers • Thumbnail bios • 24 chapter links.
1997 (R) 92m/C Steve Railsback, Athena Massey, James Farentino, Eb Lottimer; **D:** Fred Gallo; **W:** Fred Gallo, Charles Philip Moore; **C:** Eugeny Guslinsky; **M:** Deddy Tzur.

Terminator 2: Judgment Day [2 SE]

Demonstrating how quickly digital technology is changing, this "ultimate" edition eclipses both the earlier laserdisc and DVD versions of Cameron's film. Remarkably, this double-sided dual-layer disc contains both the theatrical release and the special version previously available only on laserdisc. A third "extended special edition" is included as an "Easter egg." To access it, go to the Special Edition menu and press 82997 on your remote. (You may have to press enter after each digit.) The words "The Future Is Not Set" will appear on the right and you will be directed to the film. Along with those three versions are hours of supplemental material, all brought together in a really cool package wrapped in a brushed aluminum slipcase. At the DVD 2000 Entertainment Awards, Michelle Friedman and Van Ling won awards for their work on this disc. —*MM*
Movie: 🎬🎬🎬½ **DVD:** 🎬🎬🎬🎬
Artisan Entertainment (Cat #10967, UPC #012236109679). Widescreen (2.35:1) letterboxed. Dolby Digital 5.1 Surround Stereo; DD Surround Stereo; DTS 5.1 Stereo. $39.98. Keepcase. *LANG:* English. *FEATURES:* 72 chapter links (theatrical release) • 80 chapter links (special edition) • 32-page booklet • Commentary: 26 cast and crew • Cast and crew thumbnails • Three "making of" featurettes • Teasers, trailers, screenplay • 700+ storyboard illustrations.
1991 (R) 139m/C Arnold Schwarzenegger, Linda Hamilton, Edward Furlong, Robert Patrick, Earl Boen, Joe Morton; **D:** James Cameron; **W:** James Cameron; **C:** Adam Greenberg; **M:** Brad Fiedel. *AWARDS:* Oscars '91: Makeup, Sound, Sound FX Editing, Visual FX; MTV Movie Awards '92: Film, Male Perf. (Schwarzenegger), Female Perf. (Hamilton), Breakthrough Perf. (Furlong), Most Desirable Female (Hamilton), Action Seq; *NOM:* Oscars '91: Cinematog., Film Editing.

Terms of Endearment

In his debut, director James L. Brooks adapts Larry McMurtry's novel about the changing relationship between a young woman (Winger) and her mother (MacLaine) over a 30-year period. It begins as a comedy and turns serious as the years go by. Superb supporting cast is headed by Nicholson's slyly charming neighbor/astronaut, though even he has trouble taking the film from the stars. This one has never been much to speak of in visual terms, and so the most important feature of the DVD is the commentary track by Brooks, his co-producer Penney Finkelman Cox, and production designer Polly Platt. Working from memory, they sound conversational and spontaneous. —*MM*
Movie: 🎬🎬🎬 **DVD:** 🎬🎬🎬
Paramount Home Video (Cat #01407, UPC #097360140743). Widescreen anamorphic. Dolby Digital 5.1 Surround Stereo; Restored Mono. $24.99. Keepcase. *LANG:* English; French. *SUB:* English. *FEATURES:* 16 chapter links • Trailer • Commentary: Brooks, Penney Finkelman Cox, Polly Platt.
1983 (PG) 132m/C Shirley MacLaine, Jack Nicholson, Debra Winger, John Lithgow, Jeff Daniels, Danny DeVito; **D:** James L. Brooks; **W:** James L. Brooks; **C:** Andrzej Bartkowiak; **M:** Michael Gore. *AWARDS:* Oscars '83: Actress (MacLaine), Adapt. Screenplay, Director (Brooks), Picture, Support. Actor (Nicholson); Directors Guild '83: Director (Brooks); Golden Globes '84: Actress—Drama (MacLaine), Film—Drama, Screenplay, Support. Actor (Nicholson); L.A. Film Critics '83: Actress (MacLaine), Director (Brooks), Film, Screenplay, Support. Actor (Nicholson); Natl. Bd. of Review '83: Actress (MacLaine), Director (Brooks), Support. Actor (Nicholson); N.Y. Film Critics '83: Actress (MacLaine), Film, Support. Actor (Nicholson); Natl. Soc. Film Critics '83: Actress (Winger), Support. Actor (Nicholson); Writers Guild '83: Adapt. Screenplay; *NOM:* Oscars '83: Actress (Winger), Art Dir./Set Dec., Film Editing, Sound, Support. Actor (Lithgow), Orig. Score.

Terror by Night

Holmes and Watson (Rathbone and Bruce) attempt to solve the murder of the owner of a gigantic beautiful jewel. Their investigation must be completed before their train arrives at its destination where the murderer can escape. The film marks Hoey's final appearance as Inspector Lestrade. Though this is one of the better entries in the FOCUSfilm series, it's still far less than perfect. The image ranges between fair and good, and lacks detail. The most interesting extra is an interview with Holmes's creator Arthur Conan Doyle, filmed in 1927. He talks about his detective and his interest in spiritualism. The disc is part of the "Evening with Sherlock Holmes" boxed set. —*MM*
Movie: 🎬🎬½ **DVD:** 🎬🎬½
FOCUSfilm (Cat #FF7826, UPC #6830707 82627). Full frame. $69.99. Keepcase. *LANG:* English. *FEATURES:* 7 chapter links • Episodes 24-30 of *New Adventures of Sherlock Holmes* radio show • Photo gallery • Arthur Conan Doyle interview.
1946 60m/B Basil Rathbone, Nigel Bruce, Alan Mowbray, Dennis Hoey, Renee Godfrey; **D:** Roy William Neill; **W:** Frank Gruber; **C:** Maury Gertsman.

Terror Firmer [SE]

In the opening minutes, it is obvious that Lloyd Kaufman will go to any extreme to

offend his viewers. Of course, he's offending them with the cheapest special effects money can buy, so the level of disgust is never too high. The plot, which is perhaps the least important part of the film, revolves around a series of murders committed while a blind director (Kaufman) is trying to make a Troma movie. It's very sexy, very violent, very funny. Most of the extras are on the second disc in the set. Overall, the image is remarkably sharp. Remember, though, sharpness has nothing to do with polish. The film is rough, profane, and in the poorest taste possible. Certainly the auteur's most ambitious work to date. —MM
Movie: 🎬🎬🎬 **DVD:** 🎬🎬🎬½
Troma Team Video (Cat #9020, UPC #7903 57902033). Full frame. $24.99. Keepcase boxed set. LANG: English. FEATURES: 27 chapter links • Commentary: director • Deleted scenes • Alternate scenes • Auditions • Bloopers • Comic book to film comparisons • Trailers • "Making of" documentary • "Terror Firmer" video game • Music videos • Intro to The TromaDance Film Festival • "Easter eggs" ("Troma turds") • Gyno talk with Alyce LaTourelle • Chat with Charlotte Kaufman.
2000 114m/C Alyce LaTourelle, Lloyd (Samuel Weil) Kaufman, Debbie Rochon, Will Keenan, Trent Haaga, Sheri Wenden; **D:** Lloyd (Samuel Weil) Kaufman; **W:** Patrick Cassidy, Douglas Buck, Lloyd (Samuel Weil) Kaufman; **C:** Brendan Flynt.

Terror Tract

Please see review for *Cherry Falls / Terror Tract.*
Movie: 🎬🎬
2000 (R) 97m/C John Ritter, Marcus Bagwell, Bryan Cranston, Will Estes, Brenda Strong, Rachel York, Allison Smith, Carmine D. Giovinazzo, David DeLuise, Wade Andrew Williams, Frederic Lane; **D:** Geoffrey Wright, Lance Dreesen, Clint Hutchison; **W:** Clint Hutchison; **C:** Ken Blakey; **M:** Brian Tyler.

The Terrorist

Revolutionary Malli (Dharker) is a seasoned fighter at 19. She is chosen by her leaders to be a suicide bomber in an important mission. The film explores the changes she goes through as she leaves the jungle and goes to the city where her target will be. It's an astonishingly moving portrait, told mostly in unblinking close-ups. After some inconsequential registration problems in the opening credits, DVD image and sound quality are the equal of the best Hollywood action pictures. (So are the acting, direction, and integration of music.) Much of the action takes place outdoors and the natural world has seldom been displayed so strongly in any film. Those who equate Asian films with harsh colors and thin production values will be happily surprised. This one is very good on every level. —MM **AKA:** Malli.
Movie: 🎬🎬🎬½ **DVD:** 🎬🎬🎬½

Winstar Home Entertainment (Cat #FLV52 57, UPC #720917525723). Widescreen (1.85:1) letterboxed. $24.98. Keepcase. LANG: Tamil. SUB: English. FEATURES: 16 chapter links • 2 trailers • Filmographies • Production credits.
1998 95m/C IN Ayesha Dharker; **D:** Santosh Sivan; **W:** Santosh Sivan; **C:** Santosh Sivan; **M:** Sonu Sisupal. AWARDS: NOM: Ind. Spirit '01: Foreign Film.

Terry Pratchett's Discworld: Wyrd Sisters

It's hard to top the wondrous computer-generated image of a flat planet borne across the cosmos on the back of a titanically huge turtle and supported by four mammoth blue elephants; and nothing in this six-part animated series developed for British television does come close. But even those who have not read Terry Pratchett's beloved *Discworld* books will find themselves captivated by the story, sly humor, and colorful, idiosyncratic characters who put a veddy British spin on the fantasy genre. The Wyrd Sisters are three witches who become embroiled in palace intrigue after the good king is murdered and they are compelled to raise his infant heir. The distinguished voice cast includes Christopher Lee as a very droll Death and Jane Horrocks as the ditziest of the witch sisters. Image quality is good. The extras are helpful in orienting new initiates into Pratchett's cockeyed universe. —DL
Movie: 🎬🎬🎬 **DVD:** 🎬🎬🎬
Acorn Media Publishing (Cat #8374, UPC #5496183749). Full frame. Dolby Digital. $39.95. Keepcase. LANG: English. CAP: English. FEATURES: Terry Pratchett bio • "Welcome to the Discworld" pilot video • Wyrd Sisters characters • Wyrd Sisters storyboards • Discworld books • Weblinks • 12 chapter links.
1996 140m/C GB **V:** Christopher Lee, Jane Horrocks.

The Texas Chainsaw Massacre 2

Ridiculous magnified sequel posits that the family in the first film has been traveling across Texas and winning chili cook-offs. Dennis Hopper looks silly beneath a gigantic cowboy hat. Only improvement over VHS tape is the option of screen ratios. —MM
Movie: woof **DVD:** 🎬🎬½
MGM Home Entertainment (Cat #10008 37, UPC #027616851536). Widescreen letterboxed; full frame. Dolby Digital Surround Stereo. $19.98. Keepcase. LANG: English. SUB: French; Spanish. FEATURES: 28 chapter links.
1986 (R) 90m/C Dennis Hopper, Caroline Williams, Bill Johnson, Jim Siedow, Bill Moseley, Lou Perry, John (Joe Bob Briggs) Bloom; **D:** Tobe Hooper; **W:** L.M. Kit Carson; **C:** Richard Kooris; **M:** Tobe Hooper.

Texas Chainsaw Massacre: A Family Portrait

This "appreciation" is a combination of widescreen clips from *TCM* and videotaped interviews with four of the stars about their involvement with the project. The film material is as raw-looking as it has always been, but it's far superior to the interviews, which are poorly lit and substandard in every respect. The director's name is misspelled on the box copy. —MM
Movie: 🎬 **DVD:** 🎬
MTI Home Video (Cat #1067, UPC #03941 4510676). Full frame; widescreen letterboxed. $24.95. Keepcase. LANG: English. FEATURES: 25 chapter links • Talent files • Trailers • Trivia.
1990 70m/C Gunnar Hansen, Edwin Neal, John Dugan, Jim Siedow; **D:** Brad Shellady; **W:** Brad Shellady; **C:** Bob Enlow.

That Touch of Mink

An unemployed New York secretary (Day) becomes involved with a business tycoon (Grant). You need know nothing more about the plot to get to the final clinch. Given the star power of the two leads, this one really ought to be better, though it is enjoyable enough. Much the same could be said of the DVD. It lacks the sparkle of the best romantic comedies. Image is clear but lackluster with considerable aliasing in overly bright interiors. Sound is O.K. —MM
Movie: 🎬🎬½ **DVD:** 🎬🎬
Artisan Entertainment (Cat #10082, UPC #017153100822). Widescreen (1.85:1) letterboxed. $24.99. Keepcase. LANG: English. CAP: English. FEATURES: 34 chapter links • Talent files • Trailer.
1962 99m/C Cary Grant, Doris Day, Gig Young, Audrey Meadows, John Astin, Dick Sargent; **D:** Delbert Mann; **W:** Stanley Shapiro, Nate Monaster; **C:** Russell Metty; **M:** George Duning. AWARDS: Golden Globes '63: Film—Mus./Comedy; NOM: Oscars '62: Art Dir./Set Dec., Color, Sound, Story & Screenplay.

That Uncertain Feeling [SlingShot]

Please see review of *Comedy Noir.*
Movie: 🎬🎬½
1941 86m/B Merle Oberon, Melvyn Douglas, Burgess Meredith, Alan Mowbray, Eve Arden, Sig Rumann, Harry Davenport; **D:** Ernst Lubitsch; **W:** Donald Ogden Stewart, Walter Reisch; **C:** George Barnes; **M:** Werner R. Heymann. AWARDS: NOM: Oscars '41: Orig. Dramatic Score.

That'll Be the Day

In England, 1958, dissatisfied Jim McLain (Essex) goes to live and work in a depressing seaside resort. Mike (Starr) introduces him to the wildside, and he has to choose between a life of responsibility and the rock 'n' roll scene that is coming into existence. The film is a prequel to

Stardust and is told with a rare degree of realism. DVD presents a fine image, though the film is not meant to be visually polished. It describes a rough world accurately. To have enhanced the sound would have been unfair to the material. —*MM*

Movie: 🎵🎵½ **DVD:** 🎵🎵½

Anchor Bay (Cat #DV11372, UPC #013131 137293). Widescreen (1.85:1) anamorphic. Dolby Digital Mono. $24.99. Keepcase. *LANG:* English. *FEATURES:* 28 chapter links • Trailers.

1973 (PG) 91m/C Ringo Starr, Keith Moon, David Essex, Rosemary Leach, James Booth, Billy Fury, Rosalind Ayres, Robert Lindsay, Brenda Bruce, Verna Harvey, James Ottoway, Deborah Watling, Beth Morris, Daphne Oxenford, Kim Braden, Ron Hackett, Johnny Shannon, Susan Holderness, The Debonairs; *D:* Claude Whatham; *W:* Ray Connolly; *C:* Peter Suschitzsky.

That's the Way I Like It

Homage to disco (gasp!) is set in the East. It's 1977 and Singapore store clerk Hock (Pang) wants to win a dance tournament so he can buy a motorcycle. He drops his usual partner (Tang) for the flashier Julie (Francis) and the rivalry between teams becomes intense. But Hock has the spirit of the legendary *Saturday Night Fever* studster (Pace), or a reasonable facsimile thereof, to advise him. The excellent image is all too faithful to the style and substance of its subject matter for my taste. The clothes, the flashing lights—they're presented in all their tasteless glory. Ditto, alas, the music. —*MM*

Movie: 🎵🎵🎵 **DVD:** 🎵🎵🎵

Miramax Pictures Home Video (Cat #18280, UPC #717951004703). Widescreen (1.85:1) anamorphic. Dolby Digital 5.1 Surround Stereo. $24.99. Keepcase. *LANG:* English. *CAP:* English. *FEATURES:* 26 chapter links • Trailer.

1999 (PG-13) 92m/C Adrian Pang, Anna Belle Francis, Dominic Pace, Madeline Tang, Caleb Goh; *D:* Glen Goei; *W:* Glen Goei; *C:* Brian J. Breheny; *M:* Guy Gross.

There's No Business Like Show Business

Unlike modern stars, Marilyn Monroe sometimes had no choice about what she played in for Fox, and this film is not one of her brightest moments. Shoe-horned into a semi-minor role in what is really Ethel Merman's starring vehicle, Marilyn acquits herself well. Yet the production is rather garish and empty (an awful lot of wide screens full of billowing, sequined drapes) and does no favors to talents like Donald O'Connor, who deserved better. The story is so light it's almost not there, and although MM is paired with Donald, it's totally by convention—romantically involved, they hardly seem to know each other. I know this is supposed to be the gaudy world of vaudeville, and I'm no judge of costumes, but the final kiss of death is that a lot of the stuff they have her wearing here is just plain ugly. The Irving Berlin musical numbers are of course the draw, and Ethel Merman is marvelous in one of her last big shows, belting out the title tune from her stage success *Annie Get Your Gun,* brassier than Judy Galand or Betty Hutton ever could. But it's not a great movie, and it's certainly not good Marilyn. —*GE*

Movie: 🎵🎵🎵 **DVD:** 🎵🎵🎵½

20th Century Fox Home Entertainment (Cat #2001445). Widescreen (2.35:1) anamorphic. Dolby Digital 4.0 Surround Stereo; Dolby Digital Stereo. $24.98. Keepcase. *LANG:* English. *FEATURES:* Trailers.

1954 117m/C Ethel Merman, Donald O'Connor, Marilyn Monroe, Dan Dailey, Johnny Ray, Mitzi Gaynor, Frank McHugh, Hugh O'Brian; *D:* Walter Lang; *W:* Phoebe Ephron, Henry Ephron; *C:* Leon Shamroy; *M:* Irving Berlin, Lionel Newman, Alfred Newman. *AWARDS: NOM:* Oscars '54: Costume Des. (C), Story, Scoring/Musical.

They Call Me Mr. Tibbs!

Uneven follow-up to Best Picture–winner *In the Heat of the Night.* This time around, Philadelphia detective Virgil Tibbs has been transplanted from the rural south to the big city of San Francisco, where he serves as a homicide detective assigned the seemingly routine investigation of the murder of a prostitute. Prime suspect turns out to be Martin Landau, a crusading political reformer. Is it a set-up, or is he the real killer? Of note, one year after the release of this film, another San Francisco detective by the name of Harry Callahan would get a case of his own and change the face of detective thrillers. In the alternative cinematic universe, one has to wonder if Virgil Tibbs and Dirty Harry ever worked a case together? A rough and scratchy theatrical trailer is the only special feature included. —*RT*

Movie: 🎵🎵½ **DVD:** 🎵🎵½

MGM Home Entertainment (Cat #10014 74, UPC #027616857941). Widescreen (1.85:1) anamorphic. Dolby Digital Stereo. $19.98. Keepcase. *LANG:* English; French; Spanish. *SUB:* French; Spanish. *CAP:* French; Spanish. *FEATURES:* Theatrical trailer.

1970 (R) 108m/C Sidney Poitier, Barbara McNair, Martin Landau, Juano Hernandez, Anthony Zerbe, Ed Asner, Norma Crane, Jeff Corey; *D:* Gordon Douglas; *W:* Alan R. Trustman; *C:* Gerald Perry Finnerman; *M:* Quincy Jones.

They Made Me a Criminal

Please see review of *Cinema's Dark Side Collection.* *AKA:* I Became a Criminal; They Made Me a Fugitive.

Movie: 🎵🎵½

1939 92m/B John Garfield, Ann Sheridan, Claude Rains, Leo Gorcey, Huntz Hall, Gabriel Dell, Bobby Jordan, Billy Halop; *D:* Busby Berkeley; *W:* Sig Herzig; *C:* James Wong Howe; *M:* Max Steiner.

Thick As Thieves

Alec Baldwin neatly underplays his role as a professional thief in a crime drama that will remind viewers of Elmore Leonard and Tarantino. Macklin (Baldwin) pulls a job-for-hire in Detroit but local boss Pointy Williams (White) tries to doublecross him. Macklin then has to take time away from his beloved collection of jazz on vinyl to get what's coming to him. But he does not leave his equally beloved dog at home. The characters are interesting; the supporting cast is first-rate (Braugher, White, DeMornay) and the plotting is occasionally unconventional. With production values that are adequate but not superior, the DVD image and sound are both fine. A treat for fans of the genre. —*MM*

Movie: 🎵🎵🎵 **DVD:** 🎵🎵½

USA Home Entertainment (Cat #96306009 7-2). Widescreen letterboxed; full frame. Dolby Digital 5.1 Surround Stereo. $24.95. Snapper. *LANG:* English. *SUB:* English; French; Spanish. *FEATURES:* 13 chapter links • Trailer.

1999 (R) 93m/C Alec Baldwin, Michael Jai White, Rebecca DeMornay, Andre Braugher, Bruce Greenwood, David Byrd, Richard Edson, Khandi Alexander, Robert Miano, Janeane Garofalo, Julia Sweeney, Ricky Harris; *D:* Scott Sanders; *W:* Scott Sanders, Arthur Krystal; *C:* Chris Walling; *M:* Christophe Beck.

The Thief

In 1952 Russia, young widow Katya (Rednikova) is traveling with her six-year-old son Sanya (Philipchuk) on a train when she meets hunky soldier Tolyan (Mashkov). By the end of the trip, they're posing as a family. But the man has a violent streak and he's lying about his identity. It's a solid drama that's extremely well cast and acted, particularly by young Misha Philipchuk, who's a real charmer. Image is fine but is not much superior to a widescreen tape. Bright yellow subtitles are easy to read. —*MM* *AKA:* Vor.

Movie: 🎵🎵🎵 **DVD:** 🎵🎵

Columbia Tristar Home Video (Cat #03519, UPC #043396035195). Widescreen (1.85:1) letterboxed. Dolby Digital Mono. $24.98. Keepcase. *LANG:* Russian. *SUB:* English; French; Spanish. *FEATURES:* 28 chapter links • Trailer.

1997 (R) 92m/C *RU* Vladimir Mashkov, Ekaterina Rednikova, Misha Philipchuk; *D:* Pavel Chukhrai; *W:* Pavel Chukhrai; *C:* Vladimir Klimov; *M:* Vladimir Dashkevich. *AWARDS: NOM:* Oscars '97: Foreign Film; Golden Globes '98: Foreign Film.

The Thing with Two Heads

The inspired box copy says it all: "They share the same body...but hate each other's guts!" Max Kirshner (Milland), a white racist surgeon, plans to cheat death by having his head attached to another body. Imagine his surprise when he finds his noggin stitched onto black Jack Moss

(Grier), right next to the original head. Nobody involved is taking the material too seriously. On DVD, some grain is evident but it comes from well-preserved original elements. —*MM*
Movie: 🎵🎵½ ***DVD:*** 🎵🎵½
MGM Home Entertainment (Cat #1002021, UPC #027616862624). Widescreen (1.85: 1) letterboxed. Dolby Digital Mono. $14.95. Keepcase. *LANG:* English. *SUB:* French; Spanish. *CAP:* English. *FEATURES:* 16 chapter links ▪ Trailer.
1972 (PG) 93m/C Ray Milland, Roosevelt "Rosie" Grier, Don Marshall, Roger Perry, Kathrine Baumann, Lee Frost, Wes Bishop, Rick Baker; **D:** Lee Frost; **W:** James Gordon White; **C:** Jack Steely; **M:** Robert O. Ragland.

Things to Come

Scientists use technology to rebuild the world after a lengthy war that's followed by a plague and other unfortunate events. Massey and Scott each play two roles in different generations. This sf has held up remarkably well over the years. I've seen it in a theatrical screening and on tape, and this DVD is by far the best of the three. The image is very good, with only slight registration problems and wear. —*MM*
Movie: 🎵🎵🎵½ ***DVD:*** 🎵🎵🎵
Image Entertainment (Cat #ID9879CODVD, UPC #014381987928). Full frame. Dolby Digital Mono. $24.99. Snapper. *LANG:* English. *FEATURES:* 14 chapter links ▪ Trailer.
1936 92m/B *GB* Raymond Massey, Margaretta Scott, Ralph Richardson, Cedric Hardwicke, Derrick DeMarney, Maurice Braddell; **D:** William Cameron Menzies; **W:** H.G. Wells; **C:** Georges Perinal; **M:** Arthur Bliss.

Third World Cop

Tough cop Capone (Campbell) is transferred back to his hometown of Kingston, Jamaica, and finds that his friends of old have become criminals to the local mob. Ratty (Danvers) has risen to become the right hand of the don, and suddenly the two face a huge dilemma that leads to a violent inevitable ending. The transfer is clear and clean, without blemishes or defects. The sunlit outdoor scenes look neutral. Blacks are deep and solid in the transfer but highlights appear slightly muted. Some slight compression artifacts are visible in the form of occasional pixelation and banding, resulting in a loss of detail in various scenes. Audio is defined by the multitude of powerful and pumping reggae tracks. Well integrated and with good dynamics, the music creates a vibrant world and firmly rooting the Jamaican setting. Dialogue is always understandable, although the heavy accents that tinge the film make the subtitles a welcome addition. —*GH/MM*
Movie: 🎵🎵🎵 ***DVD:*** 🎵🎵🎵
Full frame. Dolby Digital 5.1 Surround Stereo. *LANG:* English. *SUB:* English; Spanish. *FEATURES:* "Making of" featurette.

1999 (R) 98m/C *JM* Paul Campbell, Carl Bradshaw, Mark Danvers, Audrey Reid; **D:** Christopher Browne; **W:** Christopher Browne, Suzanne Fenn, Chris Salewicz; **C:** Richard Lannaman; **M:** Sly Dunbar, Robbie Shakespeare.

32 Short Films about Glenn Gould

Perceptive docudrama examines the iconoclastic Canadian classical pianist who secluded himself in the studio, forsaking live performances for much of his career. The filmmakers use a combination of dramatic re-creation, archival material, and interviews to reveal the driven artist who died at 50. Feore is memorable in the title role, especially since he is never shown playing the piano. The title and structure refer to Bach's "Goldberg" Variations, a recording that made Gould's reputation. A bit of minor aliasing is not a problem. Visually, the disc is fine; the excellent reproduction of the score is even more important and this one sounds terrific. —*MM*
Movie: 🎵🎵🎵½ ***DVD:*** 🎵🎵🎵
Columbia Tristar Home Video (Cat #74359, UPC #043396743595). Widescreen (1.85: 1) anamorphic; full frame. Dolby Digital Surround Stereo. $29.95. Keepcase. *LANG:* English. *SUB:* English; Spanish. *FEATURES:* 32 chapter links ▪ Trailers ▪ Talent files ▪ Production notes.
1993 94m/C *CA* Colm Feore, Gale Garnett, David Hughes, Katya Ladan, Gerry Quigley, Carlo Rota, Peter Millard, Yehudi Menuhin, Bruno Monsaingeon; **D:** Francois Girard; **W:** Don McKellar, Francois Girard; **C:** Alan Dostie. *AWARDS:* Genie '93: Cinematog., Director (Girard), Film, Film Editing; *NOM:* Ind. Spirit '95: Foreign Film.

This Is Spinal Tap [MGM]

The original rock "mockumentary" makes an inspired transition to DVD. Visually, the film is no better than any other early '80s production. The 5.1 remix sounds very good, and the subtitles are particularly useful to decipher those hard-to-understand bits of mumbled dialogue. The most important addition, though, is the commentary track by band members Nigel Tufnel (Guest), David St. Hubbins (McKean), and Derek Smalls (Shearer). They stay in character throughout and add a new level of humor for long-time fans. The rest of the extras on the disc are well-chosen. They may not be enough to convert those who aren't tuned in to the filmmakers' dry sense of humor, which has been copied so many times since. —*MM* *AKA:* Spinal Tap.
Movie: 🎵🎵🎵½ ***DVD:*** 🎵🎵🎵🎵
MGM Home Entertainment (Cat #1000973, UPC #027616852809). Widescreen anamorphic. Dolby Digital 5.1 Surround Stereo. $26.98. Keepcase. *LANG:* English. *SUB:* English. *FEATURES:* Commentary: Tap ▪ Interview with Rob Reiner ▪ Outtakes ▪ 6 TV commercials ▪ 4 music videos ▪ 29 chapter links ▪ Group appearance on *The*

Joe Franklin Show ▪ Flower People Press Conference ▪ Heavy Metal memories ▪ Original theatrical trailers.
1984 (R) 82m/C Michael McKean, Christopher Guest, Harry Shearer, Tony Hendra, Bruno Kirby, Rob Reiner, June Chadwick, Howard Hesseman, Billy Crystal, Dana Carvey, Ed Begley Jr., Patrick Macnee, Fran Drescher, Paul Shaffer, Anjelica Huston, Fred Willard, Paul Benedict, Archie Hahn; **D:** Rob Reiner; **W:** Michael McKean, Christopher Guest, Harry Shearer, Rob Reiner; **C:** Peter Smokler; **M:** Michael McKean, Christopher Guest, Harry Shearer, Rob Reiner.

This Night I'll Possess Your Corpse

This sequel begins at the moment that *At Midnight I'll Take Your Soul* ends. Coffin Joe (Marins) continues his search for a bride and son. It's mid-'60s Grand Guignol horror that actually loses a little something on DVD. With the added clarity of the image—and this black-and-white picture is sharp—you can clearly see that one of the snakes in a torture scene has its mouth taped shut. Even so, there are enough spiders and serpents to make viewers nervous. As a filmmaker Marins combines elements of Ed Wood Jr. and David Lynch. He is certainly not to all tastes. —*MM*
AKA: Tonight I Will Eat Your Corpse; Tonight I Will Make Your Corpse Turn Red; Tonight I Will Paint in Flesh Colour.
Movie: 🎵🎵½ ***DVD:*** 🎵🎵½
Fantoma Films (Cat #FAN0603DVD, UPC #014381060324). Widescreen (1.66:1) letterboxed. Dolby Digital Mono. $24.95. Keepcase. *LANG:* Portuguese. *SUB:* English. *FEATURES:* 12 chapter links ▪ Interview with Jose Mojica Marins ▪ Trailers ▪ Comic book.
1966 107m/C *BR* Jose Mojica Marins; **D:** Jose Mojica Marins; **W:** Jose Mojica Marins; **C:** Giorgio Attili.

Thomas and the Magic Railroad

The TV series animated with models makes a successful transition to a longer form. Alec Baldwin makes a fine Mr. Conductor. The film maintains both the innocent spirit of the original along with the bright primary colors and the familiar locomotives with real people. Many adults won't have the patience to sit through a feature-length visit with the trains, but younger kids will watch it again and again. DVD image is appropriately bright, sharp, and shiny. Sound is fine for the short set. —*MM*
Movie: 🎵🎵½ ***DVD:*** 🎵🎵🎵
Columbia Tristar Home Video (Cat #05426, UPC #043396054264). Full frame. Dolby Digital 5.1 Surround Stereo; Dolby Digital Surround. $24.95. Keepcase. *LANG:* English; Spanish. *SUB:* English; Spanish. *FEATURES:* 28 chapter links ▪ Deleted scene: "Sundae Surprise" ▪ DVD-ROM weblink ▪ Talent files ▪ Theatrical trailers.

2000 (G) 84m/C Mara Wilson, Alec Baldwin, Peter Fonda, Didi Conn; **D:** Britt Allcroft; **W:** Britt Allcroft; **C:** Paul Ryan; **M:** Hummie Mann.

Thou Shalt Not Kill . . . Except

A Vietnam vet seeks revenge against the cult leader (director Sam Raimi) who kidnapped his girlfriend in this legendary low-budget cult favorite. The DVD image is very clear, especially considering the budget of the project. It shows few defects from the source print and only features a minute amount of grain. It also suffers slightly from excesses of light and darkness. There are no obvious problems with compression or artifacts. Audio is adequate. —*ML/MM* **AKA:** Stryker's War.
Movie: 🦴🦴½ **DVD:** 🦴🦴½
Anchor Bay (Cat #11487). Widescreen (1.66:1) anamorphic. Dolby Digital Mono. $24.98. Keepcase. *LANG:* English. *FEATURES:* Commentary: Josh Becker and Bruce Campbell • Deleted scene • Alternate title section • Theatrical trailer.
1987 84m/C Brian Schulz, Robert Rickman, John Manfredi, Tim Quill, Cheryl Hansen, Sam Raimi, Perry Mallette, Theodore (Ted) Raimi, Glenn Barr, Scott Spiegel, Bruce Campbell, Paul Grabke; **D:** Josh Becker; **W:** Josh Becker, Scott Spiegel; **C:** Josh Becker; **M:** Joseph LoDuca.

The Thousand Eyes of Dr. Mabuse

Lang's last film is a return to his pre-war German character, the evil Dr. Mabuse. A series of murders occur in Berlin and police believe that the killer thinks he's the re-creation of the doctor. It ends with a crackling action setpiece that integrates all of the several crazy subplots. The film has been transferred to disc in largely excellent black and white with an image-clarifying 16:9 enhancement. The picture is fine and crisp, until the last two minutes or so, which switch to a clean but softer source. This flaw doesn't harm the impact of the finale, but is still a disappointment, considering how absolutely perfect the rest looks. (The original materials must have had a damaged reel.) The English dub track isn't recommended but is there for those who simply can't abide subtitles. An informative commentary track by David Kalat provides a wealth of insight on Mabuse the Legend and *Thousand Eyes*. —*MM/GE* **AKA:** The Secret of Dr. Mabuse; The Diabolical Dr. Mabuse; The Shadow Versus the Thousand Eyes of Dr. Mabuse; Die Tausend Augen des Dr. Mabuse.
Movie: 🦴🦴🦴½ **DVD:** 🦴🦴🦴
Image Entertainment (Cat #ADED9649, UPC #01438196492). Full frame. Dolby Digital Mono. $29.99. Keepcase. *LANG:* German; English. *SUB:* English. *FEATURES:* Commentary: David Kalat • Trailers • Featurette • Posters.
1960 103m/B *GE* Dawn Addams, Peter Van Eyck, Gert Frobe, Wolfgang Preiss; **D:** Fritz Lang; **W:** Fritz Lang, Jan Fethke, Heinz Oskar Wuttig; **C:** Karl Lob; **M:** Gerhard Becker, Bert Grund.

Three Businessmen

Bizarre independent production is virtually an experimental film. The box copy compares it to Samuel Beckett and that's accurate enough in describing its absurdism. Two businessmen, Bennie Reyes (Sandoval) and Frank King (director Cox), are staying in a Liverpool hotel. They meet in the place's empty dining room and go out to search for a meal, leading to a long night's journey. The film appears to have been made with natural or minimal lighting and so the grain is so excessive that it leads to thick artifacts in many scenes. Some of the darker scenes are so murky that the screen virtually turns black. It's difficult to muster up much interest in the proceedings. —*MM*
Movie: 🦴 **DVD:** 🦴
Anchor Bay (Cat #DV11395, UPC #013131 139594). Widescreen (1.78:1) anamorphic. Dolby Digital Mono. $24.99. Keepcase. *LANG:* English. *FEATURES:* 20 chapter links • Commentary: Alex Cox, Tod Davies • Poster • Liner notes.
1999 81m/C Miguel Sandoval, Robert Wisdom, Alex Cox, Isabel Ampudia, Andrew Schofield, Tomoroh Taguchi; **D:** Alex Cox; **W:** Tod Davies; **C:** Robert Tregenza.

The Three Caballeros

Donald Duck stars in this journey through Latin America, produced by Disney to promote Pan-American unity during World War II. It's a collection of shorter cartoons that are filled with music, variety, and live-action/animated sequences. The DVD image seems flatter than the normal Disney fare from that era and the colors aren't as vibrant as one might expect given the subject matter. Other than that, there are very few imperfections and this is probably as good a picture as the source materials will allow. The audio is a very good mono track that is split between the two front speakers. The dialogue is always clear and the abundant music comes across very well. —*MP/MM*
Movie: 🦴🦴🦴 **DVD:** 🦴🦴½
Artisan Entertainment (Cat #19599). Full frame. Dolby Digital Mono. $29.99. Keepcase. *LANG:* English; French; Spanish. *SUB:* English. *FEATURES:* Theatrical trailer • Bonus cartoons.
1945 (G) 71m/C *D:* Norman Ferguson; **V:** Sterling Holloway, Aurora Miranda. *AWARDS: NOM:* Oscars '45: Sound, Scoring/Musical.

The Three Stooges: All the World's a Stooge

These short films have been well preserved. The quality of image and sound is directly proportional to the age of the work. Black-and-white photography of the 1930s was not nearly as sharp as it was in the following decades. The movies look as good as anyone could expect. I find the subtitles a help to understand much of the Stoogian verbal sparring. Contents: "Grips, Grunts, and Groans" (1936), "All the World's a Stooge" (1941), "3 Dumb Clucks" (1937), "Three Little Pirates" (1946), "Uncivil War Brides" (1946), "Back to the Woods" (1937), and "Violent Is the Word for Curly" (1938). —*MM*
Movie: 🦴🦴🦴 **DVD:** 🦴🦴🦴
Columbia Tristar Home Video (Cat #04761, UPC #043396047617). Full frame. Dolby Digital Mono. $19.99. Keepcase. *LANG:* English; Spanish; Portuguese. *SUB:* English; Spanish; Portuguese. *FEATURES:* 7 chapter links. —*MM*
2000 124m/B Moe Howard, Curly Howard, Larry Fine.

The Three Stooges: Merry Mavericks

Please see review of *Three Stooges: All The World's a Stooge* for critical comments. Contents: "Cactus Makes Perfect" (1942), "Out West" (1947), "Vagabond Loafers" (1949), "Dopey Dicks" (1950), "Punchy Cowpunchers" (1950), and "Merry Mavericks" (1951). —*MM*
Movie: 🦴🦴🦴 **DVD:** 🦴🦴🦴
Columbia Tristar Home Video (Cat #06047, UPC #043396060470). Full frame. Dolby Digital Mono. $19.99. Keepcase. *LANG:* English; Spanish; Portuguese. *SUB:* English; French; Spanish; Portuguese. *FEATURES:* 6 chapter links.
2001 99m/B Moe Howard, Larry Fine, Curly Howard, Shemp Howard.

The Three Stooges: Nutty but Nice

Please see review of *Three Stooges: All The World's a Stooge* for critical comments. Contents: "A Ducking They Did Go" (1939), "Hoi Polloi" (1935), "Half-Wits Holiday" (1947), "Higher Than a Kite" (1943), "False Alarms" (1936), and "Nutty but Nice" (1940). —*MM*
Movie: 🦴🦴🦴 **DVD:** 🦴🦴🦴
Columbia Tristar Home Video (Cat #05494, UPC #043396054943). Full frame. Dolby Digital Mono. $19.99. Keepcase. *LANG:* English; Spanish; Portuguese. *SUB:* English; French; Spanish; Portuguese. *FEATURES:* 6 chapter links.
2000 105m/B Moe Howard, Curly Howard, Larry Fine.

The Three Stooges: Spook Louder

Please see review of *Three Stooges: All The World's a Stooge* for critical comments. Contents: "Spook Louder" (1943), "Mummy's Dummies" (1948), "Shivering Sherlocks" (1947), "The Ghost Talks" (1949), "Hokus Pokus" (1949), and "Fright Night" (1947). —*MM*
Movie: 🦴🦴🦴 **DVD:** 🦴🦴🦴
Columbia Tristar Home Video (Cat #05427, UPC #043396054271). Full frame. Dolby Digital Mono. $19.99. Keepcase. *LANG:*

English; Spanish; Portuguese. *SUB:* English; Spanish; Portuguese. *FEATURES:* 6 chapter links.
2000 99m/B Moe Howard, Larry Fine, Curly Howard, Shemp Howard.

Three Strikes
Two-time loser Rob is released from jail determined to stay straight and thus avoid the harsh sentencing of California's "Three Strikes" law. But as luck—and a lame script filled with fart jokes, swear words, and little else—would have it, his buddy picks him up from jail in a stolen car and promptly gets in a gunfight with the cops. On the run from the police and gang members, Rob tries to finds a way to clear himself and get home. There's not much to redeem this disaster of a flick, unless you find embarrassingly stereotypical characters and *In Living Color*–reject jokes amusing. An impressive video transfer is highlighted by above-average color definition and minimal loss of clarity in darker scenes. The soundtrack is also quite well done. But there isn't a second that goes by in this film that isn't offensive or ignorant, which makes the quality of the soundtrack and video transfer a tragic waste. —*MJT*
Movie: woof *DVD:* ♪♪½
MGM Home Entertainment (Cat #1000830, UPC #027616851369). Full frame; widescreen (1.85:1) anamorphic. Dolby Digital 5.1 Surround; Dolby Digital Stereo Surround. $24.98. Keepcase. *LANG:* English; Spanish. *SUB:* French; Spanish. *FEATURES:* 28 chapter links • Theatrical trailer • Music videos by Da Howg, featuring Li'l Zane, Kam & Solo, Choclair.
2000 (R) 83m/C Brian Hooks, N'Bushe Wright, Faizon Love, Starletta DuPois, David Alan Grier, Dean Norris, Meagan Good, De'Aundre Bonds, Antonio Fargas, Vincent Schiavelli, David Leisure, Gerald S. O'Loughlin, George Wallace, E40, Barima McNight, Mo'Nique; *D:* DJ Pooh; *W:* DJ Pooh; *C:* Johnny Simmons; *M:* Aaron Anderson, Andrew Slack.

Threesome
College student Eddy (Charles) is uncertain about his sexual orientation. Stuart (Baldwin) is a hunka-hunka burnin' stud muffin. They're roommates and then a housing administration screw-up throws sexy Alex (Boyle) into their room. She's attracted to Eddy, Eddy's attracted to Stuart, Stuart's.... You get the picture. At its best, the picture does capture the intense insularity and intensity of a small clique. On his soft-spoken commentary track, which is candid and honest to a point, Fleming admits that the story is in part autobiographical, but he spends almost as much time talking about the trials of low-budget filmmaking. This was supposed to be a video premiere that somehow found its way into theatres. The disc looks good, considering the film's origins. His comments are the best extra. —*MM*
Movie: ♪♪ *DVD:* ♪♪½

Columbia Tristar Home Video (Cat #05856, UPC #043396058569). Widescreen (1.85:1) anamorphic; full frame. Dolby Digital Surround. $24.99. Keepcase. *LANG:* English; Spanish; French; Portuguese. *SUB:* English; Spanish; French; Portuguese; Chinese; Korean; Thai. *FEATURES:* 28 chapter links • Talent files • Alternative ending with commentary • Trailer • Commentary: Andrew Fleming.
1994 (R) 93m/C Lara Flynn Boyle, Stephen Baldwin, Josh Charles, Alexis Arquette, Mark Arnold, Martha Gehman, Michelle Matheson; *D:* Andrew Fleming; *W:* Andrew Fleming; *C:* Alexander Grusynski; *M:* Thomas Newman.

Thrill Seekers
Tabloid reporter Tom Merrick (Van Dien) discovers the same man in photographs of disasters that occurred many years apart. Then he meets the same guy on an airliner in flight. Yikes! Very similar ideas have been handled better in other science-fiction films. This one, made for the TBS cable channel, looks good on DVD. In fact, the clarity of the medium makes the corners cut in special effects scenes all the more obvious. Surround sound is much better than broadcast. —*MM* *AKA:* The Timeshifters.
Movie: ♪♪ *DVD:* ♪♪½
York Entertainment (Cat #YPD-1052, UPC #750723105222). Full frame. DTS Surround Stereo; Dolby Digital 5.1 Surround Stereo. $14.98. Keepcase. *LANG:* English. *SUB:* Spanish. *FEATURES:* 30 chapter links • Trailer • Filmographies.
1999 (PG-13) 92m/C Casper Van Dien, Catherine Bell, Peter Outerbridge, Theresa Saldana, Martin Sheen, Mimi Kuzyk, Lawrence Dane, Catherine Van Dien; *D:* Mario Azzopardi; *W:* Kurt Inderbitzin, Gay Walch; *C:* Derick Underschultz; *M:* Fred Mollin.

Throw Down
Ex-Marine martial artist Max Finister (Wingster) comes home to find that drug pushers have taken over the neighborhood. The rest of the story follows the familiar formula. This is an unusually inept action picture. The fights (directed by Wingster) tend to be slow and director Cyrus Beyzavi tends to cut people's heads off. Image quality is equal to an EP VHS tape. There is no menu. —*MM*
Movie: ♪ *DVD:* ♪
York Entertainment (Cat #YPD-1034, UPC #750723103426). Widescreen letterboxed. $14.99. Keepcase. *LANG:* English. *FEATURES:* 15 chapter links.
2000 90m/C La'Mard J. Wingster, Mark G. Young, Maribel Velez, Wendy Fajardo, John "Kato" Hollis, Patrick "Gun" Ryan; *D:* Cyrus Beyzavi; *C:* Mike Dolgetta.

Thug Immortal
Documentary about rapper Tupac Shakur who was murdered in 1996 is made up of interviews with people who knew him,

news tape, and even surveillance camera footage. It also includes two interviews, though his last, with Rob Marriott, is audio only. The DVD image is no better than the source material and most of that is only a short step up from home movies. Most of the interviews appear to have been taped without special lighting or sound equipment, and so the quality ranges between very poor and fair. For the most dedicated fans only. —*MM*
Movie: ♪♪½ *DVD:* ♪♪
Xenon Entertainment (Cat #1085, UPC #00799108529). Full frame. $19.99. Keepcase. *LANG:* English. *FEATURES:* 12 chapter links • Trailers.
1997 90m/C Tupac Shakur; *D:* Toby Russell.

Thug Life
Houston is the setting for another slice of violent life in the 'hood. Thomas Miles actually does a fairly good job in the lead, but the action scenes are embarrassingly lame. DVD image is exceptionally dark and grainy, giving rise to heavy pixels and artifacts. Sound is O.K. —*MM*
Movie: ♪♪ *DVD:* ♪♪
York Entertainment (Cat #YP-354, UPC #75072303543). Full frame. Dolby Digital 5.1 Surround Stereo. $14.99. Keepcase. *LANG:* English. *SUB:* Spanish. *FEATURES:* Trailers • Filmographies • Music credits.
2000 98m/C Thomas Miles, Gregory Stewart, The Lady of Rage, Napoleon, Willie D., *D:* Greg Carter; *W:* Greg Carter, Keith Kjornes; *C:* Mark David.

Thumbelina
Ornery little girl named Mia is magically sucked into the pages of the storybook she's reading and finds all sorts of adventures. Loose adaptation of Hans Christian Andersen's "Thumbelina" by Bluth is lackluster with acceptable songs. It's not up to the level of the best Disney animated features, but pleasant enough for the kids. DVD presents a fine re-creation of an average theatrical image. —*MM* *AKA:* Hans Christian Andersen's Thumbelina.
Movie: ♪♪½ *DVD:* ♪♪½
Warner Home Video, Inc. (Cat #24000). Widescreen (1.85:1) letterboxed; full frame. Dolby Digital Stereo. $19.98. Snapper. *LANG:* English; French. *SUB:* French. *CAP:* English. *FEATURES:* Trailer • 32 chapter links.
1994 (G) 86m/C *D:* Don Bluth, Gary Goldman; *W:* Don Bluth; *M:* William Ross, Barry Manilow, Barry Manilow, Jack Feldman, Bruce Sussman; *V:* Jodi Benson, Gary Imhoff, Charo, Gilbert Gottfried, Carol Channing, John Hurt, Will Ryan, June Foray, Kenneth Mars. *AWARDS:* Golden Raspberries '94: Worst Song ("Marry the Mole").

Thunderbolt & Lightfoot
Doherty (Eastwood) is an ex-thief on the run from his partners (Kennedy and Lewis)

who believe he's made off with the loot from their last job. He joins up with drifter Lightfoot (Bridges) and eventually all four decide to pull the job again. Car chases, shootouts, and many explosions ensue, but none are more impressive than the polyester shirts the two stars wear. They seem constantly to be in motion, even when the wearers are immobile, and when they do move, the shirts are likely to burst into psychedelic patterns. Otherwise, the film appears to have been perfectly preserved with an image that shows no serious signs of wear. —MM
Movie: 🎬🎬🎬 **DVD:** 🎬🎬½
MGM Home Entertainment (Cat #908102, UPC #027616810229). Widescreen letterboxed. Dolby Digital Mono. $24.99. Keepcase. *LANG:* English; Spanish. *SUB:* French; Spanish. *CAP:* English. *FEATURES:* 32 chapter links ▪ Liner notes ▪ Trailer.
1974 (R) 115m/C Clint Eastwood, Jeff Bridges, George Kennedy, Geoffrey Lewis, Gary Busey; *D:* Michael Cimino; *W:* Michael Cimino; *C:* Frank Stanley; *M:* Dee Barton. *AWARDS: NOM:* Oscars '74: Support. Actor (Bridges).

Thunderheart
Ray (Kilmer), a young FBI agent, is sent to an Oglala Sioux reservation to investigate a murder. He is part Sioux but resents being chosen for the assignment because of it. He's aided by a veteran partner (Shepard) and a shrewd local tribal police officer (Greene in top form). Set in the late 1970s and filmed (beautifully by cinematographer Roger Deakins) on the Pine Ridge Reservation in South Dakota, the film is loosely based on director Apted's documentary about Leonard Peltier, *Incident at Oglala,* which might have made a good extra or companion piece. Instead, the frills-free DVD delivers a very good image. Sound is even more impressive. —MM
Movie: 🎬🎬½ **DVD:** 🎬🎬🎬
Columbia Tristar Home Video (Cat #70699, UPC #043396706996). Widescreen (1.85:1) letterboxed; full frame. Dolby Digital Stereo. $29.95. Keepcase. *LANG:* English; French. *SUB:* French. *CAP:* English. *FEATURES:* Trailer ▪ 28 chapter links.
1992 (R) 118m/C Val Kilmer, Sam Shepard, Graham Greene, Fred Ward, Fred Dalton Thompson, Sheila Tousey, Chief Ted Thin Elk, John Trudell, Dennis Banks, David Crosby; *D:* Michael Apted; *W:* John Fusco; *C:* Roger Deakins; *M:* James Horner.

The Tic Code
Twelve-year-old prodigy Miles (Marquette) tries to set his mother (Draper, who also wrote the script) up with jazz saxophonist Tyrone Pike (Hines). Given the unpolished look of the independent production, it gains little on DVD. Sound is a significant improvement, though, and the jazz score deserves the best. Also, the real points are the characters and the acting. —MM
Movie: 🎬🎬🎬 **DVD:** 🎬🎬½

Universal Studios Home Video (Cat #21105, UPC #025192110528). Full frame. Dolby Digital Surround Stereo. $24.98. Keepcase. *LANG:* English. *CAP:* English. *FEATURES:* 18 chapter links.
1999 (R) 91m/C Gregory Hines, Polly Draper, James McCaffrey, Christopher Marquette, Carol Kane, Bill Nunn, Tony Shalhoub, Desmond Robertson, Fisher Stevens, Camryn Manheim, David Johansen; *D:* Gary Winick; *W:* Polly Draper; *C:* Wolfgang Held; *M:* Michael Wolff.

Tie Me Up! Tie Me Down!
Ricky (Banderas), a psychiatric patient, kidnaps Scream Queen Marina (Abril) and holds her captive to win her love. This curiously comic love story is a showcase for filmmaker Almodovar's famously quirky predilections. It is also extremely well acted and photographed. Some fairly explicit sexual material has earned it an "NC-17" rating. Disc presents the film with eye-popping clarity. If the color scheme isn't quite as bright as *All About My Mother,* it is just as engaging. The film is certainly not to all tastes. Fans looking for something outside the mainstream and challenging should give it a look. —MM *AKA:* Atame!.
Movie: 🎬🎬🎬 **DVD:** 🎬🎬🎬
Anchor Bay (Cat #DV11267, UPC #013131126792). Widescreen (1.85:1) anamorphic. Dolby Digital Mono. $24.99. Keepcase. *LANG:* Spanish. *SUB:* English. *FEATURES:* Trailer ▪ 32 chapter links.
1990 (NC-17) 105m/C SP Victoria Abril, Antonio Banderas, Loles Leon, Francesco Rabal, Julieta Serrano, Maria Barranco, Rossy de Palma; *D:* Pedro Almodovar; *W:* Pedro Almodovar; *C:* Jose Luis Alcaine; *M:* Ennio Morricone.

The Tie That Binds
Insipid thriller is a cheap imitation of its cousin *The Hand That Rocks the Cradle* (made by the same producers). Leanne and John Netherwood (Hannah and Carradine) are the psycho parents out to reclaim their daughter from the couple (Spano and Kelly) who adopted her. Of all the kids out there, they choose the one who likes to sleep with a butcher knife under her pillow! Every "family threatened by a psychotic" cliché is trotted out. The image is generally very good with no significant flaws beyond the usual aliasing. Sound is fine. —MM
Movie: 🎬 **DVD:** 🎬🎬½
Hollywood Pictures Home Video (Cat #17636, UPC #717951003461). Widescreen (1.85:1) letterboxed. Dolby Digital Surround Stereo. $29.99. Keepcase. *LANG:* English; French. *CAP:* English. *FEATURES:* 16 chapter links ▪ Trailers.
1995 (R) 98m/C Daryl Hannah, Keith Carradine, Moira Kelly, Vincent Spano, Julia Devin, Ray Reinhardt, Cynda Williams; *D:* Wesley Strick; *W:* Michael Auerbach; *C:* Bobby Bukowski; *M:* Graeme Revell.

Tierra
Metaphysical messiness. Mystery exterminator Angel (Gomez) comes to Aragon, a land of red soil and lightning strikes, to fumigate the woodlice infesting the vineyards. He recruits locals and gypsies to help while becoming involved with two women—shy Angela (Suarez) and hot Mari (Klein). The picture is clear, and never muddy, but there is a substantial amount of grain throughout most of the film. Also, at times, the colors appear to be washed-out, but given the alien landscape, this may be intentional. Overall, the transfer is adequate, but it would have been nice to see a less grainy print. The audio offers a nice balance between dialogue and sound effects. The English subtitles are printed in white and they appear on the picture, making them difficult to read at times. —ML/MM *AKA:* Earth.
Movie: 🎬🎬 **DVD:** 🎬🎬½
Vanguard International Cinema, Inc. (Cat #1006). Widescreen (2.35:1) letterboxed. Dolby Digital Stereo. $29.95. Keepcase. *LANG:* Spanish. *SUB:* English. *FEATURES:* Trailer.
1995 122m/C SP Carmelo Gomez, Emma Suarez, Silke Klein, Karra Elejalde, Nancho Novo, Txema Blasco; *D:* Julio Medem; *W:* Julio Medem; *C:* Javier Aguirresarobe; *M:* Alberto Iglesias.

Tigerland
As a group of young army recruits is finishing boot camp, a highly intelligent southerner, Bozz (Farrell), rebels against the training and the thought-processes that go into it. By studying the military laws, Bozz is able to have several fellow recruits discharged for family hardship and other technicalities but finds he is unable to prevent himself from going off to war. At the war-like training facility "Tigerland," conflicts between Bozz and a fellow recruit come to a head. A war film without the war, this one plays at times like the first half of *Full Metal Jacket,* but earns points for its thought-provoking ideology. Farrell (who is Irish) is excellent as Bozz. The disc is sharp with a dynamic and involving sound mix, though it's a bit difficult to assess due to the muted, drab colors and intentionally grainy photography. The screen tests with Colin Farrell are interesting, though the "making of" featurette is little more than a padded commercial. The audio commentary is excellent; Schumacher is an intelligent, revealing commentator and he dissects the production with interest and enthusiasm. —DG
Movie: 🎬🎬🎬 **DVD:** 🎬🎬🎬½
20th Century Fox Home Entertainment (Cat #2001659, UPC #02454301659). Widescreen (1.85:1) anamorphic. Dolby Surround 5.1; Dolby Surround. $29.98. Keepcase. *LANG:* English. *SUB:* English; Spanish. *CAP:* English. *FEATURES:* 24 chapter links ▪ Insert card with chapter listing ▪ Commentary: Schumacher ▪ Casting sessions with Colin Farrell ▪ "Making of" featurette ▪ Theatrical trailer and TV spots.

2000 (R) 101m/C Colin Farrell, Matthew Davis, Clifton (Gonzalez) Collins Jr., Tom Guiry, Russell Richardson, Cole Hauser, Shea Whigham; **D:** Joel Schumacher; **W:** Ross Klaven, Michael McGruther; **C:** Matthew Libatique; **M:** Nathan Larsen. *AWARDS: NOM:* Ind. Spirit '01: Support. Actor (Hauser).

The Tigger Movie

Feeling lonely because no one wants to bounce with him, Tigger decides that he will find his family of Tiggers. All his friends in the Hundred Acre Wood—Winnie the Pooh, Roo, Piglet, Eeyore, Kanga, Rabbit, and Owl—pitch in to help. (A word of warning for parents: The subject matter of the film may not bode well with adopted children.) The quality of the animation lies somewhere between Disney's usual theatrical releases and Saturday morning cartoon fare. The colors are nice, and there are some multi-plane shots, but for the most part, the animation is simply average. The film is slowly paced at the beginning, so some youngsters may get bored. The seven original songs are mostly catchy and fun. The image is crystal clear and there are no obvious defects in the source print. Dialogue is always clear and the songs sound especially nice. —*ML/MM*
Movie: 🐾🐾½ **DVD:** 🐾🐾🐾
Artisan Entertainment (Cat #19302). Widescreen (1.66:1) letterboxed. Dolby Digital 5.1 Surround Stereo; Dolby Digital Stereo. $29.99. Keepcase. *LANG:* English; French; Spanish. *SUB:* English. *FEATURES:* Trailer • Trivia game • Thingamajigger game • Family tree maker • Music video • DVD storybook • Singalong "Round Your Family Tree."
2000 (G) 77m/C D: Jun Falkenstein; **W:** Jun Falkenstein; **M:** Harry Gregson-Williams; **V:** Jim (Jonah) Cummings.

Till the Clouds Roll By

In typical Hollywood fashion, this all-star high-gloss biography of songwriter Jerome Kern (Walker) bears little resemblance to the composer's real life. But it is filled with wonderful songs from his Broadway hit. Songs: Showboat Medley: Till the Clouds Roll By; Howja Like to Spoon with Me?; The Last Time I Saw Paris; They Didn't Believe Me; I Won't Dance; Why Was I Born?; Who?; Sunny. The grainy color image contains a few scratches and flecks. Sound is good but not spectacular, considering the quality of the music and singing. —*MM*
Movie: 🐾🐾½ **DVD:** 🐾🐾½
Madacy Entertainment (Cat #99008, UPC #056775004491). Full frame. Dolby Digital Mono. $9.99. Keepcase. *LANG:* English. *FEATURES:* Judy Garland thumbnail bio • Production credits • 9 chapter links. Also available from Parade (cat. # 55276), for $17.98.
1946 137m/C Robert Walker, Van Heflin, Judy Garland, Frank Sinatra, Lucille Bremer, Kathryn Grayson, June Allyson, Dinah Shore, Lena Horne, Virginia O'Brien, Tony Martin; **D:** Richard Whorf; **W:** Myles Connolly, Jean Holloway; **C:** Harry Stradling Sr.; **M:** Conrad Salinger, Roger Edens, Lennie Hayton.

Time Code

Mike Figgis's challenging real-time comic/thriller tells a story from four points of view and four separate images that sometimes overlap. It took 15 attempts to get it right. The final, theatrical release (called version 15 on this disc) was filmed with high-definition video cameras in four continuous takes at 3:00, Friday, Nov. 19, 1999. The story concerns an alcoholic Hollywood studio executive (Skarsgard), his wife (Burrows), his lover (Hayek), and her lesbian partner (Tripplehorn). The screen is divided into quarters; sound intensifies from frame to frame to guide the viewer to the important action. That's one option; you can also choose to listen to the frame of your choice. The disc also includes the first version of the film. Both have commentary by Figgis explaining what he was trying to do, and where the ideas came from. For my money, it's an intriguing experiment that's less than completely successful. The various stories never quite rose above the gimmick level. Perhaps because the four images are so small (at least on my TV), I could not see the characters well enough to generate any real empathy for them. Or was it because my attention was never fully engaged for one storyline long enough? In either case, this is no *Run, Lola, Run.* Those criticisms notwithstanding, Figgis and the DVD producers take full advantage of the medium. At some time in the future (when all of us have huge wall-sized monitors), this disc may be seen as a landmark that pointed the direction in which DVD was going to grow. —*MM* **AKA:** Timecode.
Movie: 🐾🐾½ **DVD:** 🐾🐾🐾🐾
Columbia Tristar Home Video (Cat #05608, UPC #043396056084). Full frame. Dolby Digital 5.1 Surround Stereo; Dolby Surround Stereo. $24.95. Keepcase. *LANG:* English. *CAP:* English. *FEATURES:* 15 chapter links • 2 commentary tracks • Audio interactivity • Mike Figgis's video diary • DVD-ROM features • Theatrical trailer • Production notes.
2000 (R) 97m/C Stellan Skarsgard, Saffron Burrows, Salma Hayek, Jeanne Tripplehorn, Richard Edson, Julian Sands, Xander Berkeley, Glenne Headly, Holly Hunter, Danny Huston, Kyle MacLachlan, Alessandro Nivola, Steven Weber, Viveka Davis, Aimee Graham, Andrew Heckler, Daphna Kastner, Leslie Mann, Mia Maestro; **D:** Mike Figgis; **W:** Mike Figgis; **C:** Patrick Alexander Stewart; **M:** Mike Figgis, Anthony Marinelli.

The Time Machine

Rod Taylor plays George, an inventor in Victorian England who throws a dinner party on New Year's Eve 1899 to announce that he's created a machine for traveling through time. His friends are unimpressed and don't understand what use time travel could have for mankind. Frustrated, George climbs into his machine after the guests leave and experiences adventures at various points in history (all at the very same location in England). After quick stops at both world wars and a future nuclear war (in 1966!), he finally goes far ahead into the year 802,701 where he finds humanity divided into two groups: the normal-looking Eloi, and the Morlocks, disfigured mutants who live underground. The Eloi are helpless, passive, and ignorant, and George is horrified to learn that they are essentially being used as livestock for the cannibalistic Morlocks. He falls in love with a beautiful Eloi named Weena (Mimieux) and decides to help free her people. Warner has done a stunning job in bringing this 40-year-old film to DVD. The print used is very clean with only a few white specks appearing on the source material. Colors are deep and solid, with strong blacks. The image is very crisp, detailed, and sharp. There are almost no flaws in this transfer, aside from occasional (and almost unnoticeable) grain. This transfer is amazing and hopefully will be a benchmark for future transfers of older films. Of the extras, the entertaining 50-minute documentary "The Time Machine: The Journey Back," hosted by star Rod Taylor, is an informative feature containing interviews with cast members and explanations of the impressive special effect work. Unfortunately, the isolated music track that is promised on the DVD packaging is not provided. —*GE*
Movie: 🐾🐾🐾½ **DVD:** 🐾🐾🐾½
Warner Home Video, Inc. (Cat #65231, UPC #012569523128). Widescreen (1.78:1) anamorphic. $24.98. Snapper. *LANG:* English. *SUB:* English; French. *FEATURES:* Documentary: "The Time Machine: The Journey Back" • Theatrical trailer.
1960 103m/C Rod Taylor, Yvette Mimieux, Whit Bissell, Sebastian Cabot, Alan Young, Paul Frees, Bob Barran, Doris Lloyd; **D:** George Pal; **W:** David Duncan; **C:** Paul Vogel; **M:** Russell Garcia.

Timeless

Hart's experimental feature debut uses Super-8, 16mm, and 35mm to tell a familiar story. Eighteen-year-old Terry (Bryne) hangs out on the streets of Queens doing various odd jobs for a variety of small-time gamblers, dealers, and mobsters. He falls for Lyrica (Duge) and gets her away from an abusive lover. DVD picture is notably sharp and clear, showing only a fine amount of grain at times. (This doesn't count the scenes that are intentionally grainy.) The source print shows relatively few defects, and those present are very minor. The film's color palette is very natural, although a bit washed-out at times. (Once again, this may have been intentional on the part of the filmmakers.) This is no overt artifacting or noise on the image. Monaural soundtrack gives us clear dialogue that is never overpowered by the sound effects. —*ML*

Movie: 🎬🎬🎬 **DVD:** 🎬🎬½
Vanguard International Cinema, Inc. (Cat #VF0114, UPC #658769011432). Widescreen (1.85:1) letterboxed. Dolby Digital Mono. $29.95. Keepcase. *LANG:* English.
1996 90m/C Peter Byrne, Michael Griffiths, Melissa Duge; *D:* Chris Hart; *W:* Chris Hart.

Timelock

If you have a couple of hours to spare to watch a slightly strange low-budget sci-fi prison break-out movie, this is the one for you. Ayre Gross plays Riley, a computer hacker being shuttled to a prison asteroid for his hacking crimes. He should be going to Alpha 1, a minimum security spot, but instead is going to Alpha 4, where the really bad people go. D'Abo is Teegs, the sexy captain of the ship that makes its money transporting prisoners to Alphas 1–4. The villain, named Villum (Meeks), is a southern belle of a man, occasionally fanning himself between killing people. Of course, a prison break occurs just as they land. Of course, Teegs and Riley fall in love while trying to get back to the ship (more out of script considerations than chemistry it seems.) And of course, Riley proves himself to be a hero instead of just a whiney nerd. It's a shame that Ayre Gross, who is a fine actor, is reduced to playing dorks in low-budget films and it's a shame that d'Abo, a former Bond girl is oh, never mind. *Timelock* is neither bad, nor good; it is instead the kind of film they invented the word "mediocre" for. The disc looks and sounds average. —CA
Movie: 🎬½ **DVD:** 🎬🎬
MTI Home Video (Cat #MTI1053DVD, UPC #039414030532). Full frame. $24.95. Keepcase. *LANG:* English. *FEATURES:* Trailers • Previews.
1999 100m/C Maryam D'Abo, Arye Gross, Jeff Speakman, Jeffrey Meek, Martin Kove; *D:* Robert Munic; *W:* Joseph John Barmettler Jr.; *C:* Steve Adcock.

Times Square

Privileged 13-year-old Pammy (Alvarado) learns about life on her own when she teams up with rebellious Nicky (Johnson) in New York before the raunchy parts of midtown were Disneyfied. It's unrealistic in its shameless glamorization of unappealing characters. Only Tim Curry's DJ generates any interest. The rock score is dated. DVD can do nothing to improve the low-budget shot-on-location image. —MM
Movie: 🎬🎬 **DVD:** 🎬🎬
Anchor Bay (Cat #DV11373, UPC #013131 137392). Widescreen (1.85:1) anamorphic. Dolby Digital 5.1 Surround Stereo. $24.99. Keepcase. *LANG:* English. *FEATURES:* 29 chapter links • Trailer • Commentary: Alan Moyle, Robin Johnson.
1980 (R) 111m/C Tim Curry, Trini Alvarado, Robin Johnson, Peter Coffield, Elizabeth Pena, Anna Maria Horsford; *D:* Allan Moyle; *W:* Jacob Brackman; *C:* James A. Contner.

Titan A.E.

An alien race, composed of living energy, destroys the Earth. Years later, a young salvage-man, Cale (voice of Damon) discovers that he holds the key to finding his father's lost ship, the *Titan*. Legend has it that the ship holds the secret to mankind's salvation. Pursued by the aliens, Cale joins up with the crew of the *Valkyrie* in an effort to find the ship. Though this animated film is colorful, exciting, and features several breathtaking sequences, it is somehow unsatisfying. The voice casting of the leads is probably too low-key and the betrayal of one character is manipulative and unconvincing. The disc is mostly excellent; the picture is sharp and clear, but somewhat grainy and prone to ghosting in some of the red sequences. The Surround track is excellent. The deleted scenes and featurettes are interesting, but the audio commentary is a bit dull and often hard to distinguish the voices of the two commentators. —DG
Movie: 🎬🎬½ **DVD:** 🎬🎬🎬½
Fox/Lorber Home Video (Cat #2000924, UPC #02454300924). Widescreen (2.35:1) anamorphic. DTS; 5.1 Surround, Dolby Surround. $22.98. Keepcase. *LANG:* English; French. *SUB:* English; Spanish. *CAP:* English. *FEATURES:* Commentary: director • *Quest for the Titan* FOX TV special • Music video • Still gallery • Trailers and TV spots • Deleted scenes • 20 chapter links • Insert card with chapter guide.
2000 (PG) 95m/C *D:* Don Bluth, Gary Goldman; *W:* Ben Edlund, John August, Joss Whedon; *M:* Graeme Revell; *V:* Matt Damon, Drew Barrymore, Bill Pullman, Nathan Lane, Janeane Garofalo, John Leguizamo, Tone Loc, Ron Perlman, Alex D. Linz, Jim Breuer.

Titanic 2000

The availability of more affordable computer-generated effects has made it possible for cheap exploitation to be much more ambitious. Here, with a nearly non-existent budget, the filmmakers are able to create cartoon-like shots of a digital ocean liner. The alleged plot has to do with a vampire (Parks) who is hidden in the hold of said ship, and her nubile young prey (Krause). Filling out the running time are supporting characters (who could be refugees from a weekend cable-TV horror show) who tell bad jokes. The DVD has the dim, grainy look of bargain-basement video, but then nobody's going to watch this kind of cheesy unapologetic exploitation for technical quality. —MM
Movie: 🎬½ **DVD:** 🎬
El Independent Cinema (Cat #sc-1002-dvd, UPC #612385100291). Full frame. $19.98. Keepcase. *LANG:* English. *FEATURES:* 14 chapter links • 7 short E.I. Independent films • Stills gallery • Trailers.
2000 90m/C Tammy Parks, Tina Krause, Michael Thomas, Thomas Jacob Bogert, John P. Fedele, David Fine, Roxanna Michaels; *D:* John P. Fedele; *W:* Clancy Fitzsimmons; *C:* Timothy Healy.

Tito and Me

In Belgrade, 1954, ten-year-old Zoran is fascinated with Yugoslavian leader Marshall Tito. Then there's romance; Zoran has a crush on a taller classmate who breaks up with him when she is chosen as one of Tito's Young Pioneers, which means a two-week trip to the country. If that weren't enough, Zoran lives in a crowded apartment with his extended family. In his debut role, young Vojnov is superb, even supplying a deadpan voice-over narration. Optional subtitles are easy to read, and overall, the DVD image is excellent for an import. Recommended. —MM *AKA:* Tito i Ja; Tito and I.
Movie: 🎬🎬🎬 **DVD:** 🎬🎬🎬
Winstar Home Entertainment (Cat #FLV52 78, UPC #720917527826). $24.99. Keepcase. *LANG:* Serbo-Croatian. *SUB:* English. *FEATURES:* 16 chapter links • Filmographies and awards • Production credits.
1992 104m/C *YU* Dimitrie Vojnov, Lazar Ristovski, Anica Dobra, Predrag Manojlovic, Olivera Markovic; *D:* Goran Markovic; *W:* Goran Markovic; *C:* Radoslav Vladic; *M:* Zoran Simjanovic.

Titus

Julie Taymor adapts a flashy version of Shakespeare's gory lesser-known play *Titus Andronicus*. Victorious Roman general Titus (Hopkins) has just defeated the Goths and captured Tamora (Lange), the Goth queen, and her sons, one of whom he promptly sacrifices to appease the gods. Decadent Emperor Saturninus (Cumming) claims Tamora for his queen; her daughter Lavinia (Fraser) suffers a fate worse than death; Tamora wants revenge; Titus wants revenge; there's a villainous Moor (Lennix) and a lot of campy fantasy and blood. Film arrives on DVD as a two-disc set. The first presents the film—in near-perfect visual form, of course—along with two commentary tracks. On one, Taymor talks about her experiences; the second is for Hopkins and Lennix, who are not nearly as verbose. (A separate index takes you to the scenes they're discussing.) The other extras are on the second disc. —MM
Movie: 🎬🎬½ **DVD:** 🎬🎬🎬½
20th Century Fox Home Entertainment (Cat #2000540). Widescreen (2.35:1) anamorphic. Dolby Digital 5.1 Surround; Dolby Surround. $34.98. Keepcase. *LANG:* English. *SUB:* English; Spanish. *FEATURES:* 2 commentary tracks • Isolated music track with commentary • Interview with Taymor • "Making of" documentary • "Penny Arcade nightmares" featurette • Stills gallery • "American Cinematographer" articles • Trailers and TV spots.
1999 (R) 162m/C Anthony Hopkins, Jessica Lange, Alan Cumming, Harry J. Lennix, Colm Feore, Laura Fraser, James Frain, Angus Macfadyen, Jonathan Rhys Meyers, Geraldine McEwan, Matthew Rhys; *D:* Julie Taymor; *W:* Julie Taymor; *C:* Luciano Tovoli; *M:* Elliot Goldenthal. *AWARDS: NOM:* Oscars '99: Costume Des.

Tokyo Raiders

This is a remarkably stylish Hong Kong action flick. Director Jingle Ma brings a music video sensibility to the proceedings. The plot concerns a detective (Tony Leung) and his hunt for a gangster, but that's a negligible excuse for a series of cleverly choreographed action scenes. The physical violence is carefully modulated for a young audience, and many gadgets are employed. The film looks great on DVD because so much care was taken with the production design (credit Yee Chung Man) that's done in shades of hard gray. I noticed no serious visual flaws, but I might have missed them because the slow-motion effects are so neat. For my money, this one's a lot more fun than either of the similar *Mission: Impossible* extravaganzas. —MM

Movie: 🎬🎬🎬 **DVD:** 🎬🎬🎬
Columbia Tristar Home Video (Cat #05677, UPC #043396056770). Widescreen (1.85:1) letterboxed; full frame. Dolby Digital 5.1 Surround Stereo; Dolby Digital Surround. $19.99. Keepcase. *LANG:* Cantonese; English. *SUB:* English; Spanish; Portuguese. *FEATURES:* 28 chapter links • "Making of" featurette.
2000 (PG-13) 100m/C *HK* Tony Leung Chiu-Wai, Ekin Cheng, Toru Nakamura, Hiroshi Abe, Kelly Chen, Kumiko Endo, Minami Shirakawa, Majyu Ozawa, Cecilia Cheung; **D:** Jingle Ma; **W:** Susan Chan, Felix Chong; **C:** Jingle Ma, Chan Chi Ying; **M:** Peter Kam.

Tom & Jerry's Greatest Chases

This collection contains 14 "Tom & Jerry" cartoons plus the famous "Anchors Aweigh" number where Jerry dances with Gene Kelly. Sadly, the prints used for the DVD show signs of wear with speckles, scratches, and dust visible almost throughout. Fortunately, however, the furious action on the screen quickly—and completely—distracts from those deficiencies. The transfer is strong in its color reproduction and appears balanced with solid blacks. Although the compression is generally good, some digital artifacts are evident in the presentation. While the audio is mostly free of noise, as expected, its age is undeniable. With a limited frequency response and no bass extension, the music and sound effects are often harsh sounding. —GH/MM
Movie: 🎬🎬🎬 **DVD:** 🎬🎬½
Warner Home Video, Inc. (Cat #65306). Full frame. Dolby Digital Mono. $24.98. Snapper. *LANG:* English.
1945 ?m/C

Tom Jones [MGM]

Brilliant bawdy comedy based on Henry Fielding's novel about a rustic playboy's wild life in 18th-century England is one of the highpoints of '60s cinema. It's hilarious, clever, and not at all dated, with a grand performance by Finney. The grainy

look comes from the original. Some might complain about the lack of a Surround remix during the famous hunt scene (Chapter 4), but it might well have been out of step with the rest of the action. And would that really have done anything to enhance the evocation of the past as a real place, or the characters? I doubt it. Even though MGM has chosen to make this a bare-bones DVD, it's well worth owning. —MM
Movie: 🎬🎬🎬🎬 **DVD:** 🎬🎬🎬
MGM Home Entertainment (Cat #10020 67, UPC #027616862976). Widescreen (1.66:1) letterboxed. Dolby Digital Mono. $19.98. Keepcase. *LANG:* English; French; Spanish. *SUB:* French; Spanish. *FEATURES:* 16 chapter links • Trailer.
1963 121m/C *GB* Albert Finney, Susannah York, Hugh Griffith, Edith Evans, Joan Greenwood, Diane Cilento, George Devine, David Tomlinson, Joyce Redman, Lynn Redgrave, Julian Glover, Peter Bull, David Warner; **D:** Tony Richardson; **W:** John Osborne; **C:** Walter Lassally; **M:** John Addison. *AWARDS:* Oscars '63: Adapt. Screenplay, Director (Richardson), Picture, Orig. Score; British Acad. '63: Film, Screenplay; Directors Guild '63: Director (Richardson); Golden Globes '64: Film—Mus./Comedy, Foreign Film; Natl. Bd. of Review '63: Director (Richardson); N.Y. Film Critics '63: Director (Richardson), Film; *NOM:* Oscars '63: Actor (Finney), Art Dir./Set Dec., Color, Support. Actor (Griffith), Support. Actress (Cilento, Evans, Redman).

Tom Thumb

George Pal fantasy casts Tamblyn as the titular diminutive boy who saves village treasury from bad guys Sellers and Thomas; adapted from the classic Grimm fairy tale. A bit episodic but still a delight today thanks to Pal's charming special effects, which combine live actors, animation, and puppets, and make excellent use of perspective camera tricks. The DVD presentation is sharp enough, but a slight drabness of the color takes away from some of the viewing enjoyment, as does what appears to be a slight overcropping on the widescreen side and the resulting loss of image on the top and bottom. At times, the full-frame version is preferable. The mono sound is super crisp with very little distortion and at least adequate fidelity for this vintage of film. Some supplementals on the special effect technology of the time would have been a great addition. —JO
Movie: 🎬🎬🎬 **DVD:** 🎬🎬½
Warner Home Video, Inc. (Cat #65401, UPC #012569540125). Widescreen (1.85:1) anamorphic; full frame. Dolby Digital Mono. $24.98. Snapper. *LANG:* English; French. *SUB:* English; French. *CAP:* English. *FEATURES:* 22 chapter links • 2 theatrical trailers • Commentary: Christopher Lee, Sarah Lawson.
1958 92m/C *GB* Russ Tamblyn, Peter Sellers, Terry-Thomas; **D:** George Pal; **W:** Ladislas Fodor; **C:** Georges Perinal; **M:** Douglas Gamley.

Tommy

The years have been ruthless to the Ken Russell adaptation of the Who's rock opera. The story of an abused child (Daltrey) who becomes a messiah is reduced to posturing silliness. In the wake of *The Rocky Horror Picture Show*, its campiness seems forced and false. It lacks the musical and visual complexity of *Pink Floyd: The Wall*. The parade of rock stars lip-syncing covers of the songs is a bit embarrassing. (At times, Elton John sounds like he's been inhaling helium.) No huge flaws are apparent in either image or sound, but they're not that terrific, either. —MM **AKA:** The Who's Tommy.
Movie: 🎬🎬 **DVD:** 🎬🎬
Columbia Tristar Home Video (Cat #2611). Widescreen (1.85:1) anamorphic; full frame. Dolby Digital 5.0 Surround; Dolby Digital Surround. $24.95. Keepcase. *LANG:* English. *SUB:* English; French; Spanish. *FEATURES:* Talent files • 28 chapter links.
1975 (PG) 108m/C *GB* Ann-Margret, Elton John, Oliver Reed, Tina Turner, Roger Daltrey, Eric Clapton, Keith Moon, Pete Townshend, Jack Nicholson, Robert Powell, Paul Nicholas, Barry Winch, Victoria Russell, Ben Aris, Mary Holland, Jennifer Baker, Susan Baker, Arthur Brown, John Entwhistle; **D:** Ken Russell; **W:** Ken Russell, Keith Moon, John Entwhistle; **C:** Ronnie Taylor, Dick Bush; **M:** Pete Townshend, John Entwhistle. *AWARDS:* Golden Globes '76: Actress—Mus./Comedy (Ann-Margret); *NOM:* Oscars '75: Actress (Ann-Margret), Orig. Score.

Tomorrow the World

This bizarre little wartime drama is dated in almost every respect. Emil Bruckner (Homeier) is a Hitler Youth who's sent to live with his uncle (March) in America. The conflict between a fascist mindset and liberal tolerance is painted with very broad strokes. Both acting and writing have an extravagant quality that contemporary audiences will have trouble accepting. The DVD was created from damaged materials. The soundtrack is thin and static-filled, and parts of the print are heavily scratched. —MM
Movie: 🎬🎬🎬 **DVD:** 🎬🎬
Image Entertainment (Cat #ID9800VMDVD, UPC #014381980028). Full frame. Dolby Digital Mono. $24.99. Snapper. *LANG:* English. *FEATURES:* 12 chapter links.
1944 86m/B Fredric March, Betty Field, Agnes Moorehead, Skip Homeier, Joan Carroll, Boots Brown, Edit Angold, Rudy Wiesler, Marvin Davis, Patsy Ann Thompson, Mary Newton, Tom Fadden; **D:** Leslie Fenton; **W:** Ring Lardner Jr., Leopold Atlas; **C:** Henry Sharp.

Tonight or Never

Delightful romantic comedy makes a belated but welcome arrival to home video on disc. Gloria Swanson is the opera diva who falls for a man of mystery (Melvyn Douglas). He appears to be a smooth-talking gigolo, but she might not care. The film has been preserved by the UCLA Film and

Television Archives and the Mary Pickford Foundation and so the image is exceptionally sharp and finely detailed. Gregg Toland's black-and-white cinematography is some of the best of the early 1930s. Some light snow and static appear from time to time but they do little to dim the sparkle of these attractive characters in their snappy, sexy duds, courtesy of Coco Chanel. Recommended. —*MM*
Movie: 🎞🎞🎞 **DVD:** 🎞🎞🎞
Image Entertainment (Cat #ID9200MLSD-VD, UPC #014381920024). Full frame. Dolby Digital Mono. $24.99. Snapper. *LANG:* English. *FEATURES:* 12 chapter links.
1931 80m/B Gloria Swanson, Melvyn Douglas, Ferdinand Gottschalk, Alison Skipworth, Boris Karloff, Robert Greig; **D:** Mervyn LeRoy; **W:** Ernest Vajda, Frederic Hatton, Fanny Hatton; **C:** Gregg Toland; **M:** Alfred Newman.

Tootsie

Intense and often unemployed New York actor Michael Dorsey (Hoffman) disguises himself as a woman to get a role on a soap opera. As his popularity on TV mounts, his love life becomes increasingly soap-operatic. That's only the beginning of this brilliant comedy that does more with gender assumptions than any movie since *Some Like It Hot*. Superb performances all around. Why, then, is the commentary track that director Lumet did for the laserdisc not included here? No matter, the film stands on its own just fine. Image and sound, of course, are first-rate. —*MM*
Movie: 🎞🎞🎞🎞 **DVD:** 🎞🎞🎞½
Columbia Tristar Home Video (Cat #03747, UPC #043396037472). Widescreen anamorphic; full frame. Dolby Digital 5.1; Dolby Surround; Mono. $24.95. Keepcase. *LANG:* English; French. *SUB:* English; French; Spanish; Portuguese; Chinese; Korean; Thai. *FEATURES:* 28 chapter links • Filmographies • Trailers.
1982 (PG) 110m/C Dustin Hoffman, Jessica Lange, Teri Garr, Dabney Coleman, Bill Murray, Charles Durning, Geena Davis, George Gaynes, Estelle Getty, Christine Ebersole, Sydney Pollack; **D:** Sydney Pollack; **W:** Larry Gelbart, Murray Schisgal, Don McGuire; **C:** Owen Roizman; **M:** Dave Grusin. *AWARDS:* Oscars '82: Support. Actress (Lange); AFI '98: Top 100; British Acad. '83: Actor (Hoffman); Golden Globes '83: Actor—Mus./Comedy (Hoffman), Film—Mus./Comedy, Support. Actress (Lange); L.A. Film Critics '82: Screenplay, Natl. Film Reg. '98; N.Y. Film Critics '82: Director (Pollack), Screenplay, Support. Actress (Lange); Natl. Soc. Film Critics '82: Actor (Hoffman), Film, Screenplay, Support. Actress (Lange); Writers Guild '82: Orig. Screenplay; *NOM:* Oscars '82: Actor (Hoffman), Cinematog., Director (Pollack), Film Editing, Orig. Screenplay, Picture, Song ("It Might Be You"), Sound, Support. Actress (Garr).

Topaz

In his "appreciation" extra, critic Leonard Maltin mounts a solid defense for this oft-maligned suspense film. The story concerns efforts of American and French intelligence services to find information about Soviet espionage in Cuba. Reputation notwithstanding, the film has been given the usual careful treatment by Universal, though the widescreen transfer is not anamorphic. Overall, the image is very good compared to other films of the era. Mono sound is fine. —*MM*
Movie: 🎞🎞🎞 **DVD:** 🎞🎞🎞½
Universal Studios Home Video (Cat #20674, UPC #025192067426). Widescreen (1.85:1) letterboxed. Dolby Digital Mono. $29.98. Keepcase. *LANG:* English. *SUB:* French; Spanish. *CAP:* English. *FEATURES:* 18 chapter links • "Appreciation" by Leonard Maltin • 3 alternate endings • Storyboards • Production notes and photographs • Trailer • Talent files.
1969 (PG) 126m/C John Forsythe, Frederick Stafford, Philippe Noiret, Karin Dor, Michel Piccoli; **D:** Alfred Hitchcock; **W:** Samuel A. Taylor; **C:** Jack Hildyard; **M:** Maurice Jarre. *AWARDS:* Natl. Bd. of Review '69: Director (Hitchcock), Support. Actor (Noiret).

Topper Returns

In the sassy words of Joan Blondell, this third and final entry in the "Topper" series is "a cheerful little eyeful." Blondell stars as a wisecracking ghost who recruits the hapless Cosmo Topper (Young) to help solve the mystery of her own murder. Billie Burke (Glinda, the good witch of the North in *The Wizard of Oz*) also returns as Topper's clueless wife. Eddie "Rochester" Anderson gets the best lines as Topper's hilariously haunted assistant. The image clarity varies, but this is a crisp transfer from the original camera negative. —*DL*
Movie: 🎞🎞🎞 **DVD:** 🎞🎞½
Image Entertainment (Cat #9460, UPC #014381946024). Full frame. Dolby Digital Mono. $24.99. Snapper. *LANG:* English. *FEATURES:* Original trailer • 6 chapter links.
1941 87m/B Roland Young, Joan Blondell, Dennis O'Keefe, Carole Landis, Eddie Anderson, H.B. Warner, Billie Burke; **D:** Roy Del Ruth; **W:** Gordon Douglas, Jonathan Latimer; **C:** Norbert Brodine. *AWARDS: NOM:* Oscars '41: Sound.

Topsy Turvy

The very contemporary Leigh takes a pass at Victorian England for his very long and chatty look at life in the theatre. His focus is on the comic-opera partnership of irascible lyricist W.S. Gilbert (Broadbent) and pleasure-loving composer, Sir Arthur Sullivan (Corduner). Their latest creation (after 10 hits) is a flop, causing a serious rift, but Gilbert, after a visit to a Japanese art exhibit, is inspired to write *The Mikado* and pulls Sullivan back in. The film then follows the production of the opera from rehearsal to the 1885 premiere with all its difficulties and triumphs. This is a beautiful DVD. The colors are phenomenal, especially the more vibrant hues used for the stage scenes. Sharpness is also excellent and the disc is free from digital grain and artifacts. The audio highlight of the film is the Gilbert and Sullivan music and it's never sounded better than on the 5.1 tracks. The sound is rich with full fidelity and reinforced with a solid low end that is never overbearing. During the theatre sequences, the viewer is placed in the center of the audience as the rear Surround channels kick in. A short but informative featurette is included, in which director Leigh and some of the cast are interviewed. —*JO*
Movie: 🎞🎞🎞½ **DVD:** 🎞🎞🎞½
USA Home Entertainment (Cat #9630600192, UPC #696306001928). Widescreen (1.85:1) anamorphic. Dolby Digital 5.1; Dolby Surround. $19.95. Keepcase. *LANG:* English. *SUB:* Spanish; French. *CAP:* English. *FEATURES:* 39 chapter links • Theatrical trailer • TV spots • "Making of" featurette • Talent files • Photo gallery • Gilbert and Sullivan information.
1999 (R) 160m/C *GB* Jim Broadbent, Allan Corduner, Leslie Manville, Eleanor David, Ron Cook, Timothy Spall, Kevin McKidd, Mark Benton, Shirley Henderson, Martin Savage, Jessie Bond; **D:** Mike Leigh; **W:** Mike Leigh; **C:** Dick Pope; **M:** Carl Davis. *AWARDS:* Oscars '99: Costume Des., Makeup; British Acad. '99: Makeup; N.Y. Film Critics '99: Director (Leigh), Film; Natl. Soc. Film Critics '99: Director (Leigh), Film; *NOM:* Oscars '99: Art Dir./Set Dec., Orig. Screenplay; British Acad. '99: Actor (Broadbent), Film, Orig. Screenplay, Support. Actor (Spall); Ind. Spirit '00: Foreign Film.

Tora! Tora! Tora! [2 SE]

Darryl Zanuck and Elmo Williams's blow-by-blow account of December 7, 1941, was filmed from both points of view by separate American and Japanese units, and the result is an accurate, exciting, but dramatically lacking picture of a prelude to disaster. The path to war is one bad decision after another for the Yanks, and a field day for the Japanese; *Tora! Tora! Tora!* (the code words for "attack") was controversial because it clearly showed how the Japanese "sneak attack" was an unintentional blunder of diplomatic delay. Thanks to the Oscar-winning special effects of A.D. Flowers and L.B. Abbott, the action scenes manage a high pitch of chaos and havoc. The full-scale clash of ships and planes has an immediacy and believability lacking in today's CGI. Yet most of the dialogue is so purely expository, so the overall feeling is more educational than dramatic. Earlier parts of the film tend toward dullness, with every scene flat-lit. Anachronistic '70s female hairstyles, typical of Hollywood at this time, break up the mood. Good work by a large company of character actors: Jason Robards is suitably hissable as a wrongheaded Army commander, and Martin Balsam sympathetic as the Navy chieftain who has a very, very bad day. The DVD boasts the same beautiful

16:9 transfer from the earlier non–special edition disc. The remixed 5.1 audio makes Jerry Goldsmith's music shimmer with tension, and the battle action even more exciting. A short documentary debates the issues of the attack with the help of several knowledgeable historians. The feature-length commentary hosted by Japanese film historian Stuart Galbraith IV asks all the right questions of director Richard Fleischer, and most of the time gets interesting stories from him in return. A rather foolish trailer ("The sun rose! The bombs fell!") is included. Overall, an A+ for historic accuracy and spiritual fidelity to the real-life events portrayed. —GE

Movie: 🎧🎧½ **DVD:** 🎧🎧½
20th Century Fox Home Entertainment (UPC #024543013174). Widescreen (2.35:1) anamorphic. Dolby Digital, THX. $24.98. Keepcase. *LANG:* English; French. *SUB:* English; Spanish. *CAP:* English. *FEATURES:* 20-minute documentary, "Day of Infamy" ⚬ Commentary: director Richard Fleischer, historian Stuart Galbraith IV ⚬ Theatrical trailer.
1970 (G) 144m/C Martin Balsam, So Yamamura, Joseph Cotten, E.G. Marshall, Tatsuya Mihashi, Wesley Addy, Jason Robards Jr., James Whitmore, Leon Ames, George Macready, Takahiro Tamura, Eijiro Tono, Shogo Shimada, Koreya Senda, Jun Usami, Richard Anderson, Kazuo Kitamura, Keith Andes, Edward Andrews, Neville Brand, Leora Dana, Walter Brooke, Norman Alden, Ron Masak, Edmon Ryan, Asao Uchida, Frank Aletter, Jerry Fogel; *D:* Richard Fleischer, Toshio Masuda, Kinji Fukasaku; *W:* Ryuzo Kikushima, Hideo Oguni, Larry Forrester; *C:* Sinsaku Himeda, Charles F. Wheeler, Osamu Furuya; *M:* Jerry Goldsmith. *AWARDS:* Oscars '70: Visual FX; *NOM:* Oscars '70: Art Dir./Set Dec., Cinematog., Film Editing, Sound.

Torn Curtain

This suspense film has been known for its troubled production. Hitchcock reportedly did not get along with his stars; shooting had to be rushed to accommodate schedules and so the script was not fully polished. Finally, the filmmaker quarreled with his longtime music collaborator Bernard Herrmann, who was replaced by John Addison. (Some of Herrmann's score is included here.) But even if it's not the Master's best, it contains some very good scenes. American physicist Michael Armstrong (Newman) poses as a defector to East Germany to uncover details of the Soviet missile program. His fiancée Sarah Sherman (Andrews) follows and they must escape together. Image looks very good, particularly when compared to the full-frame Universal laserdisc. Sound is acceptable. —MM

Movie: 🎧🎧🎧 **DVD:** 🎧🎧🎧
Universal Studios Home Video (Cat #206 60, UPC #025192066023). Widescreen (1.85:1) anamorphic. Dolby Digital Mono. $29.98. Keepcase. *LANG:* English; French. *SUB:* Spanish. *CAP:* English. *FEATURES:* "Making of" featurette ⚬ Scenes scored

by Bernard Herrmann ⚬ Production photos and notes ⚬ Trailer ⚬ Talent files.
1966 125m/C Paul Newman, Julie Andrews, Lila Kedrova, David Opatoshu; *D:* Alfred Hitchcock; *W:* Brian Moore; *C:* John F. Warren; *M:* John Addison.

Touch of Evil [SE]

Welles spins a complex, perverse story of murder, kidnapping, and police corruption in a Mexican border town. He also stars as Hank Quinlan, the corpulent cop whose sweaty face reveals decades of sin. His opposite number is Vargas (Heston), a stand-up Mexican detective. This DVD is made from the 1998 Walter Murch restoration. Working from Welles's voluminous notes (included), he re-edited the film to something approaching the state that Welles himself had requested. It was taken from him by Universal studio executives who didn't understand what he was trying to do. They shot new footage and changed things considerably, most notably in the famous opening shot. All of that is set forth in more detail in the disc's production notes. Both image and sound are every bit as sharp as the '98 theatrical release. A commentary track by Murch would have been superfluous. His work speaks for itself. By the way, don't miss Janet Leigh's wonderful cheesecake scene in Chapter 8. —MM

Movie: 🎧🎧🎧🎧 **DVD:** 🎧🎧🎧🎧
Universal Studios Home Video (Cat #204 70, UPC #025192047022). Widescreen (1.85:1) anamorphic. Dolby Digital Mono. $29.98. Keepcase. *LANG:* English. *SUB:* French; Spanish. *CAP:* English. *FEATURES:* 18 chapter links ⚬ Welles's memo ⚬ Trailer ⚬ Production notes ⚬ Talent files.
1958 101m/B Charlton Heston, Orson Welles, Janet Leigh, Joseph Calleia, Akim Tamiroff, Marlene Dietrich, Valentin de Vargas, Dennis Weaver, Joanna Moore, Mort Mills, Victor Millan, Ray Collins; *Cameos:* Joi Lansing, Zsa Zsa Gabor, Mercedes McCambridge, Joseph Cotten; *D:* Orson Welles; *W:* Orson Welles; *C:* Russell Metty; *M:* Henry Mancini. *AWARDS:* Natl. Film Reg. '93.

Tourist Trap

In the tradition of *Psycho, Halloween,* and *Texas Chainsaw Massacre,* a group of kids go searching for a missing friend and are stranded at the remote Slausen's Desert Oasis motel. Slausen (Connors) is an affable fellow but warns them away from the house where "Davey" lives. Guess what they do. The picture is clear, but there are many obvious defects (scratches and dirt) on the source print. Some heavy graininess intrudes at times. However, some scenes (such as the nudity-free skinny dip) are very clear and defect free. The audio is well-balanced for the most part, with the dialogue clear and understandable. —MM/ML

Movie: 🎧🎧🎧 **DVD:** 🎧🎧½
Full Moon Pictures (Cat #8022). Widescreen (1.85:1) letterboxed. Dolby Digital

Stereo. $14.98. Keepcase. *LANG:* English. *FEATURES:* Commentary: director ⚬ Filmographies ⚬ Trailers ⚬ Interview.
1979 (PG) 90m/C Tanya Roberts, Chuck Connors, Robin Sherwood, Jocelyn Jones, Jon Van Ness, Dawn Jeffory, Keith McDermott; *D:* David Schmoeller; *W:* David Schmoeller; *C:* Nicholas Josef von Sternberg; *M:* Pino Donaggio.

Tower of Song: The Canadian Music Hall of Fame

This TV special is a compilation of short interviews with and musical numbers by members of the Canadian Music Hall of Fame. Interspersed among the talking-heads are bits of aerial footage highlighting the country's natural wonders. Subjects range from Glenn Gould and Oscar Peterson to Neil Young and Paul Anka. New footage is crystalline; archival footage varies in quality. Sound is fine. —MM

Movie: 🎧🎧½ **DVD:** 🎧🎧
Image Entertainment (Cat #ID9695CDDVD, UPC #014381969528). Full frame. Dolby Digital Stereo. $24.99. Snapper. *LANG:* English. *FEATURES:* 28 chapter links.
2001 90m/C D: Mark Hall; *W:* Mark Hall, Martin Melhish; *C:* Gordon Judges, Richard Saint-Pierre; *M:* Dominic Troiano, Howard Ayers; *Nar:* Peter Gzowski.

A Town Has Turned to Dust

Lame remake of a 1958 Rod Serling script for *Playhouse 90.* Serling's story was set in the old west; this version goes for sci-fi and a post-apocalyptic desert town called Carbon run by mob boss Pearlman who controls the water supply and the scrap metal mining industry. But when he hangs an innocent man, drunken sheriff Lang is finally moved to take action. Sound and the yellow-tinted image are acceptable but no improvement over VHS tape. —MM

Movie: 🎧½ **DVD:** 🎧🎧
MTI Home Video (Cat #BP50019DVD, UPC #619935001930). Full frame. $24.95. Keepcase. *LANG:* English. *FEATURES:* 20 chapter links ⚬ Talent files.
1998 91m/C Ron Perlman, Stephen Lang, Gabriel Olds, Judy Collins; *W:* Rod Serling.

Toy Story

The first feature-length film created wholly by computer animation is a bit of a mixed bag. In its depiction of plastic toys and their world, it's fine, but when the focus shifts to human or animal characters, the shortcomings of the medium become more apparent. That said, the characters of Woody (Hanks), a cowboy doll, and Buzz Lightyear (Allen), an action figure, are fully developed and the plot zips right along at a speedy pace. Since the film is a digital creation, it looks as sharp and flawless on DVD as it does in theatres. Sound is better. (See review of *Toy Story 2.*) My only complaint remains that the image is somehow too bright and antiseptic. That said, the Disney people have done their usual no-limits work providing extras. The RSDL is simply crammed, beginning with the lively commentary of seven filmmakers and a sound effects–only track. The project's development is traced on sections devoted to history, story, design, computer animation, sound and music, deleted footage, and publicity. Of course, kids—the primary audience—are simply going to want to watch the movie over and over again. (The title is also available in a two-disc set with the sequel, catalog #20992, for $39.99.) —MM

Movie: 🎵🎵🎵 **DVD:** 🎵🎵🎵🎵
Buena Vista Home Entertainment (Cat #22 336, UPC #786936151053). Widescreen (1.77:1) anamorphic. Dolby Digital 5.1 Surround Stereo. $29.99. Keepcase. *LANG:* English; French. *FEATURES:* 30 chapter links ▪ Filmmakers commentary track ▪ On-set interviews with Woody and Buzz ▪ Sound effects track ▪ Short film "Tin Toy."
1995 (G) 84m/C D: John Lasseter; **W:** Joss Whedon, Joel Cohen, Alec Sokolow; **M:** Randy Newman; **V:** Tom Hanks, Tim Allen, Annie Potts, John Ratzenberger, Wallace Shawn, Jim Varney, Don Rickles, John Morris, R. Lee Ermey, Laurie Metcalf, Erik von Detten. *AWARDS:* NOM: Oscars '95: Orig. Screenplay, Song ("You've Got a Friend"), Orig. Score; Golden Globes '96: Film—Mus./Comedy, Song ("You Got a Friend in Me"); MTV Movie Awards '96: On-Screen Duo (Tom Hanks/Tim Allen).

Toy Story 2

This sequel does what *Godfather II* did; it surpasses the original. First, the animation is noticeably sharper in the human and animal characters (though still not perfect). Sound is much better than the theatrical release (or is the multiplex near me the only one that doesn't deliver on that count?). The conflicts are deeper. The plot is more involving and the pace moves even faster. (Check out the breathless *Raiders*-style opening to get a real visual-auditory rush.) Buzz (Allen) leads the other toys on a rescue mission after Woody (Hanks) is kidnapped by a greedy collector who's ready to sell him to the highest bidder. Like the first film, the disc is loaded with all of the extras anyone could ask for. Disney is famous for giving its hit films the royal treatment on disc. This is some of the studio's best work. (The title is also available in a two-disc set with the original, catalog #20992, for $39.99.) —MM
Movie: 🎵🎵🎵🎵 **DVD:** 🎵🎵🎵🎵
Buena Vista Home Entertainment (Cat #22 337, UPC #786936151060). Widescreen (1.77:1) anamorphic. Dolby Digital 5.1 Surround Stereo. $29.99. Keepcase. *LANG:* English; French. *FEATURES:* 35 chapter links ▪ Commentary: filmmakers ▪ Outtakes ▪ Previews ▪ Short film "Luxo Jr."
1999 (G) 92m/C D: John Lasseter, Lee Unkrich, Ash Bannon; **W:** Ash Bannon, Rita Hsiao, Doug Chamberlin, Chris Webb, Andrew Stanton; **M:** Randy Newman; **V:** Tom Hanks, Tim Allen, Joan Cusack, Don

Rickles, John Ratzenberger, Annie Potts, Wayne Knight, Laurie Metcalf, Jim Varney, Estelle Harris, Kelsey Grammer, Wallace Shawn, John Morris, R. Lee Ermey, Jodi Benson, Jonathan Harris, Joe Ranft, Andrew Stanton, Robert Goulet. *AWARDS:* Golden Globes '00: Film—Mus./Comedy; *NOM:* Oscars '99: Song ("When She Loved Me"); Golden Globes '00: Song ("When She Loved Me"); MTV Movie Awards '00: On-Screen Duo (Tim Allen/Tom Hanks).

Toy Story: The Ultimate Toybox

This boxed set contains both *Toy Story* features and a supplemental disc of more than 5 hours of extra material. It really has everything that a fan could want to know about the two films in a very cool container. The features are much too numerous to list. Trust me, it's all there from an introduction by the filmmakers to 3-D tours of the films' digital sets. —MM
Movie: 🎵🎵🎵🎵 **DVD:** 🎵🎵🎵🎵
Buena Vista Home Entertainment (Cat #18 668, UPC #717951005816). Widescreen letterboxed. Dolby Digital 5.1 Surround Stereo. $39.99. Keepcase, boxed set. *LANG:* English; French.
2000 546m/C

The Tracker

Retired gunman/tracker Noble Adams (Kristofferson) is called upon to capture murderous religious maniac Red Jack Stilwell (Wilson, as another scene-stealing villain). Adams's college-educated son (Moses), recently returned from back east, joins him. Actually, the story is much more engaging than it sounds in synopsis. Disc looks fine, but the image is soft because director Guillermin uses so much golden light. Light print damage is evident, too. —MM **AKA:** Dead or Alive.
Movie: 🎵🎵½ **DVD:** 🎵🎵½
HBO Home Video (Cat #90158, UPC #026 359015823). Widescreen anamorphic. $19.98. Snapper. *LANG:* English. *SUB:* English; French; Spanish. *FEATURES:* 12 chapter links ▪ Talent files.
1988 102m/C Kris Kristofferson, Scott Wilson, Mark Moses, David Huddleston, John Quade, Don Swayze, Brynn Thayer; **D:** John Guillermin; **M:** Sylvester Levay.

Traffic

Steven Soderbergh's unnerving, sprawling mosaic about the international war on drugs interweaves three stories from varying levels of the food chain. The first introduces Del Toro as Javier Rodriguez, an honest but struggling Tijuana policeman continually thwarted by his peers in ebbing the flow of drugs out of his country. The American government side involves Douglas as Robert Wakefield, a Ohio state justice named the new "drug czar" by the President, only to find his daughter Caroline (Christensen) has become addicted to crack cocaine. The third story revolves around Helena Ayala (Zeta Jones), preg-

nant wife of suspected drug trafficker Carlos Ayala (Bauer). When Carlos is arrested by two DEA agents (Cheadle and Guzman), she learns of her husband's activities and plays into the endless cycle of supply and demand, addiction into alienation, and commerce versus conscience. Soderbergh masterfully juggles these stories, never crossing but always swirling around each other. For its two and a half-hour running time, the film just whizzes by. Despite the ensemble cast structure, Del Toro clearly emerges as the film's emotional core, winning his Supporting Actor Oscar hands down. His Rodriguez is a moral man caught in a universe where ethical behavior only burdens. The 1.85 anamorphic transfer coalesces the disparate photographic styles (grainy film stock for the Mexico scenes, blues and grays pervade the Wakefield episode) into a consistently cohesive image. Colors are accurate and sharp. Deep black levels are evident in scenes where back-lit light sources create foreground contrast yet still yield details. Fleshtones, when not obfuscated, look natural and the source elements exhibit no blemishes or imperfections. Despite the gritty image and complex hues, digital or compression artifacts are absent. The 5.1 sound mix is rather low-key, creating a wide front soundstage without resorting to gimmicky, showy sound effect pans. Despite the presence of explosions and gunfire, it is Cliff Martinez's score that activates the LFE for maximum ominous effect. By contrast, the Dolby Surround track is much more assertive: the dialogue plays louder and sound effects have an edgier feel. Three trailers, five TV spots, and a documentary constitute the extras. *Traffic* unfolds like a densely plotted novel, teeming with characters chained together by a heinous and seemingly invulnerable—umbilical cord. —EP
Movie: 🎵🎵🎵½ **DVD:** 🎵🎵🎵
USA Home Entertainment (Cat #0518, UPC #696306010124). Widescreen (1.85:1) anamorphic. Dolby Digital 5.1; Dolby Digital Surround Stereo. $26.95. Keepcase. *LANG:* English. *SUB:* French; Spanish. *CAP:* English. *FEATURES:* 68 chapter links ▪ Theatrical trailers ▪ TV spots ▪ Photo gallery ▪ Documentary: "Inside Traffic."
2000 (R) 147m/C Michael Douglas, Catherine Zeta-Jones, Benicio Del Toro, Dennis Quaid, Benjamin Bratt, Albert Finney, Amy Irving, Don Cheadle, Luis Guzman, Steven Bauer, James Brolin, Erika Christensen, Clifton (Gonzalez) Collins Jr., Miguel Ferrer, Tomas Milian, D.W. Moffett, Marisol Padilla Sanchez, Peter Riegert, Jacob Vargas, Rena Sofer, Stacy Travis, Salma Hayek, Topher Grace, Beau Holden; **D:** Steven Soderbergh; **W:** Stephen Gaghan; **C:** Peter Andrews; **M:** Cliff Martinez. *AWARDS:* Oscars '00: Adapt. Screenplay, Director (Soderbergh), Film Editing, Support. Actor (Del Toro); British Acad. '00: Adapt. Screenplay, Support. Actor (Del Toro); Golden Globes '01: Screenplay, Support. Actor (Del Toro); L.A. Film Critics '00: Director (Soderbergh); Natl. Bd. of Review '00: Director (Soder-

Trail Beyond

See review for *Dawn Rider / Trail Beyond.*
Movie: 🐾½
1934 57m/B John Wayne, Noah Beery Sr., Verna Hillie, Noah Beery Jr.; **D:** Robert North Bradbury; **W:** Lindsley Parsons.

Traitor's Heart

Standard-issue video-premiere action flick revolves around amnesia victim Nick Brody (Genesse). Bad guys come looking for him and lots of stuff blows up. The explosions are appropriately loud. DVD image is very crisp, making the most of South African locations. —*MM*
Movie: 🐾🐾 **DVD:** 🐾🐾½
Image Entertainment (Cat #ID6362NGDVD, UPC #014381636222). Full frame. Dolby Digital Surround Stereo. $24.99. Snapper. *LANG:* English. *FEATURES:* 12 chapter links.
1998 95m/C Bryan Genesse, Kimberley Kates, Ron Smerczak; **D:** Dan Lerner; **W:** Dan Lerner, Cline Lien; **C:** Yossi Wein; **M:** Serge Colbert.

Transformers: The Movie

Full-length animated film features the universe-defending robots fighting the powers of evil. Since the robots' first incarnation was as toys, there is some marketing going on. The bombastic storytelling style seems more than a little dated now, but it is perennially popular with the short set who will enjoy this one on disc. The image is fine but the major advance over tape is the beefed-up Dolby stereo. —*MM*
Movie: 🐾 **DVD:** 🐾🐾½
Rhino Home Video (Cat #R2 976644, UPC #603497664429). Full frame. Dolby Digital 5.1 Surround Stereo. $19.95. Keepcase. *LANG:* English. *SUB:* English. *FEATURES:* 20 chapter links • Storyboards • Interview with composer Vince DiCola.
1986 (G) 85m/C D: Nelson Shin; **M:** Vince DiCola; **V:** Orson Welles, Eric Idle, Judd Nelson, Leonard Nimoy, Robert Stack.

Traveller

Deriving its name from a real group of Irish-American conmen who prowl the Southeast, this view into the lives and clannish ways of its members may have you checking that new driveway sealant. Their philosophy is: if you're not one of us, we can steal your money. Bokky (Paxton) is the jack-of-all-trades who takes the younger Pat (Wahlberg) under his wing after the boy is shunned by the rest of the group. (Pat's father married outside the clan and that's not allowed.) Bokky falls into the same trap when he meets a beautiful bartender (Margulies). Rather violent ending dims the good feeling that builds and may leave you feeling...well, cheated. Film is the directorial debut of longtime Clint Eastwood cinematographer Jack Green. Unfortunately, his work gains nothing on DVD. The full-frame image is no significant improvement over VHS tape. —*MM*
Movie: 🐾🐾🐾 **DVD:** 🐾🐾
Artisan Entertainment (Cat #10047, UPC #707729100478). Full frame. $24.99. Keepcase. *LANG:* English. *FEATURES:* 30 chapter links • Production notes • Trailer.
1996 (R) 100m/C Bill Paxton, Mark Wahlberg, Julianna Margulies, James Gammon, Luke Askew, Michael Shaner, Nikki Deloach, Danielle Wiener; **D:** Jack N. Green; **W:** Jim McGlynn; **C:** Jack N. Green; **M:** Andy Paley.

Treasures from the American Film Archives: 50 Preserved Films

This four-disc boxed set is a compact history of film in America. The works included were made between 1893 and 1985, and range in length from a few seconds to more than an hour. Much of the material is non-fiction: newsreels, home movies, peep shows, early camera experiments, travel films, training films, political ads. Considering that some of the material is more than a century old, the preservationists have done a remarkable job. Of course, some works are worn but they all have something significant to reveal, even if the subject is a man bouncing on a slack wire in what appears to be his back yard. The invaluable accompanying book by Scott Simmon and Martin Marks attempts to put the various works and their music in context. Contents: "The Original Movie" (1922), Three Early Films from the Edison Company (1893-1906), "Princess Nicotine; or The Smoke Fairy" (1909), "The Confederate Ironclad" (1912), "Hell's Hinges" (1916), "The Fall of the House of Usher" (1928), From "Groucho Marx's Home Movies" (ca. 1933), "Running Around San Francisco for an Education" (1938), From "Tevye" (1939), "Cologne: From the Diary of Ray and Esther" (1939), Private Snafu "Spies" (1943), "OffOn" (1968), "Star Theater" (1901), "Move On" (1903), "Dog Factory" (1904), "The Lonedale Operator" (1911), "Her Crowning Glory," (1911), "The Toll of the Sea" (1922), From "Accuracy First" (ca. 1928), From "West Virginia, the State Beautiful" (1929), "One-Room Schoolhouses" (ca. 1935), From "Early Amateur Sound Film" (1936–37), "Composition 1 (Themis)" (1940), "The Battle of San Pietro" (1945), "Negro Leagues Baseball" (1946), "Battery Film" (1985), "The Thieving Hand" (1908), "White Fawn's Devotion" (1910), "The Chechahcos" (1924), From "Japanese American Communities" (1927–32), From Rare Aviation Films "The Keystone 'Patrician'" (1928) and "The Zeppelin 'Hindenburg'" (1936), "We Work Again" (1937), From "La Valse" (1951), "The Wall" (1962), "George Dumpson's Place" (1965), 2 Peepshow Kinetoscopes (1894), "Interior New York Subway" (1905), "The Land Beyond the Sunset" (1912), "I'm Insured" (1916), "Snow White" (1916), From "Beautiful Japan" (1918), From "Rural Life in Maine" (ca. 1930), "The News Parade of 1934" (1934), "Rose Hobart" (1936), "The Autobiography of a Jeep" (1943), From "Marian Anderson: The Lincoln Memorial Concert" (1939). —*MM*
Movie: 🐾🐾🐾🐾 **DVD:** 🐾🐾🐾🐾
Image Entertainment (Cat #9706, UPC #01 4381970623). Full frame. Dolby Digital Stereo. $99.99. Boxed set. *LANG:* English. *SUB:* English. *FEATURES:* 50 chapter links.
2000 642m/C Nar: Laurence "Larry" Fishburne.

Tribulation

Police detective Tom Canboro (Busey) goes up against the evil Messiah (Mancuso) in another entry in the "Left Behind" series of adventures based on the Book of Revelation. Again, production values are on a direct-to-video level, making DVD a scant improvement over tape. There's little here to attract those who have not accepted a conservative Christian point of view. —*MM*
Movie: 🐾 **DVD:** 🐾🐾
Cloud Ten Pictures (Cat #7453800830). Full frame. $29.99. Keepcase. *LANG:* English. *FEATURES:* 8 chapter links • Talent files • Trailers • Weblink • Busey interview.
2000 97m/C Gary Busey, Howie Mandel, Margot Kidder, Nick Mancuso, Sherry Miller, Leigh Lewis; **D:** Andre Van Heerden; **W:** Peter LaLonde, Paul LaLonde; **C:** George Tirl.

Triumph of the Will

This is a cinematically augmented representation of the Nuremberg National Socialist rally of 1934, a week-long gathering of Germans under their brand new Fuhrer Adolf Hitler. Starting with Hitler descending Godlike from the clouds, the film is two hours of parades, adoring crowds, torchlit serenades, and massed reviews of what look like hundreds of thousands of regimented workers, Hitler youth, and party members. Hitler makes several bombastic speeches, along with pieces of speeches and testimonials by other top party members. Creating a controlled "truth" seemed to be exactly the aim of Riefenstahl and her Nazi producers, who created and ran the giant rally as much to make this propaganda tool as for its own purpose. The giant stadiums were designed to accommodate special cameras (you can see little elevators for camera buckets going up and down the colossal bannered columns) and many shots were obviously accomplished by repeatedly restaging ostensibly "candid" scenes. Because of camera placement and sound recording, it's more than probable that key "dialogue" scenes were actually shot totally separately, including whole speeches by Hitler himself. Synapse's DVD adds a dynamic to the movie that makes this disc more "useful" than seeing the film projected on a screen. Watching the show with only its own few titles as a guide, it's easy to get lost; you wish you had a college professor sitting next to you to identify all the historical villains on-screen, and the significance of whole rallies, as well as details like insignia (Who are those guys carrying shovels instead of guns? Are there any girls in the Hitler youth?). The DVD provides this extra dimension through the pleasant-sounding Dr. Anthony R. Santoro, whose running commentary is priceless. His explanations of basic facts are clear and well-timed. Without making weighted judgments, he points out the sources and the ironies of Hitler's power, remarking that everything in the rallies was chosen to bolster weaknesses in the party's rule. (Hitler had just assumed full control of the state; a major party leader had just been purged.) Finally, he makes the vital distinction between autocratic power, which wants to control your actions, and totalitarian power, which wants control over your actions and your thoughts. Thought control of masses of people wasn't possible until the 20th century and modern communications; this film pretty much proves the theory that the most powerful tool of thought control is the Cinema. —GE **AKA:** Triumph des Willens.

Movie: 🎝🎝🎝½ **DVD:** 🎝🎝🎝½
Synapse (Cat #SFD0015, UPC #65493030 1593). Widescreen letterboxed. Dolby Digital Mono. $34.98. Keepcase. LANG: German. SUB: English. FEATURES: Leni Riefenstahl short film, "Day of Freedom" ● Commentary: Dr. Anthony R. Santoro.
1934 115m/B GE **D:** Leni Riefenstahl; **W:** Leni Riefenstahl; **C:** Sepp Allgeier; **M:** Herbert Windt.

The Trouble with Harry

When a little boy (TV's Beaver, Jerry Mathers) finds a dead body in the woods near a Vermont town, it causes all kinds of problems for the community, though nobody really minds that Harry is deceased. In this comedy, everybody thinks they're guilty. As Herrmann's score (his first for Hitchcock) suggests, the tone is light and humorous throughout. It's also MacLaine's big-screen debut. Compared to the Master's other color work of the period (Man Who Knew Too Much, Rear Window), this one looks very good with a softish image that's appropriate to a New England autumn. Mono sound is fine and Universal has done its usual good job with the extras. —MM
Movie: 🎝🎝🎝 **DVD:** 🎝🎝🎝½
Universal Studios Home Video (Cat #206 70, UPC #025192067020). Widescreen (1.85:1) anamorphic. Dolby Digital Mono. $29.98. Keepcase. LANG: English; Span-

ish. SUB: French. CAP: English. FEATURES: 18 chapter links ● "Making of" featurette ● Trailer ● Production notes and photos ● Talent files.
1955 (PG) 90m/C John Forsythe, Shirley MacLaine, Edmund Gwenn, Jerry Mathers, Mildred Dunnock, Mildred Natwick, Royal Dano; **D:** Alfred Hitchcock; **W:** John Michael Hayes; **C:** Robert Burks; **M:** Bernard Herrmann.

Truck Turner

Truck Turner (Hayes) is a black bounty hunter who's up against a threadbare plot, but the sight of Yaphet Kotto in full pimp regalia is not to be missed. His outfits and Hayes's cool score are worth the price of a rental all by themselves. The low-budget image gains little on DVD. The image is gritty; sound is scratchy; colors are washed-out. —MM
Movie: 🎝🎝½ **DVD:** 🎝🎝
MGM Home Entertainment (Cat #1001471, UPC #027616087910). Widescreen (1.85:1) anamorphic. Dolby Digital Mono. $24.99. Keepcase. LANG: English. SUB: French; Spanish. CAP: English. FEATURES: Trailer ● 16 chapter links.
1974 (R) 91m/C Isaac Hayes, Yaphet Kotto, Annazette Chase, Nichelle Nichols, Scatman Crothers, Dick Miller; **D:** Jonathan Kaplan; **W:** Leigh Chapman; **C:** Charles F. Wheeler; **M:** Isaac Hayes.

True Believer

Good, solid crime thriller with Woods as Eddie Dodd, a once-idealistic lawyer out to change the world, who has become a cynical pot-smoking defender of the drug dealers. Enter Robert Downey Jr., an idealistic young law student who has come to work with Dodd, the civil rights lawyer, only to find Dodd, the cynic. At Downey's insistence, they reopen an eight-year-old murder case, and Dodd's thirst for justice is awakened when he realizes that he can once again make a difference. Yuji Okumoto turns in a great performance as Shu Kai Kim, the man falsely accused of murder, who is cold from his years in prison when we first see him but slowly begins to melt in the light of the hope offered him. The picture and sound are average, probably owing to the age of the masters. There are A- and B-sides for full-frame or widescreen presentation. —CA
Movie: 🎝🎝🎝 **DVD:** 🎝🎝🎝
Columbia Tristar Home Video (Cat #05849, UPC #043396058491). Widescreen (1.85:1) letterboxed; full frame. Dolby Surround. $19.95. Keepcase. LANG: English; French; Spanish; Portuguese. SUB: English; French; Spanish; Portuguese; Chinese; Korean; Thai. FEATURES: 28 chapter links ● Trailers ● Talent files.
1989 (R) 103m/C James Woods, Robert Downey Jr., Yuji Okumoto, Margaret Colin, Kurtwood Smith, Tom Bower, Miguel Fernandes, Charles Hallahan; **D:** Joseph Ruben; **W:** Wesley Strick; **C:** John Lindley; **M:** Brad Fiedel.

The Truth about Cats and Dogs

Funny, intelligent Abby (Garofalo) hosts a popular radio call-in show for pet lovers. When handsome Brit photographer Brian (Chaplin) phones in with a Great Dane problem involving roller skates, he becomes intrigued by her voice and asks for a date. Insecure about her looks, Abby asks her beautiful-but-dim neighbor Noelle (Thurman) to fill in. Naturally, both women fall for the shy guy. The charming updated variation on the Cyrano theme works through strong performances, particularly Garofalo, who steals the show. Since this is such a character- and dialogue-driven piece, it really gains little on DVD, and the addition of a commentary track would have been intrusive. On any medium, this is terrific. —MM
Movie: 🎝🎝🎝 **DVD:** 🎝🎝½
20th Century Fox Home Entertainment (Cat #2001380, UPC #024543013808). Widescreen (1.85:1) anamorphic. Dolby Digital 5.1 Surround Stereo; Dolby Digital Surround. $24.99. Keepcase. LANG: English; French. SUB: English; Spanish. FEATURES: 20 chapter links ● Trailers and TV spots.
1996 (PG-13) 97m/C Janeane Garofalo, Uma Thurman, Ben Chaplin, Jamie Foxx, Richard Coca, Stanley DeSantis; **D:** Michael Lehmann; **W:** Audrey Wells; **C:** Robert Brinkmann; **M:** Howard Shore. AWARDS: NOM: MTV Movie Awards '97: Comedic Perf. (Garofalo).

Tucker: The Man and His Dream

Portrait of Preston Tucker (Bridges), entrepreneur and industrial idealist, who in 1946 tried to build the car of the future and was effectively run out of business by the powers-that-were. Coppola's version of the story is a ravishing, ultra-nostalgic lullaby to the American Dream. Watch for Jeff's dad, Lloyd, in a bit role. The video transfer is very impressive; colors are vibrant and crisp, and blacks are extremely well defined. Even the muted, period look of some scenes is breathtaking. The audio is similarly impressive with no distortion or loss of clarity. The disc's supplements are a treat as well, with the 1948 promo film being a clear standout. —MJT
Movie: 🎝🎝🎝 **DVD:** 🎝🎝🎝½
Paramount Home Video (Cat #32144, UPC #097363214441). Widescreen (2.35:1) anamorphic. Dolby Digital 5.1 Surround; Dolby Surround. $29.99. Keepcase. LANG: English; French. SUB: English. FEATURES: 15 chapter links ● Tucker: The Man and the Car 1948 promo film ● "Under the Hood: Making Tucker" featurette ● Commentary: Francis Ford Coppola.
1988 (PG) 111m/C Jeff Bridges, Martin Landau, Dean Stockwell, Frederic Forrest, Mako, Joan Allen, Christian Slater, Lloyd Bridges, Elias Koteas, Nina Siemaszko, Corin "Corky" Nemec, Marshall Bell, Don Novello, Peter Donat, Dean Goodman, Patti Austin; **D:** Francis Ford Coppola; **W:** Arnold Schulman, David Seidler; **M:** Joe

Jackson, Carmine Coppola. *AWARDS:* Golden Globes '89: Support. Actor (Landau); N.Y. Film Critics '88: Support. Actor (Stockwell); *NOM:* Oscars '88: Art Dir./Set Dec., Costume Des., Support. Actor (Landau).

Tuff Turf

Morgan Hiller (Spader) is the new kid in town when his family moves to a low-class section of Los Angeles. He makes enemies immediately when he puts a move on a gang leader's girlfriend (Richards). The cast is so young and pretty that it's impossible to believe that they're capable of any real violence. Even so, the image is exceptionally rough. Grain comes from the original, not the transfer. Sound is average. —*MM*

Movie: ♫♫ **DVD:** ♫♫
Anchor Bay (Cat #DV11377, UPC #013131 137798). Widescreen (1.85:1) anamorphic. Dolby Digital Mono. $24.99. Keepcase. *LANG:* English. *FEATURES:* Trailer • 26 chapter links.
1985 (R) 113m/C James Spader, Kim Richards, Paul Mones, Matt Clark, Olivia Barash, Robert Downey Jr., Catya Sassoon; *D:* Fritz Kiersch; *W:* Jette Rinck; *C:* Willy Kurant; *M:* Jonathan Elias.

Tumbleweeds

Charming indie about a Southern mom (British stage actress Janet McTeer in an Oscar-nominated performance), whose pattern of life lessons usually comes from the back hand of a boyfriend or husband. Fleeing yet another abusive relationship, Mary Jo Walker takes to the road with her worldly-wise but weary 12-year-old daughter Ava (the equally mesmerizing Kimberly J. Brown) in the hopes of finding a new life. Settling on San Diego as their latest pitstop, both mother and daughter come to realize their commitment to each other and learn that even "tumbleweeds" must eventually find rest. What easily could have been cloying sentimental goo reads genuine scene after scene. McTeer and Brown, aided by a supporting cast including Jay O. Sanders as a sympathetic co-worker, director/writer O'Connor as a loutish trucker, and wispy gnome Michael J. Pollard as an unctuous boss, interact so naturally with each other and everyone else that one feels the camera just happened to catch their lives at the right moment. Much of that sincerity stems from the commitment to the material by director/co-writer O'Connor, as evidenced in his very entertaining and quite personal commentary. His free-form observations swing from his distaste for acting classes to the politics of film schools to problem solving on the set. O'Connor does not hold back in explaining when he had to get tough with Kimberly in some of the rougher emotional scenes and he gets just as inwardly analytical in describing his fervent connection to the story. The disc offers both an anamorphic widescreen and full-frame version of the film. As a single-sided, dual-layer DVD, rather than flipping the disc for either format, the menu allows the viewer to select screen shape. Both transfers exhibit solid black levels and natural-looking color fidelity. The source is free from blemishes and there are no discernible digital artifacts. While the widescreen version does restore some lost side information (only a sliver from what I measured), the pan-and-scan edition brings the actors' faces up close, magnifying their wonderful strutting upon a stage (Shakespeare references abound in the film). Surround sound is fine, with intelligible dialogue cleanly reproduced and occasional ambient sound effects when appropriate. You know you have watched something special when the movie is over and you feel sadness about having to leave the characters, despite the story ending where it should. *Tumbleweeds* is one such gem. —*EP*

Movie: ♫♫♫½ **DVD:** ♫♫♫½
New Line Home Video (Cat #N5026, UPC #9404330262). Widescreen (1.85:1) anamorphic; full frame. Dolby Digital Stereo Surround. $24.98. Snapper. *LANG:* English. *CAP:* English. *FEATURES:* 30 chapter links • Commentary: director • Theatrical trailer • Cast and crew filmographies • DVD-ROM Features: "Script to Screen" screenplay access • Original theatrical website.
1998 (PG-13) 104m/C Janet McTeer, Kimberly J. Brown, Gavin O'Connor, Jay O. Sanders, Lois Smith, Laurel Holloman, Michael J. Pollard, Noah Emmerich; *D:* Gavin O'Connor; *W:* Angela Shelton, Gavin O'Connor; *C:* Dan Stoloff; *M:* David Mansfield. *AWARDS:* Golden Globes '00: Actress—Mus./Comedy (McTeer); Ind. Spirit '00: Debut Perf. (Brown); Natl. Bd. of Review '99: Actress (McTeer); Sundance '99: Filmmakers Trophy; *NOM:* Oscars '99: Actress (McTeer); Ind. Spirit '00: Actress (McTeer); Screen Actors Guild '99: Actress (McTeer).

Turbo: A Power Rangers Movie

The Power Rangers must battle the evil Divatox (Turner) who's kidnapped the wizard Lerigot so she can use his power to free her even more evil boyfriend Maligore. The makeup, costumes, and effects might well have been found in a Crackerjacks box but they're consistent with the film's juvenile humor and energy. Neither image nor sound gain much on DVD, but the film does come as the second half of a double bill with *Mighty Morphin Power Rangers: The Movie* (reviewed in first edition) and so it's a good deal for parents of the target audience. —*MM*

Movie: ♫♫ **DVD:** ♫♫
20th Century Fox Home Entertainment (Cat #2001322, UPC #024543013228). Widescreen (1.85:1) anamorphic. Dolby Digital 5.1 Surround Stereo; Dolby Digital Surround. $24.98. Keepcase. *LANG:* English. *SUB:* English. *FEATURES:* 16 chapter links • Trailer • "Making of" featurette.

1996 (PG) 99m/C Jason David Frank, Stephen Antonio Cardenas, John Yong Bosch, Catherine Sutherland, Nakia Burrise, Blake Foster, Paul Schrier, Jason Narvy, Amy Jo Johnson, Austin St. John, Hilary Shepard Turner, Jon Simanton; *D:* David Winning, Shuki Levy; *W:* Shuki Levy, Shell Danielson; *C:* Ilan Rosenberg; *M:* Shuki Levy.

Turkish Delight

On his commentary track, director Verhoeven mounts an effective defense of this early work. He explains what he was trying to do and claims that it is something more than artsy soft-core. Erik Vonk (Hauer) is a sculptor who falls for Olga (Van De Ven). Their story, told in flashback, certainly shows elements that would appear later in *Basic Instinct, Show Girls,* and others. Perhaps the most remarkable thing about this disc is the quality of the image. The film looks as good as or better than Hollywood films that were made in 1972. Sound is not as strong but the optional subtitles are easy to read. —*MM*

Movie: ♫♫½ **DVD:** ♫♫♫
Anchor Bay (Cat #DV11252, UPC #013131 125290). Widescreen (1.66:1) anamorphic. Dolby Digital Mono. $24.99. Keepcase. *LANG:* Dutch. *SUB:* English. *FEATURES:* Commentary: Paul Verhoeven • Trailer • Stills gallery • 29 chapter links • Talent files.
1973 100m/C NL Monique Van De Ven, Rutger Hauer, Tonny Huurdeman, Wim Van Den Brink; *D:* Paul Verhoeven; *W:* Gerard Soeteman; *C:* Jan De Bont. *AWARDS:* *NOM:* Oscars '73: Foreign Film.

Turn It Up

Diamond (Pras) is trying to break into the music business when his buddy Gage (Ja Rule) involves him in a drug shootout that comes across as a retread from a John Woo Hong Kong action movie. After that, the film does attempt to become more serious, but there's little to recommend this one to anyone but fans of the stars' music. Since that music is so important to the story, the Surround mix is very active. Overall, the image is dark but properly detailed. —*MM*

Movie: ♫♫ **DVD:** ♫♫½
New Line Home Video (Cat #N5189, UPC #794043518928). Widescreen (1.85:1) anamorphic; full frame. Dolby Digital 5.1 Surround Stereo; Dolby Digital Surround Stereo. $24.98. Snapper. *LANG:* English. *SUB:* English. *FEATURES:* 20 chapter links • Talent files.
2000 (R) 87m/C Pras, Vondie Curtis-Hall, Ja Rule, Tamala Jones; *D:* Robert Adetuyi; *W:* Robert Adetuyi; *C:* Hubert Taczanowski; *M:* Gary Jones, Happy Walter.

The Tuskegee Airmen

Cable drama is based on the formation and WWII achievements of the U.S. Army Air Corps first squadron of black combat fighter pilots, the "Fighting 99th" of the

332nd Fighter Group. They were nick-named after the segregated military outpost where they trained in Tuskegee, Alabama. The central figure is Hannibal Lee (Fishburne) but the story is a conventional "unit picture." The image is generally good, so good that the inclusion of real combat is even more jarring and noticeable. A commentary track or documentary about the truths behind the film would be a worthwhile extra. —*MM*

Movie: 🎵🎵🎵 **DVD:** 🎵🎵🎵
HBO Home Video (Cat #91285, UPC #026 359128523). Widescreen letterboxed. Dolby Digital Surround Stereo; Dolby Stereo; Mono. $19.98. Snapper. *LANG:* English; French; Spanish. *SUB:* English; French; Spanish. *FEATURES:* 15 chapter links ▪ Talent files.
1995 (PG-13) 107m/C Laurence "Larry" Fishburne, Cuba Gooding Jr., Allen Payne, Malcolm Jamal Warner, Courtney B. Vance, Andre Braugher, John Lithgow, Rosemary Murphy, Christopher McDonald, Vivica A. Fox, Daniel Hugh-Kelly, David Harrod, Eddie Braun, Bennet Guillory; *D:* Robert Markowitz; *W:* Paris Qualles, Ron Hutchinson, Trey Ellis; *C:* Ronald Orieux; *M:* Lee Holdridge.

Twelve Angry Men

Fonda sounds the voice of reason as a jury inclines toward a quick-and-dirty verdict against a boy on trial for his life. Lumet's feature debut stands up quite well for two reasons. First, he had an outstanding ensemble cast to work with. Second, the black-and-white cinematography sparkles. The film looks terrific and it has been transferred to DVD with no flaws worth mentioning. Mono sound is true to the era and the subject. —*MM*

Movie: 🎵🎵🎵🎵 **DVD:** 🎵🎵🎵½
MGM Home Entertainment (Cat #1001590, UPC #027616859006). Widescreen (1.66:1) letterboxed. Dolby Digital Mono. $19.98. Keepcase. *LANG:* English; French. *SUB:* French; Spanish. *CAP:* English. *FEATURES:* 16 chapter links ▪ Trailer.
1957 95m/B Henry Fonda, Martin Balsam, Lee J. Cobb, E.G. Marshall, Jack Klugman, Robert Webber, Ed Begley Sr., John Fiedler, Jack Warden, George Voskovec, Edward Binns, Joseph Sweeney; *D:* Sidney Lumet; *W:* Reginald Rose; *C:* Boris Kaufman; *M:* Kenyon Hopkins. *AWARDS:* Berlin Intl. Film Fest. '57: Golden Berlin Bear; British Acad. '57: Actor (Fonda); *NOM:* Oscars '57: Adapt. Screenplay, Director (Lumet), Picture.

20th Century Fox: The First 50 Years

James Coburn narrates this feature-length documentary about the formation, growth, and legacy of 20th Century Fox. As clipfests go, this one tenders a more-than-generous helping of snippets from the studio catalog, primarily focused on its films from 1915 through 1965. Writer/director Kevin Burns gives equal and ample time in examining the boxoffice failures of the stu-dio (and near shutdown in the early 1960s) as well as showcasing its triumphs. Coburn's signature voice is a welcome tonic to the sometimes-glossy narration (e.g. Hitchcock's *Lifeboat* extolled as "continuing the studio's commitment to socially conscious cinema"). The video transfer, sporting both full-frame and letterboxed clips when appropriate, exhibits good image quality. With few exceptions, the archival sources look surprisingly clean with solid colors and deep shadow delineation in the black-and-white sections. The soundtrack does a good job of mixing audio sources of varying fidelity for well-balanced playback. The DVD is a flipper, side one housing the documentary and side two containing almost two hours of supplemental extras, mainly promotional reels from the 1930s and the 1950s. While not the caliber of the Kevin Brownlow documentaries, the DVD makes for a entertaining stroll through the studio that gave us such classic but disparate American films as *How Green Was My Valley* and *Star Wars.* —*EP*

Movie: 🎵🎵🎵 **DVD:** 🎵🎵🎵½
Image Entertainment (Cat #ID8767FSDVD, UPC #1438187672). Full frame and widescreen. Dolby Digital Stereo. $24.99. Snapper. *LANG:* English. *FEATURES:* 20 chapter links (documentary) ▪ 13 chapter links (supplemental features) ▪ "The Robe" presentation reel ▪ 20th Century Fox promotional reel (1936) ▪ 20th Century Fox studio tour (1937) ▪ "The Big Show" promotional feature (1958).
1996 129m/C Julie Andrews, Red Buttons, Alice Faye, Roddy McDowall, Don Murray, Robert Wagner, Robert Wise; *D:* Kevin Burns; *W:* Kevin Burns; *Nar:* James Coburn.

28 Days [SE]

Hard-partying New York journalist Gwen (Bullock) manages to destroy her sister's wedding reception when she gets drunk and is arrested for DUI. The film's title refers to the amount of time Gwen must spend at a rehab clinic. Naturally, Gwen doesn't really believe she has a problem and that's the first attitude adjustment she has to make. Clichés galore although Bullock is welcomingly spiky rather than sweet. Everything seems just right with this DVD transfer. The image is sharp and the colors accurate even in the scenes where video was used for effect. The outdoors scenes are lushly beautiful and the colors become even more vibrant. Surround effects are subtle yet very effective, especially in the outdoor sequences, where the ambience really opens the scene up. Richard Gibbs's score, which may be the real highlight of the film, is also offered on its own isolated track. Unfortunately, the commentary is hard to get through, even when what's being talked about is of some interest. —*JO*

Movie: 🎵🎵½ **DVD:** 🎵🎵🎵
Columbia Tristar Home Video (Cat #05064, UPC #043396050648). Widescreen (1.85:) anamorphic. Dolby Digital 5.1; Dolby Sur-round. $24.95. Keepcase. *LANG:* English. *SUB:* English. *CAP:* English. *FEATURES:* 28 chapter links ▪ Theatrical trailer ▪ Talent files ▪ Production notes ▪ Commentary: Betty Thomas, Richard Gibbs, Peter Teschner, Jenno Topping ▪ "Making of" featurette ▪ Isolated music score ▪ *Santa Cruz,* the lost episodes ▪ Guitar Guy's lost songs.
2000 (PG-13) 103m/C Sandra Bullock, Viggo Mortensen, Dominic West, Diane Ladd, Elizabeth Perkins, Steve Buscemi, Alan Tudyk, Reni Santoni, Marianne Jean-Baptiste, Michael O'Malley, Azura Skye, Margo Martindale; *D:* Betty Thomas; *W:* Susannah Grant; *C:* Declan Quinn; *M:* Richard Gibbs.

Twin Falls Idaho

Eerie romantic drama revolves around a lonely pair of conjoined twins, Francis (Michael Polish) and Blake (Mark Polish) Falls. The handsome 25-year-olds are celebrating their birthday in a shabby hotel room on Idaho Street when hooker Penny (Hicks) shows up. Blake, the strong twin, intends her as a present for the fragile Francis, whose weakening heart is kept beating by Blake's sheer will. Initially repulsed, Penny becomes fascinated by the situation and begins to fall for Blake. (The talented Polish brothers are identical but not "Siamese" twins.) The transfer is generally clean, although some scratches and speckles in the film print are visible. To underscore the oftentimes somber tone, the movie has a muted color scheme almost throughout, one that dwells in dark shades. The soundtrack is well produced and restores many of the subtle ambient sounds found in the film. It has a natural quality with a good bass and high-end extension. —*GH/MM*

Movie: 🎵🎵🎵 **DVD:** 🎵🎵🎵
Columbia Tristar Home Video (Cat #4367). Widescreen (1.85:1) anamorphic. Dolby Digital 5.1 Surround Stereo; Dolby Digital Surround Stereo. $27.95. Keepcase. *LANG:* English. *SUB:* English; French; Spanish. *FEATURES:* Commentary: Polish twins ▪ Production notes ▪ Theatrical trailer.
1999 (R) 110m/C Michael Polish, Mark Polish, Michele Hicks, Jonathan (Jon Francis) Gries, Patrick Bauchau, Garrett Morris, William Katt, Lesley Ann Warren, Teresa Hill, Holly Woodlawn; *D:* Michael Polish; *W:* Michael Polish, Mark Polish; *C:* M. David Mullen; *M:* Stuart Matthewman. *AWARDS: NOM:* Ind. Spirit '00: Cinematog., First Feature.

Twin Warriors

Dubbed, rescored version of *Tai-Chi Master* follows two young boys who are trained together but become rivals when one of them joins the military. The martial arts sequences are a thrill to behold and Li convinces with his tremendous skills. The film contains some of the most elaborately choreographed group fight scenes you'll ever watch; they have an almost Busby Berkeley geometric precision that's fascinating. Though excellent, this intense,

kinetic film becomes exhausting after the one-hour mark. The dubbing is atrocious and an insult to the film. Replacing Wai Lap Wu's ethnic score cripples the pacing and gives the film a feeling of cheapness that jars with the epic visuals. The disc is colorful, but grainy and not 16x9 enhanced. The sound is adequate but undistinguished. Seek out the original version instead. That version rates three bones. —DG/MM **AKA:** The Tai-Chi Master; Tai ji Zhang San Feng.
Movie: 🦴🦴½ **DVD:** 🦴🦴
Buena Vista Home Entertainment (Cat #18 541, UPC #71795100555). Widescreen (1.85:1) letterboxed. Dolby Digital 5.1 Surround Stereo. $29.99. Keepcase. *LANG:* English. *CAP:* English. *FEATURES:* 20 chapter links ▪ Insert card with chapter listings.
1993 (R) 94m/C *HK* Jet Li, Chin Siu Ho, Michelle Yeoh; **D:** Woo-ping Yuen; **W:** Kwong Kim Yip; **C:** Tom Lau; **M:** Wai Lap Wu.

Twitch of the Death Nerve
Typically overwrought Bava horror is perhaps his most excessive. The disc even contains a separate menu to take the curious viewer directly to each of the film's 13 gory murders. Now, that's entertainment! What plot there is serves only to introduce the characters, separate them from the others, and inventively kill them off. Then there's the "surprise" ending. The DVD probably makes the film look as good as it could, despite harsh colors and exceptionally dark interiors. Initially, the score is scratchy and distorted but that clears up to a degree later. —MM **AKA:** Bay of Blood; Last House on the Left, Part 2; Carnage.
Movie: 🦴🦴 **DVD:** 🦴🦴½
Image Entertainment (Cat #ID5945AODVD, UPC #014381594522). Widescreen (1.78:1) anamorphic. Dolby Digital Mono. $24.99. Snapper. *LANG:* English. *FEATURES:* 12 chapter links ▪ "Murder" menu ▪ Photos and poster gallery ▪ Bava thumbnail bio and filmography ▪ Trailer ▪ Radio spots ▪ Extensive liner notes by Tim Lucas.
1971 (R) 87m/C *IT* Claudine Auger, Chris Avran, Isa Miranda, Laura Betti, Luigi Pistilli, Sergio Canvari, Anna M. Rosati; **D:** Mario Bava; **W:** Mario Bava, Filippo Ottoni, Joseph McLee, Gene Luotto; **C:** Mario Bava; **M:** Stelvio Cipriano.

2 G's and a Key
A pair of "G's"—that's this low-budget movie's shorthand for gangsters—battle for the control of neighborhood drug profits. The conflict is between Curtis, an ex-con, and Sadd Dogg, the pusher he previously double-crossed. Fairly run-of-the-mill urban action is punctuated by a few good moments (including a rousing chase sequence) and a distinct editing style. It looks as though the film was shot on video, and the frequently noisy image is plagued on DVD by excessive digital artifacts. The Dolby Digital 2.0 sound is O.K.,

but there are no extras at all. In fact, even the most basic of DVD menus to navigate the chapter stops is not present. —MB
Movie: 🦴🦴 **DVD:** 🦴½
York Entertainment (Cat #YPD1036, UPC #750723103624). Full frame. Dolby Digital Stereo. $14.99. Keepcase. *LANG:* English. *FEATURES:* 15 chapter links.
2000 97m/C Conroe Brooks, Aaron Spears, Kiki Watson; **D:** Paul Wynne.

Two If by Sea
Small-time hood Frank (Leary) and his girlfriend Ros (Bullock) hole up in a New England mansion after Frank steals a valuable Matisse painting. Between verbal sparring matches, the two try to mingle with the upper crusty residents with predictable results. The film tries to be a caper/romantic comedy but fails to deliver. Nova Scotia turns in a fine performance as New England. While the color reproduction is quite good in the transfer and the framing appears to be accurate, the compression is just plain bad. Riddled with compression artifacts of all sorts, the result is a flat image without detail and definition. The kinetic use of the camera in this film doesn't make things better as the image blurs with almost every movement. Sound is natural with a good frequency response. —GH/MM **AKA:** Stolen Hearts.
Movie: 🦴½ **DVD:** 🦴½
Warner Home Video, Inc. (Cat #14159). Widescreen (1.85:1) letterboxed. Dolby Digital 5.1 Surround Stereo. $24.98. Snapper. *LANG:* English; French. *FEATURES:* Trailer ▪ Featurette ▪ Talent files ▪ Soundtrack section.
1995 (R) 96m/C Sandra Bullock, Denis Leary, Stephen (Dillon) Dillane, Yaphet Kotto, Wayne Robson, Jonathan Tucker, Mike Starr, Michael Badalucco, Lenny Clarke, John Friesen; **D:** Bill Bennett; **W:** Denis Leary, Michael Armstrong; **C:** Andrew Lesnie.

Two Moon Junction
Soon-to-be-wed Southern debutante April DeLongpre (Fenn) sets out on one last fling with carnival roustabout Perry (Tyson). All the expected naughtiness, violence, and intrigue ensues between these "lite" versions of Blanche Dubois and Stanley Kowalski. Along with *Body Heat*, this film virtually created the "erotic thriller" genre that has flourished (along with director King's career) on home video. The well-photographed image is generally bright and clear though heavy artifacts surface in the many foggy (i.e. shower) scenes. The many shades of white that are used throughout tend to glow, as they always have. Sound is fine. —MM
Movie: 🦴🦴½ **DVD:** 🦴🦴½
Columbia Tristar Home Video (Cat #9669). Widescreen (1.85:1) letterboxed; full frame. Dolby Digital Stereo. $24.95. Keepcase. *LANG:* English. *SUB:* English; French; Spanish. *FEATURES:* 28 chapter links.
1988 (R) 104m/C Sherilyn Fenn, Richard Tyson, Louise Fletcher, Burl Ives, Kristy

McNichol, Millie Perkins, Don Galloway, Herve Villechaize, Dabbs Greer, Screamin' Jay Hawkins; **D:** Zalman King; **W:** Zalman King; **C:** Mark Plummer; **M:** Jonathan Elias. *AWARDS:* Golden Raspberries '88: Worst Support. Actress (McNichol).

Tycus
A huge comet is about to slam into the Earth! Is it the big-budget *Deep Impact* or *Armageddon*? No, it's a tiny-budget video premiere that gamely tries to deliver the goods. Journalist Jake Lowe (Onarati) investigates a suspicious mining company and learns that billionaire Peter Crawford (Hopper) is preparing for something. The various explosive digital effects are kind of cool in a weirdly transparent way, but they are never remotely convincing. Sound is good and on his commentary track, director Putch talks about the difficulties of attempting to do a lot with a little. —MM
Movie: 🦴🦴½ **DVD:** 🦴🦴½
Paramount Home Video (Cat #83977, UPC #097368397774). Full frame. Dolby Digital 5.1 Surround Stereo; Dolby Digital Surround. $24.99. Keepcase. *LANG:* English. *SUB:* English. *FEATURES:* 20 chapter links ▪ Commentary: Putch ▪ Talent files ▪ Trailer.
1998 (R) 94m/C Dennis Hopper, Peter Onorati, Finola Hughes, Chick Vennera; **D:** John Putch; **W:** Michael C. Goetz, Kevin Goetz; **C:** Ross Berryman; **M:** Alexander Baker, Clair Marlo.

U-571 [CE]
Every World War II sub cliché is trotted out and the whole mix flies along at such a snappy pace that viewers never have a chance to worry about how ridiculous it all is. The wild plot is based on a true story but has little to do with reality. A U.S. sub steals an Enigma encryption device from a damaged German sub, but the Americans are forced to take over the enemy boat to get back home. The film lacks the authenticity of *Das Boot*, but it's still more than acceptable escapism. DVD handles the often dark action with no glaring flaws, but the disc really shines in the audio department. The depth charge attack in Chapter 15 sounds much more impressive with the 5.1 track than it was in theatres. —MM
Movie: 🦴🦴🦴 **DVD:** 🦴🦴🦴½
Universal Studios Home Video (Cat #207 85, UPC #02519207852). Widescreen (2.35:1) anamorphic. Dolby Digital 5.1 Surround Stereo; DTS 5.1 Surround; DD Surround. $26.98. Keepcase. *LANG:* English; French. *SUB:* English. *FEATURES:* 20 chapter links ▪ "Making of" featurette ▪ Commentary: Jonathan Mostow ▪ DVD-ROM features ▪ Featurettes on real WWII events ▪ Theatrical trailer.
2000 (PG-13) 116m/C Matthew McConaughey, Bill Paxton, Harvey Keitel, Jon Bon Jovi, Jake Weber, David Keith, Terrence "T.C." Carson, Jack Noseworthy, Tom Guiry, Thomas Kretschmann, Erik Palladino, Will Estes, Matthew Settle, Dave Power, Derk Cheetwood; **D:** Jonathan Mostow; **W:**

Jonathan Mostow, David Ayer, Sam Montgomery; *C:* Oliver Wood; *M:* Rick Marvin.

Ultimate Attraction

Sexual fantasy-comedy is based on a comic book by Milo Manara. Two employees (Hall and Chielens) of the Body Beautiful health spa discover a gizmo that triggers orgasms. They use it to boost membership and keep the business open. This one boasts a much clearer image than most Alain Siritzky productions. He's also responsible for the *Emmanuelle in Space* cable series. Production values and overall intentions are about the same here. Most of the image is very grainy. Some sex scenes are shot on video and look sharper. —*MM*

Movie: ♫♫ *DVD:* ♫♫½
New Concorde (Cat #NH2649U D, UPC #736991664999). Full frame. Stereo. $14.98. Keepcase. *LANG:* English. *FEATURES:* 24 chapter links • Talent files • Trailers.
1998 91m/C Gabriella Hall, David Chielens, Robert Donovan, Jacqueline Lovell, Nina Leichtling, Rick Jordan, Jennifer Burton; *D:* Rafael Glenn; *W:* Rolfe Kanefsky; *C:* Nils Erickson; *M:* Blaise Smith.

Ulysses

James Joyce's probably unfilmable novel is given a noble effort in this flawed adaptation covering a day in the life of Leopold Bloom as he wanders through Dublin. Shot in Ireland with a primarily Irish cast. The disc features decent definition of blacks. However, most of the edits in the film feature a glitch—more like a bad edit that results in a flash of a scene not completely cut from the final film—which I am at a loss to explain (unless it was intentional). It quickly becomes very bothersome. The soundtrack is a bit muffled and, at times, makes dialogue hard to understand (particularly with the thick accents of the actors). —*MJT*

Movie: ♫♫½ *DVD:* ♫♫½
Image Entertainment (Cat #ID9522RLDVD, UPC #014381952223). Widescreen (1.85:1) letterboxed. Dolby Digital Mono. $29.99. Snapper. *LANG:* English. *FEATURES:* 12 chapter links.
1967 140m/B Milo O'Shea, Maurice Roeves, T.P. McKenna, Martin Dempsey, Sheila O'Sullivan, Barbara Jefford; *D:* Joseph Strick; *W:* Joseph Strick, Fred Haines; *C:* Wolfgang Suschitzky; *M:* Stanley Myers. *AWARDS: NOM:* Oscars '67: Adapt. Screenplay.

The Unbelievable Truth

Ex-con Josh Hutton (Burke) meets Armageddon-obsessed model Audry (Shelley) and sparks fly until a bizarre murder occurs. Hartley's early work is a quirky black comedy that was filmed in less than two weeks. The picture is sharp and clear for the most part. There is a fine grain to the film, however, and there are also some

very minor noticeable flaws from the source print. The colors are rich and true, but some scenes appear to have been overlit, so there tends to be an overt brightness to certain shots. —*MM/ML*

Movie: ♫♫½ *DVD:* ♫♫½
Anchor Bay (Cat #DV11398, UPC #013131 139891). Widescreen (1.85:1) anamorphic. Dolby Digital Mono. $24.99. Keepcase. *LANG:* English. *FEATURES:* Hal Hartley interview • Trailer.
1990 (R) 100m/C Adrienne Shelly, Robert John Burke, Christopher Cooke, Julia Mueller, Julia McNeal, Mark Bailey, Gary Sauer, Kathrine Mayfield; *D:* Hal Hartley; *W:* Hal Hartley; *C:* Michael Spiller; *M:* Jim Coleman.

Uncensored Bosko, Vol. 1

The value of these cartoons is almost entirely historic. As important early works of animation, they are certainly worthy of study. They also reveal the racism of the 1920s and '30s. Bosko is a young black character who refers to his creator as "boss" and likes to dance and sing. The earlier works are barely watchable with very smeary blacks. Quality of the later films is greatly improved. Almost all of them show signs of wear. Contents: "Bosko the Talk-Ink Kid," "Congo Jazz," "Big Man from the North," "Ups 'N Downs," "Yodeling Yokels," "The Tree's Knees," "Bosko the Doughboy," "Bosko's Fox Hunt," "Battling Bosko," "Sinkin' in the Bathtub," "Hold Anything," "Box Car Blues," "Ain't Nature Grand!," and "Dumb Patrol." —*MM*

Movie: ♫♫ *DVD:* ♫♫
Image Entertainment (Cat #ID9572BDVD, UPC #014381957228). Full frame. Dolby Digital Mono. $24.99. Snapper. *FEATURES:* 14 chapter links.
1991 67m/B

Uncensored Bosko, Vol. 2

The entries in this volume are slightly clearer than the ones in the first volume. Otherwise, they're about the same. Accessibility of individual cartoons is the main improvement over VHS tape. Contents: "Bosko's Holiday," "Bosko Shipwrecked!," "Bosko's Soda Fountain," "Bosko at the Zoo," "The Booze Hangs High," "Big-Hearted Bosko," "Bosko and Bruno," "Bosko's Party," "Bosko's Dog Race," "Bosko at the Beach," "Bosko's Store," "Bosko the Lumberjack," "Bosko and Honey." —*MM*

Movie: ♫♫ *DVD:* ♫♫½
Image Entertainment (Cat #ID5738BKDVD, UPC #014381957327). Full frame. Dolby Digital Mono. $24.99. Snapper. *FEATURES:* 13 chapter links.
1991 67m/B

Uncommon Valor

After useless appeals to the government for information on his son listed as "missing in action," Col. Rhodes (Hackman)

takes matters into his own hands. This is one of the first of the revisionist Vietnamese-are-holding-our-boys action flicks. For those who can ignore the claptrap, it's an acceptable adventure. DVD presents a well-preserved image with no serious flaws. —*MM*

Movie: ♫♫½ *DVD:* ♫♫½
Paramount Home Video (Cat #01657, UPC #097360165746). Widescreen anamorphic. Dolby Digital 5.1 Surround Stereo; Dolby Digital Surround; Mono. $29.99. Keepcase. *LANG:* English; French. *SUB:* English. *FEATURES:* 18 chapter links.
1983 (R) 105m/C Gene Hackman, Fred Ward, Reb Brown, Randall "Tex" Cobb, Robert Stack, Patrick Swayze, Harold Sylvester, Tim Thomerson; *D:* Ted Kotcheff; *C:* Stephen Burum; *M:* James Horner.

Under Oath

Cops Nick Hollit (Scalia, looking and sounding more than ever like the lost Baldwin brother) and Ray Ramirez (Velez) decide to pull a heist, but things go wrong. Eventually, they're assigned to investigate a crime they committed. For a video premiere, this DVD boasts a very nice look. Many interiors have a careful sepia tone. There is heavy grain in some night exteriors, but overall, the image is fine. —*MM*
AKA: Urban Justice; Blood Money.
Movie: ♫♫♫ *DVD:* ♫♫½
New Concorde (Cat #NH20664 D, UPC #73 6991466494). Full frame. Stereo. $19.99. Keepcase. *LANG:* English. *FEATURES:* 24 chapter links • Talent files • Trailers.
1997 (R) 89m/C Jack Scalia, James Russo, Eddie Velez, Richard Lynch, Abraham Benrubi, Beth Grant, Clint Howard, Robert LaSardo; *D:* Dave Payne; *W:* Scott Sandin; *C:* Mike Michiewicz; *M:* Roger Neil.

Under Suspicion

Gene Hackman is tax attorney Henry Hearst, on his way to deliver a speech at a black-tie dinner when his friend, police detective Victor Benezet (Freeman), calls to say that they need to talk. Henry found the body of a murdered young girl and the cops need to straighten out a few "minor details." Add in Henry's much younger knock-out wife Chantal (Bellucci) and the final ingredient is in place. Actually the generic title is the only thing that's really wrong with this well-constructed mystery. Director Stephen Hopkins uses some tricky editing and narrative techniques to open up the action. This one's a solid sleeper with the expected fine performances from the two stars, who also serve as executive producers. Hopkins uses a deliberately pale image and undersaturated colors to make the most of the Puerto Rican locations. Sound is fine. —*MM*

Movie: ♫♫♫½ *DVD:* ♫♫♫
Columbia Tristar Home Video (Cat #06059, UPC #043396060593). Widescreen (1.85:1) anamorphic; full frame. Dolby Digital 5.1 Surround Stereo; Dolby Digital Surround. $24.95. Keepcase. *LANG:* English. *SUB:* English; Spanish; Chinese. *CAP:* English.

FEATURES: 28 chapter links • Commentary: Hopkins and Freeman • Trailer.
2000 (R) 110m/C Morgan Freeman, Gene Hackman, Thomas Jane, Monica Bellucci; **D:** Stephen Hopkins; **W:** W. Peter Iliff, Tom Provost; **C:** Peter Levy.

The Undertaker and His Pals

A mortician teams up with diner owners in a murder scheme to improve his business and to expand their menu options. It's silly stuff that attempts to work with the gruesome subjects that Herschell Gordon Lewis was filming at the same time. But these auteurs had even less money for effects and so the levels of blood and gore are considerably lower. The yellowish cast at the beginning gives way to full color. The image is very grainy but overall the disc delivers a good reproduction of a cheap original image. —*MM*
Movie: ♪ **DVD:** ♪
VCI Home Video (Cat #8244, UPC #08985 9824425). Full frame. Dolby Digital Mono. $19.99. Keepcase. *LANG:* English. *FEATURES:* 12 chapter links • Trailers • Talent files.
1967 70m/C Ray Dannis, Brad Fulton, Larrene Ott, Robert Lowery, Sally Frei; **D:** David C. Graham; **C:** Andrew Janczak.

Uninvited Guest

Debbie (Morrow) and Howard (Jackson) have already been fighting on their 3rd anniversary when Silk (Phifer) finagles his way into their house, and puts some strong moves on her. It could be the premise for any number of "erotic thrillers." The difference here is that the cast is black. DVD boasts a very good image. Many of the interiors have a warm amber cast that flatters the actors. Sound is good. —*MM* **AKA:** An Invited Guest.
Movie: ♪♪ **DVD:** ♪♪½
Trimark Home Video (Cat #7512D, UPC #031398751229). Widescreen letterboxed. Dolby Digital 5.1 Surround Stereo. $24.99. Keepcase. *LANG:* English. *SUB:* English; French; Spanish. *FEATURES:* 24 chapter links • Trailer.
1999 (R) 103m/C Mekhi Phifer, Mari Morrow, Mel Jackson, Kim Fields, Malinda Williams; **D:** Timothy Wayne Folsome; **W:** Timothy Wayne Folsome; **C:** Wayne Sells; **M:** Gregory Darryl Smith.

U.S. Seals

Absolutely undistinguished action flick pits a team of Navy SEALs against pirates from Kazahkstan. The heroes are jut-jawed guys with crewcuts and cute kids. Lots of stuff blows up. Production values are strictly of the made-for-cable quality. DVD looks exactly like tape. —*MM*
Movie: ♪♪ **DVD:** ♪♪
Image Entertainment (Cat #ID6378NGDVD, UPC #014381637823). Full frame. Dolby Digital Stereo. $24.99. Snapper. *LANG:* English. *FEATURES:* 15 chapter links • Trailer.

1998 (R) 90m/C Jim Fitzpatrick, Greg Collins, J. Kenneth Campbell; **D:** Yossi Wein.

Unmade Beds

Four real New Yorkers—Brenda Monte, Aimee Copp, Michael Russo, Michael De Stefano—were filmed for nine months and their adventures in dating were recorded for posterity. The resulting documentary is shockingly funny, honest, and fascinating. Though the image quality is nothing special, it looks fine and DVD offers the filmmakers the opportunity to toss in several intriguing extras—outtakes, the original casting tapes, and an album of New York window photographs, illustrating one of the unapologetically voyeuristic approach that director Nicholas Barker employs. By the way, chapter links are grouped by character. —*MM*
Movie: ♪♪½ **DVD:** ♪♪♪
New Yorker Video (Cat #72400, UPC #717 119724047). Widescreen (1.66:1) letterboxed. $29.95. Keepcase. *LANG:* English. *FEATURES:* 21 chapter links • Trailer • Outtakes • Windows of New York City album • Director profile and interview • Original casting tapes.
2000 (R) 95m/C Aimee Copp, Michael De Stefano, Brenda Monte, Mikey Russo; **D:** Nicholas Barker; **W:** Nicholas Barker; **C:** William Rexer.

The Unsinkable Molly Brown

The last gasp of the MGM musical begins with Debbie Reynolds yelling and screaming at the Rocky Mountains and she doesn't stop for 135 minutes. It's big, colorful, loud, and vulgar in the family-safe way that all movies were in 1964. The picture has never looked better in (finally) restored color and 16x9 enhancement. For extras there's a peppy trailer and a moronic studio short subject about the creation of a dress for Reynolds to wear in the film; with the kind of regal insensitivity one associates with Marie Antoinette, we're supposed to be impressed by how many underpaid seamstresses, for how many untold hours, can be worked to create a dress for an exalted star. —*GE*
Movie: ♪♪ **DVD:** ♪♪♪½
Warner Home Video, Inc. (Cat #65201). Widescreen (2.35:1) anamorphic. Dolby Digital 5.1 Surround Stereo. $19.98. Snapper. *LANG:* English. *FEATURES:* Trailers • "Story of a Dress" short subject • Screen tests.
1964 128m/C Debbie Reynolds, Harve Presnell, Ed Begley Sr., Martita Hunt, Hermione Baddeley; **D:** Charles Walters; **C:** Daniel F. Fapp; **M:** Meredith Willson. *AWARDS: NOM:* Oscars '64: Actress (Reynolds), Adapt. Score, Art Dir./Set Dec., Color, Color Cinematog., Costume Des. (C), Sound.

Unspeakable

James (Cline) and Alice Fhelleps have a nasty, unsatisfying marriage until a car accident turns their life together into a

true horror. From that premise, Chad Ferrin spins out a relatively realistic tale of madness and murder. Since the film was made on a severely restricted budget, it gains little visually on DVD, but the grainy, harshly lit images are fine for such a grim story. For hard-core horror fans only. —*MM*
Movie: ♪♪½ **DVD:** ♪♪
Troma Team Video (Cat #9009, UPC #7903 57900930). Widescreen (1.66:1) letterboxed. $24.99. Keepcase. *LANG:* English. *FEATURES:* 10 chapter links • Commentary: director Ferrin, star Muskatell • Short film, "Bloodbath" • Interview • Trailers • DVD credits.
2000 81m/C Robert Cline, Timothy Muskatell, Tina Birchfield, Wolf Dangler; **D:** Chad Ferrin; **W:** Chad Ferrin; **C:** Nicholas Loizides.

Untamed Heart

Adam (Slater), the painfully shy busboy with a heart condition, loves Caroline (Tomei), the bubbly waitress from afar. She doesn't notice him until he saves her from some would-be rapists and their love blooms in the coffee shop where they work. Tomei and Slater are strong in the leads and Perez, as Caroline's best buddy Cindy, hurls comic barbs with ease. Charmingly familiar surroundings (filmed on location in Minneapolis) help set this formulaic romance apart. While darker colors do tend to be a little clouded, the video transfer is, for the most part, quite good, particularly with brighter colors. The soundtrack is adequate and features clear, understandable dialogue. —*MJT*
Movie: ♪♪½ **DVD:** ♪♪½
MGM Home Entertainment (Cat #10014 59, UPC #027616857798). Widescreen (1.85:1) anamorphic. Dolby Digital Surround Stereo. $19.98. Keepcase. *LANG:* English; French; Spanish. *SUB:* French; Spanish. *FEATURES:* 16 chapter links • Theatrical trailer.
1993 (PG-13) 102m/C Christian Slater, Marisa Tomei, Rosie Perez, Kyle Secor, Willie Garson; **D:** Tony Bill; **W:** Tom Sierchio; **C:** Jost Vacano; **M:** Cliff Eidelman. *AWARDS:* MTV Movie Awards '93: Most Desirable Male (Slater), Kiss (Christian Slater/Marisa Tomei).

The Untouchables

On one hand are the extremely effective scenes of violence—Capone's (De Niro) famous baseball bat execution, the opening explosion, the train station shoot-out—on the other are moments of alleged sweetness involving Elliott Ness (Costner) and his happy little family at home. Those are nauseating. Surfacing occasionally in between is a moderately entertaining big-budget gangster movie. The casting could hardly be better. The good guys (Connery, Garcia, Smith) are an interesting, likeable lot, and the big moments work well. In the end, though, like almost all of DePalma's overrated work, the film is less than the sum of its parts. The image has never been particularly bright and the DVD reflects that with a certain pasty cast to the colors. Surround effects are acceptable but not overpowering, as they should be. —*MM*

Movie: 🐾🐾 *DVD:* 🐾🐾½

Paramount Home Video (Cat #01886, UPC #097360188646). Widescreen anamorphic. Dolby Digital 5.1 Surround Stereo; Dolby Digital Surround. $29.99. Keepcase. *LANG:* English; French. *SUB:* English. *FEATURES:* 24 chapter links ➡ Theatrical trailer.

1987 (R) 119m/C Kevin Costner, Sean Connery, Robert De Niro, Andy Garcia, Charles Martin Smith, Billy Drago, Richard Bradford, Jack Kehoe; *D:* Brian DePalma; *W:* David Mamet; *C:* Stephen Burum; *M:* Ennio Morricone. *AWARDS:* Oscars '87: Support. Actor (Connery); Golden Globes '88: Support. Actor (Connery); Natl. Bd. of Review '87: Support. Actor (Connery); *NOM:* Oscars '87: Art Dir./Set Dec., Costume Des., Orig. Score.

Up at the Villa

In Florence, Italy, 1938, British widow Mary Panton (Thomas) and American expatriate Rowley Flint (Penn, at his most engaging) find themselves caught up in a tangle of deception. If the stars aren't completely comfortable with the material, adapted from a Somerset Maugham novella, they handle it well enough. DVD delivers very good image and sound, capturing a proper amount of detail, even in nocturnal exteriors. Sound is fine. —*MM*

Movie: 🐾🐾½ *DVD:* 🐾🐾½

USA Home Entertainment (Cat #963 060 101-2, UPC #696306010128). Widescreen (1.78:1) letterboxed. Dolby Digital 5.1 Surround Stereo; Dolby Digital Surround. $26.95. Keepcase. *LANG:* English. *SUB:* French; Spanish. *CAP:* English. *FEATURES:* 16 chapter links ➡ Talent files ➡ Trailer.

2000 (PG-13) 115m/C *GB* Kristin Scott Thomas, Sean Penn, Anne Bancroft, Derek Jacobi, Jeremy Davies, James Fox, Massimo Ghini; *D:* Philip Haas; *W:* Belinda Haas; *C:* Maurizio Calvesi; *M:* Pino Donaggio.

Up in Mabel's Room

This is a dated, silly bedroom farce about squabbling couples snowed in at a lodge. It's one of those stories that's built around people hiding under beds and in closets and climbing out of windows so they won't be caught in the wrong place. The so-so black-and-white image has a curious olive/sepia tint. Sound is good. —*MM*

Movie: 🐾🐾 *DVD:* 🐾🐾

VCI Home Video (Cat #8264, UPC #08985 9826429). Full frame. Dolby Digital Mono. $19.99. Keepcase. *LANG:* English. *FEATURES:* 18 chapter links ➡ Short comedy, "Rough on Rents" ➡ Talent files.

1944 77m/B Dennis O'Keefe, Marjorie Reynolds, Gail Patrick, Mischa Auer, Lee Bowman, Charlotte Greenwood; *D:* Allan Dwan; *W:* Tom Reed, Isabel Dawn; *C:* Charles Lawton Jr.; *M:* Edward Paul.

Urban Legends 2: Final Cut

Generic horror sequel lacks even the limited wit of the original. It's a mess of clichés, beginning with the movie-within-a-movie opening. The rest has to do with filmmaking students. Image and sound are without serious flaws. On his commentary track, young director Ottman certainly sounds cheery. —*MM*

Movie: 🐾 *DVD:* 🐾🐾

Columbia Tristar Home Video (Cat #05666, UPC #043396056664). Widescreen (2.35:1) anamorphic; full frame. Dolby Digital 5.1 Surround Stereo; Dolby Digital Surround. $19.95. Keepcase. *LANG:* English; French. *SUB:* English; French. *FEATURES:* 28 chapter links ➡ 7 deleted scenes ➡ Trailers ➡ Talent files ➡ Gag reel ➡ "Making of" featurette ➡ Commentary: director John Ottman.

2000 (R) 94m/C Jenny Morrison, Anthony Anderson, Joseph Lawrence, Matthew Davis, Hart Bochner, Loretta Devine, Marco Hofschneider, Eva Mendez, Michael Bacall, Anson Mount, Jessica Cauffiel, Chas Lawther; *D:* John Ottman; *W:* Paul Harris Boardman, Scott Derrickson; *C:* Brian Pearson; *M:* John Ottman.

Utopia

Laurel and Hardy inherit a paradisiacal island but their peace is disturbed when uranium is discovered. Final screen appearance of the team is diminished by poor direction, script, and production values. The original image is grainy and poorly focused; sound is muddy. The title is available on a double feature with *The Flying Deuces*. —*MM* *AKA:* Atoll K; Robinson Crusoeland; Escapade.

Movie: 🐾🐾 *DVD:* 🐾½

Digital Disc Entertainment (Cat #585, UPC #056775037192). Full frame. Dolby Digital Mono. $9.99. Keepcase. *LANG:* English. *FEATURES:* 8 chapter links ➡ Oliver Hardy thumbnail bio ➡ Laurel and Hardy filmography ➡ Trivia.

1951 82m/B *FR* Stan Laurel, Oliver Hardy, Suzy Delair, Max Elloy; *D:* Leo Joannon; *W:* Rene Wheeler, Piero Tellini; *C:* Louis Nee, Armand Thirard; *M:* Paul Misraki.

U2: Rattle and Hum

Concert and tour documentary is virtually an hour and a half of MTV without the zit cream commercials. Director Joanou never gets beneath the surface of the reserved Irish group. Whenever the band members try to talk about what they're doing, their comments are brief and inarticulate. Almost all of the film is concert footage, shot during an American tour, or recording sessions: one at a Harlem church and one at the famous Sun studios in Memphis. For most of the running time, the screen is filled with the now-familiar shots of rock musicians on stage: circling cameras, low angles, slow motion, intense spotlights, lots of backlighting, smoke, strutting, and posturing. The night concert in Tempe, Ari-

zona, was filmed in color; the rest is grainy black and white. The group's social commitment and strong religious background are apparent throughout. Fans could hardly ask for more; there are 17 songs in the film. Both image and sound are either equal to or better than the theatrical release, as I remember it. Another plus are the subtitles, which clear up difficult-to-understand accents and lyrics. —*MM*

Movie: 🐾🐾🐾 *DVD:* 🐾🐾🐾

Paramount Home Video (Cat #32228, UPC #097363222873). Widescreen letterboxed. Dolby Digital 5.1 Surround Stereo; Dolby Digital Surround Stereo. $29.99. Keepcase. *LANG:* English. *FEATURES:* 20 chapter links ➡ Trailer.

1988 (PG-13) 90m/C *D:* Phil Joanou; *C:* Robert Brinkmann, Jordan Cronenweth.

The Vampire Bat

Please see review of *Fay Wray Collection.*

Movie: 🐾🐾½

1932 69m/B Lionel Atwill, Fay Wray, Melvyn Douglas, Dwight Frye, Maude Eburne, George E. Stone; *D:* Frank Strayer; *W:* Edward T. Lowe; *C:* Ira Morgan.

The Vampire Happening

American actress Betty Williams (Degermark) travels to Transylvania to sell the family castle and discovers that her ancestors were vampires and one of them is still alive. She unknowingly releases them to party hearty on the locals. Directed by veteran Freddie Francis, this one is a combination of *Laugh-In* and a Hammer horror. The DVD image is crisp and shows only slight grain and defects from the source material. Mono sound is fine. —*ML/MM*

Movie: 🐾½ *DVD:* 🐾🐾½

Anchor Bay (Cat #11100). Widescreen (1.85:1) anamorphic. Dolby Digital Mono. $29.98. Keepcase. *LANG:* English. *FEATURES:* Trailer.

1971 (R) 101m/C *GE* Ferdinand "Ferdy" Mayne, Pia Degermark, Thomas Hunter, Yvor Murillo, Ingrid van Bergen, Raul Retzer; *D:* Freddie Francis; *W:* Karl Heinz Hummel, August Rieger; *C:* Gerard Vandenburg; *M:* Jerry Van Rooyen.

Vampire Hunter D [SE]

The foreword says that the story is set "in a distant future when mutants and demons slither through a world of darkness," and fans of Japanese anime know what to expect—grotesque transformations, characters who can suddenly fly, bloody violence. With his cape and hat, the title character looks like The Shadow, but the filmmakers borrow freely from many other sources. The simple plot pits the laconic D against the vampire Magnus Lee and his monstrous gang. The dark inventive visuals are not really much sharper on DVD than they are on VHS tape. The main difference between the two lies in the language and subtitle options. —MM

Movie: 🎬🎬🎬 **DVD:** 🎬🎬½
Urban Vision Entertainment (Cat #UV1064, UPC #638652106407). Full frame. $29.95. Keepcase. *LANG:* English; Japanese. *SUB:* English. *FEATURES:* 11 chapter links • Trailers • "Making of" featurette • Image gallery • Weblinks.
1985 80m/C *JP D:* Toyoo Ashida.

Vamps: Deadly Dreamgirls

The umpteenth vampires-in-a-strip joint is a Cincinnati production featuring lots of mostly naked girls and the expected love scenes. The acting is on the amateur side; production values are slender. —MM

Movie: 🎬 **DVD:** 🎬
El Independent Cinema (Cat #so-5034-dvd, UPC #612385503498). Full frame. $19.98. Keepcase. *LANG:* English. *FEATURES:* 21 chapter links • Jenny Wallace featurette • Trailers.
1995 90m/C Lorissa McComas, Jennifer Huss, Paul Morris, Jenny Wallace, Amber Newman; *D:* Jeff Barklage; *C:* Jeff Barklage.

Vampyres

The sexiest horror movie ever made is a terrific DVD. Previous tape incarnations have been barely watchable. This one has been cleaned up admirably (it's a massive improvement over older VHS), and director Larraz and producer Brian Smedley-Aston provide a wonderfully bawdy commentary track. Ted (Murray Brown) picks up Fran (Marianne Morris), an attractive hitchhiker. At her moldering country estate, he allows himself to be seduced by her and her lover Miriam (Anulka), who are lesbian vampires. The combination of athletic sex, desire, and violence is certainly too strong for some tastes, making this one of the great guilty pleasures. —MM *AKA:* Vampyres, Daughters of Dracula; Blood Hunger; Satan's Daughters; Daughters of Dracula; Vampire Orgy.

Movie: 🎬🎬🎬½ **DVD:** 🎬🎬🎬½
Anchor Bay (Cat #DV11101, UPC #013131 110197). Widescreen (1.85:1) anamorphic. Dolby Digital Mono. $24.98. Keepcase. *LANG:* English. *FEATURES:* 21 chapter links • Commentary: Joseph Larraz, producer Brian Smedley-Aston • Larraz thumbnail bio • 2 trailers • Stills gallery.
1974 (R) 90m/C *GB* Marianne Morris, Anulka, Murray Brown, Brian Deacon, Sally Faulkner, Michael Byrne, Karl Lanchbury, Bessie Love, Elliott Sullivan; *D:* Joseph (Jose Ramon) Larraz; *W:* Diane Daubeney; *C:* Harry Waxman; *M:* James Clark.

Vampyros Lesbos

A lesbian vampire (Miranda) lures female victims to a remote island to love and feast on them, and to eventually kill them in one of prolific director Jess Franco's early erotic horrors. The transfer is not

enhanced for 16x9 televisions. The source print from which this transfer has been made appears to be in pretty bad shape, which is hardly surprising given the film's low budget and small stature in the market. As a result a large amount of grain is evident throughout the film's length and the entire movie has a very soft look that often becomes almost foggy. —GH/MM

Movie: 🎬½ **DVD:** 🎬½
Synapse (Cat #SYNA3). Widescreen (1.66:1) letterboxed. Dolby Digital Mono. $29.95. Keepcase. *LANG:* German. *SUB:* English. *FEATURES:* Trailer.
1970 90m/C Soledad Miranda, Dennis Price, Ewa Stromberg; *D:* Jess (Jesus) Franco.

The Vanishing American

This epic Paramount western begins in the Stone Age, follows with a mythic tale of an Indian conquest, then sweeps us into the 20th century, where we meet Nophaie (Dix), a Navajo chieftain who must reconcile his heritage with the modern age. Inept and corrupt government agents are the villains of this Zane Grey adaptation, strikingly filmed in Monument Valley and the Betatakin Cliff Dwellings of Arizona. The climactic Indian uprising is especially thrilling. The print is remarkably clean for its age and is nicely tinted, but the image flickers regrettably. Muri's organ score is effective, even though the live recording allows us the peculiar experience of hearing an audience's reactions to the film, complete with laughter and applause. —SS

Movie: 🎬🎬🎬 **DVD:** 🎬🎬
Image Entertainment (Cat #ID9229DSDVD, UPC #014381922929). Full frame. Dolby Digital Stereo. $24.99. Snapper. *LANG:* English. *FEATURES:* 16 chapter links • Organ score (recorded live) by John Muri.
1925 109m/B Richard Dix, Noah Beery Sr., Lois Wilson; *D:* George B. Seitz; *W:* Lucien Hubbard, Ethel Doherty; *C:* Harry Perry, Charles E. Schoenbaum.

Varietease

This companion piece to *Teaserama* contains similar "mild nudity" that's really no nudity at all. The film is a re-creation of a '50s burlesque show complete with a baggy pants comedian whose patterned sport coat does strange things. The real highlight of the tape is the wild comic dance routine by Baro and Rogers in Chapter 12. Surface damage and abrupt changes in color values come from the original elements. —MM

Movie: 🎬🎬 **DVD:** 🎬🎬½
Image Entertainment (Cat #ID6101SWDVD, UPC #014381610123). Full frame. Dolby Digital Mono. $24.98. Snapper. *LANG:* English. *FEATURES:* 20 chapter links • Trailers • Bettie Page arcade loop (B&W) • Commentary: Dave Friedman, Mike Vraney.
1954 72m/C Bettie (Betty) Page, Lili St. Cyr, Cass Franklin, Monica Lane, Bobby Shields; *D:* Irving Klaw.

Variety Lights

A beautiful young girl, Lily (Del Poggio), runs away with a traveling vaudeville troupe and soon becomes its main attraction as a dancer. The group's aging comic Checco sees the potential, falls for Lily, and soon dumps his longtime girlfriend Melina (Masina), deciding to make his new love a star. *Variety Lights* is filled with Fellini's now-familiar delight in the bizarre and sawdust/tinsel entertainment. Even though Criterion's DVD looks very good, Fellini's first (albeit joint) directorial effort would have benefitted greatly from some sort of supplemental section—there is none. The transfer looks good and the only flaws can be attributed to the preprint material itself. Overall, very sharp with little grain, nice contrast, and very good blacks. The mono soundtrack has more body than most transfers of this vintage film and as a result, the music sounds much better than expected, yet manages to maintain an even and distinct delivery of the dialogue. —JO *AKA:* Luci del Varieta; Lights of Variety.

Movie: 🎬🎬🎬½ **DVD:** 🎬🎬🎬
Criterion Collection (Cat #040, UPC #0374 29150023). Full frame. Dolby Digital Mono. $29.95. Keepcase. *LANG:* English. *FEATURES:* 22 chapter links.
1951 93m/B *IT* Giulietta Masina, Peppino de Filippo, Carla Del Poggio, Folco Lulli; *D:* Federico Fellini, Alberto Lattuada; *W:* Federico Fellini, Tullio Pinelli, Ennio Flaiano, Alberto Lattuada; *C:* Otello Martelli; *M:* Felice Lattuada.

The Vault

Mr. Burnett (Lyde), a teacher, takes four students—Dezaray (Pride), Willy (Priester), Zipper (Walker), and Kyle (Davis)—to visit an old high school, which is scheduled to be demolished. (The four kids fit the stereotypes of cheerleader, jock, nerd, and tough guy.) The school was originally a way-station for slaves and the group hopes to rescue some historical items (or something like that). Once they arrive at the school, they meet the eerie security guard Spangler (Papi), who warns them to not venture into the basement. You see, there's a very old locked door in the basement, and behind that door is...ultimate evil. Unfortunately, the film ends just as it's beginning to get interesting. The image is sharp and clear, showing only a minute amount of grain during the daylight scenes. There are no overt defects from the source print. The colors are natural and true, with the darker scenes being nicely balanced. The 2-channel Surround mix brings us clear and audible dialogue, coupled with nice usage of the Surround speakers for musical cues and ambient sound effects. —ML

Movie: 🎬🎬 **DVD:** 🎬🎬½
Full Moon Pictures (Cat #8074). Widescreen (1.85:1) letterboxed. Dolby Digital Surround Stereo. Keepcase. *LANG:* English. *FEATURES:* Commentary: director Black, producer J.R. Bookwalter • "Making of" featurette • Profile of Black • "Galaxy of

the Dinosaurs" 60-minute feature ▪ 13 trailers.

2000 (R) ?m/C Ted Lyde, Shani Pride, Austin Priester, Kyle Walker, Michael Cory Davis, Leopold Papi; **D:** James Black.

Velocity

This bizarre little curiosity begins and ends with a contemporary story about auto racing. Sandwiched between is most of a colorized version of Jack Nicholson's 1960 *The Wild Ride.* Colors are so false—apparently intentionally so—that the two parts look alike. Sort of, if you don't pay a lot of attention. Presumably it was done so that a shot of the young Nicholson's mug could be plastered across the box cover. The whole thing looks so nauseatingly "off" that it's impossible to judge the image by meaningful standards. —*MM*
Movie: 𝄢𝄢 **DVD:** 𝄢𝄢
New Concorde (Cat #NH20727D, UPC #73 6991372795). Full frame. $19.98. Keepcase. *LANG:* English. *FEATURES:* 24 chapter links ▪ Trailers ▪ Thumbnail bios.
1999 (PG-13) 114m/C Jack Nicholson, Georgianna Carter, Joe Richards, Harrison Young, Bernard Zilinskas, Candace Reid, Jason Sudeikis, Melinda Hill, Curtis Cofer, Peter Soby; **D:** David Wolfe, Harvey Berman; **W:** David Wolfe, Marion Rothman, Ann Porter; **C:** Taylor Sloan, Michael Mickens; **M:** David Tweedie, Rand Singer.

Velocity Trap

In 2150, electronic crime and piracy run rampant throughout the galaxy. Cop Raymond Stokes (Gruner) is assigned to escort a federal banking ship through a section of space known as the Velocity Run. It's the equivalent of the Bermuda Triangle. Along with the ship's navigator Beth Sheffield (Coppola), he must prevent thieves from grabbing the loot and keep an asteroid from destroying the ship. The image is generally dark, so dark that the picture loses detail in shadows. The aggressive 5.1 mix has a very wide frequency response with a good low end and brilliant highs. —*GH/MM*
Movie: 𝄢𝄢 **DVD:** 𝄢𝄢½
Columbia Tristar Home Video (Cat #4839). Widescreen (1.85:1) letterboxed. Dolby Digital 5.1 Surround Stereo; Dolby Digital Stereo. $27.95. Keepcase. *LANG:* English. *SUB:* English; Spanish. *FEATURES:* Commentary ▪ Trailers ▪ Talent files.
1999 (R) 90m/C Olivier Gruner, Alicia Coppola, Ken Olandt, Bruce Weitz, Craig Wasson; **D:** Phillip J. Roth; **W:** Phillip J. Roth.

Vengeance

Thin spaghetti (cappellini?) western from producer Alfredo Leone (no relation to Sergio) finds outlaw Rocco (Harrison) hunting down the five desperadoes who betrayed him after a gold heist and killed his partner, drawn and quartered in the opening scene. Scar-faced villains, cackling henchmen, close-ups of steely eyed glances,

and a saloon floozy falling in love comprise some of the obstacles Rocco crosses in his quest for revenge. Single-minded story tenders a few compelling embellishments (every time he dispenses "justice," Rocco leaves behind a scrap from the ropes used to kill his friend) and a couple of plot twists that actually surprise. Distractions include the standard atrocious ADR / dubbing and a shoot-out climax ten minutes too long. Good transfer, but print scratches and speckles plague the entire presentation. Colors are sharp and clean, with solid black levels and occasionally high contrast. Mono sound is adequate. Soundtrack highlight is the title song by Don Powell (?), playing like a Mantovani selection on an "AM gold" compilation. —*EP* **AKA:** Joko Invoca Dio...e Muori.
Movie: 𝄢𝄢½ **DVD:** 𝄢𝄢½
Image Entertainment (Cat #ALF9858DVD, UPC #014381985825). Widescreen (2.35:1) anamorphic. $24.99. Snapper. *LANG:* English. *FEATURES:* 12 chapter links.
1968 (PG) 100m/C *IT GE* Richard Harrison, Paolo Gozlino, Claudio Camaso, Werner Pochath; **D:** Anthony (Antonio Margheriti) Dawson; **W:** Anthony (Antonio Margheriti) Dawson, Renato Savino; **C:** Riccardo (Pallton) Pallottini.

Venus in Furs

Severin (Van Noord) and the lovely Wanda (Van Der Ven) enter into a contract where he agrees to be her slave. It's a loose adaptation of Leopold von Sacher-Masoch's 1869 novel. The film is deliberately slow and measured, creating a hypnotic atmosphere. Even though it contains abundant nudity, the level of sexual activity and kinkiness is considerably less graphic than late-night cable. Co-directors Maartje Seyferth and Victor E. Nieuwenhuijs are attempting to combine the cerebral with the erotic. They largely succeed, too, because the film is so beautifully photographed in black and white on a few austere but impressive sets. DVD reproduces that very dark image with no flaws that I could see. Orchestral score is very strong and everyday sounds are heightened. The film is certainly not to all tastes, but it is a serious work, recommended to the adventurous videophile. —*MM*
Movie: 𝄢𝄢𝄢 **DVD:** 𝄢𝄢𝄢
Cult Epics (Cat #DVD007, UPC #0633900 10073). Full frame. Keepcase. *LANG:* English. *SUB:* English; French; German; Spanish; Italian; Dutch; Chinese. *FEATURES:* Credits ▪ Synopsis ▪ 12 chapter links.
1994 70m/B *NL* Anne Van Der Ven, Andre Arend Van Noord, Raymond Thiery, Hilt de Vos, Claire Mijnals; **D:** Victor Nieuwenhuijs, Maartje Seyferth; **W:** Victor Nieuwenhuijs, Maartje Seyferth, Ian Kerkhof; **C:** Victor Nieuwenhuijs.

Vera Cruz

Ben Trane (Cooper) and Joe Erin (Lancaster, at his toothiest), two soldiers of fortune, become involved in the Mexican Revolution of 1866, a stolen shipment of

gold, divided loyalties, and gun battles. It's certainly not the finest moment for the stars or director Aldrich but it is an enjoyable outing. Unfortunately, the DVD leaves much to be desired. Many scenes are marred by heavy grain; sound is often distorted and brief registration jitters are annoying. —*MM*
Movie: 𝄢𝄢𝄢 **DVD:** 𝄢𝄢
MGM Home Entertainment (Cat #1001597, UPC #027616859075). Widescreen (2:1) anamorphic. Dolby Digital Mono. $19.99. Keepcase. *LANG:* English; French; Spanish. *SUB:* French; Spanish. *CAP:* English. *FEATURES:* 16 chapter links ▪ Trailer.
1953 94m/C Gary Cooper, Burt Lancaster, Denise Darcel, Cesar Romero, George Macready, Ernest Borgnine, Charles Bronson, Jack Elam; **D:** Robert Aldrich; **W:** Roland Kibbee, James R. Webb; **C:** Ernest Laszlo; **M:** Hugo Friedhofer.

Vertical Limit

The very idea of people attempting to climb K-2 with nitroglycerin strapped to their backs is so ridiculous that nobody should take this live-action cartoon seriously. That said, director Martin Campbell and a whiz-bang team of computer effects experts have created some neat visuals. On the commentary track, Campbell and producer Lloyd Phillips talk about how those effects were achieved. All that digital work translates fine to DVD with an image that is really much too sharp and clear for the subject matter (but not too clear for a cartoon). An attractive cast makes all the right facial expressions in reaction to the effects. Sound is very good. —*MM*
Movie: 𝄢𝄢 **DVD:** 𝄢𝄢𝄢½
Columbia Tristar Home Video (Cat #05066, UPC #043396050662). Widescreen anamorphic. Dolby Digital 5.1 Surround Stereo; Dolby Digital Surround. $27.96. Keepcase. *LANG:* English. *SUB:* English; French. *FEATURES:* 28 chapter links ▪ "Making of" featurette ▪ Special effects featurette ▪ National Geographic Channel's "Quest for K-2" ▪ Trailer ▪ Filmographies.
2000 (PG-13) 126m/C Chris O'Donnell, Robin Tunney, Bill Paxton, Scott Glenn, Izabela Scorupco, Temuera Morrison, Stuart Wilson, Nicholas Lea, Alexander Siddig, Robert Taylor, Roshan Seth, David Hayman, Ben Mendelsohn, Steve Le Marquand; **D:** Martin Campbell; **W:** Robert King, Terry Hayes; **C:** David Tattersall; **M:** James Newton Howard.

Vice Girls

Undercover cops Jan Cooper (Clarkson), Edith Bloch (Goodson), and Mindy Turner (Roberts) are on the trail of another serial killer in this ultra-low-budget comedy. Charlie's Angels they ain't. DVD image ranges between poor and fair. —*MM*
Movie: 𝄢½ **DVD:** 𝄢½
New Concorde (Cat #NH20621 D, UPC #736991462199). Full frame. Stereo. $19.99. Keepcase. *LANG:* English. *FEATURES:* 24 chapter links ▪ Talent files ▪ Trailers.

1996 (R) 85m/C Lana Clarkson, Liat Goodson, Kimberly Roberts, A. Michael Baldwin, Richard Gabai, Caroline Keenan, Hoke Howell; **D:** Richard Gabai; **W:** A. Michael Baldwin; **C:** Gary Graver.

Vietnam: The Ten Thousand Day War

This made-for-TV miniseries documentary is an ambitious attempt to show how America entered the civil war in Vietnam and then was unable to leave. It is even-handed enough to anger partisans on both sides of the conflict, and, with a running time of more than 10 hours, it's long enough to include the important details. It would be pointless to criticize the image, though it is always as good as the source material. This set is valuable for its content and the accessibility that DVD affords. —*MM*
Movie: 🎬🎬🎬 **DVD:** 🎬🎬🎬
Image Entertainment (Cat #ID5574BVDVD, UPC #014381557428). Full frame. Dolby Digital Mono. $89.99. Snapper boxed set. *LANG:* English. *FEATURES:* 105 chapter links.
1980 624m/C W: Peter Arnett; **Nar:** Richard Basehart.

A View to a Kill [SE]

This James Bond mission takes him to the United States, where he must stop the evil Max Zorin from destroying California's Silicon Valley. Feeble and unexciting plot with unscary villain. Duran Duran performs the catchy title tune. It's Moore's last performance as 007. The impressive video transfer features sharp, bright, vibrant colors that accent extremely well-defined blacks (you can even count the cracks in Moore's skin when he smiles). The soundtrack is similarly excellent, featuring crisp dialogue and bold sound effects. The abundance of supplements is highlighted by the extremely entertaining "Music of James Bond" featurette. Sadly, both the commentary track and the "making of" featurette amount to little more than self-glorification by the filmmakers. The film is also available as part of *The James Bond Collection, Vol. 3* (UPC #027616853912). —*MJT*
Movie: 🎬 **DVD:** 🎬🎬🎬½
MGM Home Entertainment (Cat #1001096, UPC #027616853967). Widescreen (2.35:1) anamorphic. Dolby Digital 5.1 Surround; Dolby Digital Surround. $26.98. Keepcase. *LANG:* English; Spanish. *SUB:* French; Spanish. *FEATURES:* 32 chapter links • Commentary: director John Glen, cast, crew • "Inside *A View to a Kill*" featurette • "The Music of James Bond" featurette • Deleted scenes • "A View to a Kill" music video • Theatrical trailers • Television spots • Collectible "making-of" booklet.
1985 (PG) 131m/C GB Roger Moore, Christopher Walken, Tanya Roberts, Grace Jones, Patrick Macnee, Lois Maxwell, Dolph Lundgren, Desmond Llewelyn; **D:** John Glen; **W:** Michael G. Wilson; **C:** Alan Hume; **M:** John Barry.

Village of the Giants

Director Bert I. Gordon *(Attack of the Puppet People, The Amazing Colossal Man)* combines cheesy sci-fi with mid-1960s "go go" music and ends up with a concoction as odd as child-star Ron Howard's chemistry workshop products. Nicknamed "Genius," Howard mixes up a batch of edible super-growth "goo," which ends up in the hands of mixed-up teens (Beau Bridges, Johnny Crawford, etc), who grow to gargantuan size. Results can be summed up in a single word: silly. No-frills DVD presentation oddly delivers French and Spanish subtitles, but nothing for English. —*RJT*
Movie: 🎬🎬 **DVD:** 🎬🎬
MGM Home Entertainment (Cat #1002022, UPC #027616862631). Full frame. Dolby Digital Surround. $14.95. Keepcase. *LANG:* English; French; Spanish. *SUB:* French; Spanish. *CAP:* French; Spanish. *FEATURES:* 16 chapter markers.
1965 82m/C Ron Howard, Johnny Crawford, Tommy Kirk, Beau Bridges, Freddy Cannon, Beau Brummel, Tisha Sterling, Tim Rooney, Charla Doherty, Joe Turkel; **D:** Bert I. Gordon; **W:** Alan Caillou; **C:** Paul Vogel; **M:** Jack Nitzsche.

The Vineyard

James Hong, the man we all know and love as David Lo Pan from *Big Trouble in Little China,* co-wrote, co-directed, and stars in this train wreck of a movie. He is Dr. Elsen Po, a famous winemaker who serves as a sort of Mr. Rourke, as he welcomes a group of young actors to his island home. They are supposedly there to audition for Mr. Po, who produces movies in his spare time, but he has other plans involving young women chained in his basement, and a bunch of zombies shuffling through his vineyard. One scene involving spiders is sort of creepy, but that's not enough to even come close to rescuing this horrible movie. The image is very clear, showing only a slight amount of grain, and there are few defects visible from the source print. The colors are natural and bright, and the shading is always on target. There are no overt problems from artifacting or compression. Monaural audio provides clear dialogue, which isn't overpowered by the sound effects. (I listened to some of the film through headphones, and there is unlooped dialogue audible on this track!) —*ML*
Movie: 🎬 **DVD:** 🎬🎬½
Anchor Bay (Cat #DV11401). Widescreen (1.85:1) anamorphic. Dolby Digital Mono. $24.98. Keepcase. *LANG:* English. *FEATURES:* Trailer.
1989 (R) 95m/C James Hong, Karen Witter, Michael Wong; **D:** James Hong, Bill Rice.

The Violent Years / Girl Gang

In the first half of this "drive-in double feature," spoiled Paula Parkins (Weeks) leads three of her high-school chums on an orgy of gas-station hold-ups and sexual assaults on terrified heterosexual males. Such fare could only come from the immortal Ed Wood Jr. In the second feature, the gals form a car thief ring and steal to get money for "reefers." Both films were made in fairly pale black and white. Exteriors in *Years* are muddy; interiors are better. *Girl Gang* is marred by heavy snow in places. Sound is adequate to the task. The "Let's Go to the Drive-In" plays the films as they might have been shown originally, beginning with the "5 minutes till showtime" countdown. —*MM*
AKA: *Female.*
Movie: 🎬🎬½ **DVD:** 🎬🎬½
Image Entertainment (Cat #ID9753SWDVD, UPC #014381975321). Full frame. Dolby Digital Mono. $24.99. Snapper. *LANG:* English. *FEATURES:* 24 chapter links • Archival shorts, intermission ads, and trailers • Gallery of drive-in exploitation art.
1956 60m/B Jean Moorehead, Barbara Weeks, Glenn Corbett, Theresa Hancock, I. Stanford Jolley, Arthur Millan; **D:** Edward D. Wood Jr., Franz Eichhorn, William M. Morgan; **W:** Edward D. Wood Jr.; **C:** William C. Thompson.

The Virgin Suicides

As suggested by the title, which has a vaguely Greek tragedy feel to it, this is a story about myth. Narrated by a young neighborhood boy, the tragedy of the five Lisbon sisters is played out as imagined by the people around them. They are seen as the icons of perfect teen beauty: five stunningly pretty girls who all live in one household. Parented by a bookish, science teacher for a father (Woods) and a seemingly overly religious prude for a mother (Turner), the girls are kept just out of reach of the boys who long for them, and can only become the stuff that dreams are made of. When the youngest girl commits suicide they go from dream material to pure myth, and when the final four girls commit suicide, they become something that none of the observers can ever understand. Beautifully adapted and directed by Sofia Coppola, the story is revealed more than told. The storyline is no mystery for anyone who knows the title of the film. Under Coppola's deft direction we are made horribly aware of the part of the story that is missing: the story the girls would tell if they weren't being spoken for by desirous boys and doting mothers. The disc is beautiful, capturing the sunlit haze of the neighborhood and the stark interiors of the '70s households in all their glory. The sound is also good, with the dreamy score by Air lulling us through the fairy tale. —*CA*
Movie: 🎬🎬🎬½ **DVD:** 🎬🎬½
Paramount Home Video (Cat #33817, UPC #097363381747). Widescreen anamorphic. Dolby Digital Surround; Dolby Digital 5.1 Surround. $29.99. Keepcase. *LANG:* English; French. *CAP:* English. *FEATURES:* 16 chapter links • Theatrical trailer • "Making of" featurette • Music videos.
1999 (R) 97m/C Kirsten Dunst, Kathleen Turner, James Woods, Josh Hartnett,

Hanna Hall, Chelse Swain, A.J. Cook, Leslie Hayman, Danny DeVito, Scott Glenn, Jonathan Tucker, Anthony DeSimone; **D:** Sofia Coppola; **W:** Sofia Coppola; **C:** Edward Lachman; **Nar:** Giovanni Ribisi.

Voodoo Academy [DC]

Imagine an episode of *Scooby Doo* crossed with a Calvin Klein ad and you'll get the idea of what video veteran Dave DeCoteau is doing in what he calls "the first horror film made for girls." A Bible college is a front for voodoo activity. The all-male students run around in their underwear trying to figure out what's going on. The DVD features the director's cut of the film that runs 23 minutes longer but feels a bit padded at times, and is way too talky. The image is grainy but the special effects would make Ed Wood wince, so that's unimportant. Dialogue is clear with only a slight hiss in the background. —*ML/MM*
Movie: 🐾🐾 **DVD:** 🐾🐾½
Full Moon Pictures (UPC #763843806863). Full frame. Dolby Digital Stereo. $24.99. Keepcase. *LANG:* English. *FEATURES:* Commentary: Dave DeCoteau • Behind-the-scenes footage • Trailers • Blooper reel.
2000 100m/C Riley Smith, Chad Burns, Debra Meyer; **D:** David DeCoteau.

Voyage to the Bottom of the Sea / Fantastic Voyage

During its maiden voyage, the crew of an experimental submarine witnesses the formation of a deadly radiation asteroid belt around the Earth. As the world begins to bake in the ever-increasing heat, Nelson (Pidgeon), the admiral who invented the sub, embarks on a treasonous journey to launch missiles at the belt in an effort to save the world. Episodic adventure has enough subplots for several films, and some hilarious unintentionally camp moments. Pidgeon is appropriately stodgy as Nelson, but the main threat is never satisfactorily explained and the good cast is mostly wasted. (Poor Joan Fontaine!) Later spawned a TV series (which used most of the special effects shots from this film). In *Fantastic Voyage*, a group of scientists and a submarine are reduced to microscopic size and injected into a dying scientist to repair damage to his brain. This psychedelic, thought-provoking science-fiction film features excellent special effects and suspenseful sequences, but its characters are underwritten and the buildup is too long. The cast is fine, though underutilized. Kennedy has some nice soliloquies (though whoever talked him into wearing an ill-fitting wetsuit should be shot) and Pleasence is suitably nutty. Though a scientist, Welch has barely any dialogue and is there mostly so the audience can ogle her. Watch as the entire male cast gropes her after she is attacked by white corpuscles! A somewhat cold but interesting film. These themes were later

explored in *Innerspace.* Both widescreen films (unwatchable in pan and scan) are given sharp, clear, and colorful transfers but they're recorded at low-bit rates and subject to moderate digital grain. The sound has more presence than usual for older tracks and is satisfying. —*DG*
Movie: 🐾🐾½ **DVD:** 🐾🐾🐾½
20th Century Fox Home Entertainment (Cat #2000580, UPC #02454200580). Widescreen (2.35:1) anamorphic. Dolby 4.0 Surround; Dolby Surround; Mono. $24.98. Keepcase. *LANG:* English; French. *SUB:* English; Spanish. *CAP:* English. *FEATURES:* 28 chapter links *(Voyage to the Bottom of the Sea)* • 24 chapter links *(Fantastic Voyage)* • Insert card with chapter links • Trailers.
1961 106m/C Walter Pidgeon, Joan Fontaine, Barbara Eden, Peter Lorre, Robert Sterling, Michael Ansara, Frankie Avalon; **D:** Irwin Allen; **W:** Charles Bennett, Irwin Allen; **C:** Winton C. Hoch; **M:** Paul Sawtell, Bert Shefter.

The Waiting Game

Yet another independent film explores the lives of a group of quirky slackers in New York City. But, strangely enough, this movie is pretty good. It focuses on a group of struggling actors who work as waiters. Lenny (Arnette) is the nice-guy bartender whose failure as an actor is hurting his relationship with his girlfriend. Dan (Riordan) is the intense waiter whose failure as an actor is making him insane. Andi (Matthews) is the smart waitress whose failure as an actor has led to jobs trying to seduce men to test their fidelity. These intriguing characters and funny moments save the film, as it fails on its mission to introduce us to the world of waiters or struggling actors. The image is very sharp and clear, showing only a minimal amount of grain. The film has a natural look, so the subdued lighting and neutral color palette come across well in this digital transfer. Sound is clear though muffled at times. The dialogue is always understandable, but the music and effects sound canned. —*ML/MM*
Movie: 🐾🐾½ **DVD:** 🐾🐾½
Vanguard International Cinema, Inc. (Cat #VF0052, UPC #658769005233). Widescreen (1.85:1) letterboxed. Dolby Digital Mono. $29.95. Keepcase. *LANG:* English. *FEATURES:* "Making of featurette" • Theatrical trailer • Deleted scene.
1999 81m/C Michael Raynor, Will Arnett, Terumi Mathews, Dan Riordan, Debbon Ayer; **D:** Ken Liotti; **W:** Ken Liotti; **C:** Rich Eliano; **M:** Jim Farmer.

Waking the Dead

Director Gordon's uneven but earnest adaptation of the Scott Spenser novel is also somewhat similar to Stephen King's *Hearts in Atlantis.* Aspiring politician Fielding Pierce (Crudup) is haunted by the death years before of his activist girlfriend Sarah (Connelly) in a car bombing. As Fielding begins a run for Congress, he repeatedly sees Sarah in crowds. Is she

alive or is he questioning the compromises that he has made to reach his current position? The pace is dreamily slow and the plot moves back and forth in time. The dialogue is sometimes too political and didactic, but that is true to the characters and the times. While some criticized that structure during the theatrical release, it is easy to follow on home video. DVD captures the polished sterile Hollywood look of the production. Both image and sound are unblemished and unspectacular. The disc also contains more than 45 minutes of deleted scenes that might have been reincorporated but are presented separately. —*MM*
Movie: 🐾🐾🐾 **DVD:** 🐾🐾🐾
USA Home Entertainment (Cat #963 060 099-2, UPC #696306009924). Widescreen letterboxed. Dolby Digital 5.1 Surround Stereo; Dolby Digital Surround Stereo. $24.95. Keepcase. *LANG:* English. *SUB:* Spanish. *CAP:* English. *FEATURES:* 23 chapter links • Deleted scenes • Commentary: Keith Gordon • Trailer • "Making of" featurette • Talent files.
2000 (R) 105m/C Billy Crudup, Jennifer Connelly, Molly Parker, Janet McTeer, Paul Hipp, Sandra Oh, Hal Holbrook, Lawrence Dane; **D:** Keith Gordon; **W:** Robert Dillon; **C:** Tom Richmond; **M:** Tomandandy.

A Walk in the Clouds

Piero Tellini's 1942 Italian screenplay *Quattro Passi Fra le Nuvole,* has been updated as a romantic star vehicle for Keanu Reeves with mixed results. Neatly divided into four "acts," the film bubbles along under the direction of Alfonso Arau (*Like Water for Chocolate*) for three of the four parts before running offtrack to a disastrous and inane wrap-up. The film opens well enough with Reeves, returning home from World War II, meeting a young woman on the train (Aitana Sanchez-Gijon) and agreeing to be her "husband" for a few days upon her return home to her family's wine-making estate in Napa Valley. It seems she's pregnant and her family would disapprove of this if she were not married. They eventually fall in love, only to see their world shattered by a series of contrived plot twists during the ill-conceived finale. Nice DVD presentation, with quality sound, picture, and support material. An audio commentary from director Alfonso Arau explaining the scriptwriting decision-making process would have been a welcome feature. —*RJT*
Movie: 🐾🐾½ **DVD:** 🐾🐾🐾
20th Century Fox Home Entertainment (UPC #024543008019). Widescreen (1.85:1). Dolby Digital 5.1 Surround; Dolby Digital Surround. $29.99. Keepcase. *LANG:* English. *SUB:* English; Spanish. *CAP:* English. *FEATURES:* 20 chapter markers • Theatrical trailer • Featurette • 5 cross-promotional trailers.
1995 (PG-13) 103m/C Keanu Reeves, Aitana Sanchez-Gijon, Giancarlo Giannini, Anthony Quinn, Angelica Aragon, Evangelina Elizondo, Freddy Rodriguez, Debra Messing; **D:** Alfonso Arau; **W:** Robert Mark

Kamen; **C:** Emmanuel Lubezki; **M:** Leo Brower. *AWARDS:* Golden Globes '96: Score; *NOM:* MTV Movie Awards '96: Most Desirable Male (Reeves), Kiss (Keanu Reeves/Aitana Sanchez-Gijon).

A Walk in the Sun

Some unfortunate devices and a poor transfer to DVD rob Lewis Milestone's second great war film (the first is *All Quiet on the Western Front*) of much of its power. The story follows an American platoon from its landing in Sicily to an isolated farmhouse. The ensemble cast is excellent; so is the writing; the DVD is not. Extremely large artifacts appear at random. Even without those, the image ranges between poor and fair. The soundtrack is often filled with static. *—MM* **AKA:** Salerno Beachhead.

Movie: 🦴🦴🦴 **DVD:** 🦴
Madacy Entertainment (Cat #DVD-9-9029, UPC #056775006594). Full frame. $9.95. Keepcase. *LANG:* English. *FEATURES:* 9 chapter links ▪ Dana Andrews thumbnail bio ▪ Production credits.
1946 117m/B Dana Andrews, Richard Conte, John Ireland, Lloyd Bridges, Sterling Holloway, George Tyne, Norman Lloyd, Herbert Rudley, Richard Benedict, Huntz Hall, James B. Cardwell, George Offerman Jr., Steve Brodie, Matt Willis, Alvin Hammer, Chris Drake, Victor Cutler, Jay Norris; **D:** Lewis Milestone; **W:** Robert Rossen, Harry Brown; **C:** Russell Harlan; **M:** Freddie Rich, Earl Robinson.

Walking the Edge

A widow (Kwan) hires part-time cabbie (and numbers runner) Jason Walk (Forster) to help her get even with the drug dealers who killed her son and husband. An unusually good cast differentiates this entry from dozens of other mid-budget '80s crime films. Also, this one looks very good on DVD; actually, it's amazingly sharp for a work of this age and budget. The commentary track is not out of place either. *—MM*

Movie: 🦴🦴½ **DVD:** 🦴🦴🦴
Anchor Bay (Cat #DV11312, UPC #013131 131291). Widescreen (1.85:1) anamorphic. Dolby Digital Mono. $24.99. Keepcase. *LANG:* English. *FEATURES:* 27 chapter links ▪ Commentary: Meisel, Kwan, Forster, mediator Dave Trilken ▪ Trailer ▪ Talent files.
1983 (R) 94m/C Robert Forster, Nancy Kwan, Joe Spinell, Aarika Wells; **D:** Norbert Meisel; **W:** Curt Allen; **C:** Ernie Poulos; **M:** Jay Chattaway.

Wall Street

Naive stockbroker Sheen is seduced into insider trading by sleek entrepreneur Douglas, much to his blue-collar father's chagrin. Douglas's Gordon Gekko character is greed personified, in Stone's energetic and high-minded movie about illegal trading practices and corporate raiding. That so many 1980s Wall Street types found

Gekko to be heroic is scarier than anything in the movie. A fast-moving drama of '80s materialism with a mesmerizing, award-winning performance by Douglas. Expert direction by Stone, whose father was a broker. The father-son relationship is a theme, with Sheen interacting with real-life dad Martin Sheen (playing his father on camera) as well as Douglas, his mentor in greed. The anamorphic treatment always is appreciated by owners of widescreen display devices, but any decent display is likely to reveal the image here to be on the soft side. The source material appears to have a few nicks and scratches, too, but overall is not too bad in that regard. Not a movie to give a workout to your subwoofer or Surround speakers, but the dialogue is distinct and the front mix provides a solid soundstage for the music. The best extras are a nicely done documentary and Stone's revealing commentary track. *—MB*

Movie: 🦴🦴🦴 **DVD:** 🦴🦴🦴
(Cat #2000631, UPC #024543006312). Widescreen (1.85:1) anamorphic. Dolby Digital 5.1. $29.98. Keepcase. *LANG:* English; French. *SUB:* English; Spanish. *CAP:* English. *FEATURES:* 20 chapter links ▪ Commentary: director ▪ "Making of" documentary ▪ Theatrical trailers ▪ TV spots.
1987 (R) 126m/C Michael Douglas, Charlie Sheen, Martin Sheen, Daryl Hannah, Sean Young, James Spader, Hal Holbrook, Terence Stamp, Richard Dysart, John C. McGinley, Saul Rubinek, James Karen, Josh Mostel, Millie Perkins, Cecilia Peck, Grant Shaud, Franklin Cover, Oliver Stone; **D:** Oliver Stone; **W:** Stanley Weiser, Oliver Stone; **C:** Robert Richardson; **M:** Stewart Copeland. *AWARDS:* Oscars '87: Actor (Douglas); Golden Globes '88: Actor—Drama (Douglas); Natl. Bd. of Review '87: Actor (Douglas); Golden Raspberries '87: Worst Support. Actress (Hannah).

The War Zone

Actor Roth's directorial debut is a harrowing and uncompromising look at a working class British family torn apart by incest and abuse. Dad (Winstone) has just moved the family to a small Devon town—a move resented by his children, 18-year-old Jessie (Belmont) and 15-year-old Tom (Cunliffe). Mom (Swinton) is too busy with a new baby to see what's going on but lonely Tom gradually (and later graphically) realizes that something not right is happening between his father and his sister. DVD faithfully translates Roth's cold blues and grays to the small screen. More importantly, the disc contains a help and information guide about incest as one of the extras. *—MM*

Movie: 🦴🦴🦴½ **DVD:** 🦴🦴🦴½
New Yorker Video (Cat #76600, UPC #717 119766047). Widescreen letterboxed. $29.95. Keepcase. *LANG:* English. *FEATURES:* 12 chapter links ▪ Commentary: director ▪ "Making of" featurette ▪ About the production ▪ Talent files ▪ Incest help and information guide.

1998 99m/C *GB* Ray Winstone, Tilda Swinton, Lara Belmont, Freddie Cunliffe, Aisling O'Sullivan, Colin Farrell, Annabelle Apsion, Kate Ashfield; **D:** Tim Roth; **W:** Alexander Stuart; **C:** Seamus McGarvey; **M:** Simon Boswell.

Warlock: The Armageddon

Sequel boasts better effects than the original and a plot that's just as nonsensical. The titular supernatural creature (Sands) tries to collect special runestones to bring his daddy Satan into the world, etc., etc. Small-town teens Kenny (Young) and Samantha (Marshall) must stop him. The inventive, graphic violence is leavened with equally bloody humor. Similar stuff is found in the 1995 *Prophecy* and *Buffy, the Vampire Slayer*. The overachieving little horror looks very nice on DVD. Sound is good, too. A commentary track might have been fun. *—MM*

Movie: 🦴🦴🦴 **DVD:** 🦴🦴🦴
Trimark Home Video (Cat #7076, UPC #031398707639). Widescreen anamorphic. Dolby Digital Surround Stereo. $24.99. Keepcase. *LANG:* English. *SUB:* French; Spanish. *CAP:* English. *FEATURES:* Cast and crew thumbnail bios ▪ Trailer ▪ 24 chapter links.
1993 (R) 93m/C Julian Sands, Chris Young, Paula Marshall, Steve Kahan, Charles Hallahan, R.G. Armstrong, Bruce Glover, Zach Galligan, Dawn Ann Billings, Joanna Pacula; **D:** Anthony Hickox; **W:** Kevin Rock, Sam Bernard; **C:** Gerry Lively; **M:** Mark McKenzie.

The Warriors

Seminal '70s action film begins with the ludicrous premise that New York street gangs stage a truce and call a meeting where nine members of each gang are in attendance. When the messianic leader is killed, everybody thinks that the Warriors from Coney Island did it. They've got to make their way back with all the others—including a gang of mimes!—after them. The costumes, hairstyles, and even the artfully choreographed fight scenes have dated themselves, but the film still looks terrific. Though almost all of the action is set at night, the image is clear and the dark areas are as detailed as they have ever been. And is it just the added clarity of DVD that makes the cast look so incredibly young? A commentary track with director Hill might have been nice. *—MM*

Movie: 🦴🦴🦴 **DVD:** 🦴🦴🦴
Paramount Home Video (Cat #01122, UPC #097360112245). Widescreen anamorphic. Dolby Digital Mono. $24.99. Snapper. *LANG:* English; French. *SUB:* English. *FEATURES:* 14 chapter links ▪ Trailer.
1979 (R) 94m/C Michael Beck, James Remar, Deborah Van Valkenburgh, Thomas G. Waites, David Patrick Kelly, Mercedes Ruehl, Dorsey Wright, David Harris, Brian Tyler, Tom McKitterick; **D:** Walter Hill; **W:** Walter Hill, David Shaber; **C:** Andrew Laszlo; **M:** Barry de Vorzon.

The Wasp Woman

In her quest for eternal beauty, corporate executive Janice Starling (Cabot) uses a potion made from wasp enzymes. Naturally, she turns into a monster at night, but it takes almost an hour for the laughable makeup effects to make an appearance. Actually, the film is more interesting as an early feminist work from Corman. The DVD image is acceptable but really no better than a decent tape. The jazz score is screechy. Title is part of the "Roger Corman Retrospective, Vol. 1" triple feature. —MM

Movie: ♫♫½ **DVD:** ♫½
SlingShot Entertainment (Cat #TDVD9114, UPC #017078911428). Full frame. $19.99. Large jewelcase. *LANG:* English. *FEATURES:* 18 chapter links.
1959 84m/B Susan Cabot, Anthony Eisley, Barboura Morris, Michael Marks, William Roerick, Frank Gerstle, Bruno VeSota, Frank Wolff, Lynn Cartwright, Roy Gordon; **D:** Roger Corman; **W:** Leo Gordon; **C:** Harry Neumann; **M:** Fred Katz.

The Watcher

This stylized thriller stars Keanu Reeves as serial killer David Allen Griffin. He has followed Los Angeles homicide detective Joel Campbell (Spader) to Chicago, where Campbell has fled to have migraines and sleepless nights lamenting the fact that he couldn't save Griffin's last victim. He is seeing a counselor named Polly (Tomei) who becomes the inevitable pawn in the twisted cop/killer relationship. The hook in the storyline is that Griffin feels a yin-yang link with Campbell and sends a picture of his next victim to him before each kill, giving him 24 hours to find and save the girl. The club of alienation in the big city is used to beat the audience over the head several times as the police come closer and closer to finding the unfortunate girl each time, only to fail at the last minute because people don't notice each other anymore. The tension would have been much more convincing if they had cast someone as the killer who was a threat to more than the art of acting. The script, direction, and cinematography all give the film a chance as a rental favorite, but Reeves comes across as scary as one of the rabbits in *Night of the Lepus* and the rest of the cast seems miscast. Spader sleepwalks through his role with every one of his actions seeming to say, "I should have been cast as the killer." Tomei has a dull look in her eye that hints at her worst nightmare: that her Oscar was a mistake. The film uses a lot of tricky camerawork and cool film processing techniques and so it looks really good on the disc and sounds above average. —CA

Movie: ♫ **DVD:** ♫♫½
Universal Studios Home Video (Cat #211 37, UPC #0215192113727). Widescreen (1.85:1) letterboxed. Dolby Digital 5.1 Surround. $26.98. Keepcase. *LANG:* English; French. *CAP:* English. *FEATURES:* 18 chapter links • Cast and crew filmographies

• Production notes • DVD-ROM features • Theatrical trailers.
2000 (R) 97m/C Keanu Reeves, James Spader, Marisa Tomei, Ernie Hudson, Chris Ellis, Robert Cicchini, Jenny McShane, Yvonne Niami, Gina Alexander, Joe Sikora, Rebekah Louise Smith; **D:** Joe Charbanic; **W:** Joe Charbanic, David Elliott, Clay Ayers; **C:** Michael Chapman; **M:** Marco Beltrami. *AWARDS: NOM:* Golden Raspberries '00: Worst Support. Actor (Reeves).

The Watermelon Woman

Cheryl Dunye has fashioned a "mockumentary" that rekindles the previously lost feel of independent features. With adequate skill and a story to tell (as opposed to a story to sell), Dunye presents herself and her world with fresh honesty. Never talking down to her audience, she presents real issues in a friendly non-proselytizing tone that shares understanding. In the story, Dunye happens across some films from the 1930s featuring "the Watermelon Woman," and her interest is piqued to the point of researching the old actress's life. The Watermelon Woman's history as a talented actress and young black lesbian gives inspiration to Dunye as she creates a documentary about her new-found hero. It is a bit disheartening to find in the end that Dunye created the Watermelon Woman. If a real person could have been found, it would have provided the tale a deeper impact. But one of her points is that if such a story existed, it might have been destroyed. The transfer to DVD has not damaged the low-budget feel of used celluloid. —JAS

Movie: ♫♫♫ **DVD:** ♫♫
First Run Features (Cat #FRF909273D, UPC #72022990273). Full frame. $29.95. Keepcase. *LANG:* English. *FEATURES:* Interview with Cheryl Dunye • 9 chapter links.
1997 85m/C Cheryl Dunye, Valerie Walker, Guinevere Turner, Lisa Marie Bronson; **D:** Cheryl Dunye; **W:** Cheryl Dunye; **C:** Michelle Crenshaw; **M:** Bill Coleman.

Wax Mask

Liner notes state that this loose remake of *House of Wax* was to have been directed by Lucio Fulci (*Zombie*, *The Black Cat*) who died before he could begin work. It was produced in part by Dario Argento, but the important thing for horror fans to know is that this one owes just as much to Stuart Gordon's *Re-Animator*. It takes the same gleeful approach to outrageous medical horror and sex, though overall, it is a much more polished-looking film with expensive production values, an attractive (if unknown in America) young cast, and a sharply focused image. The setting is Paris and Rome in the early 20th century. Sonia (Mondello) witnessed the brutal murder of her parents as a child. Years later, she goes to work for Boris Volkoff (Hossein), whose macabre wax museum hides terrible secrets. Director Sergio Stivaletti came to the job through special effects expertise and his work here (in both capacities) is very good. This is a man to watch. The plot goes much too far for the film ever to find a large mainstream audience, and that's the point of Grand Guignol horror. Minor aliasing and edge enhancement are visible and the Surround stereo makes the dubbing more apparent than it might be, but those are inconsequential flaws. *Wax Mask* is one of the great guilty pleasures. —MM *AKA:* M.D.C. Maschera di Cera.

Movie: ♫♫♫½ **DVD:** ♫♫♫½
Image Entertainment (Cat #ID8745RPDVD, UPC #014381874525). Widescreen (1.78:1) letterboxed. Dolby Digital Surround Stereo. $24.99. Snapper. *LANG:* English. *FEATURES:* 16 chapter links • Photo gallery.
1997 98m/C *IT FR* Robert Hossein, Romina Mondello, Ricardo Serventi Longhi; **D:** Sergio Stivaletti; **W:** Lucio Fulci; **C:** Sergio Salvati.

Way of the Gun

Phillippe and Del Toro are small-time crooks who go after big money by kidnapping a young surrogate mother (Lewis) when they learn she has been hired to carry to term the child of a filthy-rich couple. Their plan goes awry when it turns out the rich man is a big-time crime boss. The plot unfolds amid multiple twists involving irony and much bloodshed. In another time, it would have been a rousing, if complicated, western—provided it had the requisite horses and cowboy hats, of course. A top-notch cast is smartly directed by McQuarrie (despite his protestations to the contrary on the commentary track), who follows his own script. Caan's seasoned "bagman" character is a bit of a cliché, but his connection to one of the main players and professional respect for Del Toro are nice twists. Also worth noting is Geoffrey Lewis (real-life father of Juliette), who does a big job of playing a small part. This is the kind of DVD that will get played more than once, if for no other reason than to make sure all the plot turns are accounted for. However, you'll be tempted to skip through the more tedious parts upon repeat viewings. First-time director McQuarrie also scripted *The Usual Suspects*. The video quality is first-rate, with no signs of artifacts anywhere in the wide frame. Anamorphic enhancement will guarantee current and future compatibility with widescreen TV sets. The clean Dolby Digital 5.1 soundtrack is a plus, although you'll be turning down the gunshots for late-night viewing. The extras are plentiful. You can choose to view plans for a never-shot scene alternately by looking at storyboards or script segments, but the approach is more novel than engaging. Animated menus took a lot of work and are flashy, but they can be cumbersome to navigate. —MB

Movie: ♫♫♫ **DVD:** ♫♫♫½
Artisan Entertainment (Cat #10418, UPC #012236104186). Widescreen (1.85:1)

anamorphic. Dolby Digital 5.1 Surround Stereo. $24.98. Keepcase. *LANG:* English. *CAP:* English. *FEATURES:* 28 chapter links ● Commentary: director/writer McQuarrie, composer Joe Kraemer ● Isolated music track with commentary by Kraemer ● Cast and crew interviews ● Storyboards and script for a never-filmed scene ● Theatrical trailer ● TV spots ● Cast and crew information ● Production notes.
2000 (R) 118m/C Ryan Phillippe, Benicio Del Toro, Juliette Lewis, James Caan, Taye Diggs, Nicky Katt, Scott Wilson, Kristen Lehman, Geoffrey Lewis, Dylan Kussman; **D:** Christopher McQuarrie; **W:** Christopher McQuarrie; **C:** Dick Pope; **M:** Joe Kraemer.

The Way We Were [SE]

Boxoffice hit captures the two stars at their most attractive and follows a love story between opposites from the 1930s to the '50s. Streisand is a Jewish communist who meets the handsome WASP Redford at college. They're attracted to each other but World War II separates them and then brings them back together. The old-fashioned story is curiously constructed and on his commentary track, director Sydney Pollack addresses the various problems that it caused. His ideas are solid and his presentation is appropriately low-keyed. A bit of wear-related snow is visible at first, but overall the image is a flawless re-creation of the theatrical presentation. It's not particularly sharp, but then it never has been, and, for this story, it shouldn't be. The film remains a favorite. Well worth another look. —*MM*
Movie: ♪♪♪½ **DVD:** ♪♪♪½
Columbia Tristar Home Video (Cat #2850). Widescreen (2.35:1) anamorphic. Dolby Digital 5.1 Surround Stereo; Dolby Digital Surround. $24.95. Keepcase. *LANG:* English. *SUB:* English; Spanish; Portuguese; Chinese; Korean; Thai. *FEATURES:* "Making of" documentary ● Trailers ● Talent files ● 28 chapter links ● Commentary: Sydney Pollack.
1973 (PG) 118m/C Barbra Streisand, Robert Redford, Bradford Dillman, Viveca Lindfors, Herb Edelman, Murray Hamilton, Patrick O'Neal, James Woods, Sally Kirkland; **D:** Sydney Pollack; **W:** Arthur Laurents; **C:** Harry Stradling Jr.; **M:** Marvin Hamlisch. *AWARDS:* Oscars '73: Song ("The Way We Were"), Orig. Dramatic Score; Golden Globes '74: Song ("The Way We Were"); *NOM:* Oscars '73: Actress (Streisand), Art Dir./Set Dec., Cinematog., Costume Des.

W.C. Fields 6 Short Films

The five famous Fields two-reelers (20-minute shorts) are assembled here: "The Golf Specialist" (1930) allows Fields to showcase some of his famous gags on the greens as he chases a married flirt; "The Dentist" (1932) features Fields as a cranky dentist who suggestively mounts a horse-faced female patient in need of a

tooth pullin'; "The Fatal Glass of Beer" (1933) finds Fields as a prospector in Northern Canada; "The Pharmacist" (1933) has Fields as the ornery druggist whose equally irritated by friends, family, and customers; and "The Barber Shop" (1933), where the barber (guess who) does more yarn spinnin' than hair cuttin' and eventually gets himself involved with a bank robber. Also included is Fields's first film, the 10-minute silent "Pool Sharks" (1915). Some of these have appeared on other low-budget DVDs and have looked pretty atrocious. This Criterion disc is the best these historical (and hysterical) comedies have ever looked, and that includes when they were available in 16mm from Blackhawk Films years ago. The transfer itself is very sharp, with good contrast. Sure, there are some scratches, jitters, and even a few blurred scenes, but overall the vintage shorts look terrific, and you'll be laughing so hard you'll never notice. The soundtrack is clean but squawky, sharp, and flat, and occasionally reveals a warped sound element, but this is mostly due to the low fidelity of the original sound recording equipment. Of immense value are the optional English subtitles, which reveal several of Fields's (previously unintelligible) muttered double entendres. —*JO/DG*
Movie: ♪♪♪♪ **DVD:** ♪♪♪½
Criterion Collection (Cat #79, UPC #71551 5010726). Full frame. Dolby Digital Mono. $29.95. Keepcase. *LANG:* English. *FEATURES:* 79 chapter links.
1933 100m/B W.C. Fields, Elise Cavanna, Harry Watson, Dagmar Oakland, Frank Yaconelli, Marjorie "Babe" Kane, Grady Sutton, Bud Jamison, Zedna Farley, Rosemary Theby, George Chandler, Richard Cramer, Dorothy Granger, Arnold Gray; **D:** Arthur Ripley, Leslie Pearce, Clyde Bruckman, Edwin Middleton; **W:** W.C. Fields.

Weather Woman

Bizarre sex comedy is based on a popular manga. Keiko Nakadai (Mizutani and voice of Lee) is a TV weatherwoman who livens up the broadcast by flashing her panties at the audience. From there, she embarks on a series of sexual experiments that become steadily more tasteless. Cultural differences between Japan and America dilute the film's eroticism and shock value. DVD image ranges between fair and good with a lot of aliasing in brighter scenes. Dubbing has a colloquial sound and is a cut above the norm. —*MM*
Movie: ♪♪ **DVD:** ♪♪
Central Park Media/U.S. Manga Corps (Cat #APCD1974, UPC #719987197428). Widescreen letterboxed. $29.99. Keepcase. *LANG:* Japanese; English. *SUB:* English. *FEATURES:* 10 chapter links ● DVD-ROM features.
1999 84m/C Kei Mizutani, Wendee Lee, Takashi Sumida, Lex Lang, Yasuyo Shirashima, Barbara Goodson, Ren Osugi, Dylan Tully, Hideyo Amamoto, William Knight; **D:** Tomoaki Hosoyama; **W:** Tomoaki Hosoyama; **M:** Kunihiko Ida.

Welcome II the Terrordome

After a static historical introduction tinted yellow, this low-budget effort turns into post-apocalyptic sf agitprop revolving around Jodie (Burrows), who causes trouble for her black boyfriend because she's white. The film was produced in part by Britain's Channel 4 and is so grainy that it is virtually unwatchable on DVD or any other medium. —*MM*
Movie: ♪½ **DVD:** ♪
MTI Home Video (Cat #7012, UPC #03941 4570120). Full frame. $24.95. Keepcase. *LANG:* English. *SUB:* Spanish. *FEATURES:* 20 chapter links ● Saffron Burrows thumbnail bio ● Trailers.
1995 (R) 98m/C *GB* Saffron Burrows, Valentine Nonyela, Suzette Llewellyn, Felix Joseph; **D:** Ngozi Onwurah; **W:** Ngozi Onwurah.

We'll Meet Again

Clichéd, but well-made and touching miniseries (on four discs) is set in a quiet English town in 1943. At least, the town was quiet until the arrival of a B-17 bomber group from the U.S. Army Eighth Air Force. Soon, the Yanks are chasing the local girls and getting into trouble while their commander (Shannon) finds himself falling for a married doctor (York). Like most British TV productions, this one has a very soft image and pastel color scheme. Night scenes are heavily grained. The lack of sharpness in the image makes the incorporation of actual aerial combat footage fairly seamless. Sound is fine. Overall, DVD is only a small step up from broadcast quality. —*MM*
Movie: ♪♪½ **DVD:** ♪♪
BFS Video (Cat #95186-D, UPC #0668059 11866). Full frame. Dolby Digital Mono. $79.98. Keepcase boxed set. *LANG:* English. *FEATURES:* 78 chapter links.
1982 690m/C *GB* Michael J. Shannon, Susannah York, Ronald Hines, Ed Devereaux, Christopher Malcolm, Patrick O'Connell, Joris Stuyck; **D:** Christopher Hodson.

Went to Coney Island on a Mission from God...Be Back by Five

When Daniel (Cryer) and Stan (Stear) learn that their childhood friend Richie (Baez) may be homeless on Coney Island, they head out to find him. This is a simpler story than the producers' previous effort, *The Pompatus of Love,* but it is exceptionally well told with a strong sense of place. Unfortunately, the DVD is not all it could be. Though the box claims a widescreen transfer, it's full frame. The commentary track is marred by an annoying hum throughout. —*MM*
Movie: ♪♪♪ **DVD:** ♪♪
Vanguard International Cinema, Inc. (UPC #658769008036). Full frame. $29.98. Keepcase. *LANG:* English. *FEATURES:* 12

chapter links • Commentary: Schenkman, Cryer • Behind-the-scenes footage. **1998 (R) 94m/C** Jon Cryer, Rick Stear, Rafael Baez, Ione Skye, Frank Whaley, Peter Gerety, Akili Prince, Aesha Waks, Dominic Chianese; **D:** Richard Schenkman; **W:** Richard Schenkman, Jon Cryer; **C:** Adam Beekman; **M:** Midge Ure.

Wham–Bam, Thank You Spaceman

Though the box copy claims a 1985 copyright, other sources date it at 1975 and this burlesque comedy looks like it came from the mid-'70s. It's very silly stuff about aliens with fiberglass heads and balloon ears that inflate when they become excited. They transport themselves to Earth in a tiny set decorated with tinfoil where most of the action takes place. Their mission: to impregnate Earth women to save their race. Though the female nudity is abundant, the sexual action is pretty tame by today's standards. The image is miraculously clear, given the age and budget. The disc comes with all of the usual Something Weird bells and whistles. —*MM*
Movie: 🐾½ **DVD:** 🐾🐾½
Image Entertainment (Cat #ID9748SWDVD, UPC #014381974829). Full frame. Dolby Digital Mono. $24.99. Snapper. *LANG:* English. *FEATURES:* 12 chapter links • 2 short films • Theatrical previews for 6 Harry Novak exploitation movies • Trailer • Gallery of exploitation art.
1975 (R) 79m/C Jay Rasumny, Samuel Mann, Dyanne Thorne, Maria Arnold, Valda Hansen, Sandy Carey, John Ireland Jr.; **D:** William A. Levey; **W:** Shlomo D. Weinstein; **C:** David Platnik; **M:** Miles Goodman, David White.

What about Bob?

Bob (Murray), a ridiculously neurotic patient, follows his psychiatrist (Dreyfuss) on vacation, turning his life upside down. Fine work from both stars. The source print shows many defects, including scratches and white "blotches." Also, the digital transfer reveals a great deal of grain on the image, making this transfer look only slightly better than a VHS copy. The Dolby 2-channel Surround audio mix is adequate, especially as it highlights the whimsical score by Miles Goodman. —*ML/MM*
Movie: 🐾🐾🐾 **DVD:** 🐾🐾½
Artisan Entertainment (Cat #18362). Widescreen (1.85:1) letterboxed. Dolby Stereo. $29.99. Keepcase. *LANG:* English; French. *FEATURES:* Trailer.
1991 (PG) 99m/C Richard Dreyfuss, Bill Murray, Julie Hagerty, Charlie Korsmo, Tom Aldredge, Roger Bowen, Fran Brill, Kathryn Erbe, Doris Belack, Susan Willis; **D:** Frank Oz; **W:** Tom Schulman, Alvin Sargent; **C:** Michael Ballhaus; **M:** Miles Goodman.

What Lies Beneath

Is Claire Spencer (Pfeiffer) simply experiencing "empty nest syndrome" after her daughter goes off to college, or is the next door neighbor trying to murder his wife? Her professor hubby Norman (Ford) is solicitous, but might he not be involved in something untoward, too? It's best not to know much more about the plot of this slickly produced Hitchcock homage (complete with Alan Silvestri's Bernard Herrmann-esque score). It's very stylish, intelligent entertainment that knows exactly what it is and what it's trying to do. Director Zemeckis and his co-producers admit as much on their commentary track, but they refuse to say how they accomplished some of the astonishing camera tricks in the last reels. (You'll want to go back and listen to the commentary there after you've been through the film once.) Even though the running time is more than two hours, the pace zips right along. Image and sound are first-rate throughout, even during the trickier special effects. Grand fun. —*MM*
Movie: 🐾🐾🐾½ **DVD:** 🐾🐾🐾½
DreamWorks Home Entertainment (Cat #8 6406, UPC #667068640625). Widescreen (2.35:1) anamorphic. DTS 5.1 Surround; Dolby Digital 5.1 Surround Stereo; DD Surround. $26.99. Keepcase. *LANG:* English. *SUB:* English. *CAP:* English. *FEATURES:* 24 chapter links • "Making of" featurette • Trailer • Commentary: Zemeckis, producers Steve Starkey and Jack Rapke • Talent files • Production notes.
2000 (PG-13) 130m/C Harrison Ford, Michelle Pfeiffer, Diana Scarwid, Joe Morton, James Remar, Miranda Otto, Amber Valletta, Katharine Towne, Victoria Birdwell; **D:** Robert Zemeckis; **W:** Clark Gregg; **C:** Don Burgess; **M:** Alan Silvestri.

What Planet Are You From?

Two jokes, no waiting! Comedian and TV star Shandling's feature debut tries to comment on how men and women view sex and relationships differently, but it spends most of its time with a humming penis. Shandling is H1449-6, an alien sent from a planet of test tube males to impregnate an Earth woman, once he has been given the proper equipment (which has the previously mentioned unfortunate feature). He is conveniently (too conveniently) mistaken for Harold, a bank executive, and receives dating tips from a philandering co-worker (Kinnear). His direct approach somehow attracts a recovering alcoholic (Bening, who also appears before the credits as the Columbia woman). The other joke (and the better of the two) involves an FAA inspector (Goodman) who's suspicious of Harold's origins. The star's limited range won't really carry a full-length film, even a heavy-handed satiric comedy. The few-frills disc is not a significant improvement over VHS tape. —*MM*
Movie: 🐾🐾 **DVD:** 🐾🐾½
Columbia Tristar Home Video (Cat #5062). Widescreen letterboxed; full frame. Dolby Digital Surround Stereo; Dolby Digital 5.1 Surround Stereo. $24.95. Keepcase. *LANG:* English. *FEATURES:* 28 chapter links

• Isolated music score • Cast and crew thumbnail bios • "Making of" featurette. **2000 (R) 107m/C** Garry Shandling, Annette Bening, Greg Kinnear, Ben Kingsley, Linda Fiorentino, John Goodman, Richard Jenkins, Caroline Aaron, Judy Greer, Nora Dunn, Ann Cusack, Camryn Manheim, Janeane Garofalo; **D:** Mike Nichols; **W:** Garry Shandling, Michael Leeson, Edward Solomon, Peter Tolan; **C:** Michael Ballhaus; **M:** Carter Burwell.

What Women Want

Nick Marshall (Gibson) is a Chicago adman and all around male-chauvinist womanizing bad boy. After he's passed over for a promotion that goes to Darcy McGuire (Hunt), he experiences one of those accidents that happen only in movies and, Presto!, he can hear women's thoughts. It's light, fluffy, and makes the most of its leads' undeniable charm. DVD image is everything you'd expect of a big-budget, big-star romantic comedy produced by a mainstream studio. Of course, sound is fine, too. —*MM*
Movie: 🐾🐾🐾 **DVD:** 🐾🐾🐾½
Paramount Home Video (Cat #33838, UPC #09736338384). Widescreen anamorphic. Dolby Digital 5.1 Surround Stereo; Dolby Digital Surround. $29.99. Keepcase. *LANG:* English; French. *SUB:* English. *FEATURES:* 17 chapter links • 2 trailers • Cast and crew interviews • Two featurettes • Commentary: director Meyers, production designer Jon Hutman.
2000 (PG-13) 123m/C Mel Gibson, Helen Hunt, Marisa Tomei, Lauren Holly, Bette Midler, Mark Feuerstein, Ashley Johnson, Judy Greer, Alan Alda, Delta Burke, Valerie Perrine, Lisa Edelstein, Sarah Paulson, Ana Gasteyer, Loretta Devine; **D:** Nancy Meyers; **W:** Josh Goldsmith, Cathy Yuspa; **C:** Dean Cundey; **M:** Alan Silvestri.

Whatever Happened to Aunt Alice?

After murdering her husband to inherit his estate, poor eccentric widow Claire Marrable (Page) develops an awful habit: she hires maids only to murder them and steal their savings. The only evidence is the growing number of trees by the drive. Sleuth Alice Dimmock (Gordon, at her quirky best) and her nephew (Fuller) set out to solve the mystery. The image has a slightly pale, overexposed look that may be intentional to heighten the sunwashed Tucson locations. No important signs of wear are evident. —*MM*
Movie: 🐾🐾🐾 **DVD:** 🐾🐾½
Anchor Bay (Cat #DV11191, UPC #013131 119190). Widescreen (1.85:1) anamorphic. Dolby Digital Mono. $24.99. Keepcase. *LANG:* English. *FEATURES:* 22 chapter links • Trailer.
1969 (PG) 101m/C Geraldine Page, Ruth Gordon, Rosemary Forsyth, Robert Fuller, Mildred Dunnock; **D:** Lee H. Katzin; **W:** Theodore Apstein; **C:** Joseph Biroc; **M:** Gerald Fried.

Whatever It Takes

Dopey teen romancer, with the usual attractive cast, tries to be a modern version of *Cyrano de Bergerac*. Ya got cutie boy-next-door-type Ryan (West) and his sensitive best pal Maggie (Sokoloff), who is, of course, his unknown soulmate. But Ryan pines for snobby hottie Ashley (O'Keefe). Meanwhile, Maggie has won the eye of jock Chris (Franco). So Chris and Ryan team up so that each can get their dream girl before the prom. You know how everything turns out. Here we go again: the quality of the DVD is far more than this film deserves. Everything looks great here. Vibrant colors populate the screen whether indoors or out. The image is extremely sharp. There is an instance of artifacts, but if you blink at all you'll probably miss it. The sound is also top-notch, and often the viewer feels as if in the center of a crowd of students with non-stop jabbering coming from all around. The pop-rock soundtrack comes through with plenty of energy and great fidelity. If there is any reason to buy (or at least rent) this DVD, it's the commentary which is more entertaining and definitely less clichéd than the movie itself. —JO

Movie: ♫½ **DVD:** ♫♫♫
Columbia Tristar Home Video (Cat #05285, UPC #043396052857). Widescreen (1.85:1) anamorphic; full frame. Dolby Digital 5.1; Dolby Surround. $24.95. Keepcase. *LANG:* English. *SUB:* English. *CAP:* English. *FEATURES:* 28 chapter links • Theatrical trailer • Talent files • Production notes • "Making of" featurette • Commentaries: director David Raynr, cast • Isolated music score.
2000 (PG-13) 94m/C Marla Sokoloff, Jodi Lyn O'Keefe, Shane West, James Franco, Julia Sweeney, Richard Schiff, Aaron Paul, Colin Hanks; *D:* David Raynr; *W:* Mark Schwahn; *C:* Tim Suhrstedt; *M:* Ed Shearmur.

What's Cooking?

A well-told tale of the horror and splendor that is a family Thanksgiving. The film is a little heavy-handed in its attempt to show the differences and similarities between Americans from different backgrounds, and how ultimately everyone has a prejudice against some other race or orientation even if it is seemingly good-natured. There is the Chinese family headed by Chen, the Mexican family with Ruehl, the Black family with Woodard, and the Jewish family headed by Kazan with the lesbian daughter (Sedgwick) for good measure. The families cross each in the grocery store and on a few personal levels. It's notable that Margolis and Sedgwick play the lesbian couple like a real couple rather than heterosexual actresses playing gay. The cooking scenes are amazing with beautifully photographed, mouth-watering food from four continents gracing the screen and some of the recipes gracing the disc extras. The color on the disc is fabulous, which only makes the food more appealing and the sound is good. —CA

Movie: ♫♫½ **DVD:** ♫♫♫
Trimark Home Video (Cat #VM#7540D, UPC #031398754022). Widescreen letterboxed. Dolby Digital 5.1 Surround. $24.99. Keepcase. *LANG:* English. *SUB:* English; Spanish; French. *CAP:* English. *FEATURES:* 24 chapter links • Commentary: director • Recipes • Cast and crew interviews • Trailers.
2000 (PG-13) 109m/C Alfre Woodard, Joan Chen, Julianna Margulies, Mercedes Ruehl, Kyra Sedgwick, Lainie Kazan, Dennis Haysbert, Victor Rivers, Douglas Spain, A. Martinez, Maury Chaykin, Estelle Harris, Will Yun Lee, Kristy Wu; *D:* Gurinder Chadha; *W:* Gurinder Chadha, Paul Mayeda Berges; *C:* Jong Lin; *M:* Craig Preuss.

When Harry Met Sally... [SE]

Romantic comedy follows the long relationship between two adults who try throughout the changes in their lives (and their mates) to remain platonic friends— and what happens when they don't. Wry and enjoyable script is enhanced by wonderful performances. Another directorial hit for Reiner, and a tour de force of comic screenwriting for Ephron, with improvisational help from Crystal. Great songs by Sinatra sound-alike Connick. A decent video transfer is accented by crisp (though not flawless) color and black definition. Likewise, the soundtrack is clear and discernable. But the lack of a 5.1 remix is a disappointment. The charming documentary included on the disc is both informative and enjoyable, yet director Reiner seems a bit detached and uninterested during his commentary track; however, he eventually comes out of this funk and delivers some truly interesting anecdotes and behind-the-scenes insights. —MJT

Movie: ♫♫♫ **DVD:** ♫♫♫
MGM Home Entertainment (Cat #1001460, UPC #027616857804). Widescreen (1.85:1) anamorphic. Dolby Digital Surround Stereo. $24.98. Keepcase. *LANG:* English. *SUB:* French; Spanish. *FEATURES:* 16 chapter links • Commentary: director Rob Reiner • "How Harry Met Sally" documentary • "It Had to be You" music video by Harry Connick Jr. • Deleted scenes • Theatrical trailer • Additional Rob Reiner film trailers.
1989 (R) 96m/C Billy Crystal, Meg Ryan, Carrie Fisher, Bruno Kirby, Steven Ford, Lisa Jane Persky, Michelle Nicastro, Harley Jane Kozak; *D:* Rob Reiner; *W:* Nora Ephron; *C:* Barry Sonnenfeld; *M:* Harry Connick Jr., Marc Shaiman. *AWARDS:* British Acad. '89: Orig. Screenplay; *NOM:* Oscars '89: Orig. Screenplay.

Where the Heart Is

Pregnant 17-year-old Novalee Nation (Portman) is on her way to California with her no-good boyfriend (Bruno), who abandons her at an Oklahoma WalMart. Without friends or funds, she hides out there until she gives birth. After she becomes a local celebrity, she finds shelter with eccentric Sister Husband (Channing) and becomes best pals with fecund single mom Lexi (Judd). The transfer is a sparkling rendition of the film, boasting a very high level of detail and an image that is razor sharp and stable without ever appearing artificially enhanced. The 5.1 soundtrack is just as impressive. —GH/MM *AKA:* Home Is Where the Heart Is.

Movie: ♫♫ **DVD:** ♫♫♫½
20th Century Fox Home Entertainment (Cat #2000634). Widescreen anamorphic. Dolby Digital 5.1 Surround Stereo; Dolby Digital Surround Stereo. $34.98. Keepcase. *LANG:* English; French. *SUB:* English; Spanish. *FEATURES:* Music Video • Trailers and TV spots.
2000 (PG-13) 115m/C Natalie Portman, Ashley Judd, Stockard Channing, James Frain, Dylan Bruno, Joan Cusack, Keith David, Richard Jones, Sally Field; *D:* Matt Williams; *W:* Lowell Ganz, Babaloo Mandel; *C:* Richard Greatrex; *M:* Mason Daring.

Where the Money Is

Famed bank robber Henry Manning (Newman) fakes a stroke so he can be transferred from prison to a nursing home. Carol (Fiorentino) is the bored former prom queen who knows he's faking and enlists his help in pulling one more job. The characters and the superb actors playing them are the main reasons to see this one. The transfer is clean and without blemishes, although in occasional shots some grain is indeed evident. The colors are vibrant and lively, creating a powerfully rendered image that reproduces strong hues and tinges. Audio is well rounded and balanced. The Surround track is equally good but appears to be optimized for home viewing, creating a noticeably tighter sound image. —MM/GH

Movie: ♫♫½ **DVD:** ♫♫♫
USA Home Entertainment (Cat #96306 0100-2). Widescreen (1.78:1) anamorphic. Dolby Digital 5.0 Surround Stereo; Dolby Digital Surround Stereo. $26.98. Keepcase. *LANG:* English. *SUB:* English; French; Spanish. *FEATURES:* Trailer.
2000 (PG-13) 90m/C Paul Newman, Linda Fiorentino, Dermot Mulroney, Susan Barnes, Bruce MacVittie, Dorothy Gordon, Anne Pioniak, Irma St. Paul; *D:* Marek Kanievska; *W:* E. Max Frye, Topper Lilien, Carroll Cartwright; *C:* Thomas Burstyn; *M:* Mark Isham.

The Whip and the Body

Mario Bava's 19th-century ghost/love/revenge story makes a belated arrival on home video. Nevena (Lavi) is about to be married when her ex-lover Kurt (Lee), soon to be her brother-in-law, shows up. The rest of the action is almost pure Gothic with a moody castle for a setting, secret passages, ladies wandering the hallways late at night in their diaphanous gowns. Though the story doesn't quite live up to the title, it is very sexually charged for its time and Lee turns in an aggressive performance. A lot of care was taken with the transfer to

disc. Heavy black shadows are more atmospheric than detailed but the image is essentially free of blemishes. Sound is very good too, and the extras are well-chosen. The director's fans will see echoes of *Black Sunday* and *Black Sabbath.* —*MM*
AKA: Night Is the Phantom; What.
Movie: 🎬🎬½ **DVD:** 🎬🎬🎬½
VCI Home Video (Cat #8269, UPC #08955 9826924). Widescreen (1.85:1) anamorphic. Dolby Digital Mono. $24.99. Keepcase. *LANG:* English; Italian. *SUB:* English; Spanish. *FEATURES:* 18 chapter links • Commentary: *Video Watchdog* editor Tim Lucas • Music soundtrack by Carlo Rustichelli • Talent files • Original American titles • Photo gallery • Trailers.
1963 88m/C *IT* Christopher Lee, Daliah Lavi, Tony Kendall, Harriet Medin, Isli Oberon; ***D:*** Mario Bava; ***W:*** Ernesto Gastaldi, Ugo Guerra, Luciano Martino; ***C:*** Ubaldo Terzano; ***M:*** Carlo Rustichelli.

Whipped

Three New York bachelors meet at a diner once a week and talk about women. Each, unbeknownst to the others, starts dating the lovely Mia (Peet), and she seems to fall for each of them. The male characters are such bobos that it's impossible to believe that an attractive woman would have anything to do with them. DVD image ranges between very good and excellent. Same for sound, though this kind of comedy doesn't exactly overtax the Surround capabilities. —*MM*
Movie: 🎬 **DVD:** 🎬🎬🎬
Columbia Tristar Home Video (Cat #05500, UPC #043396055001). Widescreen (1.85: 1) anamorphic; full frame. Dolby Digital 5.1 Surround Stereo; Dolby Digital Surround. $24.95. Keepcase. *LANG:* English. *SUB:* English; French; Spanish. *FEATURES:* 28 chapter links • Commentary: director • Trailers • Talent files.
2000 (R) 82m/C Amanda Peet, Brian Van Holt, Judah Domke, Zorie Barber, Jonathan Abrahams, Callie (Calliope) Thorne; ***D:*** Peter M. Cohen; ***W:*** Peter M. Cohen; ***C:*** Peter B. Kowalsk; ***M:*** Michael Montes.

White Christmas

Vista Vision remake of *Holiday Inn* lacks the color and scope of the original. Army buddies Phil and Bob (Kaye and Crosby) go to Vermont to chase the singing Haynes sisters and end up saving the inn owned by their old friend General Waverly (Jagger). The dance numbers are unremarkable, except for the Minstrel show number, which borders on unbelievable, but it's worth noting that Kaye and Crosby do quite a bit of cross-dressing. Irving Berlin's work is showcased much better in films like *Easter Parade* and *Top Hat.* The disc is good to look at, though the colors are a little too unrestrained in the red spectrum. The sound is decent. —*CA*
Movie: 🎬🎬 **DVD:** 🎬🎬
Paramount Home Video (Cat #06104, UPC #097360610420). Widescreen anamorphic. Dolby Digital 5.1 Surround; Dolby Digi-

tal Mono. $29.99. Keepcase. *LANG:* English; French. *SUB:* English. *FEATURES:* 19 chapter links • Commentary: Rosemary Clooney • 2 theatrical trailers • Retrospective interview with Rosemary Clooney.
1954 120m/C Bing Crosby, Danny Kaye, Rosemary Clooney, Vera-Ellen, Dean Jagger; ***D:*** Michael Curtiz; ***W:*** Norman Panama; ***C:*** Loyal Griggs. AWARDS: NOM: Oscars '54: Song ("Count Your Blessings Instead of Sheep").

White Lies

College freshman Catherine Chapman (Polley) feels alienated and finds a place for herself at an internet chatroom. She is increasingly involved with the National Identity Movement and becomes its spokesperson before she understands that it's really a neo-Nazi group. This Canadian television film takes a fairly simplistic look at the roots of rage that fuel rightwing anger, though it is dramatically effective and Sarah Polley is fine in the lead. DVD captures director Skogland's ambitious visual effects quite well and delivers a very good image throughout. —*MM*
Movie: 🎬🎬 **DVD:** 🎬🎬½
MTI Home Video (Cat #BE50035DVD, UPC #619935403536). Full frame. $24.95. Keepcase. *LANG:* English. *SUB:* Spanish. *FEATURES:* 12 chapter links • Synopsis • "Telling of" featurette • Talent files.
1998 (R) 92m/C *CA* Sarah Polley, Tanya Allen, Johnathan Scarfe, Lynn Redgrave, Joseph Kell, Albert Schultz; ***D:*** Keri Skogland; ***W:*** Dennis Foon.

The White Lioness

Updated version of *Day of the Jackal* (the excellent 1973 original, not the 1997 Willis-Gere abomination) tells the intricate story of an assassination attempt that begins in South Africa but leads to Sweden where the murder of a young woman involves a small town policeman in the international intrigue. Image quality is seldom better than good, with all the defects coming from the original, not the transfer. Recommended. —*MM* **AKA:** Den Vita Lejoninnan.
Movie: 🎬🎬🎬 **DVD:** 🎬🎬
Vanguard International Cinema, Inc. (Cat #1-892649-47-X, UPC #658769003239). Widescreen (1.66:1) letterboxed. $29.95. Keepcase. *LANG:* English; Afrikaans; Swedish. *SUB:* English. *FEATURES:* 16 chapter links.
1996 104m/C *SW* Rolf Lassgard, Basil Appollis, Jesper Christensen, Nelson Mandela; ***D:*** Per (Pelle) Berglund; ***W:*** Lars Bjorkman; ***C:*** Tony Forsberg; ***M:*** Thomas Lindahl.

White Men Can't Jump

Small-time con man Harrelson stands around looking like a big nerd until someone dares him to play basketball and he proves to be more adept than he looks. After he beats Snipes, they become

friends and start hustling together. Fast-paced obscenity-laced dialogue does not cover up the fact that the story hovers between dull and dismal, redeemed only by the surreal *Jeopardy* game show sequence and the convincing hoops action. On the whole, the picture is quite good. Colors, brightness, sharpness, and contrast are all spot on (maybe a little too spot on as the garish colors of those early '90s bicycle shorts everyone is sporting get to be a bit overwhelming!) The main advertised extra is a deleted scene that has been cut back into the movie. Unfortunately, I'm not a big enough fan of the film to be able to recognize where exactly this additional material appears. —*MP/MM*
Movie: 🎬🎬 **DVD:** 🎬🎬½
20th Century Fox Home Entertainment (Cat #2000534). Widescreen (1.85:1) anamorphic. Dolby Digital Surround Stereo. $29.98. Keepcase. *LANG:* English; French. *SUB:* English; Spanish. *FEATURES:* Deleted scene • Music video • Theatrical trailer.
1992 (R) 115m/C Wesley Snipes, Woody Harrelson, Rosie Perez, Tyra Ferrell, Cylk Cozart, Kadeem Hardison, Ernest Harden, John Jones; ***D:*** Ron Shelton; ***W:*** Ron Shelton; ***C:*** Russell Boyd; ***M:*** Bennie Wallace.

White Wolves 2: Legend of the Wild

Troubled teens are on a school assignment involving a conservation foundation's rescue of a pair of young wolves. They must overcome lots of obstacles, including their mutual loathing. It's an average teens-in-the-woods adventure. DVD image is far less than razor sharp. Excessive graininess does no favors for either the scenery or the cute furry forest creatures. —*MM*
Movie: 🎬🎬 **DVD:** 🎬🎬
New Concorde (Cat #NH20527 D, UPC #73 6991252790). Full frame. Stereo. $14.98. Keepcase. *LANG:* English. *FEATURES:* 24 chapter links • Trailers • Talent files.
1994 (PG) 95m/C Corin "Corky" Nemec, Justin Whalin, Jeremy London, Elizabeth Berkley, Ernie Reyes Jr., Ele Keats; ***D:*** Terence H. Winkless; ***C:*** John Aronson.

White Wolves 3: Cry of the White Wolf

A plane crash strands two teens (Cain and McNab) in the Sierra mountain wilderness where they must depend on themselves and a mystical white wolf for survival. It's typically woozy outdoors drivel. Grain is slightly less of a problem here than it is in *2.* Otherwise, image and sound are about equal to tape. —*MM*
Movie: 🎬🎬 **DVD:** 🎬🎬
New Concorde (Cat #NH20716 D, UPC #73 6991271692). Full frame. Stereo. $14.98. Keepcase. *LANG:* English. *FEATURES:* 24 chapter links • Talent files • Trailers.
1998 (PG) 82m/C Rodney A. Grant, Mercedes McNab, Robin Clarke, Tracy Brooks Swope, Mick Cain, Margaret Howell; ***D:*** Victoria Muspratt.

Whity

In 1970, the controversial German filmmaker Fassbinder set his anarchic eye on the American western and created perhaps the strangest oater ever committed to film. After languishing for years in obscurity, it returns with a DVD featuring a positively tactile widescreen transfer and a revelatory commentary track. It recounts the malevolent machinations of the Nicholsons, a wealthy family in the old American West. The titular character is their mulatto slave/butler (Gunther Kaufman), both exploited and embraced by the ghoulish clan, whose pallid fleshtones suggest ghosts in the making. Love, death, transvestitism, homosexuality, and the conventions of the western merge into a complex narrative that defies any attempt at precise description. The transfer achieves practically perfect color fidelity, capturing elements as disparate as Whity's blood-red servants' uniform and the minutiae of azure-blue kitchen tile. Blacks are deep and solid, allowing for excellent contrast delineation and shadow detail. Except for some mild grain and a few color shifts, the source is pristine. —EP/MM

Movie: ♫♫♫ **DVD:** ♫♫♫

Fantoma Films (Cat #7011). Widescreen (2.35:1) anamorphic. Dolby Digital Mono. $29.95. Keepcase. LANG: German. SUB: English. FEATURES: Commentary: Fassbinder, Michael Ballhaus, Ulli Lommel • Liner notes.

1970 102m/C GE Rainer Werner Fassbinder, Gunther Kaufman, Hanna Schygulla, Ulli Lommel, Harry Baer; **D:** Rainer Werner Fassbinder; **W:** Rainer Werner Fassbinder; **C:** Michael Ballhaus; **M:** Peer Raben.

The Whole Nine Yards

Wimpy dentist Oz (Perry) has his life turned to chaos when former hitman Jimmy (Willis) moves in next door, inspiring his wife Sophie (Arquette), who's bored and wants Oz dead for the insurance money, and Jill, Oz's receptionist, who aspires to be a hitwoman herself. While it's true that nearly all the elements are not only ridiculous but cribbed from other mob comedies, this one works because all involved seem to be having such a good time. Warner Bros. has done right by this one on DVD, presenting both widescreen and full-frame images that are properly detailed and free of error. Sound is fine, and director Lynn's commentary track sticks to the business at hand. —MM

Movie: ♫♫1/2 **DVD:** ♫♫♫

Warner Home Video, Inc. (Cat #18381). Widescreen (1.85:1) anamorphic; full frame. Dolby Digital 5.1; Dolby Digital Surround. $24.98. Snapper. LANG: English; French. SUB: English; French. FEATURES: Commentary: director • Interviews • Talent files • Trailer.

2000 (PG-13) 101m/C Bruce Willis, Matthew Perry, Michael Clarke Duncan, Natasha Henstridge, Amanda Peet, Rosanna Arquette, Kevin Pollak, Harland Williams; **D:** Jonathan Lynn; **W:** Mitchell Kapner; **C:** David Franco; **M:** Randy Edelman.

Wicked City [SE]

Wild and woolly anime is similar in tone to a James Bond movie. In fact, the whole production has a mid-'60s look. A young man named Taki is picked up by a sexy woman in a bar and regrets his decision when she does one of those really icky transformations. Seems she's a visitor from the parallel Black World of monsters. He's an agent of the Black Guard, a secret intelligence organization that protects the Earth from these supernatural bad guys. The story revolves around Guiseppi Mayart, a strange little character who looks (and acts!) like an oversexed E.T., and is the key to a treaty between the two worlds. Taki and his reluctant female partner Makea are assigned to guard the debauched diplomat. The 5.1 mix is very active and is the only real difference between the disc and VHS tape. —MM

Movie: ♫♫♫ **DVD:** ♫♫1/2

Urban Vision Entertainment (Cat #UV1065, UPC #638652106506). Full frame. Dolby Digital 5.1 Surround Stereo; Dolby Stereo. $24.95. Keepcase. LANG: English; Japanese. SUB: English. FEATURES: 10 chapter links • Character profiles • Weblink • Interview with director Kawajiri.

1989 82m/C JP **D:** Yoshiaki Kawajiri; **W:** Kisei Choo.

Wide Awake

This sleeper of a flick is about a little boy (Cross) who is in search of God. Actually, he just wants to make sure his grandpa is O.K. after gramps has died. To reach that end, he asks difficult questions of his parents (Leary and Delaney) and teachers, including O'Donnell as a sports-obsessed nun. He explores Judaism, Islam, and Buddhism, as well as Christianity. Finally, he has an encounter with an angel who restores his faith. The pace is slow and methodical, and some of the performances by the kids aren't very good. Cross is just fine in the lead role, however. This is a non-anamorphic transfer, with pixelation apparent in the backgrounds of many scenes. Also, viewers who look close will spot little nicks and dirt on the film element used. You get a matrixed Surround soundtrack, so don't strain your ears listening for five discrete channels. Extras? Nothing but a trailer. A year later, director Shyamalan would release blockbuster The Sixth Sense. —MB

Movie: ♫♫1/2 **DVD:** ♫♫

Miramax Pictures Home Video (Cat #18371, UPC #717951005281). Widescreen (1.85:1) letterboxed. Dolby Digital Surround. $29.99. Keepcase. LANG: English; French. SUB: Spanish. CAP: English. FEATURES: 14 chapter links • Theatrical trailer.

1997 (PG) 88m/C Joseph Cross, Dana Delany, Rosie O'Donnell, Denis Leary, Robert Loggia, Dan Lauria, Timothy Reifsnyder, Camryn Manheim; **D:** M. Night Shyamalan; **W:** M. Night Shyamalan; **C:** Adam Holender; **M:** Edmund Choi.

The Wild Angels

The film that first made Peter Fonda on a motorcycle an icon of the 1960s is a trip back to a time when gas was 28.9 cents a gallon. Actually, it's a damning early portrait of a hedonistic generation that refuses to take responsibility for its actions. Gang leader Heavenly Blues (Fonda) makes one mistake after another in his attempts to get his friend Loser's (Dern) stolen motorcycle back. In visual terms, the film stands up as one of Corman's best. His feel for the Southern California landscape is excellent, ranging from stark desert vistas to oilfield wastelands. Overall, the film looks much better than any low-budget biker flick from the '60s ought to look. The only thing that's missing is a commentary track from the filmmaker. Those who are curious about the details of the production should check out his autobiography, How I Made a Hundred Movies in Hollywood and Never Lost a Dime. —MM

Movie: ♫♫1/2 **DVD:** ♫♫♫

MGM Home Entertainment (Cat #1001547, UPC #027616858573). Widescreen (2.35:1) anamorphic. Dolby Digital Mono. $19.98. Keepcase. LANG: English; French. SUB: French; Spanish. FEATURES: 16 chapter links • Trailer.

1966 (PG) 124m/C Peter Fonda, Nancy Sinatra, Bruce Dern, Diane Ladd, Michael J. Pollard, Gayle Hunnicutt, Peter Bogdanovich, Dick Miller; **D:** Roger Corman; **W:** Charles B. Griffith, Peter Bogdanovich; **C:** Richard Moore; **M:** Michael Curb.

Wild Bill

Severely underrated western looks very good on DVD. All that's missing is a commentary track, but given the film's poor reception, it's easy to understand why that is lacking. In Deadwood, South Dakota, Bill Hickok (Bridges at his best) tries to deal with his status as living legend and is haunted by opium-fueled dreams of his past and a lost love (Lane). Meanwhile, young Jack McCall (Arquette) has vowed to go down in history as the man who shot Wild Bill. The whole thing is almost stolen by Christina Applegate as Lurline, a hooker who's as tough as any man and smarter than most. The image does justice to Lloyd Ahern's subtle, evocative photography and the 5.1 sound field works well around John Hurt's voice-over narration. The grain in the black-and-white sequences comes from the original. A real bargain at the price. —MM

Movie: ♫♫♫1/2 **DVD:** ♫♫♫

MGM Home Entertainment (Cat #1001598, UPC #027616859082). Widescreen (1.85:1) anamorphic. Dolby Digital 5.1 Surround Stereo; Dolby Digital Surround. $19.98. Keepcase. LANG: English; French; Spanish. SUB: French; Spanish. CAP: English. FEATURES: 16 chapter links • Trailer.

1995 (R) 97m/C Jeff Bridges, Ellen Barkin, John Hurt, Diane Lane, Keith Carradine, Christina Applegate, Bruce Dern, James Gammon, David Arquette, Marjoe Gortner; **D:** Walter Hill; **W:** Walter Hill; **C:** Lloyd Ahern; **M:** Van Dyke Parks.

Wilderness

Excellent adaptation of Dennis Danvers's fine novel can be seen as a British companion piece to Jack Nicholson's *Wolf* or an updating of Paul Schrader's *Cat People,* which it quotes. Librarian Alice (Ooms) believes that during the full moon, she becomes a wolf. At least, that's what she tells her psychiatrist (Kitchen, understatedly brilliant as usual). Of course, he does not believe her. But he thinks that her belief might have something to do with her unusually predatory sexual habits. The film treats the subject and the characters seriously. If the special effects aren't as spectacular as some, they're fine. The filmmakers were smart to invest in a solid script and a first-rate cast instead. Image is a bit dim and grainy, but close-ups are O.K. DVD gains little visually over tape. Fans should try to find this one on any medium. —*MM*
Movie: 🎬🎬🎬 **DVD:** 🎬🎬½
MTI Home Video (Cat #50041DVD, UPC #6 19935404137). Full frame. $14.98. Keepcase. *LANG:* English. *SUB:* Spanish. *FEATURES:* 20 chapter links ☛ *Fangoria* magazine article ☛ Trailers.
1996 (R) 90m/C *GB* Amanda Ooms, Michael Kitchen, Owen Teale, Gemma Jones; **D:** Ben Bolt; **W:** Andrew Davies, Bernadette Davis.

Winds of the Wasteland

In the first film on this disc, Wayne and Chandler are Pony Express contractors who race rivals to land government work. In the second, Wayne is a tough Easterner who goes west and finds himself involved with miners and claim jumpers. These short B-movies helped to put the Duke on the Hollywood map, but you'd hardly be able to tell it from this disc. *Winds* looks O.K. but contains an extremely annoying background hiss. *Lucky Texan* is an unwatchable copy of a poor dupe. —*MM*
Movie: 🎬🎬½ **DVD:** 🎬
Madacy Entertainment (Cat #990035, UPC #056775002497). Full frame. Dolby Digital Mono. $9.99. Keepcase. *LANG:* English. *FEATURES:* Thumbnail bios.
1936 54m/B John Wayne, Phyllis Fraser, Lane Chandler, Yakima Canutt; **D:** Mack V. Wright; **W:** Joseph Poland; **C:** William Nobles.

Winner Takes All

Semi-professional Louisville production follows the lives of two young black men from their first involvement with crime in the late '70s, through their separation in the '80s when one goes straight, and their coming back together in the '90s. The general level of acting isn't very good, and the film has a very rough quality, particularly noticeable in the poorly recorded dialogue. But it is energetic and ambitious, and so fans of the hip-hop cast are likely to be entertained. DVD only heightens the shortcomings of both image and sound. —*MM*
Movie: 🎬🎬½ **DVD:** 🎬🎬
MTI Home Video (Cat #D7001, UPC #0394 14570014). Full frame. $24.95. Keepcase. *LANG:* English. *FEATURES:* 20 chapter links ☛ Talent files.
1998 103m/C Alfred "Rubin" Thompson, Robert Hayes III, Joe Estevez, Daniel Zirilli, AMG, B-Real, Rappin 4-Tay, Reegus Flenory, Flesh N Bone; **D:** Daniel Zirilli; **W:** Marlon Parry, Robert Hayes III, Daniel Zirilli; **C:** David West.

Winter People

Widower Wayland Jackson (Russell) and his young daughter take shelter with unmarried Collie Wright (McGillis) and her baby son during a cold Appalachian winter during the Depression. They must face feuding families when they fall in love. Both stars try gamely with fairly unforgiving material. Russell, in particular, sounds embarrassed when he's called upon to deliver this deathless line: "I'm a clockmaker. I make clocks." Grainy image is an accurate reproduction of the theatrical release, as I remember it. Same for sound. —*MM*
Movie: 🎬🎬 **DVD:** 🎬🎬
MGM Home Entertainment (Cat #1001853, UPC #027616861214). Widescreen (2.35:1) anamorphic. Dolby Digital Surround; Mono. $14.98. Keepcase. *LANG:* English; French. *SUB:* French; Spanish. *CAP:* English. *FEATURES:* 16 chapter links ☛ Trailer.
1989 (PG-13) 109m/C Kurt Russell, Kelly McGillis, Lloyd Bridges, Mitchell Ryan, Jeffrey Meek, Eileen Ryan, Amelia Burnette; **D:** Ted Kotcheff; **W:** Carol Sobieski; **M:** John Scott.

Winter Sleepers

Tom Tykwer's film was made before *Run, Lola, Run.* While it lacks the kinetic energy of that ground-breaking title, it is a solid psychological mystery, worthy of comparison to the best work of Atom Egoyan, particularly *The Sweet Hereafter* in setting and one key plot device, if not in intention. The plot involves five people—a ski instructor, his translator girlfriend, her housemate who's also a nurse, a film projectionist, and a farmer who's nearly destitute. Over the New Year's holiday in a small mountain town, their lives intersect, separate, reconnect, and change. When it's over, one of them will be dead. The steady revelation of their characters is much more important than any single event, though Tykwer makes the film work beautifully on the simple what's-going-to-happen-next level. If in the end, he overindulges in a penchant for the symbolic, it's a forgivable sin. The widescreen image is fine, but on the soft side. Characters are identified by colors and all the reds are intentionally blurry. Ochre tints soften many of the snowy exteriors. Optional English subtitles are easy to read. Fans of *Lola* won't be blown away, but they will find their patience handsomely rewarded. —*MM* **AKA:** *Winterschlafer.*
Movie: 🎬🎬🎬 **DVD:** 🎬🎬🎬
Winstar Home Entertainment (Cat #FLV52 55, UPC #720917525525). Widescreen letterboxed. Dolby Digital Stereo. $24.99. Keepcase. *LANG:* German. *SUB:* English. *FEATURES:* 16 chapter links ☛ Filmographies ☛ Production credits ☛ Trailers.
1997 124m/C *GE* Heino Ferch, Floriane Daniel, Ulrich Matthes, Marie-Lou Sellem, Josef Bierbichler; **D:** Tom Tykwer; **W:** Tom Tykwer, Anne-Francois Pyszora; **C:** Frank Griebe; **M:** Tom Tykwer, Johnny Klimek, Reinhold Heil.

Wishful Thinking

A romance told from three sides. Max (LeGros) is in love with Elizabeth (Beals), who may or may not be cheating with an old high school chum of hers. Lena (Barrymore) is in love with her long-time friend Max and decides to encourage him to believe the worst about Elizabeth. Each character gets screen time to tell his or her side and the result is a fun, watchable, romantic comedy that is a good way to waste 89 minutes of your life. A must-see for Barrymore fans as she has a funky new outfit in every scene and looks great. The disc is great with vibrant color and good sound. —*CA*
Movie: 🎬🎬 **DVD:** 🎬🎬🎬
Miramax Pictures Home Video (Cat #202 39, UPC #717951009777). Widescreen (185:1) anamorphic. Dolby Surround. $29.99. Keepcase. *LANG:* English. *SUB:* Spanish. *CAP:* English. *FEATURES:* 22 chapter links.
1992 94m/C Murray Langston, Michelle Johnson, Ruth Buzzi, Billy Barty, Johnny Dark, Ray "Boom Boom" Mancini, Vic Dunlop, Kip Addotta; **D:** Murray Langston.

The Witches

Gwen Mayfield (Fontaine) accepts a teaching position at Haddaby School. She wants to put terrifying memories of work in Africa behind her, but finds that the bucolic English country town is just as dangerous. The sense of menace isn't as strong as it is in the similar *Wicker Man,* and the film isn't one of the strongest entries from the Hammer Studio, but it is up to their high standards in terms of production values and acting. On disc, colors seem slightly undersaturated or lacking in brightness, but the image is otherwise unblemished. —*MM* **AKA:** *The Devil's Own.*
Movie: 🎬🎬½ **DVD:** 🎬🎬½
Anchor Bay (Cat #DV10689, UPC #013131 068993). Widescreen (1.66:1) anamorphic. Dolby Digital Mono. $24.99. Keepcase. *LANG:* English. *FEATURES:* 24 chapter links ☛ Trailer and TV spots ☛ *World of Hammer* episode, "Wicked Women."
1966 90m/C Joan Fontaine, Kay Walsh, Alec McCowen, Ann Bell, John Collin, Michele Dotrice, Gwen Ffrangcon Davies, Ingrid Brett; **D:** Cyril Frankel; **W:** Nigel Kneale; **C:** Arthur Grant; **M:** Richard Rodney Bennett.

Witchouse 2: Blood Coven

Students from Boston University (actually Bucharest), accompany their professor to a town infamous for its witch trials. They investigate four bodies which have recently been unearthed. The bodies turn out to be witches who are out for vengeance. The rest of this overachieving low-budget horror borrows from *The Blair Witch Project*, *The Fog*, and even *Jurassic Park*. The image is very clear, showing few defects from the source print and hardly any grain. While the sound field achieved by the 5.1 mix is only average, it makes good use of the rear speakers to help create tension in the film. The only flaw in the presentation comes when video footage is used in the movie. At those points in the film, the volume drops off and one must scramble for the volume control in order to hear the dialogue. —*ML/MM*
Movie: 🎬🎬🎬 *DVD:* 🎬🎬🎬
Full Moon Pictures (Cat #8069R, UPC #76 3843806962). Widescreen (1.85:1) anamorphic. Dolby Digital 5.1 Surround Stereo. $24.98. Keepcase. *LANG:* English. *FEATURES:* Commentary • Deleted scene • Alternate title sequence • Trailer • "Making of" featurette • "Bucharest or Bust!: A Tour of Romania" featurette.
2000 (R) 82m/C Ariauna Albright, Andrew Prine, Nicholas Lanier, Elizabeth Hopgood; *D:* J.R. Bookwalter.

A Woman Called Moses

Cicely Tyson plays Harriet Ross Tubman, who bought her freedom from slavery, founded the underground railroad, and helped lead hundreds of slaves to freedom before the Civil War. The star is excellent but the miniseries is bogged down by a so-so script. The DVD was made from a very poor print. Its faded and dark interiors dissolve into murky black grain. —*MM*
Movie: 🎬🎬½ *DVD:* 🎬
Xenon Entertainment (Cat #1026, UPC #000799102626). Full frame. $19.98. Keepcase. *LANG:* English. *FEATURES:* 20 chapter links • Trailers.
1978 200m/C Cicely Tyson, Dick Anthony Williams, Will Geer, Robert Hooks, Hari Rhodes, James Wainwright; *D:* Paul Wendkos; *W:* Lonnie Elder III; *M:* Coleridge-Taylor Perkinson.

A Woman Called Sada Abe

This curious erotic drama is based on the same true story that inspired *In the Realm of the Senses*. Geisha Sada Abe (Junko Miyashita) becomes completely obsessed with restaurateur Kichizo (Hideaki Ezumi), and he with her. Their mutual lust eventually turns to madness, and their descent is harrowing. Despite differences in culture, the two leads do believable work in demanding roles. The roughness of the DVD image appears to come from the original. Interiors and costumes tend toward warm, glaring reds. Darker interiors lose some detail, but overall, the film doesn't look much better or worse than similarly budgeted American productions from the mid-'70s. Yellow subtitles are easy to read. —*MM* *AKA:* Jitsuroku Abe Sada.
Movie: 🎬🎬½ *DVD:* 🎬🎬
Image Entertainment (Cat #ID9733KIDVD, UPC #014381973327). Widescreen (2:1) letterboxed. Dolby Digital Mono. $24.95. Snapper. *LANG:* Japanese. *SUB:* English. *FEATURES:* 8 chapter links.
1975 85m/C *JP* Junko Miyashita, Hideaki Ezumi, Koizumi Ikonosuke; *D:* Noboru Tanaka; *W:* Akio Ido; *C:* Masaru Mori; *M:* Koichi Sakata.

A Woman, Her Men and Her Futon

Trying to put her life back together after a divorce, Helen (Rubin) has to make certain compromises. She's trying to write and sell a screenplay, but when men show interest, do they want her work or her? Eventually, this is a movie about movies, about making movies, about love and sex, lies and hope, individual responsibility. It gets better and more complicated as it goes along. Director Sibay is especially good at showing the uncomfortable moments between people. Overall, the writing is better than the direction or the acting. The full-frame image is identical to VHS tape. —*MM*
Movie: 🎬🎬½ *DVD:* 🎬🎬
Image Entertainment (Cat #OVED9035DVD, UPC #014381903522). Full frame. Dolby Digital Stereo. $24.99. Snapper. *LANG:* English. *FEATURES:* 12 chapter links • Trailer.
1992 (R) 90m/C Jennifer Rubin, Lance Edwards, Grant Show, Michael Ceveris, Delaune Michel, Robert Lipton; *D:* Mussef Sibay; *W:* Mussef Sibay; *C:* Michael J. Davis; *M:* Joel Goldsmith.

The Woman in Green

Murder victims are found missing index fingers, and it's up to Holmes and Watson (Rathbone and Bruce) to find out why. Could Prof. Moriarty (Daniell) be behind the dastardly crimes? Both DVD image and sound are fair. The disc is part of the "Evening with Sherlock Holmes" boxed set. —*MM* *AKA:* Sherlock Holmes and the Woman in Green.
Movie: 🎬🎬 *DVD:* 🎬🎬
FOCUSfilm (Cat #FF7944, UPC #6830707 94422). Full frame. $69.99. Keepcase. *LANG:* English. *FEATURES:* 12 chapter links • Episodes 1-8 of *New Adventures of Sherlock Holmes* radio show • Photo gallery.
1945 68m/B Basil Rathbone, Nigel Bruce, Hillary Brooke, Henry Daniell, Paul Cavanagh, Frederick Worlock, Mary Gordon, Billy Bevan; *D:* Roy William Neill; *W:* Bertram Millhauser; *C:* Virgil Miller.

The Woman in Green/ Dressed to Kill

In the first film on this double feature, murder victims are found with missing index fingers. In the second, Holmes finds that music boxes hold the key to plates stolen from the Bank of England. It's also the final teaming of Rathbone and Bruce as the famous characters. Sadly, the DVD presentation from Marengo Films is even worse in quality than the previous release by Focus Films. Both discs seem to come from the same print, but apart from the same problems in the source material, this image is visibly overcompressed. Every bit of detail is lost as a result, giving the image a very flat and lifeless quality without definition and an extremely soft look. Compression artifacts such as pixelation can be found even in shots with little or no movement at all, and most images show banding artifacts destroying the smooth black-and-white fall-off the original image contained. To make matters worse, a 2.5-minute promotional studio trailer that cannot be skipped at all comes up every time you insert the disc in your player. —*GH/MM* *AKA:* Sherlock Holmes and the Woman in Green.
Movie: 🎬🎬½ *DVD:* woof
Marengo Films (Cat #8). Full frame. Dolby Digital Mono. $15.98. Keepcase. *LANG:* English.
1945 68m/B Basil Rathbone, Nigel Bruce, Hillary Brooke, Henry Daniell, Paul Cavanagh, Frederick Worlock, Mary Gordon, Billy Bevan; *D:* Roy William Neill; *W:* Bertram Millhauser; *C:* Virgil Miller.

Woman on Top

A curious syndrome makes Isabella (Cruz) unusually sensitive to motion sickness, thus explaining the title. She's also a terrific cook. But after she catches her husband Toninho (Benicio) fooling around, she heads for San Francisco where she attracts the attention of a producer (Feuerstein) and becomes a celebrity TV chef. The filmmakers are aiming for the delicate magical realism that made *Like Water for Chocolate* so wonderful, but even with the presence of the delightful star, they can't make it work. That said, DVD presents an accurate reproduction of an often riotous color scheme. Sound is very good, too. —*MM*
Movie: 🎬🎬½ *DVD:* 🎬🎬½
20th Century Fox Home Entertainment (Cat #2001488, UPC #024543014881). Widescreen (1.85:1) anamorphic. Dolby Digital 5.1 Surround Stereo; Dolby Digital Surround. $24.98. Keepcase. *LANG:* English; French. *SUB:* English; Spanish. *FEATURES:* 16 chapter links • Recipe booklet • 2 trailers • 3 TV spots.
2000 (R) 93m/C Penelope Cruz, Harold Perrineau Jr., Mark Feuerstein, Murilo Benicio, John de Lancie; *D:* Fina Torres; *W:* Vera Blasi; *C:* Thierry Arbogast; *M:* Luis Bacalov.

A Woman under the Influence

Like most of Cassavetes's films, this story of a woman disintegrating under the pressure of living is hard to watch. Gena Rowlands is Mabel, a high-strung housewife, mother of two, and wife to a hard-working construction foreman (Falk). She is probably manic-depressive, but her diagnosis is never given. Her husband loves her for her unusual behavior, but also wants her to be normal and appropriate when guests or his mother are over. Falk is amazing as the man who realizes he will never understand his wife, but loves her so much it is almost irrational, and Rowlands's portrayal of Mabel garnered her an Academy Award nomination. Cassavetes is almost cruel in his ability to show the slice of life behind the closed doors of this particular American family, and the film is not for everyone. Critically, this is a perfect film, but those seeking escapist fare should move along. The disc looks better than the VHS and the sound quality is good. —CA

Movie: 𝄞𝄞𝄞 **DVD:** 𝄞𝄞½
Pioneer Entertainment (Cat #PSE 98 161, UPC #01302302890). Full frame. Stereo. $24.99. Keepcase. LANG: English. FEATURES: 11 chapter links ☞ 2-sided disc.
1974 (R) 147m/C Gena Rowlands, Peter Falk, Matthew Cassel, Matthew Laborteaux, Christina Grisanti; **D:** John Cassavetes; **W:** John Cassavetes; **C:** Caleb Deschanel, Mitch Breit. AWARDS: Golden Globes '75: Actress—Drama (Rowlands); Natl. Bd. of Review '74: Actress (Rowlands), Natl. Film Reg. '90; NOM: Oscars '74: Actress (Rowlands), Director (Cassavetes).

The Womaneater

This '50s oddity makes a belated appearance on home video. Dr. James Moran (Coulouris) returns from the depths of the Amazon jungle (obviously a set filled with plastic plants) with a miraculous tree that's a close cousin of "Audrey" in the original Little Shop of Horrors. To maintain its healing powers, the doctor must feed it a steady diet of young women. Not a good sign for his sexy housekeeper Sally (Day). It's every bit as silly as it sounds, swiftly paced and short. DVD exhibits very light signs of wear. Overall, the black-and-white image ranges between very good and excellent. —MM

Movie: 𝄞𝄞 **DVD:** 𝄞𝄞½
Image Entertainment (Cat #ID8172GODVD, UPC #014381817225). Widescreen (1.66: 1) letterboxed. Dolby Digital Mono. $24.99. Snapper. LANG: English. FEATURES: 16 chapter links.
1959 71m/B GB Vera Day, George Coulouris, Robert MacKenzie, Norman Claridge, Marpessa Dawn, Jimmy Vaughan; **D:** Charles Saunders; **W:** Brandon Fleming; **C:** Ernest Palmer; **M:** Edwin Astley.

Women

Five professionally and emotionally intense women have their secrets, fears, and desires woven into a close web of friendship. After several angst-filled episodes, the women form a safety net for each other. It plays like a headier Waiting to Exhale. The video transfer is good, although blacks do tend to lose definition throughout. The soundtrack is similarly

hindered by occasionally muddied dialogue. Overall, however, both video and audio hold their own. —MJT **AKA:** Elles.
Movie: 𝄞𝄞𝄞 **DVD:** 𝄞𝄞½
Fox/Lorber Home Video (Cat #FLV5227, UPC #720917522722). Widescreen (1.85: 1) letterboxed. Dolby Digital Stereo. $29.98. Keepcase. LANG: French. SUB: English. FEATURES: 16 chapter links ☞ Production credits ☞ Filmographies and awards ☞ Weblinks.
1997 94m/C FR Carmen Maura, Miou-Miou, Marthe Keller, Marisa Berenson, Guesch Patti, Joaquim de Almeida, Didier Flamand, Morgan Perez; **D:** Luis Galvao Teles; **W:** Don Bohlinger, Luis Galvao Teles; **C:** Alfredo Mayo; **M:** Alejandro Masso.

The Women of Brewster Place

Seven black women living in a tenement fight to gain control of their lives. (Men, in general, don't come off too well.) An excellent, complex script gives each actress time in the limelight. The fine ensemble is headed by executive producer Winfrey in her TV dramatic debut. DVD image and sound are no better than VHS tape. —MM
Movie: 𝄞𝄞𝄞 **DVD:** 𝄞𝄞
Xenon Entertainment (Cat #1092, UPC #000799109229). Full frame. Stereo. $19.99. Keepcase. LANG: English. FEATURES: 16 chapter links ☞ Trailers.
1989 180m/C Oprah Winfrey, Mary Alice, Olivia Cole, Robin Givens, Moses Gunn, Jackee, Paula Kelly, Lonette McKee, Paul Winfield, Cicely Tyson; **D:** Donna Deitch; **W:** Karen Hall; **C:** Alexander Grusynski; **M:** David Shire.

Women on the Verge of a Nervous Breakdown

Actress Pepa (Maura) learns by answering machine that her lover Ivan is dumping her, and her frantic efforts to contact him (he's splitting for Stockholm with another mistress) bring her into contact with his mental-patient wife Lucia (Serrano). Ivan's shy son Carlos (Banderas) and his fiancée Marisa (de Palma) arrive to sublet Pepa's apartment, just as Pepa's neurotic best friend Candela (Barranco) shows up in a panic because the TV news says her boyfriend is a wanted terrorist! Pedro Almodovar's breakthrough movie is less disturbing than his earlier work, but just as creative and hilariously funny. The farce builds with twisted wit (Pepa sets her bed on fire; a roomful of people are zonked out by the doped gazpacho with which she intended to commit suicide) and bitingly accurate observations on romance. The highpoint is a session where Pepa redubs Joan Crawford's voice for Johnny Guitar, beautifully restating that movie's most poignant scene. Part Doris Day, part Luis Bunuel, this eye-opener makes Madrid look like the hip center of the universe. Colors are bright and the picture sharp, far better looking than the smeary Orion

laserdisc, yet not quite as snappy as they could be. The mono sound is a big improvement on the laser. Removable subtitles make this an excellent disc for language teaching. —GE **AKA:** Mujeres al Borde de un Ataque de Nervios.
Movie: 𝄞𝄞𝄞𝄞 **DVD:** 𝄞𝄞𝄞½
MGM Home Entertainment (Cat #10017 43, UPC #027616860439). Widescreen (1.78:1) anamorphic. Dolby Digital. $19.98. Keepcase. LANG: Castilian Spanish; English; French. SUB: English; French; Spanish. CAP: English. FEATURES: 16 chapter links ☞ Orion Home Video promo.
1988 (R) 88m/C SP Carmen Maura, Fernando Guillen, Julieta Serrano, Maria Barranco, Rossy de Palma, Antonio Banderas; **D:** Pedro Almodovar; **W:** Pedro Almodovar; **C:** Jose Luis Alcaine; **M:** Bernardo Bonazzi. AWARDS: N.Y. Film Critics '88: Foreign Film; NOM: Oscars '88: Foreign Film.

Wonder Boys

The weekend after his latest wife leaves him, college professor Grady Tripp (Douglas), a resolute pothead and one-time writer of great promise, ends up on a madcap spiritual odyssey with the disparate group of people that make up his life. Tripp is propelled on this adventure of self-discovery by his editor (Downey Jr.), his mistress (McDormand), her blind dog, and one of his students (Maguire), who's a talented writer and compulsive weaver of tales. A brilliant and frequently hilarious film features perhaps Douglas's best performance and truly incredible work by the rest of the cast. Director Hanson's touch is delicate and sensitive, deftly conveying all the dramatic and comedic nuances in Kloves's marvelous script. Certainly one of the best films of the year 2000. The disc is gorgeous, conveying the muted rainy hues of the story with eye-popping clarity and accuracy. The sound is also perfect, warmly conveying Douglas's gravelly voice-overs, the excellent songs, and the atmospheric Surround sound effects. NOTE: The video and DVD release of this film is missing a small bit of dialogue from the theatrical release where Maguire's character referred to Alan Ladd's suicide. This was objected to by Ladd's family and later removed from the film by Hanson. —DG
Movie: 𝄞𝄞𝄞½ **DVD:** 𝄞𝄞𝄞𝄞
Paramount Home Video (Cat #33261, UPC #097363326144). Widescreen (2.35:1) anamorphic. Dolby Digital 5.0. $29.99. Keepcase. LANG: English; French. SUB: English; French (for extras only). CAP: English. FEATURES: Featurette including cast and crew interviews ☞ Pittsburgh interactive location map with commentary by Curtis Hanson ☞ "Things Have Changed" Bob Dylan music video ☞ Commentary on the music of Wonder Boys with Curtis Hanson ☞ Theatrical trailer ☞ 15 chapter links.
2000 (R) 112m/C Michael Douglas, Tobey Maguire, Frances McDormand, Katie Holmes, Robert Downey Jr., Richard Thomas, Rip Torn, Philip Bosco, Jane Adams; **D:** Curtis Hanson; **W:** Steven Kloves; **C:** Dante Spinotti; **M:** Christopher

Young. *AWARDS:* Oscars '00: Song ("Things Have Changed"); Golden Globes '01: Song ("Things Have Changed"); *NOM:* Oscars '00: Adapt. Screenplay, Film Editing; Writers Guild '00: Adapt. Screenplay.

Wonder Man

When a brash nightclub entertainer (Kaye) is killed by gangsters, his mild-mannered twin brother takes his place to smoke out the killers. One of Kaye's better early films is also the screen debut of Vera-Ellen and Cochran. Look for Mrs. Howell of *Gilligan's Island.* DVD presents the supersaturated colors with no significant flaws. The disc was made from a well-preserved or carefully restored original. The mono sound from the theatrical release somehow sounds more appropriate than the stereo remix. —*MM*
Movie: 🎬🎬½ *DVD:* 🎬🎬½
HBO Home Video (Cat #90663, UPC #026 359066320). Full frame. Stereo; Mono. $24.98. Snapper. *LANG:* English; French; Italian; Spanish. *SUB:* English; French; Spanish. *CAP:* English. *FEATURES:* 24 chapter links • Trailer • Talent files.
1945 98m/C Danny Kaye, Virginia Mayo, Vera-Ellen, Steve Cochran, S.Z. Sakall, Otto Kruger, Natalie Schafer; *D:* H. Bruce Humberstone; *W:* Jack Jevne, Eddie Moran, Don Hartman, Melville Shavelson, Philip Rapp; *C:* Victor Milner; *M:* Ray Heindorf. *AWARDS: NOM:* Oscars '45: Song ("So in Love"), Sound, Scoring/Musical.

Wonderland

Slice of London life covers four November days in the lives of sisters Debbie (Henderson), Nadia (McKee), and Molly (Parker) and their daily struggles—single parenthood, bad dates, pregnancy, separation, unemployment, and their equally frustrated parents. Even though the subject is finally the ability to survive and not succumb, as conventional entertainment, the story is about as enjoyable as having a boil on your butt. The naturalistic image is purposefully dark and grainy. —*MM*
Movie: 🎬🎬 *DVD:* 🎬🎬
Universal Studios Home Video (Cat #212 55, UPC #025192125522). Widescreen (2.35:1) anamorphic. Dolby Digital 5.1 Surround Stereo. $29.99. Keepcase. *LANG:* English. *SUB:* French. *CAP:* English. *FEATURES:* 18 chapter links • Trailer.
1999 108m/C *GB* Shirley Henderson, Gina McKee, Molly Parker, Ian Hart, John Simm, Stuart Townsend, Kika Markham, Jack Shepherd; *D:* Michael Winterbottom; *W:* Laurence Coriat; *C:* Sean Bobbitt; *M:* Michael Nyman. *AWARDS: NOM:* British Acad. '99: Film.

Wonderwall: The Movie

Owlish professor MacGowran spies frisky Birkin and her photographer boyfriend Quarrier through a hole in his apartment wall and becomes obsessed by the young woman. It's a slightly sexy companion piece to the Beatles' *Magical Mystery Tour* with a groovy soundtrack. Dark, heavily saturated full-frame image is about equal to tape. The short film "Reflections on Love" is presented widescreen. —*MM*
Movie: 🎬🎬 *DVD:* 🎬🎬½
Rhino Home Video (Cat #R2 970045, UPC #603497004522). Full frame. Dolby Digital 5.1 Surround Stereo. $24.98. Keepcase. *LANG:* English. *SUB:* French; Spanish. *FEATURES:* 14 chapter links, *Wonderwall* • 6 chapter links, "Reflections on Love" • John Lennon poem • Eric Clapton soundtrack • Production stills • Outtakes • Trailer.
1969 82m/C *GB* Jack MacGowran, Jane Birkin, Irene Handl; *D:* Joe Massot; *C:* Harry Waxman; *M:* George Harrison, Eric Clapton, Ravi Shankar.

Working Girl

Director Nichols blends love, wit, and the corporate career struggle in this Big Apple romantic comedy in which secretary Griffith is working her way to the top. She's got plenty of ambition to get her there, and the only thing standing in her way is a manipulative, back-stabbing boss played perfectly by Weaver. Griffith gets her chance to shine when Weaver breaks a leg while skiing. She takes over Weaver's office, her apartment, and her wardrobe, then meets investment banker Ford for business that turns to romance. A 1980s Cinderella story that's sexy, funny, and sharply written and directed. Nice work by Ford, but this is definitely Griffith's movie. The new anamorphic video transfer beats any previous home release of the film in any format, and the 2.0 sound mix is true to the original. Run-of-the-mill extras (two trailers and three TV spots) are better than nothing. —*MB*
Movie: 🎬🎬🎬 *DVD:* 🎬🎬🎬
20th Century Fox Home Entertainment (Cat #2001365, UPC #024543013655). Widescreen (1.85:1) anamorphic. Dolby Digital Surround. $24.99. Keepcase. *LANG:* English; French. *SUB:* English; Spanish. *FEATURES:* 20 chapter links • Theatrical trailers • TV spots.
1988 (R) 115m/C Melanie Griffith, Harrison Ford, Sigourney Weaver, Joan Cusack, Alec Baldwin, Philip Bosco, Ricki Lake, Nora Dunn, Olympia Dukakis, Oliver Platt, James Lally, Kevin Spacey, Robert Easton; *D:* Mike Nichols; *W:* Kevin Wade; *C:* Michael Ballhaus; *M:* Carly Simon, Rob Mounsey. *AWARDS:* Oscars '88: Song ("Let the River Run"); Golden Globes '89: Actress—Mus./Comedy (Griffith), Film—Mus./Comedy, Song ("Let the River Run"), Support. Actress (Weaver); *NOM:* Oscars '88: Actress (Griffith), Director (Nichols), Picture, Support. Actress (Cusack, Weaver).

Working Girls

Independent feminist filmmaker Borden takes a realistic look at prostitution. The sex is candid and perfunctory. The fact-based fiction centers on Molly (Goodwin), a Yale graduate and lesbian who has not told her live-in partner what she does. The rest of the film follows her and her fellow workers during a typical day. Given the film's low-budget roots, it's no surprise that the image is nothing special. The main value of the DVD is the commentary track where Borden, director of photography Julie Irola, and Goodwin talk about the characters and the problems faced by independents. —*MM*
Movie: 🎬🎬 *DVD:* 🎬🎬½
Anchor Bay (Cat #DV11392, UPC #013131 139297). Widescreen (1.66:1) anamorphic. Dolby Digital Mono. $24.99. Keepcase. *LANG:* English. *FEATURES:* 26 chapter links • Trailer • Commentary: Borden, cinematographer Julie Irola, Goodwin.
1987 93m/C Amanda Goodwin, Louise Smith, Ellen McElduff, Maurisia Zach, Janne Peters, Helen Nicholas; *D:* Lizzie Borden; *W:* Sandra Kay, Lizzie Borden; *C:* Judy Irola; *M:* David Van Tiegham.

The World Is Not Enough [SE]

In the 19th James Bond adventure, 007 (Brosnan) is sent to protect Elektra King (Marceau), daughter of a murdered oil tycoon. The threat appears to come from terrorist Renard (Carlyle), who is playing the nuclear explosion card. But Bond has science babe Dr. Christmas Jones (Richards) on his side! The stunts and effects are all that fans of the series expect, and so are the numerous extras. If the disc contains any visual or auditory flaws, I missed them, but I must admit that it's difficult to maintain complete concentration on such airy eye candy. —*MM*
Movie: 🎬🎬🎬 *DVD:* 🎬🎬🎬
MGM Home Entertainment (Cat #908130, UPC #027616813022). Widescreen (2.35:1) anamorphic. Dolby Digital 5.1 Surround Stereo. $34.98. Keepcase. *LANG:* English. *SUB:* French; Spanish. *FEATURES:* 32 chapter links • Booklet • 2 commentary tracks • "Making of" documentary • Music video • Trailer • "Secrets of 007" video options.
1999 (PG-13) 125m/C Pierce Brosnan, Sophie Marceau, Denise Richards, Robert Carlyle, Judi Dench, John Cleese, Desmond Llewelyn, Robbie Coltrane, Samantha Bond, Michael Kitchen, Colin Salmon, Maria Grazia Cucinotta, David Calder, Serena Scott Thomas, Ulrich Thomsen, Goldie; *D:* Michael Apted; *W:* Neal Purvis, Robert Wade, Bruce Feirstein; *C:* Adrian Biddle; *M:* David Arnold. *AWARDS:* Golden Raspberries '99: Worst Support. Actress (Richards).

World War II

Seven of the ten programs on these discs are the "Why We Fight" documentaries produced by the War Department during World War II. The propaganda films were made by Frank Capra and were shown to servicemen and women before they went overseas. The filmmakers combine newsreel footage with animation from the Disney studios and "re-creations" to present

a strong case for American involvement in conflicts half a world away. These were the first films to establish the popularity of such fact-based series as *Victory at Sea* and *The World at War*. Though the images are harsh and grainy, these DVDs are a definite step up from older VHS tapes. The extras include brief clips from Leni Riefenstal's *Triumph of the Will,* and concentration camp footage. Sound is acceptable. Vol. 1 (cat. #DVD9-9000-1, UPC 056775000295): "Prelude to War" and "The Nazis Strike." Vol. 2 (cat. # DVD-9-9000-2, UPC 056775000394): "Divide and Conquer" and "The Battle of Britain." Vol. 3 (cat. #DVD-9-9000-3, UPC 056775000493): "The Battle of Russia" and "The Battle of China." Vol. 4 (cat. #DVD-9-9000-4, UPC 056775000592): "War Comes to America" and "D-Day, the Normandy Invasion." Vol. 5 (cat. #DVD-9-9000-5, UPC 056775000691): "The World at War" and "Appointment in Tokyo." Each volume is $11.98 and approximately one hour long. —*MM* **AKA:** Why We Fight.
Movie: 🎬🎬🎬 *DVD:* 🎬🎬½
Madacy Entertainment (Cat #DVD9-9000-n, UPC #056775000nnn). Full frame. Dolby Digital Mono. $11.98. Keepcase. *LANG:* English. *FEATURES:* 8 chapter links • Thumbnail historical bios • Propaganda posters.
1942 300m/B D: Frank Capra.

The Wounds

Srdjan Dragojevic's mad black comedy is set within the upheaval in Bosnia. Think a political *Trainspotting*. It begins in 1996 where our narrator Pinki (Pekic) and his friend Kraut (Maric) compare their recent gunshot wounds. Flash back to 1991 to learn how they came to be so casually violent. Their story is grim, horrifying, and indescribably funny in very strange ways. It's not to all tastes, but viewers who appreciate Emir Kusturica's *Underground* will recognize the moral terrain immediately. The full-frame DVD image is exceptionally sharp, capturing a wide range of visuals styles from black and white to sepia to full color. Sound is fine, too, and the colloquial subtitles are well placed and easy to read. —*MM* **AKA:** Rane.
Movie: 🎬🎬🎬½ *DVD:* 🎬🎬🎬
First Run Features (Cat #FRF909464D, UPC #720229909464). Full frame. $29.95. Keepcase. *LANG:* Serbo-Croatian. *SUB:* English. *FEATURES:* 9 chapter links.
1998 103m/C Dragan Bjelogric, Dusan Pekic, Milan Maric, Branka Katic; **D:** Srdjan Dragojevic; **W:** Srdjan Dragojevic; **C:** Dusan Joksimovic; **M:** Aleksandar Habic.

Woyzeck

Klaus Kinski is at his manic, wild-eyed best in this chilling portrayal of a man's plunge into insanity. Woyzeck is harassed by his superiors, subjected to sadistic scientific experiments, and cuckolded by his wife (Mattes). The story is based on the oft-filmed Georg Buchner play. The DVD presents an excellent image of a very well-

made production. There's virtually no wear so the film looks as good as or better than contemporaneous Hollywood studio fare. —*MM*
Movie: 🎬🎬🎬 *DVD:* 🎬🎬½
Anchor Bay (Cat #DV11120, UPC #013131 112092). Widescreen (1.66:1) anamorphic. Dolby Digital Mono. $24.99. Keepcase. *LANG:* German. *SUB:* English. *FEATURES:* 23 chapter links • Talent files • Trailer.
1978 82m/C *GE* Klaus Kinski, Eva Mattes, Wolfgang Reichmann, Josef Bierbichler; **D:** Werner Herzog; **W:** Werner Herzog; **C:** Jorge Schmidt-Reitwein.

The X-Files: Season One [CE]

This "Collector's Edition" contains all 24 episodes from the show's inaugural 1993–1994 season, spread out over six discs. The seventh disc contains several bonus features. The episodes are each presented full-frame, as they were shot for television. For the most part, the picture is very clear on each disc, with some inconsistencies based on the location being shot (the stock footage shots of D.C. are somewhat grainier than the rest of the show). The special features are a dream come true for the *X-Files* completist. Included are two scenes deleted from the pilot featuring Agent Scully's boyfriend. —*ML/MM*
Movie: 🎬🎬🎬 *DVD:* 🎬🎬🎬
20th Century Fox Home Entertainment (Cat #2000042). Full frame. Dolby Digital Stereo. $149.95. Keepcase. *LANG:* English; French. *FEATURES:* Documentary • Cast and crew interviews • TV spots • Deleted scenes.
2000 1248m/C David Duchovny, Gillian Anderson.

The X-Files: Season Two

This handsome box-set is almost identical in appearance and special features as the first *X-Files* compilation set. The collection should please any fan who was happy with the first. Quality ranges widely among the 25 episodes spread over seven discs. The stand-out episodes in this collection include: "Humbug," featuring the Jim Rose Sideshow and Agent Scully eating a bug; "3," an interesting vampire story; "Die Hand Die Verletzt," a very creepy episode with a nice surprise ending; and, of course, "The Host," featuring Flukeman! The images are all broadcast quality or better, as the digital transfer has left us with a picture that is very crisp and clear. Keep in mind that this was a period when the show hadn't achieved "big-budget" status, so some of the episodes exhibit some grain. And despite that fact that the series has a dark look anyway, some of the episodes on the DVD set look a bit too dark. Still, this is the best that these shows are ever going to look, and that makes this set even more appealing. —*ML*
Movie: 🎬🎬½ *DVD:* 🎬🎬½

20th Century Fox Home Entertainment (Cat #2000503). Full frame. Dolby Digital Surround Stereo. $149.98. Keepcase. *LANG:* English; French. *SUB:* English; French; Spanish. *FEATURES:* Deleted scenes • 15-minute documentary • Promo spots • Behind-the-scenes interviews • 3 deleted scenes.
2000 1104m/C Gillian Anderson, David Duchovny.

X-Men

The Marvel Comics characters who were born with genetic mutations that give them superpowers make an impressive and unexpectedly thoughtful translation to the screen. Charles Xavier (Stewart) runs a school to help mutant teens learn to use their powers. He fights against "The Brotherhood," led by Magneto (McKellen). The two older stars have no trouble stealing the film from the special effects and a capable supporting cast that includes Jackman as Wolverine, Paquin as Rogue, and Janssen as Dr. Jean Grey. The DVD does a fine job with the icy blue color scheme that director Singer creates. The main addition to the disc are deleted and extended scenes that can be viewed separately or incorporated into the theatrical version. Be warned, though, using that option will cause pauses as the laser searches for the extra material, and the deleted material is rough-looking. Compared to the theatrical release, the 5.1 Surround mix is more subtle and effective, even on a modest home theatre system. —*MM*
Movie: 🎬🎬🎬 *DVD:* 🎬🎬🎬
20th Century Fox Home Entertainment (Cat #2000640, UPC #024543006404). Widescreen (2.35:1) anamorphic. Dolby Digital 5.1 Surround Stereo; Dolby Digital Surround Stereo. $19.95. Boxed slipcase. *LANG:* English; French. *SUB:* English; Spanish. *FEATURES:* 28 chapter links • 6 deleted or extended scenes • Bryan Singer interview • Hugh Jackman screen test • Stills gallery • Theatrical trailers and TV spots • 2 computer animated storyboard scenes • Special featurette.
2000 (PG-13) 104m/C Patrick Stewart, Ian McKellen, Famke Janssen, Hugh Jackman, James Marsden, Halle Berry, Rebecca Romijn-Stamos, Ray Park, Tyler Mane, Anna Paquin, Bruce Davison, Shawn Ashmore; **D:** Bryan Singer; **W:** David Hayter; **C:** Newton Thomas (Tom) Sigel; **M:** Michael Kamen.

X-Men: The Phoenix Saga

The Marvel Comic superheroes make their DVD debut through Universal Home Video's release of a six-episode animated serial. Trying to save the entire galaxy from destruction through the evil emperor D'Ken, the X-Men face a tough challenge that seems too much even for them to handle. Produced as part of the "Fox Kids" television programming, the story is well told, but the animation remains crude for the most part and without notable highlights. The image transfer seems to come from a low-resolution master, which introduces a great number of noticeable NTSC artifacts in the picture. Shimmering and aliasing are visible, and serious color bleeding causes the image to lose detail and creates blurry details. Red tones are particularly affected to the point that the character of Red Eric is sometimes indistinguishably blurry and featureless. Audio is well-produced but without mentionable highlights or problems. —GH/MM

Movie: 𝄞𝄞½ **DVD:** 𝄞
Universal Studios Home Video (Cat #21119). Full frame. Dolby Digital Stereo. $26.98. Keepcase. *LANG:* English; French. *SUB:* English.
1992 120m/C

X: The Man with X-Ray Eyes

Dr. Xavier's (Milland) experiments concerning human sight are more successful than anyone could have guessed. He develops a serum that allows people to see through solid objects (and clothes!) and tests it on himself. This is first-rate Corman material, and he sounds suitably proud of it on his commentary track. Of the other extras, the "rare prologue" combines windy narration with stock footage and is easily skipped. Overall, image and sound are amazing for a movie that cost $300,000 in 1963. —MM *AKA:* The Man with the X-Ray Eyes; X.
Movie: 𝄞𝄞𝄞 **DVD:** 𝄞𝄞½
MGM Home Entertainment (Cat #1002023, UPC #027616862648). Widescreen (1.85:1) anamorphic. Dolby Digital Mono. $14.98. Keepcase. *LANG:* English. *SUB:* French; Spanish. *CAP:* English. *FEATURES:* 16 chapter links • Prologue • Commentary: Roger Corman • Trailer.
1963 79m/C Ray Milland, Diana Van Der Vlis, Harold J. Stone, John Hoyt, Don Rickles, Dick Miller, Jonathan Haze, Morris Ankrum, Barboura Morris; **D:** Roger Corman; **W:** Ray Russell, Robert Dillon; **C:** Floyd Crosby; **M:** Les Baxter.

X The Unknown

Geologist Adam Royston (Jagger) is sent to investigate a radioactive spot where a mysterious and deadly fissure has appeared. Seems a mud monster that feeds on radiation bursts out of the earth every 50 years or so and kills. Now it's expanding its territory. Anchor Bay's DVD includes the basic high-quality accoutrements: excellent transfer, handsome animated menus (the flying red "X" is very nice!), and a trailer. —MM/GE
Movie: 𝄞𝄞½ **DVD:** 𝄞𝄞𝄞
Anchor Bay (Cat #11074). Full frame. Dolby Digital Mono. $29.98. Keepcase. *LANG:* English. *FEATURES:* "World of Hammer" documentary • Trailer.
1956 78m/B Dean Jagger, Leo McKern, Edward Chapman, John Harvey, William Lucas, Anthony Newley; **D:** Leslie Norman; **W:** Jimmy Sangster; **C:** Gerald Gibbs; **M:** James Bernard.

Xchange

In the near future, bio-technology advances allow people to transfer their minds into the bodies of others. The process called "floating" lets anyone "travel" by having his or her consciousness transmitted anywhere in the world. When anti-corporate terrorists assassinate a powerful CEO, Baldwin is called in to investigate the murder. He is transported to San Francisco, where he ends up occupying the body of the lead terrorist (MacLachlan). Then he must fight to reclaim his body. The concept is more than compelling, and the action sequences generally overcome the relative low budget of the production. This is way smarter than your typical straight-to-video fare. If this had been a major release, it probably would have gotten more tender loving care for its DVD release. Although the menus are nicely designed, black levels in the film are poor. So-so video transfer suffers from excessive grain in the darkest parts of scenes. Some shots look washed-out, while others are just fine, so the quality is uneven. The letterboxed image is not anamorphic, thus the picture will fall short on widescreen displays. There is only a two-channel Surround track, which actually doesn't sound that bad, but the action sequences (guns shots, explosions, etc.) would have benefitted from a 5.1 soundtrack. Extras? You get a trailer. —MB *AKA:* X Change.
Movie: 𝄞𝄞𝄞 **DVD:** 𝄞𝄞
Trimark Home Video (Cat #VM7632D, UPC #031398763222). Widescreen (1.85:1) letterboxed. Dolby Digital Stereo. $24.99. Keepcase. *LANG:* English. *SUB:* English; Spanish; French. *CAP:* English. *FEATURES:* 24 chapter links.
2000 (R) 110m/C CA Stephen Baldwin, Kyle MacLachlan, Kim Coates; **D:** Allan Moyle.

The Yards

Just out of the joint, Leo Handler (Wahlberg) heads home to an ailing mother (Burstyn) and, he hopes, a job with his uncle Frank (Caan) who deals with the New York subway yards. His old friend Willie (Phoenix) is working for Frank and seems to have money to burn. What follows is a carefully written, tough thriller that does all the right things. Wahlberg's restrained performance never strikes a false note. DVD is an accurate reproduction of a deliberately unspectacular image and muted color scheme. On his commentary track, director Gray admits that he likes slow movies. He's interested in characters, not splashy effects. Somehow, the film was unable to find a large audience in limited theatrical release. It's one of the best sleepers in your video store. —MM
Movie: 𝄞𝄞𝄞½ **DVD:** 𝄞𝄞𝄞½
Miramax Pictures Home Video (Cat #18276, UPC #717951004666). Widescreen (2.35:1) anamorphic. Dolby Digital 5.1 Surround Stereo; Dolby Digital Surround. $24.99. Keepcase. *LANG:* English. *SUB:* Spanish. *FEATURES:* 22 chapter links • Commentary: director James Gray • Con-

cept art • Trailers • Behind-the-scenes featurette.
2000 (R) 115m/C Mark Wahlberg, James Caan, Charlize Theron, Joaquin Rafael (Leaf) Phoenix, Ellen Burstyn, Faye Dunaway, Tony Musante, Steve Lawrence, Victor Argo, Tomas Milian, Victor Arnold, Chad Aaron, Andrew Davoli, Robert Montano; **D:** James Gray; **W:** James Gray, Matt Reeves; **C:** Harris Savides; **M:** Howard Shore. *AWARDS:* Natl. Bd. of Review '00: Support. Actor (Phoenix).

Year of the Horse

Jarmusch is so faithful to the letter and spirit of his subject than any but the most devoted fans of Neil Young and the Crazy Horse band will likely lose patience with this documentary. Looking as gritty as some of the band's riffs, the film intercuts footage from performances in '76, '86, and the '96 European and U.S. tours shot on Super-8, High Fi-8 video, and 16 mm. film. Jarmusch lets each song run full-length with complete performances intact. Since the image is so deliberately unsophisticated and unpolished, the disc's value is in the audio mix. It's loud and accurate; and again for those who don't care for this kind of rock, that's a mixed blessing. Count me among the uninitiated. —MM
Movie: 𝄞𝄞 **DVD:** 𝄞𝄞
USA Home Entertainment (Cat #96306 0144-2, UPC #696306014423). Widescreen (1.77:1) letterboxed. Dolby Digital 5.1 Surround Stereo; DTS 5.1 Surround; Dolby Digital Stereo. $24.95. Keepcase. *LANG:* English. *FEATURES:* 18 chapter links • 48 minutes of outtakes • DVD-ROM connection to website.
1997 (R) 107m/C D: Jim Jarmusch.

Yellow

On the eve of their high school graduation, seven kids agree to help their friend Sin (Soon-Teck Oh) to recover the money that he lost. (It belongs to his disapproving dad.) The film is a bit too slow and talky to be another *American Graffiti* but it is a superb effort from writer/director Chris Chan Lee. He treats the young characters seriously and he got fine performances from his cast. Even though the film was made on a limited budget, it looks very good on DVD. Sound is fine, too. —MM
Movie: 𝄞𝄞𝄞 **DVD:** 𝄞𝄞½
Vanguard International Cinema, Inc. (Cat #1-892649-78-0, UPC #658769008234). Widescreen (1.66:1) letterboxed. $29.95. Keepcase. *LANG:* English. *FEATURES:* 12 chapter links.
1998 90m/C Soon-Teck Oh, Amy Hill, Michael Chung, Burt Bulos, Angie Suh, Mia Suh, Jason J. Tobin, Lela Lee, Mary Chen, John Cho; **D:** Chris Chan Lee; **W:** Chris Chan Lee; **C:** Ted Cohen; **M:** John Oh.

Yi Yi

Edward Yang's family drama is one of the best imports of recent years. NJ Jian

(Nianzhen Wu) is at a crossroads. His wife Min-Min's (Elaine Jin) mother has just had a stroke; his teenaged daughter Ting-Ting (Kelly Lee) is becoming more curious about sex, and his young son Yang-Yang (Jonathan Chang) is constantly picked on by his older female cousins. If that weren't enough, NJ's business is facing a crisis and he has run into an old sweetheart. Though the setting is Taipei, the characters and their conflicts are fully understandable. The details of family life and such shared experiences as weddings, infidelity, hospitals, and old flames are universal. The film has a depth of feeling and understanding that is notably lacking in similar American work these days. DVD looks fine, but striking visuals are not important. This is a long (nearly three hours) meditative work. Save Yang's commentary for a second viewing. Large bright burned-in yellow subs are easy to read. Music is only slightly overstated in a few moments. Overall, it's excellent. This one comes with strongest recommendations. —MM **AKA:** A One and a Two.
Movie: 🐾🐾🐾 **DVD:** 🐾🐾🐾½
Winstar Home Entertainment (Cat #LFV5273, UPC #720917527321). Widescreen anamorphic. $24.98. Keepcase. LANG: Mandarin. SUB: English. FEATURES: 24 chapter links ▪ Filmographies ▪ Trailer ▪ Commentary: Edward Yang ▪ Weblink to Yang interview.
2000 173m/C JP TW Elaine Jin, Nianzhen Wu, Kelly Lee, Jonathan Chang, Issey Ogata, Suyun Ke; **D:** Edward Yang; **W:** Edward Yang; **C:** Weihan Yang; **M:** Kai-li Peng. AWARDS: Cannes '00: Director (Yang); L.A. Film Critics '00: Foreign Film; N.Y. Film Critics '00: Foreign Film; Natl. Soc. Film Critics '00: Film.

You Can't Do That: The Making of "A Hard Day's Night"
Please see review of Beatles: The Ultimate DVD Collection.
1994 65m/C

You Only Live Twice [SE]
007 travels to Japan to take on arch-nemesis Blofeld (Pleasence), who has been capturing Russian and American spacecraft in an attempt to start World War III. Roald Dahl's plot does tend toward the wild-and-wooly, but in light of more recent excesses in the series, that is hardly a problem. MGM has done its usual bang-up job on the DVD. Image and sound are flawless. The commentary track, like the others in the series, is thoughtfully produced and lacking in spontaneity. —MM
Movie: 🐾🐾🐾½ **DVD:** 🐾🐾🐾½
MGM Home Entertainment (Cat #1001097, UPC #027616853974). Widescreen anamorphic. Dolby Digital Mono. $26.98. Keepcase. LANG: English; Spanish. SUB: French; Spanish. CAP: English. FEATURES: 32 chapter links ▪ 3 trailers ▪ 3 radio spots ▪ TV

spot ▪ "Inside 'You Only Live Twice'" featurette ▪ "Silhouettes—The James Bond Titles" featurette ▪ Animated storyboard sequence ▪ "Making of" booklet ▪ Commentary: director Lewis Gilbert, cast, crew.
1967 (PG) 125m/C GB Sean Connery, Mie Hama, Akiko Wakabayashi, Tetsuro Tamba, Karin Dor, Charles Gray, Donald Pleasence, Tsai Chin, Bernard Lee, Lois Maxwell, Desmond Llewelyn; **D:** Lewis Gilbert; **W:** Roald Dahl; **C:** Frederick A. (Freddie) Young; **M:** John Barry.

You So Crazy
Martin Lawrence's stand-up comedy film, once threatened with an "NC-17" rating, is certainly not titillating or "obscene" by most definitions of the word. He does discuss sexual practices and bodily functions in graphic detail that will embarrass some viewers. His constant use of common profanity is unimaginative. In the end, there's not much to this one. He brings no insights to his subjects. DVD image is equal to tape. Surround effects are negligible. —MM **AKA:** Martin Lawrence You So Crazy.
Movie: 🐾 **DVD:** 🐾🐾
HBO Home Video (Cat #91142, UPC #026359114229). Full frame. Dolby Digital Surround Stereo. $19.98. Snapper. LANG: English. FEATURES: 12 chapter links ▪ Martin Lawrence thumbnail bio ▪ Trailer.
1994 85m/C Martin Lawrence; **D:** Thomas Schlamme; **W:** Martin Lawrence; **C:** Arthur Albert.

Youngblood
Skating phenom Dean Youngblood (Lowe) is ready to take the hockey world by storm, but he must learn a valuable lesson first. Completely predictable sports drama does boast a few good scenes on the ice. There's nothing particularly special about either image or sound on DVD. —MM
Movie: 🐾🐾 **DVD:** 🐾🐾
MGM Home Entertainment (Cat #1001854, UPC #027616861221). Widescreen (1.85:1) letterboxed. Dolby Digital Surround; Mono. $14.98. Keepcase. LANG: English; French; Spanish. SUB: French; Spanish. CAP: English. FEATURES: 16 chapter links ▪ Trailer.
1986 (R) 111m/C Rob Lowe, Patrick Swayze, Cynthia Gibb, Ed Lauter, George Finn, Fionnula Flanagan, Keanu Reeves; **D:** Peter Markle.

Yours, Mine & Ours
Here's the story of a lovely lady. Whoops; wrong bunch. Mike and Carol Brady have nothing on Helen North, a widow with eight children, and Frank Beardsley, a widower with 10. Based on the true story that inspired Helen's 1964 best-seller Who Gets the Drumsticks?, this somewhat dated family film chronicles this overwhelmed couple's chaotic courtship and marriage, and their wildly extended brood's efforts to coexist as a family. Lucille Ball and Henry Fonda (who costarred in the 1942 drama The Big Street)

share an effortless screen chemistry. Lucy, for the most part, plays it straight, but has one vintage drunk scene in which she is an unwitting victim of an "alcoholic Pearl Harbor" at the hands of Frank's kids. Considering the size of the Beardsley family, the full-frame pan-and-scan presentation is a disappointment. The source print is relatively clean, save for scratches and speckling at the reel changes. The colors are good, but have lost some of their luster. Tim Matheson, as Frank's eldest, later graduated to National Lampoon's Animal House. Other now-familiar faces include a very young Tracy Nelson and Morgan Brittany (billed here as Suzanne Cupito). —DL
Movie: 🐾🐾🐾 **DVD:** 🐾🐾🐾
MGM Home Entertainment (Cat #1001606, UPC #2761685916). Full frame. Dolby Digital Mono. $19.98. Keepcase. LANG: English; French; Spanish. SUB: French; Spanish. CAP: English. FEATURES: Original theatrical trailer ▪ 16 chapter links.
1968 114m/C Lucille Ball, Henry Fonda, Van Johnson, Tim Matheson, Tom Bosley, Tracy Nelson, Morgan Brittany; **D:** Melville Shavelson; **W:** Melville Shavelson; **C:** Charles F. Wheeler; **M:** Fred Karlin.

Zardoz
On his commentary track, director John Boorman does a good job of explaining what he was up to in this problematic sci-fi parable. In the future of 2293, society has been divided into strict classes: intellectuals, savages, and killers who keep order. Connery, in a ridiculous red diaper, is the man who tries to find out what is behind the false god Zardoz. (The title, Boorman says, comes from The Wizard of Oz.) His comments are genuinely instructive, and anyone who's interested in his career as a filmmaker (and who, like me, remembers this film only from a long-ago late-night viewing) ought to watch it with his commentary and the subtitles. That way you can see and understand what's happening on-screen and listen to him explain what he was trying to do. Image is fine, but the extras are more important on this one. —MM
Movie: 🐾🐾🐾 **DVD:** 🐾🐾🐾
20th Century Fox Home Entertainment (Cat #2001305, UPC #024543013051). Widescreen (2.35:1) anamorphic. Dolby Digital 3.0 Surround Stereo; Dolby Digital Mono. $24.98. Keepcase. LANG: English; French. SUB: English; Spanish. FEATURES: 24 chapter links ▪ Trailer ▪ Radio spots ▪ Commentary: Boorman ▪ Stills gallery.
1973 105m/C GB Sean Connery, Charlotte Rampling, John Alderton, Sara Kestelman, Sally Anne Newton, Niall Buggy, Christopher Casson, Bosco Hogan, Jessica Swift; **D:** John Boorman; **W:** John Boorman; **C:** Geoffrey Unsworth; **M:** David Munrow.

Zombie Lake
A skinny-dipping babe takes a swim in a pond and jump-starts underwater Nazi vampire zombies. If, however, you'd prefer to see the same young lady swimming in a

suit, that option is available on the disc. So is the scene of the girl's basketball team that stops by later. It all goes back to World War II, but nobody should be too involved in the plot of this low-budget exploitation quickie. Jean Rollin directed (under the name J.A. Lazer) after replacing Jesus Franco. As is so often the case with Image's Euroshock Collection, the DVD appears to have been made from an absolutely pristine original. The film looks terrific. Sound is fine. —*MM* **AKA:** El Lago de los Muertos Vivientes; The Lake of the Living Dead.

Movie: *♫* **DVD:** *♫♫♫*
Image Entertainment (Cat #ID9111BIDVD, UPC #014381911121). Widescreen (1.66: 1) anamorphic. Dolby Digital Mono.

$24.99. Snapper. *LANG:* English; French. *FEATURES:* 12 chapter links ● Alternate "clothed" sequences ● Trailer ● English language title sequence.
1980 90m/C *FR SP* Howard Vernon, Pierre Escourrou, Anouchka, Anthony Mayans, Nadine Pascale, Jean Rollin; ***D:*** J.A. Laser, Jean Rollin; ***W:*** A. L. Mariaux, Julian Esteban.

Zu: Warriors of the Magic Mountain

The forces of evil are plotting to take over medieval China and a warrior endures the perils of the Zu Mountains to find the Twin Swords, the only weapons that can defeat

the demons. Scratches, flecks, and fine vertical lines are visible. Overall, the image is not as bright or sharp as similar American fantasy adventures. It is on a par with other Hong Kong imports. Surround sound is very good. —*MM*

Movie: *♫♫* **DVD:** *♫♫½*
Tai Seng Video Marketing (Cat #25254). Widescreen letterboxed. Dolby Digital 5.1 Surround Stereo. $49.95. Keepcase. *LANG:* Cantonese; Mandarin. *SUB:* Bahasa Ind. & Mal.; Cantonese; English; Japanese; Korean; Mandarin; Thai; Vietnamese. *FEATURES:* 8 chapter links ● Talent files ● Trailers.
1983 98m/C *HK* Adam Cheng, Yuen Biao, Brigitte (Lin Chinag-hsia) Lin, Sammo Hung; ***D:*** Tsui Hark.

"DVD Connections" offers lists of DVD-related magazines and newsletters, books, websites (including retail and rental sources), and newsgroups to help you keep abreast of this fast-paced new technology.

Magazines/Newsletters

DVD—Laser Disc Newsletter
Laser Disc Newsletter
PO Box 420
East Rockaway, NY 11518
800-551-4914
(516)594-9307 (fax)
www.dvdlaser.com

Monthly. $35/year; $62.50/2 years in North America ($50/year; $95/2 years outside North America).

Inside DVD
Versatile Media One, Inc.
2400 N. Lincoln Ave.
Altadena, CA 91001
(626)296-6361 (fax)
insidedvd@insidevd.com

Bimonthly. $29.95/year in U.S. (Published in DVD format.)

Laser Disc Gazette
Rad Bennett
Rd. 2, Box 654
Harpers Ferry, WV 25425
(304)725-0525
(304)725-0525 (fax)

Bimonthly. $19.95/year in U.S.; $19.95 elsewhere.

Schwann DVD Advance
Schwann Publications
1280 Santa Anita Ct.
Woodland, CA 95776
1-800-792-9447
www.schwann.com

Bimonthly. $29.95/year in U.S.; $7.95/issue.

Widescreen Review
27576 Commerce Center Dr., Ste. 105
Temecula, CA 92590
(909)676-4914
(909)693-2960 (fax)
www.widescreenreview.com

Ten issues/year. $34/year in U.S. ($40/year in Canada and Mexico; $75/year elsewhere).

Websites

Ace VCD DVD
www.acevcddvd.com

Sells Asian and Japanese movies, music, adult, and animation.

Active Buyer's Guide: DVDs
www.dvdplayers.activebuyersguide.com

Consumer guide to purchasing DVD players.

Active DVD
www.activewin.com/dvd

DVD news, tips, reviews, and other related articles.

All DVD Links
www.alldvdlinks.com

DVD reviews, articles, and links.

All Star DVD
www.alldvdmovies.com

Mail-order distributor of video movies, CD-ROMS, laserdiscs, and books.

Animania
www.animania-ent.com

Mail-order anime and manga.

Anime Castle
www.animecastle.com

DVD retail.

Anime on DVD
www.animeondvd.com

Anime articles and reviews.

Apollo Movie Guide
www.apolloguide.com/dvd.htm

Includes reviews of DVDs.

Asian DVD Guide
www.asiandvdguide.com

Guide to DVD movies from Hong Kong, Japan, and Korea.

AsianXpress
www.asianxpress.net

Hong Kong DVD retailer.

Askew Reviews
www.askewreviews.com

Movie, DVD, and music reviews.

Bargain Central
www.bargain-central.com

Provides links to DVD-specific purchases.

BargainFlix
www.bargainflix.com

Source for DVD bargains and coupons on the Internet.

Bay Distributors
www.baydistribution.com

DVD retail.

BestDVD
www.bestdvd.co.uk

Region 1 and 2 DVD news and reviews.

Big Picture DVD Review Page
www.thebigpicturedvd.com/bigpicmain.shtml

DVD reviews and discussion, with emphasis on high-resolution display.

BigStar
www.bigstar.com

Retail DVD and VHS.

BinaryFlix
www.binaryflix.com

DVD discussion and menu details.

Black DVD Online
www.blackdvdonline.com

News, reviews, and discussion on African American–themed DVDs.

Blackstar
www.blackstar.co.uk

DVD retail for U.K. and international customers.

Blowout Video
www.blowoutvideo.com

Retail DVD and VHS.

BlueDVD.com
www.bluedvd.com

Adult DVD rental by mail.

C & L Internet Club
www.cnl.com

Canadian DVD retailer.

Cafe DVD
www.cafedvd.com

DVD rental.

CD Playwright
www.cdplayright.com

Sells products to protect CDs and DVDs.

Century DVD
www.centurydvd.com

DVD comparison shopping service.

Cinema Classics
www.cinemaclassics.com

DVD retail.

Cinema Laser
www.thecinemalaser.com

Laserdisc and DVD reviews and links.

DC DVD
www.dc-dvd.co.uk

Retails Region 1 DVD in the U.K.

DealCatcher.com
www.dealcatcher.com

Dean's DVD Reviews
members.spree.com/sip/dvddean/

DVD reviews.

DesiFilms.com
www.desifilms.com

Indian DVD rental.

DesiPadam.com
www.desipadam.com

Indian DVD rental.

Digibuster
www.digibuster.com

DVD rental.

Digital Bits, The
www.thedigitalbits.com

DVD reviews and other articles.

Digital Entertainment, Inc.
www.indianfilmsdvd.com

Indian DVD retail.

Digital Eyes
www.digitaleyes.net

DVD retail.

Digital Ring
www.thedigitalring.com

Movie and DVD news and reviews.

Digital Video Depot
www.dv-depot.com

DVD retail.

Digital Widescreen
www.digitalwidescreen.com

News, reviews, features, information, and links on DVD.

DiscountFlix
www.discountflix.com

DVD comparison shopping service.

DiVerse DVD
www.attrill.com

Price comparison for DVDs.

DVD Amigos
www.dvdamigos.com

DVD-related articles.

DVD Angle
www.dvdangle.com

DVD reviews.

DVD AniMania
www.ij.net/wildcoast/anime/

News and reviews on anime DVD.

The DVD Answer Man
www.dvdanswerman.com

DVD info and reviews.

DVD Arena
www.dvdarena.com

Buys and sells used DVDs.

DVD Authority
www.dvdauthority.com

DVD reviews.

DVD Bargain Update
www.dvdbargainupdate.com

Newsletter for DVD bargain hunters.

DVD Bid
www.dvd-bid.com

DVD auction.

DVD Box Office
www.dvdboxoffice.com

DVD retail.

DVD Buying Guide
www.dvdbuyingguide.com

Offers info on DVD players and related issues.

DVD Cache
www.dvdcache.com

Sells used DVDs, and offers the opportunity for purchaser to sell back after viewing.

DVD Centre
www.dvdcentre.co.uk

New and information about DVD.

DVD Channel News
www.dvdchannelnews.com

DVD reviews and news.

DVD Cinema
www.dvdcinema.com

DVD retail.

DVD Corner Net
www.dvdcorner.net

Weekly e-zine offering DVD news and reviews.

DVD Coupon Post
www.dvdcouponpost.com

Information on DVD bargains.

DVD Cyber Center
www.dvdcc.com

DVD reviews and articles.

DVD Daily
www.dvd-daily.com

DVD magazine.

DVD Demystified
www.dvddemystified.com

DVD information, including an exhaustive DVD FAQ.

DVD Digital Domain
www.dvddigital.com

DVD retail.

DVD Dynamic
www.dvddynamic.com

DVD retail.

DVD Easter Eggs
www.dvdeastereggs.com

Provides info on DVD hidden features.

DVD Empire
www.dvdempire.com

DVD retailer.

DVD ESP
www.dvdesp.com

DVD shopping service.

DVD Essentials
www.dvdessentials.co.uk

Reviews and information on Region 2 DVDs.

DVD Express
www.dvdexpress.com

DVD retailer.

DVD File
www.dvdfile.com

DVD information.

DVD Freak
www.dvdfreak.com

DVD info and reviews.

DVD Journal
www.dvdjournal.com

DVD news, reviews, and commentary.

DVD King
www.dvdking.com

DVD retail.

DVD Mon
www.dvdmon.com

DVD news, reviews, and resources.

DVD Monthly
www.dvdmonthly.com

DVD movie and hardware reviews.

DVD Movie Guide
www.dvdmg.com

DVD releases, reviews, and links.

DVD Now
www.geocities.com/Hollywood/Academy/6586

Consumer-based site for DVD technology information.

DVD Overnight
www.dvdovernight.com

DVD rental.

DVD Palace
www.dvdpalace.com

Adult DVD retail.

DVD pizza.com
www.dvdpizza.com

DVD retail.

DVD Planet
www.dvdplanet.com

DVD retail.

DVD Price Compare
www.dvdpricecompare.com

DVD bargain search service.

DVD Price Search
www.dvdpricesearch.com

Offers DVD price comparisons.

DVD Review
www.dvdreview.com

DVD reviews, news, interviews, links, and chat.

DVD Reviewer
www.dvd.reviewer.co.uk

DVD news, articles, and forums.

DVD Rumble
www.dvdrumble.co.uk

DVD Region 1 and Region 2 comparison reviews.

DVD Spotlight
www.dvdspotlight.net

DVD news and reviews.

DVD Store
www.dvd1.com

DVD retail.

DVD Street
www.dvdstreet.co.uk/

DVD retail.

DVD Superstore
www.dvdsuperstore.com

DVD retail.

DVD Talk
www.dvdtalk.com

DVD news, chats, and reviews.

DVD Time
www.dvdtime.co.uk

DVD news and info.

DVD Times
www.dvdtimes.co.uk

DVD news, reviews, and forums.

DVD TitleWaves
www.dvdtitlewaves.com

DVD retail.

DVD Tracker
www.dvdtracker.com

DVD purchase cataloging service.

DVD Verdict
www.dvdverdict.com

DVD movie and hardware reviews, forums, and news.

DVD Web
www.dvdweb.co.uk

DVD news, reviews, links, and competitions.

dvdfuture.com
www.dvdfuture.com

DVD reviews, features, and forums.

DVDinsider
www.dvdinsider.com

DVD news and reviews.

DVDirect.net
www.dvdirect.net

DVD retail.

DVDLaser.com
www.DVDLaser.com

DVD reviews, info, commentary, links, and news.

DVDLink
www.dvdlink.co.uk

Directory of DVD-related sites.

DVDs 1 2 3
www.dvds123.com

Sells used DVDs.

DVDTOWN.COM
www.dvdtown.com

DVD news and reviews.

Entertainment Warehouse
www.dvd-plus.com

Canadian DVD retail.

Fight DIVX Association
www.fightdivx.com

DVD news and links.

Guide to Current DVD
www.currentfilm.com

DVD reviews and other info.

HorrorDVDs.com
www.horrordvds.com

Horror DVD news, forums, reviews, contests, and links.

IGN DVD
www.dvd.ign.com

Includes DVD news, reviews, interviews, and special features.

Incredible DVD
www.incredibledvd.com

DVD coupons, bargains, and freebies.

Introduction to 16x9 DVDs
www.cybertheater.com/DVD/DiscData/dvd_aspect_ration.html

Explains characteristics of common DVD aspect ratios.

IVidea
www.ividea.com

DVD retail.

Jeff's Used LD/DVD Finder
www.rtr.com/~jeff/

Searches for used laserdisc and DVDs.

Ken Crane's
www.kencranes.com

DVD, laserdiscs, and DTS retail.

Kozmo
www.kozmo.com

DVD rental/retail.

Laser's Edge
www.lasersedge.com

DVD retail.

Laserific
www.laserific.com

DVD rental/retail in Orlando, FL.

LaserQuest
members.home.net/laserquest/

DVD retail.

Lasertown Video Discs, Inc.
www.lasertown.com

DVD and laserdisc retail.

Let's Get Digital
www.letsgetdigital.co.uk/

DVD news, articles, and links.

Lucy's DVDs
www.lucysdvds.com

DVD retail.

Movie Store, The
www.themovie-store.com

DVD retail.

Movietrak.com
www.movietrak.com

DVD rental in the U.K.

MyDVDsource.com
www.mydvdsource.com

New and used DVD retail.

N2Video
www.n2video.com

DVD retail.

Netflix
www.netflix.com

DVD rental.

OpenDVD Group
www.opendvd.org

Comprehensive resource for developers looking to implement DVD technology, and for users to take full advantage of all the technology it has to offer.

Play247
www.play247.com

DVD retail.

Right Stuff International
www.rightstuf.com

Anime DVD retail.

Second Chance DVDs
www.scdvd.com

Buys and sells used DVDs.

Splatterhouse
www.splatterhouse.net

Reviews and other info on horror DVDs.

Starship Industries' Laser & DVD Home Page
www.starlaser.com

DVD and laserdisc retail.

Thomas Video
www.thomasvideo.com

DVD, VHS, and laserdisc retail.

Ultimate DVD Links
www.dvdlink.8m.com

Provides links to retailers, rentals, news and reviews, studios, coupons and deals, and bargain sites.

Ultimate Guide to Anamorphic Widescreen DVD (for Dummies!)
www.thedigitalbits.com/articles/anamorphic

In simple language, explains anamorphic format and its benefits.

Undercover DVD
www.hewittco.com/bstreet/verification.tpl

Sells adult DVDs.

Video Ltd.
www.videoltd.com

DVD retail.

Video Tropic
www.videotropic.com

Guide to coupons, discounts, and promotions for DVDs.

Video Zone
www.video-zone.com

DVD retail.

Widescreen Review Magazine
www.widescreenreview.com

DVD reviews.

Yanman's DVD Reviews
www.yanman.com

DVD reviews and discussion.

Books

Desktop Digital Video Production
Frederic Jones. 1998. Prentice Hall. $49.95 (paperback).

The Dictionary of New Media: The New Digital World of Video, Audio, and Print
James Monaco. 1999. Harbor Electronic Publishing. $39.95; $19.95 (paperback).

Digital Video for Dummies
Martin Doucette. 1999. IDG Books. $24.99 (paperback w/CD-ROM).

Doug Pratt's DVD-Video Guide
Douglas Pratt. 1999. Harbor Electronic Publishing. $49.95; $19.95 (paperback).

The DVD and Digital Video Directory 2001
Bethan Cater, ed. 3rd ed., 2000. Waterlow New Media Information.

DVD Demystified
Jim Taylor. 2nd ed., 2000. McGraw Hill. $49.95 (paperback w/DVD).

DVD Player Fundamentals
John Ross. 2000. Howard W. Sams & Co. $34.95 (paperback).

DVD Production
Phil De Lancie and Mark Ely. 2001. Focal Press. $39.95 (paperback w/CD).

How to Use Digital Video
Dave Johnson. 2000. Howard W. Sams & Co. $29.99 (paperback w/CD-ROM).

A Technical Introduction to Digital Video
Charles A. Poynton. 1996. John Wiley & Sons. $44.99.

The Ultimate Widescreen DVD Movie Guide
2001. *Widescreen Review* magazine. $9.95 (paperback).

Newsgroups

alt.media.dvd.cracked
alt.video.digital-tv
alt.video.divx
alt.video.dvd
alt.video.dvd.complain
alt.video.dvd.friends-of-joe
alt.video.dvd.non-anamorphic
alt.video.dvd.software
alt.video.dvd.tech
alt.video.laserdisc
aus.dvd
rec.video.dvd
rec.video.dvd.advocacy
rec.video.dvd.marketplace
rec.video.dvd.misc.
rec.video.dvd.players
rec.video.dvd.tech
rec.video.dvd.titles
uk.media.dvd

Looking for *Spinal Tap*? You can find this entry in the Ts, because the correct title is *This Is Spinal Tap*. How would you know this? By using this handy-dandy "Alternative Titles Index." Variant and translated titles for the DVDs reviewed in this book are provided below in alphabetical order followed by a cross-reference to the appropriate entry in the main review section. Please remember that English-language initial articles ("a," "an," and "the") are ignored in the sort, but non-English initial articles (such as "la" or "el" or "das") are NOT ignored. Enjoy.

The Defender
See The Bodyguard from Beijing (1994)

Dementia
See Daughter of Horror / Dementia (1955)

The Demon Doctor
See The Awful Dr. Orlof (1962)

Demons of the Swamp
See Attack of the Giant Leeches (1959)

Den Vita Lejoninnan
See The White Lioness (1996)

Der Fluch Der Gruenen Augen
See Cave of the Living Dead (1965)

Der Mude Tod
See Destiny (1921)

Der Schweigende Stern
See First Spaceship on Venus (1960)

Der Wurger kommt auf leisen Socken
See The Mad Butcher (1972)

Detroit Heat
See Detroit 9000 (1973)

The Devil's Bride
See The Devil Rides Out (1968)

The Devil's Own
See The Witches (1966)

The Diabolical Dr. Mabuse
See The Thousand Eyes of Dr. Mabuse (1960)

Dias Contados
See Running out of Time (1994)

Die, Beautiful Marianne
See Die Screaming, Marianne (1973)

Die Marquise Von O
See The Marquise of O (1976)

Die Tausend Augen des Dr. Mabuse
See The Thousand Eyes of Dr. Mabuse (1960)

Die Vierde Man
See The 4th Man (1979)

Die Xue Shuang Xiong
See The Killer (1990)

Die Zwolfte Stunde
See Nosferatu (1922)

Djoflaeyjan
See Devil's Island (1996)

Dr. Phibes
See The Abominable Dr. Phibes (1971)

Domicile Conjugal
See Bed and Board (1970)

Dope Addict
See Reefer Madness (1938)

Doped Youth
See Reefer Madness (1938)

Dracula Contra Frankenstein
See Dracula vs. Frankenstein (1971)

Drawing Blood
See Sergio Lapel's Drawing Blood (1999)

Drunken Master 2
See The Legend of Drunken Master (1994)

Du Rififi Chez les Hommes
See Rififi (1954)

Earth
See Tierra (1995)

The East Side Kids Meet Bela Lugosi
See Ghosts on the Loose (1943)

Ein Echter Hausfrauenfreund
See Inn of 1000 Sins (1975)

Ein Toter Hing im Netz
See Horrors of Spider Island (1959)

El Abuelo
See The Grandfather (1998)

El Callejon de los Milagros
See Midaq Alley (1995)

El Lago de los Muertos Vivientes
See Zombie Lake (1980)

El Marido Perfecto
See The Perfect Husband (1992)

Ella
See Monkey Shines (1988)

Elles
See Women (1997)

Encounters of the Spooky Kind
See Spooky Encounters (1980)

Enemy from Space
See Quatermass 2 (1957)

Enemy of My Enemy
See Diplomatic Siege (1999)

The Enforcer
See Jet Li's The Enforcer (1995)

Erotikill
See Female Vampire (1973)

Escapade
See Utopia (1951)

Est-Ouest
See East-West (1999)

Everybody's Cheering
See Take Me Out to the Ball Game (1949)

The Evil Eye
See The Girl Who Knew Too Much (1963)

Except for Me and Thee
See Friendly Persuasion (1956)

Expedition Moon
See Rocketship X-M (1950)

Expose
See Footsteps (1998)

Falltime
See Fall Time (1994)

Farewell, Friend
See Honor Among Thieves (1968)

Farinelli Il Castrato
See Farinelli (1994)

Farinelli the Castrato
See Farinelli (1994)

Fashion House of Death
See Blood and Black Lace (1964)

Female
See The Violent Years / Girl Gang (1956)

Femmine Infernali
See Escape from Hell (1989)

The Fiend with the Atomic Brain
See Blood of Ghastly Horror (1972)

The Fiend with the Electronic Brain
See Blood of Ghastly Horror (1972)

50 Violins
See Music of the Heart (1999)

The Final Conflict
See Omen 3: The Final Conflict (1981)

The First Time
See The Fighter (1952)

Flying Aces
See The Flying Deuces / Utopia (1939)

Fong Sai Yuk
See The Legend (1993)

Fong Shi Yu
See The Legend (1993)

Forbrydelsens Element
See The Element of Crime (1984)

Frank Herbert's Dune
See Dune (2000)

Frankenstein Made Woman
See Frankenstein Created Woman (1966)

Frightmare 2
See Frightmare (1974)

Frozen Terror
See Macabre (1980)

Fu Gui Lie Che
See The Millionaire's Express (1986)

Fun Loving
See Quackser Fortune Has a Cousin in the Bronx (1970)

A Gai Waak
See Project A (1983)

Gamblin' Man
See Cockfighter (1974)

The Game of Death
See Robert Louis Stevenson's The Game of Death (1974)

Gangland Boss
See A Better Tomorrow, Part 1 (1986)

Gangster
See Hoodlum (1996)

The Gargon Terror
See Teenagers from Outer Space (1959)

Gei Ba Ba de Xin
See Jet Li's The Enforcer (1995)

Ghosts in the Night
See Ghosts on the Loose (1943)

The Giant Leeches
See Attack of the Giant Leeches (1959)

Girls for Rent
See I Spit on Your Corpse (1974)

Glass Bottle
See Gorgeous (1999)

The Golden Hour
See Pot o' Gold (1941)

Goliathon
See The Mighty Peking Man (1977)

Grave Robbers from Outer Space
See Plan 9 from Outer Space (1956)

Greta the Mad Butcher
See Ilsa, the Wicked Warden (1978)

Greystoke 2: Tarzan and Jane
See Tarzan and the Lost City (1998)

Gritos en la Noche
See The Awful Dr. Orlof (1962)

Hadduta Misriya
See An Egyptian Story (1982)

The Hairy Bird
See All I Wanna Do (1998)

Hana-Bi
See Fireworks (1997)

Hans Christian Andersen's Thumbelina
See Thumbelina (1994)

Happy Gigolo
See Inn of 1000 Sins (1975)

Happy Times
See The Inspector General (1949)

Hard to Die
See Crime Story (1993)

Hardball
See Bounty Hunters 2: Hardball (1997)

The Haunted and the Hunted
See Dementia 13 (1963)

The Head That Wouldn't Die
See The Brain that Wouldn't Die (1963)

Hellfire on Ice, Part 2: Escape from Hell
See Escape from Hell (1989)

Hercules Goes Bananas
See Hercules in New York (1970)

Hercules: The Movie
See Hercules in New York (1970)

Here Lies Love
See The Second Woman (1951)

Highlander 3: The Magician
See Highlander: The Final Dimension (1994)

Highlander 3: The Sorcerer
See Highlander: The Final Dimension (1994)

Hillbillies in a Haunted House
See Hillbillys in a Haunted House (1967)

HMS Defiant
See Damn the Defiant (1962)

The Hollywood Strangler
See Don't Answer the Phone (1980)

Home Is Where the Heart Is
See Where the Heart Is (2000)

Hoods
See Hoodlum (1996)

Horror Planet
See Inseminoid (1980)

Hotaru no Haka
See Grave of the Fireflies (1988)

The Hounds of Zaroff
See The Most Dangerous Game (1932)

House of Crazies
See Asylum (1972)

House of Evil
See The House on Sorority Row (1983)

House of the Dark Stairway
See A Blade in the Dark (1983)

House of Usher
See The Fall of the House of Usher (1960)

Hua Pi Zhi Yinyang Fawang
See Painted Skin (1993)

Huo Shao Dao
See The Prisoner (1990)

I Became a Criminal
See They Made Me a Criminal (1939)

I Hate Your Guts
See The Intruder (1961)

I Soliti Ignoti
See Big Deal on Madonna Street (1958)

I Tre Volti della Paura
See Black Sabbath (1964)

Il Boia Scarlatto
See The Bloody Pit of Horror (1965)

Il Diario di una Cameriera
See Diary of a Chambermaid (1964)

Il Gatto Nero
See The Black Cat (1981)

Il Pleut sur Santiago
See It's Raining on Santiago (1974)

Il Rosso Segmo della Follia
See Hatchet for the Honeymoon (1970)

Ilsa, the Absolute Power
See Ilsa, the Wicked Warden (1978)

Immediate Disaster
See The Stranger from Venus (1954)

Inconvenienced
See Held Up (2000)

An Invited Guest
See Uninvited Guest (1999)

Iskanderija, Kaman oue Kaman
See Alexandria Again and Forever (1990)

It's Hot in Paradise
See Horrors of Spider Island (1959)
Jackie Chan Is the Prisoner
See The Prisoner (1990)
Jackie Chan's Project A
See Project A (1983)
James Dean: Race with Destiny
See James Dean: Live Fast, Die Young (1997)
Jane Austen's Mafia!
See Mafia! (1998)
Jean de Florette 2
See Manon of the Spring (1987)
Jennie
See Portrait of Jennie (1948)
The Jezebels
See Switchblade Sisters (1975)
Jitsuroku Abe Sada
See A Woman Called Sada Abe (1975)
Joko Invoca Dio...e Muori
See Vengeance (1968)
Joshuu Sasori—Dai 41 Sakkyobo
See Female Convict Scorpion—Jailhouse 41 (1972)
July Pork Bellies
See For Pete's Sake (1974)
Jungle Book 2
See Rudyard Kipling's the Second Jungle Book: Mowgli and Baloo (1997)
Jurassic Park 2
See The Lost World: Jurassic Park 2 (1997)
Justice
See Backlash (1999)
Keep the Aspidistra Flying
See A Merry War (1997)
Kriget ar Slut
See La Guerre Est Finie (1966)
Kyoko
See Because of You (1995)
La Casa con la Scala Nel Buio
See A Blade in the Dark (1983)
La Chute de la Maison Usher
See Fall of the House of Usher (1928)
La Citte delle Donne
See City of Women (1981)
La Decima Vittima
See 10th Victim (1965)
La Dixieme Victime
See 10th Victim (1965)
La Fille Seule
See A Single Girl (1996)
La Lengua de las Mariposas
See Butterfly (2000)
La Mariee Etait en Noir
See The Bride Wore Black (1968)
La Nouvelle Eve
See The New Eve (1998)
La Ragazza Che Sapeva Troppo
See The Girl Who Knew Too Much (1963)
La Sindrome di Stendhal
See The Stendhal Syndrome (1995)
La Vida Segun Muriel
See Life According to Muriel (1997)
La Vie de Jesus
See The Life of Jesus (1996)
The Lake of the Living Dead
See Zombie Lake (1980)
The Land of Faraway
See Mio in the Land of Faraway (1987)
L'Argent de Poche
See Small Change (1976)
Lashou Shentan
See Hard-Boiled (1992)
The Last Horror Film
See Fanatic (1982)
Last House on the Left, Part 2
See Bay of Blood (1971); Twitch of the Death Nerve (1971)
Lazarus and the Hurricane
See The Hurricane (1999)
Le Charme Discret de la Bourgeoisie
See The Discreet Charm of the Bourgeoisie (1972)
Le Diner de Cons
See The Dinner Game (1998)
Le Grand Bleu
See The Big Blue (1988)
Le Journal d'une Femme de Chambre
See Diary of a Chambermaid (1964)
Le Sirene du Mississippi
See Mississippi Mermaid (1969)

The Legend of Fong Sai-Yuk
See The Legend (1993)
Lepa Sela, Lepo Gore
See Pretty Village, Pretty Flame (1996)
Les Avaleuses
See Female Vampire (1973)
Les Boys
See The Boys (1997)
Les Felins
See Joy House (1964)
Les Fils de Gascogne
See Son of Gascogne (1995)
Les Fruits de la Passion
See Fruits of Passion: The Story of "O" Continued (1982)
Les Noces de Papier
See A Paper Wedding (1989)
Les Somnambules
See Mon Oncle d'Amerique (1980)
Les Trois Visages de la Peur
See Black Sabbath (1964)
Les Vacances de Monsieur Hulot
See Mr. Hulot's Holiday (1953)
Letter to Daddy
See Jet Li's The Enforcer (1995)
L'Histoire d'Adele H.
See The Story of Adele H. (1975)
L'Homme Qui Aimait les Femmes
See The Man Who Loved Women (1977)
L'Humanite
See Humanity (1999)
Liebesjagd durch 7 Betten
See I Like the Girls Who Do (1973)
The Life and Loves of Beethoven
See Beethoven (1936)
Lighthouse
See Dead of Night (1999)
Lights of Variety
See Variety Lights (1951)
Lila
See Mantis in Lace (1968)
Little Miss Millions
See Home for Christmas (1993)
The Living Dead at Manchester Morgue
See Let Sleeping Corpses Lie (1974)
Lo Strangolatore di Vienna
See The Mad Butcher (1972)
Lolita 2000
See Lolida 2000 (1997)
The Loner
See Ruckus (1981)
Long Time, Nothing New
See No Looking Back (1998)
Lost Women
See Mesa of Lost Women (1952)
Lost Women of Zarpa
See Mesa of Lost Women (1952)
Louis L'Amour's "The Shadow Riders"
See The Shadow Riders (1982)
The Love Cage
See Joy House (1964)
Love Madness
See Reefer Madness (1938)
The Love Maniac
See Blood of Ghastly Horror (1972)
The Loves of Irina
See Female Vampire (1973)
Luci del Varieta
See Variety Lights (1951)
L'Uomo Dalle Due Ombre
See Cold Sweat (1971)
Lysets Hjerte
See Heart of Light (1997)
Ma Vie Sexuelle...Comment Je Me Suis Dispute
See My Sex Life...Or How I Got into an Argument (1996)
Maboroshi no Hikari
See Maborosi (1995)
The Mad Butcher of Vienna
See The Mad Butcher (1972)
Make Them Die Slowly
See Cannibal Ferox (1984)
Malli
See The Terrorist (1998)
Mamba Snakes
See Fair Game (1989)
The Man with the Synthetic Brain
See Blood of Ghastly Horror (1972)
The Man with the X-Ray Eyes
See X: The Man with X-Ray Eyes (1963)

Manon des Sources
See Manon of the Spring (1987)
Marijuana: The Devil's Weed
See Marihuana / Assassin of Youth / Reefer Madness (1936)
Marijuana, Weed with Roots in Hell
See Marihuana / Assassin of Youth / Reefer Madness (1936)
Martin Lawrence You So Crazy
See You So Crazy (1994)
Mat i Syn
See Mother and Son (1997)
M.D.C. Maschera di Cera
See Wax Mask (1997)
Meat Is Meat
See The Mad Butcher (1972)
Meet the Ghosts
See Abbott and Costello Meet Frankenstein (1948)
Mein Liebster Fiend
See My Best Fiend (1999)
Meteor Monster
See Teenage Monster (1957)
MIB
See Men in Black (1997)
Michael Angel
See The Apostate (1998)
Microscopia
See Fantastic Voyage (1966)
Miel et Cendres
See Honey & Ashes (1996)
Mifune's Last Song
See Mifune (1999)
Mifunes Sidste Sang
See Mifune (1999)
Mikhail Baryshnikov's Stories from My Childhood
See Stories from My Childhood (1998)
Mikhail Baryshnikov's Stories from My Childhood, Vol. 3
See Stories from My Childhood, Vol. 3 (1999)
Milczaca Gwiazda
See First Spaceship on Venus (1960)
Mio min Mio
See Mio in the Land of Faraway (1987)
Mirage
See Maborosi (1995)
The Mission of the Yogi
See The Indian Tomb (1921)
Monkey Shines: An Experiment in Fear
See Monkey Shines (1988)
Monsieur Hulot's Holiday
See Mr. Hulot's Holiday (1953)
Monster from Mars
See Robot Monster (1953)
Monster of Terror
See Die, Monster, Die! (1965)
Monsters from the Moon
See Robot Monster (1953)
Mother Riley Meets the Vampire
See My Son, the Vampire (1952)
Mowgli and Baloo: Jungle Book 2
See Rudyard Kipling's the Second Jungle Book: Mowgli and Baloo (1997)
Mujeres al Borde de un Ataque de Nervios
See Women on the Verge of a Nervous Breakdown (1988)
Murder One
See Death Sentence (1974)
Mutter und Sohn
See Mother and Son (1997)
My Father Is a Hero
See Jet Li's The Enforcer (1995)
My Forgotten Man
See Flynn (1996)
My Life in Pink
See Ma Vie en Rose (1997)
My Love Letters
See Love Letters (1983)
My Neighbor's Daughter
See Angel Blue (1997)
My Uncle
See Mon Oncle (1958)
My Uncle, Mr. Hulot
See Mon Oncle (1958)
Mysterious Invader
See The Astounding She-Monster (1958)
Naked Warriors
See The Arena (1973)

Nattens Engel
See Angel of the Night (1998)
Navy Diver
See Men of Honor (2000)
Neco Z Alenky
See Alice (1988)
Ned Blessing: The Story of My Life and Times
See Lone Justice 2 (1993)
Night Is the Phantom
See The Whip and the Body (1963)
Night of the Anubis
See Night of the Living Dead (1968)
Night of the Flesh Eaters
See Night of the Living Dead (1968)
Night of the Vampire
See Cave of the Living Dead (1965)
Night Shadows
See Mutant (1983)
Nightfall
See Isaac Asimov's Nightfall (2000)
Non Si Sevizia un Paperino
See Don't Torture a Duckling (1972)
Nosferatu, A Symphony of Horror
See Nosferatu (1922)
Nosferatu, A Symphony of Terror
See Nosferatu (1922)
Nosferatu, Eine Symphonie des Grauens
See Nosferatu (1922)
Nosferatu, the Vampire
See Nosferatu (1922)
Numbered Days
See Running out of Time (1994)
Ohayo
See Good Morning (1959)
Old Mother Riley Meets the Vampire
See My Son, the Vampire (1952)
A One and a Two...
See Yi Yi (2000)
Ore Ni Sawaru to Abunaize
See Black Tight Killers (1966)
Par-dela les Nuages
See Beyond the Clouds (1995)
Passion Play
See Love Letters (1983)
Perceval Le Gallois
See Perceval (1978)
Perdita Durango
See Dance with the Devil (1997)
Persons Unknown
See Big Deal on Madonna Street (1958)
Pixote: A Lei do Mais Fraco
See Pixote (1981)
Playgirl Gang
See Switchblade Sisters (1975)
Poe's Tales of Terror
See Tales of Terror (1962)
Poketto Monsutaa: Maboroshi No Pokemon X: Lugia Bakudan
See Pokemon the Movie 2000: The Power of One (2000)
The Professional
See Leon, the Professional (1994)
Psycho a Go Go!
See Blood of Ghastly Horror (1972)
Quante Volte...Quella Notte
See Four Times That Night (1969)
Quella Villa Accanto Al Cimitero
See The House by the Cemetery (1983)
Rage
See Rabid (1977)
Rane
See The Wounds (1998)
Re-Animator 2
See Bride of Re-Animator (1989)
The Red Hangman
See The Bloody Pit of Horror (1965)
The Red Sign of Madness
See Hatchet for the Honeymoon (1970)
Return of the Seven
See Return of the Magnificent Seven (1966)
The Revenge of Dracula
See Dracula vs. Frankenstein (1971)
The Revenge of Milady
See The Four Musketeers (1975)
The Revengers' Comedies
See Sweet Revenge (1998)
Ritual Dos Sadicos
See Awakenings of the Beast (1968)
Ritual of the Maniacs
See Awakenings of the Beast (1968)

Roaring Timber
See Come and Get It (1936)
Robert Louis Stevenson's The Suicide Club
See Robert Louis Stevenson's The Game of Death (1999)
Robinson Crusoeland
See Utopia (1951)
Rocket to the Moon
See Cat Women of the Moon (1953)
Rodents
See Ratas, Ratones, Rateros (1999)
Roger Corman Presents: Black Scorpion
See Black Scorpion (1995)
Room Service
See Inn of 1000 Sins (1975)
Salerno Beachhead
See A Walk in the Sun (1946)
Satan's Bloody Freaks
See Dracula vs. Frankenstein (1971)
Satan's Daughters
See Vampyres (1974)
Satyricon
See Fellini Satyricon (1969)
Scrooge
See A Christmas Carol (1951)
The Second Jungle Book: Mowgli and Baloo
See Rudyard Kipling's the Second Jungle Book: Mowgli and Baloo (1997)
The Second Lieutenant
See The Last Lieutenant (1994)
Secondloitnanten
See The Last Lieutenant (1994)
The Secret
See Catherine Cookson's The Secret (2000)
The Secret of Dr. Mabuse
See The Thousand Eyes of Dr. Mabuse (1960)
Secret Weapon
See Sherlock Holmes and the Secret Weapon (1942)
Secretos del Corazon
See Secrets of the Heart (1997)
Sei Donne per l'Assassino
See Blood and Black Lace (1964)
Se7en
See Seven (1995)
Seven Doors of Death
See The Beyond (1982)
Seven Sisters
See The House on Sorority Row (1983)
Shadow Play
See Portraits Chinois (1996)
The Shadow Versus the Thousand Eyes of Dr. Mabuse
See The Thousand Eyes of Dr. Mabuse (1960)
Shadowbuilder
See Bram Stoker's Shadowbuilder (1998)
Shaft Returns
See Shaft (2000)
Shame
See The Intruder (1961)
Shanghai Express
See The Millionaire's Express (1986)
She Demons of the Swamp
See Attack of the Giant Leeches (1959)
She Knew No Other Way
See Last Resort (1986)
She Monster of the Night
See Frankenstein's Daughter (1958)
Sherlock Holmes and the Woman in Green
See The Woman in Green (1945); The Woman in Green / Dressed to Kill (1945)
She's De Lovely
See She's So Lovely (1997)
Shin Seiki Evangelion
See Neon Genesis Evangelion Collection (1999)
Shina Ningyo
See Fruits of Passion: The Story of "O" Continued (1982)
Shinju Ten No Amijima
See Double Suicide (1969)
Shocked
See Mesmerized (1984)
Sid & Nancy: Love Kills
See Sid & Nancy (1986)
Silent Night, Evil Night
See Black Christmas (1975)

Sitting Bull's History Lesson
See Buffalo Bill & the Indians (1976)
Six Women for the Murderer
See Blood and Black Lace (1964)
Snake Fist Fighter
See Master with Cracked Fingers (1971)
Soldaat van Oranje
See Soldier of Orange (1978)
Something Is Out There
See Day of the Animals (1977)
Son of Blob
See Beware! The Blob (1972)
Sondagsengler
See The Other Side of Sunday (1996)
The Space Vampires
See The Astro-Zombies (1967)
Spinal Tap
See This Is Spinal Tap (1984)
Spirit of the Dead
See The Asphyx (1972)
Stephen King's Sleepwalkers
See Sleepwalkers (1992)
Still Smokin'
See Cheech and Chong: Still Smokin' (1983)
Stolen Hearts
See Two If by Sea (1995)
The Story of "O" Continued
See Fruits of Passion: The Story of "O" Continued (1982)
Strange Journey
See Fantastic Voyage (1966)
The Stranger
See The Intruder (1961)
Stranger in the House
See Black Christmas (1975)
The Strangler of Vienna
See The Mad Butcher (1972)
Strike!
See All I Wanna Do (1998)
Stryker's War
See Thou Shalt Not Kill . . . Except (1987)
Subspecies 4
See Bloodstorm: Subspecies 4 (1998)
Subspecies 4: Bloodstorm—The Master's Revenge
See Bloodstorm: Subspecies 4 (1998)
The Suicide Club
See Robert Louis Stevenson's The Game of Death (1999)
Svitati
See Screw Loose (1999)
The Swindle
See Il Bidone (1955)
Sydney
See Hard Eight (1996)
T & A Academy
See H.O.T.S. (1979)
The Tai-Chi Master
See Twin Warriors (1993)
Tai ji Zhang San Feng
See Twin Warriors (1993)
Tarzan and Jane
See Tarzan and the Lost City (1998)
Tejing Xinrenlei
See Gen-X Cops (1999)
Tell Your Children
See Reefer Madness (1938)
Terror of Dracula
See Nosferatu (1922)
They Made Me a Fugitive
See They Made Me a Criminal (1939)
They're Coming to Get You
See Dracula vs. Frankenstein (1971)
The Three Faces of Fear
See Black Sabbath (1964)
The Three Faces of Terror
See Black Sabbath (1964)
Ti Kniver I Hjertet
See Cross My Heart and Hope to Die (1994)
Tidal Wave
See Portrait of Jennie (1948)
The Tiger of Eschanapur
See The Indian Tomb (1921)
Tim Burton's The Nightmare before Christmas
See The Nightmare before Christmas (1993)
Timecode
See Time Code (2000)
The Timeshifters
See Thrill Seekers (1999)

Tito and I
See Tito and Me (1992)

Tito i Ja
See Tito and Me (1992)

To Koritsi Me Ta Mavra
See Girl in Black (1956)

To Telefteo Psemma
See A Matter of Dignity (1957)

Todo Sobre Mi Madre
See All About My Mother (1999)

Tonight I Will Eat Your Corpse
See This Night I'll Possess Your Corpse (1966)

Tonight I Will Make Your Corpse Turn Red
See This Night I'll Possess Your Corpse (1966)

Tonight I Will Paint in Flesh Colour
See This Night I'll Possess Your Corpse (1966)

Travels with Anita
See Lovers and Liars (1981)

Treasure of the Living Dead
See Oasis of the Zombies (1982)

A Trip with Anita
See Lovers and Liars (1981)

Triumph des Willens
See Triumph of the Will (1934)

Tsuui Kun 2
See The Legend of Drunken Master (1994)

Twelve Miles Out
See The Second Woman (1951)

Twitch of the Death Nerve
See Bay of Blood (1971)

Un Divan a New York
See A Couch in New York (1995)

Un Grand Amour de Beethoven
See Beethoven (1936)

Una Hacha para la Luna de Miel
See Hatchet for the Honeymoon (1970)

Une Liaison Pornographique
See An Affair of Love (2000)

Unsane
See Tenebre (1982)

Up in Smoke
See Cheech and Chong's Up in Smoke (1979)

Urban Justice
See Under Oath (1997)

The Usual Unidentified Thieves
See Big Deal on Madonna Street (1958)

The Vampire and the Robot
See My Son, the Vampire (1952)

The Vampire-Beast Craves Blood
See Blood Beast Terror (1967)

Vampire Orgy
See Vampyres (1974)

Vampire over London
See My Son, the Vampire (1952)

Vampire's Thirst
See The Body Beneath (1970)

Vampyres, Daughters of Dracula
See Vampyres (1974)

Vengeance: The Demon
See Pumpkinhead (1988)

The Venusian
See The Stranger from Venus (1954)

Viehjud Levi
See Jew-boy Levi (1998)

The Vienna Strangler
See The Mad Butcher (1972)

Vor
See The Thief (1997)

Wandafuru Raifu
See After Life (1998)

The War Is Over
See La Guerre Est Finie (1966)

The Way Ahead
See Immortal Battalion (1944)

The Way We Are
See Quiet Days in Hollywood (1997)

What
See The Whip and the Body (1963)

The Who's Tommy
See Tommy (1975)

Why We Fight
See World War II (1942)

Wild Drifters
See Cockfighter (1974)

The Wild McCullochs
See The McCullochs (1975)

The Wild Side
See Suburbia (1983)

Winterschlafer
See Winter Sleepers (1997)

The Wisdom of Crocodiles
See Immortality (1998)

Women in Cages
See The Big Doll House (1971)

Women's Penitentiary 1
See The Big Doll House (1971)

Wong Fei-hung
See Once Upon a Time in China (1991)

The Wrong Kind of Girl
See Bus Stop (1956)

X
See X: The Man with X-Ray Eyes (1963)

X Change
See Xchange (2000)

Yanzhi Kou
See Rouge (1987)

Ying Huang Boon Sik
See A Better Tomorrow, Part 1 (1986)

Yinghung Bunsik 2
See A Better Tomorrow, Part 2 (1988)

Zhong Nan Hai Bao Biao
See The Bodyguard from Beijing (1994)

Zhong Nan Hai Bao Biao
See The Defender (1994)

Zoot Suit Jesus
See Greaser's Palace (1972)

The Cast Index provides a listing of cast members and the DVDs in which they appeared that are covered in this book. The listings for the actor names follow an alphabetical sort by last name (although the names appear in a first name, last name format). The videographies are listed chronologically, with the most recent appearance first. A (V) beside a movie title indicates voice-over work; an (N) indicates narration.

Aaliyah
Romeo Must Die '00

Caroline Aaron
What Planet Are You From? '00
Alice '90
Edward Scissorhands [SE] '90
Crimes & Misdemeanors [MGM] '89

Chad Aaron
The Yards '00

Bruce Abbott
Bride of Re-Animator '89

Bud Abbott
Jack & the Beanstalk '52
Africa Screams / Jack and the Beanstalk '49
Abbott and Costello Meet Frankenstein '48

Kareem Abdul-Jabbar
Airplane! '80

Mirlan Abdykalykov
Beshkempir the Adopted Son '98

Hiroshi Abe
Tokyo Raiders '00
Godzilla 2000 '99

Tim Abell
The Substitute 4: Failure Is Not an Option '00
The Base '99

Ian Abercrombie
Puppet Master 3: Toulon's Revenge '91

F. Murray Abraham
Finding Forrester '00
Excellent Cadavers '99
Noah's Ark '99

Jim Abrahams
Airplane! '80

Jody Abrahams
The Quarry '98

Jon Abrahams
Meet the Parents '00
Scary Movie '00

Jonathan Abrahams
Whipped '00

Lelia Abramo
Manoushe, The Story of a Gypsy Love '98

Victoria Abril
Tie Me Up! Tie Me Down! '90

Forrest J Ackerman
Dracula vs. Frankenstein '71

Leslie Ackerman
Law and Disorder '74

Joss Ackland
Citizen X '95
Mother's Boys '94
The Object of Beauty '91
Saint Jack '79

Eric Acsell
Lolida 2000 '97

Masao Adachi
Ecstasy of the Angels '72

Jean Adair
Arsenic and Old Lace '44

Brooke Adams
Picture Windows '95
The Stuff '85
Dead Zone '83

Edie Adams
Cheech and Chong's Up in Smoke '79
The Apartment '60

Jane Adams
Wonder Boys '00
Father of the Bride Part II '95

Jason Adams
Puppet Master 4 '93

Jeb Stuart Adams
Flowers in the Attic '87

Joey Lauren Adams
Beautiful '00
Chasing Amy '97

Jonathan Adams
The Rocky Horror Picture Show '75

Julie Adams
The McCullochs '75
Away All Boats '56

Lillian Adams
Heavy Traffic '73

Mason Adams
F/X '86
Omen 3: The Final Conflict '81

Maud Adams
Jane & the Lost City '87
Octopussy '83

Nick Adams
Die, Monster, Die! '65
Hell Is for Heroes '62
Picnic '55

Polly Adams
Element of Doubt '96

Stanley Adams
Lilies of the Field '63

Thomas Adams
Fallen Angel '99

Chris(topher) Adamson
Dead of Night '99

George Adamson
An Elephant Called Slowly '69

Patrick Adamson
China O'Brien '88

Meat Loaf Aday
Crazy in Alabama '99
The Rocky Horror Picture Show '75

Dawn Addams
The Thousand Eyes of Dr. Mabuse '60

James Addams
L'Avventura '60

Kip Addotta
Wishful Thinking '92

Mark Addy
The Flintstones in Viva Rock Vegas '00

Wesley Addy
The Grissom Gang '71
Tora! Tora! Tora! [2 SE] '70
Kiss Me Deadly '55

Georges Adel
Love and Death '75

Danny Ades
Aguirre, the Wrath of God '72

Isabelle Adjani
Diabolique '96
Camille Claudel '89
Possession '81
The Story of Adele H. '75

Bill Adler
The Pom Pom Girls / The Beach Girls '76
Switchblade Sisters '75

Luther Adler
D.O.A. [Roan] '49

The Loves of Carmen '48

Mario Adorf
Smilla's Sense of Snow '96

Frank Adu
Love and Death '75

Ben Affleck
Boiler Room '00
Bounce '00
Joseph: King of Dreams '00 (V)
Reindeer Games '00
Dogma '99
Chasing Amy '97

Casey Affleck
Drowning Mona '00
Hamlet '00
Attention Shoppers '99

John Agar
Attack of the Puppet People '58
The Brain from Planet Arous '57

Nikita Ager
Shark Attack 2 '00

Kris Aguilar
Bloodfist 2 '90
Bloodfist '89

Jenny Agutter
The Eagle Has Landed '77

Lee Ahsmann
Something Weird '68

Danny Aiello
Prince of Central Park '00
Leon, the Professional '94
Mistress '91
Do the Right Thing [2] '89
The Stuff '85
Fort Apache, the Bronx '81
The Godfather, Part 2 '74

Liam Aiken
I Dreamed of Africa '00

Holly Aird
Fever Pitch '96

Isabella Aitken
The Big Tease '99

Franklin Ajaye
American Yakuza '94
Car Wash '76

Andra Akers
Desert Hearts '86

David Akin
Parasite '95

Claude Akins
Battle for the Planet of the Apes '73
Return of the Magnificent Seven '66

Michio Akiyama
Go, Go Second Time Virgin '69

Jessica Alba
Idle Hands '99

Eddie Albert
The Longest Yard '74

Shari Albert
The Brothers McMullen '94

Jack Albertson
Dead and Buried '81
The Fox and the Hound '81 (V)

Ariauna Albright
Witchouse 2: Blood Coven '00

Lola Albright
Joy House '64

Alan Alda
What Women Want '00
Canadian Bacon '94
And the Band Played On '93
Crimes & Misdemeanors [MGM] '89

Robert Alda
Love by Appointment '76

Rutanya Alda
The Souler Opposite '97

Norman Alden
Tora! Tora! Tora! [2 SE] '70
The Nutty Professor '63
The Sword in the Stone '63 (V)

John Alderman
The Erotic Adventures of Zorro '72

John Alderton
Zardoz '73

Tom Aldredge
What about Bob? '91

Rhonda Aldrich
Saturday the 14th Strikes Back '88

Alona Alegre
Black Mama, White Mama '73

Aki Aleong
Lewis and Clark and George '97

John Ales
Nutty Professor 2: The Klumps [1 CE] '00
Nutty Professor 2: The Klumps [2 Uncensored] '00
Ride with the Devil '99

Frank Aletter
Tora! Tora! Tora! [2 SE] '70

Abbott Alexander
Starry Night '99

Daniel Alexander
Shark Attack 2 '00

Gina Alexander
The Watcher '00

Jace Alexander
Mistress '91
Eight Men Out '88

Jane Alexander
The Cider House Rules '99
Glory [2 SE] '89

Jason Alexander
The Adventures of Rocky & Bullwinkle '00
Coneheads '93

John Alexander
Arsenic and Old Lace '44

Khandi Alexander
Thick As Thieves '99

Max Alexander
Roxanne '87

Peter Alexander
Seamless '00

Suzanne Alexander
Cat Women of the Moon '53

Victor Alexander
Ilsa, Harem Keeper of the Oil Sheiks '76

Charlotta Alexandra
Immoral Tales '74

Aiekos Alexandrikis
Stella '55

Nora Alexis
The Gore-Gore Girls '72

Lidia Alfonsi
Black Sabbath '64

Mary Alice
The Women of Brewster Place '89

Ana Alicia
Romero '89

Rex Allan
Charlotte's Web '73 (N)

Allegra
Hot Vampire Nights '00

Ginette Allegre
Humanity '99

Bambi Allen
Satan's Sadists '69

Barbara Jo Allen
The Sword in the Stone '63 (V)

Don Allen
Suburbia '83

Elizabeth Allen
Donovan's Reef '63

Eugene Allen
House Party 2: The Pajama Jam '91

Fiona Allen
Lord Edgeware Dies '99

Jeffrey Allen
Something Weird '68

Joan Allen
The Contender '00
It's the Rage '99
In Country '89
Tucker: The Man and His Dream '88

Jonelle Allen
The Midnight Hour '86

Karen Allen
The Perfect Storm '00
Scrooged '88
Manhattan '79

Kevin Allen
The Big Tease '99

Krista Allen
Emmanuelle: First Contact '99
Emmanuelle in Space: A World of Desire '99

Nancy Allen
Kiss Toledo Goodbye '00
The Philadelphia Experiment '84

Richard Allen
The Snows of Kilimanjaro '52

Robin Allen
Next Friday [Platinum Series] '00

Tanya Allen
White Lies '98

Tim Allen
Buzz Lightyear of Star Command: The Adventure Begins '00 (V)
Galaxy Quest '99
Toy Story 2 '99 (V)
Toy Story '95 (V)

Woody Allen
Small Time Crooks '00
Picking Up the Pieces '99
Sweet and Lowdown '99
Shadows and Fog '92
Crimes & Misdemeanors [MGM] '89
Manhattan '79
Love and Death '75
Sleeper '73
Everything You Always Wanted to Know about Sex (But Were Afraid to Ask) '72
Bananas '71

Alexander Allerson
I Like the Girls Who Do '73

Kirstie Alley
Look Who's Talking, Too '90
Runaway '84
Star Trek 2: The Wrath of Khan '82

Sara Allgood
The Spiral Staircase '46
How Green Was My Valley '41

Christopher Allport
Jack Frost 2: Revenge of the Mutant Killer Snowman '00

Corbin Allred
Diamonds '99

Astrid Allwyn
Love Affair '39

June Allyson
Good News '47
Till the Clouds Roll By '46

Maria Conchita Alonso
Footsteps '98
Fear City '85

Rafael Alonso
The Grandfather '98

Carol Alt
Revelation '00

Bruce Altman
Mr. Jones '93

Robert Altman
American Cinema: 100 Years of Filmmaking '94 (N)

Don Alvarado
Battle of the Sexes '28

Trini Alvarado
Little Women [2 SE] '94
Times Square '80

Carlos Alvarez
Sniper '92

Santiago Alvarez
Slugs '87

Gabriela Alves
The Story of O: The Series '92

Syed Alwi
Anna and the King '99

Lyle Alzado
Tapeheads '89

Natacha Amal
8 1/2 Women '99

Mathieu Amalric
My Sex Life...Or How I Got into an Argument '96

Hideyo Amamoto
Weather Woman '99

Claudio Amendola
Jesus '00

Allyson Ames
Incubus '65

Christopher Ames
Last Resort '86

Leon Ames
Tora! Tora! Tora! [2 SE] '70

AMG
Winner Takes All '98

Soshana Ami
Drop Dead Rock '95

Madchen Amick
Hangman '00
The List '99
Sleepwalkers '92

Suzy Amis
One Good Turn '95

Michael Amos
Sideshow '00

John Amplas
Martin '77

Isabel Ampudia
Three Businessmen '99

Morey Amsterdam
Beach Party '63

Radu Amzulrescu
Citizen X '95

Alexi Ananishnov
Mother and Son '97

Dominic Anciano
Love, Honour & Obey '00

Avalon Anders
The Portrait '99

Glenn Anders
The Lady from Shanghai '48

Luana Anders
Greaser's Palace '72
Dementia 13 '63
The Pit and the Pendulum '61

Rudolph Anders
She Demons '58

Gotha Andersen
The Element of Crime '84

Lotte Andersen
Nightwatch '94

Susy Andersen
Black Sabbath '64

Anthony Anderson
Big Momma's House '00
Romeo Must Die '00
Urban Legends 2: Final Cut '00
Liberty Heights '99

Bruce Anderson
Perfect Profile '90

Christian Anderson
Nunsense 2: The Sequel '94

Daniel Anderson
Sex Files: Ancient Desires '99

Dawn Anderson
Teenagers from Outer Space '59

Eddie Anderson
Topper Returns '41

Erich Anderson
Friday the 13th, Part 4: The Final Chapter '84

Gillian Anderson
House of Mirth '00
The X-Files: Season One [CE] '00
The X-Files: Season Two '00
Princess Mononoke '98 (V)

Jeff Anderson
Clerks Uncensored '00 (V)
Dogma '99

John Anderson
Eight Men Out '88
Cotton Comes to Harlem '70

Judith Anderson
The Strange Love of Martha Ivers '46

Kevin Anderson
In Country '89

Loni Anderson
All Dogs Go to Heaven '89 (V)

McKee Anderson
Night of the Living Dead '90

Melody Anderson
Dead and Buried '81

Michael Anderson Jr.
Sons of Katie Elder '65

Mitchell Anderson
If These Walls Could Talk 2 '00

Pamela Anderson
Barb Wire '96

Richard Anderson
Gettysburg '93
Tora! Tora! Tora! [2 SE] '70

Richard Dean Anderson
Stargate SG-1: Season 1 '97

Warner Anderson
Go for Broke! '51

Bibi Andersson
Babette's Feast '87
It's Raining on Santiago '74

Keith Andes
Tora! Tora! Tora! [2 SE] '70
Away All Boats '56

Mansanobu Ando
Kids Return '96

Andre the Giant
The Princess Bride '87

Ursula Andress
10th Victim '65

Simon Andreu
Sharpe's Rifles '93

Simon Andrew
Blood and Sand '89

Anthony Andrews
The Pallisers '74

Dana Andrews
In Harm's Way '65
A Walk in the Sun '46
Know Your Enemy: Japan '45 (N)

David Andrews
Hannibal '01
Cherry 2000 '88

Edward Andrews
Tora! Tora! Tora! [2 SE] '70

Harry Andrews
Mesmerized '84
Death on the Nile '78
The Story of Jacob & Joseph '74
Moby Dick '56

Julie Andrews
Relative Values '99
20th Century Fox: The First 50 Years '96
Torn Curtain '66
The Sound of Music [Five Star Collection] '65
Mary Poppins [2 SE] '64

Real Andrews
Family of Cops 2: Breach of Faith '97

Tod Andrews
In Harm's Way '65
She Demons '58

The Andrews Sisters
Melody Time '48 (V)
The Road to Rio '47

Marayat Andriane
The Sand Pebbles '66

Thomas Andrisano
Teenage Gang Debs / Teenage Strangler '66

Richie Andrusco
Little Fugitive '53

Anemone
Son of Gascogne '95

Heather Angel
Bulldog Drummond's Secret Police '39
Bulldog Drummond Escapes '37

Jean-Hugues Anglade
Maximum Risk '96
Killing Zoe '94
La Femme Nikita [MGM] '91

Edit Angold
Tomorrow the World '44

Alex Angulo
Live Flesh '97

Jennifer Aniston
She's the One '96

Morris Ankrum
X: The Man with X-Ray Eyes '63
Giant from the Unknown '58

Ann-Margret
Any Given Sunday '99
Tommy '75

Richard Attenborough
Joseph and the Amazing
   Technicolor Dreamcoat '00
The Lost World: Jurassic Park
   2 [CE] '97
Jurassic Park [CE] '93
Doctor Dolittle '67
The Sand Pebbles '66

Edward Atterton
Relative Values '99

Mike Attwell
Poldark '96

Edith Atwater
Family Plot '76

Lionel Atwill
Sherlock Holmes and the
   Secret Weapon '42
The Vampire Bat '32

Rene Auberjonois
The Patriot '00
Eyes of Laura Mars '78

Lenore Aubert
Abbott and Costello Meet
   Frankenstein '48

Danielle Aubry
Bikini Beach '64

Stephane Audran
Madeline '98
Maximum Risk '96
Son of Gascogne '95
Babette's Feast '87
Coup de Torchon '81
The Discreet Charm of the
   Bourgeoisie '72

Caroline Audret
Oasis of the Zombies '82

Mischa Auer
Up in Mabel's Room '44
The Gay Desperado '36

Claudine Auger
Bay of Blood '71
Twitch of the Death Nerve '71

Karel Augusta
Chained Heat 3: Hell Mountain '98

Ewa Aulin
Candy '68

Karen Austin
The Jagged Edge '85
Summer Rental '85

Patti Austin
Tucker: The Man and His
   Dream '88

Daniel Auteuil
La Separation '98
Jean de Florette '87
Manon of the Spring '87

Alan Autry
At Close Range '86

Frankie Avalon
Dr. Goldfoot and the Bikini
   Machine '66
Beach Blanket Bingo '65
Bikini Beach '64
Beach Party '63
Voyage to the Bottom of the
   Sea / Fantastic Voyage '61
The Alamo '60

Luis Avalos
Lone Justice 3: Showdown at
   Plum Creek '96
Lone Justice 2 '93

Erik Avari
The Mummy [2 SE] '99
The Beast '88

Joe Mari Avellana
Bloodfist 2 '90
Bloodfist '89

Hy Averback
Bob Hope: Hollywood's
   Brightest Star '97

James Avery
The Colony '98

Margaret Avery
The Lathe of Heaven '80

Val Avery
The Pope of Greenwich Vil-
   lage '84
Choices '81
The Amityville Horror '79
Black Caesar '73

Rick Aviles
Ghost '90

Mili Avital
After the Storm '01
Dead Man '95

Chris Avran
Bay of Blood '71
Twitch of the Death Nerve '71

Keiko Awaji
The Bridges at Toko-Ri '55

Debbon Ayer
The Waiting Game '99

Dan Aykroyd
House of Mirth '00
Loser '00
Diamonds '99
Canadian Bacon '94
Coneheads '93

Danielle Aykroyd
Coneheads '93

Felix Aylmer
Hamlet '48

Agnes Ayres
Affairs of Anatol '21

Lew Ayres
Damien: Omen 2 '78
Battle for the Planet of the
   Apes '73
Donovan's Brain '53

Rosalind Ayres
Beautiful People '99
That'll Be the Day '73

Hank Azaria
The Cradle Will Rock '99
Mystery, Alaska '99
Homegrown '97

Shabana Azmi
Fire '96

Charles Aznavour
Candy '68

Eloy Azorin
All About My Mother '99

B-Real
Winner Takes All '98

Obba Babatunde
Soul of the Game '96

Barbara Babcock
Space Cowboys '00

Hector Babenco
Before Night Falls '00

Lauren Bacall
Diamonds '99
Misery '90
How to Marry a Millionaire
   '53

Michael Bacall
Urban Legends 2: Final Cut
   '00

Elisa Bacanegra
Girlfight '99

Dian Bachar
The Adventures of Rocky &
   Bullwinkle '00

Steve Bacic
The 6th Day '00
Bounty Hunters 2: Hardball
   '97

Brian Backer
Fast Times at Ridgemont
   High '82

Susan Backlinie
Day of the Animals '77

Jim Backus
Pete's Dragon '77
Pat and Mike '52
The Great Lover '49

Kevin Bacon
The Hollow Man [SE] '00
My Dog Skip '99
Digging to China '98
Murder in the First '95
She's Having a Baby '88
Planes, Trains & Automobiles
   '87

Paul Bacon
The Asphyx '72

Alain Bacourt
Mon Oncle '58

Gabriel Bacquier
Manon of the Spring '87

Michael Badalucco
Two If by Sea '95
Leon, the Professional '94

Hermione Baddeley
The Aristocats '70 (V)
Mary Poppins [2 SE] '64
The Unsinkable Molly Brown
   '64
A Christmas Carol '51

Sarah Badel
Cotton Mary '99

Diedrich Bader
Buzz Lightyear of Star Com-
   mand: The Adventure
   Begins '00 (V)

Russ Badger
Shanghai Noon '00
The Gore-Gore Girls '72

Erykah Badu
The Cider House Rules '99

Caroline Baehr
Ma Vie en Rose '97

Buddy Baer
Giant from the Unknown '58
Jack & the Beanstalk '52

Dave Baer
Broken Vessels '98

G. Gordon Baer
Sideshow '00

Harry Baer
Whity '70

Max Baer Sr.
Africa Screams / Jack and
   the Beanstalk '49

Max Baer Jr.
The McCullochs '75

Joan Baez
Bob Dylan: Don't Look Back
   '67

Rafael Baez
Shanghai Noon '00
Went to Coney Island on a
   Mission from God...Be
   Back by Five '98

Regina Baff
Road Movie '72

William Bagdad
The Astro-Zombies '67

Lynne Baggett
D.O.A. [Roan] '49

Marcus Bagwell
Terror Tract '00

Maxine Bahns
Cutaway '00
Dangerous Curves '99
She's the One '96
The Brothers McMullen '94

Eion Bailey
Center Stage '00

G.W. Bailey
Jesus '00

Janet Bailey
Race to Freedom: The Story
   of the Underground Railroad '94

Mark Bailey
The Unbelievable Truth '90

Pearl Bailey
The Fox and the Hound '81
   (V)

Raymond Bailey
Picnic '55

Conrad Bain
Postcards from the Edge '90
Bananas '71

Cynthia Bain
Pumpkinhead '88

Fay Bainter
Our Town '40

Scott Bairstow
Delivered '98

Riyu Bajaj
Cotton Mary '99

Manoj Bajpai
Bandit Queen '94

Richard Bakalyan
The Fox and the Hound '81
   (V)

Carroll Baker
The Greatest Story Ever Told
   [SE] '65
The Big Country '58

David Aaron Baker
The Tao of Steve '00

Diane Baker
Imaginary Crimes '94

Dylan Baker
The Cell '00
The Last of the Mohicans '92
Planes, Trains & Automobiles
   '87

George Baker
I, Claudius '91

Jennifer Baker
Tommy '75

Jill Baker
Hope and Glory '87

Joe Baker
Pocahontas '95 (V)

Joe Don Baker
Panther '95
The Living Daylights '87
The Natural '84

Jolyon Baker
Attila '01

Kathy Baker
The Cider House Rules '99
Inventing the Abbotts '97
Edward Scissorhands [SE]
   '90

Lori Baker
Frostbiter: Wrath of the
   Wendigo '94

Rick Baker
The Thing with Two Heads '72

Simon Baker
Red Planet '00
Ride with the Devil '99
Restaurant '98

Susan Baker
Tommy '75

Timothy Baker
Bloodfist 2 '90

Tom Baker
Dungeons and Dragons '00
Golden Voyage of Sinbad '73

William "Billy" Bakewell
Battle of the Sexes '28

Brenda Bakke
Lone Justice 3: Showdown at
   Plum Creek '96
Lone Justice 2 '93

Jim Bakker
The Eyes of Tammy Faye '00

Tammy Faye Bakker
The Eyes of Tammy Faye '00

Brigitte Bako
Die! Die! Die! '00

Scott Bakula
American Beauty [SE] '99
Necessary Roughness '91

Bob Balaban
Best in Show '00
The Cradle Will Rock '99
Amos and Andrew '93
Alice '90
Close Encounters of the Third
   Kind [CE] '77
Catch-22 '70

Anna Baldaccini
Boy Meets Girl '84

Tim Baldini
The St. Francisville Experiment '00

Bea Baldur
I Like the Girls Who Do '73

A. Michael Baldwin
Phantasm 4: Oblivion '98
Vice Girls '96

Adam Baldwin
The Patriot '00
The Right Temptation '00
Blind Justice '94

Alec Baldwin
Clerks Uncensored '00 (V)
Nuremberg '00
Thomas and the Magic Rail-
   road '00
Thick As Thieves '99
The Confession '98
Malice [MGM] '93
Prelude to a Kiss '92
Alice '90
Married to the Mob '88
She's Having a Baby '88
Talk Radio '88
Working Girl '88

Daniel Baldwin
Homicide: The Movie '00
In Pursuit '00
Desert Thunder '99
Love Kills '98
On the Border '98
The Pandora Project '98
Knight Moves '93
Harley Davidson and the
   Marlboro Man '91
Born on the Fourth of July [2]
   '89

Twin Falls Idaho '99
And the Band Played On '93

Chris Bauer
Flawless '99

Michelle (McClellan) Bauer
Assault of the Party Nerds 2: Heavy Petting Detective '95
Assault of the Party Nerds '89
Lust for Frankenstein '88

Steven Bauer
For Love or Country: The Arturo Sandoval Story '00
Traffic '00
Body Count '95
The Beast '88

Ricardo Bauleo
The Curious Dr. Humpp '70

Kathrine Baumann
The Thing with Two Heads '72

Harry Baur
Beethoven '36

Marilyn Bautista
Bloodfist '89

Perla Bautista
Midnight Dancers '94

Barbara Baxley
Nashville '75

Alan Baxter
Saboteur '42

Amy Lynn Baxter
Blood Bullets Buffoons '96

Anne Baxter
Angel on My Shoulder '46

Warner Baxter
42nd Street '33

Nathalie Baye
An Affair of Love '00
And the Band Played On '93
The Man Who Loved Women '77

Shani Bayete
Nothin' 2 Lose '00

Geoffrey Bayldon
Asylum '72

Lawrence Bayne
Black Robe '91

Bojan Bazelli
Tapeheads '89

Adam Beach
The Last Stop '99

Michael Beach
A Family Thing '96
One False Move '91
Internal Affairs '90

Steven Beach
Grind '96

Stephanie Beacham
Inseminoid '80

Jennifer Beals
Something More '99

Henry Bean
A Couch in New York '95

Orson Bean
Anatomy of a Murder '59

Sean Bean
Essex Boys '99
Sharpe's Justice '97
Sharpe's Revenge '97
Sharpe's Waterloo '97
Sharpe's Mission '96
Sharpe's Regiment '96
Sharpe's Siege '96
Sharpe's Battle '94

Sharpe's Company '94
Sharpe's Enemy '94
Sharpe's Gold '94
Sharpe's Honour '94
Sharpe's Sword '94
Sharpe's Eagle '93
Sharpe's Rifles '93
The Field '90

Amanda Bearse
Fright Night '85

Emmanuelle Beart
Manon of the Spring '87

John Beasley
Lost Souls '00
Crazy in Alabama '99

Norman Beaton
The Mighty Quinn '89

Clyde Beatty
Africa Screams / Jack and the Beanstalk '49

Debra Beatty
Emmanuelle in Space: A World of Desire '99

Ned Beatty
Homicide: The Movie '00
Rudy [SE] '93
Prelude to a Kiss '92
A Cry in the Wild '90
Back to School '86
Superman 2 '80
Superman: The Movie '78
Nashville '75

Warren Beatty
The Parallax View '74

Charles Beaumont
The Intruder '61

Kathryn Beaumont
Alice in Wonderland '51 (V)

Jim Beaver
In Country '89

Louise Beavers
The Jackie Robinson Story '50

Sidney Bechet
Moon over Harlem '39

Glenn Beck
Dr. Strangelove, or: How I Learned to Stop Worrying and Love the Bomb [2 SE] '64

John Beck
Sleeper '73

Kimberly Beck
Friday the 13th, Part 4: The Final Chapter '84

Michael Beck
The Warriors '79

Graham Beckel
The '70s '00
Blue Streak '99

Gerry Becker
Donnie Brasco [2] '96

Josh Becker
Evil Dead 2: Dead by Dawn [2 THX] '87

Scotty Beckett
Love Affair '39

Tony Beckley
Get Carter '71

Trevor Beckwith
Best in Show '00

Rod Bedall
Mona Lisa '86

Irene Bedard
Pocahontas 2: Journey to a New World '98 (V)
Pocahontas '95 (V)

Bonnie Bedelia
Bad Manners '98
Somebody Has to Shoot the Picture '90

Rodney Bedell
Gruesome Twosome '67

Barbara Bedford
The Last of the Mohicans '20

Brian Bedford
Robin Hood '73 (V)

Kabir Bedi
The Beast '88
Octopussy '83

Molly Bee
Hillbillys in a Haunted House '67

David Beecroft
Octopus '00

Daniel Beer
The Last Best Sunday '98
Creepshow 2 '87

Noah Beery Sr.
Trail Beyond '34
The Vanishing American '25

Noah Beery Jr.
7 Faces of Dr. Lao '63
Rocketship X-M '50
Gung Ho! '43
Only Angels Have Wings '39
Trail Beyond '34

Wallace Beery
The Lost World [Image] '25
The Last of the Mohicans '20

Jason Beghe
Monkey Shines '88

Ed Begley Sr.
The Unsinkable Molly Brown '64
Twelve Angry Men '57

Ed Begley Jr.
Best in Show '00
I'm Losing You '98
The Crazysitter '94
This Is Spinal Tap [MGM] '84
Cockfighter '74

Melissa Behr
Perfect Tenant '99

Bernard Behrens
Mother Night '96

Yeniffer Behrens
Angel Blue '97

Doris Belack
What about Bob? '91

Shari Belafonte
The Midnight Hour '86

Eileen Beldon
Pygmalion '38

Ana Belen
The Perfect Husband '92

Christine Belford
The Groundstar Conspiracy '72

Ann Bell
The Witches '66

Catherine Bell
Thrill Seekers '99

Darryl M. Bell
School Daze '88

Drake Bell
The Jack Bull '99

George Anthony Bell
House Party 2: The Pajama Jam '91

Jamie Bell
Billy Elliot '00

Marshall Bell
Mercy '00
Black & White '99
Tucker: The Man and His Dream '88
No Way Out '87

Michael Bell
Rugrats in Paris: The Movie '00 (V)

Robert Anthony Bell
One False Move '91

Tobin Bell
The 4th Floor '99
Best of the Best: Without Warning '98

Tom Bell
Catherine Cookson's The Cinder Path '94

Bill Bellamy
Any Given Sunday '99
Love Stinks '99

Florence Bellamy
Immoral Tales '74

Ned Bellamy
Carnosaur '93

Ralph Bellamy
Rosemary's Baby '68

Clara Bellar
The First 9 1/2 Weeks '98

Harry Bellaver
The Old Man and the Sea '58
The Lemon Drop Kid '51

Kathleen Beller
Fort Apache, the Bronx '81
The Godfather, Part 2 '74

Melvin Belli
Gimme Shelter '70

Maria Bello
Coyote Ugly '00
Duets '00

Gil Bellows
Beautiful Joe '00

Monica Bellucci
Under Suspicion '00

Jean-Paul Belmondo
Mississippi Mermaid '69

Lara Belmont
The War Zone '98

Robert Beltran
El Diablo '90

James Belushi
Return to Me '00
Backlash '99
K-911 '99
The Florentine '98
Stories from My Childhood '98 (V)
Canadian Bacon '94
The Pebble and the Penguin '94 (V)
Salvador [SE] '86

Richard Belzer
Homicide: The Movie '00
Get On the Bus '96

Maggie Bemby
Angels' Wild Women '72

Paul Ben-Victor
Drowning Mona '00
Gun Shy '00
Kiss Toledo Goodbye '00
Crazy in Alabama '99
Maximum Risk '96

Peter Benchley
Jaws [CE] '75

Michael C. Bendetti
Red Shoe Diaries: Luscious Lola '00

Sherry Bendorf
Slaughterhouse '87

Caprice Benedetti
Italian Movie '93

Billy (William) Benedict
Ghosts on the Loose '43

Broc Benedict
Seamless '00

Dirk Benedict
Ruckus '81

Paul Benedict
The Addams Family '91
This Is Spinal Tap [MGM] '84

Richard Benedict
A Walk in the Sun '46

Murilo Benicio
Woman on Top '00

Annette Bening
What Planet Are You From? '00
American Beauty [SE] '99
Postcards from the Edge '90

Paul Benjamin
Hoodlum '96

Richard Benjamin
Saturday the 14th '81
Catch-22 '70

Scott Benjaminson
Rudy [SE] '93

Heinz Bennent
Possession '81

Andrew Bennett
Angela's Ashes '99 (N)

Belle Bennett
Battle of the Sexes '28

Bruce (Herman Brix) Bennett
The Cosmic Man '59
Shadow of Chinatown '36

Darlene Bennett
Another Day, Another Man '66
Bad Girls Go to Hell / Another Day, Another Man '65

Hywel Bennett
Endless Night '71

Jeff Bennett
Lady and the Tramp 2: Scamp's Adventure '01 (V)
Land Before Time 7: The Stone of Cold Fire '00 (V)

Joan Bennett
Father's Little Dividend '51

June Marie Bennett
The Adventures of Priscilla, Queen of the Desert [MGM] '94

Marjorie Bennett
Kiss Me Deadly '55

Maureen Bennett
The Mirror Crack'd '80

Nigel Bennett
Gotti '96

Rita Bennett
Another Day, Another Man '66

Jack Benny
The Great Lover '49

Abraham Benrubi
Under Oath '97

Amber Benson
The Crush '93

Lucas Black
All the Pretty Horses '00
The Miracle Worker '00
Crazy in Alabama '99

Michael Ian Black
The Bogus Witch Project '00

Shane Black
Predator [20th Century Fox]
'87

Julia Blackburn
The Head Mistress '68

Stephen Blackehart
Retro Puppet Master '99

Don Blackman
The Old Man and the Sea '58

Honor Blackman
The Avengers 1964–66 '67

Jeana Blackman
Sideshow '00

Jeremy Blackman
Magnolia '99

Sidney Blackmer
Rosemary's Baby '68

David Blackwell
China O'Brien '88

Nicola Blackwell
Billy Elliot '00

Taurean Blacque
Deepstar Six '89

Ruben Blades
All the Pretty Horses '00
The Cradle Will Rock '99
The Josephine Baker Story '90
The Lemon Sisters '90
Mo' Better Blues '90
Fatal Beauty '87

Charlene Blaine
Fugitive Champion '99

Vivian Blaine
Parasite '82
Guys and Dolls '55

Betsy Blair
Marty '55

Linda Blair
Ruckus '81

Selma Blair
Down to You '00
Girl '98

Tom Blair
The Bed You Sleep In '93

Ellen Blake
Last Resort '86

Geoffrey Blake
Castaway '00

Noah Blake
The Base '99

Colin Blakely
Evil under the Sun '82

Susan Blakely
The Perfect Nanny '00
My Mom's a Werewolf '89
The Lords of Flatbush '74

Ronee Blakley
Nashville '75

Jolene Blalock
Jason and the Argonauts '00

Dominique Blanchar
L'Avventura '60

Rachel Blanchard
Road Trip '00

Cate Blanchett
The Talented Mr. Ripley '99
Paradise Road '97

Uxia Blanco
Butterfly '00

Mark Blankfield
The Midnight Hour '86

Billy Blanks
Bloodfist '89

Txema Blasco
Tierra '95

Sylvana Blasi
Bed and Board '70

Jonah Blechman
Fall Time '94

Debra Blee
Beach Girls '82

Yasmine Bleeth
Coming Soon '99

Brian Blessed
I, Claudius '91
Henry V '89

Brenda Blethyn
Saving Grace '00

Debora Bloch
Bossa Nova '99

Robert Bloch
The Fantasy Film Worlds of
George Pal '86

Sebastian Blomberg
Anatomy [SE] '00

Joan Blondell
Opening Night '77
Support Your Local Gunfight-
er '71
Topper Returns '41

Simone Blondell
Dr. Frankenstein's Castle of
Freaks '74

Bill A. Bloom
Teenage Strangler '64

Brian Bloom
Extramarital '98

Claire Bloom
Crimes & Misdemeanors
[MGM] '89

John Bloom
Dracula vs. Frankenstein '71

**John (Joe Bob Briggs)
Bloom**
The Texas Chainsaw Mas-
sacre 2 '86

Scott Bloom
The Stuff '85

Verna Bloom
The Last Temptation of Christ
'88

Eric Blore
The Adventures of Ichabod
and Mr. Toad '49 (V)

Roberts Blossom
The Last Temptation of Christ
'88

Lisa Blount
An Officer and a Gentleman
'82
Dead and Buried '81

Monte Blue
The Marriage Circle '24
Affairs of Anatol '21

Brady Bluhm
The Crazysitter '94

Mark Blum
Desperately Seeking Susan
'85

Lothaire Bluteau
I Shot Andy Warhol '96
Black Robe '91

John Blythe
Alfred Hitchcock's Bon Voyage & Aventure Malgache
'44

Peter Blythe
Frankenstein Created Woman
'66

Brigitta Boccoli
Manhattan Baby '82

Hart Bochner
Urban Legends 2: Final Cut
'00
Batman: Mask of the Phan-
tasm '93 (V)
Supergirl '84

Lloyd Bochner
Naked Gun 2 1/2: The Smell
of Fear '91

Robert Bockstael
All I Wanna Do '98

Wolfgang Bodison
Goodbye America '97

Jenna Bodnar
Best of Intimate Sessions:
Vol. 2 '99
The Portrait '99
Sex Files: Ancient Desires
'99

Kim Bodnia
Pusher '96
Nightwatch '94

Sergei Bodrov Jr.
East-West '99

Earl Boen
Nutty Professor 2: The
Klumps [1 CE] '00
Nutty Professor 2: The
Klumps [2 Uncensored] '00
Terminator 2: Judgment Day
[2 SE] '91

Dirk Bogarde
King and Country '64
Damn the Defiant '62

Humphrey Bogart
The Barefoot Contessa '54
Beat the Devil '53
The Maltese Falcon '41
Midnight '34

Peter Bogdanovich
Rated X '00
Coming Soon '99
Saint Jack '79
The Wild Angels '66

Thomas Jacob Bogert
Titanic 2000 '00

Gail Boggs
Ghost '90

Eric Bogosian
Gossip '99
Talk Radio '88

Corinne Bohrer
Kisses in the Dark '97

Richard Bohringer
The Cook, the Thief, His Wife
& Her Lover '90

Romane Bohringer
Portraits Chinois '96

Samuel Boidin
The Life of Jesus '96

James Bolam
Crucible of Terror '72

John Bolger
Just Looking '99
Parting Glances '86

Florinda Bolkan
Don't Torture a Duckling '72
The Last Valley '71

Joseph Bologna
Blame It on Rio '84
Honor Thy Father '73

Catharine Bolt
The Brothers McMullen '94

Jon Bon Jovi
U-571 [CE] '00
No Looking Back '98
Row Your Boat '98
Homegrown '97
Moonlight and Valentino '95

Paolo Bonacelli
The Stendahl Syndrome '95

Danny Bonaduce
H.O.T.S. '79
Charlotte's Web '73 (V)

Fortunio Bonanova
An Affair to Remember '57

Derek Bond
The Stranger from Venus '54

James Bond III
School Daze '88

Jessie Bond
Topsy Turvy '99

Samantha Bond
The World Is Not Enough [SE]
'99

Steve Bond
H.O.T.S. '79

Ward Bond
The Maltese Falcon '41

Beulah Bondi
Penny Serenade '41
Our Town '40
Rain '32
Street Scene '31

De'Aundre Bonds
Three Strikes '00
Ill-Gotten Gains '97
Get On the Bus '96

Layzie Bone
Bar-B-Q '00

Peter Bonerz
Catch-22 '70

Chesley Bonestell
The Fantasy Film Worlds of
George Pal '86

Lisa Bonet
High Fidelity '00

Helena Bonham Carter
Sweet Revenge '98
A Merry War '97
Portraits Chinois '96
A Room with a View '86

Sandrine Bonnaire
East-West '99

Vivian Bonnell
The Josephine Baker Story
'90

Bill Bonner
Satan's Sadists '69

Hugh Bonneville
Mansfield Park '99

Sonny Bono
Airplane 2: The Sequel '82

Brian Bonsall
Mikey '92

Sorrell Booke
Rock-a-Doodle '92 (V)

J.R. Bookwalter
The Dead Next Door '89

Mark Boone Jr.
Animal Factory '00

Pat Boone
The Greatest Story Ever Told
[SE] '65

Richard Boone
Madron '70
The Alamo '60
Away All Boats '56

Charley Boorman
The Serpent's Kiss '97
Hope and Glory '87
The Emerald Forest '85

Katrine Boorman
Camille Claudel '89
Hope and Glory '87

Bronwyn Booth
Kayla: A Cry in the Wilderness '00

Connie Booth
Monty Python and the Holy
Grail '75

James Booth
That'll Be the Day '73

Powers Boothe
Attila '01
Men of Honor '00
Blue Sky '91
The Emerald Forest '85
Southern Comfort '81

Penny Boran
The Erotic Adventures of
Zorro '72

Lynn Borden
Black Mama, White Mama
'73

Veda Ann Borg
The Alamo '60
Guys and Dolls '55

Nelly Borgeaud
Picasso '85 (N)
The Man Who Loved Women
'77
Mississippi Mermaid '69

Alexandre Borges
Bossa Nova '99

Ernest Borgnine
All Dogs Go to Heaven 2 '95
(V)
Mistress '91
Laser Mission '90
Escape from New York '81
The Prince and the Pauper
'78
Love by Appointment '76
Law and Disorder '74
Marty '55
Demetrius and the Gladiators
'54
Vera Cruz '53

Angel Boris
Interceptor Force '99

Matt Borlenghi
The Crew '00

Max Born
Fellini Satyricon '69

Katherine Borowitz
Illuminata '98

Jesse Borrego
Blood In . . . Blood Out:
Bound by Honor '93

Christian Borromeo
Tenebre '82

Ann Bortolotti
Hanging Up '99

Bill Borzage
The Fall of the House of
Usher '60

John Yong Bosch
Turbo: A Power Rangers
Movie '96

Mauro Bosco
Five Dolls for an August
Moon '70

Philip Bosco
Shaft '00
Wonder Boys '00
Critical Care '97
Shadows and Fog '92
F/X 2: The Deadly Art of Illusion '91
Another Woman '88
Working Girl '88
Children of a Lesser God '86
The Pope of Greenwich Village '84

Tom Bosley
Yours, Mine & Ours '68

Simon Bossell
Cut '00

Barry Bostwick
The Rocky Horror Picture
Show '75
Road Movie '72

Brian Bosworth
Mach 2 '00
One Man's Justice '95

Catherine Bosworth
Remember the Titans '00

Hobart Bosworth
Eternal Love '29
Joan the Woman '16

Costa Botes
Forgotten Silver '96

Sam Bottoms
Angel Blue '97
Bronco Billy '80
The Last Picture Show [DC]
'71

Timothy Bottoms
Diamondbacks '99
The Drifter '88
Mio in the Land of Faraway
'87
The Last Picture Show [DC]
'71

Barbara Bouchet
Don't Torture a Duckling '72
Amuck! '71
In Harm's Way '65

Willis Bouchey
The Man Who Shot Liberty
Valance '62
The Horse Soldiers '59
The Bridges at Toko-Ri '55

Elodie Bouchez
Don't Let Me Die on a Sunday '99

Brittany Paige Bouck
Air Bud 3: World Pup '00

Jacques Boudet
Farinelli '94

Jean Bouise
La Femme Nikita [MGM] '91

Daniel Boulanger
Bed and Board '70
The Bride Wore Black '68

Sam Bould
The End of the Affair '99

Carole Bouquet
The Bridge '00

Michel Bouquet
Mississippi Mermaid '69
The Bride Wore Black '68

Joy Boushel
The Fly / The Fly 2 '86

Lena Bousman
The Gore-Gore Girls '72

John Bowe
Poldark '96

Michael Bowen
Magnolia '99

Roger Bowen
What about Bob? '91

Tom Bower
The Million Dollar Hotel '99
True Believer '89
River's Edge '87

David Bowie
The Last Temptation of Christ
'88

Judi Bowker
In This House of Brede '75

Peter Bowles
Endless Night '71

Don Bowman
Hillbillys in a Haunted House
'67

Lee Bowman
Up in Mabel's Room '44
Love Affair '39

Riley Bowman
Bloodfist '89

John Boxer
The Bridge on the River Kwai
[LE] '57

Bruce Boxleitner
The Perfect Nanny '00

Brandon Boyd
Asylum of Terror '98

Guy Boyd
The Jagged Edge '85

Stephen Boyd
Fantastic Voyage '66
Ben-Hur '59

Tanya Boyd
Ilsa, Harem Keeper of the Oil
Sheiks '76

Charles Boyer
Love Affair '39
The Garden of Allah '36

Katy Boyer
Tapeheads '89

Sully Boyer
Car Wash '76

Lara Flynn Boyle
Threesome '94

Lisa Boyle
The Last Marshal '99

Marc Boyle
Omen 3: The Final Conflict
'81

Peter Boyle
Death and the Compass '96

Lorraine Bracco
The Sopranos: The Complete
First Season '00
Switch '91

Alejandro Bracho
Romero '89

Ray Bradbury
The Fantasy Film Worlds of
George Pal '86

Maurice Braddell
Things to Come '36

Kim Braden
That'll Be the Day '73

Jesse Bradford
Cherry Falls / Terror Tract '00

Richard Bradford
Hoodlum '96
Internal Affairs '90
The Untouchables '87
Mean Season '85

David Bradley
Lower Level '91

Doug Bradley
Hellraiser [2] '87

Booker Bradshaw
Coffy '73

Carl Bradshaw
Third World Cop '99
Klash '95
The Harder They Come '72

Charles Bradstreet
Abbott and Costello Meet
Frankenstein '48

Orla Brady
The Magical Legend of the
Leprechauns '99

Scott Brady
Satan's Sadists '69
Mohawk '56

**Eric (Hans Gudegast)
Braeden**
Escape from the Planet of
the Apes '71

Zach Braff
The Broken Hearts Club '00

Kenneth Branagh
Love's Labour's Lost '00
The Road to El Dorado '00 (V)
Henry V '89

Larry Brand
The Drifter '88

Neville Brand
Tora! Tora! Tora! [2 SE] '70
Birdman of Alcatraz '62
Mohawk '56
D.O.A. [Roan] '49

Walter Brandi
The Bloody Pit of Horror '65

Jonathan Brandis
Ride with the Devil '99

Kevin Brando
Saturday the 14th '81

Marlon Brando
Superman: The Movie '78
The Godfather DVD Collection
'72
Candy '68
One-Eyed Jacks '61
Guys and Dolls '55

**Henry (Kleinbach)
Brandon**
The Garden of Allah '36
March of the Wooden Soldiers '34

Michael Brandon
Heavy Traffic '73

J.C. Brandy
Lucinda's Spell '00

Philip Branmer
Edvard Grieg: What Price
Immortality? '00

Victor Brant
The Head Mistress '68

Mette Bratlann
Mifune '99

Benjamin Bratt
After the Storm '01
Miss Congeniality '00
The Next Best Thing '00
Red Planet '00
Traffic '00

Blood In . . . Blood Out:
Bound by Honor '93

Simon Brauer
Ratas, Ratones, Rateros '99

Andre Braugher
A Better Way to Die '00
Duets '00
Frequency '00
Homicide: The Movie '00
It's the Rage '99
Thick As Thieves '99
Get On the Bus '96
The Tuskegee Airmen '95
Somebody Has to Shoot the
Picture '90
Glory [2 SE] '89

Eddie Braun
The Tuskegee Airmen '95

Asher Brauner
Switchblade Sisters '75

Thom Bray
Deepstar Six '89

Jay Brazeau
Air Bud 2: Golden Receiver
'98
Air Bud [2] '97

Rossano Brazzi
Fear City '85
The Far Pavilions '84
Omen 3: The Final Conflict
'81
Dr. Frankenstein's Castle of
Freaks '74
The Barefoot Contessa '54

Bunny Breckinridge
Plan 9 from Outer Space
[Passport Video] '56

Joe Breen
Angela's Ashes '99

Lucille Bremer
Till the Clouds Roll By '46

Ewen Bremner
Julien Donkey-boy '99

George Brenlin
Fight for the Title '57

Claire Brennan
She-Freak '67

Eileen Brennan
The New Adventures of Pippi
Longstocking '88
Clue '85
The Last Picture Show [DC]
'71

Walter Brennan
Hangmen Also Die '42
Meet John Doe [Image] '41
Come and Get It '36
The Invisible Man '33

Dori Brenner
For the Boys '91
Baby Boom '87

George Brent
The Spiral Staircase '46
42nd Street '33

John Brent
Catch-22 '70

Edmund Breon
Dressed to Kill '46
The Scarlet Pimpernel '34

Spencer Breslin
Disney's The Kid '00

Felix Bressart
Portrait of Jennie '48

Martin Brest
Fast Times at Ridgemont
High '82

Richard Brestoff
Car Wash '76

Danielle Brett
Rated X '00

Ingrid Brett
The Witches '66

Jeremy Brett
Moll Flanders [MGM] '96
The Adventures of Sherlock
Holmes '85

Jim Breuer
Titan A.E. '00 (V)
Dick '99

Laurence Breuls
Blackrock '97

Carol Brewster
Cat Women of the Moon '53

Paget Brewster
The Adventures of Rocky &
Bullwinkle '00
The Specials '00

Ricky Brewster
Little Fugitive '53

Jean-Claude Brialy
Portraits Chinois '96
Son of Gascogne '95
The Bride Wore Black '68

Beau Bridges
Norma Rae '79
Village of the Giants '65

Jeff Bridges
The Contender '00
Raising the Mammoth '00 (N)
Simpatico '99
Wild Bill '95
The Fisher King '91
Tucker: The Man and His
Dream '88
The Jagged Edge '85
Against All Odds '84
Rancho Deluxe '75
Thunderbolt & Lightfoot '74
The Last Picture Show [DC]
'71

Jordan Bridges
Frequency '00

Lloyd Bridges
Mafia! '98
Winter People '89
Tucker: The Man and His
Dream '88
Airplane 2: The Sequel '82
Airplane! '80
Rocketship X-M '50
Abilene Town '46
A Walk in the Sun '46

Todd Bridges
Inhumanity '00

Richard Briers
Love's Labour's Lost '00
Henry V '89

Richard Bright
The Godfather, Part 3 '90
Rancho Deluxe '75

Bruce Brighton
The Brain that Wouldn't Die
'63

Eddie Brill
Drop Dead Rock '95

Fran Brill
What about Bob? '91

Wilford Brimley
The Natural '84
Tender Mercies '83

Michele Brin
Secret Games '92

Mark Bringleson
Dead Man '95

John Brinkley
A Bucket of Blood '59
Teenage Doll '57

Bo Brinkman
Gettysburg '93

Bill Brinsfield
Slaughterhouse '87

Vera Briole
A Single Girl '96

Morgan Brittany
Yours, Mine & Ours '68

Barbara Britton
Captain Kidd '45

Connie Britton
No Looking Back '98
The Brothers McMullen '94

Pamela Britton
D.O.A. [Roan] '49

Jim Broadbent
Topsy Turvy '99
Smilla's Sense of Snow '96
Princess Caraboo '94

Kent Broadhurst
A Couch in New York '95

Peter Brocco
The Balcony '63

James Broderick
The Taking of Pelham One
Two Three '74
Alice's Restaurant '69

Matthew Broderick
Glory [2 SE] '89

Don Brodie
Detour '46

Helen Brodie
Monsoon '97

Steve Brodie
Donovan's Brain '53
A Walk in the Sun '46

Adrien Brody
Liberty Heights '99
Restaurant '98

James Brolin
Traffic '00
Goodbye America '97
Lewis and Clark and George
'97
The Amityville Horror '79
Fantastic Voyage '66

Josh Brolin
The Hollow Man [SE] '00
It's the Rage '99
Nightwatch '96

Shane Brolly
Flypaper '97

J. Edward Bromberg
The Phantom of the Opera '43

Eleanor Bron
House of Mirth '00
Alfie '66

William Bronder
Return to Me '00

Charles Bronson
Family of Cops 3 '98
Family of Cops 2: Breach of
Faith '97
Death Wish 5: The Face of
Death '94
Breakheart Pass '76
The Meanest Men in the
West '76
Death Wish '74
Cold Sweat '71
Honor Among Thieves '68
The Magnificent Seven '60
Vera Cruz '53
Pat and Mike '52

Lisa Marie Bronson
The Watermelon Woman '97

Hillary Brooke
The Man Who Knew Too
Much '56
Africa Screams / Jack and
the Beanstalk '49
The Strange Woman '46
The Woman in Green '45
The Woman in Green /
Dressed to Kill '45

Paul Brooke
Dead of Night '99

Walter Brooke
Tora! Tora! Tora! [2 SE] '70

Richard Brooker
Friday the 13th, Part 4: The
Final Chapter '84
Friday the 13th, Part 3 '82

William Brooker
Something Weird '68

Jacqueline Brookes
Naked Gun 2 1/2: The Smell
of Fear '91

Albert Brooks
Critical Care '97
Mother '96
Defending Your Life '91
Lost in America '85
Real Life '79

Carroll Brooks
Mauvais Sang '86
Boy Meets Girl '84

Conrad Brooks
The Beast of Yucca Flats '61
Plan 9 from Outer Space
[Passport Video] '56

Conroe Brooks
2 G's and a Key '00

David Allan Brooks
Castaway '00
Jack Frost 2: Revenge of the
Mutant Killer Snowman '00

Deanna Brooks
The Rowdy Girls '00

Mel Brooks
Screw Loose '99
Look Who's Talking, Too '90
(V)

Richard Brooks
Johnny B. '00

Brian Brophy
Brain Dead '89

Pierce Brosnan
Dolphins '00 (N)
Grey Owl '99
The World Is Not Enough [SE]
'99
Mister Johnson '91
The Mirror Crack'd '80

Dr. Joyce Brothers
The Naked Gun: From the
Files of Police Squad '88
Embryo '76

Ben Browder
Farscape, Vol. 3 '01

Amelda Brown
Hope and Glory '87

Andy Brown
The Daytrippers '96

Anita Brown
My 5 Wives '00

Arthur Brown
Tommy '75

Barbara Brown
Jack & the Beanstalk '52

Blair Brown
Space Cowboys '00

Boots Brown
Tomorrow the World '44

Bryan Brown
On the Border '98
F/X 2: The Deadly Art of Illu-
sion '91
F/X '86

Charisse Brown
Detention '98

Clancy Brown
The Hurricane '99

Drew Bundi Brown
Shaft's Big Score '72

Dwier Brown
Gettysburg '93
The Cutting Edge '92

Ewing Miles Brown
The Astounding She-Monster
'58

Georg Stanford Brown
House Party 2: The Pajama
Jam '91

Hajni Brown
Maniac Nurses Find Ecstasy
'94

Jim Brown
Any Given Sunday '99
I'm Gonna Git You Sucka '88
Slaughter's Big Ripoff '73

Joe Brown
Mona Lisa '86

Joe E. Brown
Some Like It Hot [SE] '59

John Brown
Robot Monster '53 (V)

Judy Brown
The Big Doll House '71

Julie Brown
Plump Fiction '97
Fist of the North Star '95
Shakes the Clown '92

Kimberly J. Brown
Tumbleweeds '98

Les Brown
Bob Hope: Hollywood's
Brightest Star '97
The Nutty Professor '63

Murray Brown
Vampyres '74
Dracula / Strange Case of Dr.
Jekyll & Mr. Hyde '73

N.D. Brown
Q: The Movie '99

Pamela Brown
In This House of Brede '75
Dracula / Strange Case of Dr.
Jekyll & Mr. Hyde '73
Cleopatra '63
I Know Where I'm Going '45

P.J. Brown
Double Parked '00

Reb Brown
The Firing Line '91
Uncommon Valor '83

Robert Brown
Finding Forrester '00

Robert Brown
The Living Daylights '87
The Abominable Snowman
'57

Vanessa Brown
The Fighter '52

W. Earl Brown
Lost Souls '00

Irene Browne
Pygmalion '38

Roscoe Lee Browne
The Pompatus of Love '95

Brenda Bruce
That'll Be the Day '73

Kitty Bruce
Switchblade Sisters '75

Nigel Bruce
Dressed to Kill '46
Terror by Night '46
The Woman in Green '45
The Woman in Green /
Dressed to Kill '45
Sherlock Holmes and the
Secret Weapon '42
The Scarlet Pimpernel '34

Pascale Bruchon
Small Change '76

Beau Brummel
Village of the Giants '65

Dylan Bruno
Where the Heart Is '00

Darryl Brunson
Tha Eastsidaz '00

Andrea Bryan
Awakenings of the Beast '68

Dora Bryan
My Son, the Vampire '52

Nana Bryant
Harvey '50

Yul Brynner
Return of the Magnificent
Seven '66
The Magnificent Seven '60

Reine Brynolfsson
Les Miserables '97

Gino Buccola
Chuck & Buck '00

Colin Buchanan
Catherine Cookson's The
Secret '00

Edgar Buchanan
Shane '53
Abilene Town '46
Penny Serenade '41

Ian Buchanan
Ivory Tower '97

Robert Buchanan
The Girl Who Knew Too Much
'63

William Buchanan
Shadow of Chinatown '36

Horst Buchholz
The Magnificent Seven '60

David Buck
The Mummy's Shroud '67

Betty Buckley
Another Woman '88
Tender Mercies '83

Julie Budd
The Devil & Max Devlin '81

Nancy Buechler
Perfect Profile '90

Jimmy Buffett
Rancho Deluxe '75

Niall Buggy
Zardoz '73

Genevieve Bujold
Eye of the Beholder '99
A Paper Wedding '89
La Guerre Est Finie '66

Joyce Bulifant
Airplane! '80

Peter Bull
Doctor Dolittle '67
Dr. Strangelove, or: How I
Learned to Stop Worrying
and Love the Bomb [2 SE]
'64
Tom Jones [MGM] '63
A Christmas Carol '51

Sandra Bullock
Gun Shy '00
Miss Congeniality '00
28 Days [SE] '00
Two If by Sea '95

Joseph Buloff
The Loves of Carmen '48

Burt Bulos
Yellow '98

Brooke Bundy
The Gay Deceivers '69

Luis Buñuel
The Discreet Charm of the
Bourgeoisie '72

Marie Buñuel
Ma Vie en Rose '97

Cara Buono
Attention Shoppers '99
Next Stop, Wonderland '98
Gladiator '92

Victor Buono
The Mad Butcher '72
Beneath the Planet of the
Apes '70

Hugh Burden
Immortal Battalion '44

Louis Burdi
Double Agent 73 '80

Ray Burdis
Love, Honour & Obey '00

Ian Burfield
Circus '00

Michael J. Burg
The Audrey Hepburn Story
'00

Gregg Burge
School Daze '88

Zlatko Buric
Pusher '96

Billie Burke
Father's Little Dividend '51
Topper Returns '41

Billy Burke
Komodo '99
Mafia! '98

Bryan Burke
Forever Together '00

David Burke
The Adventures of Sherlock
Holmes '85

Delta Burke
What Women Want '00

Kathy Burke
Love, Honour & Obey '00

Michael Reilly Burke
Red Shoe Diaries: Luscious
Lola '00

Michelle Burke
Coneheads '93

Robert John Burke
Fled '96
Rambling Rose [2 SE] '91
The Unbelievable Truth '90

Simon Burke
Pitch Black '00

Kathleen Campbell
Hard Eight '96

Ken Campbell
Breakfast of Champions '98

Neve Campbell
Drowning Mona '00
Scream 3 [CS] '00

Nicholas Campbell
Full Disclosure '00

Paul Campbell
Third World Cop '99
Klash '95

Rob Campbell
Lone Justice 2 '93

Tisha Campbell
House Party 3 '94
House Party 2: The Pajama
Jam '91
House Party '90
School Daze '88

William Campbell
Dementia 13 '63

Tony Campisi
A Home of Our Own '93

Tom Campitelli
Perfect Profile '90

Rafael Campos
The Astro-Zombies '67

Gianna Maria Canale
Go for Broke! '51

John Candy
Canadian Bacon '94
The Rescuers Down Under
'90 (V)
Planes, Trains & Automobiles
'87
Summer Rental '85
Splash '84

Severine Caneele
Humanity '99

Natalie Canerday
One False Move '91

Guillaume Canet
The Beach '00

Stephen J. Cannell
Posse '93

Freddy Cannon
Village of the Giants '65

J.D. Cannon
Cotton Comes to Harlem '70

Wanda Cannon
The 6th Day '00

Richard Cansino
Mirror, Mirror 3: The Voyeur
'96

Jo Canterbury
Teenage Strangler '64

Toni Canto
All About My Mother '99

Yakima Canutt
Winds of the Wasteland '36
Dawn Rider / Trail Beyond '35
Lucky Texan '34
Man from Utah / Sagebrush
Trail '34
The Star Packer '34
Sagebrush Trail '33

Sergio Canvari
Bay of Blood '71
Twitch of the Death Nerve '71

Peter Capaldi
Smilla's Sense of Snow '96
Local Hero '83

Kate Capshaw
Power '86

Capucine
Fellini Satyricon '69

Paul Carafotes
Choices '81

Ion Caramitru
Citizen X '95

Antony Carbone
The Pit and the Pendulum '61
A Bucket of Blood '59

Nestor Carbonell
Attention Shoppers '99

**Stephen Antonio
Cardenas**
Turbo: A Power Rangers
Movie '96

Bill "Chilly Billy" Cardille
Night of the Living Dead '90
Night of the Living Dead
[Madacy] '68
Night of the Living Dead
[Elite] '68
Night of the Living Dead [3 LE
Anchor Bay] '68

Tantoo Cardinal
Legends of the Fall [2 SE] '94
Black Robe '91

Claudia Cardinale
Big Deal on Madonna Street
'58

John Cardos
Satan's Sadists '69

Pedro Cardoso
Bossa Nova '99

Rogerio Cardoso
Bossa Nova '99

Anthony Cardoza
The Beast of Yucca Flats '61

James B. Cardwell
A Walk in the Sun '46

Harry Carey Jr.
The Long Riders '80
Alvarez Kelly '66

Joyce Carey
Brief Encounter '46

Leonard Carey
The Snows of Kilimanjaro '52

MacDonald Carey
Shadow of a Doubt '43

Olive Carey
The Alamo '60

Sandy Carey
Wham-Bam, Thank You
Spaceman '75

Timothy Carey
The Killing of a Chinese
Bookie '76
Beach Blanket Bingo '65
Bikini Beach '64
One-Eyed Jacks '61

Teheya Cariocca
Alexandria Again and Forever
'90

Len Cariou
Nuremberg '00
The Lady in White '88

Claire Carleton
The Fighter '52

George Carlin
Dogma '99
Car Wash '76

Kitty Carlisle Hart
Six Degrees of Separation
'93

Amy Carlson
If These Walls Could Talk 2
'00

Joel Carlson
Communion [CE] '89

Les Carlson
The Fly / The Fly 2 '86

Hope Marie Carlton
Slumber Party Massacre 3
'90

Rebekah Carlton
Leprechaun 4: In Space '96

Pat Carlyle
Marihuana / Assassin of
Youth / Reefer Madness
'36

Robert Carlyle
The Beach '00
Angela's Ashes '99
The World Is Not Enough [SE]
'99

Roger C. Carmel
Alvarez Kelly '66

Art Carney
Pot o' Gold '41

George Carney
I Know Where I'm Going '45

Linda Carol
Reform School Girls '86

Leslie Caron
The Last of the Blonde Bomb-
shells '00
The Man Who Loved Women
'77
Madron '70

Memmo Carotenuto
Big Deal on Madonna Street
'58

David Carpenter
Spiders '00
Gettysburg '93

John Carpenter
The Cradle Will Rock '99

Sarah Carpenter
Poldark '96

Ben Carr
High Fidelity '00

Charmian Carr
The Sound of Music [Five
Star Collection] '65

Marian Carr
The Indestructible Man / The
Amazing Transparent Man
'56

David Carradine
Isaac Asimov's Nightfall '00
Dangerous Curves '99
Animal Instincts '92
The Long Riders '80

John Carradine
The Sentinel '76
The House of Seven Corpses
'73
Blood of Ghastly Horror '72
Everything You Always Want-
ed to Know about Sex (But
Were Afraid to Ask) '72
The Astro-Zombies '67
Hillbillys in a Haunted House
'67
Munster, Go Home! '66
The Man Who Shot Liberty
Valance '62
The Cosmic Man '59
The Kentuckian '55
Captain Kidd '45
The Garden of Allah '36
The Invisible Man '33

Keith Carradine
The Tie That Binds '95
Wild Bill '95
Southern Comfort '81
The Long Riders '80
Nashville '75

Marina Carradine
Dangerous Curves '99

Robert Carradine
Dangerous Curves '99
The Kid with the X-Ray Eyes
'99
Somebody Has to Shoot the
Picture '90
The Long Riders '80
Jackson County Jail '76
The Pom Pom Girls / The
Beach Girls '76

Barbara Carrera
Embryo '76

Tia Carrere
High School High '96
My Teacher's Wife '95

Elpidia Carrillo
Predator [20th Century Fox]
'87
Salvador [SE] '86

Leo Carrillo
The Phantom of the Opera
'43
The Gay Desperado '36

Daniel Carrington
Something Weird '68

John Carrol
Mantis in Lace '68

Regina Carrol
Angels' Wild Women '72
Blood of Ghastly Horror '72
Dracula vs. Frankenstein '71
Satan's Sadists '69

Janet Carroll
The Omega Code '99

Joan Carroll
Tomorrow the World '44

John Carroll
Only Angels Have Wings '39

Justin Carroll
Stormswept '95

Leo G. Carroll
North by Northwest '59
The Snows of Kilimanjaro '52
Bulldog Drummond's Secret
Police '39

Matthew Carroll
Dance with a Stranger '85

Pat Carroll
The Little Mermaid 2: Return
to the Sea '00 (V)

Jack Carson
A Star Is Born '54
Arsenic and Old Lace '44

Lisa Nicole Carson
Aftershock: Earthquake in
New York '99

Scott Carson
Killers '97

Terrence "T.C." Carson
U-571 [CE] '00

Margit Carstensen
Possession '81

Georgianna Carter
Velocity '99

Glenn Carter
Jesus Christ Superstar '00

Jack Carter
Play It to the Bone '99

Jim Carter
The Little Vampire '00
102 Dalmatians '00
A Merry War '97
The Madness of King George
'94

Joelle Carter
High Fidelity '00

Nell Carter
The Crazysitter '94

Terry Carter
Foxy Brown '74

T.K. Carter
Southern Comfort '81
The Hollywood Knights '80

Katrin Cartlidge
Breaking the Waves '95

Charles Cartmell
Jason and the Argonauts '00

Angela Cartwright
The Sound of Music [Five
Star Collection] '65

Lynn Cartwright
The Wasp Woman '59

Veronica Cartwright
Mirror, Mirror 2: Raven Dance
'94

David Caruso
King of New York '90
An Officer and a Gentleman
'82

Betty Carvalho
Halloween 5: The Revenge of
Michael Myers '89

Caroline Carver
The Magical Legend of the
Leprechauns '99

Dana Carvey
Little Nicky '00
This Is Spinal Tap [MGM] '84

Delia Casanova
Midaq Alley '95

Max Casella
Dinosaur [CE] '00 (V)

Chiara Caselli
Beyond the Clouds '95

Bernie Casey
I'm Gonna Git You Sucka '88
Brian's Song '71

Lawrence Casey
The Gay Deceivers '69

Jeanne Casilas
Don't Let Me Die on a Sunday '99

Katrina Caspary
My Mom's a Werewolf '89

Ronnie Cass
Gruesome Twosome '67

John Cassavetes
Opening Night '77
Rosemary's Baby '68

Jean-Pierre Cassel
The Killing of a Chinese
Bookie '76
The Four Musketeers '75
The Discreet Charm of the
Bourgeoisie '72

Matthew Cassel
A Woman under the Influence
'74

Seymour Cassel
Animal Factory '00
The Crew '00
Chasers '94
Imaginary Crimes '94
It Could Happen to You '94

Leslie Cheung
Chinese Ghost Story II '90
A Better Tomorrow, Part 2
   [Anchor Bay] '88
Rouge '87
A Better Tomorrow, Part 1
   [Anchor Bay] '86

Roy Cheung
The Mission '99

Maurice Chevalier
The Sorrow and the Pity '71

Arno Chevrier
Agnes Browne '99
The Red Dwarf '99

Cecile Cheyreau
Spaceways '53

Dominic Chianese
The Sopranos: The Complete
   First Season '00
Went to Coney Island on a
   Mission from God...Be
   Back by Five '98
The Godfather, Part 2 '74

Sonny Chiba
Body Count '95
Dragon Princess '81
The Bodyguard / Dragon
   Princess '76

David Chielens
Ultimate Attraction '98

Jeremy Child
Sharpe's Enemy '94

Hazel Childers
The Cheat '15

Lois Chiles
Creepshow 2 '87
Death on the Nile '78

Joey Chin
King of New York '90

Tsai Chin
You Only Live Twice [SE] '67

William Ching
Pat and Mike '52
D.O.A. [Roan] '49

John Cho
Yellow '98

Marcus Chong
Panther '95

Rae Dawn Chong
Goodbye America '97
Hideaway '94
Fear City '85

Thomas Chong
Cheech and Chong: Still
   Smokin' '83
Cheech and Chong's Up in
   Smoke '79

**Ranjit (Chaudry)
Chowdhry**
Fire '96

Emmanuelle Chriqui
Snow Day '00

Jason Christ
Ice from the Sun '00

Erika Christensen
Traffic '00

Jesper Christensen
The White Lioness '96

Claudia Christian
Final Voyage '99

John Christian
Mob War [BFS] '88

Keely Christian
Slumber Party Massacre 3
   '90

Robert Christian
Bustin' Loose '81

Audrey Christie
Frankie and Johnny '65

Julie Christie
Power '86
Nashville '75

Heidi Christine
Gladiator Eroticus '00
Mistress Frankenstein [CE]
   '00

Eric Christmas
Air Bud [2] '97
The Philadelphia Experiment
   '84
Porky's 2: The Next Day '83
Porky's / Porky's 2: The Next
   Day '82
Harold and Maude '71

Pascale Christophe
Immoral Tales '74

Dennis Christopher
Jake Speed '86

Emily Chu
Rouge '87
A Better Tomorrow, Part 1
   [Anchor Bay] '86

Delphine Chuillot
Pola X '99

Christy Chung
The Bodyguard from Beijing
   '94
The Defender '94

Michael Chung
Yellow '98

Thomas Haden Church
The Specials '00

Eduardo Ciannelli
Monster from Green Hell '58

Eddie Cibrian
In the Beginning... '00
But I'm a Cheerleader '99

Robert Cicchini
The Watcher '00

Michael Ciccolini
Beethoven's 3rd '00

Phyllis Cicero
Steele's Law '91

Jennifer Ciesar
Red Shoe Diaries: Strip Poker
   '96

Diane Cilento
Tom Jones [MGM] '63

Augusta Ciolli
Marty '55

George Cisar
Attack of the Giant Leeches
   '59

Rhonda Claebaut
The Horrible Dr. Bones '00

Gordon Clapp
Eight Men Out '88

Eric Clapton
Tommy '75

O.B. Clarence
Pygmalion '38
The Scarlet Pimpernel '34

Norman Claridge
The Womaneater '59

Al Clark
The Adventures of Priscilla,
   Queen of the Desert
   [MGM] '94

Angela Clark
The Seven Little Foys '55

Betsy Clark
Boxing Helena '93

Blake Clark
Little Nicky '00
Shakes the Clown '92

Bob (Benjamin) Clark
Porky's / Porky's 2: The Next
   Day '82

Bobby Clark
Satan's Sadists '69

Buddy Clark
Melody Time '48 (V)

Candy Clark
Cherry Falls / Terror Tract '00
At Close Range '86

Fred Clark
Dr. Goldfoot and the Bikini
   Machine '66
The Lemon Drop Kid '51

Greydon Clark
Satan's Sadists '69

Kenneth (Ken) Clark
Attack of the Giant Leeches
   '59

Marlene Clark
The Beast Must Die '75
Switchblade Sisters '75

Matt Clark
Kiss of Fire '98
Homegrown '97
Tuff Turf '85
Love Letters '83
Ruckus '81

Scott Clark
Sideshow '00

Spencer (Treat) Clark
Gladiator '00

Susan Clark
Porky's / Porky's 2: The Next
   Day '82

Wallis (Clarke) Clark
Penny Serenade '41

Christopher Clarke
Chained Heat 3: Hell Mountain '98

Gary Clarke
Missile to the Moon '59

Graham Clarke
Laser Mission '90

Lenny Clarke
Two If by Sea '95

Mae Clarke
Pat and Mike '52

Robert Clarke
The Astounding She-Monster
   '58
The Man from Planet X '51

Robin Clarke
White Wolves 3: Cry of the
   White Wolf '98
Inseminoid '80

Lana Clarkson
Vice Girls '96

Patricia Clarkson
Joe Gould's Secret '00

Andrew Dice Clay
My 5 Wives '00

Jennifer Clay
Suburbia '83

Nicholas Clay
Evil under the Sun '82

Jill Clayburgh
Semi-Tough '77

John Cleese
Isn't She Great '00
The World Is Not Enough [SE]
   '99
Silverado [SE] '85
Monty Python and the Holy
   Grail '75

Ellen Cleghorne
Coyote Ugly '00
Little Nicky '00

Christian Clemenson
And the Band Played On '93

Alysabeth Clements
Mistress of Seduction '00

Stanley Clements
Ghosts on the Loose '43

David Clennon
And the Band Played On '93

Corinne Clery
Love by Appointment '76

Carol Cleveland
Monty Python and the Holy
   Grail '75

Edith Clever
The Marquise of O '76

Jimmy Cliff
The Harder They Come '72

Richard Clifford
Henry V '89

Montgomery Clift
The Misfits '61
Suddenly, Last Summer '59

Robert Cline
Unspeakable '00

E.E. Clive
Bulldog Drummond's Secret
   Police '39
The Little Princess '39
Bulldog Drummond Escapes
   '37
The Invisible Man '33

Al Cliver
The Black Cat '81

Kristen (Kristin) Cloke
Final Destination '00

George Clooney
O Brother Where Art Thou?
   '00
The Perfect Storm '00
From Dusk Till Dawn [2 CS]
   '95

Rosemary Clooney
White Christmas '54

Glenn Close
102 Dalmatians '00
Paradise Road '97
Mary Reilly '95
The Jagged Edge '85
The Natural '84

Martin Clunes
Saving Grace '00
Sweet Revenge '98

Kim Coates
Battlefield Earth '00
Full Disclosure '00
Xchange '00

Edmund Cobb
Tales of Terror '62

Lee J. Cobb
The Meanest Men in the
   West '74
Twelve Angry Men '57
The Fighter '52

Randall "Tex" Cobb
Uncommon Valor '83

Bill Cobbs
Air Bud [2] '97
Fluke '95
Pocahontas '95 (V)

Charles Coburn
Gentlemen Prefer Blondes
   '53

James Coburn
Marilyn Monroe: The Final
   Days '00 (N)
The Great Alaska Train Adven-
   ture (N)
Noah's Ark '99
Stories from My Childhood
   '98 (V)
20th Century Fox: The First
   50 Years '96 (N)
Candy '68
Hell Is for Heroes '62
The Magnificent Seven '60

Richard Coca
The Truth about Cats and
   Dogs '96

Leigh Cochran
The Notorious Daughter of
   Fanny Hill / Head Mistress
   '66

Steve Cochran
Wonder Man '45

Michael Cochrane
Sharpe's Regiment '96
Sharpe's Eagle '93

Rory Cochrane
Black & White '99
Flawless '99
Empire Records '95

Iron Eyes Cody
Son of Paleface '52

Barry Coe
Fantastic Voyage '66

George Coe
The Omega Code '99
Bustin' Loose '81

Curtis Cofer
Velocity '99

Scott Coffey
Tank Girl '94
Shag: The Movie '89

Kelly Coffield
The Specials '00

Peter Coffield
Times Square '80

Frederick Coffin
The Base '99
The Bedroom Window '87

Emma Cohen
Cut Throats Nine '72

Lynn Cohen
I Shot Andy Warhol '96

Scott Cohen
Gia '98

Enrico Colantoni
Galaxy Quest '99

Nicholas Colasanto
Family Plot '76

Tim Colceri
Leprechaun 4: In Space '96

Gary Cole
I'll Be Home for Christmas
   '98
Kiss the Sky '98
In the Line of Fire [2 SE] '93

George Cole
Mary Reilly '95
Gone in 60 Seconds '74
A Christmas Carol '51

Hysterical '83
Love Letters '83
Harold and Maude '71

Joe Cortese
Family Enforcer '76

Valentina Cortese
The Girl Who Knew Too Much '63
The Barefoot Contessa '54

Julia Cortez
The Adventures of Priscilla, Queen of the Desert [MGM] '94

Linda Corwin
A Nymphoid Barbarian in Dinosaur Hell [SE] '94

Bradley Coryell
My Dog Skip '99

Bill Cosby
The Devil & Max Devlin '81
I Spy '65

Howard Cosell
Sleeper '73
Bananas '71

Gerard Cosloy
Half Japanese: The Band Who Would Be King '92

James Cosmo
Braveheart '95

Paulo Costanzo
Road Trip '00

Robert Costanzo
Air Bud 2: Golden Receiver '98
Plump Fiction '97

Dolores Costello
Little Lord Fauntleroy '36

Elvis Costello
Straight to Hell '87

Lou Costello
Jack & the Beanstalk '52
Africa Screams / Jack and the Beanstalk '49
Abbott and Costello Meet Frankenstein '48

Kevin Costner
For Love of the Game '99
No Way Out '87
The Untouchables '87
Silverado [SE] '85

Tina Cote
Mean Guns '97

Joseph Cotten
The Abominable Dr. Phibes '71
Tora! Tora! Tora! [2 SE] '70
Touch of Evil [SE] '58
Portrait of Jennie '48
Shadow of a Doubt '43

Oliver Cotton
Beowulf '98

Genevieve Cottreel
The Life of Jesus '96

Marjorie Cottreel
The Life of Jesus '96

Marisa Coughlan
Gossip '99

Kevin Coughlin
The Gay Deceivers '69

George Coulouris
The Womaneater '59

Bernie Coulson
The Highway Man '99
Hard Core Logo '96

Alice Coulthard
The Cement Garden '93

Mary Count
The Arena '73

Clotilde Courau
Deterrence '00

Jason Court
A Night in the Life of Jimmy Reardon '88

Margaret Courtenay
The Mirror Crack'd '80

Tom Courtenay
King and Country '64

Alex Courtney
And the Band Played On '93

Chuck Courtney
Teenage Monster '57

Lynn Courtney
She-Freak '67

Brian Cousins
Longtime Companion '90

Franklin Cover
Wall Street '87

Allen Covert
Little Nicky '00
Bulletproof '96

Jerome Cowan
Getting Gertie's Garter '45
The Maltese Falcon '41

John Cowey
The Loss of Sexual Innocence '98

John Cowley
The Field '90

Alex Cox
Three Businessmen '99
Dance with the Devil '97

Brian Cox
Nuremberg '00
For Love of the Game '99
The Minus Man '99
Braveheart '95
Sharpe's Eagle '93
Sharpe's Rifles '93

Dave Cox
Teenage Catgirls in Heat '00

Julie Cox
Dune '00

Nikki Cox
Nutty Professor 2: The Klumps [1 CE] '00
Nutty Professor 2: The Klumps [2 Uncensored] '00

Ronny Cox
Hollywood Vice Sqaud '86

Veanne Cox
Erin Brockovich '00

Courteney Cox Arquette
Scream 3 [CS] '00

Bill Coyne
Suburbia '83

Peter Coyote
Erin Brockovich '00
Red Letters '00
Rome: Power & Glory '99 (N)
Moonlight and Valentino '95
The Jagged Edge '85
Southern Comfort '81

Cylk Cozart
Play It to the Bone '99
White Men Can't Jump '92

Buster Crabbe
Flash Gordon: Space Soldiers '36

Ruth Cracknell
Lilian's Story '95

Daniel Craig
I Dreamed of Africa '00

Richard Cramer
W.C. Fields 6 Short Films '33

Barbara Crampton
Puppet Master '89

Judith Crane
Mantis in Lace '68

Norma Crane
They Call Me Mr. Tibbs! '70

Kenneth Cranham
Deep in the Heart (of Texas) '98

Lorcan Cranitch
Deacon Brodie '98

Patrick Cranshaw
Best in Show '00
Broken Vessels '98
The Amazing Transparent Man '60

Bryan Cranston
Terror Tract '00

Noel Cravat
The 5000 Fingers of Dr. T '53

Frank Craven
Our Town '40

James Craven
Sherlock Holmes and the Secret Weapon '42

Matt Craven
Nuremberg '00

Mimi (Meyer) Craven
Mikey '92

Broderick Crawford
Il Bidone '55

Hazel Ann Crawford
Postmortem '98

Joan Crawford
Rain '32

Johnny Crawford
Village of the Giants '65

Wayne Crawford
Jake Speed '86

Charlie Creed-Miles
Essex Boys '99

Jack Creley
Dr. Strangelove, or: How I Learned to Stop Worrying and Love the Bomb [2 SE] '64

Richard Crenna
Summer Rental '85
Breakheart Pass '76
The Sand Pebbles '66

Claudia Crepeda
The Story of O: The Series '92

Tara Crespo
La Cucaracha '99

Robert W. Cresse
The Erotic Adventures of Zorro '72

Luke Cresswell
Stomp Out Loud '98

Terry Crews
The 6th Day '00

Wendy Crewson
Mercy '00
The 6th Day '00
Bicentennial Man '99

Bernard Cribbins
Frenzy '72
The Mouse on the Moon '62

Isa Crino
Lilies of the Field '63

Lou Criscuola
Family Enforcer '76

Donald Crisp
The Man from Laramie '55
How Green Was My Valley '41

Linda Cristal
The Alamo '60

Perla Cristal
The Awful Dr. Orlof '62

Criswell
Plan 9 from Outer Space [Passport Video] '56

Emma Croft
Smilla's Sense of Snow '96

Jamie Croft
Napoleon '96 (V)

Peter Crombie
Seven [2 SE] '95

Ben Crompton
102 Dalmatians '00

James Cromwell
Space Cowboys '00
Snow Falling on Cedars '99

Jeanette Cronin
Mr. Accident '99

Laurel Cronin
Beethoven '92

Hume Cronyn
The Parallax View '74
Cleopatra '63
The Phantom of the Opera '43
Shadow of a Doubt '43

Peter Crook
Bird '88

Linda Cropper
Blackrock '97

Bing Crosby
White Christmas '54
The Road to Bali '53
The Adventures of Ichabod and Mr. Toad '49 (V)
My Favorite Brunette '47
The Road to Rio '47

Cathy Lee Crosby
The Big Tease '99

David Crosby
Thunderheart '92
Gimme Shelter '70

Denise Crosby
Red Shoe Diaries: Four on the Floor '96
Pet Sematary '89
Desert Hearts '86

Mary Crosby
Body Chemistry '90
Tapeheads '89

Ben Cross
The Far Pavilions '84

Harley Cross
Shriek If You Know What I Did Last Friday the 13th '00
Dance with the Devil '97
The Fly 2 '89

Joseph Cross
Wide Awake '97

Rebecca Cross
Leprechaun 4: In Space '96

TJ Cross
Gone in 60 Seconds '00

Rupert Crosse
Ride in the Whirlwind '66

Scatman Crothers
Bronco Billy '80
Truck Turner '74
Detroit 9000 '73

Lindsay Crouse
Communion [CE] '89
House of Games '87

Sheryl Crow
The Minus Man '99

Russell Crowe
Gladiator '00
Mystery, Alaska '99
Heaven's Burning '97
Romper Stomper [SE] '92

Dermot Crowley
Falling for a Dancer '98

Michael Crowley
Broken Harvest '94

Marie Josee Croze
Captive '00

Billy Crudup
Almost Famous '00
Waking the Dead '00
Jesus' Son '99
Princess Mononoke '98 (V)
Inventing the Abbotts '97
Grind '96

Le'Mark Cruise
Social Misfits '00

Tom Cruise
Mission: Impossible 2 '00
Magnolia '99
Born on the Fourth of July [2] '89
Losin' It '82

Abigail Cruttenden
Sharpe's Justice '97
Sharpe's Revenge '97
Sharpe's Mission '96
Sharpe's Regiment '96
Sharpe's Siege '96

Carlos Cruz
Guantanamera '95

Ernesto Cruz
Midaq Alley '95

Penelope Cruz
All the Pretty Horses '00
Woman on Top '00
All About My Mother '99
Live Flesh '97

Raymond Cruz
The Last Marshal '99
Alien: Resurrection '97

Wilson Cruz
Supernova '99

Jon Cryer
Went to Coney Island on a Mission from God...Be Back by Five '99
The Pompatus of Love '95
Superman 4: The Quest for Peace '87

Billy Crystal
The Adventures of Rocky & Bullwinkle '00
City Slickers '91
When Harry Met Sally... [SE] '89
The Princess Bride '87
This Is Spinal Tap [MGM] '84

Maria Grazia Cucinotta
Picking Up the Pieces '99
The World Is Not Enough [SE] '99

Concha Cuetos
Slugs '87

Kieran Culkin
The Cider House Rules '99

Patti D'Arbanville
The Boys Next Door '85

Kim Darby
Newsbreak '00
The Last Best Sunday '98
The Grissom Gang '71

Denise Darcel
Vera Cruz '53

Alexander D'Arcy
Horrors of Spider Island '59

James D'Arcy
The Canterville Ghost '98

Severn Darden
Back to School '86
Saturday the 14th '81
Jackson County Jail '76
Battle for the Planet of the
Apes '73
Conquest of the Planet of the
Apes '72

Ruth Dardick
Don't Go in the House '80

Florence Darel
Don't Let Me Die on a Sunday '99

Alan Dargin
The Adventures of Priscilla,
Queen of the Desert
[MGM] '94

Bobby Darin
Bobby Darin: Mack Is Back!
'00
Hell Is for Heroes '62

Johnny Dark
Wishful Thinking '92

Gigi Darlene
Another Day, Another Man '66
Bad Girls Go to Hell / Anoth-
er Day, Another Man '65

Jean Darling
March of the Wooden Sol-
diers '34

James Darren
The Fantasy Worlds of Irwin
Allen '95

Tony Darrow
Small Time Crooks '00

Jane Darwell
The Lemon Drop Kid '51

Nandita Das
Fire '96

Jules Dassin
Rififi '54

Jean Daste
La Guerre Est Finie '66

Alex Datcher
Passenger 57 '92

Kristin Dattilo-Hayward
Mirror, Mirror '90

Brigitta Dau
Retro Puppet Master '99

Jerry Daugirda
Gone in 60 Seconds '74

Richard (Dick) Davalos
Kelly's Heroes '70
Pit Stop '67

Harry Davenport
December 7th: The Pearl Har-
bor Story '43
That Uncertain Feeling [Sling-
Shot] '41

Jack Davenport
The Talented Mr. Ripley '99
Immortality '98

Mary Davenport
Sisters '73

Nigel Davenport
Dracula / Strange Case of Dr.
Jekyll & Mr. Hyde '73
The Last Valley '71
A Man for All Seasons '66

Robert Davi
Body Count '95
Blind Justice '94

Eleanor David
Topsy Turvy '99

Joanna David
Cotton Mary '99

Keith David
Pitch Black '00
The Replacements '00
Requiem for a Dream '00
Where the Heart Is '00
Bird '88
Platoon [2 SE] '86

Laurence David
Midnight Dancers '94

**Lolita (David)
Davidovich**
Mystery, Alaska '99
Play It to the Bone '99
The Object of Beauty '91

Ben Davidson
Conan the Barbarian [2 CE]
'82

Eileen Davidson
The House on Sorority Row
'83

James Davidson
Parasite '82

John Davidson
Edward Scissorhands [SE]
'90

Melvin Davidson
The Firing Line '91

Tommy Davidson
Bamboozled '00
Plump Fiction '97

Embeth Davidtz
Bicentennial Man '99
Mansfield Park '99
Murder in the First '95

Dean Davies
Human Traffic '99

Gwen Ffrangcon Davies
The Devil Rides Out '68
The Witches '66

Jeremy Davies
Up at the Villa '00
The Million Dollar Hotel '99

John Davies
Positive I.D. '87

Oliver Ford Davies
The Murder of Roger Ackroyd
'99

Rudi Davies
The Object of Beauty '91

Rupert Davies
Frightmare '74

Cristina Davila
Ratas, Ratones, Rateros '99

Luis Davila
Pancho Villa '72

Ann B. Davis
Naked Gun 33 1/3: The Final
Insult '94

Bette Davis
Death on the Nile '78
Of Human Bondage '34

Billy Davis
Inhumanity '00

Charles Davis
The Big Doll House '71

Cynthia Davis
Cooley High '75

Elizabeth Davis
Gruesome Twosome '67

Essie Davis
Lilian's Story '95

Geena Davis
The Fly / The Fly 2 '86
Tootsie '82

Hope Davis
Joe Gould's Secret '00
Next Stop, Wonderland '98
The Myth of Fingerprints '97
The Daytrippers '96

Jeff Davis
Sex Files: Digital Sex '98

Jim Davis
Dracula vs. Frankenstein '71
Monster from Green Hell '58

Judy Davis
Alice '90
A Passage to India '84

Keith Davis
Family Enforcer '76

Kristen Davis
Sex and the City: The Complete Second Season '00

Liz Davis
Quackser Fortune Has a
Cousin in the Bronx '70

Mac Davis
North Dallas Forty '79

Marvin Davis
Tomorrow the World '44

Matthew Davis
Tigerland '00
Urban Legends 2: Final Cut
'00

Michael Cory Davis
The Vault '00

Nancy Davis
Donovan's Brain '53

Ossie Davis
Dinosaur [CE] '00 (V)
Get On the Bus '96
Gladiator '92
Do the Right Thing [2] '89
School Daze '88

Philip Davis
The Bounty '84

Reginald Davis
Detention '98

Sammi Davis
Hope and Glory '87
Mona Lisa '86

Sammy Davis Jr.
Cannonball Run '81

Susan Davis
Dementia '98

Suzanne Davis
Fear Runs Silent '99

Viveka Davis
Castaway '00
Time Code '00

Warwick Davis
Leprechaun 5: In the Hood
'99
Leprechaun 4: In Space '96
Leprechaun 3 '95
Leprechaun 2 '94

William B. Davis
The Proposal '00

Bruce Davison
X-Men '00
Six Degrees of Separation
'93
Longtime Companion '90
The Lathe of Heaven '80

Andrew Davoli
The Yards '00

Pam Dawber
I'll Remember April '99

Marpessa Dawn
The Womaneater '59

Kamala Dawson
Lightning Jack '94

**Kim (Kimberly Dawn)
Dawson**
Scandal: The Big Turn On '99

Lee Dawson
The Stepdaughter '00

Richard Dawson
Munster, Go Home! '66

Rosario Dawson
Down to You '00
Light It Up '99

Dennis Day
Melody Time '48 (V)

Doris Day
That Touch of Mink '62
The Man Who Knew Too
Much '56

Daniel Day-Lewis
The Last of the Mohicans '92
A Room with a View '86
The Bounty '84

Vera Day
The Womaneater '59
Quatermass 2 '57

Joaquim de Almeida
La Cucaracha '99
Women '97

Isaach de Bankole
Ghost Dog: The Way of the
Samurai '99

Brenda de Banzie
The Entertainer '60
The Man Who Knew Too
Much '56

Yvonne De Carlo
Mirror, Mirror '90
The Munsters' Revenge '81
Munster, Go Home! '66

Pedro de Cordoba
Carmen / The Cheat '15

Ted de Corsia
The Lady from Shanghai '48

Peppino de Filippo
Variety Lights '51

Manuela de Freitas
God's Comedy '95

Wanda De Jesus
Flawless '99

Geert De Jong
The 4th Man '79

Esmee De La Bretoniere
The Delivery '99

Isait de la Fuente
Social Misfits '00

Danny De La Paz
Picking Up the Pieces '99

John de Lancie
Woman on Top '00
The Fisher King '91

Semina De Laurentis
Nunsense 2: The Sequel '94

Derek De Lint
Soldier of Orange '78

Terence de Marney
Die, Monster, Die! '65

Alberto De Mendoza
Bossa Nova '99

Danielle De Metz
Return of the Fly '59

Robert De Niro
The Adventures of Rocky &
Bullwinkle '00
Meet the Parents '00
Men of Honor '00
Flawless '99
Mistress '91
The Untouchables '87
The Godfather, Part 2 '74
Born to Win '71

Rossy de Palma
Tie Me Up! Tie Me Down! '90
Women on the Verge of a
Nervous Breakdown '88

Lya de Putti
The Indian Tomb '21

Chris de Rose
Aftershock '88

Portia de Rossi
Girl '98

Anthony De Sando
A Day in Black and White '01
Double Parked '00
Kiss Me, Guido '97

Joe De Santis
It's Good to Be Alive '74

Melissa De Sousa
Miss Congeniality '00

Michael De Stefano
Unmade Beds '00

Christian de Tiliere
Bed and Board '70

Valentin de Vargas
Touch of Evil [SE] '58

Jose-Luis De Villalonga
Blood and Sand '89

Hilt de Vos
Venus in Furs '94

Brandon de Wilde
In Harm's Way '65
Shane '53

Brian Deacon
Vampyres '74

Erin J. Dean
Lolita '97

Felicity Dean
The Last of the Blonde Bombshells '00

Jack Dean
The Cheat '15

Jimmy Dean
Diamonds Are Forever [SE]
'71

Loren Dean
Space Cowboys '00

Priscilla Dean
Outside the Law / Shadows
'21

Rick Dean
Carnosaur 3: Primal Species
'96
Bloodfist 3: Forced to Fight
'92

Ron Dean
Rudy [SE] '93

Johnny DeaRenzo
Straight out of Compton '00

James DeBello
Crime and Punishment in
 Suburbia '00

David Deblinger
Intern '00

Nikki DeBoer
Rated X '00
Family of Cops 3 '98

The Debonairs
That'll Be the Day '73

Jean Debucourt
Fall of the House of Usher
 '28

Rosemary DeCamp
Saturday the 14th '81

Jan Decleir
Running Free '00

Marie Dedieu
Bed and Board '70

Frances Dee
Of Human Bondage '34

Ruby Dee
Do the Right Thing [2] '89
It's Good to Be Alive '74
The Balcony '63
A Raisin in the Sun '61
The Jackie Robinson Story
 '50

Tray Deee
Tha Eastsidaz '00

Eddie Deezen
Rock-a-Doodle '92 (V)

Mos Def
Bamboozled '00

Robert DeFranco
Telling You '98

Ellen DeGeneres
If These Walls Could Talk 2
 '00

Pia Degermark
The Vampire Happening '71

Dorothy Dehn
Marihuana / Assassin of
 Youth / Reefer Madness
 '36

John Dehner
The Jagged Edge '85
Airplane 2: The Sequel '82
Support Your Local Gunfight-
 er '71
The Hallelujah Trail '65 (N)

Nicole DeHuff
Meet the Parents '00

Albert Dekker
Suddenly, Last Summer '59
Kiss Me Deadly '55

Thomas Dekker
Land Before Time 7: The
 Stone of Cold Fire '00 (V)

Frank DeKova
Heavy Traffic '73

Maria Del Mar
Price of Glory '00

Carla Del Poggio
Variety Lights '51

Angel Del Pozo
Pancho Villa '72

Dolores Del Rio
Evangeline '29

Evelyn Del Rio
The Bank Dick '40

Alex Del Rosario
Midnight Dancers '94

Benicio Del Toro
Traffic '00
Way of the Gun '00

Suzy Delair
Utopia '51

Matthew Delamere
8 1/2 Women '99

Cassandra Delaney
Fair Game '85

Kim Delaney
Mission to Mars '00
The Drifter '88
Delta Force '86

Michael Delano
Not of This Earth '88

Dana Delany
The Right Temptation '00
The Curve '97
Wide Awake '97
Batman: Mask of the Phan-
 tasm '93 (V)

Majandra Delfino
Shriek If You Know What I Did
 Last Friday the 13th '00

Debra Deliso
Slumber Party Massacre '82

Gabriel Dell
They Made Me a Criminal '39

Esmerelda Della Rocco
Erotic Survivor '00

Michael DellaFemina
Italian Movie '93

Erik Todd Dellums
Blackmale '99

Roxann Delman
Cat Women of the Moon '53

Nikki Deloach
Traveller '96

Alain Delon
Honor Among Thieves '68
Joy House '64

Nathalie Delon
Bluebeard '72

Michael Delorenzo
Gun Shy '00

Julie Delpy
But I'm a Cheerleader '99
The Passion of Ayn Rand '99
Killing Zoe '94
Mauvais Sang '86

Claudio Deluca
Small Change '76

Frank Deluca
Small Change '76

David DeLuise
Terror Tract '00

Dom DeLuise
The Secret of NIMH 2 '98 (V)
All Dogs Go to Heaven 2 '95
 (V)
All Dogs Go to Heaven '89 (V)
Cannonball Run '81
The End '78
Sextette '78
Fail-Safe '64

Peter DeLuise
The Midnight Hour '86

William Demarest
The McCullochs '75

Derrick DeMarney
Things to Come '36

David DeMering
Plan 9 from Outer Space
 [Passport Video] '56

Jonathan Demme
Married to the Mob '88

Rebecca DeMornay
The Right Temptation '00
Thick As Thieves '99

Martin Dempsey
Ulysses '67

Patrick Dempsey
Scream 3 [CS] '00

Hugh Dempster
A Christmas Carol '51

C. Paul Demsey
Assault of the Party Nerds
 '89

Jeffrey DeMunn
Citizen X '95
Betrayed '88
Frances '82

Susan Denberg
Frankenstein Created Woman
 '66

Judi Dench
The Last of the Blonde Bomb-
 shells '00
The World Is Not Enough [SE]
 '99
Henry V '89
A Room with a View '86

Catherine Deneuve
Dancer in the Dark '99
East-West '99
Pola X '99
Mississippi Mermaid '69

Maurice Denham
Damn the Defiant '62

**Marianne (Cuau)
Denicourt**
My Sex Life...Or How I Got
 into an Argument '96

Alexis Denisof
Noah's Ark '99
Sharpe's Justice '97
Sharpe's Revenge '97
Sharpe's Waterloo '97

**Anthony John (Tony)
Denison**
Men of War '94
Crime Story: The Complete
 Saga '86

Leslie Denison
Sherlock Holmes and the
 Secret Weapon '42

David Denman
The Replacements '00

Brian Dennehy
Dish Dogs '98
Gladiator '92
F/X 2: The Deadly Art of Illu-
 sion '91
F/X '86
Silverado [SE] '85
Gorky Park '83
Never Cry Wolf '83
North Dallas Forty '79
Semi-Tough '77

Charles Denner
The Man Who Loved Women
 '77
The Bride Wore Black '68

Richard Denning
An Affair to Remember '57

Nick Dennis
Kiss Me Deadly '55

Sandy Dennis
Another Woman '88

Reginald Denny
Cat Ballou [SE] '65
My Favorite Brunette '47
Bulldog Drummond's Secret
 Police '39
Bulldog Drummond Escapes
 '37
Of Human Bondage '34

John Densmore
The Doors [2 SE] '91

Elisabeth Depardieu
Jean de Florette '87
Manon of the Spring '87

Gerard Depardieu
The Bridge '00
102 Dalmatians '00
Camille Claudel '89
Jean de Florette '87
Loulou '80
Mon Oncle d'Amerique '80

Guillaume Depardieu
Pola X '99

Johnny Depp
Before Night Falls '00
The Ninth Gate '99
Donnie Brasco [2] '96
The Source '96
Dead Man '95
Nick of Time '95
Benny & Joon '93
Edward Scissorhands [SE]
 '90
Platoon [2 SE] '86

Elisabeth Dermot-Walsh
Falling for a Dancer '98

Bruce Dern
All the Pretty Horses '00
Wild Bill '95
Family Plot '76
The Wild Angels '66

Laura Dern
Dr. T & the Women '00
Jurassic Park [CE] '93
Rambling Rose [2 SE] '91
Blue Velvet '86

Stanley DeSantis
The Truth about Cats and
 Dogs '96

Jerome Deschamps
La Separation '98

Anthony DeSimone
The Virgin Suicides '99

Paul Desmond
Legends of the Fall [2 SE] '94

Geory Desmouceaux
Small Change '76

Victor Desy
Rabid '77

Amanda Detmer
Boys and Girls '00
Final Destination '00

Patti Deutsch
The Emperor's New Groove
 [SE] '00 (V)

William Devane
The Hollow Man [SE] '00
Space Cowboys '00
Family Plot '76

Ed Devereaux
We'll Meet Again '82

Julia Devin
The Tie That Binds '95

Andy Devine
Robin Hood '73 (V)
The Man Who Shot Liberty
 Valance '62

Candy Devine
All Dogs Go to Heaven '89 (V)

George Devine
Tom Jones [MGM] '63

Loretta Devine
Urban Legends 2: Final Cut
 '00
What Women Want '00
Love Kills '98
Hoodlum '96

Danny DeVito
The Big Kahuna '00
Drowning Mona '00
Screwed '00
The Virgin Suicides '99
Terms of Endearment '83

Francis Devlaeminck
Small Change '76

Laurent Devlaeminck
Small Change '76

Tim Devlin
Grind '96

Gordon Devol
Harold and Maude '71

Richard Devon
Teenage Doll '57

Emmanuelle Devos
My Sex Life...Or How I Got
 into an Argument '96

Jon (John) DeVries
The 4th Man '79

Colleen Dewhurst
Dead Zone '83
Ice Castles '79
The Story of Jacob & Joseph
 '74

Brad Dexter
The Magnificent Seven '60

Elliott Dexter
Affairs of Anatol '21

Tony Dexter
The Phantom Planet '61

Cliff DeYoung
Carnosaur 2 '94
Dr. Giggles '92
Glory [2 SE] '89
F/X '86

Ayesha Dharker
The Terrorist '98

Andrea Di Stefano
Before Night Falls '00

Rika Dialina
Black Sabbath '64

Despo Diamantidou
Love and Death '75

Don Diamond
The Old Man and the Sea '58

Keith Diamond
Dr. Giggles '92

Reed Edward Diamond
Homicide: The Movie '00

John DiAquino
Pumpkinhead '88

Cameron Diaz
Charlie's Angels '00
Any Given Sunday '99
She's the One '96

Maria Diaz
Extramarital '98

Vic Diaz
Black Mama, White Mama
 '73

Tony DiBenedetto
The Pope of Greenwich Village '84

Luigi Diberti
The Stendahl Syndrome '95

Leonardo DiCaprio
The Beach '00

George DiCenzo
The New Adventures of Pippi
Longstocking '88

Bobby DiCicco
All Dogs Go to Heaven 2 '95
(V)
The Philadelphia Experiment
'84
Splash '84

Andy Dick
Loser '00
Road Trip '00
Picking Up the Pieces '99

Kim Dickens
The Hollow Man [SE] '00

Bonnie Dickenson
Bellyfruit '99

George Dickerson
Death Warrant '90
Blue Velvet '86

Basil Dickey
Flash Gordon: Space Soldiers
'36

Angie Dickinson
Duets '00

John Diehl
Lost Souls '00
Foxfire '96
Gettysburg '93
Mikey '92

John Dierkes
The Alamo '60

Charles Dierkop
Banzai Runner '86

Vin Diesel
Boiler Room '00
Pitch Black '00

Bo Dietle
The Curve '97

Marlene Dietrich
Touch of Evil [SE] '58
The Garden of Allah '36
Scarlet Empress '34

Anton Diffring
The Beast Must Die '75

Uschi Digart
Ilsa, She-Wolf of the SS '74

Dudley Digges
The Invisible Man '33

Taye Diggs
Way of the Gun '00

Stephen (Dillon) Dillane
Two If by Sea '95

Phyllis Diller
The Bone Yard '90
Private Navy of Sgt. O'Farrell
'68

Bradford Dillman
The Way We Were [SE] '73
Escape from the Planet of
the Apes '71
The Bridge at Remagen '69

Hugh Dillon
Hard Core Logo '96

Kevin Dillon
The Doors [2 SE] '91
Platoon [2 SE] '86

Matt Dillon
Mr. Wonderful '93
Drugstore Cowboy '89

Melinda Dillon
Magnolia '99
Close Encounters of the Third
Kind [CE] '77

Tom Dillon
Dressed to Kill '46

Mohiel Dine
An Egyptian Story '82

Paul Dinello
Plump Fiction '97

Mihai Dinvale
Bloodstorm: Subspecies 4 '98

Stefano Dionisi
Kiss of Fire '98
The Loss of Sexual Inno-
cence '98
Farinelli '94

Dante DiPaolo
Blood and Black Lace '64

Kim Director
Book of Shadows: Blair Witch
2 '00

John DiResta
Miss Congeniality '00

Darren Disney
Tap Dogs '98

Roy Edward Disney
The Fantasy Film Worlds of
George Pal '86

Walt Disney
Fun & Fancy Free '47 (V)

Divine
Lust in the Dust '85

Billy Dix
She Demons '58

Richard Dix
The Vanishing American '25

Robert Dix
Satan's Sadists '69

Ivan Dixon
Car Wash '76
A Raisin in the Sun '61

James Dixon
The Stuff '85
Black Caesar '73

MacIntyre Dixon
Gettysburg '93

Omid Djalili
The Mummy [2 SE] '99

Badja (Medu) Djola
Deterrence '00
Mississippi Burning [MGM]
'88
Penitentiary '79

DMX
Backstage '00
Romeo Must Die '00

Anica Dobra
Tito and Me '92

Peter Dobson
Drowning Mona '00
Quiet Days in Hollywood '97

Megan Dodds
Bait '00

Darrick Doerner
In God's Hands '98

Tatiana Dogileva
East-West '99

Charla Doherty
Village of the Giants '65

Shannen Doherty
Girls Just Want to Have Fun
'85

Arielle Dombasle
L'Ennui '98
Fruits of Passion: The Story
of "O" Continued '82
Perceval '78

Richard Domeier
Evil Dead 2: Dead by Dawn [2
THX] '87

Myrtle Domerel
A Bucket of Blood '59

Faith Domergue
The House of Seven Corpses
'73

Wade Dominguez
City of Industry '96

Dominique
Hot Vampire Nights '00

Judah Domke
Whipped '00

Heather Donahue
Boys and Girls '00

Troy Donahue
Assault of the Party Nerds
'89
Cockfighter '74
The Godfather, Part 2 '74

James Donald
The Bridge on the River Kwai
[LE] '57
Immortal Battalion '44

Norma Donaldson
Poetic Justice '93
9 to 5 '80

Peter Donat
Tucker: The Man and His
Dream '88
The Godfather, Part 2 '74

Len Doncheff
Nuremberg '00

Chad E. Donella
Final Destination '00

Brian Donlevy
Pit Stop '67
Quatermass 2 '57
Hangmen Also Die '42

Donal Donnelly
The Godfather, Part 3 '90

Jack Donner
Retro Puppet Master '99

Richard Donner
The Omen [SE] '76

Vincent D'Onofrio
The Cell '00
Steal This Movie! '00
Men in Black [CS] '97
Imaginary Crimes '94
Stuart Saves His Family '94
Mr. Wonderful '93
Mystic Pizza '88

Amanda Donohoe
Circus '00
In the Beginning... '00
I'm Losing You '98
The Madness of King George
'94

Donovan
Bob Dylan: Don't Look Back
'67

Elisa Donovan
Loving Jezebel '99

Jeffrey Donovan
Bait '00
Book of Shadows: Blair Witch
2 '00

Martin Donovan
Onegin '99

Robert Donovan
Passion & Romance: Double
or Nothing '00
Scandal: The Big Turn On '99
Curse of the Puppet Master:
The Human Experiment '98

Ultimate Attraction '98
Passion & Romance: Scandal
'97

Tate Donovan
October 22 '98

Bae Doo-Na
The Ring Virus '99

James Doohan
Star Trek 2: The Wrath of
Khan '82

Paul Dooley
I'll Remember April '99
Shakes the Clown '92

John Doolittle
The Clan of the Cave Bear
'86

Robert DoQui
Nashville '75
Coffy '73

Karin Dor
Die Screaming, Marianne '73
Topaz '69
You Only Live Twice [SE] '67

Ann Doran
Meet John Doe [Image] '41
Penny Serenade '41

Bruce Doran
Black Eagle '88

Richard Doran
Hollywood Boulevard '76

Edna Dore
The Canterville Ghost '98

Stephen Dorff
Cecil B. Demented '00
Earthly Possessions '99
City of Industry '96
I Shot Andy Warhol '96

David Dorfman
Bounce '00

Patrick Shane Dorian
In God's Hands '98

Tony Dorian
Dope Case Pending '00

Daniela Dorio
The Black Cat '81

Michael Dorn
Mach 2 '00
The Prophet's Game '99
The Jagged Edge '85

Thomas A. Dorsey
Say Amen, Somebody '80

Rhonda Dorton
Necromancer: Satan's Ser-
vant '88

John Dossett
Longtime Companion '90

Karen Dotrice
Mary Poppins [2 SE] '64

Michele Dotrice
The Witches '66

Roy Dotrice
The Cutting Edge '92

David Douche
The Life of Jesus '96

Darby Dougherty
Gummo '97

Donna Douglas
Frankie and Johnny '65

Freddy Douglas
The Delivery '99

Illeana Douglas
The Next Best Thing '00
Flypaper '97
Search and Destroy '94

The Last Temptation of Christ
'88

James B. Douglas
The Changeling '80

Kirk Douglas
Diamonds '99
In Harm's Way '65
Seven Days in May '64
Sparacus [Criterion] '60
The Strange Love of Martha
Ivers '46

Melvyn Douglas
The Changeling '80
Being There '79
That Uncertain Feeling [Sling-
Shot] '41
The Vampire Bat '32
Tonight or Never '31

Michael Douglas
Traffic '00
Wonder Boys '00
One Day in September '99
(N)
Wall Street '87

Santiago Douglas
Girlfight '99

Sarah Douglas
Chained Heat 3: Hell Moun-
tain '98
Puppet Master 3: Toulon's
Revenge '90
Superman 2 '80
Superman: The Movie '78
Dracula / Strange Case of Dr.
Jekyll & Mr. Hyde '73

Brad Dourif
Interceptor Force '99
Alien: Resurrection '97
Nightwatch '96
Murder in the First '95
Amos and Andrew '93
Mississippi Burning [MGM]
'88
Fatal Beauty '87
Blue Velvet '86
Eyes of Laura Mars '78

Peggy Dow
Harvey '50

Ann Dowd
It Could Happen to You '94

Ned Dowd
Southern Comfort '81

Barbara Dowling
Dementia 13 '63

Doris Dowling
The Lost Weekend '45

Lesley-Anne Down
Death Wish 5: The Face of
Death '94

Morton Downey Jr.
Body Chemistry 2: Voice of a
Stranger '91

Robert Downey Jr.
Wonder Boys '00
Black and White '99
Natural Born Killers [DC] '94
True Believer '89
Back to School '86
Tuff Turf '85

Cathy Downs
Missile to the Moon '59

Johnny Downs
March of the Wooden Sol-
diers '34

David Doyle
Charlie's Angels: Angels
Undercover '76

Brian Doyle-Murray
Bob Roberts [SE] '92
Scrooged '88

Patrick Doyle
Henry V '89

Shawn Doyle
Frequency '00

Billy Drago
Mirror, Mirror 3: The Voyeur '96
Secret Games '92
Delta Force 2: Operation Stranglehold '90
The Untouchables '87

Jessica Dragonette
Gulliver's Travels [Image] '39 (V)

Betsy Drake
The Second Woman '51

Charles Drake
Harvey '50

Chris Drake
A Walk in the Sun '46

Claudia Drake
Detour '46

Larry Drake
Dr. Giggles '92

Polly Draper
The Tic Code '99

Laura Drasbaek
Pusher '96

Fran Drescher
Picking Up the Pieces '99
This Is Spinal Tap [MGM] '84
The Hollywood Knights '80

Louise Dresser
Scarlet Empress '34

Griffin (Griffen) Drew
Best of Intimate Sessions: Vol. 2 '99
The Kid with the X-Ray Eyes '99
Dinosaur Valley Girls '96

Roland (Walter Goss) Drew
Evangeline '29

Ruth Drexel
The Marquise of O '76

Jean Claude Dreyfus
Son of Gascogne '95

Richard Dreyfuss
The Crew '00
James and the Giant Peach '96 (V)
What about Bob? '91
Postcards from the Edge '90
Stand by Me [2 SE] '86
Close Encounters of the Third Kind [CE] '77
Jaws [CE] '75
Dillinger '73

Moosie Drier
The Hollywood Knights '80

Robert Drivas
Road Movie '72

Jamie Driven
Billy Elliot '00

Minnie Driver
Beautiful '00
Return to Me '00
Princess Mononoke '98 (V)

Dinara Droukarova
Son of Gascogne '95

Alice Drummond
Joe Gould's Secret '00

James Drury
The Meanest Men in the West '76

Lisa Duane
Moving Target '00

Alexis Dubin
Madman '82

Jade DuBoir
Erotic Survivor '00
Gladiator Eroticus '00

Ja'net DuBois
I'm Gonna Git You Sucka '88

Marie DuBois
Mon Oncle d'Amerique '80

David Duchovny
Red Shoe Diaries: Luscious Lola '00
Red Shoe Diaries: Swimming Naked '00
Return to Me '00
The X-Files: Season One [CE] '00
The X-Files: Season Two '00
Red Shoe Diaries: Four on the Floor '96
Red Shoe Diaries: Strip Poker '96
Beethoven '92

Ric(k) Ducommun
MVP: Most Valuable Primate '00
Final Voyage '99

Michael Dudikoff
Bounty Hunters 2: Hardball '97
Bounty Hunters '96

Denice Duff
Bloodstorm: Subspecies 4 '98

Howard Duff
No Way Out '87
Spaceways '53

Thomas F. Duffy
The Lost World: Jurassic Park 2 [CE] '97

Georges DuFresne
Ma Vie en Rose '97

Dennis Dugan
The New Adventures of Pippi Longstocking '88
She's Having a Baby '88

John Dugan
Texas Chainsaw Massacre: A Family Portrait '90

Tom Dugan
Take Me Out to the Ball Game '49

Melissa Duge
Timeless '96

Andrew Duggan
I Spy '65

Tommy Duggan
Omen 3: The Final Conflict '81

Claire Duhamel
Bed and Board '70

Claude Duhamel
Destination Vegas '95

Olympia Dukakis
The Last of the Blonde Bombshells '00
Mafia! '98
Never Too Late '98
Look Who's Talking, Too '90
Steel Magnolias '89
Working Girl '88
Death Wish '74

Bill Duke
Predator [20th Century Fox] '87

Patty Duke
Prelude to a Kiss '92
The Miracle Worker '62

David Dukes
And the Band Played On '93
The Josephine Baker Story '90

Keir Dullea
The Audrey Hepburn Story '00
Black Christmas '75

James Dumant
Bellyfruit '99

Douglass Dumbrille
Son of Paleface '52

Dennis Dun
Big Trouble in Little China [SE] '86

Faye Dunaway
The Yards '00
The Messenger: The Story of Joan of Arc '99
Gia '98
Supergirl '84
Eyes of Laura Mars '78
The Four Musketeers '75

Archie Duncan
Ring of Bright Water '69

Kenne Duncan
The Astounding She-Monster '58

Lindsay Duncan
Mansfield Park '99

Michael Clarke Duncan
The Whole Nine Yards '00

Rachel Duncan
The Crazysitter '94

Sandy Duncan
Rock-a-Doodle '92 (V)
The Fox and the Hound '81 (V)
Pinocchio '76

Stephen Dunham
The Mummy [2 SE] '99

Vic Dunlop
Wishful Thinking '92

Ethne Dunn
Dementia 13 '63

Harvey B. Dunn
Teenagers from Outer Space '59

Kevin Dunn
Mississippi Burning [MGM] '88

Michael Dunn
Dr. Frankenstein's Castle of Freaks '74

Nora Dunn
What Planet Are You From? '00
Air Bud 2: Golden Receiver '98
Working Girl '88

Chris Dunne
Dead of Night '99

Dominique Dunne
The Shadow Riders '82

Griffin Dunne
Search and Destroy '94
The Big Blue [DC] '88

Irene Dunne
Life with Father '47
Penny Serenade '41
Love Affair '39

Debbe Dunning
Leprechaun 4: In Space '96

Mildred Dunnock
Whatever Happened to Aunt Alice? '69
Butterfield 8 '60
The Trouble with Harry '55

Kirsten Dunst
The Crow: Salvation '00
Dick '99
The Virgin Suicides '99
All I Wanna Do '98
Stories from My Childhood '98 (V)
Mother Night '96
Little Women [2 SE] '94

Cheryl Dunye
The Watermelon Woman '97

Starletta DuPois
Big Momma's House '00
Three Strikes '00

Jules Dupree
Straight out of Compton '00

Richard Durden
The First 9 1/2 Weeks '98

Marc Duret
The Big Blue [DC] '88

Shevonne Durkin
Leprechaun 2 '94

Charles Durning
Backlash '99
Jerry and Tom '98
Tootsie '82
North Dallas Forty '79
Breakheart Pass '76
Sisters '73

Dick Durock
Swamp Thing '82

Jason Durr
Sharpe's Battle '94

Andre Dussollier
Perceval '78
It's Raining on Santiago '74

Charles S. Dutton
For Love or Country: The Arturo Sandoval Story '00
Aftershock: Earthquake in New York '99
Get On the Bus '99
Nick of Time '95
Rudy [SE] '93

James Duval
Gone in 60 Seconds '00

Clea DuVall
But I'm a Cheerleader '99
Girl, Interrupted '99

Robert Duvall
Gone in 60 Seconds '00
The 6th Day '00
A Family Thing '96
Rambling Rose [2 SE] '91
The Natural '84
Tender Mercies '83
The Eagle Has Landed '77
The Conversation '74
The Godfather, Part 2 '74
The Godfather DVD Collection '72

Shelley Duvall
The 4th Floor '99
Roxanne '87
Nashville '75

Dominique Dunne
The Shadow Riders '82

Wayne Duvall
A Better Way to Die '00

Ann Dvorak
Abilene Town '46

Earl Dwire
Assassin of Youth '35
Lawless Frontier / Randy Rides Alone '35
The Star Packer '34

Leslie Dwyer
Die, Monster, Die! '65
Immortal Battalion '44

Nick Dwyer
Stomp Out Loud '98

Valentine Dyall
Horror Hotel '60
Brief Encounter '46

Dale Dye
Rules of Engagement '00
Natural Born Killers [DC] '94
Heaven and Earth '93
Sniper '92
Blue Sky '91
Born on the Fourth of July [2] '89
Platoon [2 SE] '86

Danny Dyer
Human Traffic '99

Matthew Dyktynski
Heaven's Burning '97

Bob Dylan
Bob Dylan: Don't Look Back '67

Richard Dysart
Panther '95
Wall Street '87
Being There '79
Meteor '79

Edin Dzandzanovic
Beautiful People '99

George Dzundza
The Beast '88
No Way Out '87

E40
Three Strikes '00

Jeremy Isiah Earl
The Prodigy '98

Jeff East
Pumpkinhead '88

Sister Carol East
Something Wild '86

George Eastman
Call of the Wild '72

Marilyn Eastman
Santa Claws '96
Night of the Living Dead [Madacy] '68
Night of the Living Dead [Elite] '68
Night of the Living Dead [3 LE Anchor Bay] '68

Rodney Eastman
Blue Ridge Fall '99

Michael Easton
The '70s '00

Richard Easton
Henry V '89

Robert Easton
Working Girl '88
Heavy Traffic '73

Sheena Easton
All Dogs Go to Heaven 2 '95 (V)

Alison Eastwood
Black & White '99
Breakfast of Champions '98

Clint Eastwood
Space Cowboys '00
American Cinema: 100 Years of Filmmaking '94 (N)
In the Line of Fire [2 SE] '93
Bronco Billy '80
Thunderbolt & Lightfoot '74
Kelly's Heroes '70
Away All Boats '56

Caroline Eber
Jew-boy Levi '98

Christine Ebersole
Tootsie '82

Maude Eburne
The Vampire Bat '32

Christopher Eccleston
Gone in 60 Seconds '00
Death and the Compass '96
Anchoress '93

Todd Eckert
Sex Files: Digital Sex '98

Aaron Eckhart
Erin Brockovich '00
Nurse Betty '00
Any Given Sunday '99

James Eckhouse
Joseph: King of Dreams '00
(V)

Jean-Philippe Ecoffey
Ma Vie en Rose '97
Portraits Chinois '96

Paul Eddington
The Devil Rides Out '68

Nelson Eddy
The Phantom of the Opera
'43

Sarah Jane Eddy
Stomp Out Loud '98

Herb Edelman
The Way We Were [SE] '73
The Odd Couple '68

Lisa Edelstein
Keeping the Faith '00
What Women Want '00

Sir Anthony Eden
The Sorrow and the Pity '71

Barbara Eden
The Fantasy Worlds of Irwin
Allen '95
The Fantasy Film Worlds of
George Pal '86
7 Faces of Dr. Lao '63
Voyage to the Bottom of the
Sea / Fantastic Voyage '61

**Jerome (Jerry Stallion)
Eden**
The Defilers '65

Valerie Edmond
Saving Grace '00

Dartanyan Edmonds
Rangers '00

Roy Edmonds
Sniper '92

Beatie Edney
Highlander: Endgame '00
Mister Johnson '91

Richard Edson
Time Code '00
The Million Dollar Hotel '99
Thick As Thieves '99
Posse '93
Do the Right Thing [2] '89
Eight Men Out '88
Platoon [2 SE] '86
Desperately Seeking Susan
'85

Anthony Edwards
El Diablo '90
Fast Times at Ridgemont
High '82

Barbara (Lee) Edwards
House Party 3 '94

Cliff Edwards
Fun & Fancy Free '47 (V)

David Edwards
House Party 3 '94

Glynn Edwards
Get Carter '71

James Edwards
Sex Files: Digital Sex '98

Josh Edwards
Femalien 2 '98

Lance Edwards
A Woman, Her Men and Her
Futon '92

Luke Edwards
Cheaters '00
Mother's Boys '94

Stacy Edwards
The Next Best Thing '00
Black and White '99

Michael Egan
Street Gun '96

Richard Egan
Demetrius and the Gladiators
'54

Samantha Eggar
Dead Are Alive '72
Doctor Dolittle '67

Nicole Eggert
Submerged '00

Stan(ford) Egi
Paradise Road '97

Raul Eguren
Guantanamera '95

Jennifer Ehle
Sunshine '99
Bedrooms and Hallways '98
Paradise Road '97

Paul Ehlers
Madman '82

Lisa Eichhorn
Boys and Girls '00
The Talented Mr. Ripley '99
Angel Blue '97

Gard B. Eidsvold
The Last Lieutenant '94

Lisa Eilbacher
An Officer and a Gentleman
'82

Hallie Kate Eisenberg
Beautiful '00
The Miracle Worker '00
Bicentennial Man '99

Sergei Eisenstein
Sergei Eisenstein: Autobiography '96

Anthony Eisley
Dracula vs. Frankenstein '71
Frankie and Johnny '65
The Wasp Woman '59

Carmen Ejogo
Love's Labour's Lost '00

Anita Ekberg
The Red Dwarf '99
Gold of the Amazon Women
'79
Paris Holiday '57

Britt Ekland
Asylum '72
Endless Night '71
Get Carter '71

Gosta Ekman Jr.
The Inside Man '84

John El
Lucinda's Spell '00

Nour El Chef
An Egyptian Story '82

Magda El Khatib
An Egyptian Story '82

Jack Elam
Cannonball Run '81
Support Your Local Gunfight-
er '71
Kiss Me Deadly '55
The Man from Laramie '55
Vera Cruz '53

Ron Eldard
Mystery, Alaska '99
Delivered '98

Tom Eldred
Teenage Gang Debs /
Teenage Strangler '66

George Eldredge
Sherlock Holmes and the
Secret Weapon '42

Carmen Electra
Scary Movie '00
American Vampire '97

Karra Elejalde
Tierra '95
Running out of Time '94

Erika Eleniak
Aftershock: Earthquake in
New York '99
Final Voyage '99
The Pandora Project '98
Chasers '94

John Elerick
Embryo '76

Bodhi (Pine) Elfman
Gone in 60 Seconds '00
Keeping the Faith '00

Danny Elfman
The Nightmare before Christmas [2 SE] '93 (V)

Jenna Elfman
Keeping the Faith '00

Taina Elg
Hercules in New York '70

Kimberly Elise
Bojangles '01
Bait '00

Shannon Elizabeth
Scary Movie '00
Seamless '00
Dish Dogs '98

Evangelina Elizondo
A Walk in the Clouds '95

Hector Elizondo
Getting Even with Dad '94
Necessary Roughness '91
The Taking of Pelham One
Two Three '74
Born to Win '71

Kay Elkhardt
Dr. Goldfoot and the Bikini
Machine '66

Harry Ellerbe
The Fall of the House of
Usher '60

Duke Ellington
Anatomy of a Murder '59

Alison Elliott
The Miracle Worker '00

Chris Elliott
Nutty Professor 2: The
Klumps [1 CE] '00
Nutty Professor 2: The
Klumps [2 Uncensored] '00
Snow Day '00

Denholm Elliott
September '88
A Room with a View '86
Saint Jack '79

**Strange Case of Dr. Jekyll &
Mr. Hyde '68**
Alfie '66

Jack Elliott
The Ballad of Ramblin' Jack
'00

Ross Elliott
The Indestructible Man /
The Amazing Transparent Man
'56

Sam Elliott
The Contender '00
Gettysburg '93
Fatal Beauty '87
The Shadow Riders '82

Aunjanue Ellis
Men of Honor '00

Chris Ellis
The Watcher '00

Janet Ellis
Lingerie '01 (N)

Paul Ellis
Marihuana / Assassin of
Youth / Reefer Madness
'36

Tracey Ellis
The Last of the Mohicans '92

Max Elloy
Utopia '51

Michael Elphick
The Element of Crime '84

Cary Elwes
Race Against Time '00
Shadow of the Vampire '00
The Cradle Will Rock '99
The Crush '93
Glory [2 SE] '89
The Princess Bride '87

Ethan (Randall) Embry
Empire Records '95

John Emery
Kronos '57
Rocketship X-M '50

Robert Emhardt
The Intruder '61

**(Marshall Mathers)
Eminem**
Da Hip Hop Witch '00

Noah Emmerich
Frequency '00
Crazy in Alabama '99
Tumbleweeds '98

Michael Emmet
Attack of the Giant Leeches
'59

Fern Emmett
Assassin of Youth '35

Cliff Emmich
Jackson County Jail '76

Kumiko Endo
Tokyo Raiders '00

Fred Engelberg
Dinosaurus! '60

Robert Englund
Python '00
Dead and Buried '81

John Enos
Red Shoe Diaries: Luscious
Lola '00

John Ensign
Teenage Strangler '64

John Entwhistle
Tommy '75

Nora Ephron
Crimes & Misdemeanors
[MGM] '89

Mike Epps
Bait '00
Next Friday [Platinum Series]
'00

Omar Epps
Breakfast of Champions '98
Juice '92

Sean Epps
Straight out of Compton '00

Kathryn Erbe
What about Bob? '91

Andoni Erburu
Secrets of the Heart '97

Ethan Erickson
Fear Runs Silent '99

Leif Erickson
Penitentiary 2 '82

John Ericson
7 Faces of Dr. Lao '63

Tami Erin
The New Adventures of Pippi
Longstocking '88

R. Lee Ermey
Toy Story 2 '99 (V)
Soul of the Game '96
Dead Man Walking '95
Murder in the First '95
Seven [2 SE] '95
Toy Story '95 (V)
Mississippi Burning [MGM]
'88

Melissa Errico
Frequency '00

Patrick Ersgard
Backlash '99

Richard Erskine
Marihuana / Assassin of
Youth / Reefer Madness
'36

Sylvia Esau
The Quarry '98

Pierre Escourrou
Zombie Lake '80

Bella Esperance
Lady Dragon '92

Giancarlo Esposito
Homicide: The Movie '00
Big City Blues '99
Klash '95
Amos and Andrew '93
Bob Roberts [SE] '92
King of New York '90
Mo' Better Blues '90
Do the Right Thing [2] '89
School Daze '88

Jennifer Esposito
The Proposal '00

David Essex
That'll Be the Day '73

Gloria Estefan
For Love or Country: The
Arturo Sandoval Story '00
Music of the Heart [CS] '99

Will Estes
Terror Tract '00
U-571 [CE] '00
Blue Ridge Fall '99

Emilio Estevez
Rated X '00
Freejack '92
Maximum Overdrive '86
Repo Man '83

Ines Estevez
Life According to Muriel '97

Dindo Fernando
Black Mama, White Mama
'73

Angelo Ferrari
Cyrano de Bergerac '25

Conchata Ferrell
Erin Brockovich '00
Heaven and Earth '93
Edward Scissorhands [SE]
'90
Mystic Pizza '88

Tyra Ferrell
Poetic Justice '93
White Men Can't Jump '92
Boyz N the Hood '91
School Daze '88

Will Ferrell
The Ladies Man '00
Dick '99

Andrea Ferreol
La Grande Bouffe '73

Jose Ferrer
The Sentinel '76
The Greatest Story Ever Told
[SE] '65
Lawrence of Arabia '62

Leilani Sarelle Ferrer
Shag: The Movie '89

Miguel Ferrer
Traffic '00
Deepstar Six '89

Martin Ferrero
Air Bud 3: World Pup '00
Jurassic Park [CE] '93
Planes, Trains & Automobiles
'87

Martine Ferriere
Mississippi Mermaid '69

David Ferry
The Passion of Ayn Rand '99

Gabriele Ferzetti
L'Avventura '60

Debra Feuer
The Hollywood Knights '80

Mark Feuerstein
Rules of Engagement '00
What Women Want '00
Woman on Top '00

William Fichtner
Drowning Mona '00
The Perfect Storm '00
The Settlement '99

John Fiedler
The Emperor's New Groove
[SE] '00 (V)
The Fox and the Hound '81
(V)
The Odd Couple '68
A Raisin in the Sun '61
Twelve Angry Men '57

Arabella Field
The Pompatus of Love '95

Betty Field
Birdman of Alcatraz '62
Butterfield 8 '60
Bus Stop '56
Picnic '55
Tomorrow the World '44

Chelsea Field
Harley Davidson and the
Marlboro Man '91

David Field
Mr. Accident '99
Blackrock '97

Karin (Karen) Field
The Mad Butcher '72
Cave of the Living Dead '65

Margaret Field
The Man from Planet X '51

Sallie-Anne Field
Dance with a Stranger '85

Sally Field
Where the Heart Is '00
Steel Magnolias '89
Norma Rae '79
The End '78

Shirley Anne Field
Shag: The Movie '89
Alfie '66
The Entertainer '60

Todd Field
Broken Vessels '98

Dorothy Fielding
Fright Night '85

Holly Fields
Interceptor Force '99

Kim Fields
Uninvited Guest '99

Stanley Fields
The Gay Desperado '36

W.C. Fields
The Bank Dick '40
W.C. Fields 6 Short Films '33

Joseph Fiennes
Forever Mine '99

Ralph Fiennes
The End of the Affair '99
Onegin '99
Sunshine '99

Patrick Fierry
Sharpe's Sword '94

Harvey Fierstein
Playing Mona Lisa '00
Stories from My Childhood
'98 (V)

Efrain Figueroa
The Apostate '98

Rona Figueroa
Dragonheart: A New Begin-
ning '00

Jon Finch
Death on the Nile '78
Frenzy '72

Millie Findlay
The Last of the Blonde Bombshells '00

David Fine
Titanic 2000 '00

Larry Fine
The Three Stooges: Merry
Mavericks '01
The Three Stooges: All the
World's a Stooge '00
The Three Stooges: Nutty but
Nice '00
Three Stooges: Spook Louder
'00

Ken Finkleman
Airplane 2: The Sequel '82

Frank Finlay
The Magical Legend of the
Leprechauns '99
The Four Musketeers '75
Shaft in Africa '73
I'll Never Forget What's
'Isname '67

James Finlayson
The Flying Deuces / Utopia
'39

William Finley
Sisters '73

George Finn
Youngblood '86

John Finn
Glory [2 SE] '89

Shannon Finn
Playing Mona Lisa '00

Kate Finneran
Night of the Living Dead '90

Warren Finnerty
Cockfighter '74

Albert Finney
Erin Brockovich '00
Traffic '00
Simpatico '99
Breakfast of Champions '98
Annie '82
Tom Jones [MGM] '63
The Entertainer '60

Linda Fiorentino
What Planet Are You From?
'00
Where the Money Is '00
Dogma '99
Kicked in the Head '97
Men in Black [CS] '97

Ann(e) Firbank
Asylum '72

MacKenzie Firgens
Groove '00

Colin Firth
Relative Values '99
Fever Pitch '96

Peter Firth
The Perfect Husband '92
Northanger Abbey '87

Takayo Fischer
Strawberry Fields '97

Tony Fish
Madman '82

**Laurence "Larry"
Fishburne**
Treasures from the American
Film Archives: 50 Pre-
served Films '00 (N)
Fled '96
Hoodlum '96
The Tuskegee Airmen '95
Boyz N the Hood '91
King of New York '90
School Daze '88

Carrie Fisher
Scream 3 [CS] '00
When Harry Met Sally... [SE]
'89
Hollywood Vice Sqaud '86

Eddie Fisher
Butterfield 8 '60

Frances Fisher
The Audrey Hepburn Story
'00
Gone in 60 Seconds '00
The Big Tease '99
Sudie & Simpson '90

Schuyler Fisk
Snow Day '00

Lewis Fitz-Gerald
Pitch Black '00

Barry Fitzgerald
How Green Was My Valley '41

Brendan Fitzgerald
Fantastic Voyage '66

**Colleen (Ann) (Vitamin
C) Fitzpatrick**
Da Hip Hop Witch '00

Jim Fitzpatrick
U.S. Seals '98

Paul Fix
Sons of Katie Elder '65
Sherlock Holmes and the
Secret Weapon '42

Fannie Flagg
Crazy in Alabama '99
Five Easy Pieces '70

Joe Flaherty
Stuart Saves His Family '94

Didier Flamand
Women '97

Fionnula Flanagan
For Love or Country: The
Arturo Sandoval Story '00
Youngblood '86

Tommy Flanagan
Attila '01
Gladiator '00
Braveheart '95

Sean Patrick Flanery
Body Shots '99
Eden '98
Girl '98

Maureen Flannigan
Goodbye America '97

John Flaus
Lilian's Story '95

Noah Fleiss
Double Parked '00

Rhonda Fleming
The Great Lover '49
Abilene Town '46
The Spiral Staircase '46

Jason Flemyng
Lock, Stock and 2 Smoking
Barrels '98

Robert Flemyng
Blood Beast Terror '67

Reegus Flenory
Winner Takes All '98

Flesh N Bone
Winner Takes All '98

Bramwell Fletcher
The Scarlet Pimpernel '34
The Mummy '32

Brendan Fletcher
The Five Senses '99
Air Bud [2] '97

Dexter Fletcher
Lock, Stock and 2 Smoking
Barrels '98

Jay Fletcher
Born to Win '71

Louise Fletcher
A Map of the World '99
Love Kills '98
High School High '96
Two Moon Junction '88
Flowers in the Attic '87
Brainstorm '83

Jay C. Flippen
The Lemon Drop Kid '51

Dann Florek
Beautiful Joe '00

Joy Florish
Broken Harvest '94

Med Flory
The Nutty Professor '63

George "Buck" Flower
Fallen Angel '99
Pumpkinhead '88
Escape from New York '81

Kim Flowers
Alien: Resurrection '97

Roger Floyd
Big City Blues '99

Darlanne Fluegel
Crime Story: The Complete
Saga '86

Battle Beyond the Stars '80
Eyes of Laura Mars '78

Joel Fluellen
The Jackie Robinson Story
'50

Nina Foch
Sparacus [Criterion] '60

Jerry Fogel
Tora! Tora! Tora! [2 SE] '70

Dave Foley
Dick '99

Ellen Foley
Married to the Mob '88

Scott Foley
Scream 3 [CS] '00

Abel Folk
Sharpe's Gold '94

Bridget Fonda
It Could Happen to You '94
The Godfather, Part 3 '90
Shag: The Movie '89

Henry Fonda
Meteor '79
Yours, Mine & Ours '68
In Harm's Way '65
Fail-Safe '64
Twelve Angry Men '57

Jane Fonda
9 to 5 '80
Cat Ballou [SE] '65
Joy House '64

Peter Fonda
Thomas and the Magic Rail-
road '00
The Passion of Ayn Rand '99
Cannonball Run '81
The Wild Angels '66

Phil Fondacaro
Sideshow '00
The Creeps '97

Olaf Fonss
The Indian Tomb '21

Joan Fontaine
The Witches '66
Voyage to the Bottom of the
Sea / Fantastic Voyage '61

Genevieve Fontanel
The Man Who Loved Women
'77

June Foray
The Adventures of Rocky &
Bullwinkle '00
Thumbelina '94 (V)

Bryan Forbes
Quatermass 2 '57

Michelle Forbes
Homicide: The Movie '00

Christelle Ford
Bloody Murder '99

Dorothy Ford
Jack & the Beanstalk '52

Glenn Ford
Superman: The Movie '78
The Loves of Carmen '48
Gilda '46

Harrison Ford
Foolish Wives '22
Shadows '22

Harrison Ford
What Lies Beneath '00
American Cinema: 100 Years
of Filmmaking '94 (N)
Working Girl '88
The Conversation '74

Maria Ford
Slumber Party Massacre 3 '90

Christopher Fulford
Bedrooms and Hallways '98

Dale Fuller
The Marriage Circle '24

Dolores Fuller
Mesa of Lost Women '52

Kurt Fuller
Scary Movie '00
Diamonds '99

Robert Fuller
Whatever Happened to Aunt
Alice? '69
Return of the Magnificent
Seven '66
The Brain from Planet Arous
'57

Brad Fulton
The Undertaker and His Pals
'67

**Christina (Kristina)
Fulton**
Lucinda's Spell '00
Red Shoe Diaries: Luscious
Lola '00

Garvin Funches
Blue Ridge Fall '99

Stephen Fung
Gen-X Cops '99

Annette Funicello
Dr. Goldfoot and the Bikini
Machine '66
Beach Blanket Bingo '65
Bikini Beach '64
Beach Party '63

Joseph Fuqua
Gettysburg '93

Edward Furlong
Animal Factory '00
A Home of Our Own '93
Terminator 2: Judgment Day
[2 SE] '91

Benno Furmann
Anatomy [SE] '00

Judith Furse
Black Narcissus '47

Joseph Furst
Diamonds Are Forever [SE]
'71

Stephen Furst
Buzz Lightyear of Star Com-
mand: The Adventure
Begins '00 (V)

Billy Fury
That'll Be the Day '73

Ed Fury
Dinosaur Valley Girls '96

Richard Gabai
Dear Santa '98
Vice Girls '96
Assault of the Party Nerds 2:
Heavy Petting Detective '95
Assault of the Party Nerds
'89

Clark Gable
The Misfits '61

Eva Gabor
Naked Gun 2 1/2: The Smell
of Fear '91
The Rescuers Down Under
'90 (V)
The Aristocats '70 (V)
The Last Time I Saw Paris '54

Zsa Zsa Gabor
Touch of Evil [SE] '58

Sasson Gabray
The Impossible Spy '87

Ruth Gabriel
Running out of Time '94

Monique Gabrielle
Not of This Earth '88

John Gaden
A Little Bit of Soul '97

Dick Gaffield
Something Weird '68

David Gaffney
Parasite '95

Leona Gage
Tales of Terror '62

Patricia Gage
Rabid '77

Holly Gagnier
Girls Just Want to Have Fun
'85

Boyd Gaines
The Confession '98
Porky's / Porky's: The Next
Day '82

M.C. Gainey
El Diablo '90

Courtney Gains
No Code of Conduct '98
Lust in the Dust '85
Children of the Corn '84

Charlotte Gainsbourg
The Cement Garden '93

Christine Galbo
Let Sleeping Corpses Lie '74

David Gale
Bride of Re-Animator '89

Linda Gale
Teenage Gang Debs /
Teenage Strangler '66

Johnny Galecki
Bounce '00
Playing Mona Lisa '00

Anna Galiena
Excellent Cadavers '99

Eileen Galindro
Double Parked '00

Annie Galipeau
Grey Owl '99

Bronagh Gallagher
Mary Reilly '95

Peter Gallagher
Center Stage '00
American Beauty [SE] '99
Mother's Boys '94
Malice [MGM] '93

Ely Galleani
Five Dolls for an August
Moon '70

Gina Gallego
Lust in the Dust '85

Zach Galligan
The First to Go '97
Warlock: The Armageddon
'93

Michaela Gallo
Beethoven's 3rd '00

Don Galloway
Two Moon Junction '88

Jean-François Galotte
Ma Vie en Rose '97

Rita Gam
Mohawk '56

Mason Gamble
Bad Moon '96

Michael Gambon
The Last September '99

Mary Reilly '95
The Cook, the Thief, His Wife
& Her Lover '90
The Beast Must Die '75

James Gammon
The Cell '00
Traveller '96
Wild Bill '95
The McCullochs '75

Yvonne Gamy
Manon of the Spring '87

Marguerite Gance
Fall of the House of Usher
'28

James Gandolfini
The Sopranos: The Complete
First Season '00
Dance with the Devil '97
She's So Lovely '97
Italian Movie '93

Tony Ganios
Porky's 2: The Next Day '83
Porky's / Porky's 2: The Next
Day '82

Richard Ganoung
Parting Glances '86

Richard Gant
Johnny B. '00
Nutty Professor 2: The
Klumps [1 CE] '00
Nutty Professor 2: The
Klumps [2 Uncensored] '00
Sour Grapes '98

Bruno Ganz
The Marquise of O '76

Kaz Garas
Puppet Master 5: The Latest
Chapter '94

Matthew Garber
Mary Poppins [2 SE] '64

Victor Garber
Annie '99

Adam Garcia
Coyote Ugly '00

Andy Garcia
For Love or Country: The
Arturo Sandoval Story '00
Hoodlum '96
The Godfather, Part 3 '90
Internal Affairs '90
The Untouchables '87
Mean Season '85

Eddie Garcia
Black Mama, White Mama '73

Jerry Garcia
Gimme Shelter '70

Juan Garcia
Bounce '00

Nicole Garcia
Mon Oncle d'Amerique '80

Sancho Garcia
Outlaw Justice '98

Vincent Gardenia
Death Wish '74

Reginald Gardiner
The Flying Deuces / Utopia
'39

Arthur Gardner
Assassin of Youth '35

Ava Gardner
The Kidnapping of the Presi-
dent '80
The Cassandra Crossing '76
The Sentinel '76
Seven Days in May '64
The Barefoot Contessa '54
The Snows of Kilimanjaro '52
Ghosts on the Loose '43

Jimmy Gardner
Frenzy '72

Joan Gardner
The Scarlet Pimpernel '34

Rose Gardner
Inn of 1000 Sins '75

Jennifer Gareis
Miss Congeniality '00
The 6th Day '00

Martin Dahl Garfalk
Cross My Heart and Hope to
Die '94

Allen (Goorwitz) Garfield
Diabolique '96
Nashville '75
The Conversation '74
Bananas '71
Cry Uncle '71

John Garfield
They Made Me a Criminal '39

John David Garfield
Golden Voyage of Sinbad '73

Michael Garfield
Slugs '87

Art Garfunkel
Boxing Helena '93
Catch-22 '70

William Gargan
Rain '32

Troy Garity
Steal This Movie! '00

Beverly Garland
D.O.A. [Roan] '49

Judy Garland
A Star Is Born '54
Till the Clouds Roll By '46

Lee Garlington
My Life '93

James Garner
Space Cowboys '00
Support Your Local Gunfight-
er '71

Jennifer Garner
Aftershock: Earthquake in
New York '99

Gale Garnett
32 Short Films about Glenn
Gould '93
Mr. & Mrs. Bridge '90

Janeane Garofalo
The Adventures of Rocky &
Bullwinkle '00
Steal This Movie! '00
Titan A.E. '00 (V)
What Planet Are You From?
'00
Dogma '99
The Minus Man '99
Thick As Thieves '99
The Truth about Cats and
Dogs '96

Teri Garr
Dick '99
Tootsie '82
Close Encounters of the Third
Kind [CE] '77
The Conversation '74

Martin Garralaga
The Fighter '52

Donna Garrat
Diamonds Are Forever [SE]
'71

Betty Garrett
Take Me Out to the Ball
Game '49

Hank Garrett
The Boys Next Door '85

Barbara Garrick
A Couch in New York '95

Pat Garrison
The Flying Saucer '50

Willie Garson
Play It to the Bone '99
Untamed Heart '93

Jennie Garth
Telling You '98

Lorraine Gary
Jaws: The Revenge '87
Jaws [CE] '75

Vittorio Gassman
Big Deal on Madonna Street
'58

Ana Gasteyer
What Women Want '00
Dick '99

Michael Gaston
Bless the Child '00

Larry Gates
The Sand Pebbles '66

John Gatins
Leprechaun 3 '95

James Gatsby
The Monster of Camp Sun-
shine '64

Mikkel Gaup
Breaking the Waves '95

Dyna Gauzy
The Red Dwarf '99

John Gavin
Sparacus [Criterion] '60

Cassandra Gaviola
Conan the Barbarian [2 CE]
'82

Monica Gayle
Switchblade Sisters '75

Mitch Gaylord
Animal Instincts '92

George Gaynes
Dead Men Don't Wear Plaid
'82
Tootsie '82

Mitzi Gaynor
There's No Business Like
Show Business '54

Eunice Gayson
From Russia with Love [2 SE]
'63

Ben Gazzara
The List '99
Illuminata '98
Saint Jack '79
Opening Night '77
The Killing of a Chinese
Bookie '76
The Bridge at Remagen '69
Anatomy of a Murder '59

Michael V. Gazzo
The Godfather, Part 2 '74

Karl Geary
Hamlet '00
The Book of Stars '99

Martina Gedeck
Jew-boy Levi '98

Maria Geelbooi
Running Free '00

Ellen Geer
Harold and Maude '71

Thad Geer
Sex Files: Digital Sex '98
Passion & Romance: Scandal
'97

Girl, Interrupted '99
The Magical Legend of the
 Leprechauns '99
Moonlight and Valentino '95
Ghost '90
Kiss Shot '89
Fatal Beauty '87

Jeff Goldblum
The Lost World: Jurassic Park
 2 [CE] '97
Nine Months '95
Hideaway '94
Jurassic Park [CE] '93
The Fly / The Fly 2 '86
Silverado [SE] '85
The Sentinel '76
Nashville '75
Death Wish '74

Annie Golden
The Pebble and the Penguin
 '94 (V)
Baby Boom '87
Desperately Seeking Susan
 '85

Devin Goldenberg
Fanatic '82
Cry Uncle '71

Goldie
The World Is Not Enough [SE]
 '99

Ricky Paull Goldin
Mirror, Mirror '90

Meta Golding
Quiet Days in Hollywood '97

Philippe Goldman
Small Change '76

Lelia Goldoni
Choices '81

Duke Goldstone
The Fantasy Film Worlds of
 George Pal '86

Bob(cat) Goldthwait
Stories from My Childhood,
 Vol. 3 '99 (V)
Back to Back '96
Shakes the Clown '92
Tapeheads '89
Scrooged '88

Tony Goldwyn
Bounce '00
The 6th Day '00
Ghost '90

Richard Golfier
Small Change '76

David Golub
From Mao to Mozart: Isaac
 Stern in China '80

Katerina Golubeva
Pola X '99

Carlos Gomez
Asteroid '97

Carmelo Gomez
Secrets of the Heart '97
Tierra '95
Running out of Time '94

Fernando Gomez
Butterfly '00

Thomas Gomez
Beneath the Planet of the
 Apes '70

Vincente Gomez
The Snows of Kilimanjaro '52

Augustin Gonzalez
The Grandfather '98

Pedro Gonzalez-Gonzalez
Lust in the Dust '85

Meagan Good
Three Strikes '00

Caroline Goodall
Cliffhanger [2 CS] '93

Cuba Gooding Jr.
Men of Honor '00
The Tuskegee Airmen '95
Lightning Jack '94
Gladiator '92
Boyz N the Hood '91

Dean Goodman
Tucker: The Man and His
 Dream '88

Dody Goodman
Splash '84

Greer Goodman
The Tao of Steve '00

Hazelle Goodman
Hannibal '01

Henry Goodman
Mary Reilly '95

John Goodman
The Adventures of Rocky &
 Bullwinkle '00
Coyote Ugly '00
The Emperor's New Groove
 [SE] '00 (V)
What Planet Are You From?
 '00
Bringing Out the Dead '99
The Jack Bull '99
Dirty Work '97
Mother Night '96
C.H.U.D. '84

Garry Goodrow
The Hollywood Knights '80

Barbara Goodson
Weather Woman '99

Liat Goodson
Vice Girls '96

Amanda Goodwin
Working Girls '87

Harold Goodwin
The Bridge on the River Kwai
 [LE] '57

Bob Goody
Dead of Night '99

Michael Goorjian
Deal of a Lifetime '99
Something More '99

Leo Gorcey
Ghosts on the Loose '43
They Made Me a Criminal '39

Albert Gordon
The Bloody Pit of Horror '65

Anita Gordon
Fun & Fancy Free '47 (V)

Colin Gordon
The Body Beneath '70

Don Gordon
Omen 3: The Final Conflict
 '81

Dorothy Gordon
Where the Money Is '00

Eve Gordon
I'll Be Home for Christmas
 '98
Avalon '90

James Gordon
The Last of the Mohicans '20

Keith Gordon
Back to School '86

Leo Gordon
The Intruder '61

Mary Gordon
The Woman in Green '45
The Woman in Green /
 Dressed to Kill '45

Sherlock Holmes and the
 Secret Weapon '42

Roy Gordon
The Wasp Woman '59

Ruth Gordon
Harold and Maude '71
Whatever Happened to Aunt
 Alice? '69
Rosemary's Baby '68

Todd Gordon
Red Shoe Diaries: Swimming
 Naked '00

Joseph Gordon-Levitt
Picking Up the Pieces '99

Arianna Gorini
Blood and Black Lace '64

Cliff Gorman
Ghost Dog: The Way of the
 Samurai '99

Patrick Gorman
Gettysburg '93

Frank Gorshin
Beethoven's 3rd '00
Hollywood Vice Sqaud '86

Marjoe Gortner
Wild Bill '95

Ryan Gosling
Remember the Titans '00

Louis Gossett Jr.
The Highway Man '99
Flashfire '94
El Diablo '90
The Josephine Baker Story
 '90
Sudie & Simpson '90
An Officer and a Gentleman
 '82
It's Good to Be Alive '74
A Raisin in the Sun '61

Walter Gotell
Puppet Master 3: Toulon's
 Revenge '90
The Living Daylights '87
From Russia with Love [2 SE]
 '63

Gilbert Gottfried
Thumbelina '94 (V)

Carl Gottlieb
Jaws [CE] '75

John Gottowt
Nosferatu [2] '22

Ferdinand Gottschalk
Tonight or Never '31

Michael Gough
Anna Karenina '48

Elliott Gould
Kill Shot '01
Playing Mona Lisa '00
Picking Up the Pieces '99
The Lemon Sisters '90
The Devil & Max Devlin '81
Nashville '75

Harold Gould
Romero '89
Love and Death '75

Robert Goulet
Toy Story 2 '99 (V)
Naked Gun 2 1/2: The Smell
 of Fear '91
Scrooged '88

Paolo Gozlino
Vengeance '68

Sofie Graaboel
Nightwatch '94

Paul Grabke
Thou Shalt Not Kill . . .
 Except '87

Betty Grable
How to Marry a Millionaire
 '53

Sofie Graboel
Mifune '99

April Grace
Finding Forrester '00

Helen Grace
Lord Edgeware Dies '99

Nickolas Grace
Salome's Last Dance '88

Topher Grace
Traffic '00

Elizabeth (Ward) Gracen
Lower Level '91

Don Grady
The McCullochs '75

Tom Graeff
Teenagers from Outer Space
 '59

David Graf
Suture '93

Aimee Graham
Shriek If You Know What I Did
 Last Friday the 13th '00
Time Code '00
Dance with the Devil '97
Amos and Andrew '93

Bill Graham
The Doors [2 SE] '91
Gimme Shelter '70

Gary (Rand) Graham
The Hollywood Knights '80

Gerrit Graham
Stuart Saves His Family '94
Last Resort '86
Beware! The Blob '72

Heather Graham
Desert Winds '95
Six Degrees of Separation
 '93
Drugstore Cowboy '89

Julie Graham
Bedrooms and Hallways '98

Lauren Graham
Nightwatch '96

Morland Graham
The Scarlet Pimpernel '34

Tim Graham
The Brain from Planet Arous
 '57

Kelsey Grammer
Toy Story 2 '99 (V)

Alexander Granach
Hangmen Also Die '42
Nosferatu [2] '22

Dorothy Granger
W.C. Fields 6 Short Films '33

Farley Granger
Amuck! '71
Hans Christian Andersen
 [20th Century Fox] '52
Rope '48

Toby Scott Granger
Rock-a-Doodle '92 (V)

Beth Grant
Under Oath '97
Love Field '91

Bryant Grant
Teenagers from Outer Space
 '59

Cary Grant
That Touch of Mink '62
North by Northwest '59
An Affair to Remember '57

The Bishop's Wife [MGM] '47
Arsenic and Old Lace '44
Penny Serenade '41
Only Angels Have Wings '39

David Marshall Grant
And the Band Played On '93

Faye Grant
Drive Me Crazy '99
Omen 4: The Awakening '91

Hugh Grant
Small Time Crooks '00
Nine Months '95

Kathryn Grant
Anatomy of a Murder '59

Lee Grant
Dr. T & the Women '00
Defending Your Life '91
Damien: Omen 2 '78
In the Heat of the Night '67
The Balcony '63

Richard E. Grant
The Little Vampire '00
A Christmas Carol '99
A Merry War '97
The Serpent's Kiss '97
Mountains of the Moon '90

Rodney A. Grant
The Jack Bull '99
White Wolves 3: Cry of the
 White Wolf '98

Shelby Grant
Fantastic Voyage '66

Floriella Grappini
Bloodstorm: Subspecies 4
 '98

Janice Graser
Cyborg '89

Louis Grave
The Sorrow and the Pity '71

Ernest Graves
Hercules in New York '70

Gary Graves
Teenage Catgirls in Heat '00

Peter Graves
Airplane 2: The Sequel '82
Airplane! '80

Rupert Graves
Sweet Revenge '98
The Madness of King George
 '94
A Room with a View '86

Cesare Gravina
Foolish Wives '22

Arnold Gray
W.C. Fields 6 Short Films '33

Charles Gray
The Mirror Crack'd '80
The Beast Must Die '75
The Rocky Horror Picture
 Show '75
Diamonds Are Forever [SE]
 '71
The Devil Rides Out '68
You Only Live Twice [SE] '67

Coleen Gray
The Phantom Planet '61

Eric Gray
Social Misfits '00

Spalding Gray
Coming Soon '99
Diabolique '96

Kathryn Grayson
Till the Clouds Roll By '46

Angie Green
Lucinda's Spell '00

Cora Green
Moon over Harlem '39

D.L. Green
Dear Santa '98

Jeremy Green
Creepshow 2 '87

Kerri Green
Summer Rental '85

Seth Green
Idle Hands '99
Stonebrook '98

Tom Green
Charlie's Angels '00
Road Trip '00

Angela Greene
The Cosmic Man '59

Ellen Greene
Leon, the Professional '94
Rock-a-Doodle '92 (V)
Talk Radio '88

Graham Greene
Grey Owl '99
Thunderheart '92

Leon Greene
The Devil Rides Out '68

Michael Greene
Lost in America '85

Michele Greene
Captive '00

Peter Greene
Blue Streak '99
Black Cat Run '98
The Rich Man's Wife '96

Richard Greene
The Little Princess '39

Shecky Greene
Splash '84

Kate Greenhouse
The Miracle Worker '00

David Greenle
Slumber Party Massacre 3 '90

Brad Greenquist
Lost Souls '00
Pet Sematary '89
The Bedroom Window '87

Sydney Greenstreet
The Maltese Falcon '41

Bruce Greenwood
Here on Earth '00
Rules of Engagement '00
Thick As Thieves '99
Passenger 57 '92

Charlotte Greenwood
Up in Mabel's Room '44

Joan Greenwood
Tom Jones [MGM] '63

Dabbs Greer
Two Moon Junction '88

Jane Greer
Against All Odds '84

Judy Greer
The Specials '00
What Planet Are You From? '00
What Women Want '00

Everley Gregg
Brief Encounter '46
Pygmalion '38

Ezio Greggio
Screw Loose '99

Pascal Greggory
The Messenger: The Story of Joan of Arc '99

Andre Gregory
The Last Temptation of Christ '88

James Gregory
Beneath the Planet of the Apes '70
Sons of Katie Elder '65

Paul Gregory
Henry V '89

Robert Greig
Tonight or Never '31

Kim Greist
C.H.U.D. '84

Adrian Grenier
Cecil B. Demented '00
Drive Me Crazy '99

Zach Grenier
Shaft '00
Ride with the Devil '99
Donnie Brasco [2] '96
Maximum Risk '96

Joel Gretsch
The Legend of Bagger Vance '00

Laurent Grevill
Camille Claudel '89

Jennifer Grey
Bounce '00

Joel Grey
A Christmas Carol '99
Dancer in the Dark '99
Buffalo Bill & Indians '76

Sylvie Grezel
Small Change '76

Richard Grieco
Captive '00
Die! Die! Die! '00
Final Payback '99
The Apostate '98

David Alan Grier
The Adventures of Rocky & Bullwinkle '00
Return to Me '00
Three Strikes '00
I'm Gonna Git You Sucka '88
A Soldier's Story '84

Pam Grier
Snow Day '00
Holy Smoke '99
Posse '93
Fort Apache, the Bronx '81
Friday Foster '75
Sheba, Baby '75
Foxy Brown '74
The Arena '73
Black Mama, White Mama '73
Coffy '73
The Big Doll House '71

Roosevelt "Rosie" Grier
The Thing with Two Heads '72

Jonathan (Jon Francis) Gries
Twin Falls Idaho '99
Kill Me Again '89

Joe Grifasi
Benny & Joon '93
F/X '86
The Pope of Greenwich Village '84

Anthony Griffin
The Curve '97

Eddie Griffin
Deuce Bigalow: Male Gigolo '99
Picking Up the Pieces '99

Kathy Griffin
Intern '00

Rhonda Griffin
The Creeps '97

Robert E. (Bob) Griffin
Monster from Green Hell '58

Tod Griffin
She Demons '58

Anthony Griffith
Panther '95

Charles B. Griffith
Hollywood Boulevard '76

Hugh Griffith
Doctor Phibes Rises Again '72
The Abominable Dr. Phibes '71
Tom Jones [MGM] '63
Ben-Hur '59

James Griffith
The Amazing Transparent Man '60

Kristin Griffith
Interiors '78

Melanie Griffith
Cecil B. Demented '00
Crazy in Alabama '99
Lolita '97
Cherry 2000 '88
Working Girl '88
Something Wild '86
Fear City '85

Nadine Griffith
Ninth Street '98

Rhiana Griffith
Pitch Black '00

Michael Griffiths
Timeless '96

Rachel Griffiths
Me Myself I '99

Richard Griffiths
Naked Gun 2 1/2: The Smell of Fear '91

Lea Griggs
Bar-B-Q '00

Dan Grimaldi
Don't Go in the House '80

Scott Grimes
Mystery, Alaska '99

Tammy Grimes
The Stuff '85

Christina Grisanti
A Woman under the Influence '74

Stephen Grives
Inseminoid '80

George Grizzard
Small Time Crooks '00

Czeskaw Grocholski
Citizen X '95

Charles Grodin
Beethoven '92
Last Resort '86
Real Life '79
The Meanest Men in the West '76
Catch-22 '70
Rosemary's Baby '68

Kathryn Grody
The Lemon Sisters '90

Arye Gross
Gone in 60 Seconds '00
Seven Girlfriends '00
Big City Blues '99
Timelock '99
Mother Night '96
For the Boys '91

Eva Gross
Inn of 1000 Sins '75

Larry Gross
Crime and Punishment in Suburbia '00

Mary Gross
Baby Boom '87

Michael Grossi
The Dead Next Door '89

Albert Grossman
Bob Dylan: Don't Look Back '67

Gulsham Grover
Monsoon '97
Rudyard Kipling's the Second Jungle Book: Mowgli and Baloo '97

Ioan Gruffudd
102 Dalmatians '00
Solomon and Gaenor '98
Poldark '96

Greg Grunberg
The Hollow Man [SE] '00

Olivier Gruner
Interceptor Force '99
Velocity Trap '99

Christopher Guard
Lord Edgeware Dies '99

Dominic Guard
Lord Edgeware Dies '99

Harry Guardino
Hell Is for Heroes '62

Vincent Guastaferro
Liberty Heights '99
Sweet and Lowdown '99

Amr Abdel Guelil
Alexandria Again and Forever '90

Michael Guerin
Curse of the Puppet Master: The Human Experiment '98

Ruy Guerra
Aguirre, the Wrath of God '72

Christopher Guest
Best in Show '00
The Princess Bride '87
This Is Spinal Tap [MGM] '84
The Long Riders '80

Lance Guest
Mach 2 '00
Jaws: The Revenge '87

Nicholas Guest
Puppet Master 5: The Latest Chapter '94
The Long Riders '80

Cary Guffey
Close Encounters of the Third Kind [CE] '77

Ann Guilbert
Sour Grapes '98

Paul Guilfoyle
Mother's Boys '94

Paul Guilfoyle
A Couch in New York '95

Robert Guillaume
Death Warrant '90

Peter Guillemette
Bloody Murder '99

Sophie Guillemin
L'Ennui '98

Cayetana Guillen Cuervo
The Grandfather '98

Fernando Guillen
Women on the Verge of a Nervous Breakdown '88

Bennet Guillory
The Tuskegee Airmen '95

Francis Guinan
Hannibal '01

Tim Guinee
The Pompatus of Love '95
Men of War '94

Alec Guinness
A Passage to India '84
Damn the Defiant '62
Lawrence of Arabia '62
The Bridge on the River Kwai [LE] '57

Tom Guiry
Tigerland '00
U-571 [CE] '00
Ride with the Devil '99
All I Wanna Do '98

Clu Gulager
Tapeheads '89
I'm Gonna Git You Sucka '88
The Last Picture Show [DC] '71

Sean Gullette
Requiem for a Dream '00

Dorothy Gulliver
Shadow of the Eagle '32

Devon Gummersall
Dick '99

James Gunn
The Specials '00

Janet Gunn
Carnosaur 3: Primal Species '96

Moses Gunn
The Women of Brewster Place '89
Shaft's Big Score '72

Sean Gunn
The Specials '00

Dan Gunther
Lewis and Clark and George '97

Bob Gunton
The Perfect Storm '00
Bats '99
In Pursuit of Honor '95
Glory [2 SE] '89

Neena Gupta
Cotton Mary '99

Alizia Gur
From Russia with Love [2 SE] '63

Jack Gurci
Don't Mess with My Sister! '85

Arlo Guthrie
The Ballad of Ramblin' Jack '00
Alice's Restaurant '69

Steve Guttenberg
The Bedroom Window '87

Ronald Guttman
Kisses in the Dark '97
And the Band Played On '93

DeJuan Guy
One Man's Justice '95

Jasmine Guy
Klash '95
School Daze '88

Joe Guzaldo
Hoodlum '96

Luis Guzman
Traffic '00
Mr. Wonderful '93

Paul Guzzi
A Nymphoid Barbarian in Dinosaur Hell [SE] '94

Edmund Gwenn
The Trouble with Harry '55
Life with Father '47

Anne Gwynne
Teenage Monster '57

Fred Gwynne
My Cousin Vinny '92
Shadows and Fog '92
Pet Sematary '89
The Munsters' Revenge '81
Munster, Go Home! '66

Michael C. Gwynne
Cherry 2000 '88

Maggie Gyllenhaal
Cecil B. Demented '00

Nicole A. Gyony
Maniac Nurses Find Ecstasy '94

Peter Gzowski
Tower of Song: The Canadian Music Hall of Fame '01 (N)

Trent Haaga
Terror Firmer [SE] '00

Lukas Haas
Running Free '00
Breakfast of Champions '98
Rambling Rose [2 SE] '91
The Lady in White '88

George Hackathorne
The Last of the Mohicans '20

Buddy Hackett
The Little Mermaid 2: Return to the Sea '00 (V)
Scrooged '88

Ron Hackett
That'll Be the Day '73

Penne Hackforth-Jones
Paradise Road '97

Gene Hackman
The Replacements '00
Under Suspicion '00
Postcards from the Edge '90
Another Woman '88
Mississippi Burning [MGM] '88
No Way Out '87
Superman 4: The Quest for Peace '87
Power '86
Uncommon Valor '83
Superman 2 '80
Superman: The Movie '78
The Conversation '74

Zvika Hadar
Pick a Card '97

Dayle Haddon
Cyborg '89
North Dallas Forty '79

Reed Hadley
The Bank Dick '40

Molly Hagan
Playing Mona Lisa '00

Ross Hagen
Midnight Tease 2 '95
Angels' Wild Women '72

Julie Hagerty
Held Up '00
What about Bob? '91
Lost in America '85
Airplane 2: The Sequel '82
Airplane! '80

Merle Haggard
Hillbillys in a Haunted House '67

Don Haggerty
Hell Is for Heroes '62

Larry Hagman
The Eagle Has Landed '77
Beware! The Blob '72
In Harm's Way '65
Fail-Safe '64

Archie Hahn
This Is Spinal Tap [MGM] '84

Stacy Haiduk
Desert Thunder '99

Sid Haig
Black Mama, White Mama '73
The Big Doll House '71
Pit Stop '67

Kenneth Haigh
Cleopatra '63

Jester Hairston
I'm Gonna Git You Sucka '88
The Alamo '60

Haji
Ilsa, Harem Keeper of the Oil Sheiks '76

Alan Hale
The Inspector General '49
Of Human Bondage '34

Creighton Hale
The Marriage Circle '24

Ginger Hale
The Notorious Daughter of Fanny Hill / Head Mistress '66

Jennifer Hale
Scooby-Doo and the Alien Invaders '00 (V)
Sinbad: Beyond the Veil of Mists '00 (V)

Jonathan Hale
Hangmen Also Die '42

Jackie Earle Haley
Losin' It '82

H.B. Halicki
Gone in 60 Seconds '74

Albert Hall
Get On the Bus '96
Betrayed '88

Anthony Michael Hall
Six Degrees of Separation '93
Edward Scissorhands [SE] '90

Gabriella Hall
Passion & Romance: Double or Nothing '00
The Portrait '99
Ultimate Attraction '98
Lolida 2000 '97
Passion & Romance: Scandal '97

Hanna Hall
The Virgin Suicides '99

Huntz Hall
A Walk in the Sun '46
Ghosts on the Loose '43
They Made Me a Criminal '39

Irma P. Hall
A Lesson Before Dying '99
Buddy '97
A Family Thing '96

Jerry Hall
R.P.M. '97

John Hall
Detention '98

Justin Hall
C.H.U.D. '84

Kevin Peter Hall
Predator [20th Century Fox] '87

Marissa Hall
Parasite '95

Philip Baker Hall
The Contender '00
Lost Souls '00
Rules of Engagement '00
The Cradle Will Rock '99
Let the Devil Wear Black '99
Magnolia '99
The Talented Mr. Ripley '99
Sour Grapes '98
Hard Eight '96

Porter Hall
Bulldog Drummond Escapes '37

Regina Hall
Scary Movie '00

Lillian Hall-Davis
The Last of the Mohicans '20

Charles Hallahan
The Rich Man's Wife '96
Warlock: The Armageddon '93
True Believer '89

John Hallam
The Pallisers '74

Jane Hallaren
A Night in the Life of Jimmy Reardon '88

Gisli Halldorsson
Devil's Island '96

Edmund Halley
Midnight Tease / Midnight Tease 2 '94

May Hallitt
Black Narcissus '47

Billy Halop
They Made Me a Criminal '39

Brett Halsey
Four Times That Night '69
Return of the Fly '59

Michael Halsey
Postmortem '98
Mean Guns '97

Rodger Halstead
Carnosaur 3: Primal Species '96

Julie Halston
Joe Gould's Secret '00

Charles Halton
Friendly Persuasion '56
A Star Is Born '54
Saboteur '42
Come and Get It '36

Mie Hama
You Only Live Twice [SE] '67

Mark Hamill
Batman Beyond: Return of the Joker '00 (V)
Joseph: King of Dreams '00 (V)
Scooby-Doo and the Alien Invaders '00 (V)
Sinbad: Beyond the Veil of Mists '00 (V)
Batman: Mask of the Phantasm '93 (V)
Sleepwalkers '92

Carrie Hamilton
Shag: The Movie '89

George Hamilton
The Godfather, Part 3 '90
Sextette '78

Judd Hamilton
Fanatic '82

Julie Hamilton
Holy Smoke '99

Linda Hamilton
Terminator 2: Judgment Day [2 SE] '91
Black Moon Rising '86
Children of the Corn '84

Murray Hamilton
The Amityville Horror '79
Jaws [CE] '75
The Way We Were [SE] '73
Anatomy of a Murder '59

Richard Hamilton
In Country '89

Victoria Hamilton
Mansfield Park '99

Peter Hamm
Inn of 1000 Sins '75

Hammer
One Man's Justice '95

Alvin Hammer
A Walk in the Sun '46

Nicholas Hammond
The Sound of Music [Five Star Collection] '65

Susan Hampshire
The Pallisers '74

Demetra Hampton
Red Shoe Diaries: Four on the Floor '96

Sasha Hanav
Mary Reilly '95

Lou Hancock
Evil Dead 2: Dead by Dawn [2 THX] '87

Theresa Hancock
The Violent Years / Girl Gang '56

Chip Hand
The McCullochs '75

Irene Handl
Wonderwall: The Movie '69
Brief Encounter '46

James Handy
K-911 '99
Bird '88

Colin Hanks
Whatever It Takes '00

Tom Hanks
Castaway '00
Toy Story 2 '99 (V)
Toy Story '95 (V)
Splash '84

Jimmy Hanley
Immortal Battalion '44

Peter Hanly
Braveheart '95

Adam Hann-Byrd
Diabolique '96

Daryl Hannah
Diplomatic Siege '99
The Real Blonde '97
The Tie That Binds '95
Crimes & Misdemeanors [MGM] '89
Steel Magnolias '89
Roxanne '87
Wall Street '87
The Clan of the Cave Bear '86
The Pope of Greenwich Village '84
Splash '84

John Hannah
Circus '00
The Hurricane '99
The Mummy [2 SE] '99

Page Hannah
Shag: The Movie '89
Creepshow 2 '87

Alyson Hannigan
Boys and Girls '00

Cheryl Hansen
Thou Shalt Not Kill . . . Except '87

Gunnar Hansen
Hellblock 13 '97
Texas Chainsaw Massacre: A Family Portrait '90

Valda Hansen
Wham-Bam, Thank You Spaceman '75

Kristina Hanson
Dinosaurus! '60

Daniel Hanssens
Ma Vie en Rose '97

Hisako Hara
After Life '98

Haya Harareet
Ben-Hur '59

Ernest Harden
White Men Can't Jump '92

Marcia Gay Harden
Space Cowboys '00
The Daytrippers '96

Kate Hardie
Croupier '97
Mona Lisa '86

Jerry Hardin
Cujo '83

Melora Hardin
Seven Girlfriends '00

Kadeem Hardison
Panther '95
White Men Can't Jump '92
I'm Gonna Git You Sucka '88
School Daze '88

Karl Hardman
Night of the Living Dead [Madacy] '68
Night of the Living Dead [Elite] '68
Night of the Living Dead [3 LE Anchor Bay] '68

Eloise Hardt
Incubus '65

Cedric Hardwicke
Rope '48
Things to Come '36

Jonathan Hardy
Farscape, Vol. 3 '01 (V)

Oliver Hardy
Utopia '51
The Flying Deuces / Utopia '39
March of the Wooden Soldiers '34

Robert Hardy
Northanger Abbey '87

Dorian Harewood
Hendrix '00
Kiss Shot '89
Against All Odds '84

Mickey Hargitay
The Bloody Pit of Horror '65

Doris Hargrave
The Hollywood Knights '80

Dennis Harkin
Brief Encounter '46

Mark Harmon
I'll Remember April '99
The First to Go '97

Ricci Harnett
The Object of Beauty '91

Frank Harper
Lock, Stock and 2 Smoking
   Barrels '98

Hill Harper
The Skulls '00
Loving Jezebel '99
Get On the Bus '96

Paul Harper
Deadbeat at Dawn '88

Tess Harper
The In Crowd '00
Tender Mercies '83

Valerie Harper
Blame It on Rio '84

Jim Harrell
A Family Thing '96

Woody Harrelson
Play It to the Bone '99
Natural Born Killers [DC] '94
White Men Can't Jump '92

William Harrigan
The Invisible Man '33

Desmond Harrington
The Messenger: The Story of
   Joan of Arc '99

Jay Harrington
Octopus '00

Laura Harrington
Maximum Overdrive '86

Peter Harrington
Diamond Run '00

Barbara Harris
Family Plot '76
Nashville '75

Brad Harris
The Mad Butcher '72

Bud Harris
Moon over Harlem '39

Danielle Harris
Back to Back '96
Halloween 5: The Revenge of
   Michael Myers '89

David Harris
The Warriors '79

Ed Harris
The Rock [Criterion] '96
Knightriders '81

Estelle Harris
Playing Mona Lisa '00
What's Cooking? '00
Toy Story 2 '99 (V)
Downhill Willie '96

Fox Harris
Repo Man '83

Harriet Harris
Nurse Betty '00

Jared Harris
B. Monkey '97
I Shot Andy Warhol '96
Dead Man '95

Jill Harris
Double Agent 73 '80

Jonathan Harris
Toy Story 2 '99 (V)

Julie Harris
Bad Manners '98

Julius W. Harris
The Taking of Pelham One
   Two Three '74
Black Caesar '73
Shaft's Big Score '72

Laura Harris
The Highway Man '99

Mel Harris
Suture '93

Michael (M.K.) Harris
Suture '93
Slumber Party Massacre 3
   '90

Neil Patrick Harris
The Next Best Thing '00

Phil Harris
Rock-a-Doodle '92 (V)
Robin Hood '73 (V)
The Aristocats '70 (V)

Richard Harris
Gladiator '00
Smilla's Sense of Snow '96
The Field '90
The Cassandra Crossing '76

Ricky Harris
Thick As Thieves '99

Robin Harris
Sorority House Massacre 2:
   Nighty Nightmare '92
House Party '90
Mo' Better Blues '90
I'm Gonna Git You Sucka '88

Rosemary Harris
Sunshine '99

Steve Harris
The Skulls '00

Wood Harris
Hendrix '00
Remember the Titans '00

Emily Harrison
Curse of the Puppet Master:
   The Human Experiment '98

Gregory Harrison
Air Bud 2: Golden Receiver
   '98
Body Chemistry 2: Voice of a
   Stranger '91

Kathleen Harrison
A Christmas Carol '51

Linda Harrison
Beneath the Planet of the
   Apes '70
Planet of the Apes '68

Rex Harrison
The Prince and the Pauper
   '78
Doctor Dolittle '67
Cleopatra '63

Richard Harrison
Vengeance '68

Susan Harrison
Sweet Smell of Success '57

David Harrod
The Tuskegee Airmen '95

Jamie Harrold
I Shot Andy Warhol '96

Kathryn Harrold
The '70s '00

Lisa Harrow
Omen 3: The Final Conflict
   '81
All Creatures Great and Small
   '74

Deborah Harry
Drop Dead Rock '95

Ray Harryhausen
The Fantasy Film Worlds of
   George Pal '86

Dianne Lee Hart
The Pom Pom Girls / The
   Beach Girls '76

Henry Hart
D.O.A. [Roan] '49

Ian Hart
The End of the Affair '99
Wonderland '99
B. Monkey '97

Linda Hart
Crazy in Alabama '99

Melissa Joan Hart
Batman Beyond: Return of
   the Joker '00 (V)
Drive Me Crazy '99

Susan Hart
Dr. Goldfoot and the Bikini
   Machine '66

Phil Hartman
The Crazysitter '94
Coneheads '93
Last Resort '86

Ras Daniel Hartman
The Harder They Come '72

William Hartnell
Immortal Battalion '44

Josh Hartnett
Here on Earth '00
The Virgin Suicides '99

Rainbow Harvest
Mirror, Mirror '90

Alex Harvey
Gettysburg '93

Don Harvey
Men of War '94
Tank Girl '94
The Beast '88
Eight Men Out '88

Harry Harvey Jr.
Reefer Madness '38

John Harvey
X The Unknown '56

Jonathan Harvey
The Delivery '99

Laurence Harvey
The Alamo '60
Butterfield 8 '60

Marilyn Harvey
The Astounding She-Monster
   '58

Steve Harvey
Original Kings of Comedy '00

Verna Harvey
That'll Be the Day '73

Keisha Harvin
Detention '98

Ching Has
The Dragon Chronicles '94

David Hasselhoff
The Big Tease '99
Baywatch: Nightmare Bay /
   River of No Return '94

Bob Hastings
The Munsters' Revenge '81

Magnus Hastings
Comic Act '00

Mary Hatcher
The Big Wheel '49

Shawn Hatosy
Down to You '00
Simpatico '99

Raymond Hatton
Joan the Woman '16

Rutger Hauer
Soldier of Orange '78
Turkish Delight '73

Cole Hauser
Pitch Black '00
Tigerland '00

Wings Hauser
No Safe Haven '87
A Soldier's Story '84
Mutant '83

Willo Hausman
House of Games '87

Terri Haven
Heavy Traffic '73

Phyllis Haver
Battle of the Sexes '28

Nigel Havers
Element of Doubt '96
A Passage to India '84

Keeley Hawes
The Last September '99

Ethan Hawke
Hamlet '00
Snow Falling on Cedars '99
Search and Destroy '94

John Hawkes
The Perfect Storm '00

Jack Hawkins
Lawrence of Arabia '62
Ben-Hur '59
The Bridge on the River Kwai
   [LE] '57

Screamin' Jay Hawkins
Dance with the Devil '97
Two Moon Junction '88

Wanda (Petit) Hawley
Affairs of Anatol '21

Goldie Hawn
Lovers and Liars '81

Jill Haworth
In Harm's Way '65

Nigel Hawthorne
Madeline '98
The Madness of King George
   '94
The Black Cauldron '85 (V)

Colin Hay
Heaven's Burning '97

Sessue Hayakawa
The Bridge on the River Kwai
   [LE] '57
The Cheat '15

Michael Hayden
Charming Billy '99

Sterling Hayden
9 to 5 '80
The Godfather DVD Collection
   '72
Dr. Strangelove, or: How I
   Learned to Stop Worrying
   and Love the Bomb [2 SE]
   '64

Richard Haydn
The Sound of Music [Five
   Star Collection] '65

Salma Hayek
Time Code '00
Traffic '00
Dogma '99
Fled '96
From Dusk Till Dawn [2 CS]
   '95
Midaq Alley '95

Anita Hayes
Hot Vampire Nights '00

George "Gabby" Hayes
Lawless Frontier / Randy
   Rides Alone '35
Lucky Texan '34
Man from Utah / Sagebrush
   Trail '34
Randy Rides Alone '34
The Star Packer '34

**Riders of Destiny / Star Pack-
   er '33

Helen Hayes
A Farewell to Arms '32

Isaac Hayes
Reindeer Games '00
Shaft '00
Ninth Street '98
It Could Happen to You '94
Posse '93
I'm Gonna Git You Sucka '88
Escape from New York '81
Truck Turner '74

Miss Laura Hayes
Queens of Comedy '01

Peter Lind Hayes
The 5000 Fingers of Dr. T '53

Robert Hayes III
Winner Takes All '98

Tony Haygarth
Chicken Run '00 (V)

David Hayman
Vertical Limit '00
Hope and Glory '87
Sid & Nancy [MGM] '86

Leslie Hayman
The Virgin Suicides '99

Johnny Haymer
Teenage Strangler '64

Roberta Haynes
The Fighter '52

Jim Haynie
Sleepwalkers '92

Lauren Hays
Sex Files: Digital Sex '98

Lee Hays
Alice's Restaurant '69

Robert Hays
No Dessert Dad, 'Til You Mow
   the Lawn '94
Airplane 2: The Sequel '82
Airplane! '80

Dennis Haysbert
What's Cooking? '00
The Minus Man '99
Suture '93
Love Field '91
Navy SEALS [MGM] '90

James Hayter
Four Sided Triangle '53

Louis Hayward
The Strange Woman '46

Susan Hayward
Demetrius and the Gladiators
   '54
The Snows of Kilimanjaro '52

Chris Haywood
Blackrock '97
The Navigator '88

Rita Hayworth
Pal Joey '57
The Lady from Shanghai '48
The Loves of Carmen '48
Gilda '46
Only Angels Have Wings '39

Jonathan Haze
X: The Man with X-Ray Eyes
   '63

Lena Headey
Gossip '99
Onegin '99

Glenne Headly
Time Code '00
Breakfast of Champions '98
Getting Even with Dad '94
And the Band Played On '93

Anthony Heald
Postcards from the Edge '90

David Healy
Supergirl '84
The Sign of Four '83

Mary Healy
The 5000 Fingers of Dr. T '53

Cordis Heard
C.H.U.D. '84

John Heard
Animal Factory '00
187 '97
Gladiator '92
Rambling Rose [2 SE] '91
Betrayed '88
C.H.U.D. '84

Susan Heard
The Body Beneath '70

Ann Hearn
Mirror, Mirror '90

George Hearn
All Dogs Go to Heaven 2 '95
(V)

Patty (Patricia Campbell) Hearst
Cecil B. Demented '00

Charlie Heath
Leprechaun 2 '94

Joey Heatherton
Bluebeard '72

Patricia Heaton
Beethoven '92

Heavy D
The Cider House Rules '99

Anne Heche
Donnie Brasco [2] '96

Eileen Heckart
Bus Stop '56

Andrew Heckler
Time Code '00

Dan Hedaya
The Crew '00
Shaft '00
Dick '99
The Hurricane '99
Alien: Resurrection '97
Benny & Joon '93
Mr. Wonderful '93
The Addams Family '91

Amel Hedhili
Honey & Ashes '96

David Hedison
The Fantasy Worlds of Irwin Allen '95
The Fly / Return of the Fly '58

Tippi Hedren
Footsteps '98

Van Heflin
The Greatest Story Ever Told [SE] '65
Shane '53
The Strange Love of Martha Ivers '46
Till the Clouds Roll By '46

O.P. Heggie
Midnight '34

Robert Hegyes
The Pandora Project '98

Janice Heiden
The McCullochs '75

Horace Heidt
Pot o' Gold '41

Taed Heil
Something Weird '68

Vivien Heilbron
The Murder of Roger Ackroyd '99

Amelia Heinle
Black Cat Run '98

Sandy Helberg
The Hollywood Knights '80

Marg Helgenberger
Erin Brockovich '00

Richard Hell
Desperately Seeking Susan '85

Marjorie Hellen
Missile to the Moon '59

Chip Heller
Jack Frost 2: Revenge of the Mutant Killer Snowman '00

Randee Heller
The Karate Kid '84

Katherine Helmond
The Perfect Nanny '00
The Lady in White '88
Family Plot '76

Percy Helton
Kiss Me Deadly '55

David Hemblen
Family of Cops 2: Breach of Faith '97
The Adjuster '91

Mariel Hemingway
Bad Moon '96
Superman 4: The Quest for Peace '87
Mean Season '85
Manhattan '79

David Hemmings
Gladiator '00
Gladiators: Bloodsport of the Colosseum '00 (N)

Sherman Hemsley
Screwed '00

Albert Henderson
Greaser's Palace '72

Bill Henderson
City Slickers '91
Clue '85

Dell Henderson
Love Affair '39

Florence Henderson
Shakes the Clown '92

Meredith Henderson
Kayla: A Cry in the Wilderness '00

Shirley Henderson
Topsy Turvy '99
Wonderland '99

Tony Hendra
This Is Spinal Tap [MGM] '84

Nancy Hendrickson
Mother's Day [DC] '80

Gloria Hendry
Black Caesar '73
Slaughter's Big Ripoff '73

Ian Hendry
Get Carter '71

Marilu Henner
Chasers '94

Jill(ian) Hennessey
Autumn in New York '00
Nuremberg '00
Komodo '99
Row Your Boat '98
I Shot Andy Warhol '96

Astrid Henning-Jensen
The Element of Crime '84

Sam Hennings
Drop Zone '94

Lance Henriksen
Scream 3 [CS] '00
Dead Man '95
Pumpkinhead '88
The Jagged Edge '85
Damien: Omen 2 '78

Buck Henry
Breakfast of Champions '98
I'm Losing You '98
The Real Blonde '97
Defending Your Life '91
Catch-22 '70

Charlotte Henry
March of the Wooden Soldiers '34

Emmaline Henry
Rosemary's Baby '68

Gregg Henry
Fair Game '89

Hank Henry
Pal Joey '57

Thomas B(rowne). Henry
The Brain from Planet Arous '57

William Henry
The Alamo '60

Douglas Henshall
Sharpe's Justice '97

Lisa Hensley
Paradise Road '97

Daniel Henson
Frequency '00

Elden (Ratliff) Henson
Idle Hands '99

Nicky Henson
Psychomania '73

Natasha Henstridge
A Better Way to Die '00
Bounce '00
Caracara '00
Jason and the Argonauts '00
The Whole Nine Yards '00
Maximum Risk '96

Katharine Hepburn
The Lion in Winter '68
Suddenly, Last Summer '59
Pat and Mike '52

Bernard Hepton
Get Carter '71

Charles Herbert
The Fly / Return of the Fly '58

Holmes Herbert
Sherlock Holmes and the Secret Weapon '42
The Invisible Man '33

Hugh Herbert
Sherlock Holmes and the Secret Weapon '42

Leon Herbert
Lucinda's Spell '00

Percy Herbert
The Bridge on the River Kwai [LE] '57

Eileen Herlie
Hamlet '48

Paul Herman
The Last Temptation of Christ '88

Ernesto Hernandez
Price of Glory '00

Juano Hernandez
They Call Me Mr. Tibbs! '70

Sergio Hernandez
Johnny 100 Pesos '93

Blake Heron
Cheaters '00

Mark Herrier
Porky's 2: The Next Day '83
Porky's / Porky's 2: The Next Day '82

Edward Herrmann
Critical Care '97
Soul of the Game '96

Cindy Herron
Juice '92

Barbara Hershey
Breakfast of Champions '98
The Pallbearer '95
The Last Temptation of Christ '88
The Natural '84

Jean Hersholt
Battle of the Sexes '28

Whitby Hertford
Mikey '92

Jason Hervey
Back to School '86

Werner Herzog
Julien Donkey-boy '99
My Best Fiend '99 (N)

Howard Hesseman
Home for Christmas '93
Clue '85
This Is Spinal Tap [MGM] '84
Jackson County Jail '76

Charlton Heston
Any Given Sunday '99
The Fantasy Film Worlds of George Pal '86
The Prince and the Pauper '78
The Four Musketeers '75
Call of the Wild '72
Beneath the Planet of the Apes '70
Planet of the Apes '68
The Greatest Story Ever Told [SE] '65
Ben-Hur '59
The Big Country '58
Touch of Evil [SE] '58

Lori Heuring
The In Crowd '00

Jennifer Love Hewitt
The Audrey Hepburn Story '00
Telling You '98
Home for Christmas '93

Martin Hewitt
Secret Games '92

David Hewlett
The Life Before This '99

Virginia Hey
Farscape, Vol. 3 '01

Barton Heyman
Dead Man Walking '95

Jean Heywood
Billy Elliot '00

William Hickey
The Nightmare before Christmas [2 SE] '93 (V)
Puppet Master '89

Dwayne Hickman
Dr. Goldfoot and the Bikini Machine '66
Cat Ballou [SE] '65

Dan Hicks
Evil Dead 2: Dead by Dawn [2 THX] '87

Michele Hicks
Twin Falls Idaho '99

Russell Hicks
The Bank Dick '40

Clare Higgins
Catherine Cookson's The Secret '00
Hellraiser [2] '87

Colin Higgins
Hope and Glory '87

John Michael Higgins
Best in Show '00
Bicentennial Man '99

Michael Higgins
The Conversation '74

Torri Higginson
Family of Cops 3 '98

Amy Hill
Next Friday [Platinum Series] '00
Yellow '98

Bernard Hill
Mountains of the Moon '90
The Bounty '84

Brigitte Hill
Death Mask '98

Glen Hill
Passion & Romance: Double or Nothing '00

Lauryn Hill
Restaurant '98

Marianna Hill
The Godfather, Part 2 '74

Mary Hill
Mesa of Lost Women '52

Melinda Hill
Velocity '99

Richard (Rick) Hill
Bloodfist 2 '90

Teresa Hill
Twin Falls Idaho '99
Puppet Master 5: The Latest Chapter '94
Puppet Master 4 '93

Bernard Hiller
Avalon '90

Wendy Hiller
A Man for All Seasons '66
I Know Where I'm Going '45
Pygmalion '38

John Hillerman
The Last Picture Show [DC] '71

Verna Hillie
Trail Beyond '34

Peter Youngblood Hills
The Beach '00

Art Hindle
Porky's 2: The Next Day '83
Porky's / Porky's 2: The Next Day '82

Earl Hindman
The Taking of Pelham One Two Three '74

Ciaran Hinds
Jason and the Argonauts '00
Mary Reilly '95

Damon Hines
Once Upon a Time...When We Were Colored '95

Desi Arnez Hines II
Hip Hop 2000 '00

Gregory Hines
Bojangles '01
The Tic Code '99

Robert Hines
Hellraiser [2] '87

Ronald Hines
We'll Meet Again '82

Art Hingle
Kept '01

Pat Hingle
Shaft '00
Lightning Jack '94
The Land Before Time '88 (V)
Baby Boom '87
Maximum Overdrive '86
Norma Rae '79

Ed Hinkle
Daughter of Horror / Dementia '55

Sergio Hinst
Awakenings of the Beast '68

Peter Hinwood
The Rocky Horror Picture Show '75

Bill (William Heinzman) Hinzman
Night of the Living Dead [Madacy] '68
Night of the Living Dead [Elite] '68
Night of the Living Dead [3 LE Anchor Bay] '68

Paul Hipp
Waking the Dead '00

Thora Hird
The Entertainer '60

Hallee Hirsh
Joe Gould's Secret '00

Alfred Hitchcock
Family Plot '76

Michael Hitchcock
Best in Show '00

Danny Hitt
American Vampire '97

Iben Hjejle
High Fidelity '00
Mifune '99

Chin Ho
Peace Hotel '95

Linda Ho
Hillbillys in a Haunted House '67

Rodney J. Hobbs
Nothin' 2 Lose '00

David Hockney
Superstar: The Life and Times of Andy Warhol '90

Douglas Hodge
Salome's Last Dance '88

Joseph Hodge
Isaac Asimov's Nightfall '88

Earle Hodgins
The Man Who Shot Liberty Valance '62

Dennis Hoey
Terror by Night '46
Sherlock Holmes and the Secret Weapon '42

Iris Hoey
Pygmalion '38

Abbie Hoffman
Born on the Fourth of July [2] '89

Basil Hoffman
Communion [CE] '89

Dustin Hoffman
The Messenger: The Story of Joan of Arc '99

American Buffalo '95
Tootsie '82

Gaby Hoffman
Black and White '99
Coming Soon '99
All I Wanna Do '98

Joel Hoffman
Pumpkinhead '88

Phil Hoffman
Next Stop, Wonderland '98

Philip Seymour Hoffman
Almost Famous '00
Flawless '99
Magnolia '99
The Talented Mr. Ripley '99
Hard Eight '96

Thom Hoffman
The 4th Man '79

Jutta Hoffmann
Bandits '99

Stig Hoffmeyer
Nightwatch '94

Charlie Hofheimer
Music of the Heart [CS] '99

Isabella Hofmann
Homicide: The Movie '00
The Colony '98

Marco Hofschneider
Urban Legends 2: Final Cut '00

Bosco Hogan
A Portrait of the Artist As a Young Man '77
Zardoz '73

Paul Hogan
Lightning Jack '94

B.J. Hogg
Rudyard Kipling's the Second Jungle Book: Mowgli and Baloo '97

Stacy Hogue
Perfect Tenant '99

David Holbrook
Creepshow 2 '87

Hal Holbrook
Men of Honor '00
Waking the Dead '00
Wall Street '87
The Kidnapping of the President '80

Beau Holden
Traffic '00

William Holden
Damien: Omen 2 '78
Alvarez Kelly '66
The Horse Soldiers '59
The Bridge on the River Kwai [LE] '57
The Bridges at Toko-Ri '55
Picnic '55
Our Town '40

Kris Holdenried
Hendrix '00

Geoffrey Holder
Everything You Always Wanted to Know about Sex (But Were Afraid to Ask) '72
Doctor Dolittle '67

Susan Holderness
That'll Be the Day '73

Hope Holiday
The Apartment '60

David G. Holland
Hellblock 13 '97

Mary Holland
Tommy '75

Tom Hollander
Bedrooms and Hallways '98

Kene Holliday
The Josephine Baker Story '90

Earl Holliman
Perfect Tenant '99
Sons of Katie Elder '65
The Bridges at Toko-Ri '55

John "Kato" Hollis
Throw Down '00

Laurel Holloman
Loving Jezebel '99
Tumbleweeds '98
The First to Go '97
The Myth of Fingerprints '97

Stanley Holloway
In Harm's Way '65
Hamlet '48
Brief Encounter '46
Immortal Battalion '44

Sterling Holloway
The Aristocats '70 (V)
Alice in Wonderland '51 (V)
A Walk in the Sun '46
The Three Caballeros '45 (V)

Ellen Holly
School Daze '88

Lauren Holly
What Women Want '00
Any Given Sunday '99
No Looking Back '98

Ryan Hollyman
The Audrey Hepburn Story '00

Arwen Holm
Omen 3: The Final Conflict '81

Barnaby Holm
Omen 3: The Final Conflict '81

Ian Holm
Beautiful Joe '00
Bless the Child '00
Joe Gould's Secret '00
The Last of the Blonde Bombshells '00
The Madness of King George '94
Henry V '89
Another Woman '88
Dance with a Stranger '85

Katie Holmes
Wonder Boys '00

Mark Holmes
The Adventures of Priscilla, Queen of the Desert [MGM] '94

Tina Holmes
Prince of Central Park '00

Erik Holmey
Angel of the Night '98

Patrick Holt
Psychomania '73

Sandrine Holt
Loving Jezebel '99
Black Robe '91

Arabella Holzbog
Red Shoe Diaries: Swimming Naked '00
Carnosaur 2 '94

Skip Homeier
Tomorrow the World '44

Oscar Homolka
Strange Case of Dr. Jekyll & Mr. Hyde '68
The Seven Year Itch '55

Daylan Honeycutt
My Dog Skip '99

James Hong
The Art of War '00
Broken Vessels '98
The Vineyard '89
Big Trouble in Little China [SE] '86
Airplane! '80
The Sand Pebbles '66

Andre Honore
Slumber Party Massacre '82

Brian Hooks
Nothin' 2 Lose '00
Three Strikes '00
Q: The Movie '99

Jan Hooks
Coneheads '93

Robert Hooks
Posse '93
Passenger 57 '92
A Woman Called Moses '78

Brett Hool
Steel Dawn '87

Tobe Hooper
Sleepwalkers '92

William Hootkins
The Omega Code '99

Joseph Hoover
The Astro-Zombies '67
Hell Is for Heroes '62
The Man Who Shot Liberty Valance '62

Bob Hope
Bob Hope: Hollywood's Brightest Star '97
How to Commit Marriage '69
Private Navy of Sgt. O'Farrell '68
Paris Holiday '57
The Seven Little Foys '55
The Road to Bali '53
Son of Paleface '52
The Lemon Drop Kid '51
The Great Lover '49
My Favorite Brunette '47
The Road to Rio '47

Leslie Hope
The Life Before This '99
Bram Stoker's Shadowbuilder '98
Talk Radio '88

Elizabeth Hopgood
Witchouse 2: Blood Coven '00

Anthony Hopkins
Hannibal '01
Mission: Impossible 2 '00
Titus '99
Legends of the Fall [2 SE] '94
Freejack '92
The Bounty '84
All Creatures Great and Small '74
The Lion in Winter '68

Bo Hopkins
Mutant '83

Jermaine "Huggy" Hopkins
Juice '92

Josh Hopkins
The Perfect Storm '00

Marie Hopkins
Cyberotica '00

Dennis Hopper
Jason and the Argonauts '00
Jesus' Son '99
The Prophet's Game '99
The Apostate '98
Tycus '98

The Source '96
Chasers '94
Search and Destroy '94
Superstar: The Life and Times of Andy Warhol '90
River's Edge '87
Straight to Hell '87
Blue Velvet '86
The Texas Chainsaw Massacre 2 '86
The Inside Man '84
Sons of Katie Elder '65

Leslie Horan
The Brutal Truth '99

Michael Hordern
I'll Never Forget What's 'Isname '67
The Taming of the Shrew '67
Cleopatra '63
A Christmas Carol '51

Hideyuki Hori
Darkside Blues '99 (V)

Camilla Horn
Eternal Love '29

Dimitri Horne
Girl in Black '56

Geoffrey Horne
The Bridge on the River Kwai [LE] '57

Lena Horne
Till the Clouds Roll By '46

Victoria Horne
Harvey '50

Penelope Horner
Dracula / Strange Case of Dr. Jekyll & Mr. Hyde '73

David Horovitch
102 Dalmatians '00
Solomon and Gaenor '98

Jane Horrocks
Chicken Run '00 (V)
Terry Pratchett's Discworld: Wyrd Sisters '96 (V)

Michael Horse
Passenger 57 '92

Anna Maria Horsford
Nutty Professor 2: The Klumps [1 CE] '00
Nutty Professor 2: The Klumps [2 Uncensored] '00
Times Square '80

Jochen Horst
The Cement Garden '93

Edward Everett Horton
Arsenic and Old Lace '44

Peter Horton
Children of the Corn '84

Bob Hoskins
Mermaids '90
Mona Lisa '86

Robert Hossein
Wax Mask '97

Paul Houde
The Boys '97

Djimon Hounsou
Gladiator '00
Ill-Gotten Gains '97

John Houseman
Another Woman '88
The Naked Gun: From the Files of Police Squad '88
Seven Days in May '64

Allan Houston
Black and White '99

Candice Houston
The Land Before Time '88 (V)

Anders (Tofting) Hove
Mifune '99
Bloodstorm: Subspecies 4 '98

Adrian Hoven
Cave of the Living Dead '65

Alan Howard
The Cook, the Thief, His Wife & Her Lover '90

Arliss Howard
A Map of the World '99
The Lost World: Jurassic Park 2 [CE] '97
Natural Born Killers [DC] '94
For the Boys '91
Somebody Has to Shoot the Picture '90

Clint Howard
Little Nicky '00
Under Oath '97
Barb Wire '96
Leprechaun 2 '94
Carnosaur '93

Curly Howard
The Three Stooges: Merry Mavericks '01
The Three Stooges: All the World's a Stooge '00
The Three Stooges: Nutty but Nice '00
Three Stooges: Spook Louder '00

Esther Howard
Detour '46

John Howard
Bulldog Drummond's Secret Police '39

Kevyn Major Howard
Alien Nation '88

Leslie Howard
Pygmalion '38
Of Human Bondage '34
The Scarlet Pimpernel '34

Lisa Howard
Bounty Hunters 2: Hardball '97
Bounty Hunters '96

Moe Howard
The Three Stooges: Merry Mavericks '01
The Three Stooges: All the World's a Stooge '00
The Three Stooges: Nutty but Nice '00
Three Stooges: Spook Louder '00

Ron Howard
Village of the Giants '65

Shemp Howard
The Three Stooges: Merry Mavericks '01
Three Stooges: Spook Louder '00
Africa Screams / Jack and the Beanstalk '49
The Bank Dick '40

Terrence DaShon Howard
Big Momma's House '00

Traylor Howard
Dirty Work '97

Trevor Howard
Meteor '79
Superman: The Movie '78
Brief Encounter '46

Vanessa Howard
Blood Beast Terror '67

C. Thomas Howell
The Crimson Code '00
Dilemma '97
Gettysburg '93

Hoke Howell
Vice Girls '96

Margaret Howell
White Wolves 3: Cry of the White Wolf '98

Sally Ann Howes
Anna Karenina '48

Lucille Howland
Daughter of Horror / Dementia '55

Olin Howlin
The Blob '58

Rodolfo Hoyos
The Brave One '56

Carol Hoyt
Midnight Confessions '95

John Hoyt
X: The Man with X-Ray Eyes '63
Attack of the Puppet People '58

Talun Hsu
Body Count '95

Patrick Huard
The Boys '97

David Huband
Dirty Pictures '00

Elizabeth Hubbard
Center Stage '00

Harold Huber
The Gay Desperado '36

Season Hubley
Kiss the Sky '98
Escape from New York '81

Whip Hubley
Black Scorpion 2: Ground Zero '96

Cooper Huckabee
Gettysburg '93
Love Field '91

Walter Hudd
I Know Where I'm Going '45
Rembrandt '36

David Huddleston
The Tracker '88
Santa Claus: The Movie '85

Reginald (Reggie) Hudlin
Posse '93

Warrington Hudlin
Posse '93

Brett Hudson
Hysterical '83

Ernie Hudson
Miss Congeniality '00
Red Letters '00
The Watcher '00
Interceptor Force '99
Paper Bullets '99
Best of the Best: Without Warning '98
October 22 '98
Penitentiary 2 '82

Gary Hudson
The Stepdaughter '00
Bridge of Dragons '99
Eye of the Killer '99

John Paul Hudson
Greaser's Palace '72

Kate Hudson
Almost Famous '00
Dr. T & the Women '00
Gossip '99

Mark Hudson
Hysterical '83

Rock Hudson
The Mirror Crack'd '80
Embryo '76

William (Bill) Hudson
Hysterical '83
The Screaming Skull '58

Brent Huff
Submerged '00

Kevin Huff
The Curve '97

David Huffman
Ice Castles '79

Soto Joe Hugh
The Killing of a Chinese Bookie '76

Daniel Hugh-Kelly
The Tuskegee Airmen '95
Cujo '83

Barnard Hughes
The Cradle Will Rock '99
Sisters '73

Carol Hughes
Love Affair '39

David Hughes
32 Short Films about Glenn Gould '93

Finola Hughes
Pocahontas 2: Journey to a New World '98 (V)
Tycus '98

Jason Hughes
Plain Jane '00

Julie Hughes
Stormswept '95

Kristen Hughes
Jane & the Lost City '87

Lloyd Hughes
The Lost World [Image] '25

Miko Hughes
Pet Sematary '89

Wendy Hughes
Paradise Road '97
Princess Caraboo '94

D.L. Hughley
Original Kings of Comedy '00

Dianne Hull
The New Adventures of Pippi Longstocking '88

Henry Hull
Portrait of Jennie '48
Midnight '34

Josephine Hull
Harvey '50
Arsenic and Old Lace '44

Barry Humphries
Dame Edna's Neighbourhood Watch 2 '92

Tessa Humphries
Paradise Road '97

Robert Hundar
Cut Throats Nine '72

Hui Siu Hung
Running out of Time '99

Sammo Hung
Painted Skin '93
The Prisoner '90
Eastern Condors '87
The Millionaire's Express '86
Project A '83
Zu: Warriors of the Magic Mountain '83
Spooky Encounters '80

Gayle Hunnicutt
The Wild Angels '66

Bonnie Hunt
Return to Me '00
Beethoven '92

Christopher Hunt
Idle Hands '99
The Addams Family '91

Helen Hunt
Castaway '00
Dr. T & the Women '00
What Women Want '00
Girls Just Want to Have Fun '85

Linda Hunt
The Italians '00 (N)
Pocahontas 2: Journey to a New World '98 (V)
Eat Your Heart Out '96
Pocahontas '95 (V)
Silverado [SE] '85

Lois Kelso Hunt
The House on Sorority Row '83

Martita Hunt
The Unsinkable Molly Brown '64
Anna Karenina '48

William Dennis Hunt
Flesh Gordon 2: Flesh Gordon Meets the Cosmic Cheerleaders '90

Bill Hunter
The Adventures of Priscilla, Queen of the Desert [MGM] '94

Holly Hunter
O Brother Where Art Thou? '00
Time Code '00
Jesus' Son '99

Ian Hunter
The Little Princess '39

Jeffrey Hunter
Private Navy of Sgt. O'Farrell '68

Kaki Hunter
Porky's 2: The Next Day '83
Porky's / Porky's 2: The Next Day '82

Kevin Hunter
One False Move '91

Kim Hunter
Escape from the Planet of the Apes '71
Beneath the Planet of the Apes '70
Planet of the Apes '68

Tab Hunter
Lust in the Dust '85

Thomas Hunter
The Vampire Happening '71

Raymond Huntley
Immortal Battalion '44

Isabelle Huppert
La Separation '98
Love After Love '94
The Bedroom Window '87
Coup de Torchon '81
Loulou '80

Michelle Hurd
Double Parked '00

Elizabeth Hurley
Bedazzled [SE] '00
Sharpe's Enemy '94
Passenger 57 '92

Matthew Hurley
Pumpkinhead '88

David Hurst
Kelly's Heroes '70

Marguerite Hurst
Forgotten Silver '96

Ryan Hurst
Remember the Titans '00

John Hurt
Lost Souls '00
Dead Man '95
Wild Bill '95
Thumbelina '94 (V)
I, Claudius '91
The Field '90
Jake Speed '86
The Black Cauldron '85 (V)
A Man for All Seasons '66

Mary Beth Hurt
Bringing Out the Dead '99
Six Degrees of Separation '93
Interiors '78

William Hurt
Dune '00
The 4th Floor '99
Sunshine '99
A Couch in New York '95
Mr. Wonderful '93
Alice '90
Children of a Lesser God '86
Gorky Park '83

Ferlin Husky
Hillbillys in a Haunted House '67

Jennifer Huss
Vamps: Deadly Dreamgirls '95

Olivia Hussey
Death on the Nile '78
Black Christmas '75

Francis Huster
The Dinner Game '98

Anjelica Huston
Agnes Browne '99
And the Band Played On '93
The Addams Family '91
Crimes & Misdemeanors [MGM] '89
This Is Spinal Tap [MGM] '84

Danny Huston
Time Code '00

John Huston
The Black Cauldron '85 (N)
Battle for the Planet of the Apes '73
Candy '68
Know Your Enemy: Japan '45 (N)

Walter Huston
December 7th: The Pearl Harbor Story '43
The Maltese Falcon '41
Rain '32

David Hutcheson
The Abominable Dr. Phibes '71

Will Hutchins
The Shooting '66

Josephine Hutchinson
North by Northwest '59

Doug Hutchison
Bait '00

Tracy Hutson
Rated X '00

Betty Hutton
Annie Get Your Gun '50

Jim Hutton
The Hallelujah Trail '65

Lauren Hutton
Caracara '00
Nashville '75

Jerry Jarret
Killer's Kiss '55

J.R. Jarrod
Divided We Stand '00

Graham Jarvis
Misery '90
Alice's Restaurant '69

Brent Jasmer
Leprechaun 4: In Space '96

Harvey Jason
The Lost World: Jurassic Park 2 [CE] '97

Peter Jason
Alien Nation '88

Sybil Jason
The Little Princess '39

Ricky Jay
House of Games '87

Jay-Z
Backstage '00

Michael Jayston
Element of Doubt '96

Marianne Jean-Baptiste
The Cell '00
28 Days [SE] '00

Zizi Jeanmarie
Hans Christian Andersen [20th Century Fox] '52

Marcel Jeannin
The Audrey Hepburn Story '00

Allan Jeayes
The Scarlet Pimpernel '34

Joe Jeffers
Broken Harvest '94

Herbert Jefferson Jr.
Detroit 9000 '73

Aaron Jeffery
The Interview '98

Doug Jeffery
Monsoon '97

Barbara Jefford
The Ninth Gate '99
Ulysses '67

Dawn Jeffory
Tourist Trap '79

Peter Jeffrey
Doctor Phibes Rises Again '72
The Abominable Dr. Phibes '71
Ring of Bright Water '69

Chuck Jeffreys
Aftershock '88

Ron Jeffries
Dinosaur Valley Girls '96

Hsein-Chi Jen
Gorgeous '99

Allen Jenkins
The Big Wheel '49

Burgess Jenkins
Remember the Titans '00

Ken Jenkins
And the Band Played On '93

Megs Jenkins
Asylum '72

Rebecca Jenkins
Bob Roberts [SE] '92

Richard Jenkins
What Planet Are You From? '00
Snow Falling on Cedars '99
A Couch in New York '95

It Could Happen to You '94
And the Band Played On '93

Michael Jenn
Dance with a Stranger '85

Bruce Jenner
The Big Tease '99

Brent Jennings
Blue Ridge Fall '99
A Lesson Before Dying '99
Soul of the Game '96

Waylon Jennings
Outlaw Justice '98

Salome Jens
I'm Losing You '98

Mary Jerrold
Immortal Battalion '44

Patricia Jessel
Horror Hotel '60

James Jeter
The Hollywood Knights '80

Michael Jeter
Air Bud [2] '97
Drop Zone '94
The Fisher King '91

Jewel
Ride with the Devil '99

Penn Jillette
Half Japanese: The Band Who Would Be King '92

Elaine Jin
Yi Yi '00

Jeong Jin-Young
The Ring Virus '99

Edward Jobson
The Married Virgin '18

Dan Joffre
Scary Movie '00

Zita Johann
The Mummy '32

David Johansen
The Tic Code '99
Freejack '92
Married to the Mob '88
Scrooged '88

Peter Johansen
The Brothers McMullen '94

Zizi Johari
The Killing of a Chinese Bookie '76

Domenick John
Creepshow 2 '87

Elton John
The Road to El Dorado '00 (N)
Tommy '75

Anne Johns
Family Enforcer '76

Glynis Johns
Mary Poppins [2 SE] '64

Mervyn Johns
A Christmas Carol '51

Stratford Johns
Salome's Last Dance '88
Dance with a Stranger '85

Tracy C. Johns
Mo' Better Blues '90

A.J. (Anthony) Johnson
House Party '90

Amy Jo Johnson
Turbo: A Power Rangers Movie '96

Anne-Marie Johnson
Asteroid '97
I'm Gonna Git You Sucka '88

Arte Johnson
Assault of the Party Nerds 2: Heavy Petting Detective '95

Ashley Johnson
What Women Want '00

Ben Johnson
The Evening Star '96
Cherry 2000 '88
The Shadow Riders '82
Ruckus '81
Breakheart Pass '76
Dillinger '73
The Last Picture Show [DC] '71
One-Eyed Jacks '61
Shane '53

Bill Johnson
The Texas Chainsaw Massacre 2 '86

Brad Johnson
Left Behind: The Movie '00
Lone Justice 3: Showdown at Plum Creek '96
Lone Justice 2 '93

Candy Johnson
Bikini Beach '64
Beach Party '63

Celia Johnson
Brief Encounter '46

Clark Johnson
Homicide: The Movie '00

Corey Johnson
The Mummy [2 SE] '99

Cullen Oliver Johnson
Bringing Out the Dead '99

Don Johnson
In Pursuit of Honor '95
Harley Davidson and the Marlboro Man '91

Emmanuel Johnson
Magnolia '99

George Clayton Johnson
The Intruder '61

Laura Johnson
Opening Night '77

Lynn-Holly Johnson
Ice Castles '79

Mae Johnson
The Defilers '65

Michelle Johnson
Wishful Thinking '92
Blame It on Rio '84

Noble Johnson
The Most Dangerous Game [Madacy] '32
The Mummy '32

Noel Johnson
Frenzy '72

Rebekah Johnson
Liberty Heights '99

Reggie Johnson
Platoon [2 SE] '86

Robin Johnson
Times Square '80

Ryan Thomas Johnson
Carnosaur 2 '94

Stacii Jae Johnson
Da Hip Hop Witch '00

Toni Johnson
The Screaming Skull '58

Tor Johnson
The Beast of Yucca Flats '61
Plan 9 from Outer Space [Passport Video] '56

Van Johnson
The Kidnapping of the President '80
Yours, Mine & Ours '68
End of the Affair '55
The Last Time I Saw Paris '54
Go for Broke! '51

C. Johnston
Sex Files: Digital Sex '98

Christopher Johnston
The Portrait '99

J.J. Johnston
K-911 '99

John Dennis Johnston
In Pursuit of Honor '95

Kristen Johnston
The Flintstones in Viva Rock Vegas '00

Angelina Jolie
Gone in 60 Seconds '00
Girl, Interrupted '99
Gia '98
Hell's Kitchen NYC '97
Foxfire '96

I. Stanford Jolley
The Violent Years / Girl Gang '56

Barry Jones
Demetrius and the Gladiators '54

Ben Jones
Joe Gould's Secret '00

Carolyn Jones
The Man Who Knew Too Much '56
The Seven Year Itch '55
The Road to Bali '53

Cherry Jones
Erin Brockovich '00
The Perfect Storm '00
The Cradle Will Rock '99

Claude Earl Jones
Bride of Re-Animator '89

Dean Jones
Beethoven '92

Duane Jones
Night of the Living Dead [Madacy] '68
Night of the Living Dead [Elite] '68
Night of the Living Dead [LE Anchor Bay] '68

Eddie Jones
Return to Me '00
C.H.U.D. '84

Freddie Jones
The Black Cauldron '85 (V)
Krull [SE] '83
All Creatures Great and Small '74

Gemma Jones
Cotton Mary '99
Wilderness '96

Grace Jones
Straight to Hell '87
A View to a Kill [SE] '85

Hatty Jones
Madeline '98

Henry Jones
Support Your Local Gunfighter '71

Jack Jones
Airplane 2: The Sequel '82

James Earl Jones
A Family Thing '96
Naked Gun 33 1/3: The Final Insult '94

Conan the Barbarian [2 CE] '82

Dr. Strangelove, or: How I Learned to Stop Worrying and Love the Bomb [2 SE] '64

Jennifer Jones
Beat the Devil '53
Portrait of Jennie '48

Jocelyn Jones
Tourist Trap '79

John Jones
White Men Can't Jump '92

Kidada Jones
Black and White '99

L.Q. (Justus E. McQueen) Jones
The Jack Bull '99
Lightning Jack '94
Hell Is for Heroes '62

Malik Jones
Nothin' 2 Lose '00

Marcia Mae Jones
The Little Princess '39

Mark Lewis Jones
Solomon and Gaenor '98

Martin C. Jones
Nothin' 2 Lose '00

Mickey Jones
Drop Zone '94

Orlando Jones
Bedazzled [SE] '00
The Replacements '00
Liberty Heights '99

Richard Jones
Where the Heart Is '00
Blue Sky '91

Robert Earl Jones
Cockfighter '74

Sam Jones
DaVinci's War '92
Jane & the Lost City '87

Sarah Jones
Bamboozled '00

Shelly Jones
Hot Vampire Nights '00

Shirley Jones
Shriek If You Know What I Did Last Friday the 13th '00

Tamala Jones
The Ladies Man '00
Next Friday [Platinum Series] '00
Turn It Up '00
Blue Streak '99

Terry Jones
Monty Python and the Holy Grail '75

Tom Jones
Agnes Browne '99

Tommy Lee Jones
Rules of Engagement '00
Space Cowboys '00
Men in Black [CS] '97
Natural Born Killers [DC] '94
Heaven and Earth '93
Blue Sky '91
Black Moon Rising '86
Eyes of Laura Mars '78
Jackson County Jail '76
Love Story '70

Vinnie Jones
Gone in 60 Seconds '00
Lock, Stock and 2 Smoking Barrels '98

Sigurveig Jonsdottir
Devil's Island '96

Samson Jorah
Never Cry Wolf '83

Bobby Jordan
Ghosts on the Loose '43
They Made Me a Criminal '39

France Jordan
Oasis of the Zombies '82

Katie Jordan
Erotic Witch Project 2: Book
of Seduction '00
Gladiator Eroticus '00

Marsha Jordan
The Head Mistress '68

Marvin Jordan
Hip Hop 2000 '00

Richard Jordan
Gettysburg '93
Posse '93
Romero '89
Mean Season '85
Interiors '78

Rick Jordan
Ultimate Attraction '98

William Jordan
The Doors [2 SE] '91

Victor Jory
The Miracle Worker '62
Cat Women of the Moon '53
The Loves of Carmen '48

Felix Joseph
Welcome II the Terrordome
'95

Paterson Joseph
The Beach '00

Ron Joseph
Navy SEALS [MGM] '90

Todd Joseph
Midnight Tease / Midnight
Tease 2 '94

Allyn Joslyn
Only Angels Have Wings '39

Jennifer Jostyn
Milo '98
Telling You '98
The First to Go '97
The Brothers McMullen '94

Jacques Jouanneau
Bed and Board '70

Louis Jourdan
Octopussy '83
Swamp Thing '82

Meto Jovanovski
Stalked '99

Milla Jovovich
The Claim '00
The Messenger: The Story of
Joan of Arc '99
The Million Dollar Hotel '99

Marilyn Joy
Ilsa, Harem Keeper of the Oil
Sheiks '76

Robert Joy
The '70s '00
Shadows and Fog '92
Longtime Companion '90
Desperately Seeking Susan
'85

Ella Joyce
Clockin' Green '00

Michelle Joyner
Cliffhanger [2 CS] '93

Ashley Judd
Where the Heart Is '00
Eye of the Beholder '99
Natural Born Killers [DC] '94

Edward Judd
The Day the Earth Caught
Fire '61

Christopher Judge
Stargate SG-1: Season 1 '97

Raul Julia
The Addams Family '91
Romero '89
Eyes of Laura Mars '78
The Organization '71

Janet (Johnson) Julian
King of New York '90

Lenny Juliano
Not of This Earth '88

Jorge Juliao
Pixote '81

Gordon Jump
Conquest of the Planet of the
Apes '72

Katy Jurado
One-Eyed Jacks '61

Nicholas Kadi
Navy SEALS [MGM] '90

Diane Kagan
Mr. & Mrs. Bridge '90

David Kagen
Body Chemistry '90

Steve Kahan
Warlock: The Armageddon
'93

A.J. Kahn
Erotic Witch Project 2: Book
of Seduction '00
Gladiator Eroticus '00

Madeline Kahn
Clue '85

Chen Kaige
The Emperor and the Assassin '99

Khalil Kain
Juice '92

Elizabeth Kaitan
Aftershock '88

Meiko Kaji
Female Convict Scorpion—
Jailhouse 41 '72

Helena Kallianiotes
Five Easy Pieces '70

Drew Kaluski
Tap Dogs '98

Rob Kaman
Bloodfist '89

Stanley Kamel
Escape under Pressure '00
Stonebrook '98

Kamron
House Party 2: The Pajama
Jam '91

Big Daddy Kane
Posse '93

Carol Kane
Noah's Ark '99
The Tic Code '99
The Pallbearer '95
The Crazysitter '94
The Lemon Sisters '90
Scrooged '88
The Princess Bride '87

Irene Kane
Killer's Kiss '55

Ivan Kane
Gettysburg '93
Platoon [2 SE] '86

Marjorie "Babe" Kane
W.C. Fields 6 Short Films '33

Sandra Kane
Teenage Gang Debs /
Teenage Strangler '66

Ken Kaneko
Kids Return '96

Law Hang Kang
Crime Story '93

China Kantner
The Evening Star '96

Paul Kantner
Gimme Shelter '70

John Kapelos
Cold Blooded '00
Roxanne '87

Jonathan Kaplan
Hollywood Boulevard '76

Wendy Kaplan
Halloween 5: The Revenge of
Michael Myers '89

Maria Kapnist
Dead Waters '94

Kym Karath
The Sound of Music [Five
Star Collection] '65

James Karen
Girl '98
Wall Street '87
The Jagged Edge '85
Hercules in New York '70

Vic Karis
The Arena '73

Boris Karloff
Die, Monster, Die! '65
Bikini Beach '64
Black Sabbath '64
The Mummy '32
Tonight or Never '31
The Last of the Mohicans '20

Maria Karlsen
Angel of the Night '98

Janice Karman
Switchblade Sisters '75

Sarah Rose Karr
Beethoven '92

Alex Karras
Against All Odds '84
Porky's / Porky's 2: The Next
Day '82

Sabine Karsenti
Battlefield Earth '00

Vincent Kartheiser
Crime and Punishment in
Suburbia '00
All I Wanna Do '98

Claudia Karvan
Flynn '96

Tcheky Karyo
The Patriot '00
Saving Grace '00
The Messenger: The Story of
Joan of Arc '99
And the Band Played On '93
La Femme Nikita [MGM] '91

Casey Kasem
James Dean: Live Fast, Die
Young '97

Gohki Kashiyama
Maborosi '95

John Kassir
Pocahontas '95 (V)

Daphna Kastner
Time Code '00

Kimberley Kates
Traitor's Heart '98

Branka Katic
The Wounds '98

Julia Kato
Rugrats in Paris: The Movie
'00 (V)

Andreas Katsulas
Communion [CE] '89

Keiichiro Katsumoto
The Bridge on the River Kwai
[LE] '57

Fumi Katsuragi
Evil Dead Trap '88

Nicky Katt
Boiler Room '00
Way of the Gun '00
Delivered '98

William Katt
Twin Falls Idaho '99

Judah Katz
Dirty Pictures '00

Gunther Kaufman
Whity '70

**Lloyd (Samuel Weil)
Kaufman**
Terror Firmer [SE] '00

Joseph Kaufmann
Heavy Traffic '73

Maurice Kaufmann
The Abominable Dr. Phibes
'71

Caroline Kava
Born on the Fourth of July [2]
'89

Hilary Kavanagh
Moving Target '00

John Kavanagh
Sharpe's Sword '94

Julie Kavner
Shadows and Fog '92
Alice '90

Sabu Kawahara
Scene at the Sea '91

Charles Kay
Beautiful People '99
Henry V '89

Danny Kaye
Pinocchio '76
White Christmas '54
Hans Christian Andersen
[20th Century Fox] '52
The Inspector General '49
Wonder Man '45

Norman Kaye
Heaven's Burning '97

Stubby Kaye
Cat Ballou [SE] '65
Guys and Dolls '55

Thorsten Kaye
Shark Attack 2 '00

Lainie Kazan
The Crew '00
What's Cooking? '00
Delta Force '86
Lust in the Dust '85

Ayelet Kaznelson
The Tao of Steve '00

Tim Kazurinsky
Shakes the Clown '92

Suyun Ke
Yi Yi '00

James Keach
Love Letters '83
The Long Riders '80

Stacy Keach
Fear Runs Silent '99

Batman: Mask of the Phan-
tasm '93 (V)
Saturday the 14th '81
The Long Riders '80
Cheech and Chong's Up in
Smoke '79

Staci Keanan
Downhill Willie '96

Basil Keane
The Harder They Come '72

Katie Keane
Girl Explores Girl: The Alien
Encounter [CE] '00
The Erotic Witch Project [CE]
'99

William Keane
The First 9 1/2 Weeks '98

Billy Kearns
Bed and Board '70

Harry Keatan
Girl Gang '54

Fred Keating
My 5 Wives '00

Buster Keaton
Beach Blanket Bingo '65
Buster Keaton Rides Again /
The Railrodder '65
Railrodder '65

Diane Keaton
Hanging Up '99
Father of the Bride Part II '95
The Godfather, Part 3 '90
The Lemon Sisters '90
Baby Boom '87
Manhattan '79
Interiors '78
Love and Death '75
The Godfather, Part 2 '74
Sleeper '73
The Godfather DVD Collection
'72

Michael Keaton
My Life '93

Ele Keats
White Wolves 2: Legend of
the Wild '94

Brian L. Keaulana
In God's Hands '98

Lila Kedrova
Torn Curtain '66

James Patrick Keefe
Fallen Angel '99

Andrew Keegan
The Broken Hearts Club '00

Howard Keel
Annie Get Your Gun '50

Ruby Keeler
42nd Street '33

James Keeley
Jerome '98

Geoffrey Keen
The Living Daylights '87

Noah Keen
Battle for the Planet of the
Apes '73

Monica Keena
Crime and Punishment in
Suburbia '00
All I Wanna Do '98

Caroline Keenan
Vice Girls '96

Jessica Keenan
Sideshow '00

Will Keenan
Terror Firmer [SE] '00

Tom (George Duryea) Keene
Plan 9 from Outer Space [Passport Video] '56

Catherine Keener
Simpatico '99
The Real Blonde '97

Matt Keeslar
Dune '00
Scream 3 [CS] '00
Splendor '99
Sour Grapes '98

Jack Kehler
187 '97
Desert Winds '95

Jack Kehoe
The Untouchables '87
The Pope of Greenwich Village '84
Law and Disorder '74

Danny Kei
Shark Attack 2 '00

Margaret Rose Keil
Inn of 1000 Sins '75

Andrew Keir
Cleopatra '63

Harvey Keitel
Little Nicky '00
Prince of Central Park '00
U-571 [CE] '00
Holy Smoke '99
City of Industry '96
From Dusk Till Dawn [2 CS] '95
Imaginary Crimes '94
The Last Temptation of Christ '88
Buffalo Bill & the Indians '76

Brian Keith
Meteor '79
The Hallelujah Trail '65

David Keith
Men of Honor '00
U-571 [CE] '00
An Officer and a Gentleman '82

Sheila Keith
Frightmare '74

Joseph Kell
White Lies '98

Cecil Kellaway
Harvey '50
Portrait of Jennie '48

David Henry Keller
Mob War [BFS] '88

Farah Keller
The Beyond '82

Hiram Keller
Fellini Satyricon '69

Joel S. Keller
The Life Before This '99

Marthe Keller
Women '97

Sally Kellerman
Kill Shot '01
Mirror, Mirror 2: Raven Dance '94
Back to School '86

DeForest Kelley
Star Trek 2: The Wrath of Khan '82

Kimberly Kelley
Midnight Tease 2 '95

Sheila Kelley
Nurse Betty '00

Walter Kelley
Marty '55

Mike Kellin
Sleepaway Camp '83
Hell Is for Heroes '62
At War with the Army '50

Catherine Kellner
Shaft '00
Restaurant '98
Six Degrees of Separation '93

David Patrick Kelly
The Warriors '79

Gene Kelly
Take Me Out to the Ball Game '49

Grace Kelly
The Bridges at Toko-Ri '55
Rear Window '54

Kevin Kelly
The Amazing Transparent Man '60

Moira Kelly
The Tie That Binds '95
The Cutting Edge '92

Patsy Kelly
Rosemary's Baby '68

Paula Kelly
Once Upon a Time...When We Were Colored '95
The Women of Brewster Place '89

Rae'ven (Alyia Larrymore) Kelly
Milo '98

Robyn Kelly
Flesh Gordon 2: Flesh Gordon Meets the Cosmic Cheerleaders '90

Sharon Kelly
Ilsa, Harem Keeper of the Oil Sheiks '76
Ilsa, She-Wolf of the SS '74

Pat Kelman
Dead of Night '99

Kellyann Kelso
The Emperor's New Groove [SE] '00 (V)

Edward Kemmer
Giant from the Unknown '58

Warren Kemmerling
Family Plot '76

Barbie Kemp
Another Day, Another Man '66

Gary Kemp
Killing Zoe '94

Valli Kemp
Doctor Phibes Rises Again '72

Tony Kendall
The Whip and the Body '63

Arthur Kennedy
The Sentinel '76
Let Sleeping Corpses Lie '74
Fantastic Voyage '66
Lawrence of Arabia '62
The Man from Laramie '55

Beth Kennedy
Jerome '98

Douglas Kennedy
The Amazing Transparent Man '60

George Kennedy
Naked Gun 33 1/3: The Final Insult '94
Naked Gun 2 1/2: The Smell of Fear '91
Brain Dead '89

The Naked Gun: From the Files of Police Squad '88
Creepshow 2 '87
Delta Force '86
Death on the Nile '78
Thunderbolt & Lightfoot '74
In Harm's Way '65
Sons of Katie Elder '65

Jamie Kennedy
Bait '00
Boiler Room '00
Scream 3 [CS] '00
The Specials '00

Jihmi Kennedy
Glory [2 SE] '89

Leon Isaac Kennedy
Hollywood Vice Sqaud '86
Penitentiary 2 '82
Penitentiary '79

Lyn Kennedy
Teenage Gang Debs / Teenage Strangler '66

Ryan Kennedy
Slumber Party Massacre '82

June Kenney
Teenage Doll '57

June Kenny
Attack of the Puppet People '58

Tom Kenny
Shakes the Clown '92

Patsy Kensit
Monty Python and the Holy Grail '75

Cooper Kent
Double Agent 73 '80

Gary Kent
Satan's Sadists '69

Julie Kent
Center Stage '00

Steven Kerby
China O'Brien '88

Joanna (Joanna DeVarona) Kerns
No Dessert Dad, 'Til You Mow the Lawn '94

Zora Kerova
Cannibal Ferox '84

Deborah Kerr
An Affair to Remember '57
End of the Affair '55
Black Narcissus '47

E. Katherine Kerr
Children of a Lesser God '86
Power '86

John Kerr
The Pit and the Pendulum '61

Irvin Kershner
The Last Temptation of Christ '88

Brian Kerwin
The Myth of Fingerprints '97
Love Field '91

Keskhemnu
The Arrangement '99

Sara Kestelman
Zardoz '73

Harold Key
Bad Girls Go to Hell / Another Day, Another Man '65

Evelyn Keyes
The Seven Year Itch '55

Arsinee Khanjian
The Adjuster '91

Kulbashan Kharbanda
Fire '96

Nozha Khouadra
The New Eve '98
Honey & Ashes '96

Kiatenai
Detention '98

Guy Kibbee
Our Town '40
Little Lord Fauntleroy '36
42nd Street '33
Rain '32

Kid Frost
Dope Case Pending '00

Margot Kidder
Tribulation '00
Superman 4: The Quest for Peace '87
Superman 3 '83
Superman 2 '80
The Amityville Horror '79
Superman: The Movie '78
Black Christmas '75
Sisters '73
Quackser Fortune Has a Cousin in the Bronx '70

Nicole Kidman
Malice [MGM] '93
My Life '93

Richard Kiel
Hysterical '83
The Longest Yard '74
The Phantom Planet '61

Udo Kier
Red Letters '00
Shadow of the Vampire '00
Dancer in the Dark '99
Barb Wire '96
Breaking the Waves '95

Robbie Kiger
Children of the Corn '84

Susan Kiger
H.O.T.S. '79

Terence (Terry) Kilburn
Fiend Without a Face '58

Richard Kiley
Jurassic Park [CE] '93 (V)

Killah Priest
Da Hip Hop Witch '00

Val Kilmer
Red Planet '00
Thunderheart '92
The Doors [2 SE] '91
Kill Me Again '89

Patrick Kilpatrick
The Substitute 4: Failure Is Not an Option '00
Death Warrant '90

Shirley Kilpatrick
The Astounding She-Monster '58

Dana Kimmell
Friday the 13th, Part 3 '82

Andrea King
The Lemon Drop Kid '51

Kent Masters King
Johnny B. '00
Her Name Is Cat '99

Morgana King
The Godfather, Part 2 '74
The Godfather DVD Collection '72

Perry King
Switch '91
The Lords of Flatbush '74

Regina King
If These Walls Could Talk 2 '00
Poetic Justice '93

Stephen King
Sleepwalkers '92
Pet Sematary '89
Creepshow 2 '87
Maximum Overdrive '86

Ben Kingsley
Rules of Engagement '00
What Planet Are You From? '00
The Confession '98

Alex Kingston
Essex Boys '99
Croupier '97

Sam Kinison
Back to School '86

Kathleen Kinmont
Stormswept '95
Bride of Re-Animator '89

Greg Kinnear
Loser '00
Nurse Betty '00
What Planet Are You From? '00

Roy Kinnear
The Four Musketeers '75

Jack Kinney
The Adventures of Ichabod and Mr. Toad '49 (V)

Kathy Kinney
Parting Glances '86

Terry Kinney
Save the Last Dance '01
House of Mirth '00
The Last of the Mohicans '92

Klaus Kinski
My Best Fiend '99
Fruits of Passion: The Story of "O" Continued '82
Woyzeck '78
Aguirre, the Wrath of God '72

Nastassia Kinski
The Claim '00
Red Letters '00

Grace Kip
Gen-X Cops '99

Bruno Kirby
Donnie Brasco [2] '96
City Slickers '91
When Harry Met Sally... [SE] '89
This Is Spinal Tap [MGM] '84
The Godfather, Part 2 '74

Michael Kirby
Shadows and Fog '92
Another Woman '88

James Kirk
National Lampoon's Golf Punks '99

Tommy Kirk
Blood of Ghastly Horror '72
Village of the Giants '65

Kathleen Kirkham
The Married Virgin '18

Sally Kirkland
Starry Night '99
Picture Windows '95
Love Letters '83
Breakheart Pass '76
The Way We Were [SE] '73

Jess Kirkpatrick
D.O.A. [Roan] '49

Craig Kirkwood
Remember the Titans '00

Denny Kirkwood
Groove '00

Mia Kirshner
Murder in the First '95

Ralph Laidlaw
Back to God's Country /
Something New '19

Cleo Laine
The Last of the Blonde Bombshells '00

Jenny Laird
Black Narcissus '47

Don Lake
Best in Show '00

Ricki Lake
Cecil B. Demented '00
Working Girl '88

James Lally
Critical Care '97
Working Girl '88

Bowie Lam
Hard-Boiled [Winstar] '92

Nathaniel Lamar
The Horrible Dr. Bones '00

Hedy Lamarr
The Strange Woman '46

Gil Lamb
Day of the Animals '77

Larry Lamb
Essex Boys '99

Anne Louise Lambert
Napoleon '96 (V)
Lilian's Story '95

Christopher Lambert
Highlander: Endgame '00
Beowulf '98
Mean Guns '97
Highlander: The Final Dimen-
sion '94
Knight Moves '93

Henry Lambert
Oasis of the Zombies '82

Jack Lambert
Kiss Me Deadly '55

Ellie Lambetti
A Matter of Dignity '57
Girl in Black '56

Adele Lamont
The Brain that Wouldn't Die
'63

Duncan Lamont
Frankenstein Created Woman
'66

Mark Lamos
Longtime Companion '90

Dorothy Lamour
Creepshow 2 '87
Donovan's Reef '63
The Road to Bali '53
My Favorite Brunette '47
The Road to Rio '47

Zohra Lampert
Opening Night '77

Charles Lamy
Fall of the House of Usher
'28

Burt Lancaster
Local Hero '83
Buffalo Bill & the Indians '76
The Cassandra Crossing '76
The Hallelujah Trail '65
Seven Days in May '64
Birdman of Alcatraz '62
Sweet Smell of Success '57
The Kentuckian '55
Vera Cruz '53

James Lancaster
Leprechaun 2 '94
Gettysburg '93

Stuart Lancaster
Mantis in Lace '68

Vic Lance
Mantis in Lace '68

Karl Lanchbury
Vampyres '74

Elsa Lanchester
The Inspector General '49
The Bishop's Wife [MGM] '47
The Spiral Staircase '46
Rembrandt '36

Bev Land
Social Misfits '00

David Landau
Street Scene '31

Martin Landau
In the Beginning... '00
Ready to Rumble '00
The Long Way Home '97 (N)
Mistress '91
Crimes & Misdemeanors
[MGM] '89
Tucker: The Man and His
Dream '88
Meteor '79
They Call Me Mr. Tibbs! '70
The Hallelujah Trail '65
Cleopatra '63
North by Northwest '59

David Lander
Scary Movie '00

Steve Landesburg
The Souler Opposite '97
The Crazysitter '94

Sonny Landham
Predator [20th Century Fox]
'87

Carole Landis
Topper Returns '41

Jessie Royce Landis
North by Northwest '59

John Landis
Diamonds '99
Sleepwalkers '92
Body Chemistry 2: Voice of a
Stranger '91
Battle for the Planet of the
Apes '73

Nina Landis
Komodo '99

Jeffrey Landman
Halloween 5: The Revenge of
Michael Myers '89

Joe Lando
No Code of Conduct '98

Michael Landon
Fight for the Title '57

Ruth Landshoff
Nosferatu [2] '22

Miriam Landson
Oasis of the Zombies '82

Hanna Landy
Rosemary's Baby '68

Charles Lane
Posse '93

Colin Lane
Broken Harvest '94

Diane Lane
The Perfect Storm '00
My Dog Skip '99
Wild Bill '95
Knight Moves '93

Frederic Lane
Terror Tract '00

Monica Lane
Varietease '54

Nathan Lane
Isn't She Great '00
Love's Labour's Lost '00
Titan A.E. '00 (V)

Priscilla Lane
Arsenic and Old Lace '44
Saboteur '42

Richard Lane
The Jackie Robinson Story
'50
Take Me Out to the Ball
Game '49

Laura Lanfranchi
Don't Mess with My Sister!
'85

k.d. lang
Eye of the Beholder '99

Lex Lang
Weather Woman '99

Perry Lang
Eight Men Out '88

Stephen Lang
After the Storm '01
The Proposal '00
A Town Has Turned to Dust '98
Gettysburg '93
Crime Story: The Complete
Saga '86

Sue Ane Langdon
Frankie and Johnny '65

Anne Lange
Shadows and Fog '92

Artie Lange
The 4th Floor '99
Dirty Work '97

Hope Lange
Blue Velvet '86
Death Wish '74
Bus Stop '56

Jessica Lange
Titus '99
Blue Sky '91
Frances '82
Tootsie '82

Frank Langella
Jason and the Argonauts '00
The Ninth Gate '99
I'm Losing You '98
Lolita '97

Frances Langford
Melody Time '48 (V)

Chris Langham
The Big Tease '99

Amanda Langlet
A Summer's Tale '96

Caroline Langrishe
Sharpe's Justice '96
Sharpe's Regiment '96

Murray Langston
Wishful Thinking '92

Brooke Langton
Playing Mona Lisa '00
The Replacements '00

Paul Langton
The Cosmic Man '59

Nicholas Lanier
Witchouse 2: Blood Coven
'00

Angela Lansbury
Beauty and the Beast: The
Enchanted Christmas '97
(V)
The Mirror Crack'd '80
Death on the Nile '78
Bedknobs and Broomsticks
'71
The Greatest Story Ever Told
[SE] '65

Joi Lansing
Hillbillys in a Haunted House
'67
Touch of Evil [SE] '58
The Brave One '56

Robert Lansing
The Grissom Gang '71

Walter Lantz
The Fantasy Film Worlds of
George Pal '86

Anthony LaPaglia
Autumn in New York '00
House of Mirth '00
Sweet and Lowdown '99
Empire Records '95

Jean Lapointe
Never Too Late '98

Jane Lapotaire
The Asphyx '72

John Larch
The Amityville Horror '79

Vincent Laresca
Forever Mine '99
Juice '92

Veronica Lario
Tenebre '82

Bryan Larkin
Born on the Fourth of July [2]
'89

Slim Larnaout
Honey & Ashes '96

Mary Laroche
Psychomania '73

Michele Laroque
Ma Vie en Rose '97

John Larroquette
Isn't She Great '00
Summer Rental '85

Darrell Larson
Stuart Saves His Family '94

Ryan Larson
The St. Francisville Experiment '00

Tom Larson
I Married a Strange Person
'97 (V)

Lars Andreas Larssen
The Last Lieutenant '94

Ali Larter
Final Destination '00
Drive Me Crazy '99

Jack LaRue
A Farewell to Arms '32

Robert LaSardo
Under Oath '97

Michael Laskin
Bounce '00
Eight Men Out '88

Mara Laso
The Awful Dr. Orlof '62

Dagmar Lassander
The Black Cat '81
The Frightened Woman '71
Hatchet for the Honeymoon
'70

Louise Lasser
Requiem for a Dream '00
Everything You Always Want-
ed to Know about Sex (But
Were Afraid to Ask) '72
Bananas '71

Sarah Lassez
In Pursuit '00

Rolf Lassgard
The White Lioness '96

Sydney Lassick
American Vampire '97
Shakes the Clown '92

Louise Latham
Love Field '91

Philip Latham
The Pallisers '74

Alyce LaTourelle
Terror Firmer [SE] '00

Matt Lattanzi
Roxanne '87

Andy Lau
Running out of Time '99
The Legend of Drunken Mas-
ter '94
Saviour of the Soul 2 '92

Damian Lau
Jet Li's The Enforcer [Buena
Vista] '95

Andrew Lauer
Gun Shy '00
I'll Be Home for Christmas
'98

Justin Lauer
The Creeps '97

Jack Laufer
And the Band Played On '93

John Laughlin
Back to Back '96

Charles Laughton
Sparacus [Criterion] '60
Captain Kidd '45
Rembrandt '36

Rik Launspach
The Delivery '99

Stan Laurel
Utopia '51
The Flying Deuces / Utopia
'39
March of the Wooden Sol-
diers '34

Greg Lauren
The Prophet's Game '99

Ashley Laurence
Mikey '92
Hellraiser [2] '87

Phil Laurensen
The Gore-Gore Girls '72

James Laurenson
Sharpe's Mission '96
Sharpe's Regiment '96
Sharpe's Siege '96

Dan Lauria
Full Disclosure '00
Hangman '00
Fear Runs Silent '99
Wide Awake '97

Mary Dean Lauria
Heavy Traffic '73

John Laurie
Hamlet '48
Immortal Battalion '44

Piper Laurie
Children of a Lesser God '86

Ed Lauter
Youngblood '86
Girls Just Want to Have Fun
'85
Cujo '83
Breakheart Pass '76
Family Plot '76
The Longest Yard '74

Harry Lauter
Escape from the Planet of
the Apes '71

Mark Lester
The Prince and the Pauper '78

Jared Leto
Requiem for a Dream '00
American Psycho '99
Black and White '99
Girl, Interrupted '99

Dan Lett
The Life Before This '99

Al Lettieri
The Godfather DVD Collection '72

Lau Kar Leung
The Legend of Drunken Master '94

Tony Leung Chiu-Wai
Tokyo Raiders '00
Gorgeous '99
Ashes of Time '94
Hard-Boiled [Winstar] '92
Chinese Ghost Story III '91

Tony Leung Ka-Fai
Ashes of Time '94
The Prisoner '90

Sam Levene
Sweet Smell of Success '57

Sean Levert
Dope Case Pending '00

John Levin
Bounce '00

Ilana Levine
Just Looking '99

Jerry Levine
Born on the Fourth of July [2] '89

Steve Levitt
Last Resort '86

Dr. Claude Levy
The Sorrow and the Pity '71

Eugene Levy
Best in Show '00
The Ladies Man '00
Father of the Bride Part II '95
Splash '84

Al Lewis
Married to the Mob '88
The Munsters' Revenge '81
Munster, Go Home! '66

Charlotte Lewis
Men of War '94

Clea Lewis
The Rich Man's Wife '96

David Lewis
The Apartment '60

Dawnn Lewis
Race to Freedom: The Story of the Underground Railroad '94
I'm Gonna Git You Sucka '88

Fiona Lewis
Dracula / Strange Case of Dr. Jekyll & Mr. Hyde '73
Doctor Phibes Rises Again '72

Gary Lewis
Billy Elliot '00
Postmortem '98

Geoffrey Lewis
Way of the Gun '00
The Prophet's Game '99
Double Impact '91
Lust in the Dust '85
Bronco Billy '80
Thunderbolt & Lightfoot '74

Huey Lewis
Duets '00

Jenifer Lewis
Castaway '00

Jenny Lewis
Foxfire '96

Jerry Lewis
The Nutty Professor '63
The Road to Bali '53
At War with the Army '50

Juliette Lewis
Way of the Gun '00
The 4th Floor '99
The Evening Star '96
From Dusk Till Dawn [2 CS] '95
Natural Born Killers [DC] '94

Leigh Lewis
Revelation '00
Tribulation '00

Michael Lewis
Gruesome Twosome '67

Misty Lewis
Asylum of Terror '98

Phill Lewis
Once Upon a Time...When We Were Colored '95 (N)
City Slickers '91

Ralph Lewis
Outside the Law / Shadows '21

Robert Q. Lewis
An Affair to Remember '57

Toni Lewis
Homicide: The Movie '00

Vicki Lewis
Breakfast of Champions '98

Thierry Lhermitte
The Dinner Game '98

Gong Li
The Emperor and the Assassin '99
The Dragon Chronicles '94

Jet Li
Romeo Must Die '00
New Legend of Shaolin '96
Jet Li's The Enforcer [Buena Vista] '95
The Bodyguard from Beijing '94
The Defender '94
The Legend '93
Twin Warriors '93
Once Upon a Time in China '91

Richard Libertini
Telling You '98

Richard V. Licata
Just Looking '99

Mimi Lieber
Last Resort '86

Nancy Lieberman
Perfect Profile '90

Tina Lifford
The '70s '00
Grand Canyon '91

Judith Light
Joseph: King of Dreams '00 (V)

Dennis Lill
Element of Doubt '96

Matthew Lillard
Love's Labour's Lost '00
Dish Dogs '98
Telling You '98
The Curve '97

Mario Lima
Awakenings of the Beast '68

Brigitte (Lin Chinag-hsia) Lin
The Dragon Chronicles '94
Fantasy Mission Force '84
Zu: Warriors of the Magic Mountain '83

Abbey Lincoln
Mo' Better Blues '90

Greta Lind
Rudy [SE] '93

Susie Lindemann
Lilian's Story '95

Emilio Linder
Slugs '87

Viveca Lindfors
The Way We Were [SE] '73

Audra Lindley
Desert Hearts '86

Barbara Lindley
Dracula / Strange Case of Dr. Jekyll & Mr. Hyde '73

Delroy Lindo
Gone in 60 Seconds '00
Romeo Must Die '00
The Book of Stars '99
The Cider House Rules '99
Soul of the Game '96
Blood In . . . Blood Out: Bound by Honor '93
Mr. Jones '93
Mountains of the Moon '90

Robert Lindsay
That'll Be the Day '73

George Lindsey
Robin Hood '73 (V)

Richard Lineback
Ready to Rumble '00

Rosaleen Linehan
Sharpe's Gold '94

Bai Ling
Anna and the King '99
Row Your Boat '98

Beth Linhart
Hot Vampire Nights '00

Hamish Linklater
Groove '00

Cody Linley
My Dog Skip '99

Rex Linn
Drop Zone '94
Cliffhanger [2 CS] '93

Mark Linn-Baker
Manhattan '79

Eli Russell Linnetz
The Emperor's New Groove [SE] '00 (V)

Laura Linney
House of Mirth '00

Edilson Lino
Pixote '81

Larry Linville
No Dessert Dad, 'Til You Mow the Lawn '94

Alex D. Linz
Bounce '00
Titan A.E. '00 (V)

Lio
Love After Love '94

Ray Liotta
Hannibal '01
Forever Mine '99
Inferno '99
Something Wild '86

Eugene Lipinski
Bless the Child '00

Maureen Lipman
Solomon and Gaenor '98

Jonathan Lipnicki
The Little Vampire '00

Dennis Lipscomb
Sister, Sister '87

Jack Lipson
Flash Gordon: Space Soldiers '36

Peggy Lipton
Intern '00
The '70s '00
I'm Gonna Git You Sucka '88

Robert Lipton
A Woman, Her Men and Her Futon '92

Andrea Lisa
Divided We Stand '00

Virna Lisi
Bluebeard '72

Trevor Lissauer
American Vampire '97

Tommy (Tiny) Lister
Circus '00
Little Nicky '00
Next Friday [Platinum Series] '00
Out Kold '00
Men of War '94
Posse '93

John Lithgow
Rugrats in Paris: The Movie '00 (V)
Homegrown '97
The Tuskegee Airmen '95
American Cinema: 100 Years of Filmmaking '94 (N)
Princess Caraboo '94
Cliffhanger [2 CS] '93
Santa Claus: The Movie '85
Mesmerized '84
Terms of Endearment '83

Cleavon Little
Cotton Comes to Harlem '70

Kim Little
Killers '97

Little Nell
The Rocky Horror Picture Show '75

Little Richard
Mystery, Alaska '99

Nadia Litz
The Five Senses '99

Ernest Liu
From Dusk Till Dawn [2 CS] '95

Harrison Liu
Black Robe '91

Lucy Alexis Liu
Charlie's Angels '00
Shanghai Noon '00
Play It to the Bone '99
Flypaper '97

Matty Liu
In God's Hands '98

Maurice Liu
Shadow of Chinatown '36

Jason Lively
Ghost Chase '88

Roger Livesey
The Pallisers '74
The Entertainer '60
I Know Where I'm Going '45

Barry Livingston
Invisible Mom '96

Paul Livingston
The Navigator '88

Robert "Bob" Livingston
I Spit on Your Corpse '74

Ron Livingston
Body Shots '99

Shelby Livingston
Nude on the Moon '61

Linda Ljoka
Diamond Run '00

L.L. Cool J.
Charlie's Angels '00
Any Given Sunday '99

Suzette Llewellyn
Welcome II the Terrordome '95

Desmond Llewelyn
The World Is Not Enough [SE] '99
The Living Daylights '87
A View to a Kill [SE] '85
Diamonds Are Forever [SE] '71
You Only Live Twice [SE] '67
From Russia with Love [2 SE] '63

Bernard Lloyd
A Christmas Carol '99

Christopher Lloyd
Premonition '99
The Real Blonde '97
The Addams Family '91
Eight Men Out '88
Clue '85

Doris Lloyd
The Time Machine '60

Emily Lloyd
In Country '89

Gabrielle Lloyd
Poldark '96

Norman Lloyd
The Adventures of Rocky & Bullwinkle '00
A Walk in the Sun '46
Saboteur '42

Tony LoBianco
Mafia! '98
The Story of Jacob & Joseph '74

Enrico Lo Verso
Hannibal '01
Farinelli '94

Goldie Loc
Tha Eastsidaz '00

Amy Locane
Blue Sky '91

Felix Locher
Frankenstein's Daughter '58

Sondra Locke
The Prophet's Game '99
Bronco Billy '80

Calvin Lockhart
The Beast Must Die '75
Cotton Comes to Harlem '70

Gene Lockhart
The Inspector General '49
The Strange Woman '46
Hangmen Also Die '42
Meet John Doe [Image] '41

June Lockhart
The Fantasy Worlds of Irwin Allen '95

Howard Lockie
Passion & Romance: Double or Nothing '00

Evan Lockwood
Rambling Rose [2 SE] '91

Thomas Lockyer
Jesus '00
Teenagers from Outer Space
'59

John Loder
How Green Was My Valley '41

Kathryn Loder
Foxy Brown '74
The Big Doll House '71

John Lodge
Scarlet Empress '34

Roger Lodge
Not of This Earth '88

Paul Logan
Killers '97

Robert Loggia
Return to Me '00
Flypaper '97
Wide Awake '97
Smilla's Sense of Snow '96
Gladiator '92
Necessary Roughness '91
The Jagged Edge '85
An Officer and a Gentleman
'82
The Greatest Story Ever Told
[SE] '65

Donal Logue
The Patriot '00
Reindeer Games '00
Steal This Movie! '00
The Tao of Steve '00
The Big Tease '99
The Million Dollar Hotel '99
And the Band Played On '93
Gettysburg '93

Marie Lohr
Pygmalion '38

Gina Lollobrigida
Bad Man's River '72
Private Navy of Sgt. O'Farrell
'68
Beat the Devil '53

Herbert Lom
Dead Zone '83
Asylum '72
Sparacus [Criterion] '60

Karina Lombard
Footsteps '98
Legends of the Fall [2 SE] '94

Ulli Lommel
Whity '70

Jason London
Jason and the Argonauts '00
Broken Vessels '98
My Teacher's Wife '95
Fall Time '94

Jeremy London
White Wolves 2: Legend of
the Wild '94

Lisa London
H.O.T.S. '79

Tony London
Sid & Nancy [MGM] '86

Jodi Long
Amos and Andrew '93

Nia Long
Big Momma's House '00
Boiler Room '00
The Broken Hearts Club '00
Held Up '00
If These Walls Could Talk 2
'00
Boyz N the Hood '91

Shelley Long
Dr. T & the Women '00
Losin' It '82

John Longden
Quatermass 2 '57

Jane Longenecker
The Coroner '98

Ricardo Serventi Longhi
Wax Mask '97

**Michael (Michel)
Lonsdale**
The Bride Wore Black '68

Richard Loo
The Sand Pebbles '66

Deborah Loomis
Hercules in New York '70

Anna Loos
Anatomy [SE] '00

Charo Lopez
Secrets of the Heart '97

Jennifer Lopez
The Cell '00

Perry Lopez
Kelly's Heroes '70

Priscilla Lopez
Center Stage '00

Sal Lopez
Price of Glory '00

Sergei Lopez
An Affair of Love '00
The New Eve '98

Isabel Lorca
She's Having a Baby '88

Theodore Lorch
The Last of the Mohicans '20

Traci Lords
Extramarital '98
Not of This Earth '88

Donna Loren
Bikini Beach '64

Sophia Loren
The Cassandra Crossing '76

Bethany Lorraine
Femalien 2 '98

Harry Lorraine
The Last of the Mohicans '20

Peter Lorre
Tales of Terror '62
Voyage to the Bottom of the
Sea / Fantastic Voyage '61
Beat the Devil '53
Quicksand '50
My Favorite Brunette '47
Arsenic and Old Lace '44
The Maltese Falcon '41

Diana Lorys
The Awful Dr. Orlof '62

Tilly Losch
The Garden of Allah '36

Dennis Lotis
Horror Hotel '60

Eb Lottimer
Diamondbacks '99
Termination Man '97

Louanne
A Night in the Life of Jimmy
Reardon '88

Bill Louie
The Bodyguard / Dragon
Princess '76

Anita Louise
The Little Princess '39

Marie Louise
The Arena '73

Tina Louise
How to Commit Marriage '69

Todd Louiso
High Fidelity '00

Gerard Loussine
Don't Let Me Die on a Sunday '99

Bessie Love
Vampyres '74
The Lost World [Image] '25

Courtney Love
Straight to Hell '87
Sid & Nancy [MGM] '86

Faizon Love
Inhumanity '00
The Replacements '00
Three Strikes '00

Lucretia Love
Battle of the Amazons '74
The Arena '73

Alec Lovejoy
Moon over Harlem '39

Jacqueline Lovell
Ultimate Attraction '98
Lolida 2000 '97
Femalien '96

Raymond Lovell
Immortal Battalion '44

Ray Lovelock
Let Sleeping Corpses Lie '74

David Lovgren
Something More '99

Jon Lovitz
Little Nicky '00
Small Time Crooks '00
High School High '96
Last Resort '86

Elizabeth Low
Fear Runs Silent '99

Amelia Lowdell
Essex Boys '99

Brent J. Lowe
Beowulf '98

Chad Lowe
Floating '97
Quiet Days in Hollywood '97

Patrick Lowe
Slumber Party Massacre 2
'87

Rob Lowe
Escape under Pressure '00
The Specials '00
For Hire '98
Frank and Jesse '94
Youngblood '86
Class '83

Elina Lowensohn
Immortality '98

Carolyn Lowery
Octopus '00

Robert Lowery
The Undertaker and His Pals
'67

Myrna Loy
The End '78

Manuel Lozano
Butterfly '00

Margarita Lozano
Jean de Florette '87
Manon of the Spring '87

Hedda Lubin
The Gore-Gore Girls '72

Arthur Lucan
My Son, the Vampire '52

George Lucas
American Cinema: 100 Years
of Filmmaking '94 (N)

Joshua Lucas
American Psycho '99

Laurent Lucas
Pola X '99

William Lucas
X The Unknown '56

Deborah Luce
Mother's Day [DC] '80

Dominic Luchese
If Lucy Fell '95

Fabrice Luchini
Perceval '78
Immoral Tales '74

Laurence Luckinbill
Death Sentence '74

William Lucking
The Last Best Sunday '98

Laurette Luez
D.O.A. [Roan] '49

Françoise Lugagne
Diary of a Chambermaid '64

Bela Lugosi
Plan 9 from Outer Space
[Passport Video] '56
My Son, the Vampire '52
Abbott and Costello Meet
Frankenstein '48
Ghosts on the Loose '43
Shadow of Chinatown '36

Peter Luhr
The Marquise of O '76

Jackie Lui
The Mission '99

Paul Lukather
Dinosaurus! '60

Jorge Luke
Salvador [SE] '86

Keye Luke
Alice '90
The Mighty Quinn '89

Oldrich Lukes
First Spaceship on Venus '60

Folco Lulli
Variety Lights '51

Carl Lumbly
Men of Honor '00
South Central '92
The Bedroom Window '87

Sidney Lumet
American Cinema: 100 Years
of Filmmaking '94 (N)

Joanna Lumley
James and the Giant Peach
'96 (V)

Art Lund
Black Caesar '73

Deanna Lund
Dr. Goldfoot and the Bikini
Machine '66

Christine Lunde
Hardcase and Fist '89

Dolph Lundgren
Bridge of Dragons '99
Men of War '94
Red Scorpion '89
A View to a Kill [SE] '85

Jamie Luner
Confessions of Sorority Girls
'00

Ti Lung
The Legend of Drunken Mas-
ter '94
A Better Tomorrow, Part 1
[Anchor Bay] '86

Cherie Lunghi
The Sign of Four '83

Beverly Lunsford
The Intruder '61

Ida Lupino
The Gay Desperado '36

Patti LuPone
Cold Blooded '00
Just Looking '99

John Lurie
The Last Temptation of Christ
'88

Aaron Lustig
Stuart Saves His Family '94

Kate Luyben
My 5 Wives '00

Rasmus Lyberth
Heart of Light '97

Ted Lyde
The Vault '00

Gary Lydon
The Last September '99

Jimmy Lydon
Life with Father '47

Leslie Lyles
Coming Soon '99
My Teacher's Wife '95

Will Lyman
Floating '97

John Lynch
The Quarry '98
Moll Flanders [MGM] '96
Princess Caraboo '94

John Carroll Lynch
Restaurant '98

Kelly Lynch
Charlie's Angels '00
Homegrown '97
Imaginary Crimes '94
Drugstore Cowboy '89

Pauline Lynch
Attila '01

Richard Lynch
Under Oath '97

Richard Lynch
Diamond Run '00
Destination Vegas '95
Midnight Confessions '95
Lockdown '90
Puppet Master 3: Toulon's
Revenge '90
Aftershock '88

Paul Lynde
Charlotte's Web '73 (V)
Beach Blanket Bingo '65

Amy Lyndon
Big City Blues '99

Simon Lyndon
Blackrock '97

Carol Lynley
Beware! The Blob '72

Diana Lynn
The Kentuckian '55

Randee Lynn
Satan's Sadists '69

Theresa Lynn
Psycho Sisters '98

Vickie Lynn
Teaserama '55

Melanie Lynskey
Coyote Ugly '00

Natasha Lyonne
If These Walls Could Talk 2 '00
But I'm a Cheerleader '99

Bruce Lyons
The Navigator '88

Cliff Lyons
The Horse Soldiers '59

James Lyons
I Shot Andy Warhol '96

Robert F. Lyons
The Omega Code '99

Steve Lyons
For Love of the Game '99

Susan Lyons
Napoleon '96 (V)

Wu Ma
Chinese Ghost Story II '90

Hidde Maas
The Delivery '99

Lincoln Maazel
Martin '77

Byron Mabe
The Defilers '65

Eric Mabius
The Crow: Salvation '00
The Minus Man '99
Splendor '99
Around the Fire '98
I Shot Andy Warhol '96

Bernie Mac
Original Kings of Comedy '00
Get On the Bus '96
House Party 3 '94

Ralph Macchio
Forever Together '00
The Secret of NIMH 2 '98 (V)
My Cousin Vinny '92
The Karate Kid '84

Katherine MacColl
The House by the Cemetery
[Diamond] '83
The House by the Cemetery
[Anchor Bay] '83
The Beyond '82

Simon MacCorkindale
Death on the Nile '78

Bill MacDonald
Mercy '00

Edmund MacDonald
Detour '46

James MacDonald
Sour Grapes '98

Kelly Macdonald
Splendor '99
The Loss of Sexual Inno-
cence '98

Norm MacDonald
Screwed '00
Dirty Work '97

Andie MacDowell
The Object of Beauty '91

Paul Mace
The Lords of Flatbush '74

Angus Macfadyen
Jason and the Argonauts '00
The Cradle Will Rock '99
Titus '99
The Brylcreem Boys '96
Braveheart '95

Niall MacGinnis
Anna Karenina '48

Jack MacGowran
Wonderwall: The Movie '69

Ali MacGraw
Love Story '70

Philip Machale
Slugs '87

Ignacy Machowski
First Spaceship on Venus '60

Gabriel Macht
The Audrey Hepburn Story
'00

Daniel MacIvor
The Five Senses '99

Fulton Mackay
Local Hero '83

Robert MacKenzie
The Womaneater '59

Allison Mackie
The Souler Opposite '97

**Simmone Jade
MacKinnon**
Attila '01

Steven Mackintosh
Lock, Stock and 2 Smoking
Barrels '98

Kyle MacLachlan
Hamlet '00
Time Code '00
Xchange '00
The Doors [2 SE] '91
Blue Velvet '86

Shirley MacLaine
The Evening Star '96
Postcards from the Edge '90
Steel Magnolias '89
Terms of Endearment '83
Being There '79
The Apartment '60
The Trouble with Harry '55

Barton MacLane
The Maltese Falcon '41

Ian MacLean
The Joint Is Jumpin' '00 (N)

Elizabeth MacLellan
Puppet Master 2 '90

Gavin MacLeod
Kelly's Heroes '70
The Sand Pebbles '66

Aline MacMahon
The Man from Laramie '55

Will MacMillan
Salvador [SE] '86

Fred MacMurray
The Apartment '60

Patrick Macnee
A View to a Kill [SE] '85
This Is Spinal Tap [MGM] '84
The Avengers 1964–66 '67
A Christmas Carol '51

Peter MacNicol
The Secret of NIMH 2 '98 (V)

Joseph Macolo
Shaft's Big Score '72

Elle Macpherson
If Lucy Fell '95
Alice '90

Meredith MacRae
Bikini Beach '64

Carol MacReady
102 Dalmatians '00

George Macready
Tora! Tora! Tora! [2 SE] '70
Vera Cruz '53
Gilda '46

Bruce MacVittie
Where the Money Is '00

William H. Macy
Magnolia '99
Jerry and Tom '98
The Secret of NIMH 2 '98 (V)
Murder in the First '95
Benny & Joon '93

Ciaran Madden
The Beast Must Die '75

John Madden
The Replacements '00

Peter Madden
Frankenstein Created Woman
'66

Amy Madigan
Love Letters '83

Svenvara Madoka
Naked Killer '92

Madonna
The Next Best Thing '00
Shadows and Fog '92
Desperately Seeking Susan
'85

Michael Madsen
The Florentine '98
Diary of a Serial Killer '97
Donnie Brasco [2] '96
The Doors [2 SE] '91
Iguana '89
Kill Me Again '89
The Natural '84

Virginia Madsen
Full Disclosure '00
The Florentine '98
Blue Tiger '94

Mia Maestro
For Love or Country: The
Arturo Sandoval Story '00
Time Code '00

Roma Maffia
Nick of Time '95

Patrick Magee
The Black Cat '81
Asylum '72
Die, Monster, Die! '65
Dementia 13 '63

Jad Mager
Big City Blues '99

Benoit Magimel
A Single Girl '96

Pierre Magnier
Cyrano de Bergerac '25

Ann Magnuson
Tank Girl '94
A Night in the Life of Jimmy
Reardon '88
Desperately Seeking Susan
'85

Pierre Maguelon
Bed and Board '70

Tobey Maguire
Wonder Boys '00
The Cider House Rules '99
Ride with the Devil '99

John Mahoney
The Broken Hearts Club '00
She's the One '96
In the Line of Fire [2 SE] '93
Betrayed '88
Eight Men Out '88

Norman Mailer
Mailer on Mailer '00

Steven Mailer
Ride with the Devil '99
Quiet Days in Hollywood '97

Marjorie Main
Friendly Persuasion '56

Lee Majors
Scrooged '88

Susanna Makay
Maniac Nurses Find Ecstasy
'94

Kuroudo Maki
Scene at the Sea '91

Wendy Makkena
Air Bud [2] '97

Mako
Rugrats in Paris: The Movie
'00 (V)
Highlander: The Final Dimen-
sion '94
Tucker: The Man and His
Dream '88
Conan the Barbarian [2 CE]
'82
Private Navy of Sgt. O'Farrell
'68
The Sand Pebbles '66

Dragan Maksimovic
Pretty Village, Pretty Flame
'96

Patrick Malahide
Deacon Brodie '98

Paolo Malco
The House by the Cemetery
[Diamond] '83
The House by the Cemetery
[Anchor Bay] '83

Christopher Malcolm
We'll Meet Again '82

Paula Malcomson
Hamlet '00

Karl Malden
Meteor '79
Birdman of Alcatraz '62
One-Eyed Jacks '61

Arthur Malet
The Black Cauldron '85 (V)
Munster, Go Home! '66

Wendie Malick
The Emperor's New Groove
[SE] '00 (V)
Jerome '98

Keram Malicki-Sanchez
Cherry Falls / Terror Tract '00

Art Malik
In the Beginning... '00
The Living Daylights '87

Judith Malina
The Addams Family '91

John Malkovich
Shadow of the Vampire '00
The Messenger: The Story of
Joan of Arc '99
Beyond the Clouds '95
Mary Reilly '95
In the Line of Fire [2 SE] '93
Shadows and Fog '92
The Object of Beauty '91

Miles Malleson
A Christmas Carol '51

Perry Mallette
Thou Shalt Not Kill . . .
Except '87

Brian Mallon
Gettysburg '93

Dorothy Malone
Beach Party '63

Jena Malone
Cheaters '00
The Book of Stars '99
For Love of the Game '99

Patrick Malone
Grand Canyon '91

Michael Maloney
Henry V '89

H.F. Maltby
Pygmalion '38

Leonard Maltin
Forgotten Silver '96

Robert Mammone
Heaven's Burning '97

Alex Man
Rouge '87

Cheung Man
The Dragon Chronicles '94

Melissa Manchester
For the Boys '91

**Ray "Boom Boom"
Mancini**
Wishful Thinking '92

Nick Mancuso
Revelation '00
Tribulation '00

Howie Mandel
Tribulation '00

Nelson Mandela
The White Lioness '96

Jill Mandell
Cyberotica '00

Miles Mander
The Little Princess '39

Costas Mandylor
Fist of the North Star '95
The Doors [2 SE] '91

Louis Mandylor
Price of Glory '00

Tyler Mane
X-Men '00

Larry Manetti
Body Chemistry 4: Full Exposure '95

John Manfredi
Thou Shalt Not Kill . . .
Except '87

Camryn Manheim
What Planet Are You From?
'00
The Tic Code '99
Wide Awake '97

Blu Mankuma
Premonition '99

Dudley Manlove
Plan 9 from Outer Space
[Passport Video] '56

Danny Mann
Pocahontas '95 (V)

Gabriel Mann
Cherry Falls / Terror Tract '00
Kiss of Fire '98

Leslie Mann
Time Code '00
She's the One '96

Lisa Mann
Lilies of the Field '63

Robert Mann
Assault of the Party Nerds
'89

Samuel Mann
Wham-Bam, Thank You
Spaceman '75

David Manners
The Mummy '32

Ettore Manni
City of Women '81

Karina Mano
8 1/2 Women '99

Miki Manojlovic
Portraits Chinois '96

Predrag Manojlovic
Tito and Me '92

Joe Mantegna
Liberty Heights '99

Six Degrees of Separation
'93
Mean Season '85
Semi-Tough '77

Heather Matarazzo
Scream 3 [CS] '00
All I Wanna Do '98

Julian Mateos
Return of the Magnificent
Seven '66

Jerry Mathers
The Trouble with Harry '55

Hans Matheson
Les Miserables '97
Poldark '96

Judy Matheson
Crucible of Terror '72

Michelle Matheson
Threesome '94

Tim Matheson
How to Commit Marriage '69
Yours, Mine & Ours '68

Terumi Mathews
The Waiting Game '99

Reiko Mathieu
Strawberry Fields '97

Samantha Mathis
American Psycho '99
Little Women [2 SE] '94

Julia Matias
Parasite '95

Marie Matiko
The Art of War '00

Marlee Matlin
Children of a Lesser God '86

Chieko Matsubara
Black Tight Killers '66

Tatsuya Matsumura
Madadayo '92

Megumi Matsushita
Remembering the Cosmos
Flower '99

Eva Mattes
Jew-boy Levi '98
Woyzeck '78

Walter Matthau
Hanging Up '99
The Taking of Pelham One
Two Three '74
Candy '68
The Odd Couple '68
Fail-Safe '64
The Kentuckian '55

Ulrich Matthes
Winter Sleepers '97

A.E. Matthews
Immortal Battalion '44

Dakin Matthews
And the Band Played On '93

Junius Matthews
The Sword in the Stone '63
(V)

Victor Mature
Demetrius and the Gladiators
'54

John Matuszak
North Dallas Forty '79
Semi-Tough '77

Mary Maude
Crucible of Terror '72

Roddy Maude-Roxby
The Aristocats '70 (V)

Wayne Maunder
Porky's / Porky's 2: The Next
Day '82

Carmen Maura
Women '97
Women on the Verge of a
Nervous Breakdown '88

Howard Maurer
Ilsa, the Wicked Warden '78

Paula Maurice
The Brain that Wouldn't Die
'63

Frank Maxwell
The Intruder '61

Lois Maxwell
A View to a Kill [SE] '85
Diamonds Are Forever [SE]
'71
You Only Live Twice [SE] '67
From Russia with Love [2 SE]
'63

Marilyn Maxwell
The Lemon Drop Kid '51

Roberta Maxwell
Full Disclosure '00
Dead Man Walking '95
The Changeling '80

Elaine May
Small Time Crooks '00

Jodhi May
House of Mirth '00
The Last of the Mohicans '92

Mia May
The Indian Tomb '21

Traci May
Passion & Romance: Double
or Nothing '00
Passion & Romance: Scandal
'97

Rik Mayall
Jesus Christ Superstar '00
The Canterville Ghost '98

Anthony Mayans
Zombie Lake '80

Chip Mayer
Fugitive Champion '99

Kathrine Mayfield
The Unbelievable Truth '90

Ian Maynard
Drop Dead Rock '95

**Ferdinand "Ferdy"
Mayne**
The Vampire Happening '71

Asa Maynor
Conquest of the Planet of the
Apes '72

Virginia Mayo
Wonder Man '45

Whitman Mayo
Boyz N the Hood '91

Melanie Mayron
Car Wash '76

Debi Mazar
She's So Lovely '97
Empire Records '95

Mike Mazurki
The McCullochs '75
Donovan's Reef '63
Some Like It Hot [SE] '59

Ernestine Mazurowna
Jean de Florette '87

Paul Mazursky
Crazy in Alabama '99

Joseph Mazzello
The Lost World: Jurassic Park
2 [CE] '97
Jurassic Park [CE] '93

Anndi McAfee
Land Before Time 7: The
Stone of Cold Fire '00 (V)

Andrea McArdle
Annie '99

Hugh McArthur
Marihuana / Assassin of
Youth / Reefer Madness
'36

Kimberly McArthur
Slumber Party Massacre 2
'87

Diane McBain
Puppet Master 5: The Latest
Chapter '94

Chi McBride
Disney's The Kid '00
Gone in 60 Seconds '00
Hoodlum '96

Tony McCabe
Something Weird '68

James McCaffrey
The Tic Code '99

Frances Lee McCain
Real Life '79

Irish McCalla
She Demons '58

Holt McCallany
Men of Honor '00
Creepshow 2 '87

Mercedes McCambridge
Suddenly, Last Summer '59
Touch of Evil [SE] '58

Tom McCamus
The Passion of Ayn Rand '99

Donal McCann
Illuminata '98
The Serpent's Kiss '97
The Pallisers '74

Andrew McCarthy
I'm Losing You '98
Class '83

Frank McCarthy
Dead Men Don't Wear Plaid
'82

Jenny McCarthy
Python '00
Scream 3 [CS] '00
Diamonds '99

Kevin McCarthy
The Midnight Hour '86
Buffalo Bill & the Indians '76

Tom McCarthy
Meet the Parents '00

Norma McCarty
Plan 9 from Outer Space
[Passport Video] '56

Peter McCauley
The Interview '98

Saundra McClain
Mr. & Mrs. Bridge '90

Rue McClanahan
Nunsense 2: The Sequel '94

Michael McClanathan
Alice's Restaurant '69

Eileen McCloskey
Moving Target '00

Lisa McClowry
Rugrats in Paris: The Movie
'00 (V)

Doug McClure
Tapeheads '89

Marc McClure
Superman 4: The Quest for
Peace '87

Supergirl '84
Superman 3 '83
Superman 2 '80
Superman: The Movie '78

Tane McClure
Midnight Tease 2 '95

Edie McClurg
She's Having a Baby '88
Planes, Trains & Automobiles
'87
Back to School '86

Stephen McCole
Postmortem '98

Warren McCollum
Reefer Madness '38

Lorissa McComas
Stormswept '95
Vamps: Deadly Dreamgirls
'95

Heather McComb
If These Walls Could Talk 2
'00

Matthew McConaughey
U-571 [CE] '00

David Shawn McConnell
Bats '99

Marilyn McCoo
My Mom's a Werewolf '89

Kent McCord
Airplane 2: The Sequel '82

Catherine McCormack
Shadow of the Vampire '00
Deacon Brodie '98
Braveheart '95

Eric McCormack
The Audrey Hepburn Story
'00

Mary McCormack
The Broken Hearts Club '00
Gun Shy '00
The Big Tease '99
Mystery, Alaska '99

Patty McCormack
Mommy [SE] '95
Saturday the 14th Strikes
Back '88

George McCowan
She's the One '96

Alec McCowen
Henry V '89
Frenzy '72
The Witches '66

Larry McCoy
Bulletproof '96

Matt McCoy
Forever Together '00
Rangers '00
Monsoon '97
Deepstar Six '89

Joan McCracken
Good News '47

Jody McCrea
Beach Blanket Bingo '65
Bikini Beach '64
Beach Party '63

Joel McCrea
Come and Get It '36
The Most Dangerous Game
[Madacy] '32

Bruce McCulloch
Dick '99

Bill McCutcheon
Steel Magnolias '89

Tim McDaniel
Ghost Chase '88

Dylan McDermott
In the Line of Fire [2 SE] '93
Steel Magnolias '89

Keith McDermott
Tourist Trap '79

Audra McDonald
Annie '99

Christopher McDonald
The Perfect Storm '00
Requiem for a Dream '00
The Skulls '00
Dirty Work '97
The Rich Man's Wife '96
Best of the Best 3: No Turn-
ing Back / Best of the
Best: Without Warning '95
My Teacher's Wife '95
The Tuskegee Airmen '95
The Boys Next Door '85

Grace McDonald
Gung Ho! '43

Marie McDonald
Getting Gertie's Garter '45

Jo McDonnel
The Munsters' Revenge '81

Mary McDonnell
Grand Canyon '91

Frances McDormand
Almost Famous '00
Wonder Boys '00
Madeline '98
Paradise Road '97
Mississippi Burning [MGM]
'88

Roddy McDowall
Behind the Planet of the
Apes '98 (N)
Rudyard Kipling's the Second
Jungle Book: Mowgli and
Baloo '97
20th Century Fox: The First
50 Years '96
The Fantasy Worlds of Irwin
Allen '95
Mirror, Mirror 2: Raven Dance
'94
Fright Night '85
Evil under the Sun '82
Embryo '76
Battle for the Planet of the
Apes '73
Conquest of the Planet of the
Apes '72
Bedknobs and Broomsticks
'71
Escape from the Planet of
the Apes '71
Planet of the Apes '68
The Greatest Story Ever Told
[SE] '65
Cleopatra '63
How Green Was My Valley '41

Malcolm McDowell
The First 9 1/2 Weeks '98
Fist of the North Star '95
Tank Girl '94

Nelson McDowell
The Last of the Mohicans '20

James McEachin
The Groundstar Conspiracy
'72

Ellen McElduff
Working Girls '87

Natascha McElhone
Love's Labour's Lost '00

Geraldine McEwan
Love's Labour's Lost '00
Titus '99
Henry V '89

Stephanie McFadden
Love Field '91

Hamish McFarlane
The Navigator '88

Douglas McFerran
Antitrust '00

Joe McGann
The Brylcreem Boys '96

Darren McGavin
The Natural '84

Vonetta McGee
Johnny B. '00
Repo Man '83
Shaft in Africa '73

Johnny Rae McGhee
Love Field '91

Bruce McGill
The Legend of Bagger Vance '00
My Cousin Vinny '92

Everett McGill
Iguana '89

Kelly McGillis
The Settlement '99
Winter People '89

John C. McGinley
Get Carter '00
Any Given Sunday '99
The Jack Bull '99
Flypaper '97
Mother '96
The Rock [Criterion] '96
Seven [2 SE] '95
Mother's Boys '94
Talk Radio '88
Wall Street '87
Platoon [2 SE] '86

Sean McGinley
The Claim '00
Braveheart '95
The Field '90

Ted McGinley
Dick '99

Walter McGinn
The Parallax View '74

Charlotte McGinnis
Reform School Girls '86

Mike McGlone
She's the One '96
The Brothers McMullen '94

Patrick McGoohan
Braveheart '95

Barry McGovern
Braveheart '95

Elizabeth McGovern
House of Mirth '00
She's Having a Baby '88
The Bedroom Window '87

Maureen McGovern
Joseph: King of Dreams '00 (V)
Airplane! '80

Rose McGowan
Ready to Rumble '00
The Last Stop '99
Lewis and Clark and George '97

Shane McGowan
Straight to Hell '87

Brian McGrath
Falling for a Dancer '98

Douglas McGrath
Porky's / Porky's 2: The Next Day '82

Leueen McGrath
Pygmalion '38

Matt McGrath
The Broken Hearts Club '00

Charles McGraw
Sparacus [Criterion] '60
The Bridges at Toko-Ri '55

Melinda McGraw
Nutty Professor 2: The Klumps [1 CE] '00
Nutty Professor 2: The Klumps [2 Uncensored] '00

Ewan McGregor
Eye of the Beholder '99
The Serpent's Kiss '97
Nightwatch '96

Dorothy McGuire
The Greatest Story Ever Told [SE] '65
Friendly Persuasion '56
The Spiral Staircase '46

Holden McGuire
Mother's Day [DC] '80

Michael McGuire
Bird '88

Stephen McHattie
The Highway Man '99

Darren McHugh
Broken Harvest '94

Frank McHugh
There's No Business Like Show Business '54

David McIlwraith
Caracara '99

Tim McInnery
102 Dalmatians '00

John McIntire
The Fox and the Hound '81 (V)
The Kentuckian '55

James McIntyre
Gone in 60 Seconds '74

Susan McIver
I Spit on Your Corpse '74

Elizabeth P. McKay
The Brothers McMullen '94

Michael McKean
Beautiful '00
Best in Show '00
Little Nicky '00
Coneheads '93
Planes, Trains & Automobiles '87
Clue '85
This Is Spinal Tap [MGM] '84

Gina McKee
Wonderland '99
Croupier '97
Element of Doubt '96

Lafe (Lafayette) McKee
Man from Utah / Sagebrush Trail '34

Lonette McKee
Men of Honor '00
The Women of Brewster Place '89
Detroit 9000 '73

Michael McKeever
Around the Fire '98

Don McKellar
The Passion of Ayn Rand '99
The Adjuster '91

Ian McKellen
X-Men '00
And the Band Played On '93
Six Degrees of Separation '93
Plenty '85

Scott McKenna
Jerome '98

T.P. McKenna
Red Scorpion '89
A Portrait of the Artist As a Young Man '77
All Creatures Great and Small '74
Ulysses '67

Virginia McKenna
An Elephant Called Slowly '69
Ring of Bright Water '69

Hannah McKenzie
Forgotten Silver '96

Jacqueline McKenzie
Romper Stomper [SE] '92

Leo McKern
The Omen [SE] '76
King and Country '64
The Day the Earth Caught Fire '61
X The Unknown '56

Kevin McKidd
Topsy Turvy '99
Bedrooms and Hallways '98

Bill McKinney
Lone Justice 2 '93
Against All Odds '84
Bronco Billy '80
The Parallax View '74
She-Freak '67

Mona McKinnon
Plan 9 from Outer Space [Passport Video] '56

Tom McKitterick
The Warriors '79

Ellen McLaughlin
The Bed You Sleep In '93

Gibb McLaughlin
The Scarlet Pimpernel '34

Mark McLaughlin
Crocodile '00

Maya McLaughlin
Milo '98

Lenny McLean
Lock, Stock and 2 Smoking Barrels '98

Zoe McLellan
Dungeons and Dragons '00
Stonebrook '98

Pauline McLynn
Angela's Ashes '99

Ed McMahon
Slaughter's Big Ripoff '73
Daughter of Horror / Dementia '55 (N)

Terry McMahon
Moving Target '00

Don McManus
The 6th Day '00

James McManus
La Cucaracha '99

Sue McManus
Teenage Gang Debs / Teenage Strangler '66

Kenneth McMillan
The Pope of Greenwich Village '84
The Taking of Pelham One Two Three '74

Richard McMillan
Bram Stoker's Shadowbuilder '98

John McMohon
Deadly Weapons '70

Sam McMurray
Lucky Numbers '00
Getting Even with Dad '94
C.H.U.D. '84

Mercedes McNab
White Wolves 3: Cry of the White Wolf '98

Barbara McNair
The Organization '71
They Call Me Mr. Tibbs! '70

J. Patrick McNamara
Close Encounters of the Third Kind [CE] '77

Julianne McNamara
Saturday the 14th Strikes Back '88

Pat McNamara
The Daytrippers '96

William McNamara
Paper Bullets '99
The Brylcreem Boys '96
Chasers '94

Alan McNaughton
Frankenstein Created Woman '66

Julia McNeal
The Unbelievable Truth '90

Ian McNeice
Dune '00
The Canterville Ghost '98

Claudia McNeil
A Raisin in the Sun '61

Kate McNeil
Monkey Shines '88
The House on Sorority Row '83

Scott McNeil
Casper's Haunted Christmas '00 (V)

Kristy McNichol
Two Moon Junction '88
The End '78

Barima McNight
Three Strikes '00

Billy Ray McQuade
Mother's Day [DC] '80

Kris McQuade
Billy's Holiday '95

Armelia McQueen
Ghost '90

Chad McQueen
The Karate Kid '84

Steve McQueen
The Sand Pebbles '66
Hell Is for Heroes '62
The Magnificent Seven '60
The Blob '58

Elizabeth McRae
The Conversation '74

Frank McRae
Lightning Jack '94

Peter McRobbie
And the Band Played On '93

Jenny McShane
The Watcher '00
Monsoon '97

Janet McTeer
Waking the Dead '00
Tumbleweeds '98

Tyler McVey
Attack of the Giant Leeches '59

Caroline McWilliams
Mermaids '90

Taylor Mead
Superstar: The Life and Times of Andy Warhol '90

Audrey Meadows
That Touch of Mink '62

Jayne Meadows
City Slickers '91

Joyce Meadows
The Brain from Planet Arous '57

Stephen Meadows
A Cry in the Wild '90

Tim Meadows
The Ladies Man '00

Colm Meaney
The Magical Legend of the Leprechauns '99
Mystery, Alaska '99
October 22 '98
The Last of the Mohicans '92

Kevin Meaney
Plump Fiction '97

Angela Means
House Party 3 '94

Russell Means
Black Cat Run '98
Natural Born Killers [DC] '94
The Last of the Mohicans '92

Anne Meara
The Daytrippers '96

Michael Mears
Sharpe's Rifles '93

Julio Mechoso
All the Pretty Horses '00

Kay Medford
Butterfield 8 '60

Harriet Medin
Blood and Black Lace '64
The Whip and the Body '63

Frank Medrano
The Apostate '98
Telling You '98

Michie Mee
Hendrix '00

Allison Meek
No Dessert Dad, 'Til You Mow the Lawn '94

Jeffrey Meek
Timelock '99
Winter People '89

Ralph Meeker
Kiss Me Deadly '55

Armand Meffre
Jean de Florette '87
Manon of the Spring '87

Dino Mele
Amuck! '71

Anna Melita
The Arena '73

Douglas Mellor
The Beast of Yucca Flats '61

Christopher Meloni
The Souler Opposite '97

Edith Meloni
Five Dolls for an August Moon '70

Robin Meloy
The House on Sorority Row '83

Pauline Melville
Mona Lisa '86

Murray Melvin
Alfie '66

Ben Mendelsohn
Vertical Limit '00

Pierre Mendes-France
The Sorrow and the Pity '71

Eva Mendez
Urban Legends 2: Final Cut
'00

Alex Meneses
The Flintstones in Viva Rock
Vegas '00

Adolphe Menjou
A Farewell to Arms '32
The Marriage Circle '24

Oleg Menshikov
East-West '99

Yehudi Menuhin
32 Short Films about Glenn
Gould '93

Ernest Menzer
Bed and Board '70

Heather Menzies
The Sound of Music [Five
Star Collection] '65

Doro Merande
The Seven Year Itch '55

Vivien Merchant
Frenzy '72
Alfie '66

Chantal Mercier
Small Change '76

Michele Mercier
Call of the Wild '72
Black Sabbath '64

Melina Mercouri
Stella '55

Paul Mercurio
The First 9 1/2 Weeks '98

Burgess Meredith
Santa Claus: The Movie '85
Rocky [SE] '76
The Sentinel '76
Beware! The Blob '72
In Harm's Way '65
That Uncertain Feeling [Sling-
Shot] '41

Auriele Meriel
The Delivery '99

Eda Reiss Merin
Don't Tell Mom the Babysitter's Dead '91

Lee Meriwether
The Fantasy Worlds of Irwin
Allen '95

Una Merkel
The Kentuckian '55
The Bank Dick '40
42nd Street '33

Joanna Merlin
Mystic Pizza '88

Ethel Merman
Airplane! '80
There's No Business Like
Show Business '54

Brandon Merrill
Shanghai Noon '00

Dina Merrill
Suture '93
Butterfield 8 '60

Ryan Merriman
Just Looking '99

Jane Merrow
The Lion in Winter '68

William Mesnik
Stonebrook '98

Marc Messier
The Boys '97

Debra Messing
Jesus '00
A Walk in the Clouds '95

Laurie Metcalf
Toy Story 2 '99 (V)
Toy Story '95 (V)
Mistress '91
Internal Affairs '90
Desperately Seeking Susan
'85

Mark Metcalf
Drive Me Crazy '99

Asher Metchik
Milo '98

Saul Meth
Double Agent 73 '80
Deadly Weapons '70

Method Man
Backstage '00

Art Metrano
Slaughter's Big Ripoff '73

Jim Metzler
One False Move '91
River's Edge '87

Jason Mewes
Clerks Uncensored '00 (V)
Scream 3 [CS] '00
Dogma '99
Chasing Amy '97

Breckin Meyer
Road Trip '00

Debra Meyer
Voodoo Academy [DC] '00

Dina Meyer
Bats '99

Emile Meyer
Shane '53

Hans Meyer
Mauvais Sang '86

Marlene Meyer-Dunker
School's Out '99

Clipper Miano
Smilla's Sense of Snow '96

Robert Miano
Dungeons and Dragons '00
Loser '00
Thick As Thieves '99
Donnie Brasco [2] '96

Athena Michaelidou
A Matter of Dignity '57

Bret Michaels
In God's Hands '98
No Code of Conduct '98

Michele Michaels
Slumber Party Massacre '82

Roxanna Michaels
Titanic 2000 '00

Kari Michaelsen
Saturday the 14th '81

Delaune Michel
A Woman, Her Men and Her
Futon '92

Michael Michele
Homicide: The Movie '00

Keith Michell
The Story of Jacob & Joseph
'74

Charis Michelsen
I Married a Strange Person
'97 (V)

Charles Middleton
Flash Gordon: Space Soldiers
'36

Fran Middleton
Martin '77

Ramona Midgett
Ice from the Sun '00

Dale Midkiff
Air Bud 3: World Pup '00
The Crow: Salvation '00
Pet Sematary '89

Bette Midler
Drowning Mona '00
Isn't She Great '00
What Women Want '00
For the Boys '91

Tatsuya Mihashi
Tora! Tora! Tora! [2 SE] '70

Dash Mihok
The Perfect Storm '00
Telling You '98

Claire Mijnals
Venus in Furs '94

George Miki
Go for Broke! '51

Mads Mikkelsen
Pusher '96

Izabella Miko
Coyote Ugly '00

Rentaro Mikuni
Rikyu '90
Kwaidan '64

Alyssa Milano
Lady and the Tramp 2:
Scamp's Adventure '01 (V)
Confessions of Sorority Girls
'00
Double Dragon '94

Bernard Miles
The Man Who Knew Too
Much '56

Lillian Miles
Reefer Madness '38

Maria Miles
Catherine Cookson's The Cinder Path '94

Rosalind Miles
I Spit on Your Corpse '74
Shaft's Big Score '72

Sarah Miles
Hope and Glory '87

Sylvia Miles
Superstar: The Life and
Times of Andy Warhol '90
Evil under the Sun '82
The Sentinel '76

Thomas Miles
Thug Life '00

Vera Miles
The Man Who Shot Liberty
Valance '62

**Vicki (Allison Louise
Downe) Miles**
Scum of the Earth '63

Tomas Milian
For Love or Country: The
Arturo Sandoval Story '00
Traffic '00
The Yards '00
Don't Torture a Duckling '72

Arthur Millan
The Violent Years / Girl Gang
'56

Victor Millan
Touch of Evil [SE] '58

Ray Milland
The Thing with Two Heads '72
Love Story '70
X: The Man with X-Ray Eyes
'63
The Lost Weekend '45
Bulldog Drummond Escapes
'37

Peter Millard
32 Short Films about Glenn
Gould '93

Barry Miller
Flawless '99
The Last Temptation of Christ
'88

Dick Miller
Batman: Mask of the Phan-
tasm '93 (V)
Hollywood Boulevard '76
Truck Turner '74
The Wild Angels '66
X: The Man with X-Ray Eyes
'63
A Bucket of Blood '59

Jason Miller
Mommy [SE] '95
Rudy [SE] '93

Jonny Lee Miller
Love, Honour & Obey '00
Mansfield Park '99

Joshua John Miller
River's Edge '87

Kelly Miller
Newsbreak '00

Larisa Miller
Escape under Pressure '00

Larry Miller
Best in Show '00
Buzz Lightyear of Star Com-
mand: The Adventure
Begins '00 (V)
Nutty Professor 2: The
Klumps [1 CE] '00
Nutty Professor 2: The
Klumps [2 Uncensored] '00
The Big Tease '99
The Minus Man '99

Mark Miller
Love Field '91

Mirta Miller
Battle of the Amazons '74

Penelope Ann Miller
Full Disclosure '00

Percy (Master P) Miller
Gone in 60 Seconds '00

Roger Miller
Robin Hood '73 (V)

Sarah Jane Miller
Mommy [SE] '95

Sherry Miller
Tribulation '00

Stephen E. Miller
Air Bud [2] '97

Walter Miller
Shadow of the Eagle '32

Bill Mills
Teenage Strangler '64

Brooke Mills
The Big Doll House '71

Hayley Mills
Endless Night '71

John Mills
End of the Affair '55

Mort Mills
Touch of Evil [SE] '58

Martin Milner
Sweet Smell of Success '57
Life with Father '47

Milos Milos
Incubus '65

Ernest Milton
The Scarlet Pimpernel '34

Yvette Mimieux
Jackson County Jail '76
The Time Machine '60

Esther Minciotti
Marty '55

Sal Mineo
Escape from the Planet of
the Apes '71

Jan Miner
Mermaids '90

Byron Keith Minns
South Central '92

Kylie Minogue
Cut '00

Kristin Minter
The Apostate '98
Flashfire '94

Julie Mintz
Crocodile '00

Miou-Miou
Women '97

Irene Miracle
Puppet Master '89

Aurora Miranda
The Three Caballeros '45 (V)

Isa Miranda
Bay of Blood '71
Twitch of the Death Nerve '71

Robert Miranda
Blue Streak '99
Gotti '96

Soledad Miranda
She Killed in Ecstasy '70
Vampyros Lesbos '70

Helen Mirren
The Passion of Ayn Rand '99
Critical Care '97
The Madness of King George
'94
The Cook, the Thief, His Wife
& Her Lover '90

Mr. T
Penitentiary 2 '82

Jimi Mistry
East Is East '99

Cameron Mitchell
Ride in the Whirlwind '66
Blood and Black Lace '64
How to Marry a Millionaire
'53

Chuck "Porky" Mitchell
Ghost Chase '88
Porky's / Porky's 2: The Next
Day '82
Penitentiary '79

Darryl (Chill) Mitchell
Lucky Numbers '00
Galaxy Quest '99
Quiet Days in Hollywood '97

Doug Mitchell
Teenage Gang Debs /
Teenage Strangler '66

Eddy Mitchell
Coup de Torchon '81

Elizabeth Mitchell
Frequency '00
Gia '98

Ella Mitchell
Big Momma's House '00

Heather Mitchell
A Little Bit of Soul '97

Keith Mitchell
The Fox and the Hound '81
(V)

Garrett Morris
Twin Falls Idaho '99
Black Scorpion 2: Ground
Zero '96
Black Scorpion '95
The Stuff '85
Cooley High '75

Howard Morris
Splash '84
The Munsters' Revenge '81
The Nutty Professor '63

Jeff Morris
Kelly's Heroes '70

Jessica Morris
Bloody Murder '99

John Morris
Toy Story 2 '99 (V)
Toy Story '95 (V)

Johnny Morris
Forgotten Silver '96

Jonathan Morris
Bloodstorm: Subspecies 4
'98

Marianne Morris
Vampyres '74

Paul Morris
Vamps: Deadly Dreamgirls
'95

Robert Morris
Frankenstein Created Woman
'66

Bob Morrisey
Delivered '98

Fraser Morrison
Stomp Out Loud '98

Jenny Morrison
Urban Legends 2: Final Cut
'00

John Morrison
The Beast of Yucca Flats '61

Temuera Morrison
Vertical Limit '00
Barb Wire '96

David Morrissey
Robert Louis Stevenson's
The Game of Death '99

Maximo Morrone
Red Shoe Diaries: Strip Poker
'96

Jeff Morrow
Kronos '57

Mari Morrow
Uninvited Guest '99

Marry Morrow
Red Shoe Diaries: Four on
the Floor '96

Rob Morrow
Mother '96

Scotty Morrow
The Cosmic Man '59

Susan Morrow
Cat Women of the Moon '53

Barry Morse
The Changeling '80
Asylum '72

David Morse
Bait '00
Crazy in Alabama '99
Dancer in the Dark '99
The Rock [Criterion] '96

Laila Morse
Love, Honour & Obey '00

Natalie Morse
Anchoress '93

Robin Morse
Marty '55

Victoria Morsell
Saturday the 14th Strikes
Back '88

Glenn Morshower
The Jack Bull '99

Viggo Mortensen
28 Days [SE] '00
American Yakuza '94

Emily Mortimer
Disney's The Kid '00
Love's Labour's Lost '00
Scream 3 [CS] '00
Noah's Ark '99
Sharpe's Sword '94

Alicia Morton
Annie '99

Joe Morton
Bounce '00
What Lies Beneath '00
Terminator 2: Judgment Day
[2 SE] '91

Roy Morton
Blood of Ghastly Horror '72

Samantha Morton
Jesus' Son '99
Sweet and Lowdown '99

Maurice Moscovich
Love Affair '39

David Moscow
Loving Jezebel '99
Restaurant '98

Bill Moseley
Night of the Living Dead '90
Fair Game '89
The Texas Chainsaw Mas-
sacre 2 '86

Mark Moses
Gettysburg '93
The Tracker '88
Platoon [2 SE] '86

William R. Moses
Mystic Pizza '88

Aryeh Moskona
Pick a Card '97

Bryan Mosley
Get Carter '71

Arnold Moss
The Loves of Carmen '48

Carrie-Anne Moss
The Crew '00
Red Planet '00

Elissabeth Moss
Earthly Possessions '99
Girl, Interrupted '99
Imaginary Crimes '94

Stewart Moss
In Harm's Way '65

Josh Mostel
City Slickers '91
Wall Street '87

Melissa Mounds
Flesh Gordon 2: Flesh Gor-
don Meets the Cosmic
Cheerleaders '90

Anson Mount
Urban Legends 2: Final Cut
'00

Gilberto Moura
Pixote '81

Alan Mowbray
The Man Who Knew Too
Much '56
Terror by Night '46

That Uncertain Feeling [Sling-
Shot] '41

Patrick Mower
The Devil Rides Out '68

John Mowod
Santa Claws '96

Larry Moyer
Greaser's Palace '72

Stephen Moyer
Catherine Cookson's The
Secret '00
Comic Act '00

Bridget Moynahan
Coyote Ugly '00

Bill Moynihan
The Creeps '97

Leonard Mudie
The Mummy '32

Julia Mueller
The Unbelievable Truth '90

Armin Mueller-Stahl
Jesus '00
Inferno '99
Avalon '90

Marianne Muellerleile
Return to Me '00

Anita Mui
Jet Li's The Enforcer [Buena
Vista] '95
The Legend of Drunken Mas-
ter '94
Rouge '87

Geraldine Muir
Hope and Glory '87

Oliver Muirhead
MVP: Most Valuable Primate
'00

Jack Mulcahy
The Brothers McMullen '94

Patrick Muldoon
The Crimson Code '00
Black Cat Run '98

Martin Mull
Attention Shoppers '99
Clue '85

Megan Mullally
Last Resort '86

Peter Mullan
The Claim '00

Neil Mullarkey
Comic Act '00

Paul Muller
The Arena '73
She Killed in Ecstasy '70

Bill Mullikin
Hell Is for Heroes '62

Michael Mullins
The Pom Pom Girls / The
Beach Girls '76

Dermot Mulroney
Where the Money Is '00
Longtime Companion '90

Kieran Mulroney
Gettysburg '93

Kelsey Mulrooney
She's So Lovely '97

Billy Mumy
The Fantasy Worlds of Irwin
Allen '95

Misty Mundae
Erotic Survivor '00
Gladiator Eroticus '00

Yoyo Mung
Running out of Time '99

Paul Muni
Angel on My Shoulder '46

Frankie Muniz
My Dog Skip '99

Caroline Munro
Fanatic '82
Golden Voyage of Sinbad '73
Doctor Phibes Rises Again
'72
The Abominable Dr. Phibes
'71

Janet Munro
The Day the Earth Caught
Fire '61

Lochlyn Munro
Scary Movie '00

Jules Munshin
Take Me Out to the Ball
Game '49

Silvia Munt
Secrets of the Heart '97

Maxim Munzuk
Dersu Uzala '75

Takehiro Murata
Godzilla 2000 '99

Vince Murdocco
Flesh Gordon 2: Flesh Gor-
don Meets the Cosmic
Cheerleaders '90

George Murdock
Breaker! Breaker! '77

Yvor Murillo
The Vampire Happening '71

Christopher Murney
Maximum Overdrive '86

Bill Murphy
Moving Target '00

Brittany Murphy
Cherry Falls / Terror Tract '00
Girl, Interrupted '99

Carolyn Murphy
Liberty Heights '99

Donald Murphy
Frankenstein's Daughter '58

Donna Murphy
Center Stage '00
October 22 '98

Eddie Murphy
Nutty Professor 2: The
Klumps [1 CE] '00
Nutty Professor 2: The
Klumps [2 Uncensored] '00

Kim Murphy
The In Crowd '00

Martin Murphy
Dance with a Stranger '85

Megan Murphy
Deadbeat at Dawn '88

Michael Murphy
Salvador [SE] '86
Mesmerized '84
Manhattan '79
Nashville '75

Rosemary Murphy
The Tuskegee Airmen '95
For the Boys '91

Sally Murphy
Charming Billy '99

Barbara Murray
The Pallisers '74

Bill Murray
Charlie's Angels '00
Hamlet '00
The Cradle Will Rock '99
What about Bob? '91

Scrooged '88
Tootsie '82

Billy Murray
Essex Boys '99

Christopher Murray
Nice Guys Sleep Alone '99

Don Murray
20th Century Fox: The First
50 Years '96
Conquest of the Planet of the
Apes '72
Bus Stop '56

Ken Murray
The Man Who Shot Liberty
Valance '62

Rory Murray
Falling for a Dancer '98

Stephen Murray
Four Sided Triangle '53
Pygmalion '38

Kate Murtagh
Switchblade Sisters '75

Tony Musante
The Yards '00
The Pope of Greenwich Vil-
lage '84
The Grissom Gang '71

Timothy Muskatell
Unspeakable '00

Harrison Myers
Dear Santa '98

Harry Myers
The Marriage Circle '24

Mike Myers
Mystery, Alaska '99

John Mylong
Robot Monster '53

Byron Myrick
Ninth Street '98

Samia Mzali
Honey & Ashes '96

Nadajan
The Fall of the House of
Usher '60

Elayne Nadeau
Martin '77

George Nader
Beyond Atlantis '73
Away All Boats '56
Robot Monster '53

Oussama Nadir
An Egyptian Story '82

Morgan Nagler
Bird '88

Alvaro Nagore
Secrets of the Heart '97

Joanne Nail
Switchblade Sisters '75

J. Carrol Naish
Dracula vs. Frankenstein '71
Annie Get Your Gun '50
Getting Gertie's Garter '45

Laurence Naismith
Diamonds Are Forever [SE]
'71

Takashi Naito
After Life '98
Maborosi '95

Taketoshi Naito
After Life '98

Naji Najeh
Honey & Ashes '96

Kathy Najimy
CinderElmo '00

Daughter of Horror / Dementia '55 (V)

Chelsea Noble
Left Behind: The Movie '00

Trisha Noble
The Private Eyes [SE] '80

Ulrich Noethen
Jew-boy Levi '98

Natalija Nogulich
Sister, Sister '87

Philippe Noiret
Coup de Torchon '81
La Grande Bouffe '73
Topaz '69

Bob Nolan
Melody Time '48 (V)

Jeanette Nolan
The Fox and the Hound '81 (V)
The Man Who Shot Liberty Valance '62

Lloyd Nolan
The Lemon Drop Kid '51

Robin Nolan
Teenage Gang Debs / Teenage Strangler '66

William F. Nolan
The Intruder '61

Aurelia Nolin
A Summer's Tale '96

Nick Nolte
Simpatico '99
Breakfast of Champions '98
Mother Night '96
Nightwatch '96
North Dallas Forty '79
Death Sentence '74

Valentine Nonyela
Welcome II the Terrordome '95

Tommy Noonan
A Star Is Born '54
Gentlemen Prefer Blondes '53

Ghita Norby
Babette's Feast '87 (N)

Jeffrey Nordling
And the Band Played On '93

Sandee Norman
Bad Girls Go to Hell / Another Day, Another Man '65

Ava Norring
The Snows of Kilimanjaro '52

Chuck Norris
Delta Force 2: Operation Stranglehold '90
Delta Force '86
Missing in Action '84
Breaker! Breaker! '77

Dean Norris
Three Strikes '00

Jay Norris
A Walk in the Sun '46

Alan North
Glory [2 SE] '89

J.J. North
Psycho Sisters '98
Hellblock 13 '97

Matt North
Dirty Pictures '00

Sheree North
The Organization '71

Virginia North
The Abominable Dr. Phibes '71

Ryan Northcott
Mystery, Alaska '99

Dee Dee Norton
Dakota '88

Edward Norton
Keeping the Faith '00

Jack Norton
The Bank Dick '40

Ken Norton
Dirty Work '97

Kristin Norton
The Creeps '97

Richard Norton
Nautilus '99
Lady Dragon '92
China O'Brien '88
The Millionaire's Express '86

Willie Norwood Jr.
Once Upon a Time...When We Were Colored '95

Jack Noseworthy
Cecil B. Demented '00
U-571 [CE] '00
Idle Hands '99
Barb Wire '96

Ralph Nossek
Citizen X '95

Christopher Noth
Castaway '00
Sex and the City: The Complete Second Season '00
The Confession '98
Baby Boom '87

Michael Nouri
Finding Forrester '00
American Yakuza '94
DaVinci's War '92

Kim Novak
The Mirror Crack'd '80
Pal Joey '57
Picnic '55

Boyana Novakovitch
Blackrock '97

Don Novello
The Adventures of Rocky & Bullwinkle '00
The Godfather, Part 3 '90
Tucker: The Man and His Dream '88

Nancho Novo
Tierra '95

Tom Nowicki
Kiss of Fire '98

Winston Ntshona
Tarzan and the Lost City '98

Danny Nucci
The Rock [Criterion] '96

Ted Nugent
Tapeheads '89

Bill Nunn
The Substitute 4: Failure Is Not an Option '00
The Tic Code '99
Bulletproof '96
Canadian Bacon '94
Mo' Better Blues '90
Do the Right Thing [2] '89
School Daze '88

Danny Nussbaum
Beautiful People '99

Mike Nussbaum
House of Games '87

Henry O
Dragonheart: A New Beginning '00
Romeo Must Die '00
Shanghai Noon '00

Dagmar Oakland
W.C. Fields 6 Short Films '33

Simon Oakland
The Sand Pebbles '66

Wheeler Oakman
Outside the Law / Shadows '21
Back to God's Country / Something New '19

Warren Oates
Cockfighter '74
Dillinger '73
In the Heat of the Night '67
Return of the Magnificent Seven '66
The Shooting '66

William Obanhein
Alice's Restaurant '69

Philip Ober
North by Northwest '59

Sabine Oberhorner
Edvard Grieg: What Price Immortality? '00

Isli Oberon
The Whip and the Body '63

Merle Oberon
That Uncertain Feeling [Sling-Shot] '41
The Scarlet Pimpernel '34

Jacqueline Obradors
Deuce Bigalow: Male Gigolo '99

Claudio Obregon
Midaq Alley '95

Hugh O'Brian
In Harm's Way '65
There's No Business Like Show Business '54
Rocketship X-M '50

Wesley O'Brian
Passion & Romance: Scandal '97

Dave O'Brien
Reefer Madness '38

Edmond O'Brien
Fantastic Voyage '66
Seven Days in May '64
Birdman of Alcatraz '62
The Man Who Shot Liberty Valance '62
The Barefoot Contessa '54
D.O.A. [Roan] '49

Joan O'Brien
The Alamo '60

Kieran O'Brien
Jason and the Argonauts '00

Mariah O'Brien
Diamonds '99

Maureen O'Brien
Falling for a Dancer '98

Niall O'Brien
Broken Harvest '94

Pat O'Brien
The End '78
Some Like It Hot [SE] '59

Richard O'Brien
Dungeons and Dragons '00
The Rocky Horror Picture Show '75

Shauna O'Brien
Scandal: The Big Turn On '99

Timothy Eric O'Brien
Suburbia '83

Virginia O'Brien
Till the Clouds Roll By '46

Sean O'Bryan
Nice Guys Sleep Alone '99
I'll Be Home for Christmas '98

Andrea Occhipinti
A Blade in the Dark '83

Arthur O'Connell
The Last Valley '71
Fantastic Voyage '66
7 Faces of Dr. Lao '63
Anatomy of a Murder '59
Bus Stop '56
Picnic '55

Jerry O'Connell
Mission to Mars '00
Body Shots '99
Stand by Me [2 SE] '86

Patrick O'Connell
We'll Meet Again '82

Carroll O'Connor
Return to Me '00
Law and Disorder '74
Kelly's Heroes '70
In Harm's Way '65
Cleopatra '63

Derrick O'Connor
Hope and Glory '87

Donald O'Connor
There's No Business Like Show Business '54

Frances O'Connor
Bedazzled [SE] '00
Mansfield Park '99
A Little Bit of Soul '97

Gavin O'Connor
Tumbleweeds '98

Kevin J. O'Connor
The Mummy [2 SE] '99
Black Cat Run '98
Canadian Bacon '94
Steel Magnolias '89

Mary Lou O'Connor
Girl Gang '54

Terry O'Connor
Breaker! Breaker! '77

Tim O'Connor
Naked Gun 2 1/2: The Smell of Fear '91
The Groundstar Conspiracy '72

Una O'Connor
The Invisible Man '33

Akane Oda
Remembering the Cosmos Flower '99

Erika Oda
After Life '98

Judith O'Dea
Night of the Living Dead [Madacy] '68
Night of the Living Dead [Elite] '68
Night of the Living Dead [LE Anchor Bay] '68

Devon Odessa
The Omega Code '99

Odetta
The Ballad of Ramblin' Jack '00

Cathy O'Donnell
Ben-Hur '59
The Man from Laramie '55

Chris O'Donnell
Vertical Limit '00
Blue Sky '91

Rosie O'Donnell
Wide Awake '97

Marion O'Dwyer
Agnes Browne '99

George Offerman Jr.
A Walk in the Sun '46

Nick Offerman
Groove '00

Issey Ogata
Yi Yi '00

Bulle Ogier
Son of Gascogne '95
The Discreet Charm of the Bourgeoisie '72

Ian Ogilvy
Puppet Master 5: The Latest Chapter '94

Jorgo Ognenovski
Stalked '99

Gail O'Grady
Deuce Bigalow: Male Gigolo '99

Femi Ogumbanjo
The Loss of Sexual Innocence '98

Sandra Oh
Waking the Dead '00

Soon-Teck Oh
Yellow '98
A Home of Our Own '93

Michael O'Hagan
For Love or Country: The Arturo Sandoval Story '00

Brian O'Halloran
Clerks Uncensored '00 (V)

Jack O'Halloran
Superman 2 '80
Superman: The Movie '78

Brad O'Hara
Longtime Companion '90

Catherine O'Hara
Best in Show '00
The Life Before This '99
The Nightmare before Christmas [2 SE] '93 (V)

David O'Hara
Jesus '00
Braveheart '95

Mary O'Hara
Another Day, Another Man '66

Maureen O'Hara
How Green Was My Valley '41

Paige O'Hara
Beauty and the Beast: The Enchanted Christmas '97 (V)

Michael O'Hare
C.H.U.D. '84

Cornelia Hayes O'Herlihy
Rudyard Kipling's the Second Jungle Book: Mowgli and Baloo '97

Dan O'Herlihy
Fail-Safe '64

Henry Okawa
The Bridge on the River Kwai [LE] '57

Dennis O'Keefe
Getting Gertie's Garter '45
Up in Mabel's Room '44
Hangmen Also Die '42
Topper Returns '41

Jodi Lyn O'Keefe
The Crow: Salvation '00
Whatever It Takes '00

Miles O'Keeffe
Diamondbacks '99
The Drifter '88

Yuji Okumoto
I'll Remember April '99
Mean Guns '97
True Believer '89

Ken Olandt
Interceptor Force '99
Velocity Trap '99
Darkdrive '98

Richard Oldfield
Omen 3: The Final Conflict '81

Gary Oldman
Hannibal '01
The Contender '00
Jesus '00
Murder in the First '95
Leon, the Professional '94
Sid & Nancy [MGM] '86

Gabriel Olds
A Town Has Turned to Dust '98

Adam Oliensis
The Pompatus of Love '95

Lena Olin
The Ninth Gate '99
Mr. Jones '93

Christian Oliver
Kept '01
Eat Your Heart Out '96

Gordon Oliver
The Spiral Staircase '46

Susan Oliver
Butterfield 8 '60

Federico Olivera
Life According to Muriel '97

Robert Oliveri
Edward Scissorhands [SE] '90

Laurence Olivier
The Bounty '84
The Entertainer '60
Sparacus [Criterion] '60
Hamlet '48
Fire over England '37

Silvio Oliviero
Gotti '96

Walter Olkewicz
Milo '98

May Ollis
Quackser Fortune Has a Cousin in the Bronx '70

Edward James Olmos
The Road to El Dorado '00 (V)
Gossip '00

Gerald S. O'Loughlin
Three Strikes '00
Frances '82

David Olrod
Stomp Out Loud '98

Georg Olschewski
Jew-boy Levi '98

Ashley Olsen
Our Lips Are Sealed '00

Mary-Kate Olsen
Our Lips Are Sealed '00

Moroni Olsen
Father's Little Dividend '51

James Olson
The Groundstar Conspiracy '72

Richard Taylor Olson
I'll Remember April '99

Timothy Olyphant
The Broken Hearts Club '00
Gone in 60 Seconds '00

Daragh O'Malley
Sharpe's Justice '97
Sharpe's Revenge '97
Sharpe's Waterloo '97
Sharpe's Mission '96
Sharpe's Regiment '96
Sharpe's Siege '96
Sharpe's Battle '94
Sharpe's Company '94
Sharpe's Enemy '94
Sharpe's Gold '94
Sharpe's Honour '94
Sharpe's Sword '94
Sharpe's Eagle '93
Sharpe's Rifles '93

Michael O'Malley
28 Days [SE] '00

Pat O'Malley
The Adventures of Ichabod and Mr. Toad '49 (V)

Afemo Omilami
Bringing Out the Dead '99

Patrick O'Neal
For the Boys '91
Alice '90
The Stuff '85
The Way We Were [SE] '73
Alvarez Kelly '66
In Harm's Way '65

Ryan O'Neal
Coming Soon '99
The List '99
Love Story '70

Sally O'Neil
Battle of the Sexes '28

Angela O'Neill
Sorority House Massacre '86

Dick O'Neill
The Taking of Pelham One Two Three '74

Ed O'Neill
Lucky Numbers '00

Ella O'Neill
Flash Gordon: Space Soldiers '36

Michael O'Neill
The Legend of Bagger Vance '00

Dana Ong
The Cheat '15

Julius Ongewe
First Spaceship on Venus '60

Miyuki Ono
Evil Dead Trap '88

Peter Onorati
Just Looking '99
Tycus '98

Glauco Onorato
Black Sabbath '64

Lupe Ontiveros
Chuck & Buck '00
Picking Up the Pieces '99

Michael Ontkean
Postcards from the Edge '90

Amanda Ooms
Wilderness '96

David Opatoshu
Torn Curtain '66

Alan Oppenheimer
The Groundstar Conspiracy '72

Terry O'Quinn
Rated X '00
The Cutting Edge '92

Jerry Orbach
Prince of Central Park '00

Beauty and the Beast: The Enchanted Christmas '97 (V)
Crimes & Misdemeanors [MGM] '89
F/X '86

Cyril O'Reilly
Navy SEALS [MGM] '90
Porky's 2: The Next Day '83
Porky's / Porky's 2: The Next Day '82

Kathryn O'Reilly
Puppet Master '89

Pete O'Reilly
Broken Harvest '94

Julia Ormond
Smilla's Sense of Snow '96
Legends of the Fall [2 SE] '94

Ron Ormond
Teenage Strangler '64

Ed O'Ross
Hoodlum '96

Corrinne Orr
Speed Racer: The Movie (V)

Leland Orser
Alien: Resurrection '97

Zak Orth
Down to You '00
Loser '00
My Teacher's Wife '95

John Ortiz
The Last Marshal '99

Andrew Osborn
Spaceways '53

Holmes Osborne
Crazy in Alabama '99

John Osborne
Get Carter '71

Ozzy Osbourne
Little Nicky '00

Per Oscarsson
Endless Night '71
The Last Valley '71

John O'Shea
Forgotten Silver '96

Michael O'Shea
The Big Wheel '49

Milo O'Shea
Ulysses '67

Tessie O'Shea
Immortal Battalion '44

Hiroko Oshima
Scene at the Sea '91

Yukari Oshima
The Millionaire's Express '86

Haley Joel Osment
I'll Remember April '99
Beauty and the Beast: The Enchanted Christmas '97 (V)

Donny Osmond
Joseph and the Amazing Technicolor Dreamcoat '00

Carlos Osorio
Because of You '95

Jeffery Osterhage
The Shadow Riders '82

Robert Osth
Don't Go in the House '80

Ren Osugi
Weather Woman '99
Fireworks '97

Aisling O'Sullivan
The War Zone '98

Sheila O'Sullivan
Ulysses '67

Cheri Oteri
Scary Movie '00

Leo Otero
Sergio Lapel's Drawing Blood '99

Annette O'Toole
Here on Earth '00
Imaginary Crimes '94
Superman 3 '83

Peter O'Toole
Supergirl '84
The Lion in Winter '68
Lawrence of Arabia '62

Larrene Ott
The Undertaker and His Pals '67

John Ottavino
Bob Roberts [SE] '92

Rachelle Ottley
The Cutting Edge '92

Barry Otto
Lilian's Story '95

Goetz Otto
Beowulf '98

Miranda Otto
What Lies Beneath '00
The Jack Bull '99

James Ottoway
That'll Be the Day '73

Tom Ouedraoge
L'Ennui '98

Maria Ouspenskaya
Love Affair '39

Peter Outerbridge
Mission to Mars '00
Thrill Seekers '99

Geoff Outlaw
Alice's Restaurant '69

Park Overall
Mississippi Burning [MGM] '88

Kellie Overbey
Sweet and Lowdown '99

Lynne Overman
Midnight '34

Chris Owen
Ready to Rumble '00

Clive Owen
Croupier '97
The Rich Man's Wife '96

Lloyd Owen
Catherine Cookson's The Cinder Path '94

Reginald Owen
Captain Kidd '45
Of Human Bondage '34

Ciaran Owens
Agnes Browne '99
Angela's Ashes '99

Gary Owens
I'm Gonna Git You Sucka '88

Patricia Owens
The Fly / Return of the Fly '58

Catherine Oxenberg
The Omega Code '99

Daphne Oxenford
That'll Be the Day '73

Frank Oz
CinderElmo '00 (V)

Majyu Ozawa
Tokyo Raiders '00

Dominic Pace
That's the Way I Like It '99

Judy Pace
Brian's Song '71
Cotton Comes to Harlem '70

Tom Pace
The Astro-Zombies '67

Tracy Pacheco
Bloody Murder '99

Frederico Pacifici
Fluke '95

Al Pacino
Any Given Sunday '99
Donnie Brasco [2] '97
The Godfather, Part 3 '90
And Justice for All '79
The Godfather, Part 2 '74
The Godfather DVD Collection '72

Joanna Pacula
Warlock: The Armageddon '93
Gorky Park '83

Ruben Padilla
The Alamo '59

Bettie (Betty) Page
Teaserama '55
Varietease '54

Diamond Dallas Page
Ready to Rumble '00

Geraldine Page
The Pope of Greenwich Village '84
Interiors '78
Whatever Happened to Aunt Alice? '69

Harrison Page
Carnosaur '93

Ken Page
The Nightmare before Christmas [2 SE] '93 (V)

LaWanda Page
Shakes the Clown '92

Justin Pagel
Street Gun '96

Debra Paget
Tales of Terror '62
Demetrius and the Gladiators '54

Suzee Pai
Big Trouble in Little China [SE] '86

Josh Pais
Music of the Heart [CS] '99

Holly Palance
The Omen [SE] '76

Jack Palance
City Slickers '91
Dracula / Strange Case of Dr. Jekyll & Mr. Hyde '73
Strange Case of Dr. Jekyll & Mr. Hyde '68
Shane '53

Larry Palatta
Sergio Lapel's Drawing Blood '99

Evan Palazzo
Height of the Sky '99

Jo Palermo
Ice from the Sun '00

Rachel Palieri
Red Shoe Diaries: Four on the Floor '96

Michael Palin
Monty Python and the Holy Grail '75

Erik Palladino
U-571 [CE] '00

Anita Pallenberg
Candy '68

Paul Palmer
The St. Francisville Experiment '00

Chazz Palminteri
Lady and the Tramp 2: Scamp's Adventure '01 (V)
Excellent Cadavers '99
Diabolique '96

Gwyneth Paltrow
Bounce '00
Duets '00
The Talented Mr. Ripley '99
Hard Eight '96
Moonlight and Valentino '95
The Pallbearer '95
Seven [2 SE] '95
Malice [MGM] '93

Nirmal Pandey
Bandit Queen '94

Hayden Panettiere
Dinosaur [CE] '00 (V)
Remember the Titans '00

Adrian Pang
That's the Way I Like It '99

Franklin Pangborn
The Bank Dick '40

Archie Panjabi
East Is East '99

Stuart Pankin
The Hollywood Knights '80

John Pankow
Monkey Shines '88
Talk Radio '88

Joe Pantoliano
A Better Way to Die '00
Ready to Rumble '00
Black and White '99
The Life Before This '99
El Diablo '90
Mean Season '85

Cecile Paoli
Sharpe's Revenge '97
Sharpe's Waterloo '97

Anny Papa
A Blade in the Dark '83

Irene Papas
Party '96
Don't Torture a Duckling '72

Leopold Papi
The Vault '00

Georges Pappas
A Matter of Dignity '57

Roger Papsch
Something Weird '68

Anna Paquin
Almost Famous '00
Finding Forrester '00
X-Men '00
It's the Rage '99

Kip Pardue
Remember the Titans '00

Michael Pare
October 22 '98
Bad Moon '96
The Philadelphia Experiment '84

Marisa Paredes
All About My Mother '99

Monique Parent
Tender Flesh '00
James Dean: Live Fast, Die Young '97
Mirror, Mirror 3: The Voyeur '96
Midnight Confessions '95

Sally Parfait
The Monster of Camp Sunshine '64

Judy Parfitt
Element of Doubt '96

Anne Parillaud
La Femme Nikita [MGM] '91

Jerry Paris
Marty '55

Kris Park
Drive Me Crazy '99

Peyton E. Park
The Lathe of Heaven '80

Ray Park
X-Men '00

Cecilia Parker
Riders of Destiny / Star Packer '33

Eleanor Parker
The Sound of Music [Five Star Collection] '65

F. William Parker
Hard Eight '96

Fess Parker
Hell Is for Heroes '62

Jean Parker
The Flying Deuces / Utopia '39

Kim Parker
Fiend Without a Face '58

Mary-Louise Parker
The Five Senses '99
Let the Devil Wear Black '99
Mr. Wonderful '93
Grand Canyon '91
Longtime Companion '90

Molly Parker
Waking the Dead '00
The Five Senses '99
Sunshine '99
Wonderland '99

Nicole Parker
Remember the Titans '00
Blue Streak '99

Nicole Ari Parker
Loving Jezebel '99

Noelle Parker
Newsbreak '00

Sarah Jessica Parker
Sex and the City: The Complete Second Season '00
Stories from My Childhood, Vol. 3 '99 (V)
If Lucy Fell '95
Girls Just Want to Have Fun '85

Stephen Parker
Teenage Monster '57

Shaun Parkes
Human Traffic '99

Barbara Parkins
Asylum '72

Catherine Parks
Friday the 13th, Part 3 '82

Michael Parks
From Dusk Till Dawn [2 CS] '95
Death Wish 5: The Face of Death '94

Tammy Parks
The Erotic Ghost '00
Titanic 2000 '00

Trina Parks
Diamonds Are Forever [SE] '71

Steve Parlavecchio
The First to Go '97

Lana Parrilla
Spiders '00

Estelle Parsons
For Pete's Sake '74

Karyn Parsons
The Ladies Man '00

Nancy Parsons
Porky's 2: The Next Day '83
Porky's / Porky's 2: The Next Day '82

Dolly Parton
Steel Magnolias '89
9 to 5 '80

Nadine Pascale
Zombie Lake '80

Natalie Pascaud
Mr. Hulot's Holiday '53

Adrian Pasdar
The Pompatus of Love '95

Dira Pass
The Emerald Forest '85

Vincent Pastore
The Sopranos: The Complete First Season '00
The Hurricane '99
Mafia! '98
Gotti '96

Robert Pastorelli
Bait '00

Michael Pataki
Dead and Buried '81

Wally Patch
Pygmalion '38

Bill Paterson
The Object of Beauty '91

Vincent Paterson
Dancer in the Dark '99

Mandy Patinkin
Alien Nation '88
The Princess Bride '87

Tatjana Patitz
Restraining Order '99

Jason Patric
The Beast '88

Butch Patrick
Munster, Go Home! '66

Dennis Patrick
Choices '81

Gail Patrick
Up in Mabel's Room '44

Joan Patrick
The Astro-Zombies '67

Lee Patrick
7 Faces of Dr. Lao '63
The Maltese Falcon '41

Robert Patrick
All the Pretty Horses '00
Striptease '96
Double Dragon '94
Terminator 2: Judgment Day [2 SE] '91

Elizabeth Patterson
Pal Joey '57

Lorna Patterson
Airplane! '80

Neva Patterson
An Affair to Remember '57

Rocky Patterson
Perfect Profile '90

Guesch Patti
Women '97

Bart Patton
Dementia 13 '63

Will Patton
Gone in 60 Seconds '00
Remember the Titans '00
Jesus' Son '99
Breakfast of Champions '98
Inventing the Abbotts '97
Fled '96
No Way Out '87
Desperately Seeking Susan '85

Aaron Paul
Whatever It Takes '00

Adrian Paul
Highlander: Endgame '00
Premonition '99

Richard Paul
Bloodfist 3: Forced to Fight '92

Scott Paulin
A Soldier's Story '84

Rob Paulsen
Land Before Time 7: The Stone of Cold Fire '00 (V)

Sarah Paulson
Held Up '00
What Women Want '00

Paul Pavel
An Affair of Love '00

Bill Paxton
U-571 [CE] '00
Vertical Limit '00
The Evening Star '96
Traveller '96
Frank and Jesse '94
Boxing Helena '93
One False Move '91
Navy SEALS [MGM] '90
Brain Dead '89

David Paymer
Bait '00
Bounce '00
For Love or Country: The Arturo Sandoval Story '00
The Hurricane '99
The Long Way Home '97 (N)
City Slickers '91
No Way Out '87

Allen Payne
The Perfect Storm '00
The Tuskegee Airmen '95

Bruce Payne
Dungeons and Dragons '00
Highlander: Endgame '00
One Man's Justice '95
Passenger 57 '92
Switch '91

Barbara Payton
Four Sided Triangle '53

Felipe Pazos
The Old Man and the Sea '58

Trevor Peacock
A Christmas Carol '99

Guy Pearce
Rules of Engagement '00
Flynn '96
The Adventures of Priscilla, Queen of the Desert [MGM] '94

Jacqueline Pearce
Princess Caraboo '94

Randy Pearlstein
My Teacher's Wife '95

Neil Pearson
Fever Pitch '96

Andrew Pece
Suburbia '83

Sierra Pecheur
Bronco Billy '80

Bob Peck
Smilla's Sense of Snow '96
Jurassic Park [CE] '93

Cecilia Peck
Wall Street '87

George Peck
Curse of the Puppet Master: The Human Experiment '98

Gregory Peck
The Omen [SE] '76
The Big Country '58
Moby Dick '56
The Snows of Kilimanjaro '52

Tony Peck
Carnosaur 3: Primal Species '96

Chris Pederson
Platoon [2 SE] '86
Suburbia '83

Harrison Peebles
The Monster of Camp Sunshine '64

Nia Peeples
Deepstar Six '89

Amanda Peet
Isn't She Great '00
Whipped '00
The Whole Nine Yards '00
Body Shots '99
Grind '97
She's the One '96

Cheng Pei-Pei
Crouching Tiger, Hidden Dragon '00

Nikola Pejakovic
Pretty Village, Pretty Flame '96

Dusan Pekic
The Wounds '98

Valentine Pelka
The Last of the Blonde Bombshells '00

Mark Pellegrino
Drowning Mona '00

Clara Peller
The Stuff '85

Pina Pellicer
One-Eyed Jacks '61

Meeno Peluce
The Amityville Horror '79

Jennifer Peluso
Hellblock 13 '97

Candela Pena
All About My Mother '99
Running out of Time '94

Elizabeth Pena
Seven Girlfriends '00
Times Square '80

Michael Pena
Bellyfruit '99

Austin Pendleton
The 4th Floor '99
My Cousin Vinny '92
Mr. & Mrs. Bridge '90
Catch-22 '70

Cedric Pendleton
Nothin' 2 Lose '00

Danny Pintauro
Cujo '83

Harold Pinter
Mansfield Park '99

Anne Pioniak
Where the Money Is '00

Candido Pires
Manoushe, The Story of a Gypsy Love '98

Grant Piro
Mr. Accident '99

Marie-France Pisier
Son of Gascogne '95

Luigi Pistilli
Bay of Blood '71
Twitch of the Death Nerve '71

Anne Pitoniak
Sister, Sister '87

Brad Pitt
Seven [2 SE] '95
Legends of the Fall [2 SE] '94

ZaSu Pitts
Life with Father '47

Jeremy Piven
The Crew '00
Red Letters '00
Body Chemistry 2: Voice of a Stranger '91

Mary Kay Place
Girl, Interrupted '99

Tony Plana
Backlash '99
187 '97
Romero '89
Salvador [SE] '86

Niels Platow
Heart of Light '97

Edward Platt
North by Northwest '59

Oliver Platt
CinderElmo '00
Gun Shy '00
Ready to Rumble '00
Bicentennial Man '99
Benny & Joon '93
Beethoven '92
Postcards from the Edge '90
Working Girl '88

Wellington A. Playter
Back to God's Country / Something New '19

Donald Pleasence
Shadows and Fog '92
Halloween 5: The Revenge of Michael Myers '89
Escape from New York '81
Gold of the Amazon Women '79
The Eagle Has Landed '77
You Only Live Twice [SE] '67
Fantastic Voyage '66
The Greatest Story Ever Told [SE] '65
The Hallelujah Trail '65

Suzanne Pleshette
Support Your Local Gunfighter '71

Martha Plimpton
I Shot Andy Warhol '96
Another Woman '88

Joan Plowright
Dinosaur [CE] '00 (V)
Avalon '90
The Entertainer '60

Eve Plumb
I'm Gonna Git You Sucka '88

Amanda Plummer
8 1/2 Women '99

The Million Dollar Hotel '99
October 22 '98
Freejack '92
The Fisher King '91

Christopher Plummer
Full Disclosure '00
Nuremberg '00
Rock-a-Doodle '92 (V)
The Sound of Music [Five Star Collection] '65

Glenn Plummer
Rangers '00
Interceptor Force '99
South Central '92

George Plympton
Flash Gordon: Space Soldiers '36

Werner Pochat
Laser Mission '90

Werner Pochath
Vengeance '68

Ken Pogue
The 6th Day '00
The Jack Bull '99
Bad Moon '96

Larry Poindexter
Body Chemistry 4: Full Exposure '95

Priscilla Pointer
Blue Velvet '86

Earl C. Poitier
Remember the Titans '00

Sidney Poitier
The Organization '71
They Call Me Mr. Tibbs! '70
In the Heat of the Night '67
The Greatest Story Ever Told [SE] '65
Lilies of the Field '63
A Raisin in the Sun '61

Sydney Poitier
Noah's Ark '99

Basil Poledouris
Cecil B. Demented '00

Maurice Poli
Five Dolls for an August Moon '70

Mark Polish
Twin Falls Idaho '99

Michael Polish
Twin Falls Idaho '99

Jon Polito
The Adventures of Rocky & Bullwinkle '00
Homicide: The Movie '00
Fluke '95

Vic Polizos
Light It Up '99
C.H.U.D. '84

Stephen Polk
Destination Vegas '95

Sydney Pollack
Tootsie '82

Kevin Pollak
Deterrence '00
Steal This Movie! '00
The Whole Nine Yards '00
Deal of a Lifetime '99
Canadian Bacon '94
Avalon '90

Michael J. Pollard
Tumbleweeds '98
Scrooged '88
Roxanne '87
The Wild Angels '66

Sarah Polley
The Claim '00
The Life Before This '99
White Lies '98

Daniel Pollock
Romper Stomper [SE] '92

Teri Polo
Meet the Parents '00

Rui Polonah
The Emerald Forest '85

John Polson
Mission: Impossible 2 '00

Max Pomeranc
Fluke '95

Margaret Pomeranz
The Adventures of Priscilla, Queen of the Desert [MGM] '94

Yvan Ponton
The Boys '97

Iggy Pop
Snow Day '00
Dead Man '95
Tank Girl '94
Sid & Nancy [MGM] '86

Albert "Poppy" Popwell
The Joe Louis Story '53

Marc Porel
Don't Torture a Duckling '72

Paulina Porizkova
Intern '00

Billy Porter
The Broken Hearts Club '00
Intern '00

Susie Porter
Paradise Road '97

Natalie Portman
Where the Heart Is '00
Leon, the Professional '94

Richard Portnow
Desert Thunder '99
Ghost Dog: The Way of the Samurai '99

Parker Posey
Best in Show '00
Scream 3 [CS] '00
The Daytrippers '96

Roberto Posse
Macabre '80

William Post Jr.
Sherlock Holmes and the Secret Weapon '42

Pete Postlethwaite
The Lost World: Jurassic Park 2 [CE] '97
The Serpent's Kiss '97
James and the Giant Peach '96 (V)
Sharpe's Company '94
Sharpe's Enemy '94
Anchoress '93
The Last of the Mohicans '92

Michal Postnikov
First Spaceship on Venus '60

Temple Poteat
Hip Hop 2000 '00

Franka Potente
Anatomy [SE] '00

Christian Potenza
Hendrix '00

Martin Potter
Fellini Satyricon '69

Tim Potter
A Christmas Carol '99

Gerald Potterton
Buster Keaton Rides Again / The Railrodder '65

Annie Potts
Toy Story 2 '99 (V)
Toy Story '95 (V)

Cliff Potts
The Groundstar Conspiracy '72

Sara-Jane Potts
The Canterville Ghost '98

CCH Pounder
Benny & Joon '93
Postcards from the Edge '90

Melvil Poupaud
A Summer's Tale '96

Phyllis Povah
Pat and Mike '52

Charles Powell
Grey Owl '99

Dick Powell
42nd Street '33

Robert Powell
Tommy '75
The Asphyx '72
Asylum '72

William Powell
How to Marry a Millionaire '53
Life with Father '47

Power
Black and White '99

Dave Power
U-571 [CE] '00

Taryn Power
Sinbad and the Eye of the Tiger '77

Tyrone Power Jr.
Shag: The Movie '89

Leon Pownall
Dirty Pictures '00

Jerome Pradon
Jesus Christ Superstar '00

Pras
Da Hip Hop Witch '00
Turn It Up '00

Hugo Pratt
Mauvais Sang '86

Judson Pratt
The Horse Soldiers '59

Susan May Pratt
Center Stage '00
Drive Me Crazy '99

Wolfgang Preiss
Cave of the Living Dead '65
The Thousand Eyes of Dr. Mabuse '60

Paula Prentiss
Saturday the 14th '81
The Parallax View '74
Born to Win '71
Catch-22 '70
In Harm's Way '65

Elvis Presley
Frankie and Johnny '65

Priscilla Presley
Naked Gun 33 1/3: The Final Insult '94
Naked Gun 2 1/2: The Smell of Fear '91
The Naked Gun: From the Files of Police Squad '88

Harve Presnell
The Legend of Bagger Vance '00
The Unsinkable Molly Brown '64

Jason Presson
The Lady in White '88
Saturday the 14th Strikes Back '88

Cynthia Preston
Premonition '99

Kelly Preston
Battlefield Earth '00
For Love of the Game '99
From Dusk Till Dawn [2 CS] '95

Robert Preston
Semi-Tough '77

Daniel Prevost
The Dinner Game '98

Marie Prevost
The Marriage Circle '24

Al Price
Inn of 1000 Sins '75

Alan Price
Bob Dylan: Don't Look Back '67

Dennis Price
Vampyros Lesbos '70

Molly Price
Kiss Me, Guido '97

Vincent Price
Edward Scissorhands [SE] '90
Doctor Phibes Rises Again '72
The Abominable Dr. Phibes '71
Dr. Goldfoot and the Bikini Machine '66
Beach Party '63
Tales of Terror '62
The Pit and the Pendulum '61
The Fall of the House of Usher '60
Return of the Fly '59
The Fly / Return of the Fly '58
Abbott and Costello Meet Frankenstein '48 (V)

Shani Pride
The Vault '00

Austin Priester
The Vault '00

Jason Priestley
Homicide: The Movie '00
Eye of the Beholder '99
The Highway Man '99

Louis Prima
Louis Prima: The Wildest! '99

Prime Time
Dope Case Pending '00

Alec Primrose
Teenage Gang Debs / Teenage Strangler '66

Akili Prince
Went to Coney Island on a Mission from God...Be Back by Five '98

William Prince
Family Plot '76

Andrew Prine
Witchouse 2: Blood Coven '00
Gettysburg '93
The Miracle Worker '62

Freddie Prinze Jr.
Boys and Girls '00
Down to You '00

Susan Prior
Heaven's Burning '97

Ted Prior
Hardcase and Fist '89

Juergen Prochnow
Heaven's Fire '00
The Last Stop '99

Emily Procter
Body Shots '99

Robert Prosky
Dead Man Walking '95
Rudy [SE] '93
The Natural '84

Anna Prucnall
City of Women '81

Jonathan Pryce
Robert Louis Stevenson's
The Game of Death '99

Nicholas Pryor
Brain Dead '89
Damien: Omen 2 '78

Richard Pryor
Superman 3 '83
Bustin' Loose '81
Car Wash '76

Jesus Puente
Hatchet for the Honeymoon
'70

Willard Pugh
Puppet Master 5: The Latest
Chapter '94

Benjamin Pullen
Intern '00

Bill Pullman
Lucky Numbers '00
Titan A.E. '00 (V)
Malice [MGM] '93
Brain Dead '89

Maylin Pultar
In God's Hands '98

Denise Purcell
Deadly Weapons '70

Richard Purcell
The Bank Dick '40

Edmund Purdom
Dr. Frankenstein's Castle of
Freaks '74

James Purefoy
Dead of Night '99
Mansfield Park '99
Bedrooms and Hallways '98

Om Puri
East Is East '99

Linda Purl
Perfect Tenant '99

Edna Purviance
Burlesque on Carmen '16

John Putch
The Souler Opposite '97

Denver Pyle
The Man Who Shot Liberty
Valance '62
The Alamo '60
The Horse Soldiers '59

John Pyper-Ferguson
Hard Core Logo '96

John Quade
The Tracker '88

Dennis Quaid
Frequency '00
Traffic '00
Any Given Sunday '99
Postcards from the Edge '90
The Long Riders '80

Randy Quaid
The Adventures of Rocky &
Bullwinkle '00
The Magical Legend of the
Leprechauns '99
Get On the Bus '96
The Long Riders '80
The Last Picture Show [DC]
'71

John Qualen
7 Faces of Dr. Lao '63
The Man Who Shot Liberty
Valance '62
Captain Kidd '45

DJ Qualls
Road Trip '00

Robert Quarry
Doctor Phibes Rises Again
'72

Philip Quast
Napoleon '96 (V)

Anthony Quayle
The Eagle Has Landed '77
Everything You Always Want-
ed to Know about Sex (But
Were Afraid to Ask) '72
Damn the Defiant! '62
Lawrence of Arabia '62
Hamlet '48

Queen Latifah
Hoodlum '96
My Life '93
House Party 2: The Pajama
Jam '91

Valerie Quennessen
Conan the Barbarian [2 CE]
'82

John Quentin
The Stendhal Syndrome '95

Gerry Quigley
32 Short Films about Glenn
Gould '93

Linnea Quigley
Death Mask '98
Assault of the Party Nerds 2:
Heavy Petting Detective '95
Assault of the Party Nerds
'89

Tim Quill
Thou Shalt Not Kill . . .
Except '87

Denis Quilley
Mister Johnson '91
In This House of Brede '75

Kathleen Quinlan
The Doors [2 SE] '91

Aidan Quinn
Music of the Heart [CS] '99
Legends of the Fall [2 SE] '94
Benny & Joon '93
Avalon '90
The Lemon Sisters '90
Desperately Seeking Susan
'85

Aileen Quinn
Annie '82

Anthony Quinn
Gotti '96
A Walk in the Clouds '95
Lawrence of Arabia '62

Bill Quinn
Bustin' Loose '81
Dead and Buried '81

Francesco Quinn
Platoon [2 SE] '86

Glenn Quinn
Dr. Giggles '92

Marian Quinn
Broken Harvest '94

Martha Quinn
Tapeheads '89

Pat Quinn
Alice's Restaurant '69

Patricia Quinn
The Rocky Horror Picture
Show '75

Tandra Quinn
Mesa of Lost Women '52

Jonathan Quint
Floating '97

Pauline Quirke
The Canterville Ghost '98

Francesco Rabal
Goya in Bordeaux '99
Tie Me Up! Tie Me Down! '90

Liberto Rabal
Live Flesh '97

Pamela Rabe
Paradise Road '97

Kurt Rackelmann
First Spaceship on Venus '60

Sascha Radetsky
Center Stage '00

Ken Radley
Sniper '92

Bette Rae
Confessions of Sorority Girls
'00

Charlotte Rae
Bananas '71

Raekwon
Black and White '99

Giuliano Raffaelli
Blood and Black Lace '64

Deborah Raffin
The Sentinel '76

George Raft
Sextette '78
Some Like It Hot [SE] '59

William Ragsdale
Fright Night '85

Umberto Raho
Amuck! '71

Steve Railsback
Termination Man '97
Barb Wire '96

Sam Raimi
Evil Dead 2: Dead by Dawn [2
THX] '87
Thou Shalt Not Kill . . .
Except '87

Theodore (Ted) Raimi
Stuart Saves His Family '94
Evil Dead 2: Dead by Dawn [2
THX] '87
Thou Shalt Not Kill . . .
Except '87

Christina Raines
The Sentinel '76
Nashville '75

Ford Rainey
The Sand Pebbles '66

Claude Rains
The Greatest Story Ever Told
[SE] '65
Lawrence of Arabia '62
Angel on My Shoulder '46
The Phantom of the Opera '43
They Made Me a Criminal '39
The Invisible Man '33

Prayag Raj
Cotton Mary '99

Pierre-Loup Rajot
The New Eve '98

Denis Rake
The Sorrow and the Pity '71

Christopher Ralph
Hendrix '00

Jessie Ralph
The Bank Dick '40
Little Lord Fauntleroy '36

Sheryl Lee Ralph
Deterrence '00
Mistress '91
The Mighty Quinn '89

Harold Ramis
Baby Boom '87

Charlotte Rampling
Zardoz '73
Asylum '72

Bruce Ramsay
Killing Zoe '94

Remak Ramsay
Mr. & Mrs. Bridge '90

Ward Ramsey
Dinosaurus! '60

Stacey Linn Ramsower
Tank Girl '94

Tony Randall
The Fantasy Film Worlds of
George Pal '86
Everything You Always Want-
ed to Know about Sex (But
Were Afraid to Ask) '72
7 Faces of Dr. Lao '63

Ron Randell
The Loves of Carmen '48

Mary Jo Randle
The Hollow Man [SE] '00

Jane Randolph
Abbott and Costello Meet
Frankenstein '48

John Randolph
Frances '82
Conquest of the Planet of the
Apes '72
Escape from the Planet of
the Apes '71

Salvo Randone
Fellini Satyricon '69
10th Victim '65

Joe Ranft
Toy Story 2 '99 (V)

Michael Rapaport
Bamboozled '00
Kiss Toledo Goodbye '00
Lucky Numbers '00
Men of Honor '00
The 6th Day '00
Small Time Crooks '00
Kicked in the Head '97
The Pallbearer '95

Anthony Rapp
Road Trip '00
Six Degrees of Separation
'93

Rappin 4-Tay
Winner Takes All '98

David Rasche
The Big Tease '99
The Settlement '99
Manhattan '79

Stephanie Rascoe
Positive I.D. '87

Phylicia Rashad
Loving Jezebel '99
Once Upon a Time...When We
Were Colored '95

Lisbeth Rasmussen
Pusher '96

Thalmus Rasulala
Friday Foster '75

Jay Rasumny
Wham-Bam, Thank You
Spaceman '75

Jeremy Ratchford
The Crew '00

Basil Rathbone
Hillbillys in a Haunted House
'67
Tales of Terror '62
The Adventures of Ichabod
and Mr. Toad '49 (N)
Dressed to Kill '46
Terror by Night '46
The Woman in Green '45
The Woman in Green /
Dressed to Kill '45
Sherlock Holmes and the
Secret Weapon '42
The Garden of Allah '36

Benjamin Ratner
Bounty Hunters '96

John Ratzenberger
Toy Story 2 '99 (V)
Toy Story '95 (V)

Mike Raven
Crucible of Terror '72

Christopher Ravenscroft
Henry V '89

Gina Ravera
Soul of the Game '96

Adrian Rawlins
Breaking the Waves '95

Aldo Ray
Pat and Mike '52

Connie Ray
Idle Hands '99

James Ray
She's Having a Baby '88

Joey Ray
The Old Man and the Sea '58

Johnny Ray
There's No Business Like
Show Business '54

Michel Ray
Lawrence of Arabia '62
The Brave One '56

Cyril Raymond
Brief Encounter '46

Dianne Raymond
Gruesome Twosome '67

Lee Raymond
She-Freak '67

Usher Raymond
Light It Up '99

Michael Raynor
The Waiting Game '99

Peggy Rea
Love Field '91
In Country '89

Stephen Rea
The End of the Affair '99
The Life Before This '99
Fever Pitch '96
Citizen X '95
Princess Caraboo '94

James Read
Eight Men Out '88

Rufus Read
Double Parked '00

James Rebhorn
The Adventures of Rocky &
Bullwinkle '00
Meet the Parents '00
Snow Falling on Cedars '99
The Talented Mr. Ripley '99
If Lucy Fell '95

Jeff Rector
Dinosaur Valley Girls '96

Lance Reddick
I Dreamed of Africa '00

Keith Reddin
Lolita '97

Brian Reddy
Lost Souls '00

Helen Reddy
Pete's Dragon '77

Dennis Redfield
The McCullochs '75

William Redfield
Death Wish '74
For Pete's Sake '74
Fantastic Voyage '66

Brian Redford
Cannibal Ferox '84

Robert Redford
The Natural '84
The Way We Were [SE] '73

Corin Redgrave
Plain Jane '00

Lynn Redgrave
The Next Best Thing '00
All I Wanna Do '98
White Lies '98
Everything You Always Want-
ed to Know about Sex (But
Were Afraid to Ask) '72
Tom Jones [MGM] '63

Vanessa Redgrave
If These Walls Could Talk 2 '00
The Cradle Will Rock '99
Girl, Interrupted '99
Smilla's Sense of Snow '96
Mother's Boys '94
A Man for All Seasons '66

Nick Reding
Croupier '97
Mister Johnson '91

Redman
Backstage '00

Joyce Redman
Tom Jones [MGM] '63

Siobhan Redmond
Beautiful People '99

Ekaterina Rednikova
The Thief '97

Christopher Reed
Rudy [SE] '93

Donald Reed
Evangeline '29

Donna Reed
The Last Time I Saw Paris '54

Gavin Reed
The Body Beneath '70

Kira Reed
Best of Intimate Sessions:
Vol. 2 '99

Oliver Reed
Gladiator '00
The Prince and the Pauper
'78
The Four Musketeers '75
Tommy '75
I'll Never Forget What's
'Isname '67

Pamela Reed
Bob Roberts [SE] '92
The Clan of the Cave Bear
'86
The Long Riders '80

Rachel Reed
Midnight Tease / Midnight
Tease 2 '94

Tracy Reed
Dr. Strangelove, or: How I
Learned to Stop Worrying
and Love the Bomb [2 SE]
'64

Walter Reed
The Sand Pebbles '66
The Horse Soldiers '59

Norman Reedus
Gossip '99
Floating '97

**Harry (Herbert
Streicher) Reems**
Deadly Weapons '70

Roger Rees
Blackmale '99
Next Stop, Wonderland '98
Mountains of the Moon '90

Della Reese
Dinosaur [CE] '00 (V)

Christopher Reeve
Superman 4: The Quest for
Peace '87
Superman 3 '83
Superman 2 '80
Superman: The Movie '78

George Reeves
The Great Lover '49

Keanu Reeves
The Replacements '00
The Watcher '00
A Walk in the Clouds '95
River's Edge '87
Youngblood '86

Kynaston Reeves
Fiend Without a Face '58

Lisa Reeves
The Pom Pom Girls / The
Beach Girls '76

Perrey Reeves
Red Shoe Diaries: Luscious
Lola '00

Saskia Reeves
Dune '00
A Christmas Carol '99

Duncan Regehr
Air Bud 3: World Pup '00

Serge Reggiani
Mauvais Sang '86

Nadja Regin
From Russia with Love [2 SE]
'63

Meg Register
Boxing Helena '93

Regopstann
Red Scorpion '89

Lee Reherman
Downhill Willie '96

Chris Rehmann
High Fidelity '00

Wolfgang Reichmann
Woyzeck '78

Audrey Reid
Third World Cop '99

Beryl Reid
Psychomania '73
Doctor Phibes Rises Again
'72

Candace Reid
Velocity '99

Christopher Reid
House Party 3 '94
House Party 2: The Pajama
Jam '91
House Party '90

Elliott Reid
Gentlemen Prefer Blondes
'53

R.D. Reid
Dirty Pictures '00

Tara Reid
Dr. T & the Women '00
Body Shots '99
Around the Fire '98
Girl '98

Taylor Anne Reid
The 6th Day '00

Tim Reid
Race to Freedom: The Story
of the Underground Rail-
road '94

Wallace Reid
Affairs of Anatol '21
Joan the Woman '16
Carmen / The Cheat '15

Timothy Reifsnyder
Wide Awake '97

Charles Nelson Reilly
Rock-a-Doodle '92 (V)
All Dogs Go to Heaven '89 (V)

John C. Reilly
The Perfect Storm '00
For Love of the Game '99
Magnolia '99
The Settlement '99
Hard Eight '96
Nightwatch '96

Kelly Reilly
Poldark '96

Pat Reilly
Nude on the Moon '61

Lucy Reina
Romero '89

Carl Reiner
The Adventures of Rocky &
Bullwinkle '00
Dead Men Don't Wear Plaid
'82
The End '78

Rob Reiner
Postcards from the Edge '90
This Is Spinal Tap [MGM] '84

Thomas Reiner
Blood and Black Lace '64

Ray Reinhardt
The Tie That Binds '95

Judge Reinhold
Beethoven's 3rd '00
Newsbreak '00
Homegrown '97
Fast Times at Ridgemont
High '82

Ann Reinking
Annie '82

Michelle Reis
The Legend '93
Chinese Ghost Story II '90

Paulo Reis
The Story of O: The Series
'92

Winston Rekert
The Last Stop '99

Kushal Rekhi
Fire '96

James Remar
What Lies Beneath '00
One Good Turn '95
Drugstore Cowboy '89
The Clan of the Cave Bear
'86
The Warriors '79

Erika Remberg
Cave of the Living Dead '65

Jean-François Remi
La Guerre Est Finie '66

Lee Remick
The Omen [SE] '76

The Hallelujah Trail '65
Anatomy of a Murder '59

Bert Remsen
Nashville '75

Kerry Remsen
Pumpkinhead '88

Callum Keith Rennie
The Highway Man '99
The Last Stop '99
The Life Before This '99
Hard Core Logo '96

Michael Rennie
Die Screaming, Marianne '73
Demetrius and the Gladiators
'54

Jean Reno
Beyond the Clouds '95
Leon, the Professional '94
La Femme Nikita [MGM] '91
The Big Blue [DC] '88

Maggie Renzi
Eight Men Out '88

Frank Ressel
Blood and Black Lace '64

Dale Resteghini
Da Hip Hop Witch '00
Colorz of Rage '97

Tommy Rettig
The 5000 Fingers of Dr. T '53

Mary Lou Retton
Scrooged '88

Raul Retzer
The Vampire Happening '71

Gloria Reuben
Cold Blooded '00
Inferno '99
Nick of Time '95

**Paul (Pee-wee Herman)
Reubens**
Beauty and the Beast: The
Enchanted Christmas '97
(V)
Buddy '97
The Nightmare before Christ-
mas [2 SE] '93 (V)

Clive Revill
Pinocchio '76

Rosaura Revueltas
Salt of the Earth '54

Simon Rex
Shriek If You Know What I Did
Last Friday the 13th '00

Fernando Rey
The Discreet Charm of the
Bourgeoisie '72

Ernie Reyes Jr.
White Wolves 2: Legend of
the Wild '94

Rina Reyes
Bloodfist 2 '90

Burt Reynolds
The Crew '00
Big City Blues '99
Mystery, Alaska '99
Striptease '96
All Dogs Go to Heaven '89 (V)
Cannonball Run '81
The End '78
Semi-Tough '77
The Longest Yard '74
Everything You Always Want-
ed to Know about Sex (But
Were Afraid to Ask) '72

Debbie Reynolds
Rugrats in Paris: The Movie
'00 (V)
Mother '96
Heaven and Earth '93

Charlotte's Web '73 (V)
The Unsinkable Molly Brown
'64

Greg Reynolds
Deadly Weapons '70

Jacob Reynolds
Gummo '97

Jesika Reynolds
Holiday Heart '00

Marjorie Reynolds
Up in Mabel's Room '44

Nicola Reynolds
Human Traffic '99

Robert Reynolds
Element of Doubt '96

Ryan Reynolds
Coming Soon '99
Dick '99

Omry Reznik
Red Shoe Diaries: Swimming
Naked '00

Ving Rhames
Holiday Heart '00
Mission: Impossible 2 '00
Bringing Out the Dead '99
Striptease '96

Phillip Rhee
Best of the Best: Without
Warning '98
Best of the Best 3: No Turn-
ing Back / Best of the
Best: Without Warning '95

Simon Rhee
The Substitute 4: Failure Is
Not an Option '00

Ashlie Rhey
Midnight Tease / Midnight
Tease 2 '94

Julian Rhind-Tutt
The Madness of King George
'94

Allanah Rhodes
Erotic Witch Project 2: Book
of Seduction '00

Christopher Rhodes
Gorgo '61

Cynthia Rhodes
Runaway '84

Hari Rhodes
A Woman Called Moses '78
Detroit 9000 '73
Conquest of the Planet of the
Apes '72

Busta Rhymes
Finding Forrester '00
Shaft '00

Matthew Rhys
Titus '99

John Rhys-Davies
Sinbad: Beyond the Veil of
Mists '00 (V)
The Living Daylights '87

Jonathan Rhys Meyers
Ride with the Devil '99
Titus '99
The Loss of Sexual Inno-
cence '98
B. Monkey '97

Candice Rialson
Hollywood Boulevard '76

Giovanni Ribisi
Boiler Room '00
Gone in 60 Seconds '00
It's the Rage '99
The Virgin Suicides '99 (N)

Lela Rochon
Any Given Sunday '99

Rock
Da Hip Hop Witch '00

Chris Rock
Nurse Betty '00
Dogma '99
Coneheads '93
I'm Gonna Git You Sucka '88

Sam Rockwell
Charlie's Angels '00
Galaxy Quest '99
Jerry and Tom '98

Ziva Rodann
Teenage Doll '57

James Roday
Coming Soon '99

Gene Roddenberry
The Fantasy Film Worlds of
George Pal '86

Ebbe Rode
Babette's Feast '87

Jose Lopez Rodero
The Ninth Gate '99

Kate Rodger
Chained Heat 3: Hell Mountain '98

Gaby Rodgers
Kiss Me Deadly '55

Reginald Rodgers
I Shot Andy Warhol '96

Dennis Rodman
Cutaway '00

Freddy Rodriguez
For Love or Country: The
Arturo Sandoval Story '00
A Walk in the Clouds '95

Lisa Rodriguez
Next Friday [Platinum Series]
'00

Marco Rodriguez
Angel Blue '97
Internal Affairs '90

Michelle Rodriguez
Girlfight '99

Paul Rodriguez
Price of Glory '00

Channon Roe
Girl '98

Matt Roe
Puppet Master '89

Daniel Roebuck
Final Destination '00
River's Edge '87

William Roerick
The Wasp Woman '59

Maurice Roeves
The Last of the Mohicans '92
Ulysses '67

Roger-Pierre
Mon Oncle d'Amerique '80

Bill Rogers
For Love of the Game '99
Phenomenon—The Lost
Archives: Noah's Ark
Found?/Tunguska/Stolen
Glory '99 (N)
Phenomenon—The Lost
Archives: Up for
Sale/Heavy Watergate '99
(N)
A Taste of Blood '67

Ginger Rogers
42nd Street '33

Jean Rogers
Flash Gordon: Space Soldiers
'36

Jeffrey Rogers
Friday the 13th, Part 3 '82

Mimi Rogers
Seven Girlfriends '00
The Doors [2 SE] '91
The Mighty Quinn '89

Reg Rogers
Attila '01

Roy Rogers
Son of Paleface '52

Tristan Rogers
The Rescuers Down Under
'90 (V)

Helena Rojo
Aguirre, the Wrath of God '72

Maria Rojo
Midaq Alley '95

Gilbert Roland
Captain Kidd '45

Guy Rolfe
Retro Puppet Master '99
Puppet Master 5: The Latest
Chapter '94
Puppet Master 4 '93
Puppet Master 3: Toulon's
Revenge '90

Michelle Rolia
Mr. Hulot's Holiday '53

Esther Rolle
The Mighty Quinn '89

Jean Rollin
Zombie Lake '80

Howard E. Rollins Jr.
A Soldier's Story '84

Mark Rolston
Best of the Best 3: No Turn-
ing Back / Best of the
Best: Without Warning '95

Cynthia Roman
Bringing Out the Dead '99

Leticia Roman
The Girl Who Knew Too Much
'63

Ruth Roman
Day of the Animals '77

Susan Roman
Rabid '77

Andy Romano
Drop Zone '94

Robert Romanus
Fast Times at Ridgemont
High '82

Lina Romay
Tender Flesh '00
Lust for Frankenstein '88
Ilsa, the Wicked Warden '78
Female Vampire '73

Cesar Romero
Carmen Miranda: Bananas Is
My Business '95
Lust in the Dust '85
Donovan's Reef '63
Vera Cruz '53
The Little Princess '39

George A. Romero
Martin '77
Night of the Living Dead
[Madacy] '68
Night of the Living Dead
[Elite] '68
Night of the Living Dead [LE
Anchor Bay] '68

Rebecca Romijn-Stamos
X-Men '00

Helena Ronee
Five Dolls for an August
Moon '70

Michael Rooker
Here on Earth '00
Newsbreak '00
The 6th Day '00
Bram Stoker's Shadowbuilder
'98
Back to Back '96
Cliffhanger [2 CS] '93
Eight Men Out '88
Mississippi Burning [MGM]
'88

Mickey Rooney
Lady and the Tramp 2:
Scamp's Adventure '01 (V)
The Fox and the Hound '81
(V)
Pete's Dragon '77
The Bridges at Toko-Ri '55
Quicksand '50
The Big Wheel '49
Little Lord Fauntleroy '36

Tim Rooney
Village of the Giants '65

Camilla Overbye Roos
On the Border '98

Michaela Roos
Inn of 1000 Sins '75

Amanda Root
Deep in the Heart (of Texas)
'98

Bonnie Root
Coming Soon '99

Stephen Root
Bicentennial Man '99
Monkey Shines '88

Rosanna Rory
Big Deal on Madonna Street
'58

Anna M. Rosati
Bay of Blood '71
Twitch of the Death Nerve '71

Albert Roscoe
The Last of the Mohicans '20

Deborah Rose
The Bone Yard '90

Felissa Rose
Sleepaway Camp '83

Gabrielle Rose
The Five Senses '99
The Adjuster '91

Laura Rose
Kept '01

Robin Pearson Rose
Last Resort '86

Sherrie Rose
Black Scorpion 2: Ground
Zero '96

Rose Marie
Shriek If You Know What I Did
Last Friday the 13th '00

Roseanne
Look Who's Talking, Too '90
(V)

Ben Roseman
Daughter of Horror / Dementia '55

Sarah Rosenberg
Foxfire '96

Frayne Rosenoff
Python '00

Annie Ross
Superman 3 '83

Chelcie Ross
Charming Billy '99
Amos and Andrew '93
Rudy [SE] '93

**Howard (Renato
Rossini) Ross**
Five Dolls for an August
Moon '70

Hugh Ross
For Love of the Game '99

Joe E. Ross
Teaserama '55

Katharine Ross
The Shadow Riders '82

Kimberly Ross
Pumpkinhead '88

Lanny Ross
Gulliver's Travels [Image] '39
(V)

Marion Ross
The Last Best Sunday '98
The Evening Star '96

Matt Ross
American Psycho '99

Michael Ross
D.O.A. [Roan] '49

Pamela Ross
Sorority House Massacre '86

Ron Ross
Battle Beyond the Stars '80

Rose Ross
Mother's Day [DC] '80

Isabella Rossellini
Blue Velvet '86

Leo Rossi
River's Edge '87

Kim Rossi-Stuart
Beyond the Clouds '95

Norman Rossington
Lawrence of Arabia '62

Angelo Rossitto
Dracula vs. Frankenstein '71
Daughter of Horror / Demen-
tia '55
Mesa of Lost Women '52

Rick Rossovich
Telling You '98
Black Scorpion '95
Navy SEALS [MGM] '90
Roxanne '87

Carlo Rota
32 Short Films about Glenn
Gould '93

Andrea Roth
The Stepdaughter '00

Cecilia Roth
All About My Mother '99

Gene Roth
Attack of the Giant Leeches
'59
She Demons '58

Tim Roth
Lucky Numbers '00
The Million Dollar Hotel '99
Hoodlum '96
The Perfect Husband '92
The Cook, the Thief, His Wife
& Her Lover '90

John Rothman
Gettysburg '93

Cynthia Rothrock
Lady Dragon '92
China O'Brien '88
The Millionaire's Express '86

Richard Roundtree
Antitrust '00
Shaft '00
Once Upon a Time...When We
Were Colored '95
Seven [2 SE] '95
Bloodfist 3: Forced to Fight
'92
Shaft in Africa '73
Shaft's Big Score '72

Mickey Rourke
Animal Factory '00
Get Carter '00
Fall Time '94
Harley Davidson and the
Marlboro Man '91
The Pope of Greenwich Vil-
lage '84

Deborah Roush
Assault of the Party Nerds
'89

Mireille Roussel
The New Eve '98

Jordan Routledge
East Is East '99

Kelly Rowan
187 '97

Brad Rowe
The '70s '00
Body Shots '99
Stonebrook '98

Earl Rowe
The Blob '58

Michael J. Rowe
Hard Eight '96

Nicholas Rowe
Sharpe's Enemy '94

Victoria Rowell
Barb Wire '96

Oscar Rowland
Bats '99

Rodney Rowland
The 6th Day '00

Gena Rowlands
She's So Lovely '97
Another Woman '88
Opening Night '77
A Woman under the Influence
'74

Polly Rowles
Power '86

Richard Roxburgh
Mission: Impossible 2 '00
The Last September '99
Billy's Holiday '95

Pat Royale
Reefer Madness '38

Christiane Royce
Dr. Frankenstein's Castle of
Freaks '74

Selena Royle
Robot Monster '53

Dominique Rozan
La Guerre Est Finie '66

Jan Rubes
Never Too Late '98

Jennifer Rubin
Deal of a Lifetime '99
Kisses in the Dark '97
Plump Fiction '97
The Crush '93
A Woman, Her Men and Her
Futon '92

Daphne Rubin-Vega
Flawless '99

Frania Rubinek
Liberty Heights '99

Garwin Sanford
Get Carter '00

Bernard L. Sankett
Bad Girls Go to Hell / Another Day, Another Man '65

Kathryn Sannella
The Bed You Sleep In '93

Shiro Sano
Godzilla 2000 '99

Ray Santiago
Girlfight '99

Ruben Santiago-Hudson
Shaft '00

Reni Santoni
28 Days [SE] '00
Dead Men Don't Wear Plaid '82

Joe Santos
Fear City '85
Shaft's Big Score '72

Margarita Sanz
Midaq Alley '95

Peter Sapienza
Don't Mess with My Sister! '85

Mia Sara
The Pompatus of Love '95

Barbara Sarafian
8 1/2 Women '99

Richard Sarafian
Gotti '96

Chris Sarandon
Race Against Time '00
Let the Devil Wear Black '99
The Nightmare before Christmas [2 SE] '93 (V)
The Princess Bride '87
Fright Night '85
The Sentinel '76

Susan Sarandon
Joe Gould's Secret '00
Rugrats in Paris: The Movie '00 (V)
The Cradle Will Rock '99
Earthly Possessions '99
Illuminata '98
James and the Giant Peach '96 (V)
Dead Man Walking '95
Little Women [2 SE] '94
Bob Roberts [SE] '92
The Rocky Horror Picture Show '75

Dick Sargent
Private Navy of Sgt. O'Farrell '68
That Touch of Mink '62

Michael Sarrazin
For Pete's Sake '74
The Groundstar Conspiracy '72

Gailard Sartain
The Replacements '00
Getting Even with Dad '94
Mississippi Burning [MGM] '88
The Hollywood Knights '80

Jamel Sassi
Honey & Ashes '96

Catya Sassoon
Bloodfist 4: Die Trying '92
Tuff Turf '85

Ines Sastre
Beyond the Clouds '95

Tura Satana
The Astro-Zombies '67

Paul Satterfield
Creepshow 2 '87

Gary Sauer
The Unbelievable Truth '90

Ann Savage
Detour '46

Fred Savage
The Princess Bride '87

John Savage
The Jack Bull '99
One Good Turn '95
Carnosaur 2 '94
The Godfather, Part 3 '90
Do the Right Thing [2] '89
Salvador [SE] '86

Martin Savage
Topsy Turvy '99

Tracie Savage
Friday the 13th, Part 3 '82

George Savalas
Kelly's Heroes '70

Telly Savalas
Pancho Villa '72
Kelly's Heroes '70
The Greatest Story Ever Told [SE] '65
Birdman of Alcatraz '62

John Savident
Mountains of the Moon '90

Tom Savini
From Dusk Till Dawn [2 CS] '95
Creepshow 2 '87
Knightriders '81
Martin '77

Camille Saviola
Stuart Saves His Family '94

Devon Sawa
Final Destination '00
Idle Hands '99
Around the Fire '98

Julia Sawalha
Chicken Run '00 (V)

Toni Sawyer
My Life '93

John Saxon
Final Payback '99
From Dusk Till Dawn [2 CS] '95
Animal Instincts '92
My Mom's a Werewolf '89
Aftershock '88
Tenebre '82
Battle Beyond the Stars '80
Black Christmas '75
The Girl Who Knew Too Much '63

Rolf Saxon
The Canterville Ghost '98

John Sayles
Girlfight '99
Eight Men Out '88
Something Wild '86

Raphael Sbarge
Carnosaur '93

Greta Scacchi
Cotton Mary '99
The Serpent's Kiss '97

Jack Scalia
Kill Shot '01
Chained Heat 3: Hell Mountain '98
Under Oath '97
Fear City '85

Carlo Scandiuzzi
Darkdrive '98
Killing Zoe '94

Johnathan Scarfe
White Lies '98

Hunt Scarritt
Stormswept '95

Diana Scarwid
Dirty Pictures '00
What Lies Beneath '00

Johnathon Schaech
Caracara '00
The Brutal Truth '99
Splendor '99

Joshua Schaefer
No Dessert Dad, 'Til You Mow the Lawn '94

Eric Schaeffer
If Lucy Fell '95

Natalie Schafer
Wonder Man '45

William Schallert
House Party 2: The Pajama Jam '91
Death Sentence '74
The Man from Planet X '51

Tom Schanley
Footsteps '98

Karl Schanzer
Dementia 13 '63

Florence Schauffler
Pumpkinhead '88

Ann Schedeen
Embryo '76

Staffan Scheja
Edvard Grieg: What Price Immortality? '00

Roy Scheider
The Myth of Fingerprints '97
Somebody Has to Shoot the Picture '90
Jaws [CE] '75

August Schellenberg
Black Robe '91

Richard Schenkman
October 22 '98

Melinda Scherwinski
Seamless '00

Vincent Schiavelli
Three Strikes '00
Milo '98
Back to Back '96
Ghost '90
Fast Times at Ridgemont High '82

Richard Schiff
Gun Shy '00
Lucky Numbers '00
Whatever It Takes '00
Crazy in Alabama '99
The Lost World: Jurassic Park 2 [CE] '97

Claudia Schiffer
In Pursuit '00
Black and White '99

Joseph Schildkraut
The Garden of Allah '36

Gus Schilling
The Lady from Shanghai '48

Katherine Schlesinger
Northanger Abbey '87

Niels Bruno Schmidt
School's Out '99

Christianne Schmidtmer
The Big Doll House '71

David Schneider
Comic Act '00

John Schneider
Snow Day '00

Rob Schneider
Little Nicky '00
Deuce Bigalow: Male Gigolo '99

G.H. Schnell
Nosferatu [2] '22

Michael Schoeffling
Longtime Companion '90
Mermaids '90

Andrew Schofield
Three Businessmen '99
Sid & Nancy [MGM] '86

David Schofield
Gladiator '00

Kyra Schon
Night of the Living Dead [Madacy] '68
Night of the Living Dead [Elite] '68
Night of the Living Dead [LE Anchor Bay] '68

Emmanuel Schotte
Humanity '99

Max Schreck
Nosferatu [2] '22

Avery Schreiber
Saturday the 14th Strikes Back '88

Liev Schreiber
Hamlet '00
Scream 3 [CS] '00
The Hurricane '99
The Daytrippers '96

Werner Schreyer
Bandits '99

Paul Schrier
Turbo: A Power Rangers Movie '96

Greta Schroder
Nosferatu [2] '22

Steven Schub
Footsteps '98

John Schuck
My Mom's a Werewolf '89
The New Adventures of Pippi Longstocking '88

Peter Schuck
Defending Your Life '91

Matt Schue
Femalien '96

Amanda Schull
Center Stage '00

Rebecca Schull
My Life '93

Constance Schulman
Sweet and Lowdown '99

Albert Schultz
White Lies '98

Brian Schulz
Thou Shalt Not Kill . . . Except '85

Matt Schulze
Dementia '98

Paul Schulze
Drowning Mona '00
Grind '96

Scott Schwartz
Bridge of Dragons '99

Arnold Schwarzenegger
The 6th Day '00
Terminator 2: Judgment Day [2 SE] '91
Predator [20th Century Fox] '87
Conan the Barbarian [2 CE] '82
Hercules in New York '70

Eric Schweig
The Last of the Mohicans '92

David Schwimmer
It's the Rage '99
Picking Up the Pieces '99
The Pallbearer '95

Rusty Schwimmer
The Perfect Storm '00
Lone Justice 3: Showdown at Plum Creek '96
Lone Justice 2 '93

Hanna Schygulla
Delta Force '86
Whity '70

Annabella Sciorra
Asteroid '97
Mr. Wonderful '93
Internal Affairs '90

Paul Scofield
Henry V '89
A Man for All Seasons '66

Martin Scorsese
American Cinema: 100 Years of Filmmaking '94 (N)
Search and Destroy '94

Nicolette Scorsese
Boxing Helena '93

Izabela Scorupco
Vertical Limit '00

Alex Scott
The Asphyx '72
The Abominable Dr. Phibes '71

Campbell Scott
The Daytrippers '96
Longtime Companion '90

Dougray Scott
Mission: Impossible 2 '00

Eileen Scott
Teenage Gang Debs / Teenage Strangler '66

George C. Scott
Malice [MGM] '93
The Rescuers Down Under '90 (V)
The Changeling '80
The Prince and the Pauper '78
Dr. Strangelove, or: How I Learned to Stop Worrying and Love the Bomb [2 SE] '64
Anatomy of a Murder '59

Imogen Millais Scott
Salome's Last Dance '88

Keith Scott
The Adventures of Rocky & Bullwinkle '00 (V)

Ken Scott
Fantastic Voyage '66

Kimberly Scott
Bellyfruit '99

Lizabeth Scott
The Strange Love of Martha Ivers '46

Margaretta Scott
Things to Come '36

Martha Scott
Ben-Hur '59
Our Town '40

Randolph Scott
Abilene Town '46
Captain Kidd '45
Gung Ho! '43

Sarah Scott
The Horrible Dr. Bones '00

Cybill Shepherd
Alice '90
The Last Picture Show [DC]
'71

Jack Shepherd
Wonderland '99

John Shepherd
Banzai Runner '86

Simon Shepherd
Henry V '89

Suzanne Shepherd
Lolita '97

Delia Sheppard
Animal Instincts '92
Secret Games '92

**William Morgan
Sheppard**
Gettysburg '93

Ann Sheridan
They Made Me a Criminal '39

Dave Sheridan
Scary Movie '00

Jamey Sheridan
The Cradle Will Rock '99
Let the Devil Wear Black '99

Jim Sheridan
Moll Flanders [MGM] '96

Susan Sheridan
The Black Cauldron '85 (V)

Robin Sherwood
Tourist Trap '79

Arthur Shields
How Green Was My Valley '41

Bobby Shields
Varietease '54

Brooke Shields
Black and White '99

Koji Shigaragi
Good Morning '59

Shogo Shimada
Tora! Tora! Tora! [2 SE] '70

Masahiko Shimazu
Good Morning '59

Jenny Shimizu
Foxfire '96

Sab Shimono
Paradise Road '97
Suture '93

Takashi Shimura
Kwaidan '64

Sofia Shinas
Dilemma '97

Fui-On Shing
The Killer [Winstar] '90

Sue Shiomi
Dragon Princess '81

Nell Shipman
Something New '20
Back to God's Country /
Something New '19

Kayoko Shiraishi
Female Convict Scorpion—
Jailhouse 41 '72

Minami Shirakawa
Tokyo Raiders '00

Yasuyo Shirashima
Weather Woman '99

Talia Shire
The Godfather, Part 3 '90
Rocky [SE] '76
The Godfather, Part 2 '74
The Godfather DVD Collection
'72

Kai Shishido
Remembering the Cosmos
Flower '99

Craig Shoemaker
The Love Master '97

Dan Shor
Mesmerized '84

Dinah Shore
Fun & Fancy Free '47 (N)
Till the Clouds Roll By '46

Pauly Shore
The Bogus Witch Project '00

Dorothy Short
Reefer Madness '38
Assassin of Youth '35

Martin Short
Father of the Bride Part II '95
The Pebble and the Penguin
'94 (V)

Ken Shorter
Dragonheart: A New Begin-
ning '00

Grant Show
A Woman, Her Men and Her
Futon '92

**Max (Casey Adams)
Showalter**
Bus Stop '56
The Indestructible Man / The
Amazing Transparent Man
'56

John Shrapnel
Gladiator '00

Qi Shu
Gorgeous '99
Man Called Hero '99

Elisabeth Shue
The Hollow Man [SE] '00
Blind Justice '94
The Karate Kid '84

Richard B. Shull
Splash '84
Cockfighter '74

Tan Shuzhen
From Mao to Mozart: Isaac
Stern in China '80 (N)

Josephine Siao
The Legend '93

Alexander Siddig
Vertical Limit '00

Sylvia Sidney
Damien: Omen 2 '78
Blood on the Sun '45
Street Scene '31

James Sie
Strawberry Fields '97

Maria Sieber
Scarlet Empress '34

Jim Siedow
Texas Chainsaw Massacre: A
Family Portrait '90
The Texas Chainsaw Mas-
sacre 2 '86

Casey Siemaszko
The Crew '00
Black Scorpion '95
Stand by Me [2 SE] '86
Class '83

Nina Siemaszko
The Long Way Home '97 (N)
Tucker: The Man and His
Dream '88

Beanie Sigel
Backstage '00

Catherine Siggins
Robert Louis Stevenson's
The Game of Death '99

Tom Signorelli
Kelly's Heroes '70

Lung Sihung
Crouching Tiger, Hidden Dragon '00

James B. Sikking
In Pursuit of Honor '95

Joe Sikora
The Watcher '00

Tusse Silberg
Citizen X '95

Karen Sillas
Sour Grapes '98

Henry Silva
Backlash '99
Ghost Dog: The Way of the
Samurai '99
Lust in the Dust '85

Maria Silva
The Awful Dr. Orlof '62

Frank Silvano
Double Agent 73 '80

Leonor Silveira
Party '96

Joe Silver
Rabid '77

Ron Silver
Cutaway '00
Black & White '99
Semi-Tough '77

Frank Silvera
Killer's Kiss '55
The Fighter '52

Marc Silverberg
Assault of the Party Nerds
'89

Alicia Silverstone
Love's Labour's Lost '00
Hideaway '94
The Crush '93

Ben Silverstone
Lolita '97

Alastair Sim
A Christmas Carol '51

Jon Simanton
The Creeps '97
Turbo: A Power Rangers
Movie '96

Anthony Simcoe
Farscape, Vol. 3 '01

John Simm
Human Traffic '99
Wonderland '99

Gene Simmons
Runaway '84

Jean Simmons
Sparacus [Criterion] '60
The Big Country '58
Guys and Dolls '55
Hamlet '48
Black Narcissus '47

J.K. Simmons
The Cider House Rules '99
For Love of the Game '99

Peter Simmons
Best of the Best 3: No Turn-
ing Back / Best of the
Best: Without Warning '95

Venera Simmons
Dead Waters '94

Hilda Simms
The Joe Louis Story '53

Christopher Simon
The Delivery '99

Gunther Simon
First Spaceship on Venus '60

Gwenaelle Simon
A Summer's Tale '96

Robert F. Simon
The Man Who Shot Liberty
Valance '62

Tania Simon
Peach / A Bitter Song '95

Jimmi Simpson
Loser '00

John Simpson
Night of the Living Dead
[Madacy] '68
Night of the Living Dead
[Elite] '68
Night of the Living Dead [LE
Anchor Bay] '68

O.J. Simpson
Naked Gun 33 1/3: The Final
Insult '94
Naked Gun 2 1/2: The Smell
of Fear '91
The Naked Gun: From the
Files of Police Squad '88
The Cassandra Crossing '76

Russell Simpson
The Horse Soldiers '59

Joan Sims
The Last of the Blonde Bombshells '00

Frank Sinatra
Pal Joey '57
Guys and Dolls '55
Take Me Out to the Ball
Game '49
Till the Clouds Roll By '46

Nancy Sinatra
The Wild Angels '66

Sinbad
Coneheads '93
Necessary Roughness '91

Gordon John Sinclair
The Brylcreem Boys '96

Sandy Sinclair
Scum of the Earth '63

Donald Sinden
The Canterville Ghost '98

Ngai Sing
Jet Li's The Enforcer [Buena
Vista] '95
The Bodyguard from Beijing
'94
The Defender '94

Marc Singer
Body Chemistry '90

Gary Sinise
Mission to Mars '00
Reindeer Games '00
It's the Rage '99

Dean Sipling
I, Zombie '99

Peter Siragusa
Dinosaur [CE] '00 (V)

Jamie-Lynn Sisler
The Sopranos: The Complete
First Season '00

Vera Sisson
The Married Virgin '18

Jeremy Sisto
Jesus '00
Moonlight and Valentino '95
Hideaway '94
Grand Canyon '91

Chin Siu Ho
Twin Warriors '93

Frank Sivero
The Godfather, Part 2 '74

Eva Six
Beach Party '63

Tom Sizemore
Red Planet '00
Bringing Out the Dead '99
Play It to the Bone '99
The Florentine '98
Natural Born Killers [DC] '94
Passenger 57 '92
Harley Davidson and the
Marlboro Man '91
Born on the Fourth of July [2]
'89

Jimmie F. Skaggs
Puppet Master '89

Lilia Skala
House of Games '87
Lilies of the Field '63

Stellan Skarsgard
Time Code '00
Breaking the Waves '95

Jackie Skarvellis
The Body Beneath '70

Brigitte Skay
Four Times That Night '69

Tom Skerritt
Aftershock: Earthquake in
New York '99
Knight Moves '93
Steel Magnolias '89
Dead Zone '83
Cheech and Chong's Up in
Smoke '79
Ice Castles '79

Carole Skinner
Napoleon '96 (V)

Alison Skipworth
Tonight or Never '31

Espen Skjonberg
The Last Lieutenant '94

Irene Skobline
Coup de Torchon '81

Azura Skye
28 Days [SE] '00
Dementia '98

Ione Skye
Went to Coney Island on a
Mission from God...Be
Back by Five '98
A Night in the Life of Jimmy
Reardon '88
River's Edge '87

Tristen Skylar
Book of Shadows: Blair Witch
2 '00

Christian Slater
The Contender '00
Murder in the First '95
Untamed Heart '93
Tucker: The Man and His
Dream '88

Helen Slater
The Long Way Home '97 (N)
City Slickers '91
Supergirl '84

Lance Slaughter
Gladiator '92

Victor Slezak
Lost Souls '00

Walter Slezak
The Inspector General '49

Grace Slick
Gimme Shelter '70

Helene Stanley
The Snows of Kilimanjaro '52

Kim Stanley
Frances '82

Claire Stansfield
Darkdrive '98
Drop Zone '94

Andrew Stanton
Toy Story 2 '99 (V)

Harry Dean Stanton
The Straight Story '99
She's So Lovely '97
Blue Tiger '94
The Last Temptation of Christ '88
Repo Man '83
Escape from New York '81
Rancho Deluxe '75
Cockfighter '74
The Godfather, Part 2 '74
Dillinger '73
Kelly's Heroes '70
Ride in the Whirlwind '66

Robert Stanton
Next Stop, Wonderland '98
Bob Roberts [SE] '92

Barbara Stanwyck
The Strange Love of Martha Ivers '46
Meet John Doe [Image] '41

Jean Stapleton
Pocahontas 2: Journey to a New World '98 (V)

Maureen Stapleton
Interiors '78

Jo Jo Starbuck
The Cutting Edge '92

Don Stark
Switchblade Sisters '75

Graham Stark
Alfie '66

Jonathan Stark
Fright Night '85

Koo Stark
The Rocky Horror Picture Show '75

Beau Starr
Mercy '00
Hoodlum '96
Halloween 5: The Revenge of Michael Myers '89

Blaze Starr
Blaze Starr Goes Nudist '63

Dave Starr
Teaserama '55

Fredro Starr
Save the Last Dance '01
Light It Up '99

Marlene Starr
Bad Girls Go to Hell / Another Day, Another Man '65

Mike Starr
Hoodlum '96
Two If by Sea '95

Ringo Starr
Sextette '78
That'll Be the Day '73
Candy '68

Jason Statham
Lock, Stock and 2 Smoking Barrels '98

Imelda Staunton
Chicken Run '00 (V)
Citizen X '95

Rick Stear
Went to Coney Island on a Mission from God...Be Back by Five '98

Michael Stearns
Battle for the Planet of the Apes '73

Tim Steed
Lord Edgeware Dies '99

Barbara Steele
The Pit and the Pendulum '61

Bob Steele
Giant from the Unknown '58

Karen Steele
Marty '55

Paprika Steen
Mifune '99

Mary Steenburgen
Noah's Ark '99

Benito Stefanelli
Battle of the Amazons '74

Leslie Stefanson
Beautiful '00
Delivered '98

Anthony Steffen
Escape from Hell '89

Bernice Stegers
City of Women '81
Macabre '80

Rod Steiger
Crazy in Alabama '99
The Hurricane '99
In Pursuit of Honor '95
The Amityville Horror '79
In the Heat of the Night '67

Ben Stein
Planes, Trains & Automobiles '87

Saul Stein
Grind '96

David Steinberg
The End '78

John Steiner
Tenebre '82

Angel Stephens
Because of You '95

Harvey Stephens
The Omen [SE] '76

Heather Stephens
Blue Ridge Fall '99

Robert Stephens
Henry V '89
The Asphyx '72

Toby Stephens
Onegin '99

Robert Sterling
Voyage to the Bottom of the Sea / Fantastic Voyage '61

Tisha Sterling
Village of the Giants '65

Daniel Stern
City Slickers '91
C.H.U.D. '84

Isaac Stern
From Mao to Mozart: Isaac Stern in China '80

James D. Stern
Rugrats in Paris: The Movie '00 (V)

Frances Sternhagen
Misery '90
Communion [CE] '89

Blake Steury
Nice Guys Sleep Alone '99

Jean-François Stevenin
Small Change '76

Andrew Stevens
Body Chemistry 4: Full Exposure '95
Body Chemistry 3: Point of Seduction '93
Day of the Animals '77

Brinke Stevens
Sideshow '00
The Kid with the X-Ray Eyes '99
Mommy [SE] '95
Slumber Party Massacre '82

Connie Stevens
James Dean: Live Fast, Die Young '97
Tapeheads '89
The Grissom Gang '71

Fisher Stevens
The Tic Code '99

K.T. Stevens
Missile to the Moon '59

Onslow Stevens
Angel on My Shoulder '46

Robert Stevens
Cecil B. Demented '00

Ruthelma Stevens
Scarlet Empress '34

Stella Stevens
Invisible Mom '96
Body Chemistry 4: Full Exposure '95
The Nutty Professor '63

Cynthia Stevenson
Air Bud 2: Golden Receiver '98

Venetia Stevenson
Horror Hotel '60

Alexandra Stewart
Son of Gascogne '95

French Stewart
CinderElmo '00
Love Stinks '99

Gregory Stewart
Thug Life '00

Jackie Stewart
Height of the Sky '99

James Stewart
The Man Who Shot Liberty Valance '62
Anatomy of a Murder '59
The Man Who Knew Too Much '56
The Man from Laramie '55
Rear Window '54
Harvey '50
Rope '48
Pot o' Gold '41

Kate McGregor Stewart
Father of the Bride Part II '95

Malcolm Stewart
Screwed '00

Mel Stewart
Bride of Re-Animator '89

Patrick Stewart
X-Men '00
A Christmas Carol '99
I, Claudius '91

Paul Stewart
Opening Night '77
How to Commit Marriage '69
Kiss Me Deadly '55
The Joe Louis Story '53

Ross Stewart
Cyberotica '00

Sam Stewart
Another Day, Another Man '66
Bad Girls Go to Hell / Another Day, Another Man '65

Susan Stewart
Mantis in Lace '68

Yvonne Stewart
Satan's Sadists '69

Ethan Stiefel
Center Stage '00

David Ogden Stiers
Pocahontas 2: Journey to a New World '98 (V)
Beauty and the Beast: The Enchanted Christmas '97 (V)
Pocahontas '95 (V)
Shadows and Fog '92
Another Woman '88

Julia Stiles
Save the Last Dance '01
Down to You '00
Hamlet '00

Robin Stille
Slumber Party Massacre '82

Ben Stiller
Keeping the Faith '00
Meet the Parents '00
Black and White '99
If Lucy Fell '95

Jerry Stiller
My 5 Wives '00
The Taking of Pelham One Two Three '74

Stephen Stills
Gimme Shelter '70

Sting
Lock, Stock and 2 Smoking Barrels '98
Plenty '85

Rachael Stirling
In the Beginning... '00

Brian Stirner
All Creatures Great and Small '74

Nigel Stock
The Lion in Winter '68

Laura Stockman
Bloodfist 3: Forced to Fight '92

Dean Stockwell
In Pursuit '00
Restraining Order '99
Chasers '94
Married to the Mob '88
Tucker: The Man and His Dream '88
Banzai Runner '86
Blue Velvet '86

John Stockwell
Losin' It '83

Karl Stoeber
Gruesome Twosome '67

Austin Stoker
Sheba, Baby '75
Battle for the Planet of the Apes '73

Mink Stole
Cecil B. Demented '00
Shriek If You Know What I Did Last Friday the 13th '00
But I'm a Cheerleader '99

Fred Stoller
Downhill Willie '96

Eric Stoltz
House of Mirth '00
The Passion of Ayn Rand '99
Fluke '95

Killing Zoe '94
Little Women [2 SE] '94
The Fly 2 '89
Sister, Sister '87
Fast Times at Ridgemont High '82

Winston Stona
The Harder They Come '72

Bobby Stone
Ghosts on the Loose '43

Christopher Stone
Cujo '83

Ezra Stone
The Munsters' Revenge '81

George E. Stone
42nd Street '33
The Vampire Bat '32

Harold J. Stone
The McCullochs '75
X: The Man with X-Ray Eyes '63

Lewis Stone
The Lost World [Image] '25

Michael Stone
Bloody Murder '99

Oliver Stone
American Cinema: 100 Years of Filmmaking '94 (N)
Born on the Fourth of July [2] '89
Wall Street '87
Platoon [2 SE] '86

Sharon Stone
Beautiful Joe '00
If These Walls Could Talk 2 '00
Picking Up the Pieces '99
Simpatico '99
Diabolique '96
Blood and Sand '89

Pamela Stonebrook
Saturday the 14th Strikes Back '88

Sherri Stoner
Reform School Girls '86

June Storey
The Strange Woman '46

Adam Storke
Mystic Pizza '88

Tempest Storm
Teaserama '55

Peter Stormare
Circus '00
Dancer in the Dark '99
The Million Dollar Hotel '99
The Lost World: Jurassic Park 2 [CE] '97

Ken Stott
Fever Pitch '96

Madeleine Stowe
The Last of the Mohicans '92

Michael Stoyanov
Restaurant '98

Henry Stozier
The Curve '97

Beatrice Straight
Power '86

Clarence Straight
Abbott and Costello Meet Frankenstein '48

Julie Strain
Heavy Metal 2000 [SE] '00 (V)
The Rowdy Girls '00
Battle Queen 2020 '99
Lethal Seduction '97
Midnight Confessions '95

Quentin Tarantino
Little Nicky '00
Kisses in the Dark '97
From Dusk Till Dawn [2 CS] '95
American Cinema: 100 Years of Filmmaking '94 (N)

Enzo Tarascio
Dead Are Alive '72

Rene Tardif
National Lampoon's Golf Punks '99

Emil Tarding
Mifune '99

Tom Tarpey
Lost in America '85

Chris Tashima
Strawberry Fields '97

Lincoln Tate
Battle of the Amazons '74

Reginald Tate
Immortal Battalion '44

Jacques Tati
Mon Oncle '58
Mr. Hulot's Holiday '53

Jeanne Tatum
The Astounding She-Monster '58

Vic Tayback
All Dogs Go to Heaven '89 (V)

Benedict Taylor
The Far Pavilions '84

Charles Taylor
Once Upon a Time...When We Were Colored '95

Christine Taylor
Kiss Toledo Goodbye '00

Don Taylor
Father's Little Dividend '51

Dub Taylor
Support Your Local Gunfighter '71

Elizabeth Taylor
The Mirror Crack'd '80
The Taming of the Shrew '67
Cleopatra '63
Butterfield 8 '60
Suddenly, Last Summer '59
The Last Time I Saw Paris '54
Father's Little Dividend '51
Life with Father '47

Estelle Taylor
Street Scene '31

Forrest Taylor
Riders of Destiny / Star Packer '33

Frank Hoyt Taylor
A Lesson Before Dying '99

Holland Taylor
Keeping the Faith '00
Next Stop, Wonderland '98
Alice '90
She's Having a Baby '88

Jack Taylor
The Ninth Gate '99
Female Vampire '73

Jackie Taylor
Satan's Sadists '69

Kent Taylor
I Spit on Your Corpse '74
Angels' Wild Women '72
Blood of Ghastly Horror '72
Satan's Sadists '69

Lili Taylor
High Fidelity '00
Kicked in the Head '97

I Shot Andy Warhol '96
Rudy [SE] '93
Mystic Pizza '88

Martha Taylor
Manhattan Baby '82

Meshach Taylor
The Secret of NIMH 2 '98 (V)
House of Games '87
Damien: Omen 2 '78

Mick Taylor
Gimme Shelter '70

Noah Taylor
Almost Famous '00

Regina Taylor
A Family Thing '96

Robert Taylor
Vertical Limit '00

Rod Taylor
The Fantasy Film Worlds of George Pal '86
The Time Machine '60

Troy Taylor
The St. Francisville Experiment '00

Vanessa Taylor
Femalien 2 '98
Femalien '96

Wally Taylor
Shaft's Big Score '72

Leigh Taylor-Young
The Jagged Edge '85

Marshall Teague
The Shadow Riders '82

Owen Teale
Wilderness '96

Michele Tebow
Mistress of Seduction '00

Sandor Tecsi
Angel Blue '97

Paolo Tedesco
Battle of the Amazons '74

Jill Teed
Mission to Mars '00

Maureen Teefy
Supergirl '84

Aaron Teich
Darkroom '90

Claudia Teixeira
God's Comedy '95

Manuel Tejada
Cut Throats Nine '72

Olive Tell
Scarlet Empress '34

Rut Tellefsen
The Last Lieutenant '94

Sybil Temchen
Body Shots '99
Nice Guys Sleep Alone '99
The Passion of Ayn Rand '99
Restaurant '98
Floating '97

Shirley Temple
AFI's 100 Years, 100 Stars '99 (N)
The Little Princess '39

David Tennant
The Last September '99

Victoria Tennant
Flowers in the Attic '87
Inseminoid '80

Jon Tenney
Homegrown '97

Julius Tennon
Lone Justice 2 '93

Johanna Ter Steege
Paradise Road '97

Susumu Terajima
After Life '98
Fireworks '97

Lee Tergesen
Shaft '00

Studs Terkel
Eight Men Out '88

Ken Terrell
The Brain from Planet Arous '57
The Indestructible Man / The Amazing Transparent Man '56

Malcolm Terris
The Murder of Roger Ackroyd '99

Carl Terry
The Firing Line '91

John Terry
In Country '89

Kim Terry
Slugs '87

Nigel Terry
The Lion in Winter '68

Paul Terry
James and the Giant Peach '96 (V)

Peter Terry
The Dead Next Door '89

Phillip Terry
The Lost Weekend '45

Sheila Terry
Lawless Frontier / Randy Rides Alone '35

Terry-Thomas
Robin Hood '73 (V)
Doctor Phibes Rises Again '72
The Abominable Dr. Phibes '71
Munster, Go Home! '66
The Mouse on the Moon '62
Tom Thumb '58

Robert Tessier
No Safe Haven '87

Fabio Teste
Iguana '89

Todd Tevlin
Ice from the Sun '00

Tia Texada
Bait '00

Moa Thai
The Bloody Pit of Horror '65

Eric Thal
Snow Falling on Cedars '99
Six Degrees of Separation '93

Torin Thatcher
The Snows of Kilimanjaro '52

Phyllis Thaxter
Superman: The Movie '78

Brynn Thayer
The Tracker '88

Lorna Thayer
Five Easy Pieces '70

Michael Thayer
Ilsa, Harem Keeper of the Oil Sheiks '76

Rosemary Theby
W.C. Fields 6 Short Films '33

Marie Theisen
The Other Side of Sunday '96

Serge Theriault
The Boys '97

Charlize Theron
The Legend of Bagger Vance '00
Men of Honor '00
Reindeer Games '00
The Yards '00
The Cider House Rules '99

Justin Theroux
The Broken Hearts Club '00
American Psycho '99

Ernest Thesiger
A Christmas Carol '51

David Thewlis
James and the Giant Peach '96 (V)

Sean Thibodeau
The Ladies Man '00

Raymond Thiery
Venus in Furs '94

Tiffani-Amber Thiessen
The Ladies Man '00
Shriek If You Know What I Did Last Friday the 13th '00
Love Stinks '99

Lynne Thigpen
Shaft '00
Bicentennial Man '99

Chief Ted Thin Elk
Thunderheart '92

Thinline
Dope Case Pending '00

Betty Thomas
Jackson County Jail '76

Dave Thomas
Coneheads '93

Eddie Kaye Thomas
Black and White '99

Henry Thomas
All the Pretty Horses '00
A Good Baby '99
Legends of the Fall [2 SE] '94

Jay Thomas
C.H.U.D. '84

Jeffrey Thomas
Forgotten Silver '96 (N)

Jonathan Taylor Thomas
I'll Be Home for Christmas '98

Marcus Thomas
Drowning Mona '00

Marlo Thomas
Playing Mona Lisa '00
The Real Blonde '97

Michael Thomas
Titanic 2000 '00

Richard Thomas
Wonder Boys '00
Battle Beyond the Stars '80

Sean Patrick Thomas
Save the Last Dance '01

Tamara Craig Thomas
The Curve '97

William Thomas
Solomon and Gaenor '98

Tim Thomerson
The Crimson Code '00
Submerged '00
Cherry 2000 '88
Uncommon Valor '83

Alfred "Rubin" Thompson
Winner Takes All '98

Anna Thompson
Intern '00
I Shot Andy Warhol '96

Bill Thompson
The Aristocats '70 (V)

Brian Thompson
Jason and the Argonauts '00

Emma Thompson
Henry V '89

Fred Dalton Thompson
In the Line of Fire [2 SE] '93
Thunderheart '92
No Way Out '87

Kenan Thompson
The Adventures of Rocky & Bullwinkle '00

Mark Thompson
Deterrence '00

Marshall Thompson
Fiend Without a Face '58

Patsy Ann Thompson
Tomorrow the World '44

Scott Thompson
Loser '00

Shaun Thompson
In God's Hands '98

Shawn Thompson
Bram Stoker's Shadowbuilder '98

Sophie Thompson
Relative Values '99

Ulrich Thomsen
The World Is Not Enough [SE] '99
Angel of the Night '98

Scott Thomson
Fast Times at Ridgemont High '82

Bill Thornbury
Phantasm 4: Oblivion '98

Callie (Calliope) Thorne
Double Parked '00
Homicide: The Movie '00
Whipped '00

Dyanne Thorne
Ilsa, the Wicked Warden '78
Ilsa, Harem Keeper of the Oil Sheiks '76
Wham-Bam, Thank You Spaceman '75
Ilsa, She-Wolf of the SS '74

Billy Bob Thornton
Princess Mononoke '98 (V)
Homegrown '97
Dead Man '95
One False Move '91

David Thornton
She's So Lovely '97

Sven-Ole Thorsen
Gladiator '00

Jean-Yves Thual
The Red Dwarf '99

Ingrid Thulin
The Cassandra Crossing '76
La Guerre Est Finie '66

Bill Thurman
Mountaintop Motel Massacre '86

Dechen Thurman
Hamlet '00

Uma Thurman
Sweet and Lowdown '99

Glynn Turman
Men of Honor '00
Light It Up '99
Race to Freedom: The Story of the Underground Railroad '94
Penitentiary 2 '82
Cooley High '75

Barbara Turner
Monster from Green Hell '58

Debbie Turner
The Sound of Music [Five Star Collection] '65

Guinevere Turner
American Psycho '99
Dogma '99
The Watermelon Woman '97

Hilary Shepard Turner
Turbo: A Power Rangers Movie '96

Ike Turner
Gimme Shelter '70

Janine Turner
Cliffhanger [2 CS] '93
Steel Magnolias '89
Monkey Shines '88

Kathleen Turner
Beautiful '00
Prince of Central Park '00
Stories from My Childhood, Vol. 3 '99 (V)
The Virgin Suicides '99
Stories from My Childhood '98 (V)
The Real Blonde '97
Moonlight and Valentino '95

Stephen Barker Turner
Book of Shadows: Blair Witch 2 '00

Ted Turner
Gettysburg '93

Tina Turner
Tommy '75
Gimme Shelter '70

Ben Turpin
Burlesque on Carmen '16

Aida Turturro
Bringing Out the Dead '99
Illuminata '98

John Turturro
O Brother Where Art Thou? '00
The Cradle Will Rock '99
Illuminata '98
The Source '96
Search and Destroy '94
Mo' Better Blues '90
Do the Right Thing [2] '89
Desperately Seeking Susan '85

Nicholas Turturro
Mo' Better Blues '90

Ali Twaha
An Elephant Called Slowly '69

Shannon Tweed
The Rowdy Girls '00
Body Chemistry 4: Full Exposure '95
The Firing Line '91

Billy Two Rivers
Black Robe '91

Anne Twomey
The Confession '98

Brian Tyler
The Warriors '79

Geri Tyler
Teenage Gang Debs / Teenage Strangler '66

Liv Tyler
Dr. T & the Women '00
Onegin '99
Inventing the Abbotts '97
Empire Records '95

Judy Tylor
My 5 Wives '00

George Tyne
A Walk in the Sun '46

Charles Tyner
Planes, Trains & Automobiles '87
Harold and Maude '71

Susan Tyrrell
Tapeheads '89

Barbara Tyson
Beautiful Joe '00

Cathy Tyson
Mona Lisa '86

Cicely Tyson
Aftershock: Earthquake in New York '99
A Lesson Before Dying '99
Hoodlum '96
The Women of Brewster Place '89
Bustin' Loose '81
A Woman Called Moses '78

Mike Tyson
Black and White '99

Richard Tyson
Battlefield Earth '00
Desert Thunder '99
The Pandora Project '98
Monsoon '97
Two Moon Junction '88

Margaret Tyzack
I, Claudius '91

Asao Uchida
Tora! Tora! Tora! [2 SE] '70

Fabiana Udenio
Bride of Re-Animator '89

Tracey Ullman
Small Time Crooks '00
Plenty '85

Liv Ullmann
Cold Sweat '71

Skeet Ulrich
Ride with the Devil '99

Edward Underdown
Beat the Devil '53

Blair Underwood
Rules of Engagement '00
Soul of the Game '96
Posse '93

Deborah Kara Unger
The Hurricane '99
Sunshine '99
Highlander: The Final Dimension '94

James Urbaniak
Sweet and Lowdown '99

Jun Usami
Tora! Tora! Tora! [2 SE] '70

Peter Ustinov
Evil under the Sun '82
Death on the Nile '78
Robin Hood '73 (V)
Sparacus [Criterion] '60
Immortal Battalion '44

Kenneth Utt
Something Wild '86

Zenzele Uzoma
Cecil B. Demented '00

Brenda Vaccaro
Supergirl '84
Honor Thy Father '73

Dan Vadis
Bronco Billy '80

Dominique Valadie
A Single Girl '96

Serge-Henri Valcke
The Quarry '98

Carlos Valencia
Ratas, Ratones, Rateros '99

Barbara Valentin
Horrors of Spider Island '59

Michael J. Valentine
Diamond Run '00

Scott Valentine
Carnosaur 3: Primal Species '96

Rudolph Valentino
The Married Virgin '18

Riccardo Valle
The Awful Dr. Orlof '62

Amber Valletta
What Lies Beneath '00

Mark Valley
The Next Best Thing '00

Alida Valli
The Cassandra Crossing '76

Rick Vallin
Ghosts on the Loose '43

Raf Vallone
The Godfather, Part 3 '90
Honor Thy Father '73

Vampira
Plan 9 from Outer Space [Passport Video] '56

Jim Van Bebber
Deadbeat at Dawn '88

Ingrid van Bergen
The Vampire Happening '71

Lee Van Cleef
Escape from New York '81
Bad Man's River '72
The Man Who Shot Liberty Valance '62

Jean-Claude Van Damme
Maximum Risk '96
Double Impact '91
Death Warrant '90
Cyborg '89
Black Eagle '88

Monique Van De Ven
Turkish Delight '73

Wim Van Den Brink
Turkish Delight '73

Anne Van Der Ven
Venus in Furs '94

Diana Van Der Vlis
X: The Man with X-Ray Eyes '63

Trish Van Devere
Hollywood Vice Sqaud '86
The Changeling '80

Casper Van Dien
Kill Shot '01
Cutaway '00
Python '00
The Omega Code '99
Thrill Seekers '99
On the Border '98
Tarzan and the Lost City '98
James Dean: Live Fast, Die Young '97

Catherine Van Dien
Thrill Seekers '99

Dick Van Dyke
Mary Poppins [2 SE] '64

Peter Van Eyck
The Thousand Eyes of Dr. Mabuse '60

John Van Eyssen
Quatermass 2 '57
Four Sided Triangle '53

Harry Van Gorkum
Dragonheart: A New Beginning '00
Escape under Pressure '00

Brian Van Holt
Whipped '00

Patrick Van Horn
Ivory Tower '97

Fredja Van Huet
The Delivery '99

Jon Van Ness
Tourist Trap '79

Andre Arend Van Noord
Venus in Furs '94

Dick Van Patten
The New Adventures of Pippi Longstocking '88
The Midnight Hour '86
Beware! The Blob '72

Joyce Van Patten
Monkey Shines '88

Mario Van Peebles
Love Kills '98
Panther '95
Highlander: The Final Dimension '94
Posse '93
Jaws: The Revenge '87
Last Resort '86

Melvin Van Peebles
Love Kills '98
Fist of the North Star '95
Posse '93

Dave Van Ronk
The Ballad of Ramblin' Jack '00

Edward Van Sloan
The Mummy '32

Alan Van Sprang
Steal This Movie! '00

Bert Van Tuyle
Something New '20

Deborah Van Valkenburgh
Mean Guns '97
The Warriors '79

Steve Van Wormer
Groove '00

Philip Van Zandt
Sherlock Holmes and the Secret Weapon '42

Stevie Van Zandt
The Sopranos: The Complete First Season '00

Violet Vanbrugh
Pygmalion '38

Courtney B. Vance
Space Cowboys '00
Panther '95
The Tuskegee Airmen '95
Race to Freedom: The Story of the Underground Railroad '94

Alexandra Vandernoot
The Dinner Game '98

Vanity
DaVinci's War '92

Renata Vanni
The Lady in White '88

Carrie Vanston
Teenage Catgirls in Heat '00

Norma Varden
The Sound of Music [Five Star Collection] '65

Daniel Vargas
The Arena '73

Jacob Vargas
Next Friday [Platinum Series] '00
Traffic '00

Jean Vargas
Slumber Party Massacre '82

Laszlo Vargo
The Rowdy Girls '00

Jim Varney
Toy Story 2 '99 (V)
Toy Story '95 (V)

Michael Vartan
The Next Best Thing '00
The Curve '97
The Myth of Fingerprints '97
The Pallbearer '95

Jimmy Vaughan
The Womaneater '59

Paris Vaughan
Les Miserables '97

Peter Vaughan
Mountains of the Moon '90

Alberta Vaughn
Randy Rides Alone '34

Robert Vaughn
Black Moon Rising '86
Delta Force '86
Superman 3 '83
Battle Beyond the Stars '80
The Bridge at Remagen '69
The Magnificent Seven '60

Vince Vaughn
The Cell '00
The Lost World: Jurassic Park 2 [CE] '97

Emmanuelle Vaugier
My 5 Wives '00

Lyn Vaus
Next Stop, Wonderland '98

Mary Vautin
Cyberotica '00

Ron Vawter
Internal Affairs '90

Claude Vega
Bed and Board '70

Victoria Vega
The Erotic Ghost '00
Girl Explores Girl: The Alien Encounter [CE] '00
Gladiator Eroticus '00
Mistress Frankenstein [CE] '00
The Erotic Witch Project [CE] '99

Conrad Veidt
The Indian Tomb '21

Reginald Vel Johnson
Posse '93

Patricia Velasquez
The Mummy [2 SE] '99
Beowulf '98

Eddie Velez
Under Oath '97
Romero '89

Lauren Velez
Prince of Central Park '00

Maribel Velez
Throw Down '00

The Misfits '61
The Magnificent Seven '60

Katherine Wallach
Kisses in the Dark '97

Roberta Wallach
The Hollywood Knights '80

Deborah Walley
Dr. Goldfoot and the Bikini Machine '66
Beach Blanket Bingo '65

Shani Wallis
The Pebble and the Penguin '94 (N)

Dylan Walsh
Final Voyage '99
Eden '98

Gwynyth Walsh
The Crush '93

Joey Walsh
Hans Christian Andersen [20th Century Fox] '52

J.T. Walsh
Sniper '92
House of Games '87
Power '86

Kay Walsh
The Witches '66

M. Emmet Walsh
Panther '95
The Mighty Quinn '89
Red Scorpion '89
Back to School '86
Missing in Action '84
The Pope of Greenwich Village '84
Escape from the Planet of the Apes '71
Alice's Restaurant '69

Ray Walston
Saturday the 14th Strikes Back '88
Fast Times at Ridgemont High '82
The Apartment '60

Harriet Walter
Onegin '99
Bedrooms and Hallways '98
A Merry War '97

Jessica Walter
Tapeheads '89

Tracey Walter
Drowning Mona '00
Erin Brockovich '00
City Slickers '91
Married to the Mob '88
At Close Range '86
Something Wild '86
Repo Man '83

Julie Walters
Billy Elliot '00

Luana Walters
Shadow of Chinatown '36
Assassin of Youth '35

Melora Walters
Magnolia '99
Hard Eight '96

Susan Walters
Defending Your Life '91

Thorley Walters
The Sign of Four '83
Frankenstein Created Woman '66

Barrie Walton
Gruesome Twosome '67

Bill Walton
Little Nicky '00

Lisa Waltz
Starry Night '99

I (Ai) Wan
Fallen Angel '99

Lau Ching Wan
Running out of Time '99

Sam Wanamaker
Baby Boom '87
Superman 4: The Quest for Peace '87

Zoe Wanamaker
The Magical Legend of the Leprechauns '99

Joey Wang
Painted Skin '93

David Warbeck
The Beyond '82
The Black Cat '81

Patrick Warburton
Buzz Lightyear of Star Command: The Adventure Begins '00 (V)
The Emperor's New Groove [SE] '00 (V)
Scream 3 [CS] '00

B.J. Ward
Scooby-Doo and the Alien Invaders '00 (V)

Burt Ward
Assault of the Party Nerds 2: Heavy Petting Detective '95

Colin Ward
Mother's Boys '94

Fannie Ward
The Cheat '15

Fred Ward
Circus '00
The Crimson Code '00
The Crow: Salvation '00
Full Disclosure '00
Road Trip '00
Naked Gun 33 1/3: The Final Insult '94
Bob Roberts [SE] '92
Thunderheart '92
Uncommon Valor '83
Southern Comfort '81

Lyman Ward
Mikey '92
Sleepwalkers '92
Planes, Trains & Automobiles '87

Maitland Ward
Dish Dogs '98

Megan Ward
Rated X '00

Rachel Ward
Against All Odds '84
Dead Men Don't Wear Plaid '82

Sandy Ward
Cujo '83

Simon Ward
Supergirl '84
The Four Musketeers '75
All Creatures Great and Small '74
Dracula / Strange Case of Dr. Jekyll & Mr. Hyde '73

Susan Ward
The In Crowd '00

Jack Warden
The Replacements '00
Dirty Work '97
September '88
And Justice for All '79
Being There '79
Death on the Nile '78
Brian's Song '71
Donovan's Reef '63
Twelve Angry Men '57

Herta Ware
Dakota '88

Andy Warhol
Andy Warhol '88

David Warner
The Omen [SE] '76
Tom Jones [MGM] '63

H.B. Warner
Topper Returns '41
Bulldog Drummond's Secret Police '39

Jack Warner
A Christmas Carol '51

Malcolm Jamal Warner
Restaurant '98
The Tuskegee Airmen '95
Drop Zone '94

Barry Warren
Frankenstein Created Woman '66

Gene Warren
The Fantasy Film Worlds of George Pal '86

Jennifer Warren
Mutant '84
Ice Castles '79

Jennifer Leigh Warren
Sour Grapes '98

Kiersten Warren
Duets '00
Bicentennial Man '99
Liberty Heights '99

Lesley Ann Warren
Twin Falls Idaho '99
Love Kills '98
Clue '85

James Warring
Bloodfist 2 '90

Don Warrington
Dead of Night '99

Breck Warwick
Satan's Sadists '69

Beverly Washburn
Pit Stop '67

Denzel Washington
Remember the Titans '00
The Hurricane '99
Mo' Better Blues '90
Glory [2 SE] '89
The Mighty Quinn '89
Power '86
A Soldier's Story '84

Don Washington
Ninth Street '98

Isaiah Washington
Romeo Must Die '00
Get On the Bus '96

Jascha Washington
Big Momma's House '00

Kerry Washington
Save the Last Dance '01

Isako Washio
Fist of the North Star '95

Ed Wasser
Stormswept '95

Craig Wasson
Escape under Pressure '00
Velocity Trap '99
The Last Best Sunday '98

Fumio Watanabe
Female Convict Scorpion—Jailhouse 41 '72

Tetsu Watanabe
Fireworks '97

Gillian Iliana Waters
Bamboozled '00

John Waters
Sweet and Lowdown '99
Something Wild '86

Sam Waterston
Crimes & Misdemeanors [MGM] '89
September '88
Interiors '78
Rancho Deluxe '75

Gwen Watford
In This House of Brede '75

Tuc Watkins
The Mummy [2 SE] '99

Deborah Watling
That'll Be the Day '73

Jack Watling
Immortal Battalion '44

Alberta Watson
The Life Before This '99
Gotti '96

David Watson
Beneath the Planet of the Apes '70

Debbie Watson
Munster, Go Home! '66

Emily Watson
Angela's Ashes '99
The Cradle Will Rock '99
Breaking the Waves '95

Harry Watson
W.C. Fields 6 Short Films '33

Kiki Watson
2 G's and a Key '00

Mills Watson
Cujo '83

Minor Watson
The Jackie Robinson Story '50

Richard Wattis
The Abominable Snowman '57
My Son, the Vampire '52

Chanda Watts
Bar-B-Q '00

Charlie Watts
Gimme Shelter '70

Lainie Watts
China O'Brien '88

Naomi Watts
Tank Girl '94

Al Waxman
Critical Care '97
Gotti '96

Damon Wayans
Bamboozled '00
Bulletproof '96
Look Who's Talking, Too '90 (V)
I'm Gonna Git You Sucka '88
Roxanne '87

Keenen Ivory Wayans
Scary Movie '00
I'm Gonna Git You Sucka '88

Kim Wayans
I'm Gonna Git You Sucka '88

Marlon Wayans
Dungeons and Dragons '00
Requiem for a Dream '00
Scary Movie '00

Shawn Wayans
Scary Movie '00

Kristina Wayborn
Octopussy '83

Carol Wayne
I Spy '65

David Wayne
How to Marry a Millionaire '53
Portrait of Jennie '48

John Wayne
The Greatest Story Ever Told [SE] '65
In Harm's Way '65
Sons of Katie Elder '65
Donovan's Reef '63
The Man Who Shot Liberty Valance '62
The Alamo '60
The Horse Soldiers '59
Winds of the Wasteland '36
Dawn Rider / Trail Beyond '35
Lawless Frontier / Randy Rides Alone '35
Lucky Texan '34
Man from Utah / Sagebrush Trail '34
Randy Rides Alone '34
The Star Packer '34
Trail Beyond '34
Riders of Destiny / Star Packer '33
Sagebrush Trail '33
Shadow of the Eagle '32

Keith Wayne
Night of the Living Dead [Madacy] '68
Night of the Living Dead [Elite] '68
Night of the Living Dead [LE Anchor Bay] '68

Patrick Wayne
Sinbad and the Eye of the Tiger '77
Beyond Atlantis '73
The Alamo '60

Trudy Wayne
Teaserama '55

Michael Weatherly
The Substitute 4: Failure Is Not an Option '00
The Colony '98

Carl Weathers
Little Nicky '00
Predator [20th Century Fox] '87
Semi-Tough '77
Rocky [SE] '76
Friday Foster '75

Dennis Weaver
Submerged '00
Touch of Evil [SE] '58

Fritz Weaver
Power '86
Fail-Safe '64

Sigourney Weaver
Galaxy Quest '99
A Map of the World '99
Alien: Resurrection '97
Working Girl '88

Hugo Weaving
Bedrooms and Hallways '98
The Interview '98
The Adventures of Priscilla, Queen of the Desert [MGM] '94

Chloe Webb
She's So Lovely '97
Sid & Nancy [MGM] '86

Danny Webb
Henry V '89

Greg Webb
Puppet Master 2 '90

Richard Webb
Beware! The Blob '72

Mike Wiles
Held Up '00

Bill Wiley
Porky's 2: The Next Day '83

Dianne Wilhite
Gruesome Twosome '67

Kathleen Wilhoite
Drowning Mona '00
Nurse Betty '00
Getting Even with Dad '94

Fiona Wilkes
Stomp Out Loud '98

Elizabeth Wilkinson
A Taste of Blood '67

Tom Wilkinson
The Patriot '00
Essex Boys '99
Ride with the Devil '99
Smilla's Sense of Snow '96

Daniel Will-Harris
Saturday the 14th Strikes
Back '88

Fred Willard
Best in Show '00
Idle Hands '99
Roxanne '87
This Is Spinal Tap [MGM] '84

Charles Willeford
Cockfighter '74

Chad Willet
Outlaw Justice '98

Adam Williams
North by Northwest '59

Barbara Williams
Family of Cops 3 '98
Family of Cops 2: Breach of
Faith '97
Inventing the Abbotts '97

Bill Williams
Son of Paleface '52

Billy Dee Williams
The Ladies Man '00
Fear Runs Silent '99
The Contract '98
Fear City '85
Brian's Song '71

Bob Williams
Teenagers from Outer Space
'59

Caroline Williams
Leprechaun 3 '95
The Texas Chainsaw Mas-
sacre 2 '86

Cindy Williams
The Conversation '74
Beware! The Blob '72

Clarence Williams III
Reindeer Games '00
Hoodlum '96
I'm Gonna Git You Sucka '88

Cynda Williams
The Tie That Binds '95
One False Move '91
Mo' Better Blues '90

Dick Anthony Williams
Edward Scissorhands [SE]
'90
Mo' Better Blues '90
A Woman Called Moses '78

Esther Williams
Take Me Out to the Ball
Game '49

Freedom Williams
Red Shoe Diaries: Four on
the Floor '96

Gareth Williams
The Cell '00

Gregory Alan Williams
In the Line of Fire [2 SE] '93

**Guinn "Big Boy"
Williams**
The Alamo '60

Harland Williams
The Whole Nine Yards '00

Jamie Williams
Rudyard Kipling's the Second
Jungle Book: Mowgli and
Baloo '97

Jay Williams
Little Fugitive '53

JoBeth Williams
Backlash '99
Stories from My Childhood
'98 (V)
Switch '91

Kimberly Williams
Simpatico '99
Father of the Bride Part II '95

Malinda Williams
Uninvited Guest '99
High School High '96

Michelle Williams
If These Walls Could Talk 2
'00
Dick '99

Olivia Williams
Jason and the Argonauts '00

Paul Williams
The Doors [2 SE] '91
Battle for the Planet of the
Apes '73

Peter Williams
The Bridge on the River Kwai
[LE] '57

Rhys Williams
How Green Was My Valley '41

Robin Williams
Bicentennial Man '99
Nine Months '95
Shakes the Clown '92
The Fisher King '91

Sekenia Williams
Nothin' 2 Lose '00

Sixx Williams
Asylum of Terror '98

Treat Williams
The Substitute 4: Failure Is
Not an Option '01
The Eagle Has Landed '77

**Vanessa L(ynne)
Williams**
Shaft '00
Light It Up '99
Hoodlum '96
Harley Davidson and the
Marlboro Man '91

Wade Andrew Williams
Terror Tract '00
K-911 '99

Wendy O. Williams
Reform School Girls '86

Fred Williamson
Submerged '00
From Dusk Till Dawn [2 CS]
'95
Steele's Law '91
Black Caesar '73

Mykelti Williamson
Holiday Heart '00
Soul of the Game '96

Willie D.
Thug Life '00

Noble Willingham
City Slickers '91

Bruce Willis
Disney's The Kid '00
The Whole Nine Yards '00
Breakfast of Champions '98
Look Who's Talking, Too '90
(V)
In Country '89

Matt Willis
A Walk in the Sun '46

Rumer Willis
Striptease '96

Susan Willis
What about Bob? '91

Kevin Willmott
Ninth Street '98

Chill Wills
The Alamo '60

Kimo Wills
The Tao of Steve '00

Douglas Wilmer
Golden Voyage of Sinbad '73

Rod Wilmoth
The Astro-Zombies '67

Ajita Wilson
Escape from Hell '89

Barbara Wilson
Teenage Doll '57

Brian Wilson
Beach Blanket Bingo '65
Beach Party '63

Bridgette Wilson
Beautiful '00
Love Stinks '99
The Real Blonde '97

David Wilson
The Inside Man '84

**Don "The Dragon"
Wilson**
Moving Target '00
Bloodfist 3: Forced to Fight
'92
Bloodfist 4: Die Trying '92
Bloodfist 2 '90
Bloodfist '89
Born on the Fourth of July [2]
'89

Earl Wilson
Beach Blanket Bingo '65

Elizabeth Wilson
The Addams Family '91

Flip Wilson
Pinocchio '76

Harry Wilson
Frankenstein's Daughter '58

Kirk Wilson
Sergio Lapel's Drawing Blood
'99

Kristen Wilson
Dungeons and Dragons '00
Bulletproof '96
The Pompatus of Love '95

Lambert Wilson
The Last September '99

Lisa Marie Wilson
Stalked '99

Lisle Wilson
Sisters '73

Lois Wilson
The Vanishing American '25

Luke Wilson
Charlie's Angels '00
Blue Streak '99
My Dog Skip '99

Mara Wilson
Thomas and the Magic Railroad '00

Marie Wilson
March of the Wooden Sol-
diers '34

Mark Wilson
Hangman '00

Owen C. Wilson
Meet the Parents '00
Shanghai Noon '00
The Minus Man '99
Breakfast of Champions '98

Patty Wilson
Cyberotica '00

Peta Wilson
Mercy '00

Rachel Wilson
Mystery, Alaska '99

Reno Wilson
City of Industry '96

Roger Wilson
Porky's 2: The Next Day '83
Porky's / Porky's 2: The Next
Day '82

Scott Wilson
Way of the Gun '00
The Jack Bull '99
Dead Man Walking '95
The Tracker '88
The Grissom Gang '71

Stuart Wilson
Here on Earth '00
Vertical Limit '00
The Pallisers '74

Teddy Wilson
Kiss Shot '89
Cotton Comes to Harlem '70

Tom Wilson
Mystery of the Necronomicon
'00 (V)

Trey Wilson
Married to the Mob '88

Wendy Dawn Wilson
The Scorpio Factor '90

Brian Wimmer
Tank Girl '94

Camille Winbush
Ghost Dog: The Way of the
Samurai '99

Troy Winbush
The Replacements '00

Barry Winch
Tommy '75

Paul Winchell
The Fox and the Hound '81
(V)
The Aristocats '70 (V)

Jeff Wincott
Battle Queen 2020 '99
Paper Bullets '99

Michael Wincott
Before Night Falls '00
Alien: Resurrection '97
Dead Man '95
The Doors [2 SE] '91
Talk Radio '88

William Windom
She's Having a Baby '88
Planes, Trains & Automobiles
'87
Escape from the Planet of
the Apes '71

Marie Windsor
Cat Women of the Moon '53

Janu Wine
Mantis in Lace '68

Gil Winfield
Fiend Without a Face '58

Paul Winfield
Cliffhanger [2 CS] '93
The Women of Brewster
Place '89
Star Trek 2: The Wrath of
Khan '82
It's Good to Be Alive '74

Oprah Winfrey
The Women of Brewster
Place '89

Debra Winger
Betrayed '88
Terms of Endearment '83
An Officer and a Gentleman
'82

Peter Wingfield
Highlander: Endgame '00

La'Mard J. Wingster
Throw Down '00

Henry Winkler
Down to You '00
Little Nicky '00
The Lords of Flatbush '74

Lucyna Winnicka
First Spaceship on Venus '60

Charles Winninger
Pot o' Gold '41

George Winship
Teenage Gang Debs /
Teenage Strangler '66

Kate Winslet
Quills '00
Holy Smoke '99

George Winslow
Gentlemen Prefer Blondes
'53

Ray Winstone
Love, Honour & Obey '00
Agnes Browne '99
The War Zone '98

Vincent Winter
Gorgo '61

David Winters
Fanatic '82

Jonathan Winters
The Adventures of Rocky &
Bullwinkle '00

Shelley Winters
Delta Force '86
Pete's Dragon '77
Alfie '66
The Greatest Story Ever Told
[SE] '65
The Balcony '63

Sandy Winton
Me Myself I '99

Estelle Winwood
The Misfits '61

Scott Wiper
A Better Way to Die '00

Robert Wisdom
Three Businessmen '99

Ray Wise
Bob Roberts [SE] '92
Swamp Thing '82

Robert Wise
20th Century Fox: The First
50 Years '96
The Fantasy Film Worlds of
George Pal '86

Andreas Wisniewski
The Living Daylights '87

Heather Yoshimura
Strawberry Fields '97

Ken Yoshizawa
Ecstasy of the Angels '72

Aden Young
Sniper '92
Black Robe '91

Alan Young
The Fantasy Film Worlds of
George Pal '86
The Time Machine '60

Billy Jayne Young
The Crew '00

Burt Young
Kicked in the Head '97
She's So Lovely '97
Back to School '86
The Pope of Greenwich Vil-
lage '84
Rocky [SE] '76

Carleton Young
The Man Who Shot Liberty
Valance '62
The Horse Soldiers '59
Reefer Madness '38

Chris Young
Warlock: The Armageddon
'93

Denise Young
The Bone Yard '90

Gig Young
That Touch of Mink '62

Harrison Young
The Adventures of Rocky &
Bullwinkle '00
Velocity '99

Karen Young
Mercy '00
Jaws: The Revenge '87

Loretta Young
The Bishop's Wife [MGM] '47

Mark G. Young
Throw Down '00

Mary Young
The Lost Weekend '45

Melissa Young
Asylum of Terror '98

Polly Ann Young
Man from Utah / Sagebrush
Trail '34

Robert Young
The Second Woman '51

Roland Young
The Great Lover '49
Topper Returns '41

Sean Young
No Way Out '87
Wall Street '87

Henny Youngman
The Gore-Gore Girls '72

Tom Yourk
Teenage Gang Debs /
Teenage Strangler '66

Yousra
Alexandria Again and Forever
'90

Jimmy Wang Yu
Fantasy Mission Force '84

Rongguang Yu
Jet Li's The Enforcer [Buena
Vista] '95

Roger Yuan
Shanghai Noon '00

Corey Yuen
Saviour of the Soul 2 '92

Jimmy Yuill
Love's Labour's Lost '00

Harris Yulin
The Cradle Will Rock '99
The Hurricane '99
The Million Dollar Hotel '99
Stuart Saves His Family '94
Another Woman '88
Fatal Beauty '87

Chow Yun-Fat
Crouching Tiger, Hidden Drag-
on '00
Anna and the King '99
Peace Hotel '95
Hard-Boiled [Winstar] '92
The Killer [Winstar] '90
A Better Tomorrow, Part 2
[Anchor Bay] '88
A Better Tomorrow, Part 1
[Anchor Bay] '86

Will Yun Lee
What's Cooking? '00

Rick Yune
Snow Falling on Cedars '99

Victor Sen Yung
She Demons '58

William Zabka
Back to School '86
The Karate Kid '84

Grace Zabriskie
Gone in 60 Seconds '00
A Family Thing '96
Desert Winds '95
Drop Zone '94
Drugstore Cowboy '89

Maurisia Zach
Working Girls '87

Pia Zadora
Naked Gun 33 1/3: The Final
Insult '94

Eleni Zafirou
A Matter of Dignity '57
Girl in Black '56

Steve Zahn
Hamlet '00

Esti Zakheim
Pick a Card '97

Jerry Zaks
Crimes & Misdemeanors
[MGM] '89

Roxana Zal
Big City Blues '99
Broken Vessels '98
River's Edge '87

Billy Zane
Hendrix '00
Pocahontas 2: Journey to a
New World '98 (V)
Flashfire '94
Posse '93
Sniper '92

Moon Zappa
The Brutal Truth '99
The Boys Next Door '85

Tony Zarindast
Hardcase and Fist '89

Kevin Zegers
Air Bud 3: World Pup '00
MVP: Most Valuable Primate
'00
Komodo '99
Air Bud 2: Golden Receiver
'98
Bram Stoker's Shadowbuilder
'98
Air Bud [2] '97

Renee Zellweger
Nurse Betty '00
Empire Records '95

Michael Zelniker
Bird '88

Anthony Zerbe
Asteroid '97
Steel Dawn '87
Dead Zone '83
The Parallax View '74
They Call Me Mr. Tibbs! '70

Larry Zerner
Friday the 13th, Part 3 '82

Catherine Zeta-Jones
High Fidelity '00
Traffic '00
Catherine Cookson's The Cin-
der Path '94

Stacia Zhivago
Sorority House Massacre 2:
Nighty Nightmare '92

Wang Zhiwen
The Emperor and the Assassin '99

Sun Zhou
The Emperor and the Assassin '99

Janis Zido
The House on Sorority Row
'83

Chip Zien
Breakfast of Champions '98

Bernard Zilinskas
Velocity '99

Efrem Zimbalist Jr.
Batman: Mask of the Phan-
tasm '93 (V)

Stephanie Zimbalist
The Prophet's Game '99

Angela Zimmerly
Ice from the Sun '00

Joey Zimmerman
Mother's Boys '94

Luca Zingaretti
Jesus '00

Veronica Zinny
Macabre '80

Daniel Zirilli
Winner Takes All '98

Hanns Zischler
The Cement Garden '93

Bata Zivojinovic
Pretty Village, Pretty Flame
'96

Zhang Ziyi
Crouching Tiger, Hidden Dragon '00

Claudia Zohner
Edvard Grieg: What Price
Immortality? '00

Jean-Pierre Zola
Mon Oncle '58

Zaldy Zschornack
Black Mama, White Mama
'73

David Zucker
Airplane! '80

Jerry Zucker
Airplane! '80

Ralph Zucker
The Bloody Pit of Horror '65

Daphne Zuniga
The Fly 2 '89

Jose Zuniga
The Crew '00
For Love or Country: The
Arturo Sandoval Story '00
Gun Shy '00
Next Stop, Wonderland '98

Elsa Zylberstein
Portraits Chinois '96
Farinelli '94

The Director Index provides a listing for all directors of movies reviewed in this book. The listings for the director names follow an alphabetical sort by last name (although the names appear in a first name, last name format). The videographies are listed chronologically, from most recent film to the oldest. If a director helmed more than one film in the same year, these movies are listed alphabetically within the year.

Jeff Barklage
Vamps: Deadly Dreamgirls '95

Bruno Barreto
Bossa Nova '99

Neil Barrett
Rome: Power & Glory '99

Steven Barron
Coneheads '93

Zelda Barron
Shag: The Movie '89

Paul Bartel
Lust in the Dust '85

Andrzej Bartkowiak
Romeo Must Die '00

Charles T. Barton
Africa Screams / Jack and the Beanstalk '49
Abbott and Costello Meet Frankenstein '48

Fred Barzyk
The Lathe of Heaven '80

K.C. Bascombe
The Contract '98

Bradley Battersby
Red Letters '00

Lamberto Bava
A Blade in the Dark '83
Macabre '80

Mario Bava
Bay of Blood '71
Twitch of the Death Nerve '71
Five Dolls for an August Moon '70
Hatchet for the Honeymoon '70
Four Times That Night '69
Black Sabbath '64
Blood and Black Lace '64
The Girl Who Knew Too Much '63
The Whip and the Body '63

Michael Bay
The Rock [Criterion] '96

Chris Bearde
Hysterical '83

William Beaton
Glastonbury: The Movie '95

William Beaudine
Ghosts on the Loose '43

Edith Becker
Cinema Combat: Hollywood Goes to War '98

Harold Becker
Malice [MGM] '93

Josh Becker
Thou Shalt Not Kill . . . Except '87

Ford Beebe
Shadow of the Eagle '32

Luiz Begazo
Manoushe, The Story of a Gypsy Love '98

Earl Bellamy
Munster, Go Home! '66

Jack Bender
Lone Justice 3: Showdown at Plum Creek '96
Lone Justice 2 '93
The Midnight Hour '86

Richard Benjamin
Mermaids '90

Bill Bennett
Two If by Sea '95

Bruce Beresford
Paradise Road '97
Black Robe '91
Mister Johnson '91
Tender Mercies '83

Eric Bergeron
The Road to El Dorado '00

Per (Pelle) Berglund
The White Lioness '96

Andrew Bergman
Isn't She Great '00
Striptease '96
It Could Happen to You '94

Stig Bergqvist
Rugrats in Paris: The Movie '00

Busby Berkeley
Take Me Out to the Ball Game '49
They Made Me a Criminal '39

Christopher Berkeley
Roughnecks Starship Troopers Chronicles the Pluto Campaign '99

Greg Berlanti
The Broken Hearts Club '00

Alain Berliner
Ma Vie en Rose '97

Joe Berlinger
Book of Shadows: Blair Witch 2 '00

Harvey Berman
Velocity '99

Ted Berman
The Black Cauldron '85
The Fox and the Hound '81

Edward L. Bernds
Return of the Fly '59

Claude Berri
Jean de Florette '87
Manon of the Spring '87

Luc Besson
The Messenger: The Story of Joan of Arc '99
Leon, the Professional '94
La Femme Nikita [MGM] '91
The Big Blue [DC] '88

Cyrus Beyzavi
Throw Down '00

Herbert Biberman
Salt of the Earth '54

Robert Bierman
A Merry War '97

Tony Bill
A Home of Our Own '93
Untamed Heart '93

Hans Billian
I Like the Girls Who Do '73

Andrew Birkin
The Cement Garden '93

James Black
The Vault '00

Eric Blakeney
Gun Shy '00

John Blanchard
Shriek If You Know What I Did Last Friday the 13th '00

Barry W. Blaustein
Beyond the Mat '99

Jeffrey Bloom
Flowers in the Attic '87

Andy Blumenthal
Bloodfist 2 '90

Don Bluth
Titan A.E. '00

The Pebble and the Penguin '94
Thumbelina '94
Rock-a-Doodle '92
All Dogs Go to Heaven '89
The Land Before Time '88

Hart Bochner
High School High '96

Sergei Bodrov
Running Free '00

Peter Bogdanovich
Picture Windows '95
Saint Jack '79
The Last Picture Show [DC] '71

Richard Boleslawski
The Garden of Allah '36

Craig Bolotin
Light It Up '99

Ben Bolt
Wilderness '96

J.R. Bookwalter
Witchouse 2: Blood Coven '00
The Dead Next Door '89

John Boorman
Hope and Glory '87
The Emerald Forest '85
Zardoz '73

Lizzie Borden
Working Girls '87

Robert Boris
Frank and Jesse '94

Ole Bornedal
Nightwatch '96
Nightwatch '94

Walerian Borowczyk
Immoral Tales '74

Phillip Borsos
Mean Season '85

Frank Borzage
A Farewell to Arms '32

Costa Botes
Forgotten Silver '96

Fritz Bottger
Horrors of Spider Island '59

Barry Bowles
Nothin' 2 Lose '00
Q: The Movie '99

Danny Boyle
The Beach '00

Robert North Bradbury
Dawn Rider / Trail Beyond '35
Lawless Frontier / Randy Rides Alone '35
Lucky Texan '34
Man from Utah / Sagebrush Trail '34
The Star Packer '34
Trail Beyond '34
Riders of Destiny / Star Packer '33

John Bradshaw
Full Disclosure '00

Randy Bradshaw
Cold Blooded '00

Kenneth Branagh
Love's Labour's Lost '00
Henry V '89

Larry Brand
The Drifter '88

Marlon Brando
One-Eyed Jacks '61

Michel Brault
A Paper Wedding '89

A. Brescia
Battle of the Amazons '74

Steven Brill
Little Nicky '00

Gaetan Brizzi
Fantasia/2000 '00

Paul Brizzi
Fantasia/2000 '00

Deborah Brock
Slumber Party Massacre 2 '87

Michael Brook
Crime and Punishment in Suburbia '00

Albert Brooks
Mother '96
Defending Your Life '91
Lost in America '85
Real Life '79

James L. Brooks
Terms of Endearment '83

Richard Brooks
The Last Time I Saw Paris '54

Richard Brooks
Johnny B. '00

Eric Bross
Restaurant '98

Bruce Brown
Surfing Hollow Days '61
Slippery When Wet '58

Clarence Brown
The Last of the Mohicans '20

Les Brown Jr.
Bob Hope: Hollywood's Brightest Star '97

Christopher Browne
Third World Cop '99

Tod Browning
Outside the Law / Shadows '21

Clyde Bruckman
W.C. Fields 6 Short Films '33

Bob Buchholz
Digimon: The Movie '00

Luis Bunuel
The Discreet Charm of the Bourgeoisie '72
Diary of a Chambermaid '64

Ray Burdis
Love, Honour & Obey '00

Edward Burns
No Looking Back '98
She's the One '96
The Brothers McMullen '94

Kevin Burns
Behind the Planet of the Apes '98
20th Century Fox: The First 50 Years '96

Jeff Burr
Puppet Master 5: The Latest Chapter '94
Puppet Master 4 '93

Colette Burson
Coming Soon '99

Tim Burton
Edward Scissorhands [SE] '90

Steve Buscemi
Animal Factory '00

Hendel Butoy
Fantasia/2000 '00
The Rescuers Down Under '90

Zane Buzby
Last Resort '86

Michael Cacoyannis
Attila 74: The Rape of Cyprus '75
The Story of Jacob & Joseph '74
A Matter of Dignity '57
Girl in Black '56
Stella '55

Art Camacho
Final Payback '99

James Cameron
Terminator 2: Judgment Day [2 SE] '91

Doug Campbell
Perfect Tenant '99

Martin Campbell
Vertical Limit '00

Jane Campion
Holy Smoke '99

Frank Cappello
American Yakuza '94

Frank Capra
Know Your Enemy: Japan '45
Arsenic and Old Lace '44
World War II '42
Meet John Doe [Image] '41

Leos Carax
Pola X '99
Mauvais Sang '86
Boy Meets Girl '84

John Cardos
Mutant '83

Edwin Carewe
Evangeline '29

Carlo Carlei
Fluke '95

Lewis John Carlino
Class '83

Art Carnage
The Horrible Dr. Bones '00

John Carpenter
Big Trouble in Little China [SE] '86
Escape from New York '81

Steve Carr
Next Friday [Platinum Series] '00

Lucille Carra
The Inland Sea '93

Greg Carter
Thug Life '00

Thomas Carter
Save the Last Dance '01

D.J. Caruso
Black Cat Run '98

Steve Carver
The Arena '73

John Cassavetes
Opening Night '77
The Killing of a Chinese Bookie '76
A Woman under the Influence '74

Nick Cassavetes
She's So Lovely '97

Gurinder Chadha
What's Cooking? '00

Don Chaffey
Pete's Dragon '77

Youssef Chahine
Alexandria Again and Forever '90
An Egyptian Story '82
Alexandria...Why? '78

Stanley Donen
Blame It on Rio '84

Kim Dong-Bin
The Ring Virus '99

Sean K. Donnellan
In the Flesh / Blood Bullets
Buffoons '00

Richard Donner
Scrooged '88
Superman: The Movie '78
The Omen [SE] '76

Daniel D'or
Battle Queen 2020 '99

Matt Dorff
Captive '00

Lynn Dougherty
Rome: Power & Glory '99

Gordon Douglas
Slaughter's Big Ripoff '73
They Call Me Mr. Tibbs! '70

Robert Downey
Greaser's Palace '72

Srdjan Dragojevic
The Wounds '98
Pretty Village, Pretty Flame
'96

Franco Dragone
Quidam '99

Stan Dragoti
Necessary Roughness '91

Howard P. Dratch
Roots of Rhythm '99

Tony Drazan
Imaginary Crimes '94

Lance Dreesen
Terror Tract '00

Adam Dubin
Drop Dead Rock '95

Peter Duffell
The Far Pavilions '84

Martine Dugowson
Portraits Chinois '96

Christian Duguay
The Art of War '00

John Duigan
Romero '89

Bill Duke
Hoodlum '96

Bruno Dumont
Humanity '99
The Life of Jesus '96

Peter Duncan
A Little Bit of Soul '97

Cheryl Dunye
The Watermelon Woman '97

Julien Duvivier
Anna Karenina '48

Allan Dwan
Getting Gertie's Garter '45
Up in Mabel's Room '44

Clint Eastwood
Space Cowboys '00
Bird '88
Bronco Billy '80

Uli Edel
Confessions of Sorority Girls
'00
The Little Vampire '00

Don Edmonds
Ilsa, Harem Keeper of the Oil
Sheiks '76
Ilsa, She-Wolf of the SS '74

Blake Edwards
Switch '91

Daphna Edwards
Footsteps '98

Gale Edwards
Jesus Christ Superstar '00

Atom Egoyan
The Adjuster '91

Franz Eichhorn
The Violent Years / Girl Gang
'56

Rafael Eisenman
Red Shoe Diaries: Swimming
Naked '00
Red Shoe Diaries: Four on
the Floor '96
Red Shoe Diaries: Strip Poker
'96

Tom Ellery
Pocahontas 2: Journey to a
New World '98

Aiyana Elliott
The Ballad of Ramblin' Jack
'00

Lang Elliott
The Private Eyes [SE] '80

Scott Elliott
A Map of the World '99

Stephan Elliott
Eye of the Beholder '99
The Adventures of Priscilla,
Queen of the Desert
[MGM] '94

Joseph Ellison
Don't Go in the House '80

Javier Elorrieta
Blood and Sand '89

David Elton
Jerome '98

Roland Emmerich
The Patriot '00
Ghost Chase '88

Morris Engel
Little Fugitive '53

Ray Enright
Gung Ho! '43

Nora Ephron
Lucky Numbers '00

Jean Epstein
Fall of the House of Usher
'28

George Erschbamer
Bounty Hunters 2: Hardball
'97
Bounty Hunters '96

Joakim (Jack) Ersgard
Backlash '99

Chester Erskine
Midnight '34

Dwain Esper
Marihuana / Assassin of
Youth / Reefer Madness
'36

Luis Esteban
American Vampire '97

Emilio Estevez
Rated X '00

David Evans
Fever Pitch '96

David Mickey Evans
Beethoven's 3rd '00

Ellen Evans
Sex Files: Digital Sex '98

Kim Evans
Andy Warhol '88

John Eyres
Octopus '00

Christian Faber
The Next Step '95

Jun Falkenstein
The Tigger Movie '00

Jamaa Fanaka
Penitentiary 2 '82
Penitentiary '79

Hampton Fancher
The Minus Man '99

Nadia Fares
Honey & Ashes '96

Brian Farnham
Lord Edgeware Dies '99

**Rainer Werner
Fassbinder**
Whity '70

John P. Fedele
Titanic 2000 '00

Beda Docampo Feijoo
The Perfect Husband '92

Felix Feist
Donovan's Brain '53

Federico Fellini
City of Women '81
Fellini Satyricon '69
Il Bidone '55
Variety Lights '51

Leslie Fenton
Tomorrow the World '44

Norman Ferguson
The Three Caballeros '45
Saludos Amigos '43

Guy Ferland
After the Storm '01
Delivered '98

Abel Ferrara
King of New York '90
Crime Story: The Complete
Saga '86
Fear City '85

Marco Ferreri
La Grande Bouffe '73

Chad Ferrin
Unspeakable '00

Darin Ferriola
Ivory Tower '97

Ron Field
Pinocchio '76

Sally Field
Beautiful '00

Martha Fiennes
Onegin '99

Mike Figgis
Time Code '00
The Loss of Sexual Inno-
cence '98
Mr. Jones '93
Internal Affairs '90

David Fincher
Seven [2 SE] '95

Ken Finkleman
Airplane 2: The Sequel '82

Chris Fiore
Backstage '00

Michael Fischa
My Mom's a Werewolf '89

Terence Fisher
The Devil Rides Out '68
Frankenstein Created Woman
'66

Four Sided Triangle '53
Spaceways '53

Bill Fishman
Tapeheads '89

Dave Fleischer
Gulliver's Travels [Image] '39

Richard Fleischer
The Prince and the Pauper
'78
Tora! Tora! Tora! [2 SE] '70
Doctor Dolittle '67
Fantastic Voyage '66

Andrew Fleming
Dick '99
Threesome '94

Rodman Flender
Idle Hands '99
Leprechaun 2 '94

Clive Fleury
Big City Blues '99

Isaac Florentine
Bridge of Dragons '99

James Foley
At Close Range '86

Timothy Wayne Folsome
Uninvited Guest '99

Jorge Fons
Midaq Alley '95

Frederic Fonteyne
An Affair of Love '00

Clarence (Fok) Ford
Her Name Is Cat '99

John Ford
Donovan's Reef '63
The Man Who Shot Liberty
Valance '62
The Horse Soldiers '59
December 7th: The Pearl Har-
bor Story '43
How Green Was My Valley '41

Tom Forman
Shadows '22

Rolf Forsberg
Gladiators: Bloodsport of the
Colosseum '00

Bill Forsyth
Local Hero '83

Giles Foster
Northanger Abbey '87

Pascal Franchot
Milo '98

Coleman Francis
The Beast of Yucca Flats '61

Freddie Francis
The Vampire Happening '71

Jess (Jesus) Franco
Tender Flesh '00
Lust for Frankenstein '88
Oasis of the Zombies '82
Ilsa, the Wicked Warden '78
Female Vampire '73
She Killed in Ecstasy '70
Vampyros Lesbos '70
The Awful Dr. Orlof '62

Carol Frank
Sorority House Massacre '86

Cyril Frankel
The Witches '66

John Frankenheimer
Reindeer Games '00
Seven Days in May '64
Birdman of Alcatraz '62

Carl Franklin
One False Move '91

Jeff Franklin
Love Stinks '99

Richard Franklin
F/X 2: The Deadly Art of Illusion '91

Harry Fraser
Randy Rides Alone '34

Stephen Frears
High Fidelity '00
Mary Reilly '95

Robert Freeman
The Erotic Adventures of
Zorro '72

Karl Freund
The Mummy '32

Bart Freundlich
The Myth of Fingerprints '97

Fridrik Thor Fridriksson
Devil's Island '96

William Friedkin
Rules of Engagement '00

David Friedman
The Defilers '65

Richard S. Friedman
Forever Together '00

Andy Froemke
Parasite '95

Harvey Frost
National Lampoon's Golf
Punks '99

Lee Frost
The Thing with Two Heads '72

E. Max Frye
Amos and Andrew '93

Robert Fuest
Doctor Phibes Rises Again '72
The Abominable Dr. Phibes
'71

Kinji Fukasaku
Tora! Tora! Tora! [2 SE] '70

Hiroshi Fukutomi
Art of Fighting '93

Lucio Fulci
The House by the Cemetery
[Diamond] '83
The House by the Cemetery
[Anchor Bay] '83
The Beyond '82
Manhattan Baby '82
The Black Cat '81
Don't Torture a Duckling '72

Samuel Fuller
The Meanest Men in the
West '76

Antoine Fuqua
Bait '00

Sidney J. Furie
My 5 Wives '00
Superman 4: The Quest for
Peace '87

Kazuhiro Furuhashi
Samurai X Trust '99

Yoshimichi Furukawa
Darkside Blues '99

Richard Gabai
Vice Girls '96
Assault of the Party Nerds 2:
Heavy Petting Detective '95
Assault of the Party Nerds '89

Mike Gabriel
Pocahontas '95
The Rescuers Down Under
'90

John Gale
The Firing Line '91

Arthur Hiller
Love Story '70

Arthur Hilton
Cat Women of the Moon '53

Robert Hiltzik
Sleepaway Camp '83

**Alexander Gregory
(Gregory Dark)
Hippolyte**
Animal Instincts '92
Secret Games '92

Alfred Hitchcock
Family Plot '76
Frenzy '72
Topaz '69
Torn Curtain '66
North by Northwest '59
The Man Who Knew Too
  Much '56
The Trouble with Harry '55
Rear Window '54
Rope '48
Alfred Hitchcock's Bon Voy-
  age & Aventure Malgache
  '44
Shadow of a Doubt '43
Saboteur '42

Howie Hoax
Scandal: The Big Turn On '99

Klaus Hoch
Flypaper '97

Mike Hodges
Croupier '97
Get Carter '71

Christopher Hodson
We'll Meet Again '82

Antony Hoffman
Red Planet '00

David Hogan
Barb Wire '96

James Hogan
Bulldog Drummond's Secret
  Police '39
Bulldog Drummond Escapes
  '37

Tom Holland
Fatal Beauty '87
Fright Night '85

Fred Holmes
Dakota '88

Marius Holst
Cross My Heart and Hope to
  Die '94

James Hong
The Vineyard '89

Ted Hooker
Crucible of Terror '72

Kevin Hooks
Fled '96
Passenger 57 '92

Lance Hool
Steel Dawn '87

Tobe Hooper
Crocodile '00
The Texas Chainsaw Mas-
  sacre 2 '86

Stephen Hopkins
Under Suspicion '00

Dennis Hopper
Chasers '94

Jerry Hopper
Madron '70

Michael Horowitz
Park City: The Sundance Collection '01

Tomoaki Hosoyama
Weather Woman '99

Leslie Howard
Pygmalion '38

Ron Howard
Splash '84

William K. Howard
Fire over England '37

Anthony Howarth
People of the Wind '76

Peter Howitt
Antitrust '00

Frank Howson
Flynn '96

Harry Hoyt
The Lost World [Image] '25

Chin Hsin
Master with Cracked Fingers
  '71

Talun Hsu
Body Count '95

King Hu
Painted Skin '93

**Reginald (Reggie)
Hudlin**
The Ladies Man '00
House Party '90

Hugh Hudson
I Dreamed of Africa '00

Matthew Huffman
Playing Mona Lisa '00

John Hughes
She's Having a Baby '88
Planes, Trains & Automobiles
  '87

Ken Hughes
Sextette '78

Don Hulette
Breaker! Breaker! '77

H. Bruce Humberstone
Wonder Man '45

Sammo Hung
Eastern Condors '87
The Millionaire's Express '86
Spooky Encounters '80

Bonnie Hunt
Return to Me '00

Pixote Hunt
Fantasia/2000 '00

**Max (Massimo Pupillo)
Hunter**
The Bloody Pit of Horror '65

Simon Hunter
Dead of Night '99

Tim Hunter
River's Edge '87

Owen Hurley
Casper's Haunted Christmas
  '00

Brian Desmond Hurst
A Christmas Carol '51

Waris Hussein
Quackser Fortune Has a
  Cousin in the Bronx '70

Anjelica Huston
Agnes Browne '99

John Huston
Annie '82
The Misfits '61
Moby Dick '56
Beat the Devil '53
The Maltese Falcon '41

Clint Hutchison
Terror Tract '00

Brian G. Hutton
Kelly's Heroes '70

Timothy Hutton
Digging to China '98

Nicholas Hytner
Center Stage '00
The Madness of King George
  '94

Leon Ichaso
Hendrix '00

Toshiharu Ikeda
Evil Dead Trap '88

J. Christian Ingvordsen
Mob War [BFS] '88

John Irvin
Noah's Ark '99
City of Industry '96

Kris Isacsson
Park City: The Sundance Col-
  lection '01
Down to You '00

Robert Iscove
Boys and Girls '00

Shunya Ito
Female Convict Scorpion—
  Jailhouse 41 '72

Patty Ivins
Marilyn Monroe: The Final
  Days '00

James Ivory
Mr. & Mrs. Bridge '90
A Room with a View '86

Pete Jacelone
Psycho Sisters '98

Carl Jackson
Inhumanity '00

George Jackson
House Party 2: The Pajama
  Jam '91

Peter Jackson
Forgotten Silver '96

Wilfred Jackson
Alice in Wonderland '51
Saludos Amigos '43

Alan Jacobs
Sinbad: Beyond the Veil of
  Mists '00
Diary of a Serial Killer '97

John Jacobs
The First to Go '97

Jon Jacobs
Lucinda's Spell '00

John Jacobsen
Around the Fire '98

Benoit Jacquot
A Single Girl '96

Raymond Jafelice
Babar: King of the Elephants
  '99

Jim Jarmusch
Ghost Dog: The Way of the
  Samurai '99
Year of the Horse '97
Dead Man '95

J.R. Jarrod
Divided We Stand '00

Charles Jarrott
Strange Case of Dr. Jekyll &
  Mr. Hyde '68

Jean-Pierre Jeunet
Alien: Resurrection '97

Norman Jewison
The Hurricane '99
Picture Windows '95
In Country '89
A Soldier's Story '84
And Justice for All '79
In the Heat of the Night '67

Wong Jing
New Legend of Shaolin '96

Leo Joannon
Utopia '51

Phil Joanou
U2: Rattle and Hum '88

Sande N. Johnsen
Teenage Gang Debs /
  Teenage Strangler '66

Lamont Johnson
The Groundstar Conspiracy
  '72

Thomas Johnston
Jerome '98

Amy Holden Jones
The Rich Man's Wife '96
Love Letters '83
Slumber Party Massacre '82

David Hugh Jones
A Christmas Carol '99
The Confession '98

Gary Jones
Spiders '00

Terry Jones
Monty Python and the Holy
  Grail '75

Neil Jordan
The End of the Affair '99
Mona Lisa '86

Jon Jost
The Bed You Sleep In '93

Nathan (Hertz) Juran
The Brain from Planet Arous
  '57

Cedric Kahn
L'Ennui '98

Jonathan Kahn
Girl '98

Chen Kaige
The Emperor and the Assassin '99

John Kain
Cyberotica '00

Bill Kalmenson
The Souler Opposite '97

Janusz Kaminski
Lost Souls '00

Jim Kammerud
The Little Mermaid 2: Return
  to the Sea '00

Charles Kanganis
K-911 '99

Marek Kanievska
Where the Money Is '00

Jonathan Kaplan
Picture Windows '95
Love Field '91
Truck Turner '74

Shekhar Kapur
Bandit Queen '94

Wong Kar-Wai
Ashes of Time '94

Larry Karaszewski
Screwed '00

Victor Kargan
The Bogus Witch Project '00

Pip Karmel
Me Myself I '99

Eric Karson
Black Eagle '88

Lawrence Kasdan
Grand Canyon '91
Silverado [SE] '85

Shuji Kataoka
Prisoner Maria: The Movie '95

Lee H. Katzin
Restraining Order '99
Whatever Happened to Aunt
  Alice? '69

Jonathan Kaufer
Bad Manners '98

Charles Kaufman
Mother's Day [DC] '80

**Lloyd (Samuel Weil)
Kaufman**
Terror Firmer [SE] '00

Philip Kaufman
Quills '00

Yoshiaki Kawajiri
Demon City Shinjuku '93
Wicked City [SE] '89

Stephen Kay
Get Carter '00

Diane Keaton
Hanging Up '99

Antonia Keeler
Passion & Romance: Double
  or Nothing '00

Woody Keith
Dementia '98

Nicholas (Nick) Kendall
Kayla: A Cry in the Wilderness '00

Burt Kennedy
Support Your Local Gunfight-
  er '71
Return of the Magnificent
  Seven '66

Garfield Kennedy
The Last Great Adventure '99

Chris Kentis
Grind '96

Eric Kenton
Fight for the Title '57

James V. Kern
The Second Woman '51

Sarah Kernochan
All I Wanna Do '98

Justin Kerrigan
Human Traffic '99

Irvin Kershner
Eyes of Laura Mars '78

Bruce Kessler
The Gay Deceivers '69

Fritz Kiersch
Tuff Turf '85
Children of the Corn '84

Henry King
The Snows of Kilimanjaro '52

Rob King
Something More '99

Stephen King
Maximum Overdrive '86

Zalman King
Red Shoe Diaries: Luscious
  Lola '00
Red Shoe Diaries: Swimming
  Naked '00
In God's Hands '98

Gilles Mackinnon
The Last of the Blonde Bombshells '00

Alison Maclean
Jesus' Son '99

Kurt Maetzig
First Spaceship on Venus '60

Barry Mahon
The Beast That Killed Women / The Monster of Camp Sunshine '65

Robin Mahoney
Glastonbury: The Movie '95

Rob Malenfant
The Perfect Nanny '00

David Mallet
Dralion '00
Joseph and the Amazing Technicolor Dreamcoat '00

Mark Malone
The Last Stop '99

David Mamet
House of Games '87

Rouben Mamoulian
The Gay Desperado '36

Robert Mandel
F/X '86

James Mangold
Girl, Interrupted '99

Joseph L. Mankiewicz
Cleopatra '63
Suddenly, Last Summer '59
Guys and Dolls '55
The Barefoot Contessa '54

Anthony Mann
The Man from Laramie '55

Daniel Mann
Butterfield 8 '60

Delbert Mann
That Touch of Mink '62
Marty '55

Michael Mann
The Last of the Mohicans '92

Guy Manos
Cutaway '00

Robert Marcarelli
The Omega Code '99

Terry Marcel
Jane & the Lost City '87

Joaquin Luis Romero Marchent
Cut Throats Nine '72

Dwight Marcus
News from the West

Paul Marcus
Eye of the Killer '99

Edwin L. Marin
Abilene Town '46

Peter Markle
El Diablo '90
Youngblood '86

Goran Markovic
Tito and Me '92

Robert Markowitz
The Tuskegee Airmen '95

Arthur Marks
Friday Foster '75
Detroit 9000 '73

Christian Marquand
Candy '68

Richard Marquand
The Jagged Edge '85

Jacques "Jack" Marquette
Teenage Monster '57

Joel B. Marsden
Ill-Gotten Gains '97

David Marsh
Stormswept '95

George Marshall
Pot o' Gold '41

Rob Marshall
Annie '99

William Marshall
The Phantom Planet '61

Eugenio (Gene) Martin
Bad Man's River '72
Pancho Villa '72

Michael Martin
Tha Eastsidaz '00

Richard Martin
Air Bud 2: Golden Receiver '98

Raymond Martino
DaVinci's War '92

Juan A. Mas
The Coroner '98

Andy Massagli
The Gospel According to Philip K. Dick '00

Joe Massot
Wonderwall: The Movie '69

Toshio Masuda
Tora! Tora! Tora! [2 SE] '70

Rudolph Mate
D.O.A. [Roan] '49

Hiro Matsuda
Dragon Princess '81

Sally Mattison
Slumber Party Massacre 3 '90

Joe Maxwell
The Married Virgin '18

Ronald F. Maxwell
Gettysburg '93

Bradford May
Asteroid '97

Joe May
The Indian Tomb '21

Daisy von Scherler Mayer
Madeline '98

Les Mayfield
Blue Streak '99

Archie Mayo
Angel on My Shoulder '46

Albert Maysles
Gimme Shelter '70

David Maysles
Gimme Shelter '70

Craig Mazin
The Specials '00

Des McAnuff
The Adventures of Rocky & Bullwinkle '00

Don McBrearty
Race to Freedom: The Story of the Underground Railroad '94

Howard McCain
No Dessert Dad, 'Til You Mow the Lawn '94

Rod McCall
Lewis and Clark and George '97

Leo McCarey
An Affair to Remember '57

Love Affair '39

Detrich McClure
Out Kold '00

Nelson McCormick
Kill Shot '01

Jim McCullough
Mountaintop Motel Massacre '86

Bruce McDonald
Hard Core Logo '96

Michael James McDonald
The Crazysitter '94

Edward T. McDougal
The Prodigy '98

McG
Charlie's Angels '00

Scott McGehee
Suture '93

Don McGlynn
Louis Prima: The Wildest! '99

Doug McHenry
House Party 2: The Pajama Jam '91

Patrick McKnight
Dope Case Pending '00

Duncan McLachlan
Rudyard Kipling's the Second Jungle Book: Mowgli and Baloo '97

Andrew V. McLaglen
The Shadow Riders '82

Gordon McLennan
Die! Die! Die! '00

Norman Z. McLeod
The Road to Rio '47

David McNally
Coyote Ugly '00

Steve McNicholas
Stomp Out Loud '98

Christopher McQuarrie
Way of the Gun '00

John McTiernan
Predator [20th Century Fox] '87

Joshua Meador
Make Mine Music '46

Peter Medak
The Changeling '80

Julio Medem
Tierra '95

Don Medford
The Organization '71

Deepa Mehta
Fire '96

Gus Meins
March of the Wooden Soldiers '34

Norbert Meisel
Walking the Edge '83

Christopher Menaul
The Passion of Ayn Rand '99

George Mendeluk
The Kidnapping of the President '80

Sam Mendes
American Beauty [SE] '99

Ho Meng-Hua
The Mighty Peking Man '77

William Cameron Menzies
Things to Come '36

Ismail Merchant
Cotton Mary '99

Edmund Elias Merhige
Shadow of the Vampire '00

Tom Meshelski
Bob Hope: Hollywood's Brightest Star '97

Stephen Metcalfe
Beautiful Joe '00

Alan Metter
Back to School '86
Girls Just Want to Have Fun '85

Nicholas Meyer
Star Trek 2: The Wrath of Khan '82

Nancy Meyers
What Women Want '00

Eric Meza
House Party 3 '94

Bret Michaels
No Code of Conduct '98

Edwin Middleton
W.C. Fields 6 Short Films '33

Ted V. Mikels
The Astro-Zombies '67

Lewis Milestone
The Strange Love of Martha Ivers '46
A Walk in the Sun '46
Rain '32

Eduardo Milewicz
Life According to Muriel '97

John Milius
Conan the Barbarian [2 CE] '82
Dillinger '73

Michael Miller
Jackson County Jail '76

Andy Milligan
The Body Beneath '70

Travis Milloy
Street Gun '96

Michael Miner
The Book of Stars '99

Steve Miner
Friday the 13th, Part 3 '82

Anthony Minghella
The Talented Mr. Ripley '99
Mr. Wonderful '93

Vincente Minnelli
Father's Little Dividend '51

Bob Misiorowski
On the Border '98

David Mitchell
Downhill Willie '96

Mike Mitchell
Deuce Bigalow: Male Gigolo '99

Phil Mitchell
Shadow Raiders, Vol. 1: Uncommon Hero '98

Sollace Mitchell
Row Your Boat '98

Hayao Miyazaki
Princess Mononoke '98

Seiji Mizushima
Generator 1: Gawl '00

Jose Mojica Marins
Awakenings of the Beast '68
This Night I'll Possess Your Corpse '66

Hans Petter Moland
The Last Lieutenant '94

Craig Monahan
The Interview '98

Mario Monicelli
Lovers and Liars '81
Big Deal on Madonna Street '58

Joao Cesar Monteiro
God's Comedy '95

Jorge Montesi
Omen 4: The Awakening '91

Roberto Monticello
Italian Movie '93

Michael Moore
Canadian Bacon '94

Philippe Mora
Communion [CE] '89

Andrew Morahan
Highlander: The Final Dimension '94

Christopher Morahan
Element of Doubt '96

William M. Morgan
The Violent Years / Girl Gang '56
Fun & Fancy Free '47

Takeshi Mori
Gun Smith Cats: Bulletproof '95

Louis Morneau
Bats '99
Carnosaur 2 '94

Errol Morris
Mr. Death: The Rise and Fall of Fred A. Leuchter Jr. '99

Nick Morris
Jesus Christ Superstar '00

Paul Morrison
Solomon and Gaenor '98

Amanda Moss
Bar-B-Q '00

Donny Most
The Last Best Sunday '98

Jonathan Mostow
U-571 [CE] '00

Greg Mottola
The Daytrippers '96

Malcolm Mowbray
Sweet Revenge '98

John Llewellyn Moxey
Horror Hotel '60

Allan Moyle
Xchange '00
Empire Records '95
Times Square '80

Edward (Edoardo Mulargia) Muller
Escape from Hell '89

Jag Mundhra
Monsoon '97

Robert Munic
Timelock '99

Jimmy T. Murakami
Battle Beyond the Stars '80

Ryu Murakami
Because of You '95

F.W. Murnau
Nosferatu [2] '22

Geoff Murphy
Race Against Time '00
Freejack '92

Robert Redford
The Legend of Bagger Vance '00

Crispin Reece
The Canterville Ghost '98

Carol Reed
Immortal Battalion '44

Matt Reeves
The Pallbearer '95

Nicolas Winding Refn
Pusher '96

Tim Reid
Once Upon a Time...When We Were Colored '95

Roel Reine
The Delivery '99

Carl Reiner
Summer Rental '85
Dead Men Don't Wear Plaid '82

Rob Reiner
Misery '90
When Harry Met Sally... [SE] '89
The Princess Bride '87
Stand by Me [2 SE] '86
This Is Spinal Tap [MGM] '84

Wolfgang Reitherman
Robin Hood '73
The Aristocats '70
The Sword in the Stone '63

Kimble Rendall
Cut '00

Norman Rene
Prelude to a Kiss '92
Longtime Companion '90

Alain Resnais
Mon Oncle d'Amerique '80
La Guerre Est Finie '66

Dale Resteghini
Da Hip Hop Witch '00
Colorz of Rage '97

Burt Reynolds
The End '78

Kevin Reynolds
187 '97
The Beast '88

Phillip Rhee
Best of the Best: Without Warning '98
Best of the Best 3: No Turning Back / Best of the Best: Without Warning '95

Bill Rice
The Vineyard '89

Richard Rich
The Black Cauldron '85
The Fox and the Hound '81

Cybil Richards
Femalien 2 '98
Femalien '96

Sybil Richards
Lolida 2000 '97

Tony Richardson
Blue Sky '91
Tom Jones [MGM] '63
The Entertainer '60

William Richert
A Night in the Life of Jimmy Reardon '88

Evan C. Ricks
Sinbad: Beyond the Veil of Mists '00

Leni Riefenstahl
Triumph of the Will '34

Arthur Ripley
W.C. Fields 6 Short Films '33

Guy Ritchie
Lock, Stock and 2 Smoking Barrels '99

Michael Ritchie
Semi-Tough '77

Martin Ritt
Norma Rae '79

Jay Roach
Meet the Parents '00
Mystery, Alaska '99

Brian Robbins
Ready to Rumble '00

Tim Robbins
The Cradle Will Rock '99
Dead Man Walking '95
Bob Roberts [SE] '92

Bill Roberts
Saludos Amigos '43

Steve Robman
The Audrey Hepburn Story '00

Mark Robson
The Bridges at Toko-Ri '55

Marc Rocco
Murder in the First '95

Serge Rodnunsky
Newsbreak '00
Fear Runs Silent '99
Paper Bullets '99

Robert Rodriguez
From Dusk Till Dawn [2 CS] '95

Chris Roe
Pop & Me '99

Rick Roessler
Slaughterhouse '87

Charles R. Rogers
March of the Wooden Soldiers '34

Mike Rohl
Chained Heat 3: Hell Mountain '98

Eric Rohmer
A Summer's Tale '96
Perceval '78
The Marquise of O '76

Jean Rollin
Zombie Lake '80

Eddie Romero
Beyond Atlantis '73
Black Mama, White Mama '73

George A. Romero
Monkey Shines '88
Knightriders '81
Martin '77
Night of the Living Dead [Madacy] '68
Night of the Living Dead [Elite] '68
Night of the Living Dead [LE Anchor Bay] '68

Ronnie Rondell
No Safe Haven '87

Darrell Rooney
Lady and the Tramp 2: Scamp's Adventure '01

Don Roos
Bounce '00

Dan Rosen
The Curve '97

Stuart Rosenberg
The Pope of Greenwich Village '84
The Amityville Horror '79

Mark Rosman
The House on Sorority Row '83

Eugene Rosow
Roots of Rhythm '99

Herbert Ross
Steel Magnolias '89

Phillip J. Roth
Interceptor Force '99
Velocity Trap '99
Darkdrive '98

Tim Roth
The War Zone '98

William Roth
Floating '97

William Rotsler
Mantis in Lace '68

Jeannine Roussel
Lady and the Tramp 2: Scamp's Adventure '01

Philippe Rousselot
The Serpent's Kiss '97

James Rowe
Blue Ridge Fall '99

Roy Rowland
The 5000 Fingers of Dr. T '53

Patricia Rozema
Mansfield Park '99

Joseph Ruben
True Believer '89
The Pom Pom Girls / The Beach Girls '76

Bruce Joel Rubin
My Life '93

Saul Rubinek
Jerry and Tom '98

Alan Rudolph
Breakfast of Champions '98

Josef Rusnak
Quiet Days in Hollywood '97

Yael Russcol
Extramarital '98

Chuck Russell
Bless the Child '00

Jay Russell
My Dog Skip '99

Ken Russell
Salome's Last Dance '88
Gothic '87
Tommy '75

Toby Russell
Thug Immortal '97

Gregory Russin
Park City: The Sundance Collection '01

John A. Russo
Santa Claws '96

Marti Rustam
James Dean: Live Fast, Die Young '81

Stefan Ruzowitzky
Anatomy [SE] '00

Terence Ryan
The Brylcreem Boys '96

Mark Rydell
For the Boys '91
The River '84

Paul Sabella
All Dogs Go to Heaven 2 '95

Bob Saget
Dirty Work '97

Louis Saia
The Boys '97

Gene Saks
The Odd Couple '68

Matthew Salkeld
Glastonbury: The Movie '95

David Salle
Search and Destroy '94

Mikael Salomon
Aftershock: Earthquake in New York '99

Bernard Salzman
Diamondbacks '99

Rachel Samuels
Robert Louis Stevenson's The Game of Death '99

Scott Sanders
Thick As Thieves '99

Arlene Sanford
I'll Be Home for Christmas '98

Deran Sarafian
Death Warrant '90

Joseph Sargent
Bojangles '01
For Love or Country: The Arturo Sandoval Story '00
A Lesson Before Dying '99
Jaws: The Revenge '87
The Taking of Pelham One Two Three '74

Marina Sargenti
Mirror, Mirror '90

Robert Sarkies
Forgotten Silver '96

Maurice Sarli
The Bodyguard / Dragon Princess '76

Michael Sarne
Glastonbury: The Movie '95

Oley Sassone
Bloodfist 3: Forced to Fight '92

Yuzo Sato
BioHunter [SE] '95

Charles Saunders
The Womaneater '59

Carlos Saura
Goya in Bordeaux '00

Philip Saville
Deacon Brodie '98

Vic Savin
Left Behind: The Movie '00

Tom Savini
Night of the Living Dead '90

John Sayles
Eight Men Out '88

Armand Schaefer
Sagebrush Trail '33

George Schaefer
In This House of Brede '75

Eric Schaeffer
If Lucy Fell '95

Franklin J. Schaffner
Planet of the Apes '68

Carl Schenkel
Tarzan and the Lost City '98
Knight Moves '93
The Mighty Quinn '89

Richard Schenkman
October 22 '98
Went to Coney Island on a Mission from God...Be Back by Five '98
The Pompatus of Love '95

Fred Schepisi
Six Degrees of Separation '93
Roxanne '87
Plenty '85

David Schisgall
The Lifestyle '99

Piero Schivazappa
The Frightened Woman '71

Thomas Schlamme
You So Crazy '94

John Schlesinger
The Next Best Thing '00

Rob Schmidt
Crime and Punishment in Suburbia '00

David Schmoeller
Puppet Master '89
Tourist Trap '79

Julian Schnabel
Before Night Falls '00

Ernest B. Schoedsack
The Most Dangerous Game [Madacy] '32
Chang: A Drama of the Wilderness '27

Paul Schrader
Forever Mine '99

John Schultz
Drive Me Crazy '99

Michael A. Schultz
Car Wash '76
Cooley High '75

Joel Schumacher
Tigerland '00
Flawless '99

Martin Scorsese
Bringing Out the Dead '99
The Last Temptation of Christ '88

Oz Scott
Bustin' Loose '81

Ridley Scott
Hannibal '01
Gladiator '00

Sherman Scott
The Kid with the X-Ray Eyes '99

Dick Sebast
The Secret of NIMH 2 '98

Peter Segal
Nutty Professor 2: The Klumps [1 CE] '00
Nutty Professor 2: The Klumps [2 Uncensored] '00
Naked Gun 33 1/3: The Final Insult '94

Arthur Seidelman
Hercules in New York '70

Susan Seidelman
Desperately Seeking Susan '85

George B. Seitz
The Vanishing American '25

Henry Selick
James and the Giant Peach '96
The Nightmare before Christmas [2 SE] '93

Dominic Sena
Gone in 60 Seconds '00

Yahoo Serious
Mr. Accident '99

Vernon Sewell
Blood Beast Terror '67

Douglas Trumbull
Brainstorm '83

Colburn Tseng
Park City: The Sundance Collection '01

Hatuki Tsuji
Samurai X: The Movie '95

Stanley Tucci
Joe Gould's Secret '00

Phil Tucker
Robot Monster '53

Ching Siu Tung
Chinese Ghost Story III '91
Chinese Ghost Story II '90

Jon Turteltaub
Disney's The Kid '00

John Turturro
Illuminata '98

David N. Twohy
Pitch Black '00

Tom Tykwer
Winter Sleepers '97

Edgar G. Ulmer
The Amazing Transparent Man '60
The Man from Planet X '51
Detour '46
The Strange Woman '46
Moon over Harlem '39

Ron Underwood
City Slickers '91

Lee Unkrich
Toy Story 2 '99

Yasunori Urata
Sin: The Movie '98

Imanol Uribe
Running out of Time '94

Jim Van Bebber
Deadbeat at Dawn '88

Andre Van Heerden
Revelation '00
Tribulation '00

Mario Van Peebles
Love Kills '98
Panther '95
Posse '93

Gus Van Sant
Finding Forrester '00
Drugstore Cowboy '89

Bert Van Tuyle
Something New '20

Marilyn Vance
Best of Intimate Sessions: Vol. 2 '99

Francis Veber
The Dinner Game '98

Louis Venosta
Kisses in the Dark '97

Paul Verhoeven
The Hollow Man [SE] '00
The 4th Man '79
Soldier of Orange '78
Turkish Delight '73

Stephen Verona
The Lords of Flatbush '74

Steven Vidler
Blackrock '97

Charles Vidor
Hans Christian Andersen [20th Century Fox] '52
The Loves of Carmen '48
Gilda '46

King Vidor
Street Scene '31

Emilio Vieyra
The Curious Dr. Humpp '70

Rene Villar-Rios
Social Misfits '00

Robert Vince
MVP: Most Valuable Primate '00

Christian Vincent
La Separation '98

Tony Vitale
Kiss Me, Guido '97

Katja von Garnier
Bandits '99

Akos Von Rathony
Cave of the Living Dead '65

Josef von Sternberg
Scarlet Empress '34

Erich von Stroheim
Foolish Wives '22

Lars von Trier
Dancer in the Dark '99
Breaking the Waves '95
The Element of Crime '84

Trac Vu
Park City: The Sundance Collection '01

Michel Waehniuc
The Scorpio Factor '90

Bruce Wagner
I'm Losing You '98

Kai-Fai Wai
Peace Hotel '95

Koji Wakamatsu
Ecstasy of the Angels '72
Go, Go Second Time Virgin '69

Chris Walas
The Fly 2 '89

Giles Walker
Never Too Late '98

Hal Walker
The Road to Bali '53
At War with the Army '50

Pete Walker
Frightmare '74
Die Screaming, Marianne '73

Rob Walker
Circus '00

Charles Walters
The Unsinkable Molly Brown '64
Good News '47

Sam Wanamaker
Sinbad and the Eye of the Tiger '77

Matthew Warchus
Simpatico '99

Vincent Ward
The Navigator '88

Regis Wargnier
East-West '99

Deborah Warner
The Last September '99

Paul Warner
Fall Time '94

Norman J. Warren
Inseminoid '80

David Warry-Smith
Heaven's Fire '00

John Waters
Cecil B. Demented '00

Frederick P. Watkins
Lethal Seduction '97

Keoni Waxman
The Highway Man '99

Keenen Ivory Wayans
Scary Movie '00
I'm Gonna Git You Sucka '88

John Wayne
The Alamo '60

Yossi Wein
Shark Attack 2 '00
U.S. Seals '98

Eric Weinrib
Park City: The Sundance Collection '01

Don Weis
The Munsters' Revenge '81

Orson Welles
Touch of Evil [SE] '58
Around the World with Orson Welles '55
The Lady from Shanghai '48

Wim Wenders
The Million Dollar Hotel '99
Beyond the Clouds '95

Paul Wendkos
A Woman Called Moses '78
Honor Thy Father '73

Peter Werner
The '70s '00

John West
Bar-B-Q '00

James Whale
The Invisible Man '33

Darryl Wharton
Detention '98

Claude Whatham
All Creatures Great and Small '74
That'll Be the Day '73

Jim Wheat
Pitch Black '00

Ken Wheat
Pitch Black '00

Richard Wherrett
Billy's Holiday '95

Richard Whorf
Till the Clouds Roll By '46

Billy Wilder
The Apartment '60
Some Like It Hot [SE] '59
The Seven Year Itch '55
The Lost Weekend '45

Gavin Wilding
Premonition '99

Clinton J. Williams
Sex Files: Ancient Desires '99

Jeff Williams
Dope Case Pending '00

Matt Williams
Where the Heart Is '00

Ron Williams
The Story of O: The Series '92

Fred Williamson
Steele's Law '91

Nick Willing
Jason and the Argonauts '00

Kevin Willmott
Ninth Street '98

Kurt Wimmer
One Man's Justice '95

Simon Wincer
Lightning Jack '94

Harley Davidson and the Marlboro Man '91

Jonathan Winfrey
Black Scorpion 2: Ground Zero '96
Carnosaur 3: Primal Species '96
Black Scorpion '95

Gary Winick
The Tic Code '99

Terence H. Winkless
White Wolves 2: Legend of the Wild '94
Bloodfist '89

Michael Winner
The Sentinel '76
Death Wish '74
I'll Never Forget What's 'Isname '67

David Winning
Turbo: A Power Rangers Movie '96

Terry Winsor
Essex Boys '99

Stan Winston
Pumpkinhead '88

Michael Winterbottom
The Claim '00
Wonderland '99

David Winters
Fanatic '82

Scott Wiper
A Better Way to Die '00

Herbert Wise
Brother Cadfael: The Devil's Novice '94
I, Claudius '91

Robert Wise
The Sand Pebbles '66
The Sound of Music [Five Star Collection] '65

Doris Wishman
Double Agent 73 '80
Deadly Weapons '70
Another Day, Another Man '66
Bad Girls Go to Hell / Another Day, Another Man '65
Blaze Starr Goes Nudist '63
Nude on the Moon '61

Sasha Wolf
Kisses in the Dark '97

David Wolfe
Velocity '99

David Womark
Red Shoe Diaries: Four on the Floor '96

James Wong
Final Destination '00

Kirk Wong
Crime Story '93

John Woo
Mission: Impossible 2 '00
Hard-Boiled [Winstar] '92
The Killer [Winstar] '90
A Better Tomorrow, Part 2 [Anchor Bay] '88
A Better Tomorrow, Part 1 [Anchor Bay] '86

Edward D. Wood Jr.
Plan 9 from Outer Space [Passport Video] '56
The Violent Years / Girl Gang '56

Sam Wood
Our Town '40

John Woods
Plain Jane '00

Rowan Woods
Farscape, Vol. 3 '01

Chuck Workman
The Source '96
Superstar: The Life and Times of Andy Warhol '90

David Worth
Shark Attack 2 '00
The Prophet's Game '99
Lady Dragon '92

Alexander Wright
The First 9 1/2 Weeks '98

Geoffrey Wright
Cherry Falls / Terror Tract '00
Terror Tract '00
Romper Stomper [SE] '92

Mack V. Wright
Winds of the Wasteland '36

Donald Wrye
Ice Castles '79

William Wyler
Ben-Hur '59
The Big Country '58
Friendly Persuasion '56
Come and Get It '36

Paul Wynne
2 G's and a Key '00
Destination Vegas '95

Jim Wynorski
Rangers '00
Desert Thunder '99
Final Voyage '99
The Pandora Project '98
Body Chemistry 4: Full Exposure '95
Body Chemistry 3: Point of Seduction '93
Home for Christmas '93
Sorority House Massacre 2: Nighty Nightmare '92
Not of This Earth '88

Boaz Yakin
Remember the Titans '00

Takaaki Yamashita
Digimon: The Movie '00

Edward Yang
Yi Yi '00

Jean Yarbrough
Hillbillys in a Haunted House '67
Jack & the Beanstalk '52

Peter Yates
Krull [SE] '83
For Pete's Sake '74

Steve Yeager
Divine Trash '98

Irvin S. Yeaworth Jr.
Dinosaurus! '60
The Blob '58

Harold Young
The Scarlet Pimpernel '34

Roger Young
Jesus '99
Kiss the Sky '98

Terence Young
Cold Sweat '71
From Russia with Love [2 SE] '63

Ben Younger
Boiler Room '00

Corey Yuen
Jet Li's The Enforcer [Buena Vista] '95
The Bodyguard from Beijing '94
The Defender '94
The Legend '93
Saviour of the Soul 2 '92

Woo-ping Yuen
Twin Warriors '93

Jim Yukich
Double Dragon '94

Kunihiko Yuyama
Pokemon the Movie 2000:
The Power of One '00

Brian Yuzna
Bride of Re-Animator '89

Mier Zarchi
Don't Mess with My Sister!
'85

Tony Zarindast
Hardcase and Fist '89

Franco Zeffirelli
The Taming of the Shrew '67

Yuri Zeltser
Black & White '99

Robert Zemeckis
Castaway '00
What Lies Beneath '00

Scott Ziehl
Broken Vessels '98

Howard Ziehm
Flesh Gordon 2: Flesh Gor-
don Meets the Cosmic
Cheerleaders '90

Paul Ziller
Moving Target '00
Bloodfist 4: Die Trying '92

Fred Zinnemann
A Man for All Seasons '66

Daniel Zirilli
Winner Takes All '98

Joseph Zito
Red Scorpion '89
Friday the 13th, Part 4: The
Final Chapter '84
Missing in Action '84

Ralph Zondag
Dinosaur [CE] '00

David Zucker
Naked Gun 2 1/2: The Smell
of Fear '91
The Naked Gun: From the
Files of Police Squad '88
Airplane! '80

Jerry Zucker
Ghost '90
Airplane! '80

Andrzej Zulawski
Possession '81

Guido Zurli
The Mad Butcher '72

Charlotte Zwerlin
Gimme Shelter '70

Edward Zwick
Legends of the Fall [2 SE] '94
Glory [2 SE] '89

The Screenwriter Index lists all writers with at least one credit in the DVDs reviewed in this book. The listings for the writer names follow an alphabetical sort by last name (although the names appear in a first name, last name format). The videographies are listed chronologically, from most recent film to their first. If a writer wrote (or script doctored) more than one film in the same year, these movies are listed alphabetically within the year.

Douglas Aarniokoski
Puppet Master 5: The Latest Chapter '94
Puppet Master 4 '93

Aktan Abdykalykov
Beshkempir the Adopted Son '98

Lewis Abernathy
Deepstar Six '89

Jim Abrahams
Mafia! '98
The Naked Gun: From the Files of Police Squad '88
Airplane! '80

Jack Abramoff
Red Scorpion '89

Robert Abramoff
Red Scorpion '89

Ian Adams
Cold Blooded '00

Robert Adetuyi
Turn It Up '00

Avtandil Adikulov
Beshkempir the Adopted Son '98

Alan J. Adler
Parasite '82

Duane Adler
Save the Last Dance '01

Felix Adlon
Eat Your Heart Out '96

Satoru Akahori
Sorcerer Hunters: Magical Encounters '00

Genpei Akasegawa
Rikyu '90

Chantal Akerman
A Couch in New York '95

Jeff Albert
The Base '99

Steve Alden
Fall Time '94

Will Aldis
Back to School '86

William Aldridge
Mio in the Land of Faraway '87

Scott Alexander
Screwed '00

Nellie Allard
Red Shoe Diaries: Four on the Floor '96

Britt Allcroft
Thomas and the Magic Railroad '00

Curt Allen
Walking the Edge '83

India Allen
The Rowdy Girls '00

Irwin Allen
Voyage to the Bottom of the Sea / Fantastic Voyage '61

Peter Allen
Klash '95

Woody Allen
Small Time Crooks '00
Sweet and Lowdown '99
Shadows and Fog '92
Alice '90
Crimes & Misdemeanors [MGM] '89
Another Woman '88
September '88
Manhattan '79
Interiors '78
Love and Death '75
Sleeper '73
Everything You Always Wanted to Know about Sex (But Were Afraid to Ask) '72
Bananas '71

Michael Almereyda
Hamlet '00
Search and Destroy '94
Cherry 2000 '88

Pedro Almodovar
All About My Mother '99
Live Flesh '97
Tie Me Up! Tie Me Down! '90
Women on the Verge of a Nervous Breakdown '88

Rami Alon
Choices '81

Robert Altman
Buffalo Bill & the Indians '76

Silvio Amandio
Amuck! '71

Eric Ambler
Immortal Battalion '44

Mario Amendola
Battle of the Amazons '74

Mark Amin
Diplomatic Siege '99

Chiu Tai An-Ping
Rouge '87

Dominic Anciano
Love, Honour & Obey '00

Andy Anderson
Positive I.D. '87

Brad Anderson
Next Stop, Wonderland '98

Elizabeth Anderson
The Little Mermaid 2: Return to the Sea '00

Hesper Anderson
Children of a Lesser God '86

Jace Anderson
Crocodile '00

Jane Anderson
If These Walls Could Talk 2 '00
It Could Happen to You '94

Maxwell Anderson
Rain '32

Noel Anderson
Sergio Lapel's Drawing Blood '99

Paul Thomas Anderson
Magnolia '99
Hard Eight '96

Robert Anderson
The Sand Pebbles '66

Steve (Stephen M.) Anderson
South Central '92

Will Anderson
Hip Hop 2000 '00

Mario Andreacchio
Napoleon '96

Ken Annakin
The New Adventures of Pippi Longstocking '88

Hideaki Anno
Neon Genesis Evangelion Collection '99

Brian Anthony
Behind the Planet of the Apes '98

Michelangelo Antonioni
Beyond the Clouds '95
L'Avventura '60

Theodore Apstein
Whatever Happened to Aunt Alice? '69

Yuri Arabov
Mother and Son '97

Gregg Araki
Splendor '99

Shimon Arama
Black Eagle '88

Dario Argento
The Stendahl Syndrome '95
Tenebre '82

Montxo Armendariz
Secrets of the Heart '97

Michael Armstrong
Two If by Sea '95

Scot Armstrong
Road Trip '00

Erik Arnesen
Pop & Me '99

Peter Arnett
Vietnam: The Ten Thousand Day War '80

Elliott Arnold
Alvarez Kelly '66

Darren Aronofsky
Requiem for a Dream '00

William Asher
Beach Blanket Bingo '65
Bikini Beach '64

Ray Ashley
Little Fugitive '53

Leopold Atlas
Tomorrow the World '44

Paul Attanasio
Donnie Brasco [2] '96

Pierre Aubert
Mr. Hulot's Holiday '53

Pascal Aubier
Son of Gascogne '95

Michael Auerbach
The Tie That Binds '95

John August
Charlie's Angels '00
Titan A.E. '00

Michael Austin
Princess Caraboo '94

Roger Roberts Avary
Killing Zoe '94

Antonio Avati
Macabre '80

Gabriel Axel
Babette's Feast '87

George Axelrod
Bus Stop '56
The Seven Year Itch '55

David Ayer
U-571 [CE] '00

Clay Ayers
The Watcher '00

Dan Aykroyd
Coneheads '93

Rafael Azcona
Butterfly '00
Blood and Sand '89
La Grande Bouffe '73

Thom Babbes
Body Chemistry '90

Jamie Babbit
But I'm a Cheerleader '99

Hector Babenco
Pixote '81

Jimmy Santiago Baca
Blood In . . . Blood Out: Bound by Honor '93

John Bacchus
The Erotic Ghost '00
Erotic Survivor '00
Erotic Witch Project 2: Book of Seduction '00
Girl Explores Girl: The Alien Encounter [CE] '00
Gladiator Eroticus '00
Mistress Frankenstein [CE] '00
The Erotic Witch Project [CE] '99

Kwyn Bader
Loving Jezebel '99

Jennifer Badham-Stewart
Diary of a Serial Killer '97

Dave Baer
Broken Vessels '98

Max Baer Jr.
The McCullochs '75

Frederick Bailey
Goodbye America '97

Sue Bailey
Shriek If You Know What I Did Last Friday the 13th '00

Gary L. Bain
Ice Castles '79

Mariano Baino
Dead Waters '94

Steven Baio
Fugitive Champion '99

Brydon Baker
Return of the Fly '59

Herbert Baker
Sextette '78

Noel S. Baker
Hard Core Logo '96

Ralph Bakshi
Heavy Traffic '73

John Lloyd Balderston
The Mummy '32

A. Michael Baldwin
Vice Girls '96

Earl Baldwin
Africa Screams / Jack and the Beanstalk '49

Alan Ball
American Beauty [SE] '99

Ash Bannon
Toy Story 2 '99

John Banville
The Last September '99

Laurence Ferreira Barbosa
L'Ennui '98

Joe Barilla
Blood and Black Lace '64

Leora Barish
Desperately Seeking Susan '85

Andrew Bark
Dead Waters '94

Clive Barker
Hellraiser [2] '87

Nicholas Barker
Unmade Beds '00

Jeff Barmash
Bounty Hunters 2: Hardball '97

Joseph John Barmettler Jr.
Timelock '99

Peter Barnes
A Christmas Carol '99
The Magical Legend of the Leprechauns '99
Noah's Ark '99

Jackson Barr
Body Chemistry 3: Point of Seduction '93
Body Chemistry 2: Voice of a Stranger '91
Body Chemistry '90

James Lee Barrett
The Greatest Story Ever Told [SE] '65

Neil Barrett
Rome: Power & Glory '99

H.E. Barrie
Missile to the Moon '59
She Demons '58

Julian Barry
The River '84

Simon Davis Barry
The Art of War '00

Peter Barsocchini
Drop Zone '94

Sy Bartlett
The Big Country '58

Hollis Barton
The Omega Code '99

Joel Basberg
Family of Cops 2: Breach of Faith '97

Harry Basil
My 5 Wives '00

Richard Baskin
Red Shoe Diaries: Four on the Floor '96

Ronald Bass
Snow Falling on Cedars '99

Joe Batteer
Chasers '94

Bradley Battersby
Red Letters '00

Lucio Battistrada
Dead Are Alive '72

Hans Bauer
Komodo '99

Lamberto Bava
Macabre '80

Mario Bava
Bay of Blood '71
Twitch of the Death Nerve '71
Hatchet for the Honeymoon '70
Black Sabbath '64
Blood and Black Lace '64
The Girl Who Knew Too Much '63

George L. Baxt
Horror Hotel '60

Wayne Beach
The Art of War '00

Henry Bean
Internal Affairs '90

Richard Beattie
The Highway Man '99

Jerome Beaujour
A Single Girl '96

Marcel Beaulieu
Farinelli '94

Charles Beaumont
Brain Dead '89
7 Faces of Dr. Lao '63
The Intruder '61

Josh Becker
Thou Shalt Not Kill . . . Except '87

Michael Beckerman
Erotic Witch Project 2: Book of Seduction '00
Girl Explores Girl: The Alien Encounter [CE] '00
Mistress Frankenstein [CE] '00
The Erotic Witch Project [CE] '99

Michael Frost Beckner
Sniper '92

Dick Beebe
Book of Shadows: Blair Witch 2 '00

Luiz Begazo
Manoushe, The Story of a Gypsy Love '98

Jeff Begun
Saturday the 14th '81

Peter Behrens
Kayla: A Cry in the Wilderness '00

James Warner Bellah
The Man Who Shot Liberty Valance '62

Edmund Beloin
Paris Holiday '57
The Great Lover '49
My Favorite Brunette '47

Jerry Belson
The End '78

Peter Benchley
Jaws [CE] '75

Alan Bennett
The Madness of King George '94

Charles Bennett
Voyage to the Bottom of the Sea / Fantastic Voyage '61

Jean-Louis Benoit
A Couch in New York '95

Sally Benson
Shadow of a Doubt '43

Joelle Bentolila
Red Shoe Diaries: Four on the Floor '96

Robert Benton
Superman: The Movie '78

Leonardo Bercovici
Portrait of Jennie '48
The Bishop's Wife [MGM] '47

Bruce Beresford
Paradise Road '97
Mister Johnson '91

Phil Berger
Price of Glory '00

Paul Mayeda Berges
What's Cooking? '00

Andrew Bergman
Striptease '96
It Could Happen to You '94

Eric Bergren
Frances '82

Greg Berlanti
The Broken Hearts Club '00

Alain Berliner
Ma Vie en Rose '97

Joe Berlinger
Book of Shadows: Blair Witch 2 '00

Barry Berman
Benny & Joon '93

Ted Berman
The Black Cauldron '85

Paul Bern
The Marriage Circle '24

Sam Bernard
Diplomatic Siege '99
Warlock: The Armageddon '93

Edward L. Bernds
Return of the Fly '59

Peter Berneis
Portrait of Jennie '48

Maria Bernhard
Bellyfruit '99

Kevin Bernhardt
Diplomatic Siege '99

Armyan Bernstein
The Hurricane '99

Jon Bernstein
Beautiful '00

Walter Bernstein
Semi-Tough '77
Fail-Safe '64

Eric Bernt
Romeo Must Die '00

Claude Berri
Jean de Florette '87
Manon of the Spring '87

Michael Berry
Blue Streak '99

Augustina Bessa-Luis
Party '96

Luc Besson
The Messenger: The Story of Joan of Arc '99
Leon, the Professional '94
La Femme Nikita [MGM] '91
The Big Blue [DC] '88

James Best
Death Mask '98

Alberto Bevilacqua
Black Sabbath '64

A.I. Bezzerides
Kiss Me Deadly '55

Ann Biderman
Smilla's Sense of Snow '96

Hans Billian
I Like the Girls Who Do '73

Carl Binder
Pocahontas '95

Andrew Birkin
The Messenger: The Story of Joan of Arc '99
The Cement Garden '93
Omen 3: The Final Conflict '81

Lajos Biro
The Scarlet Pimpernel '34

John Bishop
Drop Zone '94

Shem Bitterman
Halloween 5: The Revenge of Michael Myers '89

Lars Bjorkman
The White Lioness '96

David Black
The Confession '98

Debra Black
Sex Files: Digital Sex '98

J. Anderson Black
Tarzan and the Lost City '98

Eric Blakeney
Gun Shy '00

Philippe Blasband
An Affair of Love '00

Vera Blasi
Woman on Top '00

Barry W. Blaustein
Nutty Professor 2: The Klumps [1 CE] '00
Nutty Professor 2: The Klumps [2 Uncensored] '00

Robert Blees
Doctor Phibes Rises Again '72

Suzannah Blinkoff
Bellyfruit '99

William Blinn
Brian's Song '71

Stephan Bliss
The Omega Code '99

Robert Bloch
Asylum '72

Jeffrey Bloom
Flowers in the Attic '87

Stuart Blumberg
Keeping the Faith '00

John Blumenthal
Blue Streak '99

Don Bluth
Thumbelina '94
All Dogs Go to Heaven '89

Jeffrey Boam
Dead Zone '83

Paul Harris Boardman
Urban Legends 2: Final Cut '00

Sergei Bodrov
East-West '99

Peter Bogdanovich
Saint Jack '79
The Last Picture Show [DC] '71
The Wild Angels '66

Paul J.M. Bogh
Python '00

Eric Bogosian
Talk Radio '88

Endre Bohem
Monster from Green Hell '58

Don Bohlinger
Women '97

Craig Bolotin
Light It Up '99

Robert Bolt
The Bounty '84
A Man for All Seasons '66
Lawrence of Arabia '62

M. Todd Bonin
Perfect Tenant '00

J.R. Bookwalter
The Dead Next Door '89

John Boorman
Hope and Glory '87
Zardoz '73

Ian Boothby
Casper's Haunted Christmas '00

Loren Boothby
Aftershock: Earthquake in New York '99

Lizzie Borden
Working Girls '87

Robert Boris
Diplomatic Siege '99
Frank and Jesse '94

Ole Bornedal
Nightwatch '96
Nightwatch '96

Janet Borrus
Bellyfruit '99

William D. Bostjancic
Battle Queen 2020 '99

Eugenia Bostwick-Singer
Joseph: King of Dreams '00

Costa Botes
Forgotten Silver '96

Chan Kin Chung
Saviour of the Soul 2 '92

Cynthia Cidre
In Country '89

Michael Cimino
Thunderbolt & Lightfoot '74

Tony Cinciripini
Hell's Kitchen NYC '97

Bob (Benjamin) Clark
Porky's 2: The Next Day '83
Porky's / Porky's 2: The Next Day '82

Dennis Lynton Clark
In Pursuit of Honor '95

James Clavell
The Last Valley '71
The Fly / Return of the Fly '58

John Cleese
Monty Python and the Holy Grail '75

Brian Clemens
Golden Voyage of Sinbad '73

Rene Clement
Joy House '64

Laury Clemmons
The Fox and the Hound '81

Rick Cleveland
Jerry and Tom '98

Lyn Clinton
Height of the Sky '99

Robert Clouse
China O'Brien '88

Robert Cochran
Attila '01

Ethan Coen
O Brother Where Art Thou? '00

Franklin Coen
Alvarez Kelly '66

Joel Coen
O Brother Where Art Thou? '00

Lenore Coffee
End of the Affair '55

Barney Cohen
Friday the 13th, Part 4: The Final Chapter '84

Howard R. Cohen
Saturday the 14th Strikes Back '88
Saturday the 14th '81

Joel Cohen
Toy Story '95
Sister, Sister '87

Larry Cohen
The Stuff '85
Black Caesar '73
Return of the Magnificent Seven '66

Lester Cohen
Of Human Bondage '34

Peter M. Cohen
Whipped '00

Brandon Cole
Illuminata '98

Lester Cole
Blood on the Sun '45

Lewis Colick
Bulletproof '96

Max Allan Collins
Mommy [SE] '95

Joseph G. Collodi
Puppet Master '89

Chris Columbus
Nine Months '95

Ryan Combs
Straight out of Compton '00

Betty Comden
Good News '47

John Comerford
Around the Fire '98

Brian Comfort
The Asphyx '72

David Comtois
Behind the Planet of the Apes '98

Chuck Conaway
Dilemma '97

Bill Condon
F/X 2: The Deadly Art of Illusion '91
Sister, Sister '87

Joe Connelly
Munster, Go Home! '66

Myles Connolly
Till the Clouds Roll By '46

Ray Connolly
That'll Be the Day '73

Mikel Conrad
The Flying Saucer '50

Christine Conradt
The Perfect Nanny '00

Alessandro Continenza
Let Sleeping Corpses Lie '74

Tim Conway
The Private Eyes [SE] '80

Michael Cooney
Jack Frost 2: Revenge of the Mutant Killer Snowman '00

H.H. Cooper
The Arrangement '99

Merian C. Cooper
Chang: A Drama of the Wilderness '27

Natalie Cooper
Desert Hearts '86

Paul Cooper
Once Upon a Time...When We Were Colored '95

Francis Ford Coppola
The Godfather, Part 3 '90
The Conversation '74
The Godfather, Part 2 '74
The Godfather DVD Collection '72
Dementia 13 '63

Sofia Coppola
The Virgin Suicides '99

Andree Corbiau
Farinelli '94

Gerard Corbiau
Farinelli '94

Bruno Corbucci
Battle of the Amazons '74

Sebastian Cordero
Ratas, Ratones, Rateros '99

Laurence Coriat
Wonderland '99

Kevin Corrigan
Kicked in the Head '97

John W. Corrington
Isaac Asimov's Nightfall '00
The Arena '73
Battle for the Planet of the Apes '73

Joyce H. Corrington
The Arena '73
Battle for the Planet of the Apes '73

Catherine Corsini
The New Eve '98

Don A. Coscarelli
Phantasm 4: Oblivion '98

Marcello Coscia
Let Sleeping Corpses Lie '74

George P. Cosmatos
The Cassandra Crossing '76

Derrick J. Costa
Diamond Run '00

Manny Coto
Dr. Giggles '92

Frank Cottrell-Boyce
The Claim '00

Jack Couffer
Ring of Bright Water '69

Suzette Couture
Jesus '99

Noel Coward
Brief Encounter '46

Alex Cox
Death and the Compass '96
Straight to Hell '87
Sid & Nancy [MGM] '86
Repo Man '83

Jim Cox
The Rescuers Down Under '90

Frank Craven
Our Town '40

Wes Craven
Swamp Thing '82

Wayne Crawford
Jake Speed '86

James A. Creelman
The Most Dangerous Game [Madacy] '32

Michael Crichton
Jurassic Park [CE] '93
Runaway '84

Armando Crispino
Dead Are Alive '72

Michael Cristofer
Gia '98
Mr. Jones '93

David Cronenberg
The Fly / The Fly 2 '86
Rabid '77

Beverley Cross
Sinbad and the Eye of the Tiger '77

Tanja Crouch
The Joint Is Jumpin' '00

Mark Crowdy
Saving Grace '00

Cameron Crowe
Almost Famous '00
Fast Times at Ridgemont High '82

Christopher Crowe
The Last of the Mohicans '92
Mean Season '85

Le'Mark Cruise
Social Misfits '00

Jon Cryer
Went to Coney Island on a Mission from God...Be Back by Five '98
The Pompatus of Love '95

Tom Cudworth
Restaurant '98

James Cummins
The Bone Yard '90

Rusty Cundieff
House Party 2: The Pajama Jam '91

Richard Cunha
She Demons '58

Lauren Currier
Cujo '83

Valerie Curtin
And Justice for All '79

Nathaniel Curtis
Jack & the Beanstalk '52
Blood on the Sun '45

Dick Cusack
The Jack Bull '99

John Cusack
High Fidelity '00

Marc Cushman
Midnight Confessions '95

Elizabeth Cuthrell
Jesus' Son '99

Catherine Cyran
Bloodfist 2 '90
A Cry in the Wild '90
Slumber Party Massacre 3 '90

Alan J. Dachman
The Gore-Gore Girls '72

Don DaGradi
Bedknobs and Broomsticks '71

Dick Dahl
The Ballad of Ramblin' Jack '00

Jens Dahl
Pusher '96

John Dahl
Kill Me Again '89

Roald Dahl
You Only Live Twice [SE] '67

Ian Dalrymple
Pygmalion '38

Suso Cecchi D'Amico
Big Deal on Madonna Street '58

Richard Dana
The Stepdaughter '00

Clemence Dane
Fire over England '37

Rodney Dangerfield
My 5 Wives '00

Shell Danielson
Turbo: A Power Rangers Movie '97

Didi Danquart
Jew-boy Levi '98

Frank Darabont
Black Cat Run '98
The Fly 2 '89

W. Scott Darling
Sherlock Holmes and the Secret Weapon '42

Jules Dassin
Rififi '54

Kensei Date
Sin: The Movie '98

Diane Daubeney
Vampyres '74

Delmer Daves
An Affair to Remember '57
Love Affair '39

Larry David
Sour Grapes '98

Paul Davids
Starry Night '99

Gordon Davie
The Interview '98

Andrew Davies
Wilderness '96

Terence Davies
House of Mirth '00

Tod Davies
Three Businessmen '99

Valentine Davies
The Bridges at Toko-Ri '55

Bernadette Davis
Wilderness '96

Clark Davis
Teenage Strangler '64

Michael Paul Davis
Double Dragon '94

Ossie Davis
Cotton Comes to Harlem '70

Tom Davis
Coneheads '93

Isabel Dawn
Up in Mabel's Room '44

Anthony (Antonio Margheriti) Dawson
Vengeance '68

Ennio de Concini
Bluebeard '72
The Girl Who Knew Too Much '63

Claude de Givray
Bed and Board '70

Fred De Gorter
The Phantom Planet '61

Anatole de Grunwald
Pygmalion '38

Alex de la Iglesia
Dance with the Devil '97

Carlos De Los Rios
Playing Mona Lisa '00

Andre Pieyre de Mandiargues
Immoral Tales '74

Manoel de Oliveira
Party '96

Tom De Simone
Reform School Girls '86

Ralph De Vito
Family Enforcer '76

William Dear
Elephant Parts '81

David DeCoteau
Femalien 2 '96
Femalien '96

Robert DeFranco
Telling You '98

Izuru Deguchi
Ecstasy of the Angels '72
Go, Go Second Time Virgin '69

Michael deGuzman
Jaws: The Revenge '87

Paul Dehn
Conquest of the Planet of the Apes '72
Escape from the Planet of the Apes '71
Beneath the Planet of the Apes '70

Gregory Fleeman
F/X '86

Bud Fleischer
Hardcase and Fist '89

Andrew Fleming
Dick '99
Threesome '94

Brandon Fleming
The Womaneater '59

Clive Fleury
Big City Blues '99

Ladislas Fodor
Tom Thumb '58

Timothy Wayne Folsome
Uninvited Guest '99

Marcello Fondato
Black Sabbath '64
Blood and Black Lace '64

Tom Fontana
Homicide: The Movie '00

Dennis Foon
White Lies '98

Horton Foote
Tender Mercies '83

Raymond Forchon
The Horrible Dr. Bones '00

Carl Foreman
The Bridge on the River Kwai
[LE] '57

Larry Forrester
Tora! Tora! Tora! [2 SE] '70

Rolf Forsberg
Gladiators: Bloodsport of the
Colosseum '00

Bill Forsyth
Local Hero '83

Vincent Fotre
Missile to the Moon '59

Christian Fournier
The Boys '97

Finis Fox
Evangeline '29

Michael France
Cliffhanger [2 CS] '93

Pascal Franchot
Red Shoe Diaries: Luscious
Lola '00

Coleman Francis
The Beast of Yucca Flats '61

Dan Franck
La Separation '98

Jess (Jesus) Franco
Tender Flesh '00
Ilsa, the Wicked Warden '78
She Killed in Ecstasy '70
The Awful Dr. Orlof '62

Ricardo Franco
Blood and Sand '89

Carol Frank
Sorority House Massacre '86

Harriet Frank Jr.
Norma Rae '79

Hubert Frank
Call of the Wild '72

Scott Frank
Malice [MGM] '93

Al Franken
Stuart Saves His Family '94

Howard Franklin
Antitrust '00

Jeff Franklin
Love Stinks '99

Paul Franklin
Reefer Madness '38

David Franzoni
Gladiator '00

**George MacDonald
Fraser**
The Prince and the Pauper
'78
The Four Musketeers '75

Roger Fredericks
Casper's Haunted Christmas
'00

Marni Freedman
Playing Mona Lisa '00

Bart Freundlich
The Myth of Fingerprints '97

David Friedman
The Erotic Adventures of
Zorro '72
The Head Mistress '68
She-Freak '67
The Notorious Daughter of
Fanny Hill / Head Mistress
'66

R.G. Fry
Dementia '98

Rick Fry
Bride of Re-Animator '89

E. Max Frye
Where the Money Is '00
Amos and Andrew '93
Something Wild '86

Thomas Fucci
Blood and Sand '89

Robert Fuest
Doctor Phibes Rises Again
'72

Lucio Fulci
Wax Mask '97
The House by the Cemetery
[Diamond] '83
The House by the Cemetery
[Anchor Bay] '83
The Beyond '82
The Black Cat '81
Don't Torture a Duckling '72

Charles Fuller
A Soldier's Story '84

David Fuller
Necessary Roughness '91

Jules Furthman
Only Angels Have Wings '39
Come and Get It '36

Masashi Furuhashi
Samurai X Trust '99

John Fusco
Thunderheart '92

Maria Pia Fusco
Bluebeard '72

Richard Gabai
Assault of the Party Nerds 2:
Heavy Petting Detective '95

Stephen Gaghan
Rules of Engagement '00
Traffic '00

Neil Gaiman
Princess Mononoke '98

John Gale
The Firing Line '91

Henrik Galeen
Nosferatu [2] '22

Mary Gallagher
The Passion of Ayn Rand '99

Fred Gallo
Termination Man '97

Abel Gance
Beethoven '36

Lucy Gannon
Plain Jane '00

Lowell Ganz
Where the Heart Is '00
City Slickers '91
Splash '84

Jose Luis Garci
The Grandfather '98

Louis Gardel
East-West '99

Pierce Gardner
Lost Souls '00

Robert Garland
No Way Out '87

Oliver H.P. Garrett
A Farewell to Arms '32

Mick Garris
The Fly 2 '89

Ernesto Gastaldi
The Whip and the Body '63

John Gay
The Hallelujah Trail '65

Steven Gaydos
Iguana '89

Joe Gayton
Bulletproof '96

Fred Gebhardt
The Phantom Planet '61

Peter Geiger
The Colony '98

**Theodore "Dr. Seuss"
Geisel**
The 5000 Fingers of Dr. T '53

Larry Gelbart
Bedazzled [SE] '00
Blame It on Rio '84
Tootsie '82

Matt George
In God's Hands '98

Peter George
Dr. Strangelove, or: How I
Learned to Stop Worrying
and Love the Bomb [2 SE]
'64

Rob George
Fair Game '85

Maurice Geraghty
Mohawk '56

Gary Gerani
Pumpkinhead '88

Chris Gerolmo
Citizen X '95
Mississippi Burning [MGM]
'88

Vance Gerry
The Fox and the Hound '81

Sacha Gervasi
The Big Tease '99

Joe Giannone
Madman '82

Robert Gianviti
Don't Torture a Duckling '72

Gwyneth Gibby
Isaac Asimov's Nightfall '00

Mark Gibson
The In Crowd '00

William Gibson
The Miracle Worker '62

Raynold Gideon
Stand by Me [2 SE] '86

Adam Gierasch
Crocodile '00

Barry Gifford
Dance with the Devil '97

Jaime Comas Gil
Iguana '89

Gail Gilchriest
My Dog Skip '99

David Giler
Southern Comfort '81
The Parallax View '74

David Giles
Paradise Road '97

Terry Gilliam
Monty Python and the Holy
Grail '75

Sidney Gilliat
Endless Night '71

John Gilling
The Mummy's Shroud '67

David Gilman
Bad Manners '98

Dan Gilroy
Chasers '94
Freejack '92

Tom Gilroy
Bait '00

Tony Gilroy
The Cutting Edge '92

Clarence Gilyard Jr.
Left Behind: The Movie '00

Francois Girard
32 Short Films about Glenn
Gould '93

William Girdler
Sheba, Baby '75

Jonathan Glassner
Mikey '92

Benjamin Glazer
A Farewell to Arms '32

Mitch Glazer
Scrooged '88

Lasse Glomm
The Other Side of Sunday '96

Don Glut
Dinosaur Valley Girls '96

Glen Goei
That's the Way I Like It '99

Kevin Goetz
Tycus '98

Michael C. Goetz
Tycus '98

Dan Goggin
Nunsense 2: The Sequel '94

Willis Goldbeck
The Man Who Shot Liberty
Valance '62

Harris Goldberg
Deuce Bigalow: Male Gigolo
'99
I'll Be Home for Christmas
'98

Howard Goldberg
Eden '98

Marshall Goldberg
Joseph: King of Dreams '00

Marilyn Goldin
Camille Claudel '89

Gary Goldman
Navy SEALS [MGM] '90
Big Trouble in Little China
[SE] '86

James Goldman
The Lion in Winter '68

**Lawrence Louis
Goldman**
Kronos '57

William Goldman
Misery '90
The Princess Bride '87

David Goldner
The Portrait '99

George Goldsmith
Children of the Corn '84

John Goldsmith
In the Beginning... '00
Agnes Browne '99

Josh Goldsmith
What Women Want '00

Martin Goldsmith
Detour '46

Allan Goldstein
Death Wish 5: The Face of
Death '94

William Goldstein
The Abominable Dr. Phibes
'71

Bob(cat) Goldthwait
Shakes the Clown '92

Lazaro Gomez Carilles
Before Night Falls '00

Shakey Gonzaless
Angel of the Night '98

Shari Goodhartz
Dragonheart: A New Begin-
ning '00

David Zelag Goodman
Eyes of Laura Mars '78

Greer Goodman
The Tao of Steve '00

Jenniphr Goodman
The Tao of Steve '00

Joe Goodman
Left Behind: The Movie '00

Frances Goodrich
Father's Little Dividend '51

Dan Gordon
The Hurricane '99
Murder in the First '95
Passenger 57 '92
Gulliver's Travels [Image] '39

Leo Gordon
Attack of the Giant Leeches
'59
The Wasp Woman '59

Robert Gordon
Galaxy Quest '99

Ruth Gordon
Pat and Mike '52

Jill Gorey
Rugrats in Paris: The Movie
'00

Carl Gottlieb
Jaws [CE] '75

Alfred Gough
Shanghai Noon '00

Heywood Gould
Fort Apache, the Bronx '81

Peter Gould
Double Dragon '94

Bill Gove
The Apostate '98

David S. Goyer
Death Warrant '90

Gustavo Graef-Marino
Johnny 100 Pesos '93

Tom Graeff
Teenagers from Outer Space
'59

Todd Graff
Coyote Ugly '00

Bruce Graham
Steal This Movie! '00

Sam Graham
The Secret of NIMH 2 '98

James Edward Grant
Support Your Local Gunfight-
er '71
Donovan's Reef '63
The Alamo '60

John Grant
Abbott and Costello Meet
Frankenstein '48

Susannah Grant
Erin Brockovich '00
28 Days [SE] '00
Pocahontas '95

James Gray
The Yards '00

Pamela Gray
Music of the Heart [CS] '99

William Gray
The Changeling '80

Clarence Green
D.O.A. [Roan] '49

Clifford Green
Bless the Child '00

Ellen Green
Bless the Child '00

Joseph Green
The Brain that Wouldn't Die
'63

Kerri Green
Bellyfruit '99

Peter Greenaway
8 1/2 Women '99
The Cook, the Thief, His Wife
& Her Lover '90

Seth Greenland
My Teacher's Wife '95

David Greenwalt
Class '83

Clark Gregg
What Lies Beneath '00

Stephen Gregg
Seven Girlfriends '00

Babs Greyhosky
Farscape, Vol. 3 '01

Charles B. Griffith
Not of This Earth '88
The Wild Angels '66
A Bucket of Blood '59
Teenage Doll '57

Leon Griffiths
The Grissom Gang '71

Nick Grinde
March of the Wooden Sol-
diers '34

Jacob Gronlykke
Heart of Light '97

Jean Gruault
Mon Oncle d'Amerique '80
The Story of Adele H. '75

Frank Gruber
Dressed to Kill '46
Terror by Night '46

John Guare
Six Degrees of Separation
'93

Bill Gucwa
No Code of Conduct '98

Tonino Guerra
Beyond the Clouds '95
10th Victim '65
L'Avventura '60

Ugo Guerra
The Whip and the Body '63

**Jorge
Guerricaechevarria**
Dance with the Devil '97
Live Flesh '97

Mino Guerrini
The Girl Who Knew Too Much
'63

Christopher Guest
Best in Show '00
This Is Spinal Tap [MGM] '84

Val Guest
The Day the Earth Caught
Fire '61
Quatermass 2 '57

James Gunn
The Specials '00

Dan Gurskis
The Substitute 4: Failure Is
Not an Option '00

Tomas Gutierrez Alea
Guantanamera '95

Sylvain Guy
The List '99

Stephen Gyllenhaal
Homegrown '97

Belinda Haas
Up at the Villa '00

Steve Haberman
Screw Loose '99

Albert Hackett
Father's Little Dividend '51

Dennis Hackin
Bronco Billy '80

Michael Haigney
Pokemon the Movie 2000:
The Power of One '00

Fred Haines
Ulysses '67

Mervyn Haisman
Jane & the Lost City '87

Doug Hajicek
Deadly Beauty: Snow's Secret
Life '01

H.B. Halicki
Gone in 60 Seconds '74

Desmond Hall
A Day in Black and White '01

Frank Hall
The Astounding She-Monster
'58

Heidi A. Hall
Kiss of Fire '98

Karen Hall
The Women of Brewster
Place '89

Lee Hall
Billy Elliot '00

Mark Hall
Tower of Song: The Canadian
Music Hall of Fame '01

Parnell Hall
C.H.U.D. '84

Philip Halprin
The In Crowd '00

John Hamburg
Meet the Parents '00

Judd Hamilton
Fanatic '82

Roy Hamilton
Cat Women of the Moon '53

Sam Hamm
Never Cry Wolf '83

Robert Hammer
Don't Answer the Phone '80

Ellen Hammill
Don't Go in the House '80

Earl Hamner
Charlotte's Web '73

Christopher Hampton
Mary Reilly '95

Orville H. Hampton
Friday Foster '75
Detroit 9000 '73

Mark Hanna
Not of This Earth '88

Lorraine Hansberry
A Raisin in the Sun '61

Marion Hansel
The Quarry '98

Curtis Hanson
The Bedroom Window '87
Never Cry Wolf '83

David Hare
Plenty '85

Tsui Hark
A Chinese Ghost Story: The
Tsui Hark Animation '97
Chinese Ghost Story III '91
Once Upon a Time in China
'91

Robert Harling
The Evening Star '96
Steel Magnolias '89

Phil Harnage
Banzai Runner '86

Stephen Harrigan
Lone Justice 3: Showdown at
Plum Creek '96

Anthony Harris
Beware! The Blob '72

Damian Harris
Mercy '00

Eoghan Harris
Sharpe's Revenge '97
Sharpe's Mission '96
Sharpe's Regiment '96
Sharpe's Siege '96
Sharpe's Enemy '94
Sharpe's Sword '94
Sharpe's Eagle '93
Sharpe's Rifles '93

Mark Jonathan Harris
The Long Way Home '97

Greg Harrison
Groove '00

John Harrison
Dinosaur [CE] '00
Dune '00

Matthew Harrison
Kicked in the Head '97

Noel Harrison
Emmanuelle in Space: A
World of Desire '99

Paul Harrison
The House of Seven Corpses
'73

Mary Harron
American Psycho '99
I Shot Andy Warhol '96

Chris Hart
Timeless '96

Moss Hart
A Star Is Born '54
Hans Christian Andersen
[20th Century Fox] '52

Hal Hartley
The Unbelievable Truth '90

Don Hartman
Wonder Man '45

Edmund Hartmann
The Lemon Drop Kid '51

Johanna Harwood
From Russia with Love [2 SE]
'63

Katsumi Hasegawa
Maze '96

Fanny Hatton
Tonight or Never '31

Frederic Hatton
Tonight or Never '31

Werner Hauff
I Like the Girls Who Do '73

Wings Hauser
No Safe Haven '87

Anthony Havelock-Allan
Brief Encounter '46

Richard Hawley
Mother's Boys '94

John Michael Hayes
Butterfield 8 '60
The Man Who Knew Too
Much '56
The Trouble with Harry '55
Rear Window '54

Robert Hayes III
Winner Takes All '98

Terry Hayes
Vertical Limit '00

David Hayter
X-Men '00

Jack Hazan
Comic Act '00

Anne Heche
If These Walls Could Talk 2
'00

Amy Heckerling
Loser '00
Look Who's Talking, Too '90

Peter Hedges
A Map of the World '99

Kevin Heffernan
Divine Trash '98

Carol Heikkinen
Center Stage '00
Empire Records '95

Monte Hellman
Iguana '89

Axel Hellstenius
The Last Lieutenant '94

Hilary Henkin
Fatal Beauty '87

Buck Henry
Catch-22 '70
Candy '68

Todd Henschell
Puppet Master 5: The Latest
Chapter '94
Puppet Master 4 '93

Jonathan Hensleigh
The Rock [Criterion] '96

Perry Henzell
The Harder They Come '72

Tim Herlihy
Little Nicky '00

**Jaoquin Romero
Hernandez**
Cut Throats Nine '72

Barbara Herndon
Rugrats in Paris: The Movie
'00

Venabel Herndon
Alice's Restaurant '69

Gary Hershberger
Python '00

Marshall Herskovitz
Glory [2 SE] '89

Jim Herzfeld
Meet the Parents '00

Sig Herzig
They Made Me a Criminal '39

Werner Herzog
Woyzeck '78
Aguirre, the Wrath of God '72

Olivia Hetreed
The Canterville Ghost '98

Winston Hibler
The Adventures of Ichabod
and Mr. Toad '49

Scott Hicks
Snow Falling on Cedars '99

Colin Higgins
Harold and Maude '71

Kenneth Higgins
Ghosts on the Loose '43

Ethel Hill
The Little Princess '39

Jack Hill
Foxy Brown '74
Coffy '73
Pit Stop '67

James Hill
An Elephant Called Slowly '69

Richard Gilbert Hill
The Perfect Nanny '00

Walter Hill
Wild Bill '95
Southern Comfort '81
The Warriors '79

David Hilton
The Delivery '99

Robert Hiltzik
Sleepaway Camp '83

David Himmelstein
Soul of the Game '96
Power '86

Janice Hirsch
Girls Just Want to Have Fun
'85

Alfred Hitchcock
Saboteur '42

Ken Hixon
Inventing the Abbotts '97

Patrick Hobby
Hollywood Boulevard '76

Klaus Hoch
Flypaper '97

John Hodge
The Beach '00

Mike Hodges
Damien: Omen 2 '78
Get Carter '71

Arthur Hoerl
Reefer Madness '38

Samuel Hoffenstein
The Phantom of the Opera '43

Paul Hoffman
Immortality '98

Paul Hogan
Lightning Jack '94

Yau Nai Hoi
Running out of Time '99

Carlton Holder
Bridge of Dragons '99

Kees Holierhoek
Soldier of Orange '78

Tom Holland
Fright Night '85

David Hollander
Rated X '00

Jean Holloway
Till the Clouds Roll By '46

Marius Holst
Cross My Heart and Hope to Die '94

William Hooke
Shark Attack 2 '00

Ted Hooker
Crucible of Terror '72

Nick Hornby
Fever Pitch '96

Israel Horovitz
Sunshine '99

Anthony Horowitz
Lord Edgeware Dies '99

Matthew Horton
Rudyard Kipling's the Second Jungle Book: Mowgli and Baloo '97

Tomoaki Hosoyama
Weather Woman '99

A.E. Hotchner
After the Storm '01

David Howard
Galaxy Quest '99

Gregory Allen Howard
Remember the Titans '00

Matthew Howard
The Groundstar Conspiracy '72

Frank Howson
Flynn '96

Perry Howze
Mystic Pizza '88

Rita Hsiao
Toy Story 2 '99

King Hu
Painted Skin '93

Lucien Hubbard
The Vanishing American '25
Outside the Law / Shadows '21

Chris Hubbell
The Secret of NIMH 2 '98

Tom Huckabee
Deep in the Heart (of Texas) '98

Reginald (Reggie) Hudlin
House Party '90

Brett Hudson
Hysterical '83

Mark Hudson
Hysterical '83

William (Bill) Hudson
Hysterical '83

Eric Hughes
Against All Odds '84

John Hughes
Beethoven '92
She's Having a Baby '88
Planes, Trains & Automobiles '87

Terri Hughes
Idle Hands '99

Tom Hughes
Red Letters '00

Steve Hulett
The Fox and the Hound '81

William Hulkower
Battle Queen 2020 '99

Karl Heinz Hummel
The Vampire Happening '71

Sammo Hung
The Millionaire's Express '86
Spooky Encounters '80

Bonnie Hunt
Return to Me '00

Simon Hunter
Dead of Night '99

James F. Hurley
Something Weird '68

Maurice Hurley
The Proposal '00

John Huston
Moby Dick '56
Beat the Devil '53
The Maltese Falcon '41

Ron Hutchinson
The Tuskegee Airmen '95

Clint Hutchison
Terror Tract '00

Chris Hyde
Chained Heat 3: Hell Mountain '98

Jeremy Iacone
Blood In . . . Blood Out: Bound by Honor '93

Rustam Ibragimbekov
East-West '99

Ice Cube
Next Friday [Platinum Series] '00

Eric Idle
Monty Python and the Holy Grail '75

Akio Ido
A Woman Called Sada Abe '75

Michael Ignatieff
Onegin '99

W. Peter Iliff
Under Suspicion '00

Kurt Inderbitzin
Thrill Seekers '99

Raul Inglis
Premonition '99

J. Christian Ingvordsen
Mob War [BFS] '88

John Irving
The Cider House Rules '99

Kris Isacsson
Down to You '00

Takashi Ishii
Evil Dead Trap '88

Tara Ison
Don't Tell Mom the Babysitter's Dead '91

Ira Israel
Dilemma '97

Neal Israel
Look Who's Talking, Too '90

Shunya Ito
Female Convict Scorpion—Jailhouse 41 '72

Nathan Ives
Dish Dogs '98

Pete Jacelone
Psycho Sisters '98

Carl Jackson
Inhumanity '00

Peter Jackson
Forgotten Silver '96

Jake Jacobs
Midnight Confessions '95

Jon Jacobs
Lucinda's Spell '00

Michael Jacobs
Halloween 5: The Revenge of Michael Myers '89

Robert Nelson Jacobs
Dinosaur [CE] '00

Hans Jacoby
The Stranger from Venus '54

Benoit Jacquot
A Single Girl '96

Raymond Jafelice
Babar: King of the Elephants '99

Don Jakoby
The Philadelphia Experiment '84

Daniel James
Gorgo '61

Rian James
42nd Street '33

Juliann Jannus
Pop & Me '99

Karen Janszen
Digging to China '98

Sebastien Japrisot
Honor Among Thieves '68

Jim Jarmusch
Ghost Dog: The Way of the Samurai '99
Dead Man '95

Kevin Jarre
Glory [2 SE] '89

John Jarrell
Romeo Must Die '00
Restraining Order '99

Rollin Jarrett
American Vampire '97

J.R. Jarrod
Divided We Stand '00

Jim Jennewein
Getting Even with Dad '94

Anders Thomas Jensen
Mifune '99

Jack Jevne
Wonder Man '45

Ruth Prawer Jhabvala
Mr. & Mrs. Bridge '90
A Room with a View '86

Neal Jimenez
Hideaway '94
For the Boys '91
River's Edge '87

Wong Jing
Her Name Is Cat '99
New Legend of Shaolin '96

Chip Johannessen
The Crow: Salvation '00

Bayard Johnson
Tarzan and the Lost City '98
Rudyard Kipling's the Second Jungle Book: Mowgli and Baloo '97

Charles Johnson
Beyond Atlantis '73
Slaughter's Big Ripoff '73

Charles Eric Johnson
Steele's Law '91

J. Randall Johnson
The Doors [2 SE] '91

Kristine Johnson
Imaginary Crimes '94

Monica Johnson
Mother '96
Lost in America '85
Real Life '79

Nunnally Johnson
How to Marry a Millionaire '53

Randy Johnson
The Doors [2 SE] '91

Robert P. Johnson
Bojangles '01

Thomas Johnston
Jerome '98

Tony Johnston
Full Disclosure '00

Trace Johnston
Hysterical '83

Amy Holden Jones
The Rich Man's Wife '96
Beethoven '92
Mystic Pizza '88
Love Letters '83

Evan Jones
King and Country '64

Laura Jones
Angela's Ashes '99

Michael Jones
Mutant '83

Terry Jones
Monty Python and the Holy Grail '75

Neil Jordan
The End of the Affair '99
Mona Lisa '86

Jon Jost
The Bed You Sleep In '93

Adrien (Carole Eastman) Joyce
Five Easy Pieces '70
The Shooting '66

C. Courtney Joyner
Puppet Master 3: Toulon's Revenge '90

Noah Jubelirer
Family of Cops 3 '98

Steve Judson
Dolphins '00

Lenny Juliano
Desert Thunder '99

Tsai Kuo Jung
Crouching Tiger, Hidden Dragon '00

Cedric Kahn
L'Ennui '98

Chen Kaige
The Emperor and the Assassin '99

Bill Kalmenson
The Souler Opposite '97

Robert Mark Kamen
A Walk in the Clouds '95
Gladiator '92
The Karate Kid '84

Steven Kampmann
Back to School '86

Aben Kandel
The Fighter '52

Michael Kane
Southern Comfort '81

Rolfe Kanefsky
Ultimate Attraction '98

Atsuji Kaneko
Gun Smith Cats: Bulletproof '95

Ryoma Kaneko
Sin: The Movie '98

Garson Kanin
Pat and Mike '52

Michael Kanin
How to Commit Marriage '69

Hal Kanter
The Road to Bali '53

Deborah Kaplan
The Flintstones in Viva Rock Vegas '00

Mitchell Kapner
The Whole Nine Yards '00

Wong Kar-Wai
Ashes of Time '94

Einar Karason
Devil's Island '96

Larry Karaszewski
Screwed '00

Pip Karmel
Me Myself I '99

Marshall Karp
Just Looking '99

Steven E. Karr
Puppet Master 5: The Latest Chapter '94

Lawrence Kasdan
Grand Canyon '91
Silverado [SE] '85

Meg Kasdan
Grand Canyon '91

Hiroshi Kashiwabara
Godzilla 2000 '99

Jason Katims
The Pallbearer '95

Allan Aaron Katz
Diamonds '99

Steven Katz
Shadow of the Vampire '00

Charles Kaufman
Mother's Day [DC] '80

Ken Kaufman
Space Cowboys '00

Lloyd (Samuel Weil) Kaufman
Terror Firmer [SE] '00

Yoshiaki Kawajiri
BioHunter [SE] '95

Tomoko Kawasaki
Project A-ko '86

Sandra Kay
Working Girls '87

Nicholas Kazan
Bicentennial Man '99
Homegrown '97
At Close Range '86
Frances '82

James Keach
The Long Riders '80

Stacy Keach
The Long Riders '80

Lloyd Keith
Back to Back '96

Woody Keith
Dementia '98
Bride of Re-Animator '89

David E. Kelley
Mystery, Alaska '99

Karen Kelly
The Last Best Sunday '98
Body Chemistry 4: Full Expo-
sure '95

Thomas J. Kelly
The House of Seven Corpses
'73

J.J. Kendall
Deadly Weapons '70

Garfield Kennedy
The Last Great Adventure '99

Chris Kentis
Grind '96

Rob Kerchner
Heaven's Fire '00

Ian Kerkhof
Venus in Furs '94

Sarah Kernochan
All I Wanna Do '98

Justin Kerrigan
Human Traffic '99

Lyle Kessler
Gladiator '92

Ayub Khan-Din
East Is East '99

Roland Kibbee
Vera Cruz '53

Ryuzo Kikushima
Tora! Tora! Tora! [2 SE] '70

Yip Kwong Kim
Saviour of the Soul 2 '92

Chloe King
Red Shoe Diaries: Luscious
Lola '00
Red Shoe Diaries: Swimming
Naked '00
B. Monkey '97

Robert King
Vertical Limit '00
Bloodfist '89

Sierra King
Scandal: The Big Turn On '99

Stephen King
Sleepwalkers '92
Pet Sematary '89
Maximum Overdrive '86

Zalman King
Red Shoe Diaries: Swimming
Naked '00
In God's Hands '98
Red Shoe Diaries: Strip Poker
'96
Two Moon Junction '88

Dorothy Kingsley
Pal Joey '57

Ernest Kinoy
The Story of Jacob & Joseph
'74

Stephen Kinsella
Double Parked '00

Harvey C. Kirk
Phenomenon—The Lost
Archives: Noah's Ark
Found?/Tunguska/Stolen
Glory '99
Phenomenon—The Lost
Archives: Up for
Sale/Heavy Watergate '99

Karey Kirkpatrick
Chicken Run '00
The Little Vampire '00
The Rescuers Down Under
'90

Nobuaki Kishima
Art of Fighting '93

Takeshi "Beat" Kitano
Fireworks '97
Kids Return '96
Scene at the Sea '91

Martin Kitrosser
Friday the 13th, Part 3 '82

Keith Kjornes
Thug Life '00

Tom Klassen
Fanatic '82

Howard Klausner
Space Cowboys '00

Josh Klausner
The 4th Floor '99

Ross Klaven
Tigerland '00

Nicholas Klein
The Million Dollar Hotel '99

Harry Kleiner
Fantastic Voyage '66

Richard Kletter
The Colony '98

Max Kleven
Ruckus '81

Herbert Kline
The Fighter '52

Steven Kloves
Wonder Boys '00

Daniel Knauf
Blind Justice '94

Nigel Kneale
Sharpe's Gold '94
The Witches '66
Damn the Defiant '62
The Entertainer '60
The Abominable Snowman
'57
Quatermass 2 '57

**Patricia Louisianna
Knop**
Red Shoe Diaries: Strip Poker
'96

Flip Kobler
Pocahontas 2: Journey to a
New World '98
Beauty and the Beast: The
Enchanted Christmas '97

David Koepp
The Lost World: Jurassic Park
2 [CE] '97
Jurassic Park [CE] '93

Bob Koherr
Plump Fiction '97

Vincent Kok
Gorgeous '99

Manuel Komroff
Scarlet Empress '34

Norio Konami
Female Convict Scorpion—
Jailhouse 41 '72

Jeffrey Konvitz
The Sentinel '76

Jill Kopelman
Intern '00

Howard Korder
The Passion of Ayn Rand '99

Hirokazu Kore-eda
After Life '98

Rachel Koretsky
The Pebble and the Penguin
'94

Harmony Korine
Julien Donkey-boy '99
Gummo '97

Mark Kornweibel
Pop & Me '99

Ken Koser
Sudie & Simpson '90

Jerzy Kosinski
Being There '79

Tetsutomo Kosugi
Remembering the Cosmos
Flower '99

Ted Kotcheff
North Dallas Forty '79

Jim Kouf
Class '83

Steven Kovacs
Angel Blue '97

Oleg Kovalov
Sergei Eisenstein: Mexican
Fantasy '98

Soeren Kragh-Jacobsen
Mifune '99

Hans Kraly
Eternal Love '29

Earl Kress
The Fox and the Hound '81

Stu Krieger
The Land Before Time '88

Peter Krikes
Anna and the King '99

Milton Krims
Mohawk '56

Yves Kropf
Honey & Ashes '96

Ehren Kruger
Reindeer Games '00
Scream 3 [CS] '00

Elizabeth Kruger
Our Lips Are Sealed '00

Arthur Krystal
Thick As Thieves '99

Yi Kuang
The Mighty Peking Man '77

Stanley Kubrick
Dr. Strangelove, or: How I
Learned to Stop Worrying
and Love the Bomb [2 SE]
'64
Killer's Kiss '55

Harry Kurnitz
The Inspector General '49

Akira Kurosawa
Madadayo '92
Dersu Uzala '75

Diane Kurys
Love After Love '94

Karyn Kusama
Girlfight '99

Judy J. Kushner
Double Agent 73 '80

Antoine Lacomblez
Love After Love '94

Jacques Lagrange
Mr. Hulot's Holiday '53

Richard LaGravenese
The Fisher King '91

Fu Lai
The Prisoner '90

Don Lake
Return to Me '00

Frank Laloggia
The Lady in White '88

Paul LaLonde
Revelation '00
Tribulation '00

Peter LaLonde
Revelation '00
Tribulation '00

John Lamb
Postmortem '98

Neil Landau
Don't Tell Mom the Babysitter's Dead '91

Richard H. Landau
Spaceways '53

John Landis
Clue '85

Lanier Laney
Shag: The Movie '89

Fritz Lang
The Thousand Eyes of Dr.
Mabuse '60
The Indian Tomb '21

Harry Langdon
The Flying Deuces / Utopia
'39

Noel Langley
A Christmas Carol '51

Arlette Langmann
Loulou '80

Ring Lardner Jr.
Tomorrow the World '44

Gil Lasky
The Gay Deceivers '69

Jonathan Latimer
Topper Returns '41

Steve Latshaw
Mach 2 '00
Rangers '00
Submerged '00

Alberto Lattuada
Variety Lights '51

Laura Lau
Grind '96

Lindy Laub
For the Boys '91

Michael Laughlin
Mesmerized '84

Dale Launer
My Cousin Vinny '92

Arthur Laurents
The Way We Were [SE] '73
Rope '48

Marc Lawrence
Miss Congeniality '00

Martin Lawrence
You So Crazy '94

J.F. Lawton
Mistress '91

Martin Lazarus
Interceptor Force '99

Paul Lazarus
Seven Girlfriends '00

Philip LaZebnik
Pocahontas '95

Yvan Le Moine
The Red Dwarf '99

Didier Le Pecheur
Don't Let Me Die on a Sunday '99

Mark Leahy
Beowulf '98

David Lean
A Passage to India '84
Brief Encounter '46

Denis Leary
Two If by Sea '95

Bruce Leddy
My Teacher's Wife '95

Herbert J. Leder
Fiend Without a Face '58

Charles Lederer
Gentlemen Prefer Blondes
'53

Chris Chan Lee
Yellow '98

Leonard Lee
Dressed to Kill '46

Ricardo Lee
Goodbye America '97
Midnight Dancers '94

Spike Lee
Bamboozled '00
Mo' Better Blues '90
Do the Right Thing [2] '89
School Daze '88

Timothy Lee
Street Gun '96

John Leekley
Prince of Central Park '00

Robert Lees
Abbott and Costello Meet
Frankenstein '48

Michael Leeson
What Planet Are You From?
'00

Doug Lefler
Steel Dawn '87

Ernest Lehman
Family Plot '76
The Sound of Music [Five
Star Collection] '65
North by Northwest '59
Sweet Smell of Success '57

Arnold Leibovit
The Fantasy Film Worlds of
George Pal '86

Jerry Leichtling
Blue Sky '91

Mike Leigh
Topsy Turvy '99

Warren Leight
Mother's Day [DC] '80

Erwin Leiser
Mein Kampf: Hitler's Rise
and Fall '60

David Leland
Mona Lisa '86

Jonathan Lemkin
Red Planet '00

Vicente Lenero
Midaq Alley '95

Umberto Lenzi
Cannibal Ferox '84

Michael G. Leonard
In the Flesh / Blood Bullets
Buffoons '00

Amit Leor
Pick a Card '97

Dan Lerner
Traitor's Heart '98

Eric Lerner
Kiss the Sky '98

Ferenc Leroget
The Monster of Camp Sun-
shine '64

Gwendolyn J. Lester
Johnny B. '00

Sheldon Lettich
Double Impact '91

Jeremy Leven
The Legend of Bagger Vance
'00

Frank Levering
Parasite '82

Marc Levin
Madeline '98

Barry Levinson
Liberty Heights '99
Avalon '90
And Justice for All '79

Eugene Levy
Best in Show '00

Shuki Levy
Turbo: A Power Rangers
Movie '96

Cecil Lewis
Pygmalion '38

Herschell Gordon Lewis
Scum of the Earth '63

Dr. Jack Lewis
The Amazing Transparent
Man '60

Jerry Lewis
The Nutty Professor '63

Russell Lewis
Sharpe's Battle '94

Harriette Lewiston
Passion & Romance: Scandal
'97

Crash Leyland
Sniper '92

Cline Lien
Traitor's Heart '98

Jimmy Lifton
Mirror, Mirror 2: Raven Dance
'94

Topper Lilien
Dungeons and Dragons '00
Where the Money Is '00

Michael Lindsay-Hogg
The Object of Beauty '91

Wang Hui Ling
Crouching Tiger, Hidden Dragon '00

Andrew Liotta
Delivered '98

Ken Liotti
The Waiting Game '99

W.P. Lipscomb
Pygmalion '38
The Garden of Allah '36

**Jeanne Rawlings
Livingston**
The Italians '00

Gerrit J. Lloyd
Battle of the Sexes '28

Andrew Lloyd Webber
Jesus Christ Superstar '00

Robert Locash
High School High '96
Naked Gun 33 1/3: The Final
Insult '94

Nancy Locke
No Safe Haven '87

David Logan
Circus '00

John Logan
Gladiator '00
Any Given Sunday '99
Bats '99

Kenneth Lonergan
The Adventures of Rocky &
Bullwinkle '00

Sheryl Longin
Dick '99

Lisa Loomer
Girl, Interrupted '99

Ray Loriga
Live Flesh '97

Hope Loring
Shadows '22

David Loughery
Passenger 57 '92

**Harry M. (Leon P.
Howard) Love**
Maniac Nurses Find Ecstasy
'94

Edward T. Lowe
Bulldog Drummond Escapes
'37
The Vampire Bat '32

Andrew Lowery
Boys and Girls '00

Craig Lucas
Prelude to a Kiss '92
Longtime Companion '90

**Rubens Francisco
Lucchetti**
Awakenings of the Beast '68

Gene Luotto
Bay of Blood '71
Twitch of the Death Nerve '71

Rod Lurie
The Contender '00
Deterrence '00

David Lynch
Blue Velvet '86

Jennifer Lynch
Boxing Helena '93

Jonathan Lynn
Clue '85

Colin MacDonald
Sharpe's Honour '94

Alexandre Machado
Bossa Nova '99

Alistair MacLean
Breakheart Pass '76

Jeanie Macpherson
Joan the Woman '16

Kathryn MacQuarrie
Red Shoe Diaries: Swimming
Naked '00

Henry Madden
Body Count '95

Ben Maddow
The Balcony '63

Diana Maddox
The Changeling '80

Doug Magee
Somebody Has to Shoot the
Picture '90

Jeff Maguire
In the Line of Fire [2 SE] '93

John Lee Mahin
The Horse Soldiers '59

Barry Mahon
The Beast That Killed Women
/ The Monster of Camp
Sunshine '65

Richard Maibaum
The Living Daylights '87
From Russia with Love [2 SE]
'63

F.X. Maier
Switchblade Sisters '75

Gloria Maley
Inseminoid '80

Nick Maley
Inseminoid '80

David Mamet
Hannibal '01
American Buffalo '95
House of Games '87
The Untouchables '87

Babaloo Mandel
Where the Heart Is '00
City Slickers '91
Splash '84

Cory Mandell
Battlefield Earth '00

James Mangold
Girl, Interrupted '99

Joseph L. Mankiewicz
Cleopatra '63
Guys and Dolls '55
The Barefoot Contessa '54

Tom Mankiewicz
The Eagle Has Landed '77
The Cassandra Crossing '76
Diamonds Are Forever [SE]
'71

Wolf Mankowitz
The Day the Earth Caught
Fire '61

Arthur Mann
The Jackie Robinson Story '50

Michael Mann
The Last of the Mohicans '92

Stanley Mann
Meteor '79

Greg Manos
Cutaway '00

Guy Manos
Cutaway '00

**Joaquin Luis Romero
Marchent**
Cut Throats Nine '72

Cindy Marcus
Pocahontas 2: Journey to a
New World '98
Beauty and the Beast: The
Enchanted Christmas '97

Dwight Marcus
News from the West

A. L. Mariaux
Oasis of the Zombies '82
Zombie Lake '80

Richard "Cheech" Marin
Cheech and Chong: Still
Smokin' '83
Cheech and Chong's Up in
Smoke '79

Giorgio Mariuzzo
The Beyond '82

Goran Markovic
Tito and Me '92

Andrew Marlowe
The Hollow Man [SE] '00

Malcolm Marmorstein
Pete's Dragon '77

Henri Marquet
Mr. Hulot's Holiday '53

Barry Mahon
The Beast That Killed Women
/ The Monster of Camp
Sunshine '65

Joel B. Marsden
Ill-Gotten Gains '97

David Marsh
Stormswept '95

William Martell
The Base '99
Invisible Mom '96

Bill Martin
Elephant Parts '81

Steve Martin
Roxanne '87
Dead Men Don't Wear Plaid
'82

Troy Kennedy Martin
Kelly's Heroes '70

Chris Martino
Blood of Ghastly Horror '72

Luciano Martino
The Whip and the Body '63

Raymond Martino
DaVinci's War '92

Ed Masterson
No Code of Conduct '98

William Mastrosimone
The Beast '88

Richard Matheson
Dracula / Strange Case of Dr.
Jekyll & Mr. Hyde '73
The Devil Rides Out '68
Tales of Terror '62
The Pit and the Pendulum '61
The Fall of the House of
Usher '60

Hiro Matsuda
Female Convict Scorpion—
Jailhouse 41 '72

Temple Matthews
The Little Mermaid 2: Return
to the Sea '00

Burny Mattinson
The Fox and the Hound '81

Ronald F. Maxwell
Gettysburg '93

Paul Mayersberg
Croupier '00

Wendell Mayes
Death Wish '74
In Harm's Way '65
Anatomy of a Murder '59

Jill Mazursky
National Lampoon's Golf
Punks '99

Rod McCall
Lewis and Clark and George
'97

Leo McCarey
An Affair to Remember '57
Love Affair '39

Peter McCarthy
Tapeheads '89

Detrich McClure
Out Kold '00

Mark McCorkle
Buzz Lightyear of Star Com-
mand: The Adventure
Begins '00

Jim McCullough Jr.
Mountaintop Motel Massacre
'86

**Michael James
McDonald**
The Crazysitter '94

Edward T. McDougal
The Prodigy '98

Michael McDowell
The Nightmare before Christmas [2 SE] '93

Alan B. McElroy
Left Behind: The Movie '00

Scott McGehee
Suture '93

David McGillivray
Frightmare '74

Jim McGlynn
Traveller '96

Michael McGruther
Tigerland '00

Thomas McGuane
Rancho Deluxe '75

Don McGuire
Tootsie '82

Jay McInerney
Gia '98

Michael McKean
This Is Spinal Tap [MGM] '84

Don McKellar
32 Short Films about Glenn
Gould '93

David McKenna
Get Carter '00
Body Shots '99

Vince McKewin
The Replacements '00

Patrick McKnight
Dope Case Pending '00

Joseph McLee
Bay of Blood '71
Twitch of the Death Nerve '71

John McMahon
Broken Vessels '98

Lee McMahon
Madron '70

James McManus
La Cucaracha '99

Michael McManus
Mafia! '98

Larry McMurtry
The Last Picture Show [DC]
'71

Dennis McNicholas
The Ladies Man '00

Christopher McQuarrie
Way of the Gun '00

Will McRobb
Snow Day '00

Martin Meader
Paradise Road '97

Herb Meadow
The Strange Woman '46

Tim Meadows
The Ladies Man '00

Irene Mecchi
Annie '99

Julio Medem
Tierra '95

Mark Medoff
Children of a Lesser God '86

Thomas Meehan
Annie '82

Steve Meerson
Anna and the King '99

Robert T. Megginson
F/X '86

Deepa Mehta
Fire '96

Frank Melford
Blood on the Sun '45

Martin Melhish
Tower of Song: The Canadian
Music Hall of Fame '01

Aaron Mendelsohn
Air Bud 2: Golden Receiver
'98
Air Bud [2] '97

Ric Menello
Drop Dead Rock '95

Anne Meredith
Rated X '00

Monte Merrick
The Miracle Worker '00

Alex Metcalf
The Crimson Code '00

Stephen Metcalfe
Beautiful Joe '00

Kai Meyer
School's Out '99

Turi Meyer
Leprechaun 2 '94

Ashley Scott Meyers
Dish Dogs '98

Nancy Meyers
Baby Boom '87

Paul Eric Meyers
Aftershock: Earthquake in
New York '99

Bret Michaels
No Code of Conduct '98

Jean Michel Michelena
Picasso '85

Dave Michener
The Fox and the Hound '81

Romano Migliorini
The Bloody Pit of Horror '65

Ted V. Mikels
The Astro-Zombies '67

Ron Milbauer
Idle Hands '99

Eduardo Milewicz
Life According to Muriel '97

John Milius
Conan the Barbarian [2 CE]
'82
Dillinger '73

Miles Millar
Shanghai Noon '00

Andrew Miller
Boys and Girls '00

Arthur Miller
The Misfits '61

Geof Miller
Deepstar Six '89

Jeff Miller
Eye of the Killer '99
Hellblock 13 '97

Bertram Millhauser
The Woman in Green '45
The Woman in Green /
Dressed to Kill '45

Travis Milloy
Street Gun '96

Paula Milne
I Dreamed of Africa '00

David Scott Milton
Born to Win '71

Waturu Mimura
Godzilla 2000 '99

Daniel Minahan
I Shot Andy Warhol '96

David Mingay
Comic Act '00

Anthony Minghella
The Talented Mr. Ripley '99

Brad Mirman
Knight Moves '93

Craig Mitchell
Komodo '99
Milo '98

Sollace Mitchell
Row Your Boat '98

Hideki Mitsui
Sol Bianca: The Legacy '90

Yoko Mizuki
Kwaidan '64

Patrick Modiano
Son of Gascogne '95

Jose Mojica Marins
Awakenings of the Beast '68
This Night I'll Possess Your
Corpse '66

Hans Petter Moland
The Last Lieutenant '94

Craig Monahan
The Interview '98

Nate Monaster
That Touch of Mink '62

Santiago Moncada
Cut Throats Nine '72
Hatchet for the Honeymoon
'70

Mario Monicelli
Lovers and Liars '81
Big Deal on Madonna Street
'58

Eric Monte
Cooley High '75

Joao Cesar Monteiro
God's Comedy '95

Sam Montgomery
U-571 [CE] '00

Vincent Monton
Die! Die! Die! '00

Keith Moon
Tommy '75

Brian Moore
Black Robe '91
Torn Curtain '66

Charles Philip Moore
Heaven's Fire '00
Termination Man '97

Michael Moore
Canadian Bacon '94

Roy Moore
Black Christmas '75

Eddie Moran
Wonder Man '45

Glen Morgan
Final Destination '00
The Boys Next Door '85

J. Everitt Morley
Final Voyage '99

Steven Robert Morris
Stonebrook '98

Paul Morrison
Solomon and Gaenor '98

William Morrow
The Road to Bali '53

Bob Mosher
Munster, Go Home! '66

Jonathan Mostow
U-571 [CE] '00

Greg Mottola
The Daytrippers '96

Bill Motz
Lady and the Tramp 2:
Scamp's Adventure '01
Buzz Lightyear of Star Com-
mand: The Adventure
Begins '00
Beauty and the Beast: The
Enchanted Christmas '97

Oren Moverman
Jesus' Son '99

Malcolm Mowbray
Sweet Revenge '98

Robin Mukbarjee
Poldark '96

Ryu Murakami
Because of You '95

Jane Murfin
Come and Get It '36

Mario Musy
Hatchet for the Honeymoon
'70

Floyd Mutrux
Blood In . . . Blood Out:
Bound by Honor '93
The Hollywood Knights '80

Julie Marie Myatt
Red Shoe Diaries: Strip Poker
'96

Nancy Myers
Father of the Bride Part II '95

John Myhers
The Private Eyes [SE] '80

Keiju Nagasawa
Prisoner Maria: The Movie '95

Yuri Nagibin
Dersu Uzala '75

Roberto Natale
The Bloody Pit of Horror '65

Jeff Nathanson
Bait '00

Rick Natkin
Necessary Roughness '91

William T. Naud
Necromancer: Satan's Ser-
vant '88

Bill Naughton
Alfie '66

Chris Neal
Python '00

Ronald Neame
Brief Encounter '46

Joe Ned
Erotic Witch Project 2: Book
of Seduction '00
Girl Explores Girl: The Alien
Encounter [CE] '00
Mistress Frankenstein [CE]
'00
The Erotic Witch Project [CE]
'99

Jesse Negron
Pop & Me '99

Joe Nelms
Shriek If You Know What I Did
Last Friday the 13th '00

Davia Nelson
Imaginary Crimes '94

John Allen Nelson
American Yakuza '94

Vladimir Nemirovsky
Hangman '99

Berit Nesheim
The Other Side of Sunday '96

Michael Nesmith
Elephant Parts '81

Kurt Neumann
Rocketship X-M '50

Craig J. Nevius
Black Scorpion 2: Ground
Zero '96
Black Scorpion '95

David Newman
Santa Claus: The Movie '85
Superman 3 '83
Superman 2 '80
Superman: The Movie '78

David Nicholls
Simpatico '99

Jack Nicholson
Ride in the Whirlwind '66

William Nicholson
Gladiator '00
Grey Owl '99

Daryl G. Nickens
House Party 2: The Pajama
Jam '91

Michael A. Nickles
Desert Winds '95

Ted Nicolaou
Bloodstorm: Subspecies 4
'98

Victor Nieuwenhuijs
Venus in Furs '94

Caron Nightengale
Battle Queen 2020 '99

Jeff Nimoy
Digimon: The Movie '00

Kogo Noda
Good Morning '59

Sergei Nolbandov
Fire over England '37

Greg Norberg
Mafia! '98

Marsha Norman
The Audrey Hepburn Story
'00

Duncan North
The Tao of Steve '00

Edmund H. North
Damn the Defiant '62

Bill W.L. Norton
Losin' It '82

William W. Norton Sr.
Day of the Animals '77

Louis Nowra
Heaven's Burning '97

Frank Nugent
Donovan's Reef '63

Tom Nursall
I'll Be Home for Christmas
'98

Bruno Nuytten
Camille Claudel '89

Dan O'Bannon
Dead and Buried '81

Rockne S. O'Bannon
Alien Nation '88

Sean O'Bannon
The Kid with the X-Ray Eyes
'99

Richard O'Brien
The Rocky Horror Picture
Show '75

Robert O'Brien
The Lemon Drop Kid '51

Sean O'Byrne
Mystery, Alaska '99

Maurice O'Callaghan
Broken Harvest '94

Brendan O'Carroll
Agnes Browne '99

Gavin O'Connor
Tumbleweeds '98

David Odell
Supergirl '84
Cry Uncle '71

Clifford Odets
Sweet Smell of Success '57

Michael O'Donoghue
Scrooged '88

Steve Oedekerk
Nutty Professor 2: The
Klumps [1 CE] '00
Nutty Professor 2: The
Klumps [2 Uncensored] '00

Yoshihisa Ogita
Maborosi '95

Jorgo Ognenovski
Stalked '99

Hideo Oguni
Tora! Tora! Tora! [2 SE] '70

Yukiyoshi Ohashi
Samurai X: The Movie '95

Paul Ohl
Highlander: The Final Dimension '94

Kaori Okamura
Demon City Shinjuku '93

Cunningham O'Keefe
Before Night Falls '00

Joel Oliansky
Bird '88

Adam Oliensis
The Pompatus of Love '95

Johanna Olofsson
Edvard Grieg: What Price
Immortality? '00

Thomas Olofsson
Edvard Grieg: What Price
Immortality? '00

Arne Olsen
All Dogs Go to Heaven 2 '95
Red Scorpion '89

Josh Olson
On the Border '98

Ngozi Onwurah
Welcome II the Terrordome
'95

Timothy O'Rawe
Midnight Confessions '95

Wyott Ordung
Robot Monster '53

Mario Orfini
Fair Game '89

Alan Ormsby
Porky's 2: The Next Day '83

J.O.C. Orton
Alfred Hitchcock's Bon Voyage & Aventure Malgache '44

Paul Osborn
Portrait of Jennie '48

John Osborne
Tom Jones [MGM] '63
The Entertainer '60

Dominique Othenin-Girard
Halloween 5: The Revenge of Michael Myers '89

Filippo Ottoni
Bay of Blood '71
Twitch of the Death Nerve '71

Eric Overmyer
Homicide: The Movie '00

Yasujiro Ozu
Good Morning '59

David Pabian
Puppet Master 2 '90

William R. Pace
Charming Billy '99

Michele Pacitto
Mistress of Seduction '00

Martin Pako
Batman: Mask of the Phantasm '93

Michael Palin
Monty Python and the Holy Grail '75

Rospo Pallenberg
The Emerald Forest '85

Marc Palmieri
Telling You '98

Norman Panama
White Christmas '54

Christopher Panneck
The Prodigy '98

Roger Paradiso
Kisses in the Dark '97

Bill Parker
Klash '95

Christine Parker
Peach / A Bitter Song '95

John Parker
Daughter of Horror / Dementia '55

Tom S. Parker
Getting Even with Dad '94

Andrew Parkinson
I, Zombie '99

Tom Parkinson
Crucible of Terror '72

Marlon Parry
Winner Takes All '98

Marion Parsonnet
Gilda '46

Lindsley Parsons
Man from Utah / Sagebrush Trail '34
Randy Rides Alone '34
Trail Beyond '34
Sagebrush Trail '33

Ivan Passer
Law and Disorder '74
Born to Win '71

Vincent Patrick
The Pope of Greenwich Village '84

Don Michael Paul
Harley Davidson and the Marlboro Man '91

Keith Payson
Puppet Master 5: The Latest Chapter '94
Puppet Master 4 '93

Ann Peacock
A Lesson Before Dying '99

Bill Peet
The Sword in the Stone '63

Wang Peigong
The Emperor and the Assassin '99

Nikola Pejakovic
Pretty Village, Pretty Flame '96

Arthur Penn
Alice's Restaurant '69

Erdman Penner
The Adventures of Ichabod and Mr. Toad '49

Jonathan Penner
Let the Devil Wear Black '99

John Penney
In Pursuit '00

Virginia Perfili
Mirror, Mirror 2: Raven Dance '94

Mark David Perry
Captive '00

Scott Perry
Teenage Catgirls in Heat '00

Michael Pertwee
The Mouse on the Moon '62

Charlie Peters
Blame It on Rio '84

Brian Wayne Peterson
But I'm a Cheerleader '99

Elio Petri
10th Victim '65

Donald Petrie
Miss Congeniality '00

Chuck Pfarrer
Red Planet '00
Barb Wire '96

Anna Hamilton Phelan
Girl, Interrupted '99

Bill Phillips
El Diablo '90

Kate Phillips
The Blob '58

Todd Phillips
Road Trip '00

Maurice Pialat
Loulou '80

Jim Piddock
One Good Turn '95

Arthur C. Pierce
The Cosmic Man '59

Tedd Pierce
Gulliver's Travels [Image] '39

Frank Pierson
In Country '89
Cat Ballou [SE] '65

Jeremy Piksen
The Lemon Sisters '90

Tullio Pinelli
Il Bidone '55
Variety Lights '51

June Pinheiro
The Scorpio Factor '90

Steve Pink
High Fidelity '00

Jumad Pinkney
Hip Hop 2000 '00

Bret Piper
A Nymphoid Barbarian in Dinosaur Hell [SE] '94

Robert Pirosh
Hell Is for Heroes '62

Mark Pirro
My Mom's a Werewolf '89

Peter Pistor
In Pursuit '00

Angelo Pizzo
Rudy [SE] '93

Alan Plater
The Last of the Blonde Bombshells '00
A Merry War '97
The Inside Man '84

Polly Platt
A Map of the World '99

Bill Plympton
I Married a Strange Person '97

Jeremy Podeswa
The Five Senses '99

James Poe
Lilies of the Field '63

Charles Edward Pogue
The Fly / The Fly 2 '86
The Sign of Four '83

John Pogue
The Skulls '00

Gregory Poirier
Gossip '99

Joseph Poland
Winds of the Wasteland '36

Roman Polanski
The Ninth Gate '99
Rosemary's Baby '68

Mark Polish
Twin Falls Idaho '99

Michael Polish
Twin Falls Idaho '99

Stu Pollard
Nice Guys Sleep Alone '99

Jack Pollexfen
The Man from Planet X '51

Vicki Polon
Mr. Wonderful '93

DJ Pooh
Three Strikes '00

Marty Poole
Diamond Run '00

Jeff Pope
Essex Boys '99

Ann Porter
Velocity '99

Linda Post
Roots of Rhythm '99

Dick Poston
Blood of Ghastly Horror '72

Dennis Potter
Gorky Park '83

Michael Powell
Black Narcissus '47
I Know Where I'm Going '45

Dennis Pratt
Leprechaun 4: In Space '96

Emeric Pressburger
Black Narcissus '47
I Know Where I'm Going '45

Steven Pressfield
Freejack '92

Richard Price
Shaft '00

Tim Rose Price
The Serpent's Kiss '97

Barry Primus
Mistress '91

Pat Proft
High School High '96
Naked Gun 33 1/3: The Final Insult '94
Naked Gun 2 1/2: The Smell of Fear '91
The Naked Gun: From the Files of Police Squad '88

Biagio Proietti
The Black Cat '81

Mark Protosevich
The Cell '00

Tom Provost
Under Suspicion '00

Peter Pruce
Excellent Cadavers '99

Richard Pryor
Bustin' Loose '81

William Pugsley
Dracula vs. Frankenstein '71

Jack Pulman
I, Claudius '91

Daniella Purcell
Midnight Tease / Midnight Tease 2 '94

Deirdre Purcell
Falling for a Dancer '98

Neal Purvis
The World Is Not Enough [SE] '99

Stephen Purvis
Deep in the Heart (of Texas) '98

Mario Puzo
The Godfather, Part 3 '90
Superman 2 '80
Superman: The Movie '78
The Godfather, Part 2 '74
The Godfather DVD Collection '72

Anne-Francois Pyszora
Winter Sleepers '97

Paris Qualles
The Tuskegee Airmen '95

Darryl Quarles
Big Momma's House '00

Mary Quijano
Stalked '99

Joseph Quillan
Son of Paleface '52

John Quinn
Fallen Angel '99

Gene Quintano
Outlaw Justice '98

Martin Rackin
The Horse Soldiers '59

Glenda Rafelli
Passion & Romance: Double or Nothing '00

Bob Rafelson
Mountains of the Moon '90
Five Easy Pieces '70

Sam Raimi
Evil Dead 2: Dead by Dawn [2 THX] '87

Norman Reilly Raine
Captain Kidd '45

Harold Ramis
Bedazzled [SE] '00
Back to School '86

Tony Randel
Fist of the North Star '95

Joe Ranft
The Rescuers Down Under '90

Ture Rangstrom
Edvard Grieg: What Price Immortality? '00

Anne Rapp
Dr. T & the Women '00

Philip Rapp
The Inspector General '49
Wonder Man '45

Judith Rascoe
A Portrait of the Artist As a Young Man '77
Road Movie '72

Paul Rattigan
Relative Values '99

Linda Ravera
Fair Game '89

Irving Ravetch
Norma Rae '79

Kimberly A. Ray
Kept '01

Theresa Rebeck
Gossip '99

Eric Red
Bad Moon '96

Jeffrey Reddick
Final Destination '00

Keith Reddin
It's the Rage '99

Aaron Reed
The Next Step '95

Tom Reed
Up in Mabel's Room '44

Harry Reeves
The Adventures of Ichabod and Mr. Toad '49

Matt Reeves
The Yards '00
The Pallbearer '95

Michael Reeves
Batman: Mask of the Phantasm '93

Nicolas Winding Refn
Pusher '96

Brian Regan
102 Dalmatians '00

Ethan Reiff
Men of War '94

Carl Reiner
Dead Men Don't Wear Plaid '82

Rob Reiner
This Is Spinal Tap [MGM] '84

Walter Reisch
That Uncertain Feeling [SlingShot] '41

Mark Reisman
Summer Rental '85

Dean Reisner
Paris Holiday '57

Adam Resnick
Lucky Numbers '00

Patricia Resnick
9 to 5 '80

Richard Schickel
AFI's 100 Years, 100 Stars '99

Stephen Schiff
Lolita '97

Suzanne Schiffman
The Man Who Loved Women '77
Small Change '76
The Story of Adele H. '75

Alfred Schiller
The Flying Deuces / Utopia '39

Victor Schiller
The Perfect Nanny '00

Murray Schisgal
Tootsie '82

Piero Schivazappa
The Frightened Woman '71

David Schmoeller
Tourist Trap '79

Julian Schnabel
Before Night Falls '00

Charles Schnee
Butterfield 8 '60

Barry Schneider
Mother's Boys '94

Rob Schneider
Deuce Bigalow: Male Gigolo '99

Ernest B. Schoedsack
Chang: A Drama of the Wilderness '27

Robert Schooley
Buzz Lightyear of Star Command: The Adventure Begins '00

Amy Schor
Mr. Wonderful '93

Paul Schrader
Bringing Out the Dead '99
Forever Mine '99
The Last Temptation of Christ '88

Arnold Schulman
And the Band Played On '93
Tucker: The Man and His Dream '88

Tom Schulman
What about Bob? '91

Joel Schumacher
Flawless '99
Car Wash '76

Mark Schwahn
Whatever It Takes '00

Steven S. Schwartz
Critical Care '97

Allan Scott
The 5000 Fingers of Dr. T '53

Deborah Scott
Best of the Best 3: No Turning Back / Best of the Best: Without Warning '95

Ted Sears
The Adventures of Ichabod and Mr. Toad '49

Lauren Sedofsky
Pola X '99

Dan Sefton
James Dean: Live Fast, Die Young '97

Erich Segal
Love Story '70

Harry Segall
Angel on My Shoulder '46

David Seidler
Tucker: The Man and His Dream '88

Michael Seitzman
Here on Earth '00

Hubert Selby Jr.
Requiem for a Dream '00

Ken Selden
Cherry Falls / Terror Tract '00

Steven Selling
One Man's Justice '95

David Seltzer
The Omen [SE] '76

Lorenzo Semple Jr.
The Parallax View '74

Jorge Semprun
La Guerre Est Finie '66

Mala Sen
Bandit Queen '94

Al Septien
Leprechaun 2 '94

Yahoo Serious
Mr. Accident '99

Rod Serling
A Town Has Turned to Dust '98
Planet of the Apes '68
Seven Days in May '64

Edmond Seward
Gulliver's Travels [Image] '39

Timothy J. Sexton
For Love or Country: The Arturo Sandoval Story '00

Maartje Seyferth
Venus in Furs '94

Alan Seymour
Catherine Cookson's The Cinder Path '94

James Seymour
42nd Street '33

David Shaber
The Warriors '79

Tasca Shadix
The Book of Stars '99

Anthony Shaffer
Evil under the Sun '82
Death on the Nile '78
Frenzy '72

Steve Shagan
Gotti '96

Garry Shandling
What Planet Are You From? '00

Alan Shapiro
The Crush '93

Craig Shapiro
Our Lips Are Sealed '00

J. David Shapiro
Battlefield Earth '00

Stanley Shapiro
For Pete's Sake '74
That Touch of Mink '62

Jim Sharman
The Rocky Horror Picture Show '75

Melville Shavelson
Yours, Mine & Ours '68
The Seven Little Foys '55
The Great Lover '49
Wonder Man '45

George Bernard Shaw
Pygmalion '38

Harry Shearer
This Is Spinal Tap [MGM] '84
Real Life '79

Charlie Sheen
No Code of Conduct '98

David Sheffield
Nutty Professor 2: The Klumps [1 CE] '00
Nutty Professor 2: The Klumps [2 Uncensored] '00

Sidney Sheldon
Annie Get Your Gun '50

Brad Shellady
Texas Chainsaw Massacre: A Family Portrait '90

Angela Shelton
Tumbleweeds '98

Ron Shelton
Play It to the Bone '99
White Men Can't Jump '92

Jack Sher
Shane '53

Ted Sherdeman
Away All Boats '56

Bob Sheridan
Sorority House Massacre 2: Nighty Nightmare '92

Jim Sheridan
The Field '90

Sam M. Sherman
Dracula vs. Frankenstein '71

Stafford Sherman
Krull [SE] '83

R.C. Sherriff
The Invisible Man '33

Bill Sherwood
Parting Glances '86

Robert Sherwood
The Bishop's Wife [MGM] '47
The Scarlet Pimpernel '34

Susan Shilliday
I Dreamed of Africa '00
Legends of the Fall [2 SE] '94

Masahiro Shinoda
Double Suicide '69

Nell Shipman
Something New '20

Michael Shoob
Parasite '82

Takeshi Shudo
Pokemon the Movie 2000: The Power of One '00

Harold Shumate
Abilene Town '46

Ronald Shusett
Freejack '92
Dead and Buried '81

Allan Shustak
Midnight Confessions '95

M. Night Shyamalan
Wide Awake '97

Charles Shyer
Father of the Bride Part II '95
Baby Boom '87

Mussef Sibay
A Woman, Her Men and Her Futon '92

Sylvia Sichel
If These Walls Could Talk 2 '00

David Siegel
Suture '93

Tom Sierchio
Untamed Heart '93

Stirling Silliphant
Shaft in Africa '73
In the Heat of the Night '67

Karol Silverstein
Best of Intimate Sessions: Vol. 2 '99

Susana Silvestre
Life According to Muriel '97

Adam Simon
Carnosaur '93
Brain Dead '89

Ellen Simon
Moonlight and Valentino '95

J(uan) Piquer Simon
Slugs '87

Neil Simon
The Odd Couple '68

Albert Simonin
Cold Sweat '71

Theodore Simonson
The Blob '58

Byron Simpson
The Rescuers Down Under '90

Raymond Singer
Joseph: King of Dreams '00

John Singleton
Poetic Justice '93
Boyz N the Hood '91

Santosh Sivan
The Terrorist '98

Mark Skeet
Jason and the Argonauts '00

Paul Skemp
Fall Time '94

Katharine R. Sloan
Deal of a Lifetime '99

Craig Smith
Caracara '00

Grace Smith
Teenage Catgirls in Heat '00

Kevin Smith
Coyote Ugly '00
Dogma '99
Chasing Amy '97

Mark Smith
Dr. Frankenstein's Castle of Freaks '74

Michael R. Smith
Hellblock 13 '97

Murray Smith
Die Screaming, Marianne '73

Robert Smith
The Second Woman '51
Quicksand '50

Scott Marshall Smith
Men of Honor '00

Wallace Smith
The Gay Desperado '36

Norman Snider
Rated X '00

Zachary Winston Snygg
Blood Bullets Buffoons '96

Carol Sobieski
Winter People '89

Steven Soderbergh
Nightwatch '96

Gerard Soeteman
The 4th Man '79
Soldier of Orange '78
Turkish Delight '73

Jerry Sohl
Die, Monster, Die! '65

Joel Soisson
Highlander: Endgame '00
Blue Tiger '94
Lower Level '91

Alec Sokolow
Toy Story '95

Ken Solarz
City of Industry '96

Helena Solberg
Carmen Miranda: Bananas Is My Business '95

Paul Solberg
Double Parked '00

Ed Soloman
Charlie's Angels '00

Edward Solomon
What Planet Are You From? '00
Men in Black [CS] '97

Stephen Sommers
The Mummy [2 SE] '99

Aaron Sorkin
Malice [MGM] '93

Helvio Soto
It's Raining on Santiago '74

Terry Southern
Dr. Strangelove, or: How I Learned to Stop Worrying and Love the Bomb [2 SE] '64

Jack Sowards
Star Trek 2: The Wrath of Khan '82

Robert Spano
Dr. Frankenstein's Castle of Freaks '74

Izzy Sparber
Gulliver's Travels [Image] '39

Ralph Spence
The Flying Deuces / Utopia '39

Don Spencer
The Big Doll House '71

Pierre Spengler
The Prince and the Pauper '78

Penelope Spheeris
Suburbia '83

Scott Spiegel
Evil Dead 2: Dead by Dawn [2 THX] '87
Thou Shalt Not Kill . . . Except '87

Steven Spielberg
Close Encounters of the Third Kind [CE] '77

Amy Spies
Girls Just Want to Have Fun '85

Tony Spiridakis
If Lucy Fell '95

Lev L. Spiro
Robert Louis Stevenson's The Game of Death '99

Hildegarde Stadie
Marihuana / Assassin of Youth / Reefer Madness '36

Langton Stafford
Ilsa, Harem Keeper of the Oil Sheiks '76

Juan Bautista Stagnaro
The Perfect Husband '92

The Cinematographer Index lists all cinematographers, or Directors of Photography (D.P.), as they are also known, credited in at least one DVD reviewed in this book. The listings for the cinematographer names follow an alphabetical sort by last name (although the names appear in a first name, last name format). The videographies are listed chronologically, from most recent to oldest film. If a cinematographer lensed more than one film in the same year, these movies are listed alphabetically within the year.

Thomas Ackerman
The Adventures of Rocky & Bullwinkle '00
Beautiful Joe '00
Back to School '86
Girls Just Want to Have Fun '85

Barry Ackroyd
Beautiful People '99

Steve Adcock
Timelock '99

Remi Adefarasin
House of Mirth '00
Onegin '99

Philippe Agostini
Rififi '54

Javier Aguirresarobe
Secrets of the Heart '97
Tierra '95
Running out of Time '94

Lloyd Ahern
Wild Bill '95

Lloyd Ahern II
Supernova '99

Mac Ahlberg
Sideshow '00
Deepstar Six '89
Parasite '82

Martin Ahlgren
Colorz of Rage '97

Pierre Aim
Madeline '98

Arthur Albert
Dirty Work '97
You So Crazy '94
The Boys Next Door '85

Kurt Albert
Best of Intimate Sessions: Vol. 2 '99

Maryse Alberti
Joe Gould's Secret '00

Jose Luis Alcaine
Tie Me Up! Tie Me Down! '90
Women on the Verge of a Nervous Breakdown '88

John Alcott
No Way Out '87
Fort Apache, the Bronx '81

Henri Alekan
Anna Karenina '48

Howard Alk
Bob Dylan: Don't Look Back '67

Sepp Allgeier
Triumph of the Will '34

Nestor Almendros
Perceval '78
The Man Who Loved Women '77
The Marquise of O '76
The Story of Adele H. '75
Cockfighter '74
Bed and Board '70

John A. Alonzo
Internal Affairs '90
Navy SEALS [MGM] '90
Steel Magnolias '89
Runaway '84
Norma Rae '79
Harold and Maude '71

John Alton
Father's Little Dividend '51

Alex Ameri
The Gore-Gore Girls '72

Jamie Anderson
The Flintstones in Viva Rock Vegas '00
Hollywood Boulevard '76

Peter Andrews
Traffic '00

Lucien N. Andriot
The Strange Woman '46
The Gay Desperado '36

Theo Angell
Kept '01
The Kid with the X-Ray Eyes '99
Dear Santa '98

Thierry Arbogast
Woman on Top '00
The Messenger: The Story of Joan of Arc '99
She's So Lovely '97
Leon, the Professional '94
La Femme Nikita [MGM] '91

Georges Archambault
Captive '00

Edgar Arellano
Hip Hop 2000 '00

Erik Arnesen
Pop & Me '99

Steve Arnold
Mr. Accident '99

John Aronson
Beethoven's 3rd '00
In God's Hands '98
White Wolves 2: Legend of the Wild '94

Jose Luis Arredondo
Johnny 100 Pesos '93

Jerome Ash
Flash Gordon: Space Soldiers '36

William Asman
Sheba, Baby '75

Ingy Assolh
Alexandria Again and Forever '90

Yoram Astrakhan
Moving Target '00

Howard Atherton
Hanging Up '99
Lolita '97
Mermaids '90

Giorgio Atilli
Awakenings of the Beast '68

Yushun Atsuta
Good Morning '59

Giorgio Attili
This Night I'll Possess Your Corpse '66

Joseph August
Portrait of Jennie '48

John G. Avildsen
Cry Uncle '71

Joaquin Baca-Asay
Coming Soon '99

Hanania Baer
Choices '81

Christopher Baffa
Next Friday [Platinum Series] '00
Idle Hands '99
The Crazysitter '94

John Bailey
Antitrust '00
For Love of the Game '99
Forever Mine '99
In the Line of Fire [2 SE] '93
Silverado [SE] '85

The Pope of Greenwich Village '84

Bob Bailin
Family Enforcer '76

Ian Baker
Six Degrees of Separation '93
Roxanne '87
Plenty '85

Lucien Ballard
Breakheart Pass '76
Sons of Katie Elder '65

Michael Ballhaus
The Legend of Bagger Vance '00
What Planet Are You From? '00
What about Bob? '91
Postcards from the Edge '90
The Last Temptation of Christ '88
Working Girl '88
Whity '70

Lionel Banes
Fiend Without a Face '58

Larry Banks
Juice '92

Diane Baratier
A Summer's Tale '96

Craig Barden
Farscape, Vol. 3 '01

Jeff Barklage
Vamps: Deadly Dreamgirls '95

George Barnes
The Road to Bali '53
Meet John Doe [Image] '41
That Uncertain Feeling [Sling-Shot] '41
Street Scene '31

Todd Baron
Passion & Romance: Double or Nothing '00

Mario Barroso
God's Comedy '95

Michael Barrow
Row Your Boat '98

Georges Barsky
It's Raining on Santiago '74

Andrzej Bartkowiak
Gossip '99

Power '86
Terms of Endearment '83

Adolfo Bartoli
The Horrible Dr. Bones '00
Octopus '00
Bloodstorm: Subspecies 4 '98
The Creeps '97
Rudyard Kipling's The Second Jungle Book: Mowgli and Baloo '97
Puppet Master 5: The Latest Chapter '94
Puppet Master 3: Toulon's Revenge '90

Paul Barton
Positive I.D. '87

Gianlorenzo Battaglia
A Blade in the Dark '83

Michel Baudour
Anchoress '93

Jurgen Baum
American Vampire '97
Flypaper '97
One Man's Justice '95
Slumber Party Massacre 3 '90

Mario Bava
Bay of Blood '71
Twitch of the Death Nerve '71
Hatchet for the Honeymoon '70
The Girl Who Knew Too Much '63

Bojan Bazelli
Boxing Helena '93
King of New York '90
Somebody Has to Shoot the Picture '90
Tapeheads '89
Pumpkinhead '88

Alfonso Beato
Price of Glory '00
All About My Mother '99
Live Flesh '97

Josh Becker
Thou Shalt Not Kill . . . Except '87

Terry Bedford
Monty Python and the Holy Grail '75

Dion Beebe
Holy Smoke '99

Stanley Cortez
The Bridge at Remagen '69
Dinosaurus! '60

Andrew M. Costikyan
Bananas '71

Michael Coulter
Mansfield Park '99

Raoul Coutard
The Bride Wore Black '68

James A. Crabe
Sextette '78
Rocky [SE] '76

Joan Crawford
Divided We Stand '00

Michelle Crenshaw
The Watermelon Woman '97

Jordan Cronenweth
U2: Rattle and Hum '88

Floyd Crosby
Beach Blanket Bingo '65
Bikini Beach '64
X: The Man with X-Ray Eyes
   '63
Tales of Terror '62
The Pit and the Pendulum '61
The Fall of the House of
   Usher '60
The Old Man and the Sea '58
Teenage Doll '57
The Fighter '52

Nat Crosby
Northanger Abbey '87

Richard Crudo
In Pursuit '00
American Buffalo '95

Luis Cuadrado
Cut Throats Nine '72

R(aul) P. Cubero
The Grandfather '98

Dean Cundey
What Women Want '00
Jurassic Park [CE] '93
Big Trouble in Little China
   [SE] '86
Escape from New York '81
Ilsa, Harem Keeper of the Oil
   Sheiks '76

Richard Cunha
Giant from the Unknown '58

Neve Cunningham
One Day in September '99

Oliver Curtis
Immortality '98

Stefan Czapsky
Prelude to a Kiss '92
Edward Scissorhands [SE]
   '90

Laurent Dailland
East-West '99

Bernard Daillencourt
Immoral Tales '74

John Daly
Essex Boys '99

Dennis Dalzell
Bustin' Loose '81

Joe D'Amato
The Arena '73

William H. Daniels
Away All Boats '56
Pat and Mike '52
Harvey '50
Foolish Wives '22

Allen Daviau
Defending Your Life '91
Avalon '90

Mark David
Thug Life '00

Zoltan David
The Colony '98
Row Your Boat '98
My Teacher's Wife '95

Benjamin Davis
Sleepaway Camp '83

Elliot Davis
The Next Best Thing '00
Light It Up '99
Breakfast of Champions '98
Get On the Bus '96
Mother's Boys '94
The Cutting Edge '92
Shakes the Clown '92

Michael J. Davis
A Woman, Her Men and Her
   Futon '92

Ernest Day
A Passage to India '84

Jan De Bont
The Clan of the Cave Bear
   '86
Cujo '83
The 4th Man '79
Soldier of Orange '78
Turkish Delight '73

John de Borman
Hamlet '00
Saving Grace '00

Jean De Segonzac
Homicide: The Movie '00

Roger Deakins
O Brother Where Art Thou?
   '00
The Hurricane '99
Dead Man Walking '95
Thunderheart '92
Mountains of the Moon '90
Sid & Nancy [MGM] '86

Henri Decae
Joy House '64

Gina DeGirolamo
Jerome '98

Thomas Del Ruth
Asteroid '97
Look Who's Talking, Too '90
Stand by Me [2 SE] '86
Hysterical '83

Benoit Delhomme
The Loss of Sexual Inno-
   cence '98

Franco Delli Colli
Macabre '80

Tonino Delli Colli
Lovers and Liars '81

Peter Deming
If These Walls Could Talk 2
   '00
Scream 3 [CS] '00
Music of the Heart [CS] '99
Mystery, Alaska '99
My Cousin Vinny '92
House Party '90
Evil Dead 2: Dead by Dawn [2
   THX] '87

Jim Denault
Double Parked '00
A Good Baby '99

Thomas Denove
Secret Games '92
Puppet Master 2 '90
Fanatic '82

Paul Desatoff
Animal Instincts '92

Caleb Deschanel
The Patriot '00
Anna and the King '99

It Could Happen to You '94
The Natural '84
Being There '79
A Woman under the Influence
   '74

Carlo Di Palma
Shadows and Fog '92
Alice '90
September '88

Gianni Di Venanzo
10th Victim '65
Big Deal on Madonna Street
   '58

Jimmy Dibling
Relative Values '99

Ernest R. Dickerson
Mo' Better Blues '90
Do the Right Thing [2] '89
School Daze '88

Desmond Dickinson
Horror Hotel '60
Hamlet '48

Rocky Dijon
The Portrait '99
Sex Files: Digital Sex '98

Mario DiLeo
Sudie & Simpson '90
Breaker! Breaker! '77

Phillip W. Dingeldein
Mommy [SE] '95

Irl Dixon
The Bone Yard '90

Mark Dobrescu
Die! Die! Die! '00

Fyodor Dobronravov
Dersu Uzala '75

Mark Doering-Powell
Telling You '98

Sergio d'Offizi
Don't Torture a Duckling '72

Mike Dolgetta
Throw Down '00

Peter Donahue
Mr. Death: The Rise and Fall
   of Fred A. Leuchter Jr. '99

Bruce Dorfman
Bloodfist 2 '90

Alan Dostie
Nuremberg '00
32 Short Films about Glenn
   Gould '93

Roger Dowling
Napoleon '96

Christopher Doyle
Liberty Heights '99

Robert Dracup
Lethal Seduction '97

Rob Draper
Dr. Giggles '92
Halloween 5: The Revenge of
   Michael Myers '89

Randy Drummond
Louis Prima: The Wildest! '99

Stuart Dryburgh
Sex and the City: The Com-
   plete Second Season '00
Shaft '00
Peach / A Bitter Song '95

Guy Dufaux
Eye of the Beholder '99

Simon Duggan
The Interview '98

Albert J. Dunk
Flashfire '94

Bert Dunk
Family of Cops 3 '98

Andrew Dunn
The Madness of King George
   '94

Guy Durban
Immoral Tales '74

Elmer Dyer
The Flying Deuces / Utopia
   '39

Alric Edens
The Meanest Men in the
   West '76

Arthur Edeson
The Maltese Falcon '41
The Invisible Man '33
The Lost World [Image] '25

David Eggby
Pitch Black '00
Blue Streak '99
Lightning Jack '94
Harley Davidson and the
   Marlboro Man '91

Eagle Egilsson
Red Shoe Diaries: Luscious
   Lola '00
Red Shoe Diaries: Swimming
   Naked '00
Red Shoe Diaries: Strip Poker
   '96

Rich Eliano
The Waiting Game '99

Chuy Elizondo
Kiss Shot '89

Ian Elkin
The Crimson Code '00

Tom Elling
The Element of Crime '84

Paul Elliott
The Broken Hearts Club '00
If These Walls Could Talk 2
   '00
Diamonds '99
And the Band Played On '93

Frederick Elmes
Ride with the Devil '99
River's Edge '87
Blue Velvet '86
Opening Night '77
The Killing of a Chinese
   Bookie '76

Danny Elsen
The Red Dwarf '99

Robert Elswit
Bounce '00
Magnolia '99
Hard Eight '96
The Pallbearer '95
Desert Hearts '86

Morris Engel
Little Fugitive '53

Bryan England
My Mom's a Werewolf '89

Bob Enlow
Texas Chainsaw Massacre: A
   Family Portrait '90

Nils Erickson
Ultimate Attraction '98
Mirror, Mirror 3: The Voyeur
   '96

Jean-Yves Escoffier
Nurse Betty '00
The Cradle Will Rock '99
Gummo '97
Mauvais Sang '86
Boy Meets Girl '84

Lauro Escorel
Stuart Saves His Family '94

Blake T. Evans
Body Count '95

Christopher Faloona
Beowulf '98

Daniel F. Fapp
The Unsinkable Molly Brown
   '64
The Lemon Drop Kid '51

Mike Fash
The Confession '98

Etienne Fauduet
Red Shoe Diaries: Four on
   the Floor '95

Don E. Fauntleroy
The Perfect Nanny '00
Seven Girlfriends '99
Body Chemistry 3: Point of
   Seduction '93

Matt Faw
Tha Eastsidaz '00

Jim Fealy
Splendor '99

Aleksei Federov
Mother and Son '97

Zhao Fei
The Emperor and the Assas-
   sin '99
Sweet and Lowdown '99

Gerald Feil
Friday the 13th, Part 3 '82

Johann Feindt
Jew-boy Levi '98

Buzz Feitshans IV
Dragonheart: A New Begin-
   ning '00

Roger Fellous
Diary of a Chambermaid '64

Joao Fernandes
Delta Force 2: Operation
   Stranglehold '90
Red Scorpion '89
Friday the 13th, Part 4: The
   Final Chapter '84
Missing in Action '84

Juan Fernandez
Deadly Weapons '70

David Ferrara
Black and White '99

Rick Fichter
Bride of Re-Animator '89

Steven Fierberg
Attila '01
Red Letters '00

Gabriel Figueroa
Kelly's Heroes '70

William Fildew
Outside the Law / Shadows
   '21

Russell Fine
The Pompatus of Love '95

Gerald Perry Finnerman
They Call Me Mr. Tibbs! '70

Mauro Fiore
Get Carter '00
Lost Souls '00

Dick Fisher
The Brothers McMullen '94

Clancy Fitzsimmons
Girl Explores Girl: The Alien
   Encounter [CE] '00

Ray Flin
Monster from Green Hell '58

Thomas Flores Alcala
Deep in the Heart (of Texas)
   '98

Jean-Jacques Flori
Son of Gascogne '95

Brendan Flynt
Terror Firmer [SE] '00

George J. Folsey
The Balcony '63
Take Me Out to the Ball
Game '49

David Foreman
Cut '00

Tony Forsberg
The White Lioness '96

Joey Forsyte
The Curve '97

Ron Fortunato
If Lucy Fell '95

Marc Fossard
Beethoven '36

Robert Fraisse
Citizen X '95

William A. Fraker
Rules of Engagement '00
Father of the Bride Part II '95
Baby Boom '87
The Hollywood Knights '80
Rancho Deluxe '75
Rosemary's Baby '68

Freddie Francis
The Straight Story '99
Princess Caraboo '94
Glory [2 SE] '89

David Franco
The Whole Nine Yards '00
Earthly Possessions '99

Jess (Jesus) Franco
Female Vampire '73

David Frazee
Chained Heat 3: Hell Mountain '98

Tom Frazier
Midnight Confessions '95

Ellsworth Fredericks
Seven Days in May '64
Friendly Persuasion '56

Mickey Freeman
Angel Blue '97

Richard Fryer
Flash Gordon: Space Soldiers
'36

Tak Fujimoto
The Replacements '00
Gladiator '92
Married to the Mob '88
Something Wild '86

Osamu Furuya
Tora! Tora! Tora! [2 SE] '70

Ricardo Jacques Gale
Stalked '99
Bloodfist '89

Yuri Gantman
Dersu Uzala '75

Rodrigo Garcia
Body Shots '99
Gia '98

Ron Garcia
El Diablo '90

Greg Gardiner
Homegrown '97
Suture '93

Mike Garfath
Croupier '97

Andres Garreton
Darkdrive '98

Miguel Garzon
Death and the Compass '96

Eric Gautier
Pola X '99
My Sex Life...Or How I Got
into an Argument '96

Mandre Gazut
The Sorrow and the Pity '71

Harvey Genkins
H.O.T.S. '79

Geoffrey George
Black Scorpion '95

Henry W. Gerrard
Of Human Bondage '34
The Most Dangerous Game
[Madacy] '32

Merritt B. Gerstad
Bulldog Drummond's Secret
Police '39

Maury Gertsman
Dressed to Kill '46
Terror by Night '46

Gerald Gibbs
Quatermass 2 '57
X The Unknown '56

Pierre Gill
The Art of War '00

Paul Gilpin
Tarzan and the Lost City '98

Aldo Giordani
Amuck! '71

Pierre William Glenn
Coup de Torchon '81
Loulou '80
Small Change '76

Bert Glennon
Our Town '40
Scarlet Empress '34

James Glennon
Playing Mona Lisa '00

Paul Glickman
The Stuff '85
Dracula vs. Frankenstein '71

Richard C. Glouner
The Gay Deceivers '69

Agnes Godard
The New Eve '98

Stephen Goldblatt
Striptease '96
For the Boys '91

Pancho Gonzales
Johnny B. '00

Carlos Gonzalez
The Omega Code '99

Anibal Gonzalez Paz
The Curious Dr. Humpp '70

Irv Goodnoff
James Dean: Live Fast, Die
Young '97

Mark J. Gordon
Fall Time '94

Michael Gornick
Knightriders '81
Martin '77

Michael Grady
Beyond the Mat '99

Tom Graeff
Teenagers from Outer Space
'59

Arthur Grant
The Devil Rides Out '68
The Mummy's Shroud '67
Frankenstein Created Woman
'66
The Witches '66
The Abominable Snowman
'57

Gary Graver
Femalien 2 '98
James Dean: Live Fast, Die
Young '97
Invisible Mom '96
Vice Girls '96
Midnight Tease 2 '95
Dracula vs. Frankenstein '71
Satan's Sadists '69

Mark W. Gray
Back to Back '96

Richard Greatrex
The Last of the Blonde Bomb-
shells '00
Where the Heart Is '00

Eric Green
Straight out of Compton '00

Guy Green
Immortal Battalion '44

Jack N. Green
Space Cowboys '00
Girl, Interrupted '99
Traveller '96
Bird '88

Adam Greenberg
Terminator 2: Judgment Day
[2 SE] '91
Ghost '90
Alien Nation '88
Madron '70

Robbie Greenberg
Save the Last Dance '01
If These Walls Could Talk 2
'00
Snow Day '00
Swamp Thing '82
The Lathe of Heaven '80

William Howard Greene
The Phantom of the Opera
'43
The Garden of Allah '36

Jack Greenhalgh
Robot Monster '53
Reefer Madness '38

George Greenough
Blackrock '97

Frank Griebe
Winter Sleepers '97

Loyal Griggs
The Greatest Story Ever Told
[SE] '65
In Harm's Way '65
The Bridges at Toko-Ri '55
White Christmas '54
Shane '53

Marcel Grignon
Madron '70

Xavier Perez Grobet
Before Night Falls '00

Alexander Grusynski
Dick '99
Maximum Risk '96
Threesome '94
The Women of Brewster
Place '89

Changwei Gu
Autumn in New York '00

Ennio Guarnieri
The Cassandra Crossing '76

Burnett Guffey
Birdman of Alcatraz '62

David Gurfinkel
Delta Force '86

Eugeny Guslinsky
Termination Man '97

Courtney Hafela
Jazz on a Summer's Day '59

Ron Hagen
Romper Stomper [SE] '92

Rob Hahn
Loser '00

Jacques Haitkin
The Base '99
Fist of the North Star '95
One Good Turn '95
Cherry 2000 '88
The Private Eyes [SE] '80

Doug Hajicek
Deadly Beauty: Snow's Secret
Life '01

Stephen Hajnal
The Brain that Wouldn't Die
'63

Thad Halci
Teenage Catgirls in Heat '00

Conrad Hall
American Beauty [SE] '99
Incubus '65

Ernest Haller
Lilies of the Field '63

Fenton Hamilton
Black Caesar '73

Victor Hammer
Sour Grapes '98

Peter Hannan
Dance with a Stranger '85

Charles Hannawalt
Dementia 13 '63

Dean Hansen
Deadly Beauty: Snow's Secret
Life '01

Russell Harlan
A Walk in the Sun '46

Harvey Harrison
R.P.M. '97
Salome's Last Dance '88
Cheech and Chong: Still
Smokin' '83

Richard Hart
Creepshow 2 '87

Joachim Hasler
First Spaceship on Venus '60

David Hausen
Drop Dead Rock '95

Robert B. Hauser
The Odd Couple '68

Yuri Haviv
Double Agent 73 '80
Another Day, Another Man '66

Peter Hawkins
The Lifestyle '99

Robert Hayes
Hardcase and Fist '89

Timothy Healy
Titanic 2000 '00
Psycho Sisters '98

Bernd Heinl
The Little Vampire '00

Wolfgang Held
The Tic Code '99
Floating '97

Otto Heller
I'll Never Forget What's
'Isname '67
Alfie '66

David Hennings
Cheaters '00
Asteroid '97

Jonathan Herron
Prince of Central Park '00

Gregg Heschong
Heavy Traffic '73

Stuart Hetherington
A Portrait of the Artist As a
Young Man '77

David Higgs
The Canterville Ghost '98

Jack Hildyard
The Beast Must Die '75
Topaz '69
Suddenly, Last Summer '59
The Bridge on the River Kwai
[LE] '57

Erwin Hillier
I Know Where I'm Going '45

Sinsaku Himeda
Tora! Tora! Tora! [2 SE] '70

**Bill (William Heinzman)
Hinzman**
Santa Claws '96

Alec Hirschfeld
Love Letters '83

Gerald Hirschfeld
Cotton Comes to Harlem '70
Fail-Safe '64

Winton C. Hoch
Voyage to the Bottom of the
Sea / Fantastic Voyage '61

Zoran Hochstatter
The Last Best Sunday '98
Body Chemistry 4: Full Expo-
sure '95
Home for Christmas '93
Not of This Earth '88

Adam Holender
Wide Awake '97

Keith Holland
Bloody Murder '99
Carnosaur '93

Heinz Holscher
I Like the Girls Who Do '73

Brian Hooper
Perfect Profile '90

Nathan Hope
Nice Guys Sleep Alone '99

Louis Horvath
Mesmerized '84

Alex Howe
Dead Waters '94

James Wong Howe
The Old Man and the Sea '58
Sweet Smell of Success '57
Picnic '55
The Fighter '52
Hangmen Also Die '42
They Made Me a Criminal '39
Fire over England '37

Gil Hubbs
Flowers in the Attic '87

Roger Hubert
Paris Holiday '57

Tsao Hui-Chi
The Mighty Peking Man '77

Alan Hume
A View to a Kill [SE] '85
Supergirl '84
Octopussy '83

John Huneck
One Man's Justice '95

Shane Hurlbut
The Skulls '00

Tom Hurwitz
The Source '96
Creepshow 2 '97

Arthur Ibbetson
Santa Claus: The Movie '85
The Bounty '84

Ghost Chase '88

John Lindley
Lucky Numbers '00
True Believer '89

Lionel Lindon
The Meanest Men in the West '76
My Favorite Brunette '47

Harold Lipstein
Hell Is for Heroes '62
Pal Joey '57

Gerry Lively
Cutaway '00
The Brylcreem Boys '96
Warlock: The Armageddon '93

William Livingston
The Italians '00

Art Lloyd
The Flying Deuces / Utopia '39
March of the Wooden Soldiers '34

Walt Lloyd
Empire Records '95
Frank and Jesse '94

Karl Lob
The Thousand Eyes of Dr. Mabuse '60

Bryan Loftus
Jake Speed '86

Bruce Logan
Jackson County Jail '76

Dietrich Lohmann
Quiet Days in Hollywood '97
A Couch in New York '95
Knight Moves '93

Paul Lohmann
Lust in the Dust '85
Meteor '79
North Dallas Forty '79
Nashville '75
Coffy '73

Nicholas Loizides
Unspeakable '00

Raoul Lomas
Children of the Corn '84

Stanley Long
Blood Beast Terror '67

Emmanuel Lubezki
A Walk in the Clouds '95

Georges Lucas
Fall of the House of Usher '28

Jean Lucas
Fall of the House of Usher '28

Bernard Lutic
I Dreamed of Africa '00
The Quarry '98

Marc Lyons
Q: The Movie '99

Jingle Ma
Tokyo Raiders '00
The Legend of Drunken Master '94
The Legend '93

Julio Macat
Crazy in Alabama '99
Moonlight and Valentino '95

Joe MacDonald
Alvarez Kelly '66
The Sand Pebbles '66
How to Marry a Millionaire '53

Peter Macdonald
Shag: The Movie '89

Kenneth Macmillan
Inventing the Abbotts '97
Henry V '89

Glen MacPherson
Romeo Must Die '00

Tomasz Magierski
Carmen Miranda: Bananas Is My Business '95

Barry Mahon
The Beast That Killed Women / The Monster of Camp Sunshine '65

Rex Maidment
Poldark '96

David Makin
Held Up '00

Denis Maloney
The Contender '00
Bad Manners '98
Desert Winds '95

Svatopluk Maly
Alice '88

Mario Mancini
Dr. Frankenstein's Castle of Freaks '74

Guglielmo Mancori
Manhattan Baby '82

Joseph Mangine
Mother's Day [DC] '80

Teodoro Maniaci
The Tao of Steve '00

Sakis Maniatis
Attila 74: The Rape of Cyprus '75

Chris Manley
Robert Louis Stevenson's The Game of Death '99

Laurence Manly
Dangerous Curves '99

Anthony Dod Mantle
Julien Donkey-boy '99
Mifune '99

Vincenzo Marano
Portraits Chinois '96

John March
Cyberotica '00

Carlos Marcovich
Midaq Alley '95

Michael D. Margulies
Best of the Best: Without Warning '98

Barbu Marion
Phenomenon—The Lost Archives: Noah's Ark Found?/Tunguska/Stolen Glory '99
Phenomenon—The Lost Archives: Up for Sale/Heavy Watergate '99

Barry Markowitz
All the Pretty Horses '00

J. Peverell Marley
Life with Father '47

Brick Marquard
Foxy Brown '74

Jacques "Jack" Marquette
The Brain from Planet Arous '57

John Marquette
A Bucket of Blood '59

Horacio Marquinez
Loving Jezebel '99

Restaurant '98

Oliver Marsh
Rain '32
Eternal Love '29

Jack Marta
Cat Ballou [SE] '65

Otello Martelli
Il Bidone '55
Variety Lights '51

Pascal Marti
L'Ennui '98

Michael Martin
Tha Eastsidaz '00

Flavio Martinez Labiano
Dance with the Devil '97

Steve Mason
Buddy '97

Andy Massagli
The Gospel According to Philip K. Dick '00

Rudolph Mate
Gilda '46
Love Affair '39
Come and Get It '36

John Mathieson
Hannibal '01
Gladiator '00

Clark Mathis
Ready to Rumble '00

Thomas Mauch
Aguirre, the Wrath of God '72

Shawn Maurer
La Cucaracha '99

Tim Maurice-Jones
Lock, Stock and 2 Smoking Barrels '98

Robert Maxwell
The Astro-Zombies '67

Harry J. May
Friday Foster '75
Detroit 9000 '73

Mike Mayers
Lewis and Clark and George '97

Alfredo Mayo
Women '97

Marco Mazzei
Red Shoe Diaries: Four on the Floor '96

John McAleer
Diamond Run '00

Donald McAlpine
Nine Months '95
Predator [20th Century Fox] '87

Ted D. McCord
The Sound of Music [Five Star Collection] '65

David McDonald
The Harder They Come '72

Seamus McGarvey
High Fidelity '00
The Big Tease '99
A Map of the World '99
The War Zone '98

John McGlashan
Plain Jane '00

Martin McGrath
Blackrock '97
A Little Bit of Soul '97

Austin McKinney
Pit Stop '67

Robert McLachlan
Final Destination '00

Stephen McNutt
Inferno '99

John McPherson
Jaws: The Revenge '87

Steve McWilliams
No Safe Haven '87

Phil Meheux
Bicentennial Man '99
Omen 3: The Final Conflict '81

Ashok Mehta
Bandit Queen '94

Sharon Meir
Goodbye America '97

William Mellor
The Greatest Story Ever Told [SE] '65

Mark Melville
Dilemma '97

Erico Menczer
Dead Are Alive '72

Chris Menges
Local Hero '83

Peter Menzies Jr.
Bless the Child '00
Disney's The Kid '00
Posse '93

Stanley Meredith
Salt of the Earth '54

Raffaele Mertes
Jesus '00
Fluke '95

John Metcalfe
Inseminoid '80

Russell Metty
That Touch of Mink '62
The Misfits '61
Spartacus [Criterion] '60
Touch of Evil [SE] '58

Rexford Metz
The Midnight Hour '86

Richard Michalak
Body Chemistry 2: Voice of a Stranger '91

Mike Michiewicz
Under Oath '97

Anastas Michos
The Big Kahuna '00
Keeping the Faith '00

Michael Mickens
Velocity '99

Gregory Middleton
After the Storm '01
The Five Senses '99

Pierre Mignot
The 6th Day '00

Arthur C. Miller
How Green Was My Valley '41
The Little Princess '39

David J. Miller
Shriek If You Know What I Did Last Friday the 13th '00
Footsteps '98

Harry B. Miller III
Dune '00

Virgil Miller
The Woman in Green '45
The Woman in Green / Dressed to Kill '45

Alec Mills
The Living Daylights '87

Charles Mills
Boyz N the Hood '91

Victor Milner
The Strange Love of Martha Ivers '46
Wonder Man '45
Bulldog Drummond Escapes '37

Doug Milsome
Dungeons and Dragons '00
Highlander: Endgame '00
The Beast '88

Dan Mindel
Shanghai Noon '00

Leung Chi Ming
Saviour of the Soul 2 '92

Yoshio Miyajima
Kwaidan '64

Hal Mohr
The Second Woman '51
The Phantom of the Opera '43
Pot o' Gold '41

Amir M. Mokri
Coyote Ugly '00
Freejack '92

William H. Molina
Destination Vegas '95

Mike Molloy
Noah's Ark '99

George Mooradian
Bats '99
K-911 '99
Love Kills '98
Postmortem '98
Mean Guns '97

Richard Moore
Annie '82
The Wild Angels '66

Ted Moore
Sinbad and the Eye of the Tiger '77
Golden Voyage of Sinbad '73
Psychomania '73
Diamonds Are Forever [SE] '71
A Man for All Seasons '66
From Russia with Love [2 SE] '63

Donald M. Morgan
Bojangles '01
For Love or Country: The Arturo Sandoval Story '00
A Lesson Before Dying '99
Kiss the Sky '98

Ira Morgan
The Vampire Bat '32

Masaru Mori
A Woman Called Sada Abe '75

Fujio Morita
Rikyu '90

Oswald Morris
Dracula / Strange Case of Dr. Jekyll & Mr. Hyde '73
The Taming of the Shrew '67
The Entertainer '60
Moby Dick '56
Beat the Devil '53

Reginald Morris
Porky's 2: The Next Day '83
Porky's / Porky's 2: The Next Day '82
Black Christmas '75

Abhik Mukhopadhyay
Isaac Asimov's Nightfall '00

M. David Mullen
Perfect Tenant '99
Twin Falls Idaho '99

Robby Muller
Dancer in the Dark '99

Chris Roe
Pop & Me '99

Lynn Rogers
Deadly Beauty: Snow's Secret
Life '01

Owen Roizman
The Addams Family '91
Grand Canyon '91
Tootsie '82
The Taking of Pelham One
Two Three '74

Glenn Roland
Ilsa, Harem Keeper of the Oil
Sheiks '76

Andy Romanoff
Something Weird '68
A Taste of Blood '67

George A. Romero
Night of the Living Dead
[Madacy] '68
Night of the Living Dead
[Elite] '68
Night of the Living Dead [LE
Anchor Bay] '68

Guillermo Rosas
Before Night Falls '00

Ilan Rosenberg
Turbo: A Power Rangers
Movie '96

Charles Rosher
Annie Get Your Gun '50
Little Lord Fauntleroy '36

Andrea Rosotto
Emmanuelle in Space: A
World of Desire '99

Fausto Rossi
Battle of the Amazons '74

Harold Rosson
The Scarlet Pimpernel '34

Andrea V. Rossotto
Fallen Angel '99
The Pandora Project '98
Carnosaur 3: Primal Species
'96

Giuseppe Rotunno
The Stendahl Syndrome '95
City of Women '81
Fellini Satyricon '69
Candy '68

Denis Rouden
Don't Let Me Die on a Sunday '99

Patrick Rousseau
Python '00

Philippe Rousselot
Remember the Titans '00
Mary Reilly '95
Hope and Glory '87
The Emerald Forest '85

Ashley Rowe
Bedrooms and Hallways '98
B. Monkey '97

Kevin Rowley
Falling for a Dancer '98

Juan Ruiz-Anchia
The Crew '00
Mr. Jones '93
House of Games '87
At Close Range '86

John L. "Jack" Russell
The Indestructible Man / The
Amazing Transparent Man
'56
The Man from Planet X '51

Joseph Ruttenberg
Butterfield 8 '60
The Last Time I Saw Paris '54

Paul Ryan
Thomas and the Magic Railroad '00

Hermann Saalfrank
Destiny '21

Eric Saarinen
Real Life '79

Virginie Saint-Martin
An Affair of Love '00

Richard Saint-Pierre
Tower of Song: The Canadian
Music Hall of Fame '01

Takao Saito
Madadayo '92

Javier Salmones
Butterfly '00

Sergio Salvati
Wax Mask '97
Puppet Master '89
The House by the Cemetery
[Diamond] '83
The House by the Cemetery
[Anchor Bay] '83
The Beyond '82
The Black Cat '81

Rodolfo Sanchez
Pixote '81

Gregory Sandor
Sisters '73
The Shooting '66

Lenny Santiago
Backstage '00

Estaban Sapir
Life According to Muriel '97

Hrvoje Saric
Cave of the Living Dead '65

Paul Sarossy
Duets '00
Rated X '00
Jerry and Tom '98
The Adjuster '91

Harris Savides
Finding Forrester '00
The Yards '00
Illuminata '98

Malik Hassan Sayeed
Original Kings of Comedy '00

Aldo Scavarda
L'Avventura '60

Roberto Schaefer
Best in Show '00

Charles Schettler
Gulliver's Travels [Image] '39

Tobias Schliessler
Bait '00

Ronn Schmidt
Men of War '94

Jorge Schmidt-Reitwein
Woyzeck '78

Charles "Chip" Schneer
The Coroner '98

Ernest B. Schoedsack
Chang: A Drama of the
Wilderness '27

Charles E. Schoenbaum
Good News '47
The Vanishing American '25

Nancy Schreiber
Book of Shadows: Blair Witch
2 '00

Fred Schuler
Just Looking '99

Howard Schwartz
The Devil & Max Devlin '81

Jason Schwartzman
Benny & Joon '93

John Schwartzman
The Rock [Criterion] '96

Chris Seager
Fever Pitch '96

John Seale
The Perfect Storm '00
The Talented Mr. Ripley '99
Children of a Lesser God '86

John Seitz
The Lost Weekend '45

Andrzej Sekula
American Psycho '99

Wayne Sells
Uninvited Guest '99

Dean Semler
Nutty Professor 2: The
Klumps [1 CE] '00
Nutty Professor 2: The
Klumps [2 Uncensored] '00
City Slickers '91

Ben Seresin
Circus '00

Michael Seresin
Angela's Ashes '99

Viorel Sergovici Jr.
Retro Puppet Master '99

Leon Shamroy
Planet of the Apes '68
Cleopatra '63
There's No Business Like
Show Business '54
The Snows of Kilimanjaro '52

Douglas W. Shannon
The Arrangement '99

Henry Sharp
Tomorrow the World '44

Boots Shelton
Detention '98

Lawrence Sher
On the Border '98

**Newton Thomas (Tom)
Sigel**
X-Men '00
Foxfire '96

James Signorelli
Black Caesar '73

Helio Silva
Manoushe, The Story of a
Gypsy Love '98

Johnny Simmons
Three Strikes '00
Once Upon a Time...When We
Were Colored '95

Geoffrey Simpson
Center Stage '00
Little Women [2 SE] '94
Mr. Wonderful '93

Fred Singer
Teenage Strangler '64

Sandi Sissel
Soul of the Game '96

Santosh Sivan
The Terrorist '98

William V. Skall
Rope '48
Life with Father '47

Michael Slifka
Teaserama '55

Taylor Sloan
Velocity '99

Michael Slovis
The 4th Floor '99

C. Davis Smith
Bad Girls Go to Hell / Another Day, Another Man '65

David W. Smith
Starry Night '99

Keith L. Smith
Diary of a Serial Killer '97

Roland Smith
The New Adventures of Pippi
Longstocking '88

Peter Smokler
This Is Spinal Tap [MGM] '84

William E. Snyder
The Loves of Carmen '48

Morten Soborg
Pusher '96

Bing Sokolsky
Black Cat Run '98

Carl Sommers
The Firing Line '91

Barry Sonnenfeld
Misery '90
When Harry Met Sally... [SE]
'89

Elena "EZ" Sorre
Backstage '00

Robert Sorrentino
Day of the Animals '77

Leonard J. South
Family Plot '76

Mike Southon
Air Bud 2: Golden Receiver
'98
Air Bud [2] '97
Gothic '87

Peter Sova
Donnie Brasco [2] '96

Thomas E. Spalding
The Blob '58

Theodor Sparkuhl
Blood on the Sun '45

David Sperling
The Drifter '88

Michael Spiller
Search and Destroy '94
The Unbelievable Truth '90

Dante Spinotti
Wonder Boys '00
The Last of the Mohicans '92
Fair Game '89

John Spotton
Buster Keaton Rides Again /
The Railrodder '65

Frank Stanley
Car Wash '76
Thunderbolt & Lightfoot '74

Oliver Stapleton
The Cider House Rules '99

Leonard Stark
Salt of the Earth '54

Jack Steely
The Thing with Two Heads '72

Mark Steensland
The Gospel According to
Philip K. Dick '00

Ueli Steiger
Chasers '94

Peter Stein
Necessary Roughness '91
Pet Sematary '89
C.H.U.D. '84

Mack Stengler
Ghosts on the Loose '43

Alan Stenvold
Private Navy of Sgt. O'Farrell
'68

Bert Stern
Jazz on a Summer's Day '59

**Patrick Alexander
Stewart**
Time Code '00

Jacques Steyn
Kill Me Again '89
The Mighty Quinn '89

David Stockton
Red Shoe Diaries: Luscious
Lola '00

Rogier Stoffers
Quills '00

Dan Stoloff
Tumbleweeds '98

Barry Stone
Full Disclosure '00

Vittorio Storaro
Dune '00
Goya in Bordeaux '00
Picking Up the Pieces '99

Archie Stout
Abilene Town '46
Captain Kidd '45
Lucky Texan '34
Man from Utah / Sagebrush
Trail '34
The Star Packer '34
Riders of Destiny / Star Pack-
er '33
Sagebrush Trail '33

Harry Stradling Sr.
Guys and Dolls '55
Hans Christian Andersen
[20th Century Fox] '52
Till the Clouds Roll By '46
Pygmalion '38

Harry Stradling Jr.
The Way We Were [SE] '73
Support Your Local Gunfight-
er '71

Ivan Strasburg
Deacon Brodie '98
Sharpe's Eagle '93
Sharpe's Rifles '93

Karl Struss
The Fly / Return of the Fly
'58
Kronos '57
Mohawk '56
Mesa of Lost Women '52
Rocketship X-M '50
Battle of the Sexes '28
Affairs of Anatol '21

Charles Stumar
The Mummy '32

Chan Wing Su
The Prisoner '90

Tim Suhrstedt
Whatever It Takes '00
Getting Even with Dad '94
Don't Tell Mom the Babysit-
ter's Dead '91
Mystic Pizza '88
The House on Sorority Row
'83
Suburbia '83

Masayoshi Sukita
After Life '98

Bruce Surtees
The Crush '93
Conquest of the Planet of the
Apes '72

Robert L. Surtees
The Last Picture Show [DC]
'71
Doctor Dolittle '67

The Hallelujah Trail '65
Ben-Hur '59

Wolfgang Suschitzky
Get Carter '71
Ring of Bright Water '69
Ulysses '67

Peter Suschitzsky
Krull [SE] '83
The Rocky Horror Picture
  Show '75
All Creatures Great and Small
  '74
That'll Be the Day '73

Misha (Mikhail) Suslov
Black Moon Rising '86

Maida Sussman
Ivory Tower '97

Rob Sweeney
I'm Losing You '98

Hubert Taczanowski
Turn It Up '00
Eden '98

Ken Talbot
The Stranger from Venus '54

Kaz Tanaka
Remembering the Cosmos
  Flower '99

Philip Tannura
The Flying Saucer '50

Jean-Jacques Tarbes
Honor Among Thieves '68

John Tarver
The First 9 1/2 Weeks '98
Stonebrook '98

David Tattersall
Vertical Limit '00
Moll Flanders [MGM] '96

Gale Tattersall
The Jack Bull '99
Hideaway '94
Tank Girl '94

Alfred Taylor
Mutant '83

Gilbert Taylor
The Bedroom Window '87
Losin' It '82
The Omen [SE] '76
Frenzy '72
Quackser Fortune Has a
  Cousin in the Bronx '70
Dr. Strangelove, or: How I
  Learned to Stop Worrying
  and Love the Bomb [2 SE]
  '64

Ronnie Taylor
Tommy '75

Manuel Teran
Mercy '00
Red Shoe Diaries: Four on
  the Floor '96

Ubaldo Terzano
Black Sabbath '64
Blood and Black Lace '64
The Whip and the Body '63

Costa Theodorides
Stella '55

Jurgen Thieme
The Sorrow and the Pity '71

Armand Thirard
Utopia '51

John Thomas
Kicked in the Head '97

Stuart Thompson
At War with the Army '50

William C. Thompson
The Astounding She-Monster
  '58
Plan 9 from Outer Space
  [Passport Video] '56
The Violent Years / Girl Gang
  '56
Daughter of Horror / Demen-
  tia '55

Alex Thomson
Love's Labour's Lost '00
Cliffhanger [2 CS] '93
Doctor Phibes Rises Again
  '72

Donald E. Thorin
Against All Odds '84
An Officer and a Gentleman
  '82

Clive Tickner
The Magical Legend of the
  Leprechauns '99

Frank Tidy
Hoodlum '96

George Tirl
Left Behind: The Movie '00
Revelation '00
Tribulation '00
Steel Dawn '87

Dan E. Toback
Midnight Tease / Midnight
  Tease 2 '94

Gregg Toland
The Bishop's Wife [MGM] '47
December 7th: The Pearl Har-
  bor Story '43
Come and Get It '36
Tonight or Never '31

John Toll
Almost Famous '00
Simpatico '99
Braveheart '95
Legends of the Fall [2 SE] '94

Lau Mun Tong
Saviour of the Soul 2 '92

Salvatore Totino
Any Given Sunday '99

Luciano Tovoli
Titus '99
The Dinner Game '98
Tenebre '82

Luciano Trasatti
The Bloody Pit of Horror '65

Robert Tregenza
Three Businessmen '99

Simon Trevor
An Elephant Called Slowly '69

William G. Troiano
She-Freak '67

David Trulli
Dementia '98

Brian Tufano
Billy Elliot '00
East Is East '99
Element of Doubt '96

George Tutanes
Midnight Dancers '94

Masaharu Ueda
Madadayo '92

Kurt Ugland
Inhumanity '00

Frantisek Uldrich
The Perfect Husband '92

Alejandro Ulloa
Bad Man's River '72
Pancho Villa '72

Derick Underschultz
Thrill Seekers '99

Geoffrey Unsworth
Superman 2 '80
Superman: The Movie '78
Zardoz '73

Jost Vacano
The Hollow Man [SE] '00
Untamed Heart '93

Jack Vacek
Gone in 60 Seconds '74

Joseph Valentine
Rope '48
Shadow of a Doubt '43
Saboteur '42

Theo van de Sande
Little Nicky '00

**Jan van den
Nieuwenhuyzen**
The Delivery '99

Steve Van Dyne
Dope Case Pending '00

Charles Van Enger
Abbott and Costello Meet
  Frankenstein '48
The Marriage Circle '24
The Last of the Mohicans '20

Anthony Van Laast
Jesus Christ Superstar '99

Philippe Van Leeuw
The Life of Jesus '96

Kees Van Oostrum
Drive Me Crazy '99
Gettysburg '93

James Van Trees
Angel on My Shoulder '46

Walther Vanden Ende
Farinelli '94

Gerard Vandenburg
The Vampire Happening '71

Mark Vargo
Play It to the Bone '99

Carlo Varini
The Big Blue [DC] '88

Gordon Verheul
Heaven's Fire '00

Noel Very
Immoral Tales '74

Rene Verzier
Rabid '77

A.J. Vesak
Bounty Hunters '96

Mark Vicente
Dish Dogs '98

Robin Vidgeon
The Fly 2 '89
Hellraiser [2] '87

Sacha Vierny
8 1/2 Women '99
The Cook, the Thief, His Wife
  & Her Lover '90
Mon Oncle d'Amerique '80
La Guerre Est Finie '66

Reynaldo Villalobos
9 to 5 '80

Alex Vlacos
Louis Prima: The Wildest! '99

Radoslav Vladic
Tito and Me '92

Paul Vogel
Return of the Magnificent
  Seven '66
Village of the Giants '65
The Time Machine '60
Go for Broke! '51

Peter von Haller
Anatomy [SE] '00

**Nicholas Josef von
Sternberg**
Tourist Trap '79

Mario Vulpiani
La Grande Bouffe '73

Steven Wacks
Diplomatic Siege '99
Louis Prima: The Wildest! '99

Fritz Arno Wagner
Nosferatu [2] '22
Destiny '21

Roy Wagner
Nick of Time '95
Drop Zone '94

Lee Tak Wai
Saviour of the Soul 2 '92

Ric Waite
Summer Rental '85
Class '83
The Long Riders '80

Kent Wakeford
China O'Brien '88

Joseph Walker
Penny Serenade '41
Only Angels Have Wings '39
Something New '20
Back to God's Country /
  Something New '19

Chris Walling
Blue Ridge Fall '99
Thick As Thieves '99

David M. Walsh
Fatal Beauty '87
Sleeper '73
Everything You Always Want-
  ed to Know about Sex (But
  Were Afraid to Ask) '72

Wing-Heng Wang
Hard-Boiled [Winstar] '92

John Ward
Love, Honour & Obey '00

John F. Warren
Torn Curtain '66
The Cosmic Man '59

Gilbert Warrenton
Mesa of Lost Women '52

Burleigh Wartes
Superstar: The Life and
  Times of Andy Warhol '90

Norman Warwick
The Abominable Dr. Phibes
  '71

Philip Alan Waters
Cyborg '89

David Watkin
Critical Care '97
The Object of Beauty '91
The Four Musketeers '75
Catch-22 '70

Jerry Watson
Best of the Best 3: No Turn-
  ing Back / Best of the
  Best: Without Warning '95

Harry Waxman
Vampyres '74
Endless Night '71
Wonderwall: The Movie '69
The Day the Earth Caught
  Fire '61

Yossi Wein
Bridge of Dragons '99
Traitor's Heart '98

Gery Werner
Inn of 1000 Sins '75

David West
Winner Takes All '98

Tony Westman
The Last Stop '99

Haskell Wexler
The Rich Man's Wife '96
Canadian Bacon '94
Gimme Shelter '70
In the Heat of the Night '67

Howard Wexler
Newsbreak '00
Scandal: The Big Turn On '99
Sex Files: Ancient Desires
  '99
Curse of the Puppet Master:
  The Human Experiment '98
Banzai Runner '86
Reform School Girls '86

Charles F. Wheeler
Truck Turner '74
Slaughter's Big Ripoff '73
Tora! Tora! Tora! [2 SE] '70
Yours, Mine & Ours '68

John Wheeler
Flynn '96

James Whitaker
The Book of Stars '99
Let the Devil Wear Black '99

Lester White
Sherlock Holmes and the
  Secret Weapon '42

William F. Whitley
Cat Women of the Moon '53

Jack Whitman
The Shadow Riders '82

Derek Wiesehahn
Hell's Kitchen NYC '97

Joseph M. Wilcots
Mountaintop Motel Massacre
  '86

John Wilcox
The Last Valley '71

Harry Wild
Gentlemen Prefer Blondes
  '53
Son of Paleface '52

Vaughn Wilkins
Hillbillys in a Haunted House
  '67

Patrick Williams
National Lampoon's Golf
  Punks '99

Gordon Willis
Malice [MGM] '93
The Godfather, Part 3 '90
Manhattan '79
Interiors '78
The Godfather, Part 2 '74
The Parallax View '74
The Godfather DVD Collection
  '72

Ian Wilson
A Christmas Carol '99

Romain Winding
Sweet Revenge '98

Stephen Windon
In Pursuit of Honor '95

Zack Winestine
Strawberry Fields '97
The Next Step '95

David Wing
Parasite '95

Glen Winter
MVP: Most Valuable Primate
  '00
Premonition '99

Arthur Wong
Gen-X Cops '99
Crime Story '93

Once Upon a Time in China
'91

Bill Wong
Caracara '00
Rouge '87

Man-Wan Wong
The Legend of Drunken Master '94

Wing-hang Wong
Peace Hotel '95
The Killer [Winstar] '90
A Better Tomorrow, Part 1
[Anchor Bay] '86

Oliver Wood
U-571 [CE] '00
Rudy [SE] '93
Don't Go in the House '80

David Worth
The Prophet's Game '99
Lady Dragon '92
Bronco Billy '80

James W. Wrenn
Dakota '88

Alvin Wyckoff
Affairs of Anatol '21
Joan the Woman '16
Carmen / The Cheat '15

Reg Wyer
Four Sided Triangle '53
Spaceways '53

Steve Yaconelli
Blue Sky '91

Hideo Yamamoto
Fireworks '97

Yutaka Yamazaki
After Life '98

Katsumi Yanagishima
Kids Return '96

Weihan Yang
Yi Yi '00

Robert Yeoman
Beautiful '00
Down to You '00
Dogma '99
Drugstore Cowboy '89

William Yim
Naked Killer '92

Chan Chi Ying
Tokyo Raiders '00

Stephen Yip
Painted Skin '93

Kohtaro Yokoyama
Generator 1: Gawl '00

**Frederick A. (Freddie)
Young**
The Asphyx '72
You Only Live Twice [SE] '67
Lawrence of Arabia '62
Gorgo '61

Richard Yuricich
Brainstorm '83

Aldo Zappala
Gladiators: Bloodsport of the
Colosseum '00

Peter Zeitlinger
My Best Fiend '99

Fei Zhao
Small Time Crooks '00

Jerzy Zielinski
Galaxy Quest '99

John R. Zilles
Height of the Sky '99

Vilmos Zsigmond
The River '84
Close Encounters of the Third
Kind [CE] '77
Blood of Ghastly Horror '72

The Composer Index provides a listing for all composers, arrangers, lyricists, and bands that have provided an original music score for any of the DVDs reviewed in this book. The listings for the composer names follow an alphabetical sort by last name (although the names appear in a first name, last name format). The videographies are listed chronologically, from most recent film to the first. If a composer provided music for more than one film in the same year, these movies are listed alphabetically within the year.

Anton Abril
Pancho Villa '72

AC/DC
Maximum Overdrive '86

Richard Addinsell
A Christmas Carol '51
Fire over England '37

John Addison
Torn Curtain '66
Tom Jones [MGM] '63
The Entertainer '60

Larry Adler
King and Country '64

Robert Alcivar
Hysterical '83

Billy Allen
She-Freak '67

Peter Allen
Chained Heat 3: Hell Mountain '98

Woody Allen
Sleeper '73

Byron Allred
Don't Answer the Phone '80

Edward L. Alperson Jr.
Mohawk '56

Lucia Alvarez
Midaq Alley '95

William Alwyn
Immortal Battalion '44

Alejandro Amenabar
Butterfly '00

David Amram
The Source '96

Aaron Anderson
Three Strikes '00

Laurie Anderson
Something Wild '86

Pete Anderson
Chasers '94

Benny Andersson
Mio in the Land of Faraway '87

Antonio Ramirez Angel
The Awful Dr. Orlof '62

George Antheil
Daughter of Horror / Dementia '55

Paul Antonelli
China O'Brien '88

Harold Arlen
A Star Is Born '54

Desi Arnaz Sr.
Roots of Rhythm '99

David Arnold
Shaft '00
The World Is Not Enough [SE] '99

Malcolm Arnold
Suddenly, Last Summer '59
The Bridge on the River Kwai [LE] '57
Four Sided Triangle '53

Leon Aronson
Bounty Hunters 2: Hardball '97

Bent Aserud
The Other Side of Sunday '96

Spring Aspers
The Specials '00

Edwin Astley
The Womaneater '59

Sonia Atherton
A Couch in New York '95

Michael Atkinson
Heaven's Burning '97

Frederic Auburtin
The Bridge '00

Georges Auric
Rififi '54

Howard Ayers
Tower of Song: The Canadian Music Hall of Fame '01

Roy Ayers
Coffy '73

Mami Azairez
Honey & Ashes '96

Charles Aznavour
Mauvais Sang '86

Louis Babin
The List '99

Luis Bacalov
Woman on Top '00
City of Women '81

Burt Bacharach
Isn't She Great '00

Alfie '66
The Blob '58

Angelo Badalamenti
The Beach '00
Forever Mine '99
Holy Smoke '99
The Straight Story '99
Blue Velvet '86
Law and Disorder '74

Tom Bahler
The Object of Beauty '91

Alexander Baker
Tycus '98

Buddy (Norman Dale) Baker
The Puppetoon Movie '87
The Devil & Max Devlin '81
The Fox and the Hound '81

John Balamos
Hercules in New York '70

Manuel Balboa
The Grandfather '98

Richard Band
Curse of the Puppet Master: The Human Experiment '98
Puppet Master 5: The Latest Chapter '94
Puppet Master 4 '93
Puppet Master 2 '90
Puppet Master 3: Toulon's Revenge '90
Bride of Re-Animator '89
Puppet Master '89
The House on Sorority Row '83
Mutant '83
Parasite '82

Brian Banks
Internal Affairs '90

Don Banks
The Mummy's Shroud '67
Die, Monster, Die! '65

Roque Banos
Goya in Bordeaux '00

Lesley Barber
Mansfield Park '99

David Barkley
Charming Billy '99

Billy Barnes
Pinocchio '76

Nathan Barr
Beyond the Mat '99

John Barry
My Life '93
The Living Daylights '87
The Jagged Edge '85
A View to a Kill [SE] '85
Octopussy '83
Frances '82
Diamonds Are Forever [SE] '71
The Last Valley '71
The Lion in Winter '68
You Only Live Twice [SE] '67
From Russia with Love [2 SE] '63

Steve Bartek
The Crew '00
Snow Day '00

Don Barto
Divine Trash '98

Dee Barton
Thunderbolt & Lightfoot '74

Richard Baskin
Buffalo Bill & the Indians '76
Nashville '75

Kevin Bassinson
Cyborg '89

George Bassman
The Joe Louis Story '53

Tyler Bates
Get Carter '00
Rated X '00
Shriek If You Know What I Did Last Friday the 13th '00

Mike Batt
A Merry War '97

Mike Baum
Ill-Gotten Gains '97

Walter Baumgartner
Ilsa, the Wicked Warden '78

Les Baxter
Switchblade Sisters '75
The Big Doll House '71
Dr. Goldfoot and the Bikini Machine '66
Beach Blanket Bingo '65
Bikini Beach '64
Black Sabbath '64
Beach Party '63
X: The Man with X-Ray Eyes '63

Tales of Terror '62
The Pit and the Pendulum '61
The Fall of the House of Usher '60

Jeff Beal
The Passion of Ayn Rand '99

Michael Bearden
The Arrangement '99

Christophe Beck
The Broken Hearts Club '00
Thick As Thieves '99

Gerhard Becker
The Thousand Eyes of Dr. Mabuse '60

Herman Beeftink
Best of Intimate Sessions: Vol. 2 '99
Dish Dogs '98

David Bell
Lone Justice 2 '93

Gary Bell
Beautiful People '99

Marco Beltrami
The Crow: Salvation '00
Scream 3 [CS] '00
The Watcher '00
The Minus Man '99

Vassal Benford
House Party 2: The Pajama Jam '91

Arthur Benjamin
The Scarlet Pimpernel '34

Richard Rodney Bennett
The Witches '66

Cary Berger
Suture '93

Irving Berlin
There's No Business Like Show Business '54
Annie Get Your Gun '50

Carmelo A. Bernaola
Cut Throats Nine '72

James Bernard
The Devil Rides Out '68
Quatermass 2 '57
X The Unknown '56

Charles Bernstein
Cujo '83

Elmer Bernstein
Keeping the Faith '00
Bringing Out the Dead '99
Buddy '97
Bulletproof '96
Hoodlum '96
Canadian Bacon '94
Search and Destroy '94
Rambling Rose [2 SE] '91
The Field '90
A Night in the Life of Jimmy
  Reardon '88
The Black Cauldron '85
Class '83
Airplane 2: The Sequel '82
Airplane! '80
The Bridge at Remagen '69
Return of the Magnificent
  Seven '66
The Hallelujah Trail '65
Sons of Katie Elder '65
Birdman of Alcatraz '62
The Magnificent Seven '60
Sweet Smell of Success '57
Cat Women of the Moon '53
Robot Monster '53

Peter Bernstein
Canadian Bacon '94

Adam Berry
Buzz Lightyear of Star Com-
  mand: The Adventure
  Begins '00

Karl Bette
I Like the Girls Who Do '73

Harry Betts
Black Mama, White Mama
  '73

Keith Bilderbeck
Ill-Gotten Gains '97

Karl Bille
Mifune '99

Edward Bilous
Sleepaway Camp '83

Kjetil Bjerkestrand
Cross My Heart and Hope to
  Die '94

Bjork
Dancer in the Dark '99

Arnold Black
Illuminata '98

Stanley Black
The Day the Earth Caught
  Fire '61

Ruben Blades
Roots of Rhythm '99

Howard Blake
An Elephant Called Slowly '69

Terence Blanchard
Bojangles '01
Bamboozled '00
Next Friday [Platinum Series]
  '00
Gia '98
Four Little Girls '97
Get On the Bus '96

Ralph Blane
Good News '47

Arthur Bliss
Things to Come '36

Michael Boddicker
Freejack '92
F/X 2: The Deadly Art of Illu-
  sion '91

John Boegehold
Fallen Angel '99

Ed Bogas
Heavy Traffic '73

Geir Bohren
The Other Side of Sunday '96

William Bolcom
Illuminata '98

Jay Bolton
The Kid with the X-Ray Eyes
  '99

Bernardo Bonazzi
Women on the Verge of a
  Nervous Breakdown '88

Bono
The Million Dollar Hotel '99

Hal Borne
Hillbillys in a Haunted House
  '67

Simon Boswell
Circus '00
Jason and the Argonauts '00
Deacon Brodie '98
The War Zone '98
Dance with the Devil '97

Jean-Francois Bovard
Honey & Ashes '96

Richard Bowers
The Perfect Nanny '00

Christopher Brady
Our Lips Are Sealed '00

Daniel Brandt
The Red Dwarf '99

Goran Bregovic
The Serpent's Kiss '97

Leslie Bricusse
Doctor Dolittle '67

David Bridie
The Myth of Fingerprints '97

Jon Brion
Magnolia '99
Hard Eight '96

Richard Bronskill
National Lampoon's Golf
  Punks '99

Joseph Brooks
The Lords of Flatbush '74

Bruce Broughton
The Rescuers Down Under '90
Silverado [SE] '85

Leo Brower
A Walk in the Clouds '95

Alex Brown
Sheba, Baby '75
Sheba, Baby '75

Bundy Brown
Strawberry Fields '97

James Brown
Black Caesar '73
Slaughter's Big Ripoff '73

George Bruns
Robin Hood '73
The Aristocats '70
The Sword in the Stone '63

Rob Bryanton
Something More '99

David Buchbinder
Jerry and Tom '98

Victor Buchino
The Curious Dr. Humpp '70

Randy Buck
Teenage Catgirls in Heat '00

Robert Buckley
Casper's Haunted Christmas
  '00

Roy Budd
Sinbad and the Eye of the
  Tiger '77
Get Carter '71

Nonong Buenoamino
Midnight Dancers '94

Jimmy Buffett
Rancho Deluxe '75

Walter Bullock
The Little Princess '39

Justin Caine Burnett
Dungeons and Dragons '00

T Bone Burnett
O Brother Where Art Thou?
  '00

Ralph Burns
The Josephine Baker Story
  '90
All Dogs Go to Heaven '89
Annie '82

Carter Burwell
Before Night Falls '00
Book of Shadows: Blair Witch
  2 '00
Hamlet '00
What Planet Are You From?
  '00
Mystery, Alaska '99
It Could Happen to You '94
And the Band Played On '93

Artie Butler
Sextette '78
For Pete's Sake '74

David Buttolph
The Horse Soldiers '59
Rope '48

David Byrne
Married to the Mob '88
Something Wild '86

John Cale
American Psycho '99
I Shot Andy Warhol '96
Something Wild '86

Darrell Calker
The Amazing Transparent
  Man '60
The Flying Saucer '50

John Cameron
The Mirror Crack'd '80

Bruce Campbell
Plan 9 from Outer Space
  [Passport Video] '56

Al Capps
Cannonball Run '81

Philip Carli
Evangeline '29
Something New '20
Back to God's Country /
  Something New '19

Robert Carli
My 5 Wives '00

Larry Carlton
Against All Odds '84

Ralph Carmichael
The Blob '58

John Carpenter
Halloween 5: The Revenge of
  Michael Myers '89
Big Trouble in Little China
  [SE] '86
Escape from New York '81

Nicholas Carras
Missile to the Moon '59
Frankenstein's Daughter '58
She Demons '58

Gaylord Carter
Shadows '22

Kristopher Carter
Parasite '95

Patrick Cassidy
Broken Harvest '94

Teddy Castellucci
Little Nicky '00
Deuce Bigalow: Male Gigolo
  '99

**Mario Castelnuovo-
Tedesco**
The Loves of Carmen '48

Daniel Catan
I'm Losing You '98

Charlie Chan
Me Myself I '99

Gary Chang
Sniper '92
Death Warrant '90

Martin Charnin
Annie '99

Peter Chase
Portraits Chinois '96

Jay Chattaway
Red Scorpion '89
Missing in Action '84
Walking the Edge '83

To Chi Chee
Saviour of the Soul 2 '92

Edmund Choi
Down to You '00
Wide Awake '97

Michalis Christodoulidis
Attila 74: The Rape of Cyprus
  '75

David Chudnow
The Jackie Robinson Story
  '50

Tony Cinciripini
Hell's Kitchen NYC '97

Stelvio Cipriano
Bay of Blood '71
The Frightened Woman '71
Twitch of the Death Nerve '71

Chuck Cirino
Body Chemistry 3: Point of
  Seduction '93
Sorority House Massacre 2:
  Nighty Nightmare '92
Not of This Earth '88

Eric Clapton
Communion [CE] '89
Wonderwall: The Movie '69

Igor Clark
Dead Waters '94

James Clark
Vampyres '74

Nigel Clarke
The Little Vampire '00

Stanley Clarke
Romeo Must Die '00
Panther '95
Poetic Justice '93
Passenger 57 '92
Boyz N the Hood '91

Siobhan Cleary
Dangerous Curves '99

Jimmy Cliff
The Harder They Come '72

George S. Clinton
Ready to Rumble '00
Red Shoe Diaries: Luscious
  Lola '00
Red Shoe Diaries: Swimming
  Naked '00
Red Shoe Diaries: Four on
  the Floor '96
Red Shoe Diaries: Strip Poker
  '96
Mother's Boys '94
The Boys Next Door '85
Cheech and Chong: Still
  Smokin' '83

Elia Cmiral
Battlefield Earth '00

Robert Cobert
Strange Case of Dr. Jekyll &
  Mr. Hyde '68

Frank A. Coe
Mantis in Lace '68

Philippe Cohen-Solal
Don't Let Me Die on a Sunday '99

Serge Colbert
On the Border '98
Traitor's Heart '98

Bill Coleman
The Watermelon Woman '97

Cy Coleman
Power '86

Jim Coleman
The Unbelievable Truth '90

Michel Colombier
Screwed '00
Kiss of Fire '98
Barb Wire '96
Foxfire '96
Posse '93
Sudie & Simpson '90
Against All Odds '84

Joseph Conlan
The Proposal '00

Harry Connick Jr.
When Harry Met Sally... [SE]
  '89

Rick Conrad
The Drifter '88

Paolo Conte
A Couch in New York '95

Bill Conti
Napoleon '96
Blood In ... Blood Out: Bound
  by Honor '93
Necessary Roughness '91
The Big Blue [DC] '88
A Night in the Life of Jimmy
  Reardon '88
Baby Boom '87
F/X '86
The Karate Kid '84
Rocky [SE] '76

Michael Convertino
Critical Care '97
Mother Night '96
Children of a Lesser God '86
Hollywood Vice Sqaud '86

Ry Cooder
Southern Comfort '81
The Long Riders '80

Stewart Copeland
Boys and Girls '00
Simpatico '99
The Pallbearer '95
She's Having a Baby '88
Talk Radio '88
Wall Street '87

Aaron Copland
Our Town '40

Carmine Coppola
The Godfather, Part 3 '90
Tucker: The Man and His
  Dream '88
The Godfather, Part 2 '74

Normand Corbeil
The Art of War '00
The Boys '97

Frank Cordell
Ring of Bright Water '69

Violaine Corradi
Dralion '00

Whatever Happened to Aunt
Alice? '69
Killer's Kiss '55

Hugo Friedhofer
An Affair to Remember '57
Vera Cruz '53
The Bishop's Wife [MGM] '47

John (Gianni) Frizzell
Beautiful '00
Mafia! '98
Alien: Resurrection '97
The Rich Man's Wife '96

Fabio Frizzi
Manhattan Baby '82

Dominic Frontiere
Incubus '65

Parmer Fuller
Saturday the 14th Strikes
Back '88
Saturday the 14th '81

William Furst
Joan the Woman '16

Magne Furuholmen
Cross My Heart and Hope to
Die '94

Giovanni Fusco
La Guerre Est Finie '66
L'Avventura '60

Peter Gabriel
The Last Temptation of Christ
'88

John Gale
Doctor Phibes Rises Again
'72

Mazatl Galindo
Pop & Me '99

Phil Gallo
Mother's Day [DC] '80

Douglas Gamley
The Beast Must Die '75
Tom Thumb '58

Russell Garcia
The Time Machine '60

Mort Garson
Beware! The Blob '72

George Gershwin
Manhattan '79

Ira Gershwin
A Star Is Born '54

Michael Gibbs
Hard-Boiled [Winstar] '92

Richard Gibbs
Big Momma's House '00
28 Days [SE] '00
The Book of Stars '99
Dirty Work '97
Blind Justice '94
Amos and Andrew '93

Alex Gibson
Suburbia '83

Philip Giffin
Beethoven's 3rd '00

Kevin Gilbert
My Teacher's Wife '95

Dizzy Gillespie
Roots of Rhythm '99

Norman Gimbel
Lady and the Tramp 2:
Scamp's Adventure '01

Philip Glass
The Source '96

Albert Glasser
Giant from the Unknown '58
Monster from Green Hell '58

The Indestructible Man / The
Amazing Transparent Man
'56

Derek Gleeson
Moving Target '00

Patrick Gleeson
The Bedroom Window '87

Nick Glennie-Smith
Attila '01
The Rock [Criterion] '96

Jesus Gluck
Blood and Sand '89

The Goblins
Tenebre '82

Ernest Gold
The McCullochs '75
The Screaming Skull '58

Barry Goldberg
Best of the Best 3: No Turn-
ing Back / Best of the
Best: Without Warning '95

Elliot Goldenthal
Titus '99
Drugstore Cowboy '89
Pet Sematary '89

Jerry Goldsmith
Disney's The Kid '00
The Hollow Man [SE] '00
The Mummy [2 SE] '99
Malice [MGM] '93
Rudy [SE] '93
Six Degrees of Separation
'93
Love Field '91
Runaway '84
Supergirl '84
Omen 3: The Final Conflict
'81
Damien: Omen 2 '78
Breakheart Pass '76
The Cassandra Crossing '76
The Omen [SE] '76
Escape from the Planet of
the Apes '71
Tora! Tora! Tora! [2 SE] '70
Planet of the Apes '68
The Sand Pebbles '66
In Harm's Way '65
Seven Days in May '64
Lilies of the Field '63

Joel Goldsmith
Diamonds '99
One Good Turn '95
Home for Christmas '93
A Woman, Her Men and Her
Futon '92
No Safe Haven '87
Banzai Runner '86

William Goldstein
The Miracle Worker '00

Vincente Gomez
The Fighter '52

Joseph Julian Gonzalez
Price of Glory '00

Miles Goodman
Getting Even with Dad '94
What about Bob? '91
Wham-Bam, Thank You
Spaceman '75

Jim Goodwin
Darkdrive '98

Ronald Goodwin
Frenzy '72

Michael Gore
Mr. Wonderful '93
Defending Your Life '91
Terms of Endearment '83

Lallo Gori
Four Times That Night '69

Orlando Gough
Immortality '98

Gerald Gouriet
Men of War '94

Patrick Gowers
Comic Act '00

Paul Grabowsky
Noah's Ark '99

Tom Graeff
Teenagers from Outer Space
'59

Ron Grainer
The Mouse on the Moon '62

Olivia "Babsy" Grange
Klash '95

David Grant
Best of the Best: Without
Warning '98

Allan Gray
I Know Where I'm Going '45

Stephen Graziano
Highlander: Endgame '00

Johnny Green
Alvarez Kelly '66
The Inspector General '49

Walter Greene
The Brain from Planet Arous
'57
Teenage Doll '57

Richard Gregoire
Nuremberg '00

Harry Gregson-Williams
Chicken Run '00
The Tigger Movie '00
Light It Up '99
Smilla's Sense of Snow '96

Richard Gresko
The Scorpio Factor '90

Dean Grinsfelder
Stonebrook '98

Ferde Grofe Jr.
Rocketship X-M '50

Guy Gross
Cut '00
That's the Way I Like It '99
The Adventures of Priscilla,
Queen of the Desert
[MGM] '94

Larry Grossman
Pocahontas 2: Journey to a
New World '98

Lawrence Nash Groupe
The Contender '00
Deterrence '00

Louis Gruenberg
Quicksand '50

Bert Grund
The Thousand Eyes of Dr.
Mabuse '60

Dave Grusin
For the Boys '91
The Pope of Greenwich Vil-
lage '84
Tootsie '82
And Justice for All '79

Jay Gruska
Outlaw Justice '98

Anthony Guefen
The Stuff '85

Christopher Guest
This Is Spinal Tap [MGM] '84

Christopher Gunning
Lord Edgeware Dies '99
The Murder of Roger Ackroyd
'99

Arlo Guthrie
Alice's Restaurant '69

Aleksandar Habic
The Wounds '98

Manos Hadjidakis
A Matter of Dignity '57
Girl in Black '56
Stella '55

Dick Halligan
Fear City '85

Marvin Hamlisch
The Devil & Max Devlin '81
Ice Castles '79
The Way We Were [SE] '73
Bananas '71

Oscar Hammerstein
The Sound of Music [Five
Star Collection] '65

Herbie Hancock
A Soldier's Story '84
Death Wish '74

Leigh Harline
7 Faces of Dr. Lao '63

W. Franke Harling
Penny Serenade '41

Udi Harpaz
Digimon: The Movie '00

George Harrison
Wonderwall: The Movie '69

Jimmy Harry
Intern '00

Daniel Hart
Nude on the Moon '61

Lorenz Hart
Pal Joey '57

Richard Hartley
The Brylcreem Boys '96
Princess Caraboo '94
The Impossible Spy '87
Dance with a Stranger '85
The Rocky Horror Picture
Show '75

Richard Harvey
The Magical Legend of the
Leprechauns '99

Bo Harwood
Opening Night '77

Paul Haslinger
Cheaters '00

John Hassell
The Million Dollar Hotel '99

Harley Hatcher
Satan's Sadists '69

Takayuki Hattori
Godzilla 2000 '99

Wayne Hawkins
Ninth Street '98

Peter Haycock
One False Move '91

Isaac Hayes
Shaft '00
Truck Turner '74

Lennie Hayton
Till the Clouds Roll By '46

Craig Hazen
Double Parked '00

Reinhold Heil
Winter Sleepers '97

Ray Heindorf
Wonder Man '45

Joe Henry
Jesus' Son '99

Matthew Herbert
Human Traffic '99

Bernard Herrmann
Sisters '73
Endless Night '71
The Bride Wore Black '68
North by Northwest '59
The Man Who Knew Too
Much '56
The Trouble with Harry '55
The Snows of Kilimanjaro '52

Boo Hewerdine
Fever Pitch '96

Werner R. Heymann
That Uncertain Feeling [Sling-
Shot] '41

Andy Hill
Sinbad: Beyond the Veil of
Mists '00

John Hill
Drop Dead Rock '95
The Pompatus of Love '95

Peter Himmelman
The Souler Opposite '97

David Hirschfelder
Hanging Up '99
The Interview '98

Joe Hisaishi
Princess Mononoke '98
Fireworks '97
Kids Return '96

Ricky Ho
A Chinese Ghost Story: The
Tsui Hark Animation '97

Michael Hoenig
Eye of the Killer '99

Paul Hoffert
The Groundstar Conspiracy
'72

Joachim Holbek
Heart of Light '97
Nightwatch '96
Breaking the Waves '95
Nightwatch '94

Lee Holdridge
The Secret of NIMH 2 '98
The Long Way Home '97
Soul of the Game '96
The Tuskegee Airmen '95
Splash '84

Loris Holland
A Day in Black and White '01

**Frederick "Friedrich"
Hollander**
The 5000 Fingers of Dr. T '53

Derek Holt
One False Move '91

Bo Holten
The Element of Crime '84

Nigel Holton
Carnosaur '93
Bloodfist 3: Forced to Fight
'92
Body Chemistry 2: Voice of a
Stranger '91
Bloodfist 2 '90

Tobe Hooper
The Texas Chainsaw Mas-
sacre 2 '86

Kenyon Hopkins
Twelve Angry Men '57

Stephen Horelick
Madman '82

Trevor Horn
Coyote Ugly '00

James Horner
The Perfect Storm '00

Joseph LoDuca
Evil Dead 2: Dead by Dawn [2 THX] '87
Thou Shalt Not Kill...Except '87

John Loeffler
Pokemon the Movie 2000: The Power of One '00

Frank Loesser
Guys and Dolls '55
Hans Christian Andersen [20th Century Fox] '52

Mike Logan
Steele's Law '91

Alexina Louie
The Five Senses '99

Lyle Lovett
Dr. T & the Women '00

Mundell Lowe
Everything You Always Wanted to Know about Sex (But Were Afraid to Ask) '72

Richard Lowry
Mommy [SE] '95

John Lunn
Immortality '98

Evan Lurie
Joe Gould's Secret '00

Neil MacColl
Fever Pitch '96

Galt MacDermot
Mistress '91
Cotton Comes to Harlem '70

Mader
Steal This Movie! '00

Michel Magne
Cold Sweat '71

Bob Mamet
Aftershock '88
Necromancer: Satan's Servant '88

Melissa Manchester
Lady and the Tramp 2: Scamp's Adventure '01

Mark Mancina
Bait '00
Moll Flanders [MGM] '96

Henry Mancini
Switch '91
Santa Claus: The Movie '85
Touch of Evil [SE] '58

Johnny Mandel
Being There '79

Harry Manfredini
The Omega Code '99
Deepstar Six '89
Swamp Thing '82

Barry Manilow
The Pebble and the Penguin '94
Thumbelina '94

Aimee Mann
Magnolia '99

Barry Mann
All Dogs Go to Heaven 2 '95

Hummie Mann
Thomas and the Magic Railroad '00
Fall Time '94

Franco Mannino
Beat the Devil '53

Clint Mansell
Requiem for a Dream '00

David Mansfield
A Good Baby '99

Tumbleweeds '98
Floating '97

Eddy Manson
Little Fugitive '53

Kevin Manthei
Milo '98

Martia Manuel
The Firing Line '91

Marco Marinangelo
Octopus '00

Anthony Marinelli
Time Code '00
Flynn '96
One Man's Justice '95

Richard Markowitz
The Shooting '66

Clair Marlo
Tycus '98

Branford Marsalis
Mo' Better Blues '90

Jack Marshall
Munster, Go Home! '66

Phil Marshall
Kiss Toledo Goodbye '00

Hugh Martin
Good News '47

Peter Martin
Hope and Glory '87

Cliff Martinez
Traffic '00

Rick Marvin
U-571 [CE] '00

John Massari
Retro Puppet Master '99

Alejandro Masso
Women '97

Sasha Matson
Bloodfist '89

Stuart Matthewman
Twin Falls Idaho '99

Peter Matz
Lust in the Dust '85
The Private Eyes [SE] '80
In This House of Brede '75

Brian May
Dr. Giggles '92
Steel Dawn '87

Toshiro Mayuzumi
Good Morning '59

Tim McCauley
Cold Blooded '00

Albritton McClain
Dilemma '97

Brian McClelland
Ice from the Sun '00

Paul McCollough
Santa Claws '96
Night of the Living Dead '90

Maureen McElheron
I Married a Strange Person '97

David McEwan
Lingerie '01

Bill McGuffie
The Asphyx '72

David McHugh
Mystic Pizza '88

Harper Mckay
Cry Uncle '71

Michael McKean
This Is Spinal Tap [MGM] '84

Mark McKenzie
Frank and Jesse '94
Warlock: The Armageddon '93

Stephen McKeon
Falling for a Dancer '98

James McVay
Desert Winds '95

Medusa
Switchblade Sisters '75

Tina Meeks
Ill-Gotten Gains '97

Gil Melle
Gold of the Amazon Women '79
Embryo '76
The Sentinel '76
The Organization '71

Rob Mellow
Human Traffic '99

Felix Mendelssohn
The Bedroom Window '87

Alan Menken
Pocahontas '95

Marc Mergen
An Affair of Love '00

Pat Metheny
A Map of the World '99

Abe Meyer
Reefer Madness '38

Matt Meyer
Ice from the Sun '00

Randall Meyers
The Last Lieutenant '94

Franco Micalizzi
Battle of the Amazons '74

Bret Michaels
No Code of Conduct '98

Cynthia Miller
Digging to China '98

Marcus Miller
The Ladies Man '00
House Party '90

Chen Ming-Chang
Maborosi '95

Carmen Miranda
Roots of Rhythm '99

Paul Misraki
Utopia '51

Vic Mizzy
The Munsters' Revenge '81

Mamoru Mochizuki
Seamless '00

Cyril Mockridge
Donovan's Reef '63
The Man Who Shot Liberty Valance '62
Bus Stop '56

Fred Mollin
Inferno '99
Thrill Seekers '99

Deborah Mollison
East Is East '99

Paddy Moloney
Agnes Browne '99

Michael Montes
Whipped '00

Hal Mooney
The Meanest Men in the West '76

Chet Moore
The Notorious Daughter of Fanny Hill / Head Mistress '66

Mio Morales
The Next Step '95

Mark Morgan
Shark Attack 2 '00

Giorgio Moroder
Fair Game '89

Jerome Moross
The Big Country '58

Andrea Morricone
Here on Earth '00
Liberty Heights '99

Ennio Morricone
Mission to Mars '00
Lolita '97
The Stendahl Syndrome '95
In the Line of Fire [2 SE] '93
Tie Me Up! Tie Me Down! '90
The Untouchables '87
Lovers and Liars '81
Bluebeard '72

John Morris
Clue '85

Van Morrison
Beyond the Clouds '95

Thomas Morse
The Apostate '98

Povl Kristian Mortensen
Pusher '96

Carlo Moser
Cyrano de Bergerac '25

Mark Mothersbaugh
The Adventures of Rocky & Bullwinkle '00
Rugrats in Paris: The Movie '00
It's the Rage '99

Rob Mounsey
Working Girl '88

Michael Muhlfriedel
Plump Fiction '97

Dominic Muldowney
Sharpe's Eagle '93
Sharpe's Rifles '93

David Munrow
Zardoz '73

John Murphy
Lock, Stock and 2 Smoking Barrels '98

Lyn Murray
The Bridges at Toko-Ri '55

Jennie Muskett
B. Monkey '97

Stanley Myers
Frightmare '74
Ulysses '67

Irwin Nafshun
The Beast of Yucca Flats '61

Seikou Nagaoka
Sol Bianca: The Legacy '90

Takashi Nakagawa
Prisoner Maria: The Movie '95

Jack Nathan
The Abominable Dr. Phibes '71

Roger Neil
Under Oath '97

David J. Nelsen
Python '00

Steven Nelson
Last Resort '86

Willie Nelson
Ruckus '81

John Neschling
Pixote '81

Ira Newborn
Bad Manners '98
High School High '96
Naked Gun 33 1/3: The Final Insult '94
Naked Gun 2 1/2: The Smell of Fear '91
The Naked Gun: From the Files of Police Squad '88
Planes, Trains & Automobiles '87

Loren Newkirk
Jackson County Jail '76

Alfred Newman
The Greatest Story Ever Told [SE] '65
The Man Who Shot Liberty Valance '62
Bus Stop '56
The Seven Year Itch '55
There's No Business Like Show Business '54
How to Marry a Millionaire '53
December 7th: The Pearl Harbor Story '43
How Green Was My Valley '41
Come and Get It '36
The Gay Desperado '36
Rain '32
Street Scene '31
Tonight or Never '31

David Newman
Duets '00
The Flintstones in Viva Rock Vegas '00
Nutty Professor 2: The Klumps [1 CE] '00
Nutty Professor 2: The Klumps [2 Uncensored] '00
102 Dalmatians '00
Galaxy Quest '99
Coneheads '93
Don't Tell Mom the Babysitter's Dead '91

Lionel Newman
There's No Business Like Show Business '54
Gentlemen Prefer Blondes '53

Randy Newman
Meet the Parents '00
Toy Story 2 '99
James and the Giant Peach '96
Toy Story '95
Avalon '90
The Natural '84

Thomas Newman
Erin Brockovich '00
American Beauty [SE] '99
American Buffalo '95
Little Women [2 SE] '94
Threesome '94
Desperately Seeking Susan '85
Girls Just Want to Have Fun '85

Lennie Niehaus
Space Cowboys '00
The Jack Bull '99
Pocahontas 2: Journey to a New World '98
Bird '88

Jose Nieto
Guantanamera '95
Running out of Time '94
The Perfect Husband '92

Stefan Nilsson
The Inside Man '84

Shiroh Sagisu
Neon Genesis Evangelion Collection '99

Koichi Sakata
A Woman Called Sada Abe '75

Gamal Salama
An Egyptian Story '82

Gary Sales
Madman '82

Conrad Salinger
The Last Time I Saw Paris '54
Till the Clouds Roll By '46

Hans J. Salter
The 5000 Fingers of Dr. T '53
Dressed to Kill '46

Bennett Salvay
Love Stinks '99

Caleb Sampson
Mr. Death: The Rise and Fall of Fred A. Leuchter Jr. '99

Mamoru Samurakouchi
Remembering the Cosmos Flower '99

Tomas San Miguel
Big City Blues '99

Jeannot Sanavia
An Affair of Love '00

Arturo Sandoval
For Love or Country: The Arturo Sandoval Story '00

Hiroaki Sano
Mystery of the Necronomicon '00

Philippe Sarde
Coup de Torchon '81
Loulou '80
La Grande Bouffe '73

Paul Sawtell
Voyage to the Bottom of the Sea / Fantastic Voyage '61
The Cosmic Man '59
The Fly / Return of the Fly '58
Kronos '57

Walter Scharf
The Nutty Professor '63

Lalo Schifrin
F/X 2: The Deadly Art of Illusion '91
Black Moon Rising '86
Mean Season '85
The Amityville Horror '79
Day of the Animals '77
The Eagle Has Landed '77
The Four Musketeers '75
Kelly's Heroes '70
Joy House '64

Ralph Schuckett
Pokemon the Movie 2000: The Power of One '00

Walter Schumann
Africa Screams / Jack and the Beanstalk '49

Siegfried Schwab
She Killed in Ecstasy '70

Stephen Schwartz
Pocahontas '95

John Scott
Rudyard Kipling's Second Jungle Book: Mowgli and Baloo '97
Winter People '89
Inseminoid '80
North Dallas Forty '79

Tom Scott
Conquest of the Planet of the Apes '72

Humphrey Searle
The Abominable Snowman '57

Eckart Seeber
Bram Stoker's Shadowbuilder '98
The Prisoner '90

Brad Segal
Isaac Asimov's Nightfall '00

Misha Segal
The New Adventures of Pippi Longstocking '88

Ilona Sekacz
Solomon and Gaenor '98
Northanger Abbey '87

Albert Sendry
Father's Little Dividend '51

Eric Serra
The Messenger: The Story of Joan of Arc '99
Leon, the Professional '94
La Femme Nikita [MGM] '91

Derek Seward
Divided We Stand '00

Sherwood Seward
Divided We Stand '00

Paul Shaffer
Postcards from the Edge '90

Yuval Shafrir
Pick a Card '97

Marc Shaiman
Mother '96
Stuart Saves His Family '94
The Addams Family '91
City Slickers '91
Misery '90
When Harry Met Sally... [SE] '89

Robbie Shakespeare
Third World Cop '99

Bud Shank
Slippery When Wet '58

Ravi Shankar
Wonderwall: The Movie '69

Theodore Shapiro
Prince of Central Park '00
Girlfight '99
Restaurant '98

Thom Sharp
Last Resort '86

Harry Shearer
This Is Spinal Tap [MGM] '84

Ed Shearmur
Charlie's Angels '00
Miss Congeniality '00
Whatever It Takes '00
The Cement Garden '93

Bert Shefter
Voyage to the Bottom of the Sea / Fantastic Voyage '61
The Cosmic Man '59
Kronos '57

Alexei Shelegin
The Red Dwarf '99

Jaime Sheriff
Slumber Party Massacre 3 '90

Garry Sherman
Alice's Restaurant '69

Richard M. Sherman
Bednobs and Broomsticks '71
Mary Poppins [2 SE] '64

Robert B. Sherman
Bednobs and Broomsticks '71
Mary Poppins [2 SE] '64

David Shire
The Women of Brewster Place '89
Monkey Shines '88
Norma Rae '79
The Conversation '74
The Taking of Pelham One Two Three '74

Howard Shore
The Cell '00
High Fidelity '00
The Yards '00
Dogma '99
Striptease '96
The Truth about Cats and Dogs '96
Moonlight and Valentino '95
Seven [2 SE] '95
Prelude to a Kiss '92
Postcards from the Edge '90
The Fly / The Fly 2 '86

Lawrence Shragge
The Audrey Hepburn Story '00

Michael Shrieve
The Bedroom Window '87

Leo Shuken
The Flying Deuces / Utopia '39

Isaak Shvarts
Dersu Uzala '75

David Siebels
Phenomenon—The Lost Archives: Noah's Ark Found?/Tunguska/Stolen Glory '99
Phenomenon—The Lost Archives: Up for Sale/Heavy Watergate '99

Christian Sievert
Mifune '99

Carlo Siliotto
Fluke '95

Michael Silversher
The Little Mermaid 2: Return to the Sea '00

Patty Silversher
The Little Mermaid 2: Return to the Sea '00

Shel Silverstein
Postcards from the Edge '90

Alan Silvestri
Castaway '00
Reindeer Games '00
The Replacements '00
What Lies Beneath '00
What Women Want '00
Father of the Bride Part II '95
Predator [20th Century Fox] '87
The Clan of the Cave Bear '86
Delta Force '86
Summer Rental '85

Zoran Simjanovic
Tito and Me '92

Carly Simon
Postcards from the Edge '90
Working Girl '88

Marty Simon
Captive '00

Yves Simon
Love After Love '94

Claudio Simonetti
Tenebre '82

Mike Simpson
Road Trip '00

Rand Singer
Velocity '99

Scott Singer
Midnight Confessions '95

Sonu Sisupal
The Terrorist '98

Roni Skies
The Next Step '95

Frank Skinner
Away All Boats '56
Harvey '50
Abbott and Costello Meet Frankenstein '48
Saboteur '42
Sherlock Holmes and the Secret Weapon '42

Cezary Skubiszewski
Lilian's Story '95

Andrew Slack
Three Strikes '00

Michael Small
Mountains of the Moon '90
Jaws: The Revenge '87
The Lathe of Heaven '80
The Parallax View '74

Bruce Smeaton
Roxanne '87
Plenty '85

B.C. Smith
Mercy '00
Around the Fire '98

Blaise Smith
Ultimate Attraction '98

Gregory Darryl Smith
Uninvited Guest '99

Joseph Smith
Animal Instincts '92
Secret Games '92

Paul J. Smith
Fun & Fancy Free '47

Mark Snow
Dirty Pictures '00
Crazy in Alabama '99
Jake Speed '86

Curt Sobel
Alien Nation '88

Stephen Sondheim
Postcards from the Edge '90

Giuliano Sorgini
Let Sleeping Corpses Lie '74

Tim Souster
Slugs '87

Eric Spear
The Stranger from Venus '54

Eddie Sperry
The Lifestyle '99

Ivor Stanley
Spaceways '53

Andrew Stein
Hollywood Boulevard '76

Herman Stein
The Intruder '61

Ronald Stein
Dementia 13 '63
Dinosaurus! '60

Max Steiner
Life with Father '47
Arsenic and Old Lace '44
They Made Me a Criminal '39
The Garden of Allah '36
Little Lord Fauntleroy '36
Of Human Bondage '34
The Most Dangerous Game [Madacy] '32

Steven Stern
Hangman '00
Bloody Murder '99

Cat Stevens
Harold and Maude '71

James Stevens
Plan 9 from Outer Space [Passport Video] '56

Sting
Dolphins '00

Gary Stockdale
Necromancer: Satan's Servant '88

Christopher Stone
Phantasm 4: Oblivion '98
Fist of the North Star '95
Choices '81

Richard Stone
Pumpkinhead '88

Charles Strouse
Annie '99

Joe Strummer
Sid & Nancy [MGM] '86

Marty Stuart
All the Pretty Horses '00

Jule Styne
Gentlemen Prefer Blondes '53

Ron Sures
The Life Before This '99

Bruce Sussman
The Pebble and the Penguin '94
Thumbelina '94

Toru Takemitsu
The Inland Sea '93
Rikyu '90
Double Suicide '69
Kwaidan '64

Frederic Talgorn
Heavy Metal 2000 [SE] '00
Delta Force 2: Operation Stranglehold '90

Art Tatum
September '88

Michael Tavera
Drowning Mona '00
Girl '98

Barry Taylor
Kept '01

Stephen James Taylor
Holiday Heart '00

Bob Telson
Life According to Muriel '97

Nicolas Tenbroek
Isaac Asimov's Nightfall '00

Dennis Michael Tenney
Leprechaun 4: In Space '96
Leprechaun 3 '95

Mikis Theodorakis
The Story of Jacob & Joseph '74

Mark Thomas
The Big Tease '99

Ken Thorne
In the Beginning... '00

Timbaland
Romeo Must Die '00

Dimitri Tiomkin
The Alamo '60
The Old Man and the Sea '58
Friendly Persuasion '56
D.O.A. [Roan] '49
Portrait of Jennie '48
Angel on My Shoulder '46
Shadow of a Doubt '43
Meet John Doe [Image] '41
Only Angels Have Wings '39

The Category Index includes subject terms ranging from straight genre descriptions (Action-Adventure, Slapstick Comedy, etc.) to more off-the-wall themes (Alien Babes, Hurling). These terms can help you identify unifying themes (Baseball, Heists), characters (Dracula, Sherlock Holmes), settings (Period Pieces, Viva Las Vegas!), events (The Great Depression, World War II), occupations (Clowns, Cops, Serial Killers), ensembles (Monty Python, the Muppets), or suddenly animate objects (Killer Toys). You will also find categories for films produced outside the U.S. (See Foreign Films for cross references). Category terms are listed alphabetically; corresponding movie lists are also alphabetical.

Supergirl
Superman: The Movie
Superman 2
Superman 3
Superman 4: The Quest for
  Peace
What Planet Are You From?

Alien Beings—Vicious
  *See also: Alien Beings—
  Benign; Aliens Are People,
  Too; Space Operas*

Alien: Resurrection
The Astounding She-Monster
The Astro-Zombies
Battle beyond the Stars
Battlefield Earth
Beware! The Blob
The Blob
The Brain from Planet Arous
Cat Women of the Moon
The Colony
Galaxy Quest
Inseminoid
Interceptor Force
Kronos
Men in Black [CS]
Not of This Earth
The Phantom Planet
Pitch Black
Plan 9 from Outer Space
  [Passport Video]
Predator [20th Century Fox]
Quatermass 2
Robot Monster
The Secret KGB UFO Files
Stargate SG-1: Season 1
The Stranger from Venus
Superman 2
Supernova
Teenagers from Outer Space
Thrill Seekers

Aliens Are People, Too
  *See also: Alien Babes; Alien
  Beings—Benign; Alien
  Beings—Vicious*

Alien: Resurrection
Men in Black [CS]
Thrill Seekers

American Indians
  See: Native America

American South
  *See also: Miami; Nashville;
  New Orleans; Savannah;
  Southern Belles*

Big Momma's House
Blue Ridge Fall
Crazy in Alabama
A Family Thing
Fled
Four Little Girls
Gettysburg
A Good Baby
In the Heat of the Night
Kiss of Fire
A Lesson Before Dying
Mississippi Burning [MGM]
My Cousin Vinny
My Dog Skip
Norma Rae
Once Upon a Time...When We
  Were Colored
One False Move
The Patriot
Rambling Rose [2 SE]
Ride with the Devil
The St. Francisville Experi-
  ment
Shag: The Movie
Sister, Sister
Southern Comfort
Stormswept
Tigerland
Two Moon Junction
A Woman Called Moses

Kingsley Amis
That Uncertain Feeling [Sling-
  Shot]

Amnesia
Desperately Seeking Susan
Inferno
The Second Woman
Traitor's Heart

Amusement Parks
  *See also: Carnivals & Circus-
  es; Fairs & Expositions*

Dr. Giggles
Getting Even with Dad
The Lady from Shanghai
My Life

Angels
  See also: Heaven Sent

The Bishop's Wife [MGM]
Defending Your Life
Dogma
Wide Awake

Animals
  *See: Birds; Cats; Horses;
  Killer Apes & Monkeys; Killer
  Dogs; Killer Kats; Killer
  Rodents; King of Beasts
  (Dogs); Monkey Shines; Nice
  Mice; Pigs; Rabbits; Wild King-
  dom*

Animated Musicals
  *See also: Animation & Car-
  toons; Musicals*

All Dogs Go to Heaven
All Dogs Go to Heaven 2
Charlotte's Web
Fantasia/2000
Joseph: King of Dreams
Melody Time
The Nightmare before Christ-
  mas [2 SE]
The Pebble and the Penguin
Pocahontas
The Road to El Dorado
Robin Hood
Rock-a-Doodle
Thumbelina

Animation & Cartoons
  *See also: Animated Musicals;
  Anime*

The Adventures of Ichabod
  and Mr. Toad
Alice in Wonderland
Animation Greats
Animation Legend: Winsor
  McCay
The Aristocats
Babar: King of the Elephants
Batman Beyond: Return of
  the Joker
Batman: Mask of the Phan-
  tasm
Beauty and the Beast: The
  Enchanted Christmas
Beetle Bailey / Hagar the
  Horrible / Betty Boop
Best of the Best: Especially
  for Kids
Best of the Best: Romantic
  Tales
Best of the Best: Strange
  Tales of the Imagination
The Best of Zagreb Film:
  Laugh at Your Own Risk
  and For Children Only
The Black Cauldron
Blue's Big Musical Movie
Buzz Lightyear of Star Com-
  mand: The Adventure
  Begins
Cartoon Crazys: Banned &
  Censored
Cartoon Crazys Comic Book
  Heroes
Cartoon Crazys Spooky Toons

Cartoon Crazys: The Great
  Animation Studios: Famous
  Studios
Cartoon Noir
Casper's Haunted Christmas
Chicken Run
A Chinese Ghost Story: The
  Tsui Hark Animation
Clerks Uncensored
The Complete Superman Col-
  lection
Dinosaur [CE]
Dirty Duck
The Fantasia Anthology
Ferngully 2: The Magical Res-
  cue
The Fox and the Hound
Great Animation Studios:
  Fleischer Studios
Gulliver's Travels [Image]
Heavy Metal 2000 [SE]
Heavy Traffic
I Married a Strange Person
Lady and the Tramp 2:
  Scamp's Adventure
The Land Before Time
Land Before Time 7: The
  Stone of Cold Fire
The Little Mermaid 2: Return
  to the Sea
Make Mine Music
Masters of Russian Anima-
  tion, Vol. 2
Masters of Russian Anima-
  tion, Vol. 3
Masters of Russian Anima-
  tion, Vol. 4
Neurotica: Middle-Age Spread
  and Other Life Crises
Pokemon the Movie 2000:
  The Power of One
The Puppetoon Movie
Reboot: Season III
Rembrandt Films' Greatest
  Hits
The Rescuers Down Under
Roughnecks Starship Troop-
  ers Chronicles the Pluto
  Campaign
Rugrats in Paris: The Movie
Scooby-Doo and the Alien
  Invaders
The Secret of Anastasia
The Secret of NIMH 2
Shadow Raiders, Vol. 1:
  Uncommon Hero
Sinbad and the Eye of the
  Tiger
Sinbad: Beyond the Veil of
  Mists
Sorcerer Hunters: Magical
  Encounters
Speed Racer: The Movie
Stories from My Childhood
Stories from My Childhood,
  Vol. 3
The Sword in the Stone
Terry Pratchett's Discworld:
  Wyrd Sisters
The Three Caballeros
The Tigger Movie
Titan A.E.
Tom & Jerry's Greatest Chas-
  es
Tom Thumb
Toy Story
Toy Story 2
Toy Story: The Ultimate Toy-
  box
Transformers: The Movie
Uncensored Bosko, Vol. 1
Uncensored Bosko, Vol. 2
Vampire Hunter D [SE]
X-Men: The Phoenix Saga

Anime
  *See also: Animation & Car-
  toons*

Art of Fighting
BioHunter [SE]

Bubblegum Crisis Tokyo
  2040
Darkside Blues
Demon City Shinjuku
Digimon: The Movie
Gasaraki 1: The Summoning
Generator 1: Gawl
Grave of the Fireflies
Gun Smith Cats: Bulletproof
  Maze
Mystery of the Necronomicon
Neon Genesis Evangelion
  Collection
Princess Mononoke
Project A-ko
Robotech: First Contact
Samurai X: The Movie
Samurai X Trust
Sin: The Movie
Sol Bianca: The Legacy
Wicked City [SE]

Anthology
  *See also: Comedy Antholo-
  gies; Horror Anthologies; Seri-
  als*

The Best of Boys in Love:
  Award Winning Gay Short
  Films
Beyond the Clouds
Black Sabbath
Fantasia/2000
Fusion One
If These Walls Could Talk 2
Kisses in the Dark
Kwaidan
Make Mine Music
Melody Time
News from the West
Park City: The Sundance Col-
  lection
Picture Windows
Red Shoe Diaries: Four on
  the Floor
Red Shoe Diaries: Luscious
  Lola
Red Shoe Diaries: Strip Poker
Red Shoe Diaries: Swimming
  Naked
Saludos Amigos
Teasearse
Varietease

Anti-Heroes
  See also: Rebel with a Cause

Lock, Stock and 2 Smoking
  Barrels
Steal This Movie!
Traveller

Anti-War War Movies
  See also: Satire & Parody

Born on the Fourth of July 2
The Bridges at Toko-Ri
Catch-22
Dr. Strangelove, or: How I
  Learned to Stop Worrying
  and Love the Bomb [2 SE]
Glory [2 SE]
Henry V
King and Country
La Guerre Est Finie
Platoon [2 SE]
Pretty Village, Pretty Flame

Apartheid
  See also: Africa; Civil Rights

The Quarry

Archaeology
  See: Big Digs

**Argentinean
(Production)**
The Curious Dr. Humpp
Life According to Muriel

Art & Artists
Andy Warhol
A Bucket of Blood
Camille Claudel
Chasing Amy

Crucible of Terror
Dirty Pictures
The Fantasy Film Worlds of
  George Pal
Gothic
Goya in Bordeaux
I Shot Andy Warhol
If Lucy Fell
Mirror, Mirror 3: The Voyeur
Moll Flanders [MGM]
The Object of Beauty
Picasso
Picture Windows
Portrait of Jennie
Rembrandt
Starry Night
Superstar: The Life and
  Times of Andy Warhol
Two If by Sea

Asia
  See also: China; Japan

Anna and the King
The Sand Pebbles
That's the Way I Like It

Asian America
Romeo Must Die
Strawberry Fields
Yellow

Isaac Asimov
Bicentennial Man
Isaac Asimov's Nightfall

Assassinations
  *See also: Foreign Intrigue; Hit
  Men; Spies & Espionage*

Caracara
Dead Zone
The Eagle Has Landed
The Emperor and the Assas-
  sin
Excellent Cadavers
F/X
Friday Foster
From Russia with Love [2 SE]
Hangmen Also Die
I Spit on Your Corpse
In the Line of Fire [2 SE]
La Femme Nikita [MGM]
The Man Who Knew Too
  Much
Nashville
Nick of Time
The Parallax View
Red Scorpion
Seven Days in May
Steele's Law
The Terrorist
Xchange

Astronauts
  See also: Space Operas

Beneath the Planet of the
  Apes
Buzz Lightyear of Star Com-
  mand: The Adventure
  Begins
Mission to Mars
Planet of the Apes
Red Planet
Space Cowboys

Astronomy & Astrology
  See: Star Gazing

At the Movies
  See also: Behind the Scenes

The Creeps
Desperately Seeking Susan
The Last Picture Show [DC]
The Real Blonde
Scream 3 [CS]
Shadow of the Vampire

At the Video Store
  See also: At the Movies

Clerks Uncensored
The Fisher King
The Watermelon Woman

Atlanta
See also: American South

Cyborg

Atlantic City
The Lemon Sisters
Sour Grapes

Jane Austen
Mansfield Park
Northanger Abbey

Australia
See: Down Under

Australian (Production)
The Adventures of Priscilla,
   Queen of the Desert
   [MGM]
Billy's Holiday
Black Robe
Blackrock
Fair Game
Flynn
Heaven's Burning
Holy Smoke
The Interview
Komodo
Lilian's Story
A Little Bit of Soul
Me Myself I
Mesmerized
Mr. Accident
Napoleon
Romper Stomper [SE]

Austrian (Production)
Jew-boy Levi

Automobiles
*See: Checkered Flag; Motor
   Vehicle Dept.*

Babysitting
*See also: Bringing Up Baby;
   Parenthood*

Angel Blue
The Crazysitter
Don't Tell Mom the Babysit-
   ter's Dead

Bachelor Party
See also: Up All Night

House Party 3

Bad Dads
*See also: Dads; Monster
   Moms; Parenthood*

American Beauty [SE]
At Close Range
The Audrey Hepburn Story
Croupier
Die Screaming, Marianne
Getting Even with Dad
Hanging Up
Julien Donkey-boy
Lilian's Story
Magnolia
The Myth of Fingerprints
Natural Born Killers [DC]
No Looking Back
Price of Glory
Romeo Must Die
Turn It Up
The War Zone

Ballet
See also: Dance Fever

Billy Elliot
Center Stage
Nine Months

Ballooning
The Last Great Adventure
Octopussy

Baltimore
And Justice for All
Avalon
Detention
Homicide: The Movie
Liberty Heights

Bar & Grill
See also: Nightclubs

Barb Wire
The Broken Hearts Club
Coyote Ugly
Deterrence
The Florentine
From Dusk Till Dawn [2 CS]
Restaurant

Clive Barker
Hellraiser 2

Baseball
Eight Men Out
For Love of the Game
Frequency
Great Baseball Movies
Headin' Home
It's Good to Be Alive
The Jackie Robinson Story
The Natural
Soul of the Game
Take Me Out to the Ball
   Game
Wide Awake

Basketball
Air Bud 2
Black and White
Finding Forrester
Perfect Profile
White Men Can't Jump

Beach Blanket Bingo
*See also: Lifeguards; Sex on
   the Beach; Surfing; Swimming*

Baywatch: Nightmare Bay /
   River of No Return
Beach Blanket Bingo
Beach Girls
Beach Party
Bikini Beach
Shag: The Movie
A Summer's Tale

Bears
See also: Wild Kingdom

Legends of the Fall [2 SE]
Rudyard Kipling's the Second
   Jungle Book: Mowgli and
   Baloo

Beatniks
A Bucket of Blood

Beauty Pageants
See also: Dream Girls

Beautiful
Miss Congeniality
Shag: The Movie

Behind Bars
*See: Great Escapes; Men in
   Prison; Women in Prison*

Behind the Scenes
*See also: At the Movies; Film
   History*

Alexandria Again and Forever
The Audrey Hepburn Story
Behind the Planet of the
   Apes
Bob Hope: Hollywood's
   Brightest Star
Body Chemistry 3: Point of
   Seduction
Buster Keaton Rides Again /
   The Railrodder
Cecil B. Demented
Cinema Combat: Hollywood
   Goes to War
Cut
Hollywood Boulevard
The Love Master
Marilyn Monroe: The Final
   Days
Mistress
Opening Night
Portraits Chinois
Postcards from the Edge
Scream 3 [CS]

Search and Destroy
Shadow of the Vampire
Son of Gascogne
Texas Chainsaw Massacre: A
   Family Portrait
Tie Me Up! Tie Me Down!
Time Code
Tootsie
The Waiting Game
The Watermelon Woman
You Can't Do That: The Mak-
   ing of "A Hard Day's Night"

Belgian (Production)
An Affair of Love
Anchoress
A Couch in New York
The Delivery
Farinelli
Ma Vie en Rose

Peter Benchley
Jaws [CE]

Berlin
See also: Germany

Mother Night
The Thousan Eyes of Dr.
   Mabuse

Beverly Hills
The Hollywood Knights

Bible Adaptations
Jesus
Jesus Christ Superstar
Joseph and the Amazing
   Technicolor Dreamcoat
Joseph: King of Dreams
Noah's Ark
The Story of Jacob & Joseph

Big Battles
*See also: Civil War; Korean
   War; Korean War; Revolution-
   ary War; Vietnam War; World
   War I; World War II*

The Alamo
The Arena
Attila
Braveheart
Diamonds Are Forever [SE]
The Emperor and the Assas-
   sin
Gettysburg
Gladiator
Glory [2 SE]
Henry V
The Long Riders
The Magical Legend of the
   Leprechauns
The Messenger: The Story of
   Joan of Arc
Monty Python and the Holy
   Grail
The Patriot
The Sand Pebbles
Tora! Tora! Tora! [2 SE]

Big-Budget Bombs
See also: Pure Ego Vehicles

Annie
Cleopatra
Santa Claus: The Movie
Supergirl
Tora! Tora! Tora! [2 SE]

Big Digs
Dead Are Alive
The Mummy
The Mummy [2 SE]
The Mummy's Shroud

Big Rigs
*See also: Motor Vehicle Dept.;
   Road Trip*

Big Trouble in Little China
   [SE]
Breaker! Breaker!
Maximum Overdrive

Bigfoot/Yeti
The Abominable Snowman

Frostbiter: Wrath of the
   Wendigo

Bikers
Angels' Wild Women
Beach Party
Fugitive Champion
Harley Davidson and the
   Marlboro Man
Hellblock 13
Knightriders
Psychomania
Satan's Sadists
The Wild Angels

Biography
See: This Is Your Life

Birds
Birdman of Alcatraz
Chicken Run
Cockfighter
The Pebble and the Penguin
The Rescuers Down Under

Birthdays
City Slickers

Bisexuality
See also: Gays; Lesbians

Bedrooms and Hallways
Threesome

Black Comedy
*See also: Comedy; Comedy
   Drama; Satire & Parody*

The Addams Family
Alice
Arsenic and Old Lace
Beat the Devil
Beautiful People
Bringing Out the Dead
Canadian Bacon
Catch-22
The Cook, the Thief, His Wife
   & Her Lover
Coup de Torchon
Critical Care
The Curve
Delivered
Dr. Strangelove, or: How I
   Learned to Stop Worrying
   and Love the Bomb [2 SE]
The End
The 4th Man
Ghost Chase
Harold and Maude
Nurse Betty
Repo Man
Shakes the Clown
Something Wild
Sweet Revenge
Three Businessmen
Tie Me Up! Tie Me Down!
The Trouble with Harry
The Unbelievable Truth
The Whole Nine Yards
Women on the Verge of a
   Nervous Breakdown

Black Gold
Breaking the Waves
Five Easy Pieces
Local Hero
Naked Gun 2 1/2: The Smell
   of Fear
The World Is Not Enough [SE]

Blackmail
*See also: Corporate Shenani-
   gans; Crime & Criminals; Disorganized Crime; Organized
   Crime*

Blackmale
Clue
Lucky Numbers

Blaxploitation
*See also: African America;
   New Black Cinema*

Black Caesar
Coffy

Cotton Comes to Harlem
Detroit 9000
Foxy Brown
Friday Foster
Moon over Harlem
Shaft in Africa
Shaft's Big Score
Sheba, Baby
Slaughter's Big Ripoff
Truck Turner

Blindness
See also: Physical Problems

Blind Justice
Crimes & Misdemeanors
   [MGM]
Dancer in the Dark
A Family Thing
Ice Castles
The Killer [Winstar]
The Miracle Worker
The Miracle Worker

Blizzards
See also: Cold Spots

The Last Stop
Snow Day

Bloody Messages
Harold and Maude
The Jagged Edge
Seven [2 SE]
The Untouchables

Boating
See: Sail Away

Bodyguards
The Bodyguard from Beijing
The Defender
Fatal Beauty
Final Voyage
In the Line of Fire [2 SE]

James Bond
Diamonds Are Forever [SE]
From Russia with Love [2 SE]
The Living Daylights
Octopussy
A View to a Kill [SE]
The World Is Not Enough [SE]
You Only Live Twice [SE]

Books
See also: Storytelling

The Ninth Gate
The Seven Year Itch

Boom!
*See also: Action-Adventure;
   Fires*

Dr. Strangelove, or: How I
   Learned to Stop Worrying
   and Love the Bomb [2 SE]
From Dusk Till Dawn [2 CS]
Hoodlum
The Rock [Criterion]

Boomer Reunions
See also: Period Piece: 1960s

The Brutal Truth

Bosnia
Beautiful People
Pretty Village, Pretty Flame
The Wounds

Boston
Bad Manners
Love Story
Next Stop, Wonderland

Bounty Hunters
Bounty Hunters
Bounty Hunters 2: Hardball
Home for Christmas
The Tracker

The Bowery Boys
Ghosts on the Loose
They Made Me a Criminal

Bowling
Mr. Wonderful

Boxing

Fight for the Title
The Fighter
Girlfight
Gladiator
Great Boxing Movies
The Hurricane
The Joe Louis Story
Killer's Kiss
Out Kold
Penitentiary
Penitentiary 2
Play It to the Bone
Price of Glory
Rocky [2 SE]
They Made Me a Criminal

Brazilian (Production)

Awakenings of the Beast
Bossa Nova
Pixote
This Night I'll Possess Your Corpse

Bridges

The Bridge at Remagen
The Bridge on the River Kwai [LE]
The Bridges at Toko-Ri

Bringing Up Baby

See also: Parenthood; Pregnant Pauses

Baby Boom
Cotton Mary
A Good Baby
Look Who's Talking, Too
Penny Serenade
Rosemary's Baby
She's So Lovely
The War Zone

British (Production)

The Abominable Dr. Phibes
The Abominable Snowman
The Adventures of Sherlock Holmes
Agatha Christie's Poirot
Alfie
Alfred Hitchcock's Bon Voyage & Aventure Malgache
All Creatures Great and Small
Anchoress
Anna Karenina
Around the World with Orson Welles
The Asphyx
Asylum
B. Monkey
Bandit Queen
The Beast Must Die
Beautiful People
Bedrooms and Hallways
The Big Tease
Billy Elliot
The Black Cat
Black Narcissus
Blood Beast Terror
The Bridge on the River Kwai [LE]
Brief Encounter
Brother Cadfael: The Devil's Novice
The Brylcreem Boys
The Canterville Ghost
The Cassandra Crossing
Catherine Cookson's The Cinder Path
Catherine Cookson's The Secret
The Cement Garden
Chicken Run
A Christmas Carol
Circus
The Cook, the Thief, His Wife & Her Lover
Cotton Mary
Croupier
Crucible of Terror
Dame Edna's Neighbourhood Watch 2
Damn the Defiant

Dance with a Stranger
Deacon Brodie
Dead of Night
Dead Waters
Death on the Nile
The Devil Rides Out
Diamonds Are Forever [SE]
Die, Monster, Die!
Die Screaming, Marianne
Doctor Phibes Rises Again
Dr. Strangelove, or: How I Learned to Stop Worrying and Love the Bomb [2 SE]
East Is East
8 1/2 Women
Element of Doubt
An Elephant Called Slowly
End of the Affair
The End of the Affair
Endless Night
The Entertainer
Essex Boys
Evil under the Sun
Falling for a Dancer
The Far Pavilions
Fever Pitch
The Field
The Filth and the Fury
Fire over England
Four Sided Triangle
Frenzy
Frightmare
From Russia with Love [2 SE]
Get Carter
Gorgo
Grey Owl
Gumboots
Hamlet
Hellraiser 2
Henry V
Hope and Glory
Horror Hotel
House of Mirth
Human Traffic
I, Claudius
I Know Where I'm Going
Immortal Battalion
Immortality
The Impossible Spy
Inseminoid
Jane & the Lost City
King and Country
Krull [SE]
The Last September
Lawrence of Arabia
Let Sleeping Corpses Lie
Local Hero
Lock, Stock and 2 Smoking Barrels
Lord Edgeware Dies
Love, Honour & Obey
Love's Labour's Lost
Ma Vie en Rose
The Madness of King George
A Man for All Seasons
Mesmerized
The Mirror Crack'd
Mona Lisa
Monty Python and the Holy Grail
The Mouse on the Moon
The Mummy's Shroud
The Murder of Roger Ackroyd
My Best Fiend
My Son, the Vampire
Northanger Abbey
Octopussy
Onegin
The Pallisers
A Passage to India
The Perfect Husband
Plain Jane
Poldark
The Prince and the Pauper
Psychomania
Pygmalion
Quatermass 2
Relative Values
Rembrandt
Ring of Bright Water

The Rocky Horror Picture Show
A Room with a View
Saving Grace
The Scarlet Pimpernel
The Serpent's Kiss
Shadow of the Vampire
Sharpe's Battle
Sharpe's Company
Sharpe's Eagle
Sharpe's Enemy
Sharpe's Gold
Sharpe's Honour
Sharpe's Justice
Sharpe's Mission
Sharpe's Regiment
Sharpe's Revenge
Sharpe's Rifles
Sharpe's Siege
Sharpe's Sword
Sharpe's Waterloo
Sid & Nancy [MGM]
The Sign of Four
Sinbad and the Eye of the Tiger
Solomon and Gaenor
Supergirl
Sweet Revenge
Terry Pratchett's Discworld: Wyrd Sisters
Things to Come
Tom Jones [MGM]
Tom Thumb
Tommy
Topsy Turvy
Up at the Villa
Vampyres
A View to a Kill [SE]
The War Zone
Welcome II the Terrordome
We'll Meet Again
Wilderness
The Womaneater
Wonderland
Wonderwall: The Movie
You Only Live Twice [SE]
Zardoz

Brothers & Sisters

At Close Range
Benny & Joon
The Book of Stars
The Brothers McMullen
The Cement Garden
City of Industry
Double Dragon
Fall of the House of Usher
The Fall of the House of Usher
Farinelli
The Florentine
Flowers in the Attic
Frank and Jesse
From Dusk Till Dawn [2 CS]
Gladiator
Grave of the Fireflies
Grind
Hanging Up
Incubus
Interiors
Inventing the Abbotts
Julien Donkey-boy
Legends of the Fall [2 SE]
Little Nicky
The Long Riders
Midnight Dancers
Mifune
Mirror, Mirror 2: Raven Dance
Phantasm 4: Oblivion
The Pit and the Pendulum
Pola X
Price of Glory
Rated X
Relative Values
Romeo Must Die
Row Your Boat
The Shadow Riders
She's the One
Sisters
Sons of Katie Elder
The Story of Jacob and Joseph
Suture

Sweet Smell of Success
Vertical Limit
The Virgin Suicides
The War Zone
Wonderland

Buddies

See also: Buddy Cops

Abbott and Costello Meet Frankenstein
The Alamo
A Better Tomorrow, Part 1 [Anchor Bay]
A Better Tomorrow, Part 2 [Anchor Bay]
Blackrock
Blue Ridge Fall
Body Shots
Bulletproof
Chasing Amy
City Slickers
Dirty Work
Dish Dogs
Donnie Brasco 2
Donovan's Reef
The Emperor's New Groove [SE]
F/X 2: The Deadly Art of Illusion
Fled
The Flintstones in Viva Rock Vegas
Floating
Gossip
Hard Core Logo
Hard Eight
Harley Davidson and the Marlboro Man
If Lucy Fell
I'll Remember April
Juice
The Karate Kid
Keeping the Faith
The Life of Jesus
The Lords of Flatbush
Love's Labour's Lost
The Mighty Quinn
Moonlight and Valentino
Mystic Pizza
The Odd Couple
Platoon [2 SE]
Play It to the Bone
The Pompatus of Love
Ready to Rumble
Ride with the Devil
The Road to El Dorado
Road Trip
Rules of Engagement
Shag: The Movie
Some Like It Hot [SE]
The Souler Opposite
Stand by Me [2 SE]
Toy Story
Toy Story 2
Twin Warriors
Went to Coney Island on a Mission from God...Be Back by Five
Whipped
White Christmas
White Men Can't Jump

Buddy Cops

See also: Cops; Women Cops

Blue Streak
Internal Affairs
Men in Black [CS]

Buffalo Bill Cody

Buffalo Bill & the Indians

Bulldog Drummond

Bulldog Drummond Escapes
Bulldog Drummond's Secret Police

Bulgarian (Production)

It's Raining on Santiago

Buried Alive

Fall of the House of Usher
The Fall of the House of Usher

Frances Hodgson Burnett

Little Lord Fauntleroy
The Little Princess

Buses

The Adventures of Priscilla, Queen of the Desert [MGM]
Bus Stop
Get On the Bus
Love Field
Planes, Trains & Automobiles

Cabbies

The Bishop's Wife [MGM]
Escape from New York
For Hire
Scrooged
She's the One

Camelot (Old)

See also: Medieval Romps; Swashbucklers

Monty Python and the Holy Grail
The Sword in the Stone

Campus Capers

See also: Hell High School; School Daze

Assault of the Party Nerds
Back to School
Black Christmas
Boys and Girls
Confessions of Sorority Girls
The Curve
Divided We Stand
Down to You
Good News
Gossip
H.O.T.S.
The House on Sorority Row
House Party 2: The Pajama Jam
I'll Be Home for Christmas
Loser
Malice [MGM]
My Sex Life...Or How I Got into an Argument
Necessary Roughness
A Night in the Life of Jimmy Reardon
Nutty Professor 2: The Klumps [1 CE]
Nutty Professor 2: The Klumps [2 Uncensored]
The Prodigy
Red Letters
Road Trip
Rudy [SE]
School Daze
The Skulls
Sorority House Massacre
Sorority House Massacre 2: Nighty Nightmare
Stonebrook
Threesome
Urban Legends 2: Final Cut
Voodoo Academy [DC]
Waking the Dead
What Lies Beneath
Wonder Boys

Canada

See also: Cold Spots; Hockey

The Adjuster
Back to God's Country / Something New
Black Christmas
Black Robe
The Boys
Canadian Bacon
The Changeling
A Cry in the Wild
Grey Owl
Hard Core Logo
Tower of Song: The Canadian Music Hall of Fame

Canadian (Production)

The Adjuster

Went to Coney Island on a Mission from God...Be Back by Five
What's Cooking?

Comedy Mystery
See also: Black Comedy; Comedy; Comedy Drama; Genre Spoofs; Horror Comedy; Satire & Parody

Clue

Comedy Performance
See: Concert Films

Comedy Sci-Fi
See also: Comedy; Comic Adventure; Genre Spoofs; Satire & Parody; Sci Fi

Coneheads
Dinosaur Valley Girls
Galaxy Quest
Men in Black [CS]
Sleeper
Space-Thing
Wham-Bam, Thank You Spaceman

Comic Adventure
See also: Action-Adventure; Comedy

Black Tight Killers
Cannonball Run
Chasers
Jake Speed
Jane & the Lost City
Lust in the Dust
O Brother Where Art Thou?
Our Lips Are Sealed

Comics/Comic Book Adaptations
Annie
Barb Wire
BioHunter [SE]
The Crow: Salvation
Female Convict Scorpion—Jailhouse 41
Fist of the North Star
Man Called Hero
Men in Black [CS]
Superman: The Movie
Superman 2
Superman 3
Superman 4: The Quest for Peace
X-Men

Coming of Age
See also: Teen Angst

Alexandria...Why?
All I Wanna Do
Beshkempir the Adopted Son
Blue Velvet
Butterfly
Catherine Cookson's The Cinder Path
Class
Coming Soon
A Cry in the Wild
Dakota
Damien: Omen 2
Edward Scissorhands [SE]
Fast Times at Ridgemont High
Fellini Satyricon
Girl
Girlfight
Inventing the Abbotts
The Karate Kid
The Lords of Flatbush
Mystic Pizza
A Night in the Life of Jimmy Reardon
The Other Side of Sunday
The Pallbearer
Platoon [2 SE]
Rambling Rose [2 SE]
Ride with the Devil
A Room with a View
Soldier of Orange

The Sword in the Stone
Tumbleweeds
Wide Awake
Wonder Boys
Youngblood

Computers
See also: Robots & Androids; Technology—Rampant

Antitrust
Jurassic Park [CE]
Reboot: Season III
The Scorpio Factor
Superman 3

Concentration/Internment Camps
See also: Nazis & Other Paramilitary Slugs; POW/MIA

Paradise Road
Snow Falling on Cedars

Concert Films
See also: Rock Stars on Film

Gimme Shelter
Original Kings of Comedy
Queens of Comedy
U2: Rattle and Hum
Year of the Horse
You So Crazy

Contemporary Noir
See also: Film Noir

After the Storm
Against All Odds
Blue Velvet
Bringing Out the Dead
City of Industry
Croupier
Dance with a Stranger
Eyes of Laura Mars
Flypaper
Forever Mine
Hard Eight
Kill Me Again
Killing Zoe
Let the Devil Wear Black
Live Flesh
The Million Dollar Hotel
No Way Out
One False Move
The Rich Man's Wife
Simpatico
Something Wild
True Believer

Cooking
See: Edibles

Catherine Cookson
Catherine Cookson's The Cinder Path
Catherine Cookson's The Secret

James Fenimore Cooper
The Last of the Mohicans

Cops
See also: Buddy Cops; Detectives; Loner Cops; Women Cops

Alien Nation
Animal Instincts
Backlash
Bandits
Big Momma's House
Black and White
Black & White
Blue Streak
Bulletproof
Cold Blooded
Cotton Comes to Harlem
Coup de Torchon
Crime Story
Detroit 9000
Drop Zone
Drowning Mona
Eyes of Laura Mars
Family of Cops 2: Breach of Faith
Family of Cops 3

Fireworks
Flashfire
Fort Apache, the Bronx
Frequency
Gen-X Cops
Get On the Bus
Gone in 60 Seconds
Gorky Park
Hard-Boiled [Winstar]
Hardcase and Fist
Hollywood Vice Sqaud
Homicide: The Movie
Humanity
In the Heat of the Night
It Could Happen to You
It's the Rage
Jet Li's The Enforcer [Buena Vista]
K-911
The Last Marshal
The Last Stop
Law and Disorder
Les Miserables
Lethal Seduction
Lockdown
Magnolia
Maximum Risk
The Million Dollar Hotel
The Naked Gun: From the Files of Police Squad
Naked Gun 33 1/3: The Final Insult
Naked Gun 2 1/2: The Smell of Fear
Nightwatch
Nightwatch
No Code of Conduct
Paper Bullets
The Proposal
The Quarry
Scream 3 [CS]
Seven [2 SE]
Steele's Law
The Stendahl Syndrome
The Substitute 4: Failure Is Not an Option
They Call Me Mr. Tibbs!
Three Strikes
Touch of Evil [SE]
Traffic
Under Oath
The White Lioness

Corporate Shenanigans
See also: Advertising; Salespeople

Antitrust
The Apartment
Boiler Room
Empire Records
Erin Brockovich
Gorgeous
Hamlet
The Harder They Come
Ivory Tower
Let the Devil Wear Black
Local Hero
Mr. Accident
Naked Gun 2 1/2: The Smell of Fear
9 to 5
Power
Scrooged
The 6th Day
Smilla's Sense of Snow
Tucker: The Man and His Dream
Wall Street
Working Girl

Courtroom Drama
See: Order in the Court

Creepy Houses
The Amityville Horror
Angel of the Night
Asylum of Terror
The Changeling
Endless Night
Fall of the House of Usher

The Fall of the House of Usher
Flowers in the Attic
Fright Night
Malice [MGM]
Mother's Day [DC]
Munster, Go Home!
The Rocky Horror Picture Show
The St. Francisville Experiment
The Screaming Skull
Sister, Sister
Stormswept
Terror Tract

Noel Coward
Brief Encounter
Relative Values

Michael Crichton
Jurassic Park [CE]
The Lost World: Jurassic Park 2 [CE]

Crime & Criminals
See also: Crime Drama; Crime Sprees; Disorganized Crime; Fugitives; Heists; Hit Men; Organized Crime; Scams, Stings & Cons; Serial Killers; True Crime; Urban Drama; Vigilantes

Bait
Beethoven's 3rd
Black Tight Killers
Cinema's Dark Side Collection
Circus
Clockin' Green
Criminals
Cutaway
Get Carter
Gun Smith Cats: Bulletproof
Heaven's Fire
Held Up
Lucky Numbers
The Mission
Requiem for a Dream
Tokyo Raiders
The Yards

Crime Drama
See also: Drama

At Close Range
Backlash
A Better Way to Die
Blackrock
Blood In . . . Blood Out: Bound by Honor
Blue Ridge Fall
Death and the Compass
Dilemma
Dillinger
Donnie Brasco 2
Element of Doubt
Essex Boys
Family of Cops 2: Breach of Faith
Family of Cops 3
Flypaper
Get Carter
Ghost Dog: The Way of the Samurai
Girl Gang
The Godfather DVD Collection
The Godfather, Part 2
The Godfather, Part 3
Gone in 60 Seconds
The Highway Man
Honor Thy Father
Hoodlum
Inferno
Internal Affairs
Juice
The Killing of a Chinese Bookie
Killing Zoe
The Life Before This
The Maltese Falcon
Natural Born Killers [DC]
One False Move

Paper Bullets
The Pope of Greenwich Village
Pusher
Ratas, Ratones, Rateros
Reindeer Games
Romeo Must Die
Seven [2 SE]
She Killed in Ecstasy
Straight out of Compton
Street Gun
Thick As Thieves
Third World Cop
Turn It Up
The Untouchables
Way of the Gun
The Wounds
The Yards

Crime Sprees
See also: Fugitives; Lovers on the Lam

The Boys Next Door
Lewis and Clark and George
Natural Born Killers [DC]
The Tie That Binds

Crop Dusters
Broken Harvest
Chicken Run
The Field
Jean de Florette
Mifune
The River
Rock-a-Doodle

Cuba
Before Night Falls
For Love or Country: The Arturo Sandoval Story
The Godfather, Part 2
Guantanamera
The Old Man and the Sea

Cuban (Production)
Guantanamera Czech

Cults
See also: Occult; Satanism

Holy Smoke
Isaac Asimov's Nightfall
Thou Shalt Not Kill . . . Except

Culture Clash
Black Robe
Coneheads
East Is East
The Emerald Forest
Heart of Light
Lawrence of Arabia
Meet the Parents
Mister Johnson
A Passage to India
Shanghai Noon
Splash
Thunderheart

Cuttin' Heads
The Big Tease
Born to Win
Mississippi Burning [MGM]
Poetic Justice
Steel Magnolias

Cyberpunk
Cyborg
Escape from New York
Freejack
Tank Girl
Terminator 2: Judgment Day [2 SE]

Czech (Production)
Alice

Dads
See also: Bad Dads; Moms; Monster Moms; Parenthood

The Bed You Sleep In
Billy Elliot
Bloodfist 4: Die Trying
Boiler Room
Come and Get It

The Gospel According to
  Philip K. Dick
Half Japanese: The Band
  Who Would Be King
In the Flesh / Blood Bullets
  Buffoons
The Italians
The Joint Is Jumpin'
Know Your Enemy: Japan
The Last Great Adventure
The Lifestyle
The Long Way Home
Mailer on Mailer
Marilyn Monroe: The Final
  Days
Mein Kampf: Hitler's Rise
  and Fall
Mr. Death: The Rise and Fall
  of Fred A. Leuchter, Jr.
My Best Fiend
One Day in September
Pearl Harbor
Pearl Harbor: December 7,
  1941
People of the Wind
Phenomenon—The Lost
  Archives: Noah's Ark
  Found?/Tunguska/Stolen
  Glory
Phenomenon—The Lost
  Archives: Up for
  Sale/Heavy Watergate
Picasso
Pop & Me
Raising the Mammoth
Roots of Rhythm
Say Amen, Somebody
The Secret KGB UFO Files
Sergei Eisenstein: Autobiog-
  raphy
Sergei Eisenstein: Mexican
  Fantasy
Slippery When Wet
The Sorrow and the Pity
The Source
Superstar: The Life and
  Times of Andy Warhol
Surfing Hollow Days
Texas Chainsaw Massacre: A
  Family Portrait
Thug Immortal
Triumph of the Will
20th Century Fox: The First
  50 Years
Unmade Beds
Vietnam: The Ten Thousand
  Day War
World War II
Year of the Horse

Dogs
  See: King of Beasts (Dogs)

Dolls That Kill
  See: Killer Toys

Down Under
The Adventures of Priscilla,
  Queen of the Desert
  [MGM]
Blackrock
Fair Game
Heaven's Burning
Holy Smoke
A Little Bit of Soul
Mission: Impossible 2
Our Lips Are Sealed
The Rescuers Down Under

Sir Arthur Conan Doyle
The Adventures of Sherlock
  Holmes
Dressed to Kill
The Lost World [Image]
Sherlock Holmes and the
  Secret Weapon
The Sign of Four
The Woman in Green
The Woman in Green /
  Dressed to Kill

Dracula
Abbott and Costello Meet
  Frankenstein
The Creeps
Dracula / Strange Case of Dr.
  Jekyll & Mr. Hyde
Dracula vs. Frankenstein
Hysterical

Dragons
  See also: Medieval Romps

Dragonheart: A New Begin-
  ning
Dungeons and Dragons
Pete's Dragon

Drama
  *See also: Adventure Drama;
  Comedy Drama; Coming of
  Age; Crime Drama; Docudra-
  ma; Historical Drama; Musical
  Drama; Romantic Drama;
  Showbiz Drama; Sports Dra-
  mas; Tearjerkers; Tragedy;
  Urban Drama*

Confessions of Sorority Girls
The Contender
A Day in Black and White
Don't Let Me Die on a Sun-
  day
Girlfight
The Head Mistress
Jew-boy Levi
Madadayo
The Million Dollar Hotel
A Woman Called Sada Abe

Dream Girls
  See also: Beauty Pageants

The Arena
Barb Wire
Blaze Starr Goes Nudist
Bluebeard
Cannonball Run
City of Women
Deadly Weapons
Diamonds Are Forever [SE]
Dinosaur Valley Girls
Dr. Goldfoot and the Bikini
  Machine
Downhill Willie
Gold of the Amazon Women
Mirror, Mirror 3: The Voyeur
Missile to the Moon
A Nymphoid Barbarian in
  Dinosaur Hell [SE]
The Seven Year Itch
Slumber Party Massacre
Some Like It Hot [SE]
Wishful Thinking
You Only Live Twice [SE]

Drug Abuse
  See also: On the Rocks

Around the Fire
Assassin of Youth
Awakenings of the Beast
B. Monkey
The Beach
Bird
Blood Bullets Buffoons
Blood In . . . Blood Out:
  Bound by Honor
Born to Win
Bringing Out the Dead
Broken Vessels
Cheech and Chong: Still
  Smokin'
Cheech and Chong's Up in
  Smoke
Coffy
Deadbeat at Dawn
Drugstore Cowboy
Fatal Beauty
Frances
Gia
Gothic
Hell's Kitchen NYC
Hendrix
Holiday Heart
Homegrown

Human Traffic
Idle Hands
Jesus' Son
Kicked in the Head
Killing Zoe
Magnolia
Marihuana / Assassin of
  Youth / Reefer Madness
Mob War [BFS]
One False Move
One Man's Justice
The Organization
Postcards from the Edge
Pusher
Rated X
Reefer Madness
Requiem for a Dream
River's Edge
Running out of Time
Saving Grace
The '70s
Sid & Nancy [MGM]
Traffic
Wild Bill
Women on the Verge of a
  Nervous Breakdown
Wonder Boys

Drugs
  See: Drug Abuse

Dublin
  See also: Ireland

Agnes Browne
Ulysses

Alexandre Dumas
The Four Musketeers

Dutch (Production)
The Delivery
The 4th Man
Soldier of Orange
Turkish Delight
Venus in Furs

Ears!
  *See also: Eyeballs!; Renegade
  Body Parts*

Blue Velvet

Earthquakes
  *See also: Disaster Flicks;
  L.A.; San Francisco*

Aftershock: Earthquake in
  New York
Black Scorpion 2: Ground
  Zero

Eat Me
  See also: Cannibalism

The Lost World: Jurassic Park
  2 [CE]

Eating
  See: Cannibalism; Edibles

Eco-Vengeance!
  See also: Killer Bugs & Slugs

Day of the Animals
Jaws [CE]
Jaws: The Revenge
Jurassic Park [CE]

Edibles
  See also: Cannibalism

Babette's Feast
The Cook, the Thief, His Wife
  & Her Lover
The Dinner Game
Eat Your Heart Out
The Godfather DVD Collection
The Godfather, Part 2
The Godfather, Part 3
God's Comedy
La Grande Bouffe
Small Time Crooks
Tom Jones [MGM]
The Waiting Game
What's Cooking?
Woman on Top

Egypt—Ancient
Cleopatra
The Mummy
The Mummy [2 SE]

Egyptian (Production)
Alexandria Again and Forever
Alexandria...Why?
An Egyptian Story

Elephants
  *See also: Carnivals & Circus-
  es; Wild Kingdom*

Babar: King of the Elephants
An Elephant Called Slowly

Elevators
In the Line of Fire [2 SE]
Nick of Time
The Omen [SE]
Terminator 2: Judgment Day
  [2 SE]
The Untouchables
What about Bob?

Bret Easton Ellis
American Psycho

Elvisfilm
Frankie and Johnny
Rock-a-Doodle

Emerging Viruses
  *See also: Disease of the
  Week*

And the Band Played On
Mission: Impossible 2

**The Empire State
Building**
  See also: New York, New York

An Affair to Remember
Love Affair

Erotic Thrillers
  See also: Sex & Sexuality

Body Chemistry
Body Chemistry 2: Voice of a
  Stranger
Body Chemistry 3: Point of
  Seduction
Body Chemistry 4: Full Expo-
  sure
The Crush
Extramarital
Kept
Lethal Seduction
Love Letters
Maniac Nurses Find Ecstasy
Mercy
Midnight Confessions
Midnight Tease / Midnight
  Tease 2
Midnight Tease 2
Secret Games
Stormswept

Escaped Cons
  *See also: Great Escapes; Men
  in Prison*

Big Momma's House
Black Cat Run
Chasers
Dead of Night
Duets
Fled
From Dusk Till Dawn [2 CS]
The Last Marshal
Lewis and Clark and George
Next Friday [Platinum Series]
O Brother Where Art Thou?
Passenger 57
Red Letters
Where the Money Is

Ethics & Morals
And Justice for All
Blame It on Rio
Boiler Room
The Bridge on the River Kwai
  [LE]
The Contender
The Conversation

Crimes & Misdemeanors
  [MGM]
Gossip
It Could Happen to You
L'Avventura
The Man Who Shot Liberty
  Valance
Marihuana / Assassin of
  Youth / Reefer Madness
A Matter of Dignity
Midnight
Platoon [2 SE]
Sweet Smell of Success
Twelve Angry Men
Wall Street

Etiquette
Pygmalion

Evil Doctors
  *See also: Doctors & Nurses;
  Mad Scientists*

The Abominable Dr. Phibes
Anatomy [SE]
The Awful Dr. Orlof
Blackmale
The Curious Dr. Humpp
Curse of the Puppet Master:
  The Human Experiment
Dr. Frankenstein's Castle of
  Freaks
Dr. Giggles
Dr. Goldfoot and the Bikini
  Machine
Doctor Phibes Rises Again
Malice [MGM]

Executing Revenge
  *See also: Death & the After-
  life; Death Row; Men in
  Prison; Revenge*

The Indestructible Man / The
  Amazing Transparent Man

Existentialism
  See: The Meaning of Life

Exploitation
  See also: Sexploitation

Assassin of Youth
Female Convict Scorpion—
  Jailhouse 41
Foxy Brown
Reefer Madness
Slaughter's Big Ripoff
Something Weird
Teenage Doll

Explorers
Mountains of the Moon

Extraordinary Pairings
Abbott and Costello Meet
  Frankenstein
Dracula vs. Frankenstein

Eyeballs!
  See also: Hearts!

Damien: Omen 2
Evil Dead 2: Dead by Dawn [2
  THX]
Eyes of Laura Mars
Friday the 13th, Part 3
The Godfather DVD Collection
Idle Hands
Nightwatch
Pitch Black
Rocky [2 SE]
X: The Man with X-Ray Eyes

Fairs & Expositions
  *See also: Amusement Parks;
  Carnivals & Circuses*

Shag: The Movie

Fairy Tale Adaptations
CinderElmo
Fun & Fancy Free
Hans Christian Andersen
  [20th Century Fox]
Jack & the Beanstalk

Golden Voyage of Sinbad
Leprechaun 2
Monty Python and the Holy Grail

Food
See: Edibles

Football
Air Bud 2: Golden Receiver
Any Given Sunday
Blue Ridge Fall
Brian's Song
Good News
The Longest Yard
Necessary Roughness
North Dallas Forty
Remember the Titans
The Replacements
Rudy [SE]
Semi-Tough

Foreign Films
See also: Algerian (Production); Argentinian (Production); Austrian (Production); Australian (Production); Belgian (Production); Brazilian (Production); British (Production); Canadian (Production); Chinese (Production); Colombian (Production); Cuban (Production); Czech (Production); Danish (Production); Dutch (Production); Filipino (Production); Finnish (Production); French (Production); German (Production); Greek (Production); Hong Kong (Production); Hungarian (Production); Icelandic (Production); Indian (Production); Iranian (Production); Irish (Production); Israeli (Production); Italian (Production); Japanese (Production); Korean (Production); Lithuanian (Production); Macedonian (Production); Mexican (Production); New Zealand (Production); Nicaraguan (Production); Norwegian (Production); Polish (Production); Portuguese (Production); Russian (Production); South African (Production); Spanish (Production); Swedish (Production); Swiss (Production); Turkish (Production); Taiwanese (Production); Vietnamese (Production); Venezuelan (Production); Yugoslavian (Production).

Foreign Intrigue
See also: Spies & Espionage

Diamonds Are Forever [SE]
The Man Who Knew Too Much
Topaz
Torn Curtain

Foreign Legion
See: Desert War/Foreign Legion

E.M. Forster
A Passage to India
A Room with a View

Four-Bone DVDs
See also: Four-Bone Movies

Alien: Resurrection
Batman: Mask of the Phantasm
The Beatles: The Ultimate DVD Collection
Before Night Falls
Beshkempir the Adopted Son
Big Deal on Madonna Street
Black Narcissus
Blue's Big Musical Movie
The Bridge on the River Kwai [LE]

Buster Keaton Rides Again / The Railrodder
Castaway
Chasing Amy
Chicken Run
The Conversation
The Crow: Salvation
Diary of a Chambermaid
Dinosaur [CE]
Do the Right Thing [2]
Dr. Strangelove, or: How I Learned to Stop Worrying and Love the Bomb [2 SE]
Dogma
Dralion
Drowning Mona
The Fantasia Anthology
Final Destination
Frenzy
From Russia with Love [2 SE]
Glory [2 SE]
The Godfather DVD Collection
Groove
Hannibal
Hellraiser [2]
James and the Giant Peach
Jazz on a Summer's Day
Jerry and Tom
Lady and the Tramp 2: Scamp's Adventure
L'Avventura
Little Women [SE]
Mary Poppins [SE]
Men of Honor
The Messenger: The Story of Joan of Arc
Mother Night
The Mummy
Nashville
North by Northwest
The Replacements
Requiem for a Dream
The Rock [criterion]
The Rocky Horror Picture Show
Rome: Power & Glory
Salvador [SE]
Seven [2 SE]
Some Like It Hot [SE]
The Sopranos: The Complete First Season
The Sorrow and the Pity
Spartacus [2]
Speed Racer: The Movie
Stonebrook
Terminator 2: Judgment Day [2 SE]
This Is Spinal Tap [MGM]
Time Code
Touch of Evil [SE]
Toy Story
Toy Story 2
Toy Story: The Ultimate Toy-box
Treasures from the American Film Archives: 50 Preserved Films
Wonder Boys

Four-Bone Movies
See also: Four-Bone DVDs

After Life
Aguirre, the Wrath of God
Airplane!
American Beauty [SE]
Anatomy of a Murder
Arsenic and Old Lace
The Avengers 1964–1967
The Bank Dick
The Beatles: The Ultimate DVD Collection
Black Narcissus
Blue's Big Musical Movie
Brian's Song
The Bridge on the River Kwai [LE]
Brief Encounter
Buster Keaton Rides Again / The Railrodder
Chicken Run
The Conversation

Th Cook, the Thief, His Wife & Her Lover
Dead and Buried
Do the Right Thing
Dr. Strangelove, or: How I Learned to Stop Worrying and Love the Bomb [2 SE]
Fantasia Anthology
Fellini Satyricon
Five Easy Pieces
From Russia with Love
Gimme Shelter
Glory [2 SE]
The Godfather DVD Collection
The Godfather, Part 2
Harold and Maude
Henry V
Hope and Glory
I, Claudius
James and the Giant Peach
Jaws
Jazz on a Summer's Day
Kwaidan
The Last Picture Show [DC]
The Last Temptation of Christ
Lawrence of Arabia
The Lion in Winter
Little Women [2 SE]
Local Hero
Longtime Companion
The Lost Weekend
The Magnificent Seven
The Maltese Falcon
Manhattan
Martin
Mr. & Mrs. Bridge
Mon Oncle
Mother Night
Nashville
The Natural
North by Northwest
Nosferatu [2]
Only Angels Have Wings
Origins of Film
Pixote
A Raisin in the Sun
Rear Window
Requiem for a Dream
The Rocky Horror Picture Show
A Room with a View
Rosemary's Baby
Small Change
Some Like It Hot [SE]
The Sopranos: The Complete First Season
The Sorrow and the Pity
Spartacus [Criterion]
Steal This Movie!
The Straight Story
Sweet Smell of Success
Tom Jones [MGM]
Tootsie
Touch of Evil [SE]
Toy Story 2
Toy Story: The Ultimate Toy Box
Treasures from the American Film Archives: 50 Preserved Films
Twelve Angry Men
W.C. Fields 6 Short Films
Women on the Verge of a Nervous Breakdown
Yi Yi

Frame-Ups
The Art of War
Death Sentence
F/X
The Mighty Quinn
Moving Target
My Cousin Vinny
Nightwatch
Nightwatch
North by Northwest
The Rich Man's Wife
Shakes the Clown
Thick As Thieves
The Yards

France
See also: Paris

Gentlemen Prefer Blondes
Killing Zoe
The Last Time I Saw Paris
Les Miserables
Maximum Risk
The Scarlet Pimpernel
A Summer's Tale

Frankenstein
Abbott and Costello Meet Frankenstein
The Creeps
Dr. Frankenstein's Castle of Freaks
Dracula vs. Frankenstein
Frankenstein Created Woman
Frankenstein's Daughter
Gothic
Lust for Frankenstein
The Munsters' Revenge
Nosferatu 2

Fraternities & Sororities
See also: Campus Capers

Black Christmas
H.O.T.S.
Sorority House Massacre
Sorority House Massacre 2: Nighty Nightmare

French (Production)
An Affair of Love
The Awful Dr. Orlof
Babar: King of the Elephants
Babette's Feast
Bed and Board
Beethoven
Beyond the Clouds
Black Sabbath
Blood and Black Lace
Boy Meets Girl
Breaking the Waves
The Bride Wore Black
The Bridge
Camille Claudel
Candy
The Cement Garden
Cold Sweat
A Couch in New York
Coup de Torchon
Cyrano de Bergerac
Dancer in the Dark
Diary of a Chambermaid
The Dinner Game
The Discreet Charm of the Bourgeoisie
Don't Let Me Die on a Sunday
East-West
Fall of the House of Usher
Farinelli
Fellini Satyricon
Female Vampire
Fruits of Passion: The Story of "O" Continued
Honor Among Thieves
Humanity
Immoral Tales
It's Raining on Santiago
Jean de Florette
La Femme Nikita [MGM]
La Grande Bouffe
La Guerre Est Finie
La Separation
The Last September
L'Ennui
Leon, the Professional
The Life of Jesus
Live Flesh
Loulou
Love After Love
Ma Vie en Rose
The Man Who Loved Women
Manon of the Spring
The Marquise of O
Mauvais Sang
Mississippi Mermaid
Mr. Hulot's Holiday
Mon Oncle

Mon Oncle d'Amerique
My Sex Life...Or How I Got into an Argument
The New Eve
The Ninth Gate
Oasis of the Zombies
Party
Perceval
Pola X
Portraits Chinois
Possession
The Red Dwarf
Rififi
The Serpent's Kiss
A Single Girl
Small Change
Son of Gascogne
The Sorrow and the Pity
The Story of Adele H.
A Summer's Tale
Sweet Revenge
Utopia [Digital Disc]
Wax Mask
Women
Zombie Lake

Friendship
See: Buddies

Front Page
See also: Mass Media; Shutterbugs

Cold Blooded
Diary of a Serial Killer
Don't Torture a Duckling
Extramarital
Footsteps
Full Disclosure
Joe Gould's Secret
Mean Season
Meet John Doe [Image]
Newsbreak
Premonition
Salvador [SE]
Snow Falling on Cedars
Superman: The Movie
Sweet Smell of Success

Fugitives
See also: Lovers on the Lam

Fled
Frank and Jesse
North by Northwest
Posse
The Quarry
Three Strikes

Funerals
See also: Death & the Afterlife

The Addams Family
The Evening Star
Guantanamera
Harold and Maude
The Pallbearer
Steel Magnolias
Terms of Endearment

Gambling
See also: Viva Las Vegas!

The Boys
Circus
Cockfighter
Croupier
Diamonds Are Forever [SE]
Eight Men Out
Frankie and Johnny
Gilda
Guys and Dolls
Hard Eight
Hoodlum
House of Games
The Lemon Drop Kid
Liberty Heights
Lock, Stock and 2 Smoking Barrels
Lost in America
Sour Grapes

Game Adaptations
Art of Fighting

Angel on My Shoulder
The Bishop's Wife [MGM]
Defending Your Life
Dogma
Ghost
Wide Awake

Heists
See also: Scams, Stings & Cons

The Amazing Transparent Man
The Bank Dick
Big Deal on Madonna Street
Black Moon Rising
Blind Justice
City of Industry
Croupier
Diamond Run
Getting Even with Dad
Gone in 60 Seconds
Harley Davidson and the Marlboro Man
Kelly's Heroes
Killing Zoe
Lightning Jack
Lock, Stock and 2 Smoking Barrels
On the Border
Reindeer Games
Rififi
R.P.M.
Thick As Thieves
Two If by Sea
Velocity Trap
Where the Money Is

Hell
All Dogs Go to Heaven
Hellraiser 2
Little Nicky

Hell High School
See also: Campus Capers; School Daze; Teen Angst

Cheaters
Class
Coneheads
Cooley High
Deal of a Lifetime
Detention
Fast Times at Ridgemont High
High School High
Light It Up
Mirror, Mirror
187
Porky's / Porky's 2: The Next Day
Porky's 2: The Next Day
School's Out
Shriek If You Know What I Did Last Friday the 13th
Teenage Strangler

The Help: Female
Cotton Mary
Diary of a Chambermaid

The Help: Male
Clue
Screwed

Ernest Hemingway
After the Storm
A Farewell to Arms
The Old Man and the Sea
The Snows of Kilimanjaro

Hide the Dead Guy
Blue Ridge Fall
The Trouble with Harry
Up at the Villa

High School Reunions
See also: School Daze

Something Wild

Highest Grossing Films of All Time
Ghost
Jaws [CE]
Jurassic Park [CE]

Terminator 2: Judgment Day [2 SE]

Patricia Highsmith
The Talented Mr. Ripley

Historical Detectives
The Sign of Four

Historical Drama
See also: Medieval Romps; Period Piece

The Alamo
Attila
Ben-Hur
Black Robe
The Bounty
Braveheart
Cleopatra
Demetrius and the Gladiators
The Emperor and the Assassin
Fellini Satyricon
Fire over England
Gettysburg
Glory [2 SE]
The Greatest Story Ever Told [SE]
Henry V
I Shot Andy Warhol
Ill-Gotten Gains
The Last Valley
Lawrence of Arabia
The Lion in Winter
A Man for All Seasons
The Marquise of O
The Messenger: The Story of Joan of Arc
Moll Flanders [MGM]
New Legend of Shaolin
The Patriot
Rikyu
Scarlet Empress
The Scarlet Pimpernel
Soldier of Orange
Soul of the Game
Spartacus [Criterion]
A Woman Called Moses

Hit Men
See also: Assassinations

Back to Back
Big City Blues
Body Count
The Contract
DaVinci's War
Destination Vegas
Full Disclosure
Ghost Dog: The Way of the Samurai
Hard-Boiled [Winstar]
Her Name Is Cat
Jerry and Tom
The Killer [Winstar]
La Femme Nikita [MGM]
Leon, the Professional
Nurse Betty
Prisoner Maria: The Movie
Thrill Seekers
The Whole Nine Yards

Hockey
See also: Skating

The Boys
The Cutting Edge
Love Story
MVP: Most Valuable Primate
Mystery, Alaska
Youngblood

Sherlock Holmes
The Adventures of Sherlock Holmes
Dressed to Kill
Sherlock Holmes and the Secret Weapon
The Sign of Four
Terror by Night
The Woman in Green
The Woman in Green / Dressed to Kill

The Holocaust
See also: Germany; Judaism; Nazis & Other Paramilitary Slugs; World War II

The Long Way Home
Mr. Death: The Rise and Fall of Fred A. Leuchter, Jr.
Sunshine

Home Alone
See also: Childhood Visions

Don't Tell Mom the Babysitter's Dead

The Homefront: England
See also: World War II

Hope and Glory
The Last of the Blonde Bombshells

The Homefront: U.S./Canada
See also: World War II

I'll Remember April
Saboteur

Homeless
See also: Great Depression; Hard Knock Life; Yuppie Nightmares

The Fisher King
Joe Gould's Secret
Times Square

Homosexuality
See: Bisexuality; Gays; Lesbians

Hong Kong
See also: Asia; China

The Art of War
A Better Tomorrow, Part 1 [Anchor Bay]
Double Impact
Gen-X Cops
Romeo Must Die

Hong Kong (Production)
A Better Tomorrow, Part 1 [Anchor Bay]
A Better Tomorrow, Part 2 [Anchor Bay]
The Bodyguard from Beijing
Chinese Ghost Story II
Chinese Ghost Story III
A Chinese Ghost Story: The Tsui Hark Animation
Crime Story
The Defender
The Dragon Chronicles
Eastern Condors
Fantasy Mission Force
Gen-X Cops
Gorgeous
Hard-Boiled [Winstar]
Her Name Is Cat
Jet Li's The Enforcer [Buena Vista]
The Killer [Winstar]
The Legend
Man Called Hero
Master with Cracked Fingers
The Mighty Peking Man
The Millionaire's Express
The Mission
Naked Killer
New Legend of Shaolin
Once Upon a Time in China
Painted Skin
Peace Hotel
The Prisoner
Project A
Rouge
Running out of Time
Spooky Encounters
Tokyo Raiders
Twin Warriors
Zu: Warriors of the Magic Mountain

Horrible Holidays
See also: Christmas

Black Christmas
Halloween 5: The Revenge of Michael Myers
Mother's Day [DC]
The Myth of Fingerprints

Horror
See: Classic Horror; Horror Anthologies; Horror Comedy; Supernatural Horror

Horror Anthologies
Asylum
Creepshow 2
Hellblock 13
Tales of Terror
Terror Tract

Horror Comedy
American Vampire
The Bogus Witch Project
The Bone Yard
Bride of Re-Animator
A Bucket of Blood
C.H.U.D.
The Creeps
Ghosts on the Loose
Hillbillys in a Haunted House
Hysterical
Idle Hands
Jack Frost 2: Revenge of the Mutant Killer Snowman
The Little Vampire
Mistress Frankenstein [CE]
My Mom's a Werewolf
My Son, the Vampire
Saturday the 14th
Saturday the 14th Strikes Back
The Stuff
Terror Firmer [SE]
The Thing with Two Heads
Titanic 2000
The Undertaker and His Pals
The Vampire Happening

Horse Racing
See: Gambling; Horses

Horses
All the Pretty Horses
The Flying Deuces / Utopia
In Pursuit of Honor
The Lemon Drop Kid
The Misfits
Running Free
Simpatico
Winds of the Wasteland

Hospitals & Medicine
See also: Disease of the Week; Doctors & Nurses; Emerging Viruses; Sanity Check; Shrinks

Bringing Out the Dead
Critical Care
Hard-Boiled [Winstar]
Nine Months
28 Days [SE]

Hostage!
See also: Kidnapped!; Missing Persons

Amos and Andrew
Cold Sweat
Diplomatic Siege
Escape from New York
Fall Time
Held Up
Johnny 100 Pesos
Light It Up
Nick of Time
The Taking of Pelham One Two Three
Uninvited Guest

Housekeepers
See: The Help: Female

Houston
The Evening Star
Terms of Endearment
Thug Life

Victor Hugo
Les Miserables

Hungarian (Production)
Sunshine

Hunted!
See also: Survival

Freejack
Maximum Risk
The Most Dangerous Game [Madacy]
Southern Comfort

Hunting
See also: Go Fish

Frostbiter: Wrath of the Wendigo

Hurling
Car Wash
The Cutting Edge
Jaws [CE]
Stand by Me [2 SE]
This Is Spinal Tap [MGM]

Icelandic (Production)
Devil's Island

Immigration
Avalon
Dancer in the Dark
East Is East

Impending Retirement
K-911
Seven [2 SE]

In-Laws
The Grandfather
Meet the Parents

Incest
See also: Family Ties

The Cement Garden
Natural Born Killers [DC]
Pola X
The War Zone

India
Bandit Queen
Black Narcissus
Cotton Mary
The Far Pavilions
Fire
The Indian Tomb
Monsoon
Octopussy
A Passage to India

Indian (Production)
Bandit Queen
The Terrorist

Interracial Affairs
Colorz of Rage
Heaven and Earth
Love Field
Pocahontas
Restaurant
Romeo Must Die
Save the Last Dance
Snow Falling on Cedars
The Tic Code
The Watermelon Woman
Welcome II the Terrordome

Interviews
See also: This Is Your Life

Dirty Pictures
The Filth and the Fury
Texas Chainsaw Massacre: A Family Portrait

Inventors & Inventions
See also: Mad Scientists; Science & Scientists

Invisible Mom

Korean (Production)
The Ring Virus

Korean War
The Bridges at Toko-Ri
For the Boys
The Last Picture Show [DC]

Kung Fu
See: Martial Arts

L.A.
See also: Earthquakes
Bellyfruit
Best of the Best: Without Warning
The Big Tease
Black Scorpion 2: Ground Zero
Blue Streak
The Boys Next Door
The Broken Hearts Club
Broken Vessels
Bulletproof
City of Industry
Fast Times at Ridgemont High
Get On the Bus
Grand Canyon
Hanging Up
Internal Affairs
K-911
Let the Devil Wear Black
The Next Best Thing
Nick of Time
187
Paper Bullets
Quiet Days in Hollywood
Scream 3 [CS]
Seamless
The Souler Opposite
Splendor
Starry Night
Telling You
Three Strikes
Time Code
Whatever It Takes
Yellow

Labor & Unions
See also: Miners & Mining
Norma Rae
North Dallas Forty
Salt of the Earth

Louis L'Amour
The Shadow Riders

Las Vegas
See: Viva Las Vegas!

Late Bloomin' Love
See also: Growing Older
Brief Encounter
Harold and Maude

Laurel & Hardy
The Flying Deuces / Utopia
Utopia [Digital Disc]

Law & Lawyers
See also: Order in the Court
Anatomy of a Murder
And Justice for All
Body Chemistry 4: Full Exposure
The Confession
Critical Care
Destination Vegas
Erin Brockovich
In Pursuit
It's the Rage
The Jagged Edge
King and Country
Love Stinks
Murder in the First
My Cousin Vinny
Nuremberg
Restraining Order
True Believer
Twelve Angry Men

Leprechauns
Leprechaun 2
Leprechaun 3
Leprechaun 4: In Space
Leprechaun 5: In the Hood
The Magical Legend of the Leprechauns

Lesbians
See also: Bisexuality; Gays; Gender Bending
But I'm a Cheerleader
Chasing Amy
Chuck & Buck
Desert Hearts
Fire
Foxfire
Gia
If These Walls Could Talk 2
Peach / A Bitter Song
Reform School Girls
The Souler Opposite
Vampyres
Vampyros Lesbos
The Watermelon Woman
What's Cookin'?
Working Girls

Ira Levin
Rosemary's Baby

Libraries and Librarians
The Creeps
Good News
Hard-Boiled [Winstar]
The Mummy [2 SE]
7 Faces of Dr. Lao
Wilderness

Lifeguards
See also: Beach Blanket Bingo; Swimming
Baywatch: Nightmare Bay / River of No Return

London
See also: Great Britain; Royalty
Alfie
B. Monkey
Beautiful People
Bedrooms and Hallways
Croupier
An Egyptian Story
End of the Affair
The End of the Affair
Fever Pitch
Frenzy
Hope and Glory
Immortality
The Little Princess
Mary Poppins [2 SE]
Mary Reilly
A Merry War
Moll Flanders [MGM]
Pocahontas 2: Journey to a New World
Poldark
Robert Louis Stevenson's The Game of Death
Topsy Turvy
Wonderland

Jack London
Call of the Wild
The Fighter

Loneliness
See: Only the Lonely

Loner Cops
See also: Cops
In the Heat of the Night

Look Ma! I'm on TV!
See also: Mass Media
Eat Your Heart Out
Magnolia
Unmade Beds
Woman on Top

Lost Worlds
See also: Parallel Universes

Beyond Atlantis
Gold of the Amazon Women
Jane & the Lost City
The Lost World [Image]

Lottery Winners
Babette's Feast
It Could Happen to You
Lucky Numbers
Next Friday [Platinum Series]

Lovable Loonies
See also: Shrinks
Benny & Joon
Best in Show
The Fisher King
What about Bob?

H.P. Lovecraft
Bride of Re-Animator
Die, Monster, Die!

Lovers on the Lam
See also: Fugitives
Heaven's Burning
Natural Born Killers [DC]
Two If by Sea

Luxembourg (Production)
An Affair of Love

Alistair MacLean
Breakheart Pass

Mad Scientists
See also: Inventors & Inventions; Science & Scientists
The Amazing Transparent Man
Attack of the Puppet People
Bloodstorm: Subspecies 4
The Brain that Wouldn't Die
Bride of Re-Animator
The Creeps
The Dead Next Door
Dr. Frankenstein's Castle of Freaks
Dr. Goldfoot and the Bikini Machine
Donovan's Brain
Embryo
Frankenstein's Daughter
The Hollow Man [SE]
The Indestructible Man / The Amazing Transparent Man
The Invisible Man
Jurassic Park [CE]
The Munsters' Revenge
Shadow of Chinatown
She Demons
Strange Case of Dr. Jekyll & Mr. Hyde
The Vampire Bat

Made for Television
See: TV Pilot Movies; TV Series

Mafia
See: Organized Crime

Magic
See also: Magic Carpet Rides; Occult
Bedknobs and Broomsticks
The Black Cauldron
Don't Torture a Duckling
Dungeons and Dragons
Pick a Card

Magic Carpet Rides
Golden Voyage of Sinbad
Sinbad and the Eye of the Tiger

Mail-Order Brides
See also: Marriage; Wedding Bells
Mississippi Mermaid

Marriage
See also: Divorce; Otherwise Engaged; War Between the Sexes; Wedding Bells; Wedding Hell
The Adjuster
Affairs of Anatol
American Beauty [SE]
Bad Manners
Battle of the Sexes
Blue Sky
Body Chemistry
Breaking the Waves
Circus
Cotton Mary
The Daytrippers
Deep in the Heart (of Texas)
East Is East
East-West
Element of Doubt
The End of the Affair
The Entertainer
Falling for a Dancer
Fireworks
For Love or Country: The Arturo Sandoval Story
For Pete's Sake
How to Commit Marriage
How to Marry a Millionaire
I Married a Strange Person
Isn't She Great
It's the Rage
The Lion in Winter
Loulou
Maborosi
Magnolia
A Map of the World
The Marquise of O
The Marriage Circle
Marty
A Matter of Dignity
Me Myself I
Mr. Wonderful
Moon over Harlem
My 5 Wives
One Good Turn
The Pallisers
A Paper Wedding
Party
The Passion of Ayn Rand
Prelude to a Kiss
Return to Me
The Rich Man's Wife
The Seven Year Itch
She's Having a Baby
She's So Lovely
She's the One
Small Time Crooks
That Uncertain Feeling [Sling-Shot]
Ulysses
A Walk in the Clouds
What Lies Beneath
Woman on Top
A Woman under the Influence
Yours, Mine & Ours

Martial Arts
Ashes of Time
Best of the Best 3: No Turning Back / Best of the Best: Without Warning
Best of the Best: Without Warning
Big Trouble in Little China [SE]
Black Eagle
Bloodfist
Bloodfist 2
Bloodfist 3: Forced to Fight
Bloodfist 4: Die Trying
The Bodyguard / Dragon Princess
Breaker! Breaker!
China O'Brien
Crime Story
Crouching Tiger, Hidden Dragon
Death Warrant
Demon City Shinjuku
Double Dragon

Double Impact
The Dragon Chronicles
Dragon Princess
Fantasy Mission Force
Jet Li's The Enforcer [Buena Vista]
The Karate Kid
Lady Dragon
The Legend of Drunken Master
Master with Cracked Fingers
Maximum Risk
The Millionaire's Express
Moving Target
Naked Killer
New Legend of Shaolin
The Prisoner
Project A
Romeo Must Die
Samurai X: The Movie
Samurai X Trust
Throw Down
Tokyo Raiders
Twin Warriors

Martyred Pop Icons
See also: Rock Stars on Film
Bob Dylan: Don't Look Back
Bus Stop
The Doors [2 SE]
I Shot Andy Warhol
The Seven Year Itch

Mass Media
See also: Front Page; Radio
Baywatch: Nightmare Bay / River of No Return
Intern
Natural Born Killers [DC]
Scrooged
The Stuff
Superstar: The Life and Times of Andy Warhol

Masseurs
Love Kills

Richard Matheson
Cold Sweat

W. Somerset Maugham
Of Human Bondage
Rain
Up at the Villa

May–December Romance
See also: Coming of Age; Growing Older; Romantic Adventures; Romantic Comedy; Romantic Drama
Autumn in New York
Harold and Maude
The Pallbearer

Ian McEwan
The Cement Garden

Larry McMurtry
The Last Picture Show [DC]
Terms of Endearment

The Meaning of Life
Love and Death
My Life

Medieval Romps
See also: Camelot (Old); Historical Drama; Period Piece; Swashbucklers
Braveheart
Brother Cadfael: The Devil's Novice
Dragonheart: A New Beginning
The Lion in Winter
Monty Python and the Holy Grail
The Navigator
Perceval
Robin Hood
Sinbad: Beyond the Veil of Mists

The Sword in the Stone

Meltdown
See also: Disaster Flicks

The Day the Earth Caught Fire
Dr. Strangelove, or: How I Learned to Stop Worrying and Love the Bomb [2 SE]
Fail-Safe
First Spaceship on Venus
A Nymphoid Barbarian in Dinosaur Hell [SE]
Seven Days in May
Slugs
Superman 4: The Quest for Peace
Utopia [Digital Disc]
Voyage to the Bottom of the Sea / Fantastic Voyage
The World Is Not Enough [SE]

Herman Melville
Moby Dick
Pola X

Memoirs or Diary Adaptations
Angela's Ashes
Anna and the King
Bandit Queen
Girl, Interrupted
The Passion of Ayn Rand

Men
See also: Dads; Repressed Men; War Between the Sexes

City Slickers
La Grande Bouffe
Planet of the Apes

Men in Prison
See also: Fugitives; Great Escapes; POW/MIA; Women in Prison

All the Pretty Horses
Animal Factory
Bait
Before Night Falls
Birdman of Alcatraz
Darkdrive
Death Warrant
Tha Eastsidaz
Escape from New York
Fled
The Hurricane
In God's Hands
Les Miserables
A Lesson Before Dying
Live Flesh
The Longest Yard
Murder in the First
Penitentiary
Penitentiary 2
The Prisoner
The Rock [Criterion]
Timelock

Mental Retardation
See also: Physical Problems; Savants

Digging to China
Mifune

Metamorphosis
See also: Genetics; Werewolves

The Fly / Return of the Fly
The Fly / The Fly 2
The Fly 2
Miss Congeniality
Nutty Professor 2: The Klumps [1 CE]
Nutty Professor 2: The Klumps [2 Uncensored]

Meteors, Asteroids, and Comets
See also: Alien Beings—Vicious; Disaster Flicks; Space Operas

The Blob

Die, Monster, Die!
Dinosaur [CE]
Meteor
Teenage Monster
Tycus

Mexican (Production)
Dance with the Devil
Death and the Compass
Midaq Alley

Mexico
See also: Central America

Against All Odds
All the Pretty Horses
From Dusk Till Dawn [2 CS]
In Pursuit
La Cucaracha
The Magnificent Seven
Midaq Alley
The Road to El Dorado
Sergei Eisenstein: Mexican Fantasy
Touch of Evil [SE]
Traffic
Vera Cruz
Way of the Gun

MGM Musicals
Annie Get Your Gun
Good News
Take Me Out to the Ball Game
Till the Clouds Roll By
The Unsinkable Molly Brown

Miami
See also: American South

Any Given Sunday
The Crew
Forever Mine
The Last Marshal

James Michener
The Bridges at Toko-Ri

Middle East
See also: Desert War/Foreign Legion; Deserts; Islam; Israel; Terrorism

Desert Thunder
Ilsa, Harem Keeper of the Oil Sheiks
Lawrence of Arabia
One Day in September

Military: Air Force
See also: Airborne

Desert Thunder
Mach 2
Space Cowboys

Military: Army
The Base
The Gay Deceivers
Gettysburg
In Pursuit of Honor
Platoon [2 SE]
Rangers
A Soldier's Story
Tigerland
We'll Meet Again

Military Comedy
See also: Comedy; War, General

At War with the Army
The Flying Deuces / Utopia
Private Navy of Sgt. O'Farrell

Military: Foreign
The Beast
The Brylcreem Boys
I'll Remember April
The Indian Tomb
King and Country
The Last Lieutenant
The Last September
The Marquise of O
Pretty Village, Pretty Flame
Soldier of Orange
Traffic

Military: Marines
Leprechaun 4: In Space
Platoon [2 SE]
The Rock [Criterion]
Rules of Engagement

Military: Navy
See also: Sail Away

The Bridges at Toko-Ri
Chasers
Men of Honor
Navy SEALS [MGM]
No Way Out
An Officer and a Gentleman
Private Navy of Sgt. O'Farrell
The Sand Pebbles
Submerged
U-571 [CE]
U.S. Seals

Miners & Mining
Billy Elliot
Chained Heat 3: Hell Mountain
The Claim
The Hallelujah Trail
How Green Was My Valley
Lucky Texan
Poldark
Salt of the Earth
Smilla's Sense of Snow
Solomon and Gaenor

Minnesota
Ice Castles
The Long Riders
Untamed Heart

Missing Persons
See also: Hostage!; Kidnapped!

The Emerald Forest
Home for Christmas
Misery

Missionaries
See also: Nuns & Priests; Religion; Religious Epics

Black Robe
Paradise Road

Mistaken Identity
See also: Amnesia; Gender Bending; Role Reversal

Amos and Andrew
Being There
A Better Way to Die
A Couch in New York
F/X 2: The Deadly Art of Illusion
The Inspector General
Mississippi Mermaid
North by Northwest
Prelude to a Kiss
Reindeer Games
Support Your Local Gunfighter
Suture
The Truth about Cats and Dogs

Model Citizens
Eyes of Laura Mars
Gia

Modern Cowboys
See also: Western Comedy; Westerns

All the Pretty Horses
Bronco Billy
City Slickers
Toy Story
Toy Story 2

Moms
See also: Bad Dads; Dads; Monster Moms; Parenthood

Agnes Browne
All About My Mother
Baby Boom
Beautiful
The Daytrippers

Digging to China
Double Parked
Gia
A Home of Our Own
Invisible Mom
Little Women [2 SE]
Me Myself I
Mermaids
Mother
Mother and Son
Postcards from the Edge
Relative Values
Requiem for a Dream
She's Having a Baby
Striptease
Terms of Endearment
Tumbleweeds
The Yards

Monkeyshines
See also: Jungle Stories; Wild Kingdom

Buddy
Monkey Shines
MVP: Most Valuable Primate
Terror Tract

Monster Moms
See also: Bad Dads; Dads; Moms; Parenthood

Gorgo
A Matter of Dignity
Mommy [SE]
Mother's Boys
Mother's Day [DC]
Sleepwalkers

Monsters, General
See: Bigfoot/Yeti; Ghosts, Ghouls, & Goblins; Giants; Killer Beasts; Killer Bugs & Slugs; Killer Plants; Killer Reptiles; Killer Sea Critters; Killer Toys; Mad Scientists; Mummies; Robots & Androids; Vampires; Werewolves; Zombies

Montreal
See also: Canada

The Whole Nine Yards

Brian Moore
Black Robe

Moscow
See also: Russia/USSR

Gorky Park

Motor Vehicle Dept.
See also: Bikers; Checkered Flag; Killer Cars

Black Cat Run
Black Moon Rising
Car Wash
Gone in 60 Seconds
The Hollywood Knights
Maximum Overdrive
Repo Man
R.P.M.
Tucker: The Man and His Dream

Mountaineering
The Abominable Snowman
Cliffhanger [2 CS]
Vertical Limit

Mummies
See also: Zombies

The Creeps
The Mummy
The Mummy [2 SE]
The Mummy's Shroud

The Muppets
CinderElmo

Murderous Children
See also: Childhood Visions

Children of the Corn
Damien: Omen 2

Gummo
Milo
The Omen [SE]

Museums
Abbott and Costello Meet Frankenstein
Crucible of Terror
Dirty Pictures

Musical Comedy
See also: Musicals

The Adventures of Priscilla, Queen of the Desert [MGM]
Beach Blanket Bingo
Beach Party
Bikini Beach
Elephant Parts
Frankie and Johnny
The Gay Desperado
Gentlemen Prefer Blondes
Good News
Guys and Dolls
Nunsense 2: The Sequel
Pal Joey
The Road to Bali
The Road to Rio
The Seven Little Foys
Sextette
Take Me Out to the Ball Game
There's No Business Like Show Business
The Unsinkable Molly Brown
White Christmas
Wonder Man

Musical Drama
See also: Musicals

42nd Street
The Harder They Come
Jesus Christ Superstar
The Josephine Baker Story
The Sound of Music [Five Star Collection]
Tommy

Musical Fantasy
See also: Musicals

Bedknobs and Broomsticks
Dancer in the Dark
Doctor Dolittle
The 5000 Fingers of Dr. T
March of the Wooden Soldiers
Mary Poppins [2 SE]
The New Adventures of Pippi Longstocking
Wonderwall: The Movie

Musicals
See also: Animated Musicals; Disco Musicals; MGM Musicals; Musical Comedy; Musical Drama; Musical Fantasy; Opera; Showbiz Musicals

Annie
Annie
Annie Get Your Gun
Billy's Holiday
Hans Christian Andersen [20th Century Fox]
Hillbillys in a Haunted House
Joseph and the Amazing Technicolor Dreamcoat
The Josephine Baker Story
Love's Labour's Lost
Moon over Harlem
Pinocchio
The Seven Little Foys
Till the Clouds Roll By

Musician Biopics
Bird
The Doors [2 SE]
For Love or Country: The Arturo Sandoval Story
Hendrix
Sweet and Lowdown

Mutiny
See also: Deep Blue; Sail Away; Sea Disasters; Shipwrecked

The Bounty

Mystery & Suspense
See also: Psycho-Thriller

The Adventures of Sherlock Holmes
Agatha Christie's Poirot
Animal Instincts
The Bedroom Window
Betrayed
The Black Cat
Blood on the Sun
Blue Velvet
Body Chemistry
Body Chemistry 3: Point of Seduction
Breakheart Pass
The Bride Wore Black
Brother Cadfael: The Devil's Novice
Bulldog Drummond's Secret Police
The Conversation
Daughter of Horror / Dementia
Dead Zone
Death on the Nile
Death Sentence
Death Warrant
Die Screaming, Marianne
D.O.A. Roan
Don't Go in the House
Don't Torture a Duckling
Dressed to Kill
Endless Night
Evil under the Sun
Eyes of Laura Mars
F/X
Fail-Safe
Family Plot
Fear City
Five Dolls for an August Moon
Flashfire
Flowers in the Attic
For Hire
Frenzy
Gorky Park
In the Heat of the Night
In the Line of Fire [2 SE]
The Inside Man
The Jagged Edge
Joy House
The Kidnapping of the President
The Lady from Shanghai
The Lady in White
Lower Level
Malice [MGM]
The Man Who Knew Too Much
Midnight
The Mirror Crack'd
The Most Dangerous Game [Madacy]
Mother's Boys
No Way Out
North by Northwest
The Parallax View
Positive I.D.
Rear Window
The Rich Man's Wife
Rififi
Rope
Saboteur
The Scorpio Factor
The Second Woman
Shadow of a Doubt
Sherlock Holmes and the Secret Weapon
The Sign of Four
Sister, Sister
Smilla's Sense of Snow
Somebody Has to Shoot the Picture
Spaceways
Swamp Thing

Tenebre
Terror by Night
They Call Me Mr. Tibbs!
Topaz
Torn Curtain
Touch of Evil [SE]
Tourist Trap
The Trouble with Harry
True Believer
Whatever Happened to Aunt Alice?
The Woman in Green
The Woman in Green / Dressed to Kill

Vladimir Nabokov
Lolita

Nannies & Governesses
See also: Babysitting; Bringing Up Baby; The Help: Female; Parenthood

Mary Poppins [2 SE]
The Perfect Nanny
The Sound of Music [Five Star Collection]

Nashville
See also: American South

Nashville
Tender Mercies

Native America
Black Robe
Dead Man
The Last of the Mohicans
Pocahontas
Pocahontas 2: Journey to a New World
Thunderheart
The Vanishing American

Nazis & Other Paramilitary Slugs
See also: Germany; The Holocaust; Judaism; World War II

Bedknobs and Broomsticks
Hangmen Also Die
Ilsa, Harem Keeper of the Oil Sheiks
Ilsa, She-Wolf of the SS
Jew-boy Levi
Mein Kampf: Hitler's Rise and Fall
Mother Night
Nuremberg
Oasis of the Zombies
Puppet Master 3: Toulon's Revenge
She Demons
Soldier of Orange
The Sorrow and the Pity
The Sound of Music [Five Star Collection]
Tomorrow the World
Triumph of the Will
Zombie Lake

Negative Utopia
See also: Post Apocalypse; Technology—Rampant

10th Victim
Zardoz

New Black Cinema
See also: African America; Blaxploitation

Bamboozled
Boyz N the Hood
Do the Right Thing 2
Get On the Bus
I'm Gonna Git You Sucka
Mo' Better Blues
Poetic Justice
Posse
School Daze

New Orleans
See also: American South

Crazy in Alabama
Dead Man Walking
The First 9 1/2 Weeks

Suddenly, Last Summer

New Year's Eve
See also: Christmas; Horrible Holidays

The Art of War
When Harry Met Sally... [SE]

New York, New York
See also: The Empire State Building

An Affair to Remember
Aftershock: Earthquake in New York
Alice
American Psycho
Annie
Annie
Another Woman
The Apartment
The Art of War
Autumn in New York
Because of You
Before Night Falls
Bless the Child
Boiler Room
Born to Win
Bringing Out the Dead
Center Stage
City Slickers
Coming Soon
A Couch in New York
Coyote Ugly
The Cradle Will Rock
Crimes & Misdemeanors [MGM]
The Daytrippers
Desperately Seeking Susan
Do the Right Thing 2
Donnie Brasco 2
Down to You
Escape from New York
Eyes of Laura Mars
F/X
Finding Forrester
The Fisher King
Flawless
Fort Apache, the Bronx
42nd Street
Frequency
Ghost
The Godfather DVD Collection
The Godfather, Part 2
The Godfather, Part 3
Gossip
Gotti
Guys and Dolls
Hamlet
Hanging Up
Highlander: Endgame
Hoodlum
House of Mirth
Illuminata
Intern
It Could Happen to You
Italian Movie
Joe Gould's Secret
Juice
Keeping the Faith
Kicked in the Head
King of New York
Kiss Me, Guido
Look Who's Talking, Too
The Lords of Flatbush
Loser
Love Story
Manhattan
Marty
Maximum Risk
Misery
Mo' Better Blues
Music of the Heart [CS]
The Natural
The Ninth Gate
The Odd Couple
The Pompatus of Love
The Pope of Greenwich Village
Portrait of Jennie
Prince of Central Park
A Raisin in the Sun

The Real Blonde
Rear Window
Rosemary's Baby
Scrooged
Seven [2 SE]
The Seven Year Itch
Sex and the City: The Complete Second Season
Shadows and Fog
Shaft
She's the One
Six Degrees of Separation
Small Time Crooks
Something Wild
Splash
Street Scene
Sweet Smell of Success
The Taking of Pelham One Two Three
The Tic Code
Timeless
Times Square
Tootsie
Untamed Heart
The Waiting Game
Wall Street
The Way We Were [SE]
When Harry Met Sally... [SE]
Whipped
Working Girl
X-Men
The Yards

New Zealand
See: Down Under

New Zealand (Production)
Forgotten Silver
Mesmerized
The Navigator

Newspapers
See: Front Page

Nice Mice
The Rescuers Down Under
Road Trip
The Secret of NIMH 2

Nightclubs
Animal Instincts
Body Shots
Bus Stop
The Killing of a Chinese Bookie
The Nutty Professor

Ninjitsu
See: Martial Arts

No-Exit Motel
See also: Grand Hotel

Mountaintop Motel Massacre

Norwegian (Production)
Cross My Heart and Hope to Die
The Last Lieutenant
Mio in the Land of Faraway
The Other Side of Sunday

Not-So-True Identity
Big Momma's House
Blue Streak
Forever Mine
Grey Owl
Gun Shy
Homegrown
Les Miserables
Mother Night
The Quarry
The Rowdy Girls
The Talented Mr. Ripley
The Thief

Nuclear Disaster
See: Disaster Flicks; Meltdown

Nuns & Priests
See also: Missionaries; Religion; Religious Epics

All About My Mother
Anchoress
The Apostate
Black Narcissus
Black Robe
Dead Man Walking
Dead Waters
The End of the Affair
In This House of Brede
Keeping the Faith
Lilies of the Field
Madeline
Nunsense 2: The Sequel
The Sound of Music [Five Star Collection]
Wide Awake

Joyce Carol Oates
Foxfire

Obsessive Love
Against All Odds
Anna Karenina
Beyond the Clouds
Brief Encounter
The Crush
Cyrano de Bergerac
8 1/2 Women
End of the Affair
The End of the Affair
Eye of the Beholder
Ghost
L'Ennui
Live Flesh
The Phantom of the Opera
Roxanne

Occult
See also: Demons & Wizards; Satanism; Witchcraft

The Black Cat
Bless the Child
Damien: Omen 2
Dance with the Devil
Donovan's Brain
Evil Dead 2: Dead by Dawn [2 THX]
Horror Hotel
Lost Souls
Mirror, Mirror
Mirror, Mirror 2: Raven Dance
Necromancer: Satan's Servant
Omen 3: The Final Conflict
Psychomania
Puppet Master
Rosemary's Baby
The Sentinel
Supergirl

Oceans
See: Deep Blue; Go Fish; Killer Sea Critters; Mutiny; Scuba; Shipwrecked; Submarines

Office Surprise
La Femme Nikita [MGM]
Misery
9 to 5

John O'Hara
Butterfield 8
Pal Joey

Oil
See: Black Gold

Oldest Profession
See also: Women in Prison

American Psycho
The Balcony
Big City Blues
The Book of Stars
Butterfield 8
Coffy
Deuce Bigalow: Male Gigolo
Diamonds
Foxy Brown
Fruits of Passion: The Story of "O" Continued
Hollywood Vice Squad

Rated X
The '70s
Steal This Movie!
That's the Way I Like It
Tigerland
The Virgin Suicides
Waking the Dead

Period Piece: The 1980s
American Psycho
Billy Elliot
Fever Pitch
Forever Mine
The Replacements
Waking the Dead

Astrid Lindgren
The New Adventures of Pippi
Longstocking

Philadelphia
Rocky [2 SE]
The Watermelon Woman

Philanthropy
See: Kindness of Strangers

Phone Sex
*See also: Sex & Sexuality;
Sexploitation*

The Truth about Cats and
Dogs

Phone Terror
Black Sabbath
Don't Answer the Phone
Scream 3 [CS]

Photography
See: Shutterbugs

Physical Problems
*See also: Blindness; Deaf-
ness; Mental Retardation;
Savants*

An Affair to Remember
Born on the Fourth of July 2
Breaking the Waves
Choices
Diamonds
Double Parked
Eden
Fireworks
Flawless
Floating
It's Good to Be Alive
Lewis and Clark and George
Lightning Jack
Love Affair
The Miracle Worker
The Miracle Worker
Monkey Shines
Of Human Bondage
The Phantom of the Opera
Rear Window
The Red Dwarf
Roxanne
The Spiral Staircase
Sweet and Lowdown
Twin Falls Idaho
Untamed Heart
X-Men

Pigs
The Amityville Horror
The Black Cauldron
Charlotte's Web
The Tigger Movie

Pirates
*See also: Island Fare; Sail
Away; Swashbucklers*

Captain Kidd
The Princess Bride

Pittsburgh
Bob Roberts [SE]
Diabolique
Wonder Boys

The Planet of the Apes
Battle for the Planet of the
Apes

Behind the Planet of the
Apes
Beneath the Planet of the
Apes
Conquest of the Planet of the
Apes
Escape from the Planet of
the Apes
Planet of the Apes

Edgar Allan Poe
The Black Cat
Fall of the House of Usher
The Fall of the House of
Usher
The Pit and the Pendulum
Tales of Terror

Poem Adaptations
Beowulf
Braveheart
Evangeline
Perceval

Poetry
Before Night Falls
News from the West
Poetic Justice

Poisons
Arsenic and Old Lace
D.O.A. Roan

Police Detectives
The Element of Crime
The Gore-Gore Girls
Kept

Polish (Production)
First Spaceship on Venus

Politics
See also: Presidency

And the Band Played On
Animal Instincts
The Art of War
Attila
Attila 74: The Rape of Cyprus
Being There
Bob Roberts [SE]
Canadian Bacon
The Contender
The Cradle Will Rock
The Emperor and the Assas-
sin
Friday Foster
Gladiator
In the Line of Fire [2 SE]
It's Raining on Santiago
Les Miserables
A Little Bit of Soul
The Man Who Shot Liberty
Valance
Nick of Time
The Pallisers
Poldark
Salt of the Earth
The '70s
Striptease
Tito and Me
Up at the Villa

Pool
See also: Gambling

Kiss Shot

Pornography
*See also: Sex & Sexuality;
Sexploitation*

Dirty Pictures
Heavy Traffic
Hollywood Vice Sqaud
Rated X

Portuguese (Production)
God's Comedy
Party

Post Apocalypse
*See also: Negative Utopia;
Technology—Rampant*

Battle for the Planet of the
Apes
Battle Queen 2020

Beneath the Planet of the
Apes
Chained Heat 3: Hell Moun-
tain
Cyborg
Double Dragon
The Element of Crime
First Spaceship on Venus
Nautilus
Planet of the Apes
Steel Dawn
Tank Girl
Terminator 2: Judgment Day
[2 SE]
Things to Come
Titan A.E.
Welcome II the Terrordome

Postwar
See also: Veterans

Born on the Fourth of July 2
Foolish Wives
Grave of the Fireflies
The Last Time I Saw Paris
Lilies of the Field
Mother Night
Plenty
Sunshine
A Walk in the Clouds

POW/MIA
*See also: Vietnam War; War,
General; World War II*

The Beast
The Bridge on the River Kwai
[LE]
The Brylcreem Boys
Missing in Action
Paradise Road

Pregnant Pauses
See also: Bringing Up Baby

All About My Mother
Beautiful People
Bellyfruit
Earthly Possessions
Falling for a Dancer
Father of the Bride Part II
Father's Little Dividend
Julien Donkey-boy
The Marquise of O
My Life
Nine Months
She's Having a Baby
A Single Girl
Solomon and Gaenor
Splendor
Turn It Up
A Walk in the Clouds
Way of the Gun
What Planet Are You From?
Where the Heart Is
Wonder Boys

Presidency
See also: Politics

Deterrence
Dick
Escape from New York
In the Line of Fire [2 SE]
The Kidnapping of the Presi-
dent
Meteor

Price of Fame
See also: Rags to Riches

Frances
It Could Happen to You
Mistress
Postcards from the Edge
Rocky [2 SE]
Shakes the Clown
A Star Is Born
Tucker: The Man and His
Dream

Princes/Princesses
See: Royalty

Prison
*See: Great Escapes; Men in
Prison; POW/MIA; Women in
Prison*

Private Eyes
The Maltese Falcon
The Right Temptation
Shaft in Africa
Shaft's Big Score

Prom
*See also: Hell High School;
School Daze*

Drive Me Crazy
Whatever It Takes

Propaganda
*See also: Patriotism & Para-
noia; Politics*

Alfred Hitchcock's Bon Voy-
age & Aventure Malgache
Blood on the Sun
Hangmen Also Die
Know Your Enemy: Japan
Reefer Madness
World War II

Prostitutes
See: Oldest Profession

Protests
See also: Rebel with a Cause

Born on the Fourth of July 2
Norma Rae
Panther

Psychiatry
See: Shrinks

Psycho-Thriller
*See also: Mystery & Sus-
pense*

Body Chemistry 2: Voice of a
Stranger
The Crush
Darkroom
Diabolique
Diary of a Serial Killer
Don't Answer the Phone
The Drifter
Eye of the Beholder
Fair Game
The 4th Floor
House of Games
Knight Moves
Mean Season
Midnight Tease / Midnight
Tease 2
Misery
The Most Dangerous Game
[Madacy]
Nightwatch
One Good Turn
Perfect Tenant
Postmortem
Secret Games
Seven [2 SE]
The Spiral Staircase
Suture
The Tie That Binds

Psychotics/Sociopaths
*See also: Roommates from
Hell*

Boxing Helena
The Boys Next Door
The Crush
Death Sentence
Dr. Giggles
Don't Answer the Phone
The Drifter
Fear City
From Dusk Till Dawn [2 CS]
In the Line of Fire [2 SE]
Killing Zoe
Mother's Boys
One Good Turn
The Rich Man's Wife
Scream 3 [CS]

Puppets
See also: Killer Toys; Toys

Bear in the Big Blue House:
Party Time with Bear
Bear in the Big Blue House:
Shapes, Sounds & Colors
Curse of the Puppet Master:
The Human Experiment
Puppet Master
Puppet Master 2
Puppet Master 4
Puppet Master 5: The Latest
Chapter
Retro Puppet Master
The Sound of Music [Five
Star Collection]

Pure Ego Vehicles
*See also: Big-Budget Bombs;
Rock Stars on Film*

Get Carter
Gummo

Mario Puzo
The Godfather DVD Collection
The Godfather, Part 2
The Godfather, Part 3

Queens
See: Royalty

Rabbits
Alice
Alice in Wonderland
Harvey
Mona Lisa
Monty Python and the Holy
Grail

Race Against Time
D.O.A. Roan
Fail-Safe
I'll Be Home for Christmas
In Pursuit of Honor
Nick of Time
Octopussy
Race Against Time
Somebody Has to Shoot the
Picture
Tycus

Radio
See also: Mass Media

The Fisher King
Midnight Confessions
Pot o' Gold
Talk Radio
The Truth about Cats and
Dogs

Rags to Riches
*See also: Price of Fame;
Wrong Side of the Tracks*

Annie
It Could Happen to You
Little Lord Fauntleroy
Meet John Doe [Image]
The Object of Beauty
The Prince and the Pauper
Pygmalion
Rocky [2 SE]
The Unsinkable Molly Brown
Working Girl

Rape
See also: Sexual Abuse

And Justice for All
Bandit Queen
Blackrock
Body Shots
Dead Man Walking
Death Wish
Divided We Stand
Gossip
Jackson County Jail
The Marquise of O
Necromancer: Satan's Ser-
vant
A Passage to India
Positive I.D.
Quiet Days in Hollywood
Titus

The Violent Years / Girl Gang

Rebel with a Cause
*See also: Rebel without a
Cause; The Resistance*

Alice's Restaurant
The Blob
Boyz N the Hood
Braveheart
The Fighter
The Firing Line
Foxfire
James Dean: Live Fast, Die
　Young
Lawrence of Arabia
Light It Up
Norma Rae
One-Eyed Jacks
A Raisin in the Sun
The Rock [Criterion]
The Sand Pebbles
The Scarlet Pimpernel
Somebody Has to Shoot the
　Picture
Tank Girl
True Believer

Rebel without a Cause
See also: Rebel with a Cause

The Boys Next Door
Cheech and Chong's Up in
　Smoke
Five Easy Pieces
Inventing the Abbotts
Kicked in the Head
Suburbia
Velocity
The Violent Years / Girl Gang
The Wild Angels

**Recycled
Footage/Redubbed
Dialogue**
Dead Men Don't Wear Plaid
The Legend of Drunken Mas-
　ter

Red Scare
See also: Russia/USSR

Tito and Me

Rehab
*See also: Drug Abuse; On the
Rocks*

Bounce
Jesus' Son
28 Days [SE]

Reincarnation
*See also: Death & the After-
life*

Angel on My Shoulder
Fluke
The Mummy [2 SE]
Switch

Religion
*See also: Islam; Judaism;
Missionaries; Nuns & Priests;
Religious Epics*

Anchoress
Breaking the Waves
Brother Cadfael: The Devil's
　Novice
Dead Man Walking
Dogma
The End of the Affair
Friendly Persuasion
The Godfather, Part 3
Greaser's Palace
The Greatest Story Ever Told
　[SE]
Jesus Christ Superstar
The Last Temptation of Christ
Left Behind: The Movie
The Loss of Sexual Inno-
　cence
A Man for All Seasons
The Other Side of Sunday
Picking Up the Pieces
The Quarry

Rain
Revelation
Romero
Tribulation
Wide Awake

Religious Epics
*See also: Bible Adaptations,
Religion*

Ben-Hur
Cleopatra
Demetrius and the Gladiators
In the Beginning...
Jesus
Noah's Ark
The Story of Jacob & Joseph

Ruth Rendell
Live Flesh

Renegade Body Parts
See also: Killer Brains

The Addams Family
Blood of Ghastly Horror
The Brain that Wouldn't Die
Evil Dead 2: Dead by Dawn [2
　THX]
Idle Hands
Picking Up the Pieces
The Thing with Two Heads

Repressed Men
See also: Men

American Beauty [SE]
Kiss the Sky
The Red Dwarf
Yi Yi

Rescue Missions
*See also: Rescue Missions
Involving Time Travel*

The Magnificent Seven
Missing in Action
Mission to Mars
Navy SEALS [MGM]
Red Planet
The Rescuers Down Under
The Rock [Criterion]
Rules of Engagement
The Secret of NIMH 2
Shanghai Noon
Stargate SG-1: Season 1
Submerged
Supernova
Toy Story
Toy Story 2
Uncommon Valor
Vertical Limit
The World Is Not Enough [SE]

**Rescue Missions
Involving Time Travel**
See also: Rescue Missions

Disney's The Kid
Frequency
The Navigator
Superman: The Movie
Terminator 2: Judgment Day
　[2 SE]

The Resistance
See also: World War II

Alfred Hitchcock's Bon Voy-
　age & Aventure Malgache
Hangmen Also Die
The Last Lieutenant
Soldier of Orange

Revealing Swimwear
Beach Girls
Horrors of Spider Island
Slumber Party Massacre 2

Revenge
See also: Vigilantes

All Dogs Go to Heaven
American Buffalo
Asylum
Banzai Runner
Black Scorpion
Bloodfist

Blue Tiger
Body Count
Broken Harvest
Coffy
Cold Sweat
The Contract
Creepshow 2
The Crow: Salvation
DaVinci's War
Dawn Rider / Trail Beyond
Deadbeat at Dawn
Death Wish
Dirty Work
Drop Zone
Fair Game
The Fall of the House of
　Usher
The Fighter
The Four Musketeers
Get Carter
Get Carter
Gladiator
The Godfather DVD Collection
The Godfather, Part 2
Hamlet
Hannibal
Hardcore and Fist
Heavy Metal 2000 [SE]
Highlander: Endgame
The Highway Man
The Indestructible Man / The
　Amazing Transparent Man
The Indian Tomb
Jack Frost 2: Revenge of the
　Mutant Killer Snowman
Lady Dragon
The Lady in White
Leon, the Professional
Live Flesh
The Man from Laramie
Manon of the Spring
Necromancer: Satan's Ser-
　vant
No Safe Haven
One-Eyed Jacks
One Man's Justice
Paper Bullets
The Patriot
Positive I.D.
Posse
Pumpkinhead
Puppet Master 3: Toulon's
　Revenge
Return of the Magnificent
　Seven
Ride with the Devil
Sharpe's Eagle
She-Freak
She Killed in Ecstasy
The Shooting
Slaughter's Big Ripoff
Sons of Katie Elder
Sour Grapes
Star Trek 2: The Wrath of
　Khan
Sweet Revenge
Thou Shalt Not Kill . . .
　Except
Titus
Truck Turner
Walking the Edge
Wild Bill
Wonder Man
Zombie Lake

Revolutionary War
The Patriot

Rio
Blame It on Rio
Bossa Nova
The Road to Rio

Road Trip
*See also: Bikers; Checkered
Flag; Motor Vehicle Dept.*

The Adventures of Priscilla,
　Queen of the Desert
　[MGM]
Beautiful Joe
Because of You
Beethoven's 3rd

Bustin' Loose
Cannonball Run
Chasers
Crazy in Alabama
The Daytrippers
The Delivery
Detour
Diamonds
Earthly Possessions
Eye of the Beholder
From Dusk Till Dawn [2 CS]
Get On the Bus
Guantanamera
Hard Core Logo
Heaven's Burning
The Highway Man
I'll Be Home for Christmas
Jerome
Lewis and Clark and George
Lolita
Lost in America
Natural Born Killers [DC]
Nurse Betty
Planes, Trains & Automobiles
Play It to the Bone
Ride in the Whirlwind
Road Movie
The Road to Bali
The Road to El Dorado
The Road to Rio
Road Trip
Something Wild
The Straight Story
Strawberry Fields

Robots & Androids
*See also: Technology—Ram-
pant*

Alien: Resurrection
The Astro-Zombies
Bicentennial Man
Cyborg
Dr. Goldfoot and the Bikini
　Machine
Edward Scissorhands [SE]
Kronos
Neon Genesis Evangelion
　Collection
Robot Monster
Robotech: First Contact
Runaway
Terminator 2: Judgment Day
　[2 SE]

Rock Stars on Film
*See also: Concert Films; Mar-
tyred Pop Icons; Pure Ego
Vehicles*

The Beatles: The Ultimate
　DVD Collection
Frankie and Johnny
The Harder They Come
The Last Temptation of Christ
Lock, Stock and 2 Smoking
　Barrels
Moonlight and Valentino
No Looking Back
Poetic Justice
Runaway
That'll Be the Day
Tommy
Traveller

Rodeos
See also: Westerns

Man from Utah / Sagebrush
　Trail
The Misfits

Rodgers & Hammerstein
The Sound of Music [Five
　Star Collection]

Role Reversal
See also: Gender Bending

Angel on My Shoulder
The Bank Dick
Desperately Seeking Susan
Doctor Dolittle
La Femme Nikita [MGM]
The Prince and the Pauper

The Scarlet Pimpernel
Switch
Tootsie
Wonder Man

Romance
*See: Late Bloomin' Love;
Lovers on the Lam;
May–December Romance;
Romantic Adventures; Roman-
tic Comedy; Romantic Drama;
Romantic Triangles*

Romantic Adventures
Back to God's Country /
　Something New
Crouching Tiger, Hidden Drag-
　on
The Last of the Mohicans
Pocahontas
Something New

Romantic Comedy
Almost Famous
The Apartment
The Arrangement
Baby Boom
Beautiful Joe
Bedrooms and Hallways
Benny & Joon
Blame It on Rio
Bossa Nova
Boys and Girls
Chasing Amy
Coming Soon
A Couch in New York
Defending Your Life
Desperately Seeking Susan
Dish Dogs
Dr. T & the Women
Down to You
Drive Me Crazy
Eat Your Heart Out
Fever Pitch
The First to Go
Forever Together
High Fidelity
How to Marry a Millionaire
I Know Where I'm Going
If Lucy Fell
It Could Happen to You
Keeping the Faith
Kiss Shot
Look Who's Talking, Too
Love by Appointment
Love Stinks
Lovers and Liars
Love's Labour's Lost
Loving Jezebel
The Man Who Loved Women
Manhattan
Married to the Mob
Mr. Wonderful
My Sex Life...Or How I Got
　into an Argument
The New Eve
Next Stop, Wonderland
Nice Guys Sleep Alone
Nothin' 2 Lose
The Pallbearer
Paris Holiday
Party
Pat and Mike
Pick a Card
Playing Mona Lisa
The Pompatus of Love
Prelude to a Kiss
Quackser Fortune Has a
　Cousin in the Bronx
Relative Values
Return to Me
Roxanne
Seven Girlfriends
The Seven Year Itch
She's Having a Baby
She's the One
Something More
Son of Gascogne
The Souler Opposite
Splash
Splendor
A Summer's Tale

The Taming of the Shrew
The Tao of Steve
That Touch of Mink
That Uncertain Feeling [Sling-Shot]
Threesome
Tom Jones [MGM]
The Truth about Cats and Dogs
Two If by Sea
What Women Want
Whatever It Takes
When Harry Met Sally... [SE]
Whipped
Wishful Thinking
Woman on Top
Working Girl

Romantic Drama
An Affair of Love
An Affair to Remember
Against All Odds
Alice
All the Pretty Horses
Anna Karenina
Beyond the Clouds
Blood and Sand
Bounce
The Bridge
Brief Encounter
The Brylcreem Boys
Camille Claudel
Carmen / The Cheat
Catherine Cookson's The Secret
Children of a Lesser God
Come and Get It
The Cutting Edge
Cyrano de Bergerac
Desert Hearts
Desert Winds
End of the Affair
The End of the Affair
Eternal Love
Evangeline
Falling for a Dancer
The Far Pavilions
A Farewell to Arms
Fire
Ghost
Girl in Black
Here on Earth
Ice Castles
Iguana
Inventing the Abbotts
Kiss of Fire
La Separation
The Last Time I Saw Paris
Legends of the Fall [2 SE]
Loulou
Love Affair
Love After Love
Love Letters
The Loves of Carmen
Mansfield Park
Marty
Mississippi Mermaid
Mr. Jones
Monsoon
No Looking Back
Northanger Abbey
Of Human Bondage
An Officer and a Gentleman
A Paper Wedding
The Perfect Husband
Picnic
Plain Jane
Poetic Justice
Portrait of Jennie
Portraits Chinois
Romper Stomper [SE]
A Room with a View
Rouge
Running out of Time
The Serpent's Kiss
Solomon and Gaenor
Stella
Street Scene
Tender Mercies
Timeless
Tonight or Never
Twin Falls Idaho

Two Moon Junction
Untamed Heart
A Walk in the Clouds
The Way We Were [SE]
We'll Meet Again
Winter People

Romantic Triangles
See also: Otherwise Engaged

The Brylcreem Boys
The Cook, the Thief, His Wife & Her Lover
Diabolique
End of the Affair
The End of the Affair
Forever Mine
Grind
Here on Earth
It Could Happen to You
Keeping the Faith
Kiss the Sky
The Last of the Mohicans
Legends of the Fall [2 SE]
The Married Virgin
Mo' Better Blues
The Pallbearer
Plain Jane
Play It to the Bone
Portraits Chinois
Quiet Days in Hollywood
A Room with a View
The Serpent's Kiss
She's So Lovely
Simpatico
Something More
Splendor
Stella
Threesome
The Truth about Cats and Dogs
The Whole Nine Yards

Rome—Ancient
See also: Historical Drama; Italy

Attila
Ben-Hur
Cleopatra
Demetrius and the Gladiators
Fellini Satyricon
Gladiator
Gladiators: Bloodsport of the Colosseum
I, Claudius
Spartacus [Criterion]
Titus

Rome—Modern
See also: Italy

The Frightened Woman
The Godfather, Part 3
The Stendahl Syndrome
The Talented Mr. Ripley

Roommates from Hell
See also: Psychotics/Sociopaths

Malice [MGM]
Perfect Tenant

Royalty
See also: Historical Drama; Medieval Romps; Period Piece; Royalty, British; Royalty, Russian

Anna and the King
The Black Cauldron
Cleopatra
Dune
The Emperor and the Assassin
The Emperor's New Groove [SE]
Farinelli
Gladiator
The Indian Tomb
Jason and the Argonauts
Love's Labour's Lost
The Prince and the Pauper
Princess Caraboo
Shanghai Noon

Titus

Royalty, British
See also: Great Britain; Historical Drama; Medieval Romps; Period Piece; Royalty

Braveheart
Henry V
The Lion in Winter
The Madness of King George
A Man for All Seasons

Royalty, Russian
See also: Historical Drama; Medieval Romps; Period Piece; Royalty; Russia/USSR

Scarlet Empress

Damon Runyon
Guys and Dolls

Russia/USSR
See also: Moscow; Red Scare, St. Petersburg

Citizen X
Dersu Uzala
East-West
Gorky Park
Laser Mission
Love and Death
Mother and Son
Scarlet Empress
The Thief

Russian (Production)
Beshkempir the Adopted Son
Dead Waters
Dersu Uzala
Masters of Russian Animation, Vol. 2
Masters of Russian Animation, Vol. 3
Masters of Russian Animation, Vol. 4
Mother and Son
Sergei Eisenstein: Autobiography
The Thief

Sail Away
See also: Deep Blue; Go Fish; Killer Sea Critters; Mutiny; Scuba; Shipwrecked; Submarines

An Affair to Remember
Away All Boats
Beat the Devil
The Bounty
Damn the Defiant
Escape under Pressure
Final Voyage
The Great Lover
Jason and the Argonauts
Jaws [CE]
Love Affair
The Perfect Storm
The Sand Pebbles
The Talented Mr. Ripley
Titanic 2000
The Unsinkable Molly Brown

St. Peterburg (Russia)
See also: Russia/USSR

Anna Karenina
Onegin

Salespeople
See also: Corporate Shenanigans

The Big Kahuna
Breakfast of Champions
A Good Baby

San Francisco
See also: Earthquakes

All Dogs Go to Heaven 2
Big Trouble in Little China [SE]
The Conversation
Groove
The Maltese Falcon

Nine Months
Playing Mona Lisa
Rated X
The Rock [Criterion]
Woman on Top

Sanity Check
See also: Doctors & Nurses; Hospitals & Medicine; Shrinks

Aguirre, the Wrath of God
American Psycho
Arsenic and Old Lace
Asylum
Asylum of Terror
A Blade in the Dark
Body Chemistry
Boxing Helena
Brain Dead
Bringing Out the Dead
Camille Claudel
Cecil B. Demented
The Cell
The Confession
Cotton Mary
Crazy in Alabama
Darkroom
Dementia 13
Die Screaming, Marianne
Dr. Frankenstein's Castle of Freaks
Dr. Strangelove, or: How I Learned to Stop Worrying and Love the Bomb [2 SE]
Don't Go in the House
Don't Mess with My Sister!
Endless Night
Eye of the Beholder
The Fall of the House of Usher
The Fisher King
The 4th Man
Frances
Girl, Interrupted
Hannibal
Harvey
Interiors
Joe Gould's Secret
Julien Donkey-boy
Lilian's Story
Lower Level
Macabre
Mr. Jones
Murder in the First
Nurse Betty
The Perfect Nanny
The Pit and the Pendulum
Scarlet Empress
Screw Loose
Seven Days in May
Sisters
The Story of Adele H.
Stuart Saves His Family
Titus
What about Bob?
A Woman under the Influence

Satanism
See also: Demons & Wizards; Devils; Occult

Bless the Child
Damien: Omen 2
The Devil Rides Out
A Little Bit of Soul
Lost Souls
Necromancer: Satan's Servant
The Ninth Gate
The Omen [SE]
Omen 3: The Final Conflict
Rosemary's Baby
The Sentinel
Warlock: The Armageddon

Satire & Parody
See also: Black Comedy; Comedy; Genre Spoofs

Aftershock
Airplane!
Airplane 2: The Sequel
American Psycho
The Apartment

Bamboozled
Bananas
Beautiful
Being There
Best in Show
Big Deal on Madonna Street
The Big Tease
Big Trouble in Little China [SE]
Bob Roberts [SE]
The Bogus Witch Project
Breakfast of Champions
But I'm a Cheerleader
Canadian Bacon
Candy
Cecil B. Demented
Cherry Falls / Terror Tract
Dead Men Don't Wear Plaid
Diary of a Chambermaid
Dick
The Discreet Charm of the Bourgeoisie
Forgotten Silver
Gentlemen Prefer Blondes
Greaser's Palace
Hard Core Logo
High School High
I'm Gonna Git You Sucka
Intern
Love and Death
Monty Python and the Holy Grail
The Mouse on the Moon
The Naked Gun: From the Files of Police Squad
Naked Gun 33 1/3: The Final Insult
Naked Gun 2 1/2: The Smell of Fear
Natural Born Killers [DC]
Northanger Abbey
The Nutty Professor
The Princess Bride
The Rocky Horror Picture Show
Scary Movie
Scream 3 [CS]
Scrooged
Search and Destroy
Shriek If You Know What I Did Last Friday the 13th
Sleeper
The Specials
Straight to Hell
Tapeheads
This Is Spinal Tap [MGM]
Three Businessmen
Weather Woman

Savannah
The Legend of Bagger Vance

Savants
See also: Mental Retardation

Being There
Doctor Dolittle

Scams, Stings & Cons
See also: Heists

American Buffalo
Beautiful Joe
Circus
The Conversation
Cotton Comes to Harlem
Croupier
F/X
F/X 2: The Deadly Art of Illusion
House of Games
Il Bidone
The Lemon Drop Kid
Lock, Stock and 2 Smoking Barrels
Love Kills
No Way Out
The Parallax View
The Road to El Dorado
The Settlement
Simpatico
Six Degrees of Separation

Support Your Local Gunfighter

Tootsie

Traveller

Where the Money Is

White Men Can't Jump

School Daze
See also: Campus Capers; Hell High School

All I Wanna Do
Around the Fire
Back to School
Black Narcissus
Blue Ridge Fall
Children of a Lesser God
Diabolique
Doctor Dolittle
Drive Me Crazy
Eden
Finding Forrester
High School High
Idle Hands
Liberty Heights
The Little Princess
Music of the Heart [CS]
My Teacher's Wife
187
Porky's / Porky's 2: The Next Day
Save the Last Dance
The Substitute 4: Failure Is Not an Option
Whatever It Takes

Arthur Schnitzler
Affairs of Anatol

Sci Fi
See also: Anime; Comedy Sci-Fi; Fantasy; Sci-Fi Westerns

Aftershock
Alien Nation
Alien: Resurrection
The Asphyx
The Astounding She-Monster
The Astro-Zombies
Attack of the Giant Leeches
Barb Wire
Battle beyond the Stars
Battle for the Planet of the Apes
Battle Queen 2020
The Beast of Yucca Flats
Beneath the Planet of the Apes
Bicentennial Man
Black Scorpion
The Blob
The Brain from Planet Arous
Brainstorm
Bubblegum Crisis Tokyo 2040
Cat Women of the Moon
Cherry 2000
Close Encounters of the Third Kind [CE]
The Colony
Communion [CE]
Conquest of the Planet of the Apes
The Cosmic Man
Cyborg
Darkdrive
Darkside Blues
The Day the Earth Caught Fire
Deepstar Six
Dinosaurus!
Dr. Goldfoot and the Bikini Machine
Donovan's Brain
Dune
The Element of Crime
Embryo
Escape from New York
Escape from the Planet of the Apes
Fantastic Voyage
The Fantasy Worlds of Irwin Allen

Farscape, Vol. 2
Farscape, Vol. 3
Femalien
Femalien 2
Fiend without a Face
First Spaceship on Venus
Flash Gordon: Space Soldiers
Flesh Gordon 2: Flesh Gordon Meets the Cosmic Cheerleaders
The Fly / Return of the Fly
The Fly / The Fly 2
The Fly 2
The Flying Saucer
Four Sided Triangle
Freejack
Frequency
Girl Explores Girl: The Alien Encounter [CE]
Gorgo
The Gospel According to Philip K. Dick
The Groundstar Conspiracy
Heavy Metal 2000 [SE]
Inseminoid
Isaac Asimov's Nightfall
Kronos
Krull [SE]
The Lathe of Heaven
Leprechaun 4: In Space
Lolida 2000
The Man from Planet X
Mesa of Lost Women
Missile to the Moon
Monster from Green Hell
Neon Genesis Evangelion Collection
Not of This Earth
Nude on the Moon
Parasite
The Phantom Planet
The Philadelphia Experiment
Pitch Black
Plan 9 from Outer Space [Passport Video]
Planet of the Apes
Predator [20th Century Fox]
Project A-ko
Quatermass 2
Race Against Time
Return of the Fly
Robot Monster
Robotech: First Contact
Rocketship X-M
Runaway
Shadow Raiders, Vol. 1: Uncommon Hero
Sol Bianca: The Legacy
Star Trek 2: The Wrath of Khan
Stargate SG-1: Season 1
The Stranger from Venus
Swamp Thing
Teenage Monster
Teenagers from Outer Space
10th Victim
Terminator 2: Judgment Day [2 SE]
Things to Come
The Time Machine
Timelock
Titan A.E.
A Town Has Turned to Dust
Velocity Trap
Village of the Giants
Voyage to the Bottom of the Sea / Fantastic Voyage
The Womaneater
The X-Files: Season One [CE]
The X-Files: Season Two
X: The Man with X-Ray Eyes
Xchange
Zardoz

Sci-Fi Westerns
See also: Sci Fi; Westerns

Battle beyond the Stars
Teenage Monster

Science & Scientists
See also: Genetics; Inventors & Inventions; Mad Scientists

Beach Party
Dead Men Don't Wear Plaid
The Dead Next Door
Die, Monster, Die!
Doctor Dolittle
Fantastic Voyage
The Fly / Return of the Fly
The Fly / The Fly 2
The Fly 2
Four Sided Triangle
Jurassic Park [CE]
A Little Bit of Soul
The Lost World: Jurassic Park 2 [CE]
Mary Reilly
Return of the Fly
The Rocky Horror Picture Show
Smilla's Sense of Snow
Spaceways
Swamp Thing
Things to Come

Scotland
See also: Great Britain

Braveheart
Breaking the Waves
Deacon Brodie
Highlander: Endgame
I Know Where I'm Going
Local Hero
Ring of Bright Water

Screwball Comedy
See also: Comedy; Romantic Comedy; Slapstick Comedy

Assault of the Party Nerds
Back to School
Everything You Always Wanted to Know about Sex (But Were Afraid to Ask)
The Gay Deceivers
Harvey
The Marriage Circle
The Munsters' Revenge
My Favorite Brunette
Some Like It Hot [SE]
Wonder Boys

Scuba
See also: Deep Blue

The Big Blue [DC]
Men of Honor
Navy SEALS [MGM]

Sculptors
See also: Art & Artists

A Bucket of Blood
Camille Claudel

Sea Disasters
See also: Air Disasters; Deep Blue; Disaster Flicks; Ship-wrecked

Deepstar Six
Men of Honor
The Unsinkable Molly Brown

Serial Killers
See also: Crime & Criminals; Crime Sprees

American Psycho
The Apostate
The Awful Dr. Orlof
Black & White
The Cell
Cherry Falls / Terror Tract
Citizen X
Cold Blooded
The Coroner
The Crimson Code
Delivered
Diary of a Serial Killer
The Element of Crime
Eye of the Beholder
Eye of the Killer
Eyes of Laura Mars
Frequency
The Girl Who Knew Too Much
Hangman
Hannibal

Hideaway
Inhumanity
Mercy
The Minus Man
Natural Born Killers [DC]
Nightwatch
Nightwatch
Postmortem
The Prophet's Game
Scary Movie
Scream 3 [CS]
Seven [2 SE]
The Stendahl Syndrome
Vice Girls
The Watcher

Serials
Flash Gordon: Space Soldiers
Shadow of Chinatown
Shadow of the Eagle

Sex & Sexuality
See also: Erotic Thrillers; Pornography; Sex on the Beach; Sexploitation

The Adjuster
An Affair of Love
Affairs of Anatol
Alfie
American Beauty [SE]
Angel Blue
Animal Instincts
The Apartment
Battle of the Sexes
Beach Girls
Black & White
Blaze Starr Goes Nudist
Body Shots
Boxing Helena
Breaking the Waves
Butterfield 8
Chasing Amy
Cheech and Chong's Up in Smoke
Cherry Falls / Terror Tract
Cherry 2000
Chuck & Buck
Class
Coming Soon
Cry Uncle
Dance with the Devil
Diary of a Chambermaid
Double Suicide
Everything You Always Wanted to Know about Sex (But Were Afraid to Ask)
Farinelli
Fast Times at Ridgemont High
Female Vampire
Femalien
Femalien 2
Fire
The 4th Man
Frenzy
Gentlemen Prefer Blondes
Gilda
Girl
God's Comedy
Gothic
Holy Smoke
Humanity
Ilsa, Harem Keeper of the Oil Sheiks
Immoral Tales
Inventing the Abbotts
Just Looking
The Ladies Man
Last Resort
L'Ennui
The Life of Jesus
The Lifestyle
Lolida 2000
Lolita
The Loss of Sexual Innocence
Loulou
Love After Love
Love Letters
Magnolia
The Man Who Loved Women
Mirror, Mirror 3: The Voyeur

Mo' Better Blues
My Sex Life...Or How I Got into an Argument
My Teacher's Wife
The Passion of Ayn Rand
Picnic
Quiet Days in Hollywood
Rain
Rambling Rose [2 SE]
Red Shoe Diaries: Four on the Floor
Red Shoe Diaries: Luscious Lola
Red Shoe Diaries: Strip Poker
Red Shoe Diaries: Swimming Naked
The Right Temptation
The Rocky Horror Picture Show
The Rowdy Girls
The '70s
Sex and the City: The Complete Second Season
Sextette
She Killed in Ecstasy
Tom Jones [MGM]
Turkish Delight
Ultimate Attraction
Venus in Furs
A View to a Kill [SE]
What Planet Are You From?
Winter Sleepers
A Woman, Her Men and Her Futon
Women on the Verge of a Nervous Breakdown
Working Girls

Sex on the Beach
See also: Island Fare

Against All Odds
Airplane!
The Beach

Sexcapades
Blue Velvet
Candy
The Cook, the Thief, His Wife & Her Lover
8 1/2 Women
The Erotic Adventures of Zorro
Fellini Satyricon
The First 9 1/2 Weeks
Four Times That Night
The Frightened Woman
Kiss the Sky
Tie Me Up! Tie Me Down!
Two Moon Junction
Up in Mabel's Room
Whipped

Sexploitation
See also: Erotic Thrillers; Exploitation

Another Day, Another Man
Bad Girls Go to Hell / Another Day, Another Man
Battle of the Amazons
The Beast That Killed Women / The Monster of Camp Sunshine
Best of Intimate Sessions: Vol. 2
The Big Doll House
The Curious Dr. Humpp
Cyberotica
Emmanuelle: First Contact
Emmanuelle in Space: A World of Desire
The Erotic Ghost
Erotic Survivor
The Erotic Witch Project [CE]
Erotic Witch Project 2: Book of Seduction
Fallen Angel
Flesh Gordon 2: Flesh Gordon Meets the Cosmic Cheerleaders
Fruits of Passion: The Story of "O" Continued

Girl Explores Girl: The Alien
    Encounter [CE]
Gladiator Eroticus
Go, Go Second Time Virgin
The Head Mistress
H.O.T.S.
I Like the Girls Who Do
Ilsa, She-Wolf of the SS
Ilsa, the Wicked Warden
In the Flesh / Blood Bullets
    Buffoons
Inn of 1000 Sins
Mistress Frankenstein [CE]
Mistress of Seduction
The Monster of Camp Sun-
    shine
Naked Killer
Nude on the Moon
Passion & Romance: Double
    or Nothing
Passion & Romance: Scandal
Scandal: The Big Turn On
Scum of the Earth
Sex Files: Ancient Desires
Sex Files: Digital Sex
Slumber Party Massacre 3
Space-Thing
The Story of O: The Series
Teaserama
Tender Flesh
Vamps: Deadly Dreamgirls
Varietease
Wham-Bam, Thank You
    Spaceman

Sexual Abuse
    *See also: Rape; Spousal
    Abuse*

The Bed You Sleep In
Boxing Helena
Ilsa, Harem Keeper of the Oil
    Sheiks
Mesmerized
Romper Stomper [SE]

Sexual Harrassment
Foxfire

William Shakespeare
Hamlet
Hamlet
Henry V
Love's Labour's Lost
Silent Shakespeare
The Taming of the Shrew
Titus

George Bernard Shaw
Pygmalion

Sam Shepard
Simpatico

Ships
    *See: Deep Blue; Mutiny; Sail
    Away; Shipwrecked; Sub-
    marines*

Shipwrecked
    See also: Sea Disasters

Dead of Night
The Most Dangerous Game
    [Madacy]
Princess Caraboo

Shops & Shopping
Attention Shoppers
Where the Heart Is

Showbiz Comedy
Bamboozled
Comic Act
Galaxy Quest
Postcards from the Edge
The Real Blonde
The Souler Opposite
Tapeheads
There's No Business Like
    Show Business

Showbiz Dramas
The Audrey Hepburn Story
The Barefoot Contessa
The Cradle Will Rock

For the Boys
Frances
I'm Losing You
Isn't She Great
James Dean: Live Fast, Die
    Young
The Next Step
Postcards from the Edge
Shadow of the Vampire
A Star Is Born
Time Code
Topsy Turvy

Showbiz Musicals
    *See also: Musical Fantasy;
    Musicals; Showbiz Comedy*

There's No Business Like
    Show Business

Showbiz Thrillers
F/X
F/X 2: The Deadly Art of Illu-
    sion
The House of Seven Corpses

Shrinks
    *See also: Doctors & Nurses;
    Sanity Check*

Body Chemistry 2: Voice of a
    Stranger
The Cell
A Couch in New York
The Evening Star
Gun Shy
Hangman
House of Games
If Lucy Fell
Mercy
Mr. Jones
The Myth of Fingerprints
Stuart Saves His Family
The Watcher
Wilderness

Shutterbugs
    See also: Front Page

Darkroom
Don't Answer the Phone
Eyes of Laura Mars
Footsteps
Joe Gould's Secret
The Portrait
Rear Window
Somebody Has to Shoot the
    Picture
The Truth about Cats and
    Dogs
The Watcher

Silent Films
Burlesque on Carmen
Buster Keaton Rides Again /
    The Railrodder
The Cheat
Destiny
Evangeline
Fall of the House of Usher
Foolish Wives
Headin' Home
The Last of the Mohicans
The Lost World [Image]
The Marriage Circle
Nosferatu 2
Outside the Law / Shadows
Shadows
The Vanishing American

Neil Simon
The Odd Couple

Single Parents
    *See also: Bringing Up Baby;
    Parenthood*

Air Bud 2: Golden Receiver
All About My Mother
Baby Boom
Beautiful
Dancer in the Dark
Double Parked
Erin Brockovich
Girlfight
Life According to Muriel

Music of the Heart [CS]
Rugrats in Paris: The Movie
The Tic Code
Where the Heart Is

Singles
    See also: Dates from Hell

Mr. Wonderful
Mystic Pizza
That Touch of Mink
When Harry Met Sally... [SE]

The '60s
    See: Period Piece: 1960s

Skateboarding
Gummo Skating

Skating
    See also: Hockey

The Cutting Edge
Ice Castles

Skiing
Downhill Willie

Skinheads
    *See also: Nazis & Other Para-
    military Slugs*

Romper Stomper [SE]
The Substitute 4: Failure Is
    Not an Option
White Lies

Skydiving
Cutaway
Drop Zone

Slapstick Comedy
    *See also: Comedy; Screwball
    Comedy*

Abbott and Costello Meet
    Frankenstein
Africa Screams / Jack and
    the Beanstalk
Amos and Andrew
At War with the Army
The Bank Dick
Beethoven
Buster Keaton Rides Again /
    The Railrodder
Cheech and Chong: Still
    Smokin'
Cheech and Chong's Up in
    Smoke
The Flying Deuces / Utopia
The Great Lover
Jack & the Beanstalk
Mr. Hulot's Holiday
Railrodder
The Three Stooges: All the
    World's a Stooge
The Three Stooges: Merry
    Mavericks
The Three Stooges: Nutty but
    Nice
The Three Stooges: Spook
    Louder
Utopia [Digital Disc]
W.C. Fields 6 Short Films
The Whole Nine Yards

Slavery
    See also: Civil Rights

The Arena
Gladiator
Race to Freedom: The Story
    of the Underground Rail-
    road
Ride with the Devil
Shaft in Africa
Spartacus [Criterion]
A Woman Called Moses

Smuggler's Blues
    *See also: Crime & Criminals;
    Drug Abuse*

Tha Eastsidaz
Essex Boys
2 G's and a Key

Snakes
    See also: Wild Kingdom

Lewis and Clark and George
Natural Born Killers [DC]
Python

Soccer
Air Bud 3: World Pup
Bossa Nova
Fever Pitch

**South African
(Production)**
The Quarry

South America
    See also: Central America

Aguirre, the Wrath of God
Bananas
The Emerald Forest
Johnny 100 Pesos
Only Angels Have Wings
Ratas, Ratones, Rateros
Saludos Amigos
The Three Caballeros

Southern Belles
    See also: American South

Nashville
Steel Magnolias

Space Operas
    *See also: Alien Beings—
    Benign; Alien Beings—Vicious*

Battle beyond the Stars
Cat Women of the Moon
First Spaceship on Venus
Inseminoid
Laser Mission
Mission to Mars
The Mouse on the Moon
Nude on the Moon
Planet of the Apes
Red Planet
Robotech: First Contact
Rocketship X-M
Space Cowboys
Star Trek 2: The Wrath of
    Khan
Supernova
Titan A.E.
Velocity Trap

Spain
The Grandfather
Live Flesh
Running out of Time
Tierra

Spanish (Production)
All About My Mother
The Awful Dr. Orlof
Bad Man's River
Battle of the Amazons
Butterfly
Cut Throats Nine
Dance with the Devil
Dracula vs. Frankenstein
Escape from Hell
Female Vampire
Goya in Bordeaux
The Grandfather
Hatchet for the Honeymoon
Live Flesh
The Ninth Gate
Oasis of the Zombies
Pancho Villa
The Perfect Husband
Running out of Time
Secrets of the Heart
She Killed in Ecstasy
Tender Flesh
Tie Me Up! Tie Me Down!
Tierra
Women on the Verge of a
    Nervous Breakdown
Zombie Lake

Spies & Espionage
    *See also: Feds; Foreign
    Intrigue; Terrorism*

The Adventures of Rocky &
    Bullwinkle
Alfred Hitchcock's Bon Voy-
    age & Aventure Malgache
The Art of War
Black Eagle
Bulldog Drummond Escapes
Diamonds Are Forever [SE]
Fire over England
From Russia with Love [2 SE]
The Groundstar Conspiracy
Hillbillys in a Haunted House
I Spy
The Impossible Spy
The Inside Man
The Kid with the X-Ray Eyes
Laser Mission
The Living Daylights
Mission: Impossible 2
Mother Night
My Favorite Brunette
No Way Out
North by Northwest
Octopussy
Saboteur
Topaz
Torn Curtain
A View to a Kill [SE]
You Only Live Twice [SE]

Sports
    *See: Baseball; Basketball;
    Boxing; Football; Golf; Hockey;
    The Olympics; Scuba; Skating;
    Skiing; Skydiving; Soccer;
    Sports Comedy; Sports Dra-
    mas; Surfing; Swimming*

Sports Comedy
Air Bud 2
Air Bud 2: Golden Receiver
Air Bud 3: World Pup
The Boys
Downhill Willie
Fever Pitch
The Longest Yard
Mystery, Alaska
National Lampoon's Golf
    Punks
Necessary Roughness
North Dallas Forty
Pat and Mike
The Replacements
Semi-Tough
White Men Can't Jump

Sports Dramas
Any Given Sunday
The Big Blue [DC]
Brian's Song
The Cutting Edge
Eight Men Out
Fight for the Title
For Love of the Game
Gladiator
Ice Castles
The Joe Louis Story
The Legend of Bagger Vance
The Natural
Price of Glory
Remember the Titans
Rocky [2 SE]
Rudy [SE]
Soul of the Game
Youngblood

Spousal Abuse
    See also: Sexual Abuse

Honey & Ashes
Mesmerized

Stagestruck
    *See also: Showbiz Comedy;
    Showbiz Dramas; Showbiz
    Thrillers*

The Cradle Will Rock
Illuminata
Kiss Me, Guido
The Next Step
Topsy Turvy

Stalked!
See also: Obsessive Love

Chuck & Buck

Star Gazing
Local Hero
Roxanne

Stepparents
See also: Family Ties; Parenthood

Home for Christmas
The Stepdaughter

Robert Louis Stevenson
Robert Louis Stevenson's
The Game of Death
Strange Case of Dr. Jekyll &
Mr. Hyde

Stewardesses
See also: Airborne

Airplane!
Passenger 57

Bram Stoker
Bram Stoker's Shadowbuilder
Dracula / Strange Case of Dr.
Jekyll & Mr. Hyde
Nosferatu 2

Stolen from Asia
The Magnificent Seven

Stolen from Europe
Nightwatch
A Walk in the Clouds

Stolen from France
Blame It on Rio
Diabolique
Nine Months
Under Suspicion

Storytelling
The Princess Bride

Strained Suburbia
See also: Yuppie Nightmares

American Beauty [SE]
The Amityville Horror
Amos and Andrew
Blue Velvet
Coneheads
Crime and Punishment in
Suburbia
Don't Tell Mom the Babysitter's Dead
Edward Scissorhands [SE]
Grand Canyon
Gummo
Jaws [CE]
Next Friday [Platinum Series]
The Virgin Suicides
The Whole Nine Yards

Strippers
Dogma
From Dusk Till Dawn [2 CS]
Kiss of Fire
Midnight Tease / Midnight
Tease 2
Midnight Tease 2
Striptease

Struggling Musicians
Mo' Better Blues
Tender Mercies
This Is Spinal Tap [MGM]

Stupid Is...
Being There
The Dinner Game
Drowning Mona
Fast Times at Ridgemont
High
Idle Hands
Little Nicky
Lock, Stock and 2 Smoking
Barrels
Mr. Accident
The Nutty Professor
Ready to Rumble
Road Trip

Submarines
See also: Deep Blue

The Inside Man
Nautilus
Octopus
U-571 [CE]
Voyage to the Bottom of the
Sea / Fantastic Voyage
You Only Live Twice [SE]

Subways
See also: Trains

Next Stop, Wonderland
The Taking of Pelham One
Two Three
The Warriors

Suicide
*See also: Death & the After-
life*

The Curve
Double Suicide
The End
Harold and Maude
Maborosi
The Pallbearer
Robert Louis Stevenson's
The Game of Death
The Virgin Suicides

Summer Camp
Blaze Starr Goes Nudist
Bloody Murder
But I'm a Cheerleader
Friday the 13th, Part 3
Friday the 13th, Part 4: The
Final Chapter
Mother's Day [DC]
Sleepaway Camp

Super Heroes
Batman: Mask of the Phantasm
Black Scorpion
Bubblegum Crisis Tokyo
2040
Cartoon Crazys Comic Book
Heroes
The Complete Superman Collection
The Specials
Supergirl
Superman: The Movie
Superman 2
Superman 3
Superman 4: The Quest for
Peace
Turbo: A Power Rangers
Movie
X-Men
X-Men: The Phoenix Saga

Supernatural Comedy
See also: Comedy

Bedazzled [SE]
Dear Santa
The Devil & Max Devlin
Hillbillys in a Haunted House
Saturday the 14th
Saturday the 14th Strikes
Back
Topper Returns
Wishful Thinking

Supernatural Horror
*See also: Bloody Mayhem;
Classic Horror; Horror Come-
dy; Supernatural Comedy*

The Amityville Horror
Asylum of Terror
Attack of the Puppet People
The Black Cat
Bless the Child
Book of Shadows: Blair Witch
2
The Crow: Salvation
Damien: Omen 2
Dead and Buried
Dead Are Alive
Death Mask
The Devil Rides Out

Die, Monster, Die!
Dr. Frankenstein's Castle of
Freaks
Doctor Phibes Rises Again
Evil Dead Trap
Female Vampire
From Dusk Till Dawn [2 CS]
Giant from the Unknown
Hellraiser 2
The Horrible Dr. Bones
Horror Hotel
The House by the Cemetery
[Diamond]
The House by the Cemetery
[Anchor Bay]
The House of Seven Corpses
Ice from the Sun
The Indestructible Man / The
Amazing Transparent Man
Kwaidan
Lost Souls
Manhattan Baby
Mirror, Mirror
The Mummy's Shroud
Necromancer: Satan's Ser-
vant
The Omen [SE]
Omen 3: The Final Conflict
Omen 4: The Awakening
Parasite
Pet Sematary
Premonition
Psychomania
Pumpkinhead
Spooky Encounters
Unspeakable
Vampyros Lesbos
The Vault
Voodoo Academy [DC]
The Whip and the Body
The Witches

**Supernatural Martial
Arts**
Zu: Warriors of the Magic
Mountain

Surfing
*See also: Beach Blanket
Bingo*

Beach Blanket Bingo
Beach Party
Bikini Beach
Blackrock
In God's Hands
Slippery When Wet
Surfing Hollow Days

Survival
*See also: Hunted!; Negative
Utopia; Post Apocalypse*

Battlefield Earth
The Bridge on the River Kwai
[LE]
Castaway
Cliffhanger [2 CS]
The Colony
Escape from Hell
Grave of the Fireflies
Heaven and Earth
The Most Dangerous Game
[Madacy]
Pitch Black
Seven Days in May
Sniper
White Wolves 3: Cry of the
White Wolf

Swashbucklers
*See also: Action-Adventure;
Medieval Romps*

Bluebeard
Captain Kidd
The Four Musketeers
The Princess Bride
Project A
Robin Hood
The Scarlet Pimpernel
Sinbad and the Eye of the
Tiger

Swedish (Production)
Dancer in the Dark
The Inside Man
La Guerre Est Finie
Mio in the Land of Faraway
Smilla's Sense of Snow
The White Lioness

Jonathan Swift
Gulliver's Travels [Image]

Swimming
*See also: Deep Blue; Go Fish;
Island Fare; Killer Sea Crit-
ters; Lifeguards; Pacific
Islands*

The Bridges at Toko-Ri
Jaws [CE]
Splash

Swiss (Production)
Honey & Ashes
Iguana
Jew-boy Levi

Sword & Sandal
Gladiator
Gladiators: Bloodsport of the
Colosseum

Sydney
See also: Down Under

Lilian's Story
Me Myself I
Napoleon

Taiwanese (Production)
Yi Yi

Tattoos
Blue Tiger
Foxfire
Lust in the Dust

Team Efforts
The Alamo
The Cutting Edge
The Magnificent Seven
Necessary Roughness
Remember the Titans
Silverado [SE]
Uncommon Valor
The Untouchables

Tearjerkers
An Affair to Remember
All About My Mother
All Dogs Go to Heaven
Autumn in New York
Brian's Song
The Cheat
Choices
The Evening Star
The Garden of Allah
Ghost
Heaven and Earth
Here on Earth
A Home of Our Own
Ice Castles
Legends of the Fall [2 SE]
The Little Princess
Love Affair
Love Story
Moon over Harlem
Only Angels Have Wings
Paradise Road
Penny Serenade
Quicksand
Steel Magnolias
Terms of Endearment
Untamed Heart

Technology—Rampant
*See also: Computers; Robots
& Androids*

Bicentennial Man
Diamonds Are Forever [SE]
Dr. Goldfoot and the Bikini
Machine
Fail-Safe
The Fly / Return of the Fly
The Fly / The Fly 2
The Fly 2
Maximum Overdrive

Mon Oncle
The Munsters' Revenge
The Philadelphia Experiment
Runaway
Things to Come
Zardoz

*See also: Coming of Age; Hell
High School*

American Beauty [SE]
Around the Fire
Beach Blanket Bingo
Beach Party
Bellyfruit
Bikini Beach
Boyz N the Hood
But I'm a Cheerleader
Candy
The Cement Garden
Cherry Falls / Terror Tract
Choices
Class
Coneheads
The Crush
A Cry in the Wild
Deal of a Lifetime
The Defilers
Detention
Dick
Don't Tell Mom the Babysit-
ter's Dead
Drive Me Crazy
Empire Records
Fall Time
Fast Times at Ridgemont
High
Fear Runs Silent
Final Destination
The Fly 2
Foxfire
Girl
Girl, Interrupted
Girls Just Want to Have Fun
Gummo
Here on Earth
The Hollywood Knights
A Home of Our Own
I'll Be Home for Christmas
Imaginary Crimes
Johnny 100 Pesos
Just Looking
The Last Best Sunday
Light It Up
Losin' It
Mermaids
Mirror, Mirror
My Teacher's Wife
Mystic Pizza
A Night in the Life of Jimmy
Reardon
The Other Side of Sunday
The Pom Pom Girls / The
Beach Girls
Porky's / Porky's 2: The Next
Day
Porky's 2: The Next Day
Rambling Rose [2 SE]
Remembering the Cosmos
Flower
River's Edge
Save the Last Dance
Scary Movie
Seamless
Shag: The Movie
Shriek If You Know What I Did
Last Friday the 13th
Social Misfits
Strawberry Fields
Suburbia
Teenage Doll
Teenage Strangler
Teenagers from Outer Space
They Made Me a Criminal
Timeless
Times Square
Village of the Giants
The Virgin Suicides
The War Zone
Whatever It Takes

White Wolves 2: Legend of the Wild
White Wolves 3: Cry of the White Wolf
The Wounds
X-Men
Yellow
Youngblood

Television
See: Mass Media; TV Pilot Movies; TV Series

Television Adaptations
The Addams Family
The Adventures of Rocky & Bullwinkle
Batman: Mask of the Phantasm
Charlie's Angels
Coneheads
Cooley High
The Flintstones in Viva Rock Vegas
Mission: Impossible 2
Munster, Go Home!
The Naked Gun: From the Files of Police Squad
Naked Gun 33 1/3: The Final Insult
Naked Gun 2 1/2: The Smell of Fear
Star Trek 2: The Wrath of Khan
Stuart Saves His Family
Thomas and the Magic Railroad
The Untouchables

Terminal Illness
See also: Disease of the Week

Because of You
The End of the Affair
Here on Earth
Magnolia
The Settlement
Terms of Endearment

Terrorism
See also: Crime & Criminals; Foreign Intrigue; Spies & Espionage

The Cassandra Crossing
Delta Force
Desert Thunder
Diplomatic Siege
Escape under Pressure
Final Voyage
Full Disclosure
The Kidnapping of the President
Naked Gun 33 1/3: The Final Insult
Navy SEALS [MGM]
Passenger 57
Rangers
The Rock [Criterion]
Running out of Time
Submerged
The Taking of Pelham One Two Three
Termination Man
The Terrorist
The White Lioness
Women on the Verge of a Nervous Breakdown
The World Is Not Enough [SE]
You Only Live Twice [SE]

Thanksgiving
Avalon
The Myth of Fingerprints
Planes, Trains & Automobiles
What's Cooking?

Paul Theroux
Saint Jack

The 3rd Degree
The Interview

This Is My Life
See also: This Is Your Life

The Jackie Robinson Story

This Is Your Life
See also: Musician Biopics

Andy Warhol
Attila
The Audrey Hepburn Story
Bandit Queen
Beethoven
Before Night Falls
Bird
Bob Hope: Hollywood's Brightest Star
Bojangles
Born on the Fourth of July 2
Buster Keaton Rides Again / The Railrodder
Camille Claudel
Carmen Miranda: Bananas Is My Business
Dance with a Stranger
Dillinger
The Doors [2 SE]
Edvard Grieg: What Price Immortality?
The Eyes of Tammy Faye
Farinelli
Flynn
Gia
Gothic
Gotti
Goya in Bordeaux
The Greatest Story Ever Told [SE]
Grey Owl
Hans Christian Andersen [20th Century Fox]
Headin' Home
Heaven and Earth
I Shot Andy Warhol
Isn't She Great
It's Good to Be Alive
The Jackie Robinson Story
James Dean: Live Fast, Die Young
Jesus
The Joe Louis Story
The Josephine Baker Story
Lawrence of Arabia
Louis Prima: The Wildest!
Men of Honor
The Miracle Worker
The Miracle Worker
Mr. Death: The Rise and Fall of Fred A. Leuchter, Jr.
Mo' Better Blues
Pancho Villa
The Passion of Ayn Rand
Rated X
Rembrandt
Ring of Bright Water
Romero
Sergei Eisenstein: Autobiography
The Seven Little Foys
Sid & Nancy [MGM]
Steal This Movie!
The Story of Adele H.
32 Short Films about Glenn Gould
Till the Clouds Roll By
Topsy Turvy
Wild Bill
A Woman Called Moses

Jim Thompson
Coup de Torchon

3-D Flicks
Cat Women of the Moon
Friday the 13th, Part 3
Parasite
Robot Monster

Thumbs Up
Creepshow 2
The Drifter
Jerome

Time Travel
See also: Rescue Missions Involving Time Travel

Battle for the Planet of the Apes
Beneath the Planet of the Apes
Conquest of the Planet of the Apes
Dinosaur Valley Girls
Escape from the Planet of the Apes
Freejack
Hercules in New York
Highlander: The Final Dimension
Nautilus
The Navigator
Phantasm 4: Oblivion
The Philadelphia Experiment
Planet of the Apes
Terminator 2: Judgment Day [2 SE]
Thrill Seekers
The Time Machine

Time Warped
Disney's The Kid

Titanic
The Unsinkable Molly Brown

Tokyo
See also: Japan

Demon City Shinjuku
Godzilla 2000

Leo Tolstoy
Anna Karenina

Torn in Two (or More)
Mary Reilly
The Nutty Professor
Nutty Professor 2: The Klumps [1 CE]
Nutty Professor 2: The Klumps [2 Uncensored]
Tierra

Toronto
See also: Canada

The Life Before This

Torrid Love Scenes
See also: Sex & Sexuality; Sex on the Beach; Sexploitation

Against All Odds
Blue Velvet
The Cook, the Thief, His Wife & Her Lover
Five Easy Pieces
Live Flesh
An Officer and a Gentleman
Something Wild
Threesome

Toys
See also: Killer Toys

Toy Story
Toy Story 2

Tragedy
See also: Drama; Tearjerkers

Evangeline
Girl in Black
Hamlet
I Dreamed of Africa
Love Story
A Map of the World
Mother Night
Onegin
The Perfect Storm
Solomon and Gaenor
Stella
Turkish Delight
The War Zone

Trains
See also: Subways

Breakheart Pass
The Cassandra Crossing

From Russia with Love [2 SE]
The Great Alaska Train Adventure
The Millionaire's Express
Railroader
Some Like It Hot [SE]
Thomas and the Magic Railroad

Transvestites & Transsexuals
See: Gender Bending

Trapped with a Killer!
See also: Psychotics/Sociopaths

Clue
Misery
The Tie That Binds

Treasure Hunt
After the Storm
Diamonds
Escape under Pressure
Kelly's Heroes
Lewis and Clark and George
Lust in the Dust
The Mummy [2 SE]

Trees & Forests
See also: Wilderness

Fear Runs Silent

Troma Films
Cry Uncle
Escape from Hell
Frostbiter: Wrath of the Wendigo
Maniac Nurses Find Ecstasy
A Nymphoid Barbarian in Dinosaur Hell [SE]
Sergio Lapel's Drawing Blood
Teenage Catgirls in Heat
Terror Firmer [SE]
Unspeakable

True Crime
See also: Crime & Criminals; This Is Your Life; True Stories

At Close Range
Blackrock
Citizen X
Dillinger
Essex Boys
Excellent Cadavers
Gotti
Johnny 100 Pesos
The Life Before This
The Untouchables

True Stories
See also: This Is Your Life; True Crime

The Alamo
Alvarez Kelly
The Amityville Horror
Anchoress
And the Band Played On
Away All Boats
The Bounty
Brian's Song
The Bridge at Remagen
Buddy
Cheaters
Citizen X
Communion [CE]
The Cradle Will Rock
Dance with a Stranger
Delta Force
Dillinger
Dirty Pictures
Donnie Brasco 2
Drugstore Cowboy
East-West
Eight Men Out
The Emerald Forest
Erin Brockovich
Farinelli
For Love or Country: The Arturo Sandoval Story
Frances
Gia

Grey Owl
A Home of Our Own
Honor Thy Father
The Horse Soldiers
The Hurricane
I Dreamed of Africa
I Shot Andy Warhol
The Impossible Spy
In Pursuit of Honor
It's Good to Be Alive
Men of Honor
The Miracle Worker
The Miracle Worker
Murder in the First
Music of the Heart [CS]
Norma Rae
Nuremberg
The Perfect Storm
A Portrait of the Artist As a Young Man
Pretty Village, Pretty Flame
Princess Caraboo
Rated X
Ring of Bright Water
River's Edge
Rudy [SE]
Sid & Nancy [MGM]
Six Degrees of Separation
Soul of the Game
The Sound of Music [Five Star Collection]
Spartacus [Criterion]
The Straight Story
Till the Clouds Roll By
The Tuskegee Airmen
Yours, Mine & Ours

TV Pilot Movies
Stargate SG-1: Season 1
The Women of Brewster Place

TV Series
Crime Story: The Complete Saga

Mark Twain
The Prince and the Pauper

Twins
See also: Family Ties

The Crazysitter
Maximum Risk
Sisters
Twin Falls Idaho
Urban Legends 2: Final Cut

Anne Tyler
Earthly Possessions

UFOs
See: Alien Beings—Benign; Alien Beings—Vicious; Space Operas

Unexplained Phenomena
Book of Shadows: Blair Witch 2
Dead Zone
Die, Monster, Die!
Eyes of Laura Mars
The House of Seven Corpses
Maximum Overdrive
Phenomenon—The Lost Archives: Noah's Ark Found?/Tunguska/Stolen Glory
Phenomenon—The Lost Archives: Up for Sale/Heavy Watergate
Scooby-Doo and the Alien Invaders
The X-Files: Season One [CE]
The X-Files: Season Two
X: The Man with X-Ray Eyes

Universal Studios' Classic Horror
Abbott and Costello Meet Frankenstein
The Invisible Man
The Mummy
The Phantom of the Opera

Just Looking
Kisses in the Dark
The Little Vampire
Local Hero
Lock, Stock and 2 Smoking
  Barrels
Look Who's Talking, Too
The Lords of Flatbush
Loser
Love and Death
Madeline
Malice [MGM]
A Man for All Seasons
The Man from Laramie
Marilyn Monroe: The Dia-
  mond Collection
Married to the Mob
Maximum Risk
Mercy
Misery
Missing in Action
Mr. Accident
Mr. Jones
Mr. Wonderful
Monkey Shines
The Mouse on the Moon
The Mummy [SE]
Murder in the First
My Life
Night of the Living Dead
No Way Out
187
One False Move
Pal Joey
Panther
Park City: The Sundance Col-
  lection
Passenger 57
Phantasm 4: Oblivion
Picnic
Poetic Justice
Posse
Price of Glory
The Prince and the Pauper
The Princess Bride
A Raisin in the Sun
Rancho Deluxe
Reindeer Games
The Right Temptation
Roxanne
Rudyard Kipling's the Second
  Jungle Book: Mowgli and
  Baloo
Runaway
Running Free
Saving Grace
School Daze
7 Faces of Dr. Lao
Shaft in Africa
Shaft's Big Score
She's the One
Simpatico
Six Degrees of Separation
Sleeper
Sleepwalkers
Sniper
A Soldier's Story
Stories from Long Island
Striptease
Suddenly, Last Summer
Swamp Thing
Sweet and Lowdown
Tales of Terror
The Texas Chainsaw Mas-
  sacre 2
Texas Chainsaw Massacre: A
  Family Portrait
Thick As Thieves
32 Short Films about Glenn
  Gould
Three Strikes
Threesome
Thumbelina
Thunderheart
Tokyo Raiders
Tom Thumb
Tommy
Tootsie
True Believer
Tumbleweeds
Turn It Up

20th Century Fox: The First
  50 Years
Two Moon Junction
Under Suspicion
Urban Legends 2: Final Cut
What Planet Are You From?
Whatever It Takes
Whipped
The Whole Nine Yards

Wild Kingdom
  *See also: Bears; Birds; Cats;
  Dinosaurs; Elephants; Killer
  Beasts; Killer Bugs & Slugs;
  Killer Sea Critters; King of
  Beasts (Dogs); Monkeyshines;
  Nice Mice; Pigs; Rabbits;
  Wilderness*

All Creatures Great and Small
All Dogs Go to Heaven 2
The Beast That Killed Women
  / The Monster of Camp
  Sunshine
The Brave One
Buddy
Call of the Wild
A Cry in the Wild
Day of the Animals
Doctor Dolittle
An Elephant Called Slowly
The Emperor's New Groove
  [SE]
The Fox and the Hound
Gladiator
I Dreamed of Africa
The Mighty Peking Man
Napoleon
Never Cry Wolf
Noah's Ark
Planet of the Apes
The Rescuers Down Under
Ring of Bright Water
Rock-a-Doodle
Rudyard Kipling's the Second
  Jungle Book: Mowgli and
  Baloo
White Wolves 2: Legend of
  the Wild

Wilderness
  See also: Trees & Forests

Black Robe
Napoleon
Never Cry Wolf
White Wolves 2: Legend of
  the Wild
White Wolves 3: Cry of the
  White Wolf

Tennessee Williams
Suddenly, Last Summer

Witchcraft
  *See also: Demons & Wizards;
  Occult*

Book of Shadows: Blair Witch
  2
The Devil Rides Out
Hellblock 13
Horror Hotel
Lucinda's Spell
Something Weird
Terry Pratchett's Discworld:
  Wyrd Sisters
Warlock: The Armageddon
The Witches
Witchouse 2: Blood Coven

Women
  *See also: Dream Girls;
  Femme Fatale; Moms; Westro-
  gens; Women in Prison; Wonder Women*

Another Woman
The Astounding She-Monster
Bandit Queen
Black Scorpion
Carmen Miranda: Bananas Is
  My Business
8 1/2 Women
Fire

Gentlemen Prefer Blondes
Heaven and Earth
Honey & Ashes
How to Marry a Millionaire
I Dreamed of Africa
In This House of Brede
Isn't She Great
Little Women [2 SE]
Love After Love
Moll Flanders [MGM]
Moonlight and Valentino
9 to 5
Poetic Justice
The '70s
A Single Girl
Steel Magnolias
The Terrorist
The Women of Brewster
  Place
Women on the Verge of a
  Nervous Breakdown
Working Girl
Working Girls

Women Cops
  See also: Cops

China O'Brien
Fatal Beauty
Miss Congeniality
Vice Girls

Women in Prison
  *See also: Exploitation; Men in
  Prison; Sexploitation*

Bandits
The Big Doll House
Black Mama, White Mama
Chasers
East-West
Escape from Hell
Female Convict Scorpion—
  Jailhouse 41
Hellblock 13
Ilsa, the Wicked Warden
A Map of the World
Midnight
Paradise Road
Red Letters
Reform School Girls

Women in War
  *See also: Doctors & Nurses;
  Korean War; Vietnam War;
  Women; Wonder Women;
  World War I; World War II*

A Farewell to Arms
Paradise Road

Wonder Women
  See also: Dream Girls

Alien: Resurrection
Battle of the Amazons
Battle Queen 2020
Black Scorpion 2: Ground
  Zero
Blue Tiger
Charlie's Angels
Charlie's Angels: Angels
  Undercover
The Clan of the Cave Bear
Cleopatra
Crouching Tiger, Hidden Drag-
  on
Deadly Weapons
Heavy Metal 2000 [SE]
La Femme Nikita [MGM]
The Messenger: The Story of
  Joan of Arc
Prisoner Maria: The Movie
Pocahontas
Supergirl
Switchblade Sisters
The World Is Not Enough [SE]

World War I
Catherine Cookson's The Cin-
  der Path
A Farewell to Arms
King and Country
Lawrence of Arabia
The Legend of Bagger Vance

Legends of the Fall [2 SE]

World War II
  *See also: The Holocaust;
  Postwar; POW/MIA; The
  Resistance*

Alexandria...Why?
Alfred Hitchcock's Bon Voy-
  age & Aventure Malgache
The Audrey Hepburn Story
Away All Boats
Bedknobs and Broomsticks
Blood on the Sun
The Bridge at Remagen
The Bridge on the River Kwai
  [LE]
Brief Encounter
The Brylcreem Boys
Catch-22
December 7th: The Pearl Har-
  bor Story
The Eagle Has Landed
End of the Affair
The End of the Affair
Fight for the Title
For the Boys
Go for Broke!
Gung Ho!
Hell Is for Heroes
Hope and Glory
I'll Remember April
Immortal Battalion
In Harm's Way
Kelly's Heroes
Know Your Enemy: Japan
The Last Lieutenant
The Last of the Blonde Bomb-
  shells
Legendary WWII Movies
Mein Kampf: Hitler's Rise
  and Fall
Mother Night
Paradise Road
Pearl Harbor
Pearl Harbor: December 7,
  1941
The Philadelphia Experiment
Private Navy of Sgt. O'Farrell
Saboteur
Sherlock Holmes and the
  Secret Weapon
Soldier of Orange
A Soldier's Story
The Sorrow and the Pity
The Sound of Music [Five
  Star Collection]
Tora! Tora! Tora! [2 SE]
Triumph of the Will
The Tuskegee Airmen
U-571 [CE]
A Walk in the Sun
We'll Meet Again
World War II

Wrestling
Beyond the Mat
Ready to Rumble

Writers
  See also: This Is Your Life

Amuck!
Bamboozled
Before Night Falls
Breakfast of Champions
Croupier
The End of the Affair
Finding Forrester
For Hire
Gothic
Isn't She Great
Joe Gould's Secret
Mailer on Mailer
A Merry War
Misery
Mother
The Passion of Ayn Rand
Portraits Chinois
Postmortem
Quills
Restaurant
The Snows of Kilimanjaro

Sweet and Lowdown
Tenebre
Wonder Boys

The Wrong Man
  *See also: Frame-Ups; Mistak-
  en Identity*

The Bedroom Window
The Crow: Salvation
Delivered
Frenzy
In Pursuit
Kept
The Man Who Knew Too Much
They Made Me a Criminal

**Wrong Side of the
Tracks**
  See also: Rags to Riches

Cat Ballou [SE]
Here on Earth
The Loves of Carmen
The Pope of Greenwich Vil-
  lage
Pygmalion
Rocky [2 SE]
Suburbia

Yakuza
  *See also: Crime & Criminals;
  Japan; Organized Crime*

American Yakuza
The Bodyguard / Dragon
  Princess

**Yugoslavian
(Production)**
The Best of Zagreb Film:
  Laugh at Your Own Risk
  and For Children Only
Cave of the Living Dead
Tito and Me

Yuppie Nightmares
  See also: Strained Suburbia

Alice
Amos and Andrew
Baby Boom
Boiler Room
Desperately Seeking Susan
The Fisher King
Lost in America
Mifune
Mother's Boys
Oasis of the Zombies
The Object of Beauty
September
Six Degrees of Separation
Something Wild
Summer Rental
The Tie That Binds
Wall Street
What about Bob?

Zombies
  *See also: Death & the After-
  life; Ghosts, Ghouls, & Goblins*

The Astro-Zombies
The Beyond
Bride of Re-Animator
The Dead Next Door
The House of Seven Corpses
I, Zombie
Let Sleeping Corpses Lie
The Mummy
The Mummy [2 SE]
Night of the Living Dead
Night of the Living Dead
  [Madacy]
Night of the Living Dead
  [Elite]
Night of the Living Dead [LE
  Anchor Bay]
Oasis of the Zombies
Plan 9 from Outer Space
  [Passport Video]
Quatermass 2
The Stuff
Zombie Lake

The "Distributor Index" provides contact information for the distributors indicated within the reviews, and the DVDs reviewed in this book which they offer. Beware: DVDs sometimes change hands frequently; we've tried to provide cross-references where applicable. Also, studio distributors do not usually sell to the public—they generally act as wholesalers, selling only to retail outlets. Many video stores provide an ordering service; check out the "DVD Connections" section on p. 345 for some websites to help you track down a title.

A & E HOME VIDEO
PO Box 2284
South Burlington, VT 05407
800-625-9000
Fax: (802)864-9846

Agatha Christie's Poirot '00
Pearl Harbor '00

A-PIX ENTERTAINMENT INC.
200 Madison Ave., 24th Fl.
New York, NY 10016
(206)284-4700
800-245-6472
Fax: (206)286-4433

Around the Fire '98
Broken Vessels '98
Colorz of Rage '97
Da Hip Hop Witch '00
Dance with the Devil '97
Forever Together '00
The 4th Floor '99
The Italians '00
Jack Frost 2: Revenge of the Mutant Killer Snowman '00
Kiss Toledo Goodbye '99
Let the Devil Wear Black '99

ACORN MEDIA PUBLISHING
7910 Woodmont Ave., Ste. 350
Bethesda, MD 20814
(301)907-0030
800-999-0212
Fax: (301)907-9049

Brother Cadfael: The Devil's Novice '94
The Far Pavilions '84
The Great Alaska Train Adventure
The Pallisers '74
Terry Pratchett's Discworld: Wyrd Sisters '96

A.D.V. FILMS
5750 Bintliff, No. 216
Houston, TX 77036-2123
(713)341-7100
Fax: (713)341-7195

Bubblegum Crisis Tokyo 2040 '00
Farscape, Vol. 2 '00
Farscape, Vol. 3 '01
Gasaraki 1: The Summoning '00
Generator 1: Gawl '00
Gun Smith Cats: Bulletproof '95
Lucinda's Spell '00

Neon Genesis Evangelion Collection '99
Reboot: Season III '97
Robotech: First Contact '00
Samurai X: The Movie '95
Samurai X Trust '99
Shadow Raiders, Vol. 1: Uncommon Hero '98
Sin: The Movie '98
Sorcerer Hunters: Magical Encounters '00

ALL DAY ENTERTAINMENT
3105 Batter Sea Ln.
Alexandria, VA 22309

Edgar Ulmer Collection, Vol. 1 '00
Fall of the House of Usher '28

ANCHOR BAY
1699 Stutz Dr.
Troy, MI 48084
(248)816-0909
800-786-8777
Fax: (248)816-3335

The Abominable Snowman '57
Aguirre, the Wrath of God '72
All Creatures Great and Small '74
The Bedroom Window '87
A Better Tomorrow, Part 1 [Anchor Bay] '86
A Better Tomorrow, Part 2 [Anchor Bay] '88
The Beyond '82
Billy's Holiday '95
The Black Cat '81
Black Moon Rising '86
A Blade in the Dark '83
Bluebeard '72
The Boys Next Door '85
Candy '68
Children of the Corn '84
C.H.U.D. '84
Cockfighter '74
The Cook, the Thief, His Wife & Her Lover '90
Creepshow 2 '87
Crime Story: The Complete Saga '86
Dakota '88
The Day the Earth Caught Fire '61
Death and the Compass '96
Death on the Nile '78
The Devil & Max Devlin '81
The Devil Rides Out '68

Don't Torture a Duckling '72
An Elephant Called Slowly '69
Endless Night '71
Evil Dead 2: Dead by Dawn [2 THX] '87
Evil under the Sun '82
Fear City '85
Flowers in the Attic '87
Four Sided Triangle '53
The 4th Man '79
Frankenstein Created Woman '66
Fruits of Passion: The Story of "O" Continued '82
The Garden of Allah '36
Girls Just Want to Have Fun '85
The Grissom Gang '71
The Groundstar Conspiracy '72
Halloween 5: The Revenge of Michael Myers '89
Hellraiser 2 '87
H.O.T.S. '79
The House by the Cemetery [Anchor Bay] '83
Iguana '89
I'll Never Forget What's 'Isname '67
Ilsa, Harem Keeper of the Oil Sheiks '76
Ilsa, She-Wolf of the SS '74
Ilsa, the Wicked Warden '78
Immoral Tales '74
Jake Speed '86
Jane & the Lost City '87
Knightriders '81
The Last Valley '71
Law and Disorder '74
The Lemon Sisters '90
Let Sleeping Corpses Lie '74
Little Lord Fauntleroy '36
Lust in the Dust '85
Macabre '80
Madman '82
Manhattan Baby '82
Martin '77
Maximum Overdrive '86
The McCullochs '75
The Midnight Hour '86
Mio in the Land of Faraway '87
The Mirror Crack'd '80
Mirror, Mirror '90
Mirror, Mirror 2: Raven Dance '94
Mirror, Mirror 3: The Voyeur '96
Mountaintop Motel Massacre '86

The Mummy's Shroud '67
My Best Fiend '99
Never Cry Wolf '83
Night of the Living Dead [LE Anchor Bay] '68
Nightwatch '94
The Philadelphia Experiment '84
Pit Stop '67
Portrait of Jennie '48
Positive I.D. '87
Possession '81
The Prince and the Pauper '78
Pusher '96
Quatermass 2 '57
Reform School Girls '86
Repo Man '83
Ring of Bright Water '69
Ruckus '81
Santa Claus: The Movie '85
Sister, Sister '87
Sleepaway Camp '83
Slugs '87
Soldier of Orange '78
The Spiral Staircase '46
Straight to Hell '87
The Stuff '85
Supergirl '84
Tapeheads '89
Tenebre '82
10th Victim '65
That'll Be the Day '73
Thou Shalt Not Kill . . . Except '87
Three Businessmen '99
Tie Me Up! Tie Me Down! '90
Times Square '80
Tuff Turf '85
Turkish Delight '73
The Unbelievable Truth '90
The Vampire Happening '71
Vampyres '74
The Vineyard '89
Walking the Edge '83
Whatever Happened to Aunt Alice? '69
The Witches '66
Working Girls '87
Woyzeck '78
X The Unknown '56

ARTISAN ENTERTAINMENT
15400 Sherman Way
PO Box 10124
Van Nuys, CA 91410-0124
(818)988-5060
800-677-0789
Fax: (818)778-3259

Aftershock: Earthquake in New York '99
Bandit Queen '94
Bloody Murder '99
Bob Roberts [SE] '92
Book of Shadows: Blair Witch 2 '00
Breaking the Waves '95
Cecil B. Demented '00
Chuck & Buck '00
The Crimson Code '00
Critical Care '97
Cujo '83
Cutaway '00
Deepstar Six '89
Dr. T & the Women '00
The Doors [2 SE] '91
Drugstore Cowboy '89
Dune '00
The Eagle Has Landed '77
Final Voyage '99
Ghost Dog: The Way of the Samurai '99
Hot Boyz '99
Illuminata '98
In the Beginning... '00
Jason and the Argonauts '00
Killing Zoe '94
King of New York '90
Knight Moves '93
The Magical Legend of the Leprechauns '99
The Minus Man '99
My 5 Wives '00
The Ninth Gate '99
One Man's Justice '95
Picking Up the Pieces '99
Premonition '99
Raising the Mammoth '00
Requiem for a Dream '00
Restraining Order '99
Seamless '00
Shanghai Noon '00
Speed Racer: The Movie
Steel Dawn '87
The Substitute 4: Failure Is Not an Option '00
Terminator 2: Judgment Day [2 SE] '91
That Touch of Mink '62
The Three Caballeros '45
The Tigger Movie '00
Traveller '96
Way of the Gun '00
What about Bob? '91

ARTIST VIEW ENTERTAINMENT
12500 Riverside Dr., Ste. 201-B

North Hollywood, CA 91607
(818)752-2480
Fax: (818)752-9339

Fear Runs Silent '99

**AVALANCHE
ENTERTAINMENT**
595 Burrard St.,
Ste. 3123
Bentall Three
Vancouver, BC, Canada V7X 1J1
(416)944-0104

Big City Blues '99
National Lampoon's Golf
Punks '99

**BELL CANYON
ENTERTAINMENT INC.**
c/o Sue Procko Public
Relations
101 S. Harper Ave.
Los Angeles, CA 90048
(232)653-5153
888-379-6769

Bad Manners '98

**BEVERLY WILSHIRE
FILMWORKS**
PO Box 111, Prince Street Sta.
New York, NY 10012

The Bodyguard from Beijing
'94

BFS VIDEO
360 Newkirk Rd.
Richmond Hill, ON, Canada
L4C 3G7
(905)884-2323
Fax: (905)884-8292

The Canterville Ghost '98
Catherine Cookson's The Cin-
der Path '94
Catherine Cookson's The
Secret '00
Deacon Brodie '98
Element of Doubt '96
Falling for a Dancer '98
Great Baseball Movies '00
Great Boxing Movies '00
Great Mafia Movies '00
The Last Great Adventure '99
Legendary WWII Movies '00
Northanger Abbey '87
The Perfect Husband '92
Plain Jane '00
Poldark '96
Sharpe's Battle '94
Sharpe's Company '94
Sharpe's Eagle '93
Sharpe's Enemy '94
Sharpe's Gold '94
Sharpe's Honour '94
Sharpe's Justice '97
Sharpe's Mission '96
Sharpe's Regiment '96
Sharpe's Revenge '97
Sharpe's Rifles '93
Sharpe's Siege '96
Sharpe's Sword '94
Sharpe's Waterloo '97
We'll Meet Again '82

BITWIN CO. LTD.
14fl Daechi B/D 889-11
Daechi 4 dong Kangnam-ku
Seoul 135-284, Republic of
Korea

The Ring Virus '99

**BRENTWOOD HOME
VIDEO**
810 Lawrence Dr., Ste. 100
Newbury Park, CA 91320
(805)375-9998
Fax: (805)375-9908

Bob Hope: Hollywood's
Brightest Star '97
The Great Lover '49
How to Commit Marriage '69
The Lemon Drop Kid '51

Paris Holiday '57
Private Navy of Sgt. O'Farrell
'68
The Road to Bali '53
The Road to Rio '47
The Seven Little Foys '55
Son of Paleface '52

BRI VIDEO
2020 Broadway Ave., 2nd Fl.
Santa Monica, CA 90404
(310)829-9497
800-906-6843
Fax: (310)829-3297

The Story of O: The Series
'92

**BUENA VISTA HOME
ENTERTAINMENT**
500 S. Buena Vista St.
Burbank, CA 91521-1120
800-723-4763

*Buena Vista is responsible for
Touchstone, Disney Home
Video, Walt Disney Home
Video, Hollywood Pictures
(see separate listing), Miramax Pictures (see separate
listing), and other labels.*

The Adventures of Ichabod
and Mr. Toad '49
Air Bud [2] '97
Air Bud 2: Golden Receiver
'98
Air Bud 3: World Pup '00
Alice in Wonderland '51
All I Wanna Do '98
Annie '99
The Aristocats '70
Backstage '00
Beauty and the Beast: The
Enchanted Christmas '97
Bedknobs and Broomsticks
'71
Beowulf '98
Best of the Best 3: No Turn-
ing Back / Best of the
Best: Without Warning '95
Bicentennial Man '99
The Black Cauldron '85
Bounty Hunters '96
Bounty Hunters 2: Hardball
'97
Boys and Girls '00
Buzz Lightyear of Star Com-
mand: The Adventure
Begins '00
The Cider House Rules '99
Confessions of Sorority Girls
'00
Coyote Ugly '00
The Cradle Will Rock '99
The Crew '00
Crime Story '93
The Crow: Salvation '00
The Defender '94
Deuce Bigalow: Male Gigolo
'99
Dinosaur [CE] '00
Disney's The Kid '00
The Emperor's New Groove
[SE] '00
The Fantasia Anthology '00
Fantasia/2000 '00
Father of the Bride Part II '95
The Fox and the Hound '81
From Dusk Till Dawn [2 CS]
'95
Fun & Fancy Free '47
Gone in 60 Seconds '00
High Fidelity '00
Highlander: Endgame '00
Highlander: The Final Dimen-
sion '94
I'll Be Home for Christmas
'98
James and the Giant Peach
'96
Jet Li's The Enforcer [Buena
Vista] '95
Keeping the Faith '00

Lady and the Tramp 2:
Scamp's Adventure '01
The Legend '93
The Legend of Drunken Mas-
ter '94
The Little Mermaid 2: Return
to the Sea '00
Mafia! '98
Make Mine Music '46
Mansfield Park '99
Mary Poppins [2 SE] '64
Melody Time '48
Men of War '94
The Miracle Worker '00
Mission to Mars '00
Next Stop, Wonderland '98
The Nightmare before Christ-
mas [2 SE] '93
Nightwatch '96
No Code of Conduct '98
O Brother Where Art Thou?
'00
102 Dalmatians '00
Pete's Dragon '77
Play It to the Bone '99
Playing Mona Lisa '00
Pocahontas '95
Pocahontas 2: Journey to a
New World '98
Project A '83
The Proposal '00
Reindeer Games '00
Remember the Titans '00
The Rescuers Down Under
'90
Robin Hood '73
Saludos Amigos '43
Scream 3 [CS] '00
Splash '84
The Straight Story '99
Sweet Revenge '98
The Sword in the Stone '63
Telling You '98
Toy Story '95
Toy Story 2 '99
Toy Story: The Ultimate Toy-
box '00
Twin Warriors '93

CBS/FOX VIDEO
1330 Avenue of the Americas
New York, NY 10019
(212)373-4800
800-800-4369
Fax: (212)373-4803

Ferngully 2: The Magical Rescue '97
Men of Honor '00

**CENTRAL PARK
MEDIA/U.S. MANGA
CORPS**
250 W. 57th St., Ste. 317
New York, NY 10107
(212)977-7456
800-833-7456
Fax: (212)977-8709

Art of Fighting '93
Darkside Blues '99
Demon City Shinjuku '93
Grave of the Fireflies '88
Maze '96
Mystery of the Necronomicon
'00
Weather Woman '99

CLOUD TEN PICTURES
1 St. Paul St.
The Penthouse
St. Catherines, ON, Canada
L2R 7L2

Left Behind: The Movie '00
Revelation '00
Tribulation '00

**COLUMBIA TRISTAR
HOME VIDEO**
Sony Pictures Plz.
10202 W. Washington Blvd.
Culver City, CA 90232

(310)280-5418
Fax: (310)280-2485

Against All Odds '84
All About My Mother '99
All the Pretty Horses '00
Alvarez Kelly '66
Anatomy [SE] '00
Anatomy of a Murder '59
And Justice for All '79
Animal Factory '00
Annie '82
The Audrey Hepburn Story
'00
Avalon '00
Backlash '99
Bandits '99
Bats '99
Bear in the Big Blue House:
Party Time with Bear '00
Bear in the Big Blue House:
Shapes, Sounds & Colors
'00
The Beast '88
Beautiful '00
Beautiful Joe '00
A Better Way to Die '00
The Big Blue [DC] '88
Black and White '99
Black & White '99
Blue Streak '99
Bossa Nova '99
Boyz N the Hood '91
Brian's Song '71
The Bridge on the River Kwai
[LE] '57
The Broken Hearts Club '00
Buddy '97
Cat Ballou [SE] '65
Center Stage '00
Charlie's Angels '00
Charlie's Angels: Angels
Undercover '76
Circus '00
Cliffhanger [2 CS] '93
Close Encounters of the Third
Kind [CE] '77
Crazy in Alabama '99
Crouching Tiger, Hidden Drag-
on '00
Damn the Defiant '62
The Daytrippers '96
Dick '99
Dr. Strangelove, or: How I
Learned to Stop Worrying
and Love the Bomb [2 SE]
'64
Dogma '99
Donnie Brasco [2] '96
Dralion '00
Drowning Mona '00
East-West '99
The Emperor and the Assas-
sin '99
End of the Affair '55
The End of the Affair '99
Eye of the Beholder '99
Eyes of Laura Mars '78
Fail-Safe '64
Farinelli '94
Finding Forrester '00
The Fisher King '91
Five Easy Pieces '70
The 5000 Fingers of Dr. T '53
For Pete's Sake '74
Foxfire '96
Fright Night '85
Gen-X Cops '99
Get On the Bus '96
Gilda '46
Girl '98
Girl, Interrupted '99
Girlfight '99
Gladiator '92
Glory [2 SE] '89
Godzilla 2000 '99
Gorgeous '99
Goya in Bordeaux '00
Grey Owl '99
Groove '00
Hanging Up '99

Hangman '00
Hard Eight '96
Heavy Metal 2000 [SE] '00
Hideaway '94
High School High '96
The Hollow Man [SE] '00
The Hollywood Knights '80
Homegrown '97
House of Mirth '00
I Dreamed of Africa '00
Ice Castles '79
Idle Hands '99
If Lucy Fell '95
In God's Hands '98
In the Line of Fire [2 SE] '93
It Could Happen to You '94
It's the Rage '99
The Jagged Edge '85
Just Looking '99
The Karate Kid '84
Kept '01
Krull [SE] '83
The Lady from Shanghai '48
The Last Picture Show [DC]
'71
Lawrence of Arabia '62
Legends of the Fall [2 SE] '94
Leon, the Professional '94
Les Miserables '97
Little Women [2 SE] '94
Look Who's Talking, Too '90
The Lords of Flatbush '74
Loser '00
The Loss of Sexual Inno-
cence '98
Love Stinks '99
The Loves of Carmen '48
Ma Vie en Rose '97
Madeline '98
A Man for All Seasons '66
The Man from Laramie '55
Mary Reilly '95
Maximum Risk '96
Me Myself I '99
Men in Black [CS] '97
Mercy '00
The Messenger: The Story of
Joan of Arc '99
Mifune '99
Mr. Jones '93
Monty Python and the Holy
Grail '75
My Life '93
The Myth of Fingerprints '97
The Natural '84
The New Adventures of Pippi
Longstocking '88
Night of the Living Dead '90
Once Upon a Time in China
'91
One Day in September '99
One False Move '91
Only Angels Have Wings '39
Pal Joey '57
A Passage to India '84
The Patriot '00
Picnic '55
Poetic Justice '93
Postcards from the Edge '90
Princess Caraboo '94
The Prisoner '90
Quidam '99
A Raisin in the Sun '61
The Red Dwarf '99
The Right Temptation '00
Roughnecks Starship Troop-
ers Chronicles the Pluto
Campaign '99
Roxanne '87
Rudy [SE] '93
Rudyard Kipling's the Second
Jungle Book: Mowgli and
Baloo '97
Runaway '84
Running Free '00
School Daze '88
Screw Loose '99
Shakes the Clown '92
Silverado [SE] '85
Sinbad and the Eye of the
Tiger '77

IDEAL ENTERPRISES/VIDEO

16228 Main Ave. SE, No. 104
Prior Lake, MN 55372
(952)447-7406
Fax: (952)447-7409

Ninth Street '98

IMAGE ENTERTAINMENT

9333 Oso Ave.
Chatsworth, CA 91311
(818)407-9100
800-473-3475
Fax: (818)407-9111

Affairs of Anatol '21
AFI's 100 Years, 100 Stars '99
Aftershock '88
Alfred Hitchcock's Bon Voyage & Aventure Malgache '44
American Cinema: 100 Years of Filmmaking '94
American Yakuza '94
Andy Warhol '88
Around the World with Orson Welles '55
The Astounding She-Monster '58
The Astro-Zombies '67
Asylum '72
The Awful Dr. Orlof '62
Back to God's Country / Something New '19
Bad Girls Go to Hell / Another Day, Another Man '65
Banzai Runner '86
The Balcony '63
Battle of the Sexes '28
The Beast Must Die '75
The Beast of Yucca Flats '61
The Beast That Killed Women / The Monster of Camp Sunshine '65
Beethoven '36
Best of the Best: Especially for Kids '99
Best of the Best: Romantic Tales '99
Best of the Best: Strange Tales of the Imagination '99
The Best of Zagreb Film: Laugh at Your Own Risk and For Children Only
Beware! The Blob '72
Beyond the Clouds '95
The Big Wheel '49
Black Sabbath '64
Black Tight Killers '66
Blackmale '99
Blaze Starr Goes Nudist '63
Blood Beast Terror '67
The Bloody Pit of Horror '65
Blue Ridge Fall '99
Blue Tiger '94
The Body Beneath '70
Body Count '95
The Brain from Planet Arous '57
The British Invasion Returns '00
The Brutal Truth '99
Bulldog Drummond Escapes '37
Bulldog Drummond's Secret Police '39
Buster Keaton Rides Again / The Railrodder '65
Cannibal Ferox '84
Carmen / The Cheat '15
Cat Women of the Moon '53
Cave of the Living Dead '65
Chang: A Drama of the Wilderness '27
Cinema Combat: Hollywood Goes to War '98
Comic Act '00
Coming Soon '99

The Complete Superman Collection '43
The Cosmic Man '59
Criminals '97
Croupier '97
Crucible of Terror '72
The Curious Dr. Humpp '70
Cyrano de Bergerac '25
Dame Edna's Neighbourhood Watch 2 '92
DaVinci's War '92
Dead of Night '99
Deadly Beauty: Snow's Secret Life '01
Deadly Weapons '70
Dear Santa '98
The Defilers '65
Dementia '98
Destiny '21
Detour '46
Die Screaming, Marianne '73
Dilemma '97
Dinosaurus! '60
Dr. Frankenstein's Castle of Freaks '74
Dolphins '00
Double Agent 73 '80
Ecstasy of the Angels '72
Edvard Grieg: What Price Immortality? '00
The Erotic Adventures of Zorro '72
Eternal Love '29
Evangeline '29
Fair Game '89
Fallen Angel '99
The Fantasy Film Worlds of George Pal '86
The Fantasy Worlds of Irwin Allen '95
Female Convict Scorpion—Jailhouse 41 '72
Female Vampire '73
First Spaceship on Venus '60
Five Dolls for an August Moon '70
Flash Gordon: Space Soldiers '36
The Flying Saucer '50
Foolish Wives '22
Four Times That Night '69
Frankenstein's Daughter '58
Frightmare '74
Fugitive Champion '99
Full Disclosure '00
The Gay Deceivers '69
The Gay Desperado '36
Ghost Chase '88
Giant from the Unknown '58
The Girl Who Knew Too Much '63
Glastonbury: The Movie '95
Go, Go Second Time Virgin '69
God's Comedy '95
Gold of the Amazon Women '79
The Gore-Gore Girls '72
Greaser's Palace '72
Gruesome Twosome '67
Gulliver's Travels [Image] '39
Gumboots '00
Hardcase and Fist '89
Hatchet for the Honeymoon '70
Hell's Kitchen NYC '97
Hollywood Vice Sqaud '86
Horrors of Spider Island '59
The House of Seven Corpses '73
Hysterical '83
I, Claudius '91
I Spy '65
Il Bidone '55
The Indian Tomb '21
The Inland Sea '93
It's Raining on Santiago '74
Jew-boy Levi '98
Joan the Woman '16
The Joint Is Jumpin' '00
Joy House '64

Kicked in the Head '97
Kids Return '96
Kronos '57
La Grande Bouffe '73
La Guerre Est Finie '66
The Life Before This '99
Lingerie '01
Little Fugitive '53
Lockdown '90
Lone Justice 2 '93
Lone Justice 3: Showdown at Plum Creek '96
The Lost World [Image] '25
Louis Prima: The Wildest! '99
Love by Appointment '76
Love Kills '98
The Love Master '97
Lower Level '91
The Mad Butcher '72
Mantis in Lace '68
Marihuana / Assassin of Youth / Reefer Madness '36
The Marriage Circle '24
The Married Virgin '18
Masters of Russian Animation, Vol. 2 '97
Masters of Russian Animation, Vol. 3 '97
Masters of Russian Animation, Vol. 4 '97
Meet John Doe [Image] '41
Mesa of Lost Women '52
Midnight '34
Missile to the Moon '59
Monster from Green Hell '58
My Son, the Vampire '52
Necromancer: Satan's Servant '88
Neurotica: Middle-Age Spread and Other Life Crises '97
The New Eve '98
A Night in the Life of Jimmy Reardon '88
No Safe Haven '87
Nosferatu [2] '22
The Notorious Daughter of Fanny Hill / Head Mistress '71
Nude on the Moon '61
Nunsense 2: The Sequel '94
Oasis of the Zombies '82
October 22 '98
On the Border '98
Origins of Film '00
Outside the Law / Shadows '21
Party '96
Passion & Romance: Double or Nothing '00
Passion & Romance: Scandal '97
People of the Wind '76
The Phantom Planet '61
Phenomenon—The Lost Archives: Noah's Ark Found?/Tunguska/Stolen Glory '99
Phenomenon—The Lost Archives: Up for Sale/Heavy Watergate '99
Picasso '85
A Portrait of the Artist As a Young Man '77
Pot o' Gold '41
Project A-ko '86
Psychomania '73
The Puppetoon Movie '87
Quiet Days in Hollywood '97
Rain '32
Relative Values '99
Rembrandt Films' Greatest Hits '00
Road Movie '72
Robot Monster '53
Rocketship X-M '50
A Room with a View '86
Scandal: The Big Turn On '99
Scene at the Sea '91
Scum of the Earth '63
Sergei Eisenstein: Autobiography '96

Sergei Eisenstein: Mexican Fantasy '98
Sex Files: Ancient Desires '99
Sex Files: Digital Sex '98
She Demons '58
She-Freak '67
The Sign of Four '83
Silent Shakespeare '00
Slippery When Wet '58
Something More '99
Something Weird '68
The Sorrow and the Pity '71
Space-Thing '67
Spaceways '53
Stalked '99
Stories from My Childhood '98
Stories from My Childhood, Vol. 3 '99
The Strange Love of Martha Ivers '46
The Stranger from Venus '54
Street Gun '96
Street Scene '31
Surfing Hollow Days '61
Tap Dogs '98
A Taste of Blood '67
Teaserama '55
Teenage Doll '57
Teenage Gang Debs / Teenage Strangler '66
Teenage Monster '57
Teenagers from Outer Space '59
Things to Come '36
The Thousand Eyes of Dr. Mabuse '60
Tomorrow the World '44
Tonight or Never '31
Topper Returns '41
Tower of Song: The Canadian Music Hall of Fame '01
Traitor's Heart '98
Treasures from the American Film Archives: 50 Preserved Films '00
20th Century Fox: The First 50 Years '96
Twitch of the Death Nerve '71
Ulysses '67
Uncensored Bosko, Vol. 1 '91
Uncensored Bosko, Vol. 2 '91
U.S. Seals '98
The Vanishing American '25
Varietease '54
Vengeance '68
Vietnam: The Ten Thousand Day War '80
The Violent Years / Girl Gang '56
Wax Mask '97
Wham-Bam, Thank You Spaceman '75
A Woman Called Sada Abe '75
A Woman, Her Men and Her Futon '92
The Womaneater '59
Zombie Lake '80

INDIE DVD

708 SW 3rd Ave., 3rd Fl.
Portland, OR 97204

Fusion One '00

KINO ON VIDEO

333 W. 39th St., Ste. 503
New York, NY 10018
(212)629-6880
800-562-3330
Fax: (212)714-0871

Daughter of Horror / Dementia '55
Dersu Uzala '75
Hangmen Also Die '42

LUMINOUS FILM & VIDEO

PO Box 1047, Dept. AC
Medford, NY 11763
(516)289-1644

Amuck! '71
Battle of the Amazons '74
Cut Throats Nine '72
Dead Are Alive '72

LUMIVISION CORP.

877 Federal Blvd.
Denver, CO 80204-3212
800-776-LUMI

Video product is now distributed through SLINGSHOT ENTERTAINMENT (see separate listing).

Animation Greats '97
Animation Legend: Winsor McCay '93
The Brave One '56
Fire over England '37

LUNACY PRODUCTIONS

2612 Montana Ave., Ste. 1
Santa Monica, CA 90403
(310)449-4400
Fax: (310)449-4404

Nice Guys Sleep Alone '99

MADACY ENTERTAINMENT

3333 Graham Blvd., Ste. 102
Montreal, QC, Canada H3R 3L5
(514)341-5600

Africa Screams / Jack and the Beanstalk '49
Anna Karenina '48
Dawn Rider / Trail Beyond '35
Dementia 13 '63
Fantasy Mission Force '84
Father's Little Dividend '51
The Flying Deuces / Utopia '39
The Last Time I Saw Paris '54
Lawless Frontier / Randy Rides Alone '35
Life with Father '47
Love Affair '39
Man from Utah / Sagebrush Trail '34
Master with Cracked Fingers '71
My Favorite Brunette '47
Night of the Living Dead [Madacy] '68
One-Eyed Jacks '61
Pearl Harbor: December 7, 1941 '00
Penny Serenade '41
Reefer Madness '38
Riders of Destiny / Star Packer '33
The Scarlet Pimpernel '34
The Secret KGB UFO Files '99
The Snows of Kilimanjaro '52
Till the Clouds Roll By '46
A Walk in the Sun '46
Winds of the Wasteland '36
World War II '42

MARENGO FILMS

14881 Quorum Dr., Ste. 900
Dallas, TX 75240

Bob Hope Double Feature '00
Errol Flynn / Randolph Scott Double Feature '00
Gary Cooper Double Feature '00
Shadow of the Eagle '32
The Woman in Green / Dressed to Kill '45

MASTERTONE MULTIMEDIA, Inc.

3208 W. Lake St., Ste. 4
St. Louis Park, MN 55416

See listing for PARADE.

MEDIA BLASTERS

118 E. 28th St., Ste. 501
New York, NY 10016

Vice Girls '96
White Wolves 2: Legend of the Wild '94
White Wolves 3: Cry of the White Wolf '98

NEW LINE HOME VIDEO
116 N. Robertson Blvd.
Los Angeles, CA 90048
(310)967-6670
Fax: (310)854-0602

An Affair of Love '00
Bamboozled '00
Before Night Falls '00
Body Shots '99
Boiler Room '00
The Cell '00
Dancer in the Dark '99
Dungeons and Dragons '00
The Filth and the Fury '99
Final Destination '00
The Five Senses '99
Frequency '00
Gummo '97
House Party '90
House Party 2: The Pajama Jam '91
House Party 3 '94
Julien Donkey-boy '99
Little Nicky '00
The Little Vampire '00
Lost Souls '00
Magnolia '99
Mother Night '96
Next Friday [Platinum Series] '00
Price of Glory '00
Saving Grace '00
Seven [2 SE] '95
Simpatico '99
Tumbleweeds '98
Turn It Up '00

NEW VIDEO GROUP
126 5th Ave., 15th Fl.
New York, NY 10011
(212)206-8600
800-420-2626
Fax: (212)206-9001

The Avengers 1964–66 '67
Bob Dylan: Don't Look Back '67
From Mao to Mozart: Isaac Stern in China '80
The Lathe of Heaven '80
Roots of Rhythm '99

NEW YORKER VIDEO
16 W. 61st St., 11th Fl.
New York, NY 10023
(212)247-6110
800-447-0196
Fax: (212)307-7855

After Life '98
The Cement Garden '93
City of Women '81
Fire '96
Fireworks '97
Guantanamera '95
The Interview '98
Jazz on a Summer's Day '59
Loulou '80
Maborosi '95
Mon Oncle d'Amerique '80
Pixote '81
Running out of Time '94
Secrets of the Heart '97
Unmade Beds '00
The War Zone '98

PARADE
Address unknown.

These titles are now available through MASTERTONE MULTI-MEDIA (see separate listing).

Bad Man's River '72
Blood on the Sun '45
Mohawk '56
Pancho Villa '72

PARAMOUNT HOME VIDEO
Bluhdorn Bldg.
5555 Melrose Ave.
Los Angeles, CA 90038
(213)956-3952

The Addams Family '91
Airplane! '80
Airplane 2: The Sequel '82
Alfie '66
Angela's Ashes '99
Bless the Child '00
Blue's Big Musical Movie '00
Braveheart '95
The Bridges at Toko-Ri '55
Bringing Out the Dead '99
Catch-22 '70
Charlotte's Web '73
Cheech and Chong: Still Smokin' '83
Cheech and Chong's Up in Smoke '79
Children of a Lesser God '86
Clue '85
Coneheads '93
The Conversation '74
Dead Zone '83
Death Wish '74
Deterrence '00
Donovan's Reef '63
Drop Zone '94
The Evening Star '96
Friday the 13th, Part 3 '82
Friday the 13th, Part 4: The Final Chapter '84
Ghost '90
The Godfather DVD Collection '72
Harold and Maude '71
Hell Is for Heroes '62
In Harm's Way '65
In Pursuit '00
Internal Affairs '90
Juice '92
Kill Shot '01
Kiss Me, Guido '97
La Cucaracha '99
The Ladies Man '00
The Longest Yard '74
Love Story '70
Lucky Numbers '00
Mach 2 '00
The Man Who Shot Liberty Valance '62
Mission: Impossible 2 '00
Mother '96
The Naked Gun: From the Files of Police Squad '88
Naked Gun 33 1/3: The Final Insult '94
Naked Gun 2 1/2: The Smell of Fear '91
Nashville '75
Necessary Roughness '91
The Next Best Thing '00
Nick of Time '95
North Dallas Forty '79
The Nutty Professor '63
The Odd Couple '68
An Officer and a Gentleman '82
Original Kings of Comedy '00
The Parallax View '74
Pet Sematary '89
Planes, Trains & Automobiles '87
The Real Blonde '97
Real Life '79
Rosemary's Baby '68
Rugrats in Paris: The Movie '00
Rules of Engagement '00
Save the Last Dance '01
Scrooged '88
She's Having a Baby '88
Snow Day '00
Sons of Katie Elder '65
Star Trek 2: The Wrath of Khan '82
Stuart Saves His Family '94
Submerged '00

Summer Rental '85
Sunshine '99
The Talented Mr. Ripley '99
Terms of Endearment '83
Tucker: The Man and His Dream '88
Tycus '98
Uncommon Valor '83
The Untouchables '87
U2: Rattle and Hum '88
The Virgin Suicides '99
The Warriors '79
What Women Want '00
White Christmas '54
Wonder Boys '00

PASSPORT INTERNATIONAL PRODUCTIONS
10520 Magnolia Blvd.
North Hollywood, CA 91601
(818)505-0696

Assault of the Party Nerds '89
Assault of the Party Nerds 2: Heavy Petting Detective '95
Embryo '76
Plan 9 from Outer Space [Passport Video] '56

PIONEER ENTERTAINMENT
2265 E. 220th St.
Long Beach, CA 90810
800-526-0363

Asteroid '97
Baywatch: Nightmare Bay / River of No Return '94
Bride of Re-Animator '89
The Cassandra Crossing '76
A Chinese Ghost Story: The Tsui Hark Animation '97
Drop Dead Rock '95
Eat Your Heart Out '96
Fall Time '94
The Field '90
For Hire '98
Gothic '87
I'll Remember April '99
The Killing of a Chinese Bookie '76
Mistress '91
Mountains of the Moon '90
The Object of Beauty '91
Opening Night '77
The Pandora Project '98
Picture Windows '95
Queens of Comedy '01
Rambling Rose [2 SE] '91
Red Letters '00
R.P.M. '97
Salome's Last Dance '88
Salt of the Earth '54
Search and Destroy '94
Shaft '00
Shane '53
Sol Bianca: The Legacy '90
The Specials '00
A Woman under the Influence '74

PROGRAM POWER ENTERTAINMENT
3300 Cherry Ave.
Long Beach, CA 90807
(562)621-9090
Fax: (562)621-9090

The Bone Yard '90
Slaughterhouse '87

QUESTAR VIDEO, INC.
PO Box 11345
Chicago, IL 60611-0345
(312)266-9400
800-544-8422
Fax: (312)266-9523

Bobby Darin: Mack Is Back! '00
Gladiators: Bloodsport of the Colosseum '00

Kayla: A Cry in the Wilderness '00
Rome: Power & Glory '99

REPUBLIC PICTURES HOME VIDEO
c/o Artisan Home Entertainment
2700 Colorado Ave.
Santa Monica, CA 90404
(310)255-3700

Frances '82
Once Upon a Time...When We Were Colored '95
Plenty '85
Tender Mercies '83

RHINO HOME VIDEO
10635 Santa Monica Blvd., 2nd Fl.
Los Angeles, CA 90025-4900
(310)474-4778
800-843-3670
Fax: (310)441-6573

Beetle Bailey / Hagar the Horrible / Betty Boop '89
Don't Answer the Phone '80
The Kidnapping of the President '80
My Mom's a Werewolf '89
Plump Fiction '97
The Pom Pom Girls / The Beach Girls '76
Sextette '78
Transformers: The Movie '86
Wonderwall: The Movie '69

ROAN GROUP
361 River Sound Village
Hayesville, NC 28904

These titles are now distributed through TROMA TEAM VIDEO (see separate listing).

D.O.A. [Roan] '49
The Indestructible Man / The Amazing Transparent Man '56
The Inspector General '49
Mommy [SE] '95
Pre-Code Hollywood: Vol. 1, "Of Human Bondage" '34

SALT CITY VIDEO PRODUCTIONS
7285 Lakeshore Rd.
Cicero, NY 13039

Ice from the Sun '00

SHOWTIME NETWORKS, INC.
5120 E. La Palma, No. 103
Anaheim Hills, CA 92807

Bojangles '01
The Passion of Ayn Rand '99
Rated X '00
Red Shoe Diaries: Four on the Floor '96
Red Shoe Diaries: Luscious Lola '00
Red Shoe Diaries: Strip Poker '96
Red Shoe Diaries: Swimming Naked '00

SIMITAR ENTERTAINMENT
5555 Pioneer Creek
Maple Plain, MN 55359
(612)479-7000
800-486-TAPE
Fax: (612)479-7001

Bay of Blood '71
Darkroom '90
Diary of a Serial Killer '97
Red Scorpion '89

SLINGSHOT ENTERTAINMENT
15030 Ventura Blvd., No. 1776
Sherman Oaks, CA 91403
800-776-5864

Attack of the Giant Leeches '59
A Bucket of Blood '59
Cinema's Dark Side Collection '00
Comedy Noir '00
Fay Wray Collection '00
The Impossible Spy '87
Irene Dunne Romance Classics '00
The Last of the Mohicans '20
The Little Princess '39
News from the West
Rikyu '90
Roger Corman Retrospective, Vol. 1 '00
The Wasp Woman '59

SOMETHING WEIRD VIDEO
PO Box 33664
Seattle, WA 98133
(206)361-3759
Fax: (206)364-7526

Something Weird's titles are distributed by IMAGE ENTERTAINMENT (see separate listing).

SONY WONDER
550 Madison Ave.
New York, NY 10022-3211
(212)833-8000

CinderElmo '99

STUDIO HOME ENTERTAINMENT
11846 Ventura Blvd., 3rd Fl.
Studio City, CA 91604
(818)762-0005
Fax: (818)762-0006

Animal Instincts '92
The Base '99
Black Eagle '88
The Boys '97
Bram Stoker's Shadowbuilder '98
China O'Brien '88
The Confession '98
The First 9 1/2 Weeks '98
The Highway Man '99
I'm Losing You '98
Kiss Shot '89
Komodo '99
Lady Dragon '92
The Last Stop '99
Mikey '00
The Million Dollar Hotel '99
Milo '98
Onegin '99
Postmortem '98
Secret Games '92

SUNLAND STUDIOS
9450 Chivers Ave.
Sun Valley, CA 91352
(818)504-6332
800-934-2111
Fax: (818)504-6380

Extramarital '98
Outlaw Justice '99

SYNAPSE
PO Box 1860
Bloomington, IL 61702
(309)661-9201
Fax: (309)661-9140

The Brain that Wouldn't Die '63
Deadbeat at Dawn '88
Evil Dead Trap '88
She Killed in Ecstasy '70
Triumph of the Will '34
Vampyros Lesbos '70

TAI SENG VIDEO MARKETING
170 S. Spruce Ave., Ste. 200
South San Francisco, CA 94080
(415)871-8118

VCI HOME VIDEO
11333 E. 60th Pl.
Tulsa, OK 74146
(918)254-6337
800-331-4077
Fax: (918)254-6117

Angel on My Shoulder '46
Beyond Atlantis '73
Blood and Black Lace '64
Broken Harvest '94
A Christmas Carol '51
December 7th: The Pearl Harbor Story '43
Getting Gertie's Garter '45
Gorgo '61
Hillbillys in a Haunted House '67
In This House of Brede '75
King and Country '64
Madron '70
Mein Kampf: Hitler's Rise and Fall '60
Pinocchio '76
Quackser Fortune Has a Cousin in the Bronx '70
Ride in the Whirlwind '66
The Shooting '66
The Undertaker and His Pals '67
Up in Mabel's Room '44
The Whip and the Body '63

WARNER HOME VIDEO, INC.
5775 Linder Canyon Rd.
Westlake Village, CA 91362
(877)277-9272

Annie Get Your Gun '50
Any Given Sunday '99
Arsenic and Old Lace '44
The Art of War '00
Bad Moon '96
Bait '00
Batman Beyond: Return of the Joker '00
Batman: Mask of the Phantasm '93
Battlefield Earth '00
Being There '79
Ben-Hur '59
Best in Show '00
The Big Tease '99
Bird '88
Brainstorm '83
Bronco Billy '80
Butterfield 8 '60
Chasers '94
A Christmas Carol '99
The Clan of the Cave Bear '86

The Crush '93
Defending Your Life '91
Diabolique '96
Empire Records '95
42nd Street '33
Freejack '92
Friendly Persuasion '56
Get Carter '71
Get Carter '00
Gettysburg '93
Good News '47
Gossip '99
Heaven and Earth '93
Imaginary Crimes '94
In Country '89
The In Crowd '00
Kelly's Heroes '70
Liberty Heights '99
Local Hero '83
Lost in America '85
The Maltese Falcon '41
Miss Congeniality '00
Mr. Wonderful '93
Murder in the First '95
MVP: Most Valuable Primate '00
My Dog Skip '99
North by Northwest '59
Nuremberg '00
The Old Man and the Sea '58 187 '97
Our Lips Are Sealed '00
Passenger 57 '92
Pat and Mike '52
The Perfect Storm '00
Pokemon the Movie 2000: The Power of One '00
Power '86
Race Against Time '00
Ready to Rumble '00
Red Planet '00
The Replacements '00
Romeo Must Die '00
Scooby-Doo and the Alien Invaders '00
Seven Days in May '64
7 Faces of Dr. Lao '63
Shaft in Africa '73
Shaft's Big Score '72
Sour Grapes '98
South Central '92
Space Cowboys '00
A Star Is Born '54
Striptease '96
Superman: The Movie '78
Superman 2 '80
Superman 3 '83
Superman 4: The Quest for Peace '87
Take Me Out to the Ball Game '49

Tarzan and the Lost City '98
Thumbelina '94
The Time Machine '60
Tom & Jerry's Greatest Chases '45
Tom Thumb '58
Two If by Sea '95
The Unsinkable Molly Brown '64
The Whole Nine Yards '00

WHIRLWIND MEDIA
105 Morris St.
Sebastopol, CA 95472
(707)824-4144
Fax: (707)824-4145

Shadow of Chinatown '36

WINSTAR HOME ENTERTAINMENT
419 Park Ave. S., 20th Fl.
New York, NY 10016
(212)686-6777
Fax: (212)686-0387

Alexandria Again and Forever '90
Alexandria...Why? '78
Attila 74: The Rape of Cyprus '75
Back to Back '96
The Ballad of Ramblin' Jack '00
Bed and Board '70
Beshkempir the Adopted Son '98
The Book of Stars '99
Boy Meets Girl '84
The Bridge '00
The Brylcreem Boys '96
Carmen Miranda: Bananas Is My Business '95
Cartoon Crazys: Banned & Censored '00
Cartoon Crazys Comic Book Heroes '00
Cartoon Crazys Spooky Toons '00
Cartoon Crazys: The Great Animation Studios: Famous Studios '00
Charming Billy '99
A Couch in New York '95
Delivered '98
Devil's Island '96
Digging to China '98
Divine Trash '98
Double Parked '00
Eden '98
An Egyptian Story '82
Fist of the North Star '95
Floating '97

The Four Musketeers '75
From a Whisper to a Scream '00
Girl in Black '56
A Good Baby '99
Great Animation Studios: Fleischer Studios '00
Grind '96
Hard-Boiled [Winstar] '92
Incubus '65
Johnny 100 Pesos '93
The Killer [Winstar] '90
La Separation '98
L'Ennui '98
Lewis and Clark and George '97
The Lifestyle '99
Love After Love '94
Mailer on Mailer '00
The Marquise of O '76
A Matter of Dignity '57
Mauvais Sang '86
Midaq Alley '95
My Sex Life...Or How I Got into an Argument '96
One Good Turn '95
The Other Side of Sunday '96
Perceval '78
Pola X '99
The Pompatus of Love '95
Pretty Village, Pretty Flame '96
A Single Girl '96
The Source '96
Stella '55
A Summer's Tale '96
Superstar: The Life and Times of Andy Warhol '90
The Terrorist '98
Tito and Me '92
Winter Sleepers '97
Yi Yi '00

WORLD VIDEO & SUPPLY, INC.
150 Executive Park Blvd., No. 1600
San Francisco, CA 94134-3303
(415)468-6218
888-960-5388
Fax: (415)468-1381

Ashes of Time '94

XENON ENTERTAINMENT
1440 9th St.
Santa Monica, CA 90401
(310)451-5510
800-829-1913
Fax: (310)395-4058

A Day in Black and White '01
Tha Eastsidaz '00
Ill-Gotten Gains '97
Klash '95
Penitentiary '79
Penitentiary 2 '82
Q: The Movie '99
Race to Freedom: The Story of the Underground Railroad '94
Say Amen, Somebody '80
Sudie & Simpson '90
Thug Immortal '97
A Woman Called Moses '78
The Women of Brewster Place '89

YORK ENTERTAINMENT
16133 Ventura Blvd., Ste. 1140
Encino, CA 91436
(818)788-4050
800-84-MOVIE
Fax: (818)788-4011

American Vampire '97
Asylum of Terror '98
Bar-B-Q '00
Best of Intimate Sessions: Vol. 2 '99
Captive '00
Clockin' Green '00
Dead Waters '94
Diamondbacks '99
Dope Case Pending '00
Final Payback '99
Heaven's Fire '99
Inhumanity '00
Interceptor Force '99
Intern '00
James Dean: Live Fast, Die Young '97
The Last Marshal '99
The List '99
Nothin' 2 Lose '00
Out Kold '00
The Perfect Nanny '00
The Prophet's Game '99
Restaurant '98
Row Your Boat '98
Social Misfits '00
Straight out of Compton '00
Thrill Seekers '99
Throw Down '00
Thug Life '00
2 G's and a Key '00

Listed below are all titles covered in both "Book 1" and this volume, "Book 2." Each DVD is labelled **1** or **2** for your convenience. Note that there are duplicates of some DVDs; if the title was put out by more than one distributor, the distributor's name will be indicated. If a distributor re-released a title, then the notations [1] and [2] will appear. Finally, some titles are annotated with the codes [CE] (Collector's Edition), [CS] (Collector's Series), [DC] (Director's Cut), or [SE] (Special Edition).

At War with the Army '50 **2**
Atomic Submarine '59 **1**
Atomic Train '99 **1**
Attack of the Giant Leeches '59 **2**
Attack of the Puppet People '58 **2**
Attention Shoppers '99 **2**
Attila '01 **2**
Attila 74: The Rape of Cyprus '75 **2**
The Audrey Hepburn Story '00 **2**
Austin Powers: International Man of Mystery '97 **1**
Austin Powers 2: The Spy Who Shagged Me '99 **1**
Autopsy '78 **1**
Autumn in New York '00 **2**
Avalon '90 **2**
The Avengers 1964–66 '67 **2**
The Avengers '67 **1**
The Avengers '98 **1**
Awakening of Gabriella '99 **1**
Awakenings '90 **1**
Awakening of the Beast '68 **2**
Away All Boats '56 **2**
The Awful Dr. Orlof '62 **2**
Ayn Rand: A Sense of Life '98 **1**

B

B. Monkey '97 **2**
Babar: King of the Elephants '99 **2**
Babe '95 **1**
Babe: Pig in the City '98 **2**
The Baby '72 **1**
Babette's Feast '87 **2**
Baby Boom '87 **2**
Baby Geniuses '98 **1**
The Babysitter's Seduction '96 **1**
The Bachelor '99 **1**
Back to Back '96 **2**
Back to God's Country / Something New '19 **2**
Back to School '86 **2**
Backdraft '91 **1**
Backlash '99 **2**
Backstage '00 **2**
Bad Boys '83 **1**
Bad Boys '95 **1**
Bad Girls Go to Hell / Another Day, Another Man '65 **2**
Bad Lieutenant '92 **1**
Bad Love '95 **1**
Bad Manners '98 **2**
Bad Man's River '72 **2**
Bad Moon '96 **2**
Badlands '74 **1**
Bait '00 **2**
Baker's Hawk '76 **1**
The Balcony '63 **2**
Ball of Fire '41 **1**
The Ballad of Ramblin' Jack '00 **2**
Bamboozled '00 **2**
Bananas '71 **2**
Bandit Queen '94 **2**
Bandits '99 **2**
The Bank Dick '40 **2**
Banzai Runner '86 **2**
Baraka '93 **1**
Barb Wire '96 **2**
Barbarella '68 **1**
The Barefoot Contessa '54 **2**
Barefoot in the Park '67 **1**
Barney's Great Adventure '98 **1**
Barry Lyndon '75 **1**
Bartok the Magnificent '99 **1**
The Base '99 **2**
BASEketball '98 **1**
Basic Instinct '92 **1**
Basket Case '82 **1**
Bastard out of Carolina '96 **1**
The Bat '59 **1**
The Bat Whispers '30 **1**

Bataan '43 **1**
Batman '89 **1**
Batman and Robin '97 **1**
Batman Beyond: Return of the Joker '00 **2**
Batman Forever '95 **1**
Batman: Mask of the Phantasm '93 **2**
Batman Returns '92 **1**
Bats '99 **2**
*batteries not included '87 **1**
Battle beyond the Stars '80 **2**
Battle for the Planet of the Apes '73 **2**
Battle of the Amazons '74 **2**
Battle of the Sexes '28 **2**
Battle Queen 2020 '99 **2**
Battlecade: Extreme Fighting '95 **1**
Battlecade: Extreme Fighting 2 '96 **1**
Battlefield Earth '00 **2**
The Battleship Potemkin '25 **1**
Battlestar Galactica '78 **1**
Battling Butler '26 **1**
Bay of Blood '71 **2**
Baywatch: Nightmare Bay / River of No Return '94 **2**
The Beach '00 **2**
Beach Blanket Bingo '65 **2**
Beach Girls '82 **2**
Beach Party '63 **2**
Bean '97 **1**
Bear in the Big Blue House: Party Time with Bear '00 **2**
Bear in the Big Blue House: Shapes, Sounds & Colors '00 **2**
The Bears & I '74 **1**
The Beast '88 **2**
Beast Cops '98 **2**
The Beast Must Die '75 **2**
The Beast of Yucca Flats '61 **2**
The Beast That Killed Women / The Monster of Camp Sunshine '65 **2**
Beat the Devil '53 **2**
The Beatles: The First U.S. Visit '91 **1**
The Beatles: The Ultimate DVD Collection '00 **2**
Beau Pere '81 **1**
Beautiful '00 **2**
Beautiful Girls '96 **1**
Beautiful Joe '00 **2**
Beautiful People '99 **2**
Beauty and the Beast '46 **1**
Beauty and the Beast: The Enchanted Christmas '97 **2**
Beauty Investigator '93 **1**
Beavis and Butt-Head Do America '96 **1**
Because of You '95 **2**
Bed and Board '70 **2**
Bed of Roses '95 **1**
The Bed You Sleep In '93 **2**
Bedazzled [SE] '00 **2**
Bedknobs and Broomsticks '71 **2**
The Bedroom Window '87 **2**
Bedrooms and Hallways '98 **2**
Beethoven '36 **2**
Beethoven '92 **2**
Beethoven's 2nd '93 **1**
Beethoven's 3rd '00 **2**
Beetle Bailey / Hagar the Horrible / Betty Boop '89 **2**
Beetlejuice '88 **1**
Before Night Falls '00 **2**
Before Sunrise '94 **1**
The Beguiled '70 **1**
Behind the Planet of the Apes '98 **2**
Being John Malkovich '99 **1**
Being There '79 **2**
Bell, Book and Candle '58 **1**
Belle of the Nineties '34 **1**

The Bells / The Crazy Ray '26 **1**
The Bells of St. Mary's '45 **1**
Belly '98 **1**
Bellyfruit '99 **2**
Beloved '98 **1**
Ben-Hur '59 **2**
Beneath the Planet of the Apes '70 **2**
Beneath the 12-Mile Reef '53 **1**
Benji '74 **1**
Benny & Joon '93 **2**
Beowulf '98 **2**
Beshkempir the Adopted Son '98 **2**
Besieged '98 **1**
Best in Show '00 **2**
Best Laid Plans '99 **1**
The Best Man '99 **1**
The Best of Boys in Love: Award Winning Gay Short Films '00 **2**
The Best of British Cinema: Five Decades of Classic British Films '88 **1**
Best of Intimate Sessions: Vol. 2 '99 **2**
Best of the Best: Especially for Kids '00 **2**
Best of the Best: Romantic Tales '99 **2**
Best of the Best: Strange Tales of the Imagination '99 **2**
Best of the Best 3: No Turning Back / Best of the Best: Without Warning '95 **2**
The Best of Times '86 **1**
The Best of Zagreb Film '? **1**
The Best of Zagreb Film: Laugh at Your Own Risk and For Children Only '?? **2**
The Best Revenge '96 **1**
The Best Years of Our Lives '46 **1**
Betrayed '88 **2**
Betrayed by Innocence '86 **1**
The Betsy '78 **1**
Better Than Chocolate '99 **1**
A Better Tomorrow, Part 1 [Tai Seng] '86 **1**
A Better Tomorrow, Part 1 [Anchor Bay] '86 **2**
A Better Tomorrow, Part 2 [Tai Seng] '88 **1**
A Better Tomorrow, Part 2 [Anchor Bay] '88 **2**
A Better Way to Die '00 **2**
Beverly Hills Ninja '96 **1**
Beware! Children at Play '95 **2**
Beware! The Blob '72 **2**
The Beyond '82 **2**
Beyond Atlantis '73 **2**
Beyond Suspicion '94 **1**
Beyond the Clouds '95 **2**
Beyond the Door 2 '79 **1**
Beyond the Mat '99 **2**
Bicentennial Man '99 **2**
The Bicycle Thief '48 **1**
Big '88 **1**
Big Bad Mama '74 **1**
The Big Blue [DC] '88 **2**
The Big Brass Ring '99 **1**
Big Bullet '96 **1**
The Big Chill '83 **1**
Big City Blues '99 **2**
Big Combo '55 **1**
The Big Country '58 **2**
Big Daddy '99 **1**
Big Deal on Madonna Street '58 **2**
The Big Doll House '71 **2**
The Big Easy '87 **1**
The Big Hit '98 **1**
The Big Kahuna '00 **2**
The Big Lebowski '97 **1**
Big Momma's House '00 **1**
Big Night '95 **1**

Big Red '62 **1**
The Big Red One '80 **1**
The Big Sleep '46 **1**
The Big Squeeze '96 **1**
The Big Tease '99 **2**
Big Trouble in Little China [SE] '86 **2**
Big Wars '93 **1**
The Big Wheel '49 **2**
Bikini Beach '64 **2**
The Bikini Car Wash Company '90 **1**
Bikini Hotel '97 **1**
Billy Elliot '00 **2**
Billy Jack '71 **1**
Billy Madison '94 **1**
Billy's Holiday '95 **2**
Billy's Hollywood Screen Kiss '98 **1**
BioHunter [SE] '95 **2**
Bird '88 **2**
Bird on a Wire '90 **1**
The Bird with the Crystal Plumage '70 **1**
The Birdcage '95 **1**
Birdman of Alcatraz '62 **2**
The Birds '63 **1**
The Birth of a Nation '15 **1**
The Bishop's Wife [HBO] '47 **1**
The Bishop's Wife [MGM] '47 **2**
Black & White '99 **1**
Black and White '99 **2**
Black Caesar '73 **2**
The Black Cat '81 **2**
Black Cat '91 **1**
Black Cat Run '98 **2**
The Black Cauldron '85 **2**
Black Christmas '75 **2**
Black Circle Boys '97 **1**
Black Death '91 **1**
Black Dog '98 **1**
Black Eagle '88 **2**
The Black Hole '79 **1**
Black Mama, White Mama '73 **2**
Black Mask '96 **1**
Black Moon Rising '86 **2**
Black Narcissus '47 **2**
Black Orpheus '58 **1**
The Black Pirate '26 **1**
Black Rain '88 **1**
Black Rain '89 **1**
Black Robe '91 **2**
Black Sabbath '64 **2**
Black Scorpion '95 **2**
Black Scorpion 2: Ground Zero '96 **2**
The Black Stallion '79 **1**
Black Sunday '60 **1**
Black Tight Killers '66 **2**
Black Tights '60 **1**
Blackjack '97 **1**
Blackmale '99 **2**
Blackrock '97 **2**
Blade '98 **1**
A Blade in the Dark '83 **2**
Blade [DC] '82 **1**
The Blair Witch Project [SE] '99 **1**
Blame It on Rio '84 **2**
Blank Generation '79 **1**
Blast from the Past '99 **1**
Blaze Starr Goes Nudist '63 **2**
Blazing Saddles '74 **1**
Bless the Child '00 **2**
Blind Justice '94 **2**
The Blob '58 **2**
Blood and Black Lace '64 **2**
Blood and Sand '89 **2**
Blood Beast Terror '67 **2**
Blood Bullets Buffoons '96 **2**
Blood Feast [SE] '63 **1**
Blood, Guts, Bullets and Octane '99 **1**
Blood In . . . Blood Out: Bound by Honor '93 **2**
Blood of Ghastly Horror '72 **2**
Blood on the Sun '45 **2**
The Blood Oranges '97 **1**

The Blood Spattered Bride '72 **1**
Bloodfist '89 **2**
Bloodfist 2 '90 **2**
Bloodfist 3: Forced to Fight '92 **2**
Bloodfist 4: Die Trying '92 **2**
Bloodstone '88 **1**
Bloodstorm: Subspecies 4 '98 **2**
The Bloodsucker Leads the Dance '75 **1**
Bloodsucking Freaks '75 **1**
Bloody Murder '99 **2**
The Bloody Pit of Horror '65 **2**
Blown Away '94 **1**
Blue Collar '78 **1**
The Blue Gardenia '53 **1**
Blue Juice '95 **1**
The Blue Lagoon '80 **1**
Blue Ridge Fall '99 **2**
Blue Sky '91 **2**
Blue Streak '99 **2**
Blue Tiger '94 **2**
Blue Velvet '86 **2**
Bluebeard '72 **2**
Blue's Big Musical Movie '00 **1**
The Blues Brothers [CE] '80 **1**
The Blues Brothers 2000 '98 **1**
Bob Dylan: Don't Look Back '67 **2**
Bob Hope Double Feature '00 **2**
Bob Hope: Hollywood's Brightest Star '97 **2**
Bob Roberts [SE] '92 **2**
Bobby Darin: Mack Is Back! '00 **2**
Body Armor '96 **1**
The Body Beneath '70 **2**
Body Chemistry '90 **2**
Body Chemistry 2: Voice of a Stranger '91 **2**
Body Chemistry 3: Point of Seduction '93 **2**
Body Chemistry 4: Full Exposure '95 **2**
Body Count '95 **2**
Body Double '84 **1**
Body Heat '81 **1**
Body of Influence 2 '96 **1**
Body Puzzle '93 **1**
Body Shot '93 **1**
Body Shots '99 **2**
Body Snatchers '93 **1**
Body Strokes '95 **1**
The Bodyguard '92 **1**
The Bodyguard / Dragon Princess '76 **2**
The Bodyguard from Beijing '94 **2**
The Bogus Witch Project '00 **2**
Boiler Room '00 **2**
Boiling Point '93 **1**
Bojangles '01 **2**
The Bone Collector '99 **1**
The Bone Yard '90 **2**
The Bonfire of the Vanities '90 **1**
Bonnie & Clyde '67 **1**
The Boogey Man '80 **1**
Boogie Nights '97 **1**
Book of Shadows: Blair Witch 2 '00 **2**
The Book of Stars '99 **2**
Booty Call '96 **1**
Born in East L.A. '87 **1**
Born on the Fourth of July [1] '89 **1**
Born on the Fourth of July [2] '89 **2**
Born to Win '71 **2**
Born Yesterday '50 **1**
The Borrowers '97 **1**
Bossa Nova '99 **2**
Boston Kickout '95 **1**
The Bostonians '84 **1**

Bottle Rocket '95 **1**
Bounce '00 **2**
Bound '96 **1**
Bound and Gagged: A Love Story '93 **1**
The Bounty '84 **2**
Bounty Hunters '96 **2**
Bounty Hunters 2: Hardball '97 **2**
Bowfinger '99 **1**
Box of Moonlight '96 **1**
The Boxer '97 **1**
Boxing Helena '93 **2**
A Boy and His Dog '75 **1**
Boy Meets Girl '84 **1**
Boyfriends & Girlfriends '88 **1**
The Boys '97 **2**
Boys and Girls '00 **2**
The Boys Club '96 **1**
Boys Don't Cry '99 **1**
Boys Life '94 **1**
Boys Life 2 '98 **1**
The Boys Next Door '85 **2**
Boys on the Side '94 **1**
Boys Will Be Boys '97 **1**
Boyz N the Hood '91 **2**
Brain Damage '88 **1**
Brain Dead '89 **2**
The Brain from Planet Arous '57 **2**
The Brain that Wouldn't Die '63 **2**
Brainstorm '83 **2**
Bram Stoker's Shadowbuilder '98 **2**
Branded to Kill '67 **1**
Brassed Off '96 **1**
The Brave Frog '87 **1**
The Brave One '56 **2**
Braveheart '95 **2**
Brazil [Criterion SE] '85 **1**
Brazil [Universal] '85 **1**
The Break Up '98 **1**
Breaker! Breaker! '77 **2**
Breaker Morant '80 **1**
Breakfast at Tiffany's '61 **1**
The Breakfast Club '85 **1**
Breakfast of Champions '98 **2**
Breakheart Pass '76 **2**
Breaking the Waves '95 **2**
Breeders '97 **1**
Brenda Starr '86 **1**
Brewster's Millions '85 **1**
Brian's Song '71 **2**
Bride of Chucky '98 **1**
The Bride of Frankenstein '35 **1**
Bride of Re-Animator '89 **2**
Bride of the Monster '55 **1**
The Bride with White Hair '93 **1**
The Bride with White Hair 2 '93 **1**
The Bride Wore Black '68 **2**
The Bridge '00 **2**
The Bridge at Remagen '69 **2**
Bridge of Dragons '99 **2**
The Bridge of San Luis Rey '44 **1**
The Bridge on the River Kwai [LE] '57 **2**
A Bridge Too Far '77 **1**
The Bridges at Toko-Ri '55 **2**
The Bridges of Madison County '95 **1**
Brief Encounter '46 **2**
Brigadoon '54 **1**
A Bright Shining Lie '98 **1**
Brighton Beach Memoirs '86 **1**
Bringing Out the Dead '99 **2**
The British Invasion Returns '00 **2**
Broadcast News '87 **1**
Brokedown Palace '99 **1**
Broken Arrow '95 **1**
Broken Blossoms '19 **1**
Broken Harvest '94 **2**
The Broken Hearts Club '00 **2**

Broken Vessels '98 **2**
Bronco Billy '80 **2**
A Bronx Tale '93 **1**
Brother Cadfael: The Devil's Novice '94 **2**
Brother, Can You Spare a Dime? '75 **1**
A Brother's Kiss '97 **1**
The Brothers McMullen '94 **2**
The Brutal Truth '99 **2**
Brute Force '46 **1**
The Brute Man '46 **1**
The Brylcreem Boys '96 **2**
Bubblegum Crisis Tokyo 2040 '00 **2**
Buck Privates '41 **1**
Buck Privates Come Home '47 **1**
A Bucket of Blood '59 **2**
Buddhist Fist '80 **1**
Buddy '97 **2**
The Buddy Holly Story '78 **1**
Buena Vista Social Club '99 **1**
Buffalo Bill & the Indians '76 **2**
Buffalo 66 '97 **1**
Buffet Froid '79 **2**
Bug Buster '99 **1**
A Bug's Life [CE] '98 **1**
Bugsy '91 **1**
Bull Durham '88 **1**
Bulldog Drummond Escapes '37 **1**
Bulldog Drummond's Secret Police '39 **2**
A Bullet in the Head '90 **1**
Bulletproof '96 **2**
Bullets over Broadway '94 **1**
Bullitt '68 **1**
Bulworth '98 **1**
The 'Burbs '89 **1**
Burglar '87 **2**
Burlesque on Carmen '16 **2**
Bury Me in Niagara '93 **1**
Bus Stop '56 **2**
Buster Keaton Rides Again / The Railrodder '65 **2**
Bustin' Loose '81 **2**
But I'm a Cheerleader '99 **2**
Butch Cassidy and the Sundance Kid '69 **1**
Butterfield 8 '60 **2**
Butterfly '00 **2**
Buzz Lightyear of Star Command: The Adventure Begins '00 **2**
Bye, Bye, Birdie '63 **1**
Bye Bye Monkey '77 **1**

C
Cabaret '72 **1**
The Cabinet of Dr. Caligari '19 **1**
The Cable Guy '96 **1**
Cabo Blanco / U.S. Marshal '81 **1**
Caddyshack '80 **1**
Caddyshack 2 '88 **1**
The Caine Mutiny '54 **1**
Caligula '80 **1**
Call of the Wild '72 **2**
Camelot '67 **1**
Camille Claudel '89 **2**
Camille 2000 '69 **1**
Canadian Bacon '94 **2**
The Candidate '72 **1**
Candleshoe '78 **1**
Candy '68 **2**
Candyman '92 **1**
Cannibal Ferox '84 **2**
Cannonball Run 2 '84 **1**
Cannonball Run '81 **2**
Can't Hardly Wait '98 **1**
The Canterbury Tales '71 **1**
The Canterville Ghost '98 **2**
Capone '89 **1**
Capricorn One '78 **2**
Captain Kidd '45 **2**
Captive '00 **2**
The Car '77 **1**
Car Wash '76 **2**

Caracara '00 **2**
Career Opportunities '91 **1**
Caress of the Vampire [CE] '96 **1**
Caress of the Vampire 2: Teenage Girl a Go-Go '96 **1**
Carlito's Way '93 **1**
Carmen / The Cheat '15 **2**
Carmen, Baby '66 **1**
Carmen Miranda: Bananas Is My Business '95 **2**
Carnal Crimes '91 **1**
Carnival of Souls '98 **1**
Carnosaur '93 **2**
Carnosaur 2 '94 **2**
Carnosaur 3: Primal Species '96 **2**
Carolina Skeletons '92 **1**
Carousel '56 **1**
Cartel '90 **1**
Cartoon Crazys '97 **1**
Cartoon Crazys 2 '98 **1**
Cartoon Crazys: And the Envelope, Please '99 **1**
Cartoon Crazys: Banned & Censored '00 **2**
Cartoon Crazys Christmas '98 **1**
Cartoon Crazys Comic Book Heroes '99 **2**
Cartoon Crazys Goes to War '98 **1**
Cartoon Crazys: Kids All-Time Favorites '99 **1**
Cartoon Crazys Sci-Fi '99 **1**
Cartoon Crazys Spooky Toons '00 **2**
Cartoon Crazys: The Great Animation Studios: Famous Studios '00 **2**
Cartoon Noir '00 **2**
Casablanca '42 **1**
Casino '95 **2**
Casper's Haunted Christmas '00 **2**
The Cassandra Crossing '76 **2**
Castaway '00 **2**
The Castle '97 **1**
Castle Freak '95 **1**
Casual Sex? '88 **1**
The Cat and the Canary '27 **1**
Cat Ballou [SE] '65 **2**
Cat City '87 **1**
The Cat from Outer Space '78 **1**
Cat on a Hot Tin Roof '84 **2**
Cat People '82 **1**
Cat Women of the Moon '53 **2**
Catch-22 '70 **2**
Catherine Cookson's The Cinder Path '94 **2**
Catherine Cookson's The Secret '00 **2**
Cats '98 **1**
Caught Up '98 **1**
Cause of Death '90 **1**
Cave of the Living Dead '65 **2**
Cecil B. Demented '00 **2**
Celebrity '98 **1**
The Cell '00 **2**
The Cement Garden '93 **2**
Center Stage '91 **1**
Center Stage '00 **2**
Central Station '98 **1**
C'est la Vie, Mon Cherie '93 **1**
Chained Heat 3: Hell Mountain '98 **2**
Chairman of the Board '97 **1**
The Challenge of Flight: Disc One '?? **1**
The Chamber '96 **1**
Champions '96 **1**
Chances Are '89 **1**
Chang: A Drama of the Wilderness '27 **2**
The Changeling '80 **2**
Changing Habits '96 **1**
Chaplin '92 **1**

The Chaplin Mutuals, Vol. 1 '9? **1**
The Chaplin Mutuals, Vol. 2 '9? **1**
The Chaplin Mutuals, Vol. 3 '9? **1**
Chaplin's Art of Comedy '66 **1**
Chaplin's Essanay Comedies, Vol. 1 '9? **1**
Chaplin's Essanay Comedies, Vol. 2 '9? **1**
Chaplin's Essanay Comedies, Vol. 3 '9? **1**
Chappaqua '66 **1**
Charade '63 **1**
Chariots of Fire '81 **1**
Charles Chaplin—A First National Collection '?? **1**
Charlie, the Lonesome Cougar '67 **1**
Charlie's Angels '00 **2**
Charlie's Angels: Angels Undercover '76 **2**
Charlotte's Web '73 **2**
Charming Billy '99 **2**
Chasers '94 **2**
Chasing Amy '97 **2**
The Cheat '15 **2**
Cheaters '00 **2**
Cheech and Chong: Still Smokin' '83 **2**
Cheech and Chong's Up in Smoke '79 **2**
Cherry Falls / Terror Tract '00 **2**
Cherry 2000 '88 **2**
Chicken Run '00 **2**
Children of a Lesser God '86 **2**
Children of the Corn '84 **2**
Children of the Corn 666: Isaac's Return '99 **1**
Children Shouldn't Play with Dead Things '72 **1**
Child's Play '88 **1**
Child's Play 2 '90 **1**
China O'Brien '88 **2**
The China Syndrome '79 **1**
Chinatown '74 **1**
Chinese Box '97 **1**
Chinese Connection '73 **1**
A Chinese Ghost Story '87 **1**
A Chinese Ghost Story II '90 **2**
A Chinese Ghost Story III '91 **2**
A Chinese Ghost Story: The Tsui Hark Animation '97 **2**
Chinese Odyssey, Part One: Pandora's Box '94 **1**
Chinese Odyssey, Part Two: Cinderalla '94 **1**
Chino / Man with a Camera '75 **1**
Chitty Chitty Bang Bang '68 **1**
Chloe in the Afternoon '72 **1**
Choices '81 **2**
The Chosen One: Legend of the Raven '98 **1**
Christine '84 **1**
A Christmas Carol '51 **2**
A Christmas Carol '84 **1**
A Christmas Carol '99 **2**
A Christmas Story '83 **1**
Chronos '87 **1**
Chuck & Buck '00 **2**
C.H.U.D. '84 **2**
Chushingura '62 **1**
The Cider House Rules '99 **2**
Cinderella '97 **1**
CinderElmo '99 **2**
Cinema Combat: Hollywood Goes to War '98 **2**
Cinema's Dark Side Collection '00 **2**
Circle of Friends '94 **1**
Circus '00 **2**
The Circus '19 **1**
Citizen X '95 **2**
City Hall '95 **1**
City Hunter '92 **1**
City Lights '31 **1**

City of Angels '98 **1**
City of Industry '96 **2**
The City of Lost Children '95 **1**
City of Women '81 **2**
City on Fire '87 **1**
City Slickers '91 **2**
City War '89 **1**
A Civil Action '98 **1**
The Claim '00 **2**
Claire's Knee '71 **1**
The Clan of the Cave Bear '86 **2**
Class '83 **2**
Class of Nuke 'Em High '86 **1**
Clay Pigeons '98 **1**
Clean and Sober '88 **1**
Clear and Present Danger '94 **1**
Cleopatra '63 **2**
Cleopatra '99 **1**
Cleopatra Jones '73 **1**
Clerks '94 **1**
Clerks Uncensored '00 **2**
The Client '94 **1**
Cliffhanger [1] '93 **1**
Cliffhanger [2 CS] '93 **2**
The Climb '97 **1**
Clockers '95 **1**
Clockin' Green '00 **2**
A Clockwork Orange '71 **1**
Close Encounters of the Third Kind [CE] '77 **2**
Closer and Closer '96 **1**
Clue '85 **2**
Clueless '95 **1**
Cobra '86 **1**
Cockfighter '74 **2**
The Cocoanuts '29 **1**
Coffy '73 **2**
Cold Blooded '00 **2**
Cold Eyes of Fear '70 **1**
Cold Harvest '98 **1**
Cold Sweat '71 **2**
College '27 **1**
The Colony '98 **2**
Color Me Blood Red '64 **1**
The Color of Money '86 **1**
Color of Night '94 **1**
The Color Purple '85 **1**
Colorz of Rage '97 **2**
Coma '78 **1**
Combat Shock '84 **1**
Come and Get It '36 **2**
Comedy Noir '00 **2**
Comic Act '00 **2**
Comin' at Ya! '81 **1**
Coming Soon '99 **2**
Coming to America '88 **1**
Commando '85 **1**
The Commitments '91 **2**
Communion [CE] '89 **2**
The Complete Superman Collection '43 **2**
The Complete Uncensored Private Snafu '46 **1**
Con Air '97 **1**
The Con Artists '80 **1**
Conan the Barbarian [1] '82 **1**
Conan the Barbarian [2 CE] '82 **2**
Conan the Destroyer '84 **1**
Condorman '81 **1**
Coneheads '93 **2**
The Confession '98 **2**
Confessions of Sorority Girls '00 **2**
Confidentially Yours '83 **1**
Congo '95 **1**
The Conman '98 **1**
The Conqueror '56 **1**
Conquest of the Planet of the Apes '72 **2**
Conspiracy: The Trial of the Chicago Eight '87 **1**
Conspiracy Theory '97 **1**
Contact '97 **1**
The Contender '00 **2**
The Contract '98 **2**
The Conversation '74 **2**

Convict 762 '98 **1**
The Cook, the Thief, His Wife & Her Lover '90 **2**
Cookie's Fortune '99 **1**
Cool Hand Luke '67 **1**
Cool Runnings '93 **1**
Cooley High '75 **2**
Cop and a Half '93 **1**
Cop Land '97 **1**
Copycat '95 **1**
The Coroner '98 **2**
Corridors of Blood '58 **1**
Corrina, Corrina '94 **1**
The Corruptor '99 **1**
The Cosmic Man '59 **2**
Cost of Living '97 **1**
Cotton Comes to Harlem '70 **2**
Cotton Mary '99 **2**
A Couch in New York '95 **2**
Coup de Torchon '81 **2**
Court Jester '56 **1**
Cousin Bette '97 **1**
The Cowboy Way '94 **1**
The Cowboys '72 **1**
Coyote Ugly '00 **2**
Crackdown '88 **1**
The Cradle Will Rock '99 **2**
The Craft '96 **1**
Crash '95 **1**
Crazy in Alabama '99 **2**
The Crazy Ray '22 **1**
Crazy Six '98 **1**
The Crazysitter '94 **2**
Creator '85 **1**
Creepers '85 **1**
The Creeps '97 **2**
Creepshow '82 **1**
Creepshow 2 '87 **2**
The Crew '00 **2**
Crime and Punishment in Suburbia '00 **2**
Crime Broker '94 **1**
Crime Story '93 **2**
Crime Story: The Complete Saga '86 **2**
Crimes & Misdemeanors [Image] '89 **1**
Crimes & Misdemeanors [MGM] '89 **2**
Crimes of Passion '84 **1**
Criminals '97 **2**
The Crimson Code '00 **2**
Crimson Tide '95 **1**
Crimson Wolf '94 **1**
Critical Care '97 **2**
Crocodile '00 **2**
Crooklyn '94 **1**
Cross My Heart and Hope to Die '94 **2**
Cross of Iron '76 **1**
The Crossing Guard '94 **1**
Crossworlds '96 **1**
Crouching Tiger, Hidden Dragon '00 **2**
Croupier '97 **2**
The Crow '93 **1**
The Crow 2: City of Angels '96 **1**
The Crow: Salvation '00 **2**
Crucible of Terror '72 **2**
Cruel Intentions '98 **1**
Crumb '94 **1**
The Crush '93 **2**
Cry Freedom '87 **1**
A Cry in the Wild '90 **2**
Cry Uncle '71 **2**
The Crying Game '92 **1**
Crystal Hunt '92 **1**
Cube '98 **1**
Cujo '83 **2**
The Cunning Little Vixen '95 **1**
The Curious Dr. Humpp '70 **2**
Curse of the Puppet Master: The Human Experiment '98 **2**
Curse of the Voodoo '64 **1**
Curtain Call '97 **2**
The Curve '97 **2**
Custer of the West '67 **1**

Cut '00 **2**
Cut Throats Nine '72 **2**
Cutaway '00 **2**
Cutthroat Island '95 **1**
The Cutting Edge '92 **2**
Cybernator '91 **1**
Cyberotica '00 **2**
Cyborg '89 **2**
Cyrano de Bergerac '25 **2**

D
Da Hip Hop Witch '00 **2**
Daddy Long Legs '19 **1**
Dakota '88 **2**
Damage '92 **1**
Dame Edna's Neighbourhood Watch 2 '92 **2**
Damien: Omen 2 '78 **2**
Damn the Defiant '62 **2**
Dance with a Stranger '85 **2**
Dance with Me '98 **1**
Dance with the Devil '97 **2**
Dancer in the Dark '99 **2**
Dancer, Texas—Pop. 81 '98 **1**
Dances with Wolves '90 **1**
Dancing at Lughnasa '98 **1**
Dancing in the Dark '95 **1**
The Dandelion Crown '93 **1**
Dangerous Beauty '98 **1**
Dangerous Curves '99 **2**
Dangerous Ground '96 **1**
Dangerous Liaisons '88 **1**
Dangerous Minds '95 **1**
Daniella by Night '61 **1**
Dante's Peak '97 **1**
Dario Argento's World of Horror '85 **2**
Dark City '97 **1**
The Dark Crystal '82 **1**
The Dark Half '91 **1**
Dark Odyssey '57 **1**
Dark Planet '97 **1**
Dark Secrets '95 **1**
Dark Shadows [SE] '99 **1**
Dark Star '74 **1**
Dark Victory '39 **1**
Dark Waters '44 **1**
Darkdrive '98 **2**
Darkman '90 **1**
Darkman 2: The Return of Durant '94 **1**
Darkroom '90 **2**
Darkside Blues '99 **2**
Das Boot [DC] '81 **1**
Daughter of Horror / Dementia '55 **2**
Daughters of Darkness '71 **1**
Dave '93 **1**
David and Lisa '62 **1**
DaVinci's War '92 **2**
Dawn of the Dead '78 **1**
Dawn Rider / Trail Beyond '35 **2**
A Day in Black and White '01 **2**
Day of the Animals '77 **2**
Day of the Dead '85 **1**
The Day of the Jackal '73 **1**
The Day the Earth Caught Fire '61 **2**
Daylight '96 **1**
Days of Heaven '78 **1**
Days of Thunder '90 **1**
The Daytrippers '96 **2**
Dazed and Confused '93 **1**
Deacon Brodie '98 **2**
Dead Again '91 **1**
Dead Alive '93 **1**
Dead and Buried '81 **2**
Dead Are Alive '72 **2**
Dead Bang '89 **1**
Dead Calm '89 **1**
Dead End '98 **1**
Dead Man '95 **2**
Dead Man on Campus '97 **1**
Dead Man Walking '95 **2**
Dead Men Don't Wear Plaid '82 **2**
The Dead Next Door '89 **2**
Dead of Night '99 **2**
Dead Poets Society '89 **1**
Dead Presidents '95 **1**

Dead Ringers '88 **1**
Dead Waters '94 **2**
Dead Zone '83 **2**
Deadbeat at Dawn '88 **2**
Deadfall '93 **1**
Deadful Melody '92 **2**
Deadly Beauty: Snow's Secret Life '01 **2**
Deadly Weapons '70 **2**
Deal of a Lifetime '99 **2**
Dean Koontz's Mr. Murder '98 **1**
Dear Santa '98 **2**
Death and the Compass '96 **2**
Death Becomes Her '92 **1**
Death Mask '98 **2**
Death on the Nile '78 **2**
Death Race 2000 '75 **1**
Death Sentence '74 **2**
Death Warrant '90 **2**
Death Wish '74 **2**
Death Wish 5: The Face of Death '94 **2**
Deathtrap '82 **1**
The Decalogue '88 **1**
The Decameron '70 **1**
December 7th: The Pearl Harbor Story '43 **2**
Deconstructing Harry '97 **1**
Dee Snider's Strangeland '98 **1**
The Deep '77 **1**
Deep Blue Sea '99 **1**
Deep Cover '92 **1**
The Deep End of the Ocean '98 **1**
Deep Impact '98 **1**
Deep in the Heart (of Texas) '98 **2**
Deep Red: Hatchet Murders '75 **1**
Deep Rising '98 **1**
Deepstar Six '89 **2**
The Deer Hunter '78 **1**
Def by Temptation '90 **1**
Def Jam's How to Be a Player '97 **1**
The Defender '94 **2**
Defending Your Life '91 **2**
The Defilers '65 **2**
Deliverance '72 **1**
Delivered '98 **2**
The Delivery '99 **2**
Delta Force '86 **2**
Delta Force 2: Operation Stranglehold '90 **2**
Dementia '55 **2**
Dementia '98 **2**
Dementia 13 '63 **2**
Demetrius and the Gladiators '54 **2**
Demolition Man '93 **1**
The Demolitionist '95 **1**
Demon City Shinjuku '93 **2**
The Demoniacs '74 **1**
Demons '86 **1**
Demons 2 '87 **1**
The Dentist '96 **1**
The Dentist 2: Brace Yourself '98 **1**
Dersu Uzala '75 **2**
The Descendant of Wing Chun '78 **1**
Desecration '99 **1**
Desert Blue '98 **1**
Desert Hearts '86 **2**
Desert Heat '99 **1**
Desert Thunder '99 **2**
Desert Winds '95 **2**
The Designated Mourner '97 **1**
Desolation Angels '95 **2**
Desperado '95 **1**
Desperado / El Mariachi '95 **1**
Desperate Crimes '93 **1**
Desperate Measures '98 **1**
Desperately Seeking Susan '85 **2**
Destination Moon '50 **1**

Destination Vegas '95 **2**
Destiny '21 **2**
Detention '98 **2**
Deterrence '00 **2**
Detour '46 **2**
Detroit 9000 '73 **2**
Detroit Rock City '99 **1**
Deuce Bigalow: Male Gigolo '99 **2**
The Devil & Max Devlin '81 **2**
The Devil Bat's Daughter '46 **1**
Devil in a Blue Dress '95 **1**
Devil in the Flesh '98 **1**
The Devil Rides Out '68 **2**
The Devil's Advocate '97 **1**
Devil's Island '96 **2**
The Devil's Nightmare '71 **1**
The Devil's Own '97 **1**
Devil's Rain '75 **1**
Devonsville Terror '83 **1**
Diabolique '55 **1**
Diabolique '96 **2**
Diamond Run '00 **2**
Diamondbacks '99 **2**
Diamonds '99 **2**
Diamonds Are Forever [SE] '71 **2**
Diary of a Chambermaid '64 **2**
Diary of a Serial Killer '97 **2**
Dick '99 **2**
Die! Die! Die! '00 **2**
Die Hard '88 **1**
Die Hard 2: Die Harder '90 **1**
Die Hard: With a Vengeance '95 **1**
Die, Monster, Die! '65 **2**
Die Screaming, Marianne '73 **2**
Die Watching '93 **1**
Digging to China '98 **2**
Digimon: The Movie '00 **2**
Dilemma '97 **2**
Dillinger '73 **2**
The Dinner Game '98 **2**
Dinosaur [CE] '00 **2**
Dinosaur Valley Girls '96 **2**
Dinosaurus! '60 **2**
Diplomatic Siege '99 **2**
Dirty Dancing [1] '87 **1**
Dirty Dancing [2 CE] '87 **1**
The Dirty Dozen '67 **1**
Dirty Duck '75 **2**
The Dirty Girls '64 **1**
Dirty Harry '71 **1**
Dirty Pictures '00 **2**
Dirty Rotten Scoundrels '88 **1**
Dirty Work '97 **2**
Disclosure '94 **1**
The Discreet Charm of the Bourgeoisie '72 **2**
The Disenchanted '90 **1**
Dish Dogs '98 **2**
Disney's The Kid '00 **2**
The Distinguished Gentleman '92 **1**
Disturbing Behavior '98 **1**
Diva '92 **1**
Divided We Stand '00 **2**
Divine Madness '80 **1**
Divine Trash '98 **2**
Django '68 **1**
Django Strikes Again '87 **1**
Do the Right Thing [1] '89 **1**
Do the Right Thing [2] '89 **2**
D.O.A. [Image] '49 **1**
D.O.A. [Roan] '49 **2**
Doc Hollywood '91 **1**
Doctor Dolittle '67 **2**
Dr. Dolittle '98 **1**
Dr. Frankenstein's Castle of Freaks '74 **2**
Dr. Giggles '92 **2**
Dr. Goldfoot and the Bikini Machine '66 **2**
Dr. Jekyll and Mr. Hyde ' **1**
Dr. No [SE] '62 **1**
Doctor Phibes Rises Again '72 **2**

Dr. Strangelove, or: How I Learned to Stop Worrying and Love the Bomb [1] '64 **1**
Dr. Strangelove, or: How I Learned to Stop Worrying and Love the Bomb [2 SE] '64 **2**
Dr. T & the Women '00 **2**
Dodsworth '36 **1**
Dog Day Afternoon '75 **1**
Dogma '99 **2**
Dolemite '75 **1**
Dolores Claiborne '94 **1**
Dolphins '92 **2**
Dominion Tank Police '89 **1**
Don Juan DeMarco '94 **1**
Donnie Brasco [1] '96 **1**
Donnie Brasco [2] '96 **2**
Donovan's Brain '53 **2**
Donovan's Reef '63 **2**
Don's Party '76 **1**
Don't Answer the Phone '80 **2**
Don't Be a Menace to South Central While Drinking Your Juice in the Hood '95 **1**
Don't Do It '94 **1**
Don't Go in the House '80 **1**
Don't Let Me Die on a Sunday '99 **2**
Don't Look in the Basement '73 **1**
Don't Mess with My Sister! '85 **2**
Don't Tell Mom the Babysitter's Dead '91 **2**
Don't Torture a Duckling '72 **1**
Don't Touch the White Woman! '74 **1**
The Doors [1] '91 **1**
The Doors [2 SE] '91 **2**
Dope Case Pending '00 **2**
Double Agent 73 '80 **2**
Double Dragon '94 **2**
Double Impact '91 **2**
Double Indemnity '44 **1**
Double Jeopardy '99 **1**
Double Parked '00 **2**
Double Suicide '69 **2**
Double Team '97 **1**
Down in the Delta '98 **1**
Down to You '00 **2**
Downhill Willie '96 **2**
Dracula '73 **1**
Dracula '79 **1**
Dracula / Strange Case of Dr. Jekyll & Mr. Hyde '73 **2**
Dracula, Prince of Darkness '66 **1**
Dracula vs. Frankenstein '71 **2**
Dragnet '87 **1**
The Dragon Chronicles '94 **2**
The Dragon Fist '80 **1**
Dragon from Shaolin '96 **1**
Dragon Princess '81 **2**
Dragon: The Bruce Lee Story '93 **1**
Dragonheart [SE] '96 **1**
Dragonheart: A New Beginning '00 **2**
Dragons Forever '88 **1**
Dragons of the Orient '88 **1**
Dralion '00 **2**
The Draughtsman's Contract '82 **1**
Dream Lovers '86 **1**
The Dreamlife of Angels '98 **1**
Dreams of Gold: The Mel Fisher Story '86 **1**
Dreamscape '84 **1**
Dressed to Kill '46 **2**
The Drifter '88 **2**
Driller Killer '74 **1**
Drive '96 **1**
Drive-in Discs, Vol. 1 '00 **2**
Drive Me Crazy '99 **2**
Driving Miss Daisy '89 **1**

From Dusk Till Dawn 2: Texas Blood Money '98 **1**
From Dusk Till Dawn 3: The Hangman's Daughter '99 **1**
From Mao to Mozart: Isaac Stern in China '80 **2**
From Russia with Love [1] '63 **1**
From Russia with Love [2 SE] '63 **2**
From the Earth to the Moon '98 **1**
From the Journals of Jean Seberg '95 **1**
The Front Page '74 **1**
Frostbiter: Wrath of the Wendigo '94 **2**
Frozen '98 **1**
The Fruit Is Swelling '97 **1**
Fruits of Passion: The Story of "O" Continued '82 **2**
The Fugitive '93 **1**
Fugitive Champion '99 **2**
Full Contact '92 **1**
Full Disclosure '00 **2**
Full Metal Jacket '87 **1**
The Full Monty '96 **1**
Full Moon in Paris '84 **1**
Full Throttle '96 **1**
Fun & Fancy Free '47 **2**
The Funeral '84 **1**
The Funhouse '81 **1**
Funny Farm '88 **1**
Funny Games '97 **1**
Fusion One '00 **2**
Futuresport '98 **1**

G

Galaxy Quest '99 **2**
Gallipoli '81 **1**
The Game '97 **1**
The Garden of Allah '36 **2**
Gargoyles '72 **1**
Gary Cooper Double Feature '00 **2**
Gasaraki 1: The Summoning '00 **2**
Gattaca '97 **1**
The Gauntlet '77 **1**
The Gay Deceivers '69 **2**
The Gay Desperado '36 **2**
Gen-X Cops '99 **2**
The General '26 **1**
The General '98 **1**
The General's Daughter '99 **1**
Generator 1: Gawl '00 **2**
Gentleman's Agreement '47 **1**
Gentlemen Prefer Blondes '53 **2**
George Balanchine's The Nutcracker '93 **1**
George of the Jungle '97 **1**
Georgia '95 **1**
Geronimo: An American Legend '93 **1**
Get Carter '71 **2**
Get Carter '00 **2**
Get On the Bus '96 **2**
Get Shorty '95 **1**
The Getaway '72 **1**
The Getaway '93 **1**
Getting Even with Dad '94 **2**
Getting Gertie's Garter '45 **2**
Gettysburg '93 **2**
Ghost '90 **2**
The Ghost and the Darkness '96 **1**
Ghost Chase '88 **2**
Ghost Dog: The Way of the Samurai '99 **2**
The Ghost Goes Gear '66 **1**
Ghost in the Shell '95 **1**
Ghost Story '81 **1**
Ghostbusters '84 **1**
Ghostbusters 2 '89 **1**
Ghosts on the Loose '43 **2**
G.I. Jane '97 **1**
Gia '98 **2**
Giant from the Unknown '58 **2**
Gigi '58 **1**

Gilda '46 **2**
Gimme Shelter '70 **2**
The Gingerbread Man '97 **1**
Girl '98 **2**
Girl Explores Girl: The Alien Encounter [CE] '00 **2**
Girl Gang '54 **2**
Girl Hunters '63 **1**
Girl in Black '56 **2**
Girl, Interrupted '99 **2**
The Girl on a Motorcycle '68 **1**
The Girl Who Knew Too Much '63 **2**
Girlfight '99 **2**
Girls Just Want to Have Fun '85 **2**
Girls of the White Orchid '85 **1**
Girls School Screamers '86 **1**
Gladiator '92 **2**
Gladiator '00 **2**
Gladiator Eroticus '00 **2**
Gladiators: Bloodsport of the Colosseum '00 **2**
Glastonbury: The Movie '95 **2**
Glen or Glenda? '53 **1**
The Glimmer Man '96 **1**
Glitch! '88 **1**
Gloria '98 **1**
Glory [1] '89 **1**
Glory [2 SE] '89 **2**
Go '99 **1**
Go for Broke! '51 **2**
Go, Go Second Time Virgin '69 **2**
Go West '25 **1**
God.com '99 **1**
God of Cookery '96 **1**
God of Gamblers '89 **1**
God of Gambler's Return '94 **1**
The Godfather DVD Collection '72 **2**
The Godfather, Part 2 '74 **2**
The Godfather, Part 3 '90 **2**
Godmoney '99 **1**
Gods and Monsters '98 **1**
God's Comedy '95 **2**
Godzilla '98 **1**
Godzilla, King of the Monsters '56 **1**
Godzilla 2000 '99 **2**
Godzilla vs. Monster Zero '68 **2**
Godzilla vs. Mothra '64 **1**
Godzilla's Revenge '69 **1**
Going My Way / Holiday Inn '44 **1**
Going Overboard '89 **1**
Gold of the Amazon Women '79 **2**
The Gold Rush '25 **1**
The Golden Child '86 **1**
Golden Voyage of Sinbad '73 **2**
Goldeneye '95 **1**
Goldfinger '64 **1**
Gone in 60 Seconds '74 **2**
Gone in 60 Seconds '00 **2**
Gone with the Wind '39 **1**
A Good Baby '99 **2**
Good Luck '96 **1**
Good Morning '59 **2**
Good News '47 **2**
The Good, the Bad and the Ugly '67 **1**
Good Will Hunting '97 **1**
Goodbye America '97 **2**
Goodbye, Lover '99 **1**
Goodfellas '90 **1**
The Gore-Gore Girls '72 **2**
Gorgeous '99 **2**
Gorgo '61 **2**
Gorillas in the Mist '88 **1**
Gorky Park '83 **2**
The Gospel According to Philip K. Dick '00 **2**
The Gospel According to St. Matthew '64 **1**
Gossip '99 **2**

Gothic '87 **2**
Gotti '96 **2**
The Governess '98 **1**
Goya in Bordeaux '00 **2**
Grace of My Heart [CE] '96 **1**
Grambling's White Tiger '81 **1**
Grand Canyon '91 **2**
Grand Illusion '37 **1**
The Grandfather '98 **2**
Grandma's House '88 **1**
Grave of the Fireflies '88 **2**
Gray's Anatomy '96 **1**
Greaser's Palace '72 **2**
The Great Alaska Train Adventure '?? **2**
Great Animation Studios: Fleischer Studios '00 **2**
Great Baseball Movies '00 **2**
Great Boxing Movies '00 **2**
The Great Conqueror's Concubine '94 **1**
The Great Conqueror's Concubine, Part 2 '94 **1**
A Great Day in Harlem / The Spitball Story '94 **1**
The Great Dictator '40 **1**
The Great Escape '63 **1**
Great Expectations '46 **1**
Great Expectations '97 **1**
The Great Locomotive Chase '56 **1**
The Great Lover '49 **2**
Great Mafia Movies '00 **2**
The Great Outdoors '88 **1**
The Great Rupert '50 **1**
The Great Santini '80 **1**
The Great Train Robbery '79 **1**
The Greatest Story Ever Told [SE] '65 **2**
Greedy '94 **1**
The Green Berets '68 **1**
The Green Mile '99 **1**
Gremlins '84 **1**
Grey Owl '99 **2**
Gridlock'd '96 **1**
The Grifters '90 **1**
Grim '95 **1**
Grind '96 **2**
The Grissom Gang '71 **2**
Grizzly '76 **1**
Groove '00 **2**
Grosse Pointe Blank '97 **1**
Ground Control '98 **1**
Groundhog Day '93 **1**
The Groundstar Conspiracy '72 **2**
Gruesome Twosome '67 **2**
Grumpier Old Men '95 **1**
Grumpy Old Men '93 **1**
Guantanamera '95 **2**
The Guardian '90 **1**
Guarding Tess '94 **1**
Guess Who's Coming to Dinner '67 **1**
Guilty by Suspicion '91 **1**
Guinevere '93 **1**
Guinevere '99 **1**
Gulliver's Travels [Image] '39 **2**
Gulliver's Travels [Winstar] '39 **1**
Gumboots '00 **2**
Gummo '97 **2**
Gun Shy '00 **2**
Gun Smith Cats: Bulletproof '95 **2**
Gung Ho! '43 **2**
The Guns of Navarone '61 **1**
Gustav Mahler: To Live, I Will Die '87 **1**
Guys and Dolls '55 **2**
GWAR: Phallus in Wonderland '92 **1**

H

Habit '97 **2**
Habitat '97 **1**
Hackers '95 **1**
Hair '79 **1**
Half a Loaf of Kung Fu '85 **1**
Half-Baked '97 **1**

Half Japanese: The Band Who Would Be King '92 **2**
The Hallelujah Trail '65 **2**
Halloween '78 **1**
Halloween 2: The Nightmare Isn't Over! '81 **1**
Halloween 3: Season of the Witch '82 **1**
Halloween 4: The Return of Michael Myers '88 **1**
Halloween 5: The Revenge of Michael Myers '89 **2**
Halloween: H20 '98 **1**
Hamburger Hill '87 **1**
Hamlet '00 **2**
Hamlet '48 **2**
Hand Gun '93 **1**
The Hand that Rocks the Cradle '92 **1**
Hang 'Em High '67 **1**
Hanging Up '99 **2**
Hangman '00 **2**
Hangmen '87 **1**
Hangmen Also Die '42 **2**
Hannibal '01 **2**
Hans Christian Andersen [HBO] '52 **1**
Hans Christian Andersen [20th Century Fox] '52 **2**
The Happiest Millionaire '67 **1**
Happiness '98 **1**
Happy Gilmore '96 **1**
Happy, Texas '99 **1**
Happy Together '95 **1**
Hard-Boiled [Criterion] '92 **1**
Hard-Boiled [Winstar] '92 **2**
Hard Bounty '94 **1**
Hard Core Logo '96 **2**
A Hard Day's Night '64 **1**
Hard Drive '94 **1**
Hard Eight '96 **2**
Hard Rain '97 **1**
Hard Target '93 **1**
Hard Times '75 **1**
Hard to Kill '89 **1**
Hard Vice '94 **1**
The Hard Way '91 **1**
Hardcase and Fist '89 **2**
The Harder They Come '72 **2**
Harley Davidson and the Marlboro Man '91 **2**
Harold and Maude '71 **2**
Harvey '50 **2**
Hatchet for the Honeymoon '70 **2**
The Haunted Strangler '58 **1**
The Haunting '99 **1**
Havana '90 **1**
Hawaiian Rainbow '87 **1**
He Got Game '98 **1**
The Head Mistress '68 **2**
Headin' Home '24 **2**
Heart and Souls '93 **1**
Heart of Dragon '85 **1**
Heart of Light '97 **2**
The Heartbreak Kid '72 **1**
Heat '72 **1**
Heat '95 **1**
Heathers '89 **1**
Heaven '99 **1**
Heaven and Earth '93 **2**
Heaven Can Wait '78 **1**
Heaven's Burning '97 **2**
Heaven's Fire '00 **2**
Heavy Metal '81 **1**
Heavy Metal 2000 [SE] '00 **2**
Heavy Traffic '73 **2**
Height of the Sky '99 **2**
Held Up '00 **2**
Hell in the Pacific '69 **1**
Hell Is for Heroes '62 **2**
Hell Night '81 **1**
Hellblock 13 '97 **2**
Hellbound: Hellraiser 2 '88 **1**
Hellfighters '69 **1**
Hellraiser [1] '87 **1**
Hellraiser [2] '87 **2**
Hell's Kitchen NYC '97 **2**
Help! '65 **1**
Hendrix '00 **2**

Henry & June '90 **1**
Henry: Portrait of a Serial Killer '90 **1**
Henry: Portrait of a Serial Killer 2: Mask of Sanity '96 **1**
Henry V '44 **1**
Henry V '89 **2**
Her Alibi '88 **1**
Her Name Is Cat '99 **2**
Hercules '97 **1**
Hercules in New York '70 **2**
Here on Earth '00 **2**
A Hero Never Dies '98 **1**
The Heroic Trio '93 **1**
The Hidden '87 **1**
Hide and Seek '00 **1**
Hideaway '94 **2**
Hideous Kinky '99 **1**
Hideous Sun Demon '59 **1**
High & Low '62 **1**
High Fidelity '00 **2**
High Noon '52 **1**
High Plains Drifter '73 **1**
High Risk '95 **1**
High School High '96 **2**
High Voltage '98 **1**
Highlander [DC] '86 **1**
Highlander 2: The Quickening '91 **1**
Highlander: The Final Dimension '94 **2**
Highlander: Endgame '00 **2**
Highway Hitcher '98 **1**
The Highway Man '99 **2**
Hilary and Jackie '98 **1**
Hillbillys in a Haunted House '67 **2**
The Hindenburg '75 **1**
Hip Hop 2000 '00 **2**
His Girl Friday '40 **1**
History of the World: Part 1 '81 **1**
Hitman '98 **1**
Holiday Heart '00 **2**
Holiday Inn '42 **1**
The Hollow Man [SE] '00 **2**
Hollywood Boulevard '76 **2**
Hollywood Christmas '96 **1**
The Hollywood Knights '80 **2**
Hollywood Vice Sqaud '86 **2**
Holy Man '98 **1**
Holy Smoke '99 **2**
Home Alone '90 **1**
Home Alone 2: Lost in New York '92 **1**
Home Alone 3 '97 **1**
Home for Christmas '93 **2**
Home Fries '98 **1**
A Home of Our Own '93 **2**
Homegrown '97 **2**
Homeward Bound: The Incredible Journey '93 **1**
Homicide: The Movie '00 **2**
Honey & Ashes '96 **2**
Honeymoon in Vegas '92 **1**
Hong Kong 1941 '84 **1**
Honor Among Thieves '68 **2**
Honor Thy Father '73 **2**
The Hoodlum '51 **1**
Hoodlum '96 **2**
Hooper '78 **1**
Hoosiers '86 **1**
Hope and Glory '87 **2**
Hope Floats '98 **1**
The Horrible Dr. Bones '00 **2**
Horror Express [Image] '84 **1**
Horror Express [Simitar] '72 **1**
Horror Hospital '73 **1**
Horror Hotel '60 **1**
Horrors of Spider Island '59 **2**
Horse Feathers '32 **1**
The Horse Soldiers '59 **2**
The Horse Whisperer '97 **1**
Horton Foote's Alone '97 **1**
Hot Blooded '98 **1**
Hot Boyz '99 **2**
The Hot Spot '90 **1**

Hot Vampire Nights '00 **2**
Hot War '98 **1**
H.O.T.S. '79 **2**
The Hound of the Baskervilles '83 **1**
The House by the Cemetery [Diamond] '83 **2**
The House by the Cemetery [Anchor Bay] '83 **2**
House of Games '87 **2**
House of Mirth '00 **2**
The House of Seven Corpses '73 **2**
House of Whipcord '75 **1**
The House of Yes '97 **1**
House on Haunted Hill '58 **1**
House on Haunted Hill '99 **1**
The House on Sorority Row '83 **2**
House Party '90 **2**
House Party 2: The Pajama Jam '91 **2**
House Party 3 '94 **2**
How Green Was My Valley '41 **2**
How Stella Got Her Groove Back '98 **1**
How the West Was Won '63 **1**
How to Be a Woman and Not Die in the Attempt '91 **1**
How to Commit Marriage '69 **2**
How to Make an American Quilt '95 **1**
How to Marry a Millionaire '53 **2**
Howard's End '92 **1**
The Hubley Collection: Everybody Rides the Carousel '9? **1**
The Hubley Collection, Vol. 1 '92 **1**
The Hubley Collection, Vol. 2 '9? **1**
Hudson Hawk '91 **1**
The Hudsucker Proxy '93 **1**
Hugo Pool '97 **1**
Hum Dil De Chuke Sanam '99 **1**
The Human Condition: No Greater Love '58 **1**
The Human Condition: Road to Eternity '59 **1**
Human Traffic '99 **2**
Humanity '99 **2**
Humanoids from the Deep '80 **1**
The Hunchback of Notre Dame '39 **1**
The Hunt for Red October '90 **1**
The Hunted '94 **1**
Hunter's Moon '97 **1**
The Hurricane '37 **1**
The Hurricane '99 **2**
Hush '98 **1**
Hush Little Baby '93 **1**
Hyper Space '89 **1**
Hysterical '83 **2**

I
I, a Woman '66 **1**
I Am Cuba '64 **1**
I, Claudius '91 **2**
I Dreamed of Africa '00 **2**
I Know What You Did Last Summer '97 **1**
I Know Where I'm Going '45 **2**
I Like the Girls Who Do '73 **2**
I Like to Play Games '95 **1**
I Love Maria '88 **1**
I Love Trouble '94 **1**
I Love You, I Love You Not '97 **1**
I Married a Strange Person '97 **2**
I Saw What You Did '65 **1**
I Shot Andy Warhol '96 **2**
I Spit on Your Corpse '74 **2**
I Spit on Your Grave '77 **1**
I Spy '65 **2**

I Still Know What You Did Last Summer '98 **1**
I Was a Teenage Zombie '87 **1**
I, Zombie '99 **2**
Ice Castles '79 **2**
Ice from the Sun '00 **2**
An Ideal Husband '99 **1**
Idle Hands '99 **2**
If Lucy Fell '95 **2**
If These Walls Could Talk 2 '00 **2**
Igor & the Lunatics '85 **1**
Iguana '89 **2**
Il Bidone '55 **2**
I'll Be Home for Christmas '98 **2**
Ill-Gotten Gains '97 **2**
I'll Never Forget What's 'Isname '67 **2**
I'll Remember April '99 **2**
Illuminata '98 **2**
Ilsa, Harem Keeper of the Oil Sheiks '76 **2**
Ilsa, She-Wolf of the SS '74 **2**
Ilsa, the Wicked Warden '78 **2**
I'm Gonna Git You Sucka '88 **2**
I'm Losing You '98 **2**
I'm No Angel '33 **1**
Image of an Assassination: A New Look at the Zapruder Film '98 **1**
Imaginary Crimes '94 **2**
Immoral Tales '74 **2**
Immortal Battalion '44 **2**
Immortal Combat '94 **1**
Immortality '98 **2**
Impact '49 **1**
The Impossible Spy '87 **2**
The Imposters '98 **1**
Impulse '84 **1**
In and Out '97 **1**
In Country '89 **2**
The In Crowd '00 **2**
In Dreams '98 **1**
In God's Hands '98 **2**
In Harm's Way '65 **2**
In Love and War '96 **1**
In Pursuit '00 **2**
In Pursuit of Honor '95 **2**
In Search of Dracula '76 **1**
In the Beginning... '00 **2**
In the Company of Men '96 **1**
In the Flesh / Blood Bullets Buffoons '00 **2**
In the Heat of the Night '67 **2**
In the Line of Duty 3 '88 **1**
In the Line of Duty 4 '89 **1**
In the Line of Duty 5 '90 **1**
In the Line of Fire [1] '93 **1**
In the Line of Fire [2 SE] '93 **2**
In the Mouth of Madness '95 **1**
In the Name of the Father '93 **1**
In the Navy '41 **1**
In the Realm of Passion '80 **1**
In the Realm of the Senses '76 **1**
In the Shadows '98 **1**
In This House of Brede '75 **2**
In Too Deep '99 **1**
Incognito '97 **1**
Incubus '65 **2**
Independence Day '96 **1**
The Indestructible Man / The Amazing Transparent Man '56 **2**
The Indian Tomb '21 **2**
Indomitable Teddy Roosevelt '83 **1**
Inferno '80 **1**
Inferno '99 **2**
Infinity '96 **1**
The Inheritance '76 **1**
Inhumanity '00 **2**
The Inland Sea '93 **2**

Inn of 1000 Sins '75 **2**
Innocent Blood '92 **1**
Inseminoid '80 **2**
The Inside Man '84 **2**
The Insider '99 **1**
Insomnia '97 **1**
Inspector Gadget '99 **1**
The Inspector General '49 **2**
Inspector Wears Skirts '88 **1**
Instinct '99 **1**
Interceptor '92 **1**
Interceptor Force '99 **2**
Interiors '78 **2**
Interlocked '98 **1**
Intermezzo '36 **1**
Intern '00 **2**
Internal Affairs '90 **2**
The Interview '98 **2**
Interview with the Vampire '94 **1**
Intolerance '16 **1**
The Intruder '61 **2**
Invaders from Mars '53 **1**
Invaders from Mars '86 **1**
Invasion of the Body Snatchers '56 **1**
Invasion of the Body Snatchers '78 **1**
Inventing the Abbotts '97 **2**
The Invisible Man '33 **2**
Invisible Mom '96 **2**
The Invisible Strangler '76 **1**
The Ipcress File '65 **1**
Irene Dunne Romance Classics '00 **2**
Irma Vep '96 **1**
Iron Eagle 4 '95 **1**
Iron Giant '99 **1**
Iron Maze '91 **1**
Iron Monkey '93 **1**
Isaac Asimov's Nightfall '00 **2**
The Island at the Top of the World '74 **1**
The Island of Dr. Moreau '96 **1**
Island of Greed '97 **1**
Isn't She Great '00 **2**
It Could Happen to You '94 **2**
It Happened Here '65 **1**
It Happened One Night '34 **1**
Italian Movie '93 **2**
The Italians '00 **2**
It's a Wonderful Life '46 **1**
It's Good to Be Alive '74 **2**
It's Raining on Santiago '74 **2**
It's the Rage '99 **2**
Ivan the Terrible, Part 1 '44 **1**
Ivan the Terrible, Part 2 '46 **1**
I've Been Waiting for You '98 **1**
Ivory Tower '97 **2**

J
Jack & the Beanstalk '52 **2**
Jack Be Nimble '94 **1**
The Jack Bull '99 **2**
Jack Frost '97 **1**
Jack Frost '98 **1**
Jack Frost 2: Revenge of the Mutant Killer Snowman '00 **2**
Jack-O '95 **1**
The Jackal [CE] '97 **1**
Jackie Chan: My Story '97 **1**
Jackie Chan: My Stunts '98 **1**
Jackie Chan's First Strike '96 **1**
Jackie Chan's Who Am I '98 **1**
The Jackie Robinson Story '50 **2**
Jackson County Jail '76 **2**
Jacob's Ladder '90 **1**
Jade '95 **2**
The Jagged Edge '85 **2**
Jail Bait '54 **1**
Jailhouse Rock '57 **1**
Jake Speed '86 **2**
Jakob the Liar '99 **1**
Jamaica Inn [Delta/Laserlight] '39 **1**
Jamaica Inn [Image] '39 **1**

James and the Giant Peach '96 **2**
James Dean Double Feature: Hill Number One / I Am a Fool '51 **1**
James Dean: Live Fast, Die Young '97 **2**
James Dean Story '57 **1**
Jan Svankmajer's Faust '94 **1**
Jane & the Lost City '87 **2**
Jane Doe '96 **1**
Jane Street '96 **1**
Jason and the Argonauts '63 **1**
Jason and the Argonauts '00 **2**
Jawbreaker '98 **1**
Jaws [CE] '75 **2**
Jaws: The Revenge '87 **2**
Jazz on a Summer's Day '59 **2**
The Jazz Singer '80 **1**
Jean de Florette '87 **2**
Jeremiah Johnson '72 **1**
The Jerk '79 **1**
Jerome '98 **2**
Jerry and Tom '98 **2**
Jerry Maguire '96 **1**
Jesus '00 **2**
Jesus Christ, Superstar '73 **1**
Jesus Christ Superstar '00 **2**
Jesus' Son '99 **2**
Jet Li's The Enforcer [Tai Seng] '95 **1**
Jet Li's The Enforcer [Buena Vista] '95 **2**
Jew-boy Levi '98 **2**
Jezebel '38 **1**
JFK '91 **1**
Jingle All the Way '96 **1**
Joan of Arc '99 **1**
Joan the Woman '16 **2**
Joe Gould's Secret '00 **2**
Joe Kidd '72 **1**
The Joe Louis Story '53 **2**
Joe the King '99 **1**
Joe's Apartment '96 **1**
John Carpenter's Vampires '97 **1**
John Grisham's The Rainmaker '97 **1**
Johnny B. '00 **2**
Johnny Mnemonic '95 **1**
Johnny 100 Pesos '93 **2**
The Johnsons '92 **1**
The Joint Is Jumpin' '00 **2**
Joseph and the Amazing Technicolor Dreamcoat '00 **2**
Joseph: King of Dreams '00 **2**
The Josephine Baker Story '90 **2**
Journey to the Far Side of the Sun '69 **1**
Joy House '64 **2**
Ju Dou '90 **1**
Judge & Jury '96 **1**
Judge Dredd '95 **1**
Judgment Night '93 **1**
Juice '97 **2**
Julien Donkey-boy '99 **2**
Juliet of the Spirits '65 **1**
Jumanji [CS] '95 **1**
June Night '40 **1**
The Jungle Book '67 **1**
Jungle Boy '98 **2**
Jungle Fever '91 **1**
Jungleground '95 **1**
Junior '94 **1**
Junior Bonner '72 **1**
Junior's Groove '97 **1**
Jurassic Park [CE] '93 **2**
The Juror '96 **1**
Just a Little Harmless Sex '99 **1**
Just Cause '94 **1**
Just Looking '99 **2**
Just the Ticket '98 **1**
Just Write '97 **1**

K
K-9 '89 **1**
K-911 '99 **2**
Kalifornia '93 **1**
Kama Sutra: A Tale of Love '96 **1**
The Karate Kid '84 **2**
Kayla: A Cry in the Wilderness '00 **2**
Keeping the Faith '00 **2**
Kelly's Heroes '70 **2**
The Kentuckian '55 **2**
Kentucky Fried Movie '77 **1**
Kept '01 **2**
Key to Sex '98 **1**
Khamoshi the Musical '96 **1**
Kicked in the Head '97 **2**
The Kid / A Dog's Life '21 **1**
A Kid Called Danger '99 **1**
A Kid in Aladdin's Palace '97 **1**
The Kid with the X-Ray Eyes '99 **2**
The Kidnapping of the President '80 **2**
Kids '95 **1**
Kids Return '96 **2**
Kika '94 **1**
Kill and Kill Again '81 **1**
Kill Me Again '89 **2**
Kill Shot '01 **2**
The Killer [Criterion] '90 **1**
The Killer [Winstar] '90 **2**
Killer: A Journal of Murder '95 **1**
Killer Condom '95 **1**
The Killer Elite '75 **1**
The Killer inside Me '76 **1**
The Killer Meteors '87 **1**
Killers '97 **2**
Killer's Kiss '55 **2**
Killer's Romance '90 **1**
The Killing '56 **1**
The Killing Grounds '97 **1**
Killing Hour '84 **1**
The Killing Jar '96 **1**
The Killing Man '94 **1**
Killing Obsession '96 **1**
The Killing of a Chinese Bookie '76 **2**
The Killing of Sister George '69 **1**
Killing Zoe '94 **2**
Kindergarten Cop '90 **1**
King and Country '64 **2**
The King and I '56 **1**
The King and I '99 **1**
King Cobra '98 **1**
A King in New York / A Woman in Paris '57 **1**
King Kong '76 **1**
King of Beggars '92 **1**
King of New York '90 **2**
King of the Zombies '41 **1**
King Ralph '91 **1**
Kingpin '96 **1**
Kiss Me Deadly '55 **2**
Kiss Me, Guido '97 **2**
Kiss Me Monster '69 **1**
Kiss of Fire '98 **2**
Kiss of the Vampire '62 **1**
Kiss Shot '89 **2**
Kiss the Girls '97 **1**
Kiss the Sky '98 **2**
Kiss Toledo Goodbye '00 **2**
Kisses in the Dark '97 **2**
Kissing a Fool '98 **1**
Klash '95 **2**
Klondike Annie '36 **1**
Knight Moves '93 **2**
Knightriders '81 **2**
Knock Off '98 **1**
Know Your Enemy: Japan '45 **2**
Komodo '99 **2**
Koyla '99 **1**
Krakatoa East of Java [Anchor Bay] '66 **1**
Krakatoa East of Java [Simitar] '66 **1**
Kronos '57 **2**

Krull [SE] '83 **2**
Kull the Conqueror '97 **1**
Kuma Hula: Keepers of the Culture '89 **1**
Kundun '97 **1**
Kwaidan '64 **2**

L
La Bamba '87 **1**
La Collectionneuse '67 **1**
L.A. Confidential '97 **1**
La Cucaracha '99 **2**
La Femme Nikita [Trimark] '91 **1**
La Femme Nikita [MGM] '91 **2**
La Grande Bouffe '73 **2**
La Guerre Est Finie '66 **2**
La Separation '98 **2**
L.A. Story '91 **1**
La Traviata '82 **1**
Labyrinth '86 **1**
The Ladies Man '00 **2**
Lady and the Tramp '55 **1**
Lady and the Tramp 2: Scamp's Adventure '01 **2**
Lady Dragon '92 **2**
The Lady from Shanghai '48 **2**
The Lady in White '88 **2**
Lady Macbeth of Mtsensk '92 **1**
Lady of the Lake '98 **1**
The Lady Vanishes '38 **1**
Ladyhawke '85 **1**
The Lair of the White Worm '88 **1**
Lake Placid '99 **1**
The Land Before Time '88 **2**
Land Before Time 7: The Stone of Cold Fire '00 **2**
The Landlady '98 **1**
Landmarks of Early Film '94 **1**
Landmarks of Early Film, Vol. 2: The Magic of Melies '94 **1**
Lap Dancing '95 **1**
Laser Mission '90 **2**
Laser Moon '92 **1**
Laserblast '78 **1**
Laserhawk '99 **1**
Last Action Hero '93 **1**
The Last Assassins '96 **1**
The Last Best Sunday '98 **2**
The Last Boy Scout '91 **1**
Last Breath '96 **1**
The Last Broadcast '98 **1**
The Last Days of Disco '98 **1**
The Last Detail '73 **1**
The Last Don '97 **1**
The Last Emperor '87 **1**
The Last Flight of Noah's Ark '80 **1**
The Last Game '95 **1**
The Last Great Adventure '99 **2**
Last Hurrah '58 **1**
The Last Lieutenant '94 **2**
Last Man Standing '96 **1**
The Last Marshal '99 **2**
The Last Metro '80 **1**
Last Night '98 **1**
The Last of the Blonde Bombshells '00 **2**
The Last of the Mohicans '20 **2**
The Last of the Mohicans '92 **2**
The Last Picture Show [DC] '71 **2**
Last Resort '86 **2**
The Last September '99 **2**
The Last Starfighter '84 **1**
The Last Stop '99 **2**
Last Tango in Paris '73 **1**
The Last Temptation of Christ '88 **2**
The Last Time I Saw Paris '54 **2**
The Last Valley '71 **2**
The Last Word '95 **1**

Last Year at Marienbad '61 **1**
The Lathe of Heaven '80 **2**
Laurel and Hardy and Friends '9? **1**
Lav Kush '97 **1**
L'Avventura '60 **2**
The Law '59 **1**
Law and Disorder '74 **2**
Lawless Frontier / Randy Rides Alone '35 **2**
Lawn Dogs '96 **1**
The Lawnmower Man '92 **1**
Lawrence of Arabia '62 **2**
Lawyer Lawyer '97 **1**
Le Beau Mariage '82 **1**
The Leading Man '96 **1**
A League of Their Own '92 **1**
Lean on Me '89 **1**
Leave It to Beaver '97 **1**
Leaving Las Vegas '95 **1**
Leaving Scars '97 **1**
Lee Rock '91 **1**
Left Behind: The Movie '00 **1**
Legacy of Rage '86 **1**
Legal Eagles '86 **1**
The Legend '93 **2**
The Legend of Bagger Vance '00 **2**
The Legend of Drunken Master '94 **2**
Legend of the Drunken Tiger '92 **1**
The Legend of the 7 Golden Vampires '73 **1**
Legendary WWII Movies '00 **2**
Legends of the Fall [1] '94 **1**
Legends of the Fall [2 SE] '94 **2**
Legionnaire '98 **1**
The Lemon Drop Kid '51 **2**
The Lemon Sisters '90 **2**
L'Enfer '93 **1**
L'Ennui '98 **2**
Leon, the Professional '94 **2**
Leonard Bernstein: Reaching for the Note '98 **1**
Leprechaun '93 **1**
Leprechaun 2 '94 **2**
Leprechaun 3 '95 **2**
Leprechaun 4: In Space '96 **2**
Leprechaun 5: In the Hood '99 **2**
Les Miserables '97 **2**
A Lesson Before Dying '99 **2**
Let Sleeping Corpses Lie '74 **2**
Let the Devil Wear Black '99 **2**
Lethal Seduction '97 **2**
Lethal Weapon '87 **1**
Lethal Weapon 2 '89 **1**
Lethal Weapon 3 '92 **1**
Lethal Weapon 4 '98 **1**
Leviathan '89 **1**
Lewis and Clark and George '97 **2**
Liar Liar '96 **1**
Liberty Heights '99 **2**
License to Kill '89 **1**
The Lickerish Quartet '70 **1**
Life '99 **1**
Life According to Muriel '97 **2**
The Life Before This '99 **2**
Life Is Beautiful '98 **1**
A Life Less Ordinary '97 **1**
Life of a Gigolo '98 **1**
The Life of Jesus '96 **2**
Life with Father '47 **2**
Lifeforce '85 **1**
The Lifestyle '99 **2**
Light It Up '99 **2**
Light Sleeper '92 **1**
Lightning Jack '94 **2**
Like It Is '98 **1**
Like Water for Chocolate '93 **1**
Lilian's Story '96 **2**
Lilies of the Field '63 **2**
Limbo '99 **1**
Limelight '52 **1**

The Limey '99 **1**
Lingerie '01 **2**
The Lion in Winter '68 **2**
The Lion King: Simba's Pride '98 **1**
Lion of the Desert '81 **1**
Lionheart '90 **1**
Lips of Blood '75 **1**
Lipstick Camera '93 **1**
Lisa and the Devil / The House of Exorcism '75 **1**
The List '99 **2**
A Little Bit of Soul '97 **2**
Little Buddha '93 **1**
The Little Foxes '41 **1**
Little Fugitive '53 **2**
Little Lord Fauntleroy '36 **2**
The Little Mermaid '89 **1**
The Little Mermaid 2: Return to the Sea '00 **2**
Little Mother '71 **1**
Little Nicky '00 **2**
The Little Princess '39 **2**
A Little Princess '95 **1**
The Little Rascals '94 **1**
Little Shop of Horrors '86 **1**
The Little Vampire '00 **1**
Little Voice '98 **1**
Little Witches '96 **1**
Little Women [1] '94 **1**
Little Women [2 SE] '94 **2**
The Littlest Horse Thieves '76 **1**
Live and Let Die '73 **1**
Live Flesh '97 **2**
The Living Daylights '87 **2**
The Living Dead Girl '82 **1**
Living Out Loud '98 **1**
Local Hero '83 **2**
Lock, Stock and 2 Smoking Barrels '98 **2**
Lock Up '89 **1**
Lockdown '00 **2**
The Lodger '26 **1**
Logan's Run '76 **1**
Lola Montes '55 **1**
Lolida 2000 '97 **2**
Lolita '62 **1**
Lolita '97 **2**
Lone Justice 2 '93 **2**
Lone Justice 3: Showdown at Plum Creek '96 **2**
The Lonely Guy '84 **1**
Long Arm of the Law '84 **1**
Long Arm of the Law II '87 **1**
The Long Good Friday '80 **1**
The Long Kiss Goodnight '96 **1**
The Long Riders '80 **2**
The Long Shadow '92 **1**
The Long Way Home '97 **2**
The Longest Day '62 **1**
The Longest Nite '92 **1**
The Longest Yard '74 **2**
Longtime Companion '90 **2**
Look Who's Talking '89 **1**
Look Who's Talking, Too '90 **2**
Looking for Lola '98 **1**
Lord Edgeware Dies '99 **2**
Lord of Illusions '95 **1**
The Lords of Flatbush '74 **2**
Loser '00 **2**
Losin' It '82 **2**
The Loss of Sexual Innocence '98 **2**
Lost and Found '99 **1**
The Lost Boys '87 **1**
Lost Continent '68 **1**
The Lost Films of Laurel and Hardy, Vol. 1 '9? **1**
The Lost Films of Laurel and Hardy, Vol. 2 '9? **1**
The Lost Films of Laurel and Hardy, Vol. 3 '9? **1**
The Lost Films of Laurel and Hardy, Vol. 5 '99 **1**
The Lost Films of Laurel and Hardy, Vol. 6 '99 **1**
Lost Horizon '37 **1**
Lost in America '85 **2**
Lost in Space '98 **1**

Lost Souls '00 **2**
The Lost Weekend '45 **2**
The Lost World [SlingShot] '25 **1**
The Lost World [Image] '25 **2**
The Lost World: Jurassic Park 2 [CE] '97 **2**
Lotto Land '95 **1**
Louis Prima: The Wildest! '99 **2**
Loulou '80 **2**
Love Affair '39 **2**
Love After Love '94 **2**
Love and a .45 '94 **2**
Love and Anarchy '73 **1**
Love and Death '75 **2**
Love and Death on Long Island '98 **1**
Love by Appointment '76 **2**
Love, etc. '96 **1**
Love Field '91 **2**
The Love Goddesses '65 **1**
Love, Honour & Obey '00 **2**
Love Jones '96 **1**
Love Kills '98 **2**
The Love Letter '99 **1**
Love Letters '83 **2**
The Love Master '97 **2**
Love Stinks '99 **2**
Love Story '70 **2**
Love to Kill '97 **1**
Loveblind '98 **1**
Lover of the Last Empress '95 **1**
Lovers and Liars '81 **2**
Love's Labour's Lost '00 **2**
The Loves of Carmen '48 **2**
Lovesick '83 **1**
Loving Jezebel '99 **2**
Lower Level '91 **2**
Lucinda's Spell '00 **2**
Lucky Luke '94 **1**
Lucky Numbers '00 **2**
Lucky Texan '34 **2**
Lulu on the Bridge '98 **1**
Lumiere and Company '96 **1**
The Lumiere Brothers' First Films '97 **1**
Lupin III: The Mystery of Mamo '78 **1**
Lust for Frankenstein '88 **2**
Lust in the Dust '85 **2**

M
M '31 **1**
Ma Saison Preferee '93 **1**
Ma Vie en Rose '97 **2**
Maborosi '95 **2**
Macabre '80 **2**
Mach 2 '00 **2**
The Mad Butcher '72 **2**
Mad City '97 **1**
Mad Dog and Glory '93 **1**
Mad Love '95 **1**
Mad Max '80 **1**
Mad Max: Beyond Thunderdome '85 **1**
Madadayo '92 **2**
Made for Each Other '39 **1**
Made in America '93 **1**
Made Men '99 **1**
Madeline '98 **1**
Madigan '68 **1**
Madman '82 **2**
The Madness of King George '94 **2**
Madron '70 **2**
Mafia! '98 **2**
The Magic Voyage '93 **1**
The Magical Legend of the Leprechauns '99 **2**
Magical Mystery Tour '67 **1**
The Magnificent Seven '60 **2**
Magnificent Warriors '87 **1**
Magnolia '99 **2**
Mah Jong Dragon '97 **1**
Mahler '74 **1**
Mailer on Mailer '00 **2**
Major Payne '95 **1**
Make Mine Music '46 **2**
Male and Female '19 **1**
Malice [Polygram] '93 **1**

Malice [MGM] '93 **2**
Mallrats '95 **1**
The Maltese Falcon '41 **2**
Man Called Hero '99 **2**
A Man for All Seasons '66 **2**
The Man from Laramie '55 **2**
The Man from Planet X '51 **2**
Man from Utah / Sagebrush Trail '34 **2**
The Man in the Iron Mask '98 **1**
A Man in Uniform '93 **1**
Man of a Thousand Faces '57 **1**
Man of the Year '95 **1**
Man on the Moon '99 **1**
Man Wanted '34 **1**
The Man Who Fell to Earth '76 **1**
The Man Who Knew Too Little '97 **1**
The Man Who Knew Too Much '34 **1**
The Man Who Knew Too Much '56 **2**
The Man Who Loved Women '77 **2**
The Man Who Shot Liberty Valance '62 **2**
The Man Who Would Be King '75 **1**
The Man with the Movie Camera '29 **1**
The Man with Two Brains '83 **1**
The Manchurian Candidate '62 **1**
Mandragora '97 **1**
Manhattan '79 **2**
Manhattan Baby '82 **2**
Manhattan Murder Mystery '93 **1**
Maniac / Narcotic '34 **1**
Maniac Cop '88 **1**
Maniac Nurses Find Ecstasy '94 **2**
Manon of the Spring '87 **2**
Manoushe, The Story of a Gypsy Love '98 **2**
Mansfield Park '99 **2**
Mantis in Lace '68 **2**
The Manxman '29 **1**
A Map of the World '99 **2**
Marat/Sade '66 **2**
Marcello Mastroianni: I Remember '97 **1**
March of the Wooden Soldiers '34 **2**
Maria Stuarda '88 **1**
Marihuana / Assassin of Youth / Reefer Madness '36 **2**
Marilyn Monroe: The Diamond Collection '00 **2**
Marilyn Monroe: The Final Days '00 **2**
Mark of the Devil '69 **1**
Mark of Zorro '75 **1**
Marked for Death '90 **1**
The Marquise of O '76 **2**
The Marriage Circle '24 **2**
Married to the Mob '88 **2**
The Married Virgin '18 **2**
Mars Attacks! '96 **1**
Martin '77 **2**
Marty '55 **2**
Marvin's Room '96 **1**
Mary Poppins [1] '64 **1**
Mary Poppins [2 SE] '64 **2**
Mary Reilly '95 **2**
Mary Shelley's Frankenstein '94 **1**
Mask '85 **1**
The Mask '94 **1**
The Mask of Diijon '46 **1**
The Mask of Zorro '98 **1**
Mass Extinctions '93 **1**
Masseuse '95 **1**
The Master '92 **1**
Master with Cracked Fingers '71 **2**

Masters of Russian Animation, Vol. 1 '97 **1**
Masters of Russian Animation, Vol. 2 '97 **2**
Masters of Russian Animation, Vol. 3 '97 **2**
Masters of Russian Animation, Vol. 4 '97 **2**
The Matchmaker '97 **1**
Matilda '96 **1**
Matinee '92 **1**
The Matrix '99 **1**
A Matter of Dignity '57 **2**
Mauvais Sang '86 **2**
Maverick '94 **1**
Maximum Overdrive '86 **2**
Maximum Risk '96 **2**
Maze '96 **2**
The McCullochs '75 **2**
McLintock! '63 **1**
MD Geist [DC] '86 **1**
Me & Will '99 **1**
Me Myself I '99 **2**
Mean Guns '97 **2**
Mean Season '85 **2**
Mean Streets '73 **1**
The Meanest Men in the West '76 **2**
Meantime '81 **1**
Meatballs '79 **1**
Medicine Man '92 **1**
Meet Joe Black '98 **1**
Meet John Doe [Madacy] '41 **1**
Meet John Doe [Image] '41 **2**
Meet the Parents '00 **2**
Meet Wally Sparks '97 **1**
Megazone 23 Part 1 '85 **1**
Mein Kampf: Hitler's Rise and Fall '60 **2**
Melody Time '48 **2**
Melvin and Howard '80 **1**
Memphis Belle '90 **1**
Men '97 **1**
Men in Black [CS] '97 **2**
Men in War '57 **1**
Men of Honor '00 **2**
Men of War '94 **2**
Menace II Society '93 **1**
Mercury Rising '98 **1**
Mercy '00 **2**
Merlin '98 **1**
Mermaids '90 **2**
A Merry War '97 **2**
Mesa of Lost Women '52 **2**
Mesmer '94 **1**
Mesmerized '84 **2**
The Message '77 **1**
Message in a Bottle '98 **1**
The Messenger: The Story of Joan of Arc '99 **2**
Meteor '79 **2**
Metro '96 **1**
Metroland '97 **1**
Metropolis '26 **1**
Miami Rhapsody '95 **1**
Michael '96 **1**
Michael Collins '96 **1**
Mickey's Once upon a Christmas '99 **1**
Midaq Alley '95 **2**
Midnight '34 **2**
Midnight Confessions '95 **2**
Midnight Cowboy '69 **2**
Midnight Dancers '94 **2**
Midnight Express '78 **1**
The Midnight Hour '86 **2**
Midnight in the Garden of Good and Evil [SE] '97 **1**
Midnight Run '88 **1**
Midnight Tease / Midnight Tease 2 '94 **2**
Midway '76 **1**
Mifune '99 **2**
The Mighty '98 **1**
Mighty Aphrodite '95 **1**
The Mighty Ducks '92 **1**
Mighty Joe Young '98 **1**
The Mighty Peking Man '77 **2**
The Mighty Quinn '89 **2**
Mikey '92 **2**

Milk and Money '97 **1**
Millennium '89 **1**
The Million Dollar Hotel '99 **2**
The Millionaire's Express '86 **2**
The Millionairess '60 **1**
Milo '98 **2**
Mimic '97 **1**
Minnie and Moskowitz '71 **1**
The Minus Man '99 **1**
Mio in the Land of Faraway '87 **2**
Miracle on 34th Street '47 **1**
The Miracle Worker '62 **1**
The Miracle Worker '00 **2**
Miracles '89 **1**
The Mirror Crack'd '80 **2**
The Mirror Has Two Faces '96 **1**
Mirror, Mirror '90 **2**
Mirror, Mirror 2: Raven Dance '94 **2**
Mirror, Mirror 3: The Voyeur '96 **2**
Mischievous '96 **1**
Misery '90 **2**
Misery Brothers Y2K '95 **1**
The Misfits '61 **2**
Miss Congeniality '00 **2**
Missile to the Moon '59 **2**
Missing in Action '84 **2**
The Mission '99 **2**
Mission: Impossible '96 **1**
Mission: Impossible 2 '00 **2**
Mission to Mars '00 **2**
Mississippi Burning [Image] '88 **1**
Mississippi Burning [MGM] '88 **2**
Mississippi Mermaid '69 **2**
Mrs. Brown '97 **1**
Mrs. Dalloway '97 **1**
Mrs. Doubtfire '93 **1**
Mr. Accident '99 **2**
Mr. Ace '46 **1**
Mr. & Mrs. Bridge '90 **2**
Mr. Baseball '92 **1**
Mr. Death: The Rise and Fall of Fred A. Leuchter, Jr. '99 **2**
Mr. Holland's Opus '95 **1**
Mr. Hulot's Holiday '53 **2**
Mr. Jealousy '98 **1**
Mister Johnson '91 **2**
Mr. Jones '93 **2**
Mr. Magoo '97 **1**
Mr. Nice Guy '98 **1**
Mister Roberts '55 **1**
Mr. Saturday Night '92 **1**
Mr. Vampire '86 **1**
Mr. Wonderful '93 **2**
Mistress '91 **2**
Mistress Frankenstein [CE] '00 **2**
Mistress of Seduction '00 **2**
Mo' Better Blues '90 **2**
Mob Story '90 **1**
Mob War [Simitar] '88 **1**
Mob War [BFS] '88 **2**
Moby Dick '56 **2**
Moby Dick '98 **1**
The Mod Squad '99 **1**
Modern Times '36 **1**
Modern Vampires '98 **1**
Mohawk '52 **2**
Moll Flanders [Anchor Bay] '96 **1**
Moll Flanders [MGM] '96 **2**
Mommy [SE] '95 **2**
Mommy 2: Mommy's Day '96 **1**
Mon Oncle '58 **2**
Mon Oncle d'Amerique '80 **2**
Mona Lisa '86 **2**
Money Kings '98 **1**
Money Train '95 **1**
Monkey Business '31 **1**
Monkey Shines '88 **2**
Monsieur Verdoux '47 **1**
Monsoon '97 **2**
The Monster '96 **1**

Monster from Green Hell '58 **2**
Monster in the Closet '86 **1**
The Monster Maker '44 **1**
The Monster of Camp Sunshine '64 **2**
Montenegro '81 **1**
Monty Python and the Holy Grail '75 **2**
Monty Python's Life of Brian [Anchor Bay] '79 **1**
Monty Python's Life of Brian [Criteron] '79 **1**
Monty Python's The Meaning of Life '83 **1**
Monument Ave. '98 **1**
Moon over Harlem '39 **2**
The Moon Warriors '92 **1**
Moonlight and Valentino '95 **2**
Moonlighting '85 **1**
Moonraker [SE] '79 **1**
Moonstruck '87 **1**
Mortal Kombat 1: The Movie '95 **1**
Mortal Kombat 2: Annihilation '97 **1**
Mortal Thoughts '91 **1**
Mosquito '95 **1**
The Most Dangerous Game [Criterion] '32 **1**
The Most Dangerous Game [Madacy] '32 **2**
Most Wanted '97 **1**
Motel Blue '98 **1**
Mother '26 **1**
Mother '96 **2**
Mother and Son '97 **2**
Mother Night '96 **2**
Mother's Boys '94 **2**
Mother's Day [DC] '80 **2**
Mountains of the Moon '90 **2**
Mountaintop Motel Massacre '86 **2**
Mouse Hunt '97 **1**
The Mouse on the Moon '62 **2**
Moving Target '96 **1**
Moving Target '00 **2**
Ms. 45 '81 **1**
Much Ado about Nothing '93 **1**
Mulan '98 **1**
Multiplicity '96 **1**
Mumford '99 **1**
Mumia: A Case for Reasonable Doubt? '96 **1**
The Mummy '32 **2**
The Mummy [1] '99 **1**
The Mummy [2 SE] '99 **2**
The Mummy's Shroud '67 **2**
Munster, Go Home! '66 **2**
The Munsters' Revenge '81 **2**
Muppets from Space '99 **1**
Murder '30 **1**
Murder at 1600 '97 **1**
Murder in the First '95 **2**
A Murder of Crows '99 **1**
The Murder of Roger Ackroyd '99 **2**
The Muse '99 **1**
The Music Man '62 **1**
Music of the Heart [CS] '99 **2**
Mutant '83 **2**
MVP: Most Valuable Primate '00 **2**
My Best Fiend '99 **2**
My Best Friend's Wedding '97 **1**
My Best Girl '27 **1**
My Blue Heaven '90 **1**
My Cousin Vinny '92 **2**
My Dinner with Andre '81 **1**
My Dog Skip '99 **2**
My Fair Lady '64 **1**
My Favorite Brunette '47 **2**
My Favorite Martian '98 **1**
My Fellow Americans '96 **1**
My 5 Wives '00 **2**
My Giant '98 **1**
My Girl '91 **1**

My Left Foot '89 **1**
My Life '93 **2**
My Life As a Dog '85 **1**
My Life So Far '98 **1**
My Life to Live '62 **1**
My Lucky Stars '85 **1**
My Man Godfrey '36 **1**
My Mom's a Werewolf '89 **2**
My Night at Maud's '69 **1**
My Science Project '85 **1**
My Sex Life...Or How I Got into an Argument '96 **2**
My Son the Fanatic '97 **1**
My Son, the Vampire '52 **2**
My Stepmother Is an Alien '88 **1**
My Teacher's Wife '95 **2**
Mystery, Alaska '99 **2**
Mystery Men '99 **1**
Mystery of the Necronomicon '00 **2**
Mystery Science Theater 3000: The Movie '96 **1**
Mystic Pizza '88 **2**
The Myth of Fingerprints '97 **2**

N
The Naked City '48 **1**
The Naked Gun: From the Files of Police Squad '88 **2**
Naked Gun 2 1/2: The Smell of Fear '91 **2**
Naked Gun 33 1/3: The Final Insult '94 **2**
Naked Killer '92 **2**
Naked Kiss '64 **1**
The Naked Truth '92 **1**
Napoleon '96 **2**
Napoleon and Samantha '72 **1**
Nashville '75 **2**
National Lampoon's Animal House '78 **1**
National Lampoon's Christmas Vacation '89 **1**
National Lampoon's Class Reunion '82 **1**
National Lampoon's Golf Punks '99 **2**
National Lampoon's Loaded Weapon 1 '93 **1**
National Lampoon's Vacation '83 **1**
National Velvet '44 **1**
The Natural '84 **2**
Natural Born Killers [DC] '94 **2**
Nautilus '99 **2**
The Navigator '24 **1**
The Navigator '88 **2**
Navy SEALS [Image] '90 **1**
Navy SEALS [MGM] '90 **2**
Necessary Roughness '91 **2**
Necromancer: Satan's Servant '88 **2**
Needful Things '93 **1**
The Negotiator '98 **1**
Neil Simon's The Odd Couple 2 '98 **1**
Nemesis '93 **1**
Neon Genesis Evangelion Collection '99 **2**
The Net '95 **1**
Network '76 **1**
Neurotica: Middle-Age Spread and Other Life Crises '97 **2**
Never Been Kissed '99 **1**
Never Cry Wolf '83 **2**
Never Talk to Strangers '95 **1**
Never Too Late '98 **2**
The New Adventures of Pippi Longstocking '88 **2**
The New Eve '98 **2**
New Fist of Fury '76 **1**
New Jack City '91 **1**
New Jersey Drive '95 **1**
New Legend of Shaolin '96 **2**
New Orleans '47 **1**
New Rose Hotel '98 **1**
New World Disorder '99 **1**
New York Ripper '82 **1**

News from the West '?? **2**
Newsbreak '00 **2**
The Newton Boys '97 **1**
The Next Best Thing '00 **2**
Next Friday [Platinum Series] '00 **2**
Next of Kin '89 **1**
The Next Step '95 **2**
Next Stop, Wonderland '98 **2**
Nice Guys Sleep Alone '99 **1**
Nicholas and Alexandra '71 **2**
Nick of Time '95 **2**
Nico Icon '95 **1**
A Night at the Roxbury '98 **1**
Night Caller from Outer Space '66 **1**
Night Calls: The Movie '98 **1**
Night Calls: The Movie 2 '99 **1**
Night Falls on Manhattan '96 **2**
Night Fire '94 **1**
A Night in the Life of Jimmy Reardon '88 **2**
Night of the Hunted '69 **1**
Night of the Living Dead [Madacy] '68 **2**
Night of the Living Dead [Elite] '68 **2**
Night of the Living Dead [LE Anchor Bay] '68 **2**
Night of the Living Dead '90 **2**
Night of the Warrior '91 **1**
Night Screams '87 **1**
Night Shift '82 **1**
The Night Stalker '71 **1**
The Night Strangler '72 **1**
The Night That Never Happened '97 **1**
Night Tide '63 **1**
A Night to Remember '58 **1**
Night Train to Terror '84 **1**
Nighthawks '81 **1**
Nightmare at Noon '87 **1**
The Nightmare before Christmas [1] '93 **1**
The Nightmare before Christmas [2 SE] '93 **2**
A Nightmare on Elm Street '84 **1**
A Nightmare on Elm Street 2: Freddy's Revenge '85 **1**
A Nightmare on Elm Street 3: Dream Warriors '87 **1**
A Nightmare on Elm Street 4: Dream Master '88 **1**
A Nightmare on Elm Street 5: Dream Child '89 **1**
The "Nightmare on Elm Street" Collection '99 **1**
Nightmares '83 **1**
Nights of Cabiria '57 **1**
Nightwatch '94 **2**
Nightwatch '96 **2**
Nikki, the Wild Dog of the North '61 **1**
9 1/2 Weeks '86 **1**
Nine Months '95 **2**
9 to 5 '80 **2**
1941 '79 **1**
90 Degrees South: With Scott to the Antarctic '33 **1**
Ninja Scroll '93 **1**
The Ninth Gate '99 **2**
Ninth Street '98 **2**
Nixon '95 **1**
No Code of Conduct '98 **2**
No Dessert Dad, 'Til You Mow the Lawn '94 **2**
No Escape '94 **1**
No Looking Back '98 **2**
No Mercy '86 **1**
No Safe Haven '87 **2**
No Strings Attached '98 **1**
No Way Out '87 **2**
Noah's Ark '99 **2**
Norma Rae '79 **2**
The North Avenue Irregulars '79 **1**
North by Northwest '59 **2**

North Dallas Forty '79 **2**
Northanger Abbey '87 **2**
Nosferatu [1] '22 **1**
Nosferatu [2] '22 **2**
Nosferatu the Vampyre '79 **1**
Nostalghia '83 **1**
Not of This Earth '88 **2**
Nothin' 2 Lose '00 **2**
Nothing but Trouble '91 **1**
Nothing Sacred '37 **1**
Nothing to Lose '96 **1**
Notorious '46 **1**
The Notorious Daughter of Fanny Hill / Head Mistress '66 **2**
Notting Hill '99 **1**
Novel Desires '92 **1**
Now and Then '95 **1**
Nowhere to Run '93 **1**
Nude for Satan '74 **1**
Nude on the Moon '61 **2**
No. 17 '32 **1**
Nunsense '93 **1**
Nunsense 2: The Sequel '94 **2**
Nuremberg '00 **2**
Nurse Betty '00 **2**
The Nutt House '92 **1**
The Nutty Professor '63 **2**
The Nutty Professor '96 **1**
Nutty Professor 2: The Klumps [1 CE] '00 **2**
Nutty Professor 2: The Klumps [2 Uncensored] '00 **2**
A Nymphoid Barbarian in Dinosaur Hell [SE] '94 **2**

O
O Brother Where Art Thou? '00 **2**
Oasis of the Zombies '82 **2**
The Object of Beauty '91 **2**
Object of Obsession '95 **1**
An Occasional Hell '96 **1**
October Sky '99 **1**
October 22 '98 **2**
Octopus '00 **2**
Octopussy '83 **2**
The Odd Couple '68 **2**
Odd Man Out '47 **1**
The Odessa File '74 **1**
Of Human Bondage '34 **2**
Of Mice and Men '39 **1**
Office Space '98 **1**
An Officer and a Gentleman '82 **2**
Oklahoma '55 **1**
The Old Dark House '32 **1**
The Old Man and the Sea '58 **1**
Oliver! '68 **1**
Oliver Twist '48 **1**
The Omega Code '99 **2**
The Omen [SE] '76 **2**
Omen 3: The Final Conflict '81 **2**
Omen 4: The Awakening '91 **2**
The Omen Collection '00 **2**
On Approval '44 **1**
On Deadly Ground '94 **1**
On Golden Pond '81 **1**
On the Border '98 **2**
On the Ropes '99 **1**
Once a Thief '96 **1**
Once Upon a Time in China '91 **2**
Once Upon a Time in China II '92 **1**
Once Upon a Time in China III '93 **1**
Once Upon a Time...When We Were Colored '95 **2**
One Day in September '99 **2**
187 '97 **2**
One-Eyed Jacks '61 **2**
One False Move '91 **2**
One Flew Over the Cuckoo's Nest '75 **1**
One Good Turn '95 **2**
101 Dalmatians '61 **1**

101 Dalmatians '96 **1**
One Hundred and One Nights '94 **1**
102 Dalmatians '00 **2**
One Magic Christmas '85 **1**
One Man's Justice '95 **2**
One Night Stand '97 **1**
One True Thing '98 **1**
Onegin '99 **2**
Only Angels Have Wings '39 **2**
Only You '94 **1**
Open City '45 **1**
Opening Night '77 **2**
Operation Condor '91 **1**
Operation Condor 2: The Armour of the Gods '86 **1**
Operation Delta Force 2: Mayday '97 **1**
Operation Delta Force 3: Clear Target '98 **1**
Opposite of Sex '98 **1**
The Organization '71 **2**
Organized Crime & Triad Bureau '93 **1**
Original Kings of Comedy '00 **2**
Origins of Film '00 **2**
Orlando '92 **1**
Orphans of the Storm '21 **1**
Othello '52 **1**
The Other Side of Sunday '96 **2**
The Other Sister '98 **1**
Our Daily Bread and Other Films of the Depression '34 **1**
Our Hospitality / Sherlock Junior '23 **1**
Our Lips Are Sealed '00 **2**
Our Town '40 **2**
Out for Justice '91 **1**
Out Kold '00 **2**
Out of Sight '98 **1**
Out of the Blue '80 **1**
Out of Time '91 **1**
The Out-of-Towners '99 **1**
Outbreak '94 **1**
Outland '81 **1**
The Outlaw Josey Wales '76 **1**
Outlaw Justice '98 **2**
Outrage '93 **1**
Outrageous Fortune '87 **1**
Outside Providence '99 **1**
Outside the Law / Shadows '21 **2**
The Outsiders '83 **1**
Over the Wire '95 **1**
Overboard '87 **1**

P
Painted Skin '93 **2**
The Pajama Game '57 **1**
Pal Joey '57 **2**
Pale Rider '85 **1**
The Pallbearer '95 **2**
The Pallisers '74 **2**
Palmetto '98 **1**
Pancho Villa '72 **2**
The Pandora Project '98 **2**
Panther '95 **2**
The Paper '94 **1**
Paper Bullets '99 **2**
A Paper Wedding '89 **2**
Papillon '73 **1**
The Paradine Case '47 **1**
Paradise Road '97 **2**
The Parallax View '74 **2**
Parasite '82 **2**
Parasite '95 **2**
The Parent Trap '98 **1**
Parenthood '89 **1**
Parents '89 **1**
Paris Holiday '57 **2**
Park City: The Sundance Collection '01 **2**
Parting Glances '86 **2**
Party '96 **2**
A Passage to India '84 **2**
Passenger 57 '92 **2**

Passion & Romance: Double or Nothing '00 **2**
Passion & Romance: Scandal '97 **2**
Passion Fish '92 **1**
The Passion of Ayn Rand '99 **2**
Passion of Joan of Arc '28 **1**
Pat and Mike '52 **2**
Patch Adams [CE] '98 **1**
Paths of Glory '57 **1**
The Patriot '98 **1**
The Patriot '00 **2**
Patriot Games '92 **1**
Patriots '94 **1**
Patton '70 **1**
Paulie '98 **1**
Payback '98 **1**
Peace Hotel '95 **2**
The Peacekeeper '98 **1**
The Peacemaker '97 **1**
Peach / A Bitter Song '95 **2**
Pearl Harbor '00 **2**
Pearl Harbor: December 7, 1941 '00 **2**
The Pebble and the Penguin '94 **2**
Pecker '98 **1**
Pee-wee's Big Adventure '85 **1**
Peeping Tom '60 **1**
Peggy Sue Got Married '86 **1**
Peking Opera Blues '86 **1**
The Pelican Brief '93 **1**
Penitentiary '79 **2**
Penitentiary 2 '82 **2**
Penny Serenade '41 **2**
People of the Wind '76 **2**
The People vs. Larry Flynt '96 **1**
Perceval '78 **2**
The Perfect Husband '92 **2**
A Perfect Murder '98 **1**
The Perfect Nanny '00 **2**
Perfect Profile '90 **2**
The Perfect Storm '00 **2**
Perfect Tenant '99 **2**
Permanent Midnight '98 **1**
Pet Sematary '89 **2**
Peter Pan '24 **1**
Peter Pan '53 **1**
Pete's Dragon '77 **2**
Phantasm '79 **1**
Phantasm 4: Oblivion '98 **2**
The Phantom '96 **1**
The Phantom of the Opera '25 **1**
The Phantom of the Opera '43 **2**
The Phantom of the Opera '90 **1**
The Phantom of the Opera '98 **1**
The Phantom Planet '61 **2**
Phantoms '97 **1**
Phenomenon '96 **1**
Phenomenon—The Lost Archives: Noah's Ark Found?/Tunguska/Stolen Glory '99 **2**
Phenomenon—The Lost Archives: Up for Sale/Heavy Watergate '99 **2**
Philadelphia '93 **1**
The Philadelphia Experiment '84 **2**
The Philadelphia Story '40 **1**
Phoenix '98 **1**
Pi '97 **1**
The Piano '93 **1**
Picasso '85 **2**
Pick a Card '97 **2**
Picking Up the Pieces '99 **2**
Picnic '55 **2**
Picnic at Hanging Rock '75 **1**
Picture Perfect '96 **1**
Picture Windows '95 **2**
Pierrot le Fou '65 **1**
The Pillow Book '95 **1**
Pillow Talk '59 **1**

Pink Floyd: The Wall '82 **1**
The Pink Panther '64 **1**
The Pink Panther Strikes Again '76 **1**
Pinocchio '40 **1**
Pinocchio '76 **2**
Piranha '78 **1**
The Pit and the Pendulum '61 **2**
Pit Stop '67 **2**
Pitch Black '00 **2**
Pixote '81 **2**
Plague of the Zombies '66 **1**
Plain Jane '00 **1**
Plan 9 from Outer Space [Image] '56 **1**
Plan 9 from Outer Space [Passport Video] '56 **2**
Planes, Trains & Automobiles '87 **2**
Planet of the Apes '68 **2**
Platoon [1] '86 **1**
Platoon [2 SE] '86 **2**
Play It to the Bone '99 **2**
Play Time '94 **1**
The Player '92 **1**
The Players Club '98 **1**
Playing by Heart '98 **1**
Playing God '96 **1**
Playing Mona Lisa '00 **2**
Pleasantville '98 **1**
Plenty '85 **2**
Plump Fiction '97 **2**
Pocahontas '95 **2**
Pocahontas 2: Journey to a New World '98 **2**
Pocket Ninjas '93 **1**
Poetic Justice '93 **2**
Point Blank '67 **1**
Point of No Return '93 **1**
Poison Ivy '92 **1**
Poison Ivy 2: Lily '95 **1**
Poison Ivy 3: The Seduction '97 **1**
Pokemon the Movie 2000: The Power of One '00 **2**
Pola X '99 **2**
Poldark '96 **2**
Police Academy '84 **1**
Polish Wedding '97 **1**
Poltergeist '82 **1**
The Pom Pom Girls / The Beach Girls '76 **2**
The Pompatus of Love '95 **2**
Ponette '96 **1**
Pop & Me '99 **2**
The Pope of Greenwich Village '84 **2**
Pork Chop Hill '59 **1**
Porky's '82 **1**
Porky's / Porky's 2: The Next Day '82 **2**
The Portrait '99 **2**
Portrait of a Lady '96 **1**
Portrait of an Assassin '49 **1**
Portrait of Jennie '48 **2**
A Portrait of the Artist As a Young Man '77 **2**
Portraits Chinois '96 **2**
The Poseidon Adventure '72 **1**
Positive I.D. '87 **2**
Posse '93 **2**
Possession '81 **2**
Postcards from the Edge '90 **2**
The Postman '94 **1**
The Postman '97 **1**
The Postman Always Rings Twice '81 **2**
Postmortem '98 **2**
Pot o' Gold '41 **2**
Powder '95 **1**
Power '86 **2**
The Power of One '92 **1**
Practical Magic '98 **1**
Pre-Code Hollywood: Vol. 1, "Of Human Bondage" '34 **2**

Predator [CBS/Fox] '87 **1**
Predator [20th Century Fox] '87 **1**
Prehistoric Women '67 **1**
Prelude to a Kiss '92 **2**
Premonition '99 **2**
Presenting Felix the Cat: The Otto Mesmer Classics 1919-24 '96 **1**
Presumed Innocent '90 **1**
Pretty As a Picture: The Art of David Lynch '98 **1**
Pretty Village, Pretty Flame '96 **2**
Pretty Woman '90 **1**
A Price above Rubies '97 **1**
The Price of Desire '96 **1**
Price of Glory '00 **2**
Pride and Prejudice '95 **1**
The Pride of the Yankees '42 **1**
Priest '94 **1**
Primal Fear '96 **1**
Primary Colors '98 **1**
Prime Suspect '82 **1**
The Prince and the Pauper '78 **2**
Prince of Central Park '00 **2**
Prince of Darkness '87 **1**
Prince of Egypt '98 **1**
The Princess and the Pirate '95 **1**
The Princess Bride '87 **2**
Princess Caraboo '94 **2**
Princess Mononoke '98 **2**
Princess Warrior '90 **1**
Prison on Fire '87 **1**
The Prisoner '90 **2**
Prisoner Maria: The Movie '95 **2**
Private Benjamin '80 **1**
The Private Eyes [SE] '80 **2**
Private Navy of Sgt. O'Farrell '68 **2**
Private Obsession '94 **1**
Private Parts '96 **1**
Prizzi's Honor '85 **1**
The Prodigy '98 **2**
The Professional '94 **1**
The Professionals '66 **1**
Project A '83 **2**
Project A-ko '86 **2**
Project: Eliminator '91 **1**
Project Moon Base '53 **1**
Prom Night '80 **1**
The Prophecy '95 **1**
The Prophecy 2: Ashtown '97 **1**
The Prophecy 3: The Ascent '99 **1**
The Prophet's Game '99 **2**
The Proposal '00 **2**
Protector '97 **1**
Protocol '84 **2**
Psycho [CE] '60 **1**
Psycho '98 **1**
Psycho 3 '86 **1**
Psycho Sisters '98 **2**
Psychomania '73 **2**
Public Access '93 **1**
Pulp Fiction '94 **1**
Pump Up the Volume '90 **1**
Pumpkinhead '88 **2**
The Punisher '90 **1**
Puppet Films of Jiri Trnka '?? **1**
Puppet Master '89 **2**
Puppet Master 2 '90 **2**
Puppet Master 3: Toulon's Revenge '90 **2**
Puppet Master 4 '93 **2**
Puppet Master 5: The Latest Chapter '94 **2**
Puppet Master Collection '00 **2**
The Puppetoon Movie '87 **2**
Pure Country '92 **1**
Purple Rain '84 **1**
Pusher '96 **2**
Pushing Hands '92 **1**
Pushing Tin '99 **1**

Pyaar Kiya to Darna Kya '98 **1**
Pyar to Hona Hi Tah '98 **1**
Pygmalion '38 **2**
Python '00 **2**

Q

Q & A '90 **1**
Q: The Movie '99 **2**
Q (The Winged Serpent) '82 **1**
Quackser Fortune Has a Cousin in the Bronx '70 **2**
Quantum Leap: The Pilot Episode '89 **1**
The Quarrel '93 **1**
The Quarry '98 **2**
Quatermass and the Pit '67 **1**
Quatermass 2 '57 **2**
Queens of Comedy '01 **2**
The Quest '96 **1**
Quest for Camelot '98 **1**
The Quick and the Dead '94 **1**
Quicksand '50 **2**
Quidam '99 **2**
Quiet Days in Hollywood '97 **2**
The Quiet Man '52 **1**
Quills '00 **2**
Quiz Show '94 **1**

R

Rabid '77 **2**
Rabid Dogs '74 **1**
Race '99 **1**
Race Against Time '00 **2**
Race to Freedom: The Story of the Underground Railroad '94 **2**
Rachel's Man '75 **1**
Radioland Murders '94 **1**
The Rage: Carrie 2 '99 **1**
Raging Bull '80 **1**
Raid on Rommel '71 **1**
Railrodder '65 **2**
Rain '32 **2**
Rain Man '88 **1**
A Raisin in the Sun '61 **2**
Raising Cain '92 **1**
Raising the Mammoth '00 **2**
Rambling Rose [1] '91 **1**
Rambling Rose [2 SE] '91 **2**
Rambo: First Blood, Part 2 '85 **1**
Rambo 3 '88 **1**
Ran '85 **1**
Rancho Deluxe '75 **2**
Randy Rides Alone '34 **2**
Rangers '00 **2**
Ransom '96 **1**
Rasputin the Mad Monk '66 **1**
The Rat Pack '98 **1**
Ratas, Ratones, Rateros '99 **2**
Rated X '00 **2**
Raven '97 **1**
Ravenous '99 **1**
Raw Deal '48 **1**
Raw Deal '86 **1**
Razor Blade Smile '98 **1**
Re-Animator '84 **1**
Ready to Rumble '00 **2**
Ready to Wear '94 **1**
The Real Blonde '97 **2**
Real Life '79 **2**
The Real McCoy '93 **1**
Reality Bites '94 **1**
Reap the Wild Wind '42 **1**
Rear Window '54 **2**
Rebecca '40 **1**
Rebel without a Cause '55 **1**
Reboot: Season III '97 **2**
Record of Lodoss War '90 **1**
Red Corner '97 **1**
Red Dawn '84 **1**
The Red Desert '64 **2**
The Red Dwarf '99 **2**
Red Heat '88 **1**
The Red House '47 **1**
Red Letters '00 **2**
Red Line '96 **1**
Red Planet '00 **2**

Red River '48 **1**
Red Scorpion '89 **2**
Red Shoe Diaries: Four on the Floor '96 **2**
Red Shoe Diaries: Luscious Lola '00 **2**
Red Shoe Diaries: Strip Poker '96 **2**
Red Shoe Diaries: Swimming Naked '00 **2**
The Red Shoes '48 **1**
The Red Violin '98 **1**
Redline '97 **1**
Reefer Madness '38 **2**
Reform School Girls '86 **2**
Regina '83 **1**
Rehearsal for Murder '82 **1**
The Reincarnation of Isabel '72 **1**
Reindeer Games '00 **2**
Relative Values '99 **2**
The Relic '96 **1**
Rembrandt '36 **2**
Rembrandt Films' Greatest Hits '00 **2**
Remember the Titans '00 **2**
Remembering the Cosmos Flower '99 **2**
Rent-A-Cop '88 **1**
The Replacement Killers '98 **1**
The Replacements '00 **2**
Repo Man '83 **2**
The Reptile '66 **1**
Requiem for a Dream '00 **2**
Requiem for a Vampire '71 **1**
The Rescuers Down Under '90 **2**
Reservoir Dogs '92 **1**
Restaurant '98 **2**
Restoration '94 **1**
Restraining Order '99 **2**
Resurrection '99 **1**
Retro Puppet Master '99 **2**
The Return of Martin Guerre '83 **1**
Return of the Blind Dead '75 **1**
Return of the Boogeyman '94 **1**
Return of the Dragon '73 **1**
Return of the Fly '59 **2**
Return of the Magnificent Seven '66 **2**
Return to Me '00 **2**
Return to Oz '85 **1**
Return to Paradise '98 **1**
Revelation '00 **2**
Revenge '90 **1**
Revenge of the Pink Panther '78 **1**
Revolt of the Zombies '36 **1**
Rich and Strange '32 **1**
The Rich Man's Wife '96 **2**
Richard Pryor: Live in Concert '79 **1**
Richard Pryor: Live on the Sunset Strip '82 **1**
Ricochet '91 **1**
Ride in the Whirlwind '66 **2**
Ride with the Devil '99 **2**
Riders of Destiny / Star Packer '33 **2**
Rififi '54 **2**
The Right Stuff '83 **1**
The Right Temptation '00 **2**
Rikyu '90 **2**
The Ring '27 **1**
Ring of Bright Water '69 **2**
The Ring Virus '99 **2**
Ringmaster '98 **1**
Rio Grande '50 **1**
Rising Sun '93 **1**
Risky Business '83 **1**
Rites of Passage '99 **1**
The River '84 **2**
A River Runs Through It '92 **1**
The River Wild '94 **1**
River's Edge '87 **2**
Road Movie '72 **2**
The Road to Bali '53 **2**

The Road to El Dorado '00 **2**
The Road to Morocco '42 **1**
The Road to Rio '47 **2**
The Road to Utopia '46 **1**
Road Trip '00 **2**
The Road Warrior '82 **1**
Rob Roy '95 **1**
Robbie Robertson: Going Home '98 **1**
Robert Louis Stevenson's The Game of Death '99 **2**
Robin Hood '22 **1**
Robin Hood '73 **2**
The Robin Hood Gang '98 **1**
Robin Hood: Prince of Thieves '91 **1**
RoboCop '87 **1**
RoboCop 2 '90 **1**
RoboCop 3 '91 **1**
Robot Monster '53 **2**
Robotech: First Contact '00 **2**
The Rock [Hollywood] '96 **1**
The Rock [Criterion] '96 **2**
Rock-a-Doodle '92 **2**
Rock 'n' Roll High School '79 **1**
Rock 'n' Roll Invaders: The AM Radio DJs '9? **1**
The Rock: The People's Champ '9? **1**
The Rocketeer '91 **1**
Rocketship X-M '50 **2**
Rocky [1] '76 **1**
Rocky [2 SE] '76 **2**
Rocky 2 '79 **1**
Rocky 4 '85 **1**
The Rocky Horror Picture Show '75 **2**
Rodgers and Hammerstein: The Sound of Movies '95 **1**
Roger Corman Retrospective, Vol. 1 '00 **2**
Rogue Trader '98 **1**
Rollerball '75 **1**
Rollercoaster '77 **1**
Romance '99 **1**
Rome: Power & Glory '99 **2**
Romeo and Juliet '68 **1**
Romeo Must Die '00 **2**
Romero '89 **2**
Romper Stomper [SE] '92 **2**
Romy and Michele's High School Reunion '97 **1**
Ronin '98 **1**
A Room with a View '86 **2**
Rooster Cogburn '75 **1**
Roots of Rhythm '99 **2**
Rope '48 **2**
Rosemary's Baby '68 **2**
Rosewood '96 **1**
Rouge '87 **2**
Roughnecks Starship Troopers Chronicles the Pluto Campaign '99 **2**
Roujin Z '95 **1**
Rounders '98 **1**
Route 9 '98 **1**
Row Your Boat '98 **2**
The Rowdy Girls '00 **2**
Roxanne '87 **2**
Royal Hunt of the Sun '69 **1**
Royal Tramp '92 **1**
Royal Wedding '51 **1**
R.P.M. '97 **2**
Ruckus '81 **2**
Rude '96 **1**
Rudy [SE] '93 **2**
Rudyard Kipling's The Second Jungle Book: Mowgli and Baloo '97 **2**
Rugrats in Paris: The Movie '00 **2**
The Rugrats Movie '98 **1**
Rules of Engagement '00 **2**
Rumble Fish '83 **1**
Rumble in the Bronx '96 **1**
Run Lola Run '98 **1**
Runaway '84 **2**
Runaway Train '85 **1**
The Runner '99 **1**
Running Free '00 **2**

The Running Man '87 **1**
Running on Empty '88 **1**
Running out of Time '94 **2**
Running out of Time '99 **2**
Running Time '97 **1**
Rush Hour '98 **1**
Rush Week '88 **1**
Rushmore '98 **1**
Russell Mulcahy's Tale of the Mummy '99 **1**

S

Sabotage '36 **1**
Saboteur '42 **2**
The Sadist '63 **1**
Sagebrush Trail '33 **2**
The Saint '97 **1**
The St. Francisville Experiment '00 **2**
Saint Jack '79 **2**
Salem's Lot '79 **1**
Sally of the Sawdust '25 **1**
Salo, or the 120 Days of Sodom '75 **1**
Salome / The Forbidden '73 **1**
Salome's Last Dance '88 **2**
Salt of the Earth '54 **2**
Saludos Amigos '43 **2**
Salvador [SE] '86 **2**
Samurai 1: Musashi Miyamoto '55 **1**
Samurai 2: Duel at Ichijoji Temple '55 **1**
Samurai 3: Duel at Ganryu Island '56 **1**
Samurai X: The Movie '95 **2**
Samurai X Trust '99 **2**
Sanctuary '98 **1**
The Sand Pebbles '66 **2**
Sands of Iwo Jima '49 **1**
Sanjuro '62 **1**
Santa Claus: The Movie '85 **2**
The Santa Clause '94 **1**
Santa Claws '96 **2**
Santa Fe '97 **1**
Santa Fe Trail '40 **1**
Santa Fe Trail '79 **2**
Santo Bugito 1 '99 **1**
The Saphead '21 **1**
Sarah, Plain and Tall '91 **1**
Sarah, Plain and Tall: Winter's End '99 **1**
Sarfarosh '98 **1**
The Satanic Rites of Dracula '73 **1**
Satan's Sadists '69 **2**
Saturday the 14th '81 **2**
Saturday the 14th Strikes Back '88 **2**
Saturn 3 '80 **1**
Save the Last Dance '01 **2**
Saving Grace '00 **2**
Saving Private Ryan '98 **1**
Savior '98 **1**
Saviour of the Soul '92 **1**
Saviour of the Soul 2 '92 **2**
Say Amen, Somebody '80 **2**
Scandal: The Big Turn On '99 **2**
Scarface '83 **1**
Scarlet Empress '34 **2**
The Scarlet Pimpernel '34 **2**
Scarred City '98 **1**
Scary Movie '00 **2**
Scene at the Sea '91 **2**
Scent of a Woman '92 **1**
School Daze '88 **2**
School Ties '92 **1**
School's Out '99 **2**
The Sci-Fi Files '97 **1**
Sci-Fighters '96 **1**
Scooby-Doo and the Alien Invaders '00 **2**
Score '72 **1**
Scorned 2 '96 **1**
The Scorpio Factor '90 **2**
Scream [CS] '96 **1**
Scream 2 '97 **1**
Scream 3 [CS] '00 **2**
Screamers '96 **1**
The Screaming Skull '58 **2**

Screw Loose '99 **2**
Screwed '00 **2**
Scrooged '88 **2**
Scum of the Earth '63 **2**
Sea of Love '89 **1**
Sea Wolves '81 **1**
Seamless '00 **2**
Search and Destroy '94 **2**
The Searchers '56 **1**
The Second Woman '51 **2**
The Secret Adventures of Tom Thumb '94 **1**
The Secret Agent '36 **1**
Secret Games '92 **2**
Secret Games 3 '94 **1**
The Secret Garden '93 **1**
The Secret KGB UFO Files '99 **2**
The Secret Life of Walter Mitty '47 **1**
The Secret of Anastasia '97 **2**
The Secret of My Success '87 **1**
The Secret of NIMH 2 '98 **2**
Secrets of the Heart '97 **2**
Selena '96 **1**
Semi-Tough '77 **2**
Sense and Sensibility '95 **1**
Senseless '98 **1**
The Sentinel '76 **2**
September '88 **2**
Sgt. Bilko '95 **1**
Sgt. Kabukiman N.Y.P.D. '94 **1**
Sergei Eisenstein: Autobiography '96 **2**
Sergei Eisenstein: Mexican Fantasy '98 **2**
Sergio Lapel's Drawing Blood '99 **2**
Serial Bomber '96 **1**
Serial Mom '94 **1**
The Serpent and the Rainbow '87 **1**
The Serpent's Kiss '97 **2**
Set It Off '96 **1**
The Settlement '99 **2**
Seven [1] '95 **1**
Seven [2 SE] '95 **2**
Seven Beauties '76 **1**
Seven Brides for Seven Brothers '54 **1**
Seven Chances '25 **1**
Seven Days in May '64 **2**
7 Faces of Dr. Lao '63 **2**
Seven Girlfriends '00 **2**
The Seven Little Foys '55 **2**
The Seven-Per-Cent Solution '76 **1**
Seven Samurai '54 **1**
The Seven Year Itch '55 **2**
Seven Years in Tibet '97 **1**
The Seventh Floor '93 **1**
The Seventh Seal '56 **1**
The Seventh Sense '99 **1**
The Seventh Sign '88 **1**
The Seventh Voyage of Sinbad '58 **1**
The '70s '00 **2**
70 Years of Popeye '00 **1**
Sex and the City: The Complete Second Season '00 **1**
Sex and the Other Man '95 **1**
Sex and Zen '93 **1**
Sex Crimes '92 **1**
Sex Files: Ancient Desires '99 **2**
Sex Files: Digital Sex '98 **2**
Sex Is. . . '93 **1**
sex, lies and videotape '89 **1**
The Sex Monster '99 **1**
Sextette '78 **2**
Sexual Malice '93 **1**
Sexual Roulette '96 **1**
The Shadow '94 **1**
Shadow of a Doubt '43 **2**
Shadow of Chinatown '36 **2**
Shadow of the Eagle '32 **2**
Shadow of the Vampire '00 **2**
Shadow Raiders, Vol. 1: Uncommon Hero '98 **2**

The Shadow Riders '82 **2**
Shadowlands '93 **1**
Shadows '22 **2**
Shadows and Fog '92 **2**
Shadrach '98 **1**
Shaft '71 **1**
Shaft '00 **2**
Shaft in Africa '73 **2**
Shaft's Big Score '72 **2**
Shag: The Movie '89 **2**
Shakedown '88 **1**
Shakes the Clown '92 **2**
Shakespeare in Love [CS] '98 **1**
Shalako '68 **1**
Shallow Grave '94 **1**
Shameless '94 **1**
Shane '53 **2**
The Shanghai Gesture '42 **1**
Shanghai Noon '00 **2**
Shaolin Avengers '94 **1**
Shark Attack '99 **1**
Shark Attack 2 '00 **2**
Sharky's Machine '81 **1**
Sharpe's Battle '94 **2**
Sharpe's Company '94 **2**
Sharpe's Eagle '93 **2**
Sharpe's Enemy '94 **2**
Sharpe's Gold '94 **2**
Sharpe's Honour '94 **2**
Sharpe's Justice '97 **2**
Sharpe's Mission '96 **2**
Sharpe's Regiment '96 **2**
Sharpe's Revenge '97 **2**
Sharpe's Rifles '93 **2**
Sharpe's Siege '96 **2**
Sharpe's Sword '94 **2**
Sharpe's Waterloo '97 **2**
Shattered Image '98 **1**
The Shawshank Redemption '94 **1**
She '35 **1**
She Demons '58 **2**
She Devils in Chains '76 **1**
She-Freak '67 **2**
She Killed in Ecstasy '70 **2**
Sheba, Baby '75 **2**
Sherlock Holmes and the Secret Weapon '42 **2**
Sherlock Holmes Consulting Detective, Vol. 1 '91 **1**
She's All That '99 **1**
She's Having a Baby '88 **2**
She's So Lovely '97 **2**
She's the One '96 **2**
Shine '95 **1**
The Shining '80 **1**
The Shiver of the Vampires '70 **1**
Shock Corridor '63 **1**
Shocker '89 **1**
Shoot Out '71 **1**
Shoot the Piano Player '62 **1**
The Shooting '66 **2**
Shooting Fish '98 **1**
Short 1: Invention '?? **1**
Short 2: Dreams '?? **1**
A Shot in the Dark '64 **1**
Showdown in Little Tokyo '91 **1**
Shriek If You Know What I Did Last Friday the 13th '00 **1**
Sid & Nancy [Criterion] '86 **1**
Sid & Nancy [MGM] '86 **2**
Sideshow '00 **2**
The Siege '98 **1**
The Sign of Four '83 **2**
Silence of the Lambs '91 **1**
Silent Running '71 **1**
Silent Shakespeare '00 **2**
Silk 'n' Sabotage '94 **1**
Silkwood '83 **1**
Silverado [SE] '85 **2**
Simon Birch '98 **1**
Simon Sez '99 **1**
Simpatico '99 **2**
A Simple Plan '98 **1**
A Simple Wish '97 **1**
Simply Irresistible '99 **1**
Sin: The Movie '98 **2**

Sinbad and the Eye of the Tiger '77 **2**
Sinbad: Beyond the Veil of Mists '00 **2**
The Sinful Nuns of Saint Valentine '74 **1**
Singin' in the Rain '52 **1**
A Single Girl '96 **2**
Single White Female '92 **1**
Singles '92 **1**
Sink or Swim '97 **1**
Sirens '94 **1**
Sister Act 2: Back in the Habit '93 **1**
Sister My Sister '94 **1**
Sister, Sister '87 **2**
Sisters '73 **2**
Six Days, Seven Nights '98 **1**
Six Degrees of Separation '93 **2**
Six Ways to Sunday '99 **1**
Sixteen Candles '84 **1**
The 6th Day '00 **2**
The Sixth Sense '99 **1**
The '60s '99 **2**
Sizzle Beach U.S.A. '74 **1**
Skin Game '31 **1**
Skinner '93 **1**
The Skulls '00 **2**
Skylark '93 **1**
Slam '98 **1**
Slap Shot '77 **1**
Slaughterhouse '87 **2**
Slaughterhouse Five '72 **1**
Slaughter's Big Ripoff '73 **2**
Slave Girls from Beyond Infinity '87 **1**
Slaves to the Underground '96 **1**
SLC Punk! '99 **1**
Sleepaway Camp '83 **2**
Sleeper '73 **2**
Sleepers '96 **1**
Sleepless in Seattle '93 **1**
Sleepwalkers '92 **1**
Sleepy Hollow '99 **1**
Sleuth '72 **1**
Sliding Doors '97 **1**
Sling Blade '96 **1**
The Slipper and the Rose '76 **1**
Slippery When Wet '58 **2**
Slugs '87 **2**
Slumber Party Massacre '82 **2**
Slumber Party Massacre 2 '87 **2**
Slumber Party Massacre 3 '90 **2**
Slums of Beverly Hills '98 **1**
Small Change '76 **2**
Small Soldiers '98 **1**
Small Time Crooks '00 **2**
Smart Money '31 **1**
Smashing Time '67 **1**
Smilla's Sense of Snow '96 **2**
Smoke Signals '98 **1**
Smokey and the Bandit '77 **1**
Snake Eyes '98 **1**
Sneakers '92 **1**
Sniper '92 **2**
Snow Day '00 **2**
Snow Falling on Cedars '99 **2**
Snow White: A Tale of Terror '97 **1**
The Snows of Kilimanjaro '52 **2**
So I Married an Axe Murderer '93 **1**
Social Misfits '00 **2**
The Soft Skin '64 **1**
Sol Bianca: The Legacy '90 **2**
Solar Crisis '92 **1**
Soldier '98 **1**
Soldier of Orange '78 **2**
A Soldier's Story '84 **2**
A Soldier's Tale '91 **1**
Solo '96 **1**
Solomon and Gaenor '98 **2**
Some Like It Hot [SE] '59 **2**

Somebody Has to Shoot the Picture '90 **2**
Someone to Watch Over Me '87 **1**
Something about Sex '98 **1**
Something More '99 **2**
Something New '20 **2**
Something Weird '68 **2**
Something Wicked This Way Comes '83 **1**
Something Wild '86 **2**
Sometimes They Come Back ... For More '99 **1**
Somewhere in Time '80 **1**
Sommersby '93 **1**
Son-in-Law '93 **1**
Son of Gascogne '95 **2**
Son of Paleface '52 **2**
Sons of Katie Elder '65 **2**
Sophie's Choice '82 **1**
The Sopranos: The Complete First Season '00 **2**
Sorcerer '77 **1**
Sorcerer Hunters: Magical Encounters '00 **2**
Sorceress '94 **1**
Sorority House Massacre '86 **1**
Sorority House Massacre 2: Nighty Nightmare '92 **2**
The Sorrow and the Pity '71 **2**
Soul Food '97 **1**
Soul of the Game '96 **2**
Soultaker '90 **1**
The Sound of Music [Five Star Collection] '65 **2**
Sour Grapes '98 **2**
The Source '96 **2**
South Central '92 **2**
South Pacific '58 **1**
Southie '98 **2**
Southern Comfort '81 **2**
Space Cowboys '00 **2**
Space Jam '96 **1**
Space-Thing '67 **2**
Space Truckers '97 **1**
Spaceways '53 **2**
The Spanish Prisoner '97 **1**
Sparrows '26 **1**
Spartacus [Universal] '60 **1**
Spartacus [Criterion] '60 **1**
Spawn [SE] '97 **1**
The Specialist '94 **1**
The Specials '00 **2**
Specimen '97 **1**
Speed '94 **1**
Speed 2: Cruise Control '97 **1**
Speed Racer: The Movie '?? **2**
Spellbound '45 **1**
Sphere '97 **1**
Spice World: The Movie '97 **1**
Spider Baby '64 **1**
Spiders '18 **1**
Spiders '00 **2**
Spies Like Us '85 **1**
The Spiral Staircase '46 **2**
Spirit of the Eagle '90 **1**
Spirits of the Dead '68 **1**
Spiritual Kung Fu '78 **1**
Splash '84 **1**
Splendor '99 **2**
Spoiler '98 **1**
Spooky Encounters '80 **2**
Spring Symphony '86 **1**
Sprung '97 **2**
Spy Hard '96 **1**
The Spy Who Loved Me [SE] '77 **1**
Stagecoach '39 **1**
Stalingrad '94 **1**
Stalked '99 **2**
Stand and Deliver '88 **1**
Stand by Me [1] '86 **1**
Stand by Me [2 SE] '86 **2**
Stand-Ins '97 **1**
Star 80 '83 **1**
A Star Is Born '37 **1**
A Star Is Born '54 **2**

The Star Packer '34 **2**
Star Trek 2: The Wrath of Khan '82 **2**
Star Trek 4: The Voyage Home '86 **1**
Star Trek 5: The Final Frontier '89 **1**
Star Trek 6: The Undiscovered Country '91 **1**
Star Trek: First Contact '96 **1**
Star Trek: Generations '94 **1**
Star Trek: Insurrection '98 **1**
Stargate '94 **1**
Stargate SG-1: Season 1 '97 **2**
Starman '84 **1**
Starry Night '99 **2**
Starship Troopers '97 **1**
State Fair '45 **1**
Stay Awake '87 **1**
Steal This Movie! '00 **2**
Steamboat Bill, Jr. '28 **1**
Steel Dawn '87 **2**
Steel Magnolias '89 **2**
Steele's Law '91 **2**
Stella '55 **2**
Stella Maris '18 **1**
The Stendahl Syndrome '95 **2**
The Stepdaughter '00 **2**
The Stepford Wives '75 **1**
Stephen King's The Night Flier '96 **1**
Stephen King's The Stand '94 **1**
Stephen King's The Storm of the Century '99 **1**
Stephen King's The Tommy-knockers '93 **1**
Stephen King's Thinner '96 **1**
Stepmom '98 **1**
Stigmata '99 **1**
Still Twisted '?? **1**
The Sting '73 **1**
Stir Crazy '80 **1**
Stir of Echoes '99 **1**
Stolen Kisses '68 **1**
Stomp Out Loud '98 **2**
Stonebrook '98 **2**
Stories from Long Island '00 **2**
Stories from My Childhood '98 **2**
Stories from My Childhood, Vol. 3 '99 **2**
Storm over Asia '28 **1**
Stormswept '95 **2**
The Story Lady '93 **1**
The Story of Adele H. '75 **2**
The Story of G.I. Joe '45 **1**
The Story of Jacob & Joseph '74 **2**
The Story of O: The Series '92 **2**
The Story of Us '99 **1**
Straight out of Compton '00 **2**
The Straight Story '99 **2**
Straight to Hell '87 **2**
Strange Case of Dr. Jekyll & Mr. Hyde '68 **2**
Strange Days '95 **2**
The Strange Love of Martha Ivers '46 **2**
The Strange Woman '46 **2**
The Stranger '46 **1**
Stranger by Night '94 **1**
The Stranger from Venus '54 **2**
A Stranger in the Kingdom '98 **1**
Stranger than Fiction '99 **1**
Strangers on a Train '51 **1**
Strangler of the Swamp '46 **1**
Straw Dogs '72 **1**
Strawberry Fields '97 **2**
Street Fighter '94 **1**
Street Gun '96 **2**
Street Law '95 **1**
Street Scene '31 **2**
Street Wars '91 **1**

A Streetcar Named Desire '51 **1**
Streets of Fire '84 **1**
Striking Distance '93 **1**
Striking Resemblance '97 **1**
Strip Search '97 **1**
Stripshow '92 **1**
Striptease '96 **2**
Stroker Ace '83 **1**
Stuart Little '99 **1**
Stuart Saves His Family '94 **2**
The Stuff '85 **2**
Submerged '00 **2**
The Substitute '96 **1**
The Substitute 2: School's Out '97 **1**
The Substitute 4: Failure Is Not an Option '00 **2**
Suburbia '83 **2**
Subway '85 **1**
Succubus '69 **1**
Sucker the Vampire '98 **1**
Sudden Fear '52 **1**
Suddenly '54 **1**
Suddenly, Last Summer '59 **2**
Sudie & Simpson '90 **2**
Suicide Kings '97 **1**
Suite 16 '94 **1**
Summer '86 **1**
Summer of Sam '99 **1**
Summer Rental '85 **2**
A Summer to Remember '84 **1**
A Summer's Tale '96 **2**
Sunday in the Park with George '86 **1**
Sunset '88 **1**
Sunshine '99 **2**
Super Speedway '97 **1**
Supercop '92 **1**
Supercop 2 '93 **1**
Supergirl '84 **2**
Superman: The Movie '78 **2**
Superman 2 '80 **2**
Superman 3 '83 **2**
Superman 4: The Quest for Peace '87 **2**
The Superman Cartoons of Max & Dave Fleischer '41 **1**
Superman, the Lost Episodes '99 **1**
Supernova '99 **2**
Superstar: The Life and Times of Andy Warhol '90 **2**
Support Your Local Gunfighter '71 **2**
Supreme Sanction '99 **1**
Surf Crazy '59 **1**
Surf Nazis Must Die [DC] '87 **1**
Surfing Hollow Days '61 **2**
The Surgeon '94 **1**
Surviving the Game '94 **1**
Suspicions '95 **1**
Suture '93 **2**
Swamp Thing '82 **2**
Swashbuckler '76 **1**
Sweepers '99 **1**
Sweet and Lowdown '99 **2**
Sweet Dreams '85 **1**
Sweet Evil '99 **1**
The Sweet Hereafter '96 **1**
Sweet Justice '92 **1**
Sweet Revenge '98 **2**
Sweet Smell of Success '57 **2**
Swept Away. . . '75 **1**
Swept from the Sea '97 **1**
Swimming with Sharks '94 **1**
Swimsuit '89 **1**
Swingers '96 **1**
The Swinging Cheerleaders '74 **1**
Swiss Conspiracy '77 **1**
Switch '91 **2**
Switchback '97 **1**
Switchblade Sisters '75 **2**
The Sword in the Stone '63 **2**
Sworn Enemies '96 **1**

Urotsukidoji: Perfect Collection '89 **1**
Urusei Yatsura Movie 2: Beautiful Dreamer '84 **1**
U.S. Marshals '98 **1**
The Usual Suspects '95 **1**
Utopia '51 **1**
U2: Rattle and Hum '88 **1**

V
The Vampire Bat '32 **2**
The Vampire Happening '71 **2**
Vampire Hunter D [SE] '85 **2**
Vampire Journals '96 **1**
Vamps: Deadly Dreamgirls '95 **2**
Vampyr '31 **1**
Vampyres '74 **2**
Vampyros Lesbos '70 **2**
The Vanishing '88 **1**
The Vanishing American '25 **2**
Varietease '54 **2**
Variety Lights '51 **2**
Varsity Blues '98 **1**
The Vault '00 **2**
Vegas Vacation '96 **1**
Velocity '99 **2**
Velocity Trap '99 **2**
Velvet Goldmine '98 **1**
Vengeance '68 **2**
The Vengeance of She '68 **1**
Venus in Furs '94 **2**
The Venus Wars '89 **1**
Vera Cruz '53 **2**
Vertical Limit '00 **2**
Vertigo [CE] '58 **1**
Very Bad Things '98 **1**
A Very Natural Thing '73 **2**
The Very Thought of You '98 **1**
Vice Girls '96 **2**
Victory '81 **1**
Videodrome '83 **1**
Vietnam: The Ten Thousand Day War '80 **2**
A View to a Kill [SE] '85 **2**
Vigilante '83 **1**
The Viking Queen '67 **1**
Village of Dreams '97 **1**
Village of the Damned '95 **1**
Village of the Giants '65 **2**
The Vineyard '89 **2**
The Violent Years / Girl Gang '56 **2**
Virasat '97 **1**
The Virgin Suicides '99 **1**
Virtual Combat '95 **1**
Virtual Desire '95 **1**
Virtuosity '95 **1**
Virus '98 **1**
Vision Quest '85 **1**
Visions of Light: The Art of Cinematography '93 **1**
Vive l'Amour '94 **1**
Volcano '97 **1**
Voltage Fighters! Gowcaizer: The Movie '98 **1**
Voodoo '95 **1**
Voodoo Academy [DC] '00 **2**
Voyage to the Bottom of the Sea / Fantastic Voyage '61 **2**

W
Wag the Dog '97 **1**
Wages of Fear '55 **1**
The Waiting Game '99 **2**
Waking Ned Devine '98 **1**
Waking the Dead '00 **2**
Waking Up Horton '99 **1**
A Walk in the Clouds '95 **2**
A Walk in the Sun '46 **2**
A Walk on the Moon '99 **1**
Walkabout '71 **1**
Walking Tall '73 **1**
Walking the Edge '83 **2**
Wall Street '87 **2**
Wallace & Gromit: The First Three Adventures '99 **1**
Waltz of the Toreadors '62 **1**
Wanted '98 **1**
The War '94 **1**
The War of the Worlds '53 **1**
The War Room '93 **1**
The War Wagon '67 **1**
The War Zone '98 **2**
WarGames '83 **1**
Warlock: The Armageddon '93 **2**
Warlock 3: The End of Innocence '98 **1**
The Warriors '79 **2**
Warriors of Virtue '97 **1**
The Wasp Woman '59 **2**
Watch Me '96 **1**
The Watcher '00 **2**
The Waterboy '98 **1**
The Watermelon Woman '97 **2**
Waterworld '95 **1**
Wax Mask '97 **2**
Way Down East ' **1**
Way of the Gun '00 **2**
The Way We Were [SE] '73 **2**
W.C. Fields 6 Short Films '33 **2**
Weather Woman '99 **2**
Web of Seduction '99 **1**
The Wedding Singer '97 **1**
Weekend at Bernie's '89 **1**
Weird Science '85 **1**
Welcome to the Dollhouse '95 **1**
Welcome II the Terrordome '95 **2**
We'll Meet Again '82 **2**
Went to Coney Island on a Mission from God...Be Back by Five '98 **2**
Werewolf '95 **1**
Werther '88 **1**
Wes Craven's New Nightmare '94 **1**
West Side Story '61 **1**
The Westerner '40 **1**
Westworld '73 **1**
Wham-Bam, Thank You Spaceman '75 **2**
What about Bob? '91 **2**
What Dreams May Come '98 **1**
What Ever Happened to Baby Jane? '62 **1**
What Lies Beneath '00 **2**

What Planet Are You From? '00 **2**
What Women Want '00 **2**
Whatever Happened to Aunt Alice? '69 **2**
Whatever It Takes '97 **1**
Whatever It Takes '00 **2**
What's Cooking? '00 **2**
What's Love Got to Do with It? '93 **1**
When a Man Loves a Woman '94 **1**
When a Stranger Calls Back '93 **1**
When Harry Met Sally... [SE] '89 **2**
Where the Buffalo Roam '80 **2**
Where the Heart Is '00 **2**
Where the Money Is '00 **2**
Where the Rivers Flow North '94 **1**
While You Were Sleeping '95 **1**
The Whip and the Body '63 **2**
Whipped '00 **2**
Whisper Kill '88 **1**
White Christmas '54 **2**
White Lies '98 **2**
The White Lioness '96 **2**
White Man's Burden '95 **1**
White Men Can't Jump '92 **2**
White Palace '90 **1**
White Squall '96 **1**
White Wolves 2: Legend of the Wild '94 **2**
White Wolves 3: Cry of the White Wolf '98 **2**
Whity '70 **2**
Who Framed Roger Rabbit '88 **1**
The Whole Nine Yards '00 **2**
Who's Afraid of Virginia Woolf? '66 **1**
Why Do Fools Fall in Love? '98 **1**
Why Has Bodhi-Darma Left for the East '89 **1**
Wicked City [SE] '89 **2**
Wicked City '92 **1**
Wicked Ways '99 **1**
The Wicked, Wicked West '97 **1**
Wide Awake '97 **2**
The Wife '95 **1**
Wild America '97 **1**
The Wild Angels '66 **2**
Wild Bill '95 **2**
The Wild Bunch '69 **1**
The Wild One '54 **1**
Wild Reeds '94 **1**
Wild Things '98 **1**
Wild Wild West '99 **1**
Wilderness '96 **2**
William Shakespeare's A Midsummer Night's Dream '99 **1**
William Shakespeare's Romeo and Juliet '96 **1**
Willy Wonka & the Chocolate Factory '71 **1**

The Wind '87 **1**
A Wind Named Amnesia '93 **1**
Winds of the Wasteland '36 **2**
Wing Commander '99 **1**
The Wings of the Dove '97 **1**
Winner Takes All '98 **2**
Winstanley '75 **1**
Winter People '89 **2**
Winter Sleepers '97 **2**
Wishful Thinking '92 **2**
Wishmaster '97 **1**
Wishmaster 2: Evil Never Dies '98 **1**
Witchcraft '88 **1**
Witchcraft 2: The Temptress '90 **1**
Witchcraft 9: Bitter Flesh '96 **1**
The Witches '66 **2**
The Witches '90 **1**
The Witches of Eastwick '87 **1**
Witchouse '99 **1**
Witchouse 2: Blood Coven '00 **2**
With Byrd at the South Pole: The Story of Little America '30 **1**
With Honors '94 **1**
Within the Rock '96 **1**
Without Air '95 **1**
Without Limits '97 **1**
Witness '85 **1**
The Wiz '78 **1**
The Wizard of Gore '70 **1**
The Wizard of Oz '39 **1**
Wolf '94 **1**
The Wolf Man '41 **1**
A Woman Called Moses '78 **2**
A Woman Called Sada Abe '75 **2**
A Woman, Her Men and Her Futon '92 **2**
The Woman in Green / Dressed to Kill '45 **2**
A Woman Is a Woman '60 **1**
Woman of the Year '42 **1**
Woman on Top '00 **2**
A Woman under the Influence '74 **2**
The Woman Who Came Back '45 **1**
The Womaneater '59 **2**
Women '97 **2**
Women in Revolt '71 **1**
The Women of Brewster Place '89 **2**
Women of Valor '86 **1**
Women on the Verge of a Nervous Breakdown '88 **2**
Wonder Boys '00 **2**
Wonder Man '45 **2**
The Wonderful, Horrible Life of Leni Riefenstahl '93 **1**
Wonderland '99 **2**
Wonderwall: The Movie '69 **2**
Woodstock [DC] '70 **1**
Word of Mouth '99 **1**
Working Girl '88 **2**
Working Girls '87 **2**

The World Is Not Enough [SE] '99 **2**
World War II '42 **2**
The World's Greatest Animation '93 **1**
The Wounds '98 **2**
Woyzeck '78 **2**
Wrongfully Accused '98 **1**
Wuthering Heights '39 **1**

X
The X-Files '98 **1**
The X-Files: Season One [CE] '00 **2**
The X-Files: Season Two '00 **2**
X-Men '00 **2**
X-Men: The Phoenix Saga '92 **2**
X: The Man with X-Ray Eyes '63 **2**
X The Unknown '56 **2**
Xanadu '80 **1**
Xchange '00 **2**
Xiu Xiu: The Sent Down Girl '97 **1**
Xtro 3: Watch the Skies '95 **1**

Y
The Yards '00 **2**
The Year of Living Dangerously '82 **1**
Year of the Horse '97 **2**
Yellow '98 **2**
Yellow Submarine '68 **1**
Yes Boss! '97 **1**
Yi Yi '00 **2**
You Can't Do That: The Making of "A Hard Day's Night" '94 **2**
You Only Live Twice [SE] '67 **2**
You So Crazy '94 **2**
Young and Innocent '37 **1**
Young Frankenstein '74 **1**
Young Guns '88 **1**
Youngblood '86 **2**
Your Friends & Neighbors '98 **1**
Yours, Mine & Ours '68 **2**
You've Got Mail '98 **1**

Z
Zachariah '70 **1**
Zardoz '73 **2**
A Zed & Two Noughts '88 **1**
Zeder '83 **1**
Zeram '91 **1**
Zero Effect '97 **1**
Zeus and Roxanne '96 **1**
Ziggy Stardust and the Spiders from Mars '83 **1**
Zombie '80 **1**
Zombie Lake '80 **2**
Zu: Warriors of the Magic Mountain '83 **2**